Street by Street

LONDON

Extended Coverage of the Capital

6th edition April 2012
© AA Media Limited 2012

Original edition printed May 2001

Enabled by **OS Ordnance Survey** This product includes map data licensed from Ordnance Survey® with the permission of the Controller of Her Majesty's Stationery Office. © Crown copyright 2012. All rights reserved. Licence number: 100021153.

The copyright in all PAF is owned by Royal Mail Group plc.

RoadPilot® Information on fixed speed camera locations provided by RoadPilot © 2011 RoadPilot® Driving Technology.

Published by AA Publishing (a trading name of AA Media Limited, whose registered office is Fanum House, Basing View, Basingstoke, Hampshire RG21 4EA. Registered number 06112600)

Produced by the Mapping Services Department of The Automobile Association. (A04695)

A CIP Catalogue record for this book is available from the British Library.

Printed by Oriental Press in Dubai

Ref: MX039v

Key to map pages	ii–iii
Key to map symbols	iv–1
Enlarged map pages	2–19
Main map pages	20–181
Index – towns & villages	182
Index – streets	184–261
Index – featured places	262–283
River bus map	283
Acknowledgements	283

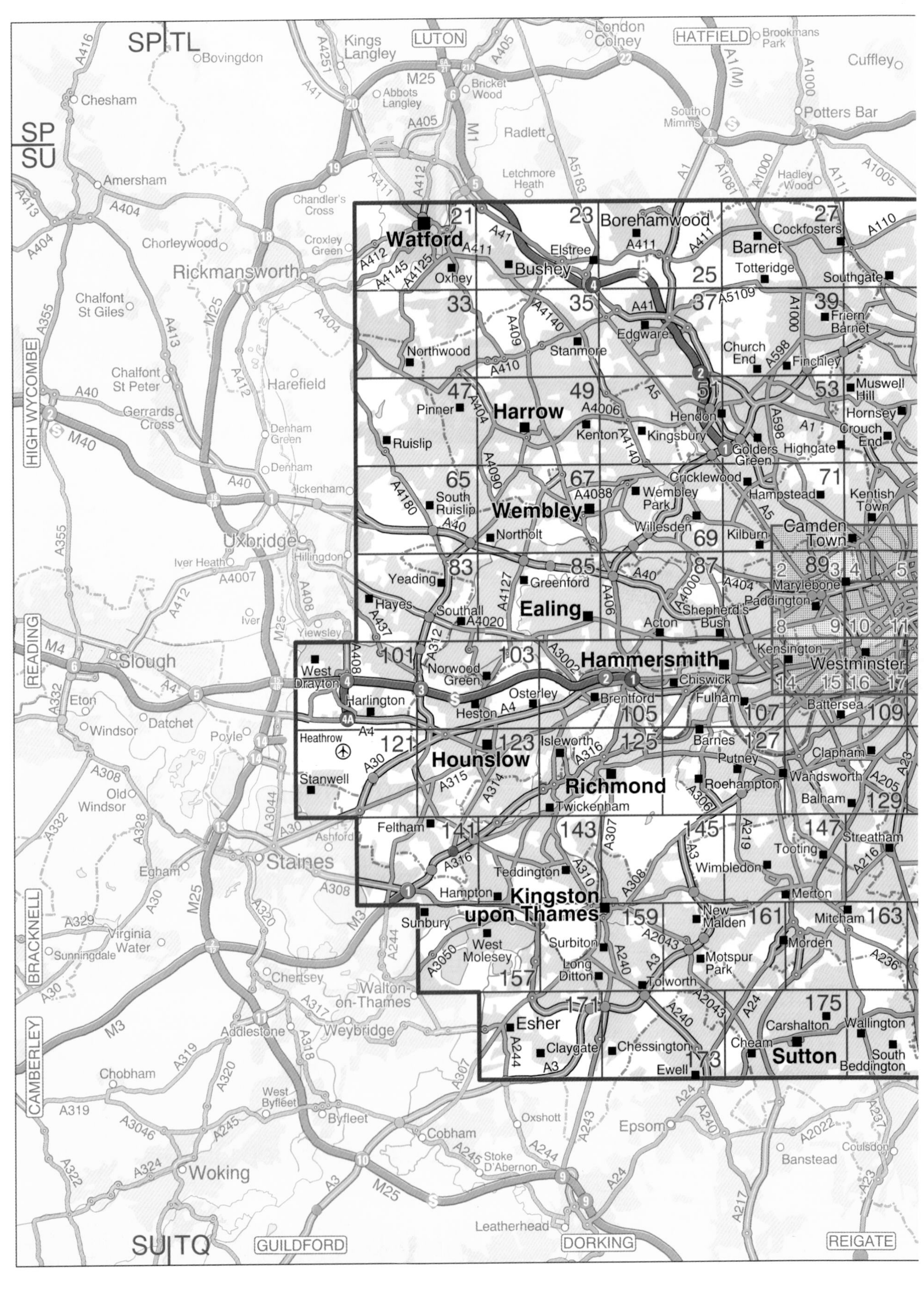

National Grid references are shown on the map frame of each page.
Red figures denote the 100 km square and blue figures the 1 km square.
Example, page 3 : Regent's Park 528 183

The reference can also be written using the National Grid two-letter prefix shown on this page, where 4 and 3 are replaced by TQ to give TQ2883.

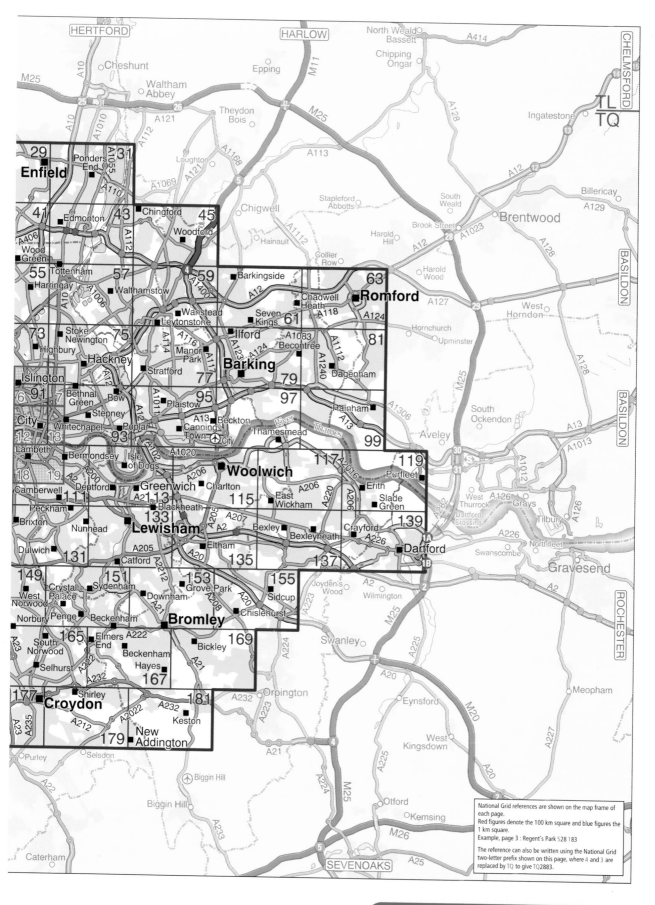

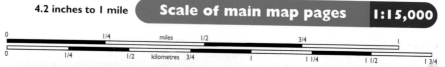

4.2 inches to 1 mile

Scale of main map pages 1:15,000

Junction 9	Motorway & junction
Service	Motorway service area
	Primary road single/dual carriageway
Service	Primary road service area
	A road single/dual carriageway
	B road single/dual carriageway
	Other road single/dual carriageway
	Minor/private road, access may be restricted
← ←	One-way street
	Pedestrian area
	Track or footpath
	Road under construction
	Road tunnel
30 **V**	Speed camera site (fixed location) with speed limit in mph or variable
40 **V**	Selection of road with two or more fixed camera sites; speed limit in mph or variable
50→ ←50	Average speed (SPECS™) camera system with speed limit in mph
P	Parking
P+	Park & Ride
	Bus/coach station

	Railway & main railway station
	Railway & minor railway station
⊖	Underground station
⊖	Docklands Light Railway (DLR) station
⊖	London Overground station
⊖	Light railway & station
+++++++++++	Preserved private railway
LC	Level crossing
•—•—•—•—	Tramway
- - - - - -	Ferry route
....	Airport runway
— · — · —	County, administrative boundary
	Congestion Charging Zone *
	Olympic Park Boundary
	Low Emission Zone (LEZ) (visit **theaa.com** for further information)
93	Page continuation 1:15,000
7	Page continuation to enlarged scale 1:10,000
	River/canal, lake, pier
	Aqueduct, lock, weir
465 ▲ Winter Hill	Peak (with height in metres)

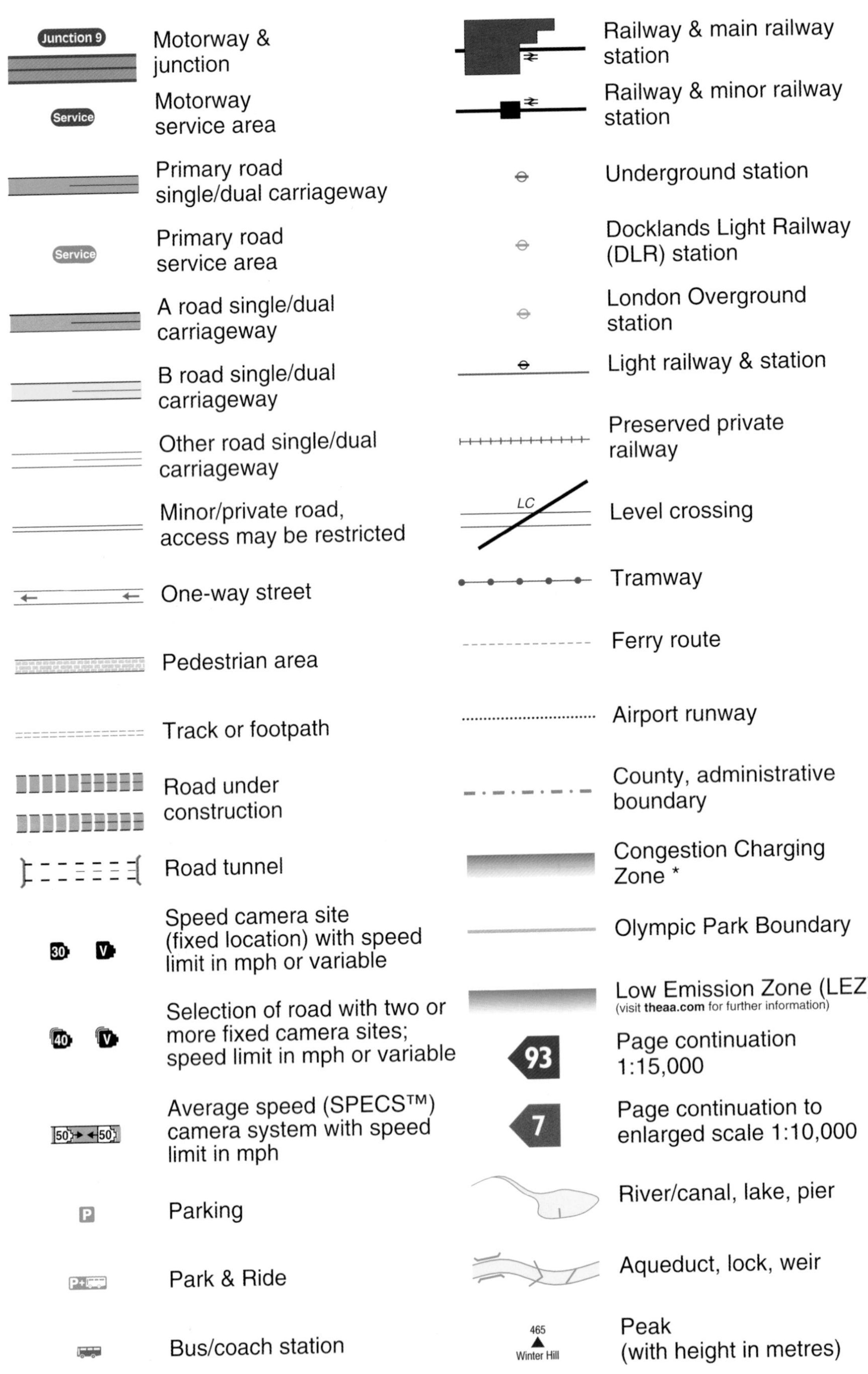

* The AA central London congestion charging map is also available

	Woodland		Golf course
	Park		Theme park
	Cemetery		Abbey, cathedral or priory
	Built-up area		Castle
	Industrial / business building		Historic house or building
	Leisure building	Wakehurst Place (NT)	National Trust property
	Retail building		Museum or art gallery
	Other building		Roman antiquity
	City wall		Ancient site, battlefield or monument
A&E	Hospital with 24-hour A&E department		Industrial interest
PO	Post Office, public library		Garden
i	Tourist Information Centre, seasonal		Garden Centre Garden Centre Association Member
	Petrol station, 24 hour Major suppliers only		Garden Centre Wyevale Garden Centre
†	Church/chapel		Arboretum
	Public toilets, with facilities for the less able		Farm or animal centre
PH	Public house AA recommended		Zoological or wildlife collection
	Restaurant AA inspected		Bird collection
Madeira Hotel	Hotel AA inspected		Nature reserve
	Theatre or performing arts centre		Aquarium
	Cinema		Visitor or heritage centre
	Camping AA inspected		Country park
	Caravan site AA inspected		Cave
	Camping & caravan site AA inspected		Windmill
			Distillery, brewery or vineyard

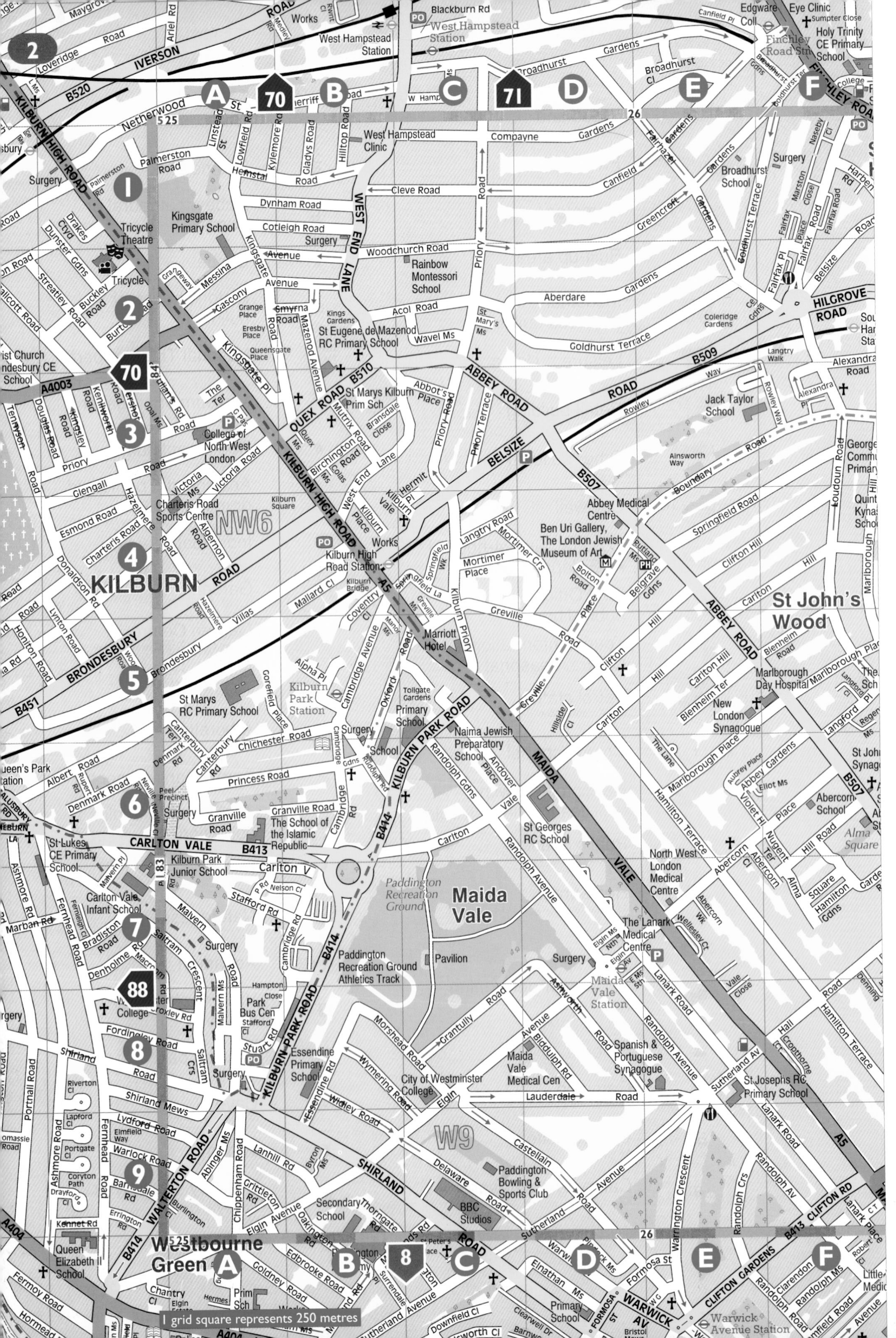

2
70
71
88
8
KILBURN
NW6
W9
St John's Wood
Maida Vale
Westbourne Green
West Hampstead Station
Kilburn High Road Station
Kilburn Park Station
Maida Vale Station
Warwick Avenue Station
Finchley Road Station
Tricycle Theatre
Paddington Recreation Ground
BBC Studios
1 grid square represents 250 metres

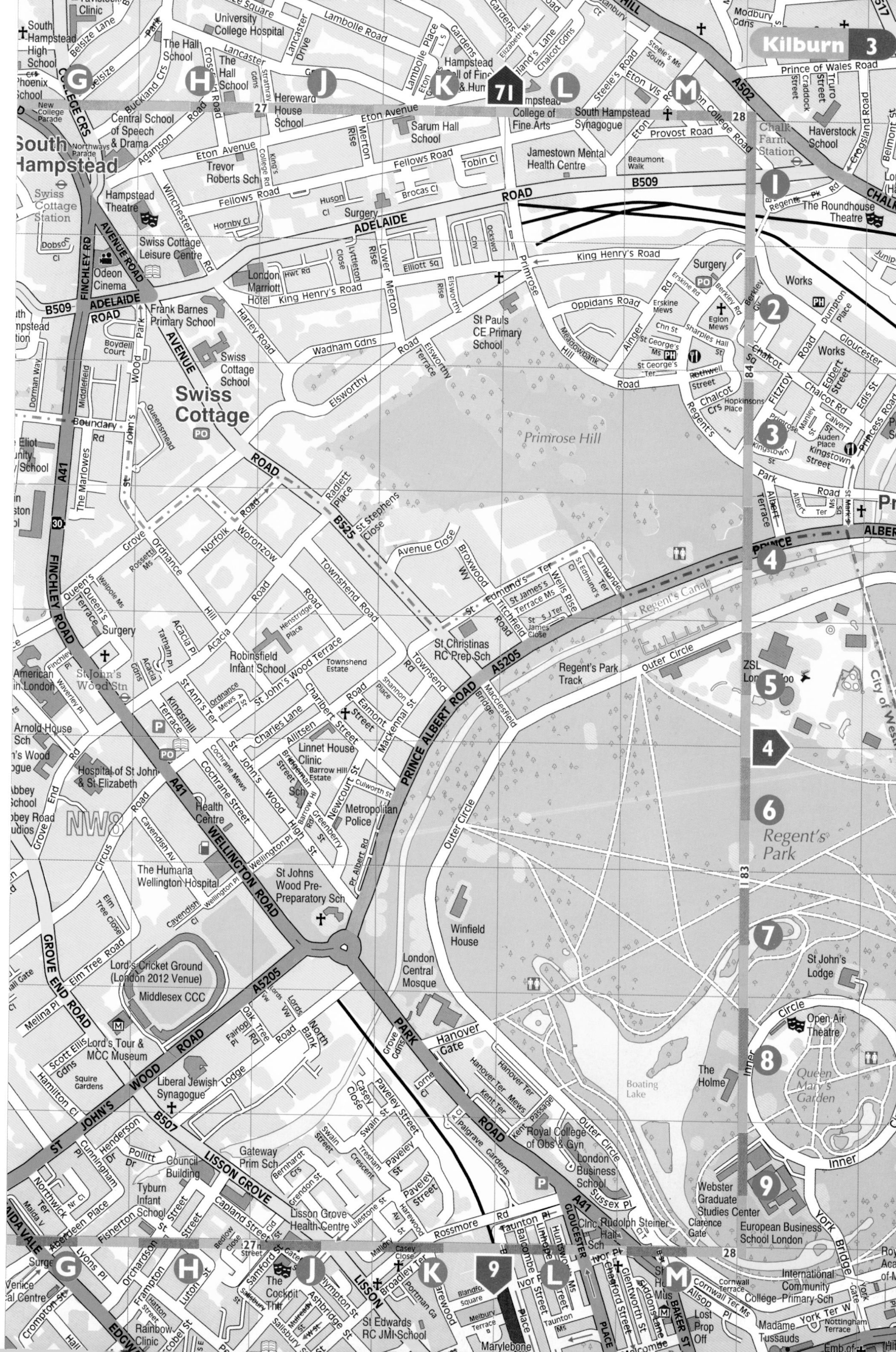
Kilburn 3
South Hampstead
Swiss Cottage Station
Swiss Cottage
Primrose Hill
Regent's Park
Chalk Farm Station
The Roundhouse Theatre
Regent's Canal
Regent's Park Track
ZSL London Zoo
Outer Circle
Inner Circle
Winfield House
London Central Mosque
Boating Lake
The Holme
St John's Lodge
Open Air Theatre
Queen Mary's Garden
Webster Graduate Studies Center
European Business School London
Clarence Gate
Hanover Gate
Royal College of Obs & Gyn
London Business School
Lord's Cricket Ground (London 2012 Venue)
Middlesex CCC
Lord's Tour & MCC Museum
Liberal Jewish Synagogue
The Humana Wellington Hospital
Hospital of St John & St Elizabeth
St Johns Wood Pre-Preparatory Sch
St John's Wood Stn
American Sch in London
Arnold House Sch
Robinsfield Infant School
St Christinas RC Prep Sch
Metropolitan Police
Linnet House Clinic
Townshend Estate
Hampstead Theatre
Swiss Cottage Leisure Centre
Odeon Cinema
Frank Barnes Primary School
Swiss Cottage School
London Marriott Hotel
St Pauls CE Primary School
University College Hospital
The Hall School
Hereward House School
Sarum Hall School
Hampstead Coll of Fine Arts & Hum
College of Fine Arts
South Hampstead Synagogue
Jamestown Mental Health Centre
Haverstock School
Trevor Roberts Sch
Central School of Speech & Drama
South Hampstead High School
Phoenix School
Gateway Prim Sch
Tyburn Infant School
Council Building
Lisson Grove Health Centre
The Cockpit Thtr
St Edwards RC JMI School
Madame Tussauds
International Community College Primary Sch
Lost Prop Off
Rudolph Steiner Hall
Marylebone
FINCHLEY ROAD
A41
WELLINGTON ROAD
PRINCE ALBERT ROAD
A5205
ST JOHN'S WOOD ROAD
LISSON GROVE
PARK ROAD
GLOUCESTER PLACE
BAKER ST
GROVE END ROAD
ADELAIDE ROAD
AVENUE ROAD
B509
B525
B507
A502
Eton Avenue
Fellows Road
King Henry's Road
Elsworthy Road
Regent's Park Road
Gloucester Avenue
Chalcot Road
Prince of Wales Road
Abbey Road
Acacia Road
Townshend Road
St John's Wood Terrace
St John's Wood High St
Circus Road
Rossmore Rd
York Bridge
NW8
G H J K L M
27 28
71
9
4
1 2 3 4 5 6 7 8 9

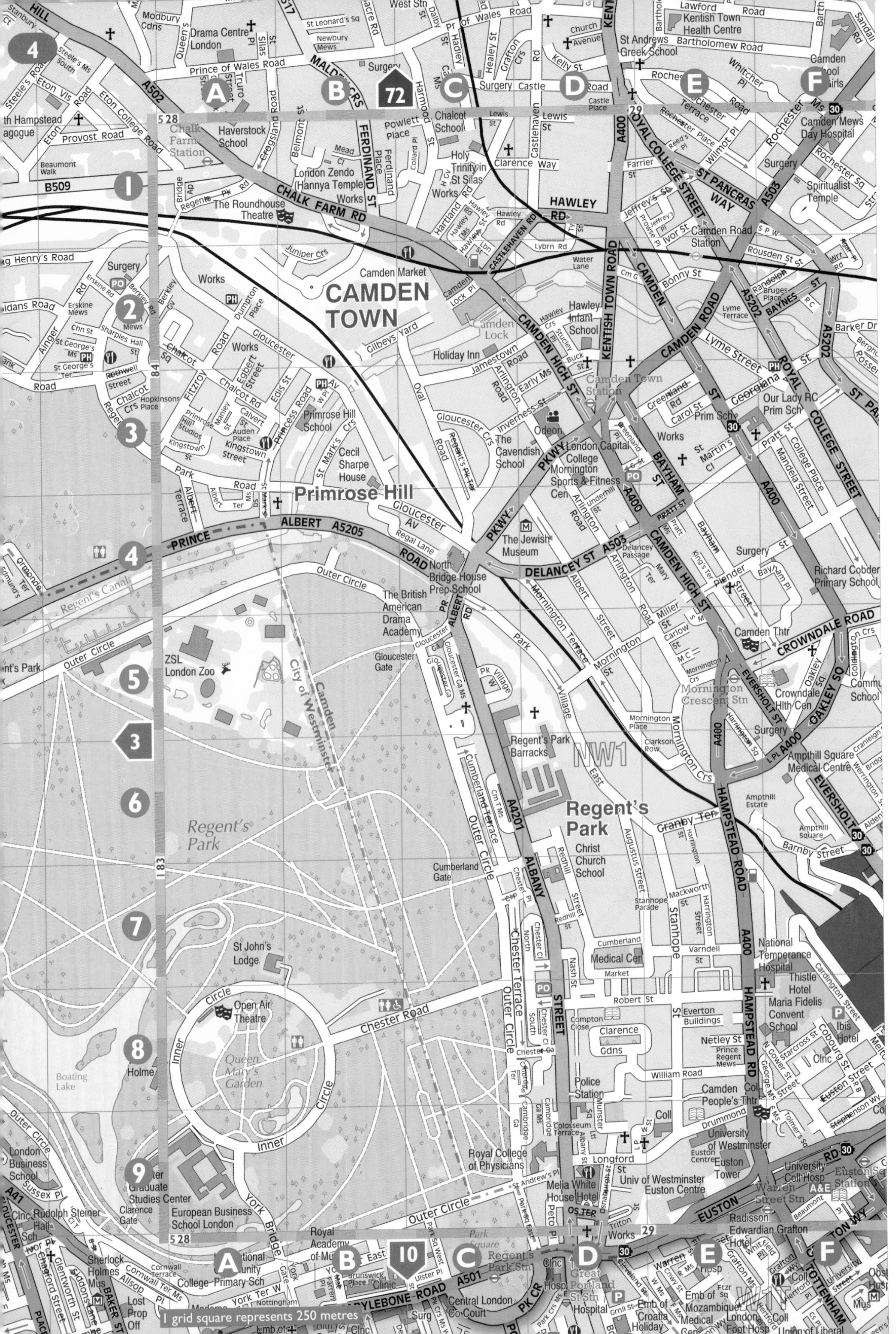
4
A
B
C
D
E
F
72
528
29
Drama Centre London
Modbury Gdns
Queen's
Prince of Wales Road
Maldenes Crs
Surgery
Harmood St
Hadley St
Healey St
Grafton Crs
Castle Road
Kelly St
Church Avenue
St Andrews Greek School
Lawford Road
Kentish Town Health Centre
Bartholomew Road
Rochester Rd
Rochester Terrace
Whitcher Pl
Camden School for Girls
Camden Mews Day Hospital
Rochester Place
Wilmot Pl
Rochester Sq
Spiritualist Temple
Steele's Road
Eton Vis
Eton College Road
A502
Hill
Provost Road
Eton Rd
Beaumont Walk
B509
Chalk Farm Station
Haverstock School
Crogsland Road
Belmont St
Ferdinand St
Ferdinand Place
Powlett Place
Chalcot School
Mead Cl
London Zendo (Hannya Temple)
Works
Holy Trinity in St Silas
Castlehaven Rd
Lewis St
Clarence Way
Farrier St
Royal College Street
St Pancras Way
A503
Hawley Rd
Hartland Rd
Jeffrey's St
Ivor St
Camden Road Station
Rousden St
Baynes St
Bruges Place
Randolph St
Regent's Pk Rd
Bridge Ap
The Roundhouse Theatre
Chalk Farm Rd
Juniper Crs
Camden Market
Camden Lock Pl
Camden Lock
Water Lane
Kentish Town Road
A400
Bonny St
Camden Road
A5202
Lyme Terrace
Lyme Street
Barker Dr
King Henry's Road
Surgery
PO
PH
Erskine Rd
Erskine Mews
Berkley Rd
Sharples Hall St
Chn St
St George's Ms
St George's Ter
Ainger Rd
Rothwell Street
Chalcot Crs
Hopkinsons Place
Regent's Park Road
Berkley Gv
Works
Dumpton Place
Chalcot Sq
Fitzroy Road
Egbert Street
Gloucester Av
Edis St
Chalcot Rd
Manley St
Calvert St
Auden Place
Primrose Hill Studios
Kingstown Street
Princess Road
Primrose Hill School
St Mark's Crs
Cecil Sharpe House
CAMDEN TOWN
Gilbeys Yard
Oval Road
Holiday Inn
Jamestown Road
Arlington Road
Early Ms
Camden High St
Hawley Infant School
Hawley Crs
Buck St
Camden Town Station
Greenland Rd
Carol St
Georgiana St
Prim Sch
Our Lady RC Prim Sch
Works
Bayham St
St Martin's Cl
Pratt St
College Place
Mandela Street
College Street
Gloucester Crs
Inverness St
Odeon
The Cavendish School
London Capital College
Mornington Sports & Fitness Cen
Regent's Pk Ter
Pkwy
Park Road
Albert Terrace
Primrose Hill
Gloucester Av
Regal Lane
Prince Albert Road
A5205
Regent's Canal
North Bridge House Prep School
The Jewish Museum
Delancey St
Delancey Passage
Mary Ter
Bayham Pl
Richard Cobden Primary School
Plender Street
Crowndale Road
Camden Thtr
Outer Circle
The British American Drama Academy
Gloucester Gate
Gloucester Ga Ms
Mornington Terrace
Albert Street
Arlington Road
Miller St
Carlow St
Mornington Crescent Stn
Eversholt St
Crowndale Hlth Cen
Oakley Sq
Goldington Crs
Comm School
ZSL London Zoo
5
3
City of Westminster
Camden
Pk Village W
Pk Village East
Mornington Pl
Clarkson Row
Mornington Crs
Surgery
Ampthill Square Medical Centre
Cranleigh St
Werrington St
6
Regent's Park Barracks
NW1
Cumberland Terrace
Cm T Ms
A4201
Albany Street
Regent's Park
Augustus Street
Granby Ter
Harrington Sq
Hampstead Road
Ampthill Estate
Ampthill Square
Barnby Street
Christ Church School
Redhill Street
Cumberland Gate
Chester Pl
Stanhope Parade
Mackworth St
Stanhope Street
Harrington Street
7
Chester Cl North
Chester Terrace
St John's Lodge
Cumberland Medical Cen
Market
Varndell St
National Temperance Hospital
Thistle Hotel
Maria Fidelis Convent School
Cardington Street
Ibis Hotel
Circle
Open Air Theatre
Chester Road
Nash St
Robert St
Everton Buildings
Netley St
Prince Regent Mews
Compton Close
Clarence Gdns
8
Holme
Boating Lake
Queen Mary's Garden
Inner Circle
Chester Ga
Cambridge Ter
William Road
Police Station
Camden People's Thtr
Drummond St
University of Westminster
Euston Street
Stephenson Wy
Starcross St
Cobourg St
N Gower St
Colosseum Terrace
Cambridge Ga
Cambridge Ga Ms
Albany St
Coll
Euston Centre
Euston Tower
9
London Business School
Sussex Pl
Graduate Studies Center
European Business School London
Clarence Gate
York Bridge
Royal College of Physicians
St Andrew's Pl
Longford St
Melia White House Hotel
Univ of Westminster Euston Centre
University Coll Hosp
Euston Station
A&E
Warren Street Stn
Euston Rd
Radisson Edwardian Grafton Hotel
Triton St
Works
Osnaburgh St
A41
Rudolph Steiner Hall
Sherlock Holmes Mus
Cornwall Ter Ms
Allsop Pl
Baker St
Glentworth St
Chagford Street
Lost Prop Off
Royal Academy of Music
National Community College Primary Sch
Park Square
Park Sq East
Park Sq West
10
Regent's Park Stn
York Ter W
York Ter East
Brunswick Place
Clinic
Ulster Pl
A501
Marylebone Road
Central London Co Court
Pk Cr
Great Portland St Stn
Hosp
Portland Hospital
Warren Ms
Grafton Ms
Whitfield Pl
Emb of Croatia
Emb of Mozambique
Holiday
Medical
London Foot Hosp
Coll
Tottenham
Beaumont Pl
1 grid square represents 250 metres

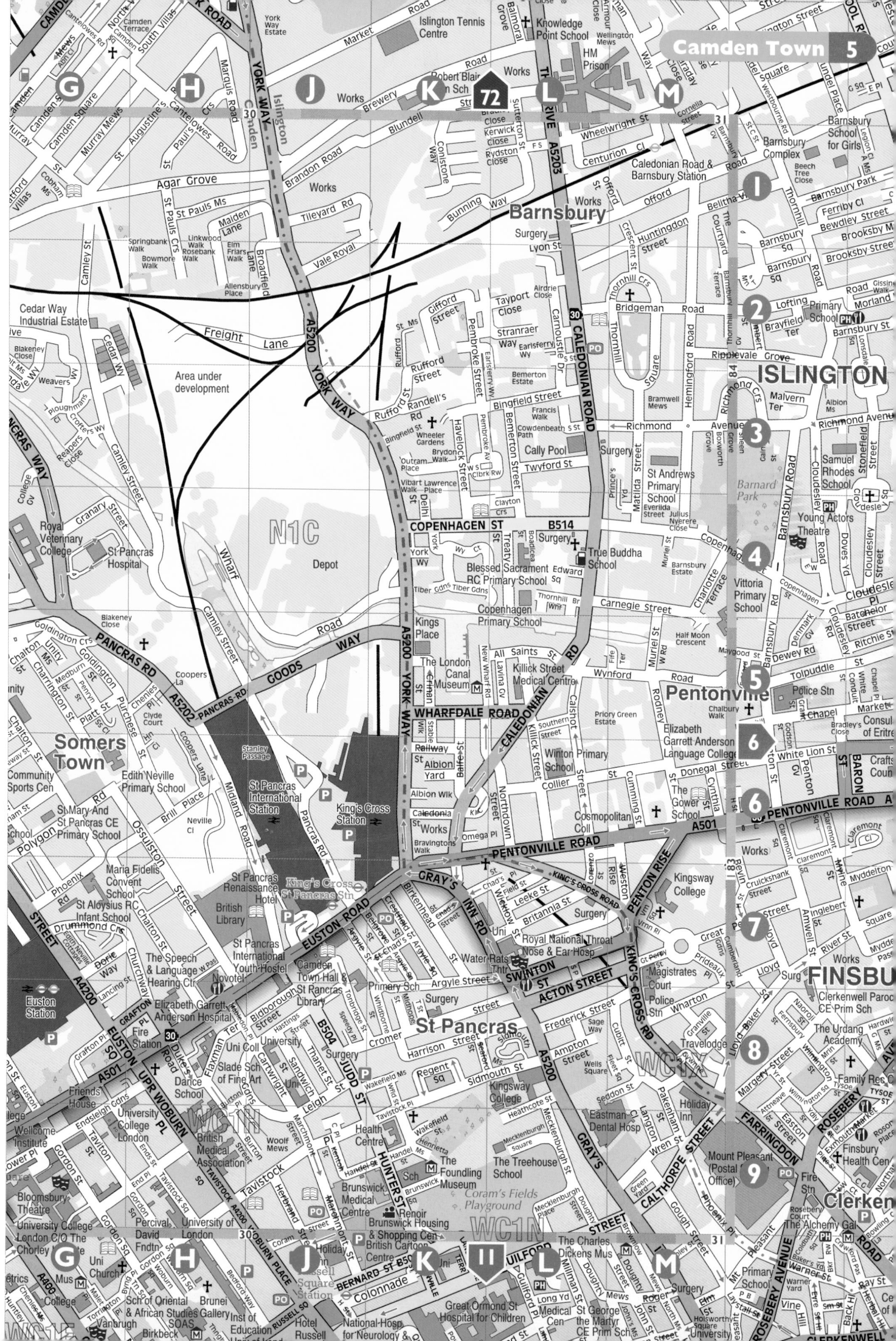
York Way Estate
Market Road
Islington Tennis Centre
Knowledge Point School
HM Prison
Robert Blair Sch
Works
72
Brewery Road
Camden Square
Murray Mews
St Augustine's Rd
St Paul's Crs
Cantelowes Road
Marquis Road
York Way
Islington
Camden
Blundell
Brandon Road
Coniston Way
Sutterton St
Kerwick Close
Rydston Close
Wheelwright St
Centurion Cl
Caledonian Road & Barnsbury Station
Agar Grove
St Pauls Ms
Maiden Lane
Tileyard Rd
Bunning Way
Barnsbury
Offord Rd
Springbank Walk
Linkwood Walk
Rosebank Walk
Elm Friars Walk
Bowmore Walk
Broadfield Lane
Vale Royal
Allensbury Place
Surgery
Lyon St
Huntingdon Street
Thornhill Crs
Bridgeman Road
Barnsbury Sq
Barnsbury Park
Ferriby Cl
Bewdley Street
Brooksby Street
Cedar Way Industrial Estate
Freight Lane
Gifford Street
Tayport Close
Stranraer Way
Pembroke Street
Carnoustie Dr
Caledonian Road
A5203
A5200
Thornhill Square
Hemingford Road
Ripplevale Grove
Lofting Road
Brayfield Ter
Primary School
Barnsbury St
ISLINGTON
Area under development
Rufford Street
Randell's Rd
Bingfield Street
Bemerton Estate
Francis Walk
Cowdenbeath Path
Richmond Avenue
Richmond Crs
Malvern Ter
Wheeler Gardens
Brydon Walk
Havelock Street
Bemerton Street
Cally Pool
Twyford St
Surgery
Matilda Street
St Andrews Primary School
Samuel Rhodes School
Barnard Park
Cloudesley Rd
Stonefield Street
Outram Place
Vibart Walk
Lawrence Place
Delhi St
Clayton Crs
Everilda Street
Julius Nyerere Close
Barnsbury Road
Young Actors Theatre
N1C
Depot
Royal Veterinary College
Granary Street
St Pancras Hospital
Camley Street
COPENHAGEN ST
B514
York Wy
Treaty St
Surgery
True Buddha School
Blessed Sacrament RC Primary School
Edward Sq
Copenhagen Street
Barnsbury Estate
Vittoria Primary School
Doves Yd
Wharf
Tiber Gdns
Thornhill Br Wlf
Carnegie Street
Charlotte Terrace
Copenhagen Primary School
Blakeney Close
Kings Place
Half Moon Crescent
Muriel St
Dewey Rd
Goldington Crs
PANCRAS RD
Goods Way
The London Canal Museum
All Saints St
New Wharf Rd
Killick Street Medical Centre
Wynford Road
Tolpuddle St
Police Stn
Pentonville
Chalbury Walk
Elizabeth Garrett Anderson Language College
Coopers La
A5202
Crinan St
Wharfdale Road
Priory Green Estate
Somers Town
Community Sports Cen
Edith Neville Primary School
Stanley Passage
St Pancras International Station
King's Cross Station
Railway St
Albion Yard
Albion Wlk
Winton Primary School
Collier St
Donegal Street
White Lion St
Penton St
Cynthia St
The Gower School
St Mary And St Pancras CE Primary School
Brill Place
Midland Road
Pancras Rd
Cosmopolitan Coll
Pentonville Road
A501
Polygon Rd
Ossulston Street
Neville Cl
Caledonia St
Works
Omega Pl
Northdown Street
Bravingtons Walk
Maria Fidelis Convent School
St Pancras Renaissance Hotel
King's Cross St Pancras Stn
Gray's Inn Rd
Birkenhead Street
Leeke St
Britannia St
King's Cross Road
Penton Rise
Kingsway College
Cruickshank Street
Myddelton Square
St Aloysius RC Infant School
British Library
Euston Road
Crestfield St
Argyle St
St Chad's St
Surgery
Royal National Throat Nose & Ear Hosp
Wicklow St
Great Percy St
Amwell St
River St
Drummond Cres
Chalton St
Churchway
The Speech & Language Hearing Ctr
St Pancras International Youth Hostel
Camden Town Hall & St Pancras Library
Water Rats Thtr
Swinton St
Acton Street
Magistrates Ct
Police Stn
Wharton St
Lloyd Sq
FINSBURY
Clerkenwell Parochial CE Prim Sch
Euston Station
A4200
Novotel
Elizabeth Garrett Anderson Hospital
Primary Sch
Argyle Street
Surgery
St Pancras
Frederick Street
Fire Station
Grafton Pl
Euston Sq
Uni Coll
University
Bidborough Street
B504
Judd St
Harrison Street
Regent Sq
Sidmouth St
Ampton Street
Wells Square
Travelodge
Lloyd Baker St
The Urdang Academy
Margery Street
Upr Woburn Pl
Dukes Road
Flaxman Ter
Slade Sch of Fine Art
Cartwright Gdns
Leigh St
Wakefield Ms
Kingsway College
Heathcote St
Seddon St
Holiday Inn
Family Rec Ctr
Friends House
Wellcome Institute
Endsleigh Gdns
University College London
Dance School
WC1H
Tavistock Pl
Health Centre
Henrietta Mews
Eastman Dental Hosp
Langton Cl
Wren St
Calthorpe Street
Farringdon Road
Rosebery Av
Finsbury Health Cen
British Medical Association
Burton Street
Woolf Mews
Marchmont Street
Hunter St
Handel St
The Foundling Museum
The Treehouse School
Mecklenburgh Square
Mount Pleasant (Postal Office)
Fire Stn
Clerkenwell
Gordon St
Bloomsbury Theatre
Tavistock Square
Brunswick Medical Centre
Renoir
Brunswick Housing & Shopping Cen
Coram's Fields Playground
WC1N
Phoenix Pl
University College London C/O The Chorley
Percival David Fndtn
University of London
Woburn Place
Herbrand Street
British Cartoon Centre
Holiday Inn
Russell Square Station
Bernard St
Colonnade
Guilford St
Great Ormond St Hospital for Children
The Charles Dickens Mus
Doughty Street
Mews
Rugby St
Long Yd
Medical Cen
St George the Martyr CE Prim Sch
Millman St
Roger St
Surgery
Gough Street
Elm St
Holsworthy Square
Mt Pleasant
Primary School
Warner St
Rosebery Avenue
The Alchemy Gal
Vine Hill
Ray St
Clerkenwell
Mus
Uni Church
Brunei Gallery
Sch of Oriental & African Studies SOAS
Inst of Education
Birkbeck
Vanbrugh
College
Hotel Russell
National Hosp for Neurology
Malet St
Torrington Pl
Russell Sq
Bedford Way
G
H
J
K
L
M
I
2
3
4
5
6
7
8
9
30
31
83
84
II

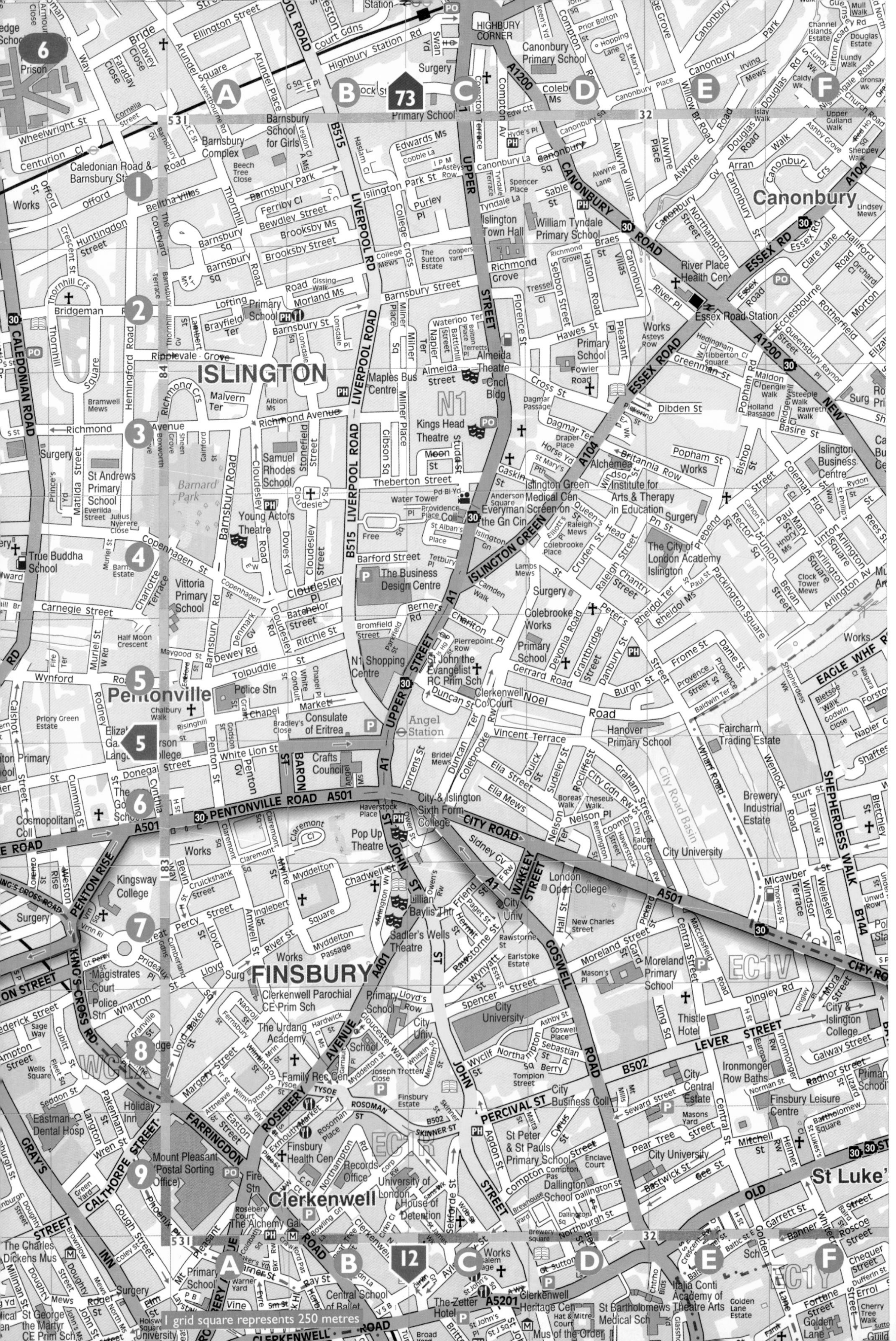

6
73
12
5
A
B
C
D
E
F
1
2
3
4
5
6
7
8
9
531
32
84
83
Prison
Ellington Street
Highbury Station Rd
Court Gdns
Arundel Square
Arundel Place
HIGHBURY CORNER
Canonbury Primary School
Surgery
Primary School
Wheelwright St
Centurion Cl
Caledonian Road & Barnsbury Stn
Offord Rd
Works
Barnsbury School for Girls
Barnsbury Complex
Beech Tree Close
Barnsbury Park
Islington Park St
Edwards Ms
Purley Pl
Canonbury La
Canonbury Sq
Sable St
Islington Town Hall
William Tyndale Primary School
CANONBURY ROAD
Canonbury
ESSEX RD
River Place Health Cen
Essex Road Station
Huntingdon Street
Thornhill Crs
Bridgeman Rd
Barnsbury Sq
Bewdley Street
Brooksby Ms
Brooksby Street
College Cross
Richmond Grove
Barnsbury Street
Primary School
Morland Ms
LIVERPOOL ROAD
UPPER STREET
Florence St
Almeida Theatre
Almeida Street
Cncl Bldg
Hawes St
Primary School
Fowler Road
Cross St
Greenman St
Dibden St
CALEDONIAN ROAD
Thornhill Square
Hemingford Road
Ripplevale Grove
ISLINGTON
Maples Bus Centre
N1
Kings Head Theatre
Moon St
Malvern Ter
Richmond Avenue
Richmond Crs
Bramwell Mews
Richmond Avenue
Barnard Park
Barnsbury Road
Samuel Rhodes School
Stonefield Street
Gibson Sq
Theberton Street
Water Tower Pl
Everyman Screen on the Gn Cin
Islington Green Medical Cen
Institute for Arts & Therapy in Education
Surgery
Alchemea
Britannia Row
Popham St
Works
Islington Business Centre
Surgery
Matilda Street
St Andrews Primary School
Everilda Street
Julius Nyerere Close
Young Actors Theatre
Cloudesley Square
Free
True Buddha School
Copenhagen St
Charlotte Terrace
Vittoria Primary School
Barford Street
The Business Design Centre
ISLINGTON GREEN
The City of London Academy Islington
Packington Square
Clock Tower Mews
Carnegie Street
Half Moon Crescent
Cloudesley Pl
Batchelor Street
Ritchie St
Dewey Rd
Bromfield Street
Parkfield St
Charlton Pl
Camden Walk
Surgery
Colebrooke Works
Primary School
Gerrard Road
Devonia Road
Grantbridge Street
Danbury St
Frome St
Dame St
Provence Street
Works
EAGLE WHF RD
Wynford Road
Pentonville
Police Stn
Tolpuddle Street
Chapel Market
N1 Shopping Centre
St John the Evangelist RC Prim Sch
Clerkenwell Co Court
Duncan St
Noel Road
Burgh St
Hanover Primary School
Faircharm Trading Estate
Priory Green Estate
Chalbury Walk
Rising Hill St
Consulate of Eritrea
Angel Station
Vincent Terrace
Wharf Road
City Road Basin
Shepherdess Wk
Wenlock Road
Brewery Industrial Estate
White Lion St
Crafts Council
Angel Ms
Torrens St
Bridel Mews
Colebrooke Row
Elia Street
Elia Mews
Quick St
Sudeley St
Rocliffe St
City Gdn Rw
Graham Street
Donegal Street
Cumming St
Cosmopolitan Coll
PENTONVILLE ROAD
A501
Haverstock Place
City & Islington Sixth Form College
CITY ROAD
Sidney Gv
Nelson Pl
City University
Claremont Sq
Pop Up Theatre
Myddelton Square
Chadwell St
Lilian Baylis Thr
Sadler's Wells Theatre
WAKLEY STREET
London Open College
City Univ
Micawber St
SHEPHERDESS WALK
Kingsway College
PENTON RISE
KING'S CROSS ROAD
Surgery
Percy Street
Lloyd St
Amwell St
Inglebert St
River St
Works
Myddelton Passage
Rawstorne St
Earlstoke Estate
GOSWELL ROAD
New Charles Street
Moreland Street
Moreland Primary School
Mason's Pl
Windsor Terrace
EC1V
Magistrates Court
Police Stn
FINSBURY
Clerkenwell Parochial CE Prim Sch
Primary School
Lloyd's Row
Spencer Street
City University
Dingley Rd
City & Islington College
The Urdang Academy
City Univ
School
Gloucester Way
Sebastian St
Wyclif St
Northampton Sq
Berry St
Thistle Hotel
LEVER STREET
Ironmonger Row Baths
Galway Street
Radnor Street
WC1X
Margery Street
Family Rec Cen
ROSEBERY AVENUE
Joseph Trotter Close
Finsbury Estate
TYSOE ST
ROSOMAN ST
SKINNER ST
PERCIVAL ST
City Business Coll
Seward Street
Central Street
City Central Estate
Masons Yard
Finsbury Leisure Centre
Seddon St
Eastman Dental Hosp
Holiday Inn
Pakenham St
Langton Cl
Wren St
CALTHORPE STREET
FARRINGDON ROAD
Exmouth Market
Finsbury Health Cen
Rosoman Place
Northampton Rd
Records Office
EC1R
St Peter & St Pauls Primary School
Compton St
Enclave Court
Pear Tree Street
City University
Bastwick St
Gee St
Mitchell St
Helmet Row
OLD STREET
St Luke's
GRAY'S INN ROAD
Mount Pleasant (Postal Sorting Office)
Fire Stn
Clerkenwell
University of London
House of Detention
Sekforde St
Dallington School
Dallington St
Northburgh St
Brewery Square
Golden Lane Estate
Garrett St
Banner St
Roscoe Street
Chequer Street
The Charles Dickens Mus
Doughty Street
Surgery
Primary School
The Alchemy Gal
Central School of Ballet
Works
Clerkenwell Heritage Cen
The Zetter Hotel
St Bartholomews Medical Sch
Italia Conti Academy of Theatre Arts
EC1Y
St George the Martyr CE Prim Sch
Mus of the Order
Golden Lane
1 grid square represents 250 metres

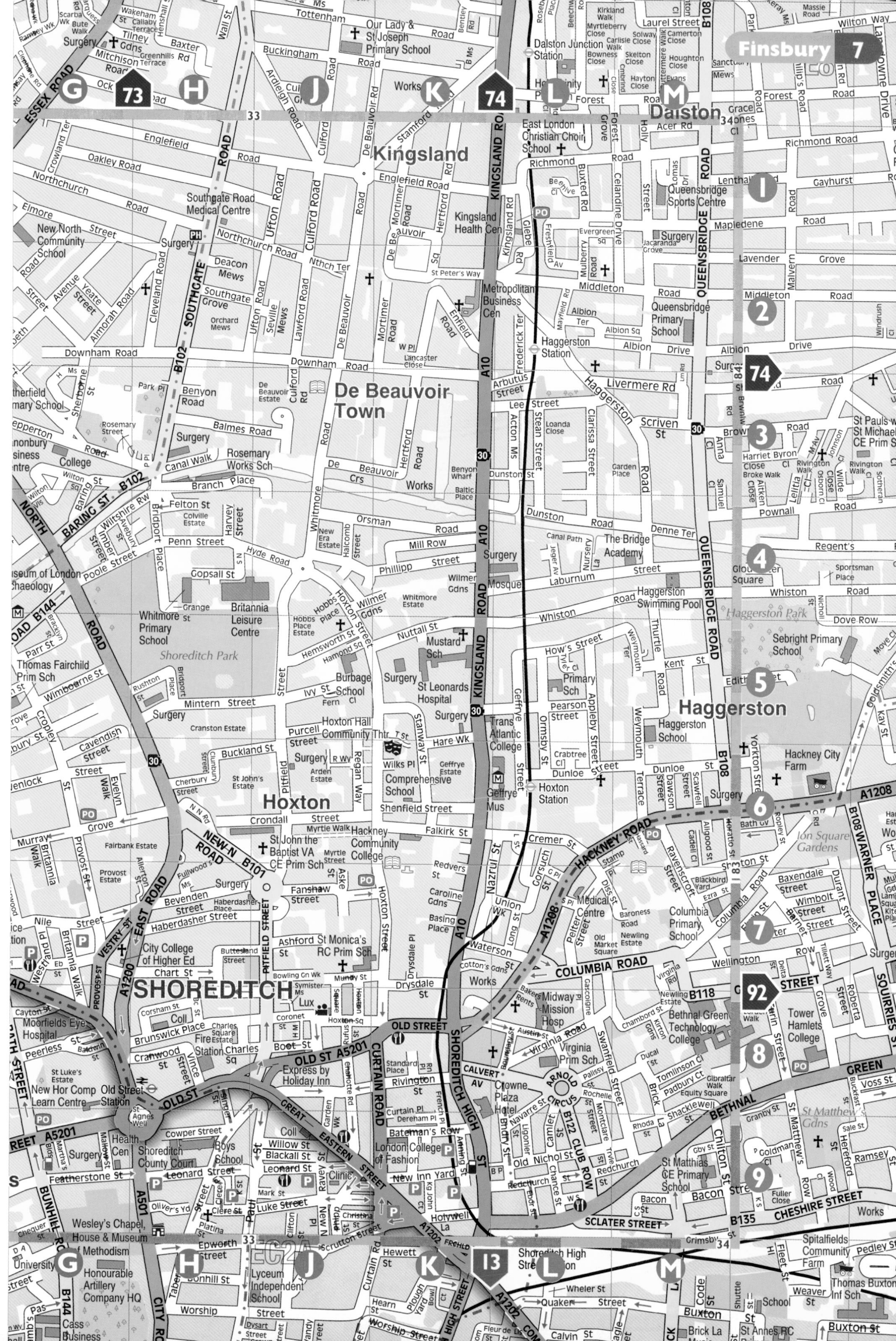
Kingsland
De Beauvoir Town
Dalston
Haggerston
Hoxton
SHOREDITCH
EC2A
73
74
92
13
G
H
J
K
L
M
1
2
3
4
5
6
7
8
9
33
34
ESSEX ROAD
SOUTHGATE ROAD
KINGSLAND ROAD
QUEENSBRIDGE ROAD
NEW NORTH ROAD
EAST ROAD
CITY ROAD
OLD STREET
HACKNEY ROAD
COLUMBIA ROAD
SHOREDITCH HIGH STREET
CURTAIN ROAD
GREAT EASTERN STREET
BETHNAL GREEN
CHESHIRE STREET
SCLATER STREET
WARNER PLACE
SQUIRRIES ST
PITFIELD STREET
BUNHILL ROW
Tottenham Road
Buckingham Road
Englefield Road
Oakley Road
Northchurch Road
Downham Road
Balmes Road
Richmond Road
Middleton Road
Albion Drive
Livermere Rd
Dunston Road
Orsman Road
Whiston Road
Laburnum Street
Regent's Row
Mintern Street
Crondall Street
Falkirk St
Haberdasher Street
Nile Street
Shenfield Street
Dalston Junction Station
Haggerston Station
Hoxton Station
Old Street Station
Shoreditch High Street Station
Queensbridge Sports Centre
Queensbridge Primary School
Britannia Leisure Centre
Whitmore Primary School
Shoreditch Park
Haggerston Park
Haggerston Swimming Pool
Haggerston School
Sebright Primary School
Hackney City Farm
Geffrye Mus
Trans Atlantic College
St Leonards Hospital
Hackney Community College
Bethnal Green Technology College
Tower Hamlets College
Moorfields Eye Hospital
Wesley's Chapel, House & Museum of Methodism
Honourable Artillery Company HQ
London College of Fashion
Crowne Plaza Hotel
Spitalfields Community Farm
St Matthew's Gdns
Ion Square Gardens
Museum of London Archaeology
Kingsland Health Cen
Metropolitan Business Cen
The Bridge Academy
Express by Holiday Inn
Shoreditch County Court
City College of Higher Ed
Lyceum Independent School
Midway Mission Hosp

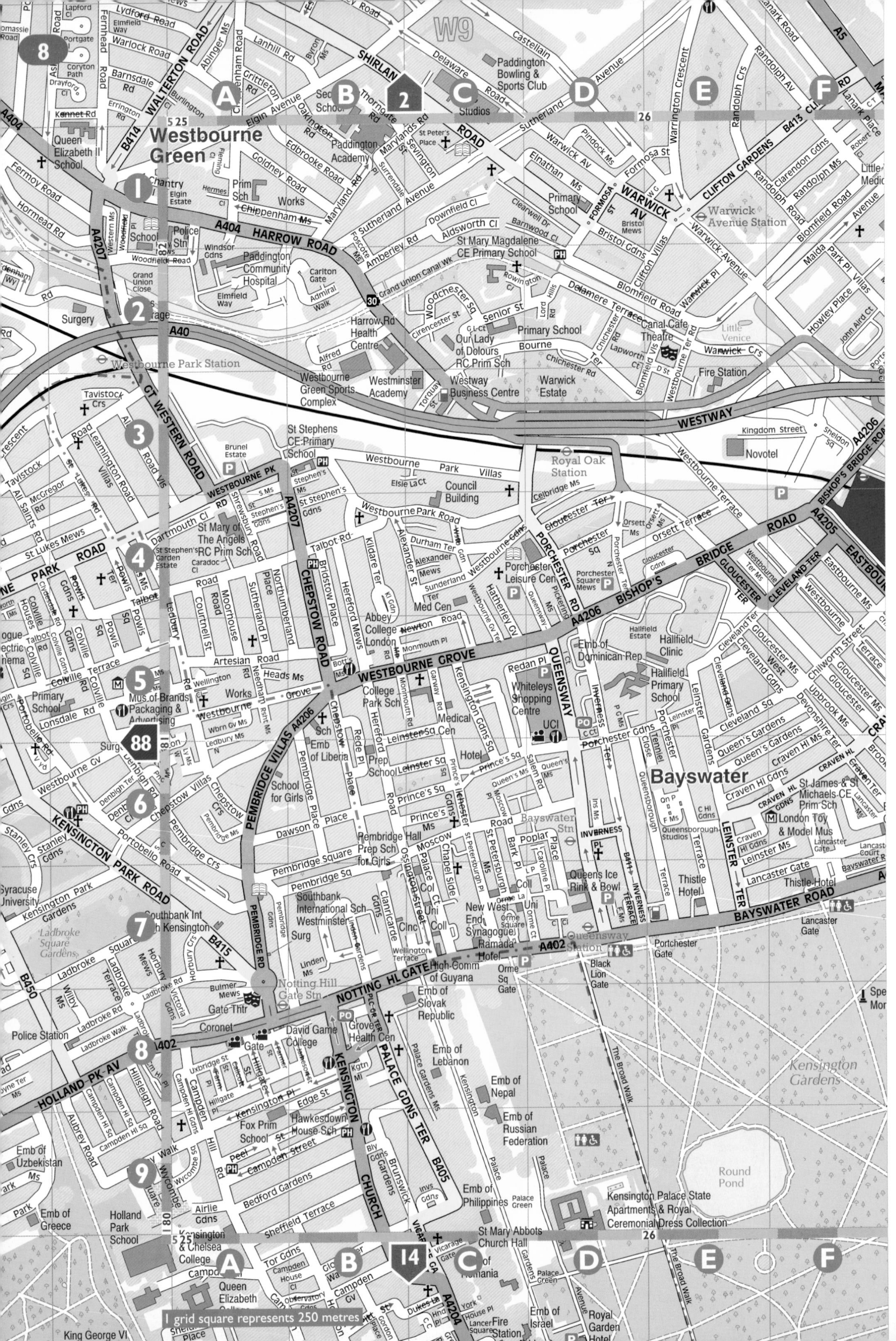
W9
8
2
A
B
C
D
E
F
525
26
Westbourne Green
Bayswater
Kensington Gardens
Round Pond
Ladbroke Square Gardens
Little Venice
Lydford Road
Elmfield Way
Warlock Road
Barnsdale Rd
Walterton Road
Fernhead Road
Shirland Road
Elgin Avenue
Delaware Road
Castellain Road
Sutherland Avenue
Warrington Crescent
Randolph Avenue
Clifton Gardens
Lanark Road
Paddington Bowling & Sports Club
Paddington Academy
Queen Elizabeth II School
Harrow Road
A404
B414
A4207
Chippenham Ms
Goldney Road
Edbrooke Road
Maryland Rd
Warwick Avenue
Warwick Avenue Station
Formosa St
Bristol Gdns
Clifton Villas
Blomfield Road
Maida Avenue
St Mary Magdalene CE Primary School
Paddington Community Hospital
Grand Union Canal Wk
Woodchester Sq
Senior St
Delamere Terrace
Canal Cafe Theatre
Warwick Crs
Fire Station
Harrow Rd Health Centre
Westminster Academy
Westbourne Green Sports Complex
Our Lady of Dolours RC Prim Sch
Westway Business Centre
Warwick Estate
Westbourne Park Station
A40
Westway
Kingdom Street
Novotel
Royal Oak Station
Westbourne Terrace
Bishop's Bridge Road
A4206
A4205
Eastbourne Ter
Gt Western Road
Westbourne Pk
St Stephens CE Primary School
Westbourne Park Villas
Council Building
Westbourne Park Road
Gloucester Ter
Orsett Terrace
Porchester Rd
Porchester Leisure Cen
Porchester Sq
Chepstow Road
Talbot Rd
All Saints Rd
St Lukes Mews
Leamington Road Villas
Tavistock Crs
Powis Sq
Colville Terrace
Artesian Road
Westbourne Grove
Queensway
Whiteleys Shopping Centre
UCI
Emb of Dominican Rep
Hallfield Clinic
Hallfield Primary School
Cleveland Gdns
Leinster Gardens
Queensborough Terrace
Inverness Terrace
Porchester Gdns
Mus of Brands Packaging & Advertising
88
Pembridge Villas
Pembridge Square
Pembridge Crs
Kensington Park Road
Ledbury Road
Chepstow Villas
Portobello Road
Westbourne Gv
Lonsdale Rd
Kensington Gdns Sq
Leinster Sq
Prince's Sq
Moscow Road
Bayswater Stn
Queens Ice Rink & Bowl
Thistle Hotel
Bayswater Road
Lancaster Gate
Leinster Ter
Craven Hl Gdns
London Toy & Model Mus
Emb of Liberia
School for Girls
Pembridge Hall Prep Sch for Girls
Southbank International Sch Westminster
New West End Synagogue
Ramada Hotel
Queensway Station
Black Lion Gate
Orme Sq Gate
Porchester Gate
High Comm of Guyana
Notting Hill Gate Stn
Notting Hl Gate
A402
Gate Thtr
Coronet
David Game College
Emb of Slovak Republic
Grove Health Cen
Emb of Lebanon
Emb of Nepal
Emb of Russian Federation
Kensington Church St
Palace Gdns Ter
B405
Ladbroke Square
Ladbroke Terrace
Ladbroke Rd
Ladbroke Walk
Police Station
Holland Pk Av
Campden Hill
Hillsleigh Road
Aubrey Road
Kensington Pl
Edge St
Fox Prim School
Hawkesdown House Sch
Campden Street
Peel St
Bedford Gardens
Sheffield Terrace
Brunswick Gardens
Emb of Uzbekistan
Emb of Greece
Holland Park School
Kensington & Chelsea College
Queen Elizabeth College
Emb of Philippines
St Mary Abbots Church Hall
Kensington Palace State Apartments & Royal Ceremonial Dress Collection
The Broad Walk
Emb of Romania
Emb of Israel
Royal Garden Hotel
Fire Station
A4204
14
King George VI
1 grid square represents 250 metres

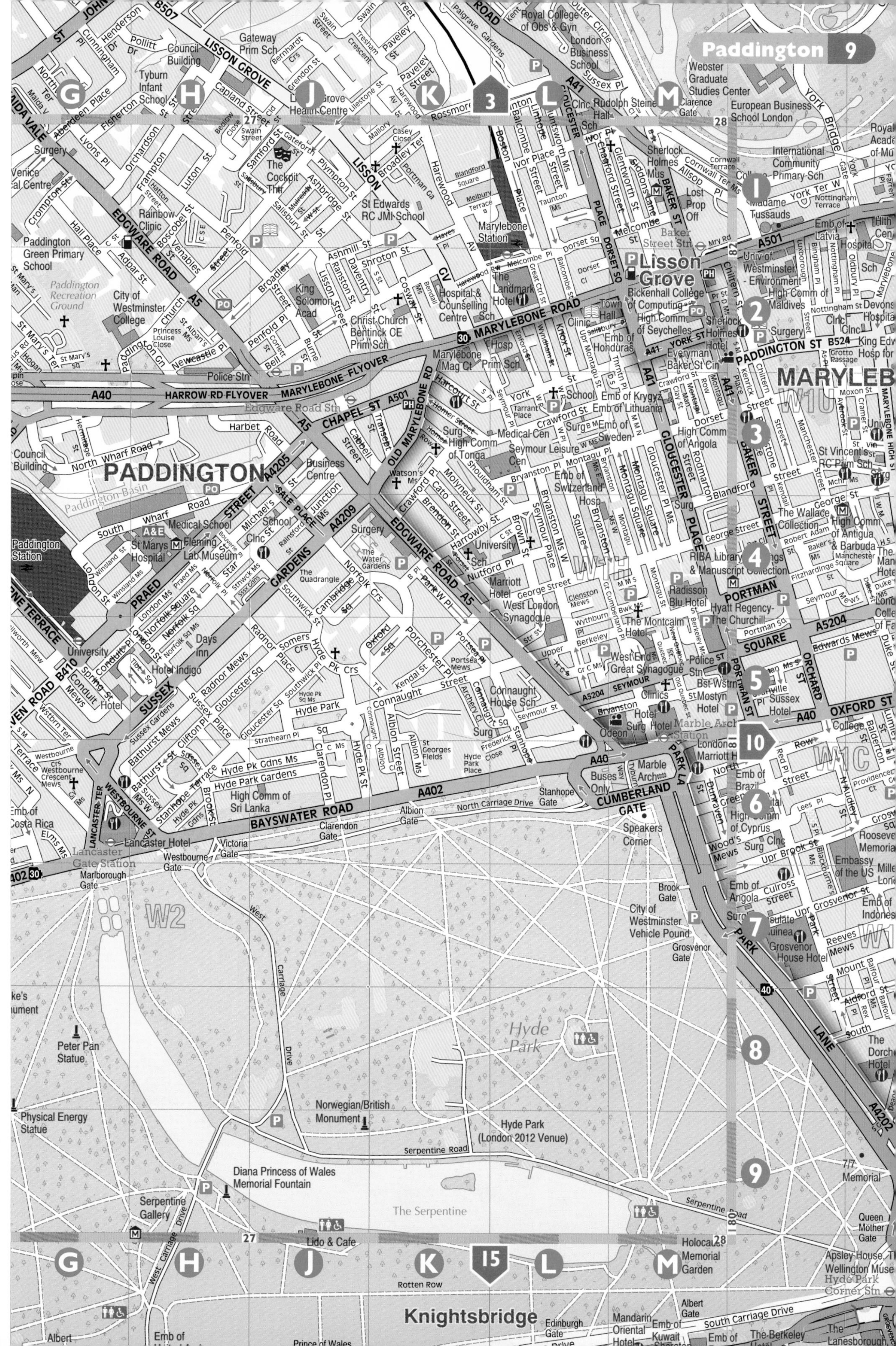
PADDINGTON
Lisson Grove
MARYLEB
Knightsbridge
Hyde Park
The Serpentine
W2
W1H
W1U
W1C
Paddington Station
Marylebone Station
Edgware Road Stn
Lancaster Gate Station
Marble Arch Station
Baker Street Stn
EDGWARE ROAD A5
MARYLEBONE ROAD
MARYLEBONE FLYOVER
HARROW RD FLYOVER
A40
BAYSWATER ROAD A402
PRAED STREET
SUSSEX GARDENS
CHAPEL ST A501
OLD MARYLEBONE RD
LISSON GROVE
GLOUCESTER PLACE
BAKER STREET
PORTMAN SQUARE
OXFORD ST
PARK LANE
CUMBERLAND GATE
SEYMOUR
Speakers Corner
Marble Arch
Peter Pan Statue
Physical Energy Statue
Norwegian/British Monument
Hyde Park (London 2012 Venue)
Diana Princess of Wales Memorial Fountain
Serpentine Gallery
Lido & Cafe
Serpentine Road
Rotten Row
South Carriage Drive
North Carriage Drive
West Carriage Drive
Holocaust Memorial Garden
7/7 Memorial
Madame Tussauds
Sherlock Holmes Mus
The Wallace Collection
St Marys Hospital
Paddington Green Primary School
Paddington Recreation Ground
City of Westminster College
Paddington Basin
The Cockpit Thtr
The Landmark Hotel
Marriott Hotel
West London Synagogue
The Montcalm Hotel
Hyatt Regency-The Churchill
Radisson Blu Hotel
Grosvenor House Hotel
Embassy of the US
Odeon
Lancaster Hotel
Hotel Indigo
Days Inn
City of Westminster Vehicle Pound
Paddington 9
G
H
J
K
L
M
27
28
3
10
15
1
2
3
4
5
6
7
8
9

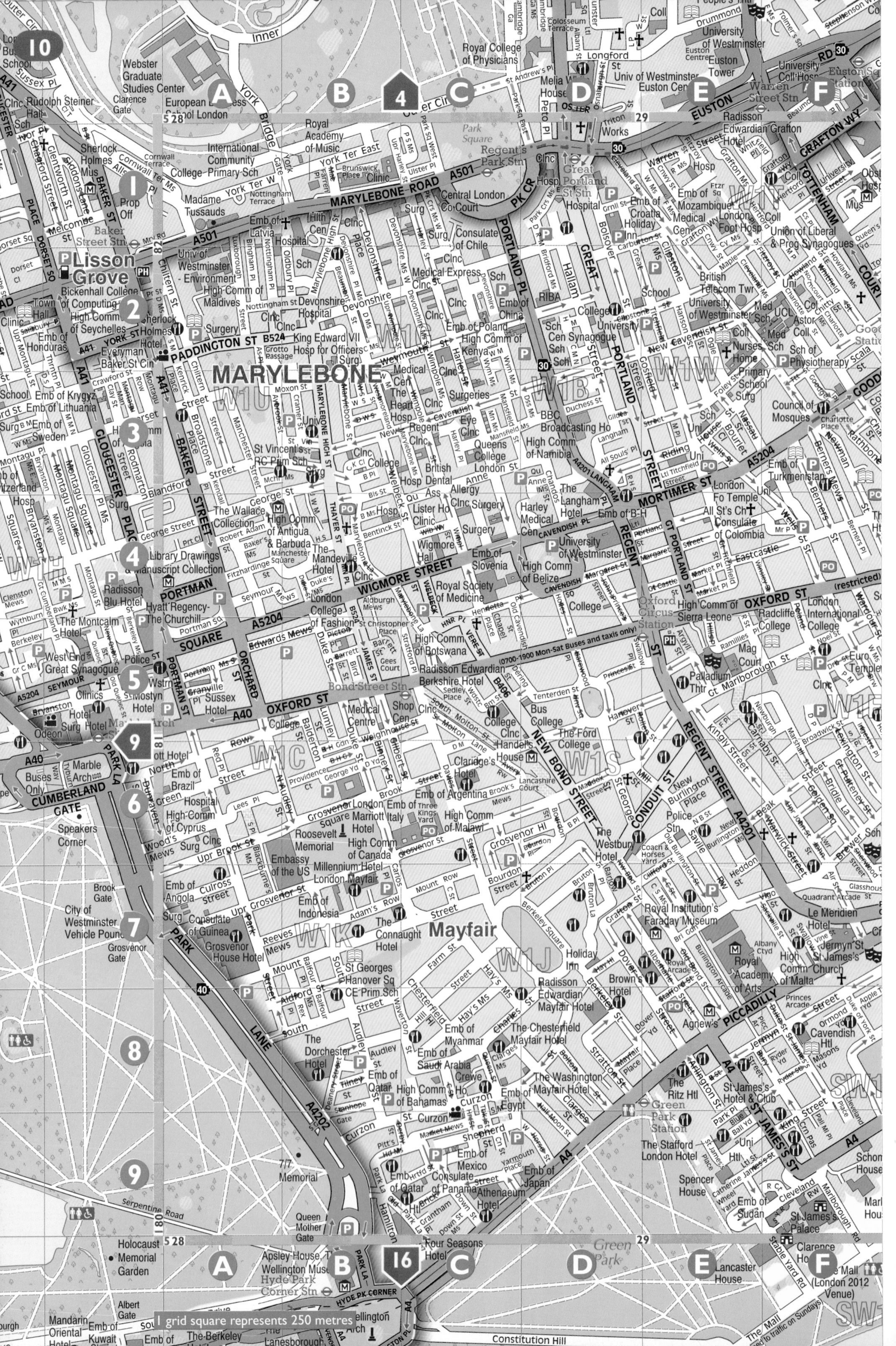

10
A
B
4
C
D
E
F
528
29
Webster Graduate Studies Center
European Business School London
Clarence Gate
York Bridge
Inner Circle
Outer Circle
Royal Academy of Music
Royal College of Physicians
Park Square
Regent's Park Stn
Univ of Westminster Euston Cen
University of Westminster
Euston Tower
Euston Centre
EUSTON RD
Warren Street Stn
Radisson Edwardian Grafton Hotel
GRAFTON WY
TOTTENHAM COURT RD
Rudolph Steiner Hall
Sherlock Holmes Mus
Baker Street Stn
BAKER ST
International Community College
Primary Sch
York Ter East
York Ter W
Madame Tussauds
MARYLEBONE ROAD
A501
Central London Co Court
PK CR
Great Portland St Stn
Hosp
Emb of Latvia
Univ of Westminster - Environment
Lisson Grove
Bickenhall College
Town of Computing Hall
High Comm of Seychelles
Emb of Honduras
YORK ST
PADDINGTON ST
B524
King Edward VII Hosp for Officers
MARYLEBONE
W1U
W1G
W1B
W1W
W1T
W1H
High Comm of Maldives
Devonshire Hospital
Medical Express Clnc
Consulate of Chile
Emb of China
Emb of Poland
High Comm of Kenya
RIBA
Cen Synagogue
PORTLAND PL
GREAT PORTLAND STREET
University of Westminster
British Telecom Twr
UCL
Med Sch
Nurses Home
Primary School
Council of Mosques
Sch of Physiotherapy
Emb of Kyrgyz
Emb of Lithuania
Emb of Sweden
GLOUCESTER PLACE
MARYLEBONE HIGH ST
St Vincent's RC Prim Sch
The Heart Hosp
Medical Cen
British Dental Ass
Queens College London
BBC Broadcasting Ho
High Comm of Namibia
The Langham Hotel
LANGHAM PL
Emb of B-H
MORTIMER ST
A5204
London Fo Temple
Emb of Turkmenistan
All St's Ch
Consulate of Colombia
The Wallace Collection
High Comm of Antigua & Barbuda
The Mandeville Hotel
Lister Ho Clinic
Wigmore Hall
Emb of Slovenia
WIGMORE STREET
Harley Medical Cen
CAVENDISH PL
High Comm of Belize
University of Westminster
REGENT ST
GT PORTLAND ST
Library Drawings & Manuscript Collection
Radisson Blu Hotel
Hyatt Regency-The Churchill
PORTMAN SQUARE
Royal Society of Medicine
London College of Fashion
Oxford Circus Station
OXFORD ST
High Comm of Sierra Leone
Radcliffe College
London International College
The Montcalm Hotel
West End Great Synagogue
Police Stn
Portman Sq
ORCHARD ST
High Comm of Botswana
Radisson Edwardian Berkshire Hotel
Bond Street Stn
Palladium Thr
Mag Court
Gt Marlborough St
SEYMOUR
A5204
Clinics
Wstmn Mostyn Hotel
Sussex Hotel
A40
Bryanston Hotel
Odeon
Marble Arch
9
Medical Centre
Shop Cen
College
Clnc Handel's House
NEW BOND STREET
Bus College
The Ford College
W1S
W1F
REGENT STREET
A4201
CONDUIT ST
New Burlington Place
Carnaby St
Kingly Street
Buses Only
CUMBERLAND GATE
PARK LA
Emb of Brazil
High Comm of Cyprus
Hospital
Claridge's Hotel
Emb of Argentina
W1C
Speakers Corner
Roosevelt Memorial
Embassy of the US
London Marriott Hotel
Emb of Italy
High Comm of Canada
High Comm of Malawi
Millennium Hotel London Mayfair
Grosvenor Sq
Grosvenor Hl
The Westbury Hotel
Police Stn
Royal Institution's Faraday Museum
Brook Gate
City of Westminster Vehicle Pound
Grosvenor Gate
Emb of Angola
Consulate of Guinea
Grosvenor House Hotel
Emb of Indonesia
The Connaught Hotel
Mayfair
W1K
W1J
Berkeley Square
Holiday Inn
Brown's Hotel
Royal Academy of Arts
Le Meridien Hotel
High Comm of Malta
St James's Church
8
PARK LANE
A4202
St Georges Hanover Sq CE Prim Sch
Radisson Edwardian Mayfair Hotel
The Chesterfield Mayfair Hotel
Emb of Myanmar
Emb of Saudi Arabia
The Dorchester Hotel
Emb of Qatar
High Comm of Bahamas
Emb of Egypt
Curzon
Curzon St
The Washington Mayfair Hotel
Agnew's
PICCADILLY
The Ritz Htl
Green Park Station
St James's Hotel & Club
Cavendish Htl
The Stafford London Hotel
A4
ST JAMES'S ST
Emb of Mexico
Consulate of Panama
Emb of Japan
Athenaeum Hotel
Emb of Qatar
Spencer House
Emb of Sudan
St James's Palace
9
Serpentine Road
7/7 Memorial
Queen Mother Gate
Holocaust Memorial Garden
Apsley House, Wellington Museum
Hyde Park Corner Stn
HYDE PK CORNER
16
Four Seasons Hotel
Green Park
Lancaster House
Clarence House
The Mall (London 2012 Venue)
Albert Gate
Mandarin Oriental Hotel
Emb of Kuwait
The Berkeley
Lanesborough
Wellington Arch
Constitution Hill
1 grid square represents 250 metres

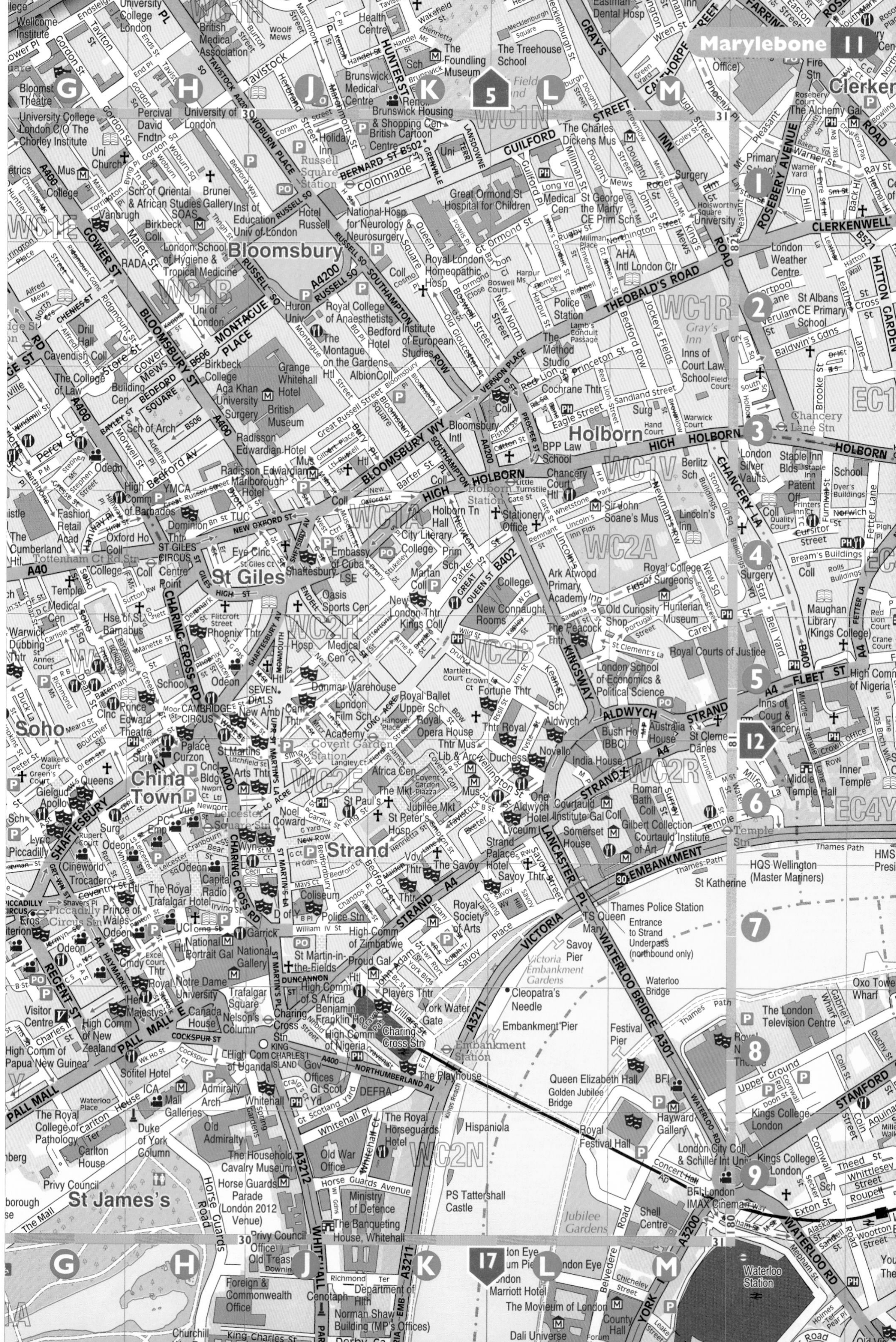
Bloomsbury
Holborn
St Giles
Soho
China Town
Strand
St James's
Clerken
WC1H
WC1N
WC1E
WC1B
WC1R
WC1V
WC1A
WC2A
WC2H
WC2B
WC2E
WC2R
WC2N
EC1
EC4Y
G
H
J
K
L
M
5
12
17
30
31
2
3
4
5
6
7
8
9
British Museum
The Foundling Museum
The Charles Dickens Mus
Great Ormond St Hospital for Children
Russell Square Station
Holborn Station
Chancery Lane Stn
Tottenham Ct Rd Stn
Covent Garden Station
Leicester Square Stn
Piccadilly Circus Stn
Charing Cross Stn
Embankment Station
Temple Stn
Waterloo Station
Sir John Soane's Mus
Royal Courts of Justice
London School of Economics & Political Science
Somerset House
Courtauld Institute Gal
National Portrait Gal
National Gallery
Trafalgar Square
Nelson's Column
St Martin-in-the-Fields
Royal Opera House
Donmar Warehouse
Royal Festival Hall
Queen Elizabeth Hall
Hayward Gallery
BFI London IMAX Cinema
Cleopatra's Needle
Embankment Pier
Festival Pier
Savoy Pier
Waterloo Bridge
Victoria Embankment Gardens
Jubilee Gardens
Old Admiralty
The Household Cavalry Museum
Horse Guards Parade
The Banqueting House, Whitehall
Ministry of Defence
Old War Office
Foreign & Commonwealth Office
Cenotaph
Norman Shaw Building (MP's Offices)
London Eye
The Movieum of London
County Hall
Dali Universe
London Marriott Hotel
HQS Wellington (Master Mariners)
Thames Police Station
The London Television Centre
Kings College London
Oxo Tower Wharf
Lincoln's Inn
Gray's Inn
Middle Temple Hall
Inner Temple
GRAY'S INN ROAD
THEOBALD'S ROAD
HIGH HOLBORN
HOLBORN
NEW OXFORD ST
KINGSWAY
ALDWYCH
STRAND
FLEET ST
VICTORIA EMBANKMENT
WATERLOO BRIDGE
WATERLOO RD
CHARING CROSS RD
SHAFTESBURY AV
GOWER ST
BLOOMSBURY ST
RUSSELL SQ
SOUTHAMPTON ROW
WOBURN PLACE
GUILFORD STREET
ROSEBERY AVENUE
CLERKENWELL
CHANCERY LA
REGENT ST
HAYMARKET
PALL MALL
WHITEHALL
NORTHUMBERLAND AV
LONG ACRE
UPPER ST MARTIN'S LA
THE MALL
STAMFORD ST
FETTER LA
HATTON GARDEN

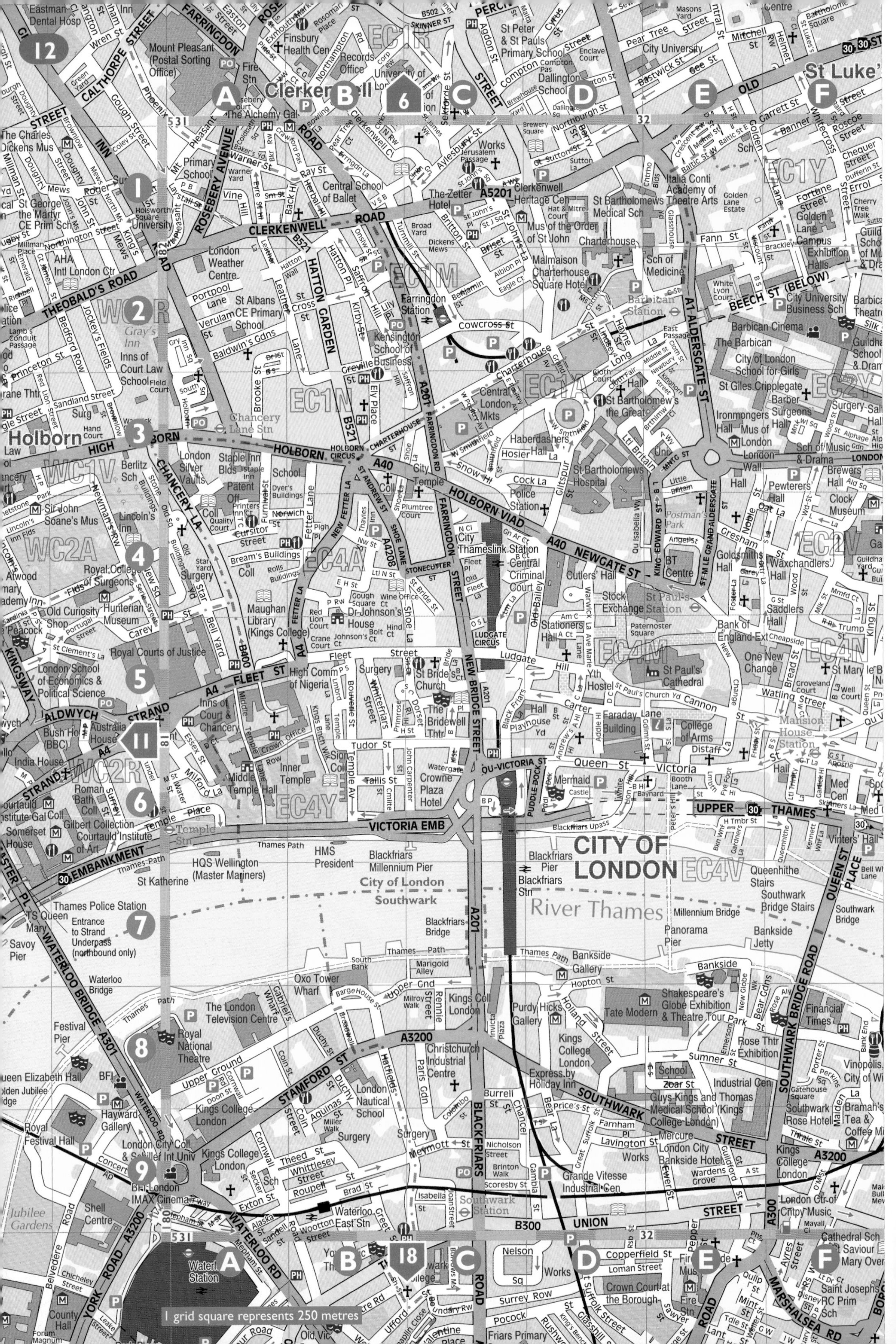

12
6
11
18
A
B
C
D
E
F
1
2
3
4
5
6
7
8
9
Eastman Dental Hosp
Mount Pleasant (Postal Sorting Office)
FARRINGDON
CALTHORPE STREET
Clerkenwell
Finsbury Health Cen
Records Office
University of London
St Peter & St Pauls Primary School
Dallington School
City University
St Luke's
OLD STREET
The Charles Dickens Mus
ROSEBERY AVENUE
Mt Pleasant
Holsworthy Square
St George the Martyr CE Prim Sch
Central School of Ballet
The Zetter Hotel
Works
Clerkenwell Heritage Cen
St Bartholomews Medical Sch
Mus of the Order of St John
Italia Conti Academy of Theatre Arts
Golden Lane Estate
CLERKENWELL ROAD
A5201
AHA Intl London Ctr
THEOBALD'S ROAD
London Weather Centre
HATTON GARDEN
EC1M
Charterhouse
Sch of Medicine
Malmaison Charterhouse Square Hotel
Barbican Station
A1 ALDERSGATE ST
BEECH ST (BELOW)
City University Business Sch
Barbican Theatre
WC1R
Gray's Inn
St Albans CE Primary School
Farringdon Station
Cowcross St
Kensington School of Business
Barbican Cinema
The Barbican
City of London School for Girls
St Giles Cripplegate
Inns of Court Law School
Baldwin's Gdns
Brooke St
EC1N
Central London Mkts
EC1A
St Bartholomew's the Great
EC2Y
Holborn
HIGH HOLBORN
HOLBORN CIRCUS
CHARTERHOUSE
A201
FARRINGDON RD
Chancery Lane Stn
London Silver Vaults
Staple Inn Blds
Haberdashers Hall
Hosier La
Ironmongers Hall
Mus of London
London Wall
WC1V
Berlitz Sch
Sir John Soane's Mus
Lincoln's Inn
CHANCERY LA
A40
City Temple
HOLBORN VIAD
Snow Hl
Cock La
Police Station
St Bartholomews Hospital
Postman's Park
Pewterers' Hall
Clock Museum
WC2A
Royal College of Surgeons
Hunterian Museum
Old Curiosity Shop
Bream's Buildings
EC4A
NEW FETTER LA
SHOE LANE
A4208
City Thameslink Station
Central Criminal Court
A40 NEWGATE ST
Cutlers' Hall
KING EDWARD ST
BT Centre
Goldsmiths Hall
Waxchandlers' Hall
EC2V
Dr Johnson's House
Maughan Library (Kings College)
Stock Exchange
St Paul's Station
Paternoster Square
Stationers Hall
Old Bailey
Bank of England Ext
Cheapside
Saddlers Hall
KINGSWAY
St Clement's La
Royal Courts of Justice
London School of Economics & Political Science
FLEET ST
A4
B400
High Comm of Nigeria
Fleet Street
St Bride's Church
LUDGATE CIRCUS
Ludgate Hill
EC4M
St Paul's Cathedral
One New Change
EC4N
ALDWYCH
STRAND
Bush Ho (BBC)
Australia House
India House
Inns of Court & Chancery
Middle Temple Hall
Inner Temple
EC4Y
The Bridewell Thtr
Crowne Plaza Hotel
Faraday Building
College of Arms
Mansion House Station
QU VICTORIA ST
Queen Victoria St
Mermaid
Cannon St
Watling Street
WC2R
Roman Bath
Somerset House
Courtauld Institute Gal
Gilbert Collection
Courtauld Institute of Art
Temple Place
Temple Stn
VICTORIA EMB
UPPER THAMES
EMBANKMENT
Thames Path
HQS Wellington (Master Mariners)
HMS President
Blackfriars Millennium Pier
Blackfriars Pier
Blackfriars Stn
CITY OF LONDON
EC4V
Queenhithe Stairs
Southwark Bridge Stairs
St Katherine
City of London
Southwark
Thames Police Station
TS Queen Mary
Entrance to Strand Underpass (northbound only)
River Thames
Millennium Bridge
Panorama Pier
Bankside Jetty
Southwark Bridge
Savoy Pier
Blackfriars Bridge
WATERLOO BRIDGE
Waterloo Bridge
Oxo Tower Wharf
Marigold Alley
Bankside Gallery
Hopton St
Tate Modern
Shakespeare's Globe Exhibition & Theatre Tour
Bankside
The London Television Centre
Kings Coll London
Purdy Hicks Gallery
Financial Times
Festival Pier
Royal National Theatre
A3200
Christchurch Industrial Centre
Kings College London
Rose Thr Exhibition
SOUTHWARK BRIDGE ROAD
Queen Elizabeth Hall
BFI
Hayward Gallery
STAMFORD ST
London Nautical School
BLACKFRIARS ROAD
Express by Holiday Inn
SOUTHWARK STREET
Guys Kings and Thomas Medical School (Kings College London)
Mercure London City Bankside Hotel
Vinopolis, City of Wine
Royal Festival Hall
London City Coll & Schiller Int Univ
BFI London IMAX Cinema
Surgery
Grande Vitesse Industrial Cen
Southwark Station
London Ctr of Contemporary Music
Jubilee Gardens
Shell Centre
WATERLOO RD
Waterloo East Stn
UNION STREET
B300
A300
Cathedral Sch of St Saviour & St Mary Overie
Waterloo Station
Nelson Sq
Works
Copperfield St
Crown Court at the Borough
County Hall
YORK ROAD
Surrey Row
Friars Primary
Saint Josephs RC Prim Sch
MARSHALSEA RD
1 grid square represents 250 metres

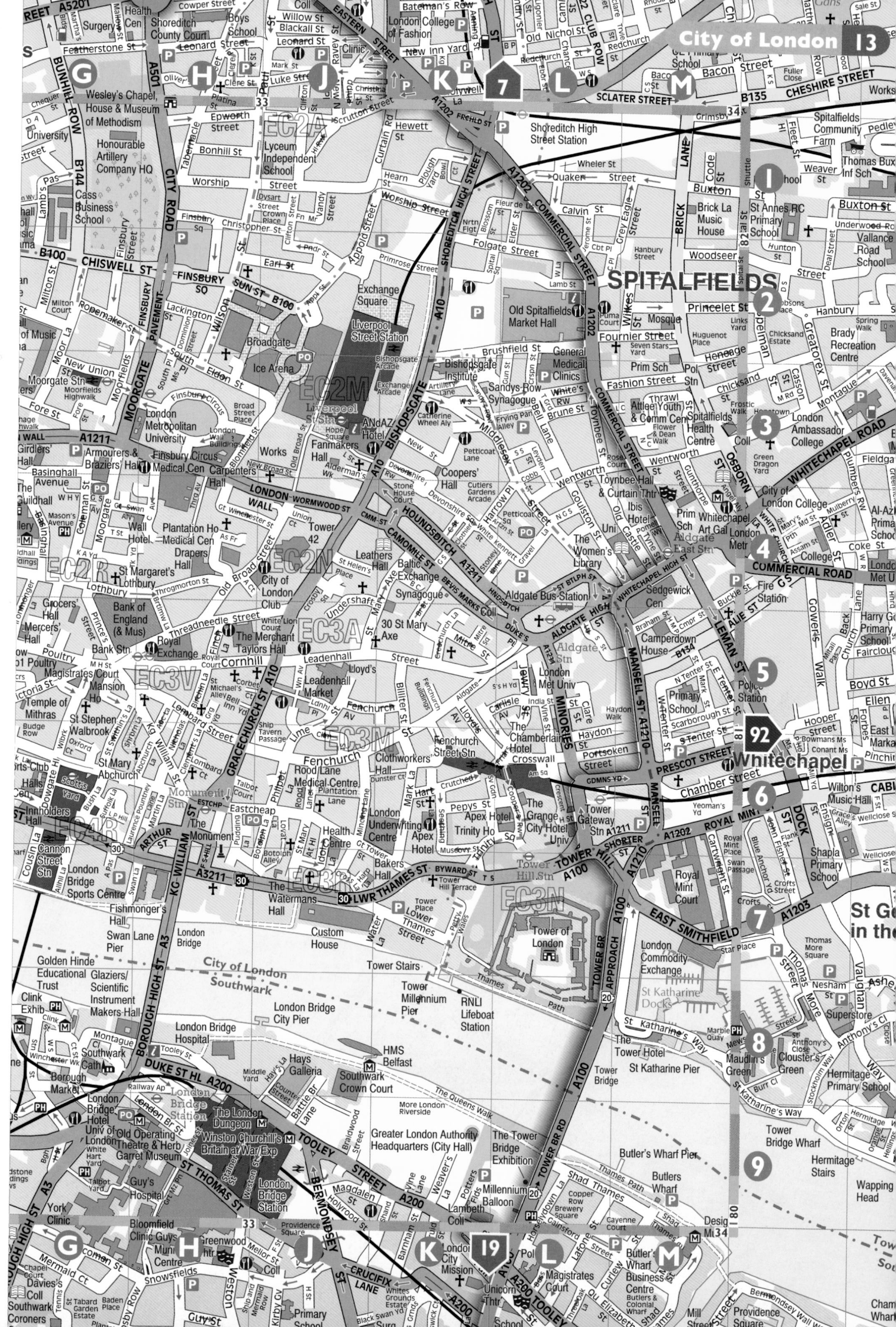
City of London
13
G
H
J
K
7
L
M
Featherstone St
Leonard Street
Leonard St
Cowper Street
Willow St
Blackall St
Boys School
Shoreditch County Court
Health Cen
Surgery
Bateman's Row
London College of Fashion
New Inn Yard
Old Nichol St
Redchurch St
CLUB ROW
Bacon Street
CHESHIRE STREET
SCLATER STREET
B135
BUNHILL ROW
A501
Wesley's Chapel, House & Museum of Methodism
Epworth Street
Bonhill St
Tabernacle
EC2A
Lyceum Independent School
Hewett St
Curtain Rd
Scrutton Street
Shoreditch High Street Station
Wheler St
Quaker Street
Spitalfields Community Farm
Weaver St
Thomas Buxton Inf Sch
Buxton St
St Annes RC Primary School
University
Honourable Artillery Company HQ
B144
Cass Business School
Finsbury Sq
Christopher St
Worship Street
Earl St
Primrose Street
Appold Street
SHOREDITCH HIGH STREET
A1202
COMMERCIAL STREET
Folgate Street
Calvin St
Brick La Music House
BRICK LANE
Hanbury Street
Woodseer St
SPITALFIELDS
B100
CHISWELL ST
FINSBURY SQ
SUN ST
Milton St
Ropemaker St
Exchange Square
Liverpool Street Station
Old Spitalfields Market Hall
Princelet St
Mosque
Fournier Street
Brady Recreation Centre
Moor La
New Union St
Moorgate Stn
MOORGATE
FINSBURY PAVEMENT
Broadgate
Ice Arena
EC2M
Bishopsgate Institute
Brushfield St
General Medical Clinics
Sandys Row Synagogue
Fashion Street
Prim Sch
Attlee Youth & Comm Cen
Spitalfields Health Centre
London Ambassador College
London Metropolitan University
Finsbury Circus
Fore St
A1211
Armourers & Braziers' Hall
Finsbury Circus Medical Cen
Carpenters' Hall
Works
Liverpool St Stn
ANdAZ Hotel
Fanmakers Hall
BISHOPSGATE
A10
Middlesex
Petticoat Lane
Coopers' Hall
Wentworth St
Toynbee Hall & Curtain Thtr
Ibis Hotel
Whitechapel Art Gal
London Metr
WHITECHAPEL ROAD
City of London College
Basinghall Avenue
The Guildhall
LONDON WALL
Plantation Ho Medical Cen
Drapers Hall
Tower 42
Leathers Hall
HOUNDSDITCH
CAMOMILE ST
Baltic Exchange
BEVIS MARKS
The Women's Library
Aldgate East Stn
WHITECHAPEL HIGH ST
COMMERCIAL ROAD
EC2R
St Margaret's Lothbury
Lothbury
Bank of England (& Mus)
City of London Club
EC2N
Synagogue
Aldgate Bus Station
Sedgewick Cen
Fire Station
Grocers' Hall
Mercers' Hall
Poultry
Threadneedle Street
Royal Exchange
The Merchant Taylors Hall
EC3A
30 St Mary Axe
ALDGATE HIGH ST
Camperdown House
LEMAN ST
Harry Gosling Primary School
Bank Stn
Cornhill
Leadenhall Street
Lloyd's
Leadenhall Market
Aldgate Stn
London Met Univ
MINORIES
MANSELL ST A1210
Primary School
Police Station
5
Boyd St
Magistrates Court
Mansion Ho
EC3V
Temple of Mithras
St Stephen Walbrook
Lombard Street
GRACECHURCH ST
Fenchurch St
Fenchurch Street Stn
EC3M
The Chamberlain Hotel
Haydon St
Crosswall
PRESCOT STREET
Chamber Street
92
Whitechapel
Wilton's Music Hall
St Mary Abchurch
Scott's Yard
Clothworkers' Hall
Rood Lane Medical Centre
Monument Stn
The Monument
Eastcheap
London Underwriting Centre
Apex Hotel
Trinity Ho
The Grange City Hotel
Tower Gateway Stn
6
ROYAL MINT ST
Royal Mint Court
Shapla Primary School
Cannon Street Stn
ARTHUR ST
KG WILLIAM
A3211
LWR THAMES ST
BYWARD ST
TOWER HILL
Tower Hill Stn
EC4R
EC3R
EC3N
London Bridge Sports Centre
Fishmonger's Hall
Swan Lane Pier
The Watermans Hall
Custom House
Lower Thames Street
Tower of London
EAST SMITHFIELD
A1203
7
London Commodity Exchange
St Katharine Docks
London Bridge
City of London
Southwark
Tower Stairs
Tower Millennium Pier
RNLI Lifeboat Station
TOWER BR APPROACH
Golden Hinde Educational Trust
Glaziers/ Scientific Instrument Makers Hall
Clink Exhib
London Bridge City Pier
London Bridge Hospital
HMS Belfast
The Tower Hotel
St Katharine Pier
8
Tower Bridge
Southwark Cath
Borough Market
BOROUGH HIGH ST A3
DUKE ST HL A200
Hays Galleria
Southwark Crown Court
The Queens Walk
More London Riverside
London Bridge Station
The London Dungeon
Winston Churchill's Britain at War Exp
Greater London Authority Headquarters (City Hall)
The Tower Bridge Exhibition
TOWER BR RD
Butler's Wharf Pier
Butlers Wharf
Tower Bridge Wharf
Hermitage Stairs
Wapping Head
9
Hermitage Primary School
London Bridge Hotel
Univ of London
Old Operating Theatre & Herb Garret Museum
Guy's Hospital
TOOLEY STREET
ST THOMAS ST
London Bridge Station
BERMONDSEY ST
Millennium Balloon
Shad Thames
York Clinic
Bloomfield Clinic Guys
Greenwood Thtr
Providence Square
G
H
J
K
19
L
M
Snowsfields
CRUCIFIX LANE
London City Mission
Magistrates Court
Butler's Wharf Business Centre
Davies's Coll
Southwark Coroners
Primary School
Mill Street
Providence Square

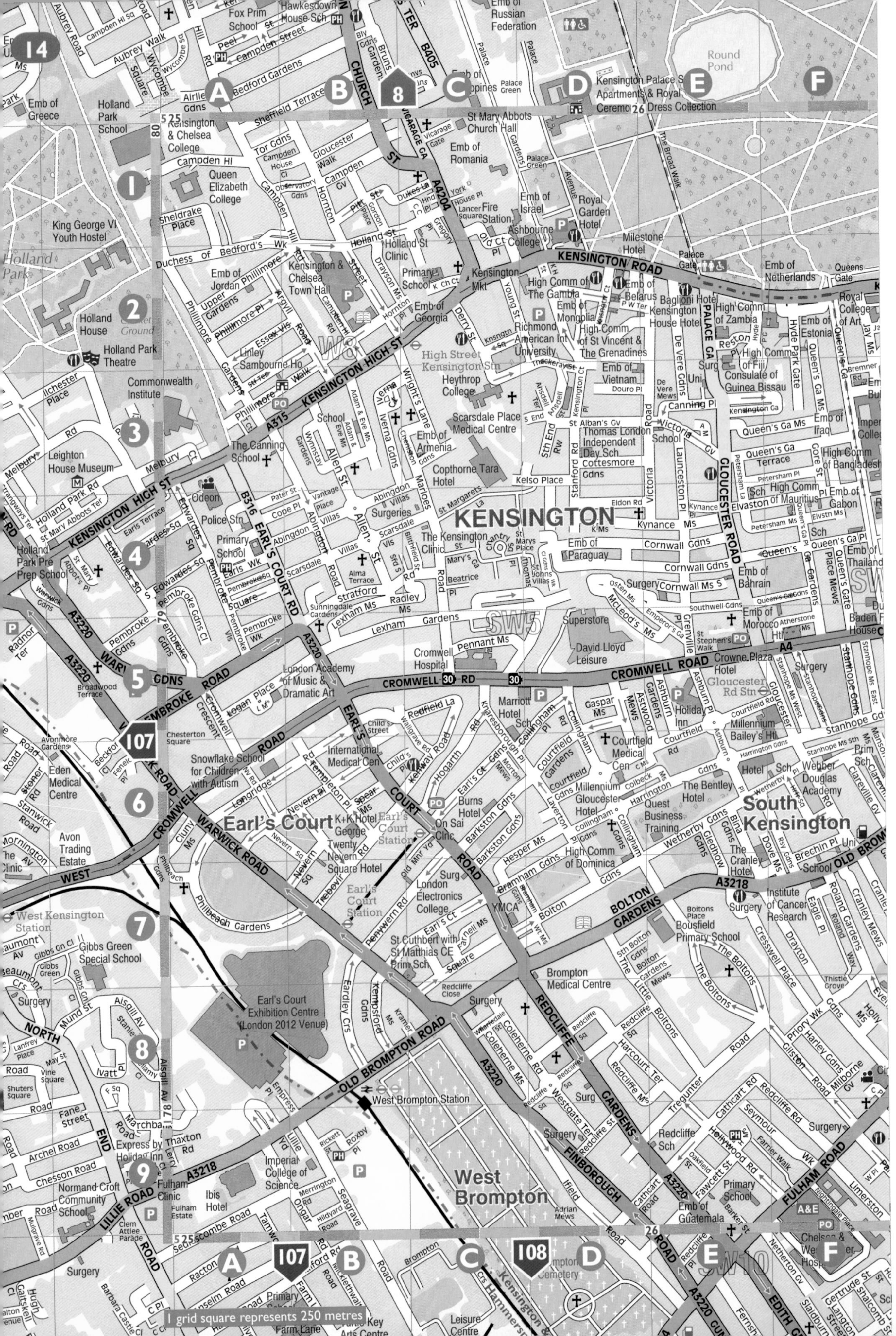

14
8
A
B
C
D
E
F
1
2
3
4
5
6
7
8
9
107
108
A
B
C
D
E
F
Fox Prim School
Hawkesdown House Sch
Campden Street
Bedford Gardens
Sheffield Terrace
Emb of Russian Federation
Round Pond
Kensington Palace State Apartments & Royal Ceremonial Dress Collection
Emb of Greece
Holland Park School
Kensington & Chelsea College
St Mary Abbots Church Hall
Emb of Romania
Queen Elizabeth College
King George VI Youth Hostel
Holland Park
Sheldrake Place
Duchess of Bedford's Wk
Emb of Israel
Royal Garden Hotel
Milestone Hotel
Fire Station
Ashbourne College
KENSINGTON ROAD
Emb of Netherlands
Queens Gate
Emb of Jordan
Kensington & Chelsea Town Hall
Holland St Clinic
Primary School
Kensington Mkt
High Comm of The Gambia
Emb of Belarus
Baglioni Hotel
Kensington House Hotel
High Comm of Zambia
Royal College of Art
Holland House
Cricket Ground
Holland Park Theatre
Emb of Georgia
KENSINGTON HIGH ST
High Street Kensington Stn
Richmond American Int University
Emb of Mongolia
High Comm of St Vincent & The Grenadines
Emb of Estonia
Linley Sambourne Ho
Heythrop College
Emb of Vietnam
Consulate of Guinea Bissau
High Comm of Fiji
Commonwealth Institute
Scarsdale Place Medical Centre
Emb of Armenia
Thomas London Independent Day Sch
Emb of Iraq
Leighton House Museum
The Canning School
Copthorne Tara Hotel
Kelso Place
GLOUCESTER ROAD
High Comm of Bangladesh
Odeon
Police Stn
KENSINGTON
High Comm of Mauritius
Emb of Gabon
Holland Park Pre Prep School
Primary School
The Kensington Clinic
Emb of Paraguay
Emb of Bahrain
Emb of Thailand
EARL'S COURT RD
Lexham Gardens
SW5
Superstore
David Lloyd Leisure
Emb of Morocco
Cromwell Hospital
London Academy of Music & Dramatic Art
CROMWELL ROAD
Crowne Plaza Hotel
Gloucester Rd Stn
Marriott Hotel
Holiday Inn
Millennium Bailey's Htl
Snowflake School for Children with Autism
International Medical Cen
Courtfield Medical Cen
Eden Medical Centre
Earl's Court
K+K Hotel George
Twenty Nevern Square Hotel
Earl's Court Station
On Sai Clinc
Burns Hotel
Millennium Gloucester Hotel
The Bentley Hotel
Quest Business Training
Webber Douglas Academy
South Kensington
Avon Trading Estate
WARWICK ROAD
WEST CROMWELL ROAD
London Electronics College
High Comm of Dominica
YMCA
BOLTON GARDENS
The Cranley Hotel
Institute of Cancer Research
West Kensington Station
Gibbs Green Special School
St Cuthbert with St Matthias CE Prim Sch
Brompton Medical Centre
Bousfield Primary School
Earl's Court Exhibition Centre (London 2012 Venue)
OLD BROMPTON ROAD
REDCLIFFE GARDENS
The Boltons
NORTH END ROAD
West Brompton Station
Express by Holiday Inn
Imperial College of Science
West Brompton
FINBOROUGH ROAD
Redcliffe Sch
Emb of Guatemala
Primary School
FULHAM ROAD
Normand Croft Community School
LILLIE ROAD
Fulham Clinic
Ibis Hotel
Chelsea & Westminster Hosp
A&E
SW10
Leisure Centre
Farm Lane
Arts Centre

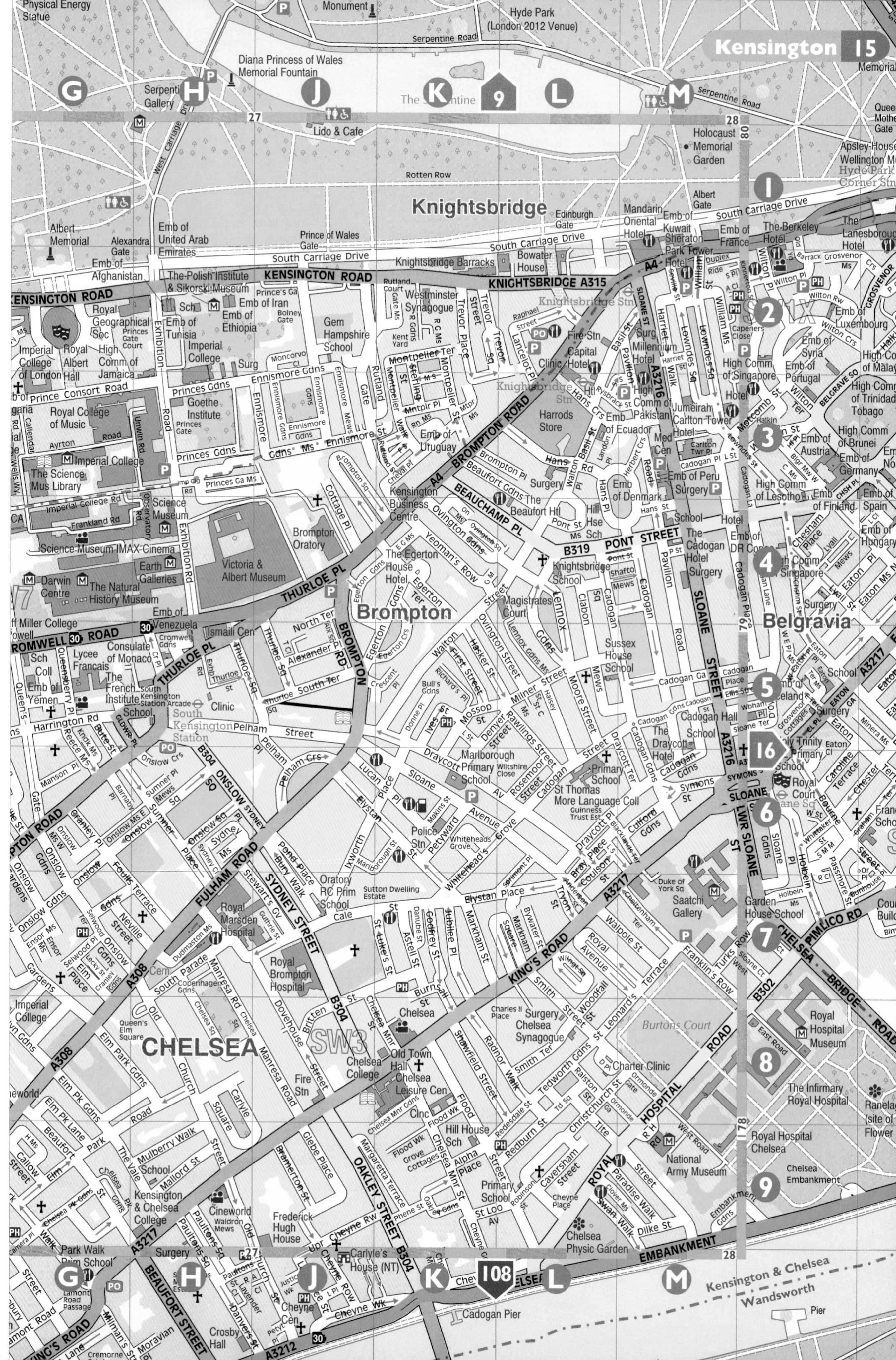

Physical Energy Statue
Monument
Hyde Park (London 2012 Venue)
Serpentine Road
Diana Princess of Wales Memorial Fountain
Serpentine Gallery
The Serpentine
9
Lido & Cafe
West Carriage Dr
Holocaust Memorial Garden
Apsley House Wellington Mu
Hyde Park Corner Stn
Rotten Row
Knightsbridge
Albert Gate
Edinburgh Gate
Mandarin Oriental Hotel
Emb of Kuwait
Sheraton Park Tower Hotel
Emb of France
The Berkeley Hotel
The Lanesborough Hotel
South Carriage Drive
Albert Memorial
Alexandra Gate
Emb of United Arab Emirates
Prince of Wales Gate
Emb of Afghanistan
Knightsbridge Barracks
Bowater House
KENSINGTON ROAD
KNIGHTSBRIDGE A315
The Polish Institute & Sikorski Museum
Royal Geographical Soc
Emb of Iran
Emb of Tunisia
Emb of Ethiopia
Imperial College
Royal Albert Hall
Imperial College of London
High Comm of Jamaica
Westminster Synagogue
Gem Hampshire School
Knightsbridge Stn
Fire Stn
Capital Hotel
Clinic
Surg Millennium Hotel
Emb of Luxembourg
Emb of Syria
Emb of Portugal
High Comm of Singapore
High Comm of Pakistan
Jumeirah Carlton Tower Hotel
High Comm of Trinidad Tobago
High Comm of Malaya
Prince Consort Road
Royal College of Music
Goethe Institute
Princes Gdns
Ennismore Gdns
Montpelier Sq
Emb of Uruguay
Harrods Store
Emb of Ecuador
Emb of Austria
High Comm of Brunei
Emb of Germany
The Science Mus Library
Imperial College
Science Museum
Science Museum IMAX Cinema
Earth Galleries
Darwin Centre
The Natural History Museum
Victoria & Albert Museum
Brompton Oratory
Kensington Business Centre
BROMPTON ROAD
BEAUCHAMP PL
The Beaufort Htl
Emb of Denmark
Emb of Peru
High Comm of Lesotho
Emb of Finland
Emb of Spain
Emb of Hungary
The Egerton House Hotel
PONT STREET
Knightsbridge School
The Cadogan Hotel
Emb of DR Congo
High Comm Singapore
Belgravia
Brompton
THURLOE PL
Emb of Venezuela
Miller College
CROMWELL ROAD
Consulate of Monaco
Lycee Francais
The French Institute School
Emb of Yemen
South Kensington Station
Clinic
Magistrates Court
Sussex House School
Cadogan Hall
The Draycott Hotel
Emb of Iceland
Holy Trinity Primary School
Royal Court
16
Marlborough Primary School
St Thomas More Language Coll
FULHAM ROAD
SYDNEY STREET
ONSLOW SQ
Royal Marsden Hospital
Oratory RC Prim School
Police Stn
Saatchi Gallery
Duke of York Sq
Garden House School
PIMLICO RD
CHELSEA BRIDGE ROAD
KING'S ROAD
Royal Brompton Hospital
Chelsea
Surgery Chelsea Synagogue
Burtons Court
Royal Hospital Museum
CHELSEA
SW3
Chelsea College
Old Town Hall
Chelsea Leisure Cen
Charter Clinic
The Infirmary Royal Hospital
Ranelagh
Imperial College
Fire Stn
Hill House Sch
Primary School
National Army Museum
Royal Hospital Chelsea
Chelsea Embankment
Kensington & Chelsea College
Cineworld
Frederick Hugh House
Chelsea Physic Garden
EMBANKMENT
Park Walk Prim School
Carlyle's House (NT)
108
Cadogan Pier
Kensington & Chelsea
Wandsworth
Pier
Crosby Hall
BEAUFORT STREET
OAKLEY STREET B304
A3212

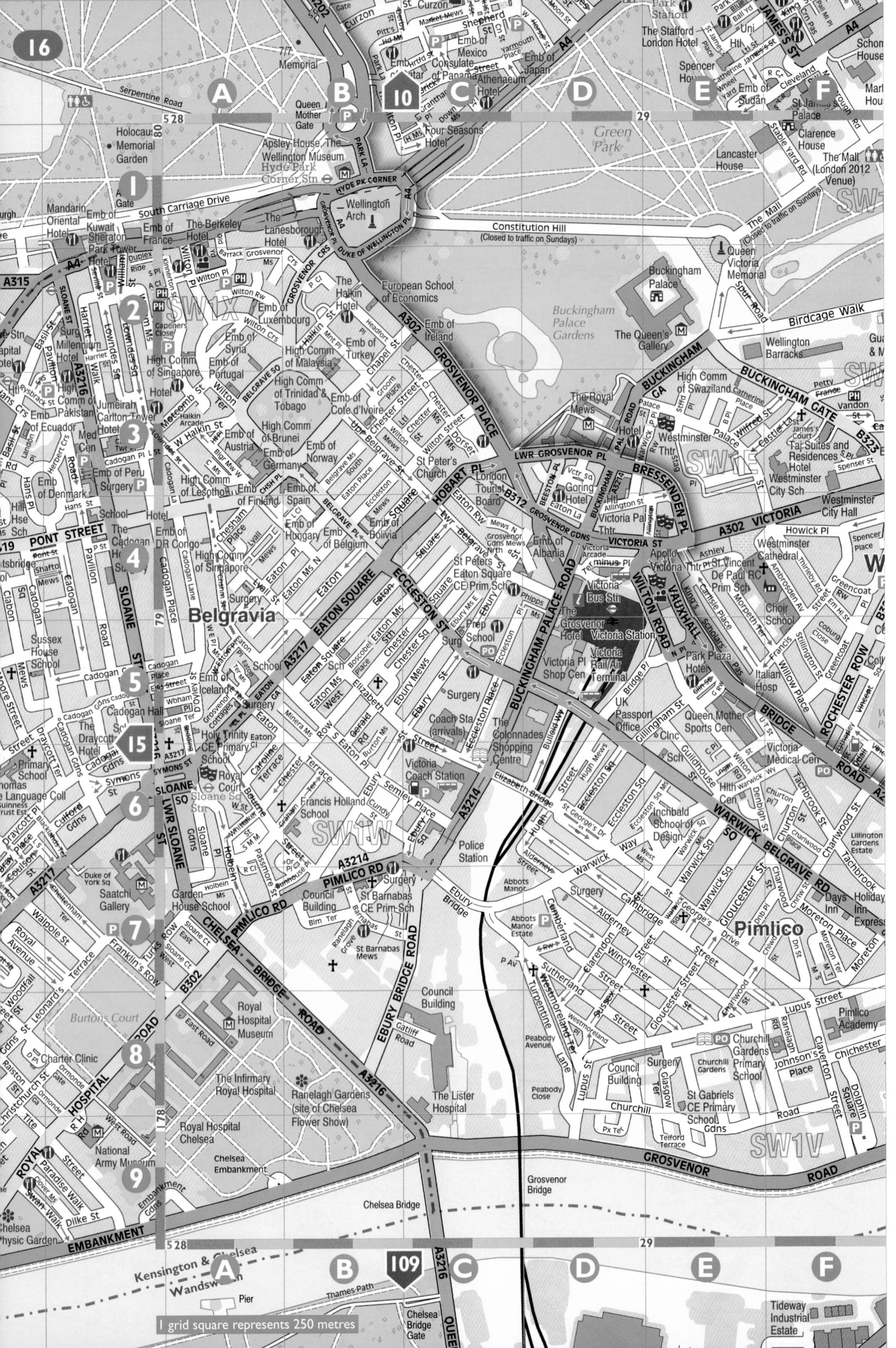

A
B
C
D
E
F
10
528
29
Serpentine Road
7/7 Memorial
Queen Mother Gate
Holocaust Memorial Garden
Apsley House, The Wellington Museum
Hyde Park Corner Stn
HYDE PK CORNER
Curzon St
Market Mews
Shepherd Market
Emb of Mexico
Consulate of Panama
Athenaeum Hotel
Emb of Japan
Yarmouth Place
Four Seasons Hotel
Green Park
Park Station
The Stafford London Hotel
Spencer House
Cleveland Row
St James's Palace
Clarence House
Stable Yard Rd
Lancaster House
The Mall (London 2012 Venue)
The Mall (Closed to traffic on Sundays)
Constitution Hill
(Closed to traffic on Sundays)
Wellington Arch
South Carriage Drive
Mandarin Oriental Hotel
Emb of Kuwait
Sheraton Park Tower Hotel
Emb of France
The Berkeley Hotel
The Lanesborough Hotel
GROSVENOR CRS
DUKE OF WELLINGTON PL
A4
A315
Queen Victoria Memorial
Buckingham Palace
Buckingham Palace Gardens
The Queen's Gallery
Spur Road
Birdcage Walk
Wellington Barracks
European School of Economics
Emb of Ireland
GROSVENOR PLACE
A302
The Halkin Hotel
Emb of Turkey
Chapel St
High Comm of Malaysia
High Comm of Trinidad & Tobago
Emb of Cote d'Ivoire
High Comm of Brunei
Emb of Norway
Emb of Germany
Emb of Austria
Emb of Luxembourg
Emb of Syria
Emb of Portugal
High Comm of Singapore
BELGRAVE SQ
Wilton Crs
Wilton Pl
Jumeirah Carlton Tower Hotel
Emb of Ecuador
Emb of Peru
Emb of Denmark
Millennium Hotel
High Comm of Pakistan
Med Cen
Surgery
Hans Pl
Hans Crs
Lowndes Sq
Harriet Walk
Basil St
Motcomb St
W Halkin St
High Comm of Lesotho
Emb of Finland
Chesham Place
Emb of Spain
Emb of Hungary
Emb of Belgium
Emb of Bolivia
Eaton Place
Belgrave Pl
Upr Belgrave St
Chester Street
Wilton Street
St Peter's Church
London Tourist Board
HOBART PL
The Royal Mews
High Comm of Swaziland
BUCKINGHAM GATE
BRESSENDEN PL
LWR GROSVENOR PL
Goring Hotel
Eaton La
B312
GROSVENOR GDNS
Emb of Albania
VICTORIA ST
Victoria Palace Thtr
Westminster Thtr
Petty France
Vandon St
Taj Suites and Residences Hotel
Westminster City Sch
Westminster City Hall
A302 VICTORIA
Howick Pl
Westminster Cathedral
St Vincent De Paul RC Prim Sch
Ashley Pl
Apollo Victoria Thtr
Bus Stn
Victoria Station
The Grosvenor Hotel
Victoria Rail/Air Terminal
Victoria Pl Shop Cen
BUCKINGHAM PALACE ROAD
WILTON ROAD
VAUXHALL
BRIDGE
ROAD
Ambrosden Av
Choir School
Greencoat Pl
ROCHESTER ROW
Park Plaza Hotel
Italian Hosp
Willow Place
Francis St
PONT STREET
SW1X
SW1E
SW1W
SW1V
Cadogan Place
Cadogan Lane
SLOANE ST
Pavilion Road
The Cadogan Hotel
Sussex House School
Cadogan Gdns
Cadogan Hall
Emb of DR Congo
High Comm of Singapore
Belgravia
EATON SQUARE
A3217
ECCLESTON ST
Eaton Sq
Emb of Iceland
Eaton Ms
Chester Sq
Elizabeth St
Ebury Mews
Ebury St
Prep School
Eccleston Place
Coach Sta (arrivals)
The Colonnades Shopping Centre
Surgery
Holy Trinity CE Primary School
Royal Court
Sloane Sq Stn
SLOANE SQ
LWR SLOANE ST
15
The Draycott Hotel
Symons St
Caroline Terrace
Chester Terrace
Francis Holland School
Semley Place
Victoria Coach Station
A3214
Police Station
Elizabeth Bridge
Eccleston Sq
UK Passport Office
Gillingham St
Queen Mother Sports Cen
Guildhouse St
Inchbald School of Design
Warwick Way
WARWICK SQ
BELGRAVE RD
Alderney Street
Cambridge St
Gloucester St
Victoria Medical Cen
Tachbrook St
Charlwood St
Lillington Gardens Estate
Days Inn
Holiday Inn Express
Moreton Place
Pimlico
Saatchi Gallery
Duke of York Sq
Garden House School
PIMLICO RD
Council Building
St Barnabas CE Prim Sch
St Barnabas Mews
Ranelagh Grove
Ebury Bridge
Abbots Manor
Abbots Manor Estate
Cumberland St
Clarendon St
Winchester St
Sutherland St
Turpentine Lane
Westmoreland Ter
Peabody Avenue
Peabody Close
Lupus Street
Pimlico Academy
Churchill Gardens Primary School
Council Building
St Gabriels CE Primary School
Churchill Gdns Road
Johnson's Place
Claverton Street
Dolphin Square
Chichester St
Telford Terrace
Walpole St
Royal Avenue
Franklin's Row
Turks Row
Burtons Court
CHELSEA BRIDGE ROAD
A3216
B302
Royal Hospital Museum
East Road
Charter Clinic
Ormonde Gate
Christchurch St
HOSPITAL ROAD
The Infirmary Royal Hospital
Ranelagh Gardens (site of Chelsea Flower Show)
Royal Hospital Chelsea
National Army Museum
West Road
EBURY BRIDGE ROAD
Council Building
Gatliff Road
The Lister Hospital
Chelsea Embankment
Grosvenor Bridge
Chelsea Bridge
GROSVENOR ROAD
ROYAL
Paradise Walk
Swan Walk
Dilke St
Chelsea Physic Garden
EMBANKMENT
Kensington & Chelsea
Wandsworth
Pier
Thames Path
109
Chelsea Bridge Gate
QUEEN
Tideway Industrial Estate
1
2
3
4
5
6
7
8
9
80
79
78
1 grid square represents 250 metres

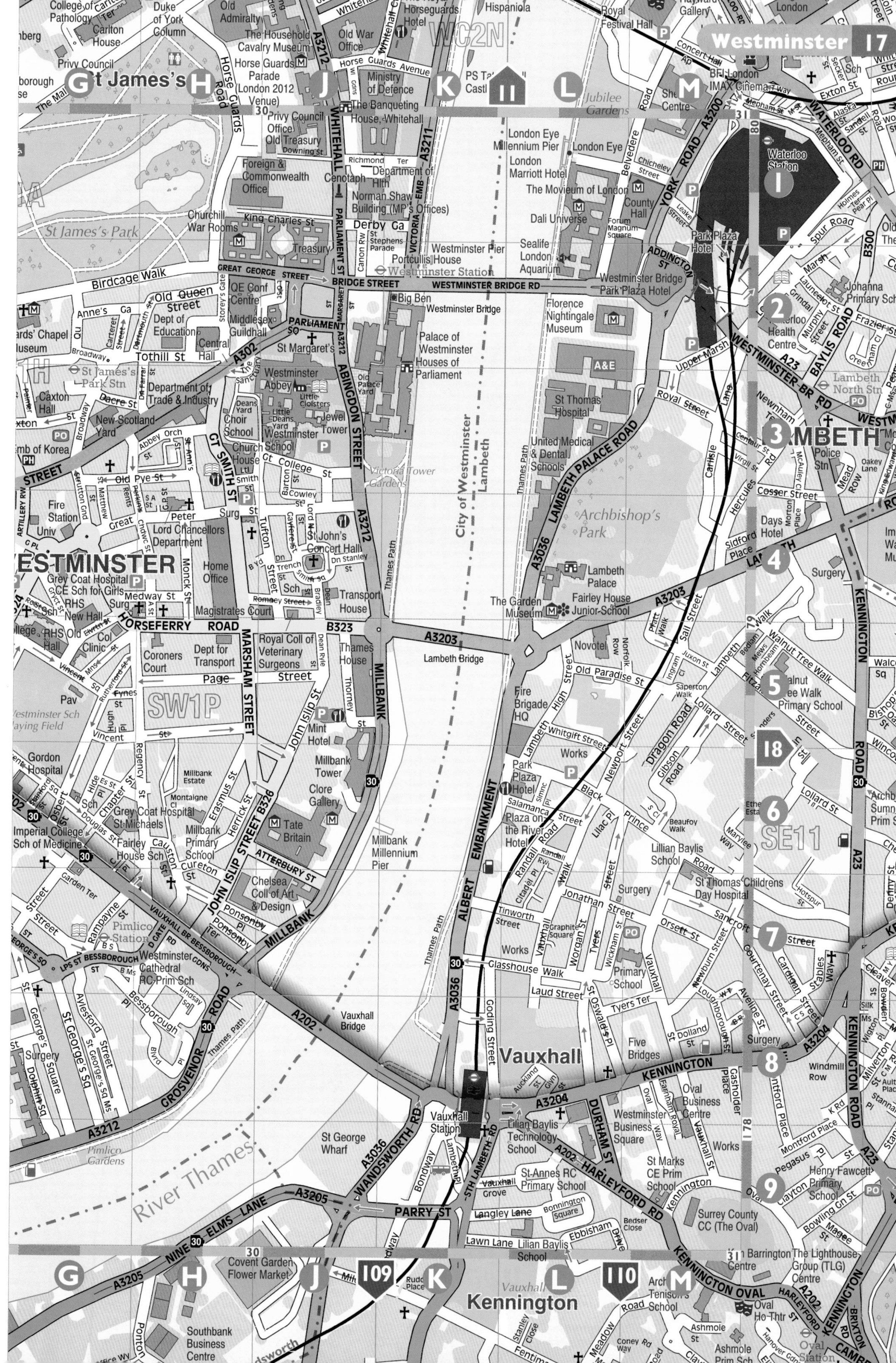
St James's Park
Horse Guards Parade
The Household Cavalry Museum
Old Admiralty
Duke of York Column
Carlton House
Privy Council
College of Pathology
Old War Office
Ministry of Defence
The Banqueting House, Whitehall
Old Treasury
Foreign & Commonwealth Office
Department of Hlth
Cenotaph
Norman Shaw Building (MP's Offices)
Churchill War Rooms
King Charles St
Treasury
Birdcage Walk
Great George Street
Bridge Street
Westminster Bridge Rd
QE Conf Centre
Middlesex Guildhall
Parliament Sq
St Margaret's
Westminster Abbey
Big Ben
Westminster Bridge
Palace of Westminster Houses of Parliament
Portcullis House
Westminster Pier
Westminster Station
London Eye
London Eye Millennium Pier
London Marriott Hotel
The Movieum of London
County Hall
Dali Universe
Sealife London Aquarium
Jubilee Gardens
Royal Festival Hall
Hayward Gallery
BFI London IMAX Cinema
Shell Centre
Waterloo Station
York Road
Waterloo Rd
Park Plaza Hotel
Westminster Bridge Park Plaza Hotel
Florence Nightingale Museum
St Thomas' Hospital
A&E
United Medical & Dental Schools
Lambeth Palace Road
Archbishop's Park
Lambeth Palace
The Garden Museum
Fairley House Junior School
Lambeth North Stn
Lambeth
Police Stn
Days Hotel
Westminster
Dept of Education
Central Hall
Tothill St
St James's Park Stn
Department of Trade & Industry
New Scotland Yard
Caxton Hall
Choir School
Westminster School
Jewel Tower
Victoria Tower Gardens
Abingdon Street
Millbank
Lord Chancellors Department
Home Office
St John's Concert Hall
Transport House
Magistrates Court
Horseferry Road
Lambeth Bridge
Dept for Transport
Royal Coll of Veterinary Surgeons
Thames House
Coroners Court
Marsham Street
SW1P
Mint Hotel
Millbank Tower
Clore Gallery
Tate Britain
Chelsea Coll of Art & Design
Millbank Millennium Pier
Grey Coat Hospital
Grey Coat Hospital St Michaels
Imperial College Sch of Medicine
Gordon Hospital
Pimlico Station
Westminster Cathedral RC Prim Sch
Vauxhall Bridge
Vauxhall Bridge Rd
Grosvenor Road
Albert Embankment
City of Westminster
Lambeth
Fire Brigade HQ
Park Plaza Hotel
Salamanca Plaza on the River Hotel
Vauxhall
Vauxhall Station
Kennington Lane
Kennington Road
Kennington Oval
Lilian Baylis Technology School
Westminster Business Square
Oval Business Centre
St Marks CE Prim School
Surrey County CC (The Oval)
Harleyford Rd
Durham St
Walnut Tree Walk Primary School
Lillian Baylis School
St Thomas Childrens Day Hospital
SE11
St George Wharf
Wandsworth Rd
Parry St
Nine Elms Lane
River Thames
Pimlico Gardens
Covent Garden Flower Market
Southbank Business Centre
Kennington
Oval Station
Henry Fawcett Primary School
The Lighthouse Group (TLG) Centre
Ashmole Prim Sch
18
109
110
11
G H J K L M
1 2 3 4 5 6 7 8 9

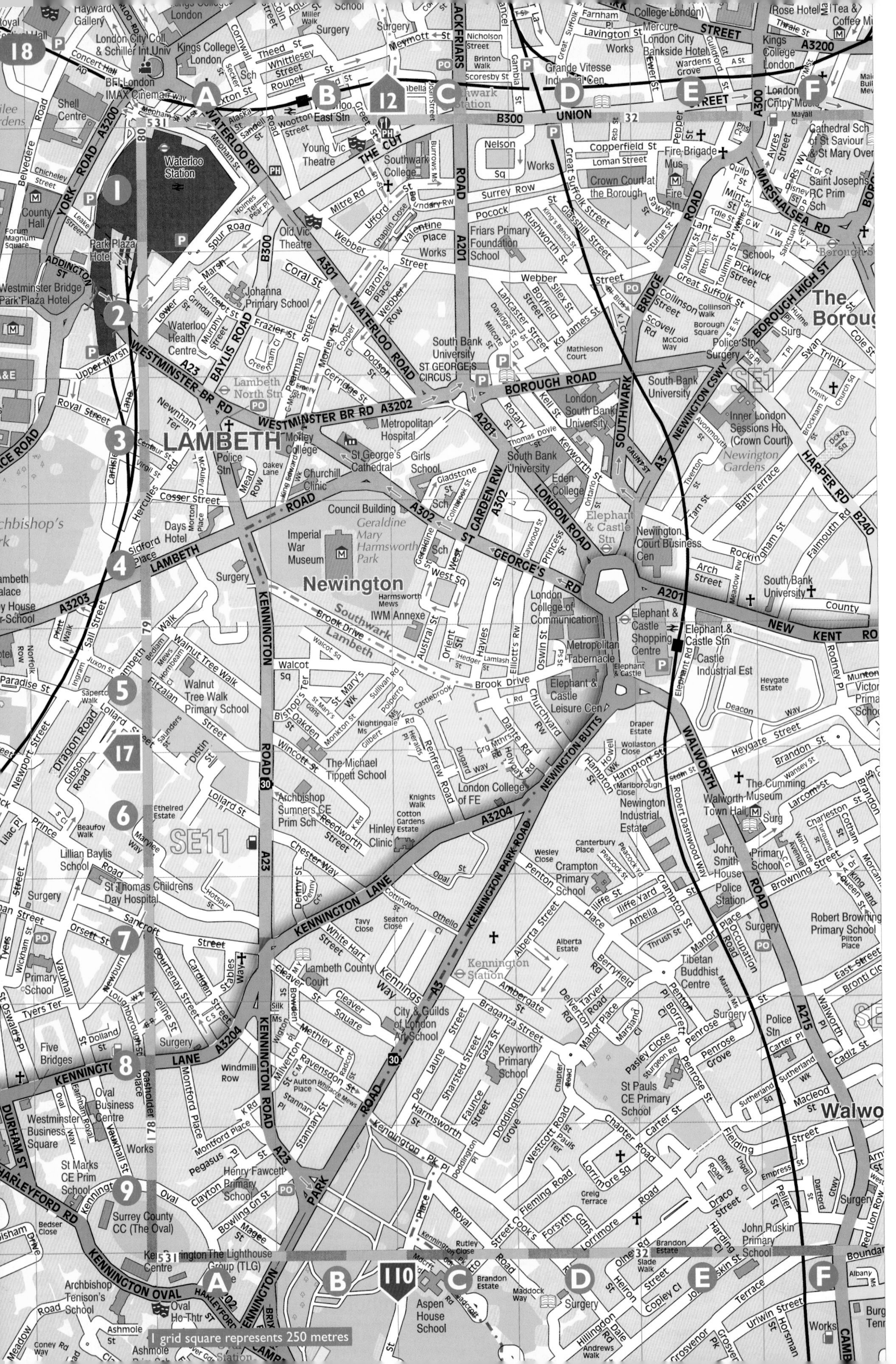
18
12
17
110
A
B
C
D
E
F
1
2
3
4
5
6
7
8
9
Hayward Gallery
London City Coll & Schiller Int Univ
Kings College London
BFI London IMAX Cinema
Shell Centre
Waterloo Station
Waterloo East Stn
Young Vic Theatre
THE CUT
Southwark College
Old Vic Theatre
County Hall
Park Plaza Hotel
Westminster Bridge Park Plaza Hotel
Johanna Primary School
Waterloo Health Centre
Lambeth North Stn
LAMBETH
Morley College
Metropolitan Hospital
St George's Cathedral
Churchill Clinic
Police Stn
Days Hotel
Council Building
Imperial War Museum
Geraldine Mary Harmsworth Park
Newington
IWM Annexe
South Bank University
ST GEORGE'S CIRCUS
London South Bank University
Eden College
Elephant & Castle Stn
Newington Court Business Cen
London College of Communication
Elephant & Castle Shopping Centre
Metropolitan Tabernacle
Elephant & Castle Leisure Cen
Castle Industrial Est
Heygate Estate
The Cumming Museum
Walworth Town Hall
Newington Industrial Estate
Crampton Primary School
Kennington Station
Keyworth Primary School
St Pauls CE Primary School
City & Guilds of London Art School
Lambeth County Court
Henry Fawcett Primary School
Surrey County CC (The Oval)
The Lighthouse Group (TLG)
Archbishop Tenison's School
Oval Ho Thtr
Aspen House School
John Ruskin Primary School
Walworth
The Borough
Borough High St
Inner London Sessions Ho (Crown Court)
Newington Gardens
Fire Brigade Mus
Crown Court at the Borough
Friars Primary Foundation School
South Bank University
Walnut Tree Walk Primary School
The Michael Tippett School
Archbishop Sumners CE Prim Sch
Hinley Clinic
London College of FE
St Thomas Childrens Day Hospital
Lillian Baylis School
Oval Business Centre
Westminster Business Square
St Marks CE Prim School
Five Bridges
Tibetan Buddhist Centre
Robert Browning Primary School
John Smith House
Police Station
SE1
SE11
WATERLOO RD
WESTMINSTER BR RD
BOROUGH ROAD
LONDON ROAD
NEW KENT RD
KENNINGTON ROAD
KENNINGTON LANE
KENNINGTON PARK ROAD
NEWINGTON BUTTS
WALWORTH ROAD
UNION STREET
KENNINGTON OVAL
HARLEYFORD RD
DURHAM ST
1 grid square represents 250 metres

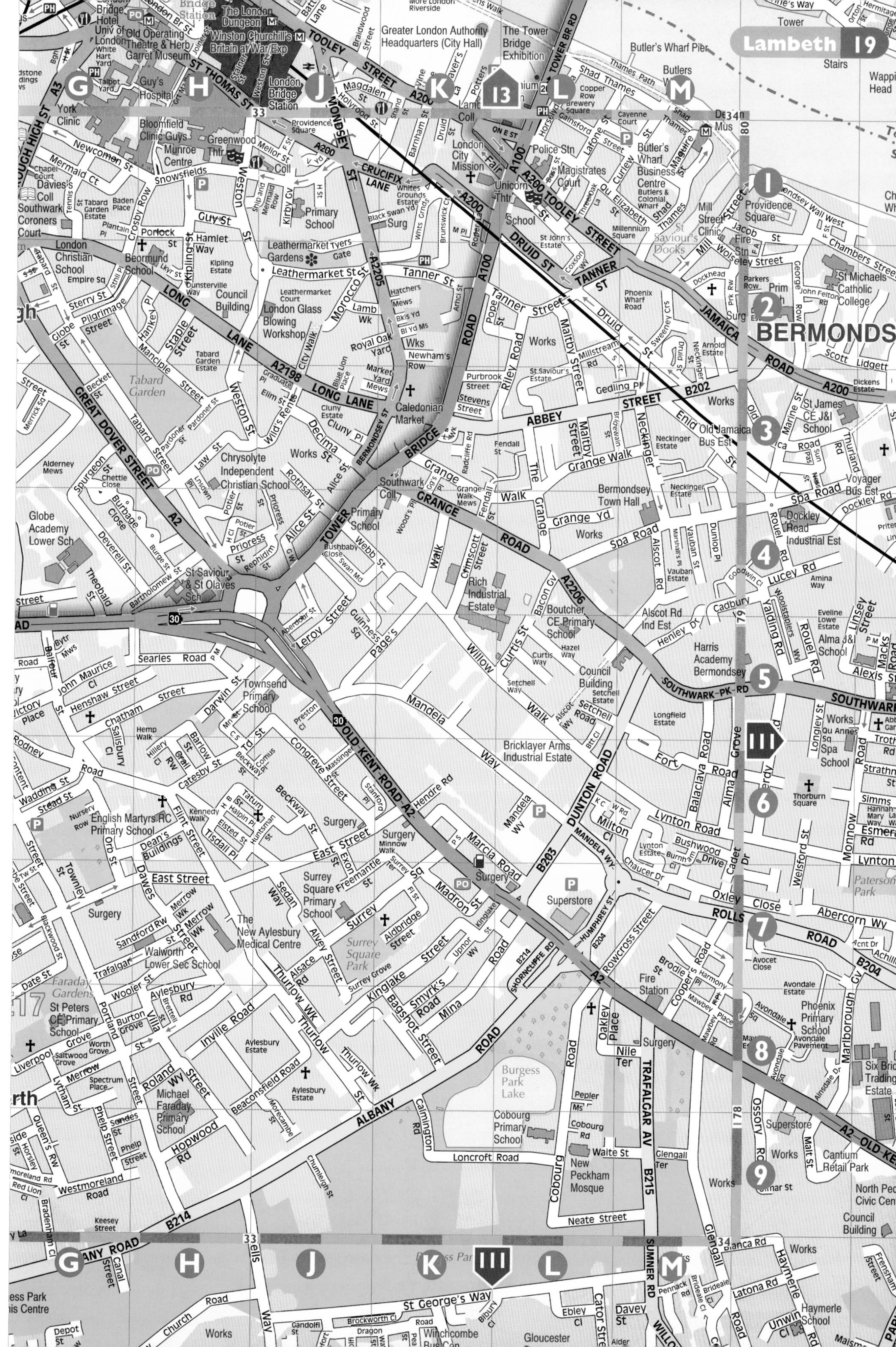

Lambeth 19
G
H
J
K
L
M
13
33
34
The London Dungeon
Winston Churchill's Britain at War Exp
Greater London Authority Headquarters (City Hall)
The Tower Bridge Exhibition
Butler's Wharf Pier
Thames Path
Butlers Wharf
Tower Stairs
Wapping Head
Hermitage
Bridge Hotel
Univ of London
Old Operating Theatre & Herb Garret Museum
Guy's Hospital
York Clinic
Bloomfield Clinic Guys
Greenwood Thtr
Munroe Centre
London Bridge Station
TOOLEY STREET
ST THOMAS ST
BOROUGH HIGH ST
A3
A200
Magdalen St
Holyrood St
Providence Square
Shad Thames
Copper Row
Brewery Square
Cayenne Court
Design Mus
Police Stn
Magistrates Court
Butler's Wharf Business Centre
Butlers & Colonial Wharf
Millennium Square
Lafone St
Curlew St
Maguire St
Horselydown La
Gainsford St
London City Mission
Unicorn Thtr
School
St John's Estate
TOOLEY STREET
DRUID ST
TANNER ST
A100
TOWER BR RD
Newcomen St
Mermaid Ct
Snowfields
Davies's Coll
Southwark Coroners Court
Tennis St
St Tabard Garden Estate
Baden Place
Crosby Row
Plantain Pl
Porlock St
Guy St
Hamlet Way
Kipling St
Kipling Estate
Dunsterville Way
Council Building
Bermondsey St
Weston St
Mellor St
Crucifix Lane
Whites Grounds Estate
Kirby Gv
Primary School
Black Swan Yd
Surg
Leathermarket Gardens
Tyers Gate
Leathermarket St
Leathermarket Court
London Glass Blowing Workshop
Morocco St
Lamb Wk
Hatchers Mews
Tanner St
Royal Oak Yard
Wks
Newham's Row
Market Yard Mews
Caledonian Market
BERMONDSEY ST
A2205
London Christian School
Bermondsey School
Empire Sq
Sterry St
Pilgrimage Street
Globe St
Hankey Pl
Staple Street
Manciple Street
Tabard Garden Estate
Tabard Garden
LONG LANE
A2198
Becket St
Tabard St
GREAT DOVER STREET
A2
Chrysolyte Independent Christian School
Law St
Decima St
Cluny Estate
Cluny Pl
Works
Alice St
Rothsay St
Prioress St
Alderney Mews
Spurgeon St
Chettle Close
Burbage Close
Deverell St
Globe Academy Lower Sch
Theobald St
St Saviour & St Olaves Sch
Bartholomew St
TOWER BRIDGE ROAD
Southwark Coll
Primary School
Webb St
Bushbaby Close
GRANGE ROAD
A2206
Grange Walk
The Grange
Grange Yd
Spa Road
Bermondsey Town Hall
Neckinger Estate
Fendall St
Radcliffe Rd
Tanner Street
Pope St
Riley Road
Maltby Street
Millstream Rd
St Saviour's Estate
Purbrook Street
Stevens Street
ABBEY STREET
B202
Gedling Pl
Phoenix Wharf Road
Sweeney Cres
Druid St
Arnold Estate
Enid St
Old Jamaica Bus Est
JAMAICA ROAD
A200
BERMONDSEY
Mill Street Clinic
Providence Square
Jacob St
Fire Stn
Wolseley Street
Dockhead
Parkers Row
Prim Sch
St Michaels Catholic College
Chambers Street
Scott Lidgett
Dickens Estate
St James CE J&I School
Marine St
Thurland Rd
Voyager Bus Est
Dockley Road Industrial Est
Rouel Rd
Lucey Rd
Amina Way
Alscot Rd
Alscot Rd Ind Est
Vauban Estate
Dunlop Pl
Cadbury Way
Henley Dr
Yalding Rd
Eveline Lowe Estate
Alma J&I School
Harris Academy Bermondsey
SOUTHWARK-PK-RD
SOUTHWARK PARK RD
Alexis St
Macks Rd
Rich Industrial Estate
Crimscott Street
Bacon Gv
Boutcher CE Primary School
Hazel Way
Curtis St
Curtis Way
Willow Walk
Council Building
Setchell Road
Setchell Estate
Longfield Estate
Fort Road
Balaclava Road
Alma Grove
Works
Qu Annes Sq
Spa School
Thorburn Square
Simms Rd
Strathnairn St
Esmeralda Rd
Lynton Rd
Paterson Park
Leroy Street
Guinness Sq
Page's Walk
Mandela Way
Bricklayer Arms Industrial Estate
DUNTON ROAD
Milton Cl
Lynton Road
Lynton Estate
Bushwood Drive
Chaucer Dr
Cadet Dr
Oxley Close
ROLLS ROAD
Abercorn Wy
Avocet Close
Avondale Estate
B204
Phoenix Primary School
Avondale Sq
Marlborough Gv
Six Bridges Trading Estate
Searles Road
John Maurice Cl
Henshaw Street
Chatham Street
Darwin St
Townsend Primary School
Preston Cl
Congreve Street
OLD KENT ROAD A2
30
Victory Place
Salisbury Cl
Rodney Road
Hemp Walk
Barlow St
Catesby St
Comus Pl
Massinger St
Stanford Pl
Hendre Rd
Wadding St
Stead St
Nursery Row
English Martyrs RC Primary School
Flint Street
Tatum St
Kennedy Walk
Huntsman St
Dean's Buildings
Tisdall Pl
Beckway St
Surgery
East Street
Exon St
Freemantle St
Surrey Square Primary School
Marcia Road
Madron St
PO
Surgery
MANDELA WY
B203
Superstore
Townley St
Dawes Street
Merrow St
Sandford Rw
Walworth Lower Sec School
The New Aylesbury Medical Centre
Sedan Way
Alvey Street
Surrey Square Park
Aldbridge Street
Surrey Grove
Kinglake Street
Upnor Wy
Humphrey St
Rowcross Street
Brodie St
Cooper's Road
Fire Station
Harmony Pl
Mawbey Place
Faraday Gardens
Date St
Trafalgar St
Wooler St
Aylesbury Rd
St Peters CE Primary School
Portland St
Burton Grove
Villa St
Inville Road
Aylesbury Estate
Thurlow St
Thurlow Wk
Alsace Rd
Bagshot Street
Smyrk's Road
Mina Road
SHORNCLIFFE RD
B214
A2
Oakley Place
Nile Ter
Surgery
TRAFALGAR AV
B215
Liverpool Grove
Saltwood Grove
Merrow St
Spectrum Place
Lytham St
Roland Wy
Michael Faraday Primary School
Beaconsfield Road
Morecambe St
Aylesbury Estate
Hopwood Rd
Queen's Rw
Horsley St
Phelp Street
Sondes St
Westmoreland Road
Westmoreland Rd
Red Lion Cl
Bradenham Cl
Keesey Street
ALBANY ROAD
B214
Calmington Rd
Burgess Park Lake
Cobourg Primary School
Cobourg Road
Pepler Ms
Cobourg Rd
Waite St
New Peckham Mosque
Loncroft Road
Chumleigh St
Neate Street
Glengall Ter
Glengall Road
Ossory Rd
Superstore
Works
Malt St
Cantium Retail Park
North Peckham Civic Centre
Council Building
Olmar St
2
3
4
5
6
7
8
9
I
Camberwell Road
Canal Street
Wells Way
Burgess Park
Sumner Rd
St George's Way
Church Road
Works
Depot St
Gandolfi St
Brockworth Cl
Dragon Road
Winchcombe Bus Cen
Bibury Cl
Ebley Cl
Cator Street
Davey St
Gloucester
Pennack Rd
Bridgeale Cl
Bianca Rd
Latona Rd
Haymerle Road
Haymerle School
Unwin Cl
Works
Frensham Street

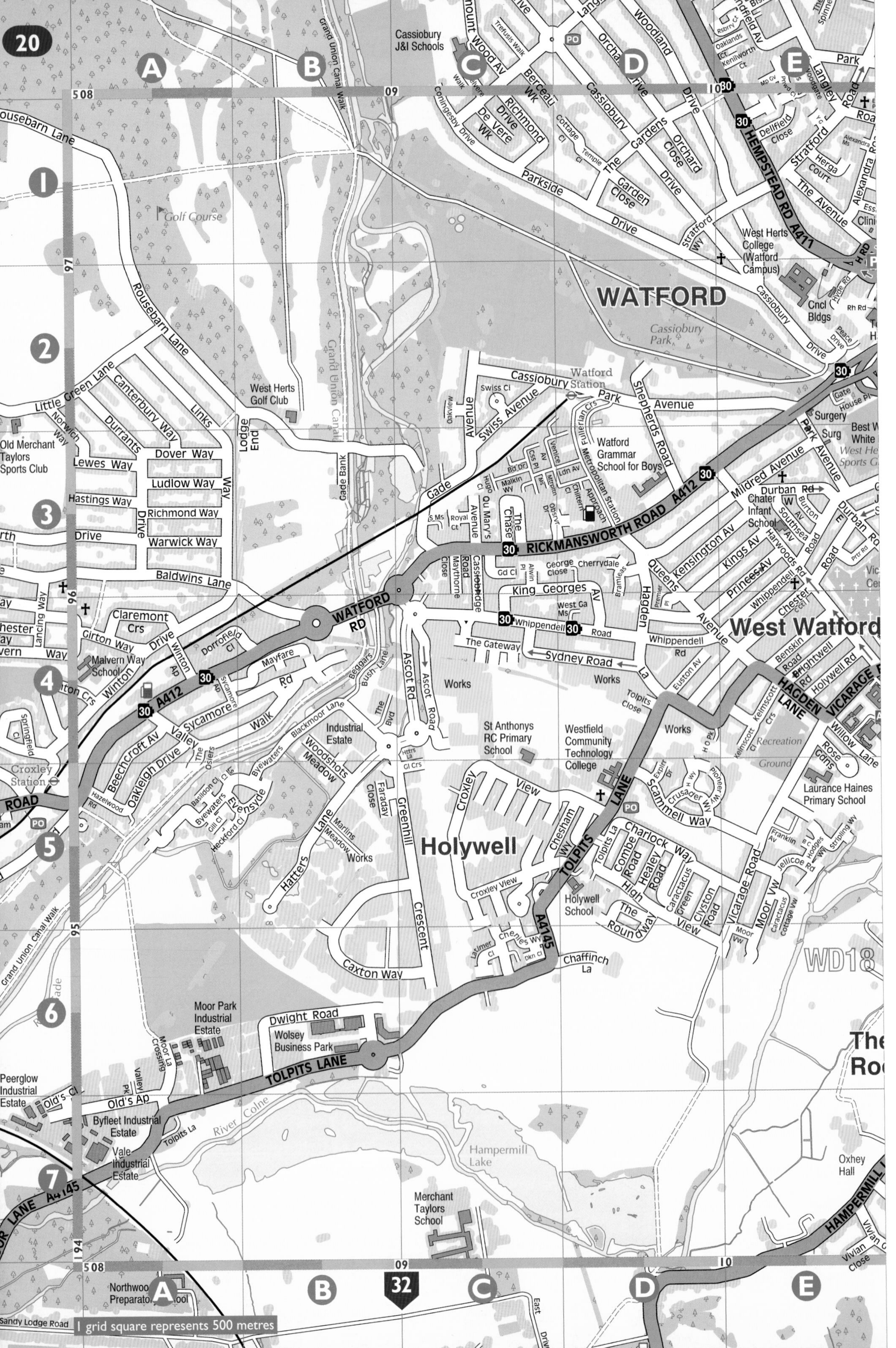

A
B
C
D
E
508
09
10
1
2
3
4
5
6
7
97
96
95
194
Cassiobury J&I Schools
Grand Union Canal Walk
Rousebarn Lane
Golf Course
West Herts Golf Club
Old Merchant Taylors Sports Club
Little Green Lane
Canterbury Way
Durrants
Links
Dover Way
Ludlow Way
Richmond Way
Warwick Way
Lewes Way
Hastings Way
Drive
Baldwins Lane
Lodge End
Way
Gade Bank
Grand Union Canal
Berceau Wk
Richmond Drive
De Vere Wk
Coningesby Drive
Orchard Drive
Woodland
Cassiobury
The Gardens
Orchard Close
Garden Close
Parkside
Drive
Stratford Wy
West Herts College (Watford Campus)
WATFORD
Cassiobury Park
Cassiobury Drive
Cncl Bldgs
HEMPSTEAD RD A411
Delffield Close
Stratford Court
Herga Court
The Avenue
Langley Road
Park
Cassiobury Park Avenue
Watford Station
Swiss Cl
Swiss Avenue
Oakview
Avenue
Shepherds Road
Watford Grammar School for Boys
Metropolitan Station Approach
Fullerian Crs
Gade
The Chase
RICKMANSWORTH ROAD A412
Mildred Avenue
Park Avenue
Surgery
Chater Infant School
Durban Rd
Kensington Av
Kings Av
Princes Av
Harwoods Rd
Southsea Av
Whippendell Rd
Chester Road
Queens Avenue
Hagden La
George Close
Cherrydale
King Georges Av
Bramleas
Cassiobridge Road
Maythorne Close
WATFORD RD
Ascot Rd
Ascot Road
Whippendell Road
The Gateway
Sydney Road
Works
Euston Av
West Watford
Benskin Road
Brightwell Rd
Holywell Rd
HAGDEN LANE
VICARAGE
Willow Lane
Rose Gdns
Recreation Ground
Laurance Haines Primary School
Claremont Crs
Girton Way
Malvern Way School
Winton Drive
Dorrofield Cl
Mayfare
Rd
A412
Sycamore Walk
Valley
Beechcroft Av
Oakleigh Drive
The Osiers
Croxley Station
ROAD
Hazelwood Rd
Lancing Way
Springfield Cl
Blackmoor Lane
Byewaters
Evensyde
Woodshots Meadow
Industrial Estate
The Bvd
Bush Lane
Beggars
Faraday Close
Greenhill Crescent
Hatters Lane
Marlins Meadow
St Anthonys RC Primary School
Westfield Community Technology College
Tolpits Close
Croxley View
Holywell
Chesham Wy
TOLPITS LANE
A4145
Scammell Way
Crusader Wy
Pioneer Wy
Charlock Way
Combe Road
Healey Road
Tolpits La
Caractacus Green
Clyston Road
High View
The Roundway
Holywell School
Vicarage Road
Moor Vw
Caxton Way
Chenies Wy
Chaffinch La
WD18
Moor Park Industrial Estate
Dwight Road
Wolsey Business Park
TOLPITS LANE
Moor La Crossing
Peerglow Industrial Estate
Old's Cl
Old's Ap
Byfleet Industrial Estate
Vale Industrial Estate
Tolpits La
River Colne
Hampermill Lake
Merchant Taylors School
Oxhey Hall
HAMPERMILL
Vivian Close
A4145
LANE
32
Northwood Preparatory School
Sandy Lodge Road
East Drive
1 grid square represents 500 metres

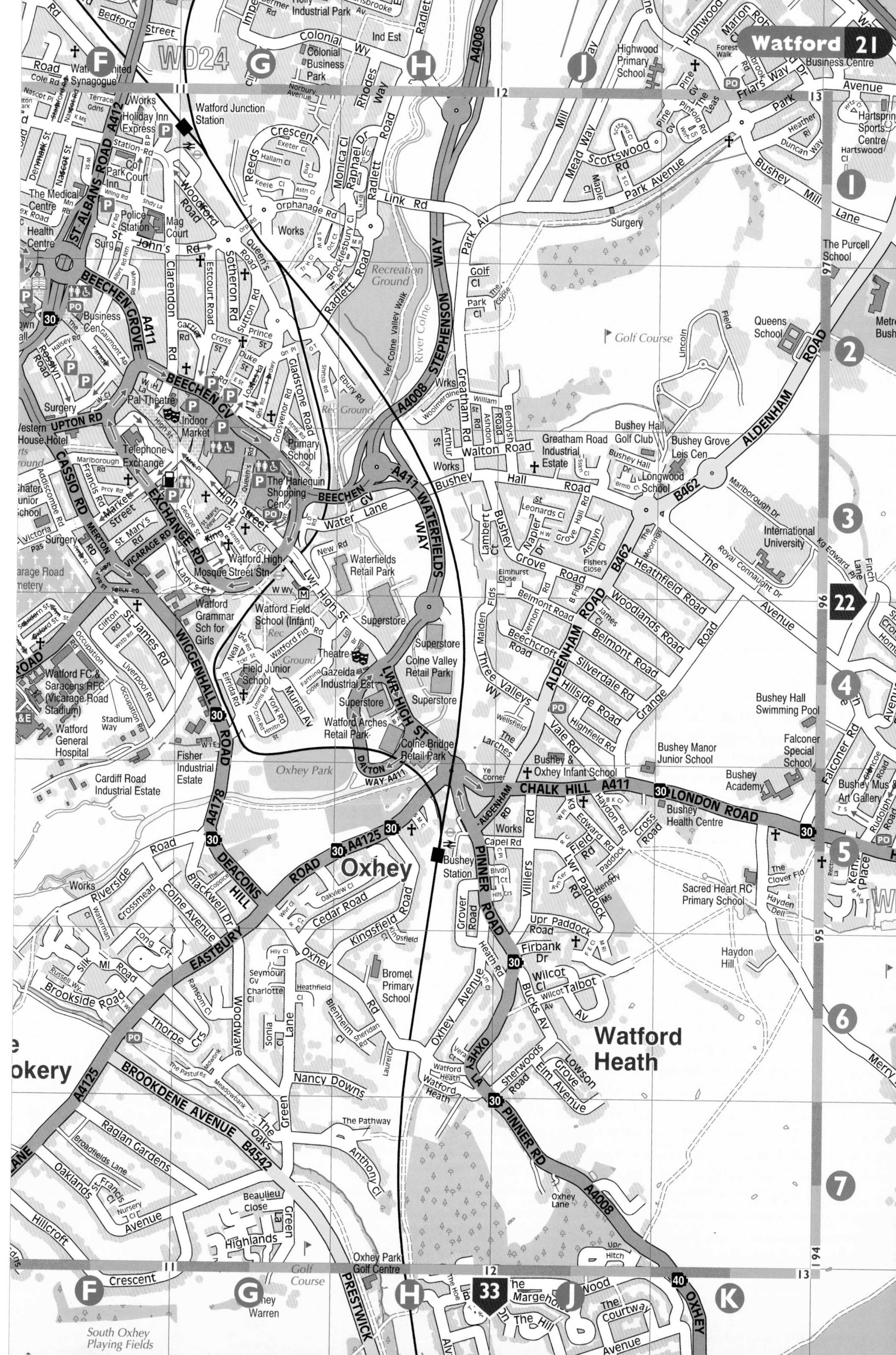
Watford Junction Station
Oxhey
Watford Heath
Bushey Station
Watford High Street Stn
Beechen Grove
Stephenson Way
Waterfields Way
Aldenham Road
Chalk Hill
London Road
Pinner Road
Eastbury Road
Brookdene Avenue
Wiggenhall Road
St Albans Road
Cassio Rd
Exchange Rd
Bushey Hall Road
Park Avenue
Golf Course
Oxhey Park
The Harlequin Shopping Cen
Watford General Hospital
Watford FC & Saracens RFC (Vicarage Road Stadium)
Watford Grammar Sch for Girls
Bushey Academy
Queens School
International University
Colne Valley Retail Park
Waterfields Retail Park
Watford Arches Retail Park
Colne Bridge Retail Park
Oxhey Park Golf Centre
South Oxhey Playing Fields
22
33

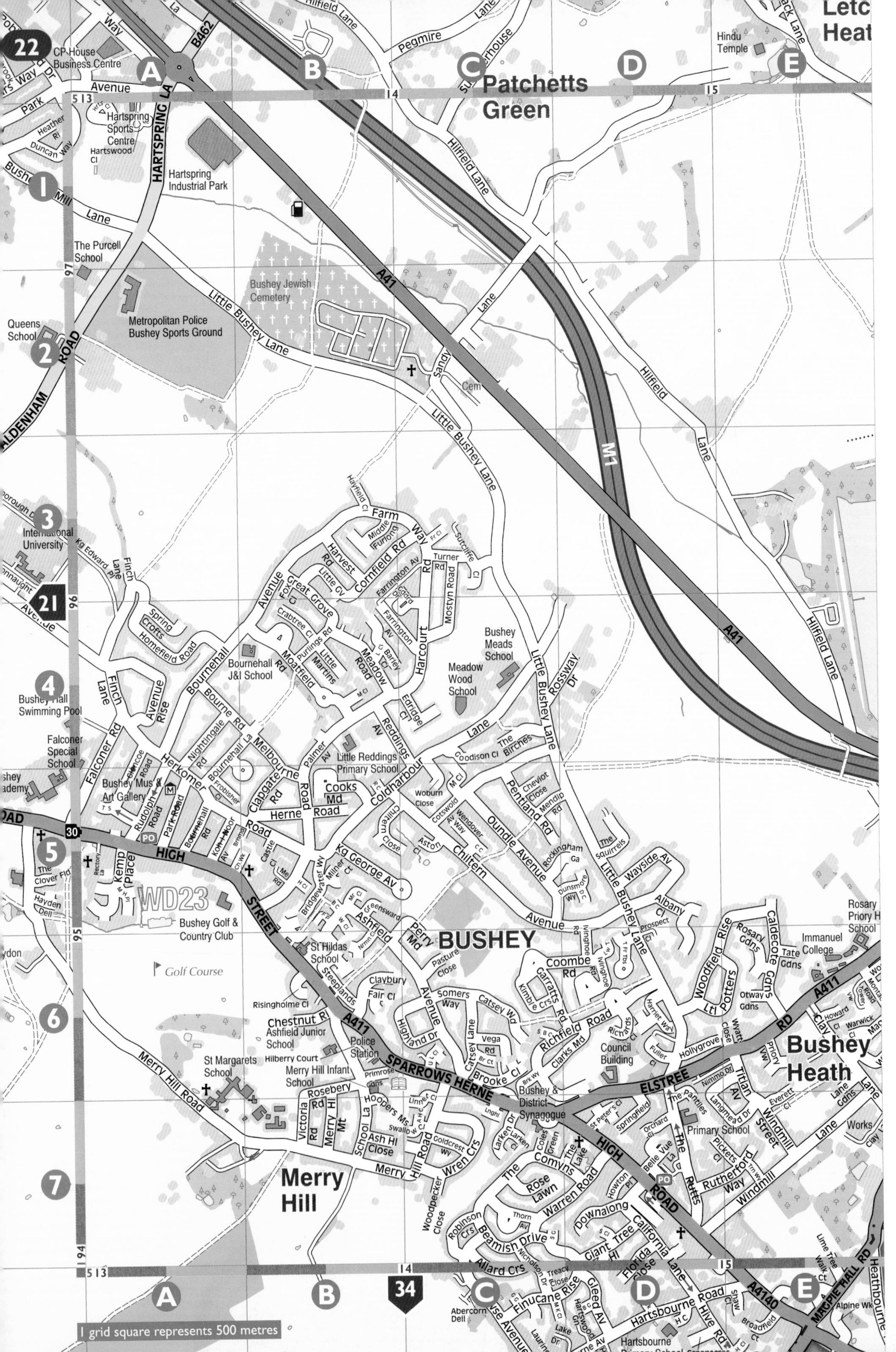

22
21
30
34
Patchetts Green
BUSHEY
Bushey Heath
Merry Hill
Hartspring Sports Centre
Hartspring Industrial Park
The Purcell School
Metropolitan Police Bushey Sports Ground
Bushey Jewish Cemetery
Queens School
International University
Bournehall J&I School
Bushey Meads School
Meadow Wood School
Little Reddings Primary School
Bushey Museum & Art Gallery
Bushey Golf & Country Club
Golf Course
St Hildas School
Ashfield Junior School
Merry Hill Infant School
St Margarets School
Police Station
Bushey & District Synagogue
Council Building
Primary School
Immanuel College
Rosary Priory High School
Hindu Temple
WD23
A41
M1
A411
A4140
B462
Sparrows Herne
Elstree Rd
High Street
High Road
Little Bushey Lane
Hilfield Lane
1 grid square represents 500 metres

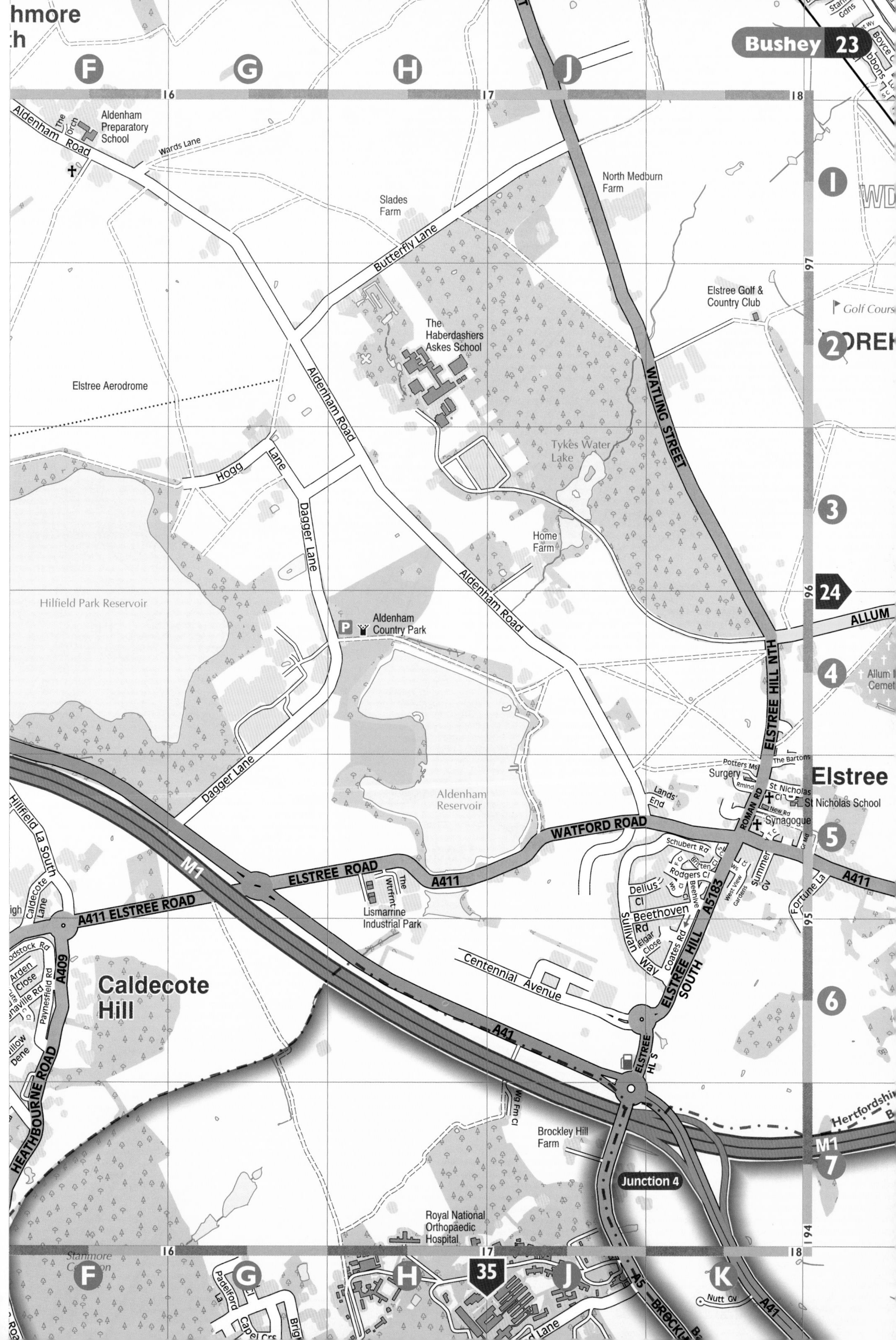
Aldenham Preparatory School
Aldenham Road
Wards Lane
Slades Farm
Butterfly Lane
North Medburn Farm
Elstree Golf & Country Club
The Haberdashers Askes School
Elstree Aerodrome
Aldenham Road
WATLING STREET
Tykes Water Lake
Hogg Lane
Dagger Lane
Home Farm
Hilfield Park Reservoir
Aldenham Country Park
Aldenham Road
ALLUM
ELSTREE HILL NTH
Dagger Lane
Aldenham Reservoir
Elstree
St Nicholas School
Synagogue
Surgery
WATFORD ROAD
ELSTREE ROAD
A411
M1
A411 ELSTREE ROAD
Lismarrine Industrial Park
Caldecote Hill
Centennial Avenue
ELSTREE HILL SOUTH
A5183
A41
HEATHBOURNE ROAD
A409
Brockley Hill Farm
Junction 4
Royal National Orthopaedic Hospital
Hertfordshire
Golf Course
Nutt Gv
Fortune La
Summer Gv
Beethoven Rd
Sullivan Way
Elgar Close
Coates Rd
Delius Cl
Rodgers Cl
Schubert Rd
Lands' End
Roman Rd
The Bartons
Potters Ms
Hilfield La South
Caldecote Lane
Paynesfield Rd
Arden Close
Willow Dene
Wg Fm Cl
Padelford La
A5

24
35

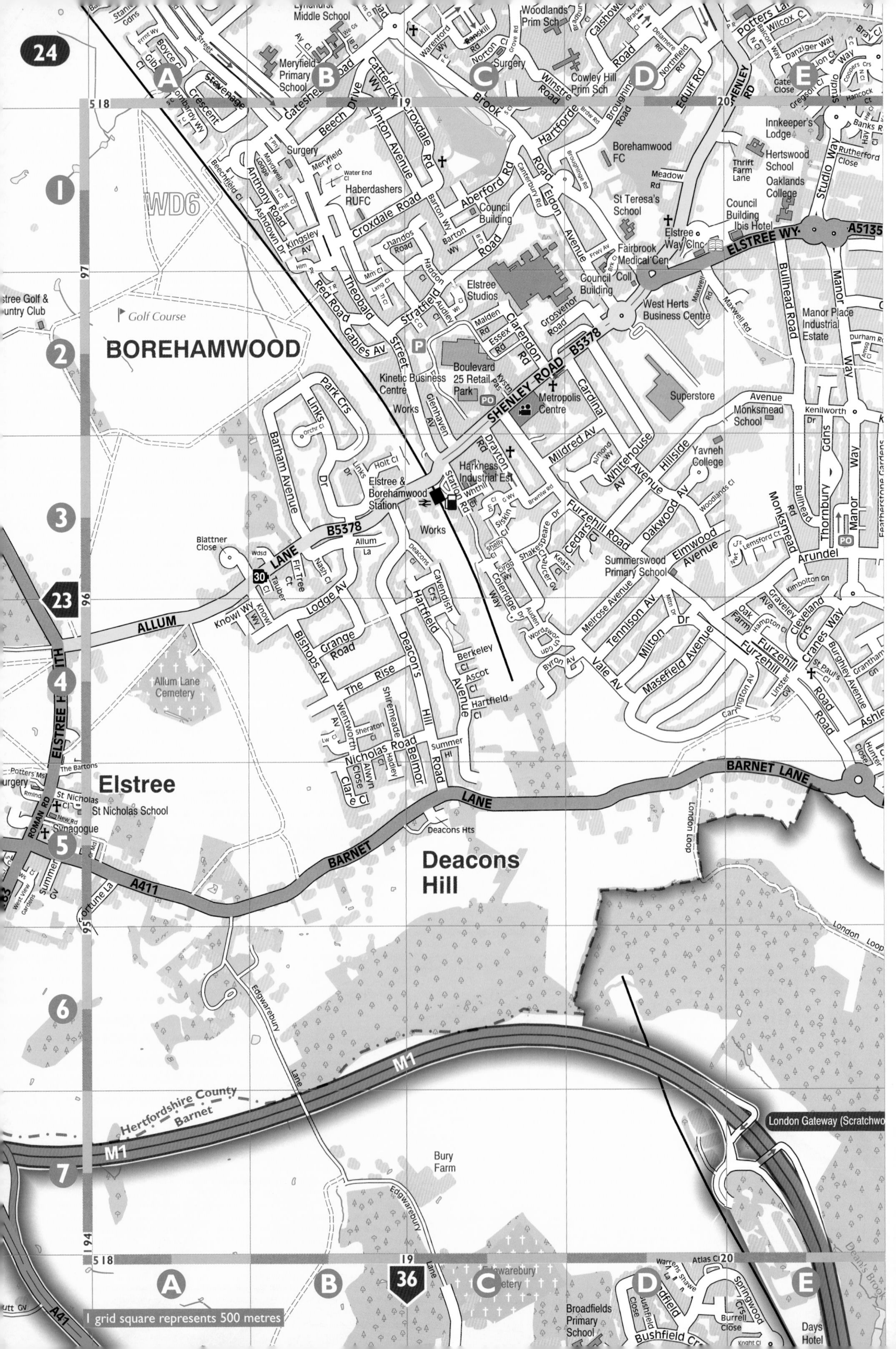
24
BOREHAMWOOD
WD6
Elstree
Deacons Hill
Golf Course
Elstree Golf & Country Club
Allum Lane Cemetery
Edgwarebury Cemetery
Meryfield Primary School
Lyndhurst Middle School
Woodlands Prim Sch
Cowley Hill Prim Sch
Haberdashers RUFC
Council Building
Elstree Studios
Borehamwood FC
St Teresa's School
Fairbrook Medical Cen
Coll
Elstree Way Clnc
Ibis Hotel
Innkeeper's Lodge
Hertswood School
Oaklands College
Thrift Farm Lane
West Herts Business Centre
Manor Place Industrial Estate
Boulevard 25 Retail Park
Kinetic Business Centre
Metropolis Centre
Superstore
Monksmead School
Yavneh College
Harkness Industrial Est
Elstree & Borehamwood Station
Works
Summerswood Primary School
St Nicholas School
Synagogue
Surgery
Deacons Hts
Bury Farm
Broadfields Primary School
Days Hotel
London Gateway (Scratchwo
London Loop
Hertfordshire County
Barnet
SHENLEY ROAD
B5378
ELSTREE WY
A5135
ALLUM LANE
BARNET LANE
A411
ELSTREE HILL
ROMAN RD
SHENLEY RD
M1
Edgwarebury Lane
Stevenage Crescent
Gateshead Road
Beech Drive
Catterick Wy
Linton Avenue
Croxdale Rd
Croxdale Road
Aberford Rd
Brook Road
Hartforde Road
Eldon Avenue
Broughinge Road
Canterbury Rd
Clarendon Rd
Grosvenor Road
Cardinal Avenue
Whitehouse Avenue
Hillside Avenue
Oakwood Av
Furzehill Road
Elmwood Avenue
Melrose Avenue
Tennison Av
Milton Dr
Masefield Avenue
Vale Av
Coleridge Way
Drayton Rd
Station Rd
Theobald Street
Stratfield Rd
Red Road
Gables Av
Anthony Road
Ashdown Dr
Kingsley Av
Barham Avenue
Links Dr
Park Crs
Lodge Av
Grange Road
Bishops Av
The Rise
Deacon's Hill Road
Hartfield Avenue
Cavendish Crs
Berkeley Cl
Ascot Cl
Hartfield Cl
Nicholas Road
Belmor
Clare Cl
Summer Hl
Bullhead Road
Manor Way
Thornbury Gdns
Monksmead Rd
Arundel
Cranes Way
Burghley Avenue
Cleveland Crs
Furzehill
Studio Way
Rutherford Close
Potters La
Danziger Way
Mildred Av
Shakespeare Dr
Cedars Cl
Byron Av
Gravelev Ave
Oak Farm
Carrington Av
Bushfield Cr
Springwood Crs
Burrell Close
Warrens Shawe La
Atlas Cl
Blattner Close
Fortune La
Summer Gv
Potters Ms
23
30
36
A B C D E
1 2 3 4 5 6 7
518 19 20
97 96 95 194
1 grid square represents 500 metres

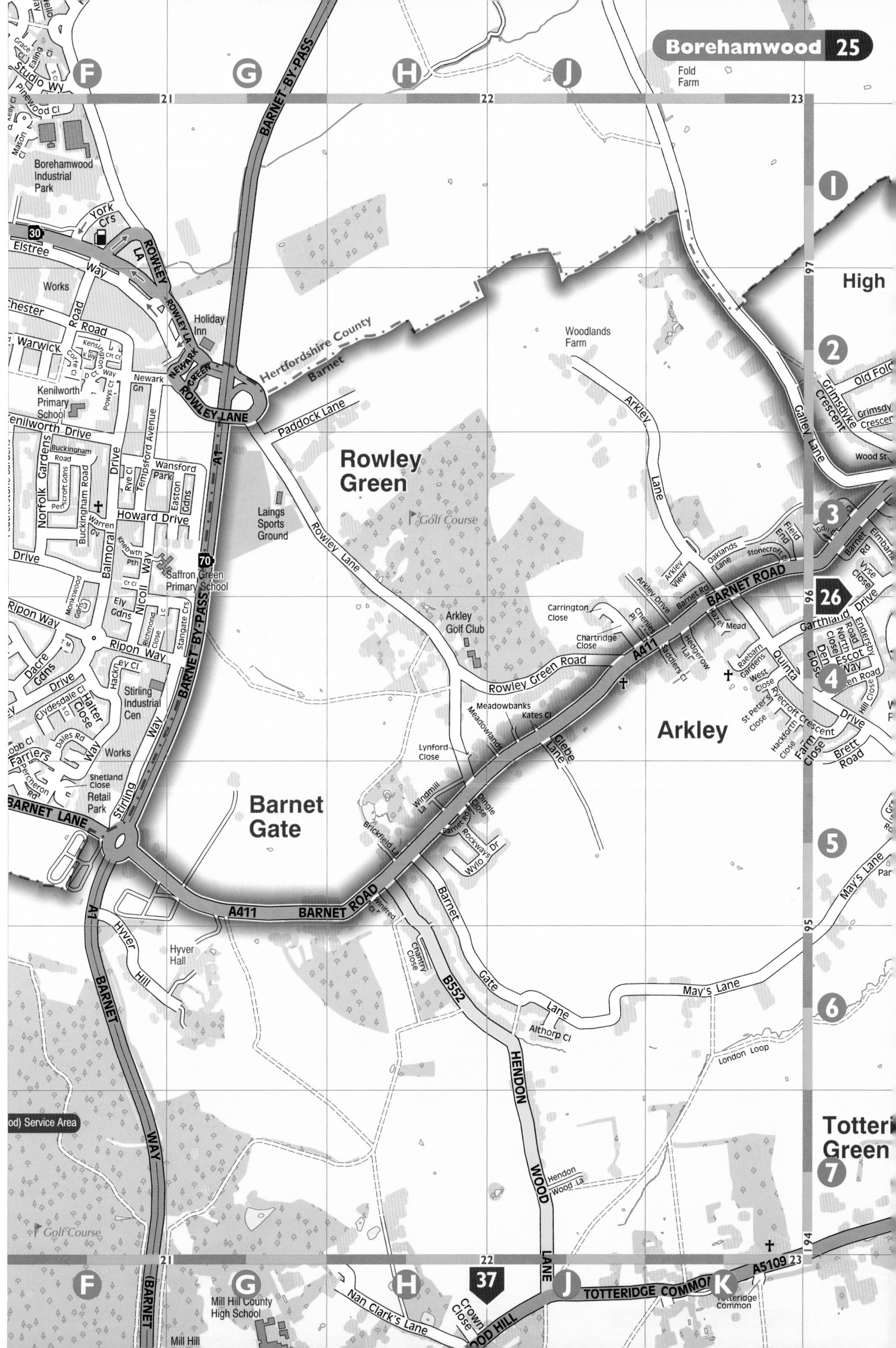
Borehamwood Industrial Park
Rowley Green
Golf Course
Laings Sports Ground
Arkley Golf Club
Woodlands Farm
Fold Farm
Barnet Gate
Arkley
Hyver Hall
Hertfordshire County
Barnet
BARNET-BY-PASS
BARNET ROAD
A411
Rowley Lane
Rowley Green Road
Arkley Lane
Galley Lane
Barnet Gate Lane
May's Lane
HENDON WOOD LANE
B552
BARNET WAY
A1
TOTTERIDGE COMMON
A5109
Holiday Inn
Saffron Green Primary School
Kenilworth Primary School
Stirling Industrial Cen
Retail Park
Mill Hill County High School
London Loop
Service Area
High
Totteridge Green
Totteridge Common
26
37
30
70

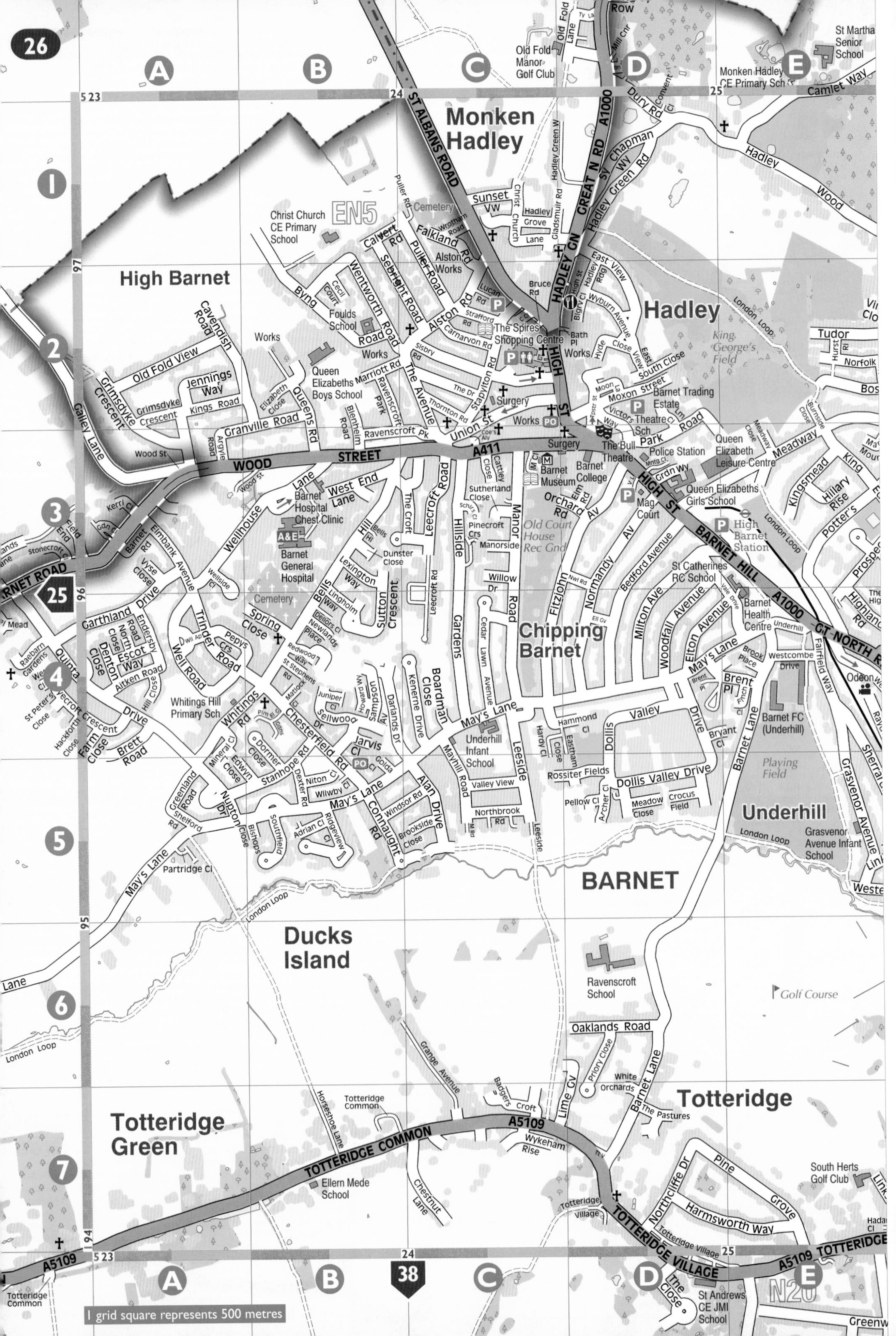
Monken Hadley
High Barnet
Hadley
Chipping Barnet
BARNET
Ducks Island
Underhill
Totteridge
Totteridge Green
EN5
N20
St Albans Road
Great North Rd
Hadley Green Rd
Wood Street
High St
Barnet Hill
Totteridge Common
Totteridge Village
Barnet Lane
May's Lane
Mays Lane
Galley Lane
Barnet Road
Christ Church CE Primary School
Foulds School
Queen Elizabeths Boys School
Barnet Hospital Chest Clinic
Barnet General Hospital
Cemetery
The Spires Shopping Centre
Barnet Museum
Barnet College
Old Court House Rec Gnd
The Bull Theatre
Police Station
Queen Elizabeth Leisure Centre
Queen Elizabeths Girls School
High Barnet Station
St Catherines RC School
Barnet Health Centre
Barnet FC (Underhill)
Playing Field
Gravenor Avenue Infant School
Underhill Infant School
Whitings Hill Primary Sch
Ravenscroft School
Golf Course
Ellern Mede School
St Andrews CE JMI School
South Herts Golf Club
Monken Hadley CE Primary Sch
St Martha Senior School
Old Fold Manor Golf Club
King George's Field
Barnet Trading Estate
London Loop
1 grid square represents 500 metres
25
38

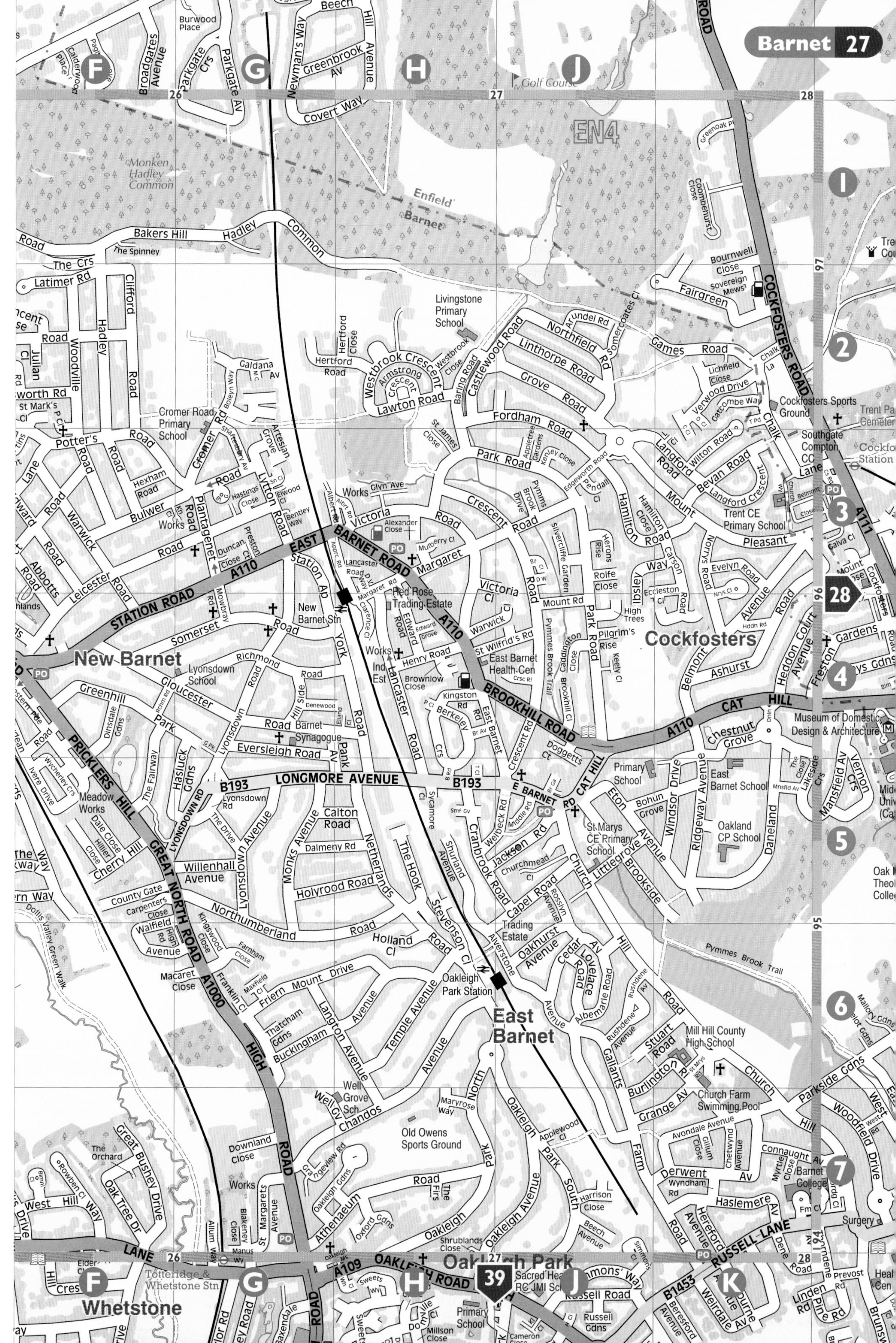

Monken Hadley Common
Enfield
Barnet
EN4
Golf Course
Hadley Common
Bakers Hill
The Spinney
Latimer Rd
Clifford Road
Hadley Road
Woodville Road
Cockfosters Road
Bournwell Close
Sovereign Mews
Fairgreen
Games Road
Livingstone Primary School
Westbrook Crescent
Armstrong Crescent
Lawton Road
Hertford Road
Hertford Close
Castlewood Road
Northfield Rd
Linthorpe Road
Grove Road
Fordham Road
Park Road
Cockfosters Sports Ground
Southgate Compton CC
Trent CE Primary School
Cromer Road Primary School
Potter's Road
Warwick Road
Bulwer Road
Plantagenet Road
Lytton Road
Hexham Road
Victoria Road
East Barnet Road
Station Road
A110
Station Ap
New Barnet Stn
Red Rose Trading Estate
Margaret Road
Crescent Road
Victoria Cl
Mount Rd
Park Road
Pymmes Brook Trail
Pilgrim's Rise
Cockfosters
Hamilton Road
Langford Crescent
Bevan Road
Mount Pleasant
Evelyn Road
Heddon Court Avenue
Ashurst
Belmont
Freston Gardens
Cat Hill
Museum of Domestic Design & Architecture
New Barnet
Somerset Road
Richmond Road
Lyonsdown School
Gloucester Road
Greenhill Park
East Barnet Health Cen
Brookhill Road
Henry Road
Lancaster Road
York Road
Kingston Rd
Berkeley Crs
Barnet Synagogue
Eversleigh Road
Longmore Avenue
B193
E Barnet Rd
Cat Hill
Chestnut Grove
East Barnet School
Primary School
Oakland CP School
Daneland
Windsor Drive
Ridgeway Avenue
Bohun Grove
Mansfield Av
Vernon Crs
Pricklers Hill
Great North Road
A1000
Lyonsdown Road
Lyonsdown Avenue
Calton Road
Dalmeny Rd
Holyrood Road
Monks Avenue
Netherlands Road
The Hook
Northumberland Road
Willenhall Avenue
Cherry Hill
Meadow Works
Cranbrook Road
Jackson Rd
Church Hill Road
Capel Road
St Marys CE Primary School
Littlegrove
Brookside
Avenue
Trading Estate
Oakhurst Avenue
Cedar Av
Lovelace Road
Albemarle Road
Rushdene Av
Pymmes Brook Trail
Stevenson Cl
Holland Cl
Alverstone Avenue
Oakleigh Park Station
East Barnet
Mill Hill County High School
Church Hill Road
Church Farm Swimming Pool
Burlington Ri
Stuart Road
Grange Av
Gallants Farm Road
Friern Mount Drive
Langton Avenue
Temple Avenue
Buckingham Road
Thatcham Gdns
Well Grove Sch
Chandos Avenue
North Road
Maryrose Way
Old Owens Sports Ground
Oakleigh Park South
Oakleigh Avenue
Applewood Cl
Harrison Close
Beech Avenue
Avondale Avenue
Derwent Av
Haslemere Av
Connaught Av
Barnet College
Surgery
Russell Lane
B1453
Parkside Gdns
Woodfield Drive
Great Bushey Drive
The Orchard
Oak Tree Dr
West Hill Way
Downland Close
Works
St Margarets Avenue
Athenaeum Road
Oakleigh Road
Oakleigh Park
Totteridge & Whetstone Stn
Whetstone
High Road
A109
Oakleigh Road
Sacred Heart RC JMI Sch
Russell Road
Russell Gdns
Primary School
Millson Close
Cameron Close
Linden Rd
Prevost Rd

28
39

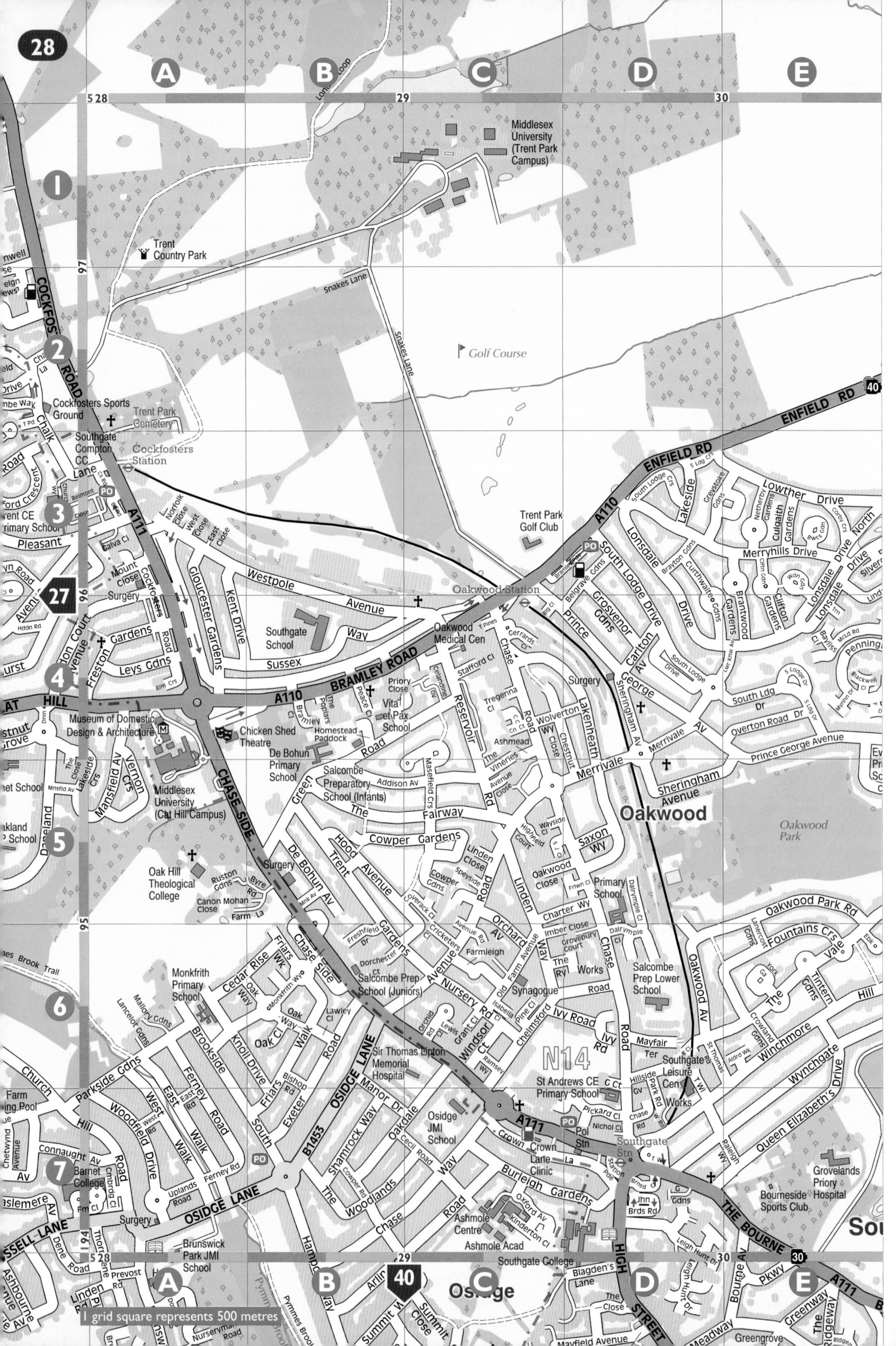

A
B
C
D
E
Middlesex University (Trent Park Campus)
Trent Country Park
Snakes Lane
Golf Course
Cockfosters Sports Ground
Trent Park Cemetery
Southgate Compton CC
Cockfosters Station
COCKFOSTERS ROAD
A111
ENFIELD RD
A110
Trent Park Golf Club
Oakwood Station
Westpole Avenue
Southgate School
Sussex Way
Gloucester Gardens
Kent Drive
BRAMLEY ROAD
Oakwood Medical Cen
Museum of Domestic Design & Architecture
Chicken Shed Theatre
De Bohun Primary School
Salcombe Preparatory School (Infants)
CHASE SIDE
Middlesex University (Cat Hill Campus)
Oak Hill Theological College
Oakwood
Oakwood Park
Lowther Drive
Merryhills Drive
South Lodge Drive
Prince George Avenue
Sheringham Avenue
Merrivale
Oakwood Park Rd
Fountains Crs
Cowper Gardens
The Fairway
Salcombe Prep Lower School
Salcombe Prep School (Juniors)
Monkfrith Primary School
Sir Thomas Lipton Memorial Hospital
N14
St Andrews CE Primary School
Southgate Leisure Cen
Osidge JMI School
OSIDGE LANE
B1453
Southgate Stn
Crown Lane Clinic
Burleigh Gardens
Ashmole Centre
Ashmole Acad
Southgate College
THE BOURNE
Grovelands Priory Hospital
Bourneside Sports Club
Wynchgate
Queen Elizabeth's Drive
Winchmore Hill
Barnet College
Brunswick Park JMI School
Osidge
HIGH STREET
Church Hill
Woodfield Drive
Ferney Road
Brookside
Chase Road
Reservoir Rd
Linden Way
Oakwood Av
Chase Side
28
29
30
97
96
95
94
27
40
1 grid square represents 500 metres

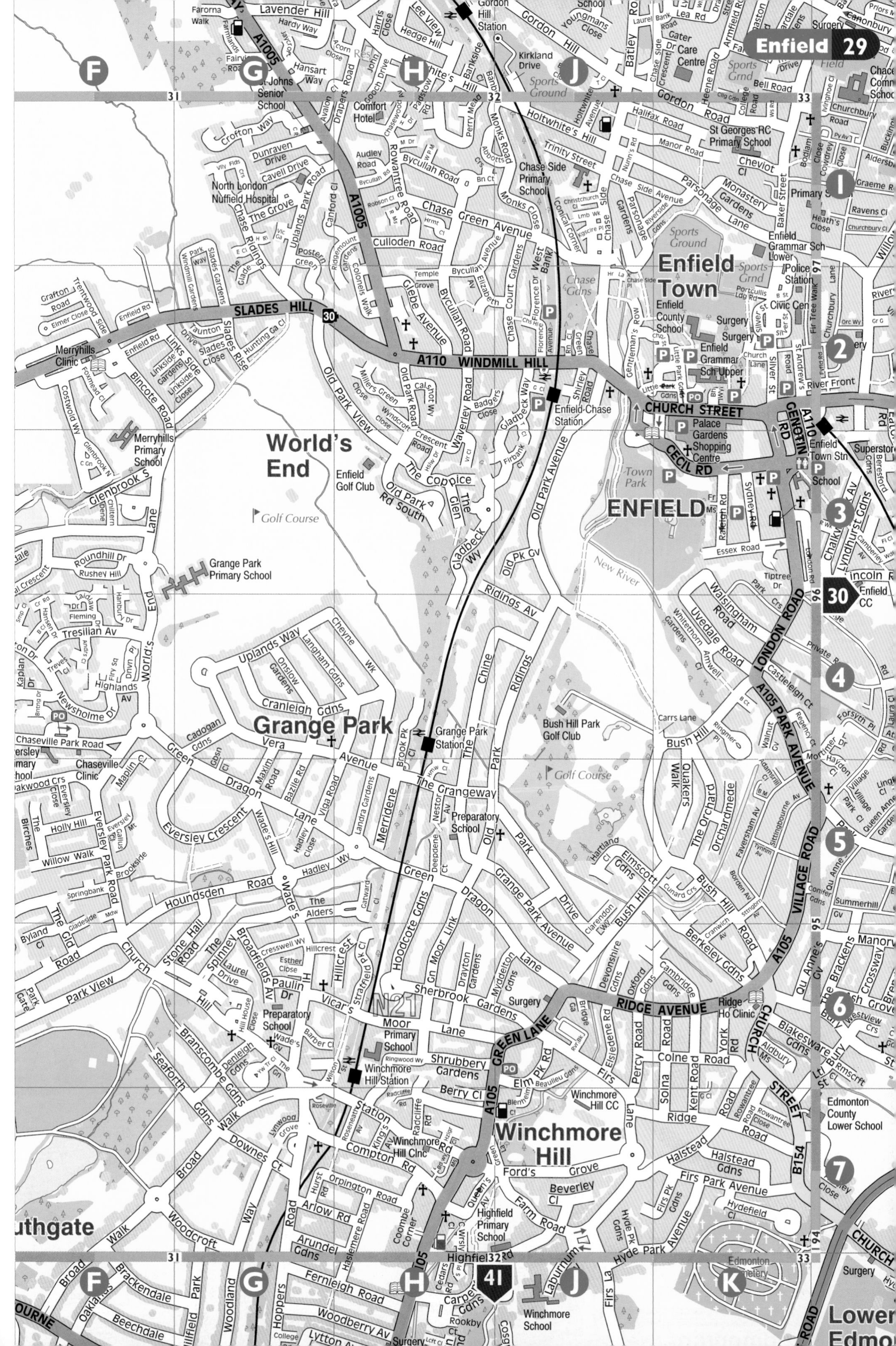
Enfield 29
Enfield Town
ENFIELD
World's End
Grange Park
Winchmore Hill
Southgate
Lower Edmonton
A110 WINDMILL HILL
SLADES HILL
CHURCH STREET
CECIL RD
GENOTIN RD
LONDON ROAD
A105 PARK AVENUE
VILLAGE ROAD
RIDGE AVENUE
GREEN LANE
CHURCH STREET
A1005
B154
Gordon Hill Station
Enfield Chase Station
Enfield Town Stn
Grange Park Station
Winchmore Hill Station
Enfield Golf Club
Golf Course
Bush Hill Park Golf Club
Merryhills Clinic
Merryhills Primary School
Grange Park Primary School
North London Nuffield Hospital
St Johns Senior School
Comfort Hotel
Chase Side Primary School
Enfield Grammar Sch Lower
Enfield Grammar Sch Upper
Enfield County School
Palace Gardens Shopping Centre
Town Park
New River
Chaseville Clinic
Preparatory School
Moor Primary School
Winchmore Hill Clnc
Winchmore Hill CC
Highfield Primary School
Winchmore School
Edmonton County Lower School
Edmonton Cemetery
Ridge Ho Clinic
Enfield CC
Lavender Hill
Gordon Hill
Holtwhite's Hill
Chase Green Avenue
Culloden Road
Old Park View
Old Park Avenue
Ridings Av
Uplands Way
Cranleigh Gdns
Vera Avenue
Green Dragon Lane
The Grangeway
Eversley Crescent
Houndsden Road
Church Hill
Vicar's Moor Lane
Sherbrook Gardens
Shrubbery Gardens
Compton Rd
Broad Walk
Woodcroft
Bush Hill
Walsingham Road
Uvedale Road
Halstead Road
Firs Park Avenue
Hyde Park Avenue
Firs Lane
Highfield Rd
Fernleigh Road
Woodberry Av
Brackendale
Beechdale
N21
30
41
F G H J K
31 32 33
94 95 96 97
1 2 3 4 5 6 7

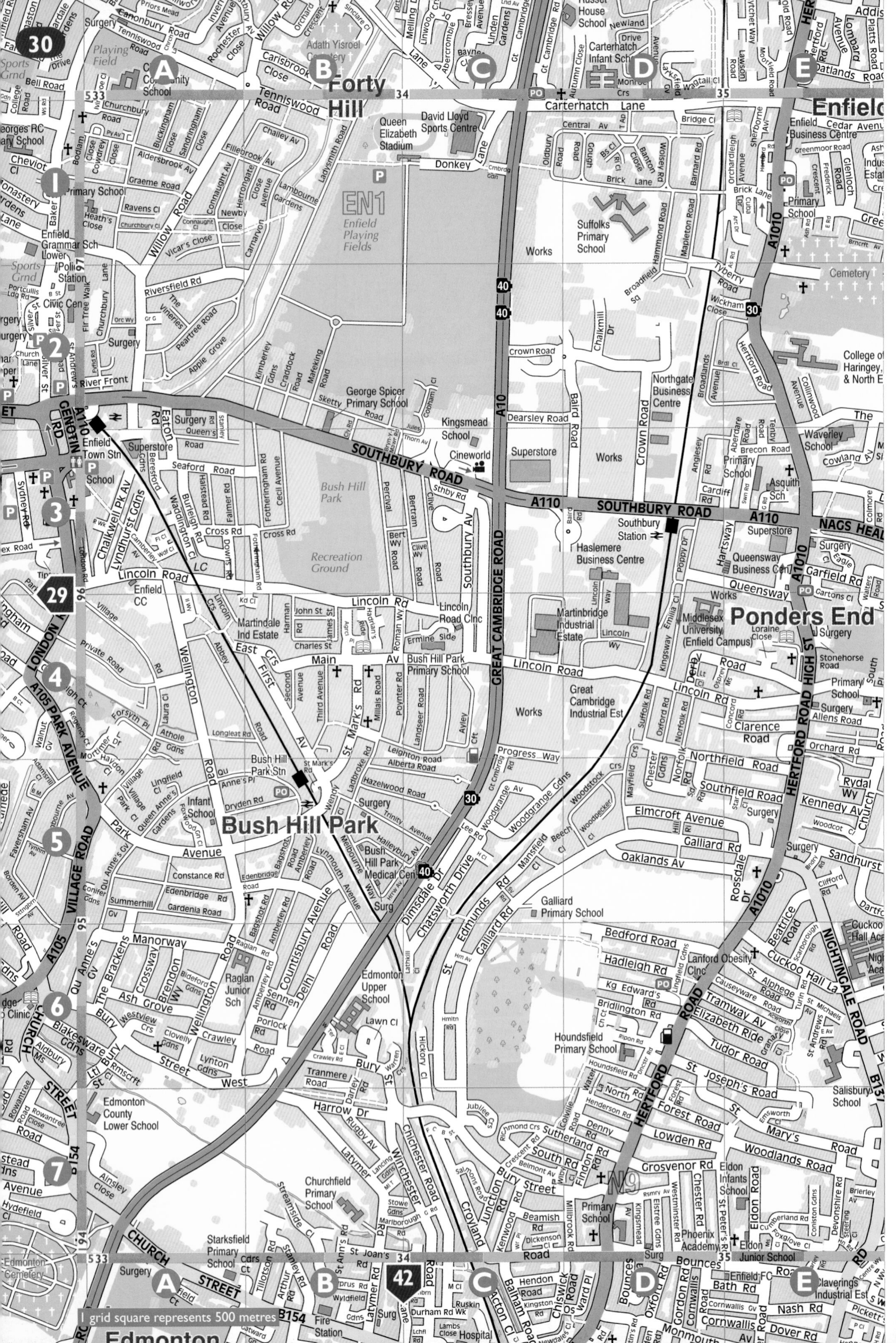

30
Forty Hill
Enfield
EN1
Enfield Playing Fields
Queen Elizabeth Stadium
David Lloyd Sports Centre
Carterhatch Lane
Donkey Lane
Brick Lane
Suffolks Primary School
Russet House School
Carterhatch Infant Sch
Adath Yisroel Cemetery
Playing Field
Community School
Tenniswood Road
Carisbrook Close
Chase Side
Enfield Grammar Sch Lower
Police Station
Civic Cen
Primary School
Riversfield Rd
Willow Road
Ladysmith Road
Lambourne Gardens
George Spicer Primary School
Kingsmead School
Cineworld
SOUTHBURY ROAD
A110
A10
A1010
GREAT CAMBRIDGE ROAD
Enfield Town Stn
Superstore
Bush Hill Park
Recreation Ground
Lincoln Road
Enfield CC
Martindale Ind Estate
Lincoln Road Clnc
Bush Hill Park Primary School
Southbury Station
Haslemere Business Centre
Martinbridge Industrial Estate
Great Cambridge Industrial Est
Works
Northgate Business Centre
Crown Road
Baird Road
Dearsley Road
Ponders End
Middlesex University (Enfield Campus)
Queensway Business Cen
Waverley School
College of Haringey, Enfield & North E
Cemetery
Enfield Business Centre
HERTFORD ROAD HIGH ST
NAGS HEAD
29
LONDON RD
A105 PARK AVENUE
VILLAGE ROAD
Bush Hill Park Stn
Bush Hill Park
Infant School
Bush Hill Park Medical Cen
Galliard Primary School
Houndsfield Primary School
Lanford Obesity Clnc
HERTFORD ROAD
NIGHTINGALE ROAD
Salisbury School
Edmonton Upper School
Raglan Junior Sch
Edmonton County Lower School
Churchfield Primary School
Starksfield Primary School
CHURCH STREET
Edmonton Cemetery
Phoenix Academy
Eldon Infants School
Eldon Junior School
Enfield FC
Claverings Industrial Est
N9
Edmonton
Fire Station
42
1 grid square represents 500 metres

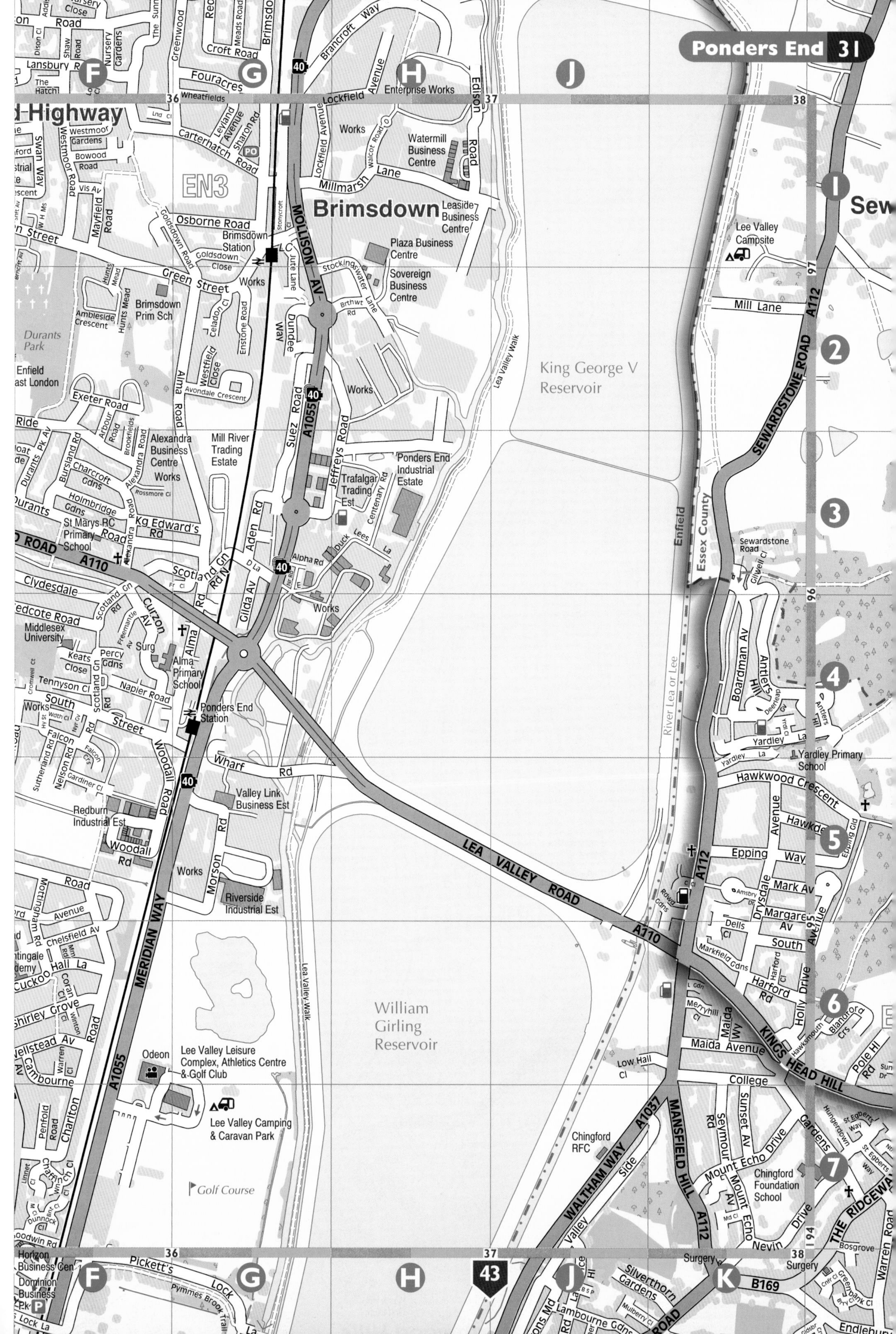

Nursery Close
The Sunn
Road
Greenwood
Red
Meads Road
Brimsdown
Brancroft Way
Croft Road
Carterhatch
Fouracres
40
Lockfield
Avenue
Enterprise Works
Edison
J
Lansbury
Dixon Cl
Shaw Road
Nursery Gardens
Wheatfields
Lockfield
36
Works
37
38
The Hatch
F
G
H
d-Highway
Westmoor
Gardens
Carterhatch Road
Sharon Rd
Works
Watermill Business Centre
I
Swan Way
Bowood Road
Leyland Avenue
PO
Road
Sew
Westmoor Road
Lea Valley Campsite
EN3
Osborne Road
Millmarsh Lane
Brimsdown
Leaside Business Centre
Mill Lane
97
A112
Mayfield Road
Goldsdown Road
Brimsdown Station
LC
Stocking
Jute Lane
Plaza Business Centre
Stockingswater Lane
2
Green Street
Goldsdown Close
Celadon Cl
Brthwt Rd
Sovereign Business Centre
Durants Park
Ambleside Crescent
Brimsdown Prim Sch
Hunts Mead
Enstone Road
Mollison Av
A1055
King George V Reservoir
Enfield East London
Westfield Close
Dundee Way
Works
3
Exeter Road
Alma Road
Avondale Crescent
40
Suez Road
Jeffreys Road
Sewardstone Road
Sewardstone Road
Essex County
Ride
Arbour Road
Brookfields
Alexandra Business Centre
Mill River Trading Estate
Ponders End Industrial Estate
Gilwell
96
Boat de
Charcroft Gdns
Alexandra Road
Works
Trafalgar Trading Est
Centenary Rd
Gilwell La
Boardman Av
Antlers
4
Durants
Holmbridge Gdns
Rossmore Cl
Duck Lees
Alpha Rd
Yardley
La
Antlers La
St Marys RC Primary School
Kg Edward's Rd
A110
Scotland
Fr Cl
40
D La
River Lea or Lee
Yardley La
Yardley Primary School
Clydesdale
Scotland Rd
Curzon Av
Freemantle
Surg
Alma
Works
Hawkwood Crescent
edcote Road
Scotland Gn
Middlesex University
Keats Close
Percy Gdns
Alma Primary School
Ponders End Station
5
Tennyson Cl
Napier Road
Epping Way
Hawkde
A112
South Works
Falcon Rd
Wharf Rd
Valley Link Business Est
Rbwd
Mark Av
Sutherland Rd
Nelson Rd
Gardiner Cl
Falcon Cl
Amsbry
Drysdale
Road
Woodall Road
Morson Rd
40
Cedars
Margaret Av
Mansfield
Redburn Industrial Est
Works
LEA VALLEY ROAD
A110
Dells Cl
South
6
Woodall Rd
Riverside Industrial Est
Markfield Gdns
Markfield Cl
Harford Rd
Holly Drive
Road
Mottingham
Chelsfield Av
Lea Valley Walk
William Girling Reservoir
Merryhill
Maida Mw
Maida Av
Blandfd Crs
Cuckoo Hall La
Coran Wilton
Shirley Grove
Meridian Way
Odeon
Lee Valley Leisure Complex, Athletics Centre & Golf Club
Maida Avenue
College
Kings Head Hill
Hawksmorth
Pole Hl Rd
Sun Dr
Wellstead Av
Cambourne
A1055
Lee Valley Camping & Caravan Park
Low Hall Cl
Mount Echo Drive
St Egberts Way
7
Charlton Road
Penfold Road
Golf Course
Chingford RFC
Waltham Way
A1057
Mansfield Hill A112
Mount Echo Av
Sevmour Rd
Sunset Av
Chingford Foundation School
St Egberts Way
Lmnt Cl
Horizon Business Cen
Pickett's Lock
Valley Side
Nevin
THE RIDGEWA
Bosgrove
Dominion Business
P
Pymmes Brook Trail
Silverthorn Gardens
K
Warren Road
Endlebur
36
37
43
B169

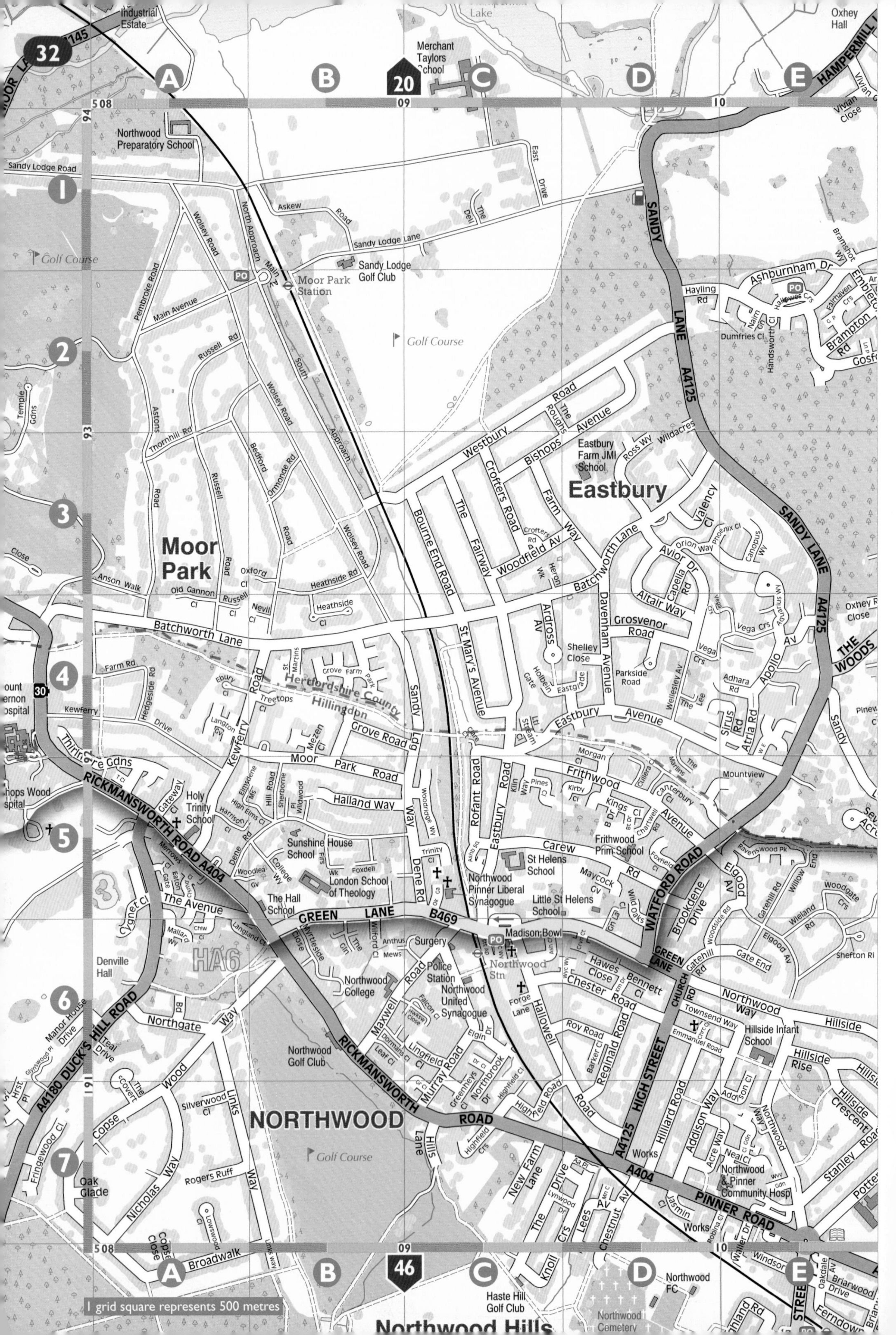
32
20
46
30
A
B
C
D
E
1
2
3
4
5
6
7
508
09
10
94
93
91
Industrial Estate
Merchant Taylors School
Oxhey Hall
HAMPERMILL LA
Vivian Close
Northwood Preparatory School
Sandy Lodge Road
Askew Road
Sandy Lodge Lane
East Drive
The Dell
Wolsey Road
North Approach
Main Av
Golf Course
Pembroke Road
Sandy Lodge Golf Club
Moor Park Station
Main Avenue
Russell Rd
South Approach
Astons Road
Temple Gdns
Thornhill Rd
Bedford
Ormonde Rd
Russell Road
Moor Park
Close
Anson Walk
Old Gannon Cl
Oxford Cl
Russell Cl
Nevil Cl
Heathside Rd
Heathside Cl
Batchworth Lane
SANDY LANE
A4125
Ashburnham Dr
Hayling Rd
Nairn Gn
Dumfries Cl
Handsworth Cl
Fairhaven Crs
Brampton Rd
Bramshot Wy
Embleton
Gosfo
Westbury Road
The Roughs
Bishops Avenue
Eastbury Farm JMI School
Ross Wy
Wildacres
Eastbury
Valency Cl
Crofters Road
Farm Way
The Fairway
Bourne End Road
Crofters Rd
Woodfield Av
Heron Wk
Batchworth Lane
Orion Way
Phoenix Cl
Canopus Wy
Avior Dr
Capella Rd
Altair Way
Aquarius Wy
Oxhey Close
Ardross Av
Davenham Avenue
Grosvenor Road
Vega Crs
Apollo Av
THE WOODS
St Mary's Avenue
Shelley Close
Parkside Road
Wellesley Av
Vega Crs
Adhara Rd
Holbein Gate
Eastgrade
The Lee
Sirus Rd
Atria Rd
Farm Rd
Hedgeside Rd
Ebury Cl
Kewferry Road
St Martins
Grove Farm Park
Hertfordshire County
Hillingdon
Treetops Cl
Sandy Ldg Way
Kewferry Drive
Langton Gv
Mezen Cl
Grove Road
Eastbury Avenue
Lt Stream Cl
Mountview
Pinew
Sandy
Moor Park Road
Rofant Road
Eastbury Road
Kiln Way
Pines Cl
Morgan Cl
Frithwood Avenue
Kirby Cl
Kings Cl
Canterbury Cl
Marlins
Thirlmere Gdns
RICKMANSWORTH ROAD A404
Gateway
Holy Trinity School
Elmsdene Ms
Hill Road
Sherborne Pl
Wildwood
Halland Way
Woodridge Wy
Chartwell Rd
High Elms Cl
Harrison Cl
Dene Rd
Sunshine House School
Trinity Cl
Carew Rd
St Helens School
Frithwood Prim School
Foxfield Cl
WATFORD ROAD
Ravenswood Pk
Elgood Av
Willow End
Woodgate Crs
Merrows Cl
Eaton Gate
College Wy
Woodlea Gv
Firs Wk
Foxdell
London School of Theology
Northwood Pinner Liberal Synagogue
Maycock Gv
Wild Oaks
Brookdene Drive
Woodside Rd
Gatehill Rd
Wieland Rd
The Avenue
Dene Rd
The Hall School
Little St Helens School
Cygnet Cl
Mallard Wy
GREEN LANE B469
Madison Bowl
Myrtleside Close
Wilford Cl
Anthus Mews
Surgery
Northwood Stn
Hawes Close
Bennett Cl
GREEN LANE
Gatehill Rd
Elgood Av
Gate End
Shefton Ri
Denville Hall
HA6
Northwood College
Police Station
Northwood United Synagogue
Forge Lane
Chester Road
CHURCH RD
Northwood Way
Hillside
Manor House Drive
A4180 DUCK'S HILL ROAD
Northgate
Way
Teal Drive
Maxwell Road
Falcon Cl
Dormans Cl
Leaf Cl
Northwood Golf Club
Lingfield Cl
Murray Road
Elgin Dr
Hallowell Road
Roy Road
Reginald Road
Barker Cl
Townsend Way
Emmanuel Road
Hillside Infant School
Hillside Rise
Hillside Crescent
Wood Links
The Covert
Silverwood Cl
Copse
Greenheys Cl
Northbrook Dr
Highfield Cl
Highfield Road
RICKMANSWORTH ROAD
A4125 HIGH STREET
Hilliard Road
Addison Way
Addison Cl
Northwood Way
NORTHWOOD
Hills Lane
Highfield Crs
Works
Acre Way
Neal Cl
Northwood & Pinner Community Hosp
Stanley Road
Fringewood Cl
Nicholas Way
Rogers Ruff
Golf Course
New Farm Lane
The Drive
Lynwood Dr
Lees Av
Chestnut Av
A404
Jasmin Cl
PINNER ROAD
Works
Oak Glade
Copse Close
Lowswood Cl
Links Way
Knoll Crs
Robina Cl
Waller Dr
Windsor
Potter
Broadwalk
Haste Hill Golf Club
Northwood FC
Northwood Cemetery
Northwood Hills
Oakdale Av
Briarwood Drive
Ferndown
STREET
1 grid square represents 500 metres

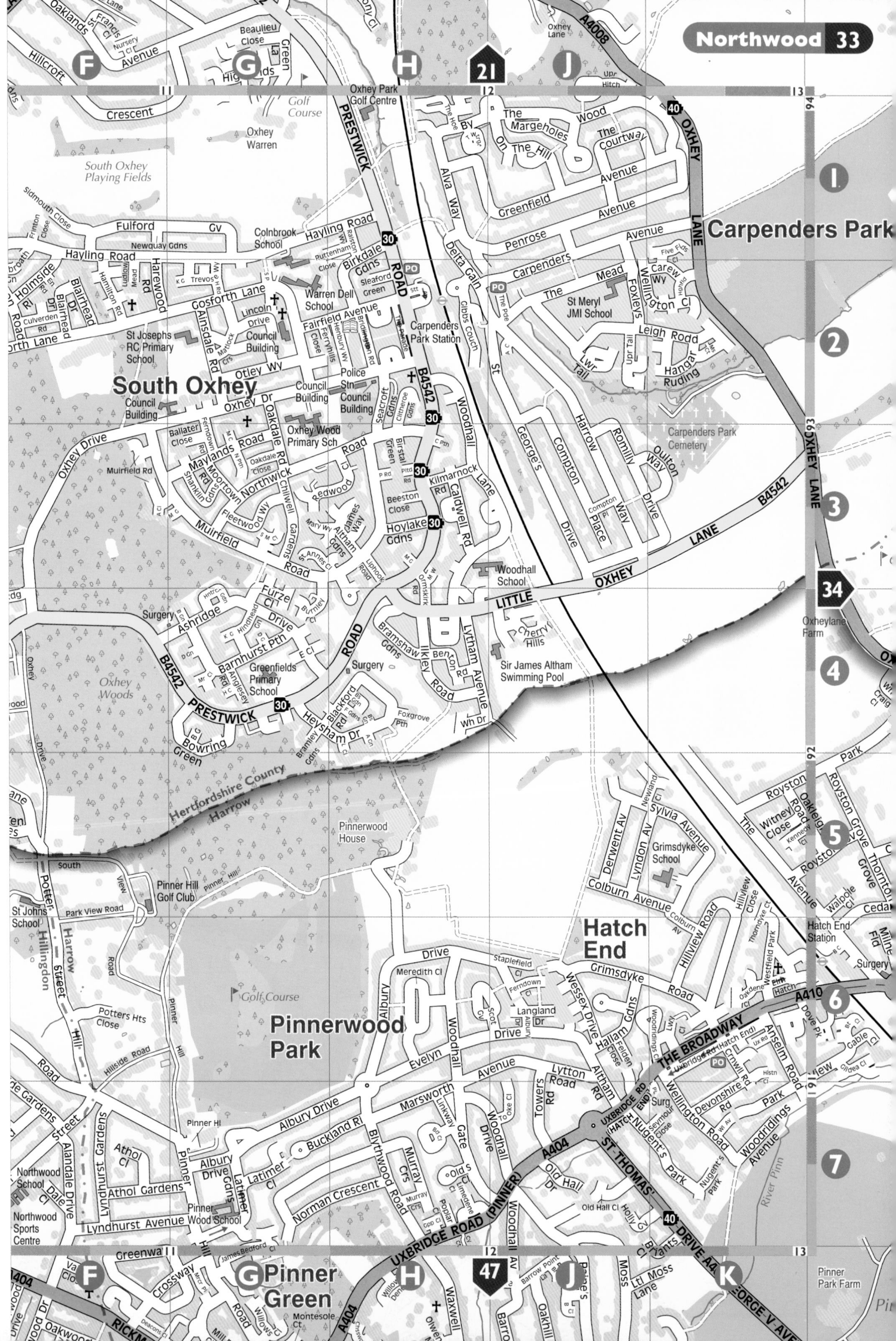

Carpenders Park
South Oxhey
Hatch End
Pinnerwood Park
Pinner Green
Oxhey Park Golf Centre
Oxhey Warren
South Oxhey Playing Fields
Carpenders Park Station
Carpenders Park Cemetery
Oxhey Woods
Hertfordshire County
Harrow
Pinnerwood House
Pinner Hill Golf Club
Golf Course
Hatch End Station
Grimsdyke School
St Meryl JMI School
Warren Dell School
Colnbrook School
St Josephs RC Primary School
Oxhey Wood Primary Sch
Greenfields Primary School
Woodhall School
Sir James Altham Swimming Pool
Northwood School
Northwood Sports Centre
Pinner Wood School
Oxheylane Farm
Pinner Park Farm
PRESTWICK ROAD
LITTLE OXHEY LANE
OXHEY LANE
UXBRIDGE ROAD (PINNER)
THE BROADWAY
ST THOMAS' DRIVE
A4008
B4542
A404
A410
21
34
47

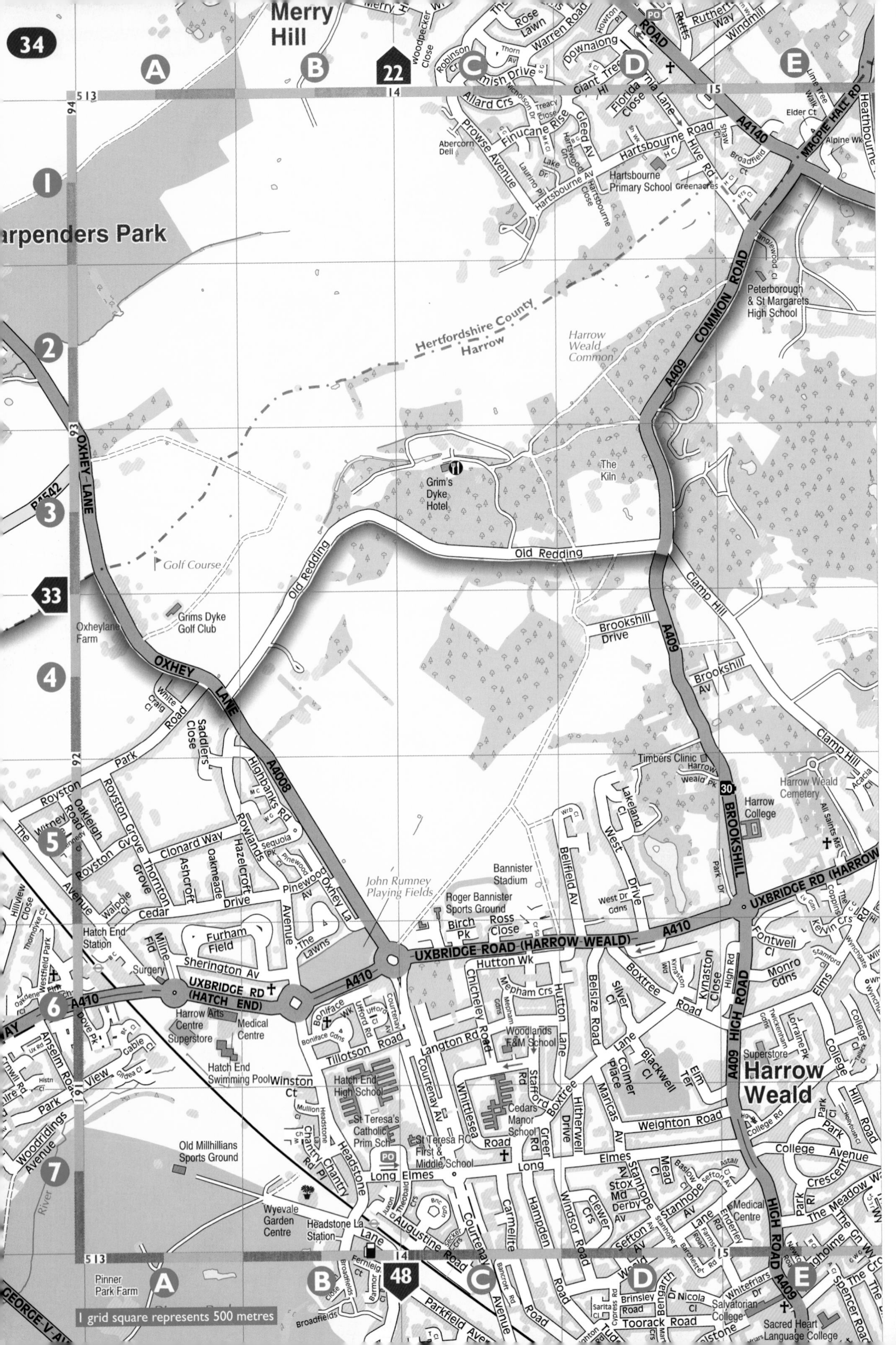

Merry Hill
Carpenders Park
Harrow Weald
Hertfordshire County
Harrow
Harrow Weald Common
Grim's Dyke Hotel
The Kiln
Old Redding
Golf Course
Grims Dyke Golf Club
Oxheylane Farm
OXHEY LANE
A4008
A409
COMMON ROAD
BROOKSHILL
Clamp Hill
Brookshill Drive
Brookshill Av
Timbers Clinic
Harrow College
Harrow Weald Cemetery
Peterborough & St Margarets High School
Hartsbourne Primary School
Hartsbourne Road
Hartsbourne Av
Prowse Avenue
Finucane Rise
Allard Crs
Warren Road
Rose Lawn
Downalong
Windmill
A4140
MAGPIE HALL RD
Heathbourne
Elder Ct
Alpine Wk
Abercorn Dell
Greenacres
Hive Rd
John Rumney Playing Fields
Bannister Stadium
Roger Bannister Sports Ground
UXBRIDGE ROAD (HARROW WEALD)
UXBRIDGE RD (HATCH END)
A410
Hatch End Station
Harrow Arts Centre
Medical Centre
Superstore
Hatch End Swimming Pool
Hatch End High School
St Teresa's Catholic Prim Sch
St Teresa RC First & Middle School
Woodlands F&M School
Cedars Manor School
Old Millhillians Sports Ground
Wyevale Garden Centre
Headstone La Station
Pinner Park Farm
Salvatorian College
Sacred Heart Language College
Weighton Road
College Avenue
HIGH ROAD
Long Elmes
Augustine Road
Courtenay Avenue
Parkfield Ave
Toorack Road
Royston Park Road
Cedar Drive
Clonard Way
Sherington Av
Furham Field
Headstone
Woodridings Avenue
A
B
C
D
E
1
2
3
4
5
6
7
22
33
48
I grid square represents 500 metres

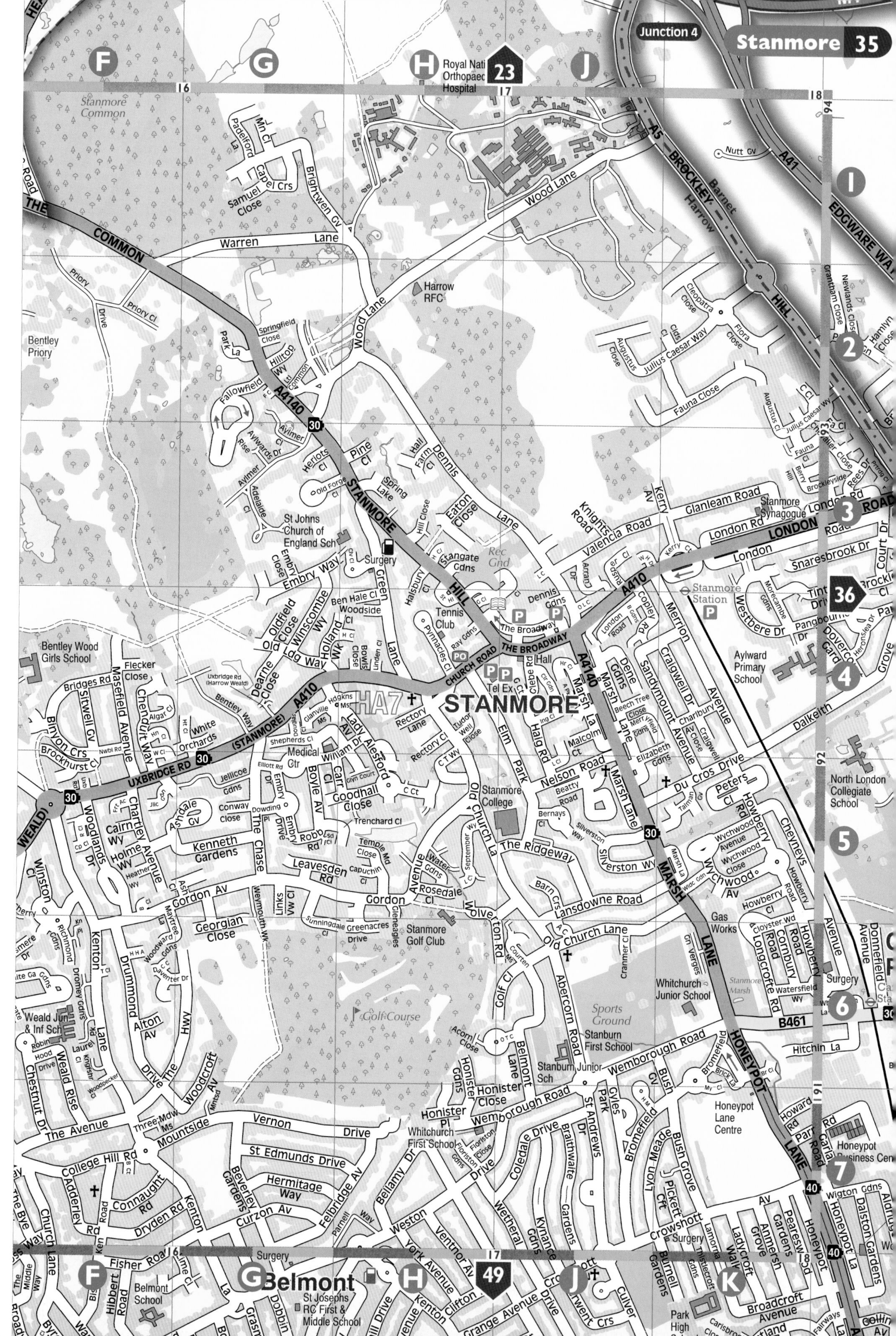
Junction 4
F
G
H
J
I
K
Royal National Orthopaedic Hospital
23
36
49
Stanmore Common
Bentley Priory
Priory Drive
Priory Cl
The Common
Warren Lane
Wood Lane
Harrow RFC
Brightwen Gv
Samuel Close
Capel Crs
Padelford La
Springfield Close
Park La
Hilltop Wy
Fallowfield
Aylmer Cl
Aylwards Rise
Aylmer Dr
Adelaide Cl
A4140
A410
A41
A5
B461
30
40
Stanmore Hill
Heriots Cl
Pine Cl
Old Forge Cl
Spring Lake
Hall Farm Cl
Dennis Lane
Eaton Close
Hill Close
Stangate Gdns
Rec Gnd
St Johns Church of England Sch
Surgery
Green Lane
Embry Way
Embry Close
Oldfield Close
Winscombe Wy
Ben Hale Cl
Woodside Cl
Holland Wk
Bowles Close
Halsbury Cl
Tennis Club
Pynnacles Cl
Ray Gdns
Church Road
The Broadway
Dennis Gdns
Valencia Road
Knights Road
Kerry Av
Glanleam Road
Stanmore Synagogue
London Road
London Rd
Snaresbrook Dr
Stanmore Station
Westbere Dr
Morecambe Gdns
Pangbourne Dr
Aylward Primary School
Dalkeith Grove
Brockley Hill
Barnet Harrow
Nutt Gv
Edgware Way
Cleopatra Close
Augustus Close
Julius Caesar Way
Flora Close
Fauna Close
Brockleyside
Rees Dr
Grantham Close
Newlands Close
Hamlyn Close
Bentley Wood Girls School
Flecker Close
Bridges Rd
Sitwell Gv
Masefield Avenue
Chenduit Way
Binyon Crs
Brockhurst Cl
Uxbridge Rd (Harrow Weald)
Bentley Way
White Orchards
Algar Cl
Dearne Close
Uxbridge Rd
(Stanmore)
HA7
STANMORE
Rectory Lane
Rectory Cl
Tudor Well Close
Lady Aylesford Av
William Dr
Carr Cl
Boyle Av
Medical Ctr
Shepherds Cl
Glanville Ms
Goodhall Close
Trenchard Cl
Jellicoe Gdns
Conway Close
Elliott Rd
Dowding Pl
Embry Drive
Robb Rd
Woodlands Dr
Chartley Avenue
Cairn Wy
Holme Wy
Ashdale Gv
Kenneth Gardens
The Chase
Leavesden Rd
Temple Md Close
Capuchin Cl
Gordon Av
Weymouth Wk
Links Vw Cl
Gordon Avenue
Rosedale Cl
Water Gdns
September Wy
Old Church La
Stanmore College
Elm Park
Haig Rd
Clebe Rd
Marsh La
Marsh Lane
Dene Gdns
Beech Tree Close
Merryfield Gdns
Elizabeth Gdns
Malcolm Ct
Nelson Road
Beatty Road
Bernays Cl
Silverston Way
Silverston Wy
The Ridgeway
Barn Crs
Lansdowne Road
Merrion Av
Copley Rd
Craigwell Dr
Sandymount Avenue
Charlbury Av
Craigwell Avenue
Du Cros Drive
Peters Cl
Howberry Rd
Howberry Road
Wychwood Avenue
Wychwood Close
Wychwood Av
Cheyneys Avenue
North London Collegiate School
Gas Works
Cloyster Wd
Cornbury Road
Longcrofte Rd
Watersfield Wy
Donnefield Avenue
Surgery
Stanmore Marsh
Marsh Lane
Honeypot Lane
Whitchurch Junior School
Sports Ground
Stanburn First School
Stanburn Junior Sch
Cranmer Cl
Abercorn Road
Old Church Lane
Wolverton Rd
Courtens Ms
Golf Cl
Belmont Lane
Acorn Close
Stanmore Golf Club
Golf Course
Greenacres Drive
Sunningdale Cl
Gleneagles
Georgian Close
Winston Cl
Kenton Lane
Richmond Gdns
Dromey Gdns
Drummond Dr
Alton Av
The Drive
Hwy
Woodcroft Av
Weald Jun & Inf Sch
Weald Rise
Chestnut Dr
Hood Drive
The Avenue
Mountside
Vernon Drive
St Edmunds Drive
Hermitage Way
Beverley Gardens
Curzon Av
Felbridge Av
College Hill Rd
Adderley Rd
Connaught Rd
Dryden Rd
Kenton Road
Church Lane
Fisher Road
Hibbert Road
Belmont School
Belmont
St Josephs RC First & Middle School
Honister Gdns
Honister Close
Honister Pl
Wemborough Road
Whitchurch First School
Floriston Drive
Coledale Drive
Braithwaite Gardens
St Andrews Dr
Cyles Park
Bromefield
Bush Gv
Bush Grove
Lyon Meade
Pickett Cft
Crowshott Av
Wetheral Dr
Kynance Gdns
Bellamy Dr
Weston Dr
Ventnor Av
York Avenue
Grange Avenue
Clifton
Culver
Burnell Gardens
Lamorna Gdns
Ladycroft Walk
Annesmere Gardens
Pearstree
Honeypot Lane Centre
Hitchin La
Howard Rd
Parr Rd
Honeypot Business Cen
Wigton Gdns
Dalston Gardens
Honeypot La
Broadcroft Avenue
Park High School
Carisbrooke Close
Fairways
Surgery

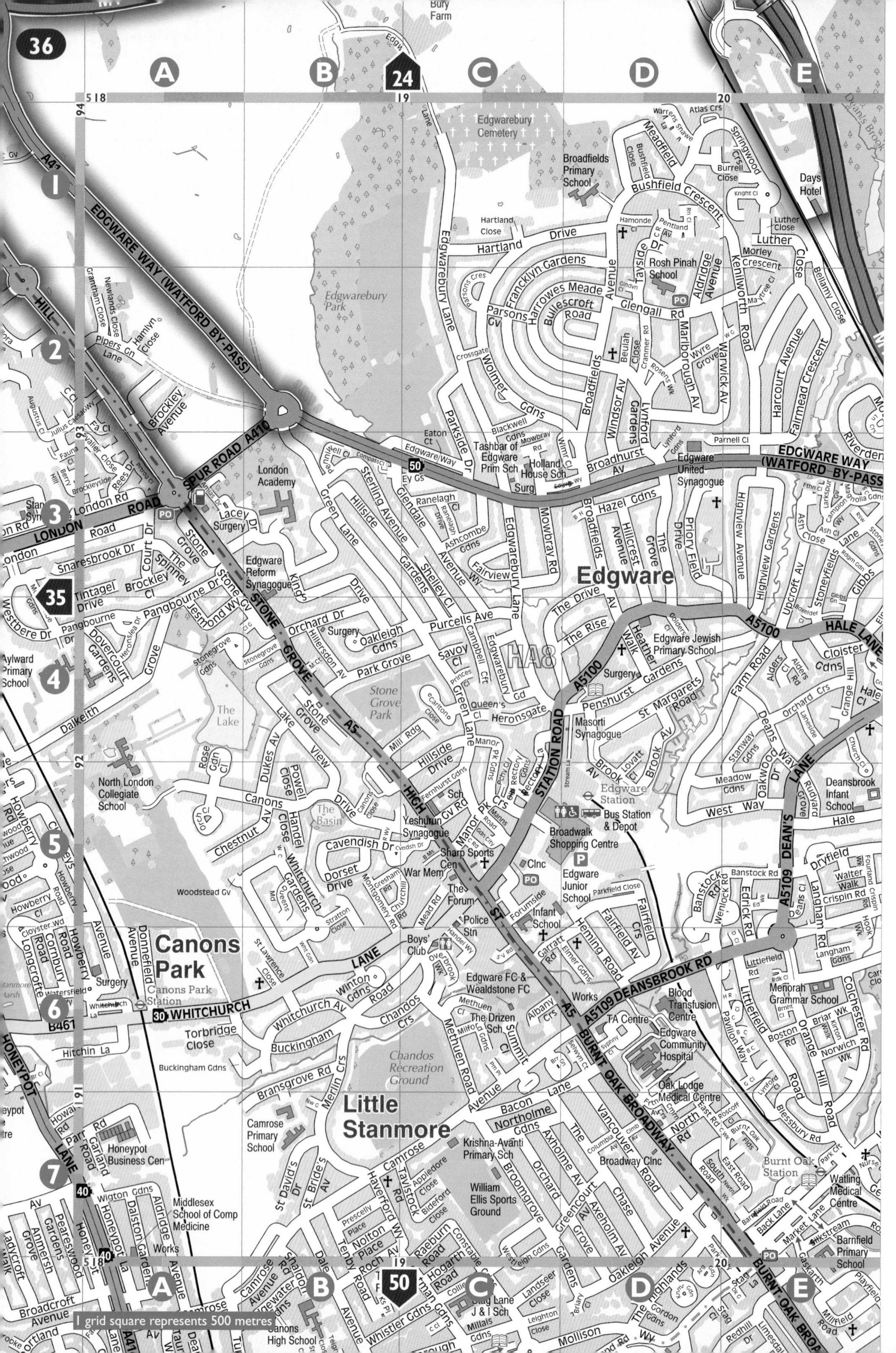

36
A
B
C
D
E
24
35
50
Bury Farm
Edgwarebury Cemetery
Broadfields Primary School
Days Hotel
Edgwarebury Park
Edgwarebury Lane
Hartland Drive
Hartland Close
Bushfield Crescent
Meadfield
Atlas Crs
Springwood Crs
Burrell Close
Luther Close
Morley Crescent
Kenilworth Road
Rosh Pinah School
Franklyn Gardens
Harrowes Meade
Bullescroft Road
Glengall Rd
Parsons Gv
Marlborough Av
Warwick Av
Harcourt Avenue
Fairmead Crescent
Bellamy Close
Wolmer Gdns
Broadfields Avenue
Windsor Av
Lynford Gardens
Parkside Dr
Tashbar of Edgware Prim Sch
Holland House Sch
Broadhurst Av
Edgware United Synagogue
EDGWARE WAY (WATFORD BY-PASS)
EDGWARE WAY (WATFORD BY-PASS)
SPUR ROAD A410
London Academy
Green Lane
Sterling Avenue
Hillside Gardens
Glendale Avenue
Shelley Cl
Ranelagh Cl
Ashcombe Gdns
Fairview Wy
Mowbray Rd
Hazel Gdns
Hillcrest Avenue
The Grove
Priory Field Drive
Highview Avenue
Highview Gardens
Edgware
HA8
LONDON ROAD
London Rd
Snaresbrook Dr
Brockley Cl
The Spinney
Stone Grove
Lacey Dr
Surgery
Edgware Reform Synagogue
Tintagel Drive
Pangbourne Dr
Jesmond Wy
Westbere Dr
Dovercourt Gardens
Aylward Primary School
Dalkeith Grove
Stonegrove Gdns
The Lake
STONE GROVE
A5
Orchard Dr
Hillersdon Av
Oakleigh Gdns
Park Grove
Purcells Ave
Savoy Cl
Campbell Cft
Edgwarebury Gd
Stone Grove Park
Carlton Close
Queen's Cl
Heronsgate
The Drive
The Rise
A5100
HALE LANE
Heather Walk
Edgware Jewish Primary School
Penshurst Gardens
St Margarets Road
Masorti Synagogue
Brook Av
Lovatt Cl
STATION ROAD
Edgware Station
Bus Station & Depot
Broadwalk Shopping Centre
Clnc
Edgware Junior School
Parkfield Close
Fairfield Crs
Farm Road
Alders Cl
Cloister Gdns
Orchard Crs
Deans Way
Stanway Gdns
Oakwood Dr
Meadow Gdns
West Way
DEAN'S LANE
Deansbrook Infant School
Hale
North London Collegiate School
Rose Gdn Cl
Dukes Av
Lake View
Powell Close
Canons Drive
Mill Rdg
Hillside Drive
Manor Pk Gdns
Rectory Gdns
HIGH ST
The Basin
Chestnut Av
Handel Close
Whitchurch Gardens
Cavendish Dr
Yeshurun Synagogue
Sharp Sports Cen
War Mem
Dorset Drive
The Forum
Police Stn
Forumside
Infant School
Garratt Rd
Heming Road
Fairfield Av
Banstock Rd
Edrick Rd
A5109 DEAN'S LANE
Dryfield Walk
Walter Walk
Crispin Rd
Langham Rd
Langham Gdns
Woodstead Gv
Canons Park
Canons Park Station
Boys' Club
Edgware FC & Wealdstone FC
Works
A5109 DEANSBROOK RD
Blood Transfusion Centre
Littlefield Rd
Menorah Grammar School
Colchester Rd
St Lawrence Close
WHITCHURCH LANE
Winton Gdns
Whitchurch Av
Chandos Crs
Torbridge Close
Buckingham
Methuen Road
The Drizen Sch
Summit Cl
Albany Crs
A5 BURNT OAK BROADWAY
TA Centre
Edgware Community Hospital
Pavilion Way
Boston Rd
Orange Hill Road
Briar Wk
Norwich Wk
Howberry Road
Donnefield Avenue
Cornbury Road
Longcroft Road
Surgery
B461
HONEYPOT LANE
Hitchin La
Buckingham Gdns
Bransgrove Rd
Merlin Crs
Chandos Recreation Ground
Little Stanmore
Camrose Primary School
Bacon Lane
Northolme Gdns
Vancouver Road
Oak Lodge Medical Centre
North Rd
East Rd
Blessbury Rd
Burnt Oak Station
Watling Medical Centre
Honeypot Business Cen
Krishna-Avanti Primary Sch
William Ellis Sports Ground
Broomgrove Gardens
Orchard Av
Axholme Av
Broadway Clnc
Middlesex School of Comp Medicine
Camrose Av
St David's Dr
St Bride's Av
Tavistock Rd
Haverford Wy
Appledore Close
Bideford Close
Prescelly Place
Nolton Place
Raeburn Road
Constable Gdns
Greencourt Av
Axeholm Av
Chase
Oakleigh Avenue
Back Lane
Market Lane
Silkstream
Barnfield Primary School
Wigton Gdns
Dalston Gardens
Aldridge Avenue
Pearswood Gardens
Amersham Grove
Broadcroft Avenue
WHITCHURCH
Hogarth Road
Stag Lane J & I Sch
Landseer Close
The Highlands
Gordon Gdns
Redhill Dr
BURNT OAK BROADWAY
Canons High School
Whistler Gdns
Mollison Wy
Playfield Road
1 grid square represents 500 metres

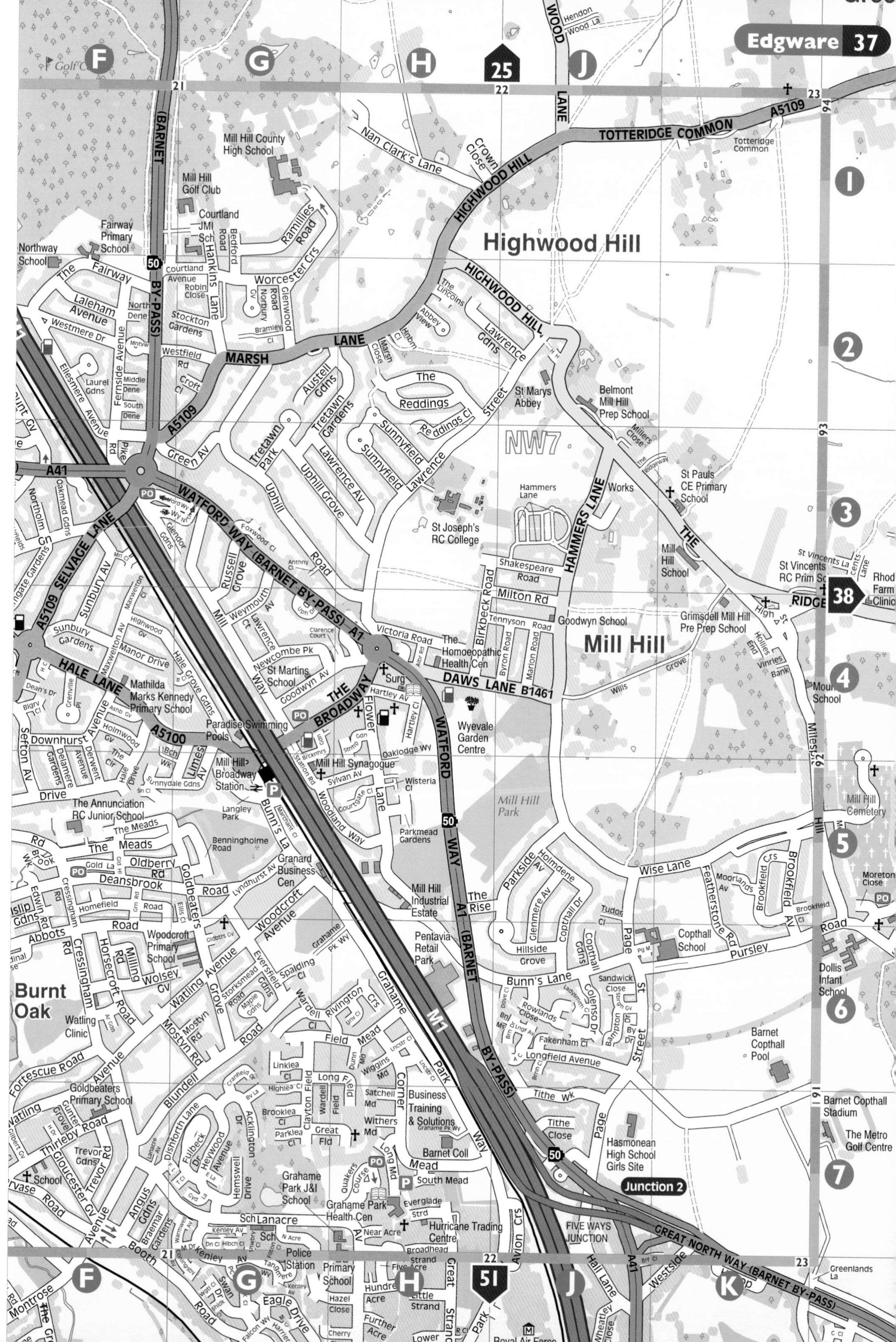

Edgware 37
25
38
51
Highwood Hill
Mill Hill
Burnt Oak
NW7
Totteridge Common
TOTTERIDGE COMMON
A5109
HIGHWOOD HILL
MARSH LANE
WOOD LANE
Hendon Wood La
Nan Clark's Lane
Crown Close
Mill Hill County High School
Mill Hill Golf Club
Courtland JMI Sch
Fairway Primary School
Northway School
The Fairway
Laleham Avenue
Westmere Dr
Ellesmere Avenue
Laurel Gdns
Fernside Avenue
Middle Dene
South Dene
North Dene
Stockton Gardens
Westfield Rd
Croft Cl
Courtland Avenue
Robin Close
Hankins Lane
Bedford Road
Ramillies Road
Worcester Crs
Norbury Gv
Glenwood Road
Bramley Cl
The Lincolns
Abbey View
Lawrence Gdns
Marsh Close
The Reddings
Reddings Cl
Sunnyfield
Lawrence Street
St Marys Abbey
Belmont Mill Hill Prep School
Millers Close
The Ridgeway
St Pauls CE Primary School
Works
Hammers Lane
HAMMERS LANE
St Joseph's RC College
Shakespeare Road
Milton Rd
Tennyson Road
Birkbeck Road
Byron Road
Marion Road
Goodwyn School
Mill Hill School
THE RIDGEWAY
St Vincents RC Prim Sch
St Vincents La
Rhodes Farm Clinic
High St
Hollies End
Vinries Bank
Grimsdell Mill Hill Pre Prep School
Wills Grove
Mount School
Milespit Hill
Mill Hill Cemetery
Moreton Close
Brookfield Crs
Brookfield Av
Moorlands Av
Featherstone Rd
Wise Lane
Pursley Road
Copthall School
Dollis Infant School
Barnet Copthall Pool
Barnet Copthall Stadium
The Metro Golf Centre
Green Av
A41
Austell Gdns
Tretawn Gardens
Tretawn Park
Uphill Road
Uphill Grove
Lawrence Av
WATFORD WAY (BARNET BY-PASS) A1
BARNET BY-PASS
SELVAGE LANE
A5109
Oakmead Gdns
Northolm Gn
Sunbury Av
Sunbury Gardens
Maxwelton Av
Maxwelton Cl
Highwood Gv
Manor Drive
Hale Grove Gdns
HALE LANE
A5100
Mathilda Marks Kennedy Primary School
Paradise Swimming Pools
Mill Hill Broadway Station
Russell Grove
Weymouth Av
Mill Way
Lawrence Ct
Newcombe Pk
St Martins School
Goodwyn Av
Victoria Road
Clarence Court
The Homoeopathic Health Cen
DAWS LANE B1461
THE BROADWAY
Flower Lane
Hartley Av
Hartley Cl
Oaklodge Wy
Surg
Mill Hill Synagogue
Sylvan Av
Station Rd
Woodland Way
Courtgate Cl
Wisteria Cl
Parkmead Gardens
Wyevale Garden Centre
Mill Hill Park
WATFORD WAY A1 (BARNET BY-PASS)
Grenville Pl
Dean's Dr
Downhurst Avenue
Sefton Av
Delamere Gardens
Derwent Avenue
Holmwood Gv
The Clr
Hale Drive
Limes Av
Sunnydale Gdns
Drive
The Annunciation RC Junior School
Langley Park
Bunn's La
Marchant Cl
Benningholme Road
The Meads
Oldberry Rd
Deansbrook Road
Goldbeaters Gv
Gold La
Cressingham Rd
Edwin Rd
Homefield Road
Abbots Road
Horsecroft Road
Milling Rd
Woodcroft Primary School
Wolsey Gv
Watling Avenue
Storksmead Road
Eversfield Gdns
Spalding Cl
Maple Gdns
Mostyn Rd
Granard Business Cen
Lyndhurst Av
Woodcroft Avenue
Grahame Pk Wy
Grahame Park Way
M1
Mill Hill Industrial Estate
The Rise
Pentavia Retail Park
Parkside
Holmdene Av
Glenmere Av
Copthall Dr
Hillside Grove
Copthall Gdns
Tudor Cl
Page Street
Bunn's Lane
Sandwick Close
Colenso Dr
Rowlands Close
Bampton Dr
Fakenham Cl
Longfield Avenue
Tithe Wk
Tithe Close
Hasmonean High School Girls Site
Junction 2
FIVE WAYS JUNCTION
GREAT NORTH WAY (BARNET BY-PASS)
Watling Clinic
Fortescue Road
Goldbeaters Primary School
Watling Avenue
Gunter Grove
Thirleby Road
Gloucester Gv
Trevor Rd
Trevor Gdns
School
Gervase Road
Angus Gdns
Braemar Gardens
Blundell Road
Dishforth Lane
Fulbeck Dr
Heywood Avenue
Acklington Dr
Hemswell Drive
Rivington Crs
Wardell Cl
Field Mead
Linklea Cl
Highlea Cl
Brooklea Cl
Parklea Cl
Clayton Field
Long Field
Wiggins Md
Satchell Md
Withers Md
Great Fld
Corner Mead
Business Training & Solutions
Barnet Coll
Long Md
South Mead
Grahame Park J&I School
Grahame Park Health Cen
Quakers Course
Everglade Strd
Hurricane Trading Centre
Near Acre
Sch Lanacre
Kenley Av
Police Station
Primary School
Five Acre
Broadhead Strand
Great Strand
Avion Crs
Hall Lane
Westside
Wheatley Close
Greenlands La
Booth Road
Montrose Av
Swan Dr
Eagle Drive
Hazel Close
Hundred Acre
Little Strand
Further Acre
Cherry Close
Lower Strand
Park Way
Royal Air Force
F
G
H
J
K
I
2
3
4
5
6
7
21
22
23
94
93
92
91

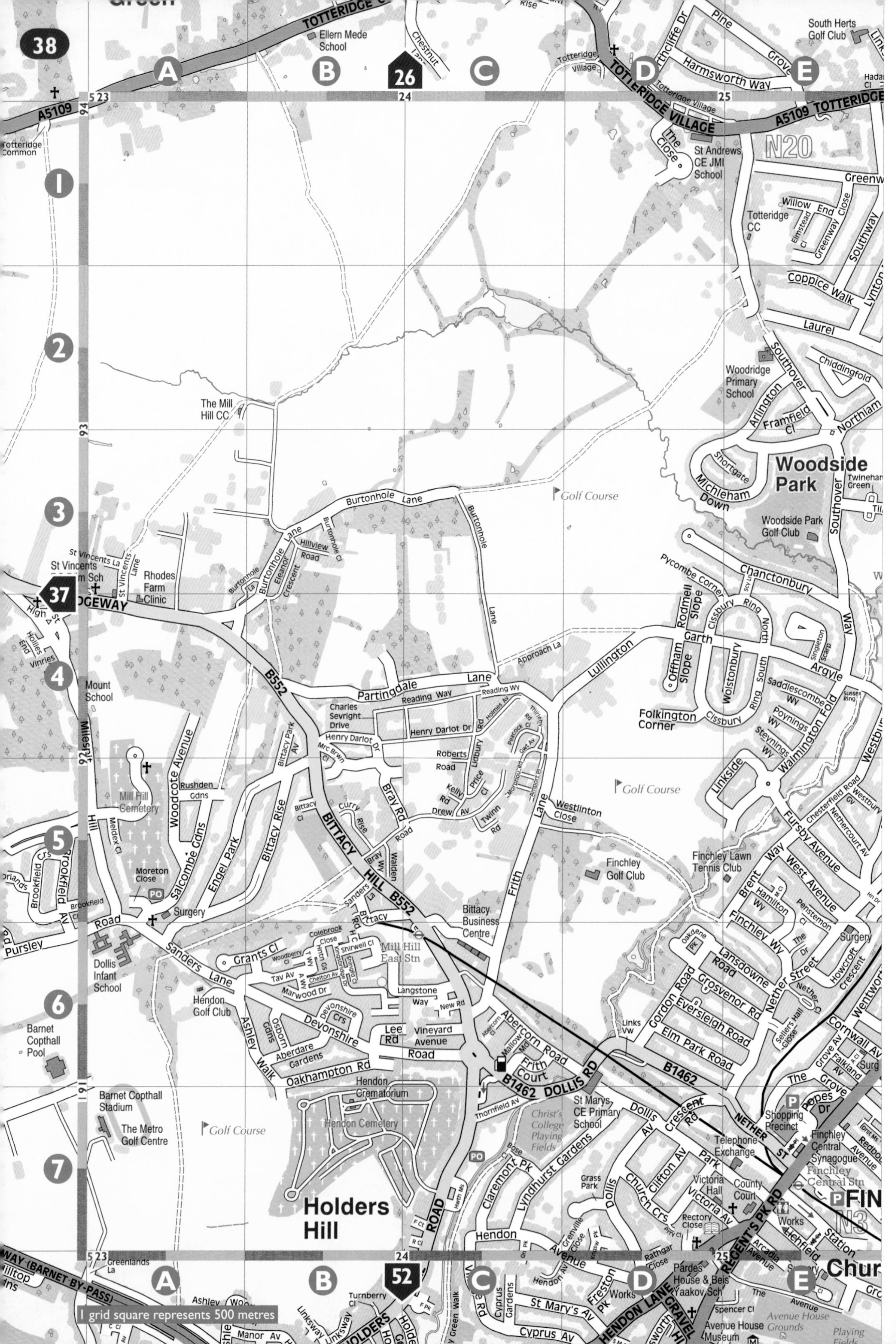

TOTTERIDGE
Ellern Mede School
Chestnut La
Totteridge Village
TOTTERIDGE VILLAGE
A5109 TOTTERIDGE
A5109
Totteridge Common
The Close
St Andrews CE JMI School
N20
South Herts Golf Club
Harmsworth Way
Pine
Grove
Totteridge CC
Willow
End
Close
Elmstead Cl
Greenway Cl
Southway
Coppice Walk
Laurel
Southover
Woodridge Primary School
Chiddingfold
Arlington
Framfield Cl
Northiam
Shortgate
Michleham Down
Woodside Park
Woodside Park Golf Club
Twinehan Green
The Mill Hill CC
Golf Course
Burtonhole Lane
Burtonhole Cl
Hillview Road
Eleanor Crescent
Burtonhole La
St Vincents La
St Vincents Lane
St Vincents RC Sch
Rhodes Farm Clinic
RIDGEWAY
High St
Hollies End
Vinries
Mount School
Milespit Hill
B552
Partingdale Lane
Approach La
Lullington
Pycombe Corner
Chanctonbury
Rodmell Slope
Cissbury Ring North
Garth
Offham Slope
Wolstonbury
Cissbury Ring South
Argyle
Saddlescombe Wy
Poynings Wy
Steynings Wy
Walmington Fold
Folkington Corner
Cissbury
Reading Way
Reading Wy
Holmes Av
Charles Sevright Drive
Henry Darlot Dr
Henry Darlot Dr
Bittacy Park Av
Roberts Road
Lidbury Rd
Peacock Cl
Thirleby
Kelly Rd
Price Cl
Drew Av
Twinn Rd
Westlinton Close
Frith Lane
Golf Course
Linkside
Chesterfield Road
Westbury
Nethercourt Av
Fursby Avenue
Brent Way
West Avenue
Finchley Lawn Tennis Club
Mill Hill Cemetery
Woodcote Avenue
Rushden Gdns
Salcombe Gdns
Engel Park
Bittacy Rise
Bittacy Cl
Curry Rise
Bray Rd
Walden Road
BITTACY HILL B552
Bray Wy
Meldex Cl
Moreton Close
PO
Surgery
Brookfield Crs
Brookfield Av
Brookfield Road
Purslev
Sanders Lane
Sanders La
Bittacy
Grants Cl
Colebrook Close
Shirwell Cl
Mill Hill East Stn
Woodberry Cl
Tav Av
Chelton Av
Marwood Dr
Langstone Way
New Rd
Bittacy Business Centre
Finchley Golf Club
Hamilton Wy
Finchley Wy
Penstemon Cl
The Dr
Surgery
Oakdene Pk
Lansdowne Road
Nether Street
Howcroft Crescent
Grosvenor Rd
Gordon Road
Eversleigh Road
Elm Park Road
Sellers Hall Close
Nether Cl
Links Vw
Dollis Infant School
Hendon Golf Club
Barnet Copthall Pool
Ashley Walk
Osborn Gdns
Devonshire Crs
Devonshire
Aberdare Gardens
Oakhampton Rd
Lee Rd
Vineyard Avenue
Road
Abercorn Road
Mallow Md
Frith Court
B1462 DOLLIS RD
B1462
Cornwall Av
Grove Av
Falkland Av
The Grove
Popes Dr
Shopping Precinct
Finchley Central Synagogue
Finchley Central Stn
Hendon Crematorium
Hendon Cemetery
Thornfield Av
Christ's College Playing Fields
St Marys CE Primary School
Dollis Av
Crescent Rd
NETHER ST
Telephone Exchange
Barnet Copthall Stadium
The Metro Golf Centre
Golf Course
Holders Hill
ROAD
Heath Ms
Bose
Claremont Pk
Lyndhurst Gardens
Grass Park
Dollis
Church Crs
Clifton Av
Park
Victoria Hall
Victoria Av
County Court
REGENT'S PK RD
Works
Lichfield
Station
FIN
N3
Chur
Hendon Avenue
Grenville Close
Rectory Close
Rathgar Close
Pardes House & Beis Yaakov Sch
Arcadia Avenue
Greenlands La
Ashley
Turnberry Cl
Linksway
Manor Av
Hendon Av
Cypress Gardens
St Mary's Av
Cyprus Avenue
Freston Pk
Works
HENDON LANE
GRAVEL HILL
Spencer Cl
Avenue House
Avenue House Grounds
Playing Fields
The Avenue
WAY (BARNET BY-PASS)
Hilltop
A
B
C
D
E
1
2
3
4
5
6
7
523
24
25
94
93
92
91

26
37
52

1 grid square represents 500 metres

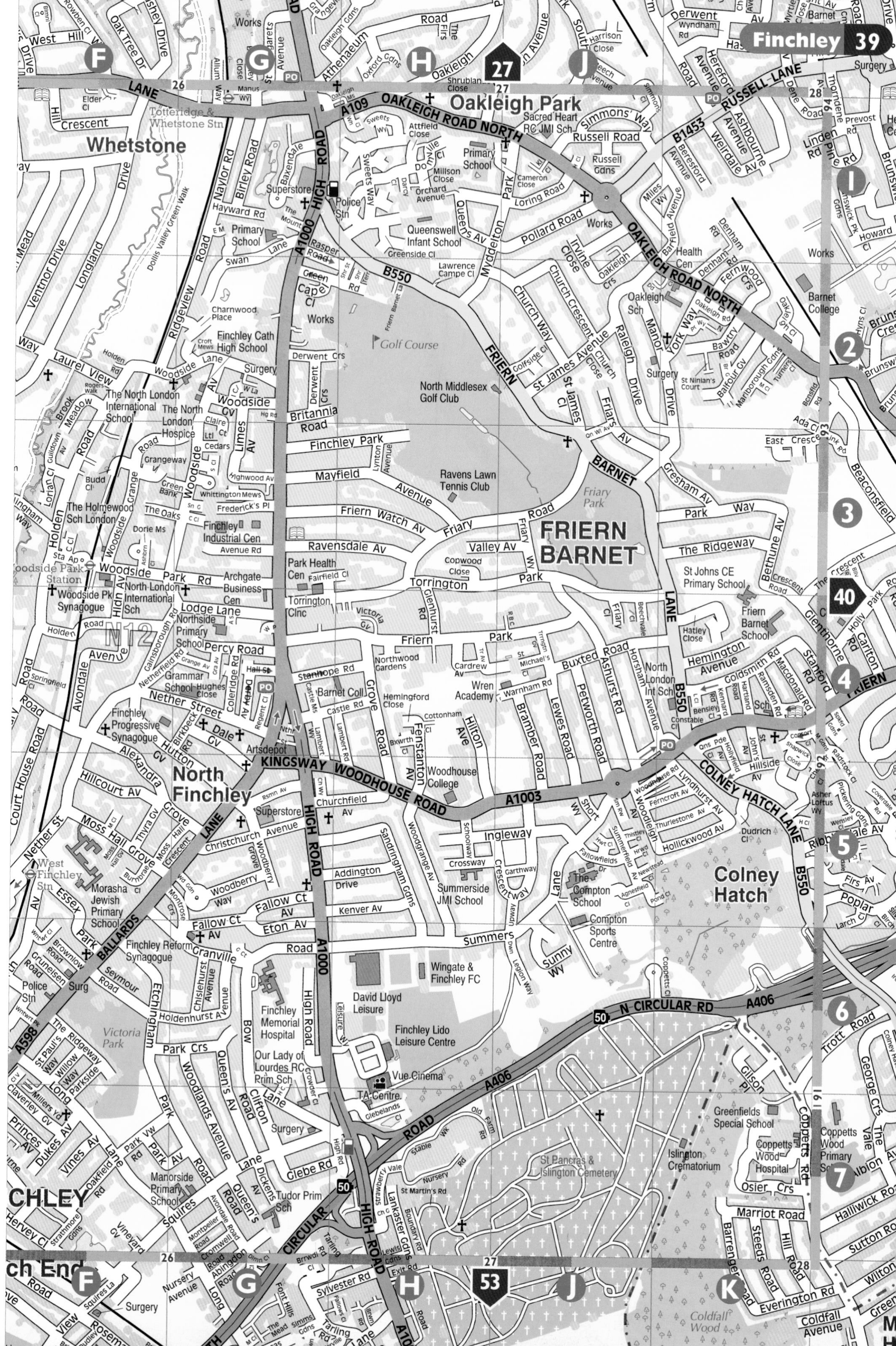
Whetstone
Oakleigh Park
FRIERN BARNET
North Finchley
Colney Hatch
N12
Totteridge & Whetstone Stn
Woodside Park Station
West Finchley Stn
OAKLEIGH ROAD NORTH
FRIERN BARNET LANE
COLNEY HATCH LANE
KINGSWAY
WOODHOUSE ROAD
BALLARDS LANE
HIGH ROAD
N CIRCULAR RD
RUSSELL LANE
A1000
A109
A1003
A406
A598
B550
B1453
Dollis Valley Green Walk
Golf Course
North Middlesex Golf Club
Ravens Lawn Tennis Club
Friary Park
Victoria Park
St Pancras & Islington Cemetery
Islington Crematorium
Coldfall Wood
Barnet College
Queenswell Infant School
Finchley Cath High School
The North London International School
The North London Hospice
The Holmewood Sch London
Woodside Pk Synagogue
North London International Sch
Northside Primary School
Grammar School
Finchley Progressive Synagogue
Finchley Industrial Cen
Archgate Business Cen
Park Health Cen
Torrington Clnc
Barnet Coll
Wren Academy
Woodhouse College
Summerside JMI School
The Compton School
Compton Sports Centre
Wingate & Finchley FC
David Lloyd Leisure
Finchley Lido Leisure Centre
Vue Cinema
TA Centre
Finchley Memorial Hospital
Our Lady of Lourdes RC Prim Sch
Tudor Prim Sch
Manorside Primary School
Morasha Jewish Primary School
Finchley Reform Synagogue
St Johns CE Primary School
Friern Barnet School
North London Int Sch
Oakleigh Sch
Sacred Heart RC JMI Sch
Primary School
Greenfields Special School
Coppetts Wood Hospital
Coppetts Wood Primary Sch
Artsdepot
Superstore
Police Stn
27
40
53
CHLEY
ch End

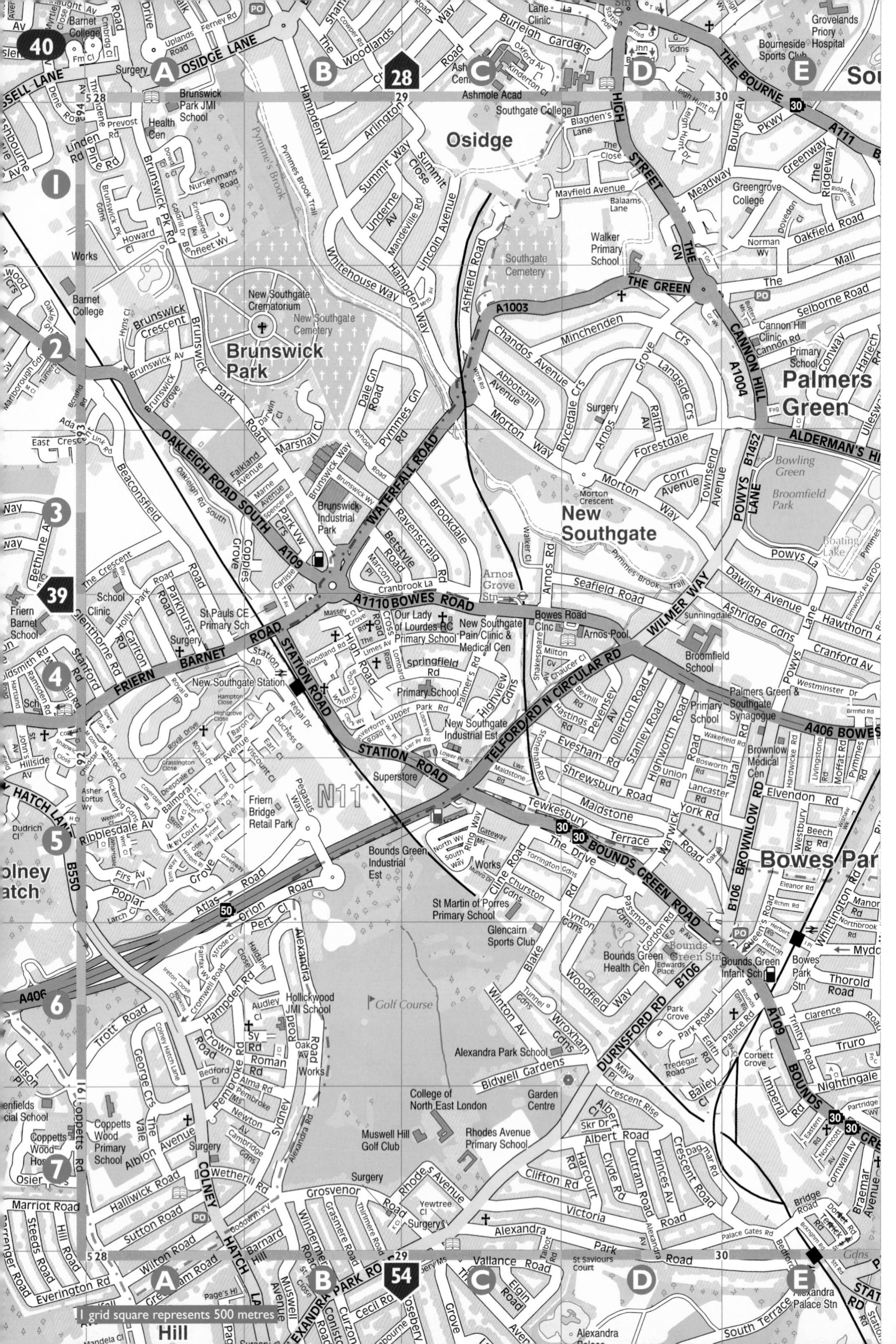

40
28
39
54
A
B
C
D
E
1
2
3
4
5
6
7
Osidge
Brunswick Park
New Southgate
Palmers Green
Bowes Par
Osidge Lane
Brunswick Park Road
Oakleigh Road South
Waterfall Road
Friern Barnet Road
Station Road
A1110 Bowes Road
Telford Rd N Circular Rd
Bounds Green Road
High Street
The Green
Cannon Hill
Alderman's Hill
Powys Lane
Wilmer Way
Brownlow Rd
Durnsford Rd
Colney Hatch Lane
Alexandra Park Road
New Southgate Crematorium
New Southgate Cemetery
Southgate Cemetery
Brunswick Park JMI School
Southgate College
Ashmole Acad
Walker Primary School
Broomfield Park
Broomfield School
New Southgate Station
Arnos Grove Stn
Bounds Green Stn
Bowes Park Stn
Alexandra Palace Stn
Friern Bridge Retail Park
Bounds Green Industrial Est
Muswell Hill Golf Club
College of North East London
Alexandra Park School
Rhodes Avenue Primary School
Coppetts Wood Primary School
Hollickwood JMI School
St Martin of Porres Primary School
Glencairn Sports Club
N11
A406
A109
A1003
A1004
B1452
B106
B550
A111
1 grid square represents 500 metres

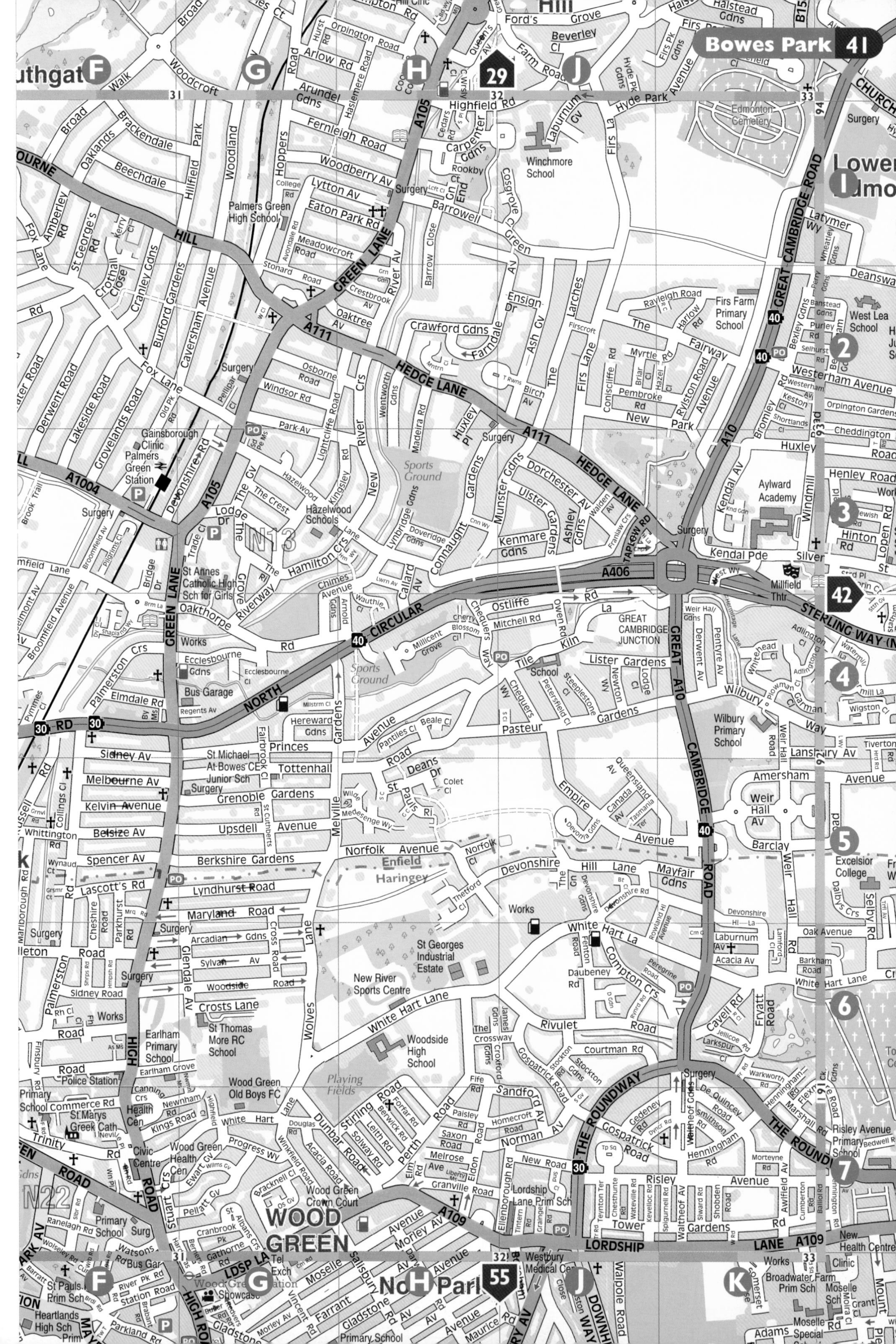
Bowes Park
41
29
42
55
F
G
H
J
K
I
2
3
4
5
6
7
Southgate
Palmers Green
Winchmore School
Palmers Green High School
Firs Farm Primary School
West Lea School
Aylward Academy
Hazelwood Schools
St Annes Catholic High Sch for Girls
Great Cambridge Junction
Wilbury Primary School
St Michael At Bowes CE Junior Sch
Excelsior College
Enfield
Haringey
St Georges Industrial Estate
New River Sports Centre
Woodside High School
St Thomas More RC School
Earlham Primary School
Wood Green Old Boys FC
Wood Green Crown Court
Wood Green
Lordship Lane Prim Sch
Broadwater Farm Prim Sch
Heartlands High Sch
Edmonton Cemetery
Millfield Thtr
Risley Avenue Primary School
North Circular Road
Hedge Lane
Great Cambridge Road
Green Lane
High Road
The Roundway
Lordship Lane
Sterling Way
N13
N22

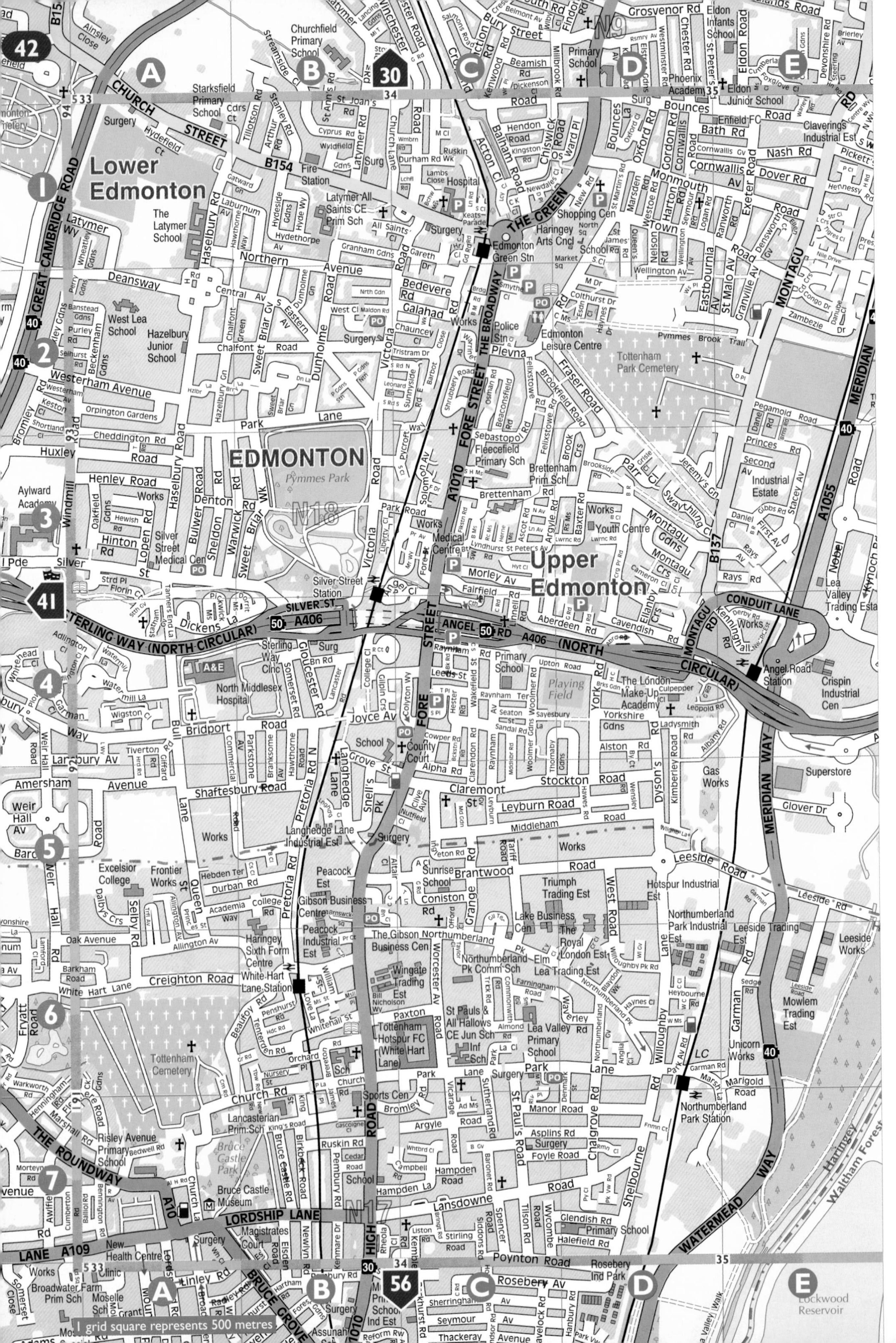

42
30
41
56
A
B
C
D
E
1
2
3
4
5
6
7
34
35
533
Lower Edmonton
EDMONTON
Upper Edmonton
Pymmes Park
N9
N18
N17
Church Street
Great Cambridge Road
Fore Street
The Broadway
The Green
High Road
Silver St
A406
Sterling Way (North Circular)
Angel Rd
Conduit Lane
Meridian Way
Watermead Way
Lordship Lane
The Roundway
Bruce Grove
Northern Avenue
Westerham Avenue
Park Lane
Montagu Rd
Church Lane
Victoria Road
Haselbury Road
Windmill Road
Edmonton Green Stn
Silver Street Station
White Hart Lane Station
Angel Road Station
Northumberland Park Station
North Middlesex Hospital
Tottenham Hotspur FC (White Hart Lane)
Tottenham Cemetery
Tottenham Park Cemetery
Bruce Castle Park
Bruce Castle Museum
Edmonton Leisure Centre
The Latymer School
Churchfield Primary School
Starksfield Primary School
West Lea School
Hazelbury Junior School
Aylward Academy
Haringey Sixth Form Centre
Excelsior College
Lea Valley Primary School
Risley Avenue Primary School
Broadwater Farm Prim Sch
Superstore
Gas Works
Crispin Industrial Cen
Lea Valley Trading Est
Lockwood Reservoir
Waltham Forest
Haringey
1 grid square represents 500 metres

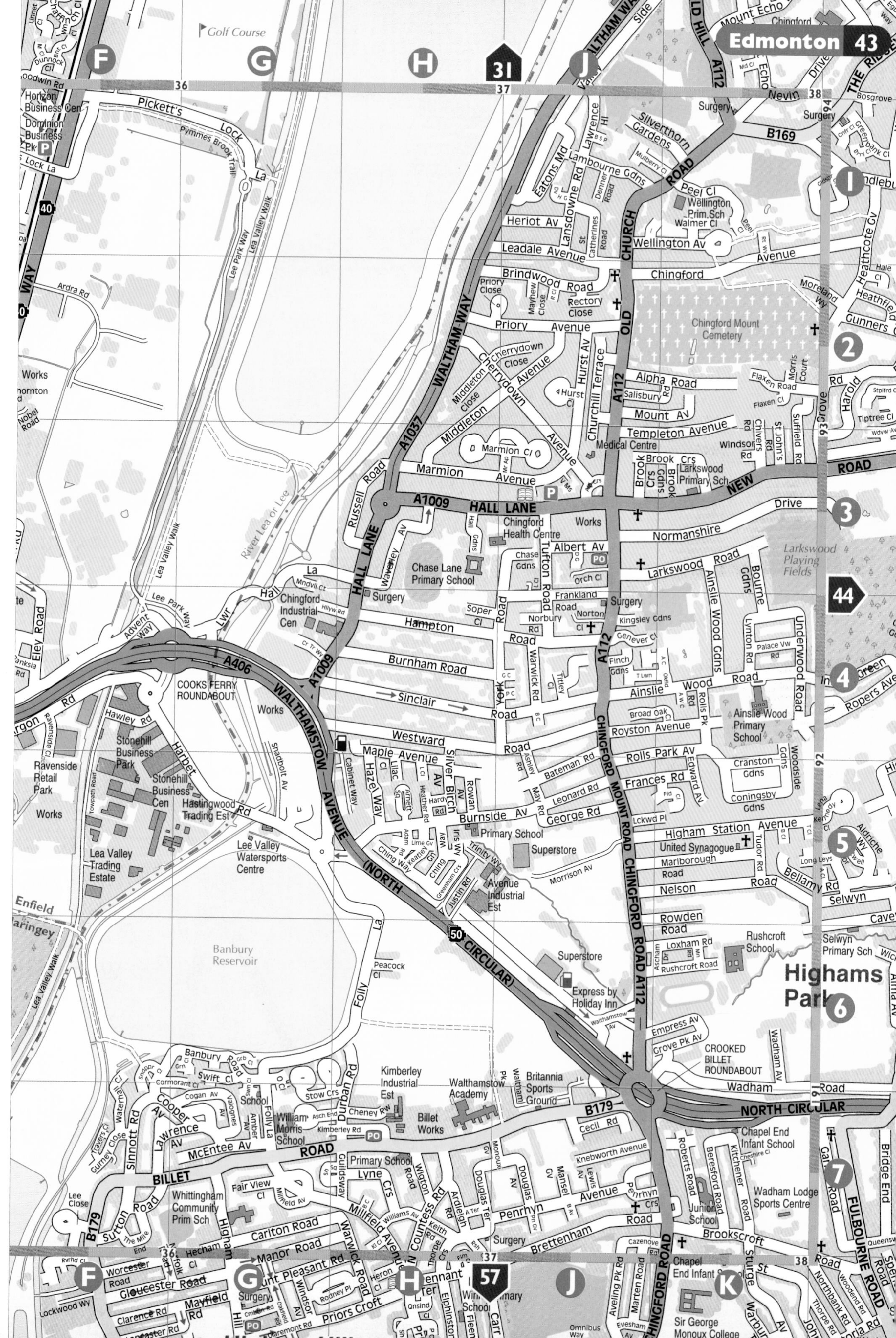
Golf Course
Horizon Business Cen
Dominion Business Pk
Pickett's Lock La
Pymmes Brook Trail
Lee Park Way
Lea Valley Walk
River Lea or Lee
Waltham Way
A1037
A1009 Hall Lane
Chingford Industrial Cen
Chase Lane Primary School
Chingford Health Centre
Old Church Road
A112
Chingford Mount Cemetery
Wellington Prim.Sch
Larkswood Primary Sch
Larkswood Playing Fields
Medical Centre
New Road
A406
Cooks Ferry Roundabout
Stonehill Business Park
Ravenside Retail Park
Lea Valley Trading Estate
Lee Valley Watersports Centre
Banbury Reservoir
Walthamstow Avenue (North Circular)
Chingford Mount Road
Ainslie Wood Primary School
Highams Park
Rushcroft School
Selwyn Primary Sch
Express by Holiday Inn
Superstore
Avenue Industrial Est
Crooked Billet Roundabout
North Circular
Kimberley Industrial Est
Walthamstow Academy
Britannia Sports Ground
Billet Works
William Morris School
Billet Road
B179
Whittingham Community Prim Sch
Chapel End Infant School
Wadham Lodge Sports Centre
Fulbourne Road
Sir George Monoux College
Chingford Road

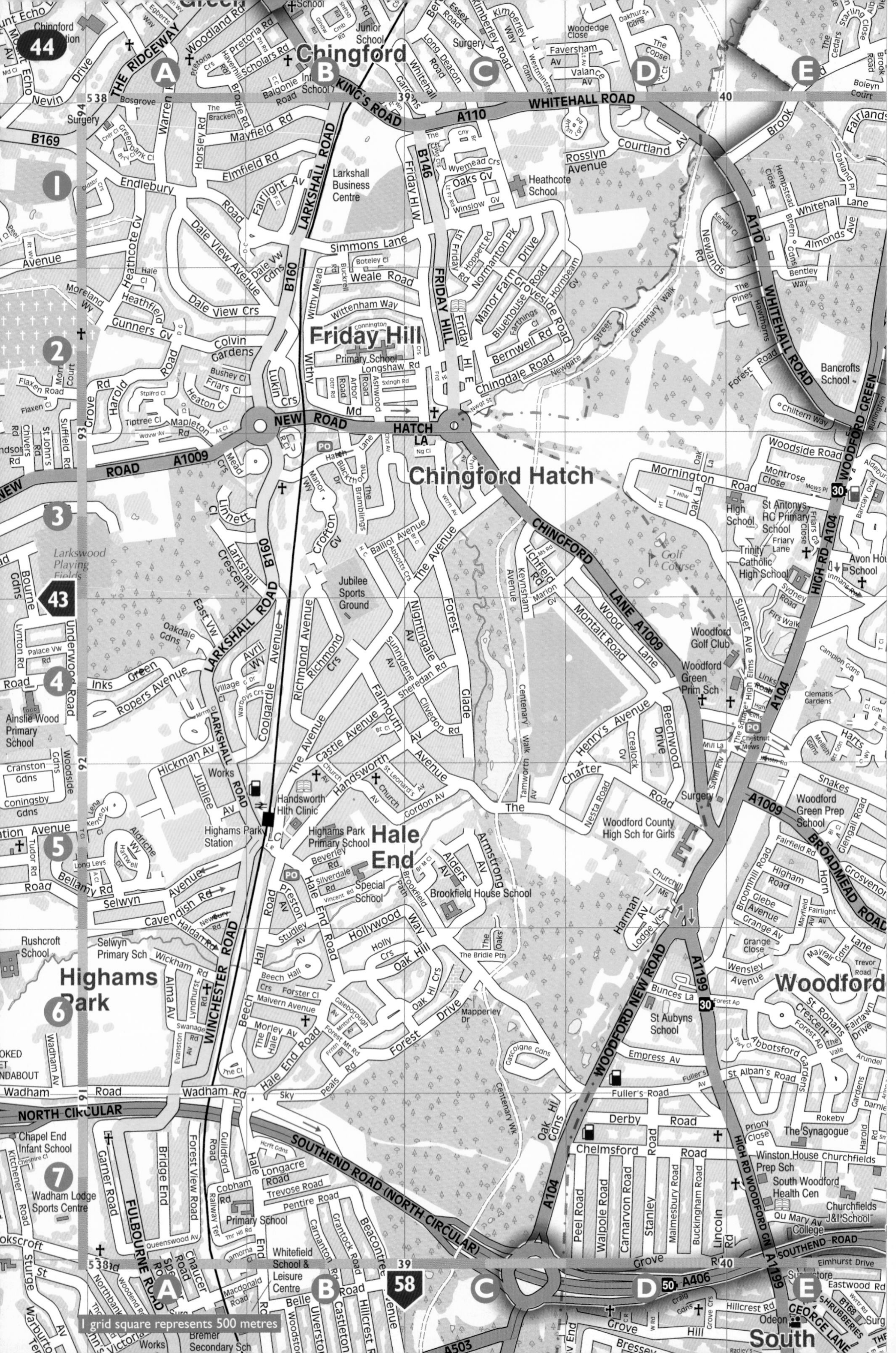

44
Chingford
Friday Hill
Chingford Hatch
Hale End
Highams Park
Woodford
South
WHITEHALL ROAD
KING'S ROAD
LARKSHALL ROAD
NEW ROAD
CHINGFORD LANE A1009
WOODFORD NEW ROAD
SOUTHEND ROAD (NORTH CIRCULAR)
NORTH CIRCULAR
WINCHESTER ROAD
HIGH RD WOODFORD GN
BROADMEAD ROAD
FULBOURNE ROAD
Larkswood Playing Fields
Jubilee Sports Ground
Larkshall Business Centre
Heathcote School
Bancrofts School
Woodford Golf Club
Woodford County High Sch for Girls
Brookfield House School
Highams Park Station
Handsworth Hlth Clinic
Highams Park Primary School
St Aubyns School
Woodford Green Prep School
Trinity Catholic High School
St Antonys RC Primary School
Wadham Lodge Sports Centre
Whitefield School & Leisure Centre
Bremer Secondary Sch
Winston House Prep Sch
South Woodford Health Cen
The Synagogue
Churchfields J&I School
43
58
1 grid square represents 500 metres

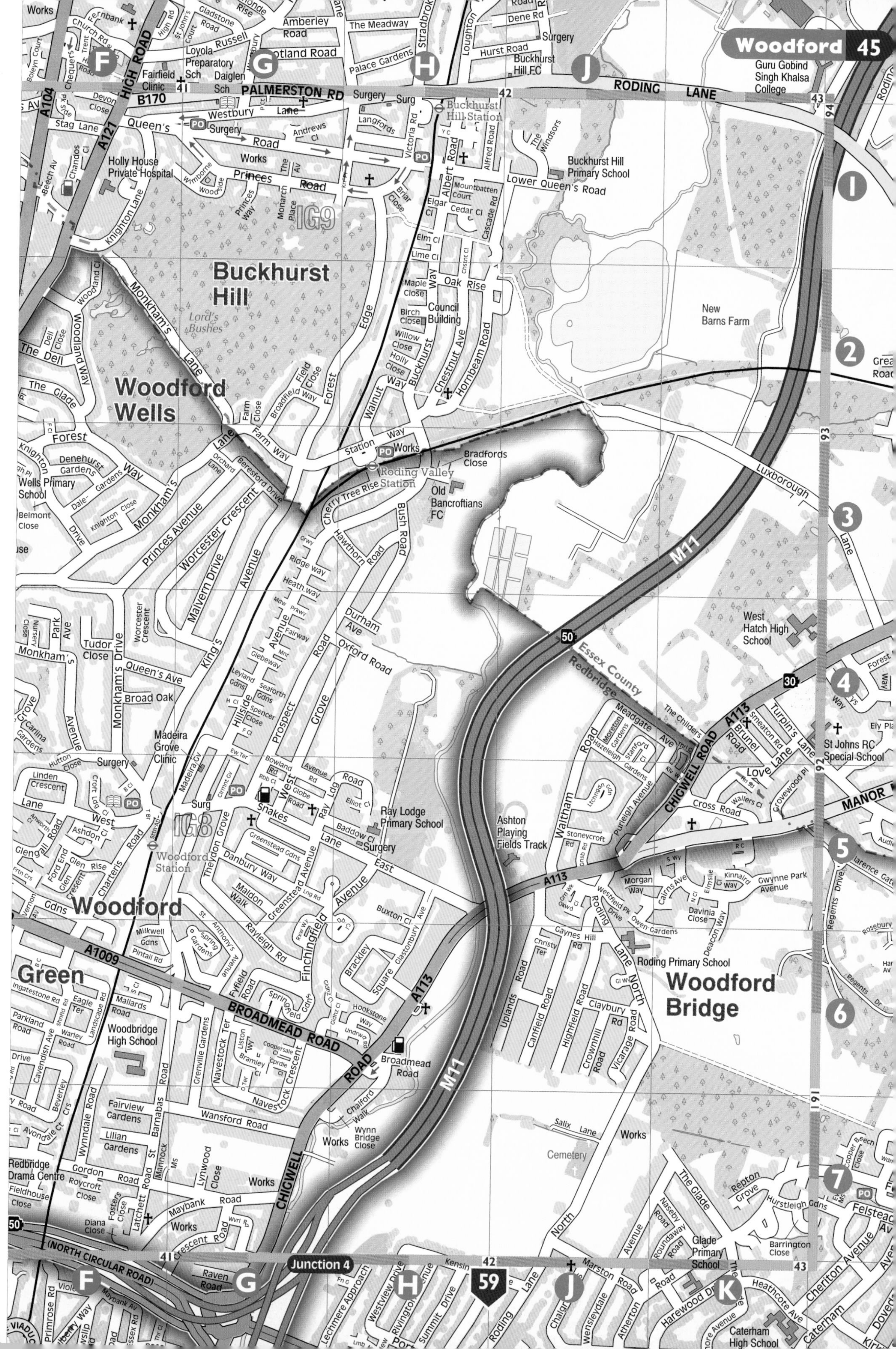
Buckhurst Hill
Woodford Wells
Woodford Green
Woodford Bridge
Buckhurst Hill Station
Roding Valley Station
Woodford Station
New Barns Farm
West Hatch High School
Ray Lodge Primary School
Roding Primary School
Woodbridge High School
Ashton Playing Fields Track
Cemetery
M11
A113
A1009
BROADMEAD ROAD
CHIGWELL ROAD
RODING LANE
PALMERSTON RD
HIGH ROAD
MANOR
Essex County
Redbridge
Junction 4
59

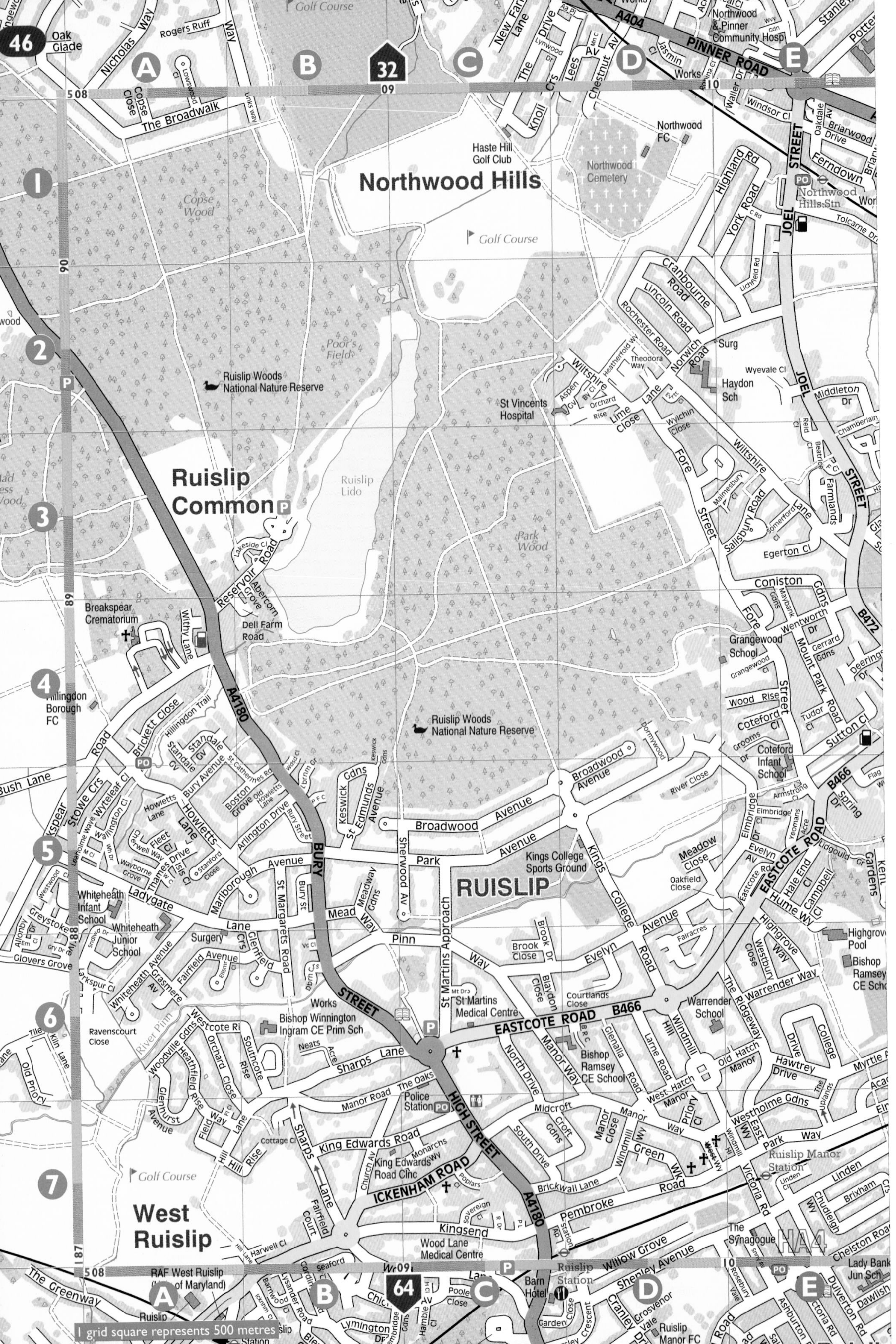
Northwood Hills
Ruislip Common
RUISLIP
West Ruislip
Ruislip Woods National Nature Reserve
Ruislip Lido
Poor's Field
Copse Wood
Park Wood
Haste Hill Golf Club
Golf Course
Northwood Cemetery
Northwood FC
Northwood & Pinner Community Hosp
Northwood Hills Stn
PINNER ROAD
A404
JOEL STREET
B472
St Vincents Hospital
Haydon Sch
Breakspear Crematorium
Hillingdon Borough FC
Grangewood School
Coteford Infant School
Kings College Sports Ground
Whiteheath Infant School
Whiteheath Junior School
Bishop Winnington Ingram CE Prim Sch
St Martins Medical Centre
EASTCOTE ROAD
B466
Bishop Ramsey CE School
Warrender School
Highgrove Pool
Police Station
King Edwards Road Clinic
ICKENHAM ROAD
HIGH STREET
BURY STREET
A4180
Ruislip Manor Station
Wood Lane Medical Centre
The Synagogue
HA4
Ruislip Station
Barn Hotel
Ruislip Manor FC
Lady Bank Jun Sch
RAF West Ruislip (Home of Maryland)
The Greenway
32
64
1 grid square represents 500 metres

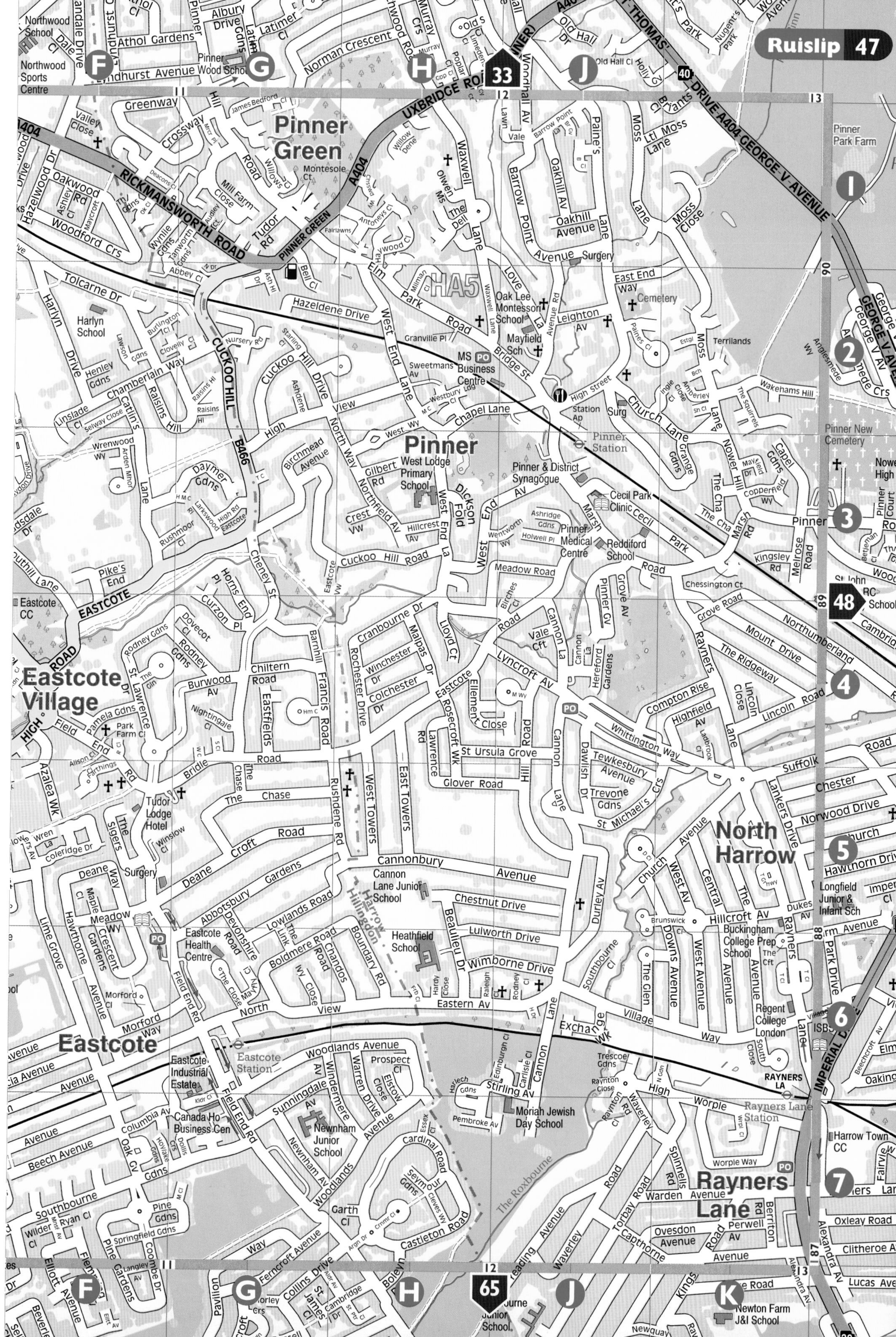

Ruislip 47
Pinner Green
Pinner
Eastcote Village
Eastcote
North Harrow
Rayners Lane
HA5
RICKMANSWORTH ROAD
UXBRIDGE ROAD
A404
PINNER GREEN
CUCKOO HILL
B466
EASTCOTE ROAD
GEORGE V AVENUE
IMPERIAL DRIVE
Pinner Station
Eastcote Station
Rayners Lane Station
Northwood Sports Centre
Northwood School
Pinner Wood School
Harlyn School
West Lodge Primary School
Pinner & District Synagogue
Cecil Park Clinic
Pinner Medical Centre
Reddiford School
MS Business Centre
Oak Lee Montessori School
Mayfield Sch
Cemetery
Pinner New Cemetery
Pinner Park Farm
Terrilands
Tudor Lodge Hotel
Eastcote Health Centre
Eastcote Industrial Estate
Canada Ho Business Cen
Newnham Junior School
Cannon Lane Junior School
Heathfield School
Moriah Jewish Day School
Longfield Junior & Infant Sch
Buckingham College Prep School
Regent College London
Harrow Town CC
Eastcote CC
Newton Farm J&I School
Harrow
Hillingdon
The Roxbourne
33
40
48
65
30

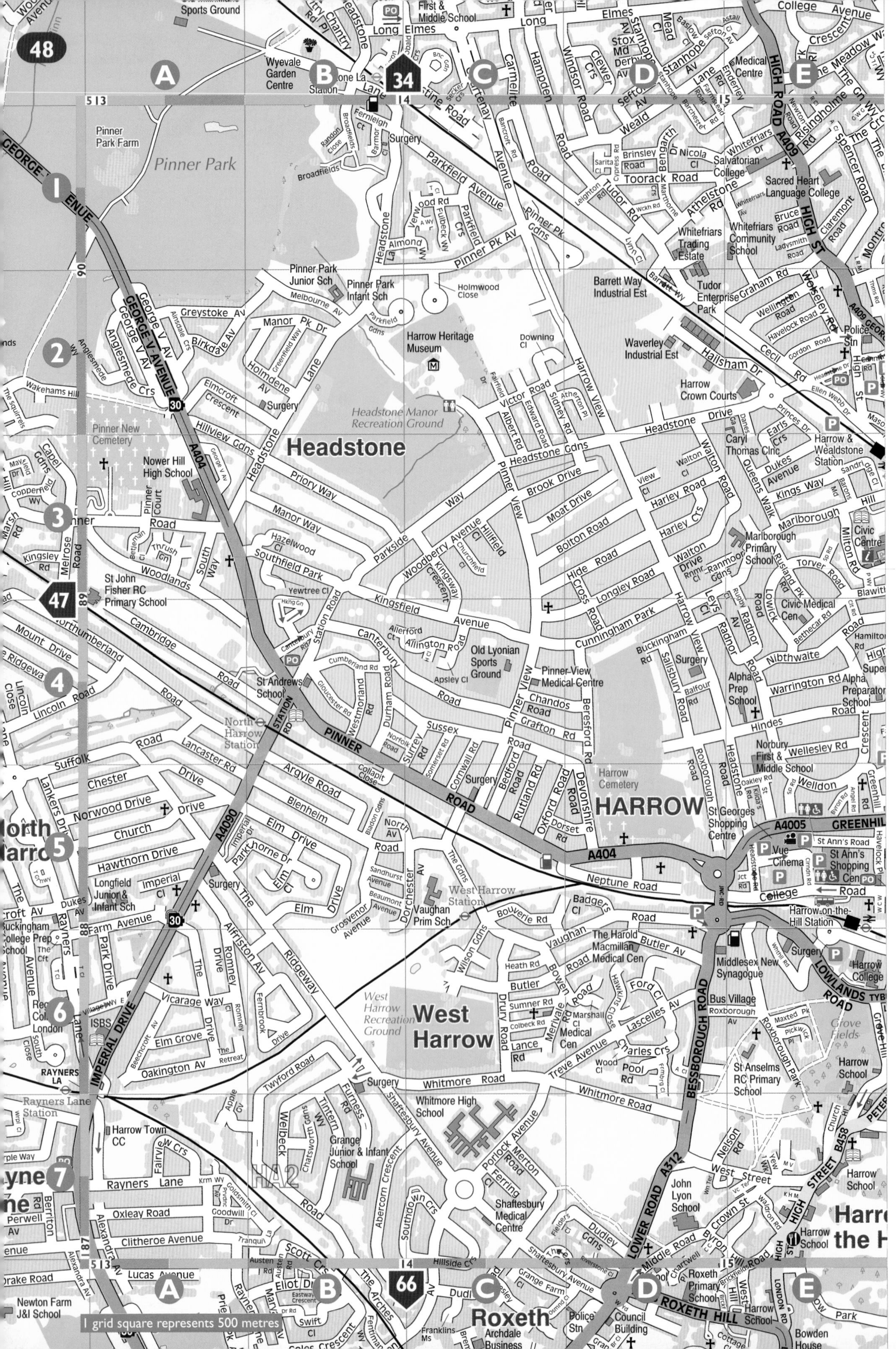
48
34
47
66
A
B
C
D
E
1
2
3
4
5
6
7
513
14
15
90
89
88
187
Sports Ground
First & Middle School
Long Elmes
Elmes
College Avenue
Wyevale Garden Centre
Medical Centre
HIGH ROAD A409
Pinner Park Farm
Pinner Park
GEORGE V AVENUE
Carmelite Road
Hampden Road
Windsor Road
Clewer Crs
Parkfield Avenue
Headstone Lane
Salvatorian College
Sacred Heart Language College
Whitefriars Trading Estate
Whitefriars Community School
Pinner Park Junior Sch
Pinner Park Infant Sch
Holmwood Close
Barrett Way Industrial Est
Tudor Enterprise Park
Harrow Heritage Museum
Waverley Industrial Est
Harrow Crown Courts
Police Stn
Pinner New Cemetery
Nower Hill High School
Headstone Manor Recreation Ground
Headstone
Headstone Drive
Harrow & Wealdstone Station
Caryl Thomas Clnc
Civic Centre
Marlborough Primary School
Civic Medical Cen
St John Fisher RC Primary School
Kingsfield Avenue
Old Lyonian Sports Ground
Pinner View Medical Centre
Alpha Prep School
Alpha Preparatory School
St Andrews School
North Harrow Station
Norbury First & Middle School
Harrow Cemetery
HARROW
St Georges Shopping Centre
PINNER ROAD
A404
A4005
GREENHILL
Vue Cinema
St Ann's Shopping Cen
North Harrow
Longfield Junior & Infant Sch
Buckingham College Prep School
West Harrow Station
Vaughan Prim Sch
The Harold Macmillan Medical Cen
Harrow-on-the-Hill Station
Middlesex New Synagogue
Harrow College
LOWLANDS ROAD
Bus Village
ISBS
West Harrow Recreation Ground
West Harrow
Marshall Medical Cen
BESSBOROUGH ROAD
Grove Fields
Harrow School
St Anselms RC Primary School
IMPERIAL DRIVE
A4090
RAYNERS LA
Rayners Lane Station
Harrow Town CC
Whitmore Road
Whitmore High School
Grange Junior & Infant School
HA2
Shaftesbury Medical Centre
John Lyon School
LOWER ROAD A312
HIGH STREET B458
Harrow on the Hill
Rayners Lane
Newton Farm J&I School
Roxeth
Roxeth Primary School
ROXETH HILL
Police Stn
Council Building
Archdale Business
Bowden House
1 grid square represents 500 metres

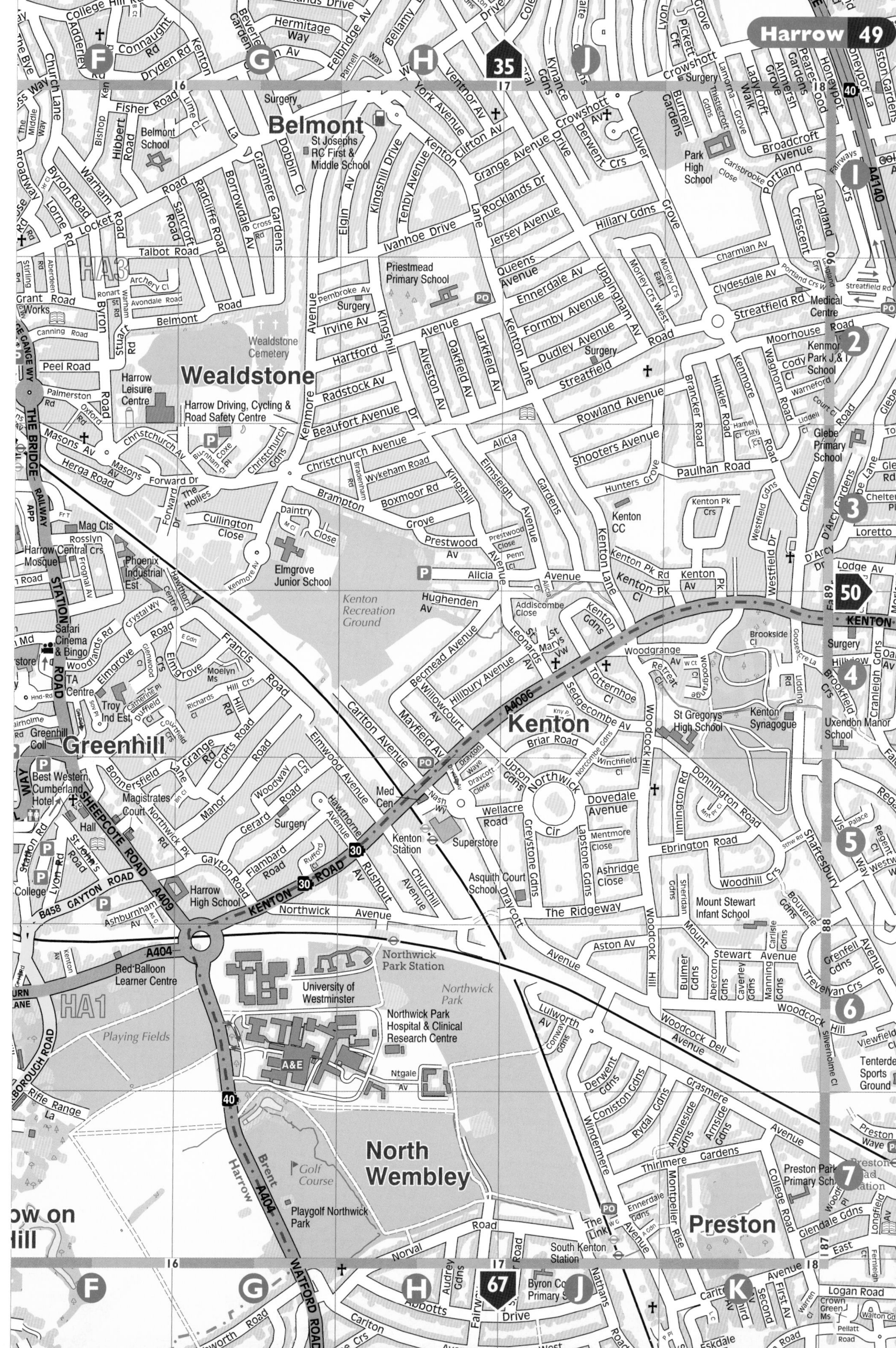
Belmont
Wealdstone
Greenhill
Kenton
North Wembley
Preston
HA3
HA1
St Josephs RC First & Middle School
Belmont School
Priestmead Primary School
Wealdstone Cemetery
Harrow Leisure Centre
Harrow Driving, Cycling & Road Safety Centre
Elmgrove Junior School
Kenton Recreation Ground
Phoenix Industrial Est
Harrow Central Mosque
Safari Cinema & Bingo
TA Centre
Troy Ind Est
Greenhill Coll
Best Western Cumberland Hotel
Magistrates Court
Harrow High School
Red Balloon Learner Centre
University of Westminster
Northwick Park Station
Northwick Park
Northwick Park Hospital & Clinical Research Centre
A&E
Playing Fields
Golf Course
Playgolf Northwick Park
Kenton Station
Superstore
Asquith Court School
St Gregorys High School
Kenton Synagogue
Mount Stewart Infant School
Park High School
Glebe Primary School
Kenmore Park J & I School
Uxendon Manor School
Kenton CC
Tenterden Sports Ground
Preston Park Primary School
South Kenton Station
Byron Court Primary School
Medical Centre
Surgery
Med Cen
KENTON ROAD
A4006
A404
A409
A4140
B458
GAYTON ROAD
SHEEPCOTE ROAD
STATION ROAD
WATFORD ROAD
THE BRIDGE
Kenton Lane
Woodcock Hill
Streatfield Road
Christchurch Avenue
Kenmore Avenue
Northwick Avenue
The Ridgeway
Preston Road
F
G
H
J
K
16
17
18
35
50
67
1
2
3
4
5
6
7

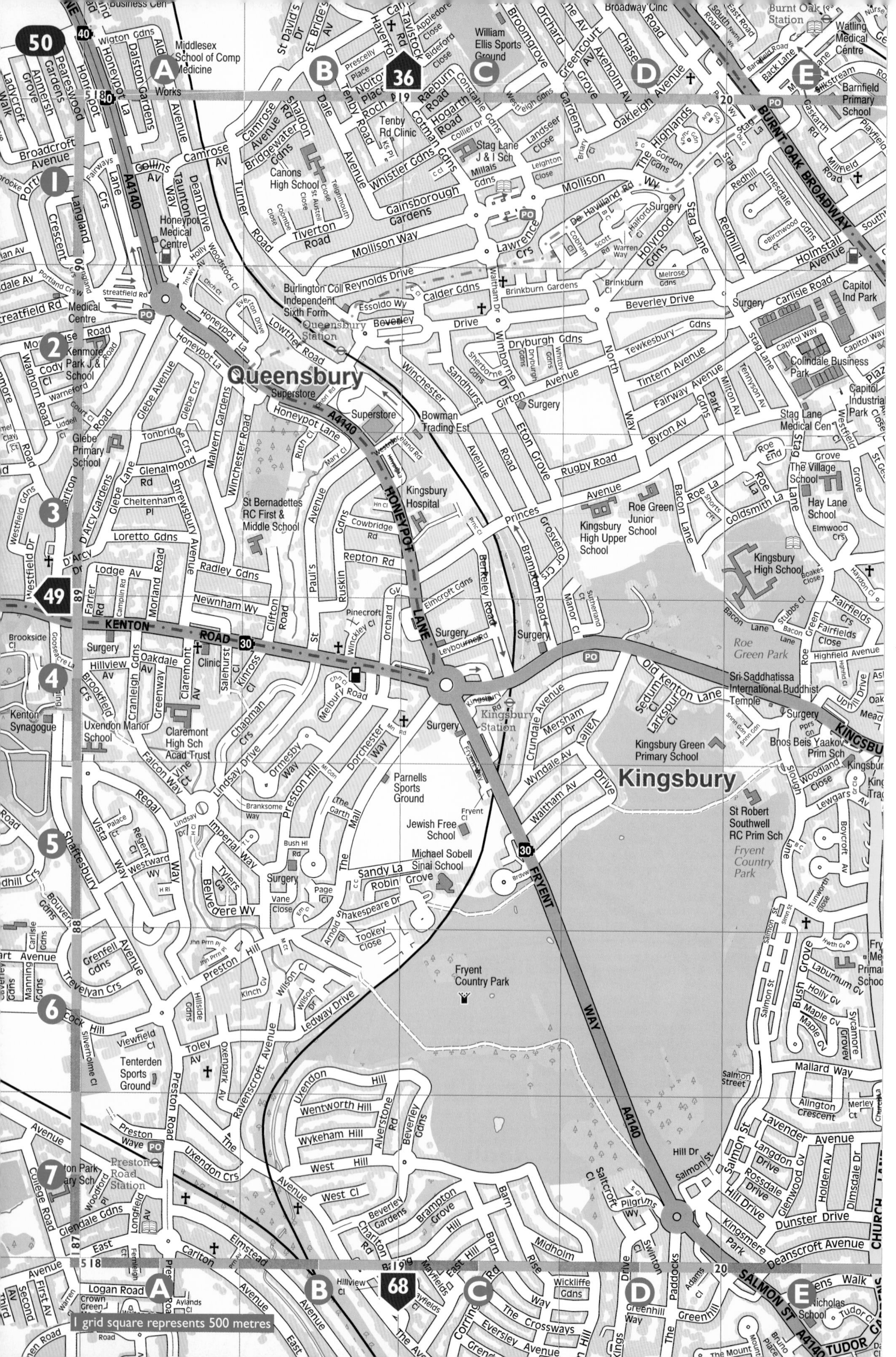

50
36
49
68
A
B
C
D
E
1
2
3
4
5
6
7
518
519
20
188
187
Queensbury
Kingsbury
Queensbury Station
Kingsbury Station
Burnt Oak Station
Preston Road Station
Kenton Road
Honeypot Lane
Fryent Way
Burnt Oak Broadway
Salmon St
A4140
Middlesex School of Comp Medicine
William Ellis Sports Ground
Canons High School
Tenby Rd Clinic
Stag Lane J & I Sch
Honeypot Medical Centre
Burlington Coll Independent Sixth Form
Kenmore Park J & I School
Glebe Primary School
St Bernadettes RC First & Middle School
Kingsbury Hospital
Bowman Trading Est
Kingsbury High Upper School
Roe Green Junior School
Kingsbury High School
The Village School
Hay Lane School
Capitol Ind Park
Colindale Business Park
Capitol Industrial Park
Stag Lane Medical Cen
Barnfield Primary School
Watling Medical Centre
Roe Green Park
Sri Saddhatissa International Buddhist Temple
Kingsbury Green Primary School
Bnos Beis Yaakov Prim Sch
St Robert Southwell RC Prim Sch
Fryent Country Park
Kenton Synagogue
Uxendon Manor School
Claremont High Sch Acad Trust
Parnells Sports Ground
Jewish Free School
Michael Sobell Sinai School
Tenterden Sports Ground
Superstore
Surgery
Clinic
Medical Centre
1 grid square represents 500 metres

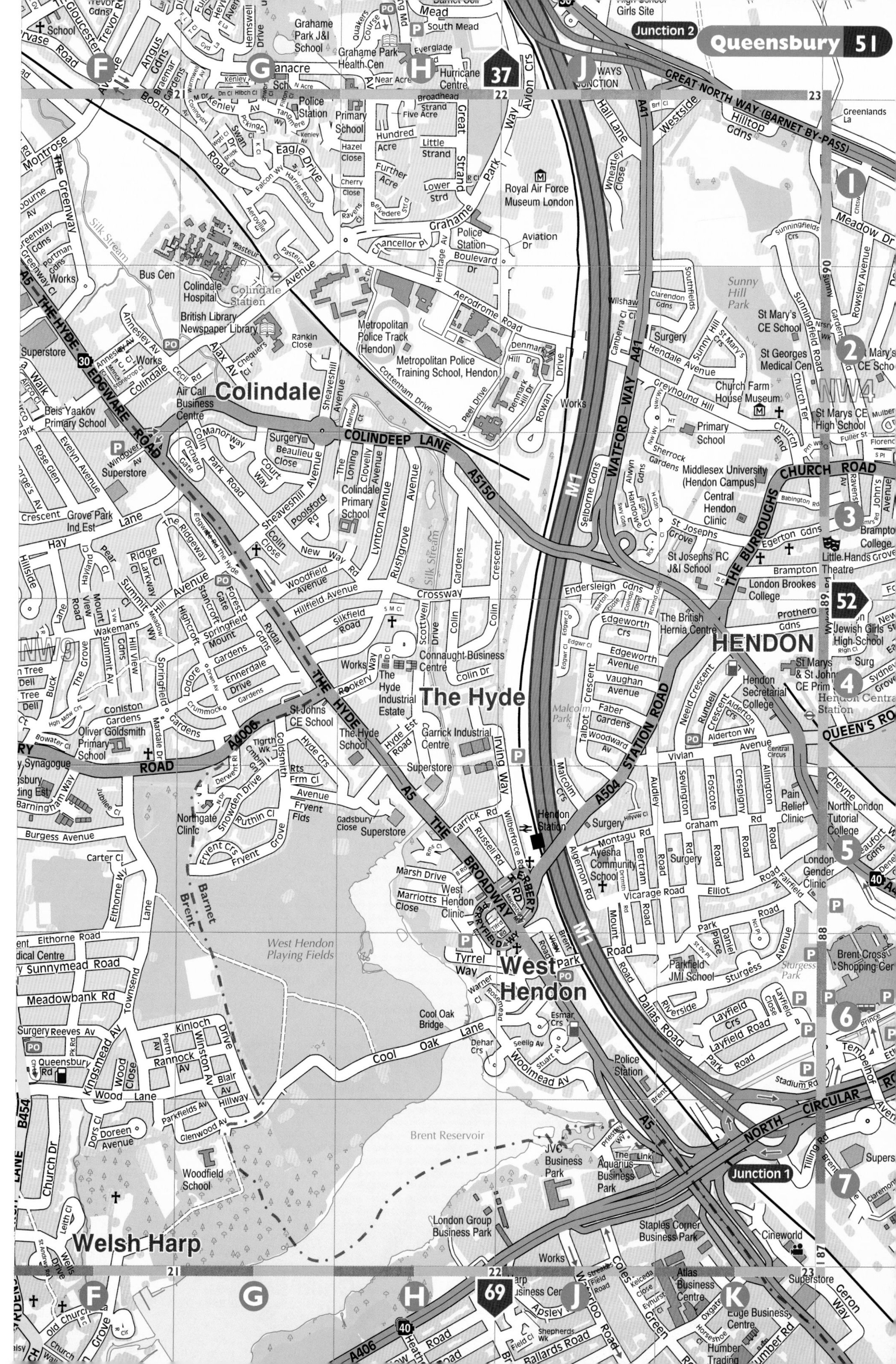
Junction 2
37
52
69
Colindale
The Hyde
HENDON
West Hendon
Welsh Harp
NW9
NW4
Grahame Park J&I School
Grahame Park Health Cen
South Mead
Everglade
Hurricane Centre
Police Station
Primary School
Royal Air Force Museum London
Aviation Dr
Aerodrome Road
Metropolitan Police Track (Hendon)
Metropolitan Police Training School, Hendon
Colindale Hospital
Colindale Station
British Library Newspaper Library
Bus Cen
Silk Stream
Superstore
EDGWARE ROAD
THE HYDE
COLINDEEP LANE
A5150
WATFORD WAY
A41
M1
GREAT NORTH WAY (BARNET BY-PASS)
Sunny Hill Park
St Mary's CE School
St Georges Medical Cen
Church Farm House Museum
St Marys CE High School
CHURCH ROAD
THE BURROUGHS
Middlesex University (Hendon Campus)
Central Hendon Clinic
St Josephs RC J&I School
London Brookes College
The British Hernia Centre
Jewish Girls High School
Hendon Secretarial College
STATION ROAD
A504
QUEEN'S RD
Beis Yaakov Primary School
Grove Park Ind Est
Colindale Primary School
Connaught Business Centre
The Hyde Industrial Estate
Garrick Industrial Centre
St Johns CE School
The Hyde School
Oliver Goldsmith Primary School
Synagogue
A4006
Northgate Clinic
Barnet Brent
West Hendon Playing Fields
Hendon Station
THE BROADWAY
West Hendon Clinic
Ayesha Community School
Parkfield JMI School
Sturgess Park
Brent Cross Shopping Cen
North London Tutorial College
London Gender Clinic
Pain Relief Clinic
Cool Oak Lane
Cool Oak Bridge
Brent Reservoir
Woodfield School
JVC Business Park
Aquarius Business Park
London Group Business Park
Staples Corner Business Park
Atlas Business Centre
Edge Business Centre
Cineworld
Superstore
NORTH CIRCULAR
Junction 1
A406
Police Station
Hendon Central Station
Little Hands Theatre
Brampton College
F
G
H
J
K
I
2
3
4
5
6
7

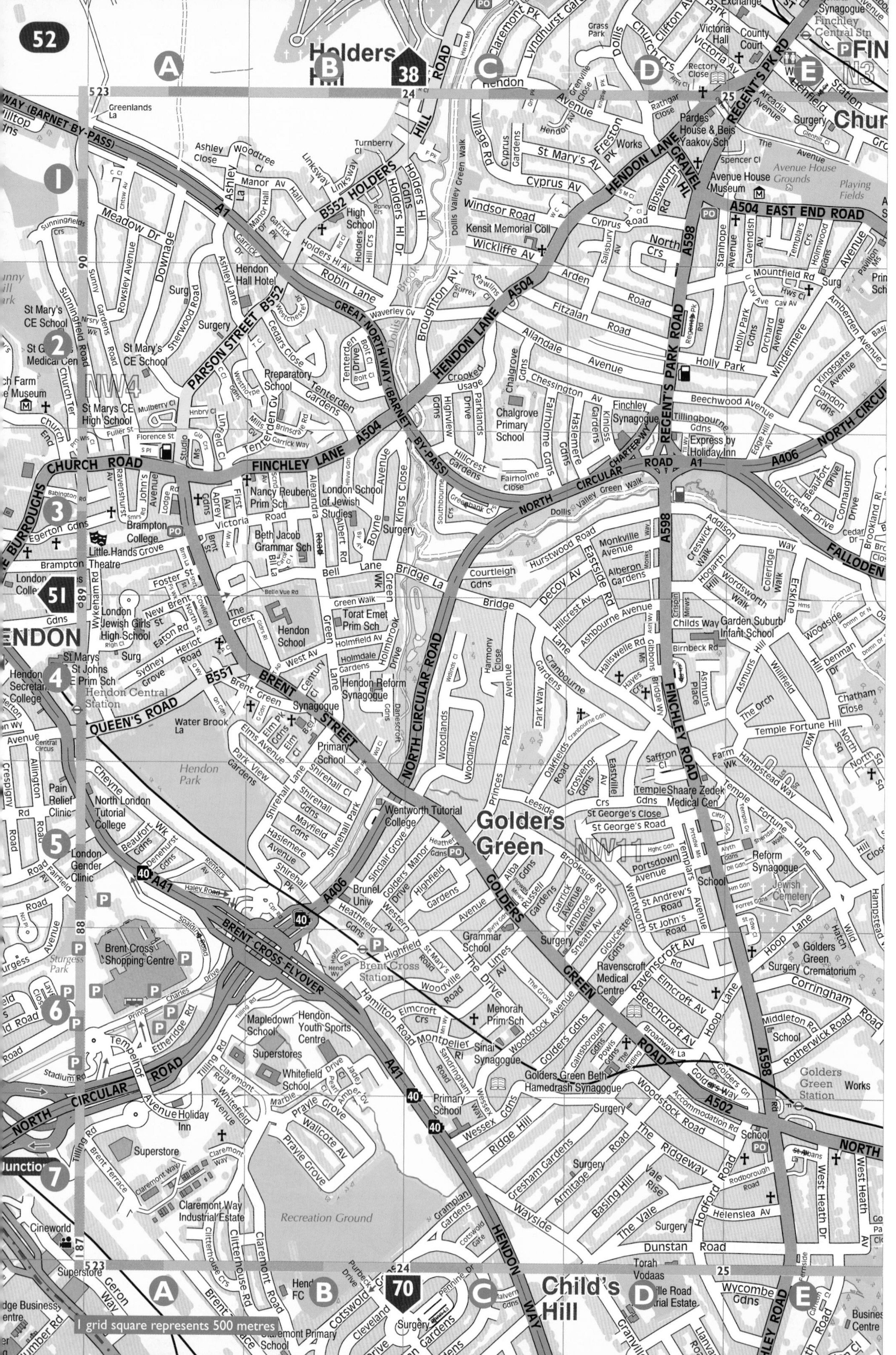
Holders Hill
38
51
70
A
B
C
D
E
1
2
3
4
5
6
7
523
24
25
90
89
88
87
Hendon
NW4
NW11
N3
Golders Green
Child's Hill
Finchley Central Stn
Church End
Great North Way (Barnet By-Pass)
A1
Holders Hill Road
B552 Holders Hill
Parson Street B552
Hendon Lane A504
Finchley Lane A504
A504 East End Road
Regent's Park Road A598
Finchley Road A598
Gravel Hill
North Circular Road
A406
Church Road
The Burroughs
Queen's Road
Brent Street B551
Golders Green Road A502
Brent Cross Flyover
A41
Hendon Way
Falloden Way
Bell Lane
Sunningfield Road
Meadow Dr
Downage
Sherwood Road
Ashley Lane
Robin Lane
Tenterden Gardens
Alexandra Road
Victoria Road
Bridge Lane
Cranbourne Gardens
Hampstead Way
Temple Fortune Lane
Temple Fortune Hill
Hoop Lane
The Ridgeway
Basing Hill
Wayside
Dunstan Road
Dollis Valley Green Walk
Dollis Brook
Hendon Park
Recreation Ground
Hendon School
Hendon Hall Hotel
Kensit Memorial Coll
Chalgrove Primary School
Finchley Synagogue
Express by Holiday Inn
Garden Suburb Infant School
Shaare Zedek Medical Cen
Reform Synagogue
Jewish Cemetery
Golders Green Crematorium
Golders Green Station
Brent Cross Station
Hendon Central Station
Brent Cross Shopping Centre
Sturgess Park
Wentworth Tutorial College
Brunel Univ
North London Tutorial College
London Gender Clinic
Menorah Prim Sch
Sinai Synagogue
Golders Green Beth Hamedrash Synagogue
Ravenscroft Medical Centre
Hendon Reform Synagogue
Torat Emet Prim Sch
London School of Jewish Studies
Nancy Reuben Prim Sch
Beth Jacob Grammar Sch
London Jewish Girls High School
Brampton College
Little Hands Theatre
St Mary's CE School
St Marys CE High School
St Marys & St Johns CE Prim Sch
Hendon Secretarial College
Avenue House Museum
Pardes House & Beis Yaakov Sch
Mapledown School
Hendon Youth Sports Centre
Whitefield School
Claremont Way Industrial Estate
Cineworld
Superstores
Superstore
Holiday Inn
Torah Vodaas
Junction 1
1 grid square represents 500 metres

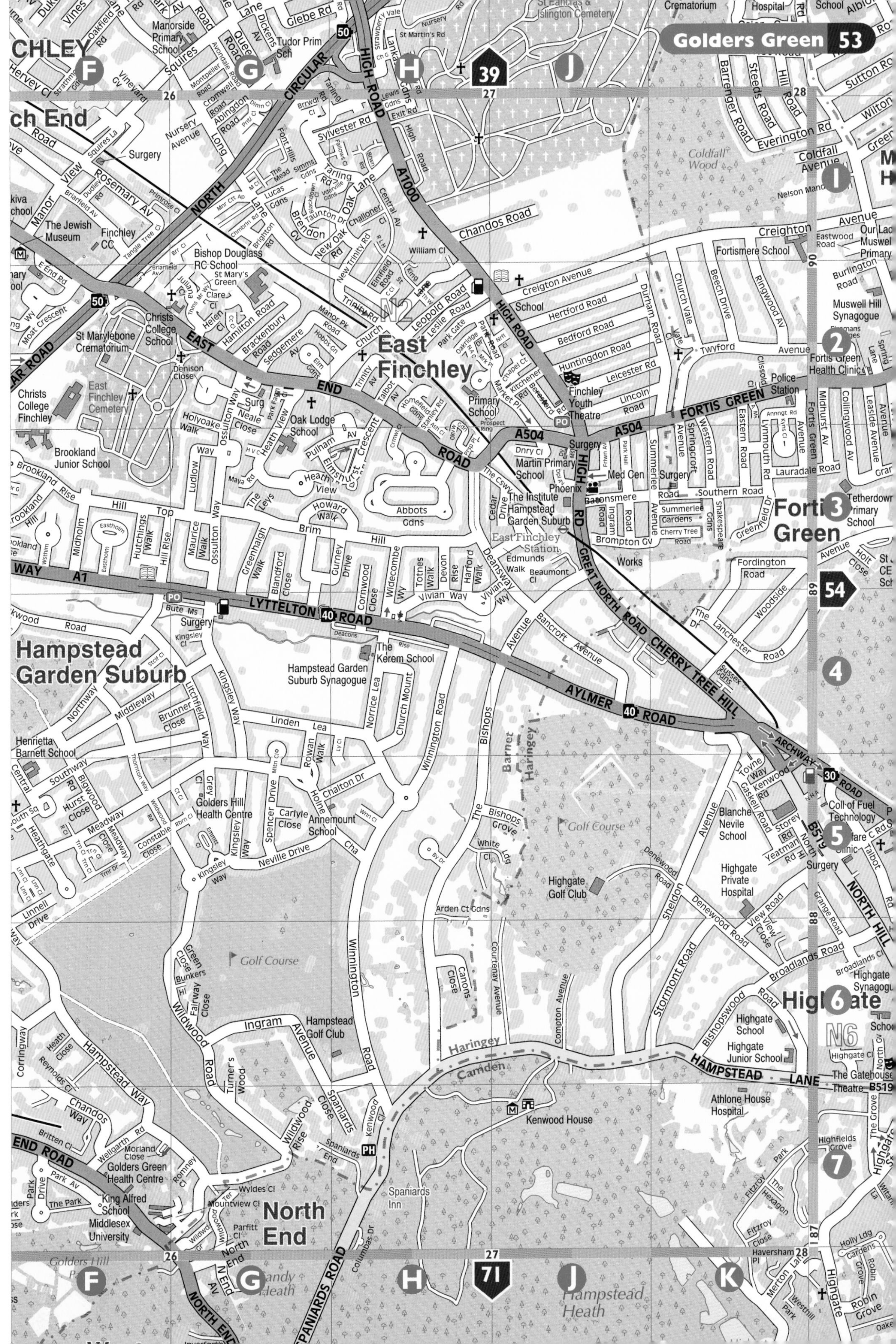

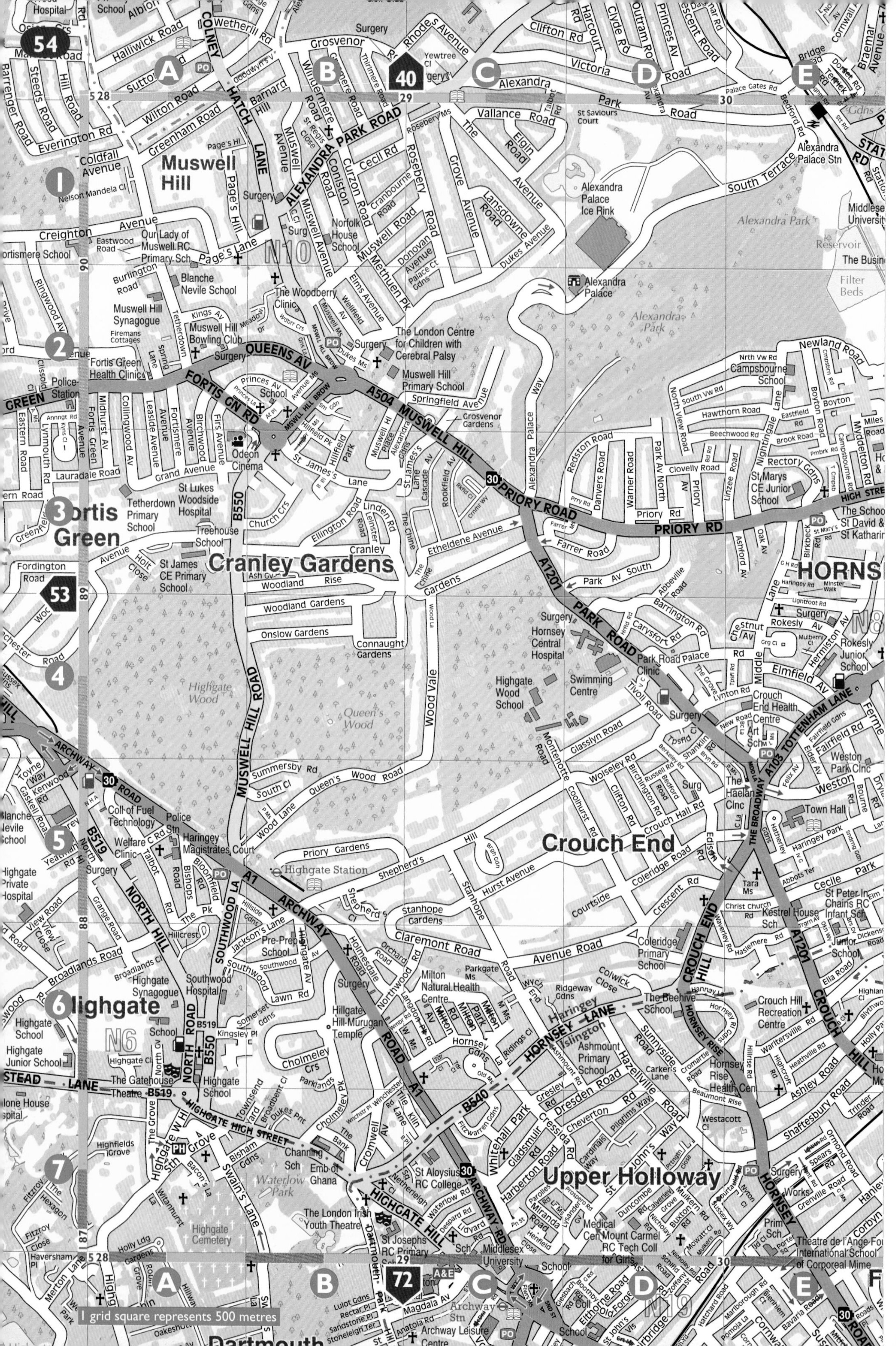

40
54
53
72
A
B
C
D
E
1
2
3
4
5
6
7
528
29
30
90
89
88
87
Muswell Hill
Fortis Green
Cranley Gardens
Highgate
Crouch End
Upper Holloway
HORNS
N10
N8
N6
N19
Alexandra Palace
Alexandra Palace Ice Rink
Alexandra Park
Alexandra Palace Stn
Highgate Wood
Queen's Wood
Waterlow Park
Highgate Cemetery
Highgate Station
Archway Stn
COLNEY HATCH LANE
ALEXANDRA PARK ROAD
QUEENS AV
FORTIS GN RD
A504 MUSWELL HILL
PRIORY ROAD
PRIORY RD
A1201 PARK ROAD
MUSWELL HILL ROAD
ARCHWAY ROAD
A1 ARCHWAY
NORTH HILL
NORTH ROAD
HIGHGATE HIGH STREET
HIGHGATE HILL
HORNSEY LANE
CROUCH END HILL
HORNSEY RISE
A103 TOTTENHAM LANE
THE BROADWAY
CROUCH HILL
Alexandra Road
Vallance Road
South Terrace
Grosvenor Road
Rhodes Avenue
Halliwick Road
Wilton Road
Greenham Road
Everington Rd
Coldfall Avenue
Creighton Avenue
Page's Lane
Page's Hill
Tetherdown
Muswell Avenue
Muswell Road
Coniston Road
Curzon Road
Cecil Rd
Rosebery Road
The Grove
Grove Avenue
Lansdowne Road
Dukes Avenue
Methuen Pk
Springfield Avenue
Etheldene Avenue
Woodland Rise
Woodland Gardens
Onslow Gardens
Connaught Gardens
Wood Vale
Queen's Wood Road
Shepherd's Hill
Hurst Avenue
Claremont Road
Avenue Road
Coleridge Road
Crescent Rd
Crouch Hall Rd
Weston Park
Haringey Park
Ashley Road
Shaftesbury Road
Cholmeley Crs
Southwood Lane
Jackson's Lane
Swain's Lane
Muswell Hill Synagogue
Muswell Hill Bowling Club
Blanche Nevile School
Odeon Cinema
Hornsey Central Hospital
Highgate Wood School
Coll of Fuel Technology
Haringey Magistrates Court
Highgate School
Highgate Synagogue
Channing Sch
St Aloysius RC College
The London Irish Youth Theatre
Middlesex University
Crouch Hill Recreation Centre
Coleridge Primary School
Ashmount Primary School
The Beehive School
Hornsey Rise Health Cen
Theatre de l'Ange Fou International School of Corporeal Mime
1 grid square represents 500 metres

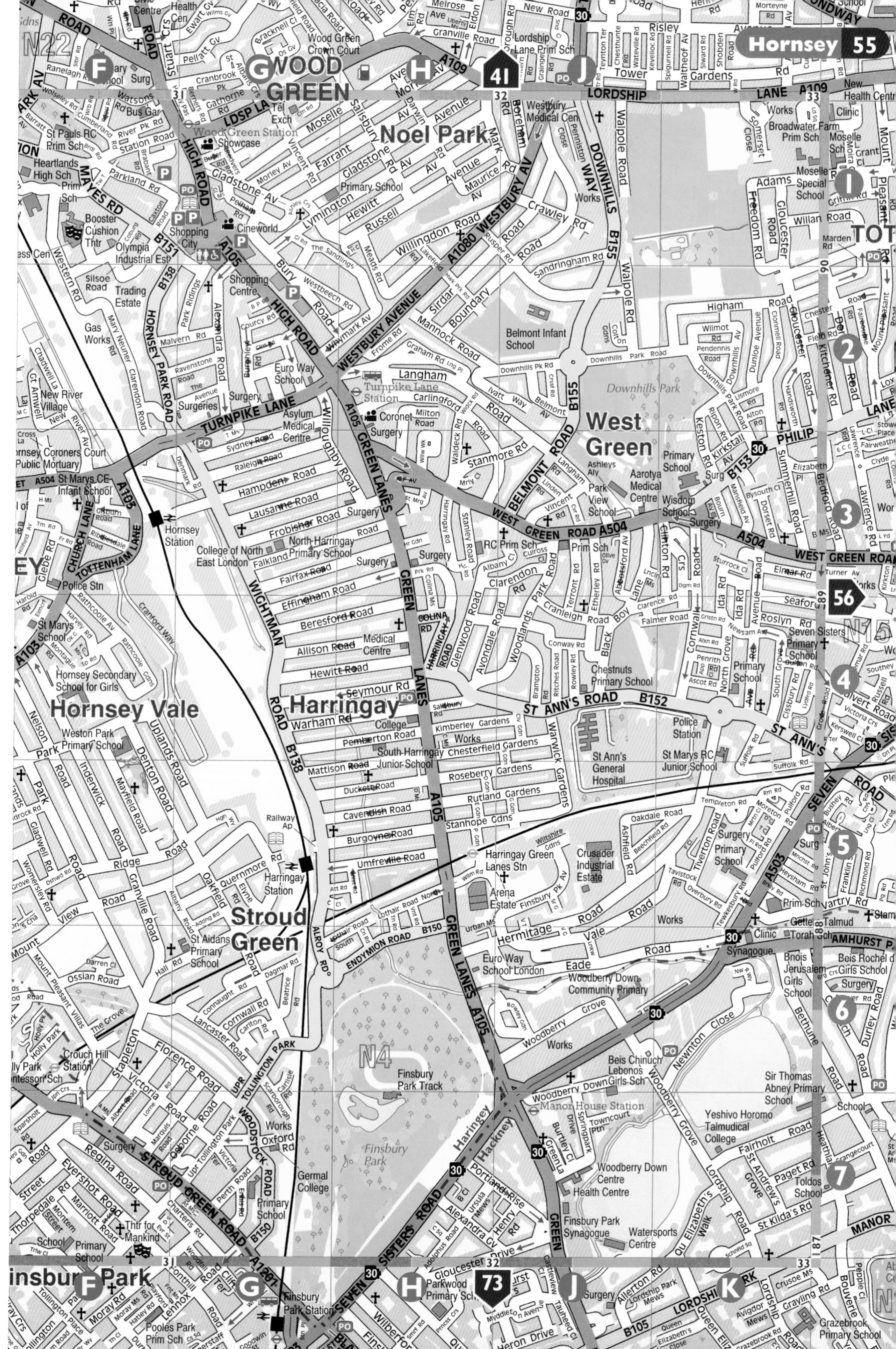

WOOD GREEN
Noel Park
West Green
Harringay
Hornsey Vale
Stroud Green
Finsbury Park
N22
N4
N15
HIGH ROAD
LORDSHIP LANE A109
WESTBURY AVENUE
A1080 WESTBURY AV
TURNPIKE LANE
GREEN LANES
A105
WEST GREEN ROAD A504
ST ANN'S ROAD B152
SEVEN SISTERS ROAD
STROUD GREEN ROAD
ENDYMION ROAD
WIGHTMAN ROAD B138
HORNSEY PARK ROAD
DOWNHILLS WAY
BELMONT ROAD
PHILIP LANE
AMHURST PARK
Wood Green Station
Turnpike Lane Station
Hornsey Station
Harringay Station
Harringay Green Lanes Stn
Manor House Station
Finsbury Park Station
Crouch Hill Station
Downhills Park
Finsbury Park
Finsbury Park Track
Wood Green Crown Court
Shopping City
Cineworld
Showcase
St Ann's General Hospital
College of North East London
Hornsey Secondary School for Girls
Belmont Infant School
Chestnuts Primary School
Arena Estate
Crusader Industrial Estate
Woodberry Down Centre
Finsbury Park Synagogue
41
56
73

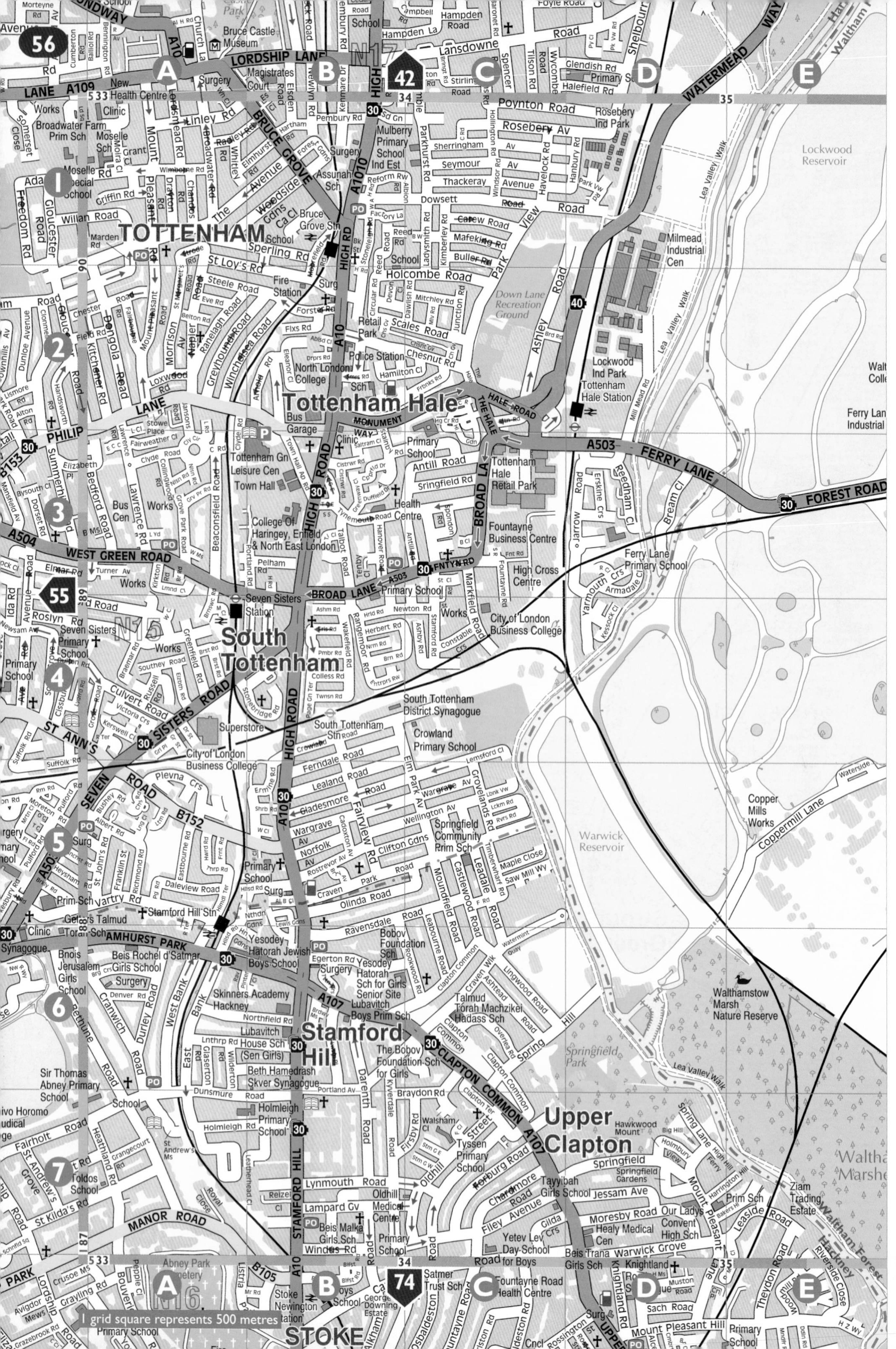

56
42
55
74
TOTTENHAM
Tottenham Hale
South Tottenham
Stamford Hill
Upper Clapton
STOKE
LORDSHIP LANE
BRUCE GROVE
HIGH RD
HIGH ROAD
A10
A1010
A109
A503
A504
A107
B152
B105
WATERMEAD WAY
FERRY LANE
FOREST ROAD
MONUMENT WAY
THE HALE
HALE ROAD
BROAD LANE
BROAD LA
FNTYN RD
WEST GREEN ROAD
PHILIP LANE
ST ANN'S ROAD
SEVEN SISTERS ROAD
AMHURST PARK
CLAPTON COMMON
MANOR ROAD
STAMFORD HILL
Bruce Castle Museum
Magistrates Court
New Health Centre
Broadwater Farm Prim Sch
Mulberry Primary School
Bruce Grove Stn
Fire Station
Police Station
North London College
Tottenham Gn Leisure Cen
Town Hall
College Of Haringey, Enfield & North East London
Down Lane Recreation Ground
Lockwood Reservoir
Milmead Industrial Cen
Lockwood Ind Park
Tottenham Hale Station
Tottenham Hale Retail Park
Fountayne Business Centre
High Cross Centre
Ferry Lane Primary School
City of London Business College
Seven Sisters Station
South Tottenham Stn
South Tottenham District Synagogue
Crowland Primary School
Superstore
Warwick Reservoir
Copper Mills Works
Coppermill Lane
Lea Valley Walk
Walthamstow Marsh Nature Reserve
Springfield Park
Springfield Community Prim Sch
Stamford Hill Stn
Skinners Academy Hackney
Beis Rochel d'Satmar Girls School
Yesodey Hatorah Jewish Boys School
Beth Hamedrash Skver Synagogue
Sir Thomas Abney Primary School
Holmleigh Primary School
Tyssen Primary School
Oldhill Medical Centre
Beis Malka Girls Sch
Abney Park Cemetery
Stoke Newington Station
Fountayne Road Health Centre
Ziam Trading Estate
Waltham Forest
Hackney
N15
N16
N17
1 grid square represents 500 metres

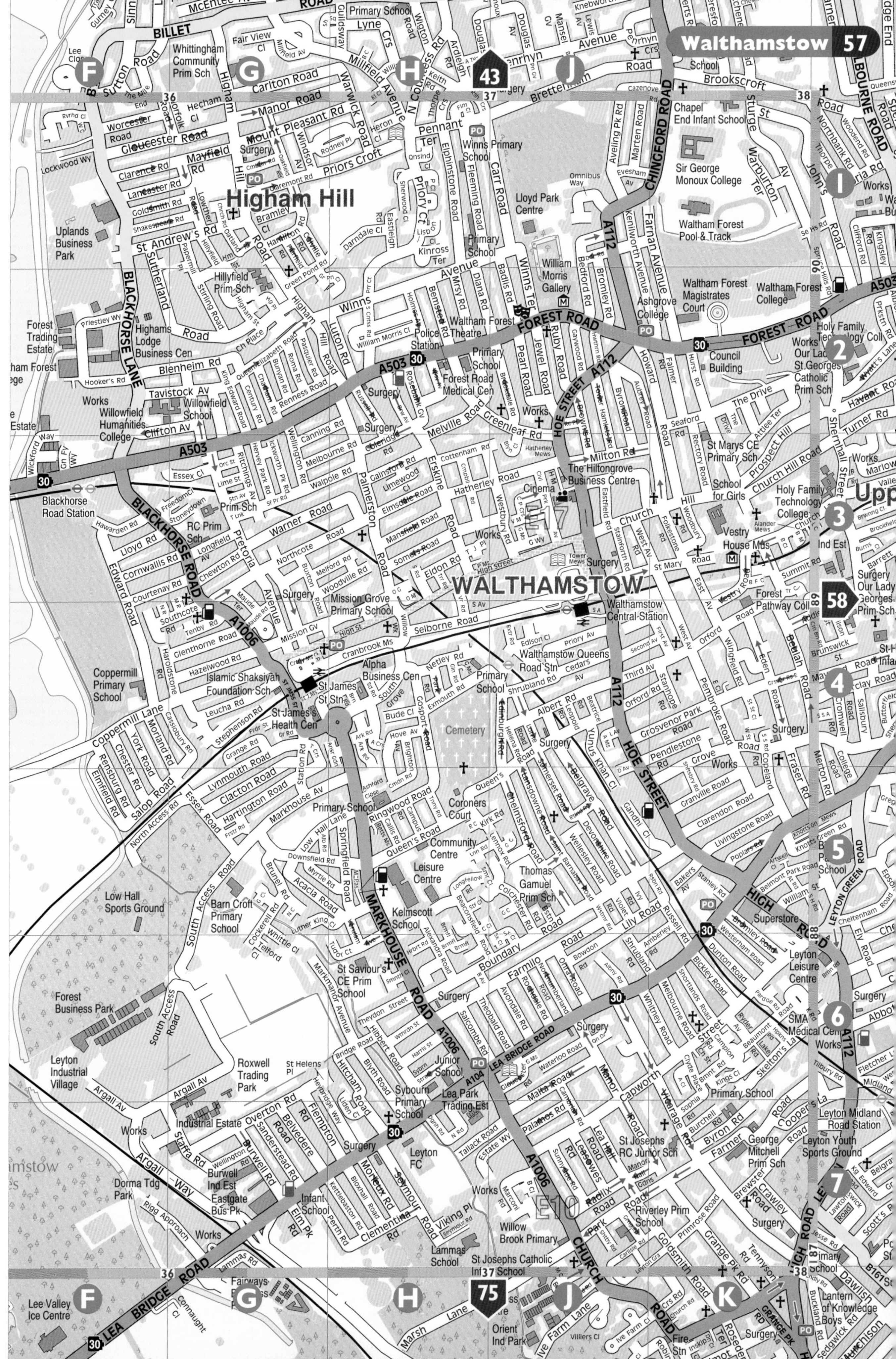

Higham Hill
WALTHAMSTOW
E17
E10
Whittingham Community Prim Sch
Fair View Cl
Primary School
Lyne Crs
Millfield Avenue
Carlton Road
Manor Road
Mount Pleasant Rd
Gloucester Road
Worcester Road
Mayfield Rd
Priors Croft
Winns Primary School
Lloyd Park Centre
Sir George Monoux College
Waltham Forest Pool & Track
Chapel End Infant School
Chingford Road
Brookscroft
Uplands Business Park
St Andrew's Rd
Sutherland Road
Hillyfield Prim Sch
Forest Trading Estate
Highams Lodge Business Cen
Blenheim Rd
Tavistock Av
Willowfield School
Willowfield Humanities College
Clifton Av
Blackhorse Lane
Blackhorse Road Station
Blackhorse Road
William Morris Gallery
Waltham Forest Magistrates Court
Waltham Forest College
Ashgrove College
Forest Road
Council Building
Holy Family Technology Coll
Waltham Forest Theatre
Police Station
Forest Road Medical Cen
Hoe Street
The Hiltongrove Business Centre
Cinema
St Marys CE Primary Sch
School for Girls
Vestry House Mus
Holy Family Technology College
Church Hill Road
Prospect Hill
Walthamstow Central Station
Walthamstow Queens Road Stn
Selborne Road
Mission Grove Primary School
Islamic Shaksiyah Foundation Sch
St James St Stn
St James's Health Cen
Alpha Business Cen
Cemetery
Coroners Court
Community Centre
Leisure Centre
Coppermill Primary School
Coppermill Lane
Low Hall Sports Ground
Barn Croft Primary School
Forest Business Park
Leyton Industrial Village
Roxwell Trading Park
Industrial Estate
Markhouse Road
A1006
Kelmscott School
St Saviour's CE Prim School
Thomas Gamuel Prim Sch
Lea Bridge Road
Junior School
Sybourn Primary School
Lea Park Trading Est
Leyton FC
Burwell Ind Est
Eastgate Bus Pk
Dorma Tdg Park
Infant School
St Josephs RC Junior Sch
Riverley Prim School
Willow Brook Primary
Lammas School
St Josephs Catholic Inf School
George Mitchell Prim Sch
Leyton Midland Road Station
Leyton Youth Sports Ground
Leyton Leisure Centre
High Road
Superstore
SMA Medical Cen
Lee Valley Ice Centre
Orient Ind Park
Marsh Lane
Church Road
Lantern of Knowledge Boys
Walthamstow Central Station
Forest Pathway Coll
Leyton Green Road

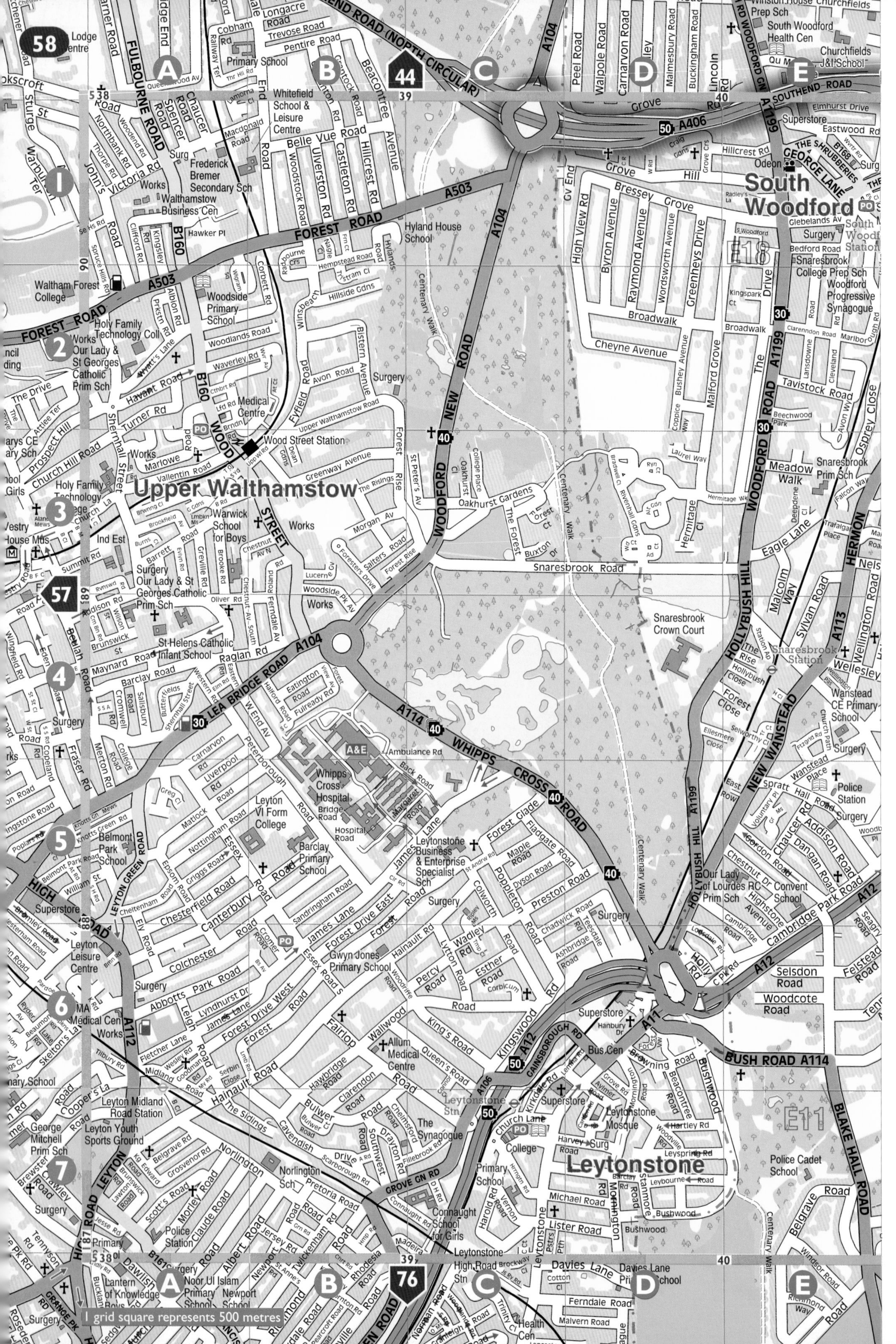
58
44
57
76
A
B
C
D
E
1
2
3
4
5
6
7
38
39
40
90
89
88
87
Upper Walthamstow
South Woodford
Leytonstone
E18
E11
FOREST ROAD
A503
FULBOURNE ROAD
NEW ROAD
A104
WOODFORD NEW ROAD
SOUTHEND ROAD (NORTH CIRCULAR)
A406
A1199
WOODFORD ROAD
GEORGE LANE
THE SHRUBBERIES
HOLLYBUSH HILL
NEW WANSTEAD
HERMON
A113
WOOD STREET
B160
LEA BRIDGE ROAD
WHIPPS CROSS ROAD
A114
HIGH ROAD
LEYTON GREEN ROAD
A112
A12
A11
A106
GAINSBOROUGH RD
BUSH ROAD A114
BLAKE HALL ROAD
GROVE GN RD
CAMBRIDGE PARK ROAD
Snaresbrook Road
Snaresbrook Crown Court
Snaresbrook Station
Wood Street Station
Leytonstone Stn
Leyton Midland Road Station
Leytonstone High Road Stn
Whipps Cross Hospital
A&E
Waltham Forest College
Holy Family Technology Coll
Woodside Primary School
Frederick Bremer Secondary Sch
Walthamstow Business Cen
Whitefield School & Leisure Centre
Hyland House School
Warwick School for Boys
St Helens Catholic Infant School
Leyton VI Form College
Barclay Primary School
Leytonstone Business & Enterprise Specialist Sch
Gwyn Jones Primary School
Allum Medical Centre
Connaught School for Girls
Leytonstone Mosque
Norlington Sch
Leyton Leisure Centre
Leyton Youth Sports Ground
George Mitchell Prim Sch
Police Station
Police Cadet School
Wanstead CE Primary School
Snaresbrook College Prep Sch
Woodford Progressive Synagogue
South Woodford Health Cen
Churchfields J&I School
Snaresbrook Prim Sch
Our Lady of Lourdes RC Prim Sch
Convent School
Belmont Park School
Davies Lane Prim School
Noor Ul Islam Primary School
Newport School
Lantern of Knowledge Boys
Superstore
Surgery
Odeon
Bus Cen
1 grid square represents 500 metres

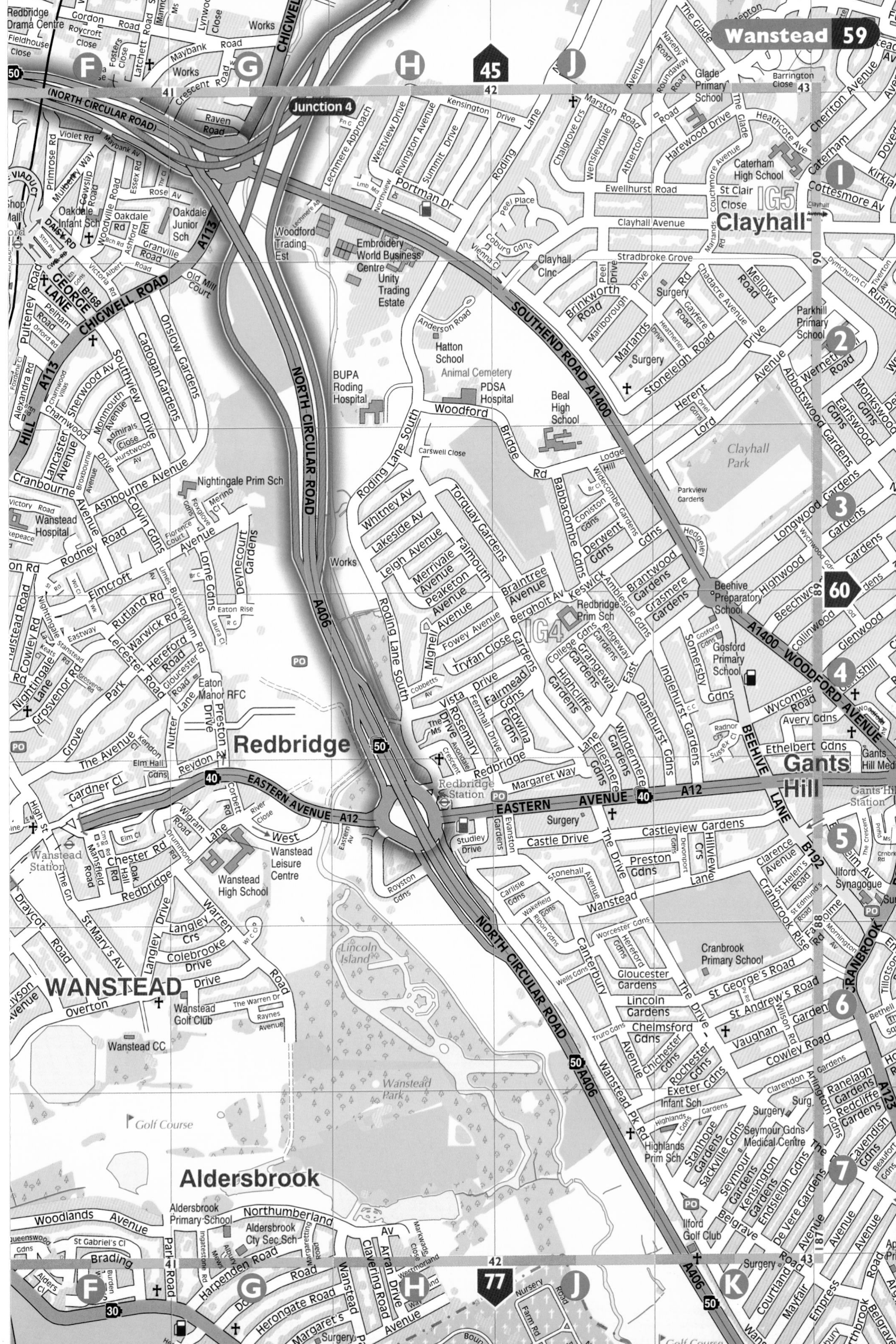

45
60
77
Junction 4
(NORTH CIRCULAR ROAD)
NORTH CIRCULAR ROAD
A406
SOUTHEND ROAD A1400
A1400 WOODFORD AVENUE
EASTERN AVENUE A12
CHIGWELL ROAD
GEORGE LANE
B168
A113
HILL
BEEHIVE LANE
B192
CRANBROOK
A123
IG4
IG5
Clayhall
Redbridge
Gants Hill
WANSTEAD
Aldersbrook
Wanstead Park
Lincoln Island
Clayhall Park
Redbridge Drama Centre
Works
Oakdale Infant Sch
Oakdale Junior Sch
Woodford Trading Est
Embroidery World Business Centre
Unity Trading Estate
Hatton School
Animal Cemetery
PDSA Hospital
BUPA Roding Hospital
Beal High School
Glade Primary School
Caterham High School
Clayhall Clnc
Surgery
Parkhill Primary School
Parkview Gardens
Nightingale Prim Sch
Wanstead Hospital
Redbridge Prim Sch
Beehive Preparatory School
Gosford Primary School
Eaton Manor RFC
Redbridge Station
Gants Hill Station
Wanstead Station
Wanstead Leisure Centre
Wanstead High School
Cranbrook Primary School
Ilford Synagogue
Wanstead Golf Club
Wanstead CC
Golf Course
Infant Sch
Highlands Prim Sch
Seymour Gdns Medical Centre
Ilford Golf Club
Aldersbrook Primary School
Aldersbrook Cty Sec Sch
Woodlands Avenue
Northumberland Av
Harpenden Road
Herongate Road
Clavering Road
Arran Drive
Wanstead Pk Rd
Cranbrook Rise
Woodford Bridge Rd
Roding Lane South
Clayhall Avenue
Ewellhurst Road
Stradbroke Grove
Castleview Gardens
Castle Drive
The Drive
Redbridge Lane
Overton Drive
Cranbourne Avenue
Ashbourne Avenue
Rodney Road
Tryfan Close
Margaret Way

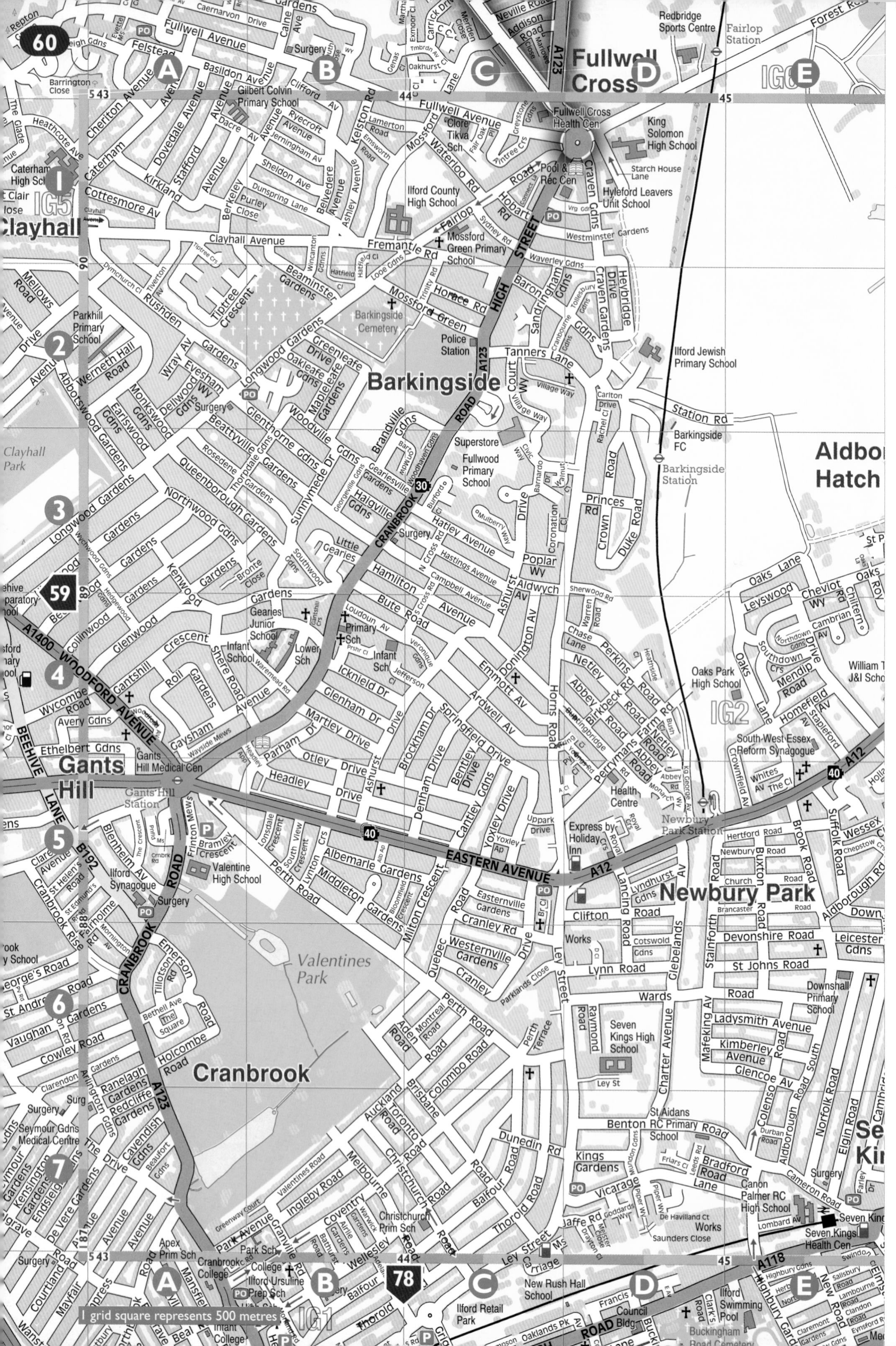

60
Fullwell Cross
Clayhall
Barkingside
Aldborough Hatch
Gants Hill
Newbury Park
Cranbrook
Valentines Park
Clayhall Park
IG5
IG6
IG2
IG1
A
B
C
D
E
1
2
3
4
5
6
7
59
78
Fullwell Avenue
Caernarvon Drive
Basildon Avenue
Gilbert Colvin Primary School
Caterham High School
Cottesmore Av
Clayhall Avenue
Fremantle Rd
Ilford County High School
Mossford Green Primary School
Barkingside Cemetery
Police Station
Fullwell Cross Health Cen
Pool & Rec Cen
King Solomon High School
Redbridge Sports Centre
Fairlop Station
Forest Rd
Hyleford Leavers Unit School
Westminster Gardens
Tanners Lane
Ilford Jewish Primary School
Station Rd
Barkingside FC
Barkingside Station
Superstore
Fullwood Primary School
Parkhill Primary School
Longwood Gardens
Woodford Avenue
A1400
Beehive Lane
Cranbrook Road
High Street
A123
A12
Eastern Avenue
Gearies Junior School
Infant School
Primary Sch
Infant Sch
Lower Sch
Gants Hill Medical Cen
Gants Hill Station
Valentine High School
Ilford Synagogue
Oaks Park High School
South West Essex Reform Synagogue
Newbury Park Station
Express by Holiday Inn
Health Centre
William T J&I Sch
Horns Road
Ley Street
Seven Kings High School
St Aidans RC Primary School
Benton Road
Canon Palmer RC High School
Seven Kings
Seven Kings Health Cen
Downshall Primary School
Christchurch Prim Sch
Apex Prim Sch
Cranbrook College
Ilford Ursuline Prep Sch
New Rush Hall School
Ilford Retail Park
Council Bldg
Ilford Swimming Pool
Buckingham Road Cemetery
Seymour Gdns Medical Centre
A118
B192
1 grid square represents 500 metres

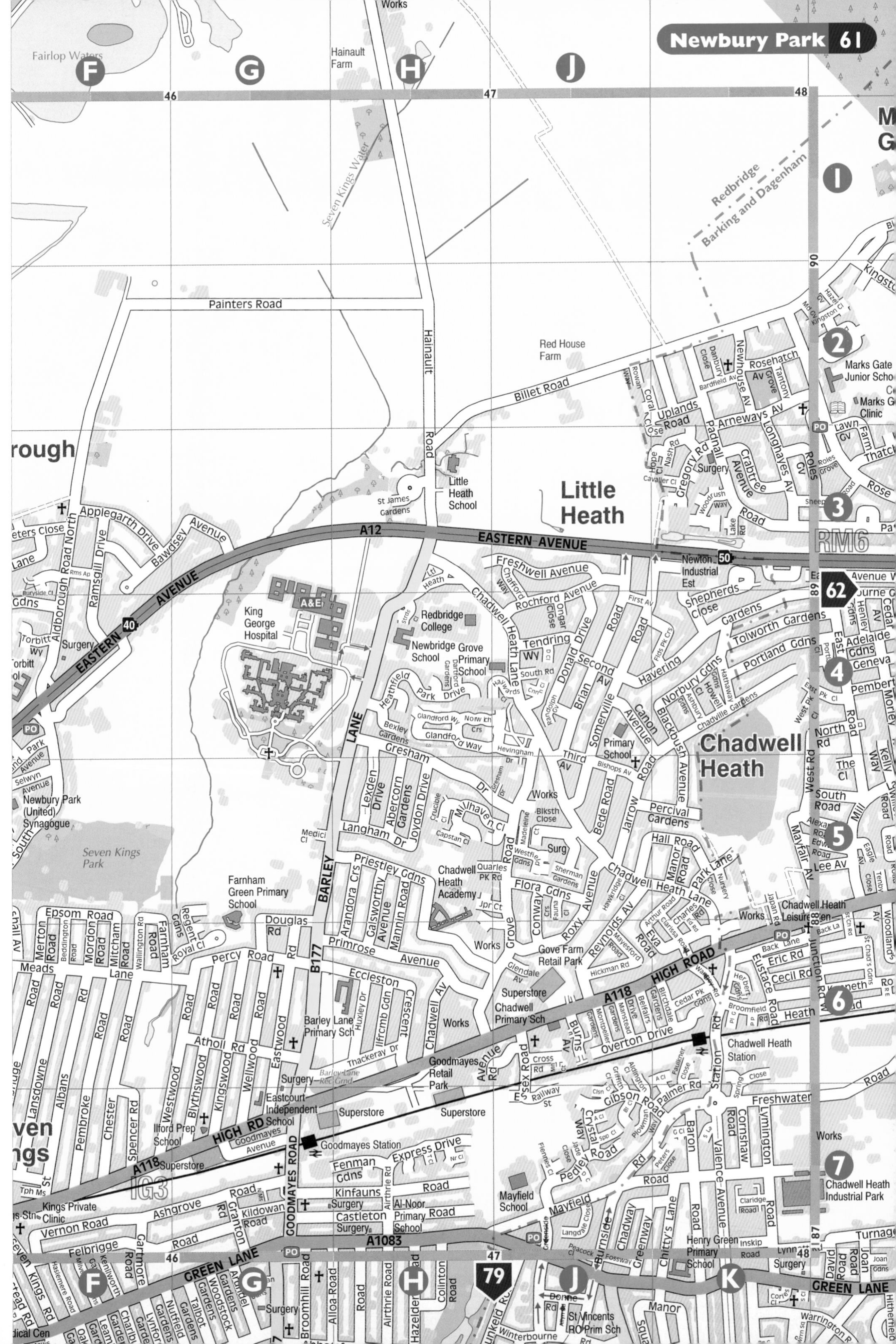
Fairlop Waters
Hainault Farm
Works
Redbridge
Barking and Dagenham
Painters Road
Hainault Road
Red House Farm
Billet Road
Little Heath
Little Heath School
St James Gardens
EASTERN AVENUE
A12
King George Hospital
A&E
Redbridge College
Newbridge School
Grove Primary School
Chadwell Heath Lane
Chadwell Heath
Newton Industrial Est
Shepherds Close
Tolworth Gardens
Portland Gdns
Marks Gate Junior School
Surgery
Seven Kings Park
Newbury Park (United) Synagogue
Farnham Green Primary School
BARLEY LANE
B177
Chadwell Heath Academy
Gove Farm Retail Park
Superstore
Chadwell Primary Sch
A118
HIGH ROAD
Goodmayes Retail Park
Chadwell Heath Station
Chadwell Heath Leisure Cen
Goodmayes Station
GOODMAYES ROAD
Barley Lane Primary Sch
Eastcourt Independent School
Ilford Prep School
Kings Private Clinic
IG3
RM6
Mayfield School
Al-Noor Primary School
A1083
GREEN LANE
Henry Green Primary School
Chadwell Heath Industrial Park
St Vincents RC Prim Sch
Junction Rd
Valence Avenue
79
62

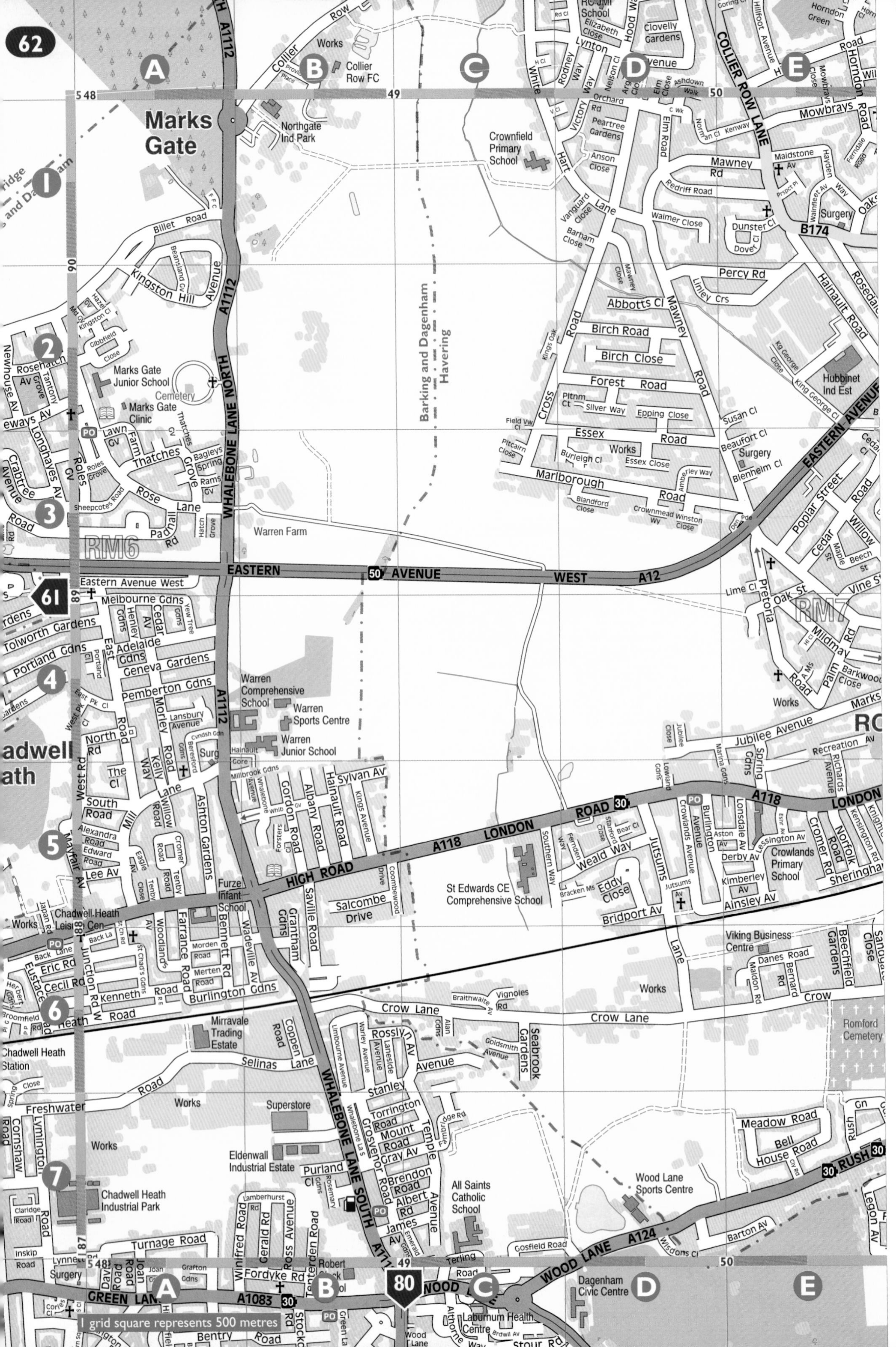

Marks Gate
Collier Row
Works
Collier Row FC
Northgate Ind Park
Crownfield Primary School
Orchard Rd
Peartree Gardens
Anson Close
Lynton Avenue
Clovelly Gardens
Rodney Way
Victory Way
Hart Lane
Elm Road
Mawney Rd
Redriff Road
Walmer Close
Dunster Cl
Dover Cl
Percy Rd
Linley Crs
Abbotts Cl
Birch Road
Birch Close
Forest Road
Silver Way
Epping Close
Essex Road
Works
Essex Close
Burleigh Cl
Marlborough Road
Blandford Close
Crownmead Wy
Winston Close
Mawney Road
Cross Road
Vanguard Close
Barham Close
Field Vw Cl
Pitcairn Close
Susan Cl
Beaufort Cl
Surgery
Blenheim Cl
COLLIER ROW LANE
Mowbrays Road
Horndon Road
Horndon Green
Hillfoot Avenue
Maidstone Av
Hayden Way
Surgery
B174
Hainault Road
Rosedale
Kg George Close
King George Cl
Hubbinet Ind Est
EASTERN AVENUE
Poplar Street
Cedar St
Willow
Beech St
Maple St
Vine St
Lime Cl
Pretoria Road
Oak St
Mildmay Rd
Palm Road
Barkwood Close
Works
RM7
Billet Road
Kingston Hill Avenue
Beansland Gv
Kingston Cl
Gibbfield Close
Rosehatch Av
Tantony Grove
Newhouse Av
Marks Gate Junior School
Cemetery
Marks Gate Clinic
PO
Lawn Farm Gv
Thatches Gv
Thatches Grove
Bagleys Spring
Rams Gv
Roles Gv
Roles Grove
Longhayes Av
Crabtree Avenue
Rose Lane
Padnall Rd
Hatch Grove
Sheepcotes Road
RM6
WHALEBONE LANE NORTH
A1112
Barking and Dagenham
Havering
Warren Farm
EASTERN AVENUE WEST A12
50
Eastern Avenue West
61
Melbourne Gdns
Henley Gdns
Cedar Av
Yew Tree Gdns
Tolworth Gardens
Adelaide Gdns
Portland Gdns
East Rd
Geneva Gardens
Pemberton Gdns
East Pk Cl
Lansbury Avenue
North Rd
Morley Road
Kelly Way
Surg
The Cl
South Road
Mill Lane
Willow Road
Alexandra Road
Edward Road
Lee Av
Eagle Close
Tenby Road
Cromer Road
Ashton Gardens
Chadwell Heath
West Rd
Mayfair Av
Warren Comprehensive School
Warren Sports Centre
Warren Junior School
Hainault Gore
Millbrook Gdns
Whalebone Avenue
Gordon Road
Albany Road
Hainault Road
Kings Avenue
Sylvan Av
Forsters Cl
Furze Infant School
HIGH ROAD
A118 LONDON ROAD
30
Salcombe Drive
Coombewood Drive
Saville Road
Grantham Gdns
St Edwards CE Comprehensive School
Southern Way
Fernden Way
Weald Way
Eddy Close
Bracken Ms
Bridport Av
Jutsums Lane
Jutsums Av
Crowlands Avenue
Burlington Avenue
Aston Av
Lonsdale Av
Derby Av
Kimberley Av
Ainsley Av
Crowlands Primary School
Cromer Rd
Norfolk Road
Sheringham
Kensington Rd
Jubilee Avenue
Spring Gdns
Recreation Av
Richards Avenue
Lowland Gdns
Marina Gdns
Works
Chadwell Heath Leisure Cen
Japan Rd
Back Lane
Eric Rd
Cecil Rd
Eustace Rd
Junction Rd W
Kenneth Road
Woodlands Av
Farrance Road
Morden Road
Merten Road
Bennett Rd
Wadeville Av
Burlington Gdns
Heath Road
Viking Business Centre
Danes Road
Bernard Rd
Maldon Rd
Beechfield Gardens
Sandgate Close
Crow Lane
Braithwaite Av
Vignoles Rd
Works
Romford Cemetery
Mirravale Trading Estate
Coppen Road
Selinas Lane
Chadwell Heath Station
Spring Close
Freshwater Road
Works
Works
Lymington Road
Cornshaw Road
Rosslyn Av
Lanesi de Avenue
Warley Avenue
Limbourne Avenue
Goldsmith Avenue
Seabrook Gardens
Stanley Avenue
Torrington Road
Mount Road
Grosvenor Road
Gray Av
Brendon Road
Albert Rd
James Av
Temple Avenue
Superstore
Eldenwall Industrial Estate
Purland Cl
Chadwell Heath Industrial Park
Claridge Road
WHALEBONE LANE SOUTH
All Saints Catholic School
Wood Lane Sports Centre
Meadow Road
Bell House Road
Rush Gn
Barton Av
Legon Av
A124 WOOD LANE
Wisdons Cl
Gosfield Road
Terling Road
Lamberhurst Road
Winifred Road
Gerald Rd
Ross Avenue
Tenterden Road
Turnage Road
Inskip Road
Lynnett Rd
Surgery
David Road
Joan Road
Grafton Gdns
Fordyke Rd
Robert Clack School
GREEN LANE
A1083
Stockd Rd
Green La
Bentry Road
80
WOOD LANE
Dagenham Civic Centre
Laburnum Health Centre
Althorne Way
Stour Rd
Wood Lane
A B C D E
1 2 3 4 5 6 7
48 49 50
87 88 89 90

1 grid square represents 500 metres

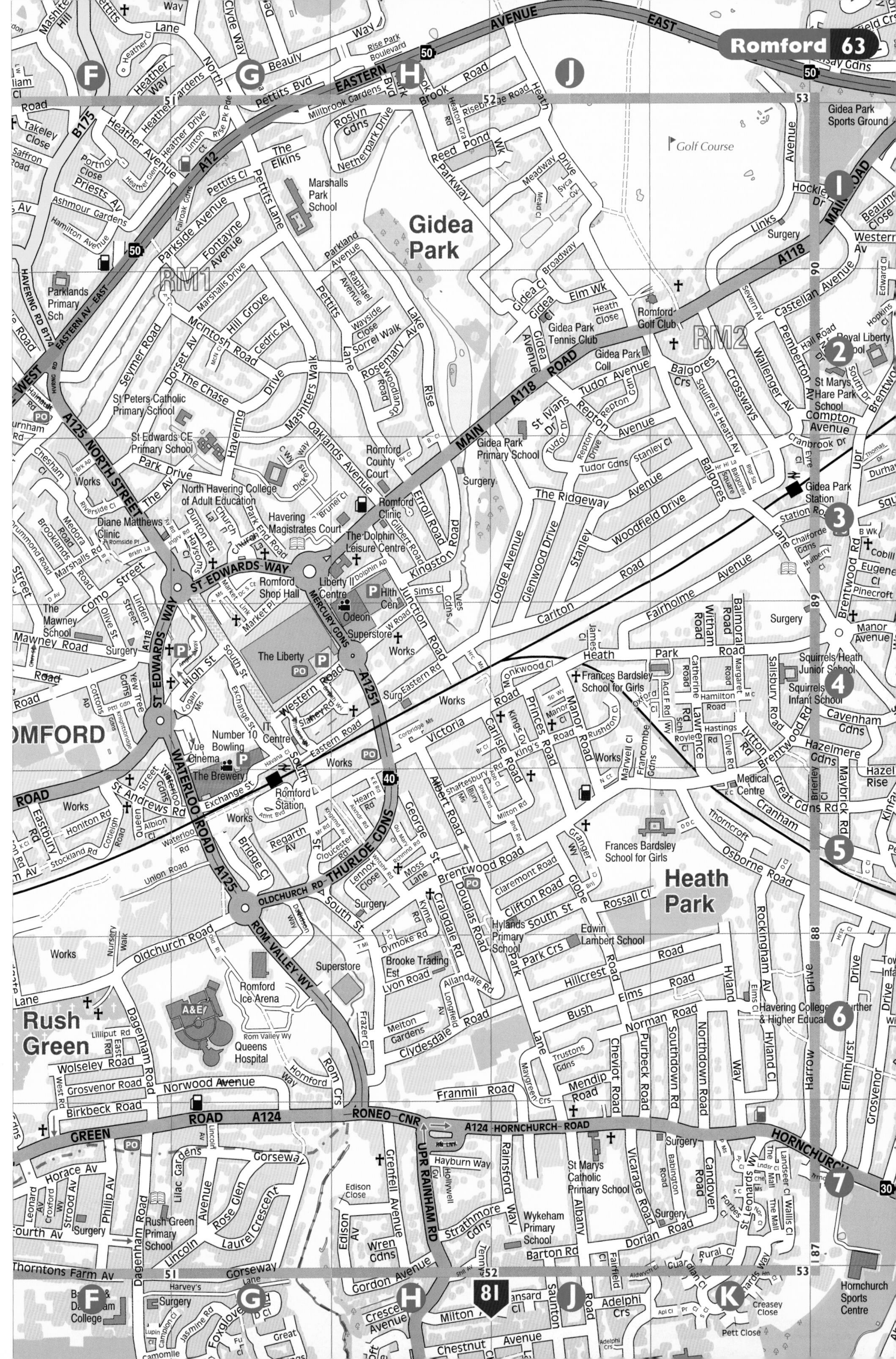

Gidea Park
Heath Park
Rush Green
ROMFORD
RM1
RM2
Golf Course
Gidea Park Sports Ground
Romford Golf Club
Gidea Park Tennis Club
Gidea Park Coll
Gidea Park Primary School
Gidea Park Station
Marshalls Park School
Parklands Primary Sch
St Peters Catholic Primary School
St Edwards CE Primary School
North Havering College of Adult Education
Diane Matthews Clinic
Havering Magistrates Court
Romford County Court
Romford Clinic
The Dolphin Leisure Centre
Romford Shop Hall
Liberty II Centre
The Liberty
Odeon
Superstore
IT Centre
Number 10 Bowling
Vue Cinema
The Brewery
Romford Station
The Mawney School
Frances Bardsley School for Girls
Squirrels Heath Junior School
Squirrels Infant School
Royal Liberty School
St Marys Hare Park School
Medical Centre
Edwin Lambert School
Hylands Primary School
Brooke Trading Est
Romford Ice Arena
Queens Hospital
Havering College Further & Higher Educat
St Marys Catholic Primary School
Wykeham Primary School
Rush Green Primary School
Barking & Dagenham College
Hornchurch Sports Centre
EASTERN AVENUE EAST
A12
A118
MAIN ROAD
A125 NORTH STREET
ST EDWARDS WAY
WATERLOO ROAD
A1251
MERCURY GDNS
OLDCHURCH RD
THURLOE GDNS
ROM VALLEY WY
A124
HORNCHURCH ROAD
RONEO CNR
UPR RAINHAM RD
GREEN ROAD
Brentwood Road
Heath Park Road
Carlton Road
Victoria Road
South Street
Dagenham Road
Oldchurch Road
Osborne Road
Balgores Lane
Main Road
81

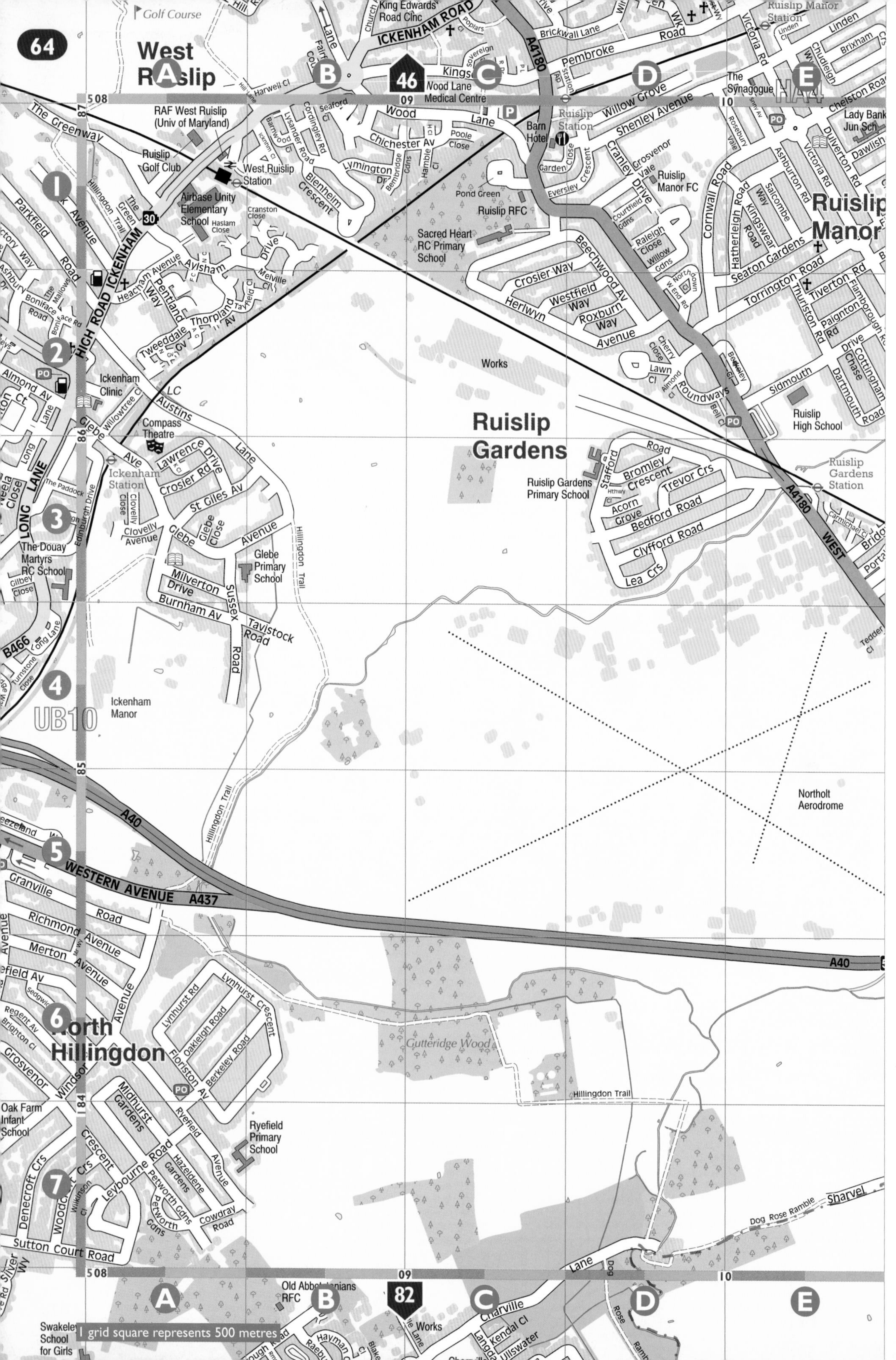

West Ruislip
Golf Course
King Edwards Road Clinc
ICKENHAM ROAD
Brickwall Lane
Pembroke Road
Victoria Rd
Ruislip Manor Station
Linden
Brixham
Chudleigh
Wood Lane Medical Centre
46
Harwell Cl
The Synagogue
HA4
Chelston Road
Willow Grove
Shenley Avenue
Wood Lane
Chichester Av
Lymington Dr
Blenheim Crescent
Poole Close
Barn Hotel
Ruislip Station
RAF West Ruislip (Univ of Maryland)
Ruislip Golf Club
West Ruislip Station
The Greenway
Airbase Unity Elementary School
Haslam Close
Cranston Close
Pond Green
Ruislip RFC
Sacred Heart RC Primary School
Lady Bank Jun Sch
Dulverton Rd
Ruislip Manor
Asburton Rd
Salcombe Way
Kingsweare Road
Cornwall Road
Hatherleigh Road
Seaton Gardens
Torrington Road
Tiverton Rd
Thurlston Rd
Paignton Rd
Flamborough Rd
Cranley Drive
Grosvenor Vale
Ruislip Manor FC
Eversley Crescent
Courtfield Gdns
Raleigh Close
Willow Gdns
Beechwood Av
Crosier Way
Herlwyn Avenue
Westfield Way
Roxburn Way
Parkfield Road
Boniface Road
HIGH ROAD ICKENHAM
Heacham Avenue
Aylsham Drive
Melville Cl
Pentland Way
Thorpland Av
Tweeddale Gv
Ickenham Clinic
Almond Av
Long Lane
Glebe Ave
Austins Lane
Compass Theatre
Ickenham Station
Lawrence Drive
Crosier Rd
St Giles Av
Clovelly Avenue
Glebe Avenue
Glebe Close
Glebe Primary School
Milverton Drive
Burnham Av
Sussex Road
Tavistock Road
Hillingdon Trail
LONG LANE
The Douay Martyrs RC School
Gilbey Close
B466
Turnstone Close
Ickenham Manor
UB10
Works
Cherry Close
Lawn Cl
Roundways
Sidmouth
Drive
Chase
Dartmouth Road
Cottingham
Ruislip High School
Ruislip Gardens
Ruislip Gardens Station
Ruislip Gardens Primary School
Stafford Road
Bromley Crescent
Trevor Crs
Acorn Grove
Bedford Road
Clyfford Road
Lea Crs
A4180 WEST
Carmichael Cl
Portal
Tedder Cl
Northolt Aerodrome
A40
WESTERN AVENUE A437
Granville Road
Richmond Avenue
Merton Avenue
Regent Av
Brighton Cl
Grosvenor
Windsor
North Hillingdon
Lynhurst Rd
Lynhurst Crescent
Oakleigh Road
Berkeley Road
Floriston Av
Ryefield Avenue
Ryefield Primary School
Midhurst Gardens
Hazeldene Gardens
Leybourne Road
Petworth Gdns
Cowdray Road
Oak Farm Infant School
Crescent
Denecroft Crs
Woodcroft Crs
Wilkinson Cl
Sutton Court Road
Gutteridge Wood
Hillingdon Trail
Dog Rose Ramble
Sharvel
Lane
Dog
Old Abbotsleigh RFC
82
Charville
Kendal Cl
Ullswater
Hayman Cl
Works
Swakeleys School for Girls
1 grid square represents 500 metres

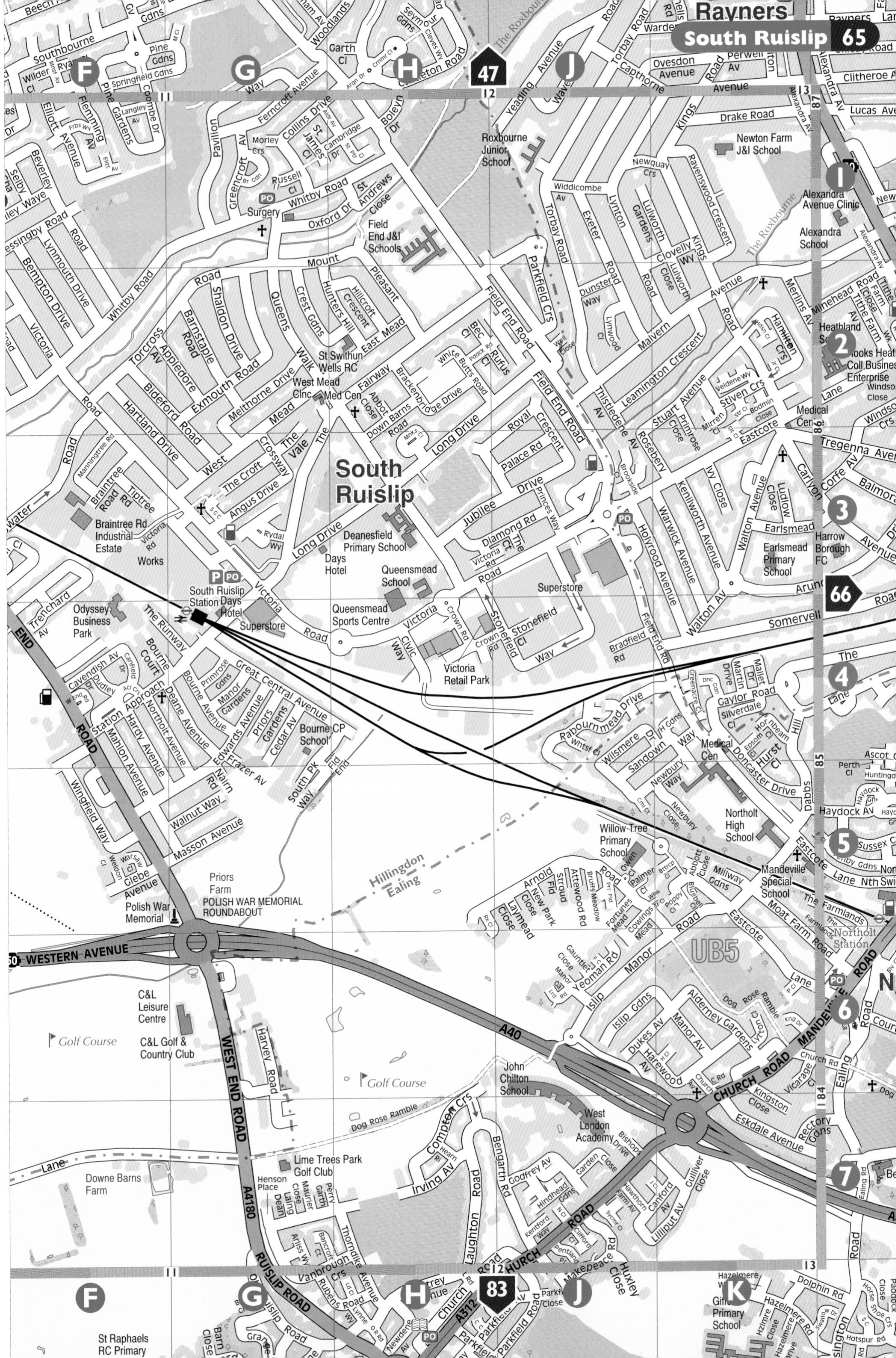
Rayners
47
66
83
South Ruislip
Roxbourne Junior School
Newton Farm J&I School
Alexandra Avenue Clinic
Alexandra School
Field End J&I Schools
St Swithun Wells RC
West Mead Clnc
Med Cen
Deanesfield Primary School
Days Hotel
Queensmead School
Queensmead Sports Centre
Superstore
Victoria Retail Park
South Ruislip Station
Braintree Rd Industrial Estate
Works
Odyssey Business Park
Bourne CP School
Earlsmead Primary School
Harrow Borough FC
Heathland School
Medical Cen
Northolt High School
Willow Tree Primary School
Mandeville Special School
Northolt Station
UB5
Priors Farm
Polish War Memorial
POLISH WAR MEMORIAL ROUNDABOUT
WESTERN AVENUE
A40
Hillingdon
Ealing
C&L Leisure Centre
C&L Golf & Country Club
Golf Course
Downe Barns Farm
Lime Trees Park Golf Club
Henson Place
John Chilton School
West London Academy
Dog Rose Ramble
WEST END ROAD
A4180
RUISLIP ROAD
CHURCH ROAD
MANDEVILLE ROAD
A312
St Raphaels RC Primary
Gifford Primary School
Victoria Road
Long Drive
Field End Road
Mount Pleasant
Whitby Road
Queens Walk
Exmouth Road
Bideford Road
Hartland Drive
Station Approach
Great Central Avenue
Somervell Road
Eastcote Lane
Church Road
Islip Manor Road
Eskdale Avenue
Kingston Close
Leamington Crescent
Malvern Avenue
Torbay Road
Yeading Avenue
Capthorne Avenue
Drake Road
Clitheroe Av
Lucas Ave
Tregenna Ave
Arundel Road
Doncaster Drive
Haydock Av
Moat Farm Road
The Farmlands

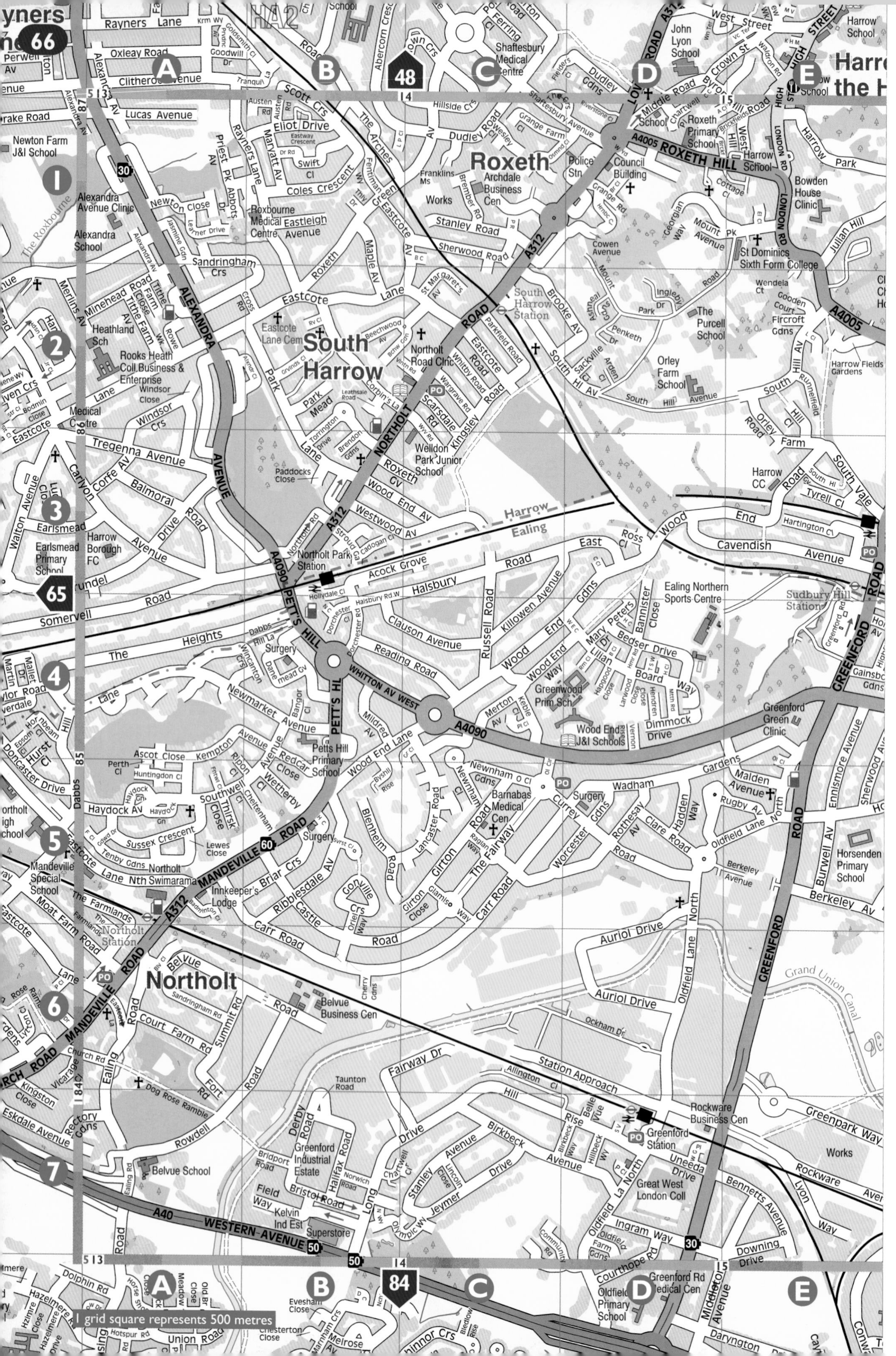
66
48
65
84
HA2
A
B
C
D
E
1
2
3
4
5
6
7
513
14
15
Rayners Lane
Oxley Road
Clitheroe Avenue
Alexandra Av
Lucas Avenue
Drake Road
Newton Farm J&I School
Newton Close
Alexandra Avenue Clinic
Alexandra School
The Roxbourne
Scott Crs
Eliot Drive
Eastway Crescent
Swift Cl
Coles Crescent
Maryatt Av
Priest Pk Av
Roxbourne Medical Centre
Eastleigh Avenue
Sandringham Crs
Abercorn Cres
Shaftesbury Medical Centre
Ferring Cl
Hillside Crs
Dudley Road
Dudley Gdns
Shaftesbury Avenue
Grange Farm Cl
Roxeth
Archdale Business Cen
Franklins Ms
Works
Brember Rd
Stanley Road
Sherwood Road
Police Stn
Council Building
A4005 ROXETH HILL
Lower Road
John Lyon School
West Street
Crown St
Middle Road
Byron Hill Road
Roxeth Primary School
Harrow School
HIGH STREET
LONDON RD
Harrow Park
Bowden House Clinic
Jullan Hill
St Dominics Sixth Form College
Mount Park Av
Georgian Way
Cowen Avenue
Ingleby Dr
The Purcell School
Penketh Dr
Orley Farm School
South Hill Av
A4005
Gooden Court
Fircroft Gdns
Harrow Fields Gardens
Runnelfield
Orley Farm Road
South Vale
Tyrell Cl
Harrow CC
Hartington Cl
Wood End Road
Cavendish Avenue
GREENFORD ROAD
Sudbury Hill Station
Ealing Northern Sports Centre
Bannister Close
Bedser Drive
Mary Peters Dr
Lilian Board Way
Greenwood Prim Sch
Wood End J&I Schools
Dimmock Drive
Greenford Green Clinic
Eastcote Lane
South Harrow
Eastcote Lane Cem
South Harrow Station
Northolt Road Clnc
Whitby Road
Eastcote Road
Parkfield Road
Scarsdale Rd
Kingsley Road
Welldon Park Junior School
Roxeth Gv
Wood End Av
Westwood Av
Paddocks Close
Park Mead
Torrington Drive
Brendon Gdns
A312 NORTHOLT ROAD
ALEXANDRA AVENUE
Minehead Road
Tithe Farm Av
Heathland Sch
Rooks Heath Coll Business & Enterprise
Windsor Close
Windsor Crs
Tregenna Avenue
Balmoral Road
Corfe Av
Carlyon Av
Drive Avenue
Earlsmead
Walton Avenue
Earlsmead Primary School
Harrow Borough FC
Arundel
Somervell Road
Harrow
Ealing
Northolt Park Station
Acock Grove
Halsbury Road
Clauson Avenue
Reading Road
Russell Road
Killowen Avenue
Wood End Gdns
Wood End Way
East Road
Ross Cl
A4090 PETT'S HILL
WHITTON AV WEST
A4090
The Heights
Dabbs Hill La
Wincanton Crs
Surgery
Newmarket Avenue
Bangor Cl
Mildred Av
Wood End Lane
Merton Av
Keble Cl
Ascot Close
Kempton Avenue
Redcar Close
Wetherby Cl
Ripon Cl
Petts Hill Primary School
Haydock Av
Southwell Close
Thirsk Close
Sussex Crescent
Lewes Close
Tenby Gdns
Northolt Swimarama
MANDEVILLE ROAD
Innkeeper's Lodge
Briar Crs
Ribblesdale Av
Castle Road
Carr Road
Gonville Crs
Blenheim Road
Lancaster Road
Newnham Gdns
Newnham Cl
Barnabas Medical Cen
The Fairway
Girton Road
Girton Close
Worcester Gdns
Currey Road
Rothesay Av
Clare Road
Hadden Way
Wadham Gardens
Malden Avenue
Rugby Av
Oldfield Lane North
Berkeley Avenue
Ennismore Avenue
Sherwood Av
Burwell Av
Horsenden Primary School
Berkeley Av
Mandeville Special School
Eastcote Lane Nth
The Farmlands
Moat Farm Road
Northolt Station
Northolt
Belvue Rd
Sandringham Rd
Summit Rd
Court Farm Rd
Fort Rd
Belvue Business Cen
Cherry Gdns
Auriol Drive
Grand Union Canal
Ockham Dr
Station Approach
Allington Cl
Fairway Dr
Taunton Road
Derby Road
Greenford Industrial Estate
Halifax Road
Bridport Road
Bristol Road
Field Way
Kelvin Ind Est
Superstore
Long Drive
Chartwell Cl
Stanley Avenue
Lincoln Close
Jeymer Drive
Birkbeck Avenue
Belle Vue Rise
Greenford Station
Uneeda Drive
Great West London Coll
Ingram Way
Oldfield La North
Rockware Business Cen
Greenpark Way
Works
Rockware Avenue
Bennetts Avenue
Lyon Way
Downing Drive
Dog Rose Ramble
Rowdell Road
Belvue School
Ealing Road
Kingston Close
Eskdale Avenue
Rectory Gdns
Vicarage
Church Rd
CHURCH ROAD
A40 WESTERN AVENUE
Dolphin Rd
Hazelmere
Union Road
Evesham Close
Chesterton Close
Melrose
Courthope Rd
Greenford Rd Medical Cen
Oldfield Primary School
Middleton Avenue
Darlington
1 grid square represents 500 metres

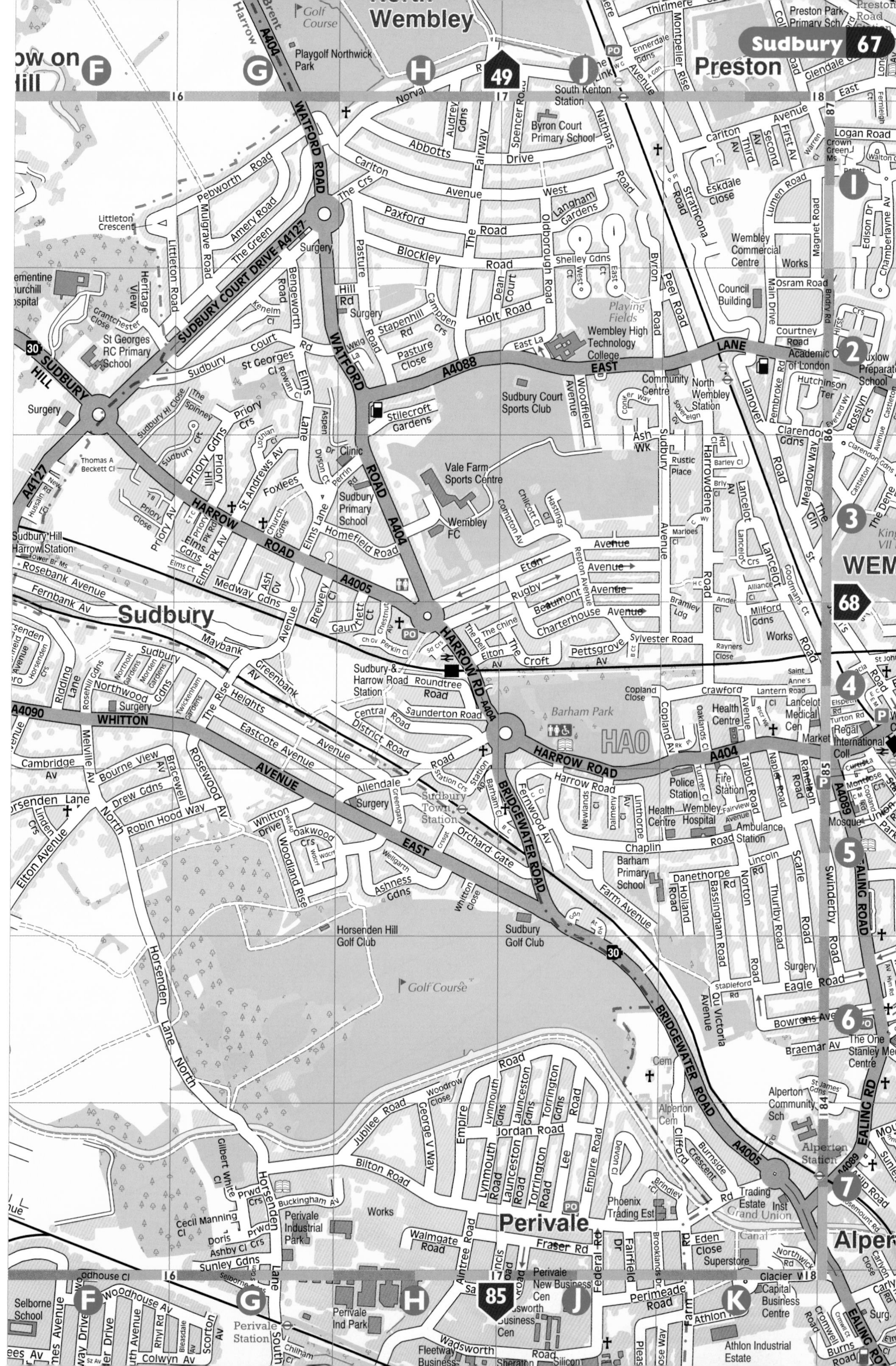

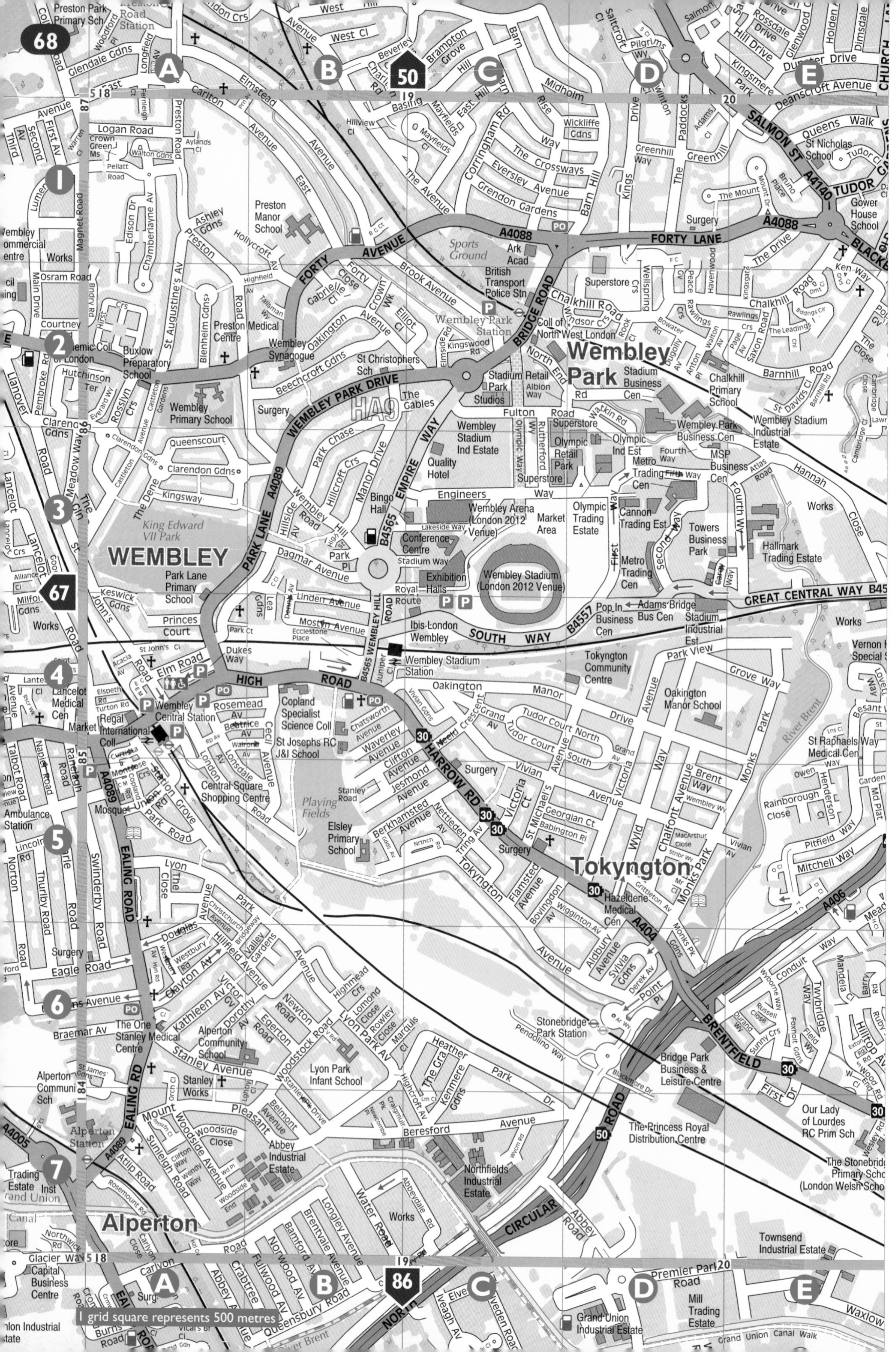

A
B
C
D
E
50
67
86
1
2
3
4
5
6
7
518
19
20
WEMBLEY
Wembley Park
Tokyngton
Alperton
HA9
Preston Park Primary Sch
Preston Road Station
Preston Manor School
Sports Ground
Ark Acad
British Transport Police Stn
Wembley Park Station
Coll of North West London
Stadium Business Cen
Chalkhill Primary School
Wembley Stadium Industrial Estate
Wembley Park Business Cen
MSP Business Cen
Wembley Stadium Ind Estate
Quality Hotel
Olympic Retail Park
Olympic Ind Est
Metro Trading Cen
Cannon Trading Est
Towers Business Park
Hallmark Trading Estate
Olympic Trading Estate
Market Area
Wembley Arena (London 2012 Venue)
Wembley Stadium (London 2012 Venue)
Conference Centre
Exhibition Halls
Bingo Hall
Ibis London Wembley
Pop In Business Cen
Adams Bridge Bus Cen
Stadium Industrial Est
Wembley Stadium Station
Tokyngton Community Centre
Oakington Manor School
St Raphaels Way Medical Cen
Copland Specialist Science Coll
St Josephs RC J&I School
Elsley Primary School
Playing Fields
Wembley Central Station
Regal International Coll
Central Square Shopping Centre
King Edward VII Park
Park Lane Primary School
Wembley Primary School
Buxlow Preparatory School
Preston Medical Centre
Wembley Synagogue
St Christophers Sch
Stadium Park Studios
Gower House School
St Nicholas School
Lancelot Medical Cen
Ambulance Station
The One Stanley Medical Centre
Alperton Community School
Stanley Works
Lyon Park Infant School
Abbey Industrial Estate
Northfields Industrial Estate
Works
Stonebridge Park Station
Bridge Park Business & Leisure Centre
The Princess Royal Distribution Centre
Our Lady of Lourdes RC Prim Sch
The Stonebridge Primary School (London Welsh School)
Townsend Industrial Estate
Mill Trading Estate
Grand Union Industrial Estate
Capital Business Centre
Alperton Station
Alperton Community Sch
Hazeldene Medical Cen
Surgery
Superstore
FORTY AVENUE
FORTY LANE
BRIDGE ROAD
EMPIRE WAY
WEMBLEY PARK DRIVE
PARK LANE
HIGH ROAD
HARROW RD
SOUTH WAY
GREAT CENTRAL WAY
EALING ROAD
NORTH CIRCULAR ROAD
BRENTFIELD
SALMON ST
TUDOR GARDENS
A4088
A4089
A4140
A404
A406
A4005
B4565
B4557
River Brent
Grand Union Canal
1 grid square represents 500 metres

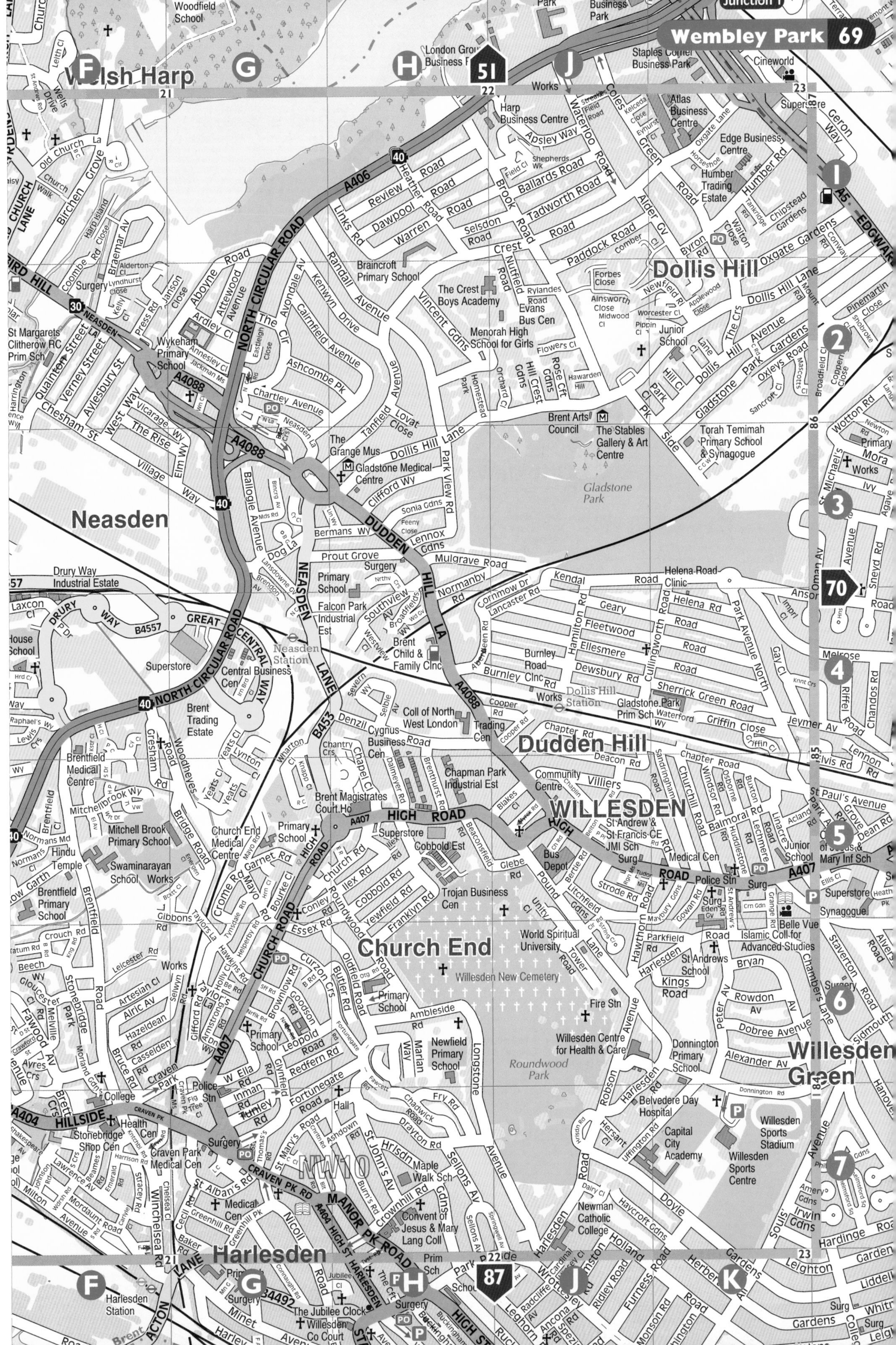
Welsh Harp
Woodfield School
London Group Business Park
51
Staples Corner Business Park
Cineworld
Junction 1
Works
Harp Business Centre
Atlas Business Centre
Edge Business Centre
Humber Trading Estate
Geron Way
EDGWARE
A5
A406
NORTH CIRCULAR ROAD
40
Review Road
Dawpool Road
Warren Road
Heather Road
Links Rd
Selsdon Road
Apsley Way
Ballards Road
Tadworth Road
Waterloo Road
Coles Green Road
Brook Road
Crest Road
Paddock Road
Alder Gv
Humber Rd
Oxgate Gardens
Oxgate Lane
Dollis Hill
Dollis Hill Lane
Dollis Hill Avenue
Gladstone Park Gardens
Oxleys Road
Braincroft Primary School
The Crest Boys Academy
Evans Bus Cen
Menorah High School for Girls
Junior School
Randall Avenue
Kenwyn Drive
Cairnfield Avenue
Avondale Av
Ashcombe Pk
Vincent Gdns
Homestead Park
Hill Crest Gdns
Rose Cft Gdns
Flowers Cl
Brent Arts Council
The Stables Gallery & Art Centre
Gladstone Park
Torah Temimah Primary School & Synagogue
Neasden
NEASDEN LA
A4088
Wykeham Primary School
St Margarets Clitherow RC Prim Sch
Quainton Street
Verney Street
Aylesbury St
Chesham St
West Way
Vicarage Wy
The Rise
Village Way
Elm Wy
Old Church La
Birchen Grove
Braemar Av
Aboyne Road
Attewood Avenue
Ardley Cl
Chartley Avenue
Tanfield Avenue
Lovat Close
The Grange Mus
Gladstone Medical Centre
Clifford Wy
Park View Rd
Dudden Hill La
Ballogie Avenue
Bermans Wy
Prout Grove
Mulgrave Road
Normanby Rd
Lennox Gdns
Primary School
Surgery
Falcon Park Industrial Est
Southview Av
Broadfields
Brent Child & Family Clnc
Neasden Station
NEASDEN LANE
Drury Way Industrial Estate
DRURY WAY
GREAT CENTRAL WAY
B4557
Superstore
Central Business Cen
Brent Trading Estate
Kendal Road
Geary Road
Fleetwood Road
Ellesmere Road
Dewsbury Rd
Burnley Road
Burnley Clnc
Helena Road
Helena Road Clinic
Cullingworth Road
Park Avenue North
Sherrick Green Road
Gladstone Park Prim Sch
Dollis Hill Station
Griffin Close
Jeymer Av
Riffel Road
Chandos Rd
Coll of North West London
Trading Cen
Cygnus Business Cen
Denzil Road
Dudden Hill
Chapter Road
Deacon Rd
Villiers
Community Centre
Chapman Park Industrial Est
B453
Brent Magistrates Court Ho
WILLESDEN
HIGH ROAD
A407
Superstore
Cobbold Est
St Andrew & St Francis CE JMI Sch
Medical Cen
Police Stn
Bus Depot
Church End
Willesden New Cemetery
World Spiritual University
Trojan Business Cen
Primary School
Newfield Primary School
Marian Way
Longstone Avenue
Roundwood Park
Willesden Centre for Health & Care
Fire Stn
Donnington Primary School
Willesden Green
Belvedere Day Hospital
Capital City Academy
Willesden Sports Stadium
Willesden Sports Centre
Newman Catholic College
Harlesden
NW10
MANOR PK ROAD
CRAVEN PK RD
HILLSIDE
A404
Stonebridge Shop Cen
Health Cen
Craven Park Medical Cen
Mitchell Brook Primary School
Swaminarayan School
Hindu Temple
Brentfield Medical Centre
Brentfield Primary School
Church End Medical Centre
College
Convent of Jesus & Mary Lang Coll
Maple Walk Sch
The Jubilee Clock
Willesden Co Court
Harlesden Station
ACTON LANE
Belle Vue
Islamic Coll for Advanced Studies
St Andrews School
Kings Road
Synagogue
Junior School
Mary Inf Sch
70
87
21
22
23
86
85
84
F
G
H
I
J
K
2
3
4
5
6
7

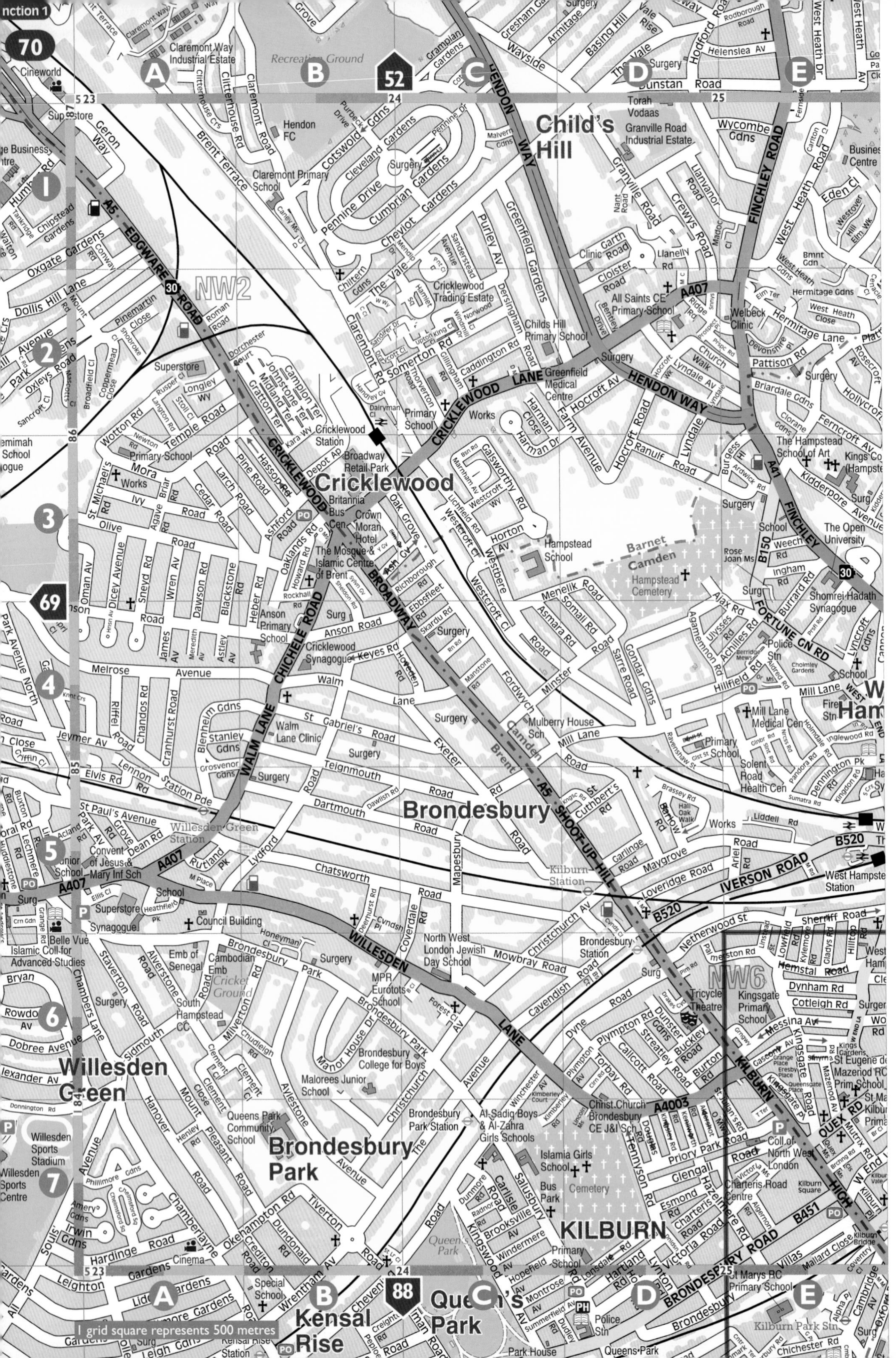
nction 1
70
52
69
88
30
A
B
C
D
E
1
2
3
4
5
6
7
523
24
25
87
86
85
84
NW2
NW6
Child's Hill
Cricklewood
Brondesbury
Willesden Green
Brondesbury Park
KILBURN
Kensal Rise
Queen's Park
Cineworld
Superstore
Claremont Way Industrial Estate
Recreation Ground
Hendon FC
Claremont Primary School
Torah Vodaas
Granville Road Industrial Estate
Cricklewood Trading Estate
All Saints CE Primary School
Welbeck Clinic
Childs Hill Primary School
Greenfield Medical Centre
Cricklewood Station
Broadway Retail Park
Britannia Bus Cen.
Crown Moran Hotel
The Mosque & Islamic Centre of Brent
Anson Primary School
Cricklewood Synagogue
Hampstead School
Hampstead Cemetery
The Hampstead School of Art
The Open University
Shomrei Hadath Synagogue
Police Stn
Mill Lane Medical Cen
Solent Road Health Cen
Mulberry House Sch
Walm Lane Clinic
Willesden Green Station
Kilburn Station
West Hampstead Station
Brondesbury Station
North West London Jewish Day School
MPR Eurotots School
Convent of Jesus & Mary Inf Sch
Council Building
Belle Vue
Islamic Coll for Advanced Studies
Emb of Senegal
Cambodian Emb
Cricket Ground
South Hampstead CC
Tricycle Theatre
Kingsgate Primary School
St Eugene de Mazenod RC Prim School
Brondesbury College for Boys
Malorees Junior School
Queens Park Community School
Brondesbury Park Station
Al-Sadiq Boys & Al-Zahra Girls Schools
Christ Church Brondesbury CE J&I Sch
Islamia Girls School
Cemetery
Coll of North West London
Kilburn Square
Willesden Sports Stadium
Willesden Sports Centre
Special School
Cinema
St Marys RC Primary School
Kilburn Park Stn
Police Stn
Park House
Queens Park
Kensal Rise Station
A5 EDGWARE ROAD
CRICKLEWOOD BROADWAY
A5 SHOOT-UP HILL
CRICKLEWOOD LANE
HENDON WAY
A407
FINCHLEY ROAD
A41
B150
FORTUNE GN RD
WALM LANE
CHICHELE ROAD
WILLESDEN LANE
IVERSON ROAD
B520
A4003
KILBURN HIGH
BRONDESBURY ROAD
B451
QUEX RD
Barnet
Camden
Brent
1 grid square represents 500 metres

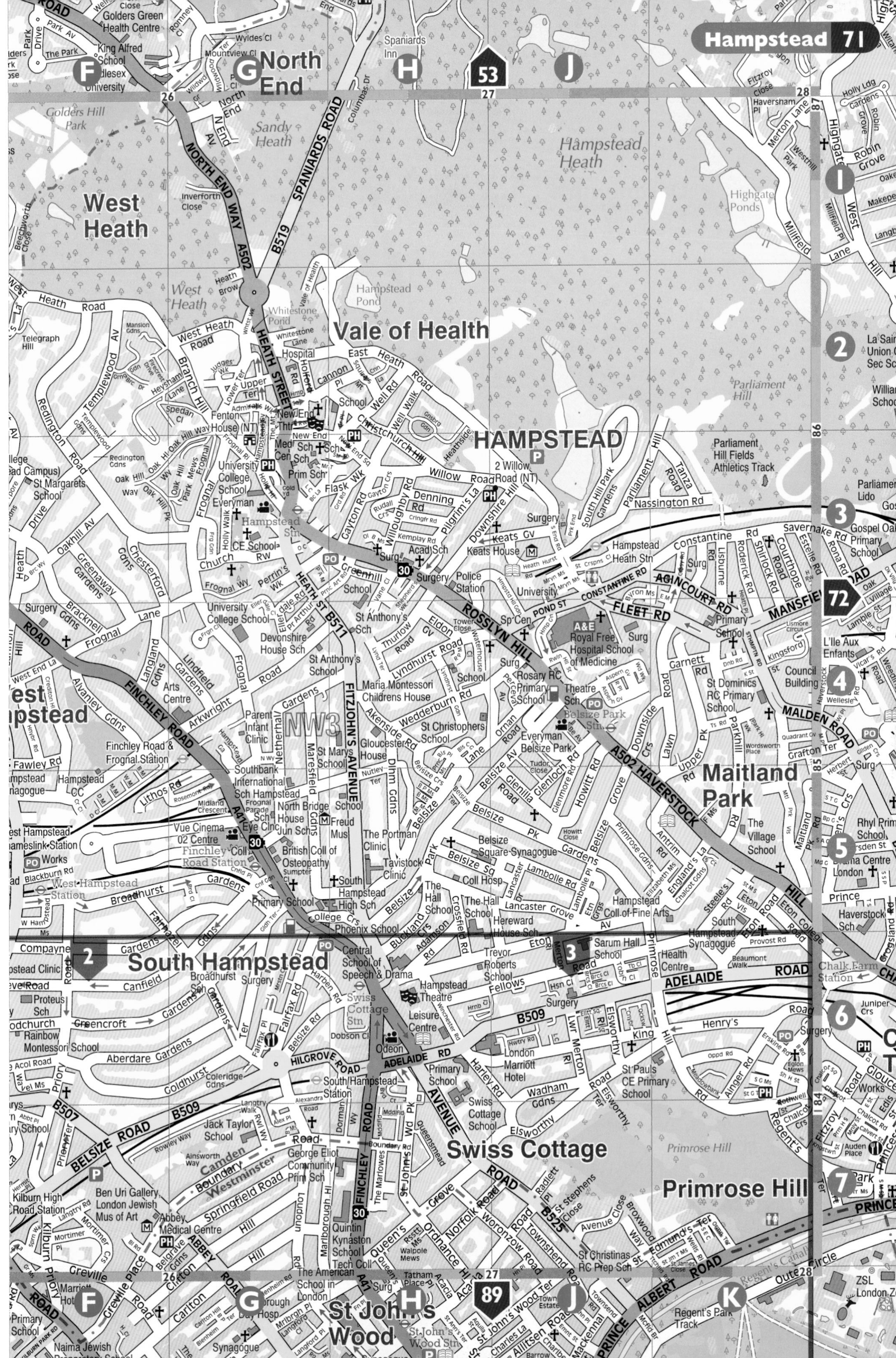
North End
West Heath
Golders Hill Park
Sandy Heath
Hampstead Heath
Spaniards Inn
Highgate Ponds
Vale of Health
Hampstead Pond
Whitestone Pond
Parliament Hill
HAMPSTEAD
Parliament Hill Fields Athletics Track
Parliament Lido
NORTH END WAY A502
SPANIARDS ROAD B519
HEATH STREET
FITZJOHN'S AVENUE
ROSSLYN HILL
A502 HAVERSTOCK HILL
FINCHLEY ROAD
BELSIZE ROAD B509
ADELAIDE ROAD
PRINCE ALBERT ROAD
Hampstead Stn
Hampstead Heath Stn
Belsize Park Stn
Finchley Road & Frognal Station
Finchley Road Station
West Hampstead Station
West Hampstead Thameslink Station
Swiss Cottage Stn
South Hampstead Station
Chalk Farm Station
St John's Wood Stn
Kilburn High Road Station
NW3
Royal Free Hospital School of Medicine
Keats House
2 Willow Road (NT)
Fenton House (NT)
Freud Mus
Hampstead Theatre
Maitland Park
South Hampstead
Swiss Cottage
Primrose Hill
St John's Wood
West Hampstead
Regent's Canal
Regent's Park
ZSL London Zoo
Ben Uri Gallery, London Jewish Mus of Art
London Marriott Hotel
Camden
Westminster
53
72
89

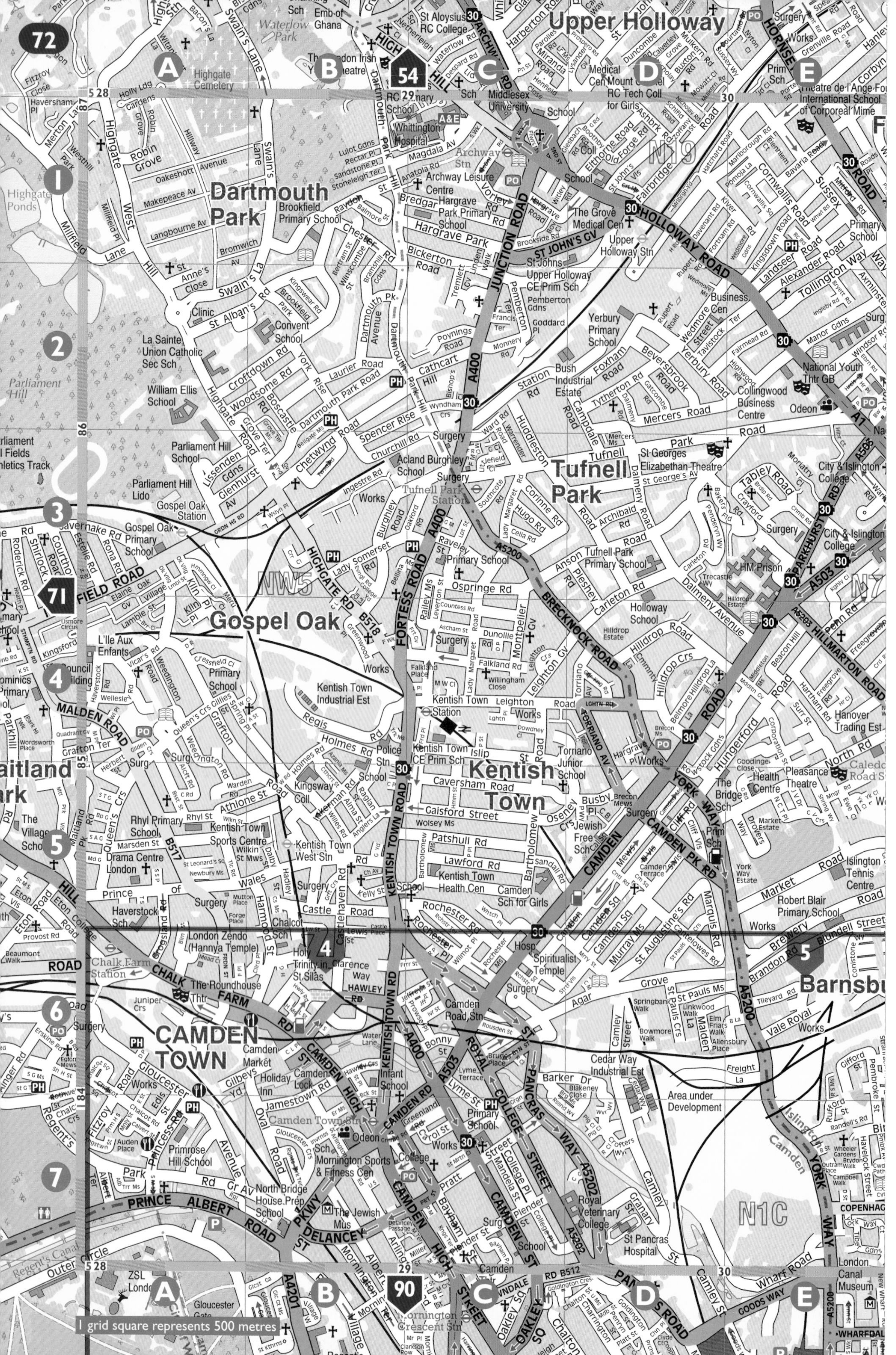
Upper Holloway
Dartmouth Park
Tufnell Park
Gospel Oak
Kentish Town
CAMDEN TOWN
Barnsbury
Highgate Cemetery
Waterlow Park
Highgate Ponds
Parliament Hill
Whittington Hospital
Archway Stn
Middlesex University
Upper Holloway Stn
Tufnell Park Station
Gospel Oak Station
Kentish Town Station
Kentish Town West Stn
Camden Road Stn
Camden Town Stn
Chalk Farm Station
Mornington Crescent Stn
HM Prison
Holloway School
The Roundhouse
Camden Market
Camden Lock
St Pancras Hospital
Royal Veterinary College
Cedar Way Industrial Est
Area under Development
London Canal Museum
JUNCTION ROAD
HOLLOWAY ROAD
FORTESS ROAD
KENTISH TOWN RD
CAMDEN HIGH ST
CAMDEN RD
BRECKNOCK ROAD
YORK WAY
HIGHGATE RD
MALDEN ROAD
PRINCE ALBERT ROAD
CHALK FARM RD
ROYAL COLLEGE ST
PANCRAS WAY
HAVERSTOCK HILL
NW5
N19
N7
N1C
A
B
C
D
E
1
2
3
4
5
6
7
54
71
90
1 grid square represents 500 metres

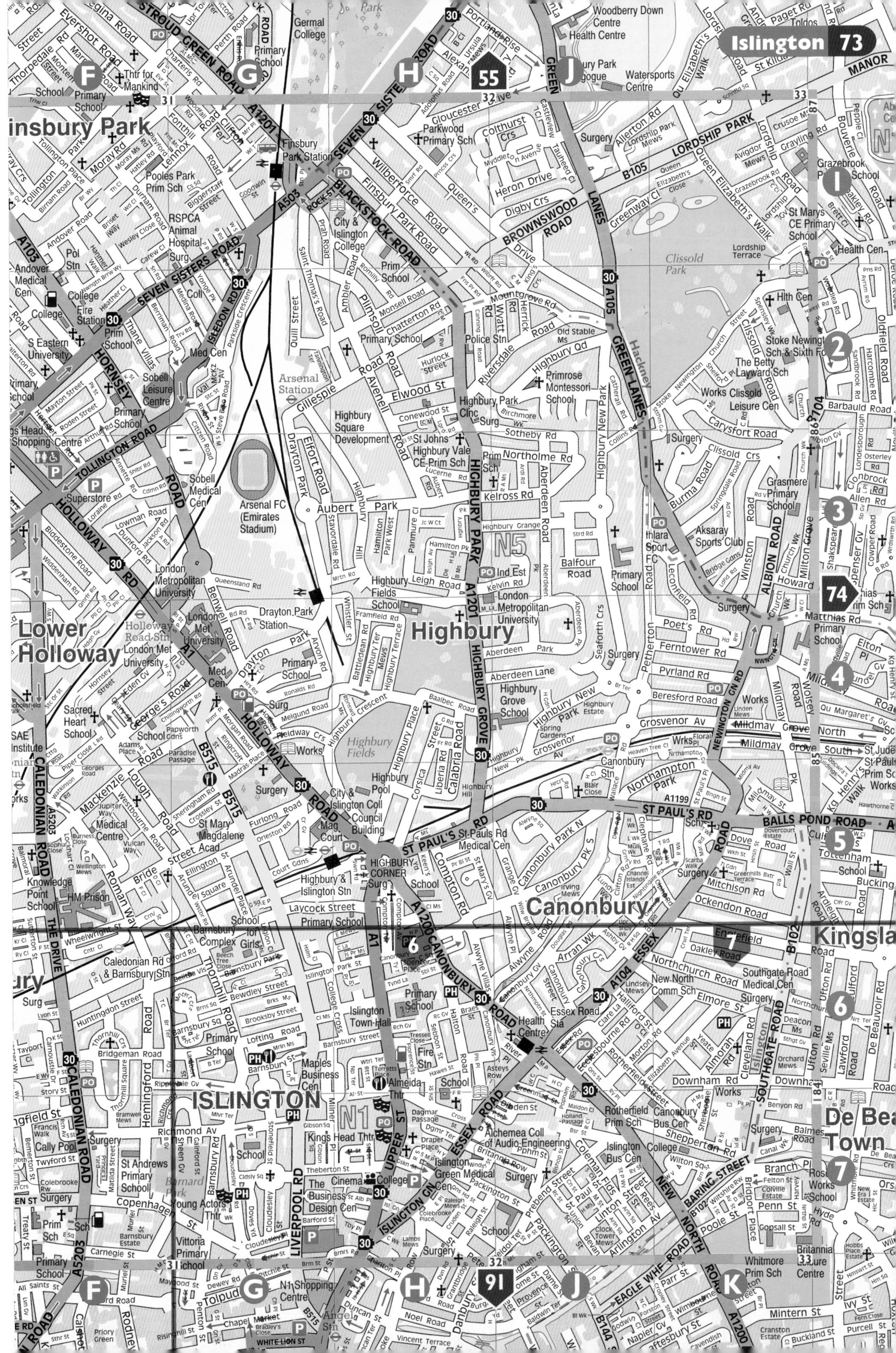
Finsbury Park
Lower Holloway
Highbury
Canonbury
ISLINGTON
Arsenal FC (Emirates Stadium)
Highbury Fields
Clissold Park
De Beauvoir Town
Kingsland
55
74
91

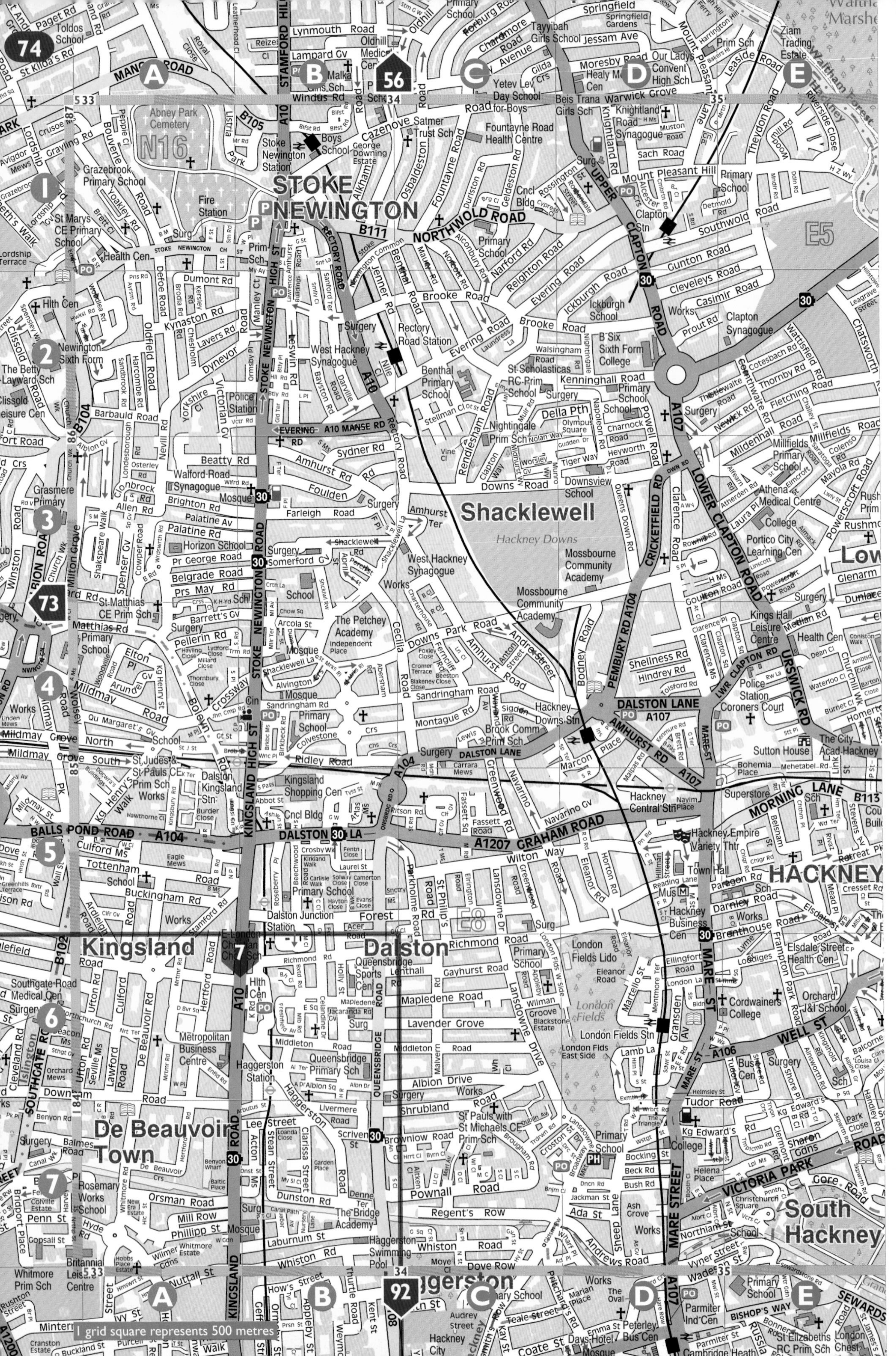
74
56
73
7
92
A
B
C
D
E
1
2
3
4
5
6
7
533
534
535
34
35
86
85
87
84
N16
E5
E8
STOKE NEWINGTON
Shacklewell
Hackney Downs
Kingsland
Dalston
De Beauvoir Town
HACKNEY
South Hackney
Haggerston
Abney Park Cemetery
Stoke Newington Station
Rectory Road Station
Clapton Stn
Hackney Downs Stn
Dalston Kingsland Stn
Dalston Junction Station
Hackney Central Stn
London Fields Stn
Haggerston Station
London Fields
London Fields Lido
Mossbourne Community Academy
Stamford Hill
Stoke Newington High St
Stoke Newington Road
Kingsland High St
Kingsland Road
Balls Pond Road
Dalston Lane
Graham Road
Amhurst Road
Rectory Road
Northwold Road
Upper Clapton Road
Lower Clapton Road
Pembury Rd A104
Cricketfield Rd
Mare Street
Morning Lane
Well St
Victoria Park Road
Queensbridge Road
Southgate Road
Manor Road
Evering Road
Brooke Road
Downs Park Road
Richmond Road
Albion Drive
Whiston Rd
Hackney Empire Variety Thtr
Town Hall
Sutton House
Hackney City
Kingsland Shopping Cen
Haggerston Swimming Pool
Britannia Leis Centre
1 grid square represents 500 metres

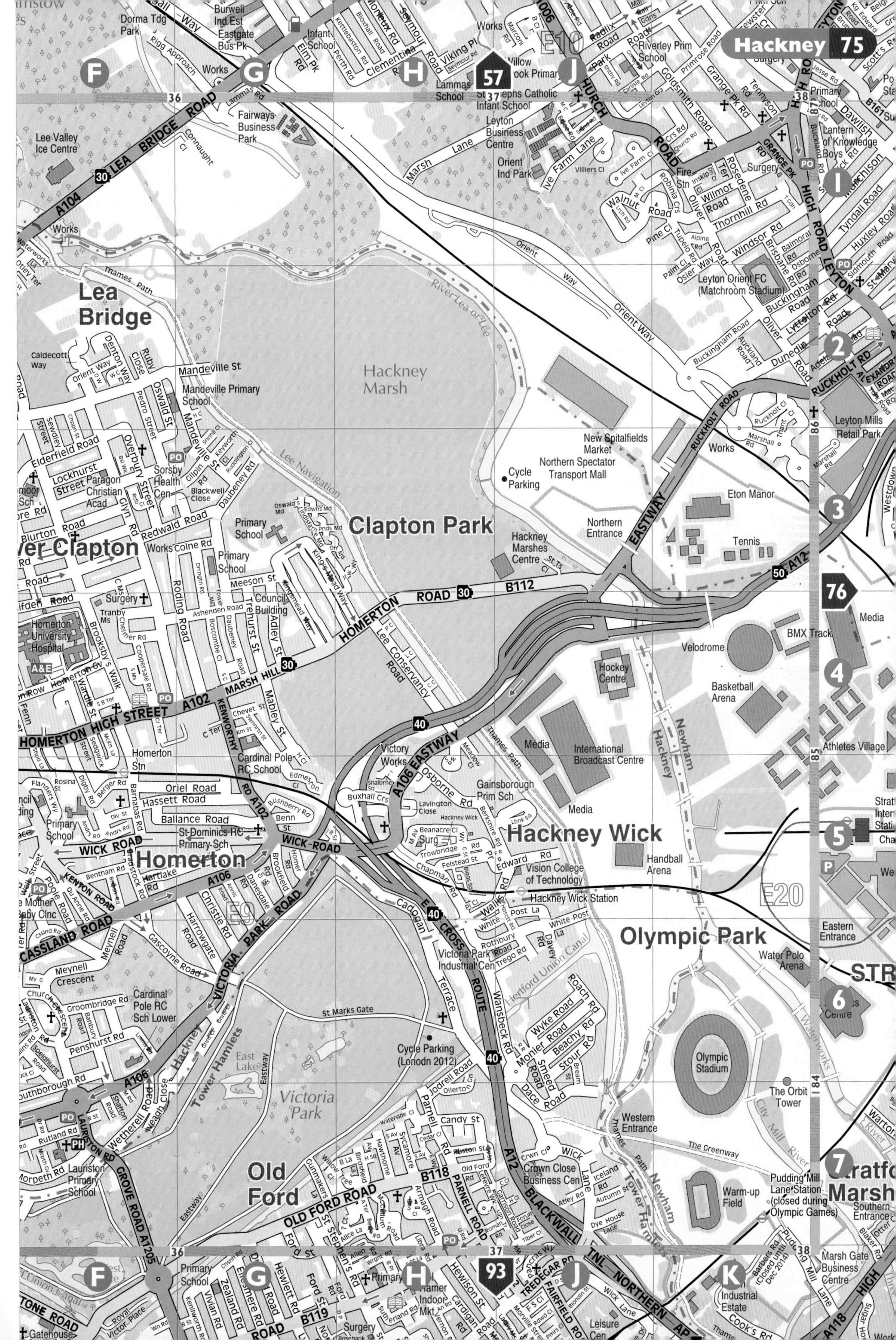

Lea Bridge
Hackney Marsh
Clapton Park
Hackney Wick
Homerton
Olympic Park
Old Ford
Victoria Park
Lee Valley Ice Centre
LEA BRIDGE ROAD
HOMERTON ROAD
HOMERTON HIGH STREET
WICK ROAD
EASTWAY
RUCKHOLT ROAD
Orient Way
Leyton Orient FC (Matchroom Stadium)
New Spitalfields Market
Northern Spectator Transport Mall
Velodrome
Hockey Centre
Basketball Arena
International Broadcast Centre
Handball Arena
Hackney Wick Station
Olympic Stadium
The Orbit Tower
Warm-up Field
Water Polo Arena
Athletes Village
Homerton University Hospital
Homerton Stn
Cycle Parking (Lonodn 2012)
OLD FORD ROAD
Pudding Mill Lane Station (closed during Olympic Games)
Leyton Mills Retail Park
Eton Manor
57
76
93

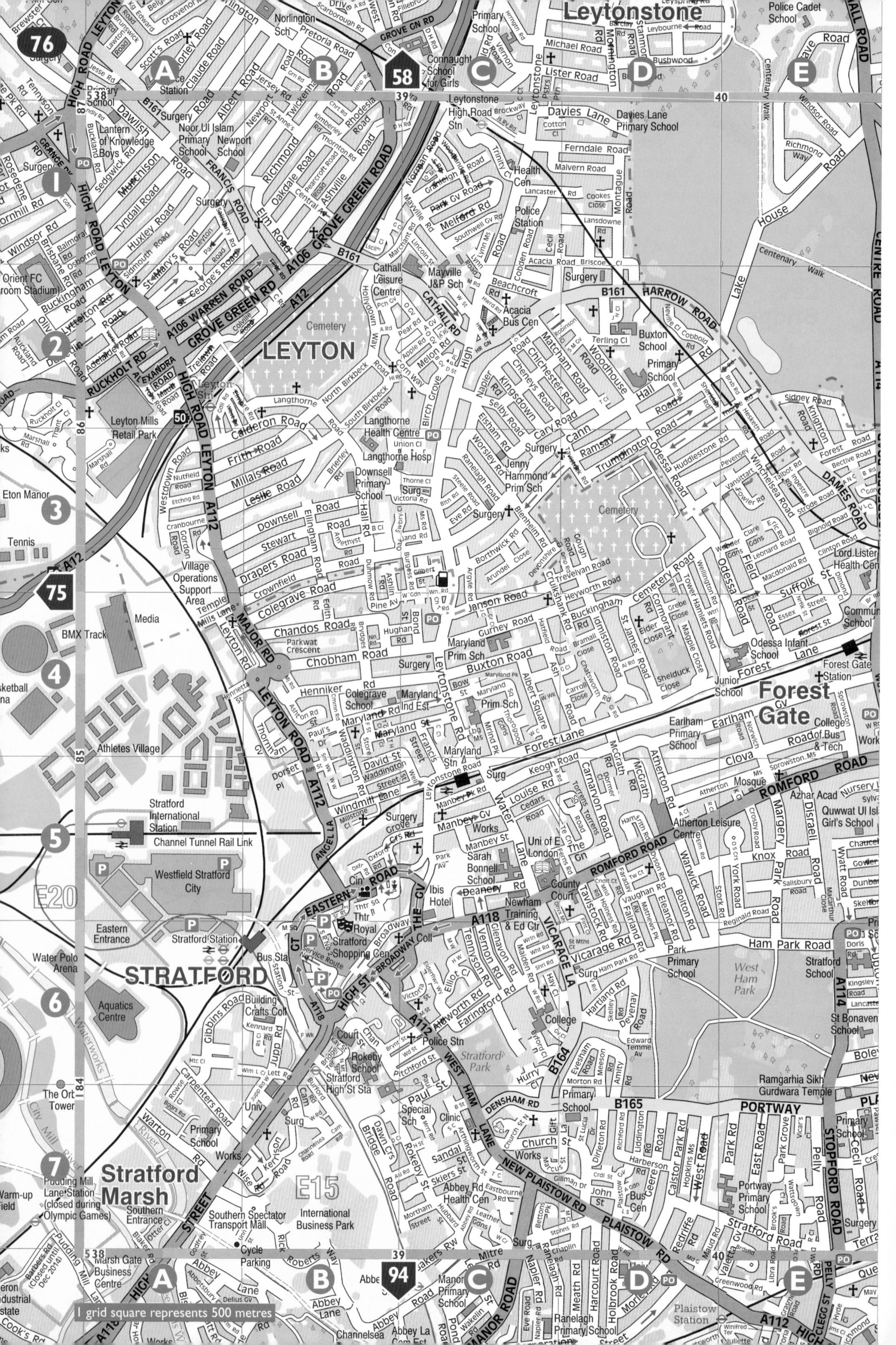

76
58
75
94
Leytonstone
LEYTON
Forest Gate
STRATFORD
Stratford Marsh
E20
E15
HIGH ROAD LEYTON
A106 GROVE GREEN ROAD
A12
ROMFORD ROAD
PORTWAY
STOPFORD ROAD
Leyton Mills Retail Park
Westfield Stratford City
Stratford International Station
Channel Tunnel Rail Link
Stratford Station
Athletes Village
Aquatics Centre
Water Polo Arena
West Ham Park
Stratford Park
International Business Park
Southern Spectator Transport Mall
Pudding Mill Lane Station (closed during Olympic Games)
1 grid square represents 500 metres

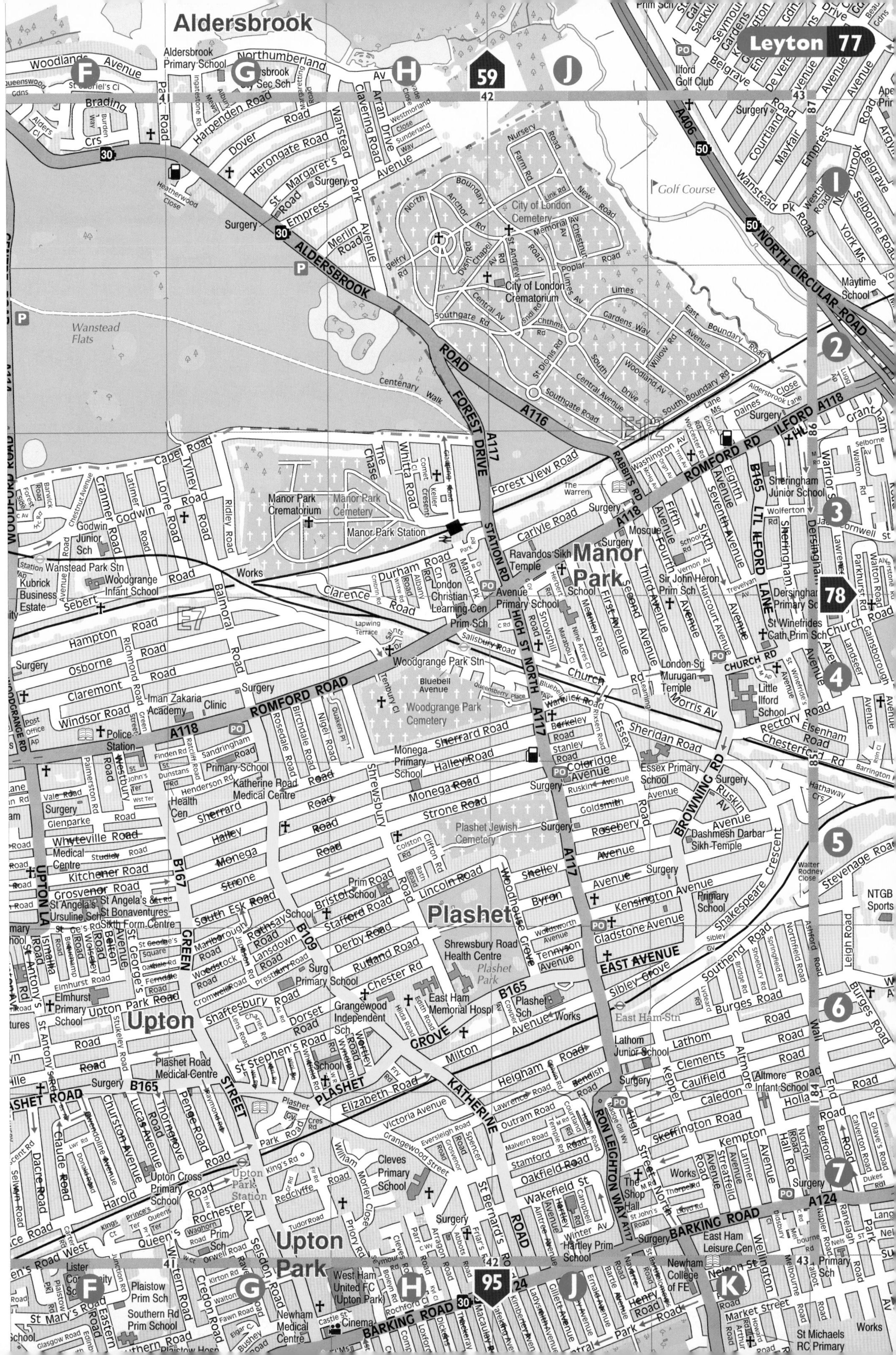

Leyton 77
59
78
95
Aldersbrook
Manor Park
Plashet
Upton
Upton Park
Wanstead Flats
City of London Cemetery
City of London Crematorium
Manor Park Crematorium
Manor Park Cemetery
Woodgrange Park Cemetery
Plashet Jewish Cemetery
Golf Course
Ilford Golf Club
Manor Park Station
Woodgrange Park Stn
Wanstead Park Stn
East Ham Stn
Upton Park Station
ALDERSBROOK ROAD
FOREST DRIVE
ROMFORD ROAD
NORTH CIRCULAR ROAD
HIGH ST NORTH
STATION RD
GREEN STREET
UPTON LA
BARKING ROAD
KATHERINE ROAD
PLASHET GROVE
EAST AVENUE
RON LEIGHTON WAY
LTL ILFORD LANE
BROWNING RD
ILFORD LANE
WOODGRANGE RD
A116
A117
A118
A124
A406
B165
B167
B109
E7
E12
F
G
H
J
K
I
2
3
4
5
6
7
41
42
43
30
50

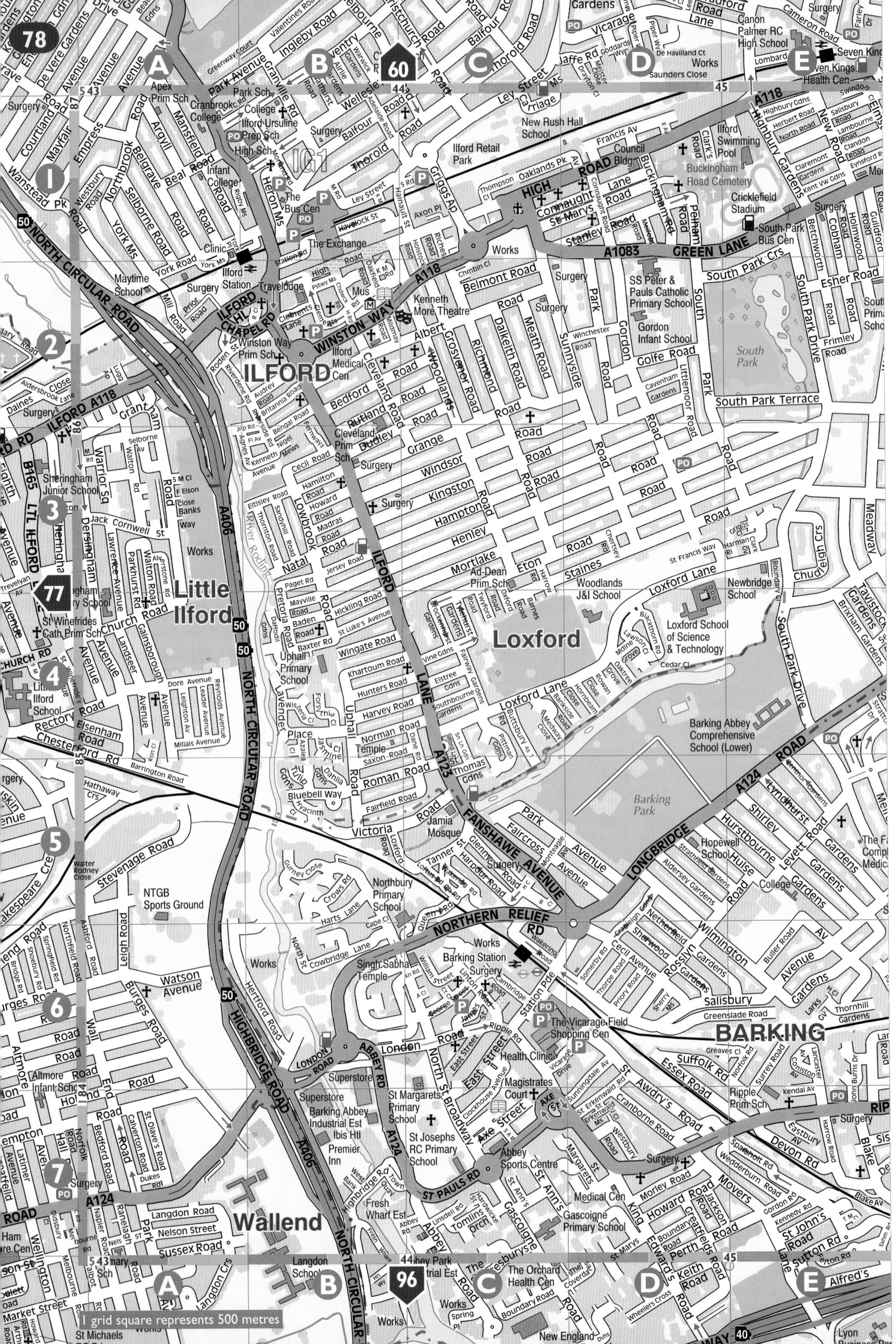

78
60
77
96
ILFORD
Little Ilford
Loxford
BARKING
Wallend
A
B
C
D
E
1
2
3
4
5
6
7
NORTH CIRCULAR ROAD
A406
A118
A1083
GREEN LANE
HIGH ROAD
A124
A123
ILFORD LANE
WINSTON WAY
FANSHAWE AVENUE
NORTHERN RELIEF RD
LONGBRIDGE ROAD
HIGHBRIDGE ROAD
ABBEY RD
ST PAULS RD
London Road
Ilford Station
Barking Station
Seven Kings
Ilford Retail Park
The Exchange
Kenneth More Theatre
Cranbrook College
Ilford Ursuline Prep Sch
Infant College
Apex Prim Sch
Maytime School
Winston Way Prim Sch
Cleveland Prim Sch
Ilford Medical Cen
Sheringham Junior School
St Winefrides Cath Prim Sch
Little Ilford School
Uphall Primary School
Ad-Dean Prim Sch
Woodlands J&I School
Loxford School of Science & Technology
Newbridge School
Barking Abbey Comprehensive School (Lower)
SS Peter & Pauls Catholic Primary School
Gordon Infant School
New Rush Hall School
Canon Palmer RC High School
Ilford Swimming Pool
Buckingham Road Cemetery
Cricklefield Stadium
South Park
Barking Park
Jamia Mosque
Northbury Primary School
NTGB Sports Ground
Singh Sabha Temple
The Vicarage Field Shopping Cen
Health Clinic
Magistrates Court
St Margarets Primary School
St Josephs RC Primary School
Abbey Sports Centre
Barking Abbey Industrial Est
Ibis Htl
Premier Inn
Fresh Wharf Est
Gascoigne Primary School
Medical Cen
Ripple Prim Sch
Hopewell School
College
Altmore Infant School
Langdon School
The Orchard Health Cen
River Roding
1 grid square represents 500 metres

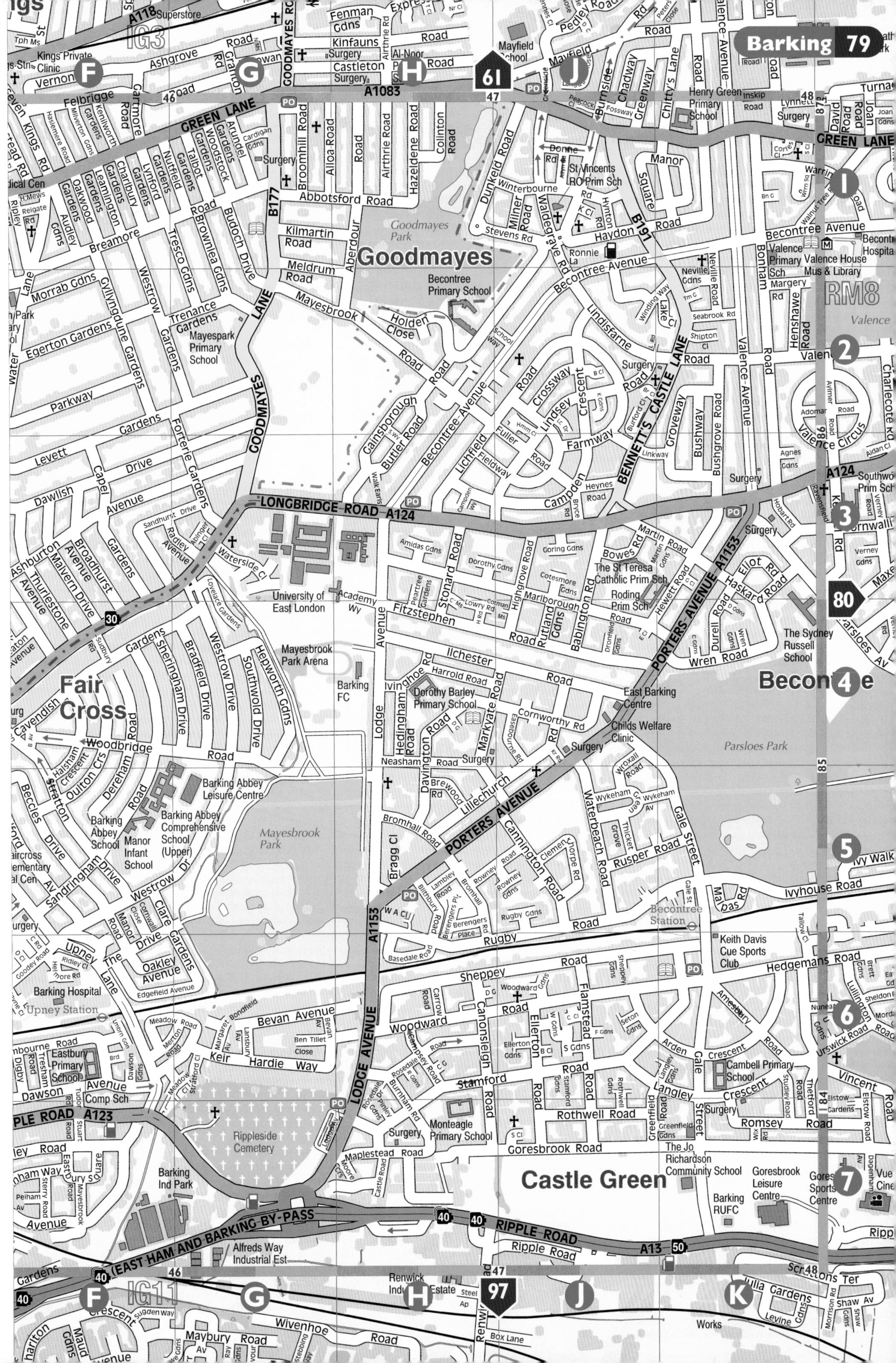
Goodmayes
Fair Cross
Castle Green
Becontree
Goodmayes Park
Mayesbrook Park
Parsloes Park
Rippleside Cemetery
University of East London
Mayesbrook Park Arena
Barking FC
Barking Abbey Leisure Centre
Barking Abbey Comprehensive School (Upper)
Barking Hospital
Upney Station
Becontree Station
LONGBRIDGE ROAD A124
GREEN LANE
GOODMAYES LANE
PORTERS AVENUE A1153
LODGE AVENUE
BENNETT'S CASTLE LANE
RIPPLE ROAD
A13
EAST HAM AND BARKING BY-PASS
RIPPLE ROAD A123
Valence House Mus & Library
Goresbrook Leisure Centre
Barking RUFC
Keith Davis Cue Sports Club
Barking Ind Park
Alfreds Way Industrial Est
Renwick Industrial Estate
RM8
IG3
IG11
61
80
97

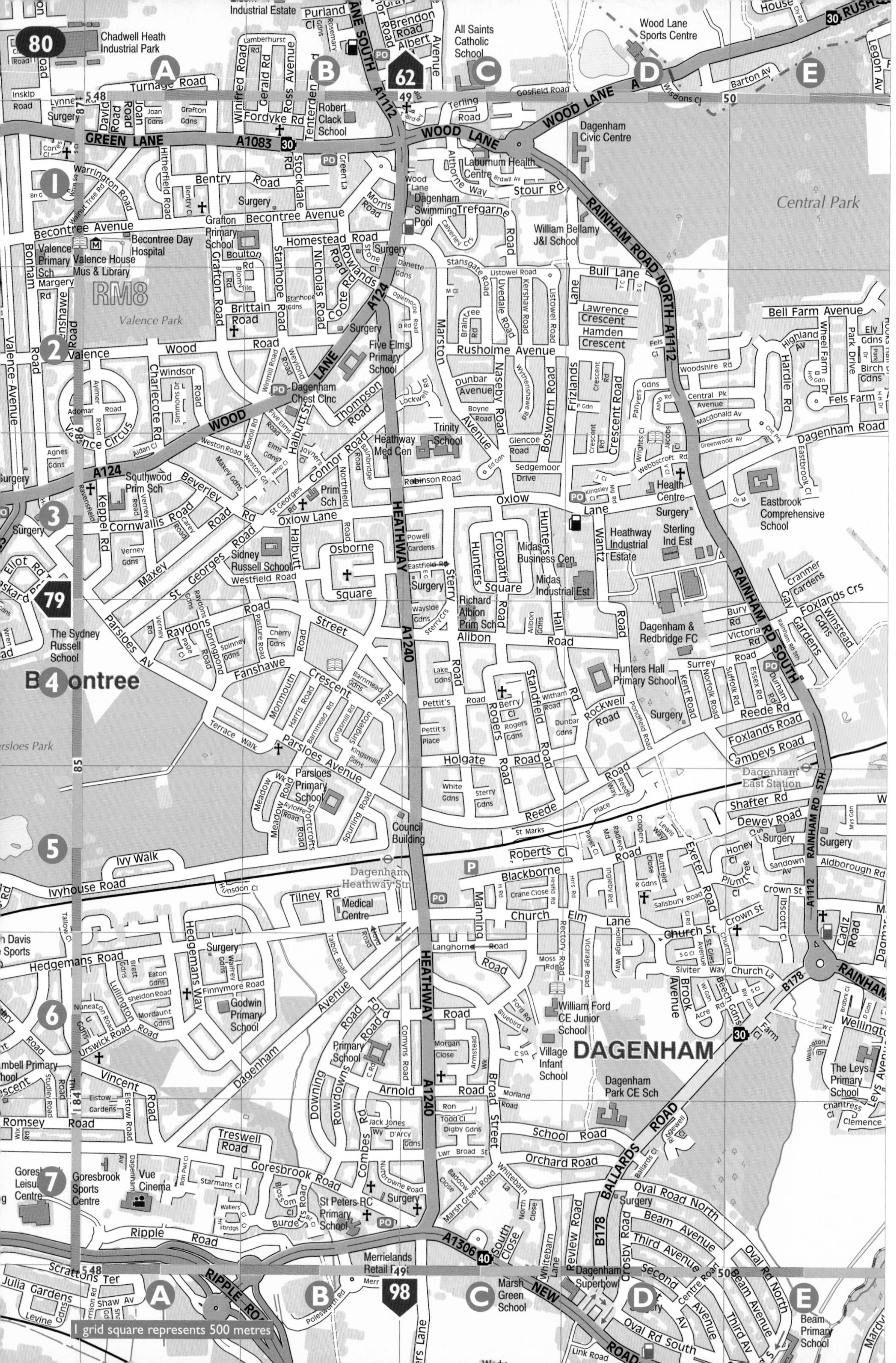

80
Industrial Estate
Chadwell Heath Industrial Park
Purland Cl
Brendon Road
Albert
62
All Saints Catholic School
Wood Lane Sports Centre
A
B
C
D
E
Turnage Road
Inskip Road
Lynnet
Surgery
David Road
Joan Road
Grafton Gdns
Winifred Road
Gerald Rd
Ross Avenue
Fordyke Rd
Tenterden Rd
Robert Clack School
Gosfield Road
Terling Road
WOOD LANE
Barton Av
Wisdons Cl
Dagenham Civic Centre
GREEN LANE
A1083
Warrington Road
Bentry Road
Stockdale Rd
Hitherfield Road
Laburnum Health Centre
Stour Rd
Central Park
Trefgarne Road
Wood Lane Dagenham Swimming Pool
Morris Road
Becontree Avenue
Grafton Primary School
Becontree Day Hospital
Valence Primary Sch
Valence House Mus & Library
Homestead Road
Nicholas Road
Rowlands Road
Stanhope Road
William Bellamy J&I School
RAINHAM ROAD NORTH A1112
Bull Lane
Lawrence Crescent
Hamden Crescent
Bell Farm Avenue
RM8
Valence Park
Brittain Road
Coote Rd
Surgery
Five Elms Primary School
Marston Avenue
Uvedale Road
Kershaw Road
Listowel Road
Rusholme Avenue
Highland Av
Park Drive
Hardie Rd
Fels Farm
Wood Road
Valence Avenue
Windsor Road
Charlecote Rd
Dagenham Chest Clnc
Thompson Road
Dunbar Avenue
Naseby Road
Bosworth Road
Frizlands
Crescent Road
Central Pk Avenue
Dagenham Road
Valence Circus
Trinity School
Heathway Med Cen
Glencoe Road
Sedgemoor Drive
Eastbrook Comprehensive School
A124
Southwood Prim Sch
Beverley Road
Connor Road
Robinson Road
Oxlow Lane
Health Centre
Surgery
Cornwallis Road
Keppel Rd
Maxey Road
St Georges Road
Prim Sch
Oxlow Lane
Halbutt St
HEATHWAY
Hunters Square
Cropath Road
Midas Business Cen
Heathway Industrial Estate
Sterling Ind Est
Eliot Rd
79
Sidney Russell School
Westfield Road
Osborne Square
Surgery
Richard Albion Prim Sch
Midas Industrial Est
Wantz Road
Cranmer Gardens
Foxlands Crs
The Sydney Russell School
Parsloes Av
Raydons Road
Street
Alibon Road
Dagenham & Redbridge FC
Bury Rd
Victoria Rd
Winstead Gdns
Gay Gardens
Becontree
Fanshawe Crescent
A1240
Hunters Hall Primary School
Surrey Road
RAINHAM RD SOUTH
Reede Rd
Foxlands Road
Cambeys Road
Parsloes Park
Terrace Walk
Parsloes Avenue
Pettit's Road
Rogers Road
Standfield Road
Rockwell Road
Surgery
Holgate Road
Dagenham East Station
Parsloes Primary School
Reede Road
Shafter Rd
Dewey Road
Surgery
Surgery
Council Building
Roberts Cl
Aldborough Rd
Ivy Walk
Ivyhouse Road
Dagenham Heathway Stn
Blackborne Road
Tilney Rd
Medical Centre
Manning Road
Church Elm Lane
Exeter Road
Crown St
Church St
Hedgemans Road
Surgery
Hedgemans Way
Finnymore Road
Godwin Primary School
Dagenham Avenue
Langhorne Road
Church La
Cadiz Road
RAINHAM
B178
William Ford CE Junior School
Village Infant School
DAGENHAM
Brook Avenue
Wellington
The Leys Primary School
Urswick Road
Vincent Road
Eistow Road
Romsey Road
Primary School
Arnold Road
Comyns Road
Morgan Close
Broad Street
Dagenham Park CE Sch
BALLARDS ROAD
School Road
Orchard Road
Treswell Road
Goresbrook Road
Goresbrook Sports Centre
Vue Cinema
Combes Rd
St Peters RC Primary School
Surgery
Oval Road North
Beam Avenue
Third Avenue
Ripple Road
A1306
NEW ROAD
Merrielands Retail Park
98
Marsh Green School
Dagenham Superbowl
Second Avenue
Oval Rd South
Beam Primary School
Scrattons Ter
Julia Gardens
RIPPLE ROAD
1 grid square represents 500 metres

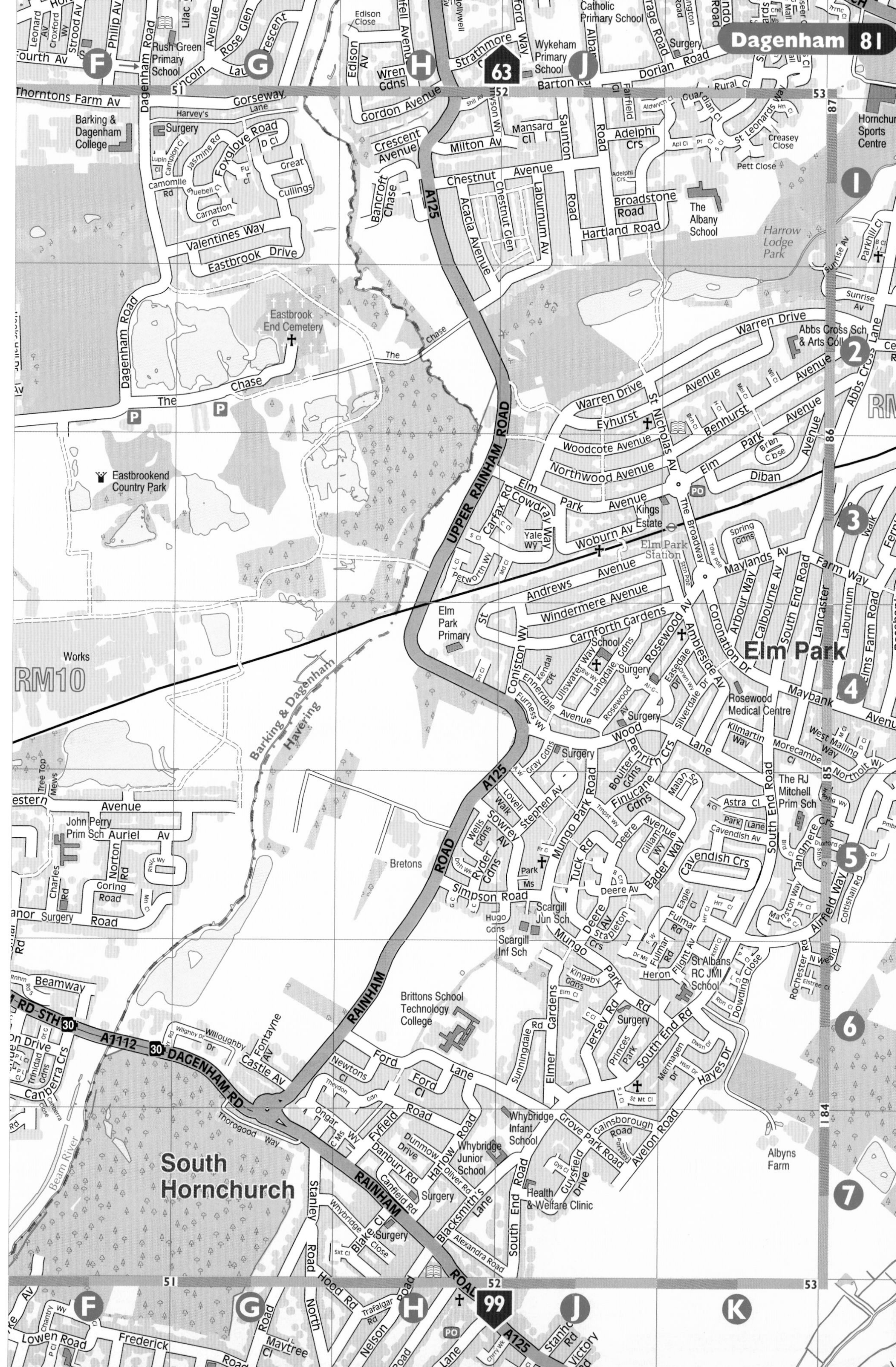

63
99
Rush Green Primary School
Wykeham Primary School
St Marys Catholic Primary School
Barking & Dagenham College
Hornchurch Sports Centre
Thorntons Farm Av
Gorseway
Dagenham Road
Valentines Way
Eastbrook Drive
Eastbrook End Cemetery
The Chase
Eastbrookend Country Park
Works
RM10
The Albany School
Harrow Lodge Park
Abbs Cross Sch & Arts Coll
Warren Drive
UPPER RAINHAM ROAD
A125
Elm Park Station
Elm Park
Elm Park Primary
Rosewood Medical Centre
The RJ Mitchell Prim Sch
St Albans RC JMI School
Barking & Dagenham
Havering
Bretons
John Perry Prim Sch
Brittons School Technology College
Whybridge Infant School
Whybridge Junior School
Health & Welfare Clinic
South Hornchurch
Albyns Farm
Beam River
A1112
DAGENHAM RD
RAINHAM ROAD
South End Road
Coronation Dr
Maylands Av
Mungo Park Road
Scargill Jun Sch
Scargill Inf Sch
Ford Lane
Gordon Avenue
Chestnut Avenue
Hartland Road
St Andrews Avenue
Windermere Avenue
Wood Lane
Airfield Way
F G H J K
51 52 53
84 85 86 87
1 2 3 4 5 6 7

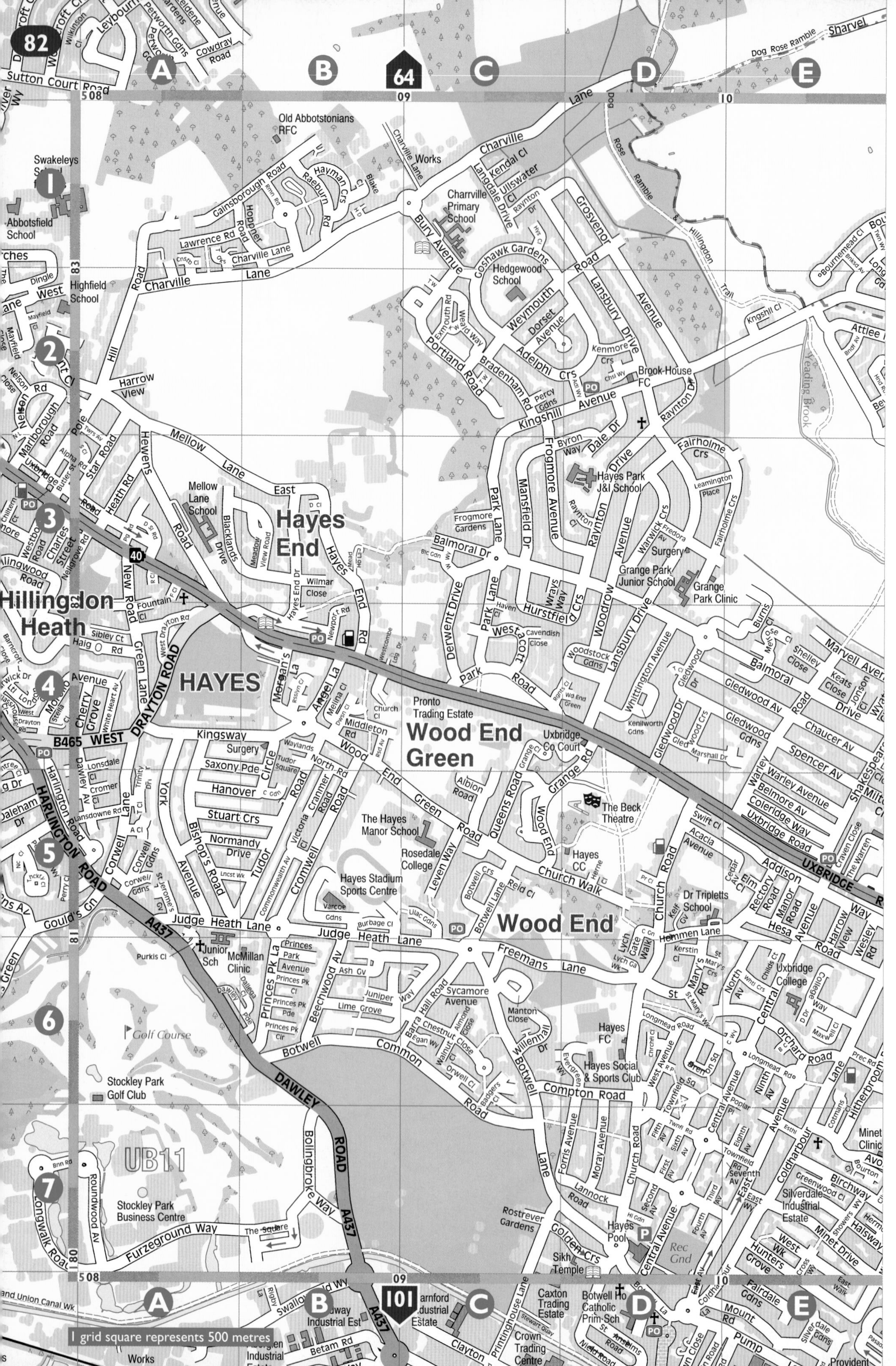

82
64
101
A
B
C
D
E
1
2
3
4
5
6
7
508
09
10
83
82
81
80
Sutton Court Road
Petworth Gdns
Cowdray Road
Leybourne
Wilkinson Cl
Dog Rose Ramble
Sharvel
Lane
Old Abbotstonians RFC
Swakeleys School
Abbotsfield School
Highfield School
Charville Lane
Works
Blake
Gainsborough Road
Hoppner Road
Hayman Crs
Raeburn Rd
Lawrence Rd
Charville Lane
Charville
Kendal Cl
Langdale Drive
Ullswater Cl
Charville Primary School
Bury Avenue
Grosvenor Road
Goshawk Gardens
Raynton Dr
Hedgewood School
Weymouth
Dorset Avenue
Lansbury Drive
Avenue
Dog Rose Ramble
Hillingdon Trail
Kingshill Cl
Bournemead Cl
Attlee
Yeading Brook
Exmouth Rd
Weald Way
Portland Road
Bradenham Rd
Adelphi Crs
Kenmore Crs
Brook House FC
Raynton Dr
Percy Gdns
Kingshill Avenue
PO
Hill Road
Harrow View
Mellow Lane
Mellow Lane East
Mellow Lane School
Blacklands Drive
Meadow View Road
Hayes End
Hayes End Rd
Hayes End Dr
Wilmar Close
Hewens Road
Heath Rd
Star Road
Pole Hill Road
Marlborough Road
Nelson Rd
Uxbridge Road
Charles Street
Westbourne Road
Hillingdon Heath
New Road
Fountain Cl
40
Byron Way
Dale Dr
Fairholme Crs
Hayes Park J&I School
Frogmore Gardens
Park Lane
Mansfield Dr
Frogmore Avenue
Raynton Cl
Raynton Drive
Woodrow Avenue
Warwick Crs
Fredora Av
Surgery
Grange Park Junior School
Grange Park Clinic
Leamington Place
Fairholme Crs
Balmoral Dr
Derwent Drive
Haven Cl
Hurstfield Crs
Wrays Way
West Acott
Cavendish Close
Woodstock Gdns
Lansbury Drive
Whittington Avenue
Gledwood Dr
Burns
Shelley Close
Marvell Avenue
Keats Close
Jonson Cl
Balmoral Road
Gledwood Av
Gledwood Gdns
Chaucer Av
Spencer Av
Drive
Sibley Ct
Haig Rd
Green Lane
West Drayton Rd
DRAYTON ROAD
HAYES
Morgan's La
Angel La
Melina Cl
Church Cl
Newport Rd
Westcombe Lodge Dr
Pronto Trading Estate
Wood End Green
Kenilworth Gdns
Uxbridge Co Court
Grange Road
Grange Rd
Gled Marshall Dr
Warley Avenue
Belmore Av
Coleridge Way
Uxbridge Road
Shakespeare
Milton
Avenue
Cherry Grove
White Heart Av
B465 WEST
Kingsway
Surgery
Saxony Pde
Hanover
Stuart Crs
Normandy Drive
Tudor Circle
Tudor Square
Waylands
North Rd
Middleton Rd
Wood End Green Road
Victoria Road
Cranmer Road
Cromwell Road
Albion Road
Queens Road
Wood End
The Beck Theatre
Swift Cl
Acacia Avenue
Church Road
Cedar Av
Elm Cl
Rectory Road
Manor Road
Avenue
UXBRIDGE RO
Addison
Craven Close
The Warren
Harrow View
Hesa Road
Wesley Rd
Harlington Road
HARLINGTON ROAD
Lonsdale
Dawley Av
Cromer Cl
Lansdowne Rd
Daleham Dr
Corwell Lane
Corwell Gdns
York Avenue
Bishop's Road
Commonwealth Av
Cromwell Cl
The Hayes Manor School
Rosedale College
Leven Way
Hayes Stadium Sports Centre
Varcoe Gdns
Hayes CC
Church Walk
Botwell Crs
Botwell Lane
Reid Cl
Dr Triplett's School
Wood End
Gould's Gn
Judge Heath Lane
A437
Junior Sch
McMillan Clinic
Purkis Cl
Burbage Cl
Lilac Gdns
PO
Princes Park Avenue
Beechwood Av
Ash Gv
Juniper Way
Lime Grove
Barra Hall Road
Sycamore Avenue
Chestnut Close
Freemans Lane
Lych Gate Walk
Hemmen Lane
Kerstin Cl
St Mary's Rd
North Av
Central Avenue
Uxbridge College
College Way
Orchard Road
Golf Course
Stockley Park Golf Club
Botwell Common Road
DAWLEY ROAD
Manton Close
Willenhall Dr
Botwell Lane
Hayes FC
Hayes Social & Sports Club
Compton Road
Evergreen Way
West Avenue
Longmead Road
Brendon Sq
Townfield Sq
Ninth Av
Longmead Rd
Hitherbroom Rd
Minet Clinic
Coldharbour Lane
UB11
Bolingbroke Way
Forris Avenue
Moray Avenue
Church Road
Lannock Road
Birchway
Greenwood Cl
Silverdale Industrial Estate
Minet Drive
Halsway
Roundwood Av
Longwalk Road
Stockley Park Business Centre
Furzeground Way
The Square
Rostrevor Gardens
Golden Crs
Sikh Temple
Hayes Pool
Rec Gnd
Central Avenue
West Wk
Hunters Grove
Fairdale Gdns
Mount Rd
Pump
Silverdale Gdns
Provident
Grand Union Canal Wk
Rigby La
Swallowfield Wy
Industrial Est
Barnford Industrial Estate
Caxton Trading Estate
Printinghouse Lane
Stewart Quay
Crown Trading Centre
Clayton
Botwell Ho Catholic Prim Sch
St Anselms
Betam Rd
Works
1 grid square represents 500 metres

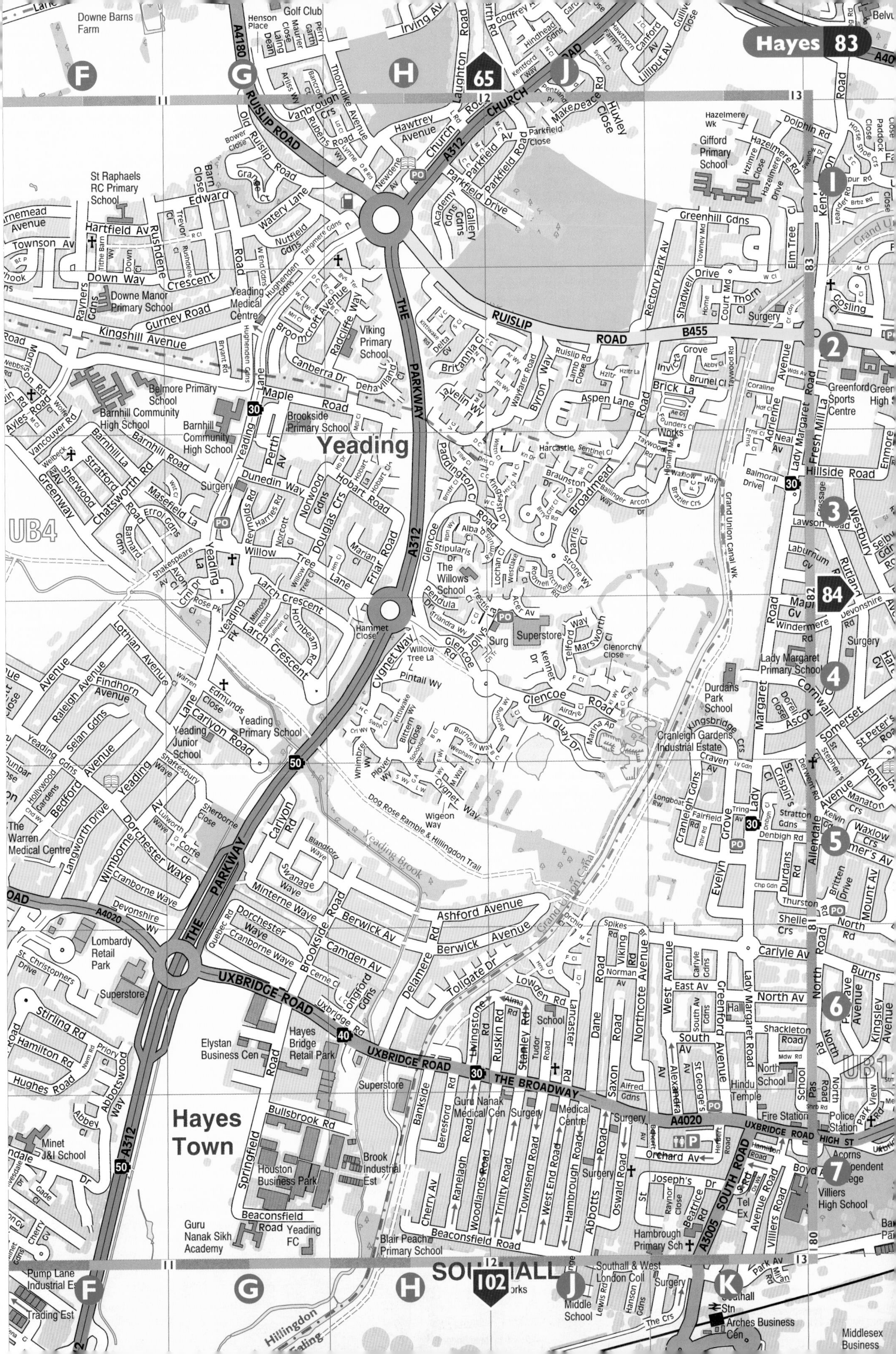

Hayes 83
65
84
102
Yeading
Hayes Town
Southall
UB4
UB1
Downe Barns Farm
Golf Club
Ruislip Road
Old Ruislip Road
Church Road
The Parkway
Uxbridge Road
The Broadway
A4180
A312
A4020
A3005
B455
South Road
Kingshill Avenue
Gurney Road
Yeading Lane
Maple Road
Willow Tree Lane
Larch Crescent
Glencoe Road
Cygnet Way
Ashford Avenue
Berwick Avenue
Brookside Road
Minterne Waye
Dorchester Waye
Cranborne Waye
Devonshire Wy
Lady Margaret Road
Greenford Avenue
North Road
Broadmead Road
Rectory Park Av
Greenhill Gdns
Shadwell Drive
Brick La
Aspen Lane
Hillside Road
Fresh Mill La
Cornwall
Carlyle Av
North Av
Beaconsfield Road
Bullsbrook Rd
Springfield Road
Lancaster Rd
Northcote Avenue
West Avenue
Saxon Road
Dane Road
Hambrough Road
West End Road
Townsend Road
Trinity Road
Woodlands Road
Ranelagh Road
Cherry Av
Abbotts Road
Oswald Road
Orchard Av
Villiers Road
Avenue Road
Park Av
St Raphaels RC Primary School
Downe Manor Primary School
Yeading Medical Centre
Viking Primary School
Belmore Primary School
Barnhill Community High School
Brookside Primary School
The Willows School
Superstore
Lady Margaret Primary School
Durdans Park School
Gifford Primary School
Greenford Sports Centre
Cranleigh Gardens Industrial Estate
Yeading Junior School
Yeading Primary School
The Warren Medical Centre
Lombardy Retail Park
Elystan Business Cen
Hayes Bridge Retail Park
Houston Business Park
Brook Industrial Est
Guru Nanak Sikh Academy
Yeading FC
Blair Peach Primary School
Guru Nanak Medical Cen
Hindu Temple
Fire Station
Police Station
Villiers High School
Hambrough Primary Sch
Southall & West London Coll
Middle School
Minet J&I School
Pump Lane Industrial Est
Trading Est
Southall Stn
Arches Business Cen
Middlesex Business
Grand Union Canal
Grand Union Canal Wk
Yeading Brook
Dog Rose Ramble & Hillingdon Trail
F
G
H
J
K
I
2
3
4
5
6
7
11
12
13
80
81
82
83

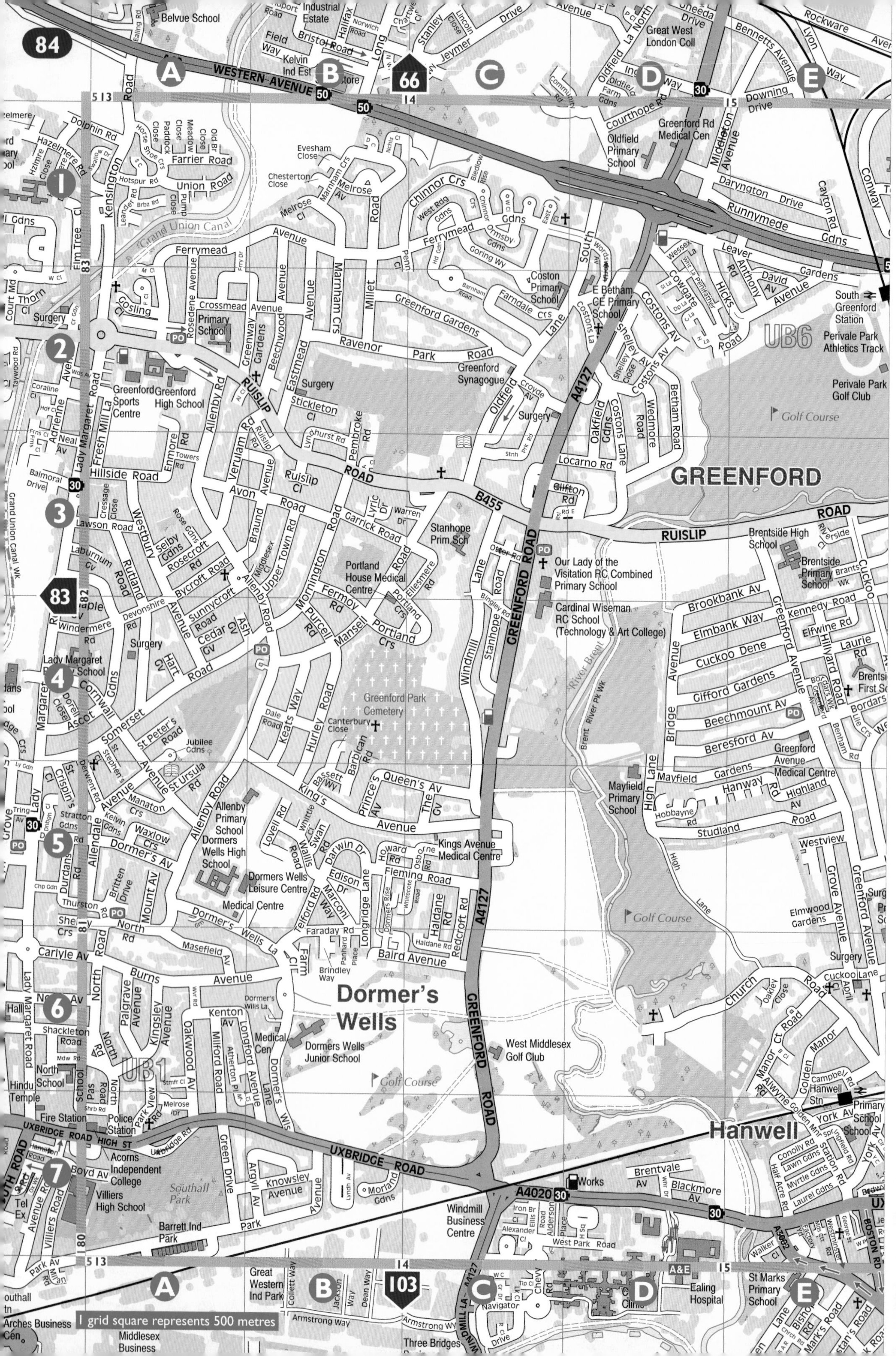
84
A
B
C
D
E
66
83
103
1
2
3
4
5
6
7
1 grid square represents 500 metres
GREENFORD
Dormer's Wells
Hanwell
UB6
UB1
WESTERN AVENUE
RUISLIP ROAD
B455
GREENFORD ROAD
A4127
UXBRIDGE ROAD
A4020
HIGH ST
Belvue School
Industrial Estate
Kelvin Ind Est
Bristol Road
Great West London Coll
Oldfield Primary School
Greenford Rd Medical Cen
Grand Union Canal
Farrier Road
Union Road
Ferrymead Avenue
Chinnor Crs
Coston Primary School
E Betham CE Primary School
Greenford Gardens
Ravenor Park Road
Greenford Synagogue
Crossmead Avenue
Primary School
Greenford Sports Centre
Greenford High School
Surgery
Hillside Road
Lady Margaret Road
Fresh Mill La
Allenby Road
Verulam Rd
Mornington Road
Portland House Medical Centre
Stanhope Prim Sch
Our Lady of the Visitation RC Combined Primary School
Cardinal Wiseman RC School (Technology & Art College)
Brentside High School
Brentside Primary School
South Greenford Station
Perivale Park Athletics Track
Perivale Park Golf Club
Golf Course
Darynqton Drive
Runnymede Gdns
Courthope Rd
Middleton Avenue
Conway
Locarno Rd
Costons Lane
Betham Road
Wedmore Road
Brookbank Av
Elmbank Way
Cuckoo Dene
Gifford Gardens
Beechmount Av
Beresford Av
Greenford Avenue Medical Centre
Mayfield Primary School
Mayfield Gardens
Hanway Rd
Studland Road
Highland Av
Greenford Avenue
Grove Avenue
Elmwood Gardens
Cuckoo Lane
Church Road
Greenford Park Cemetery
Queen's Av
King's Avenue
Kings Avenue Medical Centre
Allenby Primary School
Dormers Wells High School
Dormers Wells Leisure Centre
Medical Centre
Dormer's Wells La
Baird Avenue
Fleming Road
Burns Avenue
Carlyle Av
Dormers Wells Junior School
West Middlesex Golf Club
Somerset Road
Cornwall Road
Lady Margaret Primary School
Hindu Temple
Fire Station
Police Station
North School
Acorns Independent College
Villiers High School
Southall Park
Barrett Ind Park
Green Drive
Knowsley Avenue
Windmill Business Centre
Brentvale Av
Blackmore Av
Works
West Park Road
Ealing Hospital
A&E
Great Western Ind Park
Armstrong Way
Three Bridges
St Marks Primary School
Hanwell Stn
York Av
Primary School
Golden Manor
Boyd Av
Park Av
Arches Business Cen
Middlesex Business
513
14
15
80
81
82
83

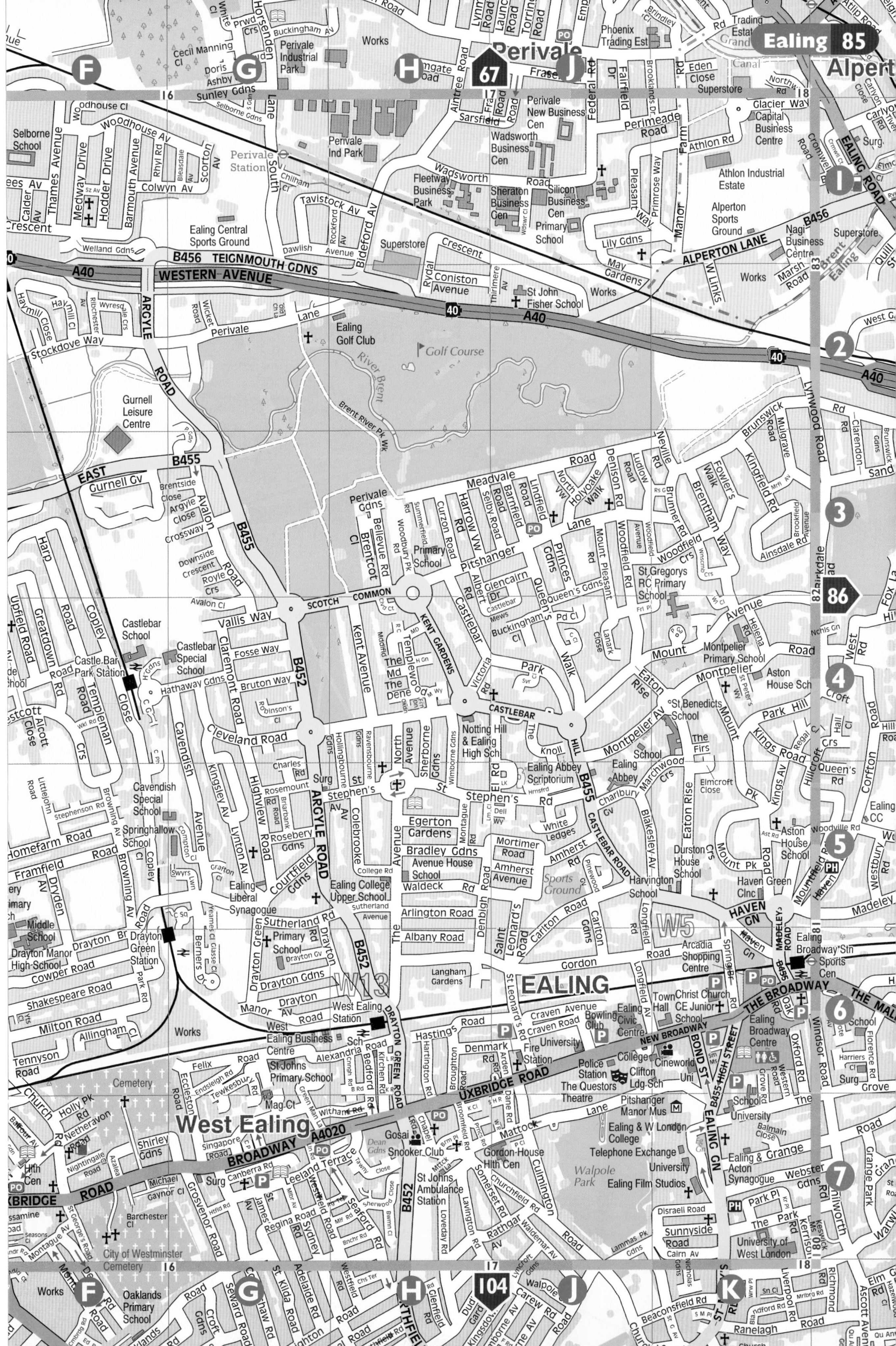
Perivale
Alperton
Perivale Industrial Park
Perivale Station
Ealing Central Sports Ground
B456 TEIGNMOUTH GDNS
WESTERN AVENUE
A40
ARGYLE ROAD
Ealing Golf Club
Golf Course
River Brent
Gurnell Leisure Centre
ALPERTON LANE
EALING ROAD
SCOTCH COMMON
KENT GARDENS
CASTLEBAR HILL
Castlebar School
Castle Bar Park Station
Drayton Green Station
West Ealing Station
ARGYLE ROAD
DRAYTON GREEN ROAD
HAVEN GN
Ealing Broadway Stn
EALING
W5
W13
THE BROADWAY
NEW BROADWAY
UXBRIDGE ROAD
West Ealing
BROADWAY A4020
Walpole Park
Ealing Film Studios
University of West London
City of Westminster Cemetery
Arcadia Shopping Centre
Ealing Broadway Centre
67
86
104

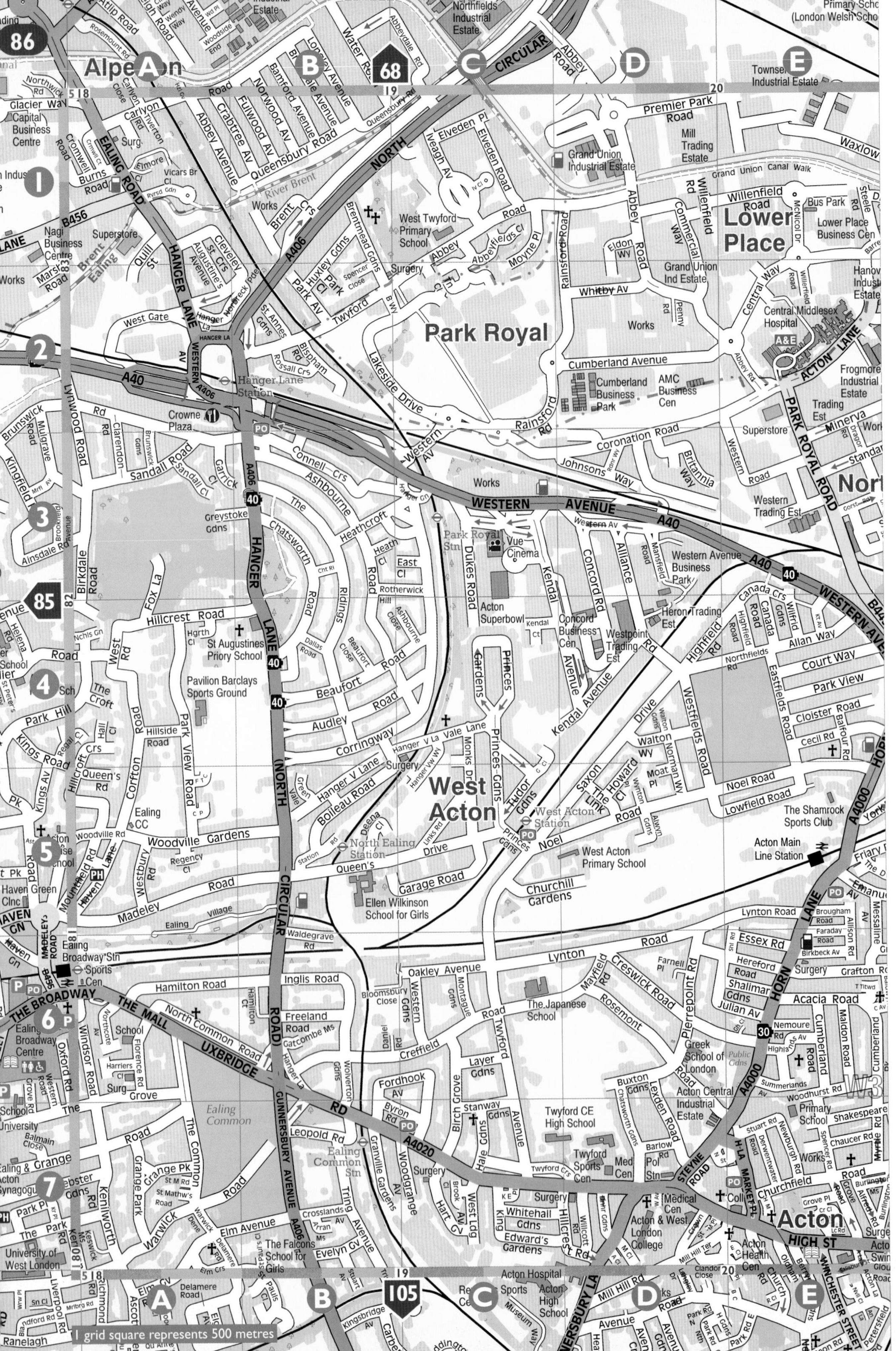
86
68
85
105
Alperton
Park Royal
Lower Place
West Acton
Acton
North Circular Road
Western Avenue
Hanger Lane
Ealing Road
Uxbridge Road
Gunnersbury Avenue
Horn Lane
Park Royal Road
High St
The Broadway
The Mall
Hanger Lane Station
Park Royal Stn
North Ealing Station
West Acton Station
Ealing Broadway Stn
Ealing Common Stn
Acton Main Line Station
Ealing Common
Central Middlesex Hospital
Acton Hospital
Northfields Industrial Estate
Grand Union Industrial Estate
Cumberland Business Park
AMC Business Cen
Western Trading Est
Heron Trading Est
Westpoint Trading Est
West Twyford Primary School
St Augustines Priory School
Pavilion Barclays Sports Ground
Ellen Wilkinson School for Girls
West Acton Primary School
The Japanese School
Twyford CE High School
Greek School of London
Acton Central Industrial Estate
Acton & West London College
The Falcons School for Girls
University of West London
The Shamrock Sports Club
Vue Cinema
Acton Superbowl
Crowne Plaza
A40
A406
A4020
A4000
B456
1 grid square represents 500 metres

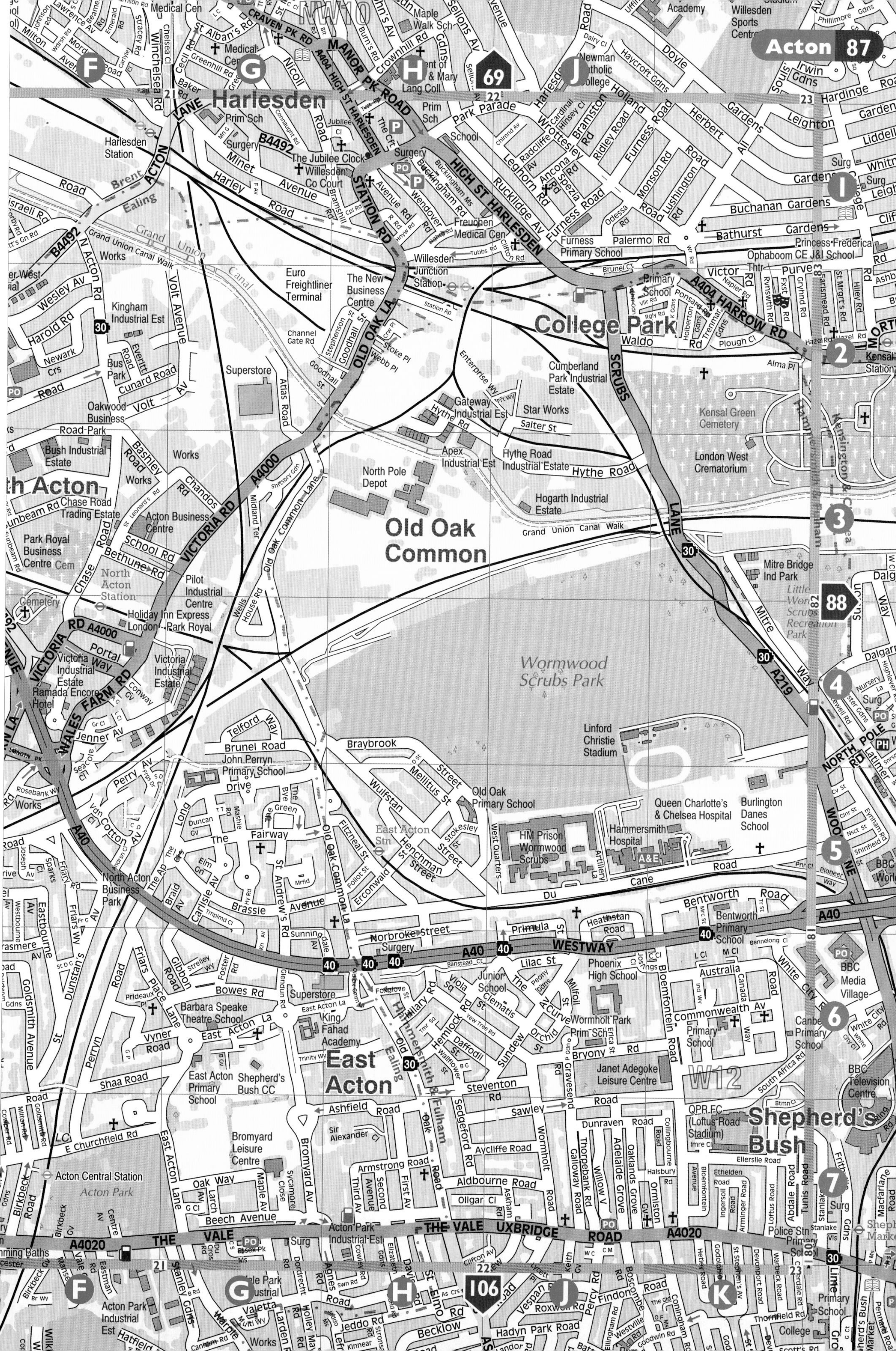
NW10
Harlesden
Harlesden Station
College Park
Old Oak Common
Wormwood Scrubs Park
East Acton
Shepherd's Bush
W12
North Acton Station
Willesden Junction Station
Kensal Green Cemetery
London West Crematorium
Acton Central Station
Acton Park
Kensal Station
Linford Christie Stadium
HM Prison Wormwood Scrubs
Hammersmith Hospital
Queen Charlotte's & Chelsea Hospital
Burlington Danes School
Old Oak Primary School
East Acton Stn
QPR FC (Loftus Road Stadium)
Janet Adegoke Leisure Centre
Phoenix High School
BBC Media Village
BBC Television Centre
Bromyard Leisure Centre
King Fahad Academy
Barbara Speake Theatre School
East Acton Primary School
Shepherd's Bush CC
Euro Freightliner Terminal
The New Business Centre
North Pole Depot
Kingham Industrial Est
Bush Industrial Estate
Acton Business Centre
Park Royal Business Centre
Pilot Industrial Centre
Victoria Industrial Estate
Holiday Inn Express London - Park Royal
Ramada Encore Hotel
Gateway Industrial Est
Apex Industrial Est
Hythe Road Industrial Estate
Hogarth Industrial Estate
Cumberland Park Industrial Estate
Star Works
Mitre Bridge Ind Park
Little Wormwood Scrubs Recreation Park
Acton Park Industrial Est
Grand Union Canal Walk
Grand Union Canal
Willesden Sports Centre
Furness Primary School
Ophaboom CE J&I School
Freuchen Medical Cen
John Perryn Primary School
Bentworth Primary School
Wormholt Park Prim Sch
Commonwealth Primary School
The Jubilee Clock
Willesden Co Court
A4000 VICTORIA RD
A404 HIGH ST HARLESDEN
A404 HARROW RD
A219
A40 WESTWAY
A4020 THE VALE
UXBRIDGE ROAD
OLD OAK LA
SCRUBS LANE
WOOD LANE
DU CANE ROAD
ACTON LANE
STATION RD
MANOR PK ROAD
CRAVEN PK RD
WALES FARM RD
NORTH POLE RD
B4492
Hammersmith & Fulham
Ealing
Brent
21
22
23
69
88
106
F
G
H
J
I
K
2
3
4
5
6
7

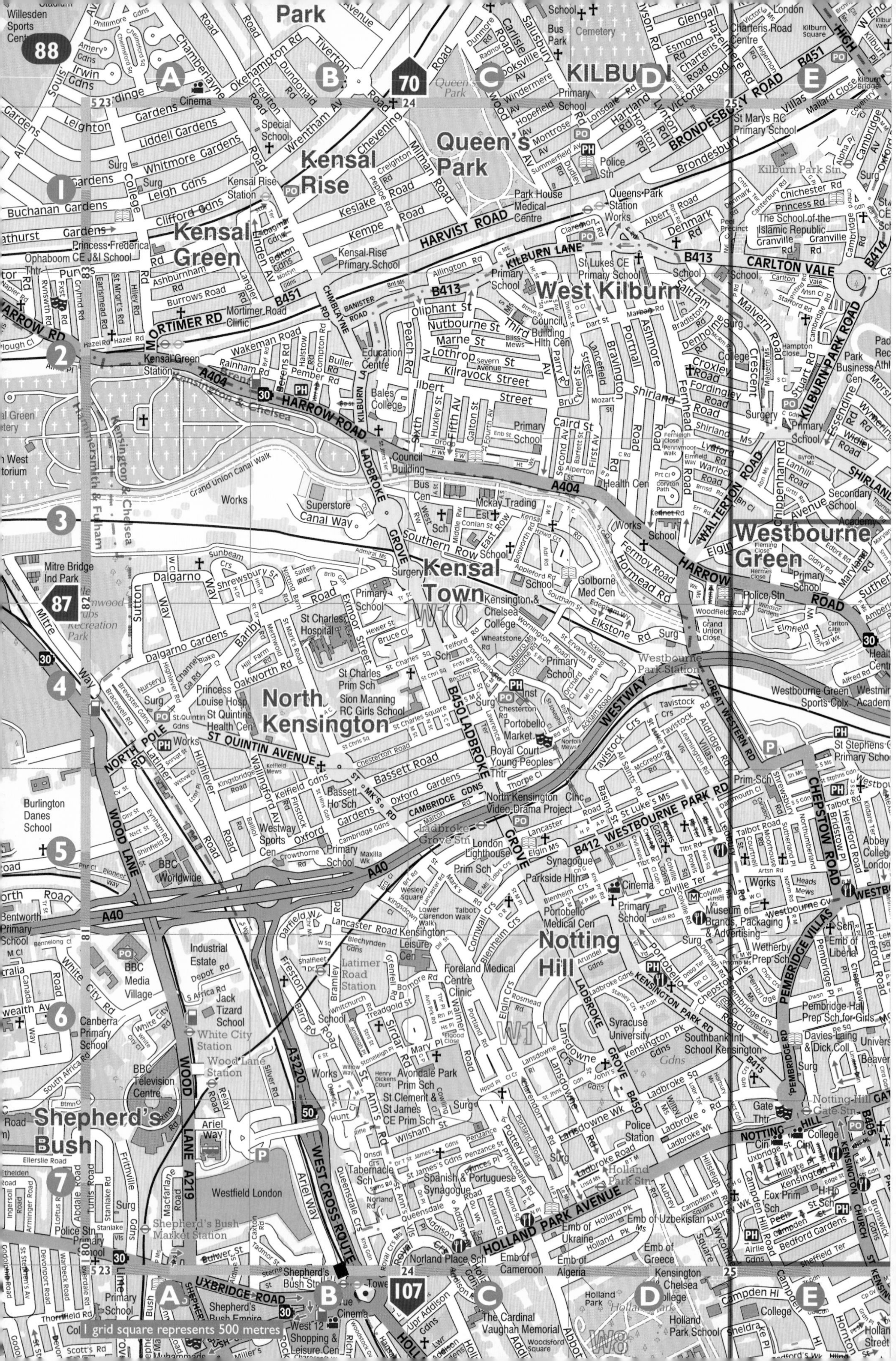
88
70
87
107
Willesden Sports Centre
Park
KILBURN
Queen's Park
Kensal Rise
Kensal Green
West Kilburn
Westbourne Green
Kensal Town
W10
North Kensington
Notting Hill
W11
Shepherd's Bush
W8
Kensal Rise Station
Kensal Green Station
Queens Park Station
Kilburn Park Stn
Westbourne Park Station
Ladbroke Grove Stn
Latimer Road Station
White City Station
Wood Lane Station
Shepherd's Bush Market Station
Holland Park Stn
Notting Hill Gate Stn
HARVIST ROAD
KILBURN LANE
CARLTON VALE
KILBURN PARK ROAD
BRONDESBURY ROAD
MORTIMER RD
HARROW ROAD
A404
B413
B451
LADBROKE GROVE
B450
WESTWAY
A40
ST QUINTIN AVENUE
NORTH POLE RD
WOOD LANE
A219
A3220
WEST CROSS ROUTE
HOLLAND PARK AVENUE
UXBRIDGE ROAD
NOTTING HILL GATE
CHEPSTOW ROAD
PEMBRIDGE VILLAS
WESTBOURNE PARK RD
B412
KENSINGTON PARK RD
PORTOBELLO
GREAT WESTERN RD
WALTERTON ROAD
CHAMBERLAYNE RD
Grand Union Canal Walk
Kensal Rise Primary School
Princess Frederica CE J&I School
Mitre Bridge Ind Park
Wormwood Scrubs Recreation Park
Burlington Danes School
BBC Worldwide
BBC Media Village
BBC Television Centre
Westfield London
Jack Tizard School
St Charles Hospital
Princess Louise Hosp
Kensington & Chelsea College
Portobello Market
Museum of Brands, Packaging & Advertising
Syracuse University
Southbank Intl School Kensington
Westbourne Green Sports Cplx
Emb of Uzbekistan
Emb of Ukraine
Emb of Cameroon
Emb of Algeria
Emb of Greece
Emb of Liberia
Holland Park School
Kensington & Chelsea College
The Cardinal Vaughan Memorial
1 grid square represents 500 metres

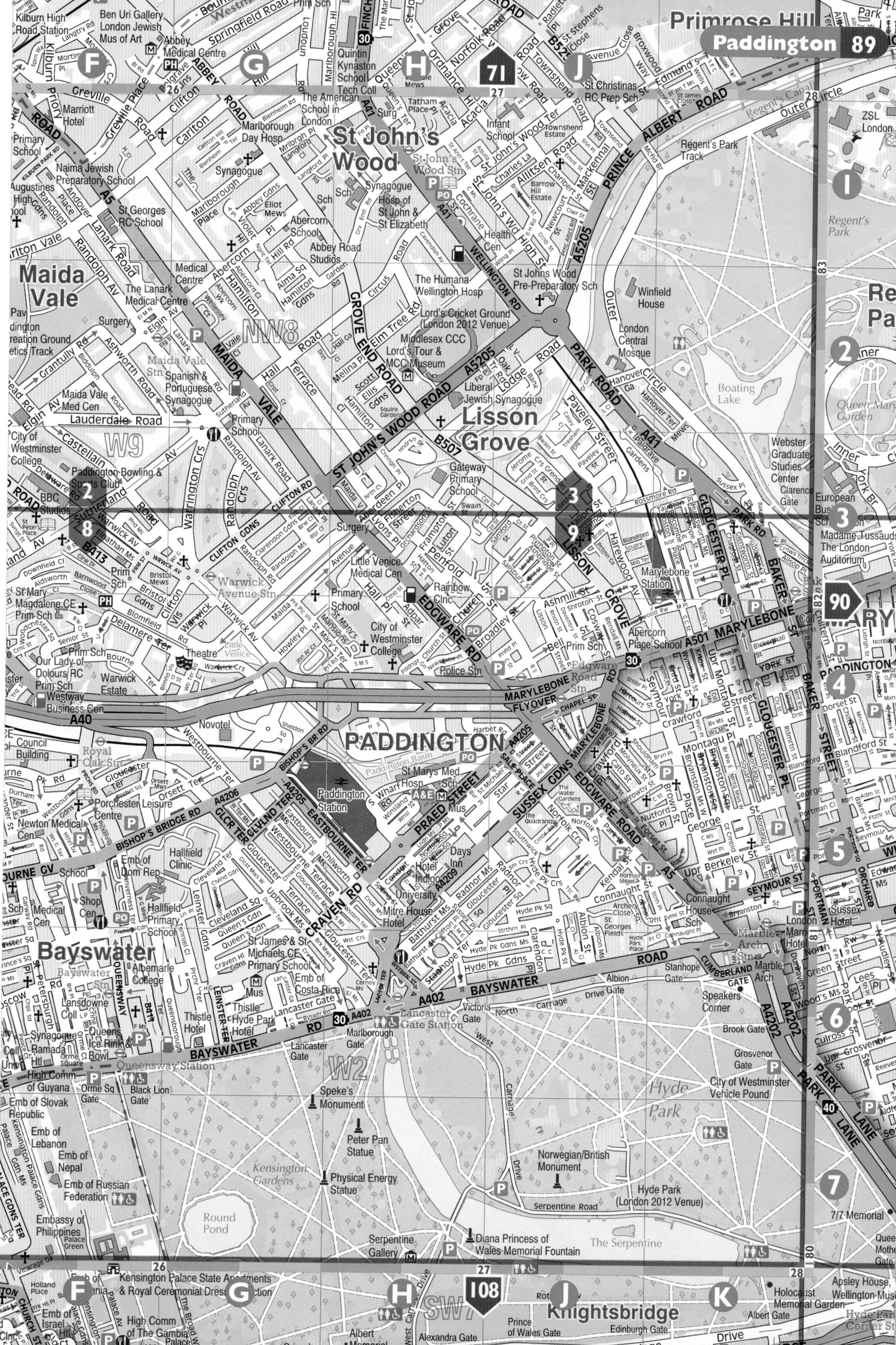
Primrose Hill
St John's Wood
Maida Vale
Lisson Grove
PADDINGTON
Bayswater
Knightsbridge
NW8
W9
W2
SW7
Regent's Park
Hyde Park
Kensington Gardens
The Serpentine
Round Pond
Boating Lake
Queen Mary Garden
Lord's Cricket Ground (London 2012 Venue)
Middlesex CCC Lord's Tour & MCC Museum
Paddington Station
Paddington Basin
Marylebone Station
Edgware Road Stn
Warwick Avenue Stn
Maida Vale Stn
Royal Oak Stn
Bayswater Stn
Queensway Station
Lancaster Gate Station
Marble Arch Stn
St John's Wood Stn
MARYLEBONE FLYOVER
A40
A5
A41
A5205
A501 MARYLEBONE RD
A402 BAYSWATER ROAD
A4202
A4205
A4206
A4209
B507
MAIDA VALE
EDGWARE RD
EDGWARE ROAD
ST JOHN'S WOOD ROAD
WELLINGTON RD
PARK ROAD
PRINCE ALBERT ROAD
GROVE END ROAD
PRAED STREET
SUSSEX GDNS
BISHOP'S BRIDGE RD
CRAVEN RD
BAKER ST
BAKER STREET
GLOUCESTER PL
PARK LANE
QUEENSWAY
CLIFTON GDNS
CUMBERLAND GATE
Madame Tussauds
The London Auditorium
London Central Mosque
Winfield House
Speakers Corner
Marble Arch
Speke's Monument
Peter Pan Statue
Physical Energy Statue
Norwegian/British Monument
Hyde Park (London 2012 Venue)
Serpentine Road
Serpentine Gallery
Diana Princess of Wales Memorial Fountain
7/7 Memorial
Holocaust Memorial Garden
Apsley House, Wellington Museum
Kensington Palace State Apartments & Royal Ceremonial Dress Collection
City of Westminster Vehicle Pound
Victoria Gate
Albion Gate
Brook Gate
Grosvenor Gate
Marlborough Gate
Lancaster Gate
Black Lion Gate
Edinburgh Gate
Albert Gate
Alexandra Gate
Prince of Wales Gate
Hallfield Clinic
Hallfield Primary School
Westway Business Cen
Novotel
Thistle Hotel
Thistle Hyde Park Hotel
Ramada Htl
Mitre House Hotel
Days Inn
Hotel Indigo
Sussex Hotel
Ben Uri Gallery London Jewish Mus of Art
Abbey Medical Centre
Marriott Hotel
Naima Jewish Preparatory School
The Humana Wellington Hosp
Hosp of St John & St Elizabeth
Abbey Road Studios
St Johns Wood Pre-Preparatory Sch
Liberal Jewish Synagogue
Gateway Primary School
Little Venice Medical Cen
City of Westminster College
Paddington Bowling & Sports Club
BBC Studios
Spanish & Portuguese Synagogue
Webster Graduate Studies Center
Emb of Slovak Republic
Emb of Lebanon
Emb of Nepal
Emb of Russian Federation
Embassy of Philippines
High Comm of Guyana
Emb of Costa Rica
Emb of Israel
High Comm of The Gambia
Emb of Dom Rep
Queens Ice Rink & Bowl
Albemarle College
St James & St Michaels CE Primary School
Council Building
Porchester Leisure Centre
ZSL London Zoo
71
90
108

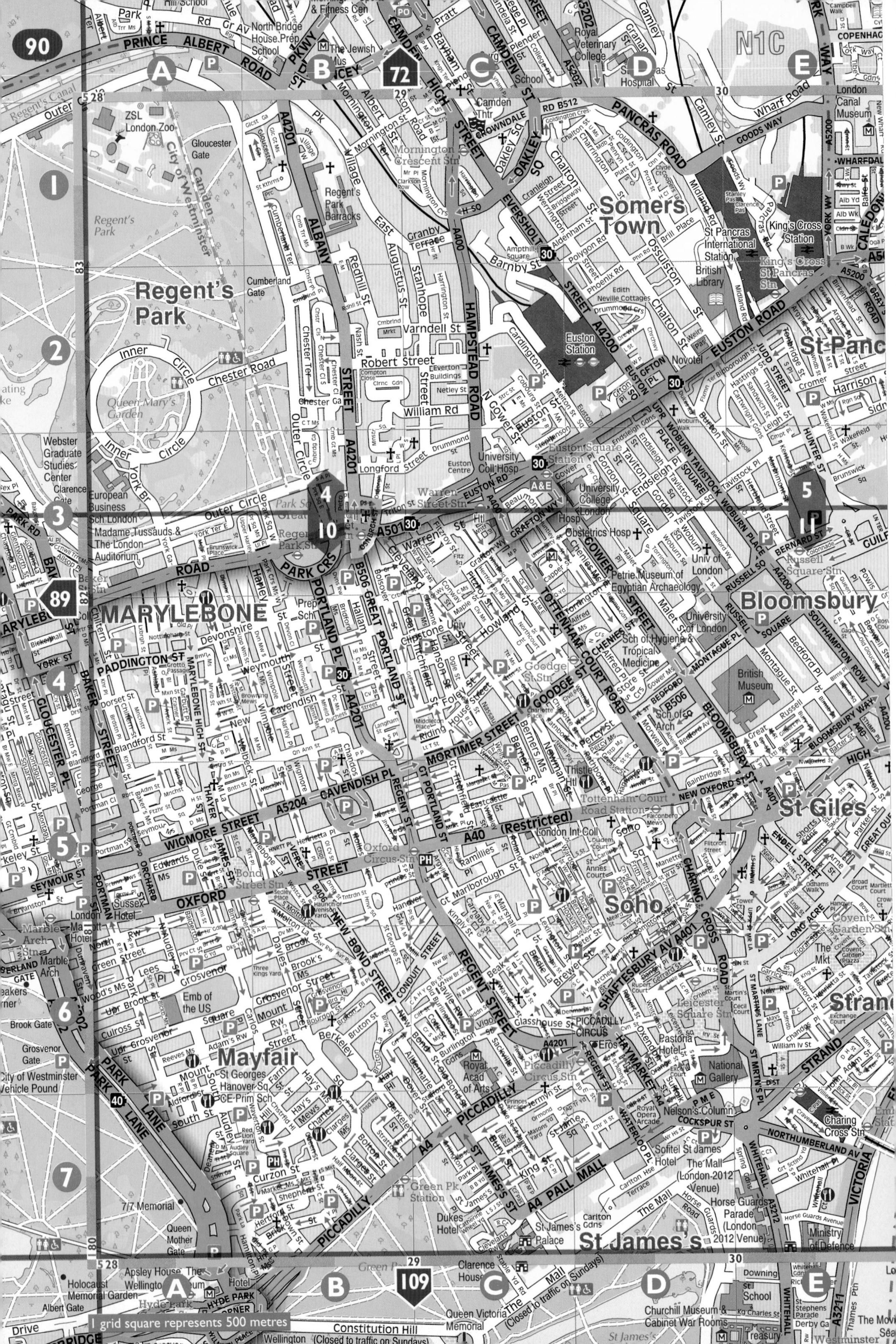
90
72
89
109
A
B
C
D
E
1
2
3
4
5
6
7
28
29
30
83
82
81
80
N1C
PRINCE ALBERT ROAD
Regent's Canal
ZSL London Zoo
Gloucester Gate
City of Westminster
Regent's Park
Cumberland Gate
Inner Circle
Chester Road
Queen Mary's Garden
Outer Circle
Webster Graduate Studies Center
Clarence Gate
European Business Sch London
Madame Tussauds & The London Auditorium
Park Sq
Great Portland St Stn
Regent's Park Stn
Baker St Stn
MARYLEBONE ROAD
MARYLEBONE
PADDINGTON ST
MARYLEBONE HIGH ST
BAKER STREET
GLOUCESTER PL
PORTMAN ST
WIGMORE STREET
CAVENDISH PL
OXFORD STREET
Bond Street Stn
Marble Arch Stn
Marble Arch
Sussex Hotel
London Marriott Hotel
NEW BOND STREET
CONDUIT STREET
REGENT STREET
Oxford Circus Stn
Mayfair
Emb of the US
Grosvenor Square
Brook Gate
Grosvenor Gate
City of Westminster Vehicle Pound
PARK LANE
7/7 Memorial
Queen Mother Gate
PICCADILLY
Green Pk Station
Royal Acad of Arts
Piccadilly Circus Stn
PICCADILLY CIRCUS
Eros
SHAFTESBURY AV
Soho
Soho Sq
CHARING CROSS ROAD
Tottenham Court Road Station
NEW OXFORD ST
St Giles
Leicester Square Stn
National Gallery
Nelson's Column
Charing Cross Stn
STRAND
WHITEHALL
NORTHUMBERLAND AV
Horse Guards Parade (London 2012 Venue)
The Mall (London 2012 Venue)
Ministry of Defence
PALL MALL
St James's Palace
St James's
Clarence House
Green Park
Constitution Hill (Closed to traffic on Sundays)
The Mall (Closed to traffic on Sundays)
Queen Victoria Memorial
Churchill Museum & Cabinet War Rooms
Apsley House The Wellington Museum
Holocaust Memorial Garden
Hyde Park Corner
Albert Gate
Downing St
1 grid square represents 500 metres
CAMDEN HIGH STREET
Camden Thtr
Mornington Crescent Stn
Somers Town
PANCRAS ROAD
St Pancras International Station
King's Cross Station
King's Cross St Pancras Stn
British Library
London Canal Museum
Euston Station
EUSTON ROAD
HAMPSTEAD ROAD
ALBANY STREET
Regent's Park Barracks
Euston Square Station
University Coll Hosp
Warren Street Stn
GOWER STREET
TOTTENHAM COURT ROAD
Goodge St Stn
University College London
Petrie Museum of Egyptian Archaeology
Univ of London
Sch of Hygiene & Tropical Medicine
Bloomsbury
RUSSELL SQUARE
Russell Square Stn
British Museum
SOUTHAMPTON ROW
St Pancras
Covent Garden Stn
LONG ACRE
ST MARTIN'S LANE
Royal Veterinary College
The Jewish Mus
North Bridge House Prep School

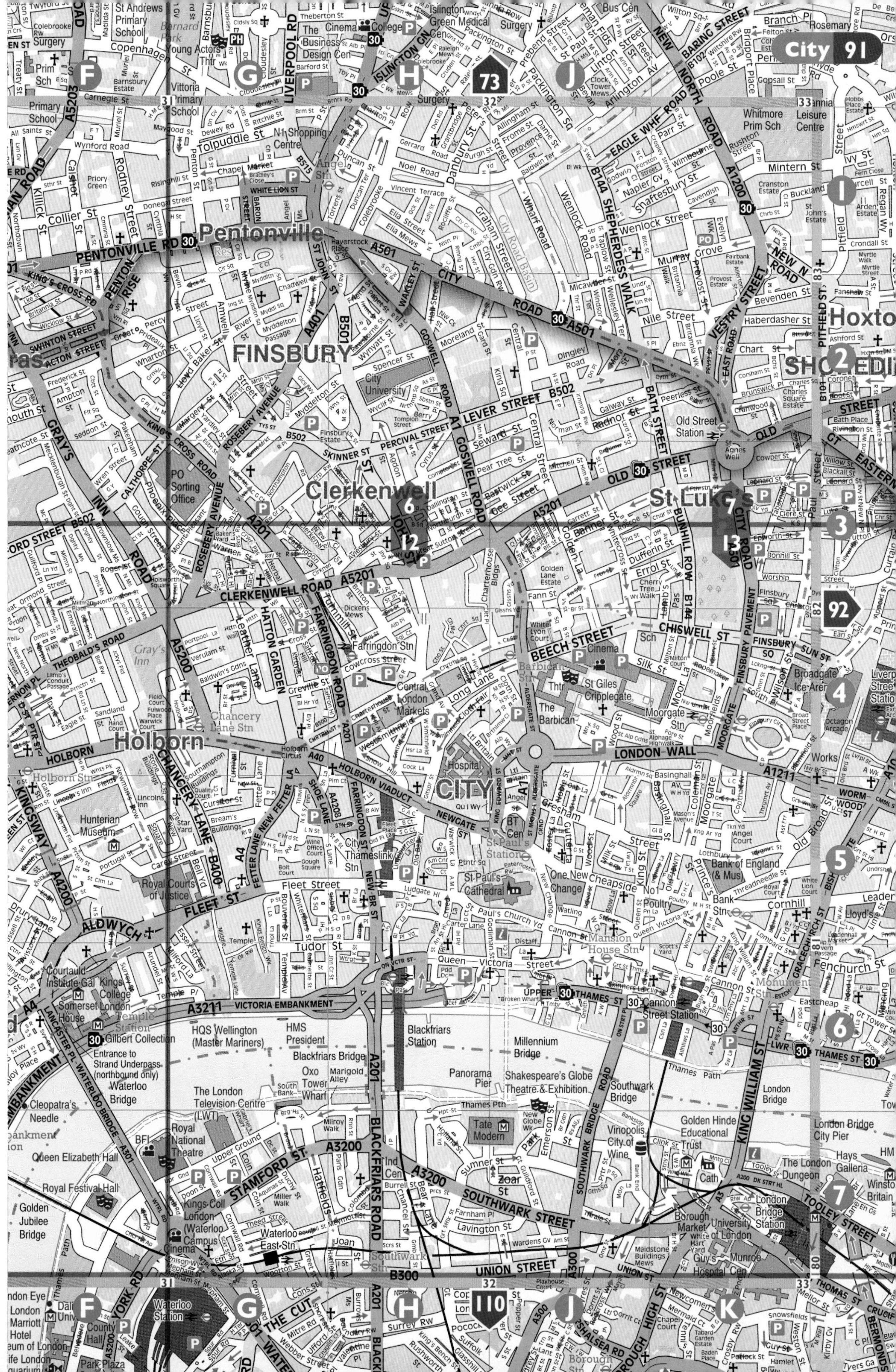
Pentonville
Finsbury
Clerkenwell
St Luke's
Hoxton
Shoreditch
Holborn
City
Pentonville Rd
King's Cross Rd
Gray's Inn Road
Rosebery Avenue
Clerkenwell Road
Farringdon Road
Goswell Road
City Road
Old Street
Bunhill Row
Finsbury Pavement
Moorgate
London Wall
Beech Street
Chiswell St
Holborn Viaduct
Newgate St
Fleet Street
Chancery Lane
Kingsway
Aldwych
Strand
Victoria Embankment
Upper Thames St
Queen Victoria Street
Cheapside
Cannon St
King William St
Gracechurch St
Southwark Street
Stamford St
Blackfriars Road
Union Street
Tooley Street
Southwark Bridge Road
Borough High St
Waterloo Bridge
Blackfriars Bridge
Millennium Bridge
Southwark Bridge
London Bridge
City University
PO Sorting Office
Farringdon Stn
Barbican Stn
Moorgate Stn
Old Street Station
Chancery Lane Stn
Holborn Stn
St Paul's Station
Blackfriars Station
Cannon Street Station
Mansion House Stn
Monument Stn
Bank Stn
London Bridge Station
Waterloo East Stn
Southwark Stn
Temple Station
City Thameslink Stn
The Barbican
St Giles Cripplegate
St Paul's Cathedral
Bank of England (& Mus)
Royal Courts of Justice
Hunterian Museum
Courtauld Institute Gal
Kings College London
Somerset House
Central London Markets
Tate Modern
Shakespeare's Globe Theatre & Exhibition
Vinopolis City of Wine
Golden Hinde Educational Trust
Borough Market
Royal National Theatre
Royal Festival Hall
Queen Elizabeth Hall
Golden Jubilee Bridge
Cleopatra's Needle
HQS Wellington (Master Mariners)
HMS President
Oxo Tower Wharf
The London Television Centre (LWT)
Waterloo Station
London Eye
The London Dungeon
Hays Galleria
London Bridge City Pier
Gray's Inn
73
92
110

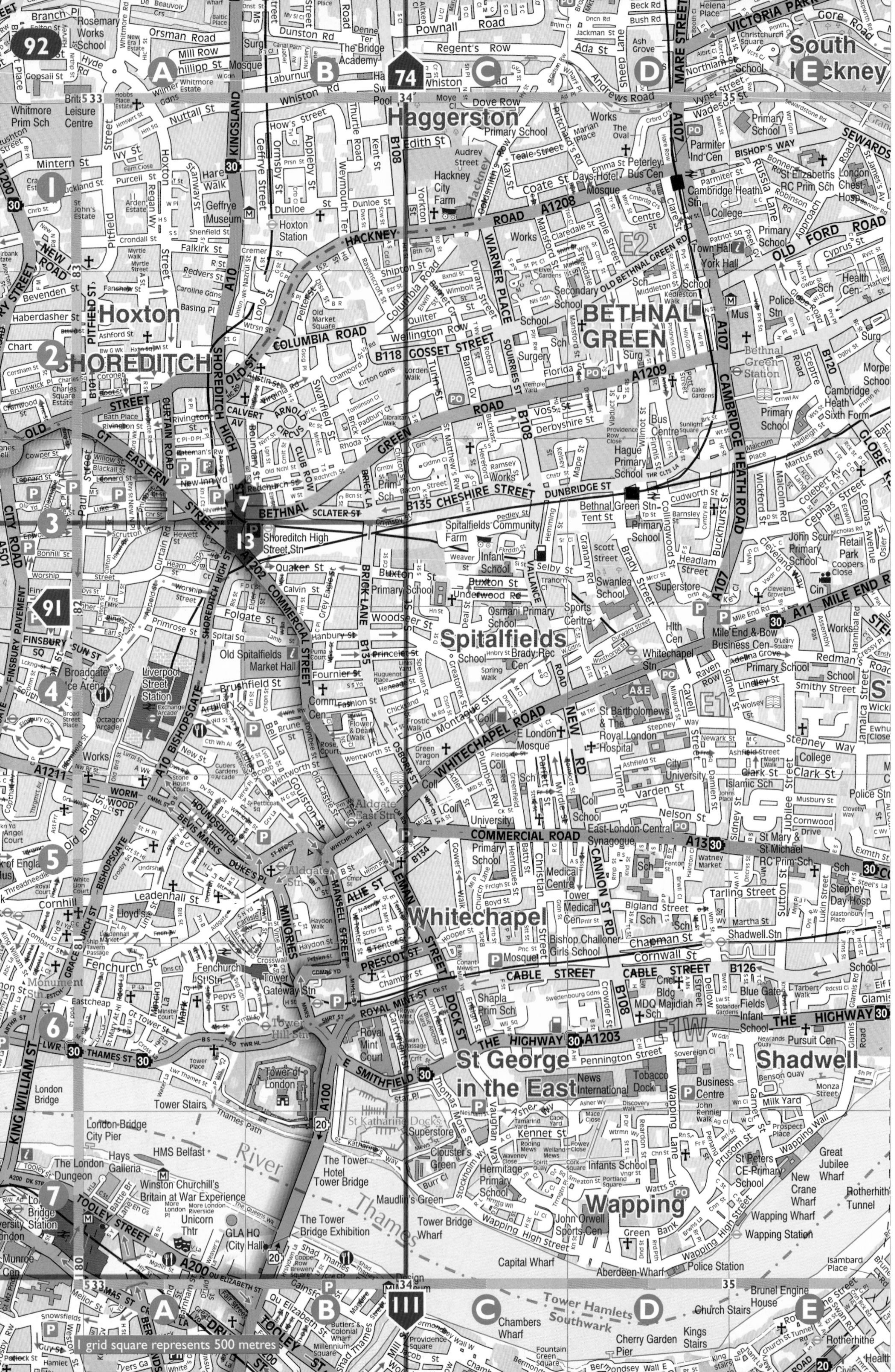

92
74
91
111
A
B
C
D
E
1
2
3
4
5
6
7
Haggerston
Hoxton
SHOREDITCH
BETHNAL GREEN
South Hackney
Spitalfields
Whitechapel
St George in the East
Shadwell
Wapping
E2
E1
E1W
VICTORIA PARK
KINGSLAND RD
SHOREDITCH HIGH ST
OLD ST
HACKNEY ROAD
COLUMBIA ROAD
B118 GOSSET STREET
A1208
A1209
GREEN ROAD
CAMBRIDGE HEATH ROAD
A107
MARE STREET
A11 MILE END RD
B135 CHESHIRE STREET
DUNBRIDGE ST
WHITECHAPEL ROAD
COMMERCIAL STREET
A1202
BRICK LANE
COMMERCIAL ROAD
A13
CABLE STREET
THE HIGHWAY
A1203
E SMITHFIELD
ROYAL MINT ST
MINORIES
LEMAN STREET
A100
TOOLEY STREET
A200
KING WILLIAM ST
CITY ROAD
A501
FINSBURY PAVEMENT
GT EASTERN STREET
CURTAIN ROAD
A10 BISHOPSGATE
HOUNDSDITCH
BEVIS MARKS
WORMWOOD ST
A1211
Fenchurch St
Leadenhall St
Cornhill
Eastcheap
LWR THAMES ST
Haggerston
Hoxton Station
Geffrye Museum
Hackney City Farm
Shoreditch High Street Stn
Liverpool Street Station
Broadgate Ice Arena
Old Spitalfields Market Hall
Spitalfields Community Farm
Bethnal Green Stn
Bethnal Green Station
Whitechapel Stn
Aldgate Stn
Aldgate East Stn
Tower Gateway Stn
Tower Hill Stn
Fenchurch St Stn
Monument Stn
London Bridge Station
Shadwell Stn
Wapping Station
Tower of London
St Katharine Docks
The Tower Hotel Tower Bridge
The Tower Bridge Exhibition
Tower Bridge Wharf
HMS Belfast
Hays Galleria
The London Dungeon
Winston Churchill's Britain at War Experience
GLA HQ (City Hall)
London Bridge City Pier
Tower Stairs
River Thames
The Royal London Hospital
St Bartholomews & The Royal London
E London Mosque
Mile End & Bow Business Cen
Tobacco Dock
News International
Royal Mint Court
Capital Wharf
Cherry Garden Pier
Rotherhithe Tunnel
Tower Hamlets
Southwark
Brunel Engine House
Great Jubilee Wharf
1 grid square represents 500 metres

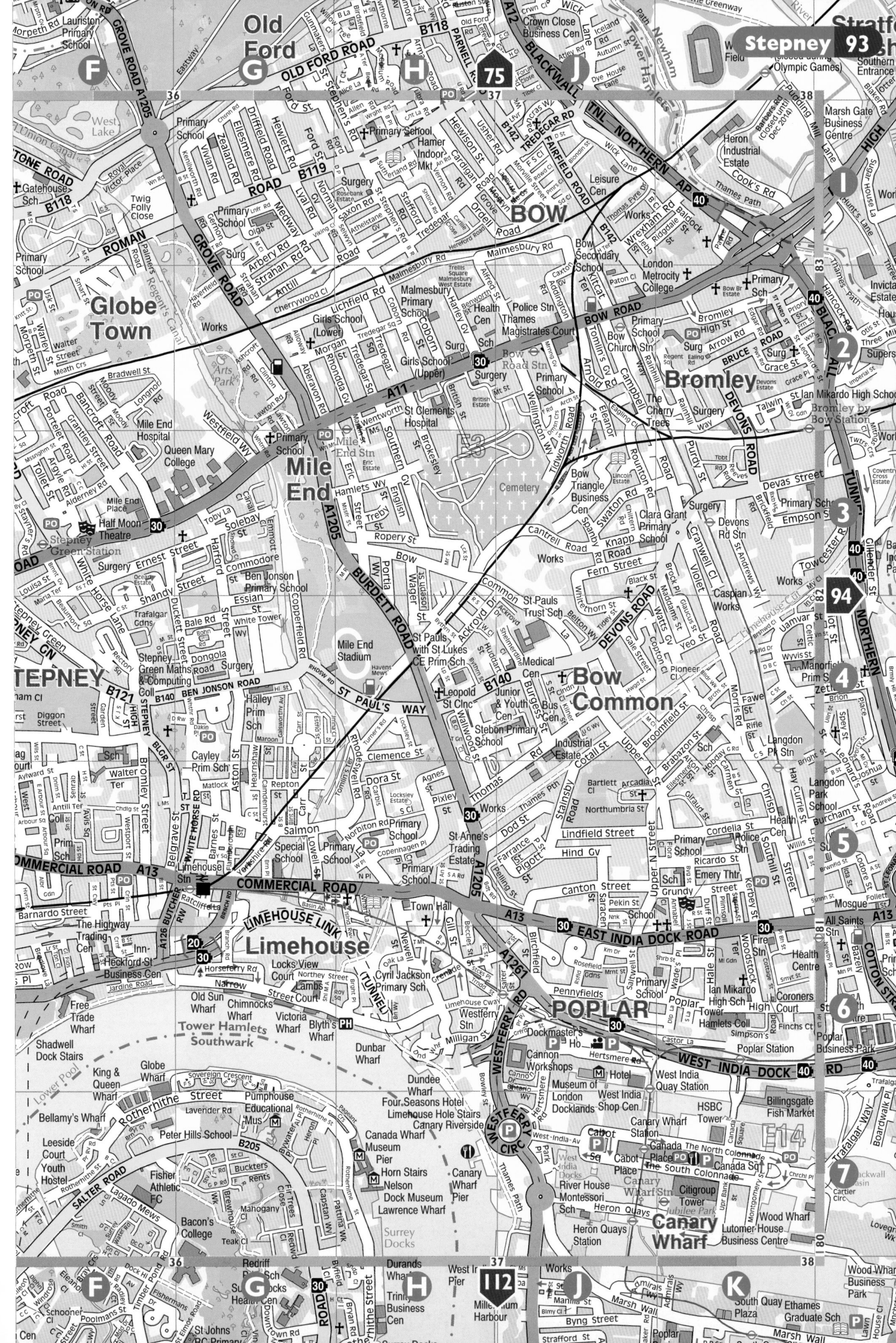
Old Ford
OLD FORD ROAD
GROVE ROAD A1205
BLACKWALL
TNL NORTHERN AP
75
Globe Town
ROMAN ROAD
BOW
BOW ROAD
A11
Bromley
DEVONS ROAD
Mile End
BURDETT ROAD
A1205
Mile End Stadium
ST PAUL'S WAY
Bow Common
STEPNEY
COMMERCIAL ROAD
A13
EAST INDIA DOCK ROAD
LIMEHOUSE LINK
Limehouse
POPLAR
WEST INDIA DOCK RD
WESTFERRY RD
WESTFERRY CIRC
Canary Wharf
E3
E14
Cemetery
Tower Hamlets
Southwark
Lower Pool
ROTHERHITHE STREET
SALTER ROAD
Surrey Docks
94
112
F
G
H
J
K
I
2
3
4
5
6
7
36
37
38
80
81
82
83

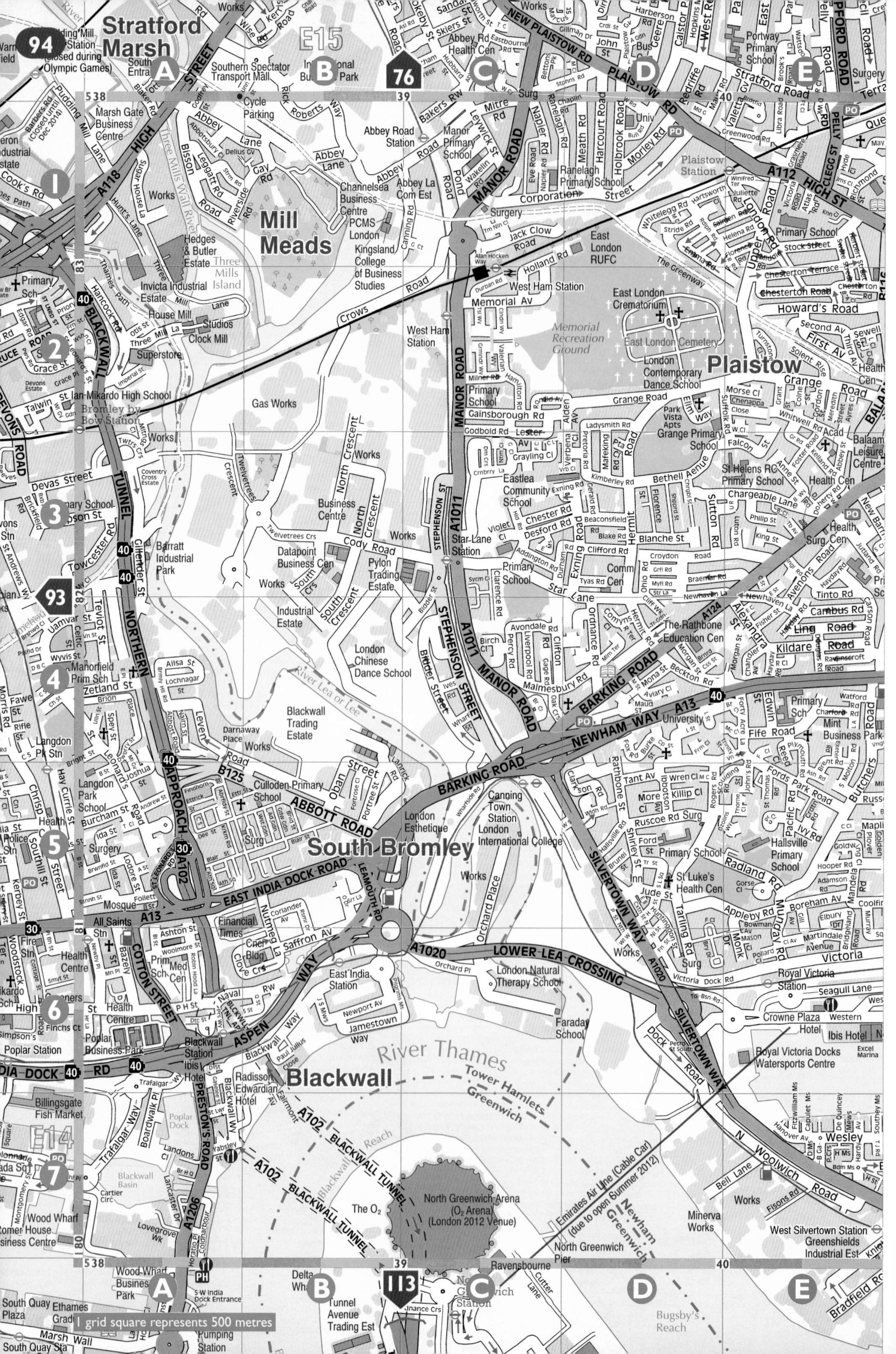

94
Stratford Marsh
Pudding Mill Lane Station (closed during Olympic Games)
E15
76
A
B
C
D
E
Southern Spectator Transport Mall
International Business Park
Abbey Rd Health Cen
NEW PLAISTOW RD
PLAISTOW RD
Portway Primary School
Stratford Road
Surgery
538
39
40
Cycle Parking
Marsh Gate Business Centre
Abbey Road Station
Manor Primary School
Univ
Plaistow Station
A112
HIGH ST
A118
HIGH STREET
Three Mills Wall River
Channelsea Business Centre
PCMS London
Kingsland College of Business Studies
Abbey La Com Est
Mill Meads
Hedges & Butler Estate
Three Mills Island
Invicta Industrial Estate
House Mill
Studios
Clock Mill
Ranelagh Primary School
Corporation Street
Surgery
Jack Clow Road
East London RUFC
West Ham Station
Primary School
East London Crematorium
East London Cemetery
Memorial Recreation Ground
London Contemporary Dance School
Plaistow
Crows Road
West Ham Station
Superstore
Bromley by Bow Station
Ian Mikardo High School
Gas Works
BLACKWALL
TUNNEL
NORTHERN
APPROACH
DEVONS ROAD
Devas Street
Primary School
Barratt Industrial Park
Works
North Crescent
Business Centre
Datapoint Business Cen
Pylon Trading Estate
Cody Road
Industrial Estate
London Chinese Dance School
MANOR ROAD
A1011
STEPHENSON STREET
Star Lane Station
Eastlea Community School
Grange Road
Grange Primary School
St Helens RC Primary School
Health Cen
Primary School
Comm Cen
Star Lane
The Rathbone Education Cen
BARKING ROAD
A124
93
Manorfield Prim Sch
Langdon Pk Stn
Langdon Park School
Blackwall Trading Estate
River Lea or Lee
Culloden Primary School
ABBOTT ROAD
BARKING ROAD
NEWHAM WAY
A13
University
Canning Town Station
London International College
London Esthetique
South Bromley
Health Cen
Police Stn
EAST INDIA DOCK ROAD
A13
Surgery
Mosque
All Saints Stn
Financial Times
Saffron Av
COTTON STREET
A102
Works
Orchard Place
SILVERTOWN WAY
A1020
LOWER LEA CROSSING
Hallsville Primary School
Primary School
St Luke's Health Cen
Radland Rd
Victoria Dock Rd
Royal Victoria Station
East India Station
Jamestown Way
London Natural Therapy School
Faraday School
Crowne Plaza Hotel
Ibis Hotel
Royal Victoria Docks Watersports Centre
Poplar Station
Poplar Business Park
Blackwall Station
Ibis Hotel
ASPEN WAY
EAST INDIA DOCK RD
Radisson Edwardian Hotel
River Thames
Blackwall
Tower Hamlets
Greenwich
Billingsgate Fish Market
E14
Poplar Dock
Blackwall Basin
PRESTON'S ROAD
A1206
A102 BLACKWALL TUNNEL
The O2
North Greenwich Arena (O2 Arena) (London 2012 Venue)
Emirates Air Line (Cable Car) (due to open Summer 2012)
Newham
Greenwich
North Greenwich Pier
N WOOLWICH ROAD
Works
Minerva Works
West Silvertown Station
Greenshields Industrial Est
Wood Wharf Business Park
113
North Greenwich Station
Tunnel Avenue Trading Est
South Quay Plaza
Marsh Wall
South Quay Sta
Pumping Station
Bugsby's Reach
1 grid square represents 500 metres

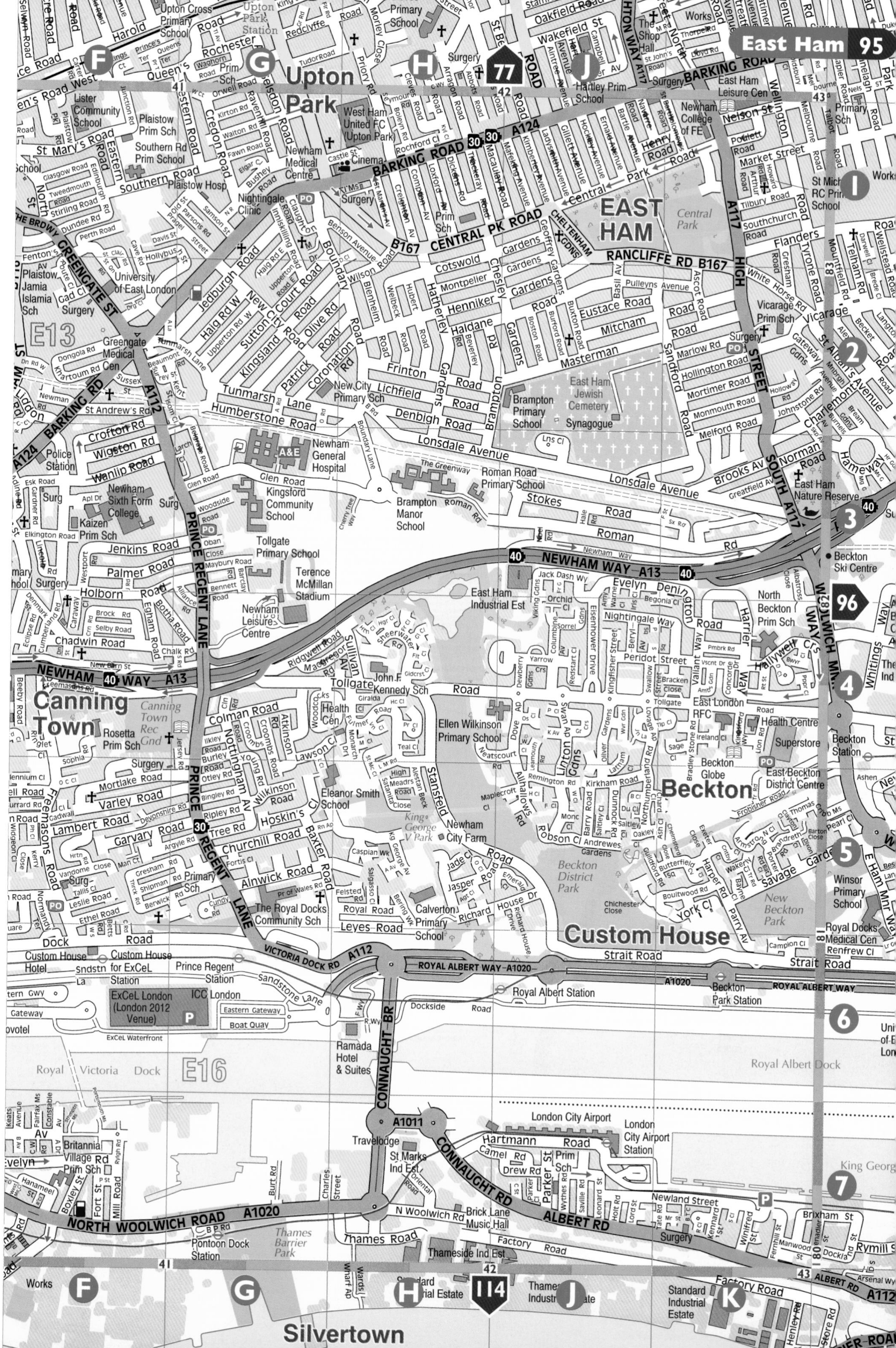
Upton Park
East Ham
Canning Town
Beckton
Custom House
Silvertown
E13
E16
Barking Road
Central Pk Road
Rancliffe Rd B167
High Street South A117
Newham Way A13
Prince Regent Lane
Victoria Dock Rd A112
Royal Albert Way A1020
Connaught Br
Connaught Rd
Albert Rd
North Woolwich Road A1020
Greengate St
Woolwich Mnr Way
West Ham United FC (Upton Park)
Newham General Hospital
East Ham Jewish Cemetery
Central Park
Royal Victoria Dock
Royal Albert Dock
London City Airport
ExCeL London (London 2012 Venue)
Beckton District Park
King George V Park
Newham City Farm
77
96
114
F G H J K
1 2 3 4 5 6 7
41 42 43

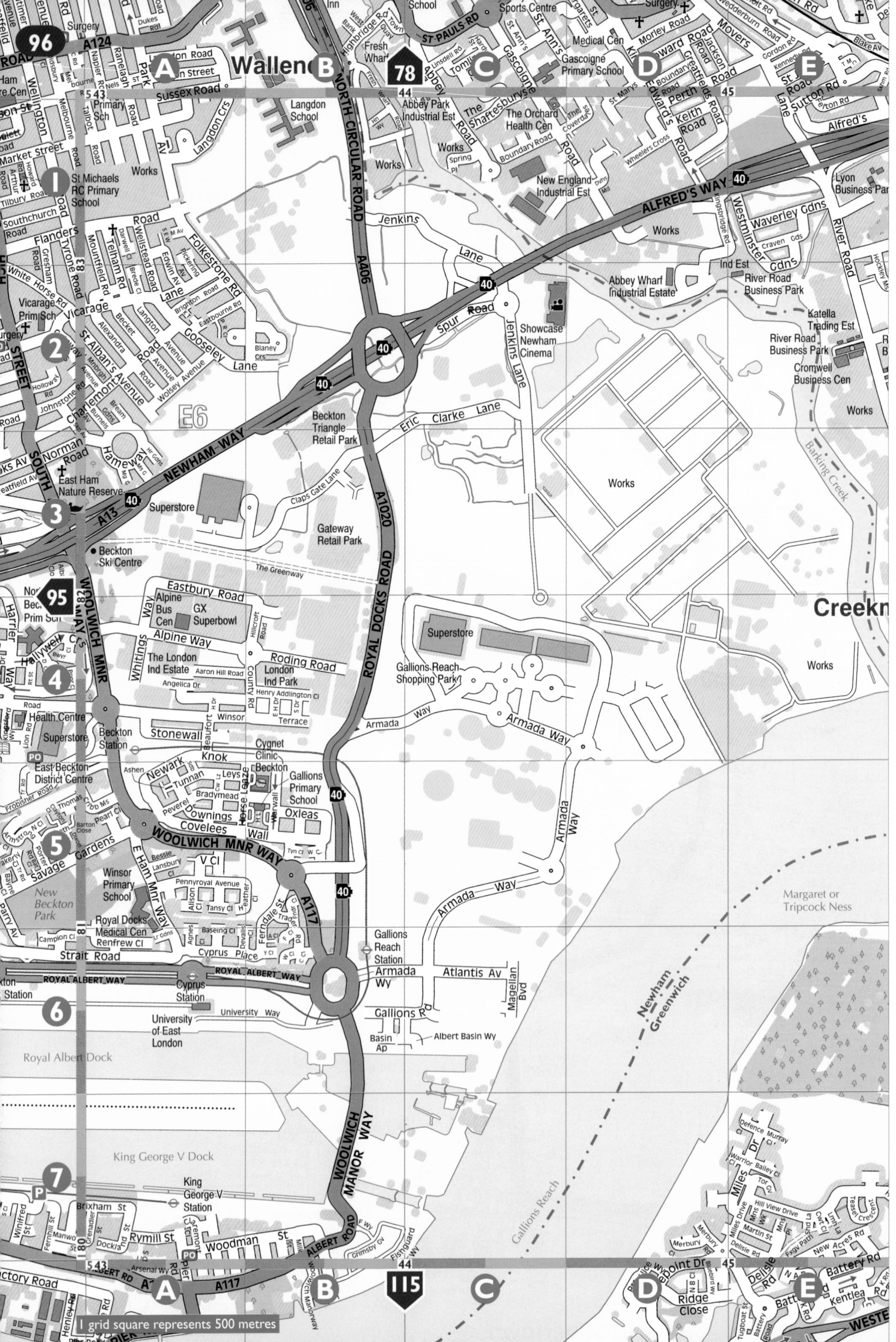

96
78
95
115
A B C D E
1 2 3 4 5 6 7
Wallend
Creekm
NORTH CIRCULAR ROAD
A406
ROYAL DOCKS ROAD
A1020
NEWHAM WAY
A13
ALFRED'S WAY
WOOLWICH MNR WAY
WOOLWICH MANOR WAY
ROYAL ALBERT WAY
A117
A124
Sussex Road
Langdon School
Abbey Park Industrial Est
The Orchard Health Cen
Gascoigne Primary School
New England Industrial Est
St Michaels RC Primary School
Abbey Wharf Industrial Estate
River Road Business Park
Katella Trading Est
Cromwell Business Cen
Showcase Newham Cinema
Beckton Triangle Retail Park
Gateway Retail Park
Eric Clarke Lane
Superstore
Beckton Ski Centre
East Ham Nature Reserve
Gallions Reach Shopping Park
Armada Way
Works
Eastbury Road
Alpine Way
Roding Road
The London Ind Estate
London Ind Park
Beckton Station
East Beckton District Centre
Gallions Primary School
Winsor Primary School
New Beckton Park
Royal Docks Medical Cen
Strait Road
Cyprus Station
University of East London
Gallions Reach Station
Atlantis Av
Royal Albert Dock
King George V Dock
King George V Station
Margaret or Tripcock Ness
Newham
Greenwich
Gallions Reach
Barking Creek
Albert Road
Ridge Close
Battery Rd
1 grid square represents 500 metres

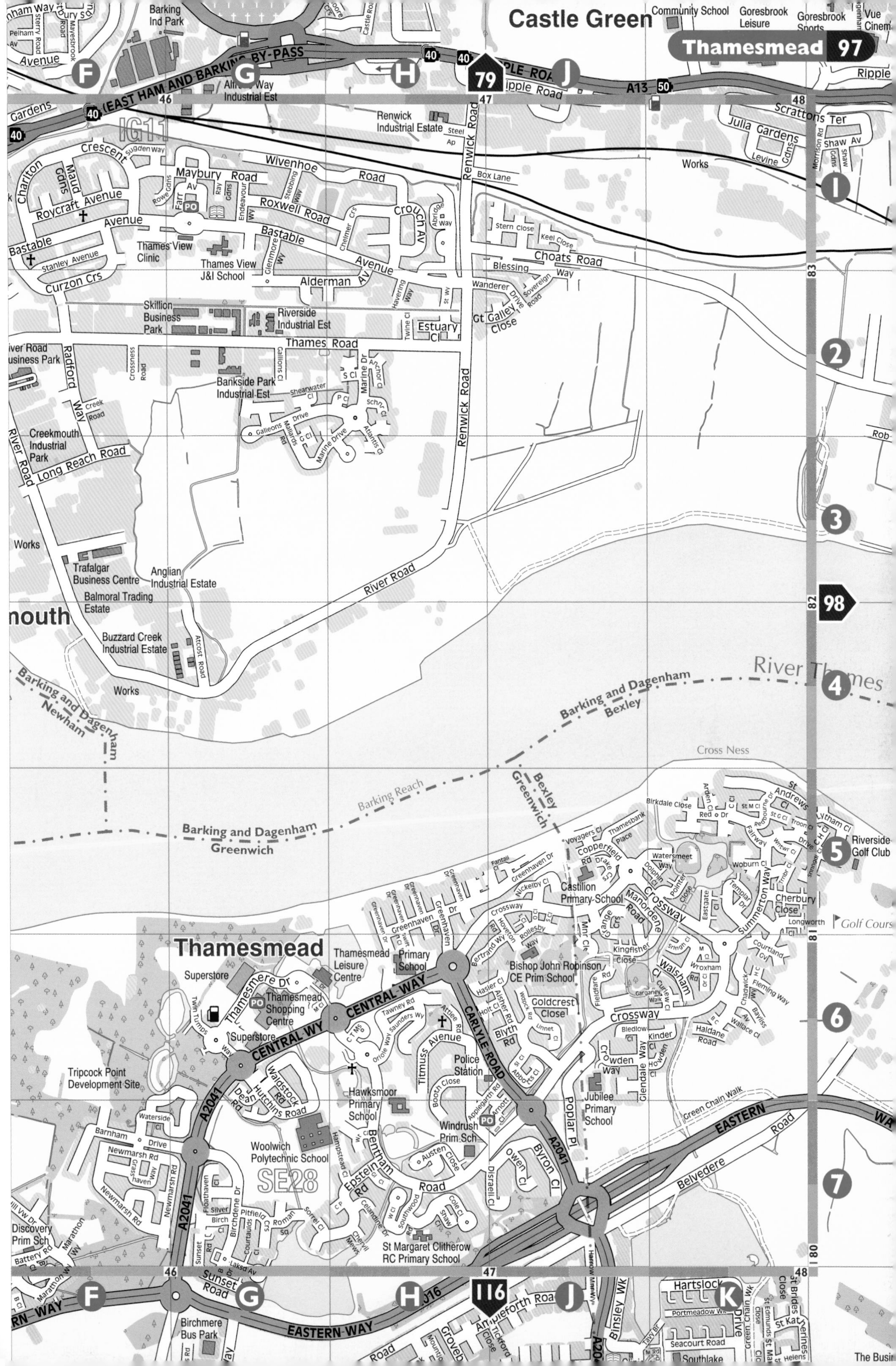
Castle Green
Barking Ind Park
Community School
Goresbrook Leisure
Goresbrook Sports
EAST HAM AND BARKING BY-PASS
Ripple Road
A13
Renwick Industrial Estate
Renwick Road
Alfreds Way Industrial Est
IG11
Maybury Road
Wivenhoe Road
Roycraft Avenue
Roxwell Road
Bastable Avenue
Crouch Av
Stern Close
Keel Close
Choats Road
Blessing Way
Thames View Clinic
Thames View J&I School
Curzon Crs
Alderman Av
Skillion Business Park
Riverside Industrial Est
Estuary Cl
Gt Galley Close
Thames Road
River Road Business Park
Radford Way
Bankside Park Industrial Est
Creekmouth Industrial Park
Long Reach Road
Marine Drive
Works
Trafalgar Business Centre
Anglian Industrial Estate
Balmoral Trading Estate
River Road
Buzzard Creek Industrial Estate
Atcost Road
River Thames
Barking and Dagenham
Newham
Bexley
Greenwich
Barking Reach
Cross Ness
Riverside Golf Club
Thamesmead
Thamesmead Leisure Centre
Primary School
Thamesmead Shopping Centre
Superstore
Central Way
Carlyle Road
Castilion Primary School
Bishop John Robinson CE Prim School
Goldcrest Close
Crossway
Tripcock Point Development Site
Hawksmoor Primary School
Police Station
Windrush Prim Sch
Woolwich Polytechnic School
SE28
Jubilee Primary School
Eastern Way
Belvedere Road
Green Chain Walk
A2041
Discovery Prim Sch
St Margaret Clitherow RC Primary School
Birchmere Bus Park
Sunset Road
Hartslock
Seacourt Road
Southlake
98
79
116

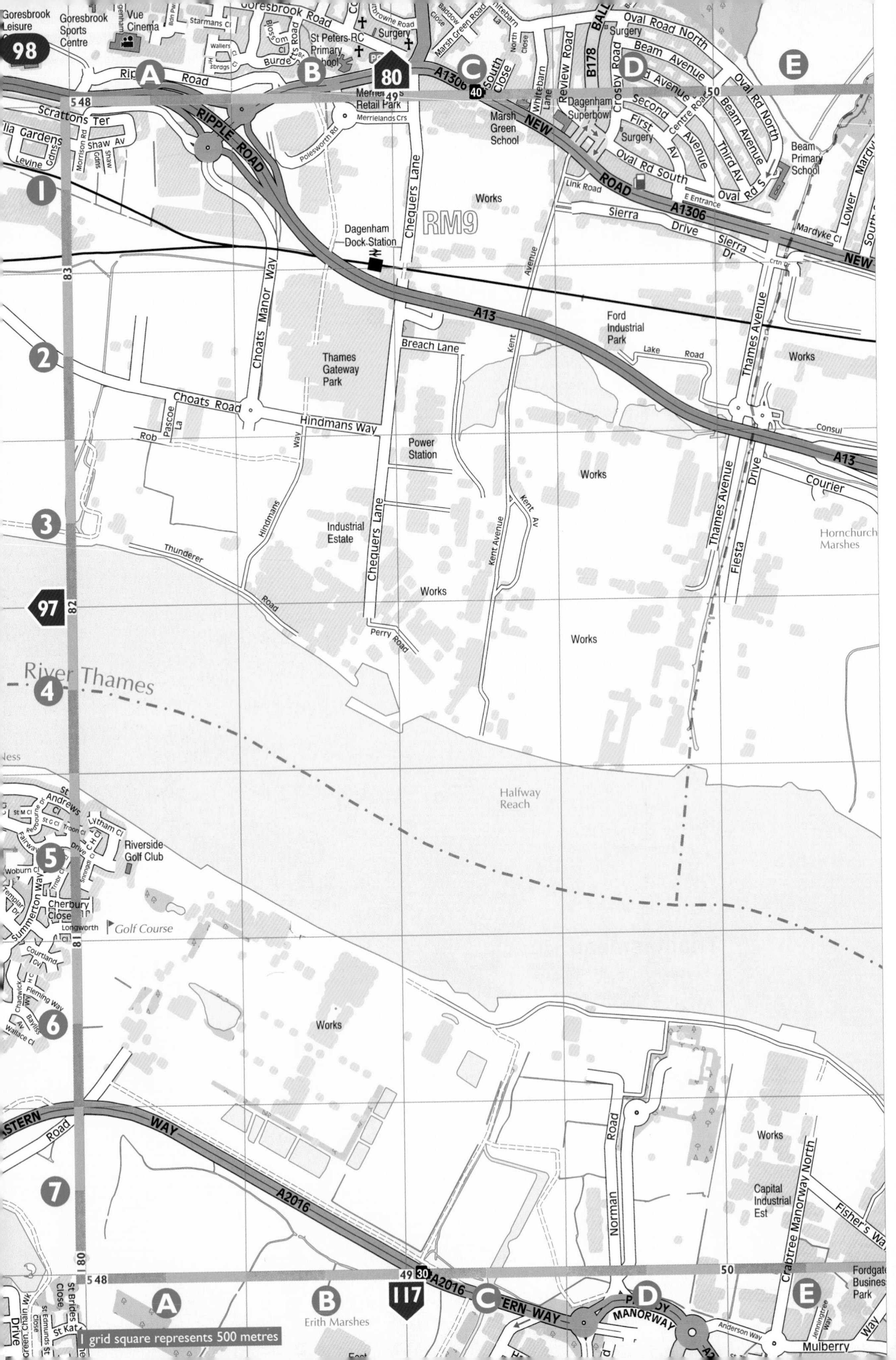

98
80
97
117
Ripple Road
Goresbrook Road
Goresbrook Sports Centre
Vue Cinema
St Peters RC Primary School
Surgery
Merrielands Retail Park
Scrattons Ter
Levine Gdns
Shaw Av
Poleswortth Rd
Merrielands Crs
A1306
New Road
Marsh Green School
Marsh Green Road
South Close
Whitebarn Lane
Review Road
Dagenham Superbowl
Crosby Road
Oval Road North
Beam Avenue
Second Avenue
First Avenue
Centre Road
Third Av
Oval Rd South
Oval Rd S
Beam Primary School
Link Road
E Entrance
Sierra Drive
Sierra Dr
Mardyke Cl
Works
RM9
Dagenham Dock Station
Chequers Lane
Choats Manor Way
A13
Ford Industrial Park
Lake Road
Thames Avenue
Breach Lane
Thames Gateway Park
Choats Road
Hindmans Way
Pascoe La
Rob
Power Station
Consul
Courier
Kent Avenue
Kent Av
Fiesta Drive
Hornchurch Marshes
Industrial Estate
Thunderer Road
Perry Road
River Thames
Halfway Reach
St Andrews Cl
Lytham Cl
Riverside Golf Club
Woburn Cl
Summerton Way
Cherbury Close
Longworth
Golf Course
Courtland Gv
Fleming Way
Chadwick Way
Bayliss Av
Wallace Cl
Eastern Way
A2016
Road
Norman Road
Capital Industrial Est
Crabtree Manorway North
Fisher's Way
Fordgate Business Park
Erith Marshes
St Brides Close
St Edmunds Close
Green Chain Wk
Manorway
Anderson Way
Jenningtree Way
Mulberry
1 grid square represents 500 metres

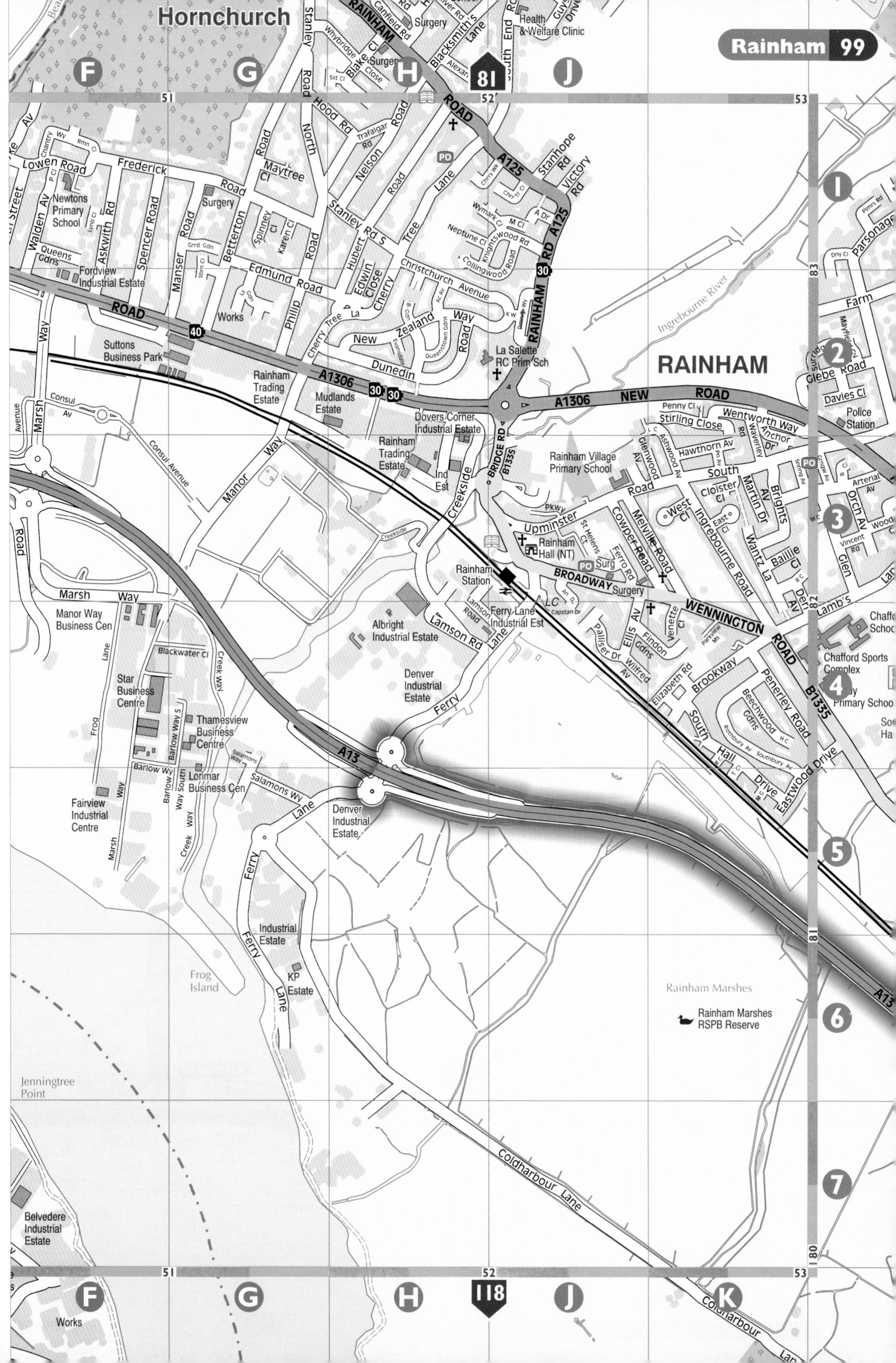

Hornchurch
RAINHAM
Rainham Marshes
Rainham Marshes RSPB Reserve
Frog Island
Jenningtree Point
Belvedere Industrial Estate
Works
Newtons Primary School
Fordview Industrial Estate
Suttons Business Park
Rainham Trading Estate
Mudlands Estate
Dovers Corner Industrial Estate
Rainham Village Primary School
Rainham Hall (NT)
Rainham Station
Ferry Lane Industrial Est
Albright Industrial Estate
Denver Industrial Estate
Manor Way Business Cen
Star Business Centre
Thamesview Business Centre
Lorimar Business Cen
Fairview Industrial Centre
KP Estate
Industrial Estate
La Salette RC Prim Sch
Health & Welfare Clinic
Police Station
Chafford Sports Complex
NEW ROAD
WENNINGTON ROAD
BROADWAY
Coldharbour Lane
A13
A1306
A125
B1335

81
118

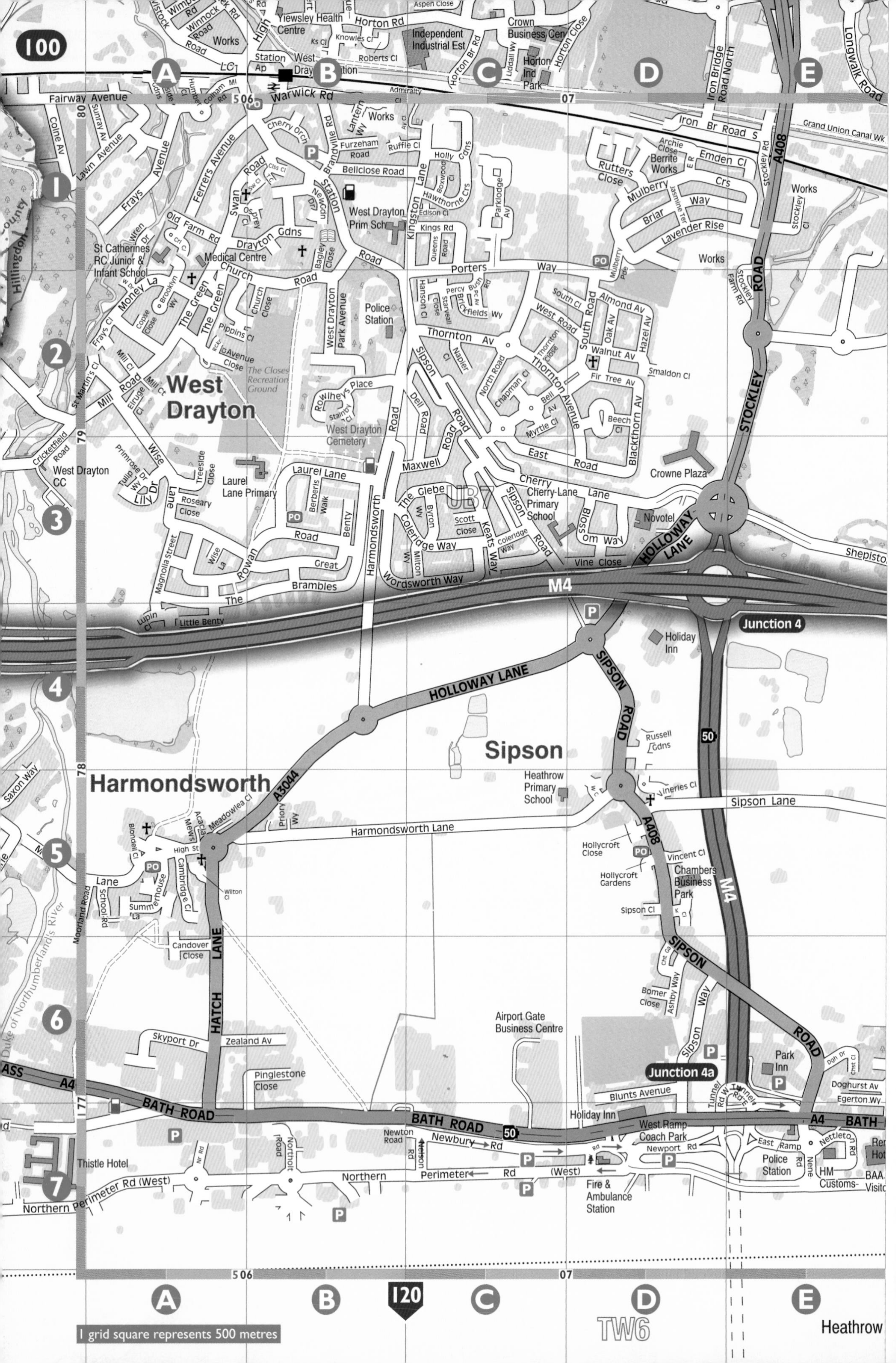
100
A
B
C
D
E
1
2
3
4
5
6
7
506
07
80
79
78
77
Yiewsley Health Centre
Horton Rd
Aspen Close
Crown Business Cen
Independent Industrial Est
Horton Close
Horton Br Rd
Horton Ind Park
Knowles Cl
Roberts Cl
Works
Winnock Rd
Road
Station Ap
West Drayton
Warwick Rd
Admiralty Cl
Fairway Avenue
Colne Av
Sunray Av
Lawn Avenue
Frays Avenue
Ferrers Avenue
Cherry Orch
Brandville Rd
Lantern Wy
Works
Furzeham Road
Ruffle Cl
Holly Gdns
Bellclose Road
Swan Road
Station Road
Kingston Lane
Boxwood Cl
Hawthorne Crs
Edison Cl
Parklodge Av
Iron Bridge Road North
Iron Br Road S
Grand Union Canal Wk
Longwalk Road
Archie Close
Berrite Works
Emden Cl
Rutters Close
Mulberry Crs
Briar Way
Jasmine Ter
Lavender Rise
Stockley Rd
A408
Stockley Cl
Works
Old Farm Rd
Osprey Cl
Drayton Gdns
West Drayton Prim Sch
Kings Rd
Queens Rd
St Catherines RC Junior & Infant School
Medical Centre
Church Road
Bagley Close
Porters Way
Mulberry Pde
Works
Stockley Farm Rd
STOCKLEY ROAD
Money La
Brooklyn Wy
Copse Close
The Green
Church Close
West Drayton Park Avenue
Police Station
Hanson Cl
Starveall Close
Percy Bush Rd
Brickfields Wy
South Cl
West Road
South Road
Almond Av
Oak Av
Hazel Av
Thornton Av
Walnut Av
Smaldon Cl
Fir Tree Av
Frays Cl
Mill Cl
Mill Road
Mill Ct
Pippins Cl
Avenue Close
The Closes Recreation Ground
West Drayton
Napier Cl
North Road
Thornton Close
Chapman Cl
Thornton Avenue
Bell Av
Myrtle Cl
Beech Cl
Blackthorn Av
St Martin's Cl
Rowlheys Place
Stainby Cl
Sipson Road
Dell Road
West Drayton Cemetery
Harmondsworth Road
Cricketfield Road
West Drayton CC
Primrose Dr
Tulip Wy
Lily Dr
Wise Lane
Treeside Close
Laurel Lane Primary
Laurel Lane
Berberis Walk
Maxwell Road
East Road
Crowne Plaza
Rosary Close
The Glebe
Byron Wy
Coleridge Wy
UB7
Sipson Road
Cherry Lane
Cherry Lane Primary School
Bloss om Way
Novotel
Scott Close
Keats Way
Coleridge Way
Milton Wy
Benty
Great
Brambles
Rowan
Magnolia Street
Wise La
Wordsworth Way
Vine Close
HOLLOWAY LANE
Shepiston
M4
The
Lupin Cl
Little Benty
Junction 4
Holiday Inn
HOLLOWAY LANE
SIPSON ROAD
Russell Gdns
Sipson
Heathrow Primary School
Harmondsworth
A3044
Meadowlea Cl
Acacia Mews
Priory Wy
Harmondsworth Lane
Vineries Cl
Sipson Lane
A408
Hollycroft Close
Hollycroft Gardens
Vincent Cl
Chambers Business Park
Sipson Cl
Saxon Way
Blondell Cl
High St
Cambridge Cl
Wilton Cl
Lane
School Rd
Summerhouse La
Moorland Road
Duke of Northumberland's River
Candover Close
HATCH LANE
SIPSON ROAD
Bomer Close
Ashby Way
Sipson Way
Airport Gate Business Centre
Skyport Dr
Zealand Av
Park Inn
Junction 4a
Doghurst Av
Egerton Wy
Pinglestone Close
Blunts Avenue
Holiday Inn
A4
BATH ROAD
BATH ROAD
West Ramp Coach Park
Tunnel Rd W
Tunnel Rd E
Thistle Hotel
Nr Rd
Northolt Road
Newton Road
Newbury Rd
Nelson Rd
Newport Rd
East Ramp
Police Station
Nene Rd
HM Customs
Northern Perimeter Rd (West)
Northern Perimeter Rd (West)
Fire & Ambulance Station
120
1 grid square represents 500 metres
TW6
Heathrow

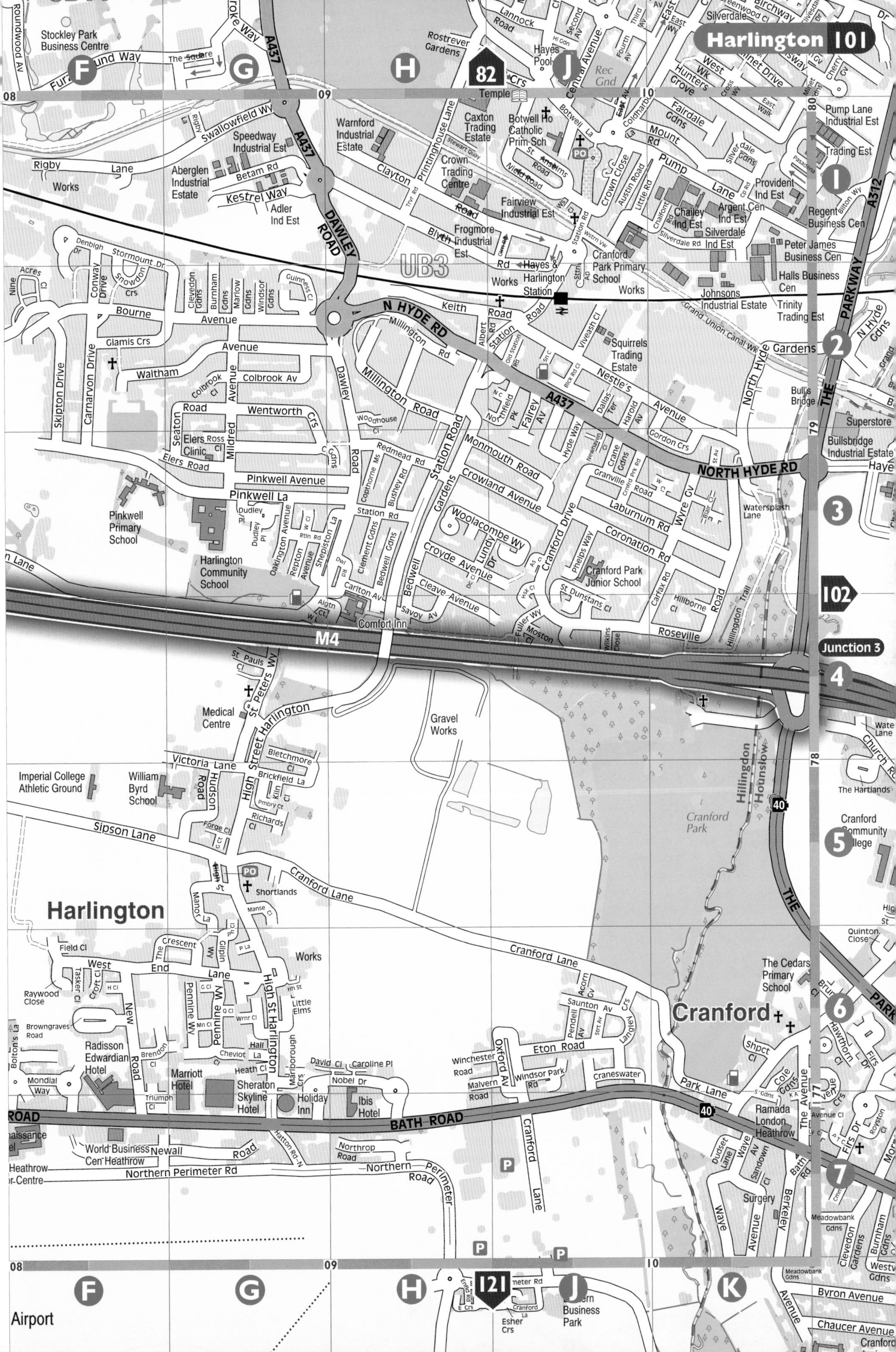
Harlington
Cranford
M4
N HYDE RD
NORTH HYDE RD
BATH ROAD
DAWLEY ROAD
THE PARKWAY
Junction 3
UB3
Stockley Park Business Centre
Hayes & Harlington Station
Harlington Community School
Pinkwell Primary School
Cranford Park
Gravel Works
Imperial College Athletic Ground
William Byrd School
Radisson Edwardian Hotel
Marriott Hotel
Sheraton Skyline Hotel
Holiday Inn
Ibis Hotel
Ramada London Heathrow
Comfort Inn

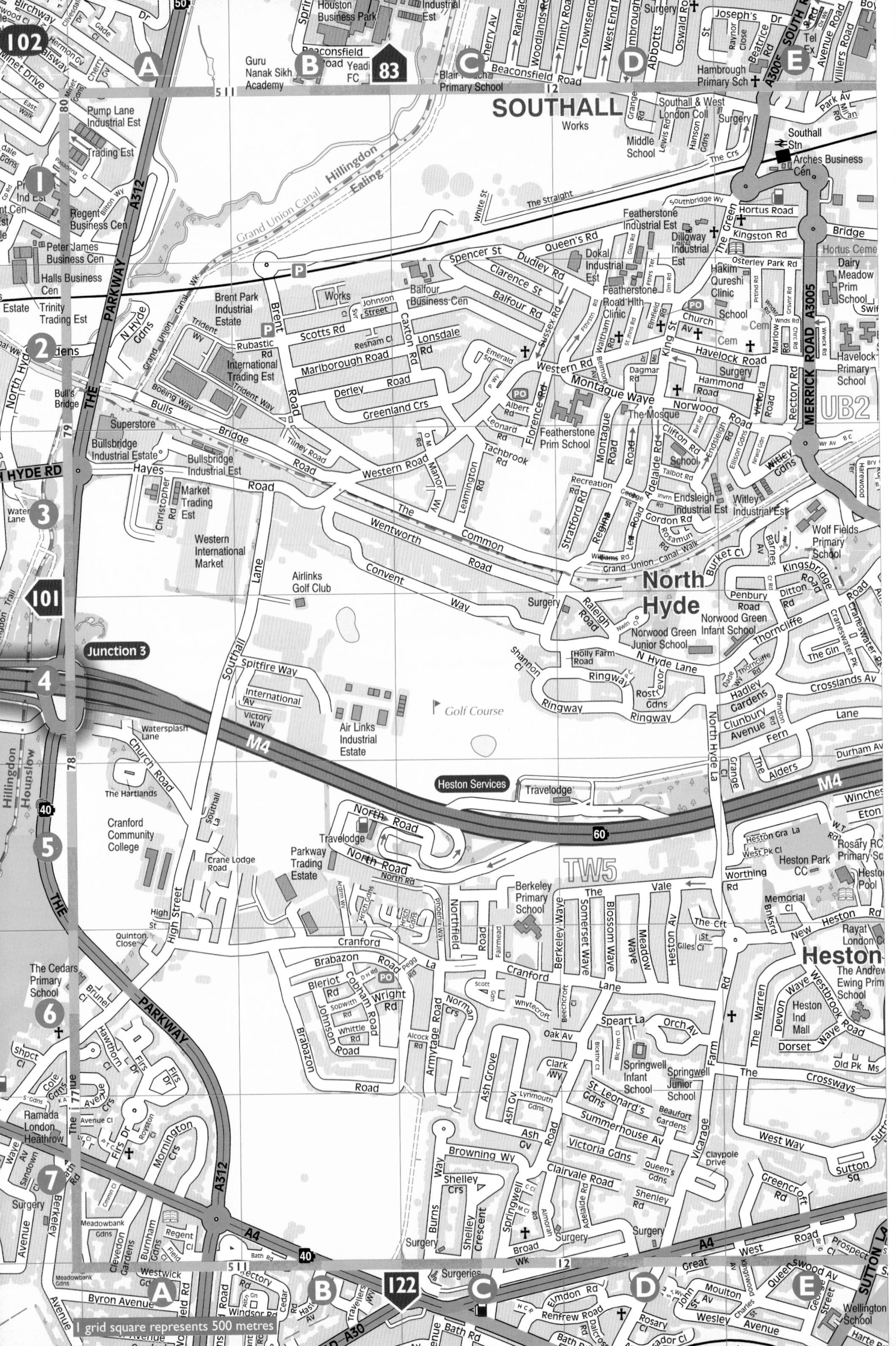

102
83
101
122
SOUTHALL
North Hyde
Heston
Junction 3
Heston Services
M4
A312
THE PARKWAY
A3005
MERRICK ROAD A3005
A4
UB2
TW5
Southall Stn
Houston Business Park
Guru Nanak Sikh Academy
Blair Peach Primary School
Beaconsfield Road
Hambrough Primary Sch
Southall & West London Coll
Middle School
Arches Business Cen
Pump Lane Industrial Est
Trading Est
Regent Business Cen
Peter James Business Cen
Halls Business Cen
Trinity Trading Est
Brent Park Industrial Estate
International Trading Est
Balfour Business Cen
Featherstone Industrial Est
Dilloway Industrial Est
Dokal Industrial Est
Featherstone Road Hlth Clinic
Hakim Qureshi Clinic
Dairy Meadow Prim School
Havelock Primary School
Featherstone Prim School
The Mosque
Endsleigh Industrial Est
Witley Industrial Est
Wolf Fields Primary School
Bullsbridge Industrial Estate
Bullsbridge Industrial Est
Superstore
Market Trading Est
Western International Market
Airlinks Golf Club
Air Links Industrial Estate
Golf Course
Norwood Green Junior School
Norwood Green Infant School
Travelodge
Parkway Trading Estate
Cranford Community College
The Hartlands
Berkeley Primary School
Heston Park CC
Rosary RC Primary Sc
The Andrew Ewing Prim School
Heston Ind Mall
Springwell Infant School
Springwell Junior School
The Cedars Primary School
Ramada London Heathrow
Grand Union Canal
Hillingdon
Ealing
Hounslow
Western Road
Hayes Road
Southall Lane
North Hyde Lane
Cranford Lane
Vicarage Farm Rd
Great West Road
Wellington School
1 grid square represents 500 metres

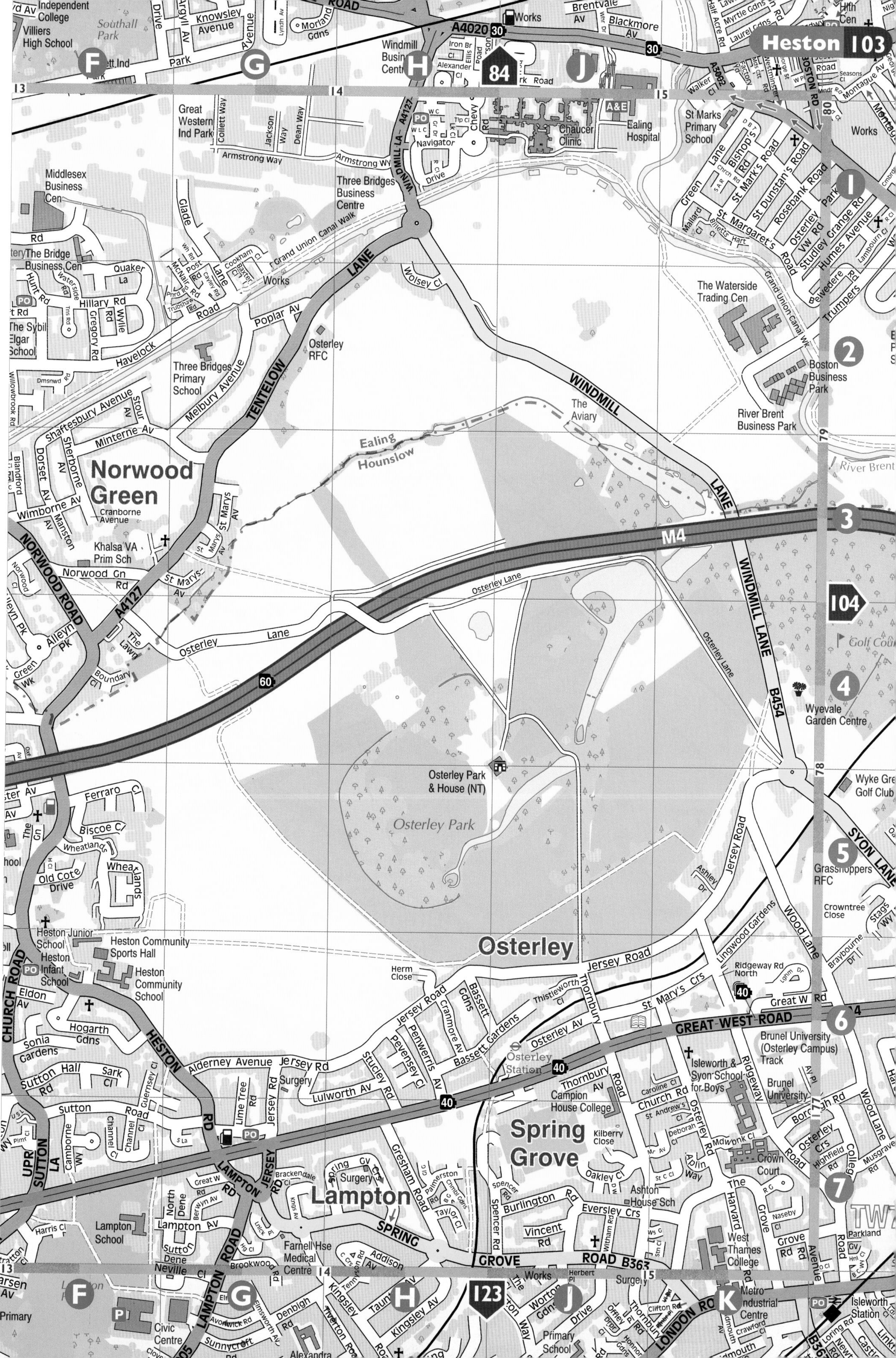

Heston 103
84
104
123
Independent College
Villiers High School
Southall Park
Great Western Ind Park
Middlesex Business Cen
The Bridge Business Cen
Three Bridges Business Centre
Grand Union Canal Walk
Windmill Business Centre
Works
A4020
A4127
A3002
B454
B363
M4
Ealing Hospital
Chaucer Clinic
A&E
St Marks Primary School
The Waterside Trading Cen
Boston Business Park
River Brent Business Park
River Brent
The Sybil Elgar School
Three Bridges Primary School
Osterley RFC
Norwood Green
Khalsa VA Prim Sch
Ealing
Hounslow
The Aviary
Osterley Park & House (NT)
Osterley Park
Osterley
Golf Course
Wyevale Garden Centre
Wyke Green Golf Club
Grasshoppers RFC
Heston Junior School
Heston Infant School
Heston Community Sports Hall
Heston Community School
Osterley Station
Isleworth & Syon School for Boys
Brunel University (Osterley Campus) Track
Brunel University
Campion House College
Spring Grove
Ashton House Sch
West Thames College
Crown Court
Lampton
Lampton School
Farnell Hse Medical Centre
Civic Centre
Primary School
Metro Industrial Centre
Isleworth Station
Surgery
TENTELOW LANE
WINDMILL LANE
NORWOOD ROAD
HESTON RD
GREAT WEST ROAD
LAMPTON ROAD
CHURCH ROAD
UPR SUTTON LA
SYON LANE
SPRING GROVE ROAD B363
LONDON ROAD
Havelock Road
Jersey Road
Osterley Lane
Wood Lane
Thornbury Road
Osterley Av
St Mary's Crs
Sutton Road
Sutton Hall Rd
Hogarth Gdns
Sonia Gardens
Alderney Avenue
Lulworth Av
Pevensey Cl
Penwerris Av
Cranmore Av
Bassett Gardens
Gresham Road
Burlington Rd
Eversley Crs
Vincent Rd
Oakley Cl
Osterley Rd
Aplin Way
Harvard Rd
Grove Rd
College Rd
Borough Rd
Osterley Crs
Ridgeway Rd North
Bravbourne Dr
Crowntree Close
Lingwood Gardens
Ashley Dr
Shaftesbury Avenue
Minterne Av
Melbury Avenue
Wimborne Av
Sherborne Av
Dorset Av
Cranborne Avenue
Norwood Gn Rd
St Marys Av
Osterley Lane
Alleyn Pk
Boundary Cl
Ferraro Cl
Biscoe Cl
Wheatlands
Old Cote Drive
Eldon Av
Lampton Av
Sutton Dene
Neville Cl
Brookwood Rd
Kingsley Av
Armstrong Way
Navigator Drive
St Margaret's Road
St Dunstan's Road
St Mark's Road
Rosebank Road
Osterley Vw Rd
Studley Grange Rd
Humes Avenue
Belvedere Rd
Trumpers
Boston Rd
Montague Av
Knowsley Avenue
Brentvale Av
Blackmore Av
30
60
40
13
14
15
F
G
H
J
K
I
2
3
4
5
6
7
77
78
79
80

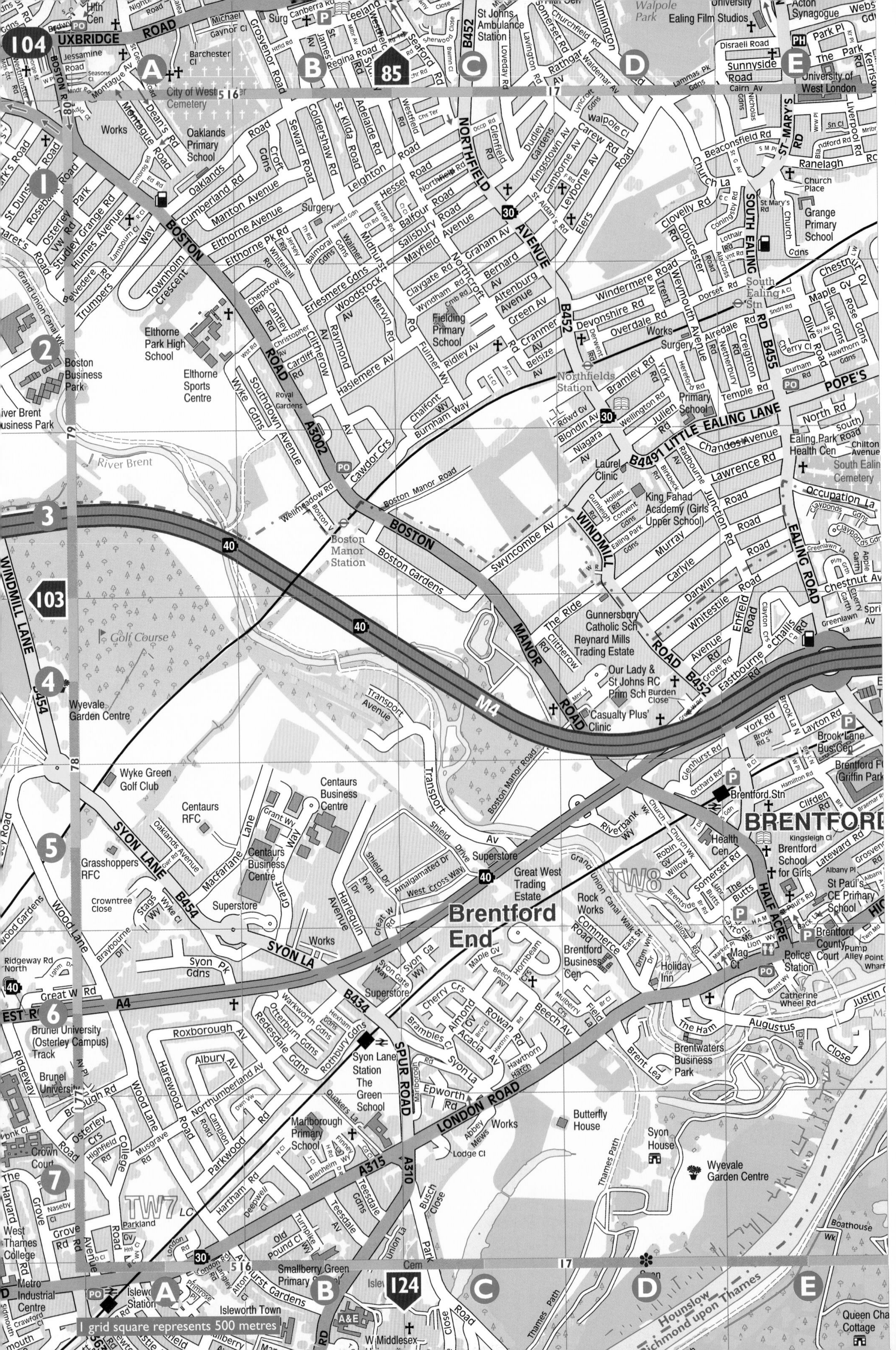

104
UXBRIDGE ROAD
85
103
124
A
B
C
D
E
1
2
3
4
5
6
7
516
17
78
79
City of Westminster Cemetery
Oaklands Primary School
Works
Barchester Cl
Jessamine Road
Seasons Cl
Montague Av
Montague Road
Dean's Rd
Boston Road
BOSTON ROAD
A3002
Cumberland Rd
Manton Avenue
Elthorne Avenue
Elthorne Pk Rd
Townholm Crescent
Elthorne Park High School
Elthorne Sports Centre
Boston Business Park
River Brent Business Park
River Brent
Grand Union Canal Wk
Grosvenor Road
Coldershaw Rd
Seward Road
St Kilda Road
Adelaide Rd
Leighton Road
Hessel Road
Balfour Road
Salisbury Road
Mayfield Avenue
Surgery
Northfield Rd
NORTHFIELD AVENUE
B452
St Johns Ambulance Station
Walpole Park
Ealing Film Studios
University of West London
Acton Synagogue
Disraeli Road
Sunnyside Road
The Park
Park Pl
Cairn Av
Lammas Pk Gdns
Walpole Cl
Carew Rd
Kingsdown Av
Leyborne Av
Camborne Av
Dudley Gardens
Glenfield Rd
Beaconsfield Rd
ST MARY'S RD
Liverpool Rd
Ranelagh
Church Place
Grange Primary School
St Mary's Church Gdns
SOUTH EALING RD
B455
South Ealing Stn
Windermere Road
Devonshire Rd
Overdale Rd
Weymouth Avenue
Gloucester Road
Clovelly Rd
Church La
Dorset Rd
Chestnut Gv
Maple Gv
Lilac Gdns
Rose Gdns
Olive Road
Cherry Cl
Hawthorn Gdns
Durham Rd
POPE'S
North Rd
South Road
Ealing Park Health Cen
Chilton Avenue
South Ealing Cemetery
Occupation La
Claypond Gdns
Chestnut Av
Greenlawn La
Northfields Station
Bramley Rd
Wellington Rd
Julien Rd
Blondin Av
Niagara Av
Primary School
B4491 LITTLE EALING LANE
Chandos Avenue
Lawrence Rd
Radbourne Av
Birkbeck Av
Laurel Clinic
King Fahad Academy (Girls Upper School)
Murray Road
Carlyle Road
Darwin Road
Whitestile Road
Junction Rd
Enfield Road
Clayton Crs
Challis Rd
EALING ROAD
WINDMILL ROAD
B452
Swyncombe Av
Ealing Park Gdns
Convent Gdns
Gumleigh Rd
Hollies Rd
Gunnersbury Catholic Sch
Reynard Mills Trading Estate
Our Lady & St Johns RC Prim Sch
Burden Close
Casualty Plus' Clinic
The Ride
Clitherow Rd
Avenue Rd
Grove Rd
Eastbourne Rd
Woodstock Av
Mervyn Rd
Raymond Av
Clitherow Av
Haslemere Av
Fulmer Wy
Ridley Av
Fielding Primary School
Claygate Rd
Northcroft Rd
Graham Av
Bernard Av
Altenburg Avenue
Green Av
Cranmer Av
Belsize Av
Chalfont Wy
Burnham Way
Cawdor Crs
Royal Gardens
Southdown Avenue
Wyke Gdns
Wellmeadow Rd
Boston Manor Road
Boston Manor Station
BOSTON MANOR ROAD
Boston Gardens
M4
40
30
WINDMILL LANE
B454
Golf Course
Wyevale Garden Centre
Wyke Green Golf Club
Grasshoppers RFC
Crowntree Close
Centaurs RFC
Centaurs Business Centre
Oaklands Avenue
Macfarlane Lane
Grant Way
Harlequin Avenue
SYON LANE
SYON LA
Superstore
Stags Wy
Wyke Cl
Braybourne Dr
Syon Pk Gdns
Works
Transport Avenue
Shield Drive
Amalgamated Dr
West Cross Way
Great West Trading Estate
Brentford End
Riverbank Wy
Grand Union Canal Walk
TW8
Rock Works
Commerce Road
Brentford Business Cen
Holiday Inn
Brentford Stn
BRENTFORD
Brentford School for Girls
St Paul's CE Primary School
Brentford County Court
Police Station
Catherine Wheel Rd
Augustus Close
The Ham
Brentwaters Business Park
Brent Lea
Health Cen
Somerset Rd
The Butts
HALF ACRE
Brook Lane Bus Cen
Layton Rd
York Rd
Glenhurst Rd
Orchard Rd
Brentford FC (Griffin Park)
Clifden Rd
Lateward Rd
Kingsleigh Cl
Albany Pl
Justin Cl
Great W Rd
A4
B434
SPUR ROAD
Syon Lane Station
The Green School
Marlborough Primary School
Quakers La
Rothbury Gdns
Redesdale Gdns
Otterburn Gdns
Warkworth Gdns
Roxborough Av
Albury Av
Northumberland Av
Harewood Road
Wood Lane
Osterley Crs
College Rd
Musgrave Rd
Campion Road
Parkwood Rd
Hartham Rd
Deepwell Cl
Old Pound Cl
Turnpike Wy
Teesdale Av
Teesdale Gdns
Epworth Rd
Syon La
Cherry Crs
Almond Gv
Acacia Av
Rowan Rd
Hawthorn Hatch
Beech Av
Brambles Cl
Maple Gv
LONDON ROAD
A315
A310
Abbey Mews
Lodge Cl
Busch Close
Park Rd
Butterfly House
Syon House
Wyevale Garden Centre
Thames Path
Boathouse Wk
Hounslow
Richmond upon Thames
Queen Charlotte's Cottage
Brunel University (Osterley Campus) Track
Brunel University
Ridgeway Rd North
Ridgeway
Crown Court
The Grove
Harvard
Naseby Cl
West Thames College
TW7
Parkland
Isleworth Station
Isleworth Town
Smallberry Green Primary School
Metro Industrial Centre
Twickenham Rd
W Middlesex
A&E
1 grid square represents 500 metres

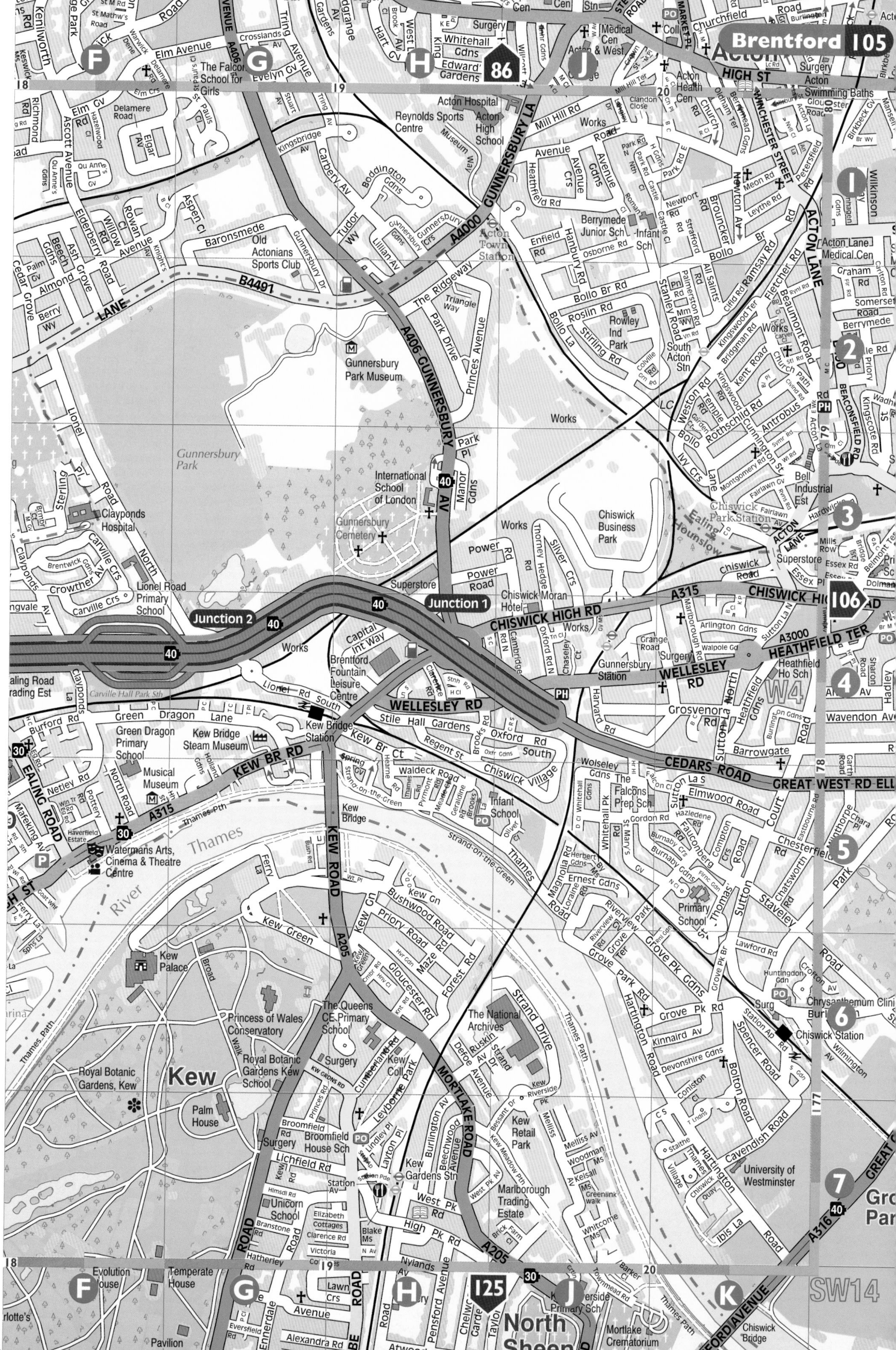

Brentford 105
86
106
125
Acton
Kew
North Sheen
W4
SW14
Acton Town Station
Acton Hospital
Reynolds Sports Centre
Acton High School
Gunnersbury Park
Gunnersbury Park Museum
International School of London
Gunnersbury Cemetery
Claypnds Hospital
Lionel Road Primary School
Old Actonians Sports Club
The Falcon School for Girls
Junction 1
Junction 2
Chiswick Business Park
Chiswick Moran Hotel
Gunnersbury Station
Chiswick Park Station
South Acton Stn
Rowley Ind Park
Berrymede Junior Sch
Infant Sch
Kew Bridge Station
Kew Bridge Steam Museum
Musical Museum
Green Dragon Primary School
Brentford Fountain Leisure Centre
Watermans Arts, Cinema & Theatre Centre
River Thames
Kew Palace
Princess of Wales Conservatory
Royal Botanic Gardens, Kew
Royal Botanic Gardens Kew School
Palm House
The Queens CE Primary School
Kew Gardens Stn
Kew Retail Park
The National Archives
Marlborough Trading Estate
Unicorn School
Chiswick Station
University of Westminster
Heathfield Ho Sch
The Falcons Prep Sch
Primary School
Infant School
Mortlake Crematorium
Chiswick Bridge
Evolution House
Temperate House
Pavilion
CHISWICK HIGH RD
GUNNERSBURY LA
GUNNERSBURY AV
KEW ROAD
KEW BR RD
MORTLAKE ROAD
WELLESLEY RD
CEDARS ROAD
GREAT WEST RD
ACTON LANE
HIGH ST
EALING ROAD
A4000
A406
A315
A205
A316
A3000
B4491

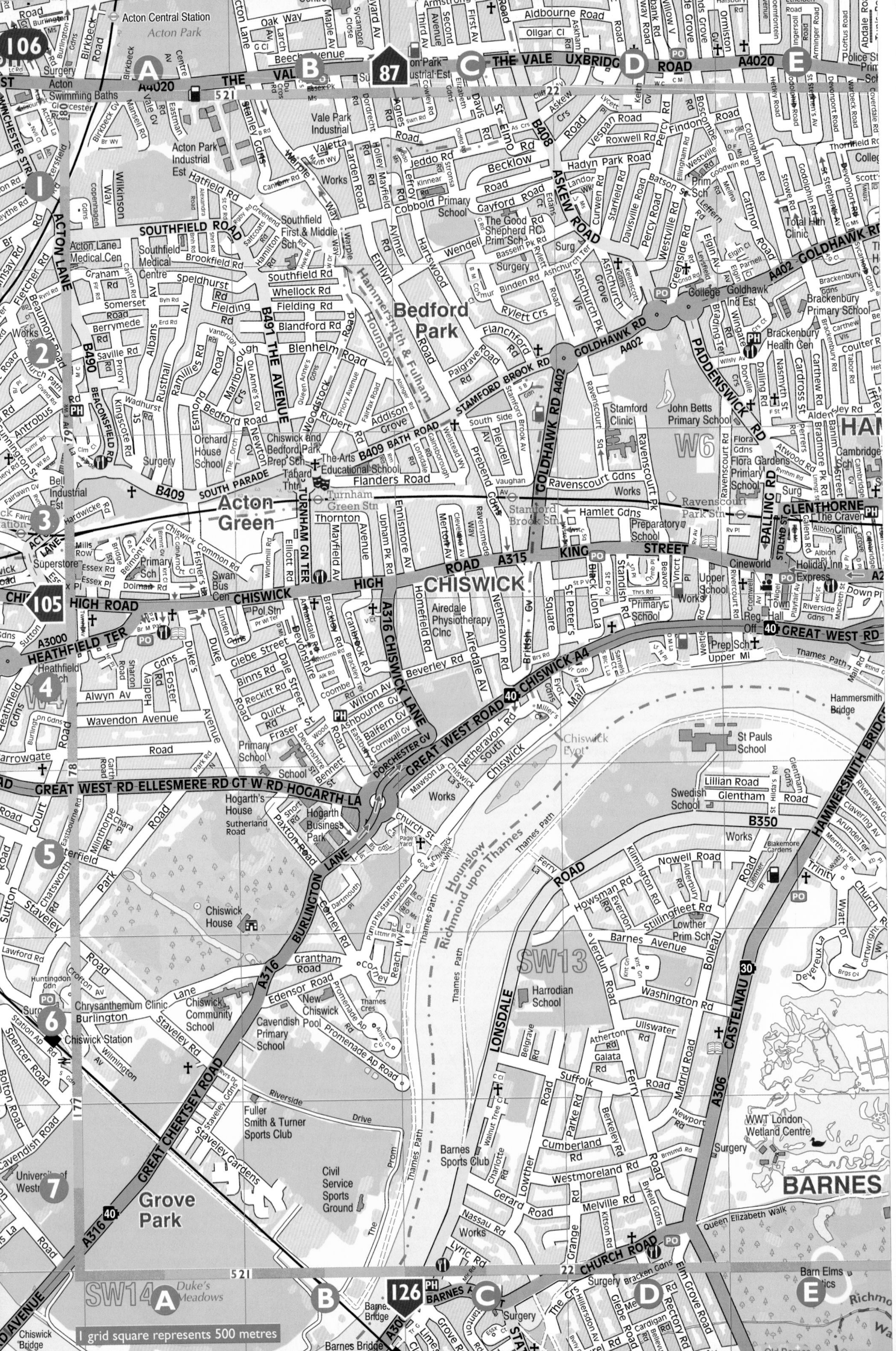
106
105
87
126
A
B
C
D
E
1
2
3
4
5
6
7
Acton Central Station
Acton Park
THE VALE
UXBRIDGE ROAD
A4020
Acton Swimming Baths
Acton Park Industrial Est
Vale Park Industrial
Works
Southfield First & Middle Sch
SOUTHFIELD ROAD
Acton Lane Medical Cen
Southfield Medical Centre
ACTON LANE
B491 THE AVENUE
Bedford Park
Hammersmith & Fulham
Hounslow
ASKEW ROAD
GOLDHAWK RD
A402
STAMFORD BROOK RD
B409 BATH ROAD
The Good Shepherd RC Prim Sch
Cobbold Primary School
Stamford Clinic
John Betts Primary School
W6
PADDENSWICK RD
Brackenbury Primary School
Brackenbury Health Cen
Total Hlth Clinic
Orchard House School
Chiswick and Bedford Park Prep Sch
The Arts Educational School
Tabard Thtr
Turnham Green Stn
Flanders Road
SOUTH PARADE
Acton Green
Bell Industrial Est
Stamford Brook Stn
Ravenscourt Park Stn
Preparatory School
GLENTHORNE
The Craven Clinic
Holiday Inn Express
KING STREET
A315
HIGH ROAD
CHISWICK
CHISWICK HIGH ROAD
Airedale Physiotherapy Clnc
Swan Bus Cen
Pol Stn
Superstore
A316 CHISWICK LANE
Upper School
Primary School
Cineworld
Town Hall
GREAT WEST RD
A3000
HEATHFIELD TER
W4
Wavendon Avenue
GREAT WEST ROAD
CHISWICK A4
GREAT WEST RD ELLESMERE RD GT W RD HOGARTH LA
Hogarth's House
Hogarth Business Park
Chiswick Eyot
Chiswick House
St Pauls School
Swedish School
Lillian Road
B350
Hounslow
Richmond upon Thames
Thames Path
SW13
LONSDALE ROAD
Harrodian School
Lowther Prim Sch
Barnes Avenue
Washington Rd
CASTELNAU
A306
HAMMERSMITH BRIDGE
Hammersmith Bridge
Burlington Lane
Chiswick Community School
Chrysanthemum Clinic
Chiswick Station
New Chiswick Pool
Cavendish Primary School
Fuller Smith & Turner Sports Club
Civil Service Sports Ground
Barnes Sports Club
WWT London Wetland Centre
BARNES
GREAT CHERTSEY ROAD
A316
Grove Park
University of West
Church Road
Queen Elizabeth Walk
Barn Elms
SW14
Duke's Meadows
Barnes Bridge
Chiswick Bridge
BARNES
1 grid square represents 500 metres

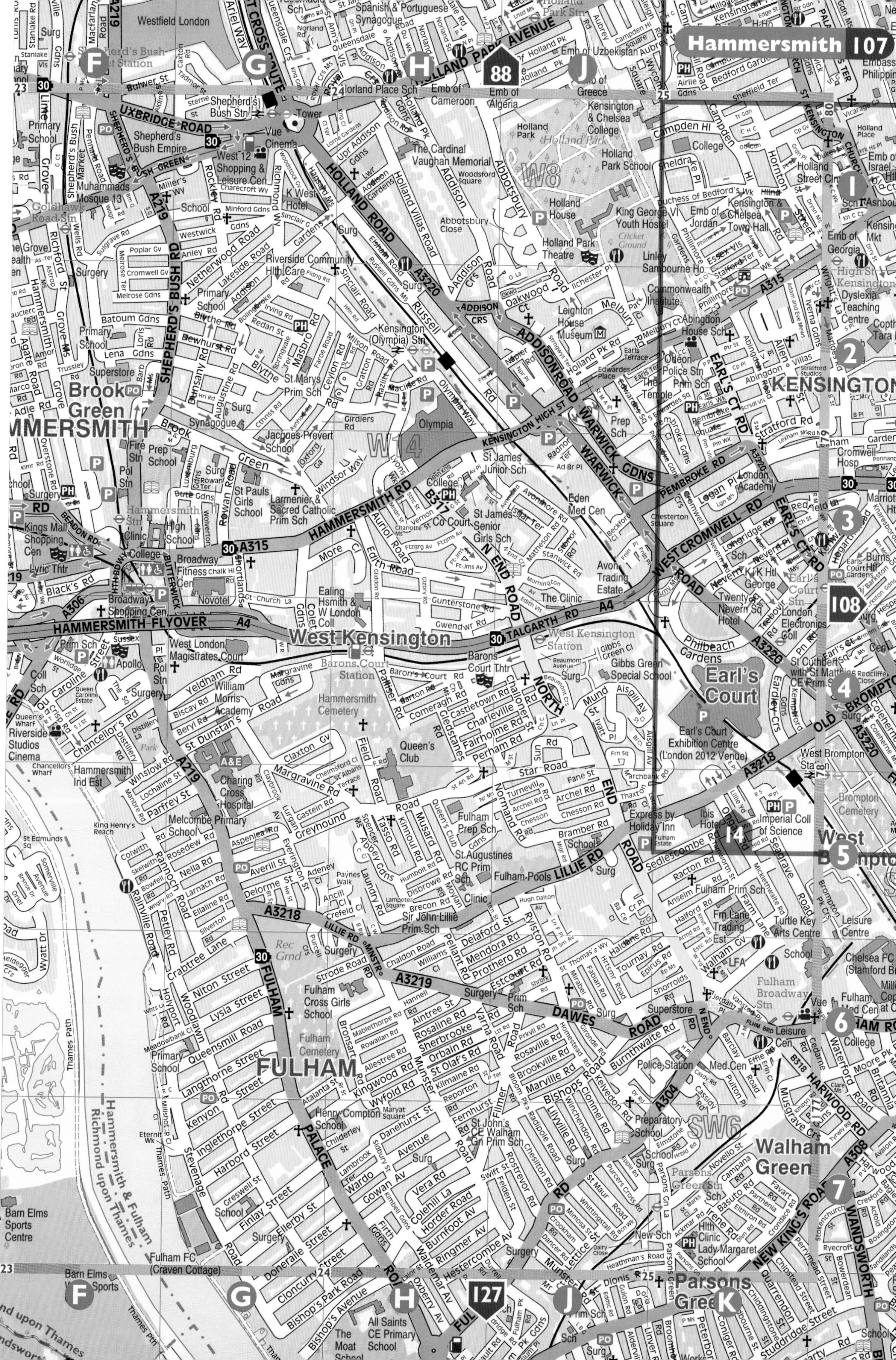
Westfield London
Shepherd's Bush Stn
Shepherd's Bush Empire
UXBRIDGE ROAD
HOLLAND PARK AVENUE
HOLLAND ROAD
Holland Park
Holland House
Kensington & Chelsea College
Holland Park School
Campden Hl
Kensington High St
KENSINGTON
Brook Green
HAMMERSMITH
Kensington (Olympia) Stn
Olympia
W14
W8
HAMMERSMITH RD
ADDISON ROAD
WARWICK GDNS
PEMBROKE RD
WEST CROMWELL ROAD
EARL'S CT RD
Earl's Court
Earl's Court Exhibition Centre (London 2012 Venue)
HAMMERSMITH FLYOVER
A4
TALGARTH RD
West Kensington
West Kensington Station
Barons Court Station
Hammersmith Cemetery
Queen's Club
Charing Cross Hospital
NORTH END ROAD
LILLIE RD
West Brompton
Brompton Cemetery
Imperial Coll of Science
FULHAM PALACE ROAD
FULHAM
DAWES ROAD
Fulham Broadway Stn
Chelsea FC (Stamford Bridge)
Walham Green
SW6
Parsons Green
NEW KING'S ROAD
WANDSWORTH BRIDGE RD
Fulham FC (Craven Cottage)
Barn Elms Sports Centre
Hammersmith & Fulham
Richmond upon Thames
Thames Path
Hammersmith Ind Est
Riverside Studios Cinema
88
108
127
F G H J K
1 2 3 4 5 6 7
23 24 25

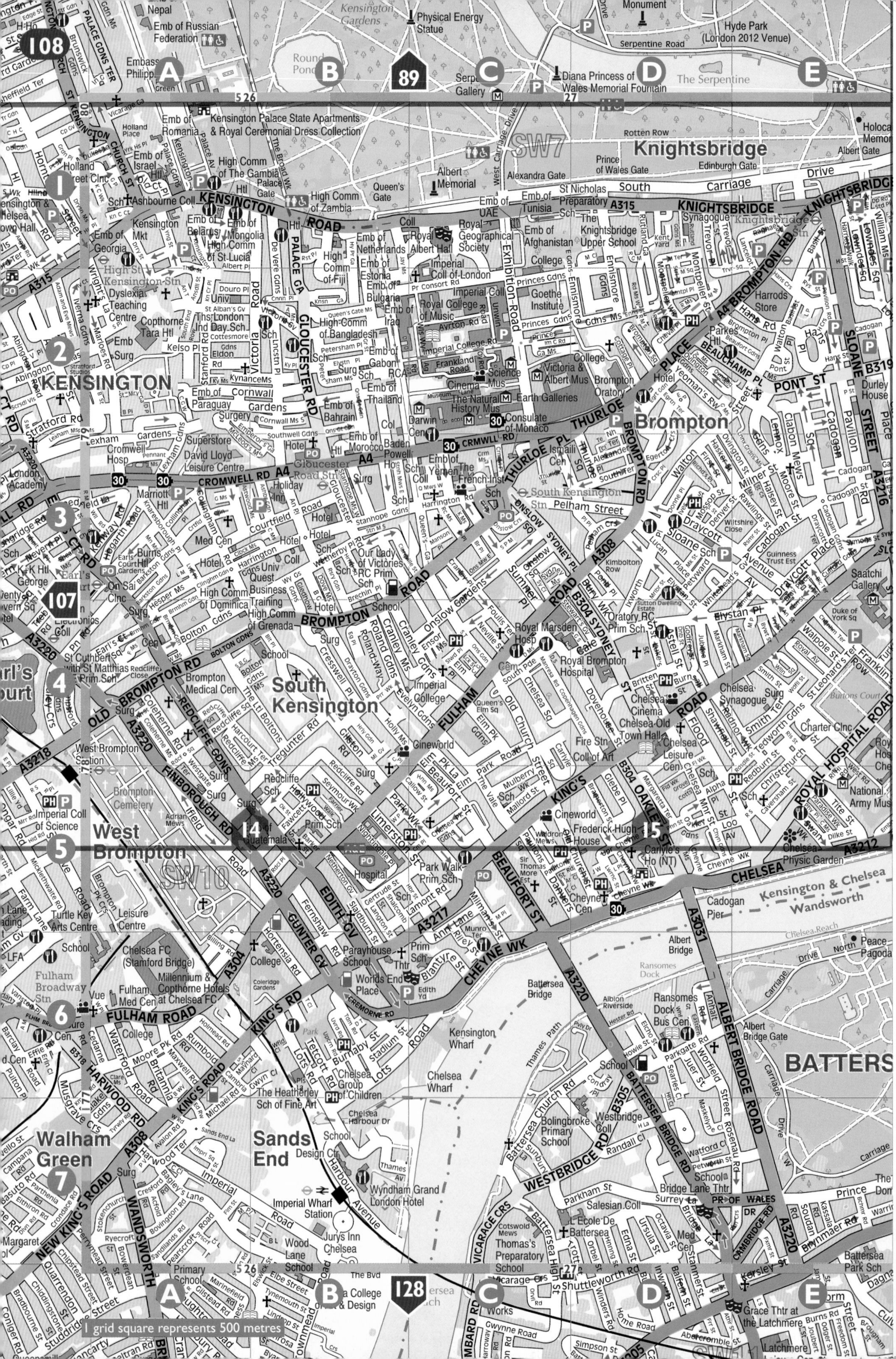
108
89
107
128
Kensington Gardens
Physical Energy Statue
Round Pond
Monument
Hyde Park (London 2012 Venue)
Serpentine Road
The Serpentine
Diana Princess of Wales Memorial Fountain
Serpentine Gallery
Kensington Palace State Apartments & Royal Ceremonial Dress Collection
Rotten Row
Knightsbridge
SW7
Albert Memorial
Alexandra Gate
Prince of Wales Gate
Edinburgh Gate
Albert Gate
South Carriage Drive
KNIGHTSBRIDGE
KENSINGTON ROAD
Royal Albert Hall
Royal Geographical Society
Imperial Coll of London
Royal College of Music
Imperial College Rd
Science Mus
Victoria & Albert Mus
The Natural History Mus
Earth Galleries
Brompton Oratory
Harrods Store
High St Kensington Stn
KENSINGTON
Holland Park
Kensington Mkt
Commonwealth Institute
GLOUCESTER RD
Gloucester Road Stn
CROMWELL RD
A4
Brompton
BROMPTON RD
South Kensington Stn
Pelham Street
THURLOE PL
SLOANE STREET
PONT ST
Sloane Sq
Cadogan Pl
Draycott Place
Saatchi Gallery
Duke of York Sq
South Kensington
BROMPTON ROAD
FULHAM ROAD
Royal Marsden Hosp
Royal Brompton Hospital
Chelsea Old Town Hall
KING'S ROAD
Cineworld
Chelsea Physic Garden
Carlyle's Ho (NT)
ROYAL HOSPITAL ROAD
National Army Mus
Earl's Court
OLD BROMPTON RD
West Brompton Station
Brompton Cemetery
West Brompton
SW10
Chelsea FC (Stamford Bridge)
Fulham Broadway Stn
FULHAM ROAD
Walham Green
NEW KING'S ROAD
WANDSWORTH BRIDGE RD
Sands End
Imperial Wharf Station
Chelsea Harbour Dr
Wyndham Grand London Hotel
Jurys Inn Chelsea
CHEYNE WK
CHELSEA EMBANKMENT
Kensington & Chelsea
Wandsworth
Cadogan Pier
Albert Bridge
Battersea Bridge
Chelsea Reach
Kensington Wharf
Chelsea Wharf
Ransomes Dock
BATTERSEA BRIDGE RD
ALBERT BRIDGE ROAD
WESTBRIDGE RD
BATTERSEA
Albert Bridge Gate
Peace Pagoda
Grace Thtr at the Latchmere
1 grid square represents 500 metres

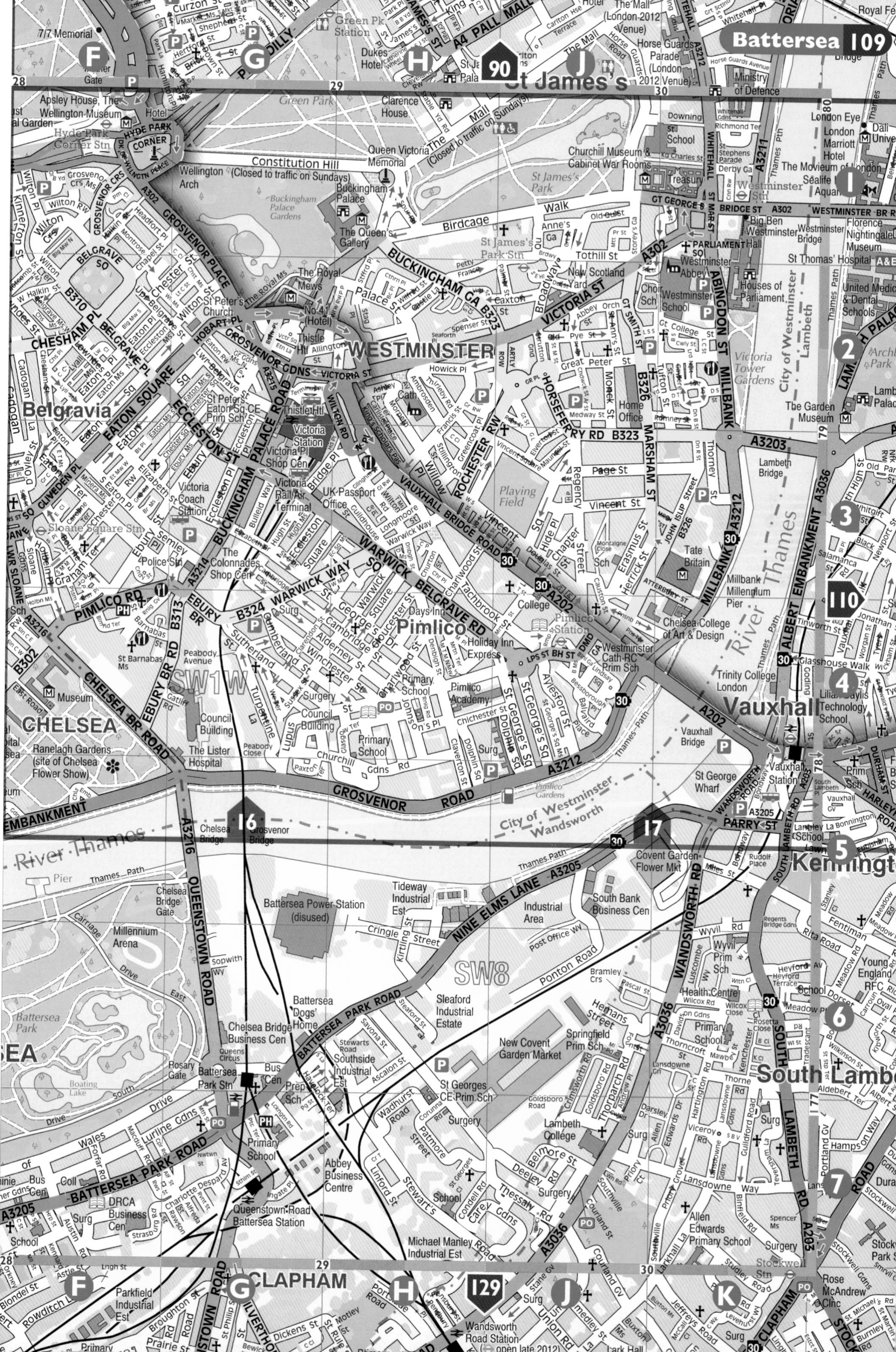

St James's
Green Park
Hyde Park Corner Stn
Apsley House, The Wellington Museum
Constitution Hill
Wellington Arch
Buckingham Palace
Buckingham Palace Gardens
The Queen's Gallery
The Royal Mews
Queen Victoria Memorial
The Mall (Closed to traffic on Sundays)
St James's Park
Birdcage Walk
Clarence House
Churchill Museum & Cabinet War Rooms
Horse Guards Parade
Ministry of Defence
Treasury
Westminster Stn
Big Ben
Westminster Bridge
Westminster Hall
Westminster Abbey
Houses of Parliament
Victoria Tower Gardens
London Eye
London Marriott Hotel
Florence Nightingale Museum
St Thomas' Hospital
The Garden Museum
Lambeth Bridge
BELGRAVE SQ
Belgravia
EATON SQUARE
GROSVENOR PLACE
WESTMINSTER
VICTORIA ST
Victoria Station
Victoria Coach Station
Westminster Cath
New Scotland Yard
HORSEFERRY RD
MILLBANK
Tate Britain
Millbank Millennium Pier
Chelsea College of Art & Design
Pimlico
Pimlico Station
VAUXHALL BRIDGE ROAD
WARWICK WAY
BELGRAVE RD
Vauxhall
Vauxhall Bridge
Vauxhall Station
St George Wharf
ALBERT EMBANKMENT
River Thames
City of Westminster
Lambeth
Wandsworth
GROSVENOR ROAD
CHELSEA BR ROAD
CHELSEA
Ranelagh Gardens (site of Chelsea Flower Show)
Chelsea Bridge
Grosvenor Bridge
EMBANKMENT
QUEENSTOWN ROAD
Battersea Power Station (disused)
NINE ELMS LANE
Covent Garden Flower Mkt
New Covent Garden Market
BATTERSEA PARK ROAD
Battersea 'Dogs' Home
Battersea Park
Battersea Park Stn
Queenstown Road Battersea Station
Millennium Arena
SW1W
SW8
WANDSWORTH RD
SOUTH LAMBETH RD
Kennington
South Lambeth
CLAPHAM
Wandsworth Road Station
Stockwell Stn

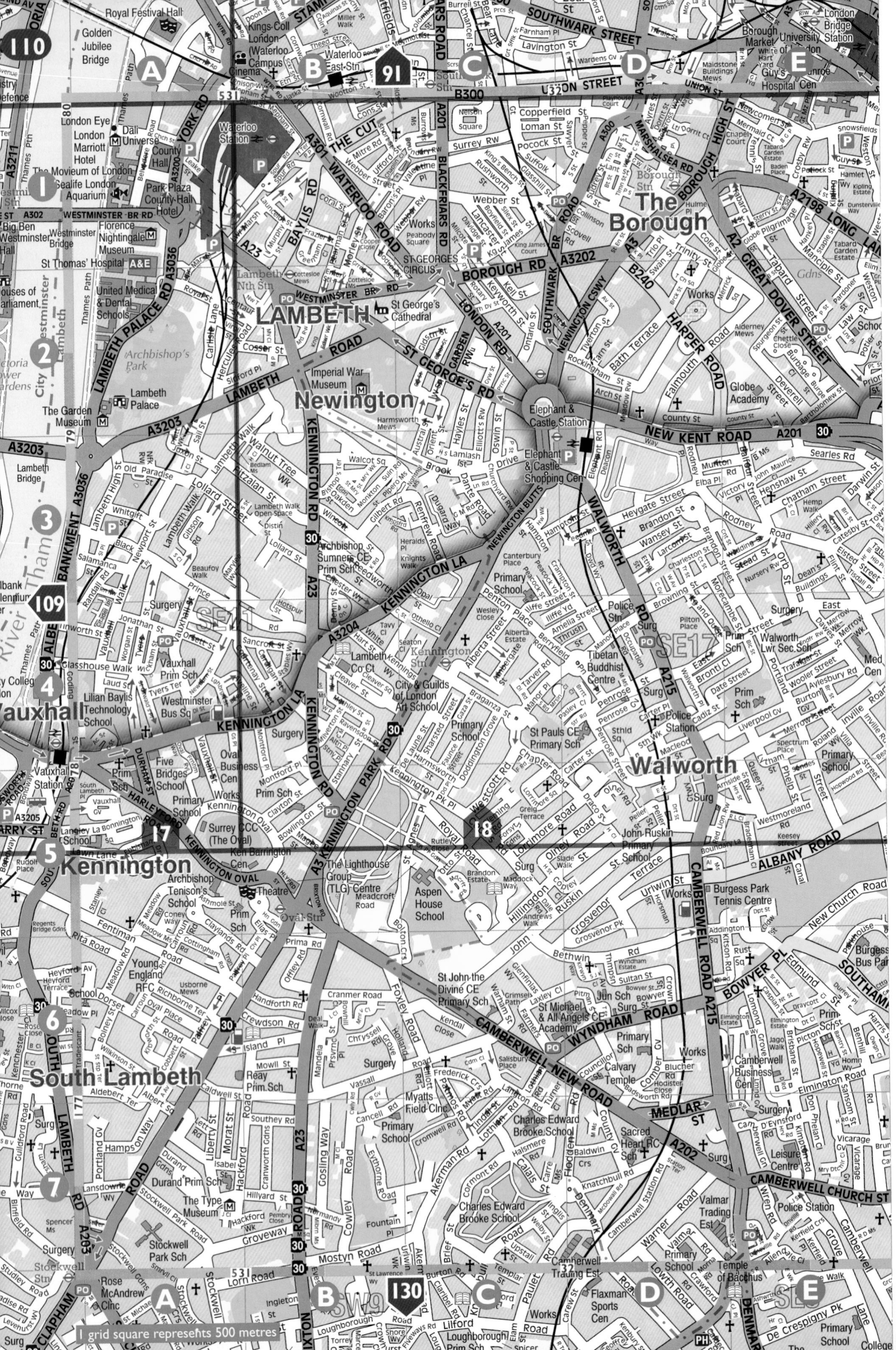
110
91
Royal Festival Hall
Golden Jubilee Bridge
Waterloo East Stn
Waterloo Station
London Eye
Dali Universe
County Hall
London Marriott Hotel
The Movieum of London
Sealife London Aquarium
Park Plaza County Hall Hotel
SOUTHWARK STREET
UNION STREET
London Bridge Station
Borough Market
Guy's Hospital
THE CUT
WATERLOO ROAD
BLACKFRIARS ROAD
BAYLIS RD
WESTMINSTER BR RD
Big Ben
Westminster Bridge
Florence Nightingale Museum
St Thomas' Hospital
Houses of Parliament
United Medical & Dental Schools
LAMBETH
St George's Cathedral
ST GEORGES CIRCUS
BOROUGH RD
The Borough
BOROUGH HIGH ST
LONG LANE
GREAT DOVER STREET
HARPER ROAD
LAMBETH PALACE RD
LAMBETH ROAD
Archbishop's Park
Lambeth Palace
The Garden Museum
Imperial War Museum
Newington
ST GEORGE'S RD
LONDON RD
Elephant & Castle Station
Elephant & Castle Shopping Cen
NEW KENT ROAD
Lambeth Bridge
KENNINGTON RD
KENNINGTON LA
NEWINGTON BUTTS
WALWORTH RD
SE11
SE17
109
Vauxhall
Vauxhall Station
Kennington Stn
City & Guilds of London Art School
Tibetan Buddhist Centre
Walworth
KENNINGTON PARK RD
Surrey CCC (The Oval)
KENNINGTON OVAL
Kennington
17
18
ALBANY ROAD
Burgess Park Tennis Centre
Oval Stn
South Lambeth
CAMBERWELL NEW ROAD
CAMBERWELL ROAD
WYNDHAM ROAD
CAMBERWELL CHURCH ST
The Type Museum
Stockwell Park Sch
Stockwell Stn
130
SW9
SE5
Temple of Bacchus
1 grid square represents 500 metres
A
B
C
D
E
1
2
3
4
5
6
7

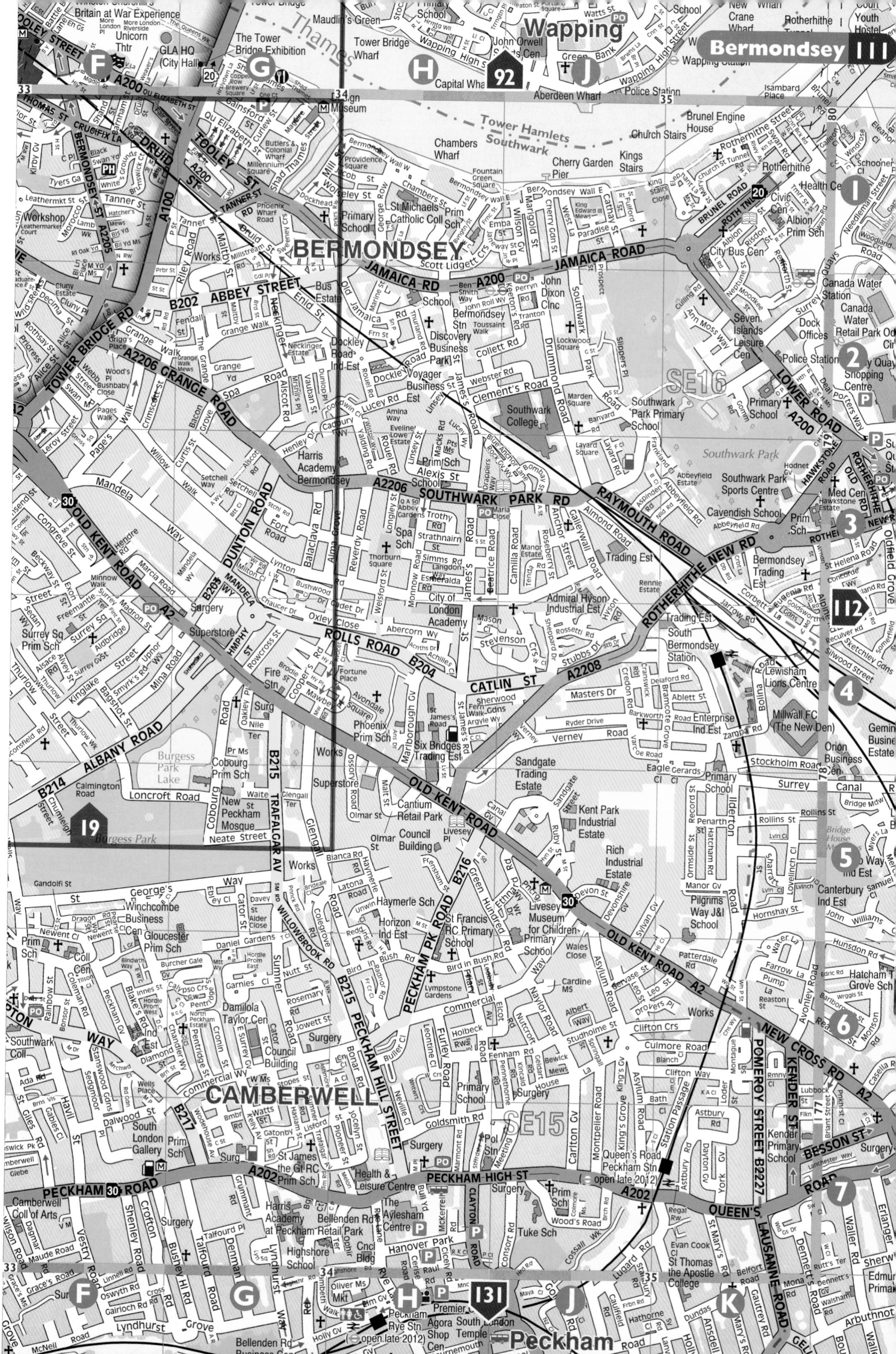
Wapping
BERMONDSEY
CAMBERWELL
Peckham
SE16
SE15
Thames
Tower Hamlets
Southwark
Britain at War Experience
Unicorn Thtr
GLA HQ (City Hall)
The Tower Bridge Exhibition
Maudlin's Green
Tower Bridge Wharf
Capital Wharf
John Orwell Sports Cen
Aberdeen Wharf
Police Station
Wapping Station
New Crane Wharf
Rotherhithe Youth Hostel
Isambard Place
Brunel Engine House
Church Stairs
Chambers Wharf
Cherry Garden Pier
Kings Stairs
Design Museum
Butlers & Colonial Wharf
Millennium Square
Providence Square
St Michaels Catholic Coll
Primary School
Rotherhithe
Health Cen
Civic Cen
Albion Prim Sch
City Bus Cen
TOOLEY STREET
TOOLEY ST
DRUID ST
BERMONDSEY ST
TOWER BRIDGE RD
A200
A100
A205
A2206 GRANGE ROAD
B202 ABBEY STREET
JAMAICA ROAD
JAMAICA RD
BRUNEL ROAD
Workshop
Leathermarket Court
Bus Estate
Scott Lidgett Crs
Bermondsey Stn
Discovery Business Park
Voyager Business Est
Dockley Road Ind Est
John Dixon Clnc
Southwark Park Rd
Southwark College
Southwark Park Primary School
Southwark Park
Seven Islands Leisure Cen
Canada Water Station
Canada Water Retail Park
Dock Offices
Police Station
Surrey Quays Shopping Centre
Primary School
LOWER ROAD
Southwark Park Sports Centre
Med Cen
Cavendish School
Harris Academy Bermondsey
A2206 SOUTHWARK PARK RD
RAYMOUTH ROAD
ROTHERHITHE NEW RD
Trading Est
Bermondsey Trading Est
Thorburn Square
City of London Academy
Admiral Hyson Industrial Est
South Bermondsey Station
Lewisham Lions Centre
Millwall FC (The New Den)
Enterprise Ind Est
Orion Business Cen
ROLLS ROAD
B204
CATLIN ST
A2208
MANDELA WY
DUNTON ROAD
OLD KENT ROAD
A2
Surgery
Superstore
Fire Stn
Phoenix Prim Sch
Six Bridges Trading Est
Sandgate Trading Estate
Kent Park Industrial Estate
Rich Industrial Estate
Pilgrims Way J&I School
Canterbury Ind Est
Burgess Park Lake
ALBANY ROAD
B214
Cobourg Prim Sch
New Peckham Mosque
Neate Street
Burgess Park
B215 TRAFALGAR AV
Cantium Retail Park
Council Building
Livesey Museum for Children
Primary School
Haymerle Sch
Horizon Ind Est
St Francis RC Primary School
Lympstone Gardens
Winchcombe Business Cen
Gloucester Prim Sch
Damilola Taylor Cen
Council Building
WILLOWBROOK RD
B215 PECKHAM HILL STREET
PECKHAM PK ROAD
B216
NEW CROSS RD
KENDER ST
POMEROY STREET B2227
Kender Primary School
BESSON ST
Southwark Coll
South London Gallery
B217
Surgery
St James the Gt RC Prim Sch
Health & Leisure Centre
PECKHAM HIGH ST
A202
PECKHAM ROAD
QUEEN'S ROAD
Queen's Road Peckham Stn
(open late 2012)
Camberwell Coll of Arts
Harris Academy at Peckham
Bellenden Rd Retail Park
The Aylesham Centre
Highshore School
Hanover Park
CLAYTON ROAD
Tuke Sch
Evan Cook Cl
St Thomas the Apostle College
LAUSANNE ROAD
Peckham Rye Stn
Premier Cen
Agora Shop Cen
South London Temple
Bellenden Rd Business Cen
92
112
19
131
F
G
H
J
K
1
2
3
4
5
6
7
33
34
35

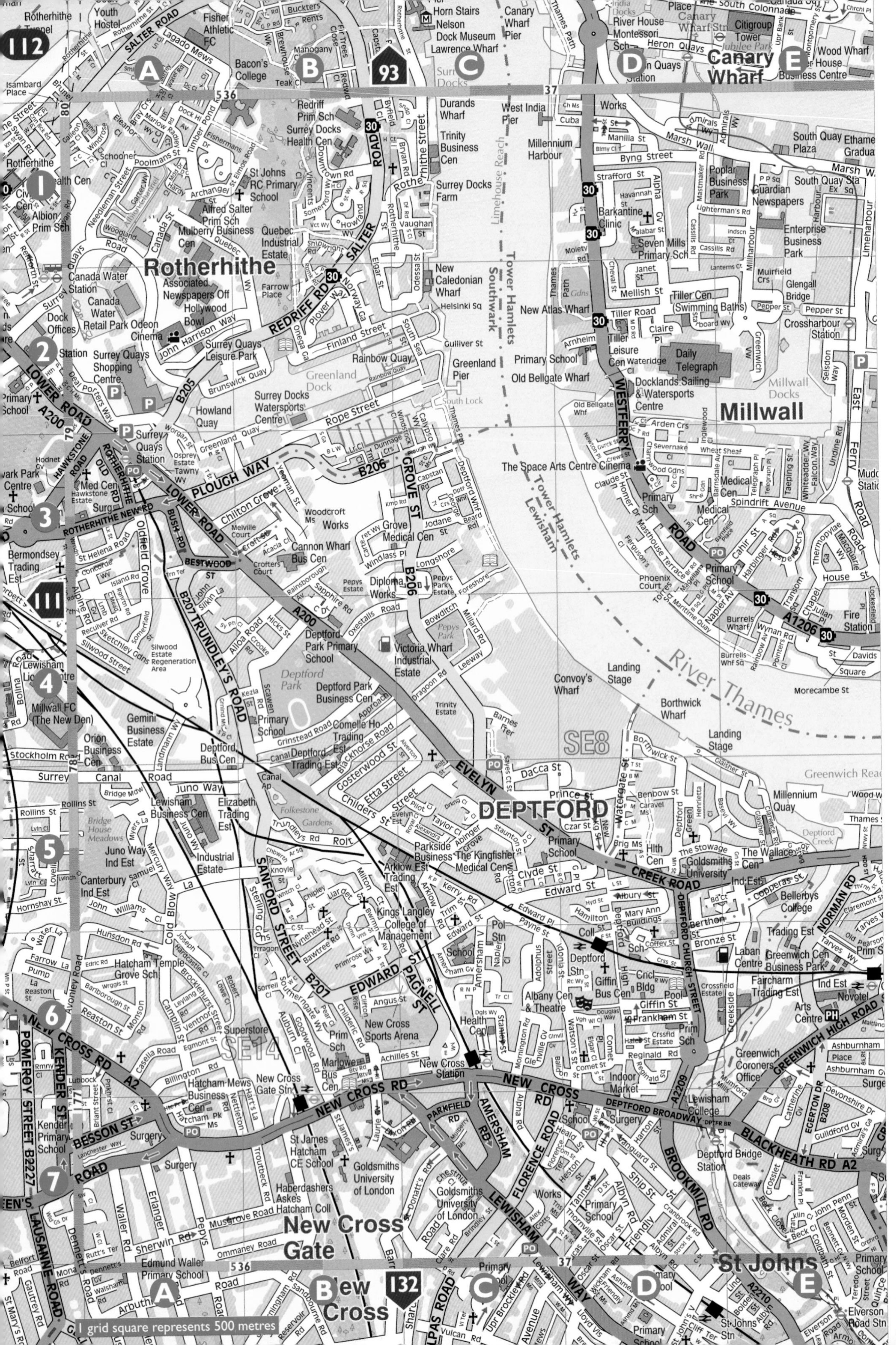

112
93
111
132
A
B
C
D
E
1
2
3
4
5
6
7
536
537
Rotherhithe
Canary Wharf
Millwall
DEPTFORD
New Cross Gate
New Cross
St Johns
SE8
SE14
River Thames
Limehouse Reach
Tower Hamlets
Southwark
Lewisham
Salter Road
Redriff Rd
Lower Road
Rotherhithe New Rd
Plough Way
Evelyn St
Grove St
Trundley's Road
Sanford Street
Edward St
Pagnell St
New Cross Rd
Amersham Rd
Lewisham Way
Florence Road
Brookmill Rd
Deptford Church Street
Creek Road
Deptford Broadway
Blackheath Rd A2
Greenwich High Road
Westferry Road
East Ferry Road
Marsh Wall
Surrey Canal Road
Besson St
Pomeroy Street B2227
Lausanne Road
Kender St
Hawkstone Road
Canada Water Station
Surrey Quays Station
Surrey Quays Shopping Centre
Surrey Docks Farm
Greenland Dock
South Dock
Surrey Docks Watersports Centre
Canada Water Retail Park
Odeon Cinema
Hollywood Bowl
Surrey Quays Leisure Park
Heron Quays
South Quay Station
Crossharbour Station
Daily Telegraph
Docklands Sailing & Watersports Centre
Millwall Docks
Millwall FC (The New Den)
Deptford Park
Deptford Park Primary School
Convoy's Wharf
Borthwick Wharf
Deptford Bridge Station
Deptford Stn
New Cross Station
New Cross Gate Stn
St Johns Stn
Goldsmiths University of London
Laban Centre
Albany Cen & Theatre
Deptford Creek
Millennium Quay
Trinity Estate
Victoria Wharf Industrial Estate
Pepys Estate
Pepys Park
Greenwich Reach
1 grid square represents 500 metres

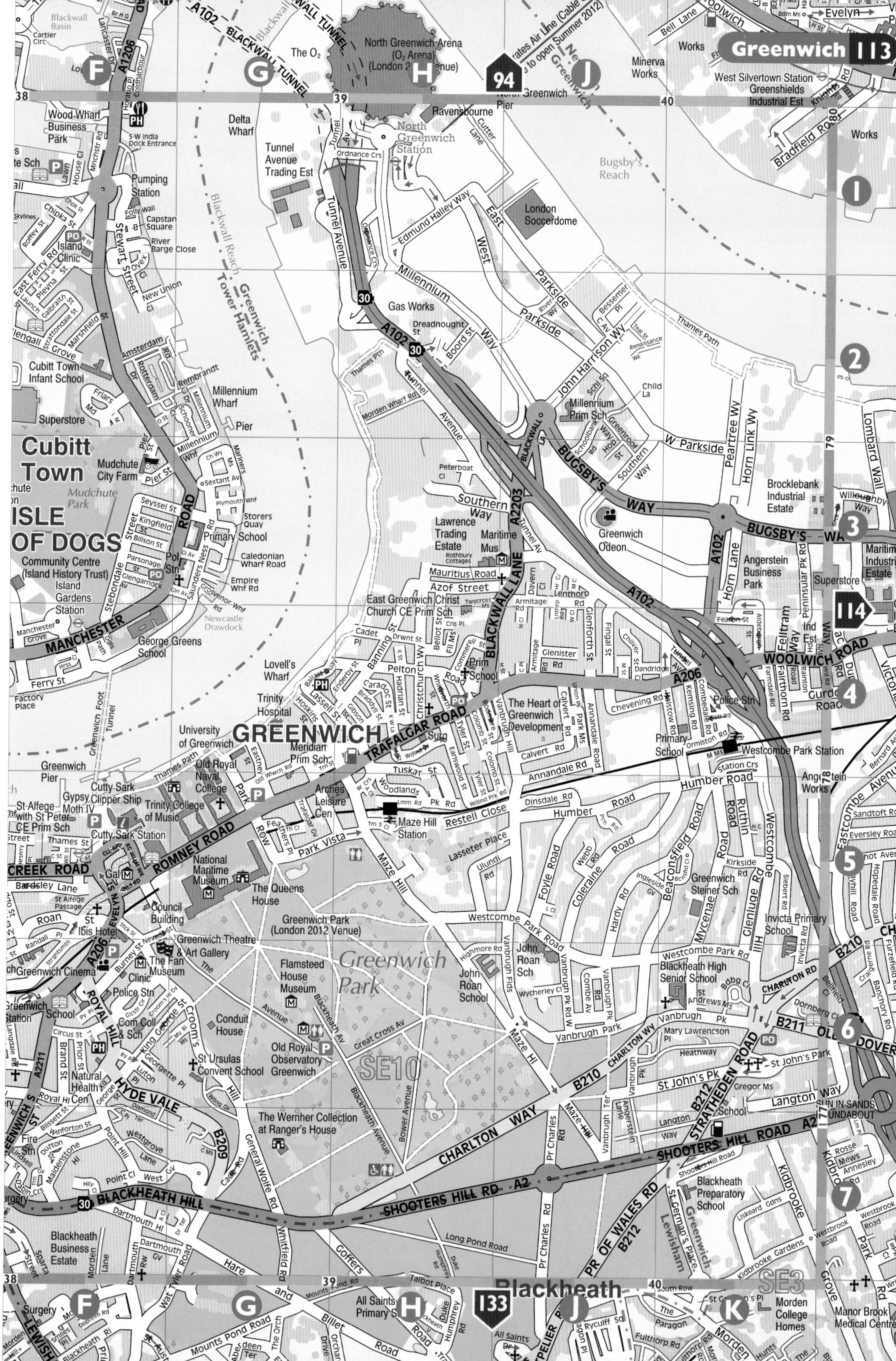
North Greenwich Arena (O2 Arena) (London 2012 Venue)
The O2
BLACKWALL TUNNEL
A102
Emirates Air Line (Cable Car) (due to open Summer 2012)
North Greenwich Pier
North Greenwich Station
Ravensbourne
Tunnel Avenue Trading Est
Delta Wharf
Wood Wharf Business Park
S W India Dock Entrance
Pumping Station
Capstan Square
River Barge Close
Minerva Works
Works
West Silvertown Station
Greenshields Industrial Est
Bradfield Rd
Bugsby's Reach
London Soccerdome
Edmund Halley Way
West Parkside
East Parkside
Millennium Way
Gas Works
Dreadnought St
Boord St
Blackwall Reach
Greenwich
Tower Hamlets
Thames Path
John Harrison Wy
Millennium Prim Sch
Cubitt Town Infant School
Superstore
Cubitt Town
Mudchute City Farm
Mudchute Park
ISLE OF DOGS
Millennium Wharf
Pier
Primary School
Caledonian Wharf Road
Empire Whf Rd
Community Centre (Island History Trust)
Island Gardens Station
George Greens School
Newcastle Drawdock
Southern Way
Lawrence Trading Estate
Maritime Mus
Mauritius Road
Azof Street
East Greenwich Christ Church CE Prim Sch
BLACKWALL LANE
A2203
Greenwich Odeon
BUGSBY'S WAY
Brocklebank Industrial Estate
Angerstein Business Park
Superstore
114
WOOLWICH ROAD
A206
Lovell's Wharf
Trinity Hospital
GREENWICH
TRAFALGAR ROAD
University of Greenwich
Meridian Prim Sch
The Heart of Greenwich Development
Westcombe Park Station
Police Stn
Primary School
Greenwich Pier
Cutty Sark Clipper Ship
Gypsy Moth IV
Old Royal Naval College
Trinity College of Music
St Alfege with St Peter CE Prim Sch
Cutty Sark Station
ROMNEY ROAD
National Maritime Museum
The Queens House
Arches Leisure Cen
Maze Hill Station
Park Vista
Humber Road
Angerstein Works
CREEK ROAD
Council Building
Greenwich Theatre & Art Gallery
The Fan Museum
Greenwich Cinema
Greenwich Park (London 2012 Venue)
Greenwich Park
Flamsteed House Museum
Greenwich Steiner Sch
Invicta Primary School
Westcombe Park Road
John Roan Sch
John Roan School
Blackheath High Senior School
St Andrews Ms
Conduit House
Old Royal Observatory Greenwich
St Ursulas Convent School
SE10
CHARLTON WAY
B210
Vanbrugh Park
St John's Pk
Mary Lawrencson Pl
HYDE VALE
B209
The Wernher Collection at Ranger's House
SHOOTERS HILL ROAD
A2
STRATHEDEN ROAD
B212
Blackheath Preparatory School
BLACKHEATH HILL
Blackheath Business Estate
Long Pond Road
PR OF WALES RD
Kidbrooke Gardens
SE3
Blackheath
133
All Saints Primary Sch
Morden College Homes
Manor Brook Medical Centre
Mounts Pond Road
Sun in Sands Roundabout

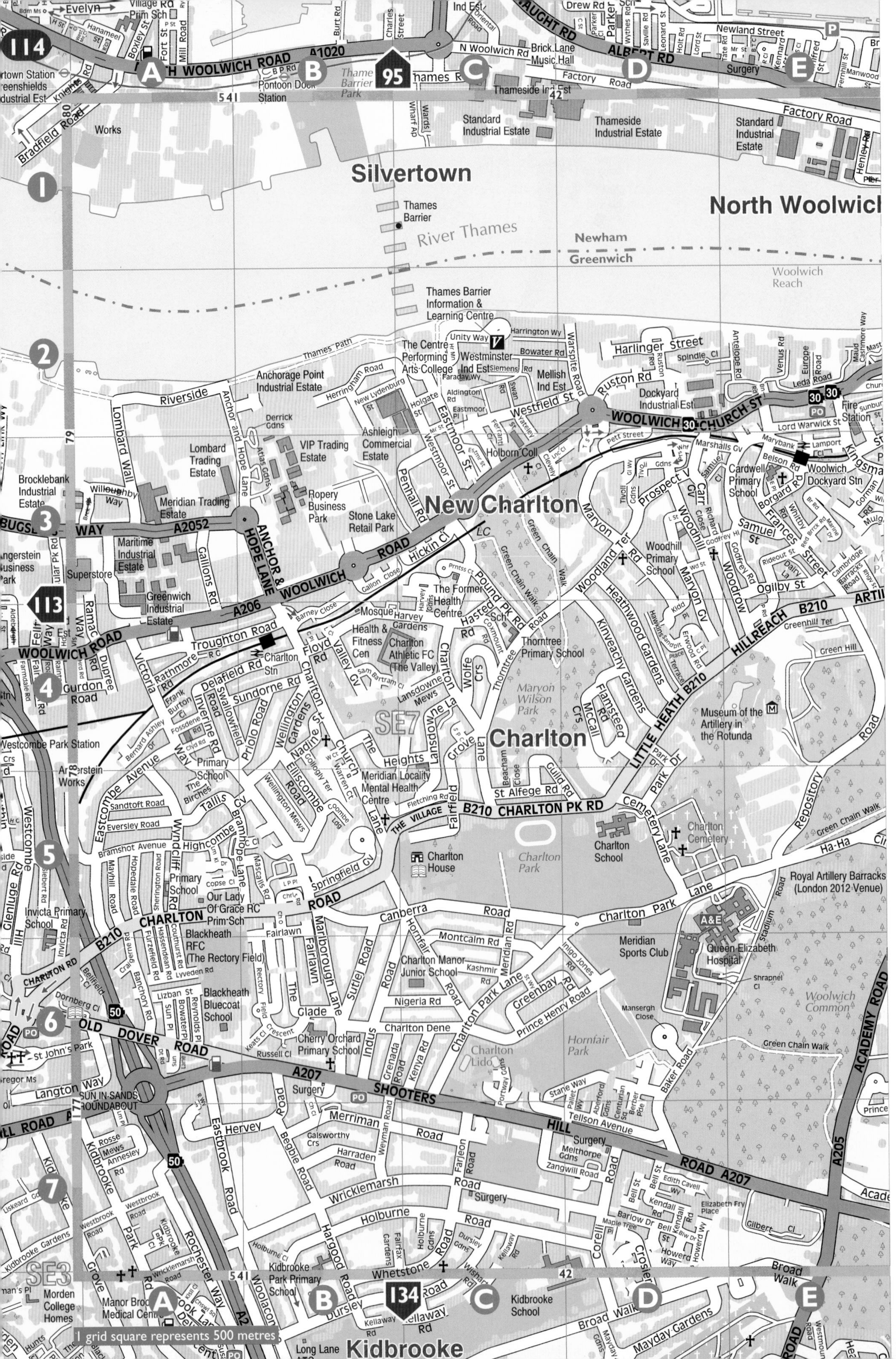

114
95
113
134
A
B
C
D
E
1
2
3
4
5
6
7
541
42
NORTH WOOLWICH ROAD A1020
ALBERT RD
Factory Road
Silvertown
North Woolwich
Thames Barrier
River Thames
Newham
Greenwich
Woolwich Reach
Thames Barrier Information & Learning Centre
Standard Industrial Estate
Thameside Industrial Estate
Works
Anchorage Point Industrial Estate
Riverside
Lombard Wall
Lombard Trading Estate
VIP Trading Estate
Ropery Business Park
Stone Lake Retail Park
Ashleigh Commercial Estate
Brocklebank Industrial Estate
Meridian Trading Estate
Maritime Industrial Estate
Greenwich Industrial Estate
Superstore
BUGSBY'S WAY A2052
ANCHOR & HOPE LANE
WOOLWICH ROAD A206
New Charlton
Westminster Ind Est
Mellish Ind Est
The Centre Performing Arts College
Harlinger Street
Dockyard Industrial Est
WOOLWICH CHURCH ST
Woolwich Dockyard Stn
Cardwell Primary School
Woodhill Primary School
Charlton Stn
Charlton Athletic FC (The Valley)
Health & Fitness Cen
The Former Health Centre
Thorntree Primary School
Maryon Wilson Park
SE7
Charlton
Meridian Locality Mental Health Centre
Museum of the Artillery in the Rotunda
LITTLE HEATH B210
HILLREACH B210
B210 CHARLTON PK RD
THE VILLAGE
Charlton House
Charlton Park
Charlton School
Charlton Cemetery
Royal Artillery Barracks (London 2012 Venue)
Queen Elizabeth Hospital
Meridian Sports Club
Charlton Manor Junior School
Woolwich Common
Hornfair Park
Charlton Lido
Green Chain Walk
Westcombe Park Station
Angerstein Works
Invicta Primary School
Our Lady Of Grace RC Prim Sch
Blackheath RFC (The Rectory Field)
Blackheath Bluecoat School
Cherry Orchard Primary School
CHARLTON ROAD
OLD DOVER ROAD
A207 SHOOTERS HILL ROAD A207
SUN IN SANDS ROUNDABOUT
ACADEMY ROAD
A205
Kidbrooke Park Primary School
Kidbrooke School
Morden College Homes
Manor Brook Medical Centre
SE3
Kidbrooke
1 grid square represents 500 metres

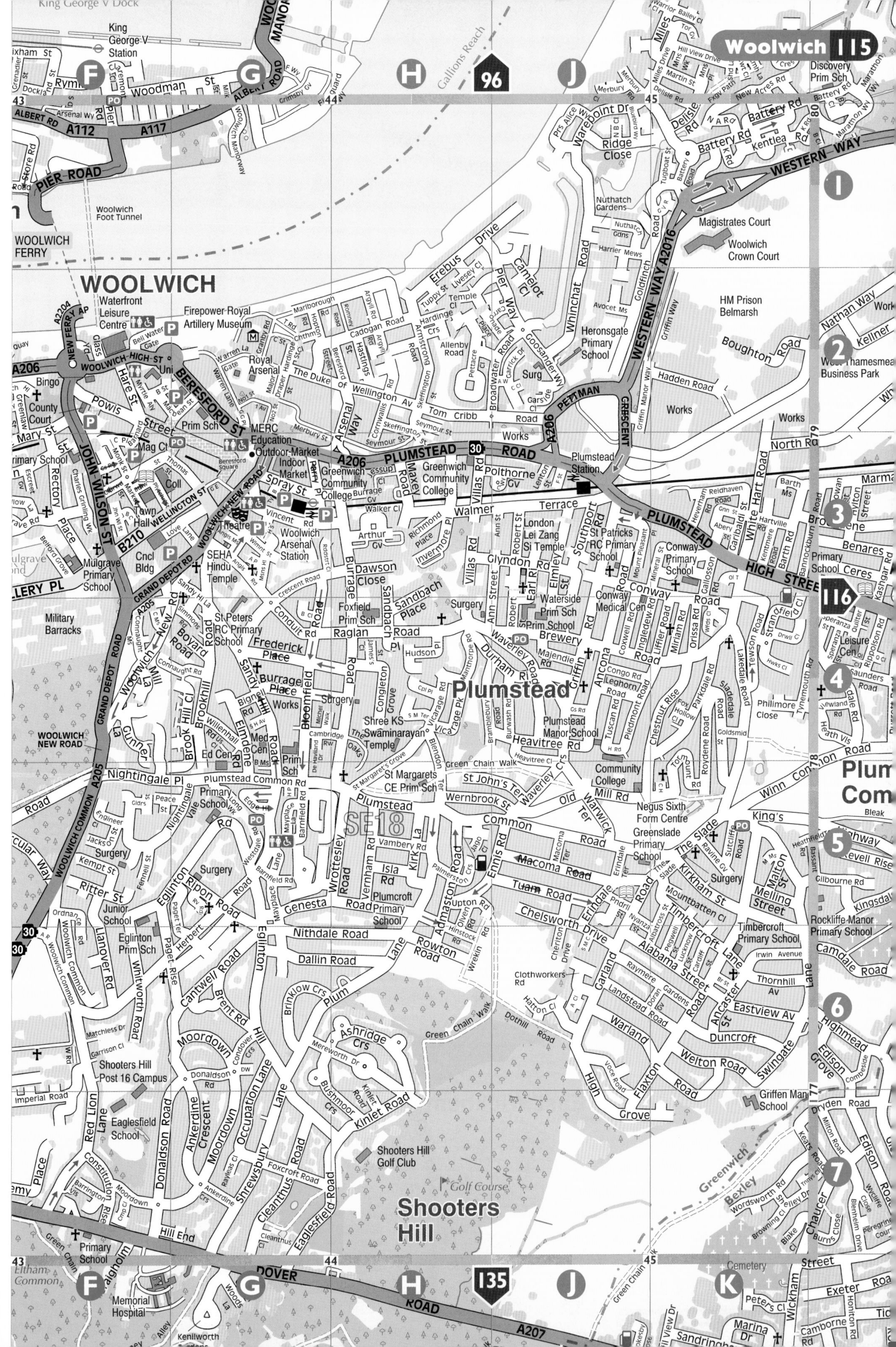
WOOLWICH
Plumstead
Shooters Hill
SE18
WOOLWICH FERRY
Woolwich Foot Tunnel
King George V Station
Woolwich Arsenal Station
Plumstead Station
HM Prison Belmarsh
Woolwich Crown Court
Magistrates Court
Firepower Royal Artillery Museum
Royal Arsenal
Waterfront Leisure Centre
Shooters Hill Golf Club
Memorial Hospital
A206 PLUMSTEAD ROAD
PLUMSTEAD HIGH STREET
WESTERN WAY A2016
GRAND DEPOT ROAD
WOOLWICH COMMON A205
DOVER ROAD A207
96
135
116

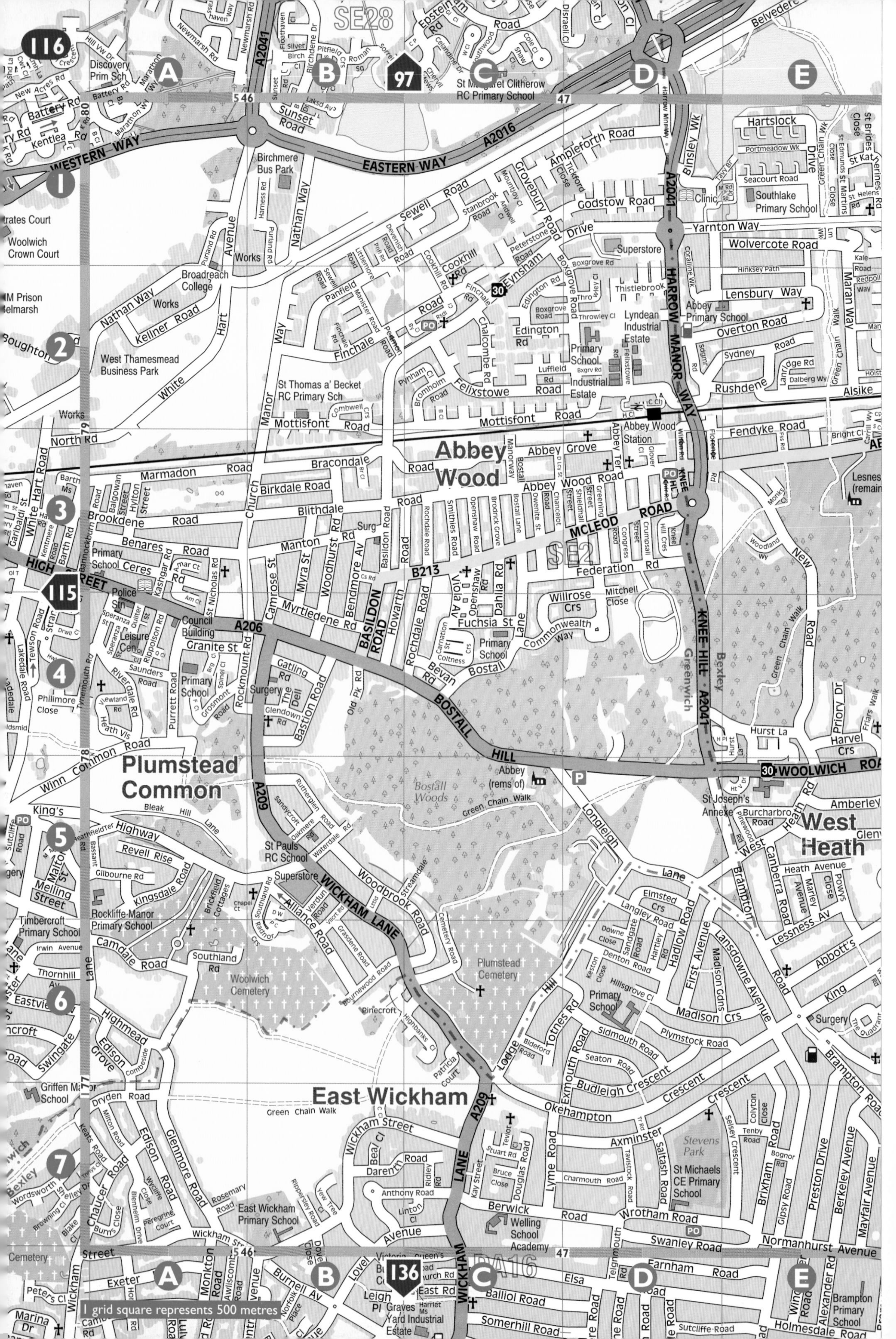
116
97
115
136
SE28
SE2
DA16
A
B
C
D
E
1
2
3
4
5
6
7
46
47
80
79
78
77
Western Way
A2016
Eastern Way
A2041
Harrow Manor Way
Knee Hill
Discovery Prim Sch
St Margaret Clitherow RC Primary School
Birchmere Bus Park
Nathan Way
Ampleforth Road
Sewell Road
Godstow Road
Yarnton Way
Wolvercote Road
Superstore
Southlake Primary School
Clinic
Hartslock
Seacourt Road
Woolwich Crown Court
HM Prison Belmarsh
Broadreach College
Works
Kellner Road
West Thamesmead Business Park
White Hart Road
Hart Avenue
Finchale Road
Eynsham Drive
Lyndean Industrial Estate
Abbey Primary School
Lensbury Way
Overton Road
Edington Rd
Primary School
Felixstowe Road
Industrial Estate
Rushdene
St Thomas a' Becket RC Primary Sch
Mottisfont Road
Abbey Wood Station
Fendyke Road
North Rd
Abbey Wood
Abbey Grove
Abbey Wood Road
Bracondale Road
Marmadon Road
Birkdale Road
Blithdale Road
Brookdene Road
McLeod Road
B213
Federation Rd
Basildon Road
Manton Rd
Woodhurst Rd
High Street
Police Stn
Council Building
A206
Leisure Cen
Granite St
Myrtledene Rd
Bostall Hill
Woolwich Road
Abbey (rems of)
Bostall Woods
Green Chain Walk
Plumstead Common
Winn Common Road
A209
Wickham Lane
St Pauls RC School
Superstore
Rockliffe Manor Primary School
Timbercroft Primary School
Woolwich Cemetery
Plumstead Cemetery
Woodbrook Road
Lesness Abbey (remains)
St Joseph's Annexe
West Heath
Brampton Road
Lansdowne Avenue
First Avenue
Hadlow Road
Madison Crs
Plymstock Road
Okehampton Crescent
Budleigh Crescent
East Wickham
Green Chain Walk
Griffen Manor School
Glenmore Road
Edison Road
Chaucer Road
East Wickham Primary School
Welling School Academy
Berwick Road
Wrotham Road
Swanley Road
Stevens Park
St Michaels CE Primary School
Normanhurst Avenue
Preston Drive
Berkeley Avenue
Mayfair Avenue
Brixham Road
Brampton Primary School
Graves Yard Industrial Estate
Wickham Street
Balliol Road
Somerhill Road
Farnham Road
Cemetery
1 grid square represents 500 metres

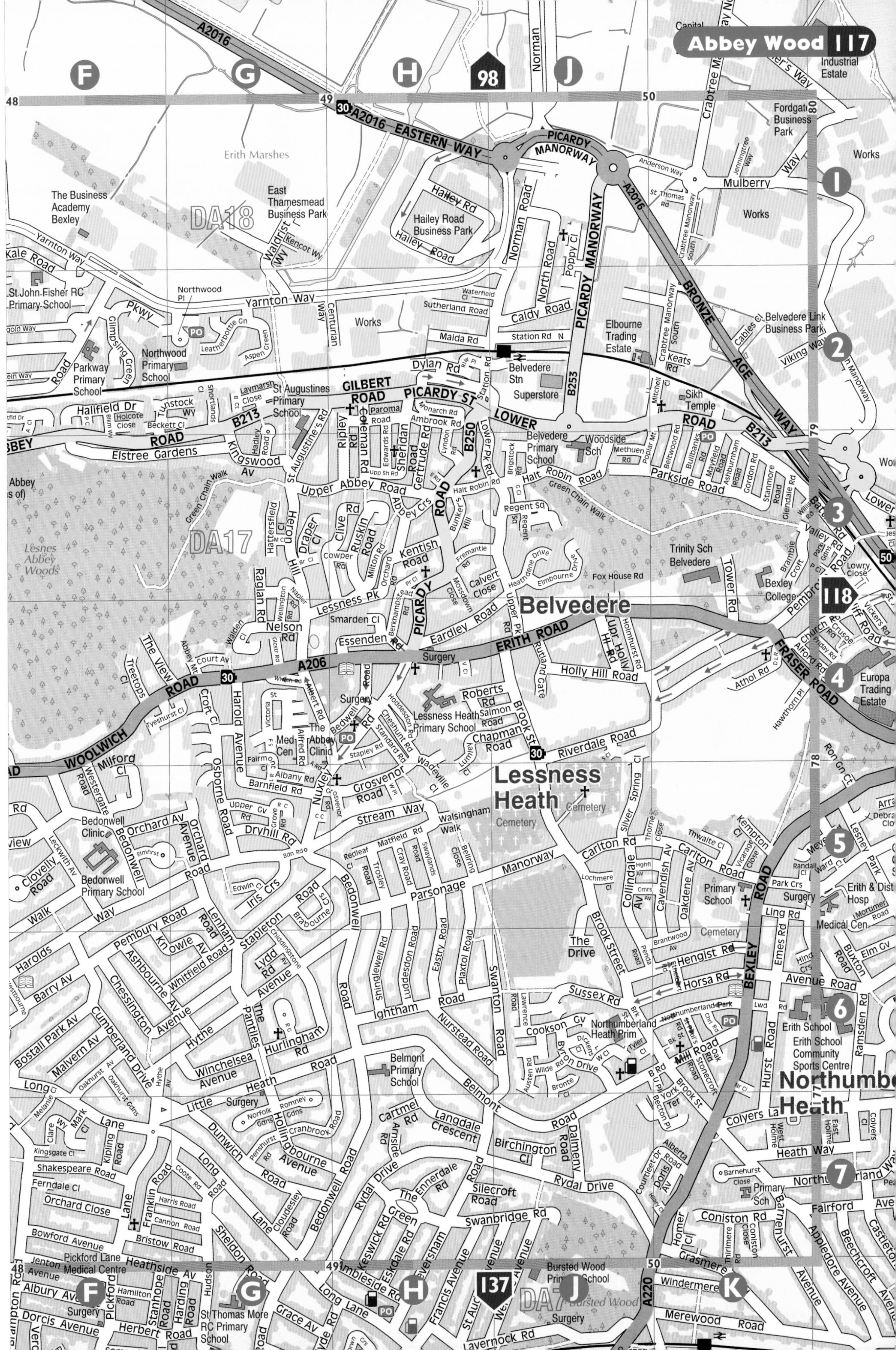
A2016
98
Norman
Capital
Industrial Estate
A2016 EASTERN WAY
PICARDY MANORWAY
Fordgate Business Park
Works
Erith Marshes
The Business Academy Bexley
DA18
East Thamesmead Business Park
Hailey Rd
Hailey Road Business Park
Norman Road
Anderson Way
Mulberry Way
St Thomas Rd
Crabtree Manorway South
BRONZE AGE WAY
Yarnton Way
Kale Road
St John Fisher RC Primary School
Northwood Pl
Waldrist Wy
Kencot Wy
Centurian Way
Waterfield Cl
Sutherland Road
Caldy Road
North Road
Poppy Cl
Elbourne Trading Estate
Belvedere Link Business Park
Cables Cl
Viking Way
Works
Maida Rd
Station Rd N
Belvedere Stn
Superstore
B253
Keats Rd
Mitchell Cl
Sikh Temple
Clumpsing Green
Parkway Primary School
Northwood Primary School
Leatherbottle Gn
Aspen Green
Gilbert Road
Picardy St
Lower Road
Dylan Rd
St Augustines Primary School
Laymarsh Close
Tunstock Wy
Halifield Dr
Holcote Close
Beckett Cl
B213
Abbey Road
Elstree Gardens
Kingswood Av
Paroma Road
Monarch Rd
Ambrook Rd
Belvedere Primary School
Woodside Sch
Methuen Rd
Beltwood Rd
Bullbanks Rd
Mayfield Road
Ashburnham Road
Gordon Rd
Stanmore Road
Glendale Rd
Parkside Road
Halt Robin Road
Upper Abbey Road
Green Chain Walk
Lesnes Abbey Woods
DA17
Hattersfield Cl
Heron Hill
Draper Cl
Clive Rd
Ruskin Road
Cowper Rd
Milton Rd
Abbey Crs
Gertrude Rd
Picardy Road
B250
Lower Pk Rd
Bunkers Hill
Regent Sq
Fremantle Rd
Kentish Road
Calvert Close
Heathdene Drive
Elmbourne Drive
Fox House Rd
Trinity Sch Belvedere
Tower Rd
Bexley College
Valley Rd
Lowry Close
118
Raglan Rd
Nelson Rd
Lessness Pk
Smarden Cl
Essenden Rd
Eardley Road
Belvedere
Upper Pk Rd
Upr Holly H Rd
Holmhurst Rd
Holly Hill Road
Rutland Gate
Church Rd
Alford Rd
Friday Rd
Crusoe Road
Fraser Road
Athol Rd
Europa Trading Estate
Hawthorn Pl
A206 Erith Road
Woolwich Road
Court Av
Abbey Mt
The View
Treetops Cl
Walden Cl
Surgery
Harold Avenue
Croft Cl
Tyeshurst Cl
Victoria St
Albert Rd
Bedwell Rd
The Abbey Clinic
Med Cen
Alfred Rd
Hoddesdon Rd
Cheshunt Rd
Standard Rd
Lessness Heath Primary School
Roberts Rd
Salmon Road
Chapman Road
Brook St
Riverdale Road
Stapley Rd
Wadeville Cl
Lumley Cl
Lessness Heath
Cemetery
Silver Spring Cl
Milford Cl
Westergate Road
Osborne Road
Fairmont Cl
Albany Rd
Barnfield Rd
Nuxley Rd
Grosvenor Road
Stream Way
Walsingham Walk
Upper Gv
Dryhill Rd
Bedonwell Clinic
Orchard Av
Orchard Avenue
Bedonwell Road
Bedonwell Primary School
Clovelly Road
Leckwith Av
Elmhurst
Redleaf Cl
Matfield Rd
Trosley Road
Cray Road
Swaylands Road
Bellring Close
Manorway
Carlton Rd
Thorne Close
Collindale Av
Cavendish Av
Oakdene Av
Thwaite Cl
Kempton Cl
Vicarage Close
Bexley Road
Randall Cl
Ward Cl
Lesney Park
Erith & District Hosp
Primary School
Park Crs
Surgery
Ling Rd
Mortimer Rd
Medical Cen
Lochmere Cl
Walk
Way
Edwin Cl
Iris Crs
Stapleton Road
Brabourne Crs
Parsonage Manorway
Pembury Road
Knowle Av
Lenham Road
Whitfield Road
Chiddingstone
Lydd Rd
Avenue
Shinglewell Rd
Woodesdon Road
Eastry Road
Plaxtol Road
Swanton Road
The Drive
Brook Street
Brantwood Av
Cemetery
Hengist Rd
Horsa Rd
Emes Rd
Hind Crs
Buxton Road
Elm Gv
Avenue Road
Harolds Road
Barry Av
Ashbourne Av
Chessington Avenue
The Pantiles
Hurlingham Rd
Ightham Road
Nurstead Road
Sussex Rd
Lawrence Road
Cookson Gv
Northumberland Heath Prim
Northumberland Park
Lwd
Erith School
Erith School Community Sports Centre
Northumberland Heath
Ramsden Rd
Bostall Park Av
Malvern Av
Cumberland Drive
Hythe Avenue
Winchelsea Avenue
Belmont Primary School
Belmont Road
Dickens Av
Byron Drive
Tyler Cl
Austen Rd
Wilde Rd
Bronte Cl
Mill Road
Oak Road
Stonecroft Road
Brook St
York Ter
Becton Pl
Hurst Road
Colyers La
West Holme
East Holme
Colyers Cl
Heath Way
Long Lane
Oakhurst Av
Oakhurst Gdns
Melanie Cl
Mark Cl
Clare Wy
Kipling Road
Kingsgate Cl
Little Heath
Surgery
Norfolk Gdns
Romney Gdns
Hollingbourne Avenue
Cranbrook Road
Dunwich Road
Cartmel Rd
Arnside Rd
Langdale Crescent
Birchington Cl
Dalmeny Road
Courtleet Dr
Alberta Road
Doris Av
Barnehurst Close
Primary Sch
Northumberland Way
Shakespeare Road
Ferndale Cl
Orchard Close
Bowford Avenue
Franklin Road
Harris Road
Cannon Road
Bristow Road
Coote Rd
Long Lane
Cloudesley Road
Bedonwell Road
Rydal Drive
The Green
Ennerdale Rd
Silecroft Road
Swanbridge Rd
Rydal Drive
Homer Cl
Coniston Rd
Thirlmere Rd
Coniston Close
Barnehurst Avenue
Fairford Av
Appledore Avenue
Beechcroft Avenue
Castleton Av
Jenton Avenue
Pickford Lane Medical Centre
Heathside Av
Albury Av
Pickford Road
Hamilton Road
Stanhope Road
Harding Road
Hudson
Sheldon Road
St Thomas More RC Primary School
Dorcis Avenue
Herbert Road
Surgery
Long Lane
Grace Av
Ambleside Rd
Keswick Rd
Eskdale Rd
Eversham
Francis Avenue
St Audrey Avenue
137
Bursted Wood Primary School
DA7
Bursted Wood
Surgery
Grasmere Rd
Windermere Rd
Merewood Road
A220
Lavernock Rd
F
G
H
J
I
K
2
3
4
5
6
7
48
49
50
77
78
79
80
30

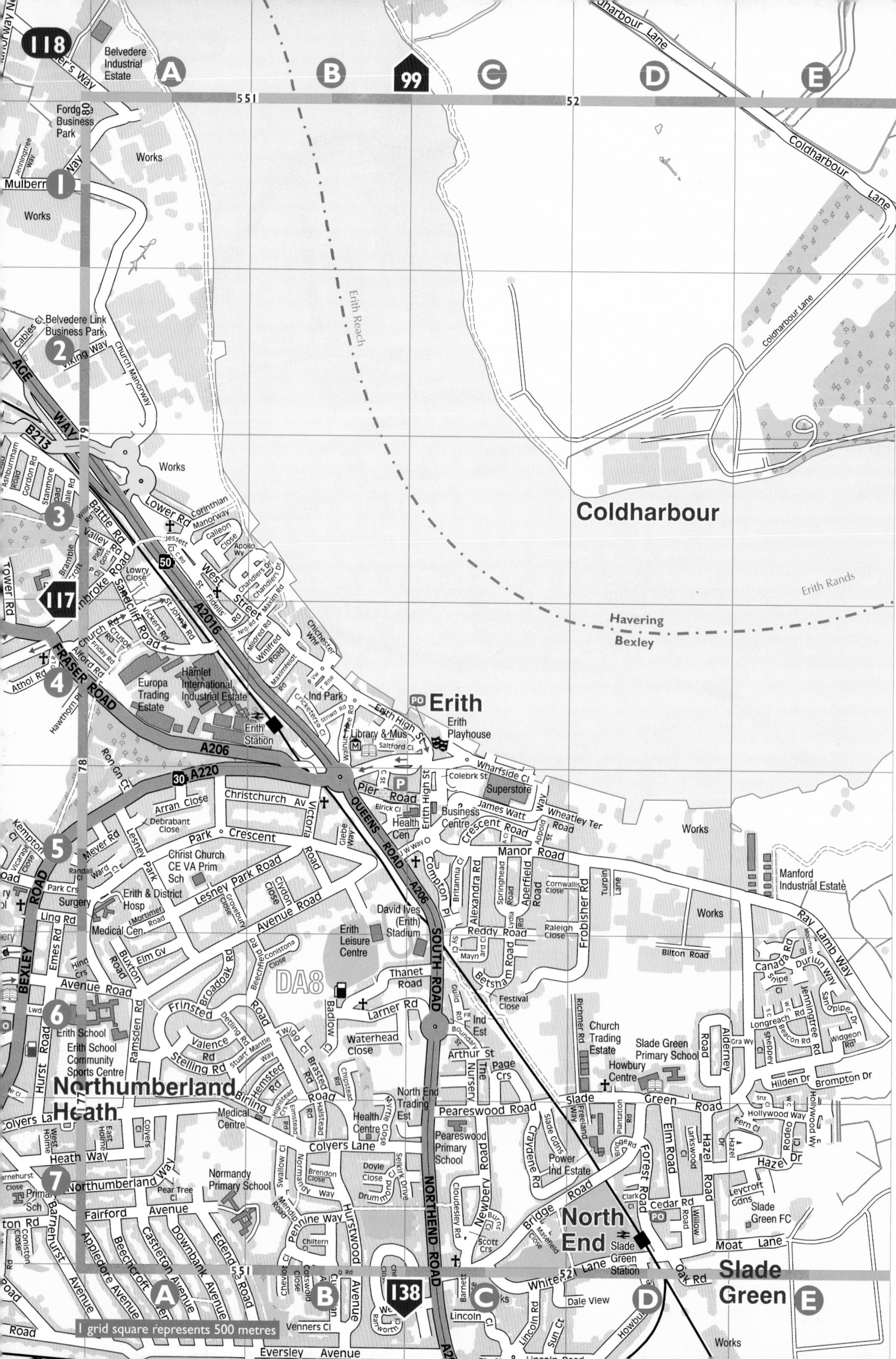

Grid references (top): A · 99 · B · C · D · E
Grid references (bottom): A · B · 138 · C · D · E
Row references (left): 118 · 1 · 2 · 3 · 117 · 4 · 30 · 5 · 6 · 7

Places and labels:

- Belvedere Industrial Estate
- Fordge Business Park
- Mulberry Way
- Works
- Belvedere Link Business Park
- Viking Way
- Church Manorway
- Erith Reach
- Coldharbour
- Coldharbour Lane
- Erith Rands
- Havering / Bexley
- B213
- Battle Road
- Lower Road
- Corinthian Manorway
- West Street
- Apollo Way
- A2016
- Tower Rd
- FRASER ROAD
- Athol Rd
- Hawthorn Rd
- Europa Trading Estate
- Hamlet International Industrial Estate
- Ind Park
- Erith Station
- A206
- A220
- Erith High St
- PO Erith
- Erith Playhouse
- Library & Mus
- Saltford Cl
- Wharfside Cl
- Colebrk St
- Superstore
- James Watt Crescent Road
- Wheatley Ter
- Pier Road
- Health Cen
- Business Centre
- Manor Road
- Works
- Manford Industrial Estate
- Christchurch Av
- QUEENS ROAD
- Victoria Road
- Park Crescent
- Arran Close
- Debrabant Close
- Meyer Rd
- Lesney Park Road
- Christ Church CE VA Prim Sch
- Erith & District Hosp
- Medical Cen
- Avenue Road
- Alexandra Rd
- Springhead
- Aperfield Road
- Cornwallis Close
- Frobisher Rd
- Turpin Lane
- Raleigh Road
- Bilton Road
- Works
- Ray Lamb Way
- Canada Rd
- Durlun Way
- Jenningtree Rd
- Longreach Rd
- Beacon Rd
- Sheppey Cl
- Widgeon Rd
- David Ives (Erith) Stadium
- Erith Leisure Centre
- DA8
- Thanet Road
- Larner Rd
- Reddy Road
- Betsham Rd
- Festival Close
- Church Trading Estate
- Howbury Centre
- Slade Green Primary School
- Hilden Dr
- Brompton Dr
- Hazel Road
- Slade Green FC
- BEXLEY ROAD
- Hurst Road
- Erith School
- Erith School Community Sports Centre
- Northumberland Heath
- Valence Rd
- Stelling Rd
- Frinsted Rd
- Broadoak Rd
- Brasted Rd
- Badlow Close
- Waterhead Close
- Arthur St
- North End Trading Est
- Peareswood Road
- Slade Green Road
- Elm Road
- Forest Road
- Leycroft Gdns
- Northumberland Way
- Normandy Primary School
- Colyers Lane
- Pennine Way
- Hurstwood Avenue
- Peareswood Primary School
- Power Ind Estate
- Craydene Rd
- Newbery Road
- NORTH END ROAD
- North End
- Slade Green Station
- Slade Green
- Moat Lane
- Oak Rd
- PO
- Cedar Rd

Scale: 1 grid square represents 500 metres

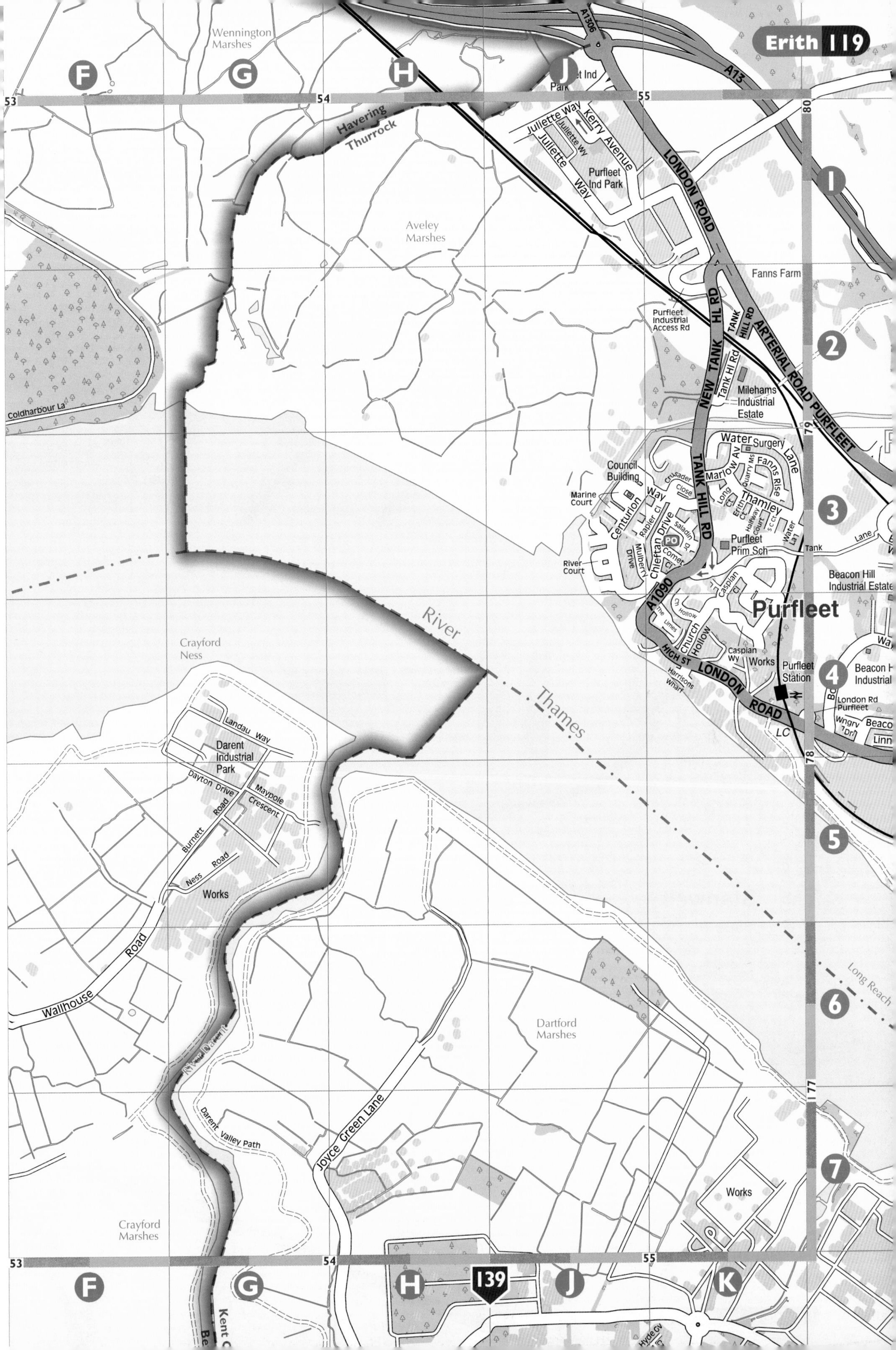

F G H J

53 54 55 80

Wennington Marshes

Havering Thurrock

Aveley Marshes

Coldharbour La

I

et Ind Park

Juliette Way
Kerry Avenue
Juliette Wy
Juliette Way

Purfleet Ind Park

LONDON ROAD

A13

Fanns Farm

Purfleet Industrial Access Rd

NEW TANK HL RD
TANK HILL RD

ARTERIAL ROAD PURFLEET

61

2

Milehams Industrial Estate

Council Building

Marine Court

Water Surgery
Marlow Av
Long Fanns Rise
Crusader
Close
Erith Ct
Halley Court
S.C.C.L.

TANK HILL RD

Centurion Way
Rapier Cl
Mulberry
Comet
Chieftan Drive
Saladin
PO
Purfleet Prim Sch

Thamley
Water La
Tank

Lane

3

River Court

Caspian Cl

A1090

The Lanes
Hollow
Church
Hollow
Works
Caspian Wy

Beacon Hill Industrial Estate

Purfleet

LONDON ROAD

Purfleet Station

HIGH ST
Harrisons Wharf

Beacon H Industrial

London Rd Purfleet

Wngrv Drf
Linn
Beac

LC

78

4

Crayford Ness

River Thames

Landau Way

Darent Industrial Park

Dayton Drive
Maypole Crescent
Burnett Road
Ness Road

Works

Wallhouse Road

River Darent

Darent Valley Path

Joyce Green Lane

Dartford Marshes

Long Reach

177

5

6

7

Works

Crayford Marshes

Kent C
Be

53 54 55

F G H **139** J K

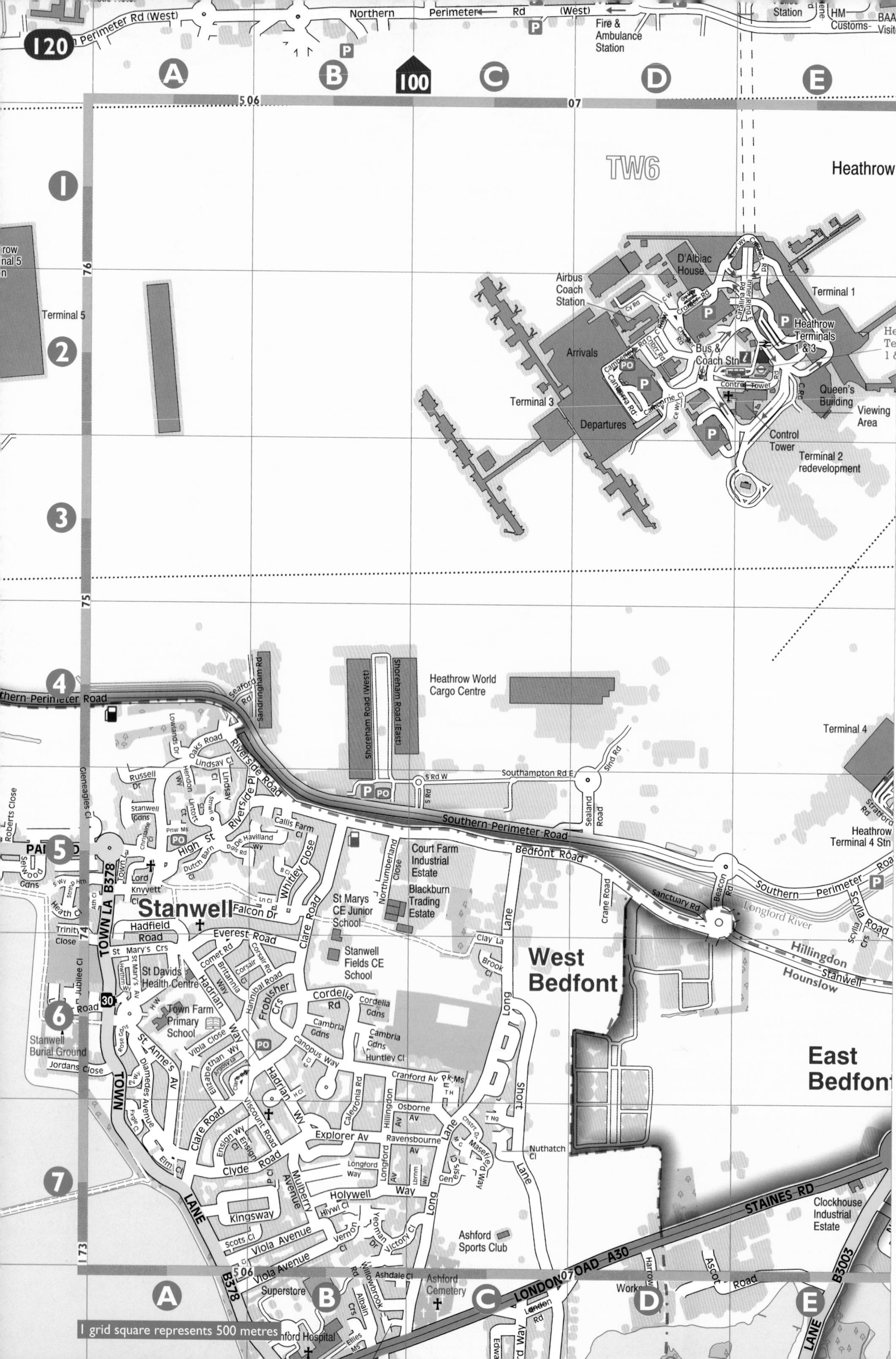

120

Northern Perimeter Rd (West)

Perimeter Rd (West)

Fire & Ambulance Station

Police Station

HM Customs

BAA Visitor

A 5.06 **B** 100 **C** 07 **D** **E**

I

TW6

Heathrow

row nal 5 n

Terminal 5

76

D'Albiac House

Airbus Coach Station

Terminal 1

2

Arrivals

Terminal 3

Bus & Coach Stn

Heathrow Terminals 1 & 3

Queen's Building

Viewing Area

Departures

Control Tower

Terminal 2 redevelopment

3

75

4

thern Perimeter Road

Seaford Rd

Sandringham Rd

Shoreham Road (West)

Shoreham Road East

Heathrow World Cargo Centre

Terminal 4

Lowlands Dr

Oaks Road

Russell Dr

Lindsay Cl

Hendon Cl

Urfort Cl

Lindsay Cl

Riverside Road

S Rd W

Southampton Rd E

Srnd Rd

Sealand Rd

Heathrow Terminal 4 Stn

Roberts Close

Gleneagles Cl

Stanwell Gdns

Christine

High St

De Havilland

Dolls Hse Cl

B Cl

Callis Farm Cl

Whitley Close

Clare Road

Northumberland Lane

Court Farm Industrial Estate

Bedfont Road

Crane Road

sanctuary Rd

Southern Perimeter Road

Longford River

Scylla Road

5

PAR RD

TOWN LA B378

74

Lord Knyvett

Dutch Barn

Ln Cl

Stanwell

Falcon Dr

St Marys CE Junior School

Blackburn Trading Estate

Clay La

Beacon

Hillingdon

West Bedfont

6

Heath Cl

Trinity Close

Jubilee Cl

30

Hadfield Road

St Mary's Crs

St David's Health Centre

Comet Rd

Britannia Way

Corsair Cl

Corsair Rd

Everest Road

Frobisher Crs

Cordelia Rd

Cordelia Gdns

Brook Cl

Stanwell Fields CE School

Cambria Rd

Cambria Gdns

Huntley Cl

Stanwell Burial Ground

Jordans Close

Town Farm Primary School

Hadrian Way

Vibia Close

Elizabethan Way

Canopus Way

Cranford Av

Pk Ms

Long Lane

Stanwell Hounslow

East Bedfont

7

TOWN LANE

173

St Anne's Av

Diamedes Avenue

Clare Road

Ensign Way

Ensign Cl

Viscount Road

Mulberry Avenue

Explorer Av

Longford Way

Caledonia Rd

Hillingdon Av

Osborne Av

Ravensbourne Av

Masefield Way

Nuthatch Cl

Short Lane

Clyde Rd

Holywell Way

Kingsway

Scots Cl

Viola Avenue

Vernon Cl

Yeoman Cl

Victory Cl

Ashdale Cl

Ashford Sports Club

LONDON ROAD A30

STAINES RD

Clockhouse Industrial Estate

B3003

A 5.06 **B** 07 **C** **D** **E**

B378

Superstore

Viola Avenue

Willowbrook

Ashford Cemetery

Londen Rd

Works

Ascot Road

LANE B3003

1 grid square represents 500 metres

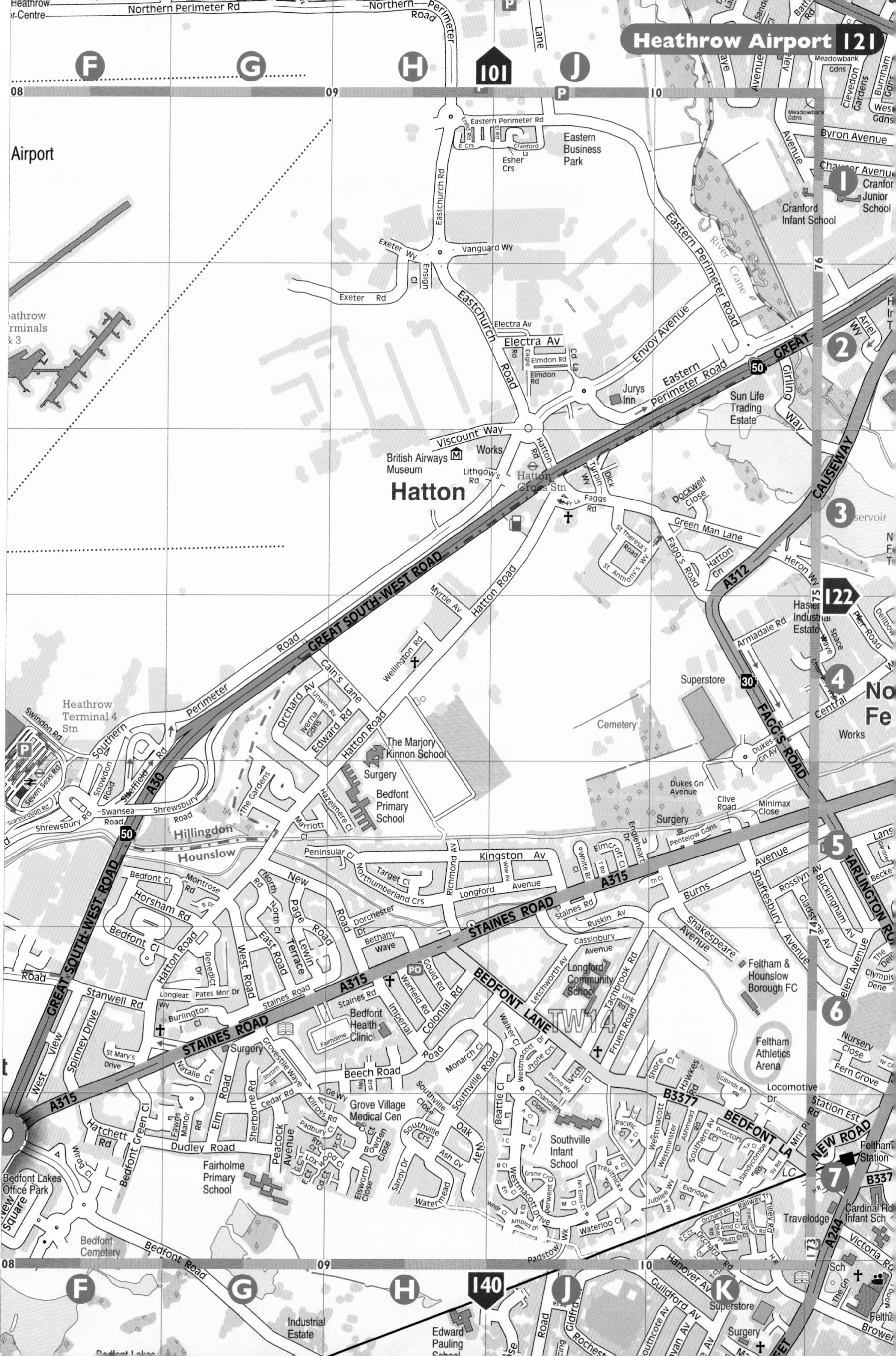
Northern Perimeter Rd
Eastern Perimeter Rd
Eastern Business Park
Eastchurch Rd
Vanguard Wy
Exeter Rd
Electra Av
Envoy Avenue
Jurys Inn
Sun Life Trading Estate
Viscount Way
British Airways Museum
Hatton
Hatton Cross Stn
Green Man Lane
Cranford Infant School
Cranford Junior School
River Crane
GREAT SOUTH-WEST ROAD
Hatton Road
Faggs Rd
Superstore
Cemetery
The Marjory Kinnon School
Surgery
Bedfont Primary School
Heathrow Terminal 4 Stn
Hillingdon
Hounslow
Kingston Av
Longford Avenue
STAINES ROAD
A315
BEDFONT LANE
TW14
Longford Community School
Feltham & Hounslow Borough FC
Feltham Athletics Arena
Bedfont Health Clinic
Grove Village Medical Cen
Southville Infant School
Fairholme Primary School
Dudley Road
Bedfont Lakes Office Park
Bedfont Cemetery
Bedfont Road
Feltham Station
NEW ROAD
Travelodge
Industrial Estate
Edward Pauling School

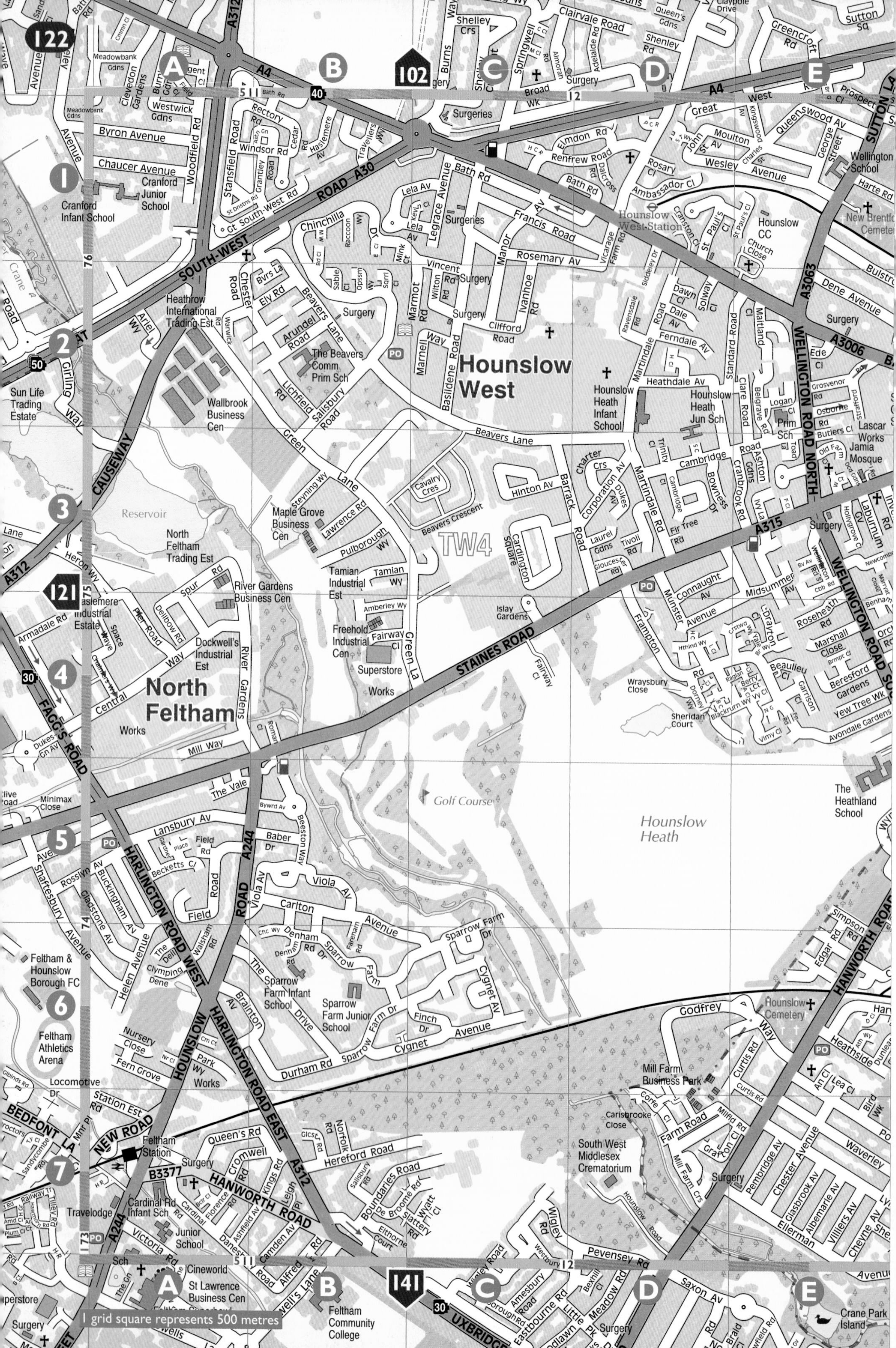
122
102
121
141
Hounslow West
North Feltham
TW4
Hounslow Heath
Golf Course
Reservoir
Hounslow West Station
Feltham Station
SOUTH-WEST ROAD A30
STAINES ROAD
WELLINGTON ROAD NORTH
HARLINGTON ROAD WEST
HARLINGTON ROAD EAST
HANWORTH ROAD
HOUNSLOW ROAD
CAUSEWAY
FAGG'S ROAD
NEW ROAD
BEDFONT LA
UXBRIDGE
A4
A312
A315
A244
A3063
A3006
B3377
Cranford Infant School
Cranford Junior School
Heathrow International Trading Est
Sun Life Trading Estate
Wallbrook Business Cen
North Feltham Trading Est
River Gardens Business Cen
Dockwell's Industrial Est
Haslemere Industrial Estate
Maple Grove Business Cen
Tamian Industrial Est
Freehold Industrial Cen
Superstore
Works
The Beavers Comm Prim Sch
Hounslow Heath Infant School
Hounslow Heath Jun Sch
Logan Prim Sch
Lascar Works
Jamia Mosque
Wellington School
Hounslow CC
The Heathland School
Hounslow Cemetery
Mill Farm Business Park
South West Middlesex Crematorium
Sparrow Farm Infant School
Sparrow Farm Junior School
Feltham & Hounslow Borough FC
Feltham Athletics Arena
Cardinal Rd Infant Sch
Junior School
Travelodge
Cineworld
St Lawrence Business Cen
Feltham Community College
Crane Park Island
1 grid square represents 500 metres

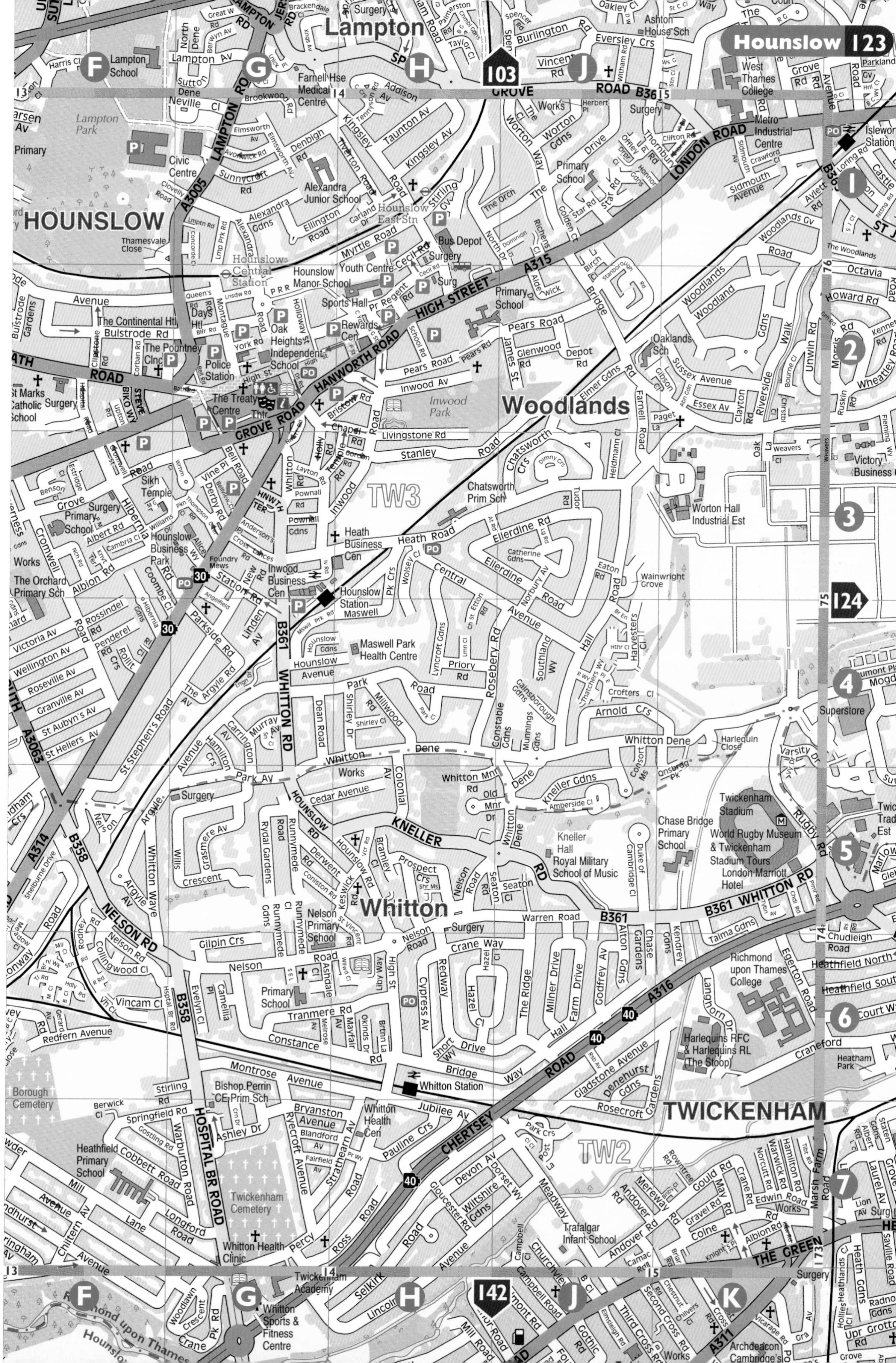
Lampton
Lampton School
Lampton Park
Lampton Av
Lampton Rd
Civic Centre
HOUNSLOW
Farnell Hse Medical Centre
103
Burlington Rd
Eversley Crs
Ashton House Sch
West Thames College
GROVE ROAD B363
Metro Industrial Centre
Isleworth Station
LONDON ROAD
Alexandra Junior School
Hounslow East Stn
Bus Depot
Surgery
Hounslow Central Station
Hounslow Manor School
Youth Centre
Sports Hall
HIGH STREET
A315
Primary School
The Continental Htl
Bulstrode Rd
Bulstrode Gardens
Days Htl
The Pountney Clnc
Police Station
Oak Heights Independent School
Rewards Cen
HANWORTH ROAD
GROVE ROAD
The Treaty Centre
Thtr
St Marks Catholic School
Surgery
Pears Road
Glenwood Rd
Depot Rd
Inwood Av
Inwood Park
Livingstone Rd
Stanley Road
Woodlands
Woodlands Gv
Oaklands Sch
Sussex Avenue
Essex Av
Riverside Walk
Octavia
Howard Rd
Wheatley Road
Victory Business C
Weavers Cl
Sikh Temple
Grove Primary School
Hounslow Business Park
Foundry Mews
Station Rd
TW3
Chatsworth Prim Sch
Heath Business Cen
Heath Road
Inwood Business Cen
Hounslow Station
Maswell
Worton Hall Industrial Est
Ellerdine Rd
Catherine Gdns
Central Avenue
Norbury Av
Wainwright Grove
124
The Orchard Primary Sch
Albion Rd
Victoria Av
Wellington Av
Roseville Av
Granville Av
St Aubyn's Av
St Hellers Av
A3063
Maswell Park Health Centre
Hounslow Avenue
B361
WHITTON RD
Rosebery Rd
Gainsborough Gdns
Crofters Cl
Arnold Crs
Superstore
Whitton Dene
Harlequin Close
Varsity Dr
Whitton Mnr Rd
Kneller Gdns
Twickenham Stadium
World Rugby Museum & Twickenham Stadium Tours
London Marriott Hotel
Chase Bridge Primary School
Kneller Hall
Royal Military School of Music
KNELLER RD
Whitton
Nelson Primary School
A314
B358
NELSON RD
Surgery
Crescent
Grasmere Av
Cedar Avenue
Colonial Av
Warren Road
B361 WHITTON RD
Richmond upon Thames College
Heathfield North
Heathfield South
Chudleigh Road
Egerton Road
Crane Way
Hazel Cl
The Ridge
Milner Drive
Hall Farm Drive
Godfrey Av
Alton Gdns
Chase Gardens
Kendrey Gdns
Talma Gdns
A316
Harlequins RFC & Harlequins RL (The Stoop)
Craneford
Heatham Park
Gilpin Crs
Vincam Cl
Redfern Avenue
Primary School
Tranmere Rd
Constance Rd
Cypress Av
Short Wy
Drive
Bridge Way
Whitton Station
Montrose Avenue
Borough Cemetery
Bishop Perrin CE Prim Sch
HOSPITAL BR ROAD
Whitton Health Cen
Jubilee Av
CHERTSEY ROAD
Gladstone Avenue
Denehurst Gdns
Rosecroft Gardens
TWICKENHAM
TW2
Heathfield Primary School
Cobbett Road
Springfield Rd
Twickenham Cemetery
Whitton Health Clinic
Percy Road
Ross Road
Gloucester Rd
Devon Av
Wiltshire Gdns
Meadway
Trafalgar Infant School
Andover Rd
Colne Rd
THE GREEN
Marsh Farm Road
Edwin Road
Surgery
Twickenham Academy
Whitton Sports & Fitness Centre
142
Richmond upon Thames
Third Cross Rd
Second Cross Rd
A311
Archdeacon Cambridge's
Heath Gdns
Radnor Gdns
Upr Grotto Rd
F
G
H
J
K
I
2
3
4
5
6
7
13
14
15
30
40

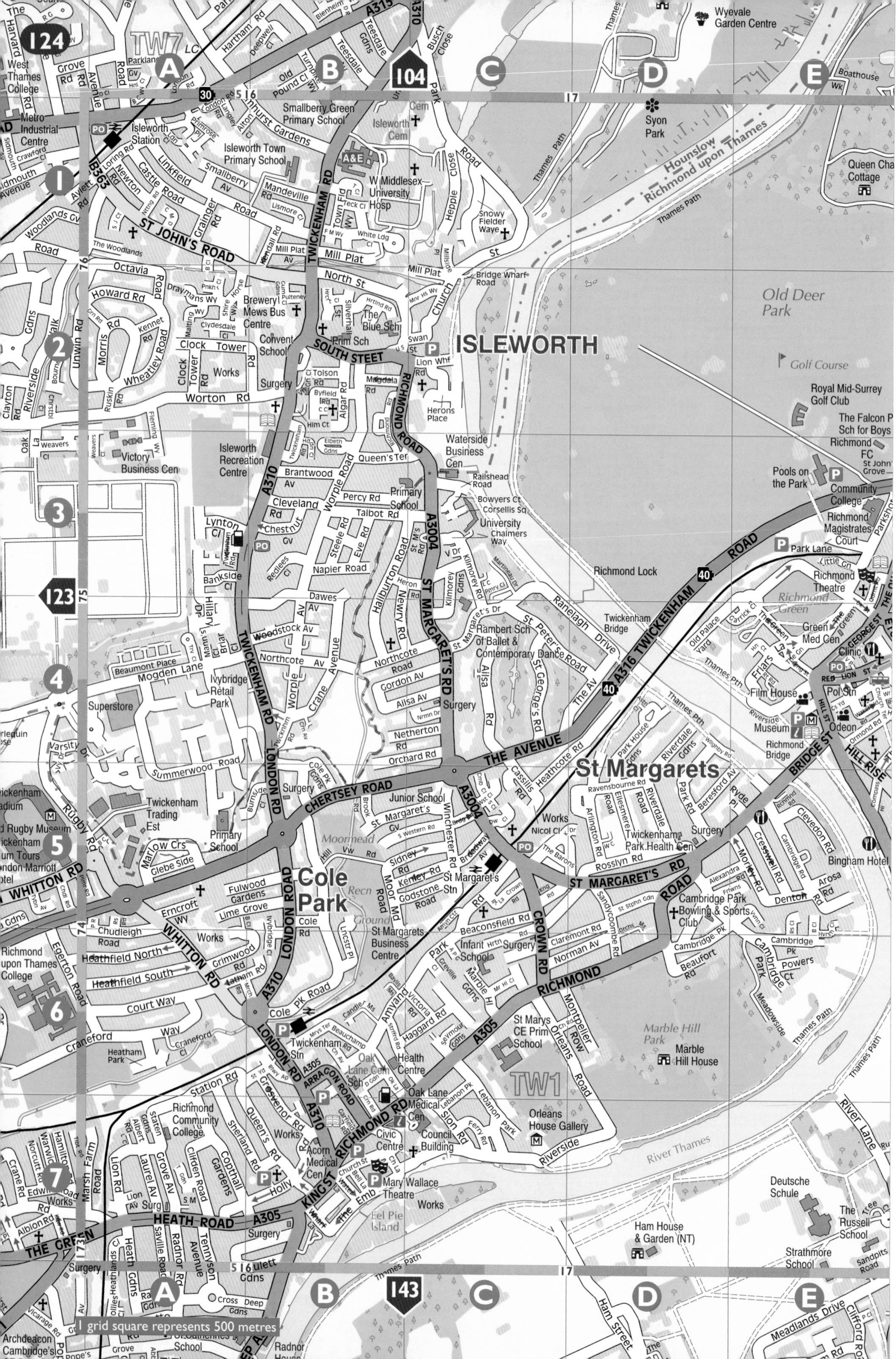
124
104
123
143
A
B
C
D
E
1
2
3
4
5
6
7
16
17
75
76
74
73
TW7
TW1
ISLEWORTH
St Margarets
Cole Park
Old Deer Park
Isleworth Station
Metro Industrial Centre
West Thames College
Smallberry Green Primary School
Isleworth Town Primary School
Isleworth Cem
W Middlesex University Hosp
Syon Park
Wyevale Garden Centre
Hounslow
Richmond upon Thames
Thames Path
Queen Charlotte's Cottage
ST JOHN'S ROAD
TWICKENHAM RD
Mill Plat
North St
SOUTH STREET
RICHMOND ROAD
Brewery Mews Bus Centre
Convent School
The Blue Sch
Prim Sch
Clock Tower Road
Worton Rd
Wheatley Road
Victory Business Cen
Isleworth Recreation Centre
Waterside Business Cen
Railshead Road
University
Golf Course
Royal Mid-Surrey Golf Club
The Falcon Pk Sch for Boys
Richmond FC
Pools on the Park
Community College
Richmond Magistrates Court
Richmond Lock
Richmond Theatre
Richmond Green
Green Med Cen
Twickenham Bridge
A316 TWICKENHAM ROAD
Ranelagh Drive
Rambert Sch of Ballet & Contemporary Dance
ST MARGARET'S RD
A3004
A310
Mogden Lane
Ivybridge Retail Park
Superstore
Summerwood Road
THE AVENUE
CHERTSEY ROAD
LONDON RD
Twickenham Trading Est
Primary School
Junior School
Moormead
Recn Ground
St Margarets Business Centre
St Margaret's Stn
ST MARGARET'S RD
Twickenham Park Health Cen
Film House
Riverside Museum
Richmond Bridge
Odeon
BRIDGE ST
HILL RISE
Bingham Hotel
Cambridge Park Bowling & Sports Club
CROWN RD
RICHMOND
A305
WHITTON RD
Rugby Rd
Twickenham Stadium
Rugby Museum
Richmond upon Thames College
Egerton Road
Heathfield North
Heathfield South
Court Way
Craneford Way
Heatham Park
Twickenham Stn
Oak Lane Cem
Health Centre
Oak Lane Medical Cen
St Marys CE Prim School
Marble Hill Park
Marble Hill House
Orleans House Gallery
Orleans Road
River Thames
Riverside
Civic Centre
Council Building
Mary Wallace Theatre
Eel Pie Island
Richmond Community College
Acorn Medical Cen
KINGST
HEATH ROAD
THE GREEN
Ham House & Garden (NT)
Deutsche Schule
The Russell School
Strathmore School
River Lane
Ham Street
Meadlands Drive
Thames Path
Station Rd
Marsh Farm Road
Surgery
Works
1 grid square represents 500 metres

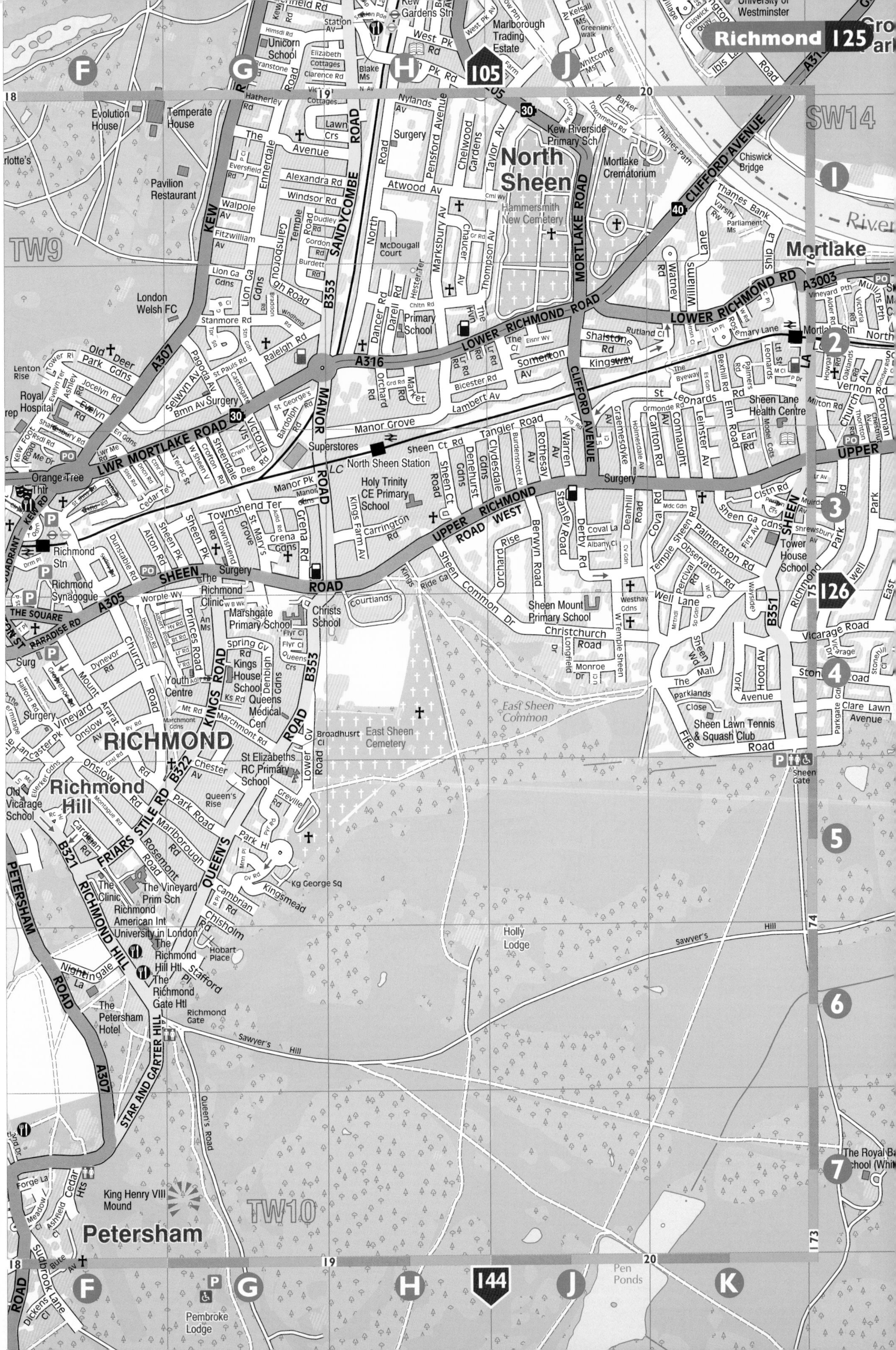
North Sheen
Mortlake
RICHMOND
Richmond Hill
Petersham
TW9
TW10
SW14
Kew Riverside Primary Sch
Mortlake Crematorium
Chiswick Bridge
Hammersmith New Cemetery
North Sheen Station
Richmond Stn
Mortlake Stn
East Sheen Cemetery
East Sheen Common
Sheen Gate
Holly Lodge
Pen Ponds
Pembroke Lodge
King Henry VIII Mound
Richmond Gate
Sawyer's Hill
LOWER RICHMOND ROAD
UPPER RICHMOND ROAD WEST
LWR MORTLAKE ROAD
SHEEN ROAD
MANOR ROAD
CLIFFORD AVENUE
MORTLAKE ROAD
SANDYCOMBE ROAD
KEW ROAD
PETERSHAM ROAD
RICHMOND HILL
STAR AND GARTER HILL
QUEEN'S ROAD
FRIARS STILE RD
KINGS ROAD
Sheen Lane Health Centre
Sheen Mount Primary School
Holy Trinity CE Primary School
Sheen Lawn Tennis & Squash Club
Richmond American Int University in London
The Petersham Hotel
Orange Tree Thtr
Royal Hospital
London Welsh FC
Evolution House
Temperate House
Pavilion Restaurant
105
126
144

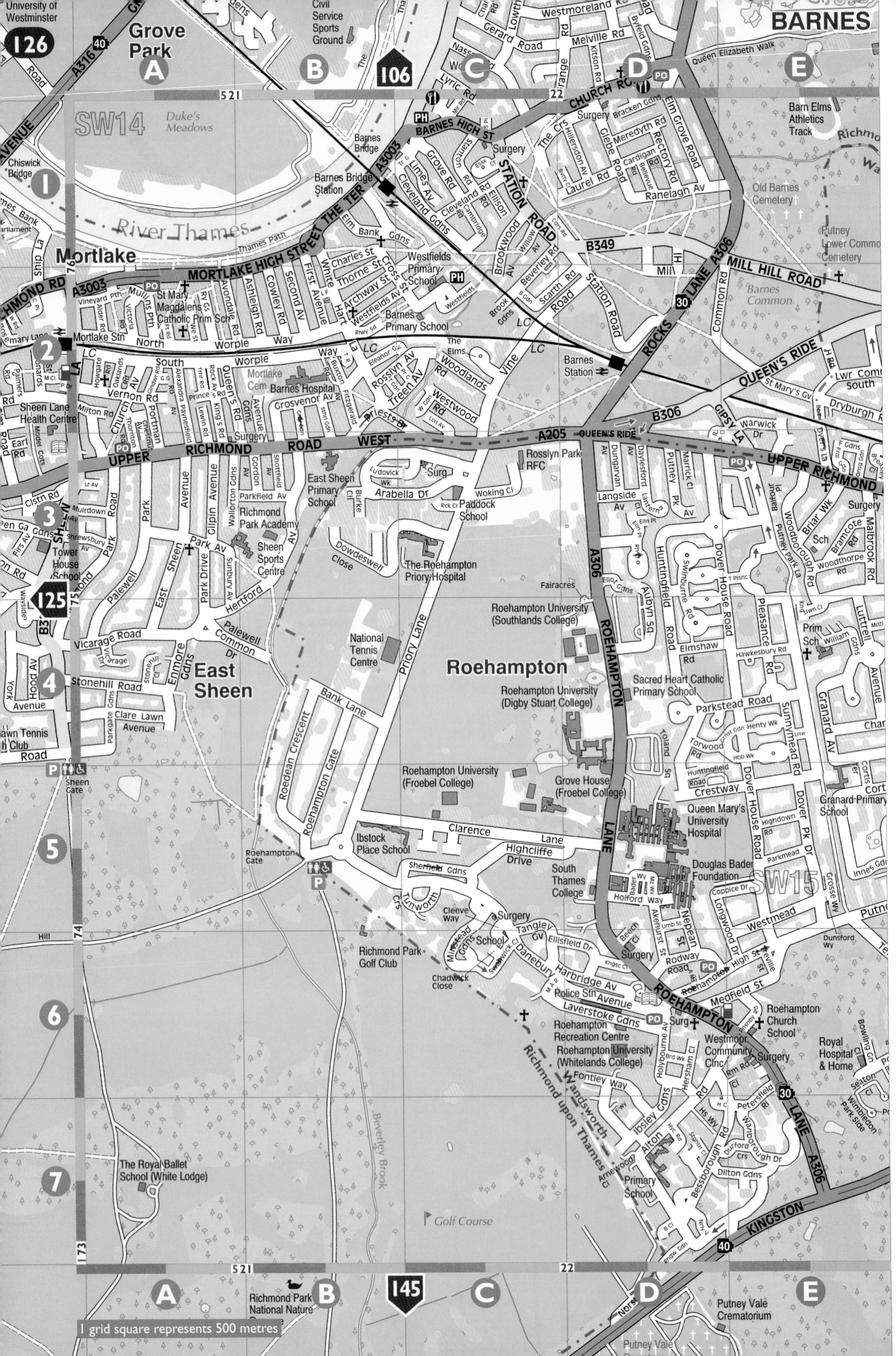

University of Westminster
126
Grove Park
Civil Service Sports Ground
106
BARNES
Queen Elizabeth Walk
SW14
Duke's Meadows
Chiswick Bridge
River Thames
Thames Path
Mortlake
MORTLAKE HIGH STREET
THE TERRACE
Barnes Bridge
Barnes Bridge Station
BARNES HIGH ST
CHURCH RD
Westmoreland Rd
Gerard Road
Melville Rd
Barn Elms Athletics Track
Old Barnes Cemetery
Putney Lower Common Cemetery
MILL HILL ROAD
Barnes Common
B349
STATION ROAD
Station Road
Barnes Station
ROCKS LANE
A306
QUEEN'S RIDE
B306
Mortlake Stn
North Worple Way
South Worple Way
Mortlake Cem
Barnes Hospital
Westfields Primary School
Barnes Primary School
St Mary Magdalens Catholic Prim Sch
Sheen Lane Health Centre
UPPER RICHMOND ROAD WEST
A205
UPPER RICHMOND ROAD
East Sheen Primary School
Richmond Park Academy
Sheen Sports Centre
Paddock School
Rosslyn Park RFC
The Roehampton Priory Hospital
Tower House School
125
East Sheen
Palewell Common Dr
Vicarage Road
Stonehill Road
Clare Lawn Avenue
National Tennis Centre
Priory Lane
Roehampton
Roehampton University (Southlands College)
Roehampton University (Digby Stuart College)
Roehampton University (Froebel College)
Grove House (Froebel College)
ROEHAMPTON LANE
Sacred Heart Catholic Primary School
Parkstead Road
Dover House Road
Queen Mary's University Hospital
Douglas Bader Foundation
SW15
Bank Lane
Roedean Crescent
Roehampton Gate
Clarence Lane
Highcliffe Drive
Ibstock Place School
South Thames College
Richmond Park Golf Club
Sheen Gate
Roehampton Gate
Roehampton Recreation Centre
Roehampton University (Whitelands College)
Richmond upon Thames
Wandsworth
Westmoor Community Clnc
Roehampton Church School
Royal Hospital & Home
Granard Primary School
Beverley Brook
Golf Course
The Royal Ballet School (White Lodge)
KINGSTON
Richmond Park National Nature Reserve
145
Putney Vale Crematorium
Putney Vale
1 grid square represents 500 metres
A B C D E
1 2 3 4 5 6 7

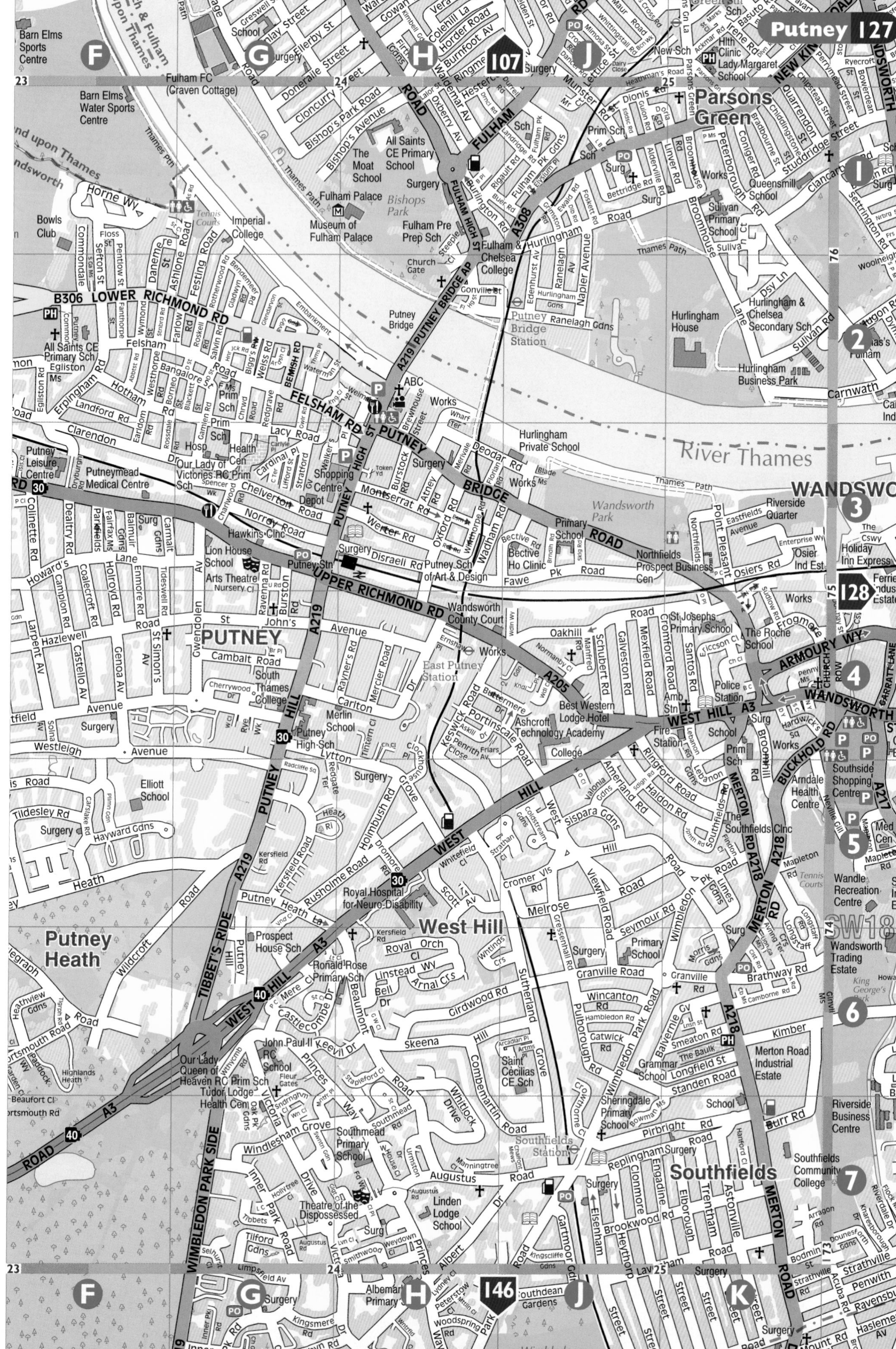

Putney 127
107
128
146
Barn Elms Sports Centre
Barn Elms Water Sports Centre
Fulham FC (Craven Cottage)
Bowls Club
Imperial College
Fulham Palace
Museum of Fulham Palace
Bishops Park
The Moat School
All Saints CE Primary School
Fulham Pre Prep Sch
Fulham & Chelsea College
Parsons Green
Queensmill School
Sulivan Primary School
Hurlingham House
Hurlingham & Chelsea Secondary Sch
Hurlingham Business Park
Putney Bridge
Putney Bridge Station
Hurlingham Private School
River Thames
Wandsworth Park
LOWER RICHMOND RD
B306
All Saints CE Primary Sch
Putney Leisure Centre
Putneymead Medical Centre
FELSHAM RD
PUTNEY BRIDGE RD
PUTNEY HIGH ST
UPPER RICHMOND RD
Putney Stn
Lion House School
Arts Theatre
Hawkins Clinic
Putney Sch of Art & Design
Wandsworth County Court
East Putney Station
PUTNEY
South Thames College
Merlin School
Putney High Sch
Elliott School
WANDSWORTH
Riverside Quarter
Holiday Inn Express
Northfields Prospect Business Cen
St Josephs Primary School
The Roche School
ARMOURY WY
WEST HILL
A3
A205
A219
A218
Best Western Lodge Hotel
Ashcroft Technology Academy
Southside Shopping Centre
Arndale Health Centre
Wandle Recreation Centre
SW18
Wandsworth Trading Estate
Royal Hospital for Neuro-Disability
West Hill
Putney Heath
Prospect House Sch
Ronald Rose Primary Sch
TIBBET'S RIDE
John Paul II RC School
Our Lady Queen of Heaven RC Prim Sch
Tudor Lodge Health Cen
Saint Cecilias CE Sch
Primary School
Sheringdale Primary School
Grammar School
Merton Road Industrial Estate
Riverside Business Centre
Southfields Community College
Southfields
Southfields Station
Southmead Primary School
Theatre of the Dispossessed
Linden Lodge School
WIMBLEDON PARK SIDE
MERTON RD
Albemarle Primary
Wimbledon Park

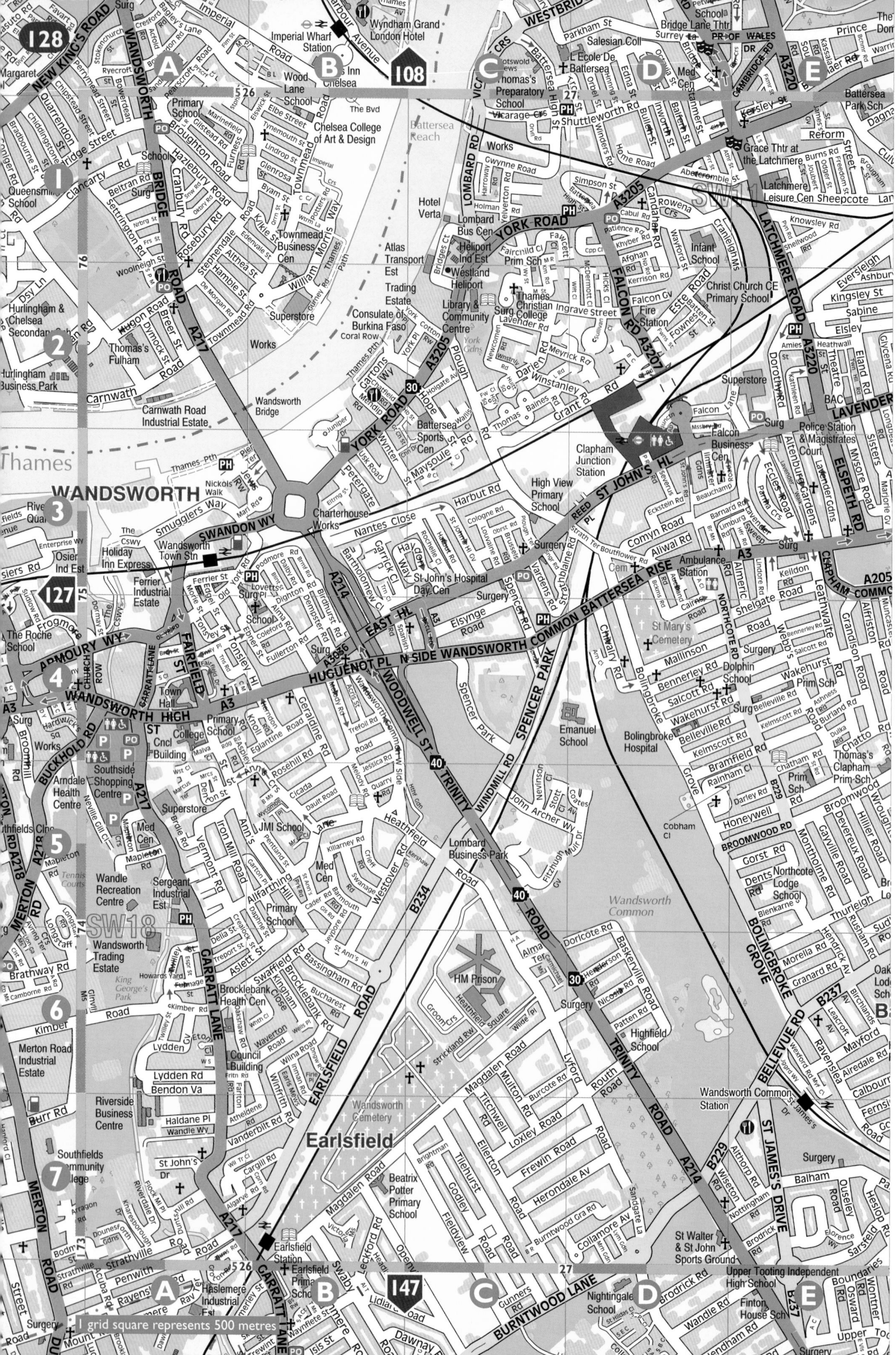

128
108
127
147
A
B
C
D
E
1
2
3
4
5
6
7
WANDSWORTH
Earlsfield
Thames
SW18
SW11
Battersea Reach
Wandsworth Common
Wandsworth Cemetery
Imperial Wharf Station
Wyndham Grand London Hotel
Chelsea College of Art & Design
Wood Lane School
Hotel Verta
Atlas Transport Est
Trading Estate
Consulate of Burkina Faso
Wandsworth Bridge
Carnwath Road Industrial Estate
Hurlingham Business Park
Hurlingham & Chelsea Secondary Sch
Queensmill School
Thomas's Fulham
Townmead Business Cen
Superstore
Works
Heliport Ind Est
Westland Heliport
Library & Community Centre
Lombard Bus Cen
Thames Christian College
Battersea Sports Cen
Clapham Junction Station
High View Primary School
Charterhouse Works
Wandsworth Town Stn
Holiday Inn Express
Ferrier Industrial Estate
Osier Ind Est
The Roche School
Town Hall
Primary School
College
Cncl Building
Southside Shopping Centre
Arndale Health Centre
Wandle Recreation Centre
Sergeant Industrial Est
Wandsworth Trading Estate
King George's Park
Merton Road Industrial Estate
Riverside Business Centre
Southfields Community College
Brocklebank Health Cen
Council Building
Lombard Business Park
HM Prison
Highfield School
Beatrix Potter Primary School
Earlsfield Station
Haslemere Industrial Est
Emanuel School
Bolingbroke Hospital
St Mary's Cemetery
Ambulance Station
Dolphin School
Thomas's Clapham Prim Sch
Northcote Lodge School
Wandsworth Common Station
St Walter & St John Sports Ground
Upper Tooting Independent High School
Finton House Sch
Nightingale School
Salesian Coll
L'Ecole De Battersea
Thomas's Preparatory School
Bridge Lane Thtr
Grace Thtr at the Latchmere
Latchmere Leisure Cen
Battersea Park Sch
Infant School
Christ Church CE Primary School
Fire Station
Police Station & Magistrates Court
Falcon Business Cen
St John's Hospital Day Cen
JMI School
NEW KING'S ROAD
WANDSWORTH BRIDGE ROAD
YORK ROAD
SWANDON WY
ARMOURY WY
WANDSWORTH HIGH ST
HUGUENOT PL
N SIDE WANDSWORTH COMMON
BATTERSEA RISE
ST JOHN'S HL
LAVENDER HILL
LATCHMERE ROAD
FALCON RD
TRINITY ROAD
WOODWELL ST
GARRATT LANE
EARLSFIELD ROAD
BURNTWOOD LANE
MERTON ROAD
BOLINGBROKE GROVE
BELLEVUE RD
ST JAMES'S DRIVE
NORTHCOTE RD
SPENCER PARK
WINDMILL RD
BUCKHOLD RD
ELSPETH RD
1 grid square represents 500 metres

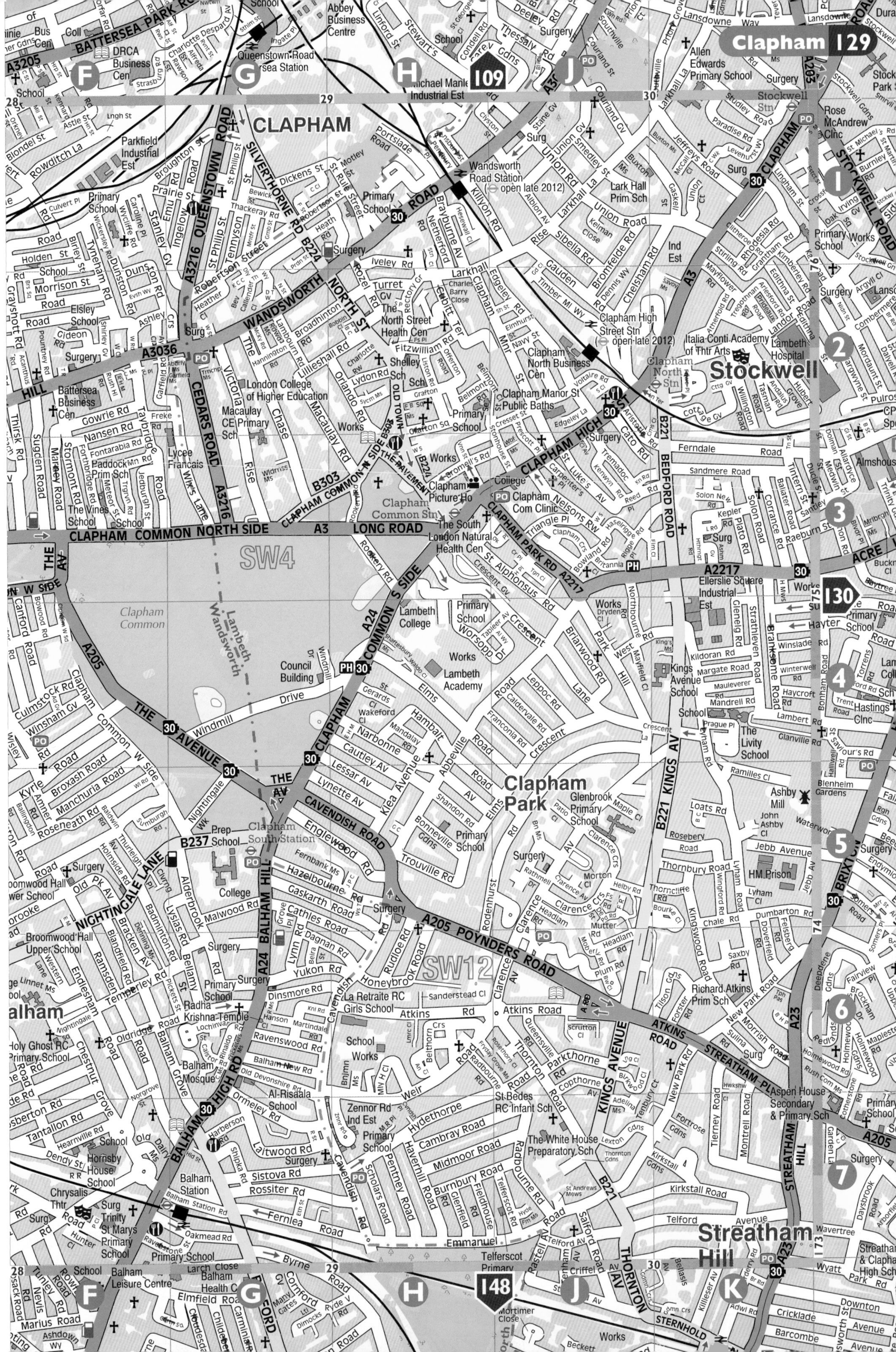

Clapham 129
CLAPHAM
Stockwell
Clapham Park
Streatham Hill
SW4
SW12
Clapham Common
109
130
148
Battersea Park Rd
Queenstown Road
Queenstown Road Battersea Station
Wandsworth Road Station
Clapham High Street Stn
Clapham North Stn
Clapham Common Stn
Clapham South Station
Balham Station
Stockwell Stn
Clapham Common North Side
Long Road
Clapham Common S Side
The Avenue
Cavendish Road
Poynders Road
Atkins Road
Streatham Pl
Kings Avenue
Bedford Road
Clapham Road
Stockwell Road
Brixton Hill
Streatham Hill
Balham Hill
Balham High Rd
Nightingale Lane
Wandsworth Road
Cedars Road
Clapham Park Rd
Acre Lane
Lambeth College
Lambeth Academy
HM Prison
Lambeth Hospital
Italia Conti Academy of Thtr Arts
Clapham Picture Ho
Clapham Manor St Public Baths
London College of Higher Education
Macaulay CE Primary Sch
Lycee Francais
Balham Leisure Centre
Balham Mosque
Radha Krishna Temple
Al-Risaala School
Hornsby House School
Aspen House Secondary & Primary Sch
The Livity School
Kings Avenue School
Richard Atkins Prim Sch
Ashby Mill
Ellerslie Square Industrial Est
Glenbrook Primary School
Wandsworth
Lambeth

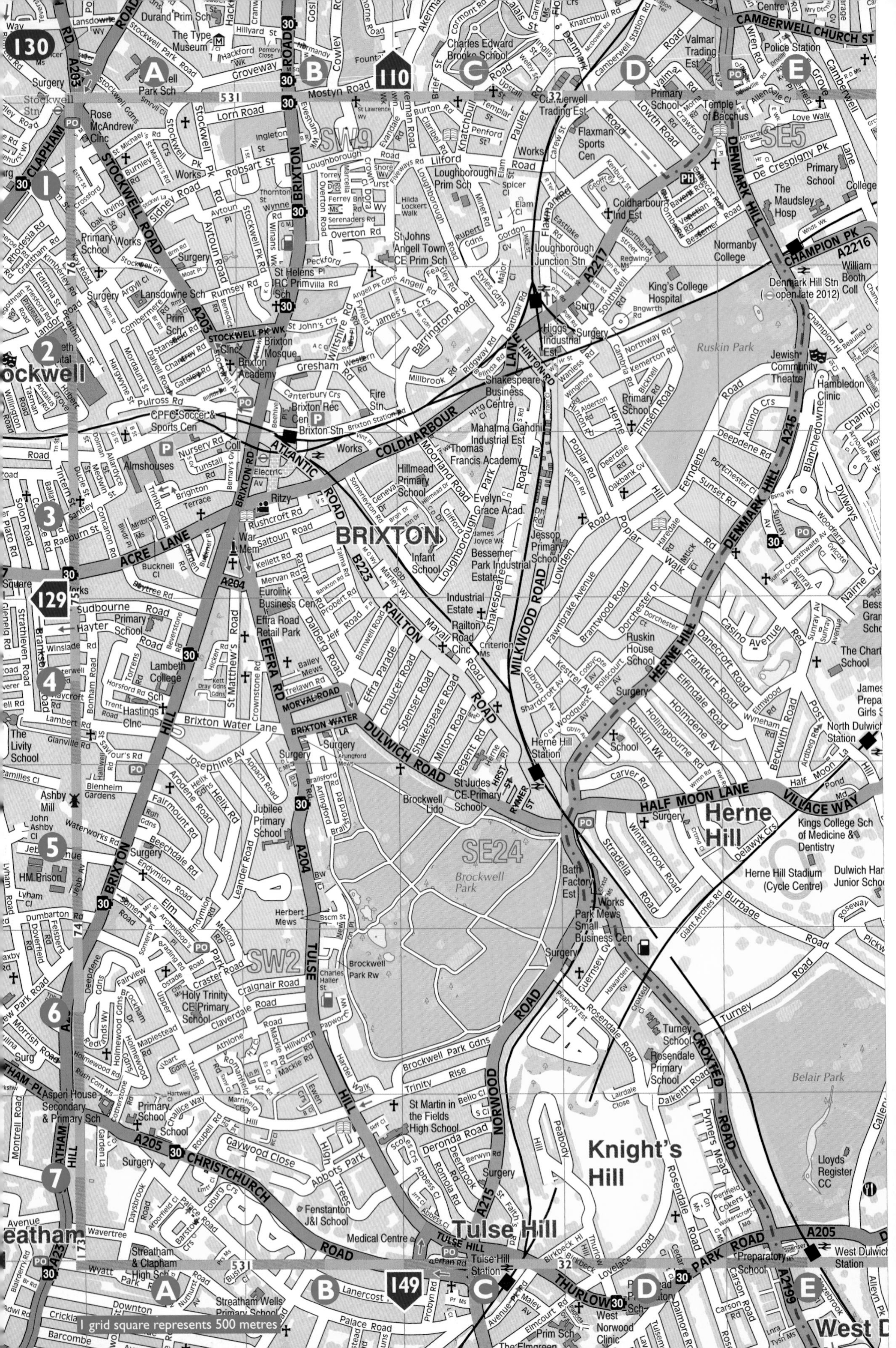
BRIXTON
Herne Hill
Knight's Hill
Tulse Hill
SW9
SE5
SE24
SW2
Brockwell Park
Ruskin Park
Belair Park
1 grid square represents 500 metres

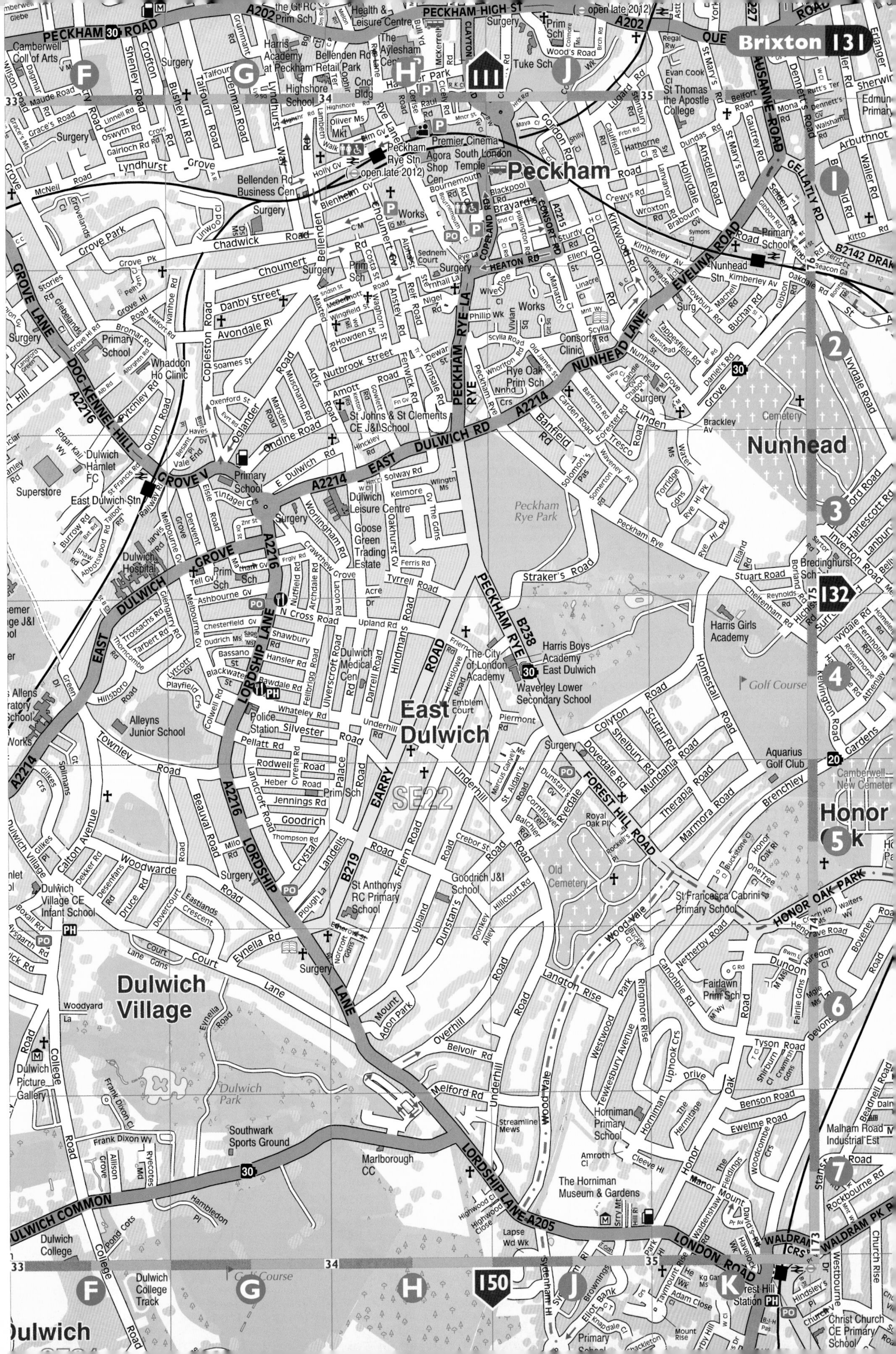
Brixton 131
132
150
Peckham
Nunhead
East Dulwich
Dulwich Village
Honor Oak
Dulwich
SE22
Peckham Rye Park
Dulwich Park
Cemetery
Golf Course
PECKHAM HIGH ST
PECKHAM ROAD
A202
RYE LANE
PECKHAM RYE
B238
EAST DULWICH RD
A2214
NUNHEAD LANE
EVELINA ROAD
GROVE LANE
DOG KENNEL HILL
A2216
LORDSHIP LANE
DULWICH GROVE
EAST DULWICH GROVE
FOREST HILL ROAD
HONOR OAK PARK
LONDON ROAD
A205
DULWICH COMMON
LAUSANNE ROAD
GELLATLY RD
B2142
BARRY ROAD
B219
Peckham Rye Stn
Nunhead Stn
East Dulwich Stn
Forest Hill Station
Dulwich Hospital
Dulwich Picture Gallery
Dulwich College
Alleyns Junior School
The City of London Academy
Harris Boys Academy East Dulwich
Harris Girls Academy
The Horniman Museum & Gardens
Southwark Sports Ground
Marlborough CC
Aquarius Golf Club
Camberwell New Cemetery
Dulwich Leisure Centre
Goose Green Trading Estate
Premier Cinema
Peckham Rye Stn
Dulwich Hamlet FC
F
G
H
I
J
K
33
34
35
1
2
3
4
5
6
7

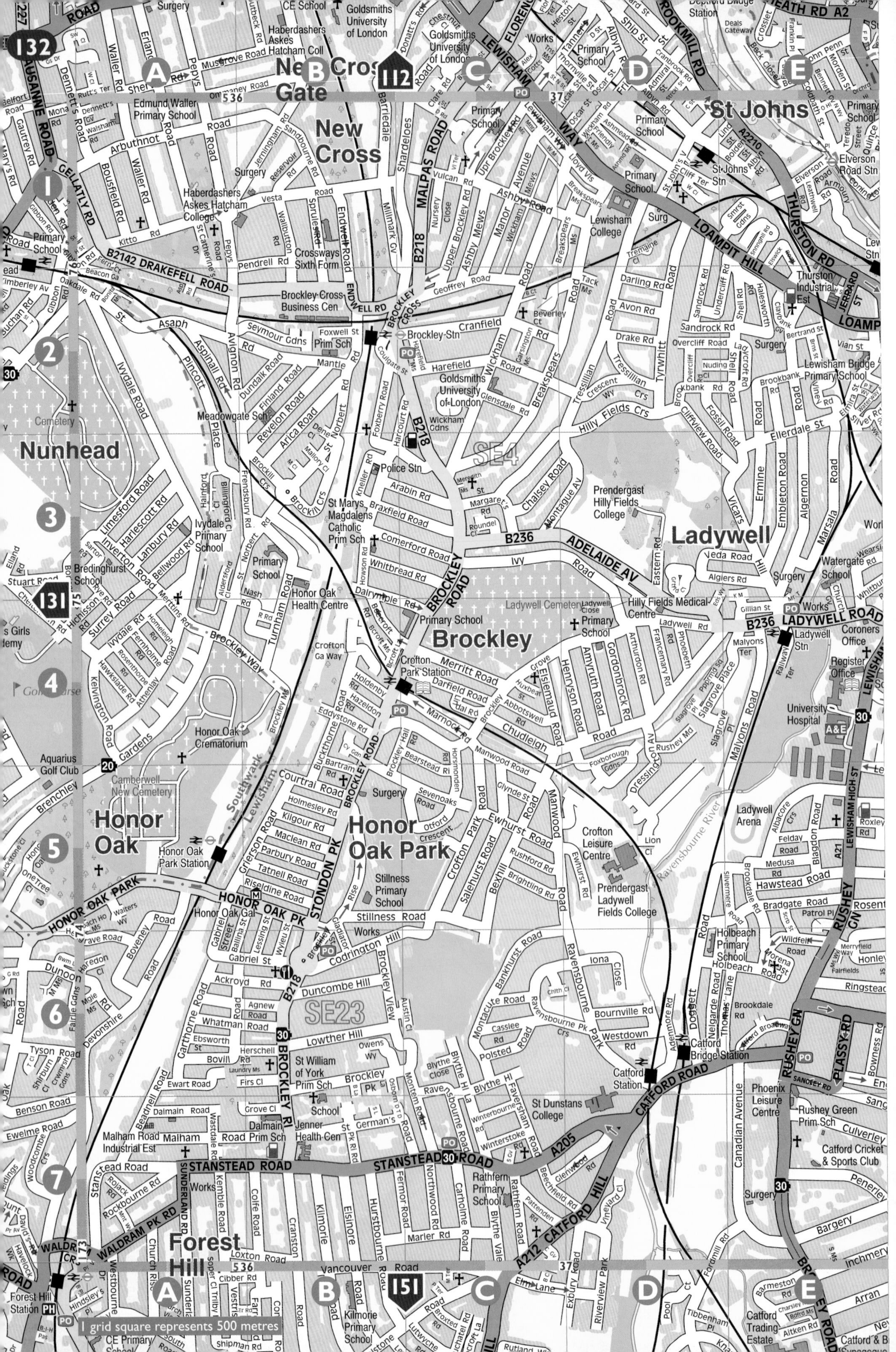

132
112
131
151
227
A
B
C
D
E
1
2
3
4
5
6
7
New Cross Gate
New Cross
St Johns
Nunhead
Ladywell
Brockley
Honor Oak
Honor Oak Park
Forest Hill
SE4
SE23
Goldsmiths University of London
Haberdashers Askes Hatcham Coll
Edmund Waller Primary School
Haberdashers Askes Hatcham College
Crossways Sixth Form
Brockley Cross Business Cen
Brockley Stn
Lewisham College
Lewisham Bridge Primary School
Thurston Industrial Est
Prendergast Hilly Fields College
Hilly Fields Medical Centre
Ladywell Cemetery
Ladywell Stn
University Hospital
Coroners Office
Register Office
Ladywell Arena
Crofton Park Station
Police Stn
St Marys Magdalens Catholic Prim Sch
Ivydale Primary School
Bredinghurst School
Honor Oak Health Centre
Honor Oak Crematorium
Camberwell New Cemetery
Aquarius Golf Club
Honor Oak Park Station
Stillness Primary School
Crofton Leisure Centre
Prendergast Ladywell Fields College
Holbeach Primary School
Catford Bridge Station
Catford Station
St Dunstans College
Phoenix Leisure Centre
Rushey Green Prim Sch
Catford Cricket & Sports Club
Rathfern Primary School
Malham Road Industrial Est
Dalmain Road Prim Sch
Jenner Health Cen
St William of York Prim Sch
Forest Hill Station
Kilmorie Primary School
Catford Trading Estate
B2142 DRAKEFELL ROAD
LEWISHAM WAY
LOAMPIT HILL
THURSTON RD
MALPAS ROAD
BROCKLEY ROAD
ADELAIDE AV
LADYWELL ROAD
STANSTEAD ROAD
CATFORD ROAD
CATFORD HILL
RUSHEY GN
HONOR OAK PARK
STONDON PK
BROCKLEY RI
LEWISHAM HIGH ST
1 grid square represents 500 metres

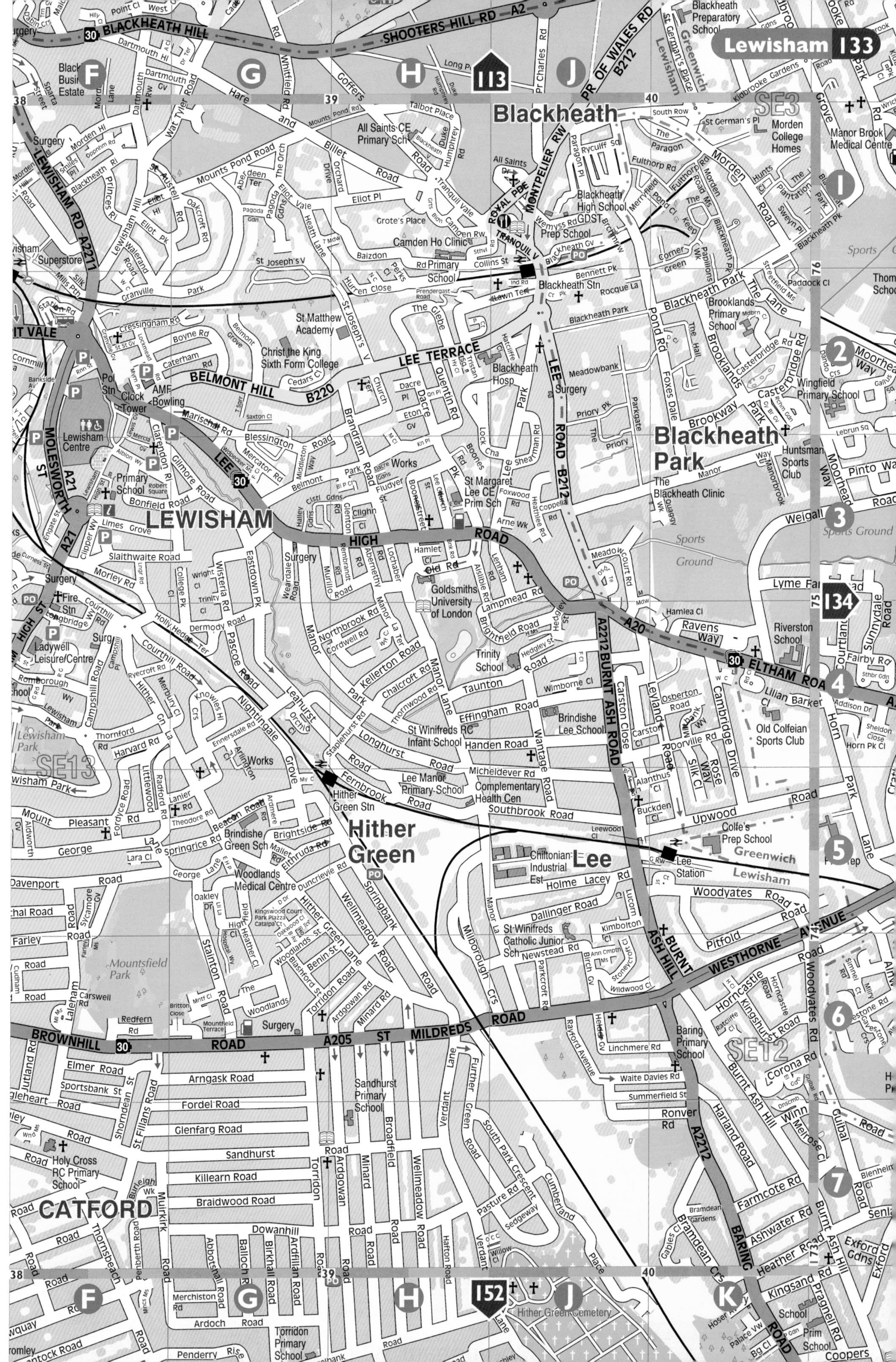

Blackheath
Blackheath Park
LEWISHAM
Hither Green
Lee
CATFORD
SE3
SE13
SE12
BLACKHEATH HILL
SHOOTERS HILL RD A2
PR OF WALES RD B212
LEWISHAM RD A2211
LEE TERRACE
BELMONT HILL B220
LEE ROAD B212
LEE HIGH ROAD
A20
ELTHAM ROAD
A2212 BURNT ASH ROAD
BURNT ASH HILL
WESTHORNE AVENUE
BROWNHILL ROAD
A205 ST MILDREDS ROAD
BARING ROAD
A2212
MOLESWORTH ST
A21
HIGH ST
Blackheath Preparatory School
All Saints CE Primary Sch
Morden College Homes
Manor Brook Medical Centre
Blackheath High School GDST
Prep School
Camden Ho Clinic
Primary School
Blackheath Stn
St Matthew Academy
Christ the King Sixth Form College
Blackheath Hosp
Brooklands Primary School
Wingfield Primary School
Huntsman Sports Club
The Blackheath Clinic
Sports Ground
Lewisham Centre
Clock Tower
AMF Bowling
Superstore
Primary School
Goldsmiths University of London
Trinity School
St Margaret Lee CE Prim Sch
Riverston School
Old Colfeian Sports Club
Brindishe Lee School
St Winifreds RC Infant School
Lee Manor Primary School
Complementary Health Cen
Hither Green Stn
Colfe's Prep School
Lee Station
Chiltonian Industrial Est
Ladywell Leisure Centre
Lewisham Park
Brindishe Green Sch
Woodlands Medical Centre
Mountsfield Park
St Winifreds Catholic Junior Sch
Baring Primary School
Sandhurst Primary School
Holy Cross RC Primary School
Torridon Primary School
Hither Green Cemetery
113
134
152
30
38
39
40
75
76
74
73
F
G
H
J
K
I
2
3
4
5
6
7

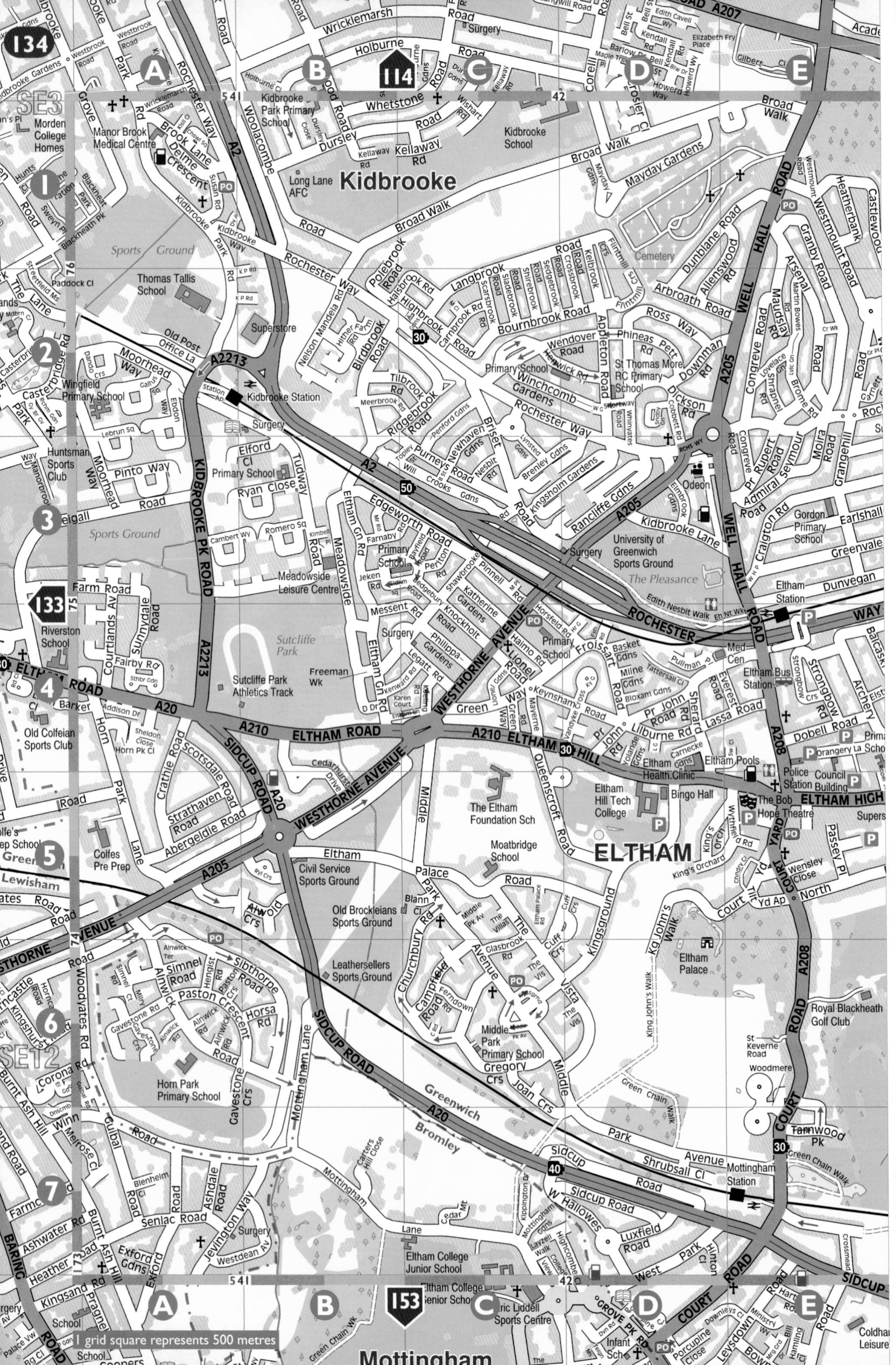

134
114
133
153
SE3
SE12
A
B
C
D
E
1
2
3
4
5
6
7
541
42
76
75
74
73
Kidbrooke
ELTHAM
Mottingham
Wricklemarsh Road
Holburne Road
Whetstone Road
Dursley Road
Kellaway Road
Kidbrooke Park Primary School
Long Lane AFC
Kidbrooke School
Broad Walk
Mayday Gardens
Rochester Way
Manor Brook Medical Centre
Morden College Homes
Brook Lane
Delme Crescent
Sports Ground
Thomas Tallis School
Superstore
Old Post Office La
Kidbrooke Station
Wingfield Primary School
Moorhead Way
Pinto Way
Huntsman Sports Club
Elford Cl
Primary School
Ryan Close
Tudway
Romero Sq
Cambert Wy
Meadowside Leisure Centre
Farm Road
Courtlands Av
Sunnydale Road
Riverston School
Fairby Rd
KIDBROOKE PK ROAD
A2213
A2
A20
A205
A210
A208
A207
Sutcliffe Park
Sutcliffe Park Athletics Track
Freeman Wk
ELTHAM ROAD
Old Colfeian Sports Club
Horn Park
Horn Pk Cl
Crathie Road
Scotsdale Road
Strathaven Road
Abergeldie Road
SIDCUP ROAD
WESTHORNE AVENUE
Cedarhurst Drive
Colfes Pre Prep
Lewisham
Civil Service Sports Ground
Old Brockleians Sports Ground
Leathersellers Sports Ground
Eltham Palace Road
Woodyates Rd
Simnel Road
Sibthorpe Road
Paston Crescent
Horsa Rd
Horn Park Primary School
Gavestone Crs
Mottingham Lane
Greenwich
Bromley
Middle Park Primary School
Moatbridge School
The Eltham Foundation Sch
Queenscroft Road
Eltham Hill Tech College
Bingo Hall
ELTHAM HILL
Eltham Pools
Health Clinic
Police Station
Council Building
The Bob Hope Theatre
ELTHAM HIGH
Eltham Palace
King John's Walk
Green Chain Walk
Royal Blackheath Golf Club
Woodmere
Tarnwood Pk
COURT ROAD
COURT YARD
WELL HALL ROAD
Mottingham Station
Eltham Station
Eltham Bus Station
Odeon
University of Greenwich Sports Ground
The Pleasance
Cemetery
Kidbrooke Lane
Gordon Primary School
St Thomas More RC Primary School
Arbroath Road
Dunblane Road
Allenswood Rd
Westmount Road
Granby Road
Ross Way
Phineas Pett Rd
Downman Rd
Dickson Rd
Bournbrook Road
Langbrook Road
Winchcomb Gardens
Rancliffe Gdns
Kingsholm Gardens
Edgeworth Road
Eltham Gn Rd
Meadowside
Katherine Gardens
Knockholt Road
Lionel Road
Froissart Road
Sidcup Road
Shrubsall Cl
Luxfield Road
West Park
Eltham College Junior School
Eltham College Senior School
Eric Liddell Sports Centre
Senlac Road
Ashdale Road
Jevington Way
Burnt Ash Hill
BARING ROAD
Kingsand Rd
Heather Road
Ashwater Rd
Exford Gdns
Carters Hill Close
Mottingham Lane
Green Chain Wk
GROVE PK RD
Porcupine Close
Leysdown Road
SIDCUP
1 grid square represents 500 metres

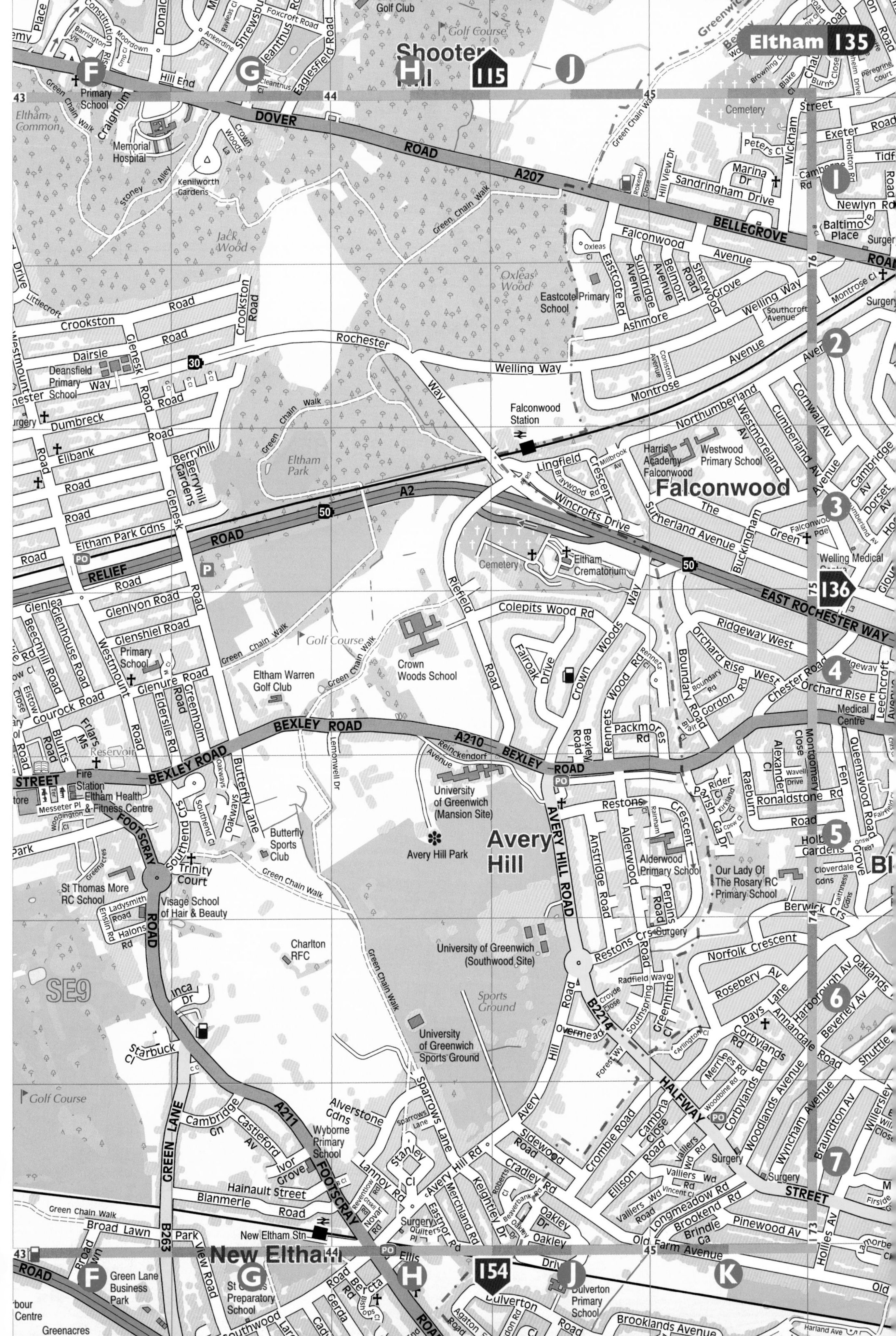
Shooters Hill
Golf Club
Golf Course
115
Constitution Rise
Barrington Vis
Moordown
Ankerdine Crs
Rayleas Cl
Shrewsbury
Foxcroft Road
Cleanthus Rd
Eaglesfield Road
Cleanthus Cl
Hill End
Primary School
Eltham Common
Green Chain Walk
Craigholm
Memorial Hospital
Crown Woods La
Kenilworth Gardens
Stoney Alley
DOVER ROAD
A207
BELLEGROVE ROAD
Jack Wood
Oxleas Wood
Green Chain Walk
Cemetery
Street
Exeter Road
Wickham
Peters Cl
Marina Dr
Sandringham Drive
Rokesby Close
Hill View Dr
Camborne Rd
Honiton Rd
Newlyn Rd
Baltimore Place
Surgery
Falconwood Avenue
Oxleas Cl
Eastcote Rd
Sundridge Avenue
Belmont Avenue
Sherwood Road
Grove
Ashmore
Welling Way
Southcroft Avenue
Montrose Cl
Eastcote Primary School
Drive
Littlecroft
Crookston Road
Dairsie Road
Glenesk Road
Deansfield Primary School
Rochester Way
Welling Way
Coniston Avenue
Montrose Avenue
Westmount
Dumbreck Road
Elibank Road
Berryhill Gardens
Berryhill
Green Chain Walk
Eltham Park
Falconwood Station
Northumberland Av
Westmoreland Av
Cumberland Av
Cornwall Av
Harris Academy Falconwood
Westwood Primary School
Lingfield Crescent
Millbrook Av
Braywood Rd
Falconwood
Cambridge Av
Dorset Av
Wincrofts Drive
Sutherland Avenue
Buckingham
The Green
Falconwood Pde
Welling Medical Centre
A2
ROAD
RELIEF ROAD
Eltham Park Gdns
50
Cemetery
Eltham Crematorium
Riefield Road
136
EAST ROCHESTER WAY
Glenlea
Glenlyon Road
Glenshiel Road
Glenhouse Road
Beechhill Road
Colepits Wood Rd
Fairoak Drive
Crown Woods Way
Rennets Wood Rd
Ridgeway West
Orchard Rise West
Boundary Rd
Boundary Road
Gordon Rd
Chester Road
Orchard Rise E
Leechcroft Avenue
Medical Centre
Golf Course
Crown Woods School
Primary School
Glenure Road
Eldersile Rd
Greenholm Road
Gourock Road
Eltham Warren Golf Club
Packmores Rd
Bexley Road
Blunts Road
Friars Ms
Reservoir
BEXLEY ROAD
A210
Reinckendorf Avenue
Lemonwell Dr
STREET
Fire Station
Eltham Health & Fitness Centre
Messeter Pl
Southend Crs
Oakways
Butterfly Lane
University of Greenwich (Mansion Site)
Avery Hill Park
Avery Hill
AVERY HILL ROAD
Restons Crescent
Anstridge Road
Alderwood Road
Alderwood Primary School
Rider Cl
Parish Ga Dr
Raeburn
Alexander Cl
Montgomery Close
Wavell Drive
Ronaldstone Rd
Queenswood Road
Fen Grove
Holbeck Gardens
Our Lady Of The Rosary RC Primary School
Cloverdale Gdns
Caithness Gdns
Berwick Crs
FOOTSCRAY ROAD
Butterfly Sports Club
Park
Greenacres
St Thomas More RC School
Trinity Court
Visage School of Hair & Beauty
Green Chain Walk
Ladysmith Road
Enslin Rd
Halons Rd
Charlton RFC
University of Greenwich (Southwood Site)
Perpins Road
Surgery
Restons Crs
Norfolk Crescent
Rosebery Av
Oaklands
Radfield Way
Greenhithe Cl
Southspring
Croyde Close
SE9
Sports Ground
Inca Dr
Starbuck Cl
Green Chain Walk
University of Greenwich Sports Ground
Overmead
B2214
Arlington Cl
Days Lane
Annandale Road
Harborough Av
Beverley Av
Corbylands Rd
Merrilees Rd
Golf Course
Cambridge Gn
Castleford Av
A211
Alverstone Gdns
Wyborne Primary School
Sparrows Lane
Avery Hill Rd
Sidewood Road
Crombie Road
Cambria Close
HALFWAY STREET
Woodlands Avenue
Wyncham Avenue
Braundton Av
Willersley Av
Shuttle
GREEN LANE
Ivor Grove
Lannoy Rd
Stanley Cl
Cradley Rd
Oakley Dr
Ellison Road
Valliers Wd Rd
Vincent Cl
Longmeadow Rd
Brookend Rd
Surgery
STREET
Hainault Street
Blanmerle Road
Green Chain Walk
Broad Lawn
B263
Park View Road
New Eltham Stn
Surgery
Merchland Rd
Keightley Dr
Brindle Ga
Pinewood Av
Hollies Av
New Eltham
Ellis
154
Old Farm Avenue
ROAD
Green Lane Business Park
St Olave's Preparatory School
Dulverton Primary School
Dulverton Rd
Brooklands Avenue
Harland Ave
Old
Centre
Greenacres
Southwood

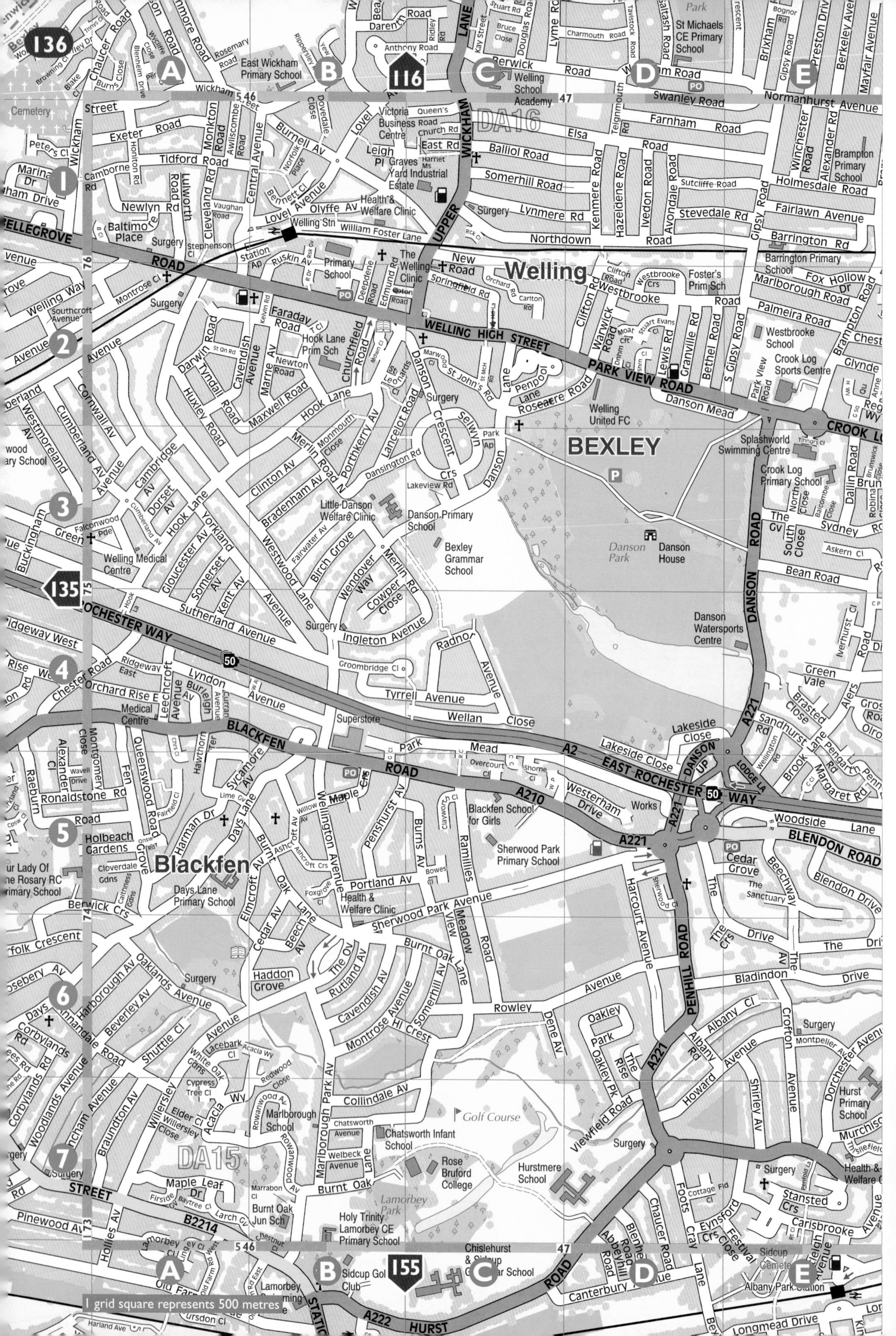

136
116
135
155
A
B
C
D
E
1
2
3
4
5
6
7
546
47
76
75
74
73
DA16
DA15
Welling
BEXLEY
Blackfen
Cemetery
East Wickham Primary School
St Michaels CE Primary School
Welling School Academy
Victoria Business Centre
Graves Yard Industrial Estate
Health & Welfare Clinic
Welling Stn
Primary School
The Welling Clinic
Foster's Prim Sch
Brampton Primary School
Barrington Primary School
Westbrooke School
Crook Log Sports Centre
Welling United FC
Splashworld Swimming Centre
Crook Log Primary School
Hook Lane Prim Sch
Little Danson Welfare Clinic
Danson Primary School
Bexley Grammar School
Danson Park
Danson House
Danson Watersports Centre
Welling Medical Centre
Medical Centre
Superstore
Blackfen School for Girls
Sherwood Park Primary School
Works
Days Lane Primary School
Health & Welfare Clinic
Marlborough School
Chatsworth Infant School
Rose Bruford College
Hurstmere School
Golf Course
Lamorbey Park
Burnt Oak Jun Sch
Holy Trinity Lamorbey CE Primary School
Sidcup Golf Club
Chislehurst & Sidcup Grammar School
Hurst Primary School
Albany Park Station
Sidcup Cemetery
Our Lady Of the Rosary RC Primary School
Surgery
WELLING HIGH STREET
PARK VIEW ROAD
BELLEGROVE ROAD
UPPER WICKHAM LANE
DANSON ROAD
ROCHESTER WAY
EAST ROCHESTER WAY
BLACKFEN ROAD
BLENDON ROAD
PENHILL ROAD
CROOK LOG
STREET
HURST
A2
A210
A221
A222
B2214
50
1 grid square represents 500 metres

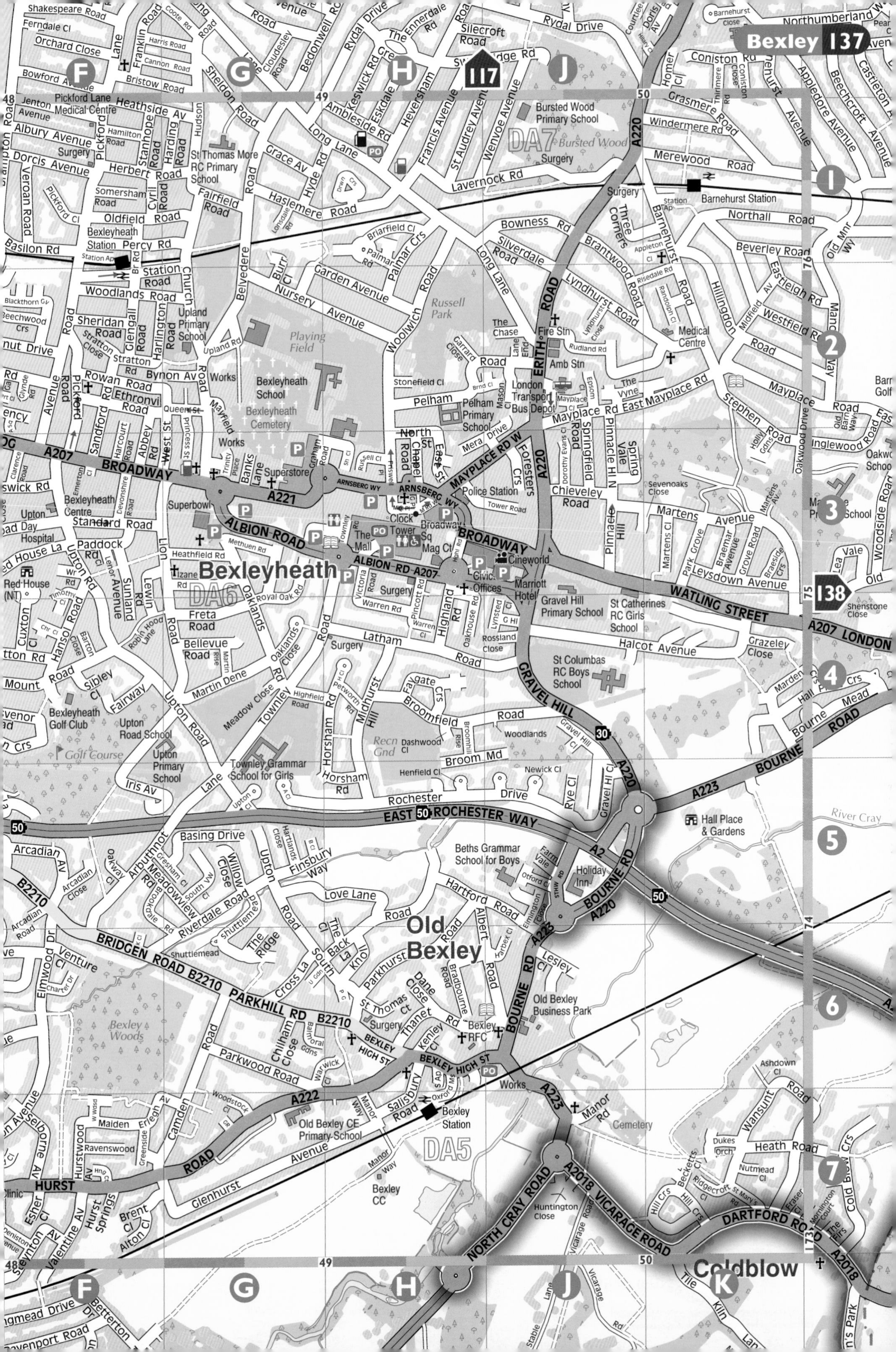

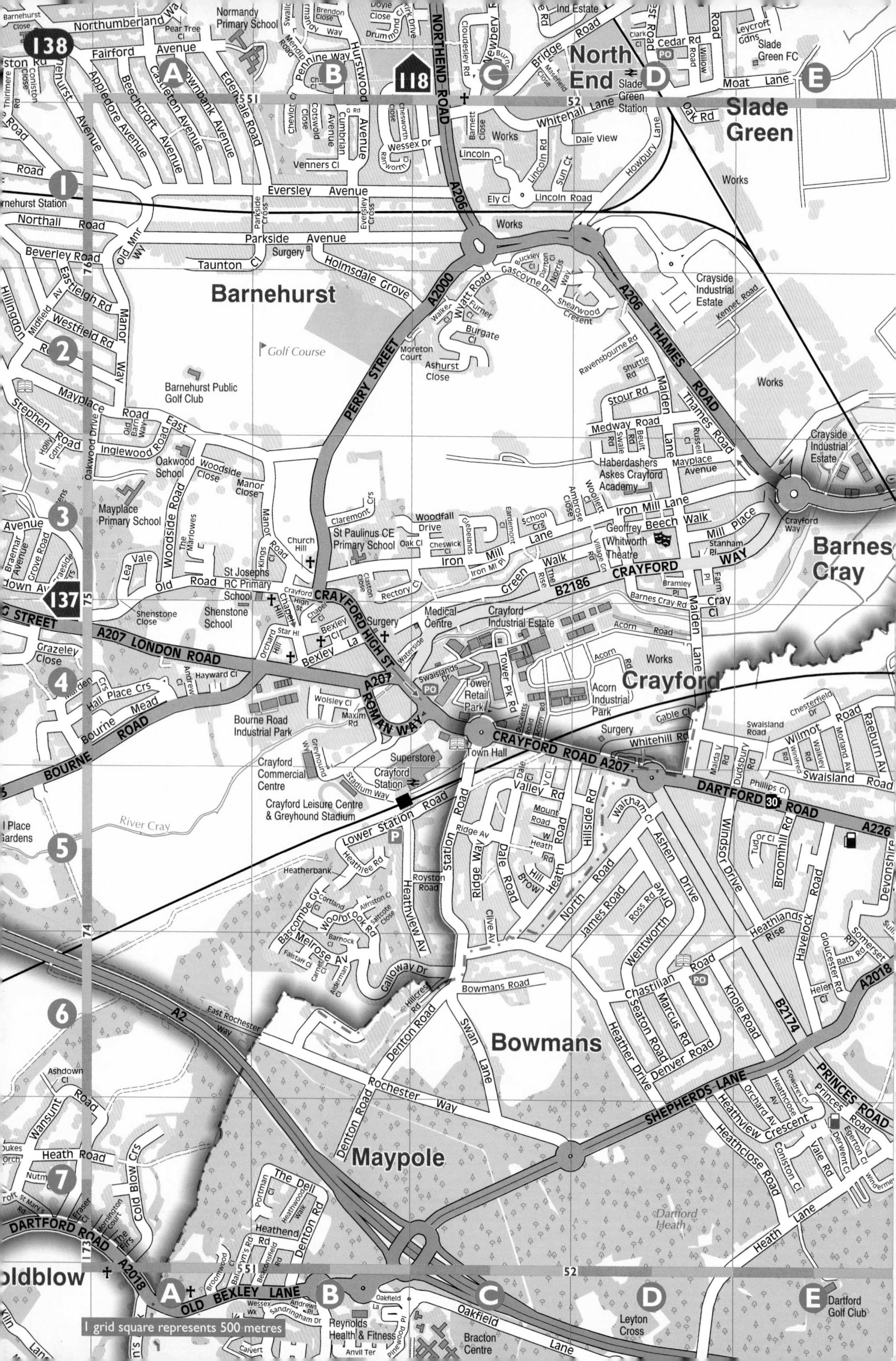

138
118
137
A
B
C
D
E
1
2
3
4
5
6
7
51
52
75
74
76
173
North End
Slade Green
Slade Green Station
Slade Green FC
Barnehurst
Barnehurst Station
Barnehurst Public Golf Club
Golf Course
Normandy Primary School
Oakwood School
Mayplace Primary School
St Paulinus CE Primary School
St Josephs RC Primary School
Shenstone School
Haberdashers Askes Crayford Academy
Geoffrey Whitworth Theatre
Barnes Cray
Crayford
Crayford Industrial Estate
Crayside Industrial Estate
Acorn Industrial Park
Bourne Road Industrial Park
Tower Retail Park
Crayford Commercial Centre
Crayford Leisure Centre & Greyhound Stadium
Crayford Station
Town Hall
Superstore
Medical Centre
Surgery
Works
River Cray
Bowmans
Maypole
Dartford Heath
Oldblow
Leyton Cross
Dartford Golf Club
Reynolds Health & Fitness
Bracton Centre
Northumberland Way
Fairford Avenue
Eversley Avenue
Parkside Avenue
Northall Road
Beverley Road
Mayplace Road East
Old Road
Iron Mill Lane
Green Walk
Crayford Way
B2186
Perry Street
A2000
Northend Road
A206
Thames Road
Maiden Lane
Crayford High St
A207 London Road
Bourne Road
Roman Way
Crayford Road A207
Dartford Road
A226
Station Road
Heath Road
North Road
Ashen Drive
Windsor Drive
B2174
Shepherds Lane
Princes Road
A2018
Rochester Way
East Rochester Way
A2
Denton Road
Swan Lane
Bowmans Road
Old Bexley Lane
Oakfield Lane
A2078
Heathclose Road
Heathview Crescent
Whitehall Lane
Lincoln Road
Moat Lane
1 grid square represents 500 metres

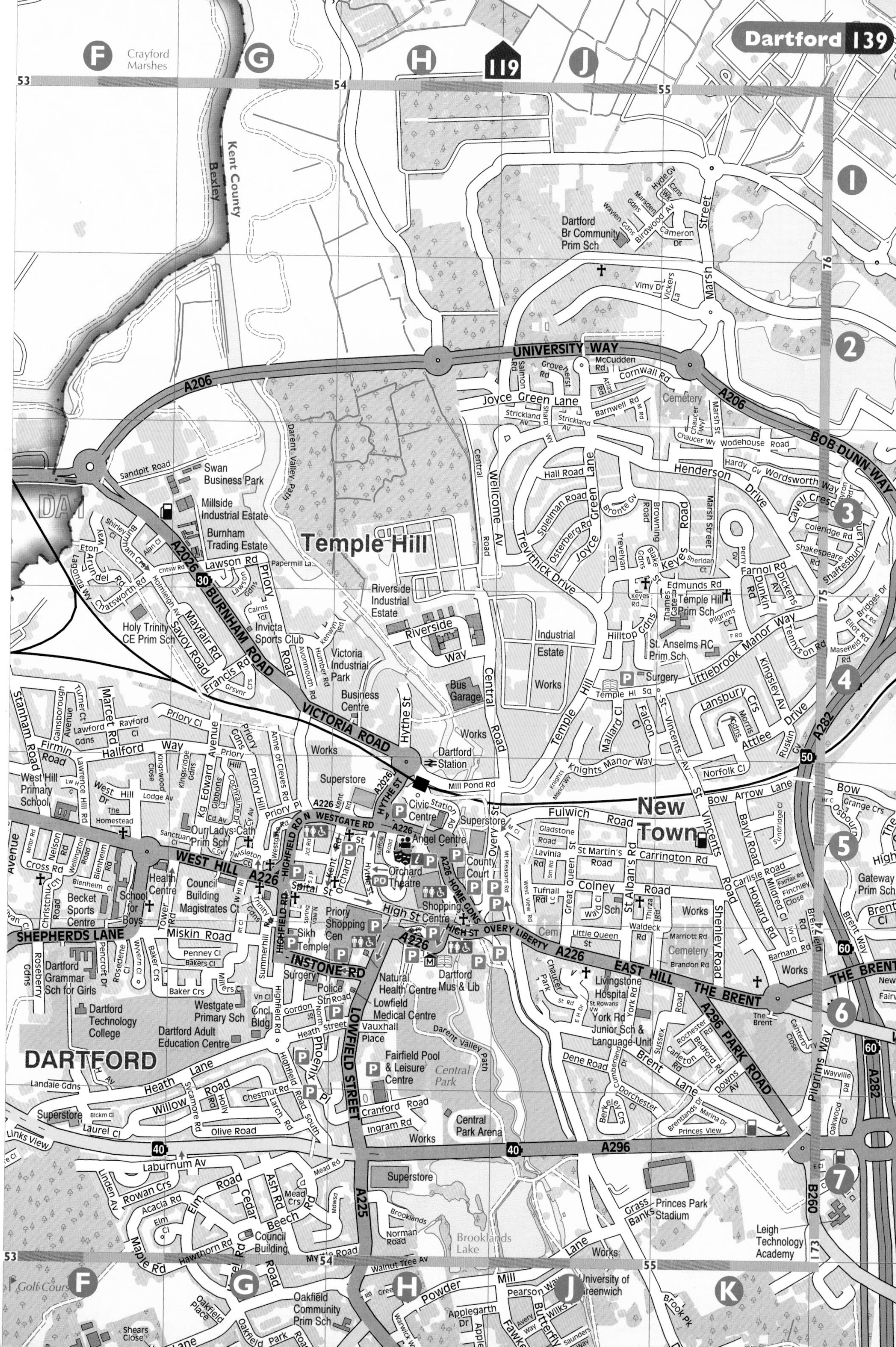
Temple Hill
New Town
DARTFORD
Crayford Marshes
University Way
A206
Bob Dunn Way
Burnham Road
Victoria Road
West Hill
East Hill
The Brent
Park Road
Lowfield Street
Dartford Station
Central Park
Princes Park Stadium
Brooklands Lake
Leigh Technology Academy
Dartford Technology College
Dartford Grammar Sch for Girls
Swan Business Park
Millside Industrial Estate
Burnham Trading Estate
Riverside Industrial Estate
Victoria Industrial Park
Orchard Theatre
Priory Shopping Cen
Livingstone Hospital
Fairfield Pool & Leisure Centre
Central Park Arena

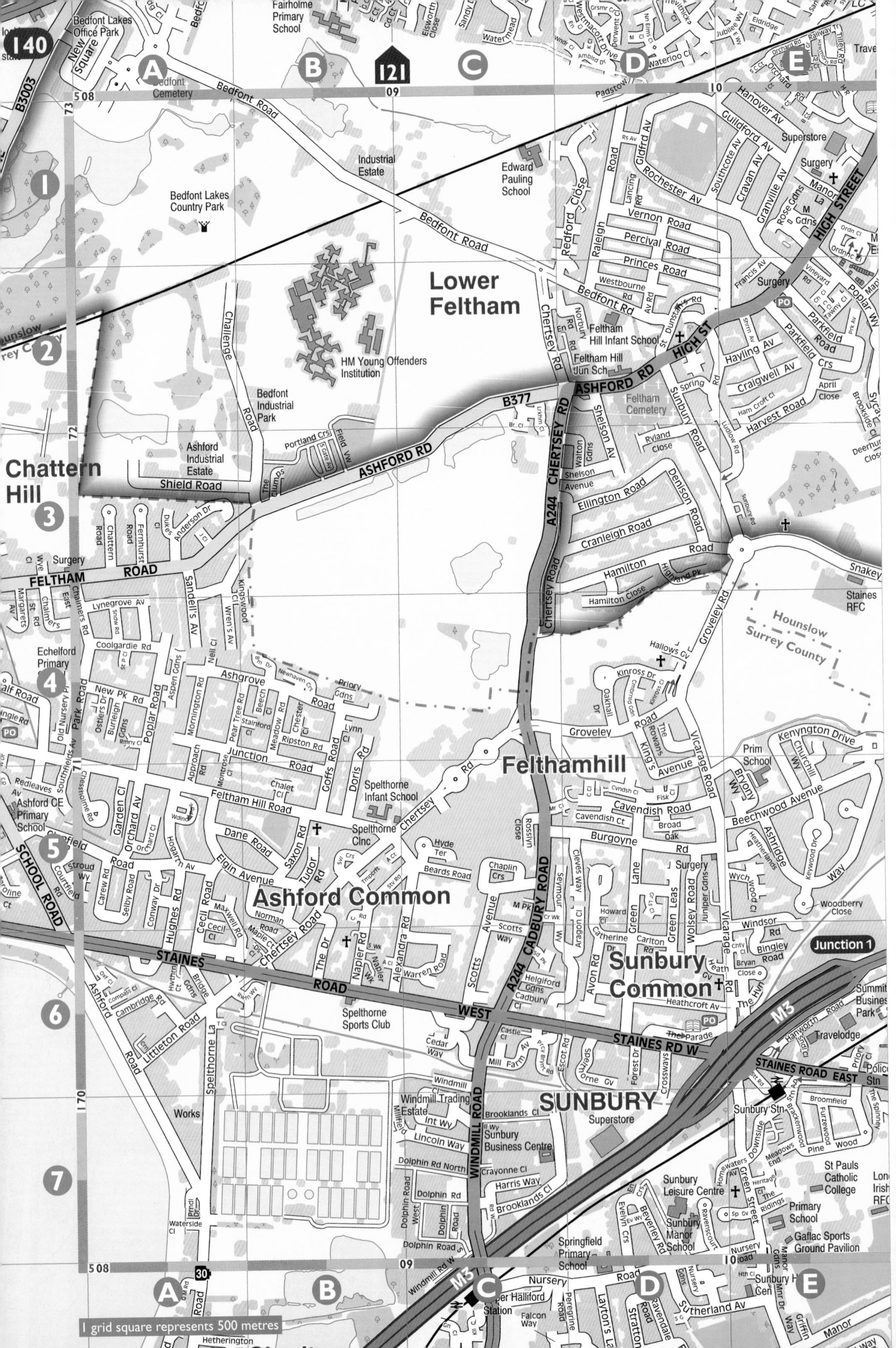

140
121
30
A
B
C
D
E
1
2
3
4
5
6
7
Bedfont Lakes Office Park
New Square
Bedfont Cemetery
Bedfont Road
Fairholme Primary School
Bedfont Lakes Country Park
Industrial Estate
Edward Pauling School
Lower Feltham
HM Young Offenders Institution
Challenge Road
Bedfont Industrial Park
Ashford Industrial Estate
Shield Road
Chattern Hill
Portland Crs
Field Vw
ASHFORD RD
B377
A244 CHERTSEY RD
HIGH ST
HIGH STREET
Feltham Hill Infant School
Feltham Hill Jun Sch
Feltham Cemetery
Sunbury Road
Denison Road
Ellington Road
Cranleigh Road
Hamilton Close
Shelson Av
Walton Gdns
Ryland Close
Harvest Road
Hayling Av
Craigwell Av
Parkfield Road
Vernon Road
Percival Road
Princes Road
Westbourne Rd
Rochester Av
Hanover Av
Guildford Av
Cravan Av
Granville Av
Southcote Av
Superstore
Surgery
Francis Av
Raleigh Road
Redford Close
Chertsey Rd
Snakey
Staines RFC
Hounslow
Surrey County
FELTHAM ROAD
Chattern Road
Fernhurst Road
Anderson Dr
Sandell's Av
Kingswood Cl
Wren's Av
Lynegrove Av
Coolgardie Rd
Echelford Primary
Ashgrove Road
New Pk Rd
Poplar Road
Mornington Rd
Junction Road
Ripston Rd
Goffs Road
Doris Rd
Priory Gdns
Chester Cl
Lynn Cl
Feltham Hill Road
Spelthorne Infant School
Spelthorne Clnc
Chertsey Rd
Groveley Road
Groveley Rd
Vicarage Road
Felthamhill
Kenyngton Drive
Churchill Wy
Prim School
Beechwood Avenue
Cavendish Road
Burgoyne Rd
Broad Oak
Kinross Dr
Ashford CE Primary School
SCHOOL ROAD
Park Road
Chalmers Rd
Garden Cl
Orchard Av
Dane Road
Elgin Avenue
Saxon Rd
Tudor Rd
Hogarth Av
Hughes Rd
Cecil Road
Conway Dr
Selby Road
Carew Rd
Courtfield Rd
Ashford Common
Beards Road
Hyde Ter
Chaplin Crs
Scotts Way
Scotts Avenue
A244 CADBURY ROAD
Seymour Way
Aragon Cl
Avon Rd
Green Lane
Green Leas
Wolsey Road
Juniper Gdns
Vicarage Rd
Windsor Rd
Bingley Road
Woodberry Close
Junction 1
Sunbury Common
Heathcroft Av
The Parade
STAINES ROAD
WEST
STAINES RD W
STAINES ROAD EAST
Summit Business Park
Travelodge
M3
Alexandra Rd
Warren Road
Napier Rd
The Dr
Chertsey Road
Norman Road
Maxwell Rd
Ashford Road
Cambridge Rd
Littleton Road
Spelthorne La
Spelthorne Sports Club
Cedar Way
Mill Farm Av
Escot Rd
Forest Dr
Crossways
Works
Windmill Trading Estate
Int Wy
Lincoln Way
Dolphin Rd North
Dolphin Road
Dolphin Rd
WINDMILL ROAD
Brooklands Cl
Sunbury Business Centre
Crayonne Cl
Harris Way
SUNBURY
Superstore
Sunbury Stn
Broomfield
Furzewood
Pine Wood
Downside
Meadows End
St Pauls Catholic College
Primary School
Gaflac Sports Ground Pavilion
Sunbury Leisure Centre
Sunbury Manor School
Springfield Primary School
Green Street
Beverley Rd
Nursery Road
Sutherland Av
Upper Halliford Station
Falcon Way
Peregrine Road
Layton's La
Ravendale Road
Stratton
Waterside Cl
Windmill Rd W
Hetherington
Manor
Griffin Way
73
72
71
170
508
09
10
1 grid square represents 500 metres

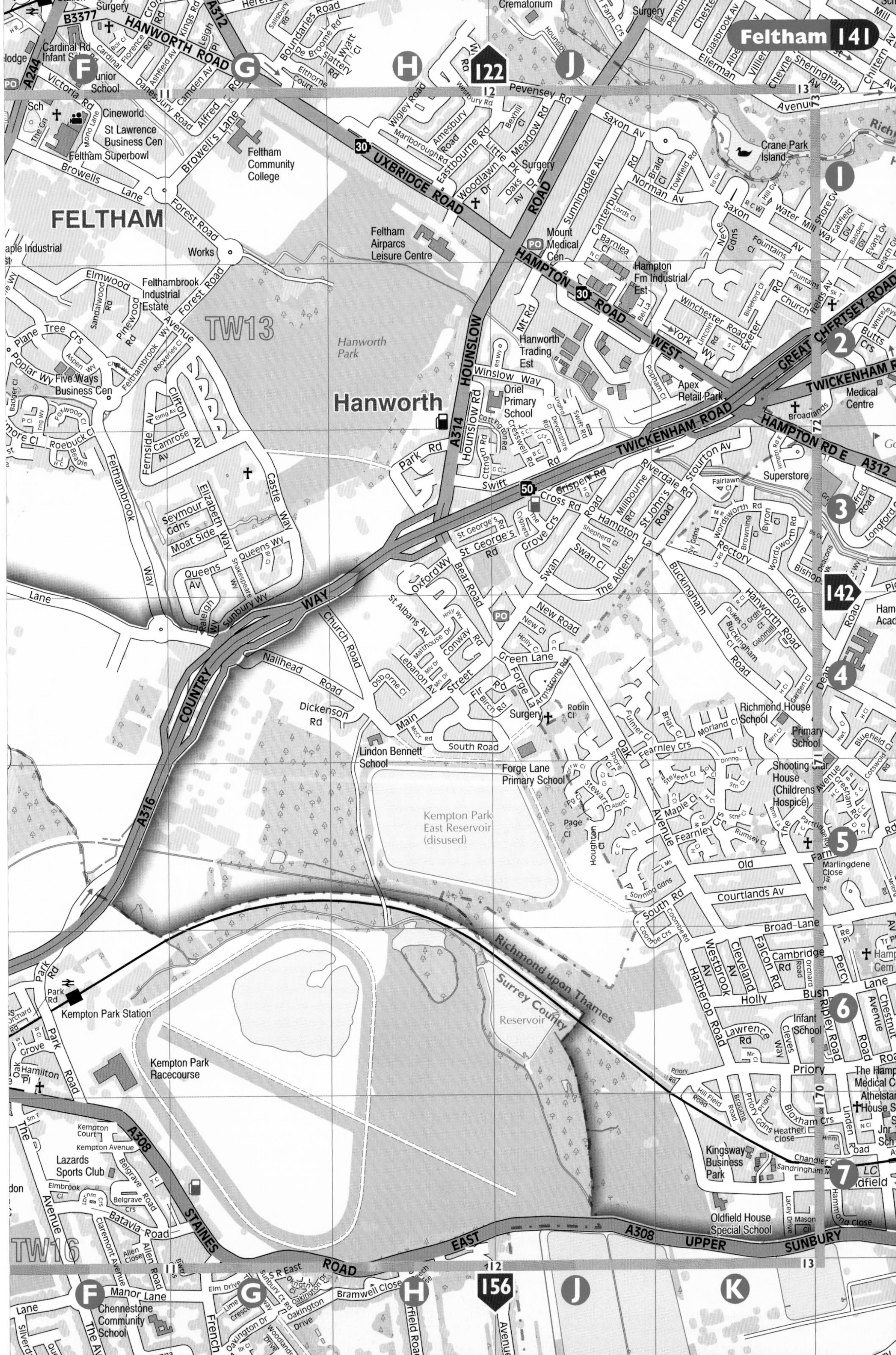
FELTHAM
Hanworth
TW13
TW16
Hanworth Park
Feltham Community College
Feltham Airparcs Leisure Centre
Cineworld
St Lawrence Business Cen
Feltham Superbowl
Felthambrook Industrial Estate
Five Ways Business Cen
Mount Medical Cen
Hampton Fm Industrial Est
Hanworth Trading Est
Apex Retail Park
Oriel Primary School
Crane Park Island
Medical Centre
Superstore
Richmond House School
Primary School
Shooting Star House (Childrens Hospice)
Forge Lane Primary School
Lindon Bennett School
Kempton Park East Reservoir (disused)
Surrey County Reservoir
Richmond upon Thames
Kempton Park Station
Kempton Park Racecourse
Lazards Sports Club
Chennestone Community School
Kingsway Business Park
Oldfield House Special School
Infant School
Crematorium
Cardinal Rd Infant Sch
Junior School
UXBRIDGE ROAD
HANWORTH ROAD
HOUNSLOW ROAD
HAMPTON ROAD WEST
TWICKENHAM ROAD
GREAT CHERTSEY ROAD
COUNTRY WAY
STAINES ROAD EAST
UPPER SUNBURY
A312
A314
A316
A308
A244
B3377
122
142
156
F
G
H
J
I
K
2
3
4
5
6
7
11
12
13
170
171
172
173

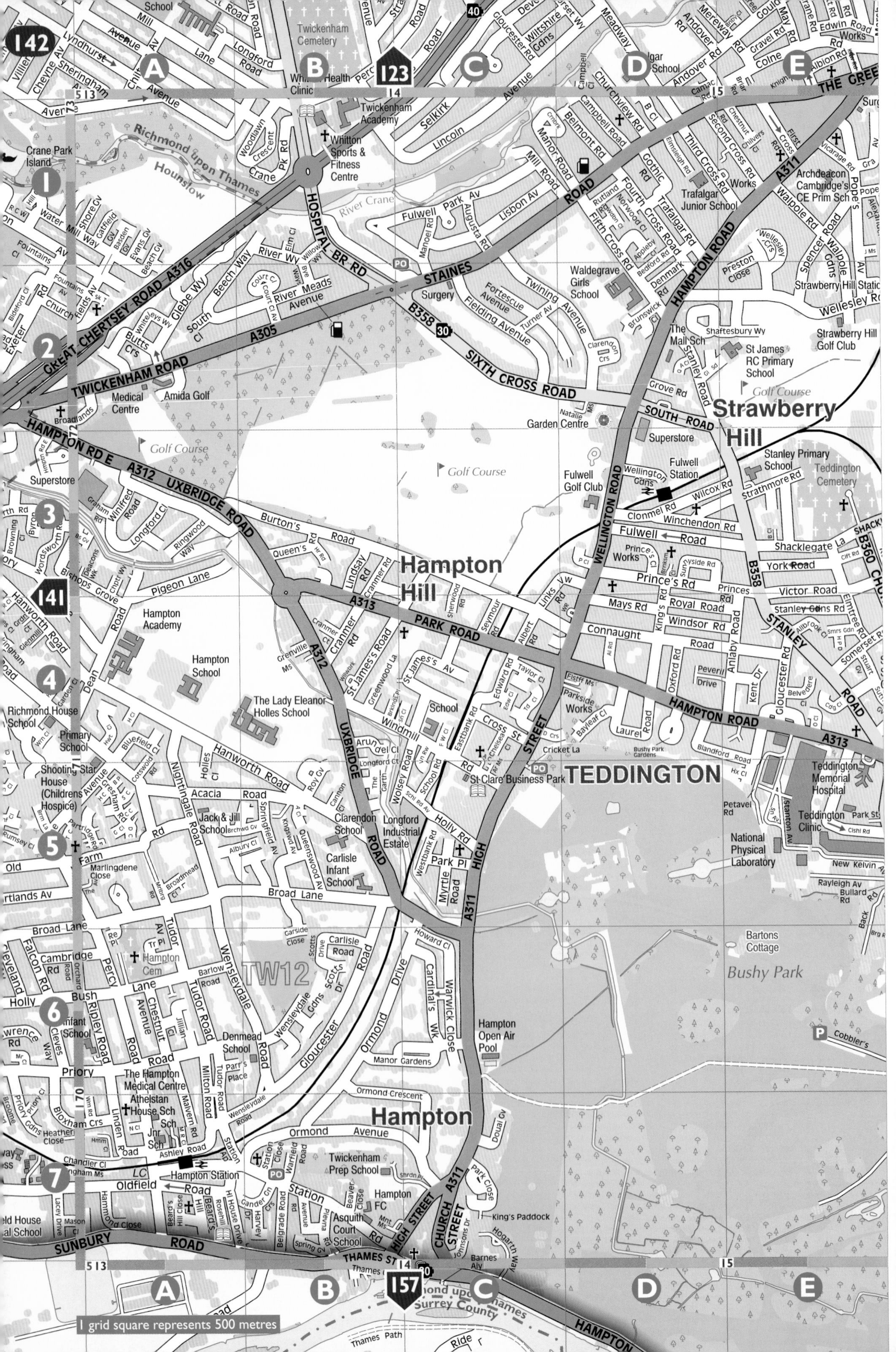
142
123
141
157
40
30
A
B
C
D
E
1
2
3
4
5
6
7
513
14
15
170
171
172
173
Twickenham Cemetery
Whitton Health Clinic
Twickenham Academy
Whitton Sports & Fitness Centre
Crane Park Island
Richmond upon Thames
Hounslow
River Crane
Great Chertsey Road A316
Twickenham Road
A305
Staines
Hospital Br Rd
B358
Sixth Cross Road
South Road
Hampton Road
A311
Archdeacon Cambridge's CE Prim Sch
Trafalgar Junior School
Waldegrave Girls School
Surgery
Medical Centre
Amida Golf
Golf Course
Hampton Rd E
A312
Uxbridge Road
Superstore
The Mall Sch
St James RC Primary School
Strawberry Hill Golf Club
Strawberry Hill Station
Strawberry Hill
Garden Centre
Fulwell Station
Fulwell Golf Club
Stanley Primary School
Teddington Cemetery
Wellington Road
Hampton Hill
A313
Park Road
Hampton Academy
Hampton School
The Lady Eleanor Holles School
Richmond House School
Primary School
Shooting Star House (Childrens Hospice)
Jack & Jill School
Clarendon School
Longford Industrial Estate
Carlisle Infant School
St Clare Business Park
TEDDINGTON
Teddington Memorial Hospital
Teddington Clinic
National Physical Laboratory
Bartons Cottage
Bushy Park
Hampton Open Air Pool
High Street
TW12
Hampton Cem
Infant School
Denmead School
The Hampton Medical Centre
Athelstan House Sch
Jnr Sch
Hampton Station
Twickenham Prep School
Hampton FC
Asquith Court School
Hampton
King's Paddock
Church Street
Sunbury Road
Thames St
Richmond upon Thames
Surrey County
Thames Path
Hampton
1 grid square represents 500 metres

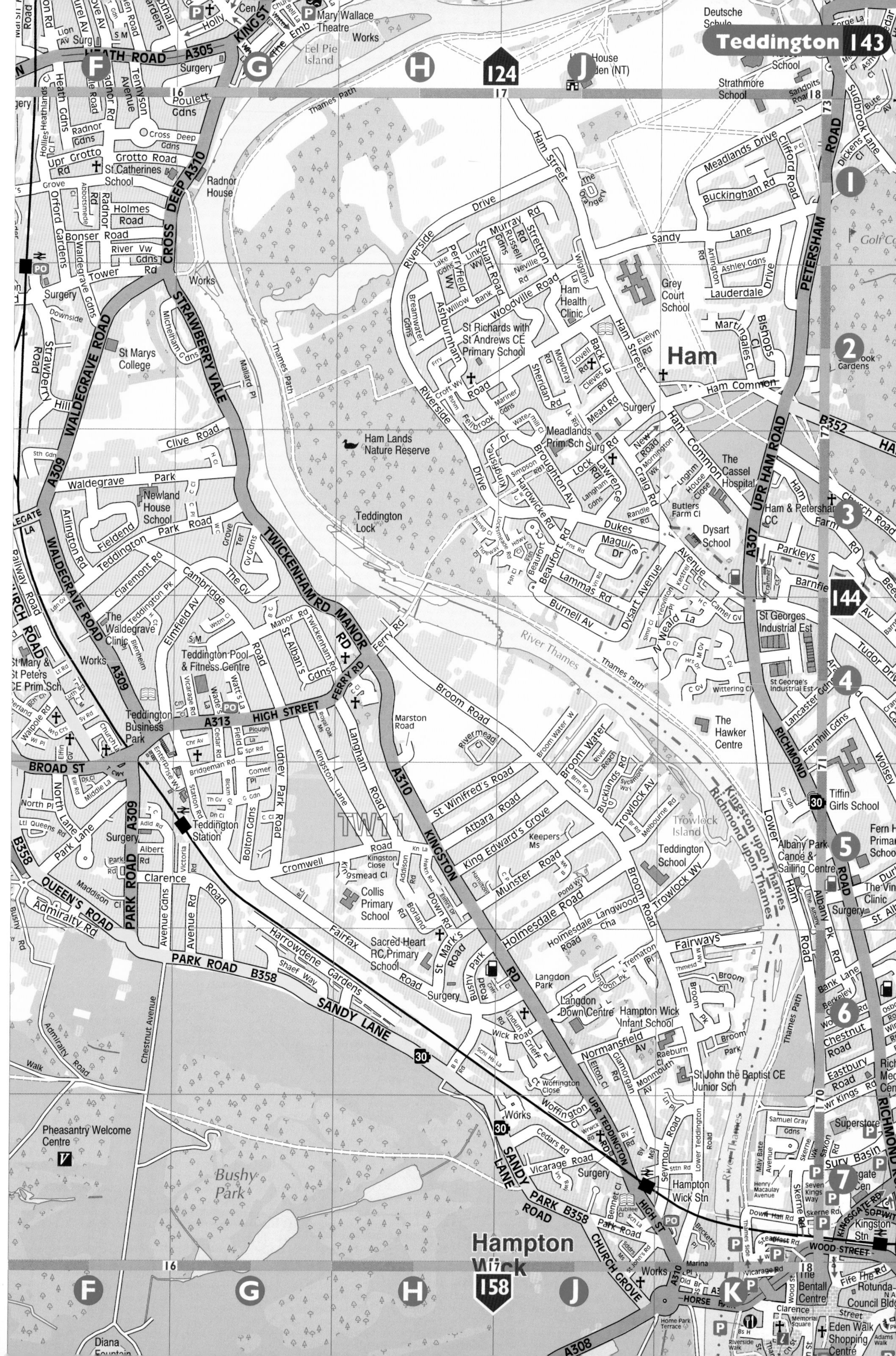
Ham
Teddington
Hampton Wick
Ham Lands Nature Reserve
Teddington Lock
River Thames
Bushy Park
Pheasantry Welcome Centre
Trowlock Island
Eel Pie Island
TW11
124
144
158

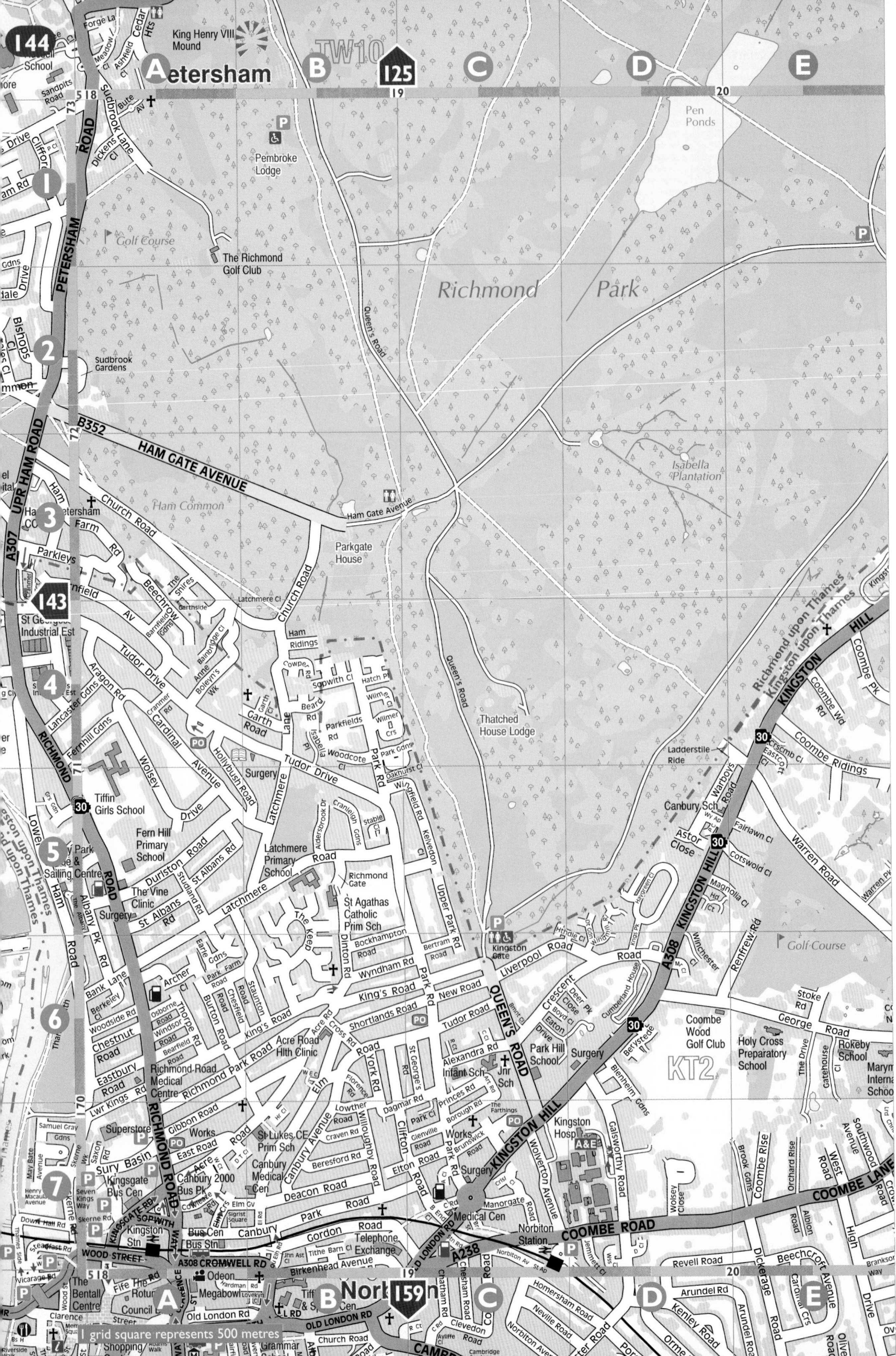
144
125
143
159
TW10
KT2
Petersham
Richmond Park
King Henry VIII Mound
Pembroke Lodge
Golf Course
The Richmond Golf Club
Pen Ponds
Isabella Plantation
Ham Common
Parkgate House
Thatched House Lodge
Sudbrook Gardens
Kingston Gate
Ham Gate Avenue
B352
HAM GATE AVENUE
PETERSHAM ROAD
UPR HAM ROAD
A307
RICHMOND ROAD
Queen's Road
QUEEN'S ROAD
KINGSTON HILL
A308
COOMBE ROAD
COOMBE LANE
A238
CAMBRIDGE ROAD
Church Road
Tudor Drive
Latchmere Road
Cardinal Avenue
Wolsey Drive
Richmond Park Road
Park Road
Liverpool Road
King's Road
Kings Road
Canbury Park Road
Birkenhead Avenue
Gordon Road
Elton Road
Deacon Road
Tiffin Girls School
Fern Hill Primary School
Latchmere Primary School
St Agathas Catholic Prim Sch
Richmond Gate
Acre Road Hlth Clinic
Richmond Medical Centre
St Lukes CE Prim Sch
Canbury Medical Cen
Canbury 2000 Bus Pk
Kingsgate Bus Cen
Kingston Stn
Bus Stn
Norbiton Station
Telephone Exchange
Kingston Hosp
A&E
Medical Cen
Park Hill School
Coombe Wood Golf Club
Holy Cross Preparatory School
Rokeby School
Canbury Sch
Infant Sch
Jnr Sch
Surgery
Superstore
Works
Odeon
Megabowl
The Bentall Centre
Richmond upon Thames
Kingston upon Thames
Golf Course
1 grid square represents 500 metres

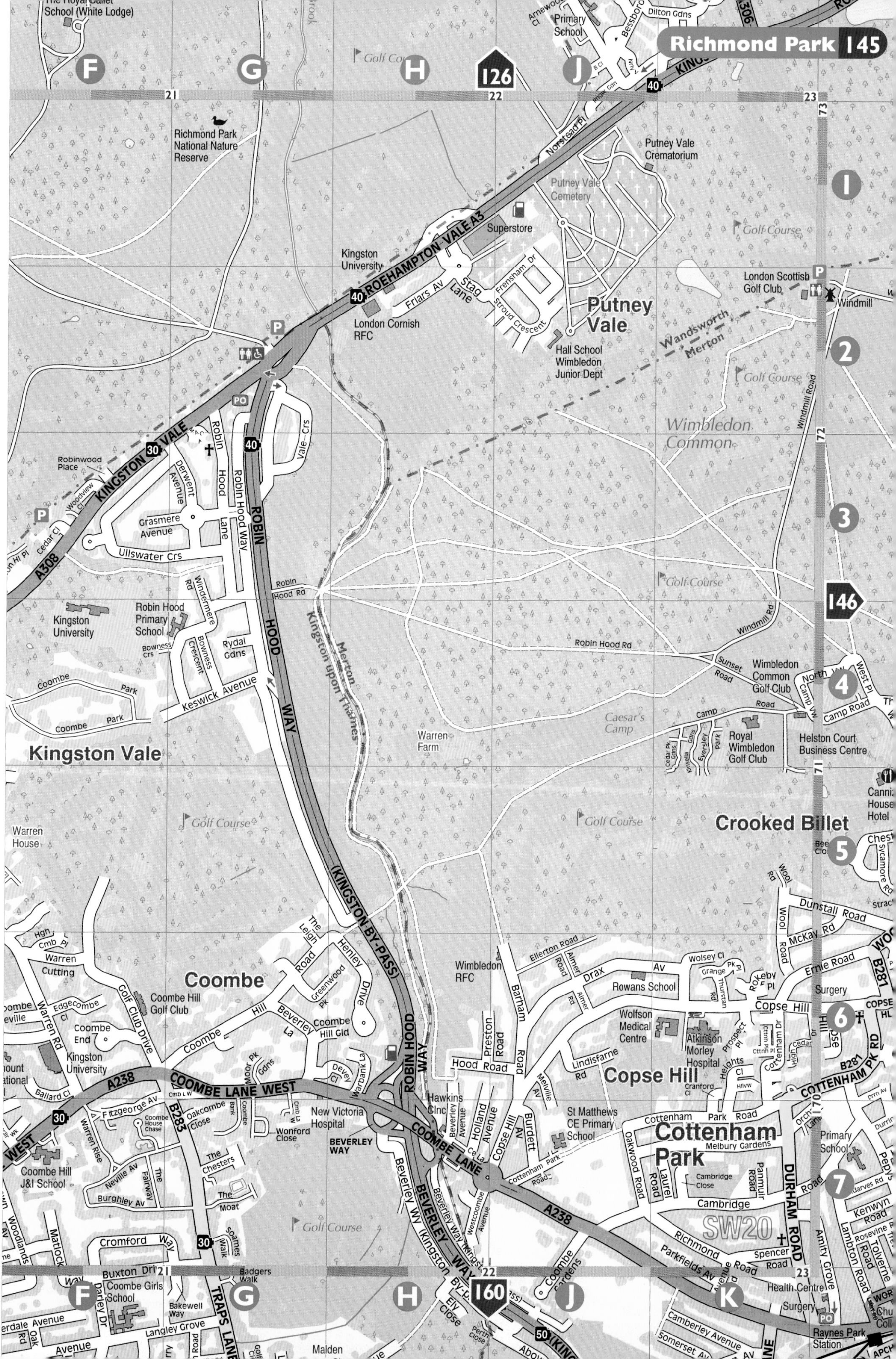

F G H 126 J 40 KINGSTON Richmond Park 145

21 22 23

The Royal Ballet
School (White Lodge)

Arnewood
Cl

Primary
School

Besboro

Dilton Gdns

A306

Golf Cor

Norstead Pl

I

Richmond Park
National Nature
Reserve

Putney Vale
Crematorium

Putney Vale
Cemetery

Golf Course

Superstore

ROEHAMPTON VALE A3

Frensham Dr

London Scottish
Golf Club

P

2

Kingston
University

Frirs Av

Stag
Lane

Stroud Crescent

Windmill

40

London Cornish
RFC

Putney
Vale

Wandsworth

Windmill Road

Merton

72

PO

Hall School
Wimbledon
Junior Dept

Wimbledon
Common

Golf Course

KINGSTON VALE

30

Robinwood
Place

Cedar Cl

Vale Crs

3

Robin
Hood
Lane

Vale Crs

Robin Hood Way

40

Robin

Derwent
Avenue

Grasmere
Avenue

Wndview

Robin
Hood Rd

146

A308

Ullswater Crs

HOOD

Windmere
Rd

Robin Hood Rd

Windmill Rd

Kingston
University

Robin Hood
Primary
School

Bowness
Crescent

Rydal
Gdns

Sunset
Road

North W

Camp

West Pl

4

Coombe
Park

Bowness
Crs

Keswick Avenue

WAY

Kingston upon Thames

Merton

Caesar's
Camp

Wimbledon
Common
Golf Club

Camp Road

71

Camp Road

Kingston Vale

Coombe
Park

Warren
Farm

Royal
Wimbledon
Golf Club

Helston Court
Business Centre

Canni
House
Hotel

Warren
House

Golf Course

Golf Course

Crooked Billet

Chest

Bee
Clo

Sycamore Rd

strac

5

Hgh
Cmb Pl

The
Leigh
Road

Henley
Drive

(KINGSTON BY-PASS)

Wimbledon
RFC

Ellerton Road

Wolsey Cl

Dunstall Road

McKay Rd

Wool
Rd

Ernie Road

B381

Woo

Warren
Cutting

Greenwood
Pk

Drax
Av

Grange
Rd

Rokeby
Pl

Surgery

Copse Hill

6

Coombe

Golf Club Drive

Coombe Hill
Golf Club

Coombe Hill Gld

Barham
Road

Rowans School

Thurstan
Rd

Copse
Hill

COPSE

Edgecombe
Cl

Coombe
Deville

Beverley
La

Coombe
Hill Gld

Wolfson
Medical
Centre

Atkinson
Morley
Hospital

Lindisfarne
Rd

Prospect
Pl

Cranford
Cl

Heights
Cl

Cedar

B281

COTTENHAM PK RD

Coombe
End

Kingston
University

Coombe

Devey
Cm

Preston
Road

Hood
Road

St Matthews
CE Primary
School

Melbury Gardens

Cottenham

Cottenham
Park
Road

Copse Hill

Cottenham
Park

COTTENHAM

Primary
School

DURHAM ROAD

7

Ballard Cl

A238

COOMBE LANE WEST

B283

Oakcombe
Close

New Victoria
Hospital

Hawkins
Clnc

Beverley
Avenue

Holland
Avenue

Laurel
Road

Cambridge
Close

Panmuir
Road

Fitzgeorge Av

Coombe
House Chase

Wonford
Close

BEVERLEY
WAY

Westcombe
Road

Cottenham
Park Road

Cambridge
Road

Richmond
Road

Spencer
Road

Kenwn
Road

Coombe Hill
J&I School

Neville Av

The
Fairway

The
Chesters

The
Moat

Burghley Av

BEVERLEY WAY (Kingston

SW20

Amity Grove

Lambton Road

Cromford
Way

30

Soanes
Walk

Golf Course

A238

Parkfields Av

Coombe
Gardens

Health Centre

Surgery

Woodlands

Buxton Drv

Coombe Girls
School

Badgers
Walk

BY-

Perth
Close

Camberley Avenue

Somerset Av

Raynes Park
Station

F G H 160 J K

21 22 23

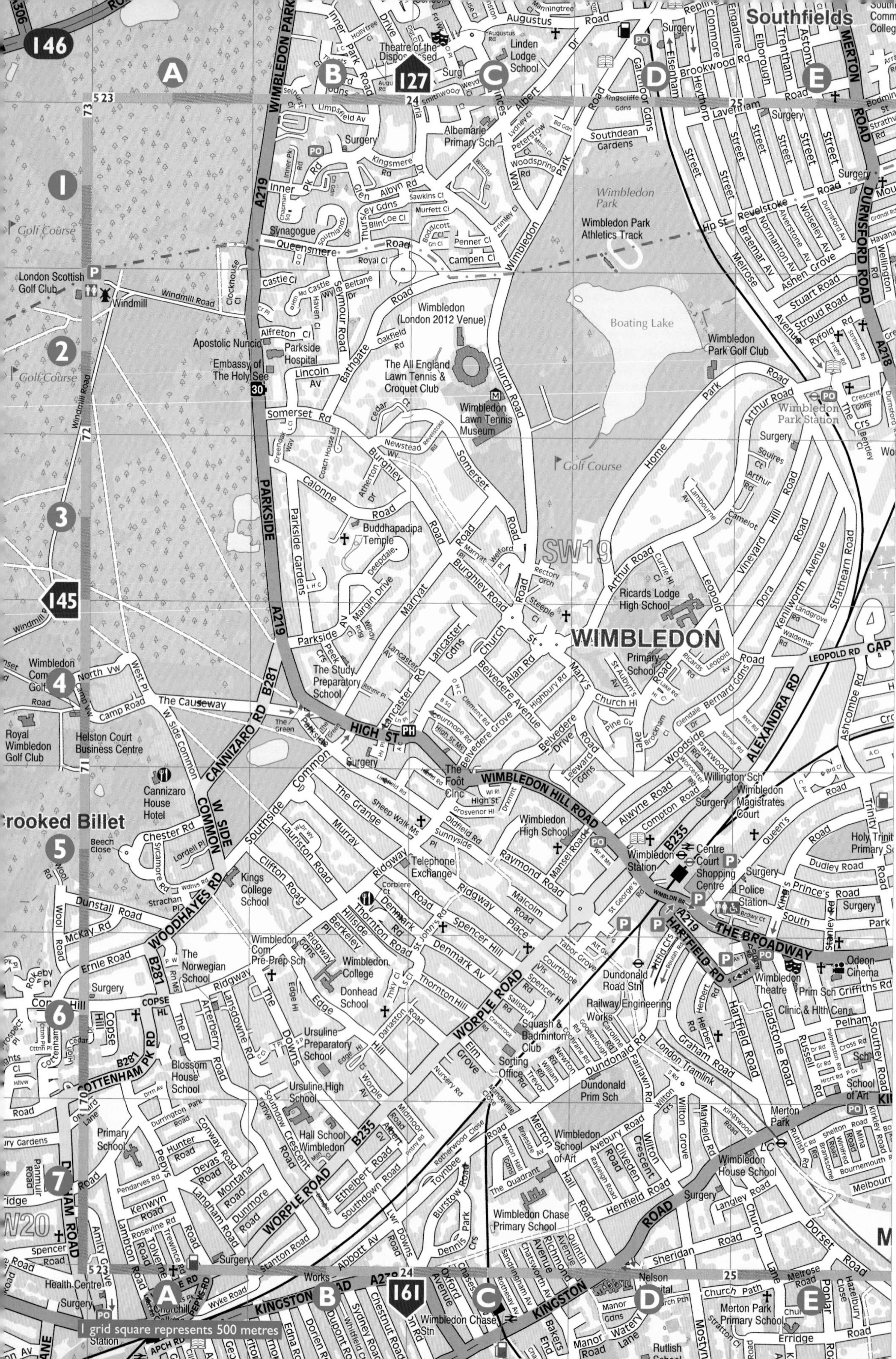
146
127
145
161
30
Southfields
Southfields Community College
A
B
C
D
E
1
2
3
4
5
6
7
523
24
25
73
72
71
70
Wimbledon Park
Wimbledon Park Athletics Track
Boating Lake
Wimbledon Park Golf Club
Wimbledon Park Station
Golf Course
London Scottish Golf Club
Windmill
Windmill Road
Windmill Rd
Queensmere Road
Clockhouse Cl
Royal Cl
Campen Cl
Penner Cl
Synagogue
Castle Cl
Seymour Road
Beltane Dr
Inner Park Road
Inner Pk Rd
Theatre of the Dispossessed
Linden Lodge School
Augustus Rd
Albemarle Primary Sch
Limpsfield Av
Kingsmere Rd
Glen Albyn Rd
Thursley Gdns
Blincoe Cl
Sawkins Cl
Murfett Cl
Peterstow Cl
Woodspring Rd
Southdean Gardens
Kingscliffe Gdns
Brookwood Rd
Elsenham St
Clonmore St
Engadine St
Elborough Street
Trentham Street
Astonville Street
Heythorp Street
Lavenham Rd
Revelstoke Road
Melrose Avenue
Braemar Av
Normanton Av
Alverstone Av
Wolseley Av
Ashen Grove
Stuart Road
Stroud Road
Ryfold Rd
Merton Road
Durnsford Road
A218
Surgery
PO
Wimbledon (London 2012 Venue)
The All England Lawn Tennis & Croquet Club
Wimbledon Lawn Tennis Museum
Church Road
Apostolic Nuncio
Embassy of The Holy See
Parkside Hospital
Alfreton Cl
Lincoln Av
Bathgate Road
Oakfield Rd
Somerset Rd
Somerset Road
Cedar Ct
Newstead Wy
Burghley Road
Calonne Road
Atherton Dr
Buddhapadipa Temple
Parkside Gardens
Margin Drive
Deepdale
Marryat Road
Marryat Pl
Welford Pl
Rectory Orch
Steeple Cl
Home Park Road
Arthur Road
Vineyard Hill Road
Dora Rd
Kenilworth Avenue
Strathearn Road
Leopold Road
Leopold Rd
Ricards Lodge High School
Camelot Cl
Lambourne Av
Squires Ct
SW19
WIMBLEDON
Parkside
A219
Wimbledon Park Side
Wimbledon Common Golf Club
Royal Wimbledon Golf Club
Helston Court Business Centre
North Vw
West Pl
Camp Road
The Causeway
W Side Common
Cannizaro Rd
Cannizaro House Hotel
B281
The Green
High St
The Study Preparatory School
Lancaster Rd
Lancaster Gdns
Church St
St Mary's Road
Alan Rd
Belvedere Avenue
Belvedere Grove
Belvedere Drive
Highbury Rd
Church Hl
Primary School
Pine Gv
Lake Rd
Brockham Cl
Alexandra Rd
Woodside
Parkwood
Bernard Gdns
Ascombe Rd
Crooked Billet
Chester Rd
Lordell Pl
Sycamore Rd
Beech Close
Woodhayes Rd
Kings College School
Southside Common
The Grange
Murray Rd
Lauriston Road
Clifton Road
Sheep Walk Ms
The Foot Clnc
Wimbledon Hill Road
Grosvenor Hl
Oldfield Rd
Sunnyside Pl
Ridgway
Telephone Exchange
Wimbledon High School
Raymond Road
Malcolm Road
Mansel Road
Alwyne Road
Compton Road
Willington Sch
Wimbledon Magistrates Court
Wimbledon Station
Centre Court Shopping Centre
Police Station
The Broadway
Hartfield Rd
Queen's Road
Holy Trinity Primary Sch
Dudley Road
Prince's Road
Kings Road
South Park
Stanley Rd
Odeon Cinema
Wimbledon Theatre
Prim Sch
Griffiths Rd
Clinic & Hlth Cen
Pelham
Dunstall Road
McKay Rd
Wool Road
Ernle Road
The Norwegian School
Wimbledon Com Pre-Prep Sch
Wimbledon College
Donhead School
Ridgway Gdns
Berkeley Pl
Hillside
Thornton Road
Thornton Hill
Denmark Rd
Denmark Av
Spencer Hill
Ridgway Place
St John's Rd
Worple Road
Tabor Grove
Courthope Vls
Dundonald Road Stn
Railway Engineering Works
Squash & Badminton Club
Sorting Office
Dundonald Prim Sch
Copse Hill
Surgery
Lansdowne Rd
Arterberry Road
The Downs
Ursuline Preparatory School
Ursuline High School
Edge Hill
Darlaston Road
Blossom House School
Cottenham Pk Rd
Durrington Park Road
Hunter Road
Conway Road
Devas Road
Montana Road
Langham Road
Dunmore Road
Primary School
Pepys Road
Kenwyn Road
Pendarves Rd
Rosevine Rd
Southdown Drive
Southdown Road
Crescent Road
Hall School Wimbledon
B235
Ethelbert Road
Midmoor Road
Elm Grove
Nursery Rd
Rotherwood Close
Toynbee Road
Burstow Road
Dennis Park Crs
Merton Hall Road
Wimbledon School of Art
The Quadrant
Wimbledon Chase Primary School
Avebury Road
Cliveden Road
Wilton Crescent
Wilton Grove
Henfield Road
Rayleigh Road
Mayfield Rd
Kingswood Road
Graham Road
London Tramlink
Merton Park
Wimbledon House School
Langley Road
Church Lane
Dorset Road
Bournemouth Rd
Melbourne
Sheridan Road
Nelson Hospital
Church Path
Merton Park Primary School
Erridge Road
Poplar Road
Hazelbury Close
Melrose Road
Kingston Road
A238
Wimbledon Chase Stn
Chatsworth Av
Richmond Avenue
Quintin Avenue
Sandringham Av
Bakers End
Manor Gdns
Watery Lane
Rutlish
Mostyn
Oxford Avenue
Chestnut Road
Sydney Road
Dupont Rd
Dorien Rd
Edna Rd
Stanton Road
Abbott Av
Lwr Downs Road
Wyke Road
Churchill Rd
Health Centre
Durham Road
Lambton Road
Amity Grove
Tolverne Rd
Panmuir Road
Spencer Road
SW20
1 grid square represents 500 metres

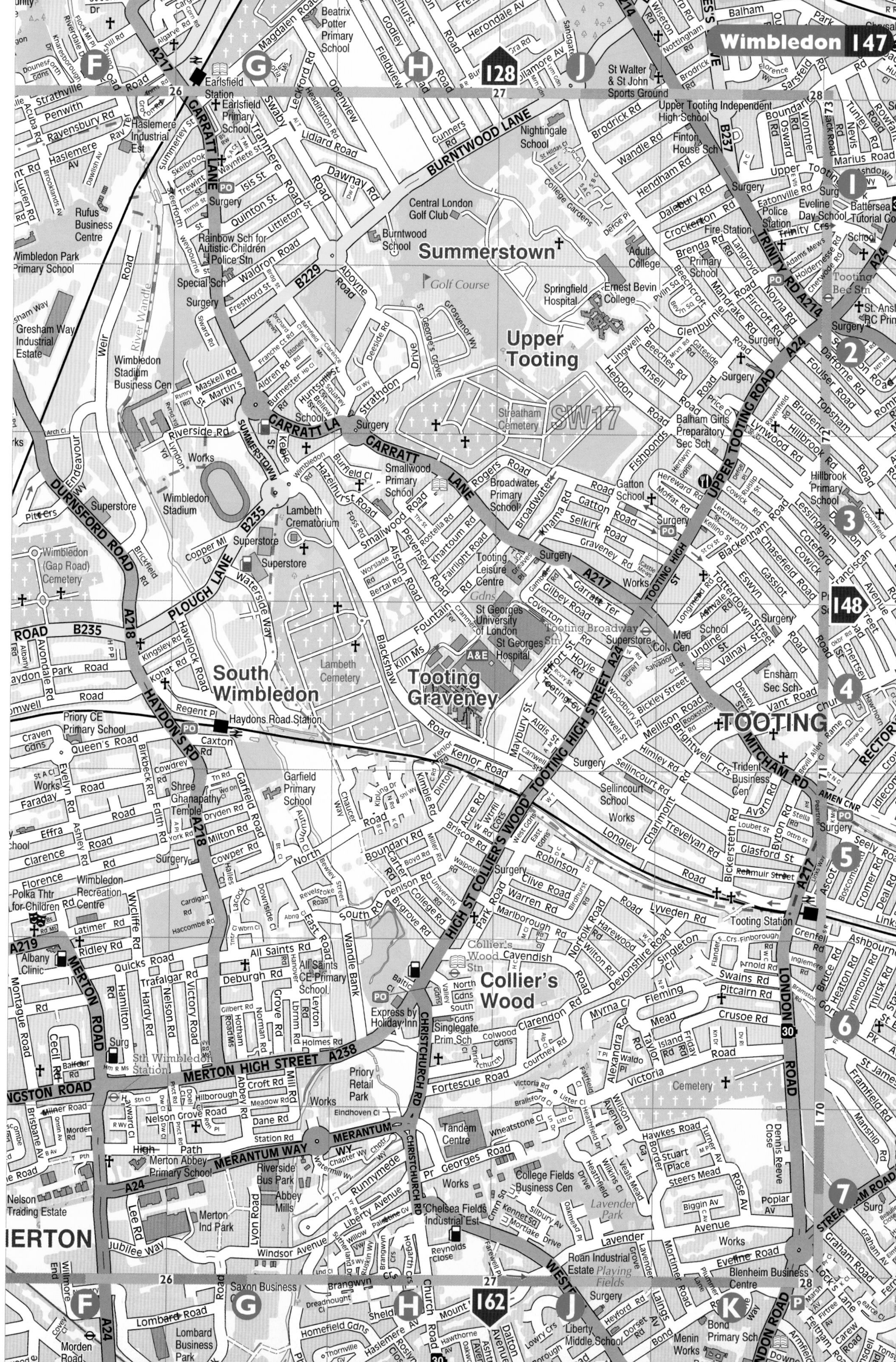
Wimbledon 147
128
148
162
F
G
H
J
K
I
2
3
4
5
6
7
26
27
28
Earlsfield Station
Earlsfield Primary School
Haslemere Industrial Est
Rufus Business Centre
Wimbledon Park Primary School
Gresham Way Industrial Estate
Wimbledon Stadium Business Cen
Wimbledon Stadium
Superstore
Wimbledon (Gap Road) Cemetery
Beatrix Potter Primary School
St Walter & St John Sports Ground
Upper Tooting Independent High School
Finton House Sch
Nightingale School
Central London Golf Club
Burntwood School
Summerstown
Golf Course
Springfield Hospital
Ernest Bevin College
Adult College
Upper Tooting
Streatham Cemetery
SW17
Rainbow Sch for Autistic Children
Police Stn
Special Sch
Surgery
Lambeth Crematorium
Smallwood Primary School
Broadwater Primary School
Tooting Leisure Centre
St Georges University of London
St Georges Hospital
A&E
Tooting Broadway
Lambeth Cemetery
South Wimbledon
Tooting Graveney
Haydons Road Station
Priory CE Primary School
Shree Ghanapathy Temple
Garfield Primary School
Wimbledon Recreation Centre
Polka Thtr for Children
Albany Clinic
All Saints CE Primary School
Express by Holiday Inn
Collier's Wood Stn
Collier's Wood
Singlegate Prim Sch
Sth Wimbledon Station
Merton High Street
Priory Retail Park
Tandem Centre
Merton Abbey Primary School
Riverside Bus Park
Abbey Mills
Merton Ind Park
Nelson Trading Estate
MERTON
College Fields Business Cen
Chelsea Fields Industrial Est
Lavender Park
Roan Industrial Estate
Playing Fields
Blenheim Business Centre
Saxon Business
Lombard Business Park
Morden Road
Liberty Middle School
Bond Primary Sch
Menin Works
Cemetery
Trident Business Cen
Sellincourt School
Ensham Sec Sch
TOOTING
Tooting Station
AMEN CNR
Hillbrook Primary School
Balham Girls Preparatory Sec Sch
Gatton School
Brenda Rd Primary School
Police Station
Fire Station
Eveline Day School
Battersea Tutorial Col
Tooting Bec Stn
St. Anselm RC Prim
Med Cen
Undine School
BURNTWOOD LANE
GARRATT LANE
GARRATT LA
DURNSFORD ROAD
PLOUGH LANE
HAYDON'S RD
MERTON ROAD
KINGSTON ROAD
MERANTUM WAY
CHRISTCHURCH RD
HIGH ST COLLIER'S WOOD
TOOTING HIGH STREET
UPPER TOOTING ROAD
TRINITY RD A214
MITCHAM RD
LONDON ROAD
A217
A218
A219
A24
A238
B229
B235
B237

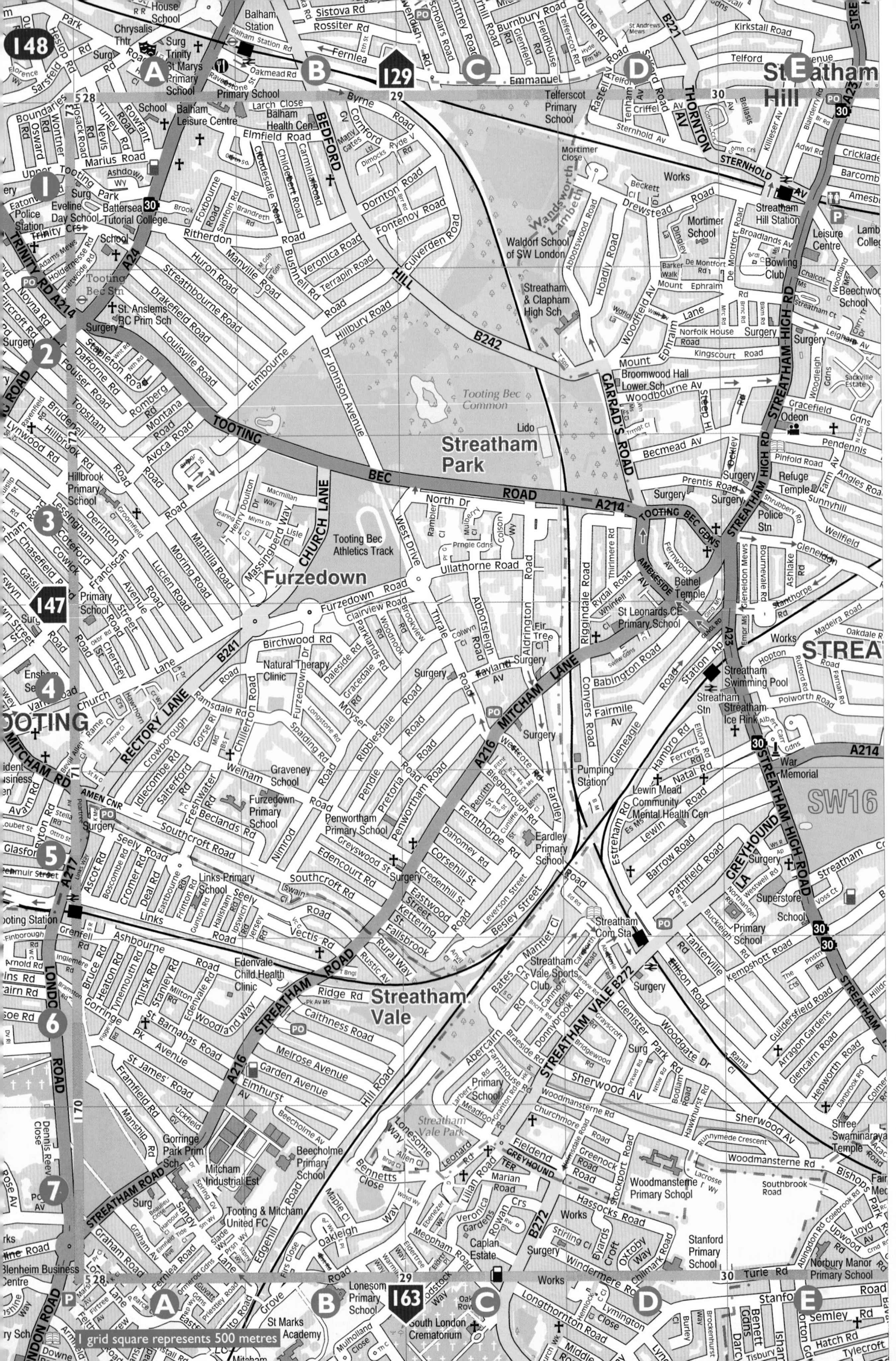
148
129
147
163
A
B
C
D
E
1
2
3
4
5
6
7
28
29
30
Balham Station
Balham Leisure Centre
Balham Health Cen
Chrysalis Thtr
Trinity St Marys Primary School
Battersea Tutorial College
Eveline Day School
Police Station
Tooting Bec Stn
St. Anslems RC Prim Sch
Hillbrook Primary School
Telferscot Primary School
Streatham Hill
Streatham Hill Station
Mortimer School
Waldorf School of SW London
Streatham & Clapham High Sch
Broomwood Hall Lower Sch
Leisure Centre
Bowling Club
Beechwood School
Tooting Bec Common
Lido
Streatham Park
Tooting Bec Athletics Track
Furzedown
Natural Therapy Clinic
Graveney School
Furzedown Primary School
Penwortham Primary School
Links Primary School
Eardley Primary School
St Leonards CE Primary School
Bethel Temple
Odeon
Refuge Temple
Police Stn
Streatham Swimming Pool
Streatham Stn
Streatham Ice Rink
War Memorial
SW16
Lewin Mead Community Mental Health Cen
Pumping Station
Streatham Com Sta
Streatham Vale Sports Club
Superstore
Primary School
Streatham Vale
Edenvale Child Health Clinic
Gorringe Park Prim Sch
Mitcham Industrial Est
Beecholme Primary School
Tooting & Mitcham United FC
Streatham Vale Park
Woodmansterne Primary School
Stanford Primary School
Norbury Manor Primary School
Caplan Estate
Lonesome Primary School
St Marks Academy
South London Crematorium
Shree Swaminarayan Temple
Blenheim Business Centre
Tooting Station
TOOTING
AMEN CNR
TOOTING BEC ROAD
A214
A24
A23
A216
A217
B241
B242
B272
B221
TRINITY RD A214
BEDFORD HILL
CHURCH LANE
RECTORY LANE
MITCHAM LANE
MITCHAM RD
GARRAD'S ROAD
STREATHAM HIGH RD
STREATHAM HIGH ROAD
STREATHAM ROAD
STREATHAM VALE B272
GREYHOUND LA
STERNHOLD AV
THORNTON AV
LONDON ROAD
Wandsworth
Lambeth
1 grid square represents 500 metres

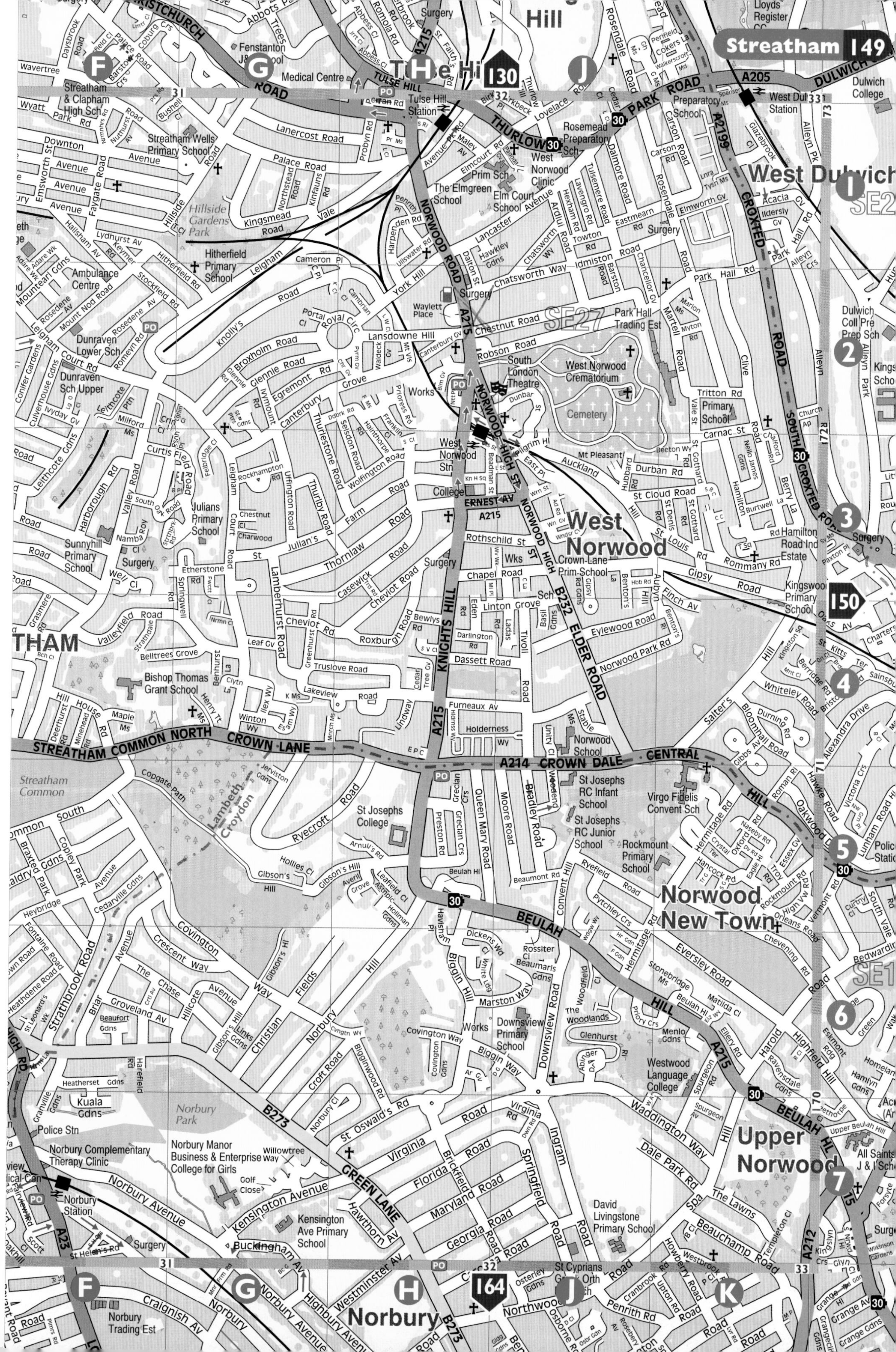

Streatham 149
130
150
164
Hill
Tulse Hill
Tulse Hill Station
West Dulwich Station
Dulwich College
West Dulwich
SE27
West Norwood
West Norwood Stn
West Norwood Crematorium
Cemetery
South London Theatre
Norwood New Town
Upper Norwood
Norbury
Norbury Station
Norbury Park
Streatham Common
Lambeth
Croydon
TULSE HILL
THURLOW PARK ROAD
NORWOOD ROAD
NORWOOD HIGH ST
KNIGHTS HILL
ELDER ROAD
CROXTED ROAD
SOUTH CROXTED ROAD
GIPSY ROAD
STREATHAM COMMON NORTH
CROWN LANE
CROWN DALE
CENTRAL HILL
BEULAH HILL
GREEN LANE
NORBURY AVENUE
A215
A205
A2199
A214
A212
A23
B232
B273
Streatham & Clapham High Sch
Streatham Wells Primary School
Hillside Gardens Park
Hitherfield Primary School
Dunraven Lower Sch
Dunraven Sch Upper
Julians Primary School
Sunnyhill Primary School
Bishop Thomas Grant School
St Josephs College
St Josephs RC Infant School
St Josephs RC Junior School
Virgo Fidelis Convent Sch
Rockmount Primary School
Norwood School
Crown Lane Prim School
Downsview Primary School
Westwood Language College
David Livingstone Primary School
Kensington Ave Primary School
Norbury Manor Business & Enterprise College for Girls
Norbury Complementary Therapy Clinic
Norbury Trading Est
Kingswood Primary School
Hamilton Road Ind Estate
Tritton Rd Primary School
Park Hall Trading Est
Rosemead Preparatory Sch
Preparatory School
The Elmgreen School
Elm Court School
West Norwood Clinic
Dulwich Coll Pre Prep Sch
All Saints J & I Sch
Police Stn
Surgery
Ambulance Centre
Medical Centre

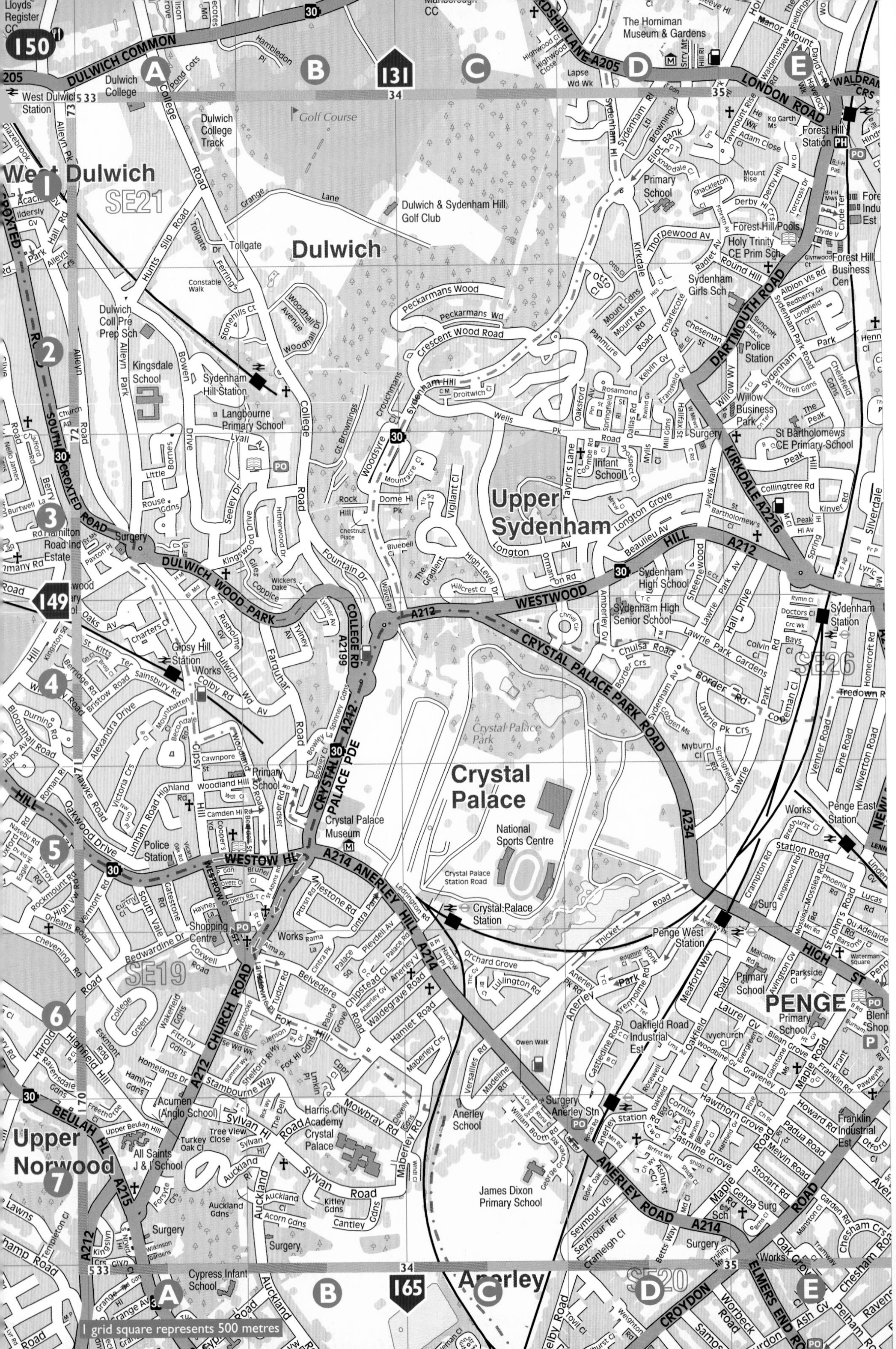

150
131
149
165
West Dulwich
SE21
Dulwich
Upper Sydenham
SE26
Crystal Palace
SE19
Upper Norwood
PENGE
Anerley
SE20
DULWICH COMMON
LONDON ROAD
DARTMOUTH ROAD
KIRKDALE A2216
WESTWOOD HILL A212
CRYSTAL PALACE PARK ROAD
DULWICH WOOD PARK
COLLEGE RD A2199
CRYSTAL PALACE PDE A212
WESTOW HL
A214 ANERLEY HILL
ANERLEY ROAD A214
CHURCH ROAD A212
BEULAH HL
SOUTH CROXTED ROAD
HIGH ST
ELMERS END RD
CROYDON
Dulwich College
West Dulwich Station
Dulwich College Track
Golf Course
Dulwich & Sydenham Hill Golf Club
The Horniman Museum & Gardens
Forest Hill Station
Forest Hill Pools
Sydenham Hill Station
Kingsdale School
Langbourne Primary School
Gipsy Hill Station
Police Station
Shopping Centre
Crystal Palace Museum
Crystal Palace Park
National Sports Centre
Crystal Palace Station
Penge West Station
Penge East Station
Sydenham Station
Sydenham High School
Sydenham Girls Sch
Anerley Stn
Anerley School
James Dixon Primary School
Harris City Academy Crystal Palace
All Saints J & I School
Cypress Infant School
Oakfield Road Industrial Est
Franklin Industrial Est
Forest Hill Business Cen
1 grid square represents 500 metres

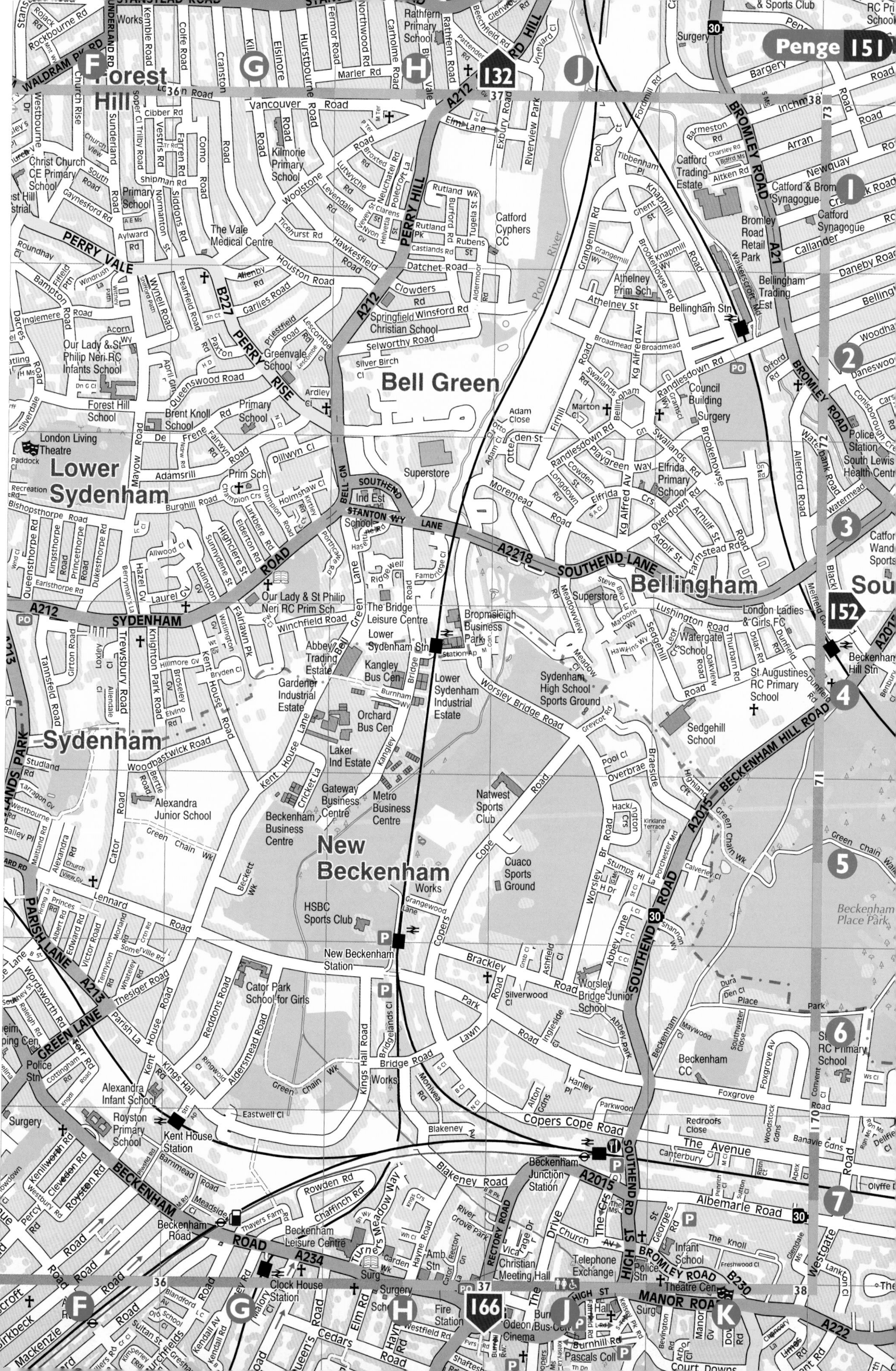

Penge 151
132
152
166
F
G
H
J
I
K
2
3
4
5
6
7
36
37
38
70
71
72
73
Forest Hill
Bell Green
Lower Sydenham
Sydenham
Bellingham
New Beckenham
Beckenham Place Park
Stanstead Road
Waldram Pk Rd
Church Rise
Westbourne Dr
Sunderland Rd
Kemble Road
Colfe Road
Cranston
Elsinore
Hurstbourne Road
Fermor Road
Northwood Rd
Carholme Road
Rathfern Primary School
Rathfern Road
Marler Rd
Vancouver Road
Perry Hill
Vineyard Cl
Riverview Park
Exbury Road
Elm Lane
Kilmorie Primary School
Christ Church CE Primary School
Gaynesford Rd
Perry Vale
Aylward Rd
Normanton St
Siddons Rd
Como Road
Woolstone
Ticehurst Rd
The Vale Medical Centre
Houston Road
Hawkesfield Road
Datchet Road
Castlands Rd
Rutland Pk
Catford Cyphers CC
Pool River
Clowders Rd
Winsford Rd
Springfield Christian School
Selworthy Road
Silver Birch Cl
Garlies Road
B227
Perry Rise
Greenvale School
Priestfield Road
Queenswood Road
Our Lady & St Philip Neri RC Infants School
Forest Hill School
Brent Knoll School
Primary School
London Living Theatre
Mayow Road
Adamsrill
Dillwyn Cl
Prim Sch
Burghill Road
Bishopsthorpe Road
Holmshaw Cl
Southend Lane
Stanton Wy
Ind Est
Superstore
A212
A2218
A21
A2015
A213
A234
B230
A222
Sydenham Road
Our Lady & St Philip Neri RC Prim Sch
Winchfield Road
The Bridge Leisure Centre
Lower Sydenham Stn
Bromsleigh Business Park
Abbey Trading Estate
Kangley Bus Cen
Gardener Industrial Estate
Lower Sydenham Industrial Estate
Orchard Bus Cen
Laker Ind Estate
Gateway Business Centre
Metro Business Centre
Beckenham Business Centre
Worsley Bridge Road
Sydenham High School Sports Ground
Natwest Sports Club
Cuaco Sports Ground
Cope Road
Woodbastwick Road
Alexandra Junior School
Green Chain Wk
Cator Road
Lennard Road
HSBC Sports Club
New Beckenham Station
Brackley Road
Park Road
Lawn Road
Cator Park School for Girls
Reddons Road
Aldersmead Road
Kings Hall Road
Bridge Road
Worsley Bridge Junior School
Silverwood Cl
Abbey Park
Southend Road
Beckenham CC
Foxgrove
Copers Cope Road
The Avenue
Beckenham Junction Station
Parish Lane
Green Lane
Thesiger Road
Kent House Road
Alexandra Infant School
Royston Primary School
Kent House Station
Beckenham Road
Beckenham Leisure Centre
Clock House Station
Blakeney Road
Rectory Road
Christian Meeting Hall
Telephone Exchange
Church Av
High St
Bromley Road
Manor Road
Theatre Cen
Fire Station
Odeon Cinema
Albemarle Road
Westgate
Police Station
Surgery
Police Stn
Infant School
Athelney Prim Sch
Athelney St
Bellingham Stn
Randlesdown Rd
Council Building
Surgery
Elfrida Primary School
Brookehowse Rd
Moremead Road
Southend Lane
Superstore
Lushington Road
Watergate School
St Augustines RC Primary School
Sedgehill School
Beckenham Hill Road
Beckenham Hill Stn
London Ladies & Girls FC
Catford Trading Estate
Bromley Road Retail Park
Bellingham Trading Est
Catford & Bromley Synagogue
Catford Synagogue
Police Station
South Lewis Health Centre
Bargery Road
Inchmery Road
Arran Road
Newquay
Callander
Daneby Road
Bromley Road
Allerford Road
Pool Cl
Overbrae
Braeside
Hackington Crs
Stumps Hill La
Abbey Lane
Calverley Cl
Dura Den Cl
Foxgrove Av
Convent Cl
Banavie Gdns
Canterbury Cl
The Knoll
Lankton Cl
Beckenham Place
Surg
Amb Stn
Turners Meadow Way
Rowden Rd
Chaffinch Rd
Westfield Rd
Burnhill Rd
Pascals Coll
Court Downs
Mackenzie
Birkbeck
Sultan St
Kendall Rd
Queen's
Cedars
Elm Rd

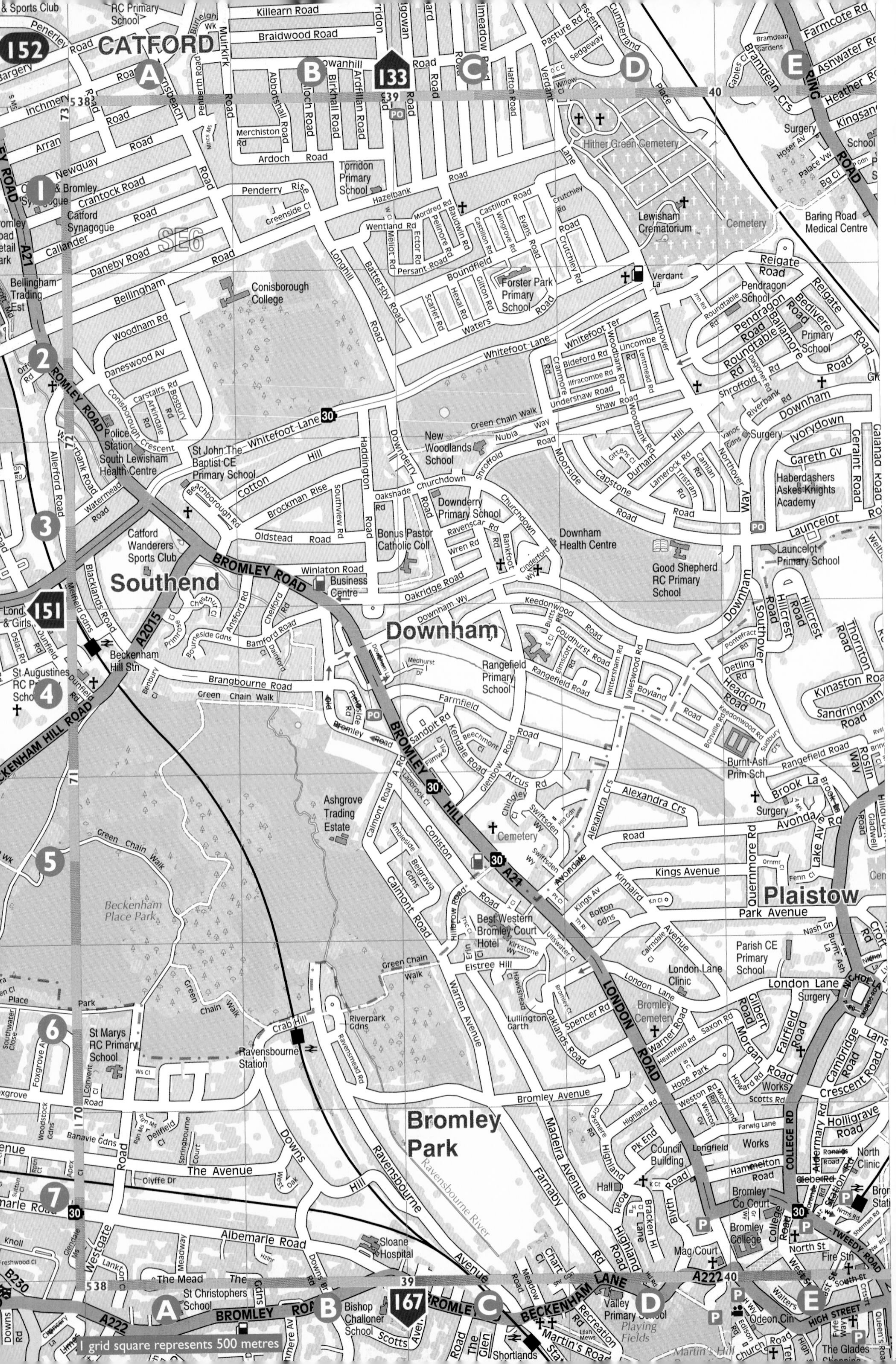
152
CATFORD
A
B
133
C
D
E
Killearn Road
Braidwood Road
Penerley Road
RC Primary School
Inchmery
Arran
Newquay
Crantock Road
Catford Synagogue
Callander Road
Daneby Road
SE6
Bellingham Trading Est
Bellingham
Conisborough College
Merchiston Rd
Ardoch Road
Torridon Primary School
Penderry Rise
Greenside Cl
Hazelbank
Longhill
Battersby Road
Wentland Rd
Mordred Rd
Castillon Road
Persant Road
Boundfield
Forster Park Primary School
Waters
Whitefoot Lane
Hither Green Cemetery
Lewisham Crematorium
Cemetery
Verdant La
Baring Road Medical Centre
Reigate Road
Pendragon School
Pendragon Road
Bedivere Road
Ballamore Road
Primary School
Roundtable Rd
Shroffold Rd
Downham
Ivorydown
Gareth Gv
Geraint Road
Galahad Road
Haberdashers Askes Knights Academy
Launcelot
Launcelot Primary School
Whitefoot Ter
Bideford Rd
Lincombe
Ilfracombe Rd
Undershaw Road
Shaw Road
Woodbank Rd
Northover
Green Chain Walk
Nubia Way
New Woodlands School
Moorside
Capstone Road
Durham Hill
Lamerock Rd
Tristram Rd
Camlan Rd
Northover Way
Surgery
Downham Health Centre
Good Shepherd RC Primary School
Woodham Rd
Daneswood Av
Carstairs Rd
Bosbury Rd
Arkindale Rd
Conisborough Crescent
Police Station
South Lewisham Health Centre
St John The Baptist CE Primary School
Cotton Hill
Haddington Road
Downderry Road
Churchdown
Oakshade Rd
Brockman Rise
Southview Rd
Oldstead Road
Beachborough Rd
Watermead Road
Allerford Road
Bonus Pastor Catholic Coll
Downderry Primary School
Ravenscar Rd
Wren Rd
Bankfoot
Cinderford Wy
Catford Wanderers Sports Club
Southend
BROMLEY ROAD
Winlaton Road
Business Centre
Oakridge Road
Downham Wy
Keedonwood Road
Coldharbour
Ansford Rd
Chelford Rd
Bamford Road
Bourneside Gdns
Downham
Rangefield Primary School
Rangefield Road
Coudhurst Road
Elmscott Rd
Wittersham Rd
Valeswood Rd
Boyland
Southover
Hillcrest Road
Thornton Road
Pontefract Rd
Detling Rd
Headcorn Road
Kynaston Road
Sandringham Road
Burnt Ash Prim Sch
Rangefield Road
Brook La
Roslin Way
151
Blacklands Road
Beckenham Hill Stn
St Augustines RC Primary School
A2015
Brangbourne Road
Green Chain Walk
Farmfield
Sandpit Rd
Kendale Road
Beechmont Cl
Glenbow Road
Arcus Rd
Chingley Cl
Swiffsden Wy
Alexandra Crs
Avondale Road
Kings Avenue
Quernmore Rd
Plaistow
Park Avenue
Bromley Road
BROMLEY HILL
Ashgrove Trading Estate
Calmont Road
Ambleside
Belgravia Gdns
Coniston Road
Cemetery
A21
Kinnaird
Bolton Gdns
Kings Av
Best Western Bromley Court Hotel
Elstree Hill
Caimdale
Parish CE Primary School
London Lane Clinic
London Lane
Bromley Cemetery
Warner Road
Saxon Rd
Gilbert Road
Morgan Road
Fairfield Road
Cambridge Road
Crescent Road
Beckenham Place Park
Green Chain Walk
Green Chain Walk
Crab Hill
Riverpark Gdns
Ravensbourne Station
Ravensmead Rd
Warren Avenue
Lullington Garth
Spencer Rd
Oaklands Road
LONDON ROAD
Hope Park
Weston Rd
Works
Scotts Rd
Farwig Lane
Longfield
Hollingrave Road
Aldermary Rd
COLLEGE RD
Council Building
Bromley Park
Ravensbourne River
Bromley Avenue
Madeira Avenue
Farnaby
Highland Road
Pk End
Hammelton Road
Bromley Co Court
Bromley College
North Clinic
St Marys RC Primary School
Foxgrove Av
Convent Cl
Woodstock Gdns
Banavie Gdns
Delifield Cl
Springbourne Court
The Avenue
Downs Hill
Ravensbourne Avenue
Olyffe Dr
Albemarle Road
Westgate Road
Meadway
Sloane Hospital
Bracken Hl
Blyth Road
Mag Court
North St
Fire Stn
TWEEDY ROAD
The Mead
St Christophers School
Bishop Challoner School
167
BROMLEY
BECKENHAM LANE
Valley Primary School
Playing Fields
Recreation
Martin's Road
Shortlands
Odeon Cin
HIGH STREET
The Glades
Martin's Hill
A222
B230
1 grid square represents 500 metres

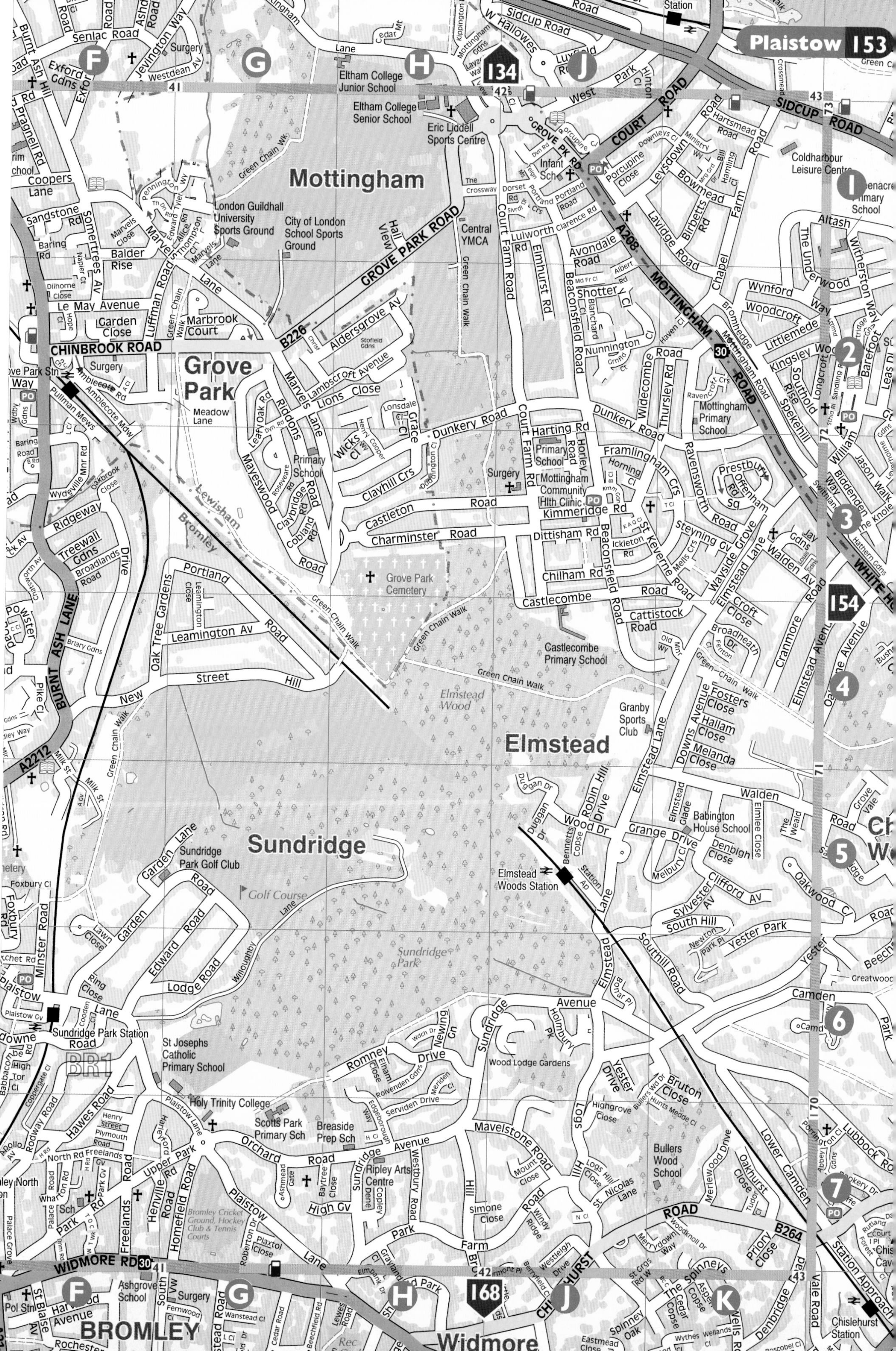

Plaistow 153
134
154
168
Mottingham
Grove Park
Sundridge
Elmstead
BROMLEY
Widmore
BR1
Eltham College Junior School
Eltham College Senior School
Eric Liddell Sports Centre
London Guildhall University Sports Ground
City of London School Sports Ground
Central YMCA
Coldharbour Leisure Centre
Mottingham Primary School
Mottingham Community Hlth Clinic
Grove Park Cemetery
Castlecombe Primary School
Granby Sports Club
Elmstead Wood
Babington House School
Elmstead Woods Station
Sundridge Park Golf Club
Golf Course
Sundridge Park
Sundridge Park Station
St Josephs Catholic Primary School
Holy Trinity College
Scotts Park Primary Sch
Breaside Prep Sch
Ripley Arts Centre
Wood Lodge Gardens
Bullers Wood School
Bromley Cricket Ground, Hockey Club & Tennis Courts
Ashgrove School
Chislehurst Station
Surgery
Station
GROVE PARK ROAD
CHINBROOK ROAD
BURNT ASH LANE
MOTTINGHAM ROAD
COURT ROAD
SIDCUP ROAD
WIDMORE RD
A208
A2212
B226
B264
Green Chain Walk
Lewisham
Bromley

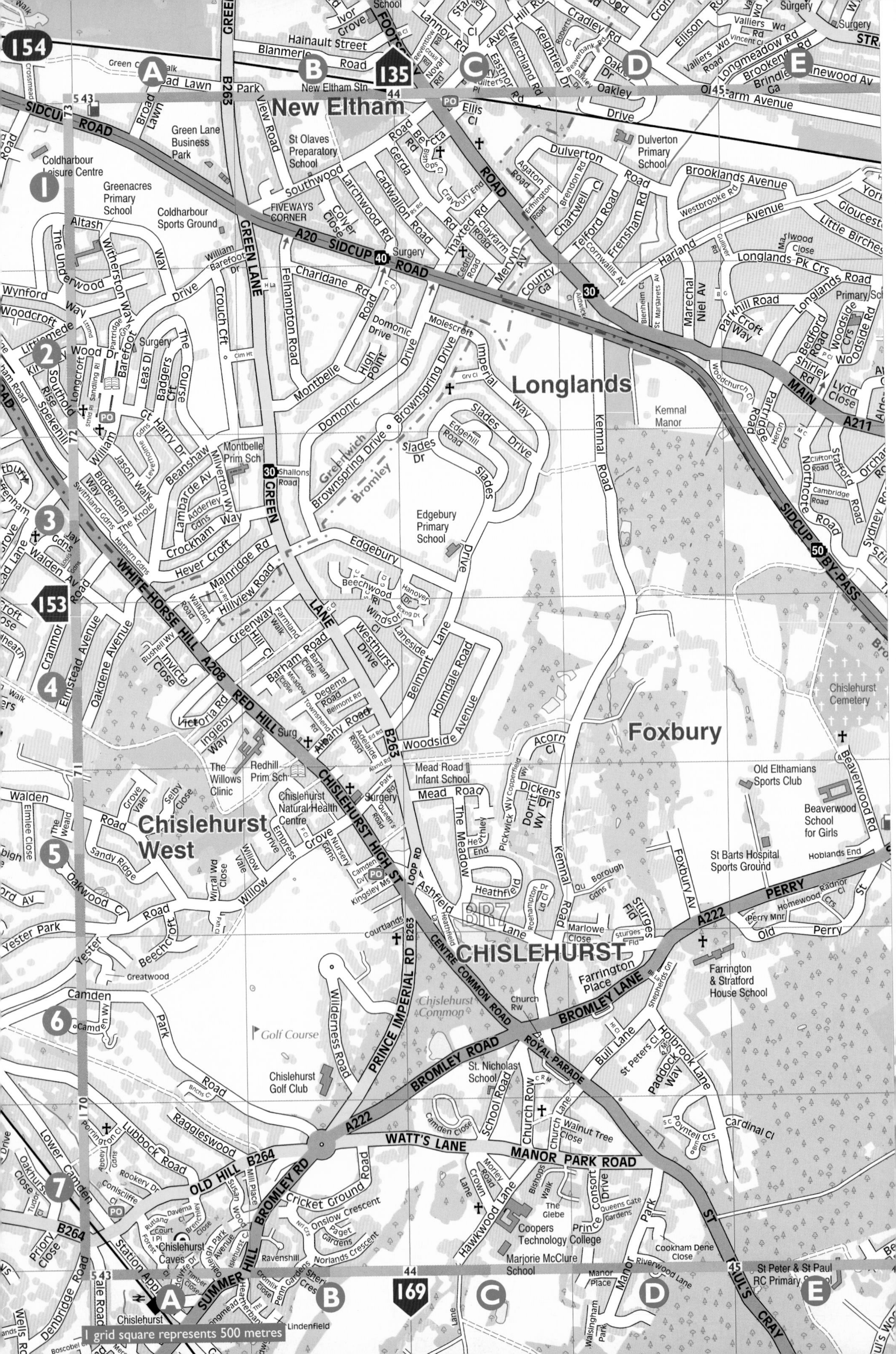
154
135
153
169
New Eltham
New Eltham Stn
Longlands
Foxbury
Chislehurst West
CHISLEHURST
BR7
A20 SIDCUP ROAD
SIDCUP ROAD
SIDCUP BY-PASS
MAIN ROAD
A211
WHITE HORSE HILL
A208 RED HILL
CHISLEHURST HIGH ST
GREEN LANE
B263
PRINCE IMPERIAL RD
CENTRE COMMON ROAD
BROMLEY ROAD
BROMLEY LANE
A222
PERRY
WATT'S LANE
MANOR PARK ROAD
OLD HILL B264
SUMMER HILL
BROMLEY RD
ROYAL PARADE
ST PAUL'S CRAY
Hainault Street
Blanmerle Road
Coldharbour Leisure Centre
Greenacres Primary School
Coldharbour Sports Ground
Green Lane Business Park
St Olaves Preparatory School
FIVEWAYS CORNER
Dulverton Primary School
Montbelle Prim Sch
Edgebury Primary School
Kemnal Manor
Chislehurst Cemetery
Old Elthamians Sports Club
Beaverwood School for Girls
St Barts Hospital Sports Ground
Mead Road Infant School
The Willows Clinic
Redhill Prim Sch
Chislehurst Natural Health Centre
Chislehurst Common
Golf Course
Chislehurst Golf Club
St. Nicholas School
Farrington & Stratford House School
Coopers Technology College
Marjorie McClure School
St Peter & St Paul RC Primary School
Chislehurst Caves
Chislehurst
Brownspring Drive
Greenwich
Bromley
Kemnal Road
Foxbury Av
Beaverwood Rd
Wilderness Road
Camden Park Road
1 grid square represents 500 metres

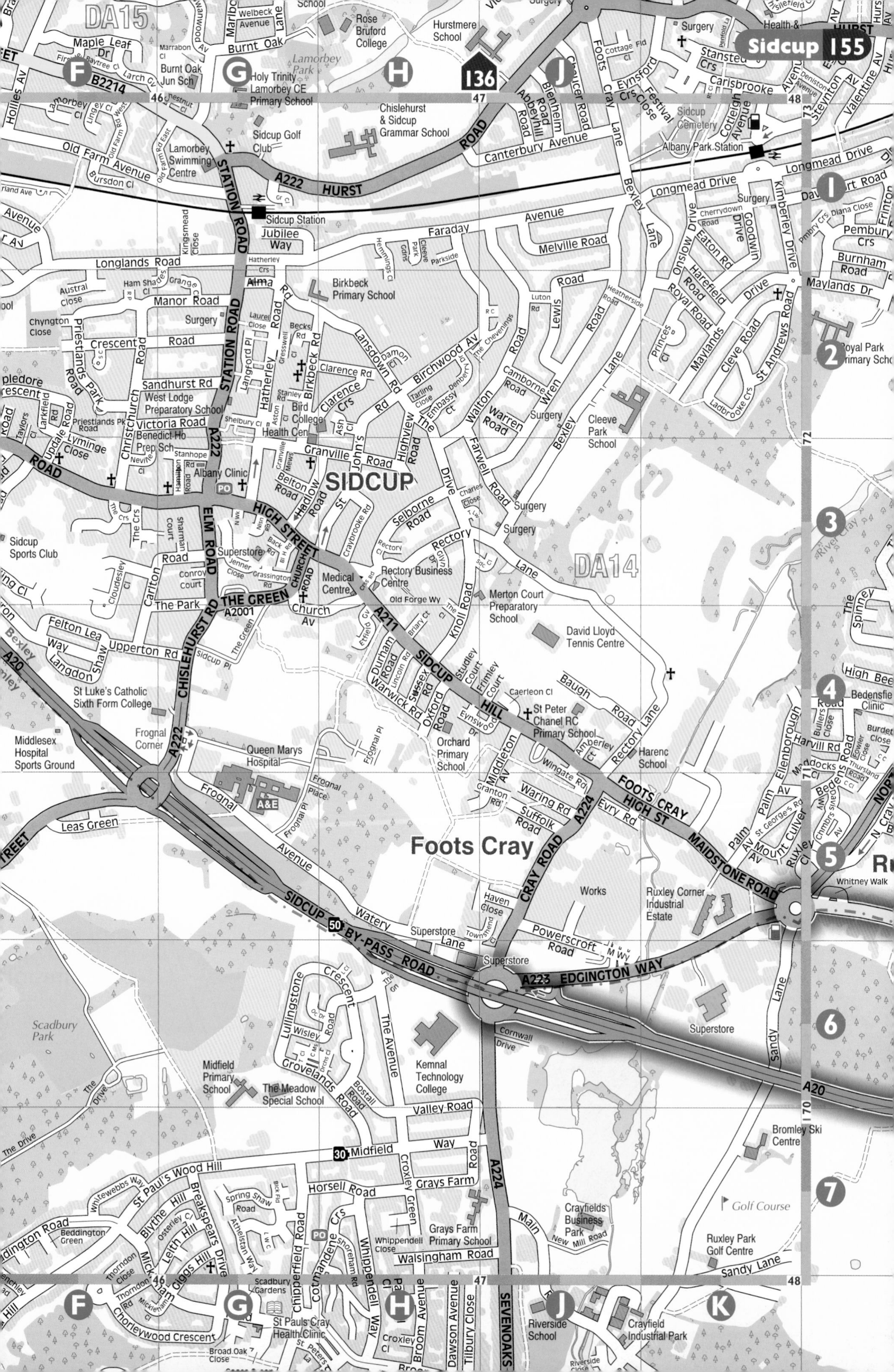
DA15
DA14
SIDCUP
Foots Cray
Sidcup Station
Albany Park Station
Rose Bruford College
Hurstmere School
Lamorbey Park
Holy Trinity Lamorbey CE Primary School
Burnt Oak Jun Sch
Chislehurst & Sidcup Grammar School
Sidcup Golf Club
Lamorbey Swimming Centre
Sidcup Cemetery
Birkbeck Primary School
West Lodge Preparatory School
Benedict Ho Prep Sch
Bird College
Health Cen
Albany Clinic
Surgery
Superstore
Medical Centre
Rectory Business Centre
Merton Court Preparatory School
David Lloyd Tennis Centre
Cleeve Park School
Royal Park Primary School
Bedensfield Clinic
St Peter Chanel RC Primary School
Harenc School
Orchard Primary School
Queen Marys Hospital
A&E
St Luke's Catholic Sixth Form College
Middlesex Hospital Sports Ground
Sidcup Sports Club
Frognal Corner
Works
Ruxley Corner Industrial Estate
Kemnal Technology College
Midfield Primary School
The Meadow Special School
Grays Farm Primary School
Crayfields Business Park
Bromley Ski Centre
Golf Course
Ruxley Park Golf Centre
Riverside School
Crayfield Industrial Park
St Pauls Cray Health Clinic
Scadbury Gardens
Scadbury Park
STATION ROAD
A222 HURST ROAD
B2214
HIGH STREET
ELM ROAD
CHISLEHURST RD
THE GREEN
A2001
A211
SIDCUP HILL
FOOTS CRAY HIGH ST
MAIDSTONE ROAD
CRAY ROAD
A224
SIDCUP BY-PASS ROAD
A20
A223 EDGINGTON WAY
SEVENOAKS
Old Farm Avenue
Longlands Road
Manor Road
Crescent Road
Sandhurst Rd
Victoria Road
Granville Road
Faraday Avenue
Melville Road
Longmead Drive
Canterbury Avenue
Bexley Lane
Lansdown Rd
Birchwood Av
Selborne Road
Rectory Lane
Frognal Avenue
Watery Lane
Powerscroft Road
Valley Road
Midfield Way
St Paul's Wood Hill
Horsell Road
Walsingham Road
Sandy Lane
Chorleywood Crescent
Main Road
New Mill Road
Grovelands Road
The Avenue
Lullingstone Crescent
Cornwall Drive
136
50
30
46
47
48
73
72
71
70
F
G
H
I
J
K
2
3
4
5
6
7

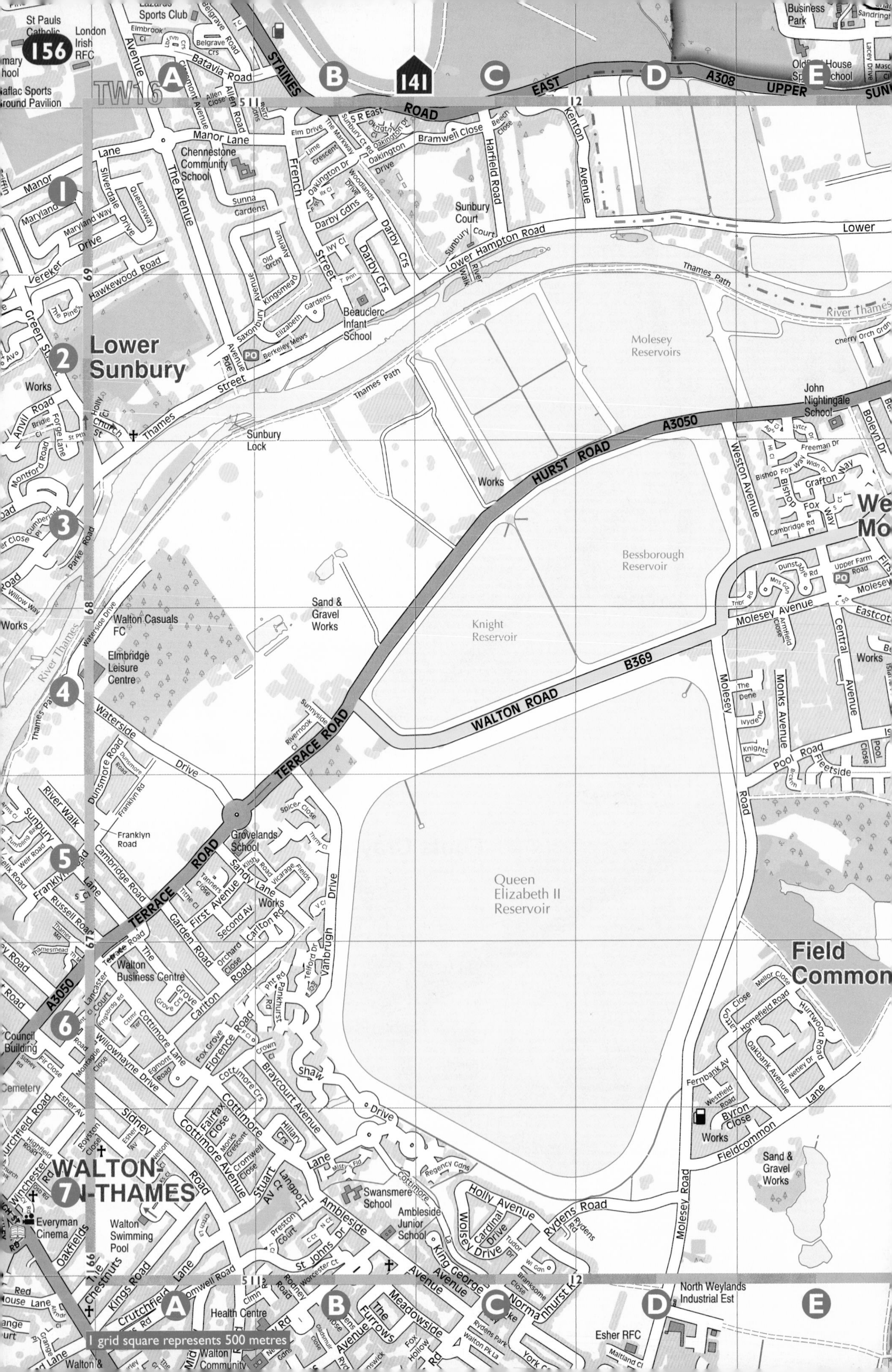

156
141
TW16
A
B
C
D
E
1
2
3
4
5
6
7
Lower Sunbury
WALTON-ON-THAMES
Field Common
Molesey Reservoirs
Bessborough Reservoir
Knight Reservoir
Queen Elizabeth II Reservoir
River Thames
Thames Path
HURST ROAD
A3050
WALTON ROAD
B369
TERRACE ROAD
STAINES ROAD
EAST
A308
UPPER
Lower Hampton Road
Sunbury Lock
Sand & Gravel Works
Walton Casuals FC
Elmbridge Leisure Centre
Chennestone Community School
Beauclerc Infant School
Grovelands School
Swansmere School
Ambleside Junior School
John Nightingale School
Walton Business Centre
Walton Swimming Pool
Everyman Cinema
Health Centre
North Weylands Industrial Est
Esher RFC
Sunbury Court
Molesey Road
Weston Avenue
Rydens Road
Fieldcommon Lane
Works
1 grid square represents 500 metres

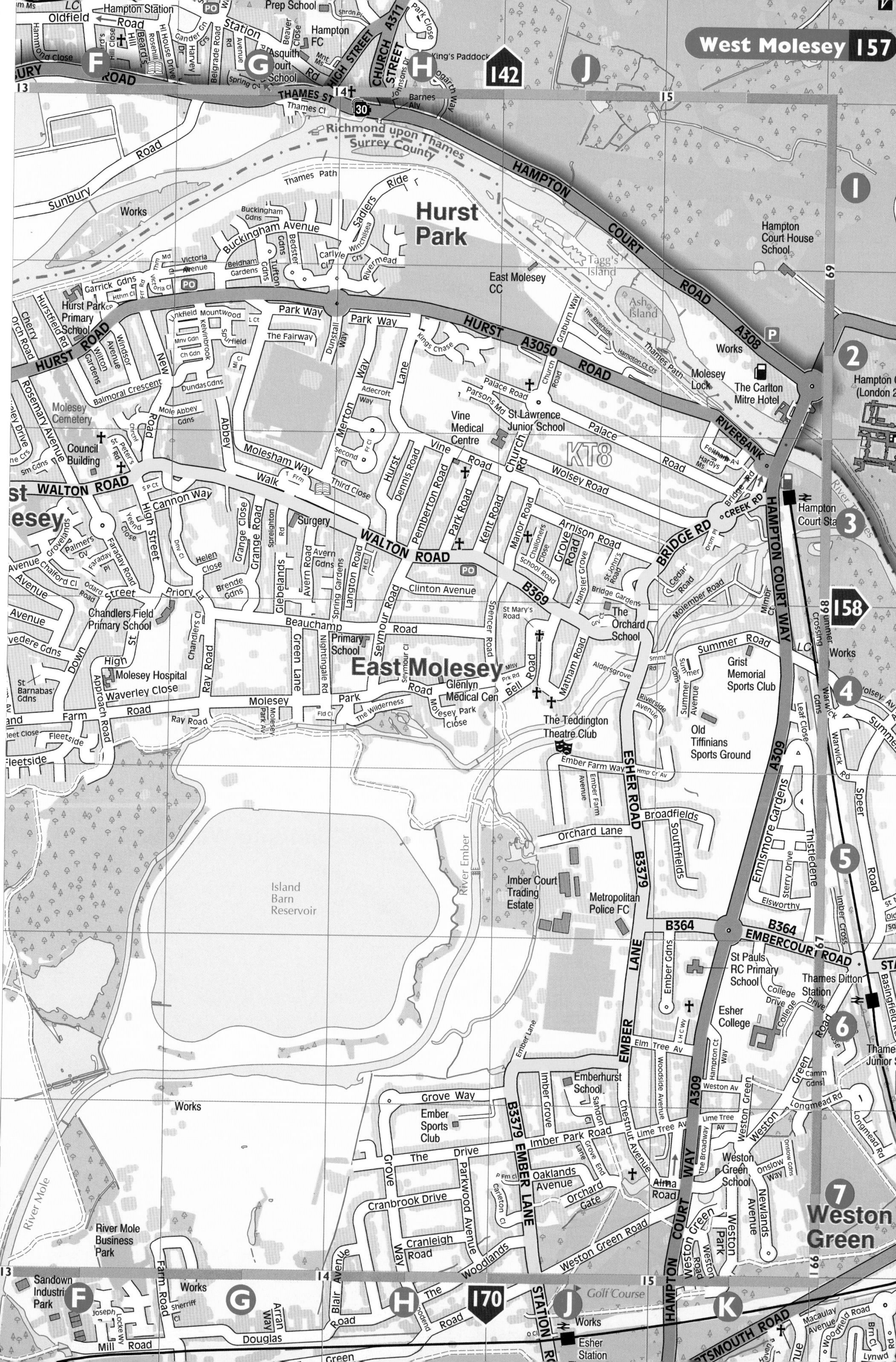
Hurst Park
East Molesey
Island Barn Reservoir
Weston Green
KT8
Hampton Court Way
Walton Road
Hurst Road
Esher Road
Ember Lane
Hampton Court Road
Molesey Lock
Tagg's Island
Ash Island
River Ember
River Mole
Thames Ditton Station
Esher Station
Hampton Court Station
142
158
170

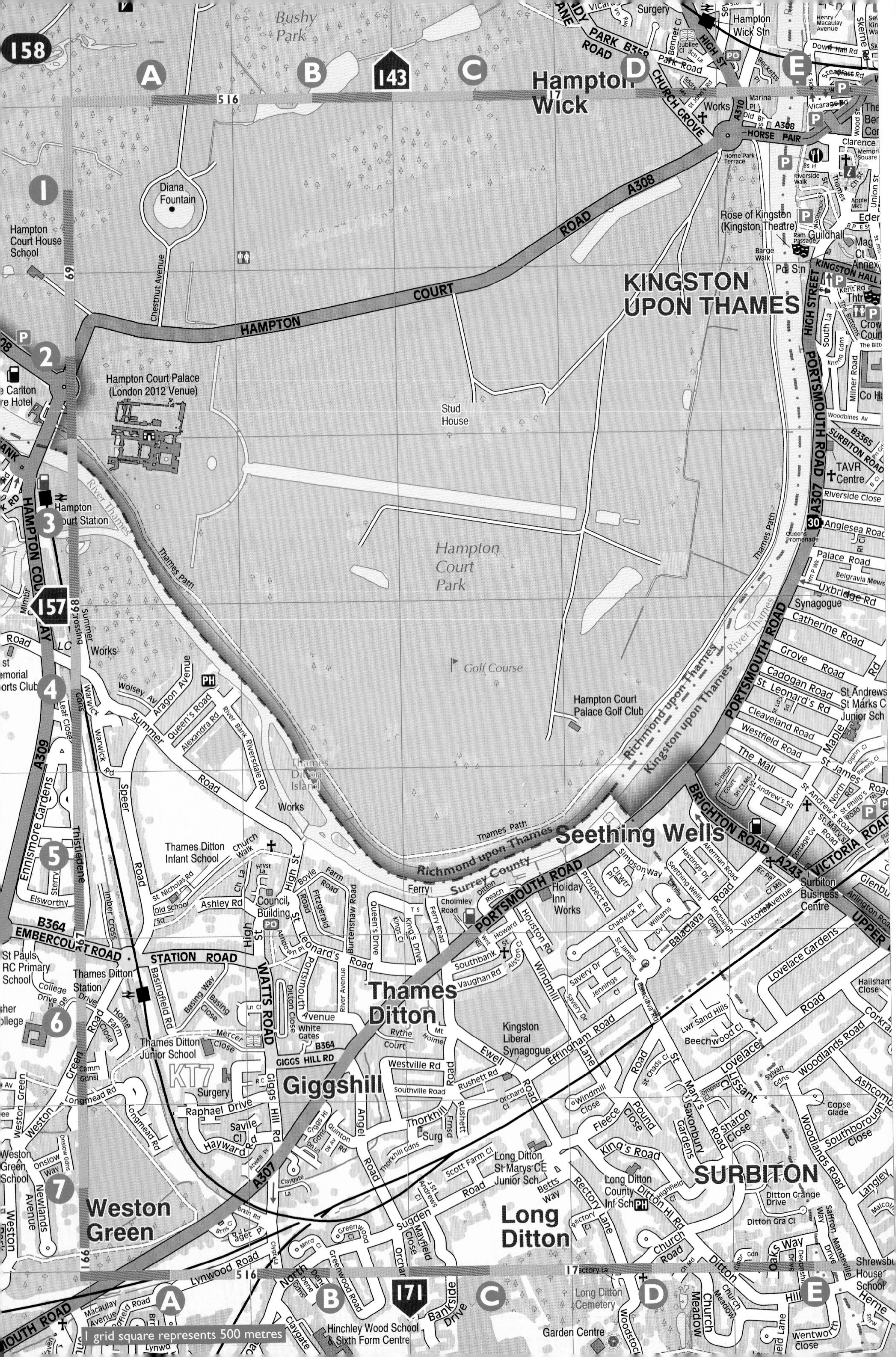

158
143
157
171
A
B
C
D
E
1
2
3
4
5
6
7
516
17
69
Bushy Park
Hampton Wick
Hampton Wick Stn
Surgery
High St
Park Road
Church Grove
A310
A308
Horse Fair
Diana Fountain
Chestnut Avenue
Hampton Court House School
Hampton Court Road
A308
Hampton Court Palace (London 2012 Venue)
Stud House
Hampton Court Park
Golf Course
Hampton Court Palace Golf Club
River Thames
Thames Path
Hampton Court Station
KINGSTON UPON THAMES
Rose of Kingston (Kingston Theatre)
Guildhall
Barge Walk
High Street
Portsmouth Road
A307
Surbiton Road
TAVR Centre
Riverside Close
Anglesea Road
Palace Road
Uxbridge Rd
Synagogue
Catherine Road
Grove Road
Cadogan Road
St Leonard's Rd
Cleaveland Road
Westfield Road
The Mall
Brighton Road
A243
Victoria Road
Surbiton Business Centre
Richmond upon Thames
Kingston upon Thames
Surrey County
Seething Wells
Thames Ditton Island
Works
Summer Road
Aragon Avenue
Queen's Road
Alexandra Rd
Riverside Rd
Speer Road
Warwick Rd
A309
Ennismore Gardens
Thistledene
Thames Ditton Infant School
Church Walk
High St
Ashley Rd
Council Building
St Leonard's Road
Portsmouth Road
Holiday Inn
Houston Rd
Windmill Lane
Effingham Road
B364
Embercourt Road
Station Road
Watts Road
St Pauls RC Primary School
Thames Ditton Station
Thames Ditton
Thames Ditton Junior School
KT7
Giggs Hill Rd
Giggshill
Westville Rd
Southville Road
Rushett Rd
Kingston Liberal Synagogue
Ewell Road
Long Ditton St Marys CE Junior Sch
Long Ditton County Inf Sch
Long Ditton
King's Road
Lovelace Gardens
Lovelace Road
Woodlands Road
SURBITON
Weston Green
Weston Green School
Longmead Rd
Raphael Drive
Hayward Rd
Lynwood Road
Greenwood Road
Sugden Road
Mayfield Close
Rectory Lane
Church Road
Ditton Hill Rd
Saffron Mandeville
Long Ditton Cemetery
Garden Centre
Hinchley Wood School & Sixth Form Centre
Woodstock
Church Meadow
Wentworth Close
1 grid square represents 500 metres

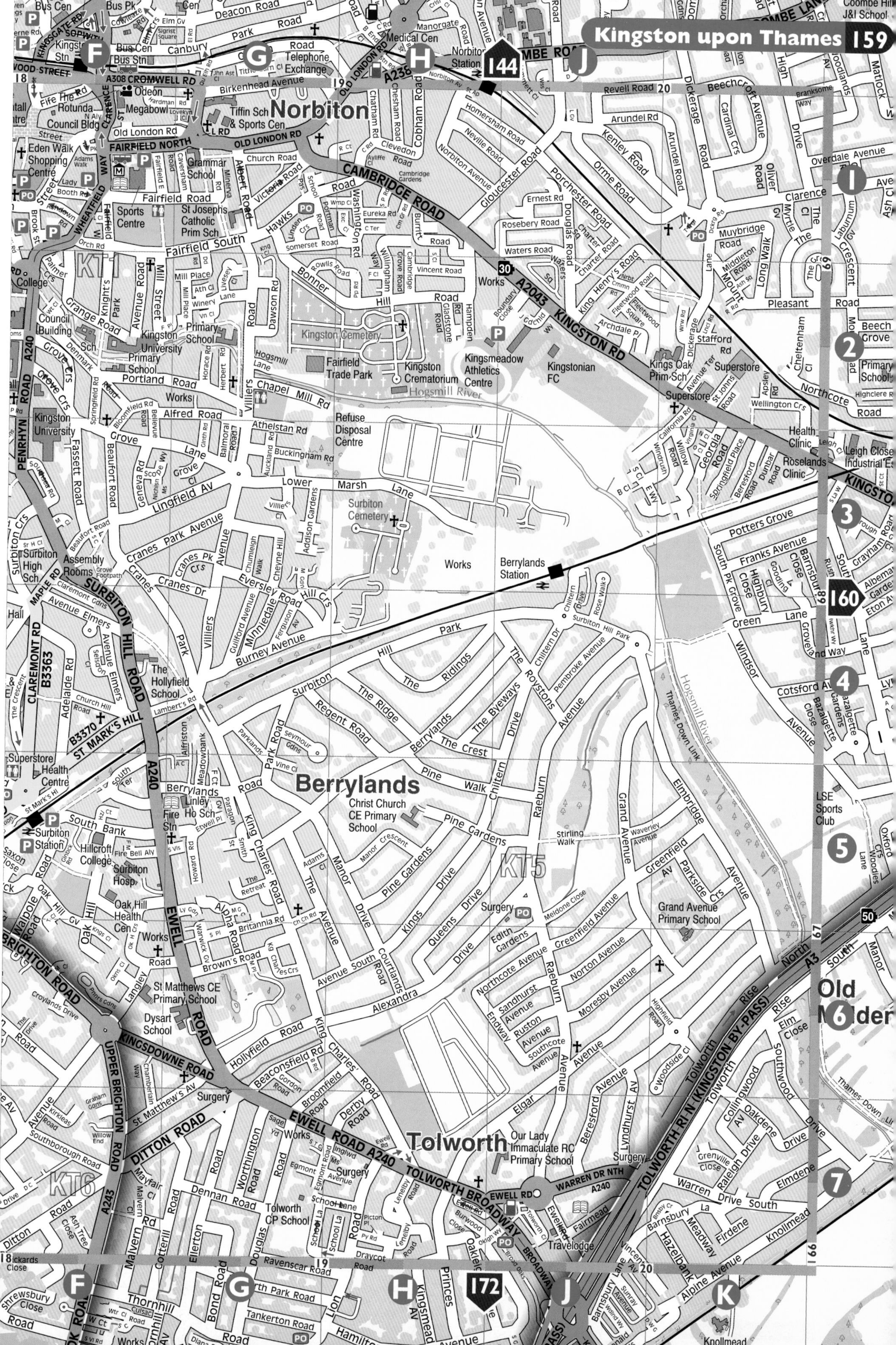
Norbiton
Berrylands
Tolworth
Old Malden
KT1
KT5
KT6
Kingston Cemetery
Kingston Crematorium
Fairfield Trade Park
Kingsmeadow Athletics Centre
Kingstonian FC
Refuse Disposal Centre
Surbiton Cemetery
Works
Berrylands Station
Norbiton Station
Surbiton Station
Hogsmill River
Thames Down Link
Tiffin Sch & Sports Cen
Grammar School
St Josephs Catholic Prim Sch
Sports Centre
Kingston University
Kingston University Primary School
Council Building
Kingston Telephone Exchange
Medical Cen
Odeon
Megabowl
Fire The Rotunda
Council Bldg
Eden Walk Shopping Centre
Kings Oak Prim Sch
Superstore
Health Clinic
Roselands Clinic
Leigh Close Industrial Est
LSE Sports Club
Grand Avenue Primary School
Christ Church CE Primary School
The Hollyfield School
Assembly Rooms
Surbiton High Sch
Hillcroft College
Surbiton Hosp
Oak Hill Health Cen
St Matthews CE Primary School
Dysart School
Our Lady Immaculate RC Primary School
Tolworth CP School
Travelodge
Coombe Hill J&I School
Primary School
CAMBRIDGE ROAD
A2043 KINGSTON RD
SURBITON HILL ROAD
A240
EWELL ROAD
EWELL ROAD A240
TOLWORTH BROADWAY
TOLWORTH RI N (KINGSTON BY-PASS)
A3
UPPER BRIGHTON ROAD
A243
BRIGHTON ROAD
KINGSDOWNE ROAD
DITTON ROAD
ST MARK'S HILL
B3370
CLAREMONT RD
B3363
PENRHYN ROAD
A240
WHEATFIELD WAY
CLARENCE
FAIRFIELD NORTH
OLD LONDON RD
A308 CROMWELL RD
A238
KINGSGATE RD
WOOD STREET
Fairfield Road
Fairfield South
Portland Road
Alfred Road
Lower Marsh Lane
Chapel Mill Rd
Cranes Park Avenue
Burney Avenue
Surbiton Hill Park
Alexandra
Raeburn Avenue
Elmbridge Avenue
Warren Drive South
Knollmead
Ravenscar Road
Hollyfield Road
King Charles' Road
Beaconsfield Rd
Princes
Kingsmead Av
Alpine Avenue
F
G
H
I
J
K
1
2
3
4
5
6
7
18
19
20
67
68
69
144
160
172
30
50

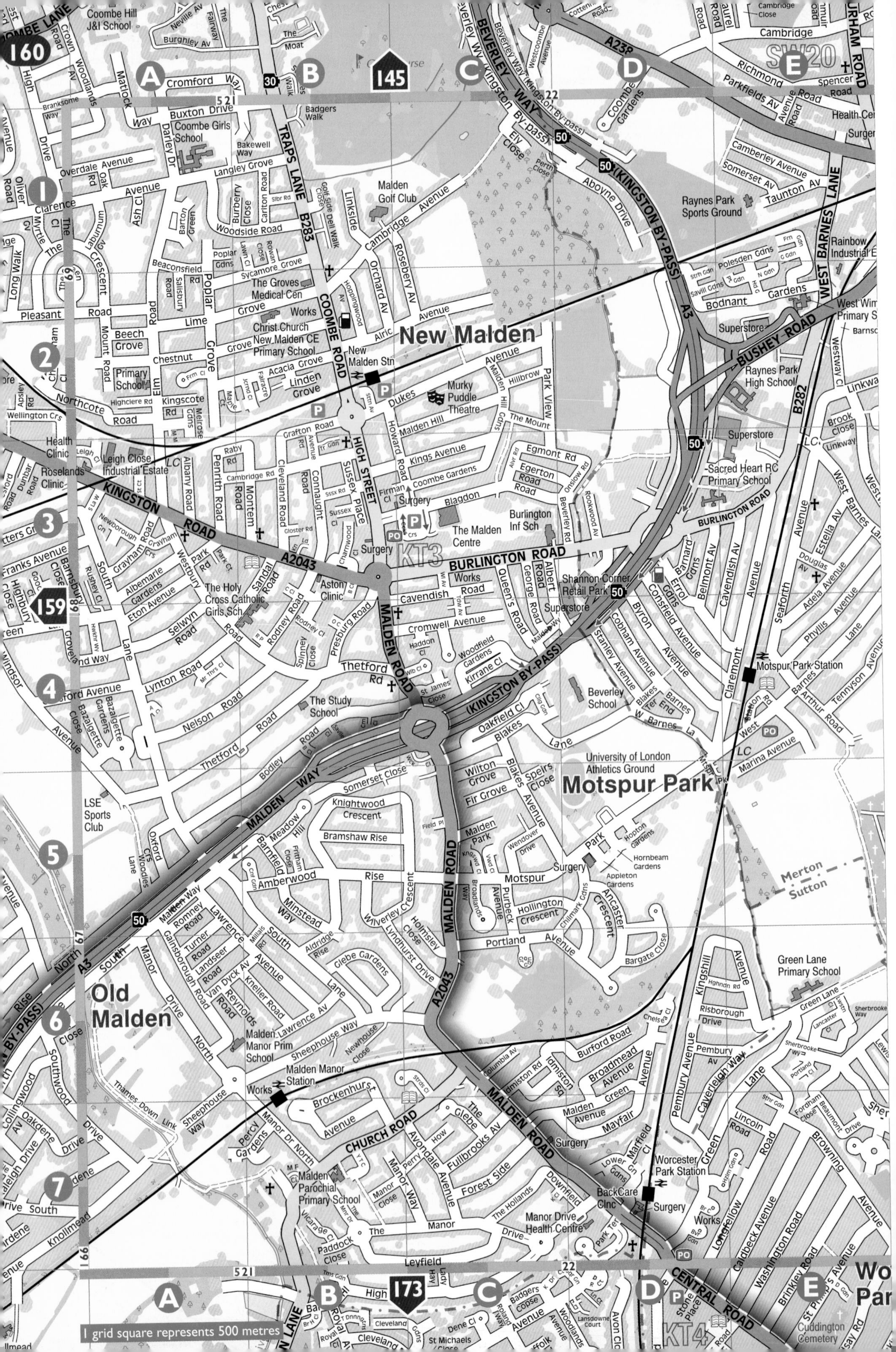
160
145
159
173
A
B
C
D
E
1
2
3
4
5
6
7
521
22
SW20
KT3
KT4
New Malden
Old Malden
Motspur Park
Coombe Lane
Coombe Hill J&I School
Coombe Girls School
Crown Road
Woodlands Av
Matlock Way
Cromford Way
Buxton Drive
Darley Dr
Bakewell Way
Badgers Walk
The Moat
Traps Lane
B283
Coombe Road
Malden Golf Club
Cambridge Avenue
Rosebery Av
Orchard Av
Linkside
Golf Side Close
Dell Walk
Beverley Way
Kingston By-pass
Kingston By-Pass
A3
A238
Coombe Gardens
Westcoombe Avenue
Ely Close
Perth Close
Aboyne Drive
Cambridge Road
Richmond Road
Parkfields Av
Spencer Road
Durham Road
Health Cen
Camberley Avenue
Somerset Av
Taunton Av
Raynes Park Sports Ground
West Barnes Lane
Rainbow Industrial E
Polesden Gdns
Bodnant Gardens
Savill Gdns
West Wim Primary S
Superstore
Bushey Road
Raynes Park High School
B282
Linkway
Brook Close
Adela Avenue
Overdale Avenue
Oak Rd
Clarence Avenue
Ash Cl
Langley Grove
Burberry Close
Carlton Road
Woodside Road
Barton Green
Laburnum Crescent
Myrtle Gv
Long Walk
The Crescent
Poplar Gdns
Beaconsfield Rd
Salisbury Road
Sycamore Grove
Rowan Close
Lawn Cl
The Groves Medical Cen
Works
Christ Church New Malden CE Primary School
Hoppingwood Av
Alric Avenue
Pleasant Road
Mount Road
Beech Grove
Lime Grove
Chestnut Grove
Primary School
Elm Road
Acacia Grove
Linden Grove
Fairacre
Kingscote Rd
Highclere Rd
Melrose Gdns
Maple Cl
Northcote Road
Apsley Rd
Wellington Crs
Health Clinic
Leigh Close Industrial Estate
Roselands Clinic
Dunbar Rd
New Malden Stn
Dukes Av
Murky Puddle Theatre
Malden Hill
Malden Hill Gdns
Hillbrow
Park View
The Mount
Egmont Rd
Egerton Road
Onslow Rd
Kings Avenue
Coombe Gardens
Howard Road
Grafton Road
High Street
Firman Cl
Surgery
Blagdon Road
The Malden Centre
Burlington Inf Sch
Beverley Rd
Rookwood Av
Burlington Road
Sacred Heart RC Primary School
Kingston Road
A2043
Albany Road
Penrith Road
Raby Rd
Cambridge Rd
Montem Road
Cleveland Road
Connaught Road
Sussex Place
Sussex Cl
Charnwood
Aston Clinic
Cavendish Road
Works Road
Queen's Road
George Road
Albert Road
Shannon Corner Retail Park
Superstore
Cromwell Avenue
Haddon Cl
Woodfield Gardens
Kirrane Cl
St James' Close
Malden Road
Barnard Gdns
Belmont Av
Cavendish Av
Claremont Avenue
Seaforth Avenue
Estella Av
Douglas Av
Phyllis Avenue
Consfield Avenue
Errol Gdns
Byron Avenue
Cobham Avenue
Stanley Avenue
Blakes Ter
W Barnes La
Barnes End
Beverley School
Motspur Park Station
Station Rd
Arthur Road
Tennyson Avenue
Marina Avenue
Franks Avenue
Barnsbury Close
Highbury Close
South Lane
Grayham Road
Grayham Crs
Albemarle Gardens
Eton Avenue
Westbury Road
Park Rd
The Holy Cross Catholic Girls Sch
Sandal Road
Selwyn Road
Rodney Road
Rodney Cl
Presburg Road
Spinney Close
Thetford Rd
Groveland Way
Lynton Road
Nelson Road
Thetford Road
Bodley Road
The Study School
Bazalgette Gardens
Bazalgette Close
Avenue
Oakfield Cl
Blakes Lane
University of London Athletics Ground
Malden Way
Somerset Close
Knightwood Crescent
Bramshaw Rise
Wilton Grove
Fir Grove
Spelrs Close
Blakes Avenue
Malden Park
Wendover Drive
Park
Hopton Gardens
Hornbeam Gardens
Appleton Gardens
Merton
Sutton
LSE Sports Club
Oxford Crs
Woodies Lane
Meadow Hill
Barnfield
Frimley Close
Amberwood Rise
Minstead Way
Waverley Crescent
Motspur Park
Broadlands
Purbeck Avenue
Hollington Crescent
Chilmark Gdns
Ancaster Crescent
Romney Road
Turner Road
Landseer Road
Lawrence Avenue
South Lane
Aldridge Rise
Lyndhurst Drive
Holmsley Close
Portland Avenue
Bargate Close
Green Lane Primary School
Kingshill Avenue
Risborough Drive
Gainsborough Road
Van Dyck Av
Reynolds Road
Kneller Road
Glebe Gardens
Manor Drive North
North Rise
Malden Manor Prim School
Sheephouse Way
Newhouse Close
Lawrence Av
Malden Manor Station
Thames Down Link
Brockenhurst Avenue
Church Road
Chelsea Cl
Burford Road
Idmiston Rd
Broadmead Avenue
Malden Green Avenue
Mayfair Avenue
Marfield Cl
Pembury Avenue
Caverleigh Way
Green Lane
Lincoln Road
Southwood Close
Collingwood Av
Oakdene Drive
Percy Gardens
Malden Parochial Primary School
Manor Way
Avondale Avenue
Fullbrooks Av
Forest Side
The Glebe
Downfield
Worcester Park Station
Surgery
BackCare Clnc
Manor Drive Health Centre
The Manor Drive
Vicarage Cl
Paddock Close
Leyfield
Knollmead
Central Road
Washington Road
Caldbeck Avenue
Brinkley Road
Browning Avenue
Longfellow
Cuddington Cemetery
High Street
Cleveland Gdns
Dene Cl
St Michaels Close
Badgers Copse
Woodlands Avenue
Stone Place
1 grid square represents 500 metres

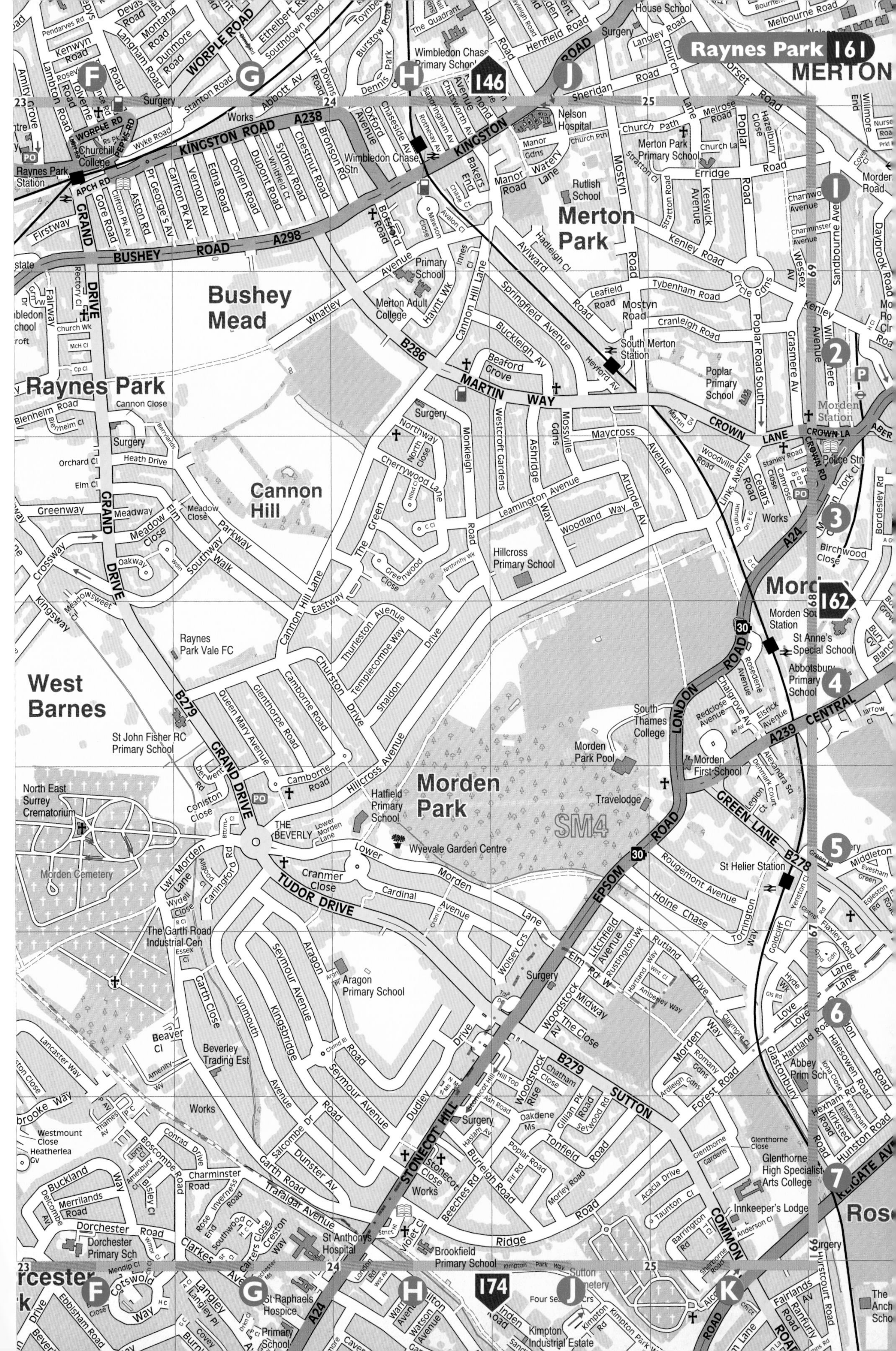

Raynes Park 161
MERTON
146
162
174
F
G
H
J
K
I
2
3
4
5
6
7
23
24
25
Raynes Park
Bushey Mead
Merton Park
Cannon Hill
West Barnes
Morden Park
Morden
SM4
Raynes Park Station
Wimbledon Chase Stn
South Merton Station
Morden South Station
St Helier Station
Morden Station
KINGSTON ROAD A238
BUSHEY ROAD A298
MARTIN WAY
B286
GRAND DRIVE
B279
LONDON ROAD
EPSOM ROAD
A24
STONECOT HILL
SUTTON COMMON ROAD
A239 CENTRAL
GREEN LANE B278
CROWN LANE
TUDOR DRIVE
WORPLE ROAD
Bushey Mead
Wimbledon Chase Primary School
Nelson Hospital
Merton Park Primary School
Rutlish School
Merton Adult College
Hillcross Primary School
Poplar Primary School
Raynes Park Vale FC
St John Fisher RC Primary School
North East Surrey Crematorium
Morden Cemetery
Hatfield Primary School
Wyevale Garden Centre
South Thames College
Morden Park Pool
Travelodge
Morden First School
St Anne's Special School
Abbotsbury Primary School
Aragon Primary School
The Garth Road Industrial Cen
Beverley Trading Est
St Anthony's Hospital
Brookfield Primary School
Dorchester Primary Sch
Glenthorne High Specialist Arts College
Innkeeper's Lodge
Abbey Prim Sch
St Raphaels Hospice
Kimpton Industrial Estate
Police Stn
THE BEVERLY

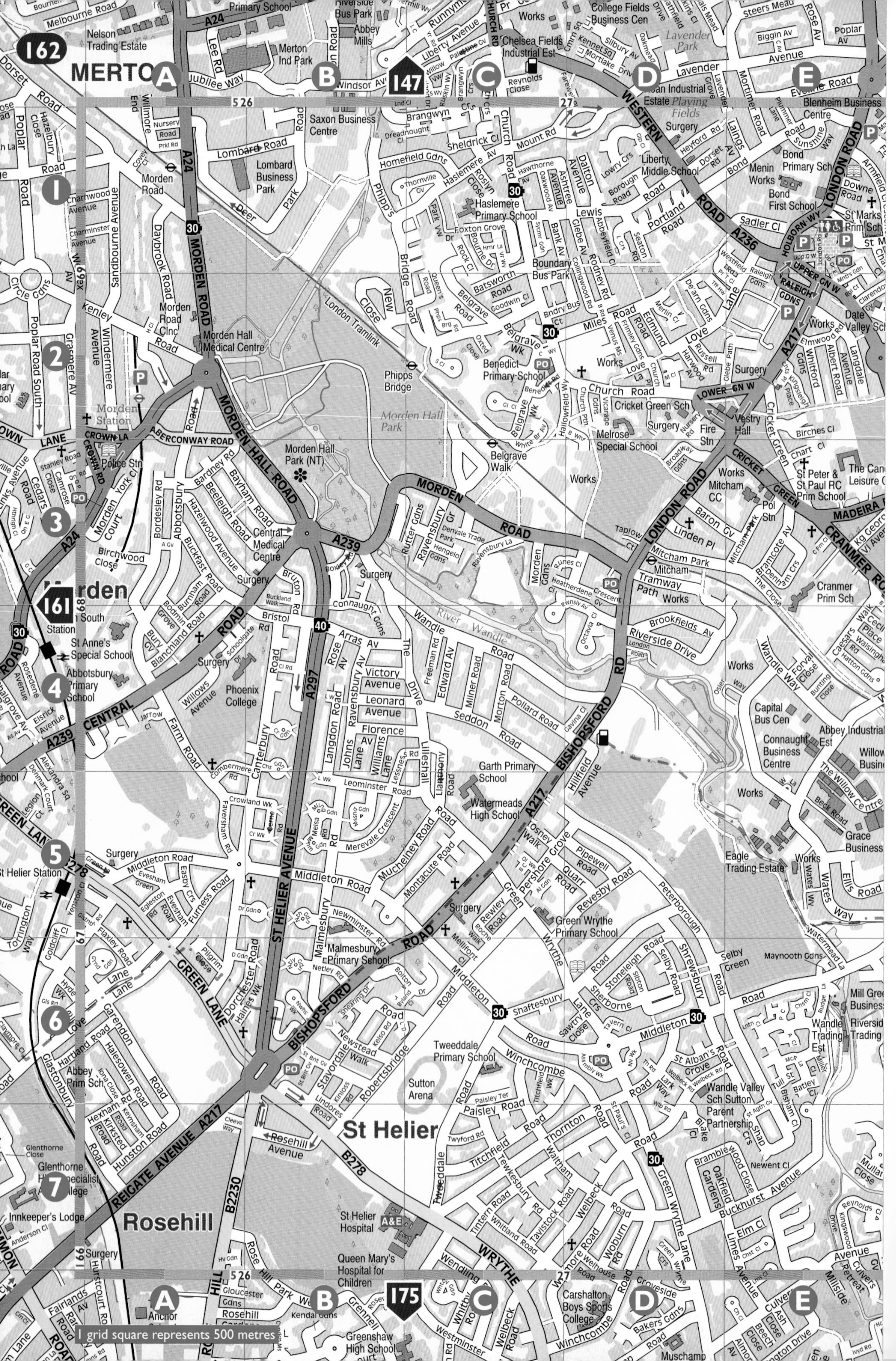
162
147
161
175
A
B
C
D
E
1
2
3
4
5
6
7
526
27
1 grid square represents 500 metres
MERTON
Morden
St Helier
Rosehill
Melbourne Road
Nelson Trading Estate
Primary School
Jubilee Way
Merton Ind Park
Abbey Mills
Windsor Av
Liberty Avenue
Chelsea Fields Industrial Est
Reynolds Close
College Fields Business Cen
Lavender Park
Steers Mead
Rose Av
Poplar Av
Biggin Av
Avenue
Lavender
Eveline Road
Blenheim Business Centre
Western Road
Playing Fields
Surgery
Liberty Middle School
Saxon Business Centre
Lombard Road
Lombard Business Park
Deer Park
Morden Road
Morden Hall Road
Morden Hall Medical Centre
Morden Road Clnc
Morden Station
Police Stn
Crown Lane
Aberconway Road
Morden Hall Park
Morden Hall Park (NT)
London Tramlink
Phipps Bridge
Phipps Bridge Road
Haslemere Primary School
Boundary Bus Park
Belgrave Walk
Benedict Primary School
Church Road
Cricket Green Sch
Melrose Special School
Mitcham CC
Vestry Hall
Fire Stn
London Road
Bond Primary Sch
Bond First School
Menin Works
St Marks Prim Sch
Holborn Wy
Upper Gn W
Lower Gn W
Raleigh Gdns
Date Valley Sch
Sadler Cl
The Canons Leisure C
St Peter & St Paul RC Prim School
Cricket Green
Madeira Rd
Cranmer Road
Cranmer Prim Sch
Mitcham Park
Mitcham
Tramway Path
Riverside Drive
Brookfields Av
Wandle Road
River Wandle
Central Road
Central Medical Centre
Abbotsbury Primary School
Abbotsbury Road
St Anne's Special School
Morden South Station
Phoenix College
Farm Road
A239 Central Road
St Helier Avenue
A297
Bishopsford Road
A217
Reigate Avenue
Garth Primary School
Watermeads High School
Green Wrythe Primary School
Middleton Road
Malmesbury Primary School
Tweeddale Primary School
Sutton Arena
St Helier Station
Green Lane
Glastonbury Road
Abbey Prim Sch
Glenthorne Close
Innkeeper's Lodge
Capital Bus Cen
Connaught Business Centre
Abbey Industrial Est
The Willow Centre
Eagle Trading Estate
Grace Business
Wandle Valley Sch Sutton Parent Partnership
Wandle Trading Est
Mill Green Business
Selby Green
Peterborough Road
Shrewsbury Road
Green Wrythe Lane
Buckhurst Avenue
Wrythe
St Helier Hospital
A&E
Queen Mary's Hospital for Children
Carshalton Boys Sports College
Greenshaw High School
Rose Hill
Gloucester Gdns
Rosehill Avenue
B278
B2230
Muschamp

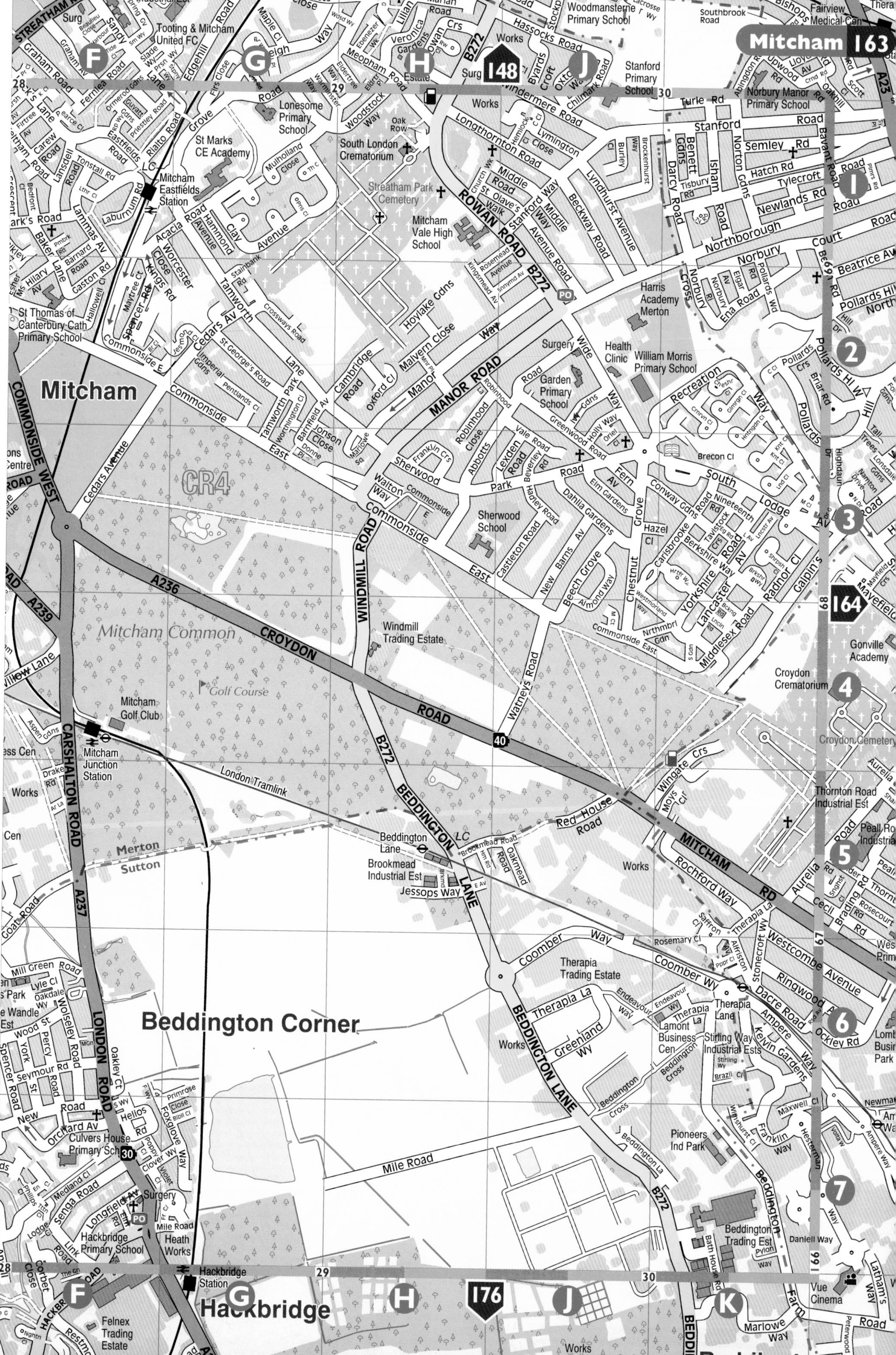
Mitcham 163
148
164
176
Mitcham
Mitcham Common
Beddington Corner
Hackbridge
Mitcham Eastfields Station
Mitcham Junction Station
Hackbridge Station
Beddington Lane
Streatham Park Cemetery
South London Crematorium
Croydon Crematorium
Croydon Cemetery
Mitcham Golf Club
Golf Course
Windmill Trading Estate
Brookmead Industrial Est
Therapia Trading Estate
Lamont Business Cen
Stirling Way Industrial Ests
Pioneers Ind Park
Beddington Trading Est
Thornton Road Industrial Est
Felnex Trading Estate
Vue Cinema
Mitcham Vale High School
Harris Academy Merton
William Morris Primary School
Garden Primary School
Sherwood School
St Marks CE Academy
Lonesome Primary School
Norbury Manor Primary School
Stanford Primary School
Woodmansterne Primary School
Gonville Academy
Hackbridge Primary School
Culvers House Primary Sch
St Thomas of Canterbury Cath Primary School
Tooting & Mitcham United FC
London Tramlink
CROYDON ROAD
A236
MITCHAM RD
COMMONSIDE WEST
CARSHALTON ROAD
LONDON ROAD
A237
A239
B272
MANOR ROAD
ROWAN ROAD
WINDMILL ROAD
BEDDINGTON LANE
Merton
Sutton
CR4

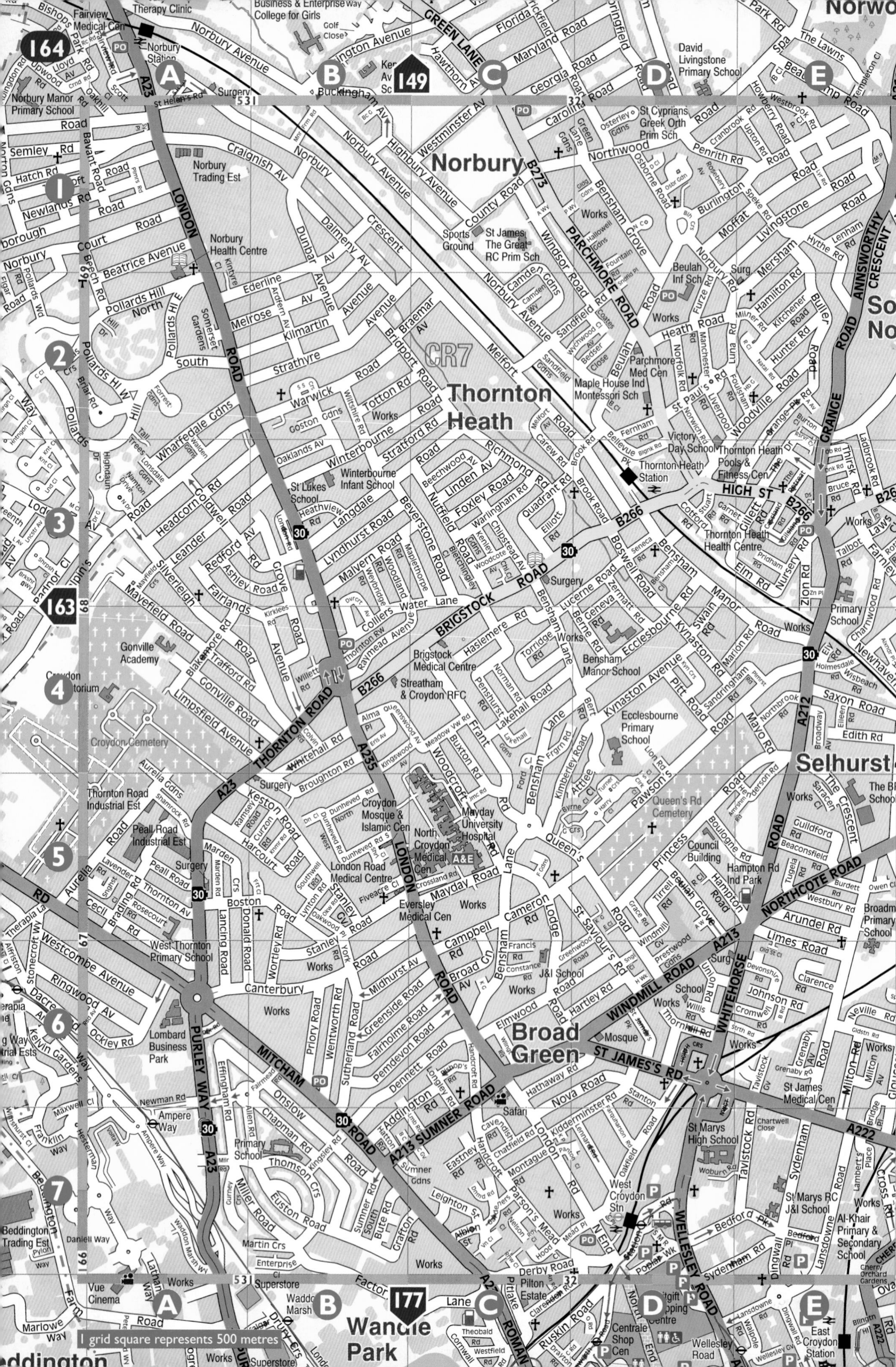
164
149
163
177
A
B
C
D
E
1
2
3
4
5
6
7
531
32
Norbury
Thornton Heath
Broad Green
Selhurst
Wandle Park
CR7
Norbury Station
Thornton Heath Station
West Croydon Stn
East Croydon Station
Therapy Clinic
Fairview Medical Cen
Norbury Manor Primary School
Business & Enterprise College for Girls
David Livingstone Primary School
St Cyprians Greek Orth Prim Sch
Norbury Trading Est
Norbury Health Centre
Sports Ground
St James The Great RC Prim Sch
Beulah Inf Sch
Parchmore Med Cen
Maple House Ind Montessori Sch
Victory Day School
Thornton Heath Pools & Fitness Cen
Thornton Heath Health Centre
Winterbourne Infant School
St Lukes School
Gonville Academy
Croydon Crematorium
Croydon Cemetery
Thornton Road Industrial Est
Peall Road Industrial Est
West Thornton Primary School
Lombard Business Park
Ampere Way
Beddington Trading Est
Vue Cinema
Superstore
Brigstock Medical Centre
Streatham & Croydon RFC
Croydon Mosque & Islamic Cen
Mayday University Hospital
North Croydon Medical Cen
A&E
London Road Medical Centre
Eversley Medical Cen
Bensham Manor School
Ecclesbourne Primary School
Queen's Rd Cemetery
Council Building
Hampton Rd Ind Park
J&I School
Mosque
Safari
Primary School
St Marys High School
St James Medical Cen
St Marys RC J&I School
Al-Khair Primary & Secondary School
Centrale Shop Cen
Whitgift Shopping Centre
Pilton Estate
LONDON ROAD
PURLEY WAY
MITCHAM ROAD
BRIGSTOCK ROAD
THORNTON ROAD
PARCHMORE ROAD
HIGH ST
GRANGE ROAD
ANNSWORTHY CRESCENT
WHITEHORSE ROAD
NORTHCOTE ROAD
WINDMILL ROAD
ST JAMES'S RD
WELLESLEY ROAD
A213 SUMNER ROAD
GREEN LANE
A23
A235
A212
A213
A222
B266
B273
1 grid square represents 500 metres

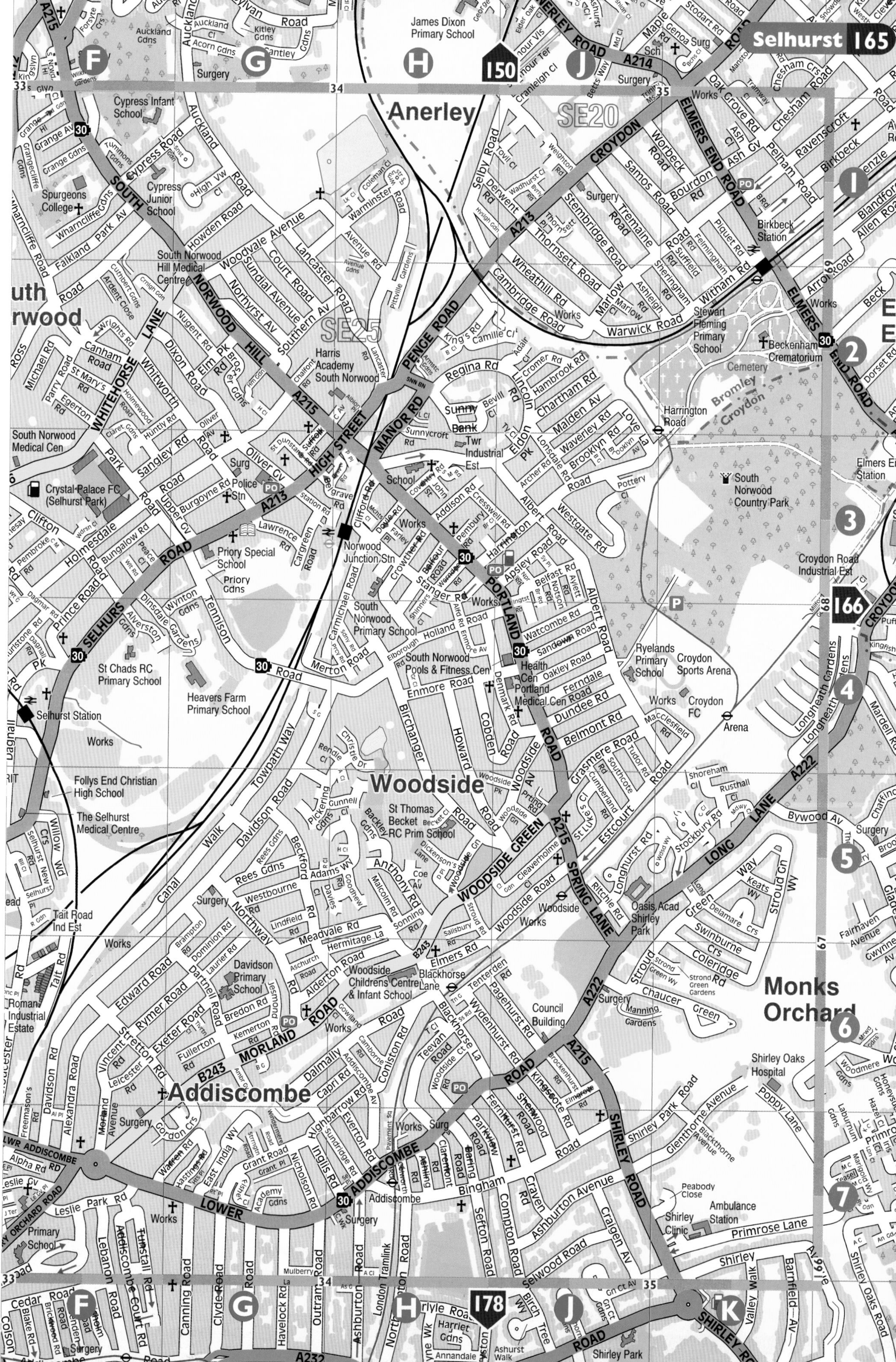
F
G
H
150
J
Anerley
SE20
James Dixon Primary School
Cypress Infant School
Cypress Junior School
Spurgeons College
South Norwood Hill Medical Centre
South Norwood
SE25
Harris Academy South Norwood
South Norwood Medical Cen
Crystal Palace FC (Selhurst Park)
Priory Special School
Norwood Junction Stn
South Norwood Primary School
South Norwood Pools & Fitness Cen
St Chads RC Primary School
Heavers Farm Primary School
Selhurst Station
Works
Follys End Christian High School
The Selhurst Medical Centre
Tait Road Ind Est
Roman Industrial Estate
Davidson Primary School
Woodside
St Thomas Becket RC Prim School
Woodside Childrens Centre & Infant School
Blackhorse Lane
Addiscombe
Health Cen Portland Medical Cen
Sunny Bank
Twr Industrial Est
Birkbeck Station
Stewart Fleming Primary School
Beckenham Crematorium
Cemetery
Bromley
Croydon
Harrington Road
South Norwood Country Park
Elmers End Station
Croydon Road Industrial Est
166
Ryelands Primary School
Croydon Sports Arena
Croydon FC
Arena
Oasis Acad Shirley Park
Council Building
Monks Orchard
Shirley Oaks Hospital
Peabody Close
Ambulance Station
Shirley Clinic
178
K
Shirley Park Golf Club
Ashurst Walk
1
2
3
4
5
6
7
33
34
35
67
68
A215
A213
A214
A222
A232
B243
30
SOUTH NORWOOD HILL
WHITEHORSE LANE
SELHURST ROAD
HIGH STREET
PENGE ROAD
MANOR RD
PORTLAND ROAD
CROYDON ROAD
ELMERS END ROAD
WOODSIDE GREEN
SPRING LANE
LONG LANE
MORLAND ROAD
LOWER ADDISCOMBE ROAD
SHIRLEY ROAD
Woodside Av
Tennison Road
Towpath Way
Canal Walk
Davidson Road
Birchanger Road
Howard Road
Cobden Road
Enmore Road
Holland Road
Albert Road
Westgate Rd
Estcourt Road
Longhurst Rd
Stroud Green Way
Chaucer Green
Ashburton Avenue
Primrose Lane
Shirley Park Road
Glenthorne Avenue
Poppy Lane
Addiscombe Court Rd
Lebanon Road
Leslie Park Rd
Canning Road
Clyde Road
Havelock Rd
Outram Rd
Ashburton Road
London Tramlink
Northampton Road
Sefton Road
Compton Road
Craven Rd
Selwood Road
Cragien Av
Bingham Rd
Addiscombe Rd
Edward Road
Rymer Road
Exeter Road
Stretton Rd
Alexandra Rd
Freemason's Rd
Warminster Road
Woodvale Avenue
Lancaster Road
Sundial Avenue
Court Road
Southern Av
Norhyrst Av
Auckland Road
Falkland Park Av
Whitworth Road
Dixon Road
Samos Road
Tremaine Road
Stembridge Road
Thornsett Road
Wheathill Rd
Cambridge Road
Warwick Road
Witham Rd
Regina Rd
Lincoln Rd
Hambrook Rd
Chartham Rd
Malden Av
Waverley Rd
Brooklyn Rd
Watcombe Rd
Sandown Road
Oakley Road
Ferndale Road
Dundee Rd
Belmont Rd
Grasmere Road
Tudor Rd
Macclesfield Rd
Longheath Gardens
Bywood Av
Keats Wy
Swinburne Crs
Coleridge Rd
Woodmere Gdns
Shirley Oaks Road
Barnfield Av
Valley Walk
Harriet Gdns
Annandale Rd
Colson Rd
Cedar Road
Blake Rd

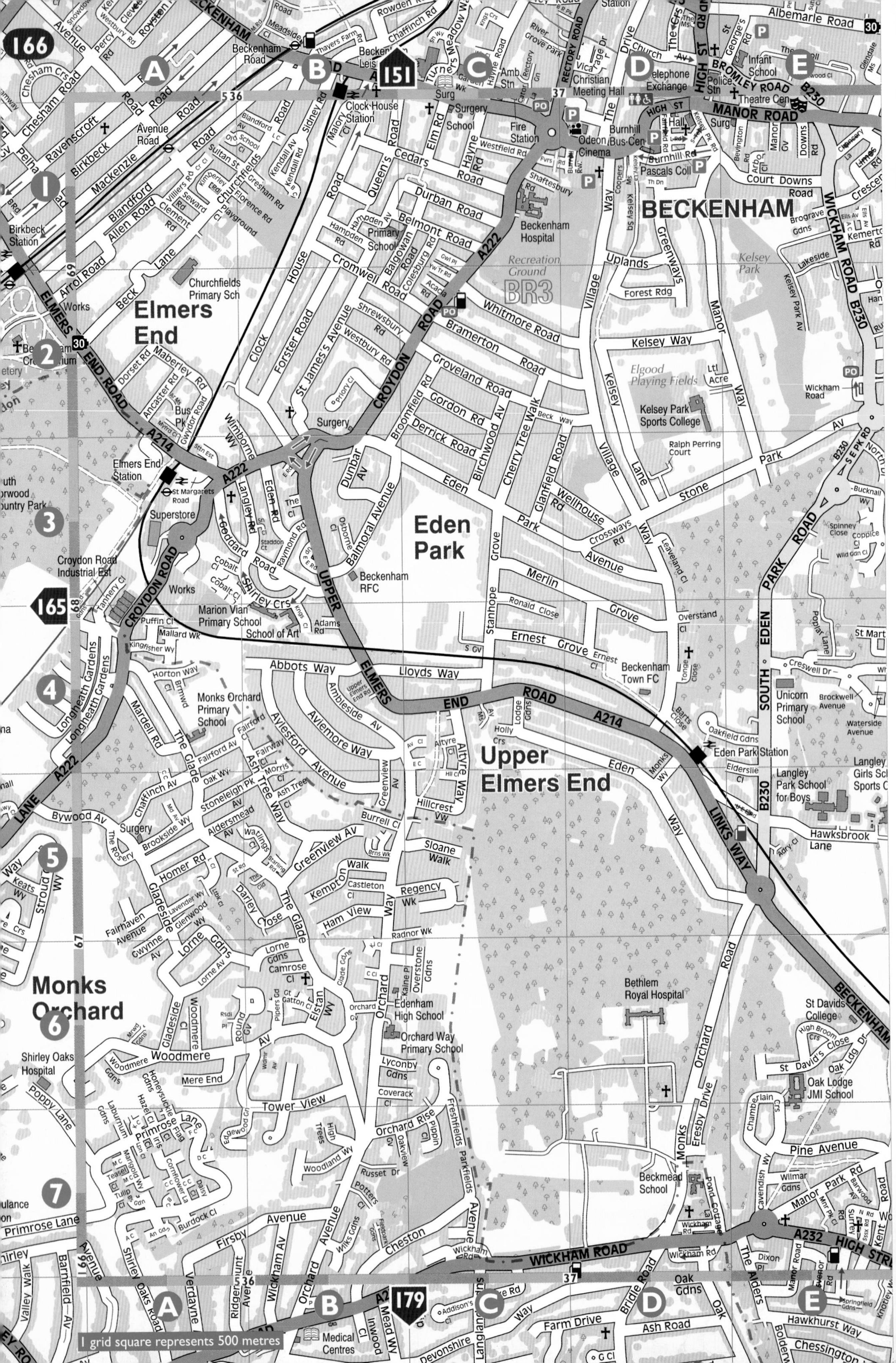

166
151
165
179
BECKENHAM
Elmers End
Eden Park
Upper Elmers End
Monks Orchard
Beckenham Hospital
Kelsey Park
Kelsey Park Sports College
Elgood Playing Fields
Churchfields Primary Sch
Elmers End Station
Clock House Station
Birkbeck Station
Eden Park Station
Beckenham RFC
Beckenham Town FC
Bethlem Royal Hospital
Monks Orchard Primary School
Marion Vian Primary School
School of Art
Edenham High School
Orchard Way Primary School
Beckmead School
Oak Lodge JMI School
St Davids College
Unicorn Primary School
Langley Park School for Boys
Shirley Oaks Hospital
Croydon Road Industrial Est
Recreation Ground
BR3
CROYDON ROAD
ELMERS END ROAD
UPPER ELMERS END ROAD
WICKHAM ROAD
SOUTH EDEN PARK ROAD
WICKHAM ROAD B230
LINKS WAY
BECKENHAM ROAD
MANOR ROAD
BROMLEY ROAD
RECTORY ROAD
HIGH ST
A222
A214
A232
B230
1 grid square represents 500 metres

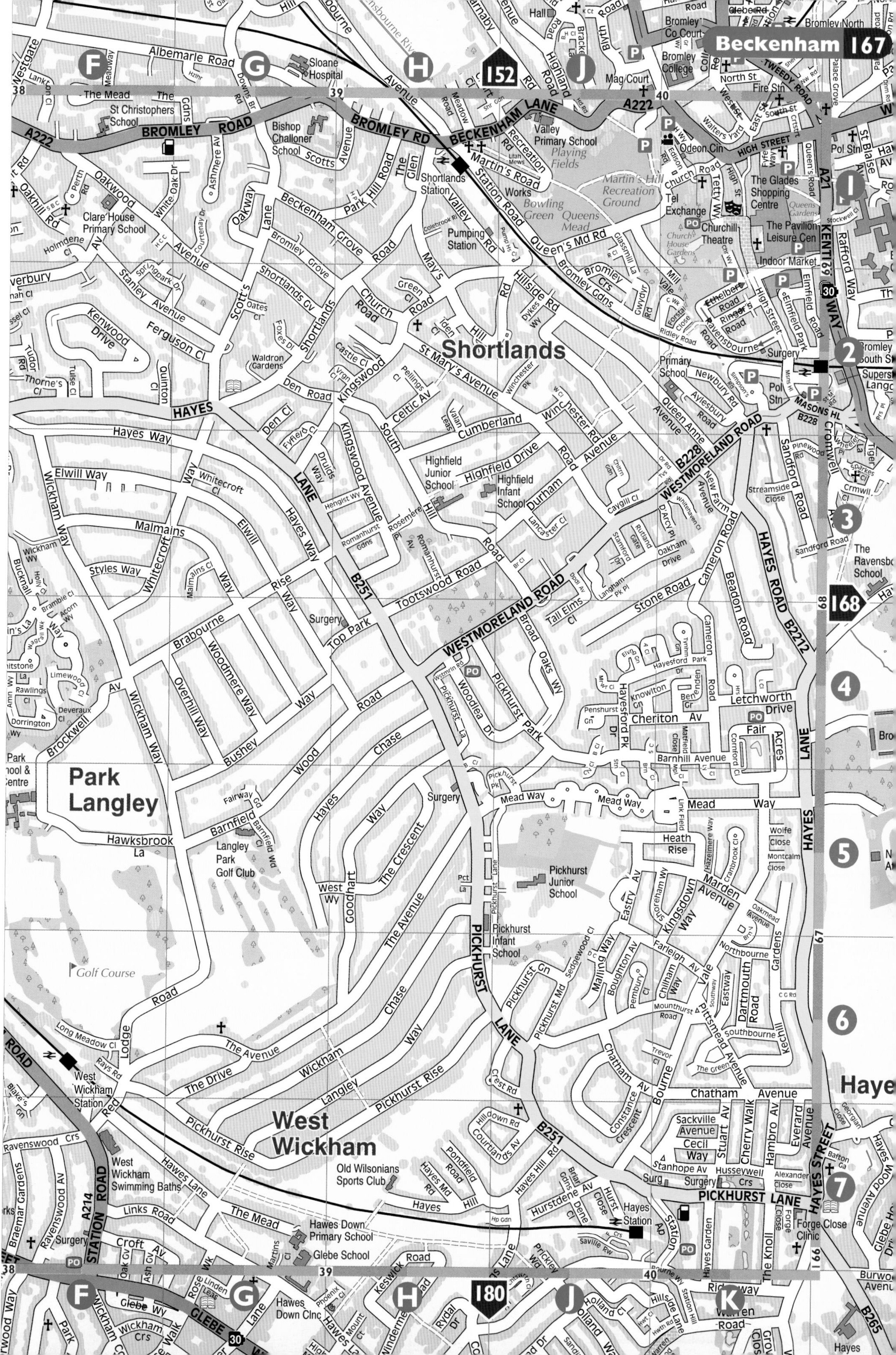

Beckenham 167
152
168
180
F
G
H
J
I
K
2
3
4
5
6
7
38
39
40
66
67
68
Shortlands
Park Langley
West Wickham
Hayes
Albemarle Road
The Mead
Westgate
Meadway
Sloane Hospital
St Christophers School
Bromley Road
A222
Bromley Rd
Beckenham Lane
Bishop Challoner School
Scotts Avenue
Shortlands Station
Martin's Road
Station Road
Recreation Rd
Valley Primary School
Playing Fields
Martin's Hill Recreation Ground
Bowling Green
Queens Mead
Queen's Md Rd
Bromley Co Court
Bromley College
Mag Court
North St
Fire Stn
Tweedy Road
High Street
Odeon Cin
Church Road
Tel Exchange
Churchill Theatre
The Glades Shopping Centre
The Pavilion Leisure Cen
Indoor Market
Kentish Way
A21
Rafford Way
Oakwood Avenue
Clare House Primary School
Oakhill Rd
Holmdene Av
Stanley Avenue
Ferguson Cl
Kenwood Drive
Scott's Lane
Oakway
Beckenham Grove
Bromley Grove
Shortlands Gv
Park Hill Road
The Glen
Valley Rd
Pumping Station
Mays Hill Rd
Church Road
Green Cl
Iden Cl
Hillside Rd
Bromley Gdns
Bromley Crs
Gwydyr Rd
Mill Vale
Ethelbert Road
Ringer's Road
Ravensbourne Road
Ridley Road
Elmfield Park
Elmfield Road
Surgery
Primary School
Newbury Rd
Aylesbury Road
Queen Anne Avenue
Masons Hl
B228
Pol Stn
Cromwell Av
Sandford Road
Streamside Close
The Ravensbourne School
St Mary's Avenue
Winchester Pk
Winchester Rd
Celtic Av
Cumberland Road
Highfield Junior School
Highfield Drive
Highfield Infant School
Durham Avenue
Lancaster Cl
Westmoreland Road
Caygill Cl
Rutland Gate
Stamford Dr
Oakham Drive
New Farm Avenue
Cameron Road
Beadon Road
Hayes Road
B2212
Stone Road
Tall Elms Cl
Langham Pk Pl
Hayes Lane
Den Road
Den Cl
Kingswood Avenue
South Hill Road
Castle Cl
Waldron Gardens
Quinton Cl
Thorne's Cl
Hayes Way
Elwill Way
Whitecroft Way
Wickham Way
Malmains Way
Styles Way
Brabourne Rise
Woodmere Way
Overhill Way
Bushey Way
Druids Way
Hengist Wy
Romanhurst Gdns
Romanhurst Av
Rosemere Pl
Tootswood Road
Top Park
B251
Wood Lodge Road
Surgery
Broad Oaks Wy
Pickhurst Park
Woodlea Dr
Pickhurst La
Hayesford Park Dr
Knowlton Gn
Cheriton Av
Letchworth Drive
Fair Acres
Barnhill Avenue
Mead Way
Link Field
Heath Rise
Wolfe Close
Montcalm Close
Hazelmere Way
Cranbrook Cl
Marden Avenue
Kingsdown Way
Eastry Av
Shoreham Wy
Oakmead Avenue
Northbourne
Pickhurst Junior School
Pickhurst Infant School
Pickhurst Lane
Pickhurst Gn
Pickhurst Md
Sedgewood Cl
Malling Way
Boughton Av
Pembury Cl
Chilham Way
Farleigh Av
Eastway
Dartmouth Road
Gardens
Mounthurst Road
Pittsmead Avenue
Southbourne
Kechill
The Green
Chatham Av
Chatham Avenue
Trevor Cl
Bourne Vale
Constance Crescent
Sackville Avenue
Cecil Way
Stuart Av
Cherry Walk
Hambro Av
Everard Avenue
Stanhope Av
Husseywell Crs
Alexander Close
Pickhurst Lane
Hayes Street
Georgian Close
Hayes Wood Avenue
Glebe Av
Burwood Avenue
B265
Barton Ga
Forge Close
Forge Clinic
Station Ap
Hayes Station
Saville Rw
Hurst Close
Dene Cl
Hurstdene Av
Hayes Hill Rd
Hilldown Rd
Courtlands Av
Crest Rd
Pondfield Road
Hayes Md Rd
Hayes Hill
Old Wilsonians Sports Club
Hayes Garden
The Knoll
Hillside Lane
Station Hill
Holland Cl
Warren Road
Ridgeway
Keswick Road
Hawes Down Primary School
Glebe School
Hawes Down Clnc
Hawes Lane
The Mead
Links Road
West Wickham Swimming Baths
Station Road
A214
Ravenswood Crs
Ravenswood Av
Braemar Gardens
Croft Av
Oak Gv
Ash Gv
Rose Wk
Linden Leas
Glebe Wy
Glebe Way
Wickham Crs
Wickham Ct
Rydal Dr
Windermere Road
Pickhurst Rise
Langley Way
Wickham Chase
Hayes Chase
The Avenue
The Drive
The Crescent
Hayes Way
Goodhart Way
West Wy
Hayes Chase
Barnfield
Barnfield Wd
Fairway Gd
Langley Park Golf Club
Hawksbrook La
Golf Course
Long Meadow Cl
Rays Rd
West Wickham Station
Red Lodge Road
Blake's Gn
Brockwell Av
Wickham Way
Wickham Wy
Bucknall
Holly Cl
Bramble Cl
Acorn Way
Limewood Cl
Rawlings Cl
Deveraux Cl
Dorrington Wy
Park School & Centre

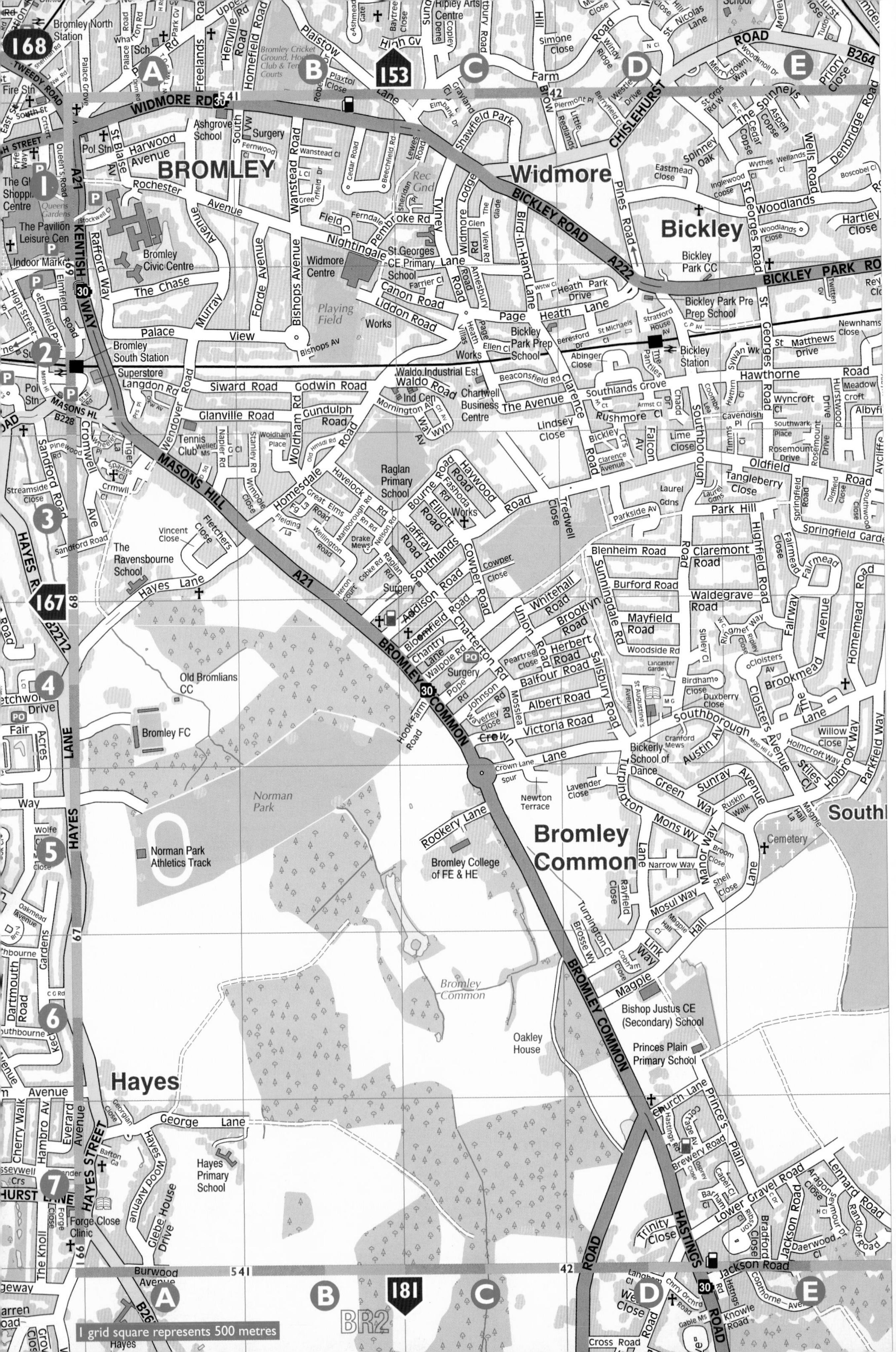
168
153
167
181
A
B
C
D
E
1
2
3
4
5
6
7
BROMLEY
Widmore
Bickley
Bromley Common
Hayes
Bromley North Station
Bromley South Station
Bickley Station
WIDMORE RD
BICKLEY ROAD
A222
A21
KENTISH WAY
MASONS HILL
BROMLEY COMMON
HASTINGS ROAD
HAYES LANE
HAYES STREET
CHISLEHURST ROAD
BICKLEY PARK ROAD
B264
B228
B2212
Bromley Civic Centre
Bromley College of FE & HE
Norman Park
Norman Park Athletics Track
Bromley FC
Old Bromlians CC
The Ravensbourne School
Raglan Primary School
Bishop Justus CE (Secondary) School
Princes Plain Primary School
Hayes Primary School
Bickley Park CC
Bickley Park Prep School
Widmore Centre
Playing Field
Oakley House
Cemetery
The Glades Shopping Centre
The Pavilion Leisure Cen
Bromley Common
Southborough Lane
Magpie Hall Lane
Turpington Lane
Crown Lane
Homesdale Road
Oldfield Road
Sandford Road
George Lane
Cross Road
Jackson Road
Lower Gravel Road
1 grid square represents 500 metres
BR2

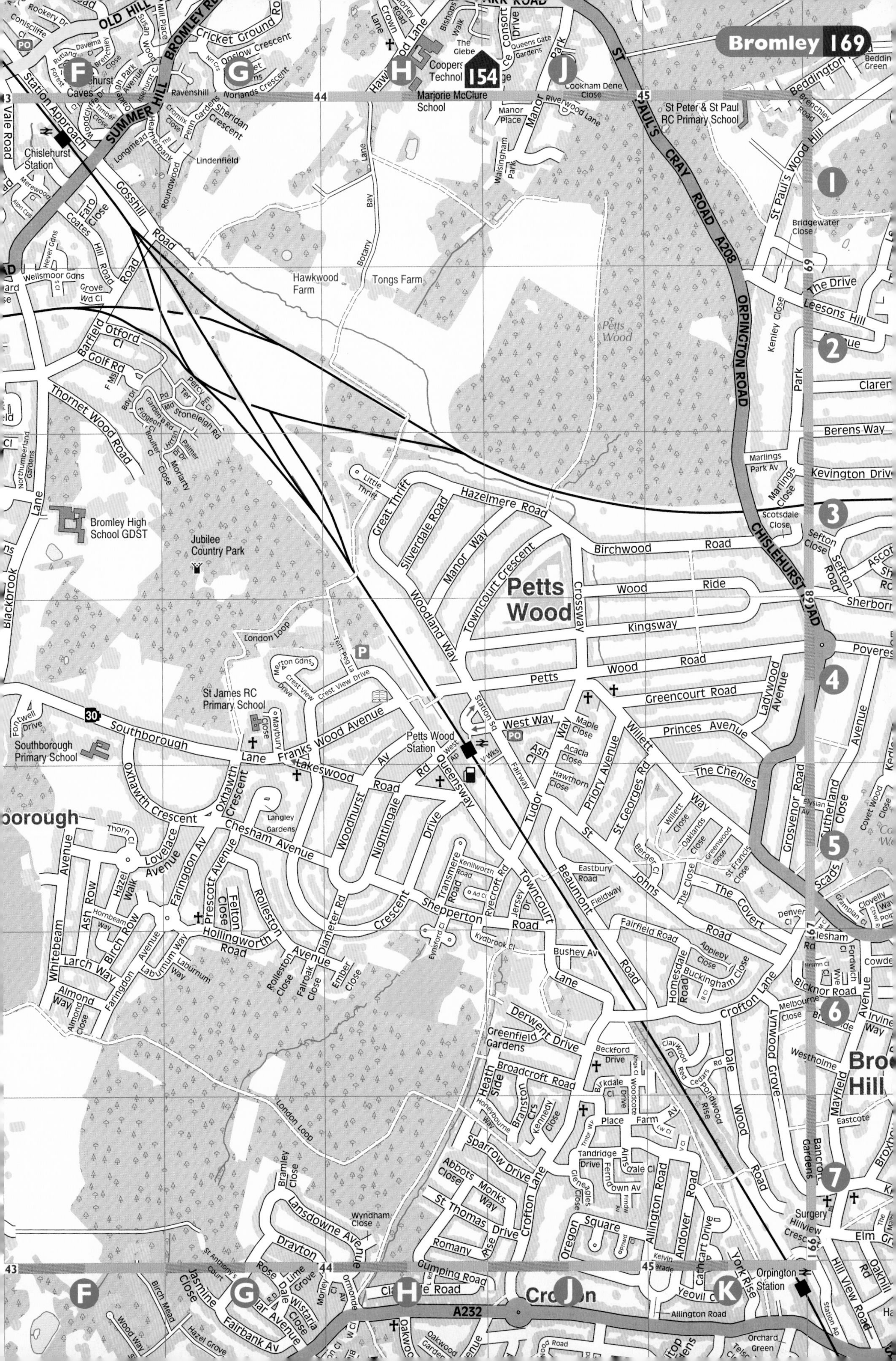
Chislehurst Station
Station Approach
Summer Hill
Bromley Rd
Old Hill
Cricket Ground Rd
Onslow Crescent
Norlands Crescent
Sheridan Crescent
Lindenfield
Gosshill Road
Hawkwood Lane
Marjorie McClure School
Cookham Dene Close
Riverwood Lane
St Peter & St Paul RC Primary School
St Paul's Cray Road A208
Orpington Road
Chislehurst Road
Hawkwood Farm
Tongs Farm
Botany Bay Lane
Petts Wood
Bromley High School GDST
Jubilee Country Park
Thornet Wood Road
Blackbrook Lane
Hazelmere Road
Birchwood Road
Wood Ride
Kingsway
Petts Wood Road
Greencourt Road
Princes Avenue
Crossway
Towncourt Crescent
Woodland Way
Silverdale Road
Manor Way
Great Thrift
Petts Wood Station
Queensway
West Way
Southborough Lane
Southborough Primary School
St James RC Primary School
Franks Wood Avenue
Lakeswood Road
Chesham Avenue
Oxhawth Crescent
Woodhurst Road
Nightingale Road
Crescent Drive
Shepperton Road
Towncourt Lane
Tudor Way
Priory Avenue
St Georges Rd
Willett Way
St Johns Road
The Covert
Beaumont Road
Crofton Lane
Dale Wood Road
Lynwood Grove
Derwent Drive
Broadcroft Road
Sparrow Drive
Place Farm Av
Allington Road
Andover Road
York Rise
Orpington Station
Lansdowne Avenue
London Loop
Whitebeam Avenue
Faringdon Avenue
Hollingworth Road
Rolleston Avenue
Crofton
A232
Broom Hill
Sherborne
Kevington Drive
Berens Way
The Drive
Leesons Hill
Bicknor Road
Westholme
Grosvenor Road
Sutherland Close
Hill View Road

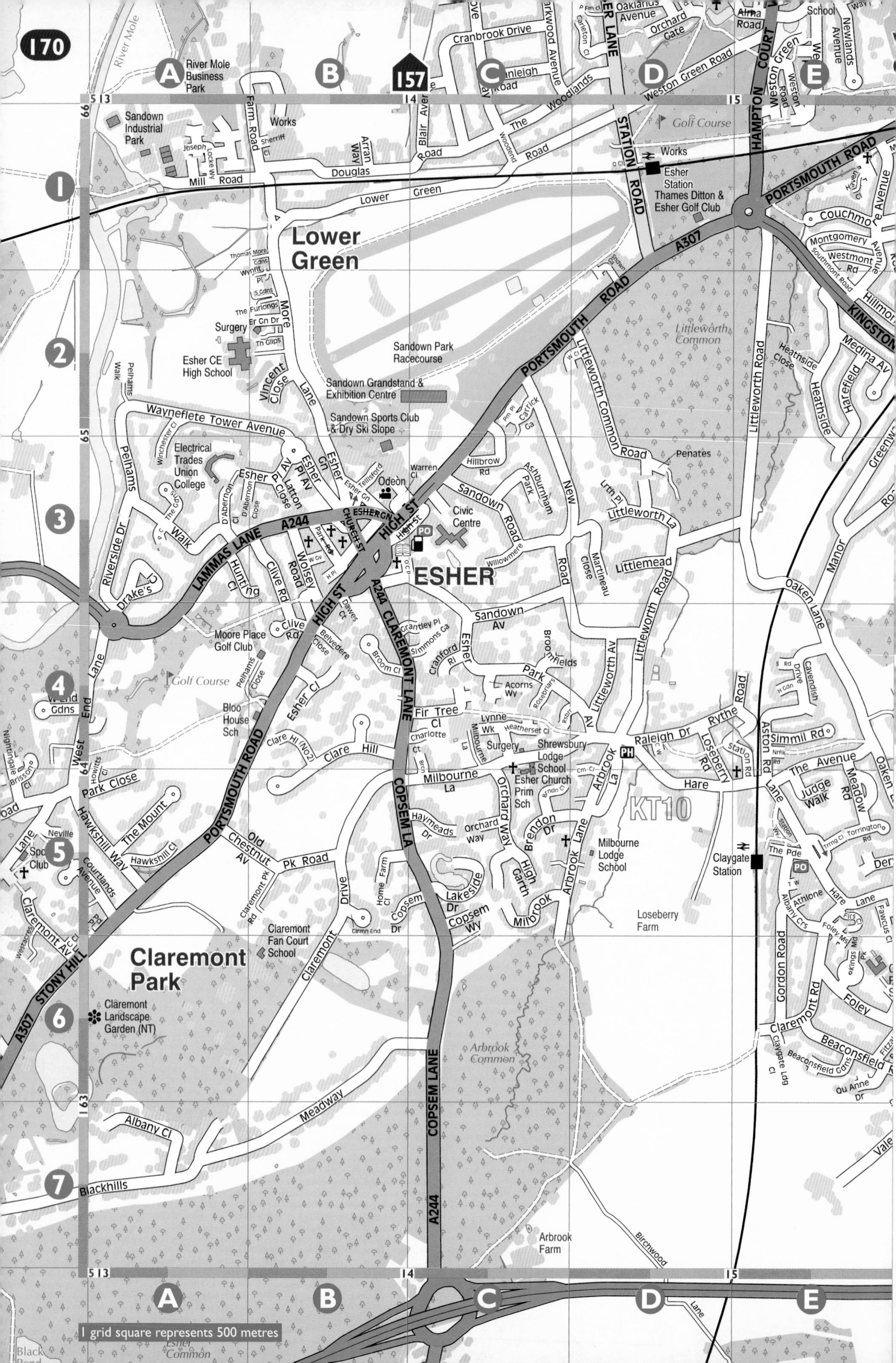
157
River Mole Business Park
Sandown Industrial Park
Works
Lower Green
Sandown Park Racecourse
Sandown Grandstand & Exhibition Centre
Sandown Sports Club & Dry Ski Slope
Esher Station
Thames Ditton & Esher Golf Club
Golf Course
Littleworth Common
Surgery
Esher CE High School
Electrical Trades Union College
Odeon
Civic Centre
ESHER
Moore Place Golf Club
Golf Course
Bloo House Sch
Penates
Surgery
Shrewsbury Lodge School
Esher Church Prim Sch
Milbourne Lodge School
KT10
Claygate Station
Loseberry Farm
Claremont Fan Court School
Claremont Park
Claremont Landscape Garden (NT)
Arbrook Common
Arbrook Farm
Esher Common
PORTSMOUTH ROAD
A307
A244
LAMMAS LANE
HIGH ST
CLAREMONT LANE
COPSEM LANE
STATION ROAD
HAMPTON COURT
KINGSTON
Littleworth Road
Littleworth Common Road
New Road
Sandown Road
Sandown Av
Milbourne La
Hare Lane
Raleigh Dr
Rythe Road
Arbrook Lane
Stony Hill
Blackhills
Meadway
Albany Cl
Douglas Road
Mill Road
Lower Green
Weston Green Road
Cranbrook Drive
The Woodlands
Wayneflete Tower Avenue
Pelhams Walk
Riverside Dr
West End Lane
Hawkshill Way
Old Chestnut Av
Pk Road
Claremont Drive
Oaken Lane
Claremont Rd
Beaconsfield Rd
Gordon Road
1 grid square represents 500 metres

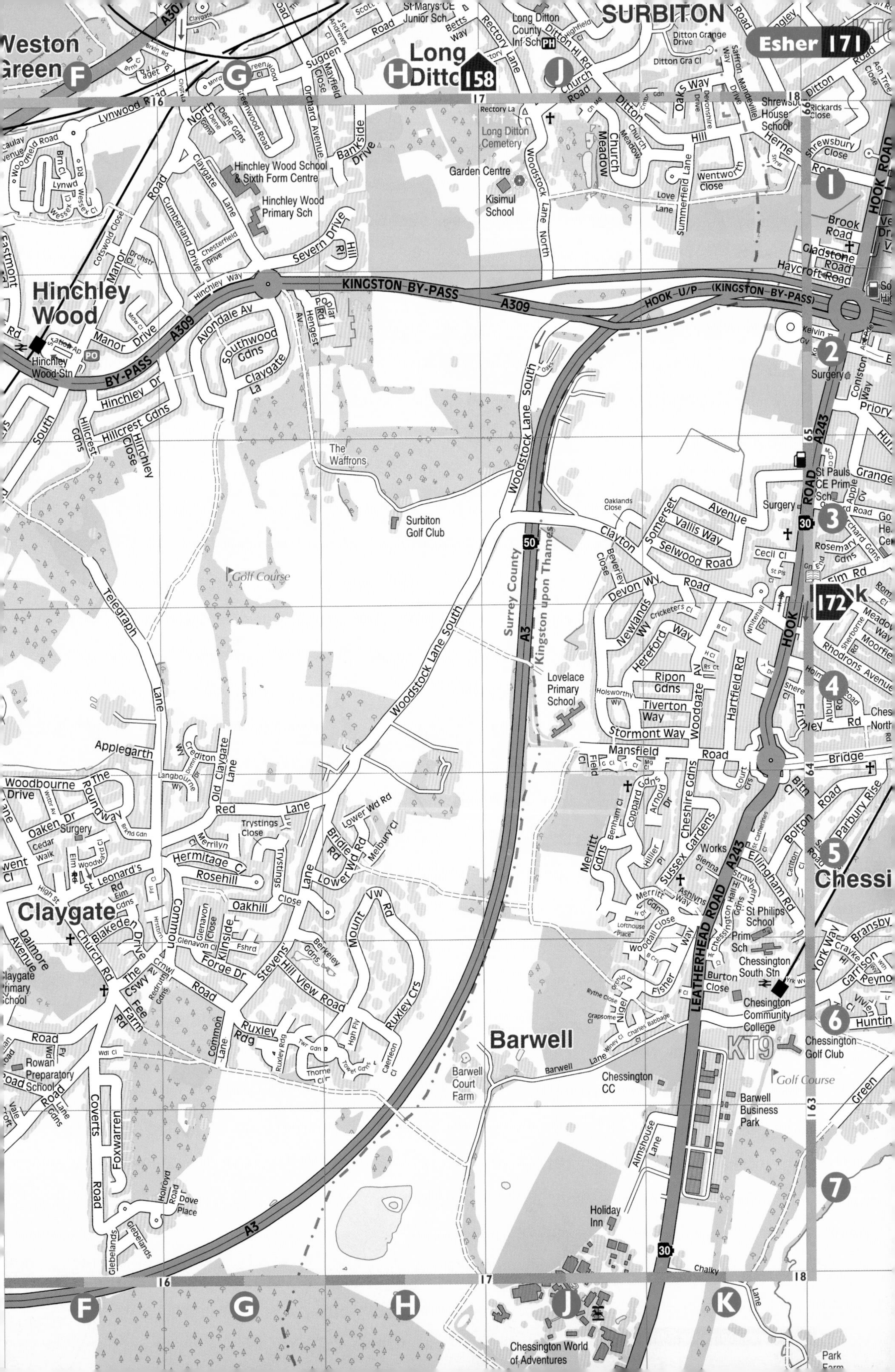
Esher 171
SURBITON
Long Ditton
158
Weston Green
Hinchley Wood
Claygate
Barwell
Chessington
172
KINGSTON BY-PASS
A309
A3
A243
HOOK ROAD
LEATHERHEAD ROAD
Woodstock Lane South
Telegraph Lane
Hinchley Wood School & Sixth Form Centre
Hinchley Wood Primary Sch
Long Ditton Cemetery
Kisimul School
Surbiton Golf Club
Golf Course
The Waffrons
Lovelace Primary School
St Philips School
Chessington South Stn
Chessington Community College
Chessington Golf Club
Barwell Business Park
Barwell Court Farm
Chessington CC
Holiday Inn
Chessington World of Adventures
Hinchley Wood Stn
Claygate Primary School
Rowan Preparatory School
Surrey County
Kingston upon Thames
KT9
16
17
18
F
G
H
J
K
1
2
3
4
5
6
7

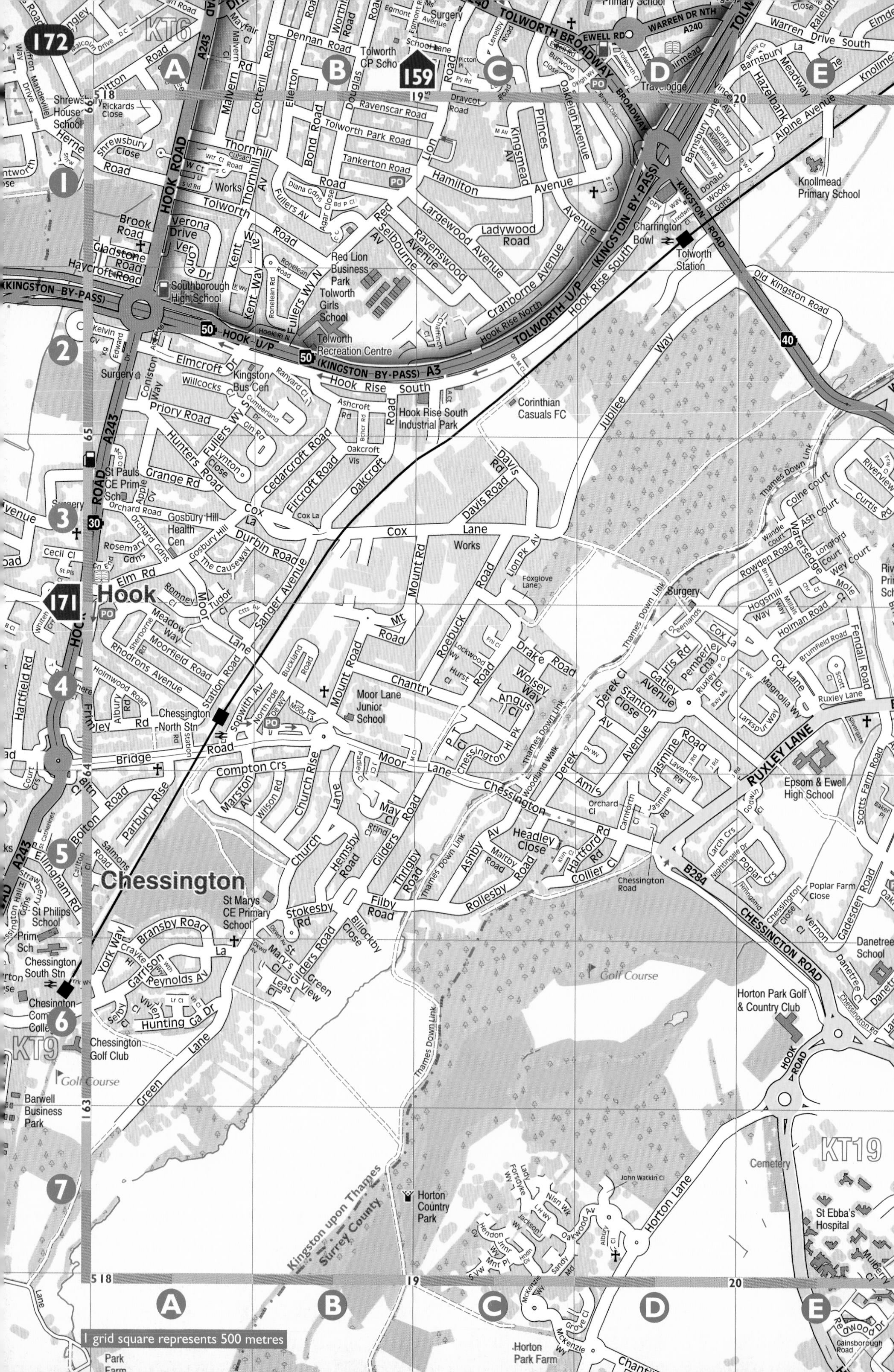

172
159
171
KT6
KT9
KT19
A
B
C
D
E
1
2
3
4
5
6
7
518
19
20
165
164
163
Hook
Chessington
HOOK ROAD
A243
TOLWORTH BROADWAY
(KINGSTON BY-PASS)
HOOK U/P
TOLWORTH U/P
A3
KINGSTON ROAD
RUXLEY LANE
CHESSINGTON ROAD
B284
Tolworth Station
Chessington North Stn
Chessington South Stn
Southborough High School
Tolworth Girls School
Tolworth Recreation Centre
Red Lion Business Park
Hook Rise South Industrial Park
Corinthian Casuals FC
Moor Lane Junior School
St Marys CE Primary School
St Pauls CE Prim Sch
Gosbury Hill Health Cen
Epsom & Ewell High School
Horton Park Golf & Country Club
Horton Country Park
Chessington Golf Club
Golf Course
Barwell Business Park
St Ebba's Hospital
Knollmead Primary School
Danetree School
Charrington Bowl
Tolworth CP Scho
Travelodge
Thames Down Link
Kingston upon Thames
Surrey County
1 grid square represents 500 metres

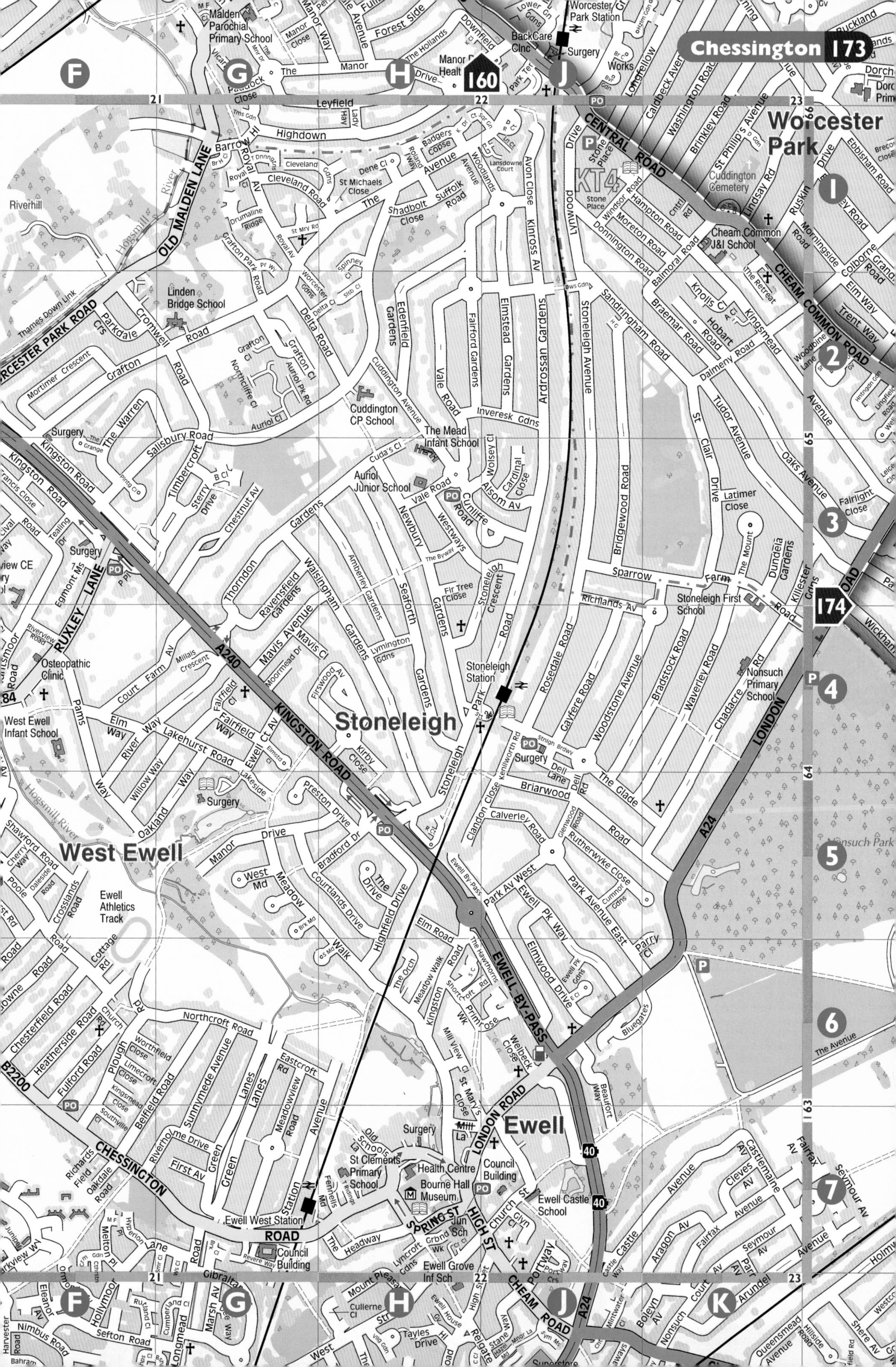
160
174
Worcester Park
Stoneleigh
West Ewell
Ewell
Riverhill
Malden Parochial Primary School
Linden Bridge School
Cuddington CP School
The Mead Infant School
Auriol Junior School
Stoneleigh Station
Stoneleigh First School
Nonsuch Primary School
Cheam Common J&I School
Cuddington Cemetery
Worcester Park Station
West Ewell Infant School
Osteopathic Clinic
Ewell Athletics Track
Ewell West Station
St Clements Primary School
Health Centre
Bourne Hall Museum
Council Building
Ewell Castle School
Ewell Grove Inf Sch
Nonsuch Park
OLD MALDEN LANE
WORCESTER PARK ROAD
CENTRAL ROAD
CHEAM COMMON ROAD
KINGSTON ROAD
A240
RUXLEY LANE
EWELL BY-PASS
LONDON ROAD
A24
CHESSINGTON ROAD
B2200
CHEAM ROAD
HIGH ST
SPRING ST
KT4

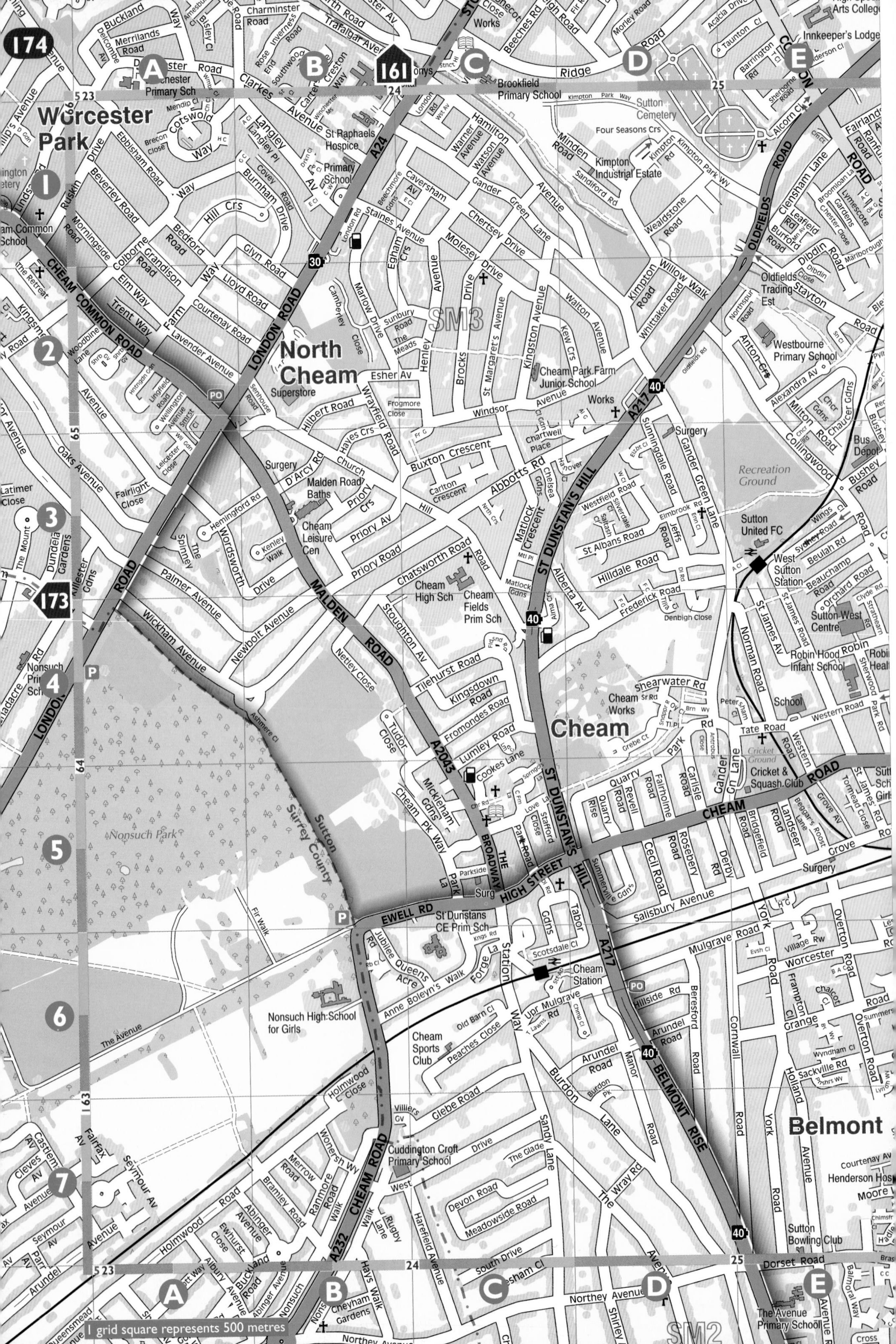
174
161
173
A
B
C
D
E
1
2
3
4
5
6
7
Worcester Park
North Cheam
Cheam
Belmont
SM3
SM2
Charminster Road
Trafalgar Ave
Merrilands Road
Buckland Way
Clarkes Avenue
Ridge Road
Brookfield Primary School
Sutton Cemetery
Kimpton Park Way
Four Seasons Crs
Minden Road
Kimpton Industrial Estate
Sandiford Rd
St Raphaels Hospice
Primary School
Cotswold Way
Ebbisham Road
Beverley Road
Langley Av
Burnham Drive
Covey Road
Hill Crs
Glyn Road
Lloyd Road
Courtenay Road
Lavender Avenue
Trent Way
Elm Way
Colborne Way
Grandison Road
Bedford Road
Morningside Road
Ruskin Drive
Cheam Common School
The Retreat
CHEAM COMMON ROAD
LONDON ROAD
A24
Staines Avenue
Caversham Av
Egham Crs
Marlow Drive
Camberley Close
Sunbury Road
The Meads
Henley Avenue
Molesey Drive
Chertsey Drive
Gander Green Lane
Hamilton Avenue
Warner Avenue
Watson Avenue
Brocks Drive
St Margaret's Avenue
Kingston Avenue
Kew Crs
Walton Avenue
Kimpton Road
Willow Walk
Whittaker Road
Wealdstone Road
OLDFIELDS ROAD
Oldfields Trading Est
Stayton Road
Dibdin Road
Westbourne Primary School
Anton Crs
Alexandra Av
Milton Road
Collingwood Road
Chaucer Gdns
Bus Depot
Busney Road
Recreation Ground
Sutton United FC
West Sutton Station
Beulah Rd
Beauchamp Road
Orchard Road
Sutton West Centre
Robin Hood Infant School
Esher Av
Superstore
Hilbert Road
Wrayfield Road
Frogmore Close
Windsor Avenue
Cheam Park Farm Junior School
Works
A217
Surgery
Sunningdale Road
Chartwell Place
Buxton Crescent
Carlton Crescent
Abbotts Rd
Hayes Crs
Church Hill Road
Malden Road Baths
Cheam Leisure Cen
Priory Crs
Priory Av
Priory Road
Chatsworth Road
Cheam High Sch
Cheam Fields Prim Sch
Matlock Crescent
Matlock Gdns
ST DUNSTAN'S HILL
Alberta Av
Westfield Road
St Albans Road
Jeffs Road
Hilldale Road
Frederick Road
Denbigh Close
Oaks Avenue
Fairlight Close
Latimer Close
The Mount
Dundela Gardens
Killester Gdns
Hemingford Rd
The Spinney
Wordsworth Drive
Kenley Walk
Palmer Avenue
Newbolt Avenue
Wickham Avenue
MALDEN ROAD
Stoughton Av
Netley Close
Tilehurst Road
Kingsdown Road
Fromondes Road
Lumley Road
Tudor Close
A2043
Nonsuch Prim Sch
Nonsuch Park
Surrey County
Sutton
Ashmere Cl
Shearwater Rd
Cheam Works
Grebe Ct
Park Rd
Gander Gn Lane
Tate Road
Cricket & Squash Club
CHEAM ROAD
Western Road
Quarry Rise
Quarry Road
Revell Road
Fairholme Road
Carlisle Road
Cookes Lane
Micklenham Gdns
Cheam Pk Way
THE BROADWAY
Love La
Stafford Close
Park Road
HIGH STREET
EWELL RD
Parkside
St Dunstans CE Prim Sch
Jubilee Rd
Queens Acre
Anne Boleyn's Walk
Forge La
Station Way
Tabor Gdns
Scotsdale Cl
Cheam Station
Summerville Gdns
Cecil Road
Rosebery Road
Derby Rd
Bridgefield Road
Landseer Road
Beggar's Roost Lane
Grove Av
Surgery
Salisbury Avenue
Mulgrave Road
Worcester Road
York Road
Overton Road
Frampton Cl
Grange Road
Chalcot Cl
Wyndham Cl
Sackville Rd
Fir Walk
The Avenue
Nonsuch High School for Girls
Cheam Sports Club
Old Barn Cl
Peaches Close
Upr Mulgrave Rd
Hillside Rd
Beresford Road
Arundel Road
Burdon Lane
Manor Road
BELMONT RISE
Cornwall Road
Holland Avenue
Holmwood Close
Glebe Road
Villiers Gv
Cuddington Croft Primary School
West Drive
The Glade
Sandy Lane
The Wray Rd
Devon Road
Meadowside Road
CHEAM ROAD
A232
Wonersh Way
Merrow Road
Bramley Road
Ranmore Road
Rugby Lane
Harefield Avenue
Fairfax Av
Seymour Av
Cleves Av
Castlemaine Avenue
Holmwood Road
Abinger Avenue
Ewhurst Close
Buckland Road
Albury Avenue
Parr Av
Arundel
Queensmead Avenue
Hays Walk
Cheyham Gardens
Northey Avenue
South Drive
Dorset Road
Balmoral Way
The Avenue Primary School
Sutton Bowling Club
Courtenay Av
Henderson Hosp
Moore
Cross
1 grid square represents 500 metres

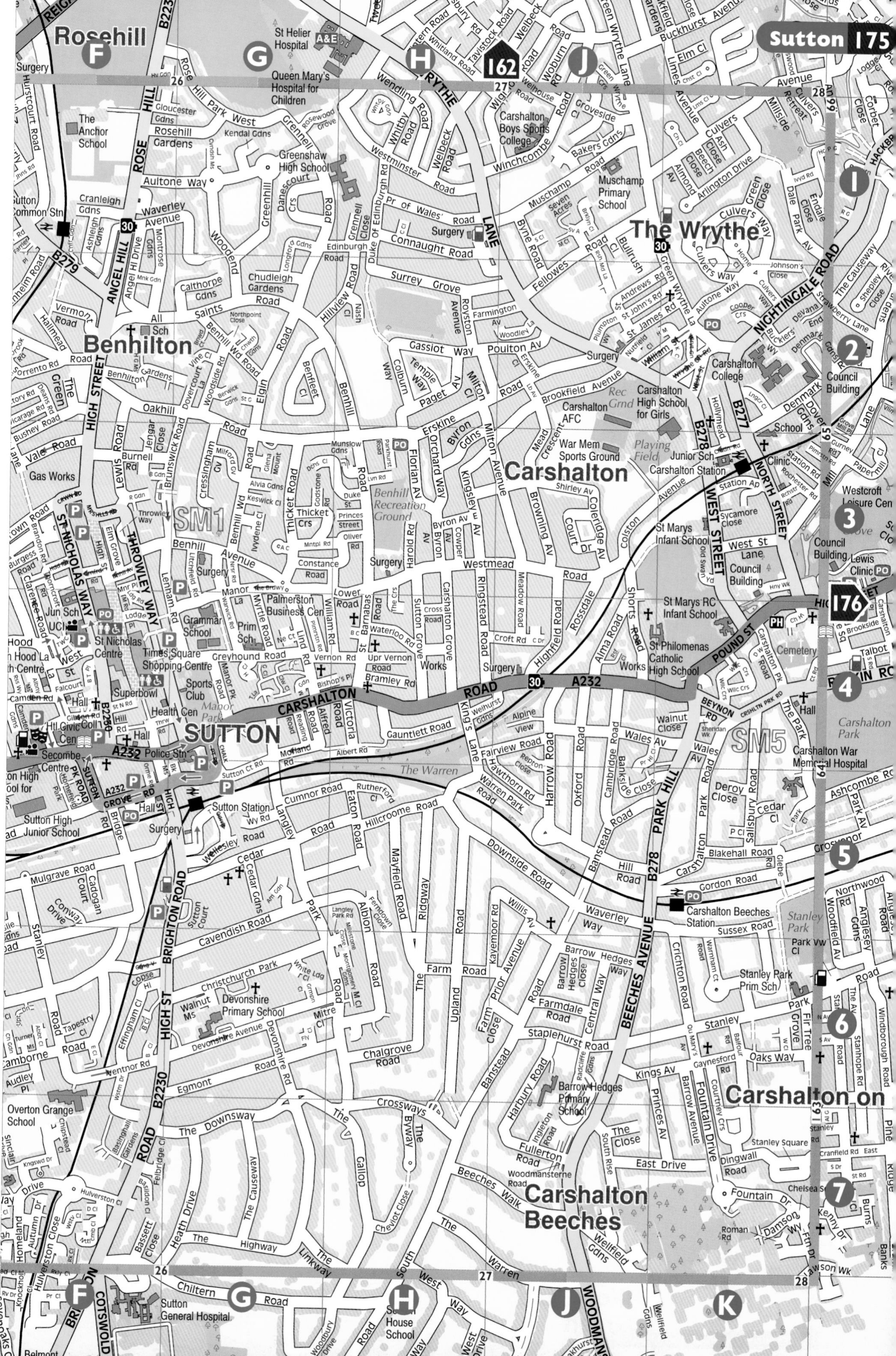

Sutton 175
Rosehill
St Helier Hospital
A&E
Queen Mary's Hospital for Children
162
The Anchor School
Rosehill Gardens
Greenshaw High School
Carshalton Boys Sports College
Muschamp Primary School
The Wrythe
Benhilton
Carshalton College
Council Building
Carshalton High School for Girls
Carshalton AFC
War Mem Sports Ground
Carshalton
Carshalton Station
Junior Sch
Benhill Recreation Ground
Westcroft Leisure Cen
St Marys Infant School
St Marys RC Infant School
St Philomenas Catholic High School
176
Gas Works
St Nicholas Centre
Times Square Shopping Centre
Grammar School
Palmerston Business Cen
Sports Club
Superbowl
Health Cen
Civic Cen
Secombe Centre
SUTTON
Police Stn
Sutton Station
Sutton High Junior School
Carshalton Road
A232
The Warren
SM1
SM5
Carshalton Park
Carshalton War Memorial Hospital
Carshalton Beeches Station
Stanley Park
Stanley Park Prim Sch
Devonshire Primary School
Barrow Hedges Primary School
Overton Grange School
Carshalton on
Carshalton Beeches
Sutton General Hospital
South House School
Brighton Road
High Street
Beeches Avenue
Park Hill
Nightingale Road
West Street
North Street
Wrythe Lane
Angel Hill
Rose Hill
Throwley Way
St Nicholas Way
Belmont

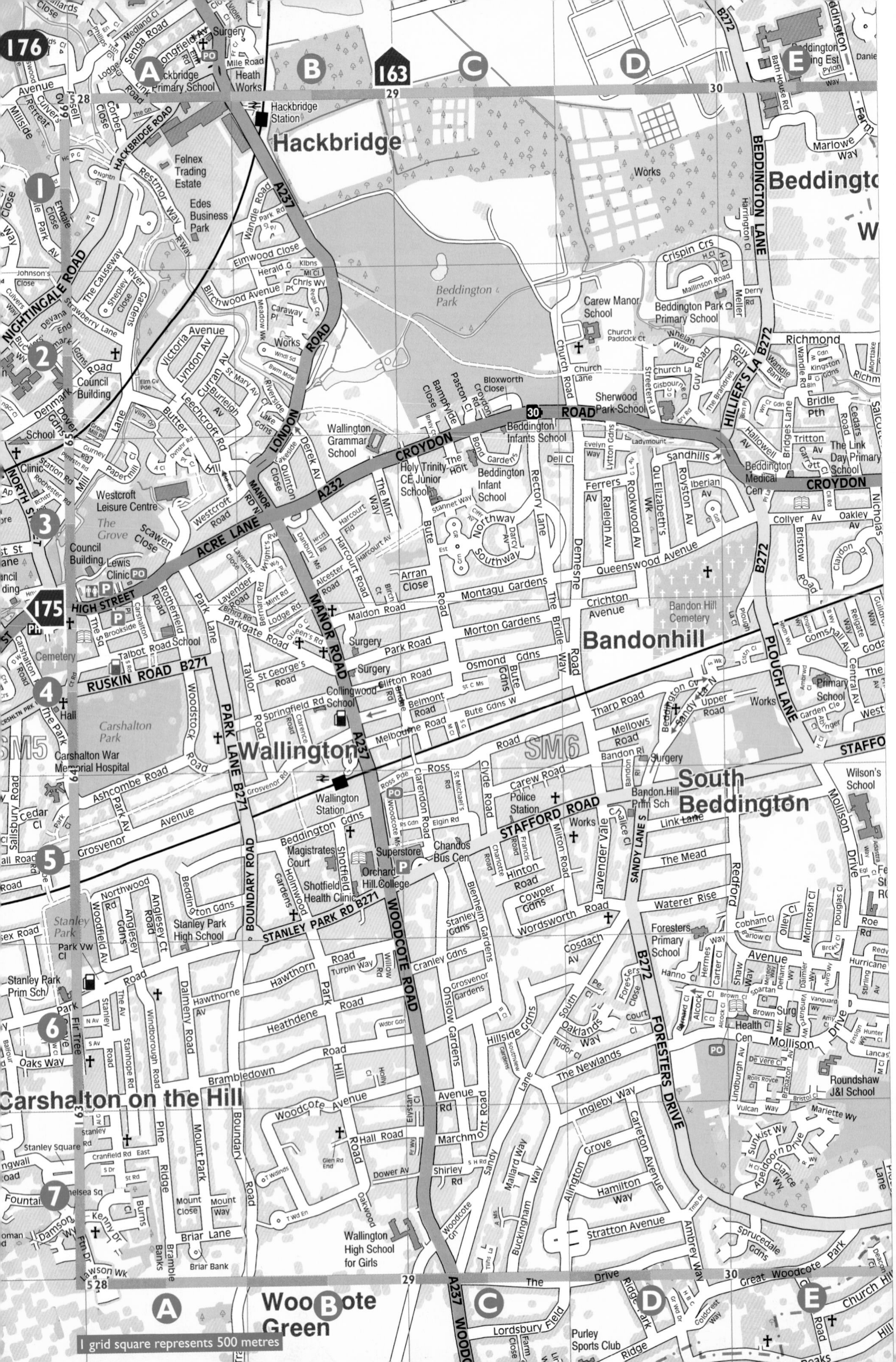

176
163
175
A
B
C
D
E
1
2
3
4
5
6
7
29
30
528
Hackbridge
Hackbridge Station
Hackbridge Primary School
Felnex Trading Estate
Edes Business Park
Beddington Park
Works
Carew Manor School
Beddington Park Primary School
Sherwood Park School
Wallington Grammar School
Beddington Infants School
Holy Trinity CE Junior School
Beddington Infant School
Westcroft Leisure Centre
The Grove
Council Building
Lewis Clinic
Bandon Hill Cemetery
Bandonhill
Carshalton Park
Carshalton War Memorial Hospital
Collingwood School
Wallington
Wallington Station
SM5
SM6
South Beddington
Wilson's School
Police Station
Bandon Hill Prim Sch
Magistrates Court
Shotfield Health Clinic
Orchard Hill College
Chandos Bus Cen
Stanley Park High School
Stanley Park Prim Sch
Foresters Primary School
Roundshaw J&I School
Carshalton on the Hill
Wallington High School for Girls
Woodcote Green
Purley Sports Club
Beddington
CROYDON ROAD
A232
ACRE LANE
HIGH STREET
MANOR ROAD
A237
LONDON ROAD
WOODCOTE ROAD
RUSKIN ROAD B271
PARK LANE B271
STANLEY PARK RD B271
BOUNDARY ROAD
STAFFORD ROAD
SANDY LANE S
FORESTERS DRIVE
B272
BEDDINGTON LANE
PLOUGH LANE
HILLIER'S LA B272
NIGHTINGALE ROAD
HACKBRIDGE ROAD
NORTH STREET
Queenswood Avenue
Montagu Gardens
Morton Gardens
Park Road
Maldon Road
Osmond Gdns
Clifton Road
Melbourne Road
Grosvenor Avenue
Ashcombe Road
Woodstock Road
Mollison Drive
Brambledown Road
Woodcote Avenue
Great Woodcote Park
The Drive
Stratton Avenue
Ingleby Way
The Newlands
I grid square represents 500 metres

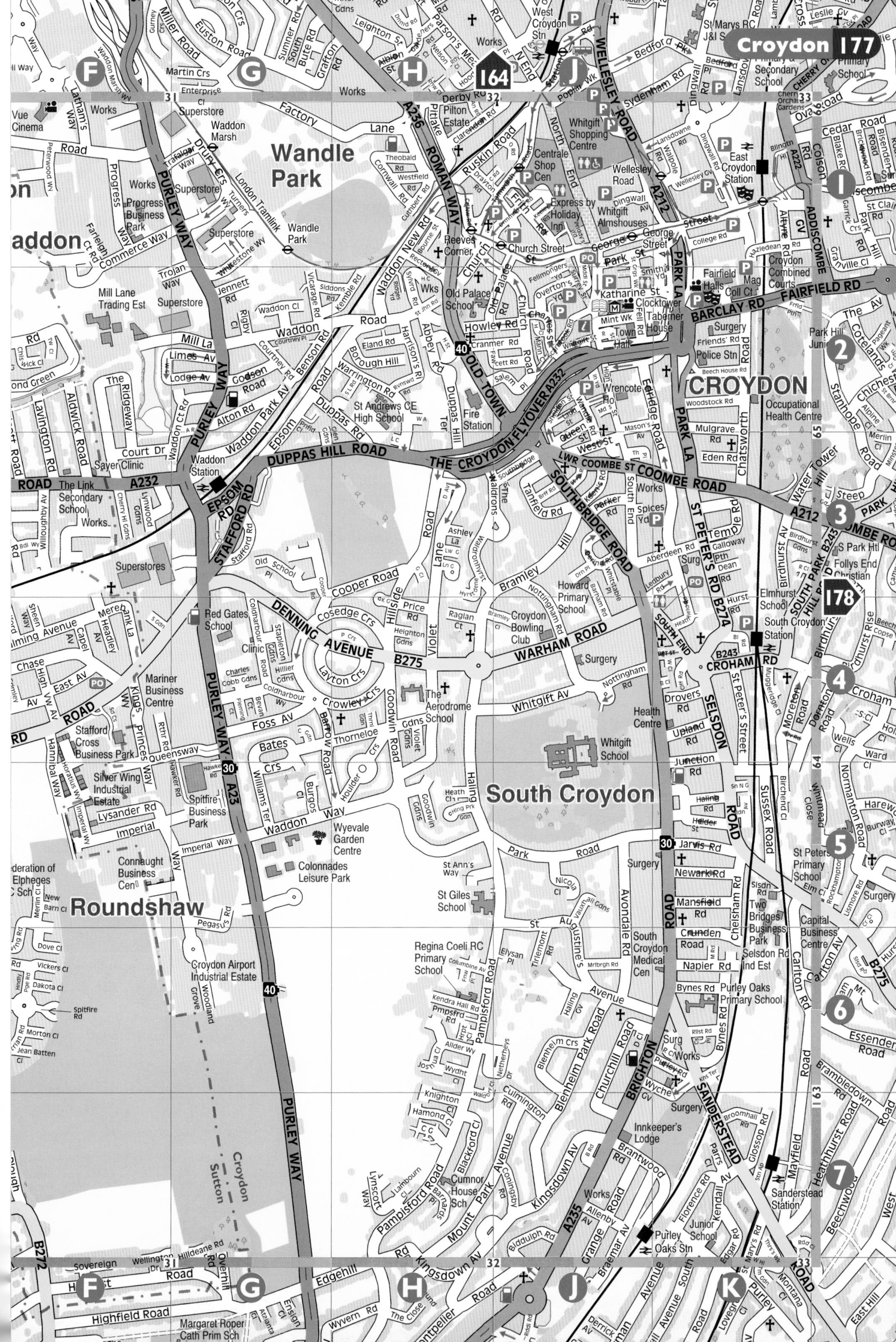
F
G
H
J
K
164
178
31
32
33
2
3
4
5
6
7
Wandle Park
Waddon
CROYDON
South Croydon
Roundshaw
West Croydon Stn
East Croydon Station
Waddon Station
South Croydon Station
Sanderstead Station
Purley Oaks Stn
Waddon Marsh
Wandle Park
Church Street
George Street
Reeves Corner
Vue Cinema
Whitgift Shopping Centre
Centrale Shop Cen
Express by Holiday Inn
Whitgift Almshouses
Fairfield Halls
Croydon Combined Courts
Clocktower
Tabernacle House
Town Hall
Police Stn
Occupational Health Centre
Old Palace School
St Andrews CE High School
Fire Station
Mill Lane Trading Est
Progress Business Park
Superstore
Superstores
Red Gates School
Mariner Business Centre
Stafford Cross Business Park
Silver Wing Industrial Estate
Spitfire Business Park
Connaught Business Cen
Croydon Airport Industrial Estate
Wyevale Garden Centre
Colonnades Leisure Park
The Aerodrome School
Croydon Bowling Club
Howard Primary School
Whitgift School
Health Centre
St Giles School
Regina Coeli RC Primary School
South Croydon Medical Cen
Purley Oaks Primary School
Two Bridges Business Park
Selsdon Rd Ind Est
Capital Business Centre
Innkeeper's Lodge
Cumnor House Sch
Junior School
Margaret Roper Cath Prim Sch
Elmhurst School
Park Hill Junior
St Peters Primary School
The Link Secondary School
Sayer Clinic
Clinic
Surgery
Works
Croydon
Sutton
PURLEY WAY
A23
ROMAN WAY
A236
OLD TOWN
THE CROYDON FLYOVER A232
DUPPAS HILL ROAD
DENNING AVENUE
B275
WARHAM ROAD
SOUTHBRIDGE ROAD
COOMBE ROAD
A212
PARK LA
ST PETER'S RD B274
BRIGHTON ROAD
A235
SANDERSTEAD ROAD
SELSDON ROAD
BARCLAY RD
FAIRFIELD RD
WELLESLEY ROAD
A212
ADDISCOMBE GV
SOUTH PARK HILL RD
B243
CROHAM RD
EPSOM RD
STAFFORD RD
B272
A222
Highfield Road
Waddon Way
Whitgift Av
Park Road
Pampisford Road
Mount Park Avenue
Kingsdown Av
Blenheim Park Road
Churchill Road
Violet Lane
Haling Park
Commerce Way
Factory Lane
Waddon Road
Mill La
Duppas Rd
Cooper Road
Foss Av
Queensway
Imperial Way
Warrington Rd
Borough Hill
Howley Rd
Cranmer Rd
Chatsworth Road
Edridge Road
Mulgrave Rd
Eden Rd
Temple Rd
Aberdeen Rd
Drovers Rd
Upland Rd
Junction Rd
Jarvis Rd
Newark Rd
Mansfield Rd
Crunden Road
Napier Rd
Bynes Rd
Avondale Rd
Sussex Road
Chelsham Rd
Carlton Rd
Normanton Road
Essenden Road
Heathhurst Road
Beechwood
Mayfield
Brantwood
Grange Road
Braemar Av
Edgehill
Wyvern Rd
Montpelier Road
Lavington Road
Aldwick Road
The Ridgeway
Progress Way
Latham's Way
Euston Road
Miller Road
Sumner Rd
Grafton Rd
Leighton St
Bedford Pk
Sydenham Rd
Dingwall Rd
Cedar Road
Water Tower Hill
Stanhope Road
Chichester Rd
Croham Rd
Edgar Rd
Purley Road
Montana Gdns

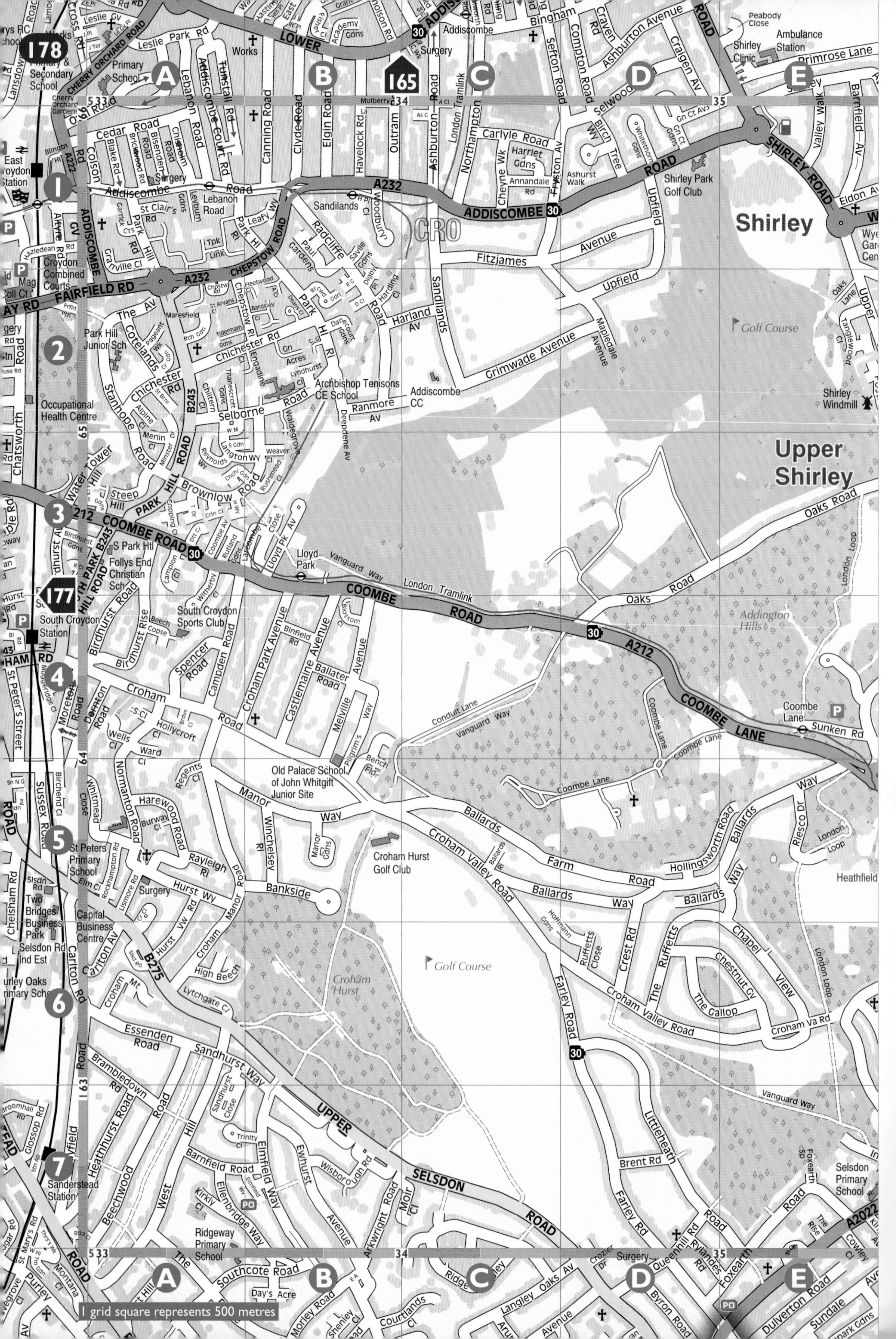

178
165
177
A
B
C
D
E
1
2
3
4
5
6
7
533
34
35
64
65
163
Shirley
Upper Shirley
CRO
Cherry Orchard Road
Leslie Park Rd
Lebanon Road
Addiscombe Court Rd
Tunstall Rd
Canning Road
Clyde Road
Elgin Road
Havelock Rd
Outram Road
Ashburton Road
London Tramlink
Northampton Road
Sefton Road
Compton Road
Ashburton Avenue
Craigen Av
Bingham
Lower Addiscombe Road
Addiscombe
Surgery
Works
Primary School
Primary & Secondary School
East Croydon Station
Cedar Road
Colson Road
Blake Rd
Brickwood Road
Bisenden Road
Chisholm Road
Addiscombe Road
Lebanon Road
Sandilands
Woodbury Cl
Radcliffe Road
Addiscombe Road
Carlyle Road
Harriet Gdns
Annandale Rd
Cheyne Wk
Fryston Av
Ashurst Walk
Birch Tree Wy
Upfield
Shirley Park Golf Club
Shirley Road
Peabody Close
Shirley Clinic
Ambulance Station
Primrose Lane
Valley Walk
Barnfield Av
Eldon Av
Fitzjames Avenue
Upfield
Croydon Combined Courts
Mag Coll Ct
Fairfield Rd
Chepstow Road
Park Hill Rd
St Clair's Rd
Granville Cl
Leafy Wy
Paul Gardens
Saville Gdns
Park Hill Ri
Harland Av
Sandilands
Grimwade Avenue
Mapledale Avenue
Golf Course
Park Hill Junior Sch
Coteland's
Chichester Rd
Stanhope Road
Engadine Cl
Acres Gn
Archbishop Tenisons CE School
Addiscombe CC
Ranmore Av
Selborne Road
Chiltern
Waldegrove
Deepdene Av
Occupational Health Centre
Chatsworth Road
Merlin Cl
Minster Dr
Langton Wy
Reynolds Wy
Weaver Cl
Rushmead Cl
Brownlow Road
Water Tower Hill
Steep Hill
Park Hill Road
B243
A212
Coombe Road
South Park Hill Road
S Park Htl
Follys End Christian Sch
Coombe Av
Rutland Gdns
Larcombe Close
Lloyd Pk Av
Lloyd Park
Vanguard Way
London Tramlink
Coombe Road
Oaks Road
Oaks Road
Addington Hills
London Loop
Shirley Windmill
Tanglewood Cl
South Croydon Sports Club
South Croydon Station
Birdhurst Road
Birdhurst Rise
Beech Copse
Spencer Road
Campden Road
Croham Park Avenue
Castlemaine Avenue
Binfield Rd
Ballater Road
Blossom Cl
Melville Avenue
Pilgrim's Way
Croham Road
Moreton Rd
Normanton Road
Hollycroft Cl
Ward Cl
Wells Cl
Harewood Road
Burway Cl
Regents Cl
Manor Way
Old Palace School of John Whitgift Junior Site
Bench Fld
Winchelsey Ri
Manor Gdns
Croham Hurst Golf Club
Conduit Lane
Coombe Lane
Coombe Lane
Sunken Rd
A212
Coombe Lane
Ballards Way
Ballards Farm Road
Hollingsworth Road
Riesco Dr
Heathfield
Croham Valley Road
Ballards Way
Crest Rd
The Ruffetts
Chapel View
Chestnut Gv
The Gallop
Croham Va Rd
Hoffmann Gdns
Ruffetts Close
Farley Road
Golf Course
Croham Hurst
St Peters Primary School
Rayleigh Ri
Hurst Wy
Surgery
Bankside
Croham Manor Road
High Beech
Lytchgate Cl
Capital Business Centre
Two Bridges Business Park
Selsdon Rd Ind Est
Purley Oaks Primary School
Sussex Road
Carlton Rd
Carlton Av
B275
Essenden Road
Brambledown Rd
Heathhurst Road
Sandhurst Way
Sandhurst Close
Upper Selsdon Road
Trinity Cl
Barnfield Road
Elmfield Way
Ewhurst Avenue
Wisborough Rd
Arkwright Road
Moir Cl
Beechwood Road
West Hill
Ellenbridge Way
Kirkly Cl
Ridgeway Primary School
Littleheath Road
Brent Rd
Farley Rd
Vanguard Way
Selsdon Primary School
Foxearth Sp
The Rise
A2022
Sanderstead Station
Glossop Rd
St Mary's Rd
Montana
Purley
The Southcote Road
Day's Acre
Morley Road
Shenley Cl
Courtlands Cl
Langley Oaks Av
Queenhill Rd
Rylandes Rd
Byron Road
Foxearth
Dulverton Road
Sundale Av
Cowley
Surgery
Crozier Dr
I grid square represents 500 metres

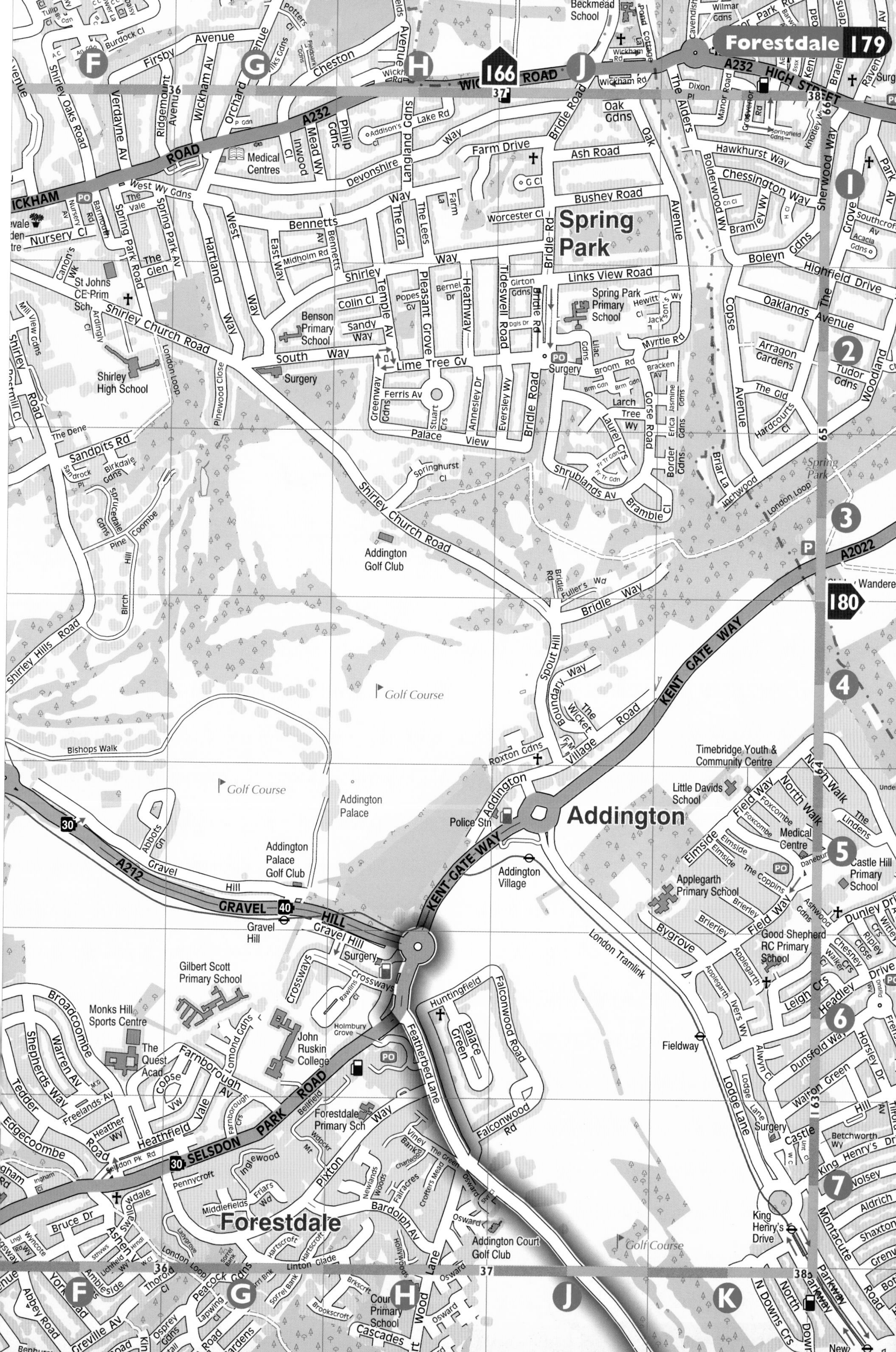

Forestdale 179
166
180
Spring Park
Addington
Forestdale
A232
WICKHAM ROAD
HIGH STREET
A2022
KENT GATE WAY
A212
GRAVEL HILL
SELSDON PARK ROAD
Shirley Church Road
Spout Hill
Featherbed Lane
Parkway
Shirley High School
St Johns CE Prim Sch
Benson Primary School
Spring Park Primary School
Addington Golf Club
Golf Course
Addington Palace
Addington Palace Golf Club
Addington Village
Police Stn
Gilbert Scott Primary School
Monks Hill Sports Centre
The Quest Acad
John Ruskin College
Forestdale Primary Sch
Addington Court Golf Club
Timebridge Youth & Community Centre
Little Davids School
Applegarth Primary School
Good Shepherd RC Primary School
Castle Hill Primary School
Medical Centre
London Tramlink
London Loop
Fieldway
King Henry's Drive
Gravel Hill
Beckmead School

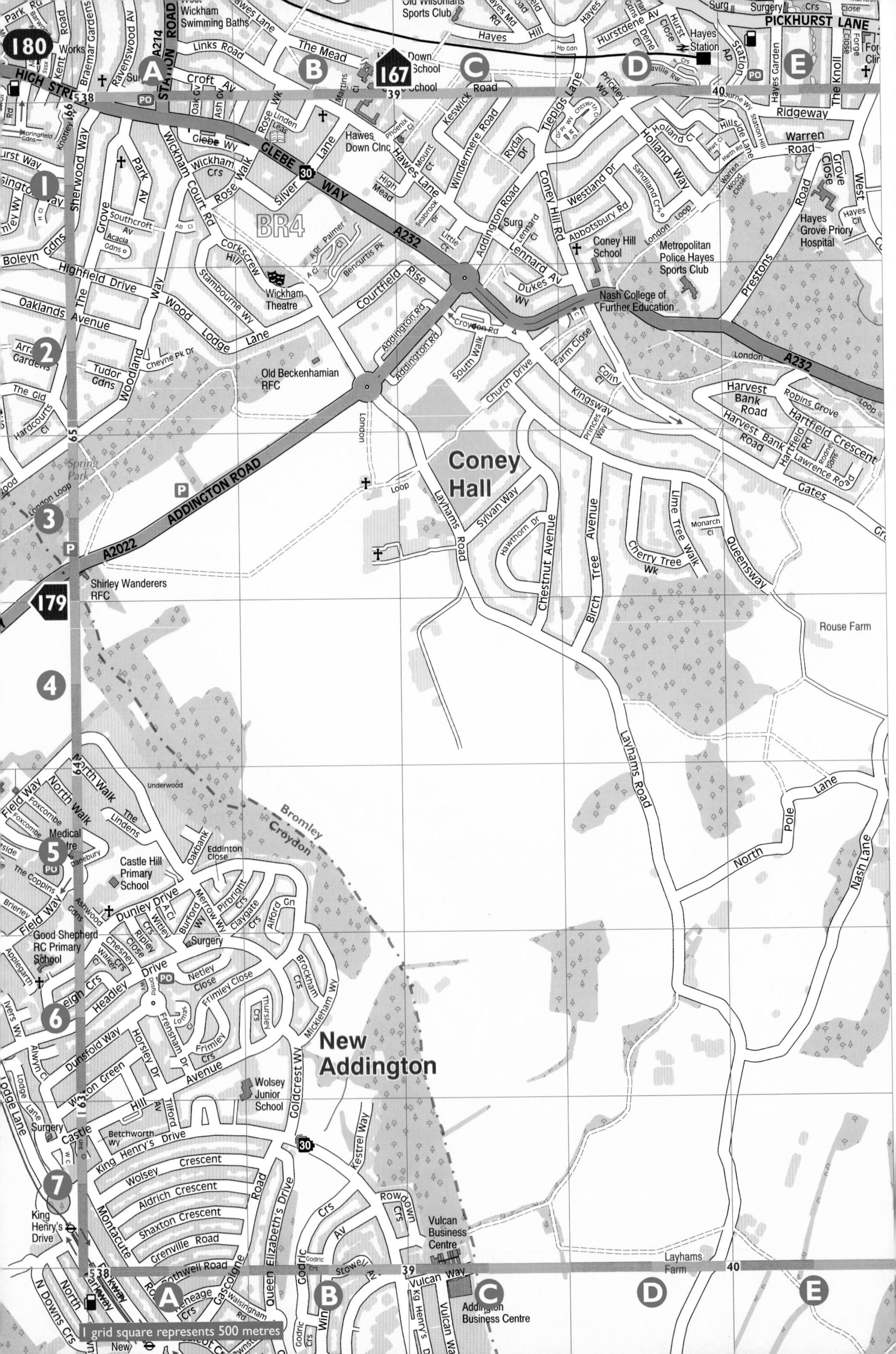

180
167
179
A
B
C
D
E
1
2
3
4
5
6
7
38
39
40
65
64
63
HIGH STREET
STATION ROAD
A214
Links Road
The Mead
Hawes Lane
Hayes
Hayes Station
PICKHURST LANE
Hurstdene Av
Station Rd
Hayes Garden
The Knoll
Ridgeway
Warren Road
Grove Close
West
Prestons Road
Hayes Grove Priory Hospital
Metropolitan Police Hayes Sports Club
Nash College of Further Education
Coney Hill School
Coney Hill Rd
Tiepigs Lane
Holland Way
Holland Cl
Hillside Lane
Westland Dr
Abbotsbury Rd
Sandiland Crs
London Loop
Keswick Road
Windermere Road
Rydal Dr
Addington Road
Lennard Av
Dukes Wy
Down School
Croft Av
Braemar Gardens
Ravenswood Av
Kent Road
Works
Sherwood Way
GLEBE WAY
A232
Glebe Wy
Wickham Crs
Rose Walk
Wickham Court Rd
Silver Lane
Hawes Down Clnc
High Mead
Mount Ct
Little Ct
BR4
Park Av
Southcroft Av
Acacia Gdns
Boleyn Gdns
Highfield Drive
Oaklands Avenue
Corkscrew Hill
Stambourne Wy
Wickham Theatre
Wood Lodge Lane
Courtfield Rise
Bencurtis Pk
Croydon Rd
South Walk
Farm Close
Church Drive
Kingsway
Princes Way
Harvest Bank Road
Robins Grove
Hartfield Crescent
Lawrence Road
Gates
Tudor Gdns
Woodland Way
Cheyne Pk Dr
Old Beckenhamian RFC
Addington Rd
Hardcourts Cl
The Gld
Spring Park
London Loop
ADDINGTON ROAD
A2022
Shirley Wanderers RFC
Coney Hall
Layhams Road
Sylvan Way
Hawthorn Dr
Chestnut Avenue
Birch Tree Avenue
Lime Tree Walk
Cherry Tree Wk
Monarch Cl
Queensway
Rouse Farm
North Pole Lane
Nash Lane
Bromley
Croydon
North Walk
Underwood
The Lindens
Field Way
Foxcombe
Medical Centre
Castle Hill Primary School
Oakbank
Eddinton Close
Dunley Drive
Burford Wy
Merrow Wy
Pirbright Crs
Claygate Crs
Alford Gn
Good Shepherd RC Primary School
Headley Drive
Netley Close
Frimley Close
Brockham Crs
Mickleham Wy
Frensham Dr
Frimley Crs
Dunsfold Way
Horsley Dr
Avenue
New Addington
Wolsey Junior School
Goldcrest Wy
Walton Green
Castle Hill Av
Tilford Av
Betchworth Wy
King Henry's Drive
Wolsey Crescent
Aldrich Crescent
Shaxton Crescent
Grenville Road
Rothwell Road
Gascoigne Road
Queen Elizabeth's Drive
Kestrel Way
Rowdown Crs
Vulcan Business Centre
Vulcan Way
Addington Business Centre
Layhams Farm
Montacute Road
Lodge Lane
Surgery
King Henry's Drive
Parkway
North Downs Crs
Godric Crs
1 grid square represents 500 metres

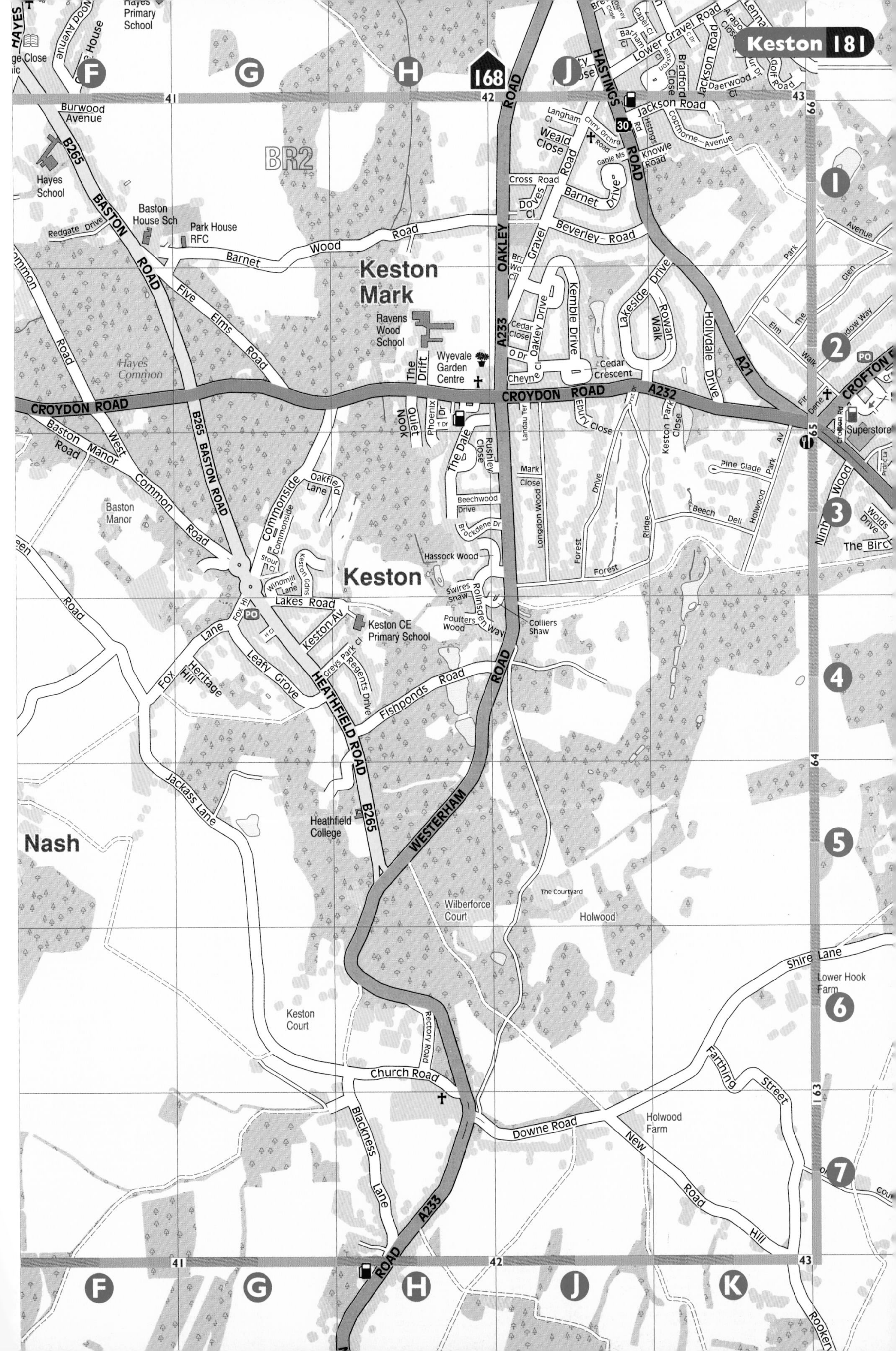
Keston
Keston Mark
Nash
BR2
CROYDON ROAD
A232
BASTON ROAD
B265
OAKLEY ROAD
A233
HASTINGS ROAD
A21
WESTERHAM ROAD
HEATHFIELD ROAD
Hayes School
Baston House Sch
Park House RFC
Barnet Wood Road
Ravens Wood School
Wyevale Garden Centre
Hayes Common
Baston Manor
Keston CE Primary School
Heathfield College
Wilberforce Court
Holwood
The Courtyard
Keston Court
Holwood Farm
Lower Hook Farm
Church Road
Downe Road
New Road Hill
Farthing Street
Shire Lane
Jackass Lane
Blackness Lane
Fishponds Road
Lakes Road
Commonside
Five Elms Road
West Common Road
Baston Manor Road
Hassock Wood
Colliers Shaw
Poulters Wood
Superstore
168
30

Abbey Wood 116 C3
Acton 86 E7
Acton Green 106 A3
Addington 179 J5
Addiscombe 165 G6
Aldborough Hatch 60 E3
Aldersbrook 59 G7
Alperton 68 A7
Anerley 165 H1
Arkley 25 K4
Ashford Common 140 B5
Avery Hill 135 H5
Balham 128 E6
Bandonhill 176 D4
Barking 78 D6
Barkingside 60 B2
Barnehurst 138 A2
Barnes 106 E7
Barnes Cray 138 E3
Barnet 26 D5
Barnet Gate 25 G5
Barnsbury 5 L1
Barwell 171 J6
Battersea 108 E6
Bayswater 8 E6
Beckenham 166 D1
Beckton 95 K5
Becontree 79 K4
Beddington 176 E1
Beddington Corner 163 F6
Bedford Park 106 C2
Belgravia 16 A5
Bell Green 151 H2
Bellingham 151 J3
Belmont 174 E7
Belmont 49 G1
Belvedere 117 J4
Benhilton 175 F2
Berrylands 159 G5
Bethnal Green 92 D2
Bexley 136 D3
Bexleyheath 137 G3
Bickley 168 D1
Blackfen 136 A5
Blackheath 133 J1
Blackheath Park 133 K3
Blackwall 94 B6
Bloomsbury 11 H2
Borehamwood 24 A2
The Borough 18 F2
Bow 93 J1
Bow Common 93 J4
Bowes Park 40 E5
Bowmans 138 C6
Brentford 104 E5
Brentford End 104 C5
Brimsdown 31 G1
Brixton 130 B3
Broad Green 164 C6
Brockley 132 C4
Bromley 168 A1
Bromley 93 K2
Bromley Common 168 C5
Bromley Park 152 C7
Brompton 15 J4
Brondesbury 70 C5
Brondesbury Park 70 B7
Brook Green 107 F2
Brunswick Park 40 A2
Buckhurst Hill 45 G2
Burnt Oak 37 F6
Bushey 22 C6
Bushey Heath 22 E6
Bushey Mead 161 G2
Bush Hill Park 30 A5
Caldecote Hill 23 F6
Camberwell 111 G7
Camden Town 4 B2
Canary Wharf 93 J7
Canning Town 95 F4
Cannon Hill 161 G3
Canonbury 6 E1
Canons Park 36 A6
Carpenders Park 33 K1
Carshalton 175 J3
Carshalton Beeches 175 J7
Carshalton on the Hill 175 K6
Castle Green 79 J7
Catford 133 F7
Chadwell Heath 61 K4
Charlton 114 C4
Cheam 174 C4
Chelsea 15 H8
Chessington 172 A5
Child's Hill 70 C1
China Town 11 H6
Chingford Hatch 44 C3
Chipping Barnet 26 C4
Chislehurst 154 C6
Chislehurst West 154 A5
Chiswick 106 C3
Church End 52 E1
Church End 69 H6
City of London 12 D6
Clapham 129 G1
Clapham Park 129 J5
Clapton Park 75 H3
Claremont Park 170 A6
Claygate 171 F5
Clayhall 59 K1
Clerkenwell 6 A9
Cockfosters 27 J4
Coldharbour 118 D3
Cole Park 124 B5
Colindale 51 G2
College Park 87 J2
Collier's Wood 147 H6
Colney Hatch 39 K5
Coney Hall 180 C3
Coombe 145 G6
Copse Hill 145 J6
Cottenham Park 145 K7
Cranbrook 60 A6
Cranford 101 K6
Cranley Gardens 54 A3
Crayford 138 D4
Creekmouth 96 E4
Cricklewood 70 B3
Crooked Billet 145 K5
Crouch End 54 C5
Croydon 177 K2
Crystal Palace 150 C5
Cubitt Town 113 F3
Custom House 95 J6
Dagenham 80 D6
Dartford 139 F6
Dartmouth Park 72 A1
Deacons Hill 24 C5
De Beauvoir Town 7 J3
Deptford 112 C5
Dollis Hill 69 K2
Dormer's Wells 84 B6
Downham 152 B4
Ducks Island 26 B6
Dudden Hill 69 J4
Dulwich 150 B1
Dulwich Village 131 F6
Ealing 85 J6
Earl's Court 14 A6
Earlsfield 128 B7
East Acton 87 H6
East Barnet 27 H6
East Bedfont 120 E6
Eastbury 32 D3
Eastcote 47 F6
Eastcote Village 47 F4
East Dulwich 131 H4
East Finchley 53 H2
East Ham 95 J1
East Molesey 157 H4
East Sheen 126 A4
East Wickham 116 B7
Eden Park 166 C3
Edgware 36 D3
Edmonton 42 A3
Elmers End 166 A2
Elm Park 81 K4
Elmstead 153 J4
Elstree 24 A5
Eltham 134 D5
Enfield 29 J3
Enfield Highway 30 E1
Enfield Town 29 K2
Erith 118 C4
Esher 170 C3
Ewell 173 J7
Fair Cross 79 F4
Falconwood 135 K3
Feltham 141 F1
Felthamhill 140 C5
Field Common 156 E6
Finchley 38 E7
Finsbury 6 A7
Finsbury Park 72 E1
Foots Cray 155 H5
Forestdale 179 G7
Forest Gate 76 E4
Forest Hill 132 A7
Fortis Green 53 K3
Foxbury 154 D4
Friday Hill 44 B2
Friern Barnet 39 J3
Fulham 107 G6
Furzedown 148 B3
Gants Hill 59 K5
Gidea Park 63 H1
Giggshill 158 B6
Globe Town 93 F2
Golders Green 52 C5
Goodmayes 79 H1
Gospel Oak 72 A4
Grange Park 29 G4
Greenford 84 D3
Greenhill 49 F4
Greenwich 113 G4
Grove Park 106 A7
Grove Park 153 G2
Hackbridge 176 B1
Hackney 74 E5
Hackney Wick 75 J5
Hadley 26 D2
Haggerston 7 M5
Hale End 44 B5
Ham 143 K2
Hammersmith 106 E3
Hampstead 71 H3
Hampstead Garden Suburb 53 F4
Hampton 142 B7
Hampton Hill 142 C3
Hampton Wick 143 H7
Hanwell 84 D7
Hanworth 141 H2
Harlesden 87 G1
Harlington 101 F5
Harmondsworth 100 A5
Harringay 55 G4
Harrow 48 D5
Harrow on the Hill 48 E7
Harrow Weald 34 E6
Hatch End 33 J6
Hatton 121 H3
Hayes 82 A4
Hayes 168 A6
Hayes End 82 B3
Hayes Town 83 G7
Headstone 48 B3
Heath Park 63 K5
Hendon 51 K4
Herne Hill 130 D5
Heston 102 E6
Higham Hill 57 G1
Highams Park 43 K6
High Barnet 26 A2
Highbury 73 H4
Highgate 53 K6
Highwood Hill 37 H1
Hinchley Wood 171 F2
Hither Green 133 H5
Holborn 11 L3
Holders Hill 38 B7
Holywell 20 C5
Homerton 75 F5
Honor Oak 132 A5
Honor Oak Park 132 B5
Hook 172 A4
Hornsey 54 E3
Hornsey Vale 55 F4
Hounslow 123 F1
Hounslow West 122 C2
Hoxton 7 J6
Hurst Park 157 H1
The Hyde 51 H4
Ilford 78 B2
Isle of Dogs 113 F3
Isleworth 124 C2
Islington 6 A3
Kennington 109 K5
Kensal Green 88 A1
Kensal Rise 88 B1
Kensal Town 88 C3
Kensington 14 C4
Kentish Town 72 C5
Kenton 49 J4
Keston 181 H3
Keston Mark 181 H2
Kew 105 G6
Kidbrooke 134 B1
Kilburn 70 C7
Kingsbury 50 D5
Kingsland 7 J1
Kingston upon Thames 158 D2
Kingston Vale 145 F4
Knightsbridge 15 K1
Knight's Hill 130 D7
Ladywell 132 D3
Lambeth 18 A3
Lampton 103 G7
Lea Bridge 75 F2
Lee 133 J5
Lessness Heath 117 J5
Lewisham 133 F3
Leyton 76 B2
Leytonstone 58 D7
Limehouse 93 G6
Lisson Grove 9 M2
Little Heath 61 J3
Little Ilford 78 A4
Little Stanmore 36 B7
Long Ditton 158 C7
Longlands 154 C2
Lower Clapton 74 E3
Lower Edmonton 42 A1
Lower Feltham 140 C2
Lower Green 170 B1
Lower Holloway 73 F4
Lower Place 86 E1
Lower Sydenham 151 F3
Loxford 78 C4
Maida Vale 2 C7
Maitland Park 71 K5
Manor Park 77 J3
Marks Gate 62 A1
Marylebone 10 A3
Mayfair 10 C7
Maypole 138 B7
Merry Hill 34 B2
Merton 146 E7
Merton Park 161 J1
Mile End 93 G3
Mill Hill 37 J4
Mill Meads 94 B1
Millwall 112 E2
Mitcham 163 F2
Monken Hadley 26 C1
Monks Orchard 165 K6
Moor Park 32 A3
Morden 161 K3
Morden Park 161 H5
Mortlake 125 K1
Motspur Park 160 D5
Mottingham 153 G1
Muswell Hill 54 A1
Nash 181 F5
Neasden 69 F3
New Addington 180 B6
New Barnet 27 F4
New Beckenham 151 G5
Newbury Park 60 D5
New Charlton 114 C3
New Cross 132 B1
New Cross Gate 112 B7
New Eltham 154 B1
Newington 18 B4
New Malden 160 C2
New Southgate 40 C3
New Town 139 J5
Noel Park 55 H1
Norbiton 159 G1
Norbury 164 C1
North Acton 86 E3
North Cheam 174 B2
North End 118 C7
North End 53 G7
North Feltham 122 A4
North Finchley 39 G5
North Harrow 47 K5
North Hyde 102 D3
North Kensington 88 B4
Northolt 66 A6
North Sheen 125 J1
Northumberland Heath 117 K6
North Wembley 49 H7
Northwood 32 A7
Northwood Hills 46 B1
North Woolwich 114 D1
Norwood Green 103 F3
Norwood New Town 149 K5
Notting Hill 88 C6
Nunhead 131 K3
Oakleigh Park 39 H1
Oakwood 28 D5
Old Bexley 137 H6
Old Ford 75 G7
Old Malden 160 A6
Old Oak Common 87 H3
Olympic Park 75 J6
Osidge 40 C1
Osterley 103 H6
Oxhey 21 H5
Paddington 9 G3
Palmers Green 40 E2
Park Langley 167 F5
Park Royal 86 C2
Parsons Green 127 K1
Peckham 131 J1
Penge 150 E6
Pentonville 5 M5
Perivale 67 J7
Petersham 125 F7
Petts Wood 169 J3
Pimlico 16 E7
Pinner 47 H3
Pinner Green 47 G1
Pinnerwood Park 33 G6
Plaistow 94 D2
Plaistow 152 E5
Plashet 77 H5
Plumstead 115 H4
Plumstead Common 116 A5
Ponders End 30 E4
Poplar 93 J6
Preston 49 K7
Primrose Hill 4 B4
Purfleet 119 K4
Putney 127 G4
Putney Heath 127 F6
Putney Vale 145 J2
Queensbury 50 A2
Queen's Park 88 C1
Rainham 99 K2
Rayners Lane 47 K7
Raynes Park 161 F2
Redbridge 59 G4
Regent's Park 4 D6
Richmond 125 F4
Richmond Hill 125 F5
Roehampton 126 C4
Romford 62 E4
The Rookery 20 E6
Rosehill 162 A7
Rotherhithe 112 A2
Roundshaw 177 F5
Rowley Green 25 H3
Roxeth 66 C1
Ruislip 46 C5
Ruislip Common 46 A3
Ruislip Gardens 64 C2
Ruislip Manor 64 E1
Rush Green 63 F6
St Giles 11 H4
St Helier 162 B7
St James's 11 G9
St Johns 132 D1
St John's Wood 2 F4
St Luke's 6 F9
St Margarets 124 D5
St Pancras 5 K8
St George in the East 92 C6
Sands End 108 B7
Seething Wells 158 C5
Selhurst 164 E4
Seven Kings 60 E7
Shacklewell 74 C3
Shadwell 92 E6
Shepherd's Bush 87 K7
Shirley 178 E1
Shooters Hill 115 H7
Shoreditch 7 H8
Shortlands 167 H2
Sidcup 155 H3
Silvertown 114 B1
Sipson 100 C4
Slade Green 138 D1
Soho 11 G5
Somers Town 5 G6
Southall 102 C1
South Beddington 176 D5
Southborough 168 E5
South Bromley 94 B5
South Croydon 177 H5
Southend 152 A3
Southfields 127 K7
Southgate 28 E7
South Hackney 74 E7
South Hampstead 2 F1
South Harrow 66 B2
South Hornchurch 81 F7
South Kensington 14 E6
South Lambeth 109 K6
South Norwood 164 E2
South Oxhey 33 F2
South Ruislip 65 H3
South Tottenham 56 A4
South Wimbledon 147 G4
South Woodford 58 E1
Spitalfields 92 C4
Spitalfields 13 L2
Spring Grove 103 J7
Spring Park 179 J1
Stamford Hill 56 B6
Stanmore 35 H4
Stanwell 120 A5
Stepney 92 E4
Stockwell 129 K2
Stoke Newington 74 B1
Stoneleigh 173 H4
Strand 11 J6
Stratford 76 A6
Stratford Marsh 76 A7
Strawberry Hill 142 D2
Streatham 148 E4
Streatham Hill 129 K7
Streatham Park 148 C3
Streatham Vale 148 B6
Stroud Green 55 G5
Sudbury 67 F4
Summerstown 147 H1
Sunbury 140 C7
Sunbury Common 140 D6
Sundridge 153 G5
Surbiton 158 D7
Sutton 175 G4
Swiss Cottage 3 H3
Sydenham 151 F4
Teddington 142 D5
Temple Hill 139 G3
Thames Ditton 158 B6
Thamesmead 97 G6
Thornton Heath 164 C2
Tokyngton 68 D5
Tolworth 159 H7
Tooting 147 K4
Tooting Graveney 147 H4
Tottenham 56 A1
Tottenham Hale 56 B2
Totteridge 26 D7
Totteridge Green 26 A7
Tufnell Park 72 C3
Tulse Hill 130 C7
Twickenham 123 K7
Underhill 26 E5
Upper Clapton 56 C7
Upper Edmonton 42 C3
Upper Elmers End 166 C4
Upper Holloway 54 C7
Upper Norwood 149 K7
Upper Shirley 178 E3
Upper Sydenham 150 C3
Upper Tooting 147 J2
Upper Walthamstow 58 A3
Upton 77 F6
Upton Park 77 G7
Vale of Health 71 H2
Vauxhall 17 K8
Waddon 176 E1
Walham Green 107 K7
Wallend 78 A7
Wallington 176 A4
Walthamstow 57 H3
Walworth 18 F8
Wandle Park 177 G1
Wandsworth 127 K3
Wanstead 59 F6
Wapping 92 D7
Watford 20 D2
Watford Heath 21 J6
Wealdstone 49 G2
Welling 136 C2
Welsh Harp 51 F7
Wembley 68 A3
Wembley Park 68 C2
West Acton 86 C5
West Barnes 161 F4
West Bedfont 120 C6
West Brompton 14 C9
West Drayton 100 A2
West Dulwich 149 K1
West Ealing 85 G7
West Ewell 173 F5
West Green 55 J2
West Hampstead 70 E4
West Harrow 48 C6
West Heath 116 E5
West Heath 71 F1
West Hendon 51 J6
West Hill 127 H6
West Kensington 107 G4
West Kilburn 88 C2
Westminster 16 F4
West Molesey 156 E3
West Norwood 149 J3
Weston Green 157 K7
West Ruislip 46 A7
West Watford 20 E4
West Wickham 167 G7
Whetstone 39 F1
Whitechapel 92 C5
Whitechapel 13 M6
Whitton 123 H5
Widmore 168 C1
Willesden 69 J5
Willesden Green 69 K6
Wimbledon 146 C4
Winchmore Hill 29 J7
Wood End 82 C5
Wood End Green 82 C4
Woodford 45 F5
Woodford Bridge 45 K6
Woodford Green 44 E6
Woodford Wells 45 F2
Wood Green 41 G7
Woodlands 123 J2
Woodside 165 H5
Woodside Park 38 E3
Woolwich 115 F2
Worcester Park 173 K1
World's End 29 G3
The Wrythe 175 J1
Yeading 83 G3

USING THE STREET INDEX

Street names are listed alphabetically. Each street name is followed by its postal town or area locality, the Postcode District, the page number, and the reference to the square in which the name is found.

Standard index entries are shown as follows:

1 Av *WOOL/PLUM* SE18.............. **115** G2

Street names and selected addresses not shown on the map due to scale restrictions are shown in the index with an asterisk:

Abbeville Ms *CLAP* SW4 * **129** J4

Entries in red indicate streets located within the London Congestion Zone. Refer to the map pages for the location of the Zone boundary

GENERAL ABBREVIATIONS

ACC	ACCESS
ALY	ALLEY
AP	APPROACH
AR	ARCADE
ASS	ASSOCIATION
AV	AVENUE
BCH	BEACH
BLDS	BUILDINGS
BND	BEND
BNK	BANK
BR	BRIDGE
BRK	BROOK
BTM	BOTTOM
BUS	BUSINESS
BVD	BOULEVARD
BY	BYPASS
CATH	CATHEDRAL
CEM	CEMETERY
CEN	CENTRE
CFT	CROFT
CH	CHURCH
CHA	CHASE
CHYD	CHURCHYARD
CIR	CIRCLE
CIRC	CIRCUS
CL	CLOSE
CLFS	CLIFFS
CMP	CAMP
CNR	CORNER
CO	COUNTY
COLL	COLLEGE
COM	COMMON
COMM	COMMISSION
CON	CONVENT
COT	COTTAGE
COTS	COTTAGES
CP	CAPE
CPS	COPSE
CR	CREEK
CREM	CREMATORIUM
CRS	CRESCENT
CSWY	CAUSEWAY
CT	COURT
CTRL	CENTRAL
CTS	COURTS

CTYD	COURTYARD
CUTT	CUTTINGS
CV	COVE
CYN	CANYON
DEPT	DEPARTMENT
DL	DALE
DM	DAM
DR	DRIVE
DRO	DROVE
DRY	DRIVEWAY
DWGS	DWELLINGS
E	EAST
EMB	EMBANKMENT
EMBY	EMBASSY
ESP	ESPLANADE
EST	ESTATE
EX	EXCHANGE
EXPY	EXPRESSWAY
EXT	EXTENSION
F/O	FLYOVER
FC	FOOTBALL CLUB
FK	FORK
FLD	FIELD
FLDS	FIELDS
FLS	FALLS
FM	FARM
FT	FORT
FTS	FLATS
FWY	FREEWAY
FY	FERRY
GA	GATE
GAL	GALLERY
GDN	GARDEN
GDNS	GARDENS
GLD	GLADE
GLN	GLEN
GN	GREEN
GND	GROUND
GRA	GRANGE
GRG	GARAGE
GT	GREAT
GTWY	GATEWAY
GV	GROVE
HGR	HIGHER
HL	HILL

HLS	HILLS
HO	HOUSE
HOL	HOLLOW
HOSP	HOSPITAL
HRB	HARBOUR
HTH	HEATH
HTS	HEIGHTS
HVN	HAVEN
HWY	HIGHWAY
IMP	IMPERIAL
IN	INLET
IND EST	INDUSTRIAL ESTATE
INF	INFIRMARY
INFO	INFORMATION
INT	INTERCHANGE
IS	ISLAND
JCT	JUNCTION
JTY	JETTY
KG	KING
KNL	KNOLL
L	LAKE
LA	LANE
LDG	LODGE
LGT	LIGHT
LK	LOCK
LKS	LAKES
LNDG	LANDING
LTL	LITTLE
LWR	LOWER
MAG	MAGISTRATE
MAN	MANSIONS
MD	MEAD
MDW	MEADOWS
MEM	MEMORIAL
MI	MILL
MKT	MARKET
MKTS	MARKETS
ML	MALL
MNR	MANOR
MS	MEWS
MSN	MISSION
MT	MOUNT
MTN	MOUNTAIN
MTS	MOUNTAINS
MUS	MUSEUM

MWY	MOTORWAY
N	NORTH
NE	NORTH EAST
NW	NORTH WEST
O/P	OVERPASS
OFF	OFFICE
ORCH	ORCHARD
OV	OVAL
PAL	PALACE
PAS	PASSAGE
PAV	PAVILION
PDE	PARADE
PH	PUBLIC HOUSE
PK	PARK
PKWY	PARKWAY
PL	PLACE
PLN	PLAIN
PLNS	PLAINS
PLZ	PLAZA
POL	POLICE STATION
PR	PRINCE
PREC	PRECINCT
PREP	PREPARATORY
PRIM	PRIMARY
PROM	PROMENADE
PRS	PRINCESS
PRT	PORT
PT	POINT
PTH	PATH
PZ	PIAZZA
QD	QUADRANT
QU	QUEEN
QY	QUAY
R	RIVER
RBT	ROUNDABOUT
RD	ROAD
RDG	RIDGE
REP	REPUBLIC
RES	RESERVOIR
RFC	RUGBY FOOTBALL CLUB
RI	RISE
RP	RAMP
RW	ROW
S	SOUTH
SCH	SCHOOL

SE	SOUTH EAST
SER	SERVICE AREA
SH	SHORE
SHOP	SHOPPING
SKWY	SKYWAY
SMT	SUMMIT
SOC	SOCIETY
SP	SPUR
SPR	SPRING
SQ	SQUARE
ST	STREET
STN	STATION
STR	STREAM
STRD	STRAND
SW	SOUTH WEST
TDG	TRADING
TER	TERRACE
THWY	THROUGHWAY
TNL	TUNNEL
TOLL	TOLLWAY
TPK	TURNPIKE
TR	TRACK
TRL	TRAIL
TWR	TOWER
U/P	UNDERPASS
UNI	UNIVERSITY
UPR	UPPER
V	VALE
VA	VALLEY
VIAD	VIADUCT
VIL	VILLA
VIS	VISTA
VLG	VILLAGE
VLS	VILLAS
VW	VIEW
W	WEST
WD	WOOD
WHF	WHARF
WK	WALK
WKS	WALKS
WLS	WELLS
WY	WAY
YD	YARD
YHA	YOUTH HOSTEL

POSTCODE TOWNS AND AREA ABBREVIATIONS

ABYW	Abbey Wood
ACT	Acton
ALP/SUD	Alperton/ Sudbury
ARCH	Archway
ASHF	Ashford (Surrey)
BAL	Balham
BANK	Bank
BAR	Barnet
BARB	Barbican
BARK	Barking
BARK/HLT	Barkingside/ Hainault
BARN	Barnes
BAY/PAD	Bayswater/ Paddington
BCTR	Becontree
BECK	Beckenham
BELMT	Belmont
BELV	Belvedere
BERM/RHTH	Bermondsey/ Rotherhithe
BETH	Bethnal Green
BFN/LL	Blackfen/Longlands
BGVA	Belgravia
BKHH	Buckhurst Hill
BKHTH/KID	Blackheath/Kidbrooke
BLKFR	Blackfriars
BMLY	Bromley
BMSBY	Bloomsbury
BORE	Borehamwood
BOW	Bow
BROCKY	Brockley
BRXN/ST	Brixton north/ Stockwell
BRXS/STRHM	Brixton south/ Streatham Hill
BRYLDS	Berrylands
BTFD	Brentford
BTSEA	Battersea
BUSH	Bushey
BXLY	Bexley
BXLYHN	Bexleyheath north
BXLYHS	Bexleyheath south
CAMTN	Camden Town
CAN/RD	Canning Town/ Royal Docks
CANST	Cannon Street station
CAR	Carshalton
CAT	Catford
CAVSQ/HST	Cavendish Square/ Harley Street
CDALE/KGS	Colindale/ Kingsbury
CEND/HSY/T	Crouch End/ Hornsey/ Turnpike Lane
CHARL	Charlton
CHCR	Charing Cross
CHDH	Chadwell Heath
CHEAM	Cheam
CHEL	Chelsea
CHIG	Chigwell
CHING	Chingford
CHSGTN	Chessington
CHST	Chislehurst
CHSWK	Chiswick
CITYW	City of London west
CLAP	Clapham
CLAY	Clayhall

CLKNW	Clerkenwell
CLPT	Clapton
CMBW	Camberwell
CONDST	Conduit Street
COVGDN	Covent Garden
CRICK	Cricklewood
CROY/NA	Croydon/ New Addington
CRW	Collier Row
DAGE	Dagenham east
DAGW	Dagenham west
DART	Dartford
DEN/HRF	Denham/ Harefield
DEPT	Deptford
DUL	Dulwich
E/WMO/HCT	East & West Molesey/ Hampton Court
EA	Ealing
EBAR	East Barnet
EBED/NFELT	East Bedfont/ North Feltham
ECT	Earl's Court
ED	Edmonton
EDGW	Edgware
EDUL	East Dulwich
EFNCH	East Finchley
EHAM	East Ham
ELTH/MOT	Eltham/ Mottingham
EMB	Embankment
EMPK	Emerson Park
EN	Enfield
ENC/FH	Enfield Chase/ Forty Hill
ERITH	Erith
ERITHM	Erith Marshes
ESH/CLAY	Esher/ Claygate
EW	Ewell
FARR	Farringdon
FBAR/BDGN	Friern Barnet/ Bounds Green
FELT	Feltham
FENCHST	Fenchurch Street
FITZ	Fitzrovia
FLST/FETLN	Fleet Street/ Fetter Lane
FNCH	Finchley
FSBYE	Finsbury east
FSBYPK	Finsbury Park
FSBYW	Finsbury west
FSTGT	Forest Gate
FSTH	Forest Hill
FUL/PGN	Fulham/Parsons Green
GDMY/SEVK	Goodmayes/ Seven Kings
GFD/PVL	Greenford/ Perivale
GINN	Gray's Inn
GLDGN	Golders Green
GNTH/NBYPK	Gants Hill/ Newbury Park
GNWCH	Greenwich
GPK	Gidea Park
GSTN	Garston
GTPST	Great Portland Street
GWRST	Gower Street
HACK	Hackney
HAMP	Hampstead

HAYES	Hayes
HBRY	Highbury
HCH	Hornchurch
HCIRC	Holborn Circus
HDN	Hendon
HDTCH	Houndsditch
HEST	Heston
HGDN/ICK	Hillingdon/ Ickenham
HGT	Highgate
HHOL	High Holborn
HMSMTH	Hammersmith
HNHL	Herne Hill
HNWL	Hanwell
HOL/ALD	Holborn/ Aldwych
HOLWY	Holloway
HOM	Homerton
HOR/WEW	Horton/West Ewell
HPTN	Hampton
HRW	Harrow
HSLW	Hounslow
HSLWW	Hounslow west
HTHAIR	Heathrow Airport
HYS/HAR	Hayes/ Harlington
IL	Ilford
IS	Islington
ISLW	Isleworth
KCROSS	King's Cross
KENS	Kensington
KIL/WHAMP	Kilburn/ West Hampstead
KTBR	Knightsbridge
KTN/HRWW/WS	Kenton/ Harrow Weald/Wealdstone
KTTN	Kentish Town
KUT/HW	Kingston upon Thames/ Hampton Wick
KUTN/CMB	Kingston upon Thames north/ Coombe
LBTH	Lambeth
LEE/GVPK	Lee/ Grove Park
LEW	Lewisham
LEY	Leyton
LINN	Lincoln's Inn
LOTH	Lothbury
LSQ/SEVD	Leicester Square/ Seven Dials
LVPST	Liverpool Street
MANHO	Mansion House
MBLAR	Marble Arch
MHST	Marylebone High Street
MLHL	Mill Hill
MNPK	Manor Park
MON	Monument
MORT/ESHN	Mortlake/ East Sheen
MRDN	Morden
MTCM	Mitcham
MUSWH	Muswell Hill
MV/WKIL	Maida Vale/ West Kilburn
MYFR/PICC	Mayfair/ Piccadilly
MYFR/PKLN	Mayfair/ Park Lane
NFNCH/WDSPK	North Finchley/ Woodside Park

NKENS	North Kensington
NOXST/BSQ	New Oxford Street/ Bloomsbury Square
NRWD	Norwood
NTGHL	Notting Hill
NTHLT	Northolt
NTHWD	Northwood
NWCR	New Cross
NWDGN	Norwood Green
NWMAL	New Malden
OBST	Old Broad Street
OLYMPICPK	Olympic Park
ORP	Orpington
OXHEY	Oxhey
OXSTW	Oxford Street west
PECK	Peckham
PEND	Ponders End
PGE/AN	Penge/ Anerley
PIM	Pimlico
PIN	Pinner
PLMGR	Palmers Green
PLSTW	Plaistow
POP/IOD	Poplar/ Isle of Dogs
PUR	Purfleet
PUR/KEN	Purley/Kenley
PUT/ROE	Putney/ Roehampton
RAIN	Rainham (Gt Lon)
RCH/KEW	Richmond/Kew
RCHPK/HAM	Richmond Park/Ham
RDART	Rural Dartford
REDBR	Redbridge
REGST	Regent Street
RKW/CH/CXG	Rickmansworth/ Chorleywood/ Croxley Green
ROM	Romford
ROMW/RG	Romford west/ Rush Green
RSLP	Ruislip
RSQ	Russell Square
RYLN/HDSTN	Rayners Lane/ Headstone
RYNPK	Raynes Park
SAND/SEL	Sanderstead/Selsdon
SCUP	Sidcup
SDTCH	Shoreditch
SEVS/STOTM	Seven Sisters/ South Tottenham
SHB	Shepherd's Bush
SHPTN	Shepperton
SKENS	South Kensington
SNWD	South Norwood
SOCK/AV	South Ockendon/ Aveley
SOHO/CST	Soho/Carnaby Street
SOHO/SHAV	Soho/ Shaftesbury Avenue
SRTFD	Stratford
STAN	Stanmore
STBT	St Bart's
STHGT/OAK	Southgate/ Oakwood
STHL	Southall
STHWK	Southwark
STJS	St James's
STJSPK	St James's Park
STJWD	St John's Wood

STKPK	Stockley Park
STLK	St Luke's
STMC/STPC	St Mary Cray/ St Paul's Cray
STNW/STAM	Stoke Newington/ Stamford Hill
STP	St Paul's
STPAN	St Pancras
STRHM/NOR	Streatham/Norbury
STWL/WRAY	Stanwell/Wraysbury
SUN	Sunbury
SURB	Surbiton
SUT	Sutton
SWFD	South Woodford
SYD	Sydenham
TEDD	Teddington
THDIT	Thames Ditton
THHTH	Thornton Heath
THMD	Thamesmead
TOOT	Tooting
TOTM	Tottenham
TPL/STR	Temple/ Strand
TRDG/WHET	Totteridge/ Whetstone
TWK	Twickenham
TWRH	Tower Hill
UED	Upper Edmonton
UX/CGN	Uxbridge/ Colham Green
VX/NE	Vauxhall/ Nine Elms
WALTH	Walthamstow
WALW	Walworth
WAN	Wanstead
WAND/EARL	Wandsworth/ Earlsfield
WAP	Wapping
WAT	Watford
WATN	Watford north
WATW	Watford west
WBLY	Wembley
WBPTN	West Brompton
WCHMH	Winchmore Hill
WCHPL	Whitechapel
WDGN	Wood Green
WDR/YW	West Drayton/ Yiewsley
WEA	West Ealing
WELL	Welling
WEST	Westminster
WESTW	Westminster west
WFD	Woodford
WHALL	Whitehall
WHTN	Whitton
WIM/MER	Wimbledon/ Merton
WKENS	West Kensington
WLGTN	Wallington
WLSDN	Willesden
WNWD	West Norwood
WOOL/PLUM	Woolwich/ Plumstead
WOT/HER	Walton-on-Thames/ Hersham
WPK	Worcester Park
WWKM	West Wickham
YEAD	Yeading

1

1 Av WOOL/PLUM SE18 115 G2

A

Aaron Hill Rd EHAM E6 96 A4
Abberley Ms BTSEA SW11 129 G2
Abbess Cl BRXS/STRHM SW2 130 C7
Abbeville Ms CLAP SW4 * 129 J4
Abbeville Rd CEND/HSY/T N8 54 D3
CLAP SW4 129 H5
Abbey Av ALP/SUD HA0 86 A1
Abbey Cl HYS/HAR UB3 83 F7
NTHLT UB5 83 K2
PIN HA5 47 F2
ROM RM1 63 H5
Abbey Crs BELV DA17 117 H3
Abbeydale Rd ALP/SUD HA0 68 B7
Abbey Dr TOOT SW17 148 A4
Abbeyfield Cl MTCM CR4 162 D1
Abbeyfield Est
BERM/RHTH SE16 111 K3
Abbeyfield Rd
BERM/RHTH SE16 111 K3
Abbeyfields Cl WLSDN NW10 86 C2
Abbey Gdns CHST BR7 154 A7
HMSMTH W6 107 H5
STHWK SE1 111 H3
STJWD NW8 2 E6
Abbey Gv ABYW SE2 116 C3
Abbeyhill Rd BFN/LL DA15 136 D7
Abbey La BECK BR3 151 J6
SRTFD E15 94 A1
Abbey Ms ISLW TW7 104 C7
WALTH E17 57 J4
Abbey Mt BELV DA17 117 G4
Abbey Orchard St WEST SW1P 17 H3
Abbey Pk BECK BR3 151 J6
Abbey Pl DART DA1 * 139 G4
Abbey Rd BARK IG11 78 B7
BELV DA17 116 E3
BXLYHN DA7 137 F3
CROY/NA CR0 177 H2
EN EN1 30 A4
GNTH/NBYPK IG2 60 D4
KIL/WHAMP NW6 2 C3
SRTFD E15 76 C7
WIM/MER SW19 147 G6
WLSDN NW10 86 D1
Abbey St PLSTW E13 94 E3
STHWK SE1 19 L3
Abbey Ter ABYW SE2 116 D2
Abbey Vw MLHL NW7 37 H2
Abbey Wk E/WMO/HCT KT8 157 G2
Abbey Wood Rd ABYW SE2 116 C3
Abbot Cl RSLP HA4 65 H2
Abbotsbury Cl SRTFD E15 94 A1
WKENS W14 107 H1
Abbotsbury Gdns PIN HA5 47 G5
Abbotsbury Ms PECK SE15 131 K2
Abbotsbury Rd MRDN SM4 162 A3
WKENS W14 107 H1
WWKM BR4 180 D1
Abbots Cl STMC/STPC BR5 169 H7
Abbots Dr RYLN/HDSTN HA2 66 A1
Abbotsford Av
SEVS/STOTM N15 55 J3
Abbotsford Gdns WFD IG8 44 E6
Abbotsford Rd
GDMY/SEVK IG3 79 G1
Abbots Gdns EFNCH N2 53 H3
Abbots Gn CROY/NA CR0 179 F5
Abbotshade Rd
BERM/RHTH SE16 * 93 F7
Abbotshall Av
STHGT/OAK N14 40 C2
Abbotshall Rd CAT SE6 133 G7
Abbotsleigh Cl BELMT SM2 175 F6
Abbotsleigh Rd
STRHM/NOR SW16 148 C3
Abbots Mnr PIM SW1V 16 C7
Abbots Manor Est PIM SW1V 16 C6
Abbotsmede Cl TWK TW1 143 F1
Abbots Pk BRXS/STRHM SW2 130 B7
Abbot's Pl KIL/WHAMP NW6 2 C3
Abbots Rd EDGW HA8 37 F6
EHAM E6 77 H7
Abbots Ter CEND/HSY/T N8 54 E5
Abbotstone Rd
PUT/ROE SW15 127 F2
Abbot St HACK E8 74 B5
Abbots Wk KENS W8 * 14 C4
Abbots Wy BECK BR3 166 B4
Abbotswell Rd BROCKY SE4 132 C4
Abbotswood Cl BELV DA17 117 F2
Abbotswood Gdns CLAY IG5 59 K2
Abbotswood Rd EDUL SE22 131 F3
STRHM/NOR SW16 148 D2
Abbotswood Wy
HYS/HAR UB3 83 F7
Abbott Av RYNPK SW20 161 G1
Abbott Cl HPTN TW12 141 J5
NTHLT UB5 65 K5
Abbott Rd POP/IOD E14 94 A4
Abbotts Cl IS N1 * 6 E1
ROMW/RG RM7 62 D2
THMD SE28 97 J6
Abbotts Crs CHING E4 44 B3
ENC/FH EN2 29 H1
Abbotts Dr ALP/SUD HA0 67 H1
Abbotts Md
RCHPK/HAM TW10 * 143 J3
Abbotts Park Rd LEY E10 58 A6
Abbotts Rd BAR EN5 27 F3
CHEAM SM3 174 C3
MTCM CR4 163 H3
STHL UB1 83 J7
Abbott's Wk BXLYHN DA7 116 E6
Abchurch La MANHO EC4N 13 H6
Abdale Rd SHB W12 87 K7
Aberavon Rd BOW E3 93 G2
Abercairn Rd
STRHM/NOR SW16 148 C6
Aberconway Rd MRDN SM4 162 A2
Abercorn Cl MLHL NW7 38 C6
STJWD NW8 2 E6
Abercorn Crs
RYLN/HDSTN HA2 48 B7
Abercorn Dell BUSH WD23 34 C1
Abercorn Gdns CHDH RM6 61 H5
KTN/HRWW/WS HA3 49 K6
Abercorn Gv RSLP HA4 46 B3
Abercorn Ms
RCHPK/HAM TW10 125 G4
Abercorn Pl STJWD NW8 2 E7
Abercorn Rd MLHL NW7 38 C6
STAN HA7 35 J6
Abercorn Wk STJWD NW8 2 E7
Abercorn Wy STHWK SE1 111 H4
Abercrombie St BTSEA SW11 128 D1
Aberdare Cl WWKM BR4 180 A1
Aberdare Gdns
KIL/WHAMP NW6 2 D2
MLHL NW7 38 B6
Aberdare Rd PEND EN3 30 E3
Aberdeen Cots STAN HA7 * 35 J6
Aberdeen La HBRY N5 73 H4
Aberdeen Pde UED N18 * 42 D4
Aberdeen Pk HBRY N5 73 H4
Aberdeen Pl BAY/PAD W2 9 G1
Aberdeen Rd CROY/NA CR0 177 J3
HBRY N5 73 J3
KTN/HRWW/WS HA3 49 F1
UED N18 42 C4
WLSDN NW10 69 H4
Aberdeen Ter BKHTH/KID SE3 133 G1
Aberdour Rd GDMY/SEVK IG3 79 H2
Aberdour St STHWK SE1 19 J5
Aberfeldy St POP/IOD E14 94 A5
Aberford Gdns
WOOL/PLUM SE18 114 D7
Aberford Rd BORE WD6 24 C1
Aberfoyle Rd
STRHM/NOR SW16 148 D6
Abergeldie Rd LEE/GVPK SE12 134 A5
Abernethy Rd LEW SE13 133 H3
Abersham Rd HACK E8 74 B4
Abery St WOOL/PLUM SE18 115 K3
Abingdon Cl WIM/MER SW19 147 G5
WPK KT4 173 K2
Abingdon Rd FNCH N3 53 G1
KENS W8 14 B4
STRHM/NOR SW16 148 E7
Abingdon St WEST SW1P 17 J2
Abingdon Vls KENS W8 14 A4
Abinger Av BELMT SM2 174 A7
Abinger Cl BMLY BR1 168 D2
CROY/NA CR0 180 A5
GDMY/SEVK IG3 79 G3
WLGTN SM6 176 E4
Abinger Dr NRWD SE19 149 J6
Abinger Gdns ISLW TW7 123 K2
Abinger Gv DEPT SE8 112 C5
Abinger Ms MV/WKIL W9 2 A9
Abinger Rd CHSWK W4 106 C2
Ablett St BERM/RHTH SE16 111 K4
Abney Park Ter
STNW/STAM N16 * 74 B1
Aboyne Dr RYNPK SW20 160 D1
Aboyne Rd TOOT SW17 147 G2
WLSDN NW10 69 G2
Abraham Cl OXHEY WD19 33 F3
Abridge Wy BARK IG11 97 H1
Abyssinia Cl BTSEA SW11 128 D3
Abyssinia Rd BTSEA SW11 * 128 D3
Acacia Av BTFD TW8 104 C6
HCH RM12 81 H1
HYS/HAR UB3 82 D5
RSLP HA4 46 E7
TOTM N17 41 K6
WBLY HA9 68 A4
Acacia Cl DEPT SE8 112 B3
STAN HA7 34 E5
STMC/STPC BR5 169 J4
Acacia Dr CHEAM SM3 161 J7
Acacia Gdns STJWD NW8 3 H5
WWKM BR4 180 A1
Acacia Gv DUL SE21 149 K1
NWMAL KT3 160 B2
Acacia Ms WDR/YW UB7 100 A5
Acacia Pl STJWD NW8 3 H5
Acacia Rd ACT W3 86 E6
BECK BR3 166 C2
DART DA1 139 F7
HPTN TW12 142 A5
MTCM CR4 163 F1
STJWD NW8 3 H5
STRHM/NOR SW16 148 E7
WALTH E17 57 G5
WAN E11 76 C1
WDGN N22 41 G7
The Acacias EBAR EN4 * 27 H4
Acacia Wy BFN/LL DA15 136 A6
Academia Wy TOTM N17 42 A5
Academy Fields Rd GPK RM2 63 K4
Academy Gdns CROY/NA CR0 165 G7
NTHLT UB5 83 H1
Academy Pl ISLW TW7 103 K6
WOOL/PLUM SE18 114 E7
Academy Rd
WOOL/PLUM SE18 114 E6
Academy Wy BCTR RM8 79 H3
Acanthus Dr STHWK SE1 111 H4
Acanthus Rd BTSEA SW11 129 F2
Accommodation Rd
GLDGN NW11 52 D6
Ace Pde CHSGTN KT9 172 A2
Acer Av YEAD UB4 83 J3
Acer Rd HACK E8 7 M1
Acfold Rd FUL/PGN SW6 108 A7
Achilles Cl STHWK SE1 111 H4
Achilles Rd KIL/WHAMP NW6 70 E4
Achilles St NWCR SE14 112 B6
Acklam Rd NKENS W10 88 D4
Acklington Dr
CDALE/KGS NW9 37 G7
Ackmar Rd FUL/PGN SW6 107 K7
Ackroyd Dr BOW E3 93 H4
Ackroyd Rd FSTH SE23 132 A6
Acland Cl WOOL/PLUM SE18 115 J6
Acland Crs CMBW SE5 130 E3
Acland Rd CRICK NW2 69 K5
Acock Gv NTHLT UB5 66 B3
Acol Crs RSLP HA4 65 F4
Acol Rd KIL/WHAMP NW6 2 B2
Acorn Cl CHING E4 43 K4
CHST BR7 154 C4
HPTN TW12 142 B5
STAN HA7 35 H6
Acorn Gdns ACT W3 87 F4
NRWD SE19 150 B7
Acorn Gv HYS/HAR UB3 101 J6
RSLP HA4 64 D3
Acorn Pde PECK SE15 * 111 J6
Acorn Rd DART DA1 138 C4
Acorns Wy ESH/CLAY KT10 170 C4
Acorn Wy BECK BR3 167 F4
FSTH SE23 151 F2
Acre Dr EDUL SE22 131 H3
Acre La BRXS/STRHM SW2 130 A3
CAR SM5 176 A3
Acre Rd DAGE RM10 80 D6
KUTN/CMB KT2 144 A7
WIM/MER SW19 147 H5
Acre Wy NTHWD HA6 32 D7
Acris St WAND/EARL SW18 128 B4
Acton Cl ED N9 42 C1
Acton Hill Ms ACT W3 * 86 D7
Acton La CHSWK W4 105 K2
WLSDN NW10 86 E2
Acton Ms HACK E8 7 L3
Acton St FSBYW WC1X 5 L8
Acuba Rd WAND/EARL SW18 147 F1
Acworth Cl ED N9 30 E6
Acworth Pl DART DA1 * 139 F5
Ada Cl FBAR/BDGN N11 39 K2
Ada Gdns POP/IOD E14 94 B5
SRTFD E15 76 D7
Adair Cl SNWD SE25 165 J2
Adair Rd NKENS W10 88 C3
Adam Cl CAT SE6 151 H3
FSTH SE23 150 E1
Adam & Eve Ms KENS W8 14 B3
Adam Rd CHING E4 43 H5
Adams Cl BRYLDS KT5 159 G5
FNCH N3 38 E6
WBLY HA9 68 D1
Adams Ct OBST EC2N 13 H4
Adams Ms TOOT SW17 147 K1
WDGN N22 41 F6
Adamson Rd CAN/RD E16 94 E5
HAMP NW3 3 H1
Adamson Wy BECK BR3 167 F4
Adams Pl HOLWY N7 73 F4
Adamsrill Cl EN EN1 29 K5
Adamsrill Rd SYD SE26 151 F3
Adams Rd BECK BR3 166 B4
TOTM N17 55 K1
Adam's Rw MYFR/PKLN W1K 10 B7
Adams Sq BXLYHS DA6 137 F2
Adam St CHCR WC2N 11 K7
Adams Wk KUT/HW KT1 159 F1
Adams Wy CROY/NA CR0 165 G5
Adam Wk FUL/PGN SW6 * 107 F6
Ada Pl BETH E2 74 C7
Adare Wk STRHM/NOR SW16 148 E1
Ada Rd ALP/SUD HA0 * 67 J2
CMBW SE5 111 F6
Adastra Wy WLGTN SM6 176 E5
Ada St HACK E8 74 D7
Adderley Gdns ELTH/MOT SE9 154 A3
Adderley Gv BTSEA SW11 129 F4
Adderley Rd
KTN/HRWW/WS HA3 35 F7
Adderley St POP/IOD E14 94 A5
Addington Dr
NFNCH/WDSPK N12 39 H5
Addington Gv SYD SE26 151 G3
Addington Rd BOW E3 93 J2
CAN/RD E16 94 C3
CROY/NA CR0 164 B7
FSBYPK N4 55 G6
WWKM BR4 180 A3
Addington Sq CMBW SE5 110 D6
Addington St STHWK SE1 17 M2
Addington Village Rd
CROY/NA CR0 179 H5
Addiscombe Av CROY/NA CR0 165 H6
Addiscombe Cl
KTN/HRWW/WS HA3 49 J4
Addiscombe Court Rd
CROY/NA CR0 165 F7
Addiscombe Gv CROY/NA CR0 177 K1
Addiscombe Rd CROY/NA CR0 178 A1
WATW WD18 21 F3
Addison Av HSLW TW3 103 H7
NTGHL W11 88 C7
STHGT/OAK N14 28 B5
Addison Bridge Pl
WKENS W14 107 J3
Addison Cl NTHWD HA6 32 E7
STMC/STPC BR5 169 H5
Addison Crs WKENS W14 107 H2
Addison Dr LEE/GVPK SE12 134 A4
Addison Gdns BRYLDS KT5 159 G3
WKENS W14 107 G2
Addison Gv CHSWK W4 106 B2
Addison Pl NTGHL W11 88 C7
Addison Rd HAYES BR2 168 C4
SNWD SE25 165 H3
TEDD TW11 143 H5
WALTH E17 57 K4
WAN E11 58 E5
WKENS W14 107 H1
Addison's Cl CROY/NA CR0 179 H1
Addison Ter CHSWK W4 * 105 K3
Addison Wy GLDGN NW11 52 D3
HYS/HAR UB3 82 E5
NTHWD HA6 32 D7
Addle Hl BLKFR EC4V 12 D6
Addle St CITYW EC2V * 12 F4
Adecroft Wy E/WMO/HCT KT8 157 H2
Adela Av NWMAL KT3 160 E4
Adelaide Av BROCKY SE4 132 D3
Adelaide Cl STAN HA7 35 G3
Adelaide Ct HNWL W7 104 A1
Adelaide Gdns CHDH RM6 62 A4
Adelaide Gv SHB W12 87 J7
Adelaide Rd CHST BR7 154 B4
HAMP NW3 3 J1
HEST TW5 102 D7
IL IG1 78 B1
LEY E10 76 A2
NWDGN UB2 102 D3
PUT/ROE SW15 127 K4
RCH/KEW TW9 125 G3
STJWD NW8 3 G2
SURB KT6 159 F4
TEDD TW11 143 F5
WEA W13 104 B1
Adelaide St CHCR WC2N * 11 J7
Adelaide Ter BTFD TW8 * 104 E4
Adela St NKENS W10 88 C3
Adelina Gv WCHPL E1 92 E4
Adelina Ms BAL SW12 129 J7
Adeline Pl RSQ WC1B 11 H3
Adeliza Cl BARK IG11 78 C6
Adelphi Crs HCH RM12 81 J1
YEAD UB4 82 C2
Adelphi Ter CHCR WC2N 11 K7
Adelphi Wy YEAD UB4 82 D2
Adeney Cl HMSMTH W6 107 G5
Aden Gv STNW/STAM N16 73 K3
Adenmore Rd CAT SE6 132 D6
Aden Rd IL IG1 60 B6
PEND EN3 31 G3
Adhara Rd NTHWD HA6 32 E4
Adie Rd HMSMTH W6 107 F2
Adine Rd PLSTW E13 94 E3
Adler St WCHPL E1 92 C4
Adley St CLPT E5 75 G4
Adlington Cl UED N18 41 K4
Admaston Rd
WOOL/PLUM SE18 115 H6
Admiral Ms NKENS W10 88 B3
Admiral Pl BERM/RHTH SE16 93 G7
Admirals Cl SWFD E18 59 F3
Admiral Seymour Rd
ELTH/MOT SE9 134 E3
Admiral's Gv GNWCH SE10 112 E7
Admiral Sq WBPTN SW10 * 108 B7
Admiral St DEPT SE8 112 D7
Admiral's Wk HAMP NW3 71 G2
Admirals Wy POP/IOD E14 112 D1
Admiralty Cl DEPT SE8 * 112 D7
Admiralty Rd TEDD TW11 143 F5
Admiralty Wy TEDD TW11 * 143 F5
Admiral Wk MV/WKIL W9 8 B2
Adnams Wk RAIN RM13 81 J4
Adolf St CAT SE6 151 J3
Adolphus Rd FSBYPK N4 73 H1
Adolphus St DEPT SE8 112 C6
Adomar Rd BCTR RM8 79 K2
Adpar St BAY/PAD W2 9 G2
Adrian Cl BAR EN5 26 B5
Adrian Ms WBPTN SW10 14 D9
Adrienne Av STHL UB1 83 K3
Advance Rd WNWD SE27 149 J3
Advent Wy UED N18 43 F4
Adys Lawn CRICK NW2 * 69 K5
Adys Rd PECK SE15 131 G2
Aerodrome Rd
CDALE/KGS NW9 51 H2
Aerodrome Wy HEST TW5 102 B5
Aeroville CDALE/KGS NW9 51 G1
Affleck St IS N1 * 5 M6
Afghan Rd BTSEA SW11 128 D1
Aftab Ter WCHPL E1 * 92 D3
Agamemnon Rd
KIL/WHAMP NW6 70 D4
Agar Cl SURB KT6 172 B1
Agar Gv CAMTN NW1 5 H1
Agar Pl CAMTN NW1 4 F2
Agar St CHCR WC2N 11 J7
Agate Cl CAN/RD E16 95 H5
Agate Rd HMSMTH W6 107 F2
Agatha Cl WAP E1W 92 D7
Agaton Rd ELTH/MOT SE9 154 C1
Agave Rd CRICK NW2 70 A3
Agdon St FSBYE EC1V 6 C9
Agincourt Rd HAMP NW3 71 K3
Agnes Av IL IG1 78 A3
Agnes Cl EHAM E6 96 A6
Agnesfield Cl
NFNCH/WDSPK N12 39 J5
Agnes Gdns BCTR RM8 79 K3
Agnes Riley Gdns CLAP SW4 * 129 H6
Agnes Rd ACT W3 106 C1
Agnes St POP/IOD E14 93 H5
Agnew Rd FSTH SE23 132 B6
Agricola Pl EN EN1 30 B4
Aidan Cl BCTR RM8 80 A3
Ailsa Av TWK TW1 124 B4
Ailsa Rd TWK TW1 124 C4
Ailsa St POP/IOD E14 94 A4
Ainger Rd HAMP NW3 3 M2
Ainsdale Cl ORP BR6 169 J7
Ainsdale Crs PIN HA5 48 A2
Ainsdale Dr STHWK SE1 111 H4
Ainsdale Rd EA W5 85 K3
OXHEY WD19 33 G2
Ainsley Av ROMW/RG RM7 62 E5
Ainsley Cl ED N9 30 A7
Ainsley St BETH E2 92 D2
Ainslie Wood Crs CHING E4 43 K4
Ainslie Wood Gdns CHING E4 43 K3
Ainslie Wood Rd CHING E4 43 J4
Ainsty St BERM/RHTH SE16 * 111 K1
Ainsworth Cl CMBW SE5 * 131 F1
CRICK NW2 69 J2
Ainsworth Rd CROY/NA CR0 164 C7
HOM E9 74 E6
Ainsworth Wy STJWD NW8 2 E3
Aintree Av EHAM E6 77 J7
Aintree Crs BARK/HLT IG6 60 C1
Aintree Rd GFD/PVL UB6 85 H1
Aintree St FUL/PGN SW6 107 H6
Airco Cl CDALE/KGS NW9 50 E2
Airdrie Cl IS N1 5 L2
YEAD UB4 83 J4
Airedale Av CHSWK W4 106 C4
Airedale Av South
CHSWK W4 * 106 C4
Airedale Rd BAL SW12 128 E6
EA W5 104 D2
Airfield Wy HCH RM12 81 K5
Airlie Gdns IL IG1 60 B7
KENS W8 8 A9
Air St REGST W1B 10 F7
Airthrie Rd GDMY/SEVK IG3 61 H7
Aisgill Av WKENS W14 107 J4
Aisher Rd THMD SE28 97 J6
Aislibie Rd LEE/GVPK SE12 133 H3
Aiten Pl HMSMTH W6 106 D3
Aitken Cl HACK E8 74 C7
MTCM CR4 162 E6
Aitken Rd BAR EN5 26 A4
CAT SE6 151 K1
Aitman Dr BTFD TW8 * 105 H4
Ajax Av CDALE/KGS NW9 51 G2
Ajax Rd KIL/WHAMP NW6 70 D3
Akabusi Cl CROY/NA CR0 165 H5
Akehurst St PUT/ROE SW15 126 D5
Akenside Rd HAMP NW3 71 H4
Akerman Rd BRXN/ST SW9 110 C7
SURB KT6 158 D5
Alabama St WOOL/PLUM SE18 115 J6
Alacross Rd EA W5 104 D1
Alan Cl DART DA1 139 F3
Alandale Dr PIN HA5 33 F7
Alander Ms WALTH E17 57 K3
Alan Dr BAR EN5 26 C5
Alan Gdns ROMW/RG RM7 62 C6
Alan Hocken Wy SRTFD E15 94 C1
Alan Rd WIM/MER SW19 146 C4
Alanthus Cl LEE/GVPK SE12 133 J5
Alaska St STHWK SE1 12 A9
Alba Cl YEAD UB4 83 H3
Albacore Crs LEW SE13 132 E5
Alba Gdns GLDGN NW11 52 C5
Albany Cl BUSH WD23 22 D5
BXLY DA5 136 D6
ESH/CLAY KT10 170 A7
MORT/ESHN SW14 125 J3
SEVS/STOTM N15 55 H3
Albany Cots HNWL W7 * 84 E7
Albany Ctyd MYFR/PICC W1J 10 E7
Albany Crs EDGW HA8 36 C6
ESH/CLAY KT10 170 E5
Albany Ms BMLY BR1 152 E5
CMBW SE5 110 D5
IS N1 6 B1
KUTN/CMB KT2 * 143 K5
SUT SM1 175 F4
Albany Pde BTFD TW8 * 105 F5
Albany Park Rd
KUTN/CMB KT2 143 K5
Albany Pl BTFD TW8 104 E5
Albany Rd BELV DA17 117 G5
BTFD TW8 104 E5
BXLY DA5 136 D6
CHDH RM6 62 B5
CHST BR7 154 B4
CMBW SE5 19 J9
FSBYPK N4 55 F5
HCH RM12 63 J7
LEY E10 57 J6
MNPK E12 77 H3
NWMAL KT3 160 A3
RCHPK/HAM TW10 * 125 G4
UED N18 42 D4
WALTH E17 57 G5
WALW SE17 110 E5
WEA W13 85 H6
WIM/MER SW19 147 F4
Albany Rw EFNCH N2 * 53 J3
Albany St CAMTN NW1 4 D7
Albany Ter
RCHPK/HAM TW10 * 125 G4
The Albany KUTN/CMB KT2 143 K5
Alba Pl NTGHL W11 88 D5
Albatross Cl EHAM E6 95 K3
Albatross St
WOOL/PLUM SE18 115 K6
Albemarle Ap
GNTH/NBYPK IG2 60 B5
Albemarle Av WHTN TW2 122 E7
Albemarle Gdns
GNTH/NBYPK IG2 60 B5
NWMAL KT3 160 A3
Albemarle Pk BECK BR3 * 151 K7
STAN HA7 35 J4
Albemarle Rd BECK BR3 151 K7
EBAR EN4 27 J6
Albemarle St CONDST W1S 10 E7
Albemarle Wy FSBYE EC1V 12 C1
Alberon Gdns GLDGN NW11 52 D3
Alberta Av SUT SM1 174 C3
Alberta Est WALW SE17 18 D7
Alberta Rd EN EN1 30 B5
ERITH DA8 117 K7
Alberta St WALW SE17 18 D7
Albert Av CHING E4 43 J3
VX/NE SW8 110 A6
Albert Basin Wy CAN/RD E16 96 C6
Albert Br BTSEA SW11 108 D6
Albert Bridge Ga BTSEA SW11 108 E6
Albert Bridge Rd BTSEA SW11 108 D6
Albert Carr Gdns
STRHM/NOR SW16 148 E4
Albert Cl HOM E9 74 D7
WDGN N22 40 D7
Albert Cots WCHPL E1 * 92 C4
Albert Crs CHING E4 43 J3
Albert Dr WIM/MER SW19 146 C1
Albert Emb STHWK SE1 17 K7
Albert Gdns WCHPL E1 93 F5
Albert Ga KTBR SW1X 15 M1
Albert Gv RYNPK SW20 146 B7
Albert Ms BROCKY SE4 * 132 C3
FSBYPK N4 55 F7
KENS W8 14 E3
POP/IOD E14 * 93 G6
Albert Pl FNCH N3 38 E7
KENS W8 * 14 D2
Albert Rd BCTR RM8 62 B7
BELV DA17 117 G4
BKHH IG9 45 H1
BXLY DA5 137 H5
CAN/RD E16 95 J7
EA W5 85 H3
EBAR EN4 27 G3
ELTH/MOT SE9 153 J2
FSBYPK N4 55 F7
HAYES BR2 168 C4
HDN NW4 52 B3
HPTN TW12 142 C4
HSLW TW3 123 F3
HYS/HAR UB3 101 H2
IL IG1 78 C2
KIL/WHAMP NW6 88 D1
KUT/HW KT1 159 G1
LEY E10 76 A1
MLHL NW7 37 H4
MTCM CR4 162 E2
NWDGN UB2 102 C2
NWMAL KT3 160 C3
PGE/AN SE20 151 F6
RCHPK/HAM TW10 125 F4
ROM RM1 63 H5
RYLN/HDSTN HA2 48 C2
SEVS/STOTM N15 56 A5
SNWD SE25 165 J3
SUT SM1 175 H4
SWFD E18 59 F2
TEDD TW11 143 F5
TWK TW1 124 A7
WALTH E17 57 J4
WDGN N22 40 D7
Albert Rd North WAT WD17 21 F2
Albert Rd South WAT WD17 * 21 F2
Albert Sq SRTFD E15 76 C4
VX/NE SW8 110 A6
Albert St CAMTN NW1 4 D4
NFNCH/WDSPK N12 39 G4
Albert Ter CAMTN NW1 4 A3
EA W5 * 85 H3
WLSDN NW10 * 69 F7
Albert Terrace Ms
CAMTN NW1 4 A3
Albert Wy PECK SE15 111 J6
Albion Av MUSWH N10 40 A7
VX/NE SW8 129 J1
Albion Cl BAY/PAD W2 9 K6
ROMW/RG RM7 63 F5
Albion Dr HACK E8 7 M2
Albion Est BERM/RHTH SE16 * 111 K1
Albion Ga BAY/PAD W2 9 K6
Albion Gv STNW/STAM N16 74 A3
Albion Ms BAY/PAD W2 9 K5
HMSMTH W6 106 E3
IS N1 6 A3
Albion Pl FARR EC1M 12 C2
HMSMTH W6 106 E3
SNWD SE25 165 H2
Albion Riverside BTSEA SW11 108 D6
Albion Rd BELMT SM2 175 H5
BXLYHS DA6 137 G3
HSLW TW3 123 F3
HYS/HAR UB3 82 C5
KUTN/CMB KT2 144 E7
STNW/STAM N16 73 K4
TOTM N17 56 B1
WALTH E17 58 A2
WHTN TW2 123 K7
Albion Sq HACK E8 7 L2
Albion St BAY/PAD W2 9 K5
BERM/RHTH SE16 111 K1
CROY/NA CR0 164 C7
Albion Ter CHING E4 * 31 K3
HACK E8 7 L2
Albion Villas Rd SYD SE26 150 E2
Albion Wk IS N1 5 K6
Albion Wy LEW SE13 133 F3
STBT EC1A 12 E3
WBLY HA9 68 C2
Albion Yd IS N1 5 K6
Albrighton Rd EDUL SE22 131 F2
Albury Av BELMT SM2 174 A7
BXLYHN DA7 137 F1

ISLW TW7 104 A6
Albury Cl HOR/WEW KT19 172 D7
HPTN TW12 142 A5
Albury Dr PIN HA5 33 G7
Albury Ms MNPK E12 59 G7
Albury Rd CHSGTN KT9 172 A4
Albury St DEPT SE8 112 D5
Albyfield BMLY BR1 168 E2
Albyn Rd DEPT SE8 112 D7
Alcester Crs CLPT E5 74 D1
Alcester Rd WLGTN SM6 176 B3
Alcock Cl WLGTN SM6 176 D6
Alcock Rd HEST TW5 102 C6
Alconbury Rd CLPT E5 74 C1
Alcorn Cl CHEAM SM3 174 E1
Alcott Cl HNWL W7 85 F4
Alcuin Ct STAN HA7 35 J6
Aldborough Rd DAGE RM10 80 E5
Aldborough Rd North
GNTH/NBYPK IG2 61 F4
Aldborough Rd South
GDMY/SEVK IG3 60 E7
Aldbourne Rd SHB W12 87 H7
Aldbridge St WALW SE17 19 K7
Aldburgh Ms MHST W1U 10 B4
Aldbury Av WBLY HA9 68 D6
Aldbury Ms ED N9 29 K6
Aldebert Ter VX/NE SW8 110 A6
Aldeburgh Pl WFD IG8 44 E3
Aldeburgh St GNWCH SE10 113 K4
Alden Av SRTFD E15 94 D2
Aldenham Rd BORE WD6 23 F1
BUSH WD23 21 J4
OXHEY WD19 21 H5
Aldenham St CAMTN NW1 4 F6
Alden Md PIN HA5 * 34 A6
Aldensley Rd HMSMTH W6 106 E2
Alderbrook Rd BAL SW12 129 G5
Alderbury Rd BARN SW13 106 D5
Alder Cl PECK SE15 111 G5
Alder Gv CRICK NW2 69 J1
Alderholt Wy PECK SE15 * 111 F6
Alderman Av BARK IG11 97 G2
Aldermanbury CITYW EC2V * 12 F4
Aldermanbury Sq CITYW EC2V 12 F3
Alderman Cl DART DA1 138 B6
Alderman Judge Ml
KUT/HW KT1 * 159 F1
Alderman's Hl PLMGR N13 40 E3
Alderman's Wk LVPST EC2M 13 J3
Aldermary Rd BMLY BR1 152 E7
Aldermoor Rd CAT SE6 151 H2
Alderney Av HEST TW5 103 G6
Alderney Gdns NTHLT UB5 65 K6
Alderney Ms STHWK SE1 19 G3
Alderney Rd ERITH DA8 118 D6
WCHPL E1 93 F3
Alderney St PIM SW1V 16 C6
Alder Rd MORT/ESHN SW14 126 A2
SCUP DA14 154 E2
Alders Av WFD IG8 44 C5
Aldersbrook Av EN EN1 30 A1
Aldersbrook Dr
KUTN/CMB KT2 144 B5
Aldersbrook La MNPK E12 77 K2
Aldersbrook Rd MNPK E12 77 G1
Alders Cl EA W5 104 E2
EDGW HA8 36 E4
WAN E11 77 F1
Aldersey Gdns BARK IG11 78 D5
Aldersford Cl BROCKY SE4 132 A3
Aldersgate St CITYW EC2V 12 E4
Aldersgrove E/WMO/HCT KT8 157 J4
Aldersgrove Av
ELTH/MOT SE9 153 G2
Aldershot Rd
KIL/WHAMP NW6 70 D7
Aldershot Ter
WOOL/PLUM SE18 * 115 F6
Aldersmead Av CROY/NA CR0 166 A5
Aldersmead Rd BECK BR3 151 G6
Alderson Pl NWDGN UB2 84 C7
Alderson St NKENS W10 88 C3
Alders Rd EDGW HA8 36 E4
The Alders FELT TW13 141 J4
HEST TW5 102 E5
STRHM/NOR SW16 * 148 C3
WCHMH N21 29 G5
WWKM BR4 166 E7
Alderton Cl WLSDN NW10 69 F2
Alderton Crs HDN NW4 51 K4
Alderton Rd CROY/NA CR0 165 G6
HNHL SE24 130 D2
Alderton Wy HDN NW4 51 K4
Alderville Rd FUL/PGN SW6 127 J1
Alderwick Dr HSLW TW3 123 J2
Alderwood Rd ELTH/MOT SE9 135 J5
Aldford St MYFR/PKLN W1K 10 A8
Aldgate FENCHST EC3M 13 K5
Aldgate Barrs WCHPL E1 * 13 M4
Aldgate High St TWRH EC3N 13 L5
Aldine St SHB W12 107 F1
Aldingham Gdns HCH RM12 81 J4
Aldington Cl CHDH RM6 61 J6
Aldington Rd CHARL SE7 114 C2
Aldis Ms TOOT SW17 147 J4
Aldis St TOOT SW17 147 J4
Aldred Rd KIL/WHAMP NW6 70 E4
Aldren Rd TOOT SW17 147 G2
Aldrich Crs CROY/NA CR0 180 A7
Aldriche Wy CHING E4 44 A5
Aldrich Gdns CHEAM SM3 174 D2
Aldrich Ter WAND/EARL SW18 147 G1
Aldridge Av EDGW HA8 36 D2
RSLP HA4 65 G1
STAN HA7 36 A7
Aldridge Ri NWMAL KT3 160 B6
Aldridge Road Vls NTGHL W11 88 D4
Aldridge Wk STHGT/OAK N14 28 E6
Aldrington Rd
STRHM/NOR SW16 148 C4
Aldsworth Cl MV/WKIL W9 8 C1
Aldwick Cl ELTH/MOT SE9 154 D2
Aldwick Rd CROY/NA CR0 177 F2
Aldworth Gv LEW SE13 133 F5
Aldworth Rd SRTFD E15 76 C6
Aldwych HOL/ALD WC2B 11 L5
Aldwych Av BARK/HLT IG6 60 C3
Aldwych Cl HCH RM12 81 J1
Alers Rd BXLYHS DA6 136 E4
Alesia Cl WDGN N22 40 E6
Alestan Beck Rd CAN/RD E16 95 H5
Alexander Av WLSDN NW10 69 K6
Alexander Cl BFN/LL DA15 135 K4
EBAR EN4 27 H3
HAYES BR2 167 K7
NWDGN UB2 84 C7
WHTN TW2 142 E1
Alexander Evans Ms
FSTH SE23 151 F1
Alexander Ms BAY/PAD W2 8 C4
Alexander Pl SKENS SW7 15 J5
Alexander Rd ARCH N19 72 E2
BXLYHN DA7 136 E1
CHST BR7 154 B5
Alexander Sq CHEL SW3 15 J5
Alexander St BAY/PAD W2 8 B4
Alexander Ter ABYW SE2 * 116 C4
Alexandra DEPT SE8 112 C5
Alexandra Av BTSEA SW11 * 109 F7
RYLN/HDSTN HA2 47 K7
STHL UB1 83 K6
SUT SM1 174 E2
WDGN N22 40 D7
Alexandra Cl ASHF TW15 140 B6
RYLN/HDSTN HA2 66 A2
Alexandra Cots NWCR SE14 112 C7
Alexandra Crs BMLY BR1 152 D5
Alexandra Dr BRYLDS KT5 159 H6
NRWD SE19 150 A4
Alexandra Gdns CAR SM5 176 A7
HSLW TW3 123 G1
MUSWH N10 54 B3
Alexandra Ga SKENS SW7 15 G1
Alexandra Gv FSBYPK N4 55 H7
NFNCH/WDSPK N12 39 F4
Alexandra Ms EFNCH N2 53 K2
WAT WD17 20 E1
Alexandra Palace Wy
CEND/HSY/T N8 54 C3
Alexandra Pde
RYLN/HDSTN HA2 * 66 B3
Alexandra Park Rd
MUSWH N10 54 B1
Alexandra Pl CROY/NA CR0 165 F7
SNWD SE25 164 E4
STJWD NW8 2 F3
Alexandra Rd ASHF TW15 140 B6
BTFD TW8 * 104 E5
CEND/HSY/T N8 55 G2
CHDH RM6 61 K5
CHSWK W4 106 A1
CROY/NA CR0 165 F7
ED N9 * 30 D6
EHAM E6 96 A2
ERITH DA8 118 C5
HDN NW4 52 B3
HSLW TW3 123 G1
KUTN/CMB KT2 144 C6
LEY E10 76 A2
MORT/ESHN SW14 126 A2
MTCM CR4 147 J6
MUSWH N10 40 B7
PEND EN3 31 F3
PGE/AN SE20 151 F5
RAIN RM13 81 H7
RCH/KEW TW9 125 G1
ROM RM1 63 H5
SEVS/STOTM N15 55 K4
STJWD NW8 2 F3
SWFD E18 59 F2
THDIT KT7 158 A4
TWK TW1 124 D5
WALTH E17 57 H5
WAT WD17 20 E1
WIM/MER SW19 146 E4
Alexandra Sq MRDN SM4 161 K4
Alexandra St CAN/RD E16 94 E4
NWCR SE14 112 B6
Alexandria Rd WEA W13 85 G6
Alexis St BERM/RHTH SE16 111 H3
Alfearn Rd CLPT E5 74 E3
Alford Gn CROY/NA CR0 180 B5
Alford Pl IS N1 * 6 F6
Alford Rd ERITH DA8 117 K4
Alfoxton Av SEVS/STOTM N15 55 H3
Alfreda St BTSEA SW11 109 G7
Alfred Cl CHSWK W4 106 A3
Alfred Gdns STHL UB1 83 J6
Alfred Ms GWRST WC1E 11 G2
Alfred Pl GWRST WC1E 11 G2
Alfred Rd ACT W3 86 E7
BAY/PAD W2 8 B2
BELV DA17 117 G4
BKHH IG9 45 H1
FELT TW13 122 B7
KUT/HW KT1 159 F2
SNWD SE25 165 H4
SRTFD E15 76 D4
SUT SM1 175 G4
Alfred's Gdns BARK IG11 96 E1
Alfred St BOW E3 93 H2
Alfred's Way (East Ham &
Barking By-Pass) BARK IG11 96 D1
Alfred Vls WALTH E17 * 58 A3
Alfreton Cl WIM/MER SW19 146 B2
Alfriston BRYLDS KT5 159 G5
Alfriston Av CROY/NA CR0 163 K6
RYLN/HDSTN HA2 48 A5
Alfriston Cl BRYLDS KT5 159 G5
DART DA1 138 B5
Alfriston Rd BTSEA SW11 128 E4
Algar Cl STAN HA7 35 F4
Algar Rd ISLW TW7 124 B2
Algarve Rd WAND/EARL SW18 128 A7
Algernon Rd HDN NW4 51 J5
KIL/WHAMP NW6 2 A4
LEW SE13 132 E2
Algiers Rd LEW SE13 132 D3
Alguin Ct STAN HA7 * 35 J5
Alibon Gdns DAGE RM10 80 C4
Alibon Rd DAGE RM10 80 C4
Alice La BOW E3 75 H7
Alice St STHWK SE1 19 J4
Alice Thompson Cl
LEE/GVPK SE12 153 G1
Alice Walker Cl HNHL SE24 * 130 C3
Alice Wy HSLW TW3 123 G3
Alicia Av KTN/HRWW/WS HA3 49 H3
Alicia Cl KTN/HRWW/WS HA3 49 J3
Alicia Gdns
KTN/HRWW/WS HA3 49 H3
Alie St WCHPL E1 13 M5
Alington Crs CDALE/KGS NW9 50 E7
Alington Gv WLGTN SM6 176 D7
Alison Cl CROY/NA CR0 166 A7
EHAM E6 96 A5
PIN HA5 47 F5
Aliwal Ms BTSEA SW11 * 128 D3
Aliwal Rd BTSEA SW11 128 D3
Alkerden Rd CHSWK W4 106 B4
Alkham Rd STNW/STAM N16 74 B1
Allan Barclay Cl
SEVS/STOTM N15 56 B5
Allan Cl NWMAL KT3 160 A4
Allandale Av FNCH N3 52 C2
Allandale Rd EMPK RM11 63 H6
Allan Wy ACT W3 86 E4
Allard Crs BUSH WD23 34 C1
Allardyce St CLAP SW4 130 A3
Allbrook Cl TEDD TW11 142 E4
Allcot Cl EBED/NFELT TW14 121 J7
Allcroft Rd KTTN NW5 72 A5
Allder Wy SAND/SEL CR2 177 H6
Allenby Av SAND/SEL CR2 177 J7
Allenby Cl GFD/PVL UB6 84 A2
Allenby Rd FSTH SE23 151 G2
STHL UB1 84 A5
WOOL/PLUM SE18 115 H2
Allen Cl MTCM CR4 148 B7
SUN TW16 141 F7
Allendale Av STHL UB1 84 A5
Allendale Cl CMBW SE5 130 E1
SYD SE26 151 F4
Allendale Rd GFD/PVL UB6 67 H5
Allen Edwards Dr VX/NE SW8 109 K7
Allen Rd BECK BR3 166 A1
BOW E3 93 H1
CROY/NA CR0 164 A6
STNW/STAM N16 74 A3
SUN TW16 141 F7
Allensbury Pl CAMTN NW1 5 H2
Allens Rd PEND EN3 30 E4
Allen St KENS W8 14 B3
Allenswood Rd ELTH/MOT SE9 134 D2
Allerford Ct HRW HA1 48 B4
Allerford Rd CAT SE6 151 K3
Allerton Rd STNW/STAM N16 73 J1
Allerton St IS N1 7 H6
Allestree Rd FUL/PGN SW6 107 H6
Alleyn Crs DUL SE21 149 K1
Alleyndale Rd BCTR RM8 79 J1
Alleyn Pk DUL SE21 149 K1
NWDGN UB2 102 E4
Alleyn Rd DUL SE21 149 K2
Allfarthing La
WAND/EARL SW18 128 B5
Allgood Cl MRDN SM4 161 G5
Allgood St BETH E2 7 M6
Allhallows La CANST EC4R 13 G7
Allhallows Rd EHAM E6 95 J5
All Hallows Rd TOTM N17 42 A7
Alliance Cl ALP/SUD HA0 67 K3
HSLWW TW4 122 E4
Alliance Rd ACT W3 86 D3
PLSTW E13 95 G3
WOOL/PLUM SE18 116 B5
Allied Wy ACT W3 * 106 B1
Allingham Cl HNWL W7 85 F6
Allington Av TOTM N17 42 A5
Allington Cl GFD/PVL UB6 66 C6
WIM/MER SW19 146 B4
Allington Rd HDN NW4 51 K4
NKENS W10 88 C2
ORP BR6 169 K7
RYLN/HDSTN HA2 48 C4
Allington St BGVA SW1W 16 D4
WESTW SW1E 16 E4
Allison Cl GNWCH SE10 113 F7
Allison Gv DUL SE21 131 F7
Allison Rd ACT W3 86 E5
CEND/HSY/T N8 55 G4
Allitsen Rd STJWD NW8 3 J6
Allnutt Wy CLAP SW4 129 J4
Alloa Rd DEPT SE8 112 A4
GDMY/SEVK IG3 79 H1
Allonby Gdns WBLY HA9 49 J7
Alloway Rd BOW E3 93 G2
Allport Ms WCHPL E1 * 92 E4
All Saints' Cl ED N9 42 B1
All Saints Dr BKHTH/KID SE3 133 J1
All Saints Ms STAN HA7 34 E5
All Saints Pas
WAND/EARL SW18 * 127 K4
All Saints Rd SUT SM1 175 F2
WIM/MER SW19 147 G6
All Saints' Rd ACT W3 105 K2
NTGHL W11 88 D4
All Saints St IS N1 5 L5
Allsop Pl CAMTN NW1 9 M1
All Souls' Av WLSDN NW10 87 K1
All Souls' Pl REGST W1B 10 D3
Allum La BORE WD6 24 A4
Allum Wy TRDG/WHET N20 27 G7
Allwood Cl SYD SE26 151 F3
Alma Av CHING E4 44 A6
Almack Rd CLPT E5 74 E3
Alma Cl MUSWH N10 * 40 B7
Alma Ct RYLN/HDSTN HA2 * 66 D1
Alma Crs SUT SM1 174 C4
Alma Gv STHWK SE1 19 M6
Alma Pl NRWD SE19 150 B6
THHTH CR7 164 B4
WLSDN NW10 87 K2
Alma Rd BFN/LL DA15 155 G2
CAR SM5 175 J4
ESH/CLAY KT10 157 K7
MUSWH N10 40 A6
PEND EN3 31 G4
STHL UB1 83 J6
WAND/EARL SW18 128 B4
Alma Rw
KTN/HRWW/WS HA3 * 34 D7
Alma Sq STJWD NW8 2 F7
Alma St KTTN NW5 72 B5
SRTFD E15 76 B5
Alma Ter BOW E3 75 H7
KENS W8 14 B4
WAND/EARL SW18 128 C6
Almeida St IS N1 6 C3
Almeric Rd BTSEA SW11 128 E3
Almer Rd RYNPK SW20 145 J6
Almington St FSBYPK N4 * 54 E7
Almond Av CAR SM5 175 K1
EA W5 105 F2
WDR/YW UB7 100 D2
Almond Cl FELT TW13 121 K7
HAYES BR2 169 F6
HYS/HAR UB3 82 C6
PECK SE15 131 H1
RSLP HA4 64 D2
Almond Gv BTFD TW8 104 C6
Almond Rd BERM/RHTH SE16 111 J3
TOTM N17 42 C6
Almonds Av BKHH IG9 44 E1
Almond Wy BORE WD6 24 D3
HAYES BR2 169 F6
MTCM CR4 163 J4
RYLN/HDSTN HA2 48 B1
Almorah Rd HEST TW5 102 C7
IS N1 7 G2
Almshouse La CHSGTN KT9 171 J7
Alnwick Gv MRDN SM4 162 A3
Alnwick Rd CAN/RD E16 95 G5
LEE/GVPK SE12 134 A6
Alnwick Ter LEE/GVPK SE12 134 A6
Alperton La ALP/SUD HA0 85 K2
Alperton St NKENS W10 88 C3
Alphabet Gdns CAR SM5 162 C5
Alpha Cl CAMTN NW1 3 K9
Alpha Est HYS/HAR UB3 * 101 H1
Alpha Gv POP/IOD E14 112 D1
Alpha Pl CHEL SW3 15 K9
KIL/WHAMP NW6 2 B5
MRDN SM4 * 161 G6
Alpha Rd BRYLDS KT5 159 G5
CHING E4 43 J2
CROY/NA CR0 165 F7
NWCR SE14 112 C7
PEND EN3 31 G3
TEDD TW11 142 D4
UED N18 42 C5
Alpha St PECK SE15 131 H1
Alphea Cl WIM/MER SW19 147 J6
Alpine Av BRYLDS KT5 172 E1
Alpine Cl CROY/NA CR0 178 A2
Alpine Copse BMLY BR1 169 F1
Alpine Gv HOM E9 74 E6
Alpine Rd BERM/RHTH SE16 111 K3
LEY E10 75 K1
Alpine Vw CAR SM5 175 J4
Alpine Wk BUSH WD23 34 E1
Alpine Wy EHAM E6 96 A4
Alric Av NWMAL KT3 160 B2
WLSDN NW10 69 F6
Alroy Rd FSBYPK N4 55 G6
Alsace Rd WALW SE17 19 J7
Alscot Rd STHWK SE1 19 M4
Alscot Wy STHWK SE1 19 L5
Alsike Rd ERITHM DA18 116 E2
Alsom Av WPK KT4 173 H3
Alston Cl SURB KT6 158 C6
Alston Rd BAR EN5 26 C2
TOOT SW17 147 H3
UED N18 42 D4
Altair Cl TOTM N17 42 B5
Altair Wy NTHWD HA6 32 D4
Altash Wy ELTH/MOT SE9 153 K1
Altenburg Av WEA W13 104 C2
Altenburg Gdns BTSEA SW11 128 E3
Alt Gv WIM/MER SW19 146 D6
Altham Ct RYLN/HDSTN HA2 * 34 B7
Altham Gdns OXHEY WD19 33 H3
Altham Rd PIN HA5 33 J6
Althea St FUL/PGN SW6 128 A1
Althorne Gdns SWFD E18 58 D3
Althorne Wy DAGE RM10 80 C1
Althorp Cl BAR EN5 25 J6
Althorpe Rd HRW HA1 * 48 C4
Althorp Rd TOOT SW17 128 E7
Altmore Av EHAM E6 77 K6
Alton Av STAN HA7 35 F6
Alton Cl BXLY DA5 137 F7
ISLW TW7 124 A1
Alton Gdns BECK BR3 151 J6
WHTN TW2 123 J5
Alton Rd CROY/NA CR0 177 G2
PUT/ROE SW15 126 D7
RCH/KEW TW9 125 F3
TOTM N17 55 K2
Alton St POP/IOD E14 93 K4
Altyre Cl BECK BR3 166 C4
Altyre Rd CROY/NA CR0 177 K1
Altyre Wy BECK BR3 166 C4
Alvanley Gdns
KIL/WHAMP NW6 71 F4
Alva Wy OXHEY WD19 33 H1
Alverstone Av EBAR EN4 27 H6
WAND/EARL SW18 146 E1
Alverstone Gdns
ELTH/MOT SE9 135 G7
Alverstone Rd CRICK NW2 70 A6
MNPK E12 78 A3
NWMAL KT3 160 C3
WBLY HA9 50 B7
Alverston Gdns SNWD SE25 165 F4
Alverton St DEPT SE8 112 C4
Alveston Av
KTN/HRWW/WS HA3 49 H2
Alveston Sq SWFD E18 * 58 E1
Alvey St WALW SE17 19 J7
Alvia Gdns SUT SM1 175 G3
Alvington Crs HACK E8 74 B4
Alway Av HOR/WEW KT19 172 E4
Alwin Pl WATW WD18 20 C3
Alwold Crs LEE/GVPK SE12 134 B5
Alwyn Av CHSWK W4 106 A4
Alwyn Cl BORE WD6 24 B5
CROY/NA CR0 179 K6
Alwyne La IS N1 6 D1
Alwyne Pl IS N1 6 E1
Alwyne Rd HNWL W7 84 E6
IS N1 6 E1
WIM/MER SW19 146 D5
Alwyne Sq IS N1 73 J5
Alwyne Vls IS N1 6 D1
Alwyn Gdns ACT W3 86 D5
HDN NW4 51 J3
Alyn Bank CEND/HSY/T N8 * 54 D5
Alyth Gdns GLDGN NW11 52 D5
Amalgamated Dr BTFD TW8 104 B5
Amanda Ms ROMW/RG RM7 62 E4
Amar Ct WOOL/PLUM SE18 116 A3
Amardeep Ct
WOOL/PLUM SE18 116 A4
Amazon St WCHPL E1 92 D5
Ambassador Cl HSLW TW3 122 D1
Ambassador Gdns EHAM E6 95 K4
Ambassador Sq POP/IOD E14 112 E3
Amber Av WALTH E17 43 G7
Amberden Av FNCH N3 52 E2
Ambergate St WALW SE17 18 C7
Amber Gv CRICK NW2 52 B7
Amberley Cl PIN HA5 47 K2
Amberley Ct SCUP DA14 155 J4
Amberley Gdns
HOR/WEW KT19 173 H3
Amberley Gv CROY/NA CR0 165 G6
SYD SE26 150 D3
Amberley Rd ABYW SE2 116 E5
EN EN1 30 B6
LEY E10 57 J6
MV/WKIL W9 8 B2
PLMGR N13 41 F1
Amberley Wy HSLWW TW4 122 B4
MRDN SM4 161 J6
ROMW/RG RM7 62 D3
Amberside Cl ISLW TW7 123 J5
Amber St SRTFD E15 * 76 B5
Amberwood Cl WLGTN SM6 176 E4
Amberwood Ri NWMAL KT3 160 B5
Amblecote Cl LEE/GVPK SE12 153 F2
Amblecote Mdw
LEE/GVPK SE12 153 F2
Amblecote Mdws
LEE/GVPK SE12 * 153 F2
Amblecote Rd LEE/GVPK SE12 153 F2
Ambler Rd FSBYPK N4 73 H2
Ambleside BMLY BR1 152 B5
Ambleside Av BECK BR3 166 B4
HCH RM12 81 K4
STRHM/NOR SW16 148 D3
WOT/HER KT12 156 B7
Ambleside Cl HOM E9 74 E4
LEY E10 57 K6
SEVS/STOTM N15 56 B2
Ambleside Crs PEND EN3 31 F2
Ambleside Dr
EBED/NFELT TW14 121 J7
Ambleside Gdns BELMT SM2 175 G5
REDBR IG4 59 J3
WBLY HA9 49 K7
Ambleside Rd BXLYHN DA7 137 H1
WLSDN NW10 69 H6
Ambrey Wy WLGTN SM6 176 D7
Ambrook Rd BELV DA17 117 H2
Ambrosden Av WEST SW1P 16 F4
Ambrose Av GLDGN NW11 52 D5
Ambrose Cl DART DA1 138 C3
Ambrose St BERM/RHTH SE16 111 J3
Ambulance Rd WAN E11 58 B4
Amelia Cl ACT W3 86 D7
Amelia St WALW SE17 18 D8
Amen Cnr STP EC4M 12 D5
TOOT SW17 148 A5
Amen Ct STP EC4M 12 D5
Amenity Wy MRDN SM4 161 F6
America Sq TWRH EC3N 13 L6
America St STHWK SE1 12 E9
Amerland Rd PUT/ROE SW15 127 J5
Amersham Av UED N18 41 K5
Amersham Gv NWCR SE14 112 C6
Amersham Rd CROY/NA CR0 164 D5
NWCR SE14 112 C7
Amersham V NWCR SE14 112 C6
Amery Gdns WLSDN NW10 69 K7
Amery Rd HRW HA1 67 G1
Amesbury Av
BRXS/STRHM SW2 148 E1
Amesbury Cl WPK KT4 161 F7
Amesbury Dr CHING E4 31 K5
Amesbury Rd BMLY BR1 168 C2
DAGW RM9 79 K6
FELT TW13 141 H1
Ames Cots POP/IOD E14 * 93 G4
Amethyst Rd SRTFD E15 76 B3
Amherst Av WEA W13 85 J5
Amherst Gdns WEA W13 * 85 J5
Amherst Rd WEA W13 85 J5
Amhurst Gdns ISLW TW7 104 A7
Amhurst Pde
STNW/STAM N16 * 56 B6
Amhurst Pk STNW/STAM N16 56 A6
Amhurst Rd STNW/STAM N16 74 B3
Amhurst Ter STNW/STAM N16 74 C3
Amias Dr EDGW HA8 36 A3
Amidas Gdns BCTR RM8 79 H3
Amiel St WCHPL E1 92 E3
Amies St BTSEA SW11 128 E2
Amina Wy BERM/RHTH SE16 111 H2
Amis Av HOR/WEW KT19 172 C5
Amity Gv RYNPK SW20 146 A7
Amity Rd SRTFD E15 76 D6
Ammanford Gn
CDALE/KGS NW9 * 51 G5
Amner Rd BTSEA SW11 129 F5
Amor Rd HMSMTH W6 107 F2
Amott Rd PECK SE15 131 H2
Ampere Wy CROY/NA CR0 163 K6
Ampleforth Rd ABYW SE2 116 C1
Amport Pl MLHL NW7 38 C5
Ampthill Est CAMTN NW1 4 E6
Ampthill Sq CAMTN NW1 4 F6
Ampton St FSBYW WC1X 5 L8
Amroth Cl FSTH SE23 131 J7
Amroth Gn CDALE/KGS NW9 * 51 G5
Amsterdam Rd POP/IOD E14 113 F2
Amwell Cl ENC/FH EN2 29 K4
Amwell St CLKNW EC1R 6 A7
Amyand Cots TWK TW1 124 C5
Amyand Park Gdns TWK TW1 124 C6
Amyand Park Rd TWK TW1 124 B6
Amy Cl WLGTN SM6 176 E6
Amyruth Rd BROCKY SE4 132 D4
Amy Warne Cl EHAM E6 95 J4
Anatola Rd ARCH N19 72 B1
Ancaster Crs NWMAL KT3 160 D5
Ancaster Ms BECK BR3 166 A2
Ancaster Rd BECK BR3 166 A2
Ancaster St WOOL/PLUM SE18 115 K6
Anchorage Cl WIM/MER SW19 146 E4
Anchor Cl BARK IG11 97 H2
Anchor Dr RAIN RM13 99 K2
Anchor & Hope La CHARL SE7 114 A2
Anchor Rd MNPK E12 77 H1
Anchor St BERM/RHTH SE16 111 J3
Anchor Ter WCHPL E1 * 92 E3
Anchor Yd FSBYE EC1V * 6 F9
Ancill Cl HMSMTH W6 107 G5
Ancona Rd WLSDN NW10 87 J1
WOOL/PLUM SE18 115 J4
Andace Park Gdns
BMLY BR1 * 153 G7
Andalus Rd BRXN/ST SW9 129 K2
Ander Cl ALP/SUD HA0 67 K3
Anderson Cl ACT W3 87 F5
CHEAM SM3 161 K7
WCHMH N21 29 F4
Anderson Dr ASHF TW15 140 A3
Anderson Rd HOM E9 75 F5
WFD IG8 59 H2
Anderson's Pl HSLW TW3 123 G3
Anderson Sq IS N1 6 C4
Anderson St CHEL SW3 15 L7
Anderson Wy BELV DA17 117 J1
Andover Av CAN/RD E16 95 H5
Andover Cl EBED/NFELT TW14 121 J7
GFD/PVL UB6 84 B3
Andover Pl KIL/WHAMP NW6 2 C6
Andover Rd HOLWY N7 73 F1
ORP BR6 169 K7
WHTN TW2 123 J7
Andover Ter HMSMTH W6 * 106 E3
Andre St HACK E8 74 C4
Andrew Borde St
LSQ/SEVD WC2H * 11 H4
Andrew Cl DART DA1 138 A4
Andrewes Gdns EHAM E6 95 J5
Andrew Pl VX/NE SW8 109 J7
Andrews Cl BKHH IG9 45 G1
HRW HA1 48 D6
WPK KT4 174 B1
Andrews Rd BETH E2 74 D7
Andrew St POP/IOD E14 94 A5
Andrews Wk WALW SE17 110 C5
Andwell Cl ABYW SE2 116 C1
Anerley Gv NRWD SE19 150 B6
Anerley Hl NRWD SE19 150 B5
Anerley Pk PGE/AN SE20 150 D5
Anerley Park Rd PGE/AN SE20 150 D6
Anerley Rd PGE/AN SE20 150 C7
Anerley Station Rd
PGE/AN SE20 150 D7
Anerley V NRWD SE19 150 B6
Anfield Cl BAL SW12 129 H6
Angela Carter Cl
BRXN/ST SW9 130 B2
Angel Alley WCHPL E1 13 M3
Angel Cl HPTN TW12 142 C4
UED N18 42 B4
Angel Corner Pde UED N18 * 42 C4
Angelfield HSLW TW3 123 G3
Angel Hl SUT SM1 175 F2
Angel Hill Dr SUT SM1 175 F2
Angelica Dr EHAM E6 96 A4

Angelica Gdns CROY/NA CR0 166 A7
Angel La HYS/HAR UB3 82 B4
SRTFD E15 76 B5
Angell Park Gdns
BRXN/ST SW9 130 B2
Angell Rd BRXN/ST SW9 130 C2
Angell Town Est
BRXN/ST SW9 * 130 B1
Angel Ms IS N1 6 B6
PUT/ROE SW15 126 D6
WCHPL E1 92 D6
Angel Pas CANST EC4R 13 G7
Angel Rd HRW HA1 48 E5
THDIT KT7 158 B7
Angel Rd (North Circular)
UED N18 42 C4
Angel Sq FSBYE EC1V * 6 C6
Angel St STBT EC1A 12 E4
Angel Wk HMSMTH W6 107 F3
Angel Wy ROM RM1 63 G4
Angerstein La BKHTH/KID SE3 113 J6
Anglers La KTTN NW5 72 B5
Anglers Reach SURB KT6 * 158 E4
Anglesea Ms
WOOL/PLUM SE18 115 G3
Anglesea Rd KUT/HW KT1 158 E3
WOOL/PLUM SE18 115 G3
Anglesey Court Rd CAR SM5 176 A5
Anglesey Dr RAIN RM13 99 J3
Anglesey Gdns CAR SM5 176 A5
Anglesey Rd OXHEY WD19 33 G4
PEND EN3 30 D3
Anglesmede Crs PIN HA5 48 A2
Anglesmede Wy PIN HA5 47 K2
Angles Rd STRHM/NOR SW16 148 E3
Anglia Cl TOTM N17 42 D6
Anglian Cl WATN WD24 21 G1
Anglian Rd WAN E11 76 B2
Anglo Rd BOW E3 93 H1
Angus Cl CHSGTN KT9 172 C4
Angus Dr RSLP HA4 65 G3
Angus Gdns CDALE/KGS NW9 37 F7
Angus Rd PLSTW E13 95 G2
Angus St NWCR SE14 112 B6
Anhalt Rd BTSEA SW11 108 D6
Ankerdine Crs
WOOL/PLUM SE18 115 G7
Anlaby Rd TEDD TW11 142 E4
Anley Rd HMSMTH W6 107 G1
Anmersh Gv STAN HA7 35 K7
Annabel Cl POP/IOD E14 93 K5
Anna Cl HACK E8 7 M3
Annandale Gv HGDN/ICK UB10 64 A2
Annandale Rd BFN/LL DA15 135 K6
CHSWK W4 106 B3
CROY/NA CR0 178 C1
GNWCH SE10 113 J4
Anna Neagle Cl FSTGT E7 76 E3
Anne Boleyn's Wk
CHEAM SM3 174 B6
KUTN/CMB KT2 144 A4
Anne Case Ms NWMAL KT3 * 160 A2
Anne Compton Ms
LEE/GVPK SE12 133 J6
Anne of Cleves Rd DART DA1 139 G4
Annesley Av CDALE/KGS NW9 51 F2
Annesley Cl WLSDN NW10 69 G2
Annesley Dr CROY/NA CR0 179 H2
Annesley Rd BKHTH/KID SE3 114 A7
Annesmere Gdns
BKHTH/KID SE3 134 C2
Anne St PLSTW E13 94 E3
Annette Cl
KTN/HRWW/WS HA3 48 E1
Annette Rd HOLWY N7 73 F3
Annie Besant Cl BOW E3 * 75 H7
Anning St WCHPL E1 7 K9
Annington Rd EFNCH N2 53 K2
Annis Rd HOM E9 75 G5
Ann La WBPTN SW10 108 C6
Ann Moss Wy
BERM/RHTH SE16 111 K2
Ann's Cl KTBR SW1X 15 M2
Ann St WOOL/PLUM SE18 115 J3
Annsworthy Av THHTH CR7 164 E2
Annsworthy Crs SNWD SE25 164 E2
Ansar Gdns WALTH E17 57 G4
Ansdell Rd PECK SE15 131 K1
Ansdell St KENS W8 14 D3
Ansdell Ter KENS W8 14 D3
Ansell Gv CAR SM5 162 E7
Ansell Rd TOOT SW17 147 J2
Anselm Cl CROY/NA CR0 178 B2
Anselm Rd FUL/PGN SW6 107 K5
PIN HA5 33 K6
Ansford Rd BMLY BR1 152 A4
Ansleigh Pl NTGHL W11 88 B6
Anson Cl ROMW/RG RM7 62 D1
Anson Rd ARCH N19 72 C3
CRICK NW2 69 K4
Anson Wk NTHWD HA6 32 A3
Anstead Dr RAIN RM13 99 J1
Anstey Rd PECK SE15 131 H2
Anstice Cl CHSWK W4 106 B6
Anstridge Rd ELTH/MOT SE9 135 J5
Antelope Rd
WOOL/PLUM SE18 114 E2
Anthony Cl MLHL NW7 37 G3
OXHEY WD19 21 H7
Anthony Rd BORE WD6 24 A1
GFD/PVL UB6 84 E1
SNWD SE25 165 H5
WELL DA16 116 B7
Anthony's Cl WAP E1W 92 C7
Anthony St WCHPL E1 92 D5
Anthus Ms NTHWD HA6 32 B6
Antill Rd BOW E3 93 G2
SEVS/STOTM N15 56 C3
Antill Ter WCHPL E1 93 F5
Antlers Hl CHING E4 31 K4
Anton Crs SUT SM1 174 E2
Antoneys Cl PIN HA5 47 H1
Anton Pl WBLY HA9 68 D2
Anton St HACK E8 74 C4
Antrim Rd HAMP NW3 71 K5
Antrobus Cl SUT SM1 174 D4
Antrobus Rd CHSWK W4 105 K3
Anvil Cl STRHM/NOR SW16 148 C6
Anworth Cl WFD IG8 45 F5
Aostle Wy THHTH CR7 164 C1
Apeldoorn Dr WLGTN SM6 176 E7
Aperfield Rd ERITH DA8 118 C5
Apex Cl BECK BR3 151 K7
Apex Pde MLHL NW7 * 37 F3
Aplin Wy ISLW TW7 103 K7
Apollo Av BMLY BR1 153 F7
NTHWD HA6 32 E4
Apollo Cl HCH RM12 81 K1
Apollo Pl WAN E11 76 C2
WBPTN SW10 * 108 C6
Apollo Wy ERITH DA8 118 A3
THMD SE28 115 J2
Apothecary St BLKFR EC4V * 12 C5
Appach Rd BRXS/STRHM SW2 130 B4
Apple Blossom Ct
VX/NE SW8 * 109 J6
Appleby Cl CHING E4 44 A5
SEVS/STOTM N15 55 K4
STMC/STPC BR5 169 K6
UX/CGN UB8 82 A5
WHTN TW2 142 D1
Appleby Gdns
EBED/NFELT TW14 * 121 J7
Appleby Rd CAN/RD E16 94 E5
HACK E8 74 C6
Appleby St BETH E2 7 L5
Appledore Av BXLYHN DA7 117 K7
RSLP HA4 65 F2
Appledore Cl EDGW HA8 36 C7
HAYES BR2 167 J4
TOOT SW17 147 K1
Appledore Crs SCUP DA14 154 E2
Appledore Wy MLHL NW7 38 B6
Appleford Rd NKENS W10 88 C3
Apple Garth BTFD TW8 104 E3
Applegarth CROY/NA CR0 179 K6
ESH/CLAY KT10 171 F4
Applegarth Dr
GNTH/NBYPK IG2 61 F3
Applegarth Rd THMD SE28 97 H7
WKENS W14 * 107 G2
Apple Gv CHSGTN KT9 172 A3
EN EN1 30 A2
RYLN/HDSTN HA2 48 A7
Apple Ldg ALP/SUD HA0 * 67 J2
Apple Market KUT/HW KT1 158 E1
Apple Rd WAN E11 76 C2
Appleton Cl BXLYHN DA7 137 J1
Appleton Gdns NWMAL KT3 160 D5
Appleton Rd ELTH/MOT SE9 134 D2
Appletree Cl PGE/AN SE20 150 D7
Appletree Gdns EBAR EN4 27 J3
Apple Tree Yd STJS SW1Y 10 F8
Applewood Cl CRICK NW2 69 K2
TRDG/WHET N20 27 J7
Applewood Dr PLSTW E13 95 F3
Appold St ERITH DA8 118 C5
SDTCH EC2A 13 J2
Apprentice Gdns NTHLT UB5 83 K2
Apprentice Wy CLPT E5 74 D3
Approach La MLHL NW7 38 C4
Approach Rd ASHF TW15 140 A5
BETH E2 92 E1
E/WMO/HCT KT8 157 F4
EBAR EN4 27 G3
RYNPK SW20 161 F1
The Approach ACT W3 87 F5
EN EN1 30 D1
HDN NW4 52 B4
Aprey Gdns HDN NW4 52 A3
April Cl FELT TW13 140 E2
HNWL W7 84 E6
April Gln FSTH SE23 151 F2
April St HACK E8 74 B3
Apsley Cl HRW HA1 48 C4
Apsley Rd NWMAL KT3 159 K2
SNWD SE25 165 J3
Apsley Wy CRICK NW2 69 J1
MYFR/PICC W1J * 10 C9
Aquarius TWK TW1 * 124 C7
Aquarius Wy NTHWD HA6 32 E4
Aquila St STJWD NW8 3 H5
Aquinas St STHWK SE1 12 B9
Arabella Dr PUT/ROE SW15 126 B3
Arabin Rd BROCKY SE4 132 B3
Aragon Av EW KT17 173 K7
THDIT KT7 158 A4
Aragon Cl HAYES BR2 168 E7
SUN TW16 140 D6
Aragon Dr RSLP HA4 47 H7
Aragon Pl MRDN SM4 161 G6
Aragon Rd KUTN/CMB KT2 144 A4
MRDN SM4 161 G6
Arandora Crs CHDH RM6 61 H6
Arbery Rd BOW E3 93 G2
Arbor Cl BECK BR3 166 E1
Arborfield Cl
BRXS/STRHM SW2 130 A7
Arbor Rd CHING E4 44 B2
Arbour Rd PEND EN3 31 F3
Arbour Sq WCHPL E1 93 F5
Arbour Wy HCH RM12 81 K4
Arbroath Gn OXHEY WD19 32 E2
Arbroath Rd ELTH/MOT SE9 134 D2
Arbrook La ESH/CLAY KT10 170 D5
Arbuthnot La BXLY DA5 137 F5
Arbuthnot Rd NWCR SE14 132 A1
Arbutus St HACK E8 7 K3
Arcade Chambers
ELTH/MOT SE9 * 135 F5
Arcade Pde CHSGTN KT9 * 172 A3
The Arcade ELTH/MOT SE9 * 135 F5
LVPST EC2M * 13 J3
WALTH E17 * 57 J3
Arcadia Av FNCH N3 38 E7
Arcadia Cl CAR SM5 176 A3
Arcadian Av BXLY DA5 137 F5
Arcadian Cl BXLY DA5 137 F5
Arcadian Gdns WDGN N22 41 G6
Arcadian Pl WAND/EARL SW18 127 H6
Arcadian Rd BXLY DA5 137 F6
Arcadia St POP/IOD E14 93 J5
Archangel St
BERM/RHTH SE16 112 A1
Archbishop's Pl
BRXS/STRHM SW2 130 A5
Archdale Pl NWMAL KT3 159 J2
Archdale Rd EDUL SE22 131 G4
Archel Rd WKENS W14 107 J5
Archer Cl BAR EN5 26 D5
KUTN/CMB KT2 144 A6
Archer Ct FELT TW13 121 K7
Archer Ms HPTN TW12 142 C5
Archer Rd SNWD SE25 165 J3
Archers Dr PEND EN3 30 E1
Archer Sq NWCR SE14 112 B5
Archer St SOHO/SHAV W1D 11 G6
Archery Cl BAY/PAD W2 9 K5
KTN/HRWW/WS HA3 49 F2
Archery Rd ELTH/MOT SE9 134 E4
The Arches CHCR WC2N * 11 K8
RYLN/HDSTN HA2 66 B1
Archibald Rd HOLWY N7 72 D3
Archibold St BOW E3 93 J2
Archie Cl WDR/YW UB7 100 D1
Arch St STHWK SE1 18 E4
Archway Cl ARCH N19 * 72 C1
NKENS W10 88 B4
WIM/MER SW19 147 F3
WLGTN SM6 * 176 E2
Archway Rd ARCH N19 54 C7
HGT N6 53 K4
Archway St BARN SW13 126 B2
Arcola St HACK E8 74 B4
Arcon Dr NTHLT UB5 83 J3
Arctic St KTTN NW5 72 B4
Arcus Rd BMLY BR1 152 C5
Ardbeg Rd HNHL SE24 130 E5
Arden Cl BUSH WD23 23 F6
HRW HA1 66 D2
THMD SE28 97 K5
WHTN TW2 122 E6
Arden Court Gdns EFNCH N2 53 H5
Arden Crs DAGW RM9 79 K6
POP/IOD E14 112 D3
Arden Est IS N1 7 J6
Arden Mhor PIN HA5 47 F3
Arden Rd FNCH N3 52 C2
WEA W13 85 J6
Ardent Cl SNWD SE25 165 F2
Ardfern Av STRHM/NOR SW16 164 B2
Ardfillan Rd CAT SE6 133 G7
Ardgowan Rd CAT SE6 133 H6
Ardilaun Rd HBRY N5 73 J3
Ardingly Cl CROY/NA CR0 179 F2
Ardleigh Gdns CHEAM SM3 161 K7
Ardleigh Rd IS N1 73 K5
WALTH E17 43 H7
Ardleigh Ter WALTH E17 43 H7
Ardley Cl CAT SE6 151 G2
WLSDN NW10 69 G2
Ardlui Rd WNWD SE27 149 J1
Ardmay Gdns SURB KT6 * 159 F4
Ardmere Rd LEW SE13 133 G5
Ardoch Rd CAT SE6 152 B1
Ardra Rd ED N9 43 F2
Ardrossan Gdns WPK KT4 173 J2
Ardross Av NTHWD HA6 32 C4
Ardshiel Cl PUT/ROE SW15 127 G2
Ardwell Av BARK/HLT IG6 60 C4
Ardwell Rd BRXS/STRHM SW2 148 E1
Ardwick Rd CRICK NW2 70 E3
Arena Est FSBYPK N4 * 55 H5
Argall Av LEY E10 57 F6
Argall Wy LEY E10 57 F7
Argenta Wy WLSDN NW10 68 D6
Argent Ct SURB KT6 * 172 C1
SURB KT6 172 C2
Argon Ms FUL/PGN SW6 107 K6
Argon Rd UED N18 42 E4
Argosy La STWL/WRAY TW19 120 A6
Argus Wy NTHLT UB5 83 J2
Argyle Av HSLW TW3 123 F5
Argyle Cl WEA W13 85 G3
Argyle Cnr WEA W13 * 85 H6
Argyle Ct WATW WD18 * 20 D3
Argyle Pl HMSMTH W6 106 E3
Argyle Rd BAR EN5 26 A3
CAN/RD E16 95 F5
GFD/PVL UB6 85 F2
HSLW TW3 123 G4
IL IG1 78 A1
NFNCH/WDSPK N12 38 E4
RYLN/HDSTN HA2 48 B5
SRTFD E15 76 C3
TOTM N17 42 C7
UED N18 42 C3
WCHPL E1 93 F3
WEA W13 85 G5
Argyle Sq STPAN WC1H 5 K7
Argyle St KCROSS N1C 5 J7
STPAN WC1H 5 K8
Argyle Wk STPAN WC1H * 5 J8
Argyle Wy BERM/RHTH SE16 111 H4
Argyll Av STHL UB1 84 B7
Argyll Cl BRXN/ST SW9 130 A2
Argyll Gdns EDGW HA8 50 D1
Argyll Rd KENS W8 14 A2
WOOL/PLUM SE18 115 H2
Argyll St SOHO/SHAV W1D 10 E5
Arhchie St STHWK SE1 19 K2
Arica Rd BROCKY SE4 132 B3
Ariel Rd KIL/WHAMP NW6 70 E5
Ariel Wy HSLWW TW4 122 A2
SHB W12 88 A7
Aristotle Rd CLAP SW4 129 J2
Arkell Gv NRWD SE19 149 H6
Arkindale Rd CAT SE6 152 A2
Arkley Crs WALTH E17 57 H4
Arkley Dr BAR EN5 25 J3
Arkley La BAR EN5 25 J2
Arkley Rd WALTH E17 57 H4
Arkley Vw BAR EN5 25 K3
Arklow Rd NWCR SE14 112 C5
Arkwright Rd HAMP NW3 71 G4
Arlesey Cl PUT/ROE SW15 127 H4
Arlesford Rd BRXN/ST SW9 129 K2
Arlingford Rd
BRXS/STRHM SW2 130 B5
Arlington NFNCH/WDSPK N12 38 E2
Arlington Av IS N1 6 F4
Arlington Cl BFN/LL DA15 135 K6
LEW SE13 133 G4
SUT SM1 174 E1
TWK TW1 * 124 D5
Arlington Ct HYS/HAR UB3 101 G4
Arlington Dr CAR SM5 175 K1
RSLP HA4 46 B5
Arlington Gdns CHSWK W4 105 K4
IL IG1 59 K6
Arlington Pde
BRXS/STRHM SW2 * 130 A3
Arlington Rd CAMTN NW1 4 C3
RCHPK/HAM TW10 143 K1
STHGT/OAK N14 40 B1
SURB KT6 158 E5
TEDD TW11 143 F3
TWK TW1 124 D5
WEA W13 85 H5
WFD IG8 44 E7
Arlington Sq IS N1 6 F4
Arlington St MYFR/PICC W1J 10 E8
Arlington Wy CLKNW EC1R 6 B7
Arliss Wy NTHLT UB5 65 G7
Arlow Rd WCHMH N21 29 G7
Armadale Cl TOTM N17 56 D3
Armadale Rd
EBED/NFELT TW14 121 K4
FUL/PGN SW6 107 K6
Armada St DEPT SE8 112 D5
Armada Wy CAN/RD E16 96 B6
Armagh Rd BOW E3 75 H7
Armfield Cl E/WMO/HCT KT8 156 E4
Armfield Crs MTCM CR4 162 E1
Arminger Rd SHB W12 87 K7
Armistice Gdns SNWD SE25 165 H2
Armitage Rd GLDGN NW11 52 C7
GNWCH SE10 113 J3
Armour Cl HOLWY N7 73 F5
Armoury Rd DEPT SE8 132 E1
Armoury Wy
WAND/EARL SW18 127 K4
Armstead Wk DAGE RM10 80 C6
Armstrong Av WFD IG8 44 C5
Armstrong Cl BCTR RM8 61 K6
BMLY BR1 168 D2
BORE WD6 24 E2
EHAM E6 95 K5
RSLP HA4 46 E5
Armstrong Crs EBAR EN4 27 H2
Armstrong Rd ACT W3 87 H7
FELT TW13 141 J4
WLSDN NW10 69 G6
WOOL/PLUM SE18 115 H2
Armstrong Wy NWDGN UB2 103 G1
Armytage Rd HEST TW5 102 C6
Arnal Crs WAND/EARL SW18 127 H6
Arncliffe Cl FBAR/BDGN N11 40 A5
Arne St LSQ/SEVD WC2H 11 K5
Arnett Sq CHING E4 43 H5
Arne Wk LEW SE13 133 J3
Arneways Av CHDH RM6 61 K3
Arneway St WEST SW1P 17 H4
Arnewood Cl PUT/ROE SW15 126 D7
Arney's La MTCM CR4 163 F5
Arngask Rd CAT SE6 133 G6
Arnheim Pl POP/IOD E14 112 D2
Arnison Rd E/WMO/HCT KT8 157 J3
Arnold Circ BETH E2 7 L8
Arnold Cl KTN/HRWW/WS HA3 50 B6
Arnold Crs ISLW TW7 123 J4
Arnold Dr CHSGTN KT9 171 K5
Arnold Est STHWK SE1 19 M2
Arnold Gdns PLMGR N13 41 H4
Arnold Rd BOW E3 93 J2
DAGW RM9 80 B6
NTHLT UB5 65 J5
SEVS/STOTM N15 56 B2
TOOT SW17 147 K6
Arnold Ter STAN HA7 * 35 F4
Arnos Gv STHGT/OAK N14 40 D3
Arnos Rd FBAR/BDGN N11 40 C4
Arnott Cl CHSWK W4 106 A3
THMD SE28 97 J7
Arnould Av CMBW SE5 130 E3
Arnsberg Wy BXLYHN DA7 137 H3
Arnside Gdns WBLY HA9 49 K7
Arnside Rd BXLYHN DA7 117 H7
Arnside St WALW SE17 18 F9
Arnulf St CAT SE6 151 K3
Arnull's Rd STRHM/NOR SW16 149 H5
Arodene Rd
BRXS/STRHM SW2 130 A5
Arosa Rd TWK TW1 124 E5
Arragon Gdns
STRHM/NOR SW16 148 E6
WWKM BR4 179 K2
Arragon Rd EHAM E6 77 H7
TWK TW1 124 B6
WAND/EARL SW18 127 K7
Arran Cl ERITH DA8 118 A5
WLGTN SM6 176 C3
Arran Dr MNPK E12 59 H7
STAN HA7 35 J3
Arran Gn OXHEY WD19 * 33 H3
Arran Ms EA W5 86 B7
Arranmore Ct BUSH WD23 * 21 J3
Arran Rd CAT SE6 151 K1
Arran Wk IS N1 6 E1
Arran Wy ESH/CLAY KT10 170 B1
Arras Av MRDN SM4 162 B4
Arrol Rd BECK BR3 165 K2
Arrow Rd BOW E3 93 K2
Arsenal Rd ELTH/MOT SE9 134 E1
Arsenal Wy CAN/RD E16 115 F1
Artemis Pl WAND/EARL SW18 127 J6
Arterberry Rd RYNPK SW20 146 A6
Arterial Rd Purfleet
SOCK/AV RM15 119 K2
Artesian Cl ROM RM1 63 H5
WLSDN NW10 69 F6
Artesian Gv BAR EN5 27 G3
Artesian Houses
BAY/PAD W2 * 8 A5
Artesian Rd BAY/PAD W2 8 A5
Arthingworth St SRTFD E15 76 C7
Arthurdon Rd BROCKY SE4 132 D4
Arthur Gv WOOL/PLUM SE18 115 H3
Arthur Rd CHDH RM6 61 J6
ED N9 42 B1
EHAM E6 95 K1
HOLWY N7 73 F3
KUTN/CMB KT2 144 C6
NWMAL KT3 160 E4
WIM/MER SW19 146 E2
Arthur St BUSH WD23 21 H2
CANST EC4R 13 H7
ERITH DA8 118 C6
Artichoke Hl WAP E1W 92 D6
Artichoke Pl CMBW SE5 * 110 E7
Artillery Cl GNTH/NBYPK IG2 60 C5
Artillery La LVPST EC2M 13 K3
SHB W12 87 J5
Artillery Pas WCHPL E1 * 13 K3
Artillery Pl WOOL/PLUM SE18 114 E4
Artillery Rw WEST SW1P 17 G4
Artisan Cl EHAM E6 96 B6
Artizan St WCHPL E1 13 K4
Artwell Cl LEY E10 57 K5
Arundel Av MRDN SM4 161 J3
Arundel Cl BTSEA SW11 128 D4
BXLY DA5 137 G5
CROY/NA CR0 * 177 H2
HPTN TW12 142 B4
SRTFD E15 76 C3
Arundel Dr BORE WD6 24 E4
RYLN/HDSTN HA2 65 K3
WFD IG8 44 E6
Arundel Gdns EDGW HA8 37 F6
GDMY/SEVK IG3 79 G1
NTGHL W11 88 D6
WCHMH N21 29 G7
Arundel Gv IS N1 74 A4
Arundel Pl HOLWY N7 73 G5
Arundel Rd BELMT SM2 174 D6
CROY/NA CR0 164 E5
DART DA1 139 F3
EBAR EN4 27 J2
HSLWW TW4 122 B2
KUT/HW KT1 159 J1
Arundel Sq HOLWY N7 73 G5
Arundel St TPL/STR WC2R 11 M6
Arundel Ter BARN SW13 106 E5
Arungford Ms
BRXS/STRHM SW2 130 B4
Arvon Rd HBRY N5 73 G4
Asbaston Ter IL IG1 78 C4
Ascalon St VX/NE SW8 109 H6
Ascham Dr CHING E4 43 K6
Ascham End WALTH E17 43 G7
Ascham St KTTN NW5 72 C4
Aschurch Rd CROY/NA CR0 165 G6
Ascot Cl BORE WD6 24 C4
NTHLT UB5 66 A4
Ascot Gdns STHL UB1 83 K4
Ascot Ms WLGTN SM6 176 C7
Ascot Pde CLAP SW4 * 129 K3
Ascot Rd EBED/NFELT TW14 120 D7
EHAM E6 95 K2
SEVS/STOTM N15 55 K4
TOOT SW17 148 A5
UED N18 42 C3
WATW WD18 20 C4
Ascott Av EA W5 105 F1
Ascott Ct PIN HA5 * 46 E3
Ashanti Ms HACK E8 * 74 D5
Ashborune Sq NTHWD HA6 32 C5
Ashbourne Av BXLYHN DA7 117 F6
GLDGN NW11 52 D4
RYLN/HDSTN HA2 * 66 D1
SWFD E18 59 F3
TRDG/WHET N20 39 K1
Ashbourne Cl EA W5 86 B4
NFNCH/WDSPK N12 39 F3
Ashbourne Gv CHSWK W4 106 B4
EDUL SE22 131 G4
MLHL NW7 37 F4
Ashbourne Pde EA W5 * 86 B3
GLDGN NW11 * 52 D3
Ashbourne Rd EA W5 86 B3
MTCM CR4 148 A5
Ashbourne Ter
WIM/MER SW19 146 E6
Ashbourne Wy GLDGN NW11 52 D4
Ashbridge Rd WAN E11 58 C6
Ashbridge St STJWD NW8 9 J1
Ashbrook EDGW HA8 * 36 B5
Ashbrook Rd ARCH N19 72 D1
DAGE RM10 80 D2
Ashburn Gdns SKENS SW7 14 E5
Ashburnham Av HRW HA1 49 F6
Ashburnham Cl EFNCH N2 53 H2
OXHEY WD19 * 32 E2
Ashburnham Dr OXHEY WD19 32 E2
Ashburnham Gdns HRW HA1 49 F5
Ashburnham Gv GNWCH SE10 112 E6
Ashburnham Pk
ESH/CLAY KT10 170 C3
Ashburnham Pl GNWCH SE10 112 E6
Ashburnham Retreat
GNWCH SE10 112 E6
Ashburnham Rd BELV DA17 117 K3
RCHPK/HAM TW10 143 H2
WBPTN SW10 * 108 B6
WLSDN NW10 88 A2
Ashburn Pl SKENS SW7 14 E5
Ashburton Av CROY/NA CR0 165 J7
GDMY/SEVK IG3 79 F3
Ashburton Cl CROY/NA CR0 165 H7
Ashburton Gdns
CROY/NA CR0 178 C1
Ashburton Rd CAN/RD E16 94 E5
CROY/NA CR0 178 C1
RSLP HA4 64 E1
Ashbury Gdns CHDH RM6 61 K4
Ashbury Pl WIM/MER SW19 147 G5
Ashbury Rd BTSEA SW11 128 E2
Ashby Av CHSGTN KT9 172 C5
Ashby Cl WWKM BR4 180 B2
Ashby Gv IS N1 6 F1
Ashby Ms BROCKY SE4 132 C2
Ashby Rd BROCKY SE4 132 C1
SEVS/STOTM N15 56 C4
Ashby St FSBYE EC1V 6 D8
Ashby Wk CROY/NA CR0 164 D5
Ashby Wy WDR/YW UB7 100 D6
Ashchurch Gv SHB W12 106 D1
Ashchurch Park Vls SHB W12 106 D2
Ashchurch Ter SHB W12 106 C2
Ash Cl CAR SM5 175 K1
EDGW HA8 36 E3
NWMAL KT3 160 A1
PGE/AN SE20 165 K1
SCUP DA14 155 H2
STAN HA7 35 G5
STMC/STPC BR5 169 J4
Ashcombe Av SURB KT6 158 E6
Ashcombe Gdns EDGW HA8 36 C3
Ashcombe Pk CRICK NW2 69 G2
Ashcombe Rd CAR SM5 176 A5
WIM/MER SW19 146 E4
Ashcombe Sq NWMAL KT3 159 K2
Ashcombe St FUL/PGN SW6 * 128 A1
Ash Ct HOR/WEW KT19 172 E3
Ashcroft PIN HA5 34 A5
Ashcroft Av BFN/LL DA15 136 B5
Ashcroft Crs BFN/LL DA15 136 B5
Ashcroft Rd BOW E3 93 G2
CHSGTN KT9 172 B2
Ashdale Cl WHTN TW2 123 G6
Ashdale Gv STAN HA7 35 F5
Ashdale Rd LEE/GVPK SE12 134 A7
Ashdene PIN HA5 47 G2
Ashdene Cl ASHF TW15 * 140 A6
Ashdon Cl WFD IG8 45 F5
Ashdon Rd BUSH WD23 21 H2
Ashdown WEA W13 * 85 H4
Ashdown Cl BECK BR3 166 E1
BXLY DA5 137 K6
Ashdown Crs KTTN NW5 * 72 A4
Ashdown Dr BORE WD6 24 B1
Ashdown Pl THDIT KT7 158 B5
Ashdown Rd KUT/HW KT1 159 F1
PEND EN3 30 E2
WLSDN NW10 69 G7
Ashdown Wy TOOT SW17 148 A1
Ashen EHAM E6 96 A5
Ashenden Rd CLPT E5 75 G4
Ashen Dr DART DA1 138 D5
Ashen Gv WIM/MER SW19 146 E2
Ashen V SAND/SEL CR2 179 F7
Asher Loftus Wy
FBAR/BDGN N11 39 K5
Asher Wy WAP E1W 92 C7
Ashfield Av BUSH WD23 22 B5
FELT TW13 122 A7
Ashfield Cl BECK BR3 151 J6
RCHPK/HAM TW10 125 F7
Ashfield Ct EA W5 * 86 A6
Ashfield La CHST BR7 154 C5
Ashfield Rd ACT W3 87 H7
FSBYPK N4 55 J5
STHGT/OAK N14 40 C2
Ashfield St WCHPL E1 92 D4
Ashfield Yd WCHPL E1 * 92 E4
Ashford Av CEND/HSY/T N8 54 E3
YEAD UB4 83 H5
Ashford Cl WALTH E17 57 H5
Ashford Crs PEND EN3 30 E1
Ashford Gn OXHEY WD19 33 H4
Ashford Ms TOTM N17 42 C7
Ashford Rd ASHF TW15 140 A6
CRICK NW2 70 B3
EHAM E6 77 K5
FELT TW13 140 B3
SWFD E18 59 F1
Ashford St IS N1 7 J7
Ash Gv ALP/SUD HA0 67 G3
CRICK NW2 70 B3
EA W5 105 F1
EBED/NFELT TW14 121 H7
EN EN1 30 A6
HACK E8 74 D7
HEST TW5 102 C7
HYS/HAR UB3 82 B6
MUSWH N10 54 B3

PGE/AN SE20 165 K1
PLMGR N13 41 J2
STHL UB1 84 A4
WWKM BR4 167 F7
Ashgrove Rd ASHF TW15 140 A4
BMLY BR1 152 B5
GDMY/SEVK IG3 61 F7
Ash Hill Cl BUSH WD23 22 B7
Ash Hill Dr PIN HA5 47 G2
Ashingdon Cl CHING E4 43 A3
Ashington Rd FUL/PGN SW6 * 127 J1
Ashlake Rd STRHM/NOR SW16 148 E3
Ashland Pl MHST W1U 10 A2
Ashlar Pl WOOL/PLUM SE18 115 G3
Ashleigh Gdns SUT SM1 175 F1
Ashleigh Rd
MORT/ESHN SW14 126 B2
PGE/AN SE20 165 J2
Ashley Av BARK/HLT IG6 60 B1
MRDN SM4 161 K4
Ashley Cl HDN NW4 52 A1
PIN HA5 47 F1
Ashley Crs BTSEA SW11 129 F2
WDGN N22 55 G1
Ashley Dr BORE WD6 24 E4
ISLW TW7 103 K5
WHTN TW2 123 G7
Ashley Gdns PLMGR N13 41 J3
RCHPK/HAM TW10 143 K2
WBLY HA9 68 A1
Ashley La CROY/NA CR0 177 H3
HDN NW4 52 A1
Ashley Pl WESTW SW1E 16 E4
Ashley Rd ARCH N19 54 E7
CHING E4 43 J4
FSTGT E7 77 G6
HPTN TW12 142 A7
PEND EN3 30 E1
RCH/KEW TW9 125 F2
THDIT KT7 158 A5
THHTH CR7 164 A3
TOTM N17 56 C2
WIM/MER SW19 147 F5
Ashleys Aly SEVS/STOTM N15 55 J3
Ashley Wk MLHL NW7 38 A6
Ashling Rd CROY/NA CR0 165 H7
Ashlin Rd SRTFD E15 76 B3
Ashlone Rd PUT/ROE SW15 127 G1
Ashlyn Cl BUSH WD23 21 J3
Ashlyns Wy CHSGTN KT9 171 K5
Ashmead STHGT/OAK N14 28 C4
Ashmead Ga BMLY BR1 153 G7
Ashmead Ms BROCKY SE4 132 D1
Ashmead Rd DEPT SE8 132 D1
EBED/NFELT TW14 121 K7
Ashmere Av BECK BR3 167 G1
Ashmere Cl CHEAM SM3 174 B4
Ashmere Gv
BRXS/STRHM SW2 129 K3
Ash Ms KTTN NW5 * 72 C4
Ashmill St STJWD NW8 9 J2
Ashmole St VX/NE SW8 110 A5
Ashmore Cl PECK SE15 111 G6
Ashmore Gv WELL DA16 135 J2
Ashmore Rd MV/WKIL W9 88 D2
Ashmount Rd
SEVS/STOTM N15 56 B4
Ashmount Ter EA W5 * 104 E3
Ashmour Gdns ROM RM1 63 F1
Ashneal Gdns HRW HA1 66 D2
Ashness Gdns GFD/PVL UB6 67 H5
Ashness Rd BTSEA SW11 128 E4
Ashridge Cl
KTN/HRWW/WS HA3 49 J5
Ashridge Crs
WOOL/PLUM SE18 115 H6
Ashridge Dr OXHEY WD19 33 G4
Ashridge Gdns PIN HA5 47 J3
PLMGR N13 40 E4
Ashridge Wy MRDN SM4 161 J3
SUN TW16 140 E5
Ash Rd CHEAM SM3 161 H7
CROY/NA CR0 179 J1
DART DA1 139 G7
SRTFD E15 76 C4
Ash Rw HAYES BR2 169 F5
Ashtead Rd STNW/STAM N16 56 C6
Ashton Cl SUT SM1 174 E3
Ashton Gdns CHDH RM6 62 A5
HSLWW TW4 122 E3
Ashton Rd SRTFD E15 76 B4
Ashton St POP/IOD E14 94 A6
Ashtree Av MTCM CR4 162 C1
Ash Tree Cl CROY/NA CR0 166 B5
SURB KT6 159 F7
Ash Tree Dell CDALE/KGS NW9 50 E4
Ash Tree Wy CROY/NA CR0 166 B4
Ashurst Cl DART DA1 138 C2
NTHWD HA6 32 C6
PGE/AN SE20 150 D7
Ashurst Dr GNTH/NBYPK IG2 60 B5
Ashurst Gdns
BRXS/STRHM SW2 * 130 B7
Ashurst Rd EBAR EN4 27 K4
NFNCH/WDSPK N12 39 J4
Ashurst Wk CROY/NA CR0 178 D1
Ashvale Rd TOOT SW17 147 K4
Ashville Rd WAN E11 76 B1
Ash Wk ALP/SUD HA0 67 J3
Ashwater Rd LEE/GVPK SE12 133 K7
Ashwell Cl EHAM E6 95 K5
Ashwin St HACK E8 74 B5
Ashwood Av RAIN RM13 99 K2
Ashwood Gdns CROY/NA CR0 179 K5
HYS/HAR UB3 101 J3
Ashwood Rd CHING E4 44 B2
Ashworth Cl CMBW SE5 130 E1
Ashworth Rd MV/WKIL W9 2 D7
Askern Cl BXLYHS DA6 136 E3
Aske St IS N1 7 J7
Askew Crs SHB W12 106 C1
Askew Rd NTHWD HA6 32 B1
SHB W12 106 C1
Askew Vls PLMGR N13 * 41 H2
Askham Rd SHB W12 87 J7
Askill Dr PUT/ROE SW15 127 H4
Askwith Rd RAIN RM13 99 F1
Asland Rd SRTFD E15 76 B7
Aslett St WAND/EARL SW18 128 A6
Asmara Rd CRICK NW2 70 C4
Asmuns Hl GLDGN NW11 52 E4
Asmuns Pl GLDGN NW11 52 D4
Asolando Dr WALW SE17 18 F7
Aspen Cl EA W5 105 G1
Aspen Copse BMLY BR1 168 E1
Aspen Ct HACK E8 * 74 C5
Aspen Dr ALP/SUD HA0 67 G2
Aspen Gdns ASHF TW15 140 A4
MTCM CR4 163 F4
Aspen Gn ERITHM DA18 117 G2
Aspen Gv PIN HA5 46 D2
Aspen La NTHLT UB5 83 J2
Aspenlea Rd HMSMTH W6 107 G5
Aspen Wy FELT TW13 141 F2
POP/IOD E14 94 A6
Aspern Gv HAMP NW3 71 J4
Aspinall Rd BROCKY SE4 132 A2
NWCR SE14 132 A2
Aspinden Rd
BERM/RHTH SE16 111 J3
Aspley Rd WAND/EARL SW18 128 A4
Asplins Rd TOTM N17 42 C7
Asplins Vls TOTM N17 * 42 C7
Asprey Ms BECK BR3 166 C4
Asquith Cl BCTR RM8 61 J7
Assam St WCHPL E1 92 C5
Assata Ms IS N1 73 H5
Assembly Pas WCHPL E1 92 E4
Assembly Wk CAR SM5 162 D6
Astall Cl KTN/HRWW/WS HA3 34 D7
Astbury Rd PECK SE15 111 K7
Astell St CHEL SW3 15 K7
Asteys Rw IS N1 6 C1
Astle St BTSEA SW11 129 F1
Astley Av CRICK NW2 70 A4
Aston Av KTN/HRWW/WS HA3 49 J6
Aston Cl BUSH WD23 22 C5
SCUP DA14 155 G2
WATN WD24 21 G1
Aston Gn HSLWW TW4 122 B1
Aston Pl STRHM/NOR SW16 149 H5
Aston Rd EA W5 85 K5
ESH/CLAY KT10 170 E4
RYNPK SW20 161 F1
Astons Rd NTHWD HA6 32 A2
Aston St POP/IOD E14 93 G5
Aston Ter BAL SW12 * 129 G5
Astonville St
WAND/EARL SW18 127 K7
Astor Av ROMW/RG RM7 62 D5
Astor Cl KUTN/CMB KT2 144 D5
Astoria Pde
STRHM/NOR SW16 * 148 E2
Astoria Wk BRXN/ST SW9 130 B2
Astra Cl HCH RM12 81 K5
Astrop Ms HMSMTH W6 107 F2
Astrop Ter HMSMTH W6 107 F2
Astwood Ms SKENS SW7 14 D5
Asylum Rd PECK SE15 111 J6
Atalanta St FUL/PGN SW6 107 G7
Atbara Rd TEDD TW11 143 H5
Atcham Rd HSLW TW3 123 H3
Atcost Rd BARK IG11 97 G4
Atheldene Rd
WAND/EARL SW18 128 A7
Athelney St CAT SE6 151 J2
Athelstane Gv BOW E3 93 H1
Athelstane Ms FSBYPK N4 55 G7
Athelstan Gdns
KIL/WHAMP NW6 * 70 C6
Athelstan Rd KUT/HW KT1 159 G3
Athelstan Wy STMC/STPC BR5 155 G7
Athelstone Rd
KTN/HRWW/WS HA3 48 D1
Athena Cl KUT/HW KT1 159 G2
RYLN/HDSTN HA2 66 D1
Athenaeum Pl MUSWH N10 54 B2
Athenaeum Rd
TRDG/WHET N20 27 G7
Athena Pl NTHWD HA6 32 D7
Athenlay Rd PECK SE15 132 A4
Athens Gdns MV/WKIL W9 * 8 A1
Atherden Rd CLPT E5 74 E3
Atherfold Rd BRXN/ST SW9 129 K2
Atherley Wy HSLWW TW4 122 E6
Atherstone Ms SKENS SW7 14 F5
Atherton Cl STWL/WRAY TW19 120 A5
Atherton Dr WIM/MER SW19 146 B3
Atherton Hts ALP/SUD HA0 67 J5
Atherton Ms FSTGT E7 76 D5
Atherton Pl RYLN/HDSTN HA2 48 C2
STHL UB1 84 A6
Atherton Rd BARN SW13 106 D6
CLAY IG5 59 J1
FSTGT E7 76 D4
Atherton St BTSEA SW11 128 D1
Athlone ESH/CLAY KT10 170 E5
Athlone Cl CLPT E5 74 D4
Athlone Ct WALTH E17 58 B2
Athlone Rd BRXS/STRHM SW2 130 A6
Athlone St KTTN NW5 72 A5
Athlon Rd ALP/SUD HA0 85 K1
Athol Cl PIN HA5 33 F7
Athole Gdns EN EN1 30 A4
Athol Gdns PIN HA5 33 F7
Atholl Rd GDMY/SEVK IG3 61 G6
Athol Rd ERITH DA8 117 K4
Athol Sq POP/IOD E14 94 A5
Atkins Dr WWKM BR4 180 B1
Atkinson Rd CAN/RD E16 95 G4
Atkins Rd BAL SW12 129 H6
LEY E10 57 K5
Atlanta Bvd ROM RM1 63 G5
Atlantic Rd BRXN/ST SW9 130 B3
Atlantis Av CAN/RD E16 96 C6
Atlantis Cl BARK IG11 97 H2
Atlas Crs EDGW HA8 36 D1
Atlas Gdns CHARL SE7 114 B3
Atlas Ms HACK E8 74 B5
Atlas Rd DART DA1 139 J2
FBAR/BDGN N11 40 A5
PLSTW E13 94 E1
WBLY HA9 68 E3
WLSDN NW10 87 G2
Atley Rd BOW E3 75 J7
Atlip Rd ALP/SUD HA0 68 A7
Atney Rd PUT/ROE SW15 127 H3
Atria Rd NTHWD HA6 32 E4
Attenborough Cl
OXHEY WD19 33 J2
Atterbury Rd FSBYPK N4 55 G5
Atterbury St WEST SW1P 17 H6
Attewood Av WLSDN NW10 69 G2
Attewood Rd NTHLT UB5 65 J5
Attfield Cl TRDG/WHET N20 39 H1
Attlee Cl THHTH CR7 164 D5
YEAD UB4 * 83 F2
Attlee Dr DART DA1 139 K4
Attlee Rd THMD SE28 97 H6
YEAD UB4 82 E2
Attlee Ter WALTH E17 57 K3
Attneave St FSBYW WC1X 6 A9
Atwell Pl THDIT KT7 158 B7
Atwell Rd PECK SE15 * 131 H1
Atwood Av RCH/KEW TW9 125 H1
Atwood Rd HMSMTH W6 106 E3
Aubert Pk HBRY N5 73 G3
Aubert Rd HBRY N5 73 H3
Aubrey Pl STJWD NW8 2 E6
Aubrey Rd CEND/HSY/T N8 * 54 E4
NTGHL W11 88 D7
WALTH E17 57 J2
Aubrey Wk KENS W8 88 D7
Auburn Cl NWCR SE14 112 B6
Aubyn Hl WNWD SE27 149 J3
Aubyn Sq PUT/ROE SW15 126 D3
Auckland Av RAIN RM13 99 H2
Auckland Cl NRWD SE19 150 B7
Auckland Gdns NRWD SE19 150 A7
Auckland Hl WNWD SE27 149 J3
Auckland Ri NRWD SE19 150 A7
Auckland Rd BTSEA SW11 128 D3
IL IG1 60 B7
KUT/HW KT1 159 G3
LEY E10 75 K2
NRWD SE19 150 B7
Auckland St LBTH SE11 17 L8
Aucuba Vls WELL DA16 * 136 C2
Audax CDALE/KGS NW9 * 51 H1
Auden Dr BORE WD6 24 C4
Auden Pl CAMTN NW1 4 A3
CHEAM SM3 * 174 A3
Audley Cl BORE WD6 24 C2
BTSEA SW11 129 F2
MUSWH N10 40 B6
Audley Ct PIN HA5 47 G1
WAN E11 58 D3
Audley Dr CAN/RD E16 95 F7
Audley Gdns GDMY/SEVK IG3 79 F1
Audley Pl BELMT SM2 175 F6
Audley Rd EA W5 86 B4
ENC/FH EN2 29 H1
HDN NW4 51 J5
RCHPK/HAM TW10 125 G4
Audley Sq MYFR/PKLN W1K * 10 B8
Audley St MYFR/PKLN W1K 10 B8
Audrey Cl BECK BR3 166 E5
Audrey Gdns ALP/SUD HA0 67 H1
Audrey Rd IL IG1 78 B2
Audrey St BETH E2 92 C1
Audric Cl KUTN/CMB KT2 144 C7
Augurs La PLSTW E13 95 F2
Augusta Cl E/WMO/HCT KT8 156 E2
Augusta Rd WHTN TW2 142 C1
Augustine Rd HMSMTH W6 107 G2
KTN/HRWW/WS HA3 34 B7
Augustus Cl BTFD TW8 104 E6
SHB W12 106 E1
STAN HA7 35 K4
Augustus Rd WIM/MER SW19 127 G7
Augustus St CAMTN NW1 4 D6
Aultone Wy CAR SM5 175 K1
SUT SM1 175 F1
Aulton Pl LBTH SE11 18 B8
Aurelia Gdns CROY/NA CR0 164 A4
Aurelia Rd CROY/NA CR0 163 K5
Auriel Av DAGE RM10 81 F5
Auriga Ms IS N1 73 K4
Auriol Cl WPK KT4 173 G2
Auriol Dr GFD/PVL UB6 66 D6
Auriol Park Rd WPK KT4 173 G2
Auriol Rd WKENS W14 107 H3
Austell Gdns MLHL NW7 37 G2
Austen Cl THMD SE28 97 H7
Austen Rd ERITH DA8 117 J6
RYLN/HDSTN HA2 66 B1
Austin Av HAYES BR2 168 D5
Austin Cl FSTH SE23 132 B6
TWK TW1 124 D4
Austin Friars OBST EC2N 13 H4
Austin Friars Sq OBST EC2N * 13 H4
Austin Rd BTSEA SW11 109 F7
HYS/HAR UB3 101 J1
Austins La HGDN/ICK UB10 64 A2
Austin St BETH E2 7 L8
Austral Cl BFN/LL DA15 155 F2
Australia Rd SHB W12 87 K6
Austral St LBTH SE11 18 C5
Austyn Gdns BRYLDS KT5 * 159 J7
Autumn Cl EN EN1 30 D1
WIM/MER SW19 147 G5
Autumn Dr BELMT SM2 175 F7
Autumn Gv BMLY BR1 153 F5
Autumn St BOW E3 75 J7
Avalon Cl ENC/FH EN2 29 G1
RYNPK SW20 161 H1
WEA W13 85 G4
Avalon Rd FUL/PGN SW6 108 A7
WEA W13 85 G3
Avarn Rd TOOT SW17 147 K5
Avebury Pk SURB KT6 * 158 E5
Avebury Rd WAN E11 58 B7
WIM/MER SW19 146 D7
Avebury St IS N1 7 G4
Aveley Cl ERITH DA8 118 C5
Aveley Rd ROM RM1 63 F3
Aveline St LBTH SE11 17 M7
Aveling Park Rd WALTH E17 57 J1
Avelon Rd RAIN RM13 81 J7
Ave Marie La STP EC4M 12 D5
Avenell Rd HBRY N5 73 H2
Avening Rd WAND/EARL SW18 127 K6
Avening Ter
WAND/EARL SW18 127 K5
Avenons Rd PLSTW E13 94 E4
Avenue Cl HEST TW5 102 A7
STHGT/OAK N14 28 C5
STJWD NW8 3 K4
WDR/YW UB7 100 A2
Avenue Crs ACT W3 105 J1
HEST TW5 102 A7
Avenue Elmers SURB KT6 159 F4
Avenue Gdns ACT W3 105 J1
HEST TW5 * 101 K6
MORT/ESHN SW14 126 B2
SNWD SE25 165 H2
TEDD TW11 143 F6
Avenue Ms MUSWH N10 54 B2
Avenue Pde SUN TW16 156 A2
WCHMH N21 * 29 K6
Avenue Park Rd WNWD SE27 149 H1
Avenue Ri BUSH WD23 22 A4
Avenue Rd ACT W3 105 J1
BTFD TW8 104 D4
BXLYHN DA7 137 F2
CHDH RM6 61 H6
ERITH DA8 117 K6
ERITH DA8 118 B5
FELT TW13 140 D2
FSTGT E7 77 F3
HAMP NW3 3 G1
HGT N6 54 C6
HPTN TW12 142 B7
ISLW TW7 103 K7
KUT/HW KT1 159 F2
NFNCH/WDSPK N12 39 G3
NWMAL KT3 160 B2
PGE/AN SE20 150 E7
PIN HA5 47 J2
RYNPK SW20 160 E1
SEVS/STOTM N15 55 K4
SNWD SE25 165 H1
STHGT/OAK N14 28 C5
STHL UB1 83 K7
STJWD NW8 3 H2
STRHM/NOR SW16 163 J1
TEDD TW11 143 G6
WFD IG8 45 G5
WLGTN SM6 176 C6
WLSDN NW10 87 H1
Avenue South BRYLDS KT5 159 G6
Avenue Ter NWMAL KT3 159 K2
OXHEY WD19 21 J5
The Avenue BAR EN5 26 C2
BECK BR3 151 K7
BELMT SM2 174 D7
BKHH IG9 45 G1
BMLY BR1 168 C2
BRYLDS KT5 159 G5
BUSH WD23 21 K3
BXLY DA5 136 E6
CAR SM5 176 A6
CEND/HSY/T N8 55 G2
CHING E4 44 B5
CHSWK W4 106 B2
CLAP SW4 129 F4
CROY/NA CR0 178 A2
ESH/CLAY KT10 170 E5
EW KT17 174 A6
FBAR/BDGN N11 40 B4
FNCH N3 52 E1
GNWCH SE10 113 G6
HEST TW5 101 K7
HPTN TW12 141 K5
HSLW TW3 123 G4
KIL/WHAMP NW6 70 C6
KTN/HRWW/WS HA3 35 F7
MUSWH N10 54 C1
NTHWD HA6 32 A5
PIN HA5 33 K5
PIN HA5 47 K5
RCH/KEW TW9 125 G1
ROM RM1 63 F3
STMC/STPC BR5 155 H6
SUN TW16 156 A1
TOTM N17 56 A1
TWK TW1 124 D4
WAN E11 59 F5
WAT WD17 20 E1
WBLY HA9 50 A7
WEA W13 85 H6
WPK KT4 173 H1
WWKM BR4 167 G6
Averil Gv STRHM/NOR SW16 149 H5
Averill St HMSMTH W6 107 G5
Avern Gdns E/WMO/HCT KT8 157 G3
Avern Rd E/WMO/HCT KT8 157 G3
Avery Farm Rw BGVA SW1W * 16 C6
Avery Gdns GNTH/NBYPK IG2 59 K4
Avery Hill Rd ELTH/MOT SE9 135 H7
Avery Rw MYFR/PKLN W1K 10 C6
Aviary Cl CAN/RD E16 94 D4
Aviation Dr CDALE/KGS NW9 51 J1
Aviemore Cl BECK BR3 166 C4
Aviemore Wy BECK BR3 166 B4
Avigdor Ms STNW/STAM N16 73 K1
Avignon Rd BROCKY SE4 132 A2
Avington Gv PGE/AN SE20 150 E6
Avington Wy PECK SE15 * 111 G6
Avion Crs CDALE/KGS NW9 51 J1
Avior Dr NTHWD HA6 32 D3
Avis Sq WCHPL E1 93 F5
Avoca Rd TOOT SW17 148 A3
Avocet Cl STHWK SE1 111 H4
Avocet Ms THMD SE28 115 J2
Avon Cl SUT SM1 175 G3
WPK KT4 173 J1
YEAD UB4 83 G3
Avon Ct PIN HA5 * 34 A6
Avondale Av CRICK NW2 69 G2
EBAR EN4 27 K7
ESH/CLAY KT10 171 G2
NFNCH/WDSPK N12 39 F4
WPK KT4 160 C7
Avondale Ct SWFD E18 45 F7
Avondale Crs PEND EN3 31 G2
REDBR IG4 59 H4
Avondale Dr HYS/HAR UB3 82 E7
Avondale Gdns HSLWW TW4 122 E4
Avondale Park Gdns
NTGHL W11 * 88 C6
Avondale Park Rd NTGHL W11 88 C6
Avondale Pavement
STHWK SE1 * 111 H4
Avondale Ri PECK SE15 131 G2
Avondale Rd BMLY BR1 152 C5
CAN/RD E16 94 C4
ELTH/MOT SE9 153 J1
FNCH N3 39 G7
KTN/HRWW/WS HA3 49 F2
MORT/ESHN SW14 126 A2
PLMGR N13 41 G1
SAND/SEL CR2 177 J5
SEVS/STOTM N15 55 H4
WALTH E17 57 J6
WELL DA16 136 D1
WIM/MER SW19 147 F4
Avondale Sq STHWK SE1 111 H4
Avonley Rd NWCR SE14 111 K6
Avonmore Gdns
WKENS W14 * 107 J3
Avonmore Pl WKENS W14 107 H3
Avonmore Rd WKENS W14 107 J3
Avonmouth Rd DART DA1 139 G4
Avonmouth St STHWK SE1 18 E3
Avon Rd BROCKY SE4 132 D2
GFD/PVL UB6 84 A3
SUN TW16 140 D6
WALTH E17 58 B2
Avon Wy SWFD E18 58 E3
Avonwick Rd HSLW TW3 123 G1
Avril Wy CHING E4 44 A4
Avro Wy WLGTN SM6 176 E6
Awberry Ct WATW WD18 * 20 B5
Awlfield Av TOTM N17 41 K7
Awliscombe Rd WELL DA16 136 A1
Axe St BARK IG11 78 C7
Axholme Av EDGW HA8 36 C7
Axis Ct GNWCH SE10 113 H5
Axminster Crs WELL DA16 116 D7
Axminster Rd HOLWY N7 72 E2
Axon Pl IL IG1 78 C1
Aybrook St MHST W1U 10 A3
Aycliff Ct KUT/HW KT1 * 159 H1
Aycliffe Cl BMLY BR1 168 E3
Aycliffe Rd SHB W12 87 H7
Aylands Cl WBLY HA9 68 A1
Aylesbury Cl FSTGT E7 76 D5
Aylesbury Est WALW SE17 19 H8
Aylesbury Rd HAYES BR2 167 K2
WALW SE17 19 H8
Aylesbury St CLKNW EC1R 12 C1
WLSDN NW10 69 F2
Aylesford Av BECK BR3 166 B4
Aylesford St PIM SW1V 17 G7
Aylesham Cl MLHL NW7 37 J6
Aylesham Rd ORP BR6 169 K6
Ayles Rd YEAD UB4 83 F2
Aylestone Av
KIL/WHAMP NW6 70 B6
Aylett Rd ISLW TW7 123 K1
SNWD SE25 165 J3
Ayley Cft EN EN1 30 C4
Ayliffe Cl KUT/HW KT1 159 H1
Aylmer Cl STAN HA7 35 G3
Aylmer Dr STAN HA7 35 G3
Aylmer Pde EFNCH N2 * 53 K4
Aylmer Rd BCTR RM8 80 A2
EFNCH N2 53 J4
SHB W12 106 B1
WAN E11 58 D6
Ayloffe Rd DAGW RM9 80 B5
Aylsham Dr HGDN/ICK UB10 64 A1
Aylton Est BERM/RHTH SE16 * 111 K1
Aylward Rd FSTH SE23 151 F1
RYNPK SW20 161 J1
Aylwards Ri STAN HA7 35 G3
Aylward St WCHPL E1 93 F5
Aynhoe Rd WKENS W14 107 G3
Aynho St WATW WD18 21 F4
Ayres Cl PLSTW E13 94 E2
Ayres Crs WLSDN NW10 69 F6
Ayres St STHWK SE1 18 F1
Ayrsome Rd STNW/STAM N16 74 A2
Ayrton Rd SKENS SW7 15 G3
Aysgarth Rd DUL SE21 130 E5
Aytoun Pl BRXN/ST SW9 130 A1
Aytoun Rd BRXN/ST SW9 130 A1
Azalea Cl HNWL W7 85 F7
IL IG1 78 B4
Azalea Ct WFD IG8 * 44 C6
Azalea Wk PIN HA5 47 F5
Azania Ms KTTN NW5 72 B4
Azenby Rd PECK SE15 131 G1
Azof St GNWCH SE10 113 H3

B

Baalbec Rd HBRY N5 73 H4
Babbacombe Cl CHSGTN KT9 171 K4
Babbacombe Gdns REDBR IG4 59 J3
Babbacombe Rd BMLY BR1 153 F7
Baber Bridge Pde
EBED/NFELT TW14 * 122 B5
Baber Dr EBED/NFELT TW14 122 B5
Babington Ri WBLY HA9 68 C5
Babington Rd BCTR RM8 79 J4
HCH RM12 63 K7
HDN NW4 51 K3
STRHM/NOR SW16 148 D4
Babmaes St STJS SW1Y 11 G8
Bache's St IS N1 7 H8
Back Church La WCHPL E1 92 C6
Back Hl CLKNW EC1R 12 B1
Back La BTFD TW8 104 E6
BXLY DA5 137 H6
CEND/HSY/T N8 54 E4
CHDH RM6 61 K6
EDGW HA8 36 E7
HAMP NW3 71 G3
RCHPK/HAM TW10 143 J2
Backley Gdns CROY/NA CR0 165 H5
Back Rd SCUP DA14 155 G3
TEDD TW11 142 E6
WALTH E17 58 A3
Bacon Gv STHWK SE1 19 L5
Bacon La CDALE/KGS NW9 50 D3
EDGW HA8 36 C7
Bacon's La HGT N6 54 A7
Bacon St BETH E2 7 M9
Bacton St BETH E2 92 E2
Baddow Cl DAGE RM10 80 C7
WFD IG8 45 H5
Baden Pl STHWK SE1 19 G1
Baden Powell Cl DAGW RM9 80 A7
SURB KT6 172 B1
Baden Rd CEND/HSY/T N8 54 D3
IL IG1 78 B4
Bader Wy PUT/ROE SW15 126 D5
RAIN RM13 81 J5
Badger Cl FELT TW13 141 F2
GNTH/NBYPK IG2 60 C5
HSLWW TW4 122 B2
Badgers Cl BORE WD6 * 24 B1
ENC/FH EN2 29 H2
HRW HA1 48 D5
HYS/HAR UB3 82 C7
Badgers Copse WPK KT4 173 H1
Badgers Ct WPK KT4 * 173 H1
Badgers Cft ELTH/MOT SE9 154 A2
TRDG/WHET N20 26 C6
Badgers Wk NWMAL KT3 160 B1
Badlis Rd WALTH E17 57 J1
Badlow Cl ERITH DA8 118 B6
Badminton Cl BORE WD6 24 C1
HRW HA1 * 48 E3
NTHLT UB5 66 A5
Badminton Ms CAN/RD E16 94 E7
Badminton Rd BAL SW12 129 F5
Badsworth Rd CMBW SE5 110 D6
Bafton Ga HAYES BR2 168 A7
Bagley Cl WDR/YW UB7 100 B1
Bagley House
WOOL/PLUM SE18 * 114 D6
Bagley's La FUL/PGN SW6 108 A7
Bagleys Spring CHDH RM6 62 A3
Bagshot Ct
WOOL/PLUM SE18 * 115 F7
Bagshot Rd EN EN1 30 B5
Bagshot St WALW SE17 19 K8
Baildon St DEPT SE8 112 C6
Bailey Cl FBAR/BDGN N11 40 D7
THMD SE28 96 E7
Bailey Cots POP/IOD E14 * 93 G4
Bailey Crs CHSGTN KT9 171 K6
Bailey House
WOOL/PLUM SE18 * 114 D6
Bailey Ms BRXS/STRHM SW2 130 B4
CHSWK W4 105 J5
Bailey Pl SYD SE26 150 E5
Baillie Cl RAIN RM13 99 K3
Bainbridge Cl
RCHPK/HAM TW10 144 A4
Bainbridge Rd DAGW RM9 80 B3
Bainbridge St
NOXST/BSQ WC1A 11 H4
Baines Cl SAND/SEL CR2 177 K4
Baird Av STHL UB1 84 B6
Baird Cl BUSH WD23 22 B5
CDALE/KGS NW9 50 E5
LEY E10 57 J7
Baird Gdns NRWD SE19 150 A3
Baird Memorial Cots
STHGT/OAK N14 * 40 D1
Baird Rd EN EN1 30 D2
Baird St STLK EC1Y 6 F9
Baizdon Rd BKHTH/KID SE3 133 H1
Baker Crs DART DA1 139 F6
Baker La MTCM CR4 163 F1
Baker Pl HOR/WEW KT19 172 E5
Baker Rd WLSDN NW10 69 G7
WOOL/PLUM SE18 114 D6

Bakers Av WALTH E17 57 K5
Bakers Cl DART DA1 139 G6
Bakers End RYNPK SW20 161 H1
Bakers Fld HOLWY N7 72 D3
Bakers Gdns CAR SM5 175 J1
Bakers Hl BAR EN5 27 F1
CLPT E5 56 D7
Baker's Ms MHST W1U 10 A4
Bakers Rents BETH E2 7 L7
Bakers Rw SRTFD E15 94 C1
Baker's Rw CLKNW EC1R 12 A1
Baker St CAMTN NW1 9 M1
EN EN1 29 K1
MHST W1U 10 A3
Baker's Yd CLKNW EC1R 12 A1
Bakery Cl BRXN/ST SW9 * 110 A6
Bakewell Wy NWMAL KT3 160 B1
Balaams La STHGT/OAK N14 40 D1
Balaam St PLSTW E13 94 E2
Balaclava Rd STHWK SE1 19 M6
SURB KT6 158 D6
Bala Gn CDALE/KGS NW9 * 51 G5
Balcaskie Rd ELTH/MOT SE9 134 E4
Balchier Rd EDUL SE22 131 J5
Balcombe Cl BXLYHS DA6 136 E3
Balcombe St CAMTN NW1 3 L9
Balcorne St HOM E9 74 E6
Balder Ri LEE/GVPK SE12 153 F1
Balderton St OXSTW W1C 10 B5
Baldock St BOW E3 93 K1
Baldry Gdns
STRHM/NOR SW16 148 E5
Baldwin Crs CMBW SE5 110 D7
Baldwin Gdns HSLW TW3 103 H7
Baldwin Rd BTSEA SW11 129 F5
Baldwin's Gdns FSBYW WC1X 12 A2
Baldwins La
RKW/CH/CXG WD3 20 A3
Baldwin St FSBYE EC1V 7 G8
Baldwin Ter IS N1 6 E5
Baldwyn Gdns ACT W3 86 E6
Bale Rd WCHPL E1 93 G4
Bales Ter ED N9 * 42 B2
Balfern Gv CHSWK W4 106 B4
Balfern St BTSEA SW11 128 D1
Balfe St IS N1 5 K6
Balfour Av HNWL W7 85 F7
Balfour Gv TRDG/WHET N20 39 K2
Balfour Ms ED N9 42 C2
MYFR/PKLN W1K 10 B8
Balfour Pl MYFR/PKLN W1K 10 B7
PUT/ROE SW15 126 E3
Balfour Rd ACT W3 86 E4
CAR SM5 175 K6
HAYES BR2 168 C4
HBRY N5 73 J3
HRW HA1 48 D4
HSLW TW3 123 G2
IL IG1 78 B1
NWDGN UB2 102 C2
SNWD SE25 165 H3
WEA W13 104 C1
WIM/MER SW19 147 F6
Balfour St STHWK SE1 19 G5
Balgores Crs GPK RM2 63 K2
Balgores La GPK RM2 63 K3
Balgores Sq GPK RM2 63 K3
Balgowan Cl NWMAL KT3 160 B3
Balgowan Rd BECK BR3 166 B2
Balgowan St
WOOL/PLUM SE18 116 A3
Balham Gv BAL SW12 129 F6
Balham High Rd BAL SW12 129 G7
Balham Hl BAL SW12 129 G6
Balham New Rd BAL SW12 129 G6
Balham Park Rd BAL SW12 128 E7
Balham Rd ED N9 42 C1
Balham Station Rd BAL SW12 129 F7
Balkan Wk WAP E1W * 92 D6
Balladier Wk POP/IOD E14 93 K4
Ballamore Rd BMLY BR1 152 E2
Ballance Rd HOM E9 75 F5
Ballantine St
WAND/EARL SW18 128 B3
Ballantyne Cl ELTH/MOT SE9 153 J3
Ballard Cl KUTN/CMB KT2 145 F6
Ballards Cl DAGE RM10 80 D7
Ballards Farm Rd
SAND/SEL CR2 178 C5
Ballards La FNCH N3 39 F6
Ballards Ms EDGW HA8 36 C5
Ballards Ri SAND/SEL CR2 178 C5
Ballards Rd CRICK NW2 69 J1
DAGE RM10 80 D7
Ballards Wy SAND/SEL CR2 178 C5
Ballast Quay GNWCH SE10 113 G4
Ballater Cl OXHEY WD19 33 G3
Ballater Rd BRXS/STRHM SW2 129 K3
SAND/SEL CR2 178 B4
Ballina St FSTH SE23 132 A6
Ballingdon Rd BTSEA SW11 129 F5
Ballinger Wy NTHLT UB5 83 J3
Balliol Av CHING E4 44 B3
Balliol Rd NKENS W10 88 A5
TOTM N17 42 A7
WELL DA16 136 C1
Balloch Rd CAT SE6 133 G7
Ballogie Av WLSDN NW10 69 G3
Ballow Cl CMBW SE5 * 110 E6
Ball's Pond Pl IS N1 * 73 K5
Balls Pond Rd IS N1 73 K5
Balmain Cl EA W5 85 K7
Balmer Rd BOW E3 93 H1
Balmes Rd IS N1 7 H3
Balmoral Av BECK BR3 166 B3
FBAR/BDGN N11 40 A5
Balmoral Cl PUT/ROE SW15 * 127 G5
Balmoral Crs
E/WMO/HCT KT8 157 F2
Balmoral Dr BORE WD6 25 F3
STHL UB1 83 K3
YEAD UB4 82 C3
Balmoral Gdns BXLY DA5 137 G6
WEA W13 104 B2
Balmoral Gv HOLWY N7 73 F5
Balmoral Ms SHB W12 106 C2
Balmoral Rd CRICK NW2 69 K5
FSTGT E7 77 G3
GPK RM2 63 K3
KUT/HW KT1 159 G3
LEY E10 75 K1
RYLN/HDSTN HA2 66 A3
WPK KT4 173 K2
Balmore Crs EBAR EN4 28 A4
Balmore St ARCH N19 72 B1
Balmuir Gdns PUT/ROE SW15 127 F3
Balnacraig Av WLSDN NW10 69 G3
Baltic Cl WIM/MER SW19 147 H6
Baltic Pl IS N1 7 K3
Baltic St East STLK EC1Y 12 E1
Baltic St West FARR EC1M 12 E1
Baltimore Pl WELL DA16 136 A1
Balvaird Pl PIM SW1V 17 H8
Balvernie Gv
WAND/EARL SW18 127 J6
Bamber Rd PECK SE15 111 G7
Bamborough Gdns SHB W12 107 F1
Bamford Av ALP/SUD HA0 68 B7
Bamford Rd BMLY BR1 152 B4
Bampfylde Cl WLGTN SM6 176 C2
Bampton Dr MLHL NW7 37 J6
Bampton Rd FSTH SE23 151 F2
Banavie Gdns BECK BR3 151 K7
Banbury Ct BELMT SM2 * 174 E6
COVGDN WC2E * 11 J6
Banbury Rd HOM E9 75 F6
WALTH E17 43 G6
Banbury St BTSEA SW11 * 128 D1
WATW WD18 20 E4
Banchory Rd BKHTH/KID SE3 114 A6
Bancroft Av EFNCH N2 53 J4
Bancroft Cha HCH RM12 81 H1
Bancroft Ct NTHLT UB5 65 G7
Bancroft Gdns
KTN/HRWW/WS HA3 34 C7
Bancroft Rd
KTN/HRWW/WS HA3 48 C1
WCHPL E1 92 E3
Bandon Ri WLGTN SM6 176 D4
Banfield Rd PECK SE15 131 J2
Bangalore St PUT/ROE SW15 127 F2
Bangor Cl NTHLT UB5 66 B4
Banim St HMSMTH W6 106 E2
Banister Rd NKENS W10 88 B2
Bank Av MTCM CR4 162 C1
Bank Blds CHING E4 * 44 B5
Bank End STHWK SE1 12 F8
Bankfoot Rd BMLY BR1 152 C3
Bankhurst Rd CAT SE6 132 C6
Bank La KUTN/CMB KT2 144 A6
PUT/ROE SW15 126 B4
Bank Ms SUT SM1 175 G5
Banksia Rd UED N18 42 E4
Bankside SAND/SEL CR2 178 B5
STHL UB1 83 H7
STHWK SE1 12 E7
Bankside Av LEW SE13 133 F2
NTHLT UB5 82 E1
Bankside Cl CAR SM5 175 J4
ISLW TW7 124 A3
Bankside Dr THDIT KT7 171 H1
Bankside Rd IL IG1 78 C4
Banks La BXLYHS DA6 137 G3
Banks Rd BORE WD6 24 E1
Banks Wy MNPK E12 78 A3
Banksyard HEST TW5 102 E5
The Bank HGT N6 54 B7
Bankton Rd
BRXS/STRHM SW2 130 B3
Bankwell Rd LEW SE13 133 H3
Banner St STLK EC1Y 12 F1
Banning St GNWCH SE10 113 H4
Bannister Cl
BRXS/STRHM SW2 130 B7
GFD/PVL UB6 66 D4
Bannockburn Rd
WOOL/PLUM SE18 115 K3
Bannow Cl HOR/WEW KT19 173 G3
Banstead Ct SHB W12 87 H6
Banstead Gdns ED N9 41 K2
Banstead Rd CAR SM5 175 H6
Banstead St PECK SE15 131 K2
Banstead Wy WLGTN SM6 176 E4
Banstock Rd EDGW HA8 36 D5
Banting Dr WCHMH N21 29 F4
Banton Cl EN EN1 30 D1
Bantry St CMBW SE5 110 E6
Banwell Rd BXLY DA5 136 E5
Banyard Rd BERM/RHTH SE16 111 J2
Baptist Gdns KTTN NW5 72 A5
Barandon Wk NTGHL W11 * 88 B6
Barbara Castle Cl
FUL/PGN SW6 107 J5
Barbara Hucklesbury Cl
WDGN N22 55 H1
Barbauld Rd STNW/STAM N16 74 A2
Barber Cl WCHMH N21 29 G6
Barbers Rd SRTFD E15 93 K1
Barbican Rd GFD/PVL UB6 84 B5
Barb Ms HMSMTH W6 107 F2
Barbon Cl BMSBY WC1N 11 K2
Barbot Cl ED N9 42 C2
Barchard St
WAND/EARL SW18 128 A4
Barchester Cl HNWL W7 85 F7
Barchester Rd
KTN/HRWW/WS HA3 34 D7
Barchester St POP/IOD E14 93 K4
Barclay Cl FUL/PGN SW6 * 107 K6
WATW WD18 20 E5
Barclay Ov WFD IG8 44 E3
Barclay Rd CROY/NA CR0 177 K2
FUL/PGN SW6 107 K6
PLSTW E13 95 G3
UED N18 41 K5
WALTH E17 58 A4
Barcombe Av
BRXS/STRHM SW2 148 E1
Barden St WOOL/PLUM SE18 115 K6
Bardfield Av CHDH RM6 61 K2
Bardney Rd MRDN SM4 162 A3
Bardolph Av CROY/NA CR0 179 H7
Bardolph Rd HOLWY N7 72 E3
RCH/KEW TW9 125 G3
Bard Rd NKENS W10 88 B6
Bardsey Pl WCHPL E1 92 E3
Bardsey Wk IS N1 * 73 J5
Bardsley Cl CROY/NA CR0 178 B2
Bardsley La GNWCH SE10 113 F5
Barfett St NKENS W10 88 D3
Barfield Av TRDG/WHET N20 39 K1
Barfield Rd BMLY BR1 169 F2
WAN E11 * 58 D7
Barford Cl HDN NW4 51 J1
Barford St IS N1 6 B4
Barforth Rd PECK SE15 131 J2
Barfreston Wy PGE/AN SE20 150 D7
Bargate Cl NWMAL KT3 160 D6
WOOL/PLUM SE18 116 A4
Barge House St STHWK SE1 12 B8
Barge La BOW E3 75 H7
Bargery Rd CAT SE6 132 E7
Barge Wk KUT/HW KT1 158 E1
Bargrove Cl PGE/AN SE20 150 C6
Bargrove Crs CAT SE6 151 H1
Barham Av BORE WD6 24 B2
Barham Cl ALP/SUD HA0 67 H5
CHST BR7 154 B4
HAYES BR2 168 D7
ROMW/RG RM7 62 D1
Barham Ct ALP/SUD HA0 67 J5
Barham Rd CHST BR7 154 B4
DART DA1 139 K6
RYNPK SW20 145 J6
SAND/SEL CR2 177 J3
Baring Cl LEE/GVPK SE12 152 E1
Baring Rd CROY/NA CR0 165 H7
EBAR EN4 27 H2
LEE/GVPK SE12 153 F3
Baring St IS N1 7 G4
Barker Cl NTHWD HA6 32 D6
NWMAL KT3 159 J3
RCH/KEW TW9 125 J1
Barker Dr CAMTN NW1 4 F2
Barker St WBPTN SW10 14 E9
Barker Wk STRHM/NOR SW16 148 D2
Barkham Rd TOTM N17 41 K6
Barking Rd CAN/RD E16 94 D4
EHAM E6 95 H1
PLSTW E13 95 F3
POP/IOD E14 94 C5
Bark Pl BAY/PAD W2 8 C6
Barkston Gdns ECT SW5 14 C6
Barkwood Cl ROMW/RG RM7 62 E4
Barkworth Rd
BERM/RHTH SE16 111 J4
Barlborough St NWCR SE14 112 A6
Barlby Gdns NKENS W10 88 B3
Barlby Rd NKENS W10 88 A4
Barley Cl ALP/SUD HA0 67 K3
BUSH WD23 22 B4
Barleycorn Wy POP/IOD E14 93 H6
Barley La GDMY/SEVK IG3 61 G5
Barley Mow Pas CHSWK W4 106 A4
Barlow Cl WLGTN SM6 176 E5
Barlow Dr BKHTH/KID SE3 114 D7
Barlow Pl MYFR/PICC W1J 10 D7
Barlow Rd ACT W3 86 D7
HPTN TW12 142 A6
KIL/WHAMP NW6 70 D5
Barlow St WALW SE17 19 H5
Barlow Wy RAIN RM13 99 F5
Barlow Wy South RAIN RM13 99 F5
Barmeston Rd CAT SE6 151 K1
Barmor Cl RYLN/HDSTN HA2 48 B1
Barmouth Av GFD/PVL UB6 85 F1
Barmouth Rd CROY/NA CR0 179 F1
WAND/EARL SW18 128 B5
Barnabas Rd HOM E9 75 F5
Barnaby Cl RYLN/HDSTN HA2 66 C1
Barnaby Pl SKENS SW7 15 G6
Barnard Cl CHST BR7 154 D7
SUN TW16 141 F6
WLGTN SM6 176 D6
WOOL/PLUM SE18 115 F3
Barnard Gdns NWMAL KT3 160 D3
YEAD UB4 83 F3
Barnard Hl MUSWH N10 54 B1
Barnard Ms BTSEA SW11 128 D3
Barnardo Dr BARK/HLT IG6 60 C3
Barnardo Gdns WCHPL E1 * 93 F5
Barnardo St WCHPL E1 93 F5
Barnard Rd BTSEA SW11 128 D3
EN EN1 30 D1
MTCM CR4 163 F2
Barnards Pl SAND/SEL CR2 177 H7
Barnby St CAMTN NW1 4 F6
SRTFD E15 76 C7
Barn Cl KTTN NW5 * 72 D4
NTHLT UB5 83 G1
Barn Crs STAN HA7 35 J5
Barneby Cl WHTN TW2 123 K7
Barnehurst Av BXLYHN DA7 117 K7
Barnehurst Cl ERITH DA8 117 K7
Barnehurst Rd BXLYHN DA7 137 K1
Barnes Aly HPTN TW12 157 H1
Barnes Av BARN SW13 106 D6
NWDGN UB2 102 E3
Barnes Br CHSWK W4 126 B1
Barnes Cl MNPK E12 77 H3
Barnes Cray Rd DART DA1 138 D3
Barnes End NWMAL KT3 160 D4
Barnes High St BARN SW13 126 C1
Barnes Rd IL IG1 78 C4
UED N18 42 E3
Barnes St POP/IOD E14 93 G5
Barnes Ter DEPT SE8 112 C4
Barnet By-Pass BORE WD6 25 G4
Barnet Dr HAYES BR2 181 J1
Barnet Gate La BAR EN5 25 H5
Barnet Gv BETH E2 92 C2
Barnet Hl BAR EN5 26 E3
Barnet La BORE WD6 24 B5
TRDG/WHET N20 26 D7
Barnet Rd BAR EN5 25 G5
Barnett Cl ERITH DA8 138 C1
Barnetts Ct
RYLN/HDSTN HA2 * 66 B2
Barnett St WCHPL E1 92 D5
Barnet Way (Barnet By-Pass)
MLHL NW7 25 F6
Barnet Wood Rd HAYES BR2 181 G1
Barney Cl CHARL SE7 114 B4
Barn Fld HAMP NW3 * 71 K4
Barnfield NWMAL KT3 160 B5
Barnfield Av CROY/NA CR0 165 K7
KUTN/CMB KT2 143 K3
MTCM CR4 163 G3
Barnfield Cl FSBYPK N4 54 E6
TOOT SW17 147 G2
Barnfield Gdns
KUTN/CMB KT2 144 A4
WOOL/PLUM SE18 * 115 G5
Barnfield Pl POP/IOD E14 112 D3
Barnfield Rd BELV DA17 117 G5
EA W5 85 J3
EDGW HA8 36 E7
SAND/SEL CR2 178 A7
WOOL/PLUM SE18 115 G5
Barnfield Wood Cl BECK BR3 167 G5
Barnfield Wood Rd BECK BR3 167 G5
Barnham Dr THMD SE28 97 F7
Barnham Rd GFD/PVL UB6 84 C2
Barnham St STHWK SE1 19 K1
Barnhill PIN HA5 47 G4
Barn Hl WBLY HA9 68 D1
Barnhill Av HAYES BR2 167 K4
Barnhill La YEAD UB4 83 F2
Barnhill Rd WBLY HA9 68 E2
YEAD UB4 83 F3
Barnhurst Pth OXHEY WD19 33 G4
Barningham Wy
CDALE/KGS NW9 50 E5
Barnlea Cl FELT TW13 141 J1
Barnmead Gdns DAGW RM9 80 B4
Barnmead Rd BECK BR3 151 F7
DAGW RM9 80 B4
Barnock Cl DART DA1 138 B6
Barn Ri WBLY HA9 50 C7
Barnsbury Cl NWMAL KT3 159 K3
Barnsbury Crs BRYLDS KT5 159 K7
Barnsbury Est IS N1 5 M4
Barnsbury Gv HOLWY N7 5 M1
Barnsbury La BRYLDS KT5 172 D1
Barnsbury Pk IS N1 6 A1
Barnsbury Rd IS N1 6 A4
Barnsbury Sq IS N1 6 A1
Barnsbury St IS N1 6 A2
Barnsbury Ter IS N1 5 M2
Barnscroft RYNPK SW20 160 E2
Barnsdale Av POP/IOD E14 112 E3
Barnsdale Rd MV/WKIL W9 88 D3
Barnsley St WCHPL E1 92 D3
Barnstaple La LEW SE13 133 F3
Barnstaple Rd RSLP HA4 65 G2
Barnston Wk IS N1 * 6 E3
Barn St STNW/STAM N16 74 A1
Barn Wy WBLY HA9 50 C7
Barnwell Rd
BRXS/STRHM SW2 130 B4
DART DA1 139 J2
Barnwood Cl MV/WKIL W9 8 C1
RSLP HA4 64 B1
Baron Cl FBAR/BDGN N11 40 A4
Baroness Rd BETH E2 7 M7
Baronet Gv TOTM N17 42 C7
Baronet Rd TOTM N17 42 C7
Baron Gdns BARK/HLT IG6 60 C2
Baron Gv MTCM CR4 162 D3
Baron Rd BCTR RM8 61 K7
Barons Cl IS N1 * 6 A5
Barons Court Rd
WKENS W14 * 107 H4
Baron's Court Rd WKENS W14 107 H4
Baronsfield Rd TWK TW1 * 124 C5
Barons Ga EBAR EN4 27 J5
Barons Keep WKENS W14 * 107 H4
Barons Md HRW HA1 48 E3
Baronsmead Rd BARN SW13 106 D7
Baronsmede EA W5 105 G1
Baronsmere Ct BAR EN5 * 26 C3
Baronsmere Rd EFNCH N2 53 J3
Baron's Pl STHWK SE1 18 B2
The Barons TWK TW1 124 C5
Baron St IS N1 6 B6
Baron's Wk CROY/NA CR0 166 B5
Barque Ms DEPT SE8 112 D5
Barrack Rd HSLWW TW4 122 C3
Barra Hall Rd HYS/HAR UB3 82 C6
Barratt Av WDGN N22 55 F1
Barratt Wy
KTN/HRWW/WS HA3 48 D2
Barrenger Rd MUSWH N10 39 K7
Barrett Rd WALTH E17 58 A3
Barrett's Green Rd
WLSDN NW10 86 E1
Barrett's Gv STNW/STAM N16 74 A4
Barrett St MHST W1U 10 B5
Barrhill Rd BRXS/STRHM SW2 148 E1
Barriedale NWCR SE14 112 B7
Barrier Point Rd CAN/RD E16 95 G7
Barringer Sq TOOT SW17 148 A3
Barrington Cl CLAY IG5 45 K7
KTTN NW5 72 A4
Barrington Rd BRXN/ST SW9 130 C2
BXLYHN DA7 136 E1
CEND/HSY/T N8 54 D4
CHEAM SM3 161 K7
MNPK E12 78 A5
Barrington Vls
WOOL/PLUM SE18 115 F7
Barrington Wk NRWD SE19 * 150 A5
Barrow Av CAR SM5 175 K6
Barrow Cl WCHMH N21 41 H2
Barrowdene Cl PIN HA5 47 J1
Barrowell Gn WCHMH N21 41 H1
Barrowgate Rd CHSWK W4 105 K4
Barrow Hedges Cl CAR SM5 175 J6
Barrow Hedges Wy CAR SM5 175 J6
Barrow Hl WPK KT4 173 G1
Barrow Hill Cl WPK KT4 173 G1
Barrow Hill Est STJWD NW8 3 J6
Barrow Hill Rd STJWD NW8 3 J6
Barrow Point Av PIN HA5 47 J1
Barrow Point La PIN HA5 47 J1
Barrow Rd CROY/NA CR0 177 G4
STRHM/NOR SW16 148 D5
Barrs Rd WLSDN NW10 69 F6
Barry Av BXLYHN DA7 117 F6
SEVS/STOTM N15 56 B5
Barry Pde EDUL SE22 * 131 H3
Barry Rd EDUL SE22 131 H5
EHAM E6 95 J5
WLSDN NW10 68 E6
Barset Rd PECK SE15 131 K2
Barsons Cl PGE/AN SE20 150 E6
Barston Rd WNWD SE27 149 J1
Barstow Crs
BRXS/STRHM SW2 130 A7
Barter St NOXST/BSQ WC1A 11 K3
Barth Ms WOOL/PLUM SE18 115 K3
Bartholomew Cl STBT EC1A 12 E3
WAND/EARL SW18 128 B3
Bartholomew La OBST EC2N 13 H4
Bartholomew Rd KTTN NW5 72 C5
Bartholomew Sq FSBYE EC1V 6 F9
Bartholomew St STHWK SE1 19 G4
Bartholomew Vls KTTN NW5 72 C5
Barth Rd WOOL/PLUM SE18 115 K3
Bartle Av EHAM E6 95 J1
Bartle Rd NTGHL W11 88 B5
Bartlett Cl POP/IOD E14 93 J5
Bartlett Ct FLST/FETLN EC4A * 12 B4
Bartlett St SAND/SEL CR2 177 K4
Barton Av ROMW/RG RM7 62 E7
Barton Cl BXLYHS DA6 137 F4
EHAM E6 95 K5
HDN NW4 51 J4
HOM E9 74 E4
PECK SE15 131 J2
Barton Gn NWMAL KT3 160 A1
Barton Mdw BARK/HLT IG6 60 B3
Barton Rd HCH RM12 63 J7
WKENS W14 107 H4
The Bartons BORE WD6 23 K5
Barton St WEST SW1P 17 J4
Barton Wy BORE WD6 24 C1
Bartram Rd BROCKY SE4 132 B4
Bartrip St HOM E9 75 G5
Barts Cl BECK BR3 166 D4
Barwell Ct CHSGTN KT9 * 171 J6
Barwell La CHSGTN KT9 171 J6
Barwick Rd FSTGT E7 77 F3
Barwood Av WWKM BR4 166 E7
Bascombe Gv DART DA1 138 B6
Bascome St
BRXS/STRHM SW2 130 B5
Basden Gv FELT TW13 142 A1
Basedale Rd DAGW RM9 79 H6
Baseing Cl EHAM E6 96 A6
Basevi Wy DEPT SE8 112 D5
Bashley Rd WLSDN NW10 87 F3
Basil Av EHAM E6 95 J2
Basildene Rd HSLWW TW4 122 C2
Basildon Cl BELMT SM2 175 F7
WATW WD18 20 A5
Basildon Rd ABYW SE2 116 B3
Basil Gdns CROY/NA CR0 166 A7
WNWD SE27 149 J4
Basilon Rd BXLYHN DA7 137 F1
Basil St CHEL SW3 15 L2
Basin Ap CAN/RD E16 96 B6
POP/IOD E14 93 G5
Basing Cl THDIT KT7 158 A6
Basing Ct PECK SE15 111 G7
Basingdon Wy CMBW SE5 130 E3
Basing Dr BXLY DA5 137 G5
Basingfield Rd THDIT KT7 158 A6
Basinghall Av CITYW EC2V 13 G4
Basinghall Gdns BELMT SM2 175 F7
Basinghall St CITYW EC2V 13 G4
Basing Hl GLDGN NW11 52 D7
WBLY HA9 68 B1
Basing Pl BETH E2 7 K7
Basing St NTGHL W11 88 D5
Basing Wy FNCH N3 52 E2
THDIT KT7 158 A6
Basire St IS N1 6 F3
Baskerville Gdns
WLSDN NW10 69 G3
Baskerville Rd
WAND/EARL SW18 128 D6
Basket Gdns ELTH/MOT SE9 134 D4
Baslow Cl
KTN/HRWW/WS HA3 34 D7
Baslow Wk CLPT E5 75 F3
Basnett Rd BTSEA SW11 * 129 F2
Bassano St EDUL SE22 131 G4
Bassant Rd WOOL/PLUM SE18 116 A5
Bassein Park Rd SHB W12 106 C1
Bassett Cl BELMT SM2 175 F7
Bassett Gdns ISLW TW7 103 H6
Bassett Rd NKENS W10 88 B5
Bassett St KTTN NW5 72 A5
Bassett Wy GFD/PVL UB6 84 B5
Bassingham Rd ALP/SUD HA0 67 K5
WAND/EARL SW18 128 B6
Basswood Cl PECK SE15 131 J2
Bastable Av BARK IG11 97 F1
Bastion Rd ABYW SE2 116 B4
Baston Manor Rd WWKM BR4 181 F2
Baston Rd HAYES BR2 181 F1
HAYES BR2 181 G3
Bastwick St FSBYE EC1V 6 D9
Basuto Rd FUL/PGN SW6 107 K7
Batavia Ms NWCR SE14 112 B6
Batavia Rd NWCR SE14 112 B6
SUN TW16 141 F7
Batchelor St IS N1 6 A5
Batchworth La NTHWD HA6 32 A4
Bateman Cl BARK IG11 78 C5
Bateman Ms CLAP SW4 129 J5
Bateman Rd CHING E4 43 J5
Bateman's Blds
SOHO/SHAV W1D 11 G5
Batemans Cnr CHSWK W4 * 106 A4
Bateman's Rw SDTCH EC2A 7 K9
Bateman St SOHO/SHAV W1D 11 G5
Bates Crs CROY/NA CR0 177 G4
STRHM/NOR SW16 148 C6
Bate St POP/IOD E14 93 H6
Bath Cl PECK SE15 111 J6
Bathgate Rd WIM/MER SW19 146 B2
Bath Gv BETH E2 92 C1
Bath House Rd CROY/NA CR0 163 K7
Bath Pas KUT/HW KT1 158 E1
Bath Pl BAR EN5 26 D2
SDTCH EC2A * 7 J8
Bath Rd CHSWK W4 106 B3
DART DA1 138 E6
ED N9 42 D1
FSTGT E7 77 H5
HTHAIR TW6 101 H7
WDR/YW UB7 100 A7
Baths Ap FUL/PGN SW6 * 107 J6
Bath St FSBYE EC1V 6 F8
Bath Ter STHWK SE1 18 E4
Bathurst Av WIM/MER SW19 147 F7
Bathurst Gdns WLSDN NW10 87 K1
Bathurst Ms BAY/PAD W2 9 H6
Bathurst Rd IL IG1 60 B7
Bathurst St BAY/PAD W2 9 H6
Bathway WOOL/PLUM SE18 115 F3
Batley Cl MTCM CR4 162 E6
Batley Pl STNW/STAM N16 74 B2
Batley Rd STNW/STAM N16 74 B2
Batman Cl SHB W12 87 K7
Batoum Gdns HMSMTH W6 107 F2
Batson St SHB W12 106 D1
Batsworth Rd MTCM CR4 162 C2
Batten Cl EHAM E6 95 K5
Batten Cots POP/IOD E14 * 93 G4
Batten St BTSEA SW11 128 D2
Battersby Rd CAT SE6 152 B1
Battersea Br WBPTN SW10 108 C6
Battersea Bridge Rd
BTSEA SW11 108 D6
Battersea Church Rd
BTSEA SW11 108 C7
Battersea High St
BTSEA SW11 128 C1
Battersea Park Rd
BTSEA SW11 109 F7
Battersea Ri BTSEA SW11 128 D4
Battersea Sq BTSEA SW11 * 108 D6
Battery Rd THMD SE28 115 K1
Battishill St IS N1 6 C2
Battle Bridge La STHWK SE1 13 J9
Battle Cl WIM/MER SW19 147 G5
Battledean Rd HBRY N5 73 H4
Battle Rd ERITH DA8 117 K3
Batty St WCHPL E1 92 C5
Baudwin Rd CAT SE6 152 C1
Baugh Rd SCUP DA14 155 J4
The Baulk WAND/EARL SW18 127 K6
Bavant Rd STRHM/NOR SW16 163 K1
Bavaria Rd ARCH N19 72 E1
Bavent Rd CMBW SE5 130 D1
Bawdale Rd EDUL SE22 131 G4
Bawdsey Av GNTH/NBYPK IG2 61 F3
Bawtree Rd NWCR SE14 112 B6
Bawtry Rd TRDG/WHET N20 39 K2
Baxendale TRDG/WHET N20 39 G1
Baxendale St BETH E2 92 C2
Baxter Cl NWDGN UB2 103 G2
Baxter Rd CAN/RD E16 95 G5
IL IG1 78 B4
IS N1 73 K5
UED N18 42 D3
Bay Ct EA W5 * 105 F2
Baycroft Cl PIN HA5 * 47 G2
Bayfield Rd ELTH/MOT SE9 134 C3
Bayford Ms HACK E8 * 74 D6
Bayford Rd WLSDN NW10 88 B2
Bayford St HACK E8 74 D6
Baygrove Ms KUT/HW KT1 143 J7
Bayham Pl CAMTN NW1 4 E4
Bayham Rd CHSWK W4 106 A2
MRDN SM4 162 A3
WEA W13 85 H6
Bayham St CAMTN NW1 4 E3
Bayhurst Dr NTHWD HA6 32 D5
Bayleaf Cl HPTN TW12 142 D4
Bayley St FITZ W1T 11 G3
Baylis Ms TWK TW1 124 B6

Baylis Rd STHWK SE1 18 A3
Bayliss Av THMD SE28 97 K6
Bayliss Cl ENC/FH EN2 28 E4
Bayly Rd DART DA1 139 K5
Bayne Cl EHAM E6 95 K5
Baynes Ms HAMP NW3 71 H5
Baynes St CAMTN NW1 4 F2
Baynham Cl BXLY DA5 137 G5
Bayonne Rd HMSMTH W6 107 H5
Bays Cl SYD SE26 150 E4
Bayshill Ri NTHLT UB5 66 B5
Bayston Rd STNW/STAM N16 74 B2
Bayswater Rd BAY/PAD W2 8 E7
Baythorne St BOW E3 93 H4
Baytree Cl BFN/LL DA15 136 A7
BMLY BR1 153 H7
Baytree Ms STHWK SE1 19 C5
Baytree Rd BRXS/STRHM SW2 130 A3
Bazalgette Cl NWMAL KT3 159 K4
Bazalgette Gdns NWMAL KT3 160 A4
Bazely St POP/IOD E14 94 A6
Bazile Rd WCHMH N21 29 G5
Beacham Cl CHARL SE7 114 C5
Beachborough Rd BMLY BR1 152 A3
Beachcroft Rd WAN E11 76 C2
Beach Gv FELT TW13 142 A2
Beachy Rd BOW E3 75 J6
Beacon Ga NWCR SE14 132 A2
Beacon Hl HOLWY N7 72 E4
Beacon Pl CROY/NA CR0 176 E2
Beacon Rd ERITH DA8 118 E6
HTHAIR TW6 120 D5
LEW SE13 133 G5
Beaconsfield Cl
BKHTH/KID SE3 113 K5
CHSWK W4 105 K4
Beaconsfield Cots
TRDG/WHET N20 * 38 E2
Beaconsfield Gdns
ESH/CLAY KT10 170 E6
Beaconsfield Rd
BKHTH/KID SE3 113 K5
BMLY BR1 168 C2
CAN/RD E16 94 D3
CHSWK W4 106 A2
CROY/NA CR0 164 E5
EA W5 104 D1
ED N9 42 C2
ELTH/MOT SE9 153 J3
ESH/CLAY KT10 170 E6
FBAR/BDGN N11 40 A3
LEY E10 * 76 A2
NWMAL KT3 160 A1
SEVS/STOTM N15 56 A3
STHL UB1 83 H7
SURB KT6 159 G6
TRDG/WHET N20 39 K2
TWK TW1 124 C5
WALTH E17 57 H5
WALW SE17 19 H9
WLSDN NW10 69 H5
YEAD UB4 83 G7
Beaconsfield Terrace Rd
WKENS W14 107 H2
Beaconsfield Wk
FUL/PGN SW6 107 J7
Beacontree Av WALTH E17 44 B7
Beacontree Rd WAN E11 58 D6
Beadlow Cl CAR SM5 162 C5
Beadman Pl WNWD SE27 * 149 H3
Beadman St WNWD SE27 149 H3
Beadnell Rd FSTH SE23 132 A7
Beadon Rd HAYES BR2 167 K3
HMSMTH W6 107 F3
Beaford Gv RYNPK SW20 161 H2
Beagle Cl FELT TW13 141 F3
Beak St REGST W1B 10 E6
Beal Cl WELL DA16 116 B7
Beale Cl PLMGR N13 41 H4
Beale Pl BOW E3 93 H1
Beale Rd BOW E3 75 H7
Beal Rd IL IG1 78 A2
Beam Av DAGE RM10 80 D7
Beames Rd WLSDN NW10 69 F7
Beaminster Gdns
BARK/HLT IG6 60 B2
Beamish Dr BUSH WD23 22 C7
Beamish Rd ED N9 30 C7
Beamway DAGE RM10 81 F6
Beanacre Cl HOM E9 75 H5
Bean Rd BXLYHS DA6 136 E3
Beanshaw ELTH/MOT SE9 154 A3
Beansland Gv CHDH RM6 62 A1
Bear Aly FLST/FETLN EC4A * 12 C4
Bear Cl ROMW/RG RM7 62 D5
Beardell St NRWD SE19 150 B5
Beardow Gv
STHGT/OAK N14 * 28 C5
Beard Rd KUTN/CMB KT2 144 B4
Beardsfield PLSTW E13 76 E7
Beard's Hl HPTN TW12 142 A7
Beard's Hill Cl HPTN TW12 142 A7
Beardsley Wy ACT W3 106 A1
Beards Rd ASHF TW15 140 C5
Bearfield Rd KUTN/CMB KT2 144 A6
Bear Gdns STHWK SE1 12 E8
Bear La STHWK SE1 12 D8
Bear Rd FELT TW13 141 H3
Bearstead Ri BROCKY SE4 132 C4
Bearstead Ter BECK BR3 * 151 J7
Bear St LSQ/SEVD WC2H 11 H6
Beasant House WATN WD24 * 21 H1
Beatrice Av
STRHM/NOR SW16 164 A2
WBLY HA9 68 A4
Beatrice Cl PIN HA5 46 E3
PLSTW E13 94 E3
Beatrice Pl KENS W8 14 C4
Beatrice Rd ED N9 30 E6
FSBYPK N4 55 G6
RCHPK/HAM TW10 125 G4
STHL UB1 83 K7
STHWK SE1 111 H3
WALTH E17 57 J4
Beattie Cl EBED/NFELT TW14 121 J6
Beattock Ri MUSWH N10 54 B3
Beatty Rd STAN HA7 35 J5
STNW/STAM N16 74 A3
Beatty St CAMTN NW1 * 4 E5
Beattyville Gdns CLAY IG5 60 A2
Beauchamp Cl CHSWK W4 105 K2
Beauchamp Pl CHEL SW3 15 K3
Beauchamp Rd BTSEA SW11 128 D3
E/WMO/HCT KT8 157 G4
FSTGT E7 77 F6
NRWD SE19 149 K7
SUT SM1 174 E4
TWK TW1 124 B6
Beauchamp St HCIRC EC1N 12 A3
Beauchamp Ter BARN SW13 126 E2
Beauclerc Rd HMSMTH W6 106 E2
Beauclerk Cl FELT TW13 122 A7
Beaufort EHAM E6 96 A4
Beaufort Av
KTN/HRWW/WS HA3 49 G3
Beaufort Cl CHING E4 43 K5
EA W5 86 B4
PUT/ROE SW15 127 F7
ROMW/RG RM7 62 E3
Beaufort Ct
RCHPK/HAM TW10 143 J3
Beaufort Dr GLDGN NW11 52 E3
Beaufort Gdns CHEL SW3 15 K3
HDN NW4 52 A5
HEST TW5 102 D7
IL IG1 60 A7
STRHM/NOR SW16 149 F6
Beaufort Rd EA W5 86 B4
KUT/HW KT1 159 F3
RCHPK/HAM TW10 143 J3
RSLP HA4 * 64 B1
TWK TW1 124 D6
Beaufort St CHEL SW3 15 G9
Beaufort Wy EW KT17 173 J6
Beaufoy Rd TOTM N17 42 A6
Beaufoy Wk LBTH SE11 17 M6
Beaulieu Av CAN/RD E16 95 F7
SYD SE26 150 D3
Beaulieu Cl CDALE/KGS NW9 51 G3
CMBW SE5 130 E2
HSLWW TW4 122 E4
MTCM CR4 148 A7
OXHEY WD19 21 G7
TWK TW1 124 E5
Beaulieu Dr PIN HA5 47 H5
Beaulieu Gdns WCHMH N21 29 J6
Beaulieu Pl CHSWK W4 105 K2
Beaumaris Gdns NRWD SE19 149 J6
Beaumaris Gn
CDALE/KGS NW9 * 51 G5
Beaumont Av ALP/SUD HA0 67 J4
RCH/KEW TW9 125 G2
RYLN/HDSTN HA2 48 B5
WKENS W14 107 J4
Beaumont Cl EFNCH N2 53 J3
KUTN/CMB KT2 144 C6
Beaumont Ct ALP/SUD HA0 67 J4
Beaumont Crs RAIN RM13 81 J5
WKENS W14 107 J4
Beaumont Dr ASHF TW15 140 B4
WPK KT4 160 E7
Beaumont Gdns HAMP NW3 70 E1
Beaumont Gv WCHPL E1 93 F3
Beaumont Ms MHST W1U * 10 B2
PIN HA5 * 47 J2
Beaumont Pl FITZ W1T 4 F9
ISLW TW7 124 A4
Beaumont Ri ARCH N19 54 D7
Beaumont Rd CHSWK W4 105 K2
LEY E10 57 K6
NRWD SE19 149 J5
PLSTW E13 95 F2
STMC/STPC BR5 169 J5
WIM/MER SW19 127 H6
Beaumont Sq WCHPL E1 93 F4
Beaumont St CAVSQ/HST W1G 10 B2
Beaumont Ter LEW SE13 * 133 H6
Beaumont Wk HAMP NW3 3 M1
Beauvais Ter NTHLT UB5 83 H2
Beauval Rd EDUL SE22 131 G5
Beaverbank Rd
ELTH/MOT SE9 135 J7
Beaver Cl HPTN TW12 142 B7
MRDN SM4 161 F6
PGE/AN SE20 * 150 C6
Beavers Crs HSLWW TW4 122 C3
Beavers La HSLWW TW4 122 B2
Beaverwood Rd CHST BR7 154 E4
Beavor La HMSMTH W6 106 D3
Bebbington Rd
WOOL/PLUM SE18 * 115 K3
Beccles Dr BARK IG11 79 F5
Beccles St POP/IOD E14 93 H5
Bec Cl RSLP HA4 65 H2
Beck Cl GNWCH SE10 112 E7
LEW SE13 112 E7
Beckenham Gdns ED N9 42 A2
Beckenham Gv HAYES BR2 167 G1
Beckenham Hill Rd
BECK BR3 151 K5
Beckenham La HAYES BR2 167 H1
Beckenham Place Pk
BECK BR3 151 K6
Beckenham Rd BECK BR3 166 E6
PGE/AN SE20 151 F7
WWKM BR4 166 E7
Becket Av EHAM E6 96 A2
Becket Cl SNWD SE25 165 H5
WIM/MER SW19 * 147 F7
Becket Fold HRW HA1 * 49 F4
Becket Rd UED N18 42 E3
Becket St STHWK SE1 19 G3
Beckett Cl BELV DA17 117 F2
STRHM/NOR SW16 148 D1
WLSDN NW10 69 F5
Becketts Cl BXLY DA5 137 K7
EBED/NFELT TW14 122 A5
Becketts Pl KUT/HW KT1 143 K7
Beckett Wk BECK BR3 151 G5
Beckford Cl WKENS W14 107 J3
Beckford Dr STMC/STPC BR5 169 J6
Beckford Pl WALW SE17 * 18 F8
Beckford Rd CROY/NA CR0 165 G5
Beck La BECK BR3 166 A2
Becklow Rd SHB W12 106 C1
Beck River Pk BECK BR3 151 H7
Beck Rd HACK E8 74 D7
MTCM CR4 162 E5
Becks Rd SCUP DA14 155 G2
Beckton Rd CAN/RD E16 94 D4
Beck Wy BECK BR3 166 C2
Beckway Rd
STRHM/NOR SW16 163 J1
Beckway St WALW SE17 19 H6
Beckwith Rd HNHL SE24 130 E5
Beclands Rd TOOT SW17 148 A5
Becmead Av
KTN/HRWW/WS HA3 49 H4
STRHM/NOR SW16 148 D3
Becondale Rd NRWD SE19 150 A4
Becontree Av BCTR RM8 79 H3
Bective Rd FSTGT E7 76 E3
PUT/ROE SW15 127 H3
Becton Pl ERITH DA8 117 J7
Bedale St STHWK SE1 * 13 G9
Beddington Cross
CROY/NA CR0 163 J7
Beddington Farm Rd
CROY/NA CR0 163 K7
Beddington Gdns WLGTN SM6 176 B5
Beddington Gn
STMC/STPC BR5 155 F7
Beddington Gv WLGTN SM6 176 D4
Beddington La CROY/NA CR0 163 H5
Beddington Rd
GDMY/SEVK IG3 61 F6
STMC/STPC BR5 154 E7
Beddington Ter
CROY/NA CR0 * 164 A6
Bede Cl PIN HA5 33 H7
Bede Rd CHDH RM6 61 J5
Bedevere Rd ED N9 42 C2
Bedfont Cl EBED/NFELT TW14 121 F5
MTCM CR4 163 F1
Bedfont Green Cl
EBED/NFELT TW14 121 F7
Bedfont La EBED/NFELT TW14 121 K7
Bedfont Rd
EBED/NFELT TW14 121 F7
STWL/WRAY TW19 120 C5
Bedford Av BAR EN5 26 D4
RSQ WC1B 11 H3
YEAD UB4 83 F5
Bedfordbury CHCR WC2N 11 J6
Bedford Cl CHSWK W4 106 B5
MUSWH N10 40 A6
Bedford Cnr CHSWK W4 * 106 B3
Bedford Ct CHCR WC2N 11 J7
Bedford Gdns KENS W8 8 A9
Bedford Hl BAL SW12 148 B1
Bedford Ms CAT SE6 151 K1
SEVS/STOTM N15 55 K3
Bedford Pk CROY/NA CR0 164 D7
Bedford Pl CROY/NA CR0 164 E7
RSQ WC1B 11 J2
Bedford Rd BFN/LL DA15 154 E2
CEND/HSY/T N8 54 D5
CHSWK W4 106 A2
CLAP SW4 129 K3
DART DA1 139 K6
ED N9 30 D6
EFNCH N2 53 J2
EHAM E6 78 A7
HRW HA1 48 C5
IL IG1 78 B2
MLHL NW7 37 G1
NTHWD HA6 32 B3
RSLP HA4 64 D3
SEVS/STOTM N15 55 K3
SWFD E18 58 E1
WALTH E17 57 J1
WDGN N22 40 E7
WEA W13 85 H6
WHTN TW2 142 D2
WPK KT4 174 A1
Bedford Rw GINN WC1R 11 M2
Bedford Sq RSQ WC1B 11 H3
Bedford St COVGDN WC2E 11 J6
Bedford Vls KUT/HW KT1 * 159 G1
Bedford Wy STPAN WC1H 11 H1
Bedgebury Gdns
WIM/MER SW19 146 C1
Bedgebury Rd ELTH/MOT SE9 134 C3
Bedivere Rd BMLY BR1 152 E2
Bedlam Ms LBTH SE11 17 M5
Bedlow Cl STJWD NW8 9 H1
Bedlow Wy CROY/NA CR0 177 F3
Bedonwell Rd BXLYHN DA7 117 G7
Bedser Cl LBTH SE11 17 M9
THHTH CR7 164 D2
Bedser Dr GFD/PVL UB6 66 D4
Bedster Gdns
E/WMO/HCT KT8 157 G1
Bedwardine Rd NRWD SE19 150 A6
Bedwell Gdns HYS/HAR UB3 101 H3
Bedwell Rd BELV DA17 117 H4
TOTM N17 42 A7
Beeby Rd CAN/RD E16 95 F4
Beech Av ACT W3 87 G7
BFN/LL DA15 136 B6
BKHH IG9 45 F1
BTFD TW8 104 C6
RSLP HA4 47 F7
TRDG/WHET N20 27 J7
Beech Cl ASHF TW15 140 B4
CAR SM5 175 K1
DEPT SE8 112 C5
ED N9 30 C5
HCH RM12 81 K2
PUT/ROE SW15 126 D6
SUN TW16 156 C1
WDR/YW UB7 100 D2
WIM/MER SW19 146 A5
Beech Copse BMLY BR1 168 E1
SAND/SEL CR2 178 A4
Beech Ct ELTH/MOT SE9 * 134 D5
Beechcroft CHST BR7 154 A6
Beechcroft Av BXLYHN DA7 118 A7
GLDGN NW11 52 D6
NWMAL KT3 144 E7
RKW/CH/CXG WD3 20 A5
RYLN/HDSTN HA2 48 A6
STHL UB1 83 J6
Beechcroft Cl HEST TW5 102 D6
STRHM/NOR SW16 149 F4
Beechcroft Gdns WBLY HA9 68 B2
Beechcroft Rd BUSH WD23 21 J4
CHSGTN KT9 172 B3
MORT/ESHN SW14 * 125 K2
SWFD E18 59 F1
TOOT SW17 147 K2
Beechdale WCHMH N21 41 F1
Beechdale Rd
BRXS/STRHM SW2 130 A5
Beech Dell HAYES BR2 181 K3
Beech Dr BORE WD6 24 B1
EFNCH N2 53 K2
Beechen Cliff Wy ISLW TW7 104 A7
Beechengrove PIN HA5 47 K2
Beechen Gv WAT WD17 21 F2
Beechen Pl FSTH SE23 150 E1
Beeches Av CAR SM5 175 J6
Beeches Cl PGE/AN SE20 150 E7
Beeches Rd CHEAM SM3 161 H7
TOOT SW17 147 J2
The Beeches HNWL W7 * 104 A1
WATW WD18 * 21 F2
Beeches Wk BELMT SM2 175 H7
Beechfield Cl BORE WD6 24 A1
Beechfield Gdns
ROMW/RG RM7 62 E6
Beechfield Rd BMLY BR1 168 B1
CAT SE6 132 C7
ERITH DA8 118 B6
FSBYPK N4 55 J5
Beech Gdns DAGE RM10 80 D6
EA W5 105 F1
Beech Gv MTCM CR4 163 J4
NWMAL KT3 160 A2
Beech Hall Crs CHING E4 44 B6
Beech Hall Rd CHING E4 44 A6
Beechhill Rd ELTH/MOT SE9 135 F4
Beech House Rd
CROY/NA CR0 177 K2
Beech Lawns
NFNCH/WDSPK N12 * 39 H4
Beechmont Cl BMLY BR1 152 C4
Beechmore Gdns CHEAM SM3 174 B1
Beechmore Rd BTSEA SW11 108 E7
Beechmount Av HNWL W7 84 D4
Beecholme Av MTCM CR4 148 B7
Beecholme Est CLPT E5 * 74 E2
Beech Rd DART DA1 139 G7
EBED/NFELT TW14 121 H6
FBAR/BDGN N11 40 E5
STRHM/NOR SW16 163 K1
Beechrow KUTN/CMB KT2 144 A3
Beech St ROMW/RG RM7 62 E3
Beech Street (Below)
BARB EC2Y 12 E2
Beech Tree Cl IS N1 6 A1
STAN HA7 35 J4
Beech Tree Pl SUT SM1 175 F4
Beechvale Cl
NFNCH/WDSPK N12 39 J4
Beech Wk DART DA1 138 D3
MLHL NW7 37 F4
Beechway BXLY DA5 136 E5
Beech Wy WHTN TW2 142 A2
WLSDN NW10 69 F6
Beechwood Av FNCH N3 52 D2
GFD/PVL UB6 84 B2
HYS/HAR UB3 82 B6
RCH/KEW TW9 105 H7
RSLP HA4 64 D1
RYLN/HDSTN HA2 66 B2
SUN TW16 140 E5
THHTH CR7 164 C3
Beechwood Cl EFNCH N2 * 53 K3
MLHL NW7 37 G4
SURB KT6 158 D6
Beechwood Crs BXLYHN DA7 136 E2
Beechwood Dr HAYES BR2 181 H3
WFD IG8 44 D4
Beechwood Gdns CLAY IG5 59 K4
RAIN RM13 99 K4
RYLN/HDSTN HA2 66 B2
Beechwood Gv ACT W3 87 G6
Beechwood Ms ED N9 42 C1
Beechwood Pk SWFD E18 58 E2
Beechwood Ri CHST BR7 154 B3
Beechwood Rd
CEND/HSY/T N8 54 D3
HACK E8 74 B5
SAND/SEL CR2 178 A7
Beechworth Cl HAMP NW3 71 F1
Beecroft La BROCKY SE4 132 B4
Beecroft Ms BROCKY SE4 132 B4
Beecroft Rd BROCKY SE4 132 B4
Beehive Cl BORE WD6 23 K5
HACK E8 7 L1
Beehive La REDBR IG4 59 K4
Beehive Pl BRXN/ST SW9 130 B2
Beeleigh Rd MRDN SM4 162 A3
Beeston Cl HACK E8 74 C4
OXHEY WD19 33 H3
Beeston Pl BGVA SW1W 16 D4
Beeston Rd EBAR EN4 27 H5
Beeston Wy
EBED/NFELT TW14 122 B5
Beethoven Rd BORE WD6 23 J6
Beethoven St NKENS W10 88 C2
Beeton Cl PIN HA5 34 A6
Beeton Wy WNWD SE27 149 J3
Begbie Rd BKHTH/KID SE3 114 B7
Beggars Bush La WATW WD18 20 B4
Beggar's Roost La SUT SM1 174 E5
Begonia Cl EHAM E6 95 J4
Begonia Pl HPTN TW12 142 A5
Beira St BAL SW12 129 G6
Bekesbourne St
POP/IOD E14 * 93 G5
Belcroft Cl BMLY BR1 152 D6
Beldham Gdns
E/WMO/HCT KT8 157 G2
Belfairs Dr CHDH RM6 61 J6
Belfairs Gdn OXHEY WD19 33 H4
Belfairs Gn OXHEY WD19 33 H4
Belfast Rd SNWD SE25 165 J3
STNW/STAM N16 74 B1
Belfield Rd HOR/WEW KT19 173 F7
Belford Gv WOOL/PLUM SE18 115 F3
Belfort Rd PECK SE15 131 K1
Belfry Cl BERM/RHTH SE16 * 111 J4
Belfry Rd MNPK E12 77 H2
Belgrade Rd HPTN TW12 142 B7
STNW/STAM N16 74 A3
Belgrave Cl ACT W3 105 K1
MLHL NW7 37 F4
STHGT/OAK N14 28 C4
Belgrave Crs SUN TW16 141 F7
Belgrave Gdns STAN HA7 35 J4
STHGT/OAK N14 28 D4
STJWD NW8 2 D4
Belgrave Ms South
KTBR SW1X 16 B3
Belgrave Ms West KTBR SW1X 16 A3
Belgrave Pl KTBR SW1X 16 B4
Belgrave Rd BARN SW13 106 C6
HSLWW TW4 122 E2
IL IG1 59 K7
LEY E10 58 A7
MTCM CR4 162 C2
PIM SW1V 16 E6
PLSTW E13 95 G3
SNWD SE25 165 G3
SUN TW16 141 F7
WALTH E17 57 J5
WAN E11 58 E7
Belgrave Sq KTBR SW1X 16 A3
Belgrave St WCHPL E1 93 F4
Belgrave Wk MTCM CR4 162 C2
Belgravia Cl BAR EN5 26 D2
Belgravia Gdns BMLY BR1 152 C5
Belgravia Ms KUT/HW KT1 158 E3
Belgrove St KCROSS N1C 5 J7
Belinda Rd BRXN/ST SW9 130 C2
Belitha Vls IS N1 5 M1
Bellamaine Cl THMD SE28 116 A1
Bellamy Cl EDGW HA8 36 E2
POP/IOD E14 112 D1
WKENS W14 107 J4
Bellamy Dr STAN HA7 35 H7
Bellamy Rd CHING E4 43 K5
ENC/FH EN2 * 29 K1
Bellamy St BAL SW12 129 G6
Bel La FELT TW13 141 J2
Bellarmine Cl THMD SE28 97 F7
Bellasis Av BRXS/STRHM SW2 129 K7
Bell Av WDR/YW UB7 100 C2
Bell Cl PIN HA5 47 G2
RSLP HA4 64 D2
Bellclose Rd WDR/YW UB7 100 B1
Bell Dr WAND/EARL SW18 127 H6
Bellefields Rd BRXN/ST SW9 130 A2
Bellegrove Cl WELL DA16 136 A1
Bellegrove Rd WELL DA16 135 K1
Bellenden Rd PECK SE15 131 G1
Belle Staines Pleasaunce
CHING E4 43 J1
Belleville Rd BTSEA SW11 128 D4
Belle Vue GFD/PVL UB6 66 D7
Belle Vue La BUSH WD23 22 D7
Bellevue Pk THHTH CR7 164 D2
Bellevue Pl WCHPL E1 * 92 E3
Belle Vue Rd HDN NW4 52 B3
WALTH E17 58 B1
Bellevue Rd BARN SW13 126 D1
BXLYHS DA6 137 G4
FBAR/BDGN N11 40 A3
KUT/HW KT1 159 F2
TOOT SW17 128 E6
WEA W13 85 H3
Bellew St TOOT SW17 147 G2
Bell Farm Av DAGE RM10 80 E2
Bellfield CROY/NA CR0 179 G7
Bellfield Av
KTN/HRWW/WS HA3 34 D5
Bellfield Cl BKHTH/KID SE3 114 A6
Bell Gdns LEY E10 * 57 J7
Bellgate Ms KTTN NW5 72 B3
Bell Gn SYD SE26 151 H3
Bell Green La SYD SE26 151 H4
Bell House Rd ROMW/RG RM7 62 E7
Bellina Ms KTTN NW5 72 B3
Bellingham Gn CAT SE6 151 J2
Bellingham Rd CAT SE6 152 A2
Bell Inn Yd BANK EC3V 13 H5
Bell La CAN/RD E16 94 D7
HDN NW4 52 B3
TWK TW1 124 B7
WBLY HA9 * 67 K1
WCHPL E1 13 L3
Bell Meadow NRWD SE19 150 A3
Bello Cl HNHL SE24 130 C7
Bellot St GNWCH SE10 113 H4
Bell Pde HSLW TW3 * 123 G3
WWKM BR4 * 180 A1
Bellring Cl BELV DA17 117 H5
Bell Rd E/WMO/HCT KT8 157 J4
HSLW TW3 123 G2
Bells Hl BAR EN5 26 B3
Bell St BAY/PAD W2 9 J2
WOOL/PLUM SE18 114 D7
Belltrees Gv
STRHM/NOR SW16 149 F4
Bellview Ct HSLW TW3 123 G3
Bell Water Ga
WOOL/PLUM SE18 115 F2
Bell Wharf La CANST EC4R 12 F7
Bellwood Rd PECK SE15 132 A3
Bell Yd LINN WC2A 12 A5
Bell Yard Ms STHWK SE1 19 K2
Belmont Av ALP/SUD HA0 68 B7
EBAR EN4 27 K4
ED N9 30 C7
NWDGN UB2 102 D2
NWMAL KT3 160 D4
PLMGR N13 40 E4
TOTM N17 55 J2
WELL DA16 135 K1
Belmont Cir
KTN/HRWW/WS HA3 * 35 H7
Belmont Cl CHING E4 44 B4
CLAP SW4 129 H2
EBAR EN4 27 K3
TRDG/WHET N20 27 F7
WFD IG8 45 F3
Belmont Gv CHSWK W4 106 A3
LEW SE13 133 G2
Belmont Hl LEW SE13 133 G2
Belmont La CHST BR7 154 C4
STAN HA7 35 J6
Belmont Pde CHST BR7 * 154 B4
GLDGN NW11 * 52 D4
Belmont Pk LEW SE13 133 G3
Belmont Park Cl LEW SE13 133 H3
Belmont Park Rd LEY E10 57 K5
Belmont Ri BELMT SM2 174 D6
Belmont Rd BECK BR3 166 B1
BUSH WD23 21 J3
CHST BR7 154 B4
CLAP SW4 129 H2
ERITH DA8 117 H6
IL IG1 78 C2
KTN/HRWW/WS HA3 49 F2
SEVS/STOTM N15 55 J3
SNWD SE25 165 J4
WHTN TW2 142 D1
WLGTN SM6 176 C4
Belmont St CAMTN NW1 4 B1
Belmont Ter CHSWK W4 106 A3
Belmor BORE WD6 24 C4
Belmore Av YEAD UB4 82 E5
Belmore La HOLWY N7 72 D4
Belmore St VX/NE SW8 109 J7
Beloe Cl PUT/ROE SW15 126 D3
Belsham St HOM E9 74 E5
Belsize Av HAMP NW3 71 H5
PLMGR N13 41 F5
WEA W13 104 C2
Belsize Court Gdns
HAMP NW3 71 H4
Belsize Crs HAMP NW3 71 H4
Belsize Gdns SUT SM1 175 F3
Belsize Gv HAMP NW3 71 J5
Belsize La HAMP NW3 71 H5
Belsize Ms HAMP NW3 * 71 H5
Belsize Pk HAMP NW3 71 H5
Belsize Park Gdns HAMP NW3 71 H5
Belsize Park Ms HAMP NW3 71 H5
Belsize Pl HAMP NW3 71 H4
Belsize Rd KIL/WHAMP NW6 2 C3
KTN/HRWW/WS HA3 34 D6
Belsize Sq HAMP NW3 71 H5
Belsize Ter HAMP NW3 71 H5
Belson Rd WOOL/PLUM SE18 114 E3
Beltane Dr WIM/MER SW19 146 B2
Belthorn Crs BAL SW12 129 H6
Belton Rd FSTGT E7 77 F6
SCUP DA14 155 G3
TOTM N17 56 A2
WAN E11 76 C3
WLSDN NW10 69 J5
Belton Wy BOW E3 93 J4
Beltran Rd FUL/PGN SW6 128 A1
Beltwood Rd BELV DA17 117 K3
Belvedere Av CLAY IG5 60 B1
WIM/MER SW19 146 C4
Belvedere Blds STHWK SE1 18 D2
Belvedere Cl ESH/CLAY KT10 170 B4
TEDD TW11 142 E4
Belvedere Ct BELV DA17 117 G2
OXHEY WD19 21 H5
Belvedere Dr WIM/MER SW19 146 C4
Belvedere Gdns
E/WMO/HCT KT8 156 E4
Belvedere Gv WIM/MER SW19 146 C4
Belvedere Ms PECK SE15 131 K2
Belvedere Pl
BRXS/STRHM SW2 130 A3
Belvedere Rd ABYW SE2 97 K7
BXLYHN DA7 137 G2
HNWL W7 103 K2
LEY E10 57 G7
NRWD SE19 150 B6

STHWK SE1 17 L1
Belvedere Sq WIM/MER SW19 146 C4
Belvedere Strd
CDALE/KGS NW9 51 H1
The Belvedere WBPTN SW10 * 108 B7
Belvedere Wy
KTN/HRWW/WS HA3 50 A5
Belvoir Rd EDUL SE22 131 H6
Belvue Cl NTHLT UB5 66 A6
Belvue Rd NTHLT UB5 66 A6
Bembridge Cl
KIL/WHAMP NW6 70 C6
Bembridge Gdns RSLP HA4 64 B1
Bemerton Est IS N1 5 L3
Bemerton St IS N1 5 L3
Bemish Rd PUT/ROE SW15 127 G2
Bempton Dr RSLP HA4 65 F1
Bemsted Rd WALTH E17 57 H2
Benares Rd WOOL/PLUM SE18 116 A3
Benbow Rd HMSMTH W6 106 E2
Benbow St DEPT SE8 112 D5
Benbury Cl BMLY BR1 152 A4
Bench Fld SAND/SEL CR2 178 B5
The Bench
RCHPK/HAM TW10 * 143 J2
Bencroft Rd
STRHM/NOR SW16 148 C6
Bencurtis Pk WWKM BR4 180 B2
Bendall Ms CAMTN NW1 9 K2
Bendemeer Rd
PUT/ROE SW15 127 G2
Bendish Rd EHAM E6 77 J6
Bendmore Av ABYW SE2 116 B4
Bendon Va WAND/EARL SW18 128 A6
Bendysh Rd BUSH WD23 21 J2
Benedict Dr
EBED/NFELT TW14 121 G6
Benedict Rd BRXN/ST SW9 130 A2
MTCM CR4 162 C2
Benedict Wy EFNCH N2 * 53 G2
Benedict Whf MTCM CR4 162 D2
Benenden Gn HAYES BR2 167 K4
Benett Gdns
STRHM/NOR SW16 163 K1
Benfleet Cl SUT SM1 175 G2
Benfleet Wy FBAR/BDGN N11 40 A1
Bengal Rd IL IG1 78 B3
Bengarth Dr
KTN/HRWW/WS HA3 48 D1
Bengarth Rd NTHLT UB5 65 H7
Bengeworth Rd CMBW SE5 130 D2
HRW HA1 67 G1
Ben Hale Cl STAN HA7 35 G4
Benham Cl CHSGTN KT9 171 J5
Benham Gdns HSLWW TW4 122 E4
Benham Rd HNWL W7 84 E4
Benhill Av SUT SM1 175 F3
Benhill Rd CMBW SE5 110 E6
SUT SM1 175 H2
Benhill Wood Rd SUT SM1 175 G3
Benhilton Gdns SUT SM1 175 F2
Benhurst Av HCH RM12 81 K3
Benhurst La
STRHM/NOR SW16 149 G4
Benin St LEW SE13 133 G6
Benjafield Cl UED N18 42 D3
Benjamin Cl EMPK RM11 63 J5
HACK E8 74 C7
Benjamin Ms BAL SW12 129 H6
Benjamin St FARR EC1M 12 C2
Ben Jonson Rd WCHPL E1 93 G4
Benledi St POP/IOD E14 94 B5
Bennelong Cl SHB W12 87 K6
Bennerley Rd BTSEA SW11 128 D4
Bennet Cl KUT/HW KT1 143 J7
Bennet's Hl BLKFR EC4V 12 D6
Bennett Cl HSLWW TW4 122 D4
NTHWD HA6 32 D6
WELL DA16 136 B1
Bennett Gv LEW SE13 112 E7
Bennett Pk BKHTH/KID SE3 133 J2
Bennett Rd BRXN/ST SW9 130 B1
CHDH RM6 62 A5
PLSTW E13 95 G3
STNW/STAM N16 74 A3
Bennetts Av CROY/NA CR0 179 G1
GFD/PVL UB6 66 E7
Bennett's Castle La BCTR RM8 79 J3
Bennetts Cl MTCM CR4 148 B7
TOTM N17 42 B5
Bennetts Copse CHST BR7 153 J5
Bennetts Fld BUSH WD23 21 J4
Bennett St CHSWK W4 106 B5
WHALL SW1A 10 E8
Bennetts Wy CROY/NA CR0 179 G1
Bennett's Yd WEST SW1P 17 H4
Benningholme Rd EDGW HA8 37 G5
Bennington Rd TOTM N17 42 A7
WFD IG8 * 44 C6
Benn St HOM E9 75 G5
Bensbury Cl PUT/ROE SW15 126 E6
Bensham Cl THHTH CR7 164 D3
Bensham Gv THHTH CR7 164 D1
Bensham La CROY/NA CR0 164 C6
THHTH CR7 164 C5
Bensham Manor Rd
THHTH CR7 164 D3
Benskin Rd WATW WD18 20 E4
Bensley Cl FBAR/BDGN N11 39 K4
Ben Smith Wy
BERM/RHTH SE16 111 H2
Benson Av PLSTW E13 95 G1
Benson Cl HSLW TW3 123 F3
Benson Quay WAP E1W 92 E6
Benson Rd CROY/NA CR0 177 G2
FSTH SE23 131 K7
Benthal Rd STNW/STAM N16 74 B1
Bentham Rd HOM E9 75 F5
THMD SE28 97 H7
Ben Tillet Cl BARK IG11 79 G6
CAN/RD E16 95 K7
Bentinck Ms MHST W1U 10 B4
Bentinck St MHST W1U 10 B4
Bentley Cl WIM/MER SW19 146 E2
Bentley Dr CRICK NW2 70 D2
GNTH/NBYPK IG2 60 C5
Bentley Ms EN EN1 29 K5
Bentley Rd IS N1 74 A5
Bentley Wy BAR EN5 27 G3
STAN HA7 35 G4
WFD IG8 44 E2
Benton Rd IL IG1 60 D7
OXHEY WD19 33 H4
Benton's La WNWD SE27 149 J3
Benton's Ri WNWD SE27 149 K4
Bentry Cl BCTR RM8 80 A1
Bentry Rd BCTR RM8 80 A1
Bentworth Rd SHB W12 87 K5
Benwell Ct SUN TW16 * 140 E7
Benwell Rd HOLWY N7 73 G3
Benwick Cl BERM/RHTH SE16 111 J3
Benwood Ct SUT SM1 175 G2
Benworth St BOW E3 93 H2
Benyon Rd IS N1 7 H3
Benyon Whf IS N1 7 K3
Berberis Wk WDR/YW UB7 100 B3
Berber Pde WOOL/PLUM SE18 114 D7
Berber Rd BTSEA SW11 * 128 E4
Bercta Rd ELTH/MOT SE9 154 C1
Berengers Pl DAGW RM9 79 H5
Berenger Wk WBPTN SW10 * 108 C6
Berens Rd WLSDN NW10 88 B2
Beresford Av ALP/SUD HA0 68 C7
BRYLDS KT5 159 J7
HNWL W7 84 D4
TRDG/WHET N20 39 K1
TWK TW1 124 D5
Beresford Dr BMLY BR1 168 C2
WFD IG8 45 G3
Beresford Gdns CHDH RM6 62 A4
EN EN1 30 A3
HSLWW TW4 122 E4
Beresford Rd BELMT SM2 174 D6
CEND/HSY/T N8 55 G4
EFNCH N2 53 J2
HBRY N5 73 K4
HRW HA1 48 D4
KUTN/CMB KT2 144 B7
NWMAL KT3 159 K3
STHL UB1 83 H6
WALTH E17 43 K7
Beresford Sq
WOOL/PLUM SE18 115 G3
Beresford St
WOOL/PLUM SE18 115 G2
Beresford Ter HBRY N5 73 J4
Berestede Rd HMSMTH W6 106 C4
Bere St WAP E1W 93 F6
Berger Cl STMC/STPC BR5 169 J5
Berger Rd HOM E9 75 F5
Berghem Ms WKENS W14 107 G2
Bergholt Av REDBR IG4 59 J4
Bergholt Crs STNW/STAM N16 56 A6
Bergholt Ms CAMTN NW1 4 F2
Bering Sq POP/IOD E14 112 D4
Bering Wk CAN/RD E16 95 H5
Berisford Ms
WAND/EARL SW18 128 B5
Berkeley Av BXLYHN DA7 116 E7
CLAY IG5 60 A1
GFD/PVL UB6 66 E5
HSLWW TW4 101 K7
Berkeley Cl BORE WD6 24 C4
KUTN/CMB KT2 144 A6
RSLP HA4 64 D2
STMC/STPC BR5 169 K6
Berkeley Ct
RKW/CH/CXG WD3 * 20 B4
WLGTN SM6 176 C2
Berkeley Crs DART DA1 139 J7
EBAR EN4 27 H4
Berkeley Dr E/WMO/HCT KT8 156 E2
Berkeley Gdns ESH/CLAY KT10 171 G6
KENS W8 8 B9
WCHMH N21 29 K6
Berkeley Ms MBLAR W1H 9 M4
SUN TW16 156 B2
Berkeley Pl WIM/MER SW19 146 B5
Berkeley Rd BARN SW13 106 D7
CDALE/KGS NW9 50 C3
CEND/HSY/T N8 54 D4
HGDN/ICK UB10 64 A6
MNPK E12 77 J4
SEVS/STOTM N15 55 K5
Berkeley Sq MYFR/PICC W1J 10 C7
The Berkeleys SNWD SE25 * 165 H3
Berkeley St MYFR/PICC W1J 10 D7
Berkeley Waye HEST TW5 102 D6
Berkhampstead Rd
BELV DA17 117 H4
Berkhamsted Av WBLY HA9 68 B5
Berkley Cl WHTN TW2 * 142 E2
Berkley Gv CAMTN NW1 4 A2
Berkley Rd CAMTN NW1 3 M2
Berkshire Gdns PLMGR N13 41 G5
UED N18 42 D4
Berkshire Rd HOM E9 75 H5
Berkshire Wy MTCM CR4 163 K3
Bermans Wy WLSDN NW10 69 G3
Bermondsey Sq STHWK SE1 * 19 K3
Bermondsey St STHWK SE1 19 J3
Bermondsey Wall East
BERM/RHTH SE16 111 H1
Bermondsey Wall West
STHWK SE1 111 H1
Bernal Cl THMD SE28 97 K6
Bernard Ashley Dr CHARL SE7 114 A4
Bernard Av WEA W13 104 C2
Bernard Cassidy St
CAN/RD E16 94 D4
Bernard Gdns
WIM/MER SW19 146 D4
Bernard Rd ROMW/RG RM7 62 E6
SEVS/STOTM N15 56 B4
WLGTN SM6 176 A4
Bernard St BMSBY WC1N 11 J1
Bernays Cl STAN HA7 35 J5
Bernay's Gv BRXN/ST SW9 130 A3
Bernel Dr CROY/NA CR0 179 H2
Berne Rd THHTH CR7 164 D4
Berners Dr WEA W13 85 G6
Berners Ms FITZ W1T 10 F3
Berners Pl FITZ W1T 10 F4
Berners Rd IS N1 6 C4
WDGN N22 41 G7
Berners St FITZ W1T 10 F3
Berner Ter WCHPL E1 * 92 C5
Berney Rd CROY/NA CR0 164 E6
Bernhardt Crs STJWD NW8 3 J9
Bernhart Cl EDGW HA8 36 E6
Bernwell Rd CHING E4 44 C2
Berridge Gn EDGW HA8 36 C6
Berridge Ms KIL/WHAMP NW6 70 E4
Berridge Rd NRWD SE19 149 K4
Berriman Rd HOLWY N7 73 F2
Berriton Rd RYLN/HDSTN HA2 47 K7
Berrybank Cl CHING E4 44 A1
Berry Cl DAGE RM10 80 C4
WCHMH N21 29 H7
Berry Cots POP/IOD E14 * 93 G5
Berry Ct HSLWW TW4 122 E4
Berrydale Rd YEAD UB4 83 J3
Berryfield Cl BMLY BR1 153 J7
Berry Field Cl WALTH E17 57 K3
Berryfield Rd WALW SE17 18 D7
Berryhill ELTH/MOT SE9 135 G3
Berry Hl STAN HA7 35 K3
Berryhill Gdns ELTH/MOT SE9 135 G3
Berrylands BRYLDS KT5 159 H4
RYNPK SW20 161 F2
Berrylands Rd BRYLDS KT5 159 G5
Berry La DUL SE21 149 K3
Berryman Cl BCTR RM8 79 J2
Berryman's La SYD SE26 151 F3
Berrymead Gdns ACT W3 86 E7
Berrymede Rd CHSWK W4 106 A2
Berry Pl FSBYE EC1V 6 D8
Berry St FSBYE EC1V 12 D1
Berry Wy EA W5 105 F2
Bertal Rd TOOT SW17 147 H3
Berthons Gdns WALTH E17 * 58 B4
Berthon St DEPT SE8 112 D6
Bertie Rd SYD SE26 151 F5
WLSDN NW10 69 J5
Bertram Rd EN EN1 30 C3
HDN NW4 51 J5
KUTN/CMB KT2 144 C6
Bertram St KTTN NW5 72 B2
Bertrand St LEW SE13 132 E2
Bertrand Wy THMD SE28 97 H6
Bert Rd THHTH CR7 164 D4
Bert Wy EN EN1 30 B3
Berwick Av YEAD UB4 83 H5
Berwick Cl STAN HA7 35 F5
WHTN TW2 123 F7
Berwick Crs BFN/LL DA15 135 K5
Berwick Gdns SUT SM1 175 G2
Berwick Rd CAN/RD E16 95 F5
WDGN N22 41 H7
WELL DA16 116 C7
Berwick St SOHO/CST W1F 10 F5
Berwyn Av HSLW TW3 103 G7
Berwyn Rd HNHL SE24 130 C7
RCHPK/HAM TW10 125 J3
Beryl Av EHAM E6 95 J4
Beryl Rd HMSMTH W6 107 G4
Berystede KUTN/CMB KT2 144 D6
Besant Cl CRICK NW2 * 70 C2
Besant Pl EDUL SE22 131 G2
Besant Rd CRICK NW2 70 C3
Besant Wy WLSDN NW10 68 E4
Besley St STRHM/NOR SW16 148 C5
Bessant Dr RCH/KEW TW9 105 J7
Bessborough Gdns PIM SW1V 17 H7
Bessborough Pl PIM SW1V 17 G8
Bessborough Rd HRW HA1 48 D7
PUT/ROE SW15 126 D7
Bessborough St PIM SW1V 17 G7
Bessemer Pl GNWCH SE10 113 J2
Bessemer Rd CMBW SE5 130 D1
Bessie Lansbury Cl EHAM E6 96 A5
Bessingby Rd RSLP HA4 64 E1
Besson St NWCR SE14 111 K7
Bessy St BETH E2 * 92 E2
Bestwood St DEPT SE8 112 A3
Beswick Ms KIL/WHAMP NW6 71 F4
Betam Rd HYS/HAR UB3 101 G1
Betchworth Cl SUT SM1 175 H4
Betchworth Rd
GDMY/SEVK IG3 78 E1
Betchworth Wy CROY/NA CR0 180 A7
Betham Rd GFD/PVL UB6 84 D2
Bethany Waye
EBED/NFELT TW14 121 H6
Bethecar Rd HRW HA1 48 E4
Bethel Cl HDN NW4 52 B4
Bethell Av CAN/RD E16 94 D3
IL IG1 60 A6
Bethel Rd WELL DA16 136 D2
Bethersden Cl BECK BR3 151 H6
Bethnal Green Rd BETH E2 7 M9
Bethune Av FBAR/BDGN N11 39 K3
Bethune Rd STNW/STAM N16 55 K6
WLSDN NW10 87 F3
Bethwin Rd CMBW SE5 110 C6
Betjeman Cl RYLN/HDSTN HA2 48 A3
Betony Cl CROY/NA CR0 166 A7
Betoyne Av CHING E4 44 C3
Betsham Rd ERITH DA8 118 C6
Betstyle Rd FBAR/BDGN N11 40 B3
Betterton Rd RAIN RM13 99 G1
Betterton St LSQ/SEVD WC2H 11 J5
Bettons Pk SRTFD E15 76 C7
Bettridge Rd FUL/PGN SW6 127 J1
Betts Cl BECK BR3 166 B1
Betts Ms WALTH E17 57 H5
Betts Rd CAN/RD E16 95 F5
Betts St WAP E1W 92 D6
Betts Wy PGE/AN SE20 165 J1
SURB KT6 158 C7
Beulah Av THHTH CR7 * 164 D1
Beulah Cl EDGW HA8 36 D2
Beulah Crs THHTH CR7 164 D1
Beulah Gv CROY/NA CR0 164 D5
Beulah Hl NRWD SE19 149 H5
Beulah Rd SUT SM1 174 E3
THHTH CR7 164 D2
WALTH E17 57 K4
WIM/MER SW19 146 D6
Beult Rd DART DA1 138 D2
Bevan Av BARK IG11 79 G6
Bevan Ct CROY/NA CR0 177 G4
Bevan House WATN WD24 21 H1
Bevan Rd ABYW SE2 116 C4
EBAR EN4 27 K3
Bevan St IS N1 6 F4
Bev Callender Cl VX/NE SW8 129 G2
Bevenden St IS N1 7 H7
Beveridge Rd WLSDN NW10 69 G6
Beverley Av BFN/LL DA15 136 A6
HSLWW TW4 122 E3
RYNPK SW20 145 H7
Beverley Cl BARN SW13 126 D1
BTSEA SW11 128 C3
CHSGTN KT9 171 J3
WCHMH N21 29 J7
Beverley Ct BROCKY SE4 132 C2
Beverley Crs WFD IG8 45 F7
Beverley Dr EDGW HA8 50 B2
Beverley Gdns BARN SW13 126 C2
GLDGN NW11 52 C6
STAN HA7 35 G7
WBLY HA9 50 B7
WPK KT4 160 D7
Beverley La KUTN/CMB KT2 145 G6
Beverley Rd BARN SW13 126 C2
BXLYHN DA7 137 K1
CHING E4 44 B5
CHSWK W4 106 C4
DAGW RM9 80 A3
EHAM E6 95 H2
HAYES BR2 181 J1
KUT/HW KT1 143 J7
MTCM CR4 163 J3
NWDGN UB2 102 D3
NWMAL KT3 160 D3
PGE/AN SE20 165 J1
RSLP HA4 65 F1
SUN TW16 140 D7
WPK KT4 174 A1
Beverley Wy RYNPK SW20 145 H7
Beverley Way (Kingston
By-Pass) NWMAL KT3 160 C1
Beversbrook Rd ARCH N19 72 D2
Beverstone Rd
BRXS/STRHM SW2 130 A4
THHTH CR7 164 B3
Beverston Ms MBLAR W1H 9 L3
Bevill Allen Cl TOOT SW17 147 K5
Bevill Cl SNWD SE25 165 H2
Bevin Cl BERM/RHTH SE16 93 G7
Bevington Rd BECK BR3 166 E1
NKENS W10 * 88 C4
Bevington St
BERM/RHTH SE16 111 H1
Bevin Rd YEAD UB4 82 E2
Bevin Sq TOOT SW17 147 K2
Bevin Wy FSBYW WC1X 6 A6
Bevis Marks HDTCH EC3A 13 K4
Bewcastle Gdns ENC/FH EN2 28 E3
Bewdley St IS N1 6 A1
Bewick Ms PECK SE15 111 J6
Bewick St VX/NE SW8 129 G1
Bewley St WCHPL E1 92 D6
WIM/MER SW19 147 G5
Bewlys Rd WNWD SE27 149 H4
Bexhill Cl FELT TW13 141 J1
Bexhill Rd BROCKY SE4 132 C5
FBAR/BDGN N11 40 D4
MORT/ESHN SW14 125 K2
Bexley Cl DART DA1 138 B4
Bexley Gdns CHDH RM6 61 H4
ED N9 41 K2
Bexley High St BXLY DA5 137 H6
Bexley La DART DA1 138 B4
SCUP DA14 155 J3
Bexley Rd ELTH/MOT SE9 135 F5
ERITH DA8 117 K6
Beynon Rd CAR SM5 175 K4
Bianca Rd PECK SE15 111 G5
Bibsworth Rd FNCH N3 52 D1
Bibury Cl PECK SE15 111 F5
Bicester Rd RCH/KEW TW9 125 H2
Bickenhall St MHST W1U 9 M2
Bickersteth Rd TOOT SW17 147 K5
Bickerton Rd ARCH N19 72 B1
Bickles Yd STHWK SE1 19 K2
Bickley Crs BMLY BR1 168 D3
Bickley Park Rd BMLY BR1 168 E2
Bickley Rd BMLY BR1 168 C1
LEY E10 57 K6
Bickley St TOOT SW17 147 J4
Bicknell Rd CMBW SE5 130 D2
Bicknor Rd ORP BR6 169 K6
Bidborough Cl HAYES BR2 167 J4
Bidborough St STPAN WC1H 5 J8
Biddenden Wy ELTH/MOT SE9 154 A3
Bidder St CAN/RD E16 94 C4
Biddestone Rd HOLWY N7 73 F3
Biddulph Rd MV/WKIL W9 2 D8
SAND/SEL CR2 177 J7
Bideford Av GFD/PVL UB6 85 H2
Bideford Cl EDGW HA8 36 C7
FELT TW13 141 K2
Bideford Gdns EN EN1 30 A6
Bideford Rd BMLY BR1 152 D2
RSLP HA4 65 F2
WELL DA16 116 C6
Bidwell Gdns FBAR/BDGN N11 40 C7
Bidwell St PECK SE15 * 111 J7
Biggerstaff Rd SRTFD E15 76 A7
Biggerstaff St FSBYPK N4 73 G1
Biggin Av MTCM CR4 147 K7
Biggin Hl NRWD SE19 149 H6
Biggin Wy NRWD SE19 149 H6
Bigginwood Rd
STRHM/NOR SW16 149 H6
Bigg's Rw PUT/ROE SW15 127 G2
Biggs Sq HOM E9 75 H5
Big Hl CLPT E5 56 D7
Bigland St WCHPL E1 92 D5
Bignell Rd WOOL/PLUM SE18 115 G4
Bignold Rd FSTGT E7 76 E3
Bigwood Rd GLDGN NW11 53 F5
Billet Rd CHDH RM6 61 J2
WALTH E17 43 F7
Billetts Hart Cl HNWL W7 103 K1
Bill Hamling Cl ELTH/MOT SE9 153 K1
Billingford Cl BROCKY SE4 132 A3
Billing Pl WBPTN SW10 * 108 A6
Billing Rd WBPTN SW10 108 A6
Billings Cl DAGW RM9 79 J6
Billing St WBPTN SW10 * 108 A6
Billington Hl CROY/NA CR0 177 K1
Billington Rd NWCR SE14 112 A6
Billiter Sq FENCHST EC3M * 13 K5
Billiter St FENCHST EC3M 13 K5
Bill Nicholson Wy TOTM N17 42 B6
Billockby Cl CHSGTN KT9 172 B5
Billson St POP/IOD E14 113 F3
Bilton Rd ERITH DA8 118 D6
GFD/PVL UB6 67 H7
Bilton Wy HYS/HAR UB3 102 A1
Bina Gdns ECT SW5 14 E6
Bincote Rd ENC/FH EN2 29 F2
Binden Rd SHB W12 106 C2
Binfield Rd CLAP SW4 109 K7
SAND/SEL CR2 178 B4
Bingfield St IS N1 5 K3
Bingham Ct IS N1 * 6 D1
Bingham Pl MHST W1U 10 A2
Bingham Rd CROY/NA CR0 165 H7
Bingham St IS N1 73 K5
Bingley Rd CAN/RD E16 95 G5
GFD/PVL UB6 84 C3
SUN TW16 140 E6
Binney St MYFR/PKLN W1K 10 B6
Binns Rd CHSWK W4 106 B4
Binsey Wk ABYW SE2 116 D1
Binstead Cl YEAD UB4 83 J4
Binyon Crs STAN HA7 35 F4
Birbetts Rd ELTH/MOT SE9 153 K1
Birchanger Rd SNWD SE25 165 H4
Birch Av PLMGR N13 41 J2
Birch Cl BKHH IG9 45 H2
BTFD TW8 104 C6
CAN/RD E16 94 C4
HSLW TW3 123 J2
ROMW/RG RM7 62 D2
TEDD TW11 143 G4
Birch Ct WLGTN SM6 176 B3
Birchdale Gdns CHDH RM6 61 K6
Birchdale Rd FSTGT E7 77 G4
Birchdene Dr THMD SE28 97 G7
Birchen Cl CDALE/KGS NW9 69 F1
Birchend Cl SAND/SEL CR2 177 K5
Birchen Gv CDALE/KGS NW9 69 F1
Birches Cl MTCM CR4 162 E2
PIN HA5 47 J4
The Birches BUSH WD23 22 C4
CHARL SE7 114 A5
CMBW SE5 * 131 F2
HSLWW TW4 * 122 D4
WCHMH N21 29 F5
Birchfield St POP/IOD E14 93 J6
Birch Gdns DAGE RM10 80 E2
Birch Gv ACT W3 86 C7
LEE/GVPK SE12 133 J6
WAN E11 76 C2
WELL DA16 136 B3
Birch Hl CROY/NA CR0 179 F4
Birchington Cl BXLYHN DA7 117 J7
Birchington Rd BRYLDS KT5 159 G6
CEND/HSY/T N8 54 D5
KIL/WHAMP NW6 2 B3
Birchin La BANK EC3V 13 H5
Birchlands Av BAL SW12 128 E6
Birchmead Av PIN HA5 47 G3
Birchmere Rw BKHTH/KID SE3 133 J1
Birchmore Wk HBRY N5 73 J2
Birch Pk KTN/HRWW/WS HA3 34 C6
Birch Rd FELT TW13 141 H4
ROMW/RG RM7 62 D2
Birch Rw HAYES BR2 169 F6
Birch Tree Av WWKM BR4 180 D4
Birch Tree Wy CROY/NA CR0 178 D1
Birch Wk MTCM CR4 148 B7
Birchway HYS/HAR UB3 82 E7
Birchwood Av BECK BR3 166 C3
MUSWH N10 54 A2
SCUP DA14 155 H2
WLGTN SM6 176 A2
Birchwood Cl MRDN SM4 162 A3
Birchwood Ct EDGW HA8 50 E1
Birchwood Dr HAMP NW3 71 F2
Birchwood Gv HPTN TW12 142 A5
Birchwood La ESH/CLAY KT10 170 D7
Birchwood Rd
STMC/STPC BR5 169 J3
TOOT SW17 148 B4
Birdbrook Cl DAGE RM10 80 E6
Birdbrook Rd BKHTH/KID SE3 134 B2
Birdcage Wk STJSPK SW1H 17 G2
WESTW SW1E 16 F2
Birdham Cl BMLY BR1 168 D4
Birdhurst Av SAND/SEL CR2 177 K3
Birdhurst Gdns SAND/SEL CR2 177 K3
Birdhurst Ri SAND/SEL CR2 178 A4
Birdhurst Rd SAND/SEL CR2 178 A4
WAND/EARL SW18 128 B3
WIM/MER SW19 147 J5
Bird In Bush Rd PECK SE15 111 H6
Bird-In-Hand La BMLY BR1 168 C1
Bird-In-Hand Ms FSTH SE23 150 E1
Bird-In-Hand Pas FSTH SE23 150 E1
Birdsfield La BOW E3 75 H7
Bird St MHST W1U 10 B5
Bird Wk WHTN TW2 122 E7
Birdwood Av DART DA1 139 J1
LEW SE13 133 G5
Birdwood Cl TEDD TW11 142 E3
Birkbeck Av ACT W3 86 E6
GFD/PVL UB6 66 C7
Birkbeck Gv ACT W3 87 F7
Birkbeck Hl DUL SE21 149 H1
Birkbeck Ms ACT W3 * 87 F6
HACK E8 74 B4
Birkbeck Pl DUL SE21 130 C7
Birkbeck Rd ACT W3 87 F7
BECK BR3 165 K1
CEND/HSY/T N8 54 E3
EA W5 104 D3
GNTH/NBYPK IG2 60 D4
HACK E8 74 B4
MLHL NW7 37 H4
NFNCH/WDSPK N12 39 G4
ROMW/RG RM7 63 F7
SCUP DA14 155 G2
TOTM N17 42 B7
WIM/MER SW19 147 F4
Birkbeck St BETH E2 92 D2
Birkbeck Wy GFD/PVL UB6 66 D7
Birkdale Av PIN HA5 48 A2
Birkdale Cl
BERM/RHTH SE16 * 111 J4
ORP BR6 169 J6
THMD SE28 97 J5
Birkdale Gdns CROY/NA CR0 179 F3
OXHEY WD19 33 H2
Birkdale Rd ABYW SE2 116 B3
EA W5 86 A3
Birkenhead Av
KUTN/CMB KT2 159 G1
Birkenhead St KCROSS N1C 5 K7
Birkhall Rd CAT SE6 133 G7
Birkwood Cl BAL SW12 129 J6
Birley Rd TRDG/WHET N20 39 G1
Birley St BTSEA SW11 129 F1
Birling Rd ERITH DA8 118 A6
Birnam Rd FSBYPK N4 73 F1
Birnbeck Rd GLDGN NW11 52 D4
Birse Crs WLSDN NW10 69 G3
Birstal Gn OXHEY WD19 33 H3
Birstall Rd SEVS/STOTM N15 56 A4
Biscay Rd HMSMTH W6 107 G4
Biscoe Cl HEST TW5 103 F5
Biscoe Wy LEW SE13 * 133 G3
Bisenden Rd CROY/NA CR0 178 A1
Bisham Cl CAR SM5 162 E6
Bisham Gdns HGT N6 54 A7
Bishop Fox Wy
E/WMO/HCT KT8 156 E3
Bishop Ken Rd
KTN/HRWW/WS HA3 49 F1
Bishop King's Rd WKENS W14 107 H3
Bishop Ramsey Cl RSLP HA4 46 D6
Bishop Rd STHGT/OAK N14 28 B6
Bishops Av BMLY BR1 168 B2
BORE WD6 24 B4
CHDH RM6 61 J5
NTHWD HA6 32 C3
PLSTW E13 77 F7
Bishop's Av FUL/PGN SW6 127 G1
The Bishops Av EFNCH N2 53 H5
Bishop's Bridge Rd
BAY/PAD W2 8 D4
Bishops Cl BAR EN5 26 B5
CHSWK W4 105 K4
ELTH/MOT SE9 154 C1
EN EN1 30 D1
RCHPK/HAM TW10 143 K2
SUT SM1 174 E2
Bishop's Cl ARCH N19 72 C2
WALTH E17 57 K3
Bishop's Ct STP EC4M 12 C4
Bishops Dr EBED/NFELT TW14 121 G5
NTHLT UB5 65 J7
Bishopsford Rd MRDN SM4 162 B6
Bishopsgate LVPST EC2M 13 K3
Bishopsgate Ar LVPST EC2M 13 J3
Bishops Gn BMLY BR1 * 153 G7
Bishops Gv EFNCH N2 53 H5
HPTN TW12 141 K3
Bishop's Hall KUT/HW KT1 158 E1
Bishops Md CMBW SE5 * 110 D6
Bishops Park Rd
STRHM/NOR SW16 148 E7
Bishop's Park Rd
FUL/PGN SW6 127 G1
Bishop's Pl SUT SM1 175 G4
Bishops Rd FUL/PGN SW6 107 J7
HGT N6 54 A5
Bishop's Rd CROY/NA CR0 164 C6
HNWL W7 103 K1
HYS/HAR UB3 82 A5

Bishop's Ter LBTH SE11 18 B5
Bishopsthorpe Rd SYD SE26 151 F3
Bishop St IS N1 6 E3
Bishops Wk CHST BR7 154 C7
CROY/NA CR0 179 F4
Bishop's Wy BETH E2 92 E1
Bishopswood Rd HGT N6 53 K6
Bishop Wilfred Wood Cl
PECK SE15 131 H1
Bisley Cl WPK KT4 161 F7
Bispham Rd WLSDN NW10 86 B2
Bisson Rd SRTFD E15 94 A1
Bistern Av WALTH E17 58 B2
Bittacy Cl MLHL NW7 38 B5
Bittacy Hl MLHL NW7 38 B5
Bittacy Park Av MLHL NW7 38 B4
Bittacy Ri MLHL NW7 38 B5
Bittacy Rd MLHL NW7 38 B5
Bittern Cl YEAD UB4 83 H4
Bittern Pl WDGN N22 * 55 F1
Bittern St STHWK SE1 18 E1
Bittoms Ct KUT/HW KT1 * 158 E2
The Bittoms KUT/HW KT1 158 E2
Bixley Cl NWDGN UB2 102 E3
Blackall St SDTCH EC2A 7 J9
Blackberry Farm Cl HEST TW5 102 D6
Blackberry Fld
STMC/STPC BR5 155 G7
Blackbird Hl WBLY HA9 68 E1
Blackbird Yd BETH E2 7 M7
Blackborne Rd DAGE RM10 80 C5
Black Boy La
SEVS/STOTM N15 55 J4
Blackbrook La HAYES BR2 169 F4
Blackburne's Ms
MYFR/PKLN W1K 10 A6
Blackburn Rd
KIL/WHAMP NW6 71 F5
Blackbush Av CHDH RM6 61 K4
Blackbush Cl BELMT SM2 175 F6
Blackdown Cl EFNCH N2 53 G1
Blackdown Ter
WOOL/PLUM SE18 * 114 E7
Blackenham Rd TOOT SW17 147 K3
Blackett St PUT/ROE SW15 127 G2
Blackfen Pde BFN/LL DA15 * 136 B5
Blackfen Rd BFN/LL DA15 136 A4
Blackford Cl SAND/SEL CR2 177 H7
Blackford Rd OXHEY WD19 33 H4
Blackfriars Br STHWK SE1 12 C7
Black Friars La BLKFR EC4V 12 C5
Blackfriars Pas BLKFR EC4V 12 C6
Blackfriars Rd STHWK SE1 12 C8
Blackfriars U/P BLKFR EC4V 12 D6
Blackheath Av GNWCH SE10 113 G6
Blackheath Gv
BKHTH/KID SE3 133 J1
Blackheath Hl GNWCH SE10 113 F7
Blackheath Pk
BKHTH/KID SE3 133 J2
Blackheath Ri LEW SE13 133 F1
Blackheath Rd GNWCH SE10 112 E7
Blackheath V BKHTH/KID SE3 133 H1
Black Horse Ct STHWK SE1 * 19 H4
Blackhorse La CROY/NA CR0 165 H6
WALTH E17 57 F2
Black Horse Pde PIN HA5 * 47 F4
Blackhorse Rd DEPT SE8 112 B5
Black Horse Rd SCUP DA14 155 G3
Blackhorse Rd WALTH E17 57 F3
Blacklands Dr YEAD UB4 82 A3
Blacklands Rd CAT SE6 152 A3
Blacklands Ter CHEL SW3 15 L6
Black Lion Ga BAY/PAD W2 8 D7
Black Lion La HMSMTH W6 106 D3
Blackmans Cl DART DA1 139 F7
Blackmans Yd WCHPL E1 * 7 M9
Blackmoor La WATW WD18 20 B4
Blackmore Av STHL UB1 84 D7
Blackmore Dr WLSDN NW10 68 D6
Blackmore's Gv TEDD TW11 143 G5
Blackness Cots HAYES BR2 * 181 H7
Blackness La HAYES BR2 181 H7
Blackpool Gdns YEAD UB4 82 C3
Blackpool Rd PECK SE15 131 J1
Black Prince Rd LBTH SE11 17 L6
Black Rod Cl HYS/HAR UB3 101 J2
Blackrurn Wy HSLWW TW4 122 D4
Blackshaw Rd TOOT SW17 147 H4
Blacksmith Cl CHDH RM6 61 J5
Blacksmith's La RAIN RM13 81 H7
Black's Rd HMSMTH W6 107 F4
Blackstock Rd FSBYPK N4 73 H1
Blackstone Est HACK E8 74 C6
Blackstone Rd CRICK NW2 70 A4
Black Swan Yd STHWK SE1 19 J1
Blackthorn Av WDR/YW UB7 100 D3
Blackthorn Ct HEST TW5 102 D6
Blackthorne Av CROY/NA CR0 165 K7
Blackthorne Dr CHING E4 44 B3
Blackthorn Gv BXLYHN DA7 137 F2
Blackthorn Rd IL IG1 78 D4
Blackthorn St BOW E3 93 J3
Blacktree Ms BRXN/ST SW9 * 130 B2
Blackwall La GNWCH SE10 113 H4
Blackwall Tnl POP/IOD E14 94 B7
Blackwall Tunnel Ap
POP/IOD E14 94 A6
Blackwall Tunnel Northern Ap
BOW E3 75 J7
BOW E3 94 A2
Blackwall Wy POP/IOD E14 94 A6
Blackwater Cl FSTGT E7 76 D3
RAIN RM13 99 F4
Blackwater St EDUL SE22 131 G4
Blackwell Cl CLPT E5 75 G3
KTN/HRWW/WS HA3 34 D6
WCHMH N21 28 E4
Blackwell Dr OXHEY WD19 21 G5
Blackwell Gdns EDGW HA8 36 C3
Blackwood St WALW SE17 19 G7
Blade Ms PUT/ROE SW15 127 J3
Bladindon Dr BXLY DA5 136 E6
Bladon Gdns
RYLN/HDSTN HA2 48 B5
Blagden's La STHGT/OAK N14 40 D1
Blagdon Rd CAT SE6 132 E5
NWMAL KT3 160 C3
Blagdon Wk TEDD TW11 143 J5
Blagrove Rd NKENS W10 88 C4
Blair Av CDALE/KGS NW9 51 G6
ESH/CLAY KT10 170 C1
Blair Cl BFN/LL DA15 135 K4
HYS/HAR UB3 101 K3
IS N1 73 J5
Blairderry Rd
BRXS/STRHM SW2 148 E1
Blairhead Dr OXHEY WD19 33 F2
Blair St POP/IOD E14 94 A5
Blake Av BARK IG11 78 E7
Blake Cl CAR SM5 162 D7
NKENS W10 88 A4
RAIN RM13 81 H7
WELL DA16 115 K7
YEAD UB4 82 B1
Blakeden Dr ESH/CLAY KT10 171 F6
Blake Gdns DART DA1 139 J3
FUL/PGN SW6 107 K7
Blakehall Rd CAR SM5 175 K5
Blake Hall Rd WAN E11 58 E7
Blake Ms RCH/KEW TW9 105 H7
Blakemore Gdns BARN SW13 106 E5
Blakemore Rd
STRHM/NOR SW16 148 E2
THHTH CR7 164 A4
Blakemore Wy BELV DA17 117 F2
Blakeney Av BECK BR3 151 H7
Blakeney Cl CAMTN NW1 5 G2
HACK E8 74 C4
TRDG/WHET N20 27 G7
Blakeney Rd BECK BR3 151 H7
Blaker Ct CHARL SE7 * 114 B6
Blake Rd CAN/RD E16 94 D3
CROY/NA CR0 178 A1
FBAR/BDGN N11 40 C6
MTCM CR4 162 D2
Blaker Rd SRTFD E15 76 A7
Blakes Av NWMAL KT3 160 C4
Blakes Cl WLSDN NW10 69 J5
Blake's Gn WWKM BR4 167 F6
Blakes La NWMAL KT3 160 C4
Blakesley Av EA W5 85 J5
Blakes Rd PECK SE15 * 111 F6
Blake's Rd PECK SE15 111 F6
Blakes Ter NWMAL KT3 160 D4
Blakesware Gdns ED N9 29 K6
Blakewood Cl FELT TW13 141 G3
Blanchard Cl ELTH/MOT SE9 153 J2
Blanchard Dr WATW WD18 20 C3
Blanchard Wy HACK E8 * 74 C5
Blanch Cl PECK SE15 111 K6
Blanchedowne CMBW SE5 130 E3
Blanche St CAN/RD E16 94 D3
Blanchland Rd MRDN SM4 162 A4
Blandfield Rd BAL SW12 129 F5
Blandford Av BECK BR3 166 B1
WHTN TW2 123 G7
Blandford Cl CROY/NA CR0 176 E2
EFNCH N2 53 G4
ROMW/RG RM7 62 D3
Blandford Rd BECK BR3 166 A1
CHSWK W4 106 B2
EA W5 104 E1
NWDGN UB2 103 F3
TEDD TW11 142 D4
Blandford Sq CAMTN NW1 9 K1
Blandford St MHST W1U 9 M4
Blandford Waye YEAD UB4 83 G5
Bland St ELTH/MOT SE9 134 C3
Blaney Crs EHAM E6 96 B2
Blanmerle Rd ELTH/MOT SE9 135 G7
Blann Cl ELTH/MOT SE9 134 C5
Blantyre St WBPTN SW10 108 C6
Blantyre Wk WBPTN SW10 * 108 C6
Blashford St LEW SE13 133 G6
Blattner Cl BORE WD6 24 A3
Blawith Rd HRW HA1 48 E3
Blaydon Cl RSLP HA4 46 C6
TOTM N17 * 42 D6
Blaydon Wk TOTM N17 42 D6
Bleak Hill La
WOOL/PLUM SE18 116 A5
Blean Gv PGE/AN SE20 150 E6
Bleasdale Av GFD/PVL UB6 85 G1
Blechynden Gdns NKENS W10 88 B6
Blechynden St NKENS W10 * 88 B6
Bledlow Cl THMD SE28 97 J6
Bledlow Ri GFD/PVL UB6 84 C1
Bleeding Heart Yd
HCIRC EC1N * 12 B3
Blegborough Rd
STRHM/NOR SW16 148 C5
Blendon Dr BXLY DA5 136 E5
Blendon Rd BXLY DA5 136 E5
Blendon Ter
WOOL/PLUM SE18 115 H4
Blendworth Wy PECK SE15 111 F6
Blenheim CDALE/KGS NW9 * 51 H1
Blenheim Av GNTH/NBYPK IG2 60 A5
Blenheim Cl DART DA1 139 F5
GFD/PVL UB6 * 84 D1
LEE/GVPK SE12 134 A7
OXHEY WD19 21 G6
ROMW/RG RM7 62 E3
RYNPK SW20 161 F2
WCHMH N21 29 J7
WLGTN SM6 176 C6
Blenheim Ct BFN/LL DA15 154 D2
WFD IG8 45 F6
Blenheim Crs NTGHL W11 88 C5
RSLP HA4 64 B1
SAND/SEL CR2 177 J6
Blenheim Dr WELL DA16 116 A7
Blenheim Gdns
BRXS/STRHM SW2 130 A5
CRICK NW2 70 A4
KUTN/CMB KT2 144 D6
WBLY HA9 68 A2
WLGTN SM6 176 C5
Blenheim Gv PECK SE15 131 G1
Blenheim Park Rd
SAND/SEL CR2 177 J7
Blenheim Pas STJWD NW8 * 2 E5
Blenheim Pl TEDD TW11 143 F4
Blenheim Ri
SEVS/STOTM N15 * 56 B3
Blenheim Rd BAR EN5 26 B2
BFN/LL DA15 136 D7
BMLY BR1 168 D3
CHSWK W4 106 B2
DART DA1 139 F5
EHAM E6 95 H2
NTHLT UB5 66 B5
PGE/AN SE20 150 E6
RYLN/HDSTN HA2 48 B5
RYNPK SW20 161 F2
STJWD NW8 2 F5
SUT SM1 174 E2
WALTH E17 57 F2
WAN E11 76 C3
Blenheim St CONDST W1S 10 C5
Blenheim Ter STJWD NW8 2 E5
Blenheim Wy ISLW TW7 104 B7
Blenhiem Ct ARCH N19 72 E1
Blenkarne Rd BTSEA SW11 128 E5
Bleriot Rd HEST TW5 102 B6
Blessbury Rd EDGW HA8 36 E7
Blessington Rd LEW SE13 133 G3
Blessing Wy BARK IG11 97 J1
Bletchingley Cl THHTH CR7 164 C3
Bletchley St IS N1 6 F6
Bletchmore Cl HYS/HAR UB3 101 G4
Bletsoe Wk IS N1 6 F5
Blincoe Cl WIM/MER SW19 146 B1
Blissett St GNWCH SE10 113 F7
Bliss Ms NKENS W10 88 C2
Blisworth Cl YEAD UB4 83 J3
Blithbury Rd DAGW RM9 79 H5
Blithdale Rd ABYW SE2 116 B3
Blithfield St KENS W8 14 C4
Blockley Rd ALP/SUD HA0 67 H1
Bloemfontein Av SHB W12 87 K7
Bloemfontein Rd SHB W12 87 K6
Blomfield Rd MV/WKIL W9 8 D2
Blomfield St LVPST EC2M 13 H3
Blomfield Vls BAY/PAD W2 8 D3
Blomville Rd BCTR RM8 80 A1
Blondell Cl WDR/YW UB7 100 A5
Blondel St BTSEA SW11 129 F1
Blondin Av EA W5 104 D3
Blondin St BOW E3 93 J1
Bloomfield Crs
GNTH/NBYPK IG2 60 B5
Bloomfield Pl
MYFR/PKLN W1K 10 D6
Bloomfield Rd HAYES BR2 168 C4
HGT N6 54 A5
KUT/HW KT1 159 F3
WOOL/PLUM SE18 115 G4
Bloomfield Ter BGVA SW1W 16 B7
Bloom Gv WNWD SE27 149 H2
Bloomhall Rd NRWD SE19 149 K4
Bloom Park Rd FUL/PGN SW6 107 J6
Bloomsbury Cl EA W5 86 B6
Bloomsbury Pl
NOXST/BSQ WC1A 11 K3
Bloomsbury Sq
NOXST/BSQ WC1A 11 K3
Bloomsbury St GWRST WC1E 11 H2
Bloomsbury Wy
NOXST/BSQ WC1A 11 J3
Blore Cl VX/NE SW8 109 J7
Blossom Cl DAGW RM9 80 B7
EA W5 105 F1
SAND/SEL CR2 178 B4
Blossom St WCHPL E1 13 K1
Blossom Wy WDR/YW UB7 100 D3
Blossom Waye HEST TW5 102 D5
Blount St POP/IOD E14 93 G5
Bloxam Gdns ELTH/MOT SE9 134 D4
Bloxhall Rd LEY E10 57 H7
Bloxham Crs HPTN TW12 141 K7
Bloxworth Cl WLGTN SM6 176 C2
Blucher Rd CMBW SE5 110 D6
Blue Anchor La
BERM/RHTH SE16 111 H3
Blue Anchor Yd WCHPL E1 92 C6
Blue Ball Yd WHALL SW1A 10 E9
Bluebell Av MNPK E12 77 H4
Bluebell Cl HOM E9 74 E7
NTHLT UB5 65 K5
ROMW/RG RM7 81 G1
SYD SE26 150 B3
WLGTN SM6 163 G7
Bluebell Wy IL IG1 78 B5
Blueberry Cl WFD IG8 44 E5
Bluebird La DAGE RM10 80 C6
Bluebird Wy THMD SE28 115 J1
Bluefield Cl HPTN TW12 142 A4
Bluegates EW KT17 173 J6
Bluehouse Rd CHING E4 44 C2
Blue Lion Pl STHWK SE1 19 J3
Blue Riband Est
CROY/NA CR0 * 177 H1
Blundell Cl HACK E8 74 C3
Blundell Rd EDGW HA8 37 F7
Blundell St HOLWY N7 5 K1
Blunden Cl BCTR RM8 61 J7
Blunt Rd SAND/SEL CR2 177 K4
Blunts Av WDR/YW UB7 100 D6
Blunts Rd ELTH/MOT SE9 135 F4
Blurton Rd CLPT E5 75 F3
Blyth Cl TWK TW1 124 A5
Blythe Cl CAT SE6 132 C6
Blythe Hl CAT SE6 132 C6
STMC/STPC BR5 155 F7
Blythe Hill La CAT SE6 132 C6
Blythe Hill Pl FSTH SE23 * 132 B6
Blythe Ms WKENS W14 * 107 G2
Blythe Rd WKENS W14 107 G2
Blythe St BETH E2 * 92 D2
Blytheswood Pl
STRHM/NOR SW16 149 F3
Blythe V CAT SE6 132 C7
Blyth Rd BMLY BR1 152 D7
HYS/HAR UB3 101 H1
THMD SE28 97 J6
WALTH E17 57 H6
Blyth's Whf POP/IOD E14 * 93 G6
Blythswood Rd
GDMY/SEVK IG3 61 G7
Blythwood Rd FSBYPK N4 54 E6
PIN HA5 33 H7
Boadicea St IS N1 5 L4
Boakes Cl CDALE/KGS NW9 50 E3
Boardman Av CHING E4 31 K4
Boardman Cl BAR EN5 26 C4
Boardwalk Pl POP/IOD E14 94 A7
Boathouse Wk PECK SE15 111 G6
RCH/KEW TW9 104 E7
Boat Lifter Wy
BERM/RHTH SE16 112 B3
Boat Quay CAN/RD E16 95 G6
Bob Anker Cl PLSTW E13 94 E2
Bobbin Cl CLAP SW4 129 H2
Bob Dunn Wy DART DA1 139 K3
Bob Marley Wy HNHL SE24 130 B3
Bockhampton Rd
KUTN/CMB KT2 144 B6
Bocking St HACK E8 74 D7
Boddicott Cl WIM/MER SW19 146 C1
Boddington Gdns ACT W3 105 H1
Bodiam Cl EN EN1 29 K1
Bodiam Rd STRHM/NOR SW16 148 D7
Bodiam Wy WLSDN NW10 86 B2
Bodicea Ms HSLWW TW4 122 E5
Bodley Cl NWMAL KT3 160 B4
Bodley Rd NWMAL KT3 160 B5
Bodmin Cl RYLN/HDSTN HA2 65 K2
Bodmin Gv MRDN SM4 162 A3
Bodmin St WAND/EARL SW18 127 K7
Bodnant Gdns RYNPK SW20 160 D2
Bodney Rd CLPT E5 74 D4
Boeing Wy NWDGN UB2 102 A2
Bofors House CHARL SE7 * 114 D6
Bognor Gdns OXHEY WD19 33 G4
Bognor Rd WELL DA16 116 E7
Bohemia Pl HACK E8 74 E5
Bohn Rd WCHPL E1 93 G4
Bohun Gv EBAR EN4 27 J5
Boileau Rd BARN SW13 106 D6
EA W5 86 B5
Bolden St DEPT SE8 132 E1
Boldero Pl STJWD NW8 * 9 J1
Bolderwood Wy WWKM BR4 179 K1
Boldmere Rd PIN HA5 47 G6
Boleyn Ct WALTH E17 57 J3
Boleyn Dr E/WMO/HCT KT8 156 E2
RSLP HA4 65 H1
Boleyn Gdns DAGE RM10 80 E6
WWKM BR4 179 K1
Boleyn Rd EHAM E6 95 H1
FSTGT E7 76 E6
STNW/STAM N16 74 A4
Boleyn Wy BAR EN5 27 G2
Bolina Rd BERM/RHTH SE16 111 K4
Bolingbroke Gv BTSEA SW11 128 D4
Bolingbroke Rd WKENS W14 107 G2
Bolingbroke Wk
BTSEA SW11 * 108 C6
Bolingbroke Wy
HYS/HAR UB3 82 B7
Bollo Bridge Rd ACT W3 105 J2
Bollo La ACT W3 105 J2
Bolney Ga SKENS SW7 15 J2
Bolney St VX/NE SW8 110 A6
Bolsover St GTPST W1W 10 D1
Bolstead Rd MTCM CR4 148 B7
Bolster Gv WDGN N22 * 40 D7
Bolt Ct FLST/FETLN EC4A 12 B5
Boltmore Cl HDN NW4 52 B2
Bolton Cl CHSGTN KT9 171 K5
Bolton Crs LBTH SE11 110 B5
Bolton Dr MRDN SM4 162 B6
Bolton Gdns BMLY BR1 152 D5
ECT SW5 14 D7
TEDD TW11 143 G5
WLSDN NW10 88 B1
Bolton Gardens Ms
WBPTN SW10 14 D7
Bolton Pl IS N1 6 C2
Bolton Rd CHSGTN KT9 171 K5
CHSWK W4 105 K6
HRW HA1 48 C3
SRTFD E15 76 D5
STJWD NW8 2 D4
UED N18 42 B4
WLSDN NW10 69 G7
Bolton's La HYS/HAR UB3 101 F6
Boltons Pl ECT SW5 14 E7
The Boltons ALP/SUD HA0 67 F3
WBPTN SW10 14 E7
WFD IG8 * 44 E3
Bolton St MYFR/PICC W1J 10 D8
Bombay St BERM/RHTH SE16 111 J3
Bomer Cl WDR/YW UB7 100 D6
Bomore Rd NTGHL W11 88 B6
Bonaparte Ms PIM SW1V 17 G7
Bonar Pl CHST BR7 153 J6
Bonar Rd PECK SE15 111 H6
Bonchester Cl CHST BR7 154 A6
Bonchurch Cl BELMT SM2 175 F6
Bonchurch Rd NKENS W10 88 C4
WEA W13 85 H7
Bondfield Av YEAD UB4 82 E2
Bond Gdns WLGTN SM6 176 C3
Bond Rd MTCM CR4 162 E1
SURB KT6 172 B1
Bond St EA W5 85 K6
SRTFD E15 76 C4
Bondway VX/NE SW8 17 K9
Boneta Rd WOOL/PLUM SE18 114 E2
Bonfield Rd LEW SE13 133 F3
Bonham Gdns BCTR RM8 79 K1
Bonham Rd BCTR RM8 79 K1
BRXS/STRHM SW2 130 A4
Bonheur Rd CHSWK W4 106 A1
Bonhill St SDTCH EC2A 13 H1
Boniface Gdns
KTN/HRWW/WS HA3 34 B6
Boniface Wk
KTN/HRWW/WS HA3 34 B6
Bonita Ms PECK SE15 132 A2
Bonner Hill Rd KUT/HW KT1 159 G2
Bonner Rd BETH E2 92 E1
Bonnersfield Cl HRW HA1 49 G5
Bonnersfield La HRW HA1 49 F5
Bonner St BETH E2 * 92 E1
Bonneville Gdns CLAP SW4 129 H5
Bonnington Sq VX/NE SW8 17 L9
Bonny St CAMTN NW1 4 E2
Bonser Rd TWK TW1 143 F1
Bonsor St CMBW SE5 111 F6
Bonville Gdns HDN NW4 51 J3
Bonville Rd BMLY BR1 152 D4
Booker Cl POP/IOD E14 93 H4
Booker Rd UED N18 42 C4
Boones Rd LEW SE13 133 H3
Boone St LEW SE13 133 H3
Boord St GNWCH SE10 113 H2
Boothby Rd ARCH N19 72 D1
Booth Cl HOM E9 74 D7
THMD SE28 97 H7
Booth La BLKFR EC4V 12 E6
Booth Rd CDALE/KGS NW9 37 F7
CROY/NA CR0 * 177 H1
Boot Pde EDGW HA8 * 36 C5
Boot St FSBYE EC1V 7 J8
Bordars Rd HNWL W7 84 E4
Bordars Wk HNWL W7 84 E4
Borden Av EN EN1 29 K5
Border Crs SYD SE26 150 D4
Border Gdns CROY/NA CR0 179 K3
Border Ga MTCM CR4 147 J7
Border Rd SYD SE26 150 D4
Bordesley Rd MRDN SM4 162 A3
Bordon Wk PUT/ROE SW15 126 D6
Boreas Wk IS N1 6 D6
Boreham Av CAN/RD E16 94 E5
Boreham Cl WAN E11 58 A7
Boreham Rd WDGN N22 41 J7
Borgard House CHARL SE7 * 114 D6
Borgard Rd WOOL/PLUM SE18 114 E3
Borland Rd PECK SE15 131 K3
TEDD TW11 143 H5
Borneo St PUT/ROE SW15 127 F2
Borough High St STHWK SE1 18 F2
Borough Hl CROY/NA CR0 177 H2
Borough Rd ISLW TW7 103 K7
KUTN/CMB KT2 144 C7
MTCM CR4 162 D1
STHWK SE1 18 C3
Borough Sq STHWK SE1 18 E2
Borrett Cl WALW SE17 18 E8
Borrodaile Rd
WAND/EARL SW18 128 A5
Borrowdale Av
KTN/HRWW/WS HA3 49 G1
Borrowdale Cl EFNCH N2 53 G1
REDBR IG4 59 J3
Borthwick Ms WAN E11 * 76 C3
Borthwick Rd
CDALE/KGS NW9 51 H5
SRTFD E15 76 C3
Borthwick St DEPT SE8 112 D4
Borwick Av WALTH E17 57 H2
Bosbury Rd CAT SE6 152 A2
Boscastle Rd KTTN NW5 72 B2
Boscobel Cl BMLY BR1 168 E1
Boscobel Pl BGVA SW1W 16 B5
Boscobel St BAY/PAD W2 9 H2
Boscombe Av LEY E10 58 B6
Boscombe Cl CLPT E5 75 G4
Boscombe Rd SHB W12 106 D1
TOOT SW17 148 A5
WIM/MER SW19 146 E7
WPK KT4 161 F7
Bose Cl FNCH N3 38 C7
Boss St STHWK SE1 19 L1
Bostall Heath ABYW SE2 * 116 D4
Bostall Hl ABYW SE2 116 C4
Bostall La ABYW SE2 116 C4
Bostall Manorway ABYW SE2 116 C3
Bostall Park Av BXLYHN DA7 117 F6
Bostall Rd STMC/STPC BR5 155 H6
Boston Gdns BTFD TW8 104 B3
CHSWK W4 106 B5
Boston Gv RSLP HA4 46 A5
Boston Manor Rd BTFD TW8 104 B3
Boston Pde HNWL W7 * 104 B3
Boston Park Rd BTFD TW8 * 104 D5
Boston Pl CAMTN NW1 9 L1
Boston Rd CROY/NA CR0 164 A5
EDGW HA8 36 E6
EHAM E6 95 J2
HNWL W7 84 E7
WALTH E17 57 J5
Bostonthorpe Rd HNWL W7 * 103 K1
Boston V HNWL W7 104 B3
Boswell Ct BMSBY WC1N 11 K2
Boswell Rd THHTH CR7 164 D3
Boswell St BMSBY WC1N 11 K2
Bosworth Cl WALTH E17 43 H7
Bosworth Rd BAR EN5 26 E2
DAGE RM10 80 C3
FBAR/BDGN N11 40 D5
NKENS W10 88 C3
Botany Bay La CHST BR7 169 H1
Botany Cl EBAR EN4 27 J3
Botany Ter PUR RM19 * 119 K4
Boteley Cl CHING E4 44 B1
Botham Cl EDGW HA8 36 E6
Botha Rd PLSTW E13 95 F4
Bothwell Cl CAN/RD E16 94 E4
Bothwell St HMSMTH W6 107 G5
Botolph Aly MON EC3R 13 J7
Botolph La MON EC3R 13 J7
Botsford Rd RYNPK SW20 161 H1
Bottonscroft Cl THHTH CR7 164 D2
Bott's Ms BAY/PAD W2 8 B5
Botwell Common Rd
HYS/HAR UB3 82 B6
Botwell Crs HYS/HAR UB3 82 C5
Botwell La HYS/HAR UB3 101 J1
Boucher Cl TEDD TW11 143 F4
Boughton Av HAYES BR2 167 J6
Boughton Rd THMD SE28 115 K2
Boulcott St WCHPL E1 93 F5
Boulevard WATW WD18 * 20 B4
Boulevard Dr CDALE/KGS NW9 51 H1
The Boulevard FUL/PGN SW6 128 B1
WATW WD18 20 B4
Boulogne Rd CROY/NA CR0 164 D5
Boulter Cl BMLY BR1 169 F2
Boulter Gdns RAIN RM13 81 J5
Boulton Rd BCTR RM8 80 A1
Boultwood Rd EHAM E6 95 K5
Bounces La ED N9 42 D1
Bounces Rd ED N9 42 D1
Boundaries Rd BAL SW12 147 K1
FELT TW13 122 B7
Boundary Av WALTH E17 57 H6
Boundary Business Ct
MTCM CR4 162 C2
Boundary Cl GDMY/SEVK IG3 78 E3
KUT/HW KT1 159 H2
NWDGN UB2 103 F4
Boundary La CMBW SE5 110 D5
PLSTW E13 95 H2
Boundary Ms STJWD NW8 * 2 F3
Boundary Pass WCHPL E1 7 L9
Boundary Rd BARK IG11 96 C1
BFN/LL DA15 135 K4
CAR SM5 176 A7
ED N9 30 E5
EFNCH N2 39 H7
PIN HA5 47 H5
PLSTW E13 95 G1
ROM RM1 63 J5
STJWD NW8 2 E4
WALTH E17 57 H6
WBLY HA9 68 A2
WDGN N22 55 H2
WIM/MER SW19 147 H5
WLGTN SM6 176 B5
Boundary Rw STHWK SE1 18 C1
Boundary St BETH E2 7 L8
ERITH DA8 118 C6
Boundary Wy CROY/NA CR0 179 J4
Boundfield Rd CAT SE6 152 C2
Bounds Green Rd
FBAR/BDGN N11 40 D5
Bourchier St SOHO/SHAV W1D 11 G6
Bourdon Pl MYFR/PKLN W1K 10 D6
Bourdon Rd PGE/AN SE20 165 K1
Bourdon St MYFR/PKLN W1K 10 C7
Bourke Cl CLAP SW4 129 K5
WLSDN NW10 69 G5
Bourlet Cl GTPST W1W 10 E3
Bourn Av EBAR EN4 27 H4
SEVS/STOTM N15 55 K3
Bournbrook Rd
BKHTH/KID SE3 134 C2
Bourne Av HYS/HAR UB3 101 F2
RSLP HA4 65 G4
STHGT/OAK N14 40 E1
Bourne Cl ISLW TW7 123 K2
THDIT KT7 171 F1
Bourne Ct RSLP HA4 65 F4
Bourne Dr MTCM CR4 162 C1
Bourne End Rd NTHWD HA6 32 C3
Bourne Est HCIRC EC1N * 12 A2
Bourne Gdns CHING E4 43 K3
Bournehall BUSH WD23 * 22 A5
Bournehall Av BUSH WD23 22 A4
Bournehall La BUSH WD23 22 A5
Bournehall Rd BUSH WD23 22 A5
Bourne Hl PLMGR N13 40 E1
Bourne Hill Cl PLMGR N13 * 41 F1
Bournemead BUSH WD23 22 A5
Bourne Md BXLY DA5 137 K4
Bournemead Av NTHLT UB5 82 E1
Bournemead Cl NTHLT UB5 82 E2
Bournemouth Cl PECK SE15 131 H1
Bournemouth Rd PECK SE15 131 H1
WIM/MER SW19 146 E7
Bourne Pde BXLY DA5 * 137 J6
Bourne Rd BUSH WD23 22 A4
BXLY DA5 137 J5
CEND/HSY/T N8 54 E5
HAYES BR2 168 C3
WAN E11 76 D2
Bourneside Crs
STHGT/OAK N14 28 D7
Bourneside Gdns CAT SE6 152 A4

Bourne St BGVA SW1W 16 A6
CROY/NA CR0 177 H1
Bourne Ter BAY/PAD W2 8 C2
The Bourne STHGT/OAK N14 28 D7
Bourne V HAYES BR2 167 K7
Bournevale Rd
STRHM/NOR SW16 148 E3
Bourne Vw GFD/PVL UB6 67 F5
Bourne Wy HAYES BR2 180 E1
HOR/WEW KT19 172 E3
SUT SM1 174 D4
Bournewood Rd
WOOL/PLUM SE18 116 B6
Bournville Rd CAT SE6 132 D6
Bournwell Cl EBAR EN4 27 K1
Bourton Cl HYS/HAR UB3 82 E7
Bousfield Rd NWCR SE14 132 A1
Boutflower Rd BTSEA SW11 128 D3
Boutique Hall LEW SE13 * 133 F3
Bouverie Gdns
KTN/HRWW/WS HA3 49 K5
Bouverie Ms STNW/STAM N16 74 A1
Bouverie Pl BAY/PAD W2 9 H4
Bouverie Rd HRW HA1 48 C5
STNW/STAM N16 74 A1
Bouverie St EMB EC4Y 12 B5
Boveney Rd FSTH SE23 132 A6
Bovill Rd FSTH SE23 132 A6
Bovingdon Av WBLY HA9 68 C5
Bovingdon La
CDALE/KGS NW9 37 G7
Bovingdon Rd FUL/PGN SW6 108 A7
Bovington Cl ARCH N19 72 C1
Bow Arrow La DART DA1 139 K5
Bowater Cl BRXS/STRHM SW2 129 K5
CDALE/KGS NW9 51 F4
Bowater Gdns SUN TW16 141 G7
Bowater Pl BKHTH/KID SE3 114 A6
Bowater Rd WBLY HA9 68 D2
WOOL/PLUM SE18 114 C2
Bow Bridge Est BOW E3 93 K2
Bow Churchyard STP EC4M * 12 F5
Bow Common La BOW E3 93 H3
Bowden Cl EBED/NFELT TW14 121 H7
Bowden St LBTH SE11 18 B7
Bowditch DEPT SE8 112 C4
Bowdon Rd WALTH E17 57 J6
Bowen Dr DUL SE21 150 A2
Bowen Rd HRW HA1 48 C6
Bowen St POP/IOD E14 93 K5
Bowens Wd CROY/NA CR0 * 179 H7
Bower Av GNWCH SE10 113 H7
Bower Cl NTHLT UB5 83 G1
Bowerdean St FUL/PGN SW6 108 A7
Bowerman Av NWCR SE14 112 B5
Bower St WCHPL E1 * 93 F5
Bowes Cl BFN/LL DA15 136 C5
Bowes Rd ACT W3 87 G6
BCTR RM8 79 J3
FBAR/BDGN N11 40 B4
Bowfell Rd HMSMTH W6 107 F5
Bowford Av BXLYHN DA7 117 F7
Bowhill Cl BRXN/ST SW9 110 B6
Bowie Cl CLAP SW4 129 J6
Bowland Rd CLAP SW4 129 J3
WFD IG8 45 G5
Bowland Yd KTBR SW1X * 15 M2
Bow La NFNCH/WDSPK N12 39 G6
STP EC4M 12 F5
Bowl Ct WCHPL E1 13 K1
Bowley Cl NRWD SE19 150 B5
Bowley La NRWD SE19 150 B4
Bowley St POP/IOD E14 93 H6
Bowling Green Cl
PUT/ROE SW15 126 E6
Bowling Green Ct WBLY HA9 68 B1
Bowling Green La
CLKNW EC1R 12 B1
Bowling Green Pl
STHWK SE1 * 19 G1
Bowling Green Rw
WOOL/PLUM SE18 * 114 E3
Bowling Green St LBTH SE11 18 A9
Bowling Green Wk IS N1 7 J7
Bow Locks BOW E3 * 94 A3
Bowls Cl STAN HA7 35 H4
Bowman Av CAN/RD E16 94 E5
Bowman Ms
WAND/EARL SW18 127 J7
Bowmans Cl WEA W13 85 H7
Bowmans Lea FSTH SE23 131 K6
Bowman's Meadow
WLGTN SM6 176 B2
Bowmans Ms WCHPL E1 92 C6
Bowman's Ms HOLWY N7 72 E2
Bowman's Pl HOLWY N7 72 E2
Bowmans Rd DART DA1 138 C6
Bowmead ELTH/MOT SE9 153 K1
Bowmore Wk CAMTN NW1 5 H2
Bowness Cl HACK E8 * 74 B5
Bowness Crs PUT/ROE SW15 145 F4
Bowness Dr HSLWW TW4 122 D3
Bowness Rd BXLYHN DA7 137 J1
CAT SE6 132 E6
Bowness Wy HCH RM12 81 J4
Bowood Rd CLAP SW4 129 F3
PEND EN3 31 F1
Bowring Gn OXHEY WD19 33 G4
Bow Rd BOW E3 93 J2
Bowrons Av ALP/SUD HA0 67 K6
Bowsley Ct FELT TW13 140 E1
Bow St COVGDN WC2E 11 K5
SRTFD E15 76 C4
Bowyer Cl EHAM E6 95 K4
Bowyer Pl CMBW SE5 110 E6
Bowyers Ct TWK TW1 124 C3
Bowyer St CMBW SE5 110 D6
Boxall Rd DUL SE21 131 F5
Boxelder Cl EDGW HA8 36 E4
Boxgrove Rd ABYW SE2 116 C1
Box La BARK IG11 97 H1
Boxley Rd MRDN SM4 162 B3
Boxley St CAN/RD E16 95 F7
Boxmoor Rd
KTN/HRWW/WS HA3 49 H3
Boxoll Rd DAGW RM9 80 B3
Boxtree La
KTN/HRWW/WS HA3 34 C7
Boxtree Rd
KTN/HRWW/WS HA3 34 D6
Boxwood Cl WDR/YW UB7 100 C1
Boxworth Cl
NFNCH/WDSPK N12 39 H4
Boxworth Gv IS N1 5 M3
Boyard Rd WOOL/PLUM SE18 115 G4
Boyce Wy PLSTW E13 94 E3
Boycroft Av CDALE/KGS NW9 50 E5
Boyd Av STHL UB1 83 K7
Boyd Cl KUTN/CMB KT2 144 C6
Boydell Ct STJWD NW8 3 G2
Boyd Rd WIM/MER SW19 147 H5
Boyd St WCHPL E1 92 C5
Boyfield St STHWK SE1 18 D2
Boyland Rd BMLY BR1 152 D4
Boyle Av STAN HA7 35 G5
Boyle Farm Rd THDIT KT7 158 B5
Boyne Av HDN NW4 52 B3
Boyne Rd DAGE RM10 80 C2
LEW SE13 133 G2
Boyne Terrace Ms NTGHL W11 88 D7
Boyton Cl CEND/HSY/T N8 54 E2
WCHPL E1 93 F3
Boyton Rd CEND/HSY/T N8 54 E2
Brabant Rd WDGN N22 55 F1
Brabazon Av WLGTN SM6 176 E6
Brabazon Rd HEST TW5 102 B6
NTHLT UB5 84 A1
Brabazon St POP/IOD E14 93 K5
Brabourne Cl NRWD SE19 150 A4
Brabourne Crs BXLYHN DA7 117 G5
Brabourne Ri BECK BR3 167 G4
Brabourn Gv PECK SE15 131 K1
Bracewell Av GFD/PVL UB6 67 F4
Bracewell Rd NKENS W10 88 A4
Bracewood Gdns
CROY/NA CR0 178 B2
Bracey St FSBYPK N4 * 72 E1
Bracken Av BAL SW12 129 F5
CROY/NA CR0 179 J2
Brackenbridge Dr RSLP HA4 65 H2
Brackenbury Gdns
HMSMTH W6 106 E2
Brackenbury Rd EFNCH N2 53 G2
HMSMTH W6 106 E2
Bracken Cl EHAM E6 95 K4
SUN TW16 * 140 D5
WHTN TW2 123 F6
Brackendale WCHMH N21 41 F1
Brackendale Cl HSLW TW3 103 G7
Bracken End ISLW TW7 123 J4
Bracken Gdns BARN SW13 126 D1
Brackenhill RSLP HA4 * 65 J3
Bracken Hill Cl BMLY BR1 152 D7
Bracken Hill La BMLY BR1 152 D7
Bracken Ms ROMW/RG RM7 62 C5
The Brackens EN EN1 30 A6
The Bracken CHING E4 44 A1
Brackenwood SUN TW16 140 E7
Brackley Av PECK SE15 131 K2
Brackley Cl WLGTN SM6 176 E6
Brackley Rd BECK BR3 151 H6
CHSWK W4 106 B3
Brackley Sq WFD IG8 45 H6
Brackley St BARB EC2Y 12 F2
Brackley Ter CHSWK W4 106 B4
Bracklyn St IS N1 7 G5
Bracknell Cl WDGN N22 41 G7
Bracknell Gdns HAMP NW3 71 F4
Bracknell Wy HAMP NW3 71 F3
Bracondale ESH/CLAY KT10 170 C4
Bracondale Rd ABYW SE2 116 B3
Bradbourne Rd BXLY DA5 137 H6
Bradbourne St FUL/PGN SW6 127 K1
Bradbury Cl NWDGN UB2 102 E3
Bradbury St STNW/STAM N16 74 A4
Braddock Cl ISLW TW7 124 A2
Braddon Ct BAR EN5 * 26 C2
Braddon Rd RCH/KEW TW9 125 G2
Braddyll St GNWCH SE10 113 H4
Bradenham Av WELL DA16 136 B3
Bradenham Cl WALW SE17 19 G9
Bradenham Rd
KTN/HRWW/WS HA3 49 H3
YEAD UB4 82 C2
Braden St MV/WKIL W9 * 8 C1
Bradfield Dr BARK IG11 79 G4
Bradfield Rd CAN/RD E16 113 K1
RSLP HA4 65 J4
Bradford Cl HAYES BR2 168 E7
SYD SE26 150 D3
TOTM N17 42 B5
Bradford Dr HOR/WEW KT19 173 H5
Bradford Rd ACT W3 106 B1
IL IG1 60 D7
Bradfords Cl BKHH IG9 45 H3
Bradgate Rd CAT SE6 132 E5
Brading Crs WAN E11 77 F1
Brading Rd BRXS/STRHM SW2 130 A6
CROY/NA CR0 164 A5
Brading Ter SHB W12 106 D2
Bradiston Rd MV/WKIL W9 88 D2
Bradley Cl HOLWY N7 5 K1
Bradley Gdns WEA W13 85 H5
Bradley Rd NRWD SE19 149 J5
WDGN N22 55 F1
Bradley's Cl IS N1 6 A5
Bradley Stone Rd EHAM E6 95 K5
Bradman Rw EDGW HA8 * 36 E6
Bradmead VX/NE SW8 * 109 G7
Bradmore Park Rd
HMSMTH W6 106 E2
Bradshaw Cl WIM/MER SW19 146 E5
Bradshaw Cots
POP/IOD E14 * 93 G5
Bradshaws Cl SNWD SE25 165 H2
Bradstock Rd EW KT17 173 K4
HOM E9 75 F5
Brad St STHWK SE1 12 B9
Bradwell Av DAGE RM10 80 C1
Bradwell Cl HCH RM12 81 K5
SWFD E18 58 D3
Bradwell Ms UED N18 42 C3
Bradwell St WCHPL E1 93 F2
Brady Dr BMLY BR1 169 F2
Bradymead EHAM E6 96 A5
Brady St WCHPL E1 92 D3
Braemar Av ALP/SUD HA0 67 K6
BXLYHN DA7 137 K3
THHTH CR7 164 B2
WDGN N22 40 E7
WIM/MER SW19 146 E1
WLSDN NW10 69 F2
Braemar Gdns BFN/LL DA15 154 D2
CDALE/KGS NW9 37 F7
WWKM BR4 167 F7
Braemar Rd BTFD TW8 104 E5
PLSTW E13 94 D3
SEVS/STOTM N15 56 A4
WPK KT4 173 K2
Braeside BECK BR3 151 J4
Braeside Av RYNPK SW20 146 C7
Braeside Cl PIN HA5 34 A6
Braeside Crs BXLYHN DA7 137 K3
Braeside Rd
STRHM/NOR SW16 148 C6
Braes St IS N1 6 D2
Braesyde Cl BELV DA17 117 G3
Brafferton Rd CROY/NA CR0 177 J3
Braganza St WALW SE17 18 C8
Bragg Cl BCTR RM8 79 H5
Bragg Rd TEDD TW11 142 E6
Braham St WCHPL E1 13 M5
Braid Av ACT W3 87 G5
Braid Cl FELT TW13 141 K1
Braidwood Rd CAT SE6 133 G7
Braidwood St STHWK SE1 13 J9
Brailsford Cl WIM/MER SW19 147 J6
Brailsford Rd
BRXS/STRHM SW2 130 B5
Brainton Av
EBED/NFELT TW14 122 A6
Braintree Av REDBR IG4 59 J4
Braintree Rd DAGE RM10 80 C2
RSLP HA4 65 F3
Braintree St BETH E2 * 92 E2
Braithwaite Av
ROMW/RG RM7 62 C6
Braithwaite Gdns STAN HA7 35 J7
Braithwaite Rd PEND EN3 31 H2
Bramall Cl SRTFD E15 76 D4
Bramber Ct EA W5 105 F3
Bramber Rd
NFNCH/WDSPK N12 39 J4
WKENS W14 107 J5
Bramble Acres Cl BELMT SM2 174 E6
Bramble Banks CAR SM5 176 A7
Bramblebury Rd
WOOL/PLUM SE18 115 J4
Bramble Cl BECK BR3 167 F4
CROY/NA CR0 179 J3
SEVS/STOTM N15 56 C3
STAN HA7 35 K6
THHTH CR7 149 K7
Bramble Cft ERITH DA8 117 K3
Brambledown Cl WWKM BR4 167 H5
Brambledown Rd CAR SM5 176 A6
SAND/SEL CR2 178 A6
Bramble Gdns SHB W12 87 H6
Bramble La HPTN TW12 141 K5
Brambles Cl ISLW TW7 104 C6
The Brambles SUT SM1 * 175 H1
WDR/YW UB7 100 A4
WIM/MER SW19 * 146 D4
Bramblewood Cl CAR SM5 162 D7
Brambling Cl BUSH WD23 21 J3
The Bramblings CHING E4 44 B3
Bramcote Av MTCM CR4 162 E3
Bramcote Gv
BERM/RHTH SE16 111 K4
Bramcote Rd PUT/ROE SW15 126 E3
Bramdean Crs LEE/GVPK SE12 133 K7
Bramdean Gdns
LEE/GVPK SE12 133 K7
Bramerton Rd BECK BR3 166 C2
Bramerton St CHEL SW3 15 J9
Bramfield Rd BTSEA SW11 128 D5
Bramford Rd
WAND/EARL SW18 128 B3
Bramham Ct NTHWD HA6 * 32 C4
Bramham Gdns CHSGTN KT9 * 171 K4
ECT SW5 14 C7
Bramhope La CHARL SE7 114 A5
Bramlands Cl BTSEA SW11 128 D2
Bramleas WATW WD18 20 D4
Bramley Cl HYS/HAR UB3 82 E6
MLHL NW7 37 G2
ORP BR6 169 G7
PIN HA5 46 D2
SAND/SEL CR2 177 H4
STHGT/OAK N14 28 B4
WALTH E17 57 G1
WFD IG8 45 G6
WHTN TW2 123 H5
Bramley Crs GNTH/NBYPK IG2 60 A5
VX/NE SW8 109 J6
Bramley Gdns OXHEY WD19 33 G5
Bramley Hl SAND/SEL CR2 177 J3
Bramley Hyrst
SAND/SEL CR2 * 177 J4
Bramley Ldg ALP/SUD HA0 67 K3
Bramley Pde STHGT/OAK N14 28 C3
Bramley Pl DART DA1 138 D3
Bramley Rd BELMT SM2 174 B7
EA W5 104 D2
NKENS W10 88 B6
STHGT/OAK N14 28 B4
SUT SM1 175 H4
Bramley Wy HSLWW TW4 122 E4
WWKM BR4 179 K1
Brampton Cl CLPT E5 74 D1
Brampton Gv HDN NW4 51 K3
KTN/HRWW/WS HA3 49 G3
WBLY HA9 50 C7
Brampton La HDN NW4 52 A3
Brampton Park Rd
WDGN N22 55 G2
Brampton Rd BXLYHN DA7 136 E2
CDALE/KGS NW9 50 C3
CROY/NA CR0 165 G6
EHAM E6 95 H3
OXHEY WD19 32 E2
SEVS/STOTM N15 55 J4
Bramshaw Gdns OXHEY WD19 33 H4
Bramshaw Ri NWMAL KT3 160 B5
Bramshaw Rd HOM E9 75 F5
Bramshill Gdns KTTN NW5 72 B2
Bramshill Rd WLSDN NW10 87 G1
Bramshot Av CHARL SE7 114 A5
Bramshott Wy OXHEY WD19 32 E1
Bramston Rd MTCM CR4 147 K6
WLSDN NW10 87 J1
Bramwell Cl SUN TW16 156 C1
Bramwell Ms IS N1 5 M3
Brancaster Dr MLHL NW7 37 J6
Brancaster Rd
GNTH/NBYPK IG2 60 D5
STRHM/NOR SW16 148 E2
Brancepeth Gdns BKHH IG9 44 E1
Branch Hl HAMP NW3 71 G2
Branch Pl IS N1 7 H3
Branch Rd POP/IOD E14 93 G5
Branch St CMBW SE5 111 F6
Brancker Rd
KTN/HRWW/WS HA3 49 K2
Brand Cl FSBYPK N4 55 H7
Brandlehow Rd
PUT/ROE SW15 127 J3
Brandon Est WALW SE17 18 E9
Brandon Ms BARB EC2Y * 13 G2
Brandon Rd DART DA1 139 K6
HOLWY N7 5 J1
NWDGN UB2 102 E4
SUT SM1 175 F3
WALTH E17 58 A3
Brandon St WALW SE17 18 F5
Brandram Ms LEW SE13 * 133 H3
Brandram Rd LEW SE13 133 H2
Brandreth Ct HRW HA1 * 49 F5
Brandreth Rd EHAM E6 95 K5
TOOT SW17 148 B1
The Brandries WLGTN SM6 176 D2
Brand St GNWCH SE10 113 F6
Brandville Gdns BARK/HLT IG6 60 B3
Brandville Rd WDR/YW UB7 100 B1
Brandy Wy BELMT SM2 174 E6
Brangbourne Rd BMLY BR1 152 A4
Brangton Rd LBTH SE11 17 M8
Brangwyn Crs
WIM/MER SW19 147 H7
Branksea St FUL/PGN SW6 107 H6
Branksome Av UED N18 42 B5
Branksome Cl TEDD TW11 142 D3
Branksome Rd
BRXS/STRHM SW2 129 K4
WIM/MER SW19 146 E7
Branksome Wy
KTN/HRWW/WS HA3 50 B5
NWMAL KT3 159 K1
Bransby Rd CHSGTN KT9 172 A6
Branscombe Gdns
WCHMH N21 29 G6
Branscombe St LEW SE13 132 E2
Bransdale Cl KIL/WHAMP NW6 2 B3
Bransgrove Rd EDGW HA8 36 B7
Branston Crs STMC/STPC BR5 169 J7
Branstone Rd RCH/KEW TW9 105 G7
Brants Wk HNWL W7 84 E3
Brantwood Av ERITH DA8 117 K6
ISLW TW7 124 B3
Brantwood Cl WALTH E17 * 57 K2
Brantwood Gdns ENC/FH EN2 28 E3
REDBR IG4 59 J4
Brantwood Rd BXLYHN DA7 137 J1
HNHL SE24 130 D4
SAND/SEL CR2 177 J7
TOTM N17 42 C5
Brasenose Dr BARN SW13 107 F5
Brasher Cl GFD/PVL UB6 66 D4
Brassey Cl
EBED/NFELT TW14 * 121 K7
Brassey Rd KIL/WHAMP NW6 70 D5
Brassey Sq BTSEA SW11 129 F2
Brassie Av ACT W3 87 G5
Brasted Cl BXLYHS DA6 136 E4
SYD SE26 150 E3
Brasted Rd ERITH DA8 118 B6
Brathway Rd
WAND/EARL SW18 127 K6
Braund Av GFD/PVL UB6 84 B3
Braundton Av BFN/LL DA15 136 A7
Braunston Dr YEAD UB4 83 J3
Bravington Pl MV/WKIL W9 88 D3
Bravington Rd MV/WKIL W9 88 D2
Bravingtons Wk IS N1 5 K6
Braxfield Rd BROCKY SE4 132 B3
Braxted Pk STRHM/NOR SW16 149 F5
Brayard's Rd PECK SE15 131 J1
Braybourne Dr ISLW TW7 104 A6
Braybrooke Gdns NRWD SE19 150 A6
Braybrook St SHB W12 87 H4
Brayburne Av VX/NE SW8 129 H1
Braycourt Av WOT/HER KT12 156 B6
Bray Crs BERM/RHTH SE16 112 A1
Braydon Rd STNW/STAM N16 56 B7
Bray Dr CAN/RD E16 94 D6
Brayfield Ter IS N1 6 A2
Brayford Sq WCHPL E1 * 92 E5
Bray Pl CHEL SW3 15 L7
Bray Rd MLHL NW7 38 B5
Brayton Gdns ENC/FH EN2 28 D3
Braywood Rd ELTH/MOT SE9 135 J3
Brazier Crs NTHLT UB5 83 K3
Brazil Cl CROY/NA CR0 163 K6
Breach La DAGW RM9 98 C2
Bread St STP EC4M 12 F5
Breakspears Dr
STMC/STPC BR5 155 G7
Breakspears Ms BROCKY SE4 132 D1
Breakspears Rd BROCKY SE4 132 C2
Bream Cl TOTM N17 56 D3
Bream Gdns EHAM E6 96 A2
Breamore Cl PUT/ROE SW15 126 D7
Breamore Rd GDMY/SEVK IG3 79 F1
Bream's Blds LINN WC2A 12 A4
Bream St BOW E3 75 J6
Breamwater Gdns
RCHPK/HAM TW10 143 H2
Brearley Cl EDGW HA8 36 E6
Breasley Cl PUT/ROE SW15 126 E3
Breasy Pl HDN NW4 * 51 K3
Brechin Pl SKENS SW7 14 F7
Brecknock Rd ARCH N19 72 C3
Brecknock Road Est
ARCH N19 * 72 D4
Brecon Cl MTCM CR4 163 K3
WPK KT4 174 A1
Brecon Gn CDALE/KGS NW9 * 51 G5
Brecon Ms KTTN NW5 72 D5
Brecon Rd HMSMTH W6 107 H5
PEND EN3 30 E3
Brede Cl EHAM E6 96 A2
Bredgar Rd ARCH N19 72 B1
Bredhurst Cl PGE/AN SE20 150 E5
Bredon Rd CROY/NA CR0 165 G6
Breer St FUL/PGN SW6 128 A2
Breezer's Hl WAP E1W * 92 C6
Bremans Rw
WAND/EARL SW18 147 G1
Brember Rd RYLN/HDSTN HA2 66 C1
Bremer Ms WALTH E17 57 K3
Bremner Rd SKENS SW7 14 F3
Brenchley Cl CHST BR7 154 A7
HAYES BR2 167 J4
Brenchley Gdns EDUL SE22 131 K5
Brenchley Rd STMC/STPC BR5 154 E7
Brenda Rd TOOT SW17 147 K1
Brende Gdns
E/WMO/HCT KT8 157 G3
Brendon SCUP DA14 * 155 G3
Brendon Av WLSDN NW10 69 G3
Brendon Cl ERITH DA8 118 B7
ESH/CLAY KT10 170 C5
HYS/HAR UB3 101 F6
Brendon Dr ESH/CLAY KT10 170 C5
Brendon Gdns
RYLN/HDSTN HA2 66 B3
Brendon Gv EFNCH N2 53 G1
Brendon Rd BCTR RM8 62 B7
ELTH/MOT SE9 154 D1
Brendon St MBLAR W1H 9 K4
Brendon Vls WCHMH N21 * 29 J7
Brendon Wy EN EN1 30 A6
Brenley Cl MTCM CR4 163 F2
Brenley Gdns ELTH/MOT SE9 134 C3
Brent Cl BXLY DA5 137 F7
Brentcot Cl WEA W13 85 H3
Brent Crs WLSDN NW10 86 B1
Brent Cross F/O HDN NW4 52 A5
Brentfield WLSDN NW10 68 D6
Brentfield Cl WLSDN NW10 69 F5
Brentfield Gdns CRICK NW2 * 52 B6
Brentfield Rd DART DA1 139 K5
WLSDN NW10 69 F5
Brentford Cl YEAD UB4 83 H3
Brent Gn HDN NW4 52 A4
Brentham Wy EA W5 85 K3
Brenthouse Rd HACK E8 74 D6
Brenthurst Rd WLSDN NW10 69 H5
Brentlands Dr DART DA1 139 K7
Brent La DART DA1 139 J6
Brent Lea BTFD TW8 104 D6
Brentmead Cl HNWL W7 84 E6
Brentmead Gdns
WLSDN NW10 86 B1
Brenton St POP/IOD E14 93 G5
Brent Park Rd
CDALE/KGS NW9 51 J7
HDN NW4 51 K6
Brent Pl BAR EN5 26 D4
Brent River Park Wk
HNWL W7 84 D4
Brent Rd BTFD TW8 104 D5
CAN/RD E16 94 E5
NWDGN UB2 102 B2
SAND/SEL CR2 178 D7
WOOL/PLUM SE18 115 G6
Brentside BTFD TW8 104 D5
Brentside Cl WEA W13 85 F3
Brent St HDN NW4 52 A3
Brent Ter CRICK NW2 70 A1
The Brent DART DA1 139 K6
Brentvale Av ALP/SUD HA0 68 B7
STHL UB1 84 D7
Brent View Rd
CDALE/KGS NW9 51 J5
Brent Wy BTFD TW8 104 E6
FNCH N3 38 E5
WBLY HA9 68 D5
Brentwick Gdns BTFD TW8 105 F3
Brentwood Cl ELTH/MOT SE9 135 H7
Brentwood Rd ROM RM1 63 H5
Brereton Rd TOTM N17 42 B6
Bressay Dr MLHL NW7 37 J6
Bressenden Pl WESTW SW1E 16 D3
Bressey Gv SWFD E18 58 D1
Brett Cl NTHLT UB5 83 H2
STNW/STAM N16 74 A1
Brett Crs WLSDN NW10 69 F7
Brettell St WALW SE17 19 H8
Brettenham Av WALTH E17 43 J7
Brettenham Rd UED N18 42 C3
WALTH E17 57 J1
Brett Gdns DAGW RM9 80 A6
Brett Pas HACK E8 74 D4
Brett Rd BAR EN5 26 A4
HACK E8 74 D4
Brett Vls ACT W3 * 87 F4
Brewer St REGST W1B 10 F6
Brewery Cl ALP/SUD HA0 67 G4
Brewery Rd HAYES BR2 168 D7
WOOL/PLUM SE18 115 J4
Brewery Sq FSBYE EC1V 12 D1
STHWK SE1 13 L9
Brewhouse La WAP E1W 92 D7
Brewhouse Rd
WOOL/PLUM SE18 114 E3
Brewhouse St PUT/ROE SW15 127 H3
Brewhouse Wk
BERM/RHTH SE16 93 G7
Brewhouse Yd FSBYE EC1V 6 C9
Brewood Rd BCTR RM8 79 H5
Brewster Gdns NKENS W10 88 A4
Brewster Rd LEY E10 57 K7
Brian Cl HCH RM12 81 K3
Brian Rd CHDH RM6 61 J4
Briants Cl PIN HA5 33 J7
Briant St NWCR SE14 112 A7
Briar Av STRHM/NOR SW16 149 F6
Briar Bank CAR SM5 176 A7
Briarbank Rd WEA W13 85 G5
Briar Cl BKHH IG9 45 H1
EFNCH N2 53 G1
HPTN TW12 141 K4
ISLW TW7 124 A4
PLMGR N13 41 J2
Briar Crs NTHLT UB5 66 B5
Briardale Gdns HAMP NW3 70 E2
Briarfield Av EFNCH N2 53 F2
Briarfield Cl BXLYHN DA7 137 H1
Briar Gdns HAYES BR2 167 J7
Briar La CAR SM5 176 A7
CROY/NA CR0 179 K3
Briar Rd CRICK NW2 70 A3
KTN/HRWW/WS HA3 49 J4
STRHM/NOR SW16 163 K2
WHTN TW2 123 K7
Briar Wk EDGW HA8 36 E6
NKENS W10 * 88 C3
PUT/ROE SW15 126 E3
Briar Wy WDR/YW UB7 100 D1
Briarwood Cl
CDALE/KGS NW9 * 50 E5
FELT TW13 140 C2
Briar Wood Cl HAYES BR2 181 J1
Briarwood Ct WPK KT4 * 160 D7
Briarwood Dr NTHWD HA6 46 E1
Briarwood Rd CLAP SW4 129 J4
EW KT17 173 J5
Briary Cl EDGW HA8 50 D1
Briary Ct SCUP DA14 155 H4
Briary Gdns BMLY BR1 153 F4
Briary La ED N9 42 A2
Brickbarn Cl WBPTN SW10 * 108 B6
Brick Ct EMB EC4Y * 12 A5
Brickett Cl RSLP HA4 46 A4
Brick Farm Cl RCH/KEW TW9 105 J7
Brickfield Cl BTFD TW8 104 D6
HOM E9 74 E5
Brickfield Cots
WOOL/PLUM SE18 116 A5
Brickfield La BAR EN5 25 H5
HYS/HAR UB3 101 G5
Brickfield Rd BOW E3 93 K3
THHTH CR7 149 H7
WIM/MER SW19 147 F3
Brickfields RYLN/HDSTN HA2 66 D1
Brickfields Wy WDR/YW UB7 100 C2
Brickfield Vls CAR SM5 * 175 J2
Brick Kiln Cl OXHEY WD19 21 J5
Brick La BETH E2 7 M8
EN EN1 30 D1
NTHLT UB5 83 K2
PEND EN3 30 E1
STAN HA7 35 K6
WCHPL E1 13 M1
Brick St MYFR/PICC W1J 10 C9
Brickwall La RSLP HA4 46 C7
Brickwood Cl SYD SE26 150 D2
Brickwood Rd CROY/NA CR0 178 A1
Brideale Cl PECK SE15 111 G5
Bride Ct EMB EC4Y 12 C5
Bride La EMB EC4Y 12 C5
Bridel Ms FSBYE EC1V 6 C6
Bride St HOLWY N7 73 F5
Bridewain St STHWK SE1 19 L3
Bridewell Pl BLKFR EC4V 12 C5
WAP E1W 92 D7
Bridford Ms GTPST W1W 10 D2
Bridge Ap CAMTN NW1 4 A1
Bridge Av HMSMTH W6 107 F4
HNWL W7 84 D4
Bridge Cl EN EN1 30 D1
NKENS W10 88 B5
ROMW/RG RM7 63 G5
Bridge Dr PLMGR N13 41 F3

Bridge End WALTH E17 44 A7
Bridge End Cl KUTN/CMB KT2 144 C7
Bridgefield Rd SUT SM1 174 E5
Bridge Gdns ASHF TW15 140 A6
E/WMO/HCT KT8 157 J3
STNW/STAM N16 73 K3
Bridge Ga WCHMH N21 29 J6
Bridgehill Cl ALP/SUD HA0 67 K7
Bridge House Quay
POP/IOD E14 94 A7
Bridgeland Rd CAN/RD E16 94 E6
Bridgelands Cl BECK BR3 151 H6
Bridge La BTSEA SW11 108 D7
HDN NW4 52 B3
Bridgeman Rd IS N1 5 M2
TEDD TW11 143 G5
Bridgeman St STJWD NW8 3 J6
Bridge Mdw NWCR SE14 112 A5
Bridgen Rd BXLY DA5 137 F6
Bridge Pde
STRHM/NOR SW16 * 148 E4
WCHMH N21 * 29 J6
Bridge Pl CROY/NA CR0 164 E7
PIM SW1V 16 D5
WAT WD17 21 H4
Bridgepoint Pl HGT N6 54 B7
Bridgeport Pl WAP E1W * 92 C7
Bridge Rd BECK BR3 151 H6
BXLYHN DA7 137 F2
CHSGTN KT9 172 A4
E/WMO/HCT KT8 157 K3
ED N9 42 C2
EHAM E6 77 K6
ERITH DA8 118 C7
HSLW TW3 123 J2
LEY E10 58 B5
NWDGN UB2 102 E1
RAIN RM13 99 J3
SRTFD E15 76 B7
SUT SM1 175 F5
TWK TW1 124 C5
WALTH E17 57 H6
WBLY HA9 68 C2
WDGN N22 40 E7
WLGTN SM6 176 B4
WLSDN NW10 69 G5
Bridge Rw CROY/NA CR0 * 164 E7
Bridges Ct BTSEA SW11 128 C2
Bridges La CROY/NA CR0 176 E3
Bridges Rd STAN HA7 35 F4
Bridges Road Ms
WIM/MER SW19 147 F5
Bridge St CHSWK W4 106 A3
PIN HA5 47 H2
TWK TW1 124 E5
WHALL SW1A 17 J2
Bridge Ter LEW SE13 * 133 G3
SRTFD E15 76 B6
The Bridge EA W5 * 86 B7
KTN/HRWW/WS HA3 49 F2
Bridgetown Cl NRWD SE19 150 A4
Bridgeview HMSMTH W6 107 F4
Bridge Vls WIM/MER SW19 * 146 E4
Bridgewater Cl
STMC/STPC BR5 169 K1
Bridgewater Gdns EDGW HA8 50 B1
Bridgewater Rd ALP/SUD HA0 67 H5
Bridgewater Sq BARB EC2Y * 12 E2
Bridgewater St BARB EC2Y 12 E2
Bridgewater Wy BUSH WD23 22 B5
Bridgeway ALP/SUD HA0 68 A6
BARK IG11 79 F6
Bridge Wy GLDGN NW11 52 D4
WHTN TW2 123 H6
Bridgeway St CAMTN NW1 4 F6
Bridge Wharf Rd ISLW TW7 124 C2
Bridgewood Cl PGE/AN SE20 150 D6
Bridgewood Rd
STRHM/NOR SW16 148 D6
WPK KT4 173 J3
Bridgford St
WAND/EARL SW18 147 G2
Bridgman Rd CHSWK W4 105 K2
Bridgwater Rd RSLP HA4 64 E3
Bridle Cl HOR/WEW KT19 172 E3
KUT/HW KT1 158 E3
Bridle La SOHO/CST W1F 10 F6
TWK TW1 124 C5
Bridle Pth CROY/NA CR0 176 E2
WAT WD17 21 F1
The Bridle Pth WFD IG8 44 C6
Bridlepath Wy
EBED/NFELT TW14 121 H6
Bridle Rd CROY/NA CR0 179 J3
ESH/CLAY KT10 171 H5
PIN HA5 47 G5
Bridle Wy CROY/NA CR0 179 J4
The Bridle Wy WLGTN SM6 176 C3
Bridlington Rd ED N9 30 D6
OXHEY WD19 33 H2
Bridport Av ROMW/RG RM7 62 D5
Bridport Pl IS N1 7 H4
Bridport Rd GFD/PVL UB6 66 B7
THHTH CR7 164 B2
UED N18 42 A4
Bridstow Pl BAY/PAD W2 8 B4
Brief St BRXN/ST SW9 110 C7
Brierley CROY/NA CR0 179 K5
Brierley Av ED N9 30 E7
Brierley Cl SNWD SE25 165 H3
Brierley Rd BAL SW12 148 C1
WAN E11 76 B3
Brierly Gdns BETH E2 * 92 E1
Brigade Cl RYLN/HDSTN HA2 66 D1
Brigade St BKHTH/KID SE3 * 133 J1
Briggeford Cl CLPT E5 74 C1
Briggs Cl MTCM CR4 148 B7
Bright Cl BELV DA17 116 E3
Brightfield Rd LEE/GVPK SE12 133 H4
Brightling Rd BROCKY SE4 132 C5
Brightlingsea Pl POP/IOD E14 93 H6
Brightman Rd
WAND/EARL SW18 128 C7
Brighton Av WALTH E17 57 H4
Brighton Dr NTHLT UB5 * 66 A5
Brighton Rd BELMT SM2 175 G6
EFNCH N2 53 G1
EHAM E6 96 A2
SAND/SEL CR2 177 J7
STNW/STAM N16 74 A3
SURB KT6 158 D5
Brighton Ter BRXN/ST SW9 130 A3
Brights Av RAIN RM13 99 K3
Brightside Rd LEW SE13 133 G5
Bright St POP/IOD E14 93 K5
Brightwell Cl CROY/NA CR0 164 B7
Brightwell Crs TOOT SW17 147 K4
Brightwell Rd WATW WD18 20 E4
Brightwen Gv STAN HA7 35 G2
Brig Ms DEPT SE8 112 D5
Brigstock Rd BELV DA17 117 J3
THHTH CR7 164 C4
Brill Pl CAMTN NW1 5 H6
Brim Hl EFNCH N2 53 G3
Brimpsfield Cl ABYW SE2 116 C2
Brindle Ga BFN/LL DA15 135 K7
Brindley Cl ALP/SUD HA0 67 J7
BXLYHN DA7 137 H2
Brindley St BROCKY SE4 112 C7
Brindley Wy BMLY BR1 152 E4
STHL UB1 84 B6
Brindwood Rd CHING E4 43 J2
Brinkburn Cl ABYW SE2 116 B3
EDGW HA8 50 D2
Brinkburn Gdns EDGW HA8 50 C2
Brinkley Rd WPK KT4 173 K1
Brinklow Crs
WOOL/PLUM SE18 115 G6
Brinkworth Rd CLAY IG5 59 J2
Brinkworth Wy HOM E9 75 H5
Brinsdale Rd HDN NW4 52 B2
Brinsley Rd
KTN/HRWW/WS HA3 48 D1
Brinsley St WCHPL E1 * 92 D5
Brinsworth Cl WHTN TW2 142 D1
Brinton Wk STHWK SE1 12 C9
Brion Pl POP/IOD E14 94 A4
Brisbane Av WIM/MER SW19 147 F7
Brisbane Rd IL IG1 60 C6
LEY E10 75 K1
Brisbane St CMBW SE5 110 E6
Briscoe Cl WAN E11 76 D1
Briscoe Rd WIM/MER SW19 147 H5
Briset Rd ELTH/MOT SE9 134 C2
Briset St FARR EC1M 12 C2
Briset Wy HOLWY N7 73 F1
Bristol Cl HSLWW TW4 123 F6
STWL/WRAY TW19 120 B5
WLGTN SM6 176 E7
Bristol Gdns MV/WKIL W9 8 D1
Bristol Ms MV/WKIL W9 8 D1
Bristol Park Rd WALTH E17 * 57 G3
Bristol Rd FSTGT E7 77 G5
GFD/PVL UB6 66 B7
MRDN SM4 162 B4
Briston Gv CEND/HSY/T N8 54 E5
Briston Ms MLHL NW7 37 J6
Bristowe Cl BRXS/STRHM SW2 130 B5
Bristow Rd BXLYHN DA7 117 F7
CROY/NA CR0 176 E3
HSLW TW3 123 G2
NRWD SE19 150 A4
Britannia Cl CLAP SW4 129 J3
ERITH DA8 118 C5
NTHLT UB5 83 H2
Britannia Ga CAN/RD E16 94 E7
Britannia La WHTN TW2 123 H6
Britannia Rd BRYLDS KT5 159 G6
FUL/PGN SW6 108 A6
IL IG1 78 B2
NFNCH/WDSPK N12 39 G2
POP/IOD E14 112 D3
Britannia Rw IS N1 6 D3
Britannia St FSBYW WC1X 5 L7
Britannia Wk IS N1 7 G6
Britannia Wy FUL/PGN SW6 108 A6
STWL/WRAY TW19 120 A6
WLSDN NW10 86 D3
British Est BOW E3 93 H2
British Gv HMSMTH W6 106 C4
British Grove Pas
CHSWK W4 * 106 C4
British Legion Rd CHING E4 44 D1
British St BOW E3 93 H2
Brittage Rd WLSDN NW10 69 G6
Brittain Rd BCTR RM8 80 A2
Britten Cl BORE WD6 23 K5
GLDGN NW11 53 F7
Britten Dr STHL UB1 84 A5
Britten St CHEL SW3 15 J8
Brittidge Rd WLSDN NW10 * 69 G6
Britton Cl CAT SE6 133 G6
Britton St FARR EC1M 12 C1
Brixham Crs RSLP HA4 46 E7
Brixham Gdns
GDMY/SEVK IG3 78 E4
Brixham Rd WELL DA16 116 E7
Brixham St CAN/RD E16 95 K7
Brixton Hl BRXS/STRHM SW2 130 A5
Brixton Hill Pl
BRXS/STRHM SW2 129 K6
Brixton Rd BRXN/ST SW9 130 B3
LBTH SE11 110 B5
Brixton Station Rd
BRXN/ST SW9 130 B2
Brixton Water La
BRXS/STRHM SW2 130 A4
Broadbent Cl HGT N6 54 B7
Broadbent St
MYFR/PKLN W1K * 10 C6
Broadberry Ct UED N18 42 D4
Broad Bridge Cl
BKHTH/KID SE3 113 K6
Broad Common Est
STNW/STAM N16 * 56 C7
Broadcoombe SAND/SEL CR2 179 F6
Broad Ct COVGDN WC2E * 11 K5
Broadcroft Av STAN HA7 49 K1
Broadcroft Rd
STMC/STPC BR5 169 J6
Broadeaves Cl SAND/SEL CR2 178 A4
Broadfield Cl CRICK NW2 70 A2
ROM RM1 63 H4
Broadfield Ct BUSH WD23 34 E1
Broadfield La CAMTN NW1 5 J2
Broadfield Pde EDGW HA8 * 36 D2
Broadfield Rd CAT SE6 133 H7
Broadfields E/WMO/HCT KT8 157 J5
RYLN/HDSTN HA2 48 B1
Broadfields Av EDGW HA8 36 D2
WCHMH N21 29 G6
Broadfields Hts EDGW HA8 36 D3
Broadfields La OXHEY WD19 21 F7
Broadfield Sq EN EN1 30 D2
Broadfields Wy WLSDN NW10 69 H4
Broadfield Wy BKHH IG9 45 G2
Broadgates Rd
WAND/EARL SW18 128 C7
Broad Green Av CROY/NA CR0 164 C6
Broadhead Strd
CDALE/KGS NW9 51 H1
Broadheath Dr CHST BR7 153 K4
Broadhinton Rd CLAP SW4 129 G2
Broadhurst Av EDGW HA8 36 D3
GDMY/SEVK IG3 79 F3
Broadhurst Cl
KIL/WHAMP NW6 71 G5
Broadhurst Gdns
KIL/WHAMP NW6 71 F5
RSLP HA4 65 G1
Broadhurst Cl
RCHPK/HAM TW10 125 G4
Broadlands FELT TW13 141 K2
Broadlands Av PEND EN3 30 D2
STRHM/NOR SW16 148 E1
Broadlands Cl HGT N6 54 A6
PEND EN3 30 D2
STRHM/NOR SW16 148 E1
Broadlands Rd BMLY BR1 153 F3
HGT N6 53 K6
Broadlands Wy NWMAL KT3 160 C5
Broad La HPTN TW12 141 K6
SEVS/STOTM N15 56 B4
Broad Lawn ELTH/MOT SE9 135 F7
Broadlawns Ct
KTN/HRWW/WS HA3 35 F7
Broadley St STJWD NW8 9 J2
Broadley Ter CAMTN NW1 9 K1
Broadmead CAT SE6 151 J2
Broadmead Av WPK KT4 160 D6
Broadmead Cl HPTN TW12 142 A5
PIN HA5 * 33 J6
Broadmead Rd WFD IG8 44 E5
YEAD UB4 83 J3
Broad Oak SUN TW16 140 D5
WFD IG8 45 F4
Broad Oak Cl CHING E4 43 J4
Broadoak Rd ERITH DA8 118 A6
Broad Oaks SURB KT6 159 J7
Broad Oaks Wy HAYES BR2 167 J4
Broadstone Pl MHST W1U 10 A3
Broadstone Rd HCH RM12 81 J1
Broad St DAGE RM10 80 C6
TEDD TW11 143 F5
Broad Street Pl LVPST EC2M 13 H3
Broadview CDALE/KGS NW9 50 C5
Broadview Rd
STRHM/NOR SW16 148 D6
Broad Wk WCHMH N21 41 F1
BKHTH/KID SE3 134 B1
HEST TW5 102 C7
RCH/KEW TW9 105 G6
Broadwalk
RYLN/HDSTN HA2 * 48 B4
SWFD E18 58 D2
Broadwalk La GLDGN NW11 52 D6
The Broad Wk BAY/PAD W2 8 D8
KENS W8 14 E1
The Broadwalk NTHWD HA6 46 A1
Broadwall STHWK SE1 12 B8
Broadwater Rd THMD SE28 115 J2
TOOT SW17 147 J3
TOTM N17 56 A1
Broadway BARK IG11 78 C7
BXLYHS DA6 137 F3
GPK RM2 63 J2
HNWL W7 84 E7
RAIN RM13 99 J3
SRTFD E15 76 B6
STJSPK SW1H 17 G2
SURB KT6 159 J7
WEA W13 85 G7
Broadway Av CROY/NA CR0 164 E4
TWK TW1 124 C5
Broadway Cl WFD IG8 45 F5
Broadway Ct WIM/MER SW19 146 E5
Broadway Gdns MTCM CR4 162 D3
Broadway Market HACK E8 74 D7
Broadway Market Ms
HACK E8 * 74 C7
Broadway Ms PLMGR N13 41 F4
STNW/STAM N16 56 B6
WCHMH N21 29 H7
Broadway Pde CHING E4 * 44 A5
HYS/HAR UB3 * 101 J1
RYLN/HDSTN HA2 * 48 B4
WDR/YW UB7 * 100 B1
The Broadway ACT W3 * 105 H1
BCTR RM8 80 B1
CDALE/KGS NW9 51 H5
CEND/HSY/T N8 54 E5
CHEAM SM3 174 C5
EA W5 85 K6
ED N9 42 C2
FBAR/BDGN N11 * 39 K4
HCH RM12 81 K3
KTN/HRWW/WS HA3 48 E1
MLHL NW7 37 G4
PIN HA5 33 K6
PLSTW E13 94 E1
RYLN/HDSTN HA2 * 66 D1
STAN HA7 35 J4
SUT SM1 175 G3
THDIT KT7 157 K7
WAT WD17 21 G2
WFD IG8 45 F5
WIM/MER SW19 146 D5
Broadwell Pde
KIL/WHAMP NW6 * 71 G5
Broadwick St SOHO/CST W1F 10 F6
Broadwood Av RSLP HA4 46 C5
Broadwood Ter WKENS W14 * 107 J3
Broad Yd FARR EC1M 12 C1
Brocas Cl HAMP NW3 3 K1
Brockdene Dr HAYES BR2 181 H3
Brockdish Av BARK IG11 79 F4
Brockenhurst
E/WMO/HCT KT8 156 E4
Brockenhurst Av WPK KT4 160 B7
Brockenhurst Gdns IL IG1 78 C4
MLHL NW7 37 G4
Brockenhurst Ms UED N18 42 C3
Brockenhurst Rd
CROY/NA CR0 165 J6
Brockenhurst Wy
STRHM/NOR SW16 163 J1
Brockham Cl WIM/MER SW19 146 D4
Brockham Crs CROY/NA CR0 180 B6
Brockham Dr
BRXS/STRHM SW2 130 A6
GNTH/NBYPK IG2 60 C5
Brockham St STHWK SE1 18 F3
Brockhurst Cl STAN HA7 35 F5
Brockill Crs BROCKY SE4 132 B3
Brocklebank Rd CHARL SE7 114 A3
WAND/EARL SW18 128 B6
Brocklehurst St NWCR SE14 112 A6
Brocklesbury Cl WATN WD24 21 G2
Brocklesby Rd SNWD SE25 165 J3
Brockley Av STAN HA7 36 A2
Brockley Cl STAN HA7 36 A3
Brockley Cross BROCKY SE4 132 B2
Brockley Gv BROCKY SE4 132 C4
Brockley Hall Rd BROCKY SE4 132 B5
Brockley Hl STAN HA7 35 K1
Brockley Ms BROCKY SE4 132 B4
Brockley Pk FSTH SE23 132 B6
Brockley Ri FSTH SE23 132 B6
Brockley Rd FSTH SE23 132 B5
Brockleyside STAN HA7 35 K3
Brockley Vw FSTH SE23 132 B6
Brockley Wy FSTH SE23 132 A4
Brockman Ri BMLY BR1 152 B3
Brock Pl BOW E3 93 K3
Brock Rd PLSTW E13 95 F4
Brocks Dr CHEAM SM3 174 C2
Brockshot Cl BTFD TW8 104 E5
Brock St PECK SE15 * 131 K2
Brockton Cl ROM RM1 63 H3
Brockway Cl WAN E11 76 C1
Brockwell Av BECK BR3 166 E4
Brockwell Park Gdns
HNHL SE24 130 C6
Brockwell Park Rw
BRXS/STRHM SW2 130 B6
Brodewater Rd BORE WD6 24 D1
Brodia Rd STNW/STAM N16 74 A2
Brodie St STHWK SE1 19 M7
Brodlove La WAP E1W 93 F6
Brodrick Gv ABYW SE2 116 C3
Brodrick Rd TOOT SW17 147 J1
Brograve Gdns BECK BR3 166 E1
Broken Whf BLKFR EC4V 12 E6
Brokesley St BOW E3 93 H3
Broke Wk HACK E8 * 74 C7
Bromar Rd CMBW SE5 131 F2
Bromborough Gn
OXHEY WD19 33 G4
Bromefield STAN HA7 35 J7
Bromehead St WCHPL E1 92 E5
Brome House CHARL SE7 * 114 D6
Bromell's Rd CLAP SW4 129 H3
Brome Rd ELTH/MOT SE9 134 E2
Bromfelde Rd CLAP SW4 129 J2
Bromfield St IS N1 6 B5
Bromhall Rd DAGW RM9 79 H5
Bromhedge ELTH/MOT SE9 153 K2
Bromholm Rd ABYW SE2 116 C2
Bromley Av BMLY BR1 152 C6
Bromley Common HAYES BR2 168 B4
Bromley Ct BMLY BR1 152 C6
Bromley Crs HAYES BR2 167 J2
RSLP HA4 64 D3
Bromley Gdns HAYES BR2 167 J1
Bromley Gv HAYES BR2 167 G1
Bromley Hall Rd POP/IOD E14 94 A4
Bromley High St BOW E3 93 K2
Bromley Hl BMLY BR1 152 B4
Bromley La CHST BR7 154 C6
Bromley Rd BECK BR3 151 J7
CAT SE6 151 K2
CHST BR7 154 B7
HAYES BR2 167 H1
LEY E10 57 K5
TOTM N17 42 B7
UED N18 41 K3
WALTH E17 57 J2
Bromley St WCHPL E1 93 F4
Brompton Ar CHEL SW3 * 15 L2
Brompton Cl HSLWW TW4 122 E4
Brompton Dr ERITH DA8 118 E6
Brompton Gv EFNCH N2 53 J3
Brompton Park Crs
FUL/PGN SW6 108 A5
Brompton Pl CHEL SW3 15 K3
Brompton Rd CHEL SW3 15 J5
Brompton Sq CHEL SW3 15 J3
Brompton Ter
WOOL/PLUM SE18 * 115 F7
Bromwich Av HGT N6 72 A1
Bromyard Av ACT W3 87 G7
Brondesbury Ms
KIL/WHAMP NW6 * 2 A2
Brondesbury Pk
KIL/WHAMP NW6 70 A6
Brondesbury Rd
KIL/WHAMP NW6 88 D1
Brondesbury Vls
KIL/WHAMP NW6 88 D1
Bronhill Ter TOTM N17 * 42 C7
Bronsart Rd FUL/PGN SW6 107 H6
Bronson Rd RYNPK SW20 161 G1
Bronte Cl ERITH DA8 117 J6
FSTGT E7 * 76 E3
GNTH/NBYPK IG2 60 A3
Bronte Gv DART DA1 139 J3
Bronti Cl WALW SE17 18 F7
Bronze Age Wy BELV DA17 117 K2
Bronze St DEPT SE8 112 D6
Brook Av DAGE RM10 80 D6
EDGW HA8 36 D5
WBLY HA9 68 B2
Brookbank Av HNWL W7 84 D4
Brookbank Rd LEW SE13 132 D2
Brook Cl ACT W3 86 C7
BORE WD6 24 D2
HOR/WEW KT19 173 G7
RSLP HA4 46 C6
RYNPK SW20 160 E2
STWL/WRAY TW19 120 C6
TOOT SW17 148 A1
Brook Ct BECK BR3 * 151 H7
Brook Crs CHING E4 43 J3
ED N9 42 D3
Brookdale FBAR/BDGN N11 40 C3
Brookdale Rd BXLY DA5 137 F5
CAT SE6 132 E5
WALTH E17 57 J2
Brookdene Av OXHEY WD19 21 F6
Brookdene Dr NTHWD HA6 32 D6
Brookdene Rd
WOOL/PLUM SE18 115 K3
Brook Dr HRW HA1 48 C3
LBTH SE11 18 B4
RSLP HA4 46 C5
Brooke Av RYLN/HDSTN HA2 66 C2
Brooke Cl BUSH WD23 22 C6
Brookehowse Rd CAT SE6 151 J1
Brookend Rd BFN/LL DA15 135 K7
Brooke Rd STNW/STAM N16 74 C2
WALTH E17 58 A3
Brooke's Market
HCIRC EC1N * 12 A2
Brooke St HCIRC EC1N 12 A3
Brooke Wy BUSH WD23 22 C6
Brookfield Av EA W5 85 K3
MLHL NW7 37 K5
SUT SM1 175 J2
WALTH E17 58 A3
Brookfield Cl MLHL NW7 37 K5
Brookfield Crs
KTN/HRWW/WS HA3 50 A4
MLHL NW7 37 K5
Brookfield Gdns
ESH/CLAY KT10 171 F5
Brookfield Pk KTTN NW5 72 B2
Brookfield Pth WFD IG8 44 B5
Brookfield Rd CHSWK W4 106 A1
ED N9 42 C2
HOM E9 75 G5
Brookfields PEND EN3 31 F3
Brookfields Av MTCM CR4 162 D4
Brook Gdns BARN SW13 126 C2
CHING E4 43 K3
KUTN/CMB KT2 144 E7
Brook Ga MYFR/PKLN W1K 9 M7
Brook Gn HMSMTH W6 107 F2
Brookhill Cl EBAR EN4 27 J4
Brook Hill Cl
WOOL/PLUM SE18 115 G4
Brookhill Rd EBAR EN4 27 H4
WOOL/PLUM SE18 115 G4
Brookhouse Gdns CHING E4 44 C3
Brooking Cl BCTR RM8 79 J2
Brooking Rd FSTGT E7 76 E4
Brookland Cl GLDGN NW11 52 E3
Brookland Garth
GLDGN NW11 52 E3
Brookland Hl GLDGN NW11 52 E3
Brookland Ri GLDGN NW11 52 E3
Brooklands DART DA1 139 H7
Brooklands Ap ROM RM1 63 F3
Brooklands Av BFN/LL DA15 154 D1
WIM/MER SW19 147 F1
Brooklands Cl ROMW/RG RM7 63 F3
SUN TW16 140 C7
Brooklands Ct
KIL/WHAMP NW6 70 D6
WCHMH N21 29 K4
Brooklands Dr GFD/PVL UB6 67 J7
Brooklands La
ROMW/RG RM7 63 F3
Brooklands Pk
BKHTH/KID SE3 133 K2
Brooklands Pl HPTN TW12 142 B4
Brooklands Rd
ROMW/RG RM7 63 F3
THDIT KT7 158 A7
The Brooklands ISLW TW7 * 103 J7
Brook La BKHTH/KID SE3 134 A1
BMLY BR1 152 E5
BXLY DA5 136 E5
Brook La North BTFD TW8 104 E4
Brooklea Cl CDALE/KGS NW9 37 G7
Brooklyn Av SNWD SE25 165 J3
Brooklyn Cl CAR SM5 175 J1
Brooklyn Gv SNWD SE25 165 J3
Brooklyn Rd HAYES BR2 168 C4
SNWD SE25 165 J3
Brooklyn Wy WDR/YW UB7 100 A2
Brookmead CROY/NA CR0 163 H5
Brook Md HOR/WEW KT19 173 G5
Brookmead Av HAYES BR2 168 E4
Brook Meadow
NFNCH/WDSPK N12 39 F3
Brook Meadow Cl WFD IG8 44 C5
Brookmead Rd CROY/NA CR0 163 H5
Brook Ms North BAY/PAD W2 8 F6
Brookmill Cl OXHEY WD19 * 21 F6
Brookmill Rd DEPT SE8 112 D7
Brook Park Cl WCHMH N21 29 H4
Brook Pl BAR EN5 26 E4
Brook Rd CEND/HSY/T N8 54 E3
CRICK NW2 69 J1
GNTH/NBYPK IG2 60 E5
GPK RM2 63 H1
SURB KT6 172 A1
THHTH CR7 164 D3
TWK TW1 124 B5
WDGN N22 * 55 F1
Brook Rd South BTFD TW8 104 E4
Brooks Av EHAM E6 95 K3
Brooksbank St HOM E9 * 75 F5
Brooksby Ms IS N1 6 A1
Brooksby St IS N1 6 A2
Brooksby's Wk HOM E9 75 F4
Brookscroft CROY/NA CR0 * 179 H7
Brookscroft Rd WALTH E17 43 K7
Brookshill
KTN/HRWW/WS HA3 34 E5
Brookshill Av
KTN/HRWW/WS HA3 34 D4
Brookshill Dr
KTN/HRWW/WS HA3 34 D4
Brookside CAR SM5 176 A4
EBAR EN4 27 J5
WCHMH N21 29 F5
Brookside Cl BAR EN5 26 B5
FELT TW13 140 E2
KTN/HRWW/WS HA3 49 K4
RSLP HA4 65 J3
Brookside Crs WPK KT4 160 D7
Brookside Rd ARCH N19 72 C1
ED N9 42 D3
GLDGN NW11 52 C5
OXHEY WD19 21 F6
UED N18 42 D3
YEAD UB4 83 G6
Brookside South EBAR EN4 28 A6
Brookside Wy CROY/NA CR0 166 A5
Brooks La CHSWK W4 105 H5
Brook's Ms MYFR/PKLN W1K 10 C6
Brooks Rd CHSWK W4 105 H4
Brook's Rd PLSTW E13 76 E7
Brook St BAY/PAD W2 9 H6
BELV DA17 117 J4
KUT/HW KT1 159 F1
MYFR/PKLN W1K 10 B6
TOTM N17 56 B1
Brooksville Av
KIL/WHAMP NW6 70 C7
Brookview Rd
STRHM/NOR SW16 148 C4
Brookville Rd FUL/PGN SW6 107 J6
Brook Wk EDGW HA8 37 F5
EFNCH N2 * 39 H7
Brook Water La HDN NW4 * 52 B4
Brookway BKHTH/KID SE3 133 K2
RAIN RM13 99 K4
Brookwood Av BARN SW13 126 C2
Brookwood Cl HAYES BR2 167 J3
Brookwood Rd HSLW TW3 123 G1
WAND/EARL SW18 127 J7
Broom Cl ESH/CLAY KT10 170 B4
HAYES BR2 168 D5
TEDD TW11 143 K6
Broomcroft Av NTHLT UB5 83 G2
Broome Rd HPTN TW12 141 K7
Broome Wy CMBW SE5 110 E6
Broomfield SUN TW16 140 E7
WALTH E17 57 H5
Broomfield Av PLMGR N13 41 F3
Broomfield Cots WEA W13 * 85 H7
Broomfield La PLMGR N13 40 E3
Broomfield Pl WEA W13 85 H7
Broomfield Rd BECK BR3 166 B3
BXLYHS DA6 137 H4
CHDH RM6 61 K6
PLMGR N13 40 E4
RCH/KEW TW9 105 G7
SURB KT6 159 G7
TEDD TW11 143 J5
WEA W13 85 H7
Broomfields ESH/CLAY KT10 170 C4
Broomfield St POP/IOD E14 93 J4
Broom Gdns CROY/NA CR0 179 J2
Broomgrove Gdns EDGW HA8 36 C7
Broomgrove Rd
BRXN/ST SW9 130 A1
Broomhall Rd SAND/SEL CR2 177 K7
Broomhill Ri BXLYHS DA6 137 H4
Broomhill Rd DART DA1 138 E5
GDMY/SEVK IG3 79 G1
WAND/EARL SW18 127 K4
WFD IG8 44 E5

Broomhouse La FUL/PGN SW6 127 K1
Broomhouse Rd
FUL/PGN SW6 127 K1
Broomloan La SUT SM1 174 E1
Broom Lock TEDD TW11 * 143 J4
Broom Md BXLYHS DA6 137 H5
Broom Pk TEDD TW11 143 K6
Broom Rd CROY/NA CR0 179 J2
TEDD TW11 143 H4
Broomsleigh St
KIL/WHAMP NW6 * 70 E4
Broom Water TEDD TW11 143 J4
Broom Water West
TEDD TW11 143 J4
Broomwood Cl CROY/NA CR0 166 A4
Broomwood Rd BTSEA SW11 128 D5
Broseley Gv SYD SE26 151 G4
Brosse Wy HAYES BR2 168 D5
Broster Gdns SNWD SE25 165 G2
Brougham Rd ACT W3 86 E5
HACK E8 74 C7
Brougham St BTSEA SW11 128 E1
Brough Cl KUTN/CMB KT2 * 143 K4
VX/NE SW8 109 K6
Broughinge Rd BORE WD6 24 D1
Broughton Av FNCH N3 52 C2
RCHPK/HAM TW10 143 J3
Broughton Dr BRXN/ST SW9 130 B3
Broughton Gdns HGT N6 54 C5
Broughton Rd FUL/PGN SW6 128 A1
THHTH CR7 164 B5
WEA W13 85 H6
Broughton Road Ap
FUL/PGN SW6 * 128 A1
Broughton St VX/NE SW8 129 F1
Brouncker Rd ACT W3 105 K1
Browells La FELT TW13 141 F1
Brown Cl WLGTN SM6 176 D6
Brownfield St POP/IOD E14 93 K5
Browngraves Rd
HYS/HAR UB3 101 F6
Brown Hart Gdns
MYFR/PKLN W1K 10 B6
Brownhill Rd CAT SE6 133 F6
Browning Av HNWL W7 85 F5
SUT SM1 175 J3
WPK KT4 160 E7
Browning Cl HPTN TW12 141 K3
MV/WKIL W9 * 8 F1
WALTH E17 58 A3
WELL DA16 115 K7
Browning Ms
CAVSQ/HST W1G * 10 B3
Browning Rd DART DA1 139 J3
MNPK E12 77 K5
WAN E11 58 D6
Browning St WALW SE17 18 F7
Browning Wy HEST TW5 102 C7
Brownlea Gdns
GDMY/SEVK IG3 79 G1
Brownlow Cl EBAR EN4 27 H4
Brownlow Ms BMSBY WC1N 5 M9
Brownlow Rd BORE WD6 24 C3
CROY/NA CR0 178 A3
FBAR/BDGN N11 40 E5
FNCH N3 39 F6
FSTGT E7 76 E3
HACK E8 7 M3
WEA W13 * 85 G7
WLSDN NW10 69 G6
Brownlow St HHOL WC1V 11 M3
Brownspring Dr
ELTH/MOT SE9 154 B2
Brown's Rd BRYLDS KT5 159 G6
WALTH E17 57 J2
Brown St MBLAR W1H 9 L4
Brownswell Rd EFNCH N2 53 H1
Brownswood Rd FSBYPK N4 73 J1
Broxash Rd BTSEA SW11 129 F5
Broxbourne Av SWFD E18 59 F3
Broxbourne House BOW E3 93 K3
Broxbourne Rd FSTGT E7 76 E2
Broxholme Cl SNWD SE25 164 E3
Broxholm Rd WNWD SE27 149 G2
Broxted Rd FSTH SE23 151 H1
Broxwood Wy STJWD NW8 3 K4
Bruce Castle Rd TOTM N17 42 B7
Bruce Cl NKENS W10 88 B4
WELL DA16 116 C7
Bruce Dr SAND/SEL CR2 179 F7
Bruce Gdns TRDG/WHET N20 39 K2
Bruce Gv TOTM N17 56 B1
Bruce Rd BAR EN5 26 C2
BOW E3 93 K2
KTN/HRWW/WS HA3 48 E1
MTCM CR4 148 A6
SNWD SE25 164 E3
WLSDN NW10 69 F6
Bruckner St NKENS W10 88 C2
Brudenell Rd TOOT SW17 147 K2
Bruffs Meadow NTHLT UB5 65 J5
Bruford Ct DEPT SE8 112 D5
Bruges Pl CAMTN NW1 4 F2
Brumfield Rd
HOR/WEW KT19 172 E4
Brunel Cl HEST TW5 102 A6
NRWD SE19 150 B5
NTHLT UB5 83 K2
ROM RM1 63 G3
Brunel Ct WLSDN NW10 87 J2
Brunel Est BAY/PAD W2 8 A3
Brunel House
WOOL/PLUM SE18 * 114 D6
Brunel Ms NKENS W10 88 B2
Brunel Rd ACT W3 87 G4
BERM/RHTH SE16 111 K1
WALTH E17 57 G5
WFD IG8 45 K4
Brunel St CAN/RD E16 94 D5
Brunel Wk WHTN TW2 123 F6
Brune St WCHPL E1 13 L3
Brunner Cl GLDGN NW11 53 F4
Brunner Rd EA W5 85 K3
WALTH E17 57 H4
Bruno Pl CDALE/KGS NW9 68 E1
Brunswick Av
FBAR/BDGN N11 40 A2
Brunswick Cl BXLYHS DA6 136 E3
PIN HA5 47 J5
THDIT KT7 158 A7
WHTN TW2 142 D2
Brunswick Ct STHWK SE1 19 K2
Brunswick Crs
FBAR/BDGN N11 40 A2
Brunswick Gdns EA W5 86 A2
KENS W8 8 B9
Brunswick Gv
FBAR/BDGN N11 40 A2
Brunswick Ms MBLAR W1H 9 M4
STRHM/NOR SW16 148 D5
Brunswick Pk CMBW SE5 110 E7
Brunswick Park Gdns
FBAR/BDGN N11 40 A1
Brunswick Park Rd
FBAR/BDGN N11 40 A2
Brunswick Pl CAMTN NW1 10 B1
IS N1 7 H8
NRWD SE19 150 C6
Brunswick Quay
BERM/RHTH SE16 112 A2
Brunswick Rd BXLYHS DA6 136 E3
EA W5 85 K3
KUTN/CMB KT2 144 C7
LEY E10 58 A7
SEVS/STOTM N15 56 A3
SUT SM1 175 F3
Brunswick Sq BMSBY WC1N 5 K9
TOTM N17 42 B5
Brunswick St WALTH E17 58 A4
Brunswick Vls CMBW SE5 111 F7
Brunswick Wy
FBAR/BDGN N11 40 B3
Brunton Pl POP/IOD E14 93 G5
Brushfield St WCHPL E1 13 K2
Brushwood Cl POP/IOD E14 93 K4
Brussels Rd BTSEA SW11 128 C3
Bruton Cl CHST BR7 153 K6
Bruton La MYFR/PICC W1J 10 D7
Bruton Pl MYFR/PICC W1J 10 D7
Bruton Rd MRDN SM4 162 B3
Bruton St MYFR/PICC W1J 10 D7
Bruton Wy WEA W13 85 G4
Bryan Av WLSDN NW10 69 K6
Bryan Cl SUN TW16 140 E6
Bryan Rd BERM/RHTH SE16 112 C1
Bryanston Av WHTN TW2 123 G7
Bryanston Cl NWDGN UB2 102 E3
Bryanstone Rd
CEND/HSY/T N8 54 D4
Bryanston Ms East
MBLAR W1H 9 L3
Bryanston Ms West
MBLAR W1H 9 L3
Bryanston Pl MBLAR W1H 9 L3
Bryanston Sq MBLAR W1H 9 L4
Bryanston St MBLAR W1H 9 L5
Bryant Cl BAR EN5 26 D4
Bryant Rd NTHLT UB5 83 G2
Bryant St SRTFD E15 76 B6
Bryantwood Rd HOLWY N7 73 G4
Brycedale Crs STHGT/OAK N14 40 D3
Bryce Rd BCTR RM8 79 J3
Bryden Cl SYD SE26 151 G4
Brydges Pl CHCR WC2N 11 J7
Brydges Rd SRTFD E15 76 B4
Brydon Wk IS N1 5 K3
Bryett Rd HOLWY N7 72 E2
Brymay Cl BOW E3 93 J1
Brynmaer Rd BTSEA SW11 108 E7
Bryn-Y-Mawr Rd EN EN1 30 B3
Bryony Rd SHB W12 87 J6
Bryony Wy SUN TW16 140 E5
Buchanan Cl WCHMH N21 29 F4
Buchanan Ct BORE WD6 * 24 E1
Buchanan Gdns WLSDN NW10 87 K1
Buchan Rd PECK SE15 131 K2
Bucharest Rd
WAND/EARL SW18 128 B6
Buckden Cl LEE/GVPK SE12 133 J5
Buckfast Rd MRDN SM4 162 A3
Buckfast St BETH E2 92 C2
Buckhold Rd
WAND/EARL SW18 127 K5
Buckhurst Av CAR SM5 162 D7
Buckhurst St WCHPL E1 92 D3
Buckhurst Wy BKHH IG9 45 H2
Buckingham Av
E/WMO/HCT KT8 157 G1
EBED/NFELT TW14 122 A5
GFD/PVL UB6 67 G7
THHTH CR7 149 G7
TRDG/WHET N20 27 G6
WELL DA16 135 K3
Buckingham Cl EA W5 85 J4
EN EN1 30 A1
HPTN TW12 141 K4
STMC/STPC BR5 169 K6
Buckingham Ct BELMT SM2 * 174 E7
Buckingham Dr CHST BR7 154 B4
Buckingham Gdns
E/WMO/HCT KT8 157 G1
STAN HA7 36 A6
THHTH CR7 164 B1
Buckingham Ga WESTW SW1E 16 E3
Buckingham La FSTH SE23 132 B6
Buckingham Ms IS N1 74 A5
WESTW SW1E * 16 E3
WLSDN NW10 87 H1
Buckingham Palace Rd
BGVA SW1W 16 C5
Buckingham Pde STAN HA7 * 35 J4
Buckingham Pl WESTW SW1E 16 E3
Buckingham Rd BORE WD6 25 F3
EDGW HA8 36 B6
HPTN TW12 141 K3
HRW HA1 48 D4
IL IG1 78 D1
IS N1 74 A5
KUT/HW KT1 159 G3
LEY E10 75 K2
MTCM CR4 163 K4
RCHPK/HAM TW10 143 K1
SRTFD E15 76 D4
SWFD E18 44 D7
WAN E11 59 F3
WDGN N22 40 E7
WLSDN NW10 87 H1
Buckingham St CHCR WC2N 11 K7
Buckingham Wy WLGTN SM6 176 C7
Buckland Crs HAMP NW3 3 G1
Buckland Ri PIN HA5 33 G7
Buckland Rd CHSGTN KT9 172 B4
LEY E10 76 A1
Bucklands OXHEY WD19 * 33 H2
Bucklands Rd TEDD TW11 143 J5
Buckland St IS N1 7 H6
Bucklands Whf KUT/HW KT1 * 158 E1
Buckland Wk MRDN SM4 162 B3
Buckland Wy WPK KT4 161 F7
Buck La CDALE/KGS NW9 51 F4
Buckleigh Av RYNPK SW20 161 J2
Buckleigh Rd
STRHM/NOR SW16 148 D5
Buckleigh Wy NRWD SE19 150 B7
Bucklersbury MANHO EC4N * 13 G5
Bucklers' Wy CAR SM5 175 K2
Buckle St WCHPL E1 13 M4
Buckley Cl DART DA1 138 C1
FSTH SE23 131 J6
Buckley Rd KIL/WHAMP NW6 70 D6
Buckmaster Rd BTSEA SW11 128 D3
Bucknall St NOXST/BSQ WC1A 11 J4
Bucknall Wy BECK BR3 166 E3
Bucknell Cl BRXS/STRHM SW2 130 A4
Buckner Rd BRXS/STRHM SW2 130 A3
Buckrell Rd CHING E4 44 B1
Bucks Av OXHEY WD19 21 J6
Buckstone Cl FSTH SE23 131 K5
Buckstone Rd UED N18 42 C5
Buck St CAMTN NW1 4 D3
Buckters Rents
BERM/RHTH SE16 93 G7
Buckthorne Rd BROCKY SE4 132 B5
Budd Cl NFNCH/WDSPK N12 39 F3
Buddings Cir WBLY HA9 68 E2
Bude Cl WALTH E17 57 H4
Budge La MTCM CR4 162 E6
Budge Rw MANHO EC4N 13 G6
Budleigh Crs WELL DA16 116 D7
Budoch Dr GDMY/SEVK IG3 79 G1
Buer Rd FUL/PGN SW6 127 H1
Bugsby's Wy GNWCH SE10 113 K3
Bulganak Rd THHTH CR7 164 D3
Bulinca St WEST SW1P * 17 J6
Bullace Rw CMBW SE5 110 E7
Bullard Rd TEDD TW11 142 E5
Bullards Pl BETH E2 93 F2
Bullbanks Rd BELV DA17 117 K3
Bulleid Wy BGVA SW1W 16 D6
Bullen St BTSEA SW11 128 D1
Buller Cl PECK SE15 111 H6
Buller Rd BARK IG11 78 E6
THHTH CR7 164 E2
TOTM N17 56 C1
WDGN N22 55 G1
WLSDN NW10 88 B2
Bullers Wood Dr CHST BR7 153 J7
Bullescroft Rd EDGW HA8 36 C2
Bullhead Rd BORE WD6 24 E3
Bullivant St POP/IOD E14 94 A6
Bull La CHST BR7 154 D6
DAGE RM10 80 D2
UED N18 42 A4
Bull Rd SRTFD E15 94 D1
Bullrush Cl CAR SM5 175 J1
CROY/NA CR0 165 F5
Bulls Aly MORT/ESHN SW14 * 126 A2
Bull's Br NWDGN UB2 101 K2
Bulls Bridge Rd NWDGN UB2 102 A2
Bullsbrook Rd YEAD UB4 83 G7
Bull's Gdns CHEL SW3 15 K5
Bull Yd PECK SE15 111 H7
Bulmer Gdns
KTN/HRWW/WS HA3 49 K6
Bulmer Ms NTGHL W11 8 A8
Bulstrode Av HSLW TW3 122 E2
Bulstrode Gdns HSLW TW3 123 F2
Bulstrode Pl MHST W1U 10 B3
Bulstrode Rd HSLW TW3 123 F2
Bulstrode St MHST W1U 10 B4
Bulwer Court Rd WAN E11 58 B7
Bulwer Gdns BAR EN5 27 G3
Bulwer Rd BAR EN5 27 F3
UED N18 42 A3
WAN E11 58 B7
Bulwer St SHB W12 88 A7
Bunces La WFD IG8 44 D6
Bungalow Rd SNWD SE25 165 F3
The Bungalows
RYLN/HDSTN HA2 * 65 K2
STRHM/NOR SW16 148 B6
Bunhill Rw STLK EC1Y 7 G9
Bunhouse Pl BGVA SW1W 16 A7
Bunkers Hl GLDGN NW11 53 G6
Bunker's Hl BELV DA17 117 H3
Bunning Wy HOLWY N7 5 K1
Bunn's La MLHL NW7 37 G5
Bunsen St BOW E3 93 G1
Buntingbridge Rd
BARK/HLT IG6 60 D4
Bunting Cl ED N9 31 F7
MTCM CR4 162 E4
Bunton St WOOL/PLUM SE18 115 F2
Bunyan Rd WALTH E17 57 G2
Burbage Cl HYS/HAR UB3 82 B5
STHWK SE1 19 G4
Burbage Rd HNHL SE24 130 E5
Burberry Cl NWMAL KT3 160 B1
Burbridge Wy TOTM N17 56 C1
Burcham St POP/IOD E14 93 K5
Burcharbro Rd ABYW SE2 116 E5
Burchell Ct BUSH WD23 22 C6
Burchell Rd LEY E10 57 K7
PECK SE15 111 J7
Burcher Gale Gv PECK SE15 111 F6
Burcote Rd WAND/EARL SW18 128 C7
Burden Cl BTFD TW8 104 D4
Burdenshott Av
RCHPK/HAM TW10 125 J3
Burden Wy WAN E11 77 F1
Burder Cl IS N1 74 A5
Burder Rd IS N1 74 A5
Burdett Av RYNPK SW20 145 J7
Burdett Cl HNWL W7 * 85 F7
Burdett Rd BOW E3 93 H3
CROY/NA CR0 164 E5
POP/IOD E14 93 H5
RCH/KEW TW9 125 G1
Burdetts Rd DAGW RM9 80 B7
Burdock Cl CROY/NA CR0 166 A7
Burdock Rd TOTM N17 56 C2
Burdon La BELMT SM2 174 C6
Burdon Pk BELMT SM2 174 D7
Burfield Cl TOOT SW17 147 G3
Burford Cl BARK/HLT IG6 60 C3
BCTR RM8 79 J2
Burford Gdns PLMGR N13 41 F2
Burford Rd BMLY BR1 168 D3
BTFD TW8 105 F4
CAT SE6 151 H1
EHAM E6 95 J2
SRTFD E15 76 B6
SUT SM1 174 E1
WPK KT4 160 D6
Burford Wk FUL/PGN SW6 * 108 A6
Burford Wy CROY/NA CR0 180 A5
Burgate Cl DART DA1 138 C2
Burges Gv BARN SW13 106 E6
Burges Rd EHAM E6 77 K6
Burgess Av CDALE/KGS NW9 51 F5
Burgess Cl FELT TW13 141 J3
Burgess Hl CRICK NW2 70 E3
Burgess Rd SRTFD E15 76 C3
SUT SM1 175 F3
Burgess St POP/IOD E14 93 J4
Burge St STHWK SE1 19 H4
Burghill Rd SYD SE26 151 F3
Burghley Av BORE WD6 24 E4
NWMAL KT3 145 F7
Burghley Hall Cl
WIM/MER SW19 * 127 H7
Burghley Pl MTCM CR4 162 E3
Burghley Rd CEND/HSY/T N8 55 G2
KTTN NW5 72 B3
WAN E11 * 58 C7
WIM/MER SW19 146 B3
Burgh St IS N1 6 D5
Burgon St BLKFR EC4V 12 D5
Burgos Cl CROY/NA CR0 177 G5
Burgos Gv GNWCH SE10 112 E7
Burgoyne Rd BRXN/ST SW9 130 A2
FSBYPK N4 55 H5
SNWD SE25 165 G3
SUN TW16 140 D5
Burham Cl PGE/AN SE20 150 E6
Burhill Gv PIN HA5 47 J1
Burke Cl PUT/ROE SW15 126 B3
Burke St CAN/RD E16 94 D4
Burket Cl NWDGN UB2 102 D3
Burland Rd BTSEA SW11 128 E4
Burleigh Av BFN/LL DA15 136 A4
WLGTN SM6 176 A2
Burleigh Cl ROMW/RG RM7 62 D3
Burleigh Ct BUSH WD23 * 21 J3
Burleigh Gdns ASHF TW15 140 A4
STHGT/OAK N14 28 C7
Burleigh Pde
STHGT/OAK N14 * 28 D7
Burleigh Pl PUT/ROE SW15 127 G4
Burleigh Rd CHEAM SM3 161 H7
EN EN1 30 A3
Burleigh St COVGDN WC2E 11 K6
Burleigh Wk CAT SE6 133 F7
Burleigh Wy ENC/FH EN2 29 K2
Burley Cl CHING E4 43 J4
STRHM/NOR SW16 163 J1
Burley Rd CAN/RD E16 95 G5
Burlington Ar CONDST W1S 10 E7
Burlington Av RCH/KEW TW9 105 H7
ROMW/RG RM7 62 D5
Burlington Cl
EBED/NFELT TW14 121 G6
EHAM E6 95 J5
MV/WKIL W9 2 A9
PIN HA5 47 F2
Burlington Gdns ACT W3 86 E7
CHDH RM6 62 A6
CHSWK W4 105 K4
CONDST W1S 10 E7
Burlington La CHSWK W4 105 K6
Burlington Ms ACT W3 86 E7
Burlington Pde CRICK NW2 * 70 B3
Burlington Pl FUL/PGN SW6 127 H1
WFD IG8 44 E2
Burlington Ri EBAR EN4 27 J7
Burlington Rd CHSWK W4 * 105 K4
FUL/PGN SW6 127 H1
ISLW TW7 103 J7
MUSWH N10 54 A2
NWMAL KT3 160 C3
THHTH CR7 164 D1
TOTM N17 42 C7
Burma Rd STNW/STAM N16 73 K3
Burma Ter NRWD SE19 * 150 A4
Burmester Rd TOOT SW17 147 G2
Burnaby Crs CHSWK W4 105 J5
Burnaby Gdns CHSWK W4 105 J5
Burnaby St WBPTN SW10 108 B6
Burnbrae Cl
NFNCH/WDSPK N12 39 F5
Burnbury Rd BAL SW12 129 H7
Burn Cl GSTN WD25 * 22 D3
Burncroft Av PEND EN3 30 E1
Burndell Wy YEAD UB4 83 H4
Burnell Av RCHPK/HAM TW10 143 J4
WELL DA16 136 B1
Burnell Gdns STAN HA7 49 K1
Burnell Rd SUT SM1 175 F3
Burnell Wk STHWK SE1 * 19 M7
Burnels Av EHAM E6 96 A2
Burness Cl HOLWY N7 73 F5
Burne St CAMTN NW1 9 J2
Burnet Cl HOM E9 74 E4
Burnett Rd ERITH DA8 119 G5
Burney Av BRYLDS KT5 159 G4
Burney St GNWCH SE10 113 F6
Burnfoot Av FUL/PGN SW6 107 H7
Burnham Av HGDN/ICK UB10 64 A3
Burnham Cl
KTN/HRWW/WS HA3 49 G3
MLHL NW7 37 J6
STHWK SE1 19 M6
Burnham Crs DART DA1 139 F3
WAN E11 59 G3
Burnham Dr WPK KT4 174 B1
Burnham Gdns CROY/NA CR0 165 G6
HSLWW TW4 102 A7
HYS/HAR UB3 101 G2
Burnham Rd CHING E4 43 H4
DAGW RM9 79 H6
DART DA1 139 G4
MRDN SM4 162 A4
ROMW/RG RM7 62 E2
Burnham St BETH E2 92 E2
KUTN/CMB KT2 144 C7
Burnham Ter DART DA1 * 139 G4
Burnham Wy SYD SE26 151 H4
WEA W13 104 C3
Burnhill Rd BECK BR3 166 D1
Burnley Cl OXHEY WD19 33 G4
Burnley Rd BRXN/ST SW9 130 A1
WLSDN NW10 69 H4
Burnsall St CHEL SW3 15 K7
Burns Av BFN/LL DA15 136 C5
CHDH RM6 61 J6
EBED/NFELT TW14 121 K5
STHL UB1 84 A6
Burns Cl CAR SM5 176 A7
ERITH DA8 118 C7
WALTH E17 58 A3
WELL DA16 116 A7
WIM/MER SW19 147 H5
YEAD UB4 82 E4
Burnside Av CHING E4 43 H5
Burnside Cl BAR EN5 26 E2
BERM/RHTH SE16 93 F7
TWK TW1 124 B5
Burnside Crs ALP/SUD HA0 67 K7
Burnside Rd BCTR RM8 79 J1
Burns Rd ALP/SUD HA0 86 A1
BTSEA SW11 128 E1
WEA W13 * 104 C1
Burn's Rd WLSDN NW10 69 H7
Burns Wy HEST TW5 102 C7
Burnt Ash Hl LEE/GVPK SE12 133 J5
Burnt Ash La BMLY BR1 152 E5
Burnt Ash Rd LEE/GVPK SE12 133 J4
Burnthwaite Rd
FUL/PGN SW6 107 J6
Burnt Oak Broadway
EDGW HA8 36 D6
Burnt Oak Flds EDGW HA8 36 E7
Burnt Oak La BFN/LL DA15 136 B7
Burntwood Cl
WAND/EARL SW18 * 128 C7
Burntwood Grange Rd
WAND/EARL SW18 128 C7
Burntwood La TOOT SW17 147 H1
Burntwood Vw NRWD SE19 * 150 B4
Buross St WCHPL E1 92 D5
Burpham Cl YEAD UB4 83 H4
Burrage Gv WOOL/PLUM SE18 115 H3
Burrage Pl WOOL/PLUM SE18 115 G4
Burrage Rd WOOL/PLUM SE18 115 H3
Burrard Rd CAN/RD E16 94 E5
KIL/WHAMP NW6 70 E4
Burr Cl BXLYHN DA7 137 G2
WAP E1W 92 C7
Burrell Cl CROY/NA CR0 166 B5
EDGW HA8 36 D1
Burrell Rw BECK BR3 166 D1
Burrell St STHWK SE1 12 C8
Burrells Wharf Sq
POP/IOD E14 112 E4
Burrels Whf POP/IOD E14 112 E4
Burritt Rd KUT/HW KT1 159 H1
Burroughs Cots
POP/IOD E14 * 93 G4
Burroughs Gdns HDN NW4 51 K3
The Burroughs HDN NW4 51 K3
Burrow Rd EDUL SE22 131 F3
Burrows Ms STHWK SE1 18 C1
Burrows Rd WLSDN NW10 88 A2
Burr Rd WAND/EARL SW18 127 K7
Bursar St STHWK SE1 * 13 J9
Bursdon Cl BFN/LL DA15 155 F1
Bursland Rd PEND EN3 31 F3
Burslem St WCHPL E1 * 92 D5
Burstock Rd PUT/ROE SW15 127 H3
Burston Rd PUT/ROE SW15 127 G4
Burstow Rd RYNPK SW20 146 C7
Burtenshaw Rd THDIT KT7 158 B6
Burtley Cl FSBYPK N4 55 J7
Burton Av WATW WD18 20 E3
Burton Bank IS N1 * 7 G2
Burton Cl CHSGTN KT9 171 K6
THHTH CR7 164 E2
Burton Gdns HEST TW5 102 E7
Burton Gv WALW SE17 19 G8
Burtonhole Cl MLHL NW7 38 B3
Burtonhole La MLHL NW7 38 B3
Burton La BRXN/ST SW9 * 130 B1
Burton Ms BGVA SW1W 16 B6
Burton Pl STPAN WC1H 5 H9
Burton Rd BRXN/ST SW9 130 B1
KIL/WHAMP NW6 70 D6
KUTN/CMB KT2 144 A6
SWFD E18 59 F2
Burtons Ct SRTFD E15 76 B6
Burton's Rd HPTN TW12 142 B3
Burton St STPAN WC1H 5 H9
Burt Rd CAN/RD E16 95 G7
Burtwell La WNWD SE27 149 K3
Burwash Rd
WOOL/PLUM SE18 115 J4
Burway Cl SAND/SEL CR2 178 A5
Burwell Av GFD/PVL UB6 66 E5
Burwell Cl WCHPL E1 92 D5
Burwell Rd LEY E10 57 G7
Burwood Av HAYES BR2 181 F1
PIN HA5 47 G4
Burwood Cl SURB KT6 159 H7
Burwood Gdns RAIN RM13 99 H2
Burwood Pl BAY/PAD W2 9 K4
Bury Av RSLP HA4 46 A5
YEAD UB4 82 C1
Bury Cl BERM/RHTH SE16 93 F7
Bury Ct HDTCH EC3A 13 K4
Bury Gv MRDN SM4 162 A4
Bury Ms ROM RM1 63 H5
Bury Pl NOXST/BSQ WC1A 11 J3
Bury Rd DAGE RM10 80 E4
WDGN N22 55 G1
Buryside Cl GNTH/NBYPK IG2 61 F4
Bury St ED N9 30 B6
HDTCH EC3A 13 K5
RSLP HA4 46 B5
STJS SW1Y 10 E8
Bury St West ED N9 30 A6
Bury Wk CHEL SW3 15 J6
Busby Pl KTTN NW5 72 D5
Busch Cl ISLW TW7 104 C7
Bushbaby Cl STHWK SE1 19 J4
Bushberry Rd HOM E9 75 G5
Bush Cl GNTH/NBYPK IG2 60 D4
Bush Cots WAND/EARL SW18 127 K4
Bushell Cl BRXS/STRHM SW2 149 F1
Bushell Gn BUSH WD23 34 D1
Bushell Wy CHST BR7 154 A4
Bush Elms Rd EMPK RM11 63 J6
Bushey Av STMC/STPC BR5 169 J6
SWFD E18 58 D2
Bushey Cl CHING E4 44 A2
Bushey Grove Rd BUSH WD23 21 H3
Bushey Hall Dr BUSH WD23 21 J3
Bushey Hall Pk BUSH WD23 * 21 J3
Bushey Hall Rd BUSH WD23 21 H3
Bushey Hill Rd CMBW SE5 111 G7
Bushey La SUT SM1 174 E2
Bushey Lees BFN/LL DA15 * 136 A5
Bushey Mill La BUSH WD23 21 K1
Bushey Rd CROY/NA CR0 179 J1
HYS/HAR UB3 101 H3
PLSTW E13 95 G1
RYNPK SW20 160 E2
SEVS/STOTM N15 56 A5
SUT SM1 174 E3
Bushey Wy BECK BR3 167 G5
Bushfield Cl EDGW HA8 36 D1
Bushfield Crs EDGW HA8 36 D1
Bush Gv CDALE/KGS NW9 50 E6
STAN HA7 35 K6
Bushgrove Rd BCTR RM8 79 K3
Bush Hl WCHMH N21 29 J6
Bush Hill Pde ED N9 * 29 K6
Bush Hill Rd
KTN/HRWW/WS HA3 50 B5
WCHMH N21 29 K5
Bush House
WOOL/PLUM SE18 * 114 D6
Bush La CANST EC4R 13 G6
Bushmead Cl
SEVS/STOTM N15 * 56 B3
Bushmoor Crs
WOOL/PLUM SE18 115 G6
Bushnell Rd TOOT SW17 148 B1
Bush Rd BKHH IG9 45 H3
DEPT SE8 112 A3
HACK E8 74 D7
RCH/KEW TW9 105 G5
WAN E11 58 D6
Bushway BCTR RM8 79 K3
Bushwood WAN E11 58 D7
Bushwood Dr STHWK SE1 19 M6
Bushwood Rd RCH/KEW TW9 105 H5
Bushy Park Gdns HPTN TW12 142 D4
Bushy Park Rd TEDD TW11 143 H6
Bushy Rd TEDD TW11 142 E5
Butcher Rw WAP E1W 93 F5
Butchers Rd CAN/RD E16 94 E5
Bute Av RCHPK/HAM TW10 144 A1
Bute Gdns HMSMTH W6 107 G3
RCHPK/HAM TW10 * 125 F7
WLGTN SM6 176 C4
Bute Gdns West WLGTN SM6 176 C4

Bute Ms GLDGN NW11 53 F4
Bute Rd BARK/HLT IG6 60 B4
CROY/NA CR0 164 B7
WLGTN SM6 176 C3
Bute St SKENS SW7 15 G5
Bute Wk IS N1 * 73 K5
Butler Av HRW HA1 48 D6
Butler Cl EDGW HA8 50 D1
Butler Rd BCTR RM8 79 H3
HRW HA1 48 C6
WLSDN NW10 69 H6
Butlers Cl HSLWW TW4 122 E3
Butlers & Colonial Whf
STHWK SE1 19 M1
Butlers Farm Cl
RCHPK/HAM TW10 143 K3
Butler St BETH E2 * 92 E2
Buttercup Cl NTHLT UB5 65 K5
Buttercup Sq
STWL/WRAY TW19 * 120 A7
Butterfield Cl
BERM/RHTH SE16 * 111 H1
TOTM N17 41 J5
TWK TW1 124 A5
Butterfield House
CHARL SE7 * 114 D6
Butterfield Ms
WOOL/PLUM SE18 115 G5
Butterfields WALTH E17 58 A4
Butterfield Sq EHAM E6 95 K5
Butterfly La BORE WD6 23 H2
ELTH/MOT SE9 135 G5
Butterfly Wk CMBW SE5 * 110 E7
Butter Hl CAR SM5 176 A2
Butteridges Cl DAGW RM9 80 B7
Buttermere Cl
EBED/NFELT TW14 121 J7
MRDN SM4 161 G5
SRTFD E15 76 B3
STHWK SE1 19 L6
Buttermere Dr
PUT/ROE SW15 127 H4
Buttermere Wk HACK E8 74 B5
Butterwick HMSMTH W6 107 F3
Butterworth Gdns WFD IG8 44 E5
Buttery Ms STHGT/OAK N14 40 E2
Buttesland St IS N1 7 H7
Buttfield Cl DAGE RM10 80 D5
Buttmarsh Cl
WOOL/PLUM SE18 115 G4
Buttsbury Rd IL IG1 78 C4
Butts Crs FELT TW13 142 A2
Buttsmead NTHWD HA6 32 A6
Butts Piece NTHLT UB5 83 F1
Butts Rd BMLY BR1 152 C4
The Butts BTFD TW8 104 E5
Buxhall Crs HOM E9 75 H5
Buxted Rd EDUL SE22 131 F3
HACK E8 7 L1
NFNCH/WDSPK N12 39 J4
Buxton Cl WFD IG8 45 H5
Buxton Crs CHEAM SM3 174 C3
Buxton Dr NWMAL KT3 160 A1
WAN E11 58 C3
Buxton Gdns ACT W3 86 D6
Buxton Ms CLAP SW4 129 J1
Buxton Pth OXHEY WD19 * 33 G2
Buxton Rd ARCH N19 54 D7
CRICK NW2 69 K5
EHAM E6 95 J2
ERITH DA8 118 A6
GNTH/NBYPK IG2 60 E5
MORT/ESHN SW14 126 B2
SRTFD E15 76 C4
THHTH CR7 164 C4
WALTH E17 57 G3
Buxton St WCHPL E1 13 M1
Byam St FUL/PGN SW6 128 B1
Byards Cft STRHM/NOR SW16 148 D7
Bychurch End TEDD TW11 * 143 F4
Bycroft Rd STHL UB1 84 A4
Bycroft St PGE/AN SE20 151 F6
Bycullah Av ENC/FH EN2 29 H2
Bycullah Rd ENC/FH EN2 29 H1
Byelands Cl BERM/RHTH SE16 93 F7
The Bye ACT W3 87 G5
Byewaters WATW WD18 20 A5
Bye Ways WHTN TW2 142 B2
The Byeways BRYLDS KT5 159 H4
The Bye Wy
KTN/HRWW/WS HA3 34 E7
The Byeway
MORT/ESHN SW14 125 K2
Byfeld Gdns BARN SW13 106 D7
Byfield Cl BERM/RHTH SE16 112 B1
Byfield Rd ISLW TW7 124 B2
Byford Cl SRTFD E15 76 C6
Bygrove CROY/NA CR0 179 K5
Bygrove Rd WIM/MER SW19 147 H5
Bygrove St POP/IOD E14 93 K5
Byland Cl ABYW SE2 116 C2
CAR SM5 162 B6
STHGT/OAK N14 29 F6
Byne Rd CAR SM5 175 J1
SYD SE26 150 E5
Bynes Rd SAND/SEL CR2 177 K6
Byng Pl GWRST WC1E 11 H1
Byng Rd BAR EN5 26 B2
Byng St POP/IOD E14 112 D1
Bynon Av BXLYHN DA7 137 F2
Byre Rd STHGT/OAK N14 28 A5
Byrne Cl CROY/NA CR0 164 C5
Byrne Rd BAL SW12 129 G7
Byron Av BORE WD6 24 C4
CDALE/KGS NW9 50 D3
HSLWW TW4 122 A1
MNPK E12 77 J5
NWMAL KT3 160 D4
SUT SM1 175 H3
SWFD E18 58 D2
Byron Av East SUT SM1 175 H3
Byron Cl HACK E8 74 C7
HPTN TW12 141 K3
PGE/AN SE20 * 165 J2
SYD SE26 * 151 G3
THMD SE28 97 J7
WOT/HER KT12 156 D7
Byron Ct ENC/FH EN2 29 H1
Byron Dr EFNCH N2 53 H5
ERITH DA8 117 J6
Byron Gdns SUT SM1 175 H3
Byron Hill Rd
RYLN/HDSTN HA2 48 D7
Byron Ms HAMP NW3 71 J4
MV/WKIL W9 2 B9
Byron Rd ALP/SUD HA0 67 J1
CRICK NW2 69 K1
EA W5 86 B7
HRW HA1 48 E5
KTN/HRWW/WS HA3 49 F1
LEY E10 57 K7
MLHL NW7 37 J4
WALTH E17 57 J2
Byron St POP/IOD E14 94 A5
Byron Ter ED N9 * 30 E6
Byron Wy NTHLT UB5 83 J2
WDR/YW UB7 100 C3
YEAD UB4 82 C3
Bysouth Cl SEVS/STOTM N15 55 K3
By The Wd OXHEY WD19 33 H1
Bythorn St BRXN/ST SW9 130 A2
Byton Rd TOOT SW17 147 K5
Byward Av EBED/NFELT TW14 122 B5
Byward St MON EC3R 13 K7
Bywater Pl BERM/RHTH SE16 93 G7
Bywater St CHEL SW3 15 L7
The Byway BELMT SM2 175 H7
HOR/WEW KT19 173 H3
Bywell Pl GTPST W1W * 10 E3
Bywood Av CROY/NA CR0 165 K5

C

Cabbell St CAMTN NW1 9 J3
Cabinet Wy CHING E4 43 H5
Cable Pl GNWCH SE10 113 F7
Cables Cl ERITH DA8 117 K2
Cable St WCHPL E1 92 C6
Cable Trade Pk CHARL SE7 * 113 K4
Cabot Sq POP/IOD E14 93 J7
Cabot Wy EHAM E6 77 H7
Cabul Rd BTSEA SW11 128 D1
Cactus Cl CMBW SE5 * 131 F1
Cadbury Cl ISLW TW7 104 B7
SUN TW16 140 C6
Cadbury Rd SUN TW16 140 C6
Cadbury Wy
BERM/RHTH SE16 19 M4
Caddington Cl EBAR EN4 27 J4
Caddington Rd CRICK NW2 70 C2
Caddis Cl STAN HA7 * 35 F6
Cadell Cl BETH E2 7 M6
Cade Rd GNWCH SE10 113 G7
Cader Rd WAND/EARL SW18 128 B5
Cadet Dr STHWK SE1 19 M7
Cadet Pl GNWCH SE10 113 H4
Cadiz Rd DAGE RM10 80 E6
Cadiz St WALW SE17 18 F8
Cadman Cl BRXN/ST SW9 110 C6
Cadmer Cl NWMAL KT3 160 B3
Cadmus Cl CLAP SW4 129 J3
Cadogan Cl HOM E9 * 75 H6
RYLN/HDSTN HA2 66 B3
TEDD TW11 142 E4
Cadogan Ct BELMT SM2 175 F5
Cadogan Gdns CHEL SW3 15 M5
FNCH N3 * 39 F7
SWFD E18 59 F2
WCHMH N21 29 G4
Cadogan Ga KTBR SW1X 15 M5
Cadogan La KTBR SW1X 16 A3
Cadogan Pl KTBR SW1X 15 M3
Cadogan Rd SURB KT6 158 E4
WOOL/PLUM SE18 115 H2
Cadogan Sq KTBR SW1X 15 L4
Cadogan St CHEL SW3 15 L6
KTBR SW1X 15 M5
Cadogan Ter HOM E9 75 H5
Cadoxton Av
SEVS/STOTM N15 56 B5
Cadwallon Rd ELTH/MOT SE9 154 B1
Caedmon Rd HOLWY N7 73 F3
Caerleon Cl ESH/CLAY KT10 171 H6
SCUP DA14 155 J4
Caernarvon Cl MTCM CR4 163 K2
Caesars Wk MTCM CR4 162 E4
Cahill St STLK EC1Y * 12 F1
Cahir St POP/IOD E14 112 E3
Cain's La EBED/NFELT TW14 121 G4
Caird St NKENS W10 88 C2
Cairn Av EA W5 85 K7
Cairndale Cl BMLY BR1 152 D6
Cairnfield Av CRICK NW2 69 G2
Cairngorm Cl TEDD TW11 143 G4
Cairns Av WFD IG8 45 K5
Cairns Cl DART DA1 139 G4
Cairns Rd BTSEA SW11 128 D4
Cairn Wy STAN HA7 35 F5
Cairo New Rd CROY/NA CR0 177 H1
Cairo Rd WALTH E17 * 57 J3
Caister Ms BAL SW12 129 G6
Caistor Park Rd SRTFD E15 76 D7
Caistor Rd BAL SW12 129 G6
Caithness Gdns BFN/LL DA15 136 A5
Caithness Rd MTCM CR4 148 B6
WKENS W14 107 G2
Calabria Rd HBRY N5 73 H5
Calais St CMBW SE5 110 C7
Calbourne Av HCH RM12 81 K4
Calbourne Rd BAL SW12 128 E6
Caldbeck Av WPK KT4 173 K1
Caldecote Gdns BUSH WD23 22 E5
Caldecote La BUSH WD23 23 F6
Caldecot Rd CMBW SE5 130 D1
Caldecott Wy CLPT E5 75 F2
Calder Av GFD/PVL UB6 85 F1
Calder Gdns EDGW HA8 50 C2
Calderon Rd WAN E11 76 A3
Calder Rd MRDN SM4 162 B4
Caldervale Rd CLAP SW4 129 J4
Calderwood St
WOOL/PLUM SE18 115 F3
Caldew St CMBW SE5 110 E6
Caldicote Gn
CDALE/KGS NW9 * 51 G5
Caldwell Rd OXHEY WD19 33 H3
Caldwell St BRXN/ST SW9 110 A6
Caldy Rd BELV DA17 117 J2
Caldy Wk IS N1 * 73 J5
Caledonian Cl
GDMY/SEVK IG3 * 61 H7
Caledonian Rd HOLWY N7 73 F4
IS N1 5 L5
Caledonian Sq CAMTN NW1 72 D5
Caledonian Wharf Rd
POP/IOD E14 113 G3
Caledonia Rd
STWL/WRAY TW19 120 B7
Caledonia St IS N1 5 K6
Caledon Rd EHAM E6 77 K7
WLGTN SM6 176 A3
Calendar Ms SURB KT6 158 E5
Cale St CHEL SW3 15 J7
Calidore Cl
BRXS/STRHM SW2 * 130 A5
California La BUSH WD23 22 D7
California Rd NWMAL KT3 159 K3
Callaby Ter IS N1 * 73 K5
Callaghan Cl LEW SE13 133 H3
Callaghan Cots WCHPL E1 * 92 E4
Callander Rd CAT SE6 151 K1
The Callanders BUSH WD23 * 22 E7
Callard Av PLMGR N13 41 H4
Callcott Rd KIL/WHAMP NW6 70 D6
Callcott St KENS W8 8 A8
Callendar Rd SKENS SW7 15 G3
Callingham Cl POP/IOD E14 93 H4
Callis Farm Cl
STWL/WRAY TW19 120 B5
Callisons Pl GNWCH SE10 113 H4
Callis Rd WALTH E17 57 H5
Callow St CHEL SW3 15 G9
Calmington Rd CMBW SE5 19 K8
Calmont Rd BMLY BR1 152 B5
Calonne Rd WIM/MER SW19 146 B3
Calshot Rd HTHAIR TW6 120 E1
Calshot St IS N1 5 L5
Calshot Wy ENC/FH EN2 29 H2
HTHAIR TW6 120 D1
Calthorpe Gdns EDGW HA8 36 B4
SUT SM1 175 G2
Calthorpe St FSBYW WC1X 5 M9
Calton Av DUL SE21 131 F5
Calton Rd BAR EN5 27 G5
Calverley Cl BECK BR3 151 K5
Calverley Crs DAGE RM10 80 C1
Calverley Gv ARCH N19 54 D7
Calverley Rd EW KT17 173 J5
Calvert Av WCHPL E1 7 K8
Calvert Cl BELV DA17 117 H3
Calverton Rd EHAM E6 78 A7
Calvert Rd BAR EN5 26 B1
GNWCH SE10 113 J4
Calvert St CAMTN NW1 4 A3
Calvin St WCHPL E1 13 L1
Calydon Rd CHARL SE7 114 A4
Calypso Crs PECK SE15 111 F6
Calypso Wy BERM/RHTH SE16 112 C2
Camac Rd WHTN TW2 123 J7
Camarthen Gn
CDALE/KGS NW9 * 51 G5
Cambalt Rd PUT/ROE SW15 127 G4
Camberley Av EN EN1 30 A3
RYNPK SW20 160 E1
Camberley Cl CHEAM SM3 174 B2
Camberley Rd HTHAIR TW6 120 D2
Cambert Wy BKHTH/KID SE3 134 A3
Camberwell Church St
CMBW SE5 110 E7
Camberwell Glebe CMBW SE5 110 E7
Camberwell Gn CMBW SE5 110 E7
Camberwell Gv CMBW SE5 110 E7
Camberwell New Rd
CMBW SE5 110 C6
Camberwell Rd CMBW SE5 110 D5
Camberwell Station Rd
CMBW SE5 110 D7
Cambeys Rd DAGE RM10 80 E4
Camborne Av WEA W13 104 C1
Camborne Cl HTHAIR TW6 120 D2
Camborne Crs HTHAIR TW6 120 D2
Camborne Ms
WAND/EARL SW18 127 K6
Camborne Rd BELMT SM2 174 E6
CROY/NA CR0 165 H6
RYNPK SW20 161 G4
SCUP DA14 155 J2
WAND/EARL SW18 127 K6
WELL DA16 135 K1
Camborne Wy HEST TW5 103 F7
HTHAIR TW6 120 D2
Cambourne Av ED N9 31 F6
Cambourne Ms NTGHL W11 88 C5
Cambray Rd BAL SW12 129 H7
Cambria Cl BFN/LL DA15 135 J7
HSLW TW3 123 F3
Cambria Ct EBED/NFELT TW14 122 A6
Cambria Gdns
STWL/WRAY TW19 120 B6
Cambrian Av GNTH/NBYPK IG2 60 E4
Cambrian Cl WNWD SE27 149 H2
Cambrian Gn CDALE/KGS NW9 51 G4
Cambrian Rd LEY E10 57 J6
RCHPK/HAM TW10 125 G5
Cambria Rd CMBW SE5 130 D2
Cambria St FUL/PGN SW6 108 A6
Cambridge Av GFD/PVL UB6 67 F4
KIL/WHAMP NW6 2 B5
NWMAL KT3 160 B1
WELL DA16 136 A3
Cambridge Barracks Rd
WOOL/PLUM SE18 114 E3
Cambridge Circ
SOHO/SHAV W1D 11 H5
Cambridge Cl EBAR EN4 28 A7
HSLWW TW4 122 D3
RYNPK SW20 145 K7
WALTH E17 57 H5
WDGN N22 * 41 G7
WDR/YW UB7 100 A5
WLSDN NW10 68 E2
Cambridge Crs BETH E2 92 D1
TEDD TW11 * 143 G4
Cambridge Dr LEE/GVPK SE12 133 K4
RSLP HA4 65 G1
Cambridge Gdns EN EN1 30 C1
KIL/WHAMP NW6 2 B5
KUT/HW KT1 159 H1
MUSWH N10 40 A7
NKENS W10 88 B5
TOTM N17 41 K6
WCHMH N21 29 K6
Cambridge Ga CAMTN NW1 4 C8
Cambridge Gate Ms
CAMTN NW1 4 D8
Cambridge Gn ELTH/MOT SE9 135 G7
Cambridge Gv HMSMTH W6 106 E3
PGE/AN SE20 * 150 D7
Cambridge Grove Rd
KUT/HW KT1 159 H1
Cambridge Heath Rd BETH E2 92 D2
Cambridge Pde EN EN1 * 30 C1
Cambridge Pk TWK TW1 124 D6
Cambridge Park Rd WAN E11 58 D6
Cambridge Pas HOM E9 74 E6
Cambridge Pl KENS W8 * 14 D2
Cambridge Rd ASHF TW15 140 A6
BARK IG11 78 C6
BARN SW13 126 C1
BMLY BR1 152 E6
BTSEA SW11 108 E7
CAR SM5 175 J5
E/WMO/HCT KT8 156 E3
GDMY/SEVK IG3 60 E7
HNWL W7 104 A1
HPTN TW12 141 K6
HSLWW TW4 122 D3
KIL/WHAMP NW6 2 B6
KUT/HW KT1 159 H1
MTCM CR4 163 H2
NWMAL KT3 160 A3
PGE/AN SE20 165 H2
RCH/KEW TW9 105 H6
RYLN/HDSTN HA2 48 A4
RYNPK SW20 145 K7
SCUP DA14 154 E3
STHL UB1 * 83 K7
TEDD TW11 143 G3
TWK TW1 124 E5
WAN E11 58 E5
WATW WD18 * 21 G3
WOT/HER KT12 156 A5
Cambridge Rd North
CHSWK W4 105 J4
Cambridge Rd South
CHSWK W4 105 J4
Cambridge Rw
WOOL/PLUM SE18 115 G4
Cambridge Sq BAY/PAD W2 9 J4
Cambridge St PIM SW1V 16 D7
Cambridge Ter CAMTN NW1 4 C8
ED N9 * 30 B6
Cambridge Terrace Ms
CAMTN NW1 * 4 D8
Cambridge Yd HNWL W7 * 104 A1
Cambus Cl YEAD UB4 83 J4
Cambus Rd CAN/RD E16 94 E4
Camdale Rd
WOOL/PLUM SE18 116 A6
Camden Av FELT TW13 141 G1
YEAD UB4 83 G6
Camden Cl CHST BR7 154 C7
Camden Gdns CAMTN NW1 4 D2
SUT SM1 175 F4
THHTH CR7 164 C2
Camden Gv CHST BR7 154 B5
Camden High St CAMTN NW1 4 D2
Camden Hill Rd NRWD SE19 150 A5
Camdenhurst St POP/IOD E14 93 G5
Camden Lock Pl CAMTN NW1 4 C2
Camden Ms CAMTN NW1 5 G1
Camden Park Rd CAMTN NW1 72 D5
CHST BR7 153 K6
Camden Pas IS N1 6 C5
Camden Rd BXLY DA5 137 G7
CAMTN NW1 4 E2
CAR SM5 175 K3
SUT SM1 175 F4
WALTH E17 57 H5
WAN E11 59 F5
Camden Rw BKHTH/KID SE3 133 H1
PIN HA5 * 47 G2
Camden Sq CAMTN NW1 5 G1
Camden St CAMTN NW1 4 D2
Camden Ter CAMTN NW1 72 D5
Camden Wk IS N1 6 C4
Camden Wy CHST BR7 153 K6
THHTH CR7 164 C2
Camelford Wk NTGHL W11 * 88 C5
Camel Gv KUTN/CMB KT2 143 K4
Camellia Pl WHTN TW2 123 G6
Camellia St VX/NE SW8 109 K6
Camelot Cl THMD SE28 115 J1
WIM/MER SW19 146 D3
Camel Rd CAN/RD E16 95 H7
Camera Pl WBPTN SW10 108 C5
Cameron Cl TRDG/WHET N20 39 J1
UED N18 42 D3
Cameron Crs EDGW HA8 36 D7
Cameron Dr DART DA1 139 J1
Cameron Pl
STRHM/NOR SW16 149 G1
Cameron Rd CAT SE6 * 151 H1
CROY/NA CR0 164 C5
GDMY/SEVK IG3 60 E7
HAYES BR2 167 K3
Cameron Sq MTCM CR4 147 J7
Cameron Ter
LEE/GVPK SE12 * 153 F2
Camerton Cl HACK E8 74 B5
Camilla Cl SUN TW16 * 140 D5
Camilla Rd BERM/RHTH SE16 111 J3
Camille Cl SNWD SE25 165 H2
Camlan Rd BMLY BR1 152 D3
Camlet St BETH E2 7 L9
Camlet Wy EBAR EN4 26 E1
Camley St CAMTN NW1 5 G3
Camm Gdns KUT/HW KT1 * 159 G1
THDIT KT7 157 K6
Camomile Av MTCM CR4 147 K7
Camomile St HDTCH EC3A 13 K4
OBST EC2N 13 J4
Camomile Rd ROMW/RG RM7 81 F1
Campana Rd FUL/PGN SW6 107 K7
Campbell Av BARK/HLT IG6 60 C3
Campbell Cl RSLP HA4 46 E5
STRHM/NOR SW16 * 148 D4
WHTN TW2 123 J7
WOOL/PLUM SE18 115 F7
Campbell Cots MTCM CR4 * 163 F1
Campbell Cft EDGW HA8 36 C4
Campbell Gordon Wy
CRICK NW2 69 K3
Campbell Rd BOW E3 93 J2
CROY/NA CR0 164 C6
EHAM E6 77 J7
HNWL W7 84 E6
SRTFD E15 76 C3
TOTM N17 42 B7
WALTH E17 57 H3
WHTN TW2 142 D1
Campbell Wk IS N1 * 5 K3
Campdale Rd HOLWY N7 72 D2
Campden Crs ALP/SUD HA0 67 H2
BCTR RM8 79 J3
Campden Gv KENS W8 14 B1
Campden Hl KENS W8 14 A1
Campden Hill Gdns KENS W8 8 A8
Campden Hill Pl NTGHL W11 * 88 D7
Campden Hill Rd KENS W8 14 A1
Campden Hill Sq KENS W8 88 D7
Campden House Cl KENS W8 14 A1
Campden House Ter
KENS W8 * 8 B9
Campden Rd SAND/SEL CR2 178 A4
Campden St KENS W8 8 A9
Campden Ter CHSWK W4 * 106 B4
Campden Wy BCTR RM8 79 H3
Campen Cl WIM/MER SW19 146 C1
Camperdown St WCHPL E1 13 M5
Campfield Rd ELTH/MOT SE9 134 C6
Campion Cl CROY/NA CR0 178 A3
EHAM E6 95 K6
KTN/HRWW/WS HA3 50 B5
ROMW/RG RM7 81 F1
Campion Ct ALP/SUD HA0 * 86 A1
Campion Gdns WFD IG8 44 E4
Campion Pl THMD SE28 97 H7
Campion Rd ISLW TW7 104 A7
LEY E10 57 K6
PUT/ROE SW15 127 F3
Campion Ter CRICK NW2 70 B2
Campion Wy EDGW HA8 36 E3
Camplin Rd
KTN/HRWW/WS HA3 50 A4
Camplin St NWCR SE14 112 A6
Camp Rd WIM/MER SW19 145 K4
Campsbourne Pde
CEND/HSY/T N8 * 54 E3
Campsbourne Rd
CEND/HSY/T N8 54 E2
The Campsbourne
CEND/HSY/T N8 54 E3
Campsey Gdns DAGW RM9 79 H6
Campsey Rd DAGW RM9 79 H6
Campshill Pl LEW SE13 133 F4
Campshill Rd LEW SE13 133 F4
Campus Rd WALTH E17 57 H5
Camp Vw WIM/MER SW19 145 K4
Cam Rd SRTFD E15 76 B7
Camrose Av EDGW HA8 50 B1
ERITH DA8 117 J5
FELT TW13 141 F3
STAN HA7 50 A1
Camrose Cl CROY/NA CR0 166 B6
MRDN SM4 161 K3
Camrose St WOOL/PLUM SE18 116 B4
Canada Av UED N18 41 J5
Canada Crs ACT W3 86 E4
Canada Park Pde EDGW HA8 * 36 D7
Canada Rd ACT W3 86 E4
ERITH DA8 118 E6
Canada Sq POP/IOD E14 93 K7
Canada St BERM/RHTH SE16 112 A1
Canada Wy SHB W12 87 K6
Canadian Av CAT SE6 132 E7
Canal Ap DEPT SE8 112 B4
Canal Bvd KTTN NW5 72 D5
Canal Cl NKENS W10 88 B3
WCHPL E1 93 G3
Canal Gv PECK SE15 111 H5
Canal Pth BETH E2 7 L4
Canal St CMBW SE5 110 E5
Canal Wk CROY/NA CR0 165 F5
IS N1 7 H3
WLSDN NW10 * 68 E6
Canal Wy NKENS W10 88 B3
Canal Whf GFD/PVL UB6 * 67 G7
Canal Yd NWDGN UB2 * 102 A3
Canberra Cl DAGE RM10 81 F6
HDN NW4 51 J2
Canberra Crs DAGE RM10 81 F6
Canberra Dr NTHLT UB5 83 G2
Canberra Rd HTHAIR TW6 120 D2
ABYW SE2 116 E5
CHARL SE7 114 B5
EHAM E6 77 K7
HTHAIR TW6 120 D2
WEA W13 85 G7
Canbury Av KUTN/CMB KT2 144 B7
Canbury Ms SYD SE26 150 B2
Canbury Park Rd
KUTN/CMB KT2 144 A7
Cancell Rd BRXN/ST SW9 110 B7
Candahar Rd BTSEA SW11 128 D1
Candle Gv PECK SE15 131 J2
Candlelight Ct SRTFD E15 76 D5
Candler Ms TWK TW1 124 B6
Candler St SEVS/STOTM N15 * 55 K5
Candover Cl WDR/YW UB7 100 A6
Candover Rd HCH RM12 63 K7
Candover St GTPST W1W * 10 E3
Candy St BOW E3 75 H7
Caney Ms CRICK NW2 70 B1
Canfield Dr RSLP HA4 65 F4
Canfield Gdns
KIL/WHAMP NW6 2 D1
Canfield Pl KIL/WHAMP NW6 71 G5
Canfield Rd RAIN RM13 81 H7
WFD IG8 45 J6
Canford Av NTHLT UB5 65 J7
Canford Cl ENC/FH EN2 29 G1
Canford Gdns NWMAL KT3 160 B5
Canford Pl TEDD TW11 143 J5
Canford Rd CLAP SW4 129 F3
Canham Rd CHSWK W4 106 B1
SNWD SE25 165 F2
Canmore Gdns
STRHM/NOR SW16 148 C6
Cann Hall Rd WAN E11 76 D3
Canning Crs WDGN N22 41 F7
Canning Cross CMBW SE5 131 F1
Canning Pas KENS W8 * 14 E3
Canning Pl KENS W8 14 E3
Canning Place Ms KENS W8 * 14 E3
Canning Rd CROY/NA CR0 178 B1
HBRY N5 73 H2
KTN/HRWW/WS HA3 48 E2
SRTFD E15 94 C1
WALTH E17 57 H2
Cannington Rd DAGW RM9 79 J5
Cannizaro Rd WIM/MER SW19 146 A5
Cannonbury Av PIN HA5 47 H5
Cannon Cl HPTN TW12 142 B5
RYNPK SW20 161 F2
Cannon Dr POP/IOD E14 93 J6
Cannon Hl KIL/WHAMP NW6 71 F4
STHGT/OAK N14 40 E2
Cannon Hill La RYNPK SW20 161 G4
Cannon La HAMP NW3 71 H2
PIN HA5 47 J6
Cannon Pl CHARL SE7 114 D4
HAMP NW3 71 G2
Cannon Rd BXLYHN DA7 117 F7
STHGT/OAK N14 40 E2
WATW WD18 21 G4
Cannon St BLKFR EC4V 12 E5
Cannon Street Rd WCHPL E1 92 D5
Cannon Wy E/WMO/HCT KT8 157 F3
Canon Av CHDH RM6 61 J4
Canon Beck Rd
BERM/RHTH SE16 111 K1
Canonbie Rd FSTH SE23 131 K6
Canonbury Crs IS N1 6 F1
Canonbury Gv IS N1 6 E1
Canonbury La IS N1 6 C1
Canonbury Pk North IS N1 73 J5
Canonbury Pk South IS N1 73 J5
Canonbury Rd IS N1 6 D1
Canonbury Sq IS N1 6 D1
Canonbury St IS N1 6 E1
Canonbury Vls IS N1 6 D2
Canon Mohan Cl
STHGT/OAK N14 28 A5
Canon Rd BMLY BR1 168 B2
Canon Rw WHALL SW1A 17 J2
Canons Cl EDGW HA8 36 B5
EFNCH N2 53 H6
Canons Cots EDGW HA8 * 36 B5
Canons Ct EDGW HA8 * 36 B5
Canons Dr EDGW HA8 36 B5
Canonsleigh Rd DAGW RM9 79 H6
Canon St IS N1 6 E4
Canon's Wk CROY/NA CR0 179 F2
Canopus Wy NTHWD HA6 32 E3
STWL/WRAY TW19 120 B6
Canrobert St BETH E2 92 D1
Cantelowes Rd CAMTN NW1 72 D5
Canterbury Av BFN/LL DA15 155 J1
IL IG1 59 J6
Canterbury Cl BECK BR3 151 K7
CMBW SE5 * 130 D1

DART DA1 139 K6
EHAM E6 95 K5
GFD/PVL UB6 84 B4
NTHWD HA6 32 D5
Canterbury Crs BRXN/ST SW9 130 B2
Canterbury Gv WNWD SE27 149 G2
Canterbury Pl WALW SE17 18 D6
Canterbury Rd BORE WD6 24 C1
CROY/NA CR0 164 A6
FELT TW13 141 J1
HRW HA1 48 B4
KIL/WHAMP NW6 2 A6
LEY E10 58 A6
MRDN SM4 162 B5
RYLN/HDSTN HA2 48 B4
WAT WD17 * 21 F1
Canterbury Ter
KIL/WHAMP NW6 2 A5
Canterbury Wy
RKW/CH/CXG WD3 20 A2
Cantley Gdns
GNTH/NBYPK IG2 60 C5
NRWD SE19 150 B7
Cantley Rd HNWL W7 104 B2
Canton St POP/IOD E14 93 J5
Cantrell Rd BOW E3 93 J3
Cantwell Rd
WOOL/PLUM SE18 115 G6
Canvey St STHWK SE1 12 E8
Cape Cl BARK IG11 78 B6
Capel Av WLGTN SM6 177 F4
Capel Cl HAYES BR2 168 D7
TRDG/WHET N20 39 G2
Capel Crs STAN HA7 35 G1
Capel Gdns GDMY/SEVK IG3 79 F3
PIN HA5 47 K3
Capella Rd NTHWD HA6 32 D4
Capel Rd EBAR EN4 27 J5
FSTGT E7 77 F3
OXHEY WD19 21 H5
Capeners Cl KTBR SW1X 15 M2
Capener's Cl KTBR SW1X * 16 A2
Capern Rd WAND/EARL SW18 128 B7
Cape Rd TOTM N17 56 C2
Cape Yd WAP E1W 92 C7
Capital Interchange Wy
BTFD TW8 105 H4
Capitol Wy CDALE/KGS NW9 50 E2
Capland St STJWD NW8 3 H9
Caple Pde WLSDN NW10 * 87 H1
Caple Rd WLSDN NW10 87 H1
Caprea Cl YEAD UB4 83 H4
Capri Rd CROY/NA CR0 165 G6
Capstan Cl CHDH RM6 61 H5
Capstan Dr RAIN RM13 99 J4
Capstan Ride ENC/FH EN2 29 G1
Capstan Rd DEPT SE8 112 C3
Capstan Sq POP/IOD E14 113 F1
Capstan Wy BERM/RHTH SE16 93 G7
Capstone Rd BMLY BR1 152 D3
Capthorne Av
RYLN/HDSTN HA2 47 J7
Capuchin Cl STAN HA7 35 H5
Capulet Ms CAN/RD E16 94 E7
Capworth St LEY E10 57 J7
Caractacus Cottage Vw
WATW WD18 20 E6
Caractacus Gn WATW WD18 20 D5
Caradoc Cl BAY/PAD W2 8 A4
Caradoc Evans Cl
FBAR/BDGN N11 * 40 B4
Caradoc St GNWCH SE10 113 H4
Caradon Ct WAN E11 58 C7
Caradon Wy
SEVS/STOTM N15 * 55 K3
Caravel Cl POP/IOD E14 112 D2
Caravel Ms DEPT SE8 112 D5
Caraway Cl PLSTW E13 95 F4
Caraway Pl WLGTN SM6 176 B2
Carberry Rd NRWD SE19 150 A5
Carbery Av ACT W3 105 G1
Carbis Rd POP/IOD E14 93 H5
Carburton St GTPST W1W 10 D2
Cardale St POP/IOD E14 113 F2
Carden Rd PECK SE15 131 J2
Cardiff Rd HNWL W7 104 B2
PEND EN3 30 D3
Cardiff St WOOL/PLUM SE18 115 K6
Cardigan Gdns
GDMY/SEVK IG3 79 G1
Cardigan Pl LEW SE13 * 133 G1
Cardigan Rd BARN SW13 126 D1
BOW E3 93 H1
RCHPK/HAM TW10 125 F5
WIM/MER SW19 147 G5
Cardigan St LBTH SE11 18 A7
Cardigan Wk IS N1 * 6 F1
Cardinal Av BORE WD6 24 D2
KUTN/CMB KT2 144 A4
MRDN SM4 161 H5
Cardinal Bourne St
STHWK SE1 * 19 H4
Cardinal Cl CHST BR7 154 D7
EDGW HA8 36 E6
MRDN SM4 161 H5
WPK KT4 173 J3
Cardinal Crs NWMAL KT3 159 K1
Cardinal Dr WOT/HER KT12 156 C7
Cardinal Hinsley Cl
WLSDN NW10 87 J1
Cardinal Pl PUT/ROE SW15 127 G3
Cardinal Rd FELT TW13 122 A7
RSLP HA4 47 H7
Cardinals Wk SUN TW16 140 C5
Cardinal's Wk HPTN TW12 142 C6
Cardinals Wy ARCH N19 54 D7
Cardinal Wy
KTN/HRWW/WS HA3 * 48 E2
Cardine Ms PECK SE15 111 J6
Cardington Sq HSLWW TW4 122 C3
Cardington St CAMTN NW1 4 F7
Cardozo Rd HOLWY N7 72 E4
Cardrew Av
NFNCH/WDSPK N12 39 H4
Cardross St HMSMTH W6 106 E2
Cardwell Rd HOLWY N7 * 72 E3
Cardwell Ter HOLWY N7 * 72 E3
Carew Cl HOLWY N7 73 F1
Carew Rd ASHF TW15 140 A5
MTCM CR4 163 F1
NTHWD HA6 32 C5
THHTH CR7 164 C2
TOTM N17 56 C1
WEA W13 104 D1
WLGTN SM6 176 C5
Carew St CMBW SE5 130 D1
Carew Wy OXHEY WD19 33 K2
Carey Gdns VX/NE SW8 109 H7
Carey La CITYW EC2V 12 E4
Carey Pl PIM SW1V 17 G6
Carey Rd DAGW RM9 80 A3
Carey St LINN WC2A 11 M5
Carey Wy WBLY HA9 68 D3
Carfax Pl CLAP SW4 129 J3
Carfax Rd HCH RM12 81 H3
HYS/HAR UB3 101 K4
The Carfax SYD SE26 * 150 E2
Carfree Cl IS N1 6 B1
Cargill Rd WAND/EARL SW18 128 B7
Cargreen Rd SNWD SE25 165 G3
Carholme Rd FSTH SE23 132 C7
Carisbrooke Av BXLY DA5 136 E7
Carisbrooke Cl HSLWW TW4 122 D7
STAN HA7 49 K1
Carisbrooke Ct NTHLT UB5 * 65 K7
Carisbrooke Gdns
PECK SE15 * 111 G6
Carisbrooke Rd HAYES BR2 168 B3
MTCM CR4 163 K3
WALTH E17 * 57 G3
Carker's La ARCH N19 54 D6
KTTN NW5 72 B4
Carleton Av WLGTN SM6 176 D7
Carleton Cl ESH/CLAY KT10 157 J7
Carleton Gdns ARCH N19 * 72 C4
Carleton Rd DART DA1 139 K6
HOLWY N7 72 D3
Carleton Vls KTTN NW5 * 72 C4
Carlile Cl BOW E3 93 H1
Carlina Gdns WFD IG8 45 F4
Carlingford Rd HAMP NW3 71 H3
MRDN SM4 161 G5
SEVS/STOTM N15 55 H2
Carlisle Av ACT W3 87 G5
TWRH EC3N 13 K5
Carlisle Cl KUTN/CMB KT2 144 C7
PIN HA5 47 J6
Carlisle Gdns IL IG1 59 J5
KTN/HRWW/WS HA3 49 K6
Carlisle La STHWK SE1 17 M3
Carlisle Pl FBAR/BDGN N11 40 B3
WEST SW1P 16 E4
Carlisle Rd CDALE/KGS NW9 50 E2
DART DA1 139 K5
FSBYPK N4 55 G7
HPTN TW12 142 B6
KIL/WHAMP NW6 70 C7
LEY E10 57 J7
ROM RM1 63 H4
SUT SM1 174 D5
Carlisle St SOHO/SHAV W1D 11 G5
Carlisle Wk HACK E8 74 B5
Carlisle Wy TOOT SW17 148 A4
Carlos Pl MYFR/PKLN W1K 10 B7
Carlow St CAMTN NW1 4 E5
Carlton Av EBED/NFELT TW14 122 B5
HYS/HAR UB3 101 H3
KTN/HRWW/WS HA3 49 H4
SAND/SEL CR2 177 K6
STHGT/OAK N14 28 D4
Carlton Av East WBLY HA9 67 K1
Carlton Av West ALP/SUD HA0 67 H1
Carlton Cl BORE WD6 25 F3
CHSGTN KT9 171 K5
EDGW HA8 36 C4
HAMP NW3 70 E1
Carlton Crs CHEAM SM3 174 C3
Carlton Dene EW KT17 * 173 K4
Carlton Dr BARK/HLT IG6 60 D2
PUT/ROE SW15 127 G4
Carlton Gdns EA W5 85 J5
Carlton Ga MV/WKIL W9 8 B2
Carlton Gn SCUP DA14 * 155 F3
Carlton Gv PECK SE15 111 J7
Carlton Hl STJWD NW8 2 D5
Carlton House Ter STJS SW1Y 11 G9
Carlton Ms KIL/WHAMP NW6 * 70 E4
Carlton Pde WBLY HA9 * 50 A7
Carlton Park Av RYNPK SW20 161 F1
Carlton Rd CHSWK W4 106 A1
EA W5 85 J6
ERITH DA8 117 J5
FBAR/BDGN N11 40 A4
FSBYPK N4 55 G6
GPK RM2 63 J4
MNPK E12 77 H3
MORT/ESHN SW14 125 K2
NWMAL KT3 160 B1
SAND/SEL CR2 177 K6
SCUP DA14 155 F4
SUN TW16 140 D6
WALTH E17 43 G7
WAN E11 58 D7
WELL DA16 136 C2
WOT/HER KT12 156 A6
Carlton Sq WCHPL E1 * 93 F3
Carlton St STJS SW1Y 11 G7
Carlton Ter SYD SE26 150 E3
UED N18 * 41 K3
WAN E11 * 59 F4
Carlton Tower Pl KTBR SW1X 15 M3
Carlton V KIL/WHAMP NW6 2 A7
Carlwell St TOOT SW17 147 J4
Carlyle Av BMLY BR1 168 C2
STHL UB1 83 K6
Carlyle Cl E/WMO/HCT KT8 157 G1
EFNCH N2 53 G5
WLSDN NW10 69 F7
Carlyle Ct WBPTN SW10 * 108 B7
Carlyle Gdns STHL UB1 83 K6
Carlyle Pl PUT/ROE SW15 127 G3
Carlyle Rd CROY/NA CR0 178 C1
EA W5 104 D3
MNPK E12 77 J3
THMD SE28 97 H6
Carlyle Sq CHEL SW3 15 H8
Carlyon Av RYLN/HDSTN HA2 65 K3
Carlyon Cl ALP/SUD HA0 68 A7
Carlyon Rd ALP/SUD HA0 86 A1
YEAD UB4 83 G4
Carlys Cl BECK BR3 166 A1
Carmalt Gdns PUT/ROE SW15 127 F3
Carmel Ct KENS W8 14 C1
Carmelite Rd
KTN/HRWW/WS HA3 34 C7
Carmelite St EMB EC4Y 12 B6
Carmel Wy RCH/KEW TW9 125 H1
Carmen St POP/IOD E14 93 K5
Carmichael Cl BTSEA SW11 * 128 C2
RSLP HA4 64 E3
Carmichael Ms
WAND/EARL SW18 128 C6
Carmichael Rd SNWD SE25 165 H4
Carminia Rd TOOT SW17 148 B1
Carnaby St SOHO/CST W1F 10 E5
Carnac St WNWD SE27 149 K3
Carnanton Rd WALTH E17 44 B7
Carnarvon Av EN EN1 30 B1
Carnarvon Dr HYS/HAR UB3 101 F2
Carnarvon Rd BAR EN5 26 C2
LEY E10 58 A4
SRTFD E15 76 D5
SWFD E18 44 D7
Carnation Cl ROMW/RG RM7 81 G1
Carnation St ABYW SE2 116 C4
Carnbrook Rd BKHTH/KID SE3 134 C2
Carnecke Gdns ELTH/MOT SE9 134 D4
Carnegie Cl SURB KT6 172 B1
Carnegie Pl WIM/MER SW19 146 B2
Carnegie St IS N1 5 L4
Carnet Cl DART DA1 138 B6
Carnforth Cl HOR/WEW KT19 172 D5
Carnforth Gdns HCH RM12 81 J4
Carnforth Rd
STRHM/NOR SW16 148 D6
Carnoustie Dr IS N1 5 L2
Carnoustie Cl THMD SE28 97 K5
Carnwath Rd FUL/PGN SW6 127 K2
Carol Cl HDN NW4 52 B3
Carolina Cl SRTFD E15 76 C4
Carolina Rd THHTH CR7 164 C1
Caroline Cl BAY/PAD W2 8 D7
CROY/NA CR0 178 A3
ISLW TW7 103 J6
MUSWH N10 54 B1
STRHM/NOR SW16 149 F2
WDR/YW UB7 100 A1
Caroline Ct STAN HA7 * 35 G5
Caroline Gdns BETH E2 7 K7
PECK SE15 * 111 J6
Caroline Pl BAY/PAD W2 8 D6
BTSEA SW11 129 F1
HYS/HAR UB3 101 H6
OXHEY WD19 21 J5
Caroline Place Ms
BAY/PAD W2 * 8 D7
Caroline Rd WIM/MER SW19 146 D6
Caroline St WCHPL E1 93 F5
Caroline Ter BGVA SW1W 16 A6
Caroline Wk HMSMTH W6 107 H5
Carol St CAMTN NW1 4 E3
Carpenders Av OXHEY WD19 33 J2
Carpenter Cl EW KT17 173 H7
Carpenter Gdns WCHMH N21 41 H1
Carpenters Ct BAR EN5 27 F5
Carpenters Ms HOLWY N7 * 72 E4
Carpenter's Pl CLAP SW4 129 J3
Carpenters Rd SRTFD E15 76 A6
Carpenter St MYFR/PKLN W1K 10 C7
Carrara Ms HACK E8 74 C4
Carr Cl STAN HA7 35 G5
Carre Ms CMBW SE5 110 C7
Carr Gv WOOL/PLUM SE18 114 D3
Carriage Dr East CHEL SW3 109 F5
Carriage Dr North
BTSEA SW11 108 E6
Carriage Dr South
BTSEA SW11 108 E7
Carriage Dr West BTSEA SW11 108 E6
Carriage Ms IL IG1 78 C1
Carrick Cl ISLW TW7 124 B2
Carrick Gdns TOTM N17 42 A6
Carrick Ga ESH/CLAY KT10 170 C2
Carrick Ms DEPT SE8 112 D5
Carrill Wy BELV DA17 116 E3
Carrington Av BORE WD6 24 D4
HSLW TW3 123 G4
Carrington Cl BAR EN5 25 J4
CROY/NA CR0 166 B6
Carrington Gdns FSTGT E7 76 E3
Carrington Pl
ESH/CLAY KT10 * 170 B3
Carrington Rd DART DA1 139 J5
RCHPK/HAM TW10 125 H3
Carrington Sq
KTN/HRWW/WS HA3 34 C6
Carrington St MYFR/PICC W1J 10 C9
Carrol Cl KTTN NW5 72 B3
Carroll Cl SRTFD E15 76 D4
Carronade Pl THMD SE28 115 H2
Carron Cl POP/IOD E14 93 K5
Carroun Rd VX/NE SW8 110 A6
Carroway La GFD/PVL UB6 84 D2
Carrow Rd DAGW RM9 79 H6
Carr Rd NTHLT UB5 66 B6
WALTH E17 57 J1
Carrs La WCHMH N21 29 K4
Carr St POP/IOD E14 93 G4
Carshalton Gv SUT SM1 175 H3
Carshalton Park Rd CAR SM5 175 K5
Carshalton Pl CAR SM5 176 A3
Carshalton Rd MTCM CR4 163 F4
SUT SM1 175 G4
Carslake Rd PUT/ROE SW15 127 F5
Carson Rd CAN/RD E16 94 E4
DUL SE21 149 J1
EBAR EN4 27 K3
Carstairs Rd CAT SE6 152 A2
Carston Cl LEE/GVPK SE12 133 J4
Carswell Cl REDBR IG4 59 H3
Carswell Rd CAT SE6 133 F6
Carter Cl CDALE/KGS NW9 51 F5
WLGTN SM6 176 D6
Carteret St STJSPK SW1H 17 G2
Carteret Wy DEPT SE8 112 B3
Carterhatch Rd PEND EN3 31 G1
Carter La BLKFR EC4V 12 D5
Carter Pl WALW SE17 18 F8
Carter Rd PLSTW E13 77 F7
WIM/MER SW19 147 H5
Carters Cl KTTN NW5 * 72 D5
WPK KT4 174 B1
Carters Hill Cl ELTH/MOT SE9 134 B7
Carter St WALW SE17 18 E9
Carters Yd
WAND/EARL SW18 * 127 K4
Carter's Yd
WAND/EARL SW18 * 127 K4
Carthew Rd HMSMTH W6 106 E2
Carthew Vls HMSMTH W6 106 E2
Carthusian St FARR EC1M 12 E2
Cartier Cir POP/IOD E14 94 A7
Carting La TPL/STR WC2R 11 K7
Cartmel Cl TOTM N17 42 D6
Cartmel Ct NTHLT UB5 65 J5
Cartmel Gdns MRDN SM4 162 B4
Cartmel Rd BXLYHN DA7 117 H7
Cartwright Gdns STPAN WC1H 5 H8
Cartwright St WCHPL E1 13 M6
Cartwright Wy BARN SW13 106 E6
Carver Cl CHSWK W4 105 K2
Carver Rd HNHL SE24 130 D5
Carville Crs BTFD TW8 105 F3
Cary Rd WAN E11 76 C3
Carysfort Rd CEND/HSY/T N8 54 D4
STNW/STAM N16 73 K2
Cascade Av MUSWH N10 54 C3
Cascade Rd BKHH IG9 45 H1
Casella Rd NWCR SE14 112 A6
Casewick Rd WNWD SE27 149 H4
Casey Cl STJWD NW8 3 J8
Casimir Rd CLPT E5 74 D2
Casino Av HNHL SE24 130 D4
Caspian Cl PUR RM19 119 K4
Caspian St CMBW SE5 110 E6
Caspian Wk CAN/RD E16 95 H5
Caspian Wy PUR RM19 119 K4
Cassandra Cl NTHLT UB5 66 D3
Casselden Rd WLSDN NW10 69 F6
Cassidy Rd FUL/PGN SW6 107 K6
Cassilda Rd ABYW SE2 116 B3
Cassilis Rd POP/IOD E14 112 D1
TWK TW1 124 C5
Cassiobridge Rd WATW WD18 20 C3
Cassiobridge Ter
RKW/CH/CXG WD3 * 20 B4
Cassiobury Av
EBED/NFELT TW14 121 J6
Cassiobury Dr WAT WD17 20 E2
Cassiobury Park Av
WATW WD18 20 C2
Cassiobury Rd WALTH E17 57 F4
Cassio Pl WATW WD18 20 C3
Cassio Rd WATW WD18 21 F3
Cassio Whf WATW WD18 * 20 B4
Cassland Rd HOM E9 75 F6
THHTH CR7 164 E3
Casslee Rd CAT SE6 132 C6
Casson St WCHPL E1 92 C4
Castellain Rd MV/WKIL W9 2 C9
Castellan Av GPK RM2 63 K2
Castellane Cl STAN HA7 35 F6
Castello Av PUT/ROE SW15 127 F4
Castelnau BARN SW13 106 E6
Casterbridge Rd
BKHTH/KID SE3 133 K2
Casterton St HACK E8 74 D5
Castile Rd WOOL/PLUM SE18 115 F3
Castillon Rd CAT SE6 152 C1
Castlands Rd CAT SE6 151 H1
Castle Av CHING E4 44 B4
EW KT17 173 J7
RAIN RM13 81 G6
Castlebar Hl WEA W13 85 H4
Castlebar Ms EA W5 85 H4
Castlebar Pk EA W5 85 H4
Castlebar Rd WEA W13 85 J5
Castle Baynard St
BLKFR EC4V 12 D6
Castlebrook Cl LBTH SE11 18 C5
Castle Cl ACT W3 105 J1
BUSH WD23 22 B5
HAYES BR2 167 H2
SUN TW16 140 C6
WIM/MER SW19 146 B2
Castlecombe Dr
WIM/MER SW19 127 G6
Castlecombe Rd
ELTH/MOT SE9 153 J4
Castle Ct BANK EC3V * 13 H5
SYD SE26 151 G3
Castledine Rd PGE/AN SE20 150 D6
Castle Dr REDBR IG4 59 J5
Castleford Av ELTH/MOT SE9 135 G7
Castleford Cl TOTM N17 42 B5
Castlegate RCH/KEW TW9 125 G2
Castlehaven Rd CAMTN NW1 4 C2
Castle Hill Av CROY/NA CR0 179 K7
Castle Hill Pde WEA W13 * 85 H6
Castle La WESTW SW1E 16 E3
Castleleigh Ct ENC/FH EN2 29 K4
Castlemaine Av EW KT17 173 K7
SAND/SEL CR2 178 B4
Castlemaine St WCHPL E1 92 D4
Castle Md CMBW SE5 * 110 D6
Castle Ms CAMTN NW1 72 B5
NFNCH/WDSPK N12 39 G4
TOOT SW17 147 J3
Castle Pde EW KT17 * 173 J6
Castle Pl CAMTN NW1 72 B5
Castlereagh St MBLAR W1H 9 L4
Castle Rd CAMTN NW1 72 B5
DAGW RM9 79 H7
ISLW TW7 124 A1
NFNCH/WDSPK N12 39 G4
NTHLT UB5 66 B5
NWDGN UB2 * 102 E2
Castle Rw CHSWK W4 * 106 A4
Castle St EHAM E6 95 G1
KUT/HW KT1 * 159 F1
Castleton Av BXLYHN DA7 118 A7
WBLY HA9 68 A3
Castleton Cl CROY/NA CR0 166 B5
Castleton Gdns WBLY HA9 68 A2
Castleton Rd ELTH/MOT SE9 153 H3
GDMY/SEVK IG3 61 H7
MTCM CR4 163 J3
RSLP HA4 47 H7
WALTH E17 58 B1
Castletown Rd WKENS W14 107 H4
Castleview Cl FSBYPK N4 55 J7
Castleview Gdns IL IG1 59 J5
Castle Vls CRICK NW2 * 69 J5
Castle Wk SUN TW16 * 156 B2
Castle Wy FELT TW13 141 G3
WIM/MER SW19 146 B2
Castlewood Dr ELTH/MOT SE9 134 E1
Castlewood Rd EBAR EN4 27 H2
STNW/STAM N16 56 C5
Castle Yd HGT N6 * 54 A6
RCH/KEW TW9 124 E4
STHWK SE1 * 12 D8
Castor La POP/IOD E14 93 K6
Catalina Rd HTHAIR TW6 120 E2
Catalpa Ct LEW SE13 133 G5
Caterham Av CLAY IG5 60 A1
Caterham Rd LEW SE13 133 F2
Catesby St WALW SE17 19 H6
Catford Broadway CAT SE6 132 E6
Catford Hl CAT SE6 132 C7
Catford Island CAT SE6 * 132 E6
Catford Rd CAT SE6 132 D7
Cathall Rd WAN E11 76 C2
Cathay St BERM/RHTH SE16 111 J1
Cathcart Hl ARCH N19 72 C2
Cathcart Rd WBPTN SW10 14 D9
Cathcart St KTTN NW5 72 B5
Cathedral St STHWK SE1 13 G8
Catherall Rd HBRY N5 73 J2
Catherine Ct STHGT/OAK N14 28 C4
Catherine Dr RCH/KEW TW9 125 F3
SUN TW16 140 D6
Catherine Gdns HSLW TW3 123 J3
Catherine Griffiths Ct
CLKNW EC1R 6 B9
Catherine Gv GNWCH SE10 112 E7
Catherine Pl HRW HA1 49 F4
WESTW SW1E 16 E3
Catherine Rd GPK RM2 63 K4
SURB KT6 158 E4
Catherines Cl WDR/YW UB7 * 100 A1
Catherine St HOL/ALD WC2B * 11 L6
Catherine Vls RYNPK SW20 * 145 K6
Catherine Wheel Aly
LVPST EC2M 13 K3
Catherine Wheel Rd
BTFD TW8 104 E6
Catherine Wheel Yd
WHALL SW1A 10 E9
Cat Hl EBAR EN4 27 J5
Cathles Rd BAL SW12 129 G5
Cathnor Rd SHB W12 106 E1
Catling Cl FSTH SE23 150 E2
Catlin's La PIN HA5 47 F2
Catlin St BERM/RHTH SE16 111 H4
Cator La BECK BR3 166 C1
Cato Rd CLAP SW4 129 J2
Cator Rd CAR SM5 175 K4
SYD SE26 151 F5
Cator St PECK SE15 111 G5
Cato St MBLAR W1H 9 K3
Catsey La BUSH WD23 22 C6
Catsey Wd BUSH WD23 22 C6
Catterick Cl FBAR/BDGN N11 40 A5
Cattistock Rd ELTH/MOT SE9 153 J4
Cattley Cl BAR EN5 26 C3
Catton St RSQ WC1B 11 L3
Caudwell Ter
WAND/EARL SW18 * 128 C5
Caulfield Rd CHSWK W4 105 K2
EHAM E6 77 K6
PECK SE15 131 J1
Causeway EBED/NFELT TW14 122 A3
The Causeway BELMT SM2 175 G7
CAR SM5 176 A2
CHSGTN KT9 172 A3
EFNCH N2 53 H3
ESH/CLAY KT10 171 F6
TEDD TW11 143 F5
WAND/EARL SW18 128 A3
WIM/MER SW19 146 A4
Causeyware Rd ED N9 30 D6
Causton Cots POP/IOD E14 * 93 G4
Causton Rd HGT N6 * 54 B6
Causton Sq DAGE RM10 80 C6
Causton St WEST SW1P 17 H6
Cautley Av CLAP SW4 129 H4
Cavalier Cl CHDH RM6 61 J3
Cavalier Gdns HYS/HAR UB3 82 B5
Cavalry Crs HSLWW TW4 122 C3
Cavalry Gdns PUT/ROE SW15 127 H4
Cavan Pl PIN HA5 * 33 K7
Cavaye Pl WBPTN SW10 14 F8
Cavell Crs DART DA1 139 K3
Cavell Dr ENC/FH EN2 29 G1
Cavell Rd TOTM N17 41 K6
Cavell St WCHPL E1 92 D4
Cavendish Av BFN/LL DA15 136 B6
ERITH DA8 117 K5
FNCH N3 52 E1
HCH RM12 81 K5
HRW HA1 66 D3
NWMAL KT3 160 E4
RSLP HA4 65 F4
STJWD NW8 3 H6
WEA W13 85 G4
WELL DA16 136 A2
WFD IG8 45 F6
Cavendish Cl
KIL/WHAMP NW6 70 D5
STJWD NW8 3 H7
SUN TW16 140 D5
UED N18 * 42 D4
YEAD UB4 82 C4
Cavendish Ct
RKW/CH/CXG WD3 * 20 B4
SUN TW16 140 D5
Cavendish Crs BORE WD6 24 C3
HCH RM12 81 K5
Cavendish Dr EDGW HA8 36 B5
ESH/CLAY KT10 170 E4
WAN E11 58 B7
Cavendish Gdns BARK IG11 79 F4
CHDH RM6 62 A4
CLAP SW4 * 129 H5
IL IG1 60 A7
Cavendish Ms SUT SM1 175 G1
Cavendish Ms North
GTPST W1W 10 D2
Cavendish Ms South
GTPST W1W * 10 D3
Cavendish Pde CLAP SW4 * 129 H3
HSLWW TW4 * 122 D1
Cavendish Pl BAL SW12 129 H7
BMLY BR1 168 E2
CAVSQ/HST W1G 10 D4
CRICK NW2 70 B5
Cavendish Rd BAL SW12 129 H6
BAR EN5 26 A2
BELMT SM2 175 G6
CHING E4 44 A5
CHSWK W4 105 K7
CLAP SW4 129 G5
CROY/NA CR0 164 C7
FSBYPK N4 55 H5
KIL/WHAMP NW6 70 C6
NWMAL KT3 160 C4
SUN TW16 140 D5
UED N18 42 D4
WIM/MER SW19 147 J6
Cavendish Sq CAVSQ/HST W1G 10 D4
Cavendish St IS N1 7 G6
Cavendish Ter BOW E3 * 93 H2
FELT TW13 * 140 E1
Cavendish Wy WWKM BR4 166 E7
Cavenham Gdns IL IG1 78 D2
Caverleigh Wy WPK KT4 160 D7
Caverley Gdns
KTN/HRWW/WS HA3 49 K6
Cave Rd PLSTW E13 95 F1
RCHPK/HAM TW10 143 J3
Caversham Av CHEAM SM3 174 C1
PLMGR N13 41 G2
Caversham Rd KTTN NW5 72 C5
KUT/HW KT1 159 G1
SEVS/STOTM N15 55 J3
Caversham St CHEL SW3 15 L9
Caverswall St SHB W12 88 A5
Cawdor Crs HNWL W7 104 B3
Cawnpore St NRWD SE19 150 A4
Caxton Gv BOW E3 93 J2
Caxton Ms BTFD TW8 104 D5
Caxton Rd NWDGN UB2 102 C2
SHB W12 88 B7
WDGN N22 55 F1
WIM/MER SW19 147 G4
The Caxtons BRXN/ST SW9 * 110 C6
Caxton St STJSPK SW1H 16 F3
Caxton St North CAN/RD E16 94 D5
Caxton Wy ROM RM1 63 G3
WATW WD18 20 B6
Cayenne Ct STHWK SE1 13 L9
Caygill Cl HAYES BR2 167 J3
Cayley Rd NWDGN UB2 103 G2
Cayton Rd GFD/PVL UB6 84 E1
Cayton St FSBYE EC1V 7 G8
Cazenove Rd
STNW/STAM N16 74 B1
WALTH E17 43 J7
Cecil Av BARK IG11 78 D6
EN EN1 30 B3
WBLY HA9 68 B4
Cecil Cl ASHF TW15 140 A5
CHSGTN KT9 171 K3
EA W5 * 85 K4

Cecil Ct BAR EN5 26 B2
LSQ/SEVD WC2H 11 H7
Cecile Pk CEND/HSY/T N8 54 E5
Cecilia Cl EFNCH N2 53 G2
Cecilia Rd HACK E8 74 B4
Cecil Manning Cl
GFD/PVL UB6 67 G7
Cecil Pk PIN HA5 47 J3
Cecil Pl MTCM CR4 162 E4
Cecil Rd ACT W3 86 E4
ASHF TW15 140 A6
CDALE/KGS NW9 51 F2
CHDH RM6 61 K6
CROY/NA CR0 163 K5
ENC/FH EN2 29 K3
HSLW TW3 123 H2
IL IG1 78 B3
KTN/HRWW/WS HA3 48 E2
MUSWH N10 54 B1
PLSTW E13 76 E7
STHGT/OAK N14 28 B7
SUT SM1 174 D5
WALTH E17 43 J7
WAN E11 76 C1
WIM/MER SW19 147 F6
WLSDN NW10 69 G7
Cecil Wy HAYES BR2 167 K7
Cedar Av BFN/LL DA15 136 B6
CHDH RM6 62 A4
EBAR EN4 27 J6
HYS/HAR UB3 82 E5
PEND EN3 30 E1
RSLP HA4 65 G4
WHTN TW2 123 G5
Cedar Cl BKHH IG9 45 H1
BOW E3 75 H7
CAR SM5 175 K5
DUL SE21 130 D7
HAYES BR2 181 J2
IL IG1 78 D4
KUTN/CMB KT2 145 F3
ROMW/RG RM7 62 E3
Cedar Copse BMLY BR1 168 E1
Cedar Ct CHARL SE7 * 114 B5
ELTH/MOT SE9 * 134 D5
WIM/MER SW19 146 B2
Cedar Crs HAYES BR2 181 J2
Cedarcroft Rd CHSGTN KT9 172 B3
Cedar Dr EFNCH N2 53 J3
GLDGN NW11 52 E3
PIN HA5 34 A5
Cedar Gdns BELMT SM2 175 G5
Cedar Gv BXLY DA5 136 E5
EA W5 104 E2
STHL UB1 84 A4
Cedar Hts RCHPK/HAM TW10 125 F7
Cedarhurst BMLY BR1 * 152 C6
Cedarhurst Dr ELTH/MOT SE9 134 B4
Cedar Lawn Av BAR EN5 26 C4
Cedar Mt ELTH/MOT SE9 134 C7
Cedarne Rd FUL/PGN SW6 107 K6
Cedar Park Gdns CHDH RM6 61 K6
WIM/MER SW19 145 K4
Cedar Pl CHARL SE7 114 B4
Cedar Ri STHGT/OAK N14 28 A6
Cedar Rd BELMT SM2 175 G5
BMLY BR1 168 B1
CRICK NW2 70 A3
CROY/NA CR0 178 A1
DART DA1 139 G7
E/WMO/HCT KT8 157 K3
EBED/NFELT TW14 121 G7
ERITH DA8 118 D7
HSLWW TW4 122 B1
OXHEY WD19 21 G5
ROMW/RG RM7 62 E3
TEDD TW11 143 G4
TOTM N17 42 B7
Cedars Av MTCM CR4 163 F3
WALTH E17 57 J4
Cedars Cl BORE WD6 24 D3
HDN NW4 52 B2
LEW SE13 133 G2
Cedars Cots PUT/ROE SW15 * 126 D5
Cedars Ct ED N9 42 A1
Cedars Ms CLAP SW4 * 129 G3
Cedars Rd BARN SW13 126 C1
BECK BR3 166 B1
CHSWK W4 105 K5
CLAP SW4 129 G2
CROY/NA CR0 176 E2
ED N9 42 C1
KUT/HW KT1 143 J7
MRDN SM4 161 K3
SRTFD E15 76 C5
WCHMH N21 41 H1
The Cedars HOM E9 * 75 F6
SRTFD E15 * 76 D7
TEDD TW11 143 F5
Cedar Ter RCH/KEW TW9 125 F3
Cedar Tree Gv WNWD SE27 149 H4
Cedarville Gdns
STRHM/NOR SW16 149 F5
Cedar Wk ESH/CLAY KT10 171 F5
Cedar Wy KCROSS N1C 5 G2
SUN TW16 140 C6
Cedric Av ROM RM1 63 G2
Cedric Rd ELTH/MOT SE9 154 C2
Celadon Cl PEND EN3 31 G2
Celandine Cl POP/IOD E14 93 J4
Celandine Dr HACK E8 7 L1
THMD SE28 97 H7
Celandine Gv STHGT/OAK N14 28 C4
Celandine Wy SRTFD E15 94 C2
Celbridge Ms BAY/PAD W2 8 D4
Celestial Gdns LEW SE13 133 G3
Celia Rd ARCH N19 72 C3
Celtic Av HAYES BR2 167 H2
Celtic St POP/IOD E14 93 K4
Cemetery La CHARL SE7 114 D5
Cemetery Rd ABYW SE2 116 C5
FSTGT E7 76 D4
TOTM N17 42 A6
Cenacle Cl HAMP NW3 70 E2
Centaur Ct BTFD TW8 * 105 F4
Centaur St STHWK SE1 17 M3
Centenary Rd PEND EN3 31 H3
Centenary Wk MNPK E12 77 H2
WAN E11 58 C3
WFD IG8 44 C6
Centennial Av BORE WD6 23 H6
Centennial Pk BORE WD6 * 23 J6
Central Av E/WMO/HCT KT8 156 E4
ED N9 42 A2
EFNCH N2 53 H1
EN EN1 30 C1
HSLW TW3 123 H3
HYS/HAR UB3 101 J1
MNPK E12 77 H2
PIN HA5 47 K5
WAN E11 76 B1
WELL DA16 136 B1
WLGTN SM6 176 E4
Central Blds EA W5 * 85 K6
Central Circ HDN NW4 51 K4
Central Hall Blds ARCH N19 * 72 C1
Central Hl NRWD SE19 149 J4
Central Pde ACT W3 * 105 H1
BFN/LL DA15 * 155 G2
E/WMO/HCT KT8 * 156 E3
GFD/PVL UB6 * 85 G2
HRW HA1 49 F4
PEND EN3 * 30 E1
PGE/AN SE20 * 151 F6
STRHM/NOR SW16 * 148 E3
SURB KT6 * 159 F5
WALTH E17 * 57 J3
Central Park Av DAGE RM10 80 D2
Central Park Est
HSLWW TW4 * 122 C3
Central Park Rd EHAM E6 95 H1
Central Pl SNWD SE25 * 165 H3
Central Rd ALP/SUD HA0 67 H4
DART DA1 139 H4
MRDN SM4 162 A4
WPK KT4 173 J1
Central Sq E/WMO/HCT KT8 156 E3
GLDGN NW11 52 E5
Central St FSBYE EC1V 6 E7
Central Ter BECK BR3 * 166 A2
Central Wy CAR SM5 175 J6
EBED/NFELT TW14 122 A4
NTHWD HA6 32 C6
THMD SE28 97 G6
WLSDN NW10 86 E2
Centre Av ACT W3 87 F7
Centre Common Rd CHST BR7 154 C6
Centre Rd DAGE RM10 98 D1
WAN E11 76 E1
Centre St BETH E2 92 D1
Centre Wy ED N9 42 E1
Centric Cl CAMTN NW1 * 4 C3
Centurian Sq
WOOL/PLUM SE18 114 D7
Centurian Wy ERITHM DA18 117 G2
Centurion Cl HOLWY N7 5 L1
Centurion Ct WLGTN SM6 * 176 B1
Centurion La BOW E3 93 H1
Centurion Sq CHARL SE7 * 114 D6
Centurion Wy PUR RM19 119 J3
Century Cl HDN NW4 52 B4
Century Ct WATW WD18 * 20 A6
Century Ms CLPT E5 * 74 E3
HBRY N5 73 H2
Century Pk WAT WD17 * 21 G4
Century Rd WALTH E17 57 G2
Cephas Av WCHPL E1 92 E3
Cephas St WCHPL E1 92 E3
Ceres Rd WOOL/PLUM SE18 116 A3
Cerise Rd PECK SE15 111 H7
Cerne Cl YEAD UB4 83 G6
Cerne Rd MRDN SM4 162 B5
Cerney Ms BAY/PAD W2 9 G6
Cervantes Ct BAY/PAD W2 8 D5
NTHWD HA6 32 D6
Ceylon Rd WKENS W14 107 G2
Chabot Dr PECK SE15 131 J2
Chadacre Av CLAY IG5 59 K2
Chadacre Rd EW KT17 173 K4
Chadbourn St POP/IOD E14 93 K4
Chad Crs ED N9 42 E2
Chadd Dr BMLY BR1 168 D2
Chadville Gdns CHDH RM6 61 K4
Chadway BCTR RM8 79 J1
Chadwell Av CHDH RM6 61 H6
Chadwell Heath La CHDH RM6 61 H3
Chadwell La CEND/HSY/T N8 55 F2
Chadwell St CLKNW EC1R 6 B7
Chadwick Av CHING E4 44 B3
WCHMH N21 * 29 F4
WIM/MER SW19 146 E5
Chadwick Cl PUT/ROE SW15 126 C6
TEDD TW11 143 G5
Chadwick Pl SURB KT6 158 D5
Chadwick Rd IL IG1 78 B2
PECK SE15 131 G1
WAN E11 58 C6
WLSDN NW10 69 H7
Chadwick St WEST SW1P 17 G4
Chadwick Wy THMD SE28 97 K6
Chadwin Rd PLSTW E13 95 F4
Chadworth Wy
ESH/CLAY KT10 170 D4
Chaffinch Av CROY/NA CR0 166 A5
Chaffinch Cl CROY/NA CR0 166 A4
ED N9 31 F7
SURB KT6 172 C2
Chaffinch La WATW WD18 20 D6
Chaffinch Rd BECK BR3 151 G7
Chafford Wy CHDH RM6 61 J3
Chagford St CAMTN NW1 9 L1
Chailey Av EN EN1 30 B1
Chailey Cl HEST TW5 102 C7
Chailey St CLPT E5 74 E2
Chalbury Wk IS N1 5 M5
Chalcombe Rd ABYW SE2 116 C2
Chalcot Cl BELMT SM2 174 E6
Chalcot Crs CAMTN NW1 3 M3
Chalcot Gdns HAMP NW3 71 K5
Chalcot Ms STRHM/NOR SW16 148 E2
Chalcot Rd CAMTN NW1 4 A3
Chalcot Sq CAMTN NW1 4 A2
Chalcott Gdns SURB KT6 * 158 D7
Chalcroft Rd LEW SE13 133 H4
Chaldon Rd FUL/PGN SW6 107 H6
Chale Rd BRXS/STRHM SW2 129 K5
Chalet Cl ASHF TW15 140 B5
Chalet Est MLHL NW7 * 37 J3
Chalfont Av WBLY HA9 68 D5
Chalfont Gn ED N9 42 A2
Chalfont Ms
WAND/EARL SW18 127 J7
Chalfont Rd ED N9 42 A2
HYS/HAR UB3 101 K1
SNWD SE25 165 G2
Chalfont Wk PIN HA5 * 47 G1
Chalfont Wy WEA W13 104 C2
Chalford Cl E/WMO/HCT KT8 157 F3
Chalforde Gdns GPK RM2 63 K3
Chalford Rd DUL SE21 149 K3
Chalford Wk WFD IG8 45 H7
Chalgrove Av MRDN SM4 161 K4
Chalgrove Crs CLAY IG5 59 J1
Chalgrove Gdns FNCH N3 52 C2
Chalgrove Rd BELMT SM2 175 H6
HOM E9 74 E5
TOTM N17 42 D7
Chalice Cl WLGTN SM6 176 D5
Chalkenden Cl PGE/AN SE20 150 D6
Chalk Farm Pde HAMP NW3 * 4 A1
Chalk Farm Rd CAMTN NW1 4 A1
Chalk Hl OXHEY WD19 21 J5
Chalk Hill Rd HMSMTH W6 107 G3
Chalkhill Rd WBLY HA9 68 C2
Chalklands WBLY HA9 68 E2
Chalk La EBAR EN4 27 K2
Chalkley Cl MTCM CR4 162 E1
Chalkmill Dr EN EN1 30 D2
Chalk Pit Rd SUT SM1 175 G4
Chalk Rd PLSTW E13 95 F4
Chalkstone Cl WELL DA16 116 B7
Chalkwell Park Av EN EN1 30 A3
Chalky La CHSGTN KT9 171 K7
Challenge Cl WLSDN NW10 69 G7
Challenge Rd ASHF TW15 140 A2
Challice Wy BRXS/STRHM SW2 130 A7
Challin St PGE/AN SE20 150 E7
Challis Rd BTFD TW8 104 E4
Challoner Cl EFNCH N2 53 H1
Challoner Crs WKENS W14 107 J4
Challoners Cl E/WMO/HCT KT8 157 J3
Challoner St WKENS W14 107 J4
Chalmers Wk WALW SE17 * 110 C5
Chalmers Wy
EBED/NFELT TW14 122 A4
TWK TW1 124 C3
Chalsey Rd BROCKY SE4 132 C3
Chalton Dr EFNCH N2 53 G5
Chalton St CAMTN NW1 5 G5
Chamberlain Cl IL IG1 78 C2
THMD SE28 115 J2
Chamberlain Cots
CMBW SE5 * 110 E7
Chamberlain Crs WWKM BR4 166 E7
Chamberlain Gdns HSLW TW3 103 H7
Chamberlain La PIN HA5 46 E3
Chamberlain Pl WALTH E17 57 G2
Chamberlain Rd EFNCH N2 53 G1
WEA W13 104 B1
Chamberlain St HAMP NW3 3 M2
Chamberlain Wy PIN HA5 47 F2
SURB KT6 159 F6
Chamberlayne Av WBLY HA9 68 A2
Chamberlayne Rd
WLSDN NW10 70 A7
Chamberlens Garages
HMSMTH W6 * 106 E3
Chambers Gdns EFNCH N2 39 H7
Chambers La WLSDN NW10 69 K6
Chambers Pl SAND/SEL CR2 177 K6
Chambers Rd HOLWY N7 72 E3
Chambers St
BERM/RHTH SE16 111 H1
Chamber St WCHPL E1 13 M6
Chambon Pl HMSMTH W6 106 D3
Chambord St BETH E2 7 M8
Champa Cl TOTM N17 56 B1
Champion Crs SYD SE26 151 G3
Champion Gv CMBW SE5 130 E2
Champion Hl CMBW SE5 130 E2
Champion Pk CMBW SE5 130 E2
Champion Rd SYD SE26 151 G3
Champness Cl WNWD SE27 149 K3
Champness Rd BARK IG11 79 F6
Champneys OXHEY WD19 * 33 J1
Champneys Cl BELMT SM2 174 D6
Chancellor Gdns
SAND/SEL CR2 177 H7
Chancellor Gv DUL SE21 149 J1
Chancellor Pl CDALE/KGS NW9 51 H1
Chancellor's Rd HMSMTH W6 107 F4
Chancellors St HMSMTH W6 107 F4
Chancellors Whf HMSMTH W6 107 F5
Chancelot Rd ABYW SE2 116 C3
Chancel St STHWK SE1 12 C8
Chancery La BECK BR3 166 E1
LINN WC2A 11 M3
Chance St BETH E2 7 L9
Chanctonbury Cl
ELTH/MOT SE9 154 B2
Chanctonbury Gdns
BELMT SM2 175 F6
Chanctonbury Wy
NFNCH/WDSPK N12 38 E3
Chandler Av CAN/RD E16 94 E4
Chandler Cl HPTN TW12 141 K7
Chandlers Av GNWCH SE10 113 J2
Chandlers Cl E/WMO/HCT KT8 157 G4
EBED/NFELT TW14 121 J6
Chandlers Ct LEE/GVPK SE12 * 153 F1
Chandlers Dr ERITH DA8 118 A3
Chandlers Ms POP/IOD E14 112 D1
Chandler St WAP E1W 92 D7
Chandlers Wy ROM RM1 63 G4
Chandler Wy PECK SE15 111 G6
Chandos Av EA W5 104 D3
STHGT/OAK N14 40 C2
TRDG/WHET N20 27 H7
WALTH E17 * 57 J1
Chandos Cl BKHH IG9 45 F1
Chandos Ct STAN HA7 35 H5
Chandos Crs EDGW HA8 36 B6
Chandos Pl CHCR WC2N 11 J7
Chandos Rd BORE WD6 24 B1
CRICK NW2 70 A4
EFNCH N2 53 H1
HRW HA1 48 C4
PIN HA5 47 G6
SRTFD E15 76 B4
TOTM N17 56 A1
WLSDN NW10 87 G3
Chandos St CAVSQ/HST W1G 10 D3
Chandos Wy GLDGN NW11 53 F7
Channel Cl HEST TW5 103 F7
Channel Gate Rd NKENS W10 88 A4
WLSDN NW10 87 G2
Channel Islands Est IS N1 73 J5
Channelsea Rd SRTFD E15 76 B7
Chantress Cl DAGE RM10 80 E7
Chantrey Rd BRXN/ST SW9 130 A2
Chantry Cl ABYW SE2 116 D2
KTN/HRWW/WS HA3 50 B4
MLHL NW7 25 H6
MV/WKIL W9 * 88 D3
SUN TW16 140 E6
Chantry Crs WLSDN NW10 69 G4
Chantry La HAYES BR2 168 C4
Chantry Pl
KTN/HRWW/WS HA3 34 B7
Chantry Rd CHSGTN KT9 172 B4
KTN/HRWW/WS HA3 34 B7
Chantry Sq KENS W8 14 C4
Chantry St IS N1 6 D4
Chantry Wy MTCM CR4 162 C2
RAIN RM13 99 F1
Chant Sq SRTFD E15 * 76 B6
Chant St SRTFD E15 76 B6
Chapel Av MNPK E12 77 H1
Chapel Cl DART DA1 138 B4
WLSDN NW10 69 H4
Chapel Ct EFNCH N2 53 J2
STHWK SE1 19 G1
WOOL/PLUM SE18 116 A5
Chapel Farm Rd
ELTH/MOT SE9 153 K2
Chapel Hl DART DA1 138 B3
Chapel House St POP/IOD E14 112 E4
Chapel La CHDH RM6 * 61 K6
PIN HA5 47 H2
Chapel Market IS N1 6 A5
Chapel Mill Rd KUT/HW KT1 159 G2
Chapel Pl CAVSQ/HST W1G 10 C4
IS N1 6 B5
TOTM N17 42 B6
Chapel Rd BXLYHN DA7 137 H3
HSLW TW3 123 G2
IL IG1 78 A2
TWK TW1 124 C6
WEA W13 85 H7
WNWD SE27 149 H3
Chapel Side BAY/PAD W2 8 C6
Chapel St BAY/PAD W2 9 J3
ENC/FH EN2 29 J2
KTBR SW1X 16 B3
Chapel Vw SAND/SEL CR2 178 E6
Chaplemount Rd WFD IG8 * 45 K5
Chaplin Cl ALP/SUD HA0 * 67 K5
STHWK SE1 18 B1
Chaplin Crs SUN TW16 140 C5
Chaplin Rd ALP/SUD HA0 67 J5
CRICK NW2 69 J5
SRTFD E15 94 C1
TOTM N17 * 56 B2
Chapman Cl WDR/YW UB7 100 C2
Chapman Crs
KTN/HRWW/WS HA3 50 A4
Chapman Rd BELV DA17 117 H4
CROY/NA CR0 164 B7
HOM E9 75 H5
Chapmans Gn WDGN N22 * 41 G7
Chapman Sq WIM/MER SW19 146 B1
Chapman St WCHPL E1 92 D6
Chapman Ter WDGN N22 * 41 H7
Chapter Cl CHSWK W4 105 K2
Chapter Rd CRICK NW2 69 J4
WALW SE17 18 D8
Chapter St WEST SW1P 17 G6
Chapter Wy HPTN TW12 142 A3
WIM/MER SW19 147 H7
Chara Pl CHSWK W4 106 A5
Charcroft Gdns PEND EN3 31 F3
Chardin Rd CHSWK W4 * 106 B3
Chardmore Rd
STNW/STAM N16 56 C7
Chardwell Cl EHAM E6 95 J5
Charecroft Wy WKENS W14 107 G1
Charford Rd CAN/RD E16 94 E4
Chargeable La PLSTW E13 94 E3
Chargeable St CAN/RD E16 94 D3
Chargrove Cl
BERM/RHTH SE16 112 A1
Charing Cross CHCR WC2N * 11 J8
Charing Cross Rd
LSQ/SEVD WC2H 11 H6
Chariot Cl BOW E3 75 J7
Charlbert St STJWD NW8 3 J5
Charlbury Av STAN HA7 35 K4
Charlbury Gdns
GDMY/SEVK IG3 79 F1
Charlbury Gv EA W5 85 J5
Charldane Rd ELTH/MOT SE9 154 B2
Charlecote Gv SYD SE26 150 D2
Charlecote Rd BCTR RM8 80 A2
Charlemont Rd EHAM E6 95 K2
Charles Babbage Cl
CHSGTN KT9 171 J6
Charles Barry Cl CLAP SW4 129 H2
Charles Cl SCUP DA14 155 H3
Charles Cobb Gdns
CROY/NA CR0 177 G4
Charles Coveney Rd
CMBW SE5 * 111 G7
Charles Crs HRW HA1 48 D6
Charles Dickens Ter
PGE/AN SE20 * 150 E6
Charlesfield ELTH/MOT SE9 153 G2
Charles Flemwell Ms
CAN/RD E16 * 94 E7
Charles Grinling Wk
WOOL/PLUM SE18 115 F3
Charles Haller St
BRXS/STRHM SW2 130 B6
Charles II Pl CHEL SW3 15 K8
Charles II St STJS SW1Y 11 G8
Charles La STJWD NW8 3 J6
Charles Pl CAMTN NW1 * 4 F8
Charles Rd CHDH RM6 61 K6
DAGE RM10 81 F5
FSTGT E7 77 G6
WEA W13 85 G5
WIM/MER SW19 146 E7
Charles Sevright Dr
MLHL NW7 38 B4
Charles Sq IS N1 7 H8
Charles Square Est IS N1 * 7 H8
Charles St BARN SW13 126 B2
CAN/RD E16 95 G7
CROY/NA CR0 177 J2
EN EN1 30 B4
HSLW TW3 122 E1
MYFR/PICC W1J 10 C8
Charleston Cl FELT TW13 140 E2
Charleston St WALW SE17 18 F6
Charles Whincup Rd
CAN/RD E16 95 F7
Charleville Circ SYD SE26 150 C4
Charleville Rd WKENS W14 107 H4
Charlieville Rd ERITH DA8 117 K6
Charlmont Rd TOOT SW17 147 J5
Charlock Wy WATW WD18 20 D5
Charlotte Cl BXLYHS DA6 137 F4
OXHEY WD19 21 G6
Charlotte Ct ESH/CLAY KT10 170 C4
Charlotte Despard Av
BTSEA SW11 109 G7
Charlotte Ms ESH/CLAY KT10 * 170 B3
FITZ W1T 10 F2
NKENS W10 88 B5
WKENS W14 107 H3
Charlotte Pde FSTH SE23 * 151 G1
Charlotte Park Av BMLY BR1 168 D2
Charlotte Pl FITZ W1T 10 F3
PIM SW1V 16 E6
Charlotte Rd BARN SW13 106 C7
SDTCH EC2A 7 J8
WLGTN SM6 176 C5
Charlotte Rw CLAP SW4 129 H2
Charlotte St FITZ W1T 10 F2
Charlotte Ter IS N1 5 M4
Charlow Cl FUL/PGN SW6 128 B1
Charlton Church La
CHARL SE7 114 B4
Charlton Crs BARK IG11 97 F1
Charlton Dene CHARL SE7 114 B6
Charlton King's Rd KTTN NW5 72 D4
Charlton La CHARL SE7 114 C4
Charlton Park La CHARL SE7 114 C6
Charlton Park Rd CHARL SE7 114 C5
Charlton Pl IS N1 6 C5
Charlton Rd BKHTH/KID SE3 113 K6
CHARL SE7 114 B5
ED N9 31 F7
KTN/HRWW/WS HA3 49 K3
WBLY HA9 50 B7
WLSDN NW10 69 G7
Charlton Wy BKHTH/KID SE3 113 J6
GNWCH SE10 113 H7
Charlwood CROY/NA CR0 179 H7
Charlwood Cl
KTN/HRWW/WS HA3 34 E5
Charlwood Pl PIM SW1V 16 F6
Charlwood Rd PUT/ROE SW15 127 G2
Charlwood St PIM SW1V 16 E8
PIM SW1V 16 F6
Charlwood Ter
PUT/ROE SW15 127 G3
Charmian Av STAN HA7 49 K2
Charminster Av
WIM/MER SW19 161 K1
Charminster Rd
ELTH/MOT SE9 153 H3
WPK KT4 161 G7
Charmouth Rd WELL DA16 116 D7
Charnock Rd CLPT E5 74 D2
Charnwood Av
WIM/MER SW19 161 K1
Charnwood Cl NWMAL KT3 160 B3
Charnwood Dr SWFD E18 59 F2
Charnwood Gdns
POP/IOD E14 112 D3
Charnwood Pl
TRDG/WHET N20 39 G2
Charnwood Rd SNWD SE25 164 E4
Charnwood St CLPT E5 * 74 C1
Charnwood Vls SWFD E18 59 F2
Charrington Rd CROY/NA CR0 177 H1
Charrington St CAMTN NW1 5 G5
Charsley Rd CAT SE6 151 K1
Chart Cl CROY/NA CR0 165 K5
HAYES BR2 152 C7
MTCM CR4 162 E3
Charter Av GNTH/NBYPK IG2 60 D7
Charter Crs HSLWW TW4 122 D3
Charter Dr BXLY DA5 137 F6
Charterhouse Av
ALP/SUD HA0 67 J4
Charterhouse Blds
FARR EC1M 12 E1
Charterhouse Ms FARR EC1M 12 D2
Charterhouse Rd HACK E8 74 C3
Charterhouse St HCIRC EC1N 12 B3
The Charterhouse
FARR EC1M * 12 D1
Charteris Rd FSBYPK N4 55 F7
KIL/WHAMP NW6 70 D7
WFD IG8 45 F5
Charter Pl WAT WD17 * 21 F3
Charter Rd KUT/HW KT1 159 J2
The Charter Rd WFD IG8 44 C5
Charters Cl NRWD SE19 150 A4
Charter Sq KUT/HW KT1 159 J1
Charter Wy FNCH N3 52 D3
STHGT/OAK N14 28 C5
Chartfield Av PUT/ROE SW15 126 E4
Chartfield Sq
PUT/ROE SW15 * 127 G4
Chartham Gv WNWD SE27 149 G2
Chartham Rd SNWD SE25 165 J2
Chart Hills Cl THMD SE28 98 A5
Chartley Av CRICK NW2 69 G2
STAN HA7 35 F5
Chartley Pde CRICK NW2 * 69 G2
Charton Cl BELV DA17 117 G5
Chartridge OXHEY WD19 * 33 H1
Chartridge Cl BAR EN5 25 J4
BUSH WD23 22 C5
Chart St IS N1 7 H7
Chartwell Cl CROY/NA CR0 164 E7
ELTH/MOT SE9 154 D1
GFD/PVL UB6 66 B7
Chartwell Gdns CHEAM SM3 174 C2
Chartwell Pl CHEAM SM3 174 C3
RYLN/HDSTN HA2 66 D1
Chartwell Rd NTHWD HA6 32 D5
Chartwell Wy PGE/AN SE20 150 D7
Charville La HGDN/ICK UB10 82 A2
Charwood STRHM/NOR SW16 149 G3
Chase Ct RYNPK SW20 161 H1
Chase Court Gdns
ENC/FH EN2 29 J2
Chasefield Rd TOOT SW17 147 K3
Chase Gdns CHING E4 43 J3
WHTN TW2 123 J5
Chase Gn ENC/FH EN2 29 J2
Chase Green Av ENC/FH EN2 29 H1
Chase Hl ENC/FH EN2 29 J2
Chase La BARK/HLT IG6 60 D4
Chaseley Ct CHSWK W4 105 J4
Chaseley St POP/IOD E14 * 93 G5
Chasemore Cl MTCM CR4 162 E6
Chasemore Gdns
CROY/NA CR0 177 G4
Chase Ridings ENC/FH EN2 29 G1
Chase Rd ACT W3 87 F3
STHGT/OAK N14 28 D7
Chase Side ENC/FH EN2 29 J1
STHGT/OAK N14 28 A5
Chase Side Av ENC/FH EN2 29 J1
Chaseside Av RYNPK SW20 146 C7
Chase Side Pl ENC/FH EN2 29 J2
The Chase BMLY BR1 168 A2
BXLYHN DA7 137 J2
CLAP SW4 129 G2
EDGW HA8 36 D7
FSTGT E7 77 H3
PIN HA5 47 G5
ROM RM1 63 G2
ROMW/RG RM7 81 F2
STAN HA7 35 G5
STRHM/NOR SW16 149 F6
SUN TW16 141 F7
WATW WD18 20 C3
WLGTN SM6 176 E4
Chaseville Pde WCHMH N21 * 29 F4
Chaseville Park Rd
WCHMH N21 29 F4
Chase Wy STHGT/OAK N14 28 B7
Chasewood Av ENC/FH EN2 29 H1
Chasewood Pk HRW HA1 * 66 E2
Chastilian Rd DART DA1 138 D6
Chatfield Rd BTSEA SW11 128 B2
CROY/NA CR0 164 C7
Chatham Av HAYES BR2 167 J6
Chatham Cl CHEAM SM3 161 J6
GLDGN NW11 52 E4
WOOL/PLUM SE18 115 G2
Chatham Pl HOM E9 74 E5
Chatham Rd BTSEA SW11 128 E5
KUT/HW KT1 159 H1
SWFD E18 58 D1
WALTH E17 57 G2
Chatham St WALW SE17 19 G5
WOOL/PLUM SE18 115 G2
Chatsfield Pl EA W5 86 A5
Chatsworth Av BFN/LL DA15 136 B7

BMLY BR1 153 F4
HDN NW4 52 A1
RYNPK SW20 146 C7
WBLY HA9 68 B4
Chatsworth Cl BORE WD6 24 C2
CHSWK W4 * 105 K5
HDN NW4 52 A1
WWKM BR4 180 D1
Chatsworth Crs HSLW TW3 123 J3
Chatsworth Dr EN EN1 30 C6
Chatsworth Est CLPT E5 * 75 F3
Chatsworth Gdns ACT W3 86 D6
NWMAL KT3 * 160 C4
RYLN/HDSTN HA2 48 B7
Chatsworth Pl MTCM CR4 162 E2
TEDD TW11 143 G3
Chatsworth Ri EA W5 86 B3
Chatsworth Rd CHEAM SM3 174 B3
CHSWK W4 105 K5
CLPT E5 74 E2
CRICK NW2 70 B5
CROY/NA CR0 177 K3
DART DA1 139 F3
EA W5 86 B3
SRTFD E15 76 D4
YEAD UB4 83 F3
Chatsworth Wy WNWD SE27 149 H2
Chattern Rd ASHF TW15 140 A3
Chatterton Ms FSBYPK N4 73 H2
Chatterton Rd FSBYPK N4 73 H2
HAYES BR2 168 C4
Chatto Rd BTSEA SW11 128 E4
Chaucer Av HSLWW TW4 122 A1
RCH/KEW TW9 125 H1
YEAD UB4 82 E4
Chaucer Cl FBAR/BDGN N11 40 C4
Chaucer Dr STHWK SE1 19 M6
Chaucer Gdns SUT SM1 174 E2
Chaucer Gn CROY/NA CR0 165 J6
Chaucer Gv BORE WD6 24 C3
Chaucer Pk DART DA1 139 J6
Chaucer Rd ACT W3 86 E7
BFN/LL DA15 136 D7
FSTGT E7 76 E5
HNHL SE24 130 B4
SUT SM1 174 E3
WALTH E17 44 A7
WAN E11 58 E5
WELL DA16 116 A7
Chaucer Wy DART DA1 139 K3
WIM/MER SW19 147 H5
Chauncey Cl ED N9 42 C2
Chaundrye Cl ELTH/MOT SE9 134 E5
Chauntler Rd CAN/RD E16 95 F5
Cheam Common Rd WPK KT4 173 K1
Cheam Man CHEAM SM3 * 174 C5
Cheam Park Wy CHEAM SM3 174 B5
Cheam Rd BELMT SM2 174 B7
Cheam St PECK SE15 * 131 J2
Cheapside CITYW EC2V 12 F5
EFNCH N2 * 53 K2
PLMGR N13 41 J3
WDGN N22 * 55 G2
Cheddar Cl FBAR/BDGN N11 39 K5
Cheddar Waye YEAD UB4 83 F5
Cheddington Rd UED N18 42 A3
Cheeseman Cl HPTN TW12 141 J5
Cheesemans Ter
WKENS W14 * 107 J4
Cheethams Rd MNPK E12 77 J2
Chelford Rd BMLY BR1 152 B4
Chelmer Crs BARK IG11 97 H1
Chelmer Rd HOM E9 75 F4
Chelmsford Cl BELMT SM2 174 E7
EHAM E6 95 K5
HMSMTH W6 107 G5
Chelmsford Gdns IL IG1 59 J6
Chelmsford Rd
STHGT/OAK N14 28 C6
SWFD E18 44 D7
WALTH E17 57 J5
Chelmsford Sq WLSDN NW10 70 A7
Chelsea Br BGVA SW1W 16 B9
Chelsea Bridge Ga VX/NE SW8 109 F5
Chelsea Bridge Rd
BGVA SW1W 16 A7
Chelsea Cl EDGW HA8 50 C1
HPTN TW12 142 C4
WLSDN NW10 69 F7
WPK KT4 160 D6
Chelsea Crs CRICK NW2 * 70 D5
WBPTN SW10 * 108 B7
Chelsea Emb CHEL SW3 16 A9
Chelsea Gdns CHEAM SM3 174 C3
WEA W13 85 F4
Chelsea Harbour Dr
WBPTN SW10 108 B7
Chelsea Manor Gdns
CHEL SW3 15 J9
Chelsea Manor St CHEL SW3 15 J7
Chelsea Ms EMPK RM11 63 K7
Chelsea Park Gdns CHEL SW3 15 G9
Chelsea Sq CAR SM5 175 K7
CHEL SW3 15 H8
Chelsea Village
FUL/PGN SW6 * 108 A6
Chelsfield Av ED N9 31 F6
Chelsfield Gdns SYD SE26 150 E2
Chelsham Rd CLAP SW4 129 J2
SAND/SEL CR2 177 K6
Chelston Rd RSLP HA4 64 E1
Chelsworth Dr
WOOL/PLUM SE18 115 J5
Cheltenham Av TWK TW1 124 B6
Cheltenham Cl NTHLT UB5 66 B5
NWMAL KT3 159 K2
Cheltenham Gdns EHAM E6 95 J1
Cheltenham Pl ACT W3 105 K1
KTN/HRWW/WS HA3 50 A3
Cheltenham Rd LEY E10 58 A5
PECK SE15 131 K3
Cheltenham Ter CHEL SW3 15 M7
Chelton Av MLHL NW7 38 B6
Chelverton Rd PUT/ROE SW15 127 G3
Chelwood Cl CHING E4 31 K5
NTHWD HA6 32 A6
Chelwood Gdns
RCH/KEW TW9 125 H1
Chenappa Cl PLSTW E13 94 E2
Chenduit Wy STAN HA7 35 F4
Cheney Rw WALTH E17 43 H7
Cheneys Rd WAN E11 76 C2
Cheney St PIN HA5 47 G3
Chenies Ms GWRST WC1E 11 G1
Chenies Pl BAR EN5 25 J4
CAMTN NW1 5 H5
Chenies St GWRST WC1E 11 G2
The Chenies ORP BR6 169 K5
Chenies Wy WATW WD18 20 C6
Cheniston Gdns KENS W8 14 B3
Chepstow Cl PUT/ROE SW15 127 H4
Chepstow Cnr BAY/PAD W2 * 8 B5
Chepstow Crs GDMY/SEVK IG3 60 E5
NTGHL W11 8 A6
Chepstow Gdns STHL UB1 83 K5
Chepstow Pl BAY/PAD W2 8 B5
Chepstow Ri CROY/NA CR0 178 A2
Chepstow Rd BAY/PAD W2 8 B4
CROY/NA CR0 178 A2
HNWL W7 104 B2
Chepstow Vls NTGHL W11 88 D6
Chequers Cl CDALE/KGS NW9 51 G2
Chequers La DAGW RM9 98 B3
Chequers Pde PLMGR N13 * 41 J4
The Chequers PIN HA5 * 47 H2
Chequer St STLK EC1Y 12 F1
Chequers Wy PLMGR N13 41 H4
Cherbury Cl THMD SE28 97 K5
Cherbury St IS N1 7 H6
Cherimoya Gdns
E/WMO/HCT KT8 157 G2
Cherington Rd HNWL W7 * 85 F7
Cheriton Av CLAY IG5 60 A1
HAYES BR2 167 J4
Cheriton Cl EA W5 85 J4
EBAR EN4 27 K2
Cheriton Ct WOT/HER KT12 156 B7
Cheriton Dr WOOL/PLUM SE18 115 J6
Cheriton Sq TOOT SW17 148 A1
Cherry Av STHL UB1 83 H7
Cherry Blossom Cl
PLMGR N13 41 H4
Cherry Cl BRXS/STRHM SW2 * 130 B6
CAR SM5 175 K1
CDALE/KGS NW9 51 H1
EA W5 104 E2
MRDN SM4 161 H3
RSLP HA4 64 D2
Cherry Ct PIN HA5 33 H7
Cherry Crs BTFD TW8 104 C6
Cherry Croft Gdns PIN HA5 * 33 K6
Cherrydale WATW WD18 20 D3
Cherrydown Av CHING E4 43 H2
Cherrydown Cl CHING E4 43 H2
Cherrydown Rd SCUP DA14 155 K1
Cherrydown Wk
ROMW/RG RM7 62 D1
Cherry Gdns DAGW RM9 80 B4
NTHLT UB5 66 B6
Cherry Garden St
BERM/RHTH SE16 111 J1
Cherry Garth BTFD TW8 104 E3
Cherry Gv HYS/HAR UB3 83 F7
UX/CGN UB8 82 A4
Cherry Hl BAR EN5 27 F5
KTN/HRWW/WS HA3 34 E5
Cherry Hill Gdns
CROY/NA CR0 177 F3
Cherry Hills OXHEY WD19 33 J4
Cherrylands Cl
CDALE/KGS NW9 * 68 E1
Cherry La WDR/YW UB7 100 C3
Cherry Orch CHARL SE7 114 B5
WDR/YW UB7 100 B1
Cherry Orchard Gdns
CROY/NA CR0 164 E7
E/WMO/HCT KT8 156 E2
Cherry Orchard Rd
CROY/NA CR0 164 E7
E/WMO/HCT KT8 157 F2
HAYES BR2 181 J1
Cherry St ROMW/RG RM7 63 F4
Cherry Tree Cl ALP/SUD HA0 67 G3
HOM E9 74 E7
RAIN RM13 99 J1
Cherry Tree Ct CHARL SE7 * 114 B5
Cherry Tree Dr
STRHM/NOR SW16 148 E2
Cherry Tree Hl EFNCH N2 53 J4
Cherry Tree La RAIN RM13 99 G2
Cherry Tree Ri BKHH IG9 45 G3
Cherry Tree Rd EFNCH N2 53 K3
SRTFD E15 76 C4
Cherry Tree Wk BECK BR3 166 C3
STLK EC1Y 12 F1
WWKM BR4 180 D3
Cherry Tree Wy PLSTW E13 95 H3
STAN HA7 35 H5
Cherry Wk HAYES BR2 167 K7
RAIN RM13 99 H1
Cherry Wy HOR/WEW KT19 173 F5
Cherrywood Cl BOW E3 93 G2
KUTN/CMB KT2 144 C6
Cherrywood Dr
PUT/ROE SW15 127 G4
Cherrywood La RYNPK SW20 161 H3
Chertsey Dr CHEAM SM3 174 C1
Chertsey Rd FELT TW13 140 C3
IL IG1 78 D3
SUN TW16 140 C5
TWK TW1 124 B5
WAN E11 76 B1
WHTN TW2 123 H7
Chertsey St TOOT SW17 148 A4
Chervil Cl FELT TW13 140 E2
Chervil Ms THMD SE28 97 H7
Cherwell Ct HOR/WEW KT19 172 E3
Cherwell Wy RSLP HA4 46 A5
Cheryls Cl FUL/PGN SW6 108 A7
Cheseman St SYD SE26 150 D2
Chesfield Rd KUTN/CMB KT2 144 A6
Chesham Av STMC/STPC BR5 169 G5
Chesham Cl KTBR SW1X * 16 A4
ROMW/RG RM7 63 F3
Chesham Crs PGE/AN SE20 150 E7
Chesham Ms KTBR SW1X 16 A3
Chesham Pl KTBR SW1X 16 A3
Chesham Rd KUT/HW KT1 159 H1
PGE/AN SE20 165 K1
WIM/MER SW19 147 H5
Chesham St KTBR SW1X 16 A4
WLSDN NW10 69 F2
Chesham Ter WEA W13 104 C1
Chesham Wy WATW WD18 20 C5
Cheshire Cl MTCM CR4 163 K2
WALTH E17 43 K7
Cheshire Gdns CHSGTN KT9 171 K5
Cheshire Rd WDGN N22 41 F6
Cheshire St BETH E2 92 C3
Chesholm Rd
STNW/STAM N16 74 A2
Cheshunt Rd BELV DA17 117 H4
FSTGT E7 77 F5
Chesilton Rd FUL/PGN SW6 107 J7
Chesil Wy YEAD UB4 82 D2
Chesley Gdns EHAM E6 95 H1
Chesney Crs CROY/NA CR0 180 A6
Chesney St BTSEA SW11 109 F7
Chesnut Av North WALTH E17 58 A3
Chesnut Gv TOTM N17 56 B2
Chesnut Rd TOTM N17 56 C2
Chesnut Rw FNCH N3 * 38 E6
Chessell Cl THHTH CR7 164 C3
Chessholme Rd ASHF TW15 140 A5
Chessington Av BXLYHN DA7 117 F6
FNCH N3 52 C2
Chessington Cl
HOR/WEW KT19 172 E5
Chessington Ct PIN HA5 47 K3
Chessington Hall Gdns
CHSGTN KT9 171 K6
Chessington Hill Pk
CHSGTN KT9 172 C5
Chessington Pde
CHSGTN KT9 * 171 K4
Chessington Rd CHSGTN KT9 172 C5
HOR/WEW KT19 172 D5
Chessington Wy WWKM BR4 179 K1
Chesson Rd WKENS W14 107 J5
Chesswood Wy PIN HA5 47 H1
Chester Av RCHPK/HAM TW10 125 G5
WHTN TW2 122 E7
Chester Cl ASHF TW15 140 B4
BARN SW13 * 126 E2
KTBR SW1X 16 B2
SUT SM1 174 E1
Chester Cl North CAMTN NW1 4 D7
Chester Cl South CAMTN NW1 4 D8
Chester Crs HACK E8 74 B4
Chester Dr RYLN/HDSTN HA2 48 A5
Chesterfield Dr DART DA1 138 E4
ESH/CLAY KT10 171 G1
Chesterfield Gdns FSBYPK N4 55 H4
GNWCH SE10 * 113 G6
MYFR/PICC W1J * 10 C8
Chesterfield Gv EDUL SE22 131 G4
Chesterfield Hl
MYFR/PKLN W1K 10 C7
Chesterfield Ms FSBYPK N4 55 H4
Chesterfield Rd BAR EN5 26 B4
CHSWK W4 105 K5
FNCH N3 38 E5
HOR/WEW KT19 173 F6
LEY E10 58 A6
Chesterfield St
MYFR/PICC W1J 10 C8
Chesterfield Wy
HYS/HAR UB3 * 101 K1
PECK SE15 111 K6
Chesterford Gdns HAMP NW3 71 F3
Chesterford Rd MNPK E12 77 K4
Chester Gdns MRDN SM4 162 B4
PEND EN3 30 D5
WEA W13 * 85 H5
Chester Ga CAMTN NW1 4 C8
Chester Ms KTBR SW1X 16 C3
Chester Pl CAMTN NW1 4 C7
NTHWD HA6 * 32 C6
Chester Rd ARCH N19 72 B1
BFN/LL DA15 135 K4
BORE WD6 24 E2
CAMTN NW1 4 B8
CAN/RD E16 94 C3
ED N9 30 D7
FSTGT E7 77 H6
GDMY/SEVK IG3 61 F7
HSLWW TW4 122 A2
HTHAIR TW6 120 D2
NTHWD HA6 32 D6
TOTM N17 55 K2
WALTH E17 57 F4
WAN E11 59 F5
WATW WD18 20 E4
WIM/MER SW19 146 A5
Chester Rw BGVA SW1W 16 A6
Chester Sq BGVA SW1W 16 B5
Chester Square Ms
BGVA SW1W * 16 C4
The Chesters NWMAL KT3 145 G7
Chester St BETH E2 92 C3
KTBR SW1X 16 B3
Chester Ter CAMTN NW1 4 C7
Chesterton Cl GFD/PVL UB6 84 B1
WAND/EARL SW18 127 K4
Chesterton Ct EA W5 * 85 K5
Chesterton Dr
STWL/WRAY TW19 120 C7
Chesterton Rd NKENS W10 88 B4
PLSTW E13 94 E2
Chesterton Sq KENS W8 107 J3
Chesterton Ter KUT/HW KT1 159 H1
PLSTW E13 94 E2
Chester Wy LBTH SE11 18 B6
Chesthunte Rd TOTM N17 41 J7
Chestnut Aly FUL/PGN SW6 * 107 J5
Chestnut Av ALP/SUD HA0 67 H4
BKHH IG9 45 H2
BTFD TW8 104 E4
CEND/HSY/T N8 54 E4
E/WMO/HCT KT8 158 A2
EDGW HA8 36 A5
ESH/CLAY KT10 157 J6
FSTGT E7 77 F3
HCH RM12 81 H1
HOR/WEW KT19 173 G3
HPTN TW12 142 A6
MNPK E12 77 J1
MORT/ESHN SW14 126 A2
NTHWD HA6 46 D1
TEDD TW11 143 F6
WWKM BR4 180 C4
Chestnut Av South
WALTH E17 58 A3
Chestnut Cl BFN/LL DA15 155 G1
BKHH IG9 45 H2
CAR SM5 162 E7
CAT SE6 152 A3
HYS/HAR UB3 82 C6
HYS/HAR UB3 100 E6
NWCR SE14 112 C7
STHGT/OAK N14 28 C4
STNW/STAM N16 73 K1
STRHM/NOR SW16 149 G3
SUN TW16 140 D5
Chestnut Cots
TRDG/WHET N20 * 26 C7
Chestnut Dr BXLYHN DA7 136 E2
KTN/HRWW/WS HA3 35 F6
PIN HA5 47 H5
WAN E11 58 E5
Chestnut Gln HCH RM12 81 H1
Chestnut Gv ALP/SUD HA0 67 H4
BAL SW12 129 F6
EA W5 104 E2
EBAR EN4 27 K4
ISLW TW7 124 B3
MTCM CR4 163 J4
NWMAL KT3 160 A2
SAND/SEL CR2 178 D6
Chestnut La TRDG/WHET N20 26 C7
Chestnut Ms WFD IG8 44 E4
Chestnut Pl SYD SE26 150 B3
Chestnut Ri BUSH WD23 22 B5
WOOL/PLUM SE18 115 K4
Chestnut Rd DART DA1 139 G7
KUTN/CMB KT2 144 A6
RYNPK SW20 161 G1
WHTN TW2 142 E1
WNWD SE27 149 H2
The Chestnuts BECK BR3 * 166 A2
PIN HA5 * 33 K6
Chestnut Ter SUT SM1 * 175 F3
Chestnut Wy FELT TW13 141 F2
Cheston Av CROY/NA CR0 166 B7
Cheswick Cl DART DA1 138 C3
Chesworth Cl ERITH DA8 118 B7
Chettle Cl STHWK SE1 19 G3
Chetwode Rd TOOT SW17 147 K2
Chetwynd Av EBAR EN4 27 K7
Chetwynd Rd KTTN NW5 72 B3
Chetwynd Vls KTTN NW5 * 72 B3
Chevalier Cl STAN HA7 35 K2
Cheval Pl SKENS SW7 15 K3
Cheval St POP/IOD E14 112 D2
Cheveney Wk HAYES BR2 167 K2
Chevening Rd GNWCH SE10 113 J4
KIL/WHAMP NW6 88 B1
NRWD SE19 149 K6
The Chevenings SCUP DA14 155 H2
Cheverton Rd ARCH N19 54 D7
Chevet St HOM E9 75 G4
Chevington CRICK NW2 * 70 D5
Cheviot Cl BELMT SM2 175 H7
BUSH WD23 22 C5
BXLYHN DA7 138 B1
ENC/FH EN2 29 K1
HYS/HAR UB3 101 G6
Cheviot Gdns CRICK NW2 70 B1
Cheviot Rd EMPK RM11 63 J6
WNWD SE27 149 G4
Cheviot Wy GNTH/NBYPK IG2 60 E4
Chevron Cl CAN/RD E16 94 E5
Chevy Rd NWDGN UB2 103 H1
Chewton Rd WALTH E17 57 G3
Cheyne Av SWFD E18 58 D2
WHTN TW2 122 E7
Cheyne Cl HAYES BR2 181 J2
Cheyne Ct BUSH WD23 * 21 J3
Cheyne Gdns CHEL SW3 15 K9
Cheyne Hl BRYLDS KT5 159 G3
Cheyne Ms CHEL SW3 108 D5
Cheyne Park Dr WWKM BR4 180 A2
Cheyne Pth HNWL W7 85 F4
Cheyne Pl CHEL SW3 15 L9
Cheyne Rd ASHF TW15 140 B5
Cheyne Rw CHEL SW3 108 D5
Cheyne Wk CHEL SW3 108 D5
CROY/NA CR0 178 C1
HDN NW4 52 A5
WBPTN SW10 108 C6
WCHMH N21 29 G4
Cheyneys Av EDGW HA8 35 K5
Chichele Gdns CROY/NA CR0 178 A3
Chichele Rd CRICK NW2 70 B4
Chicheley Rd
KTN/HRWW/WS HA3 34 C6
Chicheley St STHWK SE1 17 M1
Chichester Av RSLP HA4 64 B1
Chichester Cl BKHTH/KID SE3 114 B6
EHAM E6 95 J5
HPTN TW12 141 K5
Chichester Ct EW KT17 * 173 H7
STAN HA7 50 A2
Chichester Gdns IL IG1 59 J6
Chichester Rd BAY/PAD W2 8 D2
CROY/NA CR0 178 A2
ED N9 30 B7
KIL/WHAMP NW6 2 A6
WAN E11 76 C2
Chichester St PIM SW1V 16 F8
Chichester Wy
EBED/NFELT TW14 122 B6
POP/IOD E14 113 G3
Chichester Whf ERITH DA8 118 B4
Chicksand St WCHPL E1 13 M3
Chiddingfold
NFNCH/WDSPK N12 38 E2
Chiddingstone Av
BXLYHN DA7 117 G6
Chiddingstone St
FUL/PGN SW6 127 K1
Chieftan Dr PUR RM19 119 K3
Chieveley Pde BXLYHN DA7 * 137 J2
Chieveley Rd BXLYHN DA7 137 J3
Chignell Pl WEA W13 85 G7
Chigwell Hl WAP E1W 92 D6
Chigwell Rd SWFD E18 59 F2
WFD IG8 45 K5
Chilcott Cl ALP/SUD HA0 67 J3
Childebert Rd TOOT SW17 148 B1
Childeric Rd NWCR SE14 112 B6
Childerley St FUL/PGN SW6 107 H7
Childers St DEPT SE8 112 B5
The Childers WFD IG8 45 K4
Child La GNWCH SE10 113 J2
Childs Ct HYS/HAR UB3 82 E6
Childs La NRWD SE19 * 150 A5
Child's Ms ECT SW5 * 14 C6
Child's Pl ECT SW5 14 B6
Child's St ECT SW5 14 B5
Child's Wk ECT SW5 * 14 B5
Childs Wy GLDGN NW11 52 D5
Chilham Cl BXLY DA5 137 G6
GFD/PVL UB6 85 G1
Chilham Rd ELTH/MOT SE9 153 J3
Chilham Wy HAYES BR2 167 K6
Chillerton Rd TOOT SW17 148 A4
Chillington Dr BTSEA SW11 128 B3
Chillingworth Gdns
TWK TW1 * 143 F1
Chillingworth Rd HOLWY N7 73 F4
Chilmark Gdns NWMAL KT3 160 C5
Chilmark Rd
STRHM/NOR SW16 163 J1
Chiltern Av BUSH WD23 22 C5
WHTN TW2 123 F7
Chiltern Cl BORE WD6 24 B1
BUSH WD23 22 B5
BXLYHN DA7 118 B7
CROY/NA CR0 178 A2
WATW WD18 20 D3
WPK KT4 174 A1
Chiltern Dene ENC/FH EN2 29 F3
Chiltern Dr BRYLDS KT5 159 J5
Chiltern Gdns CRICK NW2 70 B2
HAYES BR2 167 J3
Chiltern Pl CLPT E5 74 D1
Chiltern Rd BOW E3 93 J3
GNTH/NBYPK IG2 60 E3
PIN HA5 47 G4
The Chilterns BELMT SM2 * 175 F7
Chiltern St MHST W1U 9 M2
Chiltern Wy WFD IG8 44 E2
Chilthorne Cl CAT SE6 132 C6
Chilton Av EA W5 104 E3
Chilton Gv DEPT SE8 112 A3
Chilton Rd EDGW HA8 36 C5
RCH/KEW TW9 125 H2
Chilton St BETH E2 7 M9
Chilvers Cl WHTN TW2 142 E1
Chilver St GNWCH SE10 113 J4
Chilwell Gdns OXHEY WD19 33 G3
Chilworth Gdns SUT SM1 175 G2
Chilworth Ms BAY/PAD W2 8 F5
Chilworth St BAY/PAD W2 8 F5
Chimes Av PLMGR N13 41 G3
China Hall Ms
BERM/RHTH SE16 111 K2
China Ms BRXS/STRHM SW2 130 A6
Chinbrook Crs LEE/GVPK SE12 153 F2
Chinbrook Rd LEE/GVPK SE12 153 F2
Chinchilla Dr HSLWW TW4 122 B1
The Chine ALP/SUD HA0 67 H4
MUSWH N10 54 B3
WCHMH N21 29 H5
Chingdale Rd CHING E4 44 C2
Chingford Av CHING E4 43 J2
Chingford La WFD IG8 44 C3
Chingford Mount Rd
CHING E4 43 J4
Chingford Rd CHING E4 43 J5
WALTH E17 57 K1
Chingley Cl BMLY BR1 152 C5
Ching Wy CHING E4 43 H5
Chinnor Crs GFD/PVL UB6 84 C1
Chipka St POP/IOD E14 113 F1
Chipley St NWCR SE14 112 B5
Chippendale St CLPT E5 75 F2
Chippenham Cl PIN HA5 * 46 D3
Chippenham Ms MV/WKIL W9 8 A1
Chippenham Rd MV/WKIL W9 2 A9
Chipping Cl BAR EN5 26 C2
Chipstead Av THHTH CR7 164 C3
Chipstead Cl BELMT SM2 175 F7
NRWD SE19 150 B6
Chipstead Gdns CRICK NW2 69 K1
Chipstead Rd ERITH DA8 118 B6
Chipstead St FUL/PGN SW6 107 K7
Chirk Cl YEAD UB4 83 J3
Chisenhale Rd BOW E3 93 G1
Chisholm Rd CROY/NA CR0 178 A1
RCHPK/HAM TW10 125 G5
Chislehurst Av
NFNCH/WDSPK N12 39 G6
Chislehurst High St CHST BR7 154 B5
Chislehurst Rd BMLY BR1 168 D1
RCHPK/HAM TW10 125 F5
SCUP DA14 155 G4
STMC/STPC BR5 169 K3
Chislet Cl BECK BR3 151 J6
Chisley Rd SEVS/STOTM N15 56 A5
Chiswell Sq BKHTH/KID SE3 134 A1
Chiswell St CMBW SE5 * 110 E6
STLK EC1Y 13 G2
Chiswick Br CHSWK W4 125 K1
Chiswick Cl CROY/NA CR0 177 F2
Chiswick Common Rd
CHSWK W4 106 A3
Chiswick High Rd CHSWK W4 105 H4
Chiswick House Grounds
CHSWK W4 * 106 A5
Chiswick La CHSWK W4 106 B4
Chiswick La South CHSWK W4 106 C5
Chiswick Ml CHSWK W4 106 C5
Chiswick Pk CHSWK W4 * 105 K2
Chiswick Pier CHSWK W4 * 106 C6
Chiswick Quay CHSWK W4 105 K7
Chiswick Rd CHSWK W4 105 K3
ED N9 42 C1
Chiswick Sq CHSWK W4 106 B5
Chiswick Staithe CHSWK W4 105 K7
Chiswick Village CHSWK W4 105 H5
Chiswick Whf CHSWK W4 106 C5
Chitterfield Ga WDR/YW UB7 100 D6
Chitty's La BCTR RM8 79 K1
Chitty St FITZ W1T 10 F2
Chivalry Rd BTSEA SW11 128 D4
Chivenor Gv KUTN/CMB KT2 143 K4
Chivers Rd CHING E4 43 K2
Choats Manor Wy DAGW RM9 98 B2
Choats Rd BARK IG11 97 J1
DAGW RM9 98 A2
Chobham Gdns
WIM/MER SW19 146 B1
Chobham Rd SRTFD E15 76 B4
Cholmeley Cl HGT N6 * 54 B6
Cholmeley Crs HGT N6 54 B6
Cholmeley Pk HGT N6 54 B7
Cholmley Gdns
KIL/WHAMP NW6 70 E4
Cholmley Rd THDIT KT7 158 C5
Cholmley Ter THDIT KT7 * 158 C6
Cholmley Vls THDIT KT7 * 158 C6
Cholmondeley Av
WLSDN NW10 87 J1
Chopwell Cl SRTFD E15 * 76 B6
Choumert Gv PECK SE15 131 H1
Choumert Ms PECK SE15 131 H1
Choumert Rd PECK SE15 131 G2
Chow Sq HACK E8 74 B4
HACK E8 * 74 B4
Chrislaine Cl
STWL/WRAY TW19 120 A5
Chrisp St POP/IOD E14 93 K4
Christabel Cl ISLW TW7 123 K2
Christchurch Av ALP/SUD HA0 68 A5
ERITH DA8 118 A5
KIL/WHAMP NW6 70 B7
KTN/HRWW/WS HA3 49 F3
NFNCH/WDSPK N12 39 G5
RAIN RM13 99 H1
TEDD TW11 143 G4
Christchurch Cl ENC/FH EN2 29 J1
NFNCH/WDSPK N12 * 39 H6
WIM/MER SW19 147 H6
Christchurch Gdns
KTN/HRWW/WS HA3 49 G3
Christchurch Hl HAMP NW3 71 H2
Christ Church La BAR EN5 26 C1
Christchurch Ldg EBAR EN4 * 27 K3
Christchurch Pk BELMT SM2 175 G6
Christ Church Rd BECK BR3 * 166 D1
BRYLDS KT5 159 G6
CEND/HSY/T N8 54 E5
Christchurch Rd BFN/LL DA15 155 F3
BRXS/STRHM SW2 130 A7
DART DA1 139 F6
IL IG1 60 B7
MORT/ESHN SW14 125 J4
WIM/MER SW19 147 H6
Christchurch Sq HOM E9 74 E7
Christchurch St CHEL SW3 15 L9
Christchurch Ter CHEL SW3 * 15 L9
Christchurch Wy GNWCH SE10 113 H4
Christian Flds
STRHM/NOR SW16 149 G6
Christian St WCHPL E1 92 C5
Christie Ct WATW WD18 20 E4
Christie Dr CROY/NA CR0 165 H4
Christie Rd HOM E9 75 G5
Christina Sq FSBYPK N4 55 H7
Christina St SDTCH EC2A 7 J9
Christine Worsley Cl
WCHMH N21 29 H7
Christopher Av HNWL W7 104 B2

Christopher Cl
BERM/RHTH SE16 112 A1
BFN/LL DA15 136 A4
Christopher Gdns DAGW RM9 79 K4
Christopher Pl CAMTN NW1 * 5 H7
Christopher Rd NWDGN UB2 102 A3
Christophers Ms NTGHL W11 * 88 C7
Christopher St SDTCH EC2A 13 H1
Christy Ter WFD IG8 45 J6
Chryssell Rd BRXN/ST SW9 110 B6
Chubworthy St NWCR SE14 112 B5
Chudleigh Crs GDMY/SEVK IG3 78 E3
Chudleigh Gdns SUT SM1 175 G2
Chudleigh Rd BROCKY SE4 132 C4
KIL/WHAMP NW6 70 A6
WHTN TW2 123 K5
Chudleigh St WCHPL E1 93 F5
Chudleigh Wy RSLP HA4 46 E7
Chulsa Rd SYD SE26 150 D4
Chumleigh St CMBW SE5 19 J9
Chumleigh Wk BRYLDS KT5 159 G3
Church Ap DUL SE21 149 K2
Church Av BECK BR3 151 J7
CAMTN NW1 72 B5
CHING E4 44 B5
MORT/ESHN SW14 126 A3
NTHLT UB5 65 K6
NWDGN UB2 102 D2
PIN HA5 47 J5
RSLP HA4 46 B7
SCUP DA14 155 G4
Churchbury Cl EN EN1 30 A1
Churchbury La EN EN1 30 A2
Churchbury Rd
ELTH/MOT SE9 134 C6
EN EN1 30 A1
Church Cl EDGW HA8 36 E4
HSLW TW3 122 E1
HYS/HAR UB3 82 B4
NTHWD HA6 32 D6
TRDG/WHET N20 39 J2
WDR/YW UB7 100 B2
Church Crs FNCH N3 38 D7
HOM E9 75 F6
MUSWH N10 54 B3
TRDG/WHET N20 39 J2
Churchcroft Cl BAL SW12 * 129 F6
Churchdown BMLY BR1 152 C3
Church Dr CDALE/KGS NW9 51 F7
RYLN/HDSTN HA2 48 A5
WWKM BR4 180 C2
Church Elm La DAGE RM10 80 C5
Church End HDN NW4 51 K2
WALTH E17 * 57 K3
Church Farm EBAR EN4 * 27 K6
Church Farm La CHEAM SM3 174 C5
Churchfield Av
NFNCH/WDSPK N12 39 G5
Churchfield Cl HYS/HAR UB3 82 D6
RYLN/HDSTN HA2 48 C3
Churchfield Rd ACT W3 86 E7
HNWL W7 103 K1
WEA W13 85 H7
WELL DA16 136 B2
Churchfields E/WMO/HCT KT8 157 F2
GNWCH SE10 113 F5
SWFD E18 44 E7
Churchfields Av FELT TW13 141 K2
Churchfields Rd BECK BR3 166 A1
Churchfield Wy
NFNCH/WDSPK N12 39 G5
Church Gdns ALP/SUD HA0 67 G3
EA W5 104 E1
Church Garth ARCH N19 * 72 D1
Church Ga FUL/PGN SW6 127 H2
Church Gn BRXN/ST SW9 * 130 B1
HYS/HAR UB3 82 D5
Church Gv KUT/HW KT1 143 J7
LEW SE13 132 E3
Church Hl CAR SM5 175 K4
DART DA1 138 B3
HRW HA1 48 E7
WALTH E17 57 J3
WCHMH N21 29 F6
WIM/MER SW19 146 D4
WOOL/PLUM SE18 114 E2
Church Hill Rd CHEAM SM3 174 B3
EBAR EN4 27 J5
SURB KT6 159 F4
WALTH E17 57 K3
Church Hollow PUR RM19 119 K4
Church Hyde
WOOL/PLUM SE18 115 K5
Churchill Av
KTN/HRWW/WS HA3 49 H5
Churchill Cl EBED/NFELT TW14 121 J7
Churchill Gdns ACT W3 86 C5
PIM SW1V 16 E8
Churchill Gardens Rd
PIM SW1V 16 D8
Churchill Ms WFD IG8 44 D5
Churchill Pl POP/IOD E14 93 K7
Churchill Rd CAN/RD E16 95 G5
CRICK NW2 69 K5
EDGW HA8 36 B5
KTTN NW5 72 B3
SAND/SEL CR2 177 J7
Churchill Ter CHING E4 43 J3
Churchill Wk HOM E9 74 E4
Churchill Wy BMLY BR1 167 K1
SUN TW16 140 E4
Churchlands Wy WPK KT4 174 B1
Church La CDALE/KGS NW9 50 E7
CEND/HSY/T N8 55 F3
CHSGTN KT9 172 B5
CHST BR7 154 C7
DAGE RM10 80 D5
EA W5 104 D1
ED N9 42 C1
EFNCH N2 53 H2
ENC/FH EN2 29 K2
HAYES BR2 168 D7
KTN/HRWW/WS HA3 35 F7
PIN HA5 47 J2
PUR RM19 * 119 K4
ROM RM1 63 G3
TEDD TW11 143 F4
THDIT KT7 158 A5
TOOT SW17 147 K4
TOTM N17 42 A7
TWK TW1 124 B7
WALTH E17 57 K3
WAN E11 58 C7
WIM/MER SW19 146 E7
WLGTN SM6 176 D2
Churchley Rd SYD SE26 150 D3
Church Manor Wy ABYW SE2 116 B2
Church Manorway ERITH DA8 118 A2
Church Md CMBW SE5 * 110 D6
Churchmead Cl EBAR EN4 27 J5
Church Meadow SURB KT6 171 J1
Churchmead Rd
WLSDN NW10 69 J5
Churchmore Rd
STRHM/NOR SW16 148 C7
Church Mt EFNCH N2 53 H4
Church Paddock Ct
WLGTN SM6 176 D2
Church Pas BAR EN5 * 26 D2
Church Pth CHSWK W4 105 K2
MTCM CR4 162 D2
NFNCH/WDSPK N12 * 39 G4
RYNPK SW20 161 J1
WAN E11 58 E4
WIM/MER SW19 161 J1
Church Pl EA W5 104 E1
MTCM CR4 162 D2
Church Rd LEY E10 75 K1
Church Ri CHSGTN KT9 172 B5
FSTH SE23 132 A7
Church Rd ACT W3 105 K1
BARK IG11 78 C5
BARN SW13 126 D1
BXLYHN DA7 137 G1
CHEAM SM3 174 C5
CROY/NA CR0 * 177 J3
E/WMO/HCT KT8 157 J2
ERITH DA8 117 K4
ESH/CLAY KT10 171 F5
FELT TW13 141 G4
GNTH/NBYPK IG2 60 E5
HAYES BR2 167 H2
HAYES BR2 181 H6
HDN NW4 51 K3
HEST TW5 102 A4
HGT N6 54 A5
HNWL W7 84 E6
HOR/WEW KT19 173 F6
HYS/HAR UB3 82 D7
IS N1 73 J5
ISLW TW7 103 J7
KUT/HW KT1 159 G1
LEY E10 57 J7
MNPK E12 77 J4
MTCM CR4 162 D2
NRWD SE19 150 A6
NTHLT UB5 65 K6
NTHWD HA6 32 D6
NWDGN UB2 102 E2
PEND EN3 30 E5
RCHPK/HAM TW10 125 F4
RCHPK/HAM TW10 144 A3
SCUP DA14 155 G3
STAN HA7 35 H4
SURB KT6 158 D7
TEDD TW11 142 E3
TOTM N17 42 A7
WALTH E17 57 G1
WDR/YW UB7 100 A1
WELL DA16 136 C1
WIM/MER SW19 146 C3
WIM/MER SW19 162 C1
WLGTN SM6 176 C2
WLSDN NW10 69 G5
WPK KT4 160 B7
Church Rw CHST BR7 154 C7
FUL/PGN SW6 * 108 A6
HAMP NW3 71 G3
WAND/EARL SW18 128 A4
Church Row Ms CHST BR7 154 C6
Church St BAY/PAD W2 9 H2
CHSWK W4 106 B5
CROY/NA CR0 177 H2
DAGE RM10 80 D6
ED N9 29 K6
ENC/FH EN2 29 J2
ESH/CLAY KT10 170 B3
EW KT17 173 J7
HPTN TW12 142 C7
HSLW TW3 123 H4
ISLW TW7 124 C2
KUT/HW KT1 158 E1
SRTFD E15 76 C7
TWK TW1 124 B7
WATW WD18 * 21 G3
Church Street Est
STJWD NW8 9 H1
Church St North SRTFD E15 76 C7
Church Ter BKHTH/KID SE3 133 H2
FUL/PGN SW6 * 128 A1
HDN NW4 51 K2
RCHPK/HAM TW10 124 E4
Church V EFNCH N2 53 K2
FSTH SE23 150 E1
Church Vw FSTH SE23 151 F1
Church View Gv SYD SE26 151 F5
Churchview Rd WHTN TW2 123 J7
Church Wk BTFD TW8 104 D5
BUSH WD23 22 A5
CDALE/KGS NW9 69 F1
CRICK NW2 70 D2
HYS/HAR UB3 82 C5
RYNPK SW20 161 F2
STNW/STAM N16 73 K3
STRHM/NOR SW16 163 H1
THDIT KT7 158 A5
Churchway CAMTN NW1 5 H7
Church Wy EBAR EN4 27 K3
TRDG/WHET N20 39 J2
Churchyard Rw LBTH SE11 18 D5
Churston Av PLSTW E13 77 F7
Churston Cl
BRXS/STRHM SW2 * 130 C7
Churston Dr MRDN SM4 161 G4
Churston Gdns
FBAR/BDGN N11 40 C5
Churton Pl CHSWK W4 * 105 J5
PIM SW1V 16 F6
Churton St PIM SW1V 16 F6
Chyngton Cl BFN/LL DA15 155 F2
Cibber Rd FSTH SE23 151 F1
Cicada Rd WAND/EARL SW18 128 B5
Cicely Rd PECK SE15 111 H7
Cinderford Wy BMLY BR1 152 C5
Cinema Pde EDGW HA8 * 36 C5
Cinnamon Cl CROY/NA CR0 * 163 K6
PECK SE15 111 G6
Cinnamon St WAP E1W 92 D7
Cintra Pk NRWD SE19 150 B6
Circle Gdns WIM/MER SW19 161 K2
The Circle CRICK NW2 69 G2
MLHL NW7 37 F5
The Circuits PIN HA5 47 G3
Circular Rd TOTM N17 56 B2
Circular Wy WOOL/PLUM SE18 114 E5
Circus Ms MBLAR W1H * 9 L2
Circus Pl LVPST EC2M * 13 H3
Circus Rd STJWD NW8 3 G7
Circus St GNWCH SE10 113 F6
Cirencester St BAY/PAD W2 8 C2
Cissbury Ring North
NFNCH/WDSPK N12 38 D4
Cissbury Ring South
NFNCH/WDSPK N12 38 D4
Cissbury Rd SEVS/STOTM N15 55 K4
Citadel Pl LBTH SE11 17 L7
Citizen Rd HOLWY N7 73 G2
Citron Ter PECK SE15 * 131 J2
City Barracks SHB W12 * 88 A7
City Garden Rw IS N1 6 D6
City Rd FSBYE EC1V 6 C6
STLK EC1Y 13 H1
City Wk STHWK SE1 19 J3
Civic Wy BARK/HLT IG6 60 C3
RSLP HA4 65 H4
Clabon Ms KTBR SW1X 15 L4
Clack St BERM/RHTH SE16 111 K1
Clacton Rd TOTM N17 * 56 B1
WALTH E17 57 G5
Claire Ct NFNCH/WDSPK N12 39 G2
Claire Gdns STAN HA7 35 J4
Claire Pl POP/IOD E14 112 D2
Clairvale Rd HEST TW5 102 C7
Clairview Rd
STRHM/NOR SW16 148 B4
Clairville Gdns HNWL W7 84 E7
Clamp Hl STAN HA7 34 E4
Clancarty Rd FUL/PGN SW6 127 K1
Clandon Cl ACT W3 105 J1
EW KT17 173 H5
Clandon Gdns FNCH N3 52 E2
Clandon Rd GDMY/SEVK IG3 78 E1
Clandon St DEPT SE8 132 D1
Clandon Ter RYNPK SW20 * 161 G1
Clanricarde Gdns
BAY/PAD W2 8 B7
Clapgate Rd BUSH WD23 22 B5
Clapham Common North Side
CLAP SW4 129 F3
Clapham Common South Side
CLAP SW4 129 G4
Clapham Common West Side
BTSEA SW11 128 E3
Clapham Court Ter
CLAP SW4 * 129 K4
Clapham Crs CLAP SW4 129 J3
Clapham High St CLAP SW4 129 J3
Clapham Manor St CLAP SW4 129 H2
Clapham Park Est CLAP SW4 * 129 J6
Clapham Park Rd CLAP SW4 129 H3
Clapham Park Ter
BRXS/STRHM SW2 * 129 K4
Clapham Rd BRXN/ST SW9 129 K1
Claps Gate La EHAM E6 96 B3
Clapton Common CLPT E5 56 C6
Clapton Sq CLPT E5 74 D4
Clapton Ter CLPT E5 56 C6
Clapton Wy CLPT E5 74 C3
Clara Pl WOOL/PLUM SE18 115 F3
Clare Cl BORE WD6 24 B5
EFNCH N2 53 G2
Clare Cnr ELTH/MOT SE9 135 G6
Clare Ct NTHWD HA6 32 C4
Claredale St BETH E2 92 C1
Clare Gdns BARK IG11 79 F5
FSTGT E7 76 E3
NTGHL W11 * 88 C5
Clare Hl ESH/CLAY KT10 170 B4
Clare La IS N1 6 F2
Clare Lawn Av
MORT/ESHN SW14 126 A4
Clare Ms FUL/PGN SW6 108 A6
Claremont Av
KTN/HRWW/WS HA3 50 A4
NWMAL KT3 160 E4
SUN TW16 141 F7
Claremont Cl
BRXS/STRHM SW2 130 A7
CAN/RD E16 96 A7
IS N1 6 B6
Claremont Crs DART DA1 138 B3
RKW/CH/CXG WD3 20 A4
Claremont Dr ESH/CLAY KT10 170 B6
Claremont End
ESH/CLAY KT10 170 B5
Claremont Gdns
GDMY/SEVK IG3 78 E1
SURB KT6 159 F3
Claremont Gv CHSWK W4 106 B6
WFD IG8 45 G5
Claremont House
WATW WD18 * 20 B5
Claremont La ESH/CLAY KT10 170 B4
Claremont Pk FNCH N3 38 C7
Claremont Park Rd
ESH/CLAY KT10 170 A5
Claremont Rd BMLY BR1 168 D3
CRICK NW2 52 A6
CROY/NA CR0 165 H7
EMPK RM11 63 J5
ESH/CLAY KT10 170 E6
FSTGT E7 77 F4
GLDGN NW11 70 B2
HGT N6 54 B6
KTN/HRWW/WS HA3 48 E1
MV/WKIL W9 88 C1
SURB KT6 159 F4
TEDD TW11 143 F4
TWK TW1 124 C6
WALTH E17 57 G1
WAN E11 76 B2
WEA W13 85 G4
Claremont Sq IS N1 6 A6
Claremont St GNWCH SE10 112 E5
UED N18 42 C5
Claremont Ter THDIT KT7 * 158 C6
Claremont Vls CMBW SE5 * 110 E6
KUT/HW KT1 * 159 G1
Claremont Wy CRICK NW2 52 A7
Clarence Av BMLY BR1 168 D3
CLAP SW4 129 J5
IL IG1 59 K5
NWMAL KT3 159 K1
Clarence Cl BUSH WD23 23 F6
EBAR EN4 27 H4
Clarence Ct MLHL NW7 37 G4
Clarence Crs CLAP SW4 129 J5
SCUP DA14 155 H2
Clarence Gdns CAMTN NW1 4 D8
Clarence Ga CAMTN NW1 3 M9
Clarence La PUT/ROE SW15 126 C5
Clarence Ms
BERM/RHTH SE16 93 F7
CLPT E5 74 D4
TOOT SW17 147 G2
Clarence Pas KCROSS N1C * 5 J6
Clarence Pl CLPT E5 74 D4
Clarence Rd BMLY BR1 168 D2
BXLYHS DA6 137 F3
CAN/RD E16 94 C3
CHSWK W4 105 H4
CLPT E5 74 D3
CROY/NA CR0 164 E6
DEPT SE8 112 E5
ELTH/MOT SE9 153 J1
KIL/WHAMP NW6 70 D6
MNPK E12 77 G3
PEND EN3 30 E4
RCH/KEW TW9 105 G7
SCUP DA14 155 H2
SEVS/STOTM N15 55 J4
SUT SM1 175 F3
TEDD TW11 143 F5
WALTH E17 57 F1
WDGN N22 40 E6
WIM/MER SW19 147 F5
WLGTN SM6 176 B4
Clarence St KUT/HW KT1 158 E1
NWDGN UB2 102 C2
RCH/KEW TW9 125 F3
Clarence Ter CAMTN NW1 3 M9
HSLW TW3 123 G3
Clarence Vls KUT/HW KT1 * 159 G1
Clarence Wk CLAP SW4 129 K1
Clarence Wy CAMTN NW1 4 C1
Clarendon Cl BAY/PAD W2 * 9 J6
HOM E9 74 E6
Clarendon Crs WHTN TW2 142 D2
Clarendon Cross NTGHL W11 88 C6
Clarendon Dr PUT/ROE SW15 127 F3
Clarendon Gdns HDN NW4 51 J2
IL IG1 59 K7
MV/WKIL W9 8 F1
WBLY HA9 67 K2
Clarendon Ga BAY/PAD W2 9 J6
Clarendon Gv MTCM CR4 162 E2
Clarendon Ms BAY/PAD W2 9 J6
BORE WD6 * 24 C2
Clarendon Pl BAY/PAD W2 9 J6
Clarendon Ri LEW SE13 133 F2
Clarendon Rd BORE WD6 24 C2
CEND/HSY/T N8 55 F2
CROY/NA CR0 177 H1
EA W5 86 A2
HRW HA1 48 E5
HYS/HAR UB3 101 J1
NTGHL W11 88 C6
SEVS/STOTM N15 55 H3
SWFD E18 58 E2
UED N18 42 C4
WALTH E17 57 K5
WAT WD17 21 F2
WDGN N22 * 55 F1
WIM/MER SW19 147 J6
WLGTN SM6 176 C4
Clarendon St PIM SW1V 16 D7
Clarendon Ter MV/WKIL W9 2 F9
Clarendon Wy WCHMH N21 29 J6
Clarens St CAT SE6 151 H1
Clare Pde GFD/PVL UB6 * 66 D5
Clare Rd GFD/PVL UB6 66 D5
HSLWW TW4 122 E2
NWCR SE14 132 C1
STWL/WRAY TW19 120 A6
WAN E11 58 B5
WLSDN NW10 69 J6
Clare St BETH E2 92 D1
Claret Gdns SNWD SE25 165 F3
Clareville Gv SKENS SW7 14 F6
Clareville St SKENS SW7 14 F6
Clare Wy BXLYHN DA7 117 F7
Clarges Ms MYFR/PICC W1J 10 C8
Clarges St MYFR/PICC W1J 10 D8
Claribel Rd BRXN/ST SW9 130 C1
Clarice Wy WLGTN SM6 176 E7
Claridge Rd BCTR RM8 61 K7
Clarissa Rd CHDH RM6 61 K6
Clarissa St HACK E8 7 L3
Clark Cl ERITH DA8 118 D7
Clarke Cl THHTH CR7 164 D5
Clarke Ms ED N9 42 D2
Clarkers La KTTN NW5 72 B4
Clarkes Av WPK KT4 161 G7
Clarkes Ms CAVSQ/HST W1G 10 B2
Clark Gv IL IG1 78 E3
Clarks Md BUSH WD23 22 C6
Clarkson Rd CAN/RD E16 94 D5
Clarkson Rw CAMTN NW1 4 E6
Clarkson St BETH E2 * 92 D2
Clark's Rd IL IG1 78 D1
Clark St WCHPL E1 92 E5
Clark Wy HEST TW5 102 C6
Classon Cl WDR/YW UB7 100 B1
Claston Cl DART DA1 138 B3
Claude Monet Ct EDUL SE22 * 131 H4
Claude Rd LEY E10 58 A7
PECK SE15 131 J1
PLSTW E13 77 F7
Claude St POP/IOD E14 112 D3
Claudia Pl WIM/MER SW19 127 H7
Claudius Cl STAN HA7 35 K2
Claughton Rd PLSTW E13 95 G1
Clauson Av NTHLT UB5 66 B4
Clavell St GNWCH SE10 113 F5
Claverdale Rd
BRXS/STRHM SW2 130 A6
Clavering Av BARN SW13 106 E5
Clavering Cl TEDD TW11 143 G3
Clavering Pl BAL SW12 129 F5
Clavering Rd MNPK E12 59 H7
Claverley Gv FNCH N3 38 E7
Claverley Vls FNCH N3 39 F6
Claverton St PIM SW1V 16 F8
Clave St WAP E1W 92 E7
Claxton Gv HMSMTH W6 107 G4
Clay Av MTCM CR4 163 G1
Claybank Gv LEW SE13 132 E2
Claybridge Rd LEE/GVPK SE12 153 G3
Claybrook Cl EFNCH N2 53 H2
Claybrook Rd HMSMTH W6 107 G5
Claybury BUSH WD23 22 B6
Claybury Rd WFD IG8 45 J6
Clay Ct KTN/HRWW/WS HA3 49 K3
Claydon Dr CROY/NA CR0 176 E3
Claydown Ms
WOOL/PLUM SE18 115 F4
Clayfarm Rd ELTH/MOT SE9 154 C1
Claygate Cl HCH RM12 81 J3
Claygate Crs CROY/NA CR0 180 A5
Claygate La ESH/CLAY KT10 171 G2
THDIT KT7 158 B7
Claygate Lodge Cl
ESH/CLAY KT10 170 E6
Claygate Rd WEA W13 104 C2
Clayhall Av CLAY IG5 59 J1
Clayhill Crs ELTH/MOT SE9 153 H3
Claylands Pl VX/NE SW8 110 B6
Claylands Rd VX/NE SW8 110 A5
Clay La BUSH WD23 22 E6
STWL/WRAY TW19 120 C6
Claymore Cl MRDN SM4 161 K6
Claypole Dr HEST TW5 102 D7
Claypole Rd SRTFD E15 * 94 A1
Clayponds Av BTFD TW8 105 F3
Clayponds Gdns EA W5 104 E3
Clayponds La BTFD TW8 105 F4
Clay St MHST W1U 9 M3
Clayton Av ALP/SUD HA0 68 A6
Clayton Cl EHAM E6 95 K5
Clayton Crs BTFD TW8 104 E4
IS N1 5 L4
Clayton Dr DEPT SE8 112 B4
Clayton Fld CDALE/KGS NW9 37 G7
Clayton Ms GNWCH SE10 113 G7
Clayton Rd CHSGTN KT9 171 J3
HYS/HAR UB3 101 H1
ISLW TW7 123 K2
PECK SE15 111 H7
ROMW/RG RM7 62 E7
Clayton St LBTH SE11 18 A9
Clayton Ter YEAD UB4 83 J4
Claytonville Ter BELV DA17 * 117 K1
Clay Wood Cl ORP BR6 169 K6
Clayworth Cl BFN/LL DA15 136 C5
Cleanthus Cl
WOOL/PLUM SE18 115 G7
Cleanthus Rd
WOOL/PLUM SE18 115 G7
Clearbrook Wy WCHPL E1 92 E5
Clearwater Pl SURB KT6 158 D5
Clearwater Ter NTGHL W11 107 G1
Clearwell Dr MV/WKIL W9 8 C1
Cleave Av HYS/HAR UB3 101 H3
Cleaveland Rd SURB KT6 158 E4
Cleaverholme Cl SNWD SE25 165 J5
Cleaver Sq LBTH SE11 18 B7
Cleaver St LBTH SE11 18 A7
Cleeve Ct EBED/NFELT TW14 121 H7
Cleeve Hl FSTH SE23 131 J7
Cleeve Park Gdns SCUP DA14 155 H1
Cleeve Wy PUT/ROE SW15 126 C5
SUT SM1 162 A7
Clegg St PLSTW E13 94 E1
WAP E1W 92 D7
Clematis Cots SHB W12 * 87 J6
Clematis Gdns WFD IG8 44 E4
Clematis St SHB W12 87 H6
Clem Attlee Ct FUL/PGN SW6 * 107 J5
Clem Attlee Pde
FUL/PGN SW6 * 107 J5
Clemence Rd DAGE RM10 80 E7
Clemence St POP/IOD E14 93 H4
Clement Av CLAP SW4 129 J3
Clement Cl CHSWK W4 106 A3
KIL/WHAMP NW6 70 A6
Clement Gdns HYS/HAR UB3 101 H3
Clementhorpe Rd DAGW RM9 79 J5
Clementina Rd LEY E10 57 H7
Clementine Cl WEA W13 104 C1
Clement Rd BECK BR3 166 A1
WIM/MER SW19 146 C4
Clements Av CAN/RD E16 94 E6
Clements Cl
NFNCH/WDSPK N12 39 F3
Clements La IL IG1 78 B2
Clement's La MANHO EC4N 13 H6
Clements Pl BTFD TW8 104 E4
Clements Rd
BERM/RHTH SE16 * 111 H2
EHAM E6 77 K6
IL IG1 78 B2
Clement's Rd
BERM/RHTH SE16 111 H2
Clendon Wy
WOOL/PLUM SE18 115 J3
Clennam St STHWK SE1 * 18 F1
Clensham Ct SUT SM1 174 E1
Clensham La SUT SM1 174 E1
Clenston Ms MBLAR W1H 9 L4
Cleopatra Cl STAN HA7 35 K2
Clephane Rd IS N1 73 J5
Clere Pl SDTCH EC2A 7 H9
Clere St SDTCH EC2A 7 H9
Clerkenwell Cl CLKNW EC1R 6 B9
Clerkenwell Gn CLKNW EC1R 12 C1
Clerkenwell Rd CLKNW EC1R 12 A1
Clermont Rd HOM E9 74 E7
Clevedon Gdns HEST TW5 122 A1
HYS/HAR UB3 101 G2
Clevedon Rd KUT/HW KT1 159 H1
PGE/AN SE20 151 F7
TWK TW1 124 E5
Cleveland Av CHSWK W4 106 C3
HPTN TW12 141 K6
Cleveland Crs BORE WD6 24 E4
Cleveland Gdns BARN SW13 126 C1
BAY/PAD W2 8 E5
CRICK NW2 70 B1
SEVS/STOTM N15 55 J4
WPK KT4 173 G1
Cleveland Gv WCHPL E1 92 E3
Cleveland Ms FITZ W1T 10 E2
Cleveland Park Av WALTH E17 57 J3
Cleveland Park Crs
WALTH E17 57 J3
Cleveland Pl STJS SW1Y 10 F8
Cleveland Ri MRDN SM4 161 G6
Cleveland Rd BARN SW13 126 C1
CHSWK W4 105 K2
ED N9 * 30 D6
IL IG1 78 B2
IS N1 7 H2
ISLW TW7 124 B3
NWMAL KT3 160 B3
SWFD E18 58 E2
WEA W13 85 G4
WELL DA16 136 A1
WPK KT4 173 G1
Cleveland Rw WHALL SW1A 10 F9
Cleveland Sq BAY/PAD W2 8 E5
Cleveland St CAMTN NW1 10 D1
Cleveland Ter BAY/PAD W2 8 E5
Cleveland Wy WCHPL E1 92 E3
Cleveley Crs EA W5 86 A1
Cleveleys Rd CLPT E5 74 D2
Clevely Cl CHARL SE7 114 C3
Cleverly Est SHB W12 * 87 J7
Cleve Rd KIL/WHAMP NW6 2 B1
SCUP DA14 155 K2
Cleves Av EW KT17 173 K7
Cleves Rd EHAM E6 77 H7
RCHPK/HAM TW10 143 J2
Cleves Wy HPTN TW12 141 K6
RSLP HA4 47 H7
SUN TW16 140 D5
Clewer Crs
KTN/HRWW/WS HA3 34 D7
Clifden Ms CLPT E5 75 F3
Clifden Rd BTFD TW8 104 E5
CLPT E5 74 E4
TWK TW1 124 A7
Cliffe Rd SAND/SEL CR2 177 K4
Clifford Av CHST BR7 153 K5
MORT/ESHN SW14 125 K1
RCH/KEW TW9 125 J2
WLGTN SM6 176 C3
Clifford Cl NTHLT UB5 65 J7
PLSTW E13 * 95 F2
Clifford Dr BRXN/ST SW9 130 C3
Clifford Gdns HYS/HAR UB3 101 G3
WLSDN NW10 88 A1
Clifford Rd ALP/SUD HA0 67 K7
BAR EN5 27 F2
CAN/RD E16 94 D3
ED N9 30 E5

HSLWW TW4 122 C2
RCHPK/HAM TW10 143 K1
SNWD SE25 165 H3
WALTH E17 58 A1
Clifford St CONDST W1S 10 E7
Clifford Wy WLSDN NW10 69 H3
Cliff Rd CAMTN NW1 72 D5
Cliff Ter DEPT SE8 132 D1
Cliffview Rd LEW SE13 132 D2
Cliff Vls CAMTN NW1 72 D5
Cliff Wk CAN/RD E16 94 D4
Clifton Av FELT TW13 141 G2
FNCH N3 38 D7
KTN/HRWW/WS HA3 49 H1
SHB W12 106 C1
WALTH E17 57 F3
WBLY HA9 68 B5
Clifton Ct BECK BR3 * 151 K7
Clifton Crs PECK SE15 111 J6
Clifton Gdns CHSWK W4 106 A3
ENC/FH EN2 28 E3
GLDGN NW11 52 D5
MV/WKIL W9 8 E1
SEVS/STOTM N15 56 B5
Clifton Gv HACK E8 74 C5
Clifton Hl STJWD NW8 2 D5
Clifton Ms SNWD SE25 165 F3
Clifton Pde FELT TW13 * 141 G3
Clifton Park Av RYNPK SW20 161 F1
Clifton Pl BAY/PAD W2 9 H6
BERM/RHTH SE16 111 K1
KUTN/CMB KT2 * 144 C7
Clifton Ri NWCR SE14 112 B6
Clifton Rd CAN/RD E16 94 C4
CEND/HSY/T N8 54 D5
EMPK RM11 63 J5
FNCH N3 39 G7
FSTGT E7 77 H5
GFD/PVL UB6 84 C3
GNTH/NBYPK IG2 60 D5
HTHAIR TW6 120 E2
IS N1 73 J5
ISLW TW7 123 K1
KTN/HRWW/WS HA3 50 B4
KUTN/CMB KT2 144 B7
MV/WKIL W9 2 F9
NWDGN UB2 102 D3
SCUP DA14 154 E3
SNWD SE25 165 F3
TEDD TW11 142 E3
WATW WD18 21 F4
WDGN N22 40 C7
WELL DA16 136 D2
WIM/MER SW19 146 B5
WLGTN SM6 176 B4
WLSDN NW10 87 J1
Clifton St SDTCH EC2A 13 J1
Clifton Ter FSBYPK N4 73 G1
Clifton Vls MV/WKIL W9 8 D2
Clifton Wy ALP/SUD HA0 68 A7
PECK SE15 111 K6
Cline Rd FBAR/BDGN N11 40 C5
Clink St STHWK SE1 13 G8
Clinton Av E/WMO/HCT KT8 157 H3
WELL DA16 136 B3
Clinton Rd BOW E3 93 G2
FSTGT E7 76 E3
SEVS/STOTM N15 55 K3
Clinton Ter DEPT SE8 * 112 D5
SUT SM1 * 175 G3
Clipper Cl BERM/RHTH SE16 112 A1
Clipper Wy LEW SE13 133 F3
Clippesby Cl CHSGTN KT9 * 172 B5
Clipstone Ms GTPST W1W 10 E2
Clipstone Rd HSLW TW3 123 F2
Clipstone St GTPST W1W 10 D2
Clissold Cl EFNCH N2 53 K2
Clissold Crs STNW/STAM N16 73 K3
Clissold Rd STNW/STAM N16 73 K2
Clitheroe Av RYLN/HDSTN HA2 48 A7
Clitheroe Gdns OXHEY WD19 33 H2
Clitheroe Rd BRXN/ST SW9 129 K1
Clitherow Av HNWL W7 104 B2
Clitherow Rd BTFD TW8 104 C4
Clitterhouse Crs CRICK NW2 52 A7
Clitterhouse Rd CRICK NW2 52 A7
Clive Av DART DA1 138 C5
UED N18 42 C5
Clive Ct WLSDN NW10 * 69 H6
Cliveden Cl
NFNCH/WDSPK N12 39 G3
Cliveden Pl BGVA SW1W 16 A5
Cliveden Rd WIM/MER SW19 146 D7
Clivedon Ct WEA W13 85 H4
Clivedon Rd CHING E4 44 C4
Clive Rd BELV DA17 117 H3
DUL SE21 149 K2
EBED/NFELT TW14 121 K5
EN EN1 30 C3
ESH/CLAY KT10 170 B3
GPK RM2 63 K4
TWK TW1 143 F3
WIM/MER SW19 147 J5
Clivesdale Dr HYS/HAR UB3 82 E7
Clive Wy EN EN1 30 C3
Cloak La CANST EC4R 12 F6
Clockhouse Av BARK IG11 78 C7
Clockhouse Cl
WIM/MER SW19 146 A2
Clock House Pde
PLMGR N13 * 41 G4
Clockhouse Pl PUT/ROE SW15 127 H4
Clock House Rd BECK BR3 166 B2
Clock Pde ENC/FH EN2 * 29 K4
Clocktower Ms HNWL W7 * 84 E7
Clock Tower Ms IS N1 6 F4
THMD SE28 97 H6
Clock Tower Pl HOLWY N7 * 72 E5
Clock Tower Rd ISLW TW7 124 A2
Clock View Crs HOLWY N7 72 E5
Cloister Cl RAIN RM13 99 K3
TEDD TW11 143 H4
Cloister Gdns EDGW HA8 36 E4
SNWD SE25 165 J5
Cloister Rd ACT W3 86 E4
CRICK NW2 70 D2
Cloisters Av HAYES BR2 168 E4
Clonard Wy PIN HA5 34 A5
Clonbrock Rd
STNW/STAM N16 74 A3
Cloncurry St FUL/PGN SW6 127 G1
Clonmel Cl RYLN/HDSTN HA2 48 D7
Clonmell Rd TOTM N17 55 K2
Clonmel Rd FUL/PGN SW6 107 J6
TEDD TW11 142 D3
Clonmore St
WAND/EARL SW18 127 J7
Clorane Gdns HAMP NW3 70 E2
Closemead Cl NTHWD HA6 32 A5
The Close ALP/SUD HA0 68 A5
BECK BR3 166 B3
BUSH WD23 * 22 A5
BXLY DA5 137 H5
CAR SM5 175 J7
CHDH RM6 62 A5
CHEAM SM3 161 J6
CHING E4 44 A6
EBAR EN4 27 K5
GNTH/NBYPK IG2 60 E5
ISLW TW7 123 J1
MTCM CR4 162 E3
NWMAL KT3 159 K1
PIN HA5 47 G6
RCH/KEW TW9 125 J2
SCUP DA14 155 H4
SNWD SE25 * 165 H5
STHGT/OAK N14 40 D1
STMC/STPC BR5 169 K5
SURB KT6 159 F6
TRDG/WHET N20 38 D1
WBLY HA9 68 E2
Cloth Ct STBT EC1A 12 D3
Cloth Fair STBT EC1A 12 D3
Clothier St HDTCH EC3A 13 K4
Cloth St STBT EC1A 12 E2
Clothworkers Rd
WOOL/PLUM SE18 115 J6
Cloudesdale Rd TOOT SW17 148 B1
Cloudesley Cl SCUP DA14 155 F4
Cloudesley Pl IS N1 6 B4
Cloudesley Rd BXLYHN DA7 117 G7
ERITH DA8 118 C7
IS N1 6 A3
Cloudesley Sq IS N1 6 B3
Cloudesley St IS N1 6 B4
Clouston Cl WLGTN SM6 176 E4
Clova Rd FSTGT E7 76 E4
Clove Crs POP/IOD E14 94 A6
Clovelly Av CDALE/KGS NW9 51 H3
HGDN/ICK UB10 64 A3
Clovelly Cl HGDN/ICK UB10 64 A3
PIN HA5 47 F2
Clovelly Gdns EN EN1 30 A6
NRWD SE19 150 B7
Clovelly Rd BXLYHN DA7 117 F5
CEND/HSY/T N8 54 D3
CHSWK W4 * 106 A1
EA W5 104 D1
HSLW TW3 123 F1
Clovelly Wy RYLN/HDSTN HA2 65 K2
WCHPL E1 92 E5
Clover Cl WAN E11 * 76 B1
Cloverdale Gdns BFN/LL DA15 136 A5
The Clover Fld BUSH WD23 21 K5
Clover Ms CHEL SW3 15 L9
Clover Wy WLGTN SM6 163 F7
Clove St PLSTW E13 94 E3
Clowders Rd CAT SE6 151 H2
Clowser Cl SUT SM1 175 G4
Cloysters Gn WAP E1W * 92 C7
Cloyster Wd EDGW HA8 35 K6
Club Gardens Rd HAYES BR2 167 K6
Club Rw BETH E2 7 L9
The Clumps ASHF TW15 140 B3
Clunbury Av NWDGN UB2 102 E4
Clunbury St IS N1 7 H6
Cluny Est STHWK SE1 19 J3
Cluny Ms ECT SW5 14 A6
Cluny Pl STHWK SE1 19 J3
Clutton St POP/IOD E14 93 K4
Clydach Rd EN EN1 30 B3
Clyde Circ SEVS/STOTM N15 56 A3
Clyde Ct CAMTN NW1 5 H5
Clyde Flats FUL/PGN SW6 * 107 J6
Clyde Pl LEY E10 57 K6
Clyde Rd CROY/NA CR0 178 B1
SEVS/STOTM N15 56 A3
STWL/WRAY TW19 120 A7
SUT SM1 174 E4
WDGN N22 40 D7
WLGTN SM6 176 C4
Clydesdale PEND EN3 31 F3
Clydesdale Av STAN HA7 49 K2
Clydesdale Cl BORE WD6 25 F4
ISLW TW7 124 A2
Clydesdale Gdns
RCHPK/HAM TW10 125 J3
Clydesdale Pth BORE WD6 * 25 F4
Clydesdale Rd EMPK RM11 63 H6
NTGHL W11 88 D5
Clyde St DEPT SE8 112 C5
Clyde Ter FSTH SE23 150 E1
Clyde V FSTH SE23 150 E1
Clydon Cl ERITH DA8 118 B5
Clyfford Rd RSLP HA4 64 D3
Clymping Dene
EBED/NFELT TW14 122 A6
Clyston Rd WATW WD18 20 D5
Clyston St VX/NE SW8 129 H1
Coach & Horses Yd
CONDST W1S 10 D6
Coach House La HBRY N5 * 73 H3
WIM/MER SW19 146 B3
Coach House Ms FSTH SE23 131 K5
NWCR SE14 * 112 A7
Coach House Yd
WAND/EARL SW18 * 128 A3
Coalecroft Rd PUT/ROE SW15 127 F3
Coates Av WAND/EARL SW18 128 D5
Coates Cl THHTH CR7 164 D2
Coates Hill Rd BMLY BR1 169 F1
Coates Rd BORE WD6 23 K6
Coate St BETH E2 92 C1
Cobalt Cl BECK BR3 166 A3
Cobb Cl BORE WD6 24 E4
Cobbett Rd ELTH/MOT SE9 134 D2
WHTN TW2 123 F7
Cobbetts Av REDBR IG4 59 H4
Cobbett St VX/NE SW8 110 A6
Cobble La IS N1 6 B1
Cobble Ms HBRY N5 73 J2
Cobbler's Wk TEDD TW11 142 E6
Cobblestone Pl CROY/NA CR0 164 D7
Cobbold Ms SHB W12 * 106 C1
Cobbold Rd SHB W12 106 C1
WAN E11 76 D2
WLSDN NW10 69 H5
Cobb's Rd HSLWW TW4 122 E3
Cobb St WCHPL E1 13 L4
Cobden Ms SYD SE26 150 D4
Cobden Rd SNWD SE25 165 H4
WAN E11 76 C2
Cobham Av NWMAL KT3 160 D4
Cobham Cl BFN/LL DA15 136 C5
BTSEA SW11 128 D5
EDGW HA8 50 D1
EN EN1 30 C2
HAYES BR2 168 D6
WLGTN SM6 176 E5
Cobham Ms CAMTN NW1 5 G1
Cobham Pl BXLYHS DA6 136 E4
Cobham Rd GDMY/SEVK IG3 78 E1
HEST TW5 102 B6
KUT/HW KT1 159 H1
WALTH E17 44 A7
Cobland Rd LEE/GVPK SE12 153 G3
Coborn Rd BOW E3 93 H2
Coborn St BOW E3 93 H2
Cobourg Rd CMBW SE5 19 L8
Cobourg St CAMTN NW1 4 F8
Coburg Cl WEST SW1P 16 F5
Coburg Crs BRXS/STRHM SW2 130 A7
Coburg Dwellings
WCHPL E1 * 92 E6
Coburg Gdns CLAY IG5 59 H1
Coburg Rd WDGN N22 55 F1
Cochrane Dr DART DA1 139 G5
Cochrane Ms STJWD NW8 3 H6
Cochrane Rd WIM/MER SW19 146 C6
Cochrane St STJWD NW8 3 H6
Cockcrow Hl SURB KT6 * 158 E7
Cockerell Rd WALTH E17 57 G6
Cockfosters Pde EBAR EN4 * 28 A3
Cockfosters Rd EBAR EN4 27 K2
Cock La STBT EC1A 12 C3
Cocks Crs NWMAL KT3 160 C3
Cockspur Ct STJS SW1Y 11 H8
Cockspur St STJS SW1Y 11 H8
Code St WCHPL E1 13 M1
Codling Cl WAP E1W 92 C7
Codling Wy ALP/SUD HA0 67 K3
Codrington Hl FSTH SE23 132 B6
Codrington Ms NTGHL W11 88 C5
Cody Cl KTN/HRWW/WS HA3 49 K2
WLGTN SM6 176 D6
Cody Rd CAN/RD E16 94 B3
Coe Av SNWD SE25 165 H5
Coe's Aly BAR EN5 26 C3
Coffey St DEPT SE8 112 D6
Cogan Av WALTH E17 43 G7
Coin St STHWK SE1 12 A8
Coity Rd KTTN NW5 72 A5
Cokers La DUL SE21 130 D7
Coke St WCHPL E1 92 C5
Colas Ms KIL/WHAMP NW6 2 B3
Colbeck Ms SKENS SW7 14 D6
Colbeck Rd HRW HA1 48 C6
Colberg Pl STNW/STAM N16 * 56 B6
Colborne Wy WPK KT4 174 A2
Colbrook Av HYS/HAR UB3 101 G2
Colbrook Cl HYS/HAR UB3 101 G2
Colburn Av PIN HA5 33 J5
Colburn Wy SUT SM1 175 H2
Colby Rd NRWD SE19 150 A4
Colchester Dr PIN HA5 47 H4
Colchester Rd EDGW HA8 36 E6
NTHWD HA6 46 E1
WALTH E17 57 J5
Coldbath Sq CLKNW EC1R 12 A1
Coldbath St LEW SE13 112 E7
Cold Blow Crs BXLY DA5 138 A7
Cold Blow La NWCR SE14 112 A6
Coldershaw Rd WEA W13 104 B1
Coldfall Av MUSWH N10 53 K1
Coldharbour POP/IOD E14 94 A7
Coldharbour Crest
ELTH/MOT SE9 * 154 A2
Coldharbour La BRXN/ST SW9 130 B3
BUSH WD23 22 B5
HYS/HAR UB3 101 J1
RAIN RM13 99 J7
Coldharbour Pl CMBW SE5 130 D1
Coldharbour Rd CROY/NA CR0 177 G4
Coldharbour Wy
CROY/NA CR0 177 G4
Coldstream Gdns
WAND/EARL SW18 127 J5
Colebeck Ms IS N1 73 H5
Colebert Av WCHPL E1 92 E3
Colebrook Cl MLHL NW7 38 B6
Colebrooke Av WEA W13 85 H5
Colebrooke Dr WAN E11 59 F6
Colebrooke Pl IS N1 6 D4
Colebrooke Rw IS N1 5 K3
Colebrook Ri HAYES BR2 167 H1
Colebrook Rd
STRHM/NOR SW16 148 E7
Colebrook St ERITH DA8 118 C5
Colebrook Wy
FBAR/BDGN N11 40 B4
Coleby Pth CMBW SE5 * 110 E6
Cole Cl THMD SE28 97 H7
Coledale Dr STAN HA7 35 J7
Coleford Rd
WAND/EARL SW18 128 B4
Cole Gdns HEST TW5 101 K6
Colegrave Rd SRTFD E15 76 B4
Colegrove Rd PECK SE15 111 G5
Coleherne Ms WBPTN SW10 14 C8
Coleherne Rd WBPTN SW10 14 C8
Colehill Gdns FUL/PGN SW6 * 107 H7
Colehill La FUL/PGN SW6 107 H7
Coleman Cl SNWD SE25 165 H1
Coleman Flds IS N1 6 F3
Coleman Rd BELV DA17 117 H2
CMBW SE5 111 F6
Colemans Heath
ELTH/MOT SE9 154 A2
Coleman St CITYW EC2V 13 G4
Colenso Dr MLHL NW7 37 J6
Colenso Rd CLPT E5 74 E3
GNTH/NBYPK IG2 60 E7
Cole Park Gdns TWK TW1 124 B5
Cole Park Rd TWK TW1 124 B6
Colepits Wood Rd
ELTH/MOT SE9 135 J4
Coleraine Rd BKHTH/KID SE3 113 J5
CEND/HSY/T N8 55 G2
Coleridge Av MNPK E12 77 J5
SUT SM1 175 J3
Coleridge Cl VX/NE SW8 129 G1
Coleridge Dr RSLP HA4 47 F5
Coleridge Gdns
KIL/WHAMP NW6 2 E2
WBPTN SW10 108 B6
Coleridge La CEND/HSY/T N8 54 E5
Coleridge Rd
CEND/HSY/T N8 54 D5
CROY/NA CR0 165 K6
DART DA1 139 K5
FSBYPK N4 73 G1
NFNCH/WDSPK N12 39 G4
WALTH E17 57 H3
Coleridge Sq WEA W13 85 G5
Coleridge Wk GLDGN NW11 52 E3
Coleridge Wy BORE WD6 24 C3
WDR/YW UB7 100 B3
YEAD UB4 82 E5
Cole Rd TWK TW1 124 B5
Colesburg Rd BECK BR3 166 C2
Coles Crs RYLN/HDSTN HA2 66 B1
Coles Gn BUSH WD23 22 C7
Coles Green Rd CRICK NW2 51 J7
Coleshill Rd TEDD TW11 142 E5
Colestown St BTSEA SW11 128 D1
Cole St STHWK SE1 18 F2
Colet Cl PLMGR N13 41 H5
Colet Gdns WKENS W14 107 G4
Coley St FSBYW WC1X 11 M1
Colfe & Hatcliffe Glebe
LEW SE13 * 132 E4
Colfe Rd FSTH SE23 132 B7
Colina Ms SEVS/STOTM N15 55 H3
Colina Rd CEND/HSY/T N8 55 H4
Colin Cl CDALE/KGS NW9 51 G3
CROY/NA CR0 179 H2
WWKM BR4 180 D2
Colin Crs CDALE/KGS NW9 51 H4
Colindale Av CDALE/KGS NW9 51 F2
Colindeep Gdns HDN NW4 51 J4
Colindeep La CDALE/KGS NW9 51 H3
Colin Dr CDALE/KGS NW9 51 H4
Colinette Rd PUT/ROE SW15 127 F3
Colin Gdns CDALE/KGS NW9 51 H4
Colin Park Rd
CDALE/KGS NW9 51 G2
Colinton Rd GDMY/SEVK IG3 79 H1
Coliston Rd WAND/EARL SW18 127 K6
Collamore Av
WAND/EARL SW18 128 D7
Collapit Cl HRW HA1 48 B5
Collard Pl CAMTN NW1 4 C1
College Ap GNWCH SE10 113 F5
College Av
KTN/HRWW/WS HA3 34 E7
College Cl
KTN/HRWW/WS HA3 34 E6
UED N18 42 B4
WHTN TW2 123 J7
College Ct EA W5 * 86 A6
College Crs HAMP NW3 71 G5
College Cross IS N1 6 B1
College Dr RSLP HA4 46 E6
THDIT KT7 157 K6
College East WCHPL E1 * 13 M3
College Gdns CHING E4 31 K6
NWMAL KT3 160 C4
REDBR IG4 59 J4
TOOT SW17 147 J1
UED N18 * 42 B4
College Gn NRWD SE19 150 A6
College Gv CAMTN NW1 5 G4
College Hl CANST EC4R * 12 F6
College Hill Rd
KTN/HRWW/WS HA3 34 E6
College Ms IS N1 6 B2
College Pde
KIL/WHAMP NW6 * 70 C7
College Park Cl LEW SE13 133 F3
College Pl CAMTN NW1 4 F3
WALTH E17 58 C3
WBPTN SW10 * 108 B6
College Rd BMLY BR1 152 E7
CROY/NA CR0 177 K1
DUL SE21 131 F7
ENC/FH EN2 29 K1
HRW HA1 48 E5
ISLW TW7 104 A7
KTN/HRWW/WS HA3 34 E7
NRWD SE19 150 B4
TOTM N17 42 B5
WALTH E17 58 A4
WBLY HA9 49 K7
WCHMH N21 41 G1
WEA W13 85 H5
WIM/MER SW19 147 H5
WLSDN NW10 88 A1
College St CANST EC4R * 12 F6
College Ter FNCH N3 38 D7
College Vw ELTH/MOT SE9 134 C7
College Wy HYS/HAR UB3 82 E6
NTHWD HA6 32 B5
College Yd KIL/WHAMP NW6 * 70 C7
KTTN NW5 72 B3
Collent St HOM E9 74 E5
Colless Rd SEVS/STOTM N15 56 B4
Collett Rd BERM/RHTH SE16 111 H2
Collett Wy NWDGN UB2 103 G1
Collier Cl EHAM E6 96 B6
HOR/WEW KT19 172 C5
Collier Dr EDGW HA8 50 C1
Colliers Shaw HAYES BR2 181 J4
Collier St IS N1 5 L6
Colliers Water La THHTH CR7 164 B4
Collindale Av BFN/LL DA15 136 B7
CDALE/KGS NW9 51 G2
ERITH DA8 117 J5
Collingbourne Rd SHB W12 87 K7
Collingham Gdns ECT SW5 14 D6
Collingham Pl ECT SW5 14 C6
Collingham Rd ECT SW5 14 D5
Collings Cl WDGN N22 41 F5
Collington St GNWCH SE10 * 113 G4
Collingtree Rd SYD SE26 150 E3
Collingwood Av BRYLDS KT5 159 K7
MUSWH N10 54 A2
Colling Wood Cl PGE/AN SE20 150 D7
Collingwood Cl WHTN TW2 123 F6
Collingwood Rd MTCM CR4 162 D1
RAIN RM13 99 H1
SEVS/STOTM N15 56 A3
SUT SM1 174 E3
Collingwood St WCHPL E1 92 D3
Collins Av STAN HA7 50 A1
Collins Dr RSLP HA4 65 G1
Collinson St STHWK SE1 18 E2
Collinson Wk STHWK SE1 18 E2
Collins Rd HBRY N5 73 J3
Collins Sq BKHTH/KID SE3 * 133 J2
Collins St BKHTH/KID SE3 133 H1
Collinwood Av PEND EN3 30 E2
Collinwood Gdns
GNTH/NBYPK IG2 59 K4
Collyer Av CROY/NA CR0 176 E3
Collyer Pl PECK SE15 111 H7
Collyer Rd CROY/NA CR0 176 E3
Colman Pde EN EN1 * 30 A2
Colman Rd CAN/RD E16 95 G4
Colmar Cl WCHPL E1 93 F3
Colmer Pl
KTN/HRWW/WS HA3 34 D6
Colmer Rd STRHM/NOR SW16 148 E6
Colmore Ms PECK SE15 111 J7
Colmore Rd PEND EN3 30 E3
Colnbrook St STHWK SE1 18 C4
Colne Av OXHEY WD19 21 F5
Colne Ct HOR/WEW KT19 172 E3
Colne Ldg BUSH WD23 * 21 H3
Colne Rd CLPT E5 75 F3
WCHMH N21 29 K6
WHTN TW2 123 K7
Colne St PLSTW E13 94 E2
Colney Hatch La
FBAR/BDGN N11 39 K5
Colney Rd DART DA1 139 J5
Cologne Rd BTSEA SW11 128 C3
Colombo Rd IL IG1 60 C7
Colombo St STHWK SE1 12 C9
Colomb St GNWCH SE10 113 H4
Colonels Wk ENC/FH EN2 29 H1
Colonial Av WHTN TW2 123 H5
Colonial Dr CHSWK W4 105 K3
Colonial Rd EBED/NFELT TW14 121 H6
Colonnade BMSBY WC1N 11 J1
The Colonnade DEPT SE8 * 112 C3
Colosseum Ter CAMTN NW1 4 D9
Colson Rd CROY/NA CR0 177 K1
Colson Wy STRHM/NOR SW16 148 C3
Colsterworth Rd
SEVS/STOTM N15 56 B3
Colston Av CAR SM5 175 J3
Colston Rd FSTGT E7 77 H5
MORT/ESHN SW14 125 K3
Colthurst Crs FSBYPK N4 73 H1
Colthurst Dr ED N9 42 D2
Coltness Crs ABYW SE2 116 C4
Colton Gdns TOTM N17 55 J2
Colton Rd HRW HA1 48 E4
Colts Yd WAN E11 * 58 D7
Columbas Dr HAMP NW3 71 H1
Columbia Av EDGW HA8 36 D7
RSLP HA4 47 F7
WPK KT4 160 C6
Columbia Rd BETH E2 7 L7
PLSTW E13 * 94 D3
Columbia Whf PEND EN3 * 31 G4
Columbine Av EHAM E6 95 J4
SAND/SEL CR2 177 H6
Columbine Wy LEW SE13 * 133 F1
Columbus Gdns NTHWD HA6 32 E7
Colvestone Crs HACK E8 74 B4
Colville Est IS N1 7 H4
Colville Gdns NTGHL W11 88 D5
Colville Houses NTGHL W11 88 D5
Colville Ms NTGHL W11 88 D5
Colville Pl FITZ W1T 10 F3
Colville Rd ACT W3 105 J2
ED N9 30 D7
NTGHL W11 88 D5
WALTH E17 57 G1
WAN E11 76 A2
Colville Sq NTGHL W11 * 88 D5
Colville Square Ms
NTGHL W11 * 88 D5
Colville Ter NTGHL W11 88 D5
Colvin Cl SYD SE26 150 E4
Colvin Gdns CHING E4 44 A2
SWFD E18 59 F3
Colvin Rd EHAM E6 77 J6
THHTH CR7 164 B4
Colwall Gdns WFD IG8 44 E4
Colwell Rd EDUL SE22 131 G4
Colwick Cl HGT N6 54 D6
Colwith Rd HMSMTH W6 107 F5
Colwood Gdns
WIM/MER SW19 147 H6
Colworth Gv WALW SE17 18 F6
Colworth Rd CROY/NA CR0 165 H7
WAN E11 58 C5
Colwyn Av GFD/PVL UB6 85 F1
Colwyn Cl STRHM/NOR SW16 148 C4
Colwyn Crs HSLW TW3 103 H7
Colwyn Gn CDALE/KGS NW9 * 51 G5
Colwyn Rd CRICK NW2 69 K2
Colyer Cl ELTH/MOT SE9 154 B1
Colyers Cl ERITH DA8 118 A7
Colyers La ERITH DA8 117 K7
Colyton Cl ALP/SUD HA0 67 J5
WELL DA16 116 E7
Colyton La STRHM/NOR SW16 149 G4
Colyton Rd EDUL SE22 131 J4
Colyton Wy UED N18 42 C4
Combe Av BKHTH/KID SE3 113 J6
Combedale Rd GNWCH SE10 113 K4
Combemartin Rd
WAND/EARL SW18 127 H6
Comber Cl CRICK NW2 69 J1
Comber Gv CMBW SE5 110 D6
Combermere Rd
BRXN/ST SW9 130 A2
MRDN SM4 162 A5
Combe Rd WATW WD18 20 D5
Comberton Rd CLPT E5 74 D1
Combeside WOOL/PLUM SE18 116 A6
Combes Rd DAGW RM9 80 B6
Combwell Crs ABYW SE2 116 B2
Comely Bank Rd WALTH E17 58 A4
Comeragh Ms WKENS W14 107 H4
Comeragh Rd WKENS W14 107 H4
Comerford Rd BROCKY SE4 132 B3
Comet Cl MNPK E12 77 H3
PUR RM19 119 K3
Comet Pl DEPT SE8 112 D6
Comet Rd STWL/WRAY TW19 120 A6
Comet St DEPT SE8 112 D6
Comfort St PECK SE15 111 F6
Commerce Rd BTFD TW8 104 D5
WDGN N22 41 F7
Commerce Wy CROY/NA CR0 177 F2
Commercial Rd POP/IOD E14 93 G5
UED N18 42 A4
Commercial St WCHPL E1 13 L1
Commercial Wy CMBW SE5 111 G7
WLSDN NW10 86 D1
Commerell Pl GNWCH SE10 113 J4
Commerell St GNWCH SE10 113 H4
Commodore Pde
STRHM/NOR SW16 * 149 F6
Commodore St WCHPL E1 93 F4
Commondale PUT/ROE SW15 127 F1
Common La ESH/CLAY KT10 171 G6
Common Rd BARN SW13 126 D2
ESH/CLAY KT10 171 G5
STAN HA7 34 D2
Commonside HAYES BR2 181 G3
Commonside East MTCM CR4 163 H3
Commonside West
MTCM CR4 163 F2
The Common EA W5 86 A7
NWDGN UB2 102 C3
SRTFD E15 76 D5
STAN HA7 35 F1
Commonwealth Av
HYS/HAR UB3 82 B5
SHB W12 87 K6
Commonwealth Rd
TOTM N17 42 C6
Commonwealth Wy
ABYW SE2 116 C4
Community Cl HEST TW5 102 A7
Community La HOLWY N7 72 D4
Community Rd GFD/PVL UB6 66 C7
SRTFD E15 76 B4
Como Rd FSTH SE23 151 G1
Como St ROMW/RG RM7 63 F4
Compass Ct ASHF TW15 140 A6
EDGW HA8 36 B3
Compass Hl
RCHPK/HAM TW10 124 E5
Compayne Gdns
KIL/WHAMP NW6 2 C1
Compton Av ALP/SUD HA0 67 H3
EHAM E6 95 H1
GPK RM2 63 K2
HGT N6 53 J6

IS N1	73	H5
Compton Cl CAMTN NW1	4	D8
EDGW HA8	36	E6
ESH/CLAY KT10	170	D5
GLDGN NW11	70	B2
PECK SE15	111	H6
WEA W13	85	H6
Compton Crs CHSGTN KT9	172	A5
CHSWK W4	105	K5
NTHLT UB5	65	H7
TOTM N17	41	H6
Compton Pas FSBYE EC1V	6	D9
Compton PI ERITH DA8	118	C5
OXHEY WD19	33	J3
STPAN WC1H	5	J9
Compton Ri PIN HA5	47	J4
Compton Rd CROY/NA CRO	165	J7
HYS/HAR UB3	82	C6
IS N1	73	H5
WCHMH N21	29	H7
WIM/MER SW19	146	D5
WLSDN NW10	88	B2
Compton Ter IS N1	73	H5
WCHMH N21 *	29	G7
Comus PI WALW SE17	19	J6
Comyn Rd BTSEA SW11	128	D3
Comyns Cl CAN/RD E16	94	D4
Comyns Rd DAGW RM9	80	C6
The Comyns WAT WD23	22	C7
Conant Ms WCHPL E1	92	C6
Concanon Rd CLAP SW4	130	A3
Concert Hall Ap STHWK SE1	11	M9
Concord Cl NTHLT UB5	83	H2
Concorde Cl HSLW TW3	123	G1
Concorde Dr EHAM E6	95	K4
Concorde Wy		
BERM/RHTH SE16	112	A3
Concord Rd ACT W3	86	D3
PEND EN3	30	E4
Concord Wy		
BERM/RHTH SE16 *	112	A3
Condell Rd VX/NE SW8	109	H7
Conder St POP/IOD E14	93	G5
Condover Crs		
WOOL/PLUM SE18	115	G6
Condray PI BTSEA SW11	108	D6
Conduit Ct COVGDN WC2E *	11	J6
UED N18	42	E4
Conduit Ms BAY/PAD W2	9	G5
Conduit PI BAY/PAD W2	9	G5
Conduit Rd WOOL/PLUM SE18	115	G4
Conduit St CONDST W1S	10	D6
Conduit Wy WLSDN NW10	68	G6
Conewood St HBRY N5	73	H2
Coney Burrows CHING E4	44	C1
Coney Hall Pde WWKM BR4 *	180	C1
Coney Hill Rd WWKM BR4	180	C1
Coney Wy VX/NE SW8	110	A5
Conference Cl CHING E4	44	A1
Conference Rd ABYW SE2	116	D3
Congleton Gv		
WOOL/PLUM SE18	115	H4
Congo Dr ED N9	42	E2
Congo Rd WOOL/PLUM SE18	115	J4
Congress Rd ABYW SE2	116	D3
Congreve Rd ELTH/MOT SE9	134	E2
Congreve St WALW SE17	19	J6
Conifer Gdns ENC/FH EN2	29	J1
STRHM/NOR SW16	149	F2
SUT SM1	175	F1
Conifers Cl TEDD TW11	143	H6
Conifer Wy ALP/SUD HA0	67	J2
HYS/HAR UB3	82	E6
Coniger Rd FUL/PGN SW6	127	K1
Coningham Ms SHB W12	87	J7
Coningham Rd SHB W12	106	E1
Coningsby Av		
CDALE/KGS NW9	51	G1
Coningsby Cots EA W5 *	104	E1
Coningsby Gdns CHING E4	43	K5
Coningsby Rd EA W5	104	D1
FSBYPK N4	55	H6
SAND/SEL CR2	177	J7
Conington Rd LEW SE13	132	E1
Conisbee Ct STHGT/OAK N14	28	C4
Conisborough Crs CAT SE6	152	A2
Coniscliffe Cl CHST BR7	154	A7
Coniscliffe Rd PLMGR N13	41	J2
Coniston Av BARK IG11	78	E6
GFD/PVL UB6	85	G1
WELL DA16	135	K2
Coniston Cl BARN SW13	106	C6
BXLYHN DA7	117	K3
CHSWK W4	105	K5
DART DA1	138	E7
ERITH DA8	118	B6
MRDN SM4	161	G5
Coniston Ct BAY/PAD W2 *	9	H5
Conistone Wy HOLWY N7	5	K1
Coniston Gdns BELMT SM2 *	175	H5
CDALE/KGS NW9	51	G4
ED N9	30	E7
PIN HA5	46	E3
REDBR IG4	59	J3
WBLY HA9	49	J7
Coniston Rd BMLY BR1	152	C5
BXLYHN DA7	117	K3
CROY/NA CRO	165	H6
MUSWH N10	54	B1
TOTM N17	42	C5
WHTN TW2	123	G5
Coniston Wk HOM E9	74	E4
Coniston Wy CHSGTN KT9	172	A2
HCH RM12	81	J4
Conlan St NKENS W10	88	C3
Conley Rd WLSDN NW10	69	G5
Conley St GNWCH SE10	113	H4
Connaught Av EBAR EN4	27	K7
EN EN1	30	A1
HSLWW TW4	122	D4
MORT/ESHN SW14	125	K2
Connaught Br CAN/RD E16	95	H6
CAN/RD E16	95	H7
FSBYPK N4	55	G6
IL IG1	78	D1
Connaught Cl BAY/PAD W2 *	9	J5
EN EN1	30	A1
LEY E10	75	G1
SUT SM1	175	G3
UX/CGN UB8	82	A4
Connaught Dr GLDGN NW11	52	E3
Connaught Gdns MRDN SM4	162	B4
MUSWH N10	54	B4
PLMGR N13	41	H3
Connaught La IL IG1	78	D1
Connaught Ms		
FUL/PGN SW6 *	107	H7
HAMP NW3	71	J4
WOOL/PLUM SE18	115	F4
Connaught Rd BAR EN5	26	B5
CAN/RD E16	95	H7
FSBYPK N4	55	G6
IL IG1	78	D1

KTN/HRWW/WS HA3	35	F7
NWMAL KT3	160	B3
RCHPK/HAM TW10 *	125	G4
SUT SM1	175	H1
TEDD TW11	142	D4
WALTH E17 *	57	J4
WAN E11	58	B7
WEA W13	85	H6
WLSDN NW10	87	G1
WOOL/PLUM SE18	115	F4
Connaught Sq BAY/PAD W2	9	K5
Connaught St BAY/PAD W2	9	K5
Connaught Wy PLMGR N13	41	H3
Connect La BARK/HLT IG6	60	C1
Connell Crs EA W5	86	B5
Connemara Cl BORE WD6 *	24	E5
Connington Crs CHING E4	44	C2
Connor Cl WAN E11	58	C7
Connor Rd DAGW RM9	80	B3
Connor St HOM E9	75	F7
Conolly Rd HNWL W7	84	E7
Conrad Dr WPK KT4	161	F7
Conroy Ct SCUP DA14	155	G3
Consfield Av NWMAL KT3	160	D3
Consort Cl FBAR/BDGN N11	39	K4
Consort Ms ISLW TW7	123	J5
Consort Rd PECK SE15	111	J7
Cons St STHWK SE1 *	18	B1
Constable Av CAN/RD E16	95	F7
Constable Cl FBAR/BDGN N11	39	K4
GLDGN NW11	53	F5
YEAD UB4	82	A1
Constable Crs		
SEVS/STOTM N15	56	C4
Constable Gdns EDGW HA8	36	C7
ISLW TW7	123	J4
Constable Ms BCTR RM8	79	H4
Constable Wk DUL SE21	150	A2
Constance Crs HAYES BR2	167	J7
Constance Gv DART DA1	139	G5
Constance Rd CROY/NA CRO	164	C6
EN EN1	30	A5
SUT SM1	175	G3
WHTN TW2	123	G6
Constantine Rd HAMP NW3	71	J4
Constitution HI		
MYFR/PICC W1J	16	C1
Constitution Ri		
WOOL/PLUM SE18	115	F7
Consul Av RAIN RM13	98	E3
Content St WALW SE17	18	F6
Control Tower Rd		
HTHAIR TW6	120	D2
Convent Cl BAR EN5	25	J1
BECK BR3	152	A6
Convent Gdns EA W5	104	D3
NTGHL W11	88	D5
Convent HI NRWD SE19	149	J5
Convent Wy NWDGN UB2	102	A3
Conway Cl RAIN RM13	81	J6
STAN HA7	35	G5
Conway Crs CHDH RM6	61	J6
GFD/PVL UB6	84	E1
Conway Dr ASHF TW15	140	A5
BELMT SM2	175	F5
HYS/HAR UB3	101	F2
Conway Gdns MTCM CR4	163	J3
WBLY HA9	49	J6
Conway Gv ACT W3	87	F4
Conway Ms FITZ W1T	10	E2
Conway Rd CRICK NW2	70	A1
FELT TW13	141	H4
HSLWW TW4	122	E6
RYNPK SW20	146	E1
SEVS/STOTM N15	55	J4
STHGT/OAK N14	40	E2
WOOL/PLUM SE18	115	J3
Conway St FITZ W1T	10	E1
Conybeare HAMP NW3	3	K1
Conyers Rd		
STRHM/NOR SW16	148	D4
Conyer St BOW E3 *	93	G1
Cooden Cl BMLY BR1	153	F6
Cookes Cl WAN E11	76	D1
Cookes La CHEAM SM3	174	C5
Cookham Cl NWDGN UB2	103	G2
Cookham Dene Cl CHST BR7	154	D7
Cookhill Rd ABYW SE2	116	C1
Cooks Ferry Rbt UED N18	43	G4
Cooks Md BUSH WD23	22	B5
Cookson Gv ERITH DA8	117	J6
Cooks Rd WALW SE17 *	110	C5
Cook's Rd SRTFD E15	93	K1
WALW SE17	18	C5
Coolfin Rd CAN/RD E16	94	E5
Coolgardie Av CHING E4	44	B4
Coolgardie Rd ASHF TW15	140	A4
Coolhurst Rd HGT N6	54	D5
Cool Oak Br CDALE/KGS NW9	51	H6
Cool Oak La CDALE/KGS NW9	51	H6
Coomassie Rd MV/WKIL W9	88	D3
Coombe Av CROY/NA CRO	178	A3
Coombe Bank KUTN/CMB KT2	145	G7
Coombe Cl EDGW HA8	50	B1
HSLW TW3	123	F3
Coombe Cnr WCHMH N21	29	H7
Coombe Crs HPTN TW12	141	J6
Coombe Dr RSLP HA4	47	F7
Coombe End KUTN/CMB KT2	145	F6
Coombefield Cl NWMAL KT3	160	B4
Coombe Gdns NWMAL KT3	160	D3
RYNPK SW20	160	D1
Coombe Hill Gld		
KUTN/CMB KT2	145	G6
Coombe Hill Rd		
KUTN/CMB KT2	145	G6
Coombe House Cha		
NWMAL KT3	145	F7
Coombehurst Cl EBAR EN4	27	K1
Coombe La CROY/NA CRO	178	A3
RYNPK SW20	145	H7
Coombe La West		
KUTN/CMB KT2	144	D7
Coombe Lea BMLY BR1	168	D2
Coombe Ldg CHARL SE7	114	B5
Coombe Neville		
KUTN/CMB KT2	144	E6
Coombe Pk KUTN/CMB KT2	144	E4
Coombe Ridings		
KUTN/CMB KT2	144	E4
Coombe Ri KUTN/CMB KT2	144	C7
Coombe Rd BUSH WD23	22	C6
CHSWK W4	106	B4
CROY/NA CRO	177	J3
HPTN TW12	141	K5
KUTN/CMB KT2	144	C7
NWMAL KT3	160	B3
SAND/SEL CR2	178	A3
SYD SE26	150	D3
WDGN N22	55	G1
WEA W13	104	C3
WLSDN NW10	69	F2

Coomber Wy CROY/NA CRO	163	J6
Coombe Vis		
WAND/EARL SW18 *	127	K6
Coombewood Dr CHDH RM6	62	B5
Coombe Wood Rd		
KUTN/CMB KT2	144	E4
Coombs St IS N1	6	D7
Coomer Ms FUL/PGN SW6 *	107	J5
Coomer PI FUL/PGN SW6	107	J5
Cooms Wk EDGW HA8	36	D7
Cooperage Cl TOTM N17	42	B5
Cooper Av WALTH E17	43	F7
Cooper Cl STHWK SE1	18	B2
Cooper Crs CAR SM5	175	K2
Cooperdale Cl WFD IG8	45	G5
Cooper Rd CROY/NA CRO	177	G3
HDN NW4	52	B5
WLSDN NW10	69	H4
Coopersale Cl WFD IG8	45	G6
Coopersale Rd HOM E9	75	F4
Coopers Cl DAGE RM10	80	D5
WCHPL E1	92	E3
Coopers La CAMTN NW1	5	J6
LEE/GVPK SE12	153	F1
Coopers Ms BECK BR3	166	D1
Cooper's Rd STHWK SE1	19	M8
Cooper's Rw TWRH EC3N	13	L6
Coopers Rd CAN/RD E16	94	D4
Coopers Yd IS N1 *	6	C2
Cooper's Yd NRWD SE19	150	A5
Coote Rd BCTR RM8	80	B2
BXLYHN DA7	117	G7
Copeland Rd PECK SE15	131	H1
WALTH E17	57	H4
Copeman Cl SYD SE26	150	E4
Copenhagen Gdns CHEL SW3	15	J1
CHSWK W4	106	A1
Copenhagen PI POP/IOD E14	93	H5
Copenhagen St IS N1	5	K4
Cope PI KENS W8	14	B3
Copers Cope Rd BECK BR3	151	H6
Cope St BERM/RHTH SE16	112	A3
Copford Wk IS N1 *	6	F3
Copgate Pth		
STRHM/NOR SW16	149	F5
Copland Av ALP/SUD HA0	67	K4
Copland Cl ALP/SUD HA0	67	J4
Copland Ms ALP/SUD HA0	68	A5
Copland Rd ALP/SUD HA0	68	A5
Copleston Rd PECK SE15	131	G2
Copley Cl HNWL W7	85	F3
WALW SE17	110	C5
Copley Dene BMLY BR1	153	H1
Copley Pk STRHM/NOR SW16	149	F5
Copley Rd STAN HA7	35	J4
Copley St WCHPL E1	93	F4
Coppard Gdns CHSGTN KT9	171	J5
Coppelia Rd BKHTH/KID SE3	133	J3
Coppen Rd BCTR RM8	62	B6
Copperas St DEPT SE8	112	E5
Copper Cl NRWD SE19	150	B6
Copper Rw STHWK SE1	13	L9
Copperbeech Cl HYS/HAR UB3	101	K1
Copperfield Dr		
SEVS/STOTM N15	56	B3
Copperfield Rd BOW E3	93	G3
THMD SE28	97	J3
Copperfields SUN TW16 *	140	D5
Copperfield St STHWK SE1 *	18	C1
Copperfield Wy CHST BR7	154	C5
PIN HA5	47	K3
Coppergate Cl BMLY BR1	153	F5
Coppermead Cl CRICK NW2	70	A2
Copper Mill Dr ISLW TW7	124	A1
Copper Mill La TOOT SW17	147	G3
Coppermill La WALTH E17	56	E3
Copper Rw STHWK SE1	13	L9
Coppetts Cl BMLY BR1	153	F5
Coppetts Rd MUSWH N10	39	K7
Coppice Cl BECK BR3	166	E3
RSLP HA4 *	46	A5
RYNPK SW20	161	F2
STAN HA7	35	F5
The Coppice BAR EN5 *	27	F5
ENC/FH EN2	29	H1
OXHEY WD19	21	G5
Coppice Wk TRDG/WHET N20	38	E2
Coppies Gv FBAR/BDGN N11	40	A3
Copping Cl CROY/NA CRO	178	A3
The Coppins CROY/NA CRO	179	K5
KTN/HRWW/WS HA3	34	E1
Coppock Cl BTSEA SW11	128	D1
Coppsfield E/WMO/HCT KT8	157	F2
Copse Av WWKM BR4	179	K2
Copse Cl CHARL SE7	114	A5
NTHWD HA6	32	A7
WDR/YW UB7	100	A2
Copse Gld SURB KT6	158	E7
Copse HI BELMT SM2	175	F6
RYNPK SW20	145	J7
Copsem Dr ESH/CLAY KT10	170	B5
Copsem La ESH/CLAY KT10	170	C5
Copsem Wy ESH/CLAY KT10	170	C5
The Copse BUSH WD23	21	J1
EFNCH N2 *	53	H2
Copse Vw SAND/SEL CR2	179	F6
Copsewood Wy NTHWD HA6	32	A7
Coptefield Dr BELV DA17	116	E2
Copthall Av LOTH EC2R	13	H4
Copthall Dr MLHL NW7	37	J6
Copthall Gdns MLHL NW7	37	J6
TWK TW1	124	A7
Copthorne Av BAL SW12	129	J6
HAYES BR2	181	K1
Copthorne Ms HYS/HAR UB3	101	H3
Coptic St NOXST/BSQ WC1A	11	J3
Copton Cl BOW E3	93	J4
Copwood Cl		
NFNCH/WDSPK N12	39	H3
Coral Cl CHDH RM6	61	J2
Coraline Cl STHL UB1	83	K2
Coralline Wk ABYW SE2	116	D1
Coral Rw BTSEA SW11	128	B2
Coral St STHWK SE1	18	B2
Coram St STPAN WC1H	11	J1
Coran Cl ED N9	31	F6
Corban Rd HSLW TW3	123	F2
Corbden Cl PECK SE15	111	G7
Corbet Cl WLGTN SM6	163	F7
Corbet Ct BANK EC3V	13	H5
Corbet PI WCHPL E1	13	L2
Corbett Gv FBAR/BDGN N11	40	A2
Corbett Rd WALTH E17	58	B1
WAN E11	59	F5
Corbett's La BERM/RHTH SE16 *	111	K3
Corbicum WAN E11	58	C6
Corbiere Ct WIM/MER SW19	146	B5
Corbin's La RYLN/HDSTN HA2	66	B1
Corbridge Crs BETH E2	92	D1

Corbridge Ms ROM RM1	63	H4
Corby Crs ENC/FH EN2	28	E3
Corbylands Rd BFN/LL DA15	135	K6
Corbyn St FSBYPK N4	54	E7
Corby Rd WLSDN NW10	86	E1
Corcorran Ms BOW E3	93	K5
Cordelia Gdns		
STWL/WRAY TW19	120	B6
Cordelia Rd STWL/WRAY TW19	120	B6
Cordingley Rd RSLP HA4	46	B7
Cording St POP/IOD E14	93	K4
Cordwell Rd LEW SE13	133	G4
Corelli Rd BKHTH/KID SE3	114	D7
Corfe Av RYLN/HDSTN HA2	66	A3
Corfe Cl BORE WD6	25	F2
YEAD UB4	83	H1
Corfield Rd WCHMH N21	29	F4
Corfield St BETH E2	92	D3
Corfton Rd EA W5	86	A5
Coriander Av POP/IOD E14	94	B5
Cories Cl BCTR RM8	79	K1
Corinium Cl WBLY HA9	68	B3
Corinne Rd ARCH N19	72	C3
Corinthian Manorwy		
ERITH DA8	118	A3
Corinthian Rd ERITH DA8	118	A3
Corkran Rd SURB KT6	158	E6
Cork Ms ESH/CLAY KT10 *	10	E7
Cork Sq WAP E1W	92	C7
Cork St CONDST W1S	10	E7
Cork Tree Wy CHING E4	43	G4
Corlett St CAMTN NW1	9	J2
Cormont Rd CMBW SE5	110	C7
Cormorant Cl WALTH E17	43	F7
Cormorant Rd FSTGT E7	76	D4
Cornbury Rd EDGW HA8	35	K6
Cornelia Dr YEAD UB4	83	G4
Cornelia St HOLWY N7	73	F5
Corner Fielde		
BRXS/STRHM SW2 *	130	A7
Corner Gn BKHTH/KID SE3	133	A7
Corner Md CDALE/KGS NW9	37	H6
Cornerside ASHF TW15	140	A6
The Corner EA W5 *	86	A7
Corney Reach Wy CHSWK W4	106	B6
Corney Rd CHSWK W4	106	B5
Cornfield Rd BUSH WD23	22	B3
Cornflower La CROY/NA CRO	166	A7
Cornflower Ter EDUL SE22	131	J5
Cornford Cl HAYES BR2	167	K4
Cornford Gv BAL SW12	148	B1
Cornhill BANK EC3V *	13	H5
Cornish Ct ED N9	30	D6
Cornish Gv PGE/AN SE20	150	D7
Cornmill La LEW SE13	132	E2
Cornmow Dr WLSDN NW10	69	H4
Cornshaw Rd BCTR RM8	61	K7
Cornthwaite Rd CLPT E5	74	E2
Cornwall Av BETH E2	92	E2
ESH/CLAY KT10	171	F6
FNCH N3	38	E6
STHL UB1	83	K4
WDGN N22	40	E7
WELL DA16	135	K2
Cornwall Cl BARK IG11	79	F5
Cornwall Crs NTGHL W11	88	C6
Cornwall Gdns SKENS SW7	14	C4
SNWD SE25 *	165	G3
WLSDN NW10	69	K5
Cornwall Gardens Wk		
SKENS SW7	14	D4
Cornwall Gv CHSWK W4	106	B4
Cornwallis Av ED N9	42	D1
ELTH/MOT SE9	154	D1
Cornwallis Cl ERITH DA8	118	C5
Cornwallis Gv ED N9	42	D1
Cornwallis Rd ARCH N19	72	E1
DAGW RM9	80	A3
ED N9	42	D1
WALTH E17	57	F3
WOOL/PLUM SE18	115	H3
Cornwallis Sq ARCH N19	72	E1
Cornwallis Wk ELTH/MOT SE9	134	E2
Cornwall Ms South		
SKENS SW7	14	D4
Cornwall Ms West		
SKENS SW7 *	14	C4
Cornwall Rd BELMT SM2	174	D6
CROY/NA CRO	177	H1
DART DA1	139	J2
FSBYPK N4	55	G6
HRW HA1	48	C5
PIN HA5	33	K6
RSLP HA4	64	B3
SEVS/STOTM N15	55	K4
STHWK SE1	12	A8
SUT SM1	174	D6
TWK TW1	124	B6
UED N18	42	C4
Cornwall St WCHPL E1	92	D6
Cornwall Ter CAMTN NW1	9	M1
Cornwall Terrace Ms		
CAMTN NW1	9	M1
Corn Wy WAN E11	76	B2
Cornwood Cl EFNCH N2	53	H4
Cornwood Dr WCHPL E1	92	E5
Cornworthy Rd BCTR RM8	79	J4
Corona Rd LEE/GVPK SE12	133	K6
Coronation Cl BARK/HLT IG6	60	C1
BXLY DA5	136	E5
Coronation Dr HCH RM12	81	K4
Coronation Rd HYS/HAR UB3	101	J3
PLSTW E13	95	G2
WLSDN NW10	86	D3
Coronation Vis		
WLSDN NW10 *	86	D3
Coronet Pde ALP/SUD HA0 *	68	A5
Coronet St IS N1	7	J8
Corporation Av HSLWW TW4	122	D3
Corporation Rw CLKNW EC1R	6	B9
Corporation St HOLWY N7	72	E4
SRTFD E15	94	C1
Corrance Rd		
BRXS/STRHM SW2	129	K3
Corri Av STHGT/OAK N14	40	D4
Corrib Dr SUT SM1	175	J4
Corrigan Cl HDN NW4	52	A2
Corringham Rd GLDGN NW11	52	E6
WBLY HA9	50	C7
Corringway EA W5	86	B4
GLDGN NW11	52	E6
Corris Gn CDALE/KGS NW9 *	51	G4
Corry Dr BRXN/ST SW9	130	C3
Corsair Cl STWL/WRAY TW19	120	A6
Corsair Rd STWL/WRAY TW19	120	B6
Corscombe Cl KUTN/CMB KT2	145	H4
Corsehill St STRHM/NOR SW16	148	C5
Corsellis Sq TWK TW1	124	C3
Corsham St IS N1	7	H8

Corsica St HBRY N5	73	H5
Cortayne Rd FUL/PGN SW6 *	127	J1
Cortina Dr DAGE RM10	81	F4
Cortis Rd PUT/ROE SW15	126	E5
Cortis Ter PUT/ROE SW15	126	E5
Cortland Cl DART DA1	138	B5
Corunna Rd VX/NE SW8	109	H7
Corunna Ter VX/NE SW8	109	H7
Corwell Gdns UX/CGN UB8	82	A5
Corwell La UX/CGN UB8	82	A5
Coryton Pth MV/WKIL W9	88	D3
Cosbycote Av HNHL SE24	130	D4
Cosdach Av WLGTN SM6	176	D6
Cosedge Crs CROY/NA CRO	177	G4
Cosgrove Cl WCHMH N21	41	J1
YEAD UB4	83	H3
Cosmo Pl RSQ WC1B	11	K2
Cosmur Cl SHB W12	106	C2
Cossall Wk PECK SE15	111	J7
Cossar Ms BRXS/STRHM SW2	130	B4
Cosser St STHWK SE1	18	A3
Costa St PECK SE15	131	H1
Costons Av GFD/PVL UB6	84	D2
Costons La GFD/PVL UB6	84	D2
Cosway St CAMTN NW1	9	K2
Cotall St POP/IOD E14	93	J5
Coteford Cl PIN HA5	46	E4
Coteford St TOOT SW17	147	K3
Cotelands CROY/NA CRO	178	A2
Cotesbach Rd CLPT E5	74	E2
Cotesmore Gdns BCTR RM8	79	J3
Cotford Rd THHTH CR7	164	D3
Cotham St WALW SE17	18	F6
Cotherstone HOR/WEW KT19	173	F7
Cotherstone Rd		
BRXS/STRHM SW2	130	A1
Cotleigh Av BXLY DA5	155	K1
Cotleigh Rd KIL/WHAMP NW6	2	A1
ROMW/RG RM7	63	F5
Cotman Cl GLDGN NW11	53	G5
Cotman Ms BCTR RM8	79	H4
Cotmans Cl HYS/HAR UB3	82	E7
Coton Rd WELL DA16	136	B2
Cotsford Av NWMAL KT3	159	K4
Cotswold Av BUSH WD23	22	C5
Cotswold Cl BXLYHN DA7	118	B7
ESH/CLAY KT10	171	F1
KUTN/CMB KT2	144	E5
Cotswold Gdns CRICK NW2	70	B1
EHAM E6	95	H2
GNTH/NBYPK IG2	60	C5
Cotswold Ga CRICK NW2	52	C7
Cotswold Gn ENC/FH EN2	29	F3
Cotswold Ms BTSEA SW11	108	C7
Cotswold Ri ORP BR6	169	K6
Cotswold Rd HPTN TW12	142	A5
Cotswold St WNWD SE27	149	H3
Cotswold Wy ENC/FH EN2	29	F3
WPK KT4	174	A1
Cottage Av HAYES BR2	168	D1
Cottage Cl RSLP HA4	46	B7
RYLN/HDSTN HA2	66	D1
WAT WD17	20	D1
Cottage Field Cl SCUP DA14	136	D7
Cottage Gn CMBW SE5	110	E6
Cottage Gv BRXN/ST SW9	129	K2
SURB KT6	158	E5
Cottage Pl CHEL SW3	15	J3
Cottage Rd HOLWY N7	173	F6
HOR/WEW KT19	173	F6
The Cottages		
HOR/WEW KT19 *	173	F6
Cottage St POP/IOD E14	93	K6
Cottenham Dr		
CDALE/KGS NW9	51	H2
RYNPK SW20	145	K6
Cottenham Park Rd		
RYNPK SW20	145	J7
Cottenham Pl RYNPK SW20	145	K6
Cottenham Rd WALTH E17	57	H3
Cotterill Rd SURB KT6	172	B1
Cottesbrook St NWCR SE14	112	B6
Cottesloe Ms STHWK SE1	18	B3
Cottesmore Av CLAY IG5	59	H4
Cottesmore Gdns KENS W8	14	D3
Cottimore Av WOT/HER KT12	156	A6
Cottimore Crs WOT/HER KT12	156	A6
Cottimore La WOT/HER KT12	156	A6
Cottimore Ter WOT/HER KT12	156	A6
Cottingham Cha RSLP HA4	64	D2
Cottingham Rd PGE/AN SE20	151	F6
VX/NE SW8	110	A6
Cottington Rd FELT TW13	141	H3
Cottington St LBTH SE11	18	B7
Cotton Av ACT W3	87	F5
Cotton Cl DAGW RM9	79	J6
WAN E11	76	C1
Cotton Gardens Est		
LBTH SE11	18	C6
Cottongrass Cl CROY/NA CRO	166	A7
Cottonham Cl		
NFNCH/WDSPK N12	39	H4
Cotton HI BMLY BR1	152	B3
Cotton Rw BTSEA SW11	128	B2
Cottons Ap ROMW/RG RM7	63	F4
Cotton's Gdns BETH E2	7	K7
Cotton St POP/IOD E14	94	A6
Couchmore Av CLAY IG5	59	K1
ESH/CLAY KT10	170	E1
Coulgate St BROCKY SE4	132	B2
Coulsdon Cl BCTR RM8	61	J7
Coulson Cl CHEL SW3	15	L7
Coulson St CHEL SW3	15	L7
Coulter Cl YEAD UB4	83	J3
Coulter Rd HMSMTH W6	106	E2
Councillor St CMBW SE5	110	D6
Counter Ct STHWK SE1 *	13	J8
Countess Rd KTTN NW5	72	C4
Countisbury Av EN EN1	30	B6
Country Wy FELT TW13	141	G4
County Ga BAR EN5	27	F5
ELTH/MOT SE9	154	C2
County Gv CMBW SE5	110	D7
County Pde BTFD TW8 *	104	E6
County Rd EHAM E6	96	B4
THHTH CR7	164	C1
County St STHWK SE1	18	F4
Coupland Pl		
WOOL/PLUM SE18	115	H4
Courcy Rd CEND/HSY/T N8	55	G2
Courier Rd DAGW RM9	98	E3
Courland Gv VX/NE SW8	109	J7
Courland Rd VX/NE SW8	109	J7
The Course ELTH/MOT SE9	154	A2
Courtauld Rd ARCH N19	54	D7
Courtaulds Cl THMD SE28	97	G2
Court Av BELV DA17	117	G4
Court Cl KTN/HRWW/WS HA3	49	K2
STJWD NW8 *	3	J2
WHTN TW2	142	B2
WLGTN SM6	176	D6
Court Close Av WHTN TW2	142	B2
Court Crs CHSGTN KT9	171	K5
Court Downs Rd BECK BR3	166	E1
Court Dr CROY/NA CRO	177	F3
STAN HA7	36	A3

SUT SM1 175 J3
Courtenay Av BELMT SM2 174 E7
HGT N6 53 J6
KTN/HRWW/WS HA3 34 B6
Courtenay Dr BECK BR3 167 G1
Courtenay Ms WALTH E17 57 G4
Courtenay Pl WALTH E17 57 G4
Courtenay Rd PGE/AN SE20 151 F6
WALTH E17 57 F4
WAN E11 * 76 D2
WBLY HA9 * 67 K2
WPK KT4 174 A2
Courtenay Sq LBTH SE11 18 A8
Courtenay St LBTH SE11 17 M7
Courten Ms STAN HA7 35 J6
Court Farm Av
HOR/WEW KT19 173 F4
Court Farm Rd ELTH/MOT SE9 153 H1
NTHLT UB5 66 A6
Courtfield Av HRW HA1 * 49 F4
Courtfield Crs HRW HA1 49 F4
Courtfield Gdns ECT SW5 14 D6
RSLP HA4 64 D1
WEA W13 85 G5
Courtfield Ms ECT SW5 14 D6
Courtfield Ri WWKM BR4 180 B2
Courtfield Rd SKENS SW7 14 E5
Court Gdns HOLWY N7 73 G5
Courtgate Cl MLHL NW7 37 H5
Courthill Rd LEW SE13 133 F3
Courthope Rd GFD/PVL UB6 84 D1
HAMP NW3 71 K3
WIM/MER SW19 146 C4
Courthope Vls
WIM/MER SW19 146 C6
Courthouse La
STNW/STAM N16 74 B3
Court House Rd FNCH N3 39 F5
Courtland Av CHING E4 44 D1
IL IG1 77 K1
MLHL NW7 37 F2
STRHM/NOR SW16 149 F6
Courtland Gv THMD SE28 97 K6
Courtland Rd EHAM E6 77 J7
Courtlands CHST BR7 154 B6
RCHPK/HAM TW10 125 H4
Courtlands Av HAYES BR2 167 H7
HPTN TW12 141 K5
LEE/GVPK SE12 134 A4
RCH/KEW TW9 125 J1
Courtlands Cl RSLP HA4 46 D6
Courtlands Dr
HOR/WEW KT19 173 G5
Courtlands Rd BRYLDS KT5 159 H6
Court La DUL SE21 131 G6
Court Lane Gdns DUL SE21 131 F6
Courtleet Dr BXLYHN DA7 117 J2
Courtleigh Gdns GLDGN NW11 52 C3
Courtman Rd TOTM N17 41 J6
Court Md NTHLT UB5 83 K2
Courtmead Cl HNHL SE24 130 D5
Courtnell St BAY/PAD W2 8 A4
Courtney Cl NRWD SE19 150 A5
Courtney Crs CAR SM5 175 K6
Courtney Pl CROY/NA CR0 177 G2
Courtney Rd CROY/NA CR0 177 G2
HOLWY N7 73 G4
HTHAIR TW6 120 D2
WBLY HA9 67 K2
WIM/MER SW19 147 J6
Courtney Wy HTHAIR TW6 120 D2
Courtrai Rd FSTH SE23 132 B5
Court Rd ELTH/MOT SE9 153 J1
NWDGN UB2 102 E3
SNWD SE25 165 G1
Courtside HGT N6 54 D5
SYD SE26 * 150 E2
The Courts STRHM/NOR SW16 148 E6
Courtstreet BMLY BR1 167 K1
Court St WCHPL E1 92 D4
The Court MUSWH N10 * 54 C3
RSLP HA4 65 J3
Court Vw HGT N6 * 72 B1
Court Wy ACT W3 86 E4
BARK/HLT IG6 60 C2
CDALE/KGS NW9 51 G3
WHTN TW2 124 A6
The Courtway OXHEY WD19 33 J1
Court Yd ELTH/MOT SE9 134 D5
Courtyard Ms RAIN RM13 81 H7
STMC/STPC BR5 155 G6
The Courtyards WATW WD18 * 20 B6
The Courtyard IS N1 5 M1
Cousin La CANST EC4R 13 G6
Couthurst Rd BKHTH/KID SE3 114 A5
Coutts Av CHSGTN KT9 172 A4
Coutts Crs KTTN NW5 * 72 A2
Couzins Wk DART DA1 139 J1
Coval Gdns MORT/ESHN SW14 125 J3
Coval La MORT/ESHN SW14 125 J3
Coval Rd MORT/ESHN SW14 125 J3
Covelees Wall EHAM E6 96 A5
Covent Gdn COVGDN WC2E 11 K6
Covent Garden Piazza
COVGDN WC2E 11 K6
Coventry Cl EHAM E6 95 K5
KIL/WHAMP NW6 2 B5
Coventry Cross Est BOW E3 94 A3
Coventry Rd BETH E2 * 92 D2
IL IG1 60 B7
SNWD SE25 165 H3
WCHPL E1 92 D3
Coventry St SOHO/SHAV W1D 11 G7
Coverack Cl CROY/NA CR0 166 B6
STHGT/OAK N14 28 C5
Coverdale Gdns CROY/NA CR0 178 B2
Coverdale Rd CRICK NW2 70 C6
FBAR/BDGN N11 40 A5
SHB W12 87 K7
The Coverdales BARK IG11 96 D1
Coverley Cl WCHPL E1 * 92 C4
Coverton Rd TOOT SW17 147 J3
Coverts Rd ESH/CLAY KT10 171 F6
The Covert NRWD SE19 * 150 B6
NTHWD HA6 32 A6
ORP BR6 169 K5
Covert Wy EBAR EN4 27 G1
Covey Cl WIM/MER SW19 162 A1
Covey Rd WPK KT4 174 B1
Covington Gdns
STRHM/NOR SW16 149 H6
Covington Wy
STRHM/NOR SW16 149 G6
Cowbridge La BARK IG11 78 B6
Cowbridge Rd
KTN/HRWW/WS HA3 50 B3
Cowcross St FARR EC1M 12 C2
Cowdenbeath Pth IS N1 5 L3
Cowden St CAT SE6 151 J3
Cowdray Rd HGDN/ICK UB10 64 A7
Cowdray Wy HCH RM12 81 J3
Cowdrey Cl EN EN1 30 A1
Cowdrey Ct DART DA1 138 E6
Cowdrey Rd WIM/MER SW19 147 F5
Cowen Av HRW HA1 66 D1
Cowgate Rd GFD/PVL UB6 84 D2
Cowick Rd TOOT SW17 147 K3
Cowings Md NTHLT UB5 65 J6
Cowland Av PEND EN3 30 E3
Cow La BUSH WD23 * 22 A5
Cow Leaze EHAM E6 96 A5
Cowleaze Rd KUTN/CMB KT2 144 A7
Cowley Cl SAND/SEL CR2 178 E7
Cowley Ct WAN E11 * 76 C2
Cowley La WAN E11 * 76 C2
Cowley Pl HDN NW4 52 A4
Cowley Rd ACT W3 87 H7
BRXN/ST SW9 110 B7
IL IG1 59 K6
MORT/ESHN SW14 126 B2
WAN E11 59 F4
Cowley St WEST SW1P 17 J4
Cowling Cl NTGHL W11 88 C6
Cowper Av EHAM E6 77 J6
SUT SM1 175 H3
Cowper Cl HAYES BR2 168 C3
WELL DA16 136 B4
Cowper Gdns STHGT/OAK N14 28 B5
WLGTN SM6 176 C5
Cowper Rd ACT W3 87 F7
BELV DA17 117 G3
HAYES BR2 168 C3
HNWL W7 85 F6
KUTN/CMB KT2 144 B4
RAIN RM13 99 J3
STHGT/OAK N14 28 B7
STNW/STAM N16 74 A3
UED N18 42 C4
WIM/MER SW19 147 G5
Cowper St STLK EC1Y 7 H9
Cowper Ter NKENS W10 * 88 B4
Cowslip Rd SWFD E18 59 F1
Cowthorpe Rd VX/NE SW8 109 J7
Coxe Pl KTN/HRWW/WS HA3 49 G3
Cox La CHSGTN KT9 172 A3
Coxmount Rd CHARL SE7 114 C4
Coxson Wy STHWK SE1 19 L2
Coxwell Rd NRWD SE19 150 A6
WOOL/PLUM SE18 115 J4
Crab Hl BECK BR3 152 B6
Crabtree Av ALP/SUD HA0 86 A1
CHDH RM6 61 K3
Crabtree Cl BETH E2 7 L6
BUSH WD23 22 B4
Crabtree La FUL/PGN SW6 107 G6
Crabtree Manorway North
BELV DA17 117 K1
Crabtree Manorway South
BELV DA17 117 K1
Crabtree Wk CROY/NA CR0 165 H7
Craddock Rd EN EN1 30 B2
Craddock St KTTN NW5 * 72 A5
Cradley Rd ELTH/MOT SE9 135 J7
Cragie Lea MUSWH N10 * 54 B1
Craigdale Rd EMPK RM11 63 H5
Craigen Av CROY/NA CR0 165 J7
Craigerne Rd BKHTH/KID SE3 114 A6
Craig Gdns SWFD E18 58 D1
Craigholm WOOL/PLUM SE18 135 F1
Craigmuir Pk ALP/SUD HA0 68 B7
Craignair Rd
BRXS/STRHM SW2 130 A6
Craignish Av
STRHM/NOR SW16 164 A1
Craig Park Rd UED N18 42 D3
Craig Rd RCHPK/HAM TW10 143 J3
Craig's Ct WHALL SW1A 11 J8
Craigton Rd ELTH/MOT SE9 134 E3
Craigweil Cl STAN HA7 35 K4
Craigweil Dr STAN HA7 35 K4
Craigwell Av FELT TW13 140 E2
Crail Rw WALW SE17 19 H6
Crakers Md WATW WD18 * 21 F2
Cramer St MHST W1U 10 B3
Crammond Cl HMSMTH W6 107 H5
Cramond Ct
EBED/NFELT TW14 121 G7
Crampton Rd PGE/AN SE20 150 E5
Crampton St WALW SE17 18 E7
Cranberry Cl NTHLT UB5 83 H1
Cranberry La CAN/RD E16 94 C3
Cranborne Av NWDGN UB2 103 F3
SURB KT6 172 C2
Cranborne Rd BARK IG11 78 D7
Cranborne Waye YEAD UB4 83 F5
Cranbourne Av WAN E11 59 F3
Cranbourne Cl
STRHM/NOR SW16 163 K2
Cranbourne Dr PIN HA5 47 H4
Cranbourne Gdns
BARK/HLT IG6 60 C2
GLDGN NW11 52 C4
Cranbourne Rd MNPK E12 77 J4
MUSWH N10 54 B1
NTHWD HA6 46 D2
SRTFD E15 76 B4
Cranbourn St LSQ/SEVD WC2H 11 H6
Cranbrook Cl HAYES BR2 167 K5
Cranbrook Dr ESH/CLAY KT10 157 H7
GPK RM2 63 K3
WHTN TW2 123 G7
Cranbrook La
FBAR/BDGN N11 40 B3
Cranbrook Ms WALTH E17 57 H4
Cranbrook Pk WDGN N22 41 G7
Cranbrook Ri IL IG1 59 K5
Cranbrook Rd BARK/HLT IG6 60 C2
BXLYHN DA7 117 G7
CHSWK W4 106 B4
DEPT SE8 112 D7
EBAR EN4 27 H5
GNTH/NBYPK IG2 60 A5
HSLWW TW4 122 E3
IL IG1 78 A1
THHTH CR7 164 D1
WIM/MER SW19 146 C6
Cranbrook St BETH E2 93 F1
Cranbury Rd FUL/PGN SW6 128 A1
Crane Av ACT W3 86 E6
ISLW TW7 124 B4
Cranebank Ms TWK TW1 * 124 C4
Cranebrook WHTN TW2 142 C1
Crane Cl DAGE RM10 80 C5
Crane Ct FLST/FETLN EC4A 12 B5
MORT/ESHN SW14 * 125 K3
Craneford Cl WHTN TW2 124 A6
Craneford Wy WHTN TW2 123 K6
Crane Gdns HYS/HAR UB3 101 J3
Crane Gv HOLWY N7 73 G5
Crane Lodge Rd HEST TW5 102 A5
Crane Md BERM/RHTH SE16 112 A3
Crane Park Rd WHTN TW2 142 B1
Crane Rd STWL/WRAY TW19 120 D5
WHTN TW2 123 K7
Cranesbill Cl CDALE/KGS NW9 51 F2
STRHM/NOR SW16 163 J1
Cranes Dr BRYLDS KT5 159 F3
Cranes Pk BRYLDS KT5 159 F3
Cranes Park Av BRYLDS KT5 159 F3
Cranes Park Crs BRYLDS KT5 159 G3
Crane St PECK SE15 111 G7
Craneswater HYS/HAR UB3 101 J6
Craneswater Pk NWDGN UB2 102 E4
Cranes Wy BORE WD6 24 E4
Crane Wy WHTN TW2 123 H6
Cranfield Dr CDALE/KGS NW9 37 G7
Cranfield Rd BROCKY SE4 132 C2
Cranfield Rd East CAR SM5 176 A7
Cranfield Rd West CAR SM5 * 175 K7
Cranford Av PLMGR N13 40 E4
STWL/WRAY TW19 120 B6
Cranford Cl RYNPK SW20 145 K6
STWL/WRAY TW19 120 B6
Cranford Cots WAP E1W * 93 F6
Cranford Dr HYS/HAR UB3 101 J3
Cranford La HYS/HAR UB3 101 G5
Cranford Ms HAYES BR2 168 D4
Cranford Park Rd
HYS/HAR UB3 101 J3
Cranford Ri ESH/CLAY KT10 170 C4
Cranford Rd DART DA1 139 H7
Cranford St WAP E1W 93 F6
Cranford Wy CEND/HSY/T N8 55 F4
Cranham Rd EMPK RM11 63 K5
Cranhurst Rd CRICK NW2 70 A4
Cranleigh Cl BXLY DA5 * 137 J5
PGE/AN SE20 165 J1
Cranleigh Gdns BARK IG11 78 D6
KTN/HRWW/WS HA3 50 A4
KUTN/CMB KT2 144 B5
SNWD SE25 165 F2
STHL UB1 83 K5
SUT SM1 175 F1
WCHMH N21 29 G4
Cranleigh Ms BTSEA SW11 128 D1
Cranleigh Rd ESH/CLAY KT10 157 H7
FELT TW13 140 D3
SEVS/STOTM N15 55 J4
WIM/MER SW19 161 K2
Cranleigh St CAMTN NW1 4 F6
Cranley Dr GNTH/NBYPK IG2 60 C6
RSLP HA4 64 D1
Cranley Gdns MUSWH N10 54 B3
PLMGR N13 41 F2
SKENS SW7 14 F7
WLGTN SM6 176 C6
Cranley Ms SKENS SW7 14 F7
Cranley Pl SKENS SW7 15 G6
Cranley Rd GNTH/NBYPK IG2 60 C5
PLSTW E13 95 F4
Cranley Ter HDN NW4 * 52 B1
Cranmer Av WEA W13 104 C2
Cranmer Cl MRDN SM4 161 G5
RSLP HA4 47 H7
STAN HA7 35 J6
Cranmer Ct HPTN TW12 142 B4
KUTN/CMB KT2 143 K3
Cranmer Farm Cl MTCM CR4 162 E3
Cranmer Gdns DAGE RM10 80 E3
Cranmer Rd BRXN/ST SW9 110 B6
CROY/NA CR0 177 H2
EDGW HA8 36 D2
FSTGT E7 77 F3
HPTN TW12 142 B4
HYS/HAR UB3 82 B5
KUTN/CMB KT2 144 A4
MTCM CR4 162 E3
Cranmer Ter TOOT SW17 147 H4
Cranmore Av ISLW TW7 103 H6
Cranmore Rd BMLY BR1 152 C2
CHST BR7 153 K4
Cranmore Wy MUSWH N10 54 C3
Cranston Cl HGDN/ICK UB10 64 B1
HSLW TW3 122 D1
Cranston Est IS N1 7 H5
Cranston Gdns CHING E4 43 K5
Cranston Rd FSTH SE23 132 B7
Cranswick Rd
BERM/RHTH SE16 111 J4
Crantock Rd CAT SE6 152 A1
Cranwell Cl BOW E3 93 K3
Cranwich Av WCHMH N21 29 K6
Cranwich Rd STNW/STAM N16 56 A6
Cranwood St FSBYE EC1V 7 H8
Cranworth Gdns
BRXN/ST SW9 110 B7
Craster Rd BRXS/STRHM SW2 130 A6
Crathie Rd LEE/GVPK SE12 134 A5
Cravan Av FELT TW13 140 E1
Craven Av EA W5 85 J6
STHL UB1 83 K4
Craven Cl STNW/STAM N16 * 56 C6
YEAD UB4 82 E5
Craven Gdns BARK IG11 96 E1
BARK/HLT IG6 60 D1
WIM/MER SW19 147 F4
Craven Hl BAY/PAD W2 8 F6
Craven Hill Gdns BAY/PAD W2 8 E6
Craven Hill Ms BAY/PAD W2 8 F6
Craven Ms BTSEA SW11 129 F2
Craven Pk WLSDN NW10 69 F6
Craven Park Ms WLSDN NW10 69 G6
Craven Park Rd
SEVS/STOTM N15 56 B5
WLSDN NW10 69 G7
Craven Pas CHCR WC2N 11 J8
Craven Rd BAY/PAD W2 8 F6
CROY/NA CR0 165 J7
KUTN/CMB KT2 144 B7
WEA W13 85 J6
WLSDN NW10 69 F7
Craven St CHCR WC2N 11 J8
Craven Ter BAY/PAD W2 8 F6
Craven Wk STNW/STAM N16 56 C6
Crawford Av ALP/SUD HA0 67 K4
DART DA1 139 G5
Crawford Cl ISLW TW7 123 K1
Crawford Gdns NTHLT UB5 83 K2
PLMGR N13 41 H2
Crawford Ms MBLAR W1H * 9 L3
Crawford Pas CLKNW EC1R 12 A1
Crawford Pl MBLAR W1H 9 K4
Crawford Rd CMBW SE5 130 D1
Crawford St MBLAR W1H 9 L3
MHST W1U 9 M3
WLSDN NW10 69 F6
Crawley Rd EN EN1 30 A6
LEY E10 57 K7
WDGN N22 55 J1
Crawthew Gv EDUL SE22 131 G3
Craybrooke Rd SCUP DA14 155 H3
Craybury End ELTH/MOT SE9 154 C1
Cray Cl DART DA1 138 D4
Craydene Rd ERITH DA8 118 C7
Crayford High St DART DA1 138 B3
Crayford Rd DART DA1 138 C4
HOLWY N7 72 E3
Crayford Wy DART DA1 138 D3
Crayke Hl CHSGTN KT9 172 A6
Crayleigh Ter SCUP DA14 * 155 J5
Crayonne Cl SUN TW16 140 C7
Cray Rd BELV DA17 117 H5
SCUP DA14 155 J5
Crealock Gv WFD IG8 44 D4
Crealock St WAND/EARL SW18 128 A5
Creasey Cl EMPK RM11 81 K1
Crebor St EDUL SE22 131 H5
Credenhall Dr HAYES BR2 168 E7
Credenhill St
STRHM/NOR SW16 148 C5
Crediton Hl KIL/WHAMP NW6 71 F4
Crediton Rd CAN/RD E16 94 E5
WLSDN NW10 70 B7
Crediton Wy ESH/CLAY KT10 171 G4
Credon Rd BERM/RHTH SE16 111 J4
PLSTW E13 95 G1
Creechurch La HDTCH EC3A 13 K5
Creechurch Pl HDTCH EC3A * 13 K5
Creed La BLKFR EC4V 12 D5
Creek Cots E/WMO/HCT KT8 * 157 K3
Creek Rd BARK IG11 97 F2
DEPT SE8 112 D5
E/WMO/HCT KT8 157 K3
Creekside DEPT SE8 112 E6
RAIN RM13 99 H3
Creek Wy RAIN RM13 99 G5
Creeland Gv CAT SE6 132 C7
Crefeld Cl HMSMTH W6 107 G5
Creffield Rd EA W5 86 C6
Creighton Av EFNCH N2 53 K1
EHAM E6 95 H1
Creighton Cl SHB W12 87 K6
Creighton Rd EA W5 104 E2
KIL/WHAMP NW6 88 B1
TOTM N17 42 A6
Creigton Av EFNCH N2 53 J2
Cremer St BETH E2 7 L6
Cremorne Est WBPTN SW10 * 108 C5
Cremorne Gdns
HOR/WEW KT19 173 F7
Cremorne Rd WBPTN SW10 108 B6
Crescent TWRH EC3N 13 L6
Crescent Ar GNWCH SE10 113 F5
Crescent Av HCH RM12 81 H1
Crescent Dr STMC/STPC BR5 169 H5
Crescent Gdns RSLP HA4 47 F6
WIM/MER SW19 146 E2
Crescent Gv CLAP SW4 129 H3
MTCM CR4 162 D3
Crescent La CLAP SW4 129 J4
Crescent Pl CHEL SW3 15 J5
Crescent Ri EBAR EN4 27 J4
FNCH N3 * 38 D7
WDGN N22 40 D7
Crescent Rd BECK BR3 166 E1
BFN/LL DA15 155 F2
BMLY BR1 152 E6
CEND/HSY/T N8 54 D5
DAGE RM10 80 D2
EBAR EN4 27 J5
ED N9 30 C7
EHAM E6 77 G7
ENC/FH EN2 29 H3
ERITH DA8 118 C5
FBAR/BDGN N11 39 K3
FNCH N3 38 D7
KUTN/CMB KT2 144 C6
LEY E10 75 K1
PLSTW E13 76 E7
RYNPK SW20 146 B7
SEVS/STOTM N15 * 55 H2
SWFD E18 59 G1
WDGN N22 40 D7
WOOL/PLUM SE18 115 G4
Crescent Rw STLK EC1Y 12 E1
Crescent St IS N1 5 M1
The Crescent ACT W3 87 G5
ALP/SUD HA0 67 H1
BAR EN5 27 F2
BARN SW13 126 C1
BECK BR3 151 J7
BXLY DA5 136 D6
CRICK NW2 69 K2
CROY/NA CR0 164 E5
E/WMO/HCT KT8 156 E3
FBAR/BDGN N11 39 K3
GNTH/NBYPK IG2 60 A5
HYS/HAR UB3 101 F6
NWMAL KT3 159 K1
RYLN/HDSTN HA2 48 C7
SCUP DA14 155 F3
STHL UB1 102 D1
SURB KT6 159 F4
SUT SM1 175 H4
WALTH E17 57 G4
WATW WD18 21 G3
WIM/MER SW19 146 E2
WWKM BR4 167 H5
Crescent Wy BROCKY SE4 132 D2
STRHM/NOR SW16 149 F6
Crescentway
NFNCH/WDSPK N12 39 J5
Crescent Wood Rd SYD SE26 150 C2
Cresford Rd FUL/PGN SW6 108 A7
Crespigny Rd HDN NW4 51 K5
Cressage Cl STHL UB1 84 A3
Cresset Rd HOM E9 74 E5
Cresset St CLAP SW4 129 J2
Cressfield Cl KTTN NW5 72 A4
Cressida Rd ARCH N19 54 C7
Cressingham Gv SUT SM1 175 G3
Cressingham Rd EDGW HA8 37 F5
LEW SE13 133 F2
Cressington Cl
STNW/STAM N16 74 A4
Cresswell Gdns ECT SW5 * 14 E7
Cresswell Pk BKHTH/KID SE3 133 J2
Cresswell Pl WBPTN SW10 14 E7
Cresswell Rd FELT TW13 141 J3
SNWD SE25 165 H3
TWK TW1 124 E5
Cresswell Wy WCHMH N21 29 G6
Cressy Ct HMSMTH W6 106 E2
WCHPL E1 92 E4
Cressy Houses WCHPL E1 * 92 E4
Cressy Pl WCHPL E1 92 E4
Cressy Rd HAMP NW3 71 K3
Cressys Cnr HSLW TW3 * 123 G2
Crestbrook Av PLMGR N13 41 H2
Crestbrook Pl PLMGR N13 * 41 G2
Crestfield St KCROSS N1C 5 K7
Crest Gdns RSLP HA4 65 G2
Creston Wy WPK KT4 161 G7
Crest Rd CRICK NW2 69 J1
HAYES BR2 167 J6
SAND/SEL CR2 178 D6
The Crest BRYLDS KT5 159 H4
HDN NW4 52 A4
HOLWY N7 * 72 D4
PLMGR N13 41 G3
Crest Vw PIN HA5 47 H3
Crest View Dr STMC/STPC BR5 169 G4
Crestway PUT/ROE SW15 126 D5
Creswell Wy HSLWW TW4 122 E4
Creswell Dr BECK BR3 166 E4
Creswick Rd ACT W3 86 D6
Creswick Wk GLDGN NW11 52 D3
Creukhorne Rd
WLSDN NW10 * 69 G6
Crewdson Rd BRXN/ST SW9 110 A6
Crewe Pl WLSDN NW10 87 H2
Crews St POP/IOD E14 112 D3
Crewys Rd CRICK NW2 70 D1
PECK SE15 131 J1
Crichton Av WLGTN SM6 176 D4
Crichton Rd CAR SM5 175 K6
Crichton St VX/NE SW8 * 129 H1
Cricketers Arms Rd
ENC/FH EN2 * 29 J1
Cricketers Cl CHSGTN KT9 171 K4
ERITH DA8 118 B4
STHGT/OAK N14 28 C6
Cricketers Ms BAL SW12 129 G6
WAND/EARL SW18 128 A4
Cricketers Wk SYD SE26 150 E4
Cricketfield Rd CLPT E5 74 D3
Cricket Gn MTCM CR4 162 E2
Cricket Ground Rd CHST BR7 154 B7
Cricket La BECK BR3 151 G5
HPTN TW12 142 C4
Cricket Rw EFNCH N2 * 53 H2
Cricklade Av
BRXS/STRHM SW2 148 E1
Cricklewood Broadway
CRICK NW2 70 B3
Cricklewood La CRICK NW2 70 C3
Cridland St SRTFD E15 76 D7
Crieff Ct TEDD TW11 143 J6
Crieff Rd WAND/EARL SW18 128 B5
Criffel Av BRXS/STRHM SW2 148 D1
Crimscott St STHWK SE1 19 K4
Crimsworth Rd VX/NE SW8 109 J6
Crinan St IS N1 5 K5
Cringle St VX/NE SW8 109 H6
Cripplegate St BARB EC2Y * 12 E2
Crispen Rd FELT TW13 141 J3
Crispian Cl WLSDN NW10 69 G3
Crispin Crs CROY/NA CR0 176 D1
Crispin Ms GLDGN NW11 52 D4
Crispin Rd EDGW HA8 36 E5
Crispin St WCHPL E1 13 L3
Crisp Rd HMSMTH W6 107 F4
Cristowe Rd FUL/PGN SW6 * 127 J1
Critchley Av DART DA1 139 G5
Criterion Ms ARCH N19 72 D1
HNHL SE24 130 C4
Crockerton Rd TOOT SW17 147 K1
Crockham Wy ELTH/MOT SE9 154 A3
Crocus Cl CROY/NA CR0 166 A7
Crocus Fld BAR EN5 26 D5
Croft Av WWKM BR4 167 F7
Croft Cl ABYW SE2 117 G4
CHST BR7 153 K4
HYS/HAR UB3 101 F6
MLHL NW7 37 G2
Croft Ct BORE WD6 25 F2
RSLP HA4 * 46 D7
SUT SM1 * 175 H1
Croftdown Rd KTTN NW5 72 A2
Crofters Cl ISLW TW7 123 J4
Crofters Ct DEPT SE8 112 B3
Crofters Md CROY/NA CR0 179 H7
Crofters Rd NTHWD HA6 32 C3
Crofters Wy CAMTN NW1 5 G3
Croft Gdns HNWL W7 104 B1
RSLP HA4 46 C7
Croft Lodge Cl WFD IG8 45 F5
Croft Ms NFNCH/WDSPK N12 39 G2
Crofton Av BXLY DA5 136 E6
CHSWK W4 105 K6
Crofton Gate Wy BROCKY SE4 132 B4
Crofton Gv CHING E4 44 B3
Crofton La STMC/STPC BR5 169 J7
Crofton Park Rd BROCKY SE4 132 C5
Crofton Rd CMBW SE5 111 F7
PLSTW E13 95 F3
Crofton Ter RCH/KEW TW9 125 G3
Crofton Wy BAR EN5 * 27 F5
ENC/FH EN2 29 G1
Croft Rd BMLY BR1 152 E5
STRHM/NOR SW16 149 G6
SUT SM1 175 H4
WIM/MER SW19 147 G6
Crofts Rd HRW HA1 49 G5
Croft St DEPT SE8 112 B3
WCHPL E1 92 C6
The Croft ALP/SUD HA0 67 J4
BAR EN5 26 C3
CHING E4 44 C1
EA W5 86 A4
HEST TW5 102 D6
PIN HA5 47 K6
RSLP HA4 65 G3
WLSDN NW10 87 H1
Croft Wy BFN/LL DA15 154 E2
RCHPK/HAM TW10 143 H2
Crogsland Rd CAMTN NW1 4 A1
Croham Cl SAND/SEL CR2 178 A6
Croham Manor Rd
SAND/SEL CR2 178 A6
Croham Mt SAND/SEL CR2 178 A6
Croham Park Av
SAND/SEL CR2 178 B4
Croham Rd SAND/SEL CR2 177 K4
Croham Valley Rd
SAND/SEL CR2 178 C5
Croindene Rd
STRHM/NOR SW16 148 E7
Cromartie Rd ARCH N19 54 D6
Cromarty Rd EDGW HA8 36 D1
Cromarty Vls BAY/PAD W2 * 8 E6
Crombie Cl REDBR IG4 59 K4
Crombie Ms BTSEA SW11 * 128 D1
Crombie Rd BFN/LL DA15 135 J7
Cromer Cl UX/CGN UB8 82 A5
Cromer Hyde MRDN SM4 * 162 A4
Crome Rd WLSDN NW10 69 G5
Cromer Rd BAR EN5 27 G3
CHDH RM6 62 A5
HTHAIR TW6 120 D2
LEY E10 58 B6
ROMW/RG RM7 62 E5
SNWD SE25 165 J2
TOOT SW17 148 A5
TOTM N17 56 C1
Cromer Rd West HTHAIR TW6 120 D2
Cromer St STPAN WC1H 5 K8
Cromer Ter HACK E8 74 C4
Cromer Villas Rd
WAND/EARL SW18 127 J5
Cromford Rd PUT/ROE SW15 127 J4
Cromford Wy NWMAL KT3 145 F7
Cromlix Cl CHST BR7 169 G1
Crompton St BAY/PAD W2 9 G1
Cromwell Av HAYES BR2 168 A2

HGT N6 54 B7
HMSMTH W6 106 E4
NWMAL KT3 160 C4
Cromwell Cl CHSWK W4 * 105 J4
EFNCH N2 53 H3
HAYES BR2 168 A3
WOT/HER KT12 156 A7
Cromwell Ct ALP/SUD HA0 86 A1
PEND EN3 31 F4
Cromwell Crs ECT SW5 14 A5
Cromwell Gdns SKENS SW7 15 H5
Cromwell Gv HMSMTH W6 107 F2
Cromwell Ms SKENS SW7 * 15 G5
Cromwell Pde ALP/SUD HA0 * 86 A1
Cromwell Pl ACT W3 86 E7
HGT N6 * 54 B7
MORT/ESHN SW14 125 K2
SKENS SW7 15 H5
Cromwell Rd ALP/SUD HA0 85 K1
BECK BR3 166 B1
BRXN/ST SW9 110 C7
CROY/NA CR0 164 E6
ECT SW5 14 B5
FELT TW13 122 A7
FNCH N3 53 G1
FSTGT E7 77 G6
HSLW TW3 123 F3
HYS/HAR UB3 82 B5
KUTN/CMB KT2 144 A7
MUSWH N10 40 A6
SKENS SW7 14 D5
TEDD TW11 143 G5
WALTH E17 58 A4
WIM/MER SW19 146 E4
WPK KT4 173 F2
Cromwell St HSLW TW3 123 F3
Cromwell Ter HSLW TW3 * 123 F3
Crondace Rd FUL/PGN SW6 107 K7
Crondall St IS N1 7 H6
Cronin St PECK SE15 111 G6
Crooked Billet Rbt CHING E4 43 K6
Crooked Usage FNCH N3 52 C2
Crooke Rd DEPT SE8 112 B4
Crookham Rd FUL/PGN SW6 107 J7
Crook Log BXLYHS DA6 136 F2
Crookston Rd ELTH/MOT SE9 135 F2
Croombs Rd CAN/RD E16 95 G4
Croom's Hl GNWCH SE10 113 G6
Croom's Hill Gv GNWCH SE10 113 F6
Cropley St IS N1 7 G5
Croppath Rd DAGE RM10 80 C3
Cropthorne Ct MV/WKIL W9 2 F8
Crosby Cl FELT TW13 141 J3
Crosby Rd DAGE RM10 98 D1
FSTGT E7 76 E5
Crosby Rw STHWK SE1 19 G2
Crosby Sq HDTCH EC3A 13 J5
Crosby Wk HACK E8 74 B5
Crosier Cl BKHTH/KID SE3 114 D7
Crosier Rd HGDN/ICK UB10 64 A3
Crosier Wy RSLP HA4 64 C2
Crosland Pl BTSEA SW11 129 F2
Crossbrook Rd
BKHTH/KID SE3 134 D1
Cross Deep TWK TW1 143 F2
Cross Deep Gdns TWK TW1 143 F1
Crossfield Est DEPT SE8 112 D6
Crossfield Rd HAMP NW3 71 H5
TOTM N17 55 J2
Crossfield St DEPT SE8 112 D6
Crossford St BRXN/ST SW9 130 A1
Crossgate EDGW HA8 36 C2
GFD/PVL UB6 67 H5
Cross Keys Cl ED N9 42 C1
MHST W1U 10 B3
Cross Lances Rd HSLW TW3 123 G3
Crossland Rd THHTH CR7 164 C5
Crosslands Av EA W5 86 B7
NWDGN UB2 102 E4
Crosslands Pde
NWDGN UB2 * 103 F4
Crosslands Rd
HOR/WEW KT19 173 F5
Cross La BXLY DA5 137 G6
CEND/HSY/T N8 55 F3
MON EC3R 13 J7
Crosslet St WALW SE17 19 H5
Crosslet V GNWCH SE10 112 E7
Crossley St HOLWY N7 73 G5
Crossmead ELTH/MOT SE9 134 E7
OXHEY WD19 21 F5
Crossmead Av GFD/PVL UB6 84 A2
Crossness Rd BARK IG11 97 F2
Cross Rd CHDH RM6 61 J6
CMBW SE5 131 F1
CROY/NA CR0 164 E7
DART DA1 139 F5
EN EN1 30 A3
FBAR/BDGN N11 40 B4
FELT TW13 141 J3
HAYES BR2 181 J1
HRW HA1 48 D3
KTN/HRWW/WS HA3 49 G1
KUTN/CMB KT2 144 B6
OXHEY WD19 21 J5
ROMW/RG RM7 62 C2
RYLN/HDSTN HA2 66 A2
SCUP DA14 155 H3
SUT SM1 175 H4
WDGN N22 41 G5
WFD IG8 45 K5
WIM/MER SW19 146 E6
Cross St BARN SW13 126 B1
ERITH DA8 118 B5
HPTN TW12 142 C4
IS N1 6 D3
UED N18 42 C4
WAT WD17 21 G2
Crossthwaite Av HNHL SE24 130 E3
Crosswall TWRH EC3N 13 L6
Crossway BCTR RM8 79 J2
CDALE/KGS NW9 51 H3
EN EN1 30 A6
Cross Wy HYS/HAR UB3 101 K1
Crossway NFNCH/WDSPK N12 39 H5
NWMAL KT3 161 F3
PIN HA5 47 F1
RSLP HA4 65 G3
STMC/STPC BR5 169 J3
STNW/STAM N16 74 A4
THMD SE28 97 J5
WEA W13 85 F3
Crossway Pde WDGN N22 * 41 H6
Crossways BELMT SM2 175 H7
GPK RM2 63 K2
SAND/SEL CR2 179 G6
SUN TW16 140 D7
Crossways Rd BECK BR3 166 D3
MTCM CR4 163 G2
Crossways Ter CLPT E5 * 74 E3
The Crossways BRYLDS KT5 * 159 J7
HEST TW5 102 E6
WBLY HA9 68 C1
The Cross Wy
KTN/HRWW/WS HA3 48 E1
The Crossway ELTH/MOT SE9 153 H1
WDGN N22 41 H6
Croston St HACK E8 74 C7
Crosts La WDGN N22 41 G6
Crothall Cl PLMGR N13 41 F2
Crouch Av BARK IG11 97 H1
Crouch Cl BECK BR3 151 J5
Crouch Cft ELTH/MOT SE9 154 A2
Crouch End Hl
CEND/HSY/T N8 54 D6
Crouch Hall Rd
CEND/HSY/T N8 54 D5
Crouch Hl CEND/HSY/T N8 54 E6
Crouchmans Cl SYD SE26 150 B2
Crouch Rd WLSDN NW10 69 F6
Crowborough Pth
OXHEY WD19 33 H3
Crowborough Rd TOOT SW17 148 A4
Crowden Wy THMD SE28 97 J6
Crowder Cl
NFNCH/WDSPK N12 39 G6
Crowder St WCHPL E1 92 D6
Crowfoot Cl HOM E9 75 H4
THMD SE28 96 E7
Crowhurst Cl BRXN/ST SW9 130 B1
Crowland Av HYS/HAR UB3 101 H3
Crowland Gdns
STHGT/OAK N14 28 E6
Crowland Rd
SEVS/STOTM N15 56 B4
THHTH CR7 * 164 E3
Crowlands Av ROMW/RG RM7 62 D5
Crowland Ter IS N1 7 G1
Crowland Wk MRDN SM4 162 A5
Crow La ROMW/RG RM7 62 B6
Crowley Crs CROY/NA CR0 177 G4
Crowline Wk IS N1 * 73 J5
Crowmarsh Gdns FSTH SE23 131 K6
Crown Ar KUT/HW KT1 * 158 E1
Crownbourne Ct SUT SM1 * 175 F3
Crown Cl BOW E3 75 J7
HYS/HAR UB3 101 J1
KIL/WHAMP NW6 71 F5
MLHL NW7 37 H1
WOT/HER KT12 156 B6
Crown Ct HOL/ALD WC2B 11 K5
Crown Dl NRWD SE19 149 J5
Crowndale Rd CAMTN NW1 4 F5
Crownfield Av
GNTH/NBYPK IG2 60 E4
Crownfield Rd SRTFD E15 76 B4
Crown Green Ms WBLY HA9 68 A1
Crown Hl CROY/NA CR0 * 177 J1
Crownhill Rd WFD IG8 45 J6
WLSDN NW10 69 H7
Crown La CHST BR7 154 C7
HAYES BR2 168 C4
MRDN SM4 161 K2
STHGT/OAK N14 28 C7
STRHM/NOR SW16 149 G4
Crown Lane Gdns
STRHM/NOR SW16 * 149 G4
Crown Lane Sp HAYES BR2 168 C5
Crownmead Wy
ROMW/RG RM7 62 D3
Crown Office Rw EMB EC4Y 12 A6
Crown Pde MRDN SM4 * 162 A3
STHGT/OAK N14 * 28 C7
Crown Pas STJS SW1Y 10 F9
Crown Pl KTTN NW5 72 B5
SDTCH EC2A 13 J1
Crown Rd BARK/HLT IG6 60 D3
EN EN1 30 C2
KUTN/CMB KT2 144 E7
MRDN SM4 161 K3
MUSWH N10 40 A6
RSLP HA4 65 H4
SUT SM1 174 E3
TWK TW1 124 C5
Crownstone Rd
BRXS/STRHM SW2 130 B4
Crown St ACT W3 86 D7
CMBW SE5 110 D6
DAGE RM10 80 E5
RYLN/HDSTN HA2 48 D7
Crown Ter CRICK NW2 * 70 B3
RCH/KEW TW9 125 G3
STHGT/OAK N14 * 28 D7
Crowntree Cl ISLW TW7 104 A5
Crown Vls ACT W3 * 105 K1
Crown Wk WBLY HA9 68 B2
Crown Woods La
WOOL/PLUM SE18 135 G1
Crown Woods Wy
ELTH/MOT SE9 135 J4
Crown Yd HSLW TW3 123 H2
Crowshott Av STAN HA7 35 J7
Crows Rd BARK IG11 78 B5
BOW E3 94 B2
Crowther Av BTFD TW8 105 F4
Crowther Cl FUL/PGN SW6 107 J5
Crowther Rd SNWD SE25 165 H3
Crowthorne Cl
WAND/EARL SW18 127 J6
Crowthorne Rd NKENS W10 88 B5
Croxdale Rd BORE WD6 24 B1
Croxden Cl EDGW HA8 50 C2
Croxden Wk MRDN SM4 162 B5
Croxford Gdns WDGN N22 41 H6
Croxford Wy ROMW/RG RM7 63 F7
Croxley Gn STMC/STPC BR5 155 H7
Croxley Rd MV/WKIL W9 88 D2
Croxley Vw WATW WD18 20 C5
Croxted Cl DUL SE21 130 D6
Croxted Ms HNHL SE24 130 D5
Croxted Rd DUL SE21 130 D6
Croyde Av GFD/PVL UB6 84 C2
HYS/HAR UB3 101 H3
Croyde Cl BFN/LL DA15 135 J6
The Croydon F/O
CROY/NA CR0 177 H3
Croydon Gv CROY/NA CR0 164 C7
Croydon Rd BECK BR3 166 A4
CROY/NA CR0 176 E3
HAYES BR2 181 J2
MTCM CR4 163 G4
PGE/AN SE20 165 J1
PLSTW E13 94 D3
WLGTN SM6 176 B3
WWKM BR4 180 C2
Croyland Rd ED N9 30 C7
Croylands Dr SURB KT6 159 F6
Crozier Ter HOM E9 75 F4
Crucible Cl CHDH RM6 61 H5
Crucifix La STHWK SE1 19 J1
Cruden St IS N1 6 D4
Cruickshank St FSBYW WC1X 6 A7
Cruikshank Rd SRTFD E15 76 C3
Crummock Gdns
CDALE/KGS NW9 51 G4
Crumpsall St ABYW SE2 116 D3
Crundale Av CDALE/KGS NW9 50 C4
Crunden Rd SAND/SEL CR2 177 K6
Crusader Cl PUR RM19 119 K3
Crusader Gdns CROY/NA CR0 178 A2
Crusader Wy WATW WD18 20 D5
Crusoe Ms STNW/STAM N16 73 K1
Crusoe Rd ERITH DA8 118 A4
MTCM CR4 147 K6
Crutched Friars TWRH EC3N 13 K6
Crutchfield La WOT/HER KT12 156 A7
Crutchley Rd CAT SE6 152 C1
Crystal Palace NRWD SE19 * 150 C6
Crystal Palace Pde
NRWD SE19 150 B5
Crystal Palace Park Rd
SYD SE26 150 C4
Crystal Palace Rd EDUL SE22 131 G5
Crystal Palace Station Rd
NRWD SE19 150 C5
Crystal Ter NRWD SE19 149 K5
Crystal Wy BCTR RM8 61 J7
HRW HA1 49 F4
Cuba Dr PEND EN3 30 E1
Cuba St POP/IOD E14 112 D1
Cubitt Sq NWDGN UB2 * 84 C7
Cubitt St FSBYW WC1X 5 M8
Cubitt Ter CLAP SW4 129 H2
Cuckoo Av HNWL W7 84 E3
Cuckoo Dene HNWL W7 84 D4
Cuckoo Hall La ED N9 30 E6
Cuckoo Hl PIN HA5 47 G2
Cuckoo Hill Dr PIN HA5 47 G2
Cuckoo Hill Rd PIN HA5 47 H3
Cuckoo La HNWL W7 84 E6
Cuda's Cl HOR/WEW KT19 173 H3
Cuddington Av WPK KT4 173 H2
Cudham St CAT SE6 132 E6
Cudworth St WCHPL E1 92 D3
Cuff Crs ELTH/MOT SE9 134 C6
Culford Gdns CHEL SW3 15 M6
Culford Gv IS N1 74 A5
Culford Ms IS N1 73 K5
Culford Rd IS N1 7 J1
Culgaith Gdns ENC/FH EN2 28 E3
Cullera Cl NTHWD HA6 32 D5
Culling Rd BERM/RHTH SE16 111 K2
Cullington Cl
KTN/HRWW/WS HA3 49 G3
Cullingworth Rd
WLSDN NW10 69 K4
Culloden Cl BERM/RHTH SE16 111 H4
Culloden Rd ENC/FH EN2 29 H1
Culloden St POP/IOD E14 94 A5
Cullum St FENCHST EC3M 13 J6
Culmington Pde WEA W13 * 85 J6
Culmington Rd SAND/SEL CR2 177 J6
WEA W13 85 J7
Culmore Rd PECK SE15 111 J6
Culmstock Rd BTSEA SW11 129 F4
Culpepper Cl UED N18 42 D4
Culross Cl SEVS/STOTM N15 55 J3
Culross St MYFR/PKLN W1K 10 A7
Culsac Rd SURB KT6 172 A1
Culverden Rd BAL SW12 148 C2
OXHEY WD19 33 F2
Culver Gv STAN HA7 49 J1
Culverhouse Gdns
STRHM/NOR SW16 149 F3
Culverlands Cl STAN HA7 35 H3
Culverley Rd CAT SE6 132 E7
Culvers Av CAR SM5 175 K1
Culvers Retreat CAR SM5 162 E7
Culverstone Cl HAYES BR2 167 J5
Culvers Wy CAR SM5 175 K1
Culvert Pl BTSEA SW11 129 F1
Culvert Rd BTSEA SW11 128 E1
SEVS/STOTM N15 56 A4
Culworth St STJWD NW8 3 J6
Cumberland Av WELL DA16 135 K2
WLSDN NW10 86 D2
Cumberland Cl HACK E8 74 B5
RYNPK SW20 146 B6
TWK TW1 124 C5
Cumberland Crs WKENS W14 107 H3
Cumberland Dr BXLYHN DA7 117 F6
CHSGTN KT9 172 A2
DART DA1 139 J6
ESH/CLAY KT10 171 G1
Cumberland Gdns
FSBYW WC1X 5 M7
HDN NW4 * 52 B1
Cumberland Ga BAY/PAD W2 9 L6
CAMTN NW1 4 C7
Cumberland House
KUTN/CMB KT2 144 D6
Cumberland Market
CAMTN NW1 4 D7
Cumberland Ms LBTH SE11 18 B8
Cumberland Pk ACT W3 86 E6
Cumberland Pl CAMTN NW1 4 C7
CAT SE6 133 J7
Cumberland Rd ACT W3 86 E6
BARN SW13 106 C7
ED N9 30 E7
HAYES BR2 167 H3
HNWL W7 104 A1
HRW HA1 48 B4
MNPK E12 77 H3
PLSTW E13 95 F4
RCH/KEW TW9 105 H7
SNWD SE25 165 J5
STAN HA7 50 B2
WALTH E17 57 G1
WDGN N22 55 G1
Cumberland St PIM SW1V 16 D7
Cumberland Ter CAMTN NW1 4 C6
PGE/AN SE20 * 150 D6
Cumberland Terrace Ms
CAMTN NW1 4 C6
Cumberlow Av SNWD SE25 165 H2
Cumbernauld Gdns SUN TW16 140 D4
Cumberton Rd TOTM N17 41 K7
Cumbrae Gdns SURB KT6 171 K1
Cumbrian Av BXLYHN DA7 138 B1
Cumbrian Gdns CRICK NW2 70 B1
Cumming St IS N1 5 M6
Cumnor Cl BRXN/ST SW9 * 130 A1
Cumnor Gdns EW KT17 173 J5
Cumnor Rd BELMT SM2 175 G5
Cunard Crs WCHMH N21 29 K5
Cunard Rd WLSDN NW10 87 F2
Cundy Rd CAN/RD E16 95 G5
Cundy St BGVA SW1W 16 B6
Cunliffe Rd HOR/WEW KT19 173 H3
Cunliffe St STRHM/NOR SW16 148 C5
Cunningham Cl CHDH RM6 61 J4
WWKM BR4 179 K1
Cunningham Pk HRW HA1 48 D4
Cunningham Pl STJWD NW8 3 G9
Cunningham Rd
SEVS/STOTM N15 * 56 C3
Cunnington St CHSWK W4 105 K2
Cupar Rd BTSEA SW11 109 F7
Cupola Cl BMLY BR1 153 F4
Cureton St WEST SW1P 17 H7
Curlew Cl THMD SE28 97 K6
Curlew St STHWK SE1 19 L1
Curlew Wy YEAD UB4 83 H4
Curness St LEW SE13 133 F3
Curnick's La WNWD SE27 149 J3
Curran Av BFN/LL DA15 136 A4
WLGTN SM6 176 A2
Currey Rd NTHLT UB5 66 C5
Curricle St ACT W3 87 G7
Currie Hill Cl WIM/MER SW19 146 D3
Curry Ri MLHL NW7 38 B5
Cursitor St FLST/FETLN EC4A 12 A4
Curtain Pl SDTCH EC2A 7 K8
Curtain Rd FSBYE EC1V 7 K8
SDTCH EC2A 13 J1
Curthwaite Gdns ENC/FH EN2 28 D3
Curtis Dr ACT W3 87 F5
Curtis Field Rd
STRHM/NOR SW16 149 F3
Curtis La ALP/SUD HA0 68 A5
Curtis Rd HOR/WEW KT19 172 E3
HSLWW TW4 122 E6
Curtis St STHWK SE1 19 L5
Curtis Wy STHWK SE1 19 L5
The Curve SHB W12 87 J6
Curwen Av FSTGT E7 77 F3
Curwen Rd SHB W12 106 D1
Curzon Av PEND EN3 31 F4
STAN HA7 35 G7
Curzon Crs BARK IG11 97 F2
WLSDN NW10 69 G6
Curzon Pl PIN HA5 47 G4
Curzon Rd EA W5 85 H3
MUSWH N10 54 B1
THHTH CR7 164 B5
Curzon St MYFR/PKLN W1K 10 B9
Cusack Cl TWK TW1 * 143 F3
Custom House Reach
BERM/RHTH SE16 * 112 C2
Cutcombe Rd CMBW SE5 130 D1
Cuthberga Cl BARK IG11 78 C6
Cuthbert Gdns SNWD SE25 165 F2
Cuthbert Rd CROY/NA CR0 177 H1
UED N18 42 C4
WALTH E17 58 A2
Cuthbert St BAY/PAD W2 9 G1
Cutlers Gardens Ar
LVPST EC2M 13 K4
Cutler St HDTCH EC3A 13 K4
Cutter La GNWCH SE10 113 H1
The Cut STHWK SE1 18 B1
Cuxton Cl BXLYHS DA6 137 F4
Cyclamen Cl HPTN TW12 142 A5
Cyclamen Wy HOR/WEW KT19 172 E4
Cygnet Av EBED/NFELT TW14 122 B6
Cygnet Cl NTHWD HA6 32 A6
WLSDN NW10 69 F4
The Cygnets FELT TW13 141 J3
Cygnet St WCHPL E1 7 M9
Cygnet Wy YEAD UB4 83 H4
Cymbeline Ct HRW HA1 * 49 F5
Cynthia St IS N1 5 M6
Cypress Av WHTN TW2 123 H6
Cypress Cl CLPT E5 74 C1
Cypress Gdns BROCKY SE4 132 B4
Cypress Pl FITZ W1T 10 F1
Cypress Rd
KTN/HRWW/WS HA3 48 D1
SNWD SE25 165 F1
Cypress Tree Cl BFN/LL DA15 136 A7
Cyprus Av FNCH N3 52 C1
Cyprus Cl FSBYPK N4 55 G5
Cyprus Gdns FNCH N3 52 C1
Cyprus Pl BETH E2 92 E1
EHAM E6 96 A6
Cyprus Rd ED N9 42 B1
FNCH N3 52 D1
Cyprus St BETH E2 92 E1
Cyrena Rd EDUL SE22 131 G5
Cyril Rd BXLYHN DA7 137 F1
Cyrus St FSBYE EC1V 6 D9
Czar St DEPT SE8 112 D5

D

Dabbling Cl ERITH DA8 * 118 E6
Dabbs Hill La NTHLT UB5 65 K4
D'Abernon Cl ESH/CLAY KT10 170 A3
Dabin Crs GNWCH SE10 113 F7
Dacca St DEPT SE8 112 C5
Dace Rd BOW E3 75 J7
Dacre Av CLAY IG5 60 A1
Dacre Cl GFD/PVL UB6 84 B1
Dacre Gdns BORE WD6 25 F4
LEW SE13 133 H3
Dacre Pk LEW SE13 133 H2
Dacre Pl LEW SE13 133 H2
Dacre Rd CROY/NA CR0 163 K6
PLSTW E13 77 F7
WAN E11 58 D7
Dacres Est FSTH SE23 * 151 F2
Dacres Rd FSTH SE23 151 F2
Dacre St STJSPK SW1H 17 G3
Dade Wy NWDGN UB2 102 E4
Daerwood Cl HAYES BR2 168 E7
Daffodil Cl CROY/NA CR0 166 A7
HPTN TW12 142 A5
Daffodil Gdns IL IG1 78 B4
Daffodil St SHB W12 87 H6
Dafforne Rd TOOT SW17 147 K2
Dagenham Av DAGW RM9 80 A6
Dagenham Rd DAGE RM10 80 E3
LEY E10 57 H7
RAIN RM13 81 F6
ROMW/RG RM7 81 F2
Dagger La BORE WD6 23 G5
Dagmar Av WBLY HA9 68 B3
Dagmar Gdns WLSDN NW10 88 B1
Dagmar Ms NWDGN UB2 102 D2
Dagmar Pas IS N1 6 C3
Dagmar Rd CMBW SE5 111 F7
DAGE RM10 80 E6
FSBYPK N4 55 G6
KUTN/CMB KT2 144 B7
NWDGN UB2 102 D2
SEVS/STOTM N15 55 K3
SNWD SE25 165 F3
WDGN N22 40 D7
Dagmar Ter IS N1 6 D3
Dagnall Pk SNWD SE25 165 F4
Dagnall Rd SNWD SE25 165 F4
Dagnall St BTSEA SW11 128 E1
Dagnan Rd BAL SW12 129 G6
Dagonet Rd BMLY BR1 152 E2
Dahlia Gdns IL IG1 78 B5
MTCM CR4 163 J3
Dahlia Rd ABYW SE2 116 C4
Dahomey Rd
STRHM/NOR SW16 148 C5
Daimler Wy WLGTN SM6 176 E6
Daines Cl MNPK E12 77 K2
Dainford Cl BMLY BR1 152 B4
Daintry Cl
KTN/HRWW/WS HA3 49 G3
Dairsie Rd ELTH/MOT SE9 135 F2
Dairy Cl BMLY BR1 * 153 F6
FUL/PGN SW6 107 J7
THHTH CR7 164 D1
WLSDN NW10 69 J7
Dairy La WOOL/PLUM SE18 114 E3
Dairyman Cl CRICK NW2 70 B2
Dairy Ms EFNCH N2 53 J3
Daisy Cl CDALE/KGS NW9 68 E1
CROY/NA CR0 166 A7
Daisy La FUL/PGN SW6 127 K2
Daisy Rd SWFD E18 59 F1
Dakin Pl WCHPL E1 93 G4
Dakota Cl WLGTN SM6 177 F6
Dalberg Rd BRXS/STRHM SW2 130 B4
Dalberg Wy ABYW SE2 116 E2
Dalby Rd WAND/EARL SW18 128 B3
Dalbys Crs TOTM N17 42 A5
Dalby St KTTN NW5 72 B5
Dalcross Rd HSLWW TW4 122 D1
Dale Av EDGW HA8 36 B7
HSLWW TW4 122 D2
Dalebury Rd TOOT SW17 147 K1
Dale Cl BAR EN5 27 F5
BKHTH/KID SE3 133 K2
DART DA1 138 C5
PIN HA5 33 F7
Dale Dr YEAD UB4 82 D3
Dale Gdns WFD IG8 45 F3
Dale Green Rd
FBAR/BDGN N11 40 B2
Dale Gv NFNCH/WDSPK N12 39 G4
Daleham Gdns HAMP NW3 71 H4
Daleham Ms HAMP NW3 * 71 H5
Dalemain Ms CAN/RD E16 94 E7
Dale Park Av CAR SM5 175 K1
Dale Park Rd NRWD SE19 149 J7
Dale Rd DART DA1 138 C5
KTTN NW5 72 A4
STHL UB1 84 B4
SUN TW16 * 140 D6
SUT SM1 174 D3
WALW SE17 110 C5
Dale Rw NTGHL W11 88 C5
Daleside Rd HOR/WEW KT19 173 F5
STRHM/NOR SW16 148 B4
Dales Pth BORE WD6 * 25 F4
Dales Rd BORE WD6 25 F4
Dale St CHSWK W4 106 B4
The Dale HAYES BR2 181 H3
Dale Vw BAR EN5 * 26 D2
ERITH DA8 138 D1
Dale View Av CHING E4 44 A1
Dale View Crs CHING E4 44 A2
Dale View Gdns CHING E4 44 B2
Daleview Rd
SEVS/STOTM N15 56 A5
Dalewood Gdns WPK KT4 173 K1
Dale Wood Rd ORP BR6 169 K6
Daley St HOM E9 75 F5
Daley Thompson Wy
VX/NE SW8 129 G1
Dalgarno Gdns NKENS W10 88 A4
Dalgarno Wy NKENS W10 88 A3
Dalkeith Gv STAN HA7 35 K4
Dalkeith Rd DUL SE21 130 D7
IL IG1 78 C2
Dallas Rd CHEAM SM3 174 C5
EA W5 86 B4
HDN NW4 51 J6
SYD SE26 150 D3
Dallas Ter HYS/HAR UB3 101 J2
Dallega Cl HYS/HAR UB3 82 A6
Dallinger Rd LEE/GVPK SE12 133 J5
Dalling Rd HMSMTH W6 106 E3
Dallington Sq FSBYE EC1V 6 D9
Dallington St FSBYE EC1V 6 D9
Dallin Rd BXLYHS DA6 136 E3
WOOL/PLUM SE18 115 G6
Dalmain Rd FSTH SE23 132 A7
Dalmally Rd CROY/NA CR0 165 G6
Dalmeny Av HOLWY N7 72 D3
STRHM/NOR SW16 164 B1
Dalmeny Cl ALP/SUD HA0 67 J5
Dalmeny Crs HSLW TW3 123 J3
Dalmeny Rd ARCH N19 72 D2
BAR EN5 27 G5
CAR SM5 176 A6
ERITH DA8 117 J7
HOLWY N7 72 D3
WPK KT4 173 K2
Dalmeyer Rd WLSDN NW10 69 H5
Dalmore Av ESH/CLAY KT10 171 F5
Dalmore Rd DUL SE21 149 J1
Dalrymple Cl STHGT/OAK N14 28 D5
Dalrymple Rd BROCKY SE4 132 B3
Dalston Gdns STAN HA7 36 A7
Dalston La HACK E8 74 B5
Dalton Av MTCM CR4 162 D1
Dalton Cl YEAD UB4 82 B3
Dalton St WNWD SE27 149 H1
Dalton Wy WAT WD17 21 H4
Dalwood St CMBW SE5 111 F7
Dalyell Rd BRXN/ST SW9 130 A2
Damask Crs CAN/RD E16 94 C3
Damer Ter WBPTN SW10 108 B6
Dames Rd FSTGT E7 76 E3
Dame St IS N1 6 E5
Damien St WCHPL E1 92 D4
Damon Cl SCUP DA14 155 H2
Damsel Ct BERM/RHTH SE16 * 111 H1
Damson Dr HYS/HAR UB3 82 E6
Damson Wy CAR SM5 175 K7
Damsonwood Rd
NWDGN UB2 103 F2
Danbrook Rd
STRHM/NOR SW16 148 E7
Danbury Cl CHDH RM6 61 K2
Danbury Ms WLGTN SM6 176 B3
Danbury Rd RAIN RM13 81 H7
Danbury St IS N1 6 D5
Danbury Wy WFD IG8 45 G5
Danby St PECK SE15 131 G2
Dancer Rd FUL/PGN SW6 107 J7
RCH/KEW TW9 125 H2
Dandelion Cl ROMW/RG RM7 81 G1
Dando Crs BKHTH/KID SE3 134 A2
Dandridge Cl GNWCH SE10 113 J4
Danebury CROY/NA CR0 179 K5
Danebury Av PUT/ROE SW15 126 C6
Daneby Rd CAT SE6 152 A2
Dane Cl BXLY DA5 137 H6
Danecourt Gdns
CROY/NA CR0 178 B2
Danecroft Rd HNHL SE24 130 D4
Danehurst Gdns REDBR IG4 59 J4

Danehurst St FUL/PGN SW6 107 H7
Daneland EBAR EN4 27 K5
Danemead Gv NTHLT UB5 66 B4
Danemere St PUT/ROE SW15 127 F2
Dane Pl BOW E3 93 G1
Dane Rd ASHF TW15 140 A5
IL IG1 78 C4
STHL UB1 83 J6
UED N18 42 E3
WEA W13 85 J6
WIM/MER SW19 147 G7
Danesbury Rd FELT TW13 122 A7
Danescombe LEE/GVPK SE12 133 K7
Danescourt Crs SUT SM1 175 G1
Danescroft Av HDN NW4 * 52 B4
Danescroft Gdns HDN NW4 52 B4
Danesdale Rd HOM E9 75 G5
Danes Ga HRW HA1 48 E2
Danes Rd ROMW/RG RM7 62 E6
Dane St GINN WC1R 11 L3
Daneswood Av CAT SE6 152 A2
Danethorpe Rd ALP/SUD HA0 67 K5
Danetree Cl HOR/WEW KT19 172 E6
Danetree Rd HOR/WEW KT19 172 E6
Danette Gdns DAGE RM10 80 B1
Daneville Rd CMBW SE5 110 E7
Dangan Rd WAN E11 58 E5
Daniel Bolt Cl POP/IOD E14 93 K4
Daniel Cl HSLWW TW4 122 E6
TOOT SW17 147 J5
UED N18 42 E3
Daniel Gdns PECK SE15 111 G6
Daniell Wy CROY/NA CR0 163 K7
Daniel Pl HDN NW4 51 K5
Daniel Rd EA W5 86 B6
Daniel's Rd PECK SE15 131 K2
Dan Leno Wk FUL/PGN SW6 * 108 A6
Dansey Pl SOHO/SHAV W1D 11 G6
Dansington Rd WELL DA16 136 B3
Danson Crs WELL DA16 136 C2
Danson La WELL DA16 136 C3
Danson Md WELL DA16 136 D2
Danson Rd BXLYHS DA6 136 E4
Danson U/P BFN/LL DA15 136 D5
Dante Rd LBTH SE11 18 C5
Danube Cl ED N9 42 E2
Danube St CHEL SW3 15 K7
Danvers Rd CEND/HSY/T N8 54 D3
Danvers St CHEL SW3 108 C5
Daphne Gdns CHING E4 44 A2
Daphne St WAND/EARL SW18 128 B5
Daplyn St WCHPL E1 92 C4
D'Arblay St SOHO/CST W1F 10 F5
Darby Crs SUN TW16 156 B1
Darby Gdns SUN TW16 156 B1
Darcy Av WLGTN SM6 176 C3
Darcy Cl TRDG/WHET N20 39 H1
D'Arcy Dr KTN/HRWW/WS HA3 49 K3
D'Arcy Gdns DAGW RM9 80 B7
KTN/HRWW/WS HA3 50 A3
D'Arcy Pl HAYES BR2 167 K3
Darcy Rd ISLW TW7 104 B7
STRHM/NOR SW16 163 K1
D'Arcy Rd CHEAM SM3 174 B3
Darell Rd RCH/KEW TW9 125 H2
Darenth Rd STNW/STAM N16 56 B6
WELL DA16 116 B7
Darent Valley Pth DART DA1 139 G3
Darfield Rd BROCKY SE4 132 C4
Darfield Wy NKENS W10 88 B6
Darfur St PUT/ROE SW15 127 G2
Dargate Cl NRWD SE19 150 B6
Darien Rd BTSEA SW11 128 C2
Darlands Dr BAR EN5 26 B4
Darlan Rd FUL/PGN SW6 107 J6
Darlaston Rd WIM/MER SW19 146 B6
Darley Cl CROY/NA CR0 166 A5
Darley Dr NWMAL KT3 160 A1
Darley Gdns MRDN SM4 162 A5
Darley Rd BTSEA SW11 128 E5
ED N9 30 B7
Darling Rd BROCKY SE4 132 D2
Darling Rw WCHPL E1 92 D3
Darlington Rd WNWD SE27 149 H4
Darlton Cl DART DA1 138 C1
Darmaine Cl SAND/SEL CR2 177 J6
Darnaway Pl POP/IOD E14 94 A4
Darndale Cl WALTH E17 57 H1
Darnley Rd HACK E8 74 D5
WFD IG8 44 E7
Darnley Ter NTGHL W11 88 B7
Darrell Rd EDUL SE22 131 H4
Darren Cl FSBYPK N4 55 F6
Darris Cl YEAD UB4 83 J3
Darsley Dr VX/NE SW8 109 J7
Dartford Av ED N9 30 E5
Dartford Gdns CHDH RM6 61 H4
Dartford Rd BXLY DA5 137 K7
DART DA1 138 D5
Dartford St WALW SE17 18 F9
Dartmoor Wk POP/IOD E14 * 112 D3
Dartmouth Cl NTGHL W11 88 D5
Dartmouth Gv GNWCH SE10 113 F7
Dartmouth Hl GNWCH SE10 113 F7
Dartmouth Park Av
KTTN NW5 72 B2
Dartmouth Park Hl KTTN NW5 72 B2
Dartmouth Park Rd
KTTN NW5 72 B2
Dartmouth Pl CHSWK W4 106 B5
FSTH SE23 150 E1
Dartmouth Rd CRICK NW2 70 B5
HAYES BR2 167 K6
HDN NW4 51 J5
RSLP HA4 64 E2
SYD SE26 150 D2
Dartmouth Rw GNWCH SE10 133 F1
Dartmouth St STJSPK SW1H 17 G2
Dartmouth Ter GNWCH SE10 113 G7
Dartnell Rd CROY/NA CR0 165 G6
Dartrey Wk WBPTN SW10 * 108 B6
Dart St NKENS W10 88 D2
Darville Rd STNW/STAM N16 74 B2
Darwell Cl EHAM E6 96 A1
Darwin Cl FBAR/BDGN N11 40 B2
Darwin Dr STHL UB1 84 B5
Darwin Gdns OXHEY WD19 33 G4
Darwin Rd EA W5 104 D4
WDGN N22 41 H7
WELL DA16 136 A2
Darwin St WALW SE17 19 H5
Daryngton Dr GFD/PVL UB6 84 D1
Dashwood Cl BXLYHS DA6 137 H4
Dashwood Rd
CEND/HSY/T N8 55 F5
Dassett Rd WNWD SE27 149 H4
Datchelor Pl CMBW SE5 * 110 E7
Datchet Rd CAT SE6 151 H2
Date St WALW SE17 19 G8
Daubeney Gdns TOTM N17 41 J6
Daubeney Rd CLPT E5 75 G3
TOTM N17 41 J6
Dault Rd WAND/EARL SW18 128 B5
Davema Cl CHST BR7 154 A7
Davenant Rd ARCH N19 72 D1
Davenant St WCHPL E1 92 C4
Davenham Av NTHWD HA6 32 D3
Davenport Cl TEDD TW11 * 143 G5
Davenport Rd CAT SE6 132 E5
SCUP DA14 155 K1
Daventer Dr STAN HA7 35 F6
Daventry Av WALTH E17 57 J5
Daventry St CAMTN NW1 9 J2
Davern Cl GNWCH SE10 113 J3
Davey Cl HOLWY N7 73 F5
PLMGR N13 41 F4
Davey Rd HOM E9 75 J6
Davey St PECK SE15 111 G5
David Av GFD/PVL UB6 84 E2
David Cl HYS/HAR UB3 101 G6
Davidge St STHWK SE1 18 C2
David Ms MHST W1U 9 M2
David Rd BCTR RM8 80 A1
Davidson Gdns VX/NE SW8 109 K6
Davidson Rd CROY/NA CR0 165 F7
Davidson Wy ROMW/RG RM7 63 G5
David's Rd FSTH SE23 131 K7
David St SRTFD E15 76 B5
David Twigg Cl
KUTN/CMB KT2 144 A7
Davies Cl CROY/NA CR0 165 G5
Davies La WAN E11 76 C1
Davies Ms MYFR/PKLN W1K 10 C6
Davies St MYFR/PKLN W1K 10 C6
Davies Wk ISLW TW7 103 J7
Davington Gdns BCTR RM8 79 H4
Davington Rd BCTR RM8 79 H5
Davinia Cl WFD IG8 45 K5
Davis Rd ACT W3 87 H7
CHSGTN KT9 172 C3
Davis St PLSTW E13 95 F1
Davisville Rd SHB W12 106 D1
Dawes Av ISLW TW7 124 B4
Dawes Ct ESH/CLAY KT10 170 B3
Dawes Rd FUL/PGN SW6 107 J6
Dawes St WALW SE17 19 H7
Dawley Pde HYS/HAR UB3 * 82 A6
Dawley Rd HYS/HAR UB3 82 B6
Dawlish Av GFD/PVL UB6 85 G1
PLMGR N13 40 E3
WAND/EARL SW18 147 F1
Dawlish Dr GDMY/SEVK IG3 79 F3
PIN HA5 47 J4
RSLP HA4 64 E1
Dawlish Rd CRICK NW2 70 B5
LEY E10 76 A1
TOTM N17 56 C2
Dawnay Gdns
WAND/EARL SW18 147 H1
Dawnay Rd WAND/EARL SW18 147 G1
Dawn Cl HSLWW TW4 122 D2
Dawn Crs SRTFD E15 76 B7
Dawpool Rd CRICK NW2 69 H1
Daws La MLHL NW7 37 H4
Dawson Av BARK IG11 79 F6
Dawson Cl HYS/HAR UB3 82 B4
WOOL/PLUM SE18 115 H3
Dawson Dr RAIN RM13 81 K6
Dawson Gdns BARK IG11 79 F6
Dawson Pl BAY/PAD W2 8 A6
Dawson Rd CRICK NW2 70 A4
KUT/HW KT1 159 G2
Dawson St BETH E2 7 M6
Dawson Ter ED N9 * 30 E6
Daybrook Rd WIM/MER SW19 162 A1
Daylesford Av PUT/ROE SW15 126 D3
Daymer Gdns PIN HA5 47 G3
Daysbrook Rd
BRXS/STRHM SW2 130 A7
Days La BFN/LL DA15 135 K6
Dayton Dr ERITH DA8 119 G5
Dayton Gv PECK SE15 111 K7
Deacon Cl PUR/KEN CR8 176 E7
The Deacon Est CHING E4 * 43 H5
Deacon Ms IS N1 7 H2
Deacon Rd CRICK NW2 69 J5
KUTN/CMB KT2 144 B7
Deacons Cl BORE WD6 24 C3
PIN HA5 47 F1
Deacons Hts BORE WD6 24 C5
Deacons Hl OXHEY WD19 21 G5
Deacon's Hill Rd BORE WD6 24 B4
Deacons Ri EFNCH N2 53 H4
Deacons Ter IS N1 * 73 J5
Deacons Wk HPTN TW12 142 A3
Deacon Wy WALW SE17 18 E5
WFD IG8 45 K6
Deakin Cl WATW WD18 20 C6
Deal Porters Wy
BERM/RHTH SE16 111 K2
Deal Rd TOOT SW17 148 A5
Deals Gtwy LEW SE13 112 E7
Deal St WCHPL E1 92 C4
Dealtry Rd PUT/ROE SW15 127 F3
Deal Wk BRXN/ST SW9 110 B6
Dean Bradley St WEST SW1P 17 J4
Dean Cl BERM/RHTH SE16 93 F7
HOM E9 74 E4
Dean Ct ALP/SUD HA0 67 H2
Deancross St WCHPL E1 92 E5
Dean Dr STAN HA7 50 A1
Deane Av RSLP HA4 65 F4
Deane Ct NTHWD HA6 * 32 C7
Deane Croft Rd PIN HA5 47 G5
Deanery Cl EFNCH N2 53 J3
Deanery Ms
MYFR/PKLN W1K * 10 B8
Deanery Rd SRTFD E15 76 C5
Deanery St MYFR/PKLN W1K 10 B8
Deane Wy RSLP HA4 47 F5
Dean Farrar St STJSPK SW1H 17 H3
Deanfield Gdns
CROY/NA CR0 * 177 K3
Dean Gdns WALTH E17 58 B3
Deanhill Ct
MORT/ESHN SW14 * 125 J3
Deanhill Rd MORT/ESHN SW14 125 J3
Dean Rd CRICK NW2 70 A5
CROY/NA CR0 177 K3
HPTN TW12 142 A4
HSLW TW3 123 G4
THMD SE28 97 G6
Dean Ryle St WEST SW1P 17 J5
Deansbrook Cl EDGW HA8 36 E6
Deansbrook Rd EDGW HA8 36 D6
Dean's Blds WALW SE17 19 H6
Deans Cl CHSWK W4 105 J5
CROY/NA CR0 178 B2
EDGW HA8 36 E5
Dean's Ct STP EC4M 12 D5
Deanscroft Av
CDALE/KGS NW9 68 E1
Deans Dr PLMGR N13 41 H5
Dean's Dr EDGW HA8 37 F4
Deans Gate Cl FSTH SE23 151 F2
Dean's La EDGW HA8 36 E5
Dean's Ms CAVSQ/HST W1G * 10 D4
Deans Rd SUT SM1 175 F2
Dean's Rd HNWL W7 104 A1
Dean Stanley St WEST SW1P 17 J4
Dean St FSTGT E7 76 E4
SOHO/SHAV W1D 11 G5
Deans Wy EDGW HA8 36 E4
Deansway ED N9 42 A2
EFNCH N2 53 H3
Deans Yd WEST SW1P 17 H3
Dean Trench St WEST SW1P 17 J4
Dean Wy NWDGN UB2 103 G1
Dearne Cl STAN HA7 35 G4
De'Arn Gdns MTCM CR4 162 D2
Dearsley Rd EN EN1 30 C2
Deason St SRTFD E15 * 76 A7
De Barowe Ms HBRY N5 73 H3
Debden Cl CDALE/KGS NW9 37 G7
KUTN/CMB KT2 143 K4
WFD IG8 45 H6
De Beauvoir Crs IS N1 7 J3
De Beauvoir Est IS N1 7 J3
De Beauvoir Rd IS N1 7 J1
De Beauvoir Sq IS N1 7 K2
Debnams Rd
BERM/RHTH SE16 111 K3
De Bohun Av STHGT/OAK N14 28 B5
Deborah Cl ISLW TW7 103 K7
Deborah Crs RSLP HA4 46 B6
Debrabant Cl ERITH DA8 118 A5
De Broome Rd FELT TW13 122 B7
Deburgh Rd WIM/MER SW19 147 G6
Decima St STHWK SE1 19 J3
Decimus Cl THHTH CR7 164 E3
Deck Cl BERM/RHTH SE16 93 F7
Decoy Av GLDGN NW11 52 C4
De Crespigny Pk CMBW SE5 130 E1
Deeley Rd VX/NE SW8 109 J7
Deena Cl ACT W3 86 B5
Deepdale WIM/MER SW19 146 B3
Deepdale Av HAYES BR2 167 J3
Deepdale Cl FBAR/BDGN N11 40 A5
Deepdene Av CROY/NA CR0 178 B2
Deepdene Cl WAN E11 58 E3
Deepdene Ct WCHMH N21 29 H5
Deepdene Gdns
BRXS/STRHM SW2 130 A6
Deepdene Rd HNHL SE24 130 D3
WELL DA16 136 B2
Deepwell Cl ISLW TW7 104 B7
Deepwood La GFD/PVL UB6 84 D2
Deerbrook Rd HNHL SE24 130 C7
Deerdale Rd HNHL SE24 130 D3
Deere Av RAIN RM13 81 J5
Deerfield Cl CDALE/KGS NW9 51 H4
Deerhurst Cl FELT TW13 140 E3
Deerhurst Crs HPTN TW12 142 C4
Deerhurst Rd
KIL/WHAMP NW6 70 B6
STRHM/NOR SW16 149 F4
Deerings Dr PIN HA5 46 E4
Deerleap Gv CHING E4 31 K4
Dee Rd RCH/KEW TW9 125 G3
Deer Park Cl KUTN/CMB KT2 144 D6
Deer Park Gdns MTCM CR4 * 162 C3
Deer Park Rd WIM/MER SW19 162 A1
Deer Park Wy WWKM BR4 180 D1
Deeside Rd TOOT SW17 147 H2
Dee St POP/IOD E14 94 A5
Defence Cl THMD SE28 96 E7
Defiant Wy WLGTN SM6 176 E6
Defoe Av RCH/KEW TW9 105 H6
Defoe Cl TOOT SW17 147 J5
Defoe Pl TOOT SW17 147 J1
Defoe Rd BERM/RHTH SE16 112 C1
STNW/STAM N16 74 A1
De Frene Rd SYD SE26 151 F3
De Gama Pl POP/IOD E14 112 D4
Degema Rd CHST BR7 154 B4
Dehar Crs CDALE/KGS NW9 51 H6
De Havilland Dr
WOOL/PLUM SE18 115 G4
Dehavilland Cl NTHLT UB5 83 H2
De Havilland Ct IL IG1 60 D7
De Havilland Rd EDGW HA8 50 D1
HEST TW5 102 B6
De Havilland Wy
STWL/WRAY TW19 120 A5
Dekker Rd DUL SE21 131 F5
Delacourt Rd BKHTH/KID SE3 114 A6
Delafield Rd CHARL SE7 114 A4
Delaford Rd
BERM/RHTH SE16 111 J4
Delaford St FUL/PGN SW6 107 H6
Delamare Crs CROY/NA CR0 165 K5
Delamere Gdns MLHL NW7 37 F4
Delamere Rd EA W5 86 A7
RYNPK SW20 146 B7
YEAD UB4 83 H6
Delamere St BAY/PAD W2 8 E3
Delamere Ter BAY/PAD W2 8 D2
Delancey Pas CAMTN NW1 4 D4
Delancey St CAMTN NW1 4 D4
De Laune St WALW SE17 18 C8
Delaware Rd MV/WKIL W9 2 C9
Delawyk Crs HNHL SE24 130 E5
Delcombe Av WPK KT4 161 F7
Delhi Rd EN EN1 30 B6
Delhi St IS N1 5 K4
Delia St WAND/EARL SW18 128 A6
Delisle Rd THMD SE28 96 E7
Delius Cl BORE WD6 23 J5
Delius Gv SRTFD E15 94 A1
Della Pth CLPT E5 74 C2
Dellbow Rd
EBED/NFELT TW14 122 A4
Dell Cl SRTFD E15 76 B7
WFD IG8 45 F2
WLGTN SM6 176 C3
Dell Farm Rd RSLP HA4 46 B4
Dellfield Cl BECK BR3 152 A7
WAT WD17 20 E1
Dell La EW KT17 173 J4
Dellors Cl BAR EN5 26 B4
Dellow Cl GNTH/NBYPK IG2 60 D6
Dellow St WCHPL E1 92 D6
Dell Rd EW KT17 173 J5
WDR/YW UB7 100 C2
Dells Cl CHING E4 31 K6
TEDD TW11 143 F5
Dell's Ms PIM SW1V * 16 F6
The Dell ABYW SE2 116 B4
ALP/SUD HA0 67 H4
BECK BR3 * 151 J6
BTFD TW8 104 D5
BXLY DA5 138 B7
EBED/NFELT TW14 122 A6
NRWD SE19 150 B7
NTHWD HA6 32 C1
PIN HA5 47 H1
WFD IG8 45 F2
Dell Wk NWMAL KT3 160 B1
Dell Wy WEA W13 85 J5
Dellwood Gdns CLAY IG5 60 A2
Delme Crs BKHTH/KID SE3 134 A1
Delmey Cl CROY/NA CR0 178 B2
Deloraine St DEPT SE8 112 D7
Delorme St HMSMTH W6 107 G5
Delta Cl WPK KT4 173 G2
Delta Est BETH E2 * 92 C2
Delta Gain OXHEY WD19 33 H1
Delta Gv NTHLT UB5 83 H2
Delta Rd WPK KT4 173 G2
Delta St BETH E2 * 92 C2
De Luci Rd ERITH DA8 117 K4
De Lucy St ABYW SE2 116 C3
Delvers Md DAGE RM10 80 E3
Delverton Rd WALW SE17 18 D7
Delvino Rd FUL/PGN SW6 107 K7
Demesne Rd WLGTN SM6 176 D3
Demeta Cl WBLY HA9 68 E2
De Montfort Pde
STRHM/NOR SW16 * 148 E2
De Montfort Rd
STRHM/NOR SW16 148 D1
De Morgan Rd FUL/PGN SW6 128 A2
Dempster Cl SURB KT6 158 D6
Dempster Rd
WAND/EARL SW18 128 B4
Denbar Pde ROMW/RG RM7 * 62 E3
Denberry Dr SCUP DA14 155 H2
Denbigh Cl CHST BR7 153 K5
NTGHL W11 88 D6
STHL UB1 83 K5
SUT SM1 174 D4
Denbigh Dr HYS/HAR UB3 101 F1
Denbigh Gdns
RCHPK/HAM TW10 125 G4
Denbigh Pl PIM SW1V 16 E7
Denbigh Rd EHAM E6 95 H2
HSLW TW3 123 G1
NTGHL W11 88 D6
STHL UB1 83 K5
WEA W13 85 H6
Denbigh St PIM SW1V 16 E6
Denbigh Ter NTGHL W11 88 D6
Denbridge Rd BMLY BR1 168 E1
Den Cl BECK BR3 167 G3
Dendy St BAL SW12 129 F7
Dene Av BFN/LL DA15 136 C6
HSLW TW3 122 E2
Dene Cl BROCKY SE4 132 B2
HAYES BR2 167 J7
LEY E10 75 K1
WPK KT4 173 H1
Dene Gdns STAN HA7 35 J4
THDIT KT7 171 G1
Denehurst Gdns ACT W3 86 D7
HDN NW4 52 A5
RCHPK/HAM TW10 125 H3
WFD IG8 45 F3
WHTN TW2 123 J6
Dene Rd DART DA1 139 J6
NTHWD HA6 32 A5
TRDG/WHET N20 27 K7
The Dene CROY/NA CR0 179 F3
E/WMO/HCT KT8 156 E4
WBLY HA9 68 A3
WEA W13 85 H4
Denewood BAR EN5 27 G4
Denewood Rd HGT N6 53 J5
Dengie Wk IS N1 6 E3
Denham Cl WELL DA16 136 D2
Denham Crs MTCM CR4 162 E3
Denham Dr GNTH/NBYPK IG2 60 C5
Denham Rd
EBED/NFELT TW14 122 B6
TRDG/WHET N20 39 K1
Denham Wy BARK IG11 78 E7
Denholme Rd MV/WKIL W9 88 D2
Denholme Wk RAIN RM13 81 H5
Denison Cl EFNCH N2 53 G2
Denison Rd EA W5 85 J3
FELT TW13 140 D3
WIM/MER SW19 147 H5
Deniston Av BXLY DA5 136 E7
Denleigh Gdns THDIT KT7 * 157 K5
WCHMH N21 29 G6
Denman Dr ESH/CLAY KT10 171 G4
GLDGN NW11 52 E4
Denman Dr North
GLDGN NW11 52 E4
Denman Dr South
GLDGN NW11 52 E4
Denman Rd PECK SE15 111 G7
Denman St SOHO/SHAV W1D 10 F7
Denmark Av WIM/MER SW19 146 C6
Denmark Ct MRDN SM4 161 K4
Denmark Gdns CAR SM5 175 K2
Denmark Gv IS N1 6 A5
Denmark Hl HNHL SE24 130 E3
Denmark Hill Dr
CDALE/KGS NW9 51 J2
Denmark Rd BMLY BR1 153 F7
CAR SM5 175 K2
CEND/HSY/T N8 55 F3
CMBW SE5 110 D7
KIL/WHAMP NW6 88 D1
KUT/HW KT1 159 F2
SNWD SE25 165 J4
WEA W13 85 H6
WHTN TW2 142 D2
WIM/MER SW19 146 B5
Denmark St LSQ/SEVD WC2H 11 H5
PLSTW E13 95 F4
TOTM N17 42 D7
WAN E11 76 C2
WAT WD17 21 F1
Denmark Ter EFNCH N2 * 53 K2
Denmead Rd CROY/NA CR0 164 C7
Dennan Rd SURB KT6 159 G7
Denner Rd CHING E4 43 J1
Denne Ter HACK E8 7 M4
Dennett Rd CROY/NA CR0 164 B6
Dennett's Gv NWCR SE14 132 A1
Dennett's Rd NWCR SE14 111 K7
Denning Av CROY/NA CR0 177 G4
Denning Cl HPTN TW12 141 K5
STJWD NW8 2 F7
Denning Ms BAL SW12 129 F5
Denning Rd HAMP NW3 71 H3
Dennington Park Rd
KIL/WHAMP NW6 70 E5
The Denningtons WPK KT4 173 G1
Dennis Av WBLY HA9 68 B4
Dennis Cl ASHF TW15 140 B6
Dennis Gdns STAN HA7 35 J4
Dennis La STAN HA7 35 H3
Dennis Pde STHGT/OAK N14 * 28 D7
Dennis Park Crs RYNPK SW20 146 C7
Dennis Reeve Cl MTCM CR4 147 K7
Dennis Rd E/WMO/HCT KT8 157 H3
Dennis Wy CLAP SW4 129 J2
Denny Crs LBTH SE11 18 B7
Denny Gdns DAGW RM9 79 H6
Denny Rd ED N9 30 D7
Denny St LBTH SE11 18 B7
Den Rd HAYES BR2 167 G2
Densham Rd SRTFD E15 76 C7
Densole Cl BECK BR3 * 151 G7
Densworth Gv ED N9 42 E1
Denton Cl BAR EN5 26 A4
Denton Rd BXLY DA5 138 B7
CEND/HSY/T N8 55 F4
DART DA1 138 B6
TWK TW1 124 E5
UED N18 42 A3
WELL DA16 116 D6
Denton St WAND/EARL SW18 128 A5
Denton Wy CLPT E5 75 F2
Dents Rd BTSEA SW11 128 E5
Denvale Trade Pk MTCM CR4 162 C3
Denver Cl ORP BR6 169 K5
Denver Rd DART DA1 138 D6
STNW/STAM N16 56 A6
Denyer St CHEL SW3 15 K5
Denzil Rd WLSDN NW10 69 H4
Deodar Rd PUT/ROE SW15 127 H3
Deodora Cl TRDG/WHET N20 39 J2
Depot Ap CRICK NW2 70 B3
Depot Rd HSLW TW3 123 J2
SHB W12 88 A6
Depot St CMBW SE5 110 E5
Deptford Br DEPT SE8 112 D7
Deptford Broadway
NWCR SE14 112 D7
Deptford Church St DEPT SE8 112 D5
Deptford Gn DEPT SE8 112 D5
Deptford High St DEPT SE8 112 D5
Deptford Market DEPT SE8 * 112 D6
Deptford Whf DEPT SE8 112 C3
De Quincey Ms CAN/RD E16 94 E7
De Quincey Rd TOTM N17 41 K7
Derby Av KTN/HRWW/WS HA3 34 D7
NFNCH/WDSPK N12 39 G4
ROMW/RG RM7 62 D5
Derby Ga WHALL SW1A 17 J1
Derby Hl FSTH SE23 150 E1
Derby Hill Crs FSTH SE23 150 E1
Derby Rd BRYLDS KT5 159 H7
CROY/NA CR0 177 H1
FSTGT E7 77 H6
GFD/PVL UB6 66 B7
HOM E9 75 F7
HSLW TW3 123 G3
MORT/ESHN SW14 125 J3
PEND EN3 30 D4
SUT SM1 174 D5
SWFD E18 44 D7
UED N18 42 E4
WAT WD17 21 G3
WIM/MER SW19 146 E6
Derbyshire St BETH E2 92 C2
Derby St MYFR/PICC W1J 10 B9
Dereham Pl SDTCH EC2A 7 K9
Dereham Rd BARK IG11 79 F5
Derek Av HOR/WEW KT19 172 C5
WBLY HA9 68 D6
WLGTN SM6 176 B3
Derek Cl HOR/WEW KT19 172 D4
Derek Walcott Cl HNHL SE24 * 130 C4
Deri Av RAIN RM13 99 K3
Dericote St HACK E8 74 C7
Deri Dene Cl
STWL/WRAY TW19 * 120 B5
Derifall Cl EHAM E6 95 K4
Dering Pl CROY/NA CR0 177 J3
Dering Rd CROY/NA CR0 177 J3
Dering St OXSTW W1C 10 C5
Derinton Rd TOOT SW17 148 A3
Derley Rd NWDGN UB2 102 B2
Dermody Gdns LEW SE13 * 133 G4
Dermody Rd LEW SE13 133 G4
Deronda Rd HNHL SE24 130 C7
Deroy Cl CAR SM5 175 K5
Derrick Gdns CHARL SE7 114 B2
Derrick Rd BECK BR3 166 C2
Derry Rd CROY/NA CR0 176 E2
Derry St KENS W8 14 C2
Dersingham Av MNPK E12 77 K3
Dersingham Rd CRICK NW2 70 C2
Derwent Av CDALE/KGS NW9 51 G4
EBAR EN4 27 K7
MLHL NW7 37 F4
PIN HA5 33 J5
PUT/ROE SW15 145 G3
UED N18 41 K4
Derwent Cl DART DA1 138 E7
EBED/NFELT TW14 121 J7
ESH/CLAY KT10 170 E5
Derwent Crs BXLYHN DA7 137 H1
NFNCH/WDSPK N12 39 G2
STAN HA7 49 J1
Derwent Dr STMC/STPC BR5 169 J6
YEAD UB4 82 C4
Derwent Gdns REDBR IG4 59 J3
WBLY HA9 49 J6
Derwent Gv EDUL SE22 131 G3
Derwent Ri CDALE/KGS NW9 51 G5
Derwent Rd EA W5 104 D2
PGE/AN SE20 165 H1
PLMGR N13 41 F3
RYNPK SW20 161 G5
STHL UB1 83 K5
WHTN TW2 123 G5
Derwent St GNWCH SE10 113 H4
Derwentwater Rd ACT W3 86 E7
Derwent Wy HCH RM12 81 K4
Derwent Yd EA W5 * 104 D2
De Salis Rd HGDN/ICK UB10 82 A3
Desenfans Rd DUL SE21 131 F5
Desford Rd CAN/RD E16 94 C3
Desmond St NWCR SE14 112 B5
Desmond Tutu Dr FSTH SE23 132 B7
Despard Rd ARCH N19 54 C7
Desvignes Dr LEW SE13 133 G5
Detling Rd BMLY BR1 152 E4
ERITH DA8 118 A6
Detmold Rd CLPT E5 74 D1
Devalls Cl EHAM E6 96 A6
Devana End CAR SM5 175 K2
Devas Rd RYNPK SW20 146 A7
Devas St BOW E3 93 K3
Devenay Rd SRTFD E15 76 D6
Devenish Rd ABYW SE2 116 B1
Deveraux Cl BECK BR3 167 F4
De Vere Cl WLGTN SM6 176 E6
De Vere Gdns IL IG1 59 K7
KENS W8 14 E2
Deverell St STHWK SE1 19 G4
De Vere Ms KENS W8 14 E3
Devereux Ct TPL/STR WC2R 12 A6
Devereux La BARN SW13 106 E6
Devereux Rd BTSEA SW11 128 E5
De Vere Wk WAT WD17 20 C1
Devey Cl KUTN/CMB KT2 145 H6
Devizes St IS N1 * 7 H4
Devon Av WHTN TW2 123 H7
Devon Cl BKHH IG9 45 F1

GFD/PVL UB6 .....67 J7
TOTM N17 .....56 B2
Devoncroft Gdns TWK TW1 .....124 B6
Devon Gdns FSBYPK N4 .....55 H5
Devonhurst Pl CHSWK W4 * 106 A4
Devonia Gdn UED N18 .....41 J5
Devonia Rd IS N1 .....6 D5
Devon Man
  KTN/HRWW/WS HA3 * 49 J4
Devonport Gdns IL IG1 .....59 K5
Devonport Rd SHB W12 * 87 K7
Devonport Rd SHB W12 .....87 K7
Devonport St WCHPL E1 .....92 E5
Devon Ri EFNCH N2 .....53 H3
Devon Rd BARK IG11 .....78 E7
Devons Est BOW E3 * 93 K2
Devonshire Av BELMT SM2 .....175 G6
  DART DA1 .....138 E5
Devonshire Cl
  CAVSQ/HST W1G 10 C1
  SRTFD E15 .....76 C3
Devonshire Ct FELT TW13 * 141 H1
Devonshire Crs MLHL NW7 .....38 B6
Devonshire Dr GNWCH SE10 .....112 E7
  SURB KT6 .....158 E7
Devonshire Gdns CHSWK W4 .....105 K6
  TOTM N17 .....41 J6
  WCHMH N21 .....29 J6
Devonshire Gv PECK SE15 .....111 J5
Devonshire Hill La TOTM N17 .....41 J5
Devonshire Ms CHSWK W4 .....106 B4
Devonshire Ms South
  CAVSQ/HST W1G 10 C2
Devonshire Ms West
  CAVSQ/HST W1G 10 B1
Devonshire Pl
  CAVSQ/HST W1G 10 B1
  CRICK NW2 .....70 E2
  KENS W8 * 14 C4
Devonshire Place Ms
  CAVSQ/HST W1G 10 B1
Devonshire Rd BELMT SM2 .....175 G6
  BXLYHS DA6 .....137 F3
  CAN/RD E16 .....95 F5
  CAR SM5 .....176 A3
  CHSWK W4 .....106 B4
  CROY/NA CR0 .....164 D6
  EA W5 .....104 D2
  ED N9 .....30 E7
  ELTH/MOT SE9 .....153 J1
  FELT TW13 .....141 J2
  FSTH SE23 .....132 A6
  GNTH/NBYPK IG2 .....48 D6
  HRW HA1 .....48 D6
  MLHL NW7 .....38 B6
  PIN HA5 .....47 C5
  PLMGR N13 .....41 F3
  STHL UB1 .....84 A5
  TOTM N17 .....41 J6
  WALTH E17 .....57 J5
  WIM/MER SW19 .....147 J6
Devonshire Rw LVPST EC2M 13 K3
Devonshire Row Ms
  GTPST W1W .....
  LVPST EC2M 13 K4
Devonshire Sq HAYES BR2 .....168 A3
  LVPST EC2M 13 K4
Devonshire St
  CAVSQ/HST W1G 10 B2
  CHSWK W4 .....106 B4
Devonshire Ter BAY/PAD W2 8
  EDUL SE22 * 131 H3
Devonshire Wy CROY/NA CR0 .....179 H1
  YEAD UB4 .....83 F5
Devons Rd BOW E3 .....93 J4
Devon St PECK SE15 .....111 J6
Devon Wy CHSGTN KT9 .....171 J3
  HOR/WEW KT19 .....172 D4
Devon Waye HEST TW5 .....102 E6
De Walden St
  CAVSQ/HST W1G 10 B3
Dewar St PECK SE15 .....131 H2
Dewberry Gdns EHAM E6 .....95 J4
Dewberry St POP/IOD E14 .....94 A4
Dewey La BRXS/STRHM SW2 .....130 B5
Dewey Rd DAGE RM10 .....80 D5
  IS N1 .....6 A5
Dewey St TOOT SW17 .....147 K4
Dewhurst Rd HMSMTH W6 .....107 H3
Dewsbury Cl PIN HA5 .....47 J5
Dewsbury Gdns WPK KT4 .....173 J2
Dewsbury Rd WLSDN NW10 .....69 J4
Dexter Rd BAR EN5 .....26 B5
Deyncourt Rd TOTM N17 .....41 J1
Deynecourt Gdns WAN E11 .....59 G3
D'Eynsford Rd CMBW SE5 .....110 E7
  CMBW SE5 .....110 E7
Diadem Ct SOHO/SHAV W1F * 11 G4
Diamedes Av
  STWL/WRAY TW19 .....120 A6
Diameter Rd STMC/STPC BR5 .....169 G6
Diamond Cl BCTR RM8 .....61 J7
Diamond Rd RSLP HA4 .....65 H3
Diamond St CMBW SE5 .....111 F6
  WLSDN NW10 .....69 F6
Diamond Ter GNWCH SE10 .....113 F6
Diana Cl DEPT SE8 .....112 C5
  SWFD E18 .....45 F7
Diana Gdns SURB KT6 .....172 B1
Diana Rd WALTH E17 .....57 H2
Dianne Wy EBAR EN4 .....27 J3
Dianthus Cl ABYW SE2 * 116 C4
Diban Av HCH RM12 .....81 K5
Dibden St IS N1 .....6 E3
Dibdin Cl SUT SM1 .....174 E2
Dibdin Rd SUT SM1 .....174 E2
Dicey Av CRICK NW2 .....70 A4
Dickens Av DART DA1 .....139 K3
  FNCH N3 .....39 G7
Dickens Cl ERITH DA8 .....117 J6
  HYS/HAR UB3 .....101 H3
  RCHPK/HAM TW10 .....144 A1
Dickens Est
  BERM/RHTH SE16 * 111 H2
Dickens La UED N18 .....42 A4
Dickens Ms FARR EC1M 12 C1
Dickenson Cl ED N9 .....30 C7
Dickenson Rd
  CEND/HSY/T N8 .....54 E6
  FELT TW13 .....141 G4
Dickenson's La SNWD SE25 .....165 H5
Dickenson's Pl SNWD SE25 .....165 H5
Dickens Rd EHAM E6 .....95 H1
Dickens Sq STHWK SE1 .....18 D4
Dickens St VX/NE SW8 .....129 G3
Dickens Wy ROM RM1 .....63 G3
Dickerage La NWMAL KT3 .....159 J3
Dickerage Rd NWMAL KT3 .....159 K1
Dickson Fold PIN HA5 .....47 H3
Dickson House CHARL SE7 * 114 D6
Dickson Rd ELTH/MOT SE9 .....134 D2

Dick Turpin Wy
  EBED/NFELT TW14 .....121 J3
Didsbury Cl EHAM E6 .....77 K7
Digby Crs FSBYPK N4 .....73 J1
Digby Gdns DAGE RM10 .....80 C7
Digby Pl CROY/NA CR0 .....178 B2
Digby Rd BARK IG11 .....79 F6
  HOM E9 .....75 F5
Digby St BETH E2 .....92 E2
Diggon St WCHPL E1 .....93 F4
Dighton Rd WAND/EARL SW18 .....128 B4
Dignum St IS N1 * 6 A1
Digswell St HOLWY N7 * 73 G5
Dilhorne Cl LEE/GVPK SE12 .....153 F2
Dilke St CHEL SW3 .....15 M9
Dillwyn Cl SYD SE26 .....151 G3
Dilston Cl NTHLT UB5 .....83 G2
Dilton Gdns PUT/ROE SW15 .....126 D3
Dimes Pl HMSMTH W6 .....106 E3
Dimmock Dr GFD/PVL UB6 .....66 D4
Dimond Cl FSTGT E7 .....76 E3
Dimsdale Dr CDALE/KGS NW9 .....50 A7
  EN EN1 .....30 C6
Dimsdale Wk PLSTW E13 .....76 E7
Dimson Crs BOW E3 .....93 J6
Dingle Cl BAR EN5 .....25 H5
Dingle Gdns POP/IOD E14 * 93 J6
Dingley Pl FSBYE EC1V 6 E9
Dingley Rd FSBYE EC1V 6 E8
Dingwall Av CROY/NA CR0 .....177 J2
Dingwall Gdns GLDGN NW11 .....52 E5
Dingwall Rd CAR SM5 .....175 K7
  CROY/NA CR0 .....177 K1
  WAND/EARL SW18 .....128 B6
Dinmont St BETH E2 .....92 D1
Dinsdale Gdns BAR EN5 .....27 F4
  SNWD SE25 .....165 F4
Dinsdale Rd BKHTH/KID SE3 .....113 J5
Dinsmore Rd BAL SW12 .....129 G6
Dinton Rd KUTN/CMB SE2 .....144 B2
  WIM/MER SW19 .....147 H5
Diploma Av EFNCH N2 .....53 J3
Dirleton Rd SRTFD E15 .....76 D7
Disbrowe Rd HMSMTH W6 .....107 H5
Discovery Wk WAP E1W * 92 D6
Dishforth La CDALE/KGS NW9 .....37 G3
Disney Pl STHWK SE1 * 18 F1
Disney St STHWK SE1 .....18 F1
Disraeli Cl THMD SE28 .....97 H7
  WEA W13 .....85 K7
Disraeli Rd EA W5 .....85 K7
  FSTGT E7 .....76 E5
  PUT/ROE SW15 .....127 H3
  WLSDN NW10 .....86 E1
Diss St BETH E2 .....7 L7
Distaff La BLKFR EC4V 12 E6
Distillery La HMSMTH W6 .....107 F4
Distillery Rd HMSMTH W6 .....107 F4
Distin St LBTH SE11 .....18 A6
District Rd ALP/SUD HA0 .....67 H4
Ditchburn St POP/IOD E14 .....94 A6
Ditchfield Rd YEAD UB4 .....83 J3
Dittisham Rd ELTH/MOT SE9 .....153 J3
Ditton Cl THDIT KT7 .....158 B6
Dittoncroft Cl CROY/NA CR0 .....178 A3
Ditton Grange Cl SURB KT6 .....158 E7
Ditton Grange Dr SURB KT6 .....158 E7
Ditton Hl SURB KT6 .....158 D7
Ditton Hill Rd SURB KT6 .....158 D7
Ditton Lawn THDIT KT7 .....158 B7
Ditton Pl PGE/AN SE20 * 150 D7
Ditton Reach THDIT KT7 .....158 C5
Ditton Rd BXLYHS DA6 .....136 E4
  NWDGN UB2 .....102 E4
  SURB KT6 .....159 F7
Divisional Rd MNPK E12 .....77 H2
Dixey Cots EFNCH N2 * 53 H2
Dixon Cl EHAM E6 .....95 K5
Dixon Pl WWKM BR4 .....166 E1
Dixon Rd NWCR SE14 .....112 B7
  SNWD SE25 .....165 F2
Dixon Wy WLSDN NW10 .....69 G6
Dobbin Cl
  KTN/HRWW/WS HA3 .....49 G1
Dobell Rd ELTH/MOT SE9 .....134 D4
Dobree Av WLSDN NW10 .....69 K6
Dobson Cl KIL/WHAMP NW6 .....3 H1
Dockers Tanner Rd
  POP/IOD E14 .....112 D3
Dockhead STHWK SE1 .....19 M2
Dock Hill Av BERM/RHTH SE16 .....112 A1
Dockland St CAN/RD E16 .....96 A7
Dockley Rd BERM/RHTH SE16 .....111 H2
Dock Rd BTFD TW8 * 104 E6
  CAN/RD E16 .....94 D6
Dockside Rd CAN/RD E16 .....95 H6
Dock St WCHPL E1 .....92 C6
Dockwell Cl
  EBED/NFELT TW14 .....121 K3
Doctors Cl SYD SE26 .....150 E4
Docwra's Blds IS N1 * 74 A5
Dodbrooke Rd WNWD SE27 .....149 G2
Doddington Gv WALW SE17 .....18 C9
Doddington Pl WALW SE17 .....18 C9
Dodsley Pl ED N9 .....42 E2
Dodson St STHWK SE1 .....18 B2
Dod St POP/IOD E14 .....93 J5
Doebury Wk
  WOOL/PLUM SE18 .....116 B5
Doel Cl WIM/MER SW19 .....147 G6
Doggett Rd CAT SE6 .....132 D6
Doggetts Ct EBAR EN4 .....27 J4
Doghurst Av WDR/YW UB7 .....100 B6
Doghurst Dr WDR/YW UB7 .....100 B6
Dog Kennel Hi CMBW SE5 .....131 F2
Dog La WLSDN NW10 .....69 G3
Dog Rose Ramble NTHLT UB5 .....65 H7
  YEAD UB4 .....83 H5
Dog Rose Ramble & Hillingdon
  Trail YEAD UB4 .....82 D1
Doherty Rd PLSTW E13 .....94 E3
Dolben Ct DEPT SE8 * 112 C3
Dolben St STHWK SE1 * 12 D9
Dolby Rd FUL/PGN SW6 .....127 J1
Dolland St LBTH SE11 .....17 M8
Dollary Pde KUT/HW KT1 * 159 J2
Dollis Av FNCH N3 .....38 D1
Dollis Crs RSLP HA4 .....47 G1
Dollis Hill Av CRICK NW2 .....69 J2
Dollis Hill Est CRICK NW2 * 69 H2
Dollis Hill La CRICK NW2 .....69 H3
Dollis Pk FNCH N3 .....38 D1
Dollis Rd MLHL NW7 .....38 D4
Dollis Valley Dr EBAR EN4 .....26 D5
Dollis Valley Green Wk
  FNCH N3 .....52 D3
  TRDG/WHET N20 .....39 F2
Dollis Valley Wy EBAR EN4 .....27 F4
Dolman Cl FNCH N3 * 53 G1
Dolman Rd CHSWK W4 .....106 A3
Dolman St CLAP SW4 .....130 A3
Dolphin Ap ROM RM1 .....63 H5
Dolphin Cl BERM/RHTH SE16 .....112 A1

SURB KT6 .....158 E5
THMD SE28 .....97 J5
Dolphin Est SUN TW16 * 140 C7
Dolphin La POP/IOD E14 .....93 K6
Dolphin Rd NTHLT UB5 .....83 K1
  SUN TW16 .....140 C7
Dolphin Rd North SUN TW16 .....140 B7
Dolphin Rd South SUN TW16 .....140 B7
Dolphin Rd West SUN TW16 .....140 C7
Dolphin Sq CHSWK W4 * 106 A6
  PIM SW1V 16 F8
Dolphin St KUT/HW KT1 .....159 F1
Dombey St BMSBY WC1N 11 L2
Dome Blds RCH/KEW TW9 * 124 E4
Dome Hill Pk SYD SE26 .....150 B3
Domett Cl CMBW SE5 .....130 E3
Domingo St FSBYE EC1V * 6 E9
Dominica Cl PLSTW E13 .....95 H2
Dominion Pde HRW HA1 * 49 F5
Dominion Rd CROY/NA CR0 .....165 G6
  NWDGN UB2 .....102 D2
Dominion St LVPST EC2M 13 H2
Dominion Wy RAIN RM13 .....99 J2
Domonic Dr ELTH/MOT SE9 .....154 B2
Domville Cl TRDG/WHET N20 .....39 H1
Donald Dr CHDH RM6 .....61 J4
Donald Rd CROY/NA CR0 .....164 A5
  PLSTW E13 .....77 F7
Donaldson Rd
  KIL/WHAMP NW6 .....70 D7
  WOOL/PLUM SE18 .....115 F7
Donald Woods Gdns
  BRYLDS KT5 .....172 D1
Doncaster Dr NTHLT UB5 .....65 K4
Doncaster Gdns FSBYPK N4 * 55 J5
  NTHLT UB5 .....65 K4
Doncaster Rd ED N9 .....30 D6
Donegal St IS N1 .....5 M6
Doneraile St FUL/PGN SW6 .....127 G1
Dongola Rd PLSTW E13 .....95 F2
  TOTM N17 .....56 A2
  WCHPL E1 .....93 G4
Dongola Rd West PLSTW E13 .....95 F2
Donington Av BARK/HLT IG6 .....60 C4
Donkey Aly EDUL SE22 .....131 H6
Donkey La EN EN1 .....30 C1
Donnefield Av EDGW HA8 .....36 A5
Donne Pl CHEL SW3 .....15 K5
  MTCM CR4 .....163 G3
Donne Rd BCTR RM8 .....79 J1
Donnington Rd
  KTN/HRWW/WS HA3 .....49 K5
  WLSDN NW10 .....69 K7
  WPK KT4 .....173 J1
Donnybrook Rd
  STRHM/NOR SW16 .....148 C6
Donoghue Cots
  POP/IOD E14 * 93 G4
Donovan Av MUSWH N10 .....54 B1
Donovan Pl WCHMH N21 .....29 F4
Don Phelan Cl CMBW SE5 .....110 E7
Doon St STHWK SE1 .....12 A8
Doral Wy CAR SM5 .....175 K4
Dorando Cl SHB W12 * 87 K6
Doran Gv WOOL/PLUM SE18 .....115 K6
Dora Rd WIM/MER SW19 .....146 E4
Dora St POP/IOD E14 .....93 H5
Dorchester Av BXLY DA5 .....136 E7
  PLMGR N13 .....41 J3
  RYLN/HDSTN HA2 .....48 C5
Dorchester Cl CRICK NW2 .....70 A2
  ESH/CLAY KT10 .....171 F1
  NTHLT UB5 .....66 B4
  STMC/STPC BR5 .....155 H6
Dorchester Ct CHING E4 .....43 J5
  GLDGN NW11 * 52 E5
Dorchester Dr
  EBED/NFELT TW14 .....121 H5
  HNHL SE24 .....130 D4
Dorchester Gdns CHING E4 .....43 J5
  GLDGN NW11 * 52 E5
Dorchester Ms TWK TW1 .....124 D6
Dorchester Pde
  STRHM/NOR SW16 * 148 E1
Dorchester Rd MRDN SM4 .....162 A6
  NTHLT UB5 .....66 B4
  WPK KT4 .....161 F7
Dorchester Ter HDN NW4 * 52 B1
Dorchester Wy
  KTN/HRWW/WS HA3 .....50 A4
Dorchester Waye YEAD UB4 .....83 F5
Dorcis Av BXLYHN DA7 .....137 F1
Dordrecht Rd ACT W3 .....87 G7
Dore Av MNPK E12 .....78 A4
Doreen Av CDALE/KGS NW9 .....51 F7
Dore Gdns MRDN SM4 .....162 A6
Dorell Cl STHL UB1 .....83 K4
Dorian Rd HCH RM12 .....81 J7
Doria Rd FUL/PGN SW6 .....127 J1
Doric Wy CAMTN NW1 .....5 G7
Dorie Ms NFNCH/WDSPK N12 .....39 F3
Dorien Rd RYNPK SW20 .....161 G1
Doris Ashby Cl GFD/PVL UB6 .....67 G7
Doris Av ERITH DA8 .....117 K7
Doris Rd ASHF TW15 .....140 B5
  FSTGT E7 .....76 E6
Dorking Cl DEPT SE8 .....112 C5
  WPK KT4 .....174 B1
Dorlcote Rd
  WAND/EARL SW18 .....128 C6
Dorman Pl ED N9 * 42 C1
Dormans Cl NTHWD HA6 .....32 A6
Dormay St WAND/EARL SW18 .....128 A4
Dorman Wy STJWD NW8 .....3 G3
Dormer Cl BAR EN5 .....26 B4
  SRTFD E15 .....76 D5
Dormer's Av STHL UB1 .....84 A5
Dormers Ri STHL UB1 .....84 B5
Dormer's Wells La STHL UB1 .....84 A5
Dormywood RSLP HA4 .....46 D4
Dornberg Cl BKHTH/KID SE3 .....113 K6
Dornberg Rd
  BKHTH/KID SE3 * 114 A6
Dorncliffe Rd FUL/PGN SW6 .....127 H1
Dorney Wy HSLWW TW4 .....122 D4
Dornfell St KIL/WHAMP NW6 .....70 D4
Dornton Rd BAL SW12 .....148 B1
  SAND/SEL CR2 .....177 K4
Dorothy Av ALP/SUD HA0 .....68 A6
Dorothy Evans Cl
  BXLYHN DA7 .....137 J3
Dorothy Gdns BCTR RM8 .....79 H4
Dorothy Rd BTSEA SW11 .....128 E2
Dorrington Wy BECK BR3 .....167 F4
Dorrit Ms UED N18 .....42 A4

Dorrit St STHWK SE1 * 18 F1
Dorrit Wy CHST BR7 .....154 C5
Dorrofield Cl
  RKW/CH/CXG WD3 .....20 A4
Dors Cl CDALE/KGS NW9 .....51 F7
Dorset Av NWDGN UB2 .....103 F3
  ROM RM1 .....63 J1
  WELL DA16 .....136 A3
  YEAD UB4 .....82 C2
Dorset Blds EMB EC4Y 12 C5
Dorset Dr EDGW HA8 .....36 B5
Dorset Gdns MTCM CR4 .....164 A3
Dorset Ms FNCH N3 .....38 E7
  KTBR SW1X 16 C3
Dorset Ri EMB EC4Y 12 C5
Dorset Rd BECK BR3 .....166 A2
  EA W5 .....104 D2
  ELTH/MOT SE9 .....153 J1
  FSTGT E7 .....77 G6
  HRW HA1 .....48 C5
  MTCM CR4 .....162 D1
  SEVS/STOTM N15 .....55 K3
  VX/NE SW8 .....17 M9
  WDGN N22 .....40 E7
  WIM/MER SW19 .....146 E7
Dorset Sq CAMTN NW1 .....9 L1
Dorset St MHST W1U 9 M3
Dorset Wy WHTN TW2 .....123 J7
Dorset Waye HEST TW5 .....102 E6
Dorton Cl PECK SE15 .....111 F6
Dorville Crs HMSMTH W6 .....106 E2
Dorville Rd LEE/GVPK SE12 .....133 K4
Dothill Rd WOOL/PLUM SE18 .....115 J6
Douai Gv HPTN TW12 .....142 C7
Doughty Ms BMSBY WC1N 11 J1
Douglas Av ALP/SUD HA0 .....68 A6
  NWMAL KT3 .....160 E3
  WALTH E17 .....43 J7
  WLGTN SM6 .....176 E5
Douglas Crs YEAD UB4 .....83 G3
Douglas Dr CROY/NA CR0 .....179 J2
Douglas Est IS N1 * 73 J5
Douglas Ms CRICK NW2 .....70 C2
Douglas Pth POP/IOD E14 * 113 F4
Douglas Rd CAN/RD E16 .....94 E4
  ESH/CLAY KT10 .....170 B1
  GDMY/SEVK IG3 .....61 G6
  HSLW TW3 .....123 G2
  IS N1 6
  KIL/WHAMP NW6 .....70 D7
  KUT/HW KT1 .....159 J1
  ROM RM1 .....63 H5
  STWL/WRAY TW19 .....120 A7
  SURB KT6 .....172 B1
  WDGN N22 .....41 G7
  WELL DA16 .....116 C7
Douglas Rd North IS N1 .....73 J5
Douglas Rd South IS N1 .....73 J5
Douglas Sq MRDN SM4 .....161 K5
Douglas St WEST SW1P 17 G6
Douglas Ter WALTH E17 * 43 H7
Douglas Vls KUT/HW KT1 * 159 G1
Douglas Wy NWCR SE14 .....112 B7
Doulton Ms KIL/WHAMP NW6 * 71 F5
Dounesforth Gdns
  WAND/EARL SW18 .....128 A7
Douro Pl KENS W8 .....14 D3
Douro St BOW E3 .....93 J1
Douthwaite Sq WAP E1W * 92 C7
Dove Ap EHAM E6 .....95 J4
Dove Cl MLHL NW7 .....37 H7
  NTHLT UB5 .....83 H3
  WLGTN SM6 .....177 F6
Dovecot Cl PIN HA5 .....47 F5
Dove Ct LOTH EC2R * 13 G5
Dovedale Av CLAY IG5 .....60 A1
  KTN/HRWW/WS HA3 .....49 J5
Dovedale Cl WELL DA16 .....116 B7
Dovedale Ri MTCM CR4 .....147 K6
Dovedale Rd EDUL SE22 .....131 J4
Dovedon Cl STHGT/OAK N14 .....40 E2
Dove House Gdns CHING E4 .....43 J1
Dovehouse Md BARK IG11 .....96 D1
Dovehouse St CHEL SW3 .....15 J8
Dove Ms ECT SW5 .....14 E6
Dove Pk PIN HA5 .....33 K6
Dove Pl ESH/CLAY KT10 .....171 F7
Dover Cl CRICK NW2 .....70 B1
  CRW RM5 .....62 E1
Dovercourt Av THHTH CR7 .....164 B3
Dovercourt Est IS N1 * 73 K5
Dovercourt Gdns
  STAN HA7 .....36 A4
Dovercourt La SUT SM1 .....175 G2
Dovercourt Rd DUL SE21 .....149 J2
Doverfield Rd
  BRXS/STRHM SW2 .....129 K5
Dover Gdns CAR SM5 .....175 K2
Dover House Rd
  PUT/ROE SW15 .....126 D3
Doveridge Gdns PLMGR N13 .....41 H3
Dove Rd IS N1 .....73 K5
Dove Rw BETH E2 .....7 M6
Dover Park Dr PUT/ROE SW15 .....126 E5
Dover Patrol BKHTH/KID SE3 .....114 A1
Dover Rd ED N9 .....42 E1
  EHAM E6 .....78 A7
  NRWD SE19 .....149 K5
  WOOL/PLUM SE18 .....115 F3
Dover St CONDST W1S 10 D7
Dover Ter RCH/KEW TW9 * 125 H1
Dover Wy RKW/CH/CXG WD3 .....20 A4
Dover Yd MYFR/PICC W1J 10 D8
Doves Yd IS N1 .....6 A2
Doveton Rd SAND/SEL CR2 .....177 K4
Doveton St WCHPL E1 .....92 E3
Dowanhill Rd CAT SE6 .....133 G7
Dowd Cl FBAR/BDGN N11 .....40 A1
Dowdeswell Cl
  PUT/ROE SW15 .....126 B3
Dowding Dr ELTH/MOT SE9 .....134 B4
Dowding Pl STAN HA7 .....35 G5
Dowdney Cl KTTN NW5 .....72 C4
Dower Av WLGTN SM6 .....176 B7
Dowgate Hi CANST EC4R 13 G6
Dowland St NKENS W10 .....88 C2
Dowlas St CMBW SE5 .....111 F6
Dowman Cl WIM/MER SW19 .....147 F6
Downage HDN NW4 .....52 A2
Downalong BUSH WD23 .....22 D7
Downbank Av BXLYHN DA7 .....138 A1
Down Barns Rd RSLP HA4 .....65 H2
Down Cl NTHLT UB5 .....82 B1
Downderry Rd BMLY BR1 .....152 B2
Downe Cl WELL DA16 .....116 C6
Downend WOOL/PLUM SE18 .....115 G6
Downe Rd HAYES BR2 .....181 J7

MTCM CR4 .....162 E1
Downes Cl TWK TW1 .....124 C5
Downes Ct WCHMH N21 .....29 G7
Downfield WPK KT4 .....160 C7
Downfield Cl MV/WKIL W9 .....8 C1
Down Hall Rd KUT/HW KT1 .....143 K7
Downham La BMLY BR1 .....152 B4
Downham Rd IS N1 .....7 J2
Downham Wy BMLY BR1 .....152 B4
Downhills Av TOTM N17 .....55 K2
Downhills Park Rd TOTM N17 .....55 J2
Downhills Wy TOTM N17 .....55 J2
Downhurst Av MLHL NW7 .....37 F4
Downing Cl RYLN/HDSTN HA2 .....48 C2
Downing Dr GFD/PVL UB6 .....66 E7
Downing Rd DAGW RM9 .....80 B7
Downings EHAM E6 .....96 A5
Downland Cl TRDG/WHET N20 .....27 G7
Downleys Cl ELTH/MOT SE9 .....153 J1
Downman Rd ELTH/MOT SE9 .....134 D2
Down Pl HMSMTH W6 .....106 E3
Down Rd TEDD TW11 .....143 H5
Downs Av CHST BR7 .....153 K4
  DART DA1 .....139 K6
Downs Bridge Rd BECK BR3 .....152 B7
Downs Court Pde HACK E8 * 74 D4
Downsell Rd SRTFD E15 .....76 B3
Downshall Av GDMY/SEVK IG3 .....60 E5
Downs Hi BECK BR3 .....152 B7
Downside BECK BR3 .....151 J7
  SUN TW16 .....140 D7
  TWK TW1 .....143 F2
Downside Cl WIM/MER SW19 .....147 G5
Downside Crs HAMP NW3 .....71 J4
  WEA W13 .....85 G3
Downside Rd BELMT SM2 .....175 H5
Downs La CLPT E5 .....74 D3
Downs Park Rd HACK E8 .....74 B4
Down St BECK BR3 .....166 E1
  CLPT E5 .....74 C3
  EN EN1 .....30 A4
  THHTH CR7 .....
The Downs RYNPK SW20 .....146 B6
Down St E/WMO/HCT KT8 .....157 F4
  MYFR/PICC W1J 10 C9
Downs Vw ISLW TW7 .....104 A7
Downsview Gdns NRWD SE19 .....149 G6
Downsview Rd NRWD SE19 .....149 G6
The Downsway BELMT SM2 .....175 G7
Downton Av
  BRXS/STRHM SW2 .....149 F1
Downtown Rd
  BERM/RHTH SE16 .....112 B1
Downway
  NFNCH/WDSPK N12 .....39 J3
Down Wy NTHLT UB5 .....82 B2
Dowrey St IS N1 * 6 A3
Dowsett Rd TOTM N17 .....56 C2
Dowson Cl CMBW SE5 * 130 E3
Doyce St STHWK SE1 * 18 E1
Doyle Cl ERITH DA8 .....118 B7
Doyle Gdns WLSDN NW10 .....69 K7
Doyle Rd SNWD SE25 .....165 H3
D'Oyley St BGVA SW1W 16 A5
Doynton St ARCH N19 * 72 B1
Draco Ga PUT/ROE SW15 .....127 F2
Draco St WALW SE17 .....18 E9
Dragmore St CLAP SW4 .....129 J5
Dragonfly Cl PLSTW E13 .....95 F2
Dragon Rd LBTH SE11 .....17 M6
  PECK SE15 .....111 F5
Dragoon Rd DEPT SE8 .....112 C4
Dragor Rd WLSDN NW10 .....86 E2
Drake Cl BERM/RHTH SE16 .....112 A1
Drake Crs THMD SE28 .....97 J5
Drakefell Rd NWCR SE14 .....132 A1
Drake Ms HAYES BR2 .....168 B3
  HCH RM12 .....81 J6
Drake Rd BROCKY SE4 .....132 D2
  CHSGTN KT9 .....172 C4
  CROY/NA CR0 .....164 A6
  MTCM CR4 .....163 F5
  RYLN/HDSTN HA2 .....65 K3
Drake's Cl ESH/CLAY KT10 .....170 A4
Drakes Ctyd KIL/WHAMP NW6 .....70 D6
Drake St ENC/FH EN2 .....29 H1
Drakewood Rd
  STRHM/NOR SW16 .....148 D6
Draper Cl BELV DA17 .....117 G3
  ISLW TW7 .....123 J1
Draper Est STHWK SE1 .....18 E3
Draper Pl IS N1 .....6 D3
Drapers Rd ENC/FH EN2 .....29 H1
  SRTFD E15 .....76 A3
  TOTM N17 .....56 B2
Drappers Wy
  BERM/RHTH SE16 .....111 H3
Draven Cl HAYES BR2 .....167 J6
Drawell Cl WOOL/PLUM SE18 .....115 K4
Drax Av RYNPK SW20 .....145 J6
Draxmont WIM/MER SW19 .....146 C5
Draycot Rd SURB KT6 .....159 H2
  WAN E11 .....59 F5
Draycott Av CHEL SW3 .....15 K6
  KTN/HRWW/WS HA3 .....49 H5
Draycott Cl CMBW SE5 .....110 E6
  CRICK NW2 .....70 B2
  KTN/HRWW/WS HA3 .....49 H5
Draycott Pl CHEL SW3 .....15 L6
Draycott Ter CHEL SW3 .....15 L5
Dray Ct ALP/SUD HA0 * 67 J3
Drayford Cl MV/WKIL W9 * 88 D3
Dray Gdns BRXS/STRHM SW2 .....130 A4
Draymans Ms PECK SE15 .....131 G1
Draymans Wy ISLW TW7 .....124 A2
Drayside Ms STHL UB1 * 83 K7
Drayton Av ORP BR6 .....169 G7
  WEA W13 .....85 G6
Drayton Bridge Rd HNWL W7 .....85 H6
  IL IG1 .....60 D7
Drayton Cl HSLWW TW4 .....122 E4
  IL IG1 .....60 D7
Drayton Ct WDR/YW UB7 * 100 A1
Drayton Court Chambers
  WEA W13 * 85 H6
  WCHMH N21 .....29 H7
  WDR/YW UB7 .....100 A1
  WEA W13 .....85 G6
Drayton Gdns WEA W13 .....85 G6
Drayton Green Rd WEA W13 .....85 H6
Drayton Gv WEA W13 .....85 G6
Drayton Pk HBRY N5 .....73 G4
Drayton Park Ms HOLWY N7 * 73 G4
Drayton Rd BORE WD6 .....24 C1
  CROY/NA CR0 .....177 H1
  TOTM N17 .....56 A1
  WAN E11 .....58 B7
  WEA W13 .....85 G6

WLSDN NW10 69 H7
Drayton Waye
KTN/HRWW/WS HA3 49 H5
Dreadnought Cl
WIM/MER SW19 162 B1
Dreadnought St GNWCH SE10 113 H2
Drenon Sq HYS/HAR UB3 82 D6
Dresden Cl KIL/WHAMP NW6 71 F5
Dresden Rd ARCH N19 54 C7
Dressington Av BROCKY SE4 132 D5
Drew Av MLHL NW7 38 C5
Drewery Ct BKHTH/KID SE3 * 133 H2
Drew Gdns GFD/PVL UB6 67 F5
Drew Rd CAN/RD E16 95 J7
Drews Cots
STRHM/NOR SW16 * 148 D1
Drewstead La
STRHM/NOR SW16 148 D1
Drewstead Rd
STRHM/NOR SW16 148 D1
Driffield Rd BOW E3 93 G1
The Drift HAYES BR2 181 H2
The Driftway MTCM CR4 148 A7
Drinkwater Rd
RYLN/HDSTN HA2 66 B1
Drive Ct EDGW HA8 * 36 C4
The Drive ACT W3 86 E5
ASHF TW15 140 B6
BAR EN5 26 C2
BARK IG11 79 F6
BECK BR3 166 D1
BXLY DA5 136 D5
CHST BR7 155 F6
EBED/NFELT TW14 122 A6
EDGW HA8 36 C4
ERITH DA8 117 J6
ESH/CLAY KT10 157 H7
FBAR/BDGN N11 40 C5
FNCH N3 38 E6
GLDGN NW11 52 C6
HGT N6 53 K4
HOLWY N7 73 F5
HOR/WEW KT19 173 H5
HSLW TW3 123 J1
IL IG1 59 J5
KUTN/CMB KT2 144 E6
MRDN SM4 162 B4
NTHWD HA6 32 C7
RYLN/HDSTN HA2 48 A6
RYNPK SW20 146 A6
SCUP DA14 155 H2
SURB KT6 159 F6
SWFD E18 58 E2
THHTH CR7 164 E3
WALTH E17 57 K2
WBLY HA9 68 E1
WWKM BR4 167 G6
Dr Johnson Av TOOT SW17 148 B2
Droitwich Cl SYD SE26 150 C2
Dromey Gdns
KTN/HRWW/WS HA3 35 F6
Dromore Rd PUT/ROE SW15 127 H5
Dronfield Gdns BCTR RM8 79 J4
Droop St NKENS W10 88 C3
Drovers Pl PECK SE15 111 J6
Drovers Rd SAND/SEL CR2 177 K4
Drovers Wy HOLWY N7 72 E5
Druce Rd DUL SE21 131 F5
Druid St STHWK SE1 19 K1
Druids Wy HAYES BR2 167 G3
Drumaline Rdg WPK KT4 173 G1
Drummond Av
ROMW/RG RM7 63 F3
Drummond Cl ERITH DA8 118 B7
Drummond Crs CAMTN NW1 5 G7
Drummond Dr STAN HA7 35 F6
Drummond Ga PIM SW1V 17 H7
Drummond Rd
BERM/RHTH SE16 111 J2
CROY/NA CR0 177 J1
ROMW/RG RM7 62 E3
WAN E11 59 F5
Drummonds Pl RCH/KEW TW9 125 F3
Drummond St CAMTN NW1 4 E9
Drury Crs CROY/NA CR0 177 G1
Drury La COVGDN WC2E 11 K5
Drury Rd HRW HA1 48 C6
Drury Wy WLSDN NW10 69 F4
Dryad St PUT/ROE SW15 127 G2
Dryburgh Gdns
CDALE/KGS NW9 50 C2
Dryburgh Rd PUT/ROE SW15 126 E2
Dryden Av HNWL W7 85 F5
Dryden Cl CLAP SW4 129 J4
Dryden Rd EN EN1 30 A5
KTN/HRWW/WS HA3 35 F7
WELL DA16 116 A7
WIM/MER SW19 147 G5
Dryden St COVGDN WC2E 11 K5
Dryfield Cl WLSDN NW10 68 E5
Dryfield Rd EDGW HA8 36 E5
Dryhill Rd BELV DA17 117 G5
Drylands Rd CEND/HSY/T N8 55 E5
Drysdale Av CHING E4 31 K5
Drysdale Cl NTHWD HA6 32 C6
Drysdale Dwellings HACK E8 * 74 B4
Drysdale Pl IS N1 7 K7
Drysdale St IS N1 7 K8
Dublin Av HACK E8 74 C7
Du Burstow Ter HNWL W7 103 K1
Ducal St BETH E2 7 M8
Du Cane Cl SHB W12 * 88 A5
Du Cane Rd SHB W12 87 J5
Duchess Cl FBAR/BDGN N11 40 B4
SUT SM1 175 G3
Duchess Gv BKHH IG9 * 45 F1
Duchess Ms CAVSQ/HST W1G 10 D3
Duchess of Bedford's Wk
KENS W8 107 J1
Duchess St REGST W1B 10 D2
Duchy St STHWK SE1 12 B8
Ducie St CLAP SW4 129 K3
Duckett Ms FSBYPK N4 55 H5
Duckett Rd FSBYPK N4 55 H5
Ducketts Rd DART DA1 138 C4
Duckett St WCHPL E1 93 F4
Ducking Stool Ct ROM RM1 63 G3
Duck La SOHO/CST W1F 11 G5
Duck Lees La PEND EN3 31 G3
Du Cros Dr STAN HA7 35 K5
Du Cros Rd ACT W3 87 G7
Dudden Hill La WLSDN NW10 69 H3
Dudden Hill Pde
WLSDN NW10 * 69 H3
Duddington Cl ELTH/MOT SE9 153 H3
Dudley Av
KTN/HRWW/WS HA3 49 J2
Dudley Dr MRDN SM4 161 H7
RSLP HA4 65 F4
Dudley Gdns
RYLN/HDSTN HA2 48 D7
WEA W13 104 C1
Dudley Pl HYS/HAR UB3 101 G3
Dudley Rd EBED/NFELT TW14 121 G7
FNCH N3 53 F1
IL IG1 78 B3
KIL/WHAMP NW6 88 C1
KUT/HW KT1 159 G2
NWDGN UB2 102 C1
RCH/KEW TW9 125 G1
RYLN/HDSTN HA2 66 C1
WALTH E17 57 J1
WIM/MER SW19 146 E5
Dudley St BAY/PAD W2 * 9 G3
Dudlington Rd CLPT E5 74 E1
Dudmaston Ms CHEL SW3 15 H7
Dudrich Cl
NFNCH/WDSPK N12 39 K5
Dudrich Ms EDUL SE22 131 G4
Dudsbury Rd DART DA1 138 E5
Dudset La HEST TW5 101 K7
Dufferin Av STLK EC1Y 13 G1
Dufferin St STLK EC1Y 12 F1
Duffield Cl HRW HA1 49 F4
Duffield Dr SEVS/STOTM N15 56 B3
Duff St POP/IOD E14 93 K5
Dufour's Pl SOHO/CST W1F 10 F5
Dugard Wy LBTH SE11 18 C5
Duggan Dr CHST BR7 153 J5
Dugolly Av WBLY HA9 68 D2
Duke Humphrey Rd
BKHTH/KID SE3 113 H7
Duke of Cambridge Cl
WHTN TW2 123 J5
Duke of Edinburgh Rd
SUT SM1 175 H2
The Duke of Wellington Av
WOOL/PLUM SE18 115 G2
Duke of Wellington Pl
KTBR SW1X 16 B2
Duke of York Sq CHEL SW3 15 M7
Duke of York St STJS SW1Y 10 F8
Duke Rd BARK/HLT IG6 60 D3
CHSWK W4 106 A4
Dukes Av EDGW HA8 36 B5
FNCH N3 39 F7
HRW HA1 48 E3
HSLWW TW4 122 D3
MUSWH N10 54 C2
NTHLT UB5 65 J6
NWMAL KT3 160 B2
PIN HA5 47 K5
RCHPK/HAM TW10 143 J3
Duke's Av CHSWK W4 106 A4
Dukes Cl ASHF TW15 140 A3
HPTN TW12 141 K4
Dukes Ga CHSWK W4 * 105 K3
Dukes Green Av
EBED/NFELT TW14 121 K4
Dukes La KENS W8 14 C1
Dukes Ms MUSWH N10 54 B2
Duke's Ms MHST W1U 10 B4
Dukes Orch BXLY DA5 137 K7
Duke's Pl HDTCH EC3A 13 L5
Dukes Point HGT N6 54 B7
Dukes Rd ACT W3 86 C3
EHAM E6 78 A7
Duke's Rd CAMTN NW1 5 H8
Dukesthorpe Rd SYD SE26 151 F3
Duke St MHST W1U 10 B4
RCH/KEW TW9 124 E3
SUT SM1 175 H3
WAT WD17 21 G2
Duke Street Hl STHWK SE1 13 H8
Duke Street St James's
MYFR/PICC W1J 10 F8
Dukes Wy WBLY HA9 68 A4
WWKM BR4 180 C2
Duke's Yd MYFR/PKLN W1K 10 B6
Dulas St FSBYPK N4 55 F7
Dulford St NTGHL W11 88 C6
Dulka Rd BTSEA SW11 128 E4
Dulverton Rd ELTH/MOT SE9 154 C1
RSLP HA4 64 E1
Dulwich Common DUL SE21 130 E7
The Dulwich Oaks DUL SE21 * 150 B2
Dulwich Rd HNHL SE24 130 B4
Dulwich Village DUL SE21 130 E5
Dulwich Wood Av NRWD SE19 150 A4
Dulwich Wood Pk NRWD SE19 150 A3
Dumbarton Rd
BRXS/STRHM SW2 129 K5
Dumbleton Cl KUT/HW KT1 144 D7
Dumbreck Rd ELTH/MOT SE9 135 F3
Dumfries Cl OXHEY WD19 32 E2
Dumont Rd STNW/STAM N16 74 A2
Dumpton Pl CAMTN NW1 4 A2
Dunbar Av BECK BR3 166 B3
DAGE RM10 80 C2
STRHM/NOR SW16 164 B1
Dunbar Cl YEAD UB4 82 E4
Dunbar Gdns DAGE RM10 80 C4
Dunbar Rd FSTGT E7 76 E5
NWMAL KT3 159 K3
WDGN N22 41 G7
Dunbar St WNWD SE27 149 J2
Dunblane Rd ELTH/MOT SE9 134 D2
Dunboyne Rd HAMP NW3 71 K4
Dunbridge St BETH E2 92 C3
Duncan Cl BAR EN5 27 G3
Duncan Gv ACT W3 87 G5
Duncannon St CHCR WC2N 11 J7
Duncan Rd HACK E8 74 D7
RCH/KEW TW9 125 F3
Duncan St IS N1 6 C5
Duncan Ter IS N1 6 C6
Duncan Wy BUSH WD23 21 K1
Dunch St WCHPL E1 92 D5
Duncombe Hl FSTH SE23 132 B6
Duncombe Rd ARCH N19 54 D7
Duncrievie Rd LEW SE13 133 G5
Duncroft WOOL/PLUM SE18 115 K6
Dundalk Rd BROCKY SE4 132 B2
Dundas Gdns
E/WMO/HCT KT8 157 G2
Dundas Rd PECK SE15 131 K1
Dundee Rd PLSTW E13 95 F1
SNWD SE25 165 J4
Dundee St WAP E1W 92 D7
Dundee Wy PEND EN3 31 G2
Dundee Whf POP/IOD E14 93 H6
Dundela Gdns WPK KT4 173 K3
Dundonald Cl EHAM E6 95 J5
Dundonald Rd
WIM/MER SW19 146 D6
WLSDN NW10 70 B7
Dunedin Rd IL IG1 60 C7
LEY E10 75 K2
RAIN RM13 99 H2
Dunedin Wy YEAD UB4 83 G3
Dunelm St WCHPL E1 93 F5
Dunfield Rd CAT SE6 151 K4
Dunford Rd HOLWY N7 73 F3
Dungarvan Av
PUT/ROE SW15 126 D3
Dunheved Cl THHTH CR7 164 B5
Dunheved Rd North
THHTH CR7 164 B5
Dunheved Rd South
THHTH CR7 164 B5
Dunheved Rd West
THHTH CR7 164 B5
Dunholme Gn ED N9 42 B2
Dunholme La ED N9 42 B2
Dunholme Rd ED N9 42 B2
Dunkeld Rd BCTR RM8 79 H1
SNWD SE25 164 E3
Dunkery Rd ELTH/MOT SE9 153 H3
Dunkin Rd DART DA1 139 K3
Dunkirk St WNWD SE27 * 149 J3
Dunlace Rd CLPT E5 74 E4
Dunleary Cl HSLWW TW4 122 E6
Dunley Dr CROY/NA CR0 180 A5
Dunloe Av TOTM N17 55 K2
Dunloe St BETH E2 7 L6
Dunlop Pl BERM/RHTH SE16 19 M4
Dunmore Rd
KIL/WHAMP NW6 70 C7
RYNPK SW20 146 A7
Dunmow Cl CHDH RM6 61 J4
FELT TW13 * 141 J3
Dunmow Dr RAIN RM13 81 H7
Dunmow Rd SRTFD E15 76 B3
Dunmow Wk IS N1 * 6 E3
Dunnage Crs
BERM/RHTH SE16 112 B3
Dunningford Cl HCH RM12 81 H4
Dunn Md CDALE/KGS NW9 37 H6
Dunnock Cl BORE WD6 24 C3
ED N9 31 F7
Dunnock Rd EHAM E6 95 J5
Dunn St HACK E8 74 B4
Dunollie Pl KTTN NW5 72 C4
Dunollie Rd KTTN NW5 72 C4
Dunoon Gdns FSTH SE23 * 132 A6
Dunoon Rd FSTH SE23 131 K6
Dunraven Dr ENC/FH EN2 29 G1
Dunraven Rd SHB W12 87 J7
Dunraven St MYFR/PKLN W1K 9 M6
Dunsany Rd HMSMTH W6 107 G2
Dunsbury Cl BELMT SM2 175 F7
Dunsfold Wy CROY/NA CR0 179 K6
Dunsford Wy PUT/ROE SW15 126 E6
Dunsmore OXHEY WD19 * 33 H1
Dunsmore Cl BUSH WD23 22 D5
YEAD UB4 83 H3
Dunsmore Rd WOT/HER KT12 156 A4
Dunsmore Wy BUSH WD23 22 C5
Dunsmure Rd
STNW/STAM N16 56 A7
Dunspring La CLAY IG5 60 B1
Dunstable Ms
CAVSQ/HST W1G 10 B2
Dunstable Rd
E/WMO/HCT KT8 156 E3
RCH/KEW TW9 125 F3
Dunstall Rd RYNPK SW20 145 K5
Dunstall Wy E/WMO/HCT KT8 157 G2
Dunstall Welling Est
WELL DA16 * 136 C1
Dunstan Cl EFNCH N2 * 53 G2
Dunstan Gld
STMC/STPC BR5 * 169 J5
Dunstan Houses WCHPL E1 * 92 E4
Dunstan Rd GLDGN NW11 52 D7
Dunstan's Gv EDUL SE22 131 J5
Dunstan's Rd EDUL SE22 131 H6
Dunster Av MRDN SM4 161 G7
Dunster Cl BAR EN5 26 B3
CRW RM5 62 E1
Dunster Ct BORE WD6 25 F2
MON EC3R 13 J6
Dunster Dr CDALE/KGS NW9 50 E7
Dunster Gdns
KIL/WHAMP NW6 70 D6
Dunsterville Wy STHWK SE1 19 H2
Dunster Wy RYLN/HDSTN HA2 65 J2
Dunston Rd BTSEA SW11 129 F1
HACK E8 7 L4
Dunston St HACK E8 7 K3
Dunton Cl SURB KT6 159 F7
Dunton Rd LEY E10 57 K6
ROM RM1 63 G3
STHWK SE1 19 L6
Duntshill Rd
WAND/EARL SW18 128 A7
Dunvegan Cl E/WMO/HCT KT8 157 G3
Dunvegan Rd ELTH/MOT SE9 134 E3
Dunwich Rd BXLYHN DA7 117 G7
Dunworth Ms NTGHL W11 88 D5
Duplex Ride KTBR SW1X 15 M2
Dupont Rd RYNPK SW20 161 G1
Duppas Av CROY/NA CR0 177 H3
Duppas Hill Rd CROY/NA CR0 177 G3
Duppas Hill Ter CROY/NA CR0 177 H2
Duppas Rd CROY/NA CR0 177 G2
Dupree Rd CHARL SE7 114 A4
Dura Den Cl BECK BR3 151 K6
Durand Gdns BRXN/ST SW9 110 A7
Durand Wy WLSDN NW10 68 E6
Durants Park Av PEND EN3 31 F3
Durants Rd PEND EN3 30 E3
Durant St BETH E2 92 C1
Durban Gdns DAGE RM10 80 E6
Durban Rd BECK BR3 166 C1
GNTH/NBYPK IG2 60 E7
SRTFD E15 94 C2
TOTM N17 42 A5
WALTH E17 43 H7
WNWD SE27 149 J3
Durban Rd East WATW WD18 20 E3
Durban Rd West WATW WD18 20 E3
Durbin Rd CHSGTN KT9 172 A3
Durdans Rd STHL UB1 83 K5
Durell Gdns DAGW RM9 79 K4
Durell Rd DAGW RM9 79 K4
Durfey Pl CMBW SE5 110 E6
Durford Crs PUT/ROE SW15 126 D7
Durham Av HAYES BR2 167 J3
HEST TW5 102 E5
WFD IG8 45 H4
Durham Hl BMLY BR1 152 D3
Durham House St
CHCR WC2N * 11 K7
Durham Pl CHEL SW3 15 L8
Durham Ri WOOL/PLUM SE18 115 H4
Durham Rd BORE WD6 24 E2
CAN/RD E16 94 C3
DAGE RM10 80 E4
EA W5 104 E2
EBED/NFELT TW14 122 B6
ED N9 42 C1
EFNCH N2 53 J2
HAYES BR2 167 K3
HOLWY N7 73 F1
HRW HA1 48 B4
MNPK E12 77 H3
RYNPK SW20 145 K7
SCUP DA14 155 H4
Durham Rw WCHPL E1 93 F4
Durham St LBTH SE11 17 L8
Durham Ter BAY/PAD W2 8 C4
PGE/AN SE20 * 150 D6
Durham Wharf Dr BTFD TW8 104 D6
Durham Yd BETH E2 * 92 D2
Durian Wy ERITH DA8 118 E6
Durley Av PIN HA5 47 J5
Durley Rd STNW/STAM N16 56 A6
Durlston Rd CLPT E5 74 C1
KUTN/CMB KT2 144 A5
Durnford St SEVS/STOTM N15 56 A4
Durning Rd NRWD SE19 149 K4
Durnsford Av WIM/MER SW19 146 E1
Durnsford Rd WDGN N22 40 D6
WIM/MER SW19 146 E2
Durrants Dr
RKW/CH/CXG WD3 20 A2
Durrell Rd FUL/PGN SW6 107 H7
Durrington Av RYNPK SW20 146 A6
Durrington Park Rd
RYNPK SW20 146 A7
Durrington Rd CLPT E5 75 G3
Dursley Cl BKHTH/KID SE3 134 B1
Dursley Gdns BKHTH/KID SE3 114 C7
Dursley Rd BKHTH/KID SE3 134 B1
Durward St WCHPL E1 92 D4
Durweston Ms MHST W1U * 9 M2
Durweston St MBLAR W1H 9 L3
Dutch Barn Cl
STWL/WRAY TW19 120 A5
Dutch Gdns KUTN/CMB KT2 144 D5
Dutch Yd WAND/EARL SW18 127 K4
Duthie St POP/IOD E14 94 A6
Dutton St GNWCH SE10 113 F7
Duxberry Cl HAYES BR2 168 D4
Duxford Cl HCH RM12 81 K5
Dwight Rd WATW WD18 20 B6
Dye House La BOW E3 75 J7
Dyer's Blds FLST/FETLN EC4A 12 A3
Dyers Hall Rd WAN E11 76 B1
Dyer's La PUT/ROE SW15 126 E2
Dykes Wy HAYES BR2 167 J2
Dylan Cl BORE WD6 * 23 K6
Dylan Rd BELV DA17 117 H2
HNHL SE24 130 C3
Dylways CMBW SE5 130 E3
Dymchurch Cl CLAY IG5 60 A2
Dymock St FUL/PGN SW6 128 A2
Dymoke Rd ROM RM1 63 H6
Dyneley Rd LEE/GVPK SE12 153 G3
Dyne Rd KIL/WHAMP NW6 70 D6
Dynevor Rd
RCHPK/HAM TW10 125 F4
STNW/STAM N16 74 A2
Dynham Rd KIL/WHAMP NW6 2 A1
Dyott St LSQ/SEVD WC2H 11 J4
RSQ WC1B 11 H3
Dysart Av KUTN/CMB KT2 143 J4
Dysart St SDTCH EC2A 13 H1
Dyson Ct ALP/SUD HA0 67 G3
Dyson Rd SRTFD E15 76 D5
WAN E11 58 C5
Dyson's Rd UED N18 42 D5

E

Eade Rd FSBYPK N4 55 J6
Eagans Cl EFNCH N2 * 53 H2
Eagle Av CHDH RM6 62 A5
Eagle Cl BERM/RHTH SE16 111 J4
HCH RM12 81 K5
PEND EN3 30 E3
WLGTN SM6 176 E5
Eagle Ct FARR EC1M 12 C2
Eagle Dr CDALE/KGS NW9 51 G1
Eagle Hl NRWD SE19 149 K5
Eagle House Ms CLAP SW4 129 H4
Eagle La WAN E11 58 E3
Eagle Ms IS N1 74 A5
Eagle Pl SKENS SW7 14 F7
Eagle Rd ALP/SUD HA0 67 K6
HTHAIR TW6 121 J2
Eaglesfield Rd
WOOL/PLUM SE18 115 G7
Eagle St HHOL WC1V 11 L3
Eagle Ter WFD IG8 45 F6
Eagle Wharf Rd IS N1 6 F5
Eagling Cl BOW E3 93 J2
Ealdham Sq ELTH/MOT SE9 134 B3
Ealing Golf Course
GFD/PVL UB6 * 85 G2
Ealing Gn EA W5 85 K7
Ealing Park Gdns EA W5 104 D3
Ealing Rd ALP/SUD HA0 86 A1
BOW E3 93 K2
EA W5 104 E3
NTHLT UB5 66 A6
Ealing Village EA W5 86 A5
Eamont St STJWD NW8 3 J5
Eardemont Cl DART DA1 138 C3
Eardley Crs ECT SW5 14 B7
Eardley Rd BELV DA17 117 H4
STRHM/NOR SW16 148 C5
Earl Cl FBAR/BDGN N11 40 B4
Earldom Rd PUT/ROE SW15 127 F3
Earle Gdns KUTN/CMB KT2 144 A6
Earlham Gv FSTGT E7 76 D4
WDGN N22 41 F6
Earlham St LSQ/SEVD WC2H 11 H5
Earl Ri WOOL/PLUM SE18 115 J4
Earl Rd MORT/ESHN SW14 125 K3
Earlsbury Gdns EDGW HA8 36 C3
Earl's Court Gdns ECT SW5 14 C6
Earl's Court Rd KENS W8 14 A4
Earl's Court Sq ECT SW5 14 C7
Earls Crs HRW HA1 48 E3
Earlsferry Wy IS N1 5 K2
Earlsfield Rd
WAND/EARL SW18 128 B7
Earlshall Rd ELTH/MOT SE9 134 E3
Earlsmead RYLN/HDSTN HA2 65 K3
Earlsmead Rd
SEVS/STOTM N15 56 B4
WLSDN NW10 88 A2
Earls Ms WAND/EARL SW18 128 B6
Earls Ter KENS W8 107 J2
Earlsthorpe Ms BAL SW12 129 F5
Earlsthorpe Rd SYD SE26 151 F3
Earlstoke Est FSBYE EC1V 6 C7
Earlstoke St FSBYE EC1V 6 C7
Earlston Gv HOM E9 74 D7
Earl St SDTCH EC2A 13 J2
WAT WD17 21 G2
Earls Wk BCTR RM8 79 H3
KENS W8 14 A4
Earlswood Av THHTH CR7 164 B4
Earlswood Gdns CLAY IG5 60 A2
Earlswood St GNWCH SE10 113 H4
Early Ms CAMTN NW1 4 D3
Earnshaw St
NOXST/BSQ WC1A 11 H4
Earsby St WKENS W14 107 H3
Easby Crs MRDN SM4 162 A5
Easebourne Rd BCTR RM8 79 J4
Easedale Dr HCH RM12 81 K4
East Acton Ar ACT W3 * 87 H5
East Acton La ACT W3 87 F7
East Arbour St WCHPL E1 93 F5
East Av EHAM E6 77 J6
HYS/HAR UB3 101 J1
STHL UB1 83 K6
WALTH E17 57 K3
WLGTN SM6 177 F4
East Bank STNW/STAM N16 56 A6
Eastbank Cl WALTH E17 57 K4
Eastbank Rd HPTN TW12 142 C4
East Barnet Rd BAR EN5 27 G3
East Boundary Rd MNPK E12 77 K2
Eastbourne Av ACT W3 87 F5
Eastbourne Gdns
MORT/ESHN SW14 125 K2
Eastbourne Ms BAY/PAD W2 8 F4
Eastbourne Rd BTFD TW8 104 E4
CHSWK W4 105 K5
EHAM E6 96 A2
FELT TW13 141 H1
SEVS/STOTM N15 56 A5
SRTFD E15 76 C7
TOOT SW17 148 A5
Eastbourne Ter BAY/PAD W2 8 F4
Eastbournia Av ED N9 42 D2
Eastbrook Av ED N9 30 E6
Eastbrook Cl DAGE RM10 80 E3
Eastbrook Dr ROMW/RG RM7 81 G2
Eastbrook Rd BKHTH/KID SE3 114 A7
Eastbury Av BARK IG11 78 E7
NTHWD HA6 32 C4
Eastbury Ct OXHEY WD19 * 21 G6
Eastbury Gv CHSWK W4 106 B4
Eastbury Rd EHAM E6 96 A3
KUTN/CMB KT2 144 A6
NTHWD HA6 32 C5
OXHEY WD19 21 G6
ROMW/RG RM7 63 F5
STMC/STPC BR5 169 J5
Eastbury Sq BARK IG11 79 F7
Eastbury Ter WCHPL E1 93 F3
Eastcastle St GTPST W1W 10 E4
Eastcheap FENCHST EC3M 13 H6
East Churchfield Rd ACT W3 87 F7
Eastchurch Rd HTHAIR TW6 121 H1
East Cl EA W5 86 C3
EBAR EN4 28 A3
GFD/PVL UB6 84 C1
RAIN RM13 99 K3
Eastcombe Av CHARL SE7 114 A5
Eastcote Av E/WMO/HCT KT8 156 E4
GFD/PVL UB6 67 G4
RYLN/HDSTN HA2 66 B1
Eastcote La NTHLT UB5 65 K5
Eastcote La North NTHLT UB5 65 K5
Eastcote Rd PIN HA5 47 H4
RSLP HA4 46 C6
RYLN/HDSTN HA2 66 C2
WELL DA16 135 J1
Eastcote St BRXN/ST SW9 129 K1
Eastcote Vw PIN HA5 47 G3
Eastcott Cl KUTN/CMB KT2 144 E4
East Ct ALP/SUD HA0 67 J1
East Crs EN EN1 30 A4
FBAR/BDGN N11 39 K3
Eastcroft Rd HOR/WEW KT19 173 G6
East Cross Route HOM E9 75 H5
Eastdown Pk LEW SE13 133 G3
East Dr CAR SM5 175 J7
NTHWD HA6 32 C1
East Duck Lees La PEND EN3 31 G3
East Dulwich Gv EDUL SE22 131 F4
East Dulwich Rd EDUL SE22 131 G3
East End Rd FNCH N3 52 E1
East End Wy PIN HA5 47 J2
East Entrance DAGE RM10 98 D1
Eastern Av CHDH RM6 61 H3
GNTH/NBYPK IG2 60 C5
PIN HA5 47 H6
WAN E11 59 G5
Eastern Av East ROM RM1 63 F2
Eastern Av West CHDH RM6 62 A3
Eastern Gtwy CAN/RD E16 95 G6
Eastern Perimeter Rd
HTHAIR TW6 121 H1
Eastern Rd BROCKY SE4 132 D3
EFNCH N2 53 K3
PLSTW E13 95 F1
ROM RM1 63 G4
WALTH E17 58 A4
WDGN N22 40 E7
Easternville Gdns
GNTH/NBYPK IG2 60 C5
Eastern Wy THMD SE28 116 B1
East Ferry Rd POP/IOD E14 112 E3
Eastfield Gdns DAGE RM10 80 C3
Eastfield Rd CEND/HSY/T N8 54 E2
DAGE RM10 80 C3
WALTH E17 57 J3
Eastfields PIN HA5 47 G4
Eastfields Av
WAND/EARL SW18 127 K3
Eastfields Rd ACT W3 86 E4
MTCM CR4 163 F1
Eastfield St POP/IOD E14 93 G4
East Gdns TOOT SW17 147 J5
Eastgate Cl THMD SE28 97 K5
Eastglade NTHWD HA6 32 C4
PIN HA5 47 K2
Eastham Cl BAR EN5 26 C4
East Ham Manor Wy
EHAM E6 96 A5
East Harding St
FLST/FETLN EC4A 12 B4
East Heath Rd HAMP NW3 71 H2
East Hl DART DA1 139 J6
WAND/EARL SW18 128 B4
WBLY HA9 68 C1
East Hill Dr DART DA1 139 J6
Eastholm GLDGN NW11 53 F3
East Holme ERITH DA8 118 A7
Eastholme HYS/HAR UB3 82 E7
East India Dock Rd
POP/IOD E14 93 J6
East India Wy CROY/NA CR0 165 G7
Eastlake Rd CMBW SE5 130 C1
Eastlands Crs EDUL SE22 131 G5
East La ALP/SUD HA0 67 J2
BERM/RHTH SE16 111 H1
KUT/HW KT1 158 E2
Eastlea Ms CAN/RD E16 94 C3
Eastleigh Av
RYLN/HDSTN HA2 66 B1
Eastleigh Cl BELMT SM2 175 F6
CRICK NW2 69 G2
Eastleigh Rd BXLYHN DA7 137 K1

WALTH E17 57 H1
Eastleigh Wy
EBED/NFELT TW14 121 K7
Eastman Rd ACT W3 106 A1
East Md RSLP HA4 65 H2
Eastmead Av GFD/PVL UB6 84 B2
Eastmead Cl BMLY BR1 168 D1
Eastmearn Rd WNWD SE27 149 J1
Eastmont Rd ESH/CLAY KT10 171 F1
Eastmoor Pl CHARL SE7 114 C2
Eastmoor St CHARL SE7 114 C2
WOOL/PLUM SE18 114 C3
East Mount St WCHPL E1 * 92 D4
Eastney Rd CROY/NA CR0 164 C7
Eastney St GNWCH SE10 113 G4
Eastnor Rd ELTH/MOT SE9 135 H7
Easton Gdns BORE WD6 25 G3
Easton St FSBYW WC1X 6 A9
East Park Cl CHDH RM6 61 K4
East Parkside GNWCH SE10 113 H1
East Pas STBT EC1A 12 E2
East Pl WNWD SE27 149 J3
East Pole Cots
STHGT/OAK N14 * 28 D3
East Poultry Av FARR EC1M 12 C3
East Rp HTHAIR TW6 100 E7
East Rd CHDH RM6 62 A4
CHEL SW3 16 A8
EBAR EN4 28 A7
EBED/NFELT TW14 121 G6
EDGW HA8 36 D7
IS N1 7 H7
KUTN/CMB KT2 144 A7
ROMW/RG RM7 63 F6
SRTFD E15 76 E7
WDR/YW UB7 100 C3
WELL DA16 136 C1
WIM/MER SW19 147 G5
East Rochester Wy
BFN/LL DA15 135 K4
BFN/LL DA15 136 D5
DART DA1 138 A6
East Rw NKENS W10 88 C3
WAN E11 58 E5
Eastry Av HAYES BR2 167 J5
Eastry Rd ERITH DA8 117 H6
East Sheen Av
MORT/ESHN SW14 126 A3
East Side SHB W12 * 107 F1
Eastside Rd GLDGN NW11 52 D3
East Smithfield WAP E1W 13 M7
East St BARK IG11 78 C6
BMLY BR1 167 K1
BTFD TW8 104 D6
BXLYHN DA7 137 H3
WALW SE17 18 F7
East Surrey Gv PECK SE15 111 G6
East Tenter St WCHPL E1 13 M5
East Ter BFN/LL DA15 * 135 K7
East Towers PIN HA5 47 H5
East V ACT W3 * 87 H7
East Vw BAR EN5 26 D1
CHING E4 44 A4
Eastview Av
WOOL/PLUM SE18 115 K6
Eastville Av GLDGN NW11 52 D4
East Wk EBAR EN4 28 A7
HYS/HAR UB3 101 K1
East Wy CROY/NA CR0 179 G1
HYS/HAR UB3 82 E7
RSLP HA4 46 E7
Eastway BOW E3 75 G7
HAYES BR2 167 K6
MRDN SM4 161 G4
WAN E11 59 F4
WLGTN SM6 176 C3
Eastway Crs
RYLN/HDSTN HA2 66 B1
Eastwell Cl BECK BR3 151 G7
Eastwood Cl HOLWY N7 73 G4
SWFD E18 58 E1
TOTM N17 * 42 D6
Eastwood Dr RAIN RM13 99 K5
Eastwood Rd GDMY/SEVK IG3 61 G6
MUSWH N10 54 A1
SWFD E18 58 E1
WDR/YW UB7 100 D1
Eastwood St
STRHM/NOR SW16 148 C5
Eatington Rd LEY E10 58 B4
Eaton Cl BGVA SW1W 16 A5
STAN HA7 35 H3
Eaton Ct EDGW HA8 36 C3
Eaton Dr BRXN/ST SW9 130 C3
KUTN/CMB KT2 144 C6
Eaton Gdns DAGW RM9 80 A6
Eaton Ga BGVA SW1W 16 A5
NTHWD HA6 32 A5
Eaton La BGVA SW1W 16 D4
Eaton Ms North KTBR SW1X 16 B4
Eaton Ms South BGVA SW1W 16 B5
Eaton Ms West BGVA SW1W 16 B5
Eaton Park Rd PLMGR N13 41 G1
Eaton Pl KTBR SW1X 16 A4
Eaton Ri EA W5 85 J4
WAN E11 59 G4
Eaton Rd BELMT SM2 175 H5
EN EN1 30 A2
HDN NW4 52 A4
HSLW TW3 123 J3
SCUP DA14 155 K1
Eaton Rw BGVA SW1W 16 C3
Eatons Md CHING E4 43 J1
Eaton Sq BGVA SW1W 16 B4
Eaton Ter BGVA SW1W 16 A5
BOW E3 * 93 G2
Eaton Terrace Ms BGVA SW1W 16 A5
Eatonville Rd TOOT SW17 147 K1
Eatonville Vls TOOT SW17 147 K1
Ebbisham Dr VX/NE SW8 17 L9
Ebbisham Rd WPK KT4 174 A1
Ebbsfleet Rd CRICK NW2 70 C4
Ebdon Wy BKHTH/KID SE3 134 A2
Ebenezer St IS N1 7 G7
Ebenezer Wk
STRHM/NOR SW16 148 C7
Ebley Cl PECK SE15 111 G5
Ebner St WAND/EARL SW18 128 A4
Ebor St WCHPL E1 7 L9
Ebrington Rd
KTN/HRWW/WS HA3 49 K5
Ebsworth St FSTH SE23 132 A6
Eburne Rd HOLWY N7 72 E2
Ebury Br BGVA SW1W 16 C7
Ebury Bridge Rd BGVA SW1W 16 B8
Ebury Cl HAYES BR2 181 J2
NTHWD HA6 32 A4
Ebury Ms BGVA SW1W 16 B5
Ebury Ms East BGVA SW1W 16 C5
Ebury Rd WAT WD17 21 H2
Ebury Sq BGVA SW1W 16 C6
Ebury St BGVA SW1W 16 B6
Ecclesbourne Cl PLMGR N13 41 G4
Ecclesbourne Gdns
PLMGR N13 41 G4
Ecclesbourne Rd IS N1 6 F2
THHTH CR7 164 D4
Eccles Rd BTSEA SW11 128 E3
Eccleston Cl EBAR EN4 27 J4
ORP BR6 * 169 J7
Eccleston Crs CHDH RM6 61 H6
Ecclestone Ct WBLY HA9 68 A4
Ecclestone Ms WBLY HA9 68 A4
Ecclestone Pl WBLY HA9 68 B4
Eccleston Ms KTBR SW1X 16 B4
Eccleston Pl BGVA SW1W 16 C4
Eccleston Rd WEA W13 85 G6
Eccleston Sq PIM SW1V 16 D6
Eccleston Square Ms
PIM SW1V 16 D6
Eccleston St BGVA SW1W 16 B4
Echo Hts CHING E4 * 31 K7
Eckford St IS N1 6 A5
Eckstein Rd BTSEA SW11 128 D3
Eclipse Rd PLSTW E13 95 F4
Ector Rd CAT SE6 152 C1
Edans Ct SHB W12 106 C1
Edbrooke Rd MV/WKIL W9 8 A1
Eddington Cl CROY/NA CR0 180 A5
Eddiscombe Rd FUL/PGN SW6 127 J1
Eddy Cl ROMW/RG RM7 62 D5
Eddystone Rd BROCKY SE4 132 B4
Ede Cl HSLW TW3 122 E2
Edenbridge Cl
BERM/RHTH SE16 * 111 J4
Edenbridge Rd EN EN1 30 A5
HOM E9 * 75 F6
Eden Cl ALP/SUD HA0 67 K7
HAMP NW3 70 E1
Edencourt Rd
STRHM/NOR SW16 148 B5
Edendale Rd BXLYHN DA7 118 A7
Edenfield Gdns WPK KT4 173 H2
Eden Gv HOLWY N7 73 F4
WLSDN NW10 69 K5
Edenham Wy NKENS W10 88 D3
Edenhurst Av FUL/PGN SW6 127 J2
Eden Pde BECK BR3 * 166 B3
Eden Park Av BECK BR3 166 C3
Eden Rd BECK BR3 166 B3
CROY/NA CR0 177 K3
WALTH E17 57 K4
WNWD SE27 149 H4
Edensor Rd CHSWK W4 106 B6
Eden St KUT/HW KT1 158 E1
Edenvale Rd MTCM CR4 148 A6
Edenvale St FUL/PGN SW6 128 A1
Eden Wk KUT/HW KT1 * 159 F1
Eden Wy BECK BR3 166 D4
BOW E3 75 H7
Ederline Av
STRHM/NOR SW16 164 A2
Edgar Kail Wy CMBW SE5 131 F2
Edgarley Ter FUL/PGN SW6 * 107 H7
Edgar Rd BOW E3 93 K2
HSLWW TW4 122 E6
Edgar Wallace Cl PECK SE15 111 F6
Edgbaston Rd OXHEY WD19 33 F2
Edgeborough Wy BMLY BR1 153 H7
Edgebury CHST BR7 154 B3
Edgecombe Cl KUTN/CMB KT2 145 F6
Edgecoombe SAND/SEL CR2 179 F7
Edgecote Cl ACT W3 86 E7
Edgefield Av BARK IG11 79 F6
Edge Hl WIM/MER SW19 146 B6
WOOL/PLUM SE18 115 G5
Edge Hill Av FNCH N3 52 E3
Edge Hill Ct WIM/MER SW19 146 B6
Edgehill Ct WOT/HER KT12 * 156 B7
Edgehill Gdns DAGE RM10 80 C3
Edgehill Rd CHST BR7 154 C2
MTCM CR4 148 B7
WEA W13 85 J5
Edgeley La CLAP SW4 129 J2
Edgeley Rd CLAP SW4 129 H2
Edgel St WAND/EARL SW18 128 A3
Edge Point Cl
STRHM/NOR SW16 149 H4
Edgepoint Cl WNWD SE27 * 149 H4
Edge St KENS W8 8 B8
Edgewood Gn CROY/NA CR0 166 A7
Edgeworth Av HDN NW4 51 J4
Edgeworth Cl HDN NW4 51 J4
Edgeworth Crs HDN NW4 51 J4
Edgeworth Rd EBAR EN4 27 J3
ELTH/MOT SE9 134 B3
Edgington Rd
STRHM/NOR SW16 148 D5
Edgington Wy SCUP DA14 155 J6
Edgwarebury Gdns
EDGW HA8 36 C4
Edgwarebury La EDGW HA8 24 B7
Edgware Rd BAY/PAD W2 9 G1
CDALE/KGS NW9 51 F5
CRICK NW2 70 A1
Edgware Road High St
EDGW HA8 36 C5
Edgware Road The Hyde
CDALE/KGS NW9 51 G3
Edgware Way (Watford
By-Pass) EDGW HA8 36 A1
Edinburgh Cl BETH E2 92 E1
PIN HA5 47 J6
Edinburgh Ct KUT/HW KT1 * 159 F2
Edinburgh Ga KTBR SW1X 15 L1
Edinburgh Rd HNWL W7 104 A1
PLSTW E13 95 F1
SUT SM1 175 G1
UED N18 * 42 C4
WALTH E17 57 J4
Edington Rd ABYW SE2 116 C2
PEND EN3 30 E1
Edison Av HCH RM12 63 H7
Edison Cl HCH RM12 63 H7
WDR/YW UB7 100 C1
Edison Dr STHL UB1 84 B5
WBLY HA9 68 A1
Edison Gv WOOL/PLUM SE18 116 A6
Edison Rd CEND/HSY/T N8 54 D5
HAYES BR2 167 J1
WELL DA16 116 A7
Edis St CAMTN NW1 4 A3
Edith Cavell Wy
WOOL/PLUM SE18 114 D7
Edith Gdns BRYLDS KT5 159 J6
Edith Gv WBPTN SW10 108 B5
Edithna St BRXN/ST SW9 129 K2
Edith Nesbit Wk
ELTH/MOT SE9 134 D3
Edith Neville Cots
CAMTN NW1 5 G7
Edith Rd CHDH RM6 61 K6
EHAM E6 77 H6
FBAR/BDGN N11 40 D6
SNWD SE25 164 E4
SRTFD E15 76 B4
WIM/MER SW19 147 F5
WKENS W14 107 H3
Edith Rw FUL/PGN SW6 108 A7
Edith St BETH E2 7 M5
Edith Ter WBPTN SW10 * 108 B6
Edith Vls WKENS W14 107 J3
Edith Yd WBPTN SW10 108 C6
Edlson Cl WALTH E17 57 J4
Edmansons Cl TOTM N17 56 B1
Edmeston Cl HOM E9 75 G5
Edmund Gv FELT TW13 141 K1
Edmund Halley Wy
GNWCH SE10 113 H1
Edmund Hurst Dr EHAM E6 96 B4
Edmund Rd MTCM CR4 162 D2
RAIN RM13 99 G2
WELL DA16 136 B2
Edmunds Cl YEAD UB4 83 G4
Edmund St CMBW SE5 110 E6
Edmunds Wk EFNCH N2 53 J3
Edna Rd RYNPK SW20 161 G1
Edna St BTSEA SW11 108 D7
Edrick Rd EDGW HA8 36 E5
Edrick Wk EDGW HA8 36 E5
Edric Rd NWCR SE14 112 A6
Edridge Cl BUSH WD23 22 C4
Edridge Rd CROY/NA CR0 177 J2
Edulf Rd BORE WD6 24 D1
Edward Av CHING E4 43 K4
MRDN SM4 162 C4
Edward Cl CRICK NW2 * 70 B3
ED N9 30 B6
HPTN TW12 142 C4
Edward Ct CAN/RD E16 94 E4
Edwardes Pl WKENS W14 107 J2
Edwardes Sq KENS W8 14 A4
Edward Gv EBAR EN4 27 H4
Edward Mann Cl East
WCHPL E1 * 93 F5
Edward Mann Cl West
WCHPL E1 * 93 F5
Edward Ms CAMTN NW1 * 4 D7
Edward Pl DEPT SE8 112 C5
Edward Rd BMLY BR1 153 F6
CHDH RM6 62 A5
CHST BR7 154 B4
CROY/NA CR0 165 F6
EBAR EN4 27 H4
EBED/NFELT TW14 121 G4
HPTN TW12 142 C4
NTHLT UB5 83 G1
PGE/AN SE20 151 F6
RYLN/HDSTN HA2 48 C2
WALTH E17 57 F3
Edwards Av RSLP HA4 65 G4
Edwards Cl WPK KT4 174 B1
Edwards Dr FBAR/BDGN N11 40 D6
Edward's La STNW/STAM N16 73 K1
Edwards Ms IS N1 6 B1
MHST W1U 10 A5
Edwards Pl FBAR/BDGN N11 40 D6
Edward Sq IS N1 5 L4
Edwards Rd BELV DA17 117 H3
Edward St CAN/RD E16 94 E3
NWCR SE14 112 B6
Edward's Wy BROCKY SE4 132 D4
Edward Temme Av SRTFD E15 76 D6
Edward Tyler Rd
LEE/GVPK SE12 153 F1
Edwina Gdns REDBR IG4 59 J4
Edwin Av EHAM E6 96 A1
Edwin Cl BXLYHN DA7 117 G5
RAIN RM13 99 H2
Edwin Hall Pl LEW SE13 133 G5
Edwin Pl CROY/NA CR0 164 E7
Edwin Rd EDGW HA8 37 F5
WHTN TW2 123 K7
Edwin's Md HOM E9 75 G3
Edwin St CAN/RD E16 94 E4
WCHPL E1 92 E3
Edwin Ware Ct PIN HA5 * 47 G1
Edwyn Cl BAR EN5 26 A5
Eel Brook Cl FUL/PGN SW6 * 108 A7
Effie Rd FUL/PGN SW6 107 K6
Effingham Cl BELMT SM2 175 F6
Effingham Rd
CEND/HSY/T N8 55 G4
CROY/NA CR0 164 A6
LEE/GVPK SE12 133 H4
SURB KT6 158 C6
Effort St TOOT SW17 147 J4
Effra Pde BRXS/STRHM SW2 130 B4
Effra Rd BRXS/STRHM SW2 130 B4
WIM/MER SW19 147 F5
Egan Wy HYS/HAR UB3 82 C6
Egbert St CAMTN NW1 4 A3
Egerton Cl DART DA1 138 E7
PIN HA5 46 E3
Egerton Crs CHEL SW3 15 K5
Egerton Dr GNWCH SE10 112 E7
Egerton Gdns CHEL SW3 15 J4
GDMY/SEVK IG3 79 F2
HDN NW4 51 K3
WEA W13 85 H5
WLSDN NW10 70 A7
Egerton Gardens Ms
CHEL SW3 15 K4
Egerton Pl CHEL SW3 * 15 K4
Egerton Rd ALP/SUD HA0 68 B6
NWMAL KT3 160 C3
SNWD SE25 165 F2
STNW/STAM N16 56 B6
WHTN TW2 123 K6
Egerton Ter CHEL SW3 15 K4
Egerton Wy HYS/HAR UB3 100 E6
Egham Cl CHEAM SM3 174 C1
Egham Crs CHEAM SM3 174 B2
Egham Rd PLSTW E13 95 F4
Eglantine Rd
WAND/EARL SW18 128 B4
Egleston Rd MRDN SM4 162 A5
Eglinton Hl WOOL/PLUM SE18 115 G5
Eglinton Rd
WOOL/PLUM SE18 115 F5
Egliston Ms PUT/ROE SW15 127 F2
Egliston Rd PUT/ROE SW15 127 F2
Eglon Ms CAMTN NW1 3 M2
Egmont Av SURB KT6 159 G7
Egmont Ms HOR/WEW KT19 173 F4
Egmont Rd BELMT SM2 175 G6
NWMAL KT3 160 C3
SURB KT6 159 G7
WOT/HER KT12 156 A6
Egmont St NWCR SE14 112 A6
Egremont Rd WNWD SE27 149 G2
Egret Wy YEAD UB4 83 H5
Eider Cl SRTFD E15 76 D4
Eighteenth Rd MTCM CR4 163 K3
Eighth Av HYS/HAR UB3 82 E7
MNPK E12 77 K3
Eileen Rd SNWD SE25 164 E4
Eindhoven Cl CAR SM5 163 F7
WIM/MER SW19 147 H7
Eisenhower Dr EHAM E6 95 J4
Elaine Gv KTTN NW5 72 A4
Elam Cl CMBW SE5 130 C1
Elam St CMBW SE5 130 C1
Eland Rd BTSEA SW11 128 E2
CROY/NA CR0 177 H2
Elba Pl WALW SE17 * 18 F5
Elberon Av CROY/NA CR0 163 H5
Elbe St FUL/PGN SW6 128 B1
Elborough Rd SNWD SE25 165 H4
Elborough St
WAND/EARL SW18 127 K7
Elbury Dr CAN/RD E16 94 E5
Elcho St BTSEA SW11 108 D6
Elcot Av PECK SE15 111 J6
Elder Av CEND/HSY/T N8 54 E4
Elderberry Rd EA W5 105 F1
Elder Cl BFN/LL DA15 136 A7
TRDG/WHET N20 39 F1
Elder Ct BUSH WD23 34 E1
Elderfield Rd CLPT E5 75 F3
Elderfield Wk WAN E11 59 F4
Elderflower Wy SRTFD E15 76 C6
Elder Oak Cl PGE/AN SE20 150 D7
Elder Rd WNWD SE27 149 J4
Elderslie Cl BECK BR3 166 D5
Elderslie Rd ELTH/MOT SE9 135 F4
Elder St WCHPL E1 13 L2
Elderton Rd SYD SE26 151 G3
Eldertree Pl MTCM CR4 148 C7
Eldertree Wy MTCM CR4 148 B7
Elder Wk IS N1 6 D3
Eldon Av BORE WD6 24 C1
CROY/NA CR0 178 E1
HEST TW5 103 F6
Eldon Gv HAMP NW3 71 H4
Eldon Pde WDGN N22 * 41 H7
Eldon Pk SNWD SE25 165 J3
Eldon Rd ED N9 30 E7
KENS W8 14 D4
WALTH E17 57 H3
WDGN N22 41 H7
Eldon St LVPST EC2M 13 H3
Eldon Wy WLSDN NW10 86 D1
Eldrick Ct EBED/NFELT TW14 121 G7
Eldridge Cl EBED/NFELT TW14 121 K7
Eleanora Ter SUT SM1 * 175 G4
Eleanor Cl BERM/RHTH SE16 112 A1
SEVS/STOTM N15 56 B2
Eleanor Crs MLHL NW7 38 B3
Eleanor Gdns BAR EN5 26 B4
Eleanor Gv BARN SW13 126 B2
Eleanor Rd FBAR/BDGN N11 40 E5
HACK E8 74 D5
SRTFD E15 76 D5
Eleanor St BOW E3 93 J2
Electra Av HTHAIR TW6 121 J2
Electric Av BRXN/ST SW9 130 B3
Electric La BRXN/ST SW9 * 130 B3
Electric Pde SURB KT6 158 E5
Elephant & Castle STHWK SE1 18 D5
Elephant La BERM/RHTH SE16 111 K1
Elephant Rd WALW SE17 18 E5
Elers Rd HYS/HAR UB3 101 F3
WEA W13 104 D1
Eley Rd UED N18 43 F4
Elfindale Rd HNHL SE24 130 D4
Elfin Gv TEDD TW11 143 F4
Elford Cl BKHTH/KID SE3 134 B3
Elfort Rd HBRY N5 73 G3
Elfrida Crs CAT SE6 151 J3
Elfrida Rd WATW WD18 21 G4
Elf Rw WAP E1W 92 E6
Elfwine Rd HNWL W7 84 E4
Elgar Av BRYLDS KT5 159 J7
EA W5 105 F1
STRHM/NOR SW16 163 K2
WLSDN NW10 69 F5
Elgar Cl BKHH IG9 45 H1
BORE WD6 23 J6
DEPT SE8 112 D6
PLSTW E13 95 G1
Elgar St BERM/RHTH SE16 112 B1
Elgin Av ASHF TW15 140 A5
KTN/HRWW/WS HA3 49 H1
MV/WKIL W9 8 A1
SHB W12 106 D1
Elgin Cl SHB W12 106 E1
Elgin Crs HTHAIR TW6 121 H1
NTGHL W11 88 C6
Elgin Dr NTHWD HA6 32 C6
Elgin Est MV/WKIL W9 8 A1
Elgin Ms NTGHL W11 88 C5
Elgin Ms North MV/WKIL W9 2 D7
Elgin Ms South MV/WKIL W9 2 D8
Elgin Rd CROY/NA CR0 178 B1
GDMY/SEVK IG3 60 E7
SUT SM1 175 G2
WDGN N22 54 C1
WLGTN SM6 176 C5
Elgood Av NTHWD HA6 32 E5
Elgood Cl NTGHL W11 88 C6
Elham Cl BMLY BR1 153 H6
Elia Ms IS N1 6 C6
Elias Pl VX/NE SW8 110 B5
Elia St IS N1 6 C6
Elibank Rd ELTH/MOT SE9 135 F3
Elim St STHWK SE1 19 J3
Elim Wy PLSTW E13 94 D2
Eliot Bank FSTH SE23 150 D1
Eliot Dr RYLN/HDSTN HA2 66 B1
Eliot Gdns PUT/ROE SW15 126 D3
Eliot Hl LEW SE13 133 F1
Eliot Ms STJWD NW8 2 E6
Eliot Pk LEW SE13 133 F1
Eliot Pl BKHTH/KID SE3 133 H1
Eliot Rd DAGW RM9 79 K3
Eliot V BKHTH/KID SE3 133 G1
Elizabethan Wy
STWL/WRAY TW19 120 A6
Elizabeth Av ENC/FH EN2 29 H2
IL IG1 78 D1
IS N1 6 F2
Elizabeth Barnes Ct
FUL/PGN SW6 * 128 A1
Elizabeth Br BGVA SW1W 16 C6
Elizabeth Cl BAR EN5 26 B2
MV/WKIL W9 * 8 F1
SUT SM1 174 D3
Elizabeth Clyde Cl
SEVS/STOTM N15 56 A3
Elizabeth Cots RCH/KEW TW9 105 G7
Elizabeth Fry Pl
WOOL/PLUM SE18 114 D7
Elizabeth Fry Rd HACK E8 74 D6
Elizabeth Gdns ACT W3 87 H7
ISLW TW7 124 B3
STAN HA7 35 J5
SUN TW16 156 B2
Elizabeth Ms HAMP NW3 71 J5
Elizabeth Pl SEVS/STOTM N15 55 K3
Elizabeth Ride ED N9 30 D6
Elizabeth Rd EHAM E6 77 H7
RAIN RM13 99 K4
SEVS/STOTM N15 56 A4
Elizabeth Sq
BERM/RHTH SE16 93 G6
Elizabeth St BGVA SW1W 16 B5
Elizabeth Wy FELT TW13 141 G3
NRWD SE19 149 K6
Elkanette Ms
TRDG/WHET N20 39 G1
Elkington Rd PLSTW E13 95 F3
The Elkins ROM RM1 63 G1
Elkstone Rd NKENS W10 88 D4
Ellaline Rd HMSMTH W6 107 G5
Ella Ms HAMP NW3 71 K3
Ellanby Crs UED N18 42 D4
Elland Cl BAR EN5 27 H4
Elland Rd PECK SE15 131 K3
Ella Rd CEND/HSY/T N8 54 E6
Ellement Cl PIN HA5 47 H4
Ellenborough Pl
PUT/ROE SW15 126 D3
Ellenborough Rd SCUP DA14 155 K5
WDGN N22 41 J7
Ellenbridge Wy SAND/SEL CR2 178 A7
Ellen Cl BMLY BR1 168 C2
Ellen Ct ED N9 42 E1
Ellen St WCHPL E1 * 92 C5
Ellen Webb Dr
KTN/HRWW/WS HA3 48 E2
Elleray Rd TEDD TW11 143 F5
Ellerby St FUL/PGN SW6 107 G7
Ellerdale Cl HAMP NW3 71 G4
Ellerdale Rd HAMP NW3 71 G4
Ellerdale St LEW SE13 132 E3
Ellerdine Rd HSLW TW3 123 H3
Ellerker Gdns
RCHPK/HAM TW10 125 F5
Ellerman Av WHTN TW2 122 E7
Ellerslie Rd SHB W12 87 K7
Ellerton Gdns DAGW RM9 79 J6
Ellerton Rd BARN SW13 * 106 D7
DAGW RM9 79 J6
RYNPK SW20 145 J6
SURB KT6 172 B1
WAND/EARL SW18 128 C7
Ellery Rd NRWD SE19 149 K6
Ellery St PECK SE15 131 J1
Ellesborough Cl OXHEY WD19 33 G4
Ellesmere Av BECK BR3 166 E1
MLHL NW7 37 F2
Ellesmere Cl RSLP HA4 46 A6
WAN E11 58 D4
Ellesmere Gdns REDBR IG4 59 J4
Ellesmere Gv BAR EN5 26 D4
Ellesmere Rd BOW E3 93 G1
GFD/PVL UB6 84 C3
TWK TW1 124 D5
WLSDN NW10 69 J4
Ellesmere St POP/IOD E14 93 K5
Ellingfort Rd HACK E8 74 D6
Ellingham Rd CHSGTN KT9 171 K5
SHB W12 106 D1
SRTFD E15 76 B3
Ellington Rd FELT TW13 140 D3
HSLW TW3 123 G1
MUSWH N10 54 B3
Ellington St HOLWY N7 73 G5
Elliot Cl SRTFD E15 76 C6
WBLY HA9 68 B2
WFD IG8 45 H5
Elliot Rd HDN NW4 51 K5
Elliott Av RSLP HA4 65 F1
Elliott Rd BRXN/ST SW9 110 C6
CHSWK W4 106 B3
HAYES BR2 168 C3
STAN HA7 35 G5
THHTH CR7 164 C3
Elliott's Pl IS N1 6 D4
Elliott Sq HAMP NW3 3 K2
Elliott's Rw LBTH SE11 18 D5
Ellis Av RAIN RM13 99 J4
Ellis Cl EDGW HA8 37 G5
ELTH/MOT SE9 154 C1
WLSDN NW10 70 A5
Elliscombe Mt CHARL SE7 * 114 B5
Elliscombe Rd CHARL SE7 114 B4
Ellisfield Dr PUT/ROE SW15 126 C6
Ellison Gdns NWDGN UB2 102 E3
Ellison Rd BARN SW13 126 C1
BFN/LL DA15 135 J7
STRHM/NOR SW16 148 D6
Ellis Rd MTCM CR4 162 E5
NWDGN UB2 84 C7
Ellis St KTBR SW1X 15 M5
Ellora Rd STRHM/NOR SW16 148 D4
Ellsworth St BETH E2 * 92 D2
Elmar Rd SEVS/STOTM N15 55 K3
Elm Av EA W5 86 A7
OXHEY WD19 21 J6
RSLP HA4 46 E7
Elmbank STHGT/OAK N14 28 E6
Elmbank Av BAR EN5 26 A3
Elmbank Dr BMLY BR1 168 C1
Elm Bank Gdns BARN SW13 126 B1
Elmbank Wy HNWL W7 84 D4
Elmbourne Dr BELV DA17 117 J3
Elmbourne Rd TOOT SW17 148 B2
Elmbridge Av BRYLDS KT5 159 K5
Elmbridge Cl RSLP HA4 46 E5
Elmbridge Dr RSLP HA4 46 E5
Elmbridge Wk HACK E8 * 74 C6
Elmbrook Cl SUN TW16 141 F7
Elmbrook Gdns
ELTH/MOT SE9 134 D3
Elmbrook Rd SUT SM1 174 D3
Elm Cl BKHH IG9 45 H1
BRYLDS KT5 159 K6
CAR SM5 162 E7
DART DA1 139 F7
HDN NW4 52 B4
HYS/HAR UB3 82 E5
RYLN/HDSTN HA2 48 B5
RYNPK SW20 161 F3
SAND/SEL CR2 177 K5
STWL/WRAY TW19 120 A7
WAN E11 59 F5
WHTN TW2 142 B1
Elm Cots MTCM CR4 * 162 E1
Elm Ct WAT WD17 * 21 F2
Elmcourt Rd WNWD SE27 149 H1
Elm Crs EA W5 105 F1
KUTN/CMB KT2 144 A7
Elmcroft CEND/HSY/T N8 55 F4
Elmcroft Av BFN/LL DA15 136 A6
ED N9 30 D5
GLDGN NW11 52 D6
WAN E11 59 F4
Elmcroft Cl CHSGTN KT9 * 172 A2
EA W5 85 K5
EBED/NFELT TW14 121 J5
Elmcroft Crs GLDGN NW11 52 B6
RYLN/HDSTN HA2 48 A2
Elmcroft Dr CHSGTN KT9 172 A2

Elmcroft Gdns CDALE/KGS NW9 .... 50 C4
Elmcroft St CLPT E5 .... 74 E3
Elmdale Rd PLMGR N13 .... 41 F4
Elmdene Cl BECK BR3 .... 166 C4
Elmdene Rd WOOL/PLUM SE18 .... 115 G4
Elmdon Rd HSLWW TW4 .... 122 C1
  HTHAIR TW6 .... 121 J2
Elm Dr RYLN/HDSTN HA2 .... 48 B3
  SUN TW16 .... 156 B1
Elmer Cl ENC/FH EN2 .... 29 F2
Elmer Gdns EDGW HA8 .... 36 C6
  ISLW TW7 .... 123 J3
  RAIN RM13 .... 81 J6
Elmer Rd CAT SE6 .... 133 F6
Elmer's Dr TEDD TW11 .... 143 H5
Elmers End Rd BECK BR3 .... 165 J3
Elmerside Rd BECK BR3 .... 166 B3
Elmers Rd SNWD SE25 .... 165 H6
Elmfield Av CEND/HSY/T N8 .... 54 E4
  MTCM CR4 .... 148 A7
  TEDD TW11 .... 143 F4
Elmfield Cl HRW HA1 .... 66 E1
Elmfield Pk BMLY BR1 .... 167 K3
Elmfield Rd BMLY BR1 .... 167 K2
  CHING E4 .... 44 A1
  EFNCH N2 .... 53 H2
  NWDGN UB2 .... 102 D2
  TOOT SW17 .... 148 A1
  WALTH E17 .... 57 F5
Elmfield Wy MV/WKIL W9 .... 8 A3
  SAND/SEL CR2 .... 178 B7
Elm Friars Wk CAMTN NW1 .... 5 J1
Elm Gdns EFNCH N2 .... 53 G2
  ESH/CLAY KT10 .... 171 F5
  MTCM CR4 .... 163 J3
Elmgate Av FELT TW13 .... 141 F2
Elmgate Gdns EDGW HA8 .... 36 E4
Elm Gn ACT W3 .... 87 G5
Elmgreen Cl SRTFD E15 .... 76 C7
Elm Gv CEND/HSY/T N8 .... 54 E5
  CRICK NW2 .... 70 B3
  ERITH DA8 .... 118 A6
  KUTN/CMB KT2 .... 144 A7
  PECK SE15 .... 131 H1
  RYLN/HDSTN HA2 .... 48 A6
  SUT SM1 .... 175 F3
  WIM/MER SW19 .... 146 C6
Elmgrove Crs HRW HA1 .... 49 F4
Elmgrove Gdns HRW HA1 .... 49 G4
Elm Grove Pde CAR SM5 .... 176 A2
Elm Grove Rd BARN SW13 .... 126 D1
  EA W5 .... 105 F1
Elmgrove Rd CROY/NA CR0 .... 165 J6
  HRW HA1 .... 49 F4
Elm Hall Gdns WAN E11 .... 59 F5
Elm Hatch PIN HA5 .... 33 K6
Elmhurst BELV DA17 .... 117 F5
Elmhurst Av EFNCH N2 .... 53 H2
  MTCM CR4 .... 148 A6
Elmhurst Cl BUSH WD23 .... 21 J3
Elmhurst Crs EFNCH N2 .... 53 H2
Elmhurst Dr SWFD E18 .... 58 E1
Elmhurst Rd ELTH/MOT SE9 .... 153 J1
  FSTGT E7 .... 77 F6
  TOTM N17 .... 56 A1
Elmhurst St CLAP SW4 .... 129 J2
Elmington Cl BXLY DA5 .... 137 J6
Elmington Est CMBW SE5 .... 110 D6
Elmington Rd CMBW SE5 .... 110 E7
Elmira St LEW SE13 .... 132 E2
Elm La CAT SE6 .... 151 H1
Elmlee Cl CHST BR7 .... 153 K5
Elmley St WOOL/PLUM SE18 .... 115 J3
Elmore Cl ALP/SUD HA0 .... 86 A1
Elmore Rd WAN E11 .... 76 A2
Elmore St IS N1 .... 7 G1
Elm Pde SCUP DA14 * 155 G3
Elm Pk BRXS/STRHM SW2 .... 130 A5
  STAN HA7 .... 35 H4
Elm Park Av FBAR/BDGN N11 .... 81 J3
  SEVS/STOTM N15 .... 56 B4
Elm Park Gdns HDN NW4 .... 52 B4
  WBPTN SW10 .... 15 G8
Elm Park La CHEL SW3 .... 15 G9
Elm Park Rd CHEL SW3 .... 15 G9
  FNCH N3 .... 38 D6
  LEY E10 .... 57 G6
  PIN HA5 .... 47 H2
  SNWD SE25 .... 165 G2
  WCHMH N21 .... 29 G6
Elm Pl SKENS SW7 .... 15 G7
Elm Rd BAR EN5 .... 26 D3
  BECK BR3 .... 166 C1
  CHSGTN KT9 .... 172 A3
  DART DA1 .... 139 G7
  EBED/NFELT TW14 .... 121 G7
  ERITH DA8 .... 118 D7
  ESH/CLAY KT10 .... 171 F5
  EW KT17 .... 173 H5
  FSTGT E7 .... 76 D5
  KUTN/CMB KT2 .... 144 B6
  MORT/ESHN SW14 .... 125 J2
  NWMAL KT3 .... 160 A2
  ROMW/RG RM7 .... 62 D1
  SCUP DA14 .... 155 G3
  THHTH CR7 .... 164 D3
  WALTH E17 .... 58 A4
  WBLY HA9 .... 68 A3
  WDGN N22 .... 41 H7
  WLSDN NW10 .... 69 F7
Elm Rd West CHEAM SM3 .... 161 J6
Elm Rw HAMP NW3 .... 71 G2
Elms Av HDN NW4 .... 52 B4
  MUSWH N10 .... 54 B2
Elms Cl EMPK RM11 .... 63 K6
Elmscott Gdns WCHMH N21 .... 29 J5
Elmscott Rd BMLY BR1 .... 152 C4
Elms Ct ALP/SUD HA0 .... 67 F3
Elms Crs CLAP SW4 .... 129 H5
Elmsdale Rd WALTH E17 .... 57 H3
Elmsdene Ms NTHWD HA6 .... 32 A5
Elms Gdns ALP/SUD HA0 .... 67 G3
  DAGW RM9 .... 80 B3
Elmshaw Rd PUT/ROE SW15 .... 126 D4
Elmshurst Crs EFNCH N2 .... 53 G3
Elmside CROY/NA CR0 .... 179 K5
Elmside Rd WBLY HA9 .... 68 C2
Elmslie Cl WFD IG8 .... 45 K5
Elms Ms BAY/PAD W2 .... 8 E1
Elms Park Av ALP/SUD HA0 .... 67 G3
Elms Rd CLAP SW4 .... 129 H4
  KTN/HRWW/WS HA3 .... 34 E6
Elmstead Av CHST BR7 .... 153 K4
  WBLY HA9 .... 50 A7
Elmstead Cl HOR/WEW KT19 .... 173 F5
Elmsleigh Av KTN/HRWW/WS HA3 .... 49 H3
Elmsleigh Rd WHTN TW2 .... 142 D1

TRDG/WHET N20 .... 38 E1
Elmstead Gdns WPK KT4 .... 173 J2
Elmstead Gld CHST BR7 .... 153 K5
Elmstead La CHST BR7 .... 153 J6
Elmstead Rd ERITH DA8 .... 118 B7
  GDMY/SEVK IG3 .... 78 E1
Elmstead Crs WELL DA16 .... 116 D5
The Elms BARN SW13 .... 126 C2
  ESH/CLAY KT10 * 171 F6
  NFNCH/WDSPK N12 * 39 J3
  TOOT SW17 * 148 A2
  WLGTN SM6 * 176 C3
Elm St FSBYW WC1X 11 M1
Elmsworth Av HSLW TW3 .... 123 G1
Elm Ter CRICK NW2 .... 70 E2
  ELTH/MOT SE9 .... 135 F5
  HAMP NW3 * 71 G1
Elmton Wy CLPT E5 .... 74 C1
Elm Tree Av ESH/CLAY KT10 .... 157 J6
Elm Tree Cl NTHLT UB5 .... 83 K1
  STJWD NW8 .... 3 G7
Elm Tree Ct CHARL SE7 * 114 B5
Elm Tree Rd STJWD NW8 .... 3 G7
Elmtree Rd TEDD TW11 .... 142 E4
Elm Vis HNWL W7 * 84 E6
Elm Wk GPK RM2 .... 63 J2
  HAMP NW3 .... 70 E1
  ORP BR6 .... 181 K2
  RYNPK SW20 .... 161 F3
Elm Wy FBAR/BDGN N11 .... 40 A5
  HOR/WEW KT19 .... 173 F4
  WLSDN NW10 .... 69 G3
  WPK KT4 .... 174 A2
Elmwood Av BORE WD6 .... 24 D3
  FELT TW13 .... 141 F2
  KTN/HRWW/WS HA3 .... 49 G4
  PLMGR N13 .... 40 E4
Elmwood Cl EW KT17 .... 173 J6
  WLGTN SM6 .... 176 A7
Elmwood Crs CDALE/KGS NW9 .... 50 E3
Elmwood Dr BXLY DA5 .... 137 F6
  EW KT17 .... 173 J6
Elmwood Gdns HNWL W7 .... 84 E5
Elmwood Rd CHSWK W4 .... 105 K5
  CROY/NA CR0 .... 164 C6
  HNHL SE24 .... 130 E4
  MTCM CR4 .... 162 E2
Elmworth Gv DUL SE21 .... 149 K1
Elnathan Ms MV/WKIL W9 .... 8 E1
Elphinstone Rd WALTH E17 .... 57 H1
Elphinstone St HBRY N5 .... 73 H3
Elrick Cl ERITH DA8 .... 118 B5
Elrington Rd HACK E8 .... 74 C5
  WFD IG8 .... 44 E4
Elruge Cl WDR/YW UB7 .... 100 A2
Elsa Cots POP/IOD E14 * 93 G4
Elsa Rd WELL DA16 .... 136 C1
Elsa St WCHPL E1 .... 93 G4
Elsdale St HOM E9 .... 74 E5
Elsden Ms BETH E2 * 92 E1
Elsden Rd TOTM N17 .... 42 B7
Elsenham Rd MNPK E12 .... 77 K3
Elsenham St WAND/EARL SW18 .... 127 J7
Elsham Rd WAN E11 .... 76 C2
  WKENS W14 .... 107 H1
Elsham Ter WKENS W14 * 107 H1
Elsiedene Rd WCHMH N21 .... 29 J6
Elsie Lane Ct BAY/PAD W2 .... 8 B3
Elsiemaud Rd BROCKY SE4 .... 132 C4
Elsie Rd EDUL SE22 .... 131 G3
Elsinore Av STWL/WRAY TW19 * 120 B6
Elsinore Gdns CRICK NW2 .... 70 C2
Elsinore Rd FSTH SE23 .... 132 B7
Elsinore Wy RCH/KEW TW9 .... 125 J2
Elsley Rd BTSEA SW11 .... 128 E2
Elspeth Rd ALP/SUD HA0 .... 68 A4
  BTSEA SW11 .... 128 E3
Elsrick Av MRDN SM4 .... 161 K4
Elstan Wy CROY/NA CR0 .... 166 B6
Elsted St WALW SE17 .... 19 H6
Elstow Cl ELTH/MOT SE9 .... 134 E4
  RSLP HA4 .... 47 H6
Elstow Gdns DAGW RM9 .... 80 A7
Elstow Rd DAGW RM9 .... 80 A6
Elstree Cl HCH RM12 .... 81 K6
Elstree Gdns BELV DA17 .... 117 F3
  ED N9 .... 30 D7
  IL IG1 .... 78 C4
Elstree Ga BORE WD6 * 25 F1
Elstree Hl BMLY BR1 .... 152 C6
Elstree Hl North BORE WD6 .... 23 K4
Elstree Hl South BORE WD6 .... 23 K5
Elstree Pk BORE WD6 * 25 F5
Elstree Rd BORE WD6 .... 24 E1
  BUSH WD23 .... 22 D7
Elstree Wy BORE WD6 .... 24 E1
Elswick Rd LEW SE13 .... 132 E1
Elswick St FUL/PGN SW6 .... 128 B1
Elsworth Cl EBED/NFELT TW14 .... 121 H7
Elsworthy THDIT KT7 .... 157 K5
Elsworthy Ri HAMP NW3 .... 3 K2
Elsworthy Rd HAMP NW3 .... 3 J3
Elsworthy Ter HAMP NW3 .... 3 K2
Elsynge Rd WAND/EARL SW18 .... 128 C4
Eltham Gn ELTH/MOT SE9 .... 134 B4
Eltham High St ELTH/MOT SE9 .... 134 C4
Eltham Hl ELTH/MOT SE9 .... 134 C4
Eltham Palace Rd ELTH/MOT SE9 .... 134 B5
Eltham Park Gdns ELTH/MOT SE9 .... 135 F3
  LEE/GVPK SE12 .... 133 K4
Elthiron Rd FUL/PGN SW6 .... 107 K7
Elthorne Av HNWL W7 .... 104 A1
Elthorne Ct FELT TW13 .... 122 B7
Elthorne Park Rd HNWL W7 .... 104 A1
Elthorne Rd ARCH N19 .... 72 D1
  CDALE/KGS NW9 .... 51 F1
Elthorne Wy CDALE/KGS NW9 .... 51 F2
Elthruda Rd LEW SE13 .... 133 G5
Eltisley Rd IL IG1 .... 78 B3
Elton Av ALP/SUD HA0 .... 67 H4
  BAR EN5 .... 26 D4
  GFD/PVL UB6 .... 67 F5
Elton Cl KUT/HW KT1 .... 143 J6
Elton Pl STNW/STAM N16 .... 74 A4
Elton Rd KUTN/CMB KT2 .... 144 B7
Eltringham St WAND/EARL SW18 .... 128 B3
Elvaston Ms SKENS SW7 .... 14 F4
Elvaston Pl SKENS SW7 .... 14 E4
Elveden Pl WLSDN NW10 .... 86 C1
Elveden Rd WLSDN NW10 .... 86 C1
Elvendon Rd FBAR/BDGN N11 .... 40 D5
Elver Gdns BETH E2 .... 92 C2
Elverson Ms DEPT SE8 * 112 C6
Elverson Rd DEPT SE8 .... 132 E1

Elverton St WEST SW1P 17 G5
Elvington Gn HAYES BR2 .... 167 J4
Elvington La CDALE/KGS NW9 .... 37 G3
Elvino Rd SYD SE26 .... 151 F4
Elvis Rd CRICK NW2 .... 70 A5
Elwill Wy BECK BR3 .... 167 F3
Elwood Cl BAR EN5 .... 27 G3
Elwood St HBRY N5 .... 73 H2
Elwyn Gdns LEE/GVPK SE12 .... 133 K6
Ely Cl ERITH DA8 .... 138 C1
  NWMAL KT3 .... 160 D1
Ely Gdns BORE WD6 .... 25 F4
  DAGE RM10 .... 80 E2
Elyne Rd FSBYPK N4 .... 55 G5
Ely Pl HCIRC EC1N 12 B3
Ely Rd CROY/NA CR0 .... 164 E4
  HSLWW TW4 .... 122 B2
  HTHAIR TW6 .... 121 J1
  LEY E10 .... 58 A5
Elysan Pl SAND/SEL CR2 .... 177 J5
Elysian Av STMC/STPC BR5 .... 169 K5
Elysium Pl FUL/PGN SW6 * 127 J1
Elysium Rd BXLYHN DA7 .... 117 H2
  RCH/KEW TW9 .... 125 G3
Elysium St FUL/PGN SW6 .... 127 J1
Elystan Cl WLGTN SM6 .... 176 C7
Elystan Pl CHEL SW3 .... 15 K7
Elystan St CHEL SW3 .... 15 J6
Elystan Wk IS N1 .... 6 A4
Emanuel Av ACT W3 .... 86 E5
Embankment PUT/ROE SW15 .... 127 G2
Embankment Gdns CHEL SW3 .... 15 M9
The Embankment TWK TW1 .... 124 B7
Embassy Ct SCUP DA14 .... 155 F3
  WLGTN SM6 * 176 B5
Emba St BERM/RHTH SE16 .... 111 H1
Ember Cl STMC/STPC BR5 .... 169 H6
Embercourt Rd THDIT KT7 .... 157 K5
Ember Farm Av E/WMO/HCT KT8 .... 157 J5
Ember Farm Wy E/WMO/HCT KT8 .... 157 J4
Ember Gdns THDIT KT7 .... 157 K6
Ember La ESH/CLAY KT10 .... 157 J6
Emblem Ct EDUL SE22 .... 131 H4
Embleton Rd LEW SE13 .... 132 E3
  OXHEY WD19 .... 32 E2
Embry Cl STAN HA7 .... 35 G3
Embry Dr STAN HA7 .... 35 G5
Embry Wy STAN HA7 .... 35 G4
Emden Cl WDR/YW UB7 .... 100 D1
Emden St FUL/PGN SW6 .... 108 A7
Emerald Cl CAN/RD E16 .... 95 J5
Emerald Gdns BCTR RM8 .... 62 B7
Emerald Rd WLSDN NW10 .... 69 F7
Emerald Sq NWDGN UB2 .... 102 C2
Emerald St BMSBY WC1N 11 L2
Emerson Gdns KTN/HRWW/WS HA3 .... 50 B5
Emerson Rd IL IG1 .... 60 A6
Emerson St STHWK SE1 .... 12 E8
Emerton Cl BXLYHS DA6 .... 137 F3
Emery Hill St WEST SW1P 16 F4
Emery St STHWK SE1 .... 18 B3
Emes Rd ERITH DA8 .... 117 K6
Emilia Cl PEND EN3 .... 30 D4
Emily St CAN/RD E16 .... 94 D5
Emlyn Rd SHB W12 .... 106 B1
Emma Rd PLSTW E13 .... 94 D1
Emmanuel Rd BAL SW12 .... 129 H7
  NTHWD HA6 .... 32 C5
Emma St BETH E2 .... 92 D1
Emma Ter RYNPK SW20 * 146 A6
Emmott Av BARK/HLT IG6 .... 60 C4
Emmott Cl GLDGN NW11 .... 53 G5
  WCHPL E1 .... 93 G3
Emperor's Ga SKENS SW7 .... 14 E5
Empire Av UED N18 .... 41 J5
Empire Ms STRHM/NOR SW16 .... 148 E4
Empire Pde UED N18 * 41 K5
  WBLY HA9 * 68 C2
Empire Rd GFD/PVL UB6 .... 67 H7
Empire Sq STHWK SE1 .... 19 G2
Empire Wy WBLY HA9 .... 68 B3
Empire Wharf Rd POP/IOD E14 .... 113 G3
Empress Av CHING E4 .... 43 J6
  IL IG1 .... 78 A1
  MNPK E12 .... 77 G1
  WFD IG8 .... 44 D6
Empress Dr CHST BR7 .... 154 B5
Empress Pde CHING E4 * 43 H6
Empress Pl FUL/PGN SW6 .... 14 A8
Empress St WALW SE17 .... 18 F9
Empson St BOW E3 .... 93 K3
Emsworth Cl ED N9 .... 30 E7
Emsworth Rd BARK/HLT IG6 .... 60 C1
Emsworth St BRXS/STRHM SW2 .... 149 F1
Ena Rd VX/NE SW8 .... 129 G1
Enbrook St NKENS W10 .... 88 C2
Enclave Ct EN N1 .... 6 D9
Endale Cl CAR SM5 .... 175 K1
Endeavour Wy BARK IG11 .... 97 G1
  CROY/NA CR0 .... 163 J6
  WIM/MER SW19 .... 147 F3
Endell St LSQ/SEVD WC2H 11 J4
Enderby St GNWCH SE10 .... 113 H4
Enderley Rd KTN/HRWW/WS HA3 .... 34 D7
Endersby Rd BAR EN5 .... 26 A4
Endersleigh Gdns HDN NW4 .... 51 J3
Endlebury Rd CHING E4 .... 44 A1
Endlesham Rd BAL SW12 .... 129 F6
Endsleigh Gdns IL IG1 .... 59 K7
  STPAN WC1H 5 G9
  SURB KT6 .... 158 D5
Endsleigh Pl STPAN WC1H 5 H9
Endsleigh Rd NWDGN UB2 .... 102 D3
  WEA W13 .... 85 G7
Endsleigh St STPAN WC1H 5 H9
Endway BRYLDS KT5 .... 159 H6
Endwell Rd BROCKY SE4 .... 132 B1
Endymion Rd BRXS/STRHM SW2 .... 130 A5
  FSBYPK N4 .... 55 G5
Energen Cl WLSDN NW10 .... 69 G5
Enfield Rd ACT W3 .... 105 J1
  BTFD TW8 .... 104 E4
  ENC/FH EN2 .... 28 D3
  HTHAIR TW6 .... 121 H1
  IS N1 .... 7 L2
Enford St CAMTN NW1 .... 9 L2
Engadine Cl CROY/NA CR0 .... 178 B2
Engadine St WAND/EARL SW18 .... 127 J7
Engate St LEW SE13 .... 133 F3
Engel Pk MLHL NW7 .... 38 A5
Engineer Cl WOOL/PLUM SE18 .... 115 F5
Engineers Wy WBLY HA9 .... 68 C3
England's La HAMP NW3 .... 71 K5

England Wy NWMAL KT3 .... 159 J3
Englefield Cl CROY/NA CR0 .... 164 D5
  ENC/FH EN2 .... 29 G1
Englefield Rd IS N1 .... 7 H1
Engleheart Dr EBED/NFELT TW14 .... 121 J3
Engleheart Rd CAT SE6 .... 132 E6
Englewood Rd BAL SW12 .... 129 G5
English St BOW E3 .... 93 H3
Enid St BERM/RHTH SE16 .... 19 M3
Enmore Av SNWD SE25 .... 165 H4
Enmore Gdns MORT/ESHN SW14 .... 126 A4
Enmore Rd PUT/ROE SW15 .... 127 F3
  SNWD SE25 .... 165 H4
  STHL UB1 .... 84 A3
Ennerdale Av HCH RM12 .... 81 J4
  STAN HA7 .... 49 J2
Ennerdale Cl EBED/NFELT TW14 .... 121 J2
  SUT SM1 .... 174 D3
Ennerdale Dr CDALE/KGS NW9 .... 51 G4
Ennerdale Gdns WBLY HA9 .... 49 J3
Ennerdale Rd BXLYHN DA7 .... 117 H1
  RCH/KEW TW9 .... 125 G1
Ennersdale Rd LEW SE13 .... 133 G4
Ennis Rd FSBYPK N4 .... 55 G7
  WOOL/PLUM SE18 .... 115 J5
Ennismore Av CHSWK W4 .... 106 C3
  GFD/PVL UB6 .... 66 E5
Ennismore Gdns SKENS SW7 .... 15 H3
  THDIT KT7 .... 157 K5
Ennismore Gardens Ms SKENS SW7 .... 15 H3
Ennismore Ms SKENS SW7 .... 15 H3
Ennismore St SKENS SW7 .... 15 H3
Ensign Cl HTHAIR TW6 .... 121 H1
  STWL/WRAY TW19 .... 120 A7
Ensign Dr PLMGR N13 .... 41 J2
Ensign St WCHPL E1 .... 92 C6
Ensign Wy STWL/WRAY TW19 .... 120 A7
  WLGTN SM6 .... 176 E6
Enslin Rd ELTH/MOT SE9 .... 135 F5
Ensor Ms SKENS SW7 .... 15 G7
Enstone Rd PEND EN3 .... 31 G2
Enterprise Cl CROY/NA CR0 .... 164 B7
Enterprise Rw SEVS/STOTM N15 .... 56 B4
Enterprise Wy TEDD TW11 .... 143 F4
  WAND/EARL SW18 .... 127 K3
  WLSDN NW10 .... 87 H2
Enterprise Wy DEPT SE8 * 112 C3
Envoy Av HTHAIR TW6 .... 121 K2
Epcot Ms WLSDN NW10 * 88 B2
Epirus Ms FUL/PGN SW6 .... 107 K6
Epirus Rd FUL/PGN SW6 .... 107 J6
Epping Cl POP/IOD E14 .... 112 D3
  ROMW/RG RM7 .... 62 D2
Epping Pl IS N1 .... 73 G5
Epping Wy CHING E4 .... 31 K5
Epple Rd FUL/PGN SW6 .... 107 J7
Epsom Cl BXLYHN DA7 .... 137 J2
  NTHLT UB5 .... 65 K4
Epsom Rd CHEAM SM3 * 161 J6
  CROY/NA CR0 .... 177 G3
  GDMY/SEVK IG3 .... 61 F5
  LEY E10 .... 58 A5
  MRDN SM4 .... 161 J5
Epstein Rd THMD SE28 .... 97 H7
Epworth Rd ISLW TW7 .... 104 C6
Epworth St SDTCH EC2A 13 H1
Equity Sq BETH E2 .... 7 M8
Erasmus St WEST SW1P 17 H6
Erconwald St SHB W12 .... 87 H5
Erebus Dr THMD SE28 .... 115 H2
Eresby Dr BECK BR3 .... 166 D7
Eresby Pl KIL/WHAMP NW6 .... 2 A1
Erica Gdns CROY/NA CR0 .... 179 K3
Erica St SHB W12 .... 87 J6
Eric Clarke La EHAM E6 .... 96 B7
Ericcson Cl WAND/EARL SW18 .... 127 K4
Eric Est BOW E3 .... 93 H3
Eric Rd CHDH RM6 .... 61 K6
  FSTGT E7 .... 76 E3
  WLSDN NW10 .... 69 H5
Eric St BOW E3 .... 93 H3
Eridge Rd CHSWK W4 .... 106 A2
Erin Cl BMLY BR1 .... 152 C6
  FUL/PGN SW6 .... 107 K6
Erindale WOOL/PLUM SE18 .... 115 J5
Erindale Ter WOOL/PLUM SE18 .... 115 J5
Erith Cr CHST BR7 .... 154 B5
Erith High St ERITH DA8 .... 118 A4
Erith Rd BELV DA17 .... 117 J4
  BXLYHN DA7 .... 137 J2
Erlanger Rd NWCR SE14 .... 112 A7
Erlesmere Gdns HNWL W7 .... 104 A2
Erlich Cots WCHPL E1 * 92 E4
Ermine Cl HSLWW TW4 .... 122 B1
Ermine Rd LEW SE13 .... 132 E2
  SEVS/STOTM N15 .... 56 B5
Ermine Side EN EN1 .... 30 C4
Ermington Rd ELTH/MOT SE9 .... 154 C1
Ernald Av EHAM E6 .... 95 J1
Erncroft Wy TWK TW1 .... 124 A5
Ernest Av WNWD SE27 .... 149 H3
Ernest Cl BECK BR3 .... 166 D4
Ernest Gdns CHSWK W4 .... 105 J5
Ernest Gv BECK BR3 .... 166 C4
Ernest Rd KUT/HW KT1 .... 159 J1
Ernest Sq KUT/HW KT1 .... 159 J1
Ernest St WCHPL E1 .... 93 F3
Ernle Rd RYNPK SW20 .... 145 K6
Ernshaw Pl PUT/ROE SW15 .... 127 H4
Erpingham Rd PUT/ROE SW15 .... 127 F2
Erridge Rd WIM/MER SW19 .... 161 K1
Errington Rd MV/WKIL W9 .... 88 D3
Errol Gdns NWMAL KT3 .... 160 D3
  YEAD UB4 .... 83 F3
Erroll Rd ROM RM1 .... 63 H3
Errol St STLK EC1Y 12 F1
Erskine Cl SUT SM1 .... 175 J2
Erskine Hl GLDGN NW11 .... 52 E3
Erskine Ms HAMP NW3 * 3 K1
Erskine Rd TOTM N17 .... 56 C1
  HAMP NW3 .... 3 K1
  SUT SM1 .... 175 H3
  WALTH E17 .... 57 H3
Erwood Rd CHARL SE7 .... 114 D4
Esam Wy STRHM/NOR SW16 .... 149 G4
Escot Rd SUN TW16 .... 140 C6
Escot Wy BAR EN5 .... 26 A4
Escreet Gv WOOL/PLUM SE18 .... 115 F3
Esher Av CHEAM SM3 .... 174 B2
  ROMW/RG RM7 .... 62 E4
  WOT/HER KT12 .... 156 A7
Esher Cl BXLY DA5 .... 137 F7
  ESH/CLAY KT10 .... 170 B4
Esher Crs HTHAIR TW6 .... 121 K1
Esher Gdns WIM/MER SW19 .... 127 G7
Esher Gn ESH/CLAY KT10 .... 170 B3

Esher Green Dr ESH/CLAY KT10 .... 170 A2
Esher Ms MTCM CR4 .... 163 F2
Esher Park Av ESH/CLAY KT10 .... 170 A3
Esher Place Av ESH/CLAY KT10 .... 170 A3
Esher Rd E/WMO/HCT KT8 .... 157 J4
  GDMY/SEVK IG3 .... 78 E2
Eskdale Av NTHLT UB5 .... 65 K7
Eskdale Cl WBLY HA9 .... 67 K1
Eskdale Rd BXLYHN DA7 .... 137 H1
Eskmont Rdg NRWD SE19 .... 150 A6
Esk Rd PLSTW E13 .... 95 F3
Esmar Crs CDALE/KGS NW9 .... 51 F5
Esmeralda Rd STHWK SE1 .... 111 H3
Esmond Cl RAIN RM13 .... 81 K6
Esmond Gdns CHSWK W4 .... 106 A3
Esmond Rd CHSWK W4 .... 106 A3
  KIL/WHAMP NW6 .... 70 D7
Esmond St PUT/ROE SW15 .... 127 H3
Esparto St WAND/EARL SW18 .... 128 A6
Essenden Rd BELV DA17 .... 117 H4
  SAND/SEL CR2 .... 178 A6
Essendine Rd MV/WKIL W9 .... 2 B9
Essex Av ISLW TW7 .... 123 K3
Essex Cl MRDN SM4 .... 161 G6
  ROMW/RG RM7 .... 62 D3
  RSLP HA4 .... 47 H7
  WALTH E17 .... 57 G3
Essex Ct BARN SW13 .... 126 C1
  EMB EC4Y * 12 A5
Essex Gdns FSBYPK N4 .... 55 H5
Essex Gv NRWD SE19 .... 149 K5
Essex Pk FNCH N3 .... 39 F5
Essex Park Ms ACT W3 .... 87 G7
Essex Pl CHSWK W4 .... 105 K3
Essex Place Sq CHSWK W4 * 106 A3
Essex Rd ACT W3 .... 86 E6
  BARK IG11 .... 78 D6
  BORE WD6 .... 24 C2
  CHDH RM6 .... 61 J4
  CHSWK W4 .... 106 A3
  DAGE RM10 .... 80 E4
  DART DA1 .... 139 G5
  ENC/FH EN2 .... 29 K3
  IS N1 .... 6 D3
  LEY E10 .... 58 A5
  MNPK E12 .... 77 J4
  ROMW/RG RM7 .... 62 D3
  SWFD E18 .... 59 F1
  WALTH E17 .... 57 G3
  WAT WD17 .... 20 E1
  WLSDN NW10 .... 69 G6
Essex Rd South WAN E11 .... 58 B6
Essex St FSTGT E7 .... 76 E4
  TPL/STR WC2R 12 A5
Essex Whf CLPT E5 * 75 F1
Essian St WCHPL E1 .... 93 G4
Essoldo Wy EDGW HA8 .... 50 B2
Estate Wy LEY E10 .... 57 H7
Estcourt Rd FUL/PGN SW6 .... 107 J6
  SNWD SE25 .... 165 J5
  WAT WD17 .... 21 G2
Estella Av NWMAL KT3 .... 160 E3
Estelle Rd HAMP NW3 .... 71 K3
Esterbrooke St WEST SW1P 17 G6
Este Rd BTSEA SW11 .... 128 D2
Esther Cl WCHMH N21 .... 29 G6
Esther Rd WAN E11 .... 58 C6
Estoria Cl BRXS/STRHM SW2 .... 130 B6
Estreham Rd STRHM/NOR SW16 .... 148 D5
Estridge Cl HSLW TW3 .... 123 F3
Estuary Cl BARK IG11 .... 97 H2
Eswyn Rd TOOT SW17 .... 147 K3
Etchingham Park Rd FNCH N3 .... 39 F6
Etchingham Rd SRTFD E15 .... 76 A3
Eternit Wk FUL/PGN SW6 .... 107 F7
Etfield Gv SCUP DA14 .... 155 H4
Ethelbert Gdns REDBR IG4 .... 59 K4
Ethelbert Rd BMLY BR1 .... 167 K3
  ERITH DA8 .... 117 K6
  RYNPK SW20 .... 146 B7
Ethelbert St BAL SW12 .... 129 G7
Ethelburga St BTSEA SW11 * 108 D7
Ethelden Rd SHB W12 .... 87 K7
Etheldene Av MUSWH N10 .... 54 C3
Ethelred Est LBTH SE11 .... 18 A6
Ethel Rd CAN/RD E16 .... 95 F6
Ethel St WALW SE17 .... 18 F6
Etheridge Rd CRICK NW2 .... 52 A4
Etherow St EDUL SE22 .... 131 H5
Etherstone Rd STRHM/NOR SW16 .... 149 G3
Ethnard Rd PECK SE15 .... 111 J5
Ethronvi Rd BXLYHN DA7 .... 137 F2
Etloe Rd LEY E10 .... 75 J1
Eton Av ALP/SUD HA0 .... 67 J3
  EBAR EN4 .... 27 J5
  HAMP NW3 .... 3 H1
  HEST TW5 .... 102 E5
  NFNCH/WDSPK N12 .... 39 G6
  NWMAL KT3 .... 160 A4
Eton Cl WAND/EARL SW18 .... 128 A6
Eton College Rd HAMP NW3 .... 71 K5
Eton Garages HAMP NW3 .... 71 J5
Eton Gv CDALE/KGS NW9 .... 50 C2
  LEW SE13 .... 133 H2
Eton Pl HAMP NW3 * 3 A1
Eton Ri HAMP NW3 .... 71 J6
Eton Rd HAMP NW3 .... 71 K5
  HYS/HAR UB3 .... 101 J6
  IL IG1 .... 78 C3
Eton St RCH/KEW TW9 .... 124 E4
Eton Vis HAMP NW3 .... 71 K5
Eton Wy DART DA1 .... 138 B5
Etta St DEPT SE8 .... 112 B5
Ettrick St POP/IOD E14 .... 94 A5
Etwell Pl BRYLDS KT5 .... 159 G5
Eucalyptus Ms STRHM/NOR SW16 .... 148 D5
Euesdon Cl ED N9 .... 42 D2
Eugenia Rd BERM/RHTH SE16 .... 111 K3
Eureka Rd KUT/HW KT1 .... 159 H1
Europa Pl FSBYE EC1V 6 E8
Europe Rd WOOL/PLUM SE18 .... 114 E2
Eustace Rd CHDH RM6 .... 61 K6
  EHAM E6 .... 95 J2
  FUL/PGN SW6 .... 107 K6
Euston Centre CAMTN NW1 * 4 E9
Euston Rd CAMTN NW1 .... 4 B7
  CROY/NA CR0 .... 164 B7
Euston Sq CAMTN NW1 .... 4 F8
Euston St CAMTN NW1 .... 4 E9
Evan Cook Cl PECK SE15 .... 111 K7
Evandale Rd BRXN/ST SW9 .... 130 B1
Evangelist Rd KTTN NW5 .... 72 B3

Evans Cl HACK E8 74 B5
Evansdale RAIN RM13 99 H2
Evans Gv FELT TW13 142 A1
Evans Rd CAT SE6 152 C1
Evanston Av CHING E4 44 A6
Evanston Gdns REDBR IG4 59 J5
Eva Rd CHDH RM6 61 J6
Evelina Rd PECK SE15 131 K2
PGE/AN SE20 150 E6
Eveline Lowe Est
BERM/RHTH SE16 111 H2
Eveline Rd MTCM CR4 147 K7
Evelyn Av CDALE/KGS NW9 51 F3
RSLP HA4 46 D6
Evelyn Cl WHTN TW2 123 G6
Evelyn Crs SUN TW16 140 D7
Evelyn Denington Rd
EHAM E6 95 J3
Evelyn Dr PIN HA5 33 H6
Evelyn Est DEPT SE8 112 B5
Evelyn Gdns RCH/KEW TW9 125 F3
SKENS SW7 14 F8
Evelyn Gv EA W5 86 B7
STHL UB1 83 K5
Evelyn Rd CAN/RD E16 94 E7
EBAR EN4 27 K3
RCH/KEW TW9 125 F2
RCHPK/HAM TW10 143 J2
WALTH E17 58 A3
WIM/MER SW19 147 F4
Evelyn St DEPT SE8 112 C5
GNWCH SE10 113 F5
Evelyn Ter RCH/KEW TW9 125 F2
Evelyn Wk IS N1 7 G6
Evelyn Wy SUN TW16 140 D7
WLGTN SM6 176 D3
Evensyde WATW WD18 20 A5
Evenwood Cl
PUT/ROE SW15 * 127 H4
Everard Av HAYES BR2 167 K7
Everard Wy WBLY HA9 68 A2
Everatt Cl WAND/EARL SW18 * 127 J5
Everdon Rd BARN SW13 106 D5
Everest Pl POP/IOD E14 94 A4
Everest Rd ELTH/MOT SE9 134 D4
STWL/WRAY TW19 120 A6
Everett Cl BUSH WD23 22 E7
PIN HA5 46 D2
The Everglades HSLW TW3 * 123 H2
Everglade Strd
CDALE/KGS NW9 37 H7
Evergreen Cl PGE/AN SE20 150 E6
Evergreen Ct
STWL/WRAY TW19 * 120 A6
Evergreen Sq HACK E8 7 L1
Evergreen Wy HYS/HAR UB3 82 D6
STWL/WRAY TW19 120 A6
Everilda St IS N1 5 M4
Evering Rd STNW/STAM N16 74 B2
Everington Rd MUSWH N10 53 K1
Everington St HMSMTH W6 107 G5
Everitt Rd WLSDN NW10 87 F2
Everleigh St FSBYPK N4 55 F7
Eve Rd ISLW TW7 124 B3
SRTFD E15 94 C1
TOTM N17 56 A2
WAN E11 76 C3
Eversfield Gdns EDGW HA8 37 G6
Eversfield Rd RCH/KEW TW9 125 G1
Evershed Wk CHSWK W4 105 K2
Eversholt St CAMTN NW1 4 E5
Evershot Rd FSBYPK N4 55 F7
Eversleigh Rd BAR EN5 27 G4
BTSEA SW11 128 E2
EHAM E6 77 H7
FNCH N3 38 D6
Eversley Av BXLYHN DA7 138 B1
WBLY HA9 68 C1
Eversley Cl WCHMH N21 29 F5
Eversley Crs ISLW TW7 103 J7
RSLP HA4 64 C1
WCHMH N21 29 F5
Eversley Cross BXLYHN DA7 138 B1
Eversley Mt WCHMH N21 29 F5
Eversley Pk WIM/MER SW19 145 K4
Eversley Park Rd
WCHMH N21 29 F5
Eversley Rd BRYLDS KT5 159 G3
CHARL SE7 114 A5
NRWD SE19 149 K6
Eversley Wy CROY/NA CR0 179 J2
Everthorpe Rd PECK SE15 131 G2
Everton Blds CAMTN NW1 4 E8
Everton Dr STAN HA7 50 A2
Everton Rd CROY/NA CR0 165 H7
Evesham Av WALTH E17 57 J1
Evesham Cl BELMT SM2 174 E6
GFD/PVL UB6 84 B1
Evesham Gn MRDN SM4 162 A5
Evesham Rd FBAR/BDGN N11 40 C4
MRDN SM4 162 A5
SRTFD E15 76 D6
Evesham St NTGHL W11 88 B6
Evesham Ter SURB KT6 * 158 E5
Evesham Wk BRXN/ST SW9 130 B1
CMBW SE5 130 E1
Evesham Wy BTSEA SW11 129 F2
CLAY IG5 60 A2
Evry Rd SCUP DA14 155 J5
Ewald Rd FUL/PGN SW6 127 J1
Ewanrigg Ter WFD IG8 45 G4
Ewart Gv WDGN N22 41 G7
Ewart Pl BOW E3 * 93 H1
Ewart Rd FSTH SE23 132 A6
Ewe Cl HOLWY N7 72 E5
Ewell By-Pass EW KT17 173 H5
Ewell Court Av
HOR/WEW KT19 173 G4
Ewellhurst Rd CLAY IG5 59 J1
Ewell Park Gdns EW KT17 173 J6
Ewell Park Wy EW KT17 173 J5
Ewell Rd SURB KT6 159 J7
CHEAM SM3 174 B5
SURB KT6 158 C6
Ewelme Rd FSTH SE23 131 K7
Ewen Crs BRXS/STRHM SW2 130 B6
Ewer St STHWK SE1 12 E9
Ewhurst Av SAND/SEL CR2 178 B7
Ewhurst Cl BELMT SM2 174 A7
WCHPL E1 92 E4
Ewhurst Rd BROCKY SE4 132 C5
Exbury Rd CAT SE6 151 J1
Excel Ct LSQ/SEVD WC2H 11 H7
Excel Marina CAN/RD E16 94 E6
Excelsior Cl KUT/HW KT1 159 H1
Excel Waterfront CAN/RD E16 95 F6
Exchange Ar LVPST EC2M 13 J3
Exchange Ct COVGDN WC2E * 11 K7
Exchange Rd WATW WD18 21 F3
Exchange Sq SDTCH EC2A * 13 K2
Exchange St ROMW/RG RM7 63 G5
Exchange Wk PIN HA5 47 J6
Exeter Cl EHAM E6 95 K5
WATN WD24 21 G1
Exeter Gdns IL IG1 59 K7
Exeter Ms FUL/PGN SW6 107 K6
Exeter Pde CRICK NW2 * 70 C5
Exeter Rd CAN/RD E16 94 E4
CRICK NW2 70 C4
CROY/NA CR0 165 F6
DAGE RM10 80 D5
ED N9 42 E1
FELT TW13 141 K2
HTHAIR TW6 121 H2
PEND EN3 31 F2
RYLN/HDSTN HA2 65 J1
STHGT/OAK N14 28 B7
WALTH E17 57 J4
WELL DA16 136 A1
Exeter St COVGDN WC2E 11 K6
Exeter Wy HTHAIR TW6 121 H1
NWCR SE14 112 C6
Exford Gdns LEE/GVPK SE12 134 A7
Exford Rd LEE/GVPK SE12 153 F1
Exhibition Grounds
WBLY HA9 * 68 D3
Exhibition Rd SKENS SW7 15 H4
Exit Rd EFNCH N2 53 H1
Exmoor St NKENS W10 88 B3
Exmouth Market
CLKNW EC1R 6 A9
Exmouth Ms CAMTN NW1 * 4 F8
Exmouth Pl HACK E8 74 D7
Exmouth Rd RSLP HA4 65 G2
WALTH E17 57 H4
WELL DA16 116 D7
YEAD UB4 82 C2
Exmouth St WCHPL E1 92 E5
Exning Rd CAN/RD E16 94 C3
Exon St WALW SE17 19 J6
Explorer Av STWL/WRAY TW19 120 B7
Explorer Dr WATW WD18 20 D5
Express Dr GDMY/SEVK IG3 61 H7
Exton Cl BCTR RM8 79 J4
Exton Rd WLSDN NW10 68 E6
Exton St STHWK SE1 12 A9
Eyhurst Av HCH RM12 81 J2
Eyhurst Cl CRICK NW2 69 J1
Eylewood Rd WNWD SE27 149 J4
Eynella Rd DUL SE21 131 G6
Eynham Rd SHB W12 88 A5
Eynsford Cl STMC/STPC BR5 169 H6
Eynsford Crs SCUP DA14 136 D7
Eynsford Rd GDMY/SEVK IG3 78 E1
Eynsham Dr ABYW SE2 116 C2
Eynswood Dr SCUP DA14 155 H4
Eyot Gdns HMSMTH W6 106 C4
Eyre Cl GPK RM2 63 K3
Eyre Street Hl CLKNW EC1R 12 A1
Eythorne Rd BRXN/ST SW9 110 B7
Ezra St BETH E2 7 M7

F

Faber Gdns HDN NW4 51 J4
Fabian Rd FUL/PGN SW6 107 J6
Fabian St EHAM E6 95 K3
The Facade FSTH SE23 * 150 E1
Factory La CROY/NA CR0 177 G1
TOTM N17 56 B1
Factory Pl POP/IOD E14 113 F4
Factory Rd CAN/RD E16 95 J7
Factory Yd HNWL W7 84 E7
Faggs Rd EBED/NFELT TW14 121 J3
Fairacre ISLW TW7 * 103 J7
NWMAL KT3 160 B2
Fair Acres HAYES BR2 167 K4
Fairacres CROY/NA CR0 179 H7
PUT/ROE SW15 126 C3
RSLP HA4 46 D6
Fairbank Est IS N1 * 7 G6
Fairbanks Rd TOTM N17 56 C2
Fairbourne Rd CLAP SW4 129 J5
TOTM N17 56 A2
Fairbridge Rd ARCH N19 72 D1
Fairbrook Cl PLMGR N13 41 G4
Fairby Rd LEE/GVPK SE12 134 A4
Fairchild Cl BTSEA SW11 128 C1
Fairchild Pl SDTCH EC2A * 13 K1
Fairchild St SDTCH EC2A 13 K1
Fair Cl BUSH WD23 22 B6
Fairclough Cl NTHLT UB5 83 K3
Fairclough St WCHPL E1 92 C5
Faircross Av BARK IG11 78 C5
Fairdale Gdns HYS/HAR UB3 101 K1
PUT/ROE SW15 126 E3
Fairey CDALE/KGS NW9 * 51 H1
Fairey Av HYS/HAR UB3 101 J2
Fairfax Av EW KT17 173 K7
Fairfax Cl WOT/HER KT12 156 A7
Fairfax Gdns BKHTH/KID SE3 114 B7
Fairfax Ms CAN/RD E16 95 F7
CEND/HSY/T N8 * 55 H3
PUT/ROE SW15 127 F3
Fairfax Pl KIL/WHAMP NW6 2 F1
WKENS W14 107 H2
Fairfax Rd CEND/HSY/T N8 55 G3
CHSWK W4 106 B2
DART DA1 139 K5
KIL/WHAMP NW6 2 F1
TEDD TW11 143 G6
Fairfax Wy MUSWH N10 40 A6
Fairfield Av EDGW HA8 36 D5
HDN NW4 51 K5
OXHEY WD19 33 G2
RSLP HA4 46 A6
WHTN TW2 123 G7
Fairfield Cl BFN/LL DA15 136 A5
HCH RM12 63 J7
HOR/WEW KT19 173 G4
MTCM CR4 147 J6
NFNCH/WDSPK N12 39 G3
PEND EN3 31 F3
Fairfield Cnr KUT/HW KT1 * 159 G1
Fairfield Ct RSLP HA4 46 B7
Fairfield Crs EDGW HA8 36 D5
Fairfield Dr GFD/PVL UB6 67 J7
RYLN/HDSTN HA2 48 C2
WAND/EARL SW18 128 A4
Fairfield East KUT/HW KT1 159 F1
Fairfield Gdns
CEND/HSY/T N8 54 E4
Fairfield Gv CHARL SE7 114 C5
Fairfield North
KUTN/CMB KT2 159 F1
Fairfield Pth CROY/NA CR0 177 K2
Fairfield Pl KUT/HW KT1 159 F2
Fairfield Rd BECK BR3 166 D1
BMLY BR1 152 E6
BOW E3 93 J1
BXLYHN DA7 137 G1
CEND/HSY/T N8 54 E4
CROY/NA CR0 177 K2
IL IG1 78 B5
KUT/HW KT1 159 F1
STHL UB1 83 K5
STMC/STPC BR5 169 J5
UED N18 42 C3
WALTH E17 57 G1
WFD IG8 44 E5
Fairfields CAT SE6 132 E6
Fairfields Cl CDALE/KGS NW9 50 E4
Fairfields Crs CDALE/KGS NW9 50 E3
Fairfield South KUT/HW KT1 159 F2
Fairfield St WAND/EARL SW18 128 A4
Fairfield Wy BAR EN5 26 E4
HOR/WEW KT19 173 G4
Fairfield West KUT/HW KT1 159 F1
Fairfoot Rd BOW E3 * 93 J3
Fairford Av BXLYHN DA7 117 K7
CROY/NA CR0 166 A4
Fairford Cl CROY/NA CR0 166 A4
Fairford Ct BELMT SM2 * 175 F6
Fairford Gdns WPK KT4 173 H2
Fairgreen EBAR EN4 27 K2
Fairgreen Ct EBAR EN4 * 27 K2
Fairgreen Rd THHTH CR7 164 C4
Fairhaven Av CROY/NA CR0 166 A5
Fairhaven Crs OXHEY WD19 32 E2
Fairhazel Gdns
KIL/WHAMP NW6 2 E1
Fairholme EBED/NFELT TW14 121 G6
Fairholme Av GPK RM2 63 J4
Fairholme Cl FNCH N3 52 C3
Fairholme Ct PIN HA5 * 34 A5
Fairholme Crs YEAD UB4 82 D3
Fairholme Gdns FNCH N3 52 C2
Fairholme Rd CROY/NA CR0 164 B6
HRW HA1 48 E4
IL IG1 59 K6
SUT SM1 174 D5
WKENS W14 107 H4
Fairholt Rd STNW/STAM N16 55 K7
Fairholt St SKENS SW7 15 K3
Fairland Rd SRTFD E15 76 D5
Fairlands Av BKHH IG9 44 E1
SUT SM1 174 E1
THHTH CR7 164 A3
Fairlawn CHARL SE7 114 B6
Fairlawn Av BXLYHN DA7 136 E1
CHSWK W4 105 K3
EFNCH N2 53 J3
Fairlawn Cl ESH/CLAY KT10 171 F5
FELT TW13 141 K3
KUTN/CMB KT2 144 E5
STHGT/OAK N14 28 D5
Fairlawn Ct CHARL SE7 * 114 B6
Fairlawn Dr WFD IG8 44 E6
Fairlawn Gdns STHL UB1 * 83 K6
Fairlawn Gv CHSWK W4 105 K3
Fairlawn Pk SYD SE26 151 G4
Fairlawn Rd WIM/MER SW19 146 D6
Fairlawns PIN HA5 47 G1
TWK TW1 124 D5
Fairlea Pl EA W5 85 J4
Fairlie Gdns FSTH SE23 131 K6
Fairlight Av CHING E4 44 B1
WFD IG8 44 E5
WLSDN NW10 87 G1
Fairlight Cl CHING E4 44 B1
WPK KT4 174 A3
Fairlight Rd TOOT SW17 147 H3
Fairlop Cl HCH RM12 81 K5
Fairlop Pl STJWD NW8 3 H8
Fairlop Rd BARK/HLT IG6 60 C1
WAN E11 58 B6
Fairmead BMLY BR1 168 E3
BRYLDS KT5 159 J7
Fairmead Cl BMLY BR1 168 E3
HEST TW5 102 C6
NWMAL KT3 160 A2
Fairmead Crs EDGW HA8 36 E3
Fairmead Gdns REDBR IG4 59 H4
Fairmead Rd ARCH N19 72 E2
CROY/NA CR0 164 B6
Fairmile Av STRHM/NOR SW16 148 D4
Fairmont Av POP/IOD E14 94 B6
Fairmont Cl BELV DA17 117 G4
Fairmount Rd
BRXS/STRHM SW2 130 A5
Fairoak Cl STMC/STPC BR5 169 G6
Fairoak Dr ELTH/MOT SE9 135 J4
Fairoak Gdns ROM RM1 63 G1
Fair Oak Pl BARK/HLT IG6 60 C1
Fairseat Cl BUSH WD23 34 E1
Fairstead Wk IS N1 * 6 E3
Fair St HSLW TW3 123 H2
STHWK SE1 19 K1
Fairthorn Rd CHARL SE7 113 K4
Fairview ERITH DA8 118 C6
Fairview Av ALP/SUD HA0 67 K5
Fairview Cl SYD SE26 151 G4
Fair View Cl WALTH E17 43 G7
Fairview Ct HDN NW4 * 52 B1
Fairview Crs
RYLN/HDSTN HA2 48 A7
Fairview Gdns WFD IG8 45 F7
Fairview Pl BRXS/STRHM SW2 130 A6
Fairview Rd SEVS/STOTM N15 56 B5
STRHM/NOR SW16 149 F7
SUT SM1 175 H4
Fairview Vls CHING E4 * 43 J6
Fairview Wy EDGW HA8 36 C3
Fairwater Av WELL DA16 136 B3
Fairway BXLYHS DA6 137 F4
RYNPK SW20 161 F2
STMC/STPC BR5 169 J5
WFD IG8 45 G4
Fairway Av BORE WD6 24 D1
CDALE/KGS NW9 50 D3
Fairway Cl CROY/NA CR0 166 B4
GLDGN NW11 53 G6
HOR/WEW KT19 172 E3
HSLWW TW4 122 B4
Fairway Ct MLHL NW7 * 37 F2
Fairway Dr GFD/PVL UB6 66 B6
THMD SE28 97 K5
Fairway Gdns BECK BR3 167 G5
IL IG1 78 C4
Fairways ISLW TW7 * 103 K7
STAN HA7 50 A1
TEDD TW11 143 K6
WALTH E17 * 58 A3
The Fairway ACT W3 87 G5
ALP/SUD HA0 67 H1
BAR EN5 27 F5
E/WMO/HCT KT8 157 G2
HAYES BR2 168 E4
HNWL W7 * 84 E6
MLHL NW7 37 F2
NTHLT UB5 66 C5
NTHWD HA6 32 C3
NWMAL KT3 145 F7
PLMGR N13 41 J2
RSLP HA4 65 G3
STHGT/OAK N14 28 B5
Fairweather Cl
SEVS/STOTM N15 56 A3
Fairweather Rd
STNW/STAM N16 56 C5
Fairwyn Rd SYD SE26 151 G2
Faithfield BUSH WD23 * 21 J5
Fakenham Cl MLHL NW7 37 J6
NTHLT UB5 66 A5
Fakruddin St WCHPL E1 92 C3
Falaize Av IL IG1 78 B3
Falcon Av BMLY BR1 168 D2
Falconberg Ct
SOHO/SHAV W1D * 11 G4
Falconberg Ms
SOHO/SHAV W1D 11 G4
Falcon Cl CHSWK W4 105 J5
DART DA1 139 J4
NTHWD HA6 32 C6
Falcon Ct IS N1 6 D6
Falcon Crs PEND EN3 31 F4
Falcon Dr STWL/WRAY TW19 120 A5
Falconer Rd BUSH WD23 22 A5
Falcon Gv BTSEA SW11 128 D2
Falcon La BTSEA SW11 128 D2
Falcon Rd BTSEA SW11 128 D2
HPTN TW12 141 K6
PEND EN3 31 F4
Falcon St PLSTW E13 94 E3
Falcon Ter BTSEA SW11 * 128 D2
Falcon Wy CDALE/KGS NW9 51 G1
KTN/HRWW/WS HA3 50 A4
POP/IOD E14 112 E3
WAN E11 58 E3
Falconwood Av WELL DA16 135 J1
Falconwood Pde WELL DA16 135 K3
Falconwood Rd CROY/NA CR0 179 H7
Falcourt Cl SUT SM1 175 F4
Falkirk Gdns OXHEY WD19 33 H4
Falkirk St IS N1 7 K6
Falkland Av FBAR/BDGN N11 40 A3
FNCH N3 38 E6
Falkland Park Av SNWD SE25 165 F1
Falkland Pl KTTN NW5 72 C4
Falkland Rd BAR EN5 26 C1
CEND/HSY/T N8 55 G3
KTTN NW5 72 C4
Falloden Wy GLDGN NW11 52 E3
Fallow Ct BERM/RHTH SE16 * 111 H4
Fallow Court Av
NFNCH/WDSPK N12 39 G5
Fallowfield STAN HA7 35 G2
Fallowfield Ct STAN HA7 35 G2
Fallowfields Dr
NFNCH/WDSPK N12 39 J5
Fallows Cl EFNCH N2 53 H1
Fallsbrook Rd
STRHM/NOR SW16 148 B5
Falman Cl ED N9 30 C7
Falmer Rd EN EN1 30 A3
SEVS/STOTM N15 55 J4
WALTH E17 57 K2
Falmouth Av CHING E4 44 B4
Falmouth Cl LEE/GVPK SE12 133 J4
WDGN N22 41 F6
Falmouth Gdns REDBR IG4 59 H3
Falmouth Rd STHWK SE1 18 F4
Falmouth St SRTFD E15 76 B4
Falstaff Cl DART DA1 138 B6
Falstaff Ms HPTN TW12 142 D4
Fambridge Cl SYD SE26 151 H3
Fambridge Rd BCTR RM8 62 C7
Fancourt Ms BMLY BR1 169 F2
Fane St WKENS W14 107 J5
Fanns Ri PUR RM19 119 K3
Fann St FARR EC1M 12 E1
STLK EC1Y 12 E1
Fanshawe Av BARK IG11 78 C5
Fanshawe Crs DAGW RM9 80 A4
Fanshawe Rd
RCHPK/HAM TW10 143 J3
Fanshaw St IS N1 7 J7
Fantail Cl THMD SE28 97 J5
Fanthorpe St PUT/ROE SW15 127 F2
Faraday Av SCUP DA14 155 H1
Faraday Cl HOLWY N7 73 F5
WATW WD18 20 B5
Faraday Pl E/WMO/HCT KT8 157 F3
Faraday Rd ACT W3 86 E6
E/WMO/HCT KT8 157 F3
NKENS W10 88 C4
SRTFD E15 76 D5
STHL UB1 84 B6
WELL DA16 136 B2
WIM/MER SW19 147 F5
Faraday Wy
WOOL/PLUM SE18 114 C2
Fareham Rd
EBED/NFELT TW14 122 B6
Fareham St SOHO/CST W1F * 11 G4
Farewell Pl MTCM CR4 147 H7
Faringdon Av HAYES BR2 169 F6
Faringford Rd SRTFD E15 76 C6
Farjeon Rd BKHTH/KID SE3 114 C7
Farleigh Av HAYES BR2 167 J6
Farleigh Court Rd
CROY/NA CR0 177 F1
Farleigh Pl STNW/STAM N16 74 B3
Farleigh Rd STNW/STAM N16 74 B3
Farley Dr GDMY/SEVK IG3 60 E7
Farley Ms CAT SE6 133 F6
Farley Pl SNWD SE25 165 H3
Farley Rd CAT SE6 133 F6
SAND/SEL CR2 178 C6
Farlow Rd PUT/ROE SW15 127 G2
Farlton Rd WAND/EARL SW18 128 A6
Farman Ter
KTN/HRWW/WS HA3 * 49 K3
Farm Av ALP/SUD HA0 67 J5
CRICK NW2 70 C2
RYLN/HDSTN HA2 48 A6
STRHM/NOR SW16 148 E3
Farmborough Cl HRW HA1 48 D6
Farm Cl BAR EN5 25 K4
BELMT SM2 175 H6
BKHH IG9 45 G2
DAGE RM10 80 E6
FUL/PGN SW6 * 107 K6
STHL UB1 84 B6
WWKM BR4 180 C2
Farmcote Rd LEE/GVPK SE12 133 K7
Farm Cots E/WMO/HCT KT8 * 158 B3
Farmdale Rd CAR SM5 175 J6
CHARL SE7 113 K4
Farm Dr CROY/NA CR0 179 H1
Farmer Rd LEY E10 57 K7
Farmers Rd CMBW SE5 110 C6
Farmer St KENS W8 8 A8
Farmfield Rd BMLY BR1 152 C4
Farmhouse Rd
STRHM/NOR SW16 148 C6
Farmilo Rd WALTH E17 57 J6
Farmington Av SUT SM1 175 H2
Farmlands PIN HA5 46 E3
The Farmlands NTHLT UB5 65 K5
Farmland Wk CHST BR7 154 B4
Farm La CROY/NA CR0 179 H1
FUL/PGN SW6 107 K5
STHGT/OAK N14 28 A5
Farmleigh STHGT/OAK N14 28 C6
Farm Pl DART DA1 138 D3
KENS W8 8 A8
Farm Rd BELMT SM2 175 H6
EDGW HA8 36 E4
ESH/CLAY KT10 157 F7
HSLWW TW4 122 D7
MNPK E12 77 J1
MRDN SM4 162 A4
NTHWD HA6 32 A4
WCHMH N21 29 J7
WLSDN NW10 69 F7
Farmstead Rd CAT SE6 151 K3
KTN/HRWW/WS HA3 34 D7
Farm St MYFR/PICC W1J 10 C7
The Farm WIM/MER SW19 * 127 G6
Farm V BXLY DA5 137 J5
Farm Wk GLDGN NW11 52 D4
Farmway BCTR RM8 79 J3
Farm Wy BKHH IG9 45 G3
BUSH WD23 22 B3
HCH RM12 81 K3
NTHWD HA6 32 C3
WPK KT4 174 A2
Farnaby Rd BMLY BR1 152 C7
ELTH/MOT SE9 134 B3
Farnan Av WALTH E17 57 J1
Farnan Rd STRHM/NOR SW16 148 E4
Farnborough Av
SAND/SEL CR2 179 G6
WALTH E17 * 57 G2
Farnborough Cl WBLY HA9 68 D1
Farnborough Crs HAYES BR2 167 J7
SAND/SEL CR2 179 G7
Farnborough Wy PECK SE15 * 111 F6
Farncombe St
BERM/RHTH SE16 111 H1
Farndale Av PLMGR N13 41 H2
Farndale Crs GFD/PVL UB6 84 C2
Farnell Ms ECT SW5 14 C7
Farnell Pl ACT W3 86 D6
Farnell Rd ISLW TW7 123 J2
Farnham Cl TRDG/WHET N20 27 G6
Farnham Gdns RYNPK SW20 160 E1
Farnham Pl STHWK SE1 12 D9
Farnham Rd GDMY/SEVK IG3 61 F5
WELL DA16 136 D1
Farnham Royal LBTH SE11 17 M8
Farningham Rd TOTM N17 42 C6
Farnley Rd SNWD SE25 164 E3
Farnol Rd DART DA1 139 K3
Faro Cl BMLY BR1 169 F1
Faroe Rd WKENS W14 107 G2
Farquhar Rd NRWD SE19 150 B4
WIM/MER SW19 146 E2
Farquharson Rd
CROY/NA CR0 164 D6
Farraline Rd WATW WD18 21 F3
Farrance Rd CHDH RM6 62 A5
Farrance St POP/IOD E14 93 J5
Farrant Av WDGN N22 55 G1
Farr Av BARK IG11 97 G1
Farren Rd FSTH SE23 151 G1
Farrer Ms CEND/HSY/T N8 54 C3
Farrer Rd CEND/HSY/T N8 54 C3
KTN/HRWW/WS HA3 50 A4
Farrier Cl BMLY BR1 168 C2
Farrier Pl SUT SM1 175 F2
Farrier Rd NTHLT UB5 84 A1
Farrier St CAMTN NW1 4 D1
Farriers Wy BORE WD6 25 F5
Farrier Wk WBPTN SW10 14 E9
Farringdon La CLKNW EC1R 12 B1
Farringdon Rd CLKNW EC1R 6 A9
HCIRC EC1N 12 C3
Farringdon St
FLST/FETLN EC4A 12 C4
Farrington Av BUSH WD23 22 B3
Farrington Pl CHST BR7 154 D6
Farrins Rents
BERM/RHTH SE16 93 G7
Farrow La NWCR SE14 111 K6
Farrow Pl BERM/RHTH SE16 112 B2
Farthingale Wk SRTFD E15 76 B6
Farthing Aly STHWK SE1 * 111 H1
Farthing Cl WATW WD18 21 G4
Farthing Flds WAP E1W 92 D7
Farthings Cl CHING E4 44 C2
PIN HA5 47 F5
The Farthings KUTN/CMB KT2 144 C7
Farthing St HAYES BR2 181 K6
Farwell Rd SCUP DA14 155 H3
Farwig La BMLY BR1 152 E7
Fashion St WCHPL E1 13 L3
Fashoda Rd HAYES BR2 168 C3
Fassett Rd HACK E8 74 C5
KUT/HW KT1 159 F3
Fassett Sq HACK E8 74 C5
Fauconberg Rd CHSWK W4 105 K5
Faulkner Cl BCTR RM8 61 K6
Faulkner St NWCR SE14 111 K7
Fauna Cl CHDH RM6 61 J5
STAN HA7 35 K2
Faunce St WALW SE17 18 C8
Favart Rd FUL/PGN SW6 107 K7
Faversham Av EN EN1 29 K5
Faversham Rd BECK BR3 166 C1
CAT SE6 132 C6
MRDN SM4 162 A5
Fawcett Cl BTSEA SW11 128 C1
STRHM/NOR SW16 149 G3
Fawcett Est CLPT E5 * 56 C7
Fawcett Rd CROY/NA CR0 177 H2
WLSDN NW10 69 H6
Fawcett St WBPTN SW10 14 E9
Fawcus Cl ESH/CLAY KT10 170 E5
Fawe Park Rd PUT/ROE SW15 127 J3
Fawe St POP/IOD E14 93 K4
Fawley Rd KIL/WHAMP NW6 71 F4
Fawnbrake Av HNHL SE24 130 C4
Fawn Rd PLSTW E13 95 G1
Fawns Manor Rd
EBED/NFELT TW14 121 G7
Fawood Av WLSDN NW10 69 F6
Faygate Crs BXLYHS DA6 137 H4
Faygate Rd BRXS/STRHM SW2 149 F1
Fayland Av STRHM/NOR SW16 148 C4
Fearnley Crs HPTN TW12 141 J4
Fearnley St WATW WD18 21 F3
Fearon St GNWCH SE10 113 K4
Featherbed La SAND/SEL CR2 179 H6
Feathers Pl GNWCH SE10 113 G5
Featherstone Av FSTH SE23 150 D1
Featherstone Gdns
BORE WD6 25 F3
Featherstone Rd MLHL NW7 37 K5
NWDGN UB2 102 D2
Featherstone St STLK EC1Y 7 G9

Featherstone Ter
NWDGN UB2 102 D2
Featley Rd BRXN/ST SW9 130 C2
Federal Rd GFD/PVL UB6 85 J1
Federation Rd ABYW SE2 116 D3
Fee Farm Rd ESH/CLAY KT10 171 F6
Feeny Cl WLSDN NW10 69 H3
Felbridge Av STAN HA7 35 G7
Felbridge Cl BELMT SM2 175 F7
STRHM/NOR SW16 149 G3
Felbrigge Rd GDMY/SEVK IG3 79 F1
Felday Rd LEW SE13 132 E5
Felden Cl PIN HA5 33 J6
Felden St FUL/PGN SW6 107 J7
Feldman Cl STNW/STAM N16 56 C7
Felgate Ms HMSMTH W6 106 E3
Felhampton Rd
ELTH/MOT SE9 154 B2
Felix Av CEND/HSY/T N8 55 K6
Felix Pl BRXS/STRHM SW2 130 B4
Felix Rd WEA W13 85 G6
Felixstowe Rd ABYW SE2 116 C2
ED N9 42 C2
SEVS/STOTM N15 56 B2
WLSDN NW10 87 K2
Felix St BETH E2 * 92 D1
Fellbrigg Rd EDUL SE22 131 G4
Fellbrigg St WCHPL E1 92 D3
Fellbrook RCHPK/HAM TW10 143 H2
Fellmongers Yd CROY/NA CR0 177 J2
Fellowes Cl YEAD UB4 83 H3
Fellowes Rd CAR SM5 175 J2
Fellows Rd HAMP NW3 3 H1
Fell Pth BORE WD6 * 25 F4
Fell Rd CROY/NA CR0 177 J2
Felltram Wy CHARL SE7 113 K4
Felmersham Cl CLAP SW4 129 K3
Felmingham Rd PGE/AN SE20 165 K1
Felsberg Rd
BRXS/STRHM SW2 129 K5
Fels Cl DAGE RM10 80 D2
Fels Farm Av DAGE RM10 80 E2
Felsham Ms PUT/ROE SW15 127 G2
Felsham Rd PUT/ROE SW15 127 F2
Felspar Cl WOOL/PLUM SE18 116 A4
Felstead Rd HOM E9 75 J5
WAN E11 58 E6
Felstead St HOM E9 75 H5
Felsted Rd CAN/RD E16 95 H5
Feltham Av E/WMO/HCT KT8 157 K3
Felthambrook Wy FELT TW13 141 F2
Feltham Hill Rd ASHF TW15 140 A5
Feltham Rd MTCM CR4 162 E1
Felton Cl STMC/STPC BR5 169 G5
Felton Lea SCUP DA14 155 F4
Felton Rd BARK IG11 96 E1
WEA W13 104 D1
Felton St IS N1 7 H4
Fenchurch Av FENCHST EC3M 13 J5
Fenchurch Blds
FENCHST EC3M 13 K5
Fenchurch Pl
FENCHST EC3M * 13 K6
Fenchurch St FENCHST EC3M 13 J6
Fendall Rd HOR/WEW KT19 172 E4
Fendall St STHWK SE1 19 K3
Fendt Cl CAN/RD E16 94 D5
Fendyke Rd BELV DA17 116 E3
Fenelon Pl WKENS W14 107 J3
Fen Gv BFN/LL DA15 136 A5
Fenham Rd PECK SE15 111 H6
Fenman Ct TOTM N17 42 D7
Fenman Gdns GDMY/SEVK IG3 61 H7
Fenn Cl BMLY BR1 152 E5
Fennel Cl CAN/RD E16 94 C3
CROY/NA CR0 166 A7
Fennells Md HOR/WEW KT19 173 H7
Fennell St WOOL/PLUM SE18 115 F5
Fenner Cl BERM/RHTH SE16 111 J3
Fenner Sq BTSEA SW11 * 128 C2
Fennings Rd CLAP SW4 129 J5
Fenning St STHWK SE1 19 J1
Fenn St HOM E9 75 F4
Fenstanton Av
NFNCH/WDSPK N12 39 H4
Fen St CAN/RD E16 94 D6
Fentiman Rd VX/NE SW8 110 A5
Fentiman Wy
RYLN/HDSTN HA2 66 B1
Fenton Cl BRXN/ST SW9 * 130 A1
CHST BR7 153 K4
HACK E8 74 B5
Fenton Rd TOTM N17 41 J6
Fenton's Av PLSTW E13 95 F2
Fenton St WCHPL E1 92 D5
Fenwick Gv PECK SE15 131 H2
Fenwick Pl BRXN/ST SW9 129 K2
SAND/SEL CR2 177 H6
Fenwick Rd PECK SE15 131 H2
Ferdinand Dr PECK SE15 111 F6
Ferdinand Pl CAMTN NW1 4 B1
Ferdinand St CAMTN NW1 4 B1
Ferguson Av BRYLDS KT5 159 G4
Ferguson Cl BECK BR3 167 F2
Ferguson Dr ACT W3 87 F5
Ferguson's Cl POP/IOD E14 112 D3
Fergus Rd HBRY N5 73 H4
Ferme Park Rd
CEND/HSY/T N8 54 E4
Fermor Rd FSTH SE23 132 B7
Fermoy Rd GFD/PVL UB6 84 B3
MV/WKIL W9 88 D3
Fern Av MTCM CR4 163 J3
Fernbank Av ALP/SUD HA0 67 F3
WOT/HER KT12 156 D6
Fernbank Ms BAL SW12 129 G5
Fernbrook Dr
RYLN/HDSTN HA2 48 B6
Fernbrook Rd LEW SE13 133 H5
Ferncliff Rd HACK E8 74 C4
Fern Cl ERITH DA8 118 E7
IS N1 7 J5
Fern Ct NWCR SE14 132 A1
Ferncroft Av HAMP NW3 70 E2
NFNCH/WDSPK N12 39 J5
RSLP HA4 65 G1
Ferndale BMLY BR1 168 B1
Ferndale Av HSLWW TW4 122 D2
WALTH E17 58 B4
Ferndale Cl BXLYHN DA7 117 F7
Ferndale Rd CLAP SW4 129 K3
CRW RM5 62 E1
FSTGT E7 77 F6
SEVS/STOTM N15 56 B5
SNWD SE25 165 J4
WAN E11 76 D1
Ferndale St EHAM E6 96 B6
Ferndale Ter HRW HA1 49 F3
Fern Dene WEA W13 85 H4
Ferndene Rd HNHL SE24 130 D3
Fernden Wy ROMW/RG RM7 62 D5
Ferndown NTHWD HA6 46 E1
Ferndown Av ORP BR6 169 J7
Ferndown Cl BELMT SM2 175 H5
PIN HA5 33 J6
Ferndown Rd ELTH/MOT SE9 134 C6
OXHEY WD19 33 G2
Ferney Meade Wy ISLW TW7 124 B1
Ferney Rd EBAR EN4 28 A6
Fern Gv EBED/NFELT TW14 122 A6
Fernhall Dr REDBR IG4 59 H4
Fernham Rd THHTH CR7 164 D2
Fernhead Rd MV/WKIL W9 88 D2
Fernhill Ct WALTH E17 58 B1
Fernhill Gdns KUTN/CMB KT2 143 K4
Fernhill St CAN/RD E16 95 K7
Fernholme Rd PECK SE15 132 A4
Fernhurst Gdns EDGW HA8 36 C5
Fernhurst Rd ASHF TW15 140 A3
CROY/NA CR0 165 H6
FUL/PGN SW6 107 H7
Fern La HEST TW5 102 E4
Fernlea Rd BAL SW12 129 G7
MTCM CR4 163 F1
Fernleigh Cl CROY/NA CR0 177 G3
MV/WKIL W9 88 D2
Fernleigh Ct
RYLN/HDSTN HA2 48 B1
WBLY HA9 50 A7
Fernleigh Rd WCHMH N21 41 G1
Fernley Cl PIN HA5 46 E3
Fernsbury St FSBYW WC1X 6 A8
Fernshaw Cl WBPTN SW10 * 108 B5
Fernshaw Rd WBPTN SW10 108 B5
Fernside GLDGN NW11 70 E1
THDIT KT7 158 C7
Fernside Av FELT TW13 141 F3
MLHL NW7 37 F2
Fernside Rd BAL SW12 128 E7
Ferns Rd SRTFD E15 76 C5
Fern St BOW E3 93 J3
Fernthorpe Rd
STRHM/NOR SW16 148 C5
Ferntower Rd HBRY N5 73 K4
Fern Wk BERM/RHTH SE16 111 H4
Fernways IL IG1 78 B2
Fernwood Av ALP/SUD HA0 67 J5
STRHM/NOR SW16 148 D3
Fernwood Cl BMLY BR1 168 B1
Fernwood Crs
TRDG/WHET N20 39 K2
Ferranti Cl WOOL/PLUM SE18 114 C2
Ferraro Cl HEST TW5 103 F5
Ferrers Av WDR/YW UB7 100 A1
WLGTN SM6 176 D3
Ferrers Rd STRHM/NOR SW16 148 D4
Ferrestone Rd
CEND/HSY/T N8 55 F3
Ferrey Ms BRXN/ST SW9 130 B1
Ferriby Cl IS N1 6 A1
Ferrier St WAND/EARL SW18 128 A3
Ferring Cl RYLN/HDSTN HA2 48 C7
Ferrings DUL SE21 150 A1
Ferris Av CROY/NA CR0 179 H2
Ferris Rd EDUL SE22 131 H3
Ferron Rd CLPT E5 * 74 D2
Ferro Rd RAIN RM13 99 J3
Ferryhills Cl OXHEY WD19 33 G2
Ferry La BARN SW13 106 C5
BTFD TW8 105 F5
RAIN RM13 99 G5
TOTM N17 56 D3
Ferrymead Av GFD/PVL UB6 84 A1
Ferrymead Dr GFD/PVL UB6 84 A2
Ferrymead Gdns
GFD/PVL UB6 84 C1
Ferrymoor RCHPK/HAM TW10 143 H2
Ferry Rd BARN SW13 106 D6
E/WMO/HCT KT8 157 F2
TEDD TW11 143 H4
THDIT KT7 158 C5
TWK TW1 124 C7
Ferry Sq BTFD TW8 105 F5
Ferry St POP/IOD E14 113 F4
Festing Rd PUT/ROE SW15 127 G2
Festival Cl BXLY DA5 136 E7
ERITH DA8 118 C6
Festoon Wy CAN/RD E16 95 H6
Fetter La FLST/FETLN EC4A 12 B4
Ffinch St DEPT SE8 112 D6
Fidgeon Cl BMLY BR1 169 F2
Fidler Pl BUSH WD23 22 B5
Field Cl BKHH IG9 45 G2
BMLY BR1 168 B1
CHING E4 43 K5
CHSGTN KT9 171 J4
CRICK NW2 69 J1
E/WMO/HCT KT8 157 G4
HSLWW TW4 102 A7
HYS/HAR UB3 101 F6
RSLP HA4 46 A7
Fieldcommon La
WOT/HER KT12 156 D7
Field Cots EFNCH N2 * 53 K2
FUL/PGN SW6 * 127 J1
Field Ct GINN WC1R 11 M3
Field End BAR EN5 25 K3
RSLP HA4 65 H5
Fieldend TEDD TW11 143 F3
Field End Cl OXHEY WD19 21 J6
Field End Rd PIN HA5 47 F4
RSLP HA4 65 H2
Fieldend Rd
STRHM/NOR SW16 148 C7
Fielders Cl EN EN1 30 A3
RYLN/HDSTN HA2 48 C7
Fieldfare Rd THMD SE28 97 J6
Fieldgate St WCHPL E1 92 C4
Fieldhouse Cl SWFD E18 45 F7
Fieldhouse Rd BAL SW12 129 H7
Fielding Av WHTN TW2 142 C2
Fielding La HAYES BR2 168 B3
Fielding Rd CHSWK W4 106 A2
WKENS W14 107 G2
The Fieldings FSTH SE23 131 K7
Fielding St WALW SE17 18 E9
Fielding Ter EA W5 * 86 B6
Field La BTFD TW8 104 D6
TEDD TW11 143 G4
Field Md CDALE/KGS NW9 37 G6
Fieldpark Gdns CROY/NA CR0 166 B7
Field Pl NWMAL KT3 160 C5
Field Rd EBED/NFELT TW14 122 A5
FSTGT E7 76 E3
HMSMTH W6 107 H4
OXHEY WD19 21 J5
TOTM N17 55 K2
Fieldsend Rd CHEAM SM3 174 C4
Fields Est HACK E8 * 74 C6
Fieldside Cots
TRDG/WHET N20 * 26 D6
Fieldside Rd BMLY BR1 152 B4
Fields Park Crs CHDH RM6 61 K4
Field St FSBYW WC1X 5 L7
Field Vw FELT TW13 140 B3
Fieldview WAND/EARL SW18 128 C7
Field View Cl ROMW/RG RM7 62 C2
Fieldview Cots
STHGT/OAK N14 * 40 D1
Fieldway STMC/STPC BR5 169 J5
BCTR RM8 79 H3
Field Wy CROY/NA CR0 179 K5
GFD/PVL UB6 66 B7
RSLP HA4 46 A7
WLSDN NW10 68 E6
Fieldway Crs HBRY N5 73 G4
Fiennes Cl BCTR RM8 61 J7
Fiesta Dr RAIN RM13 98 E3
Fife Rd CAN/RD E16 94 E4
KUT/HW KT1 159 F1
MORT/ESHN SW14 125 K4
WDGN N22 41 H6
Fife Ter IS N1 5 M5
Fifield Pth FSTH SE23 151 F2
Fifth Av HYS/HAR UB3 82 D7
MNPK E12 77 K3
NKENS W10 88 C3
Fifth Cross Rd WHTN TW2 142 D1
Fifth Wy WBLY HA9 68 D3
Figge's Rd MTCM CR4 148 A6
Fig Tree Cl WLSDN NW10 69 G7
Filby Rd CHSGTN KT9 172 B5
Filey Av STNW/STAM N16 56 C7
Filey Cl BELMT SM2 175 G6
Filey Waye RSLP HA4 64 E1
Fillebrook Av EN EN1 30 A1
Fillebrook Rd WAN E11 58 B7
Filmer Chambers
FUL/PGN SW6 * 107 J7
Filmer Rd FUL/PGN SW6 107 J7
Filton Cl CDALE/KGS NW9 51 G1
Finborough Rd TOOT SW17 147 K6
WBPTN SW10 14 D9
Finchale Rd ABYW SE2 116 B2
Fincham Cl HGDN/ICK UB10 64 A2
Finch Av WNWD SE27 149 K3
Finch Cl BAR EN5 26 E4
Finch Dr EBED/NFELT TW14 122 C6
Finch Gdns CHING E4 43 J4
Finchingfield Av WFD IG8 45 G6
Finch La BANK EC3V 13 H5
BUSH WD23 22 A3
Finchley Cl DART DA1 139 K5
Finchley La HDN NW4 52 B3
Finchley Pk
NFNCH/WDSPK N12 39 G3
Finchley Pl STJWD NW8 3 G5
Finchley Rd GLDGN NW11 52 D4
HAMP NW3 70 E3
STJWD NW8 3 G4
Finchley Vls
NFNCH/WDSPK N12 * 39 H3
Finchley Wy FNCH N3 38 E5
Finch Ms PECK SE15 * 111 G7
Finchs Ct POP/IOD E14 93 K6
Finden Rd FSTGT E7 77 F4
Findhorn Av YEAD UB4 83 F4
Findhorn St POP/IOD E14 94 A5
Findon Cl RYLN/HDSTN HA2 * 66 B2
WAND/EARL SW18 127 K5
Findon Gdns RAIN RM13 99 J4
Findon Rd ED N9 30 D7
SHB W12 106 D1
Fingal St GNWCH SE10 113 J4
Finland Rd BROCKY SE4 132 B2
Finland St BERM/RHTH SE16 112 B2
Finlays Cl CHSGTN KT9 172 C4
Finlay St FUL/PGN SW6 107 G7
Finney La ISLW TW7 104 B7
Finnis St BETH E2 92 D2
Finnymore Rd DAGW RM9 80 A6
Finsbury Av LVPST EC2M * 13 H3
Finsbury Circ LVPST EC2M 13 H3
Finsbury Cots WDGN N22 40 E6
Finsbury Est CLKNW EC1R 6 B8
Finsbury Market SDTCH EC2A 13 J1
Finsbury Park Av FSBYPK N4 55 J5
Finsbury Park Rd FSBYPK N4 73 H1
Finsbury Pavement
LVPST EC2M 13 H2
Finsbury Rd WDGN N22 41 F6
Finsbury Sq SDTCH EC2A 13 H1
Finsbury St STLK EC1Y 13 G2
Finsbury Wy BXLY DA5 137 G5
Finsen Rd CMBW SE5 130 D3
Finstock Rd NKENS W10 88 B5
Finucane Gdns RAIN RM13 81 J5
Finucane Ri BUSH WD23 34 C1
Finway Ct WATW WD18 * 20 D4
Fiona Ct ENC/FH EN2 * 29 H2
Firbank Cl CAN/RD E16 95 H4
ENC/FH EN2 29 J3
Firbank Dr OXHEY WD19 21 J6
Firbank Rd PECK SE15 131 J1
Fircroft Gdns HRW HA1 66 E2
Fircroft Rd CHSGTN KT9 172 B3
TOOT SW17 147 K2
Firdene BRYLDS KT5 159 K7
Fir Dene ORP BR6 181 K2
Fire Bell Aly SURB KT6 159 F5
Firebell Ms SURB KT6 159 F5
Firecrest Dr HAMP NW3 71 F2
Firefly Cl WLGTN SM6 * 176 E6
Firefly Gdns EHAM E6 95 J3
Firemans Cots EFNCH N2 54 A2
Firethorn Cl EDGW HA8 36 E3
Fir Gv NWMAL KT3 160 C5
Fir Grove Rd BRXN/ST SW9 * 130 B1
Firhill Rd CAT SE6 151 J2
Firle Pl WAND/EARL SW18 128 B6
Firman Cl NWMAL KT3 160 B3
Firmin Rd DART DA1 139 F4
Fir Rd CHEAM SM3 161 J7
FELT TW13 141 H4
Firs Av FBAR/BDGN N11 40 A5
MORT/ESHN SW14 125 K3
MUSWH N10 54 A2
Firsby Av CROY/NA CR0 166 A7
Firsby Rd STNW/STAM N16 56 B7
Firs Cl ESH/CLAY KT10 170 E5
FSTH SE23 132 A6
MTCM CR4 163 G1
Firscroft PLMGR N13 41 J2
Firs Dr HEST TW5 102 A6
Firside Gv BFN/LL DA15 136 A7
Firs La PLMGR N13 41 J2
Firs Park Av WCHMH N21 29 K7
Firs Park Gdns WCHMH N21 29 K7
First Av ACT W3 87 H7
BXLYHN DA7 116 D6
CHDH RM6 61 J4
DAGE RM10 98 D1
E/WMO/HCT KT8 156 E3
EN EN1 30 B4
HDN NW4 52 A3
HOR/WEW KT19 173 G7
HYS/HAR UB3 82 D7
MNPK E12 77 J3
MORT/ESHN SW14 126 B1
NKENS W10 88 D3
PLSTW E13 94 E2
UED N18 43 J5
WALTH E17 57 K4
WBLY HA9 67 K1
WOT/HER KT12 156 A5
First Cl E/WMO/HCT KT8 157 H3
First Cross Rd WHTN TW2 142 E1
First Dr WLSDN NW10 68 E6
The Firs BXLY DA5 138 A7
EA W5 85 K4
EBED/NFELT TW14 * 121 H5
EDGW HA8 * 37 F3
TRDG/WHET N20 27 H7
First St CHEL SW3 15 K5
Firstway RYNPK SW20 161 F1
First Wy WBLY HA9 68 D3
Firs Wk NTHWD HA6 32 B5
WFD IG8 44 E4
Firswood Av HOR/WEW KT19 173 G4
Firth Gdns FUL/PGN SW6 107 H7
Firtree Av MTCM CR4 163 F1
Fir Tree Av WDR/YW UB7 100 D2
Fir Tree Cl EA W5 86 A5
ESH/CLAY KT10 170 C4
HOR/WEW KT19 173 H3
ROM RM1 63 F2
STRHM/NOR SW16 148 C4
Fir Tree Ct BORE WD6 24 B3
Fir Tree Gdns CROY/NA CR0 179 J3
Fir Tree Gv CAR SM5 175 K6
Fir Tree Rd HSLWW TW4 122 D3
Fir Trees Cl BERM/RHTH SE16 93 G7
Fir Tree Wk EN EN1 30 A2
Fir Wk CHEAM SM3 174 B5
Fisher Cl CROY/NA CR0 165 G7
GFD/PVL UB6 84 A2
Fisherdene ESH/CLAY KT10 171 G6
Fisherman Cl
RCHPK/HAM TW10 143 J3
Fishermans Dr
BERM/RHTH SE16 112 A1
Fisher Rd KTN/HRWW/WS HA3 49 F1
Fishers Cl BUSH WD23 21 J3
STRHM/NOR SW16 148 D2
Fishers Ct NWCR SE14 112 A7
Fisher's La CHSWK W4 106 A3
Fisher St CAN/RD E16 94 E4
RSQ WC1B 11 L3
Fisher's Wy BELV DA17 98 E7
Fisherton St STJWD NW8 9 G1
Fishguard Wy CAN/RD E16 96 B7
Fishponds Rd HAYES BR2 181 H4
TOOT SW17 147 J3
Fish Street Hl MON EC3R 13 H7
Fisk Cl SUN TW16 140 D5
Fisons Rd CAN/RD E16 94 E7
Fitzalan Rd ESH/CLAY KT10 170 E6
FNCH N3 52 C2
Fitzalan St LBTH SE11 17 M5
Fitzgeorge Av NWMAL KT3 145 F7
WKENS W14 107 H3
Fitzgerald Av
MORT/ESHN SW14 126 B2
Fitzgerald Rd
MORT/ESHN SW14 126 A2
THDIT KT7 158 B5
WAN E11 58 E4
Fitzhardinge St MBLAR W1H 10 A4
Fitzhugh Gv
WAND/EARL SW18 128 C5
Fitzjames Av CROY/NA CR0 178 C1
WKENS W14 107 H3
Fitzjohn Av BAR EN5 26 C4
Fitzjohn's Av HAMP NW3 71 H4
Fitzmaurice Pl
MYFR/PICC W1J * 10 D8
Fitzneal St SHB W12 87 H5
Fitzroy Cl HGT N6 53 K7
Fitzroy Crs CHSWK W4 * 106 A6
Fitzroy Gdns NRWD SE19 150 A6
Fitzroy Ms FITZ W1T 10 E1
Fitzroy Pk HGT N6 53 K7
Fitzroy Rd CAMTN NW1 4 A3
Fitzroy Sq FITZ W1T 10 E1
Fitzroy St FITZ W1T 10 E2
Fitzstephen Rd BCTR RM8 79 H4
Fitzwarren Gdns HGT N6 54 C7
Fitzwilliam Av RCH/KEW TW9 125 G1
Fitzwilliam Cl
TRDG/WHET N20 27 K7
Fitzwilliam Ms CAN/RD E16 94 E6
Fitzwilliam Rd CLAP SW4 129 H2
Fitz Wygram Cl HPTN TW12 142 C4
Five Acre CDALE/KGS NW9 51 H1
Fiveacre Cl CROY/NA CR0 164 B5
Five Elms Rd DAGW RM9 80 B2
HAYES BR2 181 G2
Five Fields Cl OXHEY WD19 33 K1
Fiveways Cnr ELTH/MOT SE9 154 B1
Five Ways Jct HDN NW4 37 J7
Fiveways Rd BRXN/ST SW9 130 B1
Fladbury Rd SEVS/STOTM N15 55 K5
Fladgate Rd WAN E11 58 C5
Flag Cl CROY/NA CR0 166 A7
Flag Wk PIN HA5 46 E5
Flambard Rd HRW HA1 49 G5
Flamborough Rd RSLP HA4 64 E2
Flamborough St POP/IOD E14 93 G5
Flamborough Wk
POP/IOD E14 * 93 G5
Flamingo Wk HCH RM12 81 J6
Flamstead Gdns DAGW RM9 79 J6
Flamstead Rd DAGW RM9 79 J6
Flamsted Av WBLY HA9 68 C5
Flamsteed Rd CHARL SE7 114 D4
Flanchford Rd SHB W12 106 C2
Flanders Crs TOOT SW17 147 K6
Flanders Rd CHSWK W4 106 B3
EHAM E6 95 K1
Flanders Wy HOM E9 75 F5
Flank St WCHPL E1 92 C6
Flask Wk HAMP NW3 71 G3
Flather Cl STRHM/NOR SW16 148 C5
Flavell Ms GNWCH SE10 113 H4
Flaxen Cl CHING E4 43 K2
Flaxen Rd CHING E4 43 K2
Flaxley Rd MRDN SM4 162 A5
Flaxman Rd CMBW SE5 130 C1
Flaxman Ter STPAN WC1H 5 H8
Flaxton Rd WOOL/PLUM SE18 115 J7
Flecker Cl STAN HA7 35 F4
Fleece Dr ED N9 42 C3
Fleece Rd SURB KT6 158 D7
Fleece Wk HOLWY N7 * 72 E5
Fleeming Cl WALTH E17 57 H1
Fleeming Rd WALTH E17 57 H1
Fleet Cl E/WMO/HCT KT8 156 E4
RSLP HA4 46 A5
Fleet Pl FLST/FETLN EC4A 12 C4
Fleet Rd HAMP NW3 71 J4
Fleetside E/WMO/HCT KT8 156 E4
Fleet Sq FSBYW WC1X 5 L8
Fleet St EMB EC4Y 12 A5
Fleet Street Hl WCHPL E1 * 92 C3
Fleet Ter CAT SE6 * 133 F6
Fleetwood Cl CAN/RD E16 95 H4
CHSGTN KT9 171 K6
CROY/NA CR0 178 B2
Fleetwood Rd KUT/HW KT1 159 J2
WLSDN NW10 69 J4
Fleetwood Sq KUT/HW KT1 159 J2
Fleetwood St
STNW/STAM N16 74 A1
Fleetwood Wy OXHEY WD19 33 G3
Fleming Cl MV/WKIL W9 8 A1
Fleming Ct CROY/NA CR0 177 G4
Fleming Dr WCHMH N21 29 F4
Fleming Md MTCM CR4 147 J6
Fleming Rd STHL UB1 84 B5
WALW SE17 18 D9
Fleming Wk
CDALE/KGS NW9 * 51 G1
Fleming Wy ISLW TW7 124 A2
THMD SE28 97 K6
Flemming Av RSLP HA4 47 F7
Flempton Rd LEY E10 57 G7
Fletcher Cl EHAM E6 96 B6
Fletcher La LEY E10 58 A6
Fletcher Rd CHSWK W4 105 K2
Fletchers Cl HAYES BR2 168 A3
Fletcher St WCHPL E1 92 C6
Fletching Rd CHARL SE7 114 C5
CLPT E5 74 E2
Fletton Rd FBAR/BDGN N11 40 E6
Fleur De Lis St WCHPL E1 13 K1
Fleur Gates WIM/MER SW19 127 G6
Flexmere Rd TOTM N17 41 K7
Flight Ap CDALE/KGS NW9 * 37 H7
Flimwell Cl BMLY BR1 152 C4
Flint Cl SRTFD E15 76 D5
Flint Down Cl
STMC/STPC BR5 * 155 G7
Flintmill Crs BKHTH/KID SE3 134 D1
ELTH/MOT SE9 134 D2
Flinton St WALW SE17 19 K7
Flint St WALW SE17 19 H6
Flitcroft St LSQ/SEVD WC2H 11 H5
Floathaven Cl THMD SE28 97 G7
Flock Mill Pl
WAND/EARL SW18 128 A7
Flockton St BERM/RHTH SE16 111 H1
Flodden Rd CMBW SE5 110 D7
Flood La TWK TW1 * 124 B7
Flood St CHEL SW3 15 K8
Flood Wk CHEL SW3 15 K9
Flora Cl POP/IOD E14 93 K5
STAN HA7 35 K2
Flora Gdns CHDH RM6 61 J5
HMSMTH W6 106 E3
Floral Pl IS N1 73 K4
Floral St COVGDN WC2E 11 K6
Flora St BELV DA17 117 G4
Florence Av ENC/FH EN2 29 J2
MRDN SM4 162 B4
Florence Cl WOT/HER KT12 156 A6
Florence Ct WAN E11 59 F3
Florence Dr ENC/FH EN2 29 J2
Florence Elson Cl MNPK E12 78 A3
Florence Gdns CHSWK W4 105 K5
Florence Rd ABYW SE2 116 D2
BECK BR3 166 A1
BMLY BR1 152 E7
CHSWK W4 106 A2
EA W5 86 A6
EHAM E6 77 G7
FELT TW13 122 A7
FSBYPK N4 55 F6
KUTN/CMB KT2 144 B6
NWCR SE14 112 C7
NWDGN UB2 102 C3
PLSTW E13 94 E1
SAND/SEL CR2 177 K7
WIM/MER SW19 147 F5
WOT/HER KT12 156 A6
Florence St CAN/RD E16 94 D3
HDN NW4 52 A3
IS N1 6 C2
Florence Ter NWCR SE14 112 C7
Florence Vls HGT N6 * 54 B6
Florence Wy BAL SW12 128 E7
Florey Sq WCHMH N21 29 F4
Florfield Rd HACK E8 74 D5
Florian Av SUT SM1 175 H3
Florian Rd PUT/ROE SW15 127 H3
Florida Cl BUSH WD23 34 D1
Florida Rd THHTH CR7 149 H7
Florida St BETH E2 92 C2
Florin Ct UED N18 42 A3
Floris Pl CLAP SW4 129 H2
Floriston Av HGDN/ICK UB10 64 A6
Floriston Cl STAN HA7 35 H7
Floriston Gdns STAN HA7 35 H7
Floss St PUT/ROE SW15 127 F1
Flower & Dean Wk WCHPL E1 13 M3
Flower La MLHL NW7 37 H4
Flower Ms GLDGN NW11 52 C5
Flowerpot Cl
SEVS/STOTM N15 56 B5
Flowers Av RSLP HA4 46 E5
Flowers Cl CRICK NW2 69 J2
Flowers Ms ARCH N19 72 C1
Floyd Rd CHARL SE7 114 B4
Floyer Cl RCHPK/HAM TW10 125 G4
Fludyer St LEW SE13 133 H3
Foley Ms ESH/CLAY KT10 170 E5
Foley Rd ESH/CLAY KT10 170 E6
Foley St GTPST W1W 10 E3
Foley Wd ESH/CLAY KT10 171 F6
Folgate St WCHPL E1 13 K2
Foliot St SHB W12 87 H5
Folkestone Rd EHAM E6 96 A1
UED N18 42 C3
WALTH E17 57 K3
Folkingham La
CDALE/KGS NW9 37 F7
Folkington Cnr
NFNCH/WDSPK N12 38 D4
Follett St POP/IOD E14 94 A5
Folly La WALTH E17 43 G7
Folly Wall POP/IOD E14 113 F1
Fontaine Rd
STRHM/NOR SW16 149 F5
Fontarabia Rd BTSEA SW11 129 F3
Fontayne Av RAIN RM13 81 G6
ROM RM1 63 G1
Fontenoy Rd BAL SW12 148 B1
Fonteyne Gdns WFD IG8 59 H1
Fonthill Ms FSBYPK N4 73 F1
Fonthill Rd FSBYPK N4 73 F1
Font Hills EFNCH N2 53 G1
Fontley Wy PUT/ROE SW15 126 D6
Fontwell Cl
KTN/HRWW/WS HA3 34 E6
NTHLT UB5 66 A5
Fontwell Dr HAYES BR2 169 F4

The Footpath
PUT/ROE SW15 * 126 D4
Foots Cray High St
SCUP DA14 155 J5
Foots Cray La SCUP DA14 136 D7
Footscray Rd ELTH/MOT SE9 135 G7
Forbes Cl CRICK NW2 69 J2
HCH RM12 63 K7
Forbes St WCHPL E1 92 C5
Forbes Wy RSLP HA4 65 F1
Forburg Rd STNW/STAM N16 56 C7
Ford Cl BUSH WD23 22 C3
HRW HA1 48 D6
RAIN RM13 81 H6
THHTH CR7 164 C5
Forde Av BMLY BR1 168 B2
Fordel Rd CAT SE6 133 G7
Ford End WFD IG8 45 F5
Fordham Cl WPK KT4 160 E7
Fordham Rd EBAR EN4 27 H2
Fordham St WCHPL E1 92 C5
Fordhook Av EA W5 86 B6
Fordingley Rd MV/WKIL W9 88 D2
Fordington Rd HGT N6 53 K3
Ford La RAIN RM13 81 H6
Fordmill Rd CAT SE6 151 J1
Ford Rd BOW E3 93 G1
DAGW RM9 80 B6
Ford's Gv WCHMH N21 29 J7
Fords Park Rd CAN/RD E16 94 E5
Ford Sq WCHPL E1 92 D4
Ford St BOW E3 75 G7
CAN/RD E16 94 D5
Fordwych Rd CRICK NW2 70 C4
Fordyce Rd LEW SE13 133 F5
Fordyke Rd BCTR RM8 80 A1
Foreland Ct HDN NW4 38 C7
Foreland St WOOL/PLUM SE18 115 J3
Foreshore DEPT SE8 112 C4
Forest Ap WFD IG8 44 D6
Forest Cl CHST BR7 154 A7
KIL/WHAMP NW6 70 C6
WAN E11 58 D4
WFD IG8 45 F3
Forest Ct WAN E11 58 C3
Forestdale STHGT/OAK N14 40 D3
Forest Dr HAYES BR2 181 J2
MNPK E12 77 H2
SUN TW16 140 D6
WFD IG8 44 B6
Forest Dr East WAN E11 58 B6
Forest Dr West WAN E11 58 A6
Forest Edge BKHH IG9 45 G2
Forester Rd PECK SE15 131 J3
Foresters Cl WLGTN SM6 176 D6
Foresters Crs BXLYHN DA7 137 J3
Foresters Dr WALTH E17 58 B3
WLGTN SM6 176 D6
Forest Gdns TOTM N17 56 B1
Forest Ga CDALE/KGS NW9 51 G3
Forest Gld CHING E4 44 C4
WAN E11 58 C5
Forest Gv HACK E8 74 B5
Forest Hill Rd EDUL SE22 131 J5
Forestholme Cl FSTH SE23 150 E1
SYD SE26 * 150 E4
Forest La FSTGT E7 76 E4
Forest Mount Rd WFD IG8 44 B6
Fore St BARB EC2Y 13 G3
ED N9 42 C3
PIN HA5 46 D3
UED N18 42 C4
Forest Rdg BECK BR3 166 D2
HAYES BR2 181 J3
Forest Ri WALTH E17 58 B3
Forest Rd CHEAM SM3 161 K7
ED N9 30 D7
ERITH DA8 118 D7
FELT TW13 141 G1
FSTGT E7 76 E3
HACK E8 74 B5
RCH/KEW TW9 105 H6
ROMW/RG RM7 62 D2
TOTM N17 56 E3
WALTH E17 57 J2
WAN E11 58 A6
WFD IG8 44 E2
Forest Side FSTGT E7 77 F3
WPK KT4 160 C7
Forest St FSTGT E7 76 E4
The Forest WAN E11 58 C3
Forest Vw WAN E11 58 D6
Forest View Av LEY E10 58 B4
Forest View Rd MNPK E12 77 J3
WALTH E17 44 A7
Forest Wy BFN/LL DA15 135 J6
WFD IG8 45 F3
Forfar Rd BTSEA SW11 109 F7
WDGN N22 41 H7
Forge Cl HAYES BR2 167 K7
HYS/HAR UB3 101 G5
Forge Cotts EA W5 * 85 K7
Forge Dr ESH/CLAY KT10 171 G6
Forge La CHEAM SM3 174 C6
FELT TW13 141 J4
NTHWD HA6 32 C6
RCHPK/HAM TW10 125 F7
Forge Ms CROY/NA CR0 179 J4
Forge Pl CAMTN NW1 72 A5
Forman Pl STNW/STAM N16 74 B3
Formby Av
KTN/HRWW/WS HA3 49 J2
Formosa St MV/WKIL W9 8 D1
Formunt Cl CAN/RD E16 94 D4
Forres Gdns GLDGN NW11 52 E5
Forrester Pth SYD SE26 150 E3
Forrest Gdns
STRHM/NOR SW16 164 A2
Forris Av HYS/HAR UB3 82 D7
Forset St MBLAR W1H 9 K4
Forstal Cl HAYES BR2 167 K2
Forster Cl CHING E4 44 B6
Forster Rd BECK BR3 166 B2
BRXS/STRHM SW2 129 K6
TOTM N17 56 B2
WALTH E17 57 G5
Forsters Cl CHDH RM6 62 B5
Forston St IS N1 6 F5
Forsyte Crs NRWD SE19 150 A7
Forsyth Gdns WALW SE17 18 D9
Forsythia Cl IL IG1 78 B4
Forsyth Pl EN EN1 30 A4
Forterie Gdns GDMY/SEVK IG3 79 G2
Fortescue Av WHTN TW2 142 C2
Fortescue Rd EDGW HA8 37 F7
WIM/MER SW19 147 H6
Fortess Gv KTTN NW5 72 C4
Fortess Rd KTTN NW5 72 B4
Fortess Wk KTTN NW5 72 B4
Forthbridge Rd BTSEA SW11 129 F3
Fortis Cl CAN/RD E16 95 G5
Fortis Gn EFNCH N2 53 K2
Fortis Green Av EFNCH N2 54 A2
Fortis Green Rd MUSWH N10 54 A2
Fortismere Av MUSWH N10 54 A2
Fortnam Rd ARCH N19 72 D1
Fortnums Acre STAN HA7 35 F5
Fort Rd NTHLT UB5 66 A6
STHWK SE1 19 M6
Fortrose Cl POP/IOD E14 94 B5
Fortrose Gdns
BRXS/STRHM SW2 129 K7
Fort St CAN/RD E16 95 F7
WCHPL E1 * 13 K3
Fortuna Cl HOLWY N7 * 73 F5
Fortune Av EDGW HA8 36 D7
Fortunegate Rd WLSDN NW10 69 G7
Fortune Green Rd
KIL/WHAMP NW6 70 E4
Fortune La BORE WD6 23 K5
Fortune Pl STHWK SE1 19 M8
Fortunes Md NTHLT UB5 65 J5
Fortune St STLK EC1Y 12 F1
Fortune Wy WLSDN NW10 87 J2
Forty Acre La CAN/RD E16 94 E4
Forty Av WBLY HA9 68 B2
Forty Cl WBLY HA9 68 B2
Forty La WBLY HA9 68 D1
Forum Cl BOW E3 75 J7
Forum Magnum Sq
STHWK SE1 17 L1
Forumside EDGW HA8 36 C5
The Forum E/WMO/HCT KT8 157 G3
Forval Cl MTCM CR4 162 E4
Forward Dr
KTN/HRWW/WS HA3 49 F3
Fosbury Ms BAY/PAD W2 8 D7
Foscote Ms MV/WKIL W9 8 B1
Foscote Rd HDN NW4 51 K5
Foskett Rd FUL/PGN SW6 127 J1
Foss Av CROY/NA CR0 177 G4
Fossdene Rd CHARL SE7 114 A4
Fossdyke Cl YEAD UB4 83 J4
Fosse Wy WEA W13 85 G4
Fossil Rd LEW SE13 132 D2
Fossington Rd BELV DA17 116 E3
Foss Rd TOOT SW17 147 H3
Fossway BCTR RM8 79 J1
Foster La CITYW EC2V 12 E4
Foster Rd ACT W3 87 G6
CHSWK W4 106 A4
PLSTW E13 94 E3
Fosters Cl CHST BR7 153 K4
SWFD E18 45 F7
Foster St HDN NW4 52 A3
Foster Wk HDN NW4 52 A3
Fothergill Cl PLSTW E13 76 E7
Fothergill Dr WCHMH N21 28 E4
Fotheringham Rd EN EN1 30 B3
Foubert's Pl SOHO/CST W1F 10 E5
Foulden Rd STNW/STAM N16 74 B3
Foulden Ter STNW/STAM N16 74 B3
Foulis Ter SKENS SW7 15 G6
Foulser Rd TOOT SW17 147 K2
Foulsham Rd THHTH CR7 164 D2
Foundation Pl
ELTH/MOT SE9 * 135 F4
Founder Cl EHAM E6 96 B5
Founders Cl NTHLT UB5 83 K2
Founders Gdns NRWD SE19 149 J6
Foundry Cl BERM/RHTH SE16 93 G7
Foundry Ms CAMTN NW1 4 F9
HSLW TW3 123 G3
Foundry Pl
WAND/EARL SW18 * 128 A6
Fountain Cl UX/CGN UB8 82 A4
Fountain Dr CAR SM5 175 K6
NRWD SE19 150 B3
Fountain Green Sq
BERM/RHTH SE16 111 H1
Fountain Ms HAMP NW3 71 K5
Fountain Pl BRXN/ST SW9 110 B7
Fountain Rd THHTH CR7 164 D1
TOOT SW17 147 H4
Fountains Av FELT TW13 141 K2
Fountains Cl FELT TW13 141 K1
Fountains Crs
STHGT/OAK N14 28 E6
Fountayne Rd
SEVS/STOTM N15 56 C3
STNW/STAM N16 74 C1
Fount St VX/NE SW8 109 J6
Fourland Wk EDGW HA8 36 E5
Fournier St WCHPL E1 13 L2
Four Seasons Cl BOW E3 93 J1
Four Seasons Crs CHEAM SM3 174 D1
Fourth Av HYS/HAR UB3 82 D7
MNPK E12 77 K3
NKENS W10 88 C3
ROMW/RG RM7 62 E7
Fourth Cross Rd WHTN TW2 142 D1
Fourth Wy WBLY HA9 68 D3
The Four Tubs BUSH WD23 22 D6
The Four Wents CHING E4 44 B1
Fowey Av REDBR IG4 59 H4
Fowey Cl WAP E1W 92 D7
Fowler Cl BTSEA SW11 128 C2
Fowler Rd FSTGT E7 76 E3
IS N1 6 D3
Fowler's Wk EA W5 85 K3
Fownes St BTSEA SW11 128 D2
Foxberry Rd BROCKY SE4 132 B3
Foxborough Gdns
BROCKY SE4 132 D5
Foxbourne Rd TOOT SW17 148 A1
Foxbury Av CHST BR7 154 D5
Foxbury Cl BMLY BR1 153 F5
Foxbury Rd BMLY BR1 153 F5
Fox Cl BORE WD6 23 K5
BUSH WD23 22 B4
CAN/RD E16 94 E4
WCHPL E1 92 E3
Foxcombe CROY/NA CR0 179 K5
Foxcroft Rd
WOOL/PLUM SE18 115 G7
Foxdell NTHWD HA6 32 B5
Foxdene Cl SWFD E18 59 F2
Foxearth Sp SAND/SEL CR2 178 E7
Foxes Dl BKHTH/KID SE3 133 K2
HAYES BR2 167 G2
Foxfield Cl NTHWD HA6 32 D5
Foxglove Cl BFN/LL DA15 136 B5
ED N9 30 E7
STHL UB1 83 J6
STWL/WRAY TW19 120 A7
Foxglove Gdns WAN E11 59 G3
Foxglove La CHSGTN KT9 172 C3
Foxglove Pth THMD SE28 115 K1
Foxglove Rd ROMW/RG RM7 81 G1
Foxglove St ACT W3 87 H6
Foxglove Wy WLGTN SM6 163 F6
Foxgrove STHGT/OAK N14 40 E2
Fox Gv WOT/HER KT12 156 A6
Foxgrove Av BECK BR3 151 K6
Foxgrove Pth OXHEY WD19 33 H4
Foxgrove Rd BECK BR3 151 K6
Foxham Rd ARCH N19 72 D2
Fox Hl HAYES BR2 181 G4
NRWD SE19 150 B6
Fox Hill Gdns NRWD SE19 150 B6
Foxhole Rd ELTH/MOT SE9 134 D4
Fox Hollow Cl
WOOL/PLUM SE18 115 K4
Fox Hollow Dr BXLYHN DA7 136 E2
Foxholt Gdns WLSDN NW10 68 E6
Foxhome Cl CHST BR7 154 A5
Fox House Rd BELV DA17 117 J3
Fox & Knot St FARR EC1M * 12 D2
Foxlands Crs DAGE RM10 80 E4
Foxlands Rd DAGE RM10 80 E4
Fox La EA W5 86 A4
HAYES BR2 181 F4
PLMGR N13 41 F2
Foxlees ALP/SUD HA0 67 G3
Foxley Cl HACK E8 74 C4
Foxley Rd CMBW SE5 110 B6
THHTH CR7 164 C3
Foxleys OXHEY WD19 33 J2
Foxley Sq BRXN/ST SW9 * 110 C6
Foxmead Cl ENC/FH EN2 29 F2
Foxmore St BTSEA SW11 108 E7
Fox Rd CAN/RD E16 94 D4
Foxton Gv MTCM CR4 162 C1
Foxwarren ESH/CLAY KT10 171 F7
Foxwell St BROCKY SE4 132 B2
Foxwood Cl FELT TW13 141 F2
MLHL NW7 37 G3
Foxwood Green Cl EN EN1 30 A5
Foxwood Rd BKHTH/KID SE3 133 J3
Foyle Rd BKHTH/KID SE3 113 J5
TOTM N17 42 C7
Framfield Cl
NFNCH/WDSPK N12 38 E3
Framfield Rd HBRY N5 73 H4
HNWL W7 85 F5
MTCM CR4 148 A6
Framlingham Crs
ELTH/MOT SE9 153 J3
Frampton Cl BELMT SM2 174 E6
Frampton Park Rd HOM E9 74 E5
Frampton Rd HSLWW TW4 122 D4
Frampton St STJWD NW8 9 H1
Francemary Rd LEW SE13 132 D4
Frances Rd CHING E4 43 J5
Frances St WOOL/PLUM SE18 114 E3
Franche Court Rd TOOT SW17 147 G2
Francis Av BXLYHN DA7 137 H1
FELT TW13 140 E2
IL IG1 78 D1
Francis Barber Cl
STRHM/NOR SW16 * 149 F3
Francis Bentley Ms CLAP SW4 129 H2
Franciscan Rd TOOT SW17 148 A3
Francis Chichester Wy
BTSEA SW11 * 109 F7
Francis Cl HOR/WEW KT19 173 F3
Francis Gv WIM/MER SW19 146 D6
Francis Ms LEE/GVPK SE12 * 133 J5
Francis Rd CROY/NA CR0 164 C6
DART DA1 139 G4
EFNCH N2 * 53 K3
GFD/PVL UB6 85 J1
HRW HA1 49 G4
HSLWW TW4 122 C1
LEY E10 76 A1
PIN HA5 47 G4
WATW WD18 21 F3
WLGTN SM6 176 C5
Francis St SRTFD E15 76 C4
WEST SW1P 16 F5
Francis Ter ARCH N19 72 C2
Francis Wk IS N1 5 L3
Francklyn Gdns EDGW HA8 36 C2
Francombe Gdns ROM RM1 63 J5
Franconia Rd CLAP SW4 129 H4
Frank Burton Cl CHARL SE7 114 A4
Frank Dixon Cl DUL SE21 131 F6
Frank Dixon Wy DUL SE21 131 F7
Frankfurt Rd HNHL SE24 130 D4
Frankham St DEPT SE8 112 D6
Frankland Cl
BERM/RHTH SE16 111 J2
WFD IG8 45 G4
Frankland Rd CHING E4 43 J4
SKENS SW7 15 G4
Franklin Av WATW WD18 20 E5
Franklin Cl KUT/HW KT1 159 H2
LEW SE13 112 E7
TRDG/WHET N20 27 G6
WNWD SE27 149 H2
Franklin Crs MTCM CR4 163 H3
Franklin Pl GNWCH SE10 112 E7
Franklin Rd BXLYHN DA7 117 F7
PGE/AN SE20 150 E6
WAT WD17 21 F1
Franklins Ms
RYLN/HDSTN HA2 66 C1
Franklin Sq WKENS W14 107 J4
Franklins Rw CHEL SW3 * 15 M7
Franklin's Rw CHEL SW3 15 M7
Franklin St BOW E3 93 K2
SEVS/STOTM N15 56 A5
Franklin Wy CROY/NA CR0 163 K7
Franklyn Rd WLSDN NW10 69 H6
WOT/HER KT12 156 A5
Frank Ms STHWK SE1 111 J3
Franks Av NWMAL KT3 159 K3
Franks Wood Av
STMC/STPC BR5 169 G4
Franlaw Crs PLMGR N13 41 J3
Franmil Rd HCH RM12 63 H6
Fransfield Gv SYD SE26 150 D2
Franshams BUSH WD23 * 34 E1
Frant Cl PGE/AN SE20 150 E6
Frant Rd THHTH CR7 164 C4
Fraser Cl BXLY DA5 137 K7
EHAM E6 95 J5
Fraser Rd ED N9 42 D2
ERITH DA8 117 K4
GFD/PVL UB6 67 J7
WALTH E17 57 K4
Fraser St CHSWK W4 106 B4
Frating Crs WFD IG8 44 E5
Frays Av WDR/YW UB7 100 A1
Frays Cl WDR/YW UB7 100 A2
Frazer Av RSLP HA4 65 G4
Frazer Cl ROM RM1 63 H6
Frazier St STHWK SE1 18 A2
Frean St BERM/RHTH SE16 111 H2
Freda Corbett Cl PECK SE15 111 H6
Frederica St HOLWY N7 5 L1
Frederick Cl BAY/PAD W2 9 K6
SUT SM1 174 D3
Frederick Crs BRXN/ST SW9 110 C6
PEND EN3 30 E1
Frederick Gdns CROY/NA CR0 164 C5
SUT SM1 174 D4
Frederick Pl
WOOL/PLUM SE18 115 G4
Frederick Rd RAIN RM13 99 F1
SUT SM1 174 D4
WALW SE17 * 18 D8
Frederick's Pl LOTH EC2R * 13 G5
NFNCH/WDSPK N12 39 G3
Frederick Sq
BERM/RHTH SE16 93 G6
Frederick's Rw FSBYE EC1V 6 C7
Frederick St FSBYW WC1X 5 L8
Frederick Ter HACK E8 7 L3
Frederic Ms KTBR SW1X * 16 A2
Frederic St WALTH E17 57 G4
Fredora Av YEAD UB4 82 D3
Freeborne Gdns RAIN RM13 81 J5
Freedom Cl WALTH E17 57 F3
Freedom Rd TOTM N17 55 K1
Freedom St BTSEA SW11 128 E1
Freegrove Rd HOLWY N7 72 E4
Freeland Pk HDN NW4 52 C1
Freeland Rd EA W5 86 B6
Freelands Av SAND/SEL CR2 179 F7
Freelands Gv BMLY BR1 153 F7
Freelands Rd BMLY BR1 153 F7
Freeland Wy ERITH DA8 118 D7
Freeling St IS N1 * 5 L2
Freeman Cl NTHLT UB5 65 J6
Freeman Dr E/WMO/HCT KT8 156 E3
Freeman Rd MRDN SM4 162 C4
Freemans La HYS/HAR UB3 82 C6
Freemantle Av PEND EN3 31 F4
Freemantle St WALW SE17 19 J7
Freeman Wk ELTH/MOT SE9 134 B4
Freemasons Rd CAN/RD E16 95 F4
Freemason's Rd
CROY/NA CR0 165 F7
Freethorpe Cl NRWD SE19 150 A7
Freight La KCROSS N1C 5 H2
Freightmaster Est
RAIN RM13 * 118 D3
Freke Rd BTSEA SW11 129 F2
Fremantle Rd BARK/HLT IG6 60 B1
BELV DA17 117 H3
Fremont St HOM E9 74 D7
French Pl SDTCH EC2A 7 K8
French St SUN TW16 156 B1
Frendsbury Rd BROCKY SE4 132 B3
Frensham Cl STHL UB1 83 K3
Frensham Dr CROY/NA CR0 180 A6
PUT/ROE SW15 145 J1
Frensham Rd ELTH/MOT SE9 154 D1
Frensham St PECK SE15 111 H5
Frere St BTSEA SW11 128 D1
Freshfield Av HACK E8 7 L1
Freshfield Cl LEW SE13 133 G3
Freshfield Dr STHGT/OAK N14 28 B6
Freshfields CROY/NA CR0 166 C6
Freshford St TOOT SW17 147 G2
Fresh Mill La STHL UB1 84 A3
Freshwater Cl TOOT SW17 148 A5
Freshwater Rd BCTR RM8 61 K7
TOOT SW17 148 A5
Freshwell Av CHDH RM6 61 J3
Fresh Wharf Rd BARK IG11 78 B7
Freshwood Cl BECK BR3 151 K7
Freshwood Wy WLGTN SM6 176 C7
Freston Gdns EBAR EN4 28 A4
Freston Pk FNCH N3 52 D1
Freston Rd NKENS W10 88 B6
Freta Rd BXLYHS DA6 137 G4
Frewin Rd WAND/EARL SW18 128 C7
Friar Ms WNWD SE27 149 H2
Friar Rd YEAD UB4 83 H3
Friars Av PUT/ROE SW15 127 H4
TRDG/WHET N20 39 J2
Friars Cl CHING E4 44 A2
IL IG1 60 D7
NTHLT UB5 83 G2
STHWK SE1 * 12 D8
Friars Gdns ACT W3 87 F5
Friars Gate Cl WFD IG8 44 E3
Friars La RCH/KEW TW9 124 E4
Friars Md POP/IOD E14 113 F2
Friars Ms ELTH/MOT SE9 135 F4
Friars Place La ACT W3 87 F6
Friar's Rd EHAM E6 77 H7
Friars Stile Rd
RCHPK/HAM TW10 125 F5
Friars Wk ABYW SE2 116 E4
STHGT/OAK N14 28 B7
Friars Wy ACT W3 87 F5
Friars Wd CROY/NA CR0 179 G7
Friary Cl NFNCH/WDSPK N12 39 J4
Friary Est PECK SE15 * 111 H6
Friary La WFD IG8 44 E3
Friary Pk
NFNCH/WDSPK N12 * 39 J3
Friary Park Ct ACT W3 * 86 E5
Friary Rd ACT W3 86 E5
NFNCH/WDSPK N12 39 H3
PECK SE15 111 H6
Friary Wy NFNCH/WDSPK N12 39 J3
Friday Hl CHING E4 44 C2
Friday Hl East CHING E4 44 C2
Friday Hl West CHING E4 44 C1
Friday Rd ERITH DA8 118 A4
MTCM CR4 147 K6
Friday St STP EC4M 12 E6
Frideswide Pl KTTN NW5 72 C4
Friendly Pl LEW SE13 112 E7
Friendly St DEPT SE8 112 D7
Friendly Street Ms DEPT SE8 132 D1
Friendship Wy SRTFD E15 * 76 A7
Friends' Rd CROY/NA CR0 177 K2
Friend St FSBYE EC1V 6 C7
Friern Barnet La
TRDG/WHET N20 39 H2
Friern Barnet Rd
FBAR/BDGN N11 40 A4
Friern Mount Dr
TRDG/WHET N20 27 G6
Friern Pk NFNCH/WDSPK N12 39 H4
Friern Rd EDUL SE22 131 H5
Friern Watch Av
NFNCH/WDSPK N12 39 H3
Frigate Ms DEPT SE8 112 D5
Frimley Av WLGTN SM6 176 E4
Frimley Cl CROY/NA CR0 180 A6
WIM/MER SW19 146 C1
Frimley Ct SCUP DA14 155 J4
Frimley Crs CROY/NA CR0 180 A6
Frimley Gdns MTCM CR4 162 D2
Frimley Rd CHSGTN KT9 171 K4
GDMY/SEVK IG3 78 E2
Frimley Wy WCHPL E1 * 93 F3
Frinsted Rd ERITH DA8 118 A6
Frinton Cl OXHEY WD19 33 F1
Frinton Dr WFD IG8 44 B6
Frinton Ms GNTH/NBYPK IG2 60 A5
Frinton Rd EHAM E6 95 H2
SEVS/STOTM N15 56 A5
TOOT SW17 148 A5
Friston St FUL/PGN SW6 128 A1
Friswell Pl BXLYHN DA7 137 H3
Fritham Cl NWMAL KT3 160 B5
Frith Ct MLHL NW7 38 C6
Frith La MLHL NW7 38 C5
Frith Manor Farm Cots
MLHL NW7 * 38 C4
Frith Rd CROY/NA CR0 177 J1
WAN E11 76 A3
Frith St SOHO/SHAV W1D 11 G5
Frithville Gdns SHB W12 88 A7
Frithwood Av NTHWD HA6 32 D5
Frizlands La DAGE RM10 80 D2
Frobisher Cl BUSH WD23 22 A5
PIN HA5 47 H6
Frobisher Crs BARB EC2Y * 12 F2
STWL/WRAY TW19 120 B6
Frobisher Gdns LEY E10 * 57 K5
Frobisher Ms ENC/FH EN2 29 K3
Frobisher Rd CEND/HSY/T N8 55 G3
EHAM E6 95 K5
ERITH DA8 118 D6
Frog La RAIN RM13 99 F4
Frogley Rd EDUL SE22 131 G3
Frogmore WAND/EARL SW18 127 K4
Frogmore Av YEAD UB4 82 C3
Frogmore Cl CHEAM SM3 174 B2
Frogmore Est HBRY N5 * 73 J3
Frogmore Gdns CHEAM SM3 174 C3
YEAD UB4 82 C3
Frognal HAMP NW3 71 G4
Frognal Av HRW HA1 49 F3
SCUP DA14 155 G5
Frognal Cl HAMP NW3 71 G4
Frognal Gdns HAMP NW3 71 G3
Frognal La HAMP NW3 71 F4
Frognal Man HAMP NW3 * 71 G3
Frognal Pde HAMP NW3 71 G5
Frognal Pl SCUP DA14 155 G5
Frognal Ri HAMP NW3 71 G3
Frognal Wy HAMP NW3 71 G3
Frogwell Cl FSBYPK N4 55 K5
Froissart Rd ELTH/MOT SE9 134 D4
Frome Rd SEVS/STOTM N15 55 H2
Frome St IS N1 6 E5
Fromondes Rd CHEAM SM3 174 C4
Fromows Cnr CHSWK W4 * 105 K4
Frostic Wk WCHPL E1 13 M3
Froude St VX/NE SW8 129 G1
Fruen Rd EBED/NFELT TW14 121 J6
Fryatt Rd TOTM N17 41 K6
Fryday Grove Ms BAL SW12 129 H6
Fryent Cl KTN/HRWW/WS HA3 50 C5
Fryent Crs CDALE/KGS NW9 51 G5
Fryent Flds CDALE/KGS NW9 51 G5
Fryent Gv CDALE/KGS NW9 51 G5
Fryent Wy CDALE/KGS NW9 50 C4
Frying Pan Aly WCHPL E1 13 K3
Fry Rd EHAM E6 77 H6
WLSDN NW10 69 H7
Fryston Av CROY/NA CR0 178 C1
Fuchsia Cl ROMW/RG RM7 81 G1
Fuchsia St ABYW SE2 116 C4
Fulbeck Dr CDALE/KGS NW9 37 G7
Fulbeck Wy RYLN/HDSTN HA2 48 C1
Fulbourne Rd WALTH E17 44 A7
Fulbourne St WCHPL E1 92 D4
Fulbrook Ms ARCH N19 72 C3
Fulbrook Rd ARCH N19 72 C3
Fulford Gv OXHEY WD19 33 F1
Fulford Rd HOR/WEW KT19 173 F6
Fulford St BERM/RHTH SE16 111 J1
Fulham Broadway
FUL/PGN SW6 107 K6
Fulham Cl HGDN/ICK UB10 82 A3
Fulham High St FUL/PGN SW6 127 H1
Fulham Palace Rd
FUL/PGN SW6 107 G6
Fulham Park Gdns
FUL/PGN SW6 127 J1
Fulham Park Rd
FUL/PGN SW6 127 J1
Fulham Rd FUL/PGN SW6 108 A6
WBPTN SW10 14 F9
Fullbrooks Av WPK KT4 160 C7
Fuller Cl BETH E2 * 92 C3
BUSH WD23 22 D6
Fullerian Crs WATW WD18 20 D3
Fuller Rd BCTR RM8 79 J2
Fullers Av SURB KT6 172 B1
Fuller's Av SWFD E18 44 D6
Fuller's Rd SWFD E18 44 D7
Fuller St HDN NW4 52 A3
Fullers Wy North SURB KT6 172 B2
Fullers Wy South CHSGTN KT9 172 A3
Fuller's Wd CROY/NA CR0 179 J4
Fullerton Rd CAR SM5 175 J7
CROY/NA CR0 165 G6
WAND/EARL SW18 128 B4
Fuller Wy HYS/HAR UB3 101 J4
Fullwood's Ms IS N1 7 H7
Fulmar Ct BRYLDS KT5 159 G5
Fulmar Rd HCH RM12 81 J6
Fulmead St FUL/PGN SW6 108 A7
Fulmer Cl HPTN TW12 141 J4
Fulmer Rd CAN/RD E16 95 H4
Fulmer Wy WEA W13 104 C2
Fulready Rd LEY E10 58 B4
Fulstone Cl HSLWW TW4 122 E3
Fulthorp Rd BKHTH/KID SE3 133 J1
Fulton Ms BAY/PAD W2 8 E6
Fulton Rd WBLY HA9 68 C2
Fulwell Park Av WHTN TW2 142 C1
Fulwell Rd TEDD TW11 142 D3
Fulwich Rd DART DA1 139 J5
Fulwood Av ALP/SUD HA0 86 B1
Fulwood Gdns TWK TW1 124 A5
Fulwood Wk WIM/MER SW19 127 H7
Furber St HMSMTH W6 106 E2
Furham Fld PIN HA5 34 A6
Furley Rd PECK SE15 111 H6
Furlong Cl WLGTN SM6 163 G7
Furlong Rd HOLWY N7 73 G5
The Furlongs ESH/CLAY KT10 170 A2
Furmage St WAND/EARL SW18 128 A6
Furneaux Av WNWD SE27 149 H4
Furner Cl DART DA1 138 C2
Furness Rd FUL/PGN SW6 128 A1
MRDN SM4 162 A5
RYLN/HDSTN HA2 48 B6
WLSDN NW10 87 J1
Furness Wy HCH RM12 81 J4
Furnival St FLST/FETLN EC4A 12 A4
Furrow La HOM E9 74 E4
Fursby Av FNCH N3 38 E5
Further Acre CDALE/KGS NW9 51 H1
Furtherfield Cl CROY/NA CR0 164 B5
Further Green Rd CAT SE6 133 H6
Furze Cl OXHEY WD19 33 G4
Furzedown Dr TOOT SW17 148 B4
Furzedown Rd TOOT SW17 148 B4
Furze Farm Cl CHDH RM6 62 A1
Furzefield Cl CHST BR7 154 B5
Furzefield Rd BKHTH/KID SE3 114 A5
Furzeground Wy STKPK UB11 82 A7

Furzeham Rd WDR/YW UB7 100 B1
Furzehill Pde BORE WD6 * 24 C3
Furzehill Rd BORE WD6 24 D3
Furze Rd THHTH CR7 164 D2
Furze St BOW E3 * 93 J4
Furzewood SUN TW16 140 E7
Fye Foot La BLKFR EC4V 12 E6
Fyfe Wy BMLY BR1 167 K1
Fyfield Cl HAYES BR2 167 G3
Fyfield Rd BRXN/ST SW9 130 B2
EN EN1 30 A2
RAIN RM13 81 H7
WALTH E17 58 B2
WFD IG8 45 G6
Fynes St WEST SW1P 17 G5

G

Gable Cl DART DA1 138 D4
PIN HA5 34 A6
Gable Ct SYD SE26 150 D3
Gable Ms HAYES BR2 181 J1
Gables Av BORE WD6 24 B2
Gables Cl CMBW SE5 111 F7
LEE/GVPK SE12 133 K7
The Gables NRWD SE19 * 150 A7
WBLY HA9 68 B2
Gabriel Cl FELT TW13 141 J3
Gabrielle Cl WBLY HA9 68 B2
Gabriel St FSTH SE23 132 A6
Gabriel's Whf STHWK SE1 12 A8
Gad Cl PLSTW E13 95 F2
Gaddesden Av WBLY HA9 68 B5
Gade Av WATW WD18 20 C3
Gade Bank RKW/CH/CXG WD3 20 B3
Gade Cl HYS/HAR UB3 83 F7
WATW WD18 20 C3
Gadesden Rd HOR/WEW KT19 172 E5
Gadsbury Cl CDALE/KGS NW9 51 H5
Gadwall Cl CAN/RD E16 95 F5
Gage Rd CAN/RD E16 94 C4
Gage St BMSBY WC1N 11 K2
Gainford St IS N1 6 A3
Gainsboro Gdns GFD/PVL UB6 66 E4
Gainsborough Av DART DA1 139 F4
MNPK E12 78 A4
Gainsborough Cl BECK BR3 151 J6
ESH/CLAY KT10 * 157 J7
Gainsborough Ct SHB W12 107 F1
Gainsborough Gdns
EDGW HA8 50 B1
GLDGN NW11 52 D6
HAMP NW3 71 H2
HSLW TW3 123 J4
Gainsborough Ms DUL SE21 130 D7
SYD SE26 * 150 D2
Gainsborough Rd BCTR RM8 79 H3
CHSWK W4 106 C3
NFNCH/WDSPK N12 39 F4
NWMAL KT3 160 A5
RAIN RM13 81 J7
RCH/KEW TW9 125 G1
SRTFD E15 94 C2
WAN E11 58 C6
WFD IG8 45 J5
YEAD UB4 82 A1
Gainsborough Sq BXLYHS DA6 136 E2
Gainsborough St HOM E9 75 H5
Gainsborough Ter
BELMT SM2 * 174 D6
Gainsford Rd WALTH E17 57 H3
Gainsford St STHWK SE1 13 L9
Gairloch Rd CMBW SE5 131 F1
Gaisford St KTTN NW5 72 C5
Gaitskell Rd ELTH/MOT SE9 135 H7
Gaitskell Wy STHWK SE1 18 E1
Galahad Rd BMLY BR1 152 E2
ED N9 42 C1
Galata Rd BARN SW13 106 D6
Galatea Sq PECK SE15 131 J2
Galbraith St POP/IOD E14 113 F2
Galdana Av BAR EN5 27 G2
Galeborough Av WFD IG8 44 B6
Gale Cl HPTN TW12 141 J5
MTCM CR4 162 C2
Galena Rd HMSMTH W6 106 E3
Galesbury Rd
WAND/EARL SW18 128 B5
Gales Gdns BETH E2 92 D2
Gale St BOW E3 93 J4
DAGW RM9 79 K6
Gales Wy WFD IG8 45 J6
Galgate Cl WIM/MER SW19 127 G7
Gallants Farm Rd EBAR EN4 27 J6
Galleon Cl BERM/RHTH SE16 111 K1
ERITH DA8 118 A3
Galleons Dr BARK IG11 97 G2
The Galleries IS N1 * 6 C5
Gallery Gdns NTHLT UB5 83 H1
Gallery Rd DUL SE21 130 E7
Galley La BAR EN5 25 K2
Galleywall Rd
BERM/RHTH SE16 111 J3
Galliard Rd ED N9 30 C6
Gallia Rd HBRY N5 73 H4
Gallions Cl BARK IG11 97 G2
Gallions Rd CAN/RD E16 96 B6
CHARL SE7 114 A3
Gallions View Rd THMD SE28 115 K1
Gallon Cl CHARL SE7 114 B3
The Gallops ESH/CLAY KT10 170 B2
The Gallop BELMT SM2 175 H7
SAND/SEL CR2 178 D6
Gallosson Rd
WOOL/PLUM SE18 115 K3
Galloway Dr DART DA1 138 B6
Galloway Pth CROY/NA CR0 177 K3
Galloway Rd SHB W12 87 J7
Gallus Cl WCHMH N21 29 F5
Gallus Sq BKHTH/KID SE3 134 A2
Galpin's Rd THHTH CR7 163 K3
Galsworthy Av CHDH RM6 61 H6
POP/IOD E14 93 G4
Galsworthy Cl THMD SE28 97 H7
Galsworthy Crs
BKHTH/KID SE3 114 B7
Galsworthy Rd CRICK NW2 70 C3
KUTN/CMB KT2 144 D7
Galton St NKENS W10 88 C3
Galva Cl EBAR EN4 28 A3
Galveston Rd PUT/ROE SW15 127 J4
Galway Cl BERM/RHTH SE16 * 111 J4
Galway St FSBYE EC1V 6 F8
Gambetta St VX/NE SW8 129 G1
Gambia St STHWK SE1 12 D9
Gambole Rd TOOT SW17 147 J3
Games Rd EBAR EN4 27 J2
Gamlen Rd PUT/ROE SW15 127 G3
Gamuel Cl WALTH E17 57 J5
Gander Green Crs HPTN TW12 142 A7
Gander Green La CHEAM SM3 174 C1
SUT SM1 174 D5
Gandhi Cl WALTH E17 57 J5
Gandhi Ct WATN WD24 21 H1
Gandolfi St CMBW SE5 111 F5
Ganton St REGST W1B 10 E6
Ganton Wk OXHEY WD19 * 33 J3
Gantshill Crs GNTH/NBYPK IG2 60 A4
Gap Rd WIM/MER SW19 146 E4
Garage Rd ACT W3 86 C5
Garbrand Wk EW KT17 173 H7
Garbutt Pl MHST W1U * 10 B2
Garden Av BXLYHN DA7 137 G2
MTCM CR4 148 B6
Garden City EDGW HA8 36 C5
Garden Cl ASHF TW15 140 A5
BAR EN5 26 A3
CHING E4 43 J4
HPTN TW12 141 K4
LEE/GVPK SE12 153 F2
NTHLT UB5 65 J7
PUT/ROE SW15 126 E6
RSLP HA4 64 C1
WAT WD17 20 D1
WLGTN SM6 176 E4
Garden Ct CHSWK W4 105 K2
EMB EC4Y * 12 A6
HPTN TW12 141 K4
Gardeners Rd CROY/NA CR0 164 C7
Garden Flats HMSMTH W6 * 107 G5
Gardenia Rd BMLY BR1 169 F2
EN EN1 30 A5
Gardenia Wy WFD IG8 44 E5
Garden La BMLY BR1 153 F5
BRXS/STRHM SW2 130 A7
Garden Lodge Ct EFNCH N2 * 53 H2
Garden Pl HACK E8 7 L3
Garden Rd BMLY BR1 153 F6
PGE/AN SE20 150 E7
RCH/KEW TW9 125 H2
STJWD NW8 2 F7
WOT/HER KT12 156 A5
Garden Rw STHWK SE1 18 C4
The Gardens BECK BR3 167 F1
CEND/HSY/T N8 * 54 E3
CLPT E5 * 56 B6
EBED/NFELT TW14 121 G5
EDUL SE22 131 H3
ESH/CLAY KT10 170 A3
HRW HA1 48 C5
PIN HA5 * 47 K5
WAT WD17 20 D1
Garden St WCHPL E1 93 F4
Garden Studios BAY/PAD W2 * 8 E3
Gardens Wy MNPK E12 77 J2
Garden Ter PIM SW1V 17 G7
Garden Vls ESH/CLAY KT10 * 171 F6
Garden Wk BECK BR3 151 H7
SDTCH EC2A 7 J9
Garden Wy WLSDN NW10 68 E5
Gardiner Av CRICK NW2 * 70 A4
Gardiner Cl BCTR RM8 79 K3
PEND EN3 31 F5
Gardiner House CHARL SE7 * 114 D6
Gardner Cl WAN E11 59 F5
Gardner Pl EBED/NFELT TW14 122 A5
Gardner Rd PLSTW E13 95 F3
Gardners Cl FBAR/BDGN N11 40 A1
Gardners La BLKFR EC4V 12 E6
Gardnor Rd HAMP NW3 71 H3
Gard St FSBYE EC1V 6 D7
Garendon Gdns MRDN SM4 162 A6
Garendon Rd MRDN SM4 162 A6
Gareth Cl WPK KT4 174 B1
Gareth Dr ED N9 42 C1
Gareth Gv BMLY BR1 152 E3
Garfield Ms BTSEA SW11 129 G2
Garfield Rd BTSEA SW11 129 F2
PEND EN3 30 E3
PLSTW E13 94 D3
TWK TW1 124 B7
WIM/MER SW19 147 G5
Garford St POP/IOD E14 93 J6
Garganey Wk THMD SE28 97 J6
Garibaldi St WOOL/PLUM SE18 115 K3
Garland Dr HSLW TW3 123 H1
Garland Rd STAN HA7 35 K7
WOOL/PLUM SE18 115 J6
Garlick Hl BLKFR EC4V 12 F6
Garlies Rd FSTH SE23 151 G2
Garlinge Rd CRICK NW2 70 D5
Garman Cl UED N18 41 K4
Garman Rd TOTM N17 42 E6
Garnault Ms CLKNW EC1R 6 B8
Garnault Pl CLKNW EC1R 6 B8
Garner Cl BCTR RM8 61 K7
Garner Rd WALTH E17 44 A7
Garner St BETH E2 92 C1
Garnet Rd THHTH CR7 164 D3
WLSDN NW10 69 G5
Garnet St WAP E1W 92 E6
Garnett Cl ELTH/MOT SE9 134 E2
Garnett Rd HAMP NW3 71 K4
Garnham St STNW/STAM N16 74 B1
Garnies Cl PECK SE15 111 G6
Garrad's Rd
STRHM/NOR SW16 148 D2
Garrard Cl BXLYHN DA7 137 H2
CHST BR7 154 B4
Garrard Wk WLSDN NW10 * 69 G5
Garratt Cl CROY/NA CR0 176 E3
Garratt La TOOT SW17 147 G2
WAND/EARL SW18 128 A6
Garratt Rd EDGW HA8 36 C6
Garratts Rd BUSH WD23 22 C6
Garratt Ter TOOT SW17 147 J3
Garrett Cl ACT W3 87 F4
Garrett St STLK EC1Y 6 F9
Garrick Av GLDGN NW11 52 C5
Garrick Cl EA W5 86 A3
RCH/KEW TW9 124 D4
WAND/EARL SW18 128 B3
Garrick Crs CROY/NA CR0 178 A1
Garrick Dr HDN NW4 52 A1
THMD SE28 115 J2
Garrick Gdns E/WMO/HCT KT8 157 F2
Garrick Pk HDN NW4 52 B1
Garrick Rd CDALE/KGS NW9 51 H5
GFD/PVL UB6 84 B3
RCH/KEW TW9 125 H1
Garrick St COVGDN WC2E 11 J6
Garrick Wy HDN NW4 52 B3
Garrick Yd CHCR WC2N 11 J6
Garrison Cl HSLWW TW4 122 E4
WOOL/PLUM SE18 115 F6
Garrison La CHSGTN KT9 172 A6
Garrison Rd BOW E3 75 J7
Garsdale Ter WKENS W14 * 107 J4
Garside Cl HPTN TW12 142 B6
THMD SE28 115 J2
Garsington Ms BROCKY SE4 132 C2
Garter Wy BERM/RHTH SE16 112 A1
Garth Cl KUTN/CMB KT2 144 B4
MRDN SM4 161 G6
RSLP HA4 47 H7
Garthland Dr BAR EN5 25 K4
Garth Ms EA W5 * 86 A3
Garthorne Rd FSTH SE23 132 A6
Garth Rd CHSWK W4 106 A4
CRICK NW2 70 D1
KUTN/CMB KT2 144 B4
MRDN SM4 161 G7
Garthside KUTN/CMB KT2 144 A4
The Garth HPTN TW12 142 B5
KTN/HRWW/WS HA3 50 B5
NFNCH/WDSPK N12 * 39 F4
Garthway NFNCH/WDSPK N12 39 J5
Gartlet Rd WAT WD17 21 F2
Gartmoor Gdns
WIM/MER SW19 127 J7
Gartmore Rd GDMY/SEVK IG3 61 F7
Garton Pl WAND/EARL SW18 128 B5
Gartons Cl PEND EN3 30 E4
Gartons Wy BTSEA SW11 128 B2
Garvary Rd CAN/RD E16 95 F5
Garway Rd BAY/PAD W2 8 C5
Gascoigne Cl TOTM N17 42 B7
Gascoigne Gdns WFD IG8 44 C6
Gascoigne Pl BETH E2 7 L7
Gascoigne Rd BARK IG11 78 C7
Gascony Av KIL/WHAMP NW6 2 A2
Gascoyne Dr DART DA1 138 C2
Gascoyne Rd HOM E9 75 F6
Gaselee St POP/IOD E14 94 A6
Gasholder Pl LBTH SE11 17 M8
Gaskarth Rd BAL SW12 129 G5
EDGW HA8 36 E7
Gaskell Rd HGT N6 53 K5
Gaskell St CLAP SW4 129 K1
Gaskin St IS N1 6 C3
Gaspar Cl ECT SW5 * 14 D5
Gaspar Ms ECT SW5 14 D5
Gassiot Rd TOOT SW17 147 K3
Gassiot Wy SUT SM1 175 H2
Gastein Rd HMSMTH W6 107 G5
Gaston Bell Cl RCH/KEW TW9 125 G2
Gaston Rd MTCM CR4 163 F2
Gataker St BERM/RHTH SE16 111 J2
Gatcombe Ms EA W5 86 B6
Gatcombe Rd ARCH N19 72 D2
Gatcombe Wy EBAR EN4 27 K2
Gate Cots EDGW HA8 * 36 C1
Gate End NTHWD HA6 32 E6
Gateforth St STJWD NW8 9 J1
Gatehill Rd NTHWD HA6 32 D6
Gatehouse Cl KUTN/CMB KT2 144 E6
Gate House Pl WATW WD18 20 E2
Gatehouse Sq STHWK SE1 12 F8
Gateley Rd BRXN/ST SW9 130 A2
Gate Ms SKENS SW7 15 K2
Gates Green Rd WWKM BR4 180 E3
Gateshead Rd BORE WD6 24 B1
Gateside Rd TOOT SW17 147 K2
Gatestone Rd NRWD SE19 150 A5
Gate St LINN WC2A 11 L4
Gateway WALW SE17 18 F9
Gateway Ar IS N1 * 6 C5
Gateway Cl NTHWD HA6 32 A5
Gateway Gdns EHAM E6 95 K2
Gateway Ms FBAR/BDGN N11 40 C5
HACK E8 * 74 B4
The Gateways
RCH/KEW TW9 * 124 E3
The Gateway WATW WD18 20 C4
Gatfield Gv FELT TW13 142 A1
Gathorne Rd WDGN N22 55 G1
Gathorne St BETH E2 93 F1
Gatley Av HOR/WEW KT19 172 D4
Gatliff Rd BGVA SW1W 16 B8
Gatling Rd ABYW SE2 116 B4
Gatonby St PECK SE15 111 G7
Gatton Cl BELMT SM2 * 175 F7
Gatton Rd TOOT SW17 147 J3
Gatward Cl WCHMH N21 29 H5
Gatward Gn ED N9 42 A1
Gatwick Rd WAND/EARL SW18 127 J6
Gauden Cl CLAP SW4 129 J2
Gauden Rd CLAP SW4 129 J1
Gaumont Ap WAT WD17 21 F2
Gaumont Ter SHB W12 * 107 F1
Gauntlet Cl NTHLT UB5 65 J6
Gauntlett Ct ALP/SUD HA0 67 G4
Gauntlett Rd SUT SM1 175 H4
Gaunt St STHWK SE1 18 D3
Gautrey Rd PECK SE15 131 K1
Gavel St WALW SE17 * 19 H5
Gaverick St POP/IOD E14 112 D3
Gavestone Crs LEE/GVPK SE12 134 A6
Gavestone Rd LEE/GVPK SE12 134 A6
Gavina Cl MRDN SM4 162 D4
Gawain Wk ED N9 42 C2
Gawber St BETH E2 92 E2
Gawsworth Cl SRTFD E15 76 D4
Gawthorne Av MLHL NW7 38 C4
Gay Cl CRICK NW2 69 K4
Gaydon La CDALE/KGS NW9 37 G7
Gayfere Rd CLAY IG5 59 K2
EW KT17 173 J4
Gayfere St WEST SW1P 17 J4
Gayford Rd SHB W12 106 C1
Gay Gdns DAGE RM10 80 E3
Gayhurst Rd HACK E8 74 C6
Gaylor Rd NTHLT UB5 65 K4
Gaynesford Rd CAR SM5 175 K6
FSTH SE23 151 F1
Gaynes Hill Rd WFD IG8 45 J6
Gay Rd SRTFD E15 94 B1
Gaysham Av GNTH/NBYPK IG2 60 A4
Gayton Crs HAMP NW3 71 H3
Gayton Rd HAMP NW3 71 H3
HRW HA1 49 F5
Gayville Rd BTSEA SW11 128 E5
Gaywood Cl
BRXS/STRHM SW2 130 A7
Gaywood Rd WALTH E17 57 J2
Gaywood St STHWK SE1 18 D4
Gaza St WALW SE17 18 C8
Geariesville Gdns
BARK/HLT IG6 60 B3
Gearing Cl TOOT SW17 148 A3
Geary Rd WLSDN NW10 69 J4
Geary St HOLWY N7 73 F4
Geddes Pl BXLYHS DA6 137 H3
Geddes Rd BUSH WD23 * 22 C3
Gedeney Rd TOTM N17 41 J7
Gedling Pl STHWK SE1 19 L3
Geere Rd SRTFD E15 76 D7
Gees Ct MHST W1U 10 B5
Gee St FSBYE EC1V 6 E9
Geffrye Est IS N1 7 K6
Geffrye St BETH E2 7 L5
Geldart Rd PECK SE15 111 J6
Geldeston Rd CLPT E5 74 C1
Gellatly Rd NWCR SE14 131 K1
General Gordon Pl
WOOL/PLUM SE18 115 G2
General Wolfe Rd
GNWCH SE10 113 G7
Genesis Cl STWL/WRAY TW19 120 C7
Genesta Rd WOOL/PLUM SE18 115 G5
Geneva Dr BRXN/ST SW9 130 B3
Geneva Gdns CHDH RM6 62 A4
Geneva Rd KUT/HW KT1 159 F3
THHTH CR7 164 D4
Genever Cl CHING E4 43 J4
Genista Rd UED N18 42 D4
Genoa Av PUT/ROE SW15 127 F4
Genoa Rd PGE/AN SE20 150 E7
Genotin Rd EN EN1 29 K2
Gentleman's Rw ENC/FH EN2 29 J2
Geoffrey Cl CMBW SE5 130 D1
Geoffrey Gdns EHAM E6 95 J1
Geoffrey Rd BROCKY SE4 132 C2
George Beard Rd DEPT SE8 112 C3
George Cl WATW WD18 20 C3
George Crs MUSWH N10 40 A6
George Downing Est
STNW/STAM N16 74 B1
George Gange Wy
KTN/HRWW/WS HA3 48 E2
George Groves Rd
PGE/AN SE20 150 C7
George La HAYES BR2 168 A7
LEW SE13 133 F5
SWFD E18 58 E1
George Lowe Ct BAY/PAD W2 8 C2
George Mathers Rd
LBTH SE11 18 C6
George Ms BRXN/ST SW9 130 B1
CAMTN NW1 4 E8
George Rd CHING E4 43 J5
KUTN/CMB KT2 144 E6
NWMAL KT3 160 C3
George Rw BERM/RHTH SE16 111 H1
Georges Md BORE WD6 24 A5
Georges Rd HOLWY N7 73 F5
George's Rd HOLWY N7 73 F4
George St BARK IG11 78 C6
CROY/NA CR0 177 J1
HNWL W7 84 E7
HSLW TW3 122 E1
MBLAR W1H 9 L4
NWDGN UB2 102 D3
RCH/KEW TW9 124 E4
ROM RM1 63 H5
WATW WD18 21 G3
Georgetown Cl NRWD SE19 150 A4
Georgette Pl GNWCH SE10 113 F6
George V Av PIN HA5 48 A3
Georgeville Gdns
BARK/HLT IG6 60 B3
George V Wy GFD/PVL UB6 67 H6
George Wyver Cl
WIM/MER SW19 127 H6
George Yd BANK EC3V 13 H5
MYFR/PKLN W1K 10 B6
Georgiana St CAMTN NW1 4 E3
Georgian Cl HAYES BR2 168 A7
STAN HA7 35 G6
Georgian Ct WBLY HA9 68 C5
Georgian Wy HRW HA1 66 D1
Georgia Rd NWMAL KT3 159 K3
THHTH CR7 149 H7
Georgina Gdns BETH E2 * 7 M7
Geraint Rd BMLY BR1 152 E2
Geraldine Rd CHSWK W4 105 H5
WAND/EARL SW18 128 B4
Geraldine St LBTH SE11 18 C4
Gerald Rd BCTR RM8 80 B1
BGVA SW1W 16 B5
CAN/RD E16 94 D3
Gerard Av HSLWW TW4 123 F6
Gerard Gdns RAIN RM13 99 G1
Gerard Rd BARN SW13 106 C7
HRW HA1 49 G5
Gerards Cl BERM/RHTH SE16 111 K5
Gerda Rd ELTH/MOT SE9 154 B1
Germander Wy SRTFD E15 94 C2
Gernon Rd BOW E3 93 G1
Geron Wy CRICK NW2 70 A1
Gerrard Gdns PIN HA5 46 E4
Gerrard Pl SOHO/SHAV W1D * 11 H6
Gerrard Rd IS N1 6 C5
Gerrards Cl STHGT/OAK N14 28 C4
Gerrard St SOHO/SHAV W1D 11 G6
Gerridge St STHWK SE1 18 B2
Gertrude Rd BELV DA17 117 H3
Gertrude St WBPTN SW10 108 B5
Gervase Cl WBLY HA9 68 E2
Gervase Rd EDGW HA8 36 E7
Gervase St PECK SE15 111 J6
Ghent St CAT SE6 151 J1
Ghent Wy HACK E8 74 B5
Giant Arches Rd HNHL SE24 130 D6
Giant Tree Hl BUSH WD23 34 D1
Gibbfield Cl CHDH RM6 62 A2
Gibbins Rd SRTFD E15 76 A6
Gibbon Rd ACT W3 87 G6
KUTN/CMB KT2 144 A7
PECK SE15 131 K1
Gibbons La DART DA1 139 G5
Gibbons Ms GLDGN NW11 52 D4
Gibbons Rd WLSDN NW10 69 F5
Gibbon Wk PUT/ROE SW15 * 126 D3
Gibbs Av NRWD SE19 149 K5
Gibbs Cl NRWD SE19 * 149 K4
Gibbs Couch OXHEY WD19 33 H2
Gibbs Gn EDGW HA8 36 E3
WKENS W14 * 107 J4
Gibbs Green Cl WKENS W14 107 J4
Gibbs Rd UED N18 42 E3
Gibbs Sq NRWD SE19 * 149 K4
Gibraltar Wk BETH E2 7 M8
Gibson Cl CHSGTN KT9 171 J4
ISLW TW7 123 J2
WCHMH N21 29 G5
WCHPL E1 92 E3
Gibson Gdns
STNW/STAM N16 * 74 B1
Gibson Rd BCTR RM8 61 J7
LBTH SE11 17 M6
SUT SM1 175 F4
Gibson's Hl STRHM/NOR SW16 149 G6
Gibson Sq IS N1 6 B3
Gibson St GNWCH SE10 113 H4
Gidea Av GPK RM2 63 J2
Gidea Cl GPK RM2 63 J2
Gideon Cl BELV DA17 117 J3
Gideon Ms EA W5 * 104 E1
Gideon Rd BTSEA SW11 129 F2
Giesbach Rd ARCH N19 72 C1
Giffard Rd UED N18 42 A4
Giffin St DEPT SE8 112 D6
Gifford Gdns HNWL W7 84 D4
Gifford Rd WLSDN NW10 69 G6
Gifford St IS N1 5 K2
Gift La SRTFD E15 76 C7
Giggs Hill Gdns THDIT KT7 158 B7
Giggs Hill Rd THDIT KT7 158 B6
Gilbert Cl WIM/MER SW19 * 147 F7
WOOL/PLUM SE18 114 E7
Gilbert Gv EDGW HA8 36 E7
Gilbert Pl NOXST/BSQ WC1A 11 J3
Gilbert Rd BELV DA17 117 H2
BMLY BR1 152 E6
LBTH SE11 18 B5
PIN HA5 47 H3
ROM RM1 63 H3
WIM/MER SW19 147 G6
Gilbert St HSLW TW3 123 H2
MYFR/PKLN W1K 10 B5
SRTFD E15 76 C3
Gilbert White Cl GFD/PVL UB6 67 G7
Gilbey Rd TOOT SW17 147 J3
Gilbeys Yd CAMTN NW1 4 B2
Gilbourne Rd
WOOL/PLUM SE18 116 A5
Gilda Av PEND EN3 31 G4
Gilda Crs STNW/STAM N16 56 C7
Gildea Cl PIN HA5 34 A6
Gildea St GTPST W1W 10 D3
Gilden Crs KTTN NW5 72 A4
Gildersome St
WOOL/PLUM SE18 115 F5
Gilders Rd CHSGTN KT9 172 B5
Giles Coppice NRWD SE19 150 B3
Gilkes Crs DUL SE21 131 F5
Gilkes Pl DUL SE21 131 F5
Gillam Wy RAIN RM13 81 J5
Gillan Gn BUSH WD23 34 C1
Gillards Ms WALTH E17 57 J3
Gillards Wy WALTH E17 57 J3
Gill Av CAN/RD E16 94 E5
Gill Cl WATW WD18 20 A5
Gillender St BOW E3 94 A3
Gillespie Rd HBRY N5 73 G2
Gillett Av EHAM E6 95 J1
Gillett Pl HACK E8 74 A4
Gillett Rd THHTH CR7 164 E3
Gillett St STNW/STAM N16 74 A4
Gillham Ter TOTM N17 42 C5
Gillian Park Rd CHEAM SM3 161 J7
Gillian St LEW SE13 132 E4
Gillian Ter BRYLDS KT5 * 159 G5
Gillies St KTTN NW5 72 A4
Gillingham Rd CRICK NW2 70 C2
Gillingham Rw PIM SW1V 16 E5
Gillingham St PIM SW1V 16 D6
Gillison Wk
BERM/RHTH SE16 * 111 H2
Gillman Dr SRTFD E15 76 C7
Gill St POP/IOD E14 93 H5
Gillum Cl EBAR EN4 27 K7
Gilmore Rd LEW SE13 133 G3
Gilpin Av MORT/ESHN SW14 126 A3
Gilpin Cl BAY/PAD W2 8 F3
MTCM CR4 162 D1
Gilpin Crs UED N18 42 B4
WHTN TW2 123 G6
Gilpin Rd CLPT E5 75 G3
Gilpin Wy HYS/HAR UB3 101 G6
Gilroy Cl RAIN RM13 81 H5
Gilsland Rd THHTH CR7 164 E3
Gilson Pl MUSWH N10 39 K6
Gilstead Rd FUL/PGN SW6 128 A1
Gilston Rd WBPTN SW10 14 F8
Gilton Rd CAT SE6 152 C2
Giltspur St STBT EC1A 12 D4
Gilwell Cl CHING E4 31 K3
Gippeswyck Cl PIN HA5 33 H7
Gipsy Hl NRWD SE19 150 A4
Gipsy La PUT/ROE SW15 126 D2
Gipsy Rd WELL DA16 136 E1
WNWD SE27 149 K3
Gipsy Road Gdns WNWD SE27 149 J3
Giralda Cl CAN/RD E16 95 H4
Giraud St POP/IOD E14 93 K5
Girdlers Rd WKENS W14 107 H2
Girdwood Rd
WAND/EARL SW18 127 H6
Girling Wy EBED/NFELT TW14 121 K2
Gironde Rd FUL/PGN SW6 107 J6
Girton Av CDALE/KGS NW9 50 C2
Girton Cl NTHLT UB5 66 C5
Girton Gdns CROY/NA CR0 179 J2
Girton Rd NTHLT UB5 66 C5
SYD SE26 151 F4
Girton Wy RKW/CH/CXG WD3 20 A4
Gisbourne Cl WLGTN SM6 176 D2
Gisburn Rd CEND/HSY/T N8 55 F3
Gissing Wk IS N1 6 B2
Gittens Cl BMLY BR1 152 D3
Glacier Wy ALP/SUD HA0 85 K1
Gladbeck Wy ENC/FH EN2 29 H3
Gladding Rd MNPK E12 77 H3
Glade Cl SURB KT6 * 171 K1
Glade Gdns CROY/NA CR0 166 B6
Glade La NWDGN UB2 103 G1
Gladeside CROY/NA CR0 166 A6
WCHMH N21 29 F6
Gladesmore Rd
SEVS/STOTM N15 56 B5
The Glade BELMT SM2 174 C7
BMLY BR1 168 C1
CHARL SE7 114 B6
CLAY IG5 45 K7
CROY/NA CR0 166 B5
ENC/FH EN2 29 G2
EW KT17 173 J5
HACK E8 * 74 B5
NFNCH/WDSPK N12 * 39 H3
SHB W12 106 E1
WCHMH N21 29 F5
WFD IG8 45 F2
WWKM BR4 179 K2
Gladiator St FSTH SE23 132 B5
Glading Ter STNW/STAM N16 74 B2
Gladioli Cl HPTN TW12 142 A5
Gladsdale Dr PIN HA5 46 E3
Gladsmuir Rd ARCH N19 54 C7
BAR EN5 26 C1
Gladstone Av
EBED/NFELT TW14 121 K5
MNPK E12 77 J6
WDGN N22 55 H1
WHTN TW2 123 J6
Gladstone Gdns HSLW TW3 103 H7
Gladstone Ms
KIL/WHAMP NW6 * 70 D6
PGE/AN SE20 150 E6
WDGN N22 55 G1
Gladstone Pde CRICK NW2 * 70 A2
Gladstone Park Gdns
CRICK NW2 69 K2
Gladstone Pl BAR EN5 * 26 B3
E/WMO/HCT KT8 * 157 K4
Gladstone Rd CHSWK W4 * 106 A2
CROY/NA CR0 164 E6
DART DA1 139 J5
KUT/HW KT1 159 H2
NWDGN UB2 102 D1
SURB KT6 171 K1

WAT WD17 21 G2
WIM/MER SW19 146 E6
Gladstone St STHWK SE1 18 C3
Gladstone Ter VX/NE SW8 * 109 G7
WNWD SE27 * 149 J3
Gladstone Wy
KTN/HRWW/WS HA3 48 E2
Gladwell Rd BMLY BR1 152 E5
CEND/HSY/T N8 55 F5
Gladwyn Rd PUT/ROE SW15 127 G2
Gladys Rd KIL/WHAMP NW6 2 B1
Glaisher St DEPT SE8 112 D5
Glamis Crs HYS/HAR UB3 101 F2
Glamis Pl WAP E1W 92 E6
Glamis Rd WAP E1W 92 E6
Glamis Wy NTHLT UB5 66 C5
Glamorgan Cl MTCM CR4 163 K2
Glamorgan Rd KUT/HW KT1 143 J6
Glandford Wy CHDH RM6 61 H4
Glanfield Rd BECK BR3 166 C3
Glanleam Rd STAN HA7 35 K3
Glanville Ms STAN HA7 35 G4
Glanville Rd
BRXS/STRHM SW2 129 K4
HAYES BR2 168 A2
Glasbrook Av WHTN TW2 122 E7
Glasbrook Rd ELTH/MOT SE9 134 C6
Glaserton Rd
STNW/STAM N16 56 A6
Glasford St TOOT SW17 147 K5
Glasgow Rd PLSTW E13 95 F1
UED N18 42 D4
Glasgow Ter PIM SW1V 16 E8
Glaskin Ms HOM E9 75 G5
Glasse Cl WEA W13 85 G6
Glasshill St STHWK SE1 18 D1
Glasshouse Flds WAP E1W 93 F6
Glasshouse St REGST W1B 10 F7
Glasshouse Wk LBTH SE11 17 K7
Glasshouse Yd FARR EC1M 12 E1
Glasslyn Rd CEND/HSY/T N8 54 D4
Glassmill La HAYES BR2 167 J1
Glass St BETH E2 * 92 D3
Glass Yd WOOL/PLUM SE18 115 F2
Glastonbury Av WFD IG8 45 H6
Glastonbury Pl WCHPL E1 92 E5
Glastonbury Rd ED N9 30 C7
MRDN SM4 161 K5
Glastonbury St
KIL/WHAMP NW6 70 D4
Glaston Ct EA W5 * 85 K7
Glaucus St BOW E3 93 K4
Glazbury Rd WKENS W14 107 H3
Glazebrook Cl DUL SE21 149 K1
Glebe Av ENC/FH EN2 29 H2
HGDN/ICK UB10 64 A3
KTN/HRWW/WS HA3 50 A2
MTCM CR4 162 D1
RSLP HA4 65 F5
WFD IG8 44 E5
Glebe Cl CHSWK W4 * 106 B4
HGDN/ICK UB10 64 A3
Glebe Ct BKHTH/KID SE3 * 133 H2
EA W5 * 85 K7
STAN HA7 35 J4
Glebe Crs HDN NW4 52 A3
KTN/HRWW/WS HA3 50 A2
Glebe Gdns NWMAL KT3 160 B6
Glebe House Dr HAYES BR2 168 A7
Glebelands DART DA1 138 C3
E/WMO/HCT KT8 157 G4
ESH/CLAY KT10 171 F7
Glebelands Av
GNTH/NBYPK IG2 60 D6
SWFD E18 58 E1
Glebelands Cl CMBW SE5 131 F2
NFNCH/WDSPK N12 39 H7
Glebelands Rd
EBED/NFELT TW14 121 K6
Glebe La BAR EN5 25 J4
KTN/HRWW/WS HA3 50 A3
Glebe Pth MTCM CR4 162 E2
Glebe Pl CHEL SW3 15 J9
Glebe Rd BARN SW13 126 D1
BELMT SM2 174 C7
BMLY BR1 152 E7
CAR SM5 175 K5
CEND/HSY/T N8 55 F3
DAGE RM10 80 D5
FNCH N3 39 G7
HACK E8 7 L1
RAIN RM13 99 K2
STAN HA7 35 J4
WLSDN NW10 69 J5
Glebe Side TWK TW1 124 A5
Glebe Sq MTCM CR4 * 162 E2
Glebe St CHSWK W4 106 A4
The Glebe BKHTH/KID SE3 133 H2
CHST BR7 154 C7
STRHM/NOR SW16 * 148 D3
WDR/YW UB7 100 B3
WPK KT4 160 C7
Glebe Wy ERITH DA8 118 B5
FELT TW13 142 A2
Glebeway WFD IG8 45 G4
Glebe Wy WWKM BR4 180 A1
Gledhow Gdns ECT SW5 14 E6
Gledstanes Rd WKENS W14 107 H4
Gledwood Av YEAD UB4 82 E4
Gledwood Crs YEAD UB4 82 D4
Gledwood Dr YEAD UB4 82 D4
Gledwood Gdns YEAD UB4 82 E4
Gleed Av BUSH WD23 34 D1
Glegg Pl PUT/ROE SW15 * 127 G3
Glenaffric Av POP/IOD E14 113 F3
Glen Albyn Rd
WIM/MER SW19 146 B1
Glenalla Rd RSLP HA4 46 D6
Glenalmond Rd
KTN/HRWW/WS HA3 50 A3
Glenalvon Wy
WOOL/PLUM SE18 114 D3
Glena Mt SUT SM1 175 G3
Glenarm Rd CLPT E5 74 E3
Glenavon Cl ESH/CLAY KT10 171 G5
Glenavon Rd SRTFD E15 76 C6
Glenbarr Cl ELTH/MOT SE9 135 G2
Glenbow Rd BMLY BR1 152 C5
Glenbrook North ENC/FH EN2 29 F3
Glenbrook Rd
KIL/WHAMP NW6 70 E4
Glenbrook South ENC/FH EN2 29 F3
Glenbuck Rd SURB KT6 158 E5
Glenburnie Rd TOOT SW17 147 K2
Glencairn Dr EA W5 85 H3
Glencairne Cl CAN/RD E16 95 H4
Glencairn Rd
STRHM/NOR SW16 148 E6
Glencoe Av GNTH/NBYPK IG2 60 E6
Glencoe Rd BUSH WD23 22 A5
DAGE RM10 80 C3
YEAD UB4 83 H3
Glencorse Gn OXHEY WD19 * 33 H3
Glen Crs WFD IG8 45 F5
Glendale Av CHDH RM6 61 J6
EDGW HA8 36 B3
WDGN N22 41 G6
Glendale Cl ELTH/MOT SE9 135 F2
Glendale Dr WIM/MER SW19 146 D4
Glendale Gdns WBLY HA9 49 K7
Glendale Ms BECK BR3 151 K7
Glendale Rd ERITH DA8 117 K3
Glendale Wy THMD SE28 97 J7
Glendall St BRXN/ST SW9 130 A2
Glendarvon St PUT/ROE SW15 127 G2
Glendevon Cl EDGW HA8 36 D2
Glendish Rd TOTM N17 42 C7
Glendor Gdns MLHL NW7 37 F3
Glendower Gdns
MORT/ESHN SW14 126 A2
Glendower Pl SKENS SW7 15 G5
Glendower Rd
MORT/ESHN SW14 126 A2
Glendown Rd ABYW SE2 116 B4
Glendun Rd ACT W3 87 G6
Gleneagle Ms
STRHM/NOR SW16 148 D4
Gleneagle Rd
STRHM/NOR SW16 148 D4
Gleneagles STAN HA7 35 H5
Gleneagles Cl
BERM/RHTH SE16 * 111 J4
ORP BR6 169 J7
OXHEY WD19 * 33 H4
Gleneldon Ms
STRHM/NOR SW16 148 E4
Gleneldon Rd
STRHM/NOR SW16 148 E3
Glenelg Rd BRXS/STRHM SW2 129 K4
Glenesk Rd ELTH/MOT SE9 135 F3
Glenfarg Rd CAT SE6 133 G7
Glenfield Crs RSLP HA4 46 B6
Glenfield Rd BAL SW12 129 H7
WEA W13 104 C1
Glenfinlas Wy CMBW SE5 110 C6
Glenforth St GNWCH SE10 113 J3
Glengall Br POP/IOD E14 112 E2
Glengall Gv POP/IOD E14 112 E2
Glengall Pas KIL/WHAMP NW6 2 A3
Glengall Rd BXLYHN DA7 137 F2
EDGW HA8 36 D2
KIL/WHAMP NW6 70 D7
PECK SE15 19 M9
WFD IG8 44 E5
Glengall Ter PECK SE15 19 M9
Glen Gdns CROY/NA CR0 177 G2
Glengarnock Av POP/IOD E14 113 F3
Glengarry Rd EDUL SE22 131 F3
Glenham Dr GNTH/NBYPK IG2 60 B4
Glenhaven Av BORE WD6 24 C2
Glenhead Cl ELTH/MOT SE9 135 G2
Glenhill Cl FNCH N3 52 E1
Glenhouse Rd ELTH/MOT SE9 135 F4
Glenhurst Av BXLY DA5 137 G7
KTTN NW5 72 A3
RSLP HA4 46 A6
Glenhurst Ri NRWD SE19 149 J6
Glenhurst Rd BTFD TW8 104 D5
NFNCH/WDSPK N12 39 H3
Glenilla Rd HAMP NW3 71 J5
Glenister Park Rd
STRHM/NOR SW16 148 D6
Glenister Rd GNWCH SE10 113 J4
Glenlea Rd ELTH/MOT SE9 135 F4
Glenloch Rd HAMP NW3 71 J5
PEND EN3 30 E1
Glenluge Rd BKHTH/KID SE3 113 K5
Glenlyon Rd ELTH/MOT SE9 135 F4
Glenmere Av MLHL NW7 37 J6
Glenmere Rw LEE/GVPK SE12 133 J5
Glen Ms WALTH E17 57 H4
Glenmill HPTN TW12 141 K4
Glenmore Lawns WEA W13 * 85 G5
Glenmore Pde ALP/SUD HA0 * 68 A7
Glenmore Rd HAMP NW3 71 J5
WELL DA16 116 A7
Glenmore Wy BARK IG11 97 G2
Glenmore Rd WNWD SE27 149 G2
Glenny Rd BARK IG11 78 C5
Glenorchy Cl YEAD UB4 83 J4
Glenparke Rd FSTGT E7 77 F5
Glen Ri WFD IG8 45 F5
Glen Rd CHSGTN KT9 172 A2
PLSTW E13 95 G3
WALTH E17 57 H4
Glen Road End WLGTN SM6 176 B7
Glenrosa St FUL/PGN SW6 128 B1
Glenroy St SHB W12 88 A5
Glensdale Rd BROCKY SE4 132 C2
Glenshiel Rd ELTH/MOT SE9 135 F4
Glentanner Wy TOOT SW17 147 H2
Glentham Cots BARN SW13 * 106 D5
Glentham Gdns BARN SW13 106 E4
Glentham Rd BARN SW13 106 D5
The Glen BELMT SM2 * 175 G5
CROY/NA CR0 179 F2
ENC/FH EN2 29 H3
HAYES BR2 167 H1
NTHWD HA6 32 B6
NWDGN UB2 102 E4
ORP BR6 181 K2
PIN HA5 47 F4
WBLY HA9 67 K3
Glenthorne Av CROY/NA CR0 165 K7
Glenthorne Cl CHEAM SM3 161 K7
Glenthorne Gdns
BARK/HLT IG6 60 A2
CHEAM SM3 161 K7
Glenthorne Rd
FBAR/BDGN N11 39 K4
HMSMTH W6 106 E3
KUT/HW KT1 159 G3
WALTH E17 57 G4
Glenthorpe Rd MRDN SM4 161 G4
Glenton Rd LEW SE13 133 H3
Glentworth St CAMTN NW1 9 M1
Glenure Rd ELTH/MOT SE9 135 F4
Glenview ABYW SE2 116 E5
Glen View Rd BMLY BR1 168 C1
Glenville Gv DEPT SE8 112 C6
Glenville Ms
WAND/EARL SW18 128 A6
Glenville Rd KUTN/CMB KT2 144 C7
Glenwood Av
CDALE/KGS NW9 51 G7
RAIN RM13 99 J3
Glenwood Cl HRW HA1 49 F4
Glenwood Dr GPK RM2 63 J4
Glenwood Gdns
GNTH/NBYPK IG2 60 A4
Glenwood Gv
CDALE/KGS NW9 50 E7
Glenwood Rd CAT SE6 132 C7
EW KT17 173 J5
HSLW TW3 123 J2
MLHL NW7 37 G2
SEVS/STOTM N15 55 H4
Glenwood Rw NRWD SE19 * 150 B7
Glenwood Wy CROY/NA CR0 166 A5
Glenworth Av POP/IOD E14 113 G3
Gliddon Rd WKENS W14 107 H3
Glimpsing Gn ERITHM DA18 117 F2
Globe Pond Rd
BERM/RHTH SE16 93 G7
Globe Rd BETH E2 92 E2
EMPK RM11 63 J5
SRTFD E15 76 D4
WCHPL E1 92 E2
WFD IG8 45 G5
Globe St STHWK SE1 19 G2
Globe Ter BETH E2 92 E2
Glossop Rd SAND/SEL CR2 177 K7
Gloster Rd NWMAL KT3 160 B3
Gloucester Av BFN/LL DA15 154 E1
CAMTN NW1 4 A2
WELL DA16 136 A4
Gloucester Circ GNWCH SE10 113 F6
Gloucester Cl THDIT KT7 * 158 B7
WLSDN NW10 69 F6
Gloucester Ct MTCM CR4 * 163 K4
RCH/KEW TW9 * 105 H6
TWRH EC3N * 13 K7
Gloucester Crs CAMTN NW1 4 C3
Gloucester Dr FSBYPK N4 73 H1
GLDGN NW11 52 E3
Gloucester Gdns BAY/PAD W2 8 D4
EBAR EN4 28 A3
GLDGN NW11 52 D6
IL IG1 59 J6
SUT SM1 175 F1
Gloucester Ga CAMTN NW1 4 B5
Gloucester Gate Ms
CAMTN NW1 4 C5
Gloucester Gv EDGW HA8 37 F7
Gloucester Ms BAY/PAD W2 8 F5
LEY E10 57 J6
Gloucester Ms West
BAY/PAD W2 8 E5
Gloucester Pde
BFN/LL DA15 * 136 B4
HYS/HAR UB3 * 101 F2
Gloucester Pl CAMTN NW1 3 L9
MHST W1U 9 M3
Gloucester Place Ms
MHST W1U 9 M4
Gloucester Rd ACT W3 105 K1
BAR EN5 27 F4
BELV DA17 117 G4
CROY/NA CR0 164 E6
DART DA1 138 E5
EA W5 104 D1
FELT TW13 122 B7
HPTN TW12 142 B6
HRW HA1 48 B4
HSLWW TW4 122 D3
KUT/HW KT1 159 H1
LEY E10 57 J6
MNPK E12 77 K2
RCH/KEW TW9 105 H6
ROM RM1 63 G5
SKENS SW7 14 E3
TEDD TW11 142 E4
TOTM N17 55 K1
UED N18 42 B4
WALTH E17 57 F1
WAN E11 59 F4
WHTN TW2 123 H7
Gloucester Sq BAY/PAD W2 9 H5
BETH E2 74 C7
Gloucester St PIM SW1V 16 E7
Gloucester Ter BAY/PAD W2 8 D4
STHGT/OAK N14 * 28 D7
Gloucester Wk KENS W8 14 B1
Gloucester Wy CLKNW EC1R 6 B8
Glover Cl ABYW SE2 116 D3
Glover Dr UED N18 42 E5
Glover Rd PIN HA5 47 H5
Glycena Rd BTSEA SW11 128 E2
Glyn Av EBAR EN4 27 H3
Glyn Cl EW KT17 173 J7
SNWD SE25 165 F1
Glyn Ct STAN HA7 35 H5
Glynde Ms CHEL SW3 15 K4
Glynde Rd BXLYHN DA7 136 E2
Glynde St BROCKY SE4 132 C5
Glyndon Rd WOOL/PLUM SE18 115 H3
Glyn Dr SCUP DA14 155 H3
Glynfield Rd WLSDN NW10 69 G6
Glynne Rd WDGN N22 55 G1
Glyn Rd CLPT E5 75 F3
PEND EN3 30 E3
WPK KT4 174 B1
Glyn St LBTH SE11 17 L8
Glynwood Ct FSTH SE23 150 E1
Goat Rd MTCM CR4 163 F6
Goat Whf BTFD TW8 105 F5
Godalming Av WLGTN SM6 176 E4
Godalming Rd POP/IOD E14 93 K4
Godbold Rd SRTFD E15 94 C3
Goddard Dr BUSH WD23 22 B3
Goddard Pl ARCH N19 72 C2
Goddard Rd BECK BR3 166 A3
Goddards Wy IL IG1 60 D7
Godfrey Av NTHLT UB5 65 J7
WHTN TW2 123 J6
Godfrey Hl WOOL/PLUM SE18 114 D3
Godfrey Rd WOOL/PLUM SE18 114 E3
Godfrey St CHEL SW3 15 K7
SRTFD E15 94 A1
Godfrey Wy HSLWW TW4 122 D6
Goding St LBTH SE11 17 K8
Godley Rd WAND/EARL SW18 128 C7
Godliman St BLKFR EC4V 12 D5
Godman Rd PECK SE15 * 131 J1
Godolphin Cl PLMGR N13 41 H5
Godolphin Pl ACT W3 87 F6
Godolphin Rd SHB W12 87 K7
Godric Crs CROY/NA CR0 180 B7
Godson Rd CROY/NA CR0 177 G2
Godson St IS N1 6 A5
Godstone Rd SUT SM1 175 G3
TWK TW1 124 B5
Godstow Rd ABYW SE2 116 D1
Godwin Cl HOR/WEW KT19 172 E5
IS N1 6 F5
Godwin Rd FSTGT E7 77 F3
HAYES BR2 168 B2
Goffers Rd BKHTH/KID SE3 113 H7
Goffs Rd ASHF TW15 140 B5
Goidel Cl WLGTN SM6 176 D3
Golborne Gdns NKENS W10 * 88 C3
Golborne Ms NKENS W10 88 C4
Golborne Rd NKENS W10 88 C4
Golda Cl BAR EN5 26 B5
Goldbeaters Gv EDGW HA8 37 G5
Goldcliff Cl MRDN SM4 161 K6
Goldcrest Cl CAN/RD E16 95 H4
THMD SE28 97 J6
Goldcrest Ms EA W5 * 85 K4
Goldcrest Wy BUSH WD23 22 C7
CROY/NA CR0 180 B7
Golden Ct HSLW TW3 123 J1
Golden Crs HYS/HAR UB3 82 C7
Golden Cross Ms NTGHL W11 * 88 D5
Golden Hind Pl DEPT SE8 * 112 C3
Golden Jubilee Br STHWK SE1 11 L8
Golden La STLK EC1Y 6 E9
Golden Lane Est STLK EC1Y 12 E1
Golden Mnr HNWL W7 84 E6
Golden Pde WALTH E17 * 58 A2
Golden Plover Cl CAN/RD E16 94 E5
Golden Sq SOHO/CST W1F 10 F6
Golden Yd HAMP NW3 71 G3
Golders Cl EDGW HA8 36 D4
Golders Gdns GLDGN NW11 52 C6
Golders Green Crs
GLDGN NW11 52 D6
Golders Green Rd
GLDGN NW11 52 C5
Golders Hl HAMP NW3 * 71 F1
Goldersea GLDGN NW11 * 52 E7
Golders Manor Dr
GLDGN NW11 52 B5
Golders Park Cl GLDGN NW11 52 E7
Golders Ri HDN NW4 52 B4
Golders Wy GLDGN NW11 52 D6
Goldfinch Rd THMD SE28 115 J2
Goldfinch Wy BORE WD6 24 C3
Goldhawk Ms SHB W12 106 E1
Goldhawk Rd HMSMTH W6 106 C3
SHB W12 106 D2
Goldhaze Cl WFD IG8 45 G6
Gold Hl EDGW HA8 37 F5
Goldhurst Ter
KIL/WHAMP NW6 2 D2
Golding St WCHPL E1 92 C5
Goldington Crs CAMTN NW1 4 F5
Goldington St CAMTN NW1 5 G5
Gold La EDGW HA8 37 F5
Goldman Cl BETH E2 92 C3
Goldney Rd MV/WKIL W9 8 A1
Goldrill Dr FBAR/BDGN N11 40 A1
Goldsboro Rd VX/NE SW8 109 J7
Goldsborough Crs CHING E4 43 K1
Goldsdown Cl PEND EN3 31 G1
Goldsdown Rd PEND EN3 31 F1
Goldsmid St
WOOL/PLUM SE18 115 K4
Goldsmith Av ACT W3 87 F6
CDALE/KGS NW9 51 G4
MNPK E12 77 J5
ROMW/RG RM7 62 C6
Goldsmith Cl
RYLN/HDSTN HA2 48 A7
Goldsmith La CDALE/KGS NW9 50 E3
Goldsmith Pl
KIL/WHAMP NW6 * 2 C4
Goldsmith Rd ACT W3 87 F7
FBAR/BDGN N11 39 K4
LEY E10 57 K7
PECK SE15 111 H7
WALTH E17 57 F1
Goldsmiths Cl ACT W3 * 87 F7
Goldsmith's Rw BETH E2 92 C1
Goldsmith St CITYW EC2V 12 F4
Goldsworthy Gdns
BERM/RHTH SE16 111 K3
Goldwell Rd THHTH CR7 164 A3
Goldwing Cl CAN/RD E16 94 E5
Golf Cl BUSH WD23 21 H2
STAN HA7 35 J6
THHTH CR7 149 G7
Golf Club Dr KUTN/CMB KT2 145 F6
Golfe Rd IL IG1 78 D2
Golf Rd BMLY BR1 169 F2
EA W5 * 86 B5
Golf Side WHTN TW2 142 D2
Golf Side Cl NWMAL KT3 160 B1
Golfside Cl TRDG/WHET N20 39 J2
Gollogly Ter CHARL SE7 114 B4
Gomer Gdns TEDD TW11 143 G5
Gomer Pl TEDD TW11 143 G5
Gomm Rd BERM/RHTH SE16 111 K2
Gomshall Av WLGTN SM6 176 E4
Gondar Gdns CRICK NW2 70 D4
Gonson St DEPT SE8 112 E5
Gonston Cl WIM/MER SW19 146 C1
Gonville Crs NTHLT UB5 66 B5
Gonville Rd THHTH CR7 164 A4
Gonville St FUL/PGN SW6 127 H2
Goodall Rd WAN E11 76 A2
Gooden Ct HRW HA1 66 E2
Goodenough Rd
WIM/MER SW19 146 D6
Goodey Rd BARK IG11 79 F6
Goodge Pl FITZ W1T 10 F3
Goodge St FITZ W1T 10 F3
Goodhall Cl STAN HA7 35 G5
Goodhall St WLSDN NW10 87 G2
Goodhart Wy WWKM BR4 167 H5
Goodhew Rd CROY/NA CR0 165 H5
Gooding Cl NWMAL KT3 159 K3
Goodinge Cl HOLWY N7 72 E4
Goodinge Rd HOLWY N7 72 E5
Goodison Cl BUSH WD23 22 C4
Goodman Ct ALP/SUD HA0 * 67 K3
Goodman Crs
BRXS/STRHM SW2 148 D1
CROY/NA CR0 164 C5
Goodman Rd LEY E10 58 A6
Goodmans Ct ALP/SUD HA0 67 K3
Goodman's Yd TWRH EC3N 13 L6
Goodmayes Av
GDMY/SEVK IG3 61 G7
Goodmayes La
GDMY/SEVK IG3 79 G3
Goodmayes Rd
GDMY/SEVK IG3 61 G7
Goodrich Rd EDUL SE22 131 G5
Goodson Rd WLSDN NW10 69 G6
Goods Wy KCROSS N1C 5 J5
Goodway Gdns POP/IOD E14 94 B5
Goodwill Dr RYLN/HDSTN HA2 48 A7
Goodwin Cl BERM/RHTH SE16 19 M4
MTCM CR4 162 C2
Goodwin Dr SCUP DA14 155 K1
Goodwin Gdns CROY/NA CR0 177 H5
Goodwin Rd CROY/NA CR0 177 H4
ED N9 30 E7
SHB W12 106 D1
Goodwins Ct CHCR WC2N 11 J6
Goodwin St FSBYPK N4 73 G1
Goodwood Cl MRDN SM4 161 K3
Goodwood Dr NTHLT UB5 66 A5
Goodwood Pde BECK BR3 * 166 B3
Goodwood Rd NWCR SE14 112 B6
Goodwyn Av MLHL NW7 37 G4
Goodwyn's V MUSWH N10 40 A7
Goodyers Gdns HDN NW4 52 B4
Goosander Wy THMD SE28 115 J2
Gooseacre La
KTN/HRWW/WS HA3 49 K4
Gooseley La EHAM E6 96 A2
Goossens Cl SUT SM1 175 G4
Gophir La CANST EC4R * 13 G6
Gopsall St IS N1 7 H4
Gordon Av CHING E4 44 C5
HCH RM12 81 H1
MORT/ESHN SW14 126 B3
STAN HA7 35 F5
TWK TW1 124 B4
Gordonbrock Rd BROCKY SE4 132 D4
Gordon Cl WALTH E17 57 J5
Gordon Crs CROY/NA CR0 165 F7
HYS/HAR UB3 101 K3
Gordondale Rd
WIM/MER SW19 146 E1
Gordon Gdns EDGW HA8 50 D1
Gordon Gv CMBW SE5 130 C1
Gordon House Rd KTTN NW5 72 A3
Gordon Pl KENS W8 14 B1
Gordon Rd BARK IG11 78 E7
BECK BR3 166 C2
BELV DA17 117 K3
BFN/LL DA15 135 K4
BRYLDS KT5 159 G6
CAR SM5 175 K5
CHDH RM6 62 B5
CHSWK W4 105 J5
DART DA1 139 G6
EA W5 85 J6
ED N9 42 D1
ESH/CLAY KT10 170 E6
FBAR/BDGN N11 40 D6
FNCH N3 38 D6
HSLW TW3 123 H3
IL IG1 78 D2
KTN/HRWW/WS HA3 48 E2
KUTN/CMB KT2 144 B7
NWDGN UB2 102 D3
PECK SE15 131 J1
RCH/KEW TW9 125 G1
SRTFD E15 76 A3
SWFD E18 45 F7
WAN E11 58 E5
Gordon Sq STPAN WC1H 5 G9
Gordon St PLSTW E13 94 E2
STPAN WC1H 5 G9
Gordon Wy BAR EN5 26 D3
BMLY BR1 152 E7
Gorefield Pl KIL/WHAMP NW6 2 A5
Gore Rd HOM E9 74 E7
RYNPK SW20 161 F1
Goresbrook Rd DAGW RM9 79 J7
Gore St SKENS SW7 14 F3
Gorham Pl NTGHL W11 88 C6
Goring Gdns BCTR RM8 79 J3
Goring Rd DAGE RM10 81 F5
FBAR/BDGN N11 * 40 E5
Goring St HDTCH EC3A 13 K4
Goring Wy GFD/PVL UB6 84 C1
Gorleston Rd
SEVS/STOTM N15 55 K4
Gorleston St WKENS W14 107 H3
Gorman Rd WOOL/PLUM SE18 114 E3
Gorringe Park Av MTCM CR4 148 A6
Gorse Cl CAN/RD E16 94 E5
Gorse Ri TOOT SW17 148 A4
Gorse Rd CROY/NA CR0 179 J2
Gorseway ROMW/RG RM7 63 G7
Gorst Rd BTSEA SW11 128 E5
WLSDN NW10 86 E3
Gorsuch Pl BETH E2 7 L7
Gorsuch St BETH E2 7 L7
Gosberton Rd BAL SW12 128 E7
Gosbury Hl CHSGTN KT9 172 A3
Gosfield Rd BCTR RM8 62 C7
Gosfield St GTPST W1W 10 D2
Gosford Gdns REDBR IG4 59 K4
Gosforth La OXHEY WD19 32 E2
Gosforth Pth OXHEY WD19 32 E2
Goshawk Gdns YEAD UB4 82 C2
Goslett Yd SOHO/SHAV W1D 11 H4
Gosling Cl GFD/PVL UB6 84 A2
Gosling Wy BRXN/ST SW9 110 B7
Gospatrick Rd TOTM N17 41 J6
Gosport Rd WALTH E17 57 H4
Gosport Wy PECK SE15 111 G6
Gossage Rd WOOL/PLUM SE18 115 J4
Gosset St BETH E2 92 C2
Gosshill Rd BMLY BR1 169 F1
Gossington Cl CHST BR7 154 B3
Gosterwood St DEPT SE8 112 B5
Gostling Rd WHTN TW2 123 F7
Goston Gdns THHTH CR7 164 B2
Goswell Pl FSBYE EC1V 6 D8
Goswell Rd FSBYE EC1V 6 D7
Gothic Ct HYS/HAR UB3 101 G5
Gothic Rd WHTN TW2 142 D1
Gottfried Ms KTTN NW5 72 C3
Goudhurst Rd BMLY BR1 152 C4
Gough Rd EN EN1 30 D1
SRTFD E15 76 D3
Gough Sq FLST/FETLN EC4A 12 B4
Gough St FSBYW WC1X 5 M9
Goulding Gdns THHTH CR7 164 D1
Gould Rd EBED/NFELT TW14 121 H6
WHTN TW2 123 K7
Gould Ter HACK E8 74 D4
Goulston St WCHPL E1 13 L4
Goulton Rd CLPT E5 74 D4
Gourley Pl SEVS/STOTM N15 56 A4
Gourley St SEVS/STOTM N15 56 A4
Gourock Rd ELTH/MOT SE9 135 F4
Govan St BETH E2 74 C7
Govier Cl SRTFD E15 76 C6
Gowan Av FUL/PGN SW6 107 H7
Gowan Rd WLSDN NW10 69 K6
Gower Cl CLAP SW4 129 H5
Gower Ms GWRST WC1E 11 H3
Gower Pl GWRST WC1E 4 F9
Gower Rd FSTGT E7 76 E5
ISLW TW7 104 A5
Gower St GWRST WC1E 11 G1
Gower's Wk WCHPL E1 92 C5
Gowland Pl BECK BR3 166 C1
Gowlett Rd PECK SE15 131 H2
Gowland Cl CROY/NA CR0 165 H6
Gowrie Rd BTSEA SW11 129 F2
Graburn Wy E/WMO/HCT KT8 157 J2
Grace Av BXLYHN DA7 137 G1
Gracechurch St BANK EC3V 13 H6
Grace Cl EDGW HA8 36 E6
ELTH/MOT SE9 153 H2
Gracedale Rd
STRHM/NOR SW16 148 B4
Gracefield Gdns
STRHM/NOR SW16 148 E2
Grace Jones Cl HACK E8 74 B5
Grace Ms BECK BR3 151 J5
Grace Pl BOW E3 93 K2
Grace Rd CROY/NA CR0 164 D5
Graces Aly WCHPL E1 * 92 C6
Graces Ms STJWD NW8 * 2 F6
Grace's Ms CMBW SE5 130 E1

Grace's Rd CMBW SE5 131 F1
Grace St BOW E3 93 K2
The Gradient SYD SE26 150 C3
Graduate Pl STHWK SE1 19 J3
Graeme Rd EN EN1 30 A1
Graemesdyke Av
MORT/ESHN SW14 125 J2
Grafton Cl HSLWW TW4 122 D7
WEA W13 85 G5
WPK KT4 173 G2
Grafton Ct EBED/NFELT TW14 121 G7
Grafton Crs CAMTN NW1 72 B5
Grafton Gdns BCTR RM8 80 A1
FSBYPK N4 55 J5
Grafton Ms FITZ W1T 10 E1
Grafton Park Rd WPK KT4 173 G1
Grafton Pl CAMTN NW1 5 G8
Grafton Rd ACT W3 86 E6
BCTR RM8 80 A1
CROY/NA CR0 164 B7
ENC/FH EN2 29 F2
HRW HA1 48 C4
KTTN NW5 72 A4
NWMAL KT3 160 B3
WPK KT4 173 F2
Grafton Sq CLAP SW4 129 H2
Grafton St CONDST W1S 10 D7
Grafton Ter HAMP NW3 71 K4
Grafton Wy E/WMO/HCT KT8 156 E3
FITZ W1T 10 E2
Grafton Yd KTTN NW5 72 B5
Graham Av MTCM CR4 148 A7
WEA W13 104 C1
Graham Cl CROY/NA CR0 179 J1
Grahame Park Wy MLHL NW7 37 G6
Graham Gdns SURB KT6 159 F7
Graham Rd BXLYHS DA6 137 G3
CHSWK W4 106 A2
HACK E8 74 C5
HDN NW4 51 K5
HPTN TW12 142 A3
KTN/HRWW/WS HA3 48 E2
MTCM CR4 148 A7
PLSTW E13 94 E3
SEVS/STOTM N15 55 H2
WIM/MER SW19 146 D6
Graham St IS N1 6 D6
Graham Ter BFN/LL DA15 * 136 C5
BGVA SW1W 16 A6
Grainger Cl NTHLT UB5 66 C4
Grainger Rd ISLW TW7 124 A1
WDGN N22 41 J7
Gramer Cl WAN E11 76 B1
Grampian Cl BELMT SM2 175 G6
HYS/HAR UB3 101 G6
Grampian Gdns CRICK NW2 52 C7
Gramsci Wy CAT SE6 151 K2
Granada St TOOT SW17 147 K4
Granard Av PUT/ROE SW15 126 E4
Granard Rd BTSEA SW11 128 E6
Granary Cl ED N9 30 E6
Granary Rd WCHPL E1 92 D3
Granary Sq IS N1 73 G5
Granary St CAMTN NW1 5 G4
Granby Rd ELTH/MOT SE9 134 E1
WOOL/PLUM SE18 115 G2
Granby St BETH E2 7 M9
Granby Ter CAMTN NW1 4 E6
Grand Av BRYLDS KT5 159 J5
FARR EC1M 12 D2
MUSWH N10 54 A3
WBLY HA9 68 C4
Grand Av East WBLY HA9 68 D4
Grand Depot Rd
WOOL/PLUM SE18 115 F4
Grand Dr NWDGN UB2 103 H1
RYNPK SW20 161 F3
Granden Rd
STRHM/NOR SW16 * 163 K1
Grandison Rd BTSEA SW11 128 E4
WPK KT4 174 A1
Grand Junction Whf IS N1 * 6 E6
Grand Pde FSBYPK N4 * 55 H5
MORT/ESHN SW14 * 125 K3
SURB KT6 * 159 H7
WBLY HA9 * 68 D1
Grand Union Canal Wk
BTFD TW8 104 D5
MV/WKIL W9 8 B2
NTHLT UB5 83 K3
WDR/YW UB7 100 E1
WLSDN NW10 86 D1
Grand Union Cl MV/WKIL W9 88 D4
Grand Union Crs HACK E8 * 74 C7
Grand Union Wk
CAMTN NW1 * 4 D2
Grand Wk WCHPL E1 * 93 G3
Granfield St BTSEA SW11 * 108 C7
Grange Av EBAR EN4 27 J7
KTN/HRWW/WS HA3 49 H1
NFNCH/WDSPK N12 39 G4
SNWD SE25 165 F1
TRDG/WHET N20 26 C7
WFD IG8 44 E5
WHTN TW2 142 E1
Grangecliffe Gdns SNWD SE25 165 F1
Grange Cl BFN/LL DA15 155 G2
E/WMO/HCT KT8 157 G3
HEST TW5 102 E4
HYS/HAR UB3 82 C4
WFD IG8 44 E6
Grange Ct ALP/SUD HA0 * 67 J4
BELMT SM2 * 175 F6
HRW HA1 * 67 F2
NTHLT UB5 83 G1
PIN HA5 * 47 J2
WLGTN SM6 * 176 B2
Grangecourt Rd
STNW/STAM N16 56 A7
Grange Crs THMD SE28 97 J5
Grangedale Cl NTHWD HA6 32 C7
Grange Dr CHST BR7 153 J5
Grange Farm Cl
RYLN/HDSTN HA2 66 C1
Grange Gdns HAMP NW3 71 F2
PIN HA5 47 K3
SNWD SE25 165 F1
STHGT/OAK N14 28 D7
Grange Gv IS N1 73 J5
Grange Hl EDGW HA8 36 E4
SNWD SE25 165 F1
Grangehill Pl ELTH/MOT SE9 134 E2
Grangehill Rd ELTH/MOT SE9 134 E3
Grange Houses HBRY N5 * 73 J3
Grange La DUL SE21 150 B1
Grange Ms FELT TW13 * 140 B2
Grangemill Rd CAT SE6 151 J2
Grangemill Wy CAT SE6 151 J1
Grange Pk EA W5 86 A7
Grange Park Av WCHMH N21 29 H5
Grange Park Pl RYNPK SW20 145 K6
Grange Park Rd LEY E10 57 K7
THHTH CR7 164 E2
Grange Pl KIL/WHAMP NW6 2 A2
Grange Rd BARN SW13 106 D7
BELMT SM2 174 E6
BORE WD6 24 B4
BUSH WD23 21 J4
CHSGTN KT9 172 A3
CHSWK W4 105 J4
E/WMO/HCT KT8 157 G3
EA W5 85 K7
EDGW HA8 37 F5
HGT N6 54 A5
HRW HA1 49 G5
HYS/HAR UB3 82 C5
IL IG1 78 C3
KUT/HW KT1 159 F2
LEY E10 57 J7
PLSTW E13 94 D2
RYLN/HDSTN HA2 66 D1
SNWD SE25 164 E3
STHL UB1 102 D1
STHWK SE1 19 K4
TOTM N17 42 C5
WALTH E17 57 G4
WLSDN NW10 69 K5
Granger Wy ROM RM1 63 J5
Grange St IS N1 7 H4
The Grange ALP/SUD HA0 68 C6
CROY/NA CR0 179 H1
NWMAL KT3 * 160 D4
STHWK SE1 19 L3
WIM/MER SW19 146 B5
WKENS W14 * 107 J3
WPK KT4 173 F3
Grange V BELMT SM2 175 F6
Grangeview Rd
TRDG/WHET N20 27 G7
Grange Wk STHWK SE1 19 K3
Grange Walk Ms STHWK SE1 19 K4
Grange Wy ERITH DA8 118 E6
Grangeway KIL/WHAMP NW6 2 A2
NFNCH/WDSPK N12 39 F3
WFD IG8 45 G3
Grangeway Gdns REDBR IG4 59 J4
The Grangeway WCHMH N21 29 H5
Grangewood BXLY DA5 137 G7
Grangewood Cl PIN HA5 46 E4
Grangewood La BECK BR3 151 H5
Grangewood St EHAM E6 77 H7
Grange Yd STHWK SE1 19 L4
Granham Gdns ED N9 42 B1
Granite St WOOL/PLUM SE18 116 A4
Granleigh Rd WAN E11 76 C1
Gransden Av HACK E8 74 D6
Gransden Rd SHB W12 106 C1
Grantbridge St IS N1 6 D5
Grantchester KUT/HW KT1 * 159 H1
Grantchester Cl HRW HA1 67 F2
Grant Cl STHGT/OAK N14 28 C6
TOTM N17 56 A1
Grantham Cl EDGW HA8 36 A2
Grantham Gdns CHDH RM6 62 B5
Grantham Gn BORE WD6 24 E4
Grantham Pl
MYFR/PKLN W1K 10 C9
Grantham Rd BRXN/ST SW9 129 K2
CHSWK W4 106 B6
MNPK E12 78 A2
Grantley Pl ESH/CLAY KT10 170 B4
Grantley Rd HSLWW TW4 122 B1
Grantley St WCHPL E1 93 F2
Grantock Rd WALTH E17 44 B7
Granton Rd GDMY/SEVK IG3 61 G7
SCUP DA14 155 H5
STRHM/NOR SW16 148 C7
Grant Pl CROY/NA CR0 165 G7
Grant Rd BTSEA SW11 128 C2
CROY/NA CR0 165 G7
KTN/HRWW/WS HA3 48 E2
Grants Cl MLHL NW7 38 A6
Grant St IS N1 6 A5
PLSTW E13 94 E2
Grant Ter STNW/STAM N16 * 56 C6
Grantully Rd MV/WKIL W9 2 C8
Grant Wy ISLW TW7 104 B5
Granville Ar BRXN/ST SW9 * 130 B3
Granville Av ED N9 42 E2
FELT TW13 140 E1
HSLW TW3 123 F4
Granville Cl CROY/NA CR0 178 A1
Granville Gdns EA W5 86 B7
STRHM/NOR SW16 149 F7
Granville Gv LEW SE13 133 F2
Granville Ms SCUP DA14 155 G3
Granville Pk LEW SE13 133 F2
Granville Pl FUL/PGN SW6 * 108 A6
MBLAR W1H 10 A5
NFNCH/WDSPK N12 * 39 G6
PIN HA5 47 H2
Granville Rd BAR EN5 26 A3
CEND/HSY/T N8 55 F5
CRICK NW2 70 D1
HYS/HAR UB3 101 J3
IL IG1 60 B7
KIL/WHAMP NW6 2 A6
NFNCH/WDSPK N12 39 G6
PLMGR N13 41 F5
SCUP DA14 155 G3
SWFD E18 59 F1
WALTH E17 57 K5
WAND/EARL SW18 127 J6
WATW WD18 * 21 G3
WDGN N22 41 H7
WELL DA16 136 D2
WIM/MER SW19 146 E6
Granville Sq PECK SE15 * 111 F6
Granville St FSBYW WC1X 5 M8
Grape St LSQ/SEVD WC2H 11 J4
Graphite Sq LBTH SE11 17 L7
Grapsome Cl CHSGTN KT9 171 J6
Grasdene Rd
WOOL/PLUM SE18 116 B6
Grasgarth Cl ACT W3 86 E6
Grasmere Av ACT W3 86 E6
HSLW TW3 123 G5
PUT/ROE SW15 145 F3
RSLP HA4 46 A6
WBLY HA9 49 K6
WIM/MER SW19 161 K2
Grasmere Cl
EBED/NFELT TW14 121 J7
Grasmere Ct WDGN N22 41 F5
Grasmere Gdns
KTN/HRWW/WS HA3 49 G1
REDBR IG4 59 J4
Grasmere Rd BMLY BR1 152 D7
BXLYHN DA7 117 K7
MUSWH N10 40 B7
PLSTW E13 94 E1
SNWD SE25 165 J5
STRHM/NOR SW16 149 F4
TOTM N17 42 C5
Grass Banks DART DA1 139 J7
Grasshaven Wy THMD SE28 97 F7
Grassington Cl
FBAR/BDGN N11 40 A5
Grassington Rd SCUP DA14 155 G3
Grassmount FSTH SE23 150 D1
Grass Pk FNCH N3 38 D7
Grassway WLGTN SM6 176 C3
Grasvenor Av BAR EN5 26 E5
Grately Wy PECK SE15 * 111 F6
Gratton Rd WKENS W14 107 H2
Gratton Ter CRICK NW2 70 B2
Graveley Av BORE WD6 24 E3
Gravel Hl BXLYHS DA6 137 J4
CROY/NA CR0 179 F5
FNCH N3 52 D1
Gravel Hill Cl BXLYHS DA6 137 J4
Gravel La WCHPL E1 13 L4
Gravel Rd HAYES BR2 181 J1
WHTN TW2 123 K7
Gravelwood Cl CHST BR7 154 C2
Gravenel Gdns TOOT SW17 * 147 J4
Graveney Gv PGE/AN SE20 150 E6
Graveney Rd TOOT SW17 147 J3
Gravesend Rd SHB W12 87 J6
Gray Av BCTR RM8 62 B7
Gray Gdns RAIN RM13 81 J5
Grayham Crs NWMAL KT3 160 A3
Grayham Rd NWMAL KT3 160 A3
Grayland Cl BMLY BR1 153 H7
Grayling Cl CAN/RD E16 94 C3
Grayling Ct EA W5 * 85 K7
Grayling Rd STNW/STAM N16 73 K1
Grayling Sq BETH E2 * 92 C2
Grays Cots STMC/STPC BR5 * 155 J7
Grayscroft Rd
STRHM/NOR SW16 148 D6
Grays Farm Rd
STMC/STPC BR5 155 H7
Grayshott Rd BTSEA SW11 129 F2
Gray's Inn Rd FSBYW WC1X 5 K7
Gray's Inn Sq GINN WC1R 12 A2
Grayswood Gdns
RYNPK SW20 160 E1
Gray's Yd MHST W1U * 10 B5
Graywood Ct
NFNCH/WDSPK N12 39 G6
Grazebrook Rd
STNW/STAM N16 73 K1
Grazeley Cl BXLYHS DA6 137 K4
Great Amwell La
CEND/HSY/T N8 55 F2
Great Benty WDR/YW UB7 100 B3
Great Brownings DUL SE21 150 B3
Great Bushey Dr
TRDG/WHET N20 27 F7
Great Cambridge Jct
PLMGR N13 41 J4
Great Cambridge Rd EN EN1 30 C4
UED N18 41 K4
Great Castle St REGST W1B 10 E4
Great Central Av RSLP HA4 65 G4
Great Central St CAMTN NW1 9 L2
Great Central Wy WBLY HA9 68 E4
Great Chapel St
SOHO/SHAV W1D 11 G4
Great Chart St BTSEA SW11 128 B2
Great Chertsey Rd CHSWK W4 106 A7
FELT TW13 141 K2
Great Church La HMSMTH W6 107 G4
Great College St WEST SW1P 17 J3
Great Cross Av GNWCH SE10 113 H6
Great Cullings ROMW/RG RM7 81 G1
Great Cumberland Ms
MBLAR W1H 9 L5
Great Cumberland Pl
MBLAR W1H 9 L4
Great Dover St STHWK SE1 19 G3
Greatdown Rd HNWL W7 85 F4
Great Eastern Rd SRTFD E15 76 B6
Great Eastern St SDTCH EC2A 7 J8
Great Eastern Whf
BTSEA SW11 108 D6
Great Elms Rd HAYES BR2 168 B3
Great Fld CDALE/KGS NW9 37 G7
Greatfield Av EHAM E6 95 K3
Greatfield Cl ARCH N19 72 C3
BROCKY SE4 132 D3
Greatfields Rd BARK IG11 78 D7
Great Galley Cl BARK IG11 97 H2
Great Gardens Rd
EMPK RM11 63 K5
Great Gatton Cl CROY/NA CR0 166 B6
Great George St STJSPK SW1H 17 H2
Great Gv BUSH WD23 22 B3
Great Guildford St STHWK SE1 12 E9
Greatham Rd BUSH WD23 21 H2
Great Harry Dr ELTH/MOT SE9 154 A2
Great James St BMSBY WC1N 11 L2
Great Marlborough St
REGST W1B 10 E5
Great Maze Pond STHWK SE1 13 H9
Great New St
FLST/FETLN EC4A * 12 B4
Great North Rd BAR EN5 26 D1
EFNCH N2 53 J3
Great North Wy (Barnet
By-Pass) HDN NW4 37 K7
Greatorex St WCHPL E1 92 C4
Great Ormond St
BMSBY WC1N 11 K2
Great Percy St FSBYW WC1X 5 M7
Great Peter St WEST SW1P 17 G4
Great Portland St GTPST W1W 10 D2
Great Pulteney St
SOHO/CST W1F 10 F6
Great Queen St DART DA1 139 J5
HOL/ALD WC2B 11 K4
Great Russell St RSQ WC1B 11 H4
Great St Thomas Apostle
BLKFR EC4V 12 F6
Great Scotland Yd
WHALL SW1A 11 J9
Great Smith St WEST SW1P 17 H3
Great South-West Rd
EBED/NFELT TW14 121 F6
HSLWW TW4 122 A1
Great Spilmans EDUL SE22 131 F4
Great Strd CDALE/KGS NW9 51 H1
Great Suffolk St STHWK SE1 12 D9
Great Sutton St FSBYE EC1V 12 D1
Great Swan Aly LOTH EC2R 13 G4
Great Thrift STMC/STPC BR5 169 H3
Great Titchfield St
GTPST W1W 10 D2
Great Tower St MON EC3R 13 J6
Great Trinity La BLKFR EC4V 12 F6
Great Turnstile HHOL WC1V * 11 M3
Great Western Rd NTGHL W11 88 D4
Great West Rd BTFD TW8 104 B6
HEST TW5 122 D1
HMSMTH W6 106 E4
ISLW TW7 103 K6
Great West Rd Chiswick
CHSWK W4 106 C4
Great West Road Ellesmere Rd
CHSWK W4 105 K5
Great West Road Hogarth La
CHSWK W4 106 A5
Great Winchester St
OBST EC2N 13 H4
Great Windmill St
SOHO/SHAV W1D 11 G7
Greatwood CHST BR7 154 A6
Greaves Cl BARK IG11 78 D6
Greaves Cots POP/IOD E14 * 93 G4
Greaves Pl TOOT SW17 147 J3
Grebe Av YEAD UB4 83 H5
Grebe Cl BARK IG11 97 G3
FSTGT E7 76 D4
WALTH E17 43 G6
Grebe Ct SUT SM1 174 D4
Grebe Ter KUT/HW KT1 * 159 F2
Grecian Crs NRWD SE19 149 H5
Greek St SOHO/SHAV W1D 11 H5
Greenacre Cl NTHLT UB5 65 K4
Greenacre Gdns WALTH E17 58 A3
Greenacre Pl WLGTN SM6 176 B1
Green Acres CROY/NA CR0 178 B2
SCUP DA14 * 155 F3
Greenacres BUSH WD23 34 D1
ELTH/MOT SE9 135 F5
Greenacres Dr STAN HA7 35 H6
Greenacre Sq
BERM/RHTH SE16 * 112 A1
Greenacre Wk
STHGT/OAK N14 40 D2
Green Arbour Ct STBT EC1A * 12 C4
Green Av MLHL NW7 37 F3
WEA W13 104 C2
Greenaway Av UED N18 * 43 F4
Greenaway Gdns HAMP NW3 71 F3
Green Bank
NFNCH/WDSPK N12 39 F3
WAP E1W 92 D7
Greenbank Av ALP/SUD HA0 67 G4
Greenbank Cl CHING E4 44 A1
Greenbank Crs HDN NW4 52 C3
Greenbay Rd CHARL SE7 114 C6
Greenberry St STJWD NW8 3 J6
Green Chain Wk BMLY BR1 152 A4
CHARL SE7 114 C3
ELTH/MOT SE9 153 H1
SYD SE26 151 F5
THMD SE28 97 K7
WELL DA16 116 B7
Green Cl CAR SM5 175 K1
CDALE/KGS NW9 50 E5
FELT TW13 141 J4
GLDGN NW11 53 G6
HAYES BR2 167 H2
Greencoat Pl WEST SW1P 16 F5
Greencoat Rw WEST SW1P 16 F4
Green Court Av CROY/NA CR0 178 D1
Greencourt Av EDGW HA8 36 C7
Green Court Gdns
CROY/NA CR0 178 D1
Greencourt Rd
STMC/STPC BR5 169 K4
Greencroft EDGW HA8 36 E4
Greencroft Av RSLP HA4 65 G1
Greencroft Gdns EN EN1 30 A2
KIL/WHAMP NW6 2 E1
Greencroft Rd HEST TW5 102 E7
Green Dl EDUL SE22 131 F4
Green Dragon La BTFD TW8 105 F4
WCHMH N21 29 H5
Green Dragon Yd WCHPL E1 92 C4
Green Dr STHL UB1 84 A7
Green End CHSGTN KT9 171 K3
WCHMH N21 41 H1
Greenend Rd CHSWK W4 106 B1
Greenfell Man DEPT SE8 * 112 C4
Green Ferry Wy WALTH E17 57 F3
Greenfield Av BRYLDS KT5 159 J5
OXHEY WD19 33 J1
Greenfield Ct ELTH/MOT SE9 * 153 J2
Greenfield Dr BMLY BR1 168 B1
EFNCH N2 53 K3
Greenfield Gdns CRICK NW2 70 C1
DAGW RM9 79 J7
STMC/STPC BR5 169 H6
Greenfield Rd DAGW RM9 79 J7
SEVS/STOTM N15 56 A4
WCHPL E1 92 C4
Greenfields STHL UB1 84 A6
Greenfield Wy
RYLN/HDSTN HA2 48 B2
Greenford Av HNWL W7 84 E5
STHL UB1 83 K6
Greenford Gdns GFD/PVL UB6 84 B2
Greenford Rd STHL UB1 84 C6
SUT SM1 175 F3
Greengate GFD/PVL UB6 67 H5
Greengate St PLSTW E13 95 F1
Greenhalgh Wk EFNCH N2 53 G3
Greenham Cl STHWK SE1 18 A2
Greenham Crs CHING E4 43 H5
Greenham Rd MUSWH N10 54 A1
Greenhaven Dr THMD SE28 97 H5
Greenheys Cl NTHWD HA6 32 C7
Greenheys Dr SWFD E18 58 D2
Greenhill HAMP NW3 71 H3
SUT SM1 175 G1
WBLY HA9 68 D1
Green Hl WOOL/PLUM SE18 114 E4
Greenhill Ct BAR EN5 * 27 F4
Greenhill Crs WATW WD18 20 C5
Greenhill Gdns NTHLT UB5 83 K1
Greenhill Gv MNPK E12 77 J3
Greenhill Pde BAR EN5 * 27 F4
Greenhill Pk BAR EN5 27 F4
WLSDN NW10 69 G7
Greenhill Rd HRW HA1 48 E5
WLSDN NW10 69 G7
Greenhill's Rents FARR EC1M * 12 C2
Greenhills Ter IS N1 73 K5
Green Hill Ter NTHLT UB5 * 83 K1
WOOL/PLUM SE18 114 E4
Greenhill Wy HRW HA1 48 E5
WBLY HA9 68 D1
Greenhithe Cl BFN/LL DA15 135 K6
Greenholm Rd ELTH/MOT SE9 135 G4
Green Hundred Rd PECK SE15 111 H5
Greenhurst Rd WNWD SE27 149 G4
Greening St ABYW SE2 116 D3
Greenland Crs NWDGN UB2 102 B2
Greenland Ms DEPT SE8 112 A4
Greenland Pl CAMTN NW1 4 D3
Greenland Quay
BERM/RHTH SE16 112 A3
Greenland Rd BAR EN5 26 A5
CAMTN NW1 4 E3
Greenlands HOR/WEW KT19 172 D4
Greenlands La HDN NW4 52 A1
Greenland St CAMTN NW1 4 D3
Greenland Wy CROY/NA CR0 163 J6
Green La BCTR RM8 80 A1
CHSGTN KT9 172 A7
E/WMO/HCT KT8 157 G4
EDGW HA8 36 C4
ELTH/MOT SE9 135 F7
FELT TW13 141 J4
GDMY/SEVK IG3 79 G1
HDN NW4 52 B4
HNWL W7 103 K1
HSLWW TW4 122 B4
IL IG1 78 D1
MRDN SM4 161 K5
NTHWD HA6 32 B6
NWMAL KT3 159 K4
OXHEY WD19 21 G7
PGE/AN SE20 151 F6
STAN HA7 35 H3
SUN TW16 140 D6
THHTH CR7 149 H7
UX/CGN UB8 82 A4
WPK KT4 160 D7
Green Lane Cots STAN HA7 * 35 H3
Green Lane Gdns THHTH CR7 164 D1
Green Lanes FSBYPK N4 55 H5
HBRY N5 73 J2
HOR/WEW KT19 173 G7
PLMGR N13 41 F4
SEVS/STOTM N15 55 H3
WCHMH N21 29 J6
Greenlaw Ct EA W5 * 85 K5
Greenlaw Gdns NWMAL KT3 160 C6
Greenlawn La BTFD TW8 104 E3
Green Lawns
NFNCH/WDSPK N12 * 39 F5
RSLP HA4 * 47 G7
Greenlaw St
WOOL/PLUM SE18 115 F2
Green Leaf Av WLGTN SM6 176 D3
Greenleaf Cl
BRXS/STRHM SW2 * 130 B6
Greenleafe Dr BARK/HLT IG6 60 B2
Greenleaf Rd EHAM E6 77 G7
WALTH E17 57 H2
Greenleaf Wy
KTN/HRWW/WS HA3 49 F2
Greenlea Pk WIM/MER SW19 * 147 J7
Green Leas SUN TW16 140 D6
Green Leas Cl SUN TW16 140 D5
Greenlink Wk RCH/KEW TW9 105 J7
Green Man La
EBED/NFELT TW14 121 K3
WEA W13 85 G6
Greenman St IS N1 6 E2
Greenmead Cl SNWD SE25 165 H4
Green Moor Link WCHMH N21 29 H6
Greenmoor Rd PEND EN3 30 E1
Greenoak Pl EBAR EN4 27 K1
Green Oaks NWDGN UB2 * 102 C3
Greenoak Wy WIM/MER SW19 146 B3
Greenock Rd ACT W3 105 J2
STRHM/NOR SW16 148 D7
Green Pde HSLW TW3 * 123 G5
Greenpark Wy GFD/PVL UB6 66 E7
Green Pond Cl WALTH E17 57 G2
Green Pond Rd WALTH E17 57 G2
Green Rd STHGT/OAK N14 28 B5
TRDG/WHET N20 39 G2
Greenroof Wy GNWCH SE10 113 J2
Greens Ct NTGHL W11 * 88 D7
Green's Ct SOHO/CST W1F 11 G6
Greens End WOOL/PLUM SE18 115 G3
Greenshank Cl WALTH E17 43 G6
Greenside BCTR RM8 79 J1
BXLY DA5 137 F7
Greenside Cl CAT SE6 152 B1
TRDG/WHET N20 39 H1
Greenside Rd CROY/NA CR0 164 B6
SHB W12 106 D2
Greenslade Rd BARK IG11 78 D6
Greenstead Av WFD IG8 45 G5
Greenstead Gdns
PUT/ROE SW15 126 D4
WFD IG8 45 G5
Greenstone Ms WAN E11 58 E5
Green St FSTGT E7 77 F4
MYFR/PKLN W1K 9 M6
PEND EN3 30 E1
SUN TW16 140 E7
Greenstreet Hl NWCR SE14 * 132 A2
Greensward BUSH WD23 22 B5
Green Ter CLKNW EC1R 6 B8
The Green ACT W3 87 G5
BXLYHN DA7 117 H7
CAR SM5 * 176 A3
CROY/NA CR0 179 H7
ED N9 42 C1
FELT TW13 141 F1
HAYES BR2 167 K6
HEST TW5 103 F5
HGDN/ICK UB10 64 A1
HRW HA1 67 G1
MRDN SM4 161 H3
NWDGN UB2 102 E1
NWMAL KT3 159 K2
RCH/KEW TW9 124 E4
SCUP DA14 155 G4
SRTFD E15 76 D5
STHGT/OAK N14 40 D1
STMC/STPC BR5 155 H6
SUT SM1 175 F2
TOTM N17 41 J5
WAN E11 59 F5
WCHMH N21 29 G6
WDR/YW UB7 100 A2
WELL DA16 135 K3
WHTN TW2 123 K7
WIM/MER SW19 146 B4
WLGTN SM6 176 A1
Green V BXLYHS DA6 136 E4
EA W5 86 B5
Greenvale Rd ELTH/MOT SE9 134 E3
Green Verges STAN HA7 35 K6
Green Vw CHSGTN KT9 172 B6
Greenview Av BECK BR3 166 B5
CROY/NA CR0 166 B5
Greenview Cl ACT W3 87 G7
Greenview Dr RYNPK SW20 161 F2
Green Wk DART DA1 138 C3
HDN NW4 52 B3
NWDGN UB2 103 F4
RSLP HA4 46 D7
STHWK SE1 19 J4
WFD IG8 45 J5
Green Wy ELTH/MOT SE9 134 C4
HAYES BR2 168 D5
Greenway BCTR RM8 79 J1
CHST BR7 154 A4
KTN/HRWW/WS HA3 50 A4
PIN HA5 47 F1
RYNPK SW20 161 F3
STHGT/OAK N14 40 E1
TRDG/WHET N20 38 E1
WLGTN SM6 176 C3
YEAD UB4 83 F3

Greenway Av WALTH E17 58 B3
Greenway Cl
SEVS/STOTM N15 56 B3
CDALE/KGS NW9 51 F1
FBAR/BDGN N11 40 A5
FSBYPK N4 73 J1
TRDG/WHET N20 38 E1
Greenway Ct IL IG1 60 A7
SRTFD E15 94 C1
Greenway Gdns
CDALE/KGS NW9 50 E1
CROY/NA CR0 179 H2
GFD/PVL UB6 84 A2
Green Way Gdns
KTN/HRWW/WS HA3 48 E1
Greenways BECK BR3 166 D1
ESH/CLAY KT10 170 E3
NFNCH/WDSPK N12 * 39 G5
The Greenways TWK TW1 * 124 B5
The Green Wy
KTN/HRWW/WS HA3 34 E7
The Greenway
CDALE/KGS NW9 51 F1
EHAM E6 96 A3
HSLWW TW4 * 122 E3
OLYMPICPK E20 75 K7
PIN HA5 47 K5
SRTFD E15 94 D1
Greenwell St GTPST W1W 10 D1
Greenwich Church St
GNWCH SE10 * 113 F5
Greenwich Crs EHAM E6 95 J4
Greenwich Foot Tnl
GNWCH SE10 113 F4
Greenwich Hts CHARL SE7 * 114 D6
Greenwich High Rd
GNWCH SE10 112 E6
Greenwich House LEW SE13 133 G5
Greenwich Park St
GNWCH SE10 * 113 G5
Greenwich Quay DEPT SE8 * 112 D5
Greenwich South St
GNWCH SE10 112 E7
Greenwich Vw POP/IOD E14 112 E2
Greenwood Av DAGE RM10 80 D3
Greenwood Cl BFN/LL DA15 155 G1
HYS/HAR UB3 82 E7
MRDN SM4 161 H3
STMC/STPC BR5 169 K5
THDIT KT7 158 B7
Greenwood Dr CHING E4 44 A4
Greenwood Gdns PLMGR N13 41 H2
Greenwood La HPTN TW12 142 B4
Greenwood Pk
KUTN/CMB KT2 145 G6
Greenwood Pl KTTN NW5 72 B4
Greenwood Rd CROY/NA CR0 164 C6
HACK E8 74 C4
ISLW TW7 123 K2
MTCM CR4 163 J2
PLSTW E13 94 D1
THDIT KT7 158 B7
Greenwood Ter
WLSDN NW10 * 69 F7
Green Wrythe Crs CAR SM5 162 D7
Green Wrythe La CAR SM5 162 C5
Green Yd FSBYW WC1X 5 M9
Greer Rd KTN/HRWW/WS HA3 34 C7
Greet St STHWK SE1 12 B9
Greg Cl LEY E10 58 A5
Gregor Ms BKHTH/KID SE3 113 K6
Gregory Crs ELTH/MOT SE9 134 C6
Gregory Pl KENS W8 14 C1
Gregory Rd CHDH RM6 61 K3
NWDGN UB2 103 F2
Gregson Cl BORE WD6 24 E1
Greig Cl CEND/HSY/T N8 54 E4
Greig Ter WALW SE17 18 D9
Grenaby Av CROY/NA CR0 164 E6
Grenaby Rd CROY/NA CR0 164 E6
Grenada Rd BKHTH/KID SE3 114 B6
Grenade St POP/IOD E14 93 H6
Grenadier St CAN/RD E16 96 A7
Grena Gdns RCH/KEW TW9 125 G3
Grenard Cl PECK SE15 * 111 H6
Grena Rd RCH/KEW TW9 125 G3
Grendon Gdns WBLY HA9 68 C1
Grendon St STJWD NW8 3 J9
Grenfell Av HCH RM12 63 H7
Grenfell Ct MLHL NW7 * 37 K5
Grenfell Gdns
KTN/HRWW/WS HA3 50 A6
Grenfell Rd NTGHL W11 88 B6
TOOT SW17 147 K5
Grennell Cl SUT SM1 175 H1
Grennell Rd SUT SM1 175 G1
Grenoble Gdns PLMGR N13 41 G5
Grenville Cl BRYLDS KT5 159 K7
FNCH N3 38 D7
Grenville Gdns WFD IG8 45 G6
Grenville Ms ARCH N19 54 E7
HPTN TW12 142 B4
Grenville Pl MLHL NW7 37 F4
SKENS SW7 14 E5
Grenville Rd ARCH N19 54 E7
CROY/NA CR0 180 A7
Grenville St BMSBY WC1N 11 K1
Gresham Av TRDG/WHET N20 39 K3
Gresham Cl BXLY DA5 137 F5
ENC/FH EN2 29 J2
Gresham Dr CHDH RM6 61 H4
Gresham Gdns GLDGN NW11 52 C7
Gresham Rd BECK BR3 166 B1
BRXN/ST SW9 130 B2
CAN/RD E16 95 F5
EDGW HA8 36 B5
EHAM E6 95 K1
HPTN TW12 142 A5
HSLW TW3 103 H7
SNWD SE25 * 165 H3
WLSDN NW10 69 F4
Gresham St CITYW EC2V 12 E4
Gresham Wy WIM/MER SW19 146 E2
Gresley Cl SEVS/STOTM N15 * 55 K3
WALTH E17 57 G5
Gresley Rd ARCH N19 54 C7
Gressenhall Rd
WAND/EARL SW18 127 J5
Gresse St FITZ W1T 11 G3
Gresswell Cl SCUP DA14 155 G2
Greswell St FUL/PGN SW6 107 G7
Gretton Rd TOTM N17 42 A6
Greville Cl TWK TW1 124 C6
Greville Ms KIL/WHAMP NW6 2 C4
Greville Pl KIL/WHAMP NW6 2 D5
Greville Rd KIL/WHAMP NW6 2 C4
RCHPK/HAM TW10 125 G5
WALTH E17 58 A3
Greville St HCIRC EC1N 12 B3
Grey Cl GLDGN NW11 53 G5
Greycoat Pl WEST SW1P 17 G4
Greycoat St WEST SW1P 17 G4
Greycot Rd BECK BR3 151 J4
Grey Eagle St WCHPL E1 13 M1
Greyfell Cl STAN HA7 35 H4
Greyhound Hl HDN NW4 51 J2
Greyhound La
STRHM/NOR SW16 148 E5
Greyhound Rd HMSMTH W6 107 G5
SUT SM1 175 G4
TOTM N17 56 A2
WLSDN NW10 87 K2
Greyhound Ter
STRHM/NOR SW16 148 C7
Greyhound Wy DART DA1 138 B4
Greyladies Gdns
GNWCH SE10 * 133 F1
Greys Park Cl HAYES BR2 181 G4
Greystead Rd FSTH SE23 131 K6
Greystoke Av PIN HA5 48 A2
Greystoke Cots EA W5 * 86 A3
Greystoke Gdns EA W5 86 A3
ENC/FH EN2 28 D3
Greystone Gdns BARK/HLT IG6 60 C3
KTN/HRWW/WS HA3 49 J5
Greyswood Av UED N18 * 43 F4
Greyswood St
STRHM/NOR SW16 148 B5
Grierson Rd FSTH SE23 132 B5
Griffin Cl WLSDN NW10 69 K4
Griffin Manor Wy THMD SE28 115 J2
Griffin Rd TOTM N17 56 A1
WOOL/PLUM SE18 115 J4
Griffins Cl WCHMH N21 29 K7
Griffin Wy THMD SE28 115 K2
Griffith Cl CHDH RM6 61 J6
Griffiths Rd WIM/MER SW19 146 E6
Griggs Ap IL IG1 78 C1
Griggs Cl IL IG1 78 E3
Grigg's Pl STHWK SE1 19 K4
Griggs Rd LEY E10 58 A5
Grimsby Gv CAN/RD E16 96 B7
Grimsby St WCHPL E1 13 M1
Grimsdyke Crs BAR EN5 26 A2
Grimsdyke Rd PIN HA5 33 J6
Grimsel Pth CMBW SE5 110 C6
Grimshaw Cl HGT N6 * 54 A6
Grimshaw Wy ROM RM1 63 G4
Grimston Rd FUL/PGN SW6 127 J1
Grimwade Av CROY/NA CR0 178 C2
Grimwade Cl PECK SE15 131 J1
Grimwood Rd TWK TW1 124 A6
Grindall Cl CROY/NA CR0 177 H3
Grindal St STHWK SE1 18 A2
Grindleford Av
FBAR/BDGN N11 40 A1
Grindley Gdns CROY/NA CR0 * 165 G5
Grinling Pl DEPT SE8 112 D5
Grinstead Rd DEPT SE8 112 B4
Grisle Cl ED N9 42 D3
Grittleton Av WBLY HA9 68 D5
Grittleton Rd MV/WKIL W9 2 A9
Grizedale Ter FSTH SE23 150 D1
Grocers' Hall Ct LOTH EC2R * 13 G5
Groombridge Cl WELL DA16 136 B4
Groombridge Rd HOM E9 75 F6
Groom Cl HAYES BR2 168 A3
Groom Crs WAND/EARL SW18 128 C6
Groomfield Cl TOOT SW17 148 A3
Groom Pl KTBR SW1X 16 B3
Grooms Dr PIN HA5 46 E4
Grosmont Rd
WOOL/PLUM SE18 116 A4
Grosse Wy PUT/ROE SW15 126 E5
Grosvenor Av CAR SM5 175 K5
HBRY N5 73 J4
MORT/ESHN SW14 126 B2
RYLN/HDSTN HA2 48 B6
YEAD UB4 82 D1
Grosvenor Br PIM SW1V 16 D9
Grosvenor Cots KTBR SW1X 16 A5
Grosvenor Ct
RKW/CH/CXG WD3 * 20 B4
Grosvenor Crs
CDALE/KGS NW9 50 C3
DART DA1 139 G4
KTBR SW1X 16 B2
Grosvenor Crescent Ms
KTBR SW1X 16 A2
Grosvenor Gdns BGVA SW1W 16 D4
CRICK NW2 70 A5
GLDGN NW11 52 D5
KUTN/CMB KT2 143 K5
MORT/ESHN SW14 126 B2
MUSWH N10 54 C2
STHGT/OAK N14 28 D4
WFD IG8 44 E5
WLGTN SM6 176 C6
Grosvenor Gardens Ms East
BGVA SW1W * 16 D3
Grosvenor Gardens Ms North
BGVA SW1W 16 C4
Grosvenor Ga
MYFR/PKLN W1K 9 M7
Grosvenor Hl
MYFR/PKLN W1K 10 C6
WIM/MER SW19 146 C5
Grosvenor Pde EA W5 * 86 C7
Grosvenor Pk CMBW SE5 110 D6
Grosvenor Park Rd
WALTH E17 57 J4
Grosvenor Pl KTBR SW1X 16 B1
Grosvenor Ri East WALTH E17 57 K4
Grosvenor Rd BCTR RM8 62 B7
BELV DA17 117 G5
BORE WD6 24 C2
BTFD TW8 104 E5
BXLYHS DA6 136 E4
CHSWK W4 105 K4
ED N9 30 D7
FNCH N3 38 D6
FSTGT E7 77 F6
HNWL W7 85 G7
HSLWW TW4 122 E2
IL IG1 78 C2
LEY E10 58 A7
MUSWH N10 40 B7
NTHWD HA6 32 D6
NWDGN UB2 102 E2
PIM SW1V 16 D9
RCHPK/HAM TW10 125 F4
ROMW/RG RM7 63 F6
SNWD SE25 165 J3
STMC/STPC BR5 169 K5
TWK TW1 124 B6
WAN E11 59 F4
WAT WD17 21 G4
WLGTN SM6 176 B5
WWKM BR4 179 K1
Grosvenor Sq
MYFR/PKLN W1K 10 B6
Grosvenor St
MYFR/PKLN W1K 10 B6
Grosvenor Ter CMBW SE5 110 D6
Grosvenor V RSLP HA4 64 D1
Grosvenor Wy TOOT SW17 147 H2
Grosvenor Wharf Rd
POP/IOD E14 113 G3
Grote's Blds BKHTH/KID SE3 133 H1
Grote's Pl BKHTH/KID SE3 133 H1
Groton Rd WAND/EARL SW18 147 F1
Grotto Ct STHWK SE1 * 18 E1
Grotto Pas MHST W1U 10 A2
Grotto Rd TWK TW1 143 F1
Grove Av FNCH N3 38 E6
HNWL W7 84 E5
MUSWH N10 54 C1
PIN HA5 47 J3
SUT SM1 174 E5
TWK TW1 124 A7
Grove Bank OXHEY WD19 * 21 H7
Grovebury Cl ERITH DA8 118 A5
Grovebury Ct STHGT/OAK N14 28 C6
Grovebury Rd ABYW SE2 116 C1
Grove Cl FSTH SE23 132 A7
HAYES BR2 181 E1
KUT/HW KT1 159 G3
STHGT/OAK N14 * 28 B6
Grove Cots CHEL SW3 15 K9
CHSWK W4 * 106 B5
Grove Ct E/WMO/HCT KT8 157 J4
EA W5 * 86 A7
Grove Crs CDALE/KGS NW9 50 E3
FELT TW13 141 J3
KUT/HW KT1 159 F2
SWFD E18 58 D1
WOT/HER KT12 156 A6
Grove Crescent Rd SRTFD E15 76 B5
Grovedale Rd ARCH N19 72 D1
Grove Dwellings WCHPL E1 * 92 E4
Grove End KTTN NW5 72 B3
SWFD E18 58 D1
Grove End La ESH/CLAY KT10 157 J7
Grove End Rd STJWD NW8 3 G6
Grove Farm Pk NTHWD HA6 32 B4
Grove Footpath BRYLDS KT5 159 F3
Grove Gdns HDN NW4 * 51 J4
STJWD NW8 3 K8
TEDD TW11 143 G3
Grove Green Rd WAN E11 76 A2
Grove Hall Rd BUSH WD23 21 J3
Groveherst Rd DART DA1 139 J2
Grove Hl HRW HA1 48 E6
SWFD E18 58 D1
Grove Hill Rd CMBW SE5 131 F2
HRW HA1 49 F6
Grove House Rd
CEND/HSY/T N8 54 E3
Groveland Av
STRHM/NOR SW16 149 F6
Groveland Ct STP EC4M 12 F5
Groveland Rd BECK BR3 166 C2
Grovelands E/WMO/HCT KT8 157 F3
Grovelands Cl CMBW SE5 131 F1
RYLN/HDSTN HA2 66 B2
Grovelands Ct
STHGT/OAK N14 28 D6
Grovelands Rd PLMGR N13 41 F3
SEVS/STOTM N15 56 C5
STMC/STPC BR5 155 G6
Groveland Wy NWMAL KT3 159 K4
Grove La CMBW SE5 110 E7
KUT/HW KT1 159 F3
Groveley Rd SUN TW16 140 D4
Grove Market Pl
ELTH/MOT SE9 * 134 E5
Grove Ms HMSMTH W6 107 F2
Grove Mill Pl CAR SM5 176 A2
Grove Pk CDALE/KGS NW9 50 E3
CMBW SE5 131 F1
WAN E11 59 F4
Grove Park Av CHING E4 43 K6
Grove Park Br CHSWK W4 105 K6
Grove Park Gdns CHSWK W4 105 J6
Grove Park Rd CHSWK W4 105 J6
ELTH/MOT SE9 153 H2
RAIN RM13 81 J7
SEVS/STOTM N15 56 A3
Grove Park Ter CHSWK W4 105 J6
Grove Pl ACT W3 86 E7
BAL SW12 129 G5
HAMP NW3 71 H2
Grove Rd ACT W3 86 E7
BARN SW13 126 C1
BELV DA17 117 G5
BOW E3 93 G1
BTFD TW8 104 D4
BXLYHN DA7 137 K3
CHDH RM6 61 J6
CHING E4 44 A2
CRICK NW2 70 A5
E/WMO/HCT KT8 157 J3
EA W5 85 K6
EBAR EN4 27 J2
EDGW HA8 36 C5
FBAR/BDGN N11 40 B4
HOM E9 75 F7
HSLW TW3 123 F3
ISLW TW7 103 K7
MTCM CR4 163 G1
NFNCH/WDSPK N12 39 H4
NTHWD HA6 32 B4
PIN HA5 47 K4
RCHPK/HAM TW10 125 G5
SEVS/STOTM N15 56 A4
SURB KT6 158 E4
SUT SM1 174 E5
SWFD E18 58 D1
THHTH CR7 164 B3
WALTH E17 57 K4
WAN E11 58 D6
WHTN TW2 142 D2
WIM/MER SW19 147 G6
Grover Rd OXHEY WD19 21 H5
Groveside Cl ACT W3 86 C5
CAR SM5 175 J1
Groveside Rd CHING E4 44 C2
Grovestile Waye
EBED/NFELT TW14 121 G6
Grove St BERM/RHTH SE16 112 C3
UED N18 42 B4
Grove Ter KTTN NW5 72 A2
STHL UB1 * 84 A6
TEDD TW11 143 G3
Grove Terrace Ms KTTN NW5 72 B2
The Grove BXLYHS DA6 136 E3
CDALE/KGS NW9 51 F4
CEND/HSY/T N8 54 D4
EA W5 85 K7
EDGW HA8 36 D3
ENC/FH EN2 29 G1
FNCH N3 38 E6
FSBYPK N4 55 F6
GFD/PVL UB6 84 C5
GLDGN NW11 52 C6
HGT N6 54 A7
ISLW TW7 103 K7
PLMGR N13 41 G3
SRTFD E15 76 C6
TEDD TW11 143 G3
WOT/HER KT12 156 A6
WWKM BR4 180 A2
Grove V CHST BR7 154 A5
EDUL SE22 131 F3
Groveway BCTR RM8 79 K3
BRXN/ST SW9 110 A7
Grove Wy ESH/CLAY KT10 157 H6
WBLY HA9 68 E4
Grove Wood Cl BMLY BR1 169 F2
Grovewood Pl WFD IG8 45 K5
Grummant Rd PECK SE15 111 G7
Grundy St POP/IOD E14 93 K5
Gruneisen Rd FNCH N3 39 F6
Guardian Ct EMPK RM11 81 K1
Gubyon Av HNHL SE24 130 C4
Gudden Dr CLPT E5 74 D3
Guernsey Cl HEST TW5 103 F7
Guernsey Gv HNHL SE24 130 D6
Guernsey Rd IS N1 73 J5
LEY E10 58 B7
Guibal Rd LEE/GVPK SE12 133 K6
Guildersfield Rd
STRHM/NOR SW16 148 E6
Guildford Av FELT TW13 140 D1
Guildford Gv GNWCH SE10 112 E7
Guildford Rd CROY/NA CR0 164 E5
EHAM E6 95 J5
GDMY/SEVK IG3 78 E1
VX/NE SW8 109 K7
WALTH E17 44 A7
Guildford Wy WLGTN SM6 176 E4
Guildhall Blds CITYW EC2V 12 F4
Guildhall Yd CITYW EC2V 12 F4
Guildhouse St PIM SW1V 16 E6
Guildown Av
NFNCH/WDSPK N12 39 F3
Guild Rd CHARL SE7 114 C4
ERITH DA8 118 C6
Guildsway WALTH E17 43 H7
Guilford Av BRYLDS KT5 159 G4
Guilford Pl BMSBY WC1N 11 L1
Guilford St BMSBY WC1N 11 L1
Guillemot Pl WDGN N22 * 55 F1
Guinness Cl HOM E9 75 G6
HYS/HAR UB3 101 G2
Guinness Ct CROY/NA CR0 * 178 B1
Guinness Sq STHWK SE1 19 J4
Guinness Trust
STNW/STAM N16 * 56 B7
Guinness Trust Est CHEL SW3 15 L6
SRTFD E15 * 76 D7
Guion Rd FUL/PGN SW6 127 J1
Gulland Wk IS N1 * 73 J5
Gulliver Cl NTHLT UB5 65 K7
Gulliver Rd BFN/LL DA15 154 D1
Gulliver St BERM/RHTH SE16 112 C2
Gumleigh Rd EA W5 104 D3
Gumley Gdns ISLW TW7 124 B2
Gundulph Rd HAYES BR2 168 B2
Gunmakers La BOW E3 75 G7
Gunnell Cl CROY/NA CR0 165 G5
SYD SE26 * 150 C3
Gunner La WOOL/PLUM SE18 115 F4
Gunnersbury Ave ACT W3 105 H2
Gunnersbury Av (North Circular Rd) EA W5 86 B6
Gunnersbury Cl CHSWK W4 * 105 J4
Gunnersbury Crs ACT W3 105 H1
Gunnersbury Dr EA W5 105 G1
Gunnersbury Gdns ACT W3 105 H1
Gunnersbury La ACT W3 105 H1
Gunnersbury Ms CHSWK W4 105 J4
Gunners Gv CHING E4 44 A2
Gunners Rd WAND/EARL SW18 147 H1
Gunning St WOOL/PLUM SE18 115 K3
Gunstor Rd STNW/STAM N16 * 74 A3
Gun St WCHPL E1 13 L3
Gunter Gv EDGW HA8 37 F7
WBPTN SW10 108 B5
Gunterstone Rd WKENS W14 107 H4
Gunthorpe St WCHPL E1 13 M3
Gunton Rd CLPT E5 74 D2
TOOT SW17 148 A5
Gunwhale Cl
BERM/RHTH SE16 93 F7
Gunyard Ms
WOOL/PLUM SE18 * 114 D6
Gurdon Rd CHARL SE7 113 K4
Gurnell Gv WEA W13 85 F3
Gurney Cl BARK IG11 78 B5
SRTFD E15 76 C4
WALTH E17 43 F7
Gurney Crs CROY/NA CR0 164 A7
Gurney Dr EFNCH N2 53 H3
Gurney Rd CAR SM5 176 A3
FUL/PGN SW6 128 B2
NTHLT UB5 83 F2
SRTFD E15 76 C4
Guthrie St CHEL SW3 15 J7
Gutter La CITYW EC2V 12 E4
Guyatt Gdns MTCM CR4 163 F1
Guy Barnett Gv
BKHTH/KID SE3 133 K2
Guy Rd WLGTN SM6 176 D2
Guyscliff Rd LEW SE13 133 F4
Guysfield Cl RAIN RM13 81 J7
Guysfield Dr RAIN RM13 81 J7
Guy St STHWK SE1 19 H1
Gwalior Rd PUT/ROE SW15 127 G3
Gwendolen Av
PUT/ROE SW15 127 G4
Gwendoline Av PLSTW E13 77 F7
Gwendwr Rd WKENS W14 107 H4
Gweneth Cots EDGW HA8 * 36 C5
Gwillim Cl BFN/LL DA15 136 B5
Gwydor Rd BECK BR3 166 A3
Gwydyr Rd HAYES BR2 167 J2
Gwyn Cl FUL/PGN SW6 108 B6
Gwynne Av CROY/NA CR0 166 A6
Gwynne Park Av WFD IG8 45 K5
Gwynne Rd BTSEA SW11 128 C1
Gwynne Whf CHSWK W4 106 C5
Gylcote Cl CMBW SE5 130 E3
Gyles Pk STAN HA7 35 J7
Gyllyngdune Gdns
GDMY/SEVK IG3 79 F2
Gywnne Pl FSBYW WC1X 5 M8

H

Haarlem Rd WKENS W14 107 G2
Haberdasher Pl IS N1 7 H7
Haberdasher St IS N1 7 H7
Habington Cl CMBW SE5 * 110 E6
Habitat Cl PECK SE15 131 J1
Haccombe Rd
WIM/MER SW19 147 G5
Hackbridge Park Gdns
CAR SM5 175 K1
Hackbridge Rd CAR SM5 176 A1
Hackford Rd BRXN/ST SW9 110 A7
Hackford Wk BRXN/ST SW9 110 A7
Hackforth Cl BAR EN5 25 K4
Hackington Crs BECK BR3 151 J5
Hackney Cl BORE WD6 25 F4
Hackney Gv HACK E8 * 74 D5
Hackney Rd BETH E2 7 L7
Hackney Wick HOM E9 75 H5
Hadar Cl TRDG/WHET N20 26 E7
Haddenham Ct
OXHEY WD19 * 33 H2
Hadden Rd THMD SE28 115 K2
Hadden Wy GFD/PVL UB6 66 D5
Haddington Rd BMLY BR1 152 B2
Haddon Cl BORE WD6 24 C1
EN EN1 30 C5
NWMAL KT3 160 C4
Haddon Gv BFN/LL DA15 136 B6
Haddon Rd SUT SM1 175 F3
Haddo St GNWCH SE10 112 E5
Hadfield Cl STHL UB1 83 K2
Hadfield Rd
STWL/WRAY TW19 120 A5
Hadleigh Cl RYNPK SW20 161 J1
WCHPL E1 92 E3
Hadleigh Dr BELMT SM2 174 E7
Hadleigh Rd ED N9 30 D6
Hadleigh St BETH E2 92 E3
Hadley Cl BORE WD6 24 B4
WCHMH N21 29 G5
Hadley Common BAR EN5 27 G1
Hadley Gdns CHSWK W4 106 A4
NWDGN UB2 102 E4
Hadley Gn BAR EN5 26 D2
Hadley Green Rd BAR EN5 26 D1
Hadley Gn West BAR EN5 26 C1
Hadley Gv BAR EN5 26 C1
Hadley Pde BAR EN5 * 26 C2
Hadley Rdg BAR EN5 26 D2
Hadley Rd BAR EN5 27 F2
BELV DA17 117 G3
MTCM CR4 163 J3
Hadley St KTTN NW5 72 B5
Hadley Wy WCHMH N21 29 G5
Hadley Wood Rd BAR EN5 26 E1
Hadlow Pl NRWD SE19 150 C6
Hadlow Rd SCUP DA14 155 G3
WELL DA16 116 D6
Hadrian Cl BOW E3 75 J7
STWL/WRAY TW19 120 B6
Hadrian Est BETH E2 * 92 C1
Hadrian's Ride EN EN1 30 B4
Hadrian St GNWCH SE10 113 H4
Hadrian Wy STWL/WRAY TW19 120 A6
Hadyn Park Rd SHB W12 106 D1
Hafer Rd BTSEA SW11 128 E3
Hafton Rd CAT SE6 133 H7
Hagden La WATW WD18 20 D3
Haggard Rd TWK TW1 124 C6
Hagger Ct WALTH E17 * 58 B2
Haggerston Rd HACK E8 7 L3
Hague St BETH E2 92 C2
Ha-Ha Rd WOOL/PLUM SE18 114 E5
Haig Rd STAN HA7 35 J4
UX/CGN UB8 82 A4
Haig Rd East PLSTW E13 95 G2
Haig Rd West PLSTW E13 95 G2
Haigville Gdns BARK/HLT IG6 60 B3
Hailes Cl CROY/NA CR0 176 D1
WIM/MER SW19 147 G5
Haileybury Av EN EN1 30 B5
Hailey Rd ERITHM DA18 117 H1
Hailsham Av
BRXS/STRHM SW2 149 F1
Hailsham Cl SURB KT6 158 E6
Hailsham Dr HRW HA1 48 D2
Hailsham Rd TOOT SW17 148 A5
Hailsham Ter UED N18 * 41 K4
Haimo Rd ELTH/MOT SE9 134 C4
Hainault Blds LEY E10 * 58 A7
Hainault Gore CHDH RM6 62 A4
Hainault Rd CHDH RM6 61 H2
CRW RM5 62 E2
WAN E11 58 A7
Hainault St ELTH/MOT SE9 135 G7
IL IG1 78 B1
Haines Wk MRDN SM4 162 A6
Hainford Cl PECK SE15 132 A3
Haining Cl CHSWK W4 105 H4
Hainthorpe Rd WNWD SE27 149 H2
Hainton Cl WCHPL E1 92 D5
Halberd Ms CLPT E5 74 D1
Halbutt St DAGW RM9 80 B3
Halcomb St IS N1 7 J4
Halcot Av BXLYHS DA6 137 J4
Halcrow St WCHPL E1 * 92 D4
Haldane Cl MUSWH N10 40 B6
Haldane Pl WAND/EARL SW18 128 A7
Haldane Rd EHAM E6 95 H2
FUL/PGN SW6 107 J6
STHL UB1 84 C6
THMD SE28 97 K6
Haldan Rd CHING E4 44 A5
Haldon Rd WAND/EARL SW18 127 J5
Hale Cl CHING E4 44 A2
EDGW HA8 36 E4
Hale Dr MLHL NW7 36 E5
Hale End Cl RSLP HA4 46 E5
Hale End Rd WALTH E17 58 B1
Halefield Rd TOTM N17 42 C7
Hale Gdns ACT W3 86 C7
TOTM N17 56 C2
Hale Grove Gdns MLHL NW7 37 F4
Hale House
WOOL/PLUM SE18 * 114 D6
Hale La EDGW HA8 36 E4
Hale Rd EHAM E6 95 J3
TOTM N17 56 C2
Halesowen Rd MRDN SM4 162 A6
Hales St DEPT SE8 112 D6
Hale St POP/IOD E14 93 K6
Halesworth Rd LEW SE13 132 E2
The Hale CHING E4 44 B6
TOTM N17 56 C2
Haley Rd HDN NW4 52 A5
Half Acre BTFD TW8 104 E5
Half Acre Ms BTFD TW8 104 E6
Half Acre Rd HNWL W7 84 E7
Half Moon Crs IS N1 5 M5
Half Moon La HNHL SE24 130 D5
Half Moon Pas WCHPL E1 13 M5
Half Moon St MYFR/PICC W1J 10 D8
Halford Cl EDGW HA8 50 D1
Halford Rd FUL/PGN SW6 107 K5
LEY E10 58 B4
RCHPK/HAM TW10 125 F4
Halfway Ct PUR RM19 119 K3
Halfway St BFN/LL DA15 135 K7
Haliburton Rd TWK TW1 124 B4
Haliday Wk IS N1 73 K5
Halifax Cl TEDD TW11 142 E5
Halifax Rd ENC/FH EN2 29 J1

GFD/PVL UB6 66 B7
Halifax St SYD SE26 150 D2
Halifield Dr BELV DA17 117 F2
Haling Gv SAND/SEL CR2 177 J6
Haling Park Gdns
SAND/SEL CR2 177 H5
Haling Park Rd SAND/SEL CR2 177 H5
Haling Rd SAND/SEL CR2 177 K5
Halkin Ar KTBR SW1X 16 A3
Halkin Ms KTBR SW1X * 16 A3
Halkin Pl KTBR SW1X 16 A3
Halkin St KTBR SW1X 16 B2
Hallam Cl CHST BR7 153 K4
WATN WD24 21 G1
Hallam Gdns PIN HA5 33 J6
Hallam Ms GTPST W1W 10 D2
Hallam Rd BARN SW13 126 E2
SEVS/STOTM N15 55 H3
Hallam St GTPST W1W 10 D2
Halland Wy NTHWD HA6 32 B5
Hall Cl EA W5 86 A4
Hall Ct TEDD TW11 143 F4
Hall Dr SYD SE26 150 E4
Halley Gdns LEW SE13 133 G3
Halley Rd FSTGT E7 77 G5
Halley St POP/IOD E14 93 G4
Hall Farm Cl STAN HA7 35 H3
Hall Farm Dr WHTN TW2 123 J6
Hallfield Est BAY/PAD W2 8 D5
Hallford Wy DART DA1 139 F5
Hall Gdns CHING E4 43 H3
Hall Ga STJWD NW8 2 F8
Halliday Sq NWDGN UB2 84 D7
Halliford St IS N1 6 F1
Halliwell Rd
BRXS/STRHM SW2 130 A5
Halliwick Court Pde
NFNCH/WDSPK N12 * 39 K4
Halliwick Rd MUSWH N10 40 A7
Hall La CHING E4 43 H3
HDN NW4 51 J1
HYS/HAR UB3 101 G6
Hallmead Rd SUT SM1 175 F2
Hall Oak Wk KIL/WHAMP NW6 70 D5
Hallowell Av CROY/NA CR0 176 E3
Hallowell Cl MTCM CR4 163 F2
Hallowell Gdns THHTH CR7 164 D1
Hallowell Rd NTHWD HA6 32 C6
Hallowes Crs OXHEY WD19 32 E2
Hallowfield Wy MTCM CR4 162 C2
Hallows Gv SUN TW16 140 D4
Hall Pl BAY/PAD W2 9 G1
Hall Place Crs BXLY DA5 137 K4
Hall Rd CHDH RM6 61 J5
DART DA1 139 J3
EHAM E6 77 K7
GPK RM2 63 K2
ISLW TW7 123 J4
MV/WKIL W9 2 F8
SRTFD E15 76 B3
WLGTN SM6 176 B7
Hall St FSBYE EC1V 6 D7
NFNCH/WDSPK N12 39 G4
Hallsville Rd CAN/RD E16 94 D5
Hallswelle Pde GLDGN NW11 * 52 D4
Hallswelle Rd GLDGN NW11 52 D4
The Hall BKHTH/KID SE3 133 K2
Hall Vw ELTH/MOT SE9 153 H1
Hallywell Crs EHAM E6 95 K4
Halons Rd ELTH/MOT SE9 135 F6
Halpin Pl WALW SE17 19 H6
Halsbrook Rd BKHTH/KID SE3 134 B2
Halsbury Cl STAN HA7 35 H4
Halsbury Rd SHB W12 87 K7
Halsbury Rd East NTHLT UB5 66 C3
Halsbury Rd West NTHLT UB5 66 B4
Halsend HYS/HAR UB3 * 83 F7
Halsey Rd WATW WD18 21 F2
Halsey St CHEL SW3 15 L5
Halsham Crs BARK IG11 79 F5
Halsmere Rd CMBW SE5 110 C7
Halstead Cl CROY/NA CR0 177 J2
Halstead Gdns WCHMH N21 29 K7
Halstead Rd EN EN1 30 A3
ERITH DA8 118 B7
WAN E11 59 F4
WCHMH N21 29 K7
Halstow Rd GNWCH SE10 113 K4
WLSDN NW10 88 B2
Halsway HYS/HAR UB3 82 E7
Halter Cl BORE WD6 25 F4
Halton Cl FBAR/BDGN N11 39 K5
Halton Cross St IS N1 * 6 D3
Halton Pl IS N1 * 6 E3
Halton Rd IS N1 6 D2
Halt Pde CDALE/KGS NW9 * 51 F3
Halt Robin Rd BELV DA17 117 H3
Hambalt Rd CLAP SW4 129 H4
Hamble Cl RSLP HA4 64 C1
Hambledon Ct EA W5 * 86 A6
Hambledon Gdns SNWD SE25 165 G2
Hambledon Pl DUL SE21 131 G7
Hambledon Rd
WAND/EARL SW18 127 J6
Hambledown Rd
BFN/LL DA15 * 135 J6
Hamble St FUL/PGN SW6 128 A2
Hambleton Cl WPK KT4 174 A1
Hambro Av HAYES BR2 167 K7
Hambrook Rd SNWD SE25 165 J2
Hambro Rd
STRHM/NOR SW16 148 D5
Hambrough Rd STHL UB1 83 J7
Ham Common
RCHPK/HAM TW10 143 K2
Ham Croft Cl FELT TW13 140 E2
Hamden Crs DAGE RM10 80 D2
Hamel Cl KTN/HRWW/WS HA3 49 K3
Hameway EHAM E6 96 A3
Ham Farm Rd
RCHPK/HAM TW10 143 K3
Hamfrith Rd SRTFD E15 76 D5
Ham Gate Av
RCHPK/HAM TW10 144 A3
Hamilton Av BARK/HLT IG6 60 B3
CHEAM SM3 174 C1
ED N9 30 C6
ROM RM1 63 F1
SURB KT6 172 C1
Hamilton Cl BERM/RHTH SE16 112 B1
EBAR EN4 27 J3
FELT TW13 140 D4
STJWD NW8 3 G8
TEDD TW11 143 H5
TOTM N17 56 B2
Hamilton Ct EA W5 86 B6
Hamilton Crs HSLW TW3 123 G4
PLMGR N13 41 G3
RYLN/HDSTN HA2 65 K2
Hamilton Gdns STJWD NW8 2 F7
Hamilton La HBRY N5 73 H3
Hamilton Ms MYFR/PICC W1J 16 C1
Hamilton Pde FELT TW13 * 140 E3
Hamilton Pk HBRY N5 73 H3
Hamilton Pk West HBRY N5 73 H3
Hamilton Pl MYFR/PKLN W1K 10 B9
SUN TW16 141 F6
Hamilton Rd BTFD TW8 104 E5
BXLYHN DA7 137 F1
CHSWK W4 106 B2
EA W5 86 A6
EBAR EN4 27 J3
ED N9 30 C6
EFNCH N2 53 G2
FELT TW13 140 D3
GLDGN NW11 52 B6
GPK RM2 63 K4
HRW HA1 48 E4
HYS/HAR UB3 83 F6
IL IG1 78 B3
OXHEY WD19 33 F2
SCUP DA14 155 G3
SRTFD E15 94 C2
STHL UB1 83 K7
THHTH CR7 164 E2
WALTH E17 57 G1
WHTN TW2 123 K7
WIM/MER SW19 147 F6
WLSDN NW10 69 J4
WNWD SE27 149 K3
Hamilton Road Ms
WIM/MER SW19 147 F6
Hamilton Sq
NFNCH/WDSPK N12 * 39 G5
Hamilton St DEPT SE8 112 D5
WATW WD18 21 G4
Hamilton Ter STJWD NW8 2 E6
Hamilton Wy FNCH N3 38 E5
PLMGR N13 41 H3
WLGTN SM6 176 D7
Hamlea Cl LEE/GVPK SE12 133 K4
Hamlet Cl LEW SE13 133 H3
Hamlet Gdns HMSMTH W6 106 D3
Hamlet Rd NRWD SE19 150 B6
Hamlet Sq CRICK NW2 70 C2
Hamlets Wy BOW E3 93 H3
The Hamlet CMBW SE5 130 E2
Hamlet Wy STHWK SE1 19 H2
Hamlin Crs PIN HA5 47 G4
Hamlyn Cl EDGW HA8 36 A2
Hamlyn Gdns NRWD SE19 150 A6
Hammelton Rd BMLY BR1 152 E7
Hammers La MLHL NW7 37 J3
Hammersmith Br
HMSMTH W6 106 E4
Hammersmith Bridge Rd
BARN SW13 106 E4
Hammersmith Broadway
HMSMTH W6 107 F3
Hammersmith Emb
HMSMTH W6 * 107 F5
Hammersmith F/O
HMSMTH W6 107 F4
Hammersmith Gv
HMSMTH W6 * 107 F3
Hammersmith Rd
HMSMTH W6 107 G3
Hammersmith Ter
HMSMTH W6 * 106 D4
Hammet Cl YEAD UB4 83 H4
Hammett St TWRH EC3N 13 L6
Hammond Av MTCM CR4 163 G1
Hammond Cl BAR EN5 26 C4
GFD/PVL UB6 66 D4
HPTN TW12 142 A7
Hammond Rd EN EN1 30 D2
NWDGN UB2 102 D2
Hammonds Cl BCTR RM8 79 J2
Hammond St KTTN NW5 72 C5
Hamond Cl SAND/SEL CR2 177 H7
Hamonde Cl EDGW HA8 36 D1
Hamond Sq IS N1 * 7 J5
Ham Park Rd SRTFD E15 76 D6
Hampden Av BECK BR3 166 B1
Hampden Cl CAMTN NW1 5 H6
Hampden Gurney St
MBLAR W1H 9 L5
Hampden La TOTM N17 42 B7
Hampden Rd ARCH N19 72 D1
BECK BR3 166 B1
CEND/HSY/T N8 55 G3
KTN/HRWW/WS HA3 34 C7
KUT/HW KT1 159 H2
MUSWH N10 40 A6
TOTM N17 42 C7
Hampden Wy STHGT/OAK N14 40 B2
Hampermill La OXHEY WD19 20 E7
Hampshire Cl UED N18 42 D4
Hampshire Hog La
HMSMTH W6 * 106 E3
Hampshire Rd WDGN N22 41 F6
Hampshire St KTTN NW5 * 72 D5
Hampson Wy VX/NE SW8 110 A7
Hampstead Cl THMD SE28 97 H7
Hampstead Gdns
GLDGN NW11 52 E5
Hampstead Ga HAMP NW3 71 G4
Hampstead Gn HAMP NW3 71 J4
Hampstead Gv HAMP NW3 71 G3
Hampstead Hill Gdns
HAMP NW3 71 J3
Hampstead La HGT N6 53 K6
Hampstead Rd CAMTN NW1 4 E8
Hampstead Sq HAMP NW3 71 G2
Hampstead Wy GLDGN NW11 52 E5
Hampton Cl BORE WD6 24 E4
FBAR/BDGN N11 40 A4
KIL/WHAMP NW6 2 A8
RYNPK SW20 * 146 A6
Hampton Ct IS N1 73 H5
Hampton Court Av
E/WMO/HCT KT8 157 J5
Hampton Court Crs
E/WMO/HCT KT8 157 J2
Hampton Court Est
THDIT KT7 * 157 K4
Hampton Court Rd
E/WMO/HCT KT8 158 C2
HPTN TW12 157 J1
Hampton Court Wy
ESH/CLAY KT10 170 E1
Hampton La FELT TW13 141 J3
Hampton Ri
KTN/HRWW/WS HA3 50 A5
Hampton Rd CHING E4 43 H4
CROY/NA CR0 164 D5
FSTGT E7 77 F4
IL IG1 78 C3
TEDD TW11 142 D4
WAN E11 58 B7
WHTN TW2 142 D2
WPK KT4 173 J1
Hampton Rd East FELT TW13 141 K2
Hampton Rd West
FELT TW13 141 J1
Hampton St WALW SE17 18 D6
Ham Ridings
RCHPK/HAM TW10 144 B4
Ham Shades Cl BFN/LL DA15 155 F2
Ham St RCHPK/HAM TW10 143 J2
The Ham BTFD TW8 104 D6
Ham Vw CROY/NA CR0 166 B5
Ham Yd SOHO/SHAV W1D * 11 G6
Hanameel St CAN/RD E16 94 E7
Hana Ms CLPT E5 74 D3
Hanbury Cl HDN NW4 52 A2
Hanbury Ct HRW HA1 * 49 F5
Hanbury Dr WAN E11 58 D6
WCHMH N21 29 F3
Hanbury Ms IS N1 6 F4
Hanbury Rd ACT W3 105 J1
TOTM N17 56 D1
Hanbury St WCHPL E1 13 M2
Hancock Rd BOW E3 94 A2
NRWD SE19 149 K5
Handa Wk IS N1 73 J5
Hand Ct HHOL WC1V 11 M3
Handcroft Rd CROY/NA CR0 164 C6
Handel Cl EDGW HA8 36 B5
Handel Pde EDGW HA8 * 36 C5
Handel Pl WLSDN NW10 69 F5
Handel St BMSBY WC1N 5 J9
Handel Wy EDGW HA8 36 C6
Handen Rd LEE/GVPK SE12 133 H4
Handforth Rd BRXN/ST SW9 110 B6
IL IG1 78 B2
Handley Gv CRICK NW2 70 B2
Handley Page Rd WLGTN SM6 177 F6
Handley Rd HOM E9 74 E6
Handowe Cl HDN NW4 51 J3
Handside Cl WPK KT4 161 G7
Handsworth Av CHING E4 44 B5
Handsworth Cl OXHEY WD19 32 E2
Handsworth Rd TOTM N17 55 K2
Handtrough Wy BARK IG11 96 B1
Hanford Cl WAND/EARL SW18 127 K7
Hangar Ruding OXHEY WD19 33 K2
Hanger Gn EA W5 86 C3
Hanger La EA W5 86 A1
Hanger La (North Circular Rd)
EA W5 86 A2
Hanger Vale La EA W5 86 B4
Hanger View Wy ACT W3 86 C5
Hankey Pl STHWK SE1 19 H2
Hankins La MLHL NW7 37 G1
Hanley Gdns FSBYPK N4 55 F7
Hanley Pl BECK BR3 151 J6
Hanley Rd FSBYPK N4 54 E7
Hanmer Wk HOLWY N7 73 F1
Hannah Cl BECK BR3 166 E2
WLSDN NW10 68 E3
Hannah Mary Wy
STHWK SE1 * 111 H3
Hannay La ARCH N19 54 D6
Hannell Rd FUL/PGN SW6 107 H6
Hannen Rd WNWD SE27 * 149 H2
Hannibal Rd
STWL/WRAY TW19 120 B6
WCHPL E1 92 E4
Hannibal Wy CROY/NA CR0 177 F4
Hannington Rd CLAP SW4 129 G2
Hanno Cl WLGTN SM6 176 D6
Hanover Av CAN/RD E16 94 E7
FELT TW13 121 K7
Hanover Cir HYS/HAR UB3 82 A5
Hanover Cl CHEAM SM3 174 C3
RCH/KEW TW9 105 H6
Hanover Dr CHST BR7 154 C3
Hanover Gdns LBTH SE11 110 B5
Hanover Ga STJWD NW8 3 K8
Hanover Pk PECK SE15 111 H7
Hanover Pl COVGDN WC2E 11 K5
Hanover Rd SEVS/STOTM N15 56 B3
WIM/MER SW19 147 G6
WLSDN NW10 70 A6
Hanover Sq CONDST W1S 10 D5
Hanover Steps BAY/PAD W2 * 9 K5
Hanover St CONDST W1S 10 D5
CROY/NA CR0 177 H2
Hanover Ter CAMTN NW1 3 L8
Hanover Terrace Ms
CAMTN NW1 3 K8
Hanover Wy BXLYHS DA6 136 E2
Hanover Yd IS N1 * 6 D5
Hansard Ms WKENS W14 107 G1
Hans Crs KTBR SW1X 15 L3
Hanselin Cl STAN HA7 35 F4
Hansen Dr WCHMH N21 29 F4
Hanshaw Dr EDGW HA8 37 F7
Hansler Gv E/WMO/HCT KT8 157 J4
Hansler Rd EDUL SE22 131 G4
Hansol Rd BXLYHS DA6 137 F4
Hansom Ter BMLY BR1 * 153 F7
Hanson Cl BAL SW12 129 G6
BECK BR3 * 151 K5
MORT/ESHN SW14 125 K2
WDR/YW UB7 100 C2
Hanson Gdns STHL UB1 102 D1
Hanson St GTPST W1W 10 E2
Hans Pl KTBR SW1X 15 L3
Hans Rd CHEL SW3 15 L3
Hans St KTBR SW1X 15 M4
Hanway Pl FITZ W1T 11 G4
Hanway Rd HNWL W7 84 D5
Hanway St FITZ W1T 11 G4
Hanworth Rd FELT TW13 122 A7
HPTN TW12 141 K3
HSLW TW3 123 G2
HSLWW TW4 122 E6
SUN TW16 140 E6
Hanworth Ter HSLW TW3 123 G3
Hapgood Cl GFD/PVL UB6 66 D4
Harben Pde HAMP NW3 * 3 G1
Harben Rd KIL/WHAMP NW6 2 F1
Harberson Rd BAL SW12 129 G7
SRTFD E15 76 D7
Harberton Rd ARCH N19 54 C7
Harbet Rd BAY/PAD W2 9 H3
UED N18 43 F4
Harbex Cl BXLY DA5 137 J6
Harbinger Rd POP/IOD E14 112 E3
Harbledown Rd
FUL/PGN SW6 107 K7
Harbord Cl CMBW SE5 130 E1
Harbord St FUL/PGN SW6 107 G7
Harborne Cl OXHEY WD19 33 G4
Harborough Av BFN/LL DA15 135 K6
Harborough Rd
STRHM/NOR SW16 149 F3
Harbour Av WBPTN SW10 108 B7
Harbour Cl MTCM CR4 148 A7
Harbour Exchange Sq
POP/IOD E14 112 E1
Harbour Rd CMBW SE5 130 D2
Harbour Yd WBPTN SW10 * 108 B7
Harbridge Av PUT/ROE SW15 126 C6
Harbury Rd CAR SM5 175 J7
Harbut Rd BTSEA SW11 128 C3
Harcastle Cl YEAD UB4 83 J3
Harcombe Rd
STNW/STAM N16 74 A2
Harcourt Av BFN/LL DA15 136 D5
EDGW HA8 36 E2
MNPK E12 77 K3
WLGTN SM6 176 B3
Harcourt Blds EMB EC4Y * 12 A6
Harcourt Cl ISLW TW7 124 B2
Harcourt Fld WLGTN SM6 176 B3
Harcourt Ms GPK RM2 63 H4
Harcourt Rd BROCKY SE4 132 C3
BUSH WD23 22 C4
BXLYHS DA6 137 F3
SRTFD E15 94 D1
THHTH CR7 164 A5
WDGN N22 40 D7
WIM/MER SW19 146 E6
WLGTN SM6 176 B3
Harcourt St MBLAR W1H 9 K3
Harcourt Ter WBPTN SW10 14 D8
Hardcastle Cl CROY/NA CR0 165 H5
Hardcourts Cl WWKM BR4 179 K3
Hardel Wk BRXS/STRHM SW2 130 B6
Hardens Manorway
WOOL/PLUM SE18 114 C2
Harders Rd PECK SE15 131 J1
Hardess St HNHL SE24 130 D2
Hardie Cl WLSDN NW10 69 F4
Hardie Rd DAGE RM10 80 E2
Harding Cl CROY/NA CR0 178 B2
KUTN/CMB KT2 144 B7
WALW SE17 18 E9
Hardinge Crs
WOOL/PLUM SE18 115 H2
Hardinge Rd UED N18 42 A4
WLSDN NW10 70 A7
Hardinge St WCHPL E1 92 E5
WOOL/PLUM SE18 115 G2
Harding Rd BXLYHN DA7 137 G1
Hardings La PGE/AN SE20 151 F5
Hardman Rd CHARL SE7 114 A4
KUTN/CMB KT2 159 F1
Hardwick Cl STAN HA7 35 J4
Hardwicke Av HEST TW5 * 103 F7
Hardwicke Ms FSBYW WC1X * 5 M8
Hardwicke Rd CHSWK W4 105 K3
PLMGR N13 40 E4
RCHPK/HAM TW10 143 J3
Hardwicke St BARK IG11 78 C7
Hardwick Gn WEA W13 85 H4
Hardwick Pl
STRHM/NOR SW16 148 C6
Hardwick's Sq
WAND/EARL SW18 127 K4
Hardwick St CLKNW EC1R 6 B8
Hardwidge St STHWK SE1 19 J1
Hardy Av CAN/RD E16 94 E7
DART DA1 139 F6
RSLP HA4 65 F4
Hardy Cl BAR EN5 26 C4
BERM/RHTH SE16 112 A1
PIN HA5 47 H6
Hardy Cots GNWCH SE10 * 113 G5
Hardy Gv DART DA1 139 K3
Hardy Pas WDGN N22 41 F7
Hardy Rd BKHTH/KID SE3 113 J5
CHING E4 43 H5
WIM/MER SW19 147 F6
Hardys Ms E/WMO/HCT KT8 157 K3
Harebell Dr EHAM E6 96 A4
Hare & Billet Rd
BKHTH/KID SE3 113 G7
Hare Ct EMB EC4Y * 12 A5
Harecourt Rd IS N1 73 J5
Haredale Rd HNHL SE24 130 D3
Haredon Cl FSTH SE23 131 K6
Harefield ESH/CLAY KT10 170 E2
Harefield Av BELMT SM2 174 C7
Harefield Ms BROCKY SE4 132 C2
Harefield Rd BROCKY SE4 132 C2
CEND/HSY/T N8 54 D4
SCUP DA14 155 K1
STRHM/NOR SW16 149 F6
Hare Hall La GPK RM2 63 K3
Hare La ESH/CLAY KT10 170 D5
Hare Marsh BETH E2 92 C3
Harepit Cl SAND/SEL CR2 177 H6
Hare Rw BETH E2 92 D1
Haresfield Rd DAGE RM10 80 C5
Hare St WOOL/PLUM SE18 115 F2
Hare Wk IS N1 7 K6
Harewood Av CAMTN NW1 9 K1
NTHLT UB5 65 J6
STJWD NW8 3 K9
Harewood Cl NTHLT UB5 65 K6
Harewood Dr CLAY IG5 59 K1
Harewood Pl CONDST W1S 10 D5
Harewood Rd ISLW TW7 104 A6
OXHEY WD19 33 F1
SAND/SEL CR2 178 A5
WIM/MER SW19 147 J5
Harewood Rw CAMTN NW1 9 K2
Harewood Ter NWDGN UB2 102 E3
Harfield Gdns CMBW SE5 * 131 F2
Harfield Rd SUN TW16 156 C1
Harford Cl CHING E4 31 K6
Harford Rd CHING E4 31 K6
Harford St WCHPL E1 93 G3
Harford Wk EFNCH N2 53 H3
Harglaze Ter
CDALE/KGS NW9 * 51 G2
Hargood Cl
KTN/HRWW/WS HA3 50 A5
Hargood Rd BKHTH/KID SE3 114 B7
Hargrave Pk ARCH N19 72 C1
Hargrave Pl KTTN NW5 72 D4
Hargrave Rd ARCH N19 72 C1
Hargwyne St BRXN/ST SW9 130 A2
Haringey Pk CEND/HSY/T N8 54 E5
Haringey Rd CEND/HSY/T N8 54 E3
Harington Ter UED N18 * 41 K3
Harkett Cl
KTN/HRWW/WS HA3 49 F1
Harland Av BFN/LL DA15 154 D2
CROY/NA CR0 178 B2
Harland Cl WIM/MER SW19 162 A2
Harland Rd LEE/GVPK SE12 133 K7
Harlech Gdns HEST TW5 102 B5
PIN HA5 47 H6
Harlech Rd STHGT/OAK N14 40 E2
Harlequin Av BTFD TW8 104 B5
Harlequin Cl ISLW TW7 123 K4
YEAD UB4 83 H4
Harlequin Ct EA W5 * 85 J6
Harlequin Rd TEDD TW11 * 143 H6
The Harlequin WAT WD17 * 21 G3
Harlescott Rd PECK SE15 132 A3
Harlesden Gdns WLSDN NW10 69 H7
Harlesden Rd WLSDN NW10 69 J7
Harley Cl ALP/SUD HA0 * 67 K5
Harley Crs HRW HA1 48 D3
Harleyford BMLY BR1 153 G7
Harleyford Rd LBTH SE11 17 L9
Harleyford St LBTH SE11 110 B5
Harley Gdns WBPTN SW10 14 F8
Harley Gv BOW E3 93 H2
Harley Pl CAVSQ/HST W1G 10 C3
Harley Rd HAMP NW3 3 H2
HRW HA1 48 D3
WLSDN NW10 87 G1
Harley St CAVSQ/HST W1G 10 C1
Harley Vls WLSDN NW10 * 87 G1
Harlinger St
WOOL/PLUM SE18 114 D2
Harlington Cl HYS/HAR UB3 101 F6
Harlington Rd BXLYHN DA7 137 F2
Harlington Rd East
EBED/NFELT TW14 122 A6
Harlington Rd West
EBED/NFELT TW14 122 A5
Harlow Rd PLMGR N13 41 K2
RAIN RM13 81 H7
Harlyn Dr PIN HA5 47 F2
Harman Av WFD IG8 44 D6
Harman Cl CHING E4 44 B3
CRICK NW2 70 C2
STHWK SE1 * 111 H4
Harman Dr BFN/LL DA15 136 A5
CRICK NW2 70 C2
Harman Ri IL IG1 78 E3
Harman Rd EN EN1 30 B4
Harmondsworth La
WDR/YW UB7 100 B5
Harmondsworth Rd
WDR/YW UB7 100 B2
Harmony Cl GLDGN NW11 52 C4
WLGTN SM6 176 E7
Harmony Pl STHWK SE1 19 M7
Harmony Wy BMLY BR1 167 K1
HDN NW4 52 A3
Harmood Gv CAMTN NW1 4 C1
Harmood St CAMTN NW1 4 C1
Harmsworth Ms STHWK SE1 18 B4
Harmsworth St WALW SE17 18 C8
Harmsworth Wy
TRDG/WHET N20 26 D7
Harness Rd THMD SE28 116 B1
Harold Av BELV DA17 117 G4
HYS/HAR UB3 101 J2
Harold Rd CEND/HSY/T N8 55 F4
CHING E4 44 A2
NRWD SE19 149 K6
PLSTW E13 77 F7
SEVS/STOTM N15 56 B4
SUT SM1 175 H3
SWFD E18 44 E7
WAN E11 58 C7
WLSDN NW10 87 F2
Haroldstone Rd WALTH E17 57 F4
Harpenden Rd MNPK E12 77 G1
WNWD SE27 149 H1
Harper Rd EHAM E6 95 K5
STHWK SE1 18 F3
Harpers Yd ISLW TW7 * 124 A1
Harp Island Cl WLSDN NW10 69 F1
Harp La MON EC3R 13 J7
Harpley Sq WCHPL E1 92 E3
Harpour Rd BARK IG11 78 C5
Harp Rd HNWL W7 85 F3
Harpsden St BTSEA SW11 109 F7
Harpur Ms BMSBY WC1N 11 L2
Harpur St BMSBY WC1N 11 L2
Harraden Rd BKHTH/KID SE3 114 B7
Harrier Cl HCH RM12 81 K5
Harrier Ms THMD SE28 115 J1
Harrier Rd CDALE/KGS NW9 51 G1
Harriers Cl EA W5 86 A6
Harrier Wy EHAM E6 95 K4
Harries Rd YEAD UB4 83 G3
Harriet Cl HACK E8 74 C7
Harriet Gdns CROY/NA CR0 178 C1
Harriet Ms WELL DA16 136 C1
Harriet St KTBR SW1X 15 M2
Harriet Tubman Cl
BRXS/STRHM SW2 130 B6
Harriet Wk KTBR SW1X 15 M2
Harriet Wy BUSH WD23 22 D6
Harringay Gdns
CEND/HSY/T N8 55 H3
Harringay Rd
SEVS/STOTM N15 55 H4
Harrington Cl CROY/NA CR0 176 E1
WLSDN NW10 69 F2
Harrington Ct NKENS W10 * 88 D2
Harrington Gdns SKENS SW7 14 D6
Harrington Hl CLPT E5 56 D7
Harrington Rd SKENS SW7 15 G5
SNWD SE25 165 H3
WAN E11 58 C7
Harrington Sq CAMTN NW1 4 E5
Harrington St CAMTN NW1 4 E6
Harrington Wy
WOOL/PLUM SE18 114 C2
Harriott Cl GNWCH SE10 113 J3
Harris Cl HSLW TW3 103 F7
Harrison Cl NTHWD HA6 32 A5
TRDG/WHET N20 27 J7
Harrison Dr BMLY BR1 169 G3
Harrison Rd DAGE RM10 80 D5
WLSDN NW10 69 F7
Harrison's Ri CROY/NA CR0 177 H2
Harrison St STPAN WC1H 5 K8
Harrisons Whf PUR RM19 119 K4
Harris Rd BXLYHN DA7 117 F7
DAGW RM9 80 B4
Harris St CMBW SE5 110 E6
WALTH E17 57 H6
Harris Wy SUN TW16 140 C7
Harrods Gn EDGW HA8 * 36 C4
Harrogate Rd OXHEY WD19 33 G2
Harrold Rd BCTR RM8 79 H4
Harrow Av EN EN1 30 B5
Harroway Rd BTSEA SW11 128 C1
Harrowby St MBLAR W1H 9 K4
Harrow Cl CHSGTN KT9 171 K6
Harrowdene Cl ALP/SUD HA0 67 K3
Harrowdene Gdns
TEDD TW11 143 G6
Harrowdene Rd ALP/SUD HA0 67 K3
Harrow Dr ED N9 30 B7
Harrowes Meade EDGW HA8 36 C2
Harrow Fields Gdns HRW HA1 66 E2
Harrowgate Rd HOM E9 75 G5
Harrow Gn WAN E11 76 C2
Harrow La POP/IOD E14 94 A6
Harrow Manor Wy ABYW SE2 116 D2
Harrow Pk HRW HA1 66 E1
Harrow Pl WCHPL E1 13 K4
Harrow Rd ALP/SUD HA0 67 G3
CAR SM5 175 J5
EBED/NFELT TW14 120 D7
IL IG1 78 C3
MV/WKIL W9 8 A1
WAN E11 76 D2
WBLY HA9 68 C4
WLSDN NW10 87 K2

Harrow Rd F/O BAY/PAD W2 9 H3
Harrow St CAMTN NW1 * 9 K2
Harrow Vw HGDN/ICK UB10 82 A2
HRW HA1 48 D3
HYS/HAR UB3 82 E6
RYLN/HDSTN HA2 48 D2
Harrow View Rd EA W5 85 H3
Harrow Wy OXHEY WD19 33 J2
Harrow Weald Pk
KTN/HRWW/WS HA3 34 D5
Harry Cl THHTH CR7 164 D5
Harry Zeital Wy CLPT E5 74 E1
Hartcliff Ct HNWL W7 * 104 A1
Hart Cl CROY/NA CR0 177 H2
Harte Rd HSLW TW3 122 E1
Hartfield Av BORE WD6 24 C3
NTHLT UB5 83 F1
Hartfield Cl BORE WD6 24 C4
Hartfield Crs WIM/MER SW19 146 D6
WWKM BR4 180 E2
Hartfield Gv PGE/AN SE20 150 D7
Hartfield Rd CHSGTN KT9 171 K4
WIM/MER SW19 146 D5
WWKM BR4 180 E3
Hartfield Ter BOW E3 93 J1
Hartford Av
KTN/HRWW/WS HA3 49 G2
Hartforde Rd BORE WD6 24 C1
Hartford Rd BXLY DA5 137 H5
HOR/WEW KT19 172 C5
Hart Gv EA W5 86 C7
STHL UB1 84 A4
Hartham Cl HOLWY N7 72 E4
ISLW TW7 104 B7
Hartham Rd HOLWY N7 72 E4
ISLW TW7 104 A7
TOTM N17 56 B1
Harting Rd ELTH/MOT SE9 153 J3
Hartington Cl HRW HA1 66 E3
Hartington Rd CAN/RD E16 95 F5
CHSWK W4 105 J6
NWDGN UB2 * 102 D2
TWK TW1 124 C6
VX/NE SW8 109 K7
WALTH E17 57 G5
WEA W13 85 H6
Hartismere Rd FUL/PGN SW6 107 J6
Hartlake Rd HOM E9 75 F5
Hartland Cl EDGW HA8 36 C1
WCHMH N21 29 J5
Hartland Dr EDGW HA8 36 C1
RSLP HA4 65 F2
Hartland Rd CAMTN NW1 4 C1
FBAR/BDGN N11 39 K4
HCH RM12 81 J1
HPTN TW12 142 B3
ISLW TW7 124 B2
KIL/WHAMP NW6 88 D1
MRDN SM4 161 K6
SRTFD E15 76 D6
Hartland Rd Arches
CAMTN NW1 * 4 B1
Hartlands Cl BXLY DA5 137 G5
The Hartlands HEST TW5 102 A5
Hartland Wy CROY/NA CR0 179 G1
MRDN SM4 161 J6
Hartley Av EHAM E6 77 J7
MLHL NW7 37 H4
Hartley Cl BMLY BR1 168 E1
MLHL NW7 37 H4
Hartley Rd CROY/NA CR0 164 D6
WAN E11 58 D7
WELL DA16 116 D6
Hartley St BETH E2 92 E2
Hartmann Rd CAN/RD E16 95 H7
Hartnoll St HOLWY N7 73 F4
Harton Cl BMLY BR1 153 H7
Harton Rd ED N9 42 D1
Harton St DEPT SE8 112 D7
Hartsbourne Av BUSH WD23 34 C1
Hartsbourne Cl BUSH WD23 34 D1
Hartsbourne Rd BUSH WD23 34 D1
Harts Cl BUSH WD23 22 A1
Hartscroft CROY/NA CR0 179 G7
Harts Gv WFD IG8 44 E4
Hartshorn Gdns EHAM E6 96 A3
Harts La BARK IG11 78 B6
Hart's La NWCR SE14 112 B6
Hartslock Dr ABYW SE2 116 E1
Hartsmead Rd ELTH/MOT SE9 153 K1
Hartspring La BUSH WD23 22 A1
Hart Sq MRDN SM4 * 162 A4
Hart St MON EC3R 13 K6
Hartsway PEND EN3 30 D3
Hartswood Cl BUSH WD23 22 A1
Hartswood Gdns SHB W12 * 106 C2
Hartswood Gn BUSH WD23 34 D1
Hartswood Rd SHB W12 106 C1
Hartsworth Cl PLSTW E13 94 D1
Hartville Rd
WOOL/PLUM SE18 115 K3
Hartwell Cl BRXS/STRHM SW2 130 A7
Hartwell Dr CHING E4 44 A5
Hartwell St HACK E8 74 B5
Harvard Hl CHSWK W4 105 J4
Harvard Rd CHSWK W4 105 J4
ISLW TW7 103 K7
LEW SE13 133 F4
Harvel Crs ABYW SE2 116 E4
Harvest Bank Rd WWKM BR4 180 E2
Harvesters Cl ISLW TW7 123 J4
Harvest La THDIT KT7 158 B5
Harvest Rd BUSH WD23 22 B3
FELT TW13 140 E3
Harvey Dr HPTN TW12 142 B7
Harvey Gdns CHARL SE7 114 B4
Harvey Rd CEND/HSY/T N8 55 F4
CMBW SE5 110 E7
HSLWW TW4 122 E6
IL IG1 78 B4
NTHLT UB5 65 G6
WAN E11 58 C7
Harvey's La ROMW/RG RM7 81 F1
Harvey St IS N1 7 H4
Harvill Rd SCUP DA14 155 K4
Harvington Wk HACK E8 * 74 C6
Harvist Rd KIL/WHAMP NW6 88 C1
Harwell Cl RSLP HA4 46 B7
Harwood Av BMLY BR1 168 A1
MTCM CR4 162 D2
Harwood Cl ALP/SUD HA0 67 K3
NFNCH/WDSPK N12 39 J5
Harwood Ms FUL/PGN SW6 * 108 A6
Harwood Rd FUL/PGN SW6 107 K6
Harwoods Rd WATW WD18 20 E3
Harwood Ter FUL/PGN SW6 108 A7
Hascombe Ter CMBW SE5 * 130 E1
Haselbury Rd UED N18 42 A3
Haseley End FSTH SE23 * 131 K6
Haselrigge Rd CLAP SW4 129 J3
Haseltine Rd SYD SE26 151 H3
Haselwood Dr ENC/FH EN2 29 H3
Haskard Rd DAGW RM9 79 K3
Hasker St CHEL SW3 15 K5
Haslam Av CHEAM SM3 161 H7
Haslam Cl HGDN/ICK UB10 64 A1
IS N1 6 B1
Haslam St PECK SE15 111 G7
Haslemere Av EBAR EN4 27 K7
HDN NW4 52 B5
HEST TW5 122 B1
HNWL W7 104 B2
MTCM CR4 162 C1
WAND/EARL SW18 147 F1
Haslemere Cl HPTN TW12 141 K4
WLGTN SM6 176 E4
Haslemere Gdns FNCH N3 52 D2
Haslemere Heathrow Est
HSLWW TW4 * 122 A1
Haslemere Rd BXLYHN DA7 137 G1
CEND/HSY/T N8 54 E6
GDMY/SEVK IG3 79 F1
THHTH CR7 164 C4
WCHMH N21 41 H1
Hasler Cl THMD SE28 97 H6
Hasluck Gdns BAR EN5 27 G5
Hassard St BETH E2 7 M6
Hassendean Rd
BKHTH/KID SE3 114 A5
Hassett Rd HOM E9 75 F5
Hassocks Cl SYD SE26 150 D2
Hassocks Rd
STRHM/NOR SW16 148 D7
Hassock Wd HAYES BR2 181 H3
Hassop Rd CRICK NW2 70 B3
Hasted Rd CHARL SE7 114 C4
Hastings Av BARK/HLT IG6 60 C3
Hastings Cl ALP/SUD HA0 67 J3
BAR EN5 27 G3
PECK SE15 * 111 H6
Hastings Dr SURB KT6 158 D5
Hastings Pl CROY/NA CR0 165 G7
Hastings Rd CROY/NA CR0 165 G7
FBAR/BDGN N11 40 C4
GPK RM2 63 K4
HAYES BR2 168 D7
TOTM N17 * 55 K2
WEA W13 85 H6
Hastings St STPAN WC1H 5 J8
Hastings Ter
SEVS/STOTM N15 * 55 J4
Hastings Wy BUSH WD23 21 J3
Hastings St WOOL/PLUM SE18 115 H2
Hastoe Cl YEAD UB4 83 J3
Hatcham Park Ms NWCR SE14 112 A7
Hatcham Park Rd NWCR SE14 112 A7
Hatcham Rd PECK SE15 111 K5
Hatchard Rd ARCH N19 72 D1
Hatchcroft HDN NW4 51 K2
Hatchers Ms STHWK SE1 19 K2
Hatchett Rd
EBED/NFELT TW14 121 F7
Hatch Gv CHDH RM6 62 A3
Hatch La CHING E4 44 B3
WDR/YW UB7 100 A6
Hatch Pl KUTN/CMB KT2 144 B4
Hatch Rd STRHM/NOR SW16 163 K1
Hatchwoods WFD IG8 44 D3
Hatcliffe Cl BKHTH/KID SE3 133 J2
Hatcliffe St GNWCH SE10 113 J4
Hatfield Cl BARK/HLT IG6 60 B2
BELMT SM2 174 E7
MTCM CR4 * 162 C3
Hatfield Ct BKHTH/KID SE3 * 113 K6
Hatfield Rd CHSWK W4 106 A1
HNWL W7 85 G7
SRTFD E15 76 C4
Hatfields STHWK SE1 12 B8
Hathaway Cl HAYES BR2 168 E7
RSLP HA4 64 D3
STAN HA7 35 G4
Hathaway Crs MNPK E12 77 K5
Hathaway Gdns CHDH RM6 61 K4
WEA W13 85 F4
Hathaway Rd CROY/NA CR0 164 C6
Hatherleigh Cl CHSGTN KT9 171 K4
MLHL NW7 38 B6
MRDN SM4 161 K3
Hatherleigh Rd RSLP HA4 64 E1
Hatherley Crs BFN/LL DA15 155 G1
Hatherley Gdns
CEND/HSY/T N8 54 E5
EHAM E6 95 H2
Hatherley Gv BAY/PAD W2 8 C4
Hatherley Ms WALTH E17 57 J3
Hatherley Rd RCH/KEW TW9 105 G7
SCUP DA14 155 G2
WALTH E17 57 H3
Hatherley St WEST SW1P 16 F6
Hathern Gdns ELTH/MOT SE9 154 A3
Hatherop Rd HPTN TW12 141 K6
Hathorne Cl PECK SE15 131 J1
Hathorne Ter ARCH N19 * 54 D7
Hathway St PECK SE15 131 K1
Hatley Av BARK/HLT IG6 60 C3
Hatley Cl FBAR/BDGN N11 39 K4
Hatley Rd FSBYPK N4 73 F1
Hat & Mitre Ct FARR EC1M 12 D1
Hatteraick St
BERM/RHTH SE16 111 K1
Hattersfield Cl BELV DA17 117 G3
Hatters La WATW WD18 20 B5
Hatton Cl WOOL/PLUM SE18 115 J6
Hatton Cross Est
HTHAIR TW6 * 121 J3
Hatton Gdn HCIRC EC1N 12 B2
Hatton Gdns MTCM CR4 162 E4
Hatton Gn EBED/NFELT TW14 121 K3
Hatton Gv WDR/YW UB7 * 100 A1
Hatton Pl HCIRC EC1N 12 B1
Hatton Rd CROY/NA CR0 164 B7
EBED/NFELT TW14 121 F6
HTHAIR TW6 121 J3
Hatton Rd North HTHAIR TW6 101 G7
Hatton Rw STJWD NW8 * 9 H1
Hatton St STJWD NW8 9 H1
Hatton Wall HCIRC EC1N 12 A2
Haunch of Venison Yd
OXSTW W1C * 10 C5
Havana Cl ROM RM1 63 G4
Havana Rd WIM/MER SW19 146 E1
Havannah St POP/IOD E14 112 D1
Havant Rd WALTH E17 58 A2
Havelock Cl SHB W12 * 87 K6
Havelock Pl HRW HA1 48 E5
Havelock Rd BELV DA17 * 117 G3
CROY/NA CR0 178 B1
DART DA1 138 E6
HAYES BR2 168 B3
KTN/HRWW/WS HA3 48 E2
NWDGN UB2 102 D2
TOTM N17 56 C1
WIM/MER SW19 147 G4
Havelock St IL IG1 78 B1
IS N1 5 K3
Havelock Ter VX/NE SW8 109 G6
Havelock Wk FSTH SE23 131 K7
Haven Cl ELTH/MOT SE9 153 K2
ESH/CLAY KT10 170 E1
SCUP DA14 155 J5
WIM/MER SW19 146 B2
YEAD UB4 82 C4
Haven Ct BRYLDS KT5 * 159 G5
Haven Gn EA W5 85 K5
Havenhurst Ri ENC/FH EN2 29 G1
Haven La EA W5 86 A5
Havens Ms BOW E3 93 H4
Haven St CAMTN NW1 * 4 C2
Havenswood Ct
KUTN/CMB KT2 144 D5
The Haven RCH/KEW TW9 125 H2
SUN TW16 140 E6
Havenwood WBLY HA9 68 D2
Haverfield Est BTFD TW8 105 F5
Haverfield Gdns
RCH/KEW TW9 105 H6
Haverfield Rd BOW E3 93 G2
Haverford Wy EDGW HA8 36 B7
Havergal Vls
SEVS/STOTM N15 * 55 H3
Haverhill Rd BAL SW12 129 H7
Havering Dr ROM RM1 63 G3
Havering Gdns CHDH RM6 61 J4
Havering Rd ROM RM1 63 F1
Havering St WCHPL E1 93 F5
Havering Wy BARK IG11 97 H2
Haversham Cl TWK TW1 124 E6
Haversham Pl HGT N6 71 K1
Haverstock Hl HAMP NW3 71 J5
Haverstock Pl FSBYE EC1V 6 E6
Haverstock Rd KTTN NW5 72 A4
Haverstock St IS N1 6 D6
Havil St CMBW SE5 111 F7
Havisham Pl NRWD SE19 149 H5
Hawarden Gv HNHL SE24 130 D6
Hawarden Hl CRICK NW2 69 J2
Hawarden Rd WALTH E17 57 F3
Hawbridge Rd WAN E11 58 B7
Hawes Cl NTHWD HA6 32 D6
Hawes La WWKM BR4 167 F7
Hawes Rd BMLY BR1 153 F7
UED N18 42 D5
Hawes St IS N1 6 D2
Hawgood St BOW E3 93 J4
Hawkdene CHING E4 31 K5
Hawke Park Rd WDGN N22 55 H2
Hawke Pl BERM/RHTH SE16 * 112 A1
Hawke Rd NRWD SE19 149 K5
Hawker Pl WALTH E17 58 A1
Hawker Rd CROY/NA CR0 177 F5
Hawkesbury Rd
PUT/ROE SW15 126 E4
Hawkesfield Rd FSTH SE23 151 G1
Hawkesley Cl TWK TW1 143 G3
Hawkes Rd EBED/NFELT TW14 121 K6
MTCM CR4 147 J7
Hawkesworth Cl NTHWD HA6 32 C6
Hawkhurst Rd
STRHM/NOR SW16 148 D6
Hawkhurst Wy NWMAL KT3 160 A4
WWKM BR4 179 K1
Hawkins Cl BORE WD6 24 E1
EDGW HA8 37 F4
HRW HA1 48 D6
Hawkins Rd TEDD TW11 143 H5
WLSDN NW10 69 G6
Hawkins Ter CHARL SE7 114 D4
Hawkins Wy CAT SE6 151 J4
Hawkley Gdns WNWD SE27 149 H1
Hawkridge Cl CHDH RM6 61 J5
Hawksbrook La BECK BR3 166 E5
Hawkshaw Cl
BRXS/STRHM SW2 129 K6
Hawkshead Cl BMLY BR1 152 C6
Hawkshead Rd CHSWK W4 106 B2
WLSDN NW10 * 69 H6
Hawkshill Cl ESH/CLAY KT10 170 A5
Hawkshill Pl ESH/CLAY KT10 * 170 A5
Hawkslade Rd PECK SE15 132 A4
Hawksley Rd STNW/STAM N16 73 K2
Hawks Ms GNWCH SE10 * 113 F6
Hawksmoor Cl EHAM E6 95 J5
WOOL/PLUM SE18 115 K4
Hawksmoor Ms WCHPL E1 92 D6
Hawksmoor St HMSMTH W6 107 G5
Hawksmouth CHING E4 31 K6
Hawks Rd KUT/HW KT1 159 G1
Hawkstone Est
BERM/RHTH SE16 111 K3
Hawkstone Rd
BERM/RHTH SE16 111 K3
Hawkwell Wk IS N1 * 6 F3
Hawkwood Crs CHING E4 31 K5
Hawkwood La CHST BR7 154 C7
Hawkwood Mt CLPT E5 56 D7
Hawlands Dr PIN HA5 47 J6
Hawley Cl HPTN TW12 141 K5
Hawley Crs CAMTN NW1 4 D2
Hawley Ms CAMTN NW1 4 C1
Hawley Rd CAMTN NW1 4 C1
UED N18 43 F4
Hawley St CAMTN NW1 4 C2
Hawstead Rd CAT SE6 132 E5
Hawthorn Av PLMGR N13 40 E4
RAIN RM13 99 K3
THHTH CR7 149 H7
Hawthorn Centre HRW HA1 49 F3
Hawthorn Cl HEST TW5 102 A6
HPTN TW12 142 A4
STMC/STPC BR5 169 J5
Hawthorn Ct ASHF TW15 140 A6
Hawthorn Crs TOOT SW17 148 A4
Hawthornden Cl
NFNCH/WDSPK N12 39 J5
Hawthorndene Cl HAYES BR2 180 D1
Hawthorndene Rd HAYES BR2 180 E1
Hawthorn Dr
RYLN/HDSTN HA2 48 A5
WWKM BR4 180 C3
Hawthorne Av BOW E3 75 H7
CAR SM5 176 A6
KTN/HRWW/WS HA3 49 G5
MTCM CR4 162 C1
RSLP HA4 47 F5
Hawthorne Cl BMLY BR1 168 E2
IS N1 74 A5
Hawthorne Ct
STWL/WRAY TW19 * 120 A6
Hawthorne Crs WDR/YW UB7 100 C1
Hawthorne Gv
CDALE/KGS NW9 50 E6
Hawthorne Rd BMLY BR1 168 E2
UED N18 42 B5
WALTH E17 57 J2
Hawthorne Wy ED N9 42 B1
STWL/WRAY TW19 120 A6
Hawthorn Farm Av
NTHLT UB5 65 J7
Hawthorn Gdns EA W5 104 E2
Hawthorn Gv PGE/AN SE20 150 D7
Hawthorn Hatch BTFD TW8 104 C6
Hawthorn Ms MLHL NW7 38 C7
Hawthorn Pl ERITH DA8 117 K4
HYS/HAR UB3 * 82 D6
Hawthorn Rd BTFD TW8 104 C6
BXLYHS DA6 * 137 G3
CEND/HSY/T N8 54 D2
DART DA1 139 G7
FELT TW13 121 K7
SUT SM1 175 H4
WFD IG8 45 G3
WLGTN SM6 176 B6
WLSDN NW10 69 J6
Hawthorns WFD IG8 44 E2
The Hawthorns EW KT17 173 H5
Hawthorn Ter BFN/LL DA15 136 A5
Hawthorn Wk NKENS W10 88 C3
Hawtrey Av NTHLT UB5 83 H1
Hawtrey Dr RSLP HA4 46 E6
Hawtrey Rd HAMP NW3 3 J2
Haxted Rd BMLY BR1 153 F7
Hayburn Wy HCH RM12 63 H7
Hay Cl BORE WD6 24 E1
SRTFD E15 76 C6
Haycroft Gdns WLSDN NW10 69 J7
Haycroft Rd
BRXS/STRHM SW2 129 K4
SURB KT6 171 K1
Hay Currie St POP/IOD E14 93 K5
Hayday Rd CAN/RD E16 94 E3
Hayden Dell BUSH WD23 21 K5
Hayden's Pl NTGHL W11 88 D5
Hayden Wy CRW RM5 62 E1
Haydock Av NTHLT UB5 66 A5
Haydock Gn NTHLT UB5 66 A5
Haydon Cl CDALE/KGS NW9 50 E3
EN EN1 30 A5
Haydon Dell Farm
BUSH WD23 * 21 K6
Haydon Dr PIN HA5 46 E3
Haydon Park Pas
WIM/MER SW19 147 F4
Haydon Park Rd
WIM/MER SW19 146 E4
Haydon Rd BCTR RM8 79 J1
OXHEY WD19 21 J5
Haydon's Rd WIM/MER SW19 147 F4
Haydon St TWRH EC3N 13 L6
Haydon Wk WCHPL E1 13 L5
Haydon Wy WAND/EARL SW18 128 B3
Hayes Cha WWKM BR4 167 G5
Hayes Cl HAYES BR2 180 E1
Hayes Crs CHEAM SM3 174 B3
GLDGN NW11 52 D4
Hayes Dr RAIN RM13 81 K6
Hayes End Dr YEAD UB4 82 B4
Hayes End Rd YEAD UB4 82 B4
Hayesford Park Dr HAYES BR2 167 J4
Hayes Gdn HAYES BR2 180 E1
Hayes Gv EDUL SE22 131 G2
Hayes Hl HAYES BR2 167 H7
Hayes Hill Rd HAYES BR2 167 J7
Hayes La BECK BR3 167 G2
HAYES BR2 167 K5
Hayes Mead Rd HAYES BR2 167 H7
Hayes Pl CAMTN NW1 9 K1
Hayes Rd HAYES BR2 167 K3
NWDGN UB2 102 A3
Hayes St HAYES BR2 168 A7
Hayes Wy BECK BR3 167 F3
Hayes Wood Av HAYES BR2 168 A7
Hayfield Cl BUSH WD23 22 B3
Hayfield Pas WCHPL E1 92 E3
Haygarth Pl WIM/MER SW19 146 B4
Haygreen Cl KUTN/CMB KT2 144 D5
Hay Hl MYFR/PICC W1J 10 D7
Hayland Cl CDALE/KGS NW9 51 F3
Hay La CDALE/KGS NW9 51 F3
Hayles St LBTH SE11 18 C5
Haylett Gdns KUT/HW KT1 * 158 E3
Hayling Av FELT TW13 140 E2
Hayling Cl STNW/STAM N16 74 A4
Hayling Rd OXHEY WD19 32 D2
Hayman Crs YEAD UB4 82 B1
Haymarket STJS SW1Y 11 G7
Haymeads Dr ESH/CLAY KT10 170 C5
Haymer Gdns WPK KT4 173 J2
Haymerle Rd PECK SE15 111 H5
Haymill Cl GFD/PVL UB6 85 F2
Hayne Rd BECK BR3 151 H7
Haynes Cl BKHTH/KID SE3 133 H2
FBAR/BDGN N11 40 A2
TOTM N17 42 D6
Haynes Dr ED N9 42 D2
Haynes La NRWD SE19 150 A5
Haynes Rd ALP/SUD HA0 68 A6
Hayne St STBT EC1A 12 D2
Haynt Wk RYNPK SW20 161 H2
Hay's La STHWK SE1 13 J8
Haysleigh Gdns PGE/AN SE20 165 H1
Hay's Ms MYFR/PICC W1J 10 C7
Haysoms Cl ROM RM1 63 G3
Haystall Cl YEAD UB4 82 C1
Hay St BETH E2 74 C7
Hayter Rd BRXS/STRHM SW2 129 K4
Hayton Cl HACK E8 74 B5
Hayward Cl DART DA1 138 A4
WIM/MER SW19 147 F6
Hayward Gdns
PUT/ROE SW15 127 F5
Hayward Rd THDIT KT7 158 A7
TRDG/WHET N20 39 G1
Haywards Cl CHDH RM6 61 J4
Hayward's Pl CLKNW EC1R * 12 C1
Haywood Cl PIN HA5 47 H1
Haywood Rd HAYES BR2 168 C3
Hazel Av WDR/YW UB7 100 D2
Hazelbank BRYLDS KT5 159 K7
Hazelbank Rd CAT SE6 152 B1
Hazelbourne Rd BAL SW12 129 G5
Hazelbury Cl WIM/MER SW19 161 K1
Hazelbury Gn ED N9 42 A2
Hazelbury La ED N9 42 A2
Hazel Cl BTFD TW8 * 104 C6
CDALE/KGS NW9 51 H1
CROY/NA CR0 166 A6
HCH RM12 81 K2
MTCM CR4 163 J3
PLMGR N13 41 K2
WHTN TW2 123 H6
Hazelcroft PIN HA5 34 A5
Hazeldean Rd WLSDN NW10 69 F6
Hazeldene Dr PIN HA5 47 G2
Hazeldene Gdns
HGDN/ICK UB10 64 A7
Hazeldene Rd GDMY/SEVK IG3 79 H1
WELL DA16 136 D1
Hazeldon Rd BROCKY SE4 132 B4
Hazel Dr ERITH DA8 118 D7
Hazeleigh Gdns WFD IG8 45 J4
Hazel Gdns EDGW HA8 36 D3
Hazelgreen Cl WCHMH N21 29 H7
Hazel Gv ALP/SUD HA0 68 A7
CHDH RM6 62 A2
EN EN1 * 30 C5
FELT TW13 121 K7
SYD SE26 151 F3
Hazelhurst BECK BR3 152 B7
Hazelhurst Rd TOOT SW17 147 G3
Hazellville Rd ARCH N19 54 D6
Hazel Md BAR EN5 25 K4
Hazelmere Cl
EBED/NFELT TW14 121 G5
NTHLT UB5 83 K1
Hazelmere Dr NTHLT UB5 83 K1
Hazelmere Gdns EMPK RM11 63 K4
Hazelmere Rd
KIL/WHAMP NW6 2 A4
NTHLT UB5 83 K1
STMC/STPC BR5 169 H3
Hazelmere Wk NTHLT UB5 83 K1
Hazelmere Wy HAYES BR2 167 K5
Hazel Rd ERITH DA8 118 D7
SRTFD E15 * 76 C4
WLSDN NW10 87 K2
Hazel Rw
NFNCH/WDSPK N12 * 39 H4
Hazeltree La NTHLT UB5 83 J2
Hazel Wk HAYES BR2 169 F5
Hazel Wy CHING E4 43 H5
STHWK SE1 19 L5
Hazelwood Av MRDN SM4 162 A3
Hazelwood Cl CLPT E5 75 G2
EA W5 105 F1
RYLN/HDSTN HA2 48 B3
Hazelwood Ct SURB KT6 159 F5
Hazelwood Dr PIN HA5 47 F1
Hazelwood La PLMGR N13 41 G3
Hazelwood Rd EN EN1 30 B5
RKW/CH/CXG WD3 20 A5
WALTH E17 57 G4
Hazlebury Rd FUL/PGN SW6 128 A1
Hazledean Rd CROY/NA CR0 177 K1
Hazledene Rd CHSWK W4 105 K5
Hazlemere Gdns WPK KT4 160 D7
Hazlewell Rd PUT/ROE SW15 127 F4
Hazlewood Crs NKENS W10 88 C3
Hazlitt Cl FELT TW13 141 J3
Hazlitt Ms WKENS W14 * 107 H2
Hazlitt Rd WKENS W14 107 H2
Heacham Av HGDN/ICK UB10 64 A2
Headcorn Rd BMLY BR1 152 D4
THHTH CR7 164 A3
TOTM N17 42 B6
Headfort Pl KTBR SW1X 16 B2
Headingley Dr BECK BR3 151 J5
Headington Rd
WAND/EARL SW18 128 B7
Headlam Rd CLAP SW4 129 J5
Headlam St WCHPL E1 92 D3
Headley Ap GNTH/NBYPK IG2 60 A4
Headley Av WLGTN SM6 177 F4
Headley Cl CHSGTN KT9 172 C5
Headley Dr CROY/NA CR0 180 A6
GNTH/NBYPK IG2 60 B5
Heads Ms NTGHL W11 8 A5
Headstone Dr HRW HA1 48 D3
KTN/HRWW/WS HA3 48 E2
Headstone Gdns
RYLN/HDSTN HA2 48 C3
Headstone La
RYLN/HDSTN HA2 48 B1
Headstone Pde HRW HA1 * 48 D3
Headstone Rd HRW HA1 48 E4
Head St WCHPL E1 93 F5
Headway Cl
RCHPK/HAM TW10 143 J3
The Headway EW KT17 173 H7
Heald St NWCR SE14 112 C7
Healey Rd WATW WD18 20 D5
Healey St CAMTN NW1 * 72 B5
Hearne Rd CHSWK W4 105 H4
Hearn Ri NTHLT UB5 65 H7
Hearn Rd ROM RM1 63 H5
Hearn's Blds WALW SE17 19 H6
Hearnshaw St POP/IOD E14 93 G5
Hearn St SDTCH EC2A 13 K1
Hearnville Rd BAL SW12 129 F7
Heatham Pk WHTN TW2 124 A6
Heath Av BXLYHN DA7 116 E5
Heathbourne Rd BUSH WD23 34 E1
Heath Brow HAMP NW3 71 G2
Heath Cl EA W5 86 B3
GLDGN NW11 53 F6
GPK RM2 63 J2
HYS/HAR UB3 101 G6
SAND/SEL CR2 177 H5
Heathclose Av DART DA1 138 E6
Heathclose Rd DART DA1 138 D7
Heathcote Av CLAY IG5 59 K1
Heathcote Gv CHING E4 44 A2
Heathcote Rd TWK TW1 124 C5
Heathcote St BMSBY WC1N 5 L9
Heathcroft EA W5 86 B3
Heathcroft Av SUN TW16 140 D6
Heathcroft Gdns WALTH E17 44 B7
Heathdale Av HSLWW TW4 122 D2
Heathdene Dr BELV DA17 117 J3
Heathdene Rd
STRHM/NOR SW16 149 F6
WLGTN SM6 176 B6
Heath Dr BELMT SM2 175 G7
HAMP NW3 71 F3
RYNPK SW20 161 F3
Heathedge SYD SE26 * 150 D1
Heathend Rd BXLY DA5 138 B7
Heather Av ROM RM1 63 F1
Heatherbank CHST BR7 169 F1
ELTH/MOT SE9 134 E1
Heatherbank Cl DART DA1 138 B5
Heather Cl EHAM E6 96 A5
HOLWY N7 73 F2
HPTN TW12 141 K7
ISLW TW7 123 J4
LEW SE13 133 G5
VX/NE SW8 129 G2
Heatherdale Cl
KUTN/CMB KT2 144 C5
Heatherdene Cl MTCM CR4 162 C3
NFNCH/WDSPK N12 39 G7
Heather Dr DART DA1 138 D6
ENC/FH EN2 29 H1
ROM RM1 63 F1
Heatherfold Wy PIN HA5 46 D2
Heather Gdns BELMT SM2 174 E5
GLDGN NW11 52 C5
ROM RM1 63 F1
Heather Gln ROM RM1 63 F1
Heatherlands SUN TW16 140 E5
Heatherlea Gv WPK KT4 161 F7
Heatherley Dr CLAY IG5 59 K2
Heather Park Dr
ALP/SUD HA0 68 C6
Heather Park Pde
ALP/SUD HA0 * 68 B6

Heather Pl ESH/CLAY KT10 170 B3
Heather Ri BUSH WD23 21 K1
Heather Rd CHING E4 43 H5
CRICK NW2 69 H1
LEE/GVPK SE12 152 E1
Heatherset Cl ESH/CLAY KT10 170 C4
Heatherset Gdns
STRHM/NOR SW16 149 F6
Heatherside Rd
HOR/WEW KT19 173 F6
SCUP DA14 155 J2
The Heathers
STWL/WRAY TW19 120 C6
Heather Wk EDGW HA8 36 D4
NKENS W10 88 C3
Heather Wy SAND/SEL CR2 179 F7
STAN HA7 35 F5
Heatherwood Cl MNPK E12 77 F1
Heatherwood Dr YEAD UB4 82 B1
Heathfield CHING E4 44 A2
CHST BR7 154 C5
HRW HA1 * 49 F6
Heathfield Av
WAND/EARL SW18 128 C6
Heathfield Cl CAN/RD E16 95 H4
HAYES BR2 181 G4
OXHEY WD19 21 G6
Heathfield Dr MTCM CR4 147 J6
Heathfield Gdns CHSWK W4 105 K4
CROY/NA CR0 * 177 J3
GLDGN NW11 52 B5
WAND/EARL SW18 128 C5
Heathfield La CHST BR7 154 C5
Heathfield North WHTN TW2 123 K6
Heathfield Pk CRICK NW2 70 A5
Heathfield Park Dr CHDH RM6 61 H4
Heathfield Ri RSLP HA4 46 A6
Heathfield Rd ACT W3 105 J1
BMLY BR1 152 D6
BUSH WD23 21 J3
BXLYHS DA6 137 G3
HAYES BR2 181 G4
SAND/SEL CR2 177 K4
WAND/EARL SW18 128 B5
Heathfield South WHTN TW2 124 A6
Heathfield Sq
WAND/EARL SW18 128 C6
Heathfield Ter CHSWK W4 105 K4
WOOL/PLUM SE18 115 K5
Heathfield V SAND/SEL CR2 179 F7
Heath Gdns DART DA1 * 139 F7
TWK TW1 124 A7
Heathgate GLDGN NW11 53 F5
Heathgate Pl HAMP NW3 71 K3
Heath Gv PGE/AN SE20 150 E6
SUN TW16 140 D6
Heath Hurst Rd HAMP NW3 71 J3
Heathhurst Rd SAND/SEL CR2 178 A7
Heathland Rd
STNW/STAM N16 56 A7
Heathlands Cl TWK TW1 143 F1
Heathlands Ct HSLWW TW4 122 D4
Heathlands Ri DART DA1 138 E6
Heathlands Wy HSLWW TW4 122 D4
Heath La BKHTH/KID SE3 133 G1
DART DA1 138 E7
Heathlee Rd BKHTH/KID SE3 133 J3
DART DA1 138 B5
Heathley End CHST BR7 154 C5
Heath Ldg BUSH WD23 * 22 D7
Heathman's Rd FUL/PGN SW6 107 J7
Heath Md WIM/MER SW19 146 B2
Heath Park Dr BMLY BR1 168 D2
Heath Park Rd GPK RM2 63 J4
Heath Ri HAYES BR2 167 K5
PUT/ROE SW15 127 G5
Heath Rd BXLY DA5 137 K7
CHDH RM6 61 K6
DART DA1 138 C5
HGDN/ICK UB10 82 A3
HRW HA1 48 C6
HSLW TW3 123 H3
OXHEY WD19 21 H6
THHTH CR7 164 D2
TWK TW1 124 A7
VX/NE SW8 129 G1
Heath's Cl EN EN1 29 K1
Heathside ESH/CLAY KT10 170 E2
HAMP NW3 71 H3
HSLWW TW4 122 E6
Heath Side STMC/STPC BR5 169 H7
Heathside Av BXLYHN DA7 137 F1
Heathside Cl ESH/CLAY KT10 170 E2
GNTH/NBYPK IG2 60 D4
NTHWD HA6 32 B4
Heathside Rd NTHWD HA6 32 B3
Heathstan Rd SHB W12 87 J5
Heath St DART DA1 139 G6
HAMP NW3 71 G3
The Heath HNWL W7 * 103 K1
Heath Vw EFNCH N2 53 G3
Heathview Av DART DA1 138 B5
Heath View Cl EFNCH N2 53 G3
Heathview Crs DART DA1 138 D6
Heath View Dr ABYW SE2 116 E5
Heathview Gdns
PUT/ROE SW15 127 F6
Heathview Rd THHTH CR7 164 B3
Heath Vls WAND/EARL SW18 * 128 B7
WOOL/PLUM SE18 116 A4
Heathville Rd ARCH N19 54 E6
Heathwall St BTSEA SW11 128 E2
Heath Wy ERITH DA8 117 K7
Heathway BKHTH/KID SE3 113 K6
CROY/NA CR0 179 H2
DAGW RM9 80 B3
NWDGN UB2 * 102 C3
WFD IG8 45 G3
Heathwood Gdns CHARL SE7 114 D3
Heathwood Wk BXLY DA5 138 B7
Heaton Cl CHING E4 44 A2
Heaton Rd MTCM CR4 148 A6
PECK SE15 131 J2
Heaven Tree Cl IS N1 73 J4
Heaver Rd BTSEA SW11 * 128 C2
Heavitree Cl
WOOL/PLUM SE18 115 J4
Heavitree Rd
WOOL/PLUM SE18 115 J4
Hebden Ter TOTM N17 42 A5
Hebdon Rd TOOT SW17 147 J2
Heber Rd CRICK NW2 70 B4
EDUL SE22 131 G5
Hebron Rd HMSMTH W6 106 E2
Hecham Cl WALTH E17 57 G1
Heckfield Pl FUL/PGN SW6 107 K6
Heckford Cl WATW WD18 20 A5
Heckford St WAP E1W 93 F6
Hector Cl ED N9 42 C1
Hector St WOOL/PLUM SE18 * 115 K3
Heddington Gv HOLWY N7 73 F4
Heddon Cl ISLW TW7 124 B3
Heddon Court Av EBAR EN4 27 K4
Heddon Court Pde
EBAR EN4 * 28 A4
Heddon Rd EBAR EN4 27 K4
Heddon St CONDST W1S 10 E7
Hedge La PLMGR N13 41 H2
Hedgeley REDBR IG4 59 K3
Hedgemans Rd DAGW RM9 79 K6
Hedgemans Wy DAGW RM9 80 A5
Hedgerley Gdns GFD/PVL UB6 84 C1
Hedgerow La BAR EN5 25 K4
Hedger's Gv HOM E9 * 75 G5
Hedger St LBTH SE11 18 C5
Hedgeside Rd NTHWD HA6 32 A4
Hedgewood Gdns CLAY IG5 60 A3
Hedgley Ms LEE/GVPK SE12 133 J4
Hedgley St LEE/GVPK SE12 133 J4
Hedingham Cl IS N1 6 E2
Hedingham Rd BCTR RM8 79 H4
Hedley Rd WHTN TW2 123 F6
Hedley Rw HBRY N5 73 K4
Heenan Cl BARK IG11 78 C5
Heene Rd ENC/FH EN2 29 K1
Heidegger Crs BARN SW13 106 E6
Heigham Rd EHAM E6 77 J6
Heighton Gdns CROY/NA CR0 177 H4
Heights Cl RYNPK SW20 145 K6
The Heights BECK BR3 * 152 A6
CHARL SE7 114 B4
NTHLT UB5 66 A4
Heiron St WALW SE17 110 C5
Helby Rd CLAP SW4 129 J5
Helder Gv LEE/GVPK SE12 133 J6
Helder St SAND/SEL CR2 177 K5
Heldmann Cl HSLW TW3 123 J3
Helena Pl HACK E8 74 D7
Helena Rd EA W5 85 K4
PLSTW E13 94 D1
WALTH E17 57 J4
WLSDN NW10 69 K4
Helena Sq BERM/RHTH SE16 93 G6
Helen Av EBED/NFELT TW14 122 A6
Helen Cl DART DA1 138 E6
E/WMO/HCT KT8 157 G3
EFNCH N2 53 G2
Helenslea Av GLDGN NW11 52 D7
Helen's Pl BETH E2 92 E2
Helen St WOOL/PLUM SE18 115 G3
Helford Cl RSLP HA4 64 C1
Helgiford Gdns SUN TW16 140 C6
Helios Rd WLGTN SM6 163 F7
Helix Gdns BRXS/STRHM SW2 130 A5
Helix Rd BRXS/STRHM SW2 130 A5
Hellings St WAP E1W 92 C7
Helme Cl WIM/MER SW19 146 D4
Helmet Rw FSBYE EC1V 6 F9
Helmore Rd BARK IG11 79 F6
Helmsdale Cl YEAD UB4 * 83 J3
Helmsdale Rd
STRHM/NOR SW16 148 C7
Helmsley Pl HACK E8 74 D6
Helmsley St HACK E8 74 D6
Helperby Rd WLSDN NW10 69 G6
Helsinki Sq BERM/RHTH SE16 112 B2
Helston Cl PIN HA5 33 K6
Helvetia St CAT SE6 151 H1
Hemans St VX/NE SW8 109 J6
Hemery Rd GFD/PVL UB6 66 D4
Hemingford Cl
NFNCH/WDSPK N12 39 H4
Hemingford Rd CHEAM SM3 174 A3
IS N1 5 M3
Heming Rd EDGW HA8 36 D5
Hemington Av
FBAR/BDGN N11 39 K4
Hemlock Cl STRHM/NOR SW16 163 J1
Hemlock Rd SHB W12 87 H6
Hemmen La HYS/HAR UB3 82 D6
Hemming Cl HPTN TW12 142 A7
Hemmings Cl SCUP DA14 155 H1
Hemmingsmead
HOR/WEW KT19 172 E5
Hemming St WCHPL E1 92 C3
Hemmingway Cl KTTN NW5 72 A3
Hempstead Cl BKHH IG9 44 E1
Hempstead Rd WALTH E17 58 B2
WAT WD17 20 E1
Hemp Wk WALW SE17 19 H5
Hemsby Rd CHSGTN KT9 172 B5
Hemstal Rd KIL/WHAMP NW6 2 A1
Hemsted Rd ERITH DA8 118 B7
Hemswell Dr CDALE/KGS NW9 37 G7
Hemsworth St IS N1 7 J5
Henbury Wy OXHEY WD19 33 H2
Henchman St SHB W12 87 H5
Hendale Av HDN NW4 51 J2
Henderson Cl EMPK RM11 81 K1
WLSDN NW10 68 E5
Henderson Dr DART DA1 139 K3
STJWD NW8 3 G9
Henderson Rd CROY/NA CR0 164 E5
ED N9 30 D7
FSTGT E7 77 G5
WAND/EARL SW18 128 D6
YEAD UB4 82 E2
Hendham Rd TOOT SW17 147 J1
Hendon Av FNCH N3 38 C7
Hendon Gv HOR/WEW KT19 172 C7
Hendon Hall Ct HDN NW4 * 52 B2
Hendon La FNCH N3 52 C2
Hendon Park Rw
GLDGN NW11 * 52 D5
Hendon Rd ED N9 42 C1
Hendon Ter ASHF TW15 * 140 B5
Hendon Wy CRICK NW2 52 B6
STWL/WRAY TW19 120 A4
Hendon Wood La MLHL NW7 25 J7
Hendren Cl GFD/PVL UB6 66 D4
Hendre Rd STHWK SE1 19 K6
Hendrick Av BAL SW12 128 E5
Heneage St WCHPL E1 13 M2
Henfield Cl ARCH N19 54 C7
BXLY DA5 137 H5
Henfield Rd WIM/MER SW19 146 D7
Hengelo Gdns MTCM CR4 162 C3
Hengest Av ESH/CLAY KT10 171 G2
Hengist Rd ERITH DA8 117 K6
LEE/GVPK SE12 134 A6
Hengist Wy HAYES BR2 167 G3
Hengrave Rd FSTH SE23 131 K6
Hengrove Ct BXLY DA5 137 F7
Henley Av CHEAM SM3 174 C2
Henley Cl BERM/RHTH SE16 * 111 K1
GFD/PVL UB6 * 84 C1
ISLW TW7 104 A7
Henley Dr KUTN/CMB KT2 145 H6
STHWK SE1 19 M5
Henley Gdns CHDH RM6 62 A4
PIN HA5 47 F2
Henley Rd CAN/RD E16 114 E1
IL IG1 78 C3
UED N18 42 A3
WLSDN NW10 70 A7
Henley St BTSEA SW11 129 F1
Henley Wy FELT TW13 141 H4
Hennel Cl FSTH SE23 150 E2
Hennessy Rd ED N9 42 E1
Henniker Gdns EHAM E6 95 H2
Henniker Ms CHEL SW3 15 G9
Henniker Rd SRTFD E15 76 B4
Henningham Rd TOTM N17 41 K7
Henning St BTSEA SW11 108 D7
Henrietta Cl DEPT SE8 112 D5
Henrietta Ms BMSBY WC1N 5 K9
Henrietta Pl CAVSQ/HST W1G 10 C4
Henrietta St COVGDN WC2E 11 K6
SRTFD E15 76 A4
Henriques St WCHPL E1 92 C5
Henry Addlington Cl EHAM E6 96 B4
Henry Cooper Wy
ELTH/MOT SE9 153 H2
Henry Darlot Dr MLHL NW7 38 B4
Henry Dickens Ct NTGHL W11 88 B6
Henry Doulton Dr TOOT SW17 148 A3
Henry Jackson Rd
PUT/ROE SW15 127 G2
Henry Macaulay Av
KUTN/CMB KT2 143 K7
Henry Peters Dr TEDD TW11 142 E4
Henry Rd EBAR EN4 27 H4
EHAM E6 95 J1
FSBYPK N4 55 J7
Henry's Av WFD IG8 44 D4
Henryson Rd BROCKY SE4 132 D4
Henry St BMLY BR1 153 F7
Henry Tate Ms
STRHM/NOR SW16 149 G4
Hensby Ms OXHEY WD19 21 J5
Henshall St IS N1 73 K5
Henshawe Rd BCTR RM8 79 K2
Henshaw St WALW SE17 19 G5
Henslowe Rd EDUL SE22 131 H4
Henson Av CRICK NW2 70 A4
Henson Pl NTHLT UB5 65 G7
Henstridge Pl STJWD NW8 3 J5
Henty Cl BTSEA SW11 108 D6
Henty Wk PUT/ROE SW15 126 E4
Henville Rd BMLY BR1 153 F7
Henwick Rd ELTH/MOT SE9 134 C2
Henwood Side WFD IG8 45 K5
Hepburn Gdns HAYES BR2 167 J7
Hepple Cl ISLW TW7 124 C1
Hepscott Rd HOM E9 75 J6
Hepworth Gdns BARK IG11 79 G4
Hepworth Rd
STRHM/NOR SW16 148 E6
Herald Gdns WLGTN SM6 176 B2
Heralds Pl LBTH SE11 18 C5
Herald St BETH E2 92 D3
Herbal Hl CLKNW EC1R 12 B1
Herbert Crs KTBR SW1X 15 M3
Herbert Gdns CHDH RM6 61 K6
CHSWK W4 105 J5
WLSDN NW10 87 K1
Herbert Ms BRXS/STRHM SW2 130 B5
Herbert Pl ISLW TW7 123 J1
WOOL/PLUM SE18 115 G5
Herbert Rd BXLYHN DA7 137 F1
CDALE/KGS NW9 51 J5
FBAR/BDGN N11 40 E6
GDMY/SEVK IG3 78 E1
HAYES BR2 168 C4
KUT/HW KT1 159 G2
MNPK E12 77 J3
SEVS/STOTM N15 56 B4
STHL UB1 83 K7
WALTH E17 57 H6
WIM/MER SW19 146 D6
WOOL/PLUM SE18 115 G6
Herbert St KTTN NW5 72 A5
PLSTW E13 94 E1
Herbrand St BMSBY WC1N 11 J1
STPAN WC1H 5 J9
Hercules Pl HOLWY N7 72 E2
Hercules Rd STHWK SE1 17 M4
Hercules St HOLWY N7 72 E2
Hereford Av EBAR EN4 27 K7
Hereford Gdns IL IG1 59 J6
PIN HA5 47 J4
WHTN TW2 * 123 H7
Hereford Ms BAY/PAD W2 8 B4
Hereford Pl NWCR SE14 * 112 C6
Hereford Retreat PECK SE15 111 H6
Hereford Rd ACT W3 86 E6
BAY/PAD W2 8 B5
BOW E3 93 H1
EA W5 104 D2
FELT TW13 122 B7
WAN E11 59 F4
Hereford Sq SKENS SW7 14 F6
Hereford St BETH E2 92 C3
Hereford Wy CHSGTN KT9 171 J4
Herent Dr CLAY IG5 59 K2
Heretage Cl BRXN/ST SW9 130 C2
Hereward Gdns PLMGR N13 41 G4
Hereward Rd TOOT SW17 147 J3
Herga Ct WAT WD17 20 E1
Herga Rd KTN/HRWW/WS HA3 49 F3
Heriot Av CHING E4 43 J1
Heriot Rd HDN NW4 52 A4
Heriots Cl STAN HA7 35 G3
Heritage Av CDALE/KGS NW9 51 H2
Heritage Cl SUN TW16 140 E7
Heritage Hl HAYES BR2 181 G4
Heritage Pl
WAND/EARL SW18 * 128 C5
Heritage Vw HRW HA1 67 F2
Herkomer Cl BUSH WD23 22 B5
Herkomer Rd BUSH WD23 22 A4
Herlwyn Av RSLP HA4 64 C2
Herlwyn Gdns TOOT SW17 147 K3
Herm Cl ISLW TW7 103 H6
Hermes Cl MV/WKIL W9 8 A1
Hermes St IS N1 6 A6
Hermes Wy WLGTN SM6 176 D6
Hermiston Av CEND/HSY/T N8 54 E4
Hermitage Cl ABYW SE2 116 D2
ENC/FH EN2 29 H1
ESH/CLAY KT10 171 G5
RCHPK/HAM TW10 * 124 E4
SWFD E18 58 D3
Hermitage Cots STAN HA7 * 34 E4
Hermitage Gdns CRICK NW2 70 E2
NRWD SE19 149 J6
Hermitage La CRICK NW2 70 E2
CROY/NA CR0 165 G6
STRHM/NOR SW16 149 F6
UED N18 41 K4
Hermitage Rd FSBYPK N4 55 J6
NRWD SE19 149 J6
Hermitage Rw HACK E8 * 74 C4
Hermitage St BAY/PAD W2 9 G3
The Hermitage BARN SW13 * 106 C7
FELT TW13 * 140 D2
FSTH SE23 131 K7
KUT/HW KT1 * 158 E3
LEW SE13 * 133 F1
RCHPK/HAM TW10 125 F4
Hermitage Wk SWFD E18 58 D3
Hermitage Wall WAP E1W 92 C7
Hermitage Wy STAN HA7 35 G7
Hermit Pl KIL/WHAMP NW6 2 C4
Hermit Rd CAN/RD E16 94 D3
Hermit St FSBYE EC1V 6 C7
Hermon Gv HYS/HAR UB3 82 E7
Hermon Hl WAN E11 58 E3
Herndon Rd
WAND/EARL SW18 128 B4
Herne Cl HYS/HAR UB3 82 D5
WLSDN NW10 69 F4
Herne Ct BUSH WD23 * 22 C7
Herne Hl HNHL SE24 130 D4
Herne Hill Rd HNHL SE24 130 D2
Herne Ms UED N18 42 C3
Herne Pl HNHL SE24 130 C5
Herne Rd BUSH WD23 22 B5
SURB KT6 171 K1
Heron Cl WALTH E17 57 H1
WLSDN NW10 69 G5
Heron Ct HAYES BR2 168 B3
KUT/HW KT1 * 159 F2
Heron Crs SCUP DA14 154 E3
Herondale SAND/SEL CR2 179 F7
Herondale Av
WAND/EARL SW18 128 C7
Heron Dr FSBYPK N4 73 J1
Heron Flight Av HCH RM12 81 J6
Herongate Rd MNPK E12 77 G1
Heron Hl BELV DA17 117 G3
Heron Ms IL IG1 78 B1
Heron Pl BERM/RHTH SE16 93 G7
Heron Quays POP/IOD E14 93 J7
Heron Rd CROY/NA CR0 * 165 F7
HNHL SE24 130 D3
TWK TW1 124 B3
Heronsforde WEA W13 85 J5
Heronsgate EDGW HA8 36 C4
Herons Lea HGT N6 * 53 K5
Heronslea Dr STAN HA7 36 A4
Herons Pl ISLW TW7 124 C2
Herons Ri EBAR EN4 27 J3
Heron Wk NTHWD HA6 32 C3
Heron Wy
EBED/NFELT TW14 121 K3
Herrick Rd HBRY N5 73 J2
Herrick St WEST SW1P 17 H6
Herries St NKENS W10 88 C1
Herringham Rd CHARL SE7 114 B2
Herrongate Cl EN EN1 30 A1
Hersant Cl WLSDN NW10 69 J7
Herschell Rd FSTH SE23 132 A6
Hersham Cl PUT/ROE SW15 126 D6
Hershell Ct
MORT/ESHN SW14 * 125 J3
Hertford Av
MORT/ESHN SW14 126 A4
Hertford Cl EBAR EN4 27 H2
Hertford Ct STAN HA7 * 35 K6
Hertford End Ct
NTHWD HA6 * 32 C4
Hertford Pl FITZ W1T 10 E1
Hertford Rd BARK IG11 78 A6
EBAR EN4 27 G2
ED N9 30 D7
EFNCH N2 53 J2
GNTH/NBYPK IG2 60 E5
IS N1 7 K3
PEND EN3 30 E2
Hertford Road High St
PEND EN3 30 E5
Hertford St MYFR/PICC W1J 10 C8
Hertford Wy MTCM CR4 163 K3
Hertslet Rd HOLWY N7 73 F2
Hertsmere Rd POP/IOD E14 93 J6
Hertswood Ct BAR EN5 * 26 C3
Hervey Cl FNCH N3 38 E7
Hervey Park Rd WALTH E17 57 G3
Hesa Rd HYS/HAR UB3 82 E5
Hesewall Cl CLAP SW4 129 H1
Hesketh Pl NTGHL W11 88 C6
Hesketh Rd FSTGT E7 76 E2
Heslop Rd BAL SW12 128 E7
Hesper Ms ECT SW5 14 C7
Hesperus Crs POP/IOD E14 112 E3
Hessel Rd WEA W13 104 B1
Hessel St WCHPL E1 92 D5
Hesselyn Dr RAIN RM13 81 K6
Hestercombe Av
FUL/PGN SW6 127 H1
Hesterman Wy CROY/NA CR0 163 K7
Hester Rd BTSEA SW11 108 D6
UED N18 42 C4
Hester Ter RCH/KEW TW9 125 H2
Heston Av HEST TW5 102 D6
Heston Grange La HEST TW5 102 E5
Heston Rd HEST TW5 103 F6
Heston St NWCR SE14 112 C7
Heswell Gn OXHEY WD19 * 32 E2
Hetherington Rd CLAP SW4 129 K3
Hetley Rd SHB W12 87 K7
Heton Gdns HDN NW4 51 J3
Hevelius Cl GNWCH SE10 113 J4
Hever Cft ELTH/MOT SE9 154 A3
Hever Gdns BMLY BR1 169 F1
Heverham Rd
WOOL/PLUM SE18 115 K3
Heversham Rd BXLYHN DA7 137 H1
Hevingham Dr CHDH RM6 61 J4
Hewens Rd HGDN/ICK UB10 82 A2
Hewer St NKENS W10 88 B4
Hewett Cl STAN HA7 35 H3
Hewett Rd BCTR RM8 79 K4
Hewett St SDTCH EC2A 13 K1
Hewish Rd UED N18 42 A3
Hewison St BOW E3 93 H1
Hewitt Av WDGN N22 55 H1
Hewitt Cl CROY/NA CR0 179 J2
Hewitt Rd CEND/HSY/T N8 55 G4
Hewlett Rd BOW E3 93 G1
The Hexagon HGT N6 53 K7
Hexal Rd CAT SE6 152 C2
Hexham Gdns ISLW TW7 104 B6
NTHLT UB5 65 K4
Hexham Rd BAR EN5 27 F3
MRDN SM4 162 A7
WNWD SE27 149 J1
Heybourne Rd TOTM N17 42 D6
Heybridge Av
STRHM/NOR SW16 149 F5
Heybridge Dr BARK/HLT IG6 60 D2
Heybridge Wy LEY E10 57 G6
Heyford Av RYNPK SW20 161 J2
VX/NE SW8 109 K6
Heyford Rd MTCM CR4 162 D1
Heyford Ter VX/NE SW8 109 K6
Heygate Est WALW SE17 18 F5
Heygate St WALW SE17 18 E6
Heynes Rd BCTR RM8 79 J3
Heysham Dr OXHEY WD19 33 G4
Heysham La HAMP NW3 71 F2
Heysham Rd
SEVS/STOTM N15 55 K5
Heythorp St
WAND/EARL SW18 146 D1
Heywood Av CDALE/KGS NW9 37 G7
Heyworth Rd CLPT E5 74 D3
SRTFD E15 76 D3
Hibbert Rd
KTN/HRWW/WS HA3 49 F1
WALTH E17 57 H6
Hibbert St BTSEA SW11 128 B2
Hibernia Gdns HSLW TW3 123 F4
Hibernia Rd HSLW TW3 123 F3
Hichisson Rd PECK SE15 131 K4
Hicken Rd BRXS/STRHM SW2 130 A4
Hickin Cl CHARL SE7 114 C3
Hickin St POP/IOD E14 113 F2
Hickling Rd IL IG1 78 B4
Hickman Av CHING E4 44 A5
Hickman Cl CAN/RD E16 95 H4
Hickman Rd CHDH RM6 61 J6
Hickory Cl ED N9 30 C6
Hicks Av GFD/PVL UB6 84 D2
Hicks Cl BTSEA SW11 128 D2
Hicks St DEPT SE8 112 B4
Hidcote Gdns RYNPK SW20 160 E2
Hidden Cl E/WMO/HCT KT8 157 H3
Hide Pl WEST SW1P 17 G6
Hide Rd HRW HA1 48 D3
Higham Hill Rd WALTH E17 57 G2
Higham Ms NTHLT UB5 83 K3
Higham Pl WALTH E17 57 G2
Higham Rd TOTM N17 55 K2
WFD IG8 44 E5
Higham Station Av CHING E4 43 K5
The Highams WALTH E17 * 44 A7
Higham St WALTH E17 57 G1
Highbank Pl
WAND/EARL SW18 * 128 A7
Highbanks Cl WELL DA16 116 B6
Highbanks Rd PIN HA5 34 B5
Highbank Wy CEND/HSY/T N8 55 G5
Highbarrow Rd CROY/NA CR0 165 G7
High Beech SAND/SEL CR2 178 A6
Highbridge Rd BARK IG11 78 B7
Highbrook Rd BKHTH/KID SE3 134 C2
High Broom Crs WWKM BR4 166 E6
Highbury Av THHTH CR7 164 B1
Highbury Cl NWMAL KT3 159 K3
WWKM BR4 179 K1
Highbury Cnr IS N1 73 H5
Highbury Crs HBRY N5 73 G4
Highbury Est HBRY N5 73 J4
Highbury Gdns
GDMY/SEVK IG3 78 E1
Highbury Gra HBRY N5 73 H3
Highbury Gv HBRY N5 73 H4
Highbury Hl HBRY N5 73 H5
Highbury New Pk HBRY N5 73 H5
Highbury Pk HBRY N5 73 H3
Highbury Pl HBRY N5 73 H5
Highbury Qd HBRY N5 73 J2
Highbury Rd WIM/MER SW19 146 C4
Highbury Station Pde
HBRY N5 * 73 H5
Highbury Station Rd IS N1 * 73 G5
Highbury Ter HBRY N5 73 H4
Highbury Terrace Ms
HBRY N5 73 H4
High Cedar Dr RYNPK SW20 145 K6
Highclere Rd NWMAL KT3 160 A2
Highclere St SYD SE26 151 G3
Highcliffe Dr PUT/ROE SW15 126 C5
Highcliffe Gdns REDBR IG4 59 J4
Highcombe CHARL SE7 114 A5
Highcombe Cl ELTH/MOT SE9 134 C7
High Coombe Pl
KUTN/CMB KT2 145 F6
Highcroft CDALE/KGS NW9 51 G4
Highcroft Av ALP/SUD HA0 68 B6
Highcroft Gdns GLDGN NW11 52 D5
Highcroft Rd ARCH N19 54 E6
High Cross Rd TOTM N17 56 C2
Highcross Wy PUT/ROE SW15 126 D7
Highdaun Dr
STRHM/NOR SW16 164 A3
Highdown WPK KT4 173 G1
Highdown Rd PUT/ROE SW15 126 E5
High Dr NWMAL KT3 144 E7
High Elms WFD IG8 44 E4
High Elms Cl NTHWD HA6 32 A5
Highfield OXHEY WD19 33 K2
Highfield Av CDALE/KGS NW9 50 E4
ERITH DA8 117 J5
GFD/PVL UB6 66 E4
GLDGN NW11 52 B6
PIN HA5 47 K4
WBLY HA9 68 A2
Highfield Cl CDALE/KGS NW9 50 E4
LEW SE13 133 G5
NTHWD HA6 32 C7
SURB KT6 158 D7
WDGN N22 41 G7
Highfield Ct STHGT/OAK N14 28 C5
Highfield Crs NTHWD HA6 32 C7
Highfield Dr HAYES BR2 167 H3
HOR/WEW KT19 173 H6
WWKM BR4 179 K2
Highfield Gdns GLDGN NW11 52 C5
Highfield Hl NRWD SE19 149 K6
Highfield Rd ACT W3 86 D4
BMLY BR1 168 E3
BRYLDS KT5 159 K6
BUSH WD23 21 J4
BXLYHS DA6 137 G4
DART DA1 139 G6
FELT TW13 121 K7
GLDGN NW11 * 52 C5
ISLW TW7 104 A7
NTHWD HA6 32 C7
SUT SM1 175 J4
WCHMH N21 41 H1
WFD IG8 45 J6
Highfield Rd North DART DA1 139 G5
Highfield Rd South DART DA1 139 G6
Highfields Gv HGT N6 54 A7
High Foleys ESH/CLAY KT10 171 H6
High Garth ESH/CLAY KT10 170 C5
Highgate Av HGT N6 54 B6
Highgate Cl HGT N6 54 A6
Highgate Edge EFNCH N2 * 53 J4
Highgate High St HGT N6 54 A7
Highgate Hl ARCH N19 54 B7
Highgate Rd KTTN NW5 72 B3
Highgate Spinney
CEND/HSY/T N8 * 54 D5
Highgate Wk FSTH SE23 150 E1
Highgate West Hl HGT N6 54 A7
High Gv BMLY BR1 153 G7
WOOL/PLUM SE18 115 J6
Highgrove Cl CHST BR7 153 J7
FBAR/BDGN N11 40 A4
Highgrove Ms CAR SM5 175 J2

Highgrove Rd BCTR RM8 79 J4
Highgrove Wy RSLP HA4 46 E5
High Hill Ferry CLPT E5 56 D7
High Holborn HHOL WC1V 11 K4
Highland Av DAGE RM10 80 E2
HNWL W7 84 E5
Highland Cots WLGTN SM6 * 176 B3
Highland Cft BECK BR3 151 K4
Highland Dr BUSH WD23 22 B6
Highland Pk FELT TW13 140 D3
Highland Rd BMLY BR1 152 D7
BXLYHS DA6 137 H3
HAYES BR2 167 J1
NRWD SE19 150 A5
NTHWD HA6 46 E1
Highlands OXHEY WD19 21 G7
Highlands Av ACT W3 86 E6
WCHMH N21 29 F4
Highlands Cl FSBYPK N4 54 E6
HSLW TW3 103 G7
Highlands Gdns IL IG1 59 K7
Highlands Heath
PUT/ROE SW15 127 F6
Highlands Rd BAR EN5 26 E4
The Highlands BAR EN5 26 E4
EDGW HA8 50 D1
Highland Ter LEW SE13 * 132 E2
High La HNWL W7 84 D5
Highlea Cl CDALE/KGS NW9 37 G7
High Level Dr SYD SE26 150 C3
Highlever Rd NKENS W10 88 A4
High Limes NRWD SE19 * 150 A5
High Md HRW HA1 48 E4
Highmead WOOL/PLUM SE18 116 A6
High Md WWKM BR4 180 B1
Highmead Crs ALP/SUD HA0 68 B6
High Meadow Cl PIN HA5 47 F3
High Meadow Crs
CDALE/KGS NW9 51 F4
High Meads Rd CAN/RD E16 95 H5
Highmore Rd BKHTH/KID SE3 113 H6
High Mt HDN NW4 * 51 J5
The High Pde
STRHM/NOR SW16 * 148 E2
High Park Rd RCH/KEW TW9 105 H7
High Pth WIM/MER SW19 147 F7
High Point ELTH/MOT SE9 154 B2
High Rdg MUSWH N10 * 40 B7
High Rd BUSH WD23 22 D7
CHDH RM6 61 K6
EFNCH N2 53 J3
FBAR/BDGN N11 40 B4
FNCH N3 39 H7
GDMY/SEVK IG3 61 G7
IL IG1 78 B2
KTN/HRWW/WS HA3 34 E7
LEY E10 57 K5
NFNCH/WDSPK N12 39 G6
SEVS/STOTM N15 56 B4
TOTM N17 56 B2
TRDG/WHET N20 27 F6
WBLY HA9 68 A4
WDGN N22 41 F6
WDGN N22 55 G2
WLSDN NW10 69 G5
High Rd Eastcote PIN HA5 47 F4
High Rd Leyton LEY E10 75 K1
High Rd Leytonstone
WAN E11 76 C2
High Road Woodford Gn
WFD IG8 44 E3
Highshore Rd PECK SE15 131 G1
Highstead Crs ERITH DA8 118 B7
Highstone Av WAN E11 58 E5
High St ACT W3 86 E7
BAR EN5 26 C2
BARK/HLT IG6 60 C1
BECK BR3 151 J7
BELMT SM2 175 G6
BMLY BR1 167 K1
BTFD TW8 104 E5
BUSH WD23 22 A5
CAR SM5 175 K4
CEND/HSY/T N8 54 E3
CHEAM SM3 174 C5
CROY/NA CR0 177 J2
DART DA1 139 H5
E/WMO/HCT KT8 157 F4
EA W5 85 K6
ESH/CLAY KT10 170 B3
ESH/CLAY KT10 171 F5
EW KT17 173 H7
FBAR/BDGN N11 40 B4
FELT TW13 140 D2
HEST TW5 102 A5
HPTN TW12 142 B7
HRW HA1 48 E7
HSLW TW3 123 G2
HYS/HAR UB3 101 G5
KTN/HRWW/WS HA3 48 E2
KUT/HW KT1 143 J7
MLHL NW7 37 K4
NTHWD HA6 32 D7
NWMAL KT3 160 B3
PGE/AN SE20 150 E6
PIN HA5 47 J2
PLSTW E13 94 E1
PUR RM19 119 K4
ROM RM1 63 G4
RSLP HA4 46 C6
SCUP DA14 155 G3
SNWD SE25 165 G3
SRTFD E15 94 A1
STHGT/OAK N14 28 D7
STWL/WRAY TW19 120 A5
SUT SM1 175 F5
TEDD TW11 143 G4
THDIT KT7 158 B5
THHTH CR7 164 D3
WALTH E17 57 H3
WAN E11 59 F5
WAT WD17 21 F2
WBLY HA9 68 B3
WDR/YW UB7 100 A5
WHTN TW2 123 H6
WIM/MER SW19 146 B4
WWKM BR4 166 E7
High Street Collier's Wd
WIM/MER SW19 147 H6
High Street Harlesden
WLSDN NW10 69 G7
High Street Harlington
HYS/HAR UB3 101 G6
High Street Ms
WIM/MER SW19 146 C4
High St North EHAM E6 77 J7
High St South EHAM E6 95 K1
High Timber St BLKFR EC4V 12 E6
High Tor Cl BMLY BR1 153 F6
High Trees BRXS/STRHM SW2 130 B7
CROY/NA CR0 166 B7
EBAR EN4 27 J4
High Vw PIN HA5 47 G3
WATW WD18 20 D5
Highview Av EDGW HA8 36 E3
High View Av WLGTN SM6 177 F4
High View Cl NRWD SE19 165 G1
Highview Gdns EDGW HA8 36 E4
FBAR/BDGN N11 40 C4
FNCH N3 52 C2
High View Rd NRWD SE19 149 K5
SWFD E18 58 D1
Highview Rd SCUP DA14 155 H3
WEA W13 85 G5
Highview Ter DART DA1 * 139 G4
The Highway BELMT SM2 175 G7
STAN HA7 35 F7
WCHPL E1 92 C6
Highwood Av
NFNCH/WDSPK N12 39 G3
Highwood Cl EDUL SE22 131 H7
Highwood Gdns CLAY IG5 59 K4
Highwood Gv MLHL NW7 37 F4
Highwood Hl MLHL NW7 37 H1
Highwood Rd ARCH N19 72 E2
High Worple
RYLN/HDSTN HA2 47 J6
Highworth Rd
FBAR/BDGN N11 40 D5
Highworth St CAMTN NW1 * 9 K2
Hilary Av MTCM CR4 163 F2
Hilary Cl ERITH DA8 117 J7
FUL/PGN SW6 * 108 A6
Hilary Rd SHB W12 87 H6
Hilberry Ct BUSH WD23 22 B6
Hilbert Rd CHEAM SM3 174 B3
Hilborough Cl
WIM/MER SW19 147 G6
Hilborough Rd HACK E8 * 7 M2
Hilda Lockert Wk
BRXN/ST SW9 130 C1
Hilda Rd CAN/RD E16 94 C3
EHAM E6 77 H6
Hilda Ter BRXN/ST SW9 * 130 B1
Hildenborough Gdns
BMLY BR1 152 C5
Hilden Dr ERITH DA8 118 E6
Hildenlea Pl HAYES BR2 167 H1
Hildreth St BAL SW12 129 G7
Hildyard Rd FUL/PGN SW6 14 B9
Hiley Rd WLSDN NW10 88 A2
Hilfield La GSTN WD25 22 C1
Hilgrove Rd KIL/WHAMP NW6 2 F2
Hiliary Gdns STAN HA7 49 J1
Hillary Crs WOT/HER KT12 156 B7
Hillary Dr ISLW TW7 124 A3
Hillary Ri BAR EN5 26 E3
Hillary Rd NWDGN UB2 103 F2
Hillbeck Cl PECK SE15 111 K6
Hillbeck Wy GFD/PVL UB6 66 D7
Hillborne Cl HYS/HAR UB3 101 K4
Hillborough Cl
WIM/MER SW19 * 147 G6
Hillbrook Rd TOOT SW17 147 K2
Hill Brow BMLY BR1 153 H7
DART DA1 138 C5
Hillbrow NWMAL KT3 160 C2
Hillbrow Rd BMLY BR1 152 C6
ESH/CLAY KT10 170 C3
Hillbury Av
KTN/HRWW/WS HA3 49 H4
Hillbury Rd TOOT SW17 148 B2
Hill Cl BAR EN5 26 A4
CHST BR7 154 B4
CRICK NW2 69 K2
GLDGN NW11 52 E5
HRW HA1 66 E2
STAN HA7 35 H3
Hillcote Av STRHM/NOR SW16 149 G6
Hillcourt Av
NFNCH/WDSPK N12 39 F5
Hillcourt Rd EDUL SE22 131 J5
Hill Crs BRYLDS KT5 159 G4
BXLY DA5 137 K7
HRW HA1 49 G4
TRDG/WHET N20 39 F1
WPK KT4 174 A1
Hill Crest SURB KT6 * 159 F6
BFN/LL DA15 136 B6
Hillcrest HGT N6 54 A6
HNHL SE24 * 130 E3
WCHMH N21 29 G6
Hillcrest Av EDGW HA8 36 D3
GLDGN NW11 52 C4
PIN HA5 47 H3
Hillcrest Cl BECK BR3 166 C5
SYD SE26 150 C3
Hill Crest Gdns CRICK NW2 69 J2
Hillcrest Gdns ESH/CLAY KT10 171 F2
FNCH N3 52 C3
Hillcrest Rd ACT W3 86 C7
BMLY BR1 152 E3
DART DA1 138 B6
EA W5 86 A4
EMPK RM11 63 J6
WALTH E17 58 B1
Hillcrest Vw BECK BR3 166 C5
Hillcroft Av PIN HA5 47 K5
Hillcroft Crs EA W5 85 K5
OXHEY WD19 21 F7
RSLP HA4 65 H2
WBLY HA9 68 B3
Hillcroft Rd EHAM E6 96 B4
Hillcroome Rd BELMT SM2 175 H5
Hillcross Av MRDN SM4 161 H5
Hilldale Rd SUT SM1 174 D3
Hilldown Rd HAYES BR2 167 H7
STRHM/NOR SW16 148 E6
Hill Dr CDALE/KGS NW9 50 D7
STRHM/NOR SW16 164 A2
Hilldrop Crs HOLWY N7 72 D4
Hilldrop Est HOLWY N7 72 D4
Hilldrop La HOLWY N7 72 D4
Hilldrop Rd BMLY BR1 152 E5
HOLWY N7 72 D4
Hill End WOOL/PLUM SE18 115 F7
Hillersdon Av BARN SW13 126 D1
EDGW HA8 36 B4
Hillery Cl WALW SE17 19 H6
Hill Farm Rd NKENS W10 88 A4
Hillfield Av ALP/SUD HA0 68 A6
CDALE/KGS NW9 51 G4
CEND/HSY/T N8 55 F3
MRDN SM4 162 D5
Hillfield Cl RYLN/HDSTN HA2 48 C3
Hillfield La South BUSH WD23 22 B5
Hillfield Ms CEND/HSY/T N8 55 F3
Hillfield Pde MRDN SM4 * 162 C5
Hillfield Pk MUSWH N10 54 B2
WCHMH N21 41 G1
Hillfield Park Ms MUSWH N10 54 B3
Hill Field Rd HPTN TW12 141 K6
Hillfield Rd KIL/WHAMP NW6 70 D4
Hill Gardens Craven
BAY/PAD W2 * 8 E6
Hillgate Pl KENS W8 8 A8
Hillgate St KENS W8 8 A8
Hill Gv FELT TW13 141 K1
ROM RM1 63 G2
Hill House Av STAN HA7 35 F6
Hill House Cl WCHMH N21 29 G6
Hill House Dr HPTN TW12 142 A7
Hill House Rd
STRHM/NOR SW16 149 F4
Hilliard Rd NTHWD HA6 32 D7
Hilliard's Ct WAP E1W * 92 E7
Hillier Cl BAR EN5 27 F5
Hillier Gdns CROY/NA CR0 177 G4
Hillier Pl CHSGTN KT9 171 K5
Hillier Rd BTSEA SW11 128 E5
Hillier's La CROY/NA CR0 176 E2
Hillingdon Av
STWL/WRAY TW19 120 B7
Hillingdon Rd BXLYHN DA7 137 K2
Hillingdon St WALW SE17 110 C5
Hillingdon Trail
HGDN/ICK UB10 64 A5
HYS/HAR UB3 101 K4
RSLP HA4 46 A4
Hill La RSLP HA4 46 A7
Hillman Dr NKENS W10 88 A3
Hillman St HACK E8 74 D5
Hillmarton Rd HOLWY N7 72 E4
Hillmarton Ter HOLWY N7 * 72 E4
Hillmead Dr BRXN/ST SW9 130 C3
Hillmont Rd ESH/CLAY KT10 170 E2
Hillmore Gv SYD SE26 151 F4
Hillreach WOOL/PLUM SE18 114 E4
Hill Ri ED N9 30 D5
ESH/CLAY KT10 171 H1
FSTH SE23 131 J7
GFD/PVL UB6 66 C7
GLDGN NW11 53 F3
RCHPK/HAM TW10 124 E4
RSLP HA4 46 A7
Hillrise Rd ARCH N19 54 E6
Hill Rd ALP/SUD HA0 67 H2
CAR SM5 175 J5
HRW HA1 49 G4
MTCM CR4 148 B7
MUSWH N10 39 K7
NTHWD HA6 32 B5
PIN HA5 47 J5
STJWD NW8 2 F6
SUT SM1 175 F4
Hillsboro Rd EDUL SE22 131 F4
Hillsborough Gn
OXHEY WD19 * 32 E2
Hillsgrove Cl WELL DA16 116 D6
Hillside BAR EN5 * 25 J4
Hill Side BAR EN5 27 G4
Hillside CDALE/KGS NW9 51 F3
ESH/CLAY KT10 * 170 B4
WIM/MER SW19 146 B5
WLSDN NW10 69 F7
Hillside Av BORE WD6 24 D3
FBAR/BDGN N11 39 K5
WBLY HA9 68 B3
WFD IG8 45 G4
Hillside Cl MRDN SM4 161 H3
STJWD NW8 2 D5
WFD IG8 45 G4
Hillside Crs NTHWD HA6 32 E7
OXHEY WD19 21 H5
RYLN/HDSTN HA2 66 C1
Hillside Dr EDGW HA8 36 C5
Hillside Gdns BAR EN5 26 C3
BRXS/STRHM SW2 * 149 G1
EDGW HA8 36 B3
FBAR/BDGN N11 * 40 C5
HGT N6 54 A5
KTN/HRWW/WS HA3 50 A6
NTHWD HA6 32 E6
WALTH E17 58 B2
WLGTN SM6 176 C6
Hillside Gv MLHL NW7 37 J6
STHGT/OAK N14 28 D6
Hillside La HAYES BR2 180 E1
Hillside Ri NTHWD HA6 32 E6
Hillside Rd BELMT SM2 174 D6
BRXS/STRHM SW2 149 F1
BUSH WD23 21 J4
CROY/NA CR0 177 H4
DART DA1 138 D5
EA W5 86 A4
HAYES BR2 167 J2
NTHWD HA6 32 E6
SEVS/STOTM N15 56 A5
STHL UB1 84 A3
Hills La NTHWD HA6 32 C7
Hillsleigh Rd KENS W8 88 D7
Hills Ms EA W5 * 86 A6
Hills Pl SOHO/SHAV W1D 10 E5
Hillstowe St CLPT E5 74 E1
Hill St MYFR/PICC W1J 10 C8
RCH/KEW TW9 124 E4
Hill Top CHEAM SM3 161 J6
GLDGN NW11 53 F3
Hilltop WALTH E17 * 58 A2
Hilltop Av WLSDN NW10 68 E6
Hilltop Cots SYD SE26 * 150 D3
Hilltop Gdns DART DA1 139 J4
HDN NW4 51 K1
Hilltop Rd KIL/WHAMP NW6 2 B1
Hill Top Vw WFD IG8 * 45 K5
Hilltop Wy STAN HA7 35 G2
Hillview RYNPK SW20 145 K6
Hillview Av
KTN/HRWW/WS HA3 50 A4
Hillview Cl PIN HA5 33 K5
WBLY HA9 68 B1
Hillview Crs IL IG1 59 K5
ORP BR6 169 K7
Hill View Dr THMD SE28 96 E7
WELL DA16 135 K1
Hill View Gdns
CDALE/KGS NW9 51 F4
Hillview Gdns HDN NW4 52 B3
RYLN/HDSTN HA2 48 A2
Hill View Rd ESH/CLAY KT10 171 G6
TWK TW1 124 B5
Hillview Rd CHST BR7 154 A4
MLHL NW7 38 B3
PIN HA5 33 K6
SUT SM1 175 G2
Hillway CDALE/KGS NW9 51 G7
HGT N6 72 A1
Hillworth BECK BR3 * 166 E1
Hillworth Rd
BRXS/STRHM SW2 130 B6
Hillyard Rd HNWL W7 84 E4
Hillyard St BRXN/ST SW9 110 B7
Hillyfield WALTH E17 57 G1
Hillyfield Cl HOM E9 75 G4
Hilly Flds BROCKY SE4 * 132 D3
Hilly Fields Crs BROCKY SE4 132 D3
Hilsea St CLPT E5 74 E3
Hilton Av NFNCH/WDSPK N12 39 H4
Himalayan Wy WATW WD18 20 D5
Himley Rd TOOT SW17 147 J4
Hinchley Cl ESH/CLAY KT10 171 F2
Hinchley Dr ESH/CLAY KT10 171 F2
Hinchley Wy ESH/CLAY KT10 171 G2
Hinckley Rd PECK SE15 131 H3
Hind Ct FLST/FETLN EC4A 12 B5
Hind Crs ERITH DA8 117 K6
Hinde Ms MHST W1U * 10 B4
Hindes Rd HRW HA1 48 E4
Hinde St MHST W1U 10 B4
Hind Gv POP/IOD E14 93 J5
Hindhead Gdns NTHLT UB5 65 J7
Hindhead Gn OXHEY WD19 33 G4
Hindhead Wy WLGTN SM6 176 E4
Hindmans Rd EDUL SE22 131 H4
Hindmans Wy DAGW RM9 98 B2
Hindmarsh Cl WCHPL E1 * 92 C6
Hindrey Rd CLPT E5 74 D4
Hindsley's Pl FSTH SE23 150 E1
Hinkler Rd
KTN/HRWW/WS HA3 49 K2
Hinksey Pth ABYW SE2 116 E2
Hinstock Rd
WOOL/PLUM SE18 115 H6
Hinton Av HSLWW TW4 122 C3
Hinton Cl ELTH/MOT SE9 134 D7
Hinton Rd BRXN/ST SW9 130 C2
UED N18 42 A3
WLGTN SM6 176 C5
Hippodrome Pl NTGHL W11 88 C6
Hirst Crs WBLY HA9 68 A2
Hitcham Rd WALTH E17 57 H6
Hitchin La STAN HA7 35 K6
Hithe Gv BERM/RHTH SE16 111 K2
Hitherbroom Rd
HYS/HAR UB3 82 E7
Hither Farm Rd
BKHTH/KID SE3 134 B2
Hitherfield Rd BCTR RM8 80 A1
STRHM/NOR SW16 149 F1
Hither Green La LEW SE13 133 F4
Hitherwell Dr
KTN/HRWW/WS HA3 34 D7
Hitherwood Dr NRWD SE19 150 B3
Hive Cl BUSH WD23 34 D1
Hive Rd BUSH WD23 34 D1
Hoadly Rd STRHM/NOR SW16 148 D2
Hobart Cl TRDG/WHET N20 39 J1
YEAD UB4 83 H3
Hobart Dr YEAD UB4 83 H3
Hobart Gdns THHTH CR7 164 E2
Hobart La YEAD UB4 83 H3
Hobart Pl BGVA SW1W 16 C4
RCHPK/HAM TW10 125 G6
Hobart Rd BARK/HLT IG6 60 C1
DAGW RM9 79 K3
WPK KT4 173 K2
YEAD UB4 83 H3
Hobbayne Rd HNWL W7 84 D5
Hobbes Wk PUT/ROE SW15 126 E4
Hobbs Gn EFNCH N2 53 G2
Hobbs Ms GDMY/SEVK IG3 79 F1
Hobbs Pl IS N1 7 J4
Hobbs Place Est IS N1 7 J5
Hobbs Rd WNWD SE27 149 J3
Hobby St PEND EN3 31 F4
Hobday St POP/IOD E14 93 K5
Hoblands End CHST BR7 154 E5
Hobsons Pl WCHPL E1 * 92 C4
Hobury St WBPTN SW10 108 B5
Hocker St BETH E2 * 7 L8
Hockley Av EHAM E6 95 J1
Hockley Dr GPK RM2 63 K1
Hockley Ms BARK IG11 96 E1
Hocroft Av CRICK NW2 70 D2
Hocroft Rd CRICK NW2 70 D3
Hocroft Wk CRICK NW2 70 D2
Hodder Dr GFD/PVL UB6 85 F1
Hoddesdon Rd BELV DA17 117 H4
Hodes Rw HAMP NW3 71 K3
Hodford Rd GLDGN NW11 52 D7
Hodges Wy WATW WD18 20 E5
Hodgkins Cl THMD SE28 97 K6
Hodgkins Ms STAN HA7 35 G4
Hodister Cl CMBW SE5 110 D6
Hodnet Gv BERM/RHTH SE16 111 K3
Hodson Cl RYLN/HDSTN HA2 65 K2
Hoe St WALTH E17 57 J4
The Hoe OXHEY WD19 33 H1
Hoffmann Gdns
SAND/SEL CR2 178 C5
Hoffman Sq IS N1 * 7 H7
Hofland Rd WKENS W14 107 H2
Hogan Ms BAY/PAD W2 9 G2
Hogarth Av ASHF TW15 140 A5
Hogarth Cl CAN/RD E16 95 H4
EA W5 86 A4
Hogarth Crs CROY/NA CR0 164 D6
WIM/MER SW19 147 H7
Hogarth Gdns HEST TW5 103 F6
Hogarth Hl GLDGN NW11 52 D3
Hogarth Pl ECT SW5 * 14 C6
Hogarth Rd BCTR RM8 79 H4
ECT SW5 14 C6
EDGW HA8 50 C1
Hogarth Ter CHSWK W4 * 106 B5
Hogarth Wy HPTN TW12 142 C7
Hogg La BORE WD6 23 G3
Hogshead Pas WAP E1W * 92 D6
Hogsmill La KUT/HW KT1 159 G2
Hogsmill Wy HOR/WEW KT19 172 E4
Holbeach Cl CDALE/KGS NW9 37 G7
Holbeach Gdns BFN/LL DA15 135 K5
Holbeach Rd CAT SE6 132 D6
Holbeck Rw PECK SE15 111 H6
Holbein Ga NTHWD HA6 32 C4
Holbein Ms BGVA SW1W 16 A7
Holbein Pl BGVA SW1W 16 A6
Holberton Gdns WLSDN NW10 87 K2
Holborn GINN WC1R 12 A3
HCIRC EC1N 12 A3
Holborn Circ HCIRC EC1N 12 B3
Holborn Pl HHOL WC1V 11 L3
Holborn Rd PLSTW E13 95 F4
Holborn Viad STBT EC1A 12 C3
Holborn Wy MTCM CR4 162 E1
Holbrooke Ct HOLWY N7 72 E2
Holbrook La CHST BR7 154 D6
Holbrook Rd SRTFD E15 94 D1
Holbrook Wy HAYES BR2 168 E5
Holburne Cl BKHTH/KID SE3 114 B7
Holburne Gdns
BKHTH/KID SE3 114 C7
Holburne Rd BKHTH/KID SE3 114 B7
Holcombe Hl MLHL NW7 37 J2
Holcombe Rd IL IG1 60 A6
TOTM N17 56 B2
Holcombe St HMSMTH W6 106 E4
Holcote Cl BELV DA17 117 F2
Holcroft Rd HOM E9 74 E6
Holden Av CDALE/KGS NW9 50 E7
NFNCH/WDSPK N12 39 F4
Holdenby Rd BROCKY SE4 132 B4
Holden Cl BCTR RM8 79 H2
Holdenhurst Av FNCH N3 39 F6
Holden Rd
NFNCH/WDSPK N12 39 F3
Holden St BTSEA SW11 129 F1
Holdernesse Rd ISLW TW7 104 B7
TOOT SW17 147 K2
Holderness Wy WNWD SE27 149 H4
Holders Hill Av HDN NW4 52 B1
Holders Hill Crs HDN NW4 52 B1
Holders Hill Dr HDN NW4 52 B1
Holders Hill Gdns HDN NW4 52 B1
Holders Hill Pde MLHL NW7 * 38 C7
Holders Hill Rd HDN NW4 52 B1
Holford Ms FSBYW WC1X * 5 L7
Holford Rd HAMP NW3 71 G2
Holford St FSBYW WC1X 6 A7
Holford Wy PUT/ROE SW15 126 D5
Holford Yd FSBYW WC1X * 6 A6
Holgate Av BTSEA SW11 128 C2
Holgate Rd DAGE RM10 80 C4
Holgate St CHARL SE7 114 C2
Holland Av BELMT SM2 174 E6
RYNPK SW20 145 H7
Holland Cl BAR EN5 27 H6
HAYES BR2 180 D1
ROMW/RG RM7 62 E4
STAN HA7 35 H4
Holland Dr FSTH SE23 151 G2
Holland Gdns BTFD TW8 105 G4
WKENS W14 107 H2
Holland Gv BRXN/ST SW9 110 B6
Holland Pk NTGHL W11 88 D7
Holland Park Av
GDMY/SEVK IG3 60 E5
NTGHL W11 88 C7
Holland Park Gdns
WKENS W14 107 H1
Holland Park Ms NTGHL W11 88 D7
Holland Park Rd WKENS W14 107 J2
Holland Park Ter NTGHL W11 88 C7
Holland Pas IS N1 6 E3
Holland Pl KENS W8 14 C1
Holland Rd ALP/SUD HA0 67 K5
EHAM E6 77 K7
SNWD SE25 165 H4
SRTFD E15 94 C2
WKENS W14 107 G1
WLSDN NW10 69 J7
The Hollands WPK KT4 160 C7
Holland St KENS W8 14 B2
STHWK SE1 12 D8
Holland Villas Rd WKENS W14 107 H1
Holland Wk STAN HA7 35 G4
Holland Wy HAYES BR2 180 D1
Hollar Rd STNW/STAM N16 74 B2
Hollen St SOHO/CST W1F 10 F5
Holles Cl HPTN TW12 142 A5
Holles St OXSTW W1C 10 D5
Holley Rd ACT W3 106 B1
Hollickwood Av
NFNCH/WDSPK N12 39 K5
Holliday Sq BTSEA SW11 128 C2
Hollidge Wy DAGE RM10 80 D5
Hollies Av BFN/LL DA15 155 F1
Hollies Cl STRHM/NOR SW16 149 G5
TWK TW1 143 F1
Hollies End MLHL NW7 37 K4
Hollies Rd EA W5 104 D3
The Hollies BAR EN5 * 25 J4
KTN/HRWW/WS HA3 49 G3
Hollies Wy BAL SW12 * 129 F6
Holligrave Rd BMLY BR1 152 E7
Hollingbourne Av
BXLYHN DA7 117 G7
Hollingbourne Gdns WEA W13 85 G4
Hollingbourne Rd HNHL SE24 130 D4
Hollingsworth Rd
CROY/NA CR0 178 D5
Hollington Crs NWMAL KT3 160 C5
Hollington Rd EHAM E6 95 K2
TOTM N17 56 C1
Hollingworth Cl
E/WMO/HCT KT8 156 E3
Hollingworth Rd
STMC/STPC BR5 169 G6
Hollman Gdns
STRHM/NOR SW16 149 H5
Holloway La WDR/YW UB7 100 C4
Holloway Rd ARCH N19 72 D1
EHAM E6 95 K2
HOLWY N7 73 F3
WAN E11 76 B2
Holloway St HSLW TW3 123 G2
The Hollow WFD IG8 44 D3
Holly Av STAN HA7 50 A1
WOT/HER KT12 156 C7
Holly Bank MUSWH N10 * 54 C3
Hollybank Cl HPTN TW12 142 A4
Hollybrake Cl CHST BR7 154 D6
Hollybush Cl
KTN/HRWW/WS HA3 34 E7
OXHEY WD19 21 G6
WAN E11 58 E4
Hollybush Gdns BETH E2 92 D2
Hollybush Hl WAN E11 58 D5
Holly Bush La HPTN TW12 141 K6
Hollybush Pl BETH E2 92 D2
Hollybush Rd KUTN/CMB KT2 144 A4
Hollybush St PLSTW E13 95 F2
Hollybush Ter NRWD SE19 * 150 A5
Holly Bush V HAMP NW3 * 71 G3
Holly Cl BECK BR3 167 F3
BKHH IG9 45 H2
FELT TW13 141 J4
SUN TW16 156 A2
WLGTN SM6 176 B6
WLSDN NW10 69 G6
Holly Crs BECK BR3 166 C4
WFD IG8 44 B6
Hollycroft Av HAMP NW3 70 E2
WBLY HA9 68 A1
Hollycroft Cl SAND/SEL CR2 178 A4
WDR/YW UB7 100 D5
Hollycroft Gdns WDR/YW UB7 100 D5
Hollydale Cl NTHLT UB5 66 B4
Hollydale Dr HAYES BR2 181 K2
Hollydale Rd PECK SE15 131 K1
Hollydown Wy WAN E11 76 B2
Holly Dr CHING E4 31 K6
Holly Farm Rd NWDGN UB2 102 D4
Hollyfield Av FBAR/BDGN N11 39 K4
Hollyfield Rd BRYLDS KT5 159 G6
Holly Gdns BXLYHN DA7 137 K3
WDR/YW UB7 100 C1
Hollygrove BUSH WD23 22 D6
Holly Gv CDALE/KGS NW9 50 E6
PECK SE15 131 G1
PIN HA5 33 J7
Hollygrove Cl HSLW TW3 122 E3
Holly Hedge Ter LEW SE13 133 F4
Holly Hl HAMP NW3 71 G3
WCHMH N21 29 F5

Holly Hill Rd BELV DA17 117 J4
Holly Lodge Gdns HGT N6 72 A1
Hollymead CAR SM5 175 K2
Holly Ms WBPTN SW10 14 F8
Holly Mt HAMP NW3 * 71 G3
Hollymount Cl GNWCH SE10 113 F7
Holly Pk FNCH N3 52 D2
FSBYPK N4 54 E6
Holly Park Gdns FNCH N3 52 E2
Holly Park Rd
FBAR/BDGN N11 40 A4
HNWL W7 85 F7
Holly Rd CHSWK W4 * 106 A3
DART DA1 139 G7
HPTN TW12 142 C5
HSLW TW3 123 G3
TWK TW1 124 B7
WAN E11 58 D6
Hollytree Cl WIM/MER SW19 127 G7
Hollytree Pde SCUP DA14 * 155 J4
Hollyview Cl HDN NW4 51 J5
Holly Vls HMSMTH W6 * 106 E2
Holly Wk HAMP NW3 71 G3
Holly Wy MTCM CR4 163 J3
Hollywell Gv HCH RM12 63 H7
Hollywood Gdns YEAD UB4 83 F5
Hollywood Ms WBPTN SW10 14 E9
Hollywood Rd CHING E4 43 G4
WBPTN SW10 14 E9
Hollywoods CROY/NA CR0 179 H7
Hollywood Wy ERITH DA8 118 E6
WFD IG8 44 B6
Holman Ct EW KT17 * 173 J7
Holman Rd BTSEA SW11 128 C1
HOR/WEW KT19 172 E4
Holmbridge Gdns PEND EN3 31 F3
Holmbrook Dr HDN NW4 52 B4
Holmbury Cl BUSH WD23 34 E1
Holmbury Ct WIM/MER SW19 147 J6
Holmbury Gdns HYS/HAR UB3 82 D7
Holmbury Gv SAND/SEL CR2 179 H6
Holmbury Mnr SCUP DA14 * 155 G3
Holmbury Pk BMLY BR1 153 J6
Holmbury Vw CLPT E5 56 D7
Holmbush Rd PUT/ROE SW15 127 H5
Holmcote Gdns HBRY N5 73 J4
Holmcroft Wy HAYES BR2 168 E4
Holmdale Cl BORE WD6 24 B1
Holmdale Gdns HDN NW4 52 B4
Holmdale Rd CHST BR7 154 C4
KIL/WHAMP NW6 70 E4
Holmdale Ter
SEVS/STOTM N15 56 A5
Holmdene Av HNHL SE24 130 D4
MLHL NW7 37 J5
RYLN/HDSTN HA2 48 B2
Holmdene Cl BECK BR3 167 F1
Holmdene Ct BMLY BR1 168 D2
Holmead Rd FUL/PGN SW6 108 A6
Holmebury Cl BUSH WD23 * 34 E1
Holme Ct ISLW TW7 124 B2
Holme Lacey Rd
LEE/GVPK SE12 133 J5
Holme Pk BORE WD6 24 B1
Holme Rd EHAM E6 77 J7
Holmes Av MLHL NW7 38 C4
WALTH E17 57 H2
Holmes Cl EDUL SE22 131 H3
Holmesdale Av
MORT/ESHN SW14 125 J2
Holmesdale Cl SNWD SE25 165 G2
Holmesdale Rd BXLYHN DA7 136 E1
CROY/NA CR0 164 E4
HGT N6 54 B6
RCH/KEW TW9 105 G7
SNWD SE25 165 F3
TEDD TW11 143 J6
Holmesley Rd FSTH SE23 132 B5
Holmes Rd KTTN NW5 72 B4
TWK TW1 143 F1
WIM/MER SW19 147 G6
Holmes Ter STHWK SE1 18 A1
Holme Wy STAN HA7 35 F5
Holmewood Gdns
BRXS/STRHM SW2 130 A6
Holmewood Rd
BRXS/STRHM SW2 129 K6
SNWD SE25 165 F2
Holmfield Av HDN NW4 52 B4
Holmhurst Rd BELV DA17 117 J4
Holmleigh Av DART DA1 139 F3
Holmleigh Rd
STNW/STAM N16 56 A7
Holm Oak Cl PUT/ROE SW15 127 J5
Holm Oak Pk WATW WD18 20 D4
Holmsdale Gv BXLYHN DA7 138 B1
Holmshaw Cl SYD SE26 151 G3
Holmside Ri OXHEY WD19 33 F2
Holmside Rd BAL SW12 129 F5
Holmsley Cl NWMAL KT3 160 C5
Holmstall Av EDGW HA8 50 E1
Holmstall Pde EDGW HA8 * 50 E1
Holmwood Cl BELMT SM2 174 B7
NTHLT UB5 66 B5
RYLN/HDSTN HA2 48 C2
Holmwood Gdns FNCH N3 52 E1
WLGTN SM6 176 B5
Holmwood Gv MLHL NW7 37 F4
Holmwood Rd BELMT SM2 174 A7
CHSGTN KT9 172 A4
GDMY/SEVK IG3 78 E1
Holmwood Vls CHARL SE7 113 K4
Holne Cha EFNCH N2 53 G5
MRDN SM4 161 K5
Holness Rd SRTFD E15 76 D5
Holroyd Rd ESH/CLAY KT10 171 F7
PUT/ROE SW15 127 F3
Holstein Wy ERITH DA18 116 E2
Holstock Rd IL IG1 78 C1
Holsworth Cl
RYLN/HDSTN HA2 48 C4
Holsworthy Sq FSBYW WC1X 11 M1
Holsworthy Wy CHSGTN KT9 171 J4
Holt Cl BORE WD6 24 B3
MUSWH N10 54 A3
THMD SE28 97 H6
Holton St WCHPL E1 93 F3
Holt Rd ALP/SUD HA0 67 H2
CAN/RD E16 95 J7
The Holt MRDN SM4 * 161 K3
WLGTN SM6 176 C3
Holtwhite Av ENC/FH EN2 29 J1
Holwell Pl PIN HA5 47 J3
Holwood Park Av ORP BR6 181 K3
Holwood Pl CLAP SW4 129 J3
Holybourne Av
PUT/ROE SW15 126 D6
Holyoake Ct
BERM/RHTH SE16 112 B1
Holyoake Wk EA W5 85 J3
EFNCH N2 53 G2
Holyoak Rd LBTH SE11 18 C5
Holyport Rd FUL/PGN SW6 107 F6
Holyrood Av
RYLN/HDSTN HA2 65 J3
Holyrood Gdns EDGW HA8 50 D1
Holyrood Ms CAN/RD E16 94 E7
Holyrood Rd BAR EN5 27 G5
Holyrood St STHWK SE1 13 J9
Holywell Cl
BERM/RHTH SE16 * 111 J4
BKHTH/KID SE3 113 K5
STWL/WRAY TW19 120 B7
Holywell La SDTCH EC2A 7 K9
Holywell Rd WATW WD18 20 E4
Holywell Rw SDTCH EC2A 13 J1
Holywell Wy
STWL/WRAY TW19 120 B7
Home Cl CAR SM5 175 K1
NTHLT UB5 83 K2
Home Ct FELT TW13 * 121 K7
SURB KT6 * 158 E4
Homecroft Rd SYD SE26 150 E4
WDGN N22 41 H7
Home Farm Cl ESH/CLAY KT10 170 B5
THDIT KT7 158 A6
Homefarm Rd HNWL W7 84 E5
Homefield Av
GNTH/NBYPK IG2 60 E4
Homefield Cl WLSDN NW10 68 E5
YEAD UB4 83 H3
Homefield Gdns EFNCH N2 53 H2
WIM/MER SW19 162 B1
Homefield Ms BECK BR3 * 151 J7
Homefield Pk SUT SM1 175 F5
Homefield Pl CROY/NA CR0 178 B1
Homefield Rd ALP/SUD HA0 67 G3
BMLY BR1 153 G7
BUSH WD23 22 A4
CHSWK W4 106 C3
EDGW HA8 37 F5
WIM/MER SW19 146 C5
WOT/HER KT12 156 E6
Homefield St IS N1 * 7 J6
The Homefield MRDN SM4 * 161 K3
Home Gdns DAGE RM10 80 E2
DART DA1 139 H5
Homeland Dr BELMT SM2 175 F7
Homelands Dr NRWD SE19 150 A6
Homeleigh Rd PECK SE15 132 A4
Home Md STAN HA7 35 J7
Homemead Rd CROY/NA CR0 163 H5
HAYES BR2 168 E4
Home Park Ct KUT/HW KT1 * 158 E3
Home Park Rd
WIM/MER SW19 146 D3
Home Park Ter KUT/HW KT1 158 E1
Home Park Wk KUT/HW KT1 158 E3
Homer Cl BXLYHN DA7 117 K7
Homer Dr POP/IOD E14 112 D3
Home Rd BTSEA SW11 128 D1
Homer Rd CROY/NA CR0 166 A5
HOM E9 75 G5
Homer Rw CAMTN NW1 9 K3
Homersham Rd KUT/HW KT1 159 H1
Homer St MBLAR W1H 9 K3
Homerton Gv HOM E9 75 F4
Homerton High St HOM E9 75 F4
Homerton Rd HOM E9 75 H4
Homerton Rw HOM E9 74 E4
Homerton Ter HOM E9 74 E5
Homesdale Cl WAN E11 58 E4
Homesdale Rd HAYES BR2 168 B3
ORP BR6 169 K6
Homesfield GLDGN NW11 52 E4
Homestall Rd EDUL SE22 131 K4
Homestead Gdns
ESH/CLAY KT10 170 E4
Homestead Paddock
STHGT/OAK N14 28 B4
Homestead Pk CRICK NW2 69 H2
Homestead Rd BCTR RM8 80 B1
FUL/PGN SW6 107 J6
The Homestead DART DA1 139 F5
Homewaters Av SUN TW16 140 D7
Homewillow Cl WCHMH N21 29 H5
Homewood Cl HPTN TW12 141 K5
Homewood Crs CHST BR7 154 E5
Homewood Gdns
SNWD SE25 * 165 F4
Honduras St FSBYE EC1V 6 E9
Honeybourne Rd
KIL/WHAMP NW6 71 F4
Honeybourne Wy
STMC/STPC BR5 169 H7
Honeybrook Rd BAL SW12 129 H6
Honey Cl DAGE RM10 80 E5
Honeyfield Ms FSTH SE23 151 F2
Honeyman Cl CRICK NW2 70 B6
Honeypot Cl CDALE/KGS NW9 50 B3
Honeypot La CDALE/KGS NW9 50 B3
STAN HA7 35 K7
Honeysett Rd TOTM N17 56 B1
Honeysuckle Cl STHL UB1 83 J6
Honeysuckle Gdns
CROY/NA CR0 166 A6
Honeywell Rd BTSEA SW11 128 D5
Honeywood Rd ISLW TW7 * 124 B3
WLSDN NW10 87 H1
Honeywood Wk CAR SM5 175 K3
Honister Cl STAN HA7 35 H7
Honister Gdns STAN HA7 35 H6
Honister Pl STAN HA7 35 H7
Honiton Gdns MLHL NW7 38 B6
PECK SE15 * 131 K1
Honiton Rd KIL/WHAMP NW6 88 D1
ROMW/RG RM7 63 F5
WELL DA16 136 A1
Honley Rd CAT SE6 132 E6
Honnor Gdns ISLW TW7 123 J1
Honor Oak Pk FSTH SE23 131 K6
Honor Oak Ri FSTH SE23 131 K5
Honor Oak Rd FSTH SE23 131 K7
Hood Av MORT/ESHN SW14 125 K4
STHGT/OAK N14 28 B5
Hood Cl CROY/NA CR0 164 C7
Hoodcote Gdns WCHMH N21 29 H6
Hood Rd RAIN RM13 81 G7
RYNPK SW20 145 H6
Hooker's Rd WALTH E17 57 F2
Hook Farm Rd HAYES BR2 168 C4
Hooking Gn RYLN/HDSTN HA2 48 B4
Hook La WELL DA16 136 A3
Hook Ri North SURB KT6 172 B2
Hook Ri South CHSGTN KT9 172 B2
Hook Rd CHSGTN KT9 171 K4
HOR/WEW KT19 172 E6
SURB KT6 172 A1
Hooks Hall Dr DAGE RM10 80 E2
Hookstone Wy WFD IG8 45 H6
The Hook BAR EN5 27 H5
Hook Underpass (Kingston
By-Pass) SURB KT6 171 K2
Hook Wk EDGW HA8 36 E5
Hooper Rd CAN/RD E16 94 E5
Hoopers Ms BUSH WD23 22 B7
Hooper's Ms ACT W3 86 E7
Hooper St WCHPL E1 92 C6
Hoop La GLDGN NW11 52 D6
Hop Ct ALP/SUD HA0 * 67 J5
Hope Cl BTFD TW8 105 F4
CHDH RM6 61 K3
IS N1 73 J5
LEE/GVPK SE12 153 F2
SUT SM1 175 G4
Hopedale Rd CHARL SE7 114 A5
Hopefield Av
KIL/WHAMP NW6 88 C1
Hope Gdns ACT W3 105 J1
Hope La ELTH/MOT SE9 154 B2
Hope Pk BMLY BR1 152 D6
Hopes Cl HEST TW5 103 F5
Hope Sq LVPST EC2M 13 J3
Hope St BTSEA SW11 128 C2
Hopetown St WCHPL E1 * 13 M3
Hopewell St CMBW SE5 110 E6
Hopewell Yd CMBW SE5 110 E6
Hop Gdns CHCR WC2N 11 J7
Hopgood St SHB W12 88 A7
Hopkins Cl MUSWH N10 40 A6
Hopkins Ms SRTFD E15 76 D7
Hopkinsons Pl CAMTN NW1 3 M3
Hopkins Rd LEY E10 57 K6
Hopkins St SOHO/CST W1F 10 F5
Hoppers Rd WCHMH N21 41 G1
Hoppett Rd CHING E4 44 C2
Hopping La IS N1 * 73 H5
Hoppingwood Av NWMAL KT3 160 B2
Hoppner Rd YEAD UB4 82 B1
Hop St GNWCH SE10 113 J3
Hopton Gdns NWMAL KT3 160 D5
Hopton Pde
STRHM/NOR SW16 * 148 E4
Hopton Rd STRHM/NOR SW16 148 E4
WOOL/PLUM SE18 115 G2
Hoptons Gdns STHWK SE1 * 12 D8
Hopton St STHWK SE1 12 D7
Hoptree Cl
NFNCH/WDSPK N12 * 39 F3
Hopwood Cl TOOT SW17 147 G2
Hopwood Rd WALW SE17 19 H9
Hopwood Wk HACK E8 * 74 C6
Horace Av ROMW/RG RM7 63 F7
Horace Rd BARK/HLT IG6 60 C2
FSTGT E7 77 F3
KUT/HW KT1 159 G2
Horatio Pl POP/IOD E14 113 F1
Horatio St BETH E2 7 M6
Horatius Wy CROY/NA CR0 177 F5
Horbury Crs NTGHL W11 8 A7
Horbury Ms NTGHL W11 88 D6
Horder Rd FUL/PGN SW6 107 H7
Hordle Prom East PECK SE15 111 G6
Hordle Prom North
PECK SE15 111 G6
Hordle Prom West PECK SE15 111 F6
Horley Cl BXLYHS DA6 137 H4
Horley Rd ELTH/MOT SE9 153 J3
Hormead Rd MV/WKIL W9 88 D3
Hornbeam Cl IL IG1 78 D4
LBTH SE11 18 A5
MLHL NW7 37 H2
NTHLT UB5 65 K4
Hornbeam Crs BTFD TW8 104 C6
Hornbeam Gdns NWMAL KT3 160 D5
Hornbeam Gv CHING E4 44 C2
Hornbeam Rd BKHH IG9 45 H2
YEAD UB4 83 G4
Hornbeam Sq BOW E3 75 H7
Hornbeams Ri
FBAR/BDGN N11 40 A5
Hornbeam Wy HAYES BR2 169 F5
Hornbuckle Cl
RYLN/HDSTN HA2 66 D1
Hornby Cl HAMP NW3 3 H1
Horncastle Cl LEE/GVPK SE12 133 K6
Horncastle Rd LEE/GVPK SE12 133 K6
Hornchurch Cl
KUTN/CMB KT2 143 K4
Hornchurch Rd HCH RM12 63 J7
Horndean Cl PUT/ROE SW15 126 D7
Horne House CHARL SE7 * 114 D6
Horner La MTCM CR4 162 C1
The Hornets WATW WD18 21 F3
Horne Wy PUT/ROE SW15 127 F1
Hornfair Rd CHARL SE7 114 C5
Hornford Wy ROMW/RG RM7 63 G6
Horniman Dr FSTH SE23 131 J7
Horniman Gdns FSTH SE23 * 131 J7
Horning Cl ELTH/MOT SE9 153 J3
Horn La ACT W3 86 E7
GNWCH SE10 113 K3
WFD IG8 44 E5
Horn Link Wy GNWCH SE10 113 K3
Horn Park Cl LEE/GVPK SE12 134 A4
Horn Park La LEE/GVPK SE12 134 A4
Hornscroft Cl BARK IG11 78 E6
Horns End Pl PIN HA5 47 G3
Hornsey Chambers CLPT E5 * 74 D1
Hornsey La HGT N6 54 C6
Hornsey Lane Est ARCH N19 * 54 D6
Hornsey Lane Gdns HGT N6 54 C6
Hornsey Park Rd
CEND/HSY/T N8 55 F2
Hornsey Ri ARCH N19 54 D6
Hornsey Rise Gdns ARCH N19 54 D6
Hornsey Rd ARCH N19 54 E7
HOLWY N7 73 F2
Hornsey St HOLWY N7 73 F4
Hornshay St PECK SE15 111 K5
Horns Rd BARK/HLT IG6 60 C4
Hornton Pl KENS W8 14 B2
Hornton St KENS W8 14 B1
Horsa Rd ERITH DA8 117 K6
LEE/GVPK SE12 134 B6
Horsebridges Cl DAGW RM9 80 A7
Horsecroft Rd EDGW HA8 37 F6
Horse Fair KUT/HW KT1 158 E1
Horseferry Pl GNWCH SE10 113 F5
Horseferry Rd POP/IOD E14 93 G6
WEST SW1P 17 G4
Horse Guards Av WHALL SW1A 11 J9
Horse Guards Rd
WHALL SW1A 11 H9
Horse Leaze EHAM E6 96 B5
Horsell Rd HBRY N5 73 G4
STMC/STPC BR5 155 G7
Horselydown La STHWK SE1 19 L1
Horsenden Av GFD/PVL UB6 66 E4
Horsenden Crs GFD/PVL UB6 67 F4
Horsenden La North
GFD/PVL UB6 66 E5
Horsenden La South
GFD/PVL UB6 67 G7
Horseshoe Cl CRICK NW2 69 K1
POP/IOD E14 113 F4
Horse Shoe Crs NTHLT UB5 84 A1
Horseshoe La ENC/FH EN2 29 J2
TRDG/WHET N20 26 B7
Horseshoe Ms
BRXS/STRHM SW2 129 K3
Horse Yd IS N1 6 D3
Horsfeld Gdns ELTH/MOT SE9 134 D4
Horsfeld Rd ELTH/MOT SE9 134 C4
Horsford Rd
BRXS/STRHM SW2 130 A4
Horsham Av
NFNCH/WDSPK N12 39 J4
Horsham Rd BXLYHS DA6 137 G5
EBED/NFELT TW14 121 F5
Horsley Dr CROY/NA CR0 180 A6
KUTN/CMB KT2 143 K4
Horsley Rd BMLY BR1 153 F7
CHING E4 44 A1
Horsley St WALW SE17 19 G9
Horsmans Pl DART DA1 * 139 H6
Horsman St CMBW SE5 110 D5
Horsmonden Cl ORP BR6 169 K6
Horsmonden Rd BROCKY SE4 132 C4
Hortensia Rd WBPTN SW10 108 B5
Horticultural Pl CHSWK W4 106 A4
Horton Av CRICK NW2 70 C3
Horton La HOR/WEW KT19 172 D7
Horton Rd HACK E8 74 D5
Horton St LEW SE13 132 E2
Horton Wy CROY/NA CR0 166 A4
Hortus Rd NWDGN UB2 102 E1
Hosack Rd TOOT SW17 147 K1
Hoser Av LEE/GVPK SE12 152 E1
Hosier La STBT EC1A 12 C3
Hoskins Cl HYS/HAR UB3 101 J4
Hoskin's Cl CAN/RD E16 95 G5
Hoskins St GNWCH SE10 113 G4
Hospital Bridge Rd
WHTN TW2 123 F6
Hospital Rd HSLW TW3 123 F2
LEY E10 58 B5
Hospital Wy LEW SE13 133 G5
Hotham Cl E/WMO/HCT KT8 157 F2
Hotham Rd PUT/ROE SW15 127 F2
Hotham Road Ms
WIM/MER SW19 147 G6
Hotham St SRTFD E15 76 C7
Hothfield Pl BERM/RHTH SE16 111 K2
Hotspur Rd NTHLT UB5 84 A1
Hotspur St LBTH SE11 18 A7
Houblon Rd
RCHPK/HAM TW10 125 F4
Houghton Cl HACK E8 * 74 B5
HPTN TW12 141 J5
Houghton Rd
SEVS/STOTM N15 56 B3
Houghton St LINN WC2A * 11 M5
Houlder Crs CROY/NA CR0 177 H4
Houndsden Rd WCHMH N21 29 F5
Houndsditch HDTCH EC3A 13 K4
Houndsfield Rd ED N9 30 D6
Hounslow Av HSLW TW3 123 G4
Hounslow Gdns HSLW TW3 123 G4
Hounslow Rd
EBED/NFELT TW14 122 A6
Houseman Wy CMBW SE5 110 E6
Houston Rd FSTH SE23 151 G1
SURB KT6 158 C5
Hove Av WALTH E17 57 H4
Hoveden Rd CRICK NW2 70 B4
Hove Gdns SUT SM1 162 A7
Hoveton Rd THMD SE28 97 J5
Howard Av BXLY DA5 136 D7
Howard Cl ACT W3 86 D5
BUSH WD23 22 E6
CRICK NW2 * 70 C3
FBAR/BDGN N11 40 A1
HPTN TW12 142 C6
SUN TW16 140 D5
Howard Dr BORE WD6 25 F3
Howard Rd BARK IG11 78 D7
BMLY BR1 152 E6
CRICK NW2 70 B3
DART DA1 139 K5
EHAM E6 95 K1
IL IG1 78 B3
ISLW TW7 124 A2
NWMAL KT3 160 B2
PGE/AN SE20 150 E7
SEVS/STOTM N15 56 A5
SNWD SE25 165 H4
STAN HA7 35 K7
STHL UB1 84 B5
STNW/STAM N16 73 K3
SURB KT6 159 G5
WALTH E17 57 J2
WAN E11 76 C2
Howards Cl PIN HA5 * 47 F1
Howards Crest Cl BECK BR3 167 F1
Howard's La PUT/ROE SW15 127 F3
Howard's Rd PLSTW E13 94 E2
Howard St THDIT KT7 158 C6
Howards Yd
WAND/EARL SW18 128 A6
Howard Wk EFNCH N2 53 G3
Howard Wy BAR EN5 26 B4
Howarth Rd ABYW SE2 116 B4
Howberry Cl EDGW HA8 35 K5
Howberry Rd STAN HA7 35 K5
THHTH CR7 149 K7
Howbury La ERITH DA8 138 D1
Howbury Rd PECK SE15 131 K2
Howcroft Crs FNCH N3 38 E6
Howcroft La GFD/PVL UB6 84 D2
Howden Cl THMD SE28 97 J6
Howden Rd SNWD SE25 165 G1
Howden St PECK SE15 131 H2
Howell Cl CHDH RM6 61 K4
Howell Wk STHWK SE1 18 D6
Howerd Wy
WOOL/PLUM SE18 114 D7
Howes Cl FNCH N3 52 E2
Howfield Pl TOTM N17 * 56 B2
Howgate Rd
MORT/ESHN SW14 126 A2
Howick Pl WESTW SW1E 16 F4
Howie St BTSEA SW11 108 D6
Howitt Cl HAMP NW3 71 J5
Howitt Rd HAMP NW3 71 J5
Howitts Cl ESH/CLAY KT10 170 A5
Howland Ct PIN HA5 * 34 A5
Howland Ms East FITZ W1T 10 F2
Howland St FITZ W1T 10 F2
Howland Wy
BERM/RHTH SE16 112 B1
Howletts La RSLP HA4 46 A5
Howletts Rd HNHL SE24 130 D5
Howley Pl BAY/PAD W2 8 F2
Howley Rd CROY/NA CR0 177 H2
Howsman Rd BARN SW13 106 D5
Howson Rd BROCKY SE4 132 B3
Howson Ter
RCHPK/HAM TW10 * 125 F5
How's St BETH E2 7 L5
Howton Pl BUSH WD23 22 D7
Hoxton Market IS N1 7 J8
Hoxton Sq IS N1 7 J8
Hoxton St IS N1 7 J4
Hoylake Gdns MTCM CR4 163 H2
OXHEY WD19 33 H3
RSLP HA4 47 F7
Hoylake Rd ACT W3 87 G5
Hoyland Cl PECK SE15 * 111 J6
Hoyle Rd TOOT SW17 147 J4
Hoy St CAN/RD E16 94 D5
Hubbard Dr CHSGTN KT9 171 J5
Hubbard Rd WNWD SE27 149 J3
Hubbard St SRTFD E15 76 C7
Hubert Cl WIM/MER SW19 * 147 G7
Hubert Gv BRXN/ST SW9 129 K2
Hubert Rd EHAM E6 95 H2
RAIN RM13 99 H2
Huddart St BOW E3 93 H4
Huddleston Cl BETH E2 * 92 E1
Huddlestone Rd CRICK NW2 69 K5
FSTGT E7 76 D3
Huddleston Rd HOLWY N7 72 C2
Hudson Cl SHB W12 * 87 K6
Hudson Pl WOOL/PLUM SE18 115 H4
Hudson Rd BXLYHN DA7 137 G1
HYS/HAR UB3 101 G5
Huggins Pl BRXS/STRHM SW2 130 A7
Hughan Rd SRTFD E15 76 B4
Hugh Dalton Av FUL/PGN SW6 107 J5
Hughenden Av
KTN/HRWW/WS HA3 49 H4
Hughenden Gdns NTHLT UB5 83 G2
Hughenden Rd WPK KT4 160 D6
Hughes Cl NFNCH/WDSPK N12 39 G4
Hughes Rd ASHF TW15 140 A6
HYS/HAR UB3 83 F6
Hughes Ter CAN/RD E16 * 94 D4
Hughes Wk CROY/NA CR0 164 D6
Hugh Gaitskell Cl
FUL/PGN SW6 * 107 J5
Hugh Ms PIM SW1V 16 D6
Hugh Pl WEST SW1P 17 G5
Hugh St PIM SW1V 16 D6
Hugo Cl WATW WD18 20 C3
Hugo Gdns RAIN RM13 81 H5
Hugon Rd FUL/PGN SW6 128 A2
Hugo Rd ARCH N19 72 C3
Huguenot Pl
WAND/EARL SW18 128 B4
WCHPL E1 13 M2
Huitt Sq BTSEA SW11 128 C2
Hullbridge Ms IS N1 7 G3
Hull Cl BERM/RHTH SE16 * 93 F7
Hull St FSBYE EC1V 6 E8
Hulme Pl STHWK SE1 18 F2
Hulse Av BARK IG11 78 E5
Hulverston Cl BELMT SM2 175 F7
Humber Dr NKENS W10 88 B3
Humber Rd BKHTH/KID SE3 113 J5
CRICK NW2 69 K1
DART DA1 139 G4
Humberstone Rd PLSTW E13 95 G2
Humbolt Rd HMSMTH W6 107 H5
Humes Av HNWL W7 104 A2
Hume Wy RSLP HA4 46 E5
Humphrey Cl CLAY IG5 * 45 K7
Humphrey St STHWK SE1 19 L7
Humphries Cl DAGW RM9 80 B3
Hundred Acre
CDALE/KGS NW9 51 H1
Hungerford Rd HOLWY N7 72 D5
Hungerford St WCHPL E1 * 92 D5
Hunsdon Cl DAGW RM9 80 A5
Hunsdon Rd NWCR SE14 112 A6
Hunslett St BETH E2 * 92 E1
Hunston Rd MRDN SM4 162 A7
Hunt Cl BKHTH/KID SE3 * 133 K1
NTGHL W11 88 B7
Hunter Cl BAL SW12 129 F7
BORE WD6 24 E4
STHWK SE1 19 H4
WLGTN SM6 176 E6
Hunter Ct CMBW SE5 * 130 E3
Huntercrombe Gdns
OXHEY WD19 33 G4
Hunter Rd RYNPK SW20 146 A7
THHTH CR7 164 E2
Hunters Ct RCH/KEW TW9 124 E4
Hunters Gv HYS/HAR UB3 82 E7
KTN/HRWW/WS HA3 49 J3
Hunters Hall Rd DAGE RM10 80 C3
Hunters Hl RSLP HA4 65 G2
Hunters Meadow NRWD SE19 150 A3
Hunters Rd CHSGTN KT9 172 A2
IL IG1 78 B4
Hunters Sq DAGE RM10 80 C3
Hunter St BMSBY WC1N 5 K9
Hunters Wy CROY/NA CR0 178 A3
Hunting Cl ESH/CLAY KT10 170 A3
Huntingdon Cl MTCM CR4 163 K3
NTHLT UB5 66 A5
Huntingdon Gdns CHSWK W4 105 K6
WPK KT4 174 A2
Huntingdon Rd ED N9 30 E7
EFNCH N2 53 J2
Huntingdon St CAN/RD E16 94 D5
IS N1 5 M1
Huntingfield CROY/NA CR0 179 H6
Huntingfield Rd
PUT/ROE SW15 126 D5
Hunting Gate Cl ENC/FH EN2 29 G2
Hunting Gate Dr CHSGTN KT9 172 A6
Hunting Gate Ms SUT SM1 175 F2
WHTN TW2 * 123 K7
Huntings Rd DAGE RM10 80 C5
Huntington Cl BXLY DA5 137 J7
Huntland Cl RAIN RM13 99 K4
Huntley Cl STWL/WRAY TW19 120 B6
Huntley St GWRST WC1E 10 F1
Huntley Wy RYNPK SW20 * 160 D1
Huntly Dr FNCH N3 38 E5
Huntly Rd SNWD SE25 165 F2
Hunton St WCHPL E1 92 C4
Hunt Rd NWDGN UB2 103 F2
Hunts Cl BKHTH/KID SE3 133 K1
Hunt's La SRTFD E15 94 A1
Huntsman Cl FELT TW13 141 F3
Huntsman St WALW SE17 19 J6
Hunts Md PEND EN3 31 F2
Hunts Medde Cl CHST BR7 153 J6
Huntsmoor Rd
HOR/WEW KT19 173 F4
Huntspill St TOOT SW17 147 G2
Hunts Slip Rd DUL SE21 150 A1
Huntsworth Ms CAMTN NW1 3 L9
Hurdwick Pl CAMTN NW1 * 4 E5
Hurley Crs BERM/RHTH SE16 93 F7
Hurley Rd GFD/PVL UB6 84 B4
Hurlingham Gdns
FUL/PGN SW6 127 J2
Hurlingham Pk
FUL/PGN SW6 * 127 J2
Hurlingham Rd BXLYHN DA7 117 G6
FUL/PGN SW6 127 J1

Hurlingham Sq
FUL/PGN SW6 * 127 K2
Hurlock St HBRY N5 73 H2
Hurlstone Rd SNWD SE25 164 E4
Hurn Court Rd HSLWW TW4 122 C1
Huron Rd TOOT SW17 148 A1
Hurren Cl BKHTH/KID SE3 133 H2
Hurricane House
WOOL/PLUM SE18 * 114 D6
Hurricane Rd WLGTN SM6 176 E6
Hurry Cl SRTFD E15 76 C6
Hurst Av CHING E4 43 J2
HGT N6 54 C5
Hurstbourne ESH/CLAY KT10 171 F5
Hurstbourne Gdns BARK IG11 78 D5
Hurstbourne Rd FSTH SE23 132 B7
Hurst Cl CHING E4 43 J2
CHSGTN KT9 172 C4
GLDGN NW11 53 F5
HAYES BR2 167 J7
NTHLT UB5 65 K5
Hurstcourt Rd SUT SM1 162 A7
Hurstdene Av HAYES BR2 167 J7
Hurstdene Gdns
SEVS/STOTM N15 56 A6
Hurstfield HAYES BR2 167 K4
Hurstfield Crs YEAD UB4 82 C4
Hurstfield Rd
E/WMO/HCT KT8 157 F2
Hurst La ABYW SE2 116 E4
E/WMO/HCT KT8 157 H3
Hurstleigh Gdns CLAY IG5 45 K7
Hurst Pl ABYW SE2 116 D4
DART DA1 * 139 F5
Hurst Ri BAR EN5 26 E2
Hurst Rd BFN/LL DA15 155 H1
BXLY DA5 137 F7
CROY/NA CR0 177 K4
E/WMO/HCT KT8 157 F2
ERITH DA8 117 K6
WALTH E17 57 K2
WCHMH N21 29 G7
WOT/HER KT12 156 C3
Hurst Springs BXLY DA5 137 F7
Hurst St HNHL SE24 130 C5
Hurst View Rd SAND/SEL CR2 178 A6
Hurst Wy SAND/SEL CR2 178 A5
Hurstway Rd NTGHL W11 * 88 B6
Hurstway Wk NTGHL W11 * 88 B6
Hurstwood Av BXLY DA5 137 F7
ERITH DA8 118 B7
SWFD E18 59 F3
Hurstwood Dr BMLY BR1 168 E2
Hurstwood Rd GLDGN NW11 52 C3
Hurtwood Rd WOT/HER KT12 156 E6
Huson Cl HAMP NW3 3 J1
Hussain Cl HRW HA1 67 F3
Hussars Cl HSLWW TW4 122 D2
Husseywell Crs HAYES BR2 167 K7
Hutching's St POP/IOD E14 112 D1
Hutchings Wk GLDGN NW11 53 F3
Hutchins Cl SRTFD E15 76 A6
Hutchinson Ter WBLY HA9 67 K2
Hutchins Rd THMD SE28 97 G6
Hutton Cl GFD/PVL UB6 66 D4
WFD IG8 45 F5
Hutton Gv
NFNCH/WDSPK N12 39 F4
Hutton La
KTN/HRWW/WS HA3 34 C6
Hutton Rw EDGW HA8 36 E6
Hutton St EMB EC4Y 12 B5
Hutton Wk
KTN/HRWW/WS HA3 34 C6
Huxbear St BROCKY SE4 132 C4
Huxley UED N18 * 41 K4
Huxley Cl NTHLT UB5 83 J1
Huxley Dr CHDH RM6 61 H6
Huxley Gdns WLSDN NW10 86 B2
Huxley Pde UED N18 * 41 K4
Huxley Pl PLMGR N13 41 H3
Huxley Rd LEY E10 76 A1
UED N18 41 K3
WELL DA16 136 A2
Huxley Sayze UED N18 * 41 K4
Huxley St NKENS W10 88 C2
Hyacinth Cl HPTN TW12 142 A5
IL IG1 78 B5
Hyacinth Rd PUT/ROE SW15 126 D7
Hyde Cl BAR EN5 26 D2
PLSTW E13 94 E1
Hyde Crs CDALE/KGS NW9 51 G4
Hyde Estate Rd
CDALE/KGS NW9 51 H4
Hyde Farm Ms BAL SW12 129 J7
Hydefield Cl WCHMH N21 29 K7
Hydefield Ct ED N9 42 A1
Hyde Gv DART DA1 139 J1
Hyde La BTSEA SW11 108 D7
Hyde Park Av WCHMH N21 41 J1
Hyde Park Cnr
MYFR/PICC W1J 16 B1
Hyde Park Crs BAY/PAD W2 9 J5
Hyde Park Gdns BAY/PAD W2 9 H6
WCHMH N21 29 J7
Hyde Park Gardens Ms
BAY/PAD W2 9 H6
Hyde Park Ga SKENS SW7 14 E2
Hyde Park Gate Ms
SKENS SW7 * 14 F2
Hyde Park Pl BAY/PAD W2 9 K6
Hyde Park Sq BAY/PAD W2 9 J5
Hyde Park Square Ms
BAY/PAD W2 9 J5
Hyde Park St BAY/PAD W2 9 J6
Hyderabad Wy SRTFD E15 76 C6
Hyde Rd BXLYHN DA7 137 G1
IS N1 7 H4
RCHPK/HAM TW10 125 G4
WAT WD17 20 E2
Hydeside Gdns ED N9 42 B1
Hyde's Pl IS N1 6 C1
Hyde St DEPT SE8 112 D5
Hyde Ter ASHF TW15 140 C5
The Hyde CDALE/KGS NW9 * 51 F3
Hydethorpe Av ED N9 42 B1
Hydethorpe Rd BAL SW12 129 H7
Hyde V GNWCH SE10 113 F6
Hyde Wk MRDN SM4 161 K6
Hyde Wy ED N9 42 B1
HYS/HAR UB3 101 J3
Hyland Cl EMPK RM11 63 K6
Hylands Rd WALTH E17 58 B1
Hyland Wy EMPK RM11 63 K6
Hylton St WOOL/PLUM SE18 116 A3
Hyndewood FSTH SE23 * 151 F2
Hyndman St PECK SE15 111 J5
Hynton Rd BCTR RM8 79 J1
Hyperion Pl HOR/WEW KT19 173 F7
Hyrstdene SAND/SEL CR2 177 H3
Hyson Rd BERM/RHTH SE16 111 J4
Hythe Av BXLYHN DA7 117 F6
Hythe Cl UED N18 42 C3
Hythe Rd THHTH CR7 164 E1
WLSDN NW10 87 H7
Hythe St DART DA1 139 H4
Hyver Hl BAR EN5 25 F5

I

Ibbotson Av CAN/RD E16 94 D5
Ibbott St WCHPL E1 92 E3
Iberian Av WLGTN SM6 176 D3
Ibis La CHSWK W4 105 K7
Ibis Wy YEAD UB4 83 H5
Ibscott Cl DAGE RM10 80 E5
Ibsley Gdns PUT/ROE SW15 126 D7
Ibsley Wy EBAR EN4 27 J4
Iceland Rd BOW E3 75 J7
Ickburgh Est CLPT E5 * 74 D1
Ickburgh Rd CLPT E5 74 D2
Ickenham Cl RSLP HA4 64 B1
Ickenham Rd RSLP HA4 46 B7
Ickleton Rd ELTH/MOT SE9 153 J3
Icknield Dr GNTH/NBYPK IG2 60 B4
Ickworth Park Rd WALTH E17 57 G3
Ida Rd SEVS/STOTM N15 55 K4
Ida St POP/IOD E14 94 A5
Iden Cl HAYES BR2 167 H2
Idlecombe Rd TOOT SW17 148 A5
Idmiston Rd SRTFD E15 76 D4
WNWD SE27 149 J2
WPK KT4 160 C6
Idmiston Sq WPK KT4 160 C6
Idol La MON EC3R 13 J7
Idonia St DEPT SE8 112 C6
Iffley Rd HMSMTH W6 106 E2
Ifield Rd WBPTN SW10 14 D9
Ightham Rd ERITH DA8 117 H6
Ilbert St NKENS W10 88 C2
Ilchester Gdns BAY/PAD W2 8 C6
Ilchester Pl WKENS W14 107 J2
Ilchester Rd BCTR RM8 79 H4
Ildersly Gv DUL SE21 149 K1
Ilderton Rd PECK SE15 111 K5
Ilex Cl SUN TW16 156 B1
Ilex Rd WLSDN NW10 69 H5
Ilex Wy STRHM/NOR SW16 149 G4
Ilford Hl IL IG1 78 A2
MNPK E12 77 K3
Ilford La IL IG1 78 B3
Ilfracombe Gdns CHDH RM6 61 H6
Ilfracombe Rd BMLY BR1 152 D2
Iliffe St WALW SE17 18 D7
Iliffe Yd WALW SE17 18 D7
Ilkley Cl NRWD SE19 * 149 K5
Ilkley Ct FBAR/BDGN N11 40 A5
Ilkley Rd CAN/RD E16 95 G4
OXHEY WD19 33 H4
Illingworth Wy EN EN1 30 A4
Ilmington Rd
KTN/HRWW/WS HA3 49 K5
Ilminster Gdns BTSEA SW11 128 D3
Imber Cl STHGT/OAK N14 28 C6
Imber Cross THDIT KT7 158 A5
Imber Gv ESH/CLAY KT10 157 J6
Imber Park Rd ESH/CLAY KT10 157 J7
Imber St IS N1 7 G4
Imperial Av STNW/STAM N16 * 74 A3
Imperial Cl CRICK NW2 69 K4
RYLN/HDSTN HA2 48 A5
Imperial College Rd
SKENS SW7 15 G4
Imperial Crs FUL/PGN SW6 128 B1
Imperial Dr RYLN/HDSTN HA2 48 A6
Imperial Gdns MTCM CR4 163 G2
Imperial Ms EHAM E6 95 H1
Imperial Pl BORE WD6 * 24 D2
CHST BR7 154 A7
Imperial Rd
EBED/NFELT TW14 121 H6
FUL/PGN SW6 108 A7
WDGN N22 40 E6
Imperial Sq FUL/PGN SW6 108 A7
Imperial St BOW E3 94 A2
Imperial Wy CHST BR7 154 C2
CROY/NA CR0 177 F5
KTN/HRWW/WS HA3 50 A5
Imre Cl SHB W12 87 J7
Inca Dr ELTH/MOT SE9 135 G6
Inchmery Rd CAT SE6 151 K1
Inchwood CROY/NA CR0 179 K3
Independent Pl HACK E8 74 B4
Independents Rd
BKHTH/KID SE3 133 J2
Inderwick Rd CEND/HSY/T N8 55 F5
Indescon Ct POP/IOD E14 112 E1
India St TWRH EC3N 13 L5
India Wy SHB W12 87 K6
Indigo Ms POP/IOD E14 * 94 A6
STNW/STAM N16 73 K2
Indus Rd CHARL SE7 114 B6
Infant House
WOOL/PLUM SE18 * 114 D6
Ingal Rd PLSTW E13 94 E3
Ingate Pl VX/NE SW8 109 G7
Ingatestone Rd MNPK E12 59 G7
SNWD SE25 165 J4
WFD IG8 45 F6
Ingelow Rd VX/NE SW8 129 G1
Ingersoll Rd SHB W12 87 K7
Ingestre Pl SOHO/CST W1F 10 F5
Ingestre Rd FSTGT E7 76 E3
KTTN NW5 72 B3
Ingham Cl SAND/SEL CR2 179 F7
Ingham Rd KIL/WHAMP NW6 70 E3
SAND/SEL CR2 178 E7
Inglebert St CLKNW EC1R 6 A7
Ingleborough St
BRXN/ST SW9 130 B1
Ingleby Dr HRW HA1 66 D2
Ingleby Rd DAGE RM10 80 D5
HOLWY N7 72 E2
IL IG1 60 B7
Ingleby Wy CHST BR7 154 A4
WLGTN SM6 176 D7
Ingle Cl PIN HA5 47 K2
Ingledew Rd
WOOL/PLUM SE18 115 J4
Inglefield Sq WAP E1W * 92 D7
Inglehurst Gdns REDBR IG4 59 K4
Inglemere Rd FSTH SE23 151 F2
TOOT SW17 147 K6
Ingleside Cl BECK BR3 151 J6
Ingleside Gv BKHTH/KID SE3 113 J5
Inglethorpe St FUL/PGN SW6 107 G7
Ingleton Av WELL DA16 136 B4
Ingleton Rd CAR SM5 175 J7
UED N18 42 C5
Ingleton St BRXN/ST SW9 130 B1
Ingleway NFNCH/WDSPK N12 39 H5
Inglewood CROY/NA CR0 179 G7
Inglewood Cl POP/IOD E14 112 D3
Inglewood Copse BMLY BR1 168 D1
Inglewood Ms SURB KT6 159 H7
Inglewood Rd BXLYHN DA7 138 A3
KIL/WHAMP NW6 70 E4
Inglis Rd CROY/NA CR0 165 G7
EA W5 86 B6
Inglis St CMBW SE5 110 C7
Ingram Av GLDGN NW11 53 G6
Ingram Cl LBTH SE11 17 M5
STAN HA7 35 J4
Ingram Rd DART DA1 139 H7
EFNCH N2 53 J3
THHTH CR7 149 J7
Ingram Wy GFD/PVL UB6 66 D7
Ingrave Rd ROM RM1 63 F3
Ingrave St BTSEA SW11 128 C2
Ingrebourne Rd RAIN RM13 99 K3
Ingress St CHSWK W4 106 B4
Inigo Jones Rd CHARL SE7 114 C6
Inkerman Rd KTTN NW5 72 B5
Inks Gn CHING E4 44 A4
Inkwell Cl NFNCH/WDSPK N12 39 G2
Inman Rd WAND/EARL SW18 128 B6
WLSDN NW10 69 G7
Inmans Rw WFD IG8 44 E3
Inner Cir CAMTN NW1 4 A8
Inner Park Rd
WIM/MER SW19 146 B1
Inner Ring East HTHAIR TW6 120 E2
Innes Cl RYNPK SW20 161 H1
Innes Gdns PUT/ROE SW15 126 E5
Innes St PECK SE15 111 F6
Innes Yd CROY/NA CR0 177 J2
Inniskilling Rd PLSTW E13 95 G1
Innovation Cl ALP/SUD HA0 68 A7
Inskip Cl LEY E10 75 K1
Inskip Rd BCTR RM8 61 K7
Institute Pl HACK E8 74 D4
Instone Rd DART DA1 139 G6
Integer Gdns WAN E11 * 58 B6
International Av HEST TW5 102 B4
International Wy SUN TW16 140 C7
Inver Ct BAY/PAD W2 8 D5
Inveresk Gdns WPK KT4 173 H2
Inverforth Cl HAMP NW3 71 G1
Inverforth Rd
FBAR/BDGN N11 40 B4
Inverine Rd CHARL SE7 114 A4
Invermore Pl
WOOL/PLUM SE18 115 H3
Inverness Gdns KENS W8 8 C9
Inverness Ms BAY/PAD W2 8 D6
Inverness Pl BAY/PAD W2 8 D6
Inverness Rd HSLW TW3 122 E3
NWDGN UB2 102 D3
UED N18 42 D4
WPK KT4 161 G7
Inverness St CAMTN NW1 4 C3
Inverness Ter BAY/PAD W2 8 D7
WDGN N22 * 41 H7
Inverton Rd PECK SE15 132 A3
Invicta Cl CHST BR7 154 A4
EBED/NFELT TW14 121 J7
Invicta Gv NTHLT UB5 83 K2
Invicta Pde SCUP DA14 * 155 H3
Invicta Plaza STHWK SE1 12 C8
Invicta Rd BKHTH/KID SE3 113 K6
Inville Rd WALW SE17 19 H8
Inwen Ct DEPT SE8 * 112 B5
Inwood Av HSLW TW3 123 H2
Inwood Cl CROY/NA CR0 179 G1
Inwood Rd HSLW TW3 123 H3
Inworth St BTSEA SW11 128 D1
Inworth Wk IS N1 * 6 E3
Iona Cl CAT SE6 132 D6
MRDN SM4 162 A6
Ion Sq BETH E2 * 92 C1
Ipswich Rd TOOT SW17 148 A5
Ireland Cl EHAM E6 95 K4
Ireland Pl WDGN N22 40 E6
Irene Ms HNWL W7 * 85 F7
Irene Rd FUL/PGN SW6 107 K7
Ireton Cl MUSWH N10 40 A6
Ireton St BOW E3 93 J3
Iris Av BXLY DA5 137 F5
Iris Cl CROY/NA CR0 166 A7
EHAM E6 95 J4
SURB KT6 * 159 G6
Iris Crs BXLYHN DA7 117 G5
Iris Rd HOR/WEW KT19 172 D4
Iris Wy CHING E4 43 H5
Iron Bridge Cl NWDGN UB2 84 C7
WLSDN NW10 69 G4
Iron Bridge Rd South
WDR/YW UB7 100 D1
Iron Mill La DART DA1 138 C3
Iron Mill Pl DART DA1 138 C3
Iron Mill Rd WAND/EARL SW18 128 A5
Ironmonger La CITYW EC2V 13 G5
Ironmonger Rw FSBYE EC1V 6 F8
Ironmongers Pl POP/IOD E14 112 D3
Ironside Cl BERM/RHTH SE16 112 A1
Irvine Av KTN/HRWW/WS HA3 49 G2
Irvine Cl POP/IOD E14 93 K4
TRDG/WHET N20 39 J1
Irving Av NTHLT UB5 65 H7
Irving Gv BRXN/ST SW9 130 A1
Irving Ms IS N1 73 J5
Irving Rd WKENS W14 107 G2
Irving St LSQ/SEVD WC2H 11 H7
Irving Wy CDALE/KGS NW9 51 H4
Irwell Est BERM/RHTH SE16 * 111 K1
Irwin Av WOOL/PLUM SE18 115 K6
Irwin Gdns WLSDN NW10 69 K7
Isaac Wy STHWK SE1 18 F1
Isabella Cl STHGT/OAK N14 28 C6
Isabella Ct
RCHPK/HAM TW10 * 125 G5
Isabella Ms IS N1 74 A5
Isabella Pl KUTN/CMB KT2 144 B4
Isabella Rd HOM E9 * 74 E4
Isabella St STHWK SE1 12 C9
Isabel St BRXN/ST SW9 110 A7
Isambard Ms POP/IOD E14 113 F2
Isambard Pl BERM/RHTH SE16 92 E7
Isham Rd STRHM/NOR SW16 163 K1
Isis Cl PUT/ROE SW15 127 F3
RSLP HA4 46 A5
Isis St WAND/EARL SW18 147 G1
Island Farm Av
E/WMO/HCT KT8 156 E4
Island Farm Rd
E/WMO/HCT KT8 156 E4
Island Rd BERM/RHTH SE16 112 A3
MTCM CR4 147 K6
Island Rw POP/IOD E14 93 H5
Isla Rd WOOL/PLUM SE18 115 H5
Islay Gdns HSLWW TW4 122 C4
Islay Wk IS N1 * 73 J5
Islay Whf POP/IOD E14 * 94 A4
Isledon Rd HOLWY N7 73 G2
Islehurst Cl CHST BR7 154 A7
Islington Gn IS N1 6 C4
Islington High St IS N1 6 C5
Islington Park Ms IS N1 6 C1
Islington Park St IS N1 6 B1
Islip Gdns EDGW HA8 37 F5
NTHLT UB5 65 J6
Islip Manor Rd NTHLT UB5 65 J6
Islip St KTTN NW5 72 C4
Ismailia Rd FSTGT E7 77 F6
Isom Cl PLSTW E13 95 F2
Issa Rd HSLW TW3 122 E3
Ivanhoe Dr
KTN/HRWW/WS HA3 49 H1
Ivanhoe Rd CMBW SE5 131 G2
HSLWW TW4 122 C2
Ivatt Pl WKENS W14 107 J4
Ivatt Wy SEVS/STOTM N15 55 H2
Iveagh Av WLSDN NW10 86 C1
Iveagh Cl HOM E9 75 F7
WLSDN NW10 86 C1
Ivedon Rd WELL DA16 136 D1
Ive Farm Cl LEY E10 75 J1
Ive Farm La LEY E10 75 J1
Iveley Rd CLAP SW4 129 H1
Ivere Dr BAR EN5 27 F5
Iverhurst Cl BXLYHS DA6 136 E4
Iverna Ct KENS W8 14 B3
Iverna Gdns
EBED/NFELT TW14 121 G4
KENS W8 14 B3
Iverson Rd KIL/WHAMP NW6 70 D5
Ivers Wy CROY/NA CR0 179 K6
Ives Gdns ROM RM1 63 H3
Ives Rd CAN/RD E16 94 C4
Ives St CHEL SW3 15 K5
Ivimey St BETH E2 * 92 C2
Ivinghoe Cl EN EN1 30 A1
Ivinghoe Rd BCTR RM8 79 H4
BUSH WD23 22 D5
Ivor Gv ELTH/MOT SE9 135 G7
Ivor Pl CAMTN NW1 9 L1
Ivor St CAMTN NW1 4 E2
Ivory Ct FELT TW13 121 K7
Ivorydown BMLY BR1 152 E3
Ivybridge Cl TWK TW1 124 B5
Ivychurch Cl PGE/AN SE20 150 D6
Ivy Church La WALW SE17 * 19 L7
Ivy Cl DART DA1 139 K5
PIN HA5 47 G6
RYLN/HDSTN HA2 65 K3
SUN TW16 156 B1
Ivy Ct BERM/RHTH SE16 * 111 H4
Ivy Crs CHSWK W4 105 K3
Ivydale Rd CAR SM5 175 K1
PECK SE15 132 A4
Ivyday Gv STRHM/NOR SW16 149 F2
Ivydene E/WMO/HCT KT8 156 E4
Ivydene Cl SUT SM1 175 G3
Ivy Gdns CEND/HSY/T N8 54 E5
MTCM CR4 163 J2
Ivyhouse Rd DAGW RM9 79 K5
Ivy La HSLWW TW4 122 E3
Ivymount Rd WNWD SE27 149 G2
Ivy Rd BROCKY SE4 132 C3
CAN/RD E16 94 E5
CRICK NW2 70 A3
HSLW TW3 123 G3
STHGT/OAK N14 28 C6
SURB KT6 * 172 C1
TOOT SW17 147 J4
WALTH E17 57 J5
Ivy St IS N1 7 J5
Ivy Wk DAGW RM9 80 A5
NTHWD HA6 * 32 C7
Ixworth Pl CHEL SW3 15 J6
Izane Rd BXLYHS DA6 137 G3

J

Jacaranda Cl NWMAL KT3 160 B2
Jacaranda Gv HACK E8 7 M1
Jackass La HAYES BR2 181 F5
Jack Clow Rd SRTFD E15 94 C1
Jack Cornwell St MNPK E12 78 A3
Jack Dash Wy EHAM E6 95 J3
Jack Jones Wy DAGW RM9 80 B7
Jackman Ms WLSDN NW10 69 G2
Jackman St HACK E8 74 D7
Jackson Cl HOM E9 75 F6
Jackson Rd BARK IG11 78 D7
EBAR EN4 27 H5
HAYES BR2 181 J1
HOLWY N7 73 F3
Jackson's La HGT N6 54 A6
Jackson's Pl CROY/NA CR0 164 E7
Jackson St WOOL/PLUM SE18 115 F5
Jackson's Wy CROY/NA CR0 179 J2
Jackson Wy HOR/WEW KT19 172 C7
NWDGN UB2 103 G1
Jack Walker Ct HBRY N5 73 H3
Jacobs Cl DAGE RM10 80 D3
Jacob St STHWK SE1 19 M1
Jacob's Well Ms MHST W1U 10 B4
Jacqueline Cl NTHLT UB5 65 J7
Jacqueline Creft Ter HGT N6 * 54 A5
Jacqueline Vls WALTH E17 * 58 A4
Jade Cl BCTR RM8 61 J7
CAN/RD E16 95 H5
CRICK NW2 52 B6
Jade Ter KIL/WHAMP NW6 * 2 F1
Jaffe Rd IL IG1 60 C7
Jaffray Rd HAYES BR2 168 C3
Jaggard Wy BAL SW12 128 E6
Jago Cl WOOL/PLUM SE18 115 H5
Jago Wk CMBW SE5 110 E6
Jamaica Rd BERM/RHTH SE16 111 H2
STHWK SE1 19 M2
THHTH CR7 164 C5
Jamaica St WCHPL E1 92 E4
James Av BCTR RM8 62 B7
CRICK NW2 70 A4
James Bedford Cl PIN HA5 47 G1
James Cl BUSH WD23 21 J4
GLDGN NW11 * 52 C5
GPK RM2 63 J4
PLSTW E13 94 E1
James Collins Cl MV/WKIL W9 88 D3
James Gdns TOTM N17 41 J6
James Joyce Wk
BRXN/ST SW9 130 C3
James La WAN E11 58 A6
Jameson St KENS W8 8 B8
James Pl TOTM N17 42 B6
James Rd DART DA1 138 D6
James St BARK IG11 78 C6
COVGDN WC2E 11 K6
EN EN1 30 B4
HSLW TW3 123 J2
MHST W1U 10 B5
Jamestown Rd CAMTN NW1 4 C3
Jamestown Wy POP/IOD E14 94 B6
James Voller Wy WCHPL E1 92 E5
James Watt Wy ERITH DA8 118 B5
James Wy OXHEY WD19 33 H3
James Yd CHING E4 * 44 B5
Jamuna Cl POP/IOD E14 93 G4
Jane St WCHPL E1 92 D5
Janet St POP/IOD E14 112 D2
Janeway Pl BERM/RHTH SE16 111 J1
Janeway St BERM/RHTH SE16 111 H1
Janson Cl SRTFD E15 76 C4
WLSDN NW10 69 F2
Janson Rd SRTFD E15 76 C4
Jansons Rd SEVS/STOTM N15 56 A2
Japan Crs FSBYPK N4 55 F7
Japan Rd CHDH RM6 61 K5
Jardine Rd WAP E1W 93 F6
Jarrett Cl BRXS/STRHM SW2 130 C7
Jarrow Cl MRDN SM4 162 A4
Jarrow Rd BERM/RHTH SE16 111 K3
CHDH RM6 61 J5
TOTM N17 56 D3
Jarrow Wy HOM E9 75 H3
Jarvis Cl BAR EN5 26 B4
BARK IG11 78 D7
Jarvis Rd EDUL SE22 131 F3
SAND/SEL CR2 177 K5
Jasmin Cl NTHWD HA6 32 D7
Jasmine Cl IL IG1 78 B4
STHL UB1 83 J6
Jasmine Ct LEE/GVPK SE12 133 K5
Jasmine Gdns CROY/NA CR0 179 K2
RYLN/HDSTN HA2 66 A1
Jasmine Gv PGE/AN SE20 150 D7
Jasmine Rd HOR/WEW KT19 172 D5
ROMW/RG RM7 81 G1
Jasmine Ter WDR/YW UB7 100 D1
Jasmin Rd HOR/WEW KT19 172 D4
Jason Wk ELTH/MOT SE9 154 A3
Jasper Rd CAN/RD E16 95 H5
NRWD SE19 150 B5
Javelin Wy NTHLT UB5 83 H2
Jay Gdns CHST BR7 153 K3
Jay Ms SKENS SW7 14 F2
Jean Batten Cl WLGTN SM6 177 F6
Jebb Av BRXS/STRHM SW2 129 K5
Jebb St BOW E3 93 J1
Jedburgh Rd PLSTW E13 95 G2
Jedburgh St BTSEA SW11 129 F3
Jeddo Ms SHB W12 106 C1
Jeddo Rd SHB W12 106 C1
Jefferson Cl GNTH/NBYPK IG2 60 B4
WEA W13 104 C2
Jeffrey's Pl CAMTN NW1 4 E1
Jeffreys Rd CLAP SW4 129 K1
PEND EN3 31 H3
Jeffrey's St CAMTN NW1 4 D1
Jeffs Cl HPTN TW12 * 142 B5
Jeffs Rd SUT SM1 174 D3
Jeger Av BETH E2 7 L4
Jeken Rd ELTH/MOT SE9 134 B3
Jelf Rd BRXS/STRHM SW2 130 B4
Jellicoe Gdns STAN HA7 35 F5
Jellicoe Rd TOTM N17 41 K6
WATW WD18 20 E5
Jemmett Cl KUTN/CMB KT2 144 D7
Jem Paterson Ct HRW HA1 * 66 E3
Jengar Cl SUT SM1 175 F3
Jenkins La BARK IG11 96 B1
Jenkins Rd PLSTW E13 95 F3
Jenner Av ACT W3 87 F4
Jenner Cl SCUP DA14 155 G3
Jenner Pl BARN SW13 106 E5
Jenner Rd STNW/STAM N16 74 B1
Jenner Wy HOR/WEW KT19 172 C7
Jennett Rd CROY/NA CR0 177 G2
Jennifer Rd BMLY BR1 152 D2
Jennings Cl SURB KT6 158 D6
Jennings Rd EDUL SE22 131 G5
Jennings Wy BAR EN5 26 A2
Jenningtree Rd ERITH DA8 118 E6
Jenningtree Wy BELV DA17 117 K1
Jenny Hammond Cl WAN E11 76 D2
Jenson Wy NRWD SE19 150 B6
Jenton Av BXLYHN DA7 117 F7
Jephson Rd FSTGT E7 77 G6
Jephson St CMBW SE5 110 E7
Jephtha Rd WAND/EARL SW18 127 K5
Jerdan Pl FUL/PGN SW6 107 K6
Jeremiah St POP/IOD E14 93 K5
Jeremy's Gn UED N18 42 D3
Jermyn St STJS SW1Y 10 E8
Jerningham Av CLAY IG5 60 B1
Jerningham Rd NWCR SE14 132 B1
Jerome St WCHPL E1 13 L2
Jerrard St LEW SE13 132 E2
Jerrold St IS N1 * 7 K6
Jersey Av KTN/HRWW/WS HA3 49 H1
Jersey Dr STMC/STPC BR5 169 J5
Jersey Rd CAN/RD E16 95 G4
HEST TW5 103 G6
HNWL W7 104 B1
HSLW TW3 103 G7
IL IG1 78 B3
ISLW TW7 103 H6
LEY E10 58 B7
RAIN RM13 81 J6
TOOT SW17 148 B6
Jersey St BETH E2 92 D2
Jersey Vls HNWL W7 * 103 K1
Jerusalem Pas CLKNW EC1R 12 C1
Jerviston Gdns
STRHM/NOR SW16 149 G5
Jervois House
WOOL/PLUM SE18 * 114 D6
Jesmond Av WBLY HA9 68 B5
Jesmond Cl MTCM CR4 163 G2
Jesmond Dene HAMP NW3 * 71 G5
Jesmond Rd CROY/NA CR0 165 G6
Jesmond Wy STAN HA7 36 A4
Jessam Av CLPT E5 56 D7
Jessamine Rd HNWL W7 84 E7
Jesse Rd LEY E10 58 A7
Jessett Cl ERITH DA8 118 A3
Jessica Rd WAND/EARL SW18 128 B5
Jessop Av NWDGN UB2 102 E3
Jessop Sq POP/IOD E14 * 93 J7
Jessops Wy CROY/NA CR0 163 H5
Jessup Cl WOOL/PLUM SE18 115 H3
Jetstar Wy NTHLT UB5 83 J2
Jevington Wy LEE/GVPK SE12 134 A7
Jewel Rd WALTH E17 57 J2
Jewry St TWRH EC3N 13 L5
Jews Rw WAND/EARL SW18 128 A3
Jews Wk SYD SE26 150 D3
Jeymer Av WLSDN NW10 69 K4
Jeymer Dr GFD/PVL UB6 66 C7
Jeypore Rd WAND/EARL SW18 128 B6
Jillian Cl HPTN TW12 142 A6
Jim Bradley Cl
WOOL/PLUM SE18 115 F3
Jim Veal Dr HOLWY N7 72 E5
Joan Crs ELTH/MOT SE9 134 C6
Joan Gdns BCTR RM8 80 A1
Joan Rd BCTR RM8 80 A1

Joan St *STHWK* SE1 12 C9
Jocelyn Rd *RCH/KEW* TW9 125 F2
Jocelyn St *PECK* SE15 111 H7
Jockey's Flds *FSBYW* WC1X 11 M2
Jodane St *DEPT* SE8 112 C3
Jodrell Cl *ISLW* TW7 104 B7
Jodrell Rd *BOW* E3 75 H7
Joel St *PIN* HA5 46 E2
Johanna St *STHWK* SE1 * 18 A2
John Adam St *CHCR* WC2N 11 K8
John Aird Ct *BAY/PAD* W2 8 F2
John Archer Wy
WAND/EARL SW18 128 C5
John Ashby Cl
BRXS/STRHM SW2 129 K5
John Austin Cl *KUTN/CMB* KT2 144 B7
John Bradshaw Rd
STHGT/OAK N14 28 D7
John Burns Dr *BARK* IG11 78 E7
John Campbell Rd
STNW/STAM N16 74 A4
John Carpenter St *EMB* EC4Y 12 B6
John Felton Rd
BERM/RHTH SE16 * 111 H1
John Fisher St *WCHPL* E1 92 C6
John Goodchild Wy
KUT/HW KT1 159 J2
John Harrison Wy
BERM/RHTH SE16 112 A2
GNWCH SE10 113 J2
John Islip St *WEST* SW1P 17 H7
John Lamb Ct
KTN/HRWW/WS HA3 34 E7
John Maurice Cl *WALW* SE17 19 G5
John McKenna Wk
BERM/RHTH SE16 * 111 H2
John Parker Sq *BTSEA* SW11 * 128 C2
John Penn St *LEW* SE13 112 E7
John Perrin Pl
KTN/HRWW/WS HA3 50 A6
John Prince's St
CAVSQ/HST W1G 10 D4
John Rennie Wk *WAP* E1W 92 D6
John Roll Wy
BERM/RHTH SE16 111 H2
John Ruskin St *CMBW* SE5 110 C6
John's Av *HDN* NW4 52 A3
John's Cl *ASHF* TW15 140 A3
John Silkin La *DEPT* SE8 112 A4
Johns La *MRDN* SM4 162 B4
John's Ms *BMSBY* WC1N 11 M1
John Smith Av *FUL/PGN* SW6 107 J6
John Smith Ms *POP/IOD* E14 94 B6
Johnson Cl *HACK* E8 74 C7
Johnson Rd *CROY/NA* CR0 164 E6
HAYES BR2 168 C4
HEST TW5 102 B6
WLSDN NW10 69 F7
Johnson's Cl *CAR* SM5 175 K2
Johnson's Ct
FLST/FETLN EC4A 12 B5
Johnsons Dr *HPTN* TW12 142 C7
Johnson's Pl *PIM* SW1V 16 F8
Johnson St *NWDGN* UB2 102 B2
WCHPL E1 92 E5
Johnsons Wy *WLSDN* NW10 86 D3
John Spencer Sq *IS* N1 * 73 H5
Johns Pl *WCHPL* E1 92 D5
John's Ter *CROY/NA* CR0 165 F7
Johnston Cl *BRXN/ST* SW9 110 A7
Johnstone Rd *EHAM* E6 95 K2
Johnston Ter *CRICK* NW2 70 B2
Johnston Rd *WFD* IG8 44 E4
John St *BMSBY* WC1N 11 M1
EN EN1 30 B4
HSLW TW3 122 D1
SNWD SE25 165 H3
SRTFD E15 76 D7
John Trundle Highwalk
BARB EC2Y * 12 E2
John Watkin Cl
HOR/WEW KT19 172 D7
John Wesley Cl *EHAM* E6 * 95 K2
John William Cl
KUTN/CMB KT2 * 144 A7
John Williams Cl *NWCR* SE14 112 A5
John Wilson St
WOOL/PLUM SE18 115 F3
John Wooley Cl *LEW* SE13 * 133 H3
Joiners Arms Yd *CMBW* SE5 * 110 E7
Joiner St *STHWK* SE1 13 H9
Jollys La *YEAD* UB4 83 H4
Jonathan St *LBTH* SE11 17 L7
Jones Rd *PLSTW* E13 95 F3
Jonson Cl *MTCM* CR4 163 G3
YEAD UB4 82 E4
Jordan Cl *RYLN/HDSTN* HA2 65 K2
Jordan Rd *GFD/PVL* UB6 67 H7
Jordans Cl *DAGE* RM10 80 D3
Jordans Ms *WHTN* TW2 142 E1
Joseph Av *ACT* W3 87 F5
Joseph Hardcastle Cl
NWCR SE14 112 A6
Josephine Av
BRXS/STRHM SW2 130 A4
Joseph Locke Wy
ESH/CLAY KT10 170 A1
Joseph Powell Cl *BAL* SW12 129 H5
Joseph Ray Rd *WAN* E11 76 C1
Joseph St *BOW* E3 93 H4
Joseph Trotter Cl
CLKNW EC1R 6 B8
Joshua Cl *MUSWH* N10 40 B6
SAND/SEL CR2 177 H6
Joshua St *POP/IOD* E14 94 A5
Joslings Cl *SHB* W12 87 J6
Joubert St *BTSEA* SW11 128 E1
Jowett St *PECK* SE15 111 G6
Joyce Av *UED* N18 42 B4
Joyce Green La *ERITH* DA8 119 G7
Joydon Dr *CHDH* RM6 61 H5
Joyners Cl *DAGW* RM9 80 B3
Jubilee Av *CHING* E4 44 A5
ROMW/RG RM7 62 E4
WHTN TW2 123 H7
Jubilee Cl *CDALE/KGS* NW9 51 F5
KUT/HW KT1 143 J7
ROMW/RG RM7 62 D4
WLSDN NW10 87 G1
Jubilee Crs *ED* N9 30 C7
Jubilee Dr *RSLP* HA4 65 H3
Jubilee Gdns *STHL* UB1 84 A4
STHWK SE1 * 11 M9
Jubilee Pl *CHEL* SW3 15 K7
Jubilee Rd *CHEAM* SM3 174 B6
GFD/PVL UB6 67 H7
Jubilee St *WCHPL* E1 92 E5
Jubilee Ter *FUL/PGN* SW6 * 127 H1
The Jubilee *GNWCH* SE10 * 112 E6
Jubilee Vls *ESH/CLAY* KT10 * 157 K7
Jubilee Wy *CHSGTN* KT9 172 D2
EBED/NFELT TW14 121 K7
SCUP DA14 155 G1
WIM/MER SW19 147 F7
Judd St *STPAN* WC1H 5 J8
Jude St *CAN/RD* E16 94 D5
Judge Heath La *HYS/HAR* UB3 82 A5
Judges' Wk *HAMP* NW3 71 G2
Judge Wk *ESH/CLAY* KT10 170 E5
Juer St *BTSEA* SW11 108 D6
Jules Thorn Av *EN* EN1 30 C2
Julia Gdns *BARK* IG11 97 K1
Juliana Cl *EFNCH* N2 53 G2
Julian Av *ACT* W3 86 D6
Julian Cl *BAR* EN5 27 F2
Julian Hl *HRW* HA1 66 E1
Julian Pl *POP/IOD* E14 112 E4
Julian Tayler Pth *FSTH* SE23 * 150 D1
Julien Rd *EA* W5 104 D2
Juliette Rd *PLSTW* E13 94 E1
Juliette Wy *SOCK/AV* RM15 119 J1
Julius Caesar Wy *STAN* HA7 35 J2
Julius Nyerere Cl *IS* N1 5 M4
Junction Ap *BTSEA* SW11 128 D2
Junction Ms *BAY/PAD* W2 9 J4
Junction Pl *BAY/PAD* W2 * 9 H4
Junction Rd *ARCH* N19 72 C2
ASHF TW15 140 A4
DART DA1 139 G5
EA W5 104 D3
ED N9 30 C7
HRW HA1 48 D5
PLSTW E13 77 F7
ROM RM1 63 H3
SAND/SEL CR2 177 K5
TOTM N17 56 C2
Junction Rd East *CHDH* RM6 62 A6
Junction Rd West *CHDH* RM6 61 K6
Juniper Cl *BAR* EN5 26 B4
CHSGTN KT9 172 B4
HOR/WEW KT19 173 F7
WBLY HA9 68 B4
Juniper Ct *CHDH* RM6 61 H5
KTN/HRWW/WS HA3 * 35 F7
NTHWD HA6 * 32 E7
Juniper Crs *CAMTN* NW1 4 B2
Juniper Dr *WAND/EARL* SW18 128 B3
Juniper Gdns *MTCM* CR4 148 C7
SUN TW16 140 D5
Juniper La *EHAM* E6 95 J4
Juniper Rd *IL* IG1 78 A3
Juniper St *WCHPL* E1 * 92 E6
Juniper Wy *HYS/HAR* UB3 82 B6
Juno Wy *NWCR* SE14 112 A5
Jupiter Wy *HOLWY* N7 73 F5
Jupp Rd *SRTFD* E15 76 B6
Jupp Rd West *SRTFD* E15 76 B7
Justice Wk *CHEL* SW3 108 D5
Justin Cl *BTFD* TW8 104 E6
Justin Rd *CHING* E4 43 H5
Jute La *PEND* EN3 31 G1
Jutland Cl *ARCH* N19 54 E7
Jutland Rd *CAT* SE6 133 F6
PLSTW E13 94 E3
Jutsums Av *ROMW/RG* RM7 62 D5
Jutsums La *ROMW/RG* RM7 62 D5
Juxon Cl *KTN/HRWW/WS* HA3 34 B7
Juxon St *LBTH* SE11 17 M5

K

Kaduna Cl *PIN* HA5 47 F4
Kaine Pl *CROY/NA* CR0 166 C6
Kale Rd *ERITHM* DA18 116 E1
Kambala Rd *BTSEA* SW11 128 C1
Kamrans Pl *EDGW* HA8 50 B1
Kangley Bridge Rd *SYD* SE26 151 H4
Kaplan Dr *WCHMH* N21 29 F4
Kara Wy *CRICK* NW2 70 B3
Karen Cl *RAIN* RM13 99 G1
Karen Ct *BMLY* BR1 152 D7
ELTH/MOT SE9 134 B4
Karenza Ct *WBLY* HA9 * 49 J6
Karma Wy *RYLN/HDSTN* HA2 48 A7
Kashgar Rd *WOOL/PLUM* SE18 116 A4
Kashmir Rd *CHARL* SE7 114 C6
Kassala Rd *BTSEA* SW11 108 E7
Kates Cl *BAR* EN5 25 J4
Katharine St *CROY/NA* CR0 177 J2
Katherine Cl
BERM/RHTH SE16 93 F7
Katherine Gdns
ELTH/MOT SE9 134 C3
Katherine Rd *EHAM* E6 77 H6
Katherine Sq *NTGHL* W11 * 88 C7
Kathleen Av *ACT* W3 86 E4
ALP/SUD HA0 68 A6
Kathleen Rd *BTSEA* SW11 128 E2
Kayemoor Rd *BELMT* SM2 175 J6
Kay Rd *BRXN/ST* SW9 129 K1
Kays Ter *SWFD* E18 * 58 D1
Kay St *BETH* E2 92 C1
SRTFD E15 76 B6
WELL DA16 116 C7
Kean St *HOL/ALD* WC2B 11 L5
Keatley Gn *CHING* E4 43 H5
Keats Av *CAN/RD* E16 95 F7
Keats Cl *BKHTH/KID* SE3 114 B6
BORE WD6 24 C3
PEND EN3 31 F4
STHWK SE1 19 L6
WAN E11 59 F4
WIM/MER SW19 147 H5
YEAD UB4 82 E4
Keats Est *STNW/STAM* N16 * 74 B1
Keats Gv *HAMP* NW3 71 J3
Keats Pde *ED* N9 42 C1
Keats Rd *BELV* DA17 117 K2
LEY E10 57 K6
WELL DA16 115 K7
Keats Wy *CROY/NA* CR0 165 K5
GFD/PVL UB6 84 B4
WDR/YW UB7 100 C3
Keble Cl *NTHLT* UB5 66 C4
WPK KT4 160 C7
Keble Pl *BARN* SW13 106 E5
Keble St *TOOT* SW17 147 G3
Kechill Gdns *HAYES* BR2 167 K6
Kedleston Wk *BETH* E2 92 D2
Keeble Cl *WOOL/PLUM* SE18 * 115 G5
Keedonwood Rd *BMLY* BR1 152 C3
Keel Cl *BARK* IG11 97 J1
BERM/RHTH SE16 93 F7
Keele Cl *WATN* WD24 21 G1
Keeley Rd *CROY/NA* CR0 177 J1
Keeley St *HOL/ALD* WC2B 11 L5
Keeling Rd *ELTH/MOT* SE9 134 C4
Keely Cl *EBAR* EN4 27 J4
Keemor Cl
WOOL/PLUM SE18 * 115 F6
Keens Cl *STRHM/NOR* SW16 148 D4
Keen's Rd *CROY/NA* CR0 177 J3
Keen's Yd *IS* N1 73 H5
Keepers Ms *TEDD* TW11 143 J5
The Keep *BKHTH/KID* SE3 133 K1
KUTN/CMB KT2 144 B5
Keesey St *WALW* SE17 19 G9
Keeton's Rd *BERM/RHTH* SE16 111 J2
Keevil Dr *WIM/MER* SW19 127 G6
Keighley Cl *HOLWY* N7 72 E3
Keightley Dr *ELTH/MOT* SE9 135 H7
Keildon Rd *BTSEA* SW11 128 E3
Keir Hardie Est *CLPT* E5 * 56 D7
Keir Hardie Wy *BARK* IG11 79 G6
YEAD UB4 * 82 E2
Keith Connor Cl *VX/NE* SW8 129 G2
Keith Gv *SHB* W12 106 D1
Keith Rd *BARK* IG11 96 D1
HYS/HAR UB3 101 H2
WALTH E17 43 H7
Kelbrook Rd *BKHTH/KID* SE3 134 D1
Kelburn Wy *RAIN* RM13 99 J2
Kelceda Cl *CRICK* NW2 69 J1
Kelf Gv *HYS/HAR* UB3 82 D5
Kelfield Gdns *NKENS* W10 88 B5
Kelfield Ms *NKENS* W10 88 B4
Kelland Cl *CEND/HSY/T* N8 * 54 D4
Kelland Rd *PLSTW* E13 94 E3
Kellaway Rd *BKHTH/KID* SE3 134 B1
Keller Cresent *MNPK* E12 77 H3
Kellerton Rd *LEW* SE13 133 H4
Kellett Rd *BRXS/STRHM* SW2 130 B3
Kelling Gdns *CROY/NA* CR0 164 C6
Kellino St *TOOT* SW17 147 K3
Kellner Rd *THMD* SE28 116 A2
Kell St *STHWK* SE1 18 D3
Kelly Av *PECK* SE15 111 G7
Kelly Cl *BORE* WD6 25 F1
WLSDN NW10 69 F2
Kelly Ms *MV/WKIL* W9 * 88 D4
Kelly Rd *MLHL* NW7 38 C5
Kelly St *CAMTN* NW1 72 B5
Kelly Wy *CHDH* RM6 62 A4
Kelman Cl *CLAP* SW4 129 J1
Kelmore Gv *EDUL* SE22 131 H3
Kelmscott Cl *WALTH* E17 43 H7
WATW WD18 20 E5
Kelmscott Crs *WATW* WD18 20 E4
Kelmscott Gdns *SHB* W12 106 D2
Kelmscott Rd *BTSEA* SW11 128 D4
Kelross Rd *HBRY* N5 73 H3
Kelsall Cl *BKHTH/KID* SE3 134 A1
Kelsall Ms *RCH/KEW* TW9 105 J7
Kelsey La *BECK* BR3 166 D2
Kelsey Park Av *BECK* BR3 166 E2
Kelsey Park Rd *BECK* BR3 166 D1
Kelsey Sq *BECK* BR3 166 D1
Kelsey St *BETH* E2 92 C3
Kelsey Wy *BECK* BR3 166 D2
Kelso Pl *KENS* W8 14 C3
Kelso Rd *CAR* SM5 162 B6
Kelston Rd *BARK/HLT* IG6 60 B1
Kelton Vls *KUT/HW* KT1 * 159 G1
Kelvedon Cl *KUTN/CMB* KT2 144 C5
Kelvedon Rd *FUL/PGN* SW6 107 J6
Kelvedon Wy *WFD* IG8 45 K5
Kelvin Av *WDGN* N22 41 F5
Kelvinbrook *E/WMO/HCT* KT8 157 G2
Kelvin Cl *HOR/WEW* KT19 172 C5
Kelvin Crs
KTN/HRWW/WS HA3 34 E6
Kelvin Dr *TWK* TW1 124 C5
Kelvin Gdns *CROY/NA* CR0 163 K6
STHL UB1 84 A5
Kelvin Gv *CHSGTN* KT9 171 K2
SYD SE26 150 D2
Kelvington Cl *CROY/NA* CR0 166 B6
Kelvington Rd *PECK* SE15 132 A4
Kelvin Pde *ORP* BR6 169 K7
Kelvin Rd *HBRY* N5 73 H3
WELL DA16 136 B2
Kember St *IS* N1 * 5 L2
Kemble Dr *HAYES* BR2 181 J2
Kemble Rd *CROY/NA* CR0 177 H2
FSTH SE23 132 A7
TOTM N17 42 C7
Kemble St *HOL/ALD* WC2B 11 L5
Kemerton Rd *BECK* BR3 166 E1
CMBW SE5 130 D2
CROY/NA CR0 165 G6
Kemey's St *HOM* E9 75 G4
Kemnal Rd *CHST* BR7 154 C5
Kempe Rd *KIL/WHAMP* NW6 88 B1
Kemp Gdns *CROY/NA* CR0 164 D5
Kemplay Rd *HAMP* NW3 71 H3
Kemp Pl *BUSH* WD23 22 A5
Kemps Dr *NTHWD* HA6 32 D6
POP/IOD E14 93 J6
Kempsford Gdns *ECT* SW5 14 B8
Kempsford Rd *LBTH* SE11 18 B6
Kempshott Rd
STRHM/NOR SW16 148 E6
Kempson Rd *FUL/PGN* SW6 107 K7
Kempthorne Rd *DEPT* SE8 112 B3
Kempton Av *NTHLT* UB5 66 A5
SUN TW16 141 F7
Kempton Cl *ERITH* DA8 117 K5
HGDN/ICK UB10 64 A3
Kempton Ct *SUN* TW16 141 F7
Kempton Pk *SUN* TW16 * 141 G7
Kempton Rd *EHAM* E6 77 K7
Kempton Wk *CROY/NA* CR0 166 B5
Kempt St *WOOL/PLUM* SE18 115 F5
Kemsing Cl *BXLY* DA5 137 F6
THHTH CR7 * 164 D3
Kemsing Rd *GNWCH* SE10 113 K4
Kenbury St *CMBW* SE5 130 D1
Kenchester Cl *VX/NE* SW8 109 K6
Kencot Wy *ERITHM* DA18 117 G1
Kendal Av *ACT* W3 86 C4
BARK IG11 78 E7
UED N18 41 K3
Kendal Cl *BRXN/ST* SW9 110 C6
EBED/NFELT TW14 121 J7
TRDG/WHET N20 39 J1
WFD IG8 44 D1
YEAD UB4 82 C1
Kendal Ct *ACT* W3 86 C4
Kendal Cft *HCH* RM12 81 J4
Kendale Rd *BMLY* BR1 152 C4
Kendal Gdns *SUT* SM1 175 G1
UED N18 41 K3
Kendall Av *BECK* BR3 166 B1
SAND/SEL CR2 177 K7
Kendall Pl *MHST* W1U 10 A3
Kendall Rd *BECK* BR3 166 B1
ISLW TW7 124 B1
WOOL/PLUM SE18 114 D7
Kendalmere Cl *MUSWH* N10 40 B7
Kendal Pde *UED* N18 41 K3
Kendal Pl *PUT/ROE* SW15 127 J4
Kendal Rd *WLSDN* NW10 69 J3
Kendal Steps *BAY/PAD* W2 * 9 K5
Kendal St *BAY/PAD* W2 9 K5
Kender St *NWCR* SE14 111 K6
Kendoa Rd *CLAP* SW4 129 J3
Kendon Cl *WAN* E11 59 F4
Kendra Hall Rd *SAND/SEL* CR2 177 H6
Kendrey Gdns *WHTN* TW2 123 K5
Kendrick Ms *SKENS* SW7 15 G5
Kendrick Pl *SKENS* SW7 * 15 G6
Kenelm Cl *HRW* HA1 67 G2
Kenerne Dr *BAR* EN5 26 C4
Kenilford Rd *BAL* SW12 129 G6
Kenilworth Av
RYLN/HDSTN HA2 65 K3
WALTH E17 57 J1
WIM/MER SW19 146 E4
Kenilworth Dr *BORE* WD6 24 E2
Kenilworth Gdns
GDMY/SEVK IG3 79 F1
OXHEY WD19 33 G4
STHL UB1 * 83 K2
WOOL/PLUM SE18 135 G1
YEAD UB4 82 D4
Kenilworth Rd *BOW* E3 93 G1
EA W5 86 A7
EDGW HA8 36 E1
EW KT17 173 J5
KIL/WHAMP NW6 70 D7
PGE/AN SE20 151 F7
STMC/STPC BR5 169 H5
Kenilworth Ter *BELMT* SM2 * 174 E6
Kenley Av *CDALE/KGS* NW9 37 G7
Kenley Cl *BXLY* DA5 137 H6
CHST BR7 169 K2
EBAR EN4 27 J3
Kenley Gdns *THHTH* CR7 164 C3
Kenley Rd *KUT/HW* KT1 159 J1
TWK TW1 124 B5
WIM/MER SW19 161 K2
Kenley Wk *CHEAM* SM3 174 B3
NTGHL W11 * 88 C7
Kenlor Rd *TOOT* SW17 147 H4
Kenmare Dr *MTCM* CR4 147 K6
TOTM N17 56 B1
Kenmare Gdns *PLMGR* N13 41 J3
Kenmare Rd *THHTH* CR7 164 B5
Kenmere Gdns *ALP/SUD* HA0 68 C7
Kenmere Rd *WELL* DA16 136 D1
Kenmont Gdns *WLSDN* NW10 87 K2
Kenmore Av
KTN/HRWW/WS HA3 49 G4
Kenmore Crs *YEAD* UB4 82 D2
Kenmore Gdns *EDGW* HA8 50 D1
Kenmore Rd
KTN/HRWW/WS HA3 49 K2
Kenmure Rd *HACK* E8 74 D4
Kenmure Yd *HACK* E8 * 74 D4
Kennacraig Cl *CAN/RD* E16 95 F7
Kennard Rd *FBAR/BDGN* N11 39 K4
SRTFD E15 76 B6
Kennard St *BTSEA* SW11 109 F7
CAN/RD E16 95 K7
Kennedy Av *PEND* EN3 30 E5
Kennedy Cl *MTCM* CR4 163 F1
PIN HA5 33 K5
PLSTW E13 94 E1
STMC/STPC BR5 169 J7
Kennedy Rd *BARK* IG11 78 E7
HNWL W7 84 E4
Kennedy Wk *WALW* SE17 19 H6
Kennet Cl *BTSEA* SW11 128 C3
Kennet Dr *YEAD* UB4 83 J4
Kenneth Av *IL* IG1 78 B3
Kenneth Crs *CRICK* NW2 69 K4
Kenneth Gdns *STAN* HA7 35 G5
Kenneth More Rd *IL* IG1 78 B2
Kenneth Rd *CHDH* RM6 62 A6
Kennet Rd *DART* DA1 138 D2
ISLW TW7 124 A2
MV/WKIL W9 88 D3
Kennet Sq *MTCM* CR4 147 J7
Kennet St *WAP* E1W 92 C7
Kennett Wharf La
BLKFR EC4V 12 F6
Kenninghall Rd *CLPT* E5 74 D2
UED N18 42 D4
Kenning St *BERM/RHTH* SE16 111 K1
Kennings Wy *LBTH* SE11 18 B7
Kennington Gdns
KUT/HW KT1 158 E2
Kennington La *LBTH* SE11 17 M8
Kennington Ov *LBTH* SE11 17 M9
Kennington Park Gdns
LBTH SE11 18 C9
Kennington Park Pl
LBTH SE11 18 B8
Kennington Park Rd
LBTH SE11 18 C7
Kennington Rd *LBTH* SE11 18 A8
Kenny Dr *CAR* SM5 176 A7
Kenrick Pl *MHST* W1U 10 A2
Kensal Rd *NKENS* W10 88 C3
Kensal Whf *NKENS* W10 * 88 C3
Kensington Av *MNPK* E12 77 J5
THHTH CR7 149 G7
WATW WD18 20 D3
Kensington Church Ct
KENS W8 14 C2
Kensington Church St
KENS W8 8 B8
Kensington Church Wk
KENS W8 * 14 C1
Kensington Cl
FBAR/BDGN N11 * 40 A4
Kensington Ct *KENS* W8 14 D2
Kensington Court Gdns
KENS W8 * 14 D3
Kensington Court Ms
KENS W8 * 14 D3
Kensington Court Pl *KENS* W8 14 D3
Kensington Dr *WFD* IG8 59 H1
Kensington Gdns *IL* IG1 59 K7
Kensington Gardens Sq
BAY/PAD W2 8 C5
Kensington Ga *KENS* W8 14 E3
Kensington Hall Gdns
WKENS W14 * 107 J4
Kensington High St *KENS* W8 14 B3
WKENS W14 107 H3
Kensington Ml *KENS* W8 8 B8
Kensington Palace Gdns
KENS W8 8 C8
Kensington Park Gdns
NTGHL W11 88 D6
Kensington Park Ms
NTGHL W11 88 D5
Kensington Park Rd
NTGHL W11 88 D5
Kensington Pl *KENS* W8 8 A9
Kensington Rd *KENS* W8 14 D2
NTHLT UB5 84 A1
ROMW/RG RM7 62 E5
Kensington Sq *KENS* W8 14 C2
Kensington Ter *SAND/SEL* CR2 177 K6
Kensington Wy *BORE* WD6 25 F2
Kent Av *DAGW* RM9 98 C3
WEA W13 85 H4
WELL DA16 136 A4
Kent Cl *MTCM* CR4 163 K3
Kent Ct *CDALE/KGS* NW9 * 51 G1
Kent Dr *EBAR* EN4 28 A3
TEDD TW11 142 E4
Kentford Wy *NTHLT* UB5 65 J7
Kent Gdns *RSLP* HA4 46 E5
WEA W13 85 H4
Kent Gate Wy *CROY/NA* CR0 179 H5
Kent House La *BECK* BR3 151 G5
Kent House Rd *BECK* BR3 151 F6
Kentish Rd *BELV* DA17 117 H3
Kentish Town Rd *CAMTN* NW1 4 D2
Kentish Wy *BMLY* BR1 168 A1
Kentlea Rd *THMD* SE28 115 K1
Kentmere Rd
WOOL/PLUM SE18 115 K3
Kenton Av *HRW* HA1 49 F6
STHL UB1 84 A6
SUN TW16 156 C1
Kenton Gdns
KTN/HRWW/WS HA3 49 J4
Kenton La
KTN/HRWW/WS HA3 35 F6
KTN/HRWW/WS HA3 49 J2
Kenton Park Av
KTN/HRWW/WS HA3 49 K3
Kenton Park Cl
KTN/HRWW/WS HA3 49 J3
Kenton Park Crs
KTN/HRWW/WS HA3 49 K3
Kenton Park Pde
KTN/HRWW/WS HA3 * 49 J4
Kenton Park Rd
KTN/HRWW/WS HA3 49 J3
Kenton Rd *HOM* E9 75 F5
KTN/HRWW/WS HA3 49 G5
Kenton St *STPAN* WC1H 5 J9
Kenton Wy *YEAD* UB4 82 C2
Kent Pas *CAMTN* NW1 3 L9
Kent Rd *CHSWK* W4 105 K2
DAGE RM10 80 D4
DART DA1 139 H5
E/WMO/HCT KT8 157 H3
KUT/HW KT1 158 E2
RCH/KEW TW9 105 H6
WCHMH N21 29 K7
WWKM BR4 166 E7
Kent St *BETH* E2 7 M5
PLSTW E13 95 F2
Kent Ter *CAMTN* NW1 3 K8
Kent View Gdns
GDMY/SEVK IG3 78 E1
Kent Wy *SURB* KT6 172 A2
Kentwell Cl *BROCKY* SE4 * 132 B3
Kentwode Gn *BARN* SW13 106 D6
Kent Yd *SKENS* SW7 15 K2
Kenver Av
NFNCH/WDSPK N12 39 H5
Kenward Rd *ELTH/MOT* SE9 134 B4
Kenway *CRW* RM5 62 E1
Ken Wy *WBLY* HA9 68 E1
Kenway Rd *ECT* SW5 14 C6
Kenwood Cl *HAMP* NW3 53 H7
WDR/YW UB7 100 D5
Kenwood Dr *BECK* BR3 167 F2
Kenwood Gdns *CLAY* IG5 60 A3
SWFD E18 59 F2
Kenwood Rd *ED* N9 42 C1
HGT N6 53 K5
Kenworthy Rd *HOM* E9 75 G4
Kenwyn Dr *CRICK* NW2 69 G2
Kenwyn Rd *CLAP* SW4 129 J3
DART DA1 139 G4
RYNPK SW20 146 A7
Kenya Rd *CHARL* SE7 114 C6
Kenyngton Dr *SUN* TW16 140 E4
Kenyngton Pl
KTN/HRWW/WS HA3 49 J4
Kenyon St *FUL/PGN* SW6 107 G7
Keogh Rd *SRTFD* E15 76 C5
Kepler Rd *CLAP* SW4 129 K3
Keppel Rd *DAGW* RM9 80 A3
EHAM E6 77 K6
Keppel St *GWRST* WC1E 11 H2
Kerbela St *BETH* E2 92 C3
Kerbey St *POP/IOD* E14 93 K5
Kerfield Crs *CMBW* SE5 110 E7
Kerfield Pl *CMBW* SE5 110 E7
Kerri Cl *BAR* EN5 26 A3
Kerrison Pl *EA* W5 85 K7
Kerrison Rd *BTSEA* SW11 128 D2
EA W5 85 K7
SRTFD E15 76 B7
Kerry Av *SOCK/AV* RM15 119 J1
STAN HA7 35 J3
Kerry Cl *CAN/RD* E16 95 F5
PLMGR N13 41 F1
Kerry Ct *STAN* HA7 35 K3
Kerry Pth *NWCR* SE14 112 C5
Kerry Rd *NWCR* SE14 112 C5
Kersfield Rd *PUT/ROE* SW15 127 G5
WAND/EARL SW18 127 H6
Kershaw Cl
WAND/EARL SW18 128 C5
Kershaw Rd *DAGE* RM10 80 C2
Kersley Ms *BTSEA* SW11 * 108 E7
Kersley Rd *STNW/STAM* N16 74 A2
Kersley St *BTSEA* SW11 128 E1
Kerstin Cl *HYS/HAR* UB3 82 D6
Kerswell Cl *SEVS/STOTM* N15 56 A4
Kerwick Cl *HOLWY* N7 5 K1
Keslake Rd *KIL/WHAMP* NW6 88 B1
Kessock Cl *TOTM* N17 56 D4
Keston Av *HAYES* BR2 181 G4
Keston Cl *UED* N18 41 K2
WELL DA16 116 D6
Keston Gdns *HAYES* BR2 181 G3
Keston Ms *WAT* WD17 21 F1
Keston Park Cl *HAYES* BR2 181 K3
Keston Rd *PECK* SE15 131 H2
THHTH CR7 164 A5
TOTM N17 55 K2
Kestrel Av *EHAM* E6 95 J4
HNHL SE24 130 C4
Kestrel Cl *CDALE/KGS* NW9 51 G1
HCH RM12 81 K6
KUTN/CMB KT2 143 K3
WLSDN NW10 69 F4
Kestrel Pl *NWCR* SE14 * 112 B5
Kestrel Wy *CROY/NA* CR0 180 B7
HYS/HAR UB3 101 G1
Keswick Av *PUT/ROE* SW15 145 G4
WIM/MER SW19 161 K1
Keswick Cl *SUT* SM1 175 G3
Keswick Gdns *REDBR* IG4 59 J4
RSLP HA4 46 B4
WBLY HA9 68 A4
Keswick Ms *EA* W5 86 A7
Keswick Rd *BXLYHN* DA7 137 H1
PUT/ROE SW15 127 H4
WHTN TW2 123 H5
WWKM BR4 180 C1

Kettering St
  STRHM/NOR SW16 .... 148 B5
Kett Gdns BRXS/STRHM SW2 .... 130 A4
Kettlebaston Rd LEY E10 .... 57 H7
Kettlewell Cl FBAR/BDGN N11 .... 40 A5
Kevelioc Rd TOTM N17 .... 41 J1
Kevin Cl HSLWW TW4 .... 122 C1
Kew Br RCH/KEW TW9 .... 105 H5
Kew Bridge Arches
  CHSWK W4 * 105 H5
Kew Bridge Rd BTFD TW8 .... 105 H5
Kew Crs CHEAM SM3 .... 174 D2
Kewferry Rd NTHWD HA6 .... 32 A5
Kew Foot Rd RCH/KEW TW9 .... 125 F3
Kew Gardens Rd
  RCH/KEW TW9 .... 105 G6
Kew Gn RCH/KEW TW9 .... 105 G5
Kew Meadow Pth
  RCH/KEW TW9 .... 105 H7
Kew Rd RCH/KEW TW9 .... 105 J6
Kew Rd RCH/KEW TW9 .... 125 F3
Key Cl WCHPL E1 .... 92 D3
Keyes Rd CRICK NW2 .... 70 B4
  DART DA1 .... 139 J4
Keymer Rd BRXS/STRHM SW2 .... 149 F1
Keynes Cl EFNCH N2 .... 53 K2
Keynsham Av WFD IG8 .... 44 C3
Keynsham Gdns
  ELTH/MOT SE9 .... 134 D4
Keynsham Rd ELTH/MOT SE9 .... 134 D4
  MRDN SM4 .... 162 A4
Keysham Av TWST TW5 .... 101 K7
Keystone Crs IS N1 .... 5 K6
Keystone Pas BORE WD6 .... 24 C2
Keywood Dr SUN TW16 .... 140 E5
Keyworth Cl CLPT E5 .... 75 G3
Keyworth St STHWK SE1 .... 18 D3
Kezia St DEPT SE8 .... 112 B4
Khama Rd TOOT SW17 .... 147 J3
Khartoum Rd IL IG1 .... 78 B4
  PLSTW E13 .... 95 F2
  TOOT SW17 .... 147 H3
Khyber Rd BTSEA SW11 .... 128 D1
Kibworth St VX/NE SW8 .... 110 A6
Kidbrooke Gdns
  BKHTH/KID SE3 .... 133 K1
Kidbrooke Gv BKHTH/KID SE3 .... 113 K7
Kidbrooke La ELTH/MOT SE9 .... 134 D3
Kidbrooke Park Cl
  BKHTH/KID SE3 .... 114 A7
Kidbrooke Park Rd
  BKHTH/KID SE3 .... 134 A3
Kidbrooke Wy BKHTH/KID SE3 .... 134 A1
Kidderminster Pl
  CROY/NA CRO 164 C7
Kidderminster Rd
  CROY/NA CRO 164 C7
Kidderpore Av HAMP NW3 .... 70 E3
Kidderpore Gdns HAMP NW3 .... 70 E3
Kidd Pl CHARL SE7 .... 114 D4
Kiffen St SDTCH EC2A 7 F4
Kilberry Cl ISLW TW7 .... 103 J7
Kilburn Br KIL/WHAMP NW6 .... 2 B4
Kilburn High Rd
  KIL/WHAMP NW6 .... 2 B3
Kilburn La NKENS W10 .... 88 B2
Kilburn Park Rd MV/WKIL W9 .... 2 A8
Kilburn Pl KIL/WHAMP NW6 .... 2 C4
Kilburn Priory
  KIL/WHAMP NW6 .... 2 C4
Kilburn Sq KIL/WHAMP NW6 .... 2 A4
Kilburn V KIL/WHAMP NW6 .... 2 C4
Kildare Cl RSLP HA4 .... 47 G7
Kildare Gdns BAY/PAD W2 .... 8 B4
Kildare Rd CAN/RD E16 .... 94 E4
Kildare Ter BAY/PAD W2 .... 8 B4
Kildoran Rd CLAP SW4 .... 129 K4
Kildowan Rd GDMY/SEVK IG3 .... 61 G7
Kilgour Rd FSTH SE23 .... 132 B5
Kilkie St FUL/PGN SW6 .... 128 B1
Killarney Rd
  WAND/EARL SW18 .... 128 B5
Killburns Mill Cl WLGTN SM6 .... 176 B1
Killearn Rd CAT SE6 .... 133 G7
Killester Gdns WPK KT4 .... 173 K3
Killick St IS N1 .... 5 L5
Killieser Av
  BRXS/STRHM SW2 .... 148 E1
Killip Cl CAN/RD E16 .... 94 D5
Killowen Av NTHLT UB5 .... 66 C4
Killowen Rd HOM E9 * 75 F5
Killyon Rd VX/NE SW8 .... 129 H1
Kilmaine Rd FUL/PGN SW6 .... 107 H6
Kilmarnock Gdns BCTR RM8 .... 79 J2
Kilmarnock Rd OXHEY WD19 .... 33 H3
Kilmarsh Rd HMSMTH W6 .... 107 F3
Kilmartin
  STRHM/NOR SW16 .... 164 B2
Kilmartin Rd GDMY/SEVK IG3 .... 79 G1
Kilmartin Wy HCH RM12 .... 81 K3
Kilmington Rd BARN SW13 .... 106 D5
Kilmorey Gdns TWK TW1 .... 124 C3
Kilmorey Rd TWK TW1 .... 124 C3
Kilmorie Rd FSTH SE23 .... 132 B1
Kiln Cl HYS/HAR UB3 .... 101 G5
Kilner St POP/IOD E14 .... 93 J4
Kiln Ms TOOT SW17 .... 147 H4
Kilnside ESH/CLAY KT10 .... 171 G6
Kiln Wy NTHWD HA6 .... 32 C5
Kilpatrick Wy YEAD UB4 .... 83 J4
Kilravock St NKENS W10 .... 88 C2
Kilross Rd EBED/NFELT TW14 .... 121 G7
Kilsha Rd WOT/HER KT12 .... 156 A6
Kimbell Gdns FUL/PGN SW6 .... 107 H7
Kimbell Pl BKHTH/KID SE3 .... 134 B3
Kimberley Av EHAM E6 .... 95 J1
  GNTH/NBYPK IG2 .... 60 D7
  PECK SE15 .... 131 J1
  ROMW/RG RM7 .... 62 D5
Kimberley Ct
  KIL/WHAMP NW6 .... 70 C6
Kimberley Dr SCUP DA14 .... 155 K1
Kimberley Gdns EN EN1 .... 30 B1
  FSBYPK N4 .... 55 H4
Kimberley Rd BECK BR3 .... 166 A1
  BRXN/ST SW9 .... 129 K1
  CAN/RD E16 .... 94 D3
  CROY/NA CRO 164 C5
  KIL/WHAMP NW6 .... 70 C2
  TOTM N17 .... 56 C1
  WALTH E17 .... 43 G1
  WAN E11 .... 76 B2
Kimber Rd WAND/EARL SW18 .... 127 K6
Kimble Cl WATW WD18 * 20 E4
Kimble Crs BUSH WD23 .... 22 C6
Kimble Rd WIM/MER SW19 .... 147 H5
Kimbolton Cl LEE/GVPK SE12 .... 133 J5
Kimbolton Gn BORE WD6 .... 24 D2
Kimmeridge Gdns
  ELTH/MOT SE9 .... 153 J3

Kimmeridge Rd
  ELTH/MOT SE9 .... 153 J3
Kimpton Park Wy
  CHEAM SM3 .... 174 D1
Kimpton Rd CHEAM SM3 .... 174 D2
  CMBW SE5 .... 110 E7
Kinburn St
  BERM/RHTH SE16 * 112 A1
Kincaid Rd PECK SE15 .... 111 J6
Kincardine Gdns
  MV/WKIL W9 * 8 A1
Kinch Gv WBLY HA9 .... 50 B6
Kinder Cl THMD SE28 .... 97 K6
Kinder St WCHPL E1 .... 92 D5
Kinderton Ct STHGT/OAK N14 .... 28 C7
Kinfauns Rd
  BRXS/STRHM SW2 .... 149 G1
  GDMY/SEVK IG3 .... 61 H7
Kingaby Gdns RAIN RM13 .... 81 J6
King Alfred Av CAT SE6 .... 151 J3
King Arthur Cl PECK SE15 .... 111 K6
King Charles Crs BRYLDS KT5 .... 159 F6
King Charles I Island
  WHALL SW1A 11 J8
King Charles' Rd WHALL SW1A 17 H1
King Charles Ter WAP E1W * 92 D6
King Charles Wk
  WIM/MER SW19 * 127 H7
Kingcup Cl CROY/NA CRO 166 A7
King David La WCHPL E1 .... 92 E6
Kingdom St BAY/PAD W2 .... 8 D3
Kingdon Rd KIL/WHAMP NW6 .... 70 E5
King Edward Av DART DA1 .... 139 J5
King Edward Dr CHSGTN KT9 .... 172 A2
King Edward III Ms
  BERM/RHTH SE16 .... 111 J1
King Edward Pl BUSH WD23 * 21 K3
King Edward Rd BAR EN5 .... 26 E3
  LEY E10 .... 58 A7
  OXHEY WD19 .... 21 J5
  ROM RM1 .... 63 G5
  WALTH E17 .... 57 G2
King Edward's Gdns ACT W3 .... 86 C7
King Edward's Gv TEDD TW11 .... 143 H5
King Edwards Pl ACT W3 * 86 C7
King Edwards Rd RSLP HA4 .... 46 B7
King Edward's Rd BARK IG11 .... 78 D1
  ED N9 .... 30 D6
  HACK E8 .... 74 D7
  PEND EN3 .... 31 F3
  WALTH E17 * 57 G2
Kingfield Rd EA W5 .... 85 K3
Kingfield St POP/IOD E14 .... 113 F3
Kingfisher Cl
  KTN/HRWW/WS HA3 .... 35 H6
  THMD SE28 .... 97 J6
Kingfisher Dr
  RCHPK/HAM TW10 .... 143 J3
Kingfisher Ms LEW SE13 .... 132 E4
Kingfisher Pl WDGN N22 * 55 F1
Kingfisher St EHAM E6 .... 95 J4
Kingfisher Wy BECK BR3 .... 166 A4
  WLSDN NW10 * 69 F4
King Gdns CROY/NA CRO 177 H4
King Garth Ms SE23 .... 150 D1
King George Av BUSH WD23 .... 22 B5
  CAN/RD E16 .... 95 H5
  GNTH/NBYPK IG2 .... 60 D5
  WOT/HER KT12 .... 156 C7
King George Cl
  ROMW/RG RM7 .... 62 E2
  SUN TW16 * 140 C4
King George Av WATW WD18 .... 20 C4
King George Sq
  RCHPK/HAM TW10 .... 125 G5
King George VI Av MTCM CR4 .... 162 E3
Kingham Ct NTGHL W11 .... 107 H1
  WAND/EARL SW18 .... 128 B6
King Harolds Wy BXLYHN DA7 .... 116 E7
King Henry Ms HRW HA1 * 48 E7
King Henry's Dr
  KTN/HRWW/WS HA3 .... 49 H3
  NTHLT UB5 .... 83 F7
  WPK KT4 .... 160 D6
  YEAD UB4 .... 82 C2
King Henry's Reach
  HMSMTH W6 .... 107 F5
King Henry's Rd HAMP NW3 .... 3 J2
  KUT/HW KT1 .... 159 J2
King Henry St
  STNW/STAM N16 .... 74 A4
King Henry's Wk IS N1 .... 74 A5
King Henry Ter WAP E1W * 92 D6
Kinghorn St STBT EC1A 12 E3
King James Ct STHWK SE1 * 18 D2
King James St STHWK SE1 .... 18 D2
King John Ct SDTCH EC2A 7 K9
King John St WCHPL E1 .... 93 F4
King John's Wk
  ELTH/MOT SE9 .... 134 D6
Kinglake Est WALW SE17 * 19 J7
Kinglake St WALW SE17 .... 19 J8
Kinglet Cl FSTGT E7 .... 76 E5
Kingly Ct REGST W1B * 10 F6
Kingly St REGST W1B 10 E5
King & Queen Cl
  ELTH/MOT SE9 * 153 J3
King & Queen St WALW SE17 .... 18 F7
King & Queen Whf
  BERM/RHTH SE16 * 93 F7
Kingsand Rd LEE/GVPK SE12 .... 133 K2
King's Arms Yd LOTH EC2R 13 G4
Kingsash Dr YEAD UB4 .... 83 J3
Kings Av BAL SW12 .... 129 J7
  BMLY BR1 .... 152 D5
  CAR SM5 .... 175 J6
  CHDH RM6 .... 62 B5
  CLAP SW4 .... 129 K5
  EA W5 .... 85 K5
  MUSWH N10 .... 54 A2
  NWMAL KT3 .... 160 C3
  WATW WD18 .... 20 C4
King's Av WAND/EARL SW18 .... 127 K6
  HSLW TW3 .... 103 G7
  SUN TW16 .... 140 D4
  WCHMH N21 .... 29 H7
  WFD IG8 .... 45 G5
Kings Bench St STHWK SE1 .... 18 C1
Kings Bench Wk EMB EC4Y * 12 B5
Kings Bench Wk EMB EC4Y * 12 B5
Kingsbridge Av EA W5 .... 105 G1
Kingsbridge Ct POP/IOD E14 .... 112 D2
Kingsbridge Crs STHL UB1 .... 83 K5
Kingsbridge Dr ML NW7 * 38 B6
Kingsbridge Rd BARK IG11 .... 96 D1
  MRDN SM4 .... 161 G6
  NKENS W10 .... 88 A5
  NWDGN UB2 .... 102 E3
  WOT/HER KT12 .... 156 A6
Kingsbury Gn
  CDALE/KGS NW9 * 50 D4
Kingsbury Rd
  CDALE/KGS NW9 .... 50 C4
  IS N1 .... 74 A5
Kingsbury Ter IS N1 .... 74 A5
Kingsclere Cl PUT/ROE SW15 .... 126 D6
Kingsclere Pl ENC/FH EN2 .... 29 J1
Kingscliffe Gdns
  WIM/MER SW19 .... 127 J7
Kings Cl DART DA1 .... 138 B3
  HDN NW4 .... 52 B3
  LEY E10 .... 57 K6
  NTHWD HA6 .... 32 D5
  THDIT KT7 .... 158 B5
  WATW WD18 .... 21 G3
  WOT/HER KT12 .... 156 A7
Kings College Rd HAMP NW3 .... 3 H1
Kingscote Rd CHSWK W4 .... 106 A2
  CROY/NA CRO 165 J6
  NWMAL KT3 .... 160 A2
Kingscote St BLKFR EC4V 12 C6
Kingscourt Rd
  STRHM/NOR SW16 .... 148 D2
King's Crs FSBYPK N4 .... 73 J2
Kingscroft Rd CRICK NW2 .... 70 D5
King's Cross Br IS N1 * 5 K7
King's Cross Rd FSBYW WC1X 5 L7
Kingsdale Gdns NTGHL W11 .... 88 D7
Kingsdale Rd PGE/AN SE20 .... 151 F7
  WOOL/PLUM SE18 .... 116 A5
Kingsdown Av ACT W3 .... 87 G6
  SAND/SEL CR2 .... 177 J7
  WEA W13 .... 104 C1
Kingsdown Cl
  BERM/RHTH SE16 * 111 J4
  NKENS W10 .... 88 B5
Kingsdowne Rd SURB KT6 .... 159 F6
Kingsdown Rd ARCH N19 .... 72 E2
  CHEAM SM3 .... 174 C4
  WAN E11 .... 76 C2
Kingsdown Wy HAYES BR2 .... 167 K6
Kings Dr BRYLDS KT5 .... 159 H6
  EDGW HA8 .... 36 B3
  WBLY HA9 .... 68 D1
King's Dr THDIT KT7 .... 158 C5
Kingsend RSLP HA4 .... 46 C7
Kingsend Ct RSLP HA4 * 46 C7
Kings Farm WALTH E17 * 43 K7
Kings Farm Av
  RCHPK/HAM TW10 .... 125 H3
Kingsfield Av
  RYLN/HDSTN HA2 .... 48 B4
Kingsfield Rd HRW HA1 * 48 D6
  OXHEY WD19 .... 21 H6
Kingsfield Ter DART DA1 * 139 G5
Kingsford St KTTN NW5 .... 71 K4
Kingsford Wy EHAM E6 .... 95 K4
Kings Gdns IL IG1 .... 60 D7
  KIL/WHAMP NW6 * 2 B2
Kingsgate WBLY HA9 .... 68 E2
Kingsgate Av FNCH N3 .... 52 E2
Kingsgate Cl BXLYHN DA7 .... 117 F7
  IS N1 * 74 A1
Kings Gate Ms
  CEND/HSY/T N8 .... 55 F4
Kingsgate Pl
  KIL/WHAMP NW6 .... 2 A2
Kingsgate Rd
  KIL/WHAMP NW6 .... 2 A1
  KUT/HW KT1 .... 144 A7
Kingsground ELTH/MOT SE9 .... 134 C6
Kings Gv ROM RM1 .... 63 J4
King's Gv PECK SE15 .... 111 J6
Kings Hall Ms LEW SE13 * 133 F2
Kings Hall Rd BECK BR3 .... 151 F6
Kings Head HI CHING E4 .... 31 K5
King's Hwy WOOL/PLUM SE18 .... 115 K5
Kingshill Av
  KTN/HRWW/WS HA3 .... 49 H3
  NTHLT UB5 .... 83 F7
  WPK KT4 .... 160 D6
  YEAD UB4 .... 82 C2
Kingshill Cl YEAD UB4 .... 82 C2
Kingshill Ct BAR EN5 * 26 C3
Kingshill Dr
  KTN/HRWW/WS HA3 .... 49 H1
Kingshold Rd HOM E9 .... 74 E6
Kingsholm Gdns
  ELTH/MOT SE9 .... 134 C3
Kingshurst Rd LEE/GVPK SE12 .... 133 K6
Kings Keep HAYES BR2 * 167 K1
  KUT/HW KT1 * 159 F3
Kingsland Gn
  STNW/STAM N16 .... 74 A5
Kingsland High St HACK E8 .... 74 A5
Kingsland Pas HACK E8 .... 74 A5
Kingsland Rd BETH E2 .... 7 K6
  HACK E8 .... 7 L1
  PLSTW E13 .... 95 G2
King's La SUT SM1 .... 175 H4
Kingslawn Cl PUT/ROE SW15 .... 126 E4
Kingsleigh Cl BTFD TW8 * 104 E5
Kingsleigh Pl MTCM CR4 .... 162 E2
Kingsley Av BORE WD6 .... 24 B1
  DART DA1 .... 139 K4
  HSLW TW3 .... 123 H1
  STHL UB1 .... 84 A6
  SUT SM1 .... 175 H3
  WEA W13 .... 85 G5
Kingsley Cl DAGE RM10 .... 80 D3
  GLDGN NW11 .... 52 C6
Kingsley Ct EDGW HA8 .... 36 D1
Kingsley Dr WPK KT4 .... 173 H1
Kingsley Gdns CHING E4 .... 43 J4
Kingsley Ms CHST BR7 .... 154 B5
  IL IG1 .... 78 B1
  KENS W8 .... 14 C4
  WAP E1W * 92 D6
Kingsley Pl HGT N6 .... 54 A6
Kingsley Rd CROY/NA CRO 164 B7
  FSTGT E7 .... 76 E7
  HSLW TW3 .... 123 H1
  KIL/WHAMP NW6 .... 70 D7
  PIN HA5 .... 47 K3
  PLMGR N13 .... 41 G3
  RYLN/HDSTN HA2 .... 66 D2
  WALTH E17 .... 58 A1
  WIM/MER SW19 .... 146 E5
Kingsley St BTSEA SW11 .... 128 E2
Kingsley Wy EFNCH N2 .... 53 G5
Kingsley Wood Dr
  ELTH/MOT SE9 .... 153 K2
Kingslyn Crs NRWD SE19 .... 150 A7
Kings MI HMSMTH W6 * 107 H3
Kingsman St WOOL/PLUM SE18 .... 114 E3

Kingsmead BAR EN5 .... 26 E3
  RCHPK/HAM TW10 .... 125 G5
Kingsmead Av
  CDALE/KGS NW9 .... 51 F3
  ED N9 .... 30 D7
  MTCM CR4 .... 163 H2
  ROM RM1 .... 63 G5
  SUN TW16 .... 156 B2
  SURB KT6 .... 172 C1
  WPK KT4 .... 173 K2
Kingsmead Cl BFN/LL DA15 .... 155 C1
  HOR/WEW KT19 .... 173 F6
  TEDD TW11 .... 143 H5
Kingsmead Dr NTHLT UB5 .... 65 K6
Kingsmead Pde NTHLT UB5 * 65 K6
Kings Mead Pk
  ESH/CLAY KT10 .... 170 E6
Kingsmead Rd
  BRXS/STRHM SW2 .... 149 G1
Kingsmead Wy HOM E9 .... 75 G3
Kingsmere Cl PUT/ROE SW15 .... 127 G1
Kingsmere Pk
  CDALE/KGS NW9 .... 50 C7
Kingsmere Rd
  WIM/MER SW19 .... 146 B1
King's Ms BMSBY WC1N 11 M1
  CLAP SW4 .... 129 K4
Kingsmill Gdns DAGW RM9 .... 80 B4
Kingsmill Rd DAGW RM9 .... 80 B4
Kingsmill Ter STJWD NW8 .... 3 H3
Kingsnympton Pk
  KUTN/CMB KT2 .... 144 D6
Kings Oak ROMW/RG RM7 .... 62 C2
King's Orch ELTH/MOT SE9 .... 134 D5
King's Paddock HPTN TW12 .... 142 C7
Kings Pde CAR SM5 .... 175 J2
  TOTM N17 * 56 B2
  WLSDN NW10 * 70 A7
King's Pl STHWK SE1 .... 18 E2
King Sq FSBYE EC1V 6 E8
King's Quay WBPTN SW10 * 108 B7
Kings Reach EMB EC4Y * 12 B6
  WHALL SW1A 11 K9
Kings Ride Ga
  RCHPK/HAM TW10 .... 125 H3
Kingsridge Gdns DART DA1 .... 139 G5
Kings Rd BARK IG11 .... 78 C6
  CHEL SW3 .... 108 C7
  EA W5 .... 85 K4
  FELT TW13 .... 122 A7
  MTCM CR4 .... 163 F2
  RCHPK/HAM TW10 .... 125 G4
  RYLN/HDSTN HA2 .... 65 K1
  WDGN N22 .... 41 F2
  WDR/YW UB7 .... 100 C1
  WLSDN NW10 .... 69 K6
King's Rd BARK IG11 .... 78 C6
  CHEL SW3 .... 15 L7
  FUL/PGN SW6 .... 108 A7
  KUTN/CMB KT2 .... 144 B6
  MORT/ESHN SW14 .... 126 A2
  PLSTW E13 .... 77 G7
  ROM RM1 .... 63 H5
  SNWD SE25 .... 165 H2
  SURB KT6 .... 158 D7
  TEDD TW11 .... 142 E4
  TOTM N17 .... 42 B7
  TWK TW1 .... 124 C5
  UED N18 .... 42 C4
  WAN E11 .... 58 C6
  WIM/MER SW19 .... 146 E5
King's Scholars' Pas
  PIM SW1V 16 E4
King Stairs Cl
  BERM/RHTH SE16 .... 111 J1
King's Ter CAMTN NW1 .... 4 E4
Kingsthorpe Rd SYD SE26 .... 151 F3
Kingston Av CHEAM SM3 .... 174 C2
  EBED/NFELT TW14 .... 121 H5
Kingston By-Pass
  ESH/CLAY KT10 .... 170 C1
  RYNPK SW20 .... 160 D1
Kingston Cl CHDH RM6 .... 62 A3
  NTHLT UB5 .... 65 K6
  TEDD TW11 .... 143 H5
Kingston Crs BECK BR3 .... 151 H7
Kingston Gdns CROY/NA CRO 176 E2
Kingston Ga KUTN/CMB KT2 .... 144 C6
Kingston Hall Rd KUT/HW KT1 .... 158 E2
Kingston HI KUTN/CMB KT2 .... 144 D6
Kingston Hill Av CHDH RM6 .... 62 A3
Kingston Hill Pl
  KUTN/CMB KT2 .... 144 E3
Kingston House Est
  SURB KT6 * 158 D7
Kingston La TEDD TW11 .... 143 G4
  WDR/YW UB7 .... 100 C1
Kingston Ldg NWMAL KT3 * 160 B3
Kingston Pl
  KTN/HRWW/WS HA3 .... 35 F6
Kingston Rd BRYLDS KT5 .... 172 D1
  EBAR EN4 .... 27 H4
  ED N9 .... 42 C1
  HOR/WEW KT19 .... 173 F4
  IL IG1 .... 78 B2
  KUT/HW KT1 .... 159 J2
  NWDGN UB2 .... 102 E3
  NWMAL KT3 .... 160 B3
  PUT/ROE SW15 .... 126 D6
  ROM RM1 .... 63 J4
  RYNPK SW20 .... 161 F2
  TEDD TW11 .... 143 H5
  WIM/MER SW19 .... 146 B5
Kingston Sq NRWD SE19 .... 149 K4
Kingston V PUT/ROE SW15 .... 145 J3
King St CITYW EC2V 12 F4
  COVGDN WC2E 11 J3
  EFNCH N2 .... 53 H2
  HMSMTH W6 .... 106 D3
  NWDGN UB2 .... 102 D2
  PLSTW E13 .... 94 E3
  RCH/KEW TW9 .... 124 E4
  TOTM N17 .... 56 B1
  TWK TW1 .... 124 B7
  WATW WD18 .... 21 F4
  WHALL SW1A 11 H1
King Street Cloisters
  HMSMTH W6 * 106 E3
King Street Pde TWK TW1 * 124 B7
Kingswater Pl BTSEA SW11 * 108 D6
Kings Wy CROY/NA CRO 177 F3
  HRW HA1 .... 48 E3
Kingsway HOL/ALD WC2B 11 L4
  HYS/HAR UB3 .... 82 A7

  MORT/ESHN SW14 .... 125 J2
  NFNCH/WDSPK N12 .... 39 G5
  NWMAL KT3 .... 161 F3
  PEND EN3 .... 30 D4
  STMC/STPC BR5 .... 169 J4
  STWL/WRAY TW19 .... 120 A7
  WBLY HA9 .... 68 A3
  WKM BR4 .... 180 D2
Kingsway Av SAND/SEL CR2 .... 178 E7
Kingsway Crs
  RYLN/HDSTN HA2 .... 48 C3
Kingsway Pde
  STNW/STAM N16 * 73 K2
Kingsway Pl CLKNW EC1R * 6 B9
Kingsway Rd CHEAM SM3 .... 174 C6
Kingswear Rd KTTN NW5 .... 72 B2
  RSLP HA4 .... 64 E1
Kingswood Av BELV DA17 .... 117 G3
  HAYES BR2 .... 167 H2
  HPTN TW12 .... 142 B5
  HSLW TW3 .... 122 E1
  KIL/WHAMP NW6 .... 70 C7
  THHTH CR7 .... 164 B4
Kingswood Cl ASHF TW15 .... 140 A3
  BAR EN5 .... 27 G5
  DART DA1 .... 139 F5
  EN EN1 .... 30 A4
  NWMAL KT3 .... 160 C5
  STMC/STPC BR5 .... 169 J6
  SURB KT6 .... 159 F6
  VX/NE SW8 .... 109 K6
Kingswood Ct LEW SE13 .... 133 G5
Kingswood Dr BELMT SM2 .... 175 F7
  CAR SM5 .... 162 E7
  DUL SE21 .... 150 A3
Kingswood Pk FNCH N3 .... 52 D1
Kingswood Pl LEW SE13 .... 133 H3
Kingswood Rd
  BRXS/STRHM SW2 .... 129 K5
  CHSWK W4 .... 105 K2
  GDMY/SEVK IG3 .... 61 G7
  HAYES BR2 .... 167 H2
  PGE/AN SE20 .... 150 E5
  WAN E11 .... 58 C6
  WBLY HA9 .... 68 C2
  WIM/MER SW19 .... 146 D7
Kingswood Ter CHSWK W4 .... 105 K2
Kingswood Wy WLGTN SM6 .... 176 E5
Kingsworth Cl BECK BR3 .... 166 B4
Kingsworthy Cl KUT/HW KT1 .... 159 G1
Kings Yd PUT/ROE SW15 * 127 G3
  SRTFD E15 * 75 J5
Kingthorpe Rd WLSDN NW10 .... 69 F6
Kingthorpe Ter
  WLSDN NW10 * 69 F6
Kingweston Cl CRICK NW2 .... 70 C2
King William La GNWCH SE10 .... 113 H4
King William St CANST EC4R 13 H6
Kingwood Rd FUL/PGN SW6 .... 107 H6
Kinlet Rd WOOL/PLUM SE18 .... 115 H6
Kinloch Dr CDALE/KGS NW9 .... 51 G6
Kinloch St HOLWY N7 .... 73 F2
Kinloss Gdns FNCH N3 .... 52 D2
Kinloss Rd CAR SM5 .... 162 B6
Kinnaird Av BMLY BR1 .... 152 D5
  CHSWK W4 .... 105 K6
Kinnaird Cl BMLY BR1 .... 152 D5
Kinnaird Wy WFD IG8 .... 45 K5
Kinnear Rd SHB W12 .... 106 C1
Kinnerton Pl North
  KTBR SW1X * 15 M2
Kinnerton Pl South
  KTBR SW1X * 15 M2
Kinnerton St KTBR SW1X 16 A2
Kinnerton Yd KTBR SW1X * 16 A2
Kinnoul Rd HMSMTH W6 .... 107 H5
Kinross Av WPK KT4 .... 173 J1
Kinross Cl
  KTN/HRWW/WS HA3 .... 50 B4
  SUN TW16 .... 140 D4
Kinross Ter WALTH E17 .... 57 H1
Kinsale Rd PECK SE15 .... 131 G2
Kinsella Gdns WIM/MER SW19 .... 145 K5
Kintyre Cl STRHM/NOR SW16 .... 164 A1
Kinveachy Gdns CHARL SE7 .... 114 D4
Kinver Rd SYD SE26 .... 150 E3
Kipling Dr WIM/MER SW19 .... 147 H5
Kipling Est STHWK SE1 .... 19 H2
Kipling Rd BXLYHN DA7 .... 117 F7
Kipling St ED N9 * 41 K2
Kipling Ter ED N9 * 41 K2
Kippington Dr ELTH/MOT SE9 .... 134 C7
Kirby Cl HOR/WEW KT19 .... 173 H4
  NTHWD HA6 .... 32 D5
Kirby Est BERM/RHTH SE16 * 111 J2
Kirby Gv STHWK SE1 .... 19 J1
Kirby St HCIRC EC1N 12 B2
Kirchen Rd WEA W13 .... 85 H6
Kirkcaldy Gn OXHEY WD19 .... 33 G2
Kirkdale SYD SE26 .... 150 D1
Kirkdale Cnr SYD SE26 .... 150 E3
Kirkdale Rd WAN E11 .... 58 C7
Kirkfield Cl WEA W13 .... 85 H7
Kirkham Rd EHAM E6 .... 95 J5
Kirkham St WOOL/PLUM SE18 .... 115 K5
Kirkland Av CLAY IG5 .... 60 A1
Kirkland Cl BFN/LL DA15 .... 135 K5
Kirkland Ter BECK BR3 .... 151 J5
Kirkland Wk HACK E8 .... 74 B5
Kirk La WOOL/PLUM SE18 .... 115 H5
Kirkleas Rd SURB KT6 .... 159 F7
Kirklees Rd BCTR RM8 .... 79 J4
  THHTH CR7 .... 164 B4
Kirkley Rd WIM/MER SW19 .... 146 E7
Kirkly Cl SAND/SEL CR2 .... 178 A7
Kirkmichael Rd POP/IOD E14 .... 94 A5
Kirk Rd WEA W13 .... 85 H6
Kirkside Rd BKHTH/KID SE3 .... 113 K5
Kirkstall Av TOTM N17 .... 55 K3
Kirkstall Gdns
  BRXS/STRHM SW2 .... 129 J7
Kirkstall Rd BRXS/STRHM SW2 .... 129 J7
Kirkstall Rd MRDN SM4 .... 162 A7
Kirkstone Wy BMLY BR1 .... 152 D6
Kirkwall Pl BETH E2 * 92 E2
Kirkwood Rd PECK SE15 .... 131 J1
Kirn Rd WEA W13 .... 85 H6
Kirrane Cl NWMAL KT3 .... 160 C4
Kirtley Rd SYD SE26 .... 151 G3
Kirtling St VX/NE SW8 .... 109 H6
Kirton Cl CHSWK W4 .... 106 A3
Kirton Gdns BETH E2 .... 7 M8
Kirton Ldg
  WAND/EARL SW18 * 128 A5
Kirton Rd PLSTW E13 .... 95 G1
Kirton Wk EDGW HA8 .... 36 E6
Kirwyn Wy CMBW SE5 .... 110 D6
Kitcat Ter BOW E3 .... 93 J2
Kitchener Rd EFNCH N2 .... 53 J2
  FSTGT E7 .... 77 F5

THHTH CR7 164 E2
TOTM N17 56 A2
WALTH E17 43 K7
Kite Pl BETH E2 * 92 C2
Kite Yd BTSEA SW11 * 108 E7
Kitley Gdns NRWD SE19 150 B7
Kitson Rd BARN SW13 106 D7
CMBW SE5 110 D6
Kittiwake Rd NTHLT UB5 83 H2
Kittiwake Wy YEAD UB4 83 H4
Kitto Rd NWCR SE14 132 A1
Kiver Rd ARCH N19 72 D1
Kiwi Ter EHAM E6 96 A2
Klea Av CLAP SW4 129 H5
Knapdale Cl FSTH SE23 150 D1
Knapmill Rd CAT SE6 151 J1
Knapmill Wy CAT SE6 151 J1
Knapp Cl WLSDN NW10 69 G5
Knapp Rd BOW E3 93 J3
Knapton Ms TOOT SW17 148 A5
Knaresborough Dr
WAND/EARL SW18 128 A7
Knaresborough Pl ECT SW5 14 C5
Knatchbull Rd CMBW SE5 130 C1
WLSDN NW10 69 F7
Knebworth Av WALTH E17 43 J7
Knebworth Cl BAR EN5 27 F3
Knebworth Pth BORE WD6 25 F3
Knebworth Rd
STNW/STAM N16 * 74 A3
Knee Hl ABYW SE2 116 D4
Knee Hill Crs ABYW SE2 116 D3
Kneller Gdns ISLW TW7 123 J5
Kneller Rd BROCKY SE4 132 B3
NWMAL KT3 160 B6
WHTN TW2 123 H5
Knevett Ter HSLW TW3 123 F3
Knight Cl BCTR RM8 79 J1
Knighten St WAP E1W 92 D7
Knighthead Point
POP/IOD E14 * 112 D1
Knightland Rd CLPT E5 74 D1
Knighton Cl ROMW/RG RM7 63 F5
SAND/SEL CR2 177 H7
WFD IG8 45 F3
Knighton Dr WFD IG8 45 F3
Knighton La BKHH IG9 45 F1
Knighton Park Rd SYD SE26 151 F4
Knighton Rd FSTGT E7 76 E2
ROMW/RG RM7 62 E5
Knightrider Ct BLKFR EC4V * 12 D6
Knightrider St BLKFR EC4V 12 E6
Knight's Av EA W5 105 F1
Knightsbridge SKENS SW7 15 K2
Knightsbridge Gdns
ROMW/RG RM7 63 F4
Knightsbridge Gn
KTBR SW1X * 15 L2
Knights Chambers ED N9 * 42 C2
Knights Cl E/WMO/HCT KT8 156 E4
Knights Hl WNWD SE27 149 H4
Knight's Hill Sq WNWD SE27 149 H3
Knights Manor Wy
DART DA1 139 J5
Knight's Pk KUT/HW KT1 159 F2
Knight's Pl WHTN TW2 123 K7
Knights Rd CAN/RD E16 94 E7
STAN HA7 35 J3
Knights Wk LBTH SE11 18 C6
Knightswood Cl EDGW HA8 36 E1
Knightswood Rd RAIN RM13 99 H1
Knightwood Crs
NWMAL KT3 160 B5
Knivet Rd FUL/PGN SW6 107 K5
Knockholt Rd ELTH/MOT SE9 134 C4
Knole Cl CROY/NA CR0 * 165 K5
Knole Rd DART DA1 138 D6
The Knole ELTH/MOT SE9 154 A3
Knoll Crs NTHWD HA6 46 C1
Knoll Dr STHGT/OAK N14 28 A6
Knollmead BRYLDS KT5 159 K7
Knoll Rd BXLY DA5 137 H6
SCUP DA14 155 H4
WAND/EARL SW18 128 A4
Knolls Cl WPK KT4 173 K2
The Knoll BECK BR3 151 K7
EA W5 85 J4
HAYES BR2 180 E1
PIN HA5 * 47 H1
Knollys Cl
STRHM/NOR SW16 * 149 H2
Knolly's Cl
STRHM/NOR SW16 149 G2
Knolly's Rd
STRHM/NOR SW16 149 G2
Knotley Wy WWKM BR4 179 K1
Knottisford St BETH E2 93 F2
Knotts Green Ms LEY E10 57 K5
Knotts Green Rd LEY E10 57 K5
Knowle Av BXLYHN DA7 117 F6
Knowle Cl BRXN/ST SW9 130 B2
Knowle Rd HAYES BR2 181 J1
WHTN TW2 123 K7
Knowles Hill Crs LEW SE13 133 G4
Knowlton Gn HAYES BR2 167 J4
Knowl Wy BORE WD6 24 A4
Knowsley Av STHL UB1 84 B7
Knowsley Rd BTSEA SW11 128 E1
Knox Rd FSTGT E7 76 E5
Knox St CAMTN NW1 9 L2
Knoyle St NWCR SE14 112 B5
Kohat Rd WIM/MER SW19 147 F4
Koh-I-Noor Av BUSH WD23 22 A5
Kossuth St GNWCH SE10 113 H4
Kramer Ms ECT SW5 14 B8
Kreedman Wk HACK E8 * 74 C4
Kuala Gdns
STRHM/NOR SW16 149 F7
Kwesi Ms STRHM/NOR SW16 149 G4
Kydbrook Cl
STMC/STPC BR5 169 H6
Kylemore Cl EHAM E6 95 H1
Kylemore Rd
KIL/WHAMP NW6 2 A1
Kymberley Rd HRW HA1 * 48 E5
Kyme Rd ROM RM1 63 H5
Kynance Gdns STAN HA7 35 J7
Kynance Ms SKENS SW7 14 D4
Kynance Pl KENS W8 14 E4
Kynaston Av THHTH CR7 164 D4
Kynaston Cl
KTN/HRWW/WS HA3 34 D6
Kynaston Crs THHTH CR7 164 D4
Kynaston Rd BMLY BR1 152 E4
STNW/STAM N16 74 A2
THHTH CR7 164 D4
Kynaston Wd
KTN/HRWW/WS HA3 34 D6
Kynersley Cl CAR SM5 175 K2
Kynoch Rd UED N18 42 E4
Kyrle Rd BTSEA SW11 129 F5
Kyverdale Rd
STNW/STAM N16 56 B6

L

Laburnham Cl BAR EN5 26 D2
Laburnum Av DART DA1 139 F7
ED N9 42 A1
HCH RM12 81 J1
SUT SM1 175 J2
TOTM N17 41 K6
Laburnum Cl ALP/SUD HA0 68 C7
CHING E4 43 H5
PECK SE15 111 K6
Laburnum Ct STAN HA7 35 J3
Laburnum Crs SUN TW16 141 F7
Laburnum Gdns CROY/NA CR0 166 A6
Laburnum Gv
CDALE/KGS NW9 50 E6
HSLW TW3 122 E3
NWMAL KT3 160 A1
RSLP HA4 46 B5
STHL UB1 83 K3
WCHMH N21 41 J1
Laburnum Pl ELTH/MOT SE9 * 135 F4
Laburnum Rd HYS/HAR UB3 101 J3
MTCM CR4 163 F1
WIM/MER SW19 147 G6
Laburnum St BETH E2 7 L4
Laburnum Wy HAYES BR2 169 F6
STWL/WRAY TW19 120 C7
Lacebark Cl BFN/LL DA15 136 A6
Lacewing Cl PLSTW E13 94 E2
Lacey Cl ED N9 42 C1
Lacey Dr BCTR RM8 79 J2
EDGW HA8 36 A3
HPTN TW12 141 K7
Lacey Ms BOW E3 93 J1
Lackington St SDTCH EC2A 13 H2
Lacock Cl WIM/MER SW19 147 G5
Lacon Rd EDUL SE22 131 H3
Lacrosse Wy
STRHM/NOR SW16 148 D7
Lacy Rd PUT/ROE SW15 127 G3
Ladas Rd WNWD SE27 149 J4
Ladbroke Crs NTGHL W11 88 C5
Ladbroke Gdns NTGHL W11 88 D6
Ladbroke Gv NKENS W10 88 B3
NTGHL W11 88 D6
Ladbroke Ms NTGHL W11 88 C7
Ladbroke Rd EN EN1 30 B5
NTGHL W11 88 D7
Ladbroke Sq NTGHL W11 88 D6
Ladbroke Ter NTGHL W11 88 D6
Ladbroke Wk NTGHL W11 88 D7
Ladbrook Cl BMLY BR1 152 C5
PIN HA5 47 K4
Ladbrooke Crs SCUP DA14 155 K2
Ladbrook Rd SNWD SE25 164 E2
Ladderstile Ride
KUTN/CMB KT2 144 D4
Ladderswood Wy
FBAR/BDGN N11 40 C4
Lady Alesford Av STAN HA7 35 H4
Lady Booth Rd KUT/HW KT1 159 F1
Ladycroft Rd LEW SE13 132 E2
Ladycroft Wk STAN HA7 35 K7
Lady Forsdyke Wy
HOR/WEW KT19 172 C7
Ladygate La RSLP HA4 46 A5
Ladygrove CROY/NA CR0 179 G7
Lady Harewood Wy
HOR/WEW KT19 172 C7
Lady Hay WPK KT4 173 H1
Lady Margaret Rd KTTN NW5 72 C4
STHL UB1 83 K6
Ladymount WLGTN SM6 176 D3
Lady's Cl WATW WD18 21 G3
Ladyship Ter EDUL SE22 * 131 J6
Ladysmith Av EHAM E6 95 J1
GNTH/NBYPK IG2 60 D6
Ladysmith Cl MLHL NW7 37 J6
Ladysmith Rd CAN/RD E16 94 D2
ELTH/MOT SE9 135 F5
EN EN1 30 B1
KTN/HRWW/WS HA3 48 E1
TOTM N17 56 C1
Lady Somerset Rd KTTN NW5 72 B3
Ladywell Cl BROCKY SE4 132 D4
Ladywell Rd LEW SE13 132 D4
Ladywell St SRTFD E15 76 D7
Ladywell Water Tower
BROCKY SE4 * 132 C2
Ladywood Av STMC/STPC BR5 169 K4
Ladywood Rd SURB KT6 172 C1
Lafone Av FELT TW13 122 B7
Lafone St STHWK SE1 19 L1
Lagado Ms BERM/RHTH SE16 93 F7
Lagonda Wy DART DA1 139 F3
Laidlaw Dr WCHMH N21 29 F4
Laing Dean NTHLT UB5 65 G7
Laings Av MTCM CR4 162 E1
Lainlock Pl HSLW TW3 103 G7
Lainson St WAND/EARL SW18 127 K6
Lairdale Cl DUL SE21 130 D7
Lairs Cl HOLWY N7 * 72 E5
Laitwood Rd BAL SW12 129 G7
Lake Av BMLY BR1 152 E5
Lake Cl BCTR RM8 79 K2
Lakedale Rd
WOOL/PLUM SE18 115 K4
Lake Dr BUSH WD23 34 C1
Lakefield Rd WDGN N22 55 H1
Lake Gdns DAGE RM10 80 C4
RCHPK/HAM TW10 143 H2
WLGTN SM6 176 B2
Lakehall Gdns THHTH CR7 164 C4
Lakehall Rd THHTH CR7 164 C4
Lake House Rd WAN E11 76 E2
Lakehurst Rd HOR/WEW KT19 173 G4
Lakeland Cl
KTN/HRWW/WS HA3 34 D5
Lakenheath STHGT/OAK N14 28 D4
Lake Ri ROM RM1 63 H2
Lake Rd CHDH RM6 61 K3
CROY/NA CR0 179 H1
DAGW RM9 98 D2
LEY E10 57 K6
WIM/MER SW19 146 D4
Lakeside BECK BR3 166 E2
ENC/FH EN2 28 D3
HOR/WEW KT19 173 G5
WEA W13 85 J5
WLGTN SM6 176 B3
Lakeside Av REDBR IG4 59 H3
THMD SE28 97 G7
Lakeside Cl BFN/LL DA15 136 D4
RSLP HA4 46 B3
SNWD SE25 165 H1
Lakeside Crs EBAR EN4 27 K5
Lakeside Dr ESH/CLAY KT10 170 C5
HAYES BR2 181 J2
WLSDN NW10 86 B2
Lakeside Rd PLMGR N13 41 F3
WKENS W14 107 G2
Lakeside Wy WBLY HA9 68 C3
Lakes Rd HAYES BR2 181 G4
Lakeswood Rd
STMC/STPC BR5 169 G5
The Lake BUSH WD23 22 D7
Lake Vw EDGW HA8 36 B4
Lake View Est BOW E3 * 93 F1
Lakeview Rd WELL DA16 136 C3
WNWD SE27 149 G4
Lake View Ter UED N18 * 42 B3
Lakis Cl HAMP NW3 71 G3
Laleham Av MLHL NW7 37 F2
Laleham Ct SUT SM1 * 175 G4
Laleham Rd CAT SE6 133 F6
Lalor St FUL/PGN SW6 127 H1
Lambarde Av ELTH/MOT SE9 154 A3
Lamb Cl NTHLT UB5 83 J2
Lamberhurst Rd BCTR RM8 62 A7
WNWD SE27 149 G3
Lambert Av RCH/KEW TW9 125 H2
Lambert Ct BUSH WD23 21 H3
Lambert Jones Ms
BARB EC2Y * 12 E2
Lambert Rd
BRXS/STRHM SW2 129 K4
CAN/RD E16 95 F5
NFNCH/WDSPK N12 39 H4
Lambert's Pl CROY/NA CR0 164 E7
Lambert's Rd BRYLDS KT5 159 F4
Lambert St IS N1 6 A2
Lambert Wy
NFNCH/WDSPK N12 39 G4
Lambeth Br WEST SW1P 17 K5
Lambeth High St STHWK SE1 17 L6
Lambeth Hl BLKFR EC4V 12 E6
Lambeth Palace Rd
STHWK SE1 17 L4
Lambeth Rd CROY/NA CR0 164 B7
STHWK SE1 18 A4
Lambeth Wk LBTH SE11 17 M5
PECK SE15 131 G1
Lambkins Ms WALTH E17 58 A3
Lamb La HACK E8 74 D6
Lamble St KTTN NW5 72 A3
Lambley Rd DAGW RM9 79 H5
Lambolle Pl HAMP NW3 71 J5
Lambolle Rd HAMP NW3 71 J5
Lambourn Cl HNWL W7 104 A1
KTTN NW5 * 72 C3
SAND/SEL CR2 177 H7
Lambourne Av
WIM/MER SW19 146 D3
Lambourne Gdns BARK IG11 79 F6
CHING E4 43 J1
EN EN1 30 B1
Lambourne Gv
BERM/RHTH SE16 112 A4
KUT/HW KT1 159 J1
Lambourne Pl BKHTH/KID SE3 114 A7
Lambourne Rd BARK IG11 78 E6
GDMY/SEVK IG3 78 E1
WAN E11 58 A6
Lambourn Rd VX/NE SW8 129 G2
Lambrook Ter FUL/PGN SW6 107 H7
Lambs Cl ED N9 42 C1
Lamb's Conduit Pas
FSBYW WC1X 11 L2
Lamb's Conduit St
BMSBY WC1N 11 L1
Lambscroft Av ELTH/MOT SE9 153 G2
Lambs Meadow WFD IG8 59 H1
Lambs Ms IS N1 6 C4
Lamb's Pas STLK EC1Y 13 G1
Lambs Ter ED N9 * 41 K1
Lamb St WCHPL E1 13 L2
Lambs Wk ENC/FH EN2 29 J1
Lambton Pl NTGHL W11 * 88 D6
Lambton Rd ARCH N19 54 E7
RYNPK SW20 146 A7
Lamb Wk STHWK SE1 19 J2
Lamerock Rd BMLY BR1 152 D3
Lamerton Rd BARK/HLT IG6 60 B1
Lamerton St DEPT SE8 112 D5
Lamford Cl TOTM N17 41 K6
Lamington St HMSMTH W6 106 E3
Lamlash St LBTH SE11 18 C5
Lammas Av MTCM CR4 163 F1
Lammas La ESH/CLAY KT10 170 A3
Lammas Park Gdns EA W5 85 J7
Lammas Rd HOM E9 75 F6
LEY E10 75 G1
RCHPK/HAM TW10 143 J3
WATW WD18 21 G4
Lammermoor Rd BAL SW12 * 129 G6
Lamont Rd WBPTN SW10 108 C5
Lamont Road Pas
WBPTN SW10 * 108 C5
Lamorbey Cl BFN/LL DA15 155 F1
Lamorbey Pk BFN/LL DA15 * 136 C7
Lamorna Cl WALTH E17 58 A1
Lamorna Gv STAN HA7 35 K7
Lampard Gv STNW/STAM N16 56 B7
Lampern Sq BETH E2 * 92 C2
Lampeter Sq HMSMTH W6 107 H5
Lamplighter Cl WCHPL E1 92 E3
Lamplighters Cl DART DA1 139 J5
Lampmead Rd LEE/GVPK SE12 133 H4
Lamport Cl WOOL/PLUM SE18 114 E3
Lampton Av HSLW TW3 103 F7
Lampton House Cl
WIM/MER SW19 146 B3
Lampton Park Rd HSLW TW3 123 G1
Lampton Rd HSLW TW3 123 G1
Lamson Rd RAIN RM13 99 H3
Lanacre Av CDALE/KGS NW9 37 G7
EDGW HA8 37 F7
Lanadron Cl ISLW TW7 124 A1
Lanark Cl EA W5 85 J4
Lanark Pl MV/WKIL W9 2 F9
Lanark Rd MV/WKIL W9 2 E7
Lanbury Rd PECK SE15 132 A3
Lancashire Ct
MYFR/PKLN W1K 10 C6
Lancaster Av BARK IG11 78 E6
MTCM CR4 163 K3
WAN E11 59 F3
WIM/MER SW19 146 B4
WNWD SE27 149 H1
Lancaster Cl CDALE/KGS NW9 37 H6
HAYES BR2 167 J3
IS N1 7 K2
STWL/WRAY TW19 120 B5
TOTM N17 * 42 C6
WPK KT4 160 E6
Lancaster Ct BAY/PAD W2 8 F6
Lancaster Dr HAMP NW3 71 J5
HCH RM12 81 K4
POP/IOD E14 94 A7
Lancaster Garde BMLY BR1 168 D4
Lancaster Gdn KUTN/CMB KT2 143 K4
Lancaster Gdns
WIM/MER SW19 146 C4
Lancaster Ga BAY/PAD W2 8 E7
Lancaster Gv HAMP NW3 71 J5
Lancaster House
WOOL/PLUM SE18 * 114 D6
Lancaster Ms BAY/PAD W2 8 F6
RCHPK/HAM TW10 125 F5
WAND/EARL SW18 * 128 A4
Lancaster Pk
RCHPK/HAM TW10 125 F4
Lancaster Pl TPL/STR WC2R 11 L6
TWK TW1 124 B5
WIM/MER SW19 146 B4
Lancaster Rd EBAR EN4 27 H3
FBAR/BDGN N11 40 D5
FSBYPK N4 55 G6
FSTGT E7 76 E6
NKENS W10 88 B5
NTHLT UB5 66 C5
RYLN/HDSTN HA2 48 A4
SNWD SE25 165 G1
STHL UB1 83 J6
UED N18 42 B4
WALTH E17 57 F1
WAN E11 76 C1
WIM/MER SW19 146 B4
WLSDN NW10 69 H4
Lancaster Stables
HAMP NW3 * 71 J5
Lancaster St STHWK SE1 18 C2
Lancaster Ter BAY/PAD W2 9 G6
Lancaster Wk HYS/HAR UB3 82 A5
Lancaster Wy WPK KT4 161 F6
Lancaster West NTGHL W11 * 88 C5
Lancastrian Rd WLGTN SM6 176 E6
Lancefield St NKENS W10 88 D2
Lancell St STNW/STAM N16 74 A1
Lancelot Av ALP/SUD HA0 67 K3
Lancelot Crs ALP/SUD HA0 67 K3
Lancelot Gdns EBAR EN4 28 A6
Lancelot Pde ALP/SUD HA0 * 68 A4
Lancelot Pl SKENS SW7 15 L2
Lancelot Rd ALP/SUD HA0 67 K3
WELL DA16 136 B3
Lance Rd HRW HA1 48 C6
Lancer Sq KENS W8 14 C1
Lancey Cl CHARL SE7 114 C3
Lanchester Rd HGT N6 53 K4
Lanchester Wy NWCR SE14 111 K7
Lancing Gdns ED N9 30 B7
Lancing Rd CROY/NA CR0 164 A5
FELT TW13 140 D1
GNTH/NBYPK IG2 60 D5
WEA W13 85 H6
Lancing St CAMTN NW1 5 G8
Landale Gdns DART DA1 139 F7
Landau Ter HAYES BR2 181 J3
Landau Wy ERITH DA8 119 G4
Landcroft Rd EDUL SE22 131 G5
Landells Rd EDUL SE22 131 G5
Landford Rd PUT/ROE SW15 127 F2
Landgrove Rd
WIM/MER SW19 146 E4
Landleys Flds HOLWY N7 * 72 D4
Landmann Wy NWCR SE14 112 A5
Landon Pl KTBR SW1X 15 L3
Landons Cl POP/IOD E14 94 A7
Landor Rd BRXN/ST SW9 129 K2
Landor Wk SHB W12 106 D1
Landra Gdns WCHMH N21 29 H5
Landridge Rd FUL/PGN SW6 127 H1
Landrock Rd CEND/HSY/T N8 54 E5
Landscape Rd WFD IG8 45 F6
Landseer Av MNPK E12 78 A4
Landseer Cl EDGW HA8 50 C1
EMPK RM11 63 K7
WIM/MER SW19 147 G7
Landseer Rd ARCH N19 72 E2
EN EN1 30 C4
NWMAL KT3 160 A6
SUT SM1 174 E5
Lands' End BORE WD6 23 K5
Landstead Rd
WOOL/PLUM SE18 115 J6
Lane Ap MLHL NW7 * 38 C4
Lane Cl CRICK NW2 69 K2
Lane End BXLYHN DA7 137 J2
Lane Gdns BUSH WD23 22 E7
ESH/CLAY KT10 171 F6
Lane Ms MNPK E12 77 K2
Lanercost Gdns
STHGT/OAK N14 28 E5
Lanercost Rd
BRXS/STRHM SW2 149 G1
Laneside CHST BR7 154 B4
EDGW HA8 36 E4
Laneside Av BCTR RM8 62 B6
The Lane BKHTH/KID SE3 133 K2
STJWD NW8 2 E6
Laneway PUT/ROE SW15 126 E4
Lanfranc Rd BOW E3 93 G1
Lanfrey Pl WKENS W14 107 J4
Langbourne Av HGT N6 72 A1
Langbourne Wy
ESH/CLAY KT10 171 F5
Langbrook Rd BKHTH/KID SE3 134 C2
Langcroft Cl CAR SM5 175 K2
Langdale Av MTCM CR4 162 E2
Langdale Cl BCTR RM8 61 J7
MORT/ESHN SW14 125 J3
WALW SE17 18 E9
Langdale Crs BXLYHN DA7 117 H7
Langdale Dr YEAD UB4 82 C1
Langdale Gdns HCH RM12 81 J4
Langdale Pde MTCM CR4 * 162 E1
Langdale Rd GNWCH SE10 113 F6
THHTH CR7 164 B3
Langdale St WCHPL E1 * 92 D5
Langdale Ter BORE WD6 * 25 F2
Langdon Ct WLSDN NW10 69 G7
Langdon Crs EHAM E6 96 A1
Langdon Dr CDALE/KGS NW9 50 E7
Langdon House
WOOL/PLUM SE18 * 114 D6
Langdon Pk TEDD TW11 143 J6
Langdon Park Rd HGT N6 54 B6
Langdon Pl MORT/ESHN SW14 125 K2
Langdon Rd EHAM E6 78 A7
HAYES BR2 168 A2
MRDN SM4 162 B4
Langdon Shaw SCUP DA14 155 F4
Langdon Wk MRDN SM4 162 B4
Langdon Wy STHWK SE1 111 H3
Langford Cl HACK E8 74 C4
SEVS/STOTM N15 56 A5
STJWD NW8 2 F5
Langford Crs EBAR EN4 27 K3
Langford Gn CMBW SE5 131 F2
Langford Pl SCUP DA14 155 G2
STJWD NW8 2 F6
Langford Rd EBAR EN4 27 K3
FUL/PGN SW6 128 A1
WFD IG8 45 G5
Langfords BKHH IG9 45 H1
Langham Cl HAYES BR2 181 J1
Langham Ct RSLP HA4 * 65 F4
Langham Dr GDMY/SEVK IG3 61 H5
Langham Gdns ALP/SUD HA0 67 J1
EDGW HA8 36 E6
RCHPK/HAM TW10 143 J3
WCHMH N21 29 G4
WEA W13 85 H6
Langham House Cl
RCHPK/HAM TW10 143 K3
Langham Pde
SEVS/STOTM N15 * 55 H2
Langham Park Pl HAYES BR2 167 J3
Langham Pl CHSWK W4 106 B5
REGST W1B 10 D3
SEVS/STOTM N15 55 H2
Langham Rd EDGW HA8 36 E5
RYNPK SW20 146 A7
SEVS/STOTM N15 55 H2
TEDD TW11 143 H4
Langham St GTPST W1W 10 E3
REGST W1B 10 D3
Langhedge Cl UED N18 42 B5
Langhedge La UED N18 42 B4
Langholm Cl BAL SW12 129 J6
Langholme BUSH WD23 22 C7
Langhorn Dr WHTN TW2 123 K6
Langhorne Rd DAGE RM10 80 C6
Langland Ct NTHWD HA6 32 A6
Langland Crs STAN HA7 49 K1
Langland Dr PIN HA5 33 J6
Langland Gdns CROY/NA CR0 179 H1
HAMP NW3 71 F4
Langler Rd WLSDN NW10 88 A1
Langley Av RSLP HA4 65 F1
SURB KT6 158 E7
WPK KT4 174 B1
Langley Ct BECK BR3 * 166 E3
COVGDN WC2E 11 J6
Langley Crs DAGW RM9 79 J6
EDGW HA8 36 E2
HYS/HAR UB3 101 J6
WAN E11 59 F6
Langley Dr ACT W3 105 J1
WAN E11 59 F6
Langley Gdns DAGW RM9 79 K6
STMC/STPC BR5 169 G5
Langley Gv NWMAL KT3 160 A1
Langley La VX/NE SW8 17 K9
Langley Pk MLHL NW7 37 G5
Langley Park Rd BELMT SM2 175 G5
Langley Pl WPK KT4 174 B1
Langley Rd BECK BR3 166 A3
ISLW TW7 124 A1
SAND/SEL CR2 179 F7
SURB KT6 159 F6
WELL DA16 116 D5
WIM/MER SW19 146 D7
Langley St LSQ/SEVD WC2H 11 J5
Langley Wy WWKM BR4 167 G7
Langley Wd BECK BR3 * 167 H4
Langmead Dr BUSH WD23 22 D7
Langmead St WNWD SE27 149 H3
Langport Ct WOT/HER KT12 156 B7
Langridge Ms HPTN TW12 141 K5
Langroyd Rd TOOT SW17 147 K1
Langside Av PUT/ROE SW15 126 D3
Langside Crs STHGT/OAK N14 40 D2
Langstone Wy MLHL NW7 38 B6
Langston Hughes Cl
HNHL SE24 * 130 C3
Lang St WCHPL E1 92 E3
Langthorn Ct LOTH EC2R * 13 H4
Langthorne Rd WAN E11 76 B2
Langthorne St FUL/PGN SW6 107 G7
Langton Av EHAM E6 96 A2
TRDG/WHET N20 27 G6
Langton Cl FSBYW WC1X 5 M8
Langton Gv NTHWD HA6 32 A4
Langton Ri EDUL SE22 131 J6
Langton Rd BRXN/ST SW9 110 C6
CRICK NW2 70 A2
E/WMO/HCT KT8 157 H4
KTN/HRWW/WS HA3 34 C6
Langton St WBPTN SW10 108 B5
Langton Vis TOTM N17 * 42 C7
Langton Wy BKHTH/KID SE3 113 K6
CROY/NA CR0 178 A3
Langtry Rd KIL/WHAMP NW6 2 C4
NTHLT UB5 83 H1
Langtry Wk STJWD NW8 2 F2
Langwood Cha TEDD TW11 143 J5
Langworth Dr YEAD UB4 83 F5
Lanhill Rd MV/WKIL W9 2 A9
Lanier Rd LEW SE13 133 F5
Lanigan Dr HSLW TW3 123 G4
Lankaster Gdns EFNCH N2 39 H7
Lankers Dr RYLN/HDSTN HA2 47 K5
Lankton Cl BECK BR3 152 A7
Lannock Rd HYS/HAR UB3 82 D7
Lannoy Rd ELTH/MOT SE9 135 H7
Lanrick Rd POP/IOD E14 94 B4
Lanridge Rd ABYW SE2 116 E2
Lansbury Av BARK IG11 79 G6
CHDH RM6 62 A4
EBED/NFELT TW14 122 A5
UED N18 41 K4
Lansbury Cl WLSDN NW10 68 E4
Lansbury Crs DART DA1 139 K4
Lansbury Dr YEAD UB4 82 D4
Lansbury Gdns POP/IOD E14 * 94 B5
Lansbury Wy UED N18 42 A4
Lanscombe Wk VX/NE SW8 * 109 K6
Lansdell Rd MTCM CR4 163 F1
Lansdown Cl WOT/HER KT12 156 B7
Lansdowne Av BXLYHN DA7 116 D6
ORP BR6 169 G7
Lansdowne Cl BRYLDS KT5 172 D1
TWK TW1 124 A7
Lansdowne Copse WPK KT4 * 173 J1
Lansdowne Ct WPK KT4 173 J1
Lansdowne Crs NTGHL W11 88 C6
Lansdowne Dr HACK E8 74 C6
Lansdowne Gdns VX/NE SW8 109 K7
Lansdowne Gn VX/NE SW8 109 K6
Lansdowne Gv WLSDN NW10 69 G3
Lansdowne Hl WNWD SE27 149 H2
Lansdowne La CHARL SE7 114 C4
Lansdowne Ms CHARL SE7 114 C4
NTGHL W11 88 D7
Lansdowne Pl NRWD SE19 150 B6
STHWK SE1 19 H3
Lansdowne Ri NTGHL W11 88 C6
Lansdowne Rd BMLY BR1 152 E6
CHING E4 43 J1
CROY/NA CR0 164 E7
FNCH N3 38 D6
GDMY/SEVK IG3 61 F7
HACK E8 74 C5
HOR/WEW KT19 172 E6
HSLW TW3 123 G2
MUSWH N10 54 C1
NTGHL W11 88 C6
RYNPK SW20 146 A6

STAN HA7 35 J5
SWFD E18 58 E2
TOTM N17 42 C7
WALTH E17 57 J5
WAN E11 76 D1
Lansdowne Ter BMSBY WC1N 11 K1
Lansdowne Wk NTGHL W11 88 C7
Lansdowne Wy VX/NE SW8 109 K7
Lansdowne Wood Cl
WNWD SE27 149 H2
Lansdown Rd FSTGT E7 77 G6
SCUP DA14 155 H2
Lansfield Av UED N18 42 C3
Lantern Cl ALP/SUD HA0 67 K4
PUT/ROE SW15 126 D3
Lanterns Ct POP/IOD E14 112 D2
Lantern Wy WDR/YW UB7 100 B1
Lant St STHWK SE1 18 E1
Lanvanor Rd PECK SE15 131 K1
Lapford Cl MV/WKIL W9 * 88 D3
Lapse Wood Wk FSTH SE23 131 J7
Lapstone Gdns
KTN/HRWW/WS HA3 49 J5
Lapwing Cl ERITH DA8 * 118 E6
Lapwing Ter FSTGT E7 77 H4
Lapwing Wy YEAD UB4 83 H5
Lapworth Ct BAY/PAD W2 8 D2
Lara Cl CHSGTN KT9 172 A6
LEW SE13 133 F5
Larbert Rd STRHM/NOR SW16 148 C7
Larch Av ACT W3 87 G7
Larch Cl BAL SW12 148 B1
DEPT SE8 112 C5
FBAR/BDGN N11 40 A6
PLSTW E13 95 G3
Larch Crs HOR/WEW KT19 172 D5
YEAD UB4 83 G3
Larch Dr CHSWK W4 * 105 H4
Larches Av MORT/ESHN SW14 126 A3
The Larches BUSH WD23 21 J4
PLMGR N13 41 J2
Larch Gv BFN/LL DA15 136 A7
Larch Rd CRICK NW2 70 A3
DART DA1 139 G7
LEY E10 75 J1
Larch Tree Wy CROY/NA CR0 179 J2
Larch Wy HAYES BR2 169 F6
Larchwood Rd
ELTH/MOT SE9 154 B1
Larcombe Cl CROY/NA CR0 178 B3
Larcom St WALW SE17 18 F6
Larden Rd ACT W3 106 B1
Largewood Av SURB KT6 172 C1
Larkbere Rd SYD SE26 151 G3
Larken Cl BUSH WD23 22 C7
Larken Dr BUSH WD23 22 C7
Larkfield Av
KTN/HRWW/WS HA3 49 H2
Larkfield Rd RCH/KEW TW9 125 F3
SCUP DA14 155 F2
Larkhall La CLAP SW4 129 J1
Larkhall Ri CLAP SW4 129 H2
Larkham Cl FELT TW13 140 C2
Larkhill Ter
WOOL/PLUM SE18 * 115 F6
Lark Rw BETH E2 74 E7
Larks Gv BARK IG11 78 E6
Larkshall Crs CHING E4 44 A3
Larkshall Rd CHING E4 44 A4
Larkspur Cl CDALE/KGS NW9 50 D4
TOTM N17 41 K6
Larkspur Gv EDGW HA8 36 E3
Larkspur Wy HOR/WEW KT19 172 E4
Larkswood Cl ERITH DA8 118 D7
Larkswood Ri PIN HA5 47 G3
Larkswood Rd CHING E4 43 J3
Lark Wy CAR SM5 162 D6
Larkway Cl CDALE/KGS NW9 51 F3
Larnach Rd HMSMTH W6 107 G5
Larne Rd RSLP HA4 46 D6
Larner Rd ERITH DA8 118 B6
Larpent Av PUT/ROE SW15 127 F4
Larwood Cl GFD/PVL UB6 66 D4
Lascelles Av HRW HA1 48 D6
Lascelles Cl WAN E11 76 B1
Lascott's Rd WDGN N22 41 F5
Lassa Rd ELTH/MOT SE9 134 D4
Lassell St GNWCH SE10 113 G4
Lasseter Pl BKHTH/KID SE3 113 H5
Latchett Rd SWFD E18 45 F7
Latchingdon Gdns WFD IG8 45 J5
Latchmere Cl
RCHPK/HAM TW10 144 A4
Latchmere La KUTN/CMB KT2 144 B5
Latchmere Rd BTSEA SW11 128 E1
KUTN/CMB KT2 144 A5
Latchmere St BTSEA SW11 128 E1
Lateward Rd BTFD TW8 104 E5
Latham Cl EHAM E6 95 J5
Latham Rd BXLYHS DA6 137 H4
TWK TW1 124 A6
Latham's Wy CROY/NA CR0 164 A7
Lathkill Cl EN EN1 30 C6
Lathom Rd EHAM E6 77 K6
Latimer Av EHAM E6 77 K7
Latimer Cl PIN HA5 33 G7
WATW WD18 20 C6
WPK KT4 173 K3
Latimer Gdns PIN HA5 33 G7
Latimer Pl NKENS W10 88 A5
Latimer Rd BAR EN5 27 F2
CROY/NA CR0 * 177 H2
FSTGT E7 77 F3
NKENS W10 88 A4
SEVS/STOTM N15 56 A5
TEDD TW11 143 F4
WIM/MER SW19 147 F5
Latona Rd PECK SE15 111 H5
Lattimer Pl CHSWK W4 106 B6
Latton Cl ESH/CLAY KT10 170 B3
WOT/HER KT12 156 E6
Latymer Gdns FNCH N3 * 52 C1
Latymer Rd ED N9 42 B1
Latymer Wy ED N9 41 K1
Laubin Cl TWK TW1 124 C3
Lauder Cl NTHLT UB5 83 H1
Lauderdale Dr
RCHPK/HAM TW10 143 K2
Lauderdale Pde
MV/WKIL W9 * 2 C8
Lauderdale Pl BARB EC2Y * 12 F3
Lauderdale Rd MV/WKIL W9 2 D8
Laud St CROY/NA CR0 177 J2
LBTH SE11 17 L7
Laughton Rd NTHLT UB5 83 H1
Launcelot Rd BMLY BR1 152 E3
Launcelot St STHWK SE1 18 A2
Launceston Gdns
GFD/PVL UB6 67 J7
Launceston Pl KENS W8 14 E3
Launceston Rd GFD/PVL UB6 67 J7
Launch St POP/IOD E14 113 F2
Launders Ga ACT W3 * 105 J1
Laundress La
STNW/STAM N16 74 C2
Laundry Ms FSTH SE23 132 A6
Laundry Rd HMSMTH W6 107 H5
Laura Cl EN EN1 30 A4
WAN E11 59 G4
Lauradale Rd EFNCH N2 53 K3
Laura Pl CLPT E5 74 E3
Laura Ter FSBYPK N4 * 73 H1
Laurel Av TWK TW1 124 A7
Laurel Bank
NFNCH/WDSPK N12 * 39 G3
Laurel Bank Gdns
FUL/PGN SW6 127 J1
Laurel Cl BFN/LL DA15 155 G2
DART DA1 139 F7
OXHEY WD19 21 H6
TOOT SW17 147 J4
Laurel Crs CROY/NA CR0 179 J2
ROMW/RG RM7 63 G7
Laurel Dr WCHMH N21 29 G6
Laurel Gdns BMLY BR1 168 D3
CHING E4 31 K6
HNWL W7 84 E7
HSLWW TW4 122 D3
MLHL NW7 37 F2
Laurel Gv PGE/AN SE20 150 D6
SYD SE26 151 F4
Laurel La WDR/YW UB7 100 B3
Laurel Pk KTN/HRWW/WS HA3 35 F6
Laurel Rd BARN SW13 126 D1
HPTN TW12 142 D4
RYNPK SW20 145 K7
The Laurels BRXN/ST SW9 * 110 C6
BUSH WD23 * 34 E1
Laurel St HACK E8 74 B5
Laurel Vw NFNCH/WDSPK N12 39 F2
Laurel Vls HNWL W7 * 103 K1
Laurel Wy SWFD E18 58 D3
TRDG/WHET N20 38 E2
Laurence Ms SHB W12 106 D1
Laurence Pountney Hl
CANST EC4R 13 G6
Laurence Pountney La
CANST EC4R 13 G6
Laurie Gv NWCR SE14 112 B7
Laurie Rd HNWL W7 84 E4
Laurier Rd CROY/NA CR0 165 G6
KTTN NW5 72 B2
Laurimel Cl STAN HA7 35 H5
Laurino Pl BUSH WD23 34 C1
Lauriston Rd HOM E9 75 F6
WIM/MER SW19 146 B5
Lausanne Rd CEND/HSY/T N8 55 G3
PECK SE15 111 K7
Lavender Av CDALE/KGS NW9 50 E7
MTCM CR4 147 J7
WPK KT4 174 A2
Lavender Cl CAR SM5 176 A3
CHEL SW3 108 C5
CHING E4 43 J3
HAYES BR2 168 D5
Lavender Ct E/WMO/HCT KT8 157 G2
Lavender Gdns BTSEA SW11 128 E3
KTN/HRWW/WS HA3 34 E5
Lavender Gv HACK E8 74 C6
MTCM CR4 147 J7
Lavender Hl BTSEA SW11 128 E2
Lavender Pl IL IG1 78 B4
Lavender Ri WDR/YW UB7 100 D1
Lavender Rd
BERM/RHTH SE16 93 G7
BTSEA SW11 128 C2
CROY/NA CR0 164 A5
HOR/WEW KT19 172 D4
SUT SM1 175 H3
WLGTN SM6 176 A4
Lavender Sweep BTSEA SW11 128 E3
Lavender Ter BTSEA SW11 * 128 D2
Lavender V WLGTN SM6 176 D5
Lavender Wk BTSEA SW11 128 E3
Lavender Wy CROY/NA CR0 166 A5
Lavengro Rd WNWD SE27 149 J1
Lavenham Rd
WAND/EARL SW18 146 D1
Lavernock Rd BXLYHN DA7 137 H1
Lavers Rd STNW/STAM N16 74 A2
Laverstoke Gdns
PUT/ROE SW15 126 C6
Laverton Ms ECT SW5 * 14 D6
Laverton Pl ECT SW5 14 D6
Lavidge Rd ELTH/MOT SE9 153 J1
Lavina Gv IS N1 5 L5
Lavington Cl HOM E9 75 H5
Lavington Rd CROY/NA CR0 177 F2
WEA W13 85 H7
Lavington St STHWK SE1 12 D9
Lavinia Rd DART DA1 139 J5
Lawdon Gdns CROY/NA CR0 177 H3
Lawford Gdns DART DA1 139 F4
Lawford Rd CHSWK W4 105 K6
IS N1 7 J2
KTTN NW5 72 C5
Lawless St POP/IOD E14 * 93 K6
Lawley Rd STHGT/OAK N14 28 B6
Lawley St CLPT E5 74 E3
Lawn Cl BMLY BR1 153 F6
EN EN1 30 B6
NWMAL KT3 160 B1
RSLP HA4 64 D2
Lawn Crs RCH/KEW TW9 125 H1
Lawn Farm Gv CHDH RM6 62 A3
Lawn Gdns HNWL W7 84 E7
Lawn House Cl POP/IOD E14 113 F1
Lawn La VX/NE SW8 17 K9
Lawn Rd BECK BR3 151 H6
HAMP NW3 71 K4
Lawns Ct WBLY HA9 * 68 C1
The Lawns BELMT SM2 174 C6
BKHTH/KID SE3 * 133 J2
CHING E4 43 J4
NRWD SE19 149 K7
PIN HA5 34 B6
SCUP DA14 155 H3
Lawnswood BAR EN5 * 26 C4
Lawn Ter BKHTH/KID SE3 133 J2
The Lawn NWDGN UB2 103 F4
Lawn V PIN HA5 47 H1
Lawrence Av MLHL NW7 37 G3
MNPK E12 78 A3
NWMAL KT3 160 A5
PLMGR N13 41 H3
WALTH E17 43 F7
WLSDN NW10 69 F7
Lawrence Blds
STNW/STAM N16 74 B2
Lawrence Campe Cl
TRDG/WHET N20 39 H2
Lawrence Cl SEVS/STOTM N15 56 A3
SHB W12 87 K6
Lawrence Ct MLHL NW7 37 G4
OXHEY WD19 * 33 H2
Lawrence Crs DAGE RM10 80 D2
EDGW HA8 50 C1
Lawrence Dr HGDN/ICK UB10 64 A3
Lawrence Gdns MLHL NW7 37 H2
Lawrence Hl CHING E4 43 J1
Lawrence Hill Gdns DART DA1 139 F5
Lawrence Hill Rd DART DA1 139 F5
Lawrence La CITYW EC2V 12 F5
Lawrence Pde ISLW TW7 * 124 C2
Lawrence Pl IS N1 5 K3
Lawrence Rd EA W5 104 D3
EHAM E6 77 J7
ERITH DA8 117 J6
GPK RM2 63 K4
HPTN TW12 141 K6
HSLWW TW4 122 B3
PIN HA5 47 H4
PLSTW E13 77 F7
RCHPK/HAM TW10 143 J3
SEVS/STOTM N15 56 A2
SNWD SE25 165 G3
UED N18 42 D3
WWKM BR4 180 E3
YEAD UB4 82 A1
Lawrence St CAN/RD E16 94 D4
CHEL SW3 108 D5
MLHL NW7 37 H3
Lawrence Wy WLSDN NW10 68 E2
Lawrence Yd
SEVS/STOTM N15 56 A3
Lawrie Park Av SYD SE26 150 D4
Lawrie Park Crs SYD SE26 150 D4
Lawrie Park Gdns SYD SE26 150 D4
Lawrie Park Rd SYD SE26 150 E5
Laws Cl SNWD SE25 164 E3
Lawson Cl CAN/RD E16 95 G4
IL IG1 78 D4
WIM/MER SW19 146 B2
Lawson Gdns DART DA1 139 G4
PIN HA5 47 F2
Lawson Rd DART DA1 139 G3
STHL UB1 83 K3
Law St STHWK SE1 19 H3
Lawton Rd BOW E3 93 G2
EBAR EN4 27 H2
LEY E10 58 A7
Laxcon Cl WLSDN NW10 69 F4
Laxley Cl CMBW SE5 110 C6
Laxton Pl CAMTN NW1 4 D9
Layard Rd BERM/RHTH SE16 111 J3
THHTH CR7 164 E1
Layard Sq BERM/RHTH SE16 111 J3
Laycock St IS N1 73 G5
Layer Gdns ACT W3 86 C6
Layfield Cl HDN NW4 51 K6
Layfield Crs HDN NW4 51 K6
Layfield Rd HDN NW4 51 K6
Layhams Rd WWKM BR4 180 C3
Laymarsh Cl BELV DA17 117 G2
Laymead Cl NTHLT UB5 65 J5
Laystall St FSBYW WC1X 12 A1
Layton Crs CROY/NA CR0 177 G4
Layton Pl RCH/KEW TW9 105 H7
Layton Rd BTFD TW8 104 E4
HSLW TW3 123 G3
Layzell Wk ELTH/MOT SE9 134 C7
Lazenby Ct COVGDN WC2E * 11 J6
Leabank Cl HRW HA1 66 E2
Leabank Sq HOM E9 75 J5
Leabank Vw SEVS/STOTM N15 56 C5
Leabourne Rd
STNW/STAM N16 56 C5
Lea Bridge Rd LEY E10 75 F1
WALTH E17 58 A4
Lea Cl BUSH WD23 22 B4
WHTN TW2 122 E6
Lea Cots MTCM CR4 * 163 F1
Lea Crs RSLP HA4 64 D3
Leacroft Av BAL SW12 128 E6
Leacroft Cl WCHMH N21 41 H1
Leadale Av CHING E4 43 J1
Leadale Rd STNW/STAM N16 56 C5
Leadbeaters Cl
FBAR/BDGN N11 39 K4
Leadenhall Pl BANK EC3V 13 J5
Leadenhall St BANK EC3V 13 J5
Leader Av MNPK E12 78 A4
The Leadings WBLY HA9 68 E2
Leaf Cl NTHWD HA6 32 B6
THDIT KT7 157 K4
Leaf Gv WNWD SE27 149 G4
Leafield Cl STRHM/NOR SW16 149 H5
Leafield Rd RYNPK SW20 161 J2
SUT SM1 174 E1
Leafy Gv HAYES BR2 181 G4
Leafy Oak Rd LEE/GVPK SE12 153 G3
Leafy Wy CROY/NA CR0 178 B1
Lea Gdns WBLY HA9 68 B4
Leagrave St CLPT E5 74 E2
Lea Hall Gdns LEY E10 * 57 J7
Lea Hall Rd LEY E10 57 J7
Leahurst Rd LEW SE13 133 G4
Leake St STHWK SE1 17 M1
Lealand Rd SEVS/STOTM N15 56 B5
Leaming Cl MNPK E12 77 J4
Leamington Av BMLY BR1 153 G4
MRDN SM4 161 J3
WALTH E17 57 J4
Leamington Cl BMLY BR1 153 G3
HSLW TW3 123 H4
Leamington Crs
RYLN/HDSTN HA2 65 J2
Leamington Gdns
GDMY/SEVK IG3 79 F1
Leamington Pk ACT W3 87 F4
Leamington Pl YEAD UB4 82 D3
Leamington Rd NWDGN UB2 102 C3
Leamington Road Vls
NTGHL W11 88 D4
Leamore St HMSMTH W6 106 E3
Leamouth Rd EHAM E6 95 J5
POP/IOD E14 94 B5
Leander Rd BRXS/STRHM SW2 130 A5
NTHLT UB5 84 A1
THHTH CR7 164 A3
Learner Dr RYLN/HDSTN HA2 66 A1
Lea Rd BECK BR3 166 D1
NWDGN UB2 102 D3
Learoyd Gdns EHAM E6 96 A6
Leas Cl CHSGTN KT9 172 B6
Leas Dl ELTH/MOT SE9 154 A2
Leas Gn CHST BR7 155 F5
Leaside Av MUSWH N10 54 A2
Leaside Rd CLPT E5 56 E7
Leasowes Rd LEY E10 57 J7
The Leas BUSH WD23 21 K1
Leathart Cl HCH RM12 81 K6
Leatherbottle Gn
ERITHM DA18 117 G2
Leather Cl MTCM CR4 163 F1
Leatherdale St WCHPL E1 * 93 F2
Leather Gdns SRTFD E15 76 C7
Leatherhead Cl
STNW/STAM N16 56 A7
Leatherhead Rd CHSGTN KT9 171 K6
Leather La HCIRC EC1N 12 A2
Leathermarket Ct STHWK SE1 19 J2
Leathermarket St STHWK SE1 19 J2
Leather Rd
BERM/RHTH SE16 * 112 A3
Leathersellers Cl BAR EN5 * 26 C2
Leather St WAP E1W 93 F6
Leathsale Rd
RYLN/HDSTN HA2 66 B2
Leathwaite Rd BTSEA SW11 128 E3
Leathwell Rd DEPT SE8 132 E1
Lea V DART DA1 138 A3
Lea Valley Rd CHING E4 31 H5
Lea Valley Wk CLPT E5 56 D6
UED N18 43 F3
Leaveland Cl BECK BR3 166 D3
Leaver Gdns GFD/PVL UB6 84 D1
Leavesden Rd STAN HA7 35 G5
Leaway CLPT E5 * 56 E7
Lebanon Av FELT TW13 141 H4
Lebanon Gdns
WAND/EARL SW18 127 K5
Lebanon Pk TWK TW1 124 C6
Lebanon Rd CROY/NA CR0 165 F7
WAND/EARL SW18 127 K4
Lebrun Sq BKHTH/KID SE3 134 A3
Lechmere Ap WFD IG8 59 G1
Lechmere Rd CRICK NW2 69 K5
Leckford Rd
WAND/EARL SW18 147 G1
Leckhampton Pl
BRXS/STRHM SW2 130 B6
Leckwith Av ABYW SE2 117 F5
Lecky St SKENS SW7 15 G7
Leconfield Av BARN SW13 126 C2
Leconfield Rd HBRY N5 73 K3
Leda Rd WOOL/PLUM SE18 114 E2
Ledbury Ms North
NTGHL W11 8 A6
Ledbury Ms West NTGHL W11 8 A6
Ledbury Rd CROY/NA CR0 177 J3
NTGHL W11 88 D5
Ledbury St PECK SE15 111 H6
Ledrington Rd NRWD SE19 150 B5
Ledway Dr WBLY HA9 50 B6
Lee Av CHDH RM6 62 A5
Leechcroft Av BFN/LL DA15 136 A4
Leechcroft Rd WLGTN SM6 176 A2
Lee Church St LEW SE13 133 H3
Lee Cl WALTH E17 43 F7
Lee Conservancy Rd HOM E9 75 H4
Leecroft Rd BAR EN5 26 C3
Leeds Rd IL IG1 60 D7
Leeds St UED N18 42 C4
Lee High Rd LEW SE13 133 G3
Leeke St FSBYW WC1X 5 L7
Leeland Rd WEA W13 85 G7
Leeland Ter WEA W13 85 G7
Leeland Wy WLSDN NW10 69 G3
Leemount Cl HDN NW4 * 52 B3
Lee Pk BKHTH/KID SE3 133 J3
Lee Park Wy ED N9 43 G2
UED N18 43 F4
Lee Rd BKHTH/KID SE3 133 J2
EN EN1 30 C5
GFD/PVL UB6 67 J7
MLHL NW7 38 B6
WIM/MER SW19 147 F7
Lees Av NTHWD HA6 32 D7
Leeside BAR EN5 26 C4
Leeside Crs GLDGN NW11 52 C5
Leeside Rd TOTM N17 42 D5
Leeson Rd HNHL SE24 * 130 B4
Leesons Hl CHST BR7 169 K2
Lees Pl MYFR/PKLN W1K 10 A6
The Lees CROY/NA CR0 179 H1
Lee St HACK E8 7 L3
Lee Ter BKHTH/KID SE3 133 H2
The Lee NTHWD HA6 32 D4
Leeward Gdns
WIM/MER SW19 146 C5
Leeway DEPT SE8 112 C4
Leeway Cl PIN HA5 33 K6
The Leeways CHEAM SM3 * 174 C5
Leewood Cl LEE/GVPK SE12 133 J5
Lefevre Wk BOW E3 75 H7
Leffern Rd SHB W12 106 D1
Lefroy Rd SHB W12 106 C1
Left Side STHGT/OAK N14 * 28 D7
Legard Rd HBRY N5 73 H2
Legatt Rd ELTH/MOT SE9 134 C4
Leggatt Rd SRTFD E15 94 A1
Legge St LEW SE13 133 F4
Leghorn Rd WLSDN NW10 87 J1
WOOL/PLUM SE18 115 J4
Legion Cl IS N1 6 B1
Legion Ct MRDN SM4 161 K5
Legion Ter BOW E3 75 J7
Legion Wy
NFNCH/WDSPK N12 39 J6
Legon Av ROMW/RG RM7 62 E7
Legrace Av HSLWW TW4 122 C1
Leicester Av MTCM CR4 163 K3
Leicester Cl WPK KT4 174 A3
Leicester Gdns
GDMY/SEVK IG3 60 E6
Leicester Pl LSQ/SEVD WC2H * 11 H6
Leicester Rd BAR EN5 27 F4
CROY/NA CR0 165 F6
EFNCH N2 53 J2
WAN E11 59 F4
WLSDN NW10 69 F6
Leicester Sq LSQ/SEVD WC2H 11 H7
Leicester St LSQ/SEVD WC2H 11 H6
Leigham Av
STRHM/NOR SW16 148 E2
Leigham Cl STRHM/NOR SW16 149 G2
Leigham Court Rd
STRHM/NOR SW16 149 F2
Leigham Dr ISLW TW7 103 K6
Leigham Hall Pde
STRHM/NOR SW16 * 148 E2
Leigham V STRHM/NOR SW16 149 G2
Leigh Av REDBR IG4 59 H3
Leigh Cl NWMAL KT3 160 A3
Leigh Ct BORE WD6 * 25 F1
RYLN/HDSTN HA2 * 48 E7
Leigh Crs CROY/NA CR0 179 K6
Leigh Gdns WLSDN NW10 88 A1
Leigh Hunt Dr
STHGT/OAK N14 28 D7
Leigh Orchard Cl
STRHM/NOR SW16 149 F2
Leigh Pl FELT TW13 122 B7
WELL DA16 136 B1
Leigh Rd EHAM E6 78 A6
HBRY N5 73 H3
HSLW TW3 123 J3
LEY E10 58 A6
Leigh Rodd OXHEY WD19 33 J2
Leigh St STPAN WC1H 5 J9
The Leigh KUTN/CMB KT2 145 G5
Leighton Av MNPK E12 78 A4
PIN HA5 47 J2
Leighton Cl EDGW HA8 50 C1
Leighton Crs KTTN NW5 72 C4
Leighton Gdns WLSDN NW10 87 K1
Leighton Gv KTTN NW5 72 C4
Leighton Pl KTTN NW5 72 C4
Leighton Rd EN EN1 30 B4
KTN/HRWW/WS HA3 48 D1
KTTN NW5 72 C4
WEA W13 104 B1
Leighton St CROY/NA CR0 164 C7
Leila Parnell Pl CHARL SE7 114 B5
Leinster Av MORT/ESHN SW14 125 K2
Leinster Gdns BAY/PAD W2 8 E5
Leinster Ms BAY/PAD W2 8 E7
Leinster Pl BAY/PAD W2 8 E5
Leinster Rd MUSWH N10 54 B3
Leinster Sq BAY/PAD W2 8 B6
Leinster Ter BAY/PAD W2 8 E6
Leisure Wy
NFNCH/WDSPK N12 39 H6
Leith Cl CDALE/KGS NW9 51 F7
Leithcote Gdns
STRHM/NOR SW16 149 F3
Leithcote Pth
STRHM/NOR SW16 149 F2
Leith Hl STMC/STPC BR5 155 G7
Leith Rd WDGN N22 41 H7
Leith Towers BELMT SM2 * 175 F6
Leith Yd KIL/WHAMP NW6 * 2 B3
Lela Av HSLWW TW4 122 B1
Lelitia Cl HACK E8 74 C7
Leman St WCHPL E1 13 M5
Lemark Cl STAN HA7 35 J5
Le May Av LEE/GVPK SE12 153 F2
Lemmon Rd GNWCH SE10 113 H5
Lemna Rd WAN E11 58 C6
Lemonwell Dr ELTH/MOT SE9 135 G4
Lemsford Cl SEVS/STOTM N15 56 C5
Lemsford Ct BORE WD6 24 E3
Lena Crs ED N9 42 E1
Lena Gdns HMSMTH W6 107 F2
Lena Kennedy Cl CHING E4 44 A5
Lendal Ter CLAP SW4 129 J2
Lenelby Rd SURB KT6 159 H7
Len Freeman Pl FUL/PGN SW6 107 J5
Lenham Rd BXLYHN DA7 117 G5
LEE/GVPK SE12 133 J3
SUT SM1 175 F3
THHTH CR7 164 E1
Lennard Av WWKM BR4 180 C1
Lennard Cl WWKM BR4 180 C1
Lennard Rd CROY/NA CR0 164 D7
HAYES BR2 168 E7
PGE/AN SE20 151 F5
SYD SE26 150 E5
Lennard Ter PGE/AN SE20 * 151 F5
Lennon Rd CRICK NW2 70 A4
Lennox Cl ROM RM1 63 H5
Lennox Gdns CROY/NA CR0 177 H3
IL IG1 59 K7
KTBR SW1X 15 L4
WLSDN NW10 69 H3
Lennox Gardens Ms
KTBR SW1X 15 L5
Lennox Rd FSBYPK N4 73 F1
WALTH E17 57 H5
Lenor Cl BXLYHS DA6 137 F3
Lensbury Wy ABYW SE2 116 E2
Lens Rd FSTGT E7 77 G6
Lenthall Rd HACK E8 7 M1
Lenthorp Rd GNWCH SE10 113 J3
Lentmead Rd BMLY BR1 152 D2
Lenton Ri RCH/KEW TW9 125 F2
Lenton St WOOL/PLUM SE18 115 J3
Lenton Ter FSBYPK N4 * 73 G1
Leof Crs CAT SE6 151 K4
Leominster Rd MRDN SM4 162 B5
Leominster Wk MRDN SM4 162 B5
Leonard Av MRDN SM4 162 B4
ROMW/RG RM7 63 F7
Leonard Ct KENS W8 * 14 A3
Leonard Pl HAYES BR2 * 181 J2
STNW/STAM N16 74 A3
Leonard Rd CHING E4 43 J5
ED N9 42 B2
FSTGT E7 76 E3
NWDGN UB2 102 C2
STRHM/NOR SW16 148 C7
Leonard St CAN/RD E16 95 J7
SDTCH EC2A 7 H9
Leonora Tyson Ms DUL SE21 149 K1
Leontine Cl PECK SE15 111 H6
Leopold Av WIM/MER SW19 146 D4
Leopold Ms HOM E9 74 E7
Leopold Rd EA W5 86 B7
EFNCH N2 53 H2
UED N18 42 D4
WALTH E17 57 J4
WIM/MER SW19 146 D3
WLSDN NW10 69 G6
Leopold St BOW E3 93 H4
Leo St PECK SE15 111 J6
Leppoc Rd CLAP SW4 129 J4
Leroy St STHWK SE1 19 J5
Lerry Cl WKENS W14 107 J5
Lescombe Cl FSTH SE23 151 G2
Lescombe Rd FSTH SE23 151 G2
Lesley Cl BXLY DA5 137 J6
Leslie Gdns BELMT SM2 174 E6
Leslie Gv CROY/NA CR0 164 E7
Leslie Grove Pl CROY/NA CR0 165 F7
Leslie Park Rd CROY/NA CR0 165 F7
Leslie Rd CAN/RD E16 95 F5
EFNCH N2 53 H2
WAN E11 76 B3
Lesney Pk ERITH DA8 118 A5
Lesney Park Rd ERITH DA8 118 A5
Lessar Av CLAP SW4 129 H4
Lessingham Av TOOT SW17 147 K3
Lessing St FSTH SE23 132 B6
Lessington Av ROMW/RG RM7 62 E5
Lessness Av BXLYHN DA7 116 E6
Lessness Pk BELV DA17 117 G4
Lessness Rd MRDN SM4 162 B5
Lester Av SRTFD E15 94 C3
Lestock Cl SNWD SE25 165 H2
Leston Cl RAIN RM13 99 K2
Leswin Pl STNW/STAM N16 74 B2
Leswin Rd STNW/STAM N16 74 B2
Letchford Gdns WLSDN NW10 87 J2
Letchford Ms WLSDN NW10 * 87 J2
Letchford Ter
KTN/HRWW/WS HA3 * 34 B7
Letchworth Av
EBED/NFELT TW14 121 J6
Letchworth Cl HAYES BR2 167 K4
OXHEY WD19 33 H4
Letchworth Dr HAYES BR2 167 K4
Letchworth St TOOT SW17 147 K3
Letterstone Rd FUL/PGN SW6 107 J6
Lettice St FUL/PGN SW6 127 J1

Lett Rd BRXN/ST SW9 110 A7
SRTFD E15 76 B6
Leucha Rd WALTH E17 57 G4
Levana Cl WIM/MER SW19 127 H7
Levehurst Wy CLAP SW4 129 K1
Leven Cl OXHEY WD19 * 33 H4
Levendale Rd FSTH SE23 151 G1
Leven Rd POP/IOD E14 94 A4
Leven Wy HYS/HAR UB3 82 C5
Leverett St CHEL SW3 15 K5
Leverholme Gdns
ELTH/MOT SE9 154 A3
Leverson St
STRHM/NOR SW16 148 C5
Lever St FSBYE EC1V 6 E8
Leverton Pl KTTN NW5 72 C4
Leverton St KTTN NW5 72 C4
Levett Gdns GDMY/SEVK IG3 79 F3
Levett Rd BARK IG11 78 E5
Levine Gdns BARK IG11 97 K1
Lewes Cl NTHLT UB5 66 A5
Lewesdon Cl WIM/MER SW19 127 G7
Lewes Rd BMLY BR1 168 C1
NFNCH/WDSPK N12 39 J4
Leweston Pl STNW/STAM N16 56 B6
Lewgars Av CDALE/KGS NW9 50 E5
Lewing Cl ORP BR6 169 K7
Lewin Rd BXLYHS DA6 137 F3
MORT/ESHN SW14 126 A2
STRHM/NOR SW16 148 D5
Lewin Ter EBED/NFELT TW14 121 G6
Lewis Av WALTH E17 43 J7
Lewis Cl STHGT/OAK N14 28 C6
Lewis Crs WLSDN NW10 69 F4
Lewis Gdns EFNCH N2 53 H1
SEVS/STOTM N15 56 B6
Lewis Gv LEW SE13 133 F3
Lewisham High St LEW SE13 132 E4
Lewisham Hl LEW SE13 133 F1
Lewisham Pk LEW SE13 132 E5
Lewisham Rd LEW SE13 133 F1
Lewisham Wy BROCKY SE4 132 C1
Lewis Pl HACK E8 74 C4
Lewis Rd MTCM CR4 162 D1
RCH/KEW TW9 * 124 E4
SCUP DA14 155 J2
STHL UB1 102 D1
SUT SM1 175 F3
WELL DA16 136 D2
Lewis St CAMTN NW1 4 D1
Lewiston Cl WPK KT4 160 E6
Lewis Wy DAGE RM10 80 D5
Lexden Dr CHDH RM6 61 H5
Lexden Rd ACT W3 86 D6
MTCM CR4 163 J3
Lexham Gdns KENS W8 14 B5
Lexham Ms KENS W8 14 B5
Lexington Cl BORE WD6 24 B2
Lexington Pl KUT/HW KT1 143 K7
Lexington St SOHO/CST W1F 10 F5
Lexington Wy BAR EN5 26 B3
Lexton Gdns BAL SW12 129 J7
Leyborne Av WEA W13 104 D1
Leyborne Pk RCH/KEW TW9 105 H7
Leybourne Cl HAYES BR2 167 K4
Leybourne Rd CAMTN NW1 4 D2
CDALE/KGS NW9 50 C4
HGDN/ICK UB10 64 A7
WAN E11 58 D7
Leybourne St CAMTN NW1 4 C2
Leyburn Cl WALTH E17 58 A3
Leyburn Gdns CROY/NA CR0 178 A1
Leyburn Gv UED N18 42 C5
Leyburn House CHARL SE7 * 114 D6
Leyburn Rd UED N18 42 C5
Leycroft Gdns ERITH DA8 118 E7
Leyden St WCHPL E1 13 L3
Leydon Cl BERM/RHTH SE16 93 F7
Leyes Rd CAN/RD E16 95 H6
Leyfield WPK KT4 173 G1
Leyland Av PEND EN3 31 G1
Leyland Gdns WFD IG8 45 G4
Leyland Rd LEE/GVPK SE12 133 J4
Leylang Rd NWCR SE14 112 A6
Leys Av DAGE RM10 80 E7
Leys Cl DAGE RM10 80 E6
HRW HA1 48 D3
Leysdown Av BXLYHN DA7 137 K3
Leysdown Rd ELTH/MOT SE9 153 J1
Leysfield Rd SHB W12 106 D1
Leys Gdns EBAR EN4 28 A4
Leyspring Rd WAN E11 58 D7
The Leys EFNCH N2 53 G3
KTN/HRWW/WS HA3 50 B5
Ley St IL IG1 78 B1
Leyswood Dr
GNTH/NBYPK IG2 60 E4
Leythe Rd ACT W3 105 K1
Leyton Gra LEY E10 75 J1
Leyton Green Rd LEY E10 58 A5
Leyton Park Rd LEY E10 76 A1
Leyton Rd SRTFD E15 76 A4
WIM/MER SW19 147 G6
Leytonstone Rd SRTFD E15 76 C5
Leywick St SRTFD E15 94 C1
Liardet St NWCR SE14 112 B5
Liberia Rd HBRY N5 73 H5
Liberty Av WIM/MER SW19 147 H7
Liberty Cl UED N18 42 B3
WPK KT4 161 F7
Liberty Ms WDGN N22 41 H7
Liberty St BRXN/ST SW9 110 A7
Libra Rd BOW E3 75 H7
PLSTW E13 94 E1
Library Pde WLSDN NW10 * 69 G7
Library St STHWK SE1 18 D2
Library Wy WHTN TW2 123 H6
Lichfield Cl EBAR EN4 27 K2
Lichfield Gdns
RCH/KEW TW9 * 125 F4
Lichfield Gv FNCH N3 38 E7
Lichfield Rd BCTR RM8 79 H3
BOW E3 93 G2
CRICK NW2 70 C3
ED N9 42 C1
EHAM E6 95 H2
HSLWW TW4 122 B2
NTHWD HA6 46 E2
RCH/KEW TW9 105 G7
WFD IG8 44 C3
Lichfield Ter RCH/KEW TW9 * 125 F4
Lidbury Rd MLHL NW7 38 C5
Lidcote Gdns BRXN/ST SW9 * 130 B1
Liddell Cl KTN/HRWW/WS HA3 49 K2
Liddell Gdns WLSDN NW10 88 A1
Liddell Rd KIL/WHAMP NW6 70 E5
Lidding Rd
KTN/HRWW/WS HA3 49 K4
Liddington Rd SRTFD E15 76 D7
Liddon Rd BMLY BR1 168 B2
PLSTW E13 95 F2
Liden Cl LEY E10 57 H6
Lidfield Rd STNW/STAM N16 73 K3
Lidgate Rd CMBW SE5 * 111 G6
Lidgould Gv RSLP HA4 46 E5
Lidiard Rd WAND/EARL SW18 147 G1
Lidlington Pl CAMTN NW1 4 F6
Lido Sq TOTM N17 55 K1
Lidyard Rd ARCH N19 54 C7
Liffler Rd WOOL/PLUM SE18 115 K4
Lifford St PUT/ROE SW15 127 G3
Lightcliffe Rd PLMGR N13 41 G3
Lighter Cl BERM/RHTH SE16 112 B3
Lighterman Ms WCHPL E1 93 F5
Lighterman's Rd POP/IOD E14 112 D1
Lightfoot Rd CEND/HSY/T N8 54 E4
Lightley Cl ALP/SUD HA0 68 B7
Ligonier St BETH E2 7 L9
Lilac Cl CHING E4 43 H5
Lilac Gdns CROY/NA CR0 179 J2
EA W5 104 E2
HYS/HAR UB3 82 C5
ROMW/RG RM7 63 G7
Lilac Pl LBTH SE11 17 L6
Lilac St SHB W12 87 J6
Lilah Ms HAYES BR2 167 J1
Lilburne Gdns ELTH/MOT SE9 134 D4
Lilburne Rd ELTH/MOT SE9 134 D4
Lile Crs HNWL W7 84 E4
Lilestone St STJWD NW8 3 J9
Lilford Rd CMBW SE5 130 C1
Lilian Barker Cl
LEE/GVPK SE12 133 K4
Lilian Board Wy GFD/PVL UB6 66 D4
Lilian Gdns WFD IG8 45 F7
Lilian Rd STRHM/NOR SW16 148 C7
Lillechurch Rd BCTR RM8 79 H5
Lilleshall Rd MRDN SM4 162 C4
Lilley Cl WAP E1W 92 C7
Lilley La MLHL NW7 * 37 G4
Lillian Av ACT W3 105 H1
Lillian Rd BARN SW13 106 D5
Lillie Rd FUL/PGN SW6 107 G5
Lillieshall Rd CLAP SW4 129 G2
Lillie Yd FUL/PGN SW6 14 A9
Lillington Gardens Est
PIM SW1V 16 F6
Lilliput Av NTHLT UB5 65 J7
Lilliput Rd ROMW/RG RM7 63 F6
Lily Cl WKENS W14 107 H3
Lily Dr WDR/YW UB7 100 A3
Lily Gdns ALP/SUD HA0 85 J1
Lily Pl FARR EC1M 12 B2
Lily Rd WALTH E17 57 J5
Lilyville Rd FUL/PGN SW6 107 J7
Limbourne Av BCTR RM8 62 B6
Limburg Rd BTSEA SW11 128 D3
Limeburner La STP EC4M 12 C4
Lime Cl BKHH IG9 45 H1
BMLY BR1 168 D3
KTN/HRWW/WS HA3 49 G1
OXHEY WD19 21 H6
PIN HA5 46 D2
ROMW/RG RM7 62 E3
WAP E1W 92 C7
Lime Crs SUN TW16 156 B1
Limecroft Cl HOR/WEW KT19 173 F6
Limedene Cl PIN HA5 33 H7
Lime Gv BFN/LL DA15 136 A5
CHING E4 43 H5
HYS/HAR UB3 82 B6
NWMAL KT3 160 A2
RSLP HA4 47 F5
SHB W12 107 F1
TRDG/WHET N20 26 C7
TWK TW1 124 A5
Limeharbour POP/IOD E14 112 E2
Limehouse POP/IOD E14 93 J6
Limehouse Cswy
POP/IOD E14 93 H6
Limehouse Link POP/IOD E14 93 G6
Limehouse Link (Tunnel)
POP/IOD E14 93 H6
Lime Kiln Dr CHARL SE7 114 A5
Limekiln Pl NRWD SE19 150 B6
Limerick Cl BAL SW12 129 H6
Limerston St WBPTN SW10 14 F9
Limes Av BARN SW13 126 C1
CAR SM5 162 E7
CROY/NA CR0 177 F2
GLDGN NW11 52 C6
MLHL NW7 37 G5
MNPK E12 77 J2
NFNCH/WDSPK N12 39 G3
PGE/AN SE20 150 D6
WAN E11 59 F3
The Limes Av FBAR/BDGN N11 40 B4
Limes Cl CAR SM5 175 K1
FBAR/BDGN N11 * 40 C4
Limesdale Gdns EDGW HA8 50 E1
Limes Field Rd
MORT/ESHN SW14 126 B2
Limesford Rd PECK SE15 132 A3
Limes Gdns WAND/EARL SW18 127 K5
Limes Gv LEW SE13 133 F3
Limes Rd BECK BR3 166 E1
CROY/NA CR0 164 E5
The Limes CMBW SE5 * 131 F2
PUR RM19 119 K4
WAND/EARL SW18 * 127 K5
Limestone Wk ERITHM DA18 116 E1
Lime St FENCHST EC3M 13 J6
WALTH E17 57 G3
Lime Street Pas BANK EC3V * 13 J5
Limes Wk EA W5 104 E1
PECK SE15 * 131 K3
Lime Tree Av ESH/CLAY KT10 157 J7
Limetree Cl BRXS/STRHM SW2 130 A7
Lime Tree Ct PIN HA5 * 34 A6
Lime Tree Gv CROY/NA CR0 179 H2
Limetree Pl MTCM CR4 148 B7
Lime Tree Rd HEST TW5 103 G7
Lime Tree Ter CAT SE6 * 132 C7
Lime Tree Wk BUSH WD23 22 E7
WWKM BR4 180 D3
Lime Wk SRTFD E15 * 76 C7
Limewood Cl BECK BR3 167 F4
WALTH E17 57 H3
WEA W13 85 H5
Limewood Rd ERITH DA8 117 K6
Limpsfield Av THHTH CR7 164 A4
WIM/MER SW19 146 B1
Linacre Cl PECK SE15 131 J2
Linacre Rd CRICK NW2 69 K5
Linchmere Rd LEE/GVPK SE12 133 J6
Lincoln Av ROMW/RG RM7 63 F7
STHGT/OAK N14 40 C2
WHTN TW2 142 C1
WIM/MER SW19 146 B2
Lincoln Cl ERITH DA8 138 C1
GFD/PVL UB6 66 C7
RYLN/HDSTN HA2 47 K4
Lincoln Ct BORE WD6 25 F4
Lincoln Crs EN EN1 30 A4
Lincoln Dr OXHEY WD19 33 G2
Lincoln Est BOW E3 93 J3
Lincoln Fld BUSH WD23 21 K2
Lincoln Gdns IL IG1 59 J6
Lincoln Ms KIL/WHAMP NW6 70 D7
SEVS/STOTM N15 55 J3
Lincoln Pde EFNCH N2 * 53 J2
Lincoln Rd ALP/SUD HA0 67 K5
EFNCH N2 53 J2
EN EN1 30 A3
ERITH DA8 138 C1
FELT TW13 141 K2
FSTGT E7 77 H5
MTCM CR4 163 K4
NTHWD HA6 46 D2
NWMAL KT3 159 K2
PEND EN3 30 D4
PLSTW E13 95 F3
RYLN/HDSTN HA2 47 K4
SCUP DA14 155 H4
SNWD SE25 165 J2
SWFD E18 44 D7
WPK KT4 160 E7
Lincoln's Inn Flds LINN WC2A 11 L4
The Lincolns MLHL NW7 37 H2
Lincoln St CHEL SW3 15 L6
WAN E11 76 C1
Lincoln Ter BELMT SM2 * 174 E6
Lincoln Wy EN EN1 30 D4
SUN TW16 140 C7
Lincombe Rd BMLY BR1 152 D2
Lindal Crs ENC/FH EN2 28 E4
The Lindales TOTM N17 42 C5
Lindal Rd BROCKY SE4 132 C4
Lindburgh Av WLGTN SM6 176 E7
Linden Av DART DA1 139 F7
HSLW TW3 123 G4
RSLP HA4 46 E7
THHTH CR7 164 C3
WATW WD18 20 D3
WBLY HA9 68 B4
WLSDN NW10 88 B1
Linden Cl RSLP HA4 46 E7
STAN HA7 35 H4
STHGT/OAK N14 28 C5
THDIT KT7 158 B6
Linden Cots WIM/MER SW19 * 146 C5
Linden Crs GFD/PVL UB6 67 F5
KUT/HW KT1 159 G1
WFD IG8 45 F5
Lindenfield CHST BR7 169 G1
Linden Gdns BAY/PAD W2 8 B7
CHSWK W4 106 A4
Linden Gv NWMAL KT3 160 B2
PECK SE15 131 J2
SYD SE26 150 E5
TEDD TW11 143 F4
Linden Lea EFNCH N2 53 G4
PIN HA5 * 33 K6
Linden Leas WWKM BR4 180 B1
Linden Ms BAY/PAD W2 8 B7
IS N1 73 K4
Linden Pl MTCM CR4 162 D3
Linden Rd FBAR/BDGN N11 39 K1
HPTN TW12 142 A7
MUSWH N10 54 B3
SEVS/STOTM N15 55 J3
The Lindens CHSWK W4 105 K7
CROY/NA CR0 180 A5
NFNCH/WDSPK N12 * 39 H4
WALTH E17 * 57 K3
Linden St ROMW/RG RM7 63 F3
Linden Wk ARCH N19 72 C2
Linden Wy STHGT/OAK N14 28 C5
Lindfield Gdns HAMP NW3 71 G4
Lindfield Rd CROY/NA CR0 165 G5
EA W5 85 J3
Lindfield St POP/IOD E14 93 J5
Lindhill Cl PEND EN3 31 F1
Lindisfarne Md HOM E9 75 G3
Lindisfarne Rd BCTR RM8 79 J2
RYNPK SW20 145 J6
Lindley Est PECK SE15 * 111 H6
Lindley Pl RCH/KEW TW9 105 H7
Lindley Rd LEY E10 75 K1
Lindley St WCHPL E1 92 E4
Lindore Rd BTSEA SW11 128 E3
Lindores Rd CAR SM5 162 B6
Lindo St PECK SE15 131 K1
Lind Rd SUT SM1 175 G4
Lindrop St FUL/PGN SW6 128 B1
Lindsay Cl CHSGTN KT9 172 A6
STWL/WRAY TW19 120 A4
Lindsay Dr
KTN/HRWW/WS HA3 50 A5
Lindsay Rd HPTN TW12 142 B3
WPK KT4 173 K1
Lindsay Sq PIM SW1V 17 H7
Lindsell St GNWCH SE10 113 F7
Lindsey Cl BMLY BR1 168 C2
MTCM CR4 163 K3
Lindsey Gdns
EBED/NFELT TW14 * 121 G6
Lindsey Ms IS N1 6 F1
Lindsey Rd BCTR RM8 79 J2
Lindsey St FARR EC1M 12 D2
Lind St DEPT SE8 132 E1
Lindum Rd TEDD TW11 143 J6
Lindway WNWD SE27 149 H4
Linfield Cl HDN NW4 52 A2
Linford Rd WALTH E17 58 A2
Linford St VX/NE SW8 109 H7
Lingards Rd LEW SE13 133 F3
Lingey Cl BFN/LL DA15 155 F1
Lingfield Av KUT/HW KT1 159 F3
Lingfield Cl EN EN1 30 A5
NTHWD HA6 32 C6
Lingfield Ct NTHLT UB5 * 84 A1
Lingfield Crs ELTH/MOT SE9 135 J3
Lingfield Gdns ED N9 30 D6
Lingfield Rd WIM/MER SW19 146 B5
WPK KT4 174 A2
Lingham St BRXN/ST SW9 129 K1
Lingholm Wy BAR EN5 26 B4
Ling Rd CAN/RD E16 94 E4
ERITH DA8 117 K5
Lingwell Rd TOOT SW17 147 J2
Lingwood Gdns ISLW TW7 103 K6
Lingwood Rd CLPT E5 56 C6
Linhope St CAMTN NW1 3 L9
Linkfield E/WMO/HCT KT8 157 F2
Link Fld HAYES BR2 167 K5
Linkfield Rd ISLW TW7 124 A1
Link La WLGTN SM6 176 D5
Linklea Cl CDALE/KGS NW9 37 G6
Link Rd DAGW RM9 98 D1
EBED/NFELT TW14 121 J6
FBAR/BDGN N11 40 A3
MNPK E12 77 J1
WATN WD24 21 H1
WLGTN SM6 163 F7
Links Av GPK RM2 63 K1
MRDN SM4 161 K3
Links Dr BORE WD6 24 B2
TRDG/WHET N20 26 E7
Links Gdns STRHM/NOR SW16 149 G6
Linkside NFNCH/WDSPK N12 38 D5
NWMAL KT3 160 B1
Linkside Cl ENC/FH EN2 29 F2
Linkside Gdns ENC/FH EN2 29 F2
Links Rd ACT W3 86 C5
CRICK NW2 69 H1
TOOT SW17 148 A5
WFD IG8 44 E4
WWKM BR4 167 F7
Links Side ENC/FH EN2 29 F2
The Links WALTH E17 57 G3
Link St HOM E9 74 E5
Links Vw DART DA1 139 F7
FNCH N3 38 D6
Links View Cl STAN HA7 35 G5
Linksview Ct HPTN TW12 * 142 D3
Links View Rd CROY/NA CR0 179 J2
HPTN TW12 142 C4
Links Wy BECK BR3 166 D5
NTHWD HA6 32 A7
RKW/CH/CXG WD3 20 A2
TOOT SW17 147 K5
Linksway HDN NW4 52 B1
NTHWD HA6 32 B7
Links Yd WCHPL E1 13 M2
The Link ACT W3 86 D5
ALP/SUD HA0 49 J7
CRICK NW2 51 J7
NTHLT UB5 * 65 K4
PIN HA5 47 G5
Link Wy HAYES BR2 168 D6
RCHPK/HAM TW10 143 H1
Linkway BCTR RM8 79 J3
FSBYPK N4 55 J6
NWMAL KT3 160 E3
PIN HA5 33 H7
RYNPK SW20 160 E2
The Linkway BAR EN5 26 E5
BELMT SM2 175 G7
Linkwood Wk CAMTN NW1 5 H1
Linley Crs ROMW/RG RM7 62 D2
Linley Rd TOTM N17 56 A1
Linnell Cl GLDGN NW11 53 F5
Linnell Dr GLDGN NW11 53 F5
Linnell Rd CMBW SE5 131 F1
UED N18 42 C4
Linnet Cl BUSH WD23 22 C7
ED N9 31 F7
THMD SE28 97 J6
Linnet Ms BAL SW12 129 F6
Linnett Cl CHING E4 44 A3
Linom Rd CLAP SW4 129 K3
Linscott Rd CLPT E5 74 E3
Linsdell Rd BARK IG11 78 C7
Linsey St BERM/RHTH SE16 111 H2
Linslade Cl HSLWW TW4 122 D4
PIN HA5 47 F2
Linstead St KIL/WHAMP NW6 2 A1
Linstead Wy
WAND/EARL SW18 127 H6
Linster Gv BORE WD6 24 E4
Lintaine Cl HMSMTH W6 * 107 H5
Linthorpe Av ALP/SUD HA0 67 J5
Linthorpe Rd EBAR EN4 27 J2
STNW/STAM N16 56 A6
Linton Av BORE WD6 24 B1
Linton Cl CAR SM5 162 E6
CHARL SE7 114 B4
WELL DA16 116 B7
Linton Ct ROM RM1 63 G1
Linton Gdns EHAM E6 95 J5
Linton Gv WNWD SE27 149 H4
Linton Rd BARK IG11 78 C6
Linton St IS N1 6 F4
Lintott Ct STWL/WRAY TW19 120 A5
Linver Rd FUL/PGN SW6 127 J1
Linwood Cl CMBW SE5 131 G1
Linzee Rd CEND/HSY/T N8 54 E3
Lion Av TWK TW1 124 A7
Lion Cl BROCKY SE4 132 D5
Lionel Gdns ELTH/MOT SE9 134 C4
Lionel Ms NKENS W10 * 88 C4
Lionel Rd ELTH/MOT SE9 134 C4
Lionel Rd North BTFD TW8 105 F2
Lionel Rd South BTFD TW8 105 G4
Lion Gate Gdns RCH/KEW TW9 125 G2
Lion Gate Ms
WAND/EARL SW18 127 K6
Lion Mills BETH E2 * 92 C1
Lion Park Av CHSGTN KT9 172 C3
Lion Rd BXLYHS DA6 137 F3
CROY/NA CR0 164 D4
ED N9 42 C1
EHAM E6 95 K4
TWK TW1 124 A7
Lions Cl LEE/GVPK SE12 153 G2
Lion Wy BTFD TW8 104 E6
Lion Wharf Rd ISLW TW7 124 C2
Liphook Cl HCH RM12 81 H3
Liphook Crs FSTH SE23 131 K6
Liphook Rd OXHEY WD19 33 H3
Lisbon Av WHTN TW2 142 C1
Lisbon Cl WALTH E17 57 H1
Lisburne Rd HAMP NW3 71 K3
Lisford St PECK SE15 111 G7
Lisgar Ter WKENS W14 107 J3
Liskeard Cl CHST BR7 154 C5
Liskeard Gdns BKHTH/KID SE3 113 K7
Lisle Cl TOOT SW17 148 B3
Lisle St LSQ/SEVD WC2H 11 H6
Lismore WIM/MER SW19 * 146 D4
Lismore Circ KTTN NW5 71 K4
Lismore Cl ISLW TW7 124 B1
Lismore Rd SAND/SEL CR2 178 A5
TOTM N17 55 K2
Lismore Wk IS N1 73 J5
Lissant Cl SURB KT6 158 D6
Lissenden Gdns KTTN NW5 72 A3
Lisson Gv CAMTN NW1 9 J1
STJWD NW8 3 H9
Lisson St CAMTN NW1 9 J2
Lister Cl ACT W3 87 F4
MTCM CR4 147 J6
Lister Gdns UED N18 41 J4
Lister Rd WAN E11 58 C7
Liston Rd CLAP SW4 129 H2
TOTM N17 42 C7
Liston Wy WFD IG8 45 G6
Listowel Cl BRXN/ST SW9 110 B6
Listowel Rd DAGE RM10 80 C2
Listria Pk STNW/STAM N16 74 A1
Litchfield Av MRDN SM4 161 J6
SRTFD E15 * 76 C5
Litchfield Gdns WLSDN NW10 69 J5
Litchfield Rd SUT SM1 175 G3
Litchfield St LSQ/SEVD WC2H 11 H6
Litchfield Wy GLDGN NW11 53 G4
Lithgow's Rd HTHAIR TW6 121 H3
Lithos Rd HAMP NW3 71 F5
Little Acre BECK BR3 166 D2
Little Albany St CAMTN NW1 4 D9
Little Argyll St REGST W1B * 10 E5
Little Benty WDR/YW UB7 100 A4
Little Birches BFN/LL DA15 154 E1
The Little Boltons
WBPTN SW10 14 D7
Little Bornes DUL SE21 150 A3
Little Britain STBT EC1A 12 D3
Littlebrook Cl CROY/NA CR0 166 A5
Littlebrook Manor Wy
DART DA1 139 K4
Little Brownings FSTH SE23 150 D1
Littlebury Rd CLAP SW4 * 129 J2
Little Bury St ED N9 30 A6
Little Bushey La BUSH WD23 22 A2
Little Cedars
NFNCH/WDSPK N12 39 G3
Little Chester St KTBR SW1X 16 C3
Little Cloisters WEST SW1P 17 J3
Littlecombe Cl
PUT/ROE SW15 * 127 G5
Little Common STAN HA7 35 G2
Littlecote Cl WIM/MER SW19 127 G6
Littlecote Pl PIN HA5 33 J7
Little Cottage Pl
GNWCH SE10 * 112 E6
Little Ct WWKM BR4 180 C1
Littlecroft ELTH/MOT SE9 135 F2
Littledale ABYW SE2 116 B5
Little Deans Yd WEST SW1P 17 J3
Little Dimocks BAL SW12 148 B1
Little Dorrit Ct STHWK SE1 18 F1
Little Ealing La EA W5 104 D3
Little Edward St
CAMTN NW1 * 4 D7
Little Elms HYS/HAR UB3 101 G6
Little Essex St
TPL/STR WC2R * 12 A6
Little Ferry Rd TWK TW1 * 124 C7
Littlefield Cl ARCH N19 72 C3
KUT/HW KT1 159 F1
Littlefield Rd EDGW HA8 36 E6
Little Friday Rd CHING E4 44 C1
Little Gearies BARK/HLT IG6 60 B3
Little George St WEST SW1P 17 J2
Little Gn RCH/KEW TW9 124 E3
Little Green St KTTN NW5 * 72 B3
Little Gv BUSH WD23 22 B3
Littlegrove EBAR EN4 27 J5
Little Heath CHARL SE7 114 D5
CHDH RM6 61 H3
Little Heath Rd BXLYHN DA7 117 G7
Littleheath Rd SAND/SEL CR2 178 D7
Little Ilford La MNPK E12 77 K3
Littlejohn Rd HNWL W7 85 F5
Little Marlborough St
REGST W1B * 10 E5
Little Martins BUSH WD23 22 B4
Littlemead ESH/CLAY KT10 170 D3
Littlemede ELTH/MOT SE9 153 K2
Littlemoor Rd IL IG1 78 D2
Littlemore Rd ABYW SE2 116 B1
Little Moss La PIN HA5 47 J1
Little Newport St
LSQ/SEVD WC2H 11 H6
Little New St
FLST/FETLN EC4A 12 B4
Little Orchard Cl PIN HA5 * 47 J1
Little Oxhey La OXHEY WD19 33 J4
Little Park Dr FELT TW13 141 H1
Little Park Gdns ENC/FH EN2 29 J2
Little Portland St REGST W1B 10 D4
Little Potters BUSH WD23 22 D6
Little Queens Rd TEDD TW11 143 F5
Little Queen St DART DA1 139 J6
Little Redlands BMLY BR1 168 D1
Little Rd HYS/HAR UB3 101 J1
Littlers Cl WIM/MER SW19 147 H7
Little Russell St
NOXST/BSQ WC1A 11 J3
Little St James's St
WHALL SW1A 10 E9
Little St Leonards
MORT/ESHN SW14 125 K2
Little Smith St WEST SW1P 17 H3
Little Somerset St
TWRH EC3N 13 L5
Littlestone Cl BECK BR3 151 J5
Little Strd CDALE/KGS NW9 51 H1
Little Stream Cl NTHWD HA6 32 C4
Little Thrift STMC/STPC BR5 169 H3
Little Titchfield St
GTPST W1W 10 E3
Littleton Crs HRW HA1 67 F1
Littleton Rd ASHF TW15 140 A6
HRW HA1 67 F1
Littleton St WAND/EARL SW18 147 G1
Little Trinity La BLKFR EC4V 12 F6
Little Turnstile HHOL WC1V 11 L3
Littlewood LEW SE13 133 F4
Little Wood Cl
STMC/STPC BR5 155 G7
Littlewood Cl WEA W13 104 C2
Littleworth Av ESH/CLAY KT10 170 D4
Littleworth Common Rd
ESH/CLAY KT10 170 D2
Littleworth La ESH/CLAY KT10 170 D3
Littleworth Pl ESH/CLAY KT10 170 D3
Littleworth Rd ESH/CLAY KT10 170 D4
Livermere Rd HACK E8 7 L3
Liverpool Gv WALW SE17 19 G8
Liverpool Rd CAN/RD E16 94 C4
EA W5 104 E1
IS N1 6 B3
KUTN/CMB KT2 144 C6
LEY E10 58 A5
THHTH CR7 164 D2
WATW WD18 21 F4
Liverpool St LVPST EC2M 13 J3
Livesey Cl KUT/HW KT1 159 G2
THMD SE28 115 H2
Livesey Pl STHWK SE1 111 H5
Livingstone Rd BTSEA SW11 128 C2
HSLW TW3 123 H3
PLMGR N13 40 E5
STHL UB1 83 H6
THHTH CR7 164 E1
WALTH E17 57 K5
Lizard St FSBYE EC1V 6 F8
Lizban St BKHTH/KID SE3 114 A6
Llanelly Rd CRICK NW2 70 D1
Llanover Rd WBLY HA9 67 K2
WOOL/PLUM SE18 115 F6
Llanthony Rd MRDN SM4 162 C5
Llanvanor Rd CRICK NW2 70 D1
Lloyd Av STRHM/NOR SW16 148 E7
Lloyd Baker St FSBYW WC1X 6 A8
Lloyd Ct PIN HA5 47 H4
Lloyd Park Av CROY/NA CR0 178 B3
Lloyd Rd DAGW RM9 80 B5
EHAM E6 77 K7
WALTH E17 57 F3
WPK KT4 174 A2
Lloyd's Av FENCHST EC3M 13 K5
Lloyd's Pl BKHTH/KID SE3 * 133 H1

Lloyd Sq FSBYW WC1X 6 A7
Lloyd's Rw CLKNW EC1R 6 B8
Lloyd St FSBYW WC1X 6 A7
Lloyds Wy BECK BR3 166 B4
Lloyd Thomas Ct WDGN N22 * 41 F6
Lloyd Vls BROCKY SE4 132 D1
Loampit Hl LEW SE13 132 D1
Loampit V LEW SE13 132 E2
Loanda Cl HACK E8 7 L3
Loates La WAT WD17 21 G2
Loats Rd BRXS/STRHM SW2 129 K5
Local Board Rd WAT WD17 21 H4
Locarno Rd ACT W3 86 E7
GFD/PVL UB6 84 C3
Lochaber Rd LEW SE13 133 H3
Lochaline St HMSMTH W6 107 F5
Lochan Cl YEAD UB4 83 J3
Lochinvar St BAL SW12 129 G6
Lochmere Cl ERITH DA8 117 J5
Lochnagar St POP/IOD E14 94 A4
Lock Cha BKHTH/KID SE3 133 H2
Lock Cl NWDGN UB2 103 H1
Locke Cl RAIN RM13 81 H5
Lockesfield Pl POP/IOD E14 112 E3
Lockesley Sq SURB KT6 * 158 E5
Locket Rd
KTN/HRWW/WS HA3 49 F1
Locket Road Ms
KTN/HRWW/WS HA3 48 E1
Lockfield Av PEND EN3 31 G1
Lockgate Cl HOM E9 75 H4
Lockhart Cl HOLWY N7 73 F5
PEND EN3 30 D4
Lockhart St BOW E3 93 H3
Lockhurst St CLPT E5 75 F3
Lockington Rd VX/NE SW8 109 G7
Lock Keepers Cots
TOTM N17 * 56 D3
Lockmead Rd LEW SE13 133 F2
SEVS/STOTM N15 56 C5
Lock Rd RCHPK/HAM TW10 143 J2
Lock's La MTCM CR4 148 A7
Locksley Est POP/IOD E14 93 H5
Locksley St POP/IOD E14 93 H4
Locksmeade Rd
RCHPK/HAM TW10 143 H3
Lockton St NTGHL W11 * 88 B6
Lockwell Rd DAGE RM10 80 B2
Lockwood Cl EBAR EN4 27 K3
SYD SE26 151 F3
Lockwood Pl CHING E4 43 J5
Lockwood Sq
BERM/RHTH SE16 111 J2
Lockwood Wy CHSGTN KT9 172 C4
WALTH E17 57 F1
Lockyer St STHWK SE1 19 H2
Locomotive Dr
EBED/NFELT TW14 121 K6
Locton Gn BOW E3 * 75 H7
Loddiges Rd HOM E9 74 E6
Loder St PECK SE15 111 K6
Lodge Av BCTR RM8 79 H4
BORE WD6 24 B4
CROY/NA CR0 177 F2
DAGW RM9 79 G7
DART DA1 139 F5
GPK RM2 63 J4
KTN/HRWW/WS HA3 50 A3
Lodge Cl EDGW HA8 * 36 B5
ISLW TW7 104 C7
UED N18 41 J4
WLGTN SM6 163 F7
Lodge Ct ALP/SUD HA0 * 68 A4
Lodge Dr PLMGR N13 41 G3
Lodge End RKW/CH/CXG WD3 20 B3
Lodge Gdns BECK BR3 166 C4
Lodge Hl REDBR IG4 59 J3
WELL DA16 116 C6
Lodgehill Park Cl
RYLN/HDSTN HA2 66 B1
Lodge La BXLY DA5 136 E5
CROY/NA CR0 179 K6
NFNCH/WDSPK N12 39 G4
Lodge Mansions Pde
PLMGR N13 * 41 G3
Lodge Ms HBRY N5 * 73 J3
Lodge Pl SUT SM1 175 F4
Lodge Rd BMLY BR1 153 G6
CROY/NA CR0 164 C5
HDN NW4 52 A3
RKW/CH/CXG WD3 20 B3
STJWD NW8 3 H8
SUT SM1 175 F4
WLGTN SM6 176 B4
The Lodge SHB W12 * 107 G1
Lodge Vls WFD IG8 44 D6
Lodore Gdns CDALE/KGS NW9 51 G4
Lodore St POP/IOD E14 94 A5
Lofthouse Pl CHSGTN KT9 171 J5
Loftie St BERM/RHTH SE16 111 H1
Lofting Rd IS N1 6 A2
Loftus Rd BARK IG11 78 C5
SHB W12 87 K7
Loftus Vls SHB W12 * 87 K7
Logan Cl HSLWW TW4 122 E2
Logan Ms KENS W8 14 A5
ROM RM1 63 G4
Logan Pl ECT SW5 14 A5
Logan Rd ED N9 42 D1
WBLY HA9 68 A1
The Logans BAR EN5 * 26 B2
Logs Hl CHST BR7 153 J7
Logs Hill Cl CHST BR7 153 J7
Lolesworth Cl WCHPL E1 13 L3
Lollard St LBTH SE11 17 M5
Loman St STHWK SE1 18 D1
Lomas Cl CROY/NA CR0 180 A6
Lomas Dr HACK E8 7 M1
Lombard Av GDMY/SEVK IG3 60 E7
Lombard Ct MANHO EC4N 13 H6
Lombard La EMB EC4Y 12 B5
Lombard Rd BTSEA SW11 128 C1
FBAR/BDGN N11 40 B4
WIM/MER SW19 162 A1
Lombard St BANK EC3V 13 H5
Lombard Vls
FBAR/BDGN N11 * 40 B4
Lombard Wall CHARL SE7 114 A2
Lombardy Pl BAY/PAD W2 8 C7
Lomond Cl ALP/SUD HA0 68 B6
SEVS/STOTM N15 56 A3
Lomond Gdns SAND/SEL CR2 179 G6
Lomond Gv CMBW SE5 110 E6
Loncroft Rd CMBW SE5 19 K9
Londesborough Rd
STNW/STAM N16 74 A3
London Br CANST EC4R 13 H7
London Bridge St STHWK SE1 13 H9
London Bridge Wk
STHWK SE1 * 13 H8
Londonderry Pde
ERITH DA8 * 118 A6
London Flds HACK E8 * 74 D6
London Fields East Side
HACK E8 74 D6
London Fields West Side
HACK E8 74 C6
London La BMLY BR1 152 D6
HACK E8 74 D6
London Loop BAR EN5 25 K6
HAYES BR2 180 D1
ORP BR6 169 G7
SAND/SEL CR2 178 E6
London Ms BAY/PAD W2 9 H5
London Rd BARK IG11 78 B6
BMLY BR1 152 D6
BUSH WD23 21 K5
CHEAM SM3 174 B1
CROY/NA CR0 164 C7
DART DA1 138 A4
ENC/FH EN2 29 K3
EW KT17 173 H7
FSTH SE23 131 K7
HRW HA1 66 E1
ISLW TW7 123 K1
KUTN/CMB KT2 159 G1
MRDN SM4 161 K4
MTCM CR4 162 D3
PLSTW E13 94 E1
PUR RM19 119 K4
ROMW/RG RM7 62 C5
SOCK/AV RM15 119 K1
STAN HA7 35 K3
STHWK SE1 18 D3
STRHM/NOR SW16 164 A1
THHTH CR7 164 B5
TOOT SW17 147 K6
TWK TW1 124 B6
WBLY HA9 68 A4
WLGTN SM6 176 B3
London Stile CHSWK W4 105 H4
London St BAY/PAD W2 9 G4
FENCHST EC3M * 13 K6
London Ter BETH E2 * 92 C1
London Wall CITYW EC2V 12 F3
LVPST EC2M 13 H4
London Wall Blds LVPST EC2M 13 H3
Lonesome Wy MTCM CR4 148 B7
Long Acre CHCR WC2N 11 J6
COVGDN WC2E 11 J5
Long Acre Ct WEA W13 * 85 G4
Longacre Pl CAR SM5 * 176 A5
Longacre Rd WALTH E17 44 B7
Longbeach Rd BTSEA SW11 128 E2
Longboat Rw STHL UB1 83 K5
Longbridge Rd BARK IG11 78 D5
BCTR RM8 79 G3
Longbridge Wy LEW SE13 133 F4
Longcliffe Pth OXHEY WD19 32 E2
Long Ct PUR RM19 119 K3
Longcroft ELTH/MOT SE9 154 A2
Long Cft OXHEY WD19 21 F6
Longcrofte Rd EDGW HA8 35 K6
Longdon Wd HAYES BR2 181 J3
Longdown Rd CAT SE6 151 J3
Long Dr ACT W3 87 G5
GFD/PVL UB6 66 B7
RSLP HA4 65 H3
WDR/YW UB7 * 100 B1
Long Elmes
KTN/HRWW/WS HA3 34 B7
Longfellow Rd WALTH E17 57 H5
WCHPL E1 * 93 G2
WPK KT4 160 D7
Longfellow Wy STHWK SE1 * 19 M6
Longfield BMLY BR1 152 D7
Long Fld CDALE/KGS NW9 37 G6
Longfield Av EA W5 85 J6
EMPK RM11 63 H6
MLHL NW7 37 J6
WALTH E17 57 G3
WBLY HA9 50 A7
WLGTN SM6 163 F7
Longfield Crs SYD SE26 150 E2
Longfield Dr
MORT/ESHN SW14 125 J4
MTCM CR4 147 J7
Longfield Est STHWK SE1 19 M5
Longfield Rd EA W5 85 J5
Longfield St
WAND/EARL SW18 127 K6
Longford Av
EBED/NFELT TW14 121 H5
STHL UB1 84 A6
STWL/WRAY TW19 120 B7
Longford Cl FELT TW13 141 J2
HPTN TW12 142 A3
YEAD UB4 83 H6
Longford Ct HOR/WEW KT19 172 E3
HPTN TW12 142 B5
Longford Gdns SUT SM1 175 G2
YEAD UB4 83 H6
Longford Rd WHTN TW2 123 F7
Longford St CAMTN NW1 4 D9
Longford Wy
STWL/WRAY TW19 120 B7
Longhayes Av CHDH RM6 61 K2
Longheath Gdns
CROY/NA CR0 165 K4
Longhedge St BTSEA SW11 129 F1
Longhill Rd CAT SE6 152 B1
Longhook Gdns NTHLT UB5 82 E1
Longhurst Rd CROY/NA CR0 165 J5
LEW SE13 133 H4
Longland Dr TRDG/WHET N20 39 F2
Longlands Park Crs
BFN/LL DA15 154 E2
Longlands Rd BFN/LL DA15 154 E2
Long La BXLYHN DA7 117 F6
CROY/NA CR0 165 K5
FNCH N3 39 F7
STBT EC1A 12 D2
STHWK SE1 19 H2
STWL/WRAY TW19 120 C7
Longleat Rd EN EN1 30 A4
Longleat Wy
EBED/NFELT TW14 121 F6
Longleigh La ABYW SE2 116 D5
Longley Av ALP/SUD HA0 68 B7
Longley Rd CROY/NA CR0 164 C6
HRW HA1 48 D4
TOOT SW17 147 J5
Long Leys CHING E4 43 K5
Longley St STHWK SE1 111 H3
Longley Wy CRICK NW2 70 A2
Longmans Cl WATW WD18 20 A5
Long Mark Rd CAN/RD E16 95 H5
Longmarsh La THMD SE28 96 E7
Long Md CDALE/KGS NW9 37 H7
Longmead CHST BR7 169 F1
Longmead Dr SCUP DA14 155 K1
Long Meadow KTTN NW5 * 72 D5
Long Meadow Cl WWKM BR4 167 F6
Longmeadow Rd
BFN/LL DA15 135 K7
Longmead Rd HYS/HAR UB3 82 D6
THDIT KT7 157 K6
TOOT SW17 147 K4
Longmoore St PIM SW1V 16 E6
Longmore Av BAR EN5 27 G5
Longnor Rd WCHPL E1 93 F2
Long Pond Rd BKHTH/KID SE3 113 H7
Long Reach Rd BARK IG11 97 F3
Longreach Rd ERITH DA8 118 E6
Longridge La STHL UB1 84 B6
Longridge Rd ECT SW5 14 A6
Long Rd CLAP SW4 129 H3
Longshaw Rd CHING E4 44 B2
Longshore DEPT SE8 112 C3
Longstaff Crs
WAND/EARL SW18 127 K5
Longstaff Rd
WAND/EARL SW18 127 K5
Longstone Av WLSDN NW10 69 H6
Longstone Rd TOOT SW17 148 B4
Long St BETH E2 7 L6
Longthornton Rd
STRHM/NOR SW16 163 H1
Longton Av SYD SE26 150 C3
Longton Gv SYD SE26 150 D3
Longville Rd LBTH SE11 18 C5
Long Wk NWMAL KT3 159 K2
STHWK SE1 19 K3
WOOL/PLUM SE18 115 G5
Longwood Ct WPK KT4 173 J1
Longwood Dr PUT/ROE SW15 126 D5
Longwood Gdns CLAY IG5 59 K3
Longworth Cl THMD SE28 97 K5
Long Yd BMSBY WC1N 11 L1
The Loning CDALE/KGS NW9 51 H3
Lonsdale Av EHAM E6 95 H3
ROMW/RG RM7 62 E5
WBLY HA9 68 A4
Lonsdale Cl EHAM E6 95 J3
ELTH/MOT SE9 153 H2
UX/CGN UB8 82 A5
Lonsdale Crs GNTH/NBYPK IG2 60 B5
Lonsdale Dr ENC/FH EN2 28 D3
Lonsdale Dr North
ENC/FH EN2 28 E4
Lonsdale Gdns THHTH CR7 164 A3
Lonsdale Ms NTGHL W11 88 D5
RCH/KEW TW9 * 105 H7
Lonsdale Pl IS N1 6 B2
Lonsdale Rd BARN SW13 106 C6
BXLYHN DA7 137 G1
CHSWK W4 106 C3
KIL/WHAMP NW6 70 D7
NTGHL W11 88 D5
NWDGN UB2 102 C2
SNWD SE25 165 J3
WAN E11 58 D6
Lonsdale Sq IS N1 6 B2
Loobert Rd SEVS/STOTM N15 56 A2
Looe Gdns BARK/HLT IG6 60 B2
Loop Rd CHST BR7 154 C5
Lopen Rd UED N18 42 A3
Loraine Cl PEND EN3 30 E4
Loraine Cots HOLWY N7 * 73 F3
Loraine Rd CHSWK W4 105 J5
HOLWY N7 73 F3
Lord Av CLAY IG5 59 K3
Lord Chancellor Wk
KUTN/CMB KT2 144 E7
Lordell Pl WIM/MER SW19 146 A5
Lord Hills Rd BAY/PAD W2 8 D2
Lord Holland La
BRXN/ST SW9 * 130 B1
Lord Knyvett Cl
STWL/WRAY TW19 120 A5
Lord Knyvetts Ct
STWL/WRAY TW19 * 120 B5
Lord Napier Pl HMSMTH W6 106 D4
Lord North St WEST SW1P 17 J4
Lord Roberts Ms
FUL/PGN SW6 * 108 A6
Lords Cl DUL SE21 149 J1
FELT TW13 141 J1
Lordship Gv STNW/STAM N16 73 K1
Lordship La EDUL SE22 131 G5
TOTM N17 41 J7
WDGN N22 55 G1
Lordship Pk STNW/STAM N16 73 K1
Lordship Park Ms
STNW/STAM N16 73 J1
Lordship Pl CHEL SW3 108 D5
Lordship Rd NTHLT UB5 65 J6
STNW/STAM N16 55 K7
Lordship Ter STNW/STAM N16 73 K1
Lordsmead Rd TOTM N17 42 A7
Lord St CAN/RD E16 95 J7
WAT WD17 21 G2
Lords Vw STJWD NW8 3 J7
Lord Warwick St
WOOL/PLUM SE18 114 E2
Lorenzo St FSBYW WC1X 5 L7
Loretto Gdns
KTN/HRWW/WS HA3 50 A3
Lorian Cl NFNCH/WDSPK N12 39 F3
Loring Rd ISLW TW7 124 A1
TRDG/WHET N20 39 J1
Loris Rd HMSMTH W6 107 F2
Lorne Av CROY/NA CR0 166 A6
Lorne Cl STJWD NW8 3 K8
Lorne Gdns CROY/NA CR0 166 A6
NTGHL W11 107 G1
WAN E11 59 G3
Lorne Rd FSBYPK N4 55 F7
FSTGT E7 77 F3
KTN/HRWW/WS HA3 49 F1
RCHPK/HAM TW10 125 G4
WALTH E17 57 J4
Lorne Ter FNCH N3 * 52 D1
Lorn Rd BRXN/ST SW9 130 A1
Lorraine Pk
KTN/HRWW/WS HA3 34 E6
Lorrimore Rd WALW SE17 110 C5
Lorrimore Sq WALW SE17 18 D9
Loseberry Rd ESH/CLAY KT10 170 D4
Lothair Rd EA W5 104 E1
Lothair Rd North FSBYPK N4 55 H5
Lothair Rd South FSBYPK N4 55 G6
Lothbury LOTH EC2R 13 G4
Lothian Av YEAD UB4 83 F4
Lothian Cl ALP/SUD HA0 67 G3
Lothian Rd BRXN/ST SW9 110 C6
Lothrop St NKENS W10 88 C2
Lots Rd WBPTN SW10 108 B6
Loubet St TOOT SW17 147 K5
Loudoun Av BARK/HLT IG6 60 B4
Loudoun Rd STJWD NW8 2 F4
Loughborough Pk
BRXN/ST SW9 130 C3
Loughborough Rd
BRXN/ST SW9 130 B1
Loughborough St LBTH SE11 17 M7
Lough Rd HOLWY N7 73 F4
Louisa Cl HOM E9 74 E6
Louisa St WCHPL E1 93 F4
Louise Bennett Cl
HNHL SE24 * 130 C3
Louise Gdns RAIN RM13 99 G2
Louise Rd SRTFD E15 76 C5
Louis Gdns CHST BR7 153 K3
Louisville Rd TOOT SW17 148 A2
Louvaine Rd BTSEA SW11 128 C3
Lovage Ap EHAM E6 95 J4
Lovat Cl CRICK NW2 69 H2
Lovat La FENCHST EC3M 13 J6
Lovatt Cl EDGW HA8 36 D5
Loveday Rd WEA W13 85 H7
Lovegrove St STHWK SE1 111 H4
Lovegrove Wk POP/IOD E14 94 A7
Lovekyn Cl KUTN/CMB KT2 159 F1
Lovelace Av HAYES BR2 169 F5
Lovelace Gdns BARK IG11 79 G3
SURB KT6 158 E6
Lovelace Gn ELTH/MOT SE9 134 E2
Lovelace Rd DUL SE21 149 J1
EBAR EN4 27 J6
SURB KT6 158 D6
Lovelace Vls THDIT KT7 * 158 C6
Love La BXLY DA5 137 H5
CHEAM SM3 174 C5
CITYW EC2V 12 F4
MRDN SM4 161 K6
MTCM CR4 162 D2
PIN HA5 47 J2
SNWD SE25 165 J2
SURB KT6 171 K1
TOTM N17 42 B6
WFD IG8 45 K5
WOOL/PLUM SE18 115 F3
Lovel Av WELL DA16 136 B1
Lovelinch Cl PECK SE15 111 K5
Lovell Pl BERM/RHTH SE16 112 B2
Lovell Rd RCHPK/HAM TW10 143 J2
STHL UB1 84 B5
Lovell Wk RAIN RM13 81 J5
Loveridge Ms
KIL/WHAMP NW6 70 D5
Loveridge Rd
KIL/WHAMP NW6 70 D5
Lovett Dr CAR SM5 162 B6
Lovetts Pl WAND/EARL SW18 128 B3
Lovett Wy WLSDN NW10 68 E4
Love Wk CMBW SE5 130 E1
Lowbrook Rd IL IG1 78 B3
Lowden Rd ED N9 30 D7
HNHL SE24 130 C3
STHL UB1 83 J6
Lowe Av CAN/RD E16 94 E4
Lowell St POP/IOD E14 93 G5
Lowen Rd RAIN RM13 99 F1
Lower Addiscombe Rd
CROY/NA CR0 164 E7
Lower Addison Gdns
WKENS W14 107 H1
Lower Belgrave St
BGVA SW1W 16 C4
Lower Broad St DAGE RM10 80 C7
Lower Camden CHST BR7 153 K7
Lower Church St
CROY/NA CR0 * 177 H1
Lower Clapton Rd CLPT E5 74 D3
HACK E8 74 D4
Lower Clarendon Wk
NTGHL W11 88 C5
Lower Common South
PUT/ROE SW15 126 E2
Lower Coombe St
CROY/NA CR0 177 J3
Lower Derby Rd WAT WD17 21 G3
Lower Downs Rd
RYNPK SW20 146 B7
Lower Gravel Rd HAYES BR2 168 D7
Lower Green Gdns WPK KT4 160 D7
Lower Green Rd
ESH/CLAY KT10 170 B1
Lower Gn West MTCM CR4 162 D2
Lower Grosvenor Pl
BGVA SW1W 16 C3
Lower Grove Rd
RCHPK/HAM TW10 125 G5
Lower Hall La CHING E4 43 G4
Lower Hampton Rd
SUN TW16 156 C1
Lower Ham Rd
KUTN/CMB KT2 143 K5
Lower High St WAT WD17 21 G3
Lower James St
SOHO/CST W1F * 10 F6
Lower John St SOHO/CST W1F 10 F6
Lower Kenwood Av
ENC/FH EN2 28 E4
Lower Kings Rd
KUTN/CMB KT2 144 A6
Lower Lea Crossing
POP/IOD E14 94 C6
Lower Maidstone Rd
FBAR/BDGN N11 40 C5
Lower Mardyke Av
RAIN RM13 98 E1
Lower Marsh STHWK SE1 18 A2
Lower Marsh La BRYLDS KT5 159 G3
Lower Merton Ri HAMP NW3 3 J2
Lower Morden La MRDN SM4 161 F5
Lower Mortlake Rd
RCH/KEW TW9 125 F3
Lower Paddock Rd
OXHEY WD19 21 J5
Lower Park Rd BELV DA17 117 H2
FBAR/BDGN N11 40 C4
Lower Queen's Rd BKHH IG9 45 J1
Lower Richmond Rd
PUT/ROE SW15 127 F2
RCH/KEW TW9 125 H2
Lower Rd BELV DA17 117 J2
BERM/RHTH SE16 111 K1
ERITH DA8 118 A3
RYLN/HDSTN HA2 66 D1
SUT SM1 175 H4
Lower Robert St CHCR WC2N 11 K7
Lower Sand Hills SURB KT6 158 D6
Lower Sloane St BGVA SW1W 15 M6
Lower Station Rd DART DA1 138 B5
Lower Strd CDALE/KGS NW9 51 H1
Lower Sunbury Rd
E/WMO/HCT KT8 156 E1
Lower Tail OXHEY WD19 33 J2
Lower Teddington Rd
KUT/HW KT1 143 K7
Lower Ter HAMP NW3 71 G2
Lower Thames St MON EC3R 13 J7
Lower Tub BUSH WD23 22 D6
Lower Wood Rd
ESH/CLAY KT10 171 G5
Loweswater Cl WBLY HA9 67 K1
Lowfield Rd ACT W3 86 E5
KIL/WHAMP NW6 2 A1
Lowfield St DART DA1 139 H6
Low Hall Cl CHING E4 31 J6
Low Hall La WALTH E17 57 G5
Lowick Rd HRW HA1 48 E3
Lowland Gdns ROMW/RG RM7 62 D5
Lowlands Dr
STWL/WRAY TW19 120 A4
Lowlands Rd HRW HA1 48 E6
PIN HA5 47 G6
Lowman Rd HOLWY N7 73 F3
Lowndes Cl KTBR SW1X 16 B4
Lowndes Ct SOHO/CST W1F * 10 E5
Lowndes Ms
STRHM/NOR SW16 148 E1
Lowndes Pl KTBR SW1X * 16 A4
Lowndes Sq KTBR SW1X 15 M2
Lowndes St KTBR SW1X 15 M3
Lowood St WCHPL E1 92 D6
Lowry Cl ERITH DA8 118 A3
Lowry Crs MTCM CR4 162 D1
Lowry Rd BCTR RM8 79 H4
Lowson Gv OXHEY WD19 21 J6
Lowswood Cl NTHWD HA6 32 A7
Lowther Cl BORE WD6 24 B4
Lowther Dr ENC/FH EN2 28 E3
Lowther Hl FSTH SE23 132 B6
Lowther Man BARN SW13 * 106 D7
Lowther Rd BARN SW13 106 C7
HOLWY N7 * 73 G4
KUTN/CMB KT2 144 B7
STAN HA7 50 B2
WALTH E17 57 G1
Lowth Rd CMBW SE5 130 D1
Loxford Av EHAM E6 95 H1
Loxford La IL IG1 78 C4
Loxford Rd BARK IG11 78 B5
Loxham Rd CHING E4 43 K6
Loxham St STPAN WC1H * 5 K8
Loxley Cl SYD SE26 151 F4
Loxley Rd HPTN TW12 141 K3
WAND/EARL SW18 128 C7
Loxton Rd FSTH SE23 132 A7
Loxwood Cl
EBED/NFELT TW14 121 G7
Loxwood Rd TOTM N17 56 A2
Lubbock Rd CHST BR7 154 A7
Lubbock St NWCR SE14 111 K6
Lucan Pl CHEL SW3 15 J6
Lucan Rd BAR EN5 26 C2
Lucas Av PLSTW E13 77 F7
RYLN/HDSTN HA2 66 A1
Lucas Gdns EFNCH N2 53 G1
Lucas Rd PGE/AN SE20 150 E5
Lucas Sq GLDGN NW11 52 E5
Lucas St BROCKY SE4 132 D1
Lucerne Cl PLMGR N13 40 E2
Lucerne Gv WALTH E17 58 B3
Lucerne Ms KENS W8 * 8 B8
Lucerne Rd HBRY N5 73 H3
THHTH CR7 164 C4
Lucey Rd BERM/RHTH SE16 111 H2
Lucey Wy BERM/RHTH SE16 111 H2
Lucien Rd TOOT SW17 148 A3
WIM/MER SW19 147 F1
Lucknow St
WOOL/PLUM SE18 115 K6
Lucorn Cl LEE/GVPK SE12 133 J5
Luddesdon Rd ERITH DA8 117 H6
Ludford Cl CROY/NA CR0 177 H3
Ludgate Broadway
BLKFR EC4V * 12 D5
Ludgate Circ STP EC4M 12 C5
Ludgate Hl STP EC4M 12 C5
Ludgate Sq STP EC4M * 12 D5
Ludham Cl THMD SE28 97 J5
Ludlow Cl HAYES BR2 * 167 K2
RYLN/HDSTN HA2 65 K3
Ludlow Md OXHEY WD19 33 F2
Ludlow Rd EA W5 85 J3
FELT TW13 140 E2
Ludlow St FSBYE EC1V * 6 E9
Ludlow Wy EFNCH N2 53 G3
RKW/CH/CXG WD3 20 A3
Ludovick Wk PUT/ROE SW15 126 B3
Luffield Rd ABYW SE2 116 C2
Luffman Rd LEE/GVPK SE12 153 F2
Lugard Rd PECK SE15 131 J1
Lugg Ap MNPK E12 78 A2
Luke St SDTCH EC2A 7 J9
Lukin Crs CHING E4 44 B2
Lukin St WCHPL E1 92 E5
Lullingstone Cl
STMC/STPC BR5 155 H6
Lullingstone Crs
STMC/STPC BR5 155 G6
Lullingstone La LEW SE13 133 G5
Lullingstone Rd BELV DA17 117 G5
Lullington Garth BMLY BR1 152 C6
BORE WD6 * 24 E4
NFNCH/WDSPK N12 38 D4
Lullington Rd DAGW RM9 80 A6
PGE/AN SE20 150 C6
Lulot Gdns ARCH N19 72 B1
Lulworth Av HEST TW5 103 G7
WBLY HA9 49 J6
Lulworth Cl RYLN/HDSTN HA2 65 K2
Lulworth Crs MTCM CR4 162 D1
Lulworth Dr PIN HA5 47 H6
Lulworth Gdns
RYLN/HDSTN HA2 65 J1
Lulworth Rd ELTH/MOT SE9 153 J1
PECK SE15 * 131 J1
WELL DA16 136 A1
Lulworth Waye YEAD UB4 83 F5
Lumen Rd WBLY HA9 67 K1
Lumley Cl BELV DA17 117 H5
Lumley Gdns CHEAM SM3 174 C4
Lumley Rd CHEAM SM3 174 C5
Lumley St OXSTW W1C 10 B5
Luna Rd THHTH CR7 164 D2
Lundin Wk OXHEY WD19 * 33 H3
Lundy Dr HYS/HAR UB3 101 H3
Lundy Wk IS N1 73 J5
Lunham Rd NRWD SE19 150 A5
Lupin Cl BRXS/STRHM SW2 149 H1
CROY/NA CR0 166 A7
ROMW/RG RM7 81 F1
WDR/YW UB7 100 A4
Lupton Cl LEE/GVPK SE12 153 F3
Lupton St KTTN NW5 72 C3
Lupus St PIM SW1V 16 D8
Lurgan Av HMSMTH W6 107 G5
Lurline Gdns BTSEA SW11 109 F7
Luscombe Wy VX/NE SW8 109 K6
Lushington Rd CAT SE6 151 K4
WLSDN NW10 87 K1
Lushington Ter HACK E8 * 74 C4
Luther Cl EDGW HA8 36 E1
Luther King Cl WALTH E17 57 G5
Luther Ms TEDD TW11 143 F4
Luther Rd TEDD TW11 143 F4
Luton Pl GNWCH SE10 113 F6
Luton Rd PLSTW E13 94 E3
SCUP DA14 155 J2
WALTH E17 57 G2

Luton St STJWD NW8 9 H1
Luttrell Av PUT/ROE SW15 126 E4
Lutwyche Rd FSTH SE23 151 H1
Luxborough La CHIG IG7 45 K3
Luxborough St CAMTN NW1 10 A1
MHST W1U 10 A2
Luxembourg Ms SRTFD E15 76 C4
Luxemburg Gdns
HMSMTH W6 107 G3
Luxfield Rd ELTH/MOT SE9 134 D7
Luxford St BERM/RHTH SE16 112 A3
Luxmore St BROCKY SE4 112 C7
Luxor St CMBW SE5 130 D2
Lyall Av DUL SE21 150 A3
Lyall Ms KTBR SW1X 16 A4
Lyall Ms West KTBR SW1X * 16 A4
Lyall St KTBR SW1X 16 A4
Lyal Rd BOW E3 93 G1
Lycett Pl SHB W12 106 D1
Lych Gate Wk HYS/HAR UB3 82 D6
Lyconby Gdns CROY/NA CR0 166 B6
Lydd Cl BFN/LL DA15 154 E2
Lydden Gv WAND/EARL SW18 128 A6
Lydden Rd WAND/EARL SW18 128 A6
Lydd Rd BXLYHN DA7 117 G6
Lydeard Rd EHAM E6 77 K6
Lydford Cl STNW/STAM N16 74 A4
Lydford Rd CRICK NW2 70 B5
MV/WKIL W9 88 D3
SEVS/STOTM N15 55 K4
Lydhurst Av
BRXS/STRHM SW2 149 F1
Lydia Rd ERITH DA8 118 C5
Lydney Cl WIM/MER SW19 146 C1
Lydon Rd CLAP SW4 129 H2
Lydstep Rd CHST BR7 154 A3
Lyford Rd WAND/EARL SW18 128 C6
Lyford St WOOL/PLUM SE18 114 D3
Lygon Pl BGVA SW1W * 16 C4
Lyham Cl BRXS/STRHM SW2 129 K5
Lyham Rd BRXS/STRHM SW2 129 K5
Lyle Cl MTCM CR4 163 F6
Lyme Farm Rd LEE/GVPK SE12 133 K3
Lyme Gv HOM E9 74 E6
Lymer Av NRWD SE19 150 B4
Lyme Rd WELL DA16 116 C7
Lymescote Gdns SUT SM1 174 E1
Lyme St CAMTN NW1 4 E2
Lyme Ter CAMTN NW1 4 E2
Lyminge Cl SCUP DA14 155 F3
Lyminge Gdns
WAND/EARL SW18 128 D7
Lymington Av WDGN N22 55 G1
Lymington Cl
STRHM/NOR SW16 163 J1
Lymington Dr RSLP HA4 64 B1
Lymington Gdns
HOR/WEW KT19 173 H4
Lymington Rd BCTR RM8 61 K7
KIL/WHAMP NW6 * 71 F5
Lyminster Cl YEAD UB4 83 J4
Lympstone Gdns PECK SE15 111 H6
Lynbridge Gdns PLMGR N13 41 H3
Lynbrook Cl RAIN RM13 99 F1
Lynbrook Gv PECK SE15 111 F6
Lynchen Cl HEST TW5 101 K7
Lyncourt BKHTH/KID SE3 * 133 G1
Lyncroft Av PIN HA5 47 H4
Lyncroft Gdns EW KT17 173 H7
HSLW TW3 123 H4
KIL/WHAMP NW6 70 E4
WEA W13 104 D1
Lyndale CRICK NW2 70 D2
THDIT KT7 * 157 K6
Lyndale Av CRICK NW2 70 D2
Lyndale Cl BKHTH/KID SE3 113 J5
Lyndale Hampton Court Wy
ESH/CLAY KT10 157 K6
Lyndhurst Av BRYLDS KT5 159 J7
MLHL NW7 37 G5
NFNCH/WDSPK N12 39 K5
PIN HA5 33 F7
STHL UB1 84 B7
STRHM/NOR SW16 163 J1
WHTN TW2 122 E7
Lyndhurst Cl BXLYHN DA7 137 J2
CROY/NA CR0 178 B2
WLSDN NW10 69 F2
Lyndhurst Ct BELMT SM2 * 174 E6
Lyndhurst Dr LEY E10 58 A6
NWMAL KT3 160 B5
Lyndhurst Gdns BARK IG11 78 E5
EN EN1 30 A3
FNCH N3 38 C7
GNTH/NBYPK IG2 60 D5
HAMP NW3 71 H4
PIN HA5 33 F7
Lyndhurst Gv CMBW SE5 131 F1
Lyndhurst Leys HAYES BR2 * 167 G1
Lyndhurst Prior SNWD SE25 * 165 F2
Lyndhurst Rd BXLYHN DA7 137 J2
CHING E4 44 A6
GFD/PVL UB6 84 B3
HAMP NW3 71 H4
THHTH CR7 164 B3
UED N18 42 C3
WDGN N22 41 G5
Lyndhurst Sq PECK SE15 111 G7
Lyndhurst Ter HAMP NW3 71 H4
Lyndhurst Wy BELMT SM2 174 E7
PECK SE15 111 G7
Lyndon Av BFN/LL DA15 136 A4
PIN HA5 33 J5
WLGTN SM6 176 A2
Lyndon Rd BELV DA17 117 H3
Lyndon Yd TOOT SW17 147 F3
Lyne Crs WALTH E17 43 H7
Lynegrove Av ASHF TW15 140 A4
Lyneham Wk CLPT E5 * 75 G4
Lynette Av CLAP SW4 129 G5
Lynford Cl BAR EN5 25 H4
EDGW HA8 36 E7
Lynford Gdns EDGW HA8 36 D2
GDMY/SEVK IG3 79 F1
Lynford Ter ED N9 * 30 B7
Lynhurst Crs HGDN/ICK UB10 64 A6
Lynhurst Rd HGDN/ICK UB10 64 A6
Lynmere Rd WELL DA16 136 C1
Lyn Ms STNW/STAM N16 * 74 B3
Lynmouth Av EN EN1 30 B5
MRDN SM4 161 G6
Lynmouth Dr RSLP HA4 65 F1
Lynmouth Gdns GFD/PVL UB6 67 H7
HEST TW5 102 C7
Lynmouth Rd EFNCH N2 53 K2
GFD/PVL UB6 67 H7
STNW/STAM N16 56 B7
WALTH E17 57 G5
Lynn Cl ASHF TW15 140 B4
KTN/HRWW/WS HA3 48 D1
Lynnett Rd BCTR RM8 79 K1
Lynne Wk ESH/CLAY KT10 170 C4
Lynne Wy NTHLT UB5 83 H1
Lynn Ms WAN E11 76 C1
Lynn Rd BAL SW12 129 G6
GNTH/NBYPK IG2 60 D6
WAN E11 76 C1
Lynscott Wy SAND/SEL CR2 177 H7
Lynstead Cl BMLY BR1 168 B1
Lynsted Cl BXLYHS DA6 137 J4
Lynsted Ct BECK BR3 166 B1
Lynsted Gdns ELTH/MOT SE9 134 C3
Lynton Av CDALE/KGS NW9 51 H3
NFNCH/WDSPK N12 39 H3
WEA W13 85 G5
Lynton Cl CHSGTN KT9 172 A3
ISLW TW7 124 A3
WLSDN NW10 69 G4
Lynton Crs GNTH/NBYPK IG2 60 B5
Lynton Est STHWK SE1 19 M6
Lynton Gdns EN EN1 30 A6
FBAR/BDGN N11 40 D5
Lynton Md TRDG/WHET N20 38 E2
Lynton Rd ACT W3 86 C6
CEND/HSY/T N8 54 D4
CHING E4 43 K4
CROY/NA CR0 164 B5
KIL/WHAMP NW6 70 D7
NWMAL KT3 160 A4
RYLN/HDSTN HA2 65 J1
STHWK SE1 19 M6
Lynton Ter ACT W3 * 86 E5
Lynwood Cl RYLN/HDSTN HA2 65 J2
SWFD E18 45 G7
Lynwood Dr NTHWD HA6 32 C7
WPK KT4 173 J1
Lynwood Gdns CROY/NA CR0 177 F3
STHL UB1 83 K5
Lynwood Gv ORP BR6 169 K6
WCHMH N21 29 G7
Lynwood Rd EA W5 85 K2
THDIT KT7 171 F1
TOOT SW17 147 K2
Lynwood Ter
WIM/MER SW19 * 146 D7
Lyon Meade STAN HA7 35 J7
Lyon Park Av ALP/SUD HA0 68 A5
Lyon Rd HRW HA1 49 F5
ROM RM1 63 H6
WIM/MER SW19 147 G7
Lyonsdown Av BAR EN5 27 G5
Lyonsdown Rd BAR EN5 27 G4
Lyons Pl STJWD NW8 9 G1
Lyon St IS N1 5 L2
Lyons Wk WKENS W14 107 H3
Lyon Wy GFD/PVL UB6 66 D7
Lyric Dr GFD/PVL UB6 84 B3
Lyric Ms SYD SE26 150 E3
Lyric Rd BARN SW13 106 C7
Lysander CDALE/KGS NW9 * 37 H7
Lysander Gdns SURB KT6 159 G5
Lysander Gv ARCH N19 54 D7
Lysander Ms ARCH N19 54 C7
Lysander Rd CROY/NA CR0 177 F5
RSLP HA4 64 B1
Lysias Rd BAL SW12 129 F5
Lysia St FUL/PGN SW6 107 G6
Lysons Wk PUT/ROE SW15 * 126 D4
Lytchet Rd BMLY BR1 152 E6
Lytchgate Cl SAND/SEL CR2 178 A6
Lytcott Dr E/WMO/HCT KT8 156 E2
Lytcott Gv EDUL SE22 131 G4
Lytham Av OXHEY WD19 33 H4
Lytham Cl THMD SE28 98 A5
Lytham St WALW SE17 19 G8
Lyttelton Rd EFNCH N2 53 G4
LEY E10 75 K2
Lyttleton Cl HAMP NW3 3 J2
Lyttleton Rd
CEND/HSY/T N8 * 55 G2
Lytton Av PLMGR N13 41 G1
Lytton Cl EFNCH N2 53 H4
NTHLT UB5 65 K6
Lytton Gdns WLGTN SM6 176 D3
Lytton Gv PUT/ROE SW15 127 G4
Lytton Rd BAR EN5 27 G3
GPK RM2 63 K4
PIN HA5 33 J6
WAN E11 58 C6
Lyveden Rd BKHTH/KID SE3 114 A6
TOOT SW17 147 J5

M

Maberley Crs NRWD SE19 150 C6
Maberley Rd BECK BR3 166 A2
NRWD SE19 150 B7
Mabledon Pl CAMTN NW1 5 H8
Mablethorpe Rd
FUL/PGN SW6 107 H6
Mabley St HOM E9 75 G4
Macaret Cl TRDG/WHET N20 27 F6
Macarthur Cl FSTGT E7 76 E5
WBLY HA9 68 D5
Macarthur Ter CHARL SE7 * 114 C5
Macaulay Av ESH/CLAY KT10 170 E1
Macaulay Rd CLAP SW4 129 G2
EHAM E6 95 H1
Macbean St
WOOL/PLUM SE18 115 F2
Macbeth St HMSMTH W6 106 E4
Macclesfield Br STJWD NW8 3 K5
Macclesfield Rd FSBYE EC1V 6 E7
SNWD SE25 165 J4
Macclesfield St
SOHO/SHAV W1D * 11 H6
Macdonald Av DAGE RM10 80 D2
Macdonald Rd ARCH N19 72 C1
FBAR/BDGN N11 39 K4
FSTGT E7 76 E3
WALTH E17 58 A1
Macduff Rd BTSEA SW11 109 F7
Mace Cl WAP E1W 92 D7
Mace St BETH E2 93 F1
Macfarlane La ISLW TW7 104 A5
Macfarlane Rd SHB W12 88 A7
Mac Farren Pl CAMTN NW1 10 B1
Macgregor Rd CAN/RD E16 95 G4
Machell Rd PECK SE15 131 K2
Mackay Rd VX/NE SW8 129 G2
Mackennal St STJWD NW8 3 K6
Mackenzie Cl SHB W12 87 K6
Mackenzie Rd BECK BR3 166 A1
HOLWY N7 73 F5
Mackeson Rd HAMP NW3 * 71 K3
Mackie Rd BRXS/STRHM SW2 130 B6
Mackintosh La HOM E9 75 F4
Macklin St HOL/ALD WC2B * 11 K4
Macks Rd BERM/RHTH SE16 111 H2
Mackworth St CAMTN NW1 4 E7
Maclean Rd FSTH SE23 132 B5
Macleod House CHARL SE7 * 114 D6
Macleod Rd WCHMH N21 28 E4
Macleod St WALW SE17 18 F8
Maclise Rd WKENS W14 107 H2
Macmillan Wy TOOT SW17 148 B3
Macoma Rd
WOOL/PLUM SE18 115 J5
Macoma Ter
WOOL/PLUM SE18 115 J5
Maconochies Rd
POP/IOD E14 * 112 E4
Macquarie Wy POP/IOD E14 112 E3
Macroom Rd MV/WKIL W9 88 D2
Maddams St BOW E3 93 K3
Maddison Cl EFNCH N2 53 G1
TEDD TW11 143 F5
Maddocks Cl SCUP DA14 155 K5
Maddock Wy WALW SE17 110 C5
Maddox St CONDST W1S 10 D6
Madeira Av BMLY BR1 152 C7
Madeira Gv WFD IG8 45 G5
Madeira Rd MTCM CR4 162 E3
PLMGR N13 41 H3
STRHM/NOR SW16 148 E4
WAN E11 58 B7
Madeleine Ct CHDH RM6 61 J5
Madeley Rd EA W5 85 K5
Madeline Gv IL IG1 78 D4
Madeline Rd PGE/AN SE20 150 C6
Madge Gill Wy EHAM E6 77 J7
Madge Hl HNWL W7 * 84 E6
Madinah Rd HACK E8 74 C4
Madison Cl BELMT SM2 175 H6
Madison Crs BXLYHN DA7 116 D6
Madison Gdns BXLYHN DA7 116 D6
Madoc Cl CRICK NW2 70 D1
Madras Pl HOLWY N7 73 G5
Madras Rd IL IG1 78 B3
Madrid Rd BARN SW13 106 D7
Madron St WALW SE17 19 K7
Mafeking Av BTFD TW8 105 F5
EHAM E6 95 H1
GNTH/NBYPK IG2 60 D6
Mafeking Rd CAN/RD E16 94 D3
EN EN1 30 B2
TOTM N17 56 C1
Magazine Ga BAY/PAD W2 * 9 K8
Magdala Av ARCH N19 72 C1
Magdala Rd ISLW TW7 124 B2
SAND/SEL CR2 177 K6
Magdalene Gdns EHAM E6 96 A3
Magdalen Rd
WAND/EARL SW18 128 B7
Magdalen St STHWK SE1 13 J9
Magee St LBTH SE11 18 A9
Magellan Bvd CAN/RD E16 96 C6
Magellan Pl POP/IOD E14 112 D3
Magnaville Rd BUSH WD23 22 E6
Magnet Rd WBLY HA9 67 K1
Magnin Cl HACK E8 74 C7
Magnolia Cl KUTN/CMB KT2 144 D5
LEY E10 75 J1
Magnolia Ct
KTN/HRWW/WS HA3 50 B6
Magnolia Gdns EDGW HA8 36 E3
Magnolia Pl CLAP SW4 * 129 K4
EA W5 * 85 K4
Magnolia Rd CHSWK W4 105 J5
Magnolia St WDR/YW UB7 100 A3
Magnolia Wy HOR/WEW KT19 172 E4
Magnolia Whf CHSWK W4 * 105 J5
Magpie Cl CDALE/KGS NW9 51 G1
FSTGT E7 76 D4
Magpie Hall Cl HAYES BR2 168 D5
Magpie Hall La HAYES BR2 168 D6
Magpie Hall Rd STAN HA7 34 E1
Magpie Pl NWCR SE14 * 112 B5
Magri Wk WCHPL E1 92 E4
Maguire Dr RCHPK/HAM TW10 143 J3
Maguire St STHWK SE1 19 M1
Mahlon Av RSLP HA4 65 F4
Mahogany Cl
BERM/RHTH SE16 93 G7
Maida Av BAY/PAD W2 8 F2
CHING E4 31 K6
Maida Rd BELV DA17 117 H2
Maida V MV/WKIL W9 2 D6
STJWD NW8 3 G9
Maida Vale Rd DART DA1 138 D4
Maida Wy CHING E4 31 K6
Maiden Erlegh Av BXLY DA5 137 F7
Maiden La CAMTN NW1 5 H1
COVGDN WC2E 11 K6
DART DA1 138 D3
STHWK SE1 12 F9
Maiden Rd SRTFD E15 76 C6
Maidenstone Hl GNWCH SE10 113 F7
Maidstone Av CRW RM5 62 E1
Maidstone Buildings Ms
STHWK SE1 12 F9
Maidstone Rd
FBAR/BDGN N11 40 D5
SCUP DA14 155 K5
Main Av EN EN1 30 B4
NTHWD HA6 32 A2
Main Barracks
WOOL/PLUM SE18 * 114 E4
Main Dr GFD/PVL UB6 * 85 G2
WBLY HA9 67 K2
Mainridge Rd CHST BR7 154 A3
Main Rd ROM RM1 63 H3
SCUP DA14 154 E2
STMC/STPC BR5 155 J7
Main St FELT TW13 141 H4
Maise Webster Cl
STWL/WRAY TW19 * 120 A6
Maismore St PECK SE15 111 H5
The Maisonettes SUT SM1 * 174 D4
Maitland Cl GNWCH SE10 112 E6
HSLWW TW4 122 E2
Maitland Park Rd HAMP NW3 71 K5
Maitland Park Vls HAMP NW3 71 K5
Maitland Rd PGE/AN SE20 151 F5
SRTFD E15 76 D5
Majendie Rd
WOOL/PLUM SE18 115 J4
Major Cl BRXN/ST SW9 130 C2
Major Draper St
WOOL/PLUM SE18 115 G2
Major Rd BERM/RHTH SE16 * 111 H2
SRTFD E15 76 A4
Makepeace Av HGT N6 72 A1
Makepeace Rd NTHLT UB5 83 J1
WAN E11 58 E3
Makins St CHEL SW3 15 K6
Malabar St POP/IOD E14 112 D1
Malam Gdns POP/IOD E14 93 K6
Malan Sq RAIN RM13 81 K5
Malbrook Rd PUT/ROE SW15 126 E3
Malcolm Cl PGE/AN SE20 * 150 E6
Malcolm Ct STAN HA7 35 J4
Malcolm Crs HDN NW4 51 J4
Malcolm Dr SURB KT6 158 E7
Malcolm Pl BETH E2 92 E3
Malcolm Rd PGE/AN SE20 150 E6
SNWD SE25 165 H5
WCHPL E1 92 E3
WIM/MER SW19 146 C5
Malcolms Wy
STHGT/OAK N14 * 28 C4
Malcolm Wy WAN E11 58 E4
Malden Av GFD/PVL UB6 66 E5
SNWD SE25 165 J3
Malden Flds BUSH WD23 21 H4
Malden Green Av WPK KT4 160 C7
Malden Hl NWMAL KT3 160 C3
Malden Hill Gdns NWMAL KT3 160 C2
Malden Pk NWMAL KT3 160 C5
Malden Pl KTTN NW5 72 A4
Malden Rd BORE WD6 24 C2
CHEAM SM3 174 B3
KTTN NW5 71 K4
NWMAL KT3 160 B4
WAT WD17 21 F1
Malden Wy NWMAL KT3 160 A5
Maldon Cl CMBW SE5 * 131 F2
IS N1 6 E3
Maldon Rd ACT W3 86 E6
ED N9 42 B2
ROMW/RG RM7 62 E6
WLGTN SM6 176 B4
Maldon Wk WFD IG8 45 G5
Malet St GWRST WC1E 11 G1
Maley Av WNWD SE27 149 H1
Malford Gv SWFD E18 58 D2
Malfort Rd CMBW SE5 131 F2
Malham Cl FBAR/BDGN N11 40 A5
Malham Rd FSTH SE23 132 A7
Malham Ter UED N18 * 42 D5
Malins Cl BAR EN5 * 25 K4
Malkin Wy WATW WD18 20 C3
Mallams Ms BRXN/ST SW9 130 B2
Mallard Cl BAR EN5 * 27 H5
DART DA1 139 J4
HNWL W7 103 K1
KIL/WHAMP NW6 2 B4
WHTN TW2 123 F6
Mallard Ct WALTH E17 * 58 B2
Mallard Pl TWK TW1 143 G2
WDGN N22 * 55 F1
Mallards Ct OXHEY WD19 33 K2
Mallards Rd BARK IG11 97 G2
WFD IG8 45 F6
Mallard Wk BECK BR3 166 A4
Mallard Wy CDALE/KGS NW9 50 E6
NTHWD HA6 32 A6
WLGTN SM6 176 C7
Mall Chambers KENS W8 * 8 B8
Mallet Dr NTHLT UB5 65 K4
Mallet Rd LEW SE13 133 G5
Malling Cl CROY/NA CR0 * 165 K5
Malling Gdns MRDN SM4 162 B5
Malling Wy HAYES BR2 167 J6
Mallinson Rd BTSEA SW11 128 D4
CROY/NA CR0 176 D2
Mallord St CHEL SW3 15 H9
Mallory Cl BROCKY SE4 132 B3
POP/IOD E14 93 K3
Mallory Ct LEE/GVPK SE12 134 A6
Mallory Gdns EBAR EN4 28 A6
Mallory St STJWD NW8 9 K1
Mallow Cl CROY/NA CR0 166 A7
Mallow Md MLHL NW7 38 C6
Mallow St FSBYE EC1V 7 G9
Mall Rd HMSMTH W6 106 E4
The Mall BTFD TW8 * 104 E5
BXLYHS DA6 * 137 H3
EA W5 86 A6
EMPK RM11 63 K7
KTN/HRWW/WS HA3 50 B5
MORT/ESHN SW14 125 K4
SRTFD E15 * 76 B6
STHGT/OAK N14 40 E2
SURB KT6 158 E4
WHALL SW1A 16 E1
Mall Vls HMSMTH W6 * 106 E4
Malmains Cl BECK BR3 167 G4
Malmains Wy BECK BR3 167 F3
Malmesbury Cl PIN HA5 46 D3
Malmesbury Rd BOW E3 93 H1
CAN/RD E16 94 C4
MRDN SM4 162 B6
SWFD E18 44 D7
Malmesbury Ter CAN/RD E16 94 D4
Malmesbury West Est
BOW E3 93 H2
Malory Cl BECK BR3 166 B1
Malpas Dr PIN HA5 47 H4
Malpas Rd BROCKY SE4 132 C1
DAGW RM9 79 K5
HACK E8 74 D5
Malta Rd LEY E10 57 J7
Malta St FSBYE EC1V 6 C9
Maltby Rd CHSGTN KT9 172 C5
Maltby St STHWK SE1 19 L2
Malthouse Dr CHSWK W4 106 C5
FELT TW13 141 H4
Maltings Cl BOW E3 94 A2
Maltings Pl FUL/PGN SW6 108 A7
STHWK SE1 19 K1
The Maltings ROM RM1 63 H6
SNWD SE25 * 165 F2
Malting Wy ISLW TW7 124 A2
Malton Ms NKENS W10 * 88 C5
WOOL/PLUM SE18 115 K5
Malton Rd NKENS W10 88 C5
Malton St WOOL/PLUM SE18 115 K5
Maltravers St TPL/STR WC2R 11 M6
Malt St STHWK SE1 111 H5
Malva Cl WAND/EARL SW18 128 A4
Malvern Av BXLYHN DA7 117 F6
CHING E4 44 B6
RYLN/HDSTN HA2 65 J2
Malvern Cl BUSH WD23 22 C5
MTCM CR4 163 H2
NKENS W10 88 D4
SURB KT6 159 F7
Malvern Dr FELT TW13 141 H4
GDMY/SEVK IG3 79 F3
WFD IG8 45 G4
Malvern Gdns CRICK NW2 70 C1
KTN/HRWW/WS HA3 50 A3
Malvern Ms KIL/WHAMP NW6 2 A8
Malvern Pl MV/WKIL W9 * 88 D2
Malvern Rd CEND/HSY/T N8 55 F2
EHAM E6 77 J7
HACK E8 74 C6
HPTN TW12 142 A7
HYS/HAR UB3 101 H6
KIL/WHAMP NW6 2 A7
MV/WKIL W9 * 88 D2
SURB KT6 172 A1
THHTH CR7 164 B3
TOTM N17 56 C2
WAN E11 76 C1
Malvern Ter ED N9 30 B7
IS N1 6 A3
Malvern Wy WEA W13 85 H4
Malwood Rd BAL SW12 129 G5
Malyons Rd LEW SE13 132 E4
Malyons Ter LEW SE13 132 E4
Managers St POP/IOD E14 * 94 A7
Manaton Cl PECK SE15 131 J2
Manaton Crs STHL UB1 84 A5
Manbey Gv SRTFD E15 76 C5
Manbey Park Rd SRTFD E15 76 C5
Manbey Rd SRTFD E15 * 76 C5
Manbey St SRTFD E15 76 C5
Manbre Rd HMSMTH W6 107 F5
Manbrough Av EHAM E6 96 A2
Manchester Ct CAN/RD E16 95 F5
Manchester Dr NKENS W10 * 88 C3
Manchester Gv POP/IOD E14 113 F4
Manchester Ms MHST W1U 10 A3
Manchester Rd POP/IOD E14 113 F4
SEVS/STOTM N15 55 K5
THHTH CR7 164 D2
Manchester Sq MBLAR W1H 10 A4
Manchester St MHST W1U 10 A3
Manchester Wy DAGE RM10 * 80 D3
Manchuria Rd BTSEA SW11 129 F5
Manciple St STHWK SE1 19 H2
Mandalay Rd CLAP SW4 129 H4
Mandarin Wy YEAD UB4 83 H5
Mandela Cl WLSDN NW10 68 E6
Mandela Pl WATN WD24 21 H1
Mandela Rd CAN/RD E16 94 E5
Mandela St BRXN/ST SW9 110 B6
CAMTN NW1 4 F3
Mandela Wy STHWK SE1 19 K5
Mandeville Cl WIM/MER SW19 146 C6
Mandeville Ct CHING E4 43 G3
Mandeville Dr SURB KT6 158 E7
Mandeville Pl MHST W1U 10 B4
Mandeville Rd ISLW TW7 124 B1
NTHLT UB5 65 K6
STHGT/OAK N14 40 B1
Mandeville St CLPT E5 75 G2
Mandrake Rd TOOT SW17 147 K2
Mandrake Wy SRTFD E15 * 76 C6
Mandrell Rd
BRXS/STRHM SW2 129 K4
Manette St LSQ/SEVD WC2H 11 H5
Manfred Rd PUT/ROE SW15 127 J4
Manger Rd HOLWY N7 72 E5
Mangold Wy ERITHM DA18 116 E2
Manilla St POP/IOD E14 112 D1
Manister Rd ABYW SE2 116 B2
Manley Ct STNW/STAM N16 74 B2
Manley St CAMTN NW1 4 A3
Mann Cl CROY/NA CR0 177 J2
Manningford Cl FSBYE EC1V * 6 C7
Manning Gdns CROY/NA CR0 165 J6
KTN/HRWW/WS HA3 49 K6
Manning Pl RCHPK/HAM TW10 125 G5
Manning Rd DAGE RM10 80 C5
WALTH E17 57 G3
Manningtree Cl
WIM/MER SW19 127 H7
Manningtree Rd RSLP HA4 65 F3
Manningtree St WCHPL E1 92 C5
Mannin Rd CHDH RM6 61 H6
Mannock Cl CDALE/KGS NW9 51 F2
Mannock Ms SWFD E18 45 F7
Mannock Rd DART DA1 139 J2
WDGN N22 55 H2
Mann's Cl ISLW TW7 124 A4
Manns Rd EDGW HA8 36 C5
Manoel Rd WHTN TW2 142 C1
Manor Av BROCKY SE4 132 C1
HSLWW TW4 122 C2
NTHLT UB5 65 K6
Manorbrook BKHTH/KID SE3 133 K3
Manor Cl BAR EN5 26 C3
CDALE/KGS NW9 50 D3
DAGE RM10 81 F5
DART DA1 138 A3
MLHL NW7 * 37 F4
ROM RM1 63 J4
RSLP HA4 46 D7
THMD SE28 97 J5
WPK KT4 160 B7
Manor Cots NTHWD HA6 32 D7
Manor Cottages Ap
EFNCH N2 53 G1
Manor Ct ACT W3 * 105 H3
E/WMO/HCT KT8 * 157 F3
HRW HA1 * 49 F5
KUTN/CMB KT2 * 144 C7
WBLY HA9 * 68 A4
Manor Court Rd HNWL W7 84 E6
Manor Crs BRYLDS KT5 159 H5
Manor Cft EDGW HA8 * 36 C5
Manordene Cl THDIT KT7 158 B7
Manordene Rd THMD SE28 97 J5
Manor Dr BRYLDS KT5 159 H5
ESH/CLAY KT10 171 F2
FELT TW13 141 H4
HOR/WEW KT19 173 G5
MLHL NW7 37 F4
STHGT/OAK N14 28 B6
TRDG/WHET N20 39 J2
WBLY HA9 68 B3
Manor Dr North NWMAL KT3 160 A6
The Manor Dr WPK KT4 160 B7
Manor Est BERM/RHTH SE16 111 J3
Manor Farm Cl WPK KT4 160 B7
Manor Farm Dr CHING E4 44 C1
Manor Farm Rd ALP/SUD HA0 85 K1
STRHM/NOR SW16 164 B1
Manorfield Cl ARCH N19 72 C3
Manor Gdns ACT W3 105 H3
CLAP SW4 * 129 H1
HOLWY N7 72 E2
HPTN TW12 142 B6
RCH/KEW TW9 125 G3
RSLP HA4 65 G4
RYNPK SW20 161 J1
SAND/SEL CR2 178 B5
SUN TW16 140 E7
Manor Ga NTHLT UB5 65 J6
Manorgate Rd KUTN/CMB KT2 144 C7
Manor Gv BECK BR3 166 E1
PECK SE15 111 K5
RCH/KEW TW9 125 H3
Manor Hall Av HDN NW4 52 A1
Manor Hall Dr HDN NW4 52 B1
Manor Hall Gdns LEY E10 57 J7
Manor House Dr
KIL/WHAMP NW6 70 B6
Manor House Wy ISLW TW7 124 C2
Manor La FELT TW13 140 E1
HYS/HAR UB3 101 G5
LEE/GVPK SE12 133 H5
SUN TW16 156 A1
SUT SM1 175 G4
Manor Lane Ter LEW SE13 133 H3
Manor Ms BROCKY SE4 132 C1
KIL/WHAMP NW6 2 B5
Manor Mt FSTH SE23 131 K7
Manor Pde HRW HA1 * 49 F5

STNW/STAM N16 * 74 B1
Manor Pk CHST BR7 169 J1
LEW SE13 133 G4
RCH/KEW TW9 125 G3
Manor Park Cl WWKM BR4 166 E7
Manor Park Crs EDGW HA8 36 C5
Manor Park Dr
RYLN/HDSTN HA2 48 B2
Manor Park Gdns EDGW HA8 36 C4
Manor Park Rd CHST BR7 154 C7
EFNCH N2 53 G2
MNPK E12 77 H3
SUT SM1 175 G4
WLSDN NW10 69 G7
WWKM BR4 166 E7
Manor Pl BORE WD6 * 24 E2
CHST BR7 169 J1
EBED/NFELT TW14 121 K7
MTCM CR4 163 H2
SUT SM1 175 F4
WALW SE17 18 D8
Manor Rd BAR EN5 26 C3
BARK IG11 79 F5
BECK BR3 166 D1
BELMT SM2 174 D6
BFN/LL DA15 155 F2
BXLY DA5 137 J7
CAN/RD E16 94 C4
CHDH RM6 61 K5
DAGE RM10 80 E5
DART DA1 138 B3
E/WMO/HCT KT8 157 J3
ENC/FH EN2 29 K1
ERITH DA8 118 C5
HRW HA1 49 G5
HYS/HAR UB3 82 E5
LEY E10 57 J6
MTCM CR4 163 H2
RCH/KEW TW9 125 G2
ROM RM1 63 J4
RSLP HA4 46 B7
RYNPK SW20 161 J1
SNWD SE25 165 H3
SRTFD E15 94 C2
STNW/STAM N16 56 A7
TEDD TW11 143 G4
TOTM N17 42 C7
WALTH E17 57 G1
WDGN N22 40 E5
WEA W13 85 G6
WHTN TW2 142 C1
WLGTN SM6 176 B3
WWKM BR4 166 E7
Manor Rd North
ESH/CLAY KT10 171 F2
WLGTN SM6 176 B3
Manor Rd South
ESH/CLAY KT10 170 E3
Manorside BAR EN5 26 C3
Manor Sq BCTR RM8 79 J1
Manor V BTFD TW8 104 D4
Manor Vw FNCH N3 53 F1
Manor Wy WPK KT4 160 B7
BECK BR3 166 D2
BKHTH/KID SE3 133 K3
BORE WD6 24 E3
BXLY DA5 137 H7
BXLYHN DA7 138 A2
CDALE/KGS NW9 51 G3
CHING E4 44 B3
Manorway EN EN1 30 A6
Manor Wy FSTH SE23 131 K6
HAYES BR2 168 D5
MTCM CR4 163 H2
NWDGN UB2 102 C3
RAIN RM13 99 G3
RSLP HA4 46 C6
RYLN/HDSTN HA2 48 B3
SAND/SEL CR2 178 A5
STMC/STPC BR5 169 H3
Manorway WFD IG8 45 G4
The Manor Wy WLGTN SM6 176 B3
Manresa Rd CHEL SW3 15 H7
Mansard Beeches TOOT SW17 148 A4
Mansard Cl HCH RM12 81 J1
PIN HA5 47 H2
Manse Cl HYS/HAR UB3 101 G5
Mansel Gv WALTH E17 43 J7
Mansell Rd ACT W3 87 F7
GFD/PVL UB6 84 B4
Mansell St WCHPL E1 13 M5
Mansel Rd WIM/MER SW19 146 C5
Mansergh Cl CHARL SE7 114 D6
Manse Rd STNW/STAM N16 74 B2
Manser Rd RAIN RM13 99 G2
Mansfield Av EBAR EN4 27 K5
RSLP HA4 47 F7
SEVS/STOTM N15 55 K3
Mansfield Cl ED N9 30 C5
Mansfield Dr YEAD UB4 82 C3
Mansfield Hl CHING E4 31 K7
Mansfield Ms CAVSQ/HST W1G 10 C3
Mansfield Rd ACT W3 86 D3
CHSGTN KT9 171 J4
HAMP NW3 71 K4
IL IG1 78 A1
SAND/SEL CR2 177 K5
WALTH E17 57 H3
WAN E11 59 F5
Mansfield St CAVSQ/HST W1G 10 C3
Mansford St BETH E2 92 C1
Manship Rd MTCM CR4 148 A7
Mansion Cl BRXN/ST SW9 110 B7
Mansion Gdns HAMP NW3 71 F2
Mansion House Pl
MANHO EC4N * 13 G5
Mansion House St
MANHO EC4N 13 G5
Manson Ms SKENS SW7 14 F6
Manson Pl SKENS SW7 15 G6
Manstead Gdns CHDH RM6 61 J6
RAIN RM13 99 K5
Manston Av NWDGN UB2 103 F3
Manston Cl PGE/AN SE20 150 E7
Manstone Rd CRICK NW2 70 C4
Manston Gv KUTN/CMB KT2 143 K4
Manston Wy HCH RM12 81 K5
Manthorpe Rd
WOOL/PLUM SE18 115 H4
Mantilla Rd TOOT SW17 148 A3
Mantle Rd BROCKY SE4 132 B2
Mantlet Cl STRHM/NOR SW16 148 C7
Mantle Wy SRTFD E15 76 C6
Manton Av HNWL W7 104 A1
Manton Cl HYS/HAR UB3 82 C6
Manton Rd ABYW SE2 116 B3
Mantua St BTSEA SW11 128 C2
Mantus Rd WCHPL E1 92 E3
Manus Wy TRDG/WHET N20 39 G1
Manville Gdns TOOT SW17 148 B1
Manville Rd TOOT SW17 148 A1
Manwood Rd BROCKY SE4 132 C4
Manwood St CAN/RD E16 95 K7
Many Gates BAL SW12 148 B1
Mapesbury Ms
CDALE/KGS NW9 51 J5
Mapesbury Rd CRICK NW2 70 C5
Mapeshill Pl CRICK NW2 70 A5
Mape St BETH E2 92 D3
Maple Av ACT W3 87 G7
CHING E4 43 H5
RYLN/HDSTN HA2 66 B1
Maple Cl BKHH IG9 45 H2
BUSH WD23 21 J1
CLAP SW4 129 J5
FNCH N3 38 E5
HCH RM12 81 K2
HPTN TW12 141 K5
MTCM CR4 148 B7
RSLP HA4 47 F5
STMC/STPC BR5 169 J4
STNW/STAM N16 56 C5
YEAD UB4 83 H2
Maple Ct ASHF TW15 140 B5
HACK E8 * 74 C5
NWMAL KT3 160 A2
Maple Crs BFN/LL DA15 136 B5
Maplecroft Cl EHAM E6 95 H5
Mapledale Av CROY/NA CR0 178 D2
Mapledene Est HACK E8 * 74 C6
Mapledene Rd HACK E8 7 M1
Maple Gdns EDGW HA8 37 G6
Maple Gv BTFD TW8 104 C6
CDALE/KGS NW9 50 E6
EA W5 104 E2
STHL UB1 83 K4
Maplehurst Cl KUT/HW KT1 159 F3
Maple Leaf Dr BFN/LL DA15 136 A7
Mapleleafe Gdns
BARK/HLT IG6 60 B2
Maple Leaf Sq
BERM/RHTH SE16 * 112 A1
Maple Ms KIL/WHAMP NW6 * 2 C5
STRHM/NOR SW16 149 F4
Maple Pl FITZ W1T 10 F2
TOTM N17 42 C6
Maple Rd DART DA1 139 F7
PGE/AN SE20 150 D7
SURB KT6 158 E4
WAN E11 58 C5
YEAD UB4 83 G2
Maples Pl WCHPL E1 * 92 D4
Maplestead Rd
BRXS/STRHM SW2 130 A6
DAGW RM9 79 H7
The Maples ESH/CLAY KT10 * 171 G6
KUT/HW KT1 * 143 J6
Maple St BETH E2 92 C1
FITZ W1T 10 E2
ROMW/RG RM7 62 E3
Maplethorpe Rd THHTH CR7 164 B3
Mapleton Cl HAYES BR2 167 K4
Mapleton Crs
WAND/EARL SW18 128 A5
Mapleton Rd CHING E4 44 A2
EN EN1 30 D1
WAND/EARL SW18 127 K5
Maple Tree Pl BKHTH/KID SE3 114 D7
Maple Wk NKENS W10 * 88 B3
Maple Wy FELT TW13 140 E2
Maplin Cl WCHMH N21 29 F5
Maplin Rd CAN/RD E16 94 E5
Maplin St BOW E3 93 H2
Mapperley Dr WFD IG8 44 C6
Marabou Cl MNPK E12 77 J4
Maran Wy ERITHM DA18 116 E2
Marathon Wy THMD SE28 97 F7
Marban Rd MV/WKIL W9 88 D2
Marble Cl ACT W3 86 D7
Marble Dr CRICK NW2 52 B6
Marble Hill Cl TWK TW1 124 C6
Marble Hill Gdns TWK TW1 124 C6
Marble Quay WAP E1W 13 M8
Marbrook Ct LEE/GVPK SE12 153 G2
Marcella Rd BRXN/ST SW9 130 B1
Marcet Rd DART DA1 139 F4
Marchant Cl MLHL NW7 37 G5
Marchant Rd WAN E11 76 B1
Marchant St NWCR SE14 112 B5
Marchbank Rd WKENS W14 107 J5
Marchmont Gdns
RCHPK/HAM TW10 125 F4
Marchmont Rd
RCHPK/HAM TW10 125 G4
WLGTN SM6 176 C7
Marchmont St BMSBY WC1N 5 J9
STPAN WC1H 5 J9
March Rd TWK TW1 124 A6
Marchside Cl HEST TW5 102 C7
Marchwood Cl CMBW SE5 111 F6
Marchwood Crs EA W5 85 J5
Marcia Rd STHWK SE1 19 K6
Marcilly Rd WAND/EARL SW18 128 C4
Marconi Pl FBAR/BDGN N11 40 B4
Marconi Rd LEY E10 57 J7
Marconi Wy STHL UB1 84 B5
Marcon Pl HACK E8 74 D5
Marco Rd HMSMTH W6 106 E2
Marcus Garvey Ms EDUL SE22 131 J5
Marcus Garvey Wy HNHL SE24 130 B3
Marcus Rd DART DA1 138 D6
Marcus St SRTFD E15 76 C7
WAND/EARL SW18 128 A5
Marcus Ter WAND/EARL SW18 128 A5
Mardale Dr CDALE/KGS NW9 51 F4
Mardell Rd CROY/NA CR0 166 A4
Marden Av HAYES BR2 167 K5
Marden Crs BXLY DA5 137 K4
CROY/NA CR0 164 A5
Marden Rd CROY/NA CR0 164 A5
ROM RM1 63 G5
TOTM N17 56 A1
Marden Sq BERM/RHTH SE16 111 J2
Marder Rd WEA W13 104 B1
Mardyke Cl RAIN RM13 98 E1
Marechal Niel Av BFN/LL DA15 154 D2
Marechal Niel Pde
SCUP DA14 * 154 D2
Maresfield CROY/NA CR0 178 A2
Maresfield Gdns HAMP NW3 71 G4
Mare St HACK E8 74 D7
Marfield Cl WPK KT4 160 D7
Marfleet Cl CAR SM5 175 J1
Margaret Av CHING E4 31 K5
Margaret Bondfield Av
BARK IG11 79 G6
Margaret Cl GPK RM2 63 K4
Margaret Gardner Dr
ELTH/MOT SE9 153 K1
Margaret Ingram Cl
FUL/PGN SW6 * 107 J5
Margaret Lockwood Cl
KUT/HW KT1 * 159 G3
Margaret Rd BXLY DA5 136 E5
EBAR EN4 27 H3
GPK RM2 63 K4
STNW/STAM N16 * 56 B7
WAN E11 58 B5
Margaret Rutherford Pl
BAL SW12 129 H7
Margaret St GTPST W1W 10 E4
REGST W1B 10 D4
Margaretta Ter CHEL SW3 15 J9
Margaretting Rd MNPK E12 77 G1
Margaret Wy REDBR IG4 59 J5
Margate Rd
BRXS/STRHM SW2 129 K4
Margeholes OXHEY WD19 33 J1
Margery Park Rd FSTGT E7 76 E5
Margery Rd BCTR RM8 79 K2
Margery St CLKNW EC1R 6 A8
Margin Dr WIM/MER SW19 146 B4
Margravine Gdns
HMSMTH W6 107 G4
Margravine Rd HMSMTH W6 107 G5
Marguerite Vls RYNPK SW20 * 145 K6
Marham Dr CDALE/KGS NW9 51 G1
Marham Gdns MRDN SM4 162 B5
WAND/EARL SW18 128 D7
Maria Cl STHWK SE1 111 H3
Marian Cl YEAD UB4 83 H3
Marian Pl BETH E2 92 D1
Marian Rd STRHM/NOR SW16 148 C7
Marian St BETH E2 * 92 D1
Marian Wy WLSDN NW10 69 H6
Maria Ter WCHPL E1 93 F4
Maria Theresa Cl NWMAL KT3 160 A4
Maricas Av
KTN/HRWW/WS HA3 34 D7
Marie Curie CMBW SE5 * 111 F7
Marie Lloyd Wk HACK E8 * 74 C5
Mariette Wy WLGTN SM6 176 E7
Marigold Aly STHWK SE1 12 C7
Marigold Cl STHL UB1 83 J6
Marigold Rd TOTM N17 42 E6
Marigold St BERM/RHTH SE16 111 J1
Marigold Wy CROY/NA CR0 166 A7
Marina Ap YEAD UB4 83 J4
Marina Av NWMAL KT3 160 E5
Marina Dr DART DA1 139 K7
WELL DA16 135 K1
Marina Gdns ROMW/RG RM7 62 D4
Marina Pl KUT/HW KT1 158 E1
Marina Wy TEDD TW11 143 K6
Marine Ct PUR RM19 119 J3
Marine Dr BARK IG11 97 G3
WOOL/PLUM SE18 114 E3
Marinefield Rd FUL/PGN SW6 128 A1
Mariner Gdns
RCHPK/HAM TW10 143 H2
Mariner Rd MNPK E12 78 A3
Mariners Ms POP/IOD E14 113 G3
Marine St BERM/RHTH SE16 111 H2
Marion Gv WFD IG8 44 C4
Marion Ms DUL SE21 149 K2
Marion Rd MLHL NW7 37 J4
THHTH CR7 164 D4
Marischal Rd LEW SE13 133 G2
Maritime Quay POP/IOD E14 112 D4
Maritime St BOW E3 93 H3
Marius Rd TOOT SW17 148 A1
Marjorie Gv BTSEA SW11 128 E3
Mark Av CHING E4 31 K5
Mark Cl BXLYHN DA7 117 F7
HAYES BR2 181 J3
STHL UB1 84 A7
Markeston Gn OXHEY WD19 33 H3
Market Chambers
ENC/FH EN2 * 29 K2
Market Est HOLWY N7 72 E5
Market La EDGW HA8 36 E7
SHB W12 * 107 F1
Market Link ROM RM1 63 G3
Market Ms MYFR/PICC W1J 10 C9
Market Pde BMLY BR1 * 152 E7
ED N9 * 42 C1
EW KT17 * 173 H7
FELT TW13 * 141 J1
LEY E10 * 57 K5
SCUP DA14 * 155 G3
SNWD SE25 * 165 H3
STNW/STAM N16 * 56 C7
WALTH E17 * 57 H2
Market Pl ACT W3 86 E7
BERM/RHTH SE16 * 111 H3
BTFD TW8 104 D6
BXLYHS DA6 137 H3
DART DA1 139 H6
EFNCH N2 53 H2
GTPST W1W 10 E4
KUT/HW KT1 * 158 E1
ROM RM1 63 G4
WAT WD17 21 G3
Market Rd HOLWY N7 72 E5
RCH/KEW TW9 125 H2
Market Sq ED N9 42 D1
Market St EHAM E6 95 K1
WATW WD18 21 F3
WOOL/PLUM SE18 115 F3
Market Ter BTFD TW8 * 105 F5
The Market CAR SM5 * 162 B7
HNWL W7 * 104 A1
PECK SE15 * 131 H1
RCH/KEW TW9 * 124 E4
SUT SM1 * 162 B7
Market Yard Ms STHWK SE1 19 J3
Markfield Gdns CHING E4 31 K6
Markfield Rd
SEVS/STOTM N15 56 C3
Markham Cl BORE WD6 24 B2
Markham Pl CHEL SW3 * 15 L7
Markham Sq CHEL SW3 15 L7
Markham St CHEL SW3 15 K7
Markhole Cl HPTN TW12 141 K6
Markhouse Av WALTH E17 57 G5
Markhouse Pas WALTH E17 57 H5
Markhouse Rd WALTH E17 57 H5
Mark La MON EC3R 13 K6
Markmanor Av WALTH E17 57 G6
Mark Rd WDGN N22 55 H1
Marksbury Av RCH/KEW TW9 125 H2
Marks Rd ROMW/RG RM7 62 E4
Mark St SDTCH EC2A 7 J9
SRTFD E15 76 C6
Mark Ter RYNPK SW20 * 146 A6
Markwade Cl MNPK E12 59 H7
The Markway SUN TW16 156 B1
Markwell Cl SYD SE26 150 D3
Markyate Rd BCTR RM8 79 H4
Marlands Rd CLAY IG5 59 J2
Marlborogh Rd ISLW TW7 104 C7
Marlborough Av EDGW HA8 36 D2
HACK E8 74 C7
RSLP HA4 46 A5
STHGT/OAK N14 40 C2
Marlborough Cl
TRDG/WHET N20 39 K2
WALW SE17 18 D6
WIM/MER SW19 147 J5
Marlborough Ct REGST W1B * 10 E6
Marlborough Crs CHSWK W4 106 A2
HYS/HAR UB3 101 G6
Marlborough Dr BUSH WD23 21 K3
CLAY IG5 59 J2
Marlborough Gdns
TRDG/WHET N20 39 K2
Marlborough Ga BAY/PAD W2 9 G7
Marlborough Gv STHWK SE1 111 H4
Marlborough Hl HRW HA1 48 E3
STJWD NW8 2 F4
Marlborough La CHARL SE7 114 B5
Marlborough Ms
BRXS/STRHM SW2 130 A3
Marlborough Pde
FSBYPK N4 * 55 J7
Marlborough Park Av
BFN/LL DA15 136 B7
Marlborough Pl STJWD NW8 2 E6
Marlborough Rd ARCH N19 72 E1
BCTR RM8 79 J3
CHING E4 43 K5
CHSWK W4 105 K4
DART DA1 139 F5
EA W5 104 E1
ED N9 30 B7
FELT TW13 141 H1
FSTGT E7 77 G6
HAYES BR2 168 B3
HPTN TW12 142 A5
NWDGN UB2 102 B2
RCHPK/HAM TW10 125 F5
ROMW/RG RM7 62 C3
SAND/SEL CR2 177 J6
SRTFD E15 * 76 C3
SUT SM1 174 E2
SWFD E18 58 E2
WATW WD18 21 F3
WDGN N22 41 F6
WELL DA16 136 E2
WHALL SW1A 10 F9
WIM/MER SW19 147 J5
WOOL/PLUM SE18 115 G2
Marlborough St CHEL SW3 15 J6
Marlborough Yd ARCH N19 72 D1
Marler Rd FSTH SE23 132 C7
Marley Av BXLYHN DA7 116 E5
Marley Cl GFD/PVL UB6 84 A2
SEVS/STOTM N15 55 H3
Marley Rd BERM/RHTH SE16 * 112 A3
Marlin Cl SUN TW16 140 C5
Marlingdene Cl HPTN TW12 142 A5
Marlings Cl CHST BR7 169 K3
Marlings Park Av CHST BR7 169 K2
Marlins Cl SUT SM1 * 175 G4
Marlins Meadow WATW WD18 20 B5
The Marlins NTHWD HA6 32 D5
Marloes Cl ALP/SUD HA0 67 K3
Marloes Rd KENS W8 14 C3
Marlow Av PUR RM19 119 K3
Marlow Cl PGE/AN SE20 165 J2
Marlow Ct CDALE/KGS NW9 51 H2
Marlow Crs TWK TW1 124 A5
Marlow Dr CHEAM SM3 174 B2
Marlowe Cl CHST BR7 154 D5
Marlowe Rd WALTH E17 58 A3
Marlowe Sq MTCM CR4 163 H3
The Marlowes DART DA1 138 A3
STJWD NW8 3 G4
Marlowe Wy CROY/NA CR0 176 E1
Marlow Gdns HYS/HAR UB3 101 G2
Marlow Rd EHAM E6 95 K2
NWDGN UB2 102 E2
PGE/AN SE20 165 J2
Marlow Wy BERM/RHTH SE16 112 A1
Marl Rd WAND/EARL SW18 128 A3
Marlton St GNWCH SE10 113 J4
Marlwood Cl BFN/LL DA15 154 E1
Marmadon Rd
WOOL/PLUM SE18 116 A3
Marmion Ap CHING E4 43 J3
Marmion Av CHING E4 43 H3
Marmion Cl CHING E4 43 H3
Marmion Ms BTSEA SW11 * 129 F2
Marmion Rd BTSEA SW11 129 F3
Marmont Rd PECK SE15 111 H7
Marmora Rd EDUL SE22 131 K5
Marmot Rd HSLWW TW4 122 C2
Marne Av FBAR/BDGN N11 40 B3
WELL DA16 136 B2
Marnell Wy HSLWW TW4 122 C2
Marne St NKENS W10 88 C2
Marney Rd BTSEA SW11 129 F3
Marnfield Crs
BRXS/STRHM SW2 130 A7
Marnham Av CRICK NW2 70 C3
Marnham Crs GFD/PVL UB6 84 B1
Marnock Rd BROCKY SE4 132 C4
Maroon St POP/IOD E14 93 G4
Maroons Wy CAT SE6 151 J4
Marquess Rd IS N1 73 K5
Marquess Rd South IS N1 * 73 J5
Marquis Cl ALP/SUD HA0 68 B6
Marquis Rd CAMTN NW1 72 D5
FSBYPK N4 55 F7
WDGN N22 41 F5
Marrabon Cl BFN/LL DA15 136 B7
Marrick Cl PUT/ROE SW15 126 D3
Married Quarters EDGW HA8 * 36 D6
Marriner Ct HYS/HAR UB3 * 82 C6
Marriot Rd MUSWH N10 39 K7
Marriott Cl EBED/NFELT TW14 121 G5
Marriott Rd BAR EN5 26 B2
DART DA1 139 K6
FSBYPK N4 55 F7
SRTFD E15 76 C7
Marriotts Cl CDALE/KGS NW9 51 H5
Marriotts Yd BAR EN5 * 26 B2
Marryat Cl HSLWW TW4 122 E3
Marryat Pl WIM/MER SW19 146 C3
Marryat Rd WIM/MER SW19 146 B4
Marryfields Wy CAT SE6 132 E6
Marsala Rd LEW SE13 132 E3
Marsden Gdns DART DA1 139 J1
Marsden Rd ED N9 42 D1
PECK SE15 131 G2
Marsden St KTTN NW5 72 A5
Marshall Cl FBAR/BDGN N11 40 B3
HRW HA1 48 D6
HSLWW TW4 122 E4
WAND/EARL SW18 128 B5
Marshall Dr YEAD UB4 82 D4
Marshall Est MLHL NW7 * 37 J3
Marshall Rd LEY E10 75 K3
TOTM N17 41 K7
Marshalls Dr ROM RM1 63 G2
Marshalls Gv
WOOL/PLUM SE18 114 D3
Marshall's Pl
BERM/RHTH SE16 19 M4
Marshalls Rd ROMW/RG RM7 63 F3
Marshall's Rd SUT SM1 175 F3
Marshall St SOHO/CST W1F 10 F5
Marshalsea Rd STHWK SE1 18 F1
Marsham Cl CHST BR7 * 154 B4
Marsham St WEST SW1P 17 H5
Marsh Av MTCM CR4 162 E1
Marshbrook Cl
BKHTH/KID SE3 134 C2
Marsh Cl MLHL NW7 37 H2
Marsh Dr CDALE/KGS NW9 51 H5
Marsh Farm Rd WHTN TW2 124 A7
Marshfield St POP/IOD E14 113 F2
Marsh Green Rd DAGE RM10 80 C7
Marsh Hl HOM E9 75 G4
Marsh La LEY E10 75 H1
MLHL NW7 37 G2
STAN HA7 35 J4
TOTM N17 42 D6
Marsh Rd ALP/SUD HA0 85 K2
PIN HA5 47 J3
Marshside Cl ED N9 30 E7
Marsh St DART DA1 139 K2
POP/IOD E14 * 112 E3
Marsh Wall POP/IOD E14 112 D1
Marsh Wy RAIN RM13 99 F5
Marsland Cl WALW SE17 18 D8
Marston Av CHSGTN KT9 172 A5
DAGE RM10 80 C2
Marston Cl DAGE RM10 80 C2
KIL/WHAMP NW6 2 F1
Marston Ct WOT/HER KT12 * 156 B7
Marston Rd CLAY IG5 59 J1
TEDD TW11 143 H4
Marston Wy NRWD SE19 149 H6
Marsworth Av PIN HA5 33 H7
Marsworth Cl WATW WD18 * 20 C5
YEAD UB4 83 J4
Martaban Rd
STNW/STAM N16 74 A1
Martello St HACK E8 74 D6
Martell Rd DUL SE21 149 K2
Martel Pl HACK E8 74 B5
Marten Rd WALTH E17 57 J1
Martens Av BXLYHN DA7 137 K3
Martens Cl BXLYHN DA7 137 K3
Martham Cl THMD SE28 97 K6
Martha Rd SRTFD E15 76 C5
Martha's Blds FSBYE EC1V 7 G9
Martha St WCHPL E1 92 E5
Marthorne Crs
KTN/HRWW/WS HA3 48 D1
Martin Bowes Rd
ELTH/MOT SE9 134 E2
Martin Cl ED N9 31 F7
Martin Crs CROY/NA CR0 164 A7
Martindale MORT/ESHN SW14 125 K4
Martindale Av CAN/RD E16 94 E6
Martindale Rd BAL SW12 129 G6
HSLWW TW4 122 D2
Martin Dene BXLYHS DA6 137 G4
Martin Dr NTHLT UB5 65 K4
RAIN RM13 99 K3
Martineau Cl ESH/CLAY KT10 170 D3
Martineau Dr TWK TW1 124 C3
Martineau Rd HBRY N5 73 H3
Martingales Cl
RCHPK/HAM TW10 143 K2
Martin Gdns BCTR RM8 79 J3
Martin Gv MRDN SM4 161 K2
Martin La CANST EC4R 13 H6
Martin Ri BXLYHS DA6 137 G4
Martin Rd BCTR RM8 79 J3
Martins Cl WWKM BR4 180 B1
Martins Mt BAR EN5 26 E3
Martins Pl THMD SE28 96 E7
Martin's Rd HAYES BR2 167 H1
The Martins SYD SE26 150 D4
WBLY HA9 * 68 B2
Martin St THMD SE28 96 E7
Martins Wk MUSWH N10 * 40 A7
THMD SE28 96 E7
Martin Wy MRDN SM4 161 H2
Martlet Gv NTHLT UB5 83 H2
Martlett Ct HOL/ALD WC2B 11 K5
Martley Dr GNTH/NBYPK IG2 60 B4
Martock Cl
KTN/HRWW/WS HA3 49 G3
Martock Gdns
FBAR/BDGN N11 39 K4
Marton Cl CAT SE6 151 J2
Marton Rd STNW/STAM N16 * 74 A1
Martys Yd HAMP NW3 * 71 H3
Marvell Av YEAD UB4 82 E4
Marvels Cl LEE/GVPK SE12 153 F1
Marvels La LEE/GVPK SE12 153 F1
Marville Rd FUL/PGN SW6 107 J6
Marvin St HACK E8 * 74 D5
Marwell Cl ROM RM1 63 J5
WWKM BR4 180 D1
Marwood Cl WELL DA16 136 C2
Marwood Dr MLHL NW7 38 B6
Mary Adelaide Cl
PUT/ROE SW15 145 G2
Mary Ann Blds DEPT SE8 112 D5
Maryat Sq FUL/PGN SW6 107 H7
Maryatt Av RYLN/HDSTN HA2 66 B1
Marybank WOOL/PLUM SE18 114 E3
Mary Cl KTN/HRWW/WS HA3 50 B3
Mary Datchelor Cl CMBW SE5 110 E7
Mary Gn STJWD NW8 * 2 D3
Maryland Pk SRTFD E15 76 C4
Maryland Rd MV/WKIL W9 8 B1
SRTFD E15 76 B4
THHTH CR7 149 H7
WDGN N22 41 G5
Maryland Sq SRTFD E15 76 C4
Marylands Rd MV/WKIL W9 8 B1
Maryland St SRTFD E15 76 B4
Maryland Wk IS N1 * 6 E3
Mary Lawrencson Pl
BKHTH/KID SE3 113 K6
Marylebone F/O BAY/PAD W2 9 J3
Marylebone High St
CAVSQ/HST W1G 10 B3
Marylebone La MHST W1U 10 B4
Marylebone Ms
CAVSQ/HST W1G 10 B3
Marylebone Pas GTPST W1W 10 F4
Marylebone Rd CAMTN NW1 9 M1
MBLAR W1H 9 K2
Marylebone St
CAVSQ/HST W1G 10 B3
Marylee Wy LBTH SE11 17 M6
Mary Neuner Rd WDGN N22 55 F2
Maryon Gv CHARL SE7 114 D3
Maryon Ms HAMP NW3 71 J3
Maryon Rd CHARL SE7 114 D3
Mary Peters Dr GFD/PVL UB6 66 D6
Mary Pl NTGHL W11 88 C6
Mary Rose Cl HPTN TW12 142 A7
Maryrose Wy
TRDG/WHET N20 27 H7
Mary Seacole Cl HACK E8 * 7 L3
Mary Secole Cl HACK E8 * 7 L3
Mary's Ter TWK TW1 124 B6

Mary St CAN/RD E16 94 D4
IS N1 6 F4
Mary Ter CAMTN NW1 4 E4
Mary Wy OXHEY WD19 33 G3
Masbro' Rd WKENS W14 107 G2
Mascalls Rd CHARL SE7 114 B5
Mascotts Cl CRICK NW2 69 K2
Masefield Av BORE WD6 24 D4
STAN HA7 35 F4
STHL UB1 84 A6
Masefield Cl ERITH DA8 118 C7
Masefield Crs STHGT/OAK N14 28 C4
Masefield Gdns EHAM E6 96 A3
Masefield La YEAD UB4 83 F3
Masefield Rd HPTN TW12 141 K3
Masefield Wy
STWL/WRAY TW19 120 C7
Mashie Rd ACT W3 87 G5
Mashiters Wk ROM RM1 63 G2
Maskall Cl BRXS/STRHM SW2 * 130 B7
Maskell Rd TOOT SW17 147 G2
Maskelyne Cl BTSEA SW11 108 D7
Mason Cl BERM/RHTH SE16 111 H4
BORE WD6 25 F1
BXLYHN DA7 137 J2
CAN/RD E16 94 E6
HPTN TW12 141 K7
RYNPK SW20 146 B7
Mason Ct WBLY HA9 * 68 C1
Mason Rd SUT SM1 175 F4
WFD IG8 44 C3
Mason's Arms Ms
CONDST W1S * 10 D5
Masons Av
KTN/HRWW/WS HA3 48 E2
Mason's Av CITYW EC2V 13 G4
CROY/NA CR0 177 J2
Masons Ct EW KT17 * 173 J7
Masons Hl BMLY BR1 167 K2
WOOL/PLUM SE18 115 G3
Mason's Pl FSBYE EC1V 6 D7
MTCM CR4 147 K7
Mason St WALW SE17 19 H5
Masons Yd FSBYE EC1V 6 E9
STJS SW1Y 10 F8
Massey Cl FBAR/BDGN N11 40 B4
Massie Rd HACK E8 74 C5
Massingberd Wy TOOT SW17 148 B3
Massinger St WALW SE17 19 J6
Massingham St WCHPL E1 93 F3
Masson Av RSLP HA4 65 G5
Masterman Rd EHAM E6 95 J2
Masters Cl STRHM/NOR SW16 148 C5
Masters Dr BERM/RHTH SE16 111 J4
Master's St WCHPL E1 93 F4
Masthouse Ter POP/IOD E14 112 D3
Mast House Ter
POP/IOD E14 * 112 D3
Mastmaker Rd POP/IOD E14 112 D1
Mast Quay WOOL/PLUM SE18 114 E2
Maswell Park Crs HSLW TW3 123 H3
Maswell Park Rd HSLW TW3 123 G4
Matara Ms WALW SE17 18 E7
Matcham Rd WAN E11 76 C2
Matchless Dr
WOOL/PLUM SE18 115 F6
Matfield Cl HAYES BR2 167 K4
Matfield Rd BELV DA17 117 H5
Matham Gv EDUL SE22 131 G3
Matham Rd E/WMO/HCT KT8 157 J4
Matheson Rd WKENS W14 107 J3
Mathews Av EHAM E6 96 A1
Mathews Park Av SRTFD E15 76 D5
Mathews Yd
LSQ/SEVD WC2H * 11 J5
Mathieson Ct STHWK SE1 18 D2
Matilda Cl NRWD SE19 149 K6
Matilda Gdns BOW E3 93 J1
Matilda St IS N1 5 M4
Matlock Cl BAR EN5 26 B4
HNHL SE24 130 D3
Matlock Crs CHEAM SM3 174 C3
OXHEY WD19 33 G2
Matlock Gdns CHEAM SM3 174 C3
Matlock Pl CHEAM SM3 174 C3
Matlock Rd LEY E10 58 A5
Matlock St POP/IOD E14 93 G5
Matlock Wy NWMAL KT3 145 F7
Mattelen Cl WIM/MER SW19 146 C1
Matthew Cl NKENS W10 * 88 B3
Matthew Ct MTCM CR4 163 J4
Matthews Rd GFD/PVL UB6 66 D4
Matthews St BTSEA SW11 * 128 E1
Matthias Rd STNW/STAM N16 73 K4
Mattingly Wy PECK SE15 111 G6
Mattison Rd FSBYPK N4 55 G5
Mattock La WEA W13 85 H7
Maud Cashmore Wy
WOOL/PLUM SE18 114 E2
Maude Rd CMBW SE5 131 F1
WALTH E17 57 G4
Maudesville Cots HNWL W7 84 E7
Maude Ter WALTH E17 57 G3
Maud Gdns BARK IG11 97 F1
PLSTW E13 94 D1
Maudlins Gn WAP E1W * 92 C7
Maud Rd LEY E10 76 A2
PLSTW E13 94 D1
Maudslay Rd ELTH/MOT SE9 134 E2
Maud St CAN/RD E16 94 D4
Maud Wilkes Cl KTTN NW5 72 C4
Maugham Wy ACT W3 105 K2
Mauleverer Rd
BRXS/STRHM SW2 129 K4
Maundeby Wk WLSDN NW10 * 69 G4
Maunder Rd HNWL W7 84 E7
Maunsel St WEST SW1P 17 G5
Maurice Av WDGN N22 55 H1
Maurice Browne Cl
MLHL NW7 38 B4
Maurice St SHB W12 87 K5
Maurice Wk GLDGN NW11 53 G3
Maurier Cl NTHLT UB5 65 G7
Mauritius Rd GNWCH SE10 113 H3
Maury Rd STNW/STAM N16 74 C1
Mauveine Gdns HSLW TW3 123 F3
Mavelstone Rd BMLY BR1 153 H7
Maverton Rd BOW E3 * 75 J7
Mavis Av HOR/WEW KT19 173 G4
Mavis Cl HOR/WEW KT19 173 G4
Mawbey Pl STHWK SE1 19 M8
Mawbey Rd STHWK SE1 19 M8
Mawbey St VX/NE SW8 109 K6
Mawney Cl ROMW/RG RM7 62 D2
Mawney Rd ROMW/RG RM7 62 D1
Mawson Cl RYNPK SW20 161 H1
Mawson La CHSWK W4 106 C5
Maxey Gdns DAGW RM9 80 A3
Maxey Rd DAGW RM9 80 A3
WOOL/PLUM SE18 115 H3
Maxfield Cl TRDG/WHET N20 27 G6
Maxilla Wk NKENS W10 88 B5
Maximfeldt Rd ERITH DA8 118 B4
Maxim Rd DART DA1 138 B4
ERITH DA8 118 B4
WCHMH N21 29 G5
Maxted Pk HRW HA1 48 E6
Maxted Rd PECK SE15 131 G2
Maxwell Cl CROY/NA CR0 163 K7
HYS/HAR UB3 82 E6
Maxwell Ri OXHEY WD19 21 J6
Maxwell Rd ASHF TW15 140 A5
BORE WD6 24 D2
FUL/PGN SW6 108 A6
NTHWD HA6 32 B6
WDR/YW UB7 100 B3
WELL DA16 136 B3
Maxwelton Av MLHL NW7 37 F4
Maxwelton Cl MLHL NW7 37 F4
Maya Cl PECK SE15 131 J1
Mayall Cl STHWK SE1 12 F9
Mayall Rd HNHL SE24 130 C4
Maya Pl FBAR/BDGN N11 40 D6
Maya Rd EFNCH N2 53 G3
Maybank Av ALP/SUD HA0 67 G4
HCH RM12 81 K4
SWFD E18 59 F1
Maybank Gdns PIN HA5 46 E4
Maybank Rd SWFD E18 45 G7
May Bate Av KUTN/CMB KT2 143 K7
Mayberry Pl BRYLDS KT5 159 G6
Maybourne Cl SYD SE26 150 D4
Maybury Cl STMC/STPC BR5 169 G4
Maybury Gdns WLSDN NW10 69 J6
Maybury Ms HGT N6 54 C6
Maybury Rd BARK IG11 97 G1
PLSTW E13 95 G3
Maybury St TOOT SW17 147 J4
Maychurch Cl STAN HA7 35 K7
May Cl CHSGTN KT9 172 B5
Maycock Gv NTHWD HA6 32 D5
Maycroft PIN HA5 47 F1
Maycross Av MRDN SM4 161 J3
Mayday Gdns BKHTH/KID SE3 134 D1
Mayday Rd THHTH CR7 164 C5
Maydwell Ldg BORE WD6 24 B1
Mayefield Rd THHTH CR7 164 A3
Mayerne Rd ELTH/MOT SE9 134 C4
Mayesbrook Rd BARK IG11 79 F7
GDMY/SEVK IG3 79 G2
Mayesford Rd CHDH RM6 61 J6
Mayes Rd WDGN N22 55 F1
Mayeswood Rd
LEE/GVPK SE12 153 G3
Mayfair Av BXLYHN DA7 116 E7
CHDH RM6 61 K5
IL IG1 77 K1
WHTN TW2 123 H6
WPK KT4 160 D7
Mayfair Cl BECK BR3 151 K7
SURB KT6 159 F7
Mayfair Ct EDGW HA8 36 B4
Mayfair Gdns TOTM N17 41 J5
WFD IG8 44 E6
Mayfair Ms CAMTN NW1 * 3 M2
Mayfair Pl MYFR/PICC W1J 10 D8
Mayfair Rd DART DA1 139 G4
Mayfair Ter STHGT/OAK N14 28 D6
Mayfare RKW/CH/CXG WD3 20 B4
Mayfield BXLYHN DA7 137 G2
Mayfield Av CHSWK W4 106 B3
KTN/HRWW/WS HA3 49 H4
NFNCH/WDSPK N12 39 G3
STHGT/OAK N14 40 C1
WEA W13 104 C2
WFD IG8 44 E5
Mayfield Cl CLAP SW4 129 J4
PGE/AN SE20 150 D7
THDIT KT7 158 C7
Mayfield Crs ED N9 30 D5
THHTH CR7 164 A3
Mayfield Dr PIN HA5 47 K3
Mayfield Gdns HDN NW4 52 B5
HNWL W7 84 D5
Mayfield Rd ACT W3 86 D6
BCTR RM8 61 J7
BELMT SM2 175 H5
BELV DA17 117 K3
BMLY BR1 168 D4
CEND/HSY/T N8 55 F5
CHING E4 44 A1
HACK E8 7 L2
PEND EN3 31 F1
PLSTW E13 94 D3
SAND/SEL CR2 177 K7
SHB W12 106 B1
WALTH E17 57 G1
WIM/MER SW19 146 D7
Mayfields WBLY HA9 68 C1
Mayfields Cl WBLY HA9 68 C1
Mayfield Vls SCUP DA14 * 155 J5
Mayflower Cl
BERM/RHTH SE16 112 A3
RSLP HA4 46 A5
Mayflower Rd BRXN/ST SW9 129 K2
Mayflower St
BERM/RHTH SE16 111 K1
Mayfly Cl PIN HA5 47 G6
Mayford Cl BAL SW12 128 E6
BECK BR3 166 A2
Mayford Rd BAL SW12 128 E6
May Gdns ALP/SUD HA0 85 J2
Maygood St IS N1 5 M5
Maygreen Crs EMPK RM11 63 J6
Maygrove Rd
KIL/WHAMP NW6 70 D5
Mayhew Cl CHING E4 43 J2
Mayhill Rd BAR EN5 26 C4
CHARL SE7 114 A5
Maylands Av HCH RM12 81 K3
Maylands Dr SCUP DA14 155 K2
Maylands Rd OXHEY WD19 33 G3
Maynard Cl ERITH DA8 118 C6
FUL/PGN SW6 108 A6
SEVS/STOTM N15 56 A4
Maynard Rd WALTH E17 58 A4
Maynards Quay WAP E1W * 92 E6
Maynooth Gdns CAR SM5 162 E6
Mayola Rd CLPT E5 74 E3
Mayo Rd CROY/NA CR0 164 E4
WLSDN NW10 69 G5
Mayow Rd SYD SE26 151 F3
Mayplace Av DART DA1 138 D3
Mayplace Cl BXLYHN DA7 137 J2
Mayplace La
WOOL/PLUM SE18 115 G5
Mayplace Rd BXLYHN DA7 137 K2
Mayplace Rd East
BXLYHN DA7 137 J2
Mayplace Rd West
BXLYHN DA7 137 H3
Maypole Crs ERITH DA8 119 G5
May Rd CHING E4 43 J5
PLSTW E13 94 E1
WHTN TW2 123 K7
Mayroyd Av SURB KT6 172 C1
May's Buildings Ms
GNWCH SE10 113 G6
Mays Ct CHCR WC2N 11 J7
May's Hill Rd HAYES BR2 167 H1
May's La BAR EN5 25 K6
BAR EN5 26 D4
Maysoule Rd BTSEA SW11 128 C3
Mays Rd TEDD TW11 142 D4
Mayston Ms BKHTH/KID SE3 113 K4
May St WKENS W14 107 J4
Mayswood Gdns DAGE RM10 80 E5
Maythorne Cl WATW WD18 20 C3
Maythorne Cots LEW SE13 133 G5
Mayton St HOLWY N7 73 F2
Maytree Cl EDGW HA8 36 E2
RAIN RM13 99 G1
Maytree Ct MTCM CR4 163 F2
Maytree La STAN HA7 35 F5
Maytree Wk
BRXS/STRHM SW2 * 149 G1
Mayville Est
STNW/STAM N16 * 74 A4
Mayville Rd IL IG1 78 B4
WAN E11 76 C1
Maywood Cl BECK BR3 151 K6
Maze Hl BKHTH/KID SE3 113 J6
GNWCH SE10 113 H5
Mazenod Av KIL/WHAMP NW6 2 B2
Maze Rd RCH/KEW TW9 105 H6
McAdam Dr ENC/FH EN2 29 H1
McAuley Cl ELTH/MOT SE9 135 F4
STHWK SE1 18 A3
McCall Cl CLAP SW4 129 K1
McCall Crs CHARL SE7 114 D4
McCarthy Rd FELT TW13 141 H4
McCoid Wy STHWK SE1 18 E2
McCrone Ms HAMP NW3 71 H5
McCudden Rd DART DA1 139 J2
McCullum Rd BOW E3 75 H7
McDermott Cl BTSEA SW11 128 D1
McDermott Rd PECK SE15 131 H2
McDonough Cl CHSGTN KT9 172 A3
McDougall Ct RCH/KEW TW9 125 H1
McDowall Cl CAN/RD E16 94 E4
McDowall Rd CMBW SE5 110 D7
McEntee Av WALTH E17 43 G7
McEwan Wy SRTFD E15 * 76 B7
McGrath Rd SRTFD E15 76 D4
McGregor Rd NTGHL W11 88 D5
McIntosh Cl ROM RM1 63 G2
WLGTN SM6 176 E6
McIntosh Rd ROM RM1 63 G2
McKay Rd RYNPK SW20 145 K6
McKellar Cl BUSH WD23 34 C1
McKerrell Rd PECK SE15 111 H7
McKillop Wy SCUP DA14 155 J6
McLeod Rd ABYW SE2 116 D3
McLeod's Ms SKENS SW7 14 D4
McMillan St DEPT SE8 112 D5
McNair Rd NWDGN UB2 103 F2
McNeil Rd CMBW SE5 131 F1
McNicol Dr WLSDN NW10 86 E1
McRae La MTCM CR4 162 E6
Mead Cl CAMTN NW1 4 B1
GPK RM2 63 J1
KTN/HRWW/WS HA3 34 D7
Mead Ct CDALE/KGS NW9 50 E4
Mead Crs CHING E4 44 A3
DART DA1 139 G7
SUT SM1 175 J3
Meadcroft Rd LBTH SE11 110 B5
Meade Cl CHSWK W4 105 H5
Meadfield EDGW HA8 36 D1
Mead Fld RYLN/HDSTN HA2 * 65 K2
Meadfoot Rd
STRHM/NOR SW16 148 C7
Meadgate Av WFD IG8 45 J4
Mead Gv CHDH RM6 61 K2
Mead House La YEAD UB4 82 B3
Meadhurst Pk SUN TW16 140 C5
Meadlands Dr
RCHPK/HAM TW10 143 K1
Meadow Av CROY/NA CR0 166 A5
Meadowbank BKHTH/KID SE3 133 J2
BRYLDS KT5 159 G5
HAMP NW3 3 L2
OXHEY WD19 21 G6
WCHMH N21 29 F5
Meadowbank Cl
FUL/PGN SW6 107 F6
ISLW TW7 103 K7
Meadowbank Gdns
HSLWW TW4 121 K1
Meadowbank Rd
CDALE/KGS NW9 51 F6
Meadowbanks BAR EN5 25 H4
Meadow Cl BAR EN5 26 D5
BARK IG11 79 F6
BXLYHS DA6 137 G4
CAT SE6 151 J4
CHING E4 31 K7
CHST BR7 154 B4
ESH/CLAY KT10 171 F2
HOM E9 75 H4
HSLWW TW4 123 F5
NTHLT UB5 84 A1
RCHPK/HAM TW10 125 F7
RSLP HA4 46 D5
RYNPK SW20 161 F3
Meadowcourt Rd
BKHTH/KID SE3 133 J3
Meadow Cft BMLY BR1 168 E2
Meadowcroft BUSH WD23 * 22 B5
Meadowcroft Cl PLMGR N13 * 41 H1
Meadowcroft Rd PLMGR N13 41 G1
Meadow Dr HDN NW4 52 A1
MUSWH N10 54 A2
Meadowford Cl THMD SE28 97 G6
Meadow Gdns EDGW HA8 36 D5
Meadow Garth WLSDN NW10 68 E5
Meadow Hl NWMAL KT3 160 B5
Meadowlands BAR EN5 25 H4
Meadow La LEE/GVPK SE12 153 G2
Meadowlea Cl WDR/YW UB7 100 A5
Meadow Ms VX/NE SW8 110 A5
Meadow Pl CHSWK W4 * 106 B6
VX/NE SW8 109 K6
Meadow Rd ASHF TW15 140 B4
BARK IG11 79 F6
BORE WD6 24 D1
BUSH WD23 22 B4
DAGW RM9 80 B5
ESH/CLAY KT10 170 E4
FELT TW13 141 J1
HAYES BR2 152 C7
PIN HA5 47 H3
ROMW/RG RM7 62 E7
STHL UB1 83 K6
SUT SM1 175 J3
VX/NE SW8 110 A5
WIM/MER SW19 147 G6
Meadow Rw STHWK SE1 18 E4
Meadows Cl LEY E10 75 J1
Meadows End SUN TW16 140 E7
Meadowside BKHTH/KID SE3 134 B3
DART DA1 139 H7
TWK TW1 124 E6
Meadowside Rd BELMT SM2 174 C7
Meadow Stile CROY/NA CR0 177 J2
Meadowsweet Cl CAN/RD E16 95 H4
NWMAL KT3 161 F4
The Meadow CHST BR7 154 C5
Meadow Vw BFN/LL DA15 136 C5
HRW HA1 48 E7
Meadowview Rd BXLY DA5 137 F5
CAT SE6 151 J3
HOR/WEW KT19 173 G7
Meadow View Rd THHTH CR7 164 C4
YEAD UB4 82 B3
Meadow Wk DAGW RM9 80 B5
HOR/WEW KT19 173 G5
SWFD E18 58 E3
WLGTN SM6 176 B2
Meadow Wy CDALE/KGS NW9 51 F4
CHSGTN KT9 172 A4
RSLP HA4 47 F5
WBLY HA9 67 K3
Meadow Waye HEST TW5 102 D6
The Meadow Wy
KTN/HRWW/WS HA3 34 E7
Mead Pl CROY/NA CR0 164 C7
HOM E9 74 E5
Mead Plat WLSDN NW10 68 E5
Mead Rd CHST BR7 154 C5
DART DA1 139 G7
EDGW HA8 36 C5
RCHPK/HAM TW10 143 J2
Mead Rw STHWK SE1 18 A3
Meadside Cl BECK BR3 151 G7
Meads La GDMY/SEVK IG3 61 F6
Meads Rd WDGN N22 55 H1
The Meads CHEAM SM3 174 B2
EDGW HA8 37 F5
MRDN SM4 * 162 D4
The Mead BECK BR3 167 F1
EFNCH N2 53 G1
OXHEY WD19 33 J2
WEA W13 85 H4
WLGTN SM6 176 D5
WWKM BR4 167 G7
Meadvale Rd CROY/NA CR0 165 G6
EA W5 85 H3
Mead Wy BUSH WD23 21 J1
CROY/NA CR0 179 G1
HAYES BR2 167 J5
RSLP HA4 46 B5
Meadway BAR EN5 26 E3
BECK BR3 152 A7
BRYLDS KT5 159 K7
ESH/CLAY KT10 170 B7
GDMY/SEVK IG3 79 F5
GLDGN NW11 53 F5
GPK RM2 63 J1
RYNPK SW20 161 F3
STHGT/OAK N14 40 D1
WFD IG8 45 G4
WHTN TW2 123 J7
Meadway Cl BAR EN5 26 E2
GLDGN NW11 53 F5
PIN HA5 34 B5
Meadway Ct EA W5 * 86 B4
Meadway Gdns RSLP HA4 46 B5
The Meadway BKHTH/KID SE3 133 G1
Meaford Wy PGE/AN SE20 150 D6
Meanley Rd MNPK E12 77 J4
Meard St SOHO/CST W1F 11 G5
Meath Crs BETH E2 93 F2
Meath Rd IL IG1 78 C2
SRTFD E15 94 D1
Meath St BTSEA SW11 109 G7
Mecklenburgh Pl
BMSBY WC1N 5 L9
Mecklenburgh Sq
BMSBY WC1N 5 L9
Mecklenburgh St
BMSBY WC1N 5 L9
Medburn St CAMTN NW1 5 G5
Medcroft Gdns
MORT/ESHN SW14 125 K3
Medebourne Cl
BKHTH/KID SE3 133 K2
Medesenge Wy PLMGR N13 41 H5
Medfield St PUT/ROE SW15 126 D6
Medhurst Cl BOW E3 93 G1
Medhurst Dr BMLY BR1 152 C4
Median Rd CLPT E5 74 E4
Medici Cl GDMY/SEVK IG3 61 G5
Medina Av ESH/CLAY KT10 170 E2
Medina Rd HOLWY N7 73 G2
Medland Cl WLGTN SM6 163 F7
Medlar Cl NTHLT UB5 83 H1
Medlar St CMBW SE5 110 D7
Medley Rd KIL/WHAMP NW6 70 E5
Medora Rd BRXS/STRHM SW2 130 A5
ROMW/RG RM7 63 F3
Medusa Rd CAT SE6 132 E5
Medway Cl CROY/NA CR0 165 K5
IL IG1 78 C4
Medway Dr GFD/PVL UB6 85 F1
Medway Gdns ALP/SUD HA0 67 G3
Medway Pde GFD/PVL UB6 * 85 F1
Medway Rd BOW E3 93 G1
DART DA1 138 D2
Medway St WEST SW1P 17 G4
Medwin St CLAP SW4 130 A3
Meerbrook Rd BKHTH/KID SE3 134 B2
Meeson Rd SRTFD E15 76 D6
Meeson St CLPT E5 75 G3
Meesons Whf SRTFD E15 * 94 A1
Meeting Aly WAT WD17 * 21 G3
Meeting Field Pth HOM E9 * 74 E5
Meeting House Aly
WAP E1W * 92 D7
Meeting House La PECK SE15 111 J7
Mehetabel Rd HOM E9 74 E5
Meister Cl IL IG1 60 D7
Melanda Cl CHST BR7 153 K4
Melanie Cl BXLYHN DA7 117 F7
Melbourne Av PIN HA5 48 B2
WDGN N22 41 F5
WEA W13 85 G7
Melbourne Cl ORP BR6 169 K6
WLGTN SM6 176 C4
Melbourne Gdns CHDH RM6 62 A4
Melbourne Gv EDUL SE22 131 F3
Melbourne Ms BRXN/ST SW9 110 B7
CAT SE6 133 F6
Melbourne Pl HOL/ALD WC2B 11 M5
Melbourne Rd BUSH WD23 22 B4
EHAM E6 77 K7
IL IG1 60 B7
LEY E10 57 K6
TEDD TW11 143 J5
WALTH E17 57 G3
WIM/MER SW19 146 E7
WLGTN SM6 176 B4
Melbourne Sq BRXN/ST SW9 110 B7
Melbourne Ter EDUL SE22 * 131 F3
FUL/PGN SW6 * 108 A6
Melbourne Wy EN EN1 30 B5
Melbury Av NWDGN UB2 103 G2
Melbury Cl CHST BR7 153 K5
ESH/CLAY KT10 171 H5
Melbury Ct KENS W8 107 J2
Melbury Dr CMBW SE5 111 F6
Melbury Gdns RYNPK SW20 145 K7
Melbury Rd
KTN/HRWW/WS HA3 50 B4
WKENS W14 107 J2
Melbury Ter CAMTN NW1 9 K1
Melcombe Gdns
KTN/HRWW/WS HA3 50 B5
Melcombe Pl CAMTN NW1 9 L2
Melcombe St CAMTN NW1 9 M1
Meldex Cl MLHL NW7 38 A5
Meldon Cl FUL/PGN SW6 * 108 A7
Meldone Cl BRYLDS KT5 159 J5
Meldrum Rd GDMY/SEVK IG3 79 G1
Melfield Gdns CAT SE6 151 K3
Melford Av BARK IG11 78 E5
Melford Cl CHSGTN KT9 172 B4
Melford Rd EDUL SE22 131 H7
EHAM E6 95 K3
IL IG1 78 D1
WALTH E17 57 G3
WAN E11 76 C1
Melfort Av THHTH CR7 164 C2
Melfort Rd THHTH CR7 164 C2
Melgund Rd HBRY N5 73 G4
Melina Cl HYS/HAR UB3 82 B4
Melina Pl STJWD NW8 3 G8
Melina Rd SHB W12 106 E1
Melior Pl STHWK SE1 * 19 J1
Melior St STHWK SE1 19 H1
Meliot Rd CAT SE6 152 B1
Meller Cl CROY/NA CR0 176 E2
Mellifont Cl MRDN SM4 162 C5
Melling St WOOL/PLUM SE18 115 K5
Mellish Gdns WFD IG8 44 E4
Mellish St POP/IOD E14 112 D2
Mellison Rd TOOT SW17 147 J4
Melliss Av RCH/KEW TW9 105 J7
Mellitus St SHB W12 87 H5
Mellor Cl WOT/HER KT12 156 E6
Mellow La East
HGDN/ICK UB10 82 A3
Mellows Rd CLAY IG5 59 K2
WLGTN SM6 176 D4
Mells Crs ELTH/MOT SE9 153 K3
Mell St GNWCH SE10 113 H4
Melody La HBRY N5 73 H4
Melody Rd WAND/EARL SW18 128 B4
Melon Pl KENS W8 * 14 B1
Melon Rd PECK SE15 111 H7
WAN E11 76 C2
Melrose Av BORE WD6 24 D4
CRICK NW2 70 A4
DART DA1 138 B6
GFD/PVL UB6 84 B1
MTCM CR4 148 B6
STRHM/NOR SW16 164 A2
WDGN N22 41 H7
WHTN TW2 123 G6
WIM/MER SW19 146 D1
Melrose Cl GFD/PVL UB6 84 B1
LEE/GVPK SE12 133 K7
YEAD UB4 82 E4
Melrose Dr STHL UB1 84 A7
Melrose Gdns EDGW HA8 50 D2
HMSMTH W6 107 F2
NWMAL KT3 160 A2
Melrose Ms NWMAL KT3 160 A2
Melrose Rd BARN SW13 126 C1
PIN HA5 47 K3
WAND/EARL SW18 127 J5
WIM/MER SW19 161 K1
Melrose Ter HMSMTH W6 107 F1
Melrose Vls BECK BR3 * 166 D1
Melsa Rd MRDN SM4 162 B5
Melthorne Dr RSLP HA4 65 G2
Melthorpe Gdns
BKHTH/KID SE3 114 C7
Melton Cl RSLP HA4 47 G7
Melton Flds HOR/WEW KT19 173 F7
Melton Gdns ROM RM1 63 H6
Melton Pl HOR/WEW KT19 173 F7
Melton St CAMTN NW1 4 F8
Melville Av GFD/PVL UB6 67 F4
RYNPK SW20 145 J6
SAND/SEL CR2 178 B4
Melville Cl HGDN/ICK UB10 64 B2
Melville Ct DEPT SE8 112 A3
Melville Gdns PLMGR N13 41 H4
Melville Rd BARN SW13 106 D7
RAIN RM13 99 J3
SCUP DA14 155 J1
WALTH E17 57 H3
WLSDN NW10 69 F6
Melville Villas Rd ACT W3 * 87 F7
Melvin Rd PGE/AN SE20 150 E7
Memel St STLK EC1Y 12 E1
Memorial Av MNPK E12 77 J1
SRTFD E15 94 C2
Memorial Cl HEST TW5 102 E5
Memorial Sq KUT/HW KT1 158 E1
Mendez Wy PUT/ROE SW15 126 D5
Mendip Cl HYS/HAR UB3 101 G6
SYD SE26 150 E3
WPK KT4 174 A1
Mendip Dr CRICK NW2 70 C1
Mendip Houses BETH E2 * 92 E2
Mendip Rd BTSEA SW11 128 B2
BUSH WD23 22 C5
EMPK RM11 63 J6
ERITH DA8 118 B7
GNTH/NBYPK IG2 60 E4
Mendora Rd FUL/PGN SW6 107 H6
Menelik Rd CRICK NW2 70 C3
Menlo Gdns NRWD SE19 149 K6
Menon Dr ED N9 42 D2
Menotti St BETH E2 * 92 C3
Mentmore Cl
KTN/HRWW/WS HA3 49 J5
Mentmore Ter HACK E8 74 D6
Meon Rd ACT W3 105 K1
Meopham Rd MTCM CR4 148 C7
Mepham Crs
KTN/HRWW/WS HA3 34 C6
Mepham Gdns
KTN/HRWW/WS HA3 34 C6
Mepham St STHWK SE1 11 M9
Mera Dr BXLYHN DA7 137 H3
Merantum Wy
WIM/MER SW19 147 G7
Merbury Cl LEW SE13 133 F4
THMD SE28 96 D7
Merbury Rd THMD SE28 96 D7
Merbury St WOOL/PLUM SE18 115 G2
Mercator Pl POP/IOD E14 112 D4

Mercator Rd LEW SE13 133 G3
Mercer Cl THDIT KT7 158 A6
Merceron Houses BETH E2 * 92 E2
Merceron St WCHPL E1 92 D3
Mercer Pl PIN HA5 47 G1
Mercers Cl GNWCH SE10 113 J3
Mercers Cots WCHPL E1 * 93 G5
Mercers Ms ARCH N19 72 D3
Mercers Pl HMSMTH W6 107 F3
Mercers Rd ARCH N19 72 D2
Mercer St LSQ/SEVD WC2H 11 J5
Merchants Cl SNWD SE25 165 H3
Merchant St BOW E3 93 H2
Merchiston Rd CAT SE6 152 B1
Merchland Rd ELTH/MOT SE9 135 H7
Mercia Gv LEW SE13 133 F2
Mercier Rd PUT/ROE SW15 127 H4
Mercury Gdns ROM RM1 63 G3
Mercury House
HYS/HAR UB3 * 101 J1
Mercury Wy NWCR SE14 112 A5
Mercy Ter LEW SE13 132 E4
Merebank La WLGTN SM6 177 F4
Mere Cl WIM/MER SW19 127 G6
Meredith Av CRICK NW2 70 A4
Meredith Cl PIN HA5 33 H6
Meredith Ms BROCKY SE4 132 C3
Meredith St CLKNW EC1R 6 C8
PLSTW E13 94 E2
Meredyth Rd BARN SW13 126 D1
Mere End CROY/NA CR0 166 A6
Mere Rd ABYW SE2 116 D1
Mereside Pk ASHF TW15 * 140 A3
Meretone Cl BROCKY SE4 132 B3
Merevale Crs MRDN SM4 162 B5
Mereway Rd WHTN TW2 123 J7
Merewood Cl BMLY BR1 169 F1
Merewood Gdns
CROY/NA CR0 166 A6
Merewood Rd BXLYHN DA7 137 K1
Mereworth Cl HAYES BR2 167 J4
Mereworth Dr
WOOL/PLUM SE18 115 G6
Meriden Cl BMLY BR1 153 H6
Meridian Cl MLHL NW7 37 F3
Meridian Rd CHARL SE7 114 C6
Meridian Sq SRTFD E15 76 B6
Meridian Wy UED N18 42 E5
Merifield Rd ELTH/MOT SE9 134 B3
Merino Cl WAN E11 59 G3
Merivale Rd HRW HA1 48 C6
PUT/ROE SW15 127 H3
Merlewood Dr CHST BR7 153 K7
Merley Ct CDALE/KGS NW9 50 E7
Merlin Cl CROY/NA CR0 178 A3
MTCM CR4 162 D2
NTHLT UB5 83 G2
WLGTN SM6 177 F5
Merlin Crs EDGW HA8 36 B7
Merling Cl CHSGTN KT9 171 K4
Merlin Gv BECK BR3 166 C3
Merlin Rd MNPK E12 77 H1
WELL DA16 136 B3
Merlin Rd North WELL DA16 136 B3
Merlins Av RYLN/HDSTN HA2 65 K2
Merlin St FSBYW WC1X 6 A8
Mermagen Dr RAIN RM13 81 K6
Mermaid Ct STHWK SE1 19 G1
Merredene St
BRXS/STRHM SW2 130 A5
Merriam Av HOM E9 75 H5
Merriam Cl CHING E4 44 A4
Merrick Rd NWDGN UB2 102 E3
Merrick Sq STHWK SE1 19 G3
Merridene WCHMH N21 29 H5
Merrielands Crs DAGW RM9 98 B1
Merrilands Rd WPK KT4 161 F7
Merrilees Rd BFN/LL DA15 135 K6
Merrilyn Cl ESH/CLAY KT10 171 G5
Merriman Rd BKHTH/KID SE3 114 B7
Merrington Rd FUL/PGN SW6 14 B9
Merrion Av STAN HA7 35 K4
Merritt Gdns CHSGTN KT9 171 J5
Merritt Rd BROCKY SE4 132 C4
Merrivale STHGT/OAK N14 28 D4
Merrivale Av REDBR IG4 59 H3
Merrow Rd BELMT SM2 174 B7
Merrows Cl NTHWD HA6 32 A5
Merrow St WALW SE17 19 G8
Merrow Wk WALW SE17 19 H7
Merrow Wy CROY/NA CR0 180 A5
Merrydown Wy CHST BR7 153 J7
Merryfield BKHTH/KID SE3 133 J1
Merryfield Gdns STAN HA7 35 J4
Merryfield Wy CAT SE6 132 E6
Merryhill Cl CHING E4 31 K6
Merry Hill Mt BUSH WD23 22 B7
Merry Hill Rd BUSH WD23 22 A6
Merryhills Dr ENC/FH EN2 28 E3
Merryweather Cl DART DA1 139 J5
Merryweather Ct
NWMAL KT3 * 160 B4
Mersey Rd WALTH E17 57 H2
Mersham Dr CDALE/KGS NW9 50 C4
Mersham Pl PGE/AN SE20 150 D7
THHTH CR7 164 E1
Mersham Rd THHTH CR7 164 E2
Merten Rd CHDH RM6 62 A6
Merthyr Ter BARN SW13 106 E5
Merton Av CHSWK W4 106 C3
NTHLT UB5 66 C4
Merton Gdns STMC/STPC BR5 169 G4
Merton Hall Gdns
RYNPK SW20 146 C7
Merton Hall Rd
WIM/MER SW19 146 C7
Merton High St
WIM/MER SW19 147 G6
Merton La HGT N6 71 K1
Merton Pl WIM/MER SW19 * 147 G7
Merton Ri HAMP NW3 3 J1
Merton Rd BARK IG11 79 F6
GDMY/SEVK IG3 61 F6
RYLN/HDSTN HA2 48 C7
SNWD SE25 165 G4
WALTH E17 58 A4
WAND/EARL SW18 127 K7
WATW WD18 21 F3
WIM/MER SW19 147 F6
Merton Wy E/WMO/HCT KT8 157 H3
Mertoun Ter MBLAR W1H * 9 L4
Merttins Rd PECK SE15 132 A3
Meru Cl KTTN NW5 72 A3
Mervan Rd BRXS/STRHM SW2 130 B3
Mervyn Av ELTH/MOT SE9 154 C2
Mervyn Rd WEA W13 104 B2
Meryfield Cl BORE WD6 24 B1
Messaline Av ACT W3 86 E5
Messent Rd ELTH/MOT SE9 134 B4
Messeter Pl ELTH/MOT SE9 135 F5
Messina Av KIL/WHAMP NW6 2 A2
Meteor St BTSEA SW11 129 F3
Meteor Wy WLGTN SM6 176 E6
Methley St LBTH SE11 18 B8
Methuen Cl EDGW HA8 36 C6
Methuen Pk MUSWH N10 54 B1
Methuen Rd BELV DA17 117 J3
BXLYHS DA6 137 G3
EDGW HA8 36 C6
Methwold Rd NKENS W10 88 B4
Metropolitan Cl POP/IOD E14 93 J4
Metropolitan Ms WATW WD18 20 C3
Metropolitan Station Ap
WATW WD18 20 D3
Metropolitan Whf WAP E1W * 92 E7
Mews North BGVA SW1W 16 C4
Mews Pl WFD IG8 44 E3
Mews St WAP E1W 13 M8
The Mews BECK BR3 151 J7
CEND/HSY/T N8 55 G3
NFNCH/WDSPK N12 * 39 F4
REDBR IG4 59 H4
ROM RM1 63 G3
STRHM/NOR SW16 * 149 F7
TWK TW1 * 124 C5
WATW WD18 * 21 G3
Mexfield Rd PUT/ROE SW15 127 J4
Meyer Rd ERITH DA8 117 K5
Meymott St STHWK SE1 12 C9
Meynell Crs HOM E9 75 F6
Meynell Gdns HOM E9 75 F6
Meynell Rd HOM E9 75 F6
Meyrick Rd BTSEA SW11 128 C2
WLSDN NW10 69 J5
Mezen Cl NTHWD HA6 32 C6
Miah Ter WAP E1W * 92 C7
Micawber St IS N1 6 E7
Michael Gaynor Cl HNWL W7 85 F7
Michaelmas Cl RYNPK SW20 161 F2
Michael Rd FUL/PGN SW6 108 A7
SNWD SE25 165 F2
WAN E11 58 C7
Michaels Cl LEW SE13 133 H2
Micheldever Rd
LEE/GVPK SE12 133 H5
Michelham Gdns TWK TW1 143 F2
Michelsdale Dr RCH/KEW TW9 125 F3
Michel Wk WOOL/PLUM SE18 115 G4
Michigan Av MNPK E12 77 J3
Micheleham Down
NFNCH/WDSPK N12 38 D3
Mickleham Gdns CHEAM SM3 174 C5
Mickleham Rd
STMC/STPC BR5 155 F7
Mickleham Wy CROY/NA CR0 180 B6
Micklethwaite Rd
FUL/PGN SW6 107 K5
Midcroft RSLP HA4 46 C7
Middle Dartrey Wk
WBPTN SW10 * 108 B6
Middle Dene MLHL NW7 37 F2
Middlefield STJWD NW8 3 G3
Middlefielde WEA W13 85 H4
Middlefields CROY/NA CR0 179 G7
WEA W13 85 H4
Middle Furlong BUSH WD23 22 B3
Middle Green Cl BRYLDS KT5 159 G5
Middleham Gdns UED N18 42 C5
Middleham Rd UED N18 42 C5
Middle La CEND/HSY/T N8 54 E4
TEDD TW11 143 F5
Middle Lane Ms
CEND/HSY/T N8 54 E4
Middle Park Av ELTH/MOT SE9 134 C5
Middle Rd EBAR EN4 27 J5
PLSTW E13 94 E1
RYLN/HDSTN HA2 66 D1
STRHM/NOR SW16 163 H1
Middle Rw NKENS W10 88 C3
Middlesborough Rd UED N18 42 C5
Middlesex Cl STHL UB1 84 B3
Middlesex Pl HOM E9 74 E5
Middlesex Rd MTCM CR4 163 K4
Middlesex St WCHPL E1 13 K3
Middle St CROY/NA CR0 177 J1
STBT EC1A 12 E2
Middle Temple La EMB EC4Y 12 A5
Middleton Av CHING E4 43 H3
GFD/PVL UB6 84 D1
SCUP DA14 155 J5
Middleton Cl CHING E4 43 H2
Middleton Dr
BERM/RHTH SE16 112 A1
PIN HA5 46 E2
Middleton Gdns
GNTH/NBYPK IG2 60 B5
Middleton Gv HOLWY N7 72 E4
Middleton Ms HOLWY N7 72 E4
Middleton Pl GTPST W1W 10 E3
Middleton Rd CAR SM5 162 D6
GLDGN NW11 52 E6
HACK E8 7 L2
HYS/HAR UB3 82 B4
NWMAL KT3 159 K2
Middleton St BETH E2 92 D2
Middleton Wy LEW SE13 133 G3
Middleway GLDGN NW11 53 F4
Middle Wy STRHM/NOR SW16 163 J1
The Middle Wy
KTN/HRWW/WS HA3 49 F1
Middle Yd STHWK SE1 13 H8
Midfield Av BXLYHN DA7 137 K2
Midfield Wy STMC/STPC BR5 155 H7
Midford Pl FITZ W1T * 10 F1
Midholm GLDGN NW11 53 F3
WBLY HA9 50 C7
Midholm Cl GLDGN NW11 * 53 F3
Midholm Rd CROY/NA CR0 179 G2
Midhope St STPAN WC1H 5 K8
Midhurst Av CROY/NA CR0 164 B6
MUSWH N10 54 A2
Midhurst Cl HCH RM12 81 J3
Midhurst Gdns
HGDN/ICK UB10 64 A6
Midhurst Hl BXLYHS DA6 137 H4
Midhurst Pde MUSWH N10 * 54 A2
Midhurst Rd WEA W13 104 B1
Midhurst Wy CLPT E5 74 C3
Midland Arches CRICK NW2 * 69 K1
Midland Crs HAMP NW3 71 G5
Midland Rd CAMTN NW1 5 H6
LEY E10 58 A6
Midland Ter CRICK NW2 70 B2
WLSDN NW10 87 G3
Midlothian Rd BOW E3 93 H3
Midmoor Rd BAL SW12 129 H7
WIM/MER SW19 146 B7
Midship Cl BERM/RHTH SE16 * 93 F7
Midship Point POP/IOD E14 * 112 D1
Midstrath Rd WLSDN NW10 69 G3
Midsummer Av HSLWW TW4 122 E3
Midway CHEAM SM3 161 J6
Midwinter Cl WELL DA16 136 B2
Midwood Cl CRICK NW2 69 J2
Mighell Av REDBR IG4 59 H4
Milan Rd STHL UB1 102 E1
Milborne Gv WBPTN SW10 14 F8
Milborne St HOM E9 74 E5
Milborough Crs
LEE/GVPK SE12 133 H5
Milbourne La ESH/CLAY KT10 170 C4
Milbrook ESH/CLAY KT10 170 C5
Milcote St STHWK SE1 18 C2
Mildenhall Rd CLPT E5 74 E3
Mildmay Av IS N1 73 K5
Mildmay Gv North IS N1 73 K4
Mildmay Gv South IS N1 73 K4
Mildmay Pk IS N1 73 K4
Mildmay Pl STNW/STAM N16 74 A4
Mildmay Rd IL IG1 78 B2
IS N1 73 K4
ROMW/RG RM7 62 E4
Mildmay St IS N1 73 K5
Mildred Av BORE WD6 24 C3
HYS/HAR UB3 101 G3
NTHLT UB5 66 B4
WATW WD18 20 E3
Mildred Cl DART DA1 139 K5
Mildred Rd ERITH DA8 118 B4
Mile End Pl WCHPL E1 93 F3
Mile End Rd WCHPL E1 92 E4
The Mile End WALTH E17 43 F7
Mile Rd CROY/NA CR0 163 H7
WLGTN SM6 163 F7
Miles Dr THMD SE28 96 E7
Milespit Hl MLHL NW7 37 K4
Miles Pl BRYLDS KT5 * 159 G3
Miles Rd CEND/HSY/T N8 54 E2
MTCM CR4 162 D2
Miles St VX/NE SW8 109 K5
Milestone Cl BELMT SM2 175 H5
ED N9 42 C1
Milestone Rd NRWD SE19 150 B5
Miles Wy TRDG/WHET N20 39 J1
Milfoil St SHB W12 87 J6
Milford Cl ABYW SE2 117 F5
Milford Gdns ALP/SUD HA0 67 K4
CROY/NA CR0 165 K4
EDGW HA8 36 C6
Milford Gv SUT SM1 175 G3
Milford La TPL/STR WC2R 12 A6
Milford Ms STRHM/NOR SW16 149 F2
Milford Rd STHL UB1 84 A6
WEA W13 85 H7
Milk St BMLY BR1 153 F4
CAN/RD E16 96 B7
CITYW EC2V 12 F4
Milkwell Gdns WFD IG8 45 F6
Milkwell Yd CMBW SE5 110 D7
Milkwood Rd HNHL SE24 130 C4
Milk Yd WAP E1W 92 E6
Millais Av MNPK E12 78 A4
Millais Crs HOR/WEW KT19 173 G4
Millais Gdns EDGW HA8 50 C1
Millais Rd EN EN1 30 B4
NWMAL KT3 160 B6
WAN E11 76 A3
Millais Wy HOR/WEW KT19 172 E3
Millard Cl STNW/STAM N16 74 A4
Millard Rd DEPT SE8 112 C4
Millars Meadow
BKHTH/KID SE3 133 J3
Millbank WEST SW1P 17 J7
Millbank Est WEST SW1P 17 H6
Millbank Wy LEE/GVPK SE12 133 K4
Millbourne Rd FELT TW13 141 J3
Mill Br BAR EN5 * 26 D4
Millbrook Av ELTH/MOT SE9 135 J3
Millbrook Gdns CHDH RM6 62 A5
GPK RM2 63 G1
Millbrook Rd BRXN/ST SW9 130 C2
ED N9 30 D7
Mill Cl CAR SM5 * 176 A1
WDR/YW UB7 100 A2
Mill Ct WDR/YW UB7 100 A2
Millennium Br STHWK SE1 12 E7
Millennium Cl CAN/RD E16 94 E5
Millennium Dr POP/IOD E14 113 G2
Millennium Pl BETH E2 * 92 D1
Millennium Sq STHWK SE1 19 L1
Millennium Wy GNWCH SE10 113 H1
Millennium Whf POP/IOD E14 113 G3
Miller Cl BMLY BR1 152 E4
MTCM CR4 162 E6
Miller Rd CROY/NA CR0 164 A7
WIM/MER SW19 147 H5
Miller's Av HACK E8 74 B4
Millers Cl DART DA1 139 G6
MLHL NW7 37 J3
Miller's Ct CHSWK W4 106 C4
Millers Green Cl ENC/FH EN2 29 H2
Miller's Ter HACK E8 74 B4
Miller St CAMTN NW1 4 E5
Miller's Wy HMSMTH W6 107 F1
Millers Yd FNCH N3 39 F7
Miller Wk STHWK SE1 12 B9
Millet Rd GFD/PVL UB6 84 B2
Mill Farm Av SUN TW16 140 C6
Mill Farm Cl PIN HA5 47 G1
Mill Farm Crs HSLWW TW4 122 D7
Millfield SUN TW16 140 B7
Millfield Av WALTH E17 43 G7
Millfield La HGT N6 71 K1
Millfield Pl HGT N6 72 A1
Millfield Rd EDGW HA8 50 E1
HSLWW TW4 122 D7
Millfields Rd CLPT E5 74 E3
Mill Gdns SYD SE26 150 D3
Mill Gn MTCM CR4 163 F6
Mill Green Rd MTCM CR4 163 F6
Millgrove St BTSEA SW11 109 F7
Millharbour POP/IOD E14 112 E2
Millhaven Cl CHDH RM6 61 H5
Mill Hl BARN SW13 126 D2
Mill Hill Gv ACT W3 * 86 D7
Mill Hill Rd ACT W3 105 J1
BARN SW13 126 E2
Mill Hill Ter ACT W3 86 D7
Millhouse Pl WNWD SE27 149 H3
Millicent Gv PLMGR N13 41 H4
Millicent Rd LEY E10 * 57 H7
Milligan St POP/IOD E14 93 H6
Milling Rd EDGW HA8 37 F6
Millington Rd HYS/HAR UB3 101 H2
Mill La CAR SM5 176 A3
CHDH RM6 62 A5
CHING E4 31 K2
CRICK NW2 70 C4
CROY/NA CR0 177 G2
EW KT17 173 H7
KIL/WHAMP NW6 70 E4
WFD IG8 44 D4
WOOL/PLUM SE18 115 F4
Millman Ms BMSBY WC1N * 11 L1
Millman Pl BMSBY WC1N 11 L1
Millman St BMSBY WC1N 11 L1
Millmark Gv NWCR SE14 132 B1
Millmarsh La PEND EN3 31 G1
Mill Mead Rd TOTM N17 56 D2
Mill Pl CHST BR7 154 A7
DART DA1 138 D3
KUT/HW KT1 159 G2
POP/IOD E14 93 G5
Mill Plat ISLW TW7 124 B1
Mill Plat Av ISLW TW7 124 B1
Mill Pond Cl VX/NE SW8 109 J6
Millpond Est
BERM/RHTH SE16 * 111 J1
Mill Pond Rd DART DA1 139 H5
Mill Rdg EDGW HA8 36 B4
Mill Rd CAN/RD E16 95 F7
ERITH DA8 117 K6
ESH/CLAY KT10 170 A1
IL IG1 78 A2
WDR/YW UB7 100 A2
WHTN TW2 142 C1
WIM/MER SW19 147 G6
Mill Rw BXLY DA5 * 137 J6
IS N1 7 K4
Mills Gv HDN NW4 52 B2
POP/IOD E14 94 A4
Millshot Cl FUL/PGN SW6 107 F7
Millshott Cl WHALL SW1A * 11 H8
Millside CAR SM5 175 K1
Millside Pl ISLW TW7 124 C1
Millson Cl TRDG/WHET N20 39 H1
Mills Rw CHSWK W4 106 A3
Millstone Cl SRTFD E15 76 B5
Millstream Cl PLMGR N13 41 G4
Millstream Rd STHWK SE1 19 L2
Mill St CONDST W1S 10 D6
KUT/HW KT1 159 F2
STHWK SE1 19 M2
Mill V HAYES BR2 167 K2
Mill View Cl EW KT17 173 H6
Mill View Gdns CROY/NA CR0 179 F2
Millwall Dock Rd
POP/IOD E14 112 D2
Mill Wy BUSH WD23 21 J1
EBED/NFELT TW14 122 A4
MLHL NW7 37 G4
Millway Gdns NTHLT UB5 65 K5
Millwood Rd HSLW TW3 123 H4
Millwood St NKENS W10 88 C4
Mill Yd WCHPL E1 92 C6
Milman Cl PIN HA5 47 H2
Milman Rd KIL/WHAMP NW6 88 B1
Milman's St WBPTN SW10 108 C5
Milne Fld PIN HA5 34 A6
Milne Gdns ELTH/MOT SE9 134 D4
Milner Ct BUSH WD23 22 B5
Milner Dr WHTN TW2 123 J6
Milner Pl IS N1 6 B2
Milner Rd BCTR RM8 79 J1
KUT/HW KT1 158 E2
MRDN SM4 162 C4
SRTFD E15 94 C2
THHTH CR7 164 D2
WIM/MER SW19 147 F7
Milner Sq IS N1 6 B2
Milner St CHEL SW3 15 L5
Milnthorpe Rd CHSWK W4 106 A5
Milo Rd EDUL SE22 131 G5
Milroy Wk STHWK SE1 12 B8
Milson Rd WKENS W14 107 H2
Milton Av BAR EN5 26 D4
CDALE/KGS NW9 50 D2
CROY/NA CR0 164 E6
EHAM E6 77 H6
HCH RM12 81 H1
HGT N6 54 C6
SUT SM1 175 H2
WLSDN NW10 69 F7
Milton Cl EFNCH N2 53 G5
STHWK SE1 19 L6
SUT SM1 175 H2
YEAD UB4 82 E5
Milton Ct BARB EC2Y 13 G2
CHDH RM6 61 J6
Milton Court Rd NWCR SE14 112 B5
Milton Crs GNTH/NBYPK IG2 60 C6
Milton Dr BORE WD6 24 D3
Milton Gdns
STWL/WRAY TW19 120 C7
Milton Gv FBAR/BDGN N11 40 C4
STNW/STAM N16 73 K3
Milton Pk HGT N6 54 C6
Milton Rd ACT W3 87 F7
BELV DA17 117 H3
CDALE/KGS NW9 * 51 J6
CROY/NA CR0 164 E6
HGT N6 54 C6
HNHL SE24 130 C4
HNWL W7 85 F6
HPTN TW12 142 A6
HRW HA1 48 E3
MLHL NW7 37 J4
MORT/ESHN SW14 126 A2
MTCM CR4 148 A6
ROM RM1 63 J5
SEVS/STOTM N15 55 H2
SUT SM1 174 E2
WALTH E17 57 J3
WELL DA16 116 A7
WIM/MER SW19 147 G5
WLGTN SM6 176 C5
Milton St BARB EC2Y 13 G2
Milton Wy WDR/YW UB7 100 C3
Milverton Dr HGDN/ICK UB10 64 A3
Milverton Gdns
GDMY/SEVK IG3 79 F1
Milverton Rd
KIL/WHAMP NW6 70 A6
Milverton St LBTH SE11 18 B8
Milverton Wy ELTH/MOT SE9 154 A3
Milward St WCHPL E1 92 D4
Mimosa Rd YEAD UB4 83 G4
Mimosa St FUL/PGN SW6 107 J7
Minard Rd CAT SE6 133 H6
Mina Rd WALW SE17 19 K8
WIM/MER SW19 146 E7
Minchenden Crs
STHGT/OAK N14 40 D2
Mincing La MON EC3R * 13 J6
Minden Rd CHEAM SM3 174 C1
PGE/AN SE20 150 D7
Minehead Rd
RYLN/HDSTN HA2 66 A2
STRHM/NOR SW16 149 F4
Mineral Cl BAR EN5 26 A5
Mineral St WOOL/PLUM SE18 115 K3
Minera Ms BGVA SW1W 16 B5
Minerva Cl BRXN/ST SW9 110 B6
SCUP DA14 154 E3
Minerva Rd CHING E4 43 K6
KUT/HW KT1 159 G1
WLSDN NW10 86 E3
Minerva St BETH E2 92 D1
Minet Av WLSDN NW10 87 G1
Minet Dr HYS/HAR UB3 82 E7
Minet Gdns HYS/HAR UB3 83 F7
WLSDN NW10 87 G1
Minet Rd BRXN/ST SW9 130 C1
Minford Gdns WKENS W14 107 G1
Ming St POP/IOD E14 * 93 J6
Minimax Cl EBED/NFELT TW14 121 K5
Ministry Wy ELTH/MOT SE9 153 K1
Mink Ct HSLWW TW4 122 B1
Minniedale BRYLDS KT5 159 G4
Minnow Wk WALW SE17 19 K6
Minories TWRH EC3N 13 L5
Minshull Pl BECK BR3 * 151 J6
Minshull St VX/NE SW8 * 109 J7
Minson Rd HOM E9 75 F7
Minstead Gdns
PUT/ROE SW15 126 C6
Minstead Wy NWMAL KT3 160 B5
Minster Av SUT SM1 174 E1
Minster Ct MON EC3R * 13 J6
Minster Dr CROY/NA CR0 178 A3
Minster Gdns
E/WMO/HCT KT8 156 E3
Minster Rd BMLY BR1 153 F6
CRICK NW2 70 C4
Minster Wk CEND/HSY/T N8 54 E3
Minstrel Gdns BRYLDS KT5 159 G3
Mintern Cl PLMGR N13 41 H2
Minterne Av NWDGN UB2 103 F3
Minterne Rd
KTN/HRWW/WS HA3 50 B4
Minterne Waye YEAD UB4 83 G5
Mintern St IS N1 7 H5
Minton Ms KIL/WHAMP NW6 71 F5
Mint Rd WLGTN SM6 176 B4
Mint St STHWK SE1 18 E1
Mint Wk CROY/NA CR0 177 J2
Mirabel Rd FUL/PGN SW6 107 J6
Miranda Cl WCHPL E1 92 E4
Miranda Rd ARCH N19 54 C7
Mirfield St CHARL SE7 114 C2
Miriam Rd WOOL/PLUM SE18 115 K4
Mirren Cl RYLN/HDSTN HA2 65 K3
Miskin Rd DART DA1 139 F6
Missenden Cl
EBED/NFELT TW14 121 J7
Missenden Gdns MRDN SM4 162 B5
Mission Gv WALTH E17 57 G4
Mission Pl PECK SE15 111 H7
Mistletoe Cl CROY/NA CR0 166 A7
Misty's Fld WOT/HER KT12 156 B7
Mitali Pas WCHPL E1 92 C5
Mitcham La
STRHM/NOR SW16 148 C4
Mitcham Pk MTCM CR4 162 D3
Mitcham Rd CROY/NA CR0 163 K5
EHAM E6 95 J2
GDMY/SEVK IG3 61 F6
TOOT SW17 147 K4
Mitchellbrook Wy
WLSDN NW10 69 F5
Mitchell Cl ABYW SE2 116 D4
BELV DA17 117 K2
Mitchell Rd PLMGR N13 41 H4
Mitchell St FSBYE EC1V 6 E9
Mitchell Wy BMLY BR1 152 E7
WLSDN NW10 68 E5
Mitchison Rd IS N1 73 K5
Mitchley Rd TOTM N17 56 C2
Mitford Rd ARCH N19 72 E1
Mitre Cl BELMT SM2 175 G6
Mitre Rd SRTFD E15 94 C1
STHWK SE1 18 B1
Mitre Sq HDTCH EC3A 13 K5
Mitre St HDTCH EC3A 13 K5
The Mitre POP/IOD E14 93 H6
Mitre Wy NKENS W10 87 K4
Moat Cl BUSH WD23 22 B4
Moat Ct ELTH/MOT SE9 * 134 E5
Moat Crs FNCH N3 53 F2
Moat Cft WELL DA16 136 D2
Moat Dr HRW HA1 48 C3
PLSTW E13 95 G1
RSLP HA4 46 C6
Moat Farm Rd NTHLT UB5 65 K5
Moatfield Rd BUSH WD23 22 B4
Moat La ERITH DA8 118 D7
Moat Pl ACT W3 86 D5
BRXN/ST SW9 130 A2
Moat Side FELT TW13 141 G3
PEND EN3 30 E3
The Moat NWMAL KT3 145 G7
Moberly Rd CLAP SW4 129 J6
Modbury Gdns KTTN NW5 72 A5
Model Cots MORT/ESHN SW14 125 K2
WEA W13 * 104 C1
Model Farm Cl ELTH/MOT SE9 153 J2
Moelyn Ms HRW HA1 49 G4
Moffat Rd PLMGR N13 40 E5
THHTH CR7 164 D1
TOOT SW17 147 J3
Mogden La ISLW TW7 124 A4
Mohmmad Khan Rd
WAN E11 * 58 D7
Moiety Rd POP/IOD E14 112 D1
Moira Cl TOTM N17 56 A1
Moira Rd ELTH/MOT SE9 134 E3
Moir Cl SAND/SEL CR2 178 C7
Mole Abbey Gdns
E/WMO/HCT KT8 157 F2
Mole Ct HOR/WEW KT19 172 E3
Molember Ct E/WMO/HCT KT8 157 K4
Molember Rd
E/WMO/HCT KT8 157 K4
Molescroft ELTH/MOT SE9 154 C2
Molesey Av E/WMO/HCT KT8 156 E3
Molesey Dr CHEAM SM3 174 C1
Molesey Park Av
E/WMO/HCT KT8 157 G4
Molesey Park Cl
E/WMO/HCT KT8 157 H4
Molesey Park Rd
E/WMO/HCT KT8 157 G4
Molesey Rd E/WMO/HCT KT8 156 D4
WOT/HER KT12 156 D7
Molesford Rd FUL/PGN SW6 * 107 K7
Molesham Cl E/WMO/HCT KT8 157 G2
Molesham Wy
E/WMO/HCT KT8 157 G3
Molesworth St LEW SE13 133 F2
Mollison Av PEND EN3 31 G1
Mollison Dr WLGTN SM6 176 E6
Mollison Wy EDGW HA8 50 C1
Molly Huggins Cl BAL SW12 129 H6
Molyneux Dr TOOT SW17 148 B3
Molyneux St MBLAR W1H 9 K3
Monarch Cl EBED/NFELT TW14 121 H6
RAIN RM13 99 J1
WWKM BR4 180 D3
Monarch Dr CAN/RD E16 95 H4
Monarch Ms
STRHM/NOR SW16 149 G4
Monarch Pde MTCM CR4 * 162 E1
Monarch Pl BKHH IG9 45 G1
Monarch Rd BELV DA17 117 H2
Monarchs Wy RSLP HA4 46 C7

Monarch's Wy *RSLP* HA4 * 46 B7
Monarch Wy *GNTH/NBYPK* IG2 .....60 D5
Mona Rd *PECK* SE15 ....131 K1
Monastery Gdns *ENC/FH* EN2 ....29 K1
Mona St *CAN/RD* E16 ....94 D4
Monaveen Gdns
 E/WMO/HCT KT8 ....157 G2
Monck's Rw
 WAND/EARL SW18 * 127 K5
Monck St *WEST* SW1P 17 H4
Monclar Rd *CMBW* SE5 ....130 E3
Moncorvo Cl *SKENS* SW7 ....15 J2
Moncrieff Cl *EHAM* E6 ....95 J5
Moncrieff St *PECK* SE15 ....131 H1
Monday Aly *STNW/STAM* N16 ....74 B2
Mondial Wy *HYS/HAR* UB3 ....101 F6
Monega Rd *FSTGT* E7 ....77 G5
 MNPK E12 ....77 H5
Money La *WDR/YW* UB7 ....100 A2
Monica Cl *WATN* WD24 ....21 H1
Monier Rd *BOW* E3 ....75 J6
Monivea Rd *BECK* BR3 ....151 F6
Monk Dr *CAN/RD* E16 ....94 E6
Monkfrith Av *STHGT/OAK* N14 ......28 B5
Monkfrith Wy
 STHGT/OAK N14 ....28 B6
Monkham's Av *WFD* IG8 ....45 F4
Monkham's Dr *WFD* IG8 ....45 F4
Monkham's La *WFD* IG8 ....45 F3
Monkleigh Rd *MRDN* SM4 ....161 J2
Monks Av *BAR* EN5 ....27 G5
 E/WMO/HCT KT8 ....156 A4
Monks Cl *ABYW* SE2 ....116 E3
 ENC/FH EN2 ....29 J1
 RSLP HA4 ....65 H3
 RYLN/HDSTN HA2 * 66 A1
Monks Crs *WOT/HER* KT12 ....156 A7
Monksdene Gdns *SUT* SM1 ....175 F2
Monks Dr *ACT* W3 ....86 C4
Monksmead *BORE* WD6 ....24 E3
Monks Orchard Rd *BECK* BR3 ......166 D7
Monks Pk *WBLY* HA9 ....68 D4
Monks Park Gdns *WBLY* HA9 ....68 D5
Monks Rd *ENC/FH* EN2 ....29 J1
Monk St *WOOL/PLUM* SE18 ....115 F3
Monks Wy *BECK* BR3 ....166 D5
 GLDGN NW11 ....52 D3
 STMC/STPC BR5 ....169 H7
Monkswood Gdns *BORE* WD6 ....25 H4
 CLAY IG5 ....60 A2
Monk Ter *FSTH* SE23 ....151 H1
Monkton Rd *WELL* DA16 ....136 A1
Monkton St *LBTH* SE11 ....18 A3
Monkville Av *GLDGN* NW11 ....52 D3
Monkville Pde *GLDGN* NW11 * 52 D3
Monkwell Sq *BARB* EC2Y 12 D1
Monkwood Cl *ROM* RM1 ....63 J4
Monmouth Av *KUT/HW* KT1 ....143 J6
 SWFD E18 ....59 F3
Monmouth Cl *CHSWK* W4 ....106 A2
 MTCM CR4 ....163 K3
 WELL DA16 ....136 B3
Monmouth Gv *BTFD* TW8 ....105 F3
Monmouth Pl *BAY/PAD* W2 * 8 D5
Monmouth Rd *BAY/PAD* W2 ....8 D5
 DAGW RM9 ....80 B4
 ED N9 ....42 D1
 EHAM E6 ....95 K2
 HYS/HAR UB3 ....101 H3
 WAT WD17 ....21 F2
Monmouth St
 LSO/SEVD WC2H 11 J5
Monnery Rd *ARCH* N19 ....72 C2
Monnow Rd *STHWK* SE1 ....111 H4
Mono La *FELT* TW13 ....141 F1
Monoux Gv *WALTH* E17 ....43 H7
Monroe Dr *MORT/ESHN* SW14 ....125 J4
Monro Gdns
 KTN/HRWW/WS HA3 ....34 E6
Monro Pl *HOR/WEW* KT19 ....172 C7
Monsell Rd *FSBYPK* N4 ....73 H1
Monson Rd *NWCR* SE14 ....112 A6
 WLSDN NW10 ....87 J1
Mons Wy *HAYS* BR2 ....168 D5
Montacute Rd *BUSH* WD23 ....22 E6
 CAT SE6 ....132 C6
 CROY/NA CR0 ....180 A7
 MRDN SM4 ....162 C5
Montagu Crs *UED* N18 ....42 D3
Montague Av *BROCKY* SE4 ....132 C3
 HNWL W7 ....85 F7
Montague Cl *BAR* EN5 ....26 D3
 STHWK SE1 ....13 G8
Montague Gdns *EA* W5 ....86 D6
Montague Hall Pl *BUSH* WD23 ......22 A5
Montague Pl *GWRST* WC1E 11 H1
Montague Rd *CEND/HSY/T* N8 ......55 F4
 CROY/NA CR0 ....164 C7
 HACK E8 ....74 C4
 HNWL W7 ....104 A1
 HSLW TW3 ....123 G2
 NWDGN UB2 ....102 D3
 RCHPK/HAM TW10 ....125 F5
 SEVS/STOTM N15 * 56 C3
 WAN E11 ....76 D1
 WEA W13 ....85 H5
 WIM/MER SW19 ....147 F6
Montague St *RSQ* WC1B 11 J2
 STBT EC1A 12 E3
Montague Ter *HAYS* BR2 * 167 K4
Montague Waye *NWDGN* UB2 ......102 D3
Montagu Gdns *UED* N18 ....42 D3
 WLGTN SM6 ....176 C3
Montagu Man *MHST* W1U * 9 M3
Montagu Ms North
 MBLAR W1H 9 M3
Montagu Ms South
 MBLAR W1H 9 M4
Montagu Ms West
 MBLAR W1H 9 L4
Montagu Pl *MBLAR* W1H * 9 L3
Montagu Rd *ED* N9 ....42 E2
 HDN NW4 ....51 J5
 UED N18 ....42 D3
Montagu Rw *MHST* W1U 9 M3
Montagu Sq *MBLAR* W1H 9 M3
Montagu St *MBLAR* W1H 9 M4
Montaigne Cl *WEST* SW1P 17 H6
Montalt Rd *WFD* IG8 ....44 D4
Montana Gdns *SUT* SM1 ....175 G4
 SYD SE26 ....151 H4
Montana Rd *RYNPK* SW20 ....146 A7
 TOOT SW17 ....148 A2
Montbelle Rd *ELTH/MOT* SE9 ......154 B2
Montcalm Cl *HAYS* BR2 ....167 K5
 YEAD UB4 ....83 F2
Montcalm Rd *CHARL* SE7 ....114 C6
Montclare St *BETH* E2 * 7 L8
Monteagle Av *BARK* IG11 ....78 C5
Monteagle Wy *PECK* SE15 ....131 K2
Montefiore St *VX/NE* SW8 ....129 G1
Montem Rd *FSTH* SE23 ....132 C6

 NWMAL KT3 ....160 B3
Montem St *FSBYPK* N4 ....55 F7
Montenotte Rd
 CEND/HSY/T N8 ....54 C4
Montesole Ct *PIN* HA5 * 47 G1
Montesquieu Ter
 CAN/RD E16 * 94 D5
Montford Pl *LBTH* SE11 ....18 A8
Montfort Pl *WIM/MER* SW19 ....127 G7
Montgomerie Ms *FSTH* SE23 ......131 K6
Montgomery Av
 ESH/CLAY KT10 ....170 E1
Montgomery Cl *BFN/LL* DA15 .....155 K4
 MTCM CR4 ....163 K3
Montgomery Gdns
 BELMT SM2 ....175 H6
Montgomery Rd *CHSWK* W4 ....105 J3
 EDGW HA8 ....36 B5
Montholme Rd *BTSEA* SW11 ....128 E5
Monthorpe Rd *WCHPL* E1 ....92 C4
Montolieu Gdns
 PUT/ROE SW15 ....126 E4
Montpelier Av *BXLY* DA5 ....136 E6
 EA W5 ....85 J4
Montpelier Gdns *CHDH* RM6 ....61 J6
 EHAM E6 ....95 H2
Montpelier Gv *KTTN* NW5 ....72 C4
Montpelier Ms *SKENS* SW7 ....15 K3
Montpelier Pl *SKENS* SW7 ....15 K3
 WCHPL E1 ....92 E5
Montpelier Ri *GLDGN* NW11 ....52 C6
 WBLY HA9 ....49 K7
Montpelier Rd *EA* W5 ....85 K4
 FNCH N3 ....39 G7
 PECK SE15 ....111 J7
 SUT SM1 ....175 G3
Montpelier Rw
 BKHTH/KID SE3 ....133 J1
 TWK TW1 ....124 C6
Montpelier Sq *SKENS* SW7 ....15 K2
Montpelier St *SKENS* SW7 ....15 K3
Montpelier Ter *SKENS* SW7 ....15 K2
Montpelier Vis
 BKHTH/KID SE3 ....133 J1
Montpelier Wk *SKENS* SW7 ....15 K2
Montpelier Wy *GLDGN* NW11 ....52 C6
Montrave Rd *PGE/AN* SE20 ....150 E6
Montreal Pl *HOL/ALD* WC2B 11 L6
Montreal Rd *IL* IG1 ....60 D7
Montrell Rd
 BRXS/STRHM SW2 ....129 K7
Montrose Av *BFN/LL* DA15 ....136 B6
 EDGW HA8 ....51 F1
 KIL/WHAMP NW6 ....88 C1
 WELL DA16 ....135 J2
 WHTN TW2 ....123 G6
Montrose Cl *ASHF* TW15 ....140 A5
 WELL DA16 ....136 A1
 WFD IG8 ....44 E3
Montrose Crs *ALP/SUD* HA0 ....68 A5
 NFNCH/WDSPK N12 ....39 F5
Montrose Gdns *MTCM* CR4 ....162 E2
 SUT SM1 ....175 F1
Montrose Pl *KTBR* SW1X 16 B2
Montrose Rd
 EBED/NFELT TW14 ....121 G5
 KTN/HRWW/WS HA3 ....48 E1
Montrose Vls *HMSMTH* W6 * 106 D4
Montrose Wy *FSTH* SE23 ....132 A1
Montserrat Av *WFD* IG8 ....44 B6
Montserrat Cl *NRWD* SE19 ....149 K4
Montserrat Rd
 PUT/ROE SW15 ....127 H3
Monument Wy *TOTM* N17 ....56 B2
Monza St *WAP* E1W 92 E6
Moodkee St *BERM/RHTH* SE16 ...111 K2
Moody Rd *PECK* SE15 * 111 G6
Moody St *IS* N1 ....93 F2
Moon Ct *LEE/GVPK* SE12 * 133 K3
Moon La *BAR* EN5 ....26 D2
Moon St *IS* N1 ....6 C3
Moorcroft Gdns *EDGW* HA8 * 36 D7
Moorcroft Rd
 STRHM/NOR SW16 ....148 E2
Moorcroft Wy *PIN* HA5 ....47 J4
Moordown *WOOL/PLUM* SE18 .....115 F7
Moore Cl *MORT/ESHN* SW14 .....125 J1
 MTCM CR4 * 163 G1
Moore Crs *DAGW* RM9 ....79 H7
Moorefield Rd *TOTM* N17 ....56 B2
Mooreland Rd *BMLY* BR1 ....152 D6
Moore Park Rd *FUL/PGN* SW6 ....108 A6
Moore Rd *NRWD* SE19 ....149 H5
Moore St *CHEL* SW3 ....15 L5
Moore Wy *BELMT* SM2 ....174 E7
Moorey Cl *SRTFD* E15 ....76 D7
Moorfield Av *EA* W5 ....85 K3
Moorfield Rd *CHSGTN* KT9 ....172 A4
Moorfields *LVPST* EC2M 13 G2
Moorfields Highwalk
 BARB EC2Y * 13 G3
Moorgate *LOTH* EC2R * 13 G3
 LVPST EC2M 13 G2
Moorgate Pl *LOTH* EC2R * 13 G3
Moorhead Wy *BKHTH/KID* SE3 ...134 A2
Moorhen Cl *ERITH* DA8 ....118 E6
Moorhouse Rd *BAY/PAD* W2 ....8 A4
 KTN/HRWW/WS HA3 ....35 K2
The Moorings *BUSH* WD23 * 21 J3
 CHSWK W4 * 105 H5
Moorland Cl *WHTN* TW2 ....123 F6
Moorland Rd *BRXN/ST* SW9 ....130 C3
 HYS/HAR UB3 ....101 H5
Moor La *BARB* EC2Y 13 G3
 CHSGTN KT9 ....172 B4
Moor Lane Crossing
 WATW WD18 ....20 A6
Moormead Dr
 HOR/WEW KT19 ....173 G4
Moor Mead Rd *TWK* TW1 ....124 B5
Moor Park Gdns
 KUTN/CMB KT2 ....145 G6
 NTHWD HA6 ....32 A1
Moor Park Rd *NTHWD* HA6 ....32 B5
Moorside Rd *BMLY* BR1 ....152 C3
Moor St *SOHO/SHAV* W1D * 11 H5
Moortown Rd *OXHEY* WD19 ....33 G3
Moor Vw *WATW* WD18 ....20 E6
Morant Pl *POP/IOD* E14 * 93 J6
Morant Rd *CRICK* NW2 * 70 A3
Mora Rd *FSBYE* EC1V 6 D7
Morat St *BRXN/ST* SW9 ....110 A7
Moravia Av *WBPTN* SW10 ....108 A7
Moravian Pl *WBPTN* SW10 ....15 J8
Moravian St *BETH* E2 ....92 E1
Moray Av *HYS/HAR* UB3 ....82 D7
Moray Cl *EDGW* HA8 * 36 D1
Moray Ms *HOLWY* N7 ....73 F1
Moray Rd *HOLWY* N7 ....73 F1
Morcambe St *WALW* SE17 ....18 F6
Mordaunt Gdns *DAGW* RM9 ....80 A6
Mordaunt Rd *WLSDN* NW10 ....69 G7
Mordaunt St *BRXN/ST* SW9 ....130 A2

Morden Ct *MRDN* SM4 ....162 A3
Morden Court Pde
 MRDN SM4 ....162 A2
Morden Gdns *GFD/PVL* UB6 ....67 F4
 MTCM CR4 ....162 C3
Morden Hall Rd *MRDN* SM4 ....162 A2
Morden Hill *LEW* SE13 ....133 F1
Morden La *LEW* SE13 ....133 F1
 CHDH RM6 ....62 A6
 MTCM CR4 ....162 A6
 WIM/MER SW19 ....162 A1
Morden Road Ms
 BKHTH/KID SE3 ....133 K1
Morden St *LEW* SE13 ....112 E7
Morden Wy *CHEAM* SM3 ....161 K6
Morden Wharf Rd
 GNWCH SE10 ....113 H2
Mordon Rd *GDMY/SEVK* IG3 ....61 K5
Mordred Rd *CAT* SE6 ....152 C1
Morecambe Cl *HCH* RM12 ....81 K4
 WCHPL E1 * 93 F4
Morecambe Gdns *STAN* HA7 ....35 K3
Morecambe Ter *UED* N18 * 41 K3
 WALW SE17 ....19 J8
Morecambe St *POP/IOD* E14 ......112 A4
 WALW SE17 ....19 H7
More Cl *CAN/RD* E16 ....94 D5
 WKENS W14 ....107 G3
Morecoombe Cl
 KUTN/CMB KT2 ....144 D6
Moree Wy *UED* N18 ....42 C3
Moreland Cots *BOW* E3 * 93 J1
Moreland St *FSBYE* EC1V 6 D7
Moreland Wy *CHING* E4 ....43 K2
More La *ESH/CLAY* KT10 ....170 B2
Morella Rd *BTSEA* SW11 ....128 E6
More London Riverside
 STHWK SE1 ....13 K9
Moremead Rd *CAT* SE6 ....151 H3
Morena St *CAT* SE6 ....132 E6
Moresby Av *BRYLDS* KT5 ....159 J6
Moresby Rd *CLPT* E5 ....56 D7
Mores Gdn *CHEL* SW3 * 108 C5
Moreton Av *ISLW* TW7 ....103 J7
Moreton Cl *CLPT* E5 ....74 E1
 WCHPL E1 * 92 E5
 SEVS/STOTM N15 ....55 K5
Moreton Ct *DART* DA1 ....138 B2
Moreton Gdns *WFD* IG8 ....45 J4
Moreton Pl *PIM* SW1V 16 F7
 SAND/SEL CR2 ....177 K4
Moreton Rd *SAND/SEL* CR2 ....177 K4
 SEVS/STOTM N15 ....55 K5
 WPK KT4 ....173 J1
Moreton St *PIM* SW1V 16 F7
Moreton Ter *PIM* SW1V 16 F7
Moreton Terrace Ms South
 PIM SW1V * 16 F7
Morford Cl *RSLP* HA4 ....47 F6
Morford Wy *RSLP* HA4 ....47 F6
Morgan Av *WALTH* E17 ....58 B3
Morgan Cl *DAGE* RM10 ....80 C6
 NTHWD HA6 ....32 D4
Morgan Rd *BMLY* BR1 ....152 E6
 HOLWY N7 ....73 G4
 NKENS W10 ....88 D4
Morgan's La *HYS/HAR* UB3 ....82 B4
 STHWK SE1 ....13 J9
Morgan St *BOW* E3 ....93 G2
 CAN/RD E16 ....94 C4
Morgan Wy *WFD* IG8 ....45 J5
Moriarty Cl *BMLY* BR1 ....169 G3
Moriarty Cl *HOLWY* N7 ....72 E3
Morie St *WAND/EARL* SW18 ......128 A3
Morieux Rd *LEY* E10 ....57 H7
Moring Rd *TOOT* SW17 ....148 A3
Morkyns Wk *DUL* SE21 * 150 A3
Morland Av *CROY/NA* CR0 ....165 F7
Morland Cl *GLDGN* NW11 ....53 F7
 HPTN TW12 ....141 K4
 MTCM CR4 ....162 D2
Morland Est *HACK* E8 * 74 C6
Morland Gdns *STHL* UB1 ....84 B7
 WLSDN NW10 ....69 F6
Morland Ms *IS* N1 ....6 A1
Morland Rd *CROY/NA* CR0 ....165 G6
 DAGE RM10 ....80 C6
 IL IG1 ....78 B1
 KTN/HRWW/WS HA3 ....50 A4
 PGE/AN SE20 ....151 F6
 SUT SM1 ....175 G4
 WALTH E17 ....57 F4
Morley Av *CHING* E4 ....44 B6
 UED N18 ....42 C3
 WDGN N22 ....41 H7
Morley Cl *EDGW* HA8 * 36 E1
 RSLP HA4 ....65 G1
Morley Crs East *STAN* HA7 ....49 J2
Morley Crs West *STAN* HA7 ....49 J2
Morley Rd *BARK* IG11 ....78 D7
 CHDH RM6 ....62 A4
 CHEAM SM3 ....161 J7
 CHST BR7 ....154 C7
 LEW SE13 ....133 F3
 LEY E10 ....58 A7
 SRTFD E15 ....94 D1
 TWK TW1 ....124 E5
Morley St *STHWK* SE1 ....18 B2
Morna Rd *CMBW* SE5 ....130 D1
Morning La *HOM* E9 ....74 E5
Morningside Rd *WPK* KT4 ....173 K1
Mornington Av *HAYS* BR2 ....168 B2
 IL IG1 ....78 C3
 WKENS W14 ....107 J3
Mornington Ct *BXLY* DA5 ....138 A7
Mornington Crs *CAMTN* NW1 ....4 E5
 HEST TW5 ....102 A7
Mornington Gv *BOW* E3 ....93 J2
Mornington Ms *CMBW* SE5 ....110 D7
Mornington Pl *CAMTN* NW1 ....4 D5
Mornington Rd *ASHF* TW15 ....140 A4
 GFD/PVL UB6 ....84 B4
 NWCR SE14 ....112 C6
 WAN E11 ....58 D7
 WFD IG8 ....44 D3
Mornington St *CAMTN* NW1 ....4 D5
Mornington Ter *CAMTN* NW1 ....4 D4
Mornington Wk
 RCHPK/HAM TW10 ....143 J3
Morocco St *STHWK* SE1 ....19 J2
Morocco St *STHWK* SE1 ....19 J2
Morpeth Gv *HOM* E9 ....75 F7
Morpeth Rd *HOM* E9 ....74 E7
Morpeth St *BETH* E2 ....93 F2
Morpeth Ter *WEST* SW1P 16 E4
Morpeth Wk *TOTM* N17 * 42 E6
Morphou Rd *MLHL* NW7 ....38 C4
Morpington Gdns *GDMY/SEVK* IG3 ..79 F2
Morrel Ct *BAR* EN5 * 26 B2
Morrells Yd *LBTH* SE11 ....18 B7
Morris Av *MNPK* E12 ....77 K4
Morris Bishop Ter *HGT* N6 * 54 A5
Morris Cl *CROY/NA* CR0 ....166 B5
Morris Ct *CHING* E4 * 43 K2
Morris Gdns *DART* DA1 ....139 K4

 WAND/EARL SW18 ....127 K6
Morrish Rd *BRXS/STRHM* SW2 ...129 K6
Morrison Av *CHING* E4 ....43 J5
 TOTM N17 ....56 A2
Morrison Rd *BARK* IG11 ....98 A1
 YEAD UB4 ....83 F2
Morrison St *BTSEA* SW11 ....129 F2
Morris Pl *FSBYPK* N4 ....73 G1
Morris Rd *BCTR* RM8 ....80 B1
 ISLW TW7 ....124 A2
 POP/IOD E14 ....93 K4
 SRTFD E15 ....76 C3
Morris St *WCHPL* E1 ....92 D5
Morriston Cl *OXHEY* WD19 ....33 G4
Morse Cl *PLSTW* E13 ....94 E2
Morshead Rd *MV/WKIL* W9 ....2 B8
Morson Rd *PEND* EN3 ....31 G5
Morteyne Rd *TOTM* N17 ....41 K7
Mortham St *SRTFD* E15 ....76 C7
Mortimer Cl
 BUSH WD23 ....22 B5
 CRICK NW2 ....70 D2
 STRHM/NOR SW16 ....148 D1
Mortimer Crs
 KIL/WHAMP NW6 ....2 C4
 WPK KT4 ....173 F2
Mortimer Dr *EN* EN1 ....29 K4
Mortimer Pl *KIL/WHAMP* NW6 ....2 C4
Mortimer Rd *EHAM* E6 ....95 K2
 ERITH DA8 ....118 A5
 IS N1 ....7 K1
 MTCM CR4 ....147 K7
 WEA W13 ....85 J5
 WLSDN NW10 ....88 A2
Mortimer Sq *NTGHL* W11 ....88 B6
Mortimer St *GTPST* W1W 10 E2
Mortimer Ter *KTTN* NW5 * 72 B3
Mortlake Cl *CROY/NA* CR0 ....176 E3
Mortlake Dr *MTCM* CR4 ....147 J7
Mortlake High St
 MORT/ESHN SW14 ....126 A2
Mortlake Rd *CAN/RD* E16 ....95 F4
 IL IG1 ....78 C3
 MORT/ESHN SW14 ....125 J2
 RCH/KEW TW9 ....105 H6
Morton Cl *CLAP* SW4 ....129 J6
 WCHPL E1 * 92 E5
 WLGTN SM6 ....177 H6
Morton Crs *STHGT/OAK* N14 ....40 D3
Morton Gdns *WLGTN* SM6 ....176 C4
Morton Ms *ECT* SW5 ....14 C6
Morton Pl *STHWK* SE1 ....18 A4
Morton Rd *IS* N1 ....6 F2
 MRDN SM4 ....162 C4
 SRTFD E15 ....76 D6
Morton Wy *STHGT/OAK* N14 ....40 C2
Morvale Cl *BELV* DA17 ....117 G3
Morval Rd *BRXS/STRHM* SW2 ....130 B4
Morven Rd *TOOT* SW17 ....147 K2
Morville St *BOW* E3 ....93 J1
Morwell St *RSQ* WC1B 11 H3
Moscow Pl *BAY/PAD* W2 * 8 C6
Moscow Rd *BAY/PAD* W2 ....8 B6
Moselle Av *WDGN* N22 ....55 G1
Moselle Cl *CEND/HSY/T* N8 ....55 F2
Moselle Pl *TOTM* N17 * 42 B6
Moselle St *TOTM* N17 ....42 B6
Mossborough Cl
 NFNCH/WDSPK N12 ....39 F5
Mossbury Rd *BTSEA* SW11 ....128 D2
Moss Cl *PIN* HA5 ....47 K1
 WCHPL E1 ....92 C4
Mossdown Cl *BELV* DA17 ....117 H3
Mossford Gn *BARK/HLT* IG6 ....60 C1
Mossford La *BARK/HLT* IG6 ....60 C1
Mossford St *BOW* E3 ....93 H3
Moss Gdns *FELT* TW13 ....140 E1
 SAND/SEL CR2 ....179 G6
Moss Hall Crs
 NFNCH/WDSPK N12 ....39 F5
Moss Hall Gv
 NFNCH/WDSPK N12 ....39 F5
Moss La *PIN* HA5 ....47 K2
 ROM RM1 ....63 H5
Mosslea Rd *HAYS* BR2 ....168 C4
 PGE/AN SE20 ....150 E5
Mossop St *CHEL* SW3 ....15 K5
Mossville Gdns *MRDN* SM4 ....161 J2
Moston Cl *HYS/HAR* UB3 ....101 J4
Mostyn Av *WBLY* HA9 ....68 B4
Mostyn Gdns *WLSDN* NW10 ....88 B2
Mostyn Gv *BOW* E3 ....93 H1
Mostyn Rd *BRXN/ST* SW9 ....110 B7
 BUSH WD23 ....22 C5
 EDGW HA8 ....37 F6
 WIM/MER SW19 ....161 J2
Mosul Wy *HAYS* BR2 ....168 D5
Motcomb St *KTBR* SW1X 16 A3
Moth Cl *WLGTN* SM6 ....176 E6
The Mothers Sq *CLPT* E5 * 74 D3
Moth House
 WOOL/PLUM SE18 * 114 D6
Motley Av *VX/NE* SW8 ....19 H1
Motspur Pk *NWMAL* KT3 ....160 C5
Mottingham Gdns
 ELTH/MOT SE9 ....134 C7
Mottingham La
 LEE/GVPK SE12 ....134 B7
Mottingham Rd *ED* N9 ....31 F5
 ELTH/MOT SE9 ....153 J2
Mottisfont Rd *ABYW* SE2 ....116 C2
Moulins Rd *HOM* E9 ....74 E6
Moulton Av *HSLW* TW3 ....122 D1
Moundfield Rd
 STNW/STAM N16 ....56 C5
Mountacre Cl *SYD* SE26 ....150 B3
Mount Adon Pk *EDUL* SE22 ....131 H6
Mountague Pl *POP/IOD* E14 ....94 A6
Mount Angelus Rd
 PUT/ROE SW15 ....126 C6
Mount Ararat Rd
 RCHPK/HAM TW10 ....125 F4
Mount Ash Rd *SYD* SE26 ....150 D3
Mount Av *CHING* E4 ....43 J2
 EA W5 ....85 K4
 STHL UB1 ....84 A5
Mountbatten Cl *NRWD* SE19 ......150 A4
 WOOL/PLUM SE18 ....115 K5
Mountbatten Ct *BKHH* IG9 ....45 H1
Mountbel Rd *STAN* HA7 * 49 G1
Mount Cl *BMLY* BR1 ....153 J1
 CAR SM5 ....176 A7
 EA W5 ....85 H4
 EBAR EN4 ....28 A3
Mountcombe Cl *SURB* KT6 ....159 F6
Mount Cnt *WWKM* BR4 ....180 C1
Mount Culver Av *SCUP* DA14 ......155 K5
Mount Dr *RYLN/HDSTN* HA2 ....47 K4
 WBLY HA9 ....68 E2
Mountearl Gdns
 STRHM/NOR SW16 ....149 F7
Mount Echo Av *CHING* E4 ....31 K7

Mount Echo Dr *CHING* E4 ....31 K7
Mount Ephraim La
 STRHM/NOR SW16 ....148 D2
Mount Ephraim Rd
 STRHM/NOR SW16 ....148 D2
Mountfield Cl *CAT* SE6 ....133 G6
Mountfield Rd *EA* W5 ....85 K5
 EHAM E6 ....96 A1
 FNCH N3 ....52 E2
Mountfield Ter *CAT* SE6 * 133 G6
Mountfort Ter *IS* N1 * 6 A1
Mount Gdns *SYD* SE26 ....150 D2
Mount Gv *EDGW* HA8 * 37 F2
Mount Holme *THDIT* KT7 ....158 C6
Mounthurst Rd *HAYES* BR2 ....167 K6
Mountington Park Cl
 KTN/HRWW/WS HA3 ....49 K5
Mountjoy Cl *ABYW* SE2 ....116 C1
Mount Ms *HPTN* TW12 ....142 B7
Mount Mills *FSBYE* EC1V * 6 D8
Mount Nod Rd
 STRHM/NOR SW16 ....149 F2
Mount Pde *EBAR* EN4 * 27 J3
Mount Pk Av *HRW* HA1 ....66 D1
 SAND/SEL CR2 ....177 H7
Mount Park Crs *EA* W5 ....85 K5
Mount Park Rd *EA* W5 ....85 K4
 HRW HA1 ....66 D1
 PIN HA5 ....46 E4
Mount Pl *ACT* W3 * 86 D7
Mount Pleasant *ALP/SUD* HA0 .....68 A7
 EBAR EN4 ....27 J4
 FSBYW WC1X 11 M1
 HRW HA1 ....66 E1
 RSLP HA4 ....65 G2
 WNWD SE27 ....149 J3
Mount Pleasant Crs
 FSBYPK N4 * 55 F6
Mount Pleasant Hl *CLPT* E5 ....74 D1
Mount Pleasant La *CLPT* E5 ....74 D1
Mount Pleasant Pl
 WOOL/PLUM SE18 ....115 J3
Mount Pleasant Rd *DART* DA1 ....139 J5
 EA W5 ....85 J3
 LEW SE13 ....133 F5
 NWMAL KT3 ....159 K2
 TOTM N17 ....56 A2
 WALTH E17 ....57 G1
 WLSDN NW10 ....70 A6
Mount Pleasant Crs
 FSBYPK N4 ....55 F6
Mount Ri *FSTH* SE23 ....150 E1
Mount Rd *BCTR* RM8 ....62 B7
 BXLYHS DA6 ....137 F4
 CHSGTN KT9 ....172 B3
 CRICK NW2 ....69 K2
 DART DA1 ....138 C5
 EBAR EN4 ....27 J4
 FELT TW13 ....141 J2
 HDN NW4 ....51 J5
 HYS/HAR UB3 ....101 K3
 MTCM CR4 ....162 C1
 NRWD SE19 ....149 K5
 NWMAL KT3 ....160 A2
 WIM/MER SW19 ....146 E1
Mountside
 KTN/HRWW/WS HA3 ....35 F7
 STAN HA7 ....35 F7
Mounts Pond Rd
 BKHTH/KID SE3 ....133 G1
 LEW SE13 ....133 G1
The Mount Sq *HAMP* NW3 * 71 G2
Mount Stewart Av
 KTN/HRWW/WS HA3 ....49 K5
Mount Ter *WCHPL* E1 ....92 D4
The Mount *BMLY* BR1 ....153 J2
 BXLYHS DA6 ....137 J4
 CLPT E5 * 74 D1
 ESH/CLAY KT10 ....170 A5
 EW KT17 ....173 K3
 HAMP NW3 ....71 G3
 NTHLT UB5 ....66 B4
 NWMAL KT3 ....160 C2
 TRDG/WHET N20 ....39 G1
 WBLY HA9 ....68 D3
Mount Vw *NWDGN* UB2 ....102 C3
Mountview *NTHWD* HA6 * 32 D7
Mountview Cl *HAMP* NW3 ....53 J2
Mount View Rd
 CDALE/KGS NW9 ....51 F3
 ESH/CLAY KT10 ....171 H6
 FSBYPK N4 ....55 F6
Mount Vls *WNWD* SE27 ....149 H2
Mountway *CAR* SM5 ....175 J6
Mountwood *E/WMO/HCT* KT8 .....157 G2
Movers La *BARK* IG11 ....78 D7
Mowatt Cl *ARCH* N19 ....54 D7
Mowbray Gdns *NTHLT* UB5 * 66 A7
Mowbray Rd *BAR* EN5 ....27 G2
 EDGW HA8 ....36 C3
 KIL/WHAMP NW6 ....70 C1
 NRWD SE19 ....150 B7
 RCHPK/HAM TW10 ....143 H7
Mowbrays Rd *CRW* RM5 ....62 E1
Mowlem St *BETH* E2 ....92 D1
Mowll St *BRXN/ST* SW9 ....110 B6
Moxon Cl *PLSTW* E13 ....94 D1
Moxon St *BAR* EN5 ....26 D2
 MHST W1U 10 A3
Moye Cl *BETH* E2 ....92 C1
Moyers Rd *LEY* E10 ....58 A7
Moylan Rd *HMSMTH* W6 ....107 H5
Moyne Pl *WLSDN* NW10 ....86 C2
Moynihan Dr *WCHMH* N21 ....28 E4
Moys Cl *CROY/NA* CR0 ....163 K5
Moyser Rd *STRHM/NOR* SW16 ...148 B4
Mozart St *NKENS* W10 ....88 D2
Muchelney Rd *MRDN* SM4 ....162 B5
Muggeridge Cl *SAND/SEL* CR2 ...177 K4
Muggeridge Rd *DAGE* RM10 ....80 D4
Muirdown Av
 MORT/ESHN SW14 ....125 K3
Muir Dr *WAND/EARL* SW18 ....128 C5
Muirfield *ACT* W3 ....87 G5
Muirfield Cl
 BERM/RHTH SE16 * 111 J4
 OXHEY WD19 ....33 G3
Muirfield Crs *POP/IOD* E14 ....112 E2
Muirfield Grn *OXHEY* WD19 ....33 G3
Muirfield Rd *OXHEY* WD19 ....33 F3
Muirkirk Rd *CAT* SE6 ....133 F7
Muir Rd *CLPT* E5 ....74 C2
Muir St *CAN/RD* E16 ....95 K7
Mulberry Av
 STWL/WRAY TW19 ....120 B7
Mulberry Cl *CEND/HSY/T* N8 ....54 E4
 CHEL SW3 ....108 C5
 CHING E4 ....43 J1

EBAR EN4 27 H3
GPK RM2 63 K3
HDN NW4 52 A2
HOR/WEW KT19 172 E7
NTHLT UB5 83 J1
STRHM/NOR SW16 148 C3
Mulberry Crs BTFD TW8 104 C6
WDR/YW UB7 100 D1
Mulberry Dr PUR RM19 119 J3
Mulberry La CROY/NA CR0 165 G7
Mulberry Ms NWCR SE14 112 C7
Mulberry Pde WDR/YW UB7 100 D2
Mulberry Pl ELTH/MOT SE9 134 C3
HMSMTH W6 106 D4
Mulberry Rd HACK E8 7 L2
Mulberry St WCHPL E1 92 C5
Mulberry Wk CHEL SW3 15 H9
Mulberry Wy BARK/HLT IG6 60 C3
BELV DA17 117 K1
SWFD E18 59 F1
Mulgrave Rd BELMT SM2 175 F5
CROY/NA CR0 177 K2
EA W5 85 K2
HRW HA1 67 G1
WKENS W14 107 J5
WLSDN NW10 69 H3
WOOL/PLUM SE18 114 E3
Mulholland Cl MTCM CR4 163 G1
Mulkern Rd ARCH N19 54 D7
Mullards Cl MTCM CR4 162 E7
Mullet Gdns BETH E2 92 C2
Mullins Pth MORT/ESHN SW14 126 A2
Mullion Cl
KTN/HRWW/WS HA3 34 B7
Mullion Wk OXHEY WD19 33 H3
Mull Wk IS N1 73 J5
Mulready St STJWD NW8 9 J1
Multi Wy ACT W3 106 B1
Multon Rd WAND/EARL SW18 128 C6
Mumford Ct CITYW EC2V 12 F4
Mumford Mills GNWCH SE10 112 D6
Mumford Rd HNHL SE24 130 C4
Muncaster Rd CLAP SW4 128 E3
Muncies Ms CAT SE6 152 A1
Mundania Rd EDUL SE22 131 J5
Munday Rd CAN/RD E16 94 E5
Munden St WKENS W14 107 H3
Mundesly Cl OXHEY WD19 33 G3
Mundford Rd CLPT E5 74 E1
Mundon Gdns IL IG1 60 D7
Mund St WKENS W14 107 J4
Mundy St IS N1 7 J7
Mungo-Park Cl BUSH WD23 * 34 C1
Mungo Park Rd RAIN RM13 81 J5
Munnings Gdns ISLW TW7 123 J4
Munro Dr FBAR/BDGN N11 40 C5
Munroe Ter WBPTN SW10 108 C6
Munro Ms NKENS W10 88 C4
Munro Ter WBPTN SW10 108 C5
Munro Wy CLPT E5 74 C3
Munslow Gdns SUT SM1 175 G3
Munster Av HSLWW TW4 122 D3
Munster Ct FUL/PGN SW6 127 J1
Munster Gdns PLMGR N13 41 J3
Munster Ms FUL/PGN SW6 * 107 J6
Munster Rd FUL/PGN SW6 107 H6
TEDD TW11 143 J5
Munster Sq CAMTN NW1 4 D8
Munton Rd WALW SE17 18 F5
Murchison Av BXLY DA5 136 E7
Murchison Rd LEY E10 76 A1
Murdock Cl CAN/RD E16 94 D5
Murdock St PECK SE15 111 J5
Murfett Cl WIM/MER SW19 146 C1
Muriel Av WATW WD18 21 G4
Muriel St IS N1 5 M4
Murillo Rd LEW SE13 133 G3
Murphy St STHWK SE1 18 A2
Murray Av BMLY BR1 168 A2
HSLW TW3 123 G4
Murray Cl THMD SE28 96 E7
Murray Crs PIN HA5 33 H7
Murray Gv IS N1 7 G6
Murray House
WOOL/PLUM SE18 * 114 D6
Murray Ms CAMTN NW1 5 G1
Murray Rd EA W5 104 D3
NTHWD HA6 32 C7
RCHPK/HAM TW10 143 H1
WIM/MER SW19 146 B5
Murray Sq CAN/RD E16 94 E5
Murray St CAMTN NW1 4 F1
Murray Ter HAMP NW3 71 G3
Musard Rd HMSMTH W6 107 H5
Musbury St WCHPL E1 92 E5
Muscatel Pl CMBW SE5 111 F7
Muschamp Rd CAR SM5 175 J1
PECK SE15 131 G2
Muscovy St MON EC3R 13 K7
Museum St NOXST/BSQ WC1A 11 J3
Museum Wy ACT W3 105 H1
Musgrave Crs FUL/PGN SW6 107 K6
Musgrave Rd ISLW TW7 104 A7
Musgrove Rd NWCR SE14 112 A7
Musjid Rd BTSEA SW11 128 C1
Musquash Wy HSLWW TW4 122 B1
Muston Rd CLPT E5 74 D1
Muswell Av MUSWH N10 54 B1
Muswell Hl MUSWH N10 54 B2
Muswell Hill Broadway
MUSWH N10 54 B2
Muswell Hill Pl MUSWH N10 54 B3
Muswell Hill Rd HGT N6 54 A5
Muswell Ms MUSWH N10 54 B2
Muswell Rd MUSWH N10 54 B1
Mutrix Rd KIL/WHAMP NW6 2 B3
Mutter Rd CLAP SW4 129 J5
Mutton Pl CAMTN NW1 72 A5
Muybridge Rd NWMAL KT3 159 K1
Myatt Rd BRXN/ST SW9 110 C7
Mycenae Rd BKHTH/KID SE3 113 K5
Myddelton Gdns WCHMH N21 29 J6
Myddelton Pk
TRDG/WHET N20 39 H2
Myddelton Pas CLKNW EC1R 6 B7
Myddelton Rd
CEND/HSY/T N8 54 E2
Myddelton Sq CLKNW EC1R 6 B7
Myddelton St CLKNW EC1R 6 B8
Myddleton Av FSBYPK N4 73 H1
Myddleton Cl STAN HA7 35 G1
Myddleton Rd WDGN N22 40 E6
Myers La NWCR SE14 112 A5
Mylis Cl SYD SE26 150 D3
Mylne Cl HMSMTH W6 * 106 D4
Mylne St IS N1 6 A6
Myra St ABYW SE2 116 B4
Myrdle St WCHPL E1 92 C5
Myrna Cl WIM/MER SW19 147 J6
Myron Pl LEW SE13 133 F2
Myrtle Aly WOOL/PLUM SE18 115 F2
Myrtle Av EBED/NFELT TW14 121 H3
RSLP HA4 46 E6
Myrtleberry Cl HACK E8 * 74 B5
Myrtle Cl EBAR EN4 27 K7
ERITH DA8 118 B6
WDR/YW UB7 100 C3
Myrtledene Rd ABYW SE2 116 B4
Myrtle Gdns HNWL W7 84 E7
Myrtle Gv NWMAL KT3 159 K1
Myrtle Rd ACT W3 86 E7
CROY/NA CR0 179 J2
EHAM E6 77 J7
HPTN TW12 142 C5
HSLW TW3 123 H1
IL IG1 78 B1
PLMGR N13 41 J2
SUT SM1 175 G4
WALTH E17 57 G5
Myrtleside Cl NTHWD HA6 32 B6
Myrtle St IS N1 7 J6
Myrtle Wk IS N1 7 J6
Mysore Rd BTSEA SW11 128 E3
Myton Rd DUL SE21 149 K2

N

Nadine St CHARL SE7 114 B4
Nagle Cl WALTH E17 58 B1
Nag's Head La WELL DA16 136 C2
Nags Head Rd PEND EN3 30 E3
Nairne Gv HNHL SE24 130 E4
Nairn Gn OXHEY WD19 32 E2
Nairn Rd RSLP HA4 65 G5
Nairn St POP/IOD E14 94 A4
Nallhead Rd FELT TW13 141 G4
Namba Roy Cl
STRHM/NOR SW16 149 F3
Namton Dr THHTH CR7 164 A3
Nan Clark's La MLHL NW7 37 H1
Nancy Downs OXHEY WD19 21 G6
Nankin St POP/IOD E14 93 J5
Nansen Rd BTSEA SW11 129 F3
Nansen Village
NFNCH/WDSPK N12 * 39 F3
Nantes Cl WAND/EARL SW18 128 B3
Nant Rd CRICK NW2 70 D1
Nant St BETH E2 92 D2
Naoroji St FSBYW WC1X 6 A8
Napier Av FUL/PGN SW6 127 J2
POP/IOD E14 112 D4
Napier Cl DEPT SE8 112 C6
EMPK RM11 63 K7
WDR/YW UB7 100 C2
Napier Ct LEE/GVPK SE12 153 F1
Napier Dr BUSH WD23 21 J3
Napier Gv IS N1 6 F6
Napier Pl WKENS W14 107 J2
Napier Rd ALP/SUD HA0 67 K4
ASHF TW15 140 B6
BELV DA17 117 G3
EHAM E6 78 A7
HAYES BR2 168 A3
ISLW TW7 124 B3
PEND EN3 31 F4
SAND/SEL CR2 177 K6
SNWD SE25 165 J3
SRTFD E15 94 C1
TOTM N17 56 A2
WAN E11 76 C2
WKENS W14 107 J2
WLSDN NW10 87 K2
Napier Ter IS N1 6 C2
Napier Wk ASHF TW15 140 B6
Napoleon Rd CLPT E5 74 D2
TWK TW1 * 124 C6
Napton Cl YEAD UB4 83 J3
Narbonne Av CLAP SW4 129 H4
Narboro Ct ROM RM1 63 J5
Narborough Cl
HGDN/ICK UB10 64 A1
Narborough St FUL/PGN SW6 128 A1
Narcissus Rd
KIL/WHAMP NW6 70 E4
Narford Rd CLPT E5 74 C2
Narrow Boat Cl THMD SE28 115 J1
Narrow St ACT W3 86 D7
POP/IOD E14 93 G6
Narrow Wy HAYES BR2 168 D5
Nascot Pl WAT WD17 21 F1
Nascot Rd WAT WD17 21 F1
Nascot St SHB W12 88 A5
WAT WD17 21 F1
Naseby Cl ISLW TW7 103 K7
KIL/WHAMP NW6 2 F1
Naseby Rd CLAY IG5 45 K7
DAGE RM10 80 C2
NRWD SE19 149 K5
Nash Cl BORE WD6 24 B3
SUT SM1 175 H2
Nash Gn BMLY BR1 152 E6
Nash La HAYES BR2 180 E5
Nash Rd BROCKY SE4 132 B3
CHDH RM6 61 K3
ED N9 42 E1
Nash St CAMTN NW1 4 D7
Nash Wy KTN/HRWW/WS HA3 49 H5
Nasmyth St HMSMTH W6 106 E2
Nassau Rd BARN SW13 106 C7
Nassau St GTPST W1W 10 E3
Nassington Rd HAMP NW3 71 J3
Natalie Cl EBED/NFELT TW14 121 G6
Natalie Ms WHTN TW2 142 D2
Natal Rd FBAR/BDGN N11 40 E4
IL IG1 78 B3
STRHM/NOR SW16 148 D5
THHTH CR7 164 E2
Nathaniel Cl WCHPL E1 13 M3
Nathans Rd ALP/SUD HA0 67 J1
Nathan Wy ABYW SE2 116 B1
THMD SE28 116 A2
National Ter
BERM/RHTH SE16 * 111 J1
Naval Rw POP/IOD E14 94 A6
Navarino Gv HACK E8 74 C5
Navarino Rd HACK E8 74 C5
Navarre Rd EHAM E6 95 J1
Navarre St BETH E2 7 L9
Navestock Cl CHING E4 * 44 A2
Navestock Crs WFD IG8 45 G7
Navestock Ter WFD IG8 45 G6
Navigator Dr NWDGN UB2 103 H1
Navy St CLAP SW4 129 J2
Nayim Pl HACK E8 74 D5
Naylor Gv PEND EN3 31 F4
Naylor Rd PECK SE15 111 J6
TRDG/WHET N20 39 G1
Nazareth Cl PECK SE15 131 J1
Nazrul St BETH E2 7 L7
Neal Av STHL UB1 83 K3
Neal Cl NTHWD HA6 32 E7
Nealden St BRXN/ST SW9 130 A2
Neale Cl EFNCH N2 53 G2
Neal St LSQ/SEVD WC2H 11 J5
WATW WD18 21 G4
Neal Ter FSTH SE23 * 132 A7
Near Acre CDALE/KGS NW9 37 H7
Neasden Cl WLSDN NW10 69 G4
Neasden La WLSDN NW10 69 G3
Neasham Rd BCTR RM8 79 H4
Neate St CMBW SE5 19 L9
Neath Gdns MRDN SM4 162 B5
Neathouse Pl PIM SW1V 16 E5
Neats Acre RSLP HA4 46 B6
Neatscourt Rd EHAM E6 95 H4
Neckinger BERM/RHTH SE16 19 M3
Neckinger Est
BERM/RHTH SE16 19 M3
Neckinger St STHWK SE1 19 M2
Nectarine Wy LEW SE13 132 E1
Needham Rd NTGHL W11 8 A5
Needleman St
BERM/RHTH SE16 112 A1
Neeld Crs HDN NW4 51 K4
WBLY HA9 68 C4
Neil Cl ASHF TW15 140 A4
Neils Yd LSQ/SEVD WC2H * 11 J5
Nelgarde Rd CAT SE6 132 D6
Nella Rd HMSMTH W6 107 G5
Nelldale Rd BERM/RHTH SE16 111 J3
Nello James Gdns
WNWD SE27 149 K3
Nelson Cl CROY/NA CR0 164 C7
EBED/NFELT TW14 * 121 J7
KIL/WHAMP NW6 2 A7
WOT/HER KT12 156 A7
Nelson Gdns BETH E2 92 C2
HSLW TW3 123 F5
Nelson Grove Rd
WIM/MER SW19 147 F7
Nelson Mandela Cl
MUSWH N10 53 K1
Nelson Mandela Rd
BKHTH/KID SE3 134 B2
Nelson Pl IS N1 6 D6
Nelson Rd BELV DA17 117 G4
CEND/HSY/T N8 55 F4
CHING E4 43 K5
DART DA1 139 F5
ED N9 42 D2
GNWCH SE10 113 F5
HAYES BR2 168 B3
HRW HA1 48 D7
HTHAIR TW6 100 C7
NWMAL KT3 160 A4
PEND EN3 31 F5
RAIN RM13 99 H1
SCUP DA14 155 G3
SEVS/STOTM N15 56 A3
STAN HA7 35 J5
WAN E11 58 E3
WHTN TW2 123 F5
WIM/MER SW19 147 F6
Nelson Sq STHWK SE1 18 C1
Nelsons Rw CLAP SW4 129 J3
Nelson St CAN/RD E16 94 D6
EHAM E6 78 A7
WCHPL E1 92 D5
Nelson Ter FSBYE EC1V 6 D6
Nelson Wk HOR/WEW KT19 172 C7
Nemoure Rd ACT W3 86 E6
Nene Gdns FELT TW13 141 K1
Nene Rd HTHAIR TW6 100 E7
Nepaul Rd BTSEA SW11 128 D1
Nepean St PUT/ROE SW15 126 D5
Neptune Cl RAIN RM13 99 H1
Neptune Ct BORE WD6 * 24 C2
Neptune Rd HRW HA1 48 D5
HTHAIR TW6 * 101 F7
Neptune St BERM/RHTH SE16 111 K2
Nesbit Cl BKHTH/KID SE3 133 H2
Nesbit Rd ELTH/MOT SE9 134 C3
Nesbitts Aly BAR EN5 * 26 D2
Nesbitt Sq NRWD SE19 * 150 A6
Nesham St WAP E1W 92 C7
Ness Rd ERITH DA8 119 G5
Ness St BERM/RHTH SE16 111 H2
Nesta Rd WFD IG8 44 D5
Nestle's Av HYS/HAR UB3 101 J2
Nestor Av WCHMH N21 29 H5
Netheravon Rd CHSWK W4 106 C3
HNWL W7 85 F7
Netheravon Rd South
CHSWK W4 106 C5
Netherbury Rd EA W5 104 E2
Netherby Gdns ENC/FH EN2 28 E3
Netherby Rd FSTH SE23 131 K6
Nether Cl FNCH N3 38 E6
Nether Ct MLHL NW7 * 38 D5
Nethercourt Av FNCH N3 38 E5
Netherfield Gdns BARK IG11 78 D5
Netherfield Rd
NFNCH/WDSPK N12 39 F4
TOOT SW17 148 A2
Netherford Rd VX/NE SW8 129 H1
Netherhall Gdns HAMP NW3 71 G4
Netherhall Wy HAMP NW3 71 G4
Netherheys Dr SAND/SEL CR2 177 J6
Netherlands Rd BAR EN5 27 H5
Netherleigh Cl HGT N6 54 B6
Netherpark Dr GPK RM2 63 H1
Nether St FNCH N3 38 E6
Netherton Gv WBPTN SW10 108 B5
Netherton Rd
SEVS/STOTM N15 55 K5
TWK TW1 124 B4
Netherwood Pl
HMSMTH W6 * 107 G2
Netherwood Rd WKENS W14 107 G2
Netherwood St
KIL/WHAMP NW6 70 D6
Netley Cl CHEAM SM3 174 B4
CROY/NA CR0 180 A6
Netley Dr WOT/HER KT12 156 E6
Netley Gdns MRDN SM4 162 B6
Netley Rd BTFD TW8 105 F5
GNTH/NBYPK IG2 60 D4
MRDN SM4 162 B6
WALTH E17 57 H4
Netley St CAMTN NW1 4 E8
Nettlecombe Cl BELMT SM2 175 F7
Nettleden Av WBLY HA9 68 C5
Nettlefold Pl WNWD SE27 149 H2
Nettlestead Cl BECK BR3 151 H6
Nettleton Rd HTHAIR TW6 100 E7
NWCR SE14 112 A6
Nettlewood Rd
STRHM/NOR SW16 148 D6
Neuchatel Rd CAT SE6 151 H1
Nevada Cl NWMAL KT3 159 K3
Nevada St GNWCH SE10 113 F6
Nevern Pl ECT SW5 14 B6
Nevern Rd ECT SW5 14 A6
Nevern Sq ECT SW5 14 A6
Nevil Cl NTHWD HA6 32 B4
Neville Av NWMAL KT3 145 F7
Neville Cl ACT W3 105 K1
BFN/LL DA15 155 F3
CAMTN NW1 5 H6
HSLW TW3 123 F1
KIL/WHAMP NW6 88 D1
PECK SE15 111 H6
WAN E11 76 D2
Neville Dr EFNCH N2 53 G5
Neville Gdns BCTR RM8 79 K2
Neville Gill Cl
WAND/EARL SW18 127 K5
Neville Pl WDGN N22 41 F7
Neville Rd BCTR RM8 79 K1
CROY/NA CR0 164 E6
EA W5 85 K3
FSTGT E7 76 E6
KIL/WHAMP NW6 * 88 D1
KUT/HW KT1 159 H1
RCHPK/HAM TW10 143 J2
Neville St SKENS SW7 15 G7
Neville Ter SKENS SW7 * 15 G7
Neville Wk CAR SM5 162 D6
Nevill Rd STNW/STAM N16 74 A3
Nevil Wk CAR SM5 * 162 D6
Nevin Dr CHING E4 31 K7
Nevinson Cl WAND/EARL SW18 128 C5
Nevis Rd TOOT SW17 148 A1
New Acres Rd THMD SE28 96 E7
Newall Rd HTHAIR TW6 101 F7
Newark Cl WOT/HER KT12 156 B7
Newark Crs WLSDN NW10 87 F2
Newark Gn BORE WD6 25 F2
Newark Knok EHAM E6 96 A5
Newark Rd SAND/SEL CR2 177 K5
Newark St WCHPL E1 92 D4
Newark Wy HDN NW4 51 J2
New Ash Cl EFNCH N2 53 H2
New Barn Cl WLGTN SM6 177 F5
New Barns Av MTCM CR4 163 J3
New Barn St CAN/RD E16 95 F4
PLSTW E13 94 E3
Newbery Rd ERITH DA8 118 C7
Newbiggin Pth OXHEY WD19 33 G3
Newbold Cots WCHPL E1 * 92 E5
Newbolt Av CHEAM SM3 174 A4
Newbolt Rd STAN HA7 35 F5
New Bond St MYFR/PICC W1J 10 D6
Newborough Gn NWMAL KT3 160 A3
New Brent St HDN NW4 52 A4
New Bridge St EMB EC4Y 12 C5
New Broad St LVPST EC2M 13 H3
New Broadway EA W5 85 J6
Newburgh Rd ACT W3 86 E7
Newburgh St SOHO/CST W1F 10 E5
New Burlington Ms
CONDST W1S 10 E6
New Burlington Pl
CONDST W1S 10 E6
New Burlington St
CONDST W1S 10 E6
Newburn St LBTH SE11 17 M7
Newbury Cl NTHLT UB5 65 K5
Newbury Gdns
HOR/WEW KT19 173 H3
Newbury Ms KTTN NW5 72 A5
Newbury Rd CHING E4 44 A5
GNTH/NBYPK IG2 60 D5
HAYES BR2 167 K2
HTHAIR TW6 100 C7
Newbury St STBT EC1A 12 E3
Newbury Wy NTHLT UB5 65 J5
New Butt La DEPT SE8 * 112 D6
Newby Cl EN EN1 30 A1
Newby Pl POP/IOD E14 94 A6
Newby St VX/NE SW8 129 G2
Newcastle Cl
FLST/FETLN EC4A 12 C4
Newcastle Pl BAY/PAD W2 9 H3
Newcastle Rw CLKNW EC1R 12 B1
New Cavendish St
CAVSQ/HST W1G 10 B3
GTPST W1W 10 E2
New Change STP EC4M 12 E5
New Charles St FSBYE EC1V 6 D7
New Church Rd CMBW SE5 110 D6
New City Rd PLSTW E13 95 G2
New Clock Tower Pl
HOLWY N7 72 E5
New Cl FELT TW13 141 J4
WIM/MER SW19 162 B2
New College Ms IS N1 * 6 B1
New College Pde
HAMP NW3 * 71 G5
Newcombe Gdns HSLWW TW4 122 E3
Newcombe Pk ALP/SUD HA0 68 B7
MLHL NW7 37 G4
Newcombe St KENS W8 * 8 B8
Newcome Gdns
STRHM/NOR SW16 148 E3
Newcomen Rd BTSEA SW11 128 C2
WAN E11 * 76 D2
Newcomen St STHWK SE1 19 G1
New Compton St
LSQ/SEVD WC2H * 11 H5
New Ct EMB EC4Y * 12 A6
NTHLT UB5 66 B4
Newcourt St STJWD NW8 3 J6
New Crane Pl WAP E1W * 92 E7
New Crescent Yd
WLSDN NW10 * 87 H1
New Cross Rd NWCR SE14 111 K6
Newdales Cl ED N9 42 C1
Newdene Av NTHLT UB5 83 H1
Newdigate
STRHM/NOR SW16 * 149 G3
Newell St POP/IOD E14 93 H6
New End HAMP NW3 71 G3
New End Sq HAMP NW3 71 H3
Newent Cl CAR SM5 162 E7
PECK SE15 111 F6
New Era Est IS N1 * 7 J4
New Farm Av HAYES BR2 167 K3
New Farm La NTHWD HA6 32 C7
New Ferry Ap
WOOL/PLUM SE18 115 F2
New Fetter La
FLST/FETLN EC4A 12 B4
Newfield Cl HPTN TW12 142 A7
Newfield Ri CRICK NW2 69 J2
Newgale Gdns EDGW HA8 36 B7
New Garden Dr WDR/YW UB7 100 B1
Newgate CROY/NA CR0 164 D7
Newgate Cl FELT TW13 141 J1
Newgate St CHING E4 44 C2
STBT EC1A 12 D4
New Globe Wk STHWK SE1 12 E8
New Goulston St WCHPL E1 13 L4
New Green Pl
BRXS/STRHM SW2 130 B6
NRWD SE19 150 A5
Newham's Rw STHWK SE1 19 K2
Newham Wy CAN/RD E16 94 D4
EHAM E6 95 J3
Newhaven Cl HYS/HAR UB3 101 J3
Newhaven Crs ASHF TW15 140 B4
Newhaven Gdns
ELTH/MOT SE9 134 C3
Newhaven La PLSTW E13 94 D4
Newhaven Rd SNWD SE25 164 E4
New Heston Rd HEST TW5 102 E6
Newhouse Av CHDH RM6 61 K2
Newhouse Cl NWMAL KT3 160 B6
Newhouse Wk MRDN SM4 162 B6
Newick Cl BXLY DA5 137 J5
Newick Rd CLPT E5 74 D2
Newing Gn BMLY BR1 153 H6
Newington Barrow Wy
HOLWY N7 73 F2
Newington Butts WALW SE17 18 D6
Newington Cswy STHWK SE1 18 E3
Newington Gn IS N1 73 K4
Newington Green Rd IS N1 73 K4
New Inn Broadway
SDTCH EC2A * 7 K9
New Inn Sq SDTCH EC2A * 7 K9
New Inn St SDTCH EC2A * 7 K9
New Inn Yd SDTCH EC2A 7 K9
New Kelvin Av TEDD TW11 142 E5
New Kent Rd WALW SE17 18 F5
New King's Rd FUL/PGN SW6 107 K7
New King St DEPT SE8 112 D5
Newland Cl PIN HA5 33 J5
Newland Gdns WEA W13 104 B1
Newland Rd CEND/HSY/T N8 54 E2
Newlands Av THDIT KT7 157 K7
Newlands Cl ALP/SUD HA0 67 J5
EDGW HA8 36 A2
NWDGN UB2 102 D4
Newlands Pk SYD SE26 150 E5
Newlands Pl BAR EN5 26 B4
Newlands Quay WAP E1W 92 E6
Newlands Rd
STRHM/NOR SW16 163 K1
WFD IG8 44 D1
The Newlands WLGTN SM6 176 C6
Newland St CAN/RD E16 95 J7
Newlands Wy CHSGTN KT9 171 J4
Newlands Woods
CROY/NA CR0 179 H7
Newling Cl EHAM E6 95 K5
Newling Est BETH E2 7 M7
New London St MON EC3R * 13 K6
New Lydenburg St CHARL SE7 114 B2
Newlyn Gdns
RYLN/HDSTN HA2 47 K6
Newlyn Rd BAR EN5 26 D3
TOTM N17 42 B7
WELL DA16 136 A1
Newman Ms WDGN N22 41 F6
Newman Rd BMLY BR1 152 E7
CROY/NA CR0 164 A6
HYS/HAR UB3 83 F6
PLSTW E13 95 F2
WALTH E17 57 F4
Newmans La SURB KT6 158 E5
Newman's Rw LINN WC2A 11 M3
Newman St FITZ W1T 10 F3
Newman's Wy EBAR EN4 27 G1
Newmarket Av NTHLT UB5 66 A4
Newmarsh Rd THMD SE28 97 F7
New Mill Rd STMC/STPC BR5 155 J7
Newminster Ct ENC/FH EN2 * 29 H1
Newminster Rd MRDN SM4 162 B5
New Mount St SRTFD E15 76 B6
Newnham Av RSLP HA4 47 G7
Newnham Cl NTHLT UB5 66 C5
THHTH CR7 164 D1
Newnham Gdns NTHLT UB5 66 C5
Newnham Gn WDGN N22 * 41 G7
Newnham Rd WDGN N22 41 F7
Newnhams Cl BMLY BR1 168 E2
Newnham Ter STHWK SE1 18 A3
Newnham Wy
KTN/HRWW/WS HA3 50 A4
New North Pl SDTCH EC2A 7 J9
New North Rd IS N1 6 F3
New North St BMSBY WC1N 11 L2
Newnton Cl FSBYPK N4 55 K6
New Oak Rd EFNCH N2 53 G1
New Oxford St
NOXST/BSQ WC1A 11 H4
New Park Av PLMGR N13 41 J2
New Park Cl NTHLT UB5 65 J5
New Park Est UED N18 42 E4
New Park Rd ASHF TW15 140 A4
BRXS/STRHM SW2 129 K6
New Place Sq
BERM/RHTH SE16 * 111 J2
New Plaistow Rd SRTFD E15 76 C7
New Pond Pde RSLP HA4 * 64 E2
Newport Av POP/IOD E14 94 B6
Newport Ct LSQ/SEVD WC2H 11 H6
Newport Md OXHEY WD19 * 33 H3
Newport Pl
SOHO/SHAV W1D * 11 H6
Newport Rd HTHAIR TW6 100 D7
ACT W3 105 K1
BARN SW13 106 D7
HTHAIR TW6 100 D7
LEY E10 76 B1
WALTH E17 * 57 G3
YEAD UB4 82 B4
Newport St LBTH SE11 17 L6
Newquay Crs
RYLN/HDSTN HA2 65 J1
Newquay Gdns OXHEY WD19 33 F1
Newquay Rd CAT SE6 151 K1
New Quebec St MBLAR W1H 9 M5
New River Av CEND/HSY/T N8 55 F2
New River Crs PLMGR N13 41 H3
New River Wy FSBYPK N4 55 K6
New Rd ABYW SE2 116 E3
BORE WD6 23 K5
BTFD TW8 * 104 E5
CEND/HSY/T N8 54 D4
CHING E4 43 K3
DAGE RM10 98 C1
E/WMO/HCT KT8 157 F2
EBED/NFELT TW14 121 G5
ED N9 42 D1
ESH/CLAY KT10 170 C3
FELT TW13 141 J4
GDMY/SEVK IG3 78 E1
HRW HA1 67 F3
HSLW TW3 123 G3
HYS/HAR UB3 101 F6
KUTN/CMB KT2 144 C6
MLHL NW7 38 C6
MNPK E12 77 J1
MTCM CR4 163 F7
RAIN RM13 98 E2
RCHPK/HAM TW10 143 J3
TOTM N17 42 B7
UX/CGN UB8 82 A3
WAT WD17 21 G3
WCHPL E1 92 C4

WDGN N22 41 J7
WELL DA16 136 C1
New Road Hl HAYES BR2 181 J7
New Rw CHCR WC2N 11 J6
Newry Rd TWK TW1 124 B3
Newsam Av SEVS/STOTM N15 55 K4
Newsholme Dr WCHMH N21 29 F4
New Spring Gardens Wk
STHWK SE1 * 17 K8
New Sq EBED/NFELT TW14 121 F7
LINN WC2A 11 M4
Newstead Cl
NFNCH/WDSPK N12 39 J5
Newstead Ct NTHLT UB5 * 83 J2
Newstead Rd LEE/GVPK SE12 133 J6
Newstead Wk CAR SM5 162 B6
Newstead Wy
WIM/MER SW19 146 B3
New St LVPST EC2M 13 K3
WAT WD17 * 21 G3
New Street Hl BMLY BR1 153 F4
New Street Sq
FLST/FETLN EC4A 12 B4
New Tank Hill Rd PUR RM19 119 K2
Newton Av ACT W3 105 K1
MUSWH N10 40 A7
Newton Cl RYLN/HDSTN HA2 66 A1
WALTH E17 57 G5
Newton Crs BORE WD6 24 E3
Newton Gv CHSWK W4 106 B2
Newton Park Pl CHST BR7 153 K6
Newton Pl POP/IOD E14 112 D3
Newton Rd ALP/SUD HA0 68 B6
BAY/PAD W2 8 B5
CRICK NW2 70 A3
HTHAIR TW6 100 B7
ISLW TW7 124 A1
KTN/HRWW/WS HA3 34 E7
SEVS/STOTM N15 56 B4
SRTFD E15 76 B4
WELL DA16 136 B2
WIM/MER SW19 146 C6
Newtons Cl RAIN RM13 81 G6
Newton St HOL/ALD WC2B 11 K4
Newton's Yd
WAND/EARL SW18 127 K4
Newton Ter HAYES BR2 168 C5
Newton Wk EDGW HA8 36 E7
Newton Wy UED N18 41 J4
New Tower Blds WAP E1W * 92 D7
Newtown St BTSEA SW11 109 G7
New Trinity Rd EFNCH N2 53 H2
New Union Cl POP/IOD E14 113 F2
New Union St BARB EC2Y 13 G3
New Vls TOTM N17 * 42 C7
New Wanstead WAN E11 58 E5
New Way Rd CDALE/KGS NW9 51 G3
New Wharf Rd IS N1 5 K5
New Zealand Wy RAIN RM13 99 H2
Niagara Av EA W5 104 D3
Niagara Cl IS N1 6 F5
Nibthwaite Rd HRW HA1 48 E4
Nicholas Cl GFD/PVL UB6 84 B1
Nicholas Gdns EA W5 85 K7
Nicholas La MANHO EC4N 13 H6
Nicholas Rd BCTR RM8 80 B1
BORE WD6 24 B5
CROY/NA CR0 176 E3
WCHPL E1 92 E3
Nicholas Wy NTHWD HA6 32 A7
Nicholay Rd ARCH N19 54 D7
Nichol Cl STHGT/OAK N14 28 D7
Nicholes Rd HSLW TW3 123 F3
Nichol La BMLY BR1 152 E6
Nichollsfield Wk HOLWY N7 72 E4
Nicholl St BETH E2 74 C7
Nichols Cl FSBYPK N4 * 55 G7
Nichols Gn EA W5 86 A4
Nicholson Dr BUSH WD23 22 C7
Nicholson House CHARL SE7 * 114 D6
Nicholson Ms KUT/HW KT1 159 F3
Nicholson Rd CROY/NA CR0 165 G7
Nicholson St STHWK SE1 12 C9
Nickelby Cl THMD SE28 97 J5
Nickols Wk WAND/EARL SW18 128 A3
Nicola Cl KTN/HRWW/WS HA3 48 D1
SAND/SEL CR2 177 J5
Nicol Cl TWK TW1 124 C5
Nicoll Pl HDN NW4 51 K5
Nicoll Rd WLSDN NW10 69 G7
Nicoll Wy BORE WD6 25 F4
Nicosia Rd WAND/EARL SW18 128 D6
Niederwald Rd SYD SE26 151 G3
Nield Rd HYS/HAR UB3 101 J1
Nigel Cl NTHLT UB5 65 J7
Nigel Fisher Wy CHSGTN KT9 171 J6
Nigel Ms IL IG1 78 B3
Nigel Playfair Av HMSMTH W6 106 E3
Nigel Rd FSTGT E7 77 G4
PECK SE15 131 H2
Nigeria Rd CHARL SE7 114 B6
Nightingale Av CHING E4 44 C4
Nightingale Cl CAR SM5 176 A1
CHING E4 44 C3
CHSWK W4 105 K5
PIN HA5 47 G4
Nightingale Ct SUT SM1 175 G4
Nightingale Dr
HOR/WEW KT19 172 D5
Nightingale Gv LEW SE13 133 G4
Nightingale La BAL SW12 129 F5
BMLY BR1 168 B1
CEND/HSY/T N8 54 E3
RCHPK/HAM TW10 125 F6
WAN E11 59 F4
Nightingale Ms KUT/HW KT1 * 158 E2
LBTH SE11 18 B5
Nightingale Pl WBPTN SW10 14 F9
WOOL/PLUM SE18 115 F5
Nightingale Rd BUSH WD23 22 A4
CAR SM5 175 K2
CLPT E5 74 D2
E/WMO/HCT KT8 157 G4
ED N9 30 E6
HNWL W7 85 F7
HPTN TW12 142 A5
IS N1 73 J5
STMC/STPC BR5 169 H5
WDGN N22 40 E7
WLSDN NW10 87 H1
WOT/HER KT12 * 156 B6
Nightingale Sq BAL SW12 129 F6
The Nightingales
STWL/WRAY TW19 120 C7
Nightingale V
WOOL/PLUM SE18 115 F5
Nightingale Wk BAL SW12 129 G5
Nightingale Wy EHAM E6 95 J4
Nightngale Av HRW HA1 49 H6
Nile Cl STNW/STAM N16 74 B2
Nile Dr ED N9 42 E1
Nile Rd PLSTW E13 95 G1
Nile St IS N1 7 G7
Nile Ter PECK SE15 19 M8
Nimmo Dr BUSH WD23 22 D6
Nimrod Cl NTHLT UB5 83 H2
Nimrod Pas IS N1 74 A5
Nimrod Rd STRHM/NOR SW16 148 B5
Nina Mackay Cl SRTFD E15 * 76 C7
Nine Acres Cl HYS/HAR UB3 101 F2
MNPK E12 77 J4
Nine Elms Cl
EBED/NFELT TW14 121 J7
Nine Elms La VX/NE SW8 109 H6
Nineteenth Rd MTCM CR4 163 K3
Ninth Av HYS/HAR UB3 82 E6
Nipper Aly KUT/HW KT1 159 F1
Nisbett Wk SCUP DA14 155 G3
Nithdale Rd
WOOL/PLUM SE18 115 G6
Nithsdale Gv HGDN/ICK UB10 64 A2
Niton Cl BAR EN5 26 B5
Niton Rd RCH/KEW TW9 * 125 H2
Niton St FUL/PGN SW6 107 G6
No1 St WOOL/PLUM SE18 115 G2
No2 St WOOL/PLUM SE18 115 G2
Nobel Dr HYS/HAR UB3 101 H6
Nobel Rd UED N18 42 E3
Noble Cnr HEST TW5 * 103 F7
Noble St CITYW EC2V 12 E4
Noel Rd ACT W3 86 C5
EHAM E6 95 J3
IS N1 6 C5
Noel St SOHO/CST W1F 10 F5
Nolan Wy CLPT E5 74 C3
Nolton Pl EDGW HA8 36 B7
Nonsuch Pl CHEAM SM3 * 174 B6
Norbiton Av KUT/HW KT1 159 H1
KUTN/CMB KT2 144 C7
Norbiton Common Rd
KUT/HW KT1 159 J2
Norbiton Rd POP/IOD E14 93 H5
Norbreck Pde EA W5 86 A2
Norbroke St SHB W12 87 H6
Norburn St NKENS W10 88 C4
Norbury Av HSLW TW3 123 J4
STRHM/NOR SW16 149 F7
THHTH CR7 164 B1
Norbury Cl STRHM/NOR SW16 149 G7
Norbury Court Rd
STRHM/NOR SW16 163 K1
Norbury Crs
STRHM/NOR SW16 164 B1
Norbury Cross
STRHM/NOR SW16 163 K2
Norbury Gdns CHDH RM6 61 K4
Norbury Gv MLHL NW7 37 G2
Norbury Hl STRHM/NOR SW16 149 G6
Norbury Ri STRHM/NOR SW16 163 K2
Norbury Rd CHING E4 43 J4
FELT TW13 140 D2
THHTH CR7 164 D1
Norbury Vls KUT/HW KT1 * 159 G1
Norcombe Gdns
KTN/HRWW/WS HA3 49 J5
Norcott Cl YEAD UB4 83 G3
Norcott Rd STNW/STAM N16 74 C1
Norcroft Gdns EDUL SE22 131 H6
Norcutt Rd WHTN TW2 123 K7
Nordenfeldt Rd ERITH DA8 118 A4
Norfolk Av PLMGR N13 41 H5
SEVS/STOTM N15 56 B5
Norfolk Cl DART DA1 139 K5
EBAR EN4 28 A3
EFNCH N2 53 J2
PLMGR N13 41 H5
TWK TW1 * 124 C5
Norfolk Ct BAR EN5 * 26 C3
Norfolk Crs BAY/PAD W2 9 J4
BFN/LL DA15 135 K6
Norfolk Gdns BORE WD6 25 F3
BXLYHN DA7 117 G7
Norfolk House Rd
STRHM/NOR SW16 148 D2
Norfolk Ms NKENS W10 88 C4
Norfolk Pl BAY/PAD W2 9 H4
WELL DA16 136 B1
Norfolk Rd BAR EN5 26 E2
BARK IG11 78 E6
DAGE RM10 80 D4
EHAM E6 77 K7
ESH/CLAY KT10 170 E4
FELT TW13 122 B7
GDMY/SEVK IG3 60 E7
HRW HA1 48 B4
PEND EN3 30 D4
ROMW/RG RM7 62 E5
STJWD NW8 3 H4
THHTH CR7 164 D2
WALTH E17 43 F7
WIM/MER SW19 147 J6
WLSDN NW10 69 G6
Norfolk Rw STHWK SE1 17 L5
Norfolk Sq BAY/PAD W2 9 H5
Norfolk Square Ms
BAY/PAD W2 9 H5
Norfolk St FSTGT E7 76 E4
Norgrove St BAL SW12 129 F7
Norhyrst Av SNWD SE25 165 G2
Norland Pl NTGHL W11 88 C7
Norland Rd NTGHL W11 88 B7
Norlands Crs CHST BR7 154 B7
Norlands Ga CHST BR7 * 154 B7
Norland Sq NTGHL W11 88 C7
Norley V PUT/ROE SW15 126 D7
Norlington Rd LEY E10 58 A7
Norman Av FELT TW13 141 J1
STHL UB1 83 J6
TWK TW1 124 C6
WDGN N22 41 J7
Normanby Cl PUT/ROE SW15 127 J4
Normanby Rd WLSDN NW10 69 H4
Norman Cl ROMW/RG RM7 62 D1
Norman Crs HEST TW5 102 C6
PIN HA5 33 G7
Normand Gdns WKENS W14 * 107 H5
Normand Ms WKENS W14 107 H5
Normand Rd WKENS W14 107 J5
Normandy Av BAR EN5 26 D4
Normandy Cl SYD SE26 151 G2
Normandy Dr HYS/HAR UB3 82 A5
Normandy Rd BRXN/ST SW9 110 B7
Normandy Ter CAN/RD E16 95 F5
Normandy Wy ERITH DA8 118 B7
Norman Gv BOW E3 93 G1
Normanhurst Av WELL DA16 116 E7
Normanhurst Dr TWK TW1 124 C4
Normanhurst Rd
BRXS/STRHM SW2 149 F1
Norman Rd ASHF TW15 140 B5
BELV DA17 117 J1
DART DA1 139 H7
EHAM E6 95 K3
EMPK RM11 63 J6
GNWCH SE10 112 E6
IL IG1 78 B4
SEVS/STOTM N15 56 B4
SUT SM1 174 E4
THHTH CR7 164 C4
WAN E11 76 C1
WIM/MER SW19 147 G6
Normans Cl WDGN N22 * 41 J7
WLSDN NW10 69 F5
Normansfield Av KUT/HW KT1 143 J6
Normansfield Cl BUSH WD23 22 B6
Normanshire Dr CHING E4 43 J3
Normans Md WLSDN NW10 69 F5
Norman St FSBYE EC1V 6 E8
Norman Ter
KIL/WHAMP NW6 * 70 D4
Normanton Av
WAND/EARL SW18 146 E1
Normanton Pk CHING E4 44 C2
Normanton Rd SAND/SEL CR2 178 A5
Normanton St FSTH SE23 151 F1
Norman Wy ACT W3 86 D4
STHGT/OAK N14 40 E1
Normington Cl
STRHM/NOR SW16 149 G4
Norrice Lea EFNCH N2 53 H4
Norris St STJS SW1Y 11 G7
Norris Wy DART DA1 138 C2
Norroy Rd PUT/ROE SW15 127 G3
Norrys Cl EBAR EN4 27 K4
Norrys Rd EBAR EN4 27 K3
Norseman Cl GDMY/SEVK IG3 61 H7
Norseman Wy GFD/PVL UB6 66 B7
Norstead Pl PUT/ROE SW15 145 J1
North Access Rd WALTH E17 57 F5
North Acre CDALE/KGS NW9 37 G7
North Acton Rd WLSDN NW10 87 F1
Northall Rd BXLYHN DA7 137 K1
Northampton Gv IS N1 73 K4
Northampton Pk IS N1 73 J5
Northampton Rd
CLKNW EC1R 6 B9
CROY/NA CR0 178 C1
PEND EN3 31 G3
Northampton Rw
CLKNW EC1R * 6 B9
Northampton Sq FSBYE EC1V 6 C8
Northampton St IS N1 6 E1
Northanger Rd
STRHM/NOR SW16 148 E5
North Ap NTHWD HA6 32 A1
North Audley St
MYFR/PKLN W1K 10 A6
North Av CAR SM5 176 A6
HYS/HAR UB3 82 E6
RCH/KEW TW9 105 H7
RYLN/HDSTN HA2 48 B5
STHL UB1 83 K6
UED N18 42 C3
WEA W13 85 H5
North Bank STJWD NW8 3 J8
Northbank Rd WALTH E17 58 A1
North Birkbeck Rd WAN E11 76 B2
Northborough Rd
STRHM/NOR SW16 163 K1
North Boundary Rd
MNPK E12 77 H1
Northbourne HAYES BR2 167 K6
Northbourne Rd CLAP SW4 129 J3
Northbrook Dr NTHWD HA6 32 C7
Northbrook Rd BAR EN5 26 C5
CROY/NA CR0 164 E4
IL IG1 78 A1
LEW SE13 133 G4
WDGN N22 40 E5
Northburgh St FSBYE EC1V 12 D1
North Carriage Dr
BAY/PAD W2 9 K6
Northchurch Rd IS N1 7 G1
WBLY HA9 68 C5
Northchurch Ter IS N1 7 J2
North Circular PLMGR N13 41 G4
WALTH E17 43 K7
North Circular Rd BARK IG11 78 A6
CHING E4 * 43 G5
CRICK NW2 69 G2
EFNCH N2 53 G1
GLDGN NW11 52 C5
IL IG1 59 H5
MNPK E12 78 A4
NFNCH/WDSPK N12 39 J6
REDBR IG4 59 G2
WLSDN NW10 86 B1
Northcliffe Cl WPK KT4 173 G2
Northcliffe Dr
TRDG/WHET N20 26 D7
North Cl BAR EN5 26 A4
BXLYHS DA6 136 E3
DAGE RM10 80 C7
EBED/NFELT TW14 121 G5
MRDN SM4 161 H3
The North Colonnade
POP/IOD E14 93 K7
North Common Rd EA W5 86 A6
Northcote Av BRYLDS KT5 159 H6
EA W5 86 A6
ISLW TW7 124 B4
STHL UB1 83 J6
Northcote Rd BTSEA SW11 128 D3
CROY/NA CR0 164 E5
NWMAL KT3 159 K2
SCUP DA14 154 E3
TWK TW1 124 B4
WALTH E17 57 G3
WLSDN NW10 69 G6
Northcott Av WDGN N22 40 E7
North Countess Rd
WALTH E17 57 H1
Northcourt FITZ W1T 10 F2
North Crs CAN/RD E16 94 B3
FNCH N3 52 D1
GWRST WC1E 11 G2
Northcroft Rd
HOR/WEW KT19 173 G6
WEA W13 104 C1
North Cross Rd BARK/HLT IG6 60 C3
EDUL SE22 131 G4
North Dene HSLW TW3 103 G7
MLHL NW7 37 F2
Northdene Gdns
SEVS/STOTM N15 56 A5
Northdown Cl RSLP HA4 64 D2
Northdown Gdns
GNTH/NBYPK IG2 60 E4
Northdown Rd EMPK RM11 63 K6
WELL DA16 136 C1
Northdown St IS N1 5 L6
North Dr BECK BR3 166 E3
HSLW TW3 123 H1
RSLP HA4 46 C6
STRHM/NOR SW16 148 C3
North End CROY/NA CR0 164 D7
HAMP NW3 71 G1
North End Av HAMP NW3 71 G1
North End Crs WKENS W14 107 J3
Northend Rd ERITH DA8 118 C7
North End Rd FUL/PGN SW6 107 K6
GLDGN NW11 52 E7
WBLY HA9 68 C2
WKENS W14 107 H3
North End Wy HAMP NW3 71 G1
Northern Av ED N9 42 B1
Northernhay Wk MRDN SM4 161 H3
Northern Perimeter Rd
HTHAIR TW6 101 F7
Northern Perimeter Rd (West)
HTHAIR TW6 100 B7
Northern Relief Rd BARK IG11 78 C6
North Eyot Gdns
HMSMTH W6 * 106 C4
Northey St POP/IOD E14 93 G6
Northfield Av PIN HA5 47 H3
WEA W13 104 C1
Northfield Cl BMLY BR1 153 J7
HYS/HAR UB3 101 J2
Northfield Crs CHEAM SM3 174 C3
Northfield Pde
HYS/HAR UB3 * 101 J2
Northfield Pk HYS/HAR UB3 101 H2
Northfield Rd DAGW RM9 80 B3
EBAR EN4 27 J2
ED N9 * 30 D4
EHAM E6 77 K5
HEST TW5 102 C5
PEND EN3 30 D5
STNW/STAM N16 56 A6
WEA W13 104 C1
Northfields WAND/EARL SW18 127 K3
Northfields Rd ACT W3 86 E4
North Gdns WIM/MER SW19 147 H6
Northgate NTHWD HA6 32 A6
Northgate Dr
CDALE/KGS NW9 51 G5
North Gower St CAMTN NW1 4 E8
North Gv HGT N6 54 A6
SEVS/STOTM N15 55 K4
North Hl HGT N6 53 K5
North Hill Av HGT N6 53 K5
North Hyde Gdns
HYS/HAR UB3 101 K2
North Hyde La NWDGN UB2 102 D4
North Hyde Rd HYS/HAR UB3 101 H2
North Hyde Whf
NWDGN UB2 * 102 B3
Northiam NFNCH/WDSPK N12 38 E3
Northiam St HACK E8 74 D7
HOM E9 74 E7
Northington St BMSBY WC1N 11 L2
Northlands St CMBW SE5 130 D1
North La TEDD TW11 143 F5
North Lodge Cl
PUT/ROE SW15 * 127 G4
North Ms BMSBY WC1N 11 M1
North Mt TRDG/WHET N20 * 39 G1
Northolm EDGW HA8 37 F3
Northolme Gdns EDGW HA8 36 C7
Northolme Rd HBRY N5 73 J3
Northolt Av RSLP HA4 65 F4
Northolt Gdns GFD/PVL UB6 67 F4
Northolt Rd HTHAIR TW6 100 B7
RYLN/HDSTN HA2 66 B3
Northover BMLY BR1 152 D3
North Pde CHSGTN KT9 172 B4
EDGW HA8 * 50 C1
STHL UB1 * 84 A5
North Pk ELTH/MOT SE9 134 E5
North Pas WAND/EARL SW18 127 K4
North Peckham Est
PECK SE15 111 G6
North Pl MTCM CR4 147 K6
TEDD TW11 143 F5
Northpoint Cl SUT SM1 175 G2
North Pole La HAYES BR2 180 E5
North Pole Rd SHB W12 88 A5
Northport St IS N1 7 H4
North Ri BAY/PAD W2 * 9 K5
North Rd BELV DA17 117 J2
BMLY BR1 153 F7
BTFD TW8 105 F5
CHDH RM6 62 A4
DART DA1 138 C5
EA W5 104 E2
EBED/NFELT TW14 121 G5
ED N9 30 D7
EDGW HA8 36 D7
GDMY/SEVK IG3 78 E1
HEST TW5 102 B5
HGT N6 54 A6
HOLWY N7 72 E5
HYS/HAR UB3 82 B4
RCH/KEW TW9 125 H1
STHL UB1 84 A6
SURB KT6 158 E5
WDR/YW UB7 100 C2
WIM/MER SW19 147 G5
WOOL/PLUM SE18 115 K3
WWKM BR4 166 E7
Northrop Rd HTHAIR TW6 101 H7
North Rw MYFR/PKLN W1K 9 M6
North Several
BKHTH/KID SE3 * 133 G1
Northside Rd BMLY BR1 152 E7
North Side Wandsworth
Common
WAND/EARL SW18 128 B4
Northspur Rd SUT SM1 174 E2
North Sq ED N9 42 D1
GLDGN NW11 52 E4
Northstead Rd
BRXS/STRHM SW2 149 G1
North St BARK IG11 78 B6
BMLY BR1 152 E7
BXLYHN DA7 137 H3
CAR SM5 175 K3
CLAP SW4 129 G2
DART DA1 139 G6
HDN NW4 52 A4
ISLW TW7 124 B2
PLSTW E13 95 F1
ROM RM1 63 F3
North Tenter St WCHPL E1 13 M5
North Ter SKENS SW7 15 J5
Northumberland Aly
FENCHST EC3M * 13 K5
Northumberland Av
CHCR WC2N 11 J8
ISLW TW7 104 A7
MNPK E12 59 G7
WELL DA16 135 K3
Northumberland Cl
ERITH DA8 117 K6
STWL/WRAY TW19 120 B5
Northumberland Crs
EBED/NFELT TW14 121 H5
Northumberland Gdns
BMLY BR1 169 F3
ED N9 42 B2
MTCM CR4 163 J4
Northumberland Gv
TOTM N17 42 D6
Northumberland Pk
ERITH DA8 117 K6
TOTM N17 42 C6
Northumberland Pl
BAY/PAD W2 8 A4
Northumberland Rd BAR EN5 27 G5
EHAM E6 95 J5
RYLN/HDSTN HA2 47 K4
WALTH E17 57 J6
Northumberland St
CHCR WC2N 11 J8
Northumberland Wy
ERITH DA8 117 K7
Northumbria St POP/IOD E14 93 J5
North Verbena Gdns
HMSMTH W6 * 106 D4
North Vw EA W5 85 J3
PIN HA5 47 G6
WIM/MER SW19 145 K4
Northview Crs WLSDN NW10 69 H3
Northview Dr WFD IG8 59 H1
Northview Pde HOLWY N7 * 72 E2
North View Rd
CEND/HSY/T N8 54 D2
North Vls CAMTN NW1 72 D5
North Wk CROY/NA CR0 179 K4
North Wy CDALE/KGS NW9 50 D2
ED N9 42 E1
FBAR/BDGN N11 40 C5
PIN HA5 47 G2
Northway GLDGN NW11 53 F4
MRDN SM4 161 H2
WLGTN SM6 176 C3
Northway Crs MLHL NW7 37 G3
Northway Rd CMBW SE5 130 D2
CROY/NA CR0 165 G5
Northways Pde HAMP NW3 3 G1
North Weald Cl HCH RM12 81 K6
North Weald La
KUTN/CMB KT2 143 J4
North Wharf Rd BAY/PAD W2 9 G3
Northwick Av
KTN/HRWW/WS HA3 49 G5
Northwick Cir
KTN/HRWW/WS HA3 49 J5
Northwick Cl STJWD NW8 3 G9
Northwick Park Rd HRW HA1 49 F5
Northwick Rd ALP/SUD HA0 67 K7
OXHEY WD19 33 G3
Northwick Ter STJWD NW8 3 G9
Northwold Dr PIN HA5 47 G2
Northwold Rd
STNW/STAM N16 74 C1
Northwood Av HCH RM12 81 J3
Northwood Gdns CLAY IG5 60 A3
GFD/PVL UB6 67 F4
NFNCH/WDSPK N12 39 H4
Northwood Pl ERITHM DA18 117 G2
Northwood Rd CAR SM5 176 A5
FSTH SE23 132 C7
HGT N6 54 B6
HTHAIR TW6 100 A7
THHTH CR7 164 D1
Northwood Wy NTHWD HA6 32 E6
North Woolwich Rd
CAN/RD E16 94 E7
North Worple Wy
MORT/ESHN SW14 126 A2
Norton Av BRYLDS KT5 159 J6
Norton Cl CHING E4 43 J4
Norton Folgate WCHPL E1 13 K1
Norton Gdns
STRHM/NOR SW16 163 K1
Norton Rd ALP/SUD HA0 67 K5
DAGE RM10 81 F5
LEY E10 57 H7
Norval Gn BRXN/ST SW9 * 130 B1
Norval Rd ALP/SUD HA0 67 H1
Norway Ga BERM/RHTH SE16 112 B2
Norway Pl POP/IOD E14 93 H5
Norway St GNWCH SE10 112 E5
Norwich Crs CHDH RM6 61 H4
Norwich Ms GDMY/SEVK IG3 61 G7
Norwich Rd FSTGT E7 76 E4
GFD/PVL UB6 66 B7
NTHWD HA6 46 D2
THHTH CR7 164 D2
Norwich St FLST/FETLN EC4A 12 A4
Norwich Wk EDGW HA8 36 E6
Norwood Av ALP/SUD HA0 68 B7
ROMW/RG RM7 63 F6
Norwood Cl CRICK NW2 70 C2
NWDGN UB2 103 F3
WHTN TW2 142 D1
Norwood Dr
RYLN/HDSTN HA2 47 K5
Norwood Gdns NWDGN UB2 102 E3
YEAD UB4 83 G3
Norwood Green Rd
NWDGN UB2 103 F3
Norwood High St WNWD SE27 149 H2
Norwood Park Rd
WNWD SE27 149 J4
Norwood Rd HNHL SE24 130 C7
NWDGN UB2 102 D2
WNWD SE27 149 H1
Notley St CMBW SE5 110 E6
Notson Rd SNWD SE25 165 J3
Notting Barn Rd NKENS W10 88 B3
Nottingdale Sq NTGHL W11 * 88 C7
Nottingham Av CAN/RD E16 95 G4
Nottingham Ct
LSQ/SEVD WC2H 11 J5
Nottingham Pl CAMTN NW1 10 A1
Nottingham Rd ISLW TW7 124 A1
LEY E10 58 A5
SAND/SEL CR2 177 J3
TOOT SW17 128 E7
Nottingham St MHST W1U 10 A2
Nottingham Ter CAMTN NW1 10 A1
Notting Hill Ga NTGHL W11 8 B8
Nova Ms CHEAM SM3 161 H6
Nova Rd CROY/NA CR0 164 C7
Novar Rd ELTH/MOT SE9 135 H7
Novello St FUL/PGN SW6 107 K7
Nowell Rd BARN SW13 106 D5
Nower Hl PIN HA5 47 K3
Noyna Rd TOOT SW17 147 K2
Nubia Wy BMLY BR1 152 C3
Nuding Cl LEW SE13 132 D2
Nugent Rd ARCH N19 54 E7
SNWD SE25 165 G2
Nugents Ct PIN HA5 * 33 J7
Nugent's Pk PIN HA5 33 J7
Nugent Ter STJWD NW8 2 F6
Nun Ct LOTH EC2R * 13 G4
Nuneaton Rd DAGW RM9 79 K6
Nunhead Crs PECK SE15 131 J2
Nunhead Gv PECK SE15 131 J2
Nunhead La PECK SE15 131 J2
Nunnington Cl ELTH/MOT SE9 153 J2

Nunn's Rd *ENC/FH* EN2 29 J1
Nupton Dr *BAR* EN5 26 A5
Nurse Cl *EDGW* HA8 36 E7
Nursery Av *BXLYHN* DA7 137 G2
CROY/NA CR0 179 F1
FNCH N3 53 F1
Nursery Cl *BROCKY* SE4 132 C1
CHDH RM6 61 K5
CROY/NA CR0 179 F1
EBED/NFELT TW14 122 A6
OXHEY WD19 21 F7
PUT/ROE SW15 127 G4
WFD IG8 45 F4
Nursery Gdns *CHST* BR7 154 B5
HPTN TW12 141 K3
HSLWW TW4 122 E4
Nursery La *BETH* E2 7 L4
FSTGT E7 76 E5
NKENS W10 88 A4
Nurserymans Rd
FBAR/BDGN N11 40 A1
Nursery Rd *BRXN/ST* SW9 130 A3
EFNCH N2 39 H7
HOM E9 74 E5
MNPK E12 77 J1
MTCM CR4 162 D2
PIN HA5 47 G2
STHGT/OAK N14 28 C6
SUN TW16 140 E7
SUT SM1 175 G3
THHTH CR7 164 E3
WIM/MER SW19 146 C6
Nursery Rw *BAR* EN5 * 26 C2
WALW SE17 19 G6
Nursery St *TOTM* N17 42 B6
The Nursery *ERITH* DA8 118 C6
Nursery Wk *HDN* NW4 51 K2
ROMW/RG RM7 63 F6
Nurstead Rd *ERITH* DA8 117 H6
Nutbourne St *NKENS* W10 88 C2
Nutbrook St *PECK* SE15 131 G2
Nutbrowne Rd *DAGW* RM9 80 B7
Nutcroft Rd *PECK* SE15 111 J6
Nutfield Cl *CAR* SM5 175 J2
UED N18 42 C5
Nutfield Gdns *GDMY/SEVK* IG3 79 F1
NTHLT UB5 83 G1
Nutfield Rd *CRICK* NW2 69 J1
EDUL SE22 131 G4
SRTFD E15 76 A3
THHTH CR7 164 C3
Nutford Pl *MBLAR* W1H 9 K4
Nuthatch Cl
STWL/WRAY TW19 120 C7
Nuthatch Gdns *THMD* SE28 115 J1
Nuthurst Av
BRXS/STRHM SW2 149 F1
Nutley Ter *HAMP* NW3 71 H5
Nutmead Cl *BXLY* DA5 137 K7
Nutmeg Cl *CAN/RD* E16 94 C3
Nutmeg La *POP/IOD* E14 94 B5
Nuttall St *IS* N1 7 K5
Nutter La *WAN* E11 59 G4
Nutt Gv *EDGW* HA8 35 K1
Nutt St *PECK* SE15 111 G6
Nutwell St *TOOT* SW17 147 J4
Nuxley Rd *BELV* DA17 117 G5
Nyanza St *WOOL/PLUM* SE18 115 J5
Nylands Av *RCH/KEW* TW9 125 H1
Nymans Gdns *RYNPK* SW20 160 E2
Nynehead St *NWCR* SE14 112 B6
Nyon Gv *CAT* SE6 151 H1
Nyssa Cl *WFD* IG8 45 K5
Nyton Cl *ARCH* N19 54 E7

O

Oak Av *CEND/HSY/T* N8 54 E3
CROY/NA CR0 179 J1
HEST TW5 102 C6
HPTN TW12 141 J4
MUSWH N10 40 B6
TOTM N17 41 K6
WDR/YW UB7 100 D2
Oakbank *CROY/NA* CR0 180 A5
Oakbank Av *WOT/HER* KT12 156 E6
Oakbank Gv *HNHL* SE24 130 D3
Oakbrook Cl *BMLY* BR1 153 F3
Oakbury Rd *FUL/PGN* SW6 128 A1
Oak Cl *DART* DA1 138 B3
STHGT/OAK N14 28 B6
Oakcombe Cl *NWMAL* KT3 145 G7
Oak Cottage Cl *CAT* SE6 133 H7
Oak Cots *HNWL* W7 * 103 K1
Oak Crs *CAN/RD* E16 94 C4
Oakcroft Cl *PIN* HA5 47 F1
Oakcroft Rd *CHSGTN* KT9 172 B3
LEW SE13 133 G1
Oakcroft Vls *CHSGTN* KT9 172 B3
Oakdale *STHGT/OAK* N14 28 B7
Oakdale Av
KTN/HRWW/WS HA3 50 A4
NTHWD HA6 46 E1
Oakdale Cl *OXHEY* WD19 33 G3
Oakdale Gdns *CHING* E4 44 A4
Oakdale Rd *FSBYPK* N4 55 J5
FSTGT E7 77 F6
HOR/WEW KT19 173 F7
OXHEY WD19 33 G2
PECK SE15 131 K2
STRHM/NOR SW16 148 E4
SWFD E18 59 F1
WAN E11 76 B1
Oakdale Wy *MTCM* CR4 163 F6
Oakdene *WEA* W13 85 H4
Oakdene Av *CHST* BR7 154 A4
ERITH DA8 117 K5
THDIT KT7 158 B7
Oak Dene Cl *EMPK* RM11 63 K5
Oakdene Cl *PIN* HA5 33 K6
Oakdene Dr *BRYLDS* KT5 159 K7
Oakdene Ms *CHEAM* SM3 161 J7
Oakdene Pk *FNCH* N3 38 D6
Oakden St *LBTH* SE11 18 B5
Oaken Dr *ESH/CLAY* KT10 171 F5
Oaken La *ESH/CLAY* KT10 170 E4
Oakenshaw Cl *SURB* KT6 159 F6
Oakeshott Av *HGT* N6 72 A1
Oakey La *STHWK* SE1 18 A3
Oak Farm *BORE* WD6 24 E4
Oakfield *CHING* E4 43 K4
Oakfield Av
KTN/HRWW/WS HA3 49 H2
Oakfield Cl *NWMAL* KT3 160 C4
RSLP HA4 46 D5
Oakfield Ct *BORE* WD6 * 24 D3
Oakfield Gdns *BECK* BR3 166 D4
CAR SM5 162 D7
GFD/PVL UB6 84 D3
UED N18 42 A3
Oakfield La *HAYES* BR2 181 G3
Oakfield Rd *CROY/NA* CR0 164 D7
EHAM E6 77 J7
FNCH N3 39 F7
FSBYPK N4 55 G5
IL IG1 78 B2
PGE/AN SE20 150 D6
STHGT/OAK N14 40 E1
WALTH E17 57 G1
WIM/MER SW19 146 B2
Oakfields Rd *GLDGN* NW11 52 C5
Oakfield St *WBPTN* SW10 14 E9
Oakford Rd *KTTN* NW5 72 C3
Oak Gdns *CROY/NA* CR0 179 J1
EDGW HA8 50 E1
Oak Gv *CRICK* NW2 70 B3
RSLP HA4 47 F7
SUN TW16 141 F6
WWKM BR4 180 A1
Oak Grove Rd *PGE/AN* SE20 150 E7
Oakhall Dr *SUN* TW16 140 D4
Oak Hall Rd *WAN* E11 59 F5
Oakham Cl *CAT* SE6 * 151 H1
Oakham Dr *HAYES* BR2 167 K3
Oakhampton Rd *MLHL* NW7 38 B7
Oakhill *ESH/CLAY* KT10 171 G5
Oak Hl *SURB* KT6 159 F6
WFD IG8 44 B6
Oakhill Av *HAMP* NW3 71 F3
PIN HA5 47 J1
Oak Hill Crs *SURB* KT6 159 F6
WFD IG8 44 C6
Oak Hill Gdns *WFD* IG8 44 C7
Oak Hill Gv *SURB* KT6 159 F5
Oak Hill Pk *HAMP* NW3 71 F3
Oak Hill Park Ms *HAMP* NW3 71 G3
Oakhill Pl *PUT/ROE* SW15 127 K4
Oak Hill Rd *SURB* KT6 * 159 F5
Oakhill Rd *BECK* BR3 167 F1
PUT/ROE SW15 127 J4
STRHM/NOR SW16 148 E7
SUT SM1 175 F2
Oak Hill Wy *HAMP* NW3 71 F3
Oakhouse Rd *BXLYHS* DA6 137 H4
Oakhurst Av *BXLYHN* DA7 117 F6
EBAR EN4 27 J6
Oakhurst Cl *CHST* BR7 153 K7
KUTN/CMB KT2 144 B5
TEDD TW11 142 E4
WALTH E17 58 C3
Oakhurst Gdns *BXLYHN* DA7 117 F6
WALTH E17 58 C3
Oakhurst Gv *EDUL* SE22 131 H3
Oakhurst Pl *WATW* WD18 * 20 D3
Oakhurst Rd *HOR/WEW* KT19 172 E5
Oakington Av *HYS/HAR* UB3 101 G3
RYLN/HDSTN HA2 48 A6
WBLY HA9 68 B2
Oakington Cl *SUN* TW16 156 B1
Oakington Dr *SUN* TW16 156 B1
Oakington Manor Dr
WBLY HA9 68 C4
Oakington Rd *MV/WKIL* W9 2 B9
Oakington Wy
CEND/HSY/T N8 54 E5
Oakland Pl *BKHH* IG9 44 E1
Oakland Rd *SRTFD* E15 76 C3
Oaklands *WCHMH* N21 41 F1
Oaklands Av *BFN/LL* DA15 136 A6
ED N9 30 D5
ESH/CLAY KT10 157 J7
ISLW TW7 104 A5
OXHEY WD19 21 F7
ROM RM1 63 G2
THHTH CR7 164 B3
WWKM BR4 179 K2
Oaklands Cl *ALP/SUD* HA0 67 K4
BXLYHS DA6 137 G4
CHSGTN KT9 171 J3
STMC/STPC BR5 169 K5
Oaklands Dr *WHTN* TW2 123 H6
Oaklands Ga *NTHWD* HA6 32 C5
Oaklands Gv *SHB* W12 87 J7
Oaklands La *BAR* EN5 25 K3
Oaklands Ms *CRICK* NW2 70 B3
Oaklands Park Av *IL* IG1 78 C1
Oaklands Pl *CLAP* SW4 129 J3
Oaklands Rd *BMLY* BR1 152 C6
BXLYHS DA6 137 G3
CRICK NW2 70 B3
HNWL W7 104 A1
MORT/ESHN SW14 126 A2
TRDG/WHET N20 26 D6
Oaklands Wy *WLGTN* SM6 176 C6
Oakland Wy *HOR/WEW* KT19 173 F5
Oak La *EFNCH* N2 53 H1
FBAR/BDGN N11 40 D5
ISLW TW7 123 K3
POP/IOD E14 93 H6
TWK TW1 124 B6
WFD IG8 44 D3
Oakleafe Gdns *BARK/HLT* IG6 60 B2
Oakleigh Av *EDGW* HA8 50 D1
SURB KT6 159 H7
TRDG/WHET N20 27 H7
Oakleigh Cl *TRDG/WHET* N20 39 K2
Oakleigh Ct *EDGW* HA8 * 50 E1
Oakleigh Crs *TRDG/WHET* N20 39 J2
Oakleigh Dr
RKW/CH/CXG WD3 20 A5
Oakleigh Gdns *EDGW* HA8 36 B4
TRDG/WHET N20 27 G7
Oakleigh Ms *TRDG/WHET* N20 39 G1
Oakleigh Park Av *CHST* BR7 169 F1
Oakleigh Pk North
TRDG/WHET N20 27 H7
Oakleigh Pk South
TRDG/WHET N20 27 J7
Oakleigh Rd *HGDN/ICK* UB10 64 A6
PIN HA5 33 K5
Oakleigh Rd North
TRDG/WHET N20 39 H1
Oakleigh Rd South
FBAR/BDGN N11 40 A3
Oakleigh Wy *MTCM* CR4 148 B7
SURB KT6 159 H7
Oakley Av *BARK* IG11 79 F6
CROY/NA CR0 176 E3
EA W5 86 C6
Oakley Cl *CHING* E4 44 A2
EHAM E6 95 J5
HNWL W7 84 E6
ISLW TW7 103 J7
Oakley Ct *MTCM* CR4 163 F6
Oakley Crs *FSBYE* EC1V * 6 D6
Oakley Dr *CAT* SE6 133 G5
ELTH/MOT SE9 135 J7
HAYES BR2 181 J2
Oakley Gdns *CEND/HSY/T* N8 55 F4
CHEL SW3 15 K9
Oakley Pk *BXLY* DA5 136 D6
Oakley Pl *STHWK* SE1 19 L8
Oakley Rd *HAYES* BR2 181 J2
HRW HA1 48 E5
IS N1 7 G1
SNWD SE25 165 J4
Oakley Sq *CAMTN* NW1 4 F5
Oakley St *CHEL* SW3 15 J9
Oakley Yd *BETH* E2 * 7 M9
Oak Lodge Cl *STAN* HA7 35 J4
Oak Lodge Dr *WWKM* BR4 166 E6
Oaklodge Wy *MLHL* NW7 37 H5
Oakmead Av *HAYES* BR2 167 K5
Oakmeade *PIN* HA5 34 A5
Oakmead Gdns *EDGW* HA8 37 F3
Oakmead Pl *MTCM* CR4 147 J7
Oakmead Rd *BAL* SW12 129 G7
CROY/NA CR0 163 J5
Oakmere Rd *ABYW* SE2 116 B5
Oak Park Gdns
WIM/MER SW19 127 G7
Oakridge Dr *EFNCH* N2 53 H2
Oakridge Rd *BMLY* BR1 152 C3
Oak Ri *BKHH* IG9 45 H2
Oak Rd *EA* W5 85 K6
ERITH DA8 117 K6
NWMAL KT3 160 A1
Oak Rw *MTCM* CR4 163 H1
Oaks Av *CRW* RM5 62 E1
FELT TW13 141 J1
NRWD SE19 150 A4
WPK KT4 173 K3
Oaksford Av *SYD* SE26 150 D2
Oaks Gv *CHING* E4 44 C1
Oakshade Rd *BMLY* BR1 152 B3
Oakshaw Rd
WAND/EARL SW18 128 A6
Oaks La *CROY/NA* CR0 178 E2
GNTH/NBYPK IG2 60 E3
Oak Sq *BRXN/ST* SW9 130 A1
Oaks Rd *CROY/NA* CR0 178 D4
STWL/WRAY TW19 120 A4
The Oaks *CHSGTN* KT9 171 J2
FELT TW13 * 141 J1
HAYES BR2 * 169 F5
MRDN SM4 * 161 H3
NFNCH/WDSPK N12 39 F3
OXHEY WD19 21 G7
RSLP HA4 46 B6
WFD IG8 44 C6
WOOL/PLUM SE18 115 H4
YEAD UB4 82 A1
Oak St *ROMW/RG* RM7 62 E4
Oaks Wy *CAR* SM5 175 K6
SURB KT6 171 K1
Oakthorpe Rd *PLMGR* N13 41 G4
Oaktree Av *PLMGR* N13 41 G2
Oak Tree Cl *EA* W5 * 85 J5
STAN HA7 35 J6
Oak Tree Ct *BORE* WD6 * 23 K5
Oak Tree Dell *CDALE/KGS* NW9 50 E4
Oak Tree Dr *TRDG/WHET* N20 27 F7
Oak Tree Gdns *BMLY* BR1 153 F4
Oaktree Gv *IL* IG1 78 D4
Oak Tree Rd *STJWD* NW8 3 H8
Oakview *WATW* WD18 20 C2
Oakview Cl *OXHEY* WD19 21 G5
Oakview Gdns *EFNCH* N2 53 H3
Oakview Gv *CROY/NA* CR0 166 B7
Oakview Rd *CAT* SE6 151 K4
Oak Village *HAMP* NW3 72 A3
Oak Vls *GLDGN* NW11 * 52 D5
Oak Wy *ACT* W3 87 G7
CROY/NA CR0 166 A5
STHGT/OAK N14 28 A6
EBED/NFELT TW14 121 H7
Oakway *HAYES* BR2 167 G1
RYNPK SW20 161 F3
Oakway Cl *BXLY* DA5 137 F5
Oakways *ELTH/MOT* SE9 135 G5
Oakwood *WLGTN* SM6 176 B7
Oakwood Av *BECK* BR3 167 F1
BORE WD6 24 D3
CHSGTN KT9 172 A6
HAYES BR2 168 A2
MTCM CR4 162 C1
STHGT/OAK N14 28 D6
STHL UB1 84 A6
Oakwood Cl *CHST* BR7 153 K5
LEW SE13 133 G6
STHGT/OAK N14 28 C5
WFD IG8 45 J5
Oakwood Ct *WKENS* W14 107 J2
Oakwood Crs *GFD/PVL* UB6 67 G5
WCHMH N21 28 E5
Oakwood Dr *BXLYHN* DA7 137 K3
EDGW HA8 36 E5
NRWD SE19 149 K5
Oakwood Gdns
GDMY/SEVK IG3 79 F1
SUT SM1 174 E1
Oakwood La *WKENS* W14 107 J2
Oakwood Pde
STHGT/OAK N14 * 28 C4
Oakwood Park Cots
WCHMH N21 * 29 F5
Oakwood Park Rd
STHGT/OAK N14 28 E5
Oakwood Pl *CROY/NA* CR0 164 B5
Oakwood Rd *CROY/NA* CR0 164 B5
GLDGN NW11 52 E4
PIN HA5 47 F1
RYNPK SW20 145 J7
Oakworth Rd *NKENS* W10 88 A4
Oak Yd *WAT* WD17 * 21 G3
Oarsman Pl *E/WMO/HCT* KT8 157 K3
Oates Cl *HAYES* BR2 167 G2
Oatland Ri *WALTH* E17 57 G1
Oat La *CITYW* EC2V 12 E4
Oban Cl *PLSTW* E13 95 G3
Oban Rd *PLSTW* E13 95 G2
THHTH CR7 164 E3
Oban St *POP/IOD* E14 94 B5
Oberstein Rd *BTSEA* SW11 128 C3
Oborne Cl *HNHL* SE24 130 C4
Observatory Gdns *KENS* W8 14 A1
Observatory Rd
MORT/ESHN SW14 125 K3
SKENS SW7 15 H3
Observer Dr *WATW* WD18 20 C3
Occupation La *EA* W5 104 E3
WOOL/PLUM SE18 115 G7
Occupation Rd *WALW* SE17 18 E7
WATW WD18 21 F4
WEA W13 104 C1
Ocean Est *WCHPL* E1 93 F3
Ocean St *WCHPL* E1 93 F4
Ockendon Ms *IS* N1 * 73 K5
Ockendon Rd *IS* N1 73 K5
Ockham Dr *GFD/PVL* UB6 66 D6
STMC/STPC BR5 155 G6
Ockley Rd *CROY/NA* CR0 164 A6
STRHM/NOR SW16 148 E3
Octagon Ar *LVPST* EC2M * 13 J3
Octavia Cl *MTCM* CR4 162 D4
Octavia Ct *WATN* WD24 21 G1
Octavia Ms *CRICK* NW2 * 69 K5
Octavia Rd *ISLW* TW7 124 A2
Octavia St *BTSEA* SW11 108 D7
Octavius St *DEPT* SE8 112 D6
October Pl *HDN* NW4 * 52 B2
Odard Rd *E/WMO/HCT* KT8 157 F3
Odell Cl *BARK* IG11 79 F6
Odell Wk *LEW* SE13 132 E2
Odeon Pde *ELTH/MOT* SE9 * 134 D3
GFD/PVL UB6 * 67 H5
HOLWY N7 * 72 E2
ISLW TW7 * 123 K1
Odessa Rd *FSTGT* E7 76 D3
WLSDN NW10 87 J1
Odessa St *BERM/RHTH* SE16 112 C2
Odger St *BTSEA* SW11 128 E1
Odhams Wk
LSQ/SEVD WC2H * 11 J5
Odsey Vls *FSBYPK* N4 * 55 G5
Offa's Md *HOM* E9 75 G3
Offenham Rd *ELTH/MOT* SE9 153 K3
Offerton Rd *CLAP* SW4 129 H2
Offham Slope
NFNCH/WDSPK N12 38 D4
Offley Pl *ISLW* TW7 123 J1
Offley Rd *BRXN/ST* SW9 110 B6
Offord Cl *TOTM* N17 42 C6
Offord Rd *IS* N1 5 M1
Offord St *HOLWY* N7 5 L1
Ogilby St *WOOL/PLUM* SE18 114 E3
Oglander Rd *PECK* SE15 131 G3
Ogle St *GTPST* W1W 10 E2
Oglethorpe Rd *DAGE* RM10 80 B2
Ohio Rd *PLSTW* E13 94 D3
Oil Mill La *HMSMTH* W6 106 D4
Okeburn Rd *TOOT* SW17 148 A4
Okehampton Crs *WELL* DA16 116 C7
Okehampton Rd
WLSDN NW10 70 A7
Olaf St *NTGHL* W11 88 B6
Old Bailey *STP* EC4M 12 D5
Old Barn Cl *BELMT* SM2 174 C6
Old Barn Wy *BXLYHN* DA7 138 A3
Old Barrack Yd *KTBR* SW1X 16 A1
Old Bellgate Whf
POP/IOD E14 112 D2
Oldberry Rd *EDGW* HA8 37 F5
Old Bethnal Green Rd
BETH E2 92 D2
Old Bond St *CONDST* W1S 10 E7
Oldborough Rd *ALP/SUD* HA0 67 J1
Old Brewery Ms *HAMP* NW3 71 H3
Old Bridge Cl *NTHLT* UB5 84 A1
Old Bridge St *KUT/HW* KT1 158 E1
Old Broad St *OBST* EC2N 13 H4
Old Bromley Rd *BMLY* BR1 152 B4
Old Brompton Rd *ECT* SW5 14 B8
Old Blds *LINN* WC2A 12 A4
Old Burlington St
CONDST W1S 10 E6
Oldbury Pl *MHST* W1U 10 B2
Oldbury Rd *EN* EN1 30 C1
Old Castle St *WCHPL* E1 13 L4
Old Cavendish St *OXSTW* W1C 10 C5
Old Chestnut Av
ESH/CLAY KT10 170 A5
Old Church La
CDALE/KGS NW9 68 E1
GFD/PVL UB6 85 G2
STAN HA7 35 H5
Old Church Pth
ESH/CLAY KT10 170 B3
Oldchurch Ri *ROMW/RG* RM7 63 G5
Old Church Rd *CHING* E4 43 J2
Oldchurch Rd *ROMW/RG* RM7 63 F6
Old Church Rd *WCHPL* E1 * 93 F5
Old Church St *CHEL* SW3 15 H8
Old Claygate La
ESH/CLAY KT10 171 G5
Old Compton St
SOHO/SHAV W1D 11 G6
Old Cote Dr *HEST* TW5 103 F5
Old Court Pl *KENS* W8 14 C1
The Old Ctyd *BMLY* BR1 153 F7
Old Dairy Ms *BAL* SW12 129 F7
KTTN NW5 * 72 B5
Old Deer Pk *RCH/KEW* TW9 * 125 G2
Old Deer Park Gdns
RCH/KEW TW9 125 F2
Old Devonshire Rd *BAL* SW12 129 G6
Old Dock Cl *RCH/KEW* TW9 105 H5
Old Dover Rd *BKHTH/KID* SE3 113 K6
Old Farm Av *BFN/LL* DA15 135 J7
STHGT/OAK N14 28 C6
Old Farm Cl *HSLWW* TW4 122 E3
Old Farm Rd *EFNCH* N2 39 H7
HPTN TW12 141 K5
WDR/YW UB7 100 A1
Old Farm Rd East
BFN/LL DA15 155 G1
Old Farm Rd West
BFN/LL DA15 155 F1
Oldfield Cl *BMLY* BR1 168 E3
GFD/PVL UB6 66 E4
STAN HA7 35 G4
Oldfield Farm Gdns
GFD/PVL UB6 66 D7
Oldfield Gv *BERM/RHTH* SE16 112 A3
Oldfield La North
GFD/PVL UB6 66 D7
Oldfield La South
GFD/PVL UB6 84 C2
Oldfield Ms *HGT* N6 54 C6
Oldfield Rd *ACT* W3 106 C1
BMLY BR1 168 E3
BXLYHN DA7 137 F1
HPTN TW12 142 A7
STNW/STAM N16 74 A2
WIM/MER SW19 146 C5
WLSDN NW10 69 H6
Oldfields Circ *NTHLT* UB5 66 C5
Oldfields Rd *SUT* SM1 174 E1
Old Fish Street Hl
BLKFR EC4V * 12 E6
Old Fleet La *FLST/FETLN* EC4A 12 C4
Old Fold Vw *BAR* EN5 26 A2
Old Ford Lock *BOW* E3 * 75 J6
Old Ford Rd *BETH* E2 92 E1
BOW E3 75 G7
Old Forge Cl *STAN* HA7 35 G3
Old Forge Ms *SHB* W12 106 E1
Old Forge Rd *ARCH* N19 72 D1
Old Forge Wy *SCUP* DA14 155 H3
Old Gannon Cl *NTHWD* HA6 32 A3
Old Gloucester St
BMSBY WC1N 11 K2
Old Hall Cl *PIN* HA5 33 J7
Old Hall Dr *PIN* HA5 33 J7
Oldham Ter *ACT* W3 86 E7
Old Hatch Mnr *RSLP* HA4 46 D6
Old Hl *CHST* BR7 154 A7
Oldhill St *STNW/STAM* N16 56 C7
Old Homesdale Rd *HAYES* BR2 168 B3
Old Hospital Cl *BAL* SW12 * 128 E7
Old House Cl *WIM/MER* SW19 146 C4
Old House Gdns *TWK* TW1 * 124 D5
Old Howletts La *RSLP* HA4 46 B5
Old Jamaica Rd
BERM/RHTH SE16 111 H2
Old James St *PECK* SE15 131 J2
Old Jewry *LOTH* EC2R * 13 G5
Old Kenton La
CDALE/KGS NW9 50 D4
Old Kent Rd *PECK* SE15 111 J5
STHWK SE1 19 J5
Old Kingston Rd *WPK* KT4 172 E2
Old Lodge Wy *STAN* HA7 35 G4
Old London Rd
KUTN/CMB KT2 159 F1
Old Malden La *WPK* KT4 173 G1
Old Manor Dr *ISLW* TW7 123 H5
Old Manor Rd *NWDGN* UB2 102 C3
Old Manor Wy *BXLYHN* DA7 138 A1
CHST BR7 153 K4
Old Manor Yd *ECT* SW5 14 B7
Old Market Sq *BETH* E2 7 L7
Old Marylebone Rd
CAMTN NW1 9 K3
Old Mill Ct *SWFD* E18 59 G2
Old Mill Rd *WOOL/PLUM* SE18 115 J5
Old Mitre Ct *EMB* EC4Y * 12 B5
Old Montague St *WCHPL* E1 92 C4
Old Nichol St *BETH* E2 7 L9
Old North St *FSBYW* WC1X * 11 L2
Old Oak Common La
WLSDN NW10 87 G3
Old Oak La *WLSDN* NW10 87 H2
Old Oak Rd *ACT* W3 87 H6
Old Orch *SUN* TW16 156 B1
The Old Orch *HAMP* NW3 * 71 K3
Old Palace Rd *CROY/NA* CR0 177 J2
Old Palace Yd *RCH/KEW* TW9 124 D4
WHALL SW1A 17 J3
Old Paradise St *LBTH* SE11 17 L5
Old Park Av *BAL* SW12 129 F5
ENC/FH EN2 29 J3
Old Park Gv *ENC/FH* EN2 29 J3
Old Park La *MYFR/PKLN* W1K 10 B9
Old Park Ms *HEST* TW5 102 E6
Old Park Ridings *WCHMH* N21 29 H5
Old Park Rd *ABYW* SE2 116 B4
ENC/FH EN2 29 H2
PLMGR N13 41 F2
Old Park Rd South
ENC/FH EN2 29 H3
Old Park Vw *ENC/FH* EN2 29 G2
Old Pearson St *GNWCH* SE10 112 E6
Old Perry St *CHST* BR7 154 E6
Old Post Office La
BKHTH/KID SE3 134 A2
Old Pound Cl *ISLW* TW7 104 B7
Old Pye St *WEST* SW1P 17 G3
Old Quebec St *MBLAR* W1H 9 M5
Old Queen St *STJSPK* SW1H 17 H2
Old Rectory Gdns *EDGW* HA8 36 C5
Old Redding
KTN/HRWW/WS HA3 34 B4
Oldridge Rd *BAL* SW12 129 F6
Old Rd *DART* DA1 138 A3
LEW SE13 133 H3
Old Royal Free Sq *IS* N1 6 B4
Old Ruislip Rd *NTHLT* UB5 83 G1
Old's Ap *WATW* WD18 20 A7
Old School Cl *BECK* BR3 166 A1
Old School Crs *FSTGT* E7 76 E5
Old School Pl *CROY/NA* CR0 177 G3
Old Schools La *EW* KT17 173 H7
Old School Sq *THDIT* KT7 158 A5
Old School Ter *CHEAM* SM3 * 174 B6
Old Seacoal La *STP* EC4M 12 C5
Old South Cl *PIN* HA5 33 H7
Old South Lambeth Rd
VX/NE SW8 * 109 K6
Old Sq *LINN* WC2A 11 M4
Old Stable Ms *HBRY* N5 73 J2
Old Station Gdns
TEDD TW11 * 143 G5
Old Station Rd *HYS/HAR* UB3 101 J2
The Old Station Yd
WALTH E17 58 A3
Oldstead Rd *BMLY* BR1 152 B3
Old St *PLSTW* E13 95 F1
STLK EC1Y 7 H9
Old Studio Cl *CROY/NA* CR0 164 E6
Old Swan Yd *CAR* SM5 175 K3
Old Town *CLAP* SW4 129 H2
CROY/NA CR0 177 H2
Old Tramyard
WOOL/PLUM SE18 115 K3
Old Woolwich Rd
GNWCH SE10 113 G5
Old York Rd
WAND/EARL SW18 128 A4
O'Leary Sq *WCHPL* E1 92 E4
Olga St *BOW* E3 93 G1
Olinda Rd *STNW/STAM* N16 56 B5
Oliphant St *NKENS* W10 88 C2
Olive Gv *SEVS/STOTM* N15 55 J3
Oliver Av *SNWD* SE25 165 G2
Oliver Cl *CHSWK* W4 105 J5
Oliver Gdns *EHAM* E6 95 J4
Oliver Gv *SNWD* SE25 165 G3
Oliver Ms *PECK* SE15 131 H1
Olive Rd *CRICK* NW2 70 A3
DART DA1 139 G7
EA W5 104 E2
PLSTW E13 95 G2
WIM/MER SW19 * 147 G6
Oliver Rd *LEY* E10 75 K2
NWMAL KT3 159 K1
RAIN RM13 81 H7
SUT SM1 175 H3
WALTH E17 58 A4
Oliver's Yd *STLK* EC1Y 7 H9
Olive St *ROMW/RG* RM7 63 F4
Ollerton Gn *BOW* E3 75 H7
Ollerton Rd *FBAR/BDGN* N11 40 D4
Olley Cl *WLGTN* SM6 176 E6
Ollgar Cl *SHB* W12 87 H7
Olliffe St *POP/IOD* E14 113 F2
Olmar St *STHWK* SE1 111 H5
Olney Rd *WALW* SE17 18 E9
Olron Crs *BXLYHS* DA6 136 E4
Olven Rd *WOOL/PLUM* SE18 115 H6
Olveston Wk *CAR* SM5 162 C5
Olwen Ms *PIN* HA5 47 H1
Olyffe Av *WELL* DA16 136 B1
Olyffe Dr *BECK* BR3 152 A7
Olympia Wy *WKENS* W14 107 H2
Olympic Wy *GFD/PVL* UB6 66 B7
WBLY HA9 68 C2
Olympus Gv *WDGN* N22 41 G7
Olympus Sq *CLPT* E5 74 D2
Oman Av *CRICK* NW2 70 A4
O'Meara St *STHWK* SE1 12 F9
Omega Pl *IS* N1 5 K6

Omega St NWCR SE14 .....112 C7
Ommaney Rd NWCR SE14 ...112 A7
Omnibus Wy WALTH E17 ...57 J1
Ondine Rd PECK SE15 .....131 C3
Onega Ga BERM/RHTH SE16 112 D1
One Tree Cl FSTH SE23 ...131 K5
Ongar Cl CHDH RM6 ....61 J4
Ongar Rd FUL/PGN SW6 ...14 B9
Ongar Wy RAIN RM13 ......81 C7
Onra Rd WALTH E17 ....57 J6
Onslow Cl RCHPK/HAM TW10 125 F4
  NKENS W10 ....88 D2
Onslow Crs CHST BR7 .....154 B7
  SKENS SW7 ....15 H6
Onslow Dr SCUP DA14 .....155 K2
Onslow Gdns MUSWH N10 ...54 B4
  SKENS SW7 ....15 G6
  SKENS SW7 ....15 G7
  SWFD E18 ....59 F2
  THDIT KT7 ....157 K7
  WCHMH N21 ....29 G4
  WLGTN SM6 ....176 C6
Onslow Ms East SKENS SW7 15 G6
Onslow Ms West SKENS SW7 15 G6
Onslow Pde STHGT/OAK N14 * 28 B7
Onslow Rd CROY/NA CRO ...164 B6
  NWMAL KT3 ....160 D5
  RCHPK/HAM TW10 ....125 F4
Onslow Sq SKENS SW7 .....15 G6
Onslow Wy CLKNW EC1R 12 B1
Onslow Wy THDIT KT7 .....157 K7
Ontario St STHWK SE1 ....18 D4
Ontario Wy POP/IOD E14 ..93 J4
On The Hl OXHEY WD19 ....33 H1
Onyx Ms SRTFD E15 ....76 C5
Opal Cl CAN/RD E16 ......95 H5
Opal Ms KIL/WHAMP NW6 ...70 D7
Opal St LBTH SE11 ....18 C6
Openshaw Rd ABYW SE2 ....116 C3
Openview WAND/EARL SW18 .128 B7
Ophir Ter PECK SE15 .....111 H7
Opossum Wy HSLWW TW4 ...122 A1
Oppenheim Rd LEW SE13 ...133 F1
Oppidans Rd HAMP NW3 ....3 L2
Optima Pk DART DA1 ......138 D2
Orange Cl HAMP NW3 ......76 C2
Orange Hill Rd EDGW HA8 .36 E6
Orange Pl BERM/RHTH SE16 111 K2
Orangery La ELTH/MOT SE9 154 E4
The Orangery
  RCHPK/HAM TW10 ....143 J1
Orange St LSQ/SEVD WC2H .11 H7
  WAP E1W 92 C7
Oransay Rd IS N1 ....73 J3
Oratory La CHEL SW3 * ...15 H7
Orbain Rd FUL/PGN SW6 ...107 H6
Orbel St BTSEA SW11 .....108 D7
Orb St WALW SE17 ....19 G6
Orchard Av ASHF TW15 ....140 A5
  BELV DA17 ....117 F5
  CROY/NA CRO 179 J1
  DART DA1 ....138 E6
  EBED/NFELT TW14 ....121 J7
  FNCH N3 ....52 E2
  HEST TW5 ....102 D6
  MTCM CR4 ....163 F7
  NWMAL KT3 ....160 B1
  RSLP HA4 ....46 A5
  RYNPK SW20 ....161 F3
  STHGT/OAK N14 ....28 C7
  STHL UB1 ....83 J7
  THDIT KT7 ....158 B7
  TRDG/WHET N20 ....39 H1
Orchard Cl ALP/SUD HA0 ..68 A7
  ASHF TW15 ....140 A5
  BORE WD6 ....24 B3
  BUSH WD23 ....22 D7
  BXLYHN DA7 ....117 F5
  CHING E4 ....43 J3
  CRICK NW2 ....69 J2
  EDGW HA8 ....36 A5
  FSTH SE23 ....131 K5
  HOR/WEW KT19 * 172 D5
  IS N1 ....6 F2
  NKENS W10 ....88 C4
  NTHLT UB5 ....66 C5
  RSLP HA4 ....46 A6
  RYNPK SW20 ....161 F3
  THDIT KT7 ....158 C7
  WAT WD17 ....20 D1
  WOT/HER KT12 ....156 A6
Orchard Cots HYS/HAR UB3 * 101 H1
  KUTN/CMB KT2 * 144 C7
Orchard Ct WLGTN SM6 * ..176 B4
  WPK KT4 * 160 D7
Orchard Crs EDGW HA8 ....36 E4
  EN EN1 ....30 B1
Orchard Dr BKHTH/KID SE3 133 H1
  EDGW HA8 ....36 B4
Orchard Gdns CHSGTN KT9 .172 A3
Orchard Ga CDALE/KGS NW9 51 G3
  ESH/CLAY KT10 ....157 J7
  GFD/PVL UB6 ....67 H1
Orchard Gv CROY/NA CRO ..166 B6
  EDGW HA8 ....36 C7
  KTN/HRWW/WS HA3 ....50 C2
  PGE/AN SE20 ....150 C6
Orchard Hl DART DA1 .....138 E4
  LEW SE13 ....112 E7
Orchard La E/WMO/HCT KT8 157 J5
  RYNPK SW20 ....145 K7
  WFD IG8 ....45 H4
Orchardleigh Av PEND EN3 30 E1
Orchardmede WCHMH N21 ...29 K6
Orchard Ms IS N1 * 7 H2
  TOOT SW17 ....147 G2
Orchard Pl POP/IOD E14 ..94 D7
  TOTM N17 ....42 B6
Orchard Ri CROY/NA CRO ..166 B6
  KUTN/CMB KT2 ....144 E7
  PIN HA5 ....46 D2
  RCHPK/HAM TW10 ....125 J3
Orchard Ri East BFN/LL DA15 135 K4
Orchard Ri West BFN/LL DA15 135 K4
Orchard Rd BAR EN5 ......26 C3
  BELV DA17 ....117 H3
  BMLY BR1 ....153 G7
  BTFD TW8 ....104 D5
  CHSGTN KT9 ....172 A3
  DAGE RM10 ....80 C7
  FELT TW13 ....121 K7
  HPTN TW12 ....141 K6
  HSLWW TW4 ....122 E4
  HYS/HAR UB3 ....82 E6
  KUT/HW KT1 ....159 F1
  PEND EN3 ....30 E4
  RCH/KEW TW9 ....125 H2
  ROMW/RG RM7 ....62 D1
  SCUP DA14 ....154 E3
  SUN TW16 ....141 F6
  SUT SM1 ....174 B4
  TWK TW1 ....124 B4
  WELL DA16 ....136 C2
Orchardson St STJWD NW8 .9 H1

Orchard Sq WKENS W14 * ..107 J4
Orchard St DART DA1 .....139 H5
  MBLAR W1H 10 A5
  WALTH E17 ....57 G3
Orchard Ter EN EN1 * 30 C5
  WLSDN NW10 * 69 H1
The Orchard BKHTH/KID SE3 133 G1
  BORE WD6 ....23 E1
  CHSWK W4 ....106 A3
  EW KT17 ....175 H6
  GLDGN NW11 ....52 E4
  HSLW TW3 ....123 H1
  TRDG/WHET N20 ....27 F1
  WCHMH N21 ....29 K5
Orchard Vls SCUP DA14 * .155 J5
Orchard Wy CROY/NA CRO ..166 B6
  EN EN1 ....30 A2
  ESH/CLAY KT10 ....170 C5
  SUT SM1 ....175 H3
Orchid Cl CHSGTN KT9 ....171 J6
  EHAM E6 ....95 J4
  LEW SE13 ....133 G4
  STHL UB1 ....83 J5
Orchid Gdns HSLWW TW4 ...122 E3
  RYLN/HDSTN HA2 * 28 C6
Orchid St SHB W12 ....87 J6
Orde Hall St BMSBY WC1N * 11 L2
Ordell Rd BOW E3 ....93 H1
Ordnance Cl FELT TW13 ...140 E1
Ordnance Crs GNWCH SE10 .113 G1
Ordnance Hl STJWD NW8 ...3 H4
Ordnance Ms CAN/RD E16 ..94 D5
  WOOL/PLUM SE18 ....115 F5
Oregano Dr POP/IOD E14 ..94 B5
Oregon Av MNPK E12 ......77 K3
Oregon Cl NWMAL KT3 .....159 K3
Oregon Sq ORP BR6 ....169 J7
Orestes Ms KIL/WHAMP NW6 70 E4
Orford Gdns TWK TW1 .....143 F1
Orford Rd CAT SE6 ....151 K2
  SWFD E18 ....59 F2
  WALTH E17 ....57 J4
Oriel Cl MTCM CR4 ....163 J3
Oriel Ct HAMP NW3 ....71 G3
Oriel Dr BARN SW13 ......107 F5
Oriel Gdns CLAY IG5 .....59 K2
Oriel Rd HOM E9 ....75 F5
Oriel Wy NTHLT UB5 ......66 B6
Oriental Rd CAN/RD E16 ..95 H7
Oriental St POP/IOD E14 *
Orient St LBTH SE11 .....18 D4
Orient Wy CLPT E5 ....75 F2
  LEY E10 ....75 J1
Oriole Wy THMD SE28 .....97 H6
Orion Rd MUSWH N10 ......40 A5
Orion Wy NTHWD HA6 ......32 D3
Orissa Rd WOOL/PLUM SE18 115 K4
Orkney St BTSEA SW11 ....129 F1
Orlando Rd CLAP SW4 .....129 H2
Orleans Cl ESH/CLAY KT10 170 D1
Orleans Rd NRWD SE19 ....149 K5
  TWK TW1 ....124 C6
Orleston Ms HOLWY N7 * ..73 G5
Orleston Rd HOLWY N7 ....73 G5
Orley Farm Rd HRW HA1 ...66 E2
Ormanton Rd SYD SE26 ....150 C3
Orme Ct BAY/PAD W2 ......8 C7
Orme Court Ms BAY/PAD W2 * 8 C7
Ormeley Rd BAL SW12 .....129 G6
Orme Rd KUT/HW KT1 ......159 J1
  SUT SM1 ....175 F5
Ormerod Gdns MTCM CR4 ...163 F1
Ormesby Cl THMD SE28 ....97 K6
Ormesby Wy
  KTN/HRWW/WS HA3 ....50 B5
Orme Sq BAY/PAD W2 * 8 C7
Orme Square Ga BAY/PAD W2 * 8 C7
Ormiston Gv SHB W12 .....87 J7
Ormiston Rd GNWCH SE10 ..113 K4
Ormond Av HPTN TW12 .....142 C7
Ormond Cl BMSBY WC1N * ..11 K2
Ormond Crs HPTN TW12 ....142 C7
Ormond Dr HPTN TW12 .....142 B6
Ormonde Av HOR/WEW KT19 .173 F7
Ormonde Ct STJWD NW8 * ..3 L4
Ormonde Ga CHEL SW3 .....15 L8
Ormonde Pl BGVA SW1W 16 B6
Ormonde Rd
  MORT/ESHN SW14 ....125 J2
  NTHWD HA6 ....32 B3
Ormonde Ter STJWD NW8 ...3 L4
Ormond Rd ARCH N19 .....54 E7
  RCHPK/HAM TW10 ....124 E4
Ormond Yd STJS SW1Y 10 F8
Ormrod Ct WAT WD17 * 21 G1
Ormsby BELMT SM2 * 175 F6
Ormsby Gdns GFD/PVL UB6 .84 C1
Ormsby Pl STNW/STAM N16 .74 B2
Ormsby St BETH E2 ....7 L1
Ormside St PECK SE15 ....111 K5
Ormskirk Rd OXHEY WD19 ..33 H4
Ornan Rd HAMP NW3 ....71 J4
Oronsay Wk IS N1 * 73 J5
Orpheus St CMBW SE5 .....110 E7
Orpington Gdns UED N18 ..42 A1
Orpington Rd CHST BR7 ...169 K2
  WCHMH N21 ....29 G7
Orpwood Cl HPTN TW12 ....141 K5
Orsett St LBTH SE11 .....17 M7
Orsett Ter BAY/PAD W2 ...8 D5
  WFD IG8 ....45 G7
Orsman Rd IS N1 ....7 J4
Orton Gv WAP E1W 92 C7
Orville Rd BTSEA SW11 ...128 C1
Orwell Cl HYS/HAR UB3 ...82 D1
Orwell Ct WATN WD24 * ...21 H2
Orwell Rd PLSTW E15 .....95 G1

PEND EN3 ....31 G1
PLMGR N13 ....41 G2
STHL UB1 ....84 C1
THHTH CR7 ....164 D1
Osborne Sq DAGW RM9 .....80 B3
Osborne Ter TOOT SW17 * .148 A4
Osborne Wy CHSGTN KT9 ...172 A4
Osborn Gdns MLHL NW7 ....38 B6
Osborn La FSTH SE23 .....132 B6
Osborn St WCHPL E1 ......13 M1
Osborn Ter BKHTH/KID SE3 133 J5
Osbourne Ct
  RYLN/HDSTN HA2 * 48 B3
Oscar Faber Pl IS N1 * ..7 J2
Oscar St BROCKY SE4 .....132 D1
Oseney Crs KTTN NW5 .....72 C5
Osidge La STHGT/OAK N14 .28 A7
Osier Crs MUSWH N10 .....39 K7
Osiers Rd WAND/EARL SW18 127 K3
The Osiers RKW/CH/CXG WD3 20 A4
Osier St WCHPL E1 ....92 E3
Osier Wy LEY E10 ....75 K2
  MTCM CR4 ....162 D4
Oslac Rd CAT SE6 ....151 K4
Osman Cl SEVS/STOTM N15 .55 K5
Osman Rd ED N9 ....42 C2
  HMSMTH W6 ....107 F2
Osmond Cl RYLN/HDSTN HA2 66 C1
Osmond Gdns WLGTN SM6 ...176 C4
Osmund St SHB W12 ....87 H5
Osnaburgh St CAMTN NW1 ..4 D9
Osnaburgh Ter CAMTN NW1 .4 D9
Osney Wk MRDN SM4 ....162 C5
Osprey Cl EHAM E6 ....95 J4
  HAYES BR2 ....168 D7
  SUT SM1 ....174 D4
  WALTH E17 ....43 G6
  WAN E11 ....58 E3
  WDR/YW UB7 ....100 A1
Osprey Ms PEND EN3 ......30 D1
Ospringe Cl PGE/AN SE20 .150 E6
Ospringe Rd KTTN NW5 ....72 C3
Osram Rd WBLY HA9 ....67 K2
Ossian Rd FSBYPK N4 .....55 F6
Ossier Ms CHSWK W4 ......106 C5
Ossington Blds MHST W1U * 10 A2
Ossington Cl BAY/PAD W2 * 8 B7
Ossington St BAY/PAD W2 .8 B6
Ossory Rd STHWK SE1 .....111 H4
Ossulston St CAMTN NW1 ..5 H6
Ostade Rd BRXS/STRHM SW2 130 A6
Osten Ms SKENS SW7 ......14 D4
Osterley Rd DART DA1 ....139 J3
Osterley Av ISLW TW7 ....103 J6
Osterley Crs ISLW TW7 ...103 K7
Osterley Gdns THHTH CR7 .164 D1
Osterley La NWDGN UB2 ...103 H3
Osterley Park Rd NWDGN UB2 102 E2
Osterley Park View Rd
  HNWL W7 ....103 K1
Osterley Rd ISLW TW7 ....103 K6
  STNW/STAM N16 ....74 A3
Ostlers Dr ASHF TW15 ....140 A4
Ostliffe Rd PLMGR N13 ...41 H4
Oswald Rd STHL UB1 ......83 J7
Oswald's Md HOM E9 ......75 G3
Oswald St CLPT E5 ....75 F2
Oswald Ter CRICK NW2 * ..70 A2
Osward CROY/NA CRO 179 H7
Osward Pl ED N9 ....42 C1
Osward Rd BAL SW12 ......147 K1
Oswin St LBTH SE11 ......18 D5
Oswyth Rd CMBW SE5 ......131 F1
Otford Cl BMLY BR1 ......169 F2
  BXLY DA5 ....137 J5
  PGE/AN SE20 ....150 E7
Otford Crs BROCKY SE4 ...132 C5
Othello Cl LBTH SE11 ....18 C7
Otis St BOW E3 ....94 A2
Otley Cl CAT SE6 ....151 K4
Otley Dr GNTH/NBYPK IG2 .60 B5
Otley Rd CAN/RD E16 .....95 G5
Otley Ter CLPT E5 ....74 E1
Otley Wy OXHEY WD19 .....33 G2
Ottawa Gdns DAGE RM10 ...81 F6
Ottaway St CLPT E5 ......74 C2
Otterbourne Rd CHING E4 .44 B2
  CROY/NA CRO 177 J1
Otterburn Gdns ISLW TW7 .104 B6
Otterburn St TOOT SW17 ..147 K5
Otter Cl SRTFD E15 ......76 A7
Otterden St CAT SE6 .....151 J3
Otto Cl CAT SE6 ....151 H2
  SYD SE26 ....150 D1
Ottoman Ter WAT WD17 * ..21 G1
Otto St WALW SE17 ....110 C5
Otway Gdns BUSH WD23 ....22 E6
Oulton Cl THMD SE28 .....97 J5
Oulton Crs BARK IG11 ....79 F5
Oulton Rd SEVS/STOTM N15 55 K4
Oulton Wy OXHEY WD19 ....33 K3
Oundle Av BUSH WD23 ....22 C5
Ouseley Rd BAL SW12 ....128 E7
Outer Cir CAMTN NW1 ....3 K6
Outgate Rd WLSDN NW10 ..69 H6
Outram Pl IS N1 ....5 K3
Outram Rd CROY/NA CRO ...178 B1
  EHAM E6 ....77 J7
  WDGN N22 ....40 D7
Outwich St HDTCH EC3A * .13 K4
Oval Ct EDGW HA8 * 36 E6
Oval Pl VX/NE SW8 ....110 A6
Oval Rd CAMTN NW1 ....4 C4
  CROY/NA CRO 177 K1
Oval Rd North DAGE RM10 .80 D7
Oval Rd South DAGE RM10 .98 D1
The Oval BETH E2 ....92 D1
  BFN/LL DA15 ....136 B6
Oval Wy LBTH SE11 ....17 M8
Overbrae BECK BR3 ....151 J5
Overbrook Wk EDGW HA8 ...36 C6
Overbury Av BECK BR3 ....166 E2
Overbury Rd FSBYPK N4 ...55 F3
Overbury St CLPT E5 .....75 F3
Overcliff Rd BROCKY SE4 .132 A2
Overcourt Cl BFN/LL DA15 136 B6
Overdale Av NWMAL KT3 ...159 K1
Overdale Rd EA W5 ....104 D2
Overhill Cots MTCM CR4 * 163 F1
Overhill Rd EDUL SE22 ...131 H6
  PUR/KEN CR8 ....177 G4
Overhill Wy BECK BR3 ....167 G4
Overlea Rd CLPT E5 ......56 D5
Overmead ELTH/MOT SE9 ...135 J6
Overstand Cl BECK BR3 ...166 D4
Overstone Gdns
  CROY/NA CRO 166 C6

Overstone Rd HMSMTH W6 ..107 F3
Overton Cl ISLW TW7 .....104 A7
  WLSDN NW10 ....68 E5
Overton Dr CHDH RM6 .....61 J6
  WAN E11 ....59 F6
Overton Rd ABYW SE2 .....116 D2
  BELMT SM2 ....174 E6
  BRXN/ST SW9 ....130 B1
  LEY E10 ....57 F7
  STHGT/OAK N14 ....28 E4
Overton's Yd CROY/NA CRO 177 J2
Overy Liberty DART DA1 ..139 H6
Overy St DART DA1 ....139 J5
Ovesdon Av RYLN/HDSTN HA2 47 K7
Ovett Cl NRWD SE19 ......150 A5
Ovex Cl POP/IOD E14 .....113 F1
Ovington Gdns CHEL SW3 ..15 K4
Ovington Ms CHEL SW3 ....15 K4
Ovington Sq CHEL SW3 ....15 K4
Ovington St CHEL SW3 ....15 K4
Owen Cl CROY/NA CRO 164 E5
  NTHLT UB5 ....65 J6
  THMD SE28 ....97 J7
  YEAD UB4 ....83 F2
Owenite St ABYW SE2 .....116 C3
Owen Rd PLMGR N13 ......41 J4
Owens Ms WAN E11 ....76 C1
Owen's Rw FSBYE EC1V 6 C7
Owens Wy FSTH SE23 .....132 B6
Owen Wk PGE/AN SE20 ....150 C6
Owen Wy WLSDN NW10 .....68 E5
Owgan Cl CMBW SE5 ......110 E6
Oxberry Av FUL/PGN SW6 .127 H1
Oxendon St
  SOHO/SHAV W1D * 11 G7
Oxenford St PECK SE15 ...131 G2
Oxenpark Av WBLY HA9 ....50 A6
Oxestalls Rd DEPT SE8 ...112 B4
Oxford Av HEST TW5 ......103 F4
  HYS/HAR UB3 ....101 J6
  RYNPK SW20 ....161 H1
  STHGT/OAK N14 ....28 C7
Oxford Cl ASHF TW15 .....140 A6
  ED N9 ....42 D1
  GPK RM2 ....63 J4
  MTCM CR4 ....163 H2
  NTHWD HA6 ....32 A3
Oxford Crs NWMAL KT3 ....160 A5
Oxford Dr RSLP HA4 ......65 G1
Oxford Gdns CHSWK W4 ....105 H4
  NKENS W10 ....88 B5
  TRDG/WHET N20 ....27 H1
  WCHMH N21 ....29 J6
Oxford Ms BXLY DA5 ......137 H7
Oxford Rd CAR SM5 ......175 J5
  EA W5 ....85 K6
  ED N9 ....42 D1
  FSBYPK N4 ....55 G7
  HRW HA1 ....48 C5
  IL IG1 ....78 C4
  KIL/WHAMP NW6 ....2 A1
  KTN/HRWW/WS HA3 ....49 F2
  NRWD SE19 ....149 K5
  PEND EN3 ....30 D4
  PUT/ROE SW15 ....127 H3
  SCUP DA14 ....155 H4
  SRTFD E15 ....76 B5
  TEDD TW11 ....142 D4
  WFD IG8 ....45 H4
  WLGTN SM6 ....176 C4
Oxford Rd North CHSWK W4 105 J4
Oxford Rd South CHSWK W4 105 H4
Oxford Rw SUN TW16 * 156 B2
Oxford Sq BAY/PAD W2 ....9 J5
Oxford St OXSTW W1C 10 A5
  WATW WD18 ....21 F4
Oxford Wk STHL UB1 ......83 K7
Oxford Wy FELT TW13 .....141 H3
Oxgate Court Pde
  CRICK NW2 * 69 K1
Oxgate Gdns CRICK NW2 ...69 K1
Oxgate La CRICK NW2 .....69 K1
Oxhawth Crs HAYES BR2 ...169 G3
Oxhey Av OXHEY WD19 .....21 H1
Oxhey Dr NTHWD HA6 ......33 F4
Oxhey La OXHEY WD19 .....21 H1
  PIN HA5 ....34 A4
Oxhey Ridge Cl NTHWD HA6 32 E4
Oxhey Rd OXHEY WD19 .....21 H3
Oxleas EHAM E6 ....96 B5
Oxleas Cl WELL DA16 .....135 J1
Oxleay Rd RYLN/HDSTN HA2 48 A7
Oxleigh Cl NWMAL KT3 ....160 B4
Oxley Cl STHWK SE1 ......19 M7
Oxleys Rd CRICK NW2 .....69 J2
Oxlow La DAGW RM9 ......80 B3
Oxonian St EDUL SE22 ....131 G3
Oxted Cl MTCM CR4 ......162 C2
Oxtoby Wy STRHM/NOR SW16 148 D7
Oyster Catchers Cl
  CAN/RD E16 ....95 F5
Oyster Rw WCHPL E1 ......92 E5
Ozolins Wy CAN/RD E16 ...94 D5

P

Pablo Neruda HNHL SE24 ..130 C3
Pace Pl WCHPL E1 ....92 D5
Pacific Cl EBED/NFELT TW14 121 J7
Pacific Rd CAN/RD E16 ...94 E5
Packington Rd ACT W3 ....105 K2
Packington Sq IS N1 .....6 E4
Packington St IS N1 .....6 D3
Packmores Rd ELTH/MOT SE9 135 J4
Padbury Cl EBED/NFELT TW14 121 F7
Padbury Ct BETH E2 ......7 M8
Paddenswick Rd
  HMSMTH W6 ....106 D2
Paddington Cl YEAD UB4 ..83 H3
Paddington Gn BAY/PAD W2 9 G2
Paddington St MHST W1U * 10 A2
Paddock Cl BKHTH/KID SE3 133 K2
  NTHLT UB5 ....84 A1
  OXHEY WD19 ....21 J5
  SYD SE26 ....151 F3
  WPK KT4 ....160 B7
Paddock Gdns NRWD SE19 ..150 A5
Paddock La BAR EN5 * 26 A3
Paddock Rd BXLYHS DA6 ...137 F3
  CRICK NW2 ....69 J2
  RSLP HA4 ....65 H2
Paddocks Cl RYLN/HDSTN HA2 66 B3
The Paddocks EA W5 * 104 A2
  EBAR EN4 ....27 K2
  MLHL NW7 * 38 D5

WBLY HA9 ....68 D1
Paddock Wy CHST BR7 .....154 D6
  PUT/ROE SW15 ....127 F6
Padelford La STAN HA7 ...35 G1
Padfield Rd BRXN/ST SW9 .130 D2
Padley Cl CHSGTN KT9 ....172 B4
Padnall Rd CHDH RM6 .....61 K2
Padstow Rd ENC/FH EN2 ..29 H1
Padstow Wk FELT TW13 ...140 D1
Padua Rd PGE/AN SE20 ....150 E7
Pagden St VX/NE SW8 .....109 G7
Pageant Crs
  BERM/RHTH SE16 ....93 H7
Pageant Wk CROY/NA CRO .178 A2
Page Av WBLY HA9 ....68 E2
Page Cl DAGW RM9 ....80 A4
  HPTN TW12 ....141 J5
Page Crs CROY/NA CRO 177 H4
  ERITH DA8 ....118 C6
Page Green Rd
  SEVS/STOTM N15 * 56 C4
Page Green Ter
  SEVS/STOTM N15 ....56 B4
Page Heath La BMLY BR1 ..168 C2
Page Heath Vls BMLY BR1 .168 C2
Pagehurst Rd CROY/NA CRO 165 H6
Page Meadow MLHL NW7 ....37 J6
Page Rd EBED/NFELT TW14 .121 G5
Page's Hi MUSWH N10 .....54 A1
Page's La MUSWH N10 .....54 A1
Page St MLHL NW7 ....37 J7
  WEST SW1P 17 H5
Page's Wk STHWK SE1 .....19 J5
Pages Yd CHSWK W4 * 106 B5
Paget Av SUT SM1 ....175 H2
Paget Cl HPTN TW12 ......142 D3
Paget Gdns CHST BR7 .....154 B7
Paget La ISLW TW7 ....123 J2
Paget Pl KUTN/CMB KT2 * .144 E5
  THDIT KT7 ....158 A7
Paget Ri WOOL/PLUM SE18 .115 F6
  IL IG1 ....78 B3
Paget Rd HGDN/ICK UB10 ..82 A3
  IL IG1 ....78 B3
  STNW/STAM N16 ....55 K7
Paget St FSBYE EC1V 6 C7
Paget Ter WOOL/PLUM SE18 115 G5
Pagitts Gv EBAR EN4 .....27 G1
Pagnell St NWCR SE14 ....112 C6
Pagoda Av RCH/KEW TW9 ..125 G2
Pagoda Gdns BKHTH/KID SE3 133 G1
Pagoda Gv NRWD SE27 .....149 J1
Paignton Rd RSLP HA4 ....64 E2
  SEVS/STOTM N15 ....56 A5
Paines Cl PIN HA5 ....47 J2
Paine's La PIN HA5 ......47 J1
Pain's Cl MTCM CR4 ......163 G1
Painsthorpe Rd
  STNW/STAM N16 ....74 A2
Painters Ms BERM/RHTH SE16 111 H3
Painters Rd GNTH/NBYPK IG2 61 G3
Paisley Rd CAR SM5 ......162 C7
  WDGN N22 ....41 H7
Paisley Ter CAR SM5 .....162 C7
Pakeman St HOLWY N7 .....73 F2
Pakenham Cl BAL SW12 ....129 F7
Pakenham St FSBYW WC1X .5 M8
Palace Av KENS W8 ....8 D9
Palace Cl HOM E9 ....75 H5
Palace Ct BAY/PAD W2 ....8 C7
  KTN/HRWW/WS HA3 ....50 A5
Palace Court Gdns
  MUSWH N10 ....54 C2
Palace Gardens Ms KENS W8 8 C8
Palace Gardens Ter KENS W8 8 B8
Palace Ga KENS W8 ....14 E2
Palace Gates Rd WDGN N22 40 E7
Palace Gn CROY/NA CRO ...179 H6
  KENS W8 ....8 C9
Palace Gv BMLY BR1 ......153 F7
  NRWD SE19 ....150 B6
Palace Ms FUL/PGN SW6 * .107 J6
  WALTH E17 ....57 H3
Palace Pde WALTH E17 * ..57 H3
Palace Pl BGVA SW1W 16 E3
Palace Rd BMLY BR1 ......153 F7
  BRXS/STRHM SW2 ....130 A7
  CEND/HSY/T N8 ....54 D4
  E/WMO/HCT KT8 ....157 H4
  FBAR/BDGN N11 ....40 E6
  KUT/HW KT1 ....158 E3
  NRWD SE19 ....150 B6
  RSLP HA4 ....65 J3
Palace Sq NRWD SE19 .....150 B6
Palace St WESTW SW1E 16 E3
Palace Vw BMLY BR1 ......168 A2
  CROY/NA CRO 179 H3
  LEE/GVPK SE12 ....152 E1
Palace View Rd CHING E4 .43 K4
Palamos Rd LEY E10 ......57 J7
Palatine Av STNW/STAM N16 74 A3
Palatine Rd STNW/STAM N16 74 A3
Palemead Cl FUL/PGN SW6 107 G7
Palermo Rd WLSDN NW10 ..87 J1
Palestine Gv WIM/MER SW19 147 H7
Palewell Common Dr
  MORT/ESHN SW14 ....126 A4
Palewell Pk
  MORT/ESHN SW14 ....126 A4
Palfrey Pl VX/NE SW8 ....110 A6
Palgrave Av STHL UB1 ....84 A6
Palgrave Gdns CAMTN NW1 3 K9
Palgrave Rd SHB W12 ....106 C2
Palissy St BETH E2 ......7 L8
Pallant Wy WOOL/PLUM SE18 114 D7
Palliser Dr RAIN RM13 ...99 J4
Palliser Rd WKENS W14 ...107 H4
Pall MI STJS SW1Y 11 G8
Pall MI East STJS SW1Y ..11 G8
Pall Mall Pl STJS SW1Y .10 F9
Palmar Crs BXLYHN DA7 ...137 H2
Palmar Rd BXLYHN DA7 ...137 H1
Palm Av SCUP DA14 ......155 K5
Palm Cl LEY E10 ....75 K2
Palmeira Rd BXLYHN DA7 ..136 E2
Palmer Av BUSH WD23 .....22 B5
  CHEAM SM3 ....174 A4
Palmer Cl HEST TW5 ......103 F7
  NTHLT UB5 ....65 J5
  WWKM BR4 ....180 B1
Palmer Crs KUT/HW KT1 ...159 F2
Palmer Dr BMLY BR1 ......169 G3
Palmer Gdns BAR EN5 .....26 B4
Palmer Pl HOLWY N7 ......73 G4
Palmer Rd BCTR RM8 .....61 K7
  PLSTW E13 ....95 F3
Palmers Gv E/WMO/HCT KT8 157 F3
Palmers La EN EN1 ......30 D1
Palmers Rd BETH E2 ......93 F1
  MORT/ESHN SW14 ....125 K2
  STRHM/NOR SW16 ....164 A1
Palmer's Rd FBAR/BDGN N11 40 C4
Palmerston Ct BKHH IG9 ..45 G1
Palmerston Crs PLMGR N13 41 F4

WOOL/PLUM SE18 **115** H5
Palmerston Gv
WIM/MER SW19 **146** E6
Palmerston Rd *ACT* W3 **105** K2
BKHH IG9 **45** G1
CAR SM5 **175** K3
CROY/NA CR0 **164** E4
FSTGT E7 **77** F4
HSLW TW3 **103** H7
KIL/WHAMP NW6 **70** D6
KTN/HRWW/WS HA3 **49** F2
MORT/ESHN SW14 **125** K3
SUT SM1 **175** G4
WALTH E17 **57** H3
WDGN N22 **41** F6
WHTN TW2 **123** K5
WIM/MER SW19 **146** E6
Palmerston Wy *VX/NE* SW8 * **109** G6
Palmer St *STJSPK* SW1H **16** F3
Palmers Whf *KUT/HW* KT1 * **158** E1
Palm Gv *EA* W5 **105** F2
Palm Rd *ROMW/RG* RM7 **62** E4
Pamela Ct
NFNCH/WDSPK N12 * **39** F5
Pamela Gdns *PIN* HA5 **47** F4
Pampisford Rd *SAND/SEL* CR2 **177** H7
Pams Wy *HOR/WEW* KT19 **173** F4
Pancras La *MANHO* EC4N **12** F5
Pancras Rd *CAMTN* NW1 **5** G5
KCROSS N1C **5** J6
Pancras Wy *BOW* E3 **93** J1
Pandian Wy *KTTN* NW5 **72** D5
Pandora Rd *KIL/WHAMP* NW6 **70** E5
Panfield Ms *GNTH/NBYPK* IG2 **60** A5
Panfield Rd *ABYW* SE2 **116** B1
Pangbourne Av *NKENS* W10 * **88** A4
Pangbourne Dr *STAN* HA7 **35** K4
Panhard Pl *STHL* UB1 **84** B6
Pank Av *BAR* EN5 **27** H4
Pankhurst Av *CAN/RD* E16 * **95** F7
Pankhurst Cl *ISLW* TW7 **124** A2
NWCR SE14 **112** A6
Pankhurst Pl *WATN* WD24 **21** G2
Pankhurst Rd *WOT/HER* KT12 **156** B6
Pankridge *OXHEY* WD19 * **33** H1
Panmuir Rd *RYNPK* SW20 **145** K7
Panmure Cl *HBRY* N5 **73** H3
Panmure Rd *SYD* SE26 **150** D2
Pan Peninsula Sq
POP/IOD E14 **112** E1
Pansy Gdns *SHB* W12 **87** J6
Panther Dr *WLSDN* NW10 **69** F4
Pantiles Cl *PLMGR* N13 **41** H4
The Pantiles *BMLY* BR1 **168** D2
BUSH WD23 **22** D7
BXLYHN DA7 **117** G6
Panton Cl *CROY/NA* CR0 **164** C7
Panton St *STJS* SW1Y **11** H7
Panyers Gdns *DAGE* RM10 **80** D2
Paper Blds *EMB* EC4Y * **12** B6
Papermill Cl *CAR* SM5 **176** A3
Papermill La *DART* DA1 **139** G3
Papermill Pl *WALTH* E17 **57** G1
Papillons Wk *BKHTH/KID* SE3 **133** K1
Papworth Gdns *HOLWY* N7 **73** F4
Papworth Wy
BRXS/STRHM SW2 **130** B6
Parade Ms *BRXS/STRHM* SW2 **149** H1
Parade Ter *CDALE/KGS* NW9 * **51** J5
The Parade *BROCKY* SE4 * **112** C7
BTSEA SW11 * **128** C3
CAR SM5 * **175** K4
CROY/NA CR0 * **163** K5
DART DA1 * **138** C4
EA W5 * **85** K5
EDUL SE22 * **131** F2
ESH/CLAY KT10 **170** E5
FSBYPK N4 * **73** G1
GFD/PVL UB6 * **67** H5
KUT/HW KT1 * **159** F1
OXHEY WD19 **33** H2
PGE/AN SE20 * **150** E7
RCH/KEW TW9 * **125** H2
SUN TW16 **140** D6
SUT SM1 * **174** D2
SYD SE26 * **150** D3
WAT WD17 **21** F2
WLGTN SM6 * **177** F4
Paradise Pas *HOLWY* N7 **73** F4
Paradise Rd *CLAP* SW4 **129** K1
RCH/KEW TW9 **125** F4
Paradise Rw *BETH* E2 * **92** D2
Paradise St *BERM/RHTH* SE16 **111** J1
Paradise Wk *CHEL* SW3 **15** L9
Paragon Cl *CAN/RD* E16 **94** E5
Paragon Gv *BRYLDS* KT5 **159** G5
Paragon Ms *STHWK* SE1 **19** H5
Paragon Pl *BKHTH/KID* SE3 **133** J1
Paragon Rd *HACK* E8 **74** D5
The Paragon *BKHTH/KID* SE3 **133** K1
Parbury Ri *CHSGTN* KT9 **172** A5
Parbury Rd *FSTH* SE23 **132** B5
Parchmore Rd *THHTH* CR7 **164** C1
Parchmore Wy *THHTH* CR7 **164** C1
Pardoe Rd *LEY* E10 **57** K6
Pardoner St *STHWK* SE1 **19** H3
Pardon St *FSBYE* EC1V **6** D9
Parfett St *WCHPL* E1 **92** C4
Parfitt Cl *HAMP* NW3 **53** G7
Parfrey St *HMSMTH* W6 **107** F5
Parham Dr *GNTH/NBYPK* IG2 **60** B5
Paris Gdn *STHWK* SE1 **12** C8
Parish Cl *HCH* RM12 **81** K1
Parish Gate Dr *BFN/LL* DA15 **135** K5
Parish La *PGE/AN* SE20 **151** F5
Parish Whf *WOOL/PLUM* SE18 **114** D3
Park Ap *BERM/RHTH* SE16 * **111** K2
WELL DA16 **136** C3
Park Av *BARK* IG11 **78** C5
BMLY BR1 **152** E5
BUSH WD23 **21** K1
CAR SM5 **176** A5
CRICK NW2 **69** K5
EHAM E6 **78** A7
EN EN1 **29** K4
FNCH N3 **39** F7
GLDGN NW11 **53** F7
HSLW TW3 **123** G5
IL IG1 **60** A7
MORT/ESHN SW14 **126** A3
ORP BR6 **181** K1
PLMGR N13 **41** G2
RSLP HA4 **46** C5
SRTFD E15 **76** C5
STHL UB1 **102** E1
UED N18 **42** C3
WATW WD18 **20** E2
WDGN N22 **54** E1
WFD IG8 **45** F4
WLSDN NW10 **86** B2
WWKM BR4 **180** A1
Park Av East *EW* KT17 **173** J5
Park Avenue Ms *MTCM* CR4 **148** B6
Park Av North
CEND/HSY/T N8 **54** D3
WLSDN NW10 **69** K4
Park Avenue Rd *TOTM* N17 **42** D6
Park Av South
CEND/HSY/T N8 **54** D3
Park Av West *EW* KT17 **173** J5
Park Cha *WBLY* HA9 **68** B3
Park Cl *BUSH* WD23 **21** H2
CAR SM5 **175** K5
CRICK NW2 **69** J2
HOM E9 **74** E7
HPTN TW12 **142** C7
HSLW TW3 **123** H4
KTN/HRWW/WS HA3 **34** E7
KUTN/CMB KT2 **144** C7
NFNCH/WDSPK N12 * **39** H3
SKENS SW7 * **15** L2
WKENS W14 **107** J2
WLSDN NW10 **86** B2
Park Cots *FNCH* N3 * **52** D1
Park Ct *DUL* SE21 * **149** K2
NWMAL KT3 **160** A3
SYD SE26 * **150** D5
WBLY HA9 **68** A4
Park Crs *BORE* WD6 **24** B2
EMPK RM11 **63** J6
ENC/FH EN2 **29** K3
ERITH DA8 **117** K5
FNCH N3 **39** F6
KTN/HRWW/WS HA3 **34** E7
REGST W1B **10** C1
WHTN TW2 **123** J7
Park Crescent Ms East
GTPST W1W **10** D1
Park Crescent Ms West
CAVSQ/HST W1G **10** C1
Park Cft *EDGW* HA8 **36** E7
Parkcroft Rd *LEE/GVPK* SE12 **133** J6
Parkdale Crs *WPK* KT4 **173** F2
Parkdale Rd
WOOL/PLUM SE18 **115** K4
Park Dr *ACT* W3 **105** H2
CHARL SE7 **114** D4
DAGE RM10 **80** E2
GLDGN NW11 **53** F7
KTN/HRWW/WS HA3 **34** D5
MORT/ESHN SW14 **126** A4
ROM RM1 **63** F3
RYLN/HDSTN HA2 **48** A6
WCHMH N21 **29** J5
Park End *BMLY* BR1 **152** D7
HAMP NW3 **71** J3
Park End Rd *ROM* RM1 **63** G3
Parker Cl *CAN/RD* E16 **95** J7
CAR SM5 **175** K5
Parker Ms *HOL/ALD* WC2B * **11** K4
Parke Rd *BARN* SW13 **106** D7
Parker Rd *CROY/NA* CR0 **177** J3
Parker's Rw *STHWK* SE1 **19** M2
Parker St *CAN/RD* E16 **95** J7
HOL/ALD WC2B **11** K4
Parker Ter *FSTH* SE23 **151** H1
Park Farm Cl *EFNCH* N2 **53** G2
PIN HA5 **47** F4
Park Farm Rd *BMLY* BR1 **153** H7
KUTN/CMB KT2 **144** A6
Parkfield Av *FELT* TW13 **140** E2
MORT/ESHN SW14 **126** B3
NTHLT UB5 **83** H1
RYLN/HDSTN HA2 **48** C1
Parkfield Cl *EDGW* HA8 **36** D5
NTHLT UB5 **83** J1
Parkfield Crs *FELT* TW13 **140** E2
RSLP HA4 **65** J1
RYLN/HDSTN HA2 **48** C1
Parkfield Dr *NTHLT* UB5 **83** H1
Parkfield Gdns
RYLN/HDSTN HA2 **48** B2
Parkfield Pde *FELT* TW13 * **140** E2
Parkfield Rd *CLAP* SW4 **129** J5
FELT TW13 **140** E2
NTHLT UB5 **83** J1
NWCR SE14 **112** C7
RYLN/HDSTN HA2 **66** C2
WLSDN NW10 **69** J6
Parkfields *CROY/NA* CR0 **166** C7
PUT/ROE SW15 **127** F3
Parkfields Av *CDALE/KGS* NW9 **51** F7
RYNPK SW20 **145** K7
Parkfields Cl *CAR* SM5 **176** A3
Parkfields Rd *KUTN/CMB* KT2 **144** B4
Parkfield St *IS* N1 **6** B5
Parkfield Wy *HAYES* BR2 **168** E5
Park Gdns *CDALE/KGS* NW9 **50** D2
ERITH DA8 **118** A3
KUTN/CMB KT2 **144** B4
Parkgate *BKHTH/KID* SE3 **133** J2
Park Ga *EA* W5 **85** K4
EFNCH N2 **53** H2
WCHMH N21 **29** F6
Parkgate Cl *KUTN/CMB* KT2 **144** D5
Park Gate Ct *HPTN* TW12 * **142** C4
Parkgate Gdns
MORT/ESHN SW14 **126** A4
Parkgate Ms *HGT* N6 **54** C6
Parkgate Rd *BTSEA* SW11 **108** D6
WLGTN SM6 **176** A4
Park Gates
RYLN/HDSTN HA2 * **66** A3
Park Gv *BMLY* BR1 **153** F7
BXLYHN DA7 **137** K3
EDGW HA8 **36** B4
FBAR/BDGN N11 **40** D6
SRTFD E15 **76** E7
Park Grove Rd *WAN* E11 **76** C1
Park Hall Rd *DUL* SE21 **149** K1
EFNCH N2 **53** J3
Parkham St *BTSEA* SW11 **108** C7
Park Hl *BMLY* BR1 **168** D3
CAR SM5 **175** K5
CLAP SW4 **129** J4
EA W5 **85** K4
FSTH SE23 **150** D1
RCHPK/HAM TW10 **125** G5
Park Hill Cl *CAR* SM5 **175** J4
Park Hill Ri *CROY/NA* CR0 **178** A1
Park Hill Rd *CROY/NA* CR0 **178** A3
HAYES BR2 **167** H1
WLGTN SM6 **176** B6
Parkhill Rd *BFN/LL* DA15 **154** E2
BXLY DA5 **137** G6
HAMP NW3 **71** K4
Park Hill Wk *HAMP* NW3 **71** K4
Parkholme Rd *HACK* E8 **74** C5
Park House Gdns *TWK* TW1 **124** D4
Parkhouse St *CMBW* SE5 **110** E6
Parkhurst Gdns *BXLY* DA5 **137** H6
Parkhurst Rd *BXLY* DA5 **137** H6
FBAR/BDGN N11 **40** A3
HOLWY N7 **72** E3
MNPK E12 **78** A3
SUT SM1 **175** H3
TOTM N17 **56** C1
WALTH E17 * **57** G3
WDGN N22 **41** F6
Parkland Av *ROM* RM1 **63** G1
Parkland Gv *ISLW* TW7 **104** A7
Parkland Md *BMLY* BR1 **169** F2
Parkland Ms *CHST* BR7 **154** D6
Parkland Rd *WDGN* N22 **55** F1
WFD IG8 **45** F6
Parklands *BRYLDS* KT5 **159** G4
BUSH WD23 * **22** C5
HGT N6 **54** B6
Parklands Cl *GNTH/NBYPK* IG2 **60** C6
MORT/ESHN SW14 **125** K4
Parklands Dr *FNCH* N3 **52** C2
Parklands Pde *HEST* TW5 * **122** C1
Parklands Rd
STRHM/NOR SW16 **148** B4
Parklands Wy *WPK* KT4 **173** G1
Park La *CAR* SM5 **176** A3
CHDH RM6 **61** K5
CHEAM SM3 **174** C5
CROY/NA CR0 **177** K2
EMPK RM11 **63** J6
HCH RM12 **81** K5
HEST TW5 **101** K6
MYFR/PICC W1J **16** B1
OXSTW W1C **9** M6
RCH/KEW TW9 **124** E3
RYLN/HDSTN HA2 **66** B2
SRTFD E15 * **76** A7
STAN HA7 **35** G2
TEDD TW11 **143** F5
TOTM N17 **42** B6
UED N18 **42** B2
WBLY HA9 **68** B3
YEAD UB4 **82** C4
Park Lane Cl *TOTM* N17 **42** C6
Parklea Cl *CDALE/KGS* NW9 **37** G7
Parkleigh Rd *WIM/MER* SW19 **162** A1
Parkleys *RCHPK/HAM* TW10 **143** K3
Parkleys Pde
RCHPK/HAM TW10 * **143** K3
Parklodge Av *WDR/YW* UB7 **100** C1
Park Md *BFN/LL* DA15 **136** B4
Parkmead *PUT/ROE* SW15 **126** E5
Park Md *RYLN/HDSTN* HA2 **66** B2
Parkmead Gdns *MLHL* NW7 **37** H5
Park Ms *CEND/HSY/T* N8 **54** E5
GNWCH SE10 **113** J4
NKENS W10 **88** C1
RAIN RM13 **81** J5
STWL/WRAY TW19 **120** C6
Park Pde *ACT* W3 * **105** H2
HYS/HAR UB3 * **82** C5
WLSDN NW10 **87** H1
Park Piazza *LEW* SE13 **133** G5
Park Pl *ACT* W3 **105** H3
BMLY BR1 * **153** F7
EA W5 **85** K7
HPTN TW12 **142** C5
IS N1 **7** H3
POP/IOD E14 **93** J7
WBLY HA9 **68** B3
WHALL SW1A **10** E9
Park Place Vls *BAY/PAD* W2 **8** F2
Park Ridings *CEND/HSY/T* N8 **55** G2
Park Ri *KTN/HRWW/WS* HA3 **34** E7
Park Rise Rd *FSTH* SE23 **132** B7
Park Rd *ALP/SUD* HA0 **68** A5
BAR EN5 **26** D3
BECK BR3 **151** H6
BMLY BR1 **153** F7
BRYLDS KT5 **159** G5
BUSH WD23 **22** A5
CDALE/KGS NW9 **51** F6
CEND/HSY/T N8 **54** D4
CHEAM SM3 **174** C5
CHST BR7 **154** B5
CHSWK W4 **106** A5
DART DA1 **139** K6
E/WMO/HCT KT8 **157** H3
EBAR EN4 **27** H3
EFNCH N2 **53** H2
ESH/CLAY KT10 **170** B3
FBAR/BDGN N11 **40** D6
FELT TW13 **141** H3
HDN NW4 **51** K5
HNWL W7 **85** F6
HPTN TW12 **142** C4
HSLW TW3 **123** H4
IL IG1 **78** D2
ISLW TW7 **104** C7
KUT/HW KT1 **143** J7
KUTN/CMB KT2 **144** B4
LEY E10 **57** J7
MNPK E12 **59** F7
NWMAL KT3 **160** A3
PLSTW E13 **77** G7
RCHPK/HAM TW10 **125** G5
SNWD SE25 **165** F3
SRTFD E15 **76** E7
STHGT/OAK N14 **28** D6
STJWD NW8 **3** K8
SUN TW16 **141** F6
TEDD TW11 **143** F5
TWK TW1 **124** D5
UED N18 **42** B3
WALTH E17 **57** H4
WIM/MER SW19 **147** H5
WLGTN SM6 **176** B4
WLSDN NW10 * **69** G7
YEAD UB4 **82** C4
Park Rd East *ACT* W3 **105** K1
Park Rd North *ACT* W3 **105** J1
CHSWK W4 **106** A5
Park Rw *GNWCH* SE10 **113** G5
Park Royal Rd *WLSDN* NW10 **86** E2
Parkshot *RCH/KEW* TW9 **124** E3
Park Side *BKHH* IG9 **45** F1
CRICK NW2 **69** J2
HYS/HAR UB3 * **82** C6
Parkside *BECK* BR3 * **166** E1
BKHTH/KID SE3 * **113** J6
CHEAM SM3 **174** C5
FNCH N3 **39** F7
HPTN TW12 **142** D4
MLHL NW7 **37** J5
OXHEY WD19 * **21** G5
SCUP DA14 **155** H1
WIM/MER SW19 **146** B4
Parkside Av *BMLY* BR1 **168** D3
BXLYHN DA7 **138** A1
ROM RM1 **63** F1
WIM/MER SW19 **146** B4
Parkside Cl *PGE/AN* SE20 **150** E6
Parkside Crs *BRYLDS* KT5 **159** K5
HOLWY N7 **73** G2
Parkside Cross *BXLYHN* DA7 **138** B1
Parkside Dr *EDGW* HA8 **36** C2
WAT WD17 **20** C1
Parkside Est *HOM* E9 * **75** F7
Parkside Gdns *EBAR* EN4 **27** K7
WIM/MER SW19 **146** B3
Parkside Pde *DART* DA1 * **138** C1
Parkside Rd *BELV* DA17 **117** J3
HSLW TW3 **123** G4
NTHWD HA6 **32** D4
Parkside St *BTSEA* SW11 **109** F7
Parkside Ter *UED* N18 * **41** K3
Parkside Wy
RYLN/HDSTN HA2 **48** B3
Park Sq East *CAMTN* NW1 **4** C9
Park Square Ms *CAMTN* NW1 **10** C1
Park Sq West *CAMTN* NW1 **4** C9
Parkstead Rd *PUT/ROE* SW15 **126** D4
Park Steps *BAY/PAD* W2 * **9** K6
Parkstone Av *UED* N18 **42** B4
Parkstone Rd *PECK* SE15 * **131** H1
WALTH E17 **58** A2
Park St *CROY/NA* CR0 **177** J2
MYFR/PKLN W1K **10** A7
STHWK SE1 **12** E8
TEDD TW11 **142** E5
Park Ter *CAR* SM5 * **175** J2
WPK KT4 **160** D7
The Park *CAR* SM5 **175** K4
EA W5 **85** K7
GLDGN NW11 **53** F7
HGT N6 **54** A6
SCUP DA14 **155** F4
Parkthorne Cl
RYLN/HDSTN HA2 * **48** B5
Parkthorne Dr
RYLN/HDSTN HA2 **48** A5
Parkthorne Rd *BAL* SW12 **129** J6
Park Vw *ACT* W3 **86** E4
NWMAL KT3 **160** C2
PIN HA5 **33** K7
WBLY HA9 **68** D4
WCHMH N21 **29** F6
Park View Cl *CAR* SM5 **175** K6
Park View Ct
NFNCH/WDSPK N12 * **39** J3
Park View Crs
FBAR/BDGN N11 **40** B3
Parkview Crs *WPK* KT4 **161** F7
Park View Dr *MTCM* CR4 **162** C1
Park View Est *HBRY* N5 * **73** J3
Parkview Gdns *CLAY* IG5 **59** K3
Park View Gdns *HDN* NW4 **52** A4
WDGN N22 * **41** G7
Parkview Ms *RAIN* RM13 **99** K4
Park View Rd *EA* W5 **86** A4
ELTH/MOT SE9 **135** G7
FNCH N3 **39** F7
PIN HA5 **33** F5
STHL UB1 **84** A7
TOTM N17 **56** C2
WELL DA16 **136** D2
CRICK NW2 **69** H3
Parkview Rd *CROY/NA* CR0 **165** H7
Park Village East *CAMTN* NW1 **4** C5
Park Village West
CAMTN NW1 **4** C5
Park Vis *TOOT* SW17 * **147** J4
Parkville Rd *FUL/PGN* SW6 **107** J6
Park Vis *GNWCH* SE10 **113** G5
Park Vista Apartments
CAN/RD E16 **94** D2
Park Wk *WBPTN* SW10 **14** F9
Parkwat Crs *SRTFD* E15 **76** B4
Park Wy *E/WMO/HCT* KT8 **157** G2
EBED/NFELT TW14 **122** A6
EDGW HA8 **36** D7
ENC/FH EN2 **29** G1
GLDGN NW11 **52** C4
RSLP HA4 **46** E7
TRDG/WHET N20 **39** K3
Parkway *CAMTN* NW1 **4** C4
CROY/NA CR0 **180** A7
ERITHM DA18 **117** F2
GDMY/SEVK IG3 **79** F2
GPK RM2 **63** H1
RAIN RM13 **99** J3
RYNPK SW20 **161** G3
STHGT/OAK N14 **40** E1
WFD IG8 **45** G4
The Parkway *HEST* TW5 **101** K5
NTHLT UB5 **83** H2
NWDGN UB2 **102** A2
YEAD UB4 **83** G6
Park West Pl *BAY/PAD* W2 **9** K4
Parkwood *BECK* BR3 **151** J6
Parkwood Av *ESH/CLAY* KT10 **157** H7
Parkwood Ms *HGT* N6 **54** B5
Parkwood Rd *BXLY* DA5 **137** G6
ISLW TW7 **104** A7
WIM/MER SW19 **146** D4
Parliament Ct *WCHPL* E1 * **13** K3
Parliament Hl *HAMP* NW3 **71** J3
Parliament Hill Flds
KTTN NW5 * **72** A2
Parliament Ms
MORT/ESHN SW14 **125** K1
Parliament Sq *WEST* SW1P **17** J2
Parliament St *WHALL* SW1A **17** J1
Parma Crs *BTSEA* SW11 **128** E3
Parmiter St *BETH* E2 **92** D1
Parnell Cl *EDGW* HA8 **36** D3
SHB W12 **106** E2
Parnell Rd *BOW* E3 **75** H7
Parnell Wy
KTN/HRWW/WS HA3 **35** H7
Parnham Cl *BMLY* BR1 **169** G2
Parnham St *POP/IOD* E14 * **93** G5
Parolles Rd *ARCH* N19 **54** C7
Paroma Rd *BELV* DA17 **117** H2
Parr Av *EW* KT17 **173** K7
Parr Cl *ED* N9 **42** D3
Parr Rd *EHAM* E6 **77** H7
STAN HA7 **35** K7
Parrs Cl *SAND/SEL* CR2 **177** K7
Parr's Pl *HPTN* TW12 **142** A6
Parr St *IS* N1 **7** G5
Parry Av *EHAM* E6 **95** K5
Parry Cl *EW* KT17 **173** J6
Parry Pl *WOOL/PLUM* SE18 **115** G3
Parry Rd *NKENS* W10 **88** C2
SNWD SE25 **165** F2
Parry St *VX/NE* SW8 **17** K9
Parsifal Rd *KIL/WHAMP* NW6 **70** E4
Parsloes Av *DAGW* RM9 **80** A4
Parsonage Cl *HYS/HAR* UB3 **82** D5
Parsonage Gdns *ENC/FH* EN2 **29** J1
Parsonage La *ENC/FH* EN2 **29** K1
Parsonage Manorway
BELV DA17 **117** H5
Parsonage St *POP/IOD* E14 **113** F3
Parsons Crs *EDGW* HA8 **36** C2
Parsons Gn *FUL/PGN* SW6 **107** K7
Parsons Green La
FUL/PGN SW6 **107** K7
Parsons Gv *EDGW* HA8 **36** C2
Parsons Md *E/WMO/HCT* KT8 **157** H2
Parson's Md *CROY/NA* CR0 **164** C7
Parsons Rd *PLSTW* E13 **95** G1
Parson St *HDN* NW4 **52** A2
Parthenia Rd *FUL/PGN* SW6 **107** K7
Partingdale La *MLHL* NW7 **38** B4
Partington Cl *ARCH* N19 **54** D7
Partridge Cl *BAR* EN5 **26** A5
BUSH WD23 * **22** C7
CAN/RD E16 **95** H4
STAN HA7 **36** A3
Partridge Gn *ELTH/MOT* SE9 **154** A2
Partridge Rd *HPTN* TW12 **141** K5
SCUP DA14 **154** E2
Partridge Sq *EHAM* E6 **95** J4
Partridge Wy *WDGN* N22 **40** E7
Pasadena Cl *HYS/HAR* UB3 **101** K1
Pascal St *VX/NE* SW8 **109** J6
Pascoe Rd *LEW* SE13 **133** G4
Pasley Cl *WALW* SE17 **18** D8
Pasquier Rd *WALTH* E17 **57** G2
Passey Pl *ELTH/MOT* SE9 **134** E5
Passfield Dr *POP/IOD* E14 **93** K4
Passmore Gdns
FBAR/BDGN N11 **40** D5
Passmore St *BGVA* SW1W **16** A6
Pasteur Cl *CDALE/KGS* NW9 **51** G1
Pasteur Gdns *UED* N18 **41** J4
Paston Cl *WLGTN* SM6 **176** C2
Paston Crs *LEE/GVPK* SE12 **134** A6
Pastor St *LBTH* SE11 **18** D5
Pasture Cl *ALP/SUD* HA0 **67** H2
BUSH WD23 **22** C6
Pasture Rd *ALP/SUD* HA0 **67** H1
CAT SE6 **133** H7
DAGW RM9 **80** B4
Pastures Pth *WAN* E11 **58** C7
The Pastures *OXHEY* WD19 **21** F6
TRDG/WHET N20 **26** D7
Patcham Ter *VX/NE* SW8 **109** G7
Patching Wy *YEAD* UB4 **83** J4
Paternoster Sq *STP* EC4M **12** D5
Pater St *KENS* W8 **14** A4
Pates Manor Dr
EBED/NFELT TW14 **121** G6
Pathfield Rd
STRHM/NOR SW16 **148** D5
The Path *WIM/MER* SW19 **147** F7
The Pathway *OXHEY* WD19 **21** H7
Patience Rd *BTSEA* SW11 **128** D1
Patio Cl *CLAP* SW4 **129** J5
Patmore St *VX/NE* SW8 **109** H7
Patmos Rd *BRXN/ST* SW9 **110** C6
Paton Cl *BOW* E3 **93** J2
Patricia Ct *WELL* DA16 **116** C6
Patricia Vls *TOTM* N17 * **42** D7
Patrick Rd *PLSTW* E13 **95** G2
Patriot Sq *BETH* E2 **92** D1
Patrol Pl *CAT* SE6 **132** E5
Patshull Pl *KTTN* NW5 **72** C5
Patshull Rd *KTTN* NW5 **72** C5
Pattenden Rd *CAT* SE6 **132** C7
Patten Rd *WAND/EARL* SW18 **128** D6
Patterdale Cl *BMLY* BR1 **152** C5
Patterdale Rd *PECK* SE15 **111** K6
Patterson Rd *NRWD* SE19 **150** B5
Pattina Wk *BERM/RHTH* SE16 **93** G7
Pattison Rd *CRICK* NW2 **70** E2
Paul Cl *SRTFD* E15 **76** C6
Paulet Rd *CMBW* SE5 **130** C1
Paulet Wy *WLSDN* NW10 * **69** G6
Paul Gdns *CROY/NA* CR0 **178** B1
Paulhan Rd
KTN/HRWW/WS HA3 **49** K3
Paulin Dr *WCHMH* N21 **29** G6
Pauline Crs *WHTN* TW2 **123** H7
Paul Julius Cl *POP/IOD* E14 **94** B6
Paul Robeson Cl *EHAM* E6 **96** A2
Paul St *SDTCH* EC2A **7** J9
SRTFD E15 **76** C7
Paultons Sq *CHEL* SW3 **15** H9
Paultons St *CHEL* SW3 **108** C5
Pauntley St *ARCH* N19 **54** C7
Paveley Dr *BTSEA* SW11 **108** D6
Paveley St *STJWD* NW8 **3** K8
Pavement Sq *CROY/NA* CR0 **165** H7
The Pavement *CLAP* SW4 **129** H3
EA W5 * **105** F2
TEDD TW11 * **143** H6
WAN E11 * **58** A7
WIM/MER SW19 * **146** D5
WNWD SE27 * **149** J3
Pavet Cl *DAGE* RM10 **80** D5
Pavilion Ldg
RYLN/HDSTN HA2 * **48** D7
Pavilion Ms *FNCH* N3 **52** E1
Pavilion Pde *SHB* W12 * **88** A5
Pavilion Rd *IL* IG1 **59** K6
KTBR SW1X **15** M2
Pavilion St *KTBR* SW1X **15** M4
The Pavilion *VX/NE* SW8 * **109** J6
Pavilion Wy *EDGW* HA8 **36** E6
RSLP HA4 **65** G1
Pavillion Sq *TOOT* SW17 **147** J2
Pavillion Ter *SHB* W12 * **88** A5
Pawleyne Cl *PGE/AN* SE20 **150** E6
Pawsey Cl *PLSTW* E13 **76** E7
Pawson's Rd *THHTH* CR7 **164** D5
Paxford Rd *ALP/SUD* HA0 **67** H1
Paxton Cl *RCH/KEW* TW9 **125** G1
WOT/HER KT12 **156** B6
Paxton Pl *WNWD* SE27 **150** A3
Paxton Rd *BMLY* BR1 **152** E6
CHSWK W4 **106** B5
FSTH SE23 **151** G2
TOTM N17 **42** B6
Paxton Ter *PIM* SW1V **16** D9
Payne Cl *BARK* IG11 **78** E6
Paynell Ct *BKHTH/KID* SE3 **133** H2
Payne Rd *BOW* E3 **93** K1
Paynesfield Av
MORT/ESHN SW14 **126** A2
Paynesfield Rd *BUSH* WD23 **23** F6
Payne St *DEPT* SE8 **112** C5
Paynes Wk *HMSMTH* W6 **107** H5
Payzes Gdns *WFD* IG8 * **44** D5
Peabody Av *PIM* SW1V **16** C7
Peabody Cl *CROY/NA* CR0 **165** K7
GNWCH SE10 * **112** E7
PIM SW1V **16** D8
Peabody Cots *HNHL* SE24 * **130** D6
Peabody Est *BTSEA* SW11 * **128** D3
CLKNW EC1R * **12** B1
CMBW SE5 * **110** E7
HMSMTH W6 * **107** F4
HNHL SE24 **130** C6
NKENS W10 * **88** A4
STHWK SE1 * **12** B8
STLK EC1Y * **12** F1
TOTM N17 * **42** A7
Peabody Hl *DUL* SE21 **130** C7
Peabody Sq *IS* N1 * **6** E3
Peabody Ter *CLKNW* EC1R * **12** B1
Peace Cl *GFD/PVL* UB6 **66** D7
SNWD SE25 **165** F3

STHGT/OAK N14 28 B4
Peace Dr WAT WD17 20 E2
Peace Gv WBLY HA9 68 D2
Peace St WOOL/PLUM SE18 115 F5
Peaches Cl BELMT SM2 174 C6
Peach Gv WAN E11 76 B2
Peach Rd FELT TW13 121 K7
NKENS W10 88 B2
Peachum Rd BKHTH/KID SE3 113 J5
Peachy Cl EDGW HA8 36 C5
Peacock Av
EBED/NFELT TW14 121 G7
Peacock Cl BCTR RM8 61 J7
CHING E4 43 H6
MLHL NW7 38 C4
Peacock St WALW SE17 18 D6
Peacock Yd WALW SE17 18 D6
Peaketon Av REDBR IG4 59 H4
Peak Hl SYD SE26 150 E3
Peak Hill Av SYD SE26 150 E3
Peak Hill Gdns SYD SE26 * 150 E3
The Peak SYD SE26 150 E2
Peal Gdns WEA W13 85 G2
Peall Rd CROY/NA CR0 164 A5
Pearce Cl MTCM CR4 163 F1
Pearcefield Av FSTH SE23 131 K7
Pear Cl CDALE/KGS NW9 51 F3
NWCR SE14 112 B6
Pearcroft Rd WAN E11 76 B1
Peardon St VX/NE SW8 129 G2
Peareswood Gdns STAN HA7 35 K7
Peareswood Rd ERITH DA8 118 C7
Pearfield Rd FSTH SE23 151 G2
Pearing Cl WPK KT4 174 B1
Pearl Cl CRICK NW2 52 B6
EHAM E6 96 A5
Pearl Rd WALTH E17 57 J2
Pearl St WAP E1W 92 D7
Pearman St STHWK SE1 18 B3
Pear Pl STHWK SE1 18 A1
Pear Rd WAN E11 76 B2
Pearscroft Ct FUL/PGN SW6 108 A7
Pearscroft Rd FUL/PGN SW6 128 A1
Pearse St PECK SE15 111 F5
Pearson Cl BAR EN5 27 F2
Pearson's NWCR SE14 112 D7
Pearson's Rd NWCR SE14 * 112 D7
Pearson St BETH E2 7 L5
Pearson Wy MTCM CR4 148 A7
Pears Rd HSLW TW3 123 H2
Peartree Av TOOT SW17 147 K5
Pear Tree Cl CHSGTN KT9 172 C4
ERITH DA8 118 A7
MTCM CR4 162 D1
Peartree Cl HAYES BR2 168 C4
Pear Tree Ct CLKNW EC1R 12 B1
Peartree Gdns BCTR RM8 79 H4
ROMW/RG RM7 62 D1
Peartree La WAP E1W * 92 E6
Pear Tree Rd ASHF TW15 140 A4
Peartree Rd EN EN1 30 A2
Pear Tree St FSBYE EC1V 6 D9
Peartree Wy GNWCH SE10 113 K3
Pearwood Cots STAN HA7 * 35 J1
Peary Pl BETH E2 92 E2
Pease Cl HCH RM12 81 K6
Peasmead Ter CHING E4 * 44 A3
Peatfield Cl BFN/LL DA15 154 E2
Pebworth Rd HRW HA1 67 G1
Peckarmans Wd SYD SE26 150 C2
Peckett Sq HBRY N5 * 73 J3
Peckford Pl BRXN/ST SW9 130 B1
Peckham Gv PECK SE15 111 F6
Peckham High St PECK SE15 111 H7
Peckham Hill St PECK SE15 111 H6
Peckham Park Rd PECK SE15 111 H6
Peckham Rd CMBW SE5 111 F7
Peckham Rye EDUL SE22 131 H3
Pecks Yd WCHPL E1 * 13 L2
Peckwater St KTTN NW5 72 C4
Pedlars Wk HOLWY N7 * 72 E5
Pedley Rd BCTR RM8 61 J7
Pedley St WCHPL E1 92 C3
Pedro St CLPT E5 75 F2
Peek Crs WIM/MER SW19 146 B4
Peel Cl CHING E4 43 K1
ED N9 42 C2
Peel Dr CDALE/KGS NW9 51 H2
CLAY IG5 59 J2
Peel Gv BETH E2 92 E1
Peel Pas KENS W8 * 8 A9
Peel Pl CLAY IG5 59 J1
Peel Prec KIL/WHAMP NW6 88 D1
Peel Rd ALP/SUD HA0 67 J2
KTN/HRWW/WS HA3 49 F2
SWFD E18 44 D7
Peel St KENS W8 8 A9
Peerglow Est PEND EN3 * 30 E4
Peerless St FSBYE EC1V 7 G8
Pegamoid Rd UED N18 42 E2
Pegasus Cl STNW/STAM N16 * 73 K3
Pegasus Ct BTFD TW8 105 G4
Pegasus Pl FUL/PGN SW6 * 107 K7
LBTH SE11 18 A9
Pegasus Rd CROY/NA CR0 177 G5
Pegasus Wy FBAR/BDGN N11 40 B5
Pegg Rd HEST TW5 102 C6
Pegley Gdns LEE/GVPK SE12 152 E1
Pegwell St WOOL/PLUM SE18 115 K6
Pekin St POP/IOD E14 93 J5
Peldon Wk IS N1 * 6 D3
Pelham Av BARK IG11 79 F7
Pelham Cl CMBW SE5 131 F2
Pelham Cots BXLY DA5 * 137 J7
Pelham Crs SKENS SW7 15 J6
Pelham Pl SKENS SW7 15 J5
Pelham Rd BXLYHN DA7 137 H2
IL IG1 78 D1
PGE/AN SE20 165 K1
SEVS/STOTM N15 56 B3
SWFD E18 59 F2
WDGN N22 55 G1
WIM/MER SW19 146 E6
Pelhams Cl ESH/CLAY KT10 170 A4
Pelham St SKENS SW7 15 H5
Pelhams Wk ESH/CLAY KT10 170 A2
Pelier St WALW SE17 18 F9
Pelinore Rd CAT SE6 152 C1
Pellant Rd FUL/PGN SW6 107 H6
Pellatt Gv WDGN N22 41 G7
Pellatt Rd EDUL SE22 131 G4
WBLY HA9 68 A1
Pellerin Rd STNW/STAM N16 74 A4
Pellings Cl HAYES BR2 167 H2
Pelling St POP/IOD E14 93 H5
Pellipar Cl PLMGR N13 41 G2
Pellipar Rd WOOL/PLUM SE18 114 E4
Pellow Cl BAR EN5 26 D5
Pelly Rd PLSTW E13 94 E1
SRTFD E15 76 E7
Pelter St BETH E2 7 L7
Pelton Rd GNWCH SE10 113 H4
Pembar Av WALTH E17 * 57 G2
Pemberley Cha
HOR/WEW KT19 172 D4
Pemberley Cl HOR/WEW KT19 172 D4
Pember Rd WLSDN NW10 88 B2
Pemberton Av GPK RM2 63 K2
Pemberton Cl
STWL/WRAY TW19 120 B7
Pemberton Gdns ARCH N19 72 C2
CHDH RM6 62 A4
Pemberton Pl ESH/CLAY KT10 170 C2
HACK E8 74 D6
Pemberton Rd
E/WMO/HCT KT8 157 H3
FSBYPK N4 55 H4
Pemberton Rw
FLST/FETLN EC4A 12 B4
Pemberton Ter ARCH N19 72 C2
Pembridge Av WHTN TW2 122 E7
Pembridge Crs NTGHL W11 88 D6
Pembridge Gdns BAY/PAD W2 8 A7
Pembridge Ms NTGHL W11 8 A6
Pembridge Pl NTGHL W11 8 B6
Pembridge Rd NTGHL W11 8 A7
Pembridge Sq BAY/PAD W2 8 A7
Pembridge Vls BAY/PAD W2 8 A6
Pembroke Av BRYLDS KT5 159 J4
IS N1 5 K3
KTN/HRWW/WS HA3 49 G2
PIN HA5 47 H7
Pembroke Cl ERITH DA8 117 K3
KTBR SW1X 16 B2
Pembroke Gdns DAGE RM10 80 D2
KENS W8 107 J2
Pembroke Gardens Cl
KENS W8 107 J2
Pembroke Ldg STAN HA7 * 35 J5
Pembroke Ms KENS W8 * 14 A4
MUSWH N10 40 A7
Pembroke Pde ERITH DA8 * 117 K4
Pembroke Pl EDGW HA8 36 C6
ISLW TW7 123 K1
KENS W8 * 14 A4
Pembroke Rd BMLY BR1 168 B1
CEND/HSY/T N8 54 E3
EHAM E6 95 K4
ERITH DA8 117 K4
GDMY/SEVK IG3 61 F7
GFD/PVL UB6 84 B3
MTCM CR4 163 F1
MUSWH N10 40 A7
NTHWD HA6 32 A2
PLMGR N13 41 J2
RSLP HA4 46 C7
SEVS/STOTM N15 56 B4
SNWD SE25 165 F3
WALTH E17 57 K4
WBLY HA9 67 K2
Pembroke Sq KENS W8 14 A4
Pembroke St IS N1 5 K2
Pembroke Ter STJWD NW8 * 3 G4
Pembroke Vls KENS W8 14 A4
Pembroke Wk KENS W8 14 A5
Pembrook Ms BTSEA SW11 * 128 C3
Pembry Cl BRXN/ST SW9 110 B7
Pembury Av WPK KT4 160 D6
Pembury Cl CLPT E5 * 74 D4
HAYES BR2 167 J6
Pembury Ct HYS/HAR UB3 101 G5
Pembury Rd BXLYHN DA7 117 F6
CLPT E5 74 D4
SNWD SE25 165 H3
TOTM N17 42 B7
Pemdevon Rd CROY/NA CR0 164 B6
Pemell Cl WCHPL E1 92 E3
Pemerich Cl HYS/HAR UB3 * 101 J4
Pempath Pl WBLY HA9 67 K1
Penally Pl IS N1 7 H3
Penang St WAP E1W 92 D7
Penard Rd NWDGN UB2 103 F2
Penarth St PECK SE15 111 K5
Penates ESH/CLAY KT10 170 D3
Penberth Rd CAT SE6 133 F7
Penbury Rd NWDGN UB2 102 E4
Pencombe Ms NTGHL W11 88 D6
Pencraig Wy PECK SE15 111 J5
Pencroft Dr DART DA1 139 F6
Pendall Cl EBAR EN4 27 J3
Penda Rd ERITH DA8 117 J6
Pendarves Rd RYNPK SW20 146 A7
Penda's Md HOM E9 75 G3
Pendell Av HYS/HAR UB3 101 J6
Pendennis Rd
STRHM/NOR SW16 148 E3
TOTM N17 55 K2
Penderel Rd HSLW TW3 123 F4
Penderry Ri CAT SE6 152 B1
Penderyn Wy HOLWY N7 72 D3
Pendlebury House
CHARL SE7 * 114 D6
Pendle Rd STRHM/NOR SW16 148 B5
Pendlestone Rd WALTH E17 57 K4
Pendlewood Cl EA W5 85 J4
Pendolino Wy ALP/SUD HA0 68 C6
Pendragon Rd BMLY BR1 152 E2
Pendrell Rd NWCR SE14 132 B2
Pendrell St WOOL/PLUM SE18 115 J5
Pendula Dr YEAD UB4 83 H3
Pendulum Ms HACK E8 * 74 B4
Penerley Rd CAT SE6 132 E7
RAIN RM13 99 K4
Penfold Cl CROY/NA CR0 177 G2
Penfold La BXLY DA5 136 E7
Penfold Pl BAY/PAD W2 9 J2
Penfold Rd ED N9 31 F7
Penfold St STJWD NW8 9 H1
Penford Gdns ELTH/MOT SE9 134 C3
Penford St CMBW SE5 130 C1
Pengarth Rd BXLY DA5 136 E4
Penge La PGE/AN SE20 150 E6
Penge Rd PLSTW E13 77 G6
SNWD SE25 165 H2
Penhall Rd CHARL SE7 114 C3
Penhill Rd BXLY DA5 136 D6
Penifather La GFD/PVL UB6 84 D2
Peninsular Cl
EBED/NFELT TW14 121 G5
Peninsular Park Rd
CHARL SE7 113 K4
Penistone Rd
STRHM/NOR SW16 148 E6
Penketh Dr HRW HA1 66 D2
Penmon Rd ABYW SE2 116 B2
Pennack Rd PECK SE15 111 G5
Pennant Ms KENS W8 14 C5
Pennant Ter WALTH E17 57 H1
Pennard Rd SHB W12 107 F1
The Pennards SUN TW16 156 B2
Penn Cl GFD/PVL UB6 84 B1
KTN/HRWW/WS HA3 49 J3
Penner Cl WIM/MER SW19 146 C1
Penners Gdns SURB KT6 159 F6
Pennethorne Cl HOM E9 74 E7
Pennethorne Rd PECK SE15 111 J6
Penney Cl DART DA1 139 G6
Penn Gdns CHST BR7 169 G1
Pennine Dr CRICK NW2 70 B1
Pennine La CRICK NW2 70 C1
Pennine Pde CRICK NW2 * 70 C1
Pennine Wy BXLYHN DA7 118 B7
HYS/HAR UB3 101 G6
Pennington Dr WCHMH N21 28 E4
Pennington St WAP E1W 92 D6
Pennington Wy
LEE/GVPK SE12 153 F1
Penniston Cl TOTM N17 55 J1
Penniwell Cl EDGW HA8 36 B3
Penn La BXLY DA5 136 E5
Penn Rd HOLWY N7 72 E4
Penn St IS N1 7 H4
Penny Cl RAIN RM13 99 K2
Pennycroft CROY/NA CR0 179 G7
Pennyfields POP/IOD E14 93 J6
Pennymead Pl ESH/CLAY KT10 170 A5
Penny Ms WAND/EARL SW18 127 K4
Pennymoor Wk MV/WKIL W9 88 D3
Penny Rd WLSDN NW10 86 D2
Pennyroyal Av EHAM E6 96 A5
Penpoll Rd HACK E8 74 D5
Penpool La WELL DA16 136 C2
Penrhyn Av WALTH E17 43 J7
Penrhyn Crs
MORT/ESHN SW14 125 K3
WALTH E17 43 J7
Penrhyn Gdns KUT/HW KT1 158 E3
Penrhyn Gv WALTH E17 43 J7
Penrhyn Rd KUT/HW KT1 159 F2
Penrith Cl BECK BR3 151 K7
PUT/ROE SW15 127 H4
Penrith Crs HCH RM12 81 J4
Penrith Pl WNWD SE27 149 H1
Penrith Rd NWMAL KT3 160 A3
SEVS/STOTM N15 55 K4
THHTH CR7 164 D1
Penrith St STRHM/NOR SW16 148 C5
Penrose Av OXHEY WD19 33 J1
Penrose Gv WALW SE17 18 E8
Penrose St WALW SE17 18 E8
Penryn St CAMTN NW1 5 G5
Penry St STHWK SE1 19 K6
Pensbury Pl VX/NE SW8 129 H1
Pensbury St VX/NE SW8 129 H1
Penscroft Gdns BORE WD6 25 F3
Pensford Av RCH/KEW TW9 125 H1
Penshurst Av BFN/LL DA15 136 B5
Penshurst Gdns EDGW HA8 36 D4
Penshurst Gn HAYES BR2 167 J4
Penshurst Rd BXLYHN DA7 117 G7
HOM E9 75 F6
THHTH CR7 164 C4
TOTM N17 42 B6
Penshurst Wy BELMT SM2 174 E6
Pensilver Cl EBAR EN4 * 27 J3
Penstemon Cl FNCH N3 38 E5
Penta Ct BORE WD6 * 24 C3
Pentelow Gdns
EBED/NFELT TW14 121 K5
Pentire Rd WALTH E17 44 B7
Pentland Av EDGW HA8 36 D1
Pentland Cl ED N9 42 E1
GLDGN NW11 70 C1
Pentland Pl NTHLT UB5 65 J7
Pentland Rd BUSH WD23 22 C5
KIL/WHAMP NW6 2 A7
Pentlands Cl MTCM CR4 163 G2
Pentland St WAND/EARL SW18 128 B5
Pentland Wy HGDN/ICK UB10 64 A2
Pentlow St PUT/ROE SW15 127 F1
Pentney Rd BAL SW12 129 H7
RYNPK SW20 146 C7
Penton Gv IS N1 6 A6
Penton Pl WALW SE17 18 D6
Penton Ri FSBYW WC1X 5 M7
Penton St IS N1 6 A5
Pentonville Rd IS N1 5 L6
Pentridge St PECK SE15 111 G6
Pentyre Av UED N18 41 K4
Penwerris Av ISLW TW7 103 H6
Penwith Rd WAND/EARL SW18 147 F1
Penwortham Rd
STRHM/NOR SW16 148 B5
Penylan Pl EDGW HA8 * 36 C7
Penywern Rd ECT SW5 14 B7
Penzance Pl NTGHL W11 88 C7
Penzance St NTGHL W11 88 C7
Peony Gdns SHB W12 87 J6
Pepler Ms CMBW SE5 19 L8
Peploe Rd KIL/WHAMP NW6 88 B1
Pepper Cl EHAM E6 95 K4
Peppercorn Cl THHTH CR7 164 E1
Peppermead Sq LEW SE13 132 D4
Peppermint Cl CROY/NA CR0 163 K6
Peppermint Pl WAN E11 76 C2
Pepper St POP/IOD E14 112 E2
STHWK SE1 18 E1
Peppie Cl STNW/STAM N16 74 A1
Pepys Crs BAR EN5 26 A4
CAN/RD E16 94 E7
Pepys Est DEPT SE8 112 B3
Pepys Park Est DEPT SE8 112 C3
Pepys Rd NWCR SE14 132 A1
RYNPK SW20 161 F1
Pepys St TWRH EC3N 13 K6
Perceval Av HAMP NW3 71 J4
Percheron Rd BORE WD6 25 F5
Perch St HACK E8 74 B3
Percival Ct TOTM N17 42 B6
Percival Gdns CHDH RM6 61 J5
Percival Rd EN EN1 30 B3
FELT TW13 140 D1
MORT/ESHN SW14 125 K4
Percival St FSBYE EC1V 6 C9
Percival Wy HOR/WEW KT19 172 E3
Percy Bryant Rd SUN TW16 140 C6
Percy Bush Rd WDR/YW UB7 100 C2
Percy Gdns PEND EN3 31 F4
WPK KT4 160 A7
YEAD UB4 82 C2
Percy Ms FITZ W1T 11 G3
Percy Rd BXLYHN DA7 137 F1
CAN/RD E16 94 C4
GDMY/SEVK IG3 61 G6
HPTN TW12 142 A6
ISLW TW7 124 B3
MTCM CR4 163 F6
NFNCH/WDSPK N12 39 G4
PGE/AN SE20 151 F7
ROMW/RG RM7 62 E2
SHB W12 106 D1
SNWD SE25 165 G4
WAN E11 58 C6
WATW WD18 21 F3
WCHMH N21 29 J6
WHTN TW2 123 G7
Percy St FITZ W1T 11 G3
Percy Ter BMLY BR1 169 G2
Percy Wy WHTN TW2 123 H7
Peregrine Cl WLSDN NW10 69 F4
Peregrine Ct WELL DA16 116 A7
Peregrine Gdns CROY/NA CR0 179 G1
Peregrine Rd TOTM N17 41 J6
Peregrine Wy
WIM/MER SW19 146 A6
Perendale Dr SHPTN TW17 140 A7
Perham Rd WKENS W14 107 H4
Peridot St EHAM E6 95 J4
Perifield DUL SE21 130 D7
Perimeade Rd GFD/PVL UB6 85 J1
Periton Rd ELTH/MOT SE9 134 C3
Perivale Gdns WEA W13 85 H3
Perivale La GFD/PVL UB6 85 G2
Perivale Village
GFD/PVL UB6 * 85 J2
Periwood Crs GFD/PVL UB6 67 G7
Perkin Cl ALP/SUD HA0 67 H4
HSLW TW3 123 G3
Perkin's Rents WEST SW1P 17 G3
Perkins Rd BARK/HLT IG6 60 D4
Perkins Sq STHWK SE1 12 F8
Perks Cl BKHTH/KID SE3 133 H1
Perpins Rd ELTH/MOT SE9 135 K5
Perran Rd BRXS/STRHM SW2 149 H1
Perrers Rd HMSMTH W6 106 E2
Perrin Rd ALP/SUD HA0 67 G3
Perrin's Ct HAMP NW3 * 71 G3
Perrin's Wk HAMP NW3 71 G3
Perry Av ACT W3 87 F5
Perry Cl GNTH/NBYPK IG2 60 D5
RAIN RM13 99 F1
Perry Ct SEVS/STOTM N15 * 56 A5
Perryfield Wy
CDALE/KGS NW9 51 H5
RCHPK/HAM TW10 143 H1
Perry Gdns ED N9 42 A2
Perry Garth NTHLT UB5 65 G7
Perry Gv DART DA1 139 K3
Perry Hl CAT SE6 151 H1
Perry How WPK KT4 160 C7
Perry Mnr CHST BR7 154 E5
Perrymans Farm Rd
GNTH/NBYPK IG2 60 D5
Perry Md BUSH WD23 22 C5
ENC/FH EN2 29 H1
Perrymead St FUL/PGN SW6 107 K7
Perryn Rd ACT W3 87 F6
BERM/RHTH SE16 111 J2
Perry Ri FSTH SE23 151 G2
Perry Rd DAGW RM9 98 B4
Perry St CHST BR7 154 E5
DART DA1 138 B2
Perry V FSTH SE23 150 E1
Persant Rd CAT SE6 152 C2
Perseverance Pl
BRXN/ST SW9 110 B6
Pershore Cl GNTH/NBYPK IG2 60 B4
Pershore Gv CAR SM5 162 C5
Pert Cl MUSWH N10 40 B6
Perth Av CDALE/KGS NW9 51 F6
YEAD UB4 83 G3
Perth Cl NTHLT UB5 66 A5
NWMAL KT3 160 C1
Perth Rd BARK IG11 96 D1
BECK BR3 167 F1
FSBYPK N4 55 G7
GNTH/NBYPK IG2 60 B5
IL IG1 60 C6
LEY E10 57 G7
PLSTW E13 95 F1
WDGN N22 41 H7
Perth Ter GNTH/NBYPK IG2 60 C6
Perwell Av RYLN/HDSTN HA2 47 K7
Petavel Rd TEDD TW11 142 E5
Peter Av WLSDN NW10 69 K6
Peterboat Cl GNWCH SE10 113 H3
Peterborough Ms
FUL/PGN SW6 127 K1
Peterborough Rd CAR SM5 162 D5
FUL/PGN SW6 127 K1
HRW HA1 48 E7
LEY E10 58 A4
Peterborough Vls
FUL/PGN SW6 108 A7
Petergate BTSEA SW11 128 B3
Peters Cl BCTR RM8 61 K7
STAN HA7 35 K5
WELL DA16 135 K1
Petersfield Cl UED N18 41 J4
Petersfield Ri PUT/ROE SW15 126 E7
Petersfield Rd ACT W3 105 K1
Petersham Cl
RCHPK/HAM TW10 143 K1
SUT SM1 174 D4
Petersham La SKENS SW7 14 E3
Petersham Ms SKENS SW7 14 E4
Petersham Pl SKENS SW7 14 E4
Petersham Rd
RCHPK/HAM TW10 143 K2
Petersham Ter
CROY/NA CR0 * 176 E2
Peter's Hl BLKFR EC4V 12 E6
Peterstone Rd ABYW SE2 116 C1
Peterstow Cl WIM/MER SW19 146 C1
Peter St SOHO/CST W1F 11 G6
Peterwood Wy CROY/NA CR0 177 F1
Petherton Rd HBRY N5 73 J4
Petiver Cl HOM E9 * 74 E6
Petley Rd HMSMTH W6 107 F5
Peto Pl CAMTN NW1 4 D9
Peto St North CAN/RD E16 94 D5
Petrie Cl CRICK NW2 * 70 C5
Petros Gdns
KIL/WHAMP NW6 * 71 F4
Petro St South CAN/RD E16 94 D6
Pettacre Cl THMD SE28 115 H2
Pett Cl EMPK RM11 81 K1
Petticoat La WCHPL E1 13 K3
Petticoat Sq WCHPL E1 13 L4
Petticoat Tower WCHPL E1 * 13 L4
Pettits Bvd ROM RM1 63 G1
Pettits Cl ROM RM1 63 G1
Pettits La ROM RM1 63 G1
Pettit's Pl DAGE RM10 80 C4
Pettit's Rd DAGE RM10 80 C4
Pettiward Cl PUT/ROE SW15 127 F3
Pettley Gdns ROMW/RG RM7 63 F4
Pettman Crs THMD SE28 115 J2
Pettsgrove Av ALP/SUD HA0 67 J4
Pett's Hl NTHLT UB5 66 B4
RYLN/HDSTN HA2 66 B3
Pett St WOOL/PLUM SE18 114 D3
Petts Wood Rd
STMC/STPC BR5 169 J4
Petty France WESTW SW1E 16 F3
Petty Wales MON EC3R 13 K7
Petworth Cl NTHLT UB5 65 K6
Petworth Gdns
HGDN/ICK UB10 64 A7
RYNPK SW20 160 E2
Petworth Rd BXLYHS DA6 137 H4
NFNCH/WDSPK N12 39 J4
Petworth St BTSEA SW11 108 D7
Petworth Wy HCH RM12 81 H3
Petyt Pl CHEL SW3 * 108 D5
Petyward CHEL SW3 15 K6
Pevensey Av EN EN1 30 A1
FBAR/BDGN N11 40 D4
Pevensey Cl ISLW TW7 103 H6
Pevensey Rd FELT TW13 122 D7
FSTGT E7 76 E3
TOOT SW17 147 H3
Peverel EHAM E6 96 A5
Peveret Cl FBAR/BDGN N11 * 40 B4
Peveril Dr TEDD TW11 142 D4
Pewsey Cl CHING E4 43 J4
Peyton Pl GNWCH SE10 113 F6
Pharaoh Cl MTCM CR4 162 E6
Pheasant Cl CAN/RD E16 95 F5
Phelp St WALW SE17 19 G8
Phelps Wy HYS/HAR UB3 101 J3
Phene St CHEL SW3 15 K9
Philbeach Gdns ECT SW5 14 A7
Philchurch Pl WCHPL E1 92 C5
Philimore Cl
WOOL/PLUM SE18 115 K4
Philip Av ROMW/RG RM7 63 F7
Philip Gdns CROY/NA CR0 179 H1
Philip La SEVS/STOTM N15 55 K3
Philippa Gdns ELTH/MOT SE9 134 C4
Philip Rd RAIN RM13 99 G2
Philips Cl CAR SM5 163 F7
Philip St PLSTW E13 94 E3
Philip Wk PECK SE15 131 H2
Phillimore Gdns KENS W8 14 A2
WLSDN NW10 70 A7
Phillimore Gardens Cl
KENS W8 * 14 A3
Phillimore Pl KENS W8 14 A2
Phillimore Wk KENS W8 14 A3
Phillipp St IS N1 7 K4
Phillips Cl DART DA1 138 E5
Philpot La FENCHST EC3M 13 J6
Philpot St WCHPL E1 * 92 D5
Phineas Pett Rd
ELTH/MOT SE9 134 D2
Phipp's Bridge Rd
WIM/MER SW19 162 B1
Phipps Ms BGVA SW1W 16 C4
Phipp St SDTCH EC2A 7 J9
Phoebeth Rd LEW SE13 132 D4
Phoenix Cl HACK E8 * 7 L3
NTHWD HA6 32 D3
WALTH E17 57 H1
WWKM BR4 180 B1
Phoenix Ct BTFD TW8 105 F4
POP/IOD E14 112 D3
Phoenix Dr HAYES BR2 181 H2
Phoenix Pk BTFD TW8 * 104 E4
Phoenix Pl DART DA1 139 G6
FSBYW WC1X 5 M9
Phoenix Rd CAMTN NW1 5 G7
PGE/AN SE20 150 E5
Phoenix St LSQ/SEVD WC2H 11 H5
Phoenix Wy HEST TW5 102 C5
Phoenix Wharf Rd
STHWK SE1 19 M2
Phyllis Av NWMAL KT3 160 E4
Picardy Manorway
BELV DA17 117 J2
Picardy Rd BELV DA17 117 H4
Picardy St BELV DA17 117 H2
Piccadilly MYFR/PICC W1J 10 E8
Piccadilly Ar STJS SW1Y 10 E8
Piccadilly Circ REGST W1B 10 F7
Pickard Cl STHGT/OAK N14 28 D7
Pickard St FSBYE EC1V 6 D7
Pickering Av EHAM E6 96 A1
Pickering Gdns CROY/NA CR0 165 G5
FBAR/BDGN N11 40 A5
Pickering Ms BAY/PAD W2 8 D4
Pickering Pl WHALL SW1A * 10 F9
Pickering St IS N1 6 D3
Pickets Cl BUSH WD23 22 D7
Pickets St BAL SW12 129 F6
Pickett Cft STAN HA7 35 K7
Pickett's Lock La ED N9 42 E1
Pickford Cl BXLYHN DA7 137 F1
Pickford La BXLYHN DA7 137 F1
Pickford Rd BXLYHN DA7 137 F2
Pickfords Whf IS N1 * 6 E6
Pickhurst Gn HAYES BR2 167 J6
Pickhurst La WWKM BR4 167 H5
Pickhurst Md HAYES BR2 167 J6
Pickhurst Pk HAYES BR2 167 H4
Pickhurst Ri WWKM BR4 167 G7
Pickwick Cl HSLWW TW4 122 D4
Pickwick Ms UED N18 42 A4
Pickwick Pl HRW HA1 48 E6
Pickwick Rd DUL SE21 130 E6
Pickwick St STHWK SE1 18 E2
Pickwick Wy CHST BR7 154 C5
Pickworth Cl VX/NE SW8 * 109 K6
Picton Pl MHST W1U 10 B5
SURB KT6 159 H7
Picton St CMBW SE5 110 E6
Pied Bull Yd IS N1 * 6 C4
Piedmont Rd
WOOL/PLUM SE18 115 J4
Pier Head WAP E1W * 92 D7
Piermont Pl BMLY BR1 168 C1
Piermont Rd EDUL SE22 131 J4
Pierrepoint Ar IS N1 * 6 C5
Pierrepoint Rd ACT W3 86 D6
Pierrepoint Rw IS N1 6 C5
Pier Rd CAN/RD E16 114 E1
EBED/NFELT TW14 122 A4
ERITH DA8 118 B5
Pier St POP/IOD E14 113 F3
Pier Ter WAND/EARL SW18 128 A3
Pier Wy THMD SE28 115 J2
Pigeon La HPTN TW12 142 A3
Pigott St POP/IOD E14 93 J5
Pike Cl BMLY BR1 153 F4
Pike Rd MLHL NW7 37 F3
Pike's End PIN HA5 47 F3
Pikestone Cl YEAD UB4 * 83 J3
Pilgrimage St STHWK SE1 19 G2
Pilgrim Cl MRDN SM4 162 A6
Pilgrim Hl WNWD SE27 149 J3
Pilgrims Cl NTHLT UB5 66 C4
PLMGR N13 41 F3
Pilgrims Ct DART DA1 139 K4
Pilgrim's La HAMP NW3 71 H3
Pilgrims Ms POP/IOD E14 94 B6
Pilgrim's Ri EBAR EN4 27 J4
Pilgrim St BLKFR EC4V * 12 C5
Pilgrims Wy ARCH N19 54 D7
SAND/SEL CR2 * 178 B4
WBLY HA9 50 D7
Pilgrim's Wy SAND/SEL CR2 178 B5
Pilkington Rd PECK SE15 131 J1
Pilot Cl DEPT SE8 112 C5
Pilsden Cl WIM/MER SW19 * 127 G7
Piltdown Rd OXHEY WD19 33 H3

Pilton Pl WALW SE17 18 F7
Pimlico Rd BGVA SW1W 16 A7
Pinchin & Johnsons Yd
WCHPL E1 * 92 C6
Pinchin St WCHPL E1 92 C6
Pincott Pl BROCKY SE4 132 A2
Pincott Rd BXLYHS DA6 137 H4
WIM/MER SW19 147 G6
Pindar St SDTCH EC2A 13 J2
Pindock Ms MV/WKIL W9 8 D1
Pine Apple Ct WESTW SW1E * 16 E3
Pine Av SRTFD E15 76 B4
WWKM BR4 166 E7
Pine Cl LEY E10 75 J1
PGE/AN SE20 150 E7
STAN HA7 35 H3
STHGT/OAK N14 28 C6
Pine Coombe CROY/NA CR0 179 F3
Pinecroft
KTN/HRWW/WS HA3 50 B4
WOOL/PLUM SE18 116 B6
Pinecroft Crs BAR EN5 26 C3
Pinefield Cl POP/IOD E14 * 93 J6
Pine Gdns BRYLDS KT5 159 H5
RSLP HA4 47 F7
Pine Gld ORP BR6 181 K3
Pine Gv BUSH WD23 21 J1
FSBYPK N4 72 E1
TRDG/WHET N20 26 D7
WIM/MER SW19 146 D4
Pinelands Cl BKHTH/KID SE3 * 113 J6
Pinelees Ct
MORT/ESHN SW14 * 125 K3
Pinemartin Cl CRICK NW2 70 A2
Pine Rdg CAR SM5 176 A7
Pine Rd CRICK NW2 70 A3
FBAR/BDGN N11 40 A1
Pines Cl NTHWD HA6 32 C5
Pines Rd BMLY BR1 168 D1
The Pines BORE WD6 24 B1
NRWD SE19 * 149 H5
STHGT/OAK N14 28 C4
WFD IG8 44 E2
Pine St CLKNW EC1R 6 A9
Pine Tree Cl HEST TW5 102 A7
Pine Tree Wy LEW SE13 132 E2
Pine Wk BRYLDS KT5 159 H5
Pine Wd SUN TW16 140 E7
Pinewood Av BFN/LL DA15 135 K7
PIN HA5 34 B5
RAIN RM13 99 K3
Pinewood Cl CROY/NA CR0 179 G2
NTHWD HA6 32 E4
ORP BR6 169 J7
PIN HA5 34 B5
Pinewood Gv WEA W13 85 J5
Pinewood Ldg BUSH WD23 * 22 D7
Pinewood Ms
STWL/WRAY TW19 120 A5
Pinewood Pl HOR/WEW KT19 173 F3
Pinewood Rd ABYW SE2 116 E5
FELT TW13 141 F2
HAYES BR2 167 K3
Pinfold Rd BUSH WD23 21 K1
STRHM/NOR SW16 148 E3
Pinglestone Cl WDR/YW UB7 100 B6
Pinkcoat Cl FELT TW13 141 F2
Pinkwell Av HYS/HAR UB3 101 G3
Pinkwell La HYS/HAR UB3 101 G3
Pinley Gdns DAGW RM9 79 H7
Pinnacle Hl BXLYHN DA7 137 J3
Pinnacle Hl North
BXLYHN DA7 137 J2
Pinnell Rd ELTH/MOT SE9 134 C3
Pinner Ct PIN HA5 48 A3
Pinner Gn PIN HA5 47 G1
Pinner Gv PIN HA5 47 J3
Pinner Hl PIN HA5 33 F6
Pinner Hill Rd PIN HA5 33 G7
Pinner Park Av
RYLN/HDSTN HA2 48 C1
Pinner Park Gdns
RYLN/HDSTN HA2 48 C1
Pinner Rd HRW HA1 48 B4
NTHWD HA6 32 D7
OXHEY WD19 21 H5
PIN HA5 47 K3
Pinner Vw HRW HA1 48 C4
Pinn Wy RSLP HA4 46 B6
Pintail Cl EHAM E6 95 J4
Pintail Rd WFD IG8 45 F6
Pintail Wy YEAD UB4 83 H4
Pinto Cl BORE WD6 * 25 F5
Pinto Wy BKHTH/KID SE3 134 A3
Pioneer Cl BOW E3 93 K4
SHB W12 87 K5
Pioneer St PECK SE15 111 H7
Pioneer Wy SHB W12 88 A5
WATW WD18 20 D5
Piper Cl HOLWY N7 73 F5
Piper Rd KUT/HW KT1 159 H2
Pipers Gdns CROY/NA CR0 166 B6
Pipers Gn CDALE/KGS NW9 50 E4
Pipers Green La STAN HA7 36 A2
Piper Wy IL IG1 60 D7
Pipewell Rd CAR SM5 162 D5
Pippin Cl CRICK NW2 69 J2
CROY/NA CR0 166 C7
Pippins Cl WDR/YW UB7 100 A2
Piquet Rd PGE/AN SE20 165 K1
Pirbright Crs CROY/NA CR0 180 A5
Pirbright Rd
WAND/EARL SW18 127 J7
Pirie St CAN/RD E16 95 F7
Pitcairn Cl ROMW/RG RM7 62 C3
Pitcairn Rd MTCM CR4 147 K6
Pitchford St SRTFD E15 76 B6
Pitfield Crs THMD SE28 97 G7
Pitfield St IS N1 7 J7
Pitfield Wy WLSDN NW10 68 E5
Pitfold Rd LEE/GVPK SE12 133 K6
Pitlake CROY/NA CR0 177 H1
Pitman St CMBW SE5 110 D6
Pitsea Pl WCHPL E1 93 F5
Pitsea St WCHPL E1 93 F5
Pitshanger La EA W5 85 H3
Pitt Crs WIM/MER SW19 147 F3
Pittman Gdns IL IG1 78 C4
Pitt Rd RYLN/HDSTN HA2 66 C1
THHTH CR7 164 D4
Pitts Head Ms
MYFR/PICC W1J 10 B9
Pittsmead Av HAYES BR2 167 K6
Pitt St KENS W8 14 B1
Pittville Gdns SNWD SE25 165 H2
Pixley St POP/IOD E14 93 H5
Pixton Wy CROY/NA CR0 179 G7
Place Farm Av ORP BR6 169 J7
Plaistow Gv BMLY BR1 153 F6
SRTFD E15 76 D7
Plaistow La BMLY BR1 152 E6
Plaistow Park Rd PLSTW E13 95 F1
Plaistow Rd SRTFD E15 76 D7
Plane St SYD SE26 150 D2
Plane Tree Crs FELT TW13 141 F2
Plantagenet Cl WPK KT4 173 F3
Plantagenet Gdns CHDH RM6 61 K6
Plantagenet Pl CHDH RM6 61 K6
Plantagenet Rd BAR EN5 27 G3
Plantain Gdns WAN E11 * 76 B2
Plantain Pl STHWK SE1 19 G1
Plantation La FENCHST EC3M 13 J6
Plantation Rd ERITH DA8 118 D7
The Plantation
BKHTH/KID SE3 133 K1
Plashet Gv EHAM E6 77 G7
Plashet Rd PLSTW E13 76 E7
Plassy Rd CAT SE6 132 E6
Platina St SDTCH EC2A 7 H9
Platinum Ct ROMW/RG RM7 62 D2
Plato Rd BRXS/STRHM SW2 129 K3
Platt's La HAMP NW3 70 E2
Platt St CAMTN NW1 5 G5
Plawsfield Rd BECK BR3 151 F7
Plaxtol Cl BMLY BR1 153 G7
Plaxtol Rd ERITH DA8 117 H6
Playfair St HMSMTH W6 * 107 F4
Playfield Crs EDUL SE22 131 F4
Playfield Rd EDGW HA8 50 E1
Playford Rd FSBYPK N4 73 F1
Playgreen Wy CAT SE6 151 J3
Playground Cl BECK BR3 166 A1
Playhouse Ct STHWK SE1 18 E1
Playhouse Yd BLKFR EC4V 12 C5
Plaza Pde ALP/SUD HA0 * 68 A5
Plaza Wk CDALE/KGS NW9 50 E2
Pleasance Rd PUT/ROE SW15 126 E4
The Pleasance PUT/ROE SW15 126 E3
Pleasant Gv CROY/NA CR0 179 H2
Pleasant Pl IS N1 6 D2
Pleasant Vw ERITH DA8 118 B4
Pleasant Wy ALP/SUD HA0 85 J1
Plender St CAMTN NW1 4 E4
Pleshey Rd ARCH N19 72 D3
Plesman Wy WLGTN SM6 * 176 E7
Plevna Crs SEVS/STOTM N15 56 A5
Plevna Rd ED N9 42 C2
HPTN TW12 142 B7
Plevna St POP/IOD E14 113 F2
Pleydell Av HMSMTH W6 106 C2
NRWD SE19 150 B6
Pleydell Est FSBYE EC1V * 6 F8
Pleydell Gdns NRWD SE19 * 150 B5
Pleydell St EMB EC4Y 12 B5
Plimsoll Cl POP/IOD E14 93 K5
Plimsoll Rd FSBYPK N4 73 H2
Plough Cl WLSDN NW10 87 K2
Plough Farm Cl RSLP HA4 46 B5
Plough La CROY/NA CR0 176 E3
EDUL SE22 131 G5
PUR/KEN CR8 176 E7
TEDD TW11 143 G4
WIM/MER SW19 147 F4
WLGTN SM6 176 E4
Plough Lane Cl WLGTN SM6 176 E4
Ploughmans Cl CAMTN NW1 5 G3
Ploughmans End ISLW TW7 123 J4
Plough Pl FLST/FETLN EC4A 12 B4
Plough Rd BTSEA SW11 128 C2
HOR/WEW KT19 173 F6
Plough St WCHPL E1 * 92 C5
Plough Ter BTSEA SW11 128 C3
Plough Wy BERM/RHTH SE16 112 A3
Plough Yd SDTCH EC2A 13 K1
Plover Wy BERM/RHTH SE16 112 B2
YEAD UB4 83 H5
Plowden Blds EMB EC4Y * 12 A6
Plowman Cl UED N18 41 K4
Plowman Wy BCTR RM8 61 J7
Plumbers Rw WCHPL E1 92 C4
Plumbridge St GNWCH SE10 * 113 F7
Plum Cl FELT TW13 121 K7
Plum Garth BTFD TW8 104 E3
Plum La WOOL/PLUM SE18 115 G6
Plummer La MTCM CR4 147 K7
Plummer Rd CLAP SW4 129 J6
Plumpton Wy CAR SM5 175 J2
Plumstead Common Rd
WOOL/PLUM SE18 115 H5
Plumstead High St
WOOL/PLUM SE18 115 J3
Plumstead Rd
WOOL/PLUM SE18 115 H3
Plumtree Cl DAGE RM10 80 D5
WLGTN SM6 176 D6
Plumtree Ct FLST/FETLN EC4A 12 B4
Plymouth Rd BMLY BR1 153 F7
CAN/RD E16 94 E4
Plymouth Whf POP/IOD E14 113 G3
Plympton Av
KIL/WHAMP NW6 70 D6
Plympton Cl BELV DA17 117 F2
Plympton Pl STJWD NW8 * 9 J1
Plympton Rd
KIL/WHAMP NW6 70 D6
Plympton St STJWD NW8 9 J1
Plymstock Rd WELL DA16 116 D6
Pocklington Cl
CDALE/KGS NW9 51 G1
Pocock Av WDR/YW UB7 100 C2
Pocock St STHWK SE1 18 C1
Podmore Rd
WAND/EARL SW18 128 B3
Poet's Rd HBRY N5 73 K4
Poets Wy HRW HA1 48 E3
Pointalls Cl FNCH N3 53 G1
Point Cl GNWCH SE10 113 F7
Pointer Cl THMD SE28 97 K5
Pointers Cl POP/IOD E14 112 E4
Point Hl GNWCH SE10 113 F7
Point Pl WBLY HA9 68 D6
Point Pleasant
WAND/EARL SW18 127 K3
Point Wharf La BTFD TW8 104 E6
Poland St SOHO/SHAV W1D 10 F4
Polebrook Rd BKHTH/KID SE3 134 B2
Polecroft La CAT SE6 151 H1
Polesden Gdns RYNPK SW20 160 E2
Polesworth Rd DAGW RM9 98 B1
Polish War Memorial Rbt
RSLP HA4 65 G5
Pollard Cl CAN/RD E16 94 E6
HOLWY N7 73 F3
Pollard Rd MRDN SM4 162 C4
TRDG/WHET N20 39 J1
Pollard Rw BETH E2 92 C2
Pollards Crs
STRHM/NOR SW16 163 K2
Pollards Hl East
STRHM/NOR SW16 164 A2
Pollards Hl North
STRHM/NOR SW16 164 A2
Pollards Hl South
STRHM/NOR SW16 163 K2
Pollards Hl West
STRHM/NOR SW16 163 K2
Pollard St BETH E2 * 92 C2
Pollards Wood Rd
STRHM/NOR SW16 163 K1
Pollen St CONDST W1S 10 D5
Pollitt Dr STJWD NW8 3 G9
Polperro Ms LBTH SE11 18 B5
Polsted Rd CAT SE6 132 C6
Polthorne Gv
WOOL/PLUM SE18 115 H3
Polworth Rd
STRHM/NOR SW16 148 E4
Polygon Rd CAMTN NW1 5 G6
The Polygon CLAP SW4 * 129 H3
Polytechnic St
WOOL/PLUM SE18 115 F3
Pomell Wy WCHPL E1 13 M4
Pomeroy Cl TWK TW1 124 C3
Pomeroy St NWCR SE14 111 K6
Pomfret Rd CMBW SE5 130 C2
Pomoja La ARCH N19 72 E1
Pond Cl BKHTH/KID SE3 133 K1
NFNCH/WDSPK N12 39 J5
Pond Cottage La BECK BR3 166 D7
Pond Cots DUL SE21 131 F7
Ponder St HOLWY N7 * 5 L1
Pond Farm Est CLPT E5 * 74 E2
Pondfield Rd DAGE RM10 80 D4
HAYES BR2 167 H7
Pond Gn RSLP HA4 64 C1
Pond Hill Gdns CHEAM SM3 * 174 C5
Pond Lees Cl DAGE RM10 81 F6
Pond Md DUL SE21 130 E5
Pond Pl CHEL SW3 15 J6
Pond Rd BKHTH/KID SE3 133 J2
SRTFD E15 94 C1
Pondside Av WPK KT4 161 F7
Pondside Cl HYS/HAR UB3 101 G6
Pond St HAMP NW3 71 J4
Pond Wy TEDD TW11 143 J5
Pondwood Ri ORP BR6 169 K6
Ponler St WCHPL E1 92 D5
Ponsard Rd WLSDN NW10 87 K2
Ponsford St HOM E9 74 E5
Ponsonby Pl WEST SW1P 17 H7
Ponsonby Rd PUT/ROE SW15 126 E6
Ponsonby Ter WEST SW1P 17 H7
Pontefract Rd BMLY BR1 152 E4
Ponton Rd VX/NE SW8 109 J6
Pont St KTBR SW1X 15 L4
Pont Street Ms KTBR SW1X 15 L4
Pool Cl BECK BR3 151 J4
E/WMO/HCT KT8 156 E4
Pool Ct CAT SE6 151 J1
Poole Cl RSLP HA4 64 C1
Poole Court Rd HSLWW TW4 122 D1
Poole Rd HOM E9 75 F5
HOR/WEW KT19 173 F5
Pooles Blds FSBYW WC1X 12 A1
Pooles La WBPTN SW10 108 B6
Pooles Pk FSBYPK N4 73 G1
Poole St IS N1 7 G4
Poole Wy YEAD UB4 * 82 C2
Pooley Dr MORT/ESHN SW14 125 K2
Poolmans St
BERM/RHTH SE16 112 A1
Pool Rd E/WMO/HCT KT8 156 E4
HRW HA1 48 D6
Poolsford Rd CDALE/KGS NW9 51 G3
Poonah St WCHPL E1 92 E5
Pope Cl EBED/NFELT TW14 121 J7
WIM/MER SW19 * 147 H5
Pope Rd HAYES BR2 168 C4
Pope's Av WHTN TW2 142 E1
Popes Dr FNCH N3 38 E7
Popes Gv CROY/NA CR0 179 H2
Pope's Gv WHTN TW2 142 E1
Pope's La EA W5 104 E2
Pope's Rd BRXN/ST SW9 * 130 B3
Pope St STHWK SE1 19 K2
Popham Cl FELT TW13 141 J2
Popham Gdns
RCH/KEW TW9 * 125 J2
Popham Rd IS N1 6 E3
Popham St IS N1 6 E3
Popinjays Rw CHEAM SM3 * 174 B4
Poplar Av MTCM CR4 147 K7
NWDGN UB2 103 G2
Poplar Bath St POP/IOD E14 93 K6
Poplar Cl HOM E9 75 H4
PIN HA5 33 H7
Poplar Court Pde TWK TW1 * 124 D5
Poplar Crs HOR/WEW KT19 172 E5
Poplar Farm Cl
HOR/WEW KT19 172 E5
Poplar Gdns NWMAL KT3 160 A1
Poplar Gv FBAR/BDGN N11 40 A5
HMSMTH W6 107 F1
NWMAL KT3 160 A2
WBLY HA9 68 E2
Poplar High St POP/IOD E14 93 K6
Poplar La BECK BR3 166 E4
Poplar Ms SHB W12 88 A7
Poplar Mt BELV DA17 117 J3
Poplar Pl BAY/PAD W2 8 C6
HYS/HAR UB3 82 E6
THMD SE28 97 J6
Poplar Rd ASHF TW15 140 A4
CHEAM SM3 161 J7
ESH/CLAY KT10 171 G2
HNHL SE24 130 D3
MNPK E12 77 J2
WIM/MER SW19 161 K1
Poplar Rd South
WIM/MER SW19 161 K2
Poplars Cl RSLP HA4 46 C7
Poplars Rd WALTH E17 57 K5
The Poplars STHGT/OAK N14 28 B4
Poplar St ROMW/RG RM7 62 E3
Poplar Vw WBLY HA9 * 67 K1
Poplar Wk CROY/NA CR0 177 J1
HNHL SE24 130 D3
Poplar Wy BARK/HLT IG6 60 C3
FELT TW13 140 E2
Poppleton Rd WAN E11 58 C5
Poppy Cl BELV DA17 117 J2
NTHLT UB5 65 K5
WLGTN SM6 163 F7
Poppy Dr PEND EN3 30 D3
Poppy La CROY/NA CR0 165 K6
Porchester Garden Ms
BAY/PAD W2 8 D5
Porchester Gdns BAY/PAD W2 8 D6
Porchester Ga BAY/PAD W2 * 8 E7
Porchester Md BECK BR3 151 K5
Porchester Pl BAY/PAD W2 9 K5
Porchester Rd BAY/PAD W2 8 D4
KUT/HW KT1 159 J1
Porchester Sq BAY/PAD W2 8 D4
Porchester Square Ms
BAY/PAD W2 8 D4
Porchester Ter BAY/PAD W2 8 E5
Porchester Ter North
BAY/PAD W2 8 D4
Porch Wy TRDG/WHET N20 39 K2
Porcupine Cl ELTH/MOT SE9 153 J1
Porden Rd BRXS/STRHM SW2 130 A3
Porlock Av RYLN/HDSTN HA2 48 C7
Porlock Rd EN EN1 30 B6
Porlock St STHWK SE1 19 H1
Porrington Cl CHST BR7 153 K7
Portal Cl RSLP HA4 64 E3
WNWD SE27 149 G2
Portal Wy ACT W3 87 F4
Portbury Cl PECK SE15 111 H7
Portchester Cl HNHL SE24 130 D3
Portchester Ga BAY/PAD W2 * 8 E7
Portcullis Lodge Rd EN EN1 29 K2
Portelet Rd WCHPL E1 93 F2
Porten Houses WKENS W14 * 107 H2
Porten Rd WKENS W14 107 H2
Porter Rd EHAM E6 95 K5
Porters Av DAGW RM9 79 H5
Porter Sq ARCH N19 54 E7
Porter St MHST W1U 9 M2
STHWK SE1 12 F8
Porters Wk WAP E1W * 92 D6
Porters Wy WDR/YW UB7 100 C2
Porteus Rd BAY/PAD W2 8 F3
Portgate Cl MV/WKIL W9 88 D3
Porthcawe Rd SYD SE26 151 G3
Porthkerry Av WELL DA16 136 B3
Portia Wy BOW E3 93 H3
The Porticos CHEL SW3 * 108 C5
Portinscale Rd
PUT/ROE SW15 127 H4
Portland Av BFN/LL DA15 136 B5
NWMAL KT3 160 C6
STNW/STAM N16 56 B7
Portland Cl CHDH RM6 62 A4
WPK KT4 160 E6
Portland Cots CROY/NA CR0 * 163 J6
Portland Crs ELTH/MOT SE9 153 J1
FELT TW13 140 B3
GFD/PVL UB6 84 B3
STAN HA7 49 K1
Portland Crs West STAN HA7 49 K2
Portland Gdns CHDH RM6 61 K4
FSBYPK N4 55 H5
Portland Gv VX/NE SW8 110 A7
Portland Ms SOHO/CST W1F 10 F5
Portland Pl REGST W1B 10 C1
SNWD SE25 165 H3
Portland Ri FSBYPK N4 55 H7
Portland Rd BMLY BR1 153 G3
ELTH/MOT SE9 153 J1
KUT/HW KT1 159 F2
MTCM CR4 162 D1
NTGHL W11 88 C6
NWDGN UB2 102 E2
SEVS/STOTM N15 56 A3
SNWD SE25 165 H3
YEAD UB4 82 C2
Portland Sq WAP E1W 92 D7
Portland St WALW SE17 19 G8
Portland Ter RCH/KEW TW9 * 124 E3
Portman Av
MORT/ESHN SW14 126 A2
Portman Cl BXLY DA5 138 B7
BXLYHS DA6 136 E2
MBLAR W1H 10 A4
Portman Dr WFD IG8 59 H1
Portman Gdns
CDALE/KGS NW9 51 F2
Portman Ga CAMTN NW1 9 K1
Portman Ms South
MBLAR W1H 10 A5
Portman Pl BETH E2 92 E2
Portman Rd KUT/HW KT1 159 G1
Portman Sq MBLAR W1H 9 M4
Portman St MBLAR W1H 10 A5
Portmeadow Wk ABYW SE2 116 E1
Portmeers Cl WALTH E17 * 57 H5
Portnall Rd MV/WKIL W9 88 D2
Portnoi Cl ROM RM1 63 F1
Portobello Ct NTGHL W11 * 88 D6
Portobello Ms NTGHL W11 * 8 A7
Portobello Rd NKENS W10 88 C4
NTGHL W11 88 D6
Portpool La FSBYW WC1X 12 A2
Portree St POP/IOD E14 94 B5
Portsdown Av GLDGN NW11 52 D5
Portsdown Ms GLDGN NW11 52 D5
Portsea Ms BAY/PAD W2 9 K5
Portsea Pl BAY/PAD W2 9 K5
Portslade Rd VX/NE SW8 129 H1
Portsmouth Av THDIT KT7 158 B6
Portsmouth Ms CAN/RD E16 95 F6
Portsmouth Rd
ESH/CLAY KT10 170 A5
KUT/HW KT1 158 E2
PUT/ROE SW15 126 E6
THDIT KT7 158 C6
Portsmouth St LINN WC2A 11 L4
Portsoken St TWRH EC3N 13 L6
Portugal Gdns WHTN TW2 * 142 C1
Portugal St LINN WC2A 11 M5
Portway RAIN RM13 81 J7
SRTFD E15 76 E7
Portway Crs EW KT17 173 J7
Portway Gdns
WOOL/PLUM SE18 114 C7
Postern Gn ENC/FH EN2 29 G1
The Postern BARB EC2Y * 12 F3
Post La WHTN TW2 123 J7
Postmill Cl CROY/NA CR0 178 E2
Post Office Ap FSTGT E7 77 F4
Post Office Wy VX/NE SW8 109 J6
Post Rd NWDGN UB2 103 G2
Postway Ms IL IG1 78 B2
Potier St STHWK SE1 19 H4
Potter Cl MTCM CR4 * 163 G1
The Potteries BAR EN5 * 26 E4
Potterne Cl WIM/MER SW19 127 G6
Potters Cl CROY/NA CR0 166 B7
PECK SE15 * 111 F6
Potters Fld EN EN1 * 30 A3
Potters Flds STHWK SE1 13 K9
Potters Gv NWMAL KT3 159 K3
Potters Heights Cl PIN HA5 33 F6
Potter's La BAR EN5 26 E3
STRHM/NOR SW16 * 148 D5
Potters Ms BORE WD6 23 K5
Potters Rd FUL/PGN SW6 128 B1
Potter's Rd BAR EN5 27 F3
Potter St NTHWD HA6 32 E7
Potter Street Hl PIN HA5 33 F5
Pottery Cl SNWD SE25 165 J3
Pottery La NTGHL W11 88 C7
Pottery Rd BTFD TW8 105 F5
Pottery St BERM/RHTH SE16 * 111 J1
Pott St BETH E2 92 D2
Poulett Gdns TWK TW1 143 F1
Poulett Rd EHAM E6 95 K1
Poulter Pk MRDN SM4 * 162 D5
Poulters Wd HAYES BR2 181 H4
Poulton Av SUT SM1 175 H2
Poultry LOTH EC2R 13 G5
Pound Cl SURB KT6 158 D7
Pound Farm Cl
ESH/CLAY KT10 157 J7
Pound La WLSDN NW10 69 J5
Pound Park Rd CHARL SE7 114 C3
Pound Pl ELTH/MOT SE9 135 F5
Pound St CAR SM5 175 K4
Pountney Rd BTSEA SW11 129 F2
Powder Mill La WHTN TW2 122 E7
Powell Cl EDGW HA8 36 B5
Powell Gdns DAGE RM10 80 C3
Powell Rd CLPT E5 74 D2
Power Rd CHSWK W4 105 H3
Powers Ct TWK TW1 124 E6
Powerscroft Rd CLPT E5 74 E3
SCUP DA14 155 J5
Powis Ct BUSH WD23 * 22 D7
Powis Gdns GLDGN NW11 52 D6
NTGHL W11 88 D5
Powis Ms NTGHL W11 88 D5
Powis Pl BMSBY WC1N 11 K1
Powis Rd BOW E3 93 K2
Powis Sq NTGHL W11 88 D5
Powis St WOOL/PLUM SE18 115 F2
Powis Ter NTGHL W11 88 D5
Powlett Pl CAMTN NW1 4 B1
Pownall Gdns HSLW TW3 123 G3
Pownall Rd HACK E8 74 C7
HSLW TW3 123 G3
Pownsett Ter IL IG1 * 78 C4
Powster Rd BMLY BR1 152 E4
Powys Cl BXLYHN DA7 116 E5
Powys Ct BORE WD6 25 F2
Powys La PLMGR N13 40 E3
Poynders Rd CLAP SW4 129 H6
Poynings Rd ARCH N19 72 C2
Poynings Wy
NFNCH/WDSPK N12 38 E4
Poyntell Crs CHST BR7 154 D7
Poynter Rd EN EN1 30 B4
Poynton Rd TOTM N17 56 C1
Poyntz Rd BTSEA SW11 128 E1
Poyser St BETH E2 92 D1
Praed Ms BAY/PAD W2 9 H4
Praed St BAY/PAD W2 9 H4
Pragel St PLSTW E13 95 F1
Pragnell Rd LEE/GVPK SE12 153 F1
Prague Pl BRXS/STRHM SW2 129 K4
Prah Rd FSBYPK N4 73 G1
Prairie St VX/NE SW8 129 F1
Pratt Ms CAMTN NW1 4 E4
Pratt St CAMTN NW1 4 E4
Pratt Wk LBTH SE11 17 M5
Prayle Gv CRICK NW2 52 B7
Prebend Gdns HMSMTH W6 106 C3
Prebend St IS N1 6 E4
Precinct Rd HYS/HAR UB3 82 E6
The Precinct IS N1 * 6 E4
Premiere Pl POP/IOD E14 93 J6
Premier Park Rd
WLSDN NW10 86 D1
Premier Pl WATW WD18 20 D4
Prendergast Rd
BKHTH/KID SE3 133 H2
Prentis Rd
STRHM/NOR SW16 148 D3
Prentiss Ct CHARL SE7 114 C3
Presburg Rd NWMAL KT3 160 B4
Prescelly Pl EDGW HA8 36 B7
Prescot St WCHPL E1 13 M6
Prescott Av STMC/STPC BR5 169 G5
Prescott Cl EMPK RM11 63 K7
Prescott Pl CLAP SW4 129 J2
Presentation Ms
BRXS/STRHM SW2 149 F1
Presidents Dr WAP E1W 92 D7
President St FSBYE EC1V * 6 E7
Prespa Cl ED N9 42 E1
Press Rd WLSDN NW10 69 F2
Prestage Wy POP/IOD E14 94 A6
Prestbury Rd FSTGT E7 77 G6
Prestbury Sq ELTH/MOT SE9 153 K3
Prested Rd BTSEA SW11 128 D3
Preston Av CHING E4 44 B5
Preston Cl STHWK SE1 19 J5
WHTN TW2 142 E2
Preston Ct BAR EN5 27 G3
WOT/HER KT12 156 B7
Preston Dr BXLYHN DA7 116 E7
HOR/WEW KT19 173 G5
WAN E11 59 G4
Preston Gdns IL IG1 59 J5
WLSDN NW10 * 69 G5
Preston Hl
KTN/HRWW/WS HA3 50 A6
Preston Pl CRICK NW2 69 J5
Preston Rd
KTN/HRWW/WS HA3 50 A6
NRWD SE19 149 H5
RYNPK SW20 145 J6
WAN E11 58 C5
WBLY HA9 68 A1
Prestons Rd WWKM BR4 180 E2
Preston's Rd POP/IOD E14 94 A6
Preston Vls KUT/HW KT1 * 159 G1
Preston Waye
KTN/HRWW/WS HA3 50 A7
Prestwich Ter CLAP SW4 * 129 J4
Prestwick Cl NWDGN UB2 102 D4
Prestwick Rd OXHEY WD19 33 G4
Prestwood OXHEY WD19 * 33 J1
Prestwood Av
KTN/HRWW/WS HA3 49 H3
Prestwood Cl
KTN/HRWW/WS HA3 49 H3
WOOL/PLUM SE18 116 B6
Prestwood Gdns
CROY/NA CR0 164 D6
Prestwood St IS N1 * 6 F6
Pretoria Av WALTH E17 57 G3
Pretoria Pde BROCKY SE4 * 132 D1
Pretoria Rd CAN/RD E16 94 D2
IL IG1 78 B3
LEY E10 58 B7
ROMW/RG RM7 62 E3
STRHM/NOR SW16 148 B5
TOTM N17 42 B5
WATW WD18 20 E3
Pretoria Rd North UED N18 42 B5
Prevost Rd FBAR/BDGN N11 40 A1
Price Cl MLHL NW7 38 C5
TOOT SW17 147 K2
Price Rd CROY/NA CR0 177 H4
Price's St STHWK SE1 12 D9
Pricklers Hl BAR EN5 27 F4
Prickley Wd HAYES BR2 167 J7
Priddy's Yd CROY/NA CR0 177 J1
Prideaux Pl ACT W3 87 F6
FSBYW WC1X 5 M7
Prideaux Rd BRXN/ST SW9 129 K2
Pridham Rd THHTH CR7 164 E3
Priestfield Rd FSTH SE23 151 G2

Priestlands Park Rd
BFN/LL DA15 155 F2
Priestley Cl STNW/STAM N16 * 56 B6
Priestley Gdns CHDH RM6 61 H5
Priestley Rd MTCM CR4 163 F1
Priestley Wy CRICK NW2 51 J7
WALTH E17 57 F2
Priest Park Av
RYLN/HDSTN HA2 66 A1
Priests Av ROM RM1 63 F1
Priests Br MORT/ESHN SW14 126 B2
Prima Rd BRXN/ST SW9 110 B6
Primrose Av GDMY/SEVK IG3 61 G6
Primrose Cl BOW E3 93 J1
CAT SE6 152 A4
FNCH N3 53 F1
RYLN/HDSTN HA2 65 K2
WLGTN SM6 163 G7
Primrose Dr WDR/YW UB7 100 A3
Primrose Gdns BUSH WD23 22 B6
HAMP NW3 71 J5
RSLP HA4 65 G4
Primrose Hl EMB EC4Y 12 B5
Primrose Hill Rd HAMP NW3 3 L2
Primrose Hill Studios
CAMTN NW1 4 A3
Primrose La CROY/NA CR0 165 K7
Primrose Ms CAMTN NW1 * 3 M2
Primrose Pl ISLW TW7 124 A1
Primrose Rd LEY E10 57 K7
SWFD E18 59 F1
Primrose Sq HOM E9 74 E6
Primrose St SDTCH EC2A 13 J2
Primrose Wk EW KT17 173 H6
NWCR SE14 112 B6
Primrose Wy ALP/SUD HA0 85 K1
Primula St SHB W12 87 J6
Prince Albert Rd STJWD NW8 3 J7
Prince Arthur Ms HAMP NW3 71 G3
Prince Arthur Rd HAMP NW3 71 G3
Prince Charles Dr HDN NW4 52 A6
Prince Charles Rd
BKHTH/KID SE3 113 J7
Prince Charles Wy
WLGTN SM6 176 B2
Prince Consort Dr CHST BR7 154 D7
Prince Consort Rd SKENS SW7 15 G3
Princedale Rd NTGHL W11 88 C7
Prince Edward Rd HOM E9 75 H5
Prince George Av
STHGT/OAK N14 28 C4
Prince George Rd
STNW/STAM N16 74 A3
Prince George's Av
RYNPK SW20 161 F1
Prince Georges Rd
WIM/MER SW19 147 H7
Prince Henry Rd CHARL SE7 114 C6
Prince Imperial Rd CHST BR7 154 B6
WOOL/PLUM SE18 114 E7
Prince John Rd
ELTH/MOT SE9 134 D4
Princelet St WCHPL E1 13 M2
Prince of Orange La
GNWCH SE10 * 113 F6
Prince of Wales Cl HDN NW4 51 K3
Prince of Wales Dr
BTSEA SW11 108 D7
VX/NE SW8 * 109 G6
Prince of Wales Ga
SKENS SW7 15 J1
Prince of Wales Pas
CAMTN NW1 * 4 E8
Prince of Wales Rd
BKHTH/KID SE3 113 J7
CAN/RD E16 95 G5
KTTN NW5 72 A5
Prince of Wales' Rd SUT SM1 175 H1
Prince of Wales Ter
CHSWK W4 106 B4
KENS W8 14 D2
Prince Regent La CAN/RD E16 95 G5
Prince Regent Ms
CAMTN NW1 4 E8
Prince Regent Rd HSLW TW3 123 G2
Prince Rd SNWD SE25 165 F4
Prince Rupert Rd
ELTH/MOT SE9 134 E3
Princes Ar MYFR/PICC W1J 10 F8
Princes Av ACT W3 105 H2
CAR SM5 175 K6
CDALE/KGS NW9 50 C3
FNCH N3 39 F7
MUSWH N10 54 A2
PLMGR N13 41 G4
STMC/STPC BR5 169 K4
SURB KT6 172 C1
WATW WD18 20 E4
WDGN N22 40 D7
WFD IG8 45 F3
Prince's Av GFD/PVL UB6 84 B5
Princes Cl CDALE/KGS NW9 50 C3
EDGW HA8 36 C4
SCUP DA14 155 K2
Prince's Cl HPTN TW12 142 D3
Princes Ct WBLY HA9 68 A4
Princes Dr HRW HA1 48 E2
Princes Gdns ACT W3 86 C4
EA W5 85 J3
SKENS SW7 15 H3
Princes Ga SKENS SW7 15 H3
Prince's Ga SKENS SW7 15 J2
Princes Gate Ct SKENS SW7 15 G2
Princes Gate Ms SKENS SW7 15 H3
Princes La MUSWH N10 54 A2
Princes Ms HMSMTH W6 * 106 E4
HSLW TW3 123 F3
Prince's Ms BAY/PAD W2 8 C6
Princes Pde GLDGN NW11 * 52 C5
Princes Pk RAIN RM13 81 J6
Princes Park Av GLDGN NW11 52 C5
HYS/HAR UB3 82 B6
Princes Park Cir HYS/HAR UB3 82 B6
Princes Park Cl HYS/HAR UB3 82 B6
Princes Park La HYS/HAR UB3 82 B6
Princes Park Pde
HYS/HAR UB3 82 B6
Princes Pl NTGHL W11 88 C7
Prince's Pln HAYES BR2 168 D6
Princes Ri LEW SE13 133 F1
Princes Riverside Rd
BERM/RHTH SE16 93 F7
Princes Rd BARK/HLT IG6 60 D3
BKHH IG9 45 G1
DART DA1 138 E6
FELT TW13 140 D2
KUTN/CMB KT2 144 C7
PGE/AN SE20 151 F5
RCH/KEW TW9 105 G7
RCHPK/HAM TW10 125 G4
ROM RM1 63 J4
TEDD TW11 142 D3
UED N18 42 E3
WEA W13 85 H7
Prince's Rd MORT/ESHN SW14 126 A2
TEDD TW11 142 D3
WIM/MER SW19 146 E5
Princess Alice Wy THMD SE28 115 J1
Princess Av WBLY HA9 68 A1
Princess Crs FSBYPK N4 73 H1
Princesses Pde DART DA1 * 138 C4
Princess La RSLP HA4 46 C7
Princess Louise Cl
BAY/PAD W2 9 H2
Princess May Rd
STNW/STAM N16 74 A3
Princess Ms HAMP NW3 71 H5
Prince's Sq BAY/PAD W2 8 B6
Princess Rd CAMTN NW1 4 A3
CROY/NA CR0 164 D5
KIL/WHAMP NW6 2 A6
Princess St BXLYHN DA7 137 G2
STHWK SE1 18 D4
Princes St REGST W1B 10 D5
SUT SM1 175 H3
TOTM N17 42 A5
Prince's St LOTH EC2R 13 G5
RCH/KEW TW9 125 F3
Prince's Ter PLSTW E13 77 F7
Prince St DEPT SE8 112 C5
WAT WD17 21 G2
Princes Vw DART DA1 139 K7
Princes Wy BKHH IG9 45 G1
CROY/NA CR0 177 F4
RSLP HA4 65 J3
WIM/MER SW19 127 H7
WWKM BR4 180 D3
Prince's Yd IS N1 5 M4
NTGHL W11 88 C7
Princethorpe Rd SYD SE26 151 F3
Princeton St GINN WC1R 11 L3
Pringle Gdns
STRHM/NOR SW16 148 C3
Printers Inn Ct
FLST/FETLN EC4A 12 A4
Printinghouse La
HYS/HAR UB3 101 H1
Printing House Yd BETH E2 * 7 K8
Priolo Rd CHARL SE7 114 B4
Prior Av BELMT SM2 175 J6
Prior Bolton St IS N1 73 H5
Prioress Rd WNWD SE27 149 H2
Prioress St STHWK SE1 19 H4
Prior Rd IL IG1 78 A2
Priors Cft WALTH E17 57 G1
Priors Fld NTHLT UB5 65 J5
Priors Gdns RSLP HA4 65 G4
Prior St GNWCH SE10 113 F6
Priory Av ALP/SUD HA0 67 F3
CEND/HSY/T N8 54 D3
CHEAM SM3 174 B3
CHING E4 43 H2
CHSWK W4 106 B2
STMC/STPC BR5 169 J5
WALTH E17 57 J4
Priory Cl ALP/SUD HA0 67 F3
BECK BR3 166 B2
CHING E4 43 H2
CHST BR7 153 K7
DART DA1 139 F4
FNCH N3 38 D7
HPTN TW12 141 K7
HYS/HAR UB3 83 F6
RSLP HA4 46 D7
STAN HA7 35 F2
STHGT/OAK N14 28 B4
SUN TW16 140 E6
SWFD E18 44 E7
TRDG/WHET N20 26 D6
WIM/MER SW19 * 147 F7
Priory Cots EA W5 * 86 B4
Priory Ct BLKFR EC4V * 12 D5
VX/NE SW8 109 J7
WALTH E17 57 H1
Priory Crs ALP/SUD HA0 67 G2
CHEAM SM3 174 B3
NRWD SE19 149 J6
Priory Dr ABYW SE2 116 E4
STAN HA7 35 F2
Priory Field Dr EDGW HA8 36 D3
Priory Gdns ALP/SUD HA0 67 G3
ASHF TW15 140 B4
BARN SW13 126 C2
CHSWK W4 * 106 B3
DART DA1 139 G4
HGT N6 54 B5
HPTN TW12 141 K7
SNWD SE25 165 G3
Priory Green Est IS N1 5 L5
Priory Gv VX/NE SW8 109 K7
Priory Hl ALP/SUD HA0 67 G3
DART DA1 139 G5
Priory La E/WMO/HCT KT8 157 F3
PUT/ROE SW15 126 C4
Priory Leas ELTH/MOT SE9 * 134 D7
Priory Ms HCH RM12 63 K7
Priory Pk BKHTH/KID SE3 133 J2
Priory Park Rd ALP/SUD HA0 67 G3
KIL/WHAMP NW6 70 D7
Priory Pl DART DA1 139 G5
Priory Rd BARK IG11 78 D6
CEND/HSY/T N8 54 D3
CHEAM SM3 174 B3
CHSGTN KT9 172 A2
CHSWK W4 106 A2
CROY/NA CR0 164 B6
DART DA1 139 G3
EHAM E6 77 H7
HPTN TW12 141 K6
HSLW TW3 123 H4
KIL/WHAMP NW6 2 C2
MUSWH N10 54 C3
RCH/KEW TW9 105 H5
Priory St BOW E3 93 K2
Priory Ter KIL/WHAMP NW6 2 C3
The Priory BKHTH/KID SE3 133 J2
CROY/NA CR0 * 177 G2
Priory Vw BUSH WD23 22 E6
Priory Vls FBAR/BDGN N11 * 39 K5
Priory Wk WBPTN SW10 14 F8
Priory Wy NWDGN UB2 102 C2
RYLN/HDSTN HA2 48 B3
WDR/YW UB7 100 B5
Pritchard's Rd BETH E2 92 C1
Priter Rd BERM/RHTH SE16 * 111 H2
Private Rd EN EN1 29 K4
Probert Rd BRXS/STRHM SW2 130 B4
Probyn Rd BRXS/STRHM SW2 149 H1
Procter St GINN WC1R 11 L3
Proctor Cl MTCM CR4 148 A7
Proctors Cl EBED/NFELT TW14 121 K7
Progress Wy CROY/NA CR0 177 F1
EN EN1 30 C4
WDGN N22 41 G7
Promenade Approach Rd
CHSWK W4 106 B6
The Promenade CHSWK W4 106 B7
EDGW HA8 * 36 C4
Prospect Cl BELV DA17 117 H3
BUSH WD23 22 D6
HSLW TW3 102 E7
RSLP HA4 47 H6
SYD SE26 150 D3
Prospect Cots
WAND/EARL SW18 127 K3
Prospect Crs WHTN TW2 123 H5
Prospect Hl WALTH E17 57 K3
Prospect Pl CHSWK W4 106 A4
CRICK NW2 70 D2
CRW RM5 62 E1
EFNCH N2 53 H3
HAYES BR2 168 A2
RYNPK SW20 145 K6
WAP E1W 92 E7
Prospect Ring EFNCH N2 53 H2
Prospect Rd BAR EN5 26 E3
CRICK NW2 70 D2
SURB KT6 158 D5
WFD IG8 45 G4
Prospect St BERM/RHTH SE16 111 J1
Prospect V WOOL/PLUM SE18 114 D3
Prospero Rd ARCH N19 54 D7
Protea Cl CAN/RD E16 94 D3
Prothero Gdns HDN NW4 51 K4
Prothero Rd FUL/PGN SW6 107 H6
Prout Gv WLSDN NW10 69 G3
Prout Rd CLPT E5 74 D2
Provence St IS N1 6 E5
Providence Av
RYLN/HDSTN HA2 48 A7
Providence Cl HOM E9 * 75 F7
Providence Ct
MYFR/PKLN W1K 10 B6
Providence La HYS/HAR UB3 101 G6
Providence Pl IS N1 6 C4
Providence Row Cl BETH E2 92 D2
Providence Sq STHWK SE1 19 J1
Providence Yd BETH E2 * 92 C2
Provincial Ter PGE/AN SE20 * 151 F6
Provost Est IS N1 7 G7
Provost Rd HAMP NW3 3 M1
Provost St FSBYE EC1V 7 G8
IS N1 7 G6
Prowse Av BUSH WD23 34 C1
Prowse Pl CAMTN NW1 4 E1
Pruden Cl STHGT/OAK N14 * 40 C1
Prusom St WAP E1W 92 D7
Pudding La MON EC3R 13 H6
Pudding Mill La SRTFD E15 75 K7
Puddle Dock BLKFR EC4V 12 D6
Puffin Cl BARK IG11 97 H2
BECK BR3 166 A4
Pulborough Rd
WAND/EARL SW18 127 J6
Pulborough Wy HSLWW TW4 122 B3
Pulford Rd SEVS/STOTM N15 55 K5
Pulham Av EFNCH N2 53 G3
Puller Rd BAR EN5 26 B1
Pulleyns Av EHAM E6 95 J2
Pullman Gdns PUT/ROE SW15 127 F5
Pullman Ms LEE/GVPK SE12 153 F2
Pullman Pl ELTH/MOT SE9 134 D4
Pulross Rd BRXN/ST SW9 130 A2
Pulteney Cl BOW E3 75 H7
ISLW TW7 124 B2
Pulteney Rd SWFD E18 59 F2
Pulton Pl FUL/PGN SW6 107 K6
Puma Ct WCHPL E1 13 L2
Pump Aly BTFD TW8 104 E6
Pump Cl NTHLT UB5 84 A1
Pump Ct EMB EC4Y * 12 A5
Pump House Cl HAYES BR2 167 J1
Pump House Ms WCHPL E1 * 92 C6
Pumping Station Rd
CHSWK W4 106 B6
Pump La HYS/HAR UB3 101 K1
NWCR SE14 111 K6
Punderson's Gdns BETH E2 92 D2
Purbeck Av NWMAL KT3 160 C5
Purbeck Dr CRICK NW2 70 B1
Purbeck Rd EMPK RM11 63 J6
Purbrook St STHWK SE1 19 K3
Purcell Crs FUL/PGN SW6 107 G6
Purcell Ms WLSDN NW10 * 69 G6
Purcell Rd GFD/PVL UB6 84 B4
Purcells Ave EDGW HA8 36 C4
Purcell St IS N1 7 J5
Purcers Cross Rd
FUL/PGN SW6 107 J7
Purchese St CAMTN NW1 5 G5
Purdy St BOW E3 93 K3
Purelake Ms LEW SE13 * 133 G2
Purfleet Industrial Access Rd
SOCK/AV RM15 119 K2
Purkis Cl UX/CGN UB8 82 A6
Purland Cl BCTR RM8 62 B7
Purland Rd THMD SE28 116 A2
Purleigh Av WFD IG8 45 J5
Purley Av CRICK NW2 70 C1
Purley Cl CLAY IG5 60 A1
Purley Pl IS N1 6 C1
Purley Rd ED N9 41 K2
SAND/SEL CR2 177 K6
Purley Wy CROY/NA CR0 177 G7
Purlings Rd BUSH WD23 22 B4
Purneys Rd ELTH/MOT SE9 134 C3
Purrett Rd WOOL/PLUM SE18 116 A4
Pursers Cross Rd
FUL/PGN SW6 * 107 J7
Pursewardens Cl WEA W13 85 J7
Pursley Rd MLHL NW7 37 K6
Purves Rd WLSDN NW10 87 K2
Putney Br PUT/ROE SW15 127 H2
Putney Bridge Ap
FUL/PGN SW6 127 H2
Putney Bridge Rd
PUT/ROE SW15 127 H3
Putney Common
PUT/ROE SW15 127 F2
Putney Ex PUT/ROE SW15 * 127 G3
Putney Heath
PUT/ROE SW15 126 E5
Putney Heath La
PUT/ROE SW15 127 G5
Putney High St
PUT/ROE SW15 127 H3
Putney Hl PUT/ROE SW15 127 G5
Putney Park Av
PUT/ROE SW15 126 D3
Putney Park La
PUT/ROE SW15 126 E3
Puttenham Cl OXHEY WD19 33 G2
Pycombe Cnr
NFNCH/WDSPK N12 38 D3
Pycroft Wy ED N9 42 C3
Pylbrook Rd SUT SM1 174 E2
Pylon Wy CROY/NA CR0 163 K7
Pym Cl EBAR EN4 27 H4
Pymers Md DUL SE21 130 D7
Pymmes Brook Trail
EBAR EN4 27 K6
ED N9 42 D2
Pymmes Cl PLMGR N13 41 F4
TOTM N17 42 D7
Pymmes Gdns North ED N9 42 B2
Pymmes Gdns South ED N9 42 B2
Pymmes Green Rd
FBAR/BDGN N11 40 B3
Pymmes Rd PLMGR N13 40 E5
Pymms Brook Dr EBAR EN4 27 J3
Pyne Rd SURB KT6 159 H7
Pynham Cl ABYW SE2 116 B2
Pynnacles Cl STAN HA7 35 H4
Pyrland Rd HBRY N5 73 K4
RCHPK/HAM TW10 125 G5
Pyrmont Gv WNWD SE27 149 H2
Pyrmont Rd CHSWK W4 105 H5
Pytchley Crs NRWD SE19 149 J5
Pytchley Rd EDUL SE22 131 F2

Q

The Quadrangle BAY/PAD W2 9 J4
HNHL SE24 * 130 D4
WBPTN SW10 * 108 B7
Quadrant Ar REGST W1B 10 F7
Quadrant Cl HDN NW4 * 51 K4
Quadrant Gv KTTN NW5 71 K4
Quadrant Rd RCH/KEW TW9 124 E3
THHTH CR7 164 C3
The Quadrant BELMT SM2 175 G5
BXLYHN DA7 116 E6
EDGW HA8 * 36 C5
NKENS W10 * 88 B2
RCH/KEW TW9 124 E4
RYLN/HDSTN HA2 * 48 D2
RYNPK SW20 146 C7
Quad Rd WBLY HA9 * 67 K2
Quaggy Wk BKHTH/KID SE3 133 K3
Quainton St WLSDN NW10 69 F2
Quaker La NWDGN UB2 103 F2
Quakers Course
CDALE/KGS NW9 37 H7
Quakers La ISLW TW7 104 B6
Quakers Pl FSTGT E7 77 H4
Quaker St WCHPL E1 13 L1
Quakers Wk WCHMH N21 29 K5
Quality Ct LINN WC2A 12 A4
Quantock Cl HYS/HAR UB3 101 G6
Quantock Gdns CRICK NW2 * 70 B1
Quantock Ms PECK SE15 131 H1
Quantock Rd BXLYHN DA7 138 B1
Quarles Park Rd CHDH RM6 61 H5
Quarrendon St FUL/PGN SW6 107 K7
Quarr Rd CAR SM5 162 C5
Quarry Ms PUR RM19 119 K3
Quarry Park Rd SUT SM1 174 D5
Quarry Ri SUT SM1 174 D5
Quarry Rd WAND/EARL SW18 128 B5
Quatre Ports CHING E4 * 44 B4
Quay House POP/IOD E14 * 112 D1
Quebec Ms MBLAR W1H 9 M5
Quebec Rd GNTH/NBYPK IG2 60 C6
YEAD UB4 83 G6
Quebec Wy BERM/RHTH SE16 112 A1
Queen Adelaide Rd
PGE/AN SE20 150 E5
Queen Anne Av HAYES BR2 167 K2
Queen Anne Dr
ESH/CLAY KT10 170 E6
Queen Anne Ga BXLYHN DA7 136 E2
Queen Anne Ms
CAVSQ/HST W1G 10 D3
Queen Anne Rd HOM E9 75 F5
Queen Annes Cl WHTN TW2 142 D2
Queen Anne's Gdns
CHSWK W4 106 B2
EA W5 105 F1
EN EN1 30 A5
MTCM CR4 * 162 E2
Queen Anne's Ga
STJSPK SW1H 17 G2
Queen Anne's Gv CHSWK W4 106 B2
EA W5 105 F1
ED N9 29 K6
EN EN1 30 A5
Queen Anne's Pl EN EN1 30 A5
Queen Annes Sq STHWK SE1 111 H3
Queen Anne St
CAVSQ/HST W1G 10 C3
Queen Anne Ter WAP E1W * 92 D6
Queen Borough Gdns
CHST BR7 154 D5
Queenborough Gdns
GNTH/NBYPK IG2 60 A3
Queen Caroline Est
HMSMTH W6 107 F4
Queen Caroline St
HMSMTH W6 107 F4
Queen Elizabeth Blds
EMB EC4Y * 12 A6
Queen Elizabeth College
GNWCH SE10 * 113 F6
Queen Elizabeth Gdns
MRDN SM4 161 K3
Queen Elizabeth Rd
KUTN/CMB KT2 159 G1
WALTH E17 57 G2
Queen Elizabeth's Cl
STNW/STAM N16 73 K1
Queen Elizabeth's Dr
STHGT/OAK N14 28 E7
Queen Elizabeth St
STHWK SE1 19 K1
Queen Elizabeth's Wk
STNW/STAM N16 55 K7
WLGTN SM6 176 D3
Queen Elizabeth Wk
BARN SW13 106 D7
Queenhithe BLKFR EC4V 12 F7
Queen Isabella Wy STBT EC1A 12 D4
Queen Margaret's Gv IS N1 74 A4
Queen Mary Av RYNPK SW20 161 G4
SWFD E18 44 E7
Queen Mary Cl ROM RM1 63 H5
SURB KT6 172 C2
Queen Mary Rd NRWD SE19 149 H5
Queen Mary's Av CAR SM5 175 K6
WATW WD18 20 C3
Queen Mother Ga
MYFR/PICC W1J 10 B9
Queens Acre CHEAM SM3 174 B6
Queens Av FELT TW13 141 G3
KTN/HRWW/WS HA3 49 H2
MUSWH N10 54 A2
TRDG/WHET N20 39 H1
WATW WD18 20 D3
Queen's Av FNCH N3 39 G6
GFD/PVL UB6 84 B5
WCHMH N21 29 H7
WFD IG8 45 F4
Queensberry Ms West
SKENS SW7 * 15 G5
Queensberry Pl MNPK E12 77 H4
SKENS SW7 15 G5
Queensberry Wy SKENS SW7 * 15 G5
Queensborough Ms
BAY/PAD W2 * 8 E6
Queensborough Pas
BAY/PAD W2 8 E6
Queensborough Studios
BAY/PAD W2 8 E6
Queensborough Ter
BAY/PAD W2 8 D6
Queensbridge Pk ISLW TW7 123 K5
Queensbridge Rd HACK E8 7 M4
Queensbury Rd ALP/SUD HA0 86 B1
CDALE/KGS NW9 51 F6
Queensbury St IS N1 6 F2
Queens Circ VX/NE SW8 109 G6
Queens Cl ESH/CLAY KT10 * 170 B3
Queen's Cl EDGW HA8 36 C4
WLGTN SM6 176 B4
Queens Club Gdns
WKENS W14 * 107 H5
Queen's Club Gdns
WKENS W14 107 H5
Queens Club Ter
WKENS W14 * 107 J5
Queenscourt WBLY HA9 68 A3
Queens Crs RCHPK/HAM TW10 125 G4
Queen's Crs KTTN NW5 72 A4
Queenscroft Rd
ELTH/MOT SE9 134 C4
Queensdale Crs NTGHL W11 88 B7
Queensdale Pl NTGHL W11 88 C7
Queensdale Rd NTGHL W11 88 B7
Queensdale Wk NTGHL W11 88 C7
Queens Down Rd CLPT E5 74 D3
Queens Dr BRYLDS KT5 159 H6
LEY E10 57 J6
Queen's Dr EA W5 86 B5
FSBYPK N4 73 H1
THDIT KT7 158 B5
Queen's Elm Sq CHEL SW3 15 G8
Queens Gdns HDN NW4 52 A4
RAIN RM13 99 F1
Queen's Gdns BAY/PAD W2 8 E6
EA W5 85 J4
HEST TW5 102 D7
Queens Garth FSTH SE23 * 150 E1
Queens Ga SKENS SW7 14 F2
Queen's Ga SKENS SW7 14 F2
Queens Gate Gdns CHST BR7 154 D7
Queensgate Gdns
PUT/ROE SW15 126 E3
Queen's Gate Gdns
SKENS SW7 14 E4
Queen's Gate Ms SKENS SW7 14 E3
Queensgate Pl
KIL/WHAMP NW6 2 A2
Queen's Gate Pl SKENS SW7 14 F4
Queen's Gate Place Ms
SKENS SW7 14 F4
Queen's Gate Ter SKENS SW7 14 E3
Queen's Gv STJWD NW8 3 G4
Queen's Head St IS N1 6 D4
Queens Keep TWK TW1 * 124 D5
Queensland Av UED N18 41 J5
WIM/MER SW19 147 F7
Queensland Cl WALTH E17 57 H1
Queensland Rd HOLWY N7 73 G3
Queens La MUSWH N10 54 B2
Queens Md EDGW HA8 36 B5
Queensmead STJWD NW8 3 H3
Queen's Mead Rd HAYES BR2 167 J1
Queensmere Cl
WIM/MER SW19 146 B1
Queensmere Rd
WIM/MER SW19 146 B1
Queen's Ms BAY/PAD W2 8 C6
Queensmill Rd FUL/PGN SW6 107 G6
Queens Pde CEND/HSY/T N8 * 55 H3
CRICK NW2 * 70 A5
EA W5 * 86 B5
FBAR/BDGN N11 * 39 K4
HDN NW4 * 51 K4
Queens Parade Cl
FBAR/BDGN N11 39 K4
Queens Park Gdns
FELT TW13 * 140 D2
Queen's Pl MRDN SM4 161 K3
WAT WD17 21 G2
Queens Prom KUT/HW KT1 158 E3
Queen Sq BMSBY WC1N 11 K1
Queen's Ride PUT/ROE SW15 126 D3
Queen's Ri RCHPK/HAM TW10 125 G5
Queens Rd BAR EN5 26 B2
ERITH DA8 118 B5
HYS/HAR UB3 82 C5
MRDN SM4 161 K3
WDR/YW UB7 100 C1
Queen's Rd BARK IG11 78 C6
BECK BR3 166 B1
BKHH IG9 45 F1
BMLY BR1 167 K1
CHST BR7 154 B5
CROY/NA CR0 164 C5
EA W5 86 A5
ED N9 42 D1
EN EN1 30 A3
FBAR/BDGN N11 40 E6
FELT TW13 122 A7
FNCH N3 39 G7
HDN NW4 52 A4
HPTN TW12 142 B3
HSLW TW3 123 G2
KUTN/CMB KT2 144 C6
MORT/ESHN SW14 126 A2
MTCM CR4 162 C2
NWDGN UB2 102 C1
NWMAL KT3 160 C3
PECK SE15 111 K7
PLSTW E13 77 F7
RCHPK/HAM TW10 144 C4
TEDD TW11 143 F5
THDIT KT7 158 A4
TWK TW1 124 A7
WALTH E17 57 H5
WAN E11 58 C6
WAT WD17 21 G2
WELL DA16 136 C1
WIM/MER SW19 146 E5
WLGTN SM6 176 B4
Queen's Rd West PLSTW E13 94 E1
Queens Rw WALW SE17 * 19 G9
Queen's Rw WALW SE17 19 G9
Queens Ter ISLW TW7 124 B3
PLSTW E13 77 F7
THDIT KT7 * 158 B5
WCHPL E1 * 92 E3
Queen's Ter ISLW TW7 124 B3

STJWD NW8 ..... **3** G4
Queens Terrace Cots
HNWL W7 * **103** K1
Queensthorpe Ms *SYD* SE26 * **151** F3
Queensthorpe Rd *SYD* SE26 ..... **151** F3
Queenstown Gdns *RAIN* RM13 ..... **99** H2
Queenstown Rd *VX/NE* SW8 ..... **129** G1
Queen St *BXLYHN* DA7 ..... **137** G2
CROY/NA CR0 ..... **177** J3
ERITH DA8 * **118** B5
MYFR/PICC W1J **10** C8
ROMW/RG RM7 ..... **63** F5
STP EC4M **12** F5
TOTM N17 ..... **42** A5
Queen Street Pl *CANST* EC4R **12** F7
Queensville Rd *BAL* SW12 ..... **129** J6
Queens Wk *CDALE/KGS* NW9 ..... **68** E1
HRW HA1 ..... **48** E3
RSLP HA4 ..... **65** G2
Queen's Wk *EA* W5 ..... **85** J3
Queens Walk Ter *RSLP* HA4 * **65** G2
The Queens Wk *STHWK* SE1 ..... **13** K8
Queens Wy *FELT* TW13 ..... **141** G3
HDN NW4 ..... **52** A4
Queensway *BAY/PAD* W2 ..... **8** D4
CROY/NA CR0 ..... **177** F5
PEND EN3 ..... **30** E3
STMC/STPC BR5 ..... **169** H4
SUN TW16 ..... **156** A1
WWKM BR4 ..... **180** E3
Queens Well Av
TRDG/WHET N20 ..... **39** J3
Queen's Whf *HMSMTH* W6 ..... **107** F4
Queenswood Av *HPTN* TW12 ..... **142** B5
HSLW TW3 ..... **122** E1
THHTH CR7 ..... **164** B4
WALTH E17 ..... **44** A7
WLGTN SM6 ..... **176** D3
Queenswood Gdns *WAN* E11 ..... **58** E7
Queenswood Pk *FNCH* N3 ..... **52** C1
Queenswood Rd *BFN/LL* DA15 ..... **136** A4
FSTH SE23 ..... **151** G2
Queen's Wood Rd *HGT* N6 ..... **54** B5
Queen's Yd *FITZ* W1T **10** F1
Queen Victoria Av
ALP/SUD HA0 ..... **67** K6
Queen Victoria St *BLKFR* EC4V **12** C6
Queen Victoria Ter
WAP E1W * **92** D6
Quemerford Rd *HOLWY* N7 ..... **73** F4
Quentin Pl *LEW* SE13 ..... **133** H2
Quentin Rd *LEW* SE13 ..... **133** H2
Quernmore Cl *BMLY* BR1 ..... **152** E5
Quernmore Rd *BMLY* BR1 ..... **152** E5
FSBYPK N4 ..... **55** G5
Querrin St *FUL/PGN* SW6 ..... **128** B1
Quex Ms *KIL/WHAMP* NW6 ..... **2** B3
Quex Rd *KIL/WHAMP* NW6 ..... **2** B3
Quick Rd *CHSWK* W4 ..... **106** B4
Quicks Rd *WIM/MER* SW19 ..... **147** F6
Quick St *IS* N1 ..... **6** D6
Quickswood *HAMP* NW3 ..... **3** K1
Quiet Nook *HAYES* BR2 ..... **181** H2
Quill St *EA* W5 ..... **86** A2
FSBYPK N4 ..... **73** G2
Quilp St *STHWK* SE1 ..... **18** E1
Quilters Pl *ELTH/MOT* SE9 ..... **135** H7
Quilter St *BETH* E2 ..... **92** C2
WOOL/PLUM SE18 ..... **116** A4
Quince Rd *LEW* SE13 ..... **132** E1
Quinnel Cl *WOOL/PLUM* SE18 ..... **116** A4
Quinnell Cl *WOOL/PLUM* SE18 ..... **116** A4
Quinta Dr *BAR* EN5 ..... **25** K4
Quintin Av *RYNPK* SW20 ..... **146** C7
Quinton Cl *BECK* BR3 ..... **167** F2
HEST TW5 ..... **102** A6
WLGTN SM6 ..... **176** B3
Quinton Rd *THDIT* KT7 ..... **158** B7
Quinton St *WAND/EARL* SW18 ..... **147** G1
Quixley St *POP/IOD* E14 ..... **94** B6
Quorn Rd *EDUL* SE22 ..... **131** F3

R

Rabbit Rw *KENS* W8 * **8** B8
Rabbits Rd *MNPK* E12 ..... **77** J3
Rabournmead Dr *NTHLT* UB5 ..... **65** H4
Raby Rd *NWMAL* KT3 ..... **160** A3
Raby St *POP/IOD* E14 * **93** G5
Raccoon Wy *HSLWW* TW4 ..... **122** B1
Rachel Cl *BARK/HLT* IG6 ..... **60** D3
Rackham Cl *WELL* DA16 ..... **136** C1
Rackham Ms
STRHM/NOR SW16 ..... **148** C5
Racton Rd *FUL/PGN* SW6 ..... **107** K5
Radbourne Av *EA* W5 ..... **104** D3
Radbourne Cl *CLPT* E5 ..... **75** F3
Radbourne Ct
KTN/HRWW/WS HA3 * **49** H5
Radbourne Crs *WALTH* E17 ..... **58** B2
Radbourne Rd *BAL* SW12 ..... **129** H6
Radcliffe Av *WLSDN* NW10 ..... **87** J1
Radcliffe Gdns *CAR* SM5 ..... **175** J6
Radcliffe Rd *CROY/NA* CR0 ..... **178** B1
KTN/HRWW/WS HA3 ..... **49** G1
STHWK SE1 ..... **19** K3
WCHMH N21 ..... **29** H7
Radcliffe Sq *PUT/ROE* SW15 ..... **127** G5
Radcliffe Wy *NTHLT* UB5 ..... **83** H2
Radcot St *LBTH* SE11 ..... **18** B8
Raddington Rd *NKENS* W10 ..... **88** C4
Radfield Wy *BFN/LL* DA15 ..... **135** J6
Radford Est *WLSDN* NW10 * **87** G2
Radford Rd *LEW* SE13 ..... **133** F5
Radford Wy *BARK* IG11 ..... **97** F2
Radipole Rd *FUL/PGN* SW6 ..... **107** J7
Radius Pk *EBED/NFELT* TW14 * **121** J3
Radland Rd *CAN/RD* E16 ..... **94** E5
Radlet Av *SYD* SE26 ..... **150** D2
Radlett Cl *FSTGT* E7 ..... **76** D5
Radlett Pl *STJWD* NW8 ..... **3** J4
Radlett Rd *WAT* WD17 ..... **21** G2
Radley Av *GDMY/SEVK* IG3 ..... **79** F3
Radley Cl *EBED/NFELT* TW14 ..... **121** J7
Radley Ct *BERM/RHTH* SE16 ..... **112** A1
Radley Gdns
KTN/HRWW/WS HA3 ..... **50** A3
Radley Ms *KENS* W8 ..... **14** B4
Radley Rd *TOTM* N17 ..... **56** A1
Radley's La *SWFD* E18 ..... **58** E1
Radleys Md *DAGE* RM10 ..... **80** D5
Radley Sq *CLPT* E5 * **74** E1
Radley Ter *CAN/RD* E16 ..... **94** D4
Radlix Rd *LEY* E10 ..... **57** J7
Radnor Av *HRW* HA1 ..... **48** E4
WELL DA16 ..... **136** C4
Radnor Cl *CHST* BR7 ..... **154** E5
MTCM CR4 ..... **163** K4
Radnor Crs *REDBR* IG4 ..... **59** K4
WOOL/PLUM SE18 ..... **116** B6
Radnor Gdns *TWK* TW1 ..... **143** F1
Radnor Hall *BORE* WD6 * **24** A4
Radnor Ms *BAY/PAD* W2 ..... **9** H5
Radnor Pl *BAY/PAD* W2 ..... **9** J5
Radnor Rd *HRW* HA1 ..... **48** D4
KIL/WHAMP NW6 ..... **70** C7
PECK SE15 ..... **111** H6
TWK TW1 ..... **124** A7
Radnor St *FSBYE* EC1V **6** F8
Radnor Ter *WKENS* W14 ..... **107** J3
Radnor Wk *CHEL* SW3 ..... **15** K8
CROY/NA CR0 ..... **166** B6
Radnor Wy *WLSDN* NW10 ..... **86** D3
Radstock Av
KTN/HRWW/WS HA3 ..... **49** G2
Radstock Cl *FBAR/BDGN* N11 ..... **40** A4
Radstock St *BTSEA* SW11 * **108** D6
Raebarn Gdns *BAR* EN5 ..... **25** K4
Raeburn Av *BRYLDS* KT5 ..... **159** J6
DART DA1 ..... **138** E4
Raeburn Cl *GLDGN* NW11 ..... **53** G5
KUT/HW KT1 ..... **143** K6
Raeburn Rd *BFN/LL* DA15 ..... **135** K5
EDGW HA8 ..... **50** C1
YEAD UB4 ..... **82** B1
Raeburn St *BRXS/STRHM* SW2 ..... **129** K3
Rafford Wy *BMLY* BR1 ..... **168** A1
Raggleswood *CHST* BR7 ..... **154** A7
Raglan Cl *HSLWW* TW4 ..... **122** D4
Raglan Ct *SAND/SEL* CR2 ..... **177** H4
Raglan Gdns *OXHEY* WD19 ..... **21** F7
Raglan Rd *BELV* DA17 ..... **117** G3
EN EN1 ..... **30** A6
HAYES BR2 ..... **168** B3
WALTH E17 ..... **58** A4
WOOL/PLUM SE18 ..... **115** H4
Raglan St *KTTN* NW5 ..... **72** B5
Raglan Ter *RYLN/HDSTN* HA2 * **66** B3
Raglan Vls *WALTH* E17 * **58** A4
Raglan Wy *NTHLT* UB5 ..... **66** C5
Ragley Cl *ACT* W3 ..... **105** K1
Railey Ms *KTTN* NW5 ..... **72** C4
Railshead Rd *ISLW* TW7 ..... **124** C3
Railton Rd *HNHL* SE24 ..... **130** B4
Railway Ap *FSBYPK* N4 ..... **55** G5
HRW HA1 ..... **49** F3
STHWK SE1 ..... **13** G8
TWK TW1 ..... **124** B6
WLGTN SM6 * **176** B5
Railway Ar *BRXN/ST* SW9 * **130** B3
Railway Av *BERM/RHTH* SE16 ..... **111** K1
Railway Cots *HMSMTH* W6 * **107** F1
SRTFD E15 * **94** C1
WIM/MER SW19 * **147** F3
Railway Gv *NWCR* SE14 ..... **112** C6
Railway Pl *BELV* DA17 ..... **117** H2
Railway Ri *EDUL* SE22 ..... **131** F3
Railway Rd *TEDD* TW11 ..... **142** E3
Railway Side *BARN* SW13 ..... **126** B2
Railway Station Whf
LEY E10 * **57** G7
Railway St *CHDH* RM6 ..... **61** J7
IS N1 ..... **5** K6
Railway Ter *FELT* TW13 ..... **121** K7
LEW SE13 ..... **132** E4
WALTH E17 ..... **44** A7
Rainborough Cl *WBLY* HA9 ..... **68** E5
Rainbow Av *POP/IOD* E14 ..... **112** E4
Rainbow Ct *OXHEY* WD19 ..... **21** G5
Rainbow Quay
BERM/RHTH SE16 ..... **112** B2
Rainbow St *CMBW* SE5 ..... **111** F6
Raine St *WAP* E1W **92** D7
Rainham Cl *BTSEA* SW11 ..... **128** D5
ELTH/MOT SE9 ..... **135** K5
Rainham Rd *RAIN* RM13 ..... **99** J2
WLSDN NW10 ..... **88** A2
Rainham Rd North
DAGE RM10 ..... **80** D1
Rainham Rd South
DAGE RM10 ..... **80** E5
Rainhill Wy *BOW* E3 ..... **93** J2
Rainsborough Av *DEPT* SE8 ..... **112** B3
Rainsford Rd *WLSDN* NW10 ..... **86** C2
Rainsford St *BAY/PAD* W2 ..... **9** J4
Rainsford Wy *HCH* RM12 ..... **63** J7
Rainton Rd *CHARL* SE7 ..... **113** K4
Rainville Rd *HMSMTH* W6 ..... **107** F5
Raisins Hl *PIN* HA5 ..... **47** F2
Raith Av *STHGT/OAK* N14 ..... **40** D2
Raleigh Av *WLGTN* SM6 ..... **176** D3
YEAD UB4 ..... **83** F4
Raleigh Cl *ERITH* DA8 ..... **118** C5
HDN NW4 ..... **52** A4
PIN HA5 ..... **47** H6
RSLP HA4 ..... **64** D1
Raleigh Dr *BRYLDS* KT5 ..... **159** K7
ESH/CLAY KT10 ..... **170** D4
TRDG/WHET N20 ..... **39** J2
Raleigh Gdns
BRXS/STRHM SW2 ..... **130** A5
MTCM CR4 ..... **162** E1
Raleigh Ms *IS* N1 ..... **6** D4
Raleigh Rd *CEND/HSY/T* N8 ..... **55** G3
ENC/FH EN2 ..... **29** K3
FELT TW13 ..... **140** D1
NWDGN UB2 ..... **102** D4
PGE/AN SE20 ..... **151** F6
RCH/KEW TW9 ..... **125** G2
Raleigh St *IS* N1 ..... **6** D4
Raleigh Wy *FELT* TW13 ..... **141** G4
STHGT/OAK N14 ..... **28** D7
Ralph Perring Ct *BECK* BR3 ..... **166** D3
Ralston St *CHEL* SW3 ..... **15** L8
Ralston Wy *OXHEY* WD19 ..... **33** H1
Rama Cl *STRHM/NOR* SW16 ..... **148** E6
Ramac Wy *CHARL* SE7 ..... **114** A3
Rama La *NRWD* SE19 ..... **150** B6
Rambler Cl *STRHM/NOR* SW16 ..... **148** C3
Rame Cl *TOOT* SW17 ..... **148** A4
Ramilles Cl *BRXS/STRHM* SW2 ..... **129** K5
Ramillies Pl *SOHO/CST* W1F **10** E5
Ramillies Rd *BFN/LL* DA15 ..... **136** C5
CHSWK W4 ..... **106** A2
MLHL NW7 ..... **37** G1
Ramillies St *SOHO/SHAV* W1D **10** E5
Ramones Ter *MTCM* CR4 * **163** H3
Rampart St *WCHPL* E1 ..... **92** D5
Ram Pas *KUT/HW* KT1 ..... **158** E1
Rampayne St *PIM* SW1V **17** G7
Rampton Cl *CHING* E4 ..... **43** J2
Ramsay Rd *ACT* W3 ..... **105** K2
FSTGT E7 ..... **76** D3
Ramscroft Cl *ED* N9 ..... **30** A6
Ramsdale Rd *TOOT* SW17 ..... **148** A4
Ramsden Ga *BAL* SW12 * **129** G6
Ramsden Rd *BAL* SW12 ..... **129** F6
ERITH DA8 ..... **118** A6
FBAR/BDGN N11 ..... **39** K4
Ramsey Cl *CDALE/KGS* NW9 ..... **51** H5
GFD/PVL UB6 ..... **66** D4
Ramsey Rd *THHTH* CR7 ..... **164** A5
Ramsey St *BETH* E2 ..... **92** C3
Ramsey Wk *IS* N1 ..... **73** K5
Ramsey Wy *STHGT/OAK* N14 ..... **28** C6
Ramsgate Cl *CAN/RD* E16 ..... **95** F7
Ramsgate St *HACK* E8 * **74** B5
Ramsgill Ap *GNTH/NBYPK* IG2 ..... **61** F3
Ramsgill Dr *GNTH/NBYPK* IG2 ..... **61** F4
Rams Gv *CHDH* RM6 ..... **62** A3
Ramulis Dr *YEAD* UB4 ..... **83** J3
Rancliffe Gdns *ELTH/MOT* SE9 ..... **134** D3
Rancliffe Rd *EHAM* E6 ..... **95** J1
Randall Av *CRICK* NW2 ..... **69** G1
Randall Cl *BTSEA* SW11 ..... **108** D7
ERITH DA8 ..... **117** K5
Randall Pl *GNWCH* SE10 ..... **113** F6
Randall Rd *LBTH* SE11 ..... **17** L7
Randall Rw *LBTH* SE11 ..... **17** L6
Randell's Rd *IS* N1 ..... **5** K3
Randisbourne Gdns *CAT* SE6 * **151** K2
Randle Rd *RCHPK/HAM* TW10 ..... **143** J3
Randlesdown Rd *CAT* SE6 ..... **151** J3
Randolf Rd *HAYES* BR2 ..... **168** E7
Randolph Ap *CAN/RD* E16 ..... **95** G5
Randolph Av *MV/WKIL* W9 ..... **2** C6
Randolph Cl *BXLYHN* DA7 ..... **137** K2
KUTN/CMB KT2 * **144** E4
Randolph Crs *MV/WKIL* W9 ..... **8** E1
Randolph Gdns
KIL/WHAMP NW6 ..... **2** C6
Randolph Gv *CHDH* RM6 ..... **61** J4
Randolph Ms *MV/WKIL* W9 ..... **8** F1
Randolph Rd *MV/WKIL* W9 ..... **8** E1
STHL UB1 * **102** E1
WALTH E17 * **57** K4
Randolph St *CAMTN* NW1 ..... **4** E2
Randon Cl *RYLN/HDSTN* HA2 ..... **48** B1
Ranelagh Av *BARN* SW13 ..... **126** D1
FUL/PGN SW6 ..... **127** J2
Ranelagh Cl *EDGW* HA8 ..... **36** C3
Ranelagh Dr *EDGW* HA8 ..... **36** C3
TWK TW1 ..... **124** C3
Ranelagh Gdns *CHSWK* W4 ..... **105** K6
FUL/PGN SW6 ..... **127** J2
IL IG1 ..... **60** A7
WAN E11 ..... **59** G4
Ranelagh Gv *BGVA* SW1W **16** B7
Ranelagh Pl *NWMAL* KT3 ..... **160** B4
Ranelagh Rd *ALP/SUD* HA0 ..... **67** K4
EA W5 ..... **104** E1
EHAM E6 ..... **78** A7
PIM SW1V **16** F8
SRTFD E15 ..... **76** C7
STHL UB1 ..... **83** H7
TOTM N17 ..... **56** A2
WAN E11 ..... **76** C3
WDGN N22 ..... **41** F7
WLSDN NW10 ..... **87** H1
Ranfurly Rd *SUT* SM1 ..... **174** E1
Rangefield Rd *BMLY* BR1 ..... **152** C4
Rangemoor Rd
SEVS/STOTM N15 ..... **56** B4
Rangeworth Pl *BFN/LL* DA15 ..... **155** F2
Rangoon St *TWRH* EC3N * **13** L5
Rankin Cl *CDALE/KGS* NW9 ..... **51** G2
Ranleigh Gdns *BXLYHN* DA7 ..... **117** G6
Ranmere St *BAL* SW12 ..... **129** G7
Ranmoor Cl *HRW* HA1 ..... **48** D3
Ranmoor Gdns *HRW* HA1 ..... **48** D3
Ranmore Av *CROY/NA* CR0 ..... **178** B2
Ranmore Rd *BELMT* SM2 ..... **174** B7
Rannoch Cl *EDGW* HA8 ..... **36** D1
Rannoch Rd *HMSMTH* W6 ..... **107** F5
Rannock Av *CDALE/KGS* NW9 ..... **51** F6
Ransom Cl *OXHEY* WD19 ..... **21** G6
Ransom Rd *CHARL* SE7 * **114** B4
Ranston St *CAMTN* NW1 ..... **9** J2
Ranulf Rd *CRICK* NW2 ..... **70** D3
Ranwell Cl *BOW* E3 * **75** H7
Ranworth Cl *ERITH* DA8 ..... **138** B1
Ranworth Rd *ED* N9 ..... **42** E1
Ranyard Cl *CHSGTN* KT9 ..... **172** B2
Raphael Av *ROM* RM1 ..... **63** H2
Raphael Cl *KUT/HW* KT1 ..... **158** E3
Raphael Dr *THDIT* KT7 ..... **158** A7
WATN WD24 ..... **21** H1
Raphael St *SKENS* SW7 ..... **15** L2
Rapier Cl *PUR* RM19 ..... **119** J3
Rasper Rd *TRDG/WHET* N20 ..... **39** G1
Rastell Av *BRXS/STRHM* SW2 ..... **148** D1
Ratcliffe Cl *LEE/GVPK* SE12 ..... **133** K6
Ratcliffe Cross St *WCHPL* E1 * **93** F5
Ratcliffe La *POP/IOD* E14 ..... **93** G5
Ratcliff Rd *FSTGT* E7 ..... **77** G4
Rathbone Pl *FITZ* W1T **11** G3
Rathbone Sq *CROY/NA* CR0 * **177** J3
Rathbone St *CAN/RD* E16 ..... **94** D4
FITZ W1T **10** F3
Rathcoole Av *CEND/HSY/T* N8 ..... **55** F4
Rathcoole Gdns
CEND/HSY/T N8 ..... **55** F4
Rathfern Rd *CAT* SE6 ..... **132** C7
Rathgar Av *WEA* W13 ..... **85** H7
Rathgar Cl *FNCH* N3 ..... **52** D1
Rathgar Rd *BRXN/ST* SW9 ..... **130** C2
Rathmell Dr *CLAP* SW4 ..... **129** J5
Rathmore Rd *CHARL* SE7 ..... **114** A4
Rattray Rd *BRXS/STRHM* SW2 ..... **130** B3
Raul Rd *PECK* SE15 ..... **131** H1
Raveley St *KTTN* NW5 ..... **72** C3
Ravencroft Crs *ELTH/MOT* SE9 ..... **153** K2
Ravenet St *BTSEA* SW11 ..... **109** G7
Ravenfield Rd *TOOT* SW17 ..... **147** K2
Ravenhill Rd *PLSTW* E13 ..... **77** G7
Ravenna Rd *PUT/ROE* SW15 ..... **127** G4
Ravenor Park Rd
GFD/PVL UB6 ..... **84** B2
Raven Rd *SWFD* E18 ..... **59** G1
Raven Rw *WCHPL* E1 ..... **92** D4
Ravens Ait *SURB* KT6 * **158** E4
Ravensbourne Av *HAYES* BR2 ..... **152** B7
STWL/WRAY TW19 ..... **120** B7
Ravensbourne Gdns
WEA W13 ..... **85** H4
Ravensbourne Pk *CAT* SE6 ..... **132** D6
Ravensbourne Park Crs
CAT SE6 ..... **132** C6
Ravensbourne Pl *LEW* SE13 ..... **132** E1
Ravensbourne Rd *BMLY* BR1 ..... **167** K2
CAT SE6 ..... **132** C6
DART DA1 ..... **138** D2
TWK TW1 ..... **124** D5
Ravensbury Av *MRDN* SM4 ..... **162** B4
Ravensbury Gv *MTCM* CR4 ..... **162** C3
Ravensbury La *MTCM* CR4 ..... **162** C3
Ravensbury Rd
WAND/EARL SW18 ..... **147** F1
Ravensbury Ter
WAND/EARL SW18 ..... **147** F1
Ravenscar Rd *BMLY* BR1 ..... **152** C3
SURB KT6 ..... **172** B1
Ravens Cl *CDALE/KGS* NW9 ..... **51** H1
EN EN1 ..... **30** A1
HAYES BR2 ..... **167** J1
SURB KT6 ..... **158** E5
Ravenscourt *SUN* TW16 ..... **140** D7
Ravenscourt Av *HMSMTH* W6 ..... **106** D3
Ravenscourt Cl *DEN/HRF* UB9 ..... **46** A6
Ravenscourt Gdns
HMSMTH W6 ..... **106** C3
Ravenscourt Pk *HMSMTH* W6 ..... **106** D3
Ravenscourt Pl *HMSMTH* W6 ..... **106** E3
Ravenscourt Rd *HMSMTH* W6 ..... **106** E3
Ravenscourt Sq *HMSMTH* W6 ..... **106** D2
Ravenscraig Rd
FBAR/BDGN N11 ..... **40** B3
Ravenscroft Av *GLDGN* NW11 ..... **52** D6
WBLY HA9 ..... **50** A7
Ravenscroft Cl *CAN/RD* E16 ..... **94** E4
Ravenscroft Cots *BAR* EN5 * **26** E5
Ravenscroft Pk *BAR* EN5 ..... **26** B2
Ravenscroft Rd *BECK* BR3 ..... **165** K1
CAN/RD E16 ..... **94** E4
CHSWK W4 ..... **105** K3
Ravenscroft St *BETH* E2 ..... **7** M6
Ravensdale Av
NFNCH/WDSPK N12 ..... **39** G3
Ravensdale Gdns *NRWD* SE19 ..... **149** K6
Ravensdale Rd *HSLWW* TW4 ..... **122** D2
STNW/STAM N16 ..... **56** B6
Ravensdon St *LBTH* SE11 ..... **18** B8
Ravensfield *DAGW* RM9 ..... **79** K3
Ravensfield Gdns
HOR/WEW KT19 ..... **173** G4
Ravenshaw St
KIL/WHAMP NW6 ..... **70** D4
Ravenshill *CHST* BR7 ..... **154** B7
Ravenshurst Av *HDN* NW4 ..... **52** A3
Ravenside Cl *UED* N18 ..... **43** F4
Ravenslea Rd *BAL* SW12 ..... **128** E6
Ravensleigh Gdns *BMLY* BR1 ..... **152** E4
Ravensmead Rd *HAYES* BR2 ..... **152** B6
Ravensmede Wy *CHSWK* W4 ..... **106** C3
Ravens Ms *LEE/GVPK* SE12 * **133** K4
Ravenstone Rd
CDALE/KGS NW9 * **51** H5
CEND/HSY/T N8 ..... **55** F2
Ravenstone St *BAL* SW12 ..... **129** F7
Ravens Wy *LEE/GVPK* SE12 ..... **133** K4
Ravenswood *BXLY* DA5 ..... **137** F7
Ravenswood Av *SURB* KT6 ..... **172** B1
WWKM BR4 ..... **167** F7
Ravenswood Ct
KUTN/CMB KT2 * **144** E5
Ravenswood Crs
RYLN/HDSTN HA2 ..... **65** K1
WWKM BR4 ..... **167** F7
Ravenswood Gdns *ISLW* TW7 ..... **103** K7
Ravenswood Pk *NTHWD* HA6 ..... **32** E5
Ravenswood Rd *BAL* SW12 ..... **129** G6
CROY/NA CR0 ..... **177** H2
WALTH E17 ..... **58** A3
Ravensworth Rd
ELTH/MOT SE9 ..... **153** K3
WLSDN NW10 * **87** K2
Ravey St *SDTCH* EC2A **7** J9
Ravine Gv *WOOL/PLUM* SE18 ..... **115** K5
Rav Pinter Cl *STNW/STAM* N16 ..... **56** A6
Rawlings Cl *BECK* BR3 ..... **167** F4
Rawlings Crs *WBLY* HA9 ..... **68** D2
Rawlings St *CHEL* SW3 ..... **15** L5
Rawlins Cl *FNCH* N3 ..... **52** C2
SAND/SEL CR2 ..... **179** H6
Rawnsley Av *MTCM* CR4 ..... **162** C4
Rawreth Wk *IS* N1 ..... **6** F3
Rawson St *BTSEA* SW11 ..... **109** F7
Rawsthorne Cl *CAN/RD* E16 ..... **95** K7
Rawstorne Pl *FSBYE* EC1V * **6** C7
Rawstorne St *FSBYE* EC1V **6** C7
Ray Bell Ct *BROCKY* SE4 * **132** C1
Raydean Rd *BAR* EN5 ..... **26** E4
Raydons Gdns *DAGW* RM9 ..... **80** A3
Raydons Rd *DAGW* RM9 ..... **80** A4
Raydon St *ARCH* N19 ..... **72** B1
Rayfield Cl *HAYES* BR2 ..... **168** D5
Rayford Av *LEE/GVPK* SE12 ..... **133** J6
Rayford Cl *DART* DA1 ..... **139** F4
Ray Gdns *BARK* IG11 ..... **97** G1
STAN HA7 ..... **35** H4
Ray Lamb Wy *ERITH* DA8 ..... **118** E5
Rayleas Cl *WOOL/PLUM* SE18 ..... **115** G7
Rayleigh Av *TEDD* TW11 ..... **142** E5
Rayleigh Cl *PLMGR* N13 ..... **41** K2
Rayleigh Ct *KUT/HW* KT1 ..... **159** H1
Rayleigh Ri *SAND/SEL* CR2 ..... **178** A5
Rayleigh Rd *CAN/RD* E16 ..... **95** F7
PLMGR N13 ..... **41** J2
WFD IG8 ..... **45** G6
WIM/MER SW19 ..... **146** D7
Ray Lodge Rd *WFD* IG8 ..... **45** G5
Raymead Av *THHTH* CR7 ..... **164** B4
Raymere Gdns
WOOL/PLUM SE18 ..... **115** J6
Raymond Av *SWFD* E18 ..... **58** D2
WEA W13 ..... **104** B2
Raymond Blds *GINN* WC1R * **11** M2
Raymond Cl *SYD* SE26 ..... **150** E4
Raymond Rd *BECK* BR3 ..... **166** B3
GNTH/NBYPK IG2 ..... **60** D6
PLSTW E13 ..... **77** G6
WIM/MER SW19 ..... **146** C5
Raymond Wy
ESH/CLAY KT10 * **171** G5
Raymouth Rd
BERM/RHTH SE16 ..... **111** J3
Rayne Ct *SWFD* E18 ..... **58** D3
Rayners Cl *ALP/SUD* HA0 ..... **67** K4
Rayners Gdns *NTHLT* UB5 ..... **83** F2
Rayners La *PIN* HA5 ..... **47** K6
Rayner's Rd *PUT/ROE* SW15 ..... **127** H4
Raynes Av *WAN* E11 ..... **59** G6
Raynes Pk *RYNPK* SW20 ..... **161** F1
Raynham Av *UED* N18 ..... **42** C5
Raynham Rd *HMSMTH* W6 ..... **106** E3
UED N18 ..... **42** C4
Raynham Ter *UED* N18 ..... **42** C4
Raynor Cl *STHL* UB1 ..... **83** K7
Raynor Pl *IS* N1 ..... **6** F3
Raynton Cl *RYLN/HDSTN* HA2 ..... **47** J6
YEAD UB4 ..... **82** D3
Raynton Dr *YEAD* UB4 ..... **82** C1
Ray Rd *E/WMO/HCT* KT8 ..... **157** G4
Rays Av *UED* N18 ..... **42** E3
Rays Rd *UED* N18 ..... **42** E3
WWKM BR4 ..... **167** F6
Ray St *CLKNW* EC1R **12** B1
Ray Street Br *CLKNW* EC1R * **12** B1
Raywood Cl *HYS/HAR* UB3 ..... **101** F6
Reachview Cl *CAMTN* NW1 ..... **4** F2
Read Cl *THDIT* KT7 ..... **158** B6
Reading La *HACK* E8 ..... **74** D5
Reading Rd *NTHLT* UB5 ..... **66** B4
SUT SM1 ..... **175** G4
Reading Wy *MLHL* NW7 ..... **38** B4
Reads Cl *IL* IG1 ..... **78** B2
Reapers Cl *CAMTN* NW1 ..... **5** G3
Reapers Wy *ISLW* TW7 ..... **123** J4
Reardon Pth *WAP* E1W **92** D7
Reardon St *WAP* E1W **92** D7
Reaston St *NWCR* SE14 ..... **111** K6
Reckitt Rd *CHSWK* W4 ..... **106** B4
Record St *PECK* SE15 ..... **111** K5
Recovery St *TOOT* SW17 ..... **147** J4
Recreation Av *ROMW/RG* RM7 ..... **62** E4
Recreation Rd *HAYES* BR2 ..... **167** J1
NWDGN UB2 ..... **102** D3
SYD SE26 ..... **151** F3
Recreation Wy *MTCM* CR4 ..... **163** K2
Rectar Pl *ARCH* N19 ..... **72** B1
Rector St *IS* N1 ..... **6** E4
Rectory Cl *CHING* E4 ..... **43** J2
DART DA1 ..... **138** B3
FNCH N3 ..... **38** D7
RYNPK SW20 ..... **161** F1
SCUP DA14 ..... **155** H3
STAN HA7 ..... **35** H5
SURB KT6 ..... **158** D7
Rectory Field Crs *CHARL* SE7 ..... **114** B6
Rectory Gdns *BECK* BR3 * **151** J7
CEND/HSY/T N8 ..... **54** E3
CHST BR7 * **154** C7
NTHLT UB5 ..... **65** K7
Rectory Gn *BECK* BR3 ..... **151** H7
Rectory Gv *CLAP* SW4 ..... **129** H2
CROY/NA CR0 ..... **177** H1
HPTN TW12 ..... **141** K3
Rectory La *BUSH* WD23 ..... **22** A5
EDGW HA8 ..... **36** C5
SCUP DA14 ..... **155** J4
STAN HA7 ..... **35** H4
SURB KT6 ..... **158** D7
TOOT SW17 ..... **148** A4
WLGTN SM6 ..... **176** C3
Rectory Orch *WIM/MER* SW19 ..... **146** C3
Rectory Park Av *NTHLT* UB5 ..... **83** K2
Rectory Pl *CHST* BR7 * **154** C7
WOOL/PLUM SE18 ..... **115** F3
Rectory Rd *BARN* SW13 ..... **126** D1
BECK BR3 ..... **151** J7
DAGE RM10 ..... **80** C5
HAYES BR2 ..... **181** H6
HSLWW TW4 ..... **122** A1
HYS/HAR UB3 ..... **82** E5
MNPK E12 ..... **77** K4
NWDGN UB2 ..... **102** E2
STNW/STAM N16 ..... **74** B2
SUT SM1 ..... **174** E2
WALTH E17 ..... **57** K3
Rectory Sq *WCHPL* E1 ..... **93** F4
Reculver Ms *UED* N18 ..... **42** C3
Reculver Rd
BERM/RHTH SE16 ..... **112** A4
Red Anchor Cl *CHEL* SW3 ..... **108** C5
Redan Pl *BAY/PAD* W2 ..... **8** C5
Redan St *WKENS* W14 ..... **107** G2
Redan Ter *CMBW* SE5 ..... **130** C1
Red Barracks Rd
WOOL/PLUM SE18 ..... **114** E3
Redberry Gv *SYD* SE26 ..... **150** E2
Redbourne Av *FNCH* N3 ..... **38** E7
Redbourne Dr *THMD* SE28 ..... **97** K5
Redbridge Gdns *CMBW* SE5 ..... **111** F6
Redbridge La East *REDBR* IG4 ..... **59** H5
Redbridge La West *WAN* E11 ..... **59** F5
Redburn St *CHEL* SW3 ..... **15** L9
Redbury Cl *RAIN* RM13 ..... **99** K3
Redcar Cl *NTHLT* UB5 ..... **66** B4
Redcar St *CMBW* SE5 * **110** D6
Redcastle Cl *WAP* E1W **92** E6
Red Cedars Rd *ORP* BR6 ..... **169** K6
Redchurch St *BETH* E2 ..... **7** L9
WCHPL E1 ..... **7** L9
Redcliffe Cl *ECT* SW5 ..... **14** C8
Redcliffe Gdns *IL* IG1 ..... **60** A7
WBPTN SW10 ..... **14** D8
Redcliffe Ms *WBPTN* SW10 ..... **14** D8
Redcliffe Pl *WBPTN* SW10 ..... **108** B5
Redcliffe Rd *WBPTN* SW10 ..... **14** E8
Redcliffe Sq *WBPTN* SW10 ..... **14** C9
Redcliffe St *WBPTN* SW10 ..... **14** D9
Redclose Av *MRDN* SM4 ..... **161** K4
Redclyffe Rd *PLSTW* E13 ..... **77** G7
Redcroft Rd *STHL* UB1 ..... **84** C6
Redcross Wy *STHWK* SE1 ..... **18** F1
Reddings Av *BUSH* WD23 ..... **22** B4
Reddings Cl *MLHL* NW7 ..... **37** H3
The Reddings *BORE* WD6 ..... **24** B2
MLHL NW7 ..... **37** H2
Reddington Cl *SAND/SEL* CR2 ..... **177** K7
Reddins Rd *PECK* SE15 ..... **111** H6
Reddons Rd *BECK* BR3 ..... **151** G6
Reddy Rd *ERITH* DA8 ..... **118** C5
Rede Pl *BAY/PAD* W2 ..... **8** B5
Redesdale Gdns *ISLW* TW7 ..... **104** B6
Redesdale St *CHEL* SW3 ..... **15** L9
Redfern Av *HSLWW* TW4 ..... **123** F6
Redfern Rd *CAT* SE6 ..... **133** F6
WLSDN NW10 ..... **69** G6
Redfield La *ECT* SW5 ..... **14** C5
Redford Av *THHTH* CR7 ..... **164** A3
WLGTN SM6 ..... **176** E5
Redford Cl *FELT* TW13 ..... **140** D1
Redford Wk *IS* N1 * **6** D3
Redgate Dr *HAYES* BR2 ..... **181** F1
Redgate Ter *PUT/ROE* SW15 ..... **127** G5
Redgrave Cl *CROY/NA* CR0 ..... **165** G5
Redgrave Rd *PUT/ROE* SW15 ..... **127** G2
Redgrave Ter *BETH* E2 * **92** C2
Redhall Ter *EA* W5 * **86** C6
Red Hl *CHST* BR7 ..... **154** A4
Redhill Dr *EDGW* HA8 ..... **50** D1
Redhill St *CAMTN* NW1 ..... **4** D6
Red House La *BXLYHS* DA6 ..... **136** E3
Red House Rd *CROY/NA* CR0 ..... **163** J5
Red House Sq *IS* N1 ..... **6** F1
Redington Gdns *HAMP* NW3 ..... **71** F3
Redington Rd *HAMP* NW3 ..... **71** F2
Redland Gdns
E/WMO/HCT KT8 * **156** E3
Redlands Wy
BRXS/STRHM SW2 ..... **129** K6
Red La *ESH/CLAY* KT10 ..... **171** G5
Redleaf Cl *BXLYHN* DA7 ..... **117** H5
Redlees Cl *ISLW* TW7 ..... **124** B3
Red Lion Cl *WALW* SE17 ..... **19** G9
Red Lion Ct *FLST/FETLN* EC4A **12** B4
HSLW TW3 * **123** G2
Red Lion Hl *EFNCH* N2 ..... **53** H1
Red Lion La *WOOL/PLUM* SE18 ..... **115** F7
Red Lion Pde *PIN* HA5 * **47** J2
Red Lion Pl
WOOL/PLUM SE18 * **115** F7
Red Lion Rd *SURB* KT6 ..... **172** B1
Red Lion Rw *CMBW* SE5 ..... **110** D5
Red Lion Sq *GINN* WC1R **11** L3
WAND/EARL SW18 * **127** K4
Red Lion St *GINN* WC1R **11** L3
RCH/KEW TW9 ..... **124** E4
Red Lion Yd
MYFR/PKLN W1K * **10** B8
Red Lodge Rd *WWKM* BR4 ..... **167** F7

Redman Cl NTHLT UB5 83 G1
Redman's Rd WCHPL E1 92 E4
Redmead La WAP E1W 92 C7
Redmead Rd HYS/HAR UB3 101 H3
Redmore Rd HMSMTH W6 * 106 E3
Red Pl MYFR/PKLN W1K 10 A6
Redpoll Wy ERITHM DA18 116 E2
Red Post Hl HNHL SE24 130 E4
Redriffe Rd PLSTW E13 76 D7
Redriff Rd BERM/RHTH SE16 112 B2
  ROMW/RG RM7 62 D1
Red Rd BORE WD6 24 B2
Redroofs Cl BECK BR3 151 K7
Redruth Cl WDGN N22 41 F6
Redruth Gdns ESH/CLAY KT10 171 F6
Redruth Rd HOM E9 74 E7
Redsan Cl SAND/SEL CR2 177 K6
Redstart Cl EHAM E6 95 J4
  NWCR SE14 * 112 B6
Redston Rd CEND/HSY/T N8 54 D3
Redvers Rd WDGN N22 55 G1
Redvers St IS N1 7 K7
Redwald Rd CLPT E5 75 F3
Redway Dr WHTN TW2 123 H6
Redwing Ms CMBW SE5 130 D1
Redwing Rd WLGTN SM6 176 E6
Redwood Cl
  BERM/RHTH SE16 93 G7
  BFN/LL DA15 136 B7
  BOW E3 93 J1
  OXHEY WD19 33 G3
  STHGT/OAK N14 28 D6
Redwood Gdns CHING E4 31 K5
Redwood Gv EA W5 104 D2
Redwood Ms ASHF TW15 * 140 B6
  VX/NE SW8 129 G2
Redwood Wy BAR EN5 26 B4
Reece Ms SKENS SW7 15 G5
Reed Cl CAN/RD E16 94 E4
  LEE/GVPK SE12 133 K4
Reede Rd DAGE RM10 80 C5
Reede Wy DAGE RM10 80 D5
Reedham Cl TOTM N17 56 D3
Reedham St PECK SE15 * 131 H1
Reedholm Vls
  STNW/STAM N16 73 K3
Reed Pl BTSEA SW11 128 D3
  CLAP SW4 129 J3
Reed Pond Wk GPK RM2 63 H1
Reed Rd TOTM N17 56 B1
Reeds Crs WATN WD24 21 G1
Reed's Pl CAMTN NW1 4 E1
Reedworth St LBTH SE11 18 B6
Reenglass Rd STAN HA7 * 35 K3
Rees Dr STAN HA7 36 A3
Rees Gdns CROY/NA CR0 165 G5
Reesland Cl MNPK E12 78 A5
Rees St IS N1 6 F4
Reets Farm Cl
  CDALE/KGS NW9 51 G5
Reeves Av CDALE/KGS NW9 51 F6
Reeves Cnr CROY/NA CR0 * 177 H1
Reeves Ms MYFR/PKLN W1K 10 A7
Reeves Rd BOW E3 93 K3
  WOOL/PLUM SE18 115 G5
Reform Rw TOTM N17 56 B1
Reform St BTSEA SW11 128 E1
Regal Cl EA W5 85 K4
  WCHPL E1 92 C4
Regal Ct MTCM CR4 162 E2
  UED N18 42 B4
Regal Crs WLGTN SM6 176 B2
Regal Dr FBAR/BDGN N11 40 B4
Regal La CAMTN NW1 4 B4
Regal Rw PECK SE15 111 K7
Regal Wy KTN/HRWW/WS HA3 50 A5
Regan Wy IS N1 7 J6
Regarth Av ROM RM1 63 G5
Regency Cl EA W5 86 A5
  HPTN TW12 141 K4
Regency Ct EN EN1 29 K4
Regency Crs HDN NW4 52 B1
Regency Dr RSLP HA4 46 C7
Regency Gdns WOT/HER KT12 156 C7
Regency Lawn KTTN NW5 * 72 B2
Regency Ms BECK BR3 152 A7
  WLSDN NW10 69 J5
Regency Pde HAMP NW3 * 3 G2
Regency Pl WEST SW1P * 17 G5
Regency St WEST SW1P 17 H6
Regency Ter HGT N6 * 53 K5
  SEVS/STOTM N15 56 A4
  SKENS SW7 * 15 G7
Regency Wk CROY/NA CR0 166 B5
Regency Wy BXLYHS DA6 136 E2
Regeneration Rd
  BERM/RHTH SE16 112 A3
Regent Cl HSLWW TW4 102 A7
  KTN/HRWW/WS HA3 50 A5
  NFNCH/WDSPK N12 39 G4
Regent Gdns GDMY/SEVK IG3 61 G5
Regent Pde BELMT SM2 * 175 G5
  STNW/STAM N16 * 56 B6
Regent Pl CROY/NA CR0 165 G7
  WIM/MER SW19 147 G4
Regent Rd BRYLDS KT5 159 G4
  HNHL SE24 130 C5
Regents Av PLMGR N13 41 G4
Regents Bridge Gdns
  VX/NE SW8 109 K5
Regents Cl SAND/SEL CR2 178 A5
  YEAD UB4 82 C4
Regents Dr HAYES BR2 181 H4
Regents Ms STJWD NW8 2 F5
Regent's Park Rd
  CAMTN NW1 3 M3
  FNCH N3 52 D3
Regent's Park Ter
  CAMTN NW1 4 C3
Regents Plaza
  KIL/WHAMP NW6 * 2 C5
Regent Sq BELV DA17 117 J3
  BOW E3 93 K2
  STPAN WC1H 5 K8
Regent's Rw BETH E2 74 C7
Regent St CHSWK W4 105 H4
  REGST W1B 10 D4
  STJS SW1Y 11 G7
  WLSDN NW10 88 B2
Regents Whf IS N1 * 5 L5
Reginald Rd DEPT SE8 112 D6
  FSTGT E7 76 E6
  NTHWD HA6 32 D7
Reginald Sq DEPT SE8 112 D6
Regina Rd FSBYPK N4 55 F7
  NWDGN UB2 102 D3
  SNWD SE25 165 H2
  WEA W13 85 G7
Regina Ter WEA W13 85 G7
Regis Rd KTTN NW5 72 B4
Regnart Blds CAMTN NW1 4 F8
Reid Cl HYS/HAR UB3 82 C5
  PIN HA5 46 E2
Reidhaven Rd
  WOOL/PLUM SE18 115 K3
Reigate Av SUT SM1 162 A7
Reigate Rd BMLY BR1 152 E1
  GDMY/SEVK IG3 79 F1
Reigate Wy WLGTN SM6 176 E4
Reighton Rd CLPT E5 74 C2
Reinckendorf Av
  ELTH/MOT SE9 135 H4
Reindeer Cl PLSTW E13 76 E7
Reizel Cl STNW/STAM N16 56 B7
Relay Rd SHB W12 88 A6
Relf Rd PECK SE15 131 H2
Reliance Ar BRXN/ST SW9 * 130 B3
Relton Ms SKENS SW7 15 K3
Rembrandt Cl BGVA SW1W 16 A7
  POP/IOD E14 113 G2
Rembrandt Ct
  HOR/WEW KT19 173 H5
Rembrandt Rd EDGW HA8 * 50 C1
  LEW SE13 133 H3
Remington Rd EHAM E6 95 J5
  SEVS/STOTM N15 55 K5
Remington St IS N1 6 D6
Remnant St HOL/ALD WC2B 11 L4
Remus Rd BOW E3 75 J6
Renaissance Wk GNWCH SE10 113 J2
Rendle Cl CROY/NA CR0 165 G4
Rendlesham Rd CLPT E5 74 C3
Renforth St BERM/RHTH SE16 111 K1
Renfrew Cl EHAM E6 96 A6
Renfrew Rd HSLWW TW4 122 C1
  KUTN/CMB KT2 144 E6
  LBTH SE11 18 C5
Renmuir St TOOT SW17 147 K5
Rennell St LEW SE13 133 F2
Renness Rd WALTH E17 57 G2
Rennets Cl ELTH/MOT SE9 135 J4
Rennets Wood Rd
  ELTH/MOT SE9 135 J4
Rennie Est BERM/RHTH SE16 111 J3
Rennie St STHWK SE1 12 C8
Renown Cl CROY/NA CR0 164 C7
Rensburg Rd WALTH E17 57 F4
Rensburg Vls WALTH E17 * 57 F4
Renshaw Cl BELV DA17 117 G5
Renters Av HDN NW4 52 A5
Renton Cl BRXS/STRHM SW2 * 130 A5
Renwick Rd BARK IG11 97 H3
Repens Wy YEAD UB4 83 H3
Rephidim St STHWK SE1 19 H4
Replingham Rd
  WAND/EARL SW18 127 J7
Reporton Rd FUL/PGN SW6 107 H7
Repository Rd
  WOOL/PLUM SE18 114 E5
Repton Av ALP/SUD HA0 67 J3
  GPK RM2 63 J2
  HYS/HAR UB3 101 G3
Repton Cl CAR SM5 175 J4
Repton Ct BECK BR3 151 K7
Repton Dr GPK RM2 63 J3
Repton Gdns GPK RM2 63 J2
Repton Gv CLAY IG5 45 K7
Repton Rd
  KTN/HRWW/WS HA3 50 B3
Repton St POP/IOD E14 93 G5
Reservoir Cl THHTH CR7 164 E2
Reservoir Rd BROCKY SE4 132 B1
  RSLP HA4 46 A4
  STHGT/OAK N14 28 C4
Resham Cl NWDGN UB2 102 B2
Resolution Wy DEPT SE8 112 D6
Restell Cl BKHTH/KID SE3 113 H5
Restmor Wy CAR SM5 176 A1
  WLGTN SM6 176 A1
Reston Pl KENS W8 14 E2
Restons Crs ELTH/MOT SE9 135 J6
Reston Wy CAN/RD E16 95 H6
Restormel Cl HSLW TW3 123 F4
Retford St BETH E2 * 7 L7
  IS N1 * 7 K6
Retingham Wy CHING E4 43 K1
Retreat Cl
  KTN/HRWW/WS HA3 49 J4
Retreat Pl HOM E9 74 E5
Retreat Rd RCH/KEW TW9 124 E4
The Retreat BRYLDS KT5 159 G5
  CDALE/KGS NW9 51 F4
  MORT/ESHN SW14 126 B2
  RYLN/HDSTN HA2 48 A6
  THHTH CR7 164 E3
  WPK KT4 173 K1
Reunion Rw WAP E1W * 92 D6
Reveley Sq BERM/RHTH SE16 112 B1
Revell Ri WOOL/PLUM SE18 116 A5
Revell Rd KUT/HW KT1 159 J1
  SUT SM1 174 D5
Revelon Rd BROCKY SE4 132 B3
Revelstoke Rd
  WIM/MER SW19 146 C3
Reventlow Rd ELTH/MOT SE9 135 H7
Reverdy Rd STHWK SE1 111 H3
Reverend Cl RYLN/HDSTN HA2 66 B2
Revere Wy HOR/WEW KT19 173 G7
Revesby Rd CAR SM5 162 D5
Review Rd CRICK NW2 69 H1
  DAGE RM10 98 D1
Rewell St FUL/PGN SW6 * 108 B6
Rewley Rd CAR SM5 162 C5
Rex Pl MYFR/PKLN W1K 10 B8
Reydon Av WAN E11 59 G5
Reynard Cl BMLY BR1 168 E2
Reynard Dr NRWD SE19 150 B6
Reynard Pl NWCR SE14 * 112 B5
Reynardson Rd TOTM N17 41 J6
Reynolah Gdns CHARL SE7 114 A4
Reynolds Av CHDH RM6 61 J6
  CHSGTN KT9 172 A6
  MNPK E12 78 A4
Reynolds Cl CAR SM5 162 E7
  GLDGN NW11 53 F6
  WIM/MER SW19 147 H7
Reynolds Dr EDGW HA8 50 B2
Reynolds Pl BKHTH/KID SE3 114 A6
  RCHPK/HAM TW10 125 G5
Reynolds Rd CHSWK W4 105 K2
  NWMAL KT3 160 A6
  PECK SE15 131 K4
  YEAD UB4 83 G3
Reynolds Wy CROY/NA CR0 178 A3
Rheidol Ms IS N1 6 E5
Rheidol Ter IS N1 6 D5
Rheingold Wy WLGTN SM6 176 E7
Rheola Cl TOTM N17 42 B7
Rhoda St BETH E2 7 M9
Rhodes Av WDGN N22 40 C7
Rhodesia Rd BRXN/ST SW9 129 K1
  WAN E11 76 B1
Rhodes St HOLWY N7 73 F4
Rhodes Wy WATN WD24 21 H1
Rhodeswell Rd POP/IOD E14 93 G4
Rhodrons Av CHSGTN KT9 172 A4
Rhondda Gv BOW E3 93 G2
Rhyl Rd GFD/PVL UB6 85 F1
Rhyl St KTTN NW5 72 A5
Rhys Av FBAR/BDGN N11 40 D6
Rialto Rd MTCM CR4 163 F1
Ribble Cl WFD IG8 45 G5
Ribblesdale Av
  FBAR/BDGN N11 39 K5
  NTHLT UB5 66 B5
Ribblesdale Rd
  CEND/HSY/T N8 55 F3
  STRHM/NOR SW16 148 B4
Ribbon Dance Ms CMBW SE5 110 E7
Ribchester Av GFD/PVL UB6 85 F2
Ribston Cl HAYES BR2 168 E7
Ricardo St POP/IOD E14 93 K5
Ricards Rd WIM/MER SW19 146 D4
Rice Pde STMC/STPC BR5 * 169 J4
Richard Cl WOOL/PLUM SE18 114 D3
Richard House Dr
  CAN/RD E16 95 H5
Richards Av ROMW/RG RM7 62 E4
Richards Cl BUSH WD23 22 D6
  HRW HA1 49 G4
  HYS/HAR UB3 101 G5
Richards Cots CAR SM5 * 175 K4
Richards Fld HOR/WEW KT19 173 F7
Richardson Cl HACK E8 * 7 L3
Richardson Gdns DAGE RM10 80 D5
Richardson Rd SRTFD E15 * 94 C1
Richardson's Ms FITZ W1T 10 E1
Richards Pl WALTH E17 57 J2
Richard's Pl CHEL SW3 15 K5
Richbell Pl FSBYW WC1X 11 L2
Richborne Ter VX/NE SW8 110 A6
Richborough Rd CRICK NW2 70 B3
Richens Cl HSLW TW3 123 J1
Riches Rd IL IG1 78 C1
Richfield Rd BUSH WD23 22 C6
Richford Ga HMSMTH W6 * 107 F2
Richford Rd SRTFD E15 76 D7
Richford St HMSMTH W6 107 F1
Richill Ldg WHTN TW2 * 123 F5
Richlands Av EW KT17 173 J3
Richmer Rd ERITH DA8 118 D6
Richmond Av CHING E4 44 B4
  EBED/NFELT TW14 121 H5
  IS N1 5 M3
  RYNPK SW20 146 C7
Richmond Br TWK TW1 124 E4
Richmond Blds
  SOHO/SHAV W1D 11 G5
Richmond Cl BORE WD6 25 F4
  WALTH E17 57 H5
Richmond Crs CHING E4 44 B4
  ED N9 30 C7
  IS N1 5 M3
Richmond Dr WAT WD17 20 C1
Richmond Gdns HDN NW4 51 J4
  KTN/HRWW/WS HA3 35 F6
Richmond Ga KUTN/CMB KT2 144 B5
  RCHPK/HAM TW10 125 G6
Richmond Gn CROY/NA CR0 176 E2
Richmond Gv IS N1 6 C2
Richmond Hl
  RCHPK/HAM TW10 125 F5
Richmond Ms
  SOHO/SHAV W1D 11 G5
Richmond Pde TWK TW1 * 124 D5
Richmond Park Rd
  KUTN/CMB KT2 144 A6
  MORT/ESHN SW14 125 K4
Richmond Pl
  WOOL/PLUM SE18 115 H3
Richmond Rd BAR EN5 27 F4
  CROY/NA CR0 176 E2
  EA W5 105 F1
  EFNCH N2 * 53 H1
  FBAR/BDGN N11 40 E5
  FSTGT E7 77 F4
  HACK E8 7 L1
  IL IG1 78 C2
  ISLW TW7 124 B2
  KUTN/CMB KT2 143 K4
  ROM RM1 63 H5
  RYNPK SW20 145 K7
  SEVS/STOTM N15 56 A5
  THHTH CR7 164 C3
  TWK TW1 124 B7
  WAN E11 76 B1
Richmond St PLSTW E13 94 E1
Richmond Ter WHALL SW1A 17 J1
Richmond Vls WALTH E17 * 43 K7
Richmond Wy
  RKW/CH/CXG WD3 20 A3
  SHB W12 107 G1
  WAN E11 76 E1
Richmount Gdns
  BKHTH/KID SE3 133 K2
Rich St POP/IOD E14 93 H6
Rickard Cl BRXS/STRHM SW2 130 B7
  HDN NW4 51 J3
  WDR/YW UB7 100 A2
Rickards Cl SURB KT6 172 A1
Rickett St FUL/PGN SW6 14 B9
Rickman St WCHPL E1 92 E3
Rickmansworth Rd
  NTHWD HA6 32 B6
  PIN HA5 47 F1
  WATW WD18 20 C3
Rick Roberts Wy SRTFD E15 76 B7
Rickthorne Rd ARCH N19 72 E1
Ridding La GFD/PVL UB6 67 F4
Riddons Rd LEE/GVPK SE12 153 G2
Rideout St WOOL/PLUM SE18 114 E3
Rider Cl BFN/LL DA15 135 K5
The Ride BTFD TW8 104 C4
  PEND EN3 30 E2
Ridgdale St BOW E3 93 J1
Ridge Av DART DA1 138 C5
  WCHMH N21 29 J6
Ridgebrook Rd
  BKHTH/KID SE3 134 B3
Ridge Cl CDALE/KGS NW9 51 F3
  HDN NW4 52 B1
  THMD SE28 115 J1
Ridgecroft Cl BXLY DA5 137 K7
Ridge Hl GLDGN NW11 52 C7
Ridgemead Cl
  STHGT/OAK N14 40 E1
Ridgemont Gdns EDGW HA8 36 E3
Ridgemount Av CROY/NA CR0 179 F1
Ridgemount Cl PGE/AN SE20 150 D6
Ridgemount Gdns
  ENC/FH EN2 29 H2
Ridge Rd CEND/HSY/T N8 55 F5
  CHEAM SM3 161 J7
  CRICK NW2 70 D2
  MTCM CR4 148 B6
  WCHMH N21 29 K7
Ridges Yd CROY/NA CR0 177 H2
Ridge Ter WCHMH N21 * 29 J6
The Ridge BAR EN5 * 26 D4
  BRYLDS KT5 159 H4
  BXLY DA5 137 G6
  WHTN TW2 123 J6
Ridgeview Cl BAR EN5 26 B5
Ridgeview Rd
  TRDG/WHET N20 39 F2
Ridge Wy DART DA1 138 C5
  FELT TW13 141 J2
Ridgeway HAYES BR2 180 E1
  WFD IG8 45 G3
Ridgeway Av EBAR EN4 27 K5
Ridgeway Dr BMLY BR1 153 F3
Ridgeway East BFN/LL DA15 136 A4
Ridgeway Gdns HGT N6 54 C6
  REDBR IG4 59 J4
Ridgeway Rd ISLW TW7 103 K6
Ridgeway Rd North ISLW TW7 103 K6
The Ridgeway ACT W3 105 H2
  CDALE/KGS NW9 51 F3
  CROY/NA CR0 177 F2
  FBAR/BDGN N11 39 K3
  FNCH N3 39 F6
  GLDGN NW11 52 D7
  GPK RM2 63 J3
  KTN/HRWW/WS HA3 49 J5
  MLHL NW7 37 J3
  RSLP HA4 46 D6
  RYLN/HDSTN HA2 47 K4
  STAN HA7 35 K5
  STHGT/OAK N14 40 E1
Ridgeway West BFN/LL DA15 135 K4
Ridgewell Cl DAGE RM10 80 D7
  IS N1 6 F3
  SYD SE26 151 H3
Ridgmount Gdns
  GWRST WC1E 11 G2
Ridgmount Rd
  WAND/EARL SW18 128 A4
Ridgmount St GWRST WC1E 11 G2
Ridgway RCHPK/HAM TW10 * 125 F5
  WIM/MER SW19 146 A6
Ridgway Gdns
  WIM/MER SW19 146 B6
Ridgway Pl WIM/MER SW19 146 C5
Ridgway Rd BRXN/ST SW9 130 C2
The Ridgway BELMT SM2 175 H6
Ridgwell Rd CAN/RD E16 95 G4
Riding House St GTPST W1W 10 D3
Ridings Av WCHMH N21 29 H3
Ridings Cl HGT N6 54 C6
The Ridings BRYLDS KT5 159 H4
  EA W5 86 B3
  EBAR EN4 * 27 J6
  EW KT17 173 H7
  SUN TW16 140 E7
The Riding GLDGN NW11 52 D6
Ridley Av WEA W13 104 C2
Ridley Cl BARK IG11 79 F6
Ridley Rd FSTGT E7 77 G3
  HACK E8 74 B4
  HAYES BR2 167 J2
  WELL DA16 116 C7
  WIM/MER SW19 147 F6
  WLSDN NW10 87 J1
Ridsdale Rd PGE/AN SE20 150 D7
Riefield Rd ELTH/MOT SE9 135 H3
Riesco Dr CROY/NA CR0 178 E5
Riffel Rd CRICK NW2 70 A4
Rifle Pl NTGHL W11 88 B7
Rifle Range La HRW HA1 49 F7
Rifle St POP/IOD E14 93 K4
Rigault Rd FUL/PGN SW6 127 H1
Rigby Cl CROY/NA CR0 177 G2
Rigby La HYS/HAR UB3 101 F1
Rigby Ms IL IG1 78 A1
Rigden St POP/IOD E14 93 K5
Rigeley Rd WLSDN NW10 87 J2
Rigg Ap LEY E10 57 F7
Rigge Pl CLAP SW4 129 J3
Riggindale Rd
  STRHM/NOR SW16 148 D4
Right Side STHGT/OAK N14 * 28 D7
Riley Rd STHWK SE1 19 L3
Riley St WBPTN SW10 108 C6
Rinaldo Rd BAL SW12 129 G6
Ring Cl BMLY BR1 153 F6
Ringcroft St HOLWY N7 73 G4
Ringer's Rd BMLY BR1 167 K2
Ringford Rd
  WAND/EARL SW18 127 J4
Ringlet Cl CAN/RD E16 95 F4
Ringlewell Cl EN EN1 30 D1
Ringmer Av FUL/PGN SW6 107 H7
Ringmer Pl WCHMH N21 29 K4
Ringmer Wy BMLY BR1 168 E4
Ringmore Ri FSTH SE23 131 J6
Ring Rd SHB W12 88 A7
Ringslade Rd WDGN N22 55 F1
Ringstead Rd CAT SE6 132 E6
  SUT SM1 175 H3
Ring Wy FBAR/BDGN N11 40 C5
Ringway NWDGN UB2 102 C4
Ringwold Cl BECK BR3 151 G6
Ringwood Av CROY/NA CR0 163 K6
  EFNCH N2 53 K2
Ringwood Cl PIN HA5 * 47 G2
Ringwood Gdns
  PUT/ROE SW15 145 J1
Ringwood Rd WALTH E17 57 H5
Ringwood Wy HPTN TW12 142 A3
  WCHMH N21 29 H6
Ripley Cl BMLY BR1 168 E4
  CROY/NA CR0 180 A5
Ripley Gdns
  MORT/ESHN SW14 126 A2
Ripley Ms WAN E11 58 C5
Ripley Rd BELV DA17 117 H3
  CAN/RD E16 95 G5
  GDMY/SEVK IG3 78 E1
  HPTN TW12 142 A6
Ripleys Market DART DA1 * 139 H6
Ripley Vls EA W5 * 85 J5
Ripon Cl NTHLT UB5 66 A4
Ripon Gdns CHSGTN KT9 171 K4
  IL IG1 59 J5
Ripon Rd ED N9 30 D6
  TOTM N17 56 K2
  WOOL/PLUM SE18 115 G5
Ripon Wy BORE WD6 24 E4
Rippersley Rd WELL DA16 116 B7
Ripple Rd BARK IG11 78 C6
  BARK IG11 79 H7
  DAGW RM9 98 A1
Ripplevale Gv IS N1 5 M2
Rippolson Rd
  WOOL/PLUM SE18 116 A4
Ripston Rd ASHF TW15 140 B4
Risborough Cl MUSWH N10 * 54 B2
Risborough Dr WPK KT4 160 D6
Risborough St STHWK SE1 18 D1
Risdon St BERM/RHTH SE16 111 K1
Risebridge Rd GPK RM2 63 H1
Risedale Rd BXLYHN DA7 137 J2
Riseldine Rd FSTH SE23 132 B5
Rise Park Pde ROM RM1 63 G1
The Rise BORE WD6 24 B4
  BXLY DA5 136 D6
  DART DA1 138 C3
  EDGW HA8 36 D4
  GFD/PVL UB6 67 G4
  MLHL NW7 37 H5
  PLMGR N13 41 G3
  SAND/SEL CR2 178 E7
  WAN E11 58 E4
  WLSDN NW10 69 F2
Rising Hill Cl NTHWD HA6 * 32 A5
Risinghill St IS N1 6 A5
Risingholme Cl BUSH WD23 22 B6
  KTN/HRWW/WS HA3 34 E7
Risingholme Rd
  KTN/HRWW/WS HA3 48 E1
The Risings WALTH E17 58 B3
Risley Av TOTM N17 41 J7
Rita Rd VX/NE SW8 109 K6
Ritches Rd SEVS/STOTM N15 55 J4
Ritchie Rd CROY/NA CR0 165 J5
Ritchie St IS N1 6 B5
Ritchings Av WALTH E17 57 G3
Ritherdon Rd TOOT SW17 148 A1
Ritson Rd HACK E8 74 B5
Ritter St WOOL/PLUM SE18 115 F5
Rivaz Pl HOM E9 74 E5
Rivenhall Gdns SWFD E18 58 D3
River Av PLMGR N13 41 H2
  THDIT KT7 158 B6
Riverbank E/WMO/HCT KT8 157 K2
River Bank THDIT KT7 158 A4
  WCHMH N21 29 J6
Riverbank Rd BMLY BR1 152 E2
Riverbank Wy BTFD TW8 104 D5
River Barge Cl POP/IOD E14 113 F1
River Cl NWDGN UB2 103 H1
  RAIN RM13 99 K4
  RSLP HA4 46 D5
  WAN E11 59 G5
River Ct PUR RM19 119 J3
Rivercourt Rd HMSMTH W6 106 E3
River Crane Wy FELT TW13 141 K1
Riverdale Dr
  WAND/EARL SW18 128 A7
Riverdale Gdns TWK TW1 124 D4
Riverdale Rd BXLY DA5 137 G6
  ERITH DA8 117 J4
  FELT TW13 141 J3
  TWK TW1 124 D5
  WOOL/PLUM SE18 116 A4
Riverdene EDGW HA8 36 E3
Riverdene Rd IL IG1 78 A2
River Front EN EN1 29 K2
River Gdns CAR SM5 176 A1
  EBED/NFELT TW14 122 A4
River Grove Pk BECK BR3 151 H7
Riverhead Cl WALTH E17 57 F1
Riverholme Dr
  HOR/WEW KT19 173 F7
River La RCHPK/HAM TW10 124 E7
Rivermead E/WMO/HCT KT8 157 H2
  KUT/HW KT1 * 158 E4
Rivermead Cl TEDD TW11 143 H4
Rivermead Rd UED N18 * 43 F4
River Meads Av WHTN TW2 142 B2
Rivernook Cl WOT/HER KT12 156 B4
Riverpark Gdns HAYES BR2 152 B6
River Park Rd WDGN N22 55 F1
River Pl IS N1 6 E2
River Reach TEDD TW11 143 J5
River Rd BARK IG11 96 E2
Riversdale Rd HBRY N5 73 H2
  THDIT KT7 158 B4
Riversfield Rd EN EN1 30 A2
Riverside CHARL SE7 114 A2
  HDN NW4 51 K6
  RCH/KEW TW9 * 105 H5
  RCH/KEW TW9 124 E4
  SUN TW16 * 156 C1
  TWK TW1 124 C7
Riverside Av E/WMO/HCT KT8 157 J4
Riverside Cl CLPT E5 56 E7
  HNWL W7 84 E3
  KUT/HW KT1 158 E3
  ROMW/RG RM7 63 F3
  WLGTN SM6 176 B2
Riverside Ct CHING E4 * 31 K5
Riverside Dr CHSWK W4 106 A6
  ESH/CLAY KT10 170 A3
  GLDGN NW11 * 52 C5
  MTCM CR4 162 D4
  RCHPK/HAM TW10 143 H2
Riverside Gdns ALP/SUD HA0 86 A1
  ENC/FH EN2 29 J1
  HMSMTH W6 106 E4
Riverside Ms CROY/NA CR0 * 176 E2
Riverside Pl
  FBAR/BDGN N11 * 40 C2
  STWL/WRAY TW19 120 A5
Riverside Rd IL IG1 78 B2
  OXHEY WD19 21 F5
  SEVS/STOTM N15 56 C5
  SRTFD E15 94 A1
  STWL/WRAY TW19 120 A4
  TOOT SW17 147 F3
The Riverside
  E/WMO/HCT KT8 157 J2
Riverside Vls SURB KT6 * 158 D5
Riverside Wk ISLW TW7 123 K2
  KUT/HW KT1 158 E1
Riverside Wy DART DA1 139 H4
Riverside Yd TOOT SW17 147 F2
Riverstone Cl
  RYLN/HDSTN HA2 66 D1
River St CLKNW EC1R 6 A7
River Ter HMSMTH W6 107 F4
Riverton Cl MV/WKIL W9 * 88 D2
Riverview Gdns BARN SW13 106 E5
River View Gdns TWK TW1 143 F1
Riverview Gv CHSWK W4 105 J5
Riverview Pk CAT SE6 151 J1
Riverview Rd CHSWK W4 105 J6
  HOR/WEW KT19 172 E3
River Wk SUN TW16 156 C1
River Wy WHTN TW2 142 B1
  GNWCH SE10 113 J2
  HOR/WEW KT19 173 F4
Riverway PLMGR N13 41 G4
River Whf BELV DA17 * 118 A1
Riverwood La CHST BR7 169 J1
Rivington Av WFD IG8 59 H1
Rivington Crs MLHL NW7 37 G6
Rivington Pl FSBYE EC1V 7 K8
Rivington St SDTCH EC2A 7 K8
Rivington Wk HACK E8 * 74 C7
Rivulet Rd TOTM N17 41 J6
Rixon St HOLWY N7 73 G2
Rixsen Rd MNPK E12 77 J4
Roach Rd BOW E3 75 J6
Roads Pl ARCH N19 72 E1

Roan St GNWCH SE10 113 F5
Robarts Cl PIN HA5 47 F4
Robb Rd STAN HA7 35 G5
Robert Adam St MHST W1U 10 A4
Roberta St BETH E2 92 C2
Robert Cl MV/WKIL W9 8 F1
Robert Dashwood Wy
WALW SE17 18 E6
Robert Keen Cl PECK SE15 111 H7
Robert Lowe Cl NWCR SE14 112 A6
Roberton Dr BMLY BR1 168 B1
Robertsbridge Rd CAR SM5 162 B6
Roberts Cl CHEAM SM3 174 B6
DAGE RM10 80 C5
ELTH/MOT SE9 135 J7
THHTH CR7 164 E2
Roberts Ct CHSGTN KT9 171 K4
PGE/AN SE20 150 E7
WLSDN NW10 69 G5
Roberts House
WOOL/PLUM SE18 * 114 D6
Roberts Ms KTBR SW1X * 16 A4
Robertson St VX/NE SW8 129 G1
Robert's Pl CLKNW EC1R * 6 B9
Robert Sq LEW SE13 133 F3
Roberts Rd BELV DA17 117 H4
MLHL NW7 38 C4
WALTH E17 43 K7
WATW WD18 21 G4
Robert St CAMTN NW1 4 D8
CHCR WC2N 11 K7
CROY/NA CR0 177 J2
WOOL/PLUM SE18 115 J3
Robeson St BOW E3 93 H4
Robina Cl BXLYHS DA6 136 E3
NTHWD HA6 46 D1
Robin Cl FELT TW13 141 J4
MLHL NW7 37 G2
Robin Gv BTFD TW8 104 D5
HGT N6 72 A1
KTN/HRWW/WS HA3 50 B5
Robin Hill Dr CHST BR7 153 J5
Robinhood Cl MTCM CR4 163 H3
Robin Hood Dr
KTN/HRWW/WS HA3 35 F6
Robin Hood Gdns
POP/IOD E14 * 94 A6
Robin Hood La BXLYHS DA6 137 F4
POP/IOD E14 94 A6
PUT/ROE SW15 145 G2
SUT SM1 174 E4
Robinhood La MTCM CR4 163 H2
Robin Hood Rd
PUT/ROE SW15 145 G3
WIM/MER SW19 145 J4
Robin Hood Wy GFD/PVL UB6 67 F5
PUT/ROE SW15 145 G3
Robinia Cl PGE/AN SE20 150 C7
Robinia Crs LEY E10 75 K1
Robin La HDN NW4 52 B2
Robinscroft Ms GNWCH SE10 113 F7
Robins Gv WWKM BR4 180 E2
Robinson Cl ENC/FH EN2 29 J2
HCH RM12 81 K6
WAN E11 76 C2
Robinson Crs BUSH WD23 22 C7
Robinson Rd BETH E2 92 E1
DAGE RM10 80 C3
TOOT SW17 147 J5
Robinson's Cl WEA W13 85 G4
Robinson St CHEL SW3 15 L9
Robinswood Ms HBRY N5 73 H4
Robinwood Pl PUT/ROE SW15 145 F3
Rob Pascoe La DAGW RM9 98 A2
Robsart St BRXN/ST SW9 130 A1
Robson Av WLSDN NW10 69 J6
Robson Cl EHAM E6 95 J5
ENC/FH EN2 29 H1
Robson Rd WNWD SE27 149 H2
Rocastle Rd BROCKY SE4 132 B4
Roch Av EDGW HA8 50 B1
Rochdale Rd ABYW SE2 116 C4
WALTH E17 57 J6
Rochdale Wy DEPT SE8 112 D6
Rochelle Cl BTSEA SW11 128 C3
Rochelle St BETH E2 7 L8
Rochemont Wk HACK E8 * 7 M4
Roche Rd STRHM/NOR SW16 148 E7
Rochester Av BMLY BR1 168 A1
FELT TW13 140 D1
PLSTW E13 77 G7
Rochester Cl BFN/LL DA15 136 C5
STRHM/NOR SW16 * 148 E6
Rochester Dr BXLY DA5 137 H5
PIN HA5 47 H4
Rochester Gdns CROY/NA CR0 178 A2
IL IG1 59 K6
Rochester Ms CAMTN NW1 4 F1
EA W5 * 104 D3
Rochester Pde FELT TW13 * 140 E2
Rochester Pl CAMTN NW1 72 C5
Rochester Rd CAMTN NW1 72 C5
CAR SM5 175 K3
DART DA1 139 K6
HCH RM12 81 K6
NTHWD HA6 46 D2
Rochester Rw WEST SW1P 16 F5
Rochester Sq CAMTN NW1 4 F1
Rochester St WEST SW1P 17 G4
Rochester Ter CAMTN NW1 72 C5
Rochester Wk STHWK SE1 * 13 G8
Rochester Wy BKHTH/KID SE3 114 A7
DART DA1 138 B6
ELTH/MOT SE9 134 C2
Rochester Way Relief Rd
ELTH/MOT SE9 134 D4
Roche Wk CAR SM5 162 C5
Rochford Av CHDH RM6 61 J4
Rochford Cl EHAM E6 95 H1
HCH RM12 81 K5
Rochford Wk HACK E8 * 74 C6
Rochford Wy CROY/NA CR0 163 K5
Rock Av MORT/ESHN SW14 126 A2
Rockbourne Rd FSTH SE23 132 A7
Rock Cl MTCM CR4 162 C1
Rockell's Pl EDUL SE22 131 J5
Rockford Av GFD/PVL UB6 85 H1
Rock Grove Wy
BERM/RHTH SE16 111 H3
Rockhall Rd CRICK NW2 70 B3
Rockhampton Rd
SAND/SEL CR2 178 A5
STRHM/NOR SW16 149 G3
Rock Hl DUL SE21 150 B3
Rockingham Av EMPK RM11 63 K5
Rockingham Cl
PUT/ROE SW15 126 C3
Rockingham Ga BUSH WD23 22 C5
Rockingham St STHWK SE1 18 E4
Rockland Rd PUT/ROE SW15 127 H3
Rocklands Dr
KTN/HRWW/WS HA3 49 H1
Rockley Rd SHB W12 107 G1
Rockmount Rd NRWD SE19 149 K5
WOOL/PLUM SE18 116 A4
Rocks La BARN SW13 126 D2
Rock St FSBYPK N4 73 G1
Rockware Av GFD/PVL UB6 66 E7
Rockways BAR EN5 25 H5
Rockwell Gdns NRWD SE19 150 A3
Rockwell Rd DAGE RM10 80 D4
Rocliffe St IS N1 6 D6
Rocombe Crs FSTH SE23 * 131 K6
Rocque La BKHTH/KID SE3 133 J2
Rodborough Rd GLDGN NW11 52 E7
Roden Gdns CROY/NA CR0 165 F5
Rodenhurst Rd CLAP SW4 129 H6
Roden St HOLWY N7 73 F2
IL IG1 78 A2
Rodeo Cl ERITH DA8 118 E7
Roderick Rd HAMP NW3 71 K3
Rodgers Cl BORE WD6 23 K5
Roding La North WFD IG8 59 J1
Roding La South REDBR IG4 59 H3
Roding Ms WAP E1W 92 C7
Roding Rd CLPT E5 75 F3
EHAM E6 96 B4
Rodings Rw BAR EN5 * 26 C3
Rodmarton St MHST W1U 9 M3
Rodmell Cl YEAD UB4 83 J3
Rodmell Slope
NFNCH/WDSPK N12 38 D4
Rodmere St GNWCH SE10 113 H4
Rodney Cl CROY/NA CR0 164 C7
NWMAL KT3 160 B4
PIN HA5 47 J6
WOT/HER KT12 * 156 B7
Rodney Gdns PIN HA5 47 F4
WWKM BR4 180 E3
Rodney Pl STHWK SE1 18 F5
WALTH E17 57 G1
WIM/MER SW19 147 G7
Rodney Rd MTCM CR4 162 D1
NWMAL KT3 160 B4
WALW SE17 18 F6
WAN E11 59 F3
WHTN TW2 123 F6
Rodney St IS N1 5 M5
Rodway Rd BMLY BR1 153 F7
PUT/ROE SW15 126 D6
Rodwell Cl RSLP HA4 * 47 G7
Rodwell Rd EDUL SE22 131 G5
Roebuck Cl FELT TW13 141 F3
Roebuck Rd CHSGTN KT9 172 C4
Roedean Crs PUT/ROE SW15 126 B5
Roe End CDALE/KGS NW9 50 E3
Roe Gn CDALE/KGS NW9 50 E4
Roehampton Cl
PUT/ROE SW15 126 D3
Roehampton Dr CHST BR7 154 C5
Roehampton Ga
PUT/ROE SW15 126 B5
Roehampton High St
PUT/ROE SW15 126 D6
Roehampton La
PUT/ROE SW15 126 E7
Roehampton V
PUT/ROE SW15 145 H2
Roe La CDALE/KGS NW9 50 D3
Roe Rd WLGTN SM6 176 E5
Rofant Rd NTHWD HA6 32 C5
Roffey St POP/IOD E14 113 F1
Rogers Gdns DAGE RM10 80 C4
Rogers Rd CAN/RD E16 94 D5
DAGE RM10 80 C4
TOOT SW17 147 H3
Rogers Ruff NTHWD HA6 32 A7
Roger St BMSBY WC1N 11 M1
Rogers Wk
NFNCH/WDSPK N12 39 F2
Rojack Rd FSTH SE23 132 A7
Rokeby Gdns WFD IG8 44 E7
Rokeby Pl RYNPK SW20 145 K6
Rokeby Rd BROCKY SE4 * 132 C1
Rokeby St SRTFD E15 76 C7
Rokesby Cl WELL DA16 135 J1
Rokesby Pl ALP/SUD HA0 67 K4
Rokesly Av CEND/HSY/T N8 54 E4
Roland Gdns SKENS SW7 14 E7
Roland Ms WCHPL E1 * 93 F4
Roland Rd WALTH E17 58 B3
Roland Wy SKENS SW7 14 F7
WALW SE17 19 H8
WPK KT4 173 H1
Roles Gv CHDH RM6 61 K3
Rolfe Cl EBAR EN4 27 J3
Rolinsden Wy HAYES BR2 181 H3
Rollesby Rd CHSGTN KT9 172 C5
Rollesby Wy THMD SE28 97 J6
Rolleston Av STMC/STPC BR5 169 G5
Rolleston Cl STMC/STPC BR5 169 G6
Rolleston Rd SAND/SEL CR2 177 K6
Roll Gdns GNTH/NBYPK IG2 60 A4
Rollins St PECK SE15 111 K5
Rollit Crs HSLW TW3 123 F4
Rollit St HOLWY N7 73 G4
Rolls Blds FLST/FETLN EC4A 12 A4
Rollscourt Av HNHL SE24 130 D4
Rolls Park Av CHING E4 43 J5
Rolls Park Rd CHING E4 43 K4
Rolls Rd STHWK SE1 19 M7
Rolls Royce Cl WLGTN SM6 176 E6
Rolt St DEPT SE8 112 C5
NWCR SE14 112 B5
Rolvenden Gdns BMLY BR1 153 H7
Rolvenden Pl TOTM N17 42 C7
Roman Cl ACT W3 105 J1
EBED/NFELT TW14 122 B4
RAIN RM13 99 F1
Romanfield Rd
BRXS/STRHM SW2 130 A6
Romanhurst Av HAYES BR2 167 H3
Romanhurst Gdns HAYES BR2 167 H3
Roman Rd BORE WD6 23 K5
CAR SM5 175 K7
Roman Ri NRWD SE19 149 K5
Roman Rd BETH E2 93 F1
BOW E3 75 H7
CHSWK W4 106 B3
CRICK NW2 70 A2
EHAM E6 95 H3
IL IG1 78 B5
MUSWH N10 40 B6
Roman Sq THMD SE28 97 G7
Roman Wy CROY/NA CR0 177 H1
DART DA1 138 B4
EN EN1 30 B4
HOLWY N7 73 F5
Romany Gdns CHEAM SM3 161 K6
Romany Ri STMC/STPC BR5 169 H7
Roma Read Cl PUT/ROE SW15 126 E6
Roma Rd WALTH E17 57 G2
Romberg Rd TOOT SW17 148 A2
Romborough Gdns LEW SE13 133 F4
Romborough Wy LEW SE13 133 F4
Rom Crs ROMW/RG RM7 63 G6
Romeland BORE WD6 23 K5
Romero Cl BRXN/ST SW9 130 A2
Romero Sq BKHTH/KID SE3 134 B3
Romeyn Rd
STRHM/NOR SW16 149 F2
Romford Rd FSTGT E7 76 E5
MNPK E12 77 K3
SRTFD E15 76 D5
Romford St WCHPL E1 92 C4
Romilly Dr OXHEY WD19 33 J3
Romilly Rd FSBYPK N4 73 H1
Romilly St SOHO/SHAV W1D 11 H6
Rommany Rd WNWD SE27 149 K3
Romney Cl ASHF TW15 140 A4
CHSGTN KT9 172 A3
GLDGN NW11 53 G7
NWCR SE14 111 K6
RYLN/HDSTN HA2 48 A6
TOTM N17 42 D7
Romney Dr BMLY BR1 153 H6
RYLN/HDSTN HA2 48 A6
Romney Gdns BXLYHN DA7 117 G7
Romney Rd GNWCH SE10 113 F5
NWMAL KT3 160 A5
WOOL/PLUM SE18 115 H2
YEAD UB4 82 B1
Romney Rw CRICK NW2 * 70 B1
Romney St WEST SW1P 17 H4
Romola Rd HNHL SE24 130 C7
Romsey Rd DAGW RM9 79 K7
WEA W13 * 85 G6
Romside Pl ROMW/RG RM7 63 F3
Rom Valley Wy
ROMW/RG RM7 63 G5
Ronald Av SRTFD E15 94 C2
Ronald Cl BECK BR3 166 C4
Ronalds Rd BMLY BR1 152 E7
HBRY N5 73 G4
Ronaldstone Rd BFN/LL DA15 135 K5
Rona Rd HAMP NW3 72 A3
Ronart St
KTN/HRWW/WS HA3 49 F2
Rona Wk IS N1 73 K5
Rondu Rd CRICK NW2 70 C4
Ronelean Rd SURB KT6 172 B1
Roneo Cnr ROMW/RG RM7 63 H7
Roneo Link HCH RM12 63 H7
Ron Green Ct ERITH DA8 118 A4
Ron Leighton Wy EHAM E6 77 J7
Ronnie La BCTR RM8 79 J1
Ron Todd Cl DAGE RM10 80 C7
Ronver Rd LEE/GVPK SE12 133 K7
Rood La FENCHST EC3M 13 J6
Rookby Ct WCHMH N21 41 H1
Rook Cl WBLY HA9 68 D2
Rookeries Cl FELT TW13 141 F2
Rookery Dr CHST BR7 154 A7
Rookery La HAYES BR2 168 C5
Rookery Rd CLAP SW4 129 H3
The Rookery
STRHM/NOR SW16 * 149 F5
Rookery Wy CDALE/KGS NW9 51 H4
Rookfield Av MUSWH N10 54 C3
Rookfield Cl MUSWH N10 54 C3
Rookley Cl BELMT SM2 175 F7
Rooks Ter WDR/YW UB7 * 100 B1
Rookstone Rd TOOT SW17 147 K4
Rookwood Av NWMAL KT3 160 D3
WLGTN SM6 176 D4
Rookwood Gdns CHING E4 * 44 D1
Rookwood Rd
STNW/STAM N16 56 C6
Roosevelt Wy DAGE RM10 81 F5
Rootes Dr NKENS W10 88 B3
Ropemaker Rd
BERM/RHTH SE16 112 B1
Ropemaker's Flds
POP/IOD E14 * 93 H6
Ropemaker St BARB EC2Y 13 G2
Roper La STHWK SE1 19 K2
Ropers Av CHING E4 44 A4
Ropers Orch CHEL SW3 * 108 D5
Roper St ELTH/MOT SE9 134 E4
Roper Wy MTCM CR4 163 F1
Ropery St BOW E3 93 H3
Rope St BERM/RHTH SE16 112 B2
Ropewalk Gdns WCHPL E1 92 C5
Ropley St BETH E2 92 C1
Rosa Alba Ms HBRY N5 73 J3
Rosaline Rd FUL/PGN SW6 107 H6
Rosaline Ter FUL/PGN SW6 * 107 H6
Rosamond St SYD SE26 150 D2
Rosamond Vls
MORT/ESHN SW14 * 126 A3
Rosamund Cl SAND/SEL CR2 177 K3
Rosamun Rd NWDGN UB2 102 D3
Rosary Cl HSLW TW3 122 D1
Rosary Gdns BUSH WD23 22 E6
SKENS SW7 14 F6
Rosary Ga BTSEA SW11 109 G6
Rosaville Rd FUL/PGN SW6 107 J6
Roscoe St STLK EC1Y 12 F1
Roscoff Cl EDGW HA8 36 D7
Roseacre Cl WEA W13 85 H4
Roseacre Rd WELL DA16 136 C2
Rose Aly STHWK SE1 12 F8
Roseary Cl WDR/YW UB7 100 A3
Rose Av MRDN SM4 162 B4
MTCM CR4 147 K7
SWFD E18 59 F1
Rosebank PGE/AN SE20 150 D6
Rosebank Av ALP/SUD HA0 67 F3
Rose Bank Cl
NFNCH/WDSPK N12 39 J4
Rosebank Cl TEDD TW11 143 G5
Rosebank Est BOW E3 93 H1
Rosebank Gdns ACT W3 * 87 F5
BOW E3 * 93 G1
Rosebank Gv WALTH E17 57 H2
Rosebank Rd HNWL W7 103 K1
WALTH E17 57 J5
Rosebank Wk CAMTN NW1 5 H2
Rosebank Wy ACT W3 87 F5
Roseberry Gdns DART DA1 139 F6
FSBYPK N4 55 H5
Roseberry Pl HACK E8 74 B5
Roseberry St
BERM/RHTH SE16 111 J3
Rosebery Av BFN/LL DA15 135 K6
CLKNW EC1R 12 A1
MNPK E12 77 J5
NWMAL KT3 160 C1
RYLN/HDSTN HA2 66 A2
THHTH CR7 164 D1
TOTM N17 56 C1
Rosebery Cl MRDN SM4 161 G5
Rosebery Ct CLKNW EC1R 6 A9
Rosebery Gdns
CEND/HSY/T N8 * 54 E4
SUT SM1 175 F3
WEA W13 85 G5
Rosebery Ms MUSWH N10 54 C1
Rosebery Pde EW KT17 * 173 H6
Rosebery Rd BUSH WD23 22 B7
CLAP SW4 129 K5
HSLW TW3 123 H4
KUT/HW KT1 159 J1
MUSWH N10 54 C1
SUT SM1 174 D5
Rosebine Av WHTN TW2 123 J6
Rosebriars ESH/CLAY KT10 170 C4
Rosebury Rd FUL/PGN SW6 128 A1
Rosebury V RSLP HA4 64 E1
Rose Ct WCHPL E1 13 L3
Rosecourt Rd CROY/NA CR0 164 A5
Rosecroft Av HAMP NW3 70 E2
Rosecroft Ct NTHWD HA6 * 32 A5
Rose Croft Gdns CRICK NW2 69 J2
Rosecroft Gdns WHTN TW2 123 J7
Rosecroft Rd STHL UB1 84 A3
Rosecroft Wk ALP/SUD HA0 67 K4
PIN HA5 47 H4
Rose & Crown Yd STJS SW1Y * 10 F9
Rosedale Av HYS/HAR UB3 82 B4
Rosedale Cl ABYW SE2 116 C2
HNWL W7 104 A1
STAN HA7 35 H5
Rosedale Dr DAGW RM9 79 H7
Rosedale Gdns DAGW RM9 79 H6
Rosedale Pl CROY/NA CR0 166 A6
Rosedale Rd DAGW RM9 79 H6
EW KT17 173 J4
FSTGT E7 77 G4
RCH/KEW TW9 125 F3
ROM RM1 62 E2
Rosedene Av CROY/NA CR0 163 K6
GFD/PVL UB6 84 A2
MRDN SM4 161 K4
STRHM/NOR SW16 149 F2
Rosedene Cl DART DA1 139 F6
Rosedene Gdns
GNTH/NBYPK IG2 60 A3
Rosedene Ter LEY E10 75 K1
Rosedew Rd HMSMTH W6 107 G5
Rose End WPK KT4 161 G7
Rosefield POP/IOD E14 93 J6
Rosefield Cl CAR SM5 175 J4
Rosefield Gdns POP/IOD E14 93 J6
Rose Garden Cl EDGW HA8 36 A5
Rose Gdns EA W5 104 E2
FELT TW13 140 E1
STHL UB1 84 A3
STWL/WRAY TW19 120 A6
WATW WD18 20 E4
Rose Gln CDALE/KGS NW9 51 F3
ROMW/RG RM7 63 G7
Rosehart Ms NTGHL W11 8 A5
Rosehatch Av CHDH RM6 61 K2
Roseheath Rd HSLWW TW4 122 E4
Rosehill ESH/CLAY KT10 171 G5
HPTN TW12 142 A7
Rose Hl SUT SM1 175 F1
Rosehill Av SUT SM1 162 B7
Rosehill Court Pde
MRDN SM4 * 162 B6
Rosehill Gdns GFD/PVL UB6 67 F4
SUT SM1 175 F1
Rose Hill Pk West SUT SM1 162 B7
Rosehill Rd WAND/EARL SW18 128 B5
Rose Joan Ms
KIL/WHAMP NW6 70 E3
Roseland Cl TOTM N17 41 K6
Rose La CHDH RM6 62 A3
Rose Lawn BUSH WD23 22 C7
Roseleigh Av HBRY N5 73 H3
Roseleigh Cl TWK TW1 124 E5
Rosemary Av
E/WMO/HCT KT8 157 F2
ED N9 30 D7
FNCH N3 53 F1
HSLWW TW4 122 C1
ROM RM1 63 H2
Rosemary Cl CROY/NA CR0 163 K6
Rosemary Dr POP/IOD E14 94 B5
REDBR IG4 59 H4
Rosemary Gdns BCTR RM8 62 B7
CHSGTN KT9 172 A3
Rosemary La
MORT/ESHN SW14 125 K2
Rosemary Rd PECK SE15 111 G6
TOOT SW17 147 G2
WELL DA16 116 A7
Rosemary St IS N1 7 G3
Rosemead CDALE/KGS NW9 51 H6
Rosemead Av FELT TW13 140 D1
MTCM CR4 163 H2
WBLY HA9 68 A4
Rosemere Pl HAYES BR2 167 H3
Rose Ms UED N18 42 D3
Rosemont Av
NFNCH/WDSPK N12 39 G5
Rosemont Rd ACT W3 86 D6
HAMP NW3 71 G5
NWMAL KT3 159 K2
RCHPK/HAM TW10 125 F5
Rosemoor St CHEL SW3 15 L6
Rosemount Cl WFD IG8 45 K5
Rosemount Dr BMLY BR1 168 E3
Rosemount Rd ALP/SUD HA0 68 A7
WEA W13 85 G5
Rosenau Crs BTSEA SW11 108 E7
Rosenau Rd BTSEA SW11 108 D7
Rosendale Rd DUL SE21 149 J1
HNHL SE24 130 D6
Roseneath Av WCHMH N21 29 H7
Roseneath Pl
STRHM/NOR SW16 149 G3
Roseneath Rd BTSEA SW11 129 F5
Roseneath Wk EN EN1 30 A3
Rosens Wk EDGW HA8 36 D2
Rosenthal Rd CAT SE6 132 E5
Rosenthorpe Rd PECK SE15 132 A4
Rose Park Cl YEAD UB4 83 G4
Roserton St POP/IOD E14 113 F1
The Rosery CROY/NA CR0 166 A5
The Roses WFD IG8 * 44 D6
Rose St COVGDN WC2E 11 J6
Rosethorn Cl BAL SW12 129 H6
Rosetree Pl HPTN TW12 142 A6
Rosetta Cl VX/NE SW8 109 K6
Roseveare Rd LEE/GVPK SE12 153 G3
Roseville WCHMH N21 29 G7
Roseville Av HSLW TW3 123 F4
Roseville Rd HYS/HAR UB3 101 K4
Rosevine Rd RYNPK SW20 146 A7
Rose Wk BRYLDS KT5 159 J4
WWKM BR4 180 A1
Rose Wy LEE/GVPK SE12 133 K4
Roseway DUL SE21 130 E5
EDGW HA8 36 E3
Rosewell Cl PGE/AN SE20 150 D6
Rosewood Av GFD/PVL UB6 67 G4
HCH RM12 81 J4
Rosewood Cl SCUP DA14 155 J2
Rosewood Ct KUTN/CMB KT2 144 C6
Rosewood Gv SUT SM1 175 G1
Rosewood Ter PGE/AN SE20 * 150 E6
Rosher Cl SRTFD E15 76 B6
Rosina St HOM E9 75 F5
Roskell Rd PUT/ROE SW15 127 G2
Roslin Rd ACT W3 105 J2
Roslin Wy BMLY BR1 152 E4
Roslyn Cl MTCM CR4 162 C1
Roslyn Gdns GPK RM2 63 H1
Roslyn Ms SEVS/STOTM N15 * 56 A4
Roslyn Rd SEVS/STOTM N15 55 K4
Rosmead Rd NTGHL W11 88 C6
Rosoman Pl CLKNW EC1R 6 B9
Rosoman St CLKNW EC1R 6 B8
Rossall Cl EMPK RM11 63 J5
Rossall Crs WLSDN NW10 86 B2
Ross Av BCTR RM8 80 B1
Ross Cl HYS/HAR UB3 101 G3
KTN/HRWW/WS HA3 34 C6
NTHLT UB5 66 D3
Rossdale SUT SM1 175 J4
Rossdale Dr CDALE/KGS NW9 50 E7
ED N9 30 E5
Rossdale Rd PUT/ROE SW15 127 F3
Rosse Ms BKHTH/KID SE3 114 A7
Rossendale St CLPT E5 74 D1
Rossendale Wy CAMTN NW1 4 F2
Rossetti Ms STJWD NW8 3 G4
Rossetti Rd BERM/RHTH SE16 111 J4
Ross House CHARL SE7 * 114 D6
Rossignol Gdns CAR SM5 176 A1
Rossindel Rd HSLW TW3 123 F4
Rossington St CLPT E5 74 C1
Rossiter Cl NRWD SE19 149 J6
Rossiter Flds BAR EN5 26 C5
Rossiter Rd BAL SW12 129 G7
Rossland Cl BXLYHS DA6 137 H4
Rosslyn Av BARN SW13 126 B2
BCTR RM8 62 B6
CHING E4 44 D1
EBAR EN4 27 J5
EBED/NFELT TW14 121 K5
Rosslyn Cl HYS/HAR UB3 82 B4
SUN TW16 140 C5
WWKM BR4 180 D2
Rosslyn Crs HRW HA1 49 F3
WBLY HA9 68 A2
Rosslyn Hl HAMP NW3 71 H4
Rosslyn Park Ms HAMP NW3 71 H4
Rosslyn Rd BARK IG11 78 D6
TWK TW1 124 D5
WALTH E17 * 58 A3
WATW WD18 21 F2
Rossmore Cl CAMTN NW1 * 9 K1
PEND EN3 31 F3
Rossmore Rd CAMTN NW1 3 K9
Ross Pde WLGTN SM6 176 B5
Ross Rd DART DA1 138 D5
SNWD SE25 165 F2
WHTN TW2 123 H7
WLGTN SM6 176 C5
Ross Wy ELTH/MOT SE9 134 D2
NTHWD HA6 32 D3
Rossway Dr BUSH WD23 22 C4
Rosswood Gdns WLGTN SM6 176 B5
Rostella Rd TOOT SW17 147 H3
Rostrever Gdns HYS/HAR UB3 82 C7
Rostrevor Av
SEVS/STOTM N15 56 B5
Rostrevor Gdns NWDGN UB2 102 D4
Rostrevor Rd FUL/PGN SW6 107 J7
WIM/MER SW19 146 E4
Rotary St STHWK SE1 18 C3
Rothbury Av RAIN RM13 99 K4
Rothbury Cots GNWCH SE10 113 H3
Rothbury Gdns ISLW TW7 104 B6
Rothbury Rd HOM E9 75 H6
Rotherfield Rd CAR SM5 176 A3
Rotherfield St IS N1 6 F2
Rotherham Wk STHWK SE1 * 12 D9
Rotherhill Av
STRHM/NOR SW16 148 D5
Rotherhithe New Rd
BERM/RHTH SE16 111 J4
Rotherhithe Old Rd
BERM/RHTH SE16 112 A3
Rotherhithe St
BERM/RHTH SE16 112 B1
Rotherhithe Tnl
BERM/RHTH SE16 111 K1
Rothermere Rd CROY/NA CR0 177 F4
Rotherwick Hl EA W5 86 B3
Rotherwick Rd GLDGN NW11 52 E6
Rotherwood Cl RYNPK SW20 146 C7
Rotherwood Rd
PUT/ROE SW15 127 G2
Rothery St IS N1 * 6 D3
Rothery Ter BRXN/ST SW9 * 110 C6
Rothesay Av GFD/PVL UB6 66 D5
RCHPK/HAM TW10 125 J3
RYNPK SW20 161 H1
Rothesay Rd SNWD SE25 164 E3
Rothsay Rd FSTGT E7 77 G6
Rothsay St STHWK SE1 19 J3
Rothschild Rd CHSWK W4 105 K3
Rothschild St WNWD SE27 149 H3
Rothwell Gdns DAGW RM9 79 J6
Rothwell Rd DAGW RM9 79 J7
Rothwell St CAMTN NW1 3 M3
Rotterdam Dr POP/IOD E14 113 F2
Rouel Rd BERM/RHTH SE16 111 H2
Rougemont Av MRDN SM4 161 K5
The Roughs NTHWD HA6 32 C2
Roundaway Rd CLAY IG5 59 K1
Roundel Cl BROCKY SE4 132 C3
Round Gv CROY/NA CR0 166 A6
Roundhay Cl FSTH SE23 151 F1
Round Hl SYD SE26 150 D1
Roundhill Dr ENC/FH EN2 29 F3
Roundtable Rd BMLY BR1 152 D2
Roundtree Rd ALP/SUD HA0 67 H4
Roundways RSLP HA4 64 D2
The Roundway
ESH/CLAY KT10 171 F5
TOTM N17 41 J7
WATW WD18 20 D5
Roundwood CHST BR7 169 G1
Roundwood Av STKPK UB11 82 A7
Roundwood Cl RSLP HA4 * 46 B6
Roundwood Pk
WLSDN NW10 * 69 J7
Roundwood Rd WLSDN NW10 69 G5
Roundwood Ter
STNW/STAM N16 56 A6
Rounton Rd BOW E3 93 J3
Roupell Rd BRXS/STRHM SW2 130 A7
Roupell St STHWK SE1 12 B9
Rousden St CAMTN NW1 4 E2
Rousebarn La
RKW/CH/CXG WD3 20 A2
Rouse Gdns DUL SE21 150 A3
Routemaster Cl PLSTW E13 95 F2
Routh Ct EBED/NFELT TW14 121 G7
Routh Rd WAND/EARL SW18 128 D6

Routh St EHAM E6 95 K4
Rowallan Rd FUL/PGN SW6 107 H6
Rowan Av CHING E4 43 H5
Rowan Cl ALP/SUD HA0 67 G2
EA W5 105 F1
IL IG1 78 D4
NWMAL KT3 160 B1
STAN HA7 35 F5
STRHM/NOR SW16 148 C7
Rowan Crs DART DA1 139 F7
STRHM/NOR SW16 148 C7
Rowan Dr CDALE/KGS NW9 51 J2
Rowan Gdns CROY/NA CR0 178 B2
Rowan Pl HYS/HAR UB3 82 D6
Rowan Rd BTFD TW8 104 C6
BXLYHN DA7 137 F2
HMSMTH W6 107 G3
STRHM/NOR SW16 163 H1
WDR/YW UB7 100 A3
The Rowans PLMGR N13 41 J2
SUN TW16 140 D4
Rowan Ter HMSMTH W6 107 G3
PGE/AN SE20 * 150 C7
WIM/MER SW19 * 146 C6
Rowantree Cl WCHMH N21 29 K7
Rowantree Ms ENC/FH EN2 29 H1
Rowantree Rd ENC/FH EN2 29 H1
WCHMH N21 29 K7
Rowan Wk EFNCH N2 53 G5
HAYES BR2 181 K2
NKENS W10 * 88 C3
Rowan Wy CHDH RM6 61 J2
Rowanwood Av BFN/LL DA15 136 B7
Rowben Cl TRDG/WHET N20 27 F7
Rowberry Cl FUL/PGN SW6 107 G6
Rowcross St STHWK SE1 19 L7
Rowdell Rd NTHLT UB5 66 A7
Rowden Pde CHING E4 * 43 J5
Rowden Rd BECK BR3 151 G7
CHING E4 43 K5
HOR/WEW KT19 172 E3
Rowditch La BTSEA SW11 129 F1
Rowdon Av WLSDN NW10 69 K6
Rowdown Crs CROY/NA CR0 180 B7
Rowdowns Rd DAGW RM9 80 B7
Rowe Gdns BARK IG11 97 F1
Rowe La HOM E9 74 E4
Rowena Crs BTSEA SW11 128 D1
Rowe Wk RYLN/HDSTN HA2 66 A2
Rowfant Rd TOOT SW17 148 A1
Rowhill Rd CLPT E5 74 D3
Rowington Cl BAY/PAD W2 8 C2
Rowland Av
KTN/HRWW/WS HA3 49 J2
Rowland Gv SYD SE26 150 D2
Rowland Hill Av TOTM N17 41 J6
Rowland Hill St HAMP NW3 71 J4
Rowland Pl NTHWD HA6 * 32 C6
Rowlands Av PIN HA5 34 A5
Rowlands Cl HGT N6 * 54 A5
MLHL NW7 37 J6
Rowlands Rd BCTR RM8 80 B1
Rowland Wy ASHF TW15 140 A6
WIM/MER SW19 147 F7
Rowley Av BFN/LL DA15 136 C6
Rowley Cl ALP/SUD HA0 68 B6
OXHEY WD19 21 J5
Rowley Cots WKENS W14 * 107 J3
Rowley Gdns FSBYPK N4 55 J6
Rowley Green Rd BAR EN5 25 J4
Rowley La BORE WD6 25 F1
Rowley Rd SEVS/STOTM N15 55 J4
Rowley Wy STJWD NW8 2 D3
Rowlheys Pl WDR/YW UB7 100 B2
Rowlls Rd KUT/HW KT1 159 G2
Rowney Gdns DAGW RM9 79 J5
Rowney Rd DAGW RM9 79 H5
Rowntree Clifford Cl
PLSTW E13 95 F3
Rowntree Cl
KIL/WHAMP NW6 * 70 E5
Rowntree Rd WHTN TW2 123 K7
Rowse Cl SRTFD E15 76 A7
Rowsley Av HDN NW4 52 A2
Rowstock Gdns HOLWY N7 72 D5
Rowton Rd WOOL/PLUM SE18 115 H6
Roxborough Av HRW HA1 48 D6
ISLW TW7 104 A6
Roxborough Pk HRW HA1 48 E6
Roxborough Rd HRW HA1 48 D4
Roxbourne Cl NTHLT UB5 65 H5
Roxburgh Rd WNWD SE27 149 H4
Roxburn Wy RSLP HA4 64 D2
Roxby Pl FUL/PGN SW6 14 B9
Roxeth Green Av
RYLN/HDSTN HA2 66 B2
Roxeth Gv RYLN/HDSTN HA2 66 B3
Roxeth Hl RYLN/HDSTN HA2 66 D1
Roxley Rd LEW SE13 132 E5
Roxton Gdns CROY/NA CR0 179 H5
Roxwell Rd BARK IG11 97 G1
SHB W12 106 D1
Roxwell Wy WFD IG8 45 G6
Roxy Av CHDH RM6 61 J6
Royal Albert Wy EHAM E6 95 K6
Royal Ar CONDST W1S 10 E7
Royal Arsenal West
WOOL/PLUM SE18 * 115 F4
Royal Av CHEL SW3 15 L7
WPK KT4 173 G1
Royal Circ WNWD SE27 149 G2
Royal Cl DEPT SE8 112 C5
GDMY/SEVK IG3 61 G6
STNW/STAM N16 56 A7
WIM/MER SW19 146 B1
WPK KT4 173 G1
Royal College St CAMTN NW1 4 F3
Royal Connaught Dr
BUSH WD23 21 K3
Royal Ct BANK EC3V 13 H5
ELTH/MOT SE9 * 134 E7
EN EN1 * 30 A5
WATW WD18 20 C3
Royal Crs GNTH/NBYPK IG2 60 D5
NTGHL W11 107 G1
RSLP HA4 65 J3
Royal Crescent Ms
NTGHL W11 107 G1
Royal Docks Rd EHAM E6 96 B4
Royal Dr FBAR/BDGN N11 40 A4
Royal Herbert Pavilions
WOOL/PLUM SE18 * 114 E7
Royal Hl GNWCH SE10 113 F6
Royal Hospital Rd CHEL SW3 15 L9
Royal Ms BAL SW12 129 G6
Royal Mint Pl WCHPL E1 13 M6
Royal Mint St WCHPL E1 13 M6
Royal Naval Pl NWCR SE14 112 C6
Royal Oak Ms TEDD TW11 143 G4
Royal Oak Pl EDUL SE22 131 J5
Royal Oak Rd BXLYHS DA6 137 G4
HACK E8 74 D5
Royal Oak Yd STHWK SE1 19 J2
Royal Opera Ar STJS SW1Y * 11 G8
Royal Orchard Cl
WAND/EARL SW18 127 H6
Royal Pde BKHTH/KID SE3 133 J1
CHST BR7 154 C6
FUL/PGN SW6 * 107 H6
Royal Pl GNWCH SE10 113 F6
Royal Rd CAN/RD E16 95 H5
LBTH SE11 18 C9
SCUP DA14 155 K2
TEDD TW11 142 D4
Royal Route WBLY HA9 68 B3
Royal St STHWK SE1 17 M3
Royal Victor Pl BOW E3 93 F1
Roycraft Av BARK IG11 97 F1
Roycroft Cl
BRXS/STRHM SW2 * 130 B7
SWFD E18 45 F7
Roydene Rd
WOOL/PLUM SE18 115 K5
Roy Gdns GNTH/NBYPK IG2 60 E3
Roy Gv HPTN TW12 142 B5
Royle Cl GPK RM2 63 K4
Royle Crs WEA W13 85 G3
Roy Rd NTHWD HA6 32 D6
Roy Sq POP/IOD E14 93 G6
Royston Av CHING E4 43 J4
SUT SM1 175 H2
WLGTN SM6 176 D3
Royston Cl HEST TW5 102 A7
Royston Gdns IL IG1 59 H5
Royston Gv PIN HA5 33 K5
Royston Park Rd PIN HA5 33 K5
Royston Rd DART DA1 138 C5
PGE/AN SE20 151 F7
RCHPK/HAM TW10 125 F4
The Roystons BRYLDS KT5 159 J4
Royston St BETH E2 92 E1
Rozel Rd VX/NE SW8 129 H1
Rubastic Rd NWDGN UB2 102 B2
Rubens Rd NTHLT UB5 83 G1
Rubens St CAT SE6 151 H1
Ruby Cl CLPT E5 75 F2
Ruby Ms WALTH E17 * 57 J2
Ruby Rd WALTH E17 57 J2
Ruby St PECK SE15 111 J5
WLSDN NW10 68 E6
Ruby Triangle PECK SE15 * 111 J5
Ruckholt Cl LEY E10 75 K2
Ruckholt Rd LEY E10 76 A2
Rucklidge Av WLSDN NW10 87 H1
Rudall Crs HAMP NW3 71 H3
Ruddington Cl CLPT E5 75 G3
Ruddock Cl EDGW HA8 36 E6
Ruddstreet Cl
WOOL/PLUM SE18 115 G3
Rudgwick Ter STJWD NW8 * 3 K4
Rudland Rd BXLYHN DA7 137 J2
Rudloe Rd BAL SW12 129 H6
Rudolf Pl VX/NE SW8 109 K5
Rudolph Rd BUSH WD23 22 A5
KIL/WHAMP NW6 2 B6
PLSTW E13 94 D1
Rudyard Gv EDGW HA8 36 E5
Ruffetts Cl SAND/SEL CR2 178 D6
The Ruffetts SAND/SEL CR2 178 D6
Ruffle Cl WDR/YW UB7 100 B1
Rufford Cl
KTN/HRWW/WS HA3 49 G5
Rufford St IS N1 5 K3
Rufford Street Ms IS N1 5 K2
Rufus Cl RSLP HA4 65 H2
Rufus St FSBYE EC1V 7 J8
Rugby Av ALP/SUD HA0 67 J3
ED N9 30 B7
GFD/PVL UB6 66 D5
Rugby Cl HRW HA1 48 E3
Rugby Gdns DAGW RM9 79 J5
Rugby La BELMT SM2 174 B7
Rugby Rd CDALE/KGS NW9 50 C3
CHSWK W4 106 B1
DAGW RM9 79 H6
TWK TW1 123 K5
Rugby St BMSBY WC1N 11 L1
Rugg St POP/IOD E14 93 J6
Ruislip Cl GFD/PVL UB6 84 B3
Ruislip Ct RSLP HA4 * 64 D1
Ruislip Rd GFD/PVL UB6 84 A2
NTHLT UB5 83 J2
Ruislip Rd East GFD/PVL UB6 84 C3
Ruislip St TOOT SW17 147 K3
Rumbold Rd FUL/PGN SW6 108 A6
Rum Cl WAP E1W 92 D6
Rumsey Cl HPTN TW12 141 K5
Rumsey Rd BRXN/ST SW9 130 A2
Runbury Cir CDALE/KGS NW9 69 F1
Runcorn Cl TOTM N17 56 D3
Runcorn Pl NTGHL W11 88 C6
Rundell Crs HDN NW4 51 K4
Runes Cl MTCM CR4 162 C3
Runnelfield HRW HA1 66 E2
Runnymede WIM/MER SW19 147 H7
Runnymede Cl WHTN TW2 123 G5
Runnymede Crs
STRHM/NOR SW16 148 D7
Runnymede Gdns
GFD/PVL UB6 84 D1
HSLW TW3 123 G5
Runnymede Rd WHTN TW2 123 G5
Runway Cl CDALE/KGS NW9 51 H1
The Runway RSLP HA4 65 F4
Rupack St BERM/RHTH SE16 * 111 K1
Rupert Av WBLY HA9 68 A4
Rupert Ct E/WMO/HCT KT8 * 157 F3
SOHO/SHAV W1D 11 G6
Rupert Gdns BRXN/ST SW9 130 C1
Rupert Rd ARCH N19 72 D2
CHSWK W4 106 B2
KIL/WHAMP NW6 88 D1
Rupert St SOHO/SHAV W1D 11 G6
Rural Cl EMPK RM11 63 K7
Rural Wy STRHM/NOR SW16 148 B6
Rusbridge Cl HACK E8 74 C4
Ruscoe Rd CAN/RD E16 94 D5
Ruscombe Wy
EBED/NFELT TW14 121 J6
Rusham Rd BAL SW12 128 E5
Rushbridge Cl CROY/NA CR0 164 D5
Rushbrook Crs WALTH E17 43 J7
Rushbrook Rd ELTH/MOT SE9 154 C1
Rush Common Ms
BRXS/STRHM SW2 129 K6
Rushcroft Rd
BRXS/STRHM SW2 130 B3
CHING E4 43 K6
Rushden Cl NRWD SE19 149 K6
Rushdene ABYW SE2 116 D2
Rushdene Av EBAR EN4 27 J6
Rushdene Cl NTHLT UB5 83 G1
Rushdene Crs NTHLT UB5 83 F1
Rushdene Rd PIN HA5 47 G5
Rushden Gdns CLAY IG5 60 A2
MLHL NW7 38 A5
Rushdon Cl ROM RM1 63 J4
Rushett Cl THDIT KT7 158 C7
Rushett Rd THDIT KT7 158 C6
Rushey Cl NWMAL KT3 160 A3
Rushey Gn CAT SE6 132 E6
Rushey Hl ENC/FH EN2 29 F3
Rushey Md BROCKY SE4 132 D4
Rushford Rd BROCKY SE4 132 C5
Rush Green Gdns
ROMW/RG RM7 62 E7
Rush Green Rd
ROMW/RG RM7 62 E7
Rushgrove Av
CDALE/KGS NW9 51 H3
Rushgrove Pde
CDALE/KGS NW9 * 51 H4
Rushgrove St
WOOL/PLUM SE18 114 E3
Rush Hill Ms BTSEA SW11 129 F2
Rush Hill Rd BTSEA SW11 129 F2
Rushley Cl HAYES BR2 181 H3
Rushmead BETH E2 92 D2
RCHPK/HAM TW10 143 H2
Rushmead Cl CROY/NA CR0 178 B3
Rushmere Ct WPK KT4 173 J1
Rushmere Pl WIM/MER SW19 146 B4
Rushmon Pl CHEAM SM3 * 174 C5
Rushmon Vls NWMAL KT3 * 160 C3
Rushmoor Cl PIN HA5 47 F3
Rushmore Cl BMLY BR1 168 D2
Rushmore Ct WATW WD18 * 20 B5
Rushmore Rd CLPT E5 74 E3
Rusholme Av DAGE RM10 80 C2
Rusholme Gv NRWD SE19 150 A4
Rusholme Rd PUT/ROE SW15 127 G5
Rushout Av
KTN/HRWW/WS HA3 49 H5
Rushton St IS N1 7 H5
Rushworth St STHWK SE1 18 D1
Rushy Meadow La CAR SM5 175 J1
Ruskin Av EBED/NFELT TW14 121 J6
MNPK E12 77 J5
RCH/KEW TW9 105 H6
WELL DA16 136 B2
Ruskin Cl GLDGN NW11 53 F5
Ruskin Dr WELL DA16 136 B2
WPK KT4 173 K1
Ruskin Gdns EA W5 85 K3
KTN/HRWW/WS HA3 50 B4
Ruskin Gv DART DA1 139 K4
WELL DA16 136 B1
Ruskin Rd BELV DA17 117 H3
CAR SM5 176 A4
CROY/NA CR0 177 H1
ISLW TW7 124 A2
STHL UB1 83 J6
TOTM N17 42 B7
Ruskin Wk ED N9 42 C1
HAYES BR2 168 D5
HNHL SE24 130 D4
Ruskin Wy WIM/MER SW19 162 C1
Rusland Park Rd HRW HA1 48 E3
Rusper Cl CRICK NW2 70 A2
STAN HA7 35 J3
Rusper Rd DAGW RM9 79 J5
WDGN N22 55 H1
Russel Cl BECK BR3 166 E2
Russell Av WDGN N22 55 H1
Russell Cl BKHTH/KID SE3 114 B6
BXLYHN DA7 137 H3
CHSWK W4 106 C5
DART DA1 138 D2
NTHWD HA6 32 A4
RSLP HA4 65 G1
WLSDN NW10 68 E6
Russell Ct BAR EN5 * 27 G3
WHALL SW1A 10 F9
Russell Dr STWL/WRAY TW19 120 A5
Russell Gdns GLDGN NW11 52 C5
RCHPK/HAM TW10 143 J1
TRDG/WHET N20 39 J1
WDR/YW UB7 100 D4
WKENS W14 * 107 H2
Russell Gardens Ms
WKENS W14 107 H1
Russell Gv BRXN/ST SW9 110 B7
MLHL NW7 37 G4
Russell Kerr Cl CHSWK W4 * 105 K6
Russell La TRDG/WHET N20 39 K1
Russell Pde GLDGN NW11 * 52 C5
Russell Pl HAMP NW3 71 J4
Russell Rd CAN/RD E16 94 E5
CDALE/KGS NW9 51 H5
CEND/HSY/T N8 54 D5
CHING E4 43 H3
MTCM CR4 162 D2
NTHLT UB5 66 C4
NTHWD HA6 32 A2
SEVS/STOTM N15 56 A4
TRDG/WHET N20 39 J1
WALTH E17 57 K5
WDGN N22 41 F5
WHTN TW2 124 A5
WIM/MER SW19 146 E6
WKENS W14 107 H2
Russell Sq RSQ WC1B 11 H2
Russell St HOL/ALD WC2B 11 L5
Russell Wy OXHEY WD19 21 F6
SUT SM1 175 F4
Russet Cl HGDN/ICK UB10 82 A3
Russet Crs HOLWY N7 * 73 F4
Russet Dr CROY/NA CR0 166 B7
Russets Cl CHING E4 44 B3
Russia Dock Rd
BERM/RHTH SE16 * 93 G7
Russia La BETH E2 92 E1
Russia Rw CITYW EC2V 12 F5
Rusthall Av CHSWK W4 106 A2
Rusthall Cl CROY/NA CR0 165 K5
Rustic Av STRHM/NOR SW16 148 B6
Rustic Pl ALP/SUD HA0 67 K3
Rustington Wk CHEAM SM3 161 J6
Ruston Av BRYLDS KT5 159 J6
Ruston Gdns STHGT/OAK N14 28 A5
Ruston Ms NTGHL W11 * 88 C5
Ruston Rd WOOL/PLUM SE18 114 D2
Ruston St BOW E3 75 H7
Rust Sq CMBW SE5 110 E6
Rutford Rd STRHM/NOR SW16 148 E4
Ruth Cl STAN HA7 50 B3
Rutherford Cl BELMT SM2 175 H5
BORE WD6 24 E1
Rutherford St WEST SW1P 17 G5
Rutherford Wy BUSH WD23 22 D7
WBLY HA9 68 C2
Rutherglen Rd ABYW SE2 116 B5
Rutherwyke Cl EW KT17 173 J5
Ruthin Cl CDALE/KGS NW9 51 G5
Ruthin Rd BKHTH/KID SE3 113 K5
Ruthven St HOM E9 75 F7
Rutland Av BFN/LL DA15 136 B6
Rutland Cl BXLY DA5 136 E7
CHSGTN KT9 172 B5
DART DA1 139 G6
MORT/ESHN SW14 125 J2
WIM/MER SW19 147 J5
Rutland Ct CHST BR7 154 A7
SKENS SW7 15 K2
Rutland Dr MRDN SM4 161 K6
RCHPK/HAM TW10 124 E7
Rutland Gdns BCTR RM8 79 J4
CROY/NA CR0 178 A3
FSBYPK N4 55 H5
SKENS SW7 15 K2
WEA W13 * 85 G4
Rutland Gardens Ms
SKENS SW7 15 K2
Rutland Ga BELV DA17 117 J4
HAYES BR2 167 J3
SKENS SW7 15 J2
Rutland Gate Ms SKENS SW7 * 15 J2
Rutland Gv HMSMTH W6 106 E4
Rutland Ms STJWD NW8 2 D4
Rutland Ms South
SKENS SW7 * 15 J3
Rutland Pk CAT SE6 151 H1
CRICK NW2 70 A5
Rutland Pl BUSH WD23 * 22 D7
FARR EC1M * 12 D2
Rutland Rd FSTGT E7 77 H6
HOM E9 75 F7
HRW HA1 48 C5
HYS/HAR UB3 101 G3
IL IG1 78 B3
STHL UB1 84 A3
WALTH E17 57 J5
WAN E11 59 F4
WHTN TW2 142 D1
Rutland St SKENS SW7 15 K3
Rutland Wk CAT SE6 151 H1
Rutley Cl WALW SE17 18 C9
Rutlish Rd WIM/MER SW19 146 E7
Rutter Gdns MTCM CR4 162 C3
Rutters Cl WDR/YW UB7 100 D1
Rutt's Ter NWCR SE14 112 A7
The Rutts BUSH WD23 22 D7
Ruvigny Gdns PUT/ROE SW15 127 G2
Ruxley Cl HOR/WEW KT19 172 D4
SCUP DA14 155 K5
Ruxley Crs ESH/CLAY KT10 171 H6
Ruxley La HOR/WEW KT19 172 E4
Ruxley Ms HOR/WEW KT19 172 D4
Ruxley Rdg ESH/CLAY KT10 171 G6
Ruxley Towers
ESH/CLAY KT10 * 171 G6
Ryan Cl BKHTH/KID SE3 134 A3
RSLP HA4 47 F7
Ryan Ct OXHEY WD19 * 21 J6
Ryan Dr BTFD TW8 104 B5
Rycroft Wy TOTM N17 * 56 B2
Ryculff Sq BKHTH/KID SE3 133 J1
Rydal Cl HDN NW4 38 C7
Rydal Crs GFD/PVL UB6 85 H2
Rydal Dr BXLYHN DA7 117 H7
WWKM BR4 180 C1
Rydal Gdns CDALE/KGS NW9 51 G4
HSLW TW3 123 G5
PUT/ROE SW15 145 G4
WBLY HA9 49 J7
Rydal Mt HAYES BR2 * 167 J3
Rydal Rd STRHM/NOR SW16 148 D4
Rydal Wy PEND EN3 30 E5
RSLP HA4 65 G3
Ryde Pl TWK TW1 124 D5
Ryder Av LEY E10 57 K6
Ryder Cl BUSH WD23 22 B5
Ryder Dr BERM/RHTH SE16 111 J4
Ryder Gdns RAIN RM13 81 H5
Ryder St STJS SW1Y 10 F8
Ryder Yd STJS SW1Y 10 F8
Ryde Vale Rd BAL SW12 148 B1
Rydon Ms WIM/MER SW19 146 A6
Rydon St IS N1 6 F3
Rydston Cl HOLWY N7 5 K1
Rye Cl BORE WD6 25 F3
BXLY DA5 137 J5
Ryecotes Md DUL SE21 131 F7
Ryecroft Av CLAY IG5 60 B1
WHTN TW2 123 G7
Ryecroft Crs BAR EN5 25 K4
Ryecroft Rd LEW SE13 133 F4
STMC/STPC BR5 169 J5
STRHM/NOR SW16 149 G5
Ryecroft St FUL/PGN SW6 108 A7
Ryedale EDUL SE22 131 J5
Ryefield Av HGDN/ICK UB10 64 A7
Ryefield Crs PIN HA5 * 46 E1
Ryefield Pde NTHWD HA6 * 46 E1
Ryefield Rd NRWD SE19 149 J5
Rye Hill Pk PECK SE15 131 K3
Ryelands Crs LEE/GVPK SE12 134 B5
Rye La PECK SE15 131 H1
Rye Rd PECK SE15 132 A3
The Rye STHGT/OAK N14 28 C6
Rye Wk PUT/ROE SW15 127 G4
Rye Wy EDGW HA8 36 B5
Ryfold Rd WIM/MER SW19 146 E2
Ryhope Rd FBAR/BDGN N11 40 B3
Ryland Cl FELT TW13 140 D3
Rylandes Rd CRICK NW2 69 J2
SAND/SEL CR2 178 D7
Ryland Rd KTTN NW5 * 72 B5
Rylett Crs SHB W12 106 C2
Rylett Rd SHB W12 106 C1
Rylston Rd FUL/PGN SW6 107 J5
PLMGR N13 41 K2
Rymer Rd CROY/NA CR0 165 F6
Rymer St HNHL SE24 130 C5
Rymill St CAN/RD E16 96 A7
Rysbrack St CHEL SW3 15 L3
Rythe Cl CHSGTN KT9 171 J6
Rythe Ct THDIT KT7 158 B6
Rythe Rd ESH/CLAY KT10 170 D4
Ryves Cots MTCM CR4 * 163 F1

S

Sabine Rd BTSEA SW11 128 E2
Sable Cl HSLWW TW4 122 B2
Sable St IS N1 6 D1
Sach Rd CLPT E5 74 D1
Sackville Av HAYES BR2 167 K7
Sackville Cl RYLN/HDSTN HA2 66 D2
Sackville Est
STRHM/NOR SW16 148 E2
Sackville Gdns IL IG1 59 K7
Sackville Rd BELMT SM2 174 E6
Sackville St CONDST W1S 10 E7
Saddlebrook Pk SUN TW16 140 C6
Saddlers Cl BAR EN5 25 K4
BORE WD6 * 25 F4
PIN HA5 34 A4
Saddlers Ms KUT/HW KT1 143 J7
Saddlescombe Wy
NFNCH/WDSPK N12 38 E4
Sadler Cl MTCM CR4 162 E1
Sadlers Gate Ms
PUT/ROE SW15 127 F2
Sadlers Ride E/WMO/HCT KT8 157 H1
Saffron Av POP/IOD E14 94 B6
Saffron Cl CROY/NA CR0 163 K5
GLDGN NW11 52 D4
Saffron Hl HCIRC EC1N 12 B2
Saffron Rd CRW RM5 63 F1
Saffron St HCIRC EC1N 12 B2
Saffron Wy SURB KT6 158 E7
Sage Cl EHAM E6 95 K4
Sage Ms EDUL SE22 131 G4
Sage St WCHPL E1 92 E6
Sage Wy FSBYW WC1X 5 L8
Sage Yd SURB KT6 159 G7
Saigasso Cl CAN/RD E16 95 H5
Sail St LBTH SE11 17 M5
Sainfoin Rd TOOT SW17 148 A1
Sainsbury Rd NRWD SE19 150 A4
St Agatha's Gv CAR SM5 162 E7
St Agnes Cl HOM E9 * 74 E7
St Agnes Pl LBTH SE11 110 C5
St Agnes Well STLK EC1Y 7 H9
St Aidan's Rd EDUL SE22 131 J5
WEA W13 104 C1
St Albans Av CHSWK W4 106 A2
FELT TW13 141 H4
St Alban's Av EHAM E6 95 K2
St Albans Crs WDGN N22 41 G7
St Albans Farm
EBED/NFELT TW14 * 122 B4
St Alban's Gdns TEDD TW11 143 G4
St Albans Gv KENS W8 * 14 D3
St Alban's Gv CAR SM5 162 D6
KENS W8 14 D3
St Albans La GLDGN NW11 52 E7
St Alban's Ms BAY/PAD W2 9 H2
St Alban's Pl IS N1 6 C4
St Albans Rd GDMY/SEVK IG3 61 F7
KUTN/CMB KT2 144 A5
SUT SM1 174 D3
WAT WD17 21 F1
St Alban's Rd DART DA1 139 J5
KTTN NW5 72 A2
WFD IG8 44 E6
WLSDN NW10 69 G7
St Alban's St STJS SW1Y 11 G7
St Albans Ter HMSMTH W6 107 H5
St Alfege Pas GNWCH SE10 113 F5
St Alfege Rd CHARL SE7 114 C5
St Alphage Gdns BARB EC2Y 12 F3
St Alphage Highwalk
BARB EC2Y 12 F3
St Alphage Wk EDGW HA8 * 50 E1
St Alphege Rd ED N9 30 E6
St Alphonsus Rd CLAP SW4 129 H3
St Amunds Cl CAT SE6 151 J3
St Andrews Av ALP/SUD HA0 67 G3
HCH RM12 81 H4
St Andrews Cl
BERM/RHTH SE16 * 111 J4
RSLP HA4 65 H1
STAN HA7 * 49 J1
THDIT KT7 158 C7
THMD SE28 97 K5
WIM/MER SW19 147 F5
St Andrew's Cl CRICK NW2 * 69 K2
ISLW TW7 103 J7
NFNCH/WDSPK N12 * 39 G3
St Andrew's Ct
WAND/EARL SW18 147 G1
St Andrews Dr STAN HA7 35 J7
St Andrew's Gv
STNW/STAM N16 55 K7
St Andrew's Hl BLKFR EC4V 12 D5
St Andrews Ms BAL SW12 129 J7
BKHTH/KID SE3 113 K6
St Andrew's Ms
STNW/STAM N16 56 A7
St Andrew's Pl CAMTN NW1 4 C9
St Andrews Rd CAR SM5 175 J2
CDALE/KGS NW9 51 F7
ED N9 30 E6
MNPK E12 77 J1
ROMW/RG RM7 63 F5
SCUP DA14 155 K2
WKENS W14 * 107 H5
St Andrew's Rd ACT W3 87 G5
CROY/NA CR0 177 J3
EN EN1 29 K2
GLDGN NW11 52 D5
HNWL W7 103 K1
IL IG1 59 K6
PLSTW E13 95 F2
SURB KT6 158 E5
WALTH E17 57 F1
WAN E11 58 C5
WKENS W14 107 H5
WLSDN NW10 69 K5
St Andrew's Sq NTGHL W11 * 88 C5
SURB KT6 158 E5
St Andrews Ter
OXHEY WD19 * 33 G4
St Andrew St HCIRC EC1N 12 B3
St Andrews Wy BOW E3 93 K3
St Anna Rd BAR EN5 * 26 B4
St Anne's Av
STWL/WRAY TW19 120 A6
St Annes Cl OXHEY WD19 33 G3
St Anne's Cl HGT N6 72 A2
St Annes Ct SOHO/CST W1F 11 G5
St Annes Gdns WLSDN NW10 86 B2
St Anne's Pas POP/IOD E14 * 93 H5
St Anne's Rd ALP/SUD HA0 67 K4
LEY E10 76 B1
St Anne's Rw POP/IOD E14 93 H5
St Anne St POP/IOD E14 93 H5
St Ann's BARK IG11 78 C7
St Anns Ct HDN NW4 * 51 K2
St Ann's Crs
WAND/EARL SW18 128 A5
St Ann's Gdns KTTN NW5 72 A5
St Ann's Hl WAND/EARL SW18 128 A4
St Ann's Park Rd
WAND/EARL SW18 128 B5
St Anns Rd BARN SW13 * 126 C1
St Ann's Rd BARK IG11 78 C7
ED N9 42 B1
HRW HA1 48 E5
NTGHL W11 88 B6
SEVS/STOTM N15 55 J4
St Ann's St WEST SW1P 17 H3
St Ann's Ter STJWD NW8 3 H5
St Ann's Vls NTGHL W11 88 B7
St Ann's Wy CROY/NA CR0 177 H5
St Anselms Rd HYS/HAR UB3 101 J1
St Anthony's Av WFD IG8 45 G5
St Anthonys Cl TOOT SW17 147 J1
St Anthony's Cl WAP E1W * 92 C7
St Anthony's Ct ORP BR6 169 G7

St Anthony's Wy
 EBED/NFELT TW14............121 J3
St Antony's Rd FSTGT E7.........77 F6
St Arvans Cl CROY/NA CR0....178 A2
St Asaph Rd BROCKY SE4.......132 A2
St Aubyn's Av HSLW TW3.......123 F4
 WIM/MER SW19....................146 D4
St Aubyn's Rd NRWD SE19.....150 B5
St Audrey Av BXLYHN DA7......137 H1
St Augustine's Av EA W5.........86 A1
 HAYES BR2...........................168 D4
 SAND/SEL CR2......................177 J6
 WBLY HA9...............................68 A2
St Augustine's Rd BELV DA17..117 G3
 CAMTN NW1..............................5 G1
St Austell Cl EDGW HA8.........50 B1
St Austell Rd LEW SE13.........133 F1
St Awdry's Rd BARK IG11........78 D6
St Barnabas Cl BECK BR3......167 F1
 EDUL SE22...........................131 F3
St Barnabas' Gdns
 E/WMO/HCT KT8..................157 F4
St Barnabas Ms BGVA SW1W...16 B7
St Barnabas Rd MTCM CR4.....148 A6
 SUT SM1..............................175 H4
 WALTH E17.............................57 J5
 WFD IG8.................................45 F7
St Barnabas St BCVA SW1W....16 B7
St Barnabas Ter HOM E9.........75 F4
St Barnabas Vls VX/NE SW8....109 K7
St Bartholomew's Cl
 SYD SE26.............................150 E3
St Bartholomew's Rd
 EHAM E6................................77 J7
St Benets Cl TOOT SW17.......147 J1
St Benet's Gv CAR SM5.........162 B6
St Bernards CROY/NA CR0.....178 A2
St Bernards Cl WNWD SE27...149 K3
St Bernard's Rd EHAM E6.......77 H7
St Blaise Av BMLY BR1..........168 A1
St Botolph St TWRH EC3N.......13 L4
St Bride's Av EDGW HA8.........36 B7
St Brides Cl ERITHM DA18.....116 E1
St Bride St FLST/FETLN EC4A...12 C2
St Catherines Cl CHSGTN KT9..171 K5
 TOOT SW17..........................147 J1
St Catherines Ct FELT TW13...121 F4
St Catherine's Rd CHING E4....44 A1
St Catherines Ms CHEL SW3....15 J5
St Catherines Rd CHING E4.....44 A1
 RSLP HA4...............................46 A4
St Chads Cl SURB KT6...........158 D6
St Chad's Gdns CHDH RM6.....62 A6
St Chad's Pl FSBYW WC1X.......5 K7
St Chad's Rd CHDH RM6.........62 A6
St Chad's St STPAN WC1H.......5 K7
St Charles Cl NKENS W10.......88 C4
St Charles Sq NKENS W10.......88 B4
St Christopher's Cl ISLW TW7..103 K7
St Christophers Dr
 HYS/HAR UB3.........................83 F6
St Christopher's Ms
 WLGTN SM6.........................176 C4
St Christopher's Pl MHST W1U..10 B5
St Clair Cl CLAY IG5................59 K1
St Clair Dr WPK KT4..............173 K2
St Clair Rd PLSTW E13...........95 F1
St Clair's Rd CROY/NA CR0....178 A1
St Clare St TWRH EC3N..........13 L5
St Clements Ct PUR RM19......119 K3
St Clement's La LINN WC2A.....11 M3
St Clements Yd EDUL SE22....131 G4
St Cloud Rd WNWD SE27.......149 J3
St Crispins Cl HAMP NW3.......71 J3
St Crispin's Cl STHL UB1........83 K5
St Cross St HCIRC EC1N.........12 B2
St Cuthberts Gdns PIN HA5.....33 K6
St Cuthberts Rd PLMGR N13...41 K1
St Cuthbert's Rd CRICK NW2...70 D5
St Cyprian's St TOOT SW17....147 K3
St Davids Cl
 BERM/RHTH SE16 *...............111 J4
 WBLY HA9...............................68 E2
St David's Dr EDGW HA8........36 B7
St Davids Ms BOW E3 *..........93 G2
St David's Pl HDN NW4............51 K6
St Davids Sq POP/IOD E14....112 E4
St Denis Rd WNWD SE27.......149 J3
St Dionis Rd FUL/PGN SW6....107 J2
 MNPK E12..............................77 J2
St Donatt's Rd NWCR SE14....112 C7
St Dunstan's Av ACT W3..........87 F6
St Dunstans Cl HYS/HAR UB3..101 J3
St Dunstans Gdns ACT W3.......87 F6
St Dunstan's HI MON EC3R *....13 J7
 SUT SM1..............................174 C2
St Dunstan's La MON EC3R *...13 J7
St Dunstans Rd FSTGT E7......77 F5
 FELT TW13...........................140 D2
 HMSMTH W6.........................107 G4
 HNWL W7.............................103 K1
 HSLWW TW4.........................122 A4
 SNWD SE25.........................165 G3
St Edmunds Av RSLP HA4.......46 B5
St Edmunds Cl ERITHM DA18..116 E1
 TOOT SW17..........................147 J1
St Edmund's Cl STJWD NW8.....3 L4
St Edmunds Dr STAN HA7.......35 G2
St Edmunds Rd DART DA1.....139 J3
 ED N9....................................30 C6
St Edmund's Sq BARN SW13..107 H5
St Edmund's Ter STJWD NW8....3 K4
St Edward's Cl GLDGN NW11...52 E5
St Edwards Wy ROM RM1........63 G4
St Elmo Rd SHB W12.............106 D1
St Elmos Rd BERM/RHTH SE16..112 B1
St Erkenwald Ms BARK IG11 *...78 D7
St Erkenwald Rd BARK IG11....78 D7
St Ervans Rd NKENS W10........88 C4
St Faith's Rd DUL SE21.........130 C7
St Fidelis' Rd ERITH DA8.......118 A3
St Fillans Rd CAT SE6............133 F7
St Francis Cl ORP BR6...........169 K5
 OXHEY WD19..........................21 G1
St Francis Rd EDUL SE22......131 F3
St Francis Wy IL IG1...............78 D3
St Gabriel's Cl WAN E11..........59 F7
St Gabriel's Rd CRICK NW2....70 B4
St George's Av
 CDALE/KGS NW9.....................50 E3
 EA W5....................................104 E1
 FSTGT E7................................77 E5
 HOLWY N7..............................72 D3
 STHL UB1................................83 K6
St George's Circ STHWK SE1...18 C4
St Georges Ct HRW HA1..........67 G2
 THMD SE28............................97 K5
 VX/NE SW8...........................109 H7
St George's Dr OXHEY WD19...33 J2

 PIM SW1V...............................16 D6
St Georges Flds BAY/PAD W2....9 K6
St George's Gdns SURB KT6...172 D1
St George's Gv TOOT SW17....147 H2
St George's Industrial Est
 KUTN/CMB KT2......................143 K4
St George's La MON EC3R *.....13 H6
St George's Ms CHSWK W4 *..105 K5
 DEPT SE8.............................112 C3
St George's Pde CAT SE6 *....151 H1
St Georges Pde BMLY BR1....168 A1
 CHSWK W4...........................106 A1
 DAGW RM9.............................80 A4
 STMC/STPC BR5...................169 J5
St George's Rd BECK BR3.....151 K1
 FELT TW13...........................141 H3
 FSTGT E7................................77 F6
 GLDGN NW11..........................52 D5
 HNWL W7...............................85 F1
 IL IG1.....................................59 K6
 KUTN/CMB KT2......................144 B6
 LEY E10..................................76 A2
 MTCM CR4............................163 G2
 PLMGR N13.............................41 F1
 RCH/KEW TW9......................125 G2
 SCUP DA14............................155 K5
 STHL UB1................................18 C4
 TWK TW1...............................124 C4
 WIM/MER SW19....................146 D5
 WLGTN SM6.........................176 B3
St Georges Rd West
 BMLY BR1.............................168 A1
St Georges Sq NWMAL KT3 *...160 B2
St George's Sq FSTGT E7.......77 F6
 PIM SW1V...............................17 G7
St George's Square Ms
 PIM SW1V...............................17 G8
St Georges Ter PECK SE15 *..111 H6
St George St CONDST W1S......10 D6
St Georges Wk CROY/NA CR0...177 J1
St George's Wy PECK SE15 *..111 F5
St Gerards Cl CLAP SW4........129 K4
St German's Pl
 BKHTH/KID SE3....................113 K7
St German's Rd FSTH SE23....132 B1
St Giles Av DAGE RM10..........80 D6
St Giles Churchyard
 BARB EC2Y *..........................12 F3
St Giles Circ SOHO/SHAV W1D..11 H4
St Giles Cl DAGE RM10...........80 D6
 HEST TW5.............................102 D6
St Giles Ct LSQ/SEVD WC2H...11 H4
St Giles High St
 NOXST/BSQ WC1A.................11 H3
St Giles Pas LSQ/SEVD WC2H...11 H5
St Gothard Rd WNWD SE27....149 K3
St Gregory Rd RSLP HA4.........65 C3
St Helena Rd
 BERM/RHTH SE16.................112 A3
St Helena St FSBYW WC1X *.....6 A8
St Helena Ter RCH/KEW TW9 *..124 E4
St Helens Cl UX/CGN UB8........13 H6
St Helen's Crs
 STRHM/NOR SW16................149 F4
St Helen's Gdns NKENS W10...88 B5
St Helens Pl LEY E10..............57 G6
St Helen's Pl HDTCH EC3A......13 J4
St Helens Rd ERITHM DA18...116 E1
St Helen's Rd IL IG1................59 K5
 STRHM/NOR SW16................164 A1
 WEA W13.................................85 H7
St Helier Av MRDN SM4.........162 A6
St Heliers Av HSLWW TW4....123 F4
St Helier's Rd LEY E10............57 K5
St Hildas Cl
 KIL/WHAMP NW6 *..................70 B7
 TOOT SW17..........................147 J1
St Hilda's Rd BARN SW13.....106 E6
St Hughes Cl TOOT SW17 *....147 J1
St Hugh's Rd PGE/AN SE20 *..150 D7
St Ivians Dr GPK RM2..............63 J2
St James Av SUT SM1...........174 E4
 TRDG/WHET N20....................39 J2
St James Cl WEA W13.............85 G7
St James's Cl EBAR EN4..........27 H2
 STJWD NW8.............................3 L5
 TRDG/WHET N20....................39 J2
St James Gdns CHDH RM6......61 H3
St James Gdns ALP/SUD HA0..67 H3
St James Ms POP/IOD E14 *...113 F2
St James Pl DART DA1..........139 G5
St James Rd CAR SM5..........175 J2
 WATW WD18............................21 F4
St James's NWCR SE14.........112 B7
St James's Cl BECK BR3.......166 B2
 BETH E2.................................92 E1
 HPTN TW12...........................142 C4
St James's Chambers
 STJS SW1Y *..........................10 F8
St James's Cl TOOT SW17 *...147 K1
 WOOL/PLUM SE18.................115 H4
St James's Cots
 RCH/KEW TW9 *....................124 E4
St James's Ct WALTH E17 *.....57 G4
 WESTW SW1E.........................16 F3
St James's Crs BRXN/ST SW9..130 B2
St James's Dr BAL SW12........128 E2
St James's Gdns
 CAMTN NW1...........................4 E8
 NTGHL W11...........................88 D7
St James's Gv BTSEA SW11...128 E1
St James's La MUSWH N10.....54 B3
St James's Market
 STJS SW1Y *..........................11 G7
St James's Ms WALTH E17.......57 G4
St James's Pk CROY/NA CR0...164 D6
St James's Pl WHALL SW1A.....10 E1
St James's Sq SURB KT6......158 D6
St James's Rd
 BERM/RHTH SE16.................111 H4
 CROY/NA CR0.......................164 D6
 HPTN TW12...........................142 B4
St James's Rw CHSGTN KT9 *...171 K5
St James's St WALTH E17.......57 G4
 WHALL SW1A..........................10 E1
St James Sq SURB KT6.........158 D6
St James's Rd
 BERM/RHTH SE16.................111 H4
 CROY/NA CR0.......................164 D6
 HPTN TW12...........................142 B4

St James's Terrace Ms
 STJWD NW8...............................3 L4
St James St HMSMTH W6......107 F4
St James Ter BAL SW12 *.......129 F7
St James Wk CLKNW EC1R.......6 C9
St Jerome's Gv UX/CGN UB8....82 A5
St Joan's Rd ED N9..................42 B1
St John Cl FUL/PGN SW6 *....107 K6
St John's Av FBAR/BDGN N11..39 K4
 PUT/ROE SW15.....................127 G4
 WLSDN NW10..........................69 H7
St Johns Church Rd
 HOM E9 *................................74 E4
St Johns Cl STHGT/OAK N14...28 C5
St John's Cl FUL/PGN SW6 *...107 K6
 RAIN RM13.............................81 J6
 TRDG/WHET N20....................39 G1
 WBLY HA9..............................68 A4
St Johns Cots PGE/AN SE20 *..150 E6
St John's Ct ISLW TW7..........124 A1
St Johns Crs BRXN/ST SW9...130 B2
St Johns Dr WOT/HER KT12..156 B7
St John's Dr
 WAND/EARL SW18.................128 A7
St John's Est IS N1 *...............7 H4
St Johns Gdns NTGHL W11.....88 C6
St John's Gv ARCH N19..........72 C1
 BARN SW13 *........................126 C1
 RCH/KEW TW9......................124 E3
St John's HI BTSEA SW11.....128 D3
St John's Hill Gv BTSEA SW11..128 C3
St John's La FARR EC1M.........12 C1
St Johns Pde SCUP DA14 *....155 H3
St John's Pk BKHTH/KID SE3..113 K6
St John's Pl FARR EC1M..........12 C1
St Johns Rd GNTH/NBYPK IG2..60 B5
 NWMAL KT3..........................159 K2
 STMC/STPC BR5...................169 J5
St John's Rd BARK IG11...........78 E7
 BTSEA SW11.........................128 D3
 CAR/RD E16............................94 E4
 CAR SM5...............................175 J2
 CHING E4................................43 K2
 CROY/NA CR0.......................177 H2
 E/WMO/HCT KT8...................157 J3
 EHAM E6.................................77 J7
 ERITH DA8.............................118 A4
 FELT TW13...........................141 J3
 GLDGN NW11..........................52 D5
 HRW HA1................................49 F5
 ISLW TW7.............................124 A1
 KUT/HW KT1.........................158 D1
 NWDGN UB2.........................102 D2
 PGE/AN SE20........................150 E6
 RCH/KEW TW9......................125 F3
 SCUP DA14...........................155 H3
 SEVS/STOTM N15..................56 A5
 SUT SM1..............................174 E1
 WALTH E17.............................57 K1
 WAT WD17..............................21 H1
 WBLY HA9...............................67 K3
 WELL DA16............................136 C2
 WIM/MER SW19....................146 C6
St John's Sq FARR EC1M.........12 C1
St John's Ter FSTGT E7...........77 F5
 NKENS W10............................88 C3
 WOOL/PLUM SE18.................115 H5
St Johns Vls KENS W8 *..........14 D4
St Johns Vls ARCH N19...........72 D1
St John's Wy ARCH N19..........54 D7
St John's Wood High St
 STJWD NW8..............................3 H6
St John's Wood Pk
 STJWD NW8..............................3 G4
St John's Wood Rd
 STJWD NW8..............................3 G9
St John's Wood Ter
 STJWD NW8..............................3 J5
St Josephs Cl NKENS W10.......88 C4
St Joseph's Dr STHL UB1........83 J7
St Josephs Gv HDN NW4.........51 K3
St Joseph's Rd ED N9.............30 D6
St Joseph's St VX/NE SW8 *...109 G7
St Joseph's V HBTH/KID SE3..133 C1
St Jude's Rd BETH E2..............92 D1
St Jude St STNW/STAM N16.....74 A4
St Julian's Cl
 STRHM/NOR SW16 *..............149 G3
St Julian's Farm Rd
 WNWD SE27..........................149 G3
St Julian's Rd
 KIL/WHAMP NW6....................70 D7
St Katharine's Prec
 CAMTN NW1 *...........................4 C5
St Katharine's Wy WAP E1W....13 M8
St Katherines Rd
 ERITHM DA18........................116 E1
St Katherines Wk
 NTGHL W11 *..........................88 B6
St Keverne Rd ELTH/MOT SE9...153 J3
St Kilda Rd WEA W13.............104 B1
St Kilda's Rd HRW HA1............48 E5
 STNW/STAM N16....................55 K7
St Kitts Ter NRWD SE19.........150 A4
St Laurence's Cl
 KIL/WHAMP NW6....................70 B7
St Lawrence Cots
 POP/IOD E14 *........................94 A7
St Lawrence Dr PIN HA5..........47 F4
St Lawrence Ter NKENS W10...88 C4
St Lawrence Wy
 BRXN/ST SW9.......................130 B1
St Leonards Av
 KTN/HRWW/WS HA3...............49 J4
St Leonard's Av CHING E4.......44 B5
St Leonards Cl BUSH WD23....21 J3
 WELL DA16............................136 B2
St Leonards Gdns IL IG1..........78 C4
St Leonard's Gdns HEST TW5..102 C1
St Leonards Rd
 MORT/ESHN SW14.................125 J2
 CROY/NA CR0 *.....................177 H2
 ESH/CLAY KT10.....................171 J5
 POP/IOD E14...........................94 A5
 SURB KT6.............................158 D5
 THDT KT7.............................158 B5
 WEA W13................................85 H7
 WLSDN NW10..........................87 F3
St Leonard's Sq KTTN NW5 *....72 A5
 SURB KT6.............................158 C5
St Leonard's St BOW E3..........93 K2
St Leonard's Ter CHEL SW3....15 L8
St Leonards Wk
 STRHM/NOR SW16................149 F6
St Leonards Wy EMPK RM11....63 K7
St Loo Av CHEL SW3...............15 K9
St Louis Rd WNWD SE27.......149 J3

St Loy's Rd TOTM N17.............56 A1
St Lucia Dr SRTFD E15............76 D7
St Luke's Av CLAP SW4..........129 J3
 IL IG1.....................................78 B4
St Luke's Cl SNWD SE25.......165 H5
St Luke's Est FSBYE EC1V *......7 J8
St Luke's Ms NTGHL W11........88 D5
St Luke's Rd NTGHL W11........88 D4
St Lukes's Cl FSBYE EC1V.......6 F9
St Luke's Sq CAN/RD E16........94 D5
St Luke's St CHEL SW3............15 J7
St Lukes Yd MV/WKIL W9 *......88 D1
St Malo Av ED N9.....................42 E2
St Margarets BARK IG11...........78 D7
 KUTN/CMB KT2 *...................144 E4
St Margarets Av BFN/LL DA15..154 D2
 TRDG/WHET N20....................39 H2
St Margaret's Av CHEAM SM3..174 C2
 RYLN/HDSTN HA2...................66 C2
 SEVS/STOTM N15..................55 H3
St Margarets Ct
 PUT/ROE SW15.....................126 E3
St Margaret's Crs
 PUT/ROE SW15.....................126 E4
St Margaret's Dr TWK TW1....124 C4
St Margaret's Gv TWK TW1....124 D4
 WAN E11.................................76 D2
 WOOL/PLUM SE18.................115 H5
St Margarets La KENS W8.......14 C4
St Margarets Ms
 KUTN/CMB KT2......................144 E4
St Margarets Rd BECK BR3....166 A3
 EDGW HA8...............................36 D3
 RSLP HA4................................46 B5
St Margaret's Rd BROCKY SE4..132 C3
 HNWL W7.............................103 K1
 MNPK E12..............................77 G1
 TOTM N17..............................56 A2
 TWK TW1...............................124 D4
 WLSDN NW10..........................88 A2
St Margaret's Ter
 WOOL/PLUM SE18.................115 H4
St Margaret St WEST SW1P.....17 J2
St Marks Cl BAR EN5...............27 F2
St Mark's Crs CAMTN NW1 *.....4 A3
St Marks Ga HOM E9...............75 G6
St Mark's Gv WBPTN SW10 *...108 A6
St Mark's Hl SURB KT6..........159 F5
St Mark's Pl DAGE RM10.........80 C5
St Mark's Pl NTGHL W11.........88 C5
 WIM/MER SW19 *..................146 D5
St Mark's Ri HACK E8..............74 B4
St Mark's Rd EA W5.................86 A7
 EN N1......................................30 B4
 HAYES BR2...........................168 A1
 HNWL W7.............................103 K1
 MTCM CR4............................162 E1
 NKENS W10............................88 B5
 NTGHL W11............................88 C5
 SNWD SE25.........................165 H3
 TEDD TW11...........................143 H6
St Mark's Sq CAMTN NW1 *......4 A3
St Mark St WCHPL E1..............13 M5
St Marks Vls FSBYPK N4 *.......73 F1
St Martin-in-the-Fields
 CHCR WC2N *.........................11 J7
St Martins NTHWD HA6...........32 B4
St Martins Ap RSLP HA4..........46 C6
St Martin's Av EHAM E6...........95 H1
St Martins Cl ERITHM DA18...116 E1
 OXHEY WD19..........................33 G3
St Martin's Cl CAMTN NW1 *.....4 E3
St Martins Ct CHCR WC2N......11 J6
St Martin's Ct
 LSO/SEVD WC2H *..................11 J6
St Martin's La BECK BR3........166 E4
 CHCR WC2N..........................11 J6
St Martin's le Grand
 STBT EC1A.............................12 E4
St Martin's Pl CHCR WC2N.....11 J7
St Martin's Rd BRXN/ST SW9..130 A1
 DART DA1.............................139 J5
 ED N9.....................................42 D1
 EFNCH N2...............................39 H7
St Martin's St
 LSO/SEVD WC2H *..................11 H7
St Martin's Wy TOOT SW17....147 H1
St Mary Abbots Pl KENS W8 *..107 J2
St Mary Abbots Rd KENS W8 *..107 J2
St Mary Abbots Ter
 WKENS W14...........................107 J2
St Mary At Hl MON EC3R *......13 J7
St Mary Axe HDTCH EC3A.......13 J4
St Marychurch St
 BERM/RHTH SE16.................111 K1
St Mary Graces Ct WCHPL E1 *..13 M7
St Mary Rd WALTH E17............57 K3
St Marys BARK IG11.................96 D1
St Mary's Ap MNPK E12............77 K4
St Mary's Av FNCH N3..............52 C1
 HAYES BR2...........................167 H2
 NTHWD HA6............................32 C4
 STWL/WRAY TW19................120 A6
 TEDD TW11...........................143 F5
 WAN E11.................................76 C1
St Marys Cl WATW WD18 *.......21 G3
St Mary's Cl CHSGTN KT9......172 B6
 EW KT17...............................173 H6
 TOTM N17..............................42 A7
St Marys Ct HMSMTH W6......106 C2
St Mary's Crs HDN NW4...........51 K2
 HYS/HAR UB3.........................82 D6
 ISLW TW7.............................103 J6
 STWL/WRAY TW19................120 A6
St Mary's Dr
 EBED/NFELT TW14................121 F6
St Marys Est
 BERM/RHTH SE16 *...............111 K1
St Mary's Ga KENS W8............14 C4
St Mary's Gn EFNCH N2 *.........53 G2
St Mary's Gv BARN SW13......126 E2
 CHSWK W4...........................105 J5
 IS N1......................................73 H5
 RCH/KEW TW9......................125 G3
St Mary's Man BAY/PAD W2 *....9 F2
St Mary's Ms KIL/WHAMP NW6 *..2 C7
St Mary's Pth IS N1...................6 D2
 WCHPL E1 *............................92 C5
St Marys Pl KENS W8 *............14 C4
St Mary's Pl EA W5.................104 E1
St Mary's Rd BXLY DA5...........137 G3
 CEND/HSY/T N8......................54 E3
 E/WMO/HCT KT8...................157 J4
 EA W5...................................104 E1
 EBAR EN4................................27 K6
 ED N9.....................................30 B4
 GLDGN NW11..........................52 C6
 HYS/HAR UB3.........................82 D6

 LEY E10..................................76 A2
 PECK SE15............................111 K7
 PLSTW E13..............................95 F3
 SNWD SE25.........................165 F2
 SURB KT6.............................158 D6
 WAT WD18..............................21 G3
 WIM/MER SW19....................146 C5
 WLSDN NW10..........................69 G7
 WPK KT4..............................173 G1
St Mary's Sq BAY/PAD W2........9 G2
 EA W5...................................104 E1
St Marys Ter BORE WD6..........23 K5
St Mary's Ter BAY/PAD W2........9 G2
St Mary St WOOL/PLUM SE18..114 E3
St Marys Vw
 KTN/HRWW/WS HA3...............49 J4
 WATW WD18............................21 G3
St Mary's Wk HYS/HAR UB3....82 D6
 LBTH SE11..............................18 B5
St Matthew's Av SURB KT6....159 F7
St Matthews Cl OXHEY WD19...21 H5
St Matthew's Cl RAIN RM13.....81 J4
St Matthew's Ct SRTFD E15....76 B6
St Matthews Dr BMLY BR1.....168 E2
St Matthew's Rd
 BRXS/STRHM SW2.................130 A4
 EA W5...................................86 A7
St Matthew's Rw BETH E2.......92 C2
St Matthew St WEST SW1P.....17 G3
St Matthias Cl
 CDALE/KGS NW9.....................51 H4
St Maur Rd FUL/PGN SW6.....107 J7
St Meddens CHST BR7 *........154 D6
St Mellion Cl THMD SE28........97 K5
St Merryn Cl
 WOOL/PLUM SE18.................115 J6
St Michael's Aly BANK EC3V....13 H5
St Michael's Av ED N9.............30 E6
St Michael's Av WBLY HA9.......68 C5
St Michaels Cl BMLY BR1.......168 D2
 CAN/RD E16............................95 H4
 WPK KT4..............................173 G1
St Michael's Cl ERITHM DA18 *..116 E1
 FNCH N3.................................53 J1
 NFNCH/WDSPK N12...............39 J4
St Michaels Cl GLDGN NW11 *..52 D6
St Michael's Crs PIN HA5.........47 J5
St Michael's Gdns NKENS W10...88 C4
St Michael's Ms BGVA SW1W...16 A6
St Michael's Ri WELL DA16 *...116 C2
St Michael's Rd BRXN/ST SW9..130 A1
 CRICK NW2.............................70 A3
 CROY/NA CR0.......................164 D7
 WELL DA16............................136 C2
 WLGTN SM6.........................176 C5
St Michael's St BAY/PAD W2.....9 H4
St Michaels Ter HGT N6 *.........54 A7
St Michael's Ter WDGN N22.....40 E7
St Mildred's Ct LOTH EC2R *....13 H5
St Nicholas Av HCH RM12........81 J2
St Nicholas Cl BORE WD6........23 K4
St Nicholas Glebe TOOT SW17..148 A5
St Nicholas Rd SUT SM1........175 H4
 THDT KT7.............................158 A5
 WOOL/PLUM SE18.................116 A4
St Nicholas St DEPT SE8.......112 C7
St Nicholas Wy SUT SM1.......175 F3
St Nicolas La CHST BR7.........153 J7
St Ninian's Ct
 TRDG/WHET N20....................39 K2
St Norbert Rd BROCKY SE4...132 B3
St Olaf's Rd FUL/PGN SW6....107 H6
St Olave's Rd EHAM E6............78 A7
St Olave's Wk
 STRHM/NOR SW16................163 H1
St Onge Pde EN EN1 *.............29 K2
St Oswald's Pl LBTH SE11.......17 L7
St Oswald's Rd
 STRHM/NOR SW16................149 H7
St Oswulf St WEST SW1P *.......17 H6
St Pancras Gdns
 CAMTN NW1 *...........................5 G5
 KCROSS N1C *..........................5 J4
St Pancras Station Forecourt
 KCROSS N1C *..........................5 J2
St Pancras Wy CAMTN NW1 *....4 E1
St Paul's Av
 BERM/RHTH SE16 *..................93 F3
 CRICK NW2.............................69 K5
 KTN/HRWW/WS HA3...............50 B4
St Paul's Church Yd STP EC4M..12 E4
St Pauls Cl EA W5..................105 G1
 HYS/HAR UB3.......................101 G4
St Paul's Cl ASHF TW15.........140 A4
 BORE WD6...............................24 A4
 CAR SM5...............................162 D6
 CHARL SE7............................114 C4
 CHSGTN KT9.........................171 K3
 EA W5...................................105 G1
 HSLW TW3.............................122 D2
St Paul's Cray Rd CHST BR7..154 D7
St Pauls Crs CAMTN NW1 *......5 L2
 HDN NW4 *.............................52 A3
St Paul's Crs CAMTN NW1 *.....5 L2
St Paul's Dr SRTFD E15...........76 B4
St Pauls Ms CAMTN NW1 *.......5 M1
St Pauls Pl IS N1....................73 K5
St Pauls Ri PLMGR N13...........41 H5
St Pauls Rd BARK IG11............78 C7
 RCH/KEW TW9......................125 G2
St Paul's Rd BTFD TW8..........104 E5
 ERITH DA8............................117 K6
 IS N1......................................73 H5
 THHTH CR7..........................164 D2
 TOTM N17..............................56 B1
St Pauls Ter WALW SE17.........18 D9
St Paul St IS N1........................7 G1
St Paul's Wy WATN WD24.........21 G1
 FNCH N3.................................39 H5
 POP/IOD E14...........................93 H4
St Paul's Wood Hl
 STMC/STPC BR5...................169 K1
St Peter's Av BETH E2..............92 C2
 UED N18.................................42 C3
 WALTH E17.............................58 C3
St Petersburgh Ms
 BAY/PAD W2............................8 C6
St Petersburgh Pl
 BAY/PAD W2............................8 C6
St Peters Cl CHST BR7..........154 D6
 GNTH/NBYPK IG2....................60 E3
 TOOT SW17..........................147 J1
St Peter's Cl BAR EN5.............25 K4
 BETH E2.................................92 C2
 BUSH WD23............................22 D7
 RSLP HA4................................65 H1
St Peters Ct E/WMO/HCT KT8..157 F3
St Peter's Ct HDN NW4............52 A4
St Peter's Gdns WNWD SE27..149 G2
St Peter's Gv HMSMTH W6....106 D3
St Peters Ms FSBYPK N4 *......55 H4

St Peter's Pl MV/WKIL W9 8 C1
St Peters Rd KUT/HW KT1 143 H1
St Peter's Rd CROY/NA CR0 177 K3
E/WMO/HCT KT8 157 F3
ED N9 30 D7
HMSMTH W6 * 106 D4
STHL UB1 84 A4
TWK TW1 124 C4
St Peter's Sq BETH E2 * 92 C1
HMSMTH W6 106 D3
St Peter's St IS N1 6 D4
SAND/SEL CR2 177 K4
St Peter's Ter FUL/PGN SW6 107 H6
St Peter's Vls HMSMTH W6 106 D3
St Peters Wy HYS/HAR UB3 101 G4
St Peter's Wy EA W5 85 K4
IS N1 7 K2
St Philip's Av WPK KT4 173 K1
St Philip Sq VX/NE SW8 * 129 G1
St Philip's Rd HACK E8 74 C5
SURB KT6 158 E5
St Philip St VX/NE SW8 129 G1
St Philip's Wy IS N1 6 F3
St Quentin Rd WELL DA16 136 A2
St Quintin Av NKENS W10 88 A4
St Quintin Gdns NKENS W10 88 A4
St Quintin Rd PLSTW E13 95 F2
St Raphael's Wy WLSDN NW10 68 E4
St Regis Cl MUSWH N10 54 B1
St Ronans Crs WFD IG8 44 E6
St Rowans Vw DART DA1 139 J6
St Rule St VX/NE SW8 129 H1
St Saviours Ct WDGN N22 54 D1
St Saviour's Est STHWK SE1 19 L3
St Saviour's Rd
BRXS/STRHM SW2 130 A4
CROY/NA CR0 164 D5
Saints Cl WNWD SE27 149 H3
Saints Dr FSTGT E7 77 H4
St Silas Pl KTTN NW5 72 A5
St Simon's Av PUT/ROE SW15 127 F4
St Stephen's Av SHB W12 87 K7
WALTH E17 58 A4
WEA W13 85 H5
St Stephens Cl KTTN NW5 * 71 K4
STJWD NW8 3 J4
St Stephen's Cl STHL UB1 84 A4
WALTH E17 57 K4
St Stephen's Crs
BAY/PAD W2 * 8 B4
THHTH CR7 164 B2
St Stephen's Gdns
BAY/PAD W2 8 A4
TWK TW1 124 D5
St Stephen's Gv LEW SE13 133 F2
St Stephen's Ms BAY/PAD W2 8 B3
St Stephens Pde WHALL SW1A 17 J1
St Stephens Rd BAR EN5 26 B4
St Stephen's Rd BOW E3 75 G7
EHAM E6 77 G6
HSLW TW3 123 F5
WALTH E17 57 K4
WEA W13 85 H5
St Stephens Ter VX/NE SW8 * 109 K6
St Stephen's Ter VX/NE SW8 110 A6
St Stephen's Wk SKENS SW7 14 E5
St Swithin's La MANHO EC4N 13 G6
St Swithun's Rd LEW SE13 * 133 G4
St Theresas Cl HOM E9 75 J3
St Theresa's Rd
EBED/NFELT TW14 121 J3
St Thomas Cl SURB KT6 159 G7
St Thomas Ct BXLY DA5 137 H6
St Thomas Dr STMC/STPC BR5 169 H7
St Thomas' Dr PIN HA5 33 J7
STMC/STPC BR5 169 H7
St Thomas Gdns IL IG1 78 C5
St Thomas Rd BELV DA17 117 K1
CAN/RD E16 94 E5
STHGT/OAK N14 28 D6
St Thomas' Rd CHSWK W4 105 K6
St Thomas's Gdns KTTN NW5 72 A5
St Thomas's Pl HOM E9 * 74 E6
St Thomas's Rd FSBYPK N4 73 G1
WLSDN NW10 69 G7
St Thomas's Sq HOM E9 74 D6
St Thomas St STHWK SE1 13 H9
St Thomas's Wy FUL/PGN SW6 107 J6
St Ursula Gv PIN HA5 47 H4
St Ursula Rd STHL UB1 84 A5
St Vincent Cl WNWD SE27 149 H4
St Vincent Rd WHTN TW2 123 H5
St Vincents Av DART DA1 139 K4
St Vincents Cots
WATW WD18 * 21 F3
St Vincents La MLHL NW7 37 K3
St Vincents Rd DART DA1 139 K5
St Vincent St MHST W1U 10 B3
St Wilfrid's Cl EBAR EN4 * 27 J4
St Wilfrid's Rd EBAR EN4 27 H4
St Winefride's Av MNPK E12 77 K4
St Winifred's Rd TEDD TW11 143 H5
Sakura Dr WDGN N22 40 D7
Saladin Dr PUR RM19 119 K3
Salamanca Pl STHWK SE1 17 L6
Salamanca St STHWK SE1 17 L6
Salamander Cl KUTN/CMB KT2 143 J4
Salamander Quay
KUT/HW KT1 * 143 K7
Salamons Wy RAIN RM13 99 G4
Salcombe Dr CHDH RM6 62 B5
MRDN SM4 161 G7
Salcombe Gdns MLHL NW7 38 A5
Salcombe Rd
STNW/STAM N16 74 B4
WALTH E17 57 H6
Salcombe Wy RSLP HA4 64 E1
Salcott Rd BTSEA SW11 128 D4
CROY/NA CR0 176 E2
Salehurst Cl
KTN/HRWW/WS HA3 50 A4
Salehurst Rd BROCKY SE4 132 C5
Salem Pl CROY/NA CR0 177 J2
Salem Rd BAY/PAD W2 8 C6
Sale Pl BAY/PAD W2 9 J3
Sale St BETH E2 92 C3
Salford Rd BRXS/STRHM SW2 129 J7
Salhouse Cl THMD SE28 97 J5
Salisbury Av BARK IG11 78 D6
FNCH N3 52 D1
SUT SM1 174 D5
Salisbury Cl WALW SE17 19 G5
WPK KT4 173 H2
Salisbury Ct EMB EC4Y 12 B5
Salisbury Gdns
WIM/MER SW19 * 146 C6
Salisbury Pavement
FUL/PGN SW6 * 107 K6
Salisbury Pl BRXN/ST SW9 110 C6
MBLAR W1H 9 L2
Salisbury Prom
CEND/HSY/T N8 * 55 H4
Salisbury Rd BAR EN5 26 C2
BXLY DA5 137 H7
CAR SM5 175 K5
CHING E4 43 J2
DAGE RM10 80 D5
FELT TW13 122 B7
FSBYPK N4 55 H4
FSTGT E7 76 E5
GDMY/SEVK IG3 78 E1
GPK RM2 63 K4
HAYES BR2 168 D4
HRW HA1 48 D4
HSLWW TW4 122 B2
LEY E10 76 A1
MNPK E12 77 H4
NWDGN UB2 * 102 D3
NWMAL KT3 160 A2
PIN HA5 46 E3
RCH/KEW TW9 125 F3
SNWD SE25 165 H5
WALTH E17 58 A4
WDGN N22 55 H1
WEA W13 104 C1
WIM/MER SW19 146 C6
WPK KT4 173 F3
Salisbury Sq EMB EC4Y * 12 B5
Salisbury St ACT W3 105 K1
STJWD NW8 9 H1
Salisbury Ter PECK SE15 131 K2
Salisbury Wk ARCH N19 72 C1
Salix Cl SUN TW16 141 F6
Salix La WFD IG8 45 J7
Sally Murray Cl MNPK E12 78 A3
Salmen Rd PLSTW E13 94 D1
Salmond Cl STAN HA7 35 G5
Salmon La POP/IOD E14 93 G5
Salmon Ms KIL/WHAMP NW6 * 70 E4
Salmon Rd BELV DA17 117 H4
DART DA1 139 J2
Salmons Rd CHSGTN KT9 172 A5
ED N9 30 C7
Salmon St CDALE/KGS NW9 50 D7
POP/IOD E14 * 93 H5
Salomons Rd PLSTW E13 95 G4
Salop Rd WALTH E17 57 F5
Saltash Cl SUT SM1 174 D3
Saltash Rd WELL DA16 116 D7
Saltcoats Rd CHSWK W4 106 B1
Saltcote Cl DART DA1 138 B5
Saltcroft Cl WBLY HA9 50 D7
Salter Cl RYLN/HDSTN HA2 65 K2
Salterford Rd TOOT SW17 148 A5
Salter Rd BERM/RHTH SE16 112 A1
Salters' Hall Ct MANHO EC4N * 13 G6
Salter's Hl NRWD SE19 149 K4
Salters Rd NKENS W10 88 B3
WALTH E17 58 B3
Salters Rw IS N1 * 73 K5
Salter St POP/IOD E14 93 J6
WLSDN NW10 87 J2
Salterton Rd HOLWY N7 72 E2
Saltford Cl ERITH DA8 118 B4
Saltley Cl EHAM E6 95 J5
Saltoun Rd BRXS/STRHM SW2 130 B3
Saltram Cl SEVS/STOTM N15 56 B3
Saltram Crs MV/WKIL W9 2 A8
Saltwell St POP/IOD E14 93 J6
Saltwood Gv WALW SE17 19 G8
Salusbury Rd
KIL/WHAMP NW6 88 D1
Salvador TOOT SW17 147 J4
Salvia Gdns GFD/PVL UB6 85 G1
Salvin Rd PUT/ROE SW15 127 G2
Salway Cl WFD IG8 44 E6
Salway Rd SRTFD E15 76 B5
Samantha Cl WALTH E17 57 H6
Sam Bartram Cl CHARL SE7 114 B4
Sambruck Ms CAT SE6 132 E7
Samels Ct HMSMTH W6 106 D4
Samford St STJWD NW8 9 J1
Samira Cl WALTH E17 57 H5
Samos Rd PGE/AN SE20 165 J1
Sampson Av BAR EN5 26 B4
Sampson Cl BELV DA17 116 E2
Sampson St WAP E1W * 92 C7
Samson St PLSTW E13 95 G1
Samuel Cl HACK E8 7 M3
NWCR SE14 112 A5
STAN HA7 35 G1
WOOL/PLUM SE18 114 D3
Samuel Gray Gdns
KUTN/CMB KT2 143 K7
Samuel Lewis Trust Dwellings
CMBW SE5 * 110 D7
WKENS W14 * 107 H3
Samuel St WOOL/PLUM SE18 114 E3
Sancroft Cl CRICK NW2 69 K2
Sancroft Rd
KTN/HRWW/WS HA3 49 F1
Sancroft St LBTH SE11 17 M7
Sanctuary Cl DART DA1 139 F5
Sanctuary Ms HACK E8 74 B5
Sanctuary Rd HTHAIR TW6 120 D5
Sanctuary St STHWK SE1 18 F2
The Sanctuary BXLY DA5 136 E5
WEST SW1P 17 H3
Sandall Cl EA W5 86 A3
Sandall Rd EA W5 86 A3
KTTN NW5 72 C5
Sandal Rd NWMAL KT3 160 B3
UED N18 42 C4
Sandal St SRTFD E15 76 C7
Sandalwood Cl WCHPL E1 93 G3
Sandalwood Dr RSLP HA4 46 A6
Sandalwood Rd FELT TW13 141 F2
Sandbach Pl
WOOL/PLUM SE18 115 H3
Sandbourne Av
WIM/MER SW19 162 A2
Sandbourne Rd NWCR SE14 132 B1
Sandbrook Cl MLHL NW7 37 F5
Sandbrook Rd
STNW/STAM N16 74 A2
Sandby Gn ELTH/MOT SE9 134 D2
Sandcliff Rd ERITH DA8 118 A3
Sandcroft Cl PLMGR N13 41 H5
Sandell's Av ASHF TW15 140 A3
Sandell St STHWK SE1 18 A1
Sanders Cl HPTN TW12 142 C4
Sanders La MLHL NW7 38 A6
Sanderson Cl KTTN NW5 * 72 B3
Sanders Pde
STRHM/NOR SW16 * 148 E5
Sanderstead Av GLDGN NW11 70 C1
Sanderstead Cl BAL SW12 129 H6
Sanderstead Rd LEY E10 57 G7
SAND/SEL CR2 177 K6
Sandfield Gdns THHTH CR7 164 C2
Sandfield Pl THHTH CR7 164 D2
Sandfield Rd THHTH CR7 164 C2
Sandford Av WDGN N22 41 H7
Sandford Rd BXLYHS DA6 137 F3
EHAM E6 95 K2
HAYES BR2 167 K3
Sandford Rw WALW SE17 19 G7
Sandford St FUL/PGN SW6 108 A6
Sandgate Cl ROMW/RG RM7 62 E6
Sandgate La
WAND/EARL SW18 128 D7
Sandgate Rd WELL DA16 116 D6
Sandgate St PECK SE15 111 J5
Sandhills WLGTN SM6 176 D3
Sandhurst Av BRYLDS KT5 159 J6
RYLN/HDSTN HA2 48 B5
Sandhurst Cl SAND/SEL CR2 178 A7
Sandhurst Dr GDMY/SEVK IG3 79 F3
Sandhurst Market CAT SE6 * 133 F7
Sandhurst Pde CAT SE6 * 133 F7
Sandhurst Rd BFN/LL DA15 155 F2
BXLY DA5 136 E4
CAT SE6 133 G7
CDALE/KGS NW9 50 C2
ED N9 30 E5
Sandhurst Wy SAND/SEL CR2 178 A6
Sandifer Dr CRICK NW2 70 B2
Sandiford Rd CHEAM SM3 174 D1
Sandiland Crs HAYES BR2 180 D1
Sandilands CROY/NA CR0 178 C2
Sandilands Rd FUL/PGN SW6 108 A7
Sandison St PECK SE15 131 G2
Sandland St GINN WC1R 11 M3
Sandling Ri ELTH/MOT SE9 154 A2
Sandlings Cl PECK SE15 131 J1
The Sandlings WDGN N22 55 G1
Sandmartin Wy WLGTN SM6 163 F7
Sandmere Rd CLAP SW4 129 K3
Sandon Cl ESH/CLAY KT10 157 J6
Sandow Crs HYS/HAR UB3 101 J2
Sandown Av DAGE RM10 80 E5
ESH/CLAY KT10 170 C4
Sandown Cl HEST TW5 101 K7
Sandown Ct BELMT SM2 * 175 F6
SYD SE26 * 150 D2
Sandown Dr CAR SM5 176 A7
Sandown Ga ESH/CLAY KT10 170 D1
Sandown Rd ESH/CLAY KT10 170 C3
SNWD SE25 165 J4
Sandown Wy NTHLT UB5 65 J5
Sandpiper Cl
BERM/RHTH SE16 112 C1
WALTH E17 43 F6
Sandpiper Dr ERITH DA8 118 E6
Sandpiper Rd SUT SM1 174 D4
Sandpiper Ter CLAY IG5 * 60 B2
Sandpit Pl CHARL SE7 114 D4
Sandpit Rd BMLY BR1 152 C4
DART DA1 139 F3
Sandpits Rd CROY/NA CR0 179 F3
RCHPK/HAM TW10 124 E3
Sandra Cl HSLW TW3 123 G4
WDGN N22 41 J7
Sandridge Cl HRW HA1 48 E3
Sandridge St ARCH N19 72 C1
Sandringham Av RYNPK SW20 146 C7
Sandringham Cl EN EN1 30 A1
WIM/MER SW19 127 G7
Sandringham Crs
RYLN/HDSTN HA2 66 A2
Sandringham Dr WELL DA16 135 K1
Sandringham Gdns
BARK/HLT IG6 60 C2
CEND/HSY/T N8 54 E5
E/WMO/HCT KT8 157 F3
HEST TW5 101 K7
NFNCH/WDSPK N12 39 H5
Sandringham Ms EA W5 85 K6
HPTN TW12 141 K7
Sandringham Rd BARK IG11 79 F5
BMLY BR1 152 E4
CRICK NW2 69 K4
FSTGT E7 77 G4
GLDGN NW11 52 C6
HACK E8 74 B4
HTHAIR TW6 120 B4
LEY E10 58 B6
NTHLT UB5 66 A6
THHTH CR7 164 D4
WDGN N22 55 J2
WPK KT4 173 J2
Sandrock Pl CROY/NA CR0 179 F3
Sandrock Rd LEW SE13 132 D2
Sands End La FUL/PGN SW6 108 A7
Sandstone La CAN/RD E16 95 F6
Sandstone Pl ARCH N19 72 B1
Sandstone Rd LEE/GVPK SE12 153 F1
Sands Wy WFD IG8 45 K5
Sandtoft Rd CHARL SE7 114 A5
Sandwell Crs
KIL/WHAMP NW6 70 E5
Sandwich St STPAN WC1H 5 J8
Sandwick Cl MLHL NW7 37 J6
Sandycombe Rd
EBED/NFELT TW14 121 K7
RCH/KEW TW9 125 H1
Sandycoombe Rd TWK TW1 124 D5
Sandycroft ABYW SE2 116 B5
Sandy Dr EBED/NFELT TW14 121 H7
Sandy Hill Av
WOOL/PLUM SE18 115 G4
Sandy Hill La
WOOL/PLUM SE18 115 G3
Sandyhill Rd IL IG1 78 B3
Sandy Hill Rd WLGTN SM6 176 C7
WOOL/PLUM SE18 115 G4
Sandy La BELMT SM2 174 C7
BUSH WD23 22 C2
KTN/HRWW/WS HA3 50 B5
KUT/HW KT1 143 H7
MTCM CR4 148 A7
NTHWD HA6 32 E2
RCHPK/HAM TW10 143 J1
SCUP DA14 155 K6
TEDD TW11 143 G6
WOT/HER KT12 156 A5
Sandy La North WLGTN SM6 176 D4
Sandy La South WLGTN SM6 176 C7
Sandy Ldg PIN HA5 * 34 A5
Sandy Lodge Ct NTHWD HA6 * 32 A6
Sandy Lodge La NTHWD HA6 32 B1
Sandy Lodge Wy NTHWD HA6 32 C4
Sandy Md HOR/WEW KT19 172 C7
Sandymount Av STAN HA7 35 J4
Sandy Rdg CHST BR7 154 A5
Sandy's Rw WCHPL E1 13 K3
Sandy Wy CROY/NA CR0 179 H2
Sanford La STNW/STAM N16 74 B1
Sanford St NWCR SE14 112 B5
Sanford Ter STNW/STAM N16 74 B2
Sanger Av CHSGTN KT9 172 B4
Sangley Rd CAT SE6 132 E6
SNWD SE25 165 F3
Sangora Rd BTSEA SW11 128 C3
Sansom Rd WAN E11 * 76 D1
Sansom St CMBW SE5 110 E6
Sans Wk CLKNW EC1R 6 C9
Santley St CLAP SW4 129 K3
Santos Rd WAND/EARL SW18 127 K4
Saperton Wk LBTH SE11 17 M5
Sapphire Cl BCTR RM8 61 J7
Sapphire Rd DEPT SE8 112 B3
WLSDN NW10 68 E6
Saracen Cl CROY/NA CR0 164 E5
Saracen's Head Yd
FENCHST EC3M 13 K5
Saracen St POP/IOD E14 93 J5
Saratoga Rd CLPT E5 74 E3
Sardinia St HOL/ALD WC2B 11 L5
Sarita Cl KTN/HRWW/WS HA3 48 D1
Sark Cl HEST TW5 103 F6
Sarnesfield Rd
ENC/FH EN2 * 29 K3
Sarre Rd CRICK NW2 70 D4
Sarsen Av HSLW TW3 122 E1
Sarsfeld Rd BAL SW12 128 E7
Sarsfield Rd GFD/PVL UB6 85 H1
Sartor Rd PECK SE15 132 A3
Sarum Ter BOW E3 * 93 H3
Satanita Cl CAN/RD E16 95 H5
Satchell Md CDALE/KGS NW9 37 H7
Satchwell Rd BETH E2 92 C2
Sattar Ms STNW/STAM N16 * 73 K2
Sauls Gn WAN E11 76 C2
Saunders Cl IL IG1 60 D7
POP/IOD E14 * 93 H6
Saunders Ness Rd
POP/IOD E14 113 G3
Saunders Rd
WOOL/PLUM SE18 116 A4
Saunders St LBTH SE11 18 A5
Saunders Wy THMD SE28 97 H6
Saunderton Rd ALP/SUD HA0 67 H4
Saunton Av HYS/HAR UB3 101 J6
Saunton Rd HCH RM12 81 J1
Savage Gdns EHAM E6 95 K5
TWRH EC3N 13 K6
Savanah Cl PECK SE15 111 G6
Savera Cl NWDGN UB2 102 B2
Savernake Ct STAN HA7 * 35 J5
Savernake Rd ED N9 30 C5
HAMP NW3 71 K3
Savery Dr SURB KT6 158 C6
Savile Cl NWMAL KT3 160 B4
THDIT KT7 158 A7
Savile Gdns CROY/NA CR0 178 B1
Savile Rw CONDST W1S 10 E6
Saville Crs ASHF TW15 140 B5
Saville Rd CAN/RD E16 95 J7
CHDH RM6 62 B5
CHSWK W4 106 A2
TWK TW1 124 A7
Saville Rw HAYES BR2 167 J7
Savill Gdns RYNPK SW20 160 D2
Savill Rw WFD IG8 44 D5
Savona Cl WIM/MER SW19 146 B6
Savona St VX/NE SW8 109 H6
Savoy Av HYS/HAR UB3 101 H4
Savoy Cl EDGW HA8 36 C4
SRTFD E15 76 C7
Savoy Ct TPL/STR WC2R * 11 K7
Savoy Hl TPL/STR WC2R 11 L7
Savoy Ms BRXN/ST SW9 129 K2
Savoy Pde EN EN1 * 30 A2
Savoy Pl CHCR WC2N 11 K7
Savoy Rd DART DA1 139 F4
Savoy Rw TPL/STR WC2R 11 L6
Savoy Steps TPL/STR WC2R * 11 L7
Savoy St TPL/STR WC2R 11 L6
Savoy Wy TPL/STR WC2R 11 L7
Sawbill Cl YEAD UB4 83 H4
Sawkins Cl WIM/MER SW19 146 B1
Sawley Rd SHB W12 87 J7
Saw Mill Wy STNW/STAM N16 56 C5
Sawtry Cl CAR SM5 162 C6
Sawyer Cl ED N9 42 C1
Sawyers Cl DAGE RM10 80 E5
Sawyer's Hl
MORT/ESHN SW14 125 K6
RCHPK/HAM TW10 125 G6
Sawyers Lawn WEA W13 85 G5
Sawyer St STHWK SE1 18 E1
Saxby Rd BRXS/STRHM SW2 129 K6
Saxham Rd BARK IG11 78 E7
Saxlingham Rd CHING E4 44 B2
Saxon Av FELT TW13 141 J1
Saxonbury Av SUN TW16 156 A2
Saxonbury Cl MTCM CR4 162 C2
Saxonbury Gdns SURB KT6 158 D7
Saxon Cha CEND/HSY/T N8 55 F6
Saxon Cl SURB KT6 158 E5
WALTH E17 57 J6
Saxon Dr ACT W3 86 D5
Saxonfield Cl
BRXS/STRHM SW2 130 A6
Saxon Rd ASHF TW15 140 B5
BMLY BR1 152 D6
BOW E3 93 H1
EHAM E6 95 K3
IL IG1 78 B5
KUTN/CMB KT2 144 A7
SNWD SE25 164 E4
STHL UB1 83 J6
WBLY HA9 68 E2
WDGN N22 41 H7
Saxon Wy STHGT/OAK N14 28 D5
Saxony Pde HYS/HAR UB3 82 A4
Saxton Cl LEW SE13 133 G2
Sayesbury La UED N18 42 C4
Sayes Court St DEPT SE8 112 C4
Scala St FITZ W1T 10 F2
Scales Rd TOTM N17 56 B2
Scammell Wy WATW WD18 20 D5
Scampton Rd
STWL/WRAY TW19 120 C5
Scandrett St WAP E1W * 92 D7
Scarba Wk IS N1 73 K5
Scarborough Rd ED N9 30 E6
FSBYPK N4 55 G6
HTHAIR TW6 121 F5
WAN E11 58 B7
Scarborough St WCHPL E1 13 M5
Scarbrook Rd CROY/NA CR0 177 J2
Scarle Rd ALP/SUD HA0 67 K5
Scarlet Rd CAT SE6 152 C2
Scarsbrook Rd
BKHTH/KID SE3 134 C2
Scarsdale Pl KENS W8 * 14 C3
Scarsdale Rd
RYLN/HDSTN HA2 66 C2
Scarsdale Vls KENS W8 14 B4
Scarth Rd BARN SW13 126 C2
Scawen Cl CAR SM5 176 A3
Scawen Rd DEPT SE8 112 B4
Scawfell St BETH E2 7 M6
Scaynes Link
NFNCH/WDSPK N12 38 E3
Sceptre Rd BETH E2 92 E2
Scholars Cl BAR EN5 26 C3
Scholars Rd BAL SW12 129 H7
Scholars Wy GPK RM2 63 K4
Scholefield Rd ARCH N19 72 D1
Schonfeld Sq
STNW/STAM N16 73 K1
Schoolbank Rd GNWCH SE10 113 J3
School Cl DART DA1 138 C3
Schoolgate Dr MRDN SM4 162 A4
School House La TEDD TW11 143 H6
Schoolhouse La WAP E1W * 93 F6
School La BUSH WD23 22 B7
KUT/HW KT1 143 J7
PIN HA5 * 47 J3
SURB KT6 159 G7
School Pas KUT/HW KT1 159 G1
STHL UB1 83 K7
School Rd CHST BR7 154 C7
DAGE RM10 80 C7
E/WMO/HCT KT8 157 J3
HPTN TW12 142 C5
HSLW TW3 123 H2
KUT/HW KT1 * 143 J7
MNPK E12 77 K3
WDR/YW UB7 100 A5
WLSDN NW10 87 F3
School Road Av HPTN TW12 142 C5
School Sq GNWCH SE10 113 J2
School Wy BCTR RM8 79 H2
Schoolway
NFNCH/WDSPK N12 39 H5
Schooner Cl BARK IG11 97 H2
BERM/RHTH SE16 112 A1
POP/IOD E14 113 G2
Schubert Rd BORE WD6 23 K5
PUT/ROE SW15 127 J4
Sclater St WCHPL E1 7 L9
Scoble Pl STNW/STAM N16 74 B3
Scoles Crs BRXS/STRHM SW2 130 B7
Scope Wy KUT/HW KT1 159 F3
Scoresby St STHWK SE1 12 C9
Scorton Av GFD/PVL UB6 85 G1
Scotch Common WEA W13 85 G4
Scoter Cl WFD IG8 45 F6
Scot Gv PIN HA5 33 H6
Scotia Rd BRXS/STRHM SW2 130 B6
Scotland Gn TOTM N17 56 B1
Scotland Green Rd PEND EN3 31 F4
Scotland Green Rd North
PEND EN3 31 F3
Scots Cl STWL/WRAY TW19 120 A7
Scotsdale Cl CHEAM SM3 174 C6
STMC/STPC BR5 169 K3
Scotsdale Rd LEE/GVPK SE12 134 A4
Scotswood St CLKNW EC1R * 6 B9
Scotswood Wk TOTM N17 * 42 D6
Scott Av PUT/ROE SW15 127 H5
Scott Cl HOR/WEW KT19 172 E4
STRHM/NOR SW16 149 F7
WDR/YW UB7 100 C3
Scott Crs ERITH DA8 118 C7
RYLN/HDSTN HA2 48 B7
Scott Ellis Gdns STJWD NW8 3 G8
Scottes La BCTR RM8 61 K7
Scott Farm Cl THDIT KT7 158 C7
Scott Gdns HEST TW5 102 C6
Scott Lidgett Crs
BERM/RHTH SE16 111 H1
Scott Rd EDGW HA8 50 D1
Scotts Av HAYES BR2 167 G1
SUN TW16 140 C6
Scotts Dr HPTN TW12 142 B6
Scotts Farm Rd
HOR/WEW KT19 172 E5
Scott's La HAYES BR2 167 G2
Scotts Pas
WOOL/PLUM SE18 * 115 G3
Scotts Rd BMLY BR1 152 E6
NWDGN UB2 102 B2
Scott's Rd LEY E10 58 A7
SHB W12 106 E1
Scott St WCHPL E1 92 D3
Scotts Wy SUN TW16 140 C6
Scottswood Cl BUSH WD23 21 J1
Scottswood Rd BUSH WD23 21 J1
Scott's Yd MANHO EC4N 13 G6
Scott Trimmer Wy HSLW TW3 122 D1
Scottwell Dr CDALE/KGS NW9 51 H4
Scoulding Rd CAN/RD E16 94 D5
Scouler St POP/IOD E14 94 B6
Scout Wy MLHL NW7 37 F3
Scovell Crs STHWK SE1 * 18 E2
Scovell Rd STHWK SE1 18 E2
Scrattons Ter BARK IG11 97 K1
Scriven St HACK E8 7 M3
Scrooby St CAT SE6 132 E5
Scrubs La WLSDN NW10 87 J2
Scrutton Cl BAL SW12 129 J6
Scrutton St SDTCH EC2A 13 J1
Scutari Rd EDUL SE22 131 J4
Scylla Crs HTHAIR TW6 120 E6
Scylla Rd HTHAIR TW6 120 E5
PECK SE15 131 J2
Seabright St BETH E2 92 D2
Seabrook Dr WWKM BR4 180 C1
Seabrook Gdns
ROMW/RG RM7 62 C6
Seabrook Rd BCTR RM8 79 K2
Seaburn Cl RAIN RM13 99 G2
Seacole Cl ACT W3 87 F5
Seacourt Rd ABYW SE2 116 E1
Seacroft Gdns OXHEY WD19 33 H2
Seafield Rd FBAR/BDGN N11 40 D3
Seaford Cl RSLP HA4 64 B1
Seaford Rd EN EN1 30 A3
HTHAIR TW6 120 A4
SEVS/STOTM N15 55 K4
WALTH E17 57 K2
WEA W13 85 H7
Seaford St STPAN WC1H 5 K8
Seaforth Av NWMAL KT3 160 E4
Seaforth Crs HBRY N5 73 J4
Seaforth Gdns
HOR/WEW KT19 173 H3
WCHMH N21 29 F6
WFD IG8 45 G4
Seaforth Pl WESTW SW1E 16 F3
Seager Blds DEPT SE8 * 112 D7
Seagrave Cl WCHPL E1 * 93 F4
Seagrave Rd FUL/PGN SW6 14 B9
Seagry Rd WAN E11 58 E5
Seagull La CAN/RD E16 94 E6
Sealand Rd HTHAIR TW6 120 D4
Seal St HACK E8 74 B3
Searles Cl BTSEA SW11 108 D6
Searles Dr EHAM E6 96 B4
Searles Rd STHWK SE1 19 H5
Sears St CMBW SE5 110 E6
Seasons Cl HNWL W7 85 F7
Seasprite Cl NTHLT UB5 83 H2
Seaton Av GDMY/SEVK IG3 78 E4
Seaton Cl LBTH SE11 18 B7
PLSTW E13 94 E3
PUT/ROE SW15 126 E6
WHTN TW2 123 J5
Seaton Gdns RSLP HA4 64 E2
Seaton Rd ALP/SUD HA0 * 86 A1

DART DA1 138 D6
HYS/HAR UB3 101 G3
MTCM CR4 162 D1
WELL DA16 116 D6
WHTN TW2 123 H5
Seaton St UED N18 42 C4
Sebastian St FSBYE EC1V 6 D8
Sebastopol Rd ED N9 42 C3
Sebbon St IS N1 6 D2
Sebergham Gv MLHL NW7 37 J6
Sebert Rd FSTGT E7 77 F4
Sebright Rd BAR EN5 26 B1
Secker Crs
KTN/HRWW/WS HA3 34 C7
Secker St STHWK SE1 12 A9
Second Av ACT W3 87 H7
CHDH RM6 61 J4
DAGE RM10 89 D1
EN EN1 30 B4
HDN NW4 52 B3
HYS/HAR UB3 82 D7
MNPK E12 77 J3
MORT/ESHN SW14 126 B2
NKENS W10 88 C3
PLSTW E13 94 E2
UED N18 42 E3
WALTH E17 57 J4
WBLY HA9 67 K1
WOT/HER KT12 156 A5
Second Cl E/WMO/HCT KT8 157 G3
Second Cross Rd WHTN TW2 142 D1
Second Wy WBLY HA9 68 D3
Sedan Wy WALW SE17 19 J7
Sedcombe Cl SCUP DA14 155 H3
Sedcote Rd PEND EN3 30 E4
Sedding St KTBR SW1X 16 A5
Seddon Rd MRDN SM4 162 C4
Seddon St FSBYW WC1X 5 L8
Sedgebrook Rd
BKHTH/KID SE3 134 C1
Sedgecombe Av
KTN/HRWW/WS HA3 49 J4
Sedgeford Rd SHB W12 87 H7
Sedgehill Rd CAT SE6 151 J4
Sedgemere Av EFNCH N2 53 G2
Sedgemere Rd ABYW SE2 116 D2
Sedgemoor Dr DAGE RM10 80 C3
Sedge Rd TOTM N17 42 E6
Sedgeway CAT SE6 133 J7
Sedgewood Cl HAYES BR2 167 J6
Sedgmoor Pl CMBW SE5 111 F6
Sedgwick Rd LEY E10 76 A1
Sedgwick St HOM E9 75 F4
Sedleigh Rd
WAND/EARL SW18 127 J5
Sedlescombe Rd
FUL/PGN SW6 107 J5
Sedley Pl OXSTW W1C 10 C5
Sednem Ct PECK SE15 131 H1
Sedum Cl CDALE/KGS NW9 50 D4
Seeley Dr DUL SE21 150 A3
Seelig Av CDALE/KGS NW9 51 J6
Seely Rd TOOT SW17 148 A5
Seething La TWRH EC3N 13 K6
Seething Wells La SURB KT6 158 D5
Sefton Av
KTN/HRWW/WS HA3 34 D7
MLHL NW7 37 F4
Sefton Ct ENC/FH EN2 * 29 H1
Sefton Rd CROY/NA CR0 165 H7
Sefton St PUT/ROE SW15 127 F1
Sekforde St CLKNW EC1R 12 C1
Sekhon Ter FELT TW13 142 A2
Selan Gdns YEAD UB4 83 F4
Selbie Av WLSDN NW10 69 H4
Selborne Av BXLY DA5 137 F7
MNPK E12 78 A3
WALTH E17 57 H4
Selborne Gdns GFD/PVL UB6 85 G1
HDN NW4 51 J3
Selborne Rd CMBW SE5 130 E1
CROY/NA CR0 178 A2
IL IG1 78 A1
NWMAL KT3 160 B1
SCUP DA14 155 H3
STHGT/OAK N14 40 E2
WALTH E17 57 H4
WDGN N22 41 F7
Selbourne Av SURB KT6 172 B1
Selby Cha RSLP HA4 65 F1
Selby Cl CHSGTN KT9 172 A6
CHST BR7 154 A5
Selby Gdns STHL UB1 84 A3
Selby Gn CAR SM5 162 D6
Selby Rd ASHF TW15 140 A5
CAR SM5 162 D6
EA W5 85 H3
PGE/AN SE20 165 H1
PLSTW E13 95 F4
TOTM N17 42 A5
WAN E11 76 C2
Selby St WCHPL E1 92 C3
Selden Rd PECK SE15 131 K1
Selhurst Cl WIM/MER SW19 127 G7
Selhurst New Rd SNWD SE25 165 F5
Selhurst Pl SNWD SE25 165 F5
Selhurst Rd ED N9 41 K2
SNWD SE25 165 F4
Selinas La BCTR RM8 62 A6
Selkirk Dr ERITH DA8 118 B7
Selkirk Rd TOOT SW17 147 J3
WHTN TW2 142 C1
Sellers Hall Cl FNCH N3 38 E6
Sellincourt Rd TOOT SW17 147 J4
Sellindge Cl BECK BR3 151 H6
Sellons Av WLSDN NW10 69 H7
Sellwood Dr BAR EN5 26 B4
Selsdon Av SAND/SEL CR2 177 K5
Selsdon Cl SURB KT6 159 F4
Selsdon Park Rd
CROY/NA CR0 179 G7
Selsdon Rd CRICK NW2 69 H1
PLSTW E13 77 G7
SAND/SEL CR2 177 K5
WAN E11 58 E6
WNWD SE27 149 H2
Selsdon Wy POP/IOD E14 112 E2
Selsea Pl STNW/STAM N16 74 A4
Selsey Crs WELL DA16 116 E7
Selsey St BOW E3 93 J4
Selvage La MLHL NW7 37 F4
Selway Cl PIN HA5 47 F3
Selwood Pl SKENS SW7 15 G7
Selwood Rd CHEAM SM3 161 J7
CHSGTN KT9 171 K3
CROY/NA CR0 178 D1
Selwood Ter SKENS SW7 15 G7
Selworthy Cl WAN E11 58 E4
Selworthy Rd CAT SE6 151 H2
Selwyn Av CHING E4 44 A5
GDMY/SEVK IG3 61 F5
RCH/KEW TW9 125 G2
Selwyn Cl HSLWW TW4 122 D3
Selwyn Ct EDGW HA8 36 D6
Selwyn Crs WELL DA16 136 C2
Selwyn Rd BOW E3 93 H1
NWMAL KT3 160 A4
PLSTW E13 77 F7
WLSDN NW10 69 G6
Semley Pl BGVA SW1W 16 B6
STRHM/NOR SW16 164 A1
Semley Rd STRHM/NOR SW16 163 K1
Senate St PECK SE15 131 K1
Seneca Rd THHTH CR7 164 D3
Senga Rd WLGTN SM6 163 F7
Senhouse Rd CHEAM SM3 174 B2
Senior St BAY/PAD W2 8 C2
Senlac Rd LEE/GVPK SE12 134 A7
Sennen Rd EN EN1 30 B6
Senrab St WCHPL E1 93 F5
Sentamu Cl HNHL SE24 130 C7
Sentinel Cl NTHLT UB5 83 J3
September Wy STAN HA7 35 H5
Sequoia Cl BUSH WD23 22 D7
Sequoia Pk PIN HA5 34 B5
Serbin Cl LEY E10 58 A6
Serenaders Rd BRXN/ST SW9 130 B1
Serjeant's Inn EMB EC4Y * 12 B5
Serle St LINN WC2A 11 M4
Sermon La BLKFR EC4V 12 E5
Serpentine Rd SKENS SW7 15 K1
Service Route No 1
SRTFD E15 76 B6
Service Route No 2
SRTFD E15 76 B6
Service Route No 3
SRTFD E15 76 B5
Serviden Dr BMLY BR1 153 H7
Setchell Est STHWK SE1 19 L5
Setchell Rd STHWK SE1 19 L5
Setchell Wy STHWK SE1 19 L5
Seth St BERM/RHTH SE16 111 K1
Seton Gdns DAGW RM9 79 J6
Settles St WCHPL E1 92 C4
Settrington Rd FUL/PGN SW6 128 A1
Seven Acres CAR SM5 175 J1
NTHWD HA6 32 E5
Seven Dials LSQ/SEVD WC2H 11 J5
Sevenex Pde WBLY HA9 * 68 A4
Seven Kings Rd
GDMY/SEVK IG3 60 E7
Seven Kings Wy
KUTN/CMB KT2 143 K7
Sevenoaks Cl BXLYHN DA7 137 K3
Sevenoaks Rd BROCKY SE4 132 C5
Seven Seas Rd HTHAIR TW6 121 F5
Seven Sisters Rd FSBYPK N4 73 H1
HOLWY N7 73 F2
SEVS/STOTM N15 55 K5
Seven Stars Yd WCHPL E1 13 M2
Seventh Av HYS/HAR UB3 82 E7
MNPK E12 77 K3
Severnake Cl POP/IOD E14 112 D3
Severn Av GPK RM2 63 K2
NKENS W10 88 C2
Severn Dr ESH/CLAY KT10 171 G1
Severn Wy WLSDN NW10 69 H4
Severus Rd BTSEA SW11 128 D3
Seville Ms IS N1 7 J2
Seville St KTBR SW1X 15 M2
Sevington Rd HDN NW4 51 K5
Sevington St MV/WKIL W9 8 C1
Seward Rd BECK BR3 166 A1
HNWL W7 104 B1
Sewardstone Rd BETH E2 92 E1
CHING E4 31 K3
Seward St FSBYE EC1V 6 D9
Sewdley St CLPT E5 75 F2
Sewell Rd ABYW SE2 116 B1
Sewell St PLSTW E13 94 E2
Sextant Av POP/IOD E14 113 G3
Sexton Cl RAIN RM13 81 H7
Seymer Rd ROM RM1 63 F2
Seymour Av EW KT17 173 K7
MRDN SM4 161 G6
TOTM N17 56 C1
Seymour Cl E/WMO/HCT KT8 157 H4
PIN HA5 33 K7
Seymour Dr HAYES BR2 168 E7
Seymour Gdns BROCKY SE4 132 B2
BRYLDS KT5 159 G4
FELT TW13 141 F3
IL IG1 59 K7
RSLP HA4 47 H7
TWK TW1 124 C6
Seymour Gv OXHEY WD19 21 G6
Seymour Ms MBLAR W1H 10 A4
Seymour Pl MBLAR W1H 9 L3
SNWD SE25 165 J3
Seymour Rd CAR SM5 176 A4
CEND/HSY/T N8 55 H4
CHING E4 31 K7
CHSWK W4 105 K3
E/WMO/HCT KT8 157 H4
ED N9 42 D1
EHAM E6 77 H7
FNCH N3 39 F6
HPTN TW12 142 C4
KUT/HW KT1 143 K7
LEY E10 57 H7
MTCM CR4 163 F6
WAND/EARL SW18 127 J6
WIM/MER SW19 146 B2
Seymour St BAY/PAD W2 9 L5
MBLAR W1H 9 M5
WOOL/PLUM SE18 115 H2
Seymour Ter PGE/AN SE20 150 D7
Seymour Vls PGE/AN SE20 150 D7
Seymour Wk WBPTN SW10 14 E9
Seymour Wy SUN TW16 140 C5
Seyssel St POP/IOD E14 113 F3
Shaa Rd ACT W3 87 F6
Shacklegate La TEDD TW11 142 E3
Shackleton Cl FSTH SE23 150 D1
Shackleton Rd STHL UB1 83 K6
Shacklewell La HACK E8 74 B3
Shacklewell Rd
STNW/STAM N16 74 B3
Shacklewell Rw HACK E8 74 B3
Shacklewell St BETH E2 7 M9
Shadbolt Av CHING E4 43 G4
Shadbolt Cl WPK KT4 173 H1
Shad Thames STHWK SE1 13 L9
Shadwell Dr NTHLT UB5 83 K2
Shadwell Gdns WCHPL E1 * 92 E6
Shadwell Pierhead WAP E1W 92 E6
Shady Bush Cl BUSH WD23 22 D6
Shady La WAT WD17 21 F1
Shaef Wy TEDD TW11 143 G6
Shafter Rd DAGE RM10 80 E5
Shaftesbury Av BAR EN5 27 G3
EBED/NFELT TW14 121 K5
KTN/HRWW/WS HA3 49 K5
LSQ/SEVD WC2H 11 H6
NWDGN UB2 103 F3
PEND EN3 31 F1
RYLN/HDSTN HA2 48 B7
SOHO/SHAV W1D 11 G6
Shaftesbury Cir
RYLN/HDSTN HA2 * 48 C7
Shaftesbury Ct
RKW/CH/CXG WD3 * 20 A4
Shaftesbury Gdns
WLSDN NW10 87 G3
Shaftesbury Ms CLAP SW4 129 H4
KENS W8 * 14 B4
Shaftesbury Pde
RYLN/HDSTN HA2 * 48 C7
Shaftesbury Pl BARB EC2Y * 12 E3
Shaftesbury Rd ARCH N19 54 E7
BECK BR3 166 C1
CAR SM5 162 C6
FSTGT E7 77 G6
LEY E10 57 J7
RCH/KEW TW9 125 F2
ROM RM1 63 H5
UED N18 42 A5
WALTH E17 57 K4
WAT WD17 21 G2
The Shaftesburys BARK IG11 96 C1
Shaftesbury St IS N1 6 F6
Shaftesbury Ter
HMSMTH W6 * 106 C3
Shaftesbury Wy WHTN TW2 142 D2
Shaftesbury Waye YEAD UB4 83 F4
Shafteswood Ct TOOT SW17 147 K2
Shafto Ms KTBR SW1X 15 L4
Shafton Ms HOM E9 * 75 F7
Shafton Rd HOM E9 75 F7
Shakespeare Av
EBED/NFELT TW14 121 K5
FBAR/BDGN N11 40 C4
WLSDN NW10 68 E7
YEAD UB4 82 E5
Shakespeare Crs MNPK E12 77 K6
WLSDN NW10 69 F7
Shakespeare Dr BORE WD6 24 C3
KTN/HRWW/WS HA3 50 B5
Shakespeare Gdns EFNCH N2 53 K3
Shakespeare Rd ACT W3 86 E7
BXLYHN DA7 117 F7
DART DA1 139 K3
FNCH N3 * 38 E7
HNHL SE24 130 C4
HNWL W7 85 F6
MLHL NW7 37 J3
ROM RM1 63 H5
WALTH E17 57 F1
Shakespeare Ter
RCH/KEW TW9 * 125 H2
Shakespeare Wy FELT TW13 141 G3
Shakspeare Ms
STNW/STAM N16 74 A3
Shakspeare Wk
STNW/STAM N16 74 A3
Shalbourne Sq HOM E9 75 H5
Shalcomb St WBPTN SW10 108 B5
Shaldon Dr MRDN SM4 161 H4
RSLP HA4 65 G2
Shaldon Rd EDGW HA8 50 B1
Shalfleet Dr NKENS W10 88 B6
Shalford Ct IS N1 * 6 C5
Shalimar Gdns ACT W3 86 E6
Shalimar Rd ACT W3 86 E6
Shallons Rd ELTH/MOT SE9 154 B3
Shalstone Rd
MORT/ESHN SW14 125 J2
Shalston Vls SURB KT6 159 G5
Shamrock Rd CROY/NA CR0 164 A5
Shamrock St CLAP SW4 129 J2
Shamrock Wy
STHGT/OAK N14 28 B7
Shandon Rd CLAP SW4 129 H5
Shand St STHWK SE1 19 K1
Shandy St WCHPL E1 93 F4
Shanklin Gdns OXHEY WD19 33 G3
Shanklin Rd CEND/HSY/T N8 54 D4
SEVS/STOTM N15 56 C3
Shannon Cl NWDGN UB2 102 C4
Shannon Gv BRXN/ST SW9 130 A3
Shannon Pl STJWD NW8 3 K5
Shannon Wy BECK BR3 151 K5
Shap Crs CAR SM5 162 E7
Shapland Wy PLMGR N13 41 F4
Shapwick Cl FBAR/BDGN N11 39 K4
Shardcroft Av HNHL SE24 130 C4
Shardeloes Rd BROCKY SE4 * 132 C4
NWCR SE14 132 C1
Shard's Sq PECK SE15 111 H5
Sharland Cl THHTH CR7 164 B5
Sharman Ct SCUP DA14 155 G3
Sharnbrooke Cl WELL DA16 136 D2
Sharon Cl SURB KT6 158 D7
Sharon Gdns HOM E9 74 E7
Sharon Rd CHSWK W4 106 A4
PEND EN3 31 G1
Sharples Hall St CAMTN NW1 3 M2
Sharps La RSLP HA4 46 B6
Sharp Wy DART DA1 139 J2
Sharratt St PECK SE15 111 K5
Sharsted St WALW SE17 18 C8
Sharvel La YEAD UB4 64 E7
Shavers Pl MYFR/PICC W1J 11 G7
Shaw Av BARK IG11 98 A1
Shawbrooke Rd
ELTH/MOT SE9 134 C3
Shawbury Cl CDALE/KGS NW9 37 G7
Shawbury Rd EDUL SE22 131 G4
Shaw Cl BUSH WD23 34 E1
EMPK RM11 63 K7
THMD SE28 97 H7
Shaw Crs POP/IOD E14 93 G5
Shaw Dr WOT/HER KT12 156 B6
Shawfield Pk BMLY BR1 168 C1
Shawfield St CHEL SW3 15 K8
Shawford Ct PUT/ROE SW15 * 126 D6
Shawford Rd HOR/WEW KT19 173 F5
Shaw Gdns BARK IG11 98 A1
Shaw Rd BMLY BR1 152 D2
EDUL SE22 131 F3
Shaws Cots FSTH SE23 * 151 G2
Shaw's Cots FSTH SE23 151 G2
Shaw Sq WALTH E17 43 G7
The Shaw CHST BR7 * 154 C6
Shaw Wy WLGTN SM6 176 E6
Shaxton Crs CROY/NA CR0 180 A7
Sheaf Cots THDIT KT7 * 157 K7
Shearing Dr CAR SM5 162 B6
Shearling Wy HOLWY N7 72 E5
Shearman Rd BKHTH/KID SE3 133 J3
Shearwater Cl BARK IG11 97 G2
Shearwater Rd SUT SM1 174 D4
Shearwater Wy YEAD UB4 83 H5
Shearwood Crs DART DA1 138 C2
Sheaths Cots THDIT KT7 * 158 C6
Sheaveshill Av
CDALE/KGS NW9 51 G2
Sheaveshill Pde
CDALE/KGS NW9 * 51 G3
Sheen Common Dr
RCHPK/HAM TW10 125 H3
Sheen Court Rd
RCHPK/HAM TW10 125 H3
Sheendale Rd RCH/KEW TW9 125 G3
Sheenewood SYD SE26 150 D4
Sheen Ga MORT/ESHN SW14 125 K5
Sheen Gate Gdns
MORT/ESHN SW14 125 K3
Sheen Gv IS N1 6 A3
Sheen La MORT/ESHN SW14 125 K3
Sheen Pk RCH/KEW TW9 125 F3
Sheen Rd RCH/KEW TW9 125 F3
Sheen Wy WLGTN SM6 177 F4
Sheen Wd MORT/ESHN SW14 125 K4
Sheepcote Cl HEST TW5 101 K6
Sheepcote La BTSEA SW11 128 E1
Sheepcote Rd HRW HA1 49 F5
Sheepcotes Rd CHDH RM6 62 A3
Sheephouse Wy NWMAL KT3 160 A7
Sheep La HACK E8 74 D7
Sheep Walk Ms
WIM/MER SW19 146 B5
Sheerwater Rd CAN/RD E16 95 H4
Sheffield Rd HTHAIR TW6 121 F5
Sheffield St LINN WC2A * 11 L5
Sheffield Ter KENS W8 14 A1
Shefton Ri NTHWD HA6 32 E6
Shelbourne Cl PIN HA5 47 K2
Shelbourne Rd TOTM N17 42 D7
Shelburne Dr HSLWW TW4 123 F5
Shelburne Rd HOLWY N7 73 F3
Shelbury Cl SCUP DA14 155 G2
Shelbury Rd EDUL SE22 131 J4
Sheldon Av CLAY IG5 60 B1
HGT N6 53 K6
Sheldon Cl LEE/GVPK SE12 134 A4
PGE/AN SE20 150 D7
Sheldon Pl BETH E2 92 C1
Sheldon Rd BXLYHN DA7 117 G7
CRICK NW2 70 B3
DAGW RM9 80 A6
UED N18 42 A3
Sheldon Sq BAY/PAD W2 8 F3
Sheldon St CROY/NA CR0 177 J2
Sheldrake Cl CAN/RD E16 95 K7
Sheldrake Pl KENS W8 107 J1
Sheldrick Cl MTCM CR4 162 C1
Shelduck Cl SRTFD E15 76 D4
Sheldwich Ter HAYES BR2 * 168 D5
Shelford Pl STNW/STAM N16 73 K2
Shelford Ri NRWD SE19 150 A6
Shelford Rd BAR EN5 26 A5
Shelgate Rd BTSEA SW11 128 E4
Shell Cl HAYES BR2 168 D5
Shellduck Cl CDALE/KGS NW9 51 G1
Shelley Av GFD/PVL UB6 84 D2
HCH RM12 81 H1
MNPK E12 77 J5
Shelley Cl EDGW HA8 36 C3
GFD/PVL UB6 84 D2
NTHWD HA6 32 D4
PECK SE15 131 J1
YEAD UB4 82 E4
Shelley Crs HEST TW5 102 C7
STHL UB1 83 K5
Shelley Dr WELL DA16 115 K7
Shelley Gdns ALP/SUD HA0 67 J1
Shelley Rd WLSDN NW10 69 F7
Shelley Wy WIM/MER SW19 147 H5
Shellgrove Rd
STNW/STAM N16 * 74 A4
Shellness Rd CLPT E5 74 D4
Shell Rd LEW SE13 132 E2
Shellwood Rd BTSEA SW11 128 E1
Shelly Cl BORE WD6 24 C3
Shelmerdine Cl BOW E3 93 J4
Shelson Av FELT TW13 140 D2
Shelson Pde FELT TW13 * 140 D2
Shelton Rd WIM/MER SW19 146 E7
Shelton St LSQ/SEVD WC2H * 11 J5
Shenfield Rd WFD IG8 45 G6
Shenfield St IS N1 7 K6
Shenley Av RSLP HA4 64 D1
Shenley Rd BORE WD6 24 C2
CMBW SE5 111 F7
DART DA1 139 K5
HEST TW5 102 D7
Shenstone Cl DART DA1 138 A4
Shepherd Cl FELT TW13 141 J3
Shepherdess Pl FSBYE EC1V 6 F7
Shepherdess Wk IS N1 6 F5
Shepherd Market
MYFR/PICC W1J 10 C9
Shepherd's Bush Gn SHB W12 107 F1
Shepherd's Bush Market
SHB W12 107 F1
Shepherd's Bush Pl
SHB W12 * 107 G1
Shepherd's Bush Rd
HMSMTH W6 107 F2
Shepherds Cl CHDH RM6 61 K4
STAN HA7 35 G4
Shepherd's Cl HGT N6 54 B5
Shepherds Gn CHST BR7 154 D6
Shepherd's Hl HGT N6 54 B5
Shepherds La DART DA1 138 D7
THMD SE28 96 E7
Shepherd's La HOM E9 75 F4
Shepherd's Leas
ELTH/MOT SE9 * 135 J3
Shepherds Pl
MYFR/PKLN W1K 10 A6
Shepherds Rd WATW WD18 20 D2
Shepherd St MYFR/PICC W1J 10 C9
Shepherds Wk BUSH WD23 34 D1
CRICK NW2 69 J1
Shepherd's Wk HAMP NW3 71 H4
Shepherds Wy SAND/SEL CR2 179 F6
Shepiston La HYS/HAR UB3 100 E3
Shepley Cl CAR SM5 176 A2
Sheppard Cl KUT/HW KT1 159 F3
Sheppard Dr
BERM/RHTH SE16 111 J4
Sheppard St CAN/RD E16 94 D3
Shepperton Rd IS N1 6 F3
STMC/STPC BR5 169 H5
Sheppey Cl ERITH DA8 118 E6
Sheppey Gdns DAGW RM9 79 J6
Sheppey Rd DAGW RM9 79 H6
Sheppey Wk IS N1 6 F1
Shepton Houses BETH E2 * 92 E2
Sherard Rd ELTH/MOT SE9 134 D4
Sheraton Cl BORE WD6 24 B4
Sheraton Ms WATW WD18 20 C3
Sheraton St SOHO/CST W1F * 11 G5
Sherborne Av NWDGN UB2 103 F3
PEND EN3 30 E1
Sherborne Cl YEAD UB4 83 G5
Sherborne Crs CAR SM5 162 D6
Sherborne Gdns
CDALE/KGS NW9 50 C2
WEA W13 85 H5
Sherborne La MANHO EC4N 13 G6
Sherborne Pl NTHWD HA6 32 B5
Sherborne Rd CHEAM SM3 174 E1
CHSGTN KT9 172 A4
EBED/NFELT TW14 121 G6
Sherborne St IS N1 7 G3
Sherborne Vls WEA W13 * 85 H4
Sherboro Rd
SEVS/STOTM N15 56 B5
Sherbrooke Cl BXLYHN DA7 137 H3
Sherbrooke Rd FUL/PGN SW6 107 H6
Sherbrooke Ter
FUL/PGN SW6 * 107 H6
Sherbrooke Wy WPK KT4 160 E6
Sherbrook Gdns WCHMH N21 29 H6
Shere Cl CHSGTN KT9 171 K4
Sheredan Rd CHING E4 44 B4
Shere Rd GNTH/NBYPK IG2 60 A4
Sherfield Cl NWMAL KT3 159 J3
Sherfield Gdns
PUT/ROE SW15 126 C5
Sheridan Ct DART DA1 139 K3
HSLWW TW4 122 D4
Sheridan Crs CHST BR7 169 G1
Sheridan Gdns
KTN/HRWW/WS HA3 49 K5
Sheridan Ms WAN E11 59 F5
Sheridan Pl BMLY BR1 168 C1
HPTN TW12 142 B7
Sheridan Rd BELV DA17 117 H3
BXLYHN DA7 137 F2
FSTGT E7 76 D2
MNPK E12 77 J4
OXHEY WD19 21 H6
RCHPK/HAM TW10 143 J2
WIM/MER SW19 146 D7
Sheridan Ter NTHLT UB5 * 66 B4
Sheridan Wk CAR SM5 175 K4
GLDGN NW11 52 E5
Sheridan Wy BECK BR3 151 H7
Sheringham Av MNPK E12 77 K3
ROMW/RG RM7 62 E5
STHGT/OAK N14 28 D4
WHTN TW2 122 E7
Sheringham Dr BARK IG11 79 F4
Sheringham Rd HOLWY N7 73 G5
PGE/AN SE20 165 J1
Sherington Av PIN HA5 34 A6
Sherington Rd
BKHTH/KID SE3 114 A5
Sherland Rd TWK TW1 124 A7
Sherlock Ms MHST W1U 10 A2
Shermanbury Cl ERITH DA8 118 C6
Sherman Gdns CHDH RM6 61 J5
Sherman Rd BMLY BR1 152 E7
Shernhall St WALTH E17 58 A4
Sherrard Rd FSTGT E7 77 G5
Sherrards Wy BAR EN5 26 E4
Sherrick Green Rd
WLSDN NW10 69 K4
Sherriff Cl ESH/CLAY KT10 170 B1
Sherriff Rd KIL/WHAMP NW6 70 E5
Sherringham Av FELT TW13 140 E2
TOTM N17 56 C1
Sherrock Gdns HDN NW4 51 J3
Sherry Ms BARK IG11 78 D6
Sherwin Rd NWCR SE14 112 A7
Sherwood SURB KT6 171 K1
Sherwood Av GFD/PVL UB6 66 E5
RSLP HA4 46 C5
STRHM/NOR SW16 148 D6
SWFD E18 59 F2
YEAD UB4 83 F3
Sherwood Cl BXLY DA5 136 D5
WALTH E17 57 H1
WEA W13 85 H7
Sherwood Ct MBLAR W1H * 9 L3
Sherwood Gdns BARK IG11 78 D6
BERM/RHTH SE16 111 H4
POP/IOD E14 112 D3
Sherwood House
RYLN/HDSTN HA2 * 66 C2
Sherwood Park Av
BFN/LL DA15 136 B6
Sherwood Park Rd
MTCM CR4 163 H3
SUT SM1 174 E4
Sherwood Rd BARK/HLT IG6 60 D3
CROY/NA CR0 165 J6
HDN NW4 52 A2
HPTN TW12 142 C4
RYLN/HDSTN HA2 66 C1
WELL DA16 135 K2
WIM/MER SW19 146 D6
Sherwoods Rd OXHEY WD19 21 J6
Sherwood St SOHO/CST W1F 10 F6
TRDG/WHET N20 39 H2
Sherwood Ter
TRDG/WHET N20 39 H2
Sherwood Wy WWKM BR4 180 A1
Shetland Cl BORE WD6 25 F5
Shetland Rd BOW E3 93 H1
Shield Dr BTFD TW8 104 B5
Shieldhall St ABYW SE2 116 D3
Shield Rd ASHF TW15 140 A3
Shifford Pth FSTH SE23 151 F2
Shillibeer Pl MBLAR W1H 9 K3
Shillingford Cl MLHL NW7 38 B6
Shillingford St IS N1 * 6 D1
Shilling Pl HNWL W7 * 85 G7
Shinfield St SHB W12 88 A5
Shinglewell Rd ERITH DA8 117 H6
Shinners Cl SNWD SE25 165 H4
Shipka Rd BAL SW12 129 G7
Ship La MORT/ESHN SW14 125 K2
Shipman Rd CAN/RD E16 95 F5
FSTH SE23 151 F1
Ship & Mermaid Rw
STHWK SE1 19 H1
Ship St DEPT SE8 112 D7
Ship Tavern Pas BANK EC3V 13 J6
Shipton Cl BCTR RM8 79 K2
Shipton St BETH E2 7 M7
Shipwright Rd
BERM/RHTH SE16 112 B1
Shipwright Yd STHWK SE1 * 13 J9
Shirburn Cl FSTH SE23 131 K6
Shirbutt St POP/IOD E14 93 J6
Shirebrook Rd BKHTH/KID SE3 134 C1
Shire Ct EW KT17 173 H6
Shirehall Cl HDN NW4 52 B5
Shirehall Gdns HDN NW4 52 B5
Shirehall La HDN NW4 52 B5
Shirehall Pk HDN NW4 52 B5
Shire Horse Wy ISLW TW7 124 A2
Shire La ORP BR6 181 K6
Shiremeade BORE WD6 24 B4
Shire Ms WHTN TW2 123 H5
The Shires RCHPK/HAM TW10 144 A3
Shirland Ms MV/WKIL W9 88 D2
Shirland Rd MV/WKIL W9 2 B9
Shirley Av BXLY DA5 136 E6
CROY/NA CR0 165 K7

SUT SM1 175 J3
Shirley Church Rd
CROY/NA CR0 179 F2
Shirley Cl DART DA1 139 F3
HSLW TW3 123 H4
WALTH E17 * 57 K4
Shirley Crs BECK BR3 166 B3
Shirley Dr HSLW TW3 123 H4
Shirley Gdns BARK IG11 78 E5
HNWL W7 85 F7
Shirley Gv BTSEA SW11 129 F2
ED N9 30 E6
Shirley Hills Rd CROY/NA CR0 179 F4
Shirley Oaks Rd CROY/NA CR0 166 A7
Shirley Park Rd CROY/NA CR0 165 J7
Shirley Rd BFN/LL DA15 154 E2
CHSWK W4 106 A1
CROY/NA CR0 165 J7
ENC/FH EN2 29 J2
SRTFD E15 76 C6
WLGTN SM6 176 C7
Shirley Rw SNWD SE25 * 165 H1
Shirley St CAN/RD E16 94 D5
Shirley Wy CROY/NA CR0 179 H2
Shirlock Rd HAMP NW3 71 K3
Shirwell Cl MLHL NW7 38 B6
Shobden Rd TOTM N17 41 K7
Shobroke Cl CRICK NW2 70 A2
Shoebury Rd EHAM E6 77 K6
Shoe La FLST/FETLN EC4A 12 B4
Shooters Av
KTN/HRWW/WS HA3 49 J3
Shooters Hill Rd GNWCH SE10 113 H7
Shoot-Up Hl CRICK NW2 70 C5
Shops SYD SE26 * 151 F4
Shore Cl EBED/NFELT TW14 121 K6
HPTN TW12 141 J4
Shoreditch High St
FSBYE EC1V 7 K8
WCHPL E1 13 K2
Shore Gv FELT TW13 142 A1
Shoreham Cl CROY/NA CR0 165 K5
WAND/EARL SW18 128 A4
Shoreham Rd STMC/STPC BR5 155 H7
Shoreham Rd (East)
HTHAIR TW6 120 B4
Shoreham Rd (West)
HTHAIR TW6 120 B4
Shoreham Wy HAYES BR2 167 K5
Shore Pl HOM E9 74 E6
Shore Rd HOM E9 74 E6
Shore Wy BRXN/ST SW9 130 B1
Shorncliffe Rd STHWK SE1 19 L8
Shorndean St CAT SE6 133 F7
Shorne Cl BFN/LL DA15 136 C5
Shornefield Cl BMLY BR1 169 F2
Shorrolds Rd FUL/PGN SW6 107 K6
Shortcroft Rd EW KT17 173 H6
Shortcrofts Rd DAGW RM9 80 B5
Shorter St TWRH EC3N 13 L6
Shortgate
NFNCH/WDSPK N12 38 D3
Shortlands HMSMTH W6 107 G3
HYS/HAR UB3 101 G5
Shortlands Cl BELV DA17 117 G2
UED N18 41 K2
Shortlands Gdns HAYES BR2 167 H1
Shortlands Gv HAYES BR2 167 G2
Shortlands Rd HAYES BR2 167 G2
KUTN/CMB KT2 144 B6
LEY E10 57 K6
Short La STWL/WRAY TW19 120 C6
Short Rd CHSWK W4 106 B5
WAN E11 76 C1
Shorts Cft CDALE/KGS NW9 50 D3
Shorts Gdns
LSQ/SEVD WC2H * 11 J5
Shorts Rd CAR SM5 175 J3
Short St HDN NW4 52 A3
STHWK SE1 18 B1
Shortway ELTH/MOT SE9 134 D2
Short Wy NFNCH/WDSPK N12 39 J5
WHTN TW2 123 H6
Shotfield WLGTN SM6 176 B5
Shott Cl SUT SM1 175 G4
Shottendane Rd
FUL/PGN SW6 * 107 K7
Shottery Cl ELTH/MOT SE9 153 J2
Shottfield Av
MORT/ESHN SW14 126 B3
Shoulder of Mutton Aly
POP/IOD E14 93 G6
Shouldham St MBLAR W1H 9 K3
Showers Wy HYS/HAR UB3 82 E7
Shrapnel Cl WOOL/PLUM SE18 114 E6
Shrapnel Rd ELTH/MOT SE9 134 E2
Shrewsbury Av
KTN/HRWW/WS HA3 50 A3
MORT/ESHN SW14 125 K3
Shrewsbury Cl SURB KT6 172 A1
Shrewsbury Crs
WLSDN NW10 * 69 F7
Shrewsbury La
WOOL/PLUM SE18 115 G7
Shrewsbury Ms BAY/PAD W2 8 A4
Shrewsbury Rd BAY/PAD W2 8 A3
BECK BR3 166 B2
CAR SM5 162 D6
FBAR/BDGN N11 40 D5
FSTGT E7 77 H5
HTHAIR TW6 121 F5
Shrewsbury St NKENS W10 88 A3
Shrewton Rd TOOT SW17 * 147 K6
Shroffold Rd BMLY BR1 152 C3
Shropshire Cl MTCM CR4 163 K3
Shropshire Rd WDGN N22 41 F6
Shroton St CAMTN NW1 9 J2
The Shrubberies SWFD E18 58 E1
Shrubbery Gdns WCHMH N21 29 H6
Shrubbery Rd ED N9 42 C2
STHL UB1 83 K7
STRHM/NOR SW16 148 E3
The Shrubbery SURB KT6 * 159 F7
Shrubland Cl
TRDG/WHET N20 * 39 H1
Shrubland Gv WPK KT4 174 A2
Shrubland Rd HACK E8 74 C7
LEY E10 57 J6
WALTH E17 57 J4
Shrublands Av CROY/NA CR0 179 J3
Shrublands Cl SYD SE26 150 E2
TRDG/WHET N20 27 H7
Shrubsall Cl ELTH/MOT SE9 134 D7
Shubbery Cl IS N1 6 F3
Shuna Wk IS N1 * 73 K5
Shurland Av EBAR EN4 27 H5
Shurland Gdns PECK SE15 * 111 G6
Shuters Sq WKENS W14 * 107 J4
Shuttle Cl BFN/LL DA15 136 A6
Shuttlemead BXLY DA5 137 G6
Shuttle Rd DART DA1 138 D2
Shuttle St WCHPL E1 92 C3
Shuttleworth Rd BTSEA SW11 128 C1
Sibella Rd CLAP SW4 129 J1
Sibley Cl BMLY BR1 168 D4
BXLYHS DA6 137 F4
Sibley Ct UX/CGN UB8 82 A4
Sibley Gv EHAM E6 77 J6
MNPK E12 77 K6
Sibthorpe Rd LEE/GVPK SE12 134 A6
Sibthorp Rd MTCM CR4 * 162 E1
Sibton Rd CAR SM5 162 D6
Sicilian Av NOXST/BSQ WC1A * 11 K3
Sidbury St FUL/PGN SW6 107 H7
Sidcup By-Pass Rd SCUP DA14 155 G5
Sidcup Hl SCUP DA14 155 H4
Sidcup Hill Gdns SCUP DA14 * 155 J4
Sidcup Pl SCUP DA14 155 G4
Sidcup Rd ELTH/MOT SE9 134 C7
Siddeley Dr HSLWW TW4 122 D2
Siddons La CAMTN NW1 9 M1
Siddons Rd CROY/NA CR0 177 G2
FSTH SE23 151 G1
TOTM N17 42 C7
Side Rd WALTH E17 57 H4
Sidewood Rd ELTH/MOT SE9 135 J7
Sidford Pl STHWK SE1 17 M4
Sidings Ms HOLWY N7 73 G3
The Sidings WAN E11 58 A7
Sidmouth Av ISLW TW7 123 K1
Sidmouth Cl OXHEY WD19 33 F1
Sidmouth Dr RSLP HA4 64 E2
Sidmouth Ms STPAN WC1H 5 L8
Sidmouth Pde CRICK NW2 * 70 A6
Sidmouth Rd CRICK NW2 70 A6
LEY E10 76 A1
PECK SE15 111 G7
WELL DA16 116 D6
Sidmouth St STPAN WC1H 5 K8
Sidney Av PLMGR N13 41 F4
Sidney Elson Wy EHAM E6 96 A1
Sidney Gdns BTFD TW8 104 E5
Sidney Gv FSBYE EC1V 6 C6
Sidney Rd BECK BR3 166 B1
BRXN/ST SW9 130 A1
FSTGT E7 76 E2
RYLN/HDSTN HA2 48 C2
SNWD SE25 165 H4
TWK TW1 124 B5
WDGN N22 41 F6
WOT/HER KT12 156 A7
Sidney Sq WCHPL E1 * 92 E4
Sidney St WCHPL E1 92 D4
Sidworth St HACK E8 74 D6
Siebert Rd BKHTH/KID SE3 113 K5
Siemens Rd WOOL/PLUM SE18 114 C2
Sienna Cl CHSGTN KT9 171 K5
Sienna Ter CRICK NW2 * 69 J1
Sierra Dr DAGE RM10 98 D1
Sigdon Rd HACK E8 74 C4
The Sigers PIN HA5 47 F5
Signmakers Yd CAMTN NW1 * 4 D4
Sigrist Sq KUTN/CMB KT2 144 A7
Silbury Av MTCM CR4 147 J7
Silbury St IS N1 * 7 G7
Silecroft Rd BXLYHN DA7 117 H7
Silesia Blds HACK E8 74 D6
Silex St STHWK SE1 18 D2
Silk Cl LEE/GVPK SE12 133 K4
Silkfield Rd CDALE/KGS NW9 51 G4
Silkin Ms PECK SE15 111 H6
Silk Ms LBTH SE11 18 A8
Silk Mill Rd OXHEY WD19 21 F6
Silk Mills Pth LEW SE13 133 F2
Silkstream Pde EDGW HA8 * 36 E7
Silkstream Rd EDGW HA8 36 E7
Silk St BARB EC2Y 12 F2
Silsoe Rd WDGN N22 55 F2
Silver Birch Av CHING E4 43 H4
Silver Birch Cl CAT SE6 151 H2
FBAR/BDGN N11 40 A5
THMD SE28 97 G7
Silverbirch Wk HAMP NW3 * 71 K5
Silvercliffe Gdns EBAR EN4 27 J3
Silver Cl KTN/HRWW/WS HA3 34 D6
NWCR SE14 * 112 B6
Silver Crs CHSWK W4 105 J3
Silverdale ENC/FH EN2 28 E3
SYD SE26 150 E3
Silverdale Cl HNWL W7 84 E7
NTHLT UB5 65 K4
SUT SM1 174 D3
Silverdale Dr ELTH/MOT SE9 153 J1
HCH RM12 81 K4
SUN TW16 156 A1
Silverdale Gdns HYS/HAR UB3 101 K1
Silverdale Rd BUSH WD23 21 J4
BXLYHN DA7 137 J1
CHING E4 44 B5
HYS/HAR UB3 101 K1
STMC/STPC BR5 169 H3
Silverdene
NFNCH/WDSPK N12 * 39 F5
Silver Dene PUT/ROE SW15 * 127 F4
Silvergate HOR/WEW KT19 172 E4
Silverhall St ISLW TW7 124 B2
Silverholme Cl
KTN/HRWW/WS HA3 50 A6
Silver La WWKM BR4 180 B1
Silverleigh Rd THHTH CR7 164 A3
Silvermere Dr UED N18 * 43 F4
Silvermere Rd CAT SE6 132 D5
Silvermere Rw SNWD SE25 * 165 H1
Silver Pl SOHO/CST W1F 10 F5
Silver Rd LEW SE13 132 E2
NKENS W10 88 B6
Silver Spring Cl ERITH DA8 117 J5
Silverston Wy STAN HA7 35 J5
Silver St EN EN1 29 K2
UED N18 41 K3
Silverthorne Rd VX/NE SW8 129 G1
Silverthorn Gdns CHING E4 43 J1
Silverton Rd HMSMTH W6 107 G6
Silvertown Wy CAN/RD E16 94 D6
Silvertree La GFD/PVL UB6 84 D2
Silver Wy ROMW/RG RM7 62 D2
Silverwood Cl BECK BR3 151 J6
CROY/NA CR0 179 H7
NTHWD HA6 32 A7
Silvester Rd EDUL SE22 131 G4
Silvester St STHWK SE1 19 G2
Silwood Estate Regeneration
Area BERM/RHTH SE16 112 A4
Silwood St BERM/RHTH SE16 112 A4
Simmil Rd ESH/CLAY KT10 170 E4
Simmons Cl TRDG/WHET N20 27 J7
Simmons Dr BCTR RM8 80 A2
Simmons Ga ESH/CLAY KT10 170 C4
Simmons La CHING E4 44 B1
Simmons Rd
WOOL/PLUM SE18 115 G4
Simmons' Wy
TRDG/WHET N20 39 J1
Simms Cl CAR SM5 175 J1
Simms Gdns EFNCH N2 53 G1
Simms Rd STHWK SE1 111 H3
Simnel Rd LEE/GVPK SE12 134 A6
Simon Cl NTGHL W11 88 D6
Simonds Rd LEY E10 75 J1
Simone Cl BMLY BR1 153 H7
Simons Wk SRTFD E15 76 B4
Simpson Cl CROY/NA CR0 164 D5
WCHMH N21 29 F4
Simpson Dr ACT W3 87 F5
Simpson Rd HSLWW TW4 122 E5
RAIN RM13 81 H5
RCHPK/HAM TW10 143 J3
Simpson's Rd HAYES BR2 167 K2
POP/IOD E14 93 K6
Simpson St BTSEA SW11 128 D1
Simpson Wy SURB KT6 158 D5
Simrose Ct WAND/EARL SW18 127 K4
Sims Cl ROM RM1 63 H3
Sinclair Dr BELMT SM2 175 F7
Sinclair Gdns WKENS W14 107 G1
Sinclair Gv GLDGN NW11 52 B5
Sinclair Rd CHING E4 43 H4
WKENS W14 107 H2
Singapore Rd WEA W13 85 G7
Singer St FSBYE EC1V 7 H8
Singleton Cl CROY/NA CR0 164 D6
HCH RM12 81 H3
TOOT SW17 147 K6
Singleton Rd DAGW RM9 80 B4
Singleton Scarp
NFNCH/WDSPK N12 38 E4
Sinnott Rd WALTH E17 43 F7
Sion Rd TWK TW1 124 C7
Sipson Cl WDR/YW UB7 100 D5
Sipson La WDR/YW UB7 100 E5
Sipson Rd WDR/YW UB7 100 C3
Sipson Wy WDR/YW UB7 100 D6
Sir Abraham Dawes Cots
PUT/ROE SW15 * 127 H3
Sir Alexander Cl ACT W3 87 H7
Sir Cyril Black Wy
WIM/MER SW19 146 D6
Sirdar Rd MTCM CR4 148 A5
NTGHL W11 88 B6
WDGN N22 55 H2
Sir John Kirk Cl CMBW SE5 110 D6
Sir Thomas More Est
CHEL SW3 108 C5
Sirus Rd NTHWD HA6 32 E4
Sise La MANHO EC4N * 13 G5
Siskin Cl BORE WD6 24 C3
BUSH WD23 21 J3
Sisley Rd BARK IG11 78 E7
Sispara Gdns
WAND/EARL SW18 127 J5
Sissinghurst Cl BMLY BR1 152 C4
Sissinghurst Rd CROY/NA CR0 165 H6
Sister Mabels Wy PECK SE15 * 111 H6
Sisters Av BTSEA SW11 128 E3
Sistova Rd BAL SW12 129 G7
Sisulu Pl BRXN/ST SW9 130 B2
Sittingbourne Av EN EN1 29 K5
Sitwell Gv STAN HA7 35 F4
Siverst Cl NTHLT UB5 66 B5
Siviter Wy DAGE RM10 80 D6
Siward Rd HAYES BR2 168 A2
TOOT SW17 147 G2
TOTM N17 41 K7
Sixth Av HYS/HAR UB3 82 D7
MNPK E12 77 K3
NKENS W10 88 C3
Sixth Cross Rd WHTN TW2 142 C2
Skardu Rd CRICK NW2 70 C4
Skeena Hl WAND/EARL SW18 127 H6
Skeffington Rd EHAM E6 77 K7
Skeffington St
WOOL/PLUM SE18 115 H2
Skelbrook St
WAND/EARL SW18 147 F1
Skelgill Rd PUT/ROE SW15 127 J3
Skelley Rd SRTFD E15 76 D6
Skelton Cl HACK E8 * 74 B5
Skelton Rd FSTGT E7 76 E5
Skelton's La LEY E10 57 K6
Skelwith Rd HMSMTH W6 107 F5
Skerne Rd KUTN/CMB KT2 143 K7
Skerne Wk KUTN/CMB KT2 143 K7
Sketchley Gdns
BERM/RHTH SE16 112 A4
Sketty Rd EN EN1 30 B2
Skiers St SRTFD E15 76 C7
Skiffington Cl
BRXS/STRHM SW2 130 B7
Skinner Pl BGVA SW1W * 16 A6
Skinners La BLKFR EC4V 12 F6
HEST TW5 103 G7
Skinner St CLKNW EC1R 6 C9
FSBYE EC1V 6 C8
Skipsey Av EHAM E6 95 K2
Skipton Cl FBAR/BDGN N11 40 A5
Skipton Dr HYS/HAR UB3 101 F2
Skipworth Rd HOM E9 74 E7
Skylines POP/IOD E14 113 F1
Skylines Village
POP/IOD E14 * 113 F1
Sky Peals Rd WFD IG8 44 B6
Skyport Dr WDR/YW UB7 100 A6
Sladebrook Rd
BKHTH/KID SE3 134 C2
Sladedale Rd
WOOL/PLUM SE18 115 K4
Slade Gdns ERITH DA8 118 C7
Slade Green Rd ERITH DA8 118 C7
Sladen Pl CLPT E5 74 D3
Slades Cl ENC/FH EN2 29 G2
Slades Dr CHST BR7 154 C2
ELTH/MOT SE9 154 C3
Slades Gdns ENC/FH EN2 29 G1
Slades Hl ENC/FH EN2 29 G2
Slades Ri ENC/FH EN2 29 G2
The Slade WOOL/PLUM SE18 115 K5
Slade Wk WALW SE17 110 C5
Slade Wy MTCM CR4 148 A7
Slagrove Pl LEW SE13 132 D4
Slaidburn St WBPTN SW10 108 B5
Slaithwaite Rd LEW SE13 133 F3
Slaney Pl HOLWY N7 73 G4
Slaney Rd ROM RM1 63 G4
Slattery Rd FELT TW13 122 B7
Sleaford Gn OXHEY WD19 33 H2
Sleaford St VX/NE SW8 109 H6
Sledmere Ct
EBED/NFELT TW14 121 H7
Slievemore Cl CLAP SW4 129 J2
Slingsby Pl LSQ/SEVD WC2H 11 J6
Slippers Pl BERM/RHTH SE16 111 J2
Sloane Av CHEL SW3 15 K6
Sloane Ct East CHEL SW3 16 A7
Sloane Ct West CHEL SW3 15 M7
Sloane Gdns BGVA SW1W 16 A6
Sloane Sq BGVA SW1W 15 M6
Sloane St KTBR SW1X 15 M4
Sloane Ter KTBR SW1X 15 M5
Sloane Wk CROY/NA CR0 166 C5
Slocum Cl THMD SE28 97 J6
Slough La CDALE/KGS NW9 50 E5
Sly St WCHPL E1 * 92 D5
Smaldon Cl WDR/YW UB7 100 D2
Smallberry Av ISLW TW7 124 A1
Smallbrook Ms BAY/PAD W2 9 G5
Smalley Cl STNW/STAM N16 74 B2
Smallwood Rd TOOT SW17 147 H3
Smarden Cl BELV DA17 117 H4
Smart's Pl NOXST/BSQ WC1A 11 K4
UED N18 42 C4
Smart St BETH E2 93 F2
Smeaton Rd
WAND/EARL SW18 127 K6
WFD IG8 45 K4
Smeaton St WAP E1W 92 D7
Smedley St VX/NE SW8 129 J1
Smeed Rd BOW E3 75 J6
Smiles Pl LEW SE13 133 F1
Smith Cl BERM/RHTH SE16 93 F7
Smithfield St STBT EC1A 12 C3
Smithies Rd ABYW SE2 116 C3
Smith's Ct SOHO/SHAV W1D * 11 G6
Smithson Rd TOTM N17 41 K7
Smith Sq WEST SW1P 17 J4
Smith St BRYLDS KT5 159 G5
CHEL SW3 15 L7
WATW WD18 21 G3
Smith's Yd CROY/NA CR0 177 J2
Smith Ter CHEL SW3 15 L8
Smithwood Cl
WIM/MER SW19 127 H7
Smithy St WCHPL E1 92 E4
Smugglers Wy
WAND/EARL SW18 128 A3
Smyrk's Rd WALW SE17 19 K8
Smyrna Rd KIL/WHAMP NW6 2 A2
Smythe Cl ED N9 42 C2
Smythe St POP/IOD E14 93 K6
Snakes La EBAR EN4 28 B2
Snakes La East WFD IG8 45 G5
Snakes La West WFD IG8 44 E5
Snakey La FELT TW13 140 E3
Snaresbrook Dr STAN HA7 35 K3
Snaresbrook Rd WAN E11 58 C3
Snarsgate St NKENS W10 88 A4
Sneath Av GLDGN NW11 52 D6
Snell's Pk UED N18 42 B5
Sneyd Rd CRICK NW2 70 A4
Snipe Cl ERITH DA8 118 E6
Snowberry Cl SRTFD E15 76 B3
Snowbury Rd FUL/PGN SW6 128 A1
Snowden Dr CDALE/KGS NW9 51 G5
Snowdon Crs HYS/HAR UB3 101 F2
Snowdon Rd HTHAIR TW6 121 F5
Snowdown Cl PGE/AN SE20 150 E7
Snowdrop Cl HPTN TW12 142 A5
Snow Hl STBT EC1A 12 C3
Snowsfields STHWK SE1 19 H1
Snowshill Rd MNPK E12 77 J4
Snowy Fielder Waye
ISLW TW7 124 C1
Soames St PECK SE15 131 G2
Soames Wk NWMAL KT3 145 G7
Soane Cl EA W5 104 E1
Soaphouse La BTFD TW8 105 F6
Soho Sq SOHO/SHAV W1D 11 G4
Soho St SOHO/SHAV W1D 11 G4
Sojourner-Truth Cl HACK E8 74 D5
Solander Gdns WCHPL E1 92 D6
Solar Ct WATW WD18 * 20 D4
Solebay St WCHPL E1 93 G3
Solent Ri PLSTW E13 94 E2
Solent Rd KIL/WHAMP NW6 70 E4
Solna Av PUT/ROE SW15 127 F4
Solna Rd WCHMH N21 29 K7
Solomon Av UED N18 42 C3
Solomon's Pas PECK SE15 131 J3
Solon New Rd CLAP SW4 129 K3
Solon Rd BRXS/STRHM SW2 129 K3
Solway Cl HACK E8 74 B5
HSLWW TW4 122 D2
Solway Rd EDUL SE22 131 H3
WDGN N22 41 H7
Somaford Gv EBAR EN4 27 H5
Somali Rd CRICK NW2 70 D3
Somerby Rd BARK IG11 78 D6
Somercoates Cl EBAR EN4 27 J2
Somerfield Rd FSBYPK N4 73 H1
Somerfield St
BERM/RHTH SE16 112 A4
Somerford Cl PIN HA5 46 E3
Somerford Gv
STNW/STAM N16 74 B3
TOTM N17 42 C6
Somerford St WCHPL E1 * 92 D3
Somerford Wy
BERM/RHTH SE16 112 B1
Somerhill Av BFN/LL DA15 136 C6
Somerhill Rd WELL DA16 136 C1
Somerleyton Rd
BRXN/ST SW9 130 B3
Somersby Gdns REDBR IG4 59 K4
Somers Cl CAMTN NW1 5 G5
Somers Crs BAY/PAD W2 9 J5
Somerset Av CHSGTN KT9 171 K3
RYNPK SW20 160 E1
WELL DA16 136 A4
Somerset Cl CHEAM SM3 174 A2
NWMAL KT3 160 B5
TOTM N17 55 K1
WFD IG8 44 E7
Somerset Gdns HGT N6 54 A6
LEW SE13 132 E1
STRHM/NOR SW16 164 A2
TEDD TW11 142 E4
TOTM N17 * 42 A6
Somerset Rd BAR EN5 27 F4
BTFD TW8 104 D5
CHSWK W4 106 A2
DART DA1 138 E5
HDN NW4 52 A3
HRW HA1 48 C5
KUT/HW KT1 159 G1
STHL UB1 84 A4
TEDD TW11 142 E4
TOTM N17 56 B2
UED N18 42 B4
WALTH E17 57 J5
WEA W13 85 H7
WIM/MER SW19 146 B2
Somerset Sq WKENS W14 * 107 H2
Somerset Waye HEST TW5 102 D5
Somersham Rd BXLYHN DA7 137 F1
Somers Pl BRXS/STRHM SW2 130 A6
Somers Rd BRXS/STRHM SW2 130 A5
WALTH E17 57 H3
Somers Wy BUSH WD23 22 C6
Somerton Av RCH/KEW TW9 125 J2
Somerton Rd CRICK NW2 70 B2
PECK SE15 131 J3
Somertrees Av
LEE/GVPK SE12 153 F1
Somervell Rd
RYLN/HDSTN HA2 65 K4
Somerville Av BARN SW13 107 F5
Somerville Cl BRXN/ST SW9 110 A7
Somerville Rd CHDH RM6 61 J4
DART DA1 139 J5
PGE/AN SE20 151 F6
Sonderburg Rd HOLWY N7 73 F1
Sondes St WALW SE17 19 G9
Songhurst Cl CROY/NA CR0 164 A5
Sonia Cl OXHEY WD19 21 G6
Sonia Gdns HEST TW5 103 F6
NFNCH/WDSPK N12 39 G3
WLSDN NW10 69 H3
Sonning Gdns HPTN TW12 141 J5
Sonning Rd SNWD SE25 165 H5
Soper Cl CHING E4 43 H4
FSTH SE23 132 A7
Sophia Cl HOLWY N7 73 F5
Sophia Rd CAN/RD E16 95 F4
LEY E10 57 K7
Sophia Sq BERM/RHTH SE16 93 G6
Sopwith Av CHSGTN KT9 172 A4
Sopwith Cl KUTN/CMB KT2 144 B4
Sopwith Rd HEST TW5 102 B6
Sopwith Wy KUTN/CMB KT2 144 A7
VX/NE SW8 109 G6
Sorrel Bank CROY/NA CR0 * 179 G7
Sorrel Cl THMD SE28 97 G7
Sorrel Gdns EHAM E6 95 J4
Sorrel La POP/IOD E14 94 B5
Sorrell Cl BRXN/ST SW9 * 130 B1
NWCR SE14 112 B6
Sorrel Wk ROM RM1 63 H2
Sorrento Rd SUT SM1 175 F2
Sotheby Rd HBRY N5 73 J3
Sotheran Cl HACK E8 74 C7
Sotheron Rd WAT WD17 21 G1
Soudan Rd BTSEA SW11 108 E7
Souldern Rd WKENS W14 * 107 G2
Souldern St WATW WD18 21 F4
South Access Rd LEY E10 57 F6
South Africa Rd SHB W12 87 K6
Southall Ct STHL UB1 * 83 K6
Southall La HEST TW5 102 A5
Southall Pl STHWK SE1 19 G2
Southampton Blds
LINN WC2A * 12 A3
Southampton Gdns
MTCM CR4 163 K4
Southampton Ms CAN/RD E16 95 F7
Southampton Pl
NOXST/BSQ WC1A 11 K3
Southampton Rd HAMP NW3 71 K4
Southampton Rd East
HTHAIR TW6 120 C5
Southampton Rd West
HTHAIR TW6 120 C5
Southampton Rw
NOXST/BSQ WC1A 11 K2
RSQ WC1B 11 J2
Southampton St
COVGDN WC2E 11 K6
Southampton Wy CMBW SE5 110 E6
Southam St NKENS W10 88 C3
South Ap NTHWD HA6 32 B2
South Audley St
MYFR/PKLN W1K 10 B7
South Av CAR SM5 176 A6
CHING E4 31 K6
RCH/KEW TW9 * 125 H1
STHL UB1 83 K6
South Avenue Gdns STHL UB1 83 K6
South Bank STHWK SE1 12 B7
SURB KT6 159 F5
Southbank THDIT KT7 158 C6
South Bank Ter SURB KT6 * 159 F5
South Birkbeck Rd WAN E11 76 B2
South Black Lion La
HMSMTH W6 106 D4
South Bolton Gdns
WBPTN SW10 14 D7
Southborough Cl SURB KT6 158 E7
Southborough La HAYES BR2 168 D4
Southborough Rd BMLY BR1 168 D2
HOM E9 74 E7
SURB KT6 159 F7
Southborough Rd (The Lane)
SURB KT6 * 159 F7
South Boundary Rd
MNPK E12 77 K2
Southbourne HAYES BR2 167 K6
Southbourne Av
CDALE/KGS NW9 50 E1
Southbourne Cl PIN HA5 47 J6
Southbourne Crs HDN NW4 52 C3
Southbourne Gdns IL IG1 78 C4
LEE/GVPK SE12 134 A4
RSLP HA4 47 F7
Southbridge Pl CROY/NA CR0 177 J3
Southbridge Rd CROY/NA CR0 177 J3
Southbridge Wy NWDGN UB2 102 D1
Southbrook Rd
LEE/GVPK SE12 133 H5
STRHM/NOR SW16 148 E7
Southbury Av EN EN1 30 C3
RAIN RM13 99 K4
Southbury Rd EN EN1 30 B3
South Carriage Dr KTBR SW1X 15 M1
SKENS SW7 15 J2
Southchurch Rd EHAM E6 95 K1
South Cl BAR EN5 26 D2
BXLYHS DA6 136 E3
DAGE RM10 80 C7
HGT N6 54 B5
PIN HA5 47 K6
WDR/YW UB7 100 C2
WHTN TW2 142 A2
The South Colonnade
POP/IOD E14 93 J7
Southcombe St WKENS W14 107 H3
Southcote Av BRYLDS KT5 159 J6
FELT TW13 140 D1
Southcote Ri RSLP HA4 46 B6
Southcote Rd ARCH N19 72 C3
SNWD SE25 165 J4
WALTH E17 57 F4
South Countess Rd
WALTH E17 57 H2
South Crs CAN/RD E16 94 B3
Southcroft Av WELL DA16 135 K2
WWKM BR4 180 A1
Southcroft Rd TOOT SW17 148 A5
South Cross Rd BARK/HLT IG6 60 C4
South Croxted Rd DUL SE21 149 K2
Southdean Gdns
WIM/MER SW19 146 D1
South Dene MLHL NW7 37 F2
Southdown Av HNWL W7 104 B2
Southdown Crs
GNTH/NBYPK IG2 60 E4
RYLN/HDSTN HA2 48 C7
Southdown Dr RYNPK SW20 146 B6

Southdown Rd CAR SM5 176 A7
EMPK RM11 63 K6
RYNPK SW20 146 B7
Southdown Vls
SEVS/STOTM N15 * 55 H4
South Dr MNPK E12 77 J2
RSLP HA4 46 C7
South Ealing Rd EA W5 104 E1
South Eastern Av ED N9 42 B2
South Eaton Pl BGVA SW1W 16 B5
South Eden Park Rd
BECK BR3 166 E4
South Edwardes Sq KENS W8 107 J2
South End CROY/NA CR0 177 J3
KENS W8 14 D3
Southend Cl ELTH/MOT SE9 135 G5
Southend Crs ELTH/MOT SE9 135 F5
Southend La CAT SE6 151 J3
SYD SE26 151 H3
Southend Rd BECK BR3 151 J7
CLAY IG5 59 J2
EHAM E6 77 K6
South End Rd HAMP NW3 71 J3
RAIN RM13 81 J7
Southend Rd (North Circular)
WALTH E17 44 B7
Southend Rd (North Circular Rd)
SWFD E18 58 E1
South End Rw KENS W8 14 D3
Southern Av
EBED/NFELT TW14 121 K7
SNWD SE25 165 G2
Southern Down FELT TW13 * 122 B7
Southerngate Wy NWCR SE14 112 B6
Southern Gv BOW E3 93 H2
Southern Perimeter Rd
HTHAIR TW6 121 F4
STWL/WRAY TW19 120 C5
Southern Rd EFNCH N2 53 K3
PLSTW E13 95 F1
Southern Rw NKENS W10 88 B3
Southern St IS N1 5 L5
Southern Wy GNWCH SE10 113 H3
ROMW/RG RM7 62 C5
Southerton Rd HMSMTH W6 * 107 F3
South Esk Rd FSTGT E7 77 G5
Southey Rd BRXN/ST SW9 110 B7
SEVS/STOTM N15 56 A4
WIM/MER SW19 146 E6
Southey St PGE/AN SE20 151 F6
Southfield BAR EN5 26 B5
Southfield Gdns TWK TW1 143 F3
Southfield Pk
RYLN/HDSTN HA2 48 B3
Southfield Rd CHSWK W4 106 A1
PEND EN3 30 D5
Southfields E/WMO/HCT KT8 157 K5
HDN NW4 51 K2
Southfields Ms
WAND/EARL SW18 * 127 K5
Southfields Rd
WAND/EARL SW18 127 K5
South Gdns WBLY HA9 * 68 C1
WIM/MER SW19 147 H6
South Gate Av FELT TW13 140 B3
Southgate Gv IS N1 7 H2
Southgate Rd IS N1 7 H2
MNPK E12 77 H2
South Gipsy Rd WELL DA16 136 E2
South Gv HGT N6 54 A7
SEVS/STOTM N15 55 K4
WALTH E17 57 H4
South Hall Dr RAIN RM13 99 K4
South Hl CHST BR7 153 K5
NTHWD HA6 * 32 C7
South Hill Av
RYLN/HDSTN HA2 66 C2
South Hill Gv HRW HA1 66 E3
South Hill Park Gdns
HAMP NW3 71 J3
South Hill Rd HAYES BR2 167 H2
Southholme Cl NRWD SE19 150 A7
Southill La PIN HA5 46 E3
Southill Rd CHST BR7 153 J6
Southill St POP/IOD E14 93 K5
South Island Pl BRXN/ST SW9 110 A6
South Kensington Station Ar
SKENS SW7 15 H5
South Lambeth Pl VX/NE SW8 17 K9
South Lambeth Rd
VX/NE SW8 17 K9
Southland Rd
WOOL/PLUM SE18 116 B5
Southlands Dr
WIM/MER SW19 146 B1
Southlands Gv BMLY BR1 168 D2
Southlands Rd HAYES BR2 168 C3
Southland Wy HSLW TW3 123 J4
South La KUT/HW KT1 158 E2
NWMAL KT3 160 A3
South La West NWMAL KT3 160 A3
South Lodge Av MTCM CR4 163 K3
South Lodge Crs ENC/FH EN2 28 D3
South Lodge Dr
STHGT/OAK N14 28 D3
South Md CDALE/KGS NW9 37 H7
HOR/WEW KT19 173 H6
Southmead Rd
WIM/MER SW19 127 H7
Southmere Dr ABYW SE2 116 D1
South Molton La
MYFR/PKLN W1K 10 C5
South Molton Rd CAN/RD E16 94 E5
South Molton St
MYFR/PKLN W1K 10 C5
Southmont Rd
ESH/CLAY KT10 170 E1
Southmoor Wy HOM E9 75 H5
South Mt TRDG/WHET N20 * 39 G1
South Norwood Hl
SNWD SE25 150 A7
South Oak Rd
STRHM/NOR SW16 149 F3
Southold Ri ELTH/MOT SE9 153 K2
Southolm St BTSEA SW11 109 G7
Southover BMLY BR1 152 E4
NFNCH/WDSPK N12 38 E3
South Pde CHEL SW3 15 H7
CHSWK W4 106 A3
EDGW HA8 * 50 C1
WLGTN SM6 * 176 C5
South Park Crs CAT SE6 133 H7
IL IG1 78 D2
South Park Dr
GDMY/SEVK IG3 78 E4
South Park Gv NWMAL KT3 159 K3
South Park Hill Rd
SAND/SEL CR2 177 K4
South Park Ms FUL/PGN SW6 128 A2
South Park Rd IL IG1 78 D3
WIM/MER SW19 146 E5
South Park Ter IL IG1 78 D2
South Park Wy RSLP HA4 65 G5
South Pl BRYLDS KT5 159 G6
LVPST EC2M 13 H3
PEND EN3 30 E4
South Place Ms LVPST EC2M 13 H3
Southport Rd
WOOL/PLUM SE18 115 J3
Southridge Pl RYNPK SW20 146 B6
South Ri BAY/PAD W2 * 9 K6
CAR SM5 175 J7
South Rd CHDH RM6 61 J4
EA W5 104 E3
ED N9 30 C7
EDGW HA8 36 D7
ERITH DA8 118 C5
FELT TW13 141 H4
FSTH SE23 151 F1
HPTN TW12 141 J5
STHL UB1 83 K7
WDR/YW UB7 100 D2
WHTN TW2 142 D2
WIM/MER SW19 147 H5
South Rw BKHTH/KID SE3 133 K1
Southsea Av WATW WD18 20 E3
Southsea Rd KUT/HW KT1 159 F3
South Sea St
BERM/RHTH SE16 112 C2
South Side HMSMTH W6 106 C2
SEVS/STOTM N15 * 56 B3
Southside Common
WIM/MER SW19 146 B5
Southspring BFN/LL DA15 135 J6
South Sq GINN WC1R 12 A3
GLDGN NW11 52 E5
South St BMLY BR1 167 K1
EMPK RM11 63 J5
ISLW TW7 124 B2
MYFR/PKLN W1K 10 B8
PEND EN3 31 F4
RAIN RM13 98 E1
ROM RM1 63 G5
South Tenter St WCHPL E1 13 M6
South Ter SKENS SW7 15 J5
SURB KT6 159 F5
WDGN N22 54 E1
South V HRW HA1 66 E3
NRWD SE19 150 A5
Southvale Rd BKHTH/KID SE3 133 H1
South Vale Rd SURB KT6 172 A1
South Vw BMLY BR1 168 B1
Southview Av WLSDN NW10 69 H4
South View Cl BXLY DA5 137 G5
Southview Cl TOOT SW17 148 A4
South View Ct NRWD SE19 * 149 J6
South View Crs
GNTH/NBYPK IG2 60 B5
Southview Dr SWFD E18 59 F2
Southview Gdns WLGTN SM6 176 C7
Southview Rd BMLY BR1 152 B3
South View Rd
CEND/HSY/T N8 54 D2
PIN HA5 33 F5
Southviews SAND/SEL CR2 179 F7
South Vls CAMTN NW1 72 D5
Southville VX/NE SW8 109 J7
Southville Cl
EBED/NFELT TW14 121 H6
HOR/WEW KT19 173 F7
Southville Crs
EBED/NFELT TW14 121 H7
Southville Rd
EBED/NFELT TW14 121 H7
THDIT KT7 158 B6
South Wk WWKM BR4 180 C2
Southwark Br CANST EC4R 12 F7
Southwark Bridge Rd
STHWK SE1 18 D3
Southwark Park Est
BERM/RHTH SE16 * 111 J3
Southwark Park Rd
BERM/RHTH SE16 19 M5
Southwark Pl BMLY BR1 168 E2
Southwark St STHWK SE1 12 D8
Southwater Cl BECK BR3 151 K6
POP/IOD E14 93 H5
South Wy CROY/NA CR0 179 G2
ED N9 42 E1
FBAR/BDGN N11 40 C5
RYLN/HDSTN HA2 48 A3
WBLY HA9 68 C4
Southway GLDGN NW11 53 F5
HAYES BR2 167 K6
RYNPK SW20 161 G3
TRDG/WHET N20 38 E1
WLGTN SM6 176 C3
Southway Cl SHB W12 106 E1
Southwell Av NTHLT UB5 66 A5
Southwell Gdns SKENS SW7 14 E5
Southwell Grove Rd WAN E11 76 C1
Southwell Rd CMBW SE5 130 D2
CROY/NA CR0 164 B5
KTN/HRWW/WS HA3 49 K5
South Western Rd TWK TW1 124 B5
South West India Dock Entrance
POP/IOD E14 113 F1
Southwest Rd WAN E11 58 B7
South Wharf Rd BAY/PAD W2 9 G4
Southwick Ms BAY/PAD W2 9 H4
Southwick Pl BAY/PAD W2 9 J5
Southwick St BAY/PAD W2 9 J4
Southwick Yd BAY/PAD W2 * 9 K5
Southwold Dr BARK IG11 79 G4
Southwold Rd BXLY DA5 137 J5
CLPT E5 74 D1
Southwood Av HGT N6 54 B6
KUTN/CMB KT2 144 E7
Southwood Cl BMLY BR1 168 E3
WPK KT4 161 G7
Southwood Dr BRYLDS KT5 159 K6
South Woodford SWFD E18 58 E1
Southwood Gdns
ESH/CLAY KT10 171 G2
GNTH/NBYPK IG2 60 B3
Southwood La HGT N6 54 A6
Southwood Lawn Rd HGT N6 54 A6
Southwood Pk HGT N6 * 54 A6
Southwood Rd ELTH/MOT SE9 154 B1
THMD SE28 97 H7
South Worple Wy
MORT/ESHN SW14 126 A2
Southy Ms CAN/RD E16 94 E7
Sovereign Cl EA W5 85 J4
RSLP HA4 46 C7
WAP E1W 92 D6
Sovereign Ct E/WMO/HCT KT8 156 E3
Sovereign Crs
BERM/RHTH SE16 93 G6
Sovereign Gv ALP/SUD HA0 67 K2
Sovereign Ms BETH E2 * 7 L5
EBAR EN4 27 K2
Sovereign Pk WLSDN NW10 * 86 D3
Sovereign Pl HRW HA1 49 F4
Sovereign Rd BARK IG11 97 J2
Sowerby Cl ELTH/MOT SE9 134 E4
Sowrey Av RAIN RM13 81 H5
Space Waye
EBED/NFELT TW14 122 A4
Spafield St CLKNW EC1R 6 A9
Spa Green Est CLKNW EC1R * 6 B7
Spa Hl NRWD SE19 149 K7
Spalding Cl EDGW HA8 37 G6
Spalding Rd HDN NW4 52 A5
TOOT SW17 148 B4
Spanby Rd BOW E3 93 J3
Spaniards Cl GLDGN NW11 53 G7
Spaniards End HAMP NW3 53 G7
Spaniards Rd HAMP NW3 71 G1
Spanish Pl MHST W1U * 10 B4
Spanish Rd WAND/EARL SW18 128 B4
Sparkbridge Rd HRW HA1 48 E3
Sparkes Cl HAYES BR2 168 A3
Sparke Ter CAN/RD E16 * 94 D5
Sparkford Gdns
FBAR/BDGN N11 40 A4
Sparks Cl ACT W3 87 F5
BCTR RM8 79 K1
HPTN TW12 141 J5
Spa Rd BERM/RHTH SE16 19 L4
Sparrow Cl HPTN TW12 141 J5
Sparrow Dr STMC/STPC BR5 169 H7
Sparrow Farm Dr
EBED/NFELT TW14 122 B6
Sparrow Farm Rd EW KT17 173 J3
Sparrow Gn DAGE RM10 80 D2
Sparrows Herne BUSH WD23 22 B6
Sparrows La ELTH/MOT SE9 135 H6
Sparrows Wy BUSH WD23 * 22 C6
Sparrows Wick BUSH WD23 * 22 C7
Sparsholt Rd ARCH N19 55 F7
BARK IG11 78 E7
Spartan Cl WLGTN SM6 176 E6
Sparta St GNWCH SE10 113 F7
Speakers Ct CROY/NA CR0 * 164 E7
Spearman St
WOOL/PLUM SE18 * 115 F5
Spear Ms ECT SW5 14 B6
Spears Rd ARCH N19 54 E7
Speart La HEST TW5 102 D6
Spectrum Pl WALW SE17 19 G8
Spedan Cl HAMP NW3 71 F2
Speedwell St DEPT SE8 112 D6
Speedy Pl STPAN WC1H 5 J8
Speer Rd THDIT KT7 158 A5
Speirs Cl NWMAL KT3 160 C5
Spekehill ELTH/MOT SE9 153 K2
Speke Rd THHTH CR7 164 E1
Speldhurst Cl HAYES BR2 167 J4
Speldhurst Rd CHSWK W4 106 A2
HOM E9 75 F6
Spellbrook Wk IS N1 * 6 F3
Spelman St WCHPL E1 92 C4
Spelthorne Gv SUN TW16 140 D6
Spelthorne La ASHF TW15 140 A6
Spence Cl BERM/RHTH SE16 112 C1
Spencer Av PLMGR N13 41 F5
YEAD UB4 82 E4
Spencer Cl FNCH N3 52 D1
WFD IG8 45 G4
WLSDN NW10 86 B2
Spencer Dr EFNCH N2 53 G5
Spencer Gdns
MORT/ESHN SW14 125 K4
Spencer Hl WIM/MER SW19 146 C5
Spencer Hill Rd
WIM/MER SW19 146 C6
Spencer House SURB KT6 * 159 F4
Spencer Ms CLAP SW4 109 K7
HMSMTH W6 107 H5
Spencer Pk WAND/EARL SW18 128 C4
Spencer Pl CROY/NA CR0 164 E6
IS N1 6 C1
WEST SW1P 16 F4
Spencer Ri KTTN NW5 72 B3
Spencer Rd ACT W3 86 E7
ALP/SUD HA0 67 J1
BMLY BR1 152 D6
BTSEA SW11 128 C3
CEND/HSY/T N8 55 F4
CHSWK W4 105 K6
E/WMO/HCT KT8 157 H3
EHAM E6 77 H7
FBAR/BDGN N11 40 B3
GDMY/SEVK IG3 61 F7
ISLW TW7 103 J7
KTN/HRWW/WS HA3 48 E1
MTCM CR4 162 E6
RAIN RM13 99 F2
RYNPK SW20 145 K7
SAND/SEL CR2 178 A4
TOTM N17 42 C7
WALTH E17 58 A1
WHTN TW2 142 E2
Spencer St FSBYE EC1V 6 C8
NWDGN UB2 102 C2
Spencer Wk PUT/ROE SW15 127 G3
Spencer Wy WCHPL E1 92 D5
Spenser Gv STNW/STAM N16 74 A3
Spenser Ms DUL SE21 130 E7
Spenser Rd HNHL SE24 130 C4
Spenser St WESTW SW1E 16 F3
Spensley Wk STNW/STAM N16 73 K2
Speranza St
WOOL/PLUM SE18 116 A4
Sperling Rd TOTM N17 56 B1
Spert St POP/IOD E14 93 G6
Speyside STHGT/OAK N14 28 C5
Spey St POP/IOD E14 94 A4
Spezia Rd WLSDN NW10 87 J1
Spicer Cl BRXN/ST SW9 130 C1
WOT/HER KT12 156 B5
Spices Yd CROY/NA CR0 177 J3
Spielman Rd DART DA1 139 J3
Spigurnell Rd TOTM N17 41 K7
Spikes Bridge Rd STHL UB1 83 J5
Spindle Cl WOOL/PLUM SE18 114 D2
Spindlewood Gdns
CROY/NA CR0 178 A3
Spindrift Av POP/IOD E14 112 E3
Spinel Cl WOOL/PLUM SE18 116 A4
Spinnaker Cl BARK IG11 97 H2
Spinnells Rd RYLN/HDSTN HA2 47 K7
Spinney Cl BECK BR3 166 E3
NWMAL KT3 160 B4
RAIN RM13 99 G1
WPK KT4 173 H2
Spinney Dr EBED/NFELT TW14 121 F6
Spinney Gdns DAGW RM9 80 A4
ESH/CLAY KT10 170 B2
NRWD SE19 150 B4
Spinney Oak BMLY BR1 168 D1
The Spinneys BMLY BR1 168 E1
The Spinney ALP/SUD HA0 67 F2
BAR EN5 27 F1
BARN SW13 * 106 E5
CHEAM SM3 174 A3
NFNCH/WDSPK N12 * 39 G6
STAN HA7 36 A3
STRHM/NOR SW16 148 C2
SUN TW16 140 E7
WCHMH N21 29 G6
Spirit Quay WAP E1W 92 C7
Spital Sq WCHPL E1 13 K2
Spital St DART DA1 139 G5
WCHPL E1 92 C4
Spital Yd WCHPL E1 * 13 K2
Spitfire Est HEST TW5 * 102 B4
Spitfire House
WOOL/PLUM SE18 * 114 D6
Spitfire Rd WLGTN SM6 177 F6
Spitfire Wy HEST TW5 102 B4
Spode Wk KIL/WHAMP NW6 * 71 F4
Spondon Rd SEVS/STOTM N15 56 C3
Spoonbill Wy YEAD UB4 83 H4
Spooner Wk WLGTN SM6 176 D4
Sportsbank St CAT SE6 133 F6
Sportsman Pl BETH E2 74 C7
Spottons Gv TOTM N17 41 J7
Spout Hl CROY/NA CR0 179 J4
Spratt Hall Rd WAN E11 58 E5
Spray St WOOL/PLUM SE18 115 G3
Spreighton Rd
E/WMO/HCT KT8 157 G3
Sprimont Pl CHEL SW3 15 L7
Springall St PECK SE15 111 J6
Springbank WCHMH N21 29 F5
Springbank Rd LEW SE13 133 H5
Springbank Wk CAMTN NW1 5 G2
Springbourne Ct BECK BR3 152 A7
Spring Bridge Rd EA W5 85 K6
Spring Cl BAR EN5 26 B4
BCTR RM8 61 K6
BORE WD6 24 C1
Springclose La CHEAM SM3 174 C5
Spring Cnr FELT TW13 * 140 E2
Spring Cots SURB KT6 * 158 E4
Springcroft Av EFNCH N2 53 K2
Spring Crofts BUSH WD23 22 A4
Springdale Rd
STNW/STAM N16 73 K3
Spring Dr PIN HA5 46 E5
Springfield BUSH WD23 22 D7
CLPT E5 56 D7
Springfield Av HPTN TW12 142 B5
MUSWH N10 54 C2
RYNPK SW20 161 J2
Springfield Cl
NFNCH/WDSPK N12 39 F4
STAN HA7 35 G2
Springfield Dr
GNTH/NBYPK IG2 60 C4
Springfield Gdns BMLY BR1 168 E3
CDALE/KGS NW9 51 F4
CLPT E5 56 D7
RSLP HA4 47 F7
WFD IG8 45 G6
WWKM BR4 179 K1
Springfield Gv CHARL SE7 114 B5
SUN TW16 140 E7
Springfield La
KIL/WHAMP NW6 2 B4
Springfield Mt
CDALE/KGS NW9 51 G4
Springfield Parade Ms
PLMGR N13 41 G3
Springfield Pl NWMAL KT3 159 K3
Springfield Ri SYD SE26 150 D2
Springfield Rd BMLY BR1 168 E3
BXLYHN DA7 137 J2
EHAM E6 77 K6
FBAR/BDGN N11 40 C4
HNWL W7 84 E7
HRW HA1 48 E5
KUT/HW KT1 159 F3
SEVS/STOTM N15 56 C3
SRTFD E15 * 94 C2
STJWD NW8 2 E4
SYD SE26 150 D4
TEDD TW11 143 G4
THHTH CR7 149 J7
WALTH E17 57 H5
WELL DA16 136 C2
WHTN TW2 123 F7
WIM/MER SW19 146 D4
WLGTN SM6 176 B4
YEAD UB4 83 G7
Springfield Wk
KIL/WHAMP NW6 2 C4
Spring Gdns E/WMO/HCT KT8 157 H4
HBRY N5 73 J4
HCH RM12 81 K3
ROMW/RG RM7 62 E4
WFD IG8 45 G6
WHALL SW1A 11 J8
WLGTN SM6 176 C4
Spring Gv CHSWK W4 105 H4
HPTN TW12 142 B7
MTCM CR4 148 A7
Spring Grove Crs HSLW TW3 103 H7
Spring Grove Rd HSLW TW3 103 H7
RCHPK/HAM TW10 125 G4
Springhead Rd ERITH DA8 118 C5
Spring Hl CLPT E5 56 C6
SYD SE26 150 E3
Springhill Cl CMBW SE5 130 E2
Springhurst Cl CROY/NA CR0 179 H3
Spring Lake STAN HA7 35 H3
Spring La CLPT E5 56 D7
MUSWH N10 54 A2
SNWD SE25 165 J5
Spring Ms MHST W1U * 9 M2
Spring Park Av CROY/NA CR0 179 F1
Springpark Dr BECK BR3 167 F2
FSBYPK N4 55 J7
Spring Park Rd CROY/NA CR0 179 F1
Spring Pl BARK IG11 96 C1
KTTN NW5 72 A4
Springpond Rd DAGW RM9 80 A4
Springrice Rd LEW SE13 133 F5
Spring Rd FELT TW13 140 D2
Spring Shaw Rd
STMC/STPC BR5 155 G7
Spring St BAY/PAD W2 9 G5
EW KT17 173 H7
Spring Tide Cl PECK SE15 * 111 H7
Spring V BXLYHN DA7 137 J3
Springvale Av BTFD TW8 104 E4
Spring V North DART DA1 139 G6
Spring V South DART DA1 * 139 G6
Springvale Ter WKENS W14 107 G2
Spring Villa Rd EDGW HA8 36 C6
Spring Vls WEA W13 * 85 H7
Spring Wk WCHPL E1 92 C4
Springwater Cl
WOOL/PLUM SE18 * 115 F7
Springwell Av WLSDN NW10 69 H7
Springwell Rd HEST TW5 102 C7
STRHM/NOR SW16 149 F3
Springwood Cl BOW E3 93 J1
Springwood Crs EDGW HA8 36 E1
Springwood Wy ROM RM1 63 J4
Sprowston Ms FSTGT E7 76 E4
Sprowston Rd FSTGT E7 76 E4
Sprucedale Gdns
CROY/NA CR0 179 F3
WLGTN SM6 176 E7
Spruce Hills Rd WALTH E17 57 K1
Sprules Rd BROCKY SE4 132 B1
Spurfield E/WMO/HCT KT8 157 G2
Spurgeon Av NRWD SE19 149 K7
Spurgeon Rd NRWD SE19 149 K6
Spurgeon St STHWK SE1 19 G4
Spurling Rd DAGW RM9 80 B5
EDUL SE22 * 131 G3
Spur Rd BARK IG11 96 C2
EBED/NFELT TW14 122 A4
EDGW HA8 36 A3
ISLW TW7 104 B6
SEVS/STOTM N15 * 55 K3
STHWK SE1 18 A1
WHALL SW1A 16 E2
Spurstowe Rd HACK E8 74 D5
Spurstowe Ter HACK E8 74 C4
The Square CAR SM5 176 A4
HMSMTH W6 107 F4
IL IG1 60 A6
RCH/KEW TW9 125 F4
STKPK UB11 82 B7
WFD IG8 44 E4
Squarey St TOOT SW17 147 G2
Squire Gdns STJWD NW8 3 G8
Squires Ct WIM/MER SW19 146 E3
Squires La FNCH N3 39 F7
Squire's Mt HAMP NW3 71 H2
Squires Wk ASHF TW15 140 B6
Squires Wood Dr CHST BR7 * 153 K6
Squirrel Cl HSLWW TW4 122 B2
Squirrel Ms WEA W13 * 85 G6
Squirrels Cl
NFNCH/WDSPK N12 39 G3
Squirrels Gn WPK KT4 173 H1
Squirrel's Heath Av GPK RM2 63 K2
The Squirrels BUSH WD23 22 D5
LEW SE13 133 G2
PIN HA5 47 K2
Squirries St BETH E2 92 C2
Stable Cl KUTN/CMB KT2 144 B5
NTHLT UB5 84 A1
Stable Ms TWK TW1 124 A7
WNWD SE27 149 J4
Stables Wy LBTH SE11 18 A7
Stable Wk EFNCH N2 39 H7
IS N1 5 K5
Stable Wy NKENS W10 88 A5
Stable Yard Rd WHALL SW1A 10 F9
Stacey Av UED N18 42 E3
Stacey Cl LEY E10 58 B4
Stacey St HOLWY N7 73 G2
LSQ/SEVD WC2H 11 H5
Stackhouse St KTBR SW1X 15 L3
Stacy Pth CMBW SE5 * 111 F6
Staddon Cl BECK BR3 166 B3
Staddon Ct BECK BR3 166 B3
Stadium Rd HDN NW4 51 K6
WOOL/PLUM SE18 114 E6
Stadium St WBPTN SW10 108 B6
Stadium Wy DART DA1 138 B5
WATW WD18 21 F4
WBLY HA9 68 B3
Staffa Rd LEY E10 57 G7
Stafford Av CLAY IG5 60 A1
Stafford Cl CHEAM SM3 174 C5
KIL/WHAMP NW6 2 A8
STHGT/OAK N14 28 C4
WALTH E17 57 H5
Stafford Cross CROY/NA CR0 177 F4
Stafford Gdns CROY/NA CR0 177 F4
Stafford Pl RCHPK/HAM TW10 125 G6
WESTW SW1E 16 E3
Stafford Rd BOW E3 93 H1
CROY/NA CR0 177 G3
FSTGT E7 77 G6
KIL/WHAMP NW6 2 A7
KTN/HRWW/WS HA3 34 C6
NWMAL KT3 159 K2
RSLP HA4 64 D3
SCUP DA14 154 E3
WLGTN SM6 176 C5
Staffordshire St PECK SE15 111 H7
Stafford St CONDST W1S 10 E8
Stafford Ter KENS W8 14 A3
Stag Cl EDGW HA8 50 D1
Stag La BKHH IG9 45 F1
CDALE/KGS NW9 50 E2
EDGW HA8 50 D1
PUT/ROE SW15 145 H2
Stag Pl WESTW SW1E 16 E3
Stags Wy ISLW TW7 104 A5
Stainbank Rd MTCM CR4 163 G2
Stainby Cl WDR/YW UB7 100 B2
Stainby Rd TOTM N17 56 B2
Stainer St STHWK SE1 13 H9
Staines Av CHEAM SM3 174 B1
Staines Rd EBED/NFELT TW14 120 E7
EBED/NFELT TW14 122 C4
IL IG1 78 D3
WHTN TW2 142 C2
Staines Rd East SUN TW16 140 E6
Staines Rd West ASHF TW15 140 A6
Stainford Cl ASHF TW15 140 B4
Stainforth Rd
GNTH/NBYPK IG2 60 D6
WALTH E17 57 J3
Staining La CITYW EC2V 12 F4
Stainmore Cl CHST BR7 154 D7
Stainsbury St BETH E2 92 E1
Stainsby Pl POP/IOD E14 * 93 J5
Stainsby Rd POP/IOD E14 93 J5
Stainton Rd CAT SE6 133 G6
Stalbridge St CAMTN NW1 9 K2
Stalham St BERM/RHTH SE16 111 J2
Stambourne Wy NRWD SE19 150 A6
WWKM BR4 180 A2
Stambourne Woodland Wk
NRWD SE19 150 A6
Stamford Brook Av
HMSMTH W6 106 C2
Stamford Brook Gdns
HMSMTH W6 106 C2
Stamford Brook Rd
HMSMTH W6 106 C2
Stamford Cl HAMP NW3 * 71 G2
KTN/HRWW/WS HA3 34 E6
SEVS/STOTM N15 56 C3
STHL UB1 84 A6
Stamford Cots WBPTN SW10 * 108 A6
Stamford Dr HAYES BR2 167 J3
Stamford Gdns DAGW RM9 79 J6
Stamford Gv East
STNW/STAM N16 56 C7
Stamford Gv West
STNW/STAM N16 56 C7
Stamford Hl STNW/STAM N16 56 B7
Stamford Rd DAGW RM9 79 H6

EHAM E6 77 J7
IS N1 7 K1
SEVS/STOTM N15 56 C4
WAT WD17 21 F1
Stamford St STHWK SE1 12 A8
Stamp Pl BETH E2 7 L6
Stanborough Cl HPTN TW12 141 K5
Stanborough Pas HACK E8 74 B5
Stanborough Rd HSLW TW3 123 J2
Stanbridge Pl WCHMH N21 41 H1
Stanbridge Rd PUT/ROE SW15 127 F2
Stanbrook Rd ABYW SE2 116 C1
Stanbury Ct HAMP NW3 71 K5
Stanbury Rd PECK SE15 111 J7
Stancroft CDALE/KGS NW9 51 G5
Standale Gv RSLP HA4 46 A4
Standard Pl SDTCH EC2A 7 K8
Standard Rd BELV DA17 117 H4
BXLYHS DA6 137 F3
HSLW TW4 122 D2
WLSDN NW10 86 E3
Standen Rd WAND/EARL SW18 127 K6
Standfield Rd DAGE RM10 80 C4
Standish Rd HMSMTH W6 106 D3
Stane Cl WIM/MER SW19 147 F6
Stane Gv VX/NE SW8 129 J1
Stane Wy WOOL/PLUM SE18 114 C6
Stanford Cl HPTN TW12 141 K5
ROMW/RG RM7 62 D5
RSLP HA4 46 A5
WFD IG8 45 J4
Stanford Pl WALW SE17 19 J6
Stanford Rd FBAR/BDGN N11 39 K4
KENS W8 14 D4
STRHM/NOR SW16 163 K1
Stanford St PIM SW1V 17 G6
Stanford Wy
STRHM/NOR SW16 163 J1
Stangate Crs BORE WD6 25 G4
Stangate Gdns STAN HA7 35 H3
Stanger Rd SNWD SE25 165 H3
Stanham Pl DART DA1 138 D3
Stanham Rd DART DA1 139 F4
Stanhope Av FNCH N3 52 D2
HAYES BR2 167 K7
KTN/HRWW/WS HA3 34 D7
Stanhope Cl
BERM/RHTH SE16 * 112 A1
Stanhope Gdns BCTR RM8 80 B2
FSBYPK N4 55 H5
HGT N6 54 B5
IL IG1 59 K7
MLHL NW7 37 H4
SKENS SW7 14 F5
Stanhope Ga BAY/PAD W2 9 L6
MYFR/PKLN W1K 10 B9
Stanhope Gv BECK BR3 166 C4
Stanhope Ms East SKENS SW7 14 F5
Stanhope Ms South
SKENS SW7 14 F6
Stanhope Ms West
SKENS SW7 14 F5
Stanhope Pde CAMTN NW1 4 D7
Stanhope Park Rd
GFD/PVL UB6 84 C3
Stanhope Pl BAY/PAD W2 9 L5
Stanhope Rd BAR EN5 26 B5
BCTR RM8 80 B1
BFN/LL DA15 155 G3
BXLYHN DA7 137 F1
CAR SM5 176 A6
CROY/NA CR0 178 A2
GFD/PVL UB6 84 C4
HGT N6 54 C5
NFNCH/WDSPK N12 39 G4
RAIN RM13 99 J1
WALTH E17 57 K4
Stanhope Rw
MYFR/PICC W1J * 10 C9
Stanhope St CAMTN NW1 4 E7
Stanhope Ter BAY/PAD W2 9 H6
WHTN TW2 * 124 A6
Stanier Cl WKENS W14 107 J4
Stanlake Rd SHB W12 88 A7
Stanlake Vls SHB W12 88 A7
Stanley Av ALP/SUD HA0 68 A6
BARK IG11 97 F2
BCTR RM8 62 B7
BECK BR3 167 F2
GFD/PVL UB6 66 C7
GPK RM2 63 J3
NWMAL KT3 160 D4
Stanley Cl ALP/SUD HA0 68 A6
ELTH/MOT SE9 135 H7
GPK RM2 63 J3
VX/NE SW8 110 A5
Stanley Crs NTGHL W11 88 D6
Stanleycroft Cl ISLW TW7 103 K7
Stanley Gdns ACT W3 106 B1
CRICK NW2 70 A4
MTCM CR4 * 148 A5
NTGHL W11 88 D6
WLGTN SM6 176 C5
Stanley Gardens Rd
TEDD TW11 142 E4
Stanley Gv CROY/NA CR0 164 B5
VX/NE SW8 129 F1
Stanley Park Dr ALP/SUD HA0 68 B6
Stanley Park Rd CAR SM5 175 K6
WLGTN SM6 176 B6
Stanley Pas KCROSS N1C 5 H6
Stanley Rd ACT W3 105 J2
BELMT SM2 175 F5
CAR SM5 175 K7
CROY/NA CR0 164 B6
ED N9 30 B7
EFNCH N2 53 H3
EN EN1 30 A2
FBAR/BDGN N11 40 D5
HAYES BR2 168 B2
HSLW TW3 123 H3
IL IG1 78 D1
MNPK E12 77 J4
MORT/ESHN SW14 125 J3
MRDN SM4 161 K3
MTCM CR4 148 A6
MUSWH N10 40 B6
NTHWD HA6 32 E7
RYLN/HDSTN HA2 66 C1
SCUP DA14 155 G2
SEVS/STOTM N15 55 H3
STHL UB1 83 J6
SWFD E18 44 D7
TEDD TW11 142 E4
WALTH E17 57 K5
WAT WD17 21 G2
WBLY HA9 68 B5
WHTN TW2 142 D2
WIM/MER SW19 146 E6
Stanley Rd North RAIN RM13 81 G7
Stanley Rd South RAIN RM13 99 H1
Stanley Sq CAR SM5 175 K7
Stanley St DEPT SE8 112 C6
Stanley Ter ARCH N19 * 72 E1
BXLYHS DA6 * 137 H3
Stanmer St BTSEA SW11 108 D7
Stanmore Gdns
RCH/KEW TW9 125 G2
SUT SM1 175 G2
Stanmore Hl STAN HA7 35 H3
Stanmore Rd BELV DA17 117 K3
RCH/KEW TW9 125 G2
SEVS/STOTM N15 55 H3
WAN E11 58 D7
Stanmore St IS N1 5 L3
Stanmore Ter BECK BR3 166 D1
Stannard Ms HACK E8 * 74 C5
Stannard Rd HACK E8 74 C5
Stannary Pl LBTH SE11 18 B8
Stannary St LBTH SE11 18 B9
Stannet Wy WLGTN SM6 176 C3
Stansbury Sq NKENS W10 88 C2
Stansfeld Rd CAN/RD E16 95 H5
Stansfield Rd BRXN/ST SW9 130 A2
HSLWW TW4 122 A1
Stansgate Rd DAGE RM10 80 C1
Stanstead Cl HAYES BR2 167 J4
Stanstead Gv CAT SE6 132 C7
Stanstead Rd FSTH SE23 132 A7
WAN E11 59 F4
Stansted Cl HCH RM12 81 K5
Stansted Crs BXLY DA5 136 E7
Stanswood Gdns CMBW SE5 111 F6
Stanthorpe Cl
STRHM/NOR SW16 * 148 E4
Stanthorpe Rd
STRHM/NOR SW16 148 E4
Stanton Av TEDD TW11 142 E5
Stanton Cl HOR/WEW KT19 172 D4
WPK KT4 161 G7
Stanton Rd BARN SW13 126 C1
CROY/NA CR0 164 D6
RYNPK SW20 161 G1
Stanton St PECK SE15 * 111 H7
Stanton Wy SYD SE26 151 H3
Stanway Gdns ACT W3 86 C7
EDGW HA8 36 E5
Stanway St IS N1 7 K5
Stanwell Cl STWL/WRAY TW19 120 A5
Stanwell Gdns
STWL/WRAY TW19 120 A5
Stanwell Rd
EBED/NFELT TW14 121 F6
HTHAIR TW6 120 E6
Stanwick Rd WKENS W14 107 J3
Stanworth St STHWK SE1 19 L2
Stapenhill Rd ALP/SUD HA0 67 H2
Staplefield Cl
BRXS/STRHM SW2 * 129 K7
PIN HA5 33 J6
Stapleford Av
GNTH/NBYPK IG2 60 E4
Stapleford Cl CHING E4 44 A2
KUT/HW KT1 159 H1
WIM/MER SW19 127 H6
Stapleford Rd ALP/SUD HA0 67 K6
Stapleford Wy BARK IG11 97 H2
Staplehurst Rd CAR SM5 175 J6
LEW SE13 133 G4
Staple Inn HHOL WC1V 12 A3
Staples Cl BERM/RHTH SE16 93 G7
Staple St STHWK SE1 19 H2
Stapleton Crs RAIN RM13 81 J5
Stapleton Gdns CROY/NA CR0 177 G4
Stapleton Hall Rd FSBYPK N4 55 F6
Stapleton Rd BXLYHN DA7 117 G6
TOOT SW17 148 A2
Stapleton Vls
STNW/STAM N16 * 74 A3
Stapley Rd BELV DA17 117 H4
Stapylton Rd BAR EN5 26 C2
Starboard Wy POP/IOD E14 112 D2
Starbuck Cl ELTH/MOT SE9 135 F6
Starch House La
BARK/HLT IG6 60 D1
Star Cl PEND EN3 30 E5
Starcross St CAMTN NW1 4 F8
Starfield Rd SHB W12 106 D1
Star & Garter Hl
RCHPK/HAM TW10 125 F7
Star Hl DART DA1 138 B4
Star La CAN/RD E16 94 C3
Starling Cl PIN HA5 47 G2
Starling Rd CROY/NA CR0 166 B5
Starmans Cl DAGW RM9 80 A7
Star Pl WAP E1W 13 M7
Star Rd HGDN/ICK UB10 82 A3
ISLW TW7 123 J1
WKENS W14 107 J5
Star St BAY/PAD W2 9 H4
Starveall Cl WDR/YW UB7 100 C2
Star Yd LINN WC2A 12 A4
Staten Gdns TWK TW1 124 A7
Statham Gv STNW/STAM N16 73 K2
UED N18 42 A4
Station Ap ALP/SUD HA0 67 H5
BAR EN5 27 G3
BECK BR3 151 G7
BELMT SM2 174 C6
BKHH IG9 * 45 H3
BKHTH/KID SE3 134 A2
BXLY DA5 137 H6
BXLYHN DA7 137 F1
CAMTN NW1 * 10 A1
CAR SM5 175 K3
CHING E4 * 44 B5
CHST BR7 153 J5
CROY/NA CR0 * 177 K1
DART DA1 139 H5
ESH/CLAY KT10 171 F2
FBAR/BDGN N11 40 B4
FSTGT E7 77 F3
FUL/PGN SW6 * 127 H2
GFD/PVL UB6 66 C6
GLDGN NW11 * 52 B6
HAYES BR2 167 K7
HOR/WEW KT19 173 H4
HPTN TW12 142 A7
HYS/HAR UB3 101 J2
KUT/HW KT1 159 H1
NFNCH/WDSPK N12 39 F3
NTHWD HA6 32 C6
OXHEY WD19 33 H2
PIN HA5 47 J2
RCH/KEW TW9 105 H7
RSLP HA4 46 C7
RSLP HA4 65 F4
SAND/SEL CR2 177 K7
STRHM/NOR SW16 148 D4
SUN TW16 140 E7
SURB KT6 158 E5
SWFD E18 * 59 F1
SYD SE26 151 H4
WALTH E17 57 J4
WAN E11 58 E4
WAN E11 * 76 C3
WATW WD18 * 20 D3
WELL DA16 136 A1
WFD IG8 45 F5
WLSDN NW10 87 H2
Station Approach Rd
CHSWK W4 105 K6
Station Ar GTPST W1W * 10 D1
Station Av HOR/WEW KT19 173 G7
NWMAL KT3 160 B2
RCH/KEW TW9 105 H7
Station Blds HAYES BR2 * 167 K7
Station Chambers EA W5 * 86 C3
Station Cl HPTN TW12 142 B7
Station Cots WDGN N22 * 54 E1
Station Crs ALP/SUD HA0 67 H5
BKHTH/KID SE3 113 K4
SEVS/STOTM N15 55 K3
Stationers Hall Ct STP EC4M * 12 D5
Station Est BECK BR3 166 A3
Station Estate Rd
EBED/NFELT TW14 122 A7
Station Garage Ms
STRHM/NOR SW16 * 148 D5
Station Gdns CHSWK W4 105 K6
Station Gv ALP/SUD HA0 68 A5
Station Hl HAYES BR2 180 E1
Station House Ms ED N9 42 C3
Station Pde ACT W3 * 86 C5
BAL SW12 * 129 F7
BARK IG11 78 C6
BECK BR3 * 166 A3
BELMT SM2 * 175 G5
BMLY BR1 * 152 E7
BXLYHN DA7 * 137 F1
CHSWK W4 * 105 K6
CLPT E5 * 74 D2
CRICK NW2 70 A5
EA W5 * 86 B7
EBAR EN4 * 28 A3
EBED/NFELT TW14 * 122 A6
EDGW HA8 * 36 A6
EHAM E6 * 77 J6
HCH RM12 81 K3
KTN/HRWW/WS HA3 * 49 H1
NTHLT UB5 * 66 A6
PLSTW E13 * 77 G7
RCH/KEW TW9 105 H7
ROM RM1 * 63 G5
RSLP HA4 * 64 A1
RYLN/HDSTN HA2 * 66 B3
STHGT/OAK N14 28 D7
Station Pas PECK SE15 111 K7
SWFD E18 59 F1
Station Pl FSBYPK N4 73 G1
Station Ri WNWD SE27 149 H1
Station Rd BAR EN5 27 F4
BARK/HLT IG6 60 D2
BARN SW13 126 C1
BCTR RM8 61 K7
BELV DA17 117 H2
BFN/LL DA15 155 G1
BMLY BR1 152 E7
BORE WD6 24 C3
BXLYHN DA7 137 F2
CAR SM5 175 K3
CHSGTN KT9 172 A4
CROY/NA CR0 164 D7
DART DA1 138 C5
EA W5 86 B5
EDGW HA8 36 C5
ESH/CLAY KT10 170 D4
FBAR/BDGN N11 40 B4
FNCH N3 38 E7
GPK RM2 63 K3
HAYES BR2 167 H1
HDN NW4 51 J5
HNWL W7 84 E7
HOLWY N7 72 C2
HPTN TW12 142 B7
HRW HA1 48 B4
HSLW TW3 123 G3
HYS/HAR UB3 101 H3
IL IG1 78 B2
KUT/HW KT1 143 K7
KUTN/CMB KT2 144 C7
LEW SE13 133 F2
MLHL NW7 37 G5
MNPK E12 77 H3
NWMAL KT3 160 E4
PGE/AN SE20 150 E5
RYLN/HDSTN HA2 48 B4
SCUP DA14 155 G3
SNWD SE25 165 G3
SUN TW16 140 E6
TEDD TW11 143 G5
THDIT KT7 158 A6
TOTM N17 56 C2
TWK TW1 124 A7
WALTH E17 57 G5
WAT WD17 21 F1
WCHMH N21 29 H7
WDGN N22 54 E1
WDR/YW UB7 100 B1
WIM/MER SW19 147 G7
WLSDN NW10 87 H1
WWKM BR4 167 F7
Station Rd North BELV DA17 117 J2
Station Sq STMC/STPC BR5 169 H4
Station St SRTFD E15 76 B6
Station Ter CMBW SE5 110 D7
WLSDN NW10 88 B1
Station Vw GFD/PVL UB6 66 D7
Station Wy BKHH IG9 45 H3
CHEAM SM3 174 C6
ESH/CLAY KT10 170 E5
Station Yd RSLP HA4 * 64 B1
STHL UB1 * 102 E1
TWK TW1 124 B6
Staunton Rd KUTN/CMB KT2 144 B6
Staunton St DEPT SE8 112 C5
Staveley Cl HOLWY N7 * 72 E3
PECK SE15 111 K7
Staveley Gdns CHSWK W4 106 A7
Staveley Rd ASHF TW15 140 B5
CHSWK W4 105 K5
Staverton Rd CRICK NW2 70 A6
Stave Yard Rd
BERM/RHTH SE16 93 G7
Stavordale Rd CAR SM5 162 B6
HBRY N5 73 G3
Stayner's Rd WCHPL E1 93 F3
Stayton Rd SUT SM1 174 E2
Steadfast Rd KUT/HW KT1 143 K7
Stead St WALW SE17 19 G6
Steam Farm La
EBED/NFELT TW14 121 J3
Stean St HACK E8 7 L3
Stebbing Wy BARK IG11 97 G1
Stebondale St POP/IOD E14 113 F4
Stedly SCUP DA14 * 155 G3
Steed Cl EMPK RM11 81 K1
Steedman St WALW SE17 18 E6
Steeds Rd MUSWH N10 39 K7
Steel Ap BARK IG11 97 H1
Steele Rd CHSWK W4 105 K2
ISLW TW7 124 B3
TOTM N17 56 A2
WAN E11 76 C3
WLSDN NW10 86 E1
Steele's Ms North
HAMP NW3 * 71 K5
Steele's Ms South HAMP NW3 71 K5
Steele's Rd HAMP NW3 71 K5
Steeles Studios HAMP NW3 * 71 K5
Steel's La WCHPL E1 92 E5
Steep Hl CROY/NA CR0 178 A3
STRHM/NOR SW16 148 D2
Steeplands BUSH WD23 22 B6
Steeple Cl FUL/PGN SW6 127 H2
WIM/MER SW19 146 C3
Steeplestone Cl UED N18 41 J4
Steeple Wk IS N1 6 F3
Steerforth St
WAND/EARL SW18 147 F1
Steering Cl ED N9 30 E7
Steers Md MTCM CR4 147 K7
Steers Wy BERM/RHTH SE16 112 B1
Stella Rd TOOT SW17 147 K5
Stelling Rd ERITH DA8 118 A6
Stellman Cl CLPT E5 74 C2
Stembridge Rd PGE/AN SE20 165 J1
Stephan Cl HACK E8 74 C7
Stephen Av RAIN RM13 81 J5
Stephendale Rd
FUL/PGN SW6 128 A2
Stephen Ms FITZ W1T 11 G3
Stephen Pl CLAP SW4 129 H2
Stephen Rd BXLYHN DA7 137 K2
Stephenson Cl WELL DA16 136 A1
Stephenson Rd HNWL W7 85 F5
WALTH E17 57 G4
WHTN TW2 123 F6
Stephenson St CAN/RD E16 94 C3
WLSDN NW10 87 G2
Stephenson Wy BUSH WD23 21 H2
CAMTN NW1 4 F9
Stephen's Rd SRTFD E15 76 C7
Stephen St FITZ W1T 11 G4
Stepney Cswy WCHPL E1 93 F5
Stepney Gn WCHPL E1 92 E4
Stepney High St WCHPL E1 93 F4
Stepney Wy MTCM CR4 148 A7
WCHPL E1 92 D4
Sterling Av EDGW HA8 36 B3
Sterling Cl WLSDN NW10 69 J6
Sterling Gdns NWCR SE14 112 B5
Sterling Pl EA W5 105 F3
Sterling St SKENS SW7 15 K2
Sterling Way (North Circular)
UED N18 41 K4
Stern Cl BARK IG11 97 J1
Sterndale Rd DART DA1 139 J6
WKENS W14 * 107 G2
Sterne St SHB W12 107 G1
Sternhall La PECK SE15 131 H2
Sternhold Av
BRXS/STRHM SW2 148 D1
Sterry Crs DAGE RM10 80 C4
Sterry Dr HOR/WEW KT19 173 G3
THDIT KT7 157 K5
Sterry Gdns DAGE RM10 80 C5
Sterry Rd BARK IG11 79 F7
DAGE RM10 80 C3
Sterry St STHWK SE1 19 G2
Steucers La FSTH SE23 132 B7
Steve Biko La CAT SE6 151 J3
Steve Biko Rd HOLWY N7 73 G2
Steve Biko Wy HSLW TW3 123 F2
Stevedale Rd WELL DA16 136 D1
Stevedore St WAP E1W 92 D7
Stevenage Rd EHAM E6 78 A5
FUL/PGN SW6 107 G7
Stevens Av HOM E9 74 E5
Stevens Cl BECK BR3 151 J5
HPTN TW12 141 K5
PIN HA5 47 G4
Stevens Gn BUSH WD23 22 C7
Stevens' La ESH/CLAY KT10 171 G6
Stevenson Cl BAR EN5 27 H5
ERITH DA8 118 E6
Stevenson Crs
BERM/RHTH SE16 111 H4
Stevens Rd BCTR RM8 79 H1
Stevens St STHWK SE1 19 K3
Steventon Rd SHB W12 87 H6
Stewart Cl CDALE/KGS NW9 * 50 E5
CHST BR7 154 B4
HPTN TW12 141 J5
Stewart Quay HYS/HAR UB3 101 H1
Stewart Rd SRTFD E15 76 B3
Stewartsby Cl UED N18 41 J4
Stewart's Gv CHEL SW3 15 H7
Stewart's La VX/NE SW8 109 G6
Stewarts Rd VX/NE SW8 109 H6
Stewart's Rd VX/NE SW8 109 H7
Stewart St POP/IOD E14 113 F1
Steyne Rd ACT W3 86 D7
Steyning Gv ELTH/MOT SE9 153 K3
Steynings Wy
NFNCH/WDSPK N12 38 E4
Steyning Wy HSLWW TW4 122 B3
Stickland Rd BELV DA17 117 H3
Stickleton Cl GFD/PVL UB6 84 B2
Stilecroft Gdns ALP/SUD HA0 67 H2
Stile Hall Gdns CHSWK W4 105 H4
Stiles Cl ERITH DA8 117 J4
HAYES BR2 168 E5
Stillingfleet Rd BARN SW13 106 D6
Stillington St WEST SW1P 16 F5
Stillness Rd FSTH SE23 132 B5
Stipularis Dr YEAD UB4 83 H3
Stirling Av PIN HA5 47 H6
WLGTN SM6 176 E6
Stirling Cl RAIN RM13 99 K2
SCUP DA14 154 E3
STRHM/NOR SW16 148 C7
Stirling Gv HSLW TW3 123 H1
Stirling Rd ACT W3 105 J2
BRXN/ST SW9 129 K1
HYS/HAR UB3 83 F6
KTN/HRWW/WS HA3 49 F2
PLSTW E13 95 F1
TOTM N17 42 C7
WALTH E17 57 G2
WDGN N22 41 H7
WHTN TW2 123 F6
Stirling Wk BRYLDS KT5 159 J5
Stirling Wy BORE WD6 25 F5
CROY/NA CR0 163 K6
Stiven Crs RYLN/HDSTN HA2 65 K2
Stockbury Rd CROY/NA CR0 165 K5
Stockdale Rd BCTR RM8 80 B1
Stockdove Wy GFD/PVL UB6 85 F2
Stocker Gdns DAGW RM9 79 J6
Stockfield Rd ESH/CLAY KT10 170 E4
STRHM/NOR SW16 149 F2
Stockholm Rd
BERM/RHTH SE16 111 K4
Stockholm Wy WAP E1W 92 C7
Stockhurst Cl PUT/ROE SW15 127 F1
Stockingswater La PEND EN3 31 G2
Stockland Rd ROMW/RG RM7 63 F5
Stockley Cl WDR/YW UB7 100 E1
Stockley Farm Rd
WDR/YW UB7 100 E2
Stockley Rd WDR/YW UB7 100 E2
Stock Orchard Crs
HOLWY N7 * 73 F3
Stock Orchard St HOLWY N7 73 F4
Stockport Rd
STRHM/NOR SW16 148 D7
Stocksfield Rd WALTH E17 * 58 A2
Stocks Pl POP/IOD E14 93 H6
Stock St PLSTW E13 94 E1
Stockton Cl BAR EN5 27 G3
Stockton Gdns MLHL NW7 37 F2
TOTM N17 41 J6
Stockton Rd TOTM N17 41 J6
UED N18 42 C5
Stockwell Av BRXN/ST SW9 130 A2
Stockwell Cl BMLY BR1 168 A1
Stockwell Gdns BRXN/ST SW9 110 A7
Stockwell Gn BRXN/ST SW9 130 A1
Stockwell La BRXN/ST SW9 130 A1
Stockwell Park Crs
BRXN/ST SW9 130 A1
Stockwell Park Rd
BRXN/ST SW9 110 A7
Stockwell Park Wk
BRXN/ST SW9 130 A2
Stockwell Rd BRXN/ST SW9 130 A1
Stockwell St GNWCH SE10 113 F5
Stockwell Ter BRXN/ST SW9 110 A7
Stodart Rd PGE/AN SE20 150 E7
Stofield Gdns ELTH/MOT SE9 153 H2
Stoford Cl WIM/MER SW19 127 H7
Stokenchurch St
FUL/PGN SW6 108 A7
Stoke Newington Church St
STNW/STAM N16 73 K2
Stoke Newington Common
STNW/STAM N16 74 B1
Stoke Newington High St
STNW/STAM N16 74 B2
Stoke Newington Rd HACK E8 74 B4
Stoke Pl WLSDN NW10 87 H2
Stoke Rd KUTN/CMB KT2 144 E6
Stokesby Rd CHSGTN KT9 172 B5
Stokesley St SHB W12 87 H5
Stokes Ms TEDD TW11 143 G4
Stokes Rd CROY/NA CR0 166 A5
EHAM E6 95 J3
Stoll Cl CRICK NW2 70 A2
Stonard Rd BCTR RM8 79 H4
PLMGR N13 41 G2
Stondon Pk FSTH SE23 132 B5
Stonebridge Ms NRWD SE19 149 J6
Stonebridge Pk WLSDN NW10 69 F6
Stonebridge Rd
SEVS/STOTM N15 56 A4
Stonebridge Wy WBLY HA9 68 D5
Stone Blds LINN WC2A 11 M3
Stonechat Sq EHAM E6 95 J4
Stone Cl BCTR RM8 80 B1
CLAP SW4 129 H1
Stonecot Cl CHEAM SM3 161 H7
Stonecot Hl CHEAM SM3 161 H7
Stone Crs EBED/NFELT TW14 121 J6
Stonecroft Cl BAR EN5 25 K3
Stonecroft Rd ERITH DA8 117 K6
Stonecroft Wy CROY/NA CR0 163 K6
Stonecrop Cl CDALE/KGS NW9 51 F2
Stonecutter St
FLST/FETLN EC4A 12 C4
Stonefield Cl BXLYHN DA7 137 H2
RSLP HA4 65 J4
Stonefield St IS N1 6 B3
Stonefield Wy CHARL SE7 114 C6
RSLP HA4 65 H4
Stone Gv EDGW HA8 36 A3
STAN HA7 36 A3
Stonegrove Gdns EDGW HA8 36 A4
Stonehall Av IL IG1 59 J5
Stone Hall Gdns KENS W8 * 14 C4
Stone Hall Pl KENS W8 * 14 C4
Stone Hall Rd WCHMH N21 29 F6
Stoneham Rd
FBAR/BDGN N11 40 C4
Stonehill Cl MORT/ESHN SW14 126 A4
Stonehill Rd CHSWK W4 105 H4
MORT/ESHN SW14 125 K4
Stonehills Ct DUL SE21 150 A2
Stonehorse Rd PEND EN3 30 E4
Stone House Ct LVPST EC2M 13 K4
Stoneleigh Av WPK KT4 173 J2
Stoneleigh Broadway
EW KT17 173 J4
Stoneleigh Crs
HOR/WEW KT19 173 J4
Stoneleigh Park Av
CROY/NA CR0 166 A5
Stoneleigh Park Rd
HOR/WEW KT19 173 H5
Stoneleigh Pl NTGHL W11 88 B6
Stoneleigh Rd BMLY BR1 169 G2
CAR SM5 162 D6
CLAY IG5 59 J2
TOTM N17 56 B1
Stoneleigh St NTGHL W11 88 B6
Stoneleigh Ter ARCH N19 72 B1
Stonell's Rd TOOT SW17 147 G2
Stonemasons Cl
SEVS/STOTM N15 * 55 K3
Stonenest St FSBYPK N4 55 F7
Stone Park Av BECK BR3 166 D3
Stone Pl WPK KT4 173 J1
Stone Rd HAYES BR2 167 J4
Stones End St STHWK SE1 18 E2
Stonewall EHAM E6 96 A4
Stonewood Rd ERITH DA8 118 B4
Stoney Aly WOOL/PLUM SE18 135 F1
Stoneyard La POP/IOD E14 93 K6
Stoneycroft Cl LEE/GVPK SE12 133 J6
Stoneycroft Rd WFD IG8 45 J5
Stoneydown WALTH E17 57 G3
Stoneydown Av WALTH E17 57 G3
Stoneyfields Gdns EDGW HA8 36 E3
Stoneyfields La EDGW HA8 36 E4
Stoney La HDTCH EC3A 13 K4
NRWD SE19 150 B5
Stoney St STHWK SE1 13 G8
Stonhouse St CLAP SW4 129 H2
Stonnell's Rd BTSEA SW11 128 E4
Stonor Rd WKENS W14 107 J3
Stonycroft Cl PEND EN3 31 G1
Stopes St PECK SE15 111 G6
Stopford Rd PLSTW E13 76 E7
WALW SE17 * 18 D8
Store Rd CAN/RD E16 115 F1

Storers Quay POP/IOD E14 113 G3
Store St GWRST WC1E 11 G3
SRTFD E15 76 B4
Storey Rd HGT N6 53 K5
WALTH E17 57 H3
Storey's Ga STJSPK SW1H 17 H2
Stories Ms CMBW SE5 * 131 F1
Stories Rd CMBW SE5 131 F2
Stork Rd FSTGT E7 76 D5
Storksmead Rd EDGW HA8 37 G6
Storks Rd BERM/RHTH SE16 * 111 H2
Stormont Rd BTSEA SW11 129 F3
HGT N6 53 K6
Stormont Wy CHSGTN KT9 171 J4
Stormount Dr HYS/HAR UB3 101 F1
Storrington Rd CROY/NA CR0 165 G7
Story St IS N1 5 L2
Stothard St WCHPL E1 92 E3
Stott Cl WAND/EARL SW18 128 C5
Stoughton Av CHEAM SM3 174 B4
Stoughton Cl LBTH SE11 17 M6
PUT/ROE SW15 126 D7
Stour Av NWDGN UB2 103 F2
Stourcliffe St MBLAR W1H 9 L5
Stour Cl HAYES BR2 181 G3
Stourhead Cl WIM/MER SW19 127 G6
Stourhead Gdns RYNPK SW20 160 D2
Stour Rd BOW E3 75 J6
DAGE RM10 80 C1
DART DA1 138 D2
Stourton Av FELT TW13 141 K3
Stowage DEPT SE8 112 E5
The Stowage DEPT SE8 112 D5
Stow Crs WALTH E17 43 G7
Stowe Gdns ED N9 30 B7
Stowe Pl SEVS/STOTM N15 56 A2
Stowe Rd SHB W12 106 E1
Stox Md KTN/HRWW/WS HA3 34 D7
Stracey Rd WLSDN NW10 69 F7
Strachan Pl RYNPK SW20 146 A5
Stradbroke Gv CLAY IG5 59 J2
Stradbroke Rd HBRY N5 73 J3
Stradbrook Cl
RYLN/HDSTN HA2 65 K2
Stradella Rd HNHL SE24 130 D5
Strafford Rd ACT W3 105 K1
BAR EN5 26 C2
HSLW TW3 122 E2
TWK TW1 124 B6
Strafford St POP/IOD E14 112 D1
Strahan Rd BOW E3 93 G1
Straightsmouth GNWCH SE10 113 F6
The Straight NWDGN UB2 102 C1
Strait Rd EHAM E6 95 J6
Straker's Rd EDUL SE22 131 J3
Strand CHCR WC2N 11 K7
HOL/ALD WC2B 11 M5
TPL/STR WC2R 11 L6
Strand Dr RCH/KEW TW9 105 H6
Strandfield Cl
WOOL/PLUM SE18 115 K4
Strand-on-the-Green
CHSWK W4 105 H5
Strand Pl UED N18 42 A3
Strangways Ter WKENS W14 107 J2
Stranraer Wy IS N1 5 L2
Strasburg Rd BTSEA SW11 109 F7
Stratfield Park Cl
WCHMH N21 29 H6
Stratfield Rd BORE WD6 24 B2
Stratford Cl BARK IG11 79 G6
DAGE RM10 80 E6
Stratford Ct NWMAL KT3 160 A3
Stratford Gv PUT/ROE SW15 127 G3
Stratford House Av BMLY BR1 168 D2
Stratford Pl OXSTW W1C 10 C5
Stratford Rd HTHAIR TW6 120 E5
KENS W8 14 B4
NWDGN UB2 102 D3
PLSTW E13 76 E7
THHTH CR7 164 B3
WAT WD17 20 E1
YEAD UB4 83 F3
Stratford Studios KENS W8 14 B4
Stratford Vls CAMTN NW1 4 F1
Stratford Wy WAT WD17 20 D1
Strathan Cl WAND/EARL SW18 127 H5
Strathaven Rd LEE/GVPK SE12 134 A5
Strathblaine Rd BTSEA SW11 128 C4
Strathbrook Rd
STRHM/NOR SW16 149 F6
Strathcona Rd WBLY HA9 67 K1
Strathdale STRHM/NOR SW16 149 F4
Strathdon Dr TOOT SW17 147 H2
Strathearn Av HYS/HAR UB3 101 J6
WHTN TW2 123 H7
Strathearn Cots
TRDG/WHET N20 * 38 E2
Strathearn Pl BAY/PAD W2 9 J6
Strathearn Rd SUT SM1 174 E4
WIM/MER SW19 146 E4
Stratheden Rd
BKHTH/KID SE3 113 K7
Strathfield Gdns BARK IG11 78 D5
Strathleven Rd
BRXS/STRHM SW2 129 K4
Strathmore Gdns EDGW HA8 50 D1
FNCH N3 39 F7
HCH RM12 63 H7
Strathmore Rd CROY/NA CR0 164 D6
TEDD TW11 142 E3
WIM/MER SW19 146 E2
Strathnairn St STHWK SE1 111 H3
Strathray Gdns HAMP NW3 * 71 J5
Strath Ter BTSEA SW11 128 D3
Strathville Rd
WAND/EARL SW18 146 E1
Strathyre Av
STRHM/NOR SW16 164 B2
Stratton Av WLGTN SM6 176 D7
Stratton Cl BXLYHN DA7 137 F2
EDGW HA8 36 B5
HSLW TW3 102 E7
WIM/MER SW19 161 J1
WOT/HER KT12 * 156 B7
Strattondale St POP/IOD E14 113 F2
Stratton Dr BARK IG11 78 E4
Stratton Gdns STHL UB1 83 K5
Stratton Rd BXLYHN DA7 137 F2
WIM/MER SW19 161 K1
Stratton St MYFR/PICC W1J 10 D8
Strauss Rd CHSWK W4 * 106 A1
Strawberry Hl CHSGTN KT9 171 K5
Strawberry Hill Rd TWK TW1 143 F2
Strawberry La CAR SM5 175 K2
Strawberry Ter MUSWH N10 * 39 K7
Strawberry V EFNCH N2 39 H7
TWK TW1 143 F2
Streakes Field Rd CRICK NW2 69 J1
Streamdale ABYW SE2 116 C5
Stream La EDGW HA8 36 D5
Streamline Ms EDUL SE22 131 J7
Streamside Cl ED N9 30 B7
HAYES BR2 167 K3
Stream Wy BELV DA17 117 H5
Streatfeild Av EHAM E6 77 K7
Streatfeild Rd
KTN/HRWW/WS HA3 49 J2
Streatham Cl
STRHM/NOR SW16 * 148 E1
Streatham Common
STRHM/NOR SW16 * 148 D6
Streatham Common North
STRHM/NOR SW16 149 F4
Streatham Common South
STRHM/NOR SW16 148 E5
Streatham Ct
STRHM/NOR SW16 148 E2
Streatham Gn
STRHM/NOR SW16 * 148 E3
Streatham High Rd
STRHM/NOR SW16 148 E6
Streatham Hl
BRXS/STRHM SW2 129 K7
Streatham Pl
BRXS/STRHM SW2 129 K6
Streatham Rd MTCM CR4 148 A7
Streatham St
NOXST/BSQ WC1A 11 J4
Streatham V
STRHM/NOR SW16 148 C6
Streathbourne Rd TOOT SW17 148 A1
Streatleigh Pde
STRHM/NOR SW16 * 148 E1
Streatley Pl HAMP NW3 71 H3
Streatley Rd KIL/WHAMP NW6 70 D6
Streeters La WLGTN SM6 176 D2
Streetfield Ms BKHTH/KID SE3 133 K1
Streimer Rd SRTFD E15 94 A1
Strelley Wy ACT W3 87 G6
Stretton Rd CROY/NA CR0 165 F6
RCHPK/HAM TW10 143 J1
Strickland Av DART DA1 139 J2
Strickland Rw
WAND/EARL SW18 128 C6
Strickland St DEPT SE8 132 D1
Stride Rd PLSTW E13 94 D1
Strimon Cl ED N9 42 E1
Stripling Wy WATW WD18 20 E5
Strode Cl MUSWH N10 40 A6
Strode Rd FSTGT E7 76 E3
FUL/PGN SW6 107 G6
TOTM N17 56 A1
WLSDN NW10 69 J5
Strond Green Gdns
CROY/NA CR0 165 K6
Strond Green Wy
CROY/NA CR0 165 K6
Strone Rd FSTGT E7 77 G5
MNPK E12 77 H5
Strone Wy YEAD UB4 83 J3
Strongbow Crs ELTH/MOT SE9 134 E4
Strongbow Rd ELTH/MOT SE9 134 E4
Stronsa Rd SHB W12 106 C1
Strood Av ROMW/RG RM7 63 F7
Stroud Crs PUT/ROE SW15 145 H2
Stroudes Cl WPK KT4 160 C6
Stroud Fld NTHLT UB5 65 J5
Stroud Ga RYLN/HDSTN HA2 66 B3
Stroud Green Rd FSBYPK N4 55 F7
Stroud Green Wy
CROY/NA CR0 165 J6
Stroud Rd SNWD SE25 165 H5
WIM/MER SW19 146 E2
Strouds Cl CHDH RM6 61 H4
Strout's Pl BETH E2 7 L7
Strutton Gnd STJSPK SW1H 17 G3
Strype St WCHPL E1 13 L3
Stuart Av CDALE/KGS NW9 51 J6
EA W5 105 G1
HAYES BR2 167 K7
RYLN/HDSTN HA2 65 K2
WOT/HER KT12 156 B7
Stuart Ct BORE WD6 23 K5
Stuart Crs CROY/NA CR0 179 H2
HYS/HAR UB3 82 A5
WDGN N22 41 F7
Stuart Evans Cl WELL DA16 136 D2
Stuart Gv TEDD TW11 142 E4
Stuart Mantle Wy ERITH DA8 118 A6
Stuart Pl MTCM CR4 147 K7
Stuart Rd ACT W3 86 E7
BARK IG11 79 F7
EBAR EN4 27 J6
KIL/WHAMP NW6 2 A8
KTN/HRWW/WS HA3 49 F2
PECK SE15 131 K3
RCHPK/HAM TW10 143 H1
THHTH CR7 164 D3
WELL DA16 116 C7
WIM/MER SW19 146 E2
Stubbs Cl CDALE/KGS NW9 50 E4
Stubbs Dr BERM/RHTH SE16 111 J4
Stubbs Wy WIM/MER SW19 147 H7
Stucley Pl CAMTN NW1 4 D2
Stucley Rd HEST TW5 103 H6
Studdridge St FUL/PGN SW6 127 K1
Studd St IS N1 6 C3
Studholme Ct HAMP NW3 * 70 E3
Studholme St PECK SE15 111 J6
Studio Ms HDN NW4 52 A3
Studio Pl KTBR SW1X 15 M2
The Studios BUSH WD23 22 A5
Studio Wy BORE WD6 24 E1
Studland Cl BFN/LL DA15 155 F2
Studland Rd HNWL W7 84 D5
KUTN/CMB KT2 144 A5
SYD SE26 151 F4
Studland St HMSMTH W6 106 E3
Studley Av CHING E4 44 B6
Studley Cl CLPT E5 75 G4
Studley Ct SCUP DA14 155 H4
Studley Dr REDBR IG4 59 H5
Studley Grange Rd HNWL W7 103 K2
Studley Rd CLAP SW4 109 K7
DAGW RM9 79 K6
FSTGT E7 77 F5
Stukeley Rd FSTGT E7 77 F6
Stukeley St HOL/ALD WC2B 11 K4
Stumps Hill La BECK BR3 151 J5
Sturdy Rd PECK SE15 131 J1
Sturge Av WALTH E17 43 K7
Sturgeon Rd WALW SE17 18 E8
Sturges Fld CHST BR7 154 D5
Sturgess Av HDN NW4 51 K6
Sturge St STHWK SE1 18 E2
Sturmer Wy HOLWY N7 73 F4
Sturminster Cl YEAD UB4 83 G5
Sturrock Cl SEVS/STOTM N15 55 K3
Sturry St POP/IOD E14 93 K5
Sturt St IS N1 6 F6
Stutfield St WCHPL E1 92 C5
Styles Gdns BRXN/ST SW9 130 C2
Styles Wy BECK BR3 167 F3
Sudbourne Rd
BRXS/STRHM SW2 129 K4
Sudbrooke Rd BAL SW12 128 E5
Sudbrook Gdns
RCHPK/HAM TW10 144 A2
Sudbrook La
RCHPK/HAM TW10 125 F7
Sudbury EHAM E6 96 A5
Sudbury Av ALP/SUD HA0 67 J2
Sudbury Court Dr HRW HA1 67 G2
Sudbury Court Rd HRW HA1 67 G2
Sudbury Crs ALP/SUD HA0 67 H4
BMLY BR1 152 E4
Sudbury Cft ALP/SUD HA0 67 F3
Sudbury Gdns CROY/NA CR0 178 A3
Sudbury Heights Av
GFD/PVL UB6 67 F4
Sudbury Hl HRW HA1 67 F2
Sudbury Hill Cl ALP/SUD HA0 67 F2
Sudbury Rd BARK IG11 79 F4
Sudeley St IS N1 6 D6
Sudlow Rd WAND/EARL SW18 127 K3
Sudrey St STHWK SE1 18 E2
Suez Av GFD/PVL UB6 85 F1
Suez Rd PEND EN3 31 G3
Suffield Rd CHING E4 43 K2
PGE/AN SE20 165 K1
SEVS/STOTM N15 * 56 B4
Suffolk Cl BORE WD6 25 F4
Suffolk La CANST EC4R 13 G6
Suffolk Park Rd WALTH E17 57 G3
Suffolk Rd BARK IG11 78 D6
BARN SW13 106 C6
DAGE RM10 80 D4
DART DA1 139 H5
GDMY/SEVK IG3 60 E5
PEND EN3 30 D4
PLSTW E13 94 D2
RYLN/HDSTN HA2 47 K5
SCUP DA14 155 J5
SEVS/STOTM N15 55 K5
SNWD SE25 165 G3
WLSDN NW10 69 G6
WPK KT4 173 H1
Suffolk St FSTGT E7 76 E4
STJS SW1Y 11 H8
Suffolk Vls
WAND/EARL SW18 * 127 K6
Sugar House La SRTFD E15 94 A1
Sugar Loaf Wk BETH E2 * 92 E2
Sugden Rd BTSEA SW11 129 F2
THDIT KT7 158 B7
Sugden Wy BARK IG11 97 F1
Sulgrave Gdns HMSMTH W6 107 F1
Sulgrave Rd HMSMTH W6 107 F1
Sulina Rd BRXS/STRHM SW2 129 K6
Sulivan Ct FUL/PGN SW6 127 K1
Sulivan Rd FUL/PGN SW6 127 K2
Sullivan Av CAN/RD E16 95 H4
Sullivan Cl BTSEA SW11 128 D2
DART DA1 138 E5
E/WMO/HCT KT8 157 F2
YEAD UB4 83 G4
Sullivan Rd LBTH SE11 18 B5
Sullivan Wy BORE WD6 23 J5
Sultan Rd WAN E11 59 F3
Sultan St BECK BR3 166 A1
CMBW SE5 110 D6
Sumatra Rd KIL/WHAMP NW6 70 E5
Sumburgh Rd BAL SW12 129 F5
Summer Av E/WMO/HCT KT8 157 K4
Summer Crossing THDIT KT7 158 A4
Summerene Cl
STRHM/NOR SW16 148 C6
Summerfield Av
KIL/WHAMP NW6 88 C1
NFNCH/WDSPK N12 39 J5
Summerfield La SURB KT6 171 K1
Summerfield Rd EA W5 85 H3
Summerfield St
LEE/GVPK SE12 133 J6
Summer Gdns
E/WMO/HCT KT8 157 K4
Summer Gv BORE WD6 23 K5
Summer Hl BORE WD6 24 C4
CHST BR7 169 F1
Summerhill Gv EN EN1 30 A5
Summerhill Rd DART DA1 139 G6
SEVS/STOTM N15 55 K3
Summerhill Wy MTCM CR4 148 A7
Summerhouse Av HEST TW5 102 D7
Summerhouse La
WDR/YW UB7 100 A5
Summerhouse Rd
STNW/STAM N16 74 A1
Summerland Gdns
MUSWH N10 54 B2
Summerlands Av ACT W3 86 E6
Summerlee Av EFNCH N2 53 K3
Summerlee Gdns EFNCH N2 53 K3
Summerley St
WAND/EARL SW18 147 F1
Summer Pl WATW WD18 * 20 D5
Summer Rd E/WMO/HCT KT8 157 J4
THDIT KT7 158 A4
Summersby Rd HGT N6 54 B5
Summers Cl BELMT SM2 174 E6
WBLY HA9 50 D7
Summerskille Cl ED N9 42 D1
Summers La
NFNCH/WDSPK N12 39 H6
Summers Rw
NFNCH/WDSPK N12 39 J5
Summers St CLKNW EC1R 12 A1
Summerstown TOOT SW17 147 G2
Summers Wd BORE WD6 * 24 D3
Summerton Wy THMD SE28 97 K6
Summer Trees SUN TW16 141 F7
Summerville Gdns SUT SM1 174 D5
Summerwood Rd ISLW TW7 124 A5
TWK TW1 124 A5
Summit Av CDALE/KGS NW9 51 F4
Summit Cl CDALE/KGS NW9 51 F3
EDGW HA8 36 C6
STHGT/OAK N14 40 C1
Summit Dr WFD IG8 59 H1
Summit Est
STNW/STAM N16 * 56 C6
Summit Rd NTHLT UB5 66 A6
WALTH E17 57 K3
Summit Wy NRWD SE19 150 A6
STHGT/OAK N14 40 B1
Sumner Av PECK SE15 * 111 G7
Sumner Gdns CROY/NA CR0 164 B7
Sumner Pl SKENS SW7 15 H6
Sumner Place Ms SKENS SW7 15 H6
Sumner Rd CROY/NA CR0 164 C7
HRW HA1 48 C6
PECK SE15 111 G7
Sumner Rd South
CROY/NA CR0 164 B7
Sumner St STHWK SE1 12 E8
Sumpter Cl HAMP NW3 71 G5
Sunbeam Crs NKENS W10 88 A3
Sunbeam Rd WLSDN NW10 86 E3
Sunbury Av MLHL NW7 37 F4
MORT/ESHN SW14 126 A3
Sunbury Ct BAR EN5 * 26 C3
SUN TW16 156 C1
Sunbury Court Rd SUN TW16 156 B1
Sunbury Gdns MLHL NW7 37 F4
Sunbury La BTSEA SW11 108 C7
Sunbury Rd CHEAM SM3 174 B2
FELT TW13 140 D2
Sunbury St WOOL/PLUM SE18 114 E2
Sunbury Wy FELT TW13 141 G4
Sun Ct ERITH DA8 138 C1
Suncroft Pl SYD SE26 150 E2
Sundeala Cl SUN TW16 140 E6
Sunderland Mt FSTH SE23 * 151 F1
Sunderland Rd EA W5 104 E2
FSTH SE23 132 A7
Sunderland Ter BAY/PAD W2 8 C4
Sunderland Wy MNPK E12 77 H1
Sundew Av SHB W12 87 J6
Sundew Cl ALP/SUD HA0 * 86 A1
Sundial Av SNWD SE25 165 G1
Sundial Rd MNPK E12 77 J2
Sundorne Rd CHARL SE7 114 A4
Sundown Rd ASHF TW15 140 A4
Sundridge Av BMLY BR1 153 H7
WELL DA16 135 J1
Sundridge Cl DART DA1 139 K5
Sundridge Pde BMLY BR1 * 153 F6
Sundridge Pl CROY/NA CR0 165 H7
Sundridge Rd CROY/NA CR0 165 G7
Sunfields Pl BKHTH/KID SE3 114 A6
Sun in Sands Rbt
BKHTH/KID SE3 113 K6
Sunken Rd CROY/NA CR0 178 E4
Sunkist Wy WLGTN SM6 176 E7
Sunland Av BXLYHS DA6 137 F3
Sun La BKHTH/KID SE3 114 A6
Sunleigh Rd ALP/SUD HA0 68 A7
Sunley Gdns GFD/PVL UB6 85 G1
Sunlight Cl WIM/MER SW19 * 147 G5
Sunlight Sq BETH E2 92 D2
Sunna Gdns SUN TW16 156 A1
Sunningdale STHGT/OAK N14 40 D4
Sunningdale Av ACT W3 87 G6
BARK IG11 78 D7
FELT TW13 141 J1
RAIN RM13 99 K3
RSLP HA4 47 G7
Sunningdale Cl
BERM/RHTH SE16 * 111 J4
STAN HA7 35 G6
SURB KT6 172 A1
THMD SE28 98 A5
Sunningdale Gdns
CDALE/KGS NW9 50 E4
KENS W8 14 B4
Sunningdale Ldg EDGW HA8 * 36 B4
Sunningdale Rd BMLY BR1 168 D3
RAIN RM13 81 J6
SUT SM1 174 D2
Sunningfield Rd HDN NW4 51 K2
Sunningfields Crs HDN NW4 51 K1
Sunninghill Ct ACT W3 * 105 K1
Sunninghill Rd LEW SE13 132 E1
Sunny Bank SNWD SE25 165 H2
Sunny Crs WLSDN NW10 68 E6
Sunnycroft Rd HSLW TW3 123 G1
SNWD SE25 165 H3
STHL UB1 84 A4
Sunnydale Gdns MLHL NW7 37 F5
Sunnydale Rd LEE/GVPK SE12 134 A4
Sunnydene Av CHING E4 44 B4
RSLP HA4 46 E7
Sunnydene Gdns
ALP/SUD HA0 67 J5
Sunnydene St SYD SE26 151 G3
Sunnyfield MLHL NW7 37 H3
Sunny Gardens Rd HDN NW4 52 A2
Sunny Hl HDN NW4 51 K2
Sunnyhill Cl CLPT E5 75 G3
Sunnyhill Rd
STRHM/NOR SW16 148 E3
Sunnyhurst Cl SUT SM1 174 E2
Sunnymead Av MTCM CR4 163 J2
Sunnymead Rd
CDALE/KGS NW9 51 F6
PUT/ROE SW15 126 E4
Sunnymede Av
HOR/WEW KT19 173 G7
Sunnymede Dr BARK/HLT IG6 60 B3
Sunny Nook Gdns
SAND/SEL CR2 177 K5
Sunny Pl HDN NW4 52 A3
Sunnyside CAT SE6 * 132 C6
CRICK NW2 70 D2
WOT/HER KT12 156 B4
Sunnyside Pl WIM/MER SW19 146 C5
Sunnyside Rd ARCH N19 54 D6
EA W5 85 K7
IL IG1 78 C2
LEY E10 57 J7
TEDD TW11 142 D3
Sunnyside Rd East ED N9 42 C2
Sunnyside Rd North ED N9 42 B2
Sunnyside Rd South ED N9 42 B2
Sunny Vw CDALE/KGS NW9 51 F4
Sunny Wy NFNCH/WDSPK N12 39 J6
Sun Pas BERM/RHTH SE16 111 H2
Sunray Av BRYLDS KT5 172 D1
HAYES BR2 168 D5
HNHL SE24 130 E3
WDR/YW UB7 100 A1
Sunrise Cl FELT TW13 141 K2
Sun Rd WKENS W14 107 J4
Sunset Av CHING E4 31 K7
WFD IG8 44 E4
Sunset Cl ERITH DA8 118 E6
Sunset Gdns SNWD SE25 165 F1
Sunset Rd HNHL SE24 130 D3
THMD SE28 97 G7
WIM/MER SW19 145 K4
Sunset Vw BAR EN5 26 C1
Sunshine Wy MTCM CR4 162 E1
Sun St SDTCH EC2A 13 H2
Surbiton Ct SURB KT6 158 D5
Surbiton Court Ms SURB KT6 158 E5
Surbiton Crs KUT/HW KT1 159 F3
Surbiton Hall Cl KUT/HW KT1 159 F3
Surbiton Hill Pk BRYLDS KT5 159 G4
Surbiton Hill Rd SURB KT6 159 F3
Surbiton Rd KUT/HW KT1 158 E3
Surlingham Cl THMD SE28 97 K6
Surma Cl WCHPL E1 92 C3
Surmans Cl DAGW RM9 79 J7
Surrendale Pl MV/WKIL W9 8 B1
Surrey Canal Rd PECK SE15 111 K5
Surrey Cl FNCH N3 52 C2
Surrey Crs CHSWK W4 105 H4
Surrey Gdns FSBYPK N4 55 J5
Surrey Gv SUT SM1 175 H2
WALW SE17 19 J8
Surrey La BTSEA SW11 108 D7
Surrey Ms WNWD SE27 150 A3
Surrey Mt FSTH SE23 131 J7
Surrey Quays Rd
BERM/RHTH SE16 111 K2
Surrey Rd BARK IG11 78 E6
DAGE RM10 80 D4
HRW HA1 48 C5
PECK SE15 132 A4
WWKM BR4 166 E7
Surrey Rw STHWK SE1 18 C1
Surrey Sq WALW SE17 19 J7
Surrey St CROY/NA CR0 177 J2
PLSTW E13 95 F2
TPL/STR WC2R 11 M6
Surrey Ter WALW SE17 19 K6
Surrey Water Rd
BERM/RHTH SE16 93 F7
Surridge Gdns NRWD SE19 149 K5
Surr St HOLWY N7 72 E4
Sury Basin KUTN/CMB KT2 144 A7
Susan Cl ROMW/RG RM7 62 E2
Susannah St POP/IOD E14 93 K5
Susan Rd BKHTH/KID SE3 134 A1
Susan Wd CHST BR7 154 A7
Sussex Av ISLW TW7 123 K2
Sussex Cl ARCH N19 * 72 E1
NWMAL KT3 160 B3
REDBR IG4 59 K5
TWK TW1 124 C5
Sussex Crs NTHLT UB5 66 A5
Sussex Gdns BAY/PAD W2 9 H4
CHSGTN KT9 171 K5
FSBYPK N4 55 J4
HGT N6 53 K4
Sussex Ga HGT N6 * 53 K4
Sussex Ms East BAY/PAD W2 * 9 H6
Sussex Ms West BAY/PAD W2 9 H6
Sussex Pl BAY/PAD W2 9 H5
CAMTN NW1 3 L9
HMSMTH W6 107 F4
NWMAL KT3 160 B3
Sussex Ring
NFNCH/WDSPK N12 38 E4
Sussex Rd CAR SM5 175 K5
DART DA1 139 K6
EHAM E6 96 A1
ERITH DA8 117 J6
HGDN/ICK UB10 64 A3
HRW HA1 48 C4
MTCM CR4 * 163 K4
NWDGN UB2 102 C2
NWMAL KT3 160 B3
SAND/SEL CR2 177 K5
SCUP DA14 155 H4
WWKM BR4 166 E7
Sussex Sq BAY/PAD W2 9 H6
Sussex St PIM SW1V 16 D8
PLSTW E13 95 F2
Sussex Ter PGE/AN SE20 * 150 E6
Sussex Wy ARCH N19 54 D7
EBAR EN4 28 B4
Sutcliffe Cl BUSH WD23 22 C3
GLDGN NW11 53 F4
Sutcliffe Rd WELL DA16 136 D1
WOOL/PLUM SE18 115 K5
Sutherland Av HYS/HAR UB3 101 K3
MV/WKIL W9 2 E8
MV/WKIL W9 8 B1
WEA W13 85 H5
WELL DA16 135 J3
Sutherland Cl BAR EN5 26 C3
Sutherland Ct
CDALE/KGS NW9 50 D3
Sutherland Dr
WIM/MER SW19 147 H7
Sutherland Gdns
MORT/ESHN SW14 126 B2
WPK KT4 160 E7
Sutherland Gv TEDD TW11 142 E4
WAND/EARL SW18 127 J6
Sutherland House
WALTH E17 * 57 G2
Sutherland Pl BAY/PAD W2 8 A4
Sutherland Rd BELV DA17 117 H2
BOW E3 93 H1
CHSWK W4 106 A5
CROY/NA CR0 164 B6
ED N9 30 C7
PEND EN3 31 F6
STHL UB1 83 K5
TOTM N17 42 C6
WALTH E17 57 F1
WEA W13 85 G5
Sutherland Rw PIM SW1V 16 D7
Sutherland Sq WALW SE17 18 E8
Sutherland St PIM SW1V 16 D7
Sutherland Vls WEA W13 * 85 G6
Sutherland Wk WALW SE17 18 F8
Sutlej Rd CHARL SE7 114 B6
Sutterton St HOLWY N7 73 F5
Sutton Cl BECK BR3 151 K7
CHSWK W4 * 105 K5
PIN HA5 46 E4
Sutton Common Rd
CHEAM SM3 161 J6
Sutton Ct BELMT SM2 175 G6
CHSWK W4 * 105 K5
EA W5 * 86 A7
Sutton Court Rd CHSWK W4 105 K5
PLSTW E13 95 G2
SUT SM1 175 G5
Sutton Crs BAR EN5 26 B4
Sutton Dene HSLW TW3 103 G7
Sutton Dwelling Est
CHEL SW3 15 J7
Sutton Est IS N1 * 6 C1
The Sutton Est IS N1 6 C2
Sutton Gdns CROY/NA CR0 165 G4
Sutton Gv SUT SM1 175 H4
Sutton Hall Rd HEST TW5 103 F6
Sutton La FARR EC1M 12 D1
HSLW TW3 122 E1
Sutton La North CHSWK W4 105 K4
Sutton La South CHSWK W4 105 K5
Sutton Park Rd SUT SM1 175 F5
Sutton Pl HOM E9 74 E4
Sutton Rd BARK IG11 96 E1
HEST TW5 103 F7
MUSWH N10 40 A7
PLSTW E13 94 D3
WALTH E17 43 F7
WAT WD17 21 G2
Sutton Rw SOHO/SHAV W1D 11 G4
Sutton Sq HEST TW5 102 E7
HOM E9 * 74 E4
Sutton St WCHPL E1 92 E5
Sutton Wy HEST TW5 102 E7
NKENS W10 88 A4
STLK EC1Y 12 F1
Swaby Rd WAND/EARL SW18 147 G1
Swaffield Rd
WAND/EARL SW18 128 B6
Swain Cl STRHM/NOR SW16 148 B5

Swain Rd THHTH CR7 164 D4
Swains Cl WDR/YW UB7 100 B1
Swain's La HGT N6 72 A2
Swainson Rd ACT W3 106 C1
Swains Rd MTCM CR4 147 K6
Swain St STJWD NW8 3 J9
Swaisland Rd DART DA1 138 E4
Swaislands Dr DART DA1 138 C4
Swaledale Cl FBAR/BDGN N11 40 A5
Swale Rd DART DA1 138 D2
Swallands Rd CAT SE6 151 J2
Swallow Cl BUSH WD23 22 B7
ERITH DA8 118 B7
NWCR SE14 111 K7
Swallow Ct RSLP HA4 * 47 G7
Swallowdale SAND/SEL CR2 179 F7
Swallow Dr NTHLT UB5 84 A1
WLSDN NW10 69 F5
Swallowfield Rd CHARL SE7 114 A4
Swallowfield Wy
HYS/HAR UB3 101 G1
Swallow Gdns
STRHM/NOR SW16 148 D4
Swallow Pl REGST W1B 10 D5
Swallow St EHAM E6 95 J4
REGST W1B 10 F7
Swanage Rd CHING E4 44 A6
WAND/EARL SW18 128 B5
Swanage Waye YEAD UB4 83 G5
Swan Ap EHAM E6 95 J4
Swanbridge Rd BXLYHN DA7 117 H7
Swan Cl CROY/NA CR0 * 165 F6
FELT TW13 141 J3
WALTH E17 43 G7
Swandon Wy
WAND/EARL SW18 128 A3
Swan Dr CDALE/KGS NW9 51 G1
Swanfield St BETH E2 7 L8
Swan Island TWK TW1 * 143 G2
Swan La CANST EC4R 13 G7
DART DA1 138 C6
TRDG/WHET N20 39 G2
Swanley Rd WELL DA16 116 D7
Swan Md STHWK SE1 19 J4
Swan Ms BRXN/ST SW9 130 A1
Swan Pas WCHPL E1 13 M7
Swan Pl BARN SW13 126 C1
Swan Rd BERM/RHTH SE16 111 K1
FELT TW13 141 J3
STHL UB1 84 B5
WDR/YW UB7 100 A1
WOOL/PLUM SE18 114 C2
Swanscombe Rd CHSWK W4 106 B4
NTGHL W11 88 B7
Swansea Rd HTHAIR TW6 121 F5
PEND EN3 30 E3
Swanston Pth OXHEY WD19 33 G2
Swan St ISLW TW7 124 C2
STHWK SE1 18 F2
Swanton Gdns
WIM/MER SW19 127 G7
Swanton Rd ERITH DA8 117 H6
Swan Wk CHEL SW3 15 L9
Swan Wy PEND EN3 31 F1
Swanwick Cl PUT/ROE SW15 126 C6
Swan Yd IS N1 73 H5
Swaton Rd BOW E3 93 J3
Swaylands Rd BELV DA17 117 H5
Swaythling Cl UED N18 42 D3
Swedenbourg Gdns
WCHPL E1 92 C6
Sweden Ga BERM/RHTH SE16 112 B3
Sweeney Crs STHWK SE1 19 M2
Sweet Briar Gn ED N9 42 B2
Sweet Briar Gv ED N9 42 B2
Sweet Briar Wk UED N18 42 B3
Sweetmans Av PIN HA5 47 H2
Sweets Wy TRDG/WHET N20 39 H1
Swete St PLSTW E13 94 E1
Sweyn Pl BKHTH/KID SE3 133 K1
Swift Cl HYS/HAR UB3 82 D5
RYLN/HDSTN HA2 66 B1
THMD SE28 97 H5
WALTH E17 43 G6
Swift Rd FELT TW13 141 H3
NWDGN UB2 102 E2
Swiftsden Wy BMLY BR1 152 C5
Swift St FUL/PGN SW6 107 H7
Swinbrook Rd NKENS W10 88 C4
Swinburne Crs CROY/NA CR0 165 K5
Swinburne Rd PUT/ROE SW15 126 D3
Swinderby Rd ALP/SUD HA0 68 A5
Swindon Cl GDMY/SEVK IG3 78 E2
Swindon Rd HTHAIR TW6 121 F4
Swindon St SHB W12 * 87 K7
Swinfield Cl FELT TW13 141 J3
Swinford Gdns BRXN/ST SW9 130 C2
Swingate La
WOOL/PLUM SE18 115 K6
Swinnerton St HOM E9 75 G4
Swinton Cl WBLY HA9 50 D7
Swinton Pl FSBYW WC1X 5 L7
Swinton St FSBYW WC1X 5 L7
Swires Shaw HAYES BR2 181 H3
Swiss Av WATW WD18 20 C3
Swiss Cl WATW WD18 20 C2
Swithland Gdns
ELTH/MOT SE9 153 K3
Swyncombe Av EA W5 104 C3
Swynford Gdns HDN NW4 51 J3
Sybil Phoenix Cl DEPT SE8 112 A4
Sybourn St WALTH E17 57 H6
Sycamore Ap
RKW/CH/CXG WD3 20 A4
Sycamore Av BFN/LL DA15 136 A5
BOW E3 75 H7
EA W5 104 E2
HYS/HAR UB3 82 C6
Sycamore Cl ACT W3 87 G7
BUSH WD23 21 J1
CAN/RD E16 94 C3
CAR SM5 175 K3
EBAR EN4 27 H5
ED N9 42 C3
EDGW HA8 36 E3
FELT TW13 140 E2
NTHLT UB5 65 J7
SAND/SEL CR2 178 A4
Sycamore Gdns MTCM CR4 162 C1
SHB W12 106 E1
Sycamore Gv CAT SE6 133 F5
CDALE/KGS NW9 50 E6
GPK RM2 63 J1
NWMAL KT3 160 B2
PGE/AN SE20 150 C7
Sycamore Hl FBAR/BDGN N11 40 A5
Sycamore Ms CLAP SW4 129 H2
ERITH DA8 * 118 A4
Sycamore Rd DART DA1 139 G6
RKW/CH/CXG WD3 20 A4
WIM/MER SW19 146 A5
Sycamore St FSBYE EC1V 12 E1
Sycamore Wk NKENS W10 88 C3
Sycamore Wy TEDD TW11 143 J5
Sydcote DUL SE21 * 149 J1
Sydenham Av SYD SE26 150 D4
Sydenham Cl ROM RM1 63 H3
Sydenham Cots
LEE/GVPK SE12 * 153 G1
Sydenham Hl FSTH SE23 150 D1
SYD SE26 150 C2
Sydenham Pk SYD SE26 150 E2
Sydenham Park Rd SYD SE26 150 E2
Sydenham Ri FSTH SE23 150 D1
Sydenham Rd CROY/NA CR0 177 J1
SYD SE26 151 F4
Sydenham Station Ap
SYD SE26 150 E3
Sydmons Ct FSTH SE23 * 131 K6
Sydner Ms STNW/STAM N16 74 B3
Sydner Rd STNW/STAM N16 74 B3
Sydney Chapman Wy
BAR EN5 26 D1
Sydney Cl SKENS SW7 15 H6
Sydney Gv HDN NW4 52 A4
Sydney Ms CHEL SW3 15 H6
Sydney Pl SKENS SW7 15 H6
Sydney Rd ABYW SE2 116 E2
BARK/HLT IG6 60 C1
BXLYHS DA6 136 E3
CEND/HSY/T N8 55 G3
EBED/NFELT TW14 121 K7
ENC/FH EN2 29 K3
MUSWH N10 40 B7
RCH/KEW TW9 125 F3
RYNPK SW20 161 G1
SCUP DA14 154 E3
SUT SM1 174 E3
TEDD TW11 143 F4
WAN E11 59 F5
WATW WD18 20 C4
WEA W13 85 G7
WFD IG8 44 E3
Sydney St CHEL SW3 15 J7
Sydney Ter ESH/CLAY KT10 * 171 F5
Sylvan Av CHDH RM6 62 B5
MLHL NW7 37 G5
WDGN N22 41 G6
Sylvan Gdns SURB KT6 158 E6
Sylvan Gv CRICK NW2 70 B3
PECK SE15 111 J5
Sylvan Hl NRWD SE19 150 A7
Sylvan Rd FSTGT E7 76 E5
IL IG1 78 C1
NRWD SE19 150 B7
WALTH E17 * 57 J4
WAN E11 58 E4
Sylvan Ter PECK SE15 * 111 J6
Sylvan Wk BMLY BR1 168 E2
Sylvan Wy BCTR RM8 79 H2
WWKM BR4 180 C3
Sylverdale Rd CROY/NA CR0 177 H2
Sylvester Av CHST BR7 153 K5
Sylvester Pth HACK E8 * 74 D5
Sylvester Rd ALP/SUD HA0 67 J4
EFNCH N2 53 G1
HACK E8 * 74 D5
WALTH E17 * 57 H6
Sylvia Av PIN HA5 33 K5
Sylvia Gdns WBLY HA9 68 D6
Symes Ms CAMTN NW1 4 E5
Symington Ms HOM E9 75 F4
Symister Ms IS N1 7 J8
Symons Cl PECK SE15 131 K1
Symons St CHEL SW3 15 M6
KTBR SW1X 15 M6
Symphony Cl EDGW HA8 36 D6
Symphony Ms NKENS W10 88 C2
Syon Gate Wy BTFD TW8 104 B6
Syon La ISLW TW7 104 B6
Syon Pk ISLW TW7 * 124 C2
Syon Park Gdns ISLW TW7 104 A6

T

Tabard Garden Est
STHWK SE1 19 G1
Tabard St STHWK SE1 19 G2
Tabernacle Av PLSTW E13 94 E3
Tabernacle St SDTCH EC2A 13 H1
Tableer Av CLAP SW4 129 H4
Tabley Rd HOLWY N7 72 E3
Tabor Gdns CHEAM SM3 174 C5
Tabor Gv WIM/MER SW19 146 C6
Tabor Rd HMSMTH W6 106 E2
Tachbrook Rd
EBED/NFELT TW14 121 J6
NWDGN UB2 102 C3
Tachbrook St PIM SW1V 16 F6
Tack Ms BROCKY SE4 132 D2
Tadema Rd WBPTN SW10 108 B6
Tadmor St SHB W12 88 B7
Tadworth Av NWMAL KT3 160 C3
Tadworth Pde HCH RM12 81 K3
Tadworth Rd CRICK NW2 69 J1
Taeping St POP/IOD E14 112 E3
Taffy's How MTCM CR4 162 D2
Tait Ct BOW E3 75 H7
Tait Rd CROY/NA CR0 165 F6
Tait St WCHPL E1 92 D5
Takeley Cl CRW RM5 63 F1
Talacre Rd KTTN NW5 72 A5
Talbot Av EFNCH N2 53 H2
OXHEY WD19 21 J6
Talbot Cl SEVS/STOTM N15 56 B3
Talbot Ct BANK EC3V 13 H6
Talbot Crs HDN NW4 51 J4
Talbot Gdns GDMY/SEVK IG3 79 G1
Talbot Pl BKHTH/KID SE3 133 H1
Talbot Rd ALP/SUD HA0 67 K4
BAY/PAD W2 8 B4
CAR SM5 176 A4
DAGW RM9 80 B6
EDUL SE22 131 F3
EHAM E6 95 K1
FSTGT E7 76 E3
HGT N6 54 A5
ISLW TW7 124 B3
KTN/HRWW/WS HA3 49 F1
NTGHL W11 88 D5
NWDGN UB2 102 D3
SEVS/STOTM N15 56 B3
THHTH CR7 164 E3
WDGN N22 54 C1
WEA W13 * 85 G6
WHTN TW2 123 K7
Talbot Sq BAY/PAD W2 9 G5
Talbot Wk NTGHL W11 88 C5
WLSDN NW10 * 69 G5
Talbot Yd STHWK SE1 13 G9
Talcott Pth
BRXS/STRHM SW2 * 130 B7
Talehangers Cl BXLYHS DA6 136 E3
Talfourd Pl PECK SE15 111 G7
Talfourd Rd PECK SE15 111 G7
Talgarth Rd HMSMTH W6 * 107 F4
WKENS W14 107 H4
Talgarth Wk CDALE/KGS NW9 51 G4
Talisman Cl GDMY/SEVK IG3 61 H7
Talisman Sq SYD SE26 150 C3
Talisman Wy WBLY HA9 68 B2
Tallack Cl KTN/HRWW/WS HA3 34 E6
Tallack Rd LEY E10 57 H7
Tall Elms Cl HAYES BR2 167 J4
Tallis Cl CAN/RD E16 95 F5
Tallis Gv CHARL SE7 114 A5
Tallis St EMB EC4Y 12 B6
Tallis Vw WLSDN NW10 69 F5
Tallow Cl DAGW RM9 79 K5
Tallow Rd BTFD TW8 104 D5
Tall Trees STRHM/NOR SW16 164 A2
Talma Gdns WHTN TW2 123 K6
Talmage Cl FSTH SE23 131 K6
Talman Gv STAN HA7 35 K5
Talma Rd BRXS/STRHM SW2 130 B3
Talwin St BOW E3 93 K2
Tamar Cl BOW E3 * 75 H7
Tamarind Yd WAP E1W 92 C7
Tamarisk Sq SHB W12 87 H6
Tamar St CHARL SE7 114 D3
Tamesis Gdns WPK KT4 173 G1
Tamian Wy HSLWW TW4 122 B3
Tamworth Av WFD IG8 44 C5
Tamworth La MTCM CR4 163 G2
Tamworth Pk MTCM CR4 163 G3
Tamworth Pl CROY/NA CR0 * 177 J1
Tamworth Rd CROY/NA CR0 177 J1
Tamworth St FUL/PGN SW6 14 A9
Tancred Rd FSBYPK N4 55 H5
Tandridge Dr ORP BR6 169 J7
Tanfield Av CRICK NW2 69 H3
Tanfield Rd CROY/NA CR0 177 J3
Tangier Rd RCHPK/HAM TW10 125 H3
Tangleberry Cl BMLY BR1 168 E3
Tangle Tree Cl FNCH N3 53 F1
Tanglewood Cl CROY/NA CR0 178 E2
STAN HA7 34 E1
Tanglewood Wy FELT TW13 141 F2
Tangley Gv PUT/ROE SW15 126 C6
Tangley Park Rd HPTN TW12 * 141 K4
Tangmere Crs HCH RM12 81 K5
Tangmere Gdns NTHLT UB5 83 G1
Tangmere Gv KUTN/CMB KT2 143 K4
Tangmere Wy
CDALE/KGS NW9 51 G1
Tanhouse Fld KTTN NW5 * 72 D4
Tankerton Houses
STPAN WC1H * 5 K8
Tankerton Rd SURB KT6 172 B1
Tankerton St STPAN WC1H 5 K8
Tankerton Ter CROY/NA CR0 * 164 A6
Tankerville Rd
STRHM/NOR SW16 148 D6
Tank Hill Rd PUR RM19 119 K2
Tankridge Rd CRICK NW2 69 K1
The Tanneries WCHPL E1 * 92 E3
Tanners Cl WOT/HER KT12 156 A5
Tanners End La UED N18 42 A3
Tanner's Hl DEPT SE8 112 D7
Tanners La BARK/HLT IG6 60 C2
Tanners Ms DEPT SE8 112 C7
Tanner St BARK IG11 78 C5
STHWK SE1 19 K2
Tannery Cl CROY/NA CR0 166 A4
DAGE RM10 80 D2
Tannington Ter HBRY N5 73 G2
Tannoy Sq WNWD SE27 149 K3
Tannsfeld Rd SYD SE26 151 F4
Tansley Cl HOLWY N7 72 D4
Tanswell St STHWK SE1 * 18 A2
Tansy Cl EHAM E6 96 A5
Tantallon Rd BAL SW12 129 F7
Tant Av CAN/RD E16 94 D5
Tantony Gv CHDH RM6 61 K2
Tanworth Cl NTHWD HA6 32 A5
Tanworth Gdns PIN HA5 47 F1
Tan Yard La BXLY DA5 * 137 H6
Tanza Rd HAMP NW3 71 K3
Tapestry Cl BELMT SM2 175 F6
Taplow Ct MTCM CR4 162 D3
Taplow Rd PLMGR N13 41 J3
Taplow St IS N1 6 F6
Tappesfield Rd PECK SE15 131 K2
Tapping Cl KUTN/CMB KT2 * 144 C6
Tapp St WCHPL E1 92 D3
Tapster St BAR EN5 26 D2
Tara Ms CEND/HSY/T N8 54 E5
Taransay Wk IS N1 73 K5
Tara Ter BROCKY SE4 * 132 B2
Tarbert Rd EDUL SE22 131 F4
Tarbert Wk WCHPL E1 92 E6
Target Cl EBED/NFELT TW14 121 H5
Tariff Rd UED N18 42 C5
Tarleton Gdns FSTH SE23 131 J7
Tarling Cl SCUP DA14 155 H2
Tarling Rd CAN/RD E16 94 D5
EFNCH N2 39 G7
Tarling St WCHPL E1 92 D5
Tarnbank ENC/FH EN2 28 E4
Tarn St STHWK SE1 18 E4
Tarnwood Pk ELTH/MOT SE9 134 E7
Tarragon Cl NWCR SE14 112 B6
Tarragon Gv SYD SE26 151 F5
Tarrant Pl MBLAR W1H 9 L3
Tarriff Crs DEPT SE8 112 C3
Tarrington Cl
STRHM/NOR SW16 148 D3
Tarver Rd WALW SE17 18 D8
Tarves Wy GNWCH SE10 112 E6
Tash Pl FBAR/BDGN N11 * 40 B4
Tasker Cl HYS/HAR UB3 101 F6
Tasker Rd HAMP NW3 71 K4
Tasmania Ter UED N18 41 J5
Tasman Rd BRXN/ST SW9 129 K2
Tasso Rd HMSMTH W6 107 H5
Tate Gdns BUSH WD23 22 E6
Tate Rd CAN/RD E16 95 K7
SUT SM1 174 E4
Tatham Pl STJWD NW8 3 H5
Tatnell Rd FSTH SE23 132 B5
Tattersall Cl ELTH/MOT SE9 134 D4
Tatton Cl CAR SM5 163 F7
Tatton Crs CLPT E5 56 B6
Tatum Rd WLSDN NW10 68 E6
Tatum St WALW SE17 19 H6
Tauber Cl BORE WD6 24 B3
Tauheed Cl FSBYPK N4 73 J1
Taunton Av HSLW TW3 123 H1
RYNPK SW20 160 E1
Taunton Cl BXLYHN DA7 138 A2
CHEAM SM3 161 K7
Taunton Dr EFNCH N2 53 G1
ENC/FH EN2 29 G2
Taunton Ms CAMTN NW1 9 L1
Taunton Pl CAMTN NW1 3 L9
Taunton Rd GFD/PVL UB6 66 B6
LEE/GVPK SE12 133 H4
Taunton Wy STAN HA7 50 A1
Tavern Cl CAR SM5 162 D6
Taverners Cl NTGHL W11 88 C7
Taverner Sq HBRY N5 * 73 J3
Tavistock Av GFD/PVL UB6 85 G1
MLHL NW7 38 B6
WALTH E17 57 F2
Tavistock Cl
STNW/STAM N16 * 74 A4
Tavistock Ct COVGDN WC2E * 11 K6
Tavistock Crs MTCM CR4 163 K3
NTGHL W11 88 D4
Tavistock Gdns
GDMY/SEVK IG3 78 E3
Tavistock Gv CROY/NA CR0 164 E6
Tavistock Ms NTGHL W11 * 88 D5
Tavistock Pl STHGT/OAK N14 * 28 B5
STPAN WC1H 5 H9
Tavistock Rd CAR SM5 162 C7
CROY/NA CR0 164 E7
EDGW HA8 36 B7
FSBYPK N4 55 K5
HAYES BR2 167 K3
HGDN/ICK UB10 64 B4
NTGHL W11 88 D4
SRTFD E15 76 D5
SWFD E18 58 E2
WAN E11 76 D3
WELL DA16 116 D7
WLSDN NW10 87 H1
Tavistock Sq STPAN WC1H 5 H9
Tavistock St COVGDN WC2E 11 K6
HOL/ALD WC2B 11 L6
Tavistock Ter ARCH N19 72 D2
Taviton St STPAN WC1H 5 G9
Tavy Br ABYW SE2 116 D1
Tavy Cl LBTH SE11 18 B7
Tawney Rd THMD SE28 97 H6
Tawny Cl FELT TW13 140 E2
WEA W13 85 H7
Tawny Wy BERM/RHTH SE16 112 A3
Tayben Av WHTN TW2 123 K5
Taybridge Rd BTSEA SW11 129 F2
Tayburn Cl POP/IOD E14 94 A5
Tayfield Cl HGDN/ICK UB10 64 A2
Taylor Av RCH/KEW TW9 125 J1
Taylor Cl DEPT SE8 112 C5
HPTN TW12 142 C4
HSLW TW3 103 H7
TOTM N17 42 C6
Taylor Rd MTCM CR4 147 J6
WLGTN SM6 176 B4
Taylor's Blds
WOOL/PLUM SE18 115 G3
Taylors Cl SCUP DA14 155 F3
Taylors Ct FELT TW13 140 E1
Taylor's Gn ACT W3 * 87 G5
Taylors La WLSDN NW10 69 G5
Taylor's La SYD SE26 150 D3
WLSDN NW10 69 G6
Taylors Md MLHL NW7 * 37 J4
Taymount Ri FSTH SE23 150 E1
Tayport Cl IS N1 5 L2
Tayside Dr EDGW HA8 36 D2
Taywood Rd NTHLT UB5 83 J3
Teak Cl BERM/RHTH SE16 93 G7
Teal Cl CAN/RD E16 95 H4
Teal Dr NTHWD HA6 32 A6
Teale St BETH E2 92 C1
Teal Pl SUT SM1 174 D4
Tealing Dr HOR/WEW KT19 173 F3
Teal St GNWCH SE10 113 J2
Teasel Cl CROY/NA CR0 166 A7
Teasel Crs THMD SE28 96 E7
Teasel Wy SRTFD E15 94 C2
Tebworth Rd TOTM N17 42 B6
Teck Cl ISLW TW7 124 B1
Tedder Cl CHSGTN KT9 171 J4
RSLP HA4 64 E4
Tedder Rd SAND/SEL CR2 179 F6
Teddington Pk TEDD TW11 143 F4
Teddington Park Rd
TEDD TW11 143 F3
Tedworth Gdns CHEL SW3 15 L8
Tedworth Sq CHEL SW3 15 L8
Tees Av GFD/PVL UB6 84 E1
Teesdale Av ISLW TW7 104 B7
Teesdale Cl BETH E2 92 C1
Teesdale Gdns ISLW TW7 104 B7
SNWD SE25 165 F1
Teesdale Rd WAN E11 58 D5
Teesdale St BETH E2 92 D1
Teesdale Yd BETH E2 * 92 D1
The Tee ACT W3 87 G5
Teevan Cl CROY/NA CR0 165 H6
Teevan Rd CROY/NA CR0 165 H6
Teign Ms ELTH/MOT SE9 153 J1
Teignmouth Cl CLAP SW4 129 J3
EDGW HA8 50 B1
Teignmouth Gdns
GFD/PVL UB6 85 G1
Teignmouth Rd CRICK NW2 70 B4
WELL DA16 136 D1
Telcote Wy RSLP HA4 * 47 G6
Telegraph Hl HAMP NW3 71 F2
Telegraph La ESH/CLAY KT10 171 F3
Telegraph Ms GDMY/SEVK IG3 61 F7
Telegraph Pas
BRXS/STRHM SW2 129 K6
Telegraph Pl POP/IOD E14 112 E3
Telegraph Rd PUT/ROE SW15 126 E6
Telegraph St LOTH EC2R 13 G4
Telephone Pl WKENS W14 * 107 J5
Telferscot Rd BAL SW12 129 J7
Telford Av BRXS/STRHM SW2 129 J7
Telford Cl NRWD SE19 150 B5
WALTH E17 57 G6
Telford Dr WOT/HER KT12 156 B6
Telford Rd CDALE/KGS NW9 51 H5
ELTH/MOT SE9 154 D1
NKENS W10 88 C4
STHL UB1 84 B6
WHTN TW2 123 F6
Telford Rd (North Circular Rd)
FBAR/BDGN N11 40 C4
Telfords Yd WAP E1W * 92 C6
Telford Ter PIM SW1V 16 E9
Telford Wy ACT W3 87 G4
YEAD UB4 83 J4
Telham Rd EHAM E6 96 A1
Tell Gv EDUL SE22 131 G3
Tellisford ESH/CLAY KT10 170 B3
Tellson Av WOOL/PLUM SE18 114 D7
Temeraire Pl BTFD TW8 105 G4
Temeraire St
BERM/RHTH SE16 111 K1
Tempelhof Av HDN NW4 52 A6
Temperley Rd BAL SW12 129 F6
Tempest Wy RAIN RM13 81 J5
Templar Dr THMD SE28 97 K5
Templar Pl HPTN TW12 142 A6
Templars Av GLDGN NW11 52 D5
Templars Ct DART DA1 * 139 K4
Templars Crs FNCH N3 52 E1
Templars Dr
KTN/HRWW/WS HA3 * 34 D5
Templar St CMBW SE5 130 C1
Temple Av BCTR RM8 62 C7
CROY/NA CR0 179 H2
EMB EC4Y 12 B6
TRDG/WHET N20 27 H6
Temple Cl FNCH N3 52 D1
THMD SE28 115 H2
WAN E11 58 C6
WAT WD17 20 D1
Templecombe Rd HOM E9 74 E7
Templecombe Wy MRDN SM4 161 H4
Temple Dwellings BETH E2 * 92 D1
Temple Fortune Hl
GLDGN NW11 52 E4
Temple Fortune La
GLDGN NW11 52 D5
Temple Gdns BCTR RM8 79 K2
EMB EC4Y * 12 A6
GLDGN NW11 52 D5
WCHMH N21 * 41 H1
Temple Gv ENC/FH EN2 29 H2
GLDGN NW11 52 E5
Temple Hl DART DA1 139 J4
Temple Hill Sq DART DA1 139 J4
Temple La EMB EC4Y 12 B5
Templeman Rd HNWL W7 85 F4
Templemead Cl ACT W3 87 G5
Temple Mead Cl STAN HA7 35 H5
Temple Mills La SRTFD E15 76 A4
Temple Pde BAR EN5 * 27 H6
Temple Pl TPL/STR WC2R 11 M6
Temple Rd CEND/HSY/T N8 55 F3
CHSWK W4 105 K2
CRICK NW2 70 A3
CROY/NA CR0 177 K3
EA W5 104 E2
EHAM E6 77 J7
HSLW TW3 123 G3
Temple Sheen Rd
MORT/ESHN SW14 125 K3
Temple St BETH E2 92 D1
Temple Ter WDGN N22 * 55 G1
Templeton Av CHING E4 43 J3
Templeton Cl NRWD SE19 149 K7
STNW/STAM N16 * 74 A4
Templeton Pl ECT SW5 14 B6
Templeton Rd FSBYPK N4 55 K5
Temple Wy SUT SM1 175 H2
Templewood WEA W13 85 H4
Templewood Av HAMP NW3 71 F2
Templewood Gdns
HAMP NW3 71 F2
Temple Yd BETH E2 92 C2
Tempsford Av BORE WD6 25 F3
Tempsford Cl ENC/FH EN2 29 J2
Temsford Cl RYLN/HDSTN HA2 48 C1
Tenbury Cl FSTGT E7 77 H4
Tenbury Ct BAL SW12 129 J7
Tenby Av KTN/HRWW/WS HA3 49 H1
Tenby Cl CHDH RM6 62 A5
SEVS/STOTM N15 56 B3
Tenby Gdns NTHLT UB5 66 A5
Tenby Rd CHDH RM6 62 A5
EDGW HA8 36 B7
PEND EN3 30 E2
WALTH E17 57 G4
WELL DA16 116 E7
Tench St WAP E1W * 92 D7
Tenda Rd STHWK SE1 111 J3
Tendring Wy CHDH RM6 61 J4
Tenham Av BRXS/STRHM SW2 148 D1
Tenison Wy STHWK SE1 12 A9
Tenniel Cl BAY/PAD W2 8 E5
Tennison Av BORE WD6 24 D4
Tennison Rd SNWD SE25 165 G3
Tennis St STHWK SE1 19 G1
Tennyson Av CDALE/KGS NW9 50 E2
MNPK E12 77 J6
NWMAL KT3 160 E4
TWK TW1 124 A7
WAN E11 58 E6
Tennyson Cl
EBED/NFELT TW14 121 K5
PEND EN3 31 F4
WELL DA16 115 K7
Tennyson Rd DART DA1 139 K4
HNWL W7 85 F6
HSLW TW3 123 H1
KIL/WHAMP NW6 70 D7
LEY E10 57 K7
MLHL NW7 37 H4
PGE/AN SE20 151 F6
SRTFD E15 76 C6
WALTH E17 57 H5
WIM/MER SW19 147 G5
Tennyson St VX/NE SW8 129 G1
Tennyson Wy HCH RM12 63 H7
Tensing Rd NWDGN UB2 103 F2
Tentelow La NWDGN UB2 103 G2
Tenterden Cl ELTH/MOT SE9 153 K3
HDN NW4 52 B2
Tenterden Dr HDN NW4 52 B2
Tenterden Gdns CROY/NA CR0 165 H6
HDN NW4 52 B2
Tenterden Gv HDN NW4 52 A3
Tenterden Rd BCTR RM8 80 B1
CROY/NA CR0 165 H6
TOTM N17 42 B6
Tenterden St CONDST W1S 10 D5
Tenter Gnd WCHPL E1 13 L3
Tent Peg La STMC/STPC BR5 169 H4
Tent St WCHPL E1 92 D3
Teredo St LEW SE13 132 E1
Terling Cl WAN E11 76 D2
Terling Rd BCTR RM8 80 C1
Terling Wk IS N1 * 6 E3
Terminus Pl BGVA SW1W 16 D4
Terrace Gdns BARN SW13 126 C1
WAT WD17 21 F1
Terrace Rd HOM E9 75 F6
PLSTW E13 76 E7
WOT/HER KT12 156 A5
The Terrace BARN SW13 126 B1
BETH E2 * 92 E2
CHING E4 * 44 C2
DEPT SE8 * 112 C3
EFNCH N2 * 54 A3
FNCH N3 * 52 D1
FSTH SE23 * 132 B6
KIL/WHAMP NW6 2 A3
Terrace Vls HMSMTH W6 * 106 D4
Terrace Wk DAGW RM9 80 A4
Terrac St RCH/KEW TW9 125 G3
Terrapin Rd TOOT SW17 148 B2
Terretts Pl IS N1 6 C2
Terrick Rd WDGN N22 40 E7
Terrick St SHB W12 87 K5
Terrilands PIN HA5 47 K2
Terront Rd SEVS/STOTM N15 55 J4

Tessa Sanderson Wy
GFD/PVL UB6 66 D4
Testerton Rd NTGHL W11 * 88 B6
Testerton Wk NTGHL W11 * 88 B6
Tetbury Pl IS N1 6 C4
Tetcott Rd WBPTN SW10 108 B6
Tetherdown MUSWH N10 54 A2
Tetty Wy BMLY BR1 167 K1
Teversham La VX/NE SW8 109 K7
Teviot Cl WELL DA16 116 C7
Teviot St POP/IOD E14 94 A4
Tewkesbury Av FSTH SE23 131 J7
PIN HA5 47 J4
Tewkesbury Cl
SEVS/STOTM N15 55 K5
Tewkesbury Gdns
CDALE/KGS NW9 50 D2
Tewkesbury Rd CAR SM5 162 C7
SEVS/STOTM N15 55 K6
WEA W13 85 G7
Tewkesbury Ter
FBAR/BDGN N11 40 C5
Tewson Rd WOOL/PLUM SE18 115 K4
Teynham Av EN EN1 29 K5
Teynham Gn HAYES BR2 167 K4
Teynton Ter TOTM N17 41 J7
Thackeray Av TOTM N17 56 C1
Thackeray Cl ISLW TW7 124 B1
WIM/MER SW19 146 B6
Thackeray Dr CHDH RM6 61 H6
Thackeray Ms HACK E8 74 C5
Thackeray Rd EHAM E6 95 H1
VX/NE SW8 129 G1
Thackeray St KENS W8 14 D3
Thakeham Cl SYD SE26 150 D4
Thalia Cl GNWCH SE10 113 G5
Thame Rd BERM/RHTH SE16 112 A1
Thames Av DAGW RM9 98 D3
GFD/PVL UB6 85 F1
WBPTN SW10 108 B7
WPK KT4 161 F7
Thames Bank
MORT/ESHN SW14 125 K1
Thamesbank Pl THMD SE28 97 J5
Thames Cir POP/IOD E14 112 D3
Thames Cl HPTN TW12 157 G1
RAIN RM13 99 K5
Thames Crs CHSWK W4 106 B6
Thames Down Link
BRYLDS KT5 159 K4
HOR/WEW KT19 172 C6
WPK KT4 173 F2
Thames Dr RSLP HA4 46 A5
Thames Eyot TWK TW1 * 143 G1
Thames Ga DART DA1 139 K4
Thamesgate Cl
RCHPK/HAM TW10 143 H3
Thameside TEDD TW11 143 K6
Thames Meadow
E/WMO/HCT KT8 157 F2
Thamesmere Dr THMD SE28 97 G6
Thames Pth BARN SW13 106 C7
BERM/RHTH SE16 112 C2
CHEL SW3 109 F5
CLPT E5 75 F2
E/WMO/HCT KT8 158 A3
ISLW TW7 124 C1
KUTN/CMB KT2 143 J4
MORT/ESHN SW14 126 B1
PIM SW1V 17 H8
POP/IOD E14 112 D2
RCH/KEW TW9 124 D4
RCHPK/HAM TW10 143 G2
SRTFD E15 93 K1
SUN TW16 156 B2
TPL/STR WC2R 11 M7
TWK TW1 143 G1
TWRH EC3N 13 K8
VX/NE SW8 109 J5
Thames Pl PUT/ROE SW15 127 G2
Thamespoint TEDD TW11 * 143 K6
Thames Quay WBPTN SW10 * 108 B7
Thames Reach KUT/HW KT1 * 143 K7
Thames Rd BARK IG11 97 G2
CAN/RD E16 95 H7
CHSWK W4 105 H3
DART DA1 138 D2
Thames Side KUT/HW KT1 143 K7
THDIT KT7 158 C5
Thames St GNWCH SE10 112 E5
HPTN TW12 157 G1
KUT/HW KT1 158 E1
SUN TW16 156 A2
Thamesvale Cl HSLW TW3 123 F1
Thames Village CHSWK W4 105 K7
Thamley PUR RM19 119 K3
Thanescroft Gdns
CROY/NA CR0 178 A2
Thanet Dr HAYES BR2 181 H2
Thanet Pl CROY/NA CR0 177 J3
Thanet Rd BXLY DA5 137 H6
ERITH DA8 118 B6
Thanet St STPAN WC1H 5 J8
Thane Vls HOLWY N7 73 F2
Thant Cl LEY E10 75 K2
Tharp Rd WLGTN SM6 176 D4
Thatcham Gdns
TRDG/WHET N20 27 G6
Thatcher Cl WDR/YW UB7 100 B1
Thatchers Wy ISLW TW7 123 J4
Thatches Gv CHDH RM6 62 A2
Thavies Inn FLST/FETLN EC4A 12 B4
Thaxted Pl RYNPK SW20 146 B6
Thaxted Rd ELTH/MOT SE9 154 C1
Thaxton Rd WKENS W14 107 J5
Thayers Farm Rd BECK BR3 151 G7
Thayer St MHST W1U 10 B4
Theatre Sq SRTFD E15 76 B5
Theatre St BTSEA SW11 128 E2
Theberton St IS N1 6 B3
The Beverly MRDN SM4 161 G5
The Courtyard HAYES BR2 181 J5
Theed St STHWK SE1 12 A9
The Green WIM/MER SW19 146 B4
Thelma Gv TEDD TW11 143 G5
Theobald Crs
KTN/HRWW/WS HA3 34 B7
Theobald Rd CROY/NA CR0 177 H1
WALTH E17 57 H6
Theobald's Rd GINN WC1R 11 L2
Theobald St BORE WD6 24 B2
STHWK SE1 19 G4
Theodora Wy PIN HA5 46 D2
Theodore Rd LEW SE13 133 G5
Therapia La CROY/NA CR0 163 J6
Therapia Rd EDUL SE22 131 K5
Theresa Rd HMSMTH W6 106 D3
Theresa's Wk SAND/SEL CR2 177 K7
Thermopylae Ga POP/IOD E14 112 E3
Theseus Wk IS N1 6 D6
Thesiger Rd PGE/AN SE20 151 F6
Thessaly Rd VX/NE SW8 109 J7
Thetford Cl PLMGR N13 41 H5
Thetford Rd DAGW RM9 79 K6
NWMAL KT3 160 A5
Theydon Gdns RAIN RM13 81 G6
Theydon Gv WFD IG8 45 G5
Theydon Rd CLPT E5 74 E1
Theydon St WALTH E17 57 H6
Thicket Crs SUT SM1 175 G3
Thicket Gv DAGW RM9 79 J5
PGE/AN SE20 150 C6
Thicket Rd PGE/AN SE20 150 D6
SUT SM1 175 G3
Thicket Ter PGE/AN SE20 * 150 C6
Third Av ACT W3 87 H7
CHDH RM6 61 J5
DAGE RM10 80 D7
EN EN1 30 B4
HYS/HAR UB3 82 D7
MNPK E12 77 J3
NKENS W10 88 C2
PLSTW E13 94 E2
WALTH E17 57 J4
WBLY HA9 67 K1
Third Cl E/WMO/HCT KT8 157 G3
Third Cross Rd WHTN TW2 142 D1
Thirleby Rd EDGW HA8 37 F7
MLHL NW7 38 C4
WEST SW1P 16 F4
Thirlmere Av GFD/PVL UB6 85 J2
Thirlmere Gdns WBLY HA9 49 J7
Thirlmere Ri BMLY BR1 152 D5
Thirlmere Rd BXLYHN DA7 137 K1
MUSWH N10 40 B7
STRHM/NOR SW16 148 D3
Thirsk Cl NTHLT UB5 66 A5
Thirsk Rd BTSEA SW11 129 F2
MTCM CR4 148 A6
SNWD SE25 164 E3
Thirza Rd DART DA1 139 J5
Thislefield Cl BXLY DA5 136 E7
Thistlebrook ABYW SE2 116 D2
Thistlecroft Gdns STAN HA7 35 K7
Thistledene THDIT KT7 157 K5
Thistledene Av
RYLN/HDSTN HA2 65 J2
Thistle Gv WBPTN SW10 14 F8
Thistlemead CHST BR7 169 G1
Thistlewaite Rd CLPT E5 74 D2
Thistlewood Cl HOLWY N7 73 F1
Thistleworth Cl ISLW TW7 103 J6
Thistley Cl
NFNCH/WDSPK N12 39 J5
Thomas A Beckett Cl
HRW HA1 67 F3
Thomas Baines Rd
BTSEA SW11 128 C2
Thomas Cribb Ms EHAM E6 95 K5
Thomas Dean Rd SYD SE26 * 151 H3
Thomas Dinwiddy Rd
LEE/GVPK SE12 153 F1
Thomas Doyle St STHWK SE1 18 C3
Thomas Fyre Dr BOW E3 93 J1
Thomas Jacomb Pl
WALTH E17 57 H3
Thomas' La CAT SE6 132 E6
Thomas Moore St WAP E1W 92 C6
Thomas Moore Wy EFNCH N2 53 G2
Thomas More Gdns
ESH/CLAY KT10 170 A1
Thomas More St WAP E1W * 92 C6
Thomas North Ter
CAN/RD E16 * 94 D4
Thomas Pl KENS W8 14 C4
Thomas Rd POP/IOD E14 93 H5
Thomas St WOOL/PLUM SE18 115 F3
Thomas Wall Cl SUT SM1 175 F4
Thompson Av CMBW SE5 110 D6
RCH/KEW TW9 125 J2
Thompson Cl CHEAM SM3 161 K7
IL IG1 78 C1
Thompson Rd DAGW RM9 80 B2
EDUL SE22 131 G5
HSLW TW3 123 G3
Thomson Crs CROY/NA CR0 164 B7
Thomson Rd
KTN/HRWW/WS HA3 48 E2
Thorburn Sq STHWK SE1 111 H3
Thorburn Wy
WIM/MER SW19 * 147 H7
Thoresby St IS N1 6 F7
Thorkhill Gdns THDIT KT7 158 B7
Thorkhill Rd THDIT KT7 158 C7
Thornaby Gdns UED N18 42 C5
Thorn Av BUSH WD23 22 C7
Thornbury Av ISLW TW7 103 J6
Thornbury Cl
STNW/STAM N16 74 A4
Thornbury Gdns BORE WD6 24 E3
Thornbury Rd CLAP SW4 129 K5
ISLW TW7 123 J1
Thornbury Sq HGT N6 54 C7
Thornby Rd CLPT E5 74 E2
Thorncliffe Rd CLAP SW4 129 J5
NWDGN UB2 102 E4
Thorn Cl HAYES BR2 169 F5
NTHLT UB5 83 K2
Thorncombe Rd EDUL SE22 131 F4
Thorn Ct BELMT SM2 * 175 F6
Thorncroft EMPK RM11 63 K5
Thorncroft Rd SUT SM1 175 F3
Thorncroft St VX/NE SW8 109 K6
Thorndean St
WAND/EARL SW18 147 G1
Thorndene Av
TRDG/WHET N20 28 A7
Thorndike Av NTHLT UB5 65 H7
Thorndike Cl WBPTN SW10 108 B6
Thorndike Rd IS N1 73 K5
Thorndike St PIM SW1V * 17 G6
Thorndon Gdns
HOR/WEW KT19 173 G3
Thorndyke Ct PIN HA5 33 K6
Thorne Cl ASHF TW15 140 A6
CAN/RD E16 94 E5
ERITH DA8 117 J5
ESH/CLAY KT10 171 G6
WAN E11 76 C3
Thorneloe Gdns CROY/NA CR0 177 H4
Thorne Rd VX/NE SW8 109 K6
Thorne's Cl BECK BR3 167 F2
Thorne St BARN SW13 126 B2
Thornet Wood Rd BMLY BR1 169 F2
Thorney Crs BTSEA SW11 * 108 C6
Thorneycroft Cl
WOT/HER KT12 156 B5
Thorney Hedge Rd
CHSWK W4 105 J3
Thorney St WEST SW1P 17 J5
Thornfield Av MLHL NW7 38 C7
Thornfield Pde MLHL NW7 * 38 C6
Thornfield Rd SHB W12 106 E1
Thornford Rd LEW SE13 133 F4
Thorngate Rd MV/WKIL W9 2 B9
Thorngrove Rd PLSTW E13 77 F7
Thornham Gv SRTFD E15 76 B4
Thornham St GNWCH SE10 112 E5
Thornhaugh St STPAN WC1H 11 H1
Thornhill Av SURB KT6 172 A1
WOOL/PLUM SE18 115 K6
Thornhill Bridge Whf IS N1 5 L4
Thornhill Crs IS N1 5 M2
Thornhill Gdns BARK IG11 78 E6
LEY E10 75 K1
Thornhill Gv IS N1 6 A2
Thornhill Rd CROY/NA CR0 164 D6
IS N1 6 A1
LEY E10 75 K1
NTHWD HA6 32 A3
SURB KT6 172 A1
Thornhill Sq IS N1 5 M2
Thornlaw Rd WNWD SE27 149 G3
Thornley Cl TOTM N17 42 C6
Thornley Dr RYLN/HDSTN HA2 66 B1
Thornsbeach Rd CAT SE6 133 F7
Thornsett Pl PGE/AN SE20 165 J1
Thornsett Rd PGE/AN SE20 165 J1
WAND/EARL SW18 147 F1
Thornsett Ter PGE/AN SE20 * 165 J1
Thornton Av
BRXS/STRHM SW2 129 J7
CHSWK W4 106 B3
CROY/NA CR0 164 A5
WDR/YW UB7 100 C2
Thornton Cl WDR/YW UB7 100 C2
Thornton Dene BECK BR3 166 D1
Thornton Gdns BAL SW12 129 J7
Thornton Gv PIN HA5 34 A5
Thornton Hl WIM/MER SW19 146 C6
Thornton Pl MBLAR W1H 9 M2
Thornton Rd BAL SW12 129 J6
BAR EN5 26 C2
BELV DA17 * 117 J3
BMLY BR1 152 E4
CAR SM5 162 C7
IL IG1 78 B3
MORT/ESHN SW14 126 A2
THHTH CR7 164 B4
UED N18 42 E2
WAN E11 76 B1
WIM/MER SW19 146 B5
Thornton Rw THHTH CR7 164 B4
Thorntons Farm Av
ROMW/RG RM7 80 E1
Thornton St BRXN/ST SW9 130 B1
Thornton Wy GLDGN NW11 53 F4
Thorntree Rd CHARL SE7 114 C4
Thornville Gv MTCM CR4 162 B1
Thornville St DEPT SE8 112 D7
Thornwood Cl SWFD E18 59 F1
Thornwood Rd LEW SE13 133 H4
Thorogood Gdns SRTFD E15 76 C4
Thorogood Wy RAIN RM13 81 G7
Thorold Rd IL IG1 78 B1
WDGN N22 40 E6
Thorparch Rd VX/NE SW8 109 J7
Thorpebank Rd SHB W12 87 J7
Thorpe Cl NKENS W10 88 C5
SYD SE26 * 151 F3
Thorpe Ct TOOT SW17 147 J3
Thorpe Crs OXHEY WD19 21 F6
WALTH E17 57 H1
Thorpedale Gdns
GNTH/NBYPK IG2 60 A3
Thorpedale Rd FSBYPK N4 55 F7
Thorpe Hall Rd WALTH E17 44 A7
Thorpe Rd BARK IG11 78 D6
EHAM E6 77 K7
FSTGT E7 76 E2
KUTN/CMB KT2 144 A6
SEVS/STOTM N15 56 A5
WALTH E17 58 A1
Thorpewood Av SYD SE26 150 D1
Thorpland Av HGDN/ICK UB10 64 A2
Thorsden Wy NRWD SE19 * 150 A4
Thorverton Rd CRICK NW2 70 C2
Thoydon Rd BOW E3 93 G1
Thrale Rd STRHM/NOR SW16 148 C4
Thrale St STHWK SE1 12 F9
Thrasher Cl HACK E8 * 7 L3
Thrawl St WCHPL E1 13 M3
Threadneedle St LOTH EC2R 13 H5
Three Colts La BETH E2 92 D3
Three Colt St POP/IOD E14 * 93 H6
Three Corners BXLYHN DA7 137 J1
Three Kings Yd
MYFR/PKLN W1K 10 C6
Three Meadows Ms
KTN/HRWW/WS HA3 35 F7
Three Mill La BOW E3 94 A2
Three Oak La STHWK SE1 19 L1
Three Valleys Wy BUSH WD23 21 H4
Threshers Pl NTGHL W11 88 C6
Thriffwood SYD SE26 150 E2
Thrift Farm La BORE WD6 24 E1
Thrigby Rd CHSGTN KT9 172 B5
Throckmorten Rd
CAN/RD E16 95 F5
Throgmorton Av OBST EC2N 13 H4
Throgmorton St OBST EC2N 13 H4
Throwley Cl ABYW SE2 116 D2
Throwley Rd SUT SM1 175 F4
Throwley Wy SUT SM1 175 F3
Thrupp Cl MTCM CR4 163 G1
Thrush Gn RYLN/HDSTN HA2 48 A3
Thrush St WALW SE17 18 E7
Thunderer Rd DAGW RM9 98 A3
Thurbarn Rd CAT SE6 151 K4
Thurland Rd
BERM/RHTH SE16 111 H2
Thurlby Cl WFD IG8 45 K4
Thurlby Rd ALP/SUD HA0 67 K5
WNWD SE27 149 G3
Thurleigh Av BAL SW12 129 F5
Thurleigh Rd BAL SW12 128 E5
Thurleston Av MRDN SM4 161 H4
Thurlestone Av
GDMY/SEVK IG3 79 F3
NFNCH/WDSPK N12 39 K5
Thurlestone Rd WNWD SE27 149 G2
Thurloe Cl SKENS SW7 15 J5
Thurloe Gdns ROM RM1 63 G5
Thurloe Pl SKENS SW7 15 H5
Thurloe Place Ms
SKENS SW7 * 15 H5
Thurloe Sq SKENS SW7 15 J5
Thurloe St SKENS SW7 15 H5
Thurlow Cl CHING E4 43 K5
Thurlow Gdns ALP/SUD HA0 * 67 K4
Thurlow Hl DUL SE21 130 D7
Thurlow Park Rd DUL SE21 149 H1
Thurlow Rd HAMP NW3 71 H4
HNWL W7 104 B1
Thurlow St WALW SE17 19 J8
Thurlow Ter KTTN NW5 71 K4
Thurlow Wk WALW SE17 19 J7
Thurlston Rd RSLP HA4 64 E2
Thursley Crs CROY/NA CR0 180 B6
Thursley Gdns
WIM/MER SW19 146 B1
Thursley Rd ELTH/MOT SE9 153 K2
Thurso St TOOT SW17 147 H3
Thurstan Rd RYNPK SW20 145 K6
Thurston Rd DEPT SE8 132 E1
STHL UB1 83 K5
Thurtle Rd BETH E2 7 M4
Thwaite Cl ERITH DA8 117 K5
Thyra Gv NFNCH/WDSPK N12 39 F5
Tibbatt's Rd BOW E3 93 K3
Tibbenham Pl CAT SE6 151 J1
Tibberton Sq IS N1 6 E2
Tibbets Cl WIM/MER SW19 127 G7
Tibbet's Ride PUT/ROE SW15 127 G6
Tiber Cl BOW E3 75 J7
Tiber Gdns IS N1 5 K4
Ticehurst Cl STMC/STPC BR5 155 G6
Ticehurst Rd FSTH SE23 151 G1
Tickford Cl ABYW SE2 116 D1
Tidal Basin Rd CAN/RD E16 94 D6
Tide Cl MTCM CR4 148 A7
Tidenham Gdns CROY/NA CR0 178 A2
Tideswell Rd CROY/NA CR0 179 J2
PUT/ROE SW15 127 F3
Tideway Cl RCHPK/HAM TW10 143 J4
Tideway Wk VX/NE SW8 * 109 H5
Tidey St BOW E3 93 J4
Tidford Rd WELL DA16 136 A1
Tidworth Rd BOW E3 93 J2
Tiepigs La WWKM BR4 180 C1
Tierney Rd BRXS/STRHM SW2 129 K7
Tierney Ter
BRXS/STRHM SW2 * 129 K7
Tiger La HAYES BR2 168 A3
Tiger Wy CLPT E5 74 D3
Tigres Cl ED N9 42 E1
Tilbrook Rd BKHTH/KID SE3 134 B2
Tilbury Cl PECK SE15 111 G6
PIN HA5 * 33 K6
Tilbury Rd EHAM E6 95 K1
LEY E10 58 A6
Tildesley Rd PUT/ROE SW15 127 F5
Tilehouse Cl BORE WD6 24 B2
Tilehurst Rd CHEAM SM3 174 C4
WAND/EARL SW18 128 C7
Tile Kiln La HGT N6 54 B7
PLMGR N13 41 J4
Tileyard Rd HOLWY N7 5 J1
Tilford Av CROY/NA CR0 180 A6
Tilford Gdns WIM/MER SW19 127 G7
Tilia Cl SUT SM1 174 D4
Tilia Wk BRXN/ST SW9 130 C3
Tiller Rd POP/IOD E14 112 D2
Tillett Cl WLSDN NW10 68 E5
Tillet Wy BETH E2 92 C2
Tilley Rd FELT TW13 121 K7
Tillingbourne Gdns FNCH N3 52 D2
Tillingbourne Wy FNCH N3 52 D3
Tillingham Wy
NFNCH/WDSPK N12 38 E3
Tilling Rd CRICK NW2 51 K7
Tilling Wy WBLY HA9 * 67 K2
Tillman St WCHPL E1 92 D5
Tilloch St IS N1 * 5 L2
Tillotson Rd ED N9 42 B1
IL IG1 60 A6
KTN/HRWW/WS HA3 34 B6
Tilney Gdns IS N1 73 K5
Tilney Rd DAGW RM9 80 B5
NWDGN UB2 102 B3
Tilney St MYFR/PKLN W1K 10 B8
Tilson Cl CMBW SE5 111 F6
Tilson Gdns BRXS/STRHM SW2 129 K6
Tilson Rd TOTM N17 42 C7
Tilston Cl WAN E11 76 D2
Tilton St FUL/PGN SW6 107 H5
The Tiltwood ACT W3 86 E6
Tilt Yard Ap ELTH/MOT SE9 134 E5
Timber Cl CHST BR7 169 F1
Timbercroft HOR/WEW KT19 173 G3
Timbercroft La
WOOL/PLUM SE18 115 K5
Timberland Cl PECK SE15 * 111 H6
Timberland Rd WCHPL E1 * 92 D5
Timber Mill Wy CLAP SW4 129 J2
Timber Pond Rd
BERM/RHTH SE16 112 A1
Timberslip Dr WLGTN SM6 176 D7
The Timbers CHEAM SM3 * 174 C5
Timber St FSBYE EC1V * 6 E9
Timberwharf Rd
SEVS/STOTM N15 56 C5
Time Sq HACK E8 74 B4
Times Sq SUT SM1 * 175 F4
Timms Cl BMLY BR1 168 E3
Timothy Cl BXLYHS DA6 137 F4
Tindal St BRXN/ST SW9 110 C7
Tinniswood Cl HBRY N5 73 G4
HOLWY N7 * 73 G4
Tinsley Cl SNWD SE25 165 J2
Tinsley Rd WCHPL E1 92 E4
Tintagel Crs EDUL SE22 131 G3
Tintagel Dr STAN HA7 35 K4
Tintern Av CDALE/KGS NW9 50 D2
Tintern Cl PUT/ROE SW15 127 H4
WIM/MER SW19 147 G6
Tintern Gdns STHGT/OAK N14 28 E6
Tintern Rd CAR SM5 162 C7
WDGN N22 41 J7
Tintern St CLAP SW4 129 K3
Tintern Wy RYLN/HDSTN HA2 48 B7
Tinto Rd CAN/RD E16 94 E4
Tinwell Ms BORE WD6 25 F4
Tinworth St LBTH SE11 17 K7
Tipthorpe Rd BTSEA SW11 129 F2
Tipton Dr CROY/NA CR0 178 A3
Tiptree Cl CHING E4 44 A2
Tiptree Crs CLAY IG5 60 A1
Tiptree Dr ENC/FH EN2 29 K3
Tiptree Rd RSLP HA4 65 F3
Tirlemont Rd SAND/SEL CR2 177 J6
Tirrell Rd CROY/NA CR0 164 D5
Tisbury Rd STRHM/NOR SW16 163 K1
Tisdall Pl WALW SE17 19 H6
Titan Ct BTFD TW8 105 G4
Titchborne Rw BAY/PAD W2 9 K5
Titchfield Rd CAR SM5 162 C7
STJWD NW8 3 K4
Titchfield Wk CAR SM5 162 C6
Titchwell Rd
WAND/EARL SW18 128 C6
Tite St CHEL SW3 15 L9
Tithe Barn Cl KUTN/CMB KT2 144 B7
Tithe Barn Wy NTHLT UB5 83 F1
Tithe Cl MLHL NW7 37 J7
WOT/HER KT12 156 A5
YEAD UB4 82 D4
Tithe Ct HDN NW4 * 37 J7
Tithe Farm Av
RYLN/HDSTN HA2 66 A2
Tithe Farm Cl
RYLN/HDSTN HA2 66 A2
Tithe Wk MLHL NW7 37 J7
Titian Av BUSH WD23 22 E6
Titley Cl CHING E4 43 J4
Titmus Cl UX/CGN UB8 82 A5
Titmuss Av THMD SE28 97 H6
Titmuss St SHB W12 * 106 E1
Tiverton Av CLAY IG5 60 A2
Tiverton Cl CROY/NA CR0 165 G6
Tiverton Rd ALP/SUD HA0 86 A1
EDGW HA8 50 B1
HSLW TW3 123 G1
RSLP HA4 64 E2
SEVS/STOTM N15 55 K5
UED N18 42 A4
WLSDN NW10 70 B7
Tiverton St STHWK SE1 18 E3
Tiverton Wy CHSGTN KT9 171 J4
MLHL NW7 38 B6
Tivoli Gdns WOOL/PLUM SE18 114 D3
Tivoli Rd CEND/HSY/T N8 54 D4
HSLWW TW4 122 D3
WNWD SE27 149 J4
Toad La HSLWW TW4 122 E3
Tobago St POP/IOD E14 112 D1
Tobin Cl HAMP NW3 3 K1
Toby La WCHPL E1 93 G3
Toby Wy SURB KT6 172 D1
Tokenhouse Yd LOTH EC2R 13 G4
Token Yd PUT/ROE SW15 127 H3
Tokyngton Av WBLY HA9 68 C5
Toland Sq PUT/ROE SW15 126 D4
Tolcarne Dr PIN HA5 46 E1
Toley Av KTN/HRWW/WS HA3 50 A6
Tollbridge Cl NKENS W10 88 C3
Tollesbury Gdns BARK/HLT IG6 60 D2
Tollet St WCHPL E1 93 F3
Tollgate Dr DUL SE21 150 A1
YEAD UB4 83 H6
Tollgate Gdns
KIL/WHAMP NW6 2 C5
Tollgate Rd CAN/RD E16 95 G4
Tollhouse La WLGTN SM6 176 C7
Tollhouse Wy ARCH N19 72 C1
Tollington Pk FSBYPK N4 73 F1
Tollington Pl FSBYPK N4 73 F1
Tollington Rd HOLWY N7 73 F3
Tollington Wy HOLWY N7 72 E2
Tolmer's Sq CAMTN NW1 4 F9
Tolpits Cl WATW WD18 20 D4
Tolpits La WATW WD18 20 A7
Tolpuddle Av PLSTW E13 77 G7
Tolpuddle St IS N1 6 A5
Tolsford Rd HACK E8 74 D4
Tolson Rd ISLW TW7 124 B2
Tolverne Rd RYNPK SW20 146 A7
Tolworth Broadway
SURB KT6 159 H7
Tolworth Cl SURB KT6 159 J7
Tolworth Gdns CHDH RM6 61 K4
Tolworth Park Rd SURB KT6 172 B1
Tolworth Ri North
BRYLDS KT5 159 K6
Tolworth Rise North (Kingston
By-Pass) BRYLDS KT5 159 J7
Tolworth Ri South
BRYLDS KT5 159 K6
Tolworth Rd SURB KT6 172 A1
Tolworth Underpass (Kingston
By-Pass) SURB KT6 172 C2
Tom Cribb Rd
WOOL/PLUM SE18 115 H2
Tom Groves Cl SRTFD E15 76 B4
Tom Hood Cl SRTFD E15 76 B4
Tom Jenkinson Rd
CAN/RD E16 94 E7
Tomlin's Gv BOW E3 93 J2
Tomlinson Cl BETH E2 7 M8
CHSWK W4 105 J4
Tomlins Orch BARK IG11 78 C7
Tomlin's Ter POP/IOD E14 93 H5
Tom Mann Cl BARK IG11 78 E7
Tom Nolan Cl SRTFD E15 94 C1
Tompion St FSBYE EC1V 6 C8
Tom Smith Cl GNWCH SE10 113 H5
Tonbridge Crs
KTN/HRWW/WS HA3 50 A3
Tonbridge Rd
E/WMO/HCT KT8 156 D3
Tonbridge St STPAN WC1H 5 J8
Tonfield Rd CHEAM SM3 161 J7
Tonge Cl BECK BR3 166 D4
Tonsley Hl WAND/EARL SW18 128 A4
Tonsley Pl WAND/EARL SW18 128 A4
Tonsley Rd WAND/EARL SW18 128 A4
Tonsley St WAND/EARL SW18 128 A4
Tonstall Rd MTCM CR4 163 F1
Tooke Cl PIN HA5 33 J7
Tookey Cl
KTN/HRWW/WS HA3 50 B6
Took's Ct FLST/FETLN EC4A 12 A4
Tooley St STHWK SE1 13 H8
Toorack Rd
KTN/HRWW/WS HA3 48 D1
Tooting Bec Gdns
STRHM/NOR SW16 148 D3
Tooting Bec Rd TOOT SW17 148 A2
Tooting Gv TOOT SW17 147 J4
Tooting High St TOOT SW17 147 J5
Tooting Market TOOT SW17 * 147 K3
Tootswood Rd HAYES BR2 167 H4
Topham Sq TOTM N17 41 J7
Topham St CLKNW EC1R * 6 A9
Topiary Sq RCH/KEW TW9 125 G2
Topley St ELTH/MOT SE9 134 B3
Topmast Point POP/IOD E14 * 112 D1
Top Pk BECK BR3 167 H4
Topsfield Cl CEND/HSY/T N8 54 D4
Topsfield Pde
CEND/HSY/T N8 * 54 E4
Topsfield Rd CEND/HSY/T N8 54 E4
Topsham Rd TOOT SW17 147 K2
Torbay Rd KIL/WHAMP NW6 70 D6
RYLN/HDSTN HA2 65 J1
Torbay St CAMTN NW1 4 D1
Torbitt Wy GNTH/NBYPK IG2 61 F4
Torbridge Cl EDGW HA8 36 A6
Torcross Dr FSTH SE23 150 E1
Torcross Rd RSLP HA4 65 F2
Tor Gdns KENS W8 14 A1
Tor Gv THMD SE28 96 E7
Tormead Cl SUT SM1 174 E5
Tormount Rd
WOOL/PLUM SE18 115 K5
Toronto Av MNPK E12 77 K3
Toronto Rd IL IG1 60 B7
Torquay Gdns REDBR IG4 59 H3
Torquay St BAY/PAD W2 8 C3
Torrens Rd BRXS/STRHM SW2 130 A4
SRTFD E15 76 D5
Torrens Sq SRTFD E15 76 D5
Torrens St FSBYE EC1V 6 C6
Torres Sq POP/IOD E14 112 D4
Torrey Dr BRXN/ST SW9 130 B1

Torriano Av KTTN NW5 72 D4
Torriano Cots KTTN NW5 72 D4
Torridge Gdns PECK SE15 131 K3
Torridge Rd THHTH CR7 164 C4
Torridon Rd CAT SE6 133 G7
Torrington Av
NFNCH/WDSPK N12 39 H4
Torrington Cl ESH/CLAY KT10 170 E5
Torrington Dr
RYLN/HDSTN HA2 66 B3
Torrington Gdns
FBAR/BDGN N11 40 C5
GFD/PVL UB6 67 J7
Torrington Gv
NFNCH/WDSPK N12 39 J4
Torrington Pk
NFNCH/WDSPK N12 39 H3
Torrington Pl FITZ W1T 10 F2
GWRST WC1E 11 G1
WAP E1W 92 C7
Torrington Rd BCTR RM8 62 B7
ESH/CLAY KT10 170 E5
GFD/PVL UB6 67 J7
RSLP HA4 64 E2
Torrington Sq CROY/NA CR0 * 164 E6
STPAN WC1H 11 H1
Torrington Wy MRDN SM4 161 K6
Tor Rd WELL DA16 116 D7
Torr Rd PGE/AN SE20 151 F6
Torver Rd HRW HA1 48 E3
Torwood Rd PUT/ROE SW15 126 D4
Tothill St STJSPK SW1H 17 G2
Totnes Rd WELL DA16 116 C6
Totnes Vls FBAR/BDGN N11 * 40 C4
Totnes Wk EFNCH N2 53 H3
Tottan Ter WCHPL E1 * 93 F5
Tottenhall Rd PLMGR N13 41 G5
Tottenham Court Rd FITZ W1T 10 F1
Tottenham Gn East
SEVS/STOTM N15 56 B3
Tottenham Gn East South Side
SEVS/STOTM N15 56 B3
Tottenham La
CEND/HSY/T N8 54 E4
Tottenham Ms FITZ W1T * 10 F2
Tottenham Rd IS N1 74 A5
Tottenham St FITZ W1T 10 F3
Totterdown St TOOT SW17 147 K3
Totteridge Common
TRDG/WHET N20 37 J1
Totteridge La
TRDG/WHET N20 38 E1
Totteridge Village
TRDG/WHET N20 26 C7
Totternhoe Cl
KTN/HRWW/WS HA3 49 J4
Totton Rd THHTH CR7 164 B2
Toucan Cl WLSDN NW10 86 C2
Toulmin St STHWK SE1 18 E2
Toulon St CMBW SE5 110 D6
Tournay Rd FUL/PGN SW6 107 J6
Toussaint Wk
BERM/RHTH SE16 111 H2
Tovil Cl PGE/AN SE20 165 H1
Towcester Rd BOW E3 93 K3
Tower Br WAP E1W 13 L8
Tower Bridge Ap TWRH EC3N 13 L8
Tower Bridge Ms
ALP/SUD HA0 67 F3
Tower Bridge Rd STHWK SE1 19 J4
Tower Blds WAP E1W * 92 D7
Tower Cl HAMP NW3 71 H4
PGE/AN SE20 150 D6
Tower Ct LSQ/SEVD WC2H * 11 J5
Tower Gdns ESH/CLAY KT10 171 G6
Tower Gardens Rd TOTM N17 41 J7
Tower Hamlets Rd FSTGT E7 76 D3
WALTH E17 57 J2
Tower Hl TWRH EC3N 13 L7
Tower Hill Ter MON EC3R 13 K7
Tower La WBLY HA9 * 67 K2
Tower Ms CLPT E5 75 G3
WALTH E17 57 J3
Tower Mill Rd CMBW SE5 * 111 F6
Tower Park Rd DART DA1 138 C4
Tower Pl MON EC3R 13 K7
Tower Ri RCH/KEW TW9 125 F2
Tower Rd BELV DA17 117 K3
BXLYHN DA7 137 J3
DART DA1 139 F6
TWK TW1 143 F2
WLSDN NW10 69 J6
Tower Royal MANHO EC4N * 12 F6
Towers Av HGDN/ICK UB10 82 A2
Towers Ct HGDN/ICK UB10 * 82 A2
Towers Pl RCH/KEW TW9 125 F4
Towers Rd PIN HA5 33 J7
STHL UB1 84 A3
Tower St LSQ/SEVD WC2H 11 J5
Tower Ter WDGN N22 55 F1
Tower Vw BUSH WD23 22 E6
CROY/NA CR0 166 B7
Towfield Rd FELT TW13 141 K1
Towncourt Crs
STMC/STPC BR5 169 H4
Towncourt La
STMC/STPC BR5 169 J5
Towncourt Pth FSBYPK N4 55 J7
Town End Pde KUT/HW KT1 * 158 E2
Towney Md NTHLT UB5 83 K1
Town Farm Wy
STWL/WRAY TW19 * 120 A6
Townfield Rd HYS/HAR UB3 82 D7
Townfield Sq HYS/HAR UB3 82 D7
Town Field Wy ISLW TW7 124 B1
Town Hall Approach Rd
SEVS/STOTM N15 56 B3
Townhall Av CHSWK W4 106 A4
Town Hall Pde
BRXS/STRHM SW2 * 130 A3
Town Hall Rd BTSEA SW11 128 E2
Townholm Crs HNWL W7 104 A2
Town La STWL/WRAY TW19 120 A5
Townley Ct SRTFD E15 76 D5
Townley Rd BXLYHS DA6 137 G4
EDUL SE22 131 F4
Townley St WALW SE17 19 G7
Town Meadow BTFD TW8 104 E6
Townmead Rd FUL/PGN SW6 128 B2
RCH/KEW TW9 125 J1
Town Quay BARK IG11 78 B7
Town Rd ED N9 42 D1
Townsend Av STHGT/OAK N14 40 D3
Townsend La CDALE/KGS NW9 51 F6
Townsend Ms
WAND/EARL SW18 147 G1
Townsend Rd
SEVS/STOTM N15 56 B4
STHL UB1 83 J7
STJWD NW8 3 K5
WOOL/PLUM SE18 115 G2
Townsend St WALW SE17 19 H6
Townsend Wy NTHWD HA6 32 D6
Townsend Yd HGT N6 54 A7
Townshend Cl SCUP DA14 155 H5
Townshend Est STJWD NW8 3 J5
Townshend Rd CHST BR7 154 B4
RCH/KEW TW9 125 G3
STJWD NW8 3 J4
Townshend Ter
RCH/KEW TW9 125 G3
Townson Av NTHLT UB5 83 F1
Townson Wy NTHLT UB5 82 E1
Town Whf ISLW TW7 * 124 C2
Towpath Rd UED N18 43 F5
Towpath Wy CROY/NA CR0 165 G5
Towton Rd WNWD SE27 149 J1
Toynbec Cl CHST BR7 154 B3
Toynbee Rd RYNPK SW20 146 C7
Toynbee St WCHPL E1 13 L3
Toyne Wy HGT N6 53 K5
Tracey Av CRICK NW2 * 70 A4
Trade Cl PLMGR N13 41 G3
Trader Rd EHAM E6 96 B5
Tradescant Rd VX/NE SW8 109 K6
Trading Estate Rd
WLSDN NW10 * 86 E3
Trafalgar Av PECK SE15 19 M8
TOTM N17 42 A5
WPK KT4 161 G7
Trafalgar Gdns WCHPL E1 93 F4
Trafalgar Gv GNWCH SE10 113 G5
Trafalgar Ms HOM E9 * 75 H5
Trafalgar Pl UED N18 42 C4
WAN E11 58 E3
Trafalgar Rd GNWCH SE10 113 H4
RAIN RM13 99 H1
WHTN TW2 142 D1
WIM/MER SW19 147 F6
Trafalgar Sq STJS SW1Y * 11 H8
Trafalgar St WALW SE17 19 G7
Trafalgar Wy CROY/NA CR0 177 F1
POP/IOD E14 94 A6
Trafford Rd THHTH CR7 164 A4
Trahorn Cl WCHPL E1 92 C3
Tram Cl HNHL SE24 130 C2
Tramway Av ED N9 30 D6
Tramway Cl PGE/AN SE20 150 E7
Tramway Pth MTCM CR4 162 D3
Tranby Ms HOM E9 75 F4
Tranley Ms HAMP NW3 * 71 J3
Tranmere Rd ED N9 30 B6
WAND/EARL SW18 147 G1
WHTN TW2 123 G6
Tranquil La RYLN/HDSTN HA2 48 C3
Tranquil Pas BKHTH/KID SE3 * 133 J1
Tranquil Ri ERITH DA8 118 B4
Tranquil V BKHTH/KID SE3 133 H1
Transept St CAMTN NW1 9 J3
Transmere Rd
STMC/STPC BR5 169 H5
Transom Cl BERM/RHTH SE16 112 B3
Transom Sq POP/IOD E14 112 E4
Transport Av BTFD TW8 104 B4
Tranton Rd BERM/RHTH SE16 111 J2
Traps La NWMAL KT3 160 B1
Travellers Wy HSLWW TW4 122 B1
Travers Cl WALTH E17 43 F7
Travers Rd HOLWY N7 73 G2
Treacy Cl BUSH WD23 34 C1
Treadgold St NTGHL W11 88 B6
Treadway St BETH E2 92 D1
Treaty St IS N1 5 L4
Trebeck St MYFR/PICC W1J 10 C8
Trebovir Rd ECT SW5 14 B7
Treby St BOW E3 93 H3
Trecastle Wy HOLWY N7 72 D3
Tredegar Rd BOW E3 93 H1
FBAR/BDGN N11 40 D6
Tredegar Sq BOW E3 93 H2
Trederwen Rd HACK E8 74 C7
Tredown Rd SYD SE26 150 E4
Tredwell Cl BRXS/STRHM SW2 149 F1
HAYES BR2 168 C3
Tredwell Rd WNWD SE27 149 H3
Tree Cl RCHPK/HAM TW10 124 E7
Treen Av BARN SW13 126 B2
Tree Rd CAN/RD E16 95 G5
Treeside Cl WDR/YW UB7 100 A3
Tree Top Ms DAGE RM10 81 F5
Treetops Cl ABYW SE2 117 F4
NTHWD HA6 32 B4
Tree View Cl NRWD SE19 150 A7
Treewall Gdns BMLY BR1 153 F3
Trefgarne Rd DAGE RM10 80 C1
Trefoil Rd WAND/EARL SW18 128 B4
Tregaron Av CEND/HSY/T N8 54 E6
Tregaron Gdns NWMAL KT3 160 B3
Tregarvon Rd BTSEA SW11 129 F3
Tregenna Av
RYLN/HDSTN HA2 66 A3
Tregenna Cl STHGT/OAK N14 28 C4
Trego Rd HOM E9 75 J6
Tregothnan Rd BRXN/ST SW9 129 K2
Tregunter Rd WBPTN SW10 14 E9
Treherne Ct BRXN/ST SW9 * 110 C7
Trehern Rd MORT/ESHN SW14 126 A2
Trehurst St CLPT E5 75 G4
Trelawney Est HOM E9 * 74 E5
Trelawn Rd BRXS/STRHM SW2 130 B4
LEY E10 76 A2
Trelawny Cl WALTH E17 57 K3
Trellis Sq BOW E3 93 H2
Treloar Gdns NRWD SE19 149 K5
Trelwney Est HOM E9 * 74 E5
Tremadoc Rd CLAP SW4 129 J3
Tremaine Cl BROCKY SE4 132 D1
Tremaine Rd PGE/AN SE20 165 J1
Trematon Pl TEDD TW11 143 J6
Tremlett Gv ARCH N19 72 C2
Tremlett Ms ARCH N19 * 72 C2
Trenance Gdns
GDMY/SEVK IG3 79 G2
Trenchard Av RSLP HA4 65 F4
Trenchard Cl CDALE/KGS NW9 37 G7
STAN HA7 35 H5
Trenchard St GNWCH SE10 113 G4
Trenchold St VX/NE SW8 * 109 K5
Trenholme Rd PGE/AN SE20 150 D6
Trenholme Ter PGE/AN SE20 150 D6
Trenmar Gdns WLSDN NW10 87 K2
Trent Av EA W5 104 D2
Trent Ct WAN E11 58 E4
Trent Gdns STHGT/OAK N14 28 B5
Trentham St
WAND/EARL SW18 127 K7
Trent Pk EBAR EN4 * 28 C1
Trent Rd BRXS/STRHM SW2 130 A4
Trent Wy WPK KT4 174 A2
YEAD UB4 82 C2
Trentwood Side ENC/FH EN2 29 F2
Treport St WAND/EARL SW18 128 A6
Tresco Cl BMLY BR1 152 C5
Trescoe Gdns
RYLN/HDSTN HA2 47 J6
Tresco Gdns GDMY/SEVK IG3 79 F1
Tresco Rd PECK SE15 131 J3
Tresham Crs STJWD NW8 3 J9
Tresham Rd BARK IG11 79 F6
Tresilian Av WCHMH N21 29 F4
Tressel Cl IS N1 6 D2
Tressillian Crs BROCKY SE4 132 D2
Tressillian Rd BROCKY SE4 132 D2
Trestis Cl YEAD UB4 83 H3
Treswell Rd DAGW RM9 80 A7
Tretawn Gdns MLHL NW7 37 G3
Tretawn Pk MLHL NW7 37 G3
Trevanion Rd WKENS W14 * 107 H4
Treve Av HRW HA1 48 C6
Trevelyan Av MNPK E12 77 K3
Trevelyan Cl DART DA1 139 J3
Trevelyan Crs
KTN/HRWW/WS HA3 49 K6
Trevelyan Gdns
WLSDN NW10 * 70 A7
Trevelyan Rd SRTFD E15 76 C3
TOOT SW17 147 K5
Treveris St STHWK SE1 12 D9
Treverton St NKENS W10 88 B3
Treves Cl WCHMH N21 29 F4
Treville St PUT/ROE SW15 126 E6
Treviso Rd FSTH SE23 151 F1
Trevithick Cl
EBED/NFELT TW14 121 J7
Trevithick Dr DART DA1 139 J3
Trevithick St DEPT SE8 112 D5
Trevone Gdns PIN HA5 47 J5
Trevor Cl EBAR EN4 27 H5
HAYES BR2 167 J6
ISLW TW7 124 A4
KTN/HRWW/WS HA3 35 F6
NTHLT UB5 83 G1
Trevor Crs RSLP HA4 64 D3
Trevor Gdns EDGW HA8 37 F7
Trevor Pl SKENS SW7 15 K2
Trevor Rd EDGW HA8 37 F7
HYS/HAR UB3 101 H1
WFD IG8 44 E6
WIM/MER SW19 146 C6
Trevor Sq SKENS SW7 15 K2
Trevor St SKENS SW7 15 K2
Trevose Rd WALTH E17 44 B7
Trevose Wy OXHEY WD19 33 G2
Trewenna Dr CHSGTN KT9 171 K4
Trewince Rd RYNPK SW20 146 A7
Trewint St WAND/EARL SW18 147 G1
Trewsbury Rd SYD SE26 151 F4
Triandra Wy YEAD UB4 83 H4
Triangle Pas EBAR EN4 * 27 G3
Triangle Pl CLAP SW4 129 J3
Triangle Rd HACK E8 74 D7
The Triangle BFN/LL DA15 * 136 B6
HACK E8 74 D7
KUT/HW KT1 159 K1
Triangle Wy ACT W3 105 H2
Trident St BERM/RHTH SE16 112 A3
Trident Wy NWDGN UB2 102 A2
Trigon Rd VX/NE SW8 110 A6
Trilby Rd FSTH SE23 151 F1
Trim St NWCR SE14 112 C5
Trinder Rd ARCH N19 54 E7
BAR EN5 26 A4
Tring Av EA W5 86 B7
STHL UB1 83 K5
WBLY HA9 68 C5
Tring Cl GNTH/NBYPK IG2 60 C4
Trinidad Gdns DAGE RM10 81 F6
Trinidad St POP/IOD E14 93 H6
Trinity Av EFNCH N2 53 H2
EN EN1 30 B5
Trinity Buoy Whf
POP/IOD E14 * 94 B6
Trinity Church Rd BARN SW13 106 E5
Trinity Church Sq STHWK SE1 18 F3
Trinity Cl CLAP SW4 * 129 H3
HACK E8 * 74 B5
HAYES BR2 168 D7
HSLWW TW4 122 D3
LEW SE13 133 G3
NTHWD HA6 32 C5
SAND/SEL CR2 178 A7
WAN E11 76 C1
Trinity Ct ELTH/MOT SE9 135 G5
Trinity Crs TOOT SW17 147 K1
Trinity Dr UX/CGN UB8 82 A5
Trinity Est DEPT SE8 112 C4
Trinity Gdns BRXN/ST SW9 130 A3
CAN/RD E16 94 D4
DART DA1 139 G5
Trinity Gn WCHPL E1 * 92 E4
Trinity Gv GNWCH SE10 113 F7
Trinity Hall Cl WATN WD24 21 G1
Trinity Ms PGE/AN SE20 165 J1
Trinity Pde HSLW TW3 * 123 G2
Trinity Pk CHING E4 * 43 H5
Trinity Pl BXLYHS DA6 137 G3
Trinity Ri BRXS/STRHM SW2 130 C6
Trinity Rd BARK/HLT IG6 60 C2
EFNCH N2 53 H2
RCH/KEW TW9 * 125 G2
STHL UB1 83 J7
TOOT SW17 147 K1
WAND/EARL SW18 128 C5
WDGN N22 40 E6
WIM/MER SW19 146 E5
Trinity Sq TWRH EC3N 13 K7
Trinity St CAN/RD E16 94 D4
ENC/FH EN2 29 J1
STHWK SE1 18 F2
Trinity Wy ACT W3 87 G6
CHING E4 43 H5
Trio Pl STHWK SE1 18 F2
Tristan Ldg BUSH WD23 * 21 J3
Tristan Sq BKHTH/KID SE3 133 H2
Tristram Cl WALTH E17 58 B2
Tristram Dr ED N9 42 B2
Tristram Rd BMLY BR1 152 D3
Triton St CAMTN NW1 4 D9
Tritton Av CROY/NA CR0 176 E3
Tritton Rd DUL SE21 149 K2
Triumph Cl HYS/HAR UB3 101 F7
Triumph Rd EHAM E6 95 K5
Trojan Wy CROY/NA CR0 177 F2
Troon Cl BERM/RHTH SE16 * 111 J4
THMD SE28 97 K5
Troon St WCHPL E1 93 G5
Trosley Rd BELV DA17 117 H5
Trossachs Rd EDUL SE22 131 F4
Trothy Rd STHWK SE1 111 H3
Trott Rd MUSWH N10 40 A6
Trott St BTSEA SW11 108 C7
Troughton Rd CHARL SE7 114 A4
Troutbeck Rd NWCR SE14 112 B7
Trouville Rd CLAP SW4 129 H5
Trowbridge Rd HOM E9 75 H5
Trowlock Av TEDD TW11 143 J5
Trowlock Wy TEDD TW11 143 J5
Troy Ct KENS W8 14 A3
Troy Rd NRWD SE19 149 K5
Troy Town PECK SE15 131 H2
Trubshaw Rd NWDGN UB2 103 F2
Trueman Cl EDGW HA8 * 36 D6
Trulock Rd TOTM N17 42 C6
Truman's Rd STNW/STAM N16 74 A4
Trumpers Wy HNWL W7 104 A2
Trumpington Rd FSTGT E7 76 D3
Trump St CITYW EC2V 12 F5
Trundlers Wy BUSH WD23 22 E7
Trundle St STHWK SE1 18 E1
Trundleys Rd DEPT SE8 112 B5
Trundley's Rd DEPT SE8 112 A4
Trundley's Ter DEPT SE8 112 A3
Truro Gdns IL IG1 59 J6
Truro Rd WALTH E17 57 H3
WDGN N22 40 E6
Truro St KTTN NW5 72 A5
Truro Wy YEAD UB4 82 C2
Trusedale Rd EHAM E6 95 K5
Truslove Rd WNWD SE27 149 G4
Trussley Rd HMSMTH W6 107 F2
Trustons Gdns EMPK RM11 63 J6
Tryfan Cl REDBR IG4 59 H4
Tryon Crs HOM E9 74 E7
Tryon St CHEL SW3 15 L7
Trystings Cl ESH/CLAY KT10 171 G5
Tuam Rd WOOL/PLUM SE18 115 J5
Tubbs Rd WLSDN NW10 87 H1
Tucker St WATW WD18 21 G4
Tuck Rd RAIN RM13 81 J5
Tudor Av GPK RM2 63 J2
HPTN TW12 142 A5
WPK KT4 173 K2
Tudor Cl BRXS/STRHM SW2 * 130 A5
CDALE/KGS NW9 68 E1
CHEAM SM3 174 B4
CHSGTN KT9 172 A4
CHST BR7 153 K7
DART DA1 138 E5
HAMP NW3 71 J4
HGT N6 54 C6
HPTN TW12 142 C4
MLHL NW7 37 J5
PIN HA5 46 E4
WFD IG8 45 F4
WLGTN SM6 176 C6
Tudor Ct BORE WD6 24 A1
ELTH/MOT SE9 * 134 D3
WALTH E17 57 H6
Tudor Ct North WBLY HA9 68 C4
Tudor Ct South WBLY HA9 68 C4
Tudor Dr GPK RM2 63 J3
KUTN/CMB KT2 144 A4
MRDN SM4 161 G5
WOT/HER KT12 156 C7
Tudor Est WLSDN NW10 * 86 D1
Tudor Gdns ACT W3 86 C5
BARN SW13 126 B2
CDALE/KGS NW9 68 E1
GPK RM2 63 J3
TWK TW1 124 A7
WWKM BR4 180 A2
Tudor Gv HOM E9 74 E6
Tudor Ms WLSDN NW10 69 J5
Tudor Pde ELTH/MOT SE9 * 134 D3
Tudor Pl MTCM CR4 147 J6
NRWD SE19 * 150 B6
Tudor Rd ASHF TW15 140 B5
BAR EN5 26 E2
BARK IG11 79 F6
BECK BR3 167 F2
CHING E4 43 K5
ED N9 30 D6
HACK E8 74 D7
HPTN TW12 142 A6
HSLW TW3 123 J3
HYS/HAR UB3 82 B5
KTN/HRWW/WS HA3 48 D1
KUTN/CMB KT2 144 C6
NRWD SE19 150 B6
PIN HA5 47 G1
PLSTW E13 77 G7
SNWD SE25 165 J4
STHL UB1 83 J6
Tudor Sq HYS/HAR UB3 82 B4
Tudor St EMB EC4Y 12 B6
Tudor Wy ACT W3 105 H1
STHGT/OAK N14 28 D7
STMC/STPC BR5 169 J5
Tudor Well Cl STAN HA7 35 H4
Tudway Rd BKHTH/KID SE3 134 B3
Tufnail Rd DART DA1 139 J5
Tufnell Park Rd HOLWY N7 72 D3
Tufton Gdns E/WMO/HCT KT8 157 G1
Tufton Rd CHING E4 43 J3
Tufton St WEST SW1P 17 J4
Tugboat St THMD SE28 115 K1
Tugela Rd CROY/NA CR0 164 E5
Tugela St CAT SE6 151 H1
Tulip Cl CROY/NA CR0 166 A7
EHAM E6 95 J4
HPTN TW12 141 K5
NWDGN UB2 103 H1
Tulip Gdns CHING E4 * 44 B2
IL IG1 78 B5
Tulip Wy WDR/YW UB7 100 A3
Tull St CAR SM5 162 E6
Tulse Cl BECK BR3 167 F2
Tulse Hl BRXS/STRHM SW2 130 C7
Tulsemere Rd WNWD SE27 149 J1
Tummons Gdns SNWD SE25 165 F1
Tuncombe Rd UED N18 42 A3
Tunis Rd SHB W12 88 A7
Tunley Gn POP/IOD E14 93 H4
Tunley Rd TOOT SW17 148 A1
WLSDN NW10 69 G7
Tunmarsh La PLSTW E13 95 F2
Tunnan Leys EHAM E6 96 A5
Tunnel Av GNWCH SE10 113 G1
Tunnel Gdns FBAR/BDGN N11 40 C6
Tunnel Rd BERM/RHTH SE16 111 K1
Tunnel Rd East WDR/YW UB7 100 E6
Tunnel Rd West WDR/YW UB7 100 D7
Tunstall Rd BRXN/ST SW9 130 A3
CROY/NA CR0 165 F7
Tunstock Wy BELV DA17 117 F2
Tunworth Cl CDALE/KGS NW9 50 E5
Tunworth Crs PUT/ROE SW15 126 C5
Tupelo Rd LEY E10 75 K1
Tuppy St THMD SE28 115 H2
Turene Cl WAND/EARL SW18 128 B3
Turin Rd ED N9 30 E6
Turin St BETH E2 92 C2
Turkey Oak Cl NRWD SE19 150 A7
Turks Rw CHEL SW3 15 M7
Turle Rd FSBYPK N4 * 73 F1
STRHM/NOR SW16 163 K1
Turlewray Cl FSBYPK N4 55 F7
Turley Cl SRTFD E15 76 C7
Turnagain La
FLST/FETLN EC4A * 12 C4
Turnage Rd BCTR RM8 62 A7
Turnant Rd TOTM N17 41 J7
Turnberry Cl
BERM/RHTH SE16 * 111 J4
HDN NW4 52 B1
Turnberry Ct OXHEY WD19 * 33 G2
Turnberry Wy ORP BR6 169 J7
Turnbury Cl THMD SE28 97 K5
Turnchapel Ms CLAP SW4 129 G2
Turner Av MTCM CR4 147 K7
SEVS/STOTM N15 56 A3
WHTN TW2 142 C2
Turner Cl ALP/SUD HA0 67 K4
BRXN/ST SW9 110 C7
GLDGN NW11 53 F5
Turner Ct CMBW SE5 * 130 E3
DART DA1 139 F4
Turner Crs THHTH CR7 164 D5
Turner Dr GLDGN NW11 53 F5
Turner Ms BELMT SM2 175 F6
Turner Rd BUSH WD23 22 C3
EDGW HA8 50 A1
NWMAL KT3 160 A6
WALTH E17 58 A3
Turners Cl TRDG/WHET N20 39 K2
Turners Meadow Wy
BECK BR3 151 H7
Turner's Rd BOW E3 93 H4
Turner St CAN/RD E16 94 D5
WCHPL E1 92 D4
Turners Wy CROY/NA CR0 177 G1
Turner's Wd GLDGN NW11 53 G7
Turneville Rd WKENS W14 107 J5
Turney Rd DUL SE21 130 D6
Turnham Green Ter
CHSWK W4 106 B3
Turnham Rd BROCKY SE4 132 B4
Turnmill St FARR EC1M 12 B1
Turnpike Cl DEPT SE8 112 C6
WELL DA16 136 B2
Turnpike La CEND/HSY/T N8 55 G3
SUT SM1 175 G4
Turnpike Link CROY/NA CR0 178 A1
Turnpike Ms
CEND/HSY/T N8 * 55 G2
Turnpike Pde
SEVS/STOTM N15 * 55 H2
Turnpike Wy ISLW TW7 104 B7
Turnstone Cl
CDALE/KGS NW9 * 51 G1
PLSTW E13 94 E2
Turnstone Ter WEA W13 * 85 F3
Turpentine La PIM SW1V 16 D7
Turpin Cl WAP E1W 93 F6
Turpington Cl HAYES BR2 168 D5
Turpington La HAYES BR2 168 D4
Turpin La ERITH DA8 118 D5
Turpin Rd EBED/NFELT TW14 121 J5
Turpin's La WFD IG8 45 K4
Turpins Yd CRICK NW2 * 69 K1
GNWCH SE10 113 F6
Turpin Wy WLGTN SM6 176 B6
Turquand St WALW SE17 18 F6
Turret Gv CLAP SW4 129 H2
Turton Rd ALP/SUD HA0 68 A4
Turville St BETH E2 7 L9
Tuscan Rd WOOL/PLUM SE18 115 J4
Tuskar St GNWCH SE10 113 H4
Tweeddale Gv
HGDN/ICK UB10 64 A2
Tweeddale Rd CAR SM5 162 C7
Tweedmouth Rd PLSTW E13 95 F1
Tweedy Rd BMLY BR1 152 E7
Twelvetrees Crs BOW E3 94 A3
Twentyman Cl WFD IG8 44 E4
Twickenham Br TWK TW1 124 D4
Twickenham Cl CROY/NA CR0 177 F2
Twickenham Gdns
GFD/PVL UB6 67 G4
KTN/HRWW/WS HA3 34 E6
Twickenham Rd FELT TW13 141 J3
ISLW TW7 124 A3
TEDD TW11 143 G3
WAN E11 76 B1
Twig Folly Cl BETH E2 93 F1
Twig Folly Whf BETH E2 * 93 F1
Twigg Cl ERITH DA8 118 B6
Twilley St WAND/EARL SW18 128 A6
Twine Cl BARK IG11 97 H2
Twine Ct WCHPL E1 92 E6
Twineham Gn
NFNCH/WDSPK N12 38 E3
Twine Ter BOW E3 * 93 H3
Twining Av WHTN TW2 142 C2
Twinn Rd MLHL NW7 38 C5
Twin Tumps Wy THMD SE28 97 G6
Twisden Rd KTTN NW5 72 B3
Twisleton Ct DART DA1 139 G5
Twitten Gv BMLY BR1 168 E2
Twybridge Wy WLSDN NW10 68 E6
Twycross Ms GNWCH SE10 113 H3
Twyford Abbey Rd
WLSDN NW10 86 B2
Twyford Av ACT W3 86 C6
EFNCH N2 53 K2
Twyford Crs ACT W3 86 C7
Twyford Rd CAR SM5 162 C7
IL IG1 78 C4
RYLN/HDSTN HA2 48 B6
Twyford St IS N1 5 L3
Tyas Rd CAN/RD E16 94 D3
Tybenham Rd
WIM/MER SW19 161 K2
Tyberry Rd PEND EN3 30 D2
Tyburn La HRW HA1 48 E6
Tyburn Wy MBLAR W1H 9 M6
Tyers Ga STHWK SE1 19 J2
Tyers St LBTH SE11 17 L7
Tyers Ter LBTH SE11 17 L8
Tyeshurst Cl ABYW SE2 117 F4
Tylecroft Rd
STRHM/NOR SW16 163 K1
Tylehurst Gdns IL IG1 78 C4
Tyler Cl BETH E2 7 L5
ERITH DA8 117 J6
Tylers Ga KTN/HRWW/WS HA3 50 A5
Tyler St GNWCH SE10 113 H4
Tylney Av NRWD SE19 150 B4
Tylney Rd BMLY BR1 168 C1
FSTGT E7 77 G3
Tynan Cl EBED/NFELT TW14 121 K7
Tyndale La IS N1 6 C1
Tyndale Ter IS N1 6 C1
Tyndall Rd LEY E10 76 A1
WELL DA16 136 A2
Tyneham Cl BTSEA SW11 * 129 F2
Tyneham Rd BTSEA SW11 129 F1
Tynemouth Cl EHAM E6 96 B5
Tynemouth Rd MTCM CR4 148 A6
SEVS/STOTM N15 56 B3
WOOL/PLUM SE18 115 K4
Tynemouth St FUL/PGN SW6 128 B1
Tynemouth Ter
SEVS/STOTM N15 * 56 B3
Tyne St WCHPL E1 13 M4

Tynsdale Rd WLSDN NW10 69 G6
Type St BETH E2 93 F1
Tyrawley Rd FUL/PGN SW6 108 A7
Tyre La CDALE/KGS NW9 * 51 G3
Tyrell Cl HRW HA1 66 E3
Tyrone Rd EHAM E6 95 K1
Tyron Wy SCUP DA14 154 E3
Tyrrell Av WELL DA16 136 B4
Tyrrell Rd EDUL SE22 131 H3
Tyrrel Wy CDALE/KGS NW9 51 H6
Tyrwhitt Rd BROCKY SE4 132 D2
Tysoe St CLKNW EC1R 6 B8
FSBYW WC1X 6 A8
Tyson Gdns FSTH SE23 * 131 K6
Tyson Rd FSTH SE23 131 K6
Tyssen Rd STNW/STAM N16 * 74 B2
Tyssen St HACK E8 74 B5
IS N1 7 K5
Tytherton Rd ARCH N19 72 D2

U

Uamvar St POP/IOD E14 93 K4
Uckfield Gv MTCM CR4 148 A7
Udall St WEST SW1P 16 F6
Udney Park Rd TEDD TW11 143 G4
Uffington Rd WLSDN NW10 69 J7
WNWD SE27 149 G3
Ufford Cl KTN/HRWW/WS HA3 34 B6
Ufford Rd
KTN/HRWW/WS HA3 34 B6
Ufford St STHWK SE1 18 B1
Ufton Rd IS N1 7 J1
Uhura Sq STNW/STAM N16 * 74 A2
Ullathorne Rd
STRHM/NOR SW16 148 C3
Ulleswater Rd
STHGT/OAK N14 40 E3
Ulleswater Vls
STHGT/OAK N14 * 40 E3
Ullin St POP/IOD E14 94 A4
Ullswater Cl BMLY BR1 152 C5
PUT/ROE SW15 * 145 F3
YEAD UB4 82 C1
Ullswater Ct
RYLN/HDSTN HA2 * 48 A6
Ullswater Crs PUT/ROE SW15 145 F3
Ullswater Rd BARN SW13 106 D6
WNWD SE27 149 H2
Ullswater Wy HCH RM12 81 J4
Ulster Gdns PLMGR N13 41 J3
Ulster Pl CAMTN NW1 10 C1
Ulundi Rd BKHTH/KID SE3 113 H5
Ulva Rd PUT/ROE SW15 127 G3
Ulverscroft Rd EDUL SE22 131 H4
Ulverston Rd WALTH E17 58 B1
Ulysses Rd KIL/WHAMP NW6 70 D4
Umberston St WCHPL E1 * 92 C5
Umbria St PUT/ROE SW15 126 D5
Umfreville Rd FSBYPK N4 55 H5
Undercliff Rd LEW SE13 132 D2
Underhill BAR EN5 26 E4
Underhill Ct BAR EN5 * 26 E4
Underhill Rd EDUL SE22 131 H4
Underhill St CAMTN NW1 4 D4
Underne Av STHGT/OAK N14 40 B1
Undershaft HDTCH EC3A 13 J5
Undershaw Rd BMLY BR1 152 C2
Underwood CROY/NA CR0 180 A5
Underwood Rd CHING E4 43 K4
WCHPL E1 92 C3
WFD IG8 45 H6
Underwood Rw IS N1 6 F7
Underwood St IS N1 6 F7
The Underwood
ELTH/MOT SE9 153 K1
Undine Rd POP/IOD E14 112 E3
Undine St TOOT SW17 147 K4
Uneeda Dr GFD/PVL UB6 66 D7
Union Cl WAN E11 76 B3
Union Ct CLAP SW4 129 K1
OBST EC2N 13 J4
Union Dr WCHPL E1 * 93 G3
Union Gv VX/NE SW8 129 J1
Union La ISLW TW7 104 B7
Union Pk GNWCH SE10 113 J4
Union Rd ALP/SUD HA0 68 A5
CLAP SW4 129 J1
CROY/NA CR0 164 D6
FBAR/BDGN N11 40 D5
HAYES BR2 168 C4
NTHLT UB5 84 A1
ROMW/RG RM7 63 F5
VX/NE SW8 129 J1
Union Sq IS N1 6 E4
Union St BAR EN5 26 C3
KUT/HW KT1 158 E1
SRTFD E15 76 B7
STHWK SE1 12 D9
Union Wk BETH E2 7 L7
Unity Cl CROY/NA CR0 179 K7
NRWD SE19 149 J4
WLSDN NW10 69 J5
Unity Ms CAMTN NW1 5 G5
Unity Wy WOOL/PLUM SE18 114 C2
University Cl MLHL NW7 37 H6
University Gdns BXLY DA5 137 G6
University Pl ERITH DA8 117 J6
University Rd WIM/MER SW19 147 H5
University St FITZ W1T 10 F1
University Wy CAN/RD E16 96 A6
DART DA1 139 J2
Unwin Av EBED/NFELT TW14 121 G4
Unwin Cl PECK SE15 111 H5
Unwin Rd ISLW TW7 123 K2
SKENS SW7 15 H3
Upbrook Ms BAY/PAD W2 8 F5
Upcerne Rd WBPTN SW10 108 B6
Upcroft Av EDGW HA8 36 E4
Updale Rd SCUP DA14 155 F3
Upfield CROY/NA CR0 178 D1
Upfield Rd HNWL W7 85 F3
Uphall Rd IL IG1 78 B4
Upham Park Rd CHSWK W4 106 B3
Uphill Dr CDALE/KGS NW9 50 E4
MLHL NW7 37 G4
Uphill Gv MLHL NW7 37 G3
Uphill Rd MLHL NW7 37 G3
Upland Rd BELMT SM2 175 H6
BXLYHN DA7 137 G2
EDUL SE22 131 H6
PLSTW E13 94 E3
SAND/SEL CR2 177 K4
Uplands BECK BR3 166 D1
Uplands Cl MORT/ESHN SW14 125 J4
WOOL/PLUM SE18 115 G4
Uplands Park Rd ENC/FH EN2 29 G1
Uplands Rd CEND/HSY/T N8 55 F4
CHDH RM6 61 K2
EBAR EN4 28 A7
WFD IG8 45 J6
The Uplands RSLP HA4 46 E7
Uplands Wy WCHMH N21 29 G4
Upminster Rd South
RAIN RM13 99 J3
Upney La BARK IG11 79 F6
Upnor Wy WALW SE17 19 K7
Uppark Dr GNTH/NBYPK IG2 60 C5
Upper Abbey Rd BELV DA17 117 G3
Upper Addison Gdns
WKENS W14 107 H1
Upper Bank St POP/IOD E14 93 K7
Upper Bardsey Wk IS N1 * 73 J5
Upper Belgrave St KTBR SW1X 16 B3
Upper Berenger Wk
WBPTN SW10 * 108 C6
Upper Berkeley St
MBLAR W1H 9 L5
Upper Beulah Hl NRWD SE19 150 A7
Upper Blantyre Wk
WBPTN SW10 * 108 C6
Upper Brighton Rd SURB KT6 158 E5
Upper Brockley Rd
BROCKY SE4 132 C1
Upper Brook St
MYFR/PKLN W1K 10 A6
Upper Butts BTFD TW8 104 D5
Upper Caldy Wk IS N1 * 73 J5
Upper Camelford Wk
NTGHL W11 * 88 C5
Upper Cavendish Av FNCH N3 52 E2
Upper Cheyne Rw CHEL SW3 108 D5
Upper Clapton Rd CLPT E5 74 D1
Upper Clarendon Wk
NTGHL W11 * 88 C5
Upper Dartrey Wk
WBPTN SW10 * 108 B6
Upper Dengie Wk IS N1 * 6 E3
Upper Elmers End Rd
BECK BR3 166 B3
Upper Farm Rd
E/WMO/HCT KT8 156 E3
Upper Gn East MTCM CR4 162 E1
Upper Gn West MTCM CR4 162 E1
Upper Grosvenor St
MYFR/PKLN W1K 10 A7
Upper Grotto Rd TWK TW1 143 F1
Upper Gnd STHWK SE1 12 A8
Upper Gv SNWD SE25 165 F3
Upper Grove Rd BELV DA17 117 G5
Upper Gulland Wk IS N1 * 73 J5
Upper Ham Rd
RCHPK/HAM TW10 143 K3
Upper Handa Wk IS N1 * 73 K5
Upper Harley St CAMTN NW1 10 B1
Upper Hawkwell Wk IS N1 * 6 F3
Upper Hitch OXHEY WD19 21 J7
Upper Holly Hill Rd BELV DA17 117 J4
Upper John St SOHO/CST W1F 10 F6
Upper Lismore Wk IS N1 * 73 J5
Upper Ml HMSMTH W6 106 D4
Upper Marsh STHWK SE1 17 M3
Upper Montagu St
MBLAR W1H 9 L2
Upper Mulgrave Rd
BELMT SM2 174 C6
Upper North St POP/IOD E14 93 J4
Upper Paddock Rd
OXHEY WD19 21 J5
Upper Park Rd BELV DA17 117 J3
BMLY BR1 153 F7
FBAR/BDGN N11 40 B4
HAMP NW3 71 K5
KUTN/CMB KT2 144 C5
Upper Phillimore Gdns
KENS W8 14 A2
Upper Rainham Rd HCH RM12 81 H3
Upper Rawreth Wk IS N1 * 6 F3
Upper Richmond Rd
PUT/ROE SW15 126 E3
Upper Richmond Rd West
MORT/ESHN SW14 126 A3
RCHPK/HAM TW10 125 H3
Upper Rd PLSTW E13 94 E2
WLGTN SM6 176 D4
Upper St Martin's La
LSQ/SEVD WC2H 11 J5
Upper Selsdon Rd
SAND/SEL CR2 178 B7
Upper Sheppey Wk IS N1 73 J5
Upper Sheridan Rd
BELV DA17 117 H3
Upper Shirley Rd
CROY/NA CR0 178 E2
Upper Sq ISLW TW7 124 B2
Upper St IS N1 6 B5
IS N1 6 C1
Upper Sunbury Rd
HPTN TW12 141 K7
Upper Sutton La HEST TW5 103 F7
Upper Tachbrook St
PIM SW1V 16 E5
Upper Tail OXHEY WD19 33 J2
Upper Talbot Wk
NTGHL W11 * 88 C5
Upper Teddington Rd
KUT/HW KT1 143 J7
Upper Ter HAMP NW3 71 G2
Upper Thames St BLKFR EC4V 12 E6
Upper Tollington Pk
FSBYPK N4 55 G7
Upperton Rd SCUP DA14 155 F4
Upperton Rd East PLSTW E13 95 G2
Upperton Rd West PLSTW E13 95 G2
Upper Tooting Pk TOOT SW17 147 K1
Upper Tooting Rd TOOT SW17 147 K3
Upper Town Rd STHL UB1 84 B3
Upper Tulse Hl
BRXS/STRHM SW2 130 A6
Upper Vernon Rd SUT SM1 175 H4
Upper Walthamstow Rd
WALTH E17 58 B3
Upper Whistler Wk
WBPTN SW10 * 108 B6
Upper Wickham La
WELL DA16 136 C1
Upper Wimpole St
CAVSQ/HST W1G 10 B2
Upper Woburn Pl
CAMTN NW1 5 H8
STPAN WC1H 5 H9
Uppingham Av STAN HA7 49 J2
Upsdell Av PLMGR N13 41 G5
Upstall St CMBW SE5 110 C7
Upton Av FSTGT E7 76 E6
Upton Cl BXLY DA5 137 G5
CRICK NW2 70 C2
Upton Dene BELMT SM2 175 F6
Upton Gdns
KTN/HRWW/WS HA3 49 J5
Upton La FSTGT E7 77 F5
Upton Lodge Cl BUSH WD23 22 C6
Upton Park Rd FSTGT E7 77 F6
Upton Rd BXLYHS DA6 137 F3
HSLW TW3 123 F2
THHTH CR7 164 E1
UED N18 42 C4
WATW WD18 21 F3
WOOL/PLUM SE18 115 H5
Upton Rd South BXLY DA5 137 G5
Upway NFNCH/WDSPK N12 39 J6
Upwood Rd LEE/GVPK SE12 133 K5
STRHM/NOR SW16 148 E7
Urban Ms FSBYPK N4 55 H6
Urlwin St CMBW SE5 110 D5
Urlwin Wk BRXN/ST SW9 110 B7
Urmston Dr WIM/MER SW19 127 H7
Ursula Gould Wy
POP/IOD E14 93 J4
Ursula Ms FSBYPK N4 55 H7
Ursula St BTSEA SW11 108 D7
Urswick Gdns DAGW RM9 80 A6
Urswick Rd CLPT E5 74 E4
DAGW RM9 80 A6
Usborne Ms VX/NE SW8 110 A6
Usher Rd BOW E3 75 H7
Usk Rd BTSEA SW11 128 B3
Usk St BETH E2 93 F2
Uvedale Rd DAGE RM10 80 C2
ENC/FH EN2 29 K4
Uverdale Rd WBPTN SW10 108 B6
Uxbridge Rd EA W5 86 A6
FELT TW13 141 H1
HGDN/ICK UB10 82 A3
HNWL W7 84 E7
HPTN TW12 142 B4
KUT/HW KT1 158 E3
SHB W12 87 J7
STHL UB1 84 A7
WEA W13 85 H7
YEAD UB4 82 E5
Uxbridge Rd (Harrow Weald)
KTN/HRWW/WS HA3 34 C6
Uxbridge Rd (Hatch End)
PIN HA5 33 J7
Uxbridge Road High St
STHL UB1 83 K7
Uxbridge Rd (Pinner) PIN HA5 47 H1
Uxbridge Rd (Stanmore)
STAN HA7 35 F5
Uxbridge Rd The Broadway
YEAD UB4 83 H6
Uxbridge St KENS W8 8 A8
Uxendon Crs WBLY HA9 50 A7
Uxendon Hl WBLY HA9 50 B7

V

Valan Leas HAYES BR2 167 H2
Vale Av BORE WD6 24 D4
Vale Cl EFNCH N2 53 K2
MV/WKIL W9 2 E8
TWK TW1 * 143 G2
Vale Cots PUT/ROE SW15 * 145 G2
Vale Ct ACT W3 * 87 H7
Vale Crs PUT/ROE SW15 145 G3
Vale Cft ESH/CLAY KT10 171 F6
PIN HA5 47 J4
Vale Dr BAR EN5 26 D3
Vale End EDUL SE22 131 G3
Vale Gv ACT W3 87 F7
FSBYPK N4 55 J6
Vale La ACT W3 86 C4
Valence Av BCTR RM8 79 K2
Valence Circ BCTR RM8 79 K2
Valence Rd ERITH DA8 118 A6
Valence Wood Rd BCTR RM8 79 K2
Valencia Rd STAN HA7 35 J3
Valency Cl NTHWD HA6 32 D3
Valentia Pl BRXN/ST SW9 130 B3
Valentine Pl STHWK SE1 18 C1
Valentine Rd HOM E9 * 75 F5
RYLN/HDSTN HA2 66 B2
Valentines Rd IL IG1 60 B7
Valentines Wy
ROMW/RG RM7 81 G1
Vale of Health HAMP NW3 71 G2
Valerian Wy SRTFD E15 94 C2
Vale Ri GLDGN NW11 52 D7
Vale Rd BMLY BR1 169 F1
BUSH WD23 21 J4
DART DA1 138 E7
ESH/CLAY KT10 170 E7
FSBYPK N4 55 J6
FSTGT E7 77 F5
HOR/WEW KT19 173 H3
MTCM CR4 163 J2
SUT SM1 175 F3
WPK KT4 173 H2
Vale Rw HBRY N5 73 H2
Vale Royal HOLWY N7 5 J2
Vale St DUL SE21 149 K2
Valeswood Rd BMLY BR1 152 D4
Vale Ter FSBYPK N4 55 J5
The Vale ACT W3 87 F7
CHEL SW3 15 G9
CROY/NA CR0 179 F1
EBED/NFELT TW14 122 A5
GLDGN NW11 70 B2
HEST TW5 102 D5
MUSWH N10 40 A7
RSLP HA4 65 G3
SHB W12 87 H7
STHGT/OAK N14 28 E6
SUN TW16 * 140 E5
WFD IG8 44 E6
Valetta Gv PLSTW E13 94 E1
Valetta Rd ACT W3 106 B1
Valette St HACK E8 * 74 D5
Valiant Cl NTHLT UB5 83 H2
ROMW/RG RM7 62 C1
Valiant Wy EHAM E6 95 K4
Vallance Rd MUSWH N10 54 C1
WCHPL E1 92 C3
Vallentin Rd WALTH E17 58 A3
Valley Av NFNCH/WDSPK N12 39 H3
Valley Cl DART DA1 138 C5
PIN HA5 47 F1
Valley Dr CDALE/KGS NW9 50 D4
Valleyfield Rd
STRHM/NOR SW16 149 F4
Valley Fields Crs ENC/FH EN2 29 G1
Valley Gdns ALP/SUD HA0 68 B6
WIM/MER SW19 147 H6
Valley Gv CHARL SE7 114 B4
Valley Pk WATW WD18 20 A6
Valley Rd DART DA1 138 C5
ERITH DA8 117 K3
HAYES BR2 167 H1
STMC/STPC BR5 155 H7
STRHM/NOR SW16 149 F3
Valley Side CHING E4 31 J7
Valley Vw BAR EN5 26 C5
Valley Wk CROY/NA CR0 178 E1
RKW/CH/CXG WD3 20 A4
Valliere Rd WLSDN NW10 87 J2
Valliers Wood Rd
BFN/LL DA15 135 J7
Vallis Wy CHSGTN KT9 171 K3
WEA W13 85 G4
Valmar Rd CMBW SE5 110 D7
Val McKenzie Av HOLWY N7 73 G2
Valnay St TOOT SW17 147 K4
Valognes Av WALTH E17 43 G7
Valonia Gdns
WAND/EARL SW18 127 J5
Vambery Rd
WOOL/PLUM SE18 115 H5
Vanbrough Crs NTHLT UB5 83 G1
Vanbrugh Dr WOT/HER KT12 156 B6
Vanbrugh Flds
BKHTH/KID SE3 113 J5
Vanbrugh Hl GNWCH SE10 113 H4
Vanbrugh Pk BKHTH/KID SE3 113 J6
Vanbrugh Park Rd
BKHTH/KID SE3 113 J6
Vanbrugh Park Rd West
BKHTH/KID SE3 113 J6
Vanbrugh Rd CHSWK W4 106 A2
Vanbrugh Ter BKHTH/KID SE3 113 J7
Vanburgh Cl CAN/RD E16 95 H4
ORP BR6 169 K7
Vancouver Man EDGW HA8 * 36 D7
Vancouver Rd EDGW HA8 36 D7
FSTH SE23 151 G1
RCHPK/HAM TW10 143 J3
YEAD UB4 83 F3
Vanderbilt Rd
WAND/EARL SW18 128 A7
Vanderbilt Vls SHB W12 * 107 G1
Vanderville Gdns EFNCH N2 53 G1
Vandome Cl CAN/RD E16 95 F5
Vandon St STJSPK SW1H 16 F3
Van Dyck Av NWMAL KT3 160 A6
Vandyke Cl PUT/ROE SW15 127 G5
Vandyke Cross ELTH/MOT SE9 134 D4
Vandy St SDTCH EC2A 13 J1
Vane Cl HAMP NW3 71 H4
KTN/HRWW/WS HA3 50 B5
Vanessa Cl BELV DA17 117 H4
Van Gogh Cl ISLW TW7 124 B2
Vanguard CDALE/KGS NW9 * 37 G6
Vanguard Cl CAN/RD E16 94 E4
CROY/NA CR0 164 C7
ROMW/RG RM7 62 D1
Vanguard St DEPT SE8 112 D7
Vanguard Wy CROY/NA CR0 178 B3
HTHAIR TW6 121 H1
WLGTN SM6 176 E6
Vanneck Sq PUT/ROE SW15 * 126 D4
Vanoc Gdns BMLY BR1 152 E3
Vanquish Cl WHTN TW2 123 F6
Vansittart Rd FSTGT E7 76 E3
Vansittart St NWCR SE14 112 B6
Vanston Pl FUL/PGN SW6 107 K6
Vantage Pl KENS W8 14 B4
Vant Rd TOOT SW17 147 K4
Varcoe Gdns HYS/HAR UB3 82 B5
Varcoe Rd BERM/RHTH SE16 111 J4
Vardens Rd BTSEA SW11 128 C3
Varden St WCHPL E1 92 D5
Vardon Cl ACT W3 87 F5
Varley Dr TWK TW1 124 C3
Varley Rd CAN/RD E16 95 F5
Varley Wy MTCM CR4 162 C1
Varna Rd FUL/PGN SW6 107 H6
HPTN TW12 * 142 B7
Varndell St CAMTN NW1 4 E7
Varsity Dr TWK TW1 123 K4
Varsity Rw MORT/ESHN SW14 125 K1
Vartry Rd SEVS/STOTM N15 56 A5
Vassall Rd BRXN/ST SW9 110 B6
Vauban Est BERM/RHTH SE16 19 M4
Vauban St BERM/RHTH SE16 19 M4
Vaughan Av HDN NW4 51 J4
HMSMTH W6 106 C3
Vaughan Cl DART DA1 139 G6
Vaughan Est BETH E2 * 7 L7
Vaughan Gdns IL IG1 59 K6
Vaughan Rd CMBW SE5 130 D1
HRW HA1 48 C6
SRTFD E15 76 D5
THDIT KT7 158 C6
WELL DA16 136 A1
Vaughan St BERM/RHTH SE16 112 C1
Vaughan Wy WAP E1W 92 C6
Vaughan Williams Cl
DEPT SE8 112 D6
Vauxhall Br STHWK SE1 17 J8
Vauxhall Bridge Rd PIM SW1V 16 E4
WEST SW1P 17 H7
Vauxhall Gdns SAND/SEL CR2 177 J5
Vauxhall Gv VX/NE SW8 17 K9
Vauxhall Pl DART DA1 139 H6
Vauxhall St LBTH SE11 17 M7
Vauxhall Wk LBTH SE11 17 L7
Vawdrey Cl WCHPL E1 92 E3
Veals Md MTCM CR4 147 J7
Vectis Gdns TOOT SW17 148 B5
Vectis Rd TOOT SW17 148 B5
Veda Rd LEW SE13 132 D3
Vega Crs NTHWD HA6 32 D4
Vega Rd BUSH WD23 22 C6
Veitch Cl EBED/NFELT TW14 121 J6
Veldene Wy RYLN/HDSTN HA2 65 K2
Vellum Dr CAR SM5 176 A2
Venables Cl DAGE RM10 80 D3
Venables St STJWD NW8 9 H1
Vencourt Pl HMSMTH W6 106 D3
Venetian Rd CMBW SE5 130 D1
Venetia Rd EA W5 104 E1
FSBYPK N4 55 H5
Venette Cl RAIN RM13 99 K4
Venice Av WATW WD18 20 C3
Venner Rd SYD SE26 150 E5
Venners Cl BXLYHN DA7 138 B1
Venn St CLAP SW4 129 H3
Ventnor Av STAN HA7 35 H7
Ventnor Dr TRDG/WHET N20 39 F2
Ventnor Gdns BARK IG11 78 E5
Ventnor Rd BELMT SM2 175 F6
NWCR SE14 112 A6
Ventnor Ter
SEVS/STOTM N15 * 56 C3
Venture Cl BXLY DA5 137 F6
Venue St POP/IOD E14 93 K4
Venus Ms MTCM CR4 162 D2
Venus Rd WOOL/PLUM SE18 114 E2
Vera Av WCHMH N21 29 G4
Vera Ct OXHEY WD19 21 H6
Vera Lynn Cl FSTGT E7 76 E3
Vera Rd FUL/PGN SW6 107 H7
Verbena Cl CAN/RD E16 94 C3
Verbena Gdns HMSMTH W6 106 D4
Ver-Colne Valley Wk
WAT WD17 21 H2
Verdant La CAT SE6 133 H7
Verdayne Av CROY/NA CR0 166 A7
Verdun Rd BARN SW13 106 D6
WOOL/PLUM SE18 116 B5
Vereker Rd WKENS W14 * 107 H4
Vere St CAVSQ/HST W1G 10 C5
Vermont Cl ENC/FH EN2 29 H3
Vermont Rd NRWD SE19 149 K5
SUT SM1 175 F2
WAND/EARL SW18 128 A5
Verney Gdns DAGW RM9 80 A3
Verney Rd BERM/RHTH SE16 111 J4
DAGW RM9 80 A3
Verney St WLSDN NW10 69 F2
Verney Wy BERM/RHTH SE16 111 J4
Vernham Rd
WOOL/PLUM SE18 115 H5
Vernon Av MNPK E12 77 K3
RYNPK SW20 161 G1
WFD IG8 45 F5
Vernon Cl HOR/WEW KT19 172 E5
STWL/WRAY TW19 120 B7
Vernon Crs EBAR EN4 28 A4
Vernon Dr STAN HA7 35 G7
Vernon Pl FSBYW WC1X 11 K3
Vernon Ri FSBYW WC1X 5 M7
GFD/PVL UB6 66 D4
Vernon Rd BOW E3 93 H1
BUSH WD23 21 J4
CEND/HSY/T N8 * 55 G2
FELT TW13 140 D1
GDMY/SEVK IG3 61 F7
MORT/ESHN SW14 126 A2
SRTFD E15 76 C6
SUT SM1 175 G4
WALTH E17 57 H3
WAN E11 58 C7
Vernon Sq FSBYW WC1X 5 M7
Vernon St WKENS W14 107 H3
Vernon Yd NTGHL W11 88 D6
Veroan Rd BXLYHN DA7 137 F1
Verona Ct CHSWK W4 106 B4
Verona Dr SURB KT6 172 A1
Veronica Gdns
STRHM/NOR SW16 148 C7
Veronica Rd TOOT SW17 148 B2
Veronique Gdns BARK/HLT IG6 60 C4
Verran Rd BAL SW12 * 129 G6
Versailles Rd PGE/AN SE20 150 C6
Verulam Av WALTH E17 57 H5
Verulam Ct CDALE/KGS NW9 * 51 J6
Verulam Rd GFD/PVL UB6 84 A3
Verulam St FSBYW WC1X 12 A2
Verwood Dr EBAR EN4 27 K2
Verwood Rd
RYLN/HDSTN HA2 48 C1
Vespan Rd SHB W12 106 D1
Vesta Rd BROCKY SE4 132 B1
Vestris Rd FSTH SE23 151 F1
Vestry Ms CMBW SE5 111 F7
Vestry Rd CMBW SE5 111 F7
WALTH E17 57 K4
Vestry St IS N1 7 G7
Vevey St CAT SE6 151 H1
Viaduct Pl BETH E2 92 D2
Viaduct St BETH E2 92 D2
The Viaduct MUSWH N10 * 54 B3
SWFD E18 58 E1
Vian St LEW SE13 132 E2
Vibart Gdns
BRXS/STRHM SW2 130 A6
Vibart Wk IS N1 5 K3
Vibia Cl STWL/WRAY TW19 120 A6
Vicarage Cl ERITH DA8 117 K5
NTHLT UB5 65 K7
RSLP HA4 46 B6
WPK KT4 160 B7
Vicarage Ct BECK BR3 * 166 B2
Vicarage Crs BTSEA SW11 128 C1
Vicarage Dr BARK IG11 78 C6
BECK BR3 151 J7
MORT/ESHN SW14 126 A4
Vicarage Farm Rd
HSLWW TW4 122 D1
Vicarage Flds WOT/HER KT12 156 B5
Vicarage Gdns KENS W8 * 14 B1
MTCM CR4 162 D2
Vicarage Ga KENS W8 8 C9
Vicarage Gv CMBW SE5 110 E7
Vicarage La EHAM E6 95 K2
IL IG1 60 D7
SRTFD E15 76 C5
Vicarage Ms CHSWK W4 * 106 B5
Vicarage Pde
SEVS/STOTM N15 * 55 J3
Vicarage Pk
WOOL/PLUM SE18 115 H4
Vicarage Rd BXLY DA5 137 J7
CROY/NA CR0 177 G2
DAGE RM10 80 D6
HCH RM12 63 J7
HDN NW4 51 J5
KUT/HW KT1 143 J7
LEY E10 57 K6
MORT/ESHN SW14 125 K4
SRTFD E15 76 D6
SUN TW16 140 D5
SUT SM1 174 E3
TEDD TW11 143 G4
TOTM N17 42 C6
WATW WD18 20 E6
WFD IG8 45 J6
WHTN TW2 123 H5
WOOL/PLUM SE18 115 H4
Vicarage Wk BTSEA SW11 * 108 C7
Vicarage Wy
RYLN/HDSTN HA2 48 A6
WLSDN NW10 69 F2
Vicars Bridge Cl ALP/SUD HA0 86 A1
Vicar's Cl EN EN1 30 A1
HOM E9 74 E7
SRTFD E15 76 E7
Vicars Hl LEW SE13 132 E3
Vicar's Moor La WCHMH N21 29 G6
Vicars Oak Rd NRWD SE19 150 A5
Vicar's Rd KTTN NW5 72 A4
Viceroy Cl EFNCH N2 * 53 J3
Viceroy Pde EFNCH N2 * 53 J3
Viceroy Rd VX/NE SW8 109 K7
Vickers Cl WLGTN SM6 177 F6
Vickers La DART DA1 139 K2
Vickers Rd ERITH DA8 118 A4
Victor Gv ALP/SUD HA0 68 A6
Victoria Ar WESTW SW1E 16 D4
Victoria Av E/WMO/HCT KT8 157 G2
EHAM E6 77 H7
FNCH N3 38 D7
HSLW TW3 123 F4
SURB KT6 158 E5
WBLY HA9 68 D5
WLGTN SM6 176 A2
Victoria Cl E/WMO/HCT KT8 157 F2
EBAR EN4 27 H3

HRW HA1 49 F5
HYS/HAR UB3 82 B5
Victoria Cots RCH/KEW TW9 105 G7
WCHPL E1 * 92 C4
Victoria Ct WBLY HA9 68 C5
Victoria Crs NRWD SE19 150 A5
SEVS/STOTM N15 56 A4
WIM/MER SW19 * 146 D6
Victoria Dock Rd CAN/RD E16 94 D6
Victoria Dr WIM/MER SW19 127 G7
Victoria Emb EMB EC4Y 12 B6
TPL/STR WC2R 11 L7
WHALL SW1A 17 K2
Victoria Embankment Gdns
CHCR WC2N * 11 K7
Victoria Gdns HEST TW5 102 D7
NTGHL W11 88 D7
Victoria Ga BAY/PAD W2 9 H6
Victoria Gv KENS W8 14 E3
NFNCH/WDSPK N12 39 H4
Victoria Grove Ms
BAY/PAD W2 * 8 C7
Victoria La BAR EN5 26 D3
HYS/HAR UB3 101 G4
Victoria Ms KIL/WHAMP NW6 2 A4
WAND/EARL SW18 128 B7
Victorian Gv STNW/STAM N16 74 A2
Victorian Rd STNW/STAM N16 74 A2
Victoria Pde RCH/KEW TW9 * 105 H7
Victoria Park Rd HOM E9 74 E7
Victoria Park Sq BETH E2 92 E2
Victoria Park Studios
HOM E9 * 74 E5
Victoria Pas WATW WD18 21 F3
Victoria Pl RCH/KEW TW9 124 E4
Victoria Ri CLAP SW4 129 G2
Victoria Rd ACT W3 87 F4
BARK IG11 78 B5
BFN/LL DA15 155 F2
BKHH IG9 45 H1
BUSH WD23 22 B7
BXLYHS DA6 137 H3
CHST BR7 154 A4
DAGE RM10 80 E4
DART DA1 139 G4
EA W5 85 H4
EBAR EN4 27 H3
ED N9 42 B2
ERITH DA8 118 B5
FELT TW13 122 A7
FSBYPK N4 55 F6
HAYES BR2 168 C4
HDN NW4 52 A3
KENS W8 14 E4
KIL/WHAMP NW6 2 A3
KUT/HW KT1 159 G1
MLHL NW7 37 H4
MORT/ESHN SW14 126 A2
MTCM CR4 147 J6
NWDGN UB2 102 E2
PLSTW E13 94 E1
ROM RM1 63 H4
RSLP HA4 46 E7
RSLP HA4 65 F3
SEVS/STOTM N15 * 56 C3
SURB KT6 158 E5
SUT SM1 175 H4
SWFD E18 59 F2
TEDD TW11 143 G5
TWK TW1 124 C6
UED N18 42 B3
WALTH E17 58 A1
WAN E11 76 B3
WDGN N22 40 D7
WIM/MER SW19 147 J6
WLSDN NW10 87 G3
Victoria Sq BGVA SW1W 16 D3
Victoria St BELV DA17 117 G4
SRTFD E15 76 C6
WESTW SW1E 16 D4
Victoria Ter EA W5 * 85 K7
FSBYPK N4 55 G7
HRW HA1 48 E7
Victoria Vls RCH/KEW TW9 125 G2
Victoria Wy CHARL SE7 114 A4
Victoria Works
STMC/STPC BR5 169 H4
Victoria Yd WCHPL E1 * 92 C5
Victor Rd PGE/AN SE20 151 F6
RYLN/HDSTN HA2 48 C2
TEDD TW11 142 E4
WLSDN NW10 87 K2
Victors Dr HPTN TW12 * 141 J5
Victors Wy BAR EN5 26 D2
Victor Vls ED N9 * 41 K2
Victory Av MRDN SM4 162 B4
Victory Cl STWL/WRAY TW19 120 B7
Victory Pk WBLY HA9 * 67 K2
Victory Pl NRWD SE19 * 150 A5
WALW SE17 18 F5
Victory Rd RAIN RM13 99 J1
WAN E11 58 E3
WIM/MER SW19 147 G6
Victory Road Ms
WIM/MER SW19 147 G6
Victory Wy BERM/RHTH SE16 112 B1
HEST TW5 102 B4
ROMW/RG RM7 62 D1
Vienna Cl WFD IG8 59 H1
View Cl HGT N6 53 K6
HRW HA1 48 D3
View Crs CEND/HSY/T N8 54 D4
Viewfield Cl
KTN/HRWW/WS HA3 50 A6
Viewfield Rd BFN/LL DA15 136 D7
WAND/EARL SW18 127 J5
Viewland Rd
WOOL/PLUM SE18 116 A4
View Rd HGT N6 53 K6
The View ABYW SE2 117 F4
Viga Rd WCHMH N21 29 G5
Vigilant Cl SYD SE26 150 C3
Vignoles Rd ROMW/RG RM7 62 C6
Vigo St CONDST W1S 10 E7
Viking Cl BOW E3 93 G1
Viking Gdns EHAM E6 95 J4
Viking Pl LEY E10 57 H7
Viking Rd STHL UB1 83 J6
Viking Wy ERITH DA8 117 K2
Villacourt Rd
WOOL/PLUM SE18 116 B6
Village Cl CHING E4 44 A4
HAMP NW3 * 71 H4
Village Green Rd DART DA1 138 D3
Village Ms CDALE/KGS NW9 * 69 F1
Village Mt HAMP NW3 * 71 G3
Village Park Cl EN EN1 30 A5
Village Rd EN EN1 29 K5
FNCH N3 52 C1
Village Rw BELMT SM2 174 E6
The Village CHARL SE7 114 B5
HAMP NW3 * 71 G1
Village Wy BARK/HLT IG6 60 C2
BECK BR3 166 D3
DUL SE21 130 E5
PIN HA5 47 J6
WLSDN NW10 69 F3
Village Wy East PIN HA5 47 K6
Villa Rd BRXN/ST SW9 130 B2
Villas Rd WOOL/PLUM SE18 115 H3
Villa St WALW SE17 19 H8
Villiers Av BRYLDS KT5 159 G4
WHTN TW2 122 E7
Villiers Cl BRYLDS KT5 159 G3
LEY E10 75 J1
Villiers Gv BELMT SM2 174 B7
Villiers Rd BECK BR3 166 A1
CRICK NW2 69 J5
ISLW TW7 123 K1
KUT/HW KT1 159 G2
OXHEY WD19 21 J5
STHL UB1 83 K7
Villiers St CHCR WC2N 11 K8
Vimy Cl HSLWW TW4 122 E4
Vimy Dr DART DA1 139 J2
Vincam Cl WHTN TW2 123 F6
Vincennes Est WNWD SE27 * 149 K3
Vincent Av BRYLDS KT5 159 J7
Vincent Cl BAR EN5 26 E2
BFN/LL DA15 135 K7
ESH/CLAY KT10 170 B2
HAYES BR2 168 A3
WDR/YW UB7 100 D5
Vincent Gdns CRICK NW2 69 H2
Vincent Pde FSBYPK N4 * 54 E7
Vincent Rd ACT W3 105 K2
ALP/SUD HA0 68 B6
CHING E4 44 B5
CROY/NA CR0 165 F6
DAGW RM9 80 A6
HSLWW TW4 122 C2
ISLW TW7 103 J7
KUT/HW KT1 159 H2
SEVS/STOTM N15 55 J3
WDGN N22 55 G1
WOOL/PLUM SE18 115 G3
Vincent Rw HPTN TW12 142 C5
Vincents Cl BERM/RHTH SE16 112 B1
Vincent Sq WDGN N22 * 55 G1
WEST SW1P 16 F5
Vincent St CAN/RD E16 94 E4
WEST SW1P 17 G5
Vincent Ter IS N1 6 C5
Vincent Vls
SEVS/STOTM N15 * 55 J3
Vince St FSBYE EC1V 7 H8
Vine Cl BRYLDS KT5 159 G5
CLPT E5 74 C3
SUT SM1 175 G2
WDR/YW UB7 100 D3
Vine Cots HNWL W7 * 84 E7
WCHPL E1 * 92 E5
Vine Ct KTN/HRWW/WS HA3 50 A5
WCHPL E1 92 C4
Vine Gdns IL IG1 78 C4
Vinegar St WAP E1W 92 D7
Vinegar Yd STHWK SE1 19 J1
Vine Hl CLKNW EC1R 12 A1
Vine La STHWK SE1 13 K9
Vine Pl HSLW TW3 123 G3
Vineries Cl WDR/YW UB7 100 D5
The Vineries CAT SE6 * 132 D7
EN EN1 30 A2
STHGT/OAK N14 28 C5
Vine Rd BARN SW13 126 C2
E/WMO/HCT KT8 157 H3
SRTFD E15 76 D6
Vine Rw RCHPK/HAM TW10 * 125 F4
Viners Cl WOT/HER KT12 156 B5
Vines Av FNCH N3 39 F7
Vine Sq WKENS W14 * 107 J4
Vine St MYFR/PICC W1J 10 F7
ROMW/RG RM7 62 E4
TWRH EC3N 13 L5
Vine Street Br FARR EC1M 12 B1
Vine Yd STHWK SE1 18 F1
Vineyard Av MLHL NW7 38 C6
Vineyard Cl CAT SE6 132 D7
KUT/HW KT1 159 G2
Vineyard Gv FNCH N3 39 F7
Vineyard Hill Rd
WIM/MER SW19 146 E3
Vineyard Ms CLKNW EC1R * 6 A9
Vineyard Pth
MORT/ESHN SW14 126 A2
Vineyard Rd FELT TW13 140 E2
Vineyard Rw KUT/HW KT1 143 J7
The Vineyard
RCHPK/HAM TW10 124 E4
Vineyard Wk CLKNW EC1R 6 A9
Viney Bank CROY/NA CR0 179 H7
Viney Rd LEW SE13 132 E2
Vining St BRXS/STRHM SW2 130 B3
Vinries Bank MLHL NW7 37 K4
Vintage Ms CHING E4 43 J3
Vintry Ms WALTH E17 57 J3
Viola Av ABYW SE2 116 C3
EBED/NFELT TW14 122 B5
STWL/WRAY TW19 120 B7
Viola Sq SHB W12 87 H6
Violet Cl CAN/RD E16 94 C3
CHEAM SM3 161 H7
DEPT SE8 112 C5
WLGTN SM6 163 F7
Violet Gdns CROY/NA CR0 177 H4
Violet Hl STJWD NW8 2 E6
Violet La SAND/SEL CR2 177 H4
Violet Rd BOW E3 93 K3
SWFD E18 59 F1
WALTH E17 57 J5
Violet St BETH E2 92 D3
Virgil St STHWK SE1 17 M3
Virginia Cl HAYES BR2 167 H2
NWMAL KT3 159 K3
Virginia Gdns BARK/HLT IG6 60 D1
Virginia Rd BETH E2 7 L8
THHTH CR7 149 H7
Virginia St WCHPL E1 * 92 C6
Viscount Cl FBAR/BDGN N11 40 B4
Viscount Dr EHAM E6 95 K4
Viscount Gv NTHLT UB5 83 H2
Viscount Rd
STWL/WRAY TW19 120 A6
Viscount St BARB EC2Y 12 E1
Viscount Wy HTHAIR TW6 121 H3
Vista Av PEND EN3 31 F1
Vista Dr REDBR IG4 59 H4
The Vista ELTH/MOT SE9 134 C5
Vista Wy KTN/HRWW/WS HA3 50 A5
Viveash Cl HYS/HAR UB3 101 J2
Vivian Av HDN NW4 51 K4
WBLY HA9 68 C5
Vivian Cl OXHEY WD19 32 E1
Vivian Gdns OXHEY WD19 20 E7
WBLY HA9 68 C4
Vivian Rd BOW E3 93 G1
Vivian Sq PECK SE15 131 J2
Vivian Wy EFNCH N2 53 H4
Vivien Cl CHSGTN KT9 172 A6
Vivienne Cl TWK TW1 124 E5
Vixen Ms HACK E8 * 7 L3
Voce Rd WOOL/PLUM SE18 115 J6
Voewood Cl NWMAL KT3 160 C5
Voltaire Rd CLAP SW4 129 J2
Volt Av WLSDN NW10 87 F2
Volta Wy CROY/NA CR0 164 A7
Voluntary Pl WAN E11 58 E5
Vorley Rd ARCH N19 72 C1
Voss Ct STRHM/NOR SW16 148 E5
Voss St BETH E2 92 C2
Voyagers Cl THMD SE28 97 J5
Vulcan Cl EHAM E6 96 A5
Vulcan Ga ENC/FH EN2 29 G1
Vulcan Rd BROCKY SE4 132 C1
Vulcan Ter BROCKY SE4 132 C1
Vulcan Wy HOLWY N7 73 F5
WLGTN SM6 176 E7
Vyner Rd ACT W3 87 F6
Vyner St BETH E2 92 D1
The Vyne BXLYHN DA7 137 J2
Vyse Cl BAR EN5 26 A3

W

Wadbrook St KUT/HW KT1 158 E1
Wadding St WALW SE17 19 G6
Waddington Cl EN EN1 30 A3
Waddington Rd SRTFD E15 76 B4
Waddington St SRTFD E15 76 B5
Waddington Wy NRWD SE19 149 J7
Waddon Cl CROY/NA CR0 177 G2
Waddon Court Rd
CROY/NA CR0 177 G3
Waddon Marsh Wy
CROY/NA CR0 164 A7
Waddon New Rd
CROY/NA CR0 177 H2
Waddon Park Av
CROY/NA CR0 177 G3
Waddon Rd CROY/NA CR0 177 G2
Waddon Wy CROY/NA CR0 177 G5
Wade House STHWK SE1 * 111 H1
Wade's Gv WCHMH N21 29 G6
Wade's Hl WCHMH N21 29 G5
Wade's La TEDD TW11 143 G4
Wadeson St BETH E2 92 D1
Wade's Pl POP/IOD E14 93 K6
Wadeville Av CHDH RM6 62 A5
Wadeville Cl BELV DA17 117 H4
Wadham Av WALTH E17 43 K6
Wadham Gdns GFD/PVL UB6 66 D5
HAMP NW3 3 J2
Wadham Rd CHING E4 44 A7
PUT/ROE SW15 127 H3
WALTH E17 43 K7
Wadhurst Cl PGE/AN SE20 165 J1
Wadhurst Rd CHSWK W4 106 A2
VX/NE SW8 109 H7
Wadley Rd WAN E11 58 C6
Wadsworth Cl GFD/PVL UB6 85 J1
PEND EN3 31 F4
Wadsworth Rd GFD/PVL UB6 85 H1
Wager St BOW E3 93 H3
Waghorn Rd
KTN/HRWW/WS HA3 49 K2
PLSTW E13 77 G7
Waghorn St PECK SE15 131 H2
Wagner St PECK SE15 111 K6
Wagstaff Gdns DAGW RM9 79 J6
Wagtail Cl CDALE/KGS NW9 51 G1
Wagtail Wk BECK BR3 167 F4
Waid Cl DART DA1 139 J5
Waights Ct KUTN/CMB KT2 144 A7
Wainfleet Av CRW RM5 62 E1
Wainford Cl WIM/MER SW19 127 G7
Wainwright Gv ISLW TW7 123 J3
Waite Davies Rd
LEE/GVPK SE12 133 J6
Waite St CMBW SE5 19 L9
Wakefield Gdns IL IG1 59 J5
NRWD SE19 150 A6
Wakefield Ms STPAN WC1H 5 J8
Wakefield Rd
FBAR/BDGN N11 40 D4
RCHPK/HAM TW10 124 E4
SEVS/STOTM N15 56 B4
Wakefield St BMSBY WC1N 5 K9
EHAM E6 77 J7
STPAN WC1H 5 K8
UED N18 42 C4
Wakeford Cl CLAP SW4 129 H4
Wakehams Hl PIN HA5 47 K2
Wakeham St IS N1 73 K5
Wakehurst Rd BTSEA SW11 128 D4
Wakeling La ALP/SUD HA0 67 H2
Wakeling Rd HNWL W7 85 F4
Wakeling St WCHPL E1 * 93 G5
Wakelin Rd SRTFD E15 94 C1
Wakeman Rd WLSDN NW10 88 A2
Wakemans Hill Av
CDALE/KGS NW9 51 F4
Wakering Rd BARK IG11 78 C5
Wakerly Cl EHAM E6 95 K5
Wakley St FSBYE EC1V 6 C7
Walberswick St VX/NE SW8 109 K6
Walbrook MANHO EC4N 13 G6
Walburgh St WCHPL E1 92 D5
Walcorde Av WALW SE17 18 F6
Walcot Rd PEND EN3 31 H1
Walcot Sq LBTH SE11 18 B5
Walcott St WEST SW1P * 16 F5
Waldeck Gv WNWD SE27 149 H2
Waldeck Rd CHSWK W4 105 H5
DART DA1 139 J6
MORT/ESHN SW14 125 K2
SEVS/STOTM N15 55 H2
WEA W13 85 H5
Waldegrave Gdns TWK TW1 143 F1
Waldegrave Pk TWK TW1 143 F5
Waldegrave Rd BCTR RM8 79 J1
BMLY BR1 168 D4
CEND/HSY/T N8 * 55 G2
EA W5 86 B6
NRWD SE19 150 B6
TWK TW1 143 F5
Waldegrove CROY/NA CR0 178 B2
Waldemar Av FUL/PGN SW6 107 H7
WEA W13 85 J7
Waldemar Rd WIM/MER SW19 146 E4
Walden Av CHST BR7 153 K3
PLMGR N13 41 J3
RAIN RM13 99 F1
Walden Cl BELV DA17 117 G4
Walden Gdns THHTH CR7 164 A3
Walden Pde CHST BR7 * 153 K5
Walden Rd CHST BR7 153 K5
TOTM N17 41 K7
Waldenshaw Rd FSTH SE23 131 K7
Walden St WCHPL E1 * 92 D5
Walden Wy MLHL NW7 38 B5
Waldo Cl CLAP SW4 129 H4
Waldo Pl MTCM CR4 147 J6
Waldorf Cl SAND/SEL CR2 177 H7
Waldo Rd BMLY BR1 168 B2
WLSDN NW10 87 J2
Waldram Crs FSTH SE23 131 K7
Waldram Park Rd FSTH SE23 132 A7
Waldrist Wy ERITH DA18 117 G1
Waldron Gdns HAYES BR2 167 G2
Waldronhyrst CROY/NA CR0 177 H3
Waldron Ms CHEL SW3 15 H9
Waldron Rd RYLN/HDSTN HA2 48 E7
WAND/EARL SW18 147 G2
The Waldrons CROY/NA CR0 177 J3
Waldron's Yd
RYLN/HDSTN HA2 66 D1
Waldstock Rd THMD SE28 97 G6
Waleran Cl STAN HA7 35 F5
Walerand Rd LEW SE13 133 F1
Wales Av CAR SM5 175 J4
Wales Cl PECK SE15 111 J6
Wales Farm Rd ACT W3 87 F4
Waleton Acres WLGTN SM6 * 176 C5
Waley St WCHPL E1 * 93 F4
Walfield Av TRDG/WHET N20 27 F6
Walford Rd STNW/STAM N16 74 A3
Walfrey Gdns DAGW RM9 80 A6
Walham Green Ct
FUL/PGN SW6 * 108 A6
Walham Gv FUL/PGN SW6 107 K6
Walham Ri WIM/MER SW19 146 C5
Walham Yd FUL/PGN SW6 107 K6
Walkden Rd CHST BR7 154 A3
Walker Cl CROY/NA CR0 180 A6
DART DA1 138 C2
EBED/NFELT TW14 121 J6
FBAR/BDGN N11 40 C3
HNWL W7 84 E7
HPTN TW12 141 K5
WOOL/PLUM SE18 115 H3
Walker's Ct SOHO/CST W1F 11 G6
Walkerscroft Md CAT SE6 151 K1
DUL SE21 130 D7
Walker's Pl PUT/ROE SW15 127 G3
Walkley Rd DART DA1 138 E4
The Walks EFNCH N2 53 H2
The Walk PLMGR N13 * 41 G2
Wallace Cl THMD SE28 97 K6
Wallace Crs CAR SM5 175 K4
Wallace Rd IS N1 73 J5
Wallbutton Rd BROCKY SE4 132 B1
Wallcote Av CRICK NW2 52 B7
Walled Garden Cl BECK BR3 166 E3
Wall End Rd EHAM E6 78 A6
Wallenger Av GPK RM2 63 K2
Waller Dr NTHWD HA6 32 E7
Waller Rd NWCR SE14 112 A7
Wallers Cl DAGW RM9 80 A7
WFD IG8 45 K5
Wallflower St SHB W12 87 H6
Wallgrave Rd ECT SW5 14 B5
Wallhouse Rd ERITH DA8 119 F6
Wallingford Av NKENS W10 88 B4
Wallington Cl RSLP HA4 46 A5
Wallington Rd
GDMY/SEVK IG3 61 F6
Wallis Cl BTSEA SW11 128 C2
EMPK RM11 63 K7
Wallis Rd HOM E9 75 H5
STHL UB1 84 B5
Wallman Pl WDGN N22 41 F7
Wallorton Gdns
MORT/ESHN SW14 126 A3
Wallside BARB EC2Y * 12 F3
Wall St IS N1 73 K5
Wallwood Rd WAN E11 58 B6
Wallwood St POP/IOD E14 93 H4
Walmer Cl CHING E4 43 K1
ROMW/RG RM7 62 D1
Walmer Gdns WEA W13 104 B1
Walmer Pl MBLAR W1H * 9 L2
Walmer Rd NTGHL W11 88 C6
Walmer Ter WOOL/PLUM SE18 115 H3
Walmgate Rd GFD/PVL UB6 67 H7
Walmington Fold
NFNCH/WDSPK N12 38 E5
Walm La CRICK NW2 70 B4
Walney Wk IS N1 * 73 J5
Walnut Av WDR/YW UB7 100 D2
Walnut Cl BARK/HLT IG6 60 C3
CAR SM5 175 K4
DEPT SE8 112 C5
HYS/HAR UB3 82 C6
Walnut Ct EA W5 * 105 F1
Walnut Gdns SRTFD E15 76 C4
Walnut Gn BUSH WD23 21 K1
Walnut Gv EN EN1 29 K4
Walnut Ms BELMT SM2 175 G6
Walnut Rd LEY E10 75 J1
Walnut Tree Av MTCM CR4 * 162 D2
Walnut Tree Cl BARN SW13 106 C7
CHST BR7 154 C7
Walnut Tree Rd BCTR RM8 79 K1
BTFD TW8 105 F5
ERITH DA8 118 B4
GNWCH SE10 * 113 H4
HEST TW5 102 E5
Walnut Tree Wk LBTH SE11 18 A5
Walnut Wy BKHH IG9 45 H2
RSLP HA4 65 G5
Walpole Av RCH/KEW TW9 125 G1
Walpole Cl PIN HA5 34 A5
WEA W13 104 D1
Walpole Crs TEDD TW11 143 F4
Walpole Gdns CHSWK W4 105 K4
WHTN TW2 142 E1
Walpole Ms STJWD NW8 3 G4
Walpole Pl TEDD TW11 143 F4
Walpole Rd CROY/NA CR0 177 K1
EHAM E6 77 G6
HAYES BR2 168 C4
SURB KT6 159 F6
SWFD E18 44 D7
TEDD TW11 143 F4
TOTM N17 55 J1
WALTH E17 57 G3
WHTN TW2 142 E1
WIM/MER SW19 147 H5
Walpole St CHEL SW3 15 L7
Walrond Av WBLY HA9 68 A4
Walsham Cl STNW/STAM N16 56 C7
THMD SE28 97 K6
Walsham Rd
EBED/NFELT TW14 122 A6
NWCR SE14 132 A1
Walsingham Gdns
HOR/WEW KT19 173 G3
Walsingham Pk CHST BR7 169 J1
Walsingham Rd CLAP SW4 129 F5
CLPT E5 74 C2
ENC/FH EN2 29 K3
MTCM CR4 162 E4
STMC/STPC BR5 155 H7
WEA W13 * 85 G7
Walsingham Wk BELV DA17 117 H5
Walter Rodney Cl MNPK E12 77 K5
Walters Cl HYS/HAR UB3 101 J1
Walters Rd PEND EN3 30 E4
Walter's Rd SNWD SE25 165 F3
Walter St BETH E2 93 F2
KUTN/CMB KT2 * 144 A7
Walters Wy FSTH SE23 132 A5
Walters Yd BMLY BR1 167 K1
Walter Ter WCHPL E1 93 F5
Walterton Rd MV/WKIL W9 88 D3
Walter Wk EDGW HA8 36 E5
Waltham Av CDALE/KGS NW9 50 C5
HYS/HAR UB3 101 F2
Waltham Cl DART DA1 138 D5
Waltham Dr EDGW HA8 50 C1
Waltham Pk WALTH E17 43 J6
Waltham Park Wy CHING E4 * 43 J6
Waltham Rd CAR SM5 162 C7
NWDGN UB2 102 D2
WFD IG8 45 J5
Walthamstow Av CHING E4 43 J6
**Walthamstow Av (North
Circular)** CHING E4 43 G4
Waltham Wy CHING E4 43 H2
Waltheof Av TOTM N17 41 K7
Waltheof Gdns TOTM N17 41 K7
Walton Av CHEAM SM3 174 D2
NWMAL KT3 160 C3
RYLN/HDSTN HA2 65 K3
WBLY HA9 68 D2
Walton Cl CRICK NW2 69 K1
HRW HA1 48 D3
VX/NE SW8 109 K6
Walton Dr HRW HA1 48 D3
WLSDN NW10 69 F5
Walton Gdns ACT W3 86 D4
FELT TW13 140 D3
WBLY HA9 68 A1
Walton Gn CROY/NA CR0 179 K7
Walton Pl CHEL SW3 15 L3
Walton Rd BUSH WD23 21 H3
E/WMO/HCT KT8 157 F3
HRW HA1 48 D3
MNPK E12 78 A3
PLSTW E13 95 G1
SCUP DA14 155 H2
SEVS/STOTM N15 * 56 B3
WOT/HER KT12 156 C4
Walton St CHEL SW3 15 K5
Walton Vls IS N1 * 7 K2
Walton Wy ACT W3 86 D4
MTCM CR4 163 H3
Walt Whitman Cl HNHL SE24 * 130 C3
Walverns Cl OXHEY WD19 21 G5
Walworth Pl WALW SE17 18 F8
Walworth Rd STHWK SE1 18 E5
Walwyn Av BMLY BR1 168 C2
Wanborough Dr
PUT/ROE SW15 126 E7
Wanderer Dr BARK IG11 97 H2
Wandle Bank CROY/NA CR0 176 E2
WIM/MER SW19 147 H5
Wandle Ct HOR/WEW KT19 172 E3
Wandle Court Gdns
CROY/NA CR0 176 E2
Wandle Rd CROY/NA CR0 176 E2
MRDN SM4 162 C4
TOOT SW17 147 J1
WLGTN SM6 176 B1
Wandle Side CROY/NA CR0 177 F2
WLGTN SM6 176 B2
Wandle Wy MTCM CR4 162 E4
WAND/EARL SW18 128 A7
Wandsworth Br
WAND/EARL SW18 128 B2
Wandsworth Bridge Rd
FUL/PGN SW6 108 A7
**Wandsworth Common West
Side** WAND/EARL SW18 128 B4
Wandsworth High St
WAND/EARL SW18 127 K4
Wandsworth Rd VX/NE SW8 17 J9
VX/NE SW8 * 129 J1
Wangey Rd CHDH RM6 61 K6
Wanless Rd HNHL SE24 130 D2
Wanley Rd CMBW SE5 130 E3
Wanlip Rd PLSTW E13 95 F3
Wansbeck Rd HOM E9 75 H6
Wansdown Pl FUL/PGN SW6 108 A6
Wansey St WALW SE17 18 F6
Wansford Pk BORE WD6 25 F3
Wansford Rd WFD IG8 45 G7
Wanstead Cl BMLY BR1 168 B1
Wanstead La IL IG1 59 J5
Wanstead Park Av MNPK E12 77 H1
Wanstead Park Rd IL IG1 59 J6
Wanstead Pl WAN E11 58 E5
Wanstead Rd BMLY BR1 168 B1
Wansunt Rd BXLY DA5 137 K7
Wantage Rd LEE/GVPK SE12 133 J4
Wantz La RAIN RM13 99 K3
Wantz Rd DAGE RM10 80 D3
Wapping Dock St WAP E1W * 92 D7
Wapping High St WAP E1W 92 C7
Wapping La WAP E1W 92 D6
Wapping Wall WAP E1W 92 E7
Warbank La KUTN/CMB KT2 145 H6
Warbeck Rd SHB W12 87 K7
Warberry Rd WDGN N22 55 F1
Warboys Ap KUTN/CMB KT2 144 D5
Warboys Crs CHING E4 44 A4
Warboys Rd KUTN/CMB KT2 144 D5
Warburton Cl IS N1 74 A5
KTN/HRWW/WS HA3 34 D5
Warburton Rd HACK E8 74 D7
WHTN TW2 123 G7
Warburton St HACK E8 74 D7
Warburton Ter WALTH E17 57 K1
Wardalls Gv NWCR SE14 * 111 K6
Ward Cl ERITH DA8 118 A5
SAND/SEL CR2 178 A4
Wardell Cl EDGW HA8 37 G6
Wardell Fld CDALE/KGS NW9 37 G7
Warden Av RYLN/HDSTN HA2 47 J7
Warden Rd KTTN NW5 72 A5
Wardens Gv STHWK SE1 12 E9
Wardle St HOM E9 75 F4
Wardley St WAND/EARL SW18 128 A6
Wardo Av FUL/PGN SW6 107 H7
Wardour Ms SOHO/CST W1F 10 F5
Wardour St SOHO/CST W1F 10 F4
Ward Rd ARCH N19 72 C2
SRTFD E15 * 76 B7
Wardrobe Pl BLKFR EC4V * 12 D5
The Wardrobe
RCH/KEW TW9 * 124 E4
Wards La BORE WD6 23 F1

Wards Rd GNTH/NBYPK IG2 60 D6
Wards Wharf Ap CAN/RD E16 114 C1
Wareham Cl HSLW TW3 123 F3
Waremead Rd
GNTH/NBYPK IG2 60 B4
Warepoint Dr THMD SE28 115 J1
Warfield Rd
EBED/NFELT TW14 121 H6
HPTN TW12 142 B7
WLSDN NW10 88 B2
Warfield Yd WLSDN NW10 * 88 B2
Wargrave Av
SEVS/STOTM N15 56 B5
Wargrave Rd
RYLN/HDSTN HA2 66 C2
Warham Rd FSBYPK N4 55 G4
KTN/HRWW/WS HA3 49 F1
SAND/SEL CR2 177 J4
Warham St CMBW SE5 110 C6
Waring Rd SCUP DA14 155 J5
Waring St WNWD SE27 149 J3
Warkworth Gdns ISLW TW7 104 B6
Warkworth Rd TOTM N17 41 K6
Warland Rd WOOL/PLUM SE18 115 J6
Warley Av BCTR RM8 62 B6
YEAD UB4 82 E5
Warley Rd ED N9 42 E1
WFD IG8 45 F6
YEAD UB4 82 E5
Warley St BETH E2 93 F2
Warlingham Rd THHTH CR7 164 C3
Warlock Rd MV/WKIL W9 88 D3
Warlters Cl HOLWY N7 * 72 E3
Warlters Rd HOLWY N7 72 E3
Warltersville Rd ARCH N19 54 E6
Warming Cl CLPT E5 * 75 F2
Warmington Rd HNHL SE24 130 D5
Warmington St PLSTW E13 94 E3
Warminster Rd SNWD SE25 165 H1
Warminster Sq SNWD SE25 165 H1
Warminster Wy MTCM CR4 148 B7
Warmwell Av CDALE/KGS NW9 37 G7
Warndon St BERM/RHTH SE16 111 K3
Warneford Pl OXHEY WD19 21 J5
Warneford Rd
KTN/HRWW/WS HA3 49 K2
Warneford St HOM E9 74 D7
Warne Pl BFN/LL DA15 136 C5
Warner Av CHEAM SM3 174 C1
Warner Cl CDALE/KGS NW9 51 H6
HPTN TW12 141 K4
HYS/HAR UB3 101 G6
SRTFD E15 76 C4
Warner Pl BETH E2 92 C1
Warner Rd BMLY BR1 152 D6
CEND/HSY/T N8 54 D3
CMBW SE5 110 D7
WALTH E17 57 G3
Warner St CLKNW EC1R 12 A1
Warner Ter POP/IOD E14 * 93 J4
Warner Yd CLKNW EC1R 12 A1
Warnham Court Rd CAR SM5 175 K6
Warnham Rd
NFNCH/WDSPK N12 39 J4
Warple Ms ACT W3 * 106 B1
Warple Wy ACT W3 106 B1
SHB W12 106 B1
Warren Av BMLY BR1 152 C6
RCHPK/HAM TW10 125 J3
SAND/SEL CR2 179 F6
WAN E11 * 76 B2
Warren Cl BXLYHS DA6 137 H4
ED N9 31 F6
ESH/CLAY KT10 170 C3
WBLY HA9 67 K1
YEAD UB4 83 G4
Warren Ct CHARL SE7 114 B4
Warren Crs ED N9 30 B6
Warren Cutting
KUTN/CMB KT2 145 F6
Warrender Rd ARCH N19 72 C2
Warrender Wy RSLP HA4 46 E6
Warren Dr GFD/PVL UB6 84 B3
HCH RM12 81 J2
RSLP HA4 47 H6
Warren Dr North BRYLDS KT5 159 J7
Warren Dr South BRYLDS KT5 159 K7
The Warren Dr WAN E11 59 G6
Warren Flds STAN HA7 * 35 J3
Warren Gv BORE WD6 25 F3
Warren La STAN HA7 35 G1
WOOL/PLUM SE18 115 G2
Warren Lane Ga
WOOL/PLUM SE18 115 G2
Warren Ms FITZ W1T 10 E1
Warren Pk KUTN/CMB KT2 144 E5
Warren Park Rd SUT SM1 175 H5
Warren Ri KUTN/CMB KT2 145 F7
Warren Rd ASHF TW15 140 C6
BARK/HLT IG6 60 D4
BUSH WD23 22 C7
BXLYHS DA6 137 H4
CHING E4 44 A1
CRICK NW2 69 H1
CROY/NA CR0 165 F7
HAYES BR2 180 E1
KUTN/CMB KT2 144 E5
LEY E10 76 A2
SCUP DA14 155 J2
WAN E11 59 G5
WHTN TW2 123 J5
WIM/MER SW19 147 J5
Warrens Shawe La EDGW HA8 36 D1
Warren St FITZ W1T 10 E1
The Warren BELMT SM2 175 H7
HEST TW5 102 E6
MNPK E12 77 J3
WPK KT4 173 F3
YEAD UB4 82 E5
Warren Wy EDGW HA8 50 D1
Warren Wood Cl HAYES BR2 180 E1
Warriner Dr ED N9 42 C2
Warriner Gdns BTSEA SW11 108 E7
Warrington Crs MV/WKIL W9 8 E1
Warrington Gdns
MV/WKIL W9 8 E1
Warrington Pl POP/IOD E14 * 94 A7
Warrington Rd BCTR RM8 79 K1
CROY/NA CR0 177 H2
HRW HA1 48 E4
RCHPK/HAM TW10 124 E4
Warrington Sq BCTR RM8 79 K1
Warrior Cl THMD SE28 96 E7
Warrior Sq MNPK E12 78 A3
Warsaw Cl RSLP HA4 65 F5
Warspite Rd
WOOL/PLUM SE18 114 D2
Warton Rd SRTFD E15 76 A7
Warwall EHAM E6 96 B5
Warwick Av EDGW HA8 36 D2
MV/WKIL W9 8 D1
RYLN/HDSTN HA2 65 K3
Warwick Cl BUSH WD23 22 E6
BXLY DA5 137 G6
EBAR EN4 27 H4
HPTN TW12 142 C6
Warwick Ct HHOL WC1V 11 M3
SURB KT6 172 A1
Warwick Crs BAY/PAD W2 8 E2
YEAD UB4 82 D3
Warwick Dene EA W5 86 A7
Warwick Dr PUT/ROE SW15 126 E2
Warwick Gdns FSBYPK N4 55 J4
IL IG1 60 B7
THDIT KT7 158 A4
THHTH CR7 * 164 B3
WKENS W14 107 J2
Warwick Gv BRYLDS KT5 159 G6
CLPT E5 56 D7
Warwick House St STJS SW1Y 11 H8
Warwick La STP EC4M 12 D4
Warwick Pde
KTN/HRWW/WS HA3 * 49 H1
Warwick Pl BORE WD6 * 25 F2
EA W5 104 E1
MV/WKIL W9 8 E1
THDIT KT7 * 158 B5
Warwick Pl North PIM SW1V * 16 E6
Warwick Rd BAR EN5 27 F3
BORE WD6 25 F2
CHING E4 43 J4
EA W5 86 A7
ECT SW5 14 A6
FBAR/BDGN N11 40 D5
HSLWW TW4 122 A2
KUT/HW KT1 143 J7
MNPK E12 77 J4
NWDGN UB2 102 E2
NWMAL KT3 159 K2
PGE/AN SE20 165 J2
SCUP DA14 155 H4
SRTFD E15 76 D5
SUT SM1 175 G4
THDIT KT7 158 A4
THHTH CR7 164 B2
UED N18 42 A3
WALTH E17 43 H7
WAN E11 59 F4
WELL DA16 136 D2
WHTN TW2 123 K7
WKENS W14 107 J3
Warwick Rw WESTW SW1E 16 E3
Warwick Sq PIM SW1V 16 E6
STP EC4M * 12 D4
Warwick Square Ms
PIM SW1V 16 E6
Warwick St REGST W1B 10 F6
Warwick Ter WALTH E17 * 58 B4
WOOL/PLUM SE18 115 J5
Warwick Wy PIM SW1V 16 D7
RKW/CH/CXG WD3 20 A3
Warwick Yd STLK EC1Y * 12 F1
Washington Av MNPK E12 77 J3
Washington Cl BOW E3 93 K2
Washington Rd BARN SW13 106 D6
EHAM E6 77 G6
KUT/HW KT1 159 H1
SWFD E18 58 D1
WPK KT4 173 K1
Wastdale Rd FSTH SE23 132 A7
Watchfield Ct CHSWK W4 * 105 K4
The Watch
NFNCH/WDSPK N12 * 39 G3
Watcombe Rd SNWD SE25 165 J4
Waterbank Rd CAT SE6 151 K2
Waterbeach Rd DAGW RM9 79 J5
Water Brook La HDN NW4 52 A4
Watercress Pl IS N1 7 K2
Waterdale Rd ABYW SE2 116 B5
Water End Cl BORE WD6 24 B1
Waterer Ri WLGTN SM6 176 D5
Waterfall Cots
WIM/MER SW19 147 H5
Waterfall Rd FBAR/BDGN N11 40 B3
WIM/MER SW19 147 H5
Waterfall Ter TOOT SW17 147 J5
Waterfield Cl BELV DA17 117 H2
THMD SE28 97 H7
Waterfield Cots
MORT/ESHN SW14 * 125 J3
Waterfield Gdns SNWD SE25 165 F3
Waterfields Wy BUSH WD23 21 H3
Waterford Rd FUL/PGN SW6 108 A6
Waterford Wy WLSDN NW10 69 K4
The Waterfront BORE WD6 23 H5
Water Gdns STAN HA7 35 H5
The Water Gdns BAY/PAD W2 9 J4
Watergate EMB EC4Y 12 C6
Watergate St DEPT SE8 112 D5
The Watergate OXHEY WD19 33 H1
Waterhall Av CHING E4 44 C3
Waterhall Cl WALTH E17 43 F7
Waterhead Cl ERITH DA8 118 B6
Waterhouse Cl HAMP NW3 71 H4
Wateridge Cl POP/IOD E14 112 D2
Water La CAMTN NW1 4 D2
ED N9 30 D7
GDMY/SEVK IG3 79 F2
KUT/HW KT1 143 K7
MON EC3R 13 J7
NWCR SE14 111 K6
PUR RM19 119 K3
SRTFD E15 76 C5
TWK TW1 124 B7
WAT WD17 21 G3
Water Lily Cl NWDGN UB2 103 H1
Waterloo Br STHWK SE1 11 M7
TPL/STR WC2R 11 L7
Waterloo Cl
EBED/NFELT TW14 121 J7
HOM E9 74 E4
Waterloo Gdns BETH E2 92 E1
ROMW/RG RM7 63 F5
Waterloo Pl CAR SM5 * 175 K2
RCH/KEW TW9 105 H5
STJS SW1Y 11 G8
Waterloo Rd BARK/HLT IG6 60 C1
CRICK NW2 69 J1
EHAM E6 77 G6
FSTGT E7 76 D5
LEY E10 57 J6
ROMW/RG RM7 63 F4
STHWK SE1 11 M8
SUT SM1 175 H4
Waterloo Ter IS N1 6 C2
Waterlow Rd ARCH N19 54 C7
Waterman Cl OXHEY WD19 21 F5
Watermans Cl
KUTN/CMB KT2 * 144 A6
Watermans Wk EA W5 * 86 A6
Waterman Sq PGE/AN SE20 150 E6
Waterman St PUT/ROE SW15 127 G2
Waterman Wy WAP E1W 92 D7
Watermead
EBED/NFELT TW14 121 H7
Watermead La CAR SM5 162 E5
Watermeadow Cl ERITH DA8 118 E6
Watermeadow La
FUL/PGN SW6 128 B1
Watermead Rd CAT SE6 152 A3
Watermead Wy TOTM N17 42 D7
Watermens Sq PGE/AN SE20 * 150 E6
Water Ms PECK SE15 131 K3
Watermill Cl
RCHPK/HAM TW10 143 J2
Watermill La UED N18 42 A4
Water Mill Wy FELT TW13 141 K1
Watermill Wy WIM/MER SW19 147 G7
Watermint Quay
STNW/STAM N16 56 C6
Water Rd ALP/SUD HA0 68 B7
Watersedge HOR/WEW KT19 172 E3
Water's Edge FUL/PGN SW6 * 107 K7
Watersfield Wy EDGW HA8 35 K6
Waterside DART DA1 138 B4
WALTH E17 56 E5
Waterside Av BECK BR3 166 E4
Waterside Cl BARK IG11 79 G3
BERM/RHTH SE16 111 H1
BOW E3 75 H7
NTHLT UB5 83 K2
SHPTN TW17 140 A7
SURB KT6 172 A1
THMD SE28 97 F7
Waterside Ct LEW SE13 * 133 G3
Waterside Dr WOT/HER KT12 156 A4
Waterside Pl CAMTN NW1 4 B3
Waterside Rd NWDGN UB2 103 F2
Waterside Wy TOOT SW17 147 G3
Watersmeet Wy THMD SE28 97 K5
Waterson St BETH E2 7 K7
Watersplash Cl KUT/HW KT1 159 F2
Watersplash La HEST TW5 102 A4
HYS/HAR UB3 101 K3
Waters Rd CAT SE6 152 C2
KUT/HW KT1 159 J1
Waters Sq KUT/HW KT1 159 J2
Water St TPL/STR WC2R 12 A6
Water Tower Hl CROY/NA CR0 177 K3
Water Tower Pl IS N1 6 B4
Waterway Av LEW SE13 132 E2
Waterworks La CLPT E5 75 F1
Waterworks Rd
BRXS/STRHM SW2 129 K5
Watery La HYS/HAR UB3 101 G4
NTHLT UB5 83 G1
RYNPK SW20 161 J1
STMC/STPC BR5 155 H5
Wates Wy MTCM CR4 162 E5
Wateville Rd TOTM N17 41 J7
Watford Cl BTSEA SW11 108 D7
Watford Field Rd
WATW WD18 21 G4
Watford Heath OXHEY WD19 21 H6
Watford Heath Farm
OXHEY WD19 * 21 H6
Watford House La WAT WD17 21 F2
Watford Rd BORE WD6 23 J5
CAN/RD E16 94 E4
HRW HA1 67 G2
NTHWD HA6 32 D6
RKW/CH/CXG WD3 20 B4
WBLY HA0 67 K4
Watford Wy HDN NW4 51 J3
MLHL NW7 37 F3
Watford Way (Barnet By-Pass)
MLHL NW7 37 H4
Watkin Rd WBLY HA9 68 D2
Watkinson Rd HOLWY N7 73 F5
Watling Av EDGW HA8 36 E7
Watling Ct STP EC4M 12 F5
Watling Farm Cl BORE WD6 23 J7
Watlings Cl CROY/NA CR0 166 B5
Watling St BORE WD6 23 J2
BXLYHS DA6 137 K4
PECK SE15 111 F5
STP EC4M 12 E5
Watlington Gv SYD SE26 151 G4
Watney Market WCHPL E1 92 D5
Watney Rd
MORT/ESHN SW14 125 K2
Watneys Rd CROY/NA CR0 163 J4
Watney St WCHPL E1 92 D5
Watson Av CHEAM SM3 174 C1
EHAM E6 78 A6
Watson Cl STNW/STAM N16 73 K4
WIM/MER SW19 147 J5
Watson's Ms CAMTN NW1 9 K3
Watsons Rd WDGN N22 41 F7
Watson's St DEPT SE8 112 D6
Wattisfield Rd CLPT E5 74 E2
Watts Cl SEVS/STOTM N15 56 A4
Wattsdown Cl PLSTW E13 76 E7
Watts Gv BOW E3 93 J4
Watt's La CHST BR7 154 B7
TEDD TW11 143 G4
Watts Rd THDIT KT7 158 B6
Watts St PECK SE15 111 G7
WAP E1W 92 D7
Wat Tyler Rd GNWCH SE10 133 F1
Wauthier Cl PLMGR N13 41 H4
Wavell Dr BFN/LL DA15 135 K5
Wavel Ms KIL/WHAMP NW6 2 C2
Wavel Pl SYD SE26 150 B3
Wavendon Av CHSWK W4 106 A4
Waveney Av PECK SE15 131 J3
Waveney Cl WAP E1W 92 C7
Waverley Av BRYLDS KT5 159 J5
CHING E4 43 H3
SUT SM1 175 F1
WALTH E17 58 B2
WBLY HA9 68 B4
WHTN TW2 122 E7
Waverley Cl E/WMO/HCT KT8 157 F4
HAYES BR2 168 C4
HYS/HAR UB3 101 G3
Waverley Crs
WOOL/PLUM SE18 115 J5
Waverley Gdns BARK IG11 96 E1
BARK/HLT IG6 60 C1
EHAM E6 95 J4
NTHWD HA6 32 E7
Waverley Gv FNCH N3 52 B2
Waverley Pl FSBYPK N4 * 55 H7
STJWD NW8 3 G5
Waverley Rd CEND/HSY/T N8 54 D5
ENC/FH EN2 29 H3
EW KT17 173 K4
RAIN RM13 99 K2
RYLN/HDSTN HA2 65 J1
SNWD SE25 165 J3
STHL UB1 84 A6
SWFD E18 45 G7
TOTM N17 42 D6
WALTH E17 58 A2
WOOL/PLUM SE18 115 H4
Waverley Wy CAR SM5 175 J5
Waverton Rd
WAND/EARL SW18 128 B6
Waverton St MYFR/PKLN W1K 10 B8
Wavertree Rd
BRXS/STRHM SW2 130 A7
SWFD E18 58 E1
Waxlow Crs STHL UB1 84 A5
Waxlow Rd WLSDN NW10 86 E1
Waxlow Wy NTHLT UB5 83 K3
Waxwell La PIN HA5 47 H2
Wayborne Gv RSLP HA4 46 A5
Waye Av HEST TW5 101 K7
Wayfarer Rd NTHLT UB5 83 J2
Wayford St BTSEA SW11 128 D1
Wayland Av HACK E8 74 C4
Waylands HYS/HAR UB3 82 B4
Waylen Gdns DART DA1 139 J1
Waylett Pl ALP/SUD HA0 * 67 K3
WNWD SE27 149 H2
Wayneflete Pl ESH/CLAY KT10 170 A2
Wayneflete Tower Av
ESH/CLAY KT10 170 A2
Waynflete Av CROY/NA CR0 177 H2
Waynflete Sq NKENS W10 88 B6
Waynflete St
WAND/EARL SW18 147 G1
Wayside CROY/NA CR0 * 179 K5
GLDGN NW11 52 C7
MORT/ESHN SW14 125 K3
Wayside Av BUSH WD23 22 D5
Wayside Cl ROM RM1 63 H2
STHGT/OAK N14 28 C5
Wayside Ct TWK TW1 124 D5
Wayside Gdns DAGE RM10 80 C4
Wayside Gv ELTH/MOT SE9 153 K3
Wayside Ms GNTH/NBYPK IG2 60 A5
Weald Cl BERM/RHTH SE16 111 J4
HAYES BR2 181 J1
Weald La KTN/HRWW/WS HA3 48 D1
Weald Ri KTN/HRWW/WS HA3 35 F6
Weald Sq CLPT E5 * 74 D1
Wealdstone Rd CHEAM SM3 174 D1
The Weald CHST BR7 153 K5
Weald Wy ROMW/RG RM7 62 D5
YEAD UB4 82 C2
Wealdwood Gdns PIN HA5 34 B5
Weale Rd CHING E4 44 B2
Weardale Rd LEW SE13 133 G3
Wearside Rd LEW SE13 132 E3
Weatherley Cl BOW E3 93 H4
Weaver Cl CROY/NA CR0 178 B3
EHAM E6 96 B6
Weavers Cl ISLW TW7 123 K3
Weaver's La STHWK SE1 13 K9
Weavers Ter FUL/PGN SW6 * 107 K5
Weaver St WCHPL E1 92 C3
Weavers Wy CAMTN NW1 5 G3
Weaver Wk WNWD SE27 149 H3
Webb Cl NKENS W10 88 A3
Webber Cl BORE WD6 23 K5
ERITH DA8 118 E6
Webber Rw STHWK SE1 18 B2
Webber St STHWK SE1 18 B1
Webb Est CLPT E5 * 56 C6
Webb Pl WLSDN NW10 87 H2
Webb Rd BKHTH/KID SE3 113 J5
Webbscroft Rd DAGE RM10 80 D3
Webbs Rd YEAD UB4 82 E2
Webb's Rd BTSEA SW11 128 E4
Webb St STHWK SE1 19 J4
Webster Gdns EA W5 85 K7
Webster Rd BERM/RHTH SE16 111 H2
WAN E11 76 A2
Wedderburn Rd BARK IG11 78 D7
HAMP NW3 71 H4
Wedgewood Cl NTHWD HA6 * 32 A6
Wedgwood Wk
KIL/WHAMP NW6 * 71 F4
Wedgwood Wy NRWD SE19 149 J6
Wedlake St NKENS W10 88 C3
Wedmore Gdns ARCH N19 72 E1
Wedmore Ms ARCH N19 72 D2
Wedmore Rd GFD/PVL UB6 84 D2
Wedmore St ARCH N19 72 D2
Weech Rd KIL/WHAMP NW6 70 E3
Weedington Rd KTTN NW5 72 A4
Weekley Sq BTSEA SW11 * 128 C2
Weigall Rd LEE/GVPK SE12 133 K3
Weighhouse St
MYFR/PKLN W1K 10 B6
Weighton Rd
KTN/HRWW/WS HA3 34 D7
PGE/AN SE20 165 J1
Weihurst Gdns SUT SM1 175 H4
Weimar St PUT/ROE SW15 127 H2
Weirdale Av TRDG/WHET N20 39 K1
Weir Hall Av UED N18 41 K5
Weir Hall Gdns UED N18 41 K4
Weir Hall Rd UED N18 41 K4
Weir Rd BAL SW12 129 H7
WIM/MER SW19 147 F2
Weirs Pas CAMTN NW1 5 H7
Weiss Rd PUT/ROE SW15 127 G2
Welbeck Av BFN/LL DA15 136 B7
BMLY BR1 152 E3
YEAD UB4 83 F3
Welbeck Cl BORE WD6 24 C2
EW KT17 173 J6
NWMAL KT3 160 C4
Welbeck Rd CAR SM5 162 D6
EBAR EN4 27 H5
EHAM E6 95 H2
RYLN/HDSTN HA2 48 B7
SUT SM1 175 H1
Welbeck St CAVSQ/HST W1G 10 B3
Welbeck Vls WCHMH N21 * 29 J7
Welbeck Wy CAVSQ/HST W1G 10 C4
Welby Ct PLSTW E13 95 G1
Welby St CMBW SE5 110 C7
Welch Pl PIN HA5 * 33 G7
Weldon Cl RSLP HA4 65 F5
Weldon Dr E/WMO/HCT KT8 156 E3
Weld Pl FBAR/BDGN N11 40 B4
Welfare Rd SRTFD E15 76 C6
Welford Cl CLPT E5 75 F2
Welford Pl WIM/MER SW19 146 C3
Welham Rd TOOT SW17 148 A4
Welhouse Rd CAR SM5 162 D7
Wellacre Rd
KTN/HRWW/WS HA3 49 H5
Wellan Cl BFN/LL DA15 136 C4
Welland Gdns GFD/PVL UB6 85 F1
Welland Ms WAP E1W 92 C7
Wellands Cl BMLY BR1 168 E1
Welland St GNWCH SE10 113 F5
Well Ap BAR EN5 26 A4
Wellby Cl ED N9 30 C7
Well Cl RSLP HA4 65 J2
STRHM/NOR SW16 149 F3
Wellclose Sq WCHPL E1 92 C6
Wellclose St WCHPL E1 92 C6
Wellcome Av DART DA1 139 H3
Well Cottage Cl WAN E11 59 G6
Well Ct STP EC4M 12 F5
Welldon Crs HRW HA1 48 E5
Weller Ms HAYES BR2 168 A3
Weller St STHWK SE1 18 E1
Wellesley Av HMSMTH W6 106 E2
NTHWD HA6 32 D4
Wellesley Cl CHARL SE7 * 114 B4
Wellesley Ct MV/WKIL W9 2 E7
Wellesley Court Rd
CROY/NA CR0 * 177 K1
Wellesley Crs WHTN TW2 142 E1
Wellesley Gv CROY/NA CR0 177 K1
Wellesley Pde WHTN TW2 * 142 E2
Wellesley Park Ms
ENC/FH EN2 29 H1
Wellesley Pl CAMTN NW1 * 5 G8
KTTN NW5 72 A4
Wellesley Rd BELMT SM2 175 G5
CHSWK W4 105 H4
CROY/NA CR0 164 D7
HRW HA1 48 E4
IL IG1 78 B1
KTTN NW5 72 A4
WALTH E17 57 J5
WAN E11 58 E4
WHTN TW2 142 E2
WOOL/PLUM SE18 115 F6
Wellesley St WCHPL E1 93 F4
Wellesley Ter IS N1 6 F7
Wellfield Av MUSWH N10 54 B2
Wellfield Gdns CAR SM5 175 J7
Wellfield Rd
STRHM/NOR SW16 148 E3
Wellfit St HNHL SE24 130 C2
Wellgarth GFD/PVL UB6 67 H5
Wellgarth Rd GLDGN NW11 53 F7
Well Gv TRDG/WHET N20 27 G7
Well Hall Pde ELTH/MOT SE9 134 E3
Well Hall Rd ELTH/MOT SE9 134 E3
Wellhouse La BAR EN5 26 A3
Wellhouse Rd BECK BR3 166 C3
Welling High St WELL DA16 136 C2
Wellington Av BFN/LL DA15 136 B5
CHING E4 43 J1
ED N9 42 D2
HSLW TW3 123 F4
PIN HA5 33 K7
SEVS/STOTM N15 56 C5
WPK KT4 174 A2
Wellington Cl DAGE RM10 80 E6
NTGHL W11 8 A5
NWCR SE14 112 A7
OXHEY WD19 33 J2
Wellington Crs NWMAL KT3 159 K2
Wellington Dr DAGE RM10 80 E6
Wellington Gdns CHARL SE7 114 B4
WHTN TW2 142 D3
Wellington Gv GNWCH SE10 113 G6
Wellington Ms CHARL SE7 114 B5
EDUL SE22 131 H3
HOLWY N7 73 F5
STRHM/NOR SW16 148 D2
Wellington Pde
BFN/LL DA15 * 136 B4
Wellington Park Est
CRICK NW2 * 69 J1
Wellington Pas WAN E11 58 E4
Wellington Pl EFNCH N2 * 53 J4
STJWD NW8 3 H7
Wellington Rd BELV DA17 117 G4
BXLY DA5 136 E5
CROY/NA CR0 164 C6
DART DA1 139 F5
EA W5 104 D3
EBED/NFELT TW14 121 H4
EHAM E6 77 K7
EN EN1 30 A6
FSTGT E7 76 D3
HAYES BR2 168 B3
HPTN TW12 142 D3
KTN/HRWW/WS HA3 48 E2
LEY E10 57 G7
NKENS W10 * 88 B2
PIN HA5 33 K7
STJWD NW8 3 H6
WALTH E17 57 G2
WAN E11 58 E4
WAT WD17 21 F1
WIM/MER SW19 146 E1
Wellington Rd North
HSLWW TW4 122 E2
Wellington Rd South
HSLWW TW4 122 E3
Wellington Rw BETH E2 7 M7
Wellington Sq CHEL SW3 15 L7
IS N1 5 K3
Wellington St COVGDN WC2E 11 K6
WOOL/PLUM SE18 115 F3
Wellington Ter BAY/PAD W2 8 B7
CEND/HSY/T N8 * 55 G2
HRW HA1 48 D7
WAP E1W * 92 D7
Wellington Wy BOW E3 93 J2
Welling Wy ELTH/MOT SE9 135 J2
WELL DA16 135 K2
Well La MORT/ESHN SW14 125 K4
Wellmeadow Rd CAT SE6 133 H7
HNWL W7 104 B3
LEW SE13 133 H5
Well Rd BAR EN5 26 A4
HAMP NW3 71 H2
Wells Cl NTHLT UB5 83 G2
SAND/SEL CR2 178 A4
Wells Dr CDALE/KGS NW9 51 F7
Wellsfield BUSH WD23 21 J4
Wells Gdns IL IG1 59 J6
RAIN RM13 81 H5
Wells House Rd WLSDN NW10 87 G4
Wellside Cl BAR EN5 26 A3
Wellside Gdns
MORT/ESHN SW14 125 K3
Wells Ms FITZ W1T * 10 F3
Wellsmoor Gdns BMLY BR1 169 F2
Wells Park Rd SYD SE26 150 C2
Wells Pl CMBW SE5 111 F6
WAND/EARL SW18 128 B6
Wellspring Crs WBLY HA9 68 D1
Wellspring Ms SYD SE26 150 D2
Wellspring Wy WAT WD17 21 G3
Wells Ri STJWD NW8 3 L4
Wells Rd BMLY BR1 168 E1
SHB W12 107 F1
Wells Sq FSBYW WC1X 5 L8
Wells St FITZ W1T 10 F4
GTPST W1W 10 E3
Wellstead Av ED N9 30 E6
Wellstead Rd EHAM E6 96 A1
Wells Ter FSBYPK N4 73 G1
The Wells STHGT/OAK N14 28 D6
Wellstones WAT WD17 * 21 F3
Well St HOM E9 74 E6
SRTFD E15 76 C5
Wells Wy SKENS SW7 15 G3
Well Wk HAMP NW3 71 H2
Wellwood Rd GDMY/SEVK IG3 61 G7
Welsford St STHWK SE1 111 H4

Welsh Cl PLSTW E13 94 E2
Welshpool St HACK E8 * 74 C7
Welshside CDALE/KGS NW9 * 51 G4
Welstead Wy CHSWK W4 106 C2
Weltje Rd HMSMTH W6 106 D4
Welton Rd WOOL/PLUM SE18 115 K6
Welwyn Av EBED/NFELT TW14 121 J5
Welwyn St BETH E2 92 E2
Welwyn Wy YEAD UB4 82 C3
Wembley Hill Rd WBLY HA9 68 B4
Wembley Park Dr WBLY HA9 68 B3
Wembley Rd HPTN TW12 142 A7
Wembley Wy WBLY HA9 68 D5
Wemborough Rd STAN HA7 35 H7
Wembury Ms HGT N6 54 B6
Wembury Rd HGT N6 54 B6
Wemyss Rd BKHTH/KID SE3 133 J1
Wendela Ct HRW HA1 66 E2
Wendell Rd SHB W12 106 C1
Wendling Rd SUT SM1 162 C7
Wendon St BOW E3 75 H7
Wendover Cl YEAD UB4 83 H3
Wendover Dr NWMAL KT3 160 C5
Wendover Rd ELTH/MOT SE9 134 C2
HAYES BR2 168 A3
WLSDN NW10 87 H1
Wendover Wy BUSH WD23 22 C5
WELL DA16 136 B4
Wendy Cl EN EN1 30 B5
Wendy Wy ALP/SUD HA0 68 A7
Wenlock Gdns HDN NW4 * 51 J3
Wenlock Rd EDGW HA8 36 D5
IS N1 6 E6
Wenlock St IS N1 6 F6
Wennington Rd BOW E3 93 F1
RAIN RM13 99 K4
Wensley Av WFD IG8 44 E6
Wensley Cl ELTH/MOT SE9 134 E5
FBAR/BDGN N11 40 A5
Wensleydale Av CLAY IG5 59 J1
Wensleydale Gdns
HPTN TW12 142 B6
Wensleydale Rd HPTN TW12 142 A7
Wensley Rd UED N18 42 D5
Wentland Cl CAT SE6 152 B1
Wentland Rd CAT SE6 152 B1
Wentworth Av BORE WD6 24 B4
FNCH N3 38 E6
Wentworth Cl FNCH N3 39 F6
HAYES BR2 * 180 E1
MRDN SM4 161 K6
SURB KT6 171 K1
THMD SE28 97 K5
Wentworth Crs
HYS/HAR UB3 101 G2
PECK SE15 111 H6
Wentworth Dr DART DA1 138 D6
OXHEY WD19 33 H4
PIN HA5 46 E4
Wentworth Gdns PLMGR N13 41 H2
Wentworth Hl WBLY HA9 50 B7
Wentworth Ms BOW E3 93 G3
Wentworth Pk FNCH N3 39 F6
Wentworth Pl STAN HA7 * 35 H5
Wentworth Rd BAR EN5 26 B1
CROY/NA CR0 164 B6
GLDGN NW11 52 D5
MNPK E12 77 H3
NWDGN UB2 102 B3
Wentworth St WCHPL E1 13 L4
Wentworth Wy PIN HA5 47 H3
RAIN RM13 99 K2
Wenvoe Av BXLYHN DA7 137 J1
Wepham Cl YEAD UB4 83 H4
Wernbrook St
WOOL/PLUM SE18 115 H5
Werndee Rd SNWD SE25 165 H3
Werneth Hall Rd CLAY IG5 59 K2
Werrington St CAMTN NW1 4 F6
Werter Rd PUT/ROE SW15 127 H3
Wesleyan Pl KTTN NW5 72 B3
Wesley Av CAN/RD E16 94 E7
HSLW TW3 122 D1
WLSDN NW10 87 F2
Wesley Cl HOLWY N7 73 F1
RYLN/HDSTN HA2 66 C1
WALW SE17 18 D6
Wesley Rd HYS/HAR UB3 82 E6
LEY E10 58 A6
WLSDN NW10 68 E7
Wesley Sq NTGHL W11 88 B5
Wesley St CAVSQ/HST W1G 10 B3
Wessex Av WIM/MER SW19 161 K1
Wessex Cl GDMY/SEVK IG3 60 E5
KUT/HW KT1 144 D7
THDIT KT7 171 F1
Wessex Ct BECK BR3 * 151 G7
Wessex Dr ERITH DA8 138 B1
PIN HA5 33 J6
Wessex Gdns GLDGN NW11 52 C7
Wessex La GFD/PVL UB6 84 D1
Wessex St BETH E2 92 E2
Wessex Ter MTCM CR4 * 162 D4
Wessex Wy GLDGN NW11 52 C6
Wesson Md CMBW SE5 * 110 D6
Westacott YEAD UB4 82 C4
Westacott Cl ARCH N19 54 D7
West Ap STMC/STPC BR5 169 H4
West Arbour St WCHPL E1 92 E5
West Av FNCH N3 38 E5
HDN NW4 52 B4
HYS/HAR UB3 82 D6
PIN HA5 47 K5
STHL UB1 83 K6
WALTH E17 57 K4
WLGTN SM6 176 E4
West Avenue Rd WALTH E17 57 J3
West Bank BARK IG11 78 B7
ENC/FH EN2 29 J2
STNW/STAM N16 56 A6
Westbank Rd HPTN TW12 142 C5
West Barnes La NWMAL KT3 160 D4
Westbeech Rd WDGN N22 55 G2
Westbere Dr STAN HA7 35 K4
Westbere Rd CRICK NW2 70 C3
Westbourne Av ACT W3 87 F5
CHEAM SM3 174 C1
Westbourne Cl YEAD UB4 83 G3
Westbourne Crs BAY/PAD W2 9 G6
Westbourne Crescent Ms
BAY/PAD W2 9 G6
Westbourne Dr FSTH SE23 132 A7
Westbourne Gdns
BAY/PAD W2 8 C4
Westbourne Ga BAY/PAD W2 9 H6
Westbourne Gv BAY/PAD W2 8 B5
NTGHL W11 8 A5
Westbourne Grove Ms
NTGHL W11 8 A5
Westbourne Grove Ter
BAY/PAD W2 8 C4
Westbourne Park Rd
NTGHL W11 8 A4
Westbourne Park Vls
BAY/PAD W2 8 B3
Westbourne Pl ED N9 42 D2
Westbourne Rd BXLYHN DA7 116 E6
CROY/NA CR0 165 G5
FELT TW13 140 D2
HOLWY N7 73 F5
SYD SE26 151 F5
Westbourne St BAY/PAD W2 9 G6
Westbourne Ter BAY/PAD W2 8 E3
Westbourne Terrace Ms
BAY/PAD W2 8 E4
Westbourne Terrace Rd
BAY/PAD W2 8 E3
Westbridge Cl SHB W12 87 J7
Westbridge Rd BTSEA SW11 108 C7
Westbrook Av HPTN TW12 141 K6
Westbrook Cl EBAR EN4 27 H2
Westbrook Crs EBAR EN4 27 H2
Westbrooke Crs WELL DA16 136 D2
Westbrooke Rd BFN/LL DA15 154 D1
WELL DA16 136 D2
Westbrook Rd BKHTH/KID SE3 113 K7
HEST TW5 102 E6
THHTH CR7 149 K7
Westbury Ar WDGN N22 * 55 H2
Westbury Av ALP/SUD HA0 68 A6
ESH/CLAY KT10 171 F5
SEVS/STOTM N15 55 H2
STHL UB1 84 A3
WDGN N22 55 H1
Westbury Cl RSLP HA4 46 E6
Westbury Gv
NFNCH/WDSPK N12 38 E5
Westbury La BKHH IG9 45 G1
Westbury Lodge Cl PIN HA5 47 H2
Westbury Pl BTFD TW8 104 E5
Westbury Rd ALP/SUD HA0 68 A6
BARK IG11 78 D7
BECK BR3 166 B2
BMLY BR1 153 H7
CROY/NA CR0 164 E5
EA W5 86 A5
FBAR/BDGN N11 40 E5
FELT TW13 122 C7
FSTGT E7 77 F4
IL IG1 78 A1
NFNCH/WDSPK N12 38 E5
NTHWD HA6 32 C3
NWMAL KT3 160 A3
PGE/AN SE20 151 F7
WALTH E17 57 J3
WATW WD18 21 F4
Westbury Ter FSTGT E7 77 F5
West Carriage Dr
BAY/PAD W2 9 H9
West Central St
LSQ/SEVD WC2H 11 J4
West Chantry
KTN/HRWW/WS HA3 34 B7
Westchester Dr HDN NW4 52 B2
Westcliffe Vls KUT/HW KT1 * 159 G1
West Cl BAR EN5 25 K4
EBAR EN4 28 A3
ED N9 42 B2
GFD/PVL UB6 84 C1
RAIN RM13 99 K3
WBLY HA9 50 B7
Westcombe Av CROY/NA CR0 163 K5
Westcombe Dr BAR EN5 26 E4
Westcombe Hl
BKHTH/KID SE3 113 K5
Westcombe Lodge Dr
YEAD UB4 82 B4
Westcombe Park Rd
BKHTH/KID SE3 113 H5
West Common Rd HAYES BR2 180 E1
Westcoombe Av RYNPK SW20 145 H7
Westcote Ri RSLP HA4 46 A6
Westcote Rd
STRHM/NOR SW16 148 C4
Westcott Cl BMLY BR1 168 D4
CROY/NA CR0 179 K7
SEVS/STOTM N15 56 B5
Westcott Crs HNWL W7 84 E4
Westcott House
POP/IOD E14 * 93 J6
Westcott Rd WALW SE17 18 D9
West Ct ALP/SUD HA0 67 J1
Westcroft Cl CRICK NW2 70 C3
Westcroft Gdns MRDN SM4 161 J2
Westcroft Ms HMSMTH W6 * 106 D3
Westcroft Rd CAR SM5 176 A3
Westcroft Sq HMSMTH W6 106 D3
Westcroft Wy CRICK NW2 70 C3
West Cross Route NTGHL W11 88 B7
West Cross Wy BTFD TW8 104 C5
Westdale Rd
WOOL/PLUM SE18 115 G5
Westdean Av LEE/GVPK SE12 134 A7
Westdean Cl
WAND/EARL SW18 128 A5
Westdown Rd CAT SE6 132 D6
SRTFD E15 76 A3
West Drayton Park Av
WDR/YW UB7 100 B2
West Drayton Rd
UX/CGN UB8 82 A4
UX/CGN UB8 82 A4
West Dr BELMT SM2 174 B7
KTN/HRWW/WS HA3 34 D5
STRHM/NOR SW16 148 B3
West Drive Gdns
KTN/HRWW/WS HA3 34 D5
West Eaton Pl BGVA SW1W 16 A5
West Eaton Place Ms
KTBR SW1X 16 A5
West Ella Rd WLSDN NW10 69 G6
West End Av LEY E10 58 A4
PIN HA5 47 H3
West End Cl WLSDN NW10 68 E6
West End Ct PIN HA5 * 47 H3
West End Gdns NTHLT UB5 83 G1
West End La BAR EN5 26 B3
HYS/HAR UB3 101 F6
KIL/WHAMP NW6 2 B4
PIN HA5 47 H3
West End Rd NTHLT UB5 65 G6
RSLP HA4 64 D2
STHL UB1 83 J7
Westerdale Rd GNWCH SE10 113 K4
Westerfield Rd
SEVS/STOTM N15 * 56 B4
Westergate Rd ABYW SE2 117 F5
Westerham Av ED N9 41 K2
UED N18 41 K2
Westerham Dr BFN/LL DA15 136 D5
Westerham Rd HAYES BR2 181 H5
LEY E10 57 K5
Westerley Crs SYD SE26 * 151 H4
Western Av DAGE RM10 80 E5
EA W5 86 A2
GFD/PVL UB6 66 A7
GFD/PVL UB6 85 F2
GLDGN NW11 52 B5
RSLP HA4 65 F6
Western Ct FNCH N3 * 38 E5
Western Gdns EA W5 86 C6
Western Gtwy CAN/RD E16 94 E6
Western La BAL SW12 129 F6
Western Man BAR EN5 * 27 F4
Western Ms MV/WKIL W9 88 D3
Western Pde BAR EN5 26 E4
Western Pl BERM/RHTH SE16 111 K1
Western Rd BRXN/ST SW9 130 B2
EA W5 85 K6
EFNCH N2 53 K2
MTCM CR4 147 J7
NWDGN UB2 102 B3
PLSTW E13 77 F7
ROM RM1 63 G4
SUT SM1 174 E4
WALTH E17 58 A4
WDGN N22 55 F1
WLSDN NW10 86 E3
Western Ter HMSMTH W6 * 106 D4
Western Vw HYS/HAR UB3 101 J1
Westernville Gdns
GNTH/NBYPK IG2 60 C6
Western Wy BAR EN5 26 E5
THMD SE28 115 J2
Westferry Circ POP/IOD E14 93 J7
Westferry Rd POP/IOD E14 112 D2
Westfield Cl CDALE/KGS NW9 50 E2
FUL/PGN SW6 * 108 B6
PEND EN3 31 G2
SUT SM1 174 D3
WBPTN SW10 108 B6
Westfield Dr
KTN/HRWW/WS HA3 49 K4
Westfield Gdns CHDH RM6 61 J5
KTN/HRWW/WS HA3 49 K3
Westfield Pk PIN HA5 33 K6
Westfield Park Dr WFD IG8 45 J5
Westfield Rd BECK BR3 166 C1
BXLYHN DA7 137 K2
CROY/NA CR0 177 H1
DAGW RM9 80 A3
MLHL NW7 37 F2
MTCM CR4 162 D1
SURB KT6 158 E4
SUT SM1 174 D3
WEA W13 85 G7
WOT/HER KT12 156 D6
Westfields BARN SW13 126 C2
Westfields Av BARN SW13 126 B2
Westfields Rd ACT W3 86 D4
Westfield St
WOOL/PLUM SE18 114 C2
Westfield Wy RSLP HA4 64 C2
WCHPL E1 93 G2
West Gdns TOOT SW17 147 J5
WAP E1W 92 D6
West Ga EA W5 86 A2
Westgate Est
EBED/NFELT TW14 * 120 E7
West Gate Ms WATW WD18 20 C4
Westgate Rd BECK BR3 152 A7
DART DA1 139 G5
SNWD SE25 165 J3
Westgate St HACK E8 74 D7
Westgate Ter WBPTN SW10 14 D8
Westglade Ct
KTN/HRWW/WS HA3 49 K4
West Green Pl GFD/PVL UB6 66 D7
West Green Rd
SEVS/STOTM N15 55 H3
West Gv GNWCH SE10 113 F7
WFD IG8 45 G5
Westgrove La GNWCH SE10 113 F7
West Halkin St KTBR SW1X 16 A3
West Hallowes ELTH/MOT SE9 134 C7
West Ham La SRTFD E15 76 B6
West Hampstead Ms
KIL/WHAMP NW6 71 F5
West Harding St
FLST/FETLN EC4A * 12 B4
West Hatch Mnr RSLP HA4 46 D7
Westhay Gdns
MORT/ESHN SW14 125 J4
West Heath Av GLDGN NW11 52 E7
West Heath Cl DART DA1 * 138 C5
HAMP NW3 70 E2
West Heath Dr GLDGN NW11 52 E7
West Heath Gdns HAMP NW3 70 E1
West Heath Rd ABYW SE2 116 E5
DART DA1 138 C5
HAMP NW3 70 E1
West Hl DART DA1 139 G5
PUT/ROE SW15 127 H5
RYLN/HDSTN HA2 66 E1
SAND/SEL CR2 178 A7
WAND/EARL SW18 127 K4
WBLY HA9 50 B7
WIM/MER SW19 127 G6
West Hill Dr DART DA1 139 F5
Westhill Pk HGT N6 71 K1
West Hill Ri DART DA1 139 G5
West Hill Rd
WAND/EARL SW18 127 J5
West Hill Wy TRDG/WHET N20 27 F7
Westholm GLDGN NW11 53 F3
West Holme ERITH DA8 117 K7
Westholme ORP BR6 169 K6
Westholme Gdns RSLP HA4 46 E7
Westhorne Av ELTH/MOT SE9 134 B5
LEE/GVPK SE12 133 K6
Westhorpe Gdns HDN NW4 52 A2
Westhorpe Rd PUT/ROE SW15 127 F2
West House Cl
WIM/MER SW19 127 H7
Westhurst Dr CHST BR7 154 B4
West India Av POP/IOD E14 93 J7
West India Dock Rd
POP/IOD E14 93 K6
Westlake Cl PLMGR N13 41 G2
YEAD UB4 83 J3
Westland Cl
STWL/WRAY TW19 * 120 B5
Westland Dr HAYES BR2 180 D1
Westland Pl FSBYE EC1V 7 G7
Westland Rd WAT WD17 * 21 F1
Westlands Cl HYS/HAR UB3 101 K3
Westlands Ter BAL SW12 129 H5
West La BERM/RHTH SE16 111 J1
Westlea Rd HNWL W7 104 B2
Westleigh Av PUT/ROE SW15 127 F4
Westleigh Dr BMLY BR1 168 D1
Westleigh Gdns EDGW HA8 36 C7
West Links ALP/SUD HA0 85 K2
Westlinton Cl MLHL NW7 38 C5
West Lodge Av ACT W3 86 C7
West Lodge Ct ACT W3 * 86 C7
Westmacott Dr
EBED/NFELT TW14 121 J6
West Malling Wy HCH RM12 81 K4
West Md HOR/WEW KT19 173 G5
Westmead PUT/ROE SW15 126 E6
West Md RSLP HA4 65 G3
Westmead Rd SUT SM1 175 H3
Westmere Dr MLHL NW7 37 F2
West Mersea Cl CAN/RD E16 95 F7
West Ms PIM SW1V 16 D6
TOTM N17 * 42 D6
Westminster Av THHTH CR7 164 C1
Westminster Br WHALL SW1A 17 K2
Westminster Bridge Rd
WHALL SW1A 17 K2
Westminster Cl
EBED/NFELT TW14 121 K7
TEDD TW11 143 G4
Westminster Dr PLMGR N13 40 E4
Westminster Gdns BARK IG11 96 E1
BARK/HLT IG6 60 D1
Westminster Rd ED N9 30 D7
HNWL W7 84 E7
SUT SM1 175 H1
Westmoat Cl BECK BR3 152 A6
Westmont Rd ESH/CLAY KT10 170 E1
Westmoor Gdns PEND EN3 31 F1
Westmoor Rd PEND EN3 31 F1
Westmoor St CHARL SE7 114 C3
Westmoreland Av WELL DA16 135 K2
Westmoreland Dr BELMT SM2 175 F7
Westmoreland Pl BMLY BR1 * 167 K2
EA W5 * 85 K4
PIM SW1V 16 D8
Westmoreland Rd
BARN SW13 106 C7
CMBW SE5 18 F9
HAYES BR2 167 H4
KTN/HRWW/WS HA3 50 B3
WALW SE17 19 G9
WWKM BR4 167 H4
Westmoreland St
CAVSQ/HST W1G 10 B3
Westmoreland Ter
PGE/AN SE20 * 150 D6
PIM SW1V 16 D7
Westmorland Cl MNPK E12 77 H1
TWK TW1 124 C5
Westmorland Rd HRW HA1 48 B4
WALTH E17 57 J5
Westmorland Wy MTCM CR4 163 J3
Westmount Cl WPK KT4 161 F7
Westmount Ct EA W5 * 86 B4
Westmount Rd
ELTH/MOT SE9 134 E2
West Oak BECK BR3 152 B7
Westoe Rd ED N9 42 D1
Weston Av E/WMO/HCT KT8 156 D3
THDIT KT7 157 K6
Weston Dr STAN HA7 35 H7
Weston Gdns ISLW TW7 103 J7
Weston Gn DAGW RM9 80 A3
THDIT KT7 170 E1
Weston Green Rd
ESH/CLAY KT10 157 J7
Weston Gv BMLY BR1 152 D6
Weston Pk CEND/HSY/T N8 54 E5
KUT/HW KT1 159 F1
THDIT KT7 157 K7
Weston Park Cl THDIT KT7 * 157 K7
Weston Ri FSBYW WC1X 5 M7
Weston Rd BMLY BR1 152 D7
CHSWK W4 105 K2
DAGW RM9 80 A3
ENC/FH EN2 29 K1
THDIT KT7 157 K7
Weston St STHWK SE1 19 H3
Weston Wk HACK E8 74 D6
Westover Cl BELMT SM2 175 F7
Westover Hl HAMP NW3 70 E1
Westover Rd
WAND/EARL SW18 128 B5
Westow Hl NRWD SE19 150 A5
Westow St NRWD SE19 150 A5
West Pk ELTH/MOT SE9 153 J1
West Park Av RCH/KEW TW9 105 H7
West Park Cl CHDH RM6 61 K4
HEST TW5 102 E5
West Park Rd NWDGN UB2 84 C7
RCH/KEW TW9 105 H7
West Parkside GNWCH SE10 113 H1
West Pl NWDGN UB2 * 103 G3
WIM/MER SW19 146 A4
Westpole Av EBAR EN4 28 B3
Westport Rd PLSTW E13 95 F3
Westport St WCHPL E1 93 F5
West Poultry Av FARR EC1M 12 C3
West Quarters SHB W12 87 J5
West Quay Dr YEAD UB4 83 J4
West Ridge Gdns
GFD/PVL UB6 84 C1
West Ri BAY/PAD W2 * 9 K6
West Rd CHDH RM6 62 A5
CHEL SW3 15 M9
CLAP SW4 129 J4
EA W5 86 A4
EBAR EN4 28 A7
EBED/NFELT TW14 121 G6
KUTN/CMB KT2 144 E7
ROMW/RG RM7 63 F6
SRTFD E15 76 D7
TOTM N17 42 D5
WDR/YW UB7 100 C2
West Rw NKENS W10 88 C3
Westrow Dr BARK IG11 79 G4
Westrow Gdns
GDMY/SEVK IG3 79 F1
West Sheen V RCH/KEW TW9 125 G3
Westside HDN NW4 51 K1
West Side Common
WIM/MER SW19 146 A4
West Smithfield STBT EC1A 12 C3
West Sq LBTH SE11 18 C4
West St BETH E2 92 D1
BMLY BR1 152 E7
BXLYHN DA7 137 G3
CAR SM5 175 K2
CROY/NA CR0 177 J3
ERITH DA8 118 A3
HRW HA1 48 D7
LSQ/SEVD WC2H 11 H5
SUT SM1 175 F4
WALTH E17 57 K4
WAN E11 76 C2
WAT WD17 21 F1
West Street La CAR SM5 175 K3
West Street Pl CROY/NA CR0 * 177 J3
West Temple Sheen
MORT/ESHN SW14 125 J4
West Tenter St WCHPL E1 13 M5
West Ter BFN/LL DA15 * 135 K7
West Towers PIN HA5 47 H5
West Vw EBED/NFELT TW14 121 F7
Westview HNWL W7 84 E5
Westview Cl NKENS W10 88 A5
WLSDN NW10 69 H4
Westview Ct BORE WD6 23 K5
Westview Crs ED N9 30 A6
Westview Dr WFD IG8 59 H1
West View Gdns BORE WD6 23 J5
West View Rd DART DA1 139 J5
Westville Rd SHB W12 106 D1
THDIT KT7 158 B6
West Wk EBAR EN4 28 A7
HYS/HAR UB3 82 E7
Westward Rd CHING E4 43 H4
Westward Wy
KTN/HRWW/WS HA3 50 A5
West Warwick Pl PIM SW1V * 16 E6
West Wy CROY/NA CR0 179 G1
EDGW HA8 36 D5
HEST TW5 102 E7
PIN HA5 47 H2
RSLP HA4 46 D7
STMC/STPC BR5 169 J4
UED N18 41 K3
WLSDN NW10 69 F3
WWKM BR4 167 G5
Westway BAY/PAD W2 8 E3
NKENS W10 88 D4
RYNPK SW20 160 E3
SHB W12 87 J6
Westway Cl RYNPK SW20 160 E2
West Way Gdns CROY/NA CR0 179 F1
Westways HOR/WEW KT19 173 H3
Westwell Rd
STRHM/NOR SW16 148 E5
Westwell Road Ap
STRHM/NOR SW16 148 E5
Westwick Gdns HMSMTH W6 107 G1
HSLWW TW4 122 A1
Westwood Av NRWD SE19 149 J7
RYLN/HDSTN HA2 66 B3
Westwood Cl BMLY BR1 168 C2
ESH/CLAY KT10 170 C2
Westwood Gdns BARN SW13 126 C2
Westwood Hl SYD SE26 150 C4
Westwood La WELL DA16 136 B3
Westwood Pk FSTH SE23 131 J6
Westwood Pl SYD SE26 * 150 C4
Westwood Rd BARN SW13 126 C2
GDMY/SEVK IG3 61 F7
West Woodside BXLY DA5 137 F7
Wetheral Dr STAN HA7 35 H7
Wetherby Cl NTHLT UB5 66 B5
Wetherby Gdns ECT SW5 14 E6
Wetherby Ms ECT SW5 14 D7
Wetherby Pl SKENS SW7 14 E6
Wetherby Wy CHSGTN KT9 172 A6
Wetherden St WALTH E17 57 H6
Wetherell Rd HOM E9 75 F7
Wetherill Rd MUSWH N10 40 A7
Wexford Rd BAL SW12 128 E6
Weybourne St
WAND/EARL SW18 147 G1
Weybridge Ct
BERM/RHTH SE16 * 111 J4
Weybridge Rd THHTH CR7 164 B3
Wey Ct HOR/WEW KT19 172 E3
Weydown Cl WIM/MER SW19 127 H7
Weyhill Rd WCHPL E1 * 92 C5
Weylond Rd BCTR RM8 80 B2
Weyman Rd BKHTH/KID SE3 114 B7
Weymouth Av EA W5 104 D2
MLHL NW7 37 G4
Weymouth Cl EHAM E6 96 B5
Weymouth Ct BELMT SM2 * 175 F6
Weymouth Ms
CAVSQ/HST W1G 10 C2
Weymouth Rd YEAD UB4 82 C2
Weymouth St
CAVSQ/HST W1G 10 B2
Weymouth Ter BETH E2 7 M5
Weymouth Vls FSBYPK N4 * 73 F1
Weymouth Wk STAN HA7 35 G5
Whadcoat St FSBYPK N4 73 G1
Whalebone Av CHDH RM6 62 B5
Whalebone Gv CHDH RM6 62 B5
Whalebone La North
CHDH RM6 62 A3
Whalebone La South
BCTR RM8 62 B6
Whales Yd SRTFD E15 * 76 C6
Wharfdale Cl FBAR/BDGN N11 40 A5
Wharfdale Rd IS N1 5 K5
Wharfedale Gdns THHTH CR7 164 A3
Wharfedale St WBPTN SW10 14 C8
Wharf La POP/IOD E14 93 H5
TWK TW1 124 B7
Wharf Pl BETH E2 74 C7
Wharf Rd IS N1 6 E6
KCROSS N1C 5 H4
PEND EN3 31 G5
SRTFD E15 76 B7
Wharfside Cl ERITH DA8 118 C4
Wharfside Rd POP/IOD E14 94 C5
Wharf St CAN/RD E16 94 C4
Wharf Ter PUT/ROE SW15 127 H2
Wharncliffe Dr STHL UB1 84 D7
Wharncliffe Gdns SNWD SE25 165 F1
Wharncliffe Rd SNWD SE25 164 E1
Wharton Cl WLSDN NW10 69 G5
Wharton Cots FSBYW WC1X * 5 M8
Wharton Rd BMLY BR1 153 F7
Wharton St FSBYW WC1X 5 M8
Whateley Rd EDUL SE22 131 G4
PGE/AN SE20 151 F6
Whatley Av RYNPK SW20 161 G2
Whatman Rd FSTH SE23 132 A6
Wheastone Rd NKENS W10 * 88 C4
Wheatfield Wy KUT/HW KT1 159 F1
Wheathill Rd PGE/AN SE20 165 J1
Wheatlands HEST TW5 103 F5
Wheatlands Rd TOOT SW17 148 A2
Wheatley Cl HDN NW4 51 J1
Wheatley Crs HYS/HAR UB3 82 E6
Wheatley Gdns ED N9 42 A1
Wheatley Rd ISLW TW7 124 A2
Wheatley St CAVSQ/HST W1G 10 B3
Wheatley Terrace Rd
ERITH DA8 118 C5
Wheatsheaf Cl NTHLT UB5 65 J4
Wheat Sheaf Cl POP/IOD E14 112 D3
Wheatsheaf La FUL/PGN SW6 107 F6
VX/NE SW8 109 K6
Wheatsheaf Rd ROM RM1 63 H5
Wheatsheaf Ter
FUL/PGN SW6 * 107 J6
Wheatstone Cl
WIM/MER SW19 147 H7
Wheatstone Rd NKENS W10 88 C4
Wheeler Gdns IS N1 5 K3
Wheeler La WCHPL E1 13 L2
Wheeler Pl HAYES BR2 168 A3
Wheelers Cross BARK IG11 96 D1
Wheelers Dr RSLP HA4 46 A5
Wheel Farm Dr DAGE RM10 80 E2
Wheelock Cl ERITH DA8 117 J6
Wheelright Cl BUSH WD23 22 B5

Wheelwright St HOLWY N7 5 L1
Whelan Wy WLGTN SM6 176 D2
Wheler St WCHPL E1 13 L1
Whellock Rd CHSWK W4 106 B2
Whetstone Cl
TRDG/WHET N20 39 H1
Whetstone Pk LINN WC2A 11 L4
Whetstone Rd BKHTH/KID SE3 134 B1
Whewell Rd ARCH N19 72 E1
Whichcote St STHWK SE1 * 12 A9
Whidborne Cl DEPT SE8 132 D1
Whidborne St STPAN WC1H 5 K8
Whimbrel Wy YEAD UB4 83 H5
Whinchat Rd THMD SE28 115 J2
Whinfell Cl STRHM/NOR SW16 148 D4
Whinyates Rd ELTH/MOT SE9 134 D2
Whippendell Cl
STMC/STPC BR5 155 H7
Whippendell Rd WATW WD18 20 C4
Whippendell Wy
STMC/STPC BR5 155 H7
Whipps Cross Rd WAN E11 58 C4
Whiskin St CLKNW EC1R 6 C8
Whistler Gdns EDGW HA8 50 B1
Whistler Ms PECK SE15 111 G6
Whistlers Av BTSEA SW11 * 108 C6
Whistler St HBRY N5 73 H3
Whistler Wk WBPTN SW10 * 108 B6
Whiston Rd BETH E2 7 L5
Whitacre Ms LBTH SE11 18 B8
Whitbread Cl TOTM N17 42 C7
Whitbread Rd BROCKY SE4 132 B3
Whitburn Rd LEW SE13 132 E4
Whitby Av WLSDN NW10 86 D2
Whitby Gdns CDALE/KGS NW9 50 C2
SUT SM1 175 H1
Whitby Pde RSLP HA4 * 65 G1
Whitby Rd RSLP HA4 65 F2
RYLN/HDSTN HA2 66 C2
SUT SM1 175 H1
WOOL/PLUM SE18 114 E3
Whitby St WCHPL E1 7 L9
Whitcher Cl NWCR SE14 112 B5
Whitcher Pl CAMTN NW1 72 C5
Whitchurch Av EDGW HA8 36 B6
Whitchurch Cl EDGW HA8 36 B5
Whitchurch Gdns EDGW HA8 36 B5
Whitchurch La EDGW HA8 36 A6
Whitchurch Pde EDGW HA8 * 36 C6
Whitchurch Rd NKENS W10 88 B6
Whitcomb St
SOHO/SHAV W1D 11 G6
Whitcome Ms RCH/KEW TW9 105 J7
Whiteadder Wy POP/IOD E14 112 E3
Whitear Wk SRTFD E15 76 B5
Whitebarn La DAGE RM10 80 C7
Whitebeam Av HAYES BR2 169 F6
Whitebeam Cl VX/NE SW8 * 110 A6
White Bear Pl HAMP NW3 * 71 H3
White Bear Yd CLKNW EC1R * 12 A1
White Bridge Av MTCM CR4 162 C3
White Bridge Cl
EBED/NFELT TW14 121 J5
White Butts Rd RSLP HA4 65 H5
Whitechapel High St
TWRH EC3N 13 M4
Whitechapel Rd WCHPL E1 92 C5
White Church La WCHPL E1 92 C5
White City Cl SHB W12 88 A6
White City Rd SHB W12 87 K6
White Conduit St IS N1 6 B5
Whitecote Rd STHL UB1 84 C5
White Craig Cl PIN HA5 34 A4
Whitecroft Cl BECK BR3 167 G3
Whitecroft Wy BECK BR3 167 F3
Whitecross St STLK EC1Y 6 F9
Whitefield Av CRICK NW2 52 A6
Whitefield Cl PUT/ROE SW15 127 H5
Whitefoot La BMLY BR1 152 B3
Whitefoot Ter BMLY BR1 152 D2
Whitefriars Av
KTN/HRWW/WS HA3 48 E1
Whitefriars Dr
KTN/HRWW/WS HA3 48 E1
Whitefriars St EMB EC4Y 12 B5
White Gdns DAGE RM10 80 C5
White Gate Gdns
KTN/HRWW/WS HA3 34 E6
White Gates THDIT KT7 158 B6
Whitehall WHALL SW1A 11 J9
Whitehall Cl BORE WD6 24 C3
Whitehall Ct WHALL SW1A 11 J9
Whitehall Crs CHSGTN KT9 171 K4
Whitehall Gdns ACT W3 86 C7
CHSWK W4 105 J5
WHALL SW1A 11 J9
Whitehall La BKHH IG9 44 E1
ERITH DA8 138 C1
Whitehall Pk ARCH N19 54 C7
Whitehall Park Rd CHSWK W4 105 J5
Whitehall Pl WHALL SW1A 11 J9
WLGTN SM6 176 B3
Whitehall Rd CHING E4 44 C1
HAYES BR2 168 C4
HNWL W7 104 B1
HRW HA1 48 E6
THHTH CR7 164 B4
WFD IG8 44 E2
Whitehall St TOTM N17 42 B6
White Hart Av
WOOL/PLUM SE18 116 A2
White Hart La BARN SW13 126 B1
TOTM N17 41 J6
White Hart Rd
WOOL/PLUM SE18 115 K3
White Hart St LBTH SE11 18 B7
White Hart Ter TOTM N17 * 42 B6
White Hart Yd STHWK SE1 13 G9
Whitehaven Cl HAYES BR2 167 K3
Whitehaven St STJWD NW8 9 J1
Whitehead Cl UED N18 41 K4
WAND/EARL SW18 128 B6
Whiteheads Gv CHEL SW3 15 K6
Whitehead's Gv CHEL SW3 15 K7
White Heart Av UX/CGN UB8 82 A4
Whiteheath Av RSLP HA4 46 A6
White Heron Ms TEDD TW11 * 143 F5
Whitehill Rd DART DA1 138 D4
White Horse Hl CHST BR7 154 A3
Whitehorse La SNWD SE25 165 F3
White Horse La WCHPL E1 93 F4
White Horse Ms PEND EN3 31 F1
White Horse Rd EHAM E6 95 K2
WCHPL E1 93 G5
Whitehorse Rd CROY/NA CR0 164 D6
WCHPL E1 93 G4
White Horse St
MYFR/PICC W1J 10 D9
White Horse Yd LOTH EC2R 13 G4
Whitehouse Av BORE WD6 24 D3
White House Dr STAN HA7 35 J3
Whitehouse Wy
STHGT/OAK N14 40 B1
Whitehurst Dr UED N18 * 43 F4
White Kennett St
HDTCH EC3A 13 K4
Whitelands Crs
WAND/EARL SW18 127 H6
White Ledges WEA W13 85 J5
Whitelegg Rd PLSTW E13 94 D1
Whiteley Rd NRWD SE19 149 K4
Whiteleys Wy FELT TW13 142 A2
White Lion Ct LOTH EC2R 13 J5
PECK SE15 * 111 K5
White Lion Hl BLKFR EC4V 12 D6
White Lion St IS N1 6 A6
White Ldg NRWD SE19 149 H6
White Lodge Cl BELMT SM2 175 G6
EFNCH N2 53 H5
ISLW TW7 124 B1
The White Ldg BAR EN5 * 26 C2
White Lyon Ct STBT EC1A 12 E2
White Oak Dr BECK BR3 167 F1
White Oak Gdns BFN/LL DA15 136 A6
Whiteoaks La GFD/PVL UB6 84 D1
White Orchards STAN HA7 35 G4
TRDG/WHET N20 26 D6
White Post La HOM E9 75 H6
White Post St NWCR SE14 111 K6
White Rd SRTFD E15 76 C6
Whites Av GNTH/NBYPK IG2 60 E5
White's Grounds STHWK SE1 19 K1
Whites Grounds Est
STHWK SE1 19 K1
Whites Meadow BMLY BR1 * 169 F3
White's Rw WCHPL E1 13 L3
White's Sq CLAP SW4 129 J3
Whitestile Rd BTFD TW8 104 D4
Whitestone La HAMP NW3 71 G2
Whitestone Wk HAMP NW3 71 G2
Whitestone Wy CROY/NA CR0 177 G2
White St STHL UB1 102 C1
Whitethorn Gdns
CROY/NA CR0 178 D1
ENC/FH EN2 29 K4
Whitethorn St BOW E3 93 J3
White Tower Wy WCHPL E1 93 G4
Whitewebbs Wy
STMC/STPC BR5 155 F7
Whitfield Ct RYNPK SW20 161 G1
Whitfield Pl FITZ W1T 10 E1
Whitfield Rd BXLYHN DA7 117 G6
EHAM E6 77 G6
GNWCH SE10 113 G7
Whitfield St FITZ W1T 10 F2
Whitford Gdns MTCM CR4 162 E2
Whitgift Av SAND/SEL CR2 177 J4
Whitgift St CROY/NA CR0 177 J2
STHWK SE1 17 L5
Whitings Rd BAR EN5 26 A4
Whitings Wy EHAM E6 96 A4
Whitland Rd CAR SM5 162 C7
Whitley Cl STWL/WRAY TW19 120 B5
Whitley Rd TOTM N17 56 A1
Whitlock Dr WIM/MER SW19 127 H6
Whitman Rd WCHPL E1 93 G3
Whitmead Cl SAND/SEL CR2 177 K5
Whitmore Cl FBAR/BDGN N11 40 B4
Whitmore Est IS N1 7 K4
Whitmore Gdns WLSDN NW10 88 A1
Whitmore Rd BECK BR3 166 C2
HRW HA1 48 C6
IS N1 7 J4
Whitnell Wy PUT/ROE SW15 * 127 F4
Whitney Av REDBR IG4 59 H3
Whitney Rd LEY E10 57 J6
Whitstable Cl BECK BR3 151 H7
Whitstable Pl CROY/NA CR0 177 J3
Whitstone La BECK BR3 166 E4
Whittaker Av RCH/KEW TW9 * 124 E4
Whittaker Rd CHEAM SM3 174 D2
EHAM E6 77 G6
Whittaker St BGVA SW1W 16 A6
Whitta Rd MNPK E12 77 H3
Whittell Gdns SYD SE26 150 E2
Whittingstall Rd
FUL/PGN SW6 107 J7
Whittington Av BANK EC3V 13 J5
YEAD UB4 82 D4
Whittington Ms
NFNCH/WDSPK N12 39 G3
Whittington Rd WDGN N22 40 E6
Whittington Wy PIN HA5 47 J4
Whittlebury Cl CAR SM5 175 K6
Whittle Cl STHL UB1 84 B5
WALTH E17 57 G5
Whittle Rd HEST TW5 102 B6
NWDGN UB2 103 G1
Whittlesea Rd
KTN/HRWW/WS HA3 34 C6
Whittlesey St STHWK SE1 12 B9
Whitton Av East GFD/PVL UB6 67 F4
Whitton Av West NTHLT UB5 66 B4
Whitton Cl GFD/PVL UB6 67 H5
Whitton Dene HSLW TW3 123 G4
Whitton Dr GFD/PVL UB6 67 G5
Whitton Manor Rd
WHTN TW2 123 H5
Whitton Rd HSLW TW3 123 G4
WHTN TW2 123 K5
Whitton Waye HSLW TW3 123 F5
Whitwell Rd PLSTW E13 94 E2
Whitworth Rd SNWD SE25 165 F2
WOOL/PLUM SE18 115 F6
Whitworth St GNWCH SE10 113 H4
Whorlton Rd PECK SE15 131 H2
Whybridge Cl RAIN RM13 81 G7
Whymark Av WDGN N22 55 G2
Whytecroft HEST TW5 102 C6
Whyteville Rd FSTGT E7 77 F5
Wickersley Rd BTSEA SW11 129 F1
Wickers Oake NRWD SE19 150 B3
Wicker St WCHPL E1 * 92 C5
Wicket Rd GFD/PVL UB6 85 G2
The Wicket CROY/NA CR0 179 J4
Wickford St WCHPL E1 92 E3
Wickford Wy WALTH E17 57 F3
Wickham Av CHEAM SM3 174 A4
CROY/NA CR0 179 G1
Wickham Cha WWKM BR4 167 G6
Wickham Cl NWMAL KT3 160 C4
PEND EN3 30 E2
WCHPL E1 92 E4
Wickham Ct WWKM BR4 * 180 B3
Wickham Court Rd
WWKM BR4 180 A1
Wickham Crs WWKM BR4 180 A1
Wickham Gdns BROCKY SE4 132 C2
Wickham La ABYW SE2 116 B5
Wickham Ms BROCKY SE4 132 C1
Wickham Rd BECK BR3 166 E2
BROCKY SE4 132 C2
CHING E4 44 A6
CROY/NA CR0 178 E1
KTN/HRWW/WS HA3 48 D1
Wickham St LBTH SE11 17 L7
WELL DA16 116 B7
WELL DA16 135 K1
Wickham Wy BECK BR3 167 F4
Wick La BOW E3 93 J1
Wickliffe Av FNCH N3 52 C1
Wickliffe Gdns WBLY HA9 68 C1
Wicklow St FSBYW WC1X 5 L7
Wick Rd HOM E9 75 F5
TEDD TW11 143 H6
Wicks Cl LEE/GVPK SE12 153 H3
Wickwood St CMBW SE5 130 C1
Widdenham Rd HOLWY N7 73 F3
Widdicombe Av
RYLN/HDSTN HA2 65 J1
Widdin St SRTFD E15 76 C6
Widecombe Gdns REDBR IG4 59 J3
Widecombe Rd
ELTH/MOT SE9 153 J2
Widecombe Wy EFNCH N2 53 H4
Widegate St WCHPL E1 13 K3
Widenham Cl PIN HA5 47 G4
Wide Wy MTCM CR4 163 J2
Widgeon Cl CAN/RD E16 95 F5
Widgeon Rd ERITH DA8 118 E6
Widley Rd MV/WKIL W9 2 B8
Widmore Lodge Rd BMLY BR1 168 C1
Widmore Rd BMLY BR1 168 A1
Wieland Rd NTHWD HA6 32 E6
Wigeon Wy YEAD UB4 83 H5
Wiggenhall Industrial Est
WATW WD18 21 G4
Wiggenhall Rd WATW WD18 21 F4
Wiggins La RCHPK/HAM TW10 143 J1
Wiggins Md CDALE/KGS NW9 37 H6
Wigginton Av WBLY HA9 68 C5
Wightman Rd
CEND/HSY/T N8 55 G3
Wigley Rd FELT TW13 122 C7
Wigmore Pl MHST W1U * 10 C4
Wigmore Rd CAR SM5 175 H1
Wigmore St MHST W1U 10 B4
Wigram Rd WAN E11 59 G5
Wigram Sq WALTH E17 58 A2
Wigston Cl UED N18 42 A4
Wigston Rd PLSTW E13 95 F3
Wigton Gdns STAN HA7 36 A7
Wigton Pl LBTH SE11 18 B8
Wigton Rd WALTH E17 43 H7
Wilberforce Ms CLAP SW4 129 J3
Wilberforce Rd
CDALE/KGS NW9 51 J5
FSBYPK N4 73 H1
Wilberforce Wk SRTFD E15 76 C4
Wilberforce Wy
WIM/MER SW19 146 B5
Wilbraham Pl KTBR SW1X 16 A5
Wilbury Wy UED N18 41 K4
Wilby Ms NTGHL W11 88 D6
Wilcot Av OXHEY WD19 21 J6
Wilcot Cl OXHEY WD19 21 J6
Wilcox Cl VX/NE SW8 109 K6
Wilcox Rd SUT SM1 * 175 F3
TEDD TW11 142 D3
VX/NE SW8 109 K6
Wildacres NTHWD HA6 32 D3
Wild Ct HOL/ALD WC2B 11 L4
Wildcroft Gdns STAN HA7 35 K5
Wildcroft Rd PUT/ROE SW15 127 F6
Wilde Cl HACK E8 74 C7
Wilde Pl PLMGR N13 41 H5
WAND/EARL SW18 128 C6
Wilder Cl RSLP HA4 47 F7
Wilderness Ms CLAP SW4 129 G3
Wilderness Rd CHST BR7 154 B6
The Wilderness
E/WMO/HCT KT8 157 H4
HPTN TW12 * 142 B3
Wilde Rd ERITH DA8 117 J6
Wilderton Rd
STNW/STAM N16 56 A6
Wildfell Rd CAT SE6 132 E6
Wild Goose Dr NWCR SE14 111 K7
Wild Hatch GLDGN NW11 52 E5
Wild Oaks Cl NTHWD HA6 32 D5
Wild's Rents STHWK SE1 19 J3
Wild St HOL/ALD WC2B 11 K5
Wildwood NTHWD HA6 32 B5
Wildwood Cl LEE/GVPK SE12 133 J6
Wildwood Gv HAMP NW3 53 G7
Wildwood Ri GLDGN NW11 53 G7
Wildwood Rd GLDGN NW11 53 F5
Wildwood Ter HAMP NW3 53 G7
Wilford Cl ENC/FH EN2 * 29 K2
NTHWD HA6 32 B6
Wilfred Av RAIN RM13 99 J4
Wilfred Owen Cl
WIM/MER SW19 147 G5
Wilfred St WESTW SW1E 16 E3
Wilfrid Gdns ACT W3 86 E4
Wilkes Rd BTFD TW8 105 F5
Wilkes St WCHPL E1 13 M2
Wilkins Cl HYS/HAR UB3 101 J4
MTCM CR4 147 J7
Wilkinson Gdns SNWD SE25 150 A7
Wilkinson Rd CAN/RD E16 95 G5
Wilkinson St VX/NE SW8 110 A6
Wilkinson Wy CHSWK W4 106 A1
Wilkin St KTTN NW5 72 A5
Wilkin Street Ms KTTN NW5 72 A5
Wilks Gdns CROY/NA CR0 166 B7
Wilks Pl IS N1 7 K6
Willan Rd TOTM N17 55 K1
Willan Wall CAN/RD E16 94 D6
Willard St VX/NE SW8 129 G2
Willcocks Cl CHSGTN KT9 172 A2
Willcott Rd ACT W3 86 D7
Will Crooks Gdns
ELTH/MOT SE9 134 C3
Willenfield Rd WLSDN NW10 86 D1
Willenhall Av BAR EN5 27 G5
Willenhall Dr HYS/HAR UB3 82 C6
Willenhall Rd
WOOL/PLUM SE18 115 G4
Willerfield Rd WLSDN NW10 86 E2
Willersley Av BFN/LL DA15 136 A7
Willersley Cl BFN/LL DA15 136 A7
Willesden La
KIL/WHAMP NW6 70 B6
Willes Rd KTTN NW5 72 B5
Willett Cl NTHLT UB5 83 G2
STMC/STPC BR5 169 K5
Willett Rd THHTH CR7 164 B4
Willett Wy STMC/STPC BR5 169 J4
William Ash Cl DAGW RM9 79 H5
William Barefoot Dr
ELTH/MOT SE9 154 A3
William Booth Rd
PGE/AN SE20 150 C7
William Carey Wy HRW HA1 48 E5
William Cl EFNCH N2 53 H1
LEW SE13 133 F2
NWDGN UB2 103 H1
William Dr STAN HA7 35 G5
William Ellis Wy
BERM/RHTH SE16 * 111 H2
William Foster La WELL DA16 136 B1
William Gdns PUT/ROE SW15 126 E4
William Guy Gdns BOW E3 93 K2
William IV St CHCR WC2N 11 J7
William Margrie Cl
PECK SE15 * 131 H1
William Ms KTBR SW1X 15 M2
William Morley Cl EHAM E6 77 H7
William Morris Cl WALTH E17 57 H2
William Morris Wy
FUL/PGN SW6 128 B2
William Rd CAMTN NW1 4 E8
SUT SM1 175 G4
WIM/MER SW19 146 C6
Williams Av WALTH E17 43 H7
William's Blds WCHPL E1 * 92 E3
Williams Cl CEND/HSY/T N8 * 54 D5
FUL/PGN SW6 107 H6
Williams Dr HSLW TW3 123 F3
Williams Gv SURB KT6 158 D5
WDGN N22 41 G7
Williams La MORT/ESHN SW14 125 K1
MRDN SM4 162 B5
Williamson Cl GNWCH SE10 113 J4
Williamson Rd FSBYPK N4 55 H5
Williamson St HOLWY N7 * 72 E3
William Sq BERM/RHTH SE16 93 G7
Williams Rd NWDGN UB2 102 D3
William's Rd WEA W13 * 85 G7
Williams Ter CROY/NA CR0 177 G5
William St BARK IG11 78 C6
BUSH WD23 21 H2
CAR SM5 175 J2
KTBR SW1X 15 M2
LEY E10 57 K5
TOTM N17 42 B6
Willifield Wy GLDGN NW11 52 E4
Willingdon Rd WDGN N22 55 H1
Willingham Cl KTTN NW5 72 C4
Willingham Ter KTTN NW5 * 72 C4
Willingham Wy KUT/HW KT1 159 H1
Willington Rd BRXN/ST SW9 129 K2
Willis Av BELMT SM2 175 J5
Willis Rd CROY/NA CR0 164 D6
ERITH DA8 117 K3
SRTFD E15 76 D7
Willis St POP/IOD E14 93 K5
Willmore End WIM/MER SW19 147 F7
Willoughby Av CROY/NA CR0 177 F3
Willoughby Dr RAIN RM13 81 G6
Willoughby Gv TOTM N17 42 D6
Willoughby La BMLY BR1 153 G6
TOTM N17 42 D6
Willoughby Ms TOTM N17 42 D6
Willoughby Park Rd
TOTM N17 42 D6
Willoughby Rd
CEND/HSY/T N8 55 G2
HAMP NW3 71 H3
KUTN/CMB KT2 144 B7
TWK TW1 124 D4
Willoughby Wy CHARL SE7 114 A3
Willow Av BARN SW13 126 C1
BFN/LL DA15 136 B5
Willow Bank
RCHPK/HAM TW10 143 H2
Willowbay Cl BAR EN5 26 B5
Willow Bridge Rd IS N1 73 J5
Willowbrook HPTN TW12 142 B4
Willowbrook Est PECK SE15 * 111 G6
Willowbrook Rd NWDGN UB2 102 E2
PECK SE15 111 G5
STWL/WRAY TW19 120 B7
The Willow Centre MTCM CR4 162 E4
Willow Cl BKHH IG9 45 H2
BTFD TW8 104 D5
BXLY DA5 137 G5
CAT SE6 133 J7
HAYES BR2 168 E4
HCH RM12 81 K2
Willow Ct STAN HA7 * 35 K6
Willowcourt Av
KTN/HRWW/WS HA3 49 H4
Willow Dean PIN HA5 * 47 H1
Willow Dene BUSH WD23 22 E6
PIN HA5 47 H1
Willowdene HGT N6 * 53 K6
Willowdene Cl WHTN TW2 123 H6
Willow Dr BAR EN5 26 C3
Willow End NTHWD HA6 32 E5
SURB KT6 159 F7
TRDG/WHET N20 38 E1
Willowfields Cl
WOOL/PLUM SE18 115 K4
Willow Gdns HSLW TW3 * 103 F7
RSLP HA4 64 D1
Willow Gv CHST BR7 154 A5
RSLP HA4 64 D1
Willowhayne Dr
WOT/HER KT12 156 A6
Willowhayne Gdns WPK KT4 174 A3
Willow La MTCM CR4 162 E4
WATW WD18 20 E4
WOOL/PLUM SE18 114 E3
Willowmead Cl EA W5 85 K4
Willowmere ESH/CLAY KT10 170 C3
Willow Mt CROY/NA CR0 178 A3
Willow Pl WEST SW1P 16 F5
Willow Rd CHDH RM6 62 A5
DART DA1 139 F7
EA W5 105 F1
EN EN1 30 A1
ERITH DA8 118 D7
HAMP NW3 71 H3
MNPK E12 77 K2
NWMAL KT3 159 K3
WLGTN SM6 176 B6
Willows Av MRDN SM4 162 A4
Willows Cl PIN HA5 47 G1
Willows Ter WLSDN NW10 * 87 H1
The Willows BECK BR3 * 151 J7
EBAR EN4 * 27 J5
ESH/CLAY KT10 170 E5
OXHEY WD19 21 F6
Willow St ROMW/RG RM7 62 E3
SDTCH EC2A 7 J9
Willow Ter PGE/AN SE20 * 150 D7
Willow Tree Cl BOW E3 75 G7
NTHLT UB5 65 J5
WAND/EARL SW18 128 A7
YEAD UB4 83 G3
Willowtree Cl HGDN/ICK UB10 64 A2
Willow Tree La YEAD UB4 83 G3
Willow Tree Wk BMLY BR1 153 F7
Willowtree Wy THHTH CR7 149 G7
Willow V CHST BR7 154 A5
SHB W12 87 J7
Willow Vw WIM/MER SW19 147 H7
Willow Wk CHEAM SM3 174 D2
DART DA1 * 139 H4
SEVS/STOTM N15 55 H3
STHWK SE1 19 K5
WALTH E17 57 H4
WCHMH N21 29 F5
Willow Wy ALP/SUD HA0 * 67 G2
FNCH N3 39 F6
HOR/WEW KT19 173 F5
NTGHL W11 88 B6
SYD SE26 150 D2
WHTN TW2 142 B1
Willow Wood Crs SNWD SE25 165 F5
Willow Wren Whf
NWDGN UB2 * 102 A3
Will Rd KTTN NW5 72 B5
Willrose Crs ABYW SE2 116 C4
Wills Crs HSLW TW3 123 G5
Wills Gv MLHL NW7 37 J4
Wilman Gv HACK E8 74 C6
Wilmar Cl YEAD UB4 82 B3
Wilmar Gdns WWKM BR4 166 E7
Wilmer Cl KUTN/CMB KT2 144 B4
Wilmer Crs KUTN/CMB KT2 144 B4
Wilmer Gdns IS N1 7 J4
Wilmer Lea Cl SRTFD E15 76 A6
Wilmer Pl STNW/STAM N16 74 B1
Wilmer Wy FBAR/BDGN N11 40 D4
Wilmington Av CHSWK W4 106 A6
Wilmington Cl WATW WD18 21 F2
Wilmington Gdns BARK IG11 78 D6
Wilmington Sq FSBYW WC1X 6 A8
Wilmington St FSBYW WC1X 6 A8
Wilmot Cl PECK SE15 * 111 H6
Wilmot Pl CAMTN NW1 4 E1
HNWL W7 84 E7
Wilmot Rd CAR SM5 * 175 K4
DART DA1 138 E4
LEY E10 75 K1
TOTM N17 55 K2
Wilmot St BETH E2 92 D3
Wilmount St
WOOL/PLUM SE18 115 G3
Wilna Rd WAND/EARL SW18 128 B6
Wilsham St NTGHL W11 88 B7
Wilshaw Cl HDN NW4 51 J2
Wilshaw St NWCR SE14 112 D7
Wilsmere Dr
KTN/HRWW/WS HA3 34 E6
NTHLT UB5 65 J5
Wilson Av MTCM CR4 147 J6
Wilson Cl SAND/SEL CR2 177 K4
WBLY HA9 50 B6
Wilson Dr WBLY HA9 50 B6
Wilson Gdns HRW HA1 48 C6
Wilson Gv BERM/RHTH SE16 111 J1
Wilson Rd CHSGTN KT9 172 B5
CMBW SE5 110 E7
IL IG1 59 K6
PLSTW E13 95 H2
Wilson's Av TOTM N17 56 B1
Wilson's Pl POP/IOD E14 93 H5
Wilson's Rd HMSMTH W6 107 G4
Wilson St LVPST EC2M 13 H2
WALTH E17 58 A4
WCHMH N21 29 G6
Wilson Wk CHSWK W4 * 106 C3
Wilstone Cl YEAD UB4 83 J3
Wilthorne Gdns DAGE RM10 80 D6
Wilton Av CHSWK W4 106 B4
Wilton Cl WDR/YW UB7 100 A5
Wilton Crs KTBR SW1X 16 A2
WIM/MER SW19 146 D7
Wilton Est HACK E8 * 74 C5
Wilton Gdns E/WMO/HCT KT8 157 F3
WOT/HER KT12 156 C7
Wilton Gv NWMAL KT3 160 C5
WIM/MER SW19 146 D6
Wilton Ms HACK E8 * 74 D5
KTBR SW1X 16 B3
Wilton Pl KTBR SW1X 16 A1
Wilton Rd ABYW SE2 116 D2
EBAR EN4 27 K3
HSLWW TW4 122 C2
MUSWH N10 54 A1
PIM SW1V 16 D4
WIM/MER SW19 147 J6
Wilton Rw KTBR SW1X 16 A2
Wilton Sq IS N1 7 G3
Wilton St KTBR SW1X 16 C3
Wilton Ter KTBR SW1X 16 A3
Wilton Vls IS N1 7 G4
Wilton Wk FELT TW13 * 141 F1
Wilton Wy HACK E8 74 C5
Wiltshire Cl CHEL SW3 15 K6
MLHL NW7 * 37 H4
Wiltshire Gdns FSBYPK N4 55 J5
WHTN TW2 123 H7
Wiltshire La PIN HA5 46 E3
Wiltshire Rd BRXN/ST SW9 130 B2
THHTH CR7 164 B2
Wiltshire Rw IS N1 7 G4
Wilverley Crs NWMAL KT3 160 B5
Wimbart Rd
BRXS/STRHM SW2 * 130 A6
Wimbledon Br
WIM/MER SW19 146 D5
Wimbledon Hill Rd
WIM/MER SW19 146 C5
Wimbledon Park Rd
WAND/EARL SW18 127 J7
WIM/MER SW19 146 C2
Wimbledon Park Side
PUT/ROE SW15 126 E7
WIM/MER SW19 146 B1
Wimbledon Rd TOOT SW17 147 G3
Wimbolt St BETH E2 92 C2
Wimborne Av NWDGN UB2 103 F3
YEAD UB4 83 F5
Wimborne Cl BKHH IG9 45 G1
LEE/GVPK SE12 133 J4
WPK KT4 161 F7
Wimborne Dr EDGW HA8 50 C2
PIN HA5 47 H6
Wimborne Gdns WEA W13 85 H5
Wimborne Rd ED N9 42 C1
TOTM N17 56 A1
Wimborne Wy BECK BR3 166 A2
Wimbourne St IS N1 7 G5
Wimpole Cl HAYES BR2 168 B3
KUT/HW KT1 159 G1
Wimpole Ms CAVSQ/HST W1G 10 C2
Wimpole St CAVSQ/HST W1G 10 C3
Wimshurst Cl CROY/NA CR0 163 K7
Winans Wk BRXN/ST SW9 130 B1
Wincanton Crs NTHLT UB5 66 A4
Wincanton Gdns
BARK/HLT IG6 60 B2
Wincanton Rd
WAND/EARL SW18 127 J6
Winchcombe Rd CAR SM5 175 H1
Winchcomb Gdns
ELTH/MOT SE9 134 C2
Winchelsea Av BXLYHN DA7 117 G6
Winchelsea Cl PUT/ROE SW15 127 G4
Winchelsea Rd FSTGT E7 76 E3

TOTM N17 56 A2
WLSDN NW10 69 F7
Winchelsey Ri SAND/SEL CR2 178 B5
Winchendon Rd
FUL/PGN SW6 107 J6
TEDD TW11 142 D3
Winchester Av
CDALE/KGS NW9 50 B2
HEST TW5 102 E5
KIL/WHAMP NW6 70 C6
Winchester Cl EN EN1 * 30 A4
ESH/CLAY KT10 170 A3
HAYES BR2 167 J2
KUTN/CMB KT2 144 D6
LBTH SE11 * 18 D6
Winchester Dr PIN HA5 47 H4
Winchester Ms WPK KT4 174 B1
Winchester Pk HAYES BR2 167 J2
Winchester Pl HACK E8 74 B4
HGT N6 54 B7
Winchester Rd BXLYHN DA7 136 E1
CHING E4 44 A6
ED N9 30 B7
FELT TW13 141 K2
HAMP NW3 3 H1
HAYES BR2 167 J2
HGT N6 54 B7
HYS/HAR UB3 101 H6
IL IG1 78 D2
KTN/HRWW/WS HA3 50 A3
TWK TW1 124 C5
Winchester Sq STHWK SE1 13 G8
Winchester St ACT W3 86 E7
PIM SW1V 16 D7
Winchester Wk STHWK SE1 13 G8
Winchfield Cl
KTN/HRWW/WS HA3 49 J5
Winchfield Rd SYD SE26 151 G4
Winchilsea Crs
E/WMO/HCT KT8 157 H1
Winchmore Hill Rd
STHGT/OAK N14 28 D7
Winchmore Vls WCHMH N21 * 29 F6
Winckley Cl
KTN/HRWW/WS HA3 50 B4
Wincott St LBTH SE11 18 B5
Wincrofts Dr ELTH/MOT SE9 135 J3
Windall Cl NRWD SE19 150 C7
Windborough Rd CAR SM5 176 A6
Windermere Av FNCH N3 52 E1
HCH RM12 81 J4
KIL/WHAMP NW6 70 C7
RSLP HA4 47 G6
WBLY HA9 49 J7
WIM/MER SW19 162 A2
Windermere Cl DART DA1 138 E7
EBED/NFELT TW14 121 H7
Windermere Gdns REDBR IG4 59 J4
Windermere Gv WBLY HA9 49 J7
Windermere Hall EDGW HA8 * 36 B4
Windermere Rd ARCH N19 * 72 C1
BXLYHN DA7 137 K1
CROY/NA CR0 165 G7
EA W5 104 D2
MUSWH N10 40 B7
PUT/ROE SW15 145 G3
STHL UB1 83 K4
STRHM/NOR SW16 148 C7
WWKM BR4 180 C1
Winders Rd BTSEA SW11 128 D1
Windfield Cl SYD SE26 151 F3
Windham Rd RCH/KEW TW9 125 G2
Winding Wy BCTR RM8 79 J2
Windlass Pl DEPT SE8 112 B3
Windlesham Gv
WIM/MER SW19 127 G7
Windley Cl FSTH SE23 150 E1
Windmill Cl LEW SE13 * 133 F1
STHWK SE1 * 111 H3
SUN TW16 140 C6
SURB KT6 158 D7
Windmill Dr CLAP SW4 129 G4
CRICK NW2 70 C2
Windmill Gdns ENC/FH EN2 29 G1
Windmill Gv CROY/NA CR0 164 D6
Windmill Hl ENC/FH EN2 29 H2
HAMP NW3 * 71 G2
RSLP HA4 46 D6
Windmill La BAR EN5 25 H5
BUSH WD23 22 E7
GFD/PVL UB6 84 C4
HAYES BR2 181 G3
ISLW TW7 103 K3
NWDGN UB2 103 H1
SRTFD E15 76 B5
SURB KT6 158 C6
Windmill Pas CHSWK W4 * 106 B3
Windmill Ri KUTN/CMB KT2 144 D6
Windmill Rd CHSWK W4 106 B3
CROY/NA CR0 164 D6
EA W5 104 D3
HPTN TW12 142 B4
MTCM CR4 163 H4
SUN TW16 140 C7
UED N18 41 K3
WAND/EARL SW18 128 C5
WIM/MER SW19 145 K4
Windmill Rd West SUN TW16 140 C7
Windmill Rw LBTH SE11 18 A8
Windmill St BUSH WD23 22 E7
FITZ W1T 11 G3
Windmill Wk STHWK SE1 * 12 B9
Windmill Wy RSLP HA4 46 D7
Windover Av CDALE/KGS NW9 51 F3
Windrose Cl BERM/RHTH SE16 112 A1
Windrush NWMAL KT3 159 J3
Windrush Cl BTSEA SW11 * 128 C3
CHSWK W4 * 105 K6
HACK E8 74 C6
TOTM N17 42 A7
Windrush La FSTH SE23 151 F2
Windrush Rd WLSDN NW10 69 F7
Windsor Av CHEAM SM3 174 C2
E/WMO/HCT KT8 157 F2
EDGW HA8 36 D3
NWMAL KT3 159 K4
WALTH E17 57 G1
WIM/MER SW19 147 G7
Windsor Cl CHST BR7 154 B4
FNCH N3 52 C1
NTHWD HA6 46 E1
RYLN/HDSTN HA2 66 A2
WNWD SE27 149 J3
Windsor Ct PIN HA5 * 47 H2
STHGT/OAK N14 28 C6
Windsor Crs RYLN/HDSTN HA2 66 A2
WBLY HA9 68 C2
Windsor Dr DART DA1 138 D5
EBAR EN4 27 K5
Windsor Gdns CROY/NA CR0 176 E2
HYS/HAR UB3 101 G2
MV/WKIL W9 8 A2
Windsor Gv WNWD SE27 149 J3
Windsor Ms CAT SE6 133 F7
Windsor Park Rd
HYS/HAR UB3 101 J6
Windsor Rd BAR EN5 26 B5
BCTR RM8 80 A2
BXLYHS DA6 137 F3
CHING E4 43 K3
CRICK NW2 69 K5
EA W5 86 A6
FNCH N3 52 C1
FSTGT E7 77 F4
HOLWY N7 72 E2
HSLWW TW4 122 A1
IL IG1 78 C3
KTN/HRWW/WS HA3 34 C7
KUTN/CMB KT2 144 A6
LEY E10 75 K1
NWDGN UB2 102 E2
PLMGR N13 41 G2
RCH/KEW TW9 125 G1
SUN TW16 140 E6
TEDD TW11 142 D4
THHTH CR7 164 C1
TOTM N17 56 C1
WAN E11 58 E7
WPK KT4 173 J1
The Windsors BKHH IG9 45 J1
Windsor St IS N1 6 D3
Windsor Ter IS N1 6 F7
Windsor Wk CMBW SE5 130 E1
Windsor Wy WKENS W14 107 G3
Windspoint Dr PECK SE15 111 J5
Windstock Cl
BERM/RHTH SE16 112 C2
Windus Rd STNW/STAM N16 56 B7
Windy Rdg BMLY BR1 153 J7
Windy Ridge Cl
WIM/MER SW19 146 B4
Wine Cl WAP E1W 92 E6
Wine Office Ct
FLST/FETLN EC4A 12 B4
Winery La KUT/HW KT1 159 G2
Winey Cl CHSGTN KT9 171 J6
Winforton St GNWCH SE10 113 F7
Winfrith Rd WAND/EARL SW18 128 B6
Wingate Crs CROY/NA CR0 163 K5
Wingate Rd HMSMTH W6 106 E2
IL IG1 78 B4
SCUP DA14 155 J4
Wingate Sq CLAP SW4 129 H3
Wingfield Ct WATW WD18 * 20 B5
Wingfield Ms PECK SE15 131 H2
Wingfield Rd KUTN/CMB KT2 144 B5
SRTFD E15 76 C4
WALTH E17 57 K4
Wingfield St PECK SE15 131 H2
Wingfield Wy RSLP HA4 65 F5
Wingford Rd
BRXS/STRHM SW2 129 K5
Wingmore Rd HNHL SE24 130 D2
Wingrave Rd HMSMTH W6 107 F5
Wingrove Rd CAT SE6 152 C1
Wings Cl SUT SM1 174 E3
Winifred Cl BAR EN5 25 H5
Winifred Pl
NFNCH/WDSPK N12 39 G4
Winifred Rd BCTR RM8 80 A1
DART DA1 138 E4
ERITH DA8 118 B4
HPTN TW12 142 A3
WIM/MER SW19 146 E7
Winifred St CAN/RD E16 95 K7
Winifred Ter EN EN1 30 B6
PLSTW E13 94 E1
Winkfield Rd WDGN N22 41 G7
Winkley St BETH E2 92 D1
Winkworth Cots WCHPL E1 * 92 E3
Winlaton Rd BMLY BR1 152 B3
Winmill Rd BCTR RM8 80 B2
Winn Common Rd
WOOL/PLUM SE18 115 K5
Winnett St SOHO/SHAV W1D 11 G6
Winnington Cl EFNCH N2 53 H5
Winnington Rd EFNCH N2 53 H6
Winn Rd LEE/GVPK SE12 133 K7
Winns Av WALTH E17 57 H2
Winns Ms SEVS/STOTM N15 56 A3
Winns Ter WALTH E17 57 J1
Winsbeach WALTH E17 58 B2
Winscombe Crs EA W5 85 K3
Winscombe St KTTN NW5 72 B2
Winscombe Wy STAN HA7 35 G4
Winsford Rd CAT SE6 151 H2
Winsford Ter UED N18 * 41 K4
Winsham Gv BTSEA SW11 129 F4
Winslade Rd
BRXS/STRHM SW2 129 K4
Winsland Ms BAY/PAD W2 9 G4
Winsland St BAY/PAD W2 9 G4
Winsley St GTPST W1W 10 E4
Winslow Cl PIN HA5 47 F5
WLSDN NW10 69 G2
Winslow Gv CHING E4 44 C1
Winslow Rd HMSMTH W6 107 F5
Winslow Wy FELT TW13 141 H2
Winsor Ter EHAM E6 96 A4
Winstanley Rd BTSEA SW11 128 C2
Winstead Gdns DAGE RM10 80 E4
Winston Av CDALE/KGS NW9 51 G6
Winston Cl
KTN/HRWW/WS HA3 35 F5
ROMW/RG RM7 62 D3
Winston Ct
KTN/HRWW/WS HA3 34 B6
Winston House SURB KT6 * 159 F4
Winston Rd STNW/STAM N16 73 K3
Winston Wy IL IG1 78 B2
Winter Av EHAM E6 77 J7
Winterbourne Rd BCTR RM8 79 J1
CAT SE6 132 C7
THHTH CR7 164 B3
Winter Box Wk
RCHPK/HAM TW10 125 G4
Winterbrook Rd HNHL SE24 130 D5
Winterburn Cl
FBAR/BDGN N11 40 A5
Winterfold Cl WIM/MER SW19 146 C1
Winters Rd THDIT KT7 158 C6
Winterstoke Rd FSTH SE23 132 C7
Winterton Pl WBPTN SW10 14 F9
Winterwell Rd
BRXS/STRHM SW2 129 K4
Winthorpe Rd PUT/ROE SW15 127 H3
Winthorpe St WCHPL E1 92 D4
Winthrop St WCHPL E1 * 92 D4
Winton Ap RKW/CH/CXG WD3 20 A4
Winton Av FBAR/BDGN N11 40 C6
Winton Cl ED N9 31 F6
Winton Dr RKW/CH/CXG WD3 20 A4
Winton Gdns EDGW HA8 36 B6
The Wintons BUSH WD23 * 22 D7
Winton Wy STRHM/NOR SW16 149 G4
Wirral Wood Cl CHST BR7 154 A5
Wisbeach Rd CROY/NA CR0 164 E4
Wisborough Rd
SAND/SEL CR2 178 B7
Wisdons Cl DAGE RM10 62 D7
Wise La MLHL NW7 37 J5
WDR/YW UB7 100 A3
Wiseman Rd LEY E10 * 75 J1
Wise Rd SRTFD E15 76 A7
Wiseton Rd TOOT SW17 128 D7
Wishart Rd BKHTH/KID SE3 114 C7
Wishaw Wk FBAR/BDGN N11 40 E5
Wisley Rd BTSEA SW11 128 E4
STMC/STPC BR5 155 G6
Wisteria Cl IL IG1 78 B4
MLHL NW7 37 H5
Wisteria Rd LEW SE13 133 G3
Witanhurst La HGT N6 54 A7
Witan St BETH E2 92 D2
Witham Rd DAGE RM10 80 C4
GPK RM2 63 K4
ISLW TW7 103 J7
PGE/AN SE20 165 K2
WEA W13 85 G7
Witherby Cl CROY/NA CR0 178 A4
Witherington Rd HBRY N5 * 73 G4
Withers Md CDALE/KGS NW9 37 H7
Witherston Wy
ELTH/MOT SE9 154 A1
Withycombe Rd
WIM/MER SW19 127 G6
Withy La RSLP HA4 46 A4
Withy Md CHING E4 44 B2
Witley Crs CROY/NA CR0 180 A5
Witley Gdns NWDGN UB2 102 E3
Witley Rd ARCH N19 72 C1
Witney Cl PIN HA5 33 K5
Witney Pth FSTH SE23 151 F2
Wittenham Wy CHING E4 44 B2
Wittering Cl KUTN/CMB KT2 143 K4
Wittersham Rd BMLY BR1 152 D4
Wivenhoe Cl PECK SE15 131 H2
Wivenhoe Ct HSLW TW3 122 E3
Wivenhoe Rd BARK IG11 97 G1
Wiverton Rd SYD SE26 150 E5
Wix Rd DAGW RM9 79 K7
Wix's La CLAP SW4 129 G3
Woburn WEA W13 * 85 H4
Woburn Av HCH RM12 81 J3
Woburn Cl BUSH WD23 22 C5
THMD SE28 97 K5
WIM/MER SW19 147 G5
Woburn Pl STPAN WC1H 5 J9
Woburn Rd CAR SM5 162 D7
CROY/NA CR0 164 D7
Woburn Sq STPAN WC1H 11 H1
Woburn Wk STPAN WC1H * 5 H8
Wodeham Gdns WCHPL E1 92 C4
Wodehouse Av CMBW SE5 111 G7
Wodehouse Rd DART DA1 139 K3
Woffington Cl TEDD TW11 143 J6
Woking Cl PUT/ROE SW15 126 C3
Woldham Pl HAYES BR2 168 B3
Woldham Rd HAYES BR2 168 B3
Wolfe Cl HAYES BR2 167 K5
YEAD UB4 83 F2
Wolfe Crs CHARL SE7 114 C4
Wolferton Rd MNPK E12 77 K3
Wolfington Rd WNWD SE27 149 H3
Wolfram Cl LEW SE13 133 H4
Wolftencroft Cl BTSEA SW11 128 D2
Wollaston Cl STHWK SE1 18 D5
Wolmer Cl EDGW HA8 36 C3
Wolmer Gdns EDGW HA8 36 C2
Wolseley Av
WAND/EARL SW18 146 E1
Wolseley Gdns CHSWK W4 105 J5
Wolseley Rd CEND/HSY/T N8 54 D5
CHSWK W4 105 K3
FSTGT E7 77 F6
KTN/HRWW/WS HA3 48 E2
MTCM CR4 163 F6
ROMW/RG RM7 63 F6
WDGN N22 41 F7
Wolseley St STHWK SE1 19 M2
Wolsey Av EHAM E6 96 A2
THDIT KT7 158 A4
WALTH E17 57 H2
Wolsey Cl HSLW TW3 123 H3
KUTN/CMB KT2 144 D7
NWDGN UB2 103 H2
RYNPK SW20 145 K6
WPK KT4 173 J3
Wolsey Ct ELTH/MOT SE9 * 134 E5
Wolsey Crs CROY/NA CR0 180 A7
MRDN SM4 161 J6
Wolsey Dr KUTN/CMB KT2 144 A4
WOT/HER KT12 156 C7
Wolsey Gv EDGW HA8 37 F6
ESH/CLAY KT10 170 B3
Wolsey Ms KTTN NW5 72 C5
Wolsey Rd E/WMO/HCT KT8 157 J3
EN EN1 30 D1
ESH/CLAY KT10 170 B3
HPTN TW12 142 B5
IS N1 73 K4
NTHWD HA6 32 A1
SUN TW16 140 D6
Wolsey St WCHPL E1 92 E4
Wolsey Wy CHSGTN KT9 172 C4
Wolsley Cl DART DA1 138 B4
Wolstonbury
NFNCH/WDSPK N12 38 E4
Wolvercote Rd ABYW SE2 116 E1
Wolverley St BETH E2 * 92 D2
Wolverton Av
KUTN/CMB KT2 144 C7
Wolverton Gdns EA W5 86 B6
HMSMTH W6 107 G3
Wolverton Rd STAN HA7 35 H5
Wolverton Wy
STHGT/OAK N14 28 C4
Wolves La WDGN N22 41 G6
Womersley Rd
CEND/HSY/T N8 55 F5
Wonersh Wy BELMT SM2 174 B7
Wonford Cl KUTN/CMB KT2 145 G7
Wontner Cl IS N1 6 E2
Wontner Rd BAL SW12 147 K1
Woodall Cl CHSGTN KT9 171 J6
Woodall Rd PEND EN3 31 F4
Woodbank Rd BMLY BR1 152 D2
Woodbastwick Rd SYD SE26 151 F5
Woodberry Av
RYLN/HDSTN HA2 48 C3
WCHMH N21 41 G1
Woodberry Cl MLHL NW7 38 B6
SUN TW16 140 E5
Woodberry Crs MUSWH N10 54 B2
Woodberry Down FSBYPK N4 55 J7
Woodberry Gdns
NFNCH/WDSPK N12 39 G5
Woodberry Gv FSBYPK N4 55 J6
NFNCH/WDSPK N12 39 G5
Woodberry Wy
NFNCH/WDSPK N12 39 G5
Woodbine Cl WHTN TW2 142 D1
Woodbine Gv PGE/AN SE20 150 D6
Woodbine La WPK KT4 173 K2
Woodbine Pl WAN E11 58 E5
Woodbine Rd BFN/LL DA15 135 K7
Woodbines Av KUT/HW KT1 158 E2
Woodbine Ter HOM E9 74 E5
Woodborough Rd
PUT/ROE SW15 126 E3
Woodbourne Av
STRHM/NOR SW16 148 D2
Woodbourne Dr
ESH/CLAY KT10 171 F5
Woodbourne Gdns
WLGTN SM6 176 B6
Woodbridge Cl HOLWY N7 73 F1
Woodbridge Rd BARK IG11 79 F4
Woodbridge St CLKNW EC1R 6 C9
Woodbrook Rd ABYW SE2 116 B5
Woodburn Cl HDN NW4 52 B4
Woodbury Cl CROY/NA CR0 178 B1
WAN E11 59 F3
Woodbury Gdns
LEE/GVPK SE12 153 F2
Woodbury Park Rd WEA W13 85 H3
Woodbury Rd WALTH E17 57 K3
Woodbury St TOOT SW17 147 J4
Woodchester Sq BAY/PAD W2 8 C2
Woodchurch Cl SCUP DA14 154 D2
Woodchurch Dr BMLY BR1 153 H6
Woodchurch Rd
KIL/WHAMP NW6 2 B2
Wood Cl BETH E2 92 C3
CDALE/KGS NW9 51 F6
HRW HA1 48 D6
Woodclyffe Dr CHST BR7 169 F1
Woodcock Dell Av
KTN/HRWW/WS HA3 49 J6
Woodcock Hl
KTN/HRWW/WS HA3 49 J5
Woodcocks CAN/RD E16 95 G4
Woodcombe Crs FSTH SE23 131 K7
Woodcot Cl PEND EN3 30 E5
Woodcote Av HCH RM12 81 J3
MLHL NW7 38 A5
THHTH CR7 164 C3
WLGTN SM6 176 B7
Woodcote Cl KUTN/CMB KT2 144 B4
Woodcote Dr ORP BR6 169 J6
Woodcote Gn WLGTN SM6 176 C7
Woodcote Ms WLGTN SM6 176 B5
Woodcote Pl WNWD SE27 * 149 H4
Woodcote Rd WAN E11 58 E6
WLGTN SM6 176 B5
Wood Crest BELMT SM2 * 175 G6
Woodcroft ELTH/MOT SE9 153 K2
GFD/PVL UB6 67 G5
WCHMH N21 29 F7
Woodcroft Av MLHL NW7 37 G6
STAN HA7 35 G7
Woodcroft Ms DEPT SE8 112 B3
Woodcroft Rd THHTH CR7 164 C4
Wood Dene PECK SE15 * 111 J7
Wood Dr CHST BR7 153 J5
Wooden Bridge Ter
WNWD SE27 * 149 H2
Wood End HYS/HAR UB3 82 C5
Woodend ESH/CLAY KT10 170 C1
NRWD SE19 149 J5
SUT SM1 175 G1
Wood End Av
RYLN/HDSTN HA2 66 B3
Wood End Cl NTHLT UB5 66 D4
Woodend Gdns ENC/FH EN2 28 E3
Wood End Gdns NTHLT UB5 66 C4
Wood End Gn YEAD UB4 82 D4
Wood End Green Rd
HYS/HAR UB3 * 82 A5
Wood End La NTHLT UB5 66 B5
Wood End Rd HRW HA1 66 D3
Woodend Rd WALTH E17 58 A1
The Wood End WLGTN SM6 176 B7
Wood End Wy NTHLT UB5 66 C4
Wooder Gdns FSTGT E7 76 D3
Wooderson Cl SNWD SE25 165 F3
Woodfall Av BAR EN5 26 D4
Woodfall Dr DART DA1 138 C3
Woodfall Rd FSBYPK N4 55 G7
Woodfall St CHEL SW3 15 L8
Woodfarrs CMBW SE5 130 E3
Wood Fld HAMP NW3 * 71 K4
Woodfield Av ALP/SUD HA0 67 J2
CAR SM5 176 A5
CDALE/KGS NW9 51 G3
EA W5 85 J3
NTHWD HA6 32 C3
STRHM/NOR SW16 148 D2
Woodfield Cl EN EN1 30 A3
NRWD SE19 149 J6
Woodfield Crs EA W5 85 K3
Woodfield Dr EBAR EN4 28 A7
GPK RM2 63 J3
Woodfield Gdns NWMAL KT3 160 C4
Woodfield Gv
STRHM/NOR SW16 148 D2
Woodfield La
STRHM/NOR SW16 148 D2
Woodfield Pl MV/WKIL W9 88 D4
Woodfield Ri BUSH WD23 22 D6
Woodfield Rd EA W5 85 J3
HSLWW TW4 122 A1
MV/WKIL W9 88 D4
THDIT KT7 171 F1
Woodfields WATW WD18 * 21 G3
Woodfield Wy
FBAR/BDGN N11 40 D6
Woodford Av
GNTH/NBYPK IG2 59 K4
Woodford Bridge Rd
REDBR IG4 59 H2
Woodford Crs PIN HA5 47 F1
Woodford New Rd
WALTH E17 58 C2
Woodford Pl WBLY HA9 50 A7
Woodford Rd FSTGT E7 77 F3
SWFD E18 58 E3
WAT WD17 21 F1
Woodgate Av CHSGTN KT9 171 K4
Woodgate Crs NTHWD HA6 32 E5
Woodgate Dr
STRHM/NOR SW16 148 D6
Woodger Rd SHB W12 107 F1
Woodget Cl EHAM E6 95 J5
Woodgrange Av EA W5 86 B7
EN EN1 30 C5
KTN/HRWW/WS HA3 49 J4
NFNCH/WDSPK N12 39 H5
Woodgrange Cl
KTN/HRWW/WS HA3 49 K4
Woodgrange Gdns EN EN1 30 C5
Woodgrange Rd FSTGT E7 76 E4
Woodgrange Ter EN EN1 * 30 C5
Woodhall Av DUL SE21 150 B2
PIN HA5 33 J7
Woodhall Dr DUL SE21 150 B2
PIN HA5 33 H7
Woodhall Ga PIN HA5 33 H6
Woodhall La OXHEY WD19 33 H2
Woodham Ct SWFD E18 58 D3
Woodham Rd CAT SE6 152 A2
Woodhatch Cl EHAM E6 95 J4
Woodhaven Gdns
BARK/HLT IG6 60 C3
Woodhayes Rd
WIM/MER SW19 146 A5
Woodheyes Rd WLSDN NW10 69 G4
Woodhill WOOL/PLUM SE18 114 D3
Woodhill Crs
KTN/HRWW/WS HA3 49 K5
Woodhouse Av GFD/PVL UB6 85 F1
Woodhouse Cl EDUL SE22 131 H3
GFD/PVL UB6 85 F1
HYS/HAR UB3 101 H2
Woodhouse Eaves
NTHWD HA6 32 E4
Woodhouse Gv FSTGT E7 77 J5
Woodhouse Rd
NFNCH/WDSPK N12 39 G5
WAN E11 76 D2
Woodhurst Av
STMC/STPC BR5 169 H5
Woodhurst Rd ABYW SE2 116 B4
ACT W3 86 E7
Woodies La NWMAL KT3 160 A5
Woodington Cl ELTH/MOT SE9 135 F5
Woodknoll Dr CHST BR7 153 K7
Woodland Ap GFD/PVL UB6 67 G5
Woodland Av MNPK E12 77 J2
Woodland Cl CDALE/KGS NW9 50 E5
HOR/WEW KT19 * 173 G5
NRWD SE19 150 A5
WFD IG8 45 F2
Woodland Ct GLDGN NW11 * 52 C4
Woodland Crs
BERM/RHTH SE16 112 A1
GNWCH SE10 113 H5
Woodland Gdns ISLW TW7 123 K2
MUSWH N10 54 B4
Woodland Gv CROY/NA CR0 177 G6
GNWCH SE10 113 H4
Woodland Hl NRWD SE19 150 A5
Woodland Ms
STRHM/NOR SW16 148 E2
Woodland Ri GFD/PVL UB6 67 G5
MUSWH N10 54 B3
Woodland Rd
FBAR/BDGN N11 40 B4
NRWD SE19 150 A4
THHTH CR7 164 B3
Woodlands BXLYHS DA6 137 J4
GLDGN NW11 52 C4
RYLN/HDSTN HA2 48 A3
RYNPK SW20 161 F3
Woodlands Av ACT W3 86 D7
BFN/LL DA15 135 K7
CHDH RM6 62 A5
FNCH N3 39 G6
NWMAL KT3 145 F7
RSLP HA4 47 G7
WAN E11 59 F7
WPK KT4 173 H1
Woodlands Cl BMLY BR1 168 E1
BORE WD6 24 D3
ESH/CLAY KT10 171 F6
GLDGN NW11 52 C4
Woodlands Dr STAN HA7 35 F5
SUN TW16 156 B1
Woodlands Gdns
WALTH E17 * 58 C3
Woodlands Gv ISLW TW7 123 K1
Woodlands Pde ASHF TW15 140 A5
Woodlands Park Rd
GNWCH SE10 113 H5
SEVS/STOTM N15 55 J4
Woodlands Rd BARN SW13 126 C2
BMLY BR1 168 E1
BUSH WD23 21 J3
BXLYHN DA7 137 F2
ED N9 30 E7
HRW HA1 49 F4
IL IG1 78 C2
ISLW TW7 123 K2
ROM RM1 63 H2
STHL UB1 83 H7
SURB KT6 158 E6
WALTH E17 58 A2
WAN E11 76 C1
Woodlands St LEW SE13 133 G6
The Woodlands
BRXN/ST SW9 * 110 C6
ESH/CLAY KT10 170 C1
HRW HA1 * 66 E1
ISLW TW7 124 A1
LEW SE13 133 G6
NRWD SE19 149 J6
STAN HA7 * 35 H4
STHGT/OAK N14 28 B7
WLGTN SM6 176 B7
Woodland St HACK E8 * 74 B5
Woodlands Wy
PUT/ROE SW15 127 J4
Woodland Ter CHARL SE7 114 D3
Woodland Wk HAMP NW3 71 J4
HOR/WEW KT19 172 C5
Woodland Wy ABYW SE2 116 E3
BRYLDS KT5 172 D1
CROY/NA CR0 166 B7
MLHL NW7 37 G5
MRDN SM4 161 J3
MTCM CR4 148 A6
STMC/STPC BR5 169 H3
WCHMH N21 41 G1
WFD IG8 45 F2
WWKM BR4 180 A2
Wood La BCTR RM8 80 C1
CDALE/KGS NW9 51 F6
DAGW RM9 80 A2
HCH RM12 81 J4
HGT N6 54 B5
ISLW TW7 103 K5
MUSWH N10 54 C4
RSLP HA4 64 B1
SHB W12 88 A6
STAN HA7 35 H2
WFD IG8 44 D4
Woodlawn Cl PUT/ROE SW15 127 J4
Woodlawn Crs WHTN TW2 142 B1
Woodlawn Dr FELT TW13 141 H1
Woodlawn Rd FUL/PGN SW6 107 G6
Woodlea Dr HAYES BR2 167 H4
Woodlea Gv NTHWD HA6 32 A5
Woodlea Rd STNW/STAM N16 74 A2
Woodleigh Av
NFNCH/WDSPK N12 39 J5

Woodleigh Gdns
STRHM/NOR SW16 148 E2
Woodley Cl TOOT SW17 147 K6
Woodley La SUT SM1 175 J2
Wood Lodge Gdns BMLY BR1 153 J6
Wood Lodge La WWKM BR4 180 A2
Woodman Ms RCH/KEW TW9 105 J7
Woodmans Gv WLSDN NW10 69 H4
Woodmansterne Rd CAR SM5 175 J7
STRHM/NOR SW16 148 C6
Woodman St CAN/RD E16 96 A7
Wood Md TOTM N17 * 42 C5
Woodmere ELTH/MOT SE9 134 E6
Woodmere Av CROY/NA CR0 166 A6
Woodmere Cl BTSEA SW11 129 F2
CROY/NA CR0 166 A6
Woodmere Gdns
CROY/NA CR0 166 A6
Woodmere Wy BECK BR3 167 G4
Woodmill Rd CLPT E5 74 E1
Woodnook Rd
STRHM/NOR SW16 148 B4
Woodpecker Cl BUSH WD23 22 C7
ED N9 30 D5
KTN/HRWW/WS HA3 35 F7
Woodpecker Ms LEW SE13 133 G3
Woodpecker Mt
CROY/NA CR0 179 G7
Woodpecker Rd THMD SE28 97 J6
Woodquest Av HNHL SE24 130 C4
Wood Ride STMC/STPC BR5 169 J3
Woodridge Wy NTHWD HA6 32 C5
Woodridings Av PIN HA5 33 K7
Woodridings Cl PIN HA5 33 K6
Woodriffe Rd WAN E11 58 B6
Wood Ri PIN HA5 46 E4
Wood Rd WLSDN NW10 68 E6
Woodrow WOOL/PLUM SE18 114 D3
Woodrow Av YEAD UB4 82 D4
Woodrow Cl GFD/PVL UB6 67 H6
Woodrow Ct TOTM N17 42 D6
Woodrush Cl NWCR SE14 112 B6
Woodrush Wy CHDH RM6 61 K3
Woodseer St WCHPL E1 13 M2
Woodsford Sq WKENS W14 107 H1
Woodshire Rd DAGE RM10 80 D2
Woodshots Meadow
WATW WD18 20 B4
Woodside BKHH IG9 45 G1
BORE WD6 24 B3
GLDGN NW11 52 E4
WIM/MER SW19 146 D4
Woodside Av ALP/SUD HA0 68 A7
CHST BR7 154 C4
ESH/CLAY KT10 157 K6
HGT N6 53 K4
NFNCH/WDSPK N12 39 G3
SNWD SE25 165 J5
Woodside Cl ALP/SUD HA0 68 A7
BRYLDS KT5 159 K6
BXLYHN DA7 138 A3
RSLP HA4 46 B5
STAN HA7 35 G4
Woodside Ct EA W5 * 86 A7
Woodside Court Rd
CROY/NA CR0 165 H6
Woodside Crs BFN/LL DA15 154 E2
Woodside End ALP/SUD HA0 68 A7
Woodside Gdns CHING E4 43 K4
TOTM N17 56 B1
Woodside Grange Rd
NFNCH/WDSPK N12 39 F3
Woodside Gn SNWD SE25 165 H5
Woodside Gv
NFNCH/WDSPK N12 39 G2
Woodside La BXLY DA5 136 E5
TRDG/WHET N20 39 F2
Woodside Pde BFN/LL DA15 * 154 E2
Woodside Pk SNWD SE25 165 H5
Woodside Park Av WALTH E17 58 B3
Woodside Park Rd
NFNCH/WDSPK N12 39 F3
Woodside Pl ALP/SUD HA0 68 A7
Woodside Rd BFN/LL DA15 154 E2
BMLY BR1 168 D4
BXLYHN DA7 138 A3
KUTN/CMB KT2 144 A6
NTHWD HA6 32 D6
NWMAL KT3 160 A1
PLSTW E13 95 G3
SNWD SE25 165 J5
SUT SM1 175 G2
WDGN N22 41 G6
WFD IG8 44 E3
Woodside Wy CROY/NA CR0 165 K5
MTCM CR4 148 B7
Wood's Ms MYFR/PKLN W1K 9 M6
Woodsome Rd KTTN NW5 72 A2
Wood's Pl STHWK SE1 19 K4
Woodspring Rd
WIM/MER SW19 146 C1
Wood's Rd PECK SE15 111 J7
Woodstead Gv EDGW HA8 36 A5
The Woods NTHWD HA6 32 E4
Woodstock Av CHEAM SM3 161 J6
GLDGN NW11 52 C6
ISLW TW7 124 B4
STHL UB1 83 K2
WEA W13 104 B2
Woodstock Cl BXLY DA5 137 G7
STAN HA7 50 A1
Woodstock Crs ED N9 30 D5
Woodstock Gdns BECK BR3 151 K7
GDMY/SEVK IG3 79 G1
YEAD UB4 82 D4
Woodstock Gra EA W5 * 86 A7
Woodstock Gv SHB W12 107 G1
Woodstock La North
SURB KT6 171 J1
Woodstock La South
ESH/CLAY KT10 171 H4
Woodstock Ms
CAVSQ/HST W1G 10 B3
Woodstock Ri CHEAM SM3 161 J7
Woodstock Rd ALP/SUD HA0 68 B6
BUSH WD23 22 E6
CAR SM5 176 A4
CHSWK W4 106 B3
CROY/NA CR0 177 K2
FSBYPK N4 55 G7
FSTGT E7 77 G6
GLDGN NW11 52 D6
WALTH E17 58 B1
Woodstock St CAN/RD E16 94 D5
OXSTW W1C 10 C5
Woodstock Ter POP/IOD E14 93 K6
Woodstock Wy MTCM CR4 163 H1
Woodstone Av EW KT17 173 J4
Wood St BAR EN5 26 A3
BARB EC2Y 12 F3
CAN/RD E16 95 F6
CHSWK W4 106 B4
CITYW EC2V 12 F4
KUT/HW KT1 143 K7
MTCM CR4 163 F6
WALTH E17 58 A2
Woodsyre SYD SE26 150 B3
Wood Ter CRICK NW2 * 69 H1
Woodthorpe Rd
PUT/ROE SW15 126 E3
Woodtree Cl HDN NW4 52 A1
Wood V FSTH SE23 131 J7
MUSWH N10 54 C4
Woodvale Av SNWD SE25 165 G2
Woodvale Wy GLDGN NW11 70 B2
Woodview Av CHING E4 44 A3
Woodview Cl PUT/ROE SW15 145 F3
Woodville Cl LEE/GVPK SE12 133 K4
TEDD TW11 143 G3
Woodville Court Ms
WAT WD17 * 20 E1
Woodville Gdns BARK/HLT IG6 60 B5
EA W5 86 A5
RSLP HA4 46 A6
SURB KT6 * 158 E6
Woodville Gv WELL DA16 * 136 B2
Woodville Rd BAR EN5 27 F2
EA W5 86 A5
GLDGN NW11 52 C6
KIL/WHAMP NW6 * 88 D1
MRDN SM4 161 K3
RCHPK/HAM TW10 143 H2
STNW/STAM N16 74 A4
SWFD E18 59 F1
THHTH CR7 164 E2
WALTH E17 57 G3
WAN E11 58 D7
Woodville St
WOOL/PLUM SE18 114 D3
Woodward Av HDN NW4 51 J4
Woodward Cl ESH/CLAY KT10 171 F5
Woodwarde Rd EDUL SE22 131 F5
Woodward Gdns DAGW RM9 79 J6
STAN HA7 35 F6
Woodward Rd DAGW RM9 79 H6
Woodway Crs HRW HA1 49 G5
Woodwaye OXHEY WD19 21 G6
Woodwell St
WAND/EARL SW18 128 B4
Wood Whf GNWCH SE10 112 E5
Woodyard Cl KTTN NW5 72 A4
Woodyard La DUL SE21 131 F6
Woodyates Rd
LEE/GVPK SE12 133 K5
Woolacombe Rd
BKHTH/KID SE3 134 B1
Woolacombe Wy
HYS/HAR UB3 101 H3
Woolbrook Rd DART DA1 138 B5
Wooler St WALW SE17 19 G8
Woolf Cl THMD SE28 97 H7
Woolf Ms STPAN WC1H 5 J9
Woollaston Rd FSBYPK N4 55 H5
Woollett Cl DART DA1 138 D3
Woolmead Av
CDALE/KGS NW9 51 J6
Woolmerdine Ct BUSH WD23 21 H2
Woolmer Gdns UED N18 42 C5
Woolmer Rd UED N18 42 C4
Woolmore St POP/IOD E14 94 A6
Woolneigh St FUL/PGN SW6 128 A2
Woolridge Cl
EBED/NFELT TW14 121 F7
Woolridge Wy HOM E9 * 74 E6
Wool Rd RYNPK SW20 145 K5
Woolstaplers Wy
BERM/RHTH SE16 111 H2
Woolston Cl WALTH E17 57 F1
Woolstone Rd FSTH SE23 151 G1
Woolwich Church St
WOOL/PLUM SE18 114 D2
Woolwich Common
WOOL/PLUM SE18 115 F5
Woolwich Foot Tnl
CAN/RD E16 115 F1
Woolwich High St
WOOL/PLUM SE18 115 F2
Woolwich Manorway
CAN/RD E16 115 G1
Woolwich Manor Wy
EHAM E6 95 K3
Woolwich New Rd
WOOL/PLUM SE18 115 F4
Woolwich Rd ABYW SE2 116 E5
BXLYHN DA7 137 H2
CHARL SE7 114 B3
GNWCH SE10 113 K4
Wooster Gdns POP/IOD E14 94 B5
Wootton Gv FNCH N3 38 E7
Wootton St STHWK SE1 18 B1
Worbeck Rd PGE/AN SE20 165 J1
Worcester Av TOTM N17 42 C6
Worcester Cl CRICK NW2 69 J2
CROY/NA CR0 179 H1
MTCM CR4 163 F1
Worcester Crs MLHL NW7 37 G2
WFD IG8 45 G3
Worcester Dr CHSWK W4 106 B2
Worcester Gdns GFD/PVL UB6 66 C5
IL IG1 59 J6
WPK KT4 173 G2
Worcester Ms
KIL/WHAMP NW6 71 F5
Worcester Park Rd WPK KT4 172 E2
Worcester Rd BELMT SM2 174 E6
MNPK E12 77 K2
WALTH E17 57 F1
WIM/MER SW19 146 D4
Wordsworth Av GFD/PVL UB6 84 D1
MNPK E12 77 J6
SWFD E18 58 D2
Wordsworth Dr CHEAM SM3 174 A3
Wordsworth Gdns BORE WD6 24 C4
Wordsworth Pde
CEND/HSY/T N8 * 55 H3
Wordsworth Pl HAMP NW3 71 K4
Wordsworth Rd HPTN TW12 141 K3
PGE/AN SE20 151 F6
STHWK SE1 19 L6
STNW/STAM N16 74 A3
WELL DA16 115 K7
WLGTN SM6 176 C5
Wordsworth Wk
GLDGN NW11 52 D3
Wordsworth Wy DART DA1 139 K3
WDR/YW UB7 100 B3
Worfield St BTSEA SW11 108 D6
Worgan St BERM/RHTH SE16 112 A2
LBTH SE11 17 L7
Worland Rd SRTFD E15 76 C6
Worlds End Est
WBPTN SW10 * 108 C6
World's End La WCHMH N21 29 F4
Worlds End Pas
WBPTN SW10 * 108 C6
Worlidge St HMSMTH W6 107 F4
Worlingham Rd EDUL SE22 131 G3
Wormholt Rd SHB W12 87 J7
Wormholt Ter SHB W12 * 87 J7
Wormwood St OBST EC2N 13 J4
Wornington Rd NKENS W10 88 C4
Woronzow Rd STJWD NW8 3 H4
Worple Av ISLW TW7 124 B4
WIM/MER SW19 146 B6
Worple Cl RYLN/HDSTN HA2 47 K7
Worple Rd ISLW TW7 124 B3
RYNPK SW20 161 F1
WIM/MER SW19 146 C6
Worple Road Ms
WIM/MER SW19 146 D5
Worple St MORT/ESHN SW14 126 A2
Worple Wy RCHPK/HAM TW10 125 F4
RYLN/HDSTN HA2 47 K7
Worship St SDTCH EC2A 13 H1
Worslade Rd TOOT SW17 147 H3
Worsley Bridge Rd SYD SE26 151 H4
Worsley Gv CLPT E5 74 C3
Worsley Rd WAN E11 76 C3
Worsopp Dr CLAP SW4 129 H4
Worthfield Cl HOR/WEW KT19 173 F6
Worth Gv WALW SE17 19 G8
Worthing Cl SRTFD E15 76 C7
Worthing Rd HEST TW5 102 E5
Worthington Cl MTCM CR4 163 G3
Worthington Rd SURB KT6 159 G7
Wortley Rd CROY/NA CR0 164 B6
EHAM E6 77 H6
Worton Gdns ISLW TW7 123 J1
Worton Rd ISLW TW7 124 A2
Worton Wy ISLW TW7 123 J1
Wotton Rd CRICK NW2 70 A3
DEPT SE8 112 C5
Wouldham Rd CAN/RD E16 94 D5
Wragby Rd WAN E11 * 76 C2
Wrampling Pl ED N9 30 C7
Wray Av CLAY IG5 60 A2
Wray Crs FSBYPK N4 72 E1
Wrayfield Rd CHEAM SM3 174 B2
Wray Rd BELMT SM2 174 D7
Wraysbury Cl HSLWW TW4 122 D4
Wrays Wy YEAD UB4 82 C4
Wrekin Rd WOOL/PLUM SE18 115 H6
Wren Av CRICK NW2 70 A3
NWDGN UB2 102 E3
Wren Cl CAN/RD E16 94 D5
ED N9 31 F7
Wren Crs BUSH WD23 22 C7
Wren Dr WDR/YW UB7 100 A1
Wren Gdns DAGW RM9 79 K4
HCH RM12 63 H7
Wren La RSLP HA4 47 F5
Wren Ms LEW SE13 * 133 H3
Wren Rd CMBW SE5 110 E7
DAGW RM9 79 K4
SCUP DA14 155 J2
Wren's Av ASHF TW15 140 A4
Wren St FSBYW WC1X 5 M9
Wrentham Av WLSDN NW10 88 B1
Wrenthorpe Rd BMLY BR1 152 C3
Wrenwood Wy PIN HA5 47 F3
Wrexham Rd BOW E3 93 J1
Wricklemarsh Rd
BKHTH/KID SE3 134 A1
Wrigglesworth St NWCR SE14 112 A6
Wright Cl LEW SE13 133 G3
Wright Rd HEST TW5 102 B6
Wrights Cl DAGE RM10 80 D3
Wrights La KENS W8 * 14 B3
Wright's La KENS W8 14 C3
Wrights Pl WLSDN NW10 * 68 E5
Wrights Rd SNWD SE25 165 F2
Wright's Rd BOW E3 93 H1
Wright's Rw WLGTN SM6 176 B3
Wrigley Cl CHING E4 * 44 B4
Wrotham Rd BAR EN5 26 C1
CAMTN NW1 4 F2
WEA W13 85 J7
WELL DA16 116 D7
Wrottesley Rd WLSDN NW10 87 J1
WOOL/PLUM SE18 115 H5
Wroughton Rd BTSEA SW11 128 E5
Wroughton Ter HDN NW4 * 51 K3
Wroxall Rd DAGW RM9 79 J5
Wroxham Gdns
FBAR/BDGN N11 40 C6
Wroxham Rd THMD SE28 97 K6
Wroxton Rd PECK SE15 131 J1
Wrythe Gn CAR SM5 175 K2
Wrythe Green Rd CAR SM5 175 K2
Wrythe La CAR SM5 162 C7
Wulfstan St SHB W12 87 H5
Wyatt Cl BUSH WD23 22 E6
FELT TW13 122 C7
YEAD UB4 82 E4
Wyatt Dr BARN SW13 106 E5
Wyatt Park Rd
BRXS/STRHM SW2 149 F1
Wyatt Rd DART DA1 138 C2
FSTGT E7 76 E5
HBRY N5 73 J2
Wyatt's La WALTH E17 58 A2
Wybert St CAMTN NW1 4 D9
Wyborne Wy WLSDN NW10 68 E6
Wyburn Av BAR EN5 26 D2
Wychcombe Studios
HAMP NW3 * 71 K5
Wyche Gv SAND/SEL CR2 177 J6
Wych Elm Cl KUTN/CMB KT2 144 B6
Wycherley Cl BKHTH/KID SE3 113 J6
Wycherley Crs BAR EN5 27 F5
Wychwood Av EDGW HA8 35 K5
THHTH CR7 164 C2
Wychwood Cl EDGW HA8 35 K5
SUN TW16 140 E5
Wychwood End HGT N6 54 C6
Wychwood Gdns CLAY IG5 59 K3
Wychwood Wy NTHWD HA6 32 D6
Wycliffe Cl WELL DA16 116 A7
Wycliffe Rd BTSEA SW11 129 F1
WIM/MER SW19 147 F5
Wyclif St FSBYE EC1V 6 C8
Wycombe Gdns GLDGN NW11 70 D1
Wycombe Pl
WAND/EARL SW18 128 B5
Wycombe Rd ALP/SUD HA0 68 C7
GNTH/NBYPK IG2 59 K4
TOTM N17 42 C7
Wycombe Sq KENS W8 8 A9
Wydell Cl MRDN SM4 161 F5
Wydenhurst Rd CROY/NA CR0 165 H6
Wydeville Manor Rd
LEE/GVPK SE12 153 F3
Wye Cl RSLP HA4 46 A5
Wyemead Crs CHING E4 44 C1
Wye St BTSEA SW11 128 C2
Wyevale Cl NTHWD HA6 46 E2
Wyfold Rd FUL/PGN SW6 107 H7
Wyke Cl ISLW TW7 104 A5
Wyke Gdns HNWL W7 104 A2
Wykeham Av DAGW RM9 79 J5
Wykeham Cl WDR/YW UB7 100 D5
Wykeham Gn DAGW RM9 79 J5
Wykeham Hl WBLY HA9 50 B7
Wykeham Ri TRDG/WHET N20 26 C7
Wykeham Rd HDN NW4 52 A4
KTN/HRWW/WS HA3 49 H3
Wyke Rd BOW E3 75 J6
RYNPK SW20 161 F1
Wylchin Cl PIN HA5 46 D3
Wyldes Cl GLDGN NW11 53 G7
Wyldfield Gdns ED N9 42 B1
Wyld Wy WBLY HA9 68 D5
Wyleu St FSTH SE23 132 B6
Wylie Rd NWDGN UB2 103 F2
Wyllen Cl WCHPL E1 92 E3
Wylo Dr BAR EN5 25 H5
Wymark Cl RAIN RM13 99 H1
Wymering Rd MV/WKIL W9 2 B8
Wymond St PUT/ROE SW15 127 F2
Wynan Rd POP/IOD E14 112 E4
Wynaud Ct WDGN N22 41 F5
Wyncham Av BFN/LL DA15 135 K7
Wynchgate
KTN/HRWW/WS HA3 34 E6
STHGT/OAK N14 28 E6
Wyncote Wy SAND/SEL CR2 179 F7
Wyncroft Cl BMLY BR1 168 E2
Wyndale Av CDALE/KGS NW9 50 C5
Wyndcliff Rd CHARL SE7 114 A5
Wyndcroft Cl ENC/FH EN2 29 H2
Wyndham Cl BELMT SM2 174 E6
ORP BR6 169 H7
Wyndham Crs HSLWW TW4 122 E5
KTTN NW5 72 C2
Wyndham Est CMBW SE5 110 D6
Wyndham Ms MBLAR W1H 9 L3
Wyndham Pl MBLAR W1H 9 L3
Wyndham Rd CMBW SE5 110 D6
EBAR EN4 27 K7
EHAM E6 77 H6
KUTN/CMB KT2 144 B6
WEA W13 104 C2
Wyndham St CAMTN NW1 9 L2
Wyndham Yd MBLAR W1H * 9 L3
Wyndhurst Cl SAND/SEL CR2 177 H6
Wyneham Rd HNHL SE24 130 E4
Wynell Rd FSTH SE23 151 F2
Wynford Pl BELV DA17 117 H5
Wynford Rd IS N1 5 L5
Wynford Wy ELTH/MOT SE9 153 K2
Wynlie Gdns PIN HA5 47 F1
Wynn Bridge Cl WFD IG8 45 H7
Wynndale Rd SWFD E18 45 F7
Wynne Rd BRXN/ST SW9 130 B1
Wynn's Av BFN/LL DA15 136 B4
Wynnstay Gdns KENS W8 14 B3
Wynter St BTSEA SW11 128 B3
Wynton Gdns SNWD SE25 165 F4
Wynton Pl ACT W3 86 D5
Wynyard Ter LBTH SE11 17 M7
Wynyatt St FSBYE EC1V 6 C7
Wyre Gv EDGW HA8 36 D2
HYS/HAR UB3 101 K3
Wyresdale Crs GFD/PVL UB6 85 F2
Wyteleaf Cl RSLP HA4 46 A5
Wythburn Pl MBLAR W1H 9 L5
Wythenshawe Rd DAGE RM10 80 C2
Wythes Cl BMLY BR1 168 E1
Wythes Rd CAN/RD E16 95 J7
Wythfield Rd ELTH/MOT SE9 134 E5
Wyvenhoe Rd
RYLN/HDSTN HA2 66 C2
Wyvern Cl DART DA1 139 F6
Wyvern Est NWMAL KT3 * 160 D2
Wyvil Rd VX/NE SW8 109 K6
Wyvis St POP/IOD E14 93 K4

Y

Yabsley St POP/IOD E14 94 A7
Yalding Rd BERM/RHTH SE16 111 H2
Yale Cl HSLWW TW4 122 E4
Yale Wy HCH RM12 81 J3
Yarborough Rd
WIM/MER SW19 147 H7
Yardley Cl CHING E4 31 K4
Yardley La CHING E4 31 K4
Yardley St FSBYW WC1X 6 A8
Yarmouth Crs TOTM N17 56 D4
Yarmouth Pl MYFR/PICC W1J 10 C9
Yarnton Wy ABYW SE2 116 D1
ERITHM DA18 117 F1
Yarrow Crs EHAM E6 95 J4
Yateley St WOOL/PLUM SE18 114 C2
Yeading Av RYLN/HDSTN HA2 65 J1
Yeading Fk YEAD UB4 83 G4
Yeading Gdns YEAD UB4 83 F4
Yeading La YEAD UB4 83 F5
Yeames Cl WEA W13 85 G5
Yeate St IS N1 7 G2
Yeatman Rd HGT N6 53 K5
Yeats Cl HNWL W7 85 F6
LEW SE13 * 133 G1
WLSDN NW10 69 G5
Ye Cnr OXHEY WD19 21 H5
Yeend Cl E/WMO/HCT KT8 157 F3
Yeldham Rd HMSMTH W6 107 G4
Yeldham Vls HMSMTH W6 * 107 G4
Yelverton Rd BTSEA SW11 128 C1
Yenston Cl MRDN SM4 161 K5
Yeoman Cl EHAM E6 96 B6
Yeoman Dr STWL/WRAY TW19 120 B7
Yeoman Rd NTHLT UB5 65 J6
Yeomans Acre RSLP HA4 46 E5
Yeoman's Rw CHEL SW3 15 K4
Yeoman St BERM/RHTH SE16 112 B3
Yeomans Wy PEND EN3 * 30 D1
Yeoman's Yd WCHPL E1 13 M6
Yeo St BOW E3 93 K4
Yeovilton Pl KUTN/CMB KT2 143 K4
Yerbury Rd ARCH N19 72 D2
Yester Dr CHST BR7 153 J6
Yester Pk CHST BR7 153 K6
Yester Rd CHST BR7 153 K6
Yew Cl BKHH IG9 45 H1
Yewdale Cl BMLY BR1 152 C5
Yewfield Rd WLSDN NW10 69 H5
Yew Gv CRICK NW2 70 B3
Yew Tree Cl LEW SE13 133 F2
Yewtree Cl MUSWH N10 40 C7
RYLN/HDSTN HA2 48 B3
Yew Tree Cl WCHMH N21 29 G6
WELL DA16 116 B7
WPK KT4 160 B7
Yew Tree Ct BORE WD6 23 K5
Yew Tree Gdns CHDH RM6 62 A4
ROMW/RG RM7 63 F4
Yew Tree Rd BECK BR3 166 C2
SHB W12 87 H6
Yew Tree Wk HSLWW TW4 122 E4
Yew Wk HRW HA1 48 E7
Yoakley Rd STNW/STAM N16 74 A1
Yoke Cl HOLWY N7 72 E5
Yolande Gdns ELTH/MOT SE9 134 D4
Yonge Pk HOLWY N7 73 G2
York Av BFN/LL DA15 154 E1
HNWL W7 84 E7
HYS/HAR UB3 82 A5
MORT/ESHN SW14 125 K4
STAN HA7 35 H7
York Br CAMTN NW1 4 A9
York Blds CHCR WC2N 11 K7
York Cl CMBW SE5 * 130 D1
EHAM E6 95 K5
HNWL W7 84 E7
MRDN SM4 162 A3
York Crs BORE WD6 25 F1
Yorke Ga WAT WD17 20 E1
York Ga CAMTN NW1 10 B1
STHGT/OAK N14 28 E6
York Gv PECK SE15 111 K7
York Hl WNWD SE27 149 H2
York House Pl KENS W8 14 C1
Yorkland Av WELL DA16 136 A3
York Ms IL IG1 78 A1
KTTN NW5 72 B4
York Pde BTFD TW8 * 104 E4
CDALE/KGS NW9 * 51 J5
York Pl BTSEA SW11 128 B2
IL IG1 78 A1
York Ri KTTN NW5 72 B2
ORP BR6 169 K7
York Rd ACT W3 86 E5
BAR EN5 27 G4
BELMT SM2 174 E7
BTFD TW8 104 E4
BTSEA SW11 128 B3
CHING E4 43 J4
CROY/NA CR0 164 B6
DART DA1 139 J6
EA W5 104 D2
FBAR/BDGN N11 40 D5
FSTGT E7 76 E5
HSLW TW3 123 G2
IL IG1 78 A2
KUTN/CMB KT2 144 B6
LEY E10 76 A2
NTHWD HA6 46 E1
RAIN RM13 81 F6
RCHPK/HAM TW10 125 G4
STHWK SE1 17 M1
TEDD TW11 142 E3
UED N18 42 D4
WALTH E17 57 F4
WATW WD18 21 G4
WCHMH N21 29 K6
WIM/MER SW19 147 F5
Yorkshire Cl STNW/STAM N16 74 A2
Yorkshire Gdns UED N18 42 D4
Yorkshire Grey Yd
GINN WC1R * 11 L3
Yorkshire Rd MTCM CR4 163 K4
POP/IOD E14 93 G5
York Sq POP/IOD E14 93 G5
York St MBLAR W1H 9 L3
MTCM CR4 163 F6
York Street Chambers
MHST W1U * 9 M2
York Ter ERITH DA8 117 K7
York Ter East CAMTN NW1 10 B1
York Ter West CAMTN NW1 10 A1
Yorkton St BETH E2 92 C1
York Wy CHSGTN KT9 171 K6
FELT TW13 141 K2
HOLWY N7 72 D5
KCROSS N1C 5 K5
TRDG/WHET N20 39 K2
York Way Ct IS N1 5 K4
York Way Est HOLWY N7 72 E5
Young Rd CAN/RD E16 95 G5
Youngs Rd GNTH/NBYPK IG2 60 D4
Young St KENS W8 14 C2
Yoxley Ap GNTH/NBYPK IG2 60 C5
Yoxley Dr GNTH/NBYPK IG2 60 C5
Yukon Rd BAL SW12 129 G6
Yunus Khan Cl WALTH E17 57 J4

Z

Zambezie Dr ED N9 42 E2
Zampa Rd BERM/RHTH SE16 111 K4
Zander Ct BETH E2 92 C2
Zangwill Rd BKHTH/KID SE3 114 C7
Zealand Av WDR/YW UB7 100 A6
Zealand Rd BOW E3 93 G1
Zennor Rd BAL SW12 129 H7
Zenoria St EDUL SE22 131 G3
Zermatt Rd THHTH CR7 164 D3
Zetland St POP/IOD E14 94 A4
Zion Pl THHTH CR7 164 E3
Zion Rd THHTH CR7 164 E3
Zoar St STHWK SE1 12 E8
Zoffany St ARCH N19 72 D1

02 Centre
HAMP NW3............71 G5
2 Willow Road (NT)
HAMP NW3............71 J3
30 St Mary Axe
HDTCH EC3A............13 K5
41 Hotel
BGVA SW1W............16 D3
7/7 Memorial
MYFR/PKLN W1K............10 A9
Aarotya Medical Centre
SEVS/STOTM N15............55 J3
Abbey Business Centre
VX/NE SW8............109 H7
Abbey Christian School for the English Language
STJWD NW8............2 F4
The Abbey Clinic
BELV DA17............117 G4
Abbey College London
BAY/PAD W2............8 B5
Abbey Industrial Estate
ALP/SUD HA0............68 B7
MTCM CR4............162 E4
Abbey Lane Commercial Estate
SRTFD E15............94 B1
Abbey Medical Centre
STJWD NW8............2 D4
Abbey Mills
WIM/MER SW19............147 G7
Abbey Park Industrial Estate
BARK IG11............96 B1
Abbey Primary School
ABYW SE2............116 D2
MRDN SM4............161 K6
Abbey Road
SRTFD E15............94 B1
Abbey Road Health Centre
SRTFD E15............76 C7
Abbey Road Studios
STJWD NW8............2 F6
Abbey Sports Centre
BARK IG11............78 C7
Abbey Trading Estate
SYD SE26............151 G4
Abbey Wharf Industrial Estate
BARK IG11............96 D2
Abbey Wood ⇌
ABYW SE2............116 D2
Abbotsbury Primary School
MRDN SM4............161 K4
Abbs Cross School & Arts College
HCH RM12............81 K2
ABC Cinema
PUT/ROE SW15............127 H2
Abercorn Place School
CAMTN NW1............9 K2
Abercorn School
MBLAR W1H............9 L3
STJWD NW8............2 F6
Aberdeen Wharf
WAP E1W............92 D7
Aberglen Industrial Estate
HYS/HAR UB3............101 G1
Abingdon House School
KENS W8............14 B3
Abney Park Cemetery
STNW/STAM N16............74 A1
Acacia Business Centre
WAN E11............76 C2
Academic College of London
WBLY HA9............67 K2
The Academy School
HAMP NW3............71 H3
Acland Burghley School
KTTN NW5............72 B3
Acorn Industrial Park
DART DA1............138 D4
Acorn Medical Centre
TWK TW1............124 B7
Acorns Independent College
STHL UB1............84 A7
Acre Road Health Clinic
KUTN/CMB KT2............144 B6
Acton Business Centre
WLSDN NW10............87 F3
Acton Central ⇌
ACT W3............87 F7
Acton Central Industrial Estate
ACT W3............86 D6
Acton Health Centre
ACT W3............86 E7
Acton High School
ACT W3............105 H1
Acton Hospital
ACT W3............105 H1
Acton Lane Medical Centre
CHSWK W4............105 K1
Acton Main Line ⇌
ACT W3............86 E5
Acton Park Industrial Estate
ACT W3............106 A1
Acton Superbowl
ACT W3............86 C4
Acton Swimming Baths
ACT W3............86 E7
Acton Town ⊖
ACT W3............105 H1
Acton & West London College
ACT W3............86 D7
Acumen (Anglo School)
NRWD SE19............150 A7
Adams Bridge Business Centre
WBLY HA9............68 D4
Adamsrill Primary School
SYD SE26............151 G2
Ad-Dean Primary School
IL IG1............78 C3
Addey & Stanhope School
NWCR SE14............112 C7
Addington Court Golf Club
CROY/NA CR0............179 H7
Addington Golf Club
CROY/NA CR0............179 H3
Addington Palace Golf Club
CROY/NA CR0............179 G5
Addington Village ⊖
CROY/NA CR0............179 J5
Addiscombe ⊖
CROY/NA CR0............165 H7
Addiscombe CC
CROY/NA CR0............178 C2
Addison Primary School
WKENS W14............107 G2
Adelphi Theatre
COVGDN WC2E............11 K7
Adler Industrial Estate
HYS/HAR UB3............101 G1
Admiral Hyson Industrial Estate
STHWK SE1............111 J3
Admiralty Arch
STJS SW1Y............11 H8

The Adult College of Barking & Dagenham
BARK IG11............78 E5
The Aerodrome School
CROY/NA CR0............177 H4
Africa Centre
COVGDN WC2E............11 K6
Aga Khan University
CAN/RD E16............94 D4
RSQ WC1B............11 H3
Agnew's
CONDST W1S............10 E3
Agora Shopping Centre
PECK SE15............131 H1
AHA International London Centre
BMSBY WC1N............11 M2
Ainslie Wood Primary School
CHING E4............43 K4
Airbase Unity Elementary School
RSLP HA4............64 A1
Airbus Coach Station
HTHAIR TW6............120 C2
Air Call Business Centre
CDALE/KGS NW9............51 F2
Airedale Physiotherapy Clinic
CHSWK W4............106 C4
Airlinks Golf Club
NWDGN UB2............102 B3
Air Links Industrial Estate
HEST TW5............102 K4
Airport Gate Business Centre
WDR/YW UB7............100 C4
Akiva School
FNCH N3............52 E1
Aksaray Sports Club
STNW/STAM N16............73 K3
Al-Azhar Primary School
WCHPL E1............92 C5
Albany Centre & Theatre
DEPT SE8............112 C6
Albany Clinic
BFN/LL DA15............155 G3
WIM/MER SW19............147 F6
Albany Park ⇌
SCUP DA14............155 K1
Albany Park Canoe & Sailing Centre
KUTN/CMB KT2............143 K5
The Albany School
HCH RM12............81 K1
Albemarle Primary School
WIM/MER SW19............146 C1
Albert Memorial
SKENS SW7............15 G1
Albion College
RSQ WC1B............11 J3
Albion Health Centre
WCHPL E1............92 D4
Albion Primary School
BERM/RHTH SE16............111 K1
Albion Street Health Centre
BERM/RHTH SE16............111 K1
Albright Industrial Estate
RAIN RM13............99 H4
Alchemea College of Audio Engineering
IS N1............6 D3
The Alchemy Gallery
CLKNW EC1R............6 A9
Aldenham Country Park
BORE WD6............23 H4
Aldenham Preparatory School
BORE WD6............23 F1
Alderbrook Primary School
BAL SW12............129 G6
Aldersbrook County Secondary School
MNPK E12............59 G4
Aldersbrook Primary School
MNPK E12............59 F7
Alderwood Primary School
ELTH/MOT SE9............135 J1
Aldgate ⊖
TWRH EC3N............13 L5
Aldgate Bus Station
HDTCH EC3A............13 L4
Aldgate East ⊖
WCHPL E1............13 M4
Aldwych Theatre
HOL/ALD WC2B............11 L5
Alexander McLeod Primary School
ABYW SE2............116 C4
Alexandra Avenue Clinic
RYLN/HDSTN HA2............65 K1
Alexandra Business Centre
PEND EN3............31 F5
Alexandra Infant School
KUTN/CMB KT2............144 C6
PGE/AN SE20............151 F6
Alexandra Junior School
HSLW TW3............123 G1
Alexandra Palace
WDGN N22............54 D2
Alexandra Palace Ice Rink
WDGN N22............54 D1
Alexandra Park School
FBAR/BDGN N11............40 C4
Alexandra Primary School
WDGN N22............55 F1
Alexandra School
RYLN/HDSTN HA2............65 K1
Al Falah Boys School
CLPT E5............74 D2
Al Falah Primary School
CLPT E5............74 D2
Alfred Salter Primary School
BERM/RHTH SE16............112 A1
Alfreds Way Industrial Estate
BARK IG11............79 G2
Al-Khair Primary & Secondary School
CROY/NA CR0............164 D7
Allenby Primary School
STHL UB1............84 A1
Allen Edwards Primary School
CLAP SW4............109 K7
The All England Lawn Tennis & Croquet Club
WIM/MER SW19............146 B2
Alleyns Junior School
EDUL SE22............131 F4
Allfarthing JMI School
WAND/EARL SW18............128 B5
All Saints
POP/IOD E14............94 A5
All Saints Benhilton CE Primary
SUT SM1............175 F2
All Saints Catholic School
BCTR RM8............62 C7

All Saints CE Primary School
BKHTH/KID SE3............133 H1
CAR SM5............176 A4
FUL/PGN SW6............70 D2
PUT/ROE SW15............127 F2
TRDG/WHET N20............39 H1
WIM/MER SW19............147 G6
All Saints J & I School
NRWD SE19............150 A7
All Souls CE Primary School
GTPST W1W............10 E3
Allum Lane Cemetery
BORE WD6............24 A4
Allum Medical Centre
WAN E11............58 B6
Alma Primary School
BERM/RHTH SE16............111 H3
PEND EN3............31 G4
Almeida Theatre
IS N1............6 C2
Al-Noor Primary School
GDMY/SEVK IG3............61 H7
Alperton ⊖
ALP/SUD HA0............67 K7
Alperton Cemetery
ALP/SUD HA0............67 K7
Alperton Community School
ALP/SUD HA0............67 K6
Alperton Sports Ground
ALP/SUD HA0............85 K1
Alpha Business Centre
WALTH E17............57 H4
Alpha Preparatory School
HRW HA1............48 E4
Alpine Business Centre
EHAM E6............96 A4
Al-Risaala School
BAL SW12............129 G7
Al-Sadiq Boys & Al-Zahra Girls Schools
KIL/WHAMP NW6............70 C7
Alscot Road Industrial Estate
STHWK SE1............19 M5
Altmore Infant School
EHAM E6............77 K6
The Alton School
PUT/ROE SW15............126 C6
Ambler Primary School
FSBYPK N4............73 H2
Ambleside Junior School
WOT/HER KT12............156 B7
AMC Business Centre
WLSDN NW10............86 D2
American Intercontinental University
MHST W1U............10 B3
The American School in London
STJWD NW8............2 F5
AMF Bowling
LEW SE13............133 F2
Amida Golf
FELT TW13............142 A2
Ampere Way ⊖
CROY/NA CR0............164 A7
Ampthill Square Medical Centre
CAMTN NW1............4 F6
Anchorage Point Industrial Estate
CHARL SE7............114 B2
Anchor Bay Industrial Estate
ERITH DA8............118 C6
Anchor Retail Park
WCHPL E1............92 E3
The Anchor School
SUT SM1............175 F1
ANdAZ Hotel
LVPST EC2M............13 J3
Andover Medical Centre
HOLWY N7............73 F2
The Andrew Ewing Primary School
HEST TW5............102 E6
Anerley ⇌
PGE/AN SE20............150 C7
Anerley School
NRWD SE19............150 C7
Angel ⊖
IS N1............6 C5
Angel Centre
DART DA1............139 H5
Angel Road ⇌
UED N18............42 E4
Angerstein Business Park
GNWCH SE10............113 K3
Anglian Industrial Estate
BARK IG11............97 F3
Animal Cemetery
REDBR IG4............59 H2
Annemount School
EFNCH N2............53 G5
Annunciation RC Infant School
EDGW HA8............37 F7
The Annunciation RC Junior School
MLHL NW7............37 F5
Anson Primary School
CRICK NW2............70 B4
Apex Hotel
MON EC3R............13 K6
Apex Industrial Estate
WLSDN NW10............87 H3
Apex Primary School
IL IG1............60 A7
Apex Retail Park
FELT TW13............141 K2
Apollo Theatre
SOHO/CST W1F............11 G6
Apollo Victoria Theatre
PIM SW1V............16 E4
Apostolic Nuncio
WIM/MER SW19............146 A2
Applegarth Primary School
CROY/NA CR0............179 K5
Apsley House, The Wellington Museum
KTBR SW1X............16 A1
Aquarius Business Park
CRICK NW2............51 J7
Aquarius Golf Club
EDUL SE22............131 K4
Aquatics Centre
OLYMPICPK E20............76 A6
Aragon Primary School
MRDN SM4............161 H6
Arcadia Shopping Centre
EA W5............85 K6
Arcadia University
BAY/PAD W2............8 C7
Archbishop Sumners CE Primary School
LBTH SE11............18 B6

Archbishop Tenisons CE School
CROY/NA CR0............178 B2
Archbishop Tenison's School
VX/NE SW8............110 A5
Archdale Business Centre
RYLN/HDSTN HA2............66 C1
Archdeacon Cambridge's CE Primary School
WHTN TW2............142 E1
Arches Business Centre
NWDGN UB2............102 E1
Arches Leisure Centre
GNWCH SE10............113 G5
Archgate Business Centre
NFNCH/WDSPK N12............39 G3
Architectural Association School of Architecture
RSQ WC1B............11 G3
Archway ⊖
ARCH N19............72 C1
Archway Business Centre
ARCH N19............72 D2
Archway Leisure Centre
ARCH N19............72 C1
Arena ⊖
SNWD SE25............165 K4
Arena Estate
FSBYPK N4............55 H5
Argent Centre Industrial Estate
HYS/HAR UB3............101 K1
Argyle Primary School
STPAN WC1H............5 K8
Ark Academy
WBLY HA9............68 C1
Ark Atwood Primary Academy
HOL/ALD WC2B............11 L4
Arkley Golf Club
BAR EN5............25 H4
Arklow Trading Estate
NWCR SE14............112 B5
Armourers & Braziers' Hall
LOTH EC2R............13 G3
Arndale Health Centre
WAND/EARL SW18............127 K5
Arnhem Wharf Primary School
POP/IOD E14............112 C2
Arnold House School
STJWD NW8............3 C1
Arnos Grove ⊖
FBAR/BDGN N11............40 C3
Arnos Pool
FBAR/BDGN N11............40 D4
Arrivals
HTHAIR TW6............120 C2
Arsenal ⊖
HBRY N5............73 G2
Arsenal FC (Emirates Stadium)
HOLWY N7............73 G3
Artsdepot
NFNCH/WDSPK N12............39 G4
The Arts Educational School
CHSWK W4............106 B3
Arts Theatre
LSQ/SEVD WC2H............11 H6
Aragon College
KENS W8............14 C1
Ashburnham Primary School
WBPTN SW10............108 C6
Ashby Mill
BRXS/STRHM SW2............129 K5
Ashby Mill School
CLAP SW4............129 K4
Ashcroft Technology Academy
PUT/ROE SW15............127 J4
Ashfield Junior School
BUSH WD23............22 B6
Ashford Industrial Estate
ASHF TW15............140 A3
Ashford Sports Club
STWL/WRAY TW19............120 C7
Ashgrove College
WALTH E17............57 J2
Ashgrove School
BMLY BR1............168 A1
Ashgrove Trading Estate
BMLY BR1............152 B5
Ashleigh Commercial Estate
CHARL SE7............114 B3
Ashmead Primary School
BROCKY SE4............132 D1
Ashmole Academy
STHGT/OAK N14............28 C7
Ashmole Centre
STHGT/OAK N14............28 C7
Ashmole Primary School
VX/NE SW8............110 A5
Ashmount Primary School
ARCH N19............54 D6
Ashton House School
ISLW TW7............103 J7
Ashton Playing Fields Track
WFD IG8............45 J5
Aspen House School
LBTH SE11............110 C5
Aspen House Secondary & Primary School
BRXS/STRHM SW2............129 K7
Asquith Court School
HPTN TW12............142 B7
KTN/HRWW/WS HA3............49 K5
Asquith School
PEND EN3............30 E3
Associated Newspapers Offices
BERM/RHTH SE16............112 A2
Assunah School
TOTM N17............56 B1
Aston Clinic
NWMAL KT3............160 B3
Aston House School
EA W5............85 K5
Asylum Medical Centre
CEND/HSY/T N8............55 G2
Athelney Primary School
CAT SE6............151 J2
Athelstan House School
HPTN TW12............142 A7
Athenaeum Hotel
MYFR/PICC W1J............10 C9
Athena Medical Centre
CLPT E5............74 E3
Atherton Leisure Centre
SRTFD E15............76 D5
Athletes Village
OLYMPICPK E20............76 A4
Athlone House Hospital
HGT N6............53 K7
Athlon Industrial Estate
ALP/SUD HA0............85 K1
Atkinson Morley Hospital
RYNPK SW20............145 K6

Atlantic House (Richmond American International University)
KENS W8............14 E3
Atlas Business Centre
CRICK NW2............69 K1
Atlas Transport Estate
BTSEA SW11............128 B1
Attlee Youth & Community Centre
WCHPL E1............13 M3
Auriol Junior School
HOR/WEW KT19............173 H3
Australia House
HOL/ALD WC2B............11 M5
Avenue House Museum
FNCH N3............52 D1
Avenue House School
WEA W13............85 H5
Avenue Industrial Estate
CHING E4............43 H5
Avenue Pre-Preparatory School
HGT N6............54 B6
Avenue Primary School
MNPK E12............77 J3
Avenue Road ⊖
BECK BR3............166 A1
Avery Hill Park
ELTH/MOT SE9............135 H5
Avondale Park Primary School
NTGHL W11............88 B6
Avon House School
WFD IG8............44 E4
Avon Trading Estate
WKENS W14............107 J3
Ayesha Community School
HDN NW4............51 J5
The Aylesham Centre
PECK SE15............111 H7
Aylward Academy
UED N18............41 K3
Aylward Primary School
STAN HA7............35 K4
Azhar Academy
FSTGT E7............76 E5
BAA Heathrow Visitor Centre
HTHAIR TW6............100 E1
Babington House School
CHST BR7............153 K5
BackCare Clinic
WPK KT4............160 D7
Bacon's College
BERM/RHTH SE16............93 G3
Baden Powell House
SKENS SW7............14 C5
Baglioni Hotel
KENS W8............14 E2
Bakers Hall
MON EC3R............13 K7
Baker Street ⊖
CAMTN NW1............9 M1
Balaam Leisure Centre
PLSTW E13............94 E3
Bales College
NKENS W10............88 C2
Balfour Business Centre
NWDGN UB2............102 C3
Balgowan Primary School
BECK BR3............166 B1
Balham ⊖
BAL SW12............129 G6
Balham Girls Preparatory Secondary School
TOOT SW17............147 J1
Balham Health Centre
BAL SW12............148 B1
Balham Leisure Centre
TOOT SW17............148 A1
Balmoral Trading Estate
BARK IG11............97 F3
Baltic Exchange
HDTCH EC3A............13 K4
WFD IG8............44 E2
Bandon Hill Cemetery
WLGTN SM6............176 D4
Bandon Hill Primary School
WLGTN SM6............176 D4
Bangabandhu Primary School
BETH E2............92 E2
Bank ⊖
LOTH EC2R............13 G5
Bank of England Extension
CITYW EC2V............12 E5
Bank of England (& Museum)
LOTH EC2R............13 G5
Bankside Gallery
STHWK SE1............12 D7
Bankside Jetty
STHWK SE1............12 E7
Bankside Park Industrial Estate
BARK IG11............97 G2
Bannister Stadium
KTN/HRWW/WS HA3............34 C5
Bannockburn Primary School
WOOL/PLUM SE18............116 A3
The Banqueting House, Whitehall
WHALL SW1A............11 J1
Barbara Speake Theatre School
ACT W3............87 G2
Barber Surgeons' Hall
BARB EC2Y............12 F3
Barbican ⊖
FARR EC1M............12 D2
Barbican Cinema
BARB EC2Y............12 F2
Barbican Exhibition Halls
BARB EC2Y............12 E2
The Barbican
BARB EC2Y............12 F2
Barbican Theatre
BARB EC2Y............12 F2
Barclay Primary School
LEY E10............58 B5
Barham Primary School
ALP/SUD HA0............67 J5
Baring Primary School
LEE/GVPK SE12............133 K6
Baring Road Medical Centre
BMLY BR1............152 D1
Barkantine Clinic
POP/IOD E14............112 D1
Barking ⇌⊖
BARK IG11............78 C6
Barking Abbey Comprehensive School (Lower)
IL IG1............78 D4
Barking Abbey Comprehensive School (Upper)
BARK IG11............79 F5
Barking Abbey Industrial Estate
BARK IG11............78 B7

- Barking Abbey Leisure Centre *BARK* IG11 79 G5
- Barking Abbey School *BARK* IG11 79 F5
- Barking & Dagenham College *ROMW/RG* RM7 81 F1
- Barking FC *BCTR* RM8 79 H4
- Barking Hospital *BARK* IG11 79 F6
- Barking Industrial Park *BARK* IG11 79 F7
- Barking RUFC *DAGW* RM9 79 K7
- Barkingside ⊖ *BARK/HLT* IG6 60 D3
- Barkingside Cemetery *BARK/HLT* IG6 60 B2
- Barkingside FC *BARK/HLT* IG6 60 D3
- Barlby Primary School *NKENS* W10 88 B3
- Barley Lane Primary School *GDMY/SEVK* IG3 61 G6
- Barnabas Medical Centre *NTHLT* UB5 66 C5
- Barn Croft Primary School *WALTH* E17 57 G5
- Barnehurst ⇌ *BXLYHN* DA7 137 K1
- Barnehurst Primary School *ERITH* DA8 117 K7
- Barnehurst Public Golf Club *BXLYHN* DA7 138 A2
- Barn Elms Athletics Track *BARN* SW13 126 E1
- Barn Elms Sports Centre *BARN* SW13 107 F7
- Barn Elms Water Sports Centre *PUT/ROE* SW15 127 F1
- Barnes ⇌ *BARN* SW13 126 D2
- Barnes Bridge ⇌ *BARN* SW13 126 B1
- Barnes Hospital *MORT/ESHN* SW14 126 B2
- Barnes Primary School *BARN* SW13 126 B2
- Barnes Sports Club *BARN* SW13 106 C7
- Barnet College
  - *BAR* EN5 26 D3
  - *CDALE/KGS* NW9 37 H7
  - *EBAR* EN4 27 K7
  - *FBAR/BDGN* N11 39 K2
  - *NFNCH/WDSPK* N12 39 G4
- Barnet Copthall Pool *HDN* NW4 37 K6
- Barnet Copthall Stadium *HDN* NW4 38 A7
- Barnet County Court *FNCH* N3 38 E7
- Barnet FC (Underhill) *BAR* EN5 26 E4
- Barnet General Hospital *BAR* EN5 26 B3
- Barnet Health Centre *BAR* EN5 26 E4
- Barnet Hospital Chest Clinic *BAR* EN5 26 B3
- Barnet Magistrates Court *BAR* EN5 26 D3
- Barnet Museum *BAR* EN5 26 C3
- Barnet Trading Estate *BAR* EN5 26 D2
- Barnfield Primary School *EDGW* HA8 36 E7
- Barnhill Community High School *YEAD* UB4 83 F2
- Barn Hotel *RSLP* HA4 64 C1
- Barnsbury Complex *IS* N1 6 A1
- Barnsbury School for Girls *IS* N1 73 G5
- Barons Court ⊖ *HMSMTH* W6 107 G4
- Barons Court Theatre *WKENS* W14 107 H4
- Barratt Industrial Park *BOW* E3 94 A3
- Barrett Industrial Park *STHL* UB1 84 A7
- Barrett Way Industrial Estate *RYLN/HDSTN* HA2 48 D2
- Barrington Primary School *WELL* DA16 136 E1
- Barrow Hedges Primary School *CAR* SM5 175 J6
- Barrow Hill Junior School *STJWD* NW8 3 J6
- Barton House Health Centre *STNW/STAM* N16 73 K2
- Barwell Business Park *CHSGTN* KT9 171 K6
- Basketball Arena *OLYMPICPK* E20 75 K4
- Bassett House School *NKENS* W10 88 B5
- Baston House School *HAYES* BR2 181 F1
- Bath Factory Estate *HNHL* SE24 130 D5
- Battersea Arts Centre (BAC) *BTSEA* SW11 128 E2
- Battersea Business Centre *BTSEA* SW11 129 F2
- Battersea Dogs' Home *VX/NE* SW8 109 G6
- Battersea Park ⇌ *BTSEA* SW11 109 G6
- Battersea Park School *BTSEA* SW11 108 E7
- Battersea Power Station (disused) *VX/NE* SW8 109 G5
- Battersea Sports Centre *BTSEA* SW11 128 C2
- Battersea Tutorial College *TOOT* SW17 148 A1
- Bayswater ⊖ *BAY/PAD* W2 8 C6
- BBC Broadcasting House *REGST* W1B 10 D3
- BBC Media Village *SHB* W12 88 A6
- BBC Studios *MV/WKIL* W9 2 C9
- BBC Television Centre *SHB* W12 88 A6
- BBC Worldwide *SHB* W12 88 A5
- Beal High School *REDBR* IG4 59 J2
- Beam Primary School *DAGE* RM10 98 E1
- Beatrice Tate School *BETH* E2 92 D2
- Beatrix Potter Primary School *WAND/EARL* SW18 128 B7
- Beauclerc Infant School *SUN* TW16 156 B2
- The Beaufort Hotel *CHEL* SW3 15 L4
- Beaumont Primary School *LEY* E10 57 K6
- Beaver College *BAY/PAD* W2 8 C7
- The Beavers Community Primary School *HSLWW* TW4 122 B2
- Beaverwood School for Girls *CHST* BR7 154 E5
- Beckenham Business Centre *BECK* BR3 151 G5
- Beckenham Crematorium *BECK* BR3 165 K2
- Beckenham CC *BECK* BR3 151 K6
- Beckenham Hill ⇌ *CAT* SE6 152 A4
- Beckenham Hospital *BECK* BR3 166 C1
- Beckenham Junction ⇌ ⊖ *BECK* BR3 151 J7
- Beckenham Leisure Centre *BECK* BR3 151 G7
- Beckenham RFC *BECK* BR3 166 B3
- Beckenham Road ⊖ *BECK* BR3 151 F7
- Beckenham School of Art *BECK* BR3 166 B4
- Beckenham Theatre Centre *BECK* BR3 166 E1
- Beckenham Town FC *BECK* BR3 166 D4
- Becket Sports Centre *DART* DA1 139 F5
- Beckford Primary School *KIL/WHAMP* NW6 70 D4
- Beckmead School *BECK* BR3 166 D7
- The Beck Theatre *HYS/HAR* UB3 82 D5
- Beckton ⊖ *EHAM* E6 96 A4
- Beckton Park ⊖ *EHAM* E6 95 K6
- Beckton Ski Centre *EHAM* E6 96 A3
- Beckton Triangle Retail Park *EHAM* E6 96 B2
- Becontree ⊖ *DAGW* RM9 79 J5
- Becontree Day Hospital *BCTR* RM8 80 A1
- Becontree Primary School *BCTR* RM8 79 H2
- Bective House Clinic *PUT/ROE* SW15 127 J3
- Beddington Infant School *WLGTN* SM6 176 C2
- Beddington Lane ⊖ *CROY/NA* CR0 163 H5
- Beddington Medical Centre *CROY/NA* CR0 176 E3
- Beddington Park Primary School *CROY/NA* CR0 176 D2
- Beddington Trading Estate *CROY/NA* CR0 163 K7
- Bedelsford School *KUT/HW* KT1 159 F2
- Bedfont Cemetery *EBED/NFELT* TW14 121 F7
- Bedfont Health Clinic *EBED/NFELT* TW14 121 H6
- Bedfont Industrial Park *ASHF* TW15 140 B2
- Bedfont Lakes Country Park *EBED/NFELT* TW14 140 A1
- Bedfont Lakes Office Park *EBED/NFELT* TW14 121 F7
- Bedfont Primary School *EBED/NFELT* TW14 121 H5
- Bedford Hotel *RSQ* WC1B 11 J2
- Bedonwell Clinic *ABYW* SE2 117 F5
- Bedonwell Medical Centre *BELV* DA17 117 G4
- Bedonwell Primary School *BXLYHN* DA7 117 F5
- Beecholme Primary School *MTCM* CR4 148 B7
- Beechwood School *STRHM/NOR* SW16 148 E2
- Beehive Preparatory School *REDBR* IG4 59 K3
- The Beehive School *ARCH* N19 54 D6
- Beis Chinuch Lebonos Girls School *FSBYPK* N4 55 J6
- Beis Malka Girls School *STNW/STAM* N16 56 B7
- Beis Rochel d'Satmar Girls School *STNW/STAM* N16 56 A6
- Beis Trana Girls School *STNW/STAM* N16 56 C7
- Beis Yaakov Primary School *CDALE/KGS* NW9 51 F2
- Belgrave Walk ⊖ *MTCM* CR4 162 C3
- Bellamy's Wharf *BERM/RHTH* SE16 93 F7
- Bellenden Primary School *PECK* SE15 131 H2
- Bellenden Road Business Centre *PECK* SE15 131 G1
- Bellenden Road Retail Park *PECK* SE15 111 G7
- Bellerbys College *DEPT* SE8 112 E5
- Belleville Primary School *BTSEA* SW11 128 E4
- Belle Vue Cinema *WLSDN* NW10 69 K6
- Bell Industrial Estate *CHSWK* W4 105 K3
- Bellingham ⇌ *CAT* SE6 151 K2
- Bellingham Trading Estate *CAT* SE6 151 K2
- Belmont Bowling Club *STRHM/NOR* SW16 148 E2
- Belmont Infant School *TOTM* N17 55 J2
- Belmont Mill Hill Preparatory School *MLHL* NW7 37 J2
- Belmont Park School *LEY* E10 58 A5
- Belmont Primary School
  - *CHSWK* W4 106 A3
  - *ERITH* DA8 117 H6
- Belmont School *KTN/HRWW/WS* HA3 49 F1
- Belmore Primary School *YEAD* UB4 83 F2
- Belsize Park ⊖ *HAMP* NW3 71 J4
- Belvedere ⇌ *BELV* DA17 117 J2
- Belvedere Day Hospital *WLSDN* NW10 69 J7
- Belvedere Industrial Estate *BELV* DA17 99 F7
- Belvedere Link Business Park *ERITH* DA8 117 K2
- Belvedere Primary School *BELV* DA17 117 J3
- Belvue Business Centre *NTHLT* UB5 66 B6
- Belvue School *NTHLT* UB5 66 A7
- Benedict House Preparatory School *BFN/LL* DA15 155 F3
- Benedict Primary School *MTCM* CR4 162 C2
- Benjamin Franklin House *CHCR* WC2N 11 J8
- Ben Jonson Primary School *WCHPL* E1 93 G3
- Bensham Manor School *THHTH* CR7 164 D4
- Benson Primary School *CROY/NA* CR0 179 G2
- The Bentall Centre *KUT/HW* KT1 158 E1
- Benthal Primary School *STNW/STAM* N16 74 C2
- The Bentley Hotel *SKENS* SW7 14 E6
- Bentley Wood Girls School *STAN* HA7 35 F4
- Bentworth Primary School *SHB* W12 87 K5
- Ben Uri Gallery, The London Jewish Museum of Art *STJWD* NW8 2 D4
- Beormund School *STHWK* SE1 19 G2
- Beresford Square Outdoor Market *WOOL/PLUM* SE18 115 G3
- Berger Primary School *HOM* E9 75 F5
- The Berkeley Hotel *KTBR* SW1X 16 A1
- Berkeley Primary School *HEST* TW5 102 C5
- Berlitz School of Languages *HHOL* WC1V 11 M3
- Bermondsey ⊖ ⊖ *BERM/RHTH* SE16 111 H2
- Bermondsey Town Hall *STHWK* SE1 19 L4
- Bermondsey Trading Estate *BERM/RHTH* SE16 111 K4
- Berrylands ⇌ *BRYLDS* KT5 159 J3
- Berrymede Infant School *ACT* W3 105 J1
- Berrymede Junior School *ACT* W3 105 J1
- Bertram House School *TOOT* SW17 148 A1
- Bessemer Grange J & I School *HNHL* SE24 130 E4
- Bessemer Park Industrial Estate *BRXN/ST* SW9 130 C3
- Best Western Bromley Court Hotel *BMLY* BR1 152 C5
- Best Western Cumberland Hotel *HRW* HA1 49 F5
- Best Western Lodge Hotel *PUT/ROE* SW15 127 J4
- Best Western Mostyn Hotel *MBLAR* W1H 9 M5
- Best Western Phoenix Hotel *BAY/PAD* W2 8 C6
- Best Western White House Hotel *WATW* WD18 20 E3
- Beth Jacob Grammar School *HDN* NW4 52 B3
- Bethlem Royal Hospital *BECK* BR3 166 D6
- Bethnal Green ⊖
  - *BETH* E2 92 E2
  - *WCHPL* E1 92 D3
- Bethnal Green Technology College *BETH* E2 7 M8
- Beths Grammar School for Boys *BXLY* DA5 137 H5
- The Betty Layward School *STNW/STAM* N16 73 K2
- Beulah Infant School *THHTH* CR7 164 D1
- Beverley School *NWMAL* KT3 160 D4
- Beverley Trading Estate *MRDN* SM4 161 G6
- Bevington Primary School *NKENS* W10 88 C4
- Bexley ⇌ *BXLY* DA5 137 H7
- Bexley College *BELV* DA17 117 K3
- Bexley CC *BXLY* DA5 137 H7
- Bexley Grammar School *WELL* DA16 136 C3
- Bexleyheath ⇌ *BXLYHN* DA7 137 F1
- Bexleyheath Cemetery *BXLYHN* DA7 137 G2
- Bexleyheath Centre *BXLYHS* DA6 137 F3
- Bexleyheath Golf Club *BXLYHS* DA6 137 F4
- Bexleyheath Marriott Hotel *BXLYHS* DA6 137 J3
- Bexleyheath School *BXLYHN* DA7 137 G2
- Bexleyheath Superbowl *BXLYHS* DA6 137 G3
- Bexley RFC *BXLY* DA5 137 H6
- BFI *STHWK* SE1 11 M8
- BFI London IMAX Cinema *STHWK* SE1 11 M9
- Bickenhall College of Computing *CAMTN* NW1 9 M2
- Bickerly School of Dance *HAYES* BR2 168 D4
- Bickley ⇌ *BMLY* BR1 168 D2
- Bickley Park CC *BMLY* BR1 168 D1
- Bickley Park Pre-Preparatory School *BMLY* BR1 168 D2
- Bickley Park Preparatory School *BMLY* BR1 168 C2
- Big Ben *WHALL* SW1A 17 K2
- Bigland Green Primary School *WCHPL* E1 92 D5
- Billingsgate Fish Market *POP/IOD* E14 93 K7
- Bingham Hotel *TWK* TW1 124 E5
- Birchmere Business Park *THMD* SE28 116 B1
- Bird College *SCUP* DA14 155 G2
- Birkbeck ⇌ ⊖ *BECK* BR3 165 K1
- Birkbeck College
  - *GWRST* WC1E 11 H1
  - *RSQ* WC1B 11 H3
- Birkbeck Primary School *SCUP* DA14 155 H2
- Birkenhall College of Computing *MBLAR* W14 9 M2
- Bishop Challoner Catholic Collegiate School *WCHPL* E1 92 E6
- Bishop Challoner Girls School *WCHPL* E1 92 C6
- Bishop Challoner School *HAYES* BR2 167 G1
- Bishop Douglass RC School *EFNCH* N2 53 G1
- Bishop Gilpin Primary School *WIM/MER* SW19 146 D4
- Bishop John Robinson CE Primary School *THMD* SE28 97 J6
- Bishop Justus CE (Secondary) School *HAYES* BR2 168 D6
- Bishop Perrin CE Primary School *WHTN* TW2 123 G6
- Bishop Ramsey CE School *RSLP* HA4 46 D6
- Bishopsgate Institute *LVPST* EC2M 13 K3
- Bishop Thomas Grant School *STRHM/NOR* SW16 149 F4
- Bishop Winnington Ingram CE Primary School *RSLP* HA4 46 B6
- Bittacy Business Centre *MLHL* NW7 38 C5
- Blackburn Trading Estate *STWL/WRAY* TW19 120 C5
- Blackfen Medical Centre *BFN/LL* DA15 136 A4
- Blackfen School for Girls *BFN/LL* DA15 136 C5
- Blackfriars ⇌ ⊖ *BLKFR* EC4V 12 C6
- Blackfriars Millennium Pier *EMB* EC4Y 12 B6
- Blackfriars Pier *BLKFR* EC4V 12 D7
- Blackheath ⇌ *BKHTH/KID* SE3 133 J2
- Blackheath Bluecoat School *BKHTH/KID* SE3 114 A6
- Blackheath Business Estate *GNWCH* SE10 113 F7
- The Blackheath Clinic *BKHTH/KID* SE3 133 K3
- Blackheath High School GDST *BKHTH/KID* SE3 133 J1
- Blackheath High Senior School *BKHTH/KID* SE3 113 K6
- Blackheath Hospital *BKHTH/KID* SE3 133 J2
- Blackheath Preparatory School *BKHTH/KID* SE3 113 K7
- Blackheath RFC (The Rectory Field) *BKHTH/KID* SE3 114 A6
- Blackhorse ⊖ *CROY/NA* CR0 165 H6
- Blackhorse Road ⊖ ⊖ *WALTH* E17 57 F3
- Blackwall ⊖ *POP/IOD* E14 94 A6
- Blackwall Trading Estate *POP/IOD* E14 94 B4
- Blair Peach Primary School *STHL* UB1 83 H7
- Blake College *GTPST* W1W 10 E2
- Blanche Nevile School
  - *HGT* N6 53 K5
  - *MUSWH* N10 54 A2
- Blenheim Business Centre *MTCM* CR4 147 K7
- Blenheim Shopping Centre *PGE/AN* SE20 150 E6
- Blessed Dominic RC Primary School *CDALE/KGS* NW9 51 G1
- Blessed Sacrament RC Primary School *IS* N1 5 K4
- Bloo House School *ESH/CLAY* KT10 170 A4
- Bloomfield Clinic Guys *STHWK* SE1 19 H1
- Bloomsbury International *NOXST/BSQ* WC1A 11 K3
- Bloomsbury Theatre *GWRST* WC1E 5 G9
- Blossom House School *RYNPK* SW20 146 A6
- Blossoms Inn Medical Centre *BLKFR* EC4V 12 F6
- Blue Gate Fields Infant School *WCHPL* E1 92 E6
- The Blue School *ISLW* TW7 124 B2
- Blyth's Wharf *POP/IOD* E14 93 G6
- BMI Medical Centre *CAVSQ/HST* W1G 10 B3
- BMX Track *OLYMPICPK* E20 75 K4
- Bnois Jerusalem Girls School *STNW/STAM* N16 55 K6
- Bnos Beis Yaakov Primary School *CDALE/KGS* NW9 50 E4
- The Bob Hope Theatre *ELTH/MOT* SE9 134 E5
- Bobov Foundation School *STNW/STAM* N16 56 B6
- The Bobov Foundation School for Girls *CLPT* E5 56 B6
- Bodywise Natural Health Centre *BETH* E2 92 E2
- Boleyn Cinema *EHAM* E6 95 H1
- Bolingbroke Hospital *BTSEA* SW11 128 D4
- Bolingbroke Primary School *BTSEA* SW11 108 C7
- Bond First School *MTCM* CR4 162 E1
- Bond Primary School *MTCM* CR4 162 E1
- Bond Street ⊖ *OXSTW* W1C 10 B5
- Bonner Primary School *BETH* E2 93 F1
- Bonneville Primary School *CLAP* SW4 129 H5
- Bonus Pastor Catholic College *BMLY* BR1 152 B3
- Boomes Industrial Estate *RAIN* RM13 99 H3
- Booster Cushion Theatre *WDGN* N22 55 F1
- Borehamwood FC *BORE* WD6 24 D1
- Borehamwood Industrial Park *BORE* WD6 25 F1
- Borough ⊖ *STHWK* SE1 18 F2
- Borough Cemetery *HSLWW* TW4 123 F6
- Borough Market *STHWK* SE1 13 G8
- Borthwick Wharf *DEPT* SE8 112 D4
- Boston Business Park *HNWL* W7 103 K2
- Boston Manor ⊖ *HNWL* W7 104 B3
- Botwell House Catholic Primary School *HYS/HAR* UB3 101 J1
- Boulevard 25 Retail Park *BORE* WD6 24 C2
- Boundary Business Park *MTCM* CR4 162 C1
- Bounds Green ⊖ *FBAR/BDGN* N11 40 D6
- Bounds Green Health Centre *FBAR/BDGN* N11 40 D6
- Bounds Green Industrial Estate *FBAR/BDGN* N11 40 B5
- Bounds Green Infant School *FBAR/BDGN* N11 40 D6
- Bourne CP School *RSLP* HA4 65 G4
- Bourne Hall Health Centre *EW* KT17 173 H7
- Bournehall J & I School *BUSH* WD23 22 A4
- Bourne Hall Museum *EW* KT17 173 H7
- Bourne Road Industrial Park *DART* DA1 138 A4
- Bourneside Sports Club *STHGT/OAK* N14 28 E7
- Bousfield Primary School *ECT* SW5 14 E7
- Boutcher CE Primary School *STHWK* SE1 19 L4
- Bowater House *SKENS* SW7 15 L2
- Bow Church ⊖ *BOW* E3 93 J2
- Bow County Court *SRTFD* E15 76 C5
- Bowden House Clinic *HRW* HA1 66 E1
- Bowes Park ⇌ *WDGN* N22 40 E6
- Bowes Primary School *FBAR/BDGN* N11 40 D4
- Bowes Road Clinic *FBAR/BDGN* N11 40 C4
- Bow Junior & Youth Centre *BOW* E3 93 H4
- Bowman Trading Estate *CDALE/KGS* NW9 50 C2
- Bow Road ⊖ *BOW* E3 93 J2
- Bow Secondary School *BOW* E3 93 J1
- Bow Triangle Business Centre *BOW* E3 93 J3
- Boxgrove Primary School *ABYW* SE2 116 D2
- BPP Law School *HHOL* WC1V 11 L3
- Brackenbury Health Centre *HMSMTH* W6 106 E2
- Brackenbury Primary School *HMSMTH* W6 106 E2
- Brady Recreation Centre *WCHPL* E1 92 C4
- Braincroft Primary School *CRICK* NW2 69 H2
- Braintree Road Industrial Estate *RSLP* HA4 65 F3
- Bramah's Tea & Coffee Museum *STHWK* SE1 12 F9
- Brampton College *HDN* NW4 52 A3
- Brampton Manor School *EHAM* E6 95 H3

Brampton Primary School
BXLYHN DA7 .... 136 E1
EHAM E6 .... 95 J2
Brandlehow Primary School
PUT/ROE SW15 .... 127 J3
Branollys Health Centre
PLSTW E13 .... 94 E3
Breakspear Crematorium
RSLP HA4 .... 46 A4
Breaside Preparatory School
BMLY BR1 .... 153 G7
Brecknock Primary School
HOLWY N7 .... 72 D5
Bredinghurst School
PECK SE15 .... 131 K3
Brent Adult College
WLSDN NW10 .... 69 F7
Brent Arts Council
CRICK NW2 .... 69 J2
Brent Child & Family Clinic
WLSDN NW10 .... 69 H4
Brent Cross ⊖
GLDGN NW11 .... 52 B6
Brent Cross Shopping Centre
HDN NW4 .... 52 A6
Brentfield Medical Centre
WLSDN NW10 .... 69 F5
Brentfield Primary School
WLSDN NW10 .... 69 F5
Brentford ⇌
BTFD TW8 .... 104 E5
Brentford Business Centre
BTFD TW8 .... 104 D6
Brentford County Court
BTFD TW8 .... 104 E6
Brentford FC (Griffin Park)
BTFD TW8 .... 104 E5
Brentford Fountain
Leisure Centre
BTFD TW8 .... 105 G4
Brentford Health Centre
BTFD TW8 .... 104 D5
Brentford School for Girls
BTFD TW8 .... 104 E5
Brent Knoll School
FSTH SE23 .... 151 F2
Brent Magistrates Court House
WLSDN NW10 .... 69 G5
Brent Park Industrial Estate
NWDGN UB2 .... 102 A3
Brentside First School
HNWL W7 .... 84 E4
Brentside High School
HNWL W7 .... 84 E3
Brentside Primary School
HNWL W7 .... 84 E3
Brent Trading Estate
WLSDN NW10 .... 69 G4
Brentwaters Business Park
BTFD TW8 .... 104 C6
Brettenham Primary School
ED N9 .... 42 C3
Brewers' Hall
CITYW EC2V 12 F5
Brewery Industrial Estate
IS N1 .... 6 E2
Brewery Mews Business Centre
ISLW TW7 .... 124 A2
The Brewery
ROMW/RG RM7 .... 63 G5
Brick Lane Music Hall
CAN/RD E16 .... 95 H7
Brick Lane Music House
WCHPL E1 .... 13 M1
Bricklayer Arms
Industrial Estate
STHWK SE1 .... 19 L6
The Bridewell Theatre
EMB EC4Y 12 C5
The Bridge Academy
BETH E2 .... 7 L4
The Bridge Business Centre
NWDGN UB2 .... 103 F1
Bridge Lane Theatre
BTSEA SW11 .... 108 D7
The Bridge Leisure Centre
SYD SE26 .... 151 H4
Bridge Park Business &
Leisure Centre
WLSDN NW10 .... 68 D6
The Bridge School
ARCH N19 .... 72 C1
HOLWY N7 .... 72 D5
Brigham Young University
BAY/PAD W2 .... 8 C7
Bright Sparks
Montessori School
WKENS W14 .... 107 H1
Brigstock Medical Centre
THHTH CR7 .... 164 C4
Brimsdown ⇌
PEND EN3 .... 31 G1
Brimsdown Industrial Estate
PEND EN3 .... 30 E1
Brimsdown Primary School
PEND EN3 .... 31 F2
Brindishe Green School
LEW SE13 .... 133 G5
Brindishe Lee School
LEE/GVPK SE12 .... 133 J4
Britain & London Visitor Centre
STJS SW1Y 11 H7
Britannia Business Centre
CRICK NW2 .... 70 B3
Britannia College of Excellence
IS N1 .... 7 H8
Britannia Leisure Centre
IS N1 .... 7 H4
Britannia Sports Ground
WALTH E17 .... 43 J6
Britannia Village
Primary School
CAN/RD E16 .... 95 K4
British Airways Museum
HTHAIR TW6 .... 121 H3
The British American
Drama Academy
CAMTN NW1 .... 4 B4
British Cartoon Centre
BMSBY WC1N 11 K1
British College of Osteopathy
HAMP NW3 .... 71 G4
British Dental Association
CAVSO/HST W1G 10 C1
The British Hernia Centre
HDN NW4 .... 51 K4
British Library
CAMTN NW1 .... 5 H7
British Library
Newspaper Library
CDALE/KGS NW9 .... 51 G2
British Medical Association
STPAN WC1H 5 H3

British Museum
RSQ WC1B 11 J3
British Telecom Tower
GTPST W1W 10 E2
The BRIT School
SNWD SE25 .... 164 E5
Brittons School
Technology College
RAIN RM13 .... 81 H6
Brixton ⇌ ⊖
BRXN/ST SW9 .... 130 B3
Brixton Academy
BRXN/ST SW9 .... 130 B2
Brixton Recreation Centre
BRXN/ST SW9 .... 130 B2
Broadfields Primary School
EDGW HA8 .... 36 C1
Broadgate
LVPST EC2M 13 H2
Broadgate Ice Arena
LVPST EC2M 13 H1
Broadhurst School
KIL/WHAMP NW6 .... 2 E1
Broadmead Primary School
CROY/NA CR0 .... 164 E5
Broadreach College
THMD SE28 .... 116 A2
Broadwalk Shopping Centre
EDGW HA8 .... 36 C5
Broadwater Farm
Primary School
TOTM N17 .... 55 K1
Broadwater Primary School
TOOT SW17 .... 147 H3
Broadway Clinic
EDGW HA8 .... 36 D7
Broadway Retail Park
CRICK NW2 .... 70 B3
Broadway Shopping Centre
BXLYHS DA6 .... 137 H3
HMSMTH W6 .... 107 F4
Broadway Squash &
Fitness Centre
HMSMTH W6 .... 107 G3
Brocklebank Health Centre
WAND/EARL SW18 .... 128 A6
Brocklebank Industrial Estate
GNWCH SE10 .... 113 K3
Brockley ⇌ ⊖
BROCKY SE4 .... 132 C2
Brockley Cross Business Centre
BROCKY SE4 .... 132 B2
Brockley Primary School
BROCKY SE4 .... 132 C4
Brockwell Lido
HNHL SE24 .... 130 C5
Bromet Primary School
OXHEY WD19 .... 21 H6
Bromley by Bow ⊖
BOW E3 .... 93 K2
Bromley Cemetery
BMLY BR1 .... 152 D6
Bromley Civic Centre
BMLY BR1 .... 168 A1
Bromley College of
Further & Higher Education
BMLY BR1 .... 152 E7
HAYES BR2 .... 168 C5
Bromley County Court
BMLY BR1 .... 152 E7
Bromley FC
HAYES BR2 .... 168 A4
Bromley High School GDST
BMLY BR1 .... 169 F3
Bromley Industrial Centre
BMLY BR1 .... 168 C2
Bromley Mall Indoor Market
BMLY BR1 .... 167 K1
Bromley North ⇌
BMLY BR1 .... 152 E7
Bromley Road Infant School
BECK BR3 .... 151 K7
Bromley Road Retail Park
CAT SE6 .... 151 K1
Bromley Ski Centre
STMC/STPC BR5 .... 155 K7
Bromley South ⇌
BMLY BR1 .... 168 A2
Bromley Wendover Lawn
Tennis Club
HAYES BR2 .... 168 A3
Brompton Medical Centre
ECT SW5 .... 14 D7
Brompton Oratory
SKENS SW7 .... 15 J4
Bromyard Leisure Centre
ACT W3 .... 87 G7
Brondesbury ⊖
KIL/WHAMP NW6 .... 70 D6
Brondesbury
College for Boys
KIL/WHAMP NW6 .... 70 B6
Brondesbury Park ⊖
KIL/WHAMP NW6 .... 70 C7
Brook Community
Primary School
HACK E8 .... 74 C4
Brooke Trading Estate
ROM RM1 .... 63 H6
Brookfield House School
WFD IG8 .... 44 C3
Brookfield Primary School
CHEAM SM3 .... 161 H7
HGT N6 .... 72 B1
Brook House FC
YEAD UB4 .... 82 D2
Brook Industrial Estate
YEAD UB4 .... 83 H7
Brookland Junior School
GLDGN NW11 .... 53 F3
Brooklands Primary School
BKHTH/KID SE3 .... 133 K2
Brook Lane Business Centre
BTFD TW8 .... 104 E4
Brookmarsh Trading Estate
DEPT SE8 .... 112 C6
Brookmead Industrial Estate
CROY/NA CR0 .... 163 H5
Brookside Primary School
YEAD UB4 .... 83 G2
Brookfield House School
RCH/KEW TW9 .... 105 G7
Broomfield School
FBAR/BDGN N11 .... 40 D4
Broomsleigh Business Park
SYD SE26 .... 151 H4
Broomwood Hall Lower School
BAL SW12 .... 128 E5
STRHM/NOR SW16 .... 148 D2
Brownlow Medical Centre
FBAR/BDGN N11 .... 40 E4
Brown's Hotel
MYFR/PICC W1J 10 D7

Bruce Castle Museum
TOTM N17 .... 42 A7
Bruce Grove ⇌
TOTM N17 .... 56 B1
Bruce Grove Primary School
TOTM N17 .... 56 B1
Brunei Gallery
STPAN WC1H 11 H1
Brunel Engine House
BERM/RHTH SE16 .... 111 K1
Brunel University
GLDGN NW11 .... 52 B5
ISLW TW7 .... 103 K6
TWK TW1 .... 124 C3
Brunel University (Osterley
Campus) Track
ISLW TW7 .... 103 K6
Brunswick Health Centre
FBAR/BDGN N11 .... 40 A1
Brunswick Housing &
Shopping Centre
BMSBY WC1N 5 K9
Brunswick Industrial Park
FBAR/BDGN N11 .... 40 B3
Brunswick Medical Centre
BMSBY WC1N 5 J9
Brunswick Park JMI School
STHGT/OAK N14 .... 28 A7
Brunswick Park
Primary School
CMBW SE5 .... 110 E6
B Six Sixth Form College
CLPT E5 .... 74 D2
BT Centre
STBT EC1A 12 E4
Buckhurst Hill ⊖
BKHH IG9 .... 45 H1
Buckhurst Hill Primary School
BKHH IG9 .... 45 J1
Buckingham College
Preparatory School
PIN HA5 .... 47 K6
Buckingham Palace
WHALL SW1A 16 E2
Buckingham Primary School
HPTN TW12 .... 141 K4
Buckingham Road Cemetery
IL IG1 .... 78 D1
The Building Centre
GWRST WC1E 11 G3
Building Crafts College
SRTFD E15 .... 76 B6
Bullers Wood School
CHST BR7 .... 153 K7
Bullsbridge Industrial Estate
NWDGN UB2 .... 102 A3
The Bull Theatre
BAR EN5 .... 26 D3
BUPA Roding Hospital
REDBR IG4 .... 59 H2
Burbage School
IS N1 .... 7 J5
Burdett Coutts CE
Primary School
WEST SW1P 17 G4
Burgess Business Park
CMBW SE5 .... 110 E6
Burgess Park Tennis Centre
CMBW SE5 .... 110 D5
Burlington College
Independent Sixth Form
EDGW HA8 .... 50 B2
Burlington Danes School
SHB W12 .... 87 K5
Burlington Infant School
NWMAL KT3 .... 160 C3
Burney Street Clinic
GNWCH SE10 .... 113 F6
Burnham Trading Estate
DART DA1 .... 139 G3
Burnhill Business Centre
BECK BR3 .... 166 D1
Burnley Road Clinic
WLSDN NW10 .... 69 J4
Burns Hotel
ECT SW5 .... 14 C6
Burnt Ash Primary School
BMLY BR1 .... 152 E4
Burnt Oak ⊖
EDGW HA8 .... 36 E7
Burnt Oak Junior School
BFN/LL DA15 .... 136 B7
Burntwood School
TOOT SW17 .... 147 H1
Bursted Wood Primary School
BXLYHN DA7 .... 137 J1
Burwell Industrial Estate
LEY E10 .... 57 G7
Bushey ⇌
OXHEY WD19 .... 21 H5
Bushey Academy
BUSH WD23 .... 21 K5
Bushey Golf & Country Club
BUSH WD23 .... 22 A5
Bushey Grove Leisure Centre
BUSH WD23 .... 21 K3
Bushey Hall Golf Club
BUSH WD23 .... 21 J2
Bushey Hall Swimming Pool
BUSH WD23 .... 21 K4
Bushey Health Centre
BUSH WD23 .... 21 K5
Bushey Heath Primary School
BUSH WD23 .... 22 D7
Bushey Jewish Cemetery
BUSH WD23 .... 22 B2
Bushey Manor Junior School
BUSH WD23 .... 21 K4
Bushey Meads School
BUSH WD23 .... 22 C4
Bushey Museum & Art Gallery
BUSH WD23 .... 22 A5
Bushey & Oxhey Infant School
BUSH WD23 .... 21 K4
Bush Hill Park ⇌
EN EN1 .... 30 B5
Bush Hill Park Golf Club
WCHMH N21 .... 29 J4
Bush Hill Park Medical Centre
EN EN1 .... 30 A5
Bush Hill Park Primary School
EN EN1 .... 30 C4
Bush House (BBC)
HOL/ALD WC2B 11 L5
Bush Industrial Estate
ARCH N19 .... 72 C2
WLSDN NW10 .... 87 F3
The Business Academy Bexley
ERITHM DA18 .... 117 H7
The Business Centre
CEND/HSY/T N8 .... 54 E1
The Business Design Centre
IS N1 .... 6 B4

Business Training & Solutions
CDALE/KGS NW9 .... 37 H7
Bute House Preparatory School
for Girls
HMSMTH W6 .... 107 F3
Butlers Wharf
STHWK SE1 .... 13 M9
Butler's Wharf Business Centre
STHWK SE1 .... 19 M1
Butler's Wharf Pier
STHWK SE1 .... 13 M9
Butterfly Sports Club
ELTH/MOT SE9 .... 135 G5
Buxlow Preparatory School
WBLY HA9 .... 68 A2
Buxton School
WAN E11 .... 76 D2
Buzzard Creek Industrial Estate
BARK IG11 .... 97 F4
Byam Shaw School of Art
ARCH N19 .... 72 C1
Byfleet Industrial Estate
WATW WD18 .... 20 A7
Bygrove Primary School
POP/IOD E14 .... 93 K5
Byron Court Primary School
ALP/SUD HA0 .... 67 J1
Cable Car
CAN/RD E16 .... 94 D7
Cadet Place
POP/IOD E14 .... 93 J7
Cadogan Hall
CHEL SW3 .... 15 M5
The Cadogan Hotel
KTBR SW1X 15 M4
Cadogan Pier
CHEL SW3 .... 108 D5
Caledonian Market
STHWK SE1 .... 19 L3
Caledonian Road ⊖
HOLWY N7 .... 72 E4
Caledonian Road & Barnsbury ⊖
HOLWY N7 .... 5 M1
Cally Pool
IS N1 .... 5 L3
Calverton Primary School
CAN/RD E16 .... 95 H5
Cambell Primary School
DAGW RM9 .... 79 K6
Camberwell Business Centre
CMBW SE5 .... 110 E6
Camberwell College of Arts
CMBW SE5 .... 111 F7
Camberwell Leisure Centre
CMBW SE5 .... 110 E6
Camberwell New Cemetery
PECK SE15 .... 132 A3
Camberwell Trading Estate
CMBW SE5 .... 130 C1
Cambodian Embassy
CRICK NW2 .... 70 A6
Cambridge Heath ⇌
BETH E2 .... 92 D1
Cambridge Heath Sixth Form
BETH E2 .... 92 D2
Cambridge Park Bowling &
Sports Club
TWK TW1 .... 124 D5
Cambridge School
HMSMTH W6 .... 106 E3
Cambridge Theatre
LSQ/SEVD WC2H 11 J3
Camden Arts Centre
HAMP NW3 .... 71 F4
Camden House Clinic
BKHTH/KID SE3 .... 133 H1
Camden Junior School
CAR SM5 .... 175 K3
Camden Market
CAMTN NW1 .... 4 B2
Camden Mews Day Hospital
CAMTN NW1 .... 4 D1
Camden People's Theatre
CAMTN NW1 .... 4 E8
Camden Road ⊖
CAMTN NW1 .... 4 E1
Camden School for Girls
KTTN NW5 .... 72 C5
Camden Theatre
CAMTN NW1 .... 4 D2
Camden Town ⊖
CAMTN NW1 .... 4 D3
Camden Town Hall & St
Pancras Library
CAMTN NW1 .... 5 J7
Camelot Primary School
PECK SE15 .... 111 J6
Cameron House School
CHEL SW3 .... 15 H9
Camperdown House
WCHPL E1 .... 13 M5
Campion House College
ISLW TW7 .... 103 J5
Campsbourne School
CEND/HSY/T N8 .... 54 E2
Camrose Primary School
EDGW HA8 .... 36 B7
Canada House
STJS SW1Y 11 H8
Canada House Business Centre
RSLP HA4 .... 47 G7
Canada Place
POP/IOD E14 .... 93 J7
Canada Square
POP/IOD E14 .... 93 J7
Canada Water ⊖
BERM/RHTH SE16 .... 111 K2
Canada Water Retail Park
BERM/RHTH SE16 .... 111 K2
Canada Wharf Museum
BERM/RHTH SE16 .... 112 A2
Canada Wharf Museum
BERM/RHTH SE16 .... 93 H7
Canal Cafe Theatre
BAY/PAD W2 .... 8 D2
Canary Riverside
BERM/RHTH SE16 .... 93 H7
Canary Wharf ⊖
POP/IOD E14 .... 93 J7
Canary Wharf Pier
POP/IOD E14 .... 93 H7
Canberra Primary School
SHB W12 .... 87 K6
Canbury 2000 Business Park
KUTN/CMB KT2 .... 144 A7
Canbury Business Centre
KUTN/CMB KT2 .... 144 A7
Canbury Medical Centre
KUTN/CMB KT2 .... 144 B7
Canbury School
KUTN/CMB KT2 .... 144 D5
Cann Hall Primary School
WAN E11 .... 76 D2
The Canning School
ECT SW5 .... 14 C5

KENS W8 .... 14 A3
Canning Town ⊖
POP/IOD E14 .... 94 C5
Cannizaro House Hotel
WIM/MER SW19 .... 146 A5
Cannon Hill Clinic
STHGT/OAK N14 .... 40 E2
Cannon Lane Junior School
PIN HA5 .... 47 H5
Cannon Sports Club
CANST EC4R 12 F6
Cannon Street ⇌ ⊖
CANST EC4R 13 G7
Cannon Trading Estate
WBLY HA9 .... 68 D3
Cannon Wharf Business Centre
DEPT SE8 .... 112 B3
Canon Barnett Primary School
WCHPL E1 .... 13 M4
Canonbury ⇌
IS N1 .... 73 J5
Canonbury Business Centre
IS N1 .... 6 F3
Canonbury Primary School
IS N1 .... 73 H5
Canon Palmer RC High School
IL IG1 .... 60 E7
Canons High School
EDGW HA8 .... 50 B1
The Canons Leisure Centre
MTCM CR4 .... 162 E3
Canons Park ⊖
EDGW HA8 .... 36 A6
Canterbury Industrial Estate
NWCR SE14 .... 112 A5
Cantium Retail Park
STHWK SE1 .... 111 H5
Capital Business Centre
ALP/SUD HA0 .... 85 K1
MTCM CR4 .... 162 E4
SAND/SEL CR2 .... 177 K5
Capital City Academy
WLSDN NW10 .... 69 K7
The Capital Hotel
CHEL SW3 .... 15 L2
Capital Industrial Estate
BELV DA17 .... 98 E7
Capital Radio
LSQ/SEVD WC2H 11 H7
Capital Wharf
WAP E1W 92 C7
Capitol Industrial Park
CDALE/KGS NW9 .... 50 E2
Caplan Estate
MTCM CR4 .... 148 C7
Cardiff Road Industrial Estate
WATW WD18 .... 21 F5
Cardinal Pole RC School
HOM E9 .... 75 G5
Cardinal Pole RC School (Lower)
HOM E9 .... 75 F6
Cardinal Road Infant School
FELT TW13 .... 122 A7
The Cardinal Vaughan Memorial
WKENS W14 .... 107 H1
Cardinal Wiseman RC School
(Technology & Art College)
GFD/PVL UB6 .... 84 C4
Cardwell Primary School
WOOL/PLUM SE18 .... 114 E3
Carew Manor School
WLGTN SM6 .... 176 D2
Carlisle Infant School
HPTN TW12 .... 142 B5
Carlton House
STJS SW1Y 11 G9
The Carlton Mitre Hotel
E/WMO/HCT KT8 .... 157 K2
Carlton Primary School
KTTN NW5 .... 72 A4
Carlton Vale Infant School
MV/WKIL W9 .... 88 D2
Carlyle's House (NT)
CHEL SW3 .... 108 D5
Carnwath Road
Industrial Estate
FUL/PGN SW6 .... 128 A2
Carpenders Park ⊖
OXHEY WD19 .... 33 H2
Carpenders Park Cemetery
OXHEY WD19 .... 33 K3
Carpenters' Hall
OBST EC2N 13 H3
Carpenters Primary School
SRTFD E15 .... 76 A7
Carshalton ⇌
CAR SM5 .... 175 J3
Carshalton AFC
SUT SM1 .... 175 J2
Carshalton Beeches ⇌
CAR SM5 .... 175 K5
Carshalton Boys Sports College
CAR SM5 .... 175 H1
Carshalton College
CAR SM5 .... 175 J2
Carshalton
High School for Girls
CAR SM5 .... 175 J2
Carshalton War
Memorial Hospital
CAR SM5 .... 175 H5
The Cartoon Museum
RSQ WC1B 11 J3
Caryl Thomas Clinic
HRW HA1 .... 48 E3
Cass Business School
STLK EC1Y 13 G1
The Cassel Hospital
RCHPK/HAM TW10 .... 143 K3
Cassidy Medical Centre
FUL/PGN SW6 .... 107 K6
Castilion Primary School
THMD SE28 .... 97 J5
Castle Bar Park ⇌
HNWL W7 .... 85 F4
Castlebar School
HNWL W7 .... 85 F4
Castlebar Special School
WEA W13 .... 85 G4
Castlecombe Primary School
ELTH/MOT SE9 .... 153 J4
Castle Hill Primary School
CROY/NA CR0 .... 180 A5
Castle Industrial Estate
WALW SE17 .... 18 E5
Casualty Plus Clinic
BTFD TW8 .... 104 E4
Caterham High School
CLAY IG5 .... 59 K1
Catford ⇌
CAT SE6 .... 132 D6
Catford Bridge ⇌
CAT SE6 .... 132 D6

Catford Cricket & Sports Club *CAT* SE6 132 E7
Catford Cyphers CC *CAT* SE6 151 H1
Catford Trading Estate *CAT* SE6 151 K1
Catford Wanderers Sports Club *CAT* SE6 152 A3
Cathall Leisure Centre *WAN* E11 76 B2
Cathedral School of St Saviour & St Mary Overy *STHWK* SE1 18 F1
Cator Park School for Girls *BECK* BR3 151 G6
Cavendish College *FITZ* W1T 11 G2
Cavendish Hotel *STJS* SW1Y 10 F8
Cavendish Primary School *CHSWK* W4 106 B6
Cavendish School *BERM/RHTH* SE16 111 K3
The Cavendish School *CAMTN* NW1 4 C3
Cavendish Special School *HNWL* W7 85 F5
Caxton Hall *STJSPK* SW1H 17 G3
Caxton Trading Estate *HYS/HAR* UB3 101 H1
Cayley Primary School *WCHPL* E1 93 G4
Cecil Park Clinic *PIN* HA5 47 J3
Cecil Sharpe House *CAMTN* NW1 4 B3
The Cedar School *FSTGT* E7 77 G5
Cedars Manor School *KTN/HRWW/WS* HA3 34 C7
The Cedars Primary School *HEST* TW5 101 K6
Cedar Way Industrial Estate *CAMTN* NW1 5 G2
Cenotaph *WHALL* SW1A 17 J1
Centaurs Business Centre *ISLW* TW7 104 B5
Centaurs RFC *ISLW* TW7 104 A5
Central Business Centre *WLSDN* NW10 69 G4
The Central College of London *WCHPL* E1 13 M3
Central Criminal Court *STP* EC4M 12 C4
Centrale Shopping Centre *CROY/NA* CR0 177 J1
Central Foundation Boys School *SDTCH* EC2A 7 H9
Central Foundation Girls School (Lower) *BOW* E3 93 G2
Central Foundation Girls School (Upper) *BOW* E3 93 H2
Central Hall *STJSPK* SW1H 17 H2
Central Hendon Clinic *HDN* NW4 51 K3
Central London County Court *CAVSQ/HST* W1G 10 C1
Central London Golf Club *TOOT* SW17 147 H1
Central London Markets *STBT* EC1A 12 C3
Central Medical Centre *MRDN* SM4 162 B3
Central Middlesex Hospital *WLSDN* NW10 86 E2
Central Park Arena *DART* DA1 139 H7
Central Park Primary School *EHAM* E6 95 H1
Central Primary School *WAT* WD17 21 G3
Central St Martins College of Art & Design *RSQ* WC1B 11 L3
Central School of Ballet *CLKNW* EC1R 12 B1
Central School of Fashion *GTPST* W1W 10 E3
Central School of Speech & Drama *HAMP* NW3 3 G1
Central Square Shopping Centre *WBLY* HA9 68 A5
Central YMCA *ELTH/MOT* SE9 153 H1
Centre Court Shopping Centre *WIM/MER* SW19 146 D5
The Centre Performing Arts College *CHARL* SE7 114 C2
Centre Point *LSQ/SEVD* WC2H 11 H4
Chadwell Heath ⇌ *CHDH* RM6 61 K6
Chadwell Heath Academy *CHDH* RM6 61 H5
Chadwell Heath Industrial Park *BCTR* RM8 62 A7
Chadwell Heath Leisure Centre *CHDH* RM6 61 K5
Chadwell Infant & Primary School *CHDH* RM6 61 J6
Chaffinch Business Park *BECK* BR3 166 A2
Chailey Industrial Estate *HYS/HAR* UB3 101 K1
Chalcot School *CAMTN* NW1 4 C1
Chalgrove Primary School *FNCH* N3 52 C2
Chalk Farm ⊖ *HAMP* NW3 4 A1
Chalkhill Primary School *WBLY* HA9 68 D2
The Chamberlain Hotel *TWRH* EC3N 13 L6
Chambers Business Park *WDR/YW* UB7 100 D5
Chambers Wharf *BERM/RHTH* SE16 111 H1
Chancery Court Hotel *HHOL* WC1V 11 L3
Chancery Lane ⊖ *FSBYW* WC1X 12 A3
Chandlers Field Primary School *E/WMO/HCT* KT8 157 F4
Chandos Business Centre *WLGTN* SM6 176 C5
Channelsea Business Centre *SRTFD* E15 94 B1
Channing School *HGT* N6 54 B7
Chapel End Infant School *WALTH* E17 57 K1
Chapel End Junior School *WALTH* E17 43 K7
Chapman Park Industrial Estate *WLSDN* NW10 69 H5
Charing Cross ⇌ *CHCR* WC2N 11 J8
Charing Cross Hospital *HMSMTH* W6 107 G5
Charing Cross Hotel *CHCR* WC2N 11 J7
The Charles Dickens Museum *BMSBY* WC1N 11 L1
Charles Dickens Primary School *STHWK* SE1 18 E2
Charles Edward Brooke School (Lower School) *CMBW* SE5 110 C7
Charles Edward Brooke School (Upper School) *BRXN/ST* SW9 110 C7
Charlotte Sharman Primary School *LBTH* SE11 18 C4
Charlton ⇌ *CHARL* SE7 114 B4
Charlton Athletic FC (The Valley) *CHARL* SE7 114 B4
Charlton Cemetery *CHARL* SE7 114 D5
Charlton Health & Fitness Centre *CHARL* SE7 114 B4
Charlton House *CHARL* SE7 114 C5
Charlton Manor Junior School *CHARL* SE7 114 C6
Charlton RFC *ELTH/MOT* SE9 135 G6
Charlton School *CHARL* SE7 114 D5
Charrington Bowl *SURB* KT6 172 D1
Charrville Primary School *YEAD* UB4 82 C1
Charter Clinic *CHEL* SW3 15 L8
Charterhouse *FARR* EC1M 12 D1
Charteris Road Sports Centre *HAMP* NW3 71 J4
KIL/WHAMP NW6 70 D7
Charter Nightingale Hospital & Counselling Centre *CAMTN* NW1 9 K2
The Charter School *HNHL* SE24 130 E4
Chartwell Business Centre *BMLY* BR1 168 C2
Chase Bridge Primary School *WHTN* TW2 123 K5
Chase Lane Primary School *CHING* E4 43 H3
Chase Road Trading Estate *WLSDN* NW10 87 F3
Chase Side Primary School *ENC/FH* EN2 29 J1
Chaseville Clinic *WCHMH* N21 29 F5
Chater Infant School *WATW* WD18 20 E3
Chater Junior School *WATW* WD18 20 E3
Chatsworth Infant School *BFN/LL* DA15 136 B7
Chatsworth Primary School *HSLW* TW3 123 H3
Chaucer Clinic *NWDGN* UB2 103 J1
Cheam ⇌ *BELMT* SM2 174 D6
Cheam Common J & I School *WPK* KT4 173 K1
Cheam Fields Primary School *CHEAM* SM3 174 C4
Cheam High School *CHEAM* SM3 174 C3
Cheam Leisure Centre *CHEAM* SM3 174 B3
Cheam Park Farm Junior School *CHEAM* SM3 174 C2
Cheam Sports Club *CHEAM* SM3 174 C6
Chelsea Bridge Business Centre *VX/NE* SW8 109 G6
Chelsea Centre & Theatre *WBPTN* SW10 108 B6
Chelsea Cinema *CHEL* SW3 15 K8
The Chelsea Club Leisure Centre *FUL/PGN* SW6 108 A5
Chelsea College of Art & Design *CHEL* SW3 15 J8
FUL/PGN SW6 128 B1
SHB W12 106 E1
WEST SW1P 17 H7
Chelsea FC (Stamford Bridge) *FUL/PGN* SW6 108 A6
Chelsea Fields Industrial Estate *WIM/MER* SW19 147 H7
Chelsea Group of Children *WBPTN* SW10 108 B6
Chelsea Independent College *FUL/PGN* SW6 108 A6
Chelsea Leisure Centre *CHEL* SW3 15 K8
Chelsea Old Town Hall *CHEL* SW3 15 K8
Chelsea Physic Garden *CHEL* SW3 15 L9
CHEL SW3 108 E5
Chelsea & Westminster Hospital *WBPTN* SW10 108 B5
Chelsea Wharf *WBPTN* SW10 108 C6
Chennestone Community School *SUN* TW16 156 A1
Cherington House Health Centre *HNWL* W7 85 F7
Cherry Garden Pier *BERM/RHTH* SE16 111 J1
Cherry Garden School *BERM/RHTH* SE16 111 H3
Cherry Lane Primary School *WDR/YW* UB7 100 C3
Cherry Orchard Primary School *CHARL* SE7 114 B6
The Cherry Trees *BOW* E3 93 J2
Chesington Community College *CHSGTN* KT9 171 K6
Chessington CC *CHSGTN* KT9 171 J6
Chessington Golf Club *CHSGTN* KT9 171 K6
Chessington North ⇌ *CHSGTN* KT9 172 A4
Chessington South ⇌ *CHSGTN* KT9 171 K6
The Chesterfield Mayfair Hotel *MYFR/PICC* W1J 10 C8
Chesterton Primary School *BTSEA* SW11 109 F7
Chestnut Grove School *BAL* SW12 129 F7
Chestnuts Primary School *SEVS/STOTM* N15 55 J4
Cheyne Centre *CHEL* SW3 108 C5
Chicken Shed Theatre *STHGT/OAK* N14 28 A4
Childeric Primary School *NWCR* SE14 112 B6
Childrens House Upper School *IS* N1 74 A4
Childs Hill Clinic *CRICK* NW2 70 D1
Childs Hill Primary School *CRICK* NW2 70 C2
Childs Welfare Clinic *BCTR* RM8 79 J4
Chiltonian Industrial Estate *LEE/GVPK* SE12 133 J5
Chimnocks Wharf *POP/IOD* E14 93 G6
Chingford Foundation School *CHING* E4 31 K7
Chingford Hall Primary School *CHING* E4 43 H5
Chingford Health Centre *CHING* E4 43 J3
Chingford Industrial Centre *CHING* E4 43 G4
Chingford Mount Cemetery *CHING* E4 43 K2
Chingford RFC *CHING* E4 31 J7
Chisenhale Primary School *BOW* E3 93 G1
Chislehurst ⇌ *BMLY* BR1 169 F1
Chislehurst Caves *CHST* BR7 154 A7
Chislehurst Cemetery *CHST* BR7 154 E4
Chislehurst Golf Club *CHST* BR7 154 B6
Chislehurst Natural Health Centre *CHST* BR7 154 B5
Chislehurst & Sidcup Grammar School *BFN/LL* DA15 155 H1
Chiswick ⇌ *CHSWK* W4 105 K6
Chiswick & Bedford Park Preparatory School *CHSWK* W4 106 B3
Chiswick Business Park *CHSWK* W4 105 J3
Chiswick Community School *CHSWK* W4 106 A6
Chiswick House *CHSWK* W4 106 A5
Chiswick Moran Hotel *CHSWK* W4 105 J4
Chiswick Park ⊖ *CHSWK* W4 105 K3
Chrisp Street Health Centre *POP/IOD* E14 93 K5
Christ Church Bentinck CE Primary School *CAMTN* NW1 9 J2
Christ Church Brondesbury CE J & I School *KIL/WHAMP* NW6 70 D7
Christ Church CE Junior School *EA* W5 85 K6
Christ Church CE Primary School *BAR* EN5 26 B1
BRXN/ST SW9 110 B7
BRYLDS KT5 159 H5
BTSEA SW11 128 D2
CHEL SW3 15 K9
FSTH SE23 151 F1
WOOL/PLUM SE18 115 F7
Christchurch CE Primary School *HAMP* NW3 71 H2
WCHPL E1 13 M3
Christ Church CE VA Primary School *ERITH* DA8 118 A5
Christchurch Industrial Centre *STHWK* SE1 12 C8
Christ Church New Malden CE Primary School *NWMAL* KT3 160 B2
Christchurch Primary School *IL* IG1 60 B7
Christ Church Primary School *NWMAL* KT3 160 A2
Christ Church School *CAMTN* NW1 4 D6
Christian Meeting Hall *BECK* BR3 151 J7
Christopher Hatton Primary School *FSBYW* WC1X 12 A1
Christs College Finchley *FNCH* N3 53 F2
Christs College School *EFNCH* N2 53 F2
Christs School *RCHPK/HAM* TW10 125 G4
Christ the King RC Primary School *FSBYPK* N4 55 F7
Christ the King Sixth Form College *LEW* SE13 133 G2
Chrysalis Theatre *BAL* SW12 129 F7
Chrysanthemum Clinic *CHSWK* W4 105 K6
Chrysolyte Independent Christian School *STHWK* SE1 19 H3
Church Down Adult School *LEE/GVPK* SE12 152 E1
Church End Medical Centre *WLSDN* NW10 69 G5
Church Farm House Museum *HDN* NW4 51 K2
Church Farm Swimming Pool *EBAR* EN4 27 K7
Churchfield Primary School *ED* N9 30 B7
Churchfields J & I School *SWFD* E18 44 E7
Churchfields Primary School *BECK* BR3 166 A2
Church House *WEST* SW1P 17 H3
Churchill Clinic *STHWK* SE1 18 B3
Churchill College *RYNPK* SW20 161 F1
Churchill Gardens Primary School *PIM* SW1V 16 E8
Churchill Theatre *BMLY* BR1 167 K1
Churchill War Rooms *STJSPK* SW1H 17 H1
Church Stairs *BERM/RHTH* SE16 111 J1
Church Street ⊖ *CROY/NA* CR0 177 J1
Church Trading Estate *ERITH* DA8 118 D6
Cineworld *CHEL* SW3 15 H9
CRICK NW2 51 K7
EA W5 85 K6
EN EN1 30 C3
FELT TW13 141 F1
HMSMTH W6 106 E3
SOHO/SHAV W1D 11 G7
WBPTN SW10 14 F8
BXLYHS DA6 137 J3
WDGN N22 55 G1
Citigroup Tower *POP/IOD* E14 93 K7
The City Academy Hackney *HOM* E9 74 E4
City Banking College *STHWK* SE1 19 J1
City Business Centre *BERM/RHTH* SE16 111 K1
City Business College *FSBYE* EC1V 6 D8
City Central Estate *FSBYE* EC1V 6 E8
City College of Higher Education *IS* N1 7 H7
City & Guilds of London Art School *LBTH* SE11 18 B8
City Health Centre *FSBYE* EC1V 7 G9
City & Islington College *FSBYE* EC1V 6 F8
FSBYPK N4 73 H1
HBRY N5 73 G5
HOLWY N7 72 E3
HOLWY N7 73 F2
IS N1 7 G3
City & Islington Sixth Form College *FSBYE* EC1V 6 C6
City Literary College *HHOL* WC1V 11 K4
City of London Academy *STHWK* SE1 111 H4
The City of London Academy Islington *IS* N1 6 E4
The City of London Academy *EDUL* SE22 131 H4
City of London Business College *SEVS/STOTM* N15 56 A4
SEVS/STOTM N15 56 C4
City of London Cemetery *MNPK* E12 77 J1
City of London Club *OBST* EC2N 13 J4
City of London College *WCHPL* E1 92 C5
City of London Crematorium *MNPK* E12 77 J2
City of London Magistrates Court *LOTH* EC2R 13 G5
City of London School for Girls *BARB* EC2Y 12 E2
City of London School Sports Ground *LEE/GVPK* SE12 153 G1
City of Westminster Cemetery *HNWL* W7 85 F7
City of Westminster College *BAY/PAD* W2 9 G2
MV/WKIL W9 2 B8
City of Westminster Vehicle Pound *MYFR/PKLN* W1K 9 M7
City Thameslink ⇌ *FLST/FETLN* EC4A 12 C4
City University *CLKNW* EC1R 6 C8
IS N1 6 E6
STBT EC1A 12 E3
WCHPL E1 92 D4
City University Business School *BARB* EC2Y 12 F2
Civic Medical Centre *HRW* HA1 48 E4
Civil Service Sports Ground *CHSWK* W4 106 B7
LEE/GVPK SE12 134 B5
Clapham Common ⊖ *CLAP* SW4 129 H3
Clapham Common Clinic *CLAP* SW4 129 J3
Clapham High Street ⇌ ⊖ *CLAP* SW4 129 J2
Clapham Junction ⇌ ⊖ *BTSEA* SW11 128 D3
Clapham Manor Primary School *CLAP* SW4 129 H2
Clapham Manor Street Public Baths *CLAP* SW4 129 J2
Clapham North ⊖ *CLAP* SW4 129 J2
Clapham North Business Centre *CLAP* SW4 129 J2
Clapham Picture House *CLAP* SW4 129 H3
Clapham South ⊖ *CLAP* SW4 129 G5
Clapton ⇌ *CLPT* E5 74 D1
Clapton Girls Technology College *CLPT* E5 74 E3
Clara Grant Primary School *BOW* E3 93 J3
Clare House Primary School *BECK* BR3 167 F1
Claremont Clinic *FSTGT* E7 77 G4
Claremont Fan Court School *ESH/CLAY* KT10 170 B5
Claremont High School Academy Trust *KTN/HRWW/WS* HA3 50 A4
Claremont Landscape Garden (NT) *ESH/CLAY* KT10 170 A6
Claremont Primary School *CRICK* NW2 70 B1
Claremont Way Industrial Estate *CRICK* NW2 52 A7
Clarence House *WHALL* SW1A 16 F1
Clarendon Special School *HPTN* TW12 142 B5
Claridge's Hotel *MYFR/PKLN* W1K 10 C6
Claverings Industrial Estate *ED* N9 42 E1
Claygate ⇌ *ESH/CLAY* KT10 170 D5
Claygate Primary School *ESH/CLAY* KT10 170 E6
Clayhall Clinic *CLAY* IG5 59 J2
Clayponds Hospital *BTFD* TW8 105 F3
Cleeve Park School *SCUP* DA14 155 J2
Clementine Churchill Hospital *HRW* HA1 66 E2
Cleopatra's Needle *CHCR* WC2N 11 L8
Clerkenwell County Court *IS* N1 6 C5
Clerkenwell Heritage Centre *FARR* EC1M 12 C1
Clerkenwell Parochial CE Primary School *CLKNW* EC1R 6 A8
Cleveland Primary School *IL* IG1 78 B3
Cleves Primary School *EHAM* E6 77 H7
C & L Golf & Country Club *NTHLT* UB5 65 F6
Clifton Lodge School *EA* W5 85 J6
Clifton Primary School *NWDGN* UB2 102 D3
Clink Exhibition *STHWK* SE1 13 G8
Clissold Leisure Centre *STNW/STAM* N16 73 K2
Clissold Park Natural Health Centre *STNW/STAM* N16 74 A1
C & L Leisure Centre *RSLP* HA4 65 F6
Clock House ⇌ *BECK* BR3 166 B1
Clockhouse Industrial Estate *EBED/NFELT* TW14 120 E7
Clock Mill *POP/IOD* E14 94 A2
Clock Museum *CITYW* EC2V 12 F4
Cloisters Business Centre *VX/NE* SW8 109 G6
Clore Gallery *WEST* SW1P 17 J6
Clore Tikva School *BARK/HLT* IG6 60 C1
Clothworkers' Hall *FENCHST* EC3M 13 K6
Clouster's Green *WAP* E1W 92 C7
Cobbold Estate *WLSDN* NW10 69 H5
Cobourg Primary School *CMBW* SE5 19 L9
Cochrane Theatre *GINN* WC1R 11 L3
Cockfosters ⊖ *EBAR* EN4 28 A3
Cockfosters Sports Ground *EBAR* EN4 27 K2
The Cockpit Theatre *STJWD* NW8 9 J1
Coldharbour Industrial Estate *CMBW* SE5 130 D1
Coldharbour Leisure Centre *ELTH/MOT* SE9 153 K1
Coldharbour Sports Ground *ELTH/MOT* SE9 154 A1
Colebrooke Primary School *IS* N1 6 C5
Colegrave School *SRTFD* E15 76 B4
Coleraine Park Primary School *TOTM* N17 42 D7
Coleridge Primary School *HGT* N6 54 D6
Colfes Pre-Preparatory School *LEE/GVPK* SE12 134 A5
Colfe's Preparatory School *LEE/GVPK* SE12 133 K5
Colindale ⊖ *CDALE/KGS* NW9 51 G2
Colindale Business Park *CDALE/KGS* NW9 50 E2
Colindale Hospital *CDALE/KGS* NW9 51 G2
Colindale Primary School *CDALE/KGS* NW9 51 H3
Coliseum Theatre *CHCR* WC2N 11 J7
College Fields Business Centre *WIM/MER* SW19 147 J7
College of Arms *BLKFR* EC4V 12 E5
College of Central London *SDTCH* EC2A 7 J9

College of Fuel Technology
 HGT N6............................54 A5
College of Haringey, Enfield &
 North East London
 PEND EN3.........................30 E2
 SEVS/STOTM N15..................56 B3
The College of Law
 FITZ W1T..........................11 G3
 LINN WC2A........................12 A4
College of North East London
 CEND/HSY/T N8...................55 G3
 WDGN N22.........................40 C7
College of North West London
 KIL/WHAMP NW6....................2 A3
 WBLY HA9.........................68 C2
 WLSDN NW10.......................69 H4
College of Organists
 FLST/FETLN EC4A..................12 B3
College of Osteopathy
 BORE WD6.........................24 D2
College Park School
 BAY/PAD W2........................8 B5
Collier's Wood ⊖
 WIM/MER SW19.....................147 H6
Collingwood Business Centre
 ARCH N19.........................72 E2
Collingwood School
 WLGTN SM6........................176 B4
Collins Method School
 CRICK NW2........................70 A5
Collis Primary School
 TEDD TW11........................143 H5
Colnbrook School
 OXHEY WD19.......................33 G1
Colne Bridge Retail Park
 WAT WD17.........................21 H4
Colne Valley Retail Park
 WAT WD17.........................21 H4
Colonnades Leisure Park
 CROY/NA CR0......................177 G5
The Colonnades
 Shopping Centre
 BGVA SW1W........................16 C5
Colours Sports Club
 SUT SM1..........................175 G4
Columbia Primary School
 BETH E2...........................7 M7
Colvestone Primary School
 HACK E8..........................74 B4
Colville Primary School
 NTGHL W11........................88 D5
Colyers Lane Medical Centre
 ERITH DA8.......................118 A7
Comber Grove Primary School
 CMBW SE5........................110 D6
Comedy Theatre
 STJS SW1Y.........................11 G7
Comelle House Trading Estate
 DEPT SE8........................112 B4
Comfort Hotel
 EMC/FH EN2.......................29 H1
Comfort Inn
 HYS/HAR UB3.....................101 H4
Commonwealth Institute
 WKENS W14.......................107 J2
Community Arts Centre
 GNWCH SE10......................112 E6
Community Centre
 (Island History Trust)
 POP/IOD E14.....................113 F3
Community College & School
 GNWCH SE10......................113 F6
The Community College
 HACK E8..........................74 D7
Compass Theatre
 HGDN/ICK UB10....................64 A2
Complementary
 Health Centre
 LEE/GVPK SE12...................133 H5
The Compton School
 NFNCH/WDSPK N12..................39 J5
Compton Sports Centre
 NFNCH/WDSPK N12..................39 J5
Concord Business Centre
 ACT W3...........................86 D4
Conduit House
 GNWCH SE10......................113 G6
Coney Hill School
 HAYES BR2.......................180 D1
Conisborough College
 CAT SE6.........................152 B2
Connaught Business Centre
 CDALE/KGS NW9....................51 H4
 CROY/NA CR0.....................177 F5
 MTCM CR4........................162 E4
The Connaught Hotel
 MYFR/PKLN W1K....................10 B7
Connaught House School
 BAY/PAD W2........................9 K5
Connaught School for Girls
 WAN E11..........................58 C7
Consort Clinic
 PECK SE15.......................131 J2
Consulate
 General of Monaco
 SKENS SW7........................15 G5
Consulate General of The
 Republic of Guinea Bissau
 KENS W8..........................14 E3
Consulate of Burkina Faso
 BTSEA SW11......................128 B2
Consulate of Chile
 CAVSQ/HST W1G....................10 C1
Consulate of Colombia
 GTPST W1W........................10 E4
Consulate of Eritrea
 IS N1.............................6 B5
Consulate of Guinea
 MYFR/PKLN W1K....................10 A7
Consulate of Panama
 MYFR/PICC W1J....................10 C9
The Continental Hotel
 HSLW TW3........................123 F2
Convent of Jesus & Mary
 Infant School
 CRICK NW2........................70 A4
Convent of Jesus &
 Mary Language College
 WLSDN NW10.......................69 H7
Convoy's Wharf
 DEPT SE8........................112 C4
Conway Medical Centre
 WOOL/PLUM SE18..................115 J4
Conway Primary School
 WOOL/PLUM SE18..................115 K3
Coombe Girls School
 NWMAL KT3.......................160 A1
Coombe Hill Golf Club
 KUTN/CMB KT2....................145 F6
Coombe Hill J & I School
 NWMAL KT3.......................145 F6
Coombe Lane ⊖
 CROY/NA CR0.....................178 E6

Coombe Wood Golf Club
 KUTN/CMB KT2....................144 D6
Coopers' Hall
 LVPST EC2M.......................13 K3
Coopers Lane Primary School
 LEE/GVPK SE12...................152 E1
Coopers Technology College
 CHST BR7........................154 C7
Copenhagen Primary School
 IS N1.............................5 K4
Copland Specialist
 Science College
 WBLY HA9.........................68 B4
Coppermill Primary School
 WALTH E17........................57 F4
Coppetts Wood Hospital
 MUSWH N10........................39 K7
Coppetts Wood
 Primary School
 MUSWH N10........................40 A7
Copthall School
 MLHL NW7.........................37 K6
Copthorne Tara Hotel
 KENS W8..........................14 C3
Cordwainers College
 HACK E8..........................74 E6
Corinthian Casuals FC
 SURB KT6........................172 C2
Coronet Cinema
 NTGHL W11.........................8 A8
 SEVS/STOTM N15...................55 H2
Corpus Christi RC
 Primary School
 BRXS/STRHM SW2..................130 A4
Cosmopolitan College
 IS N1.............................5 L6
Coston Primary School
 GFD/PVL UB6......................84 C2
Coteford Infant School
 PIN HA5..........................46 E4
County Council Offices
 BUSH WD23........................22 D6
Courtauld Institute Gallery
 TPL/STR WC2R.....................11 L6
Courtauld Institute of Art
 TPL/STR WC2R.....................11 M6
Court Farm Industrial Estate
 STWL/WRAY TW19..................120 C5
Courtfield Medical Centre
 ECT SW5..........................14 D6
Courtland JMI School
 MLHL NW7.........................37 G1
Covent Garden ⊖
 COVGDN WC2E......................11 J6
Covent Garden Flower Market
 VX/NE SW8.......................109 J5
Covent Garden Medical Centre
 LSQ/SEVD WC2H....................11 J5
Crafts Council
 IS N1.............................6 B6
Crampton Primary School
 WALW SE17........................18 D6
Cranbrook College
 IL IG1...........................78 A1
Cranbrook Primary School
 IL IG1...........................59 K6
Crane Park Island
 Nature Reserve
 FELT TW13.......................141 K1
Cranford Community College
 HEST TW5........................102 A5
Cranford Infant School
 HSLWW TW4.......................121 K1
Cranford Junior School
 HSLWW TW4.......................122 A1
Cranford Park Junior School
 HYS/HAR UB3.....................101 J3
Cranford Park Primary School
 HYS/HAR UB3.....................101 J1
Cranleigh Gardens
 Industrial Estate
 STHL UB1.........................83 K4
The Cranley Hotel
 ECT SW5..........................14 E7
Cranmer Primary School
 MTCM CR4........................162 E3
The Craven Clinic
 HMSMTH W6.......................106 E3
Craven Park Health Centre
 WLSDN NW10.......................69 F7
Craven Park Medical Centre
 WLSDN NW10.......................69 F7
Crawford Primary School
 CMBW SE5........................110 D7
Crayfields Business Park
 STMC/STPC BR5...................155 J7
Crayford ⇌
 DART DA1........................138 B5
Crayford Commercial Centre
 DART DA1........................138 B4
Crayford Industrial Estate
 DART DA1........................138 C4
Crayford Leisure Centre &
 Greyhound Stadium
 DART DA1........................138 B5
Crayford Medical Centre
 DART DA1........................138 C4
Crayside Industrial Estate
 DART DA1........................138 D2
Creekmouth Industrial Estate
 BARK IG11........................97 F3
Creek Road Health Centre
 DEPT SE8........................112 D5
Creek Road Industrial Estate
 DEPT SE8........................112 E5
The Crest Boys Academy
 CRICK NW2........................69 H2
Crewe House
 MYFR/PICC W1J....................10 C8
Cricket Green School
 MTCM CR4........................162 D2
Cricklefield Stadium
 IL IG1...........................78 E1
Cricklewood ⇌
 CRICK NW2........................70 B2
Cricklewood Trading Estate
 CRICK NW2........................70 C2
Crispin Industrial Centre
 UED N18..........................42 E4
Criterion Theatre
 MYFR/PICC W1J....................10 F7
Crofton Leisure Centre
 BROCKY SE4......................132 D5
Crofton Park ⇌
 BROCKY SE4......................132 C4
Croham Hurst Golf Club
 SAND/SEL CR2....................178 B5
Cromer Road Primary School
 BAR EN5..........................27 F2
Cromwell Business Centre
 BARK IG11........................96 E2
Cromwell Hospital
 ECT SW5..........................14 C5

Crook Log Primary School
 BXLYHS DA6......................136 E3
Crook Log Sports Centre
 WELL DA16.......................136 E2
Crossharbour
 POP/IOD E14.....................112 C2
Crossways Sixth Form
 BROCKY SE4......................132 E3
Crouch End Art School
 CEND/HSY/T N8....................54 E4
Crouch End Health Centre
 CEND/HSY/T N8....................54 E4
Crouch Hill ⇌
 FSBYPK N4........................55 F6
Crouch Hill Recreation Centre
 CEND/HSY/T N8....................54 E6
Crowland Primary School
 SEVS/STOTM N15...................56 C4
Crowlands Primary School
 ROMW/RG RM7......................62 C5
Crown Close Business Centre
 BOW E3...........................75 J7
Crown Court at The Borough
 STHWK SE1........................18 D1
Crowndale Health Centre
 CAMTN NW1.........................4 F5
Crowne Plaza
 EA W5............................86 A2
 WDR/YW UB7......................100 A3
Crowne Plaza Hotel
 BETH E2...........................7 L8
 CAN/RD E16.......................94 E6
 EMB EC4Y.........................12 C6
 SKENS SW7........................14 E5
Crownfield Primary School
 ROMW/RG RM7......................62 C1
Crown Lane Clinic
 STHGT/OAK N14....................28 C7
Crown Lane Primary School
 WNWD SE27.......................149 J3
Crown Moran Hotel
 CRICK NW2........................70 B3
Crown Trading Centre
 HYS/HAR UB3.....................101 H1
Crown Woods School
 ELTH/MOT SE9....................135 H4
Croydon Airport
 Industrial Estate
 CROY/NA CR0.....................177 G6
Croydon Bowling Club
 SAND/SEL CR2....................177 J4
Croydon Cemetery
 CROY/NA CR0.....................164 A4
Croydon Clocktower Cinema
 CROY/NA CR0.....................177 J2
Croydon College
 CROY/NA CR0.....................177 K2
Croydon Combined Courts
 CROY/NA CR0.....................177 K2
Croydon Crematorium
 THHTH CR7.......................163 H4
Croydon Fairfield Halls Cinema
 CROY/NA CR0.....................177 K2
Croydon FC
 SNWD SE25.......................165 K4
Croydon Road
 Industrial Estate
 BECK BR3........................165 K3
Croydon Sports Arena
 SNWD SE25.......................165 K4
Crusader Industrial Estate
 FSBYPK N4........................55 J5
Crystal Palace ⇌ ⊖
 PGE/AN SE20.....................150 C5
Crystal Palace FC
 (Selhurst Park)
 SNWD SE25.......................165 F3
Crystal Palace FC Soccer &
 Sports Centre
 BRXN/ST SW9.....................130 A2
Crystal Palace Museum
 NRWD SE19.......................150 B5
Cuaco Sports Ground
 BECK BR3........................151 J5
Cubitt Town Infant School
 POP/IOD E14.....................113 F2
Cuckoo Hall Academy
 ED N9............................30 E6
Cuddington Cemetery
 WPK KT4.........................173 K1
Cuddington CP School
 WPK KT4.........................173 H2
Cuddington Croft
 Primary School
 BELMT SM2.......................174 B7
Culloden Primary School
 POP/IOD E14......................94 B5
Culvers House Primary School
 MTCM CR4........................163 F7
Cumberland Business Park
 WLSDN NW10.......................86 D2
The Cumberland Hotel
 FITZ W1T.........................11 G4
 MBLAR W1H.........................9 M5
Cumberland Park
 Industrial Estate
 WLSDN NW10.......................87 J2
The Cumming Museum
 WALW SE17........................18 E6
Cumnor House School
 SAND/SEL CR2....................177 H7
Curwen Primary School
 PLSTW E13........................94 E1
Curzon Mayfair Cinema
 MYFR/PICC W1J....................10 C9
Curzon Soho Cinema
 SOHO/SHAV W1D....................11 H6
Custom House
 MON EC3R.........................13 J7
Custom House for ExCeL ⊖
 CAN/RD E16.......................95 F6
Custom House Hotel
 CAN/RD E16.......................95 F6
Cutlers' Hall
 STP EC4M.........................12 D4
Cutty Sark ⊖
 GNWCH SE10......................113 F5
Cutty Sark Clipper Ship
 GNWCH SE10......................113 F5
Cygnet Clinic Beckton
 EHAM E6..........................96 B4
Cygnus Business Centre
 WLSDN NW10.......................69 H4
Cypress Infant School
 SNWD SE25.......................165 F1
Cypress Junior School
 SNWD SE25.......................165 F1
Cyprus ⊖
 CAN/RD E16.......................96 A6
Cyprus College of Art
 WNWD SE27.......................149 H3
Cyril Jackson Primary School
 POP/IOD E14......................93 H6

Dagenham Chest Clinic
 BCTR RM8.........................80 B2
Dagenham Civic Centre
 DAGE RM10........................80 D1
Dagenham Dock ⇌
 DAGW RM9.........................98 B1
Dagenham East ⊖
 DAGE RM10........................80 E5
Dagenham Heathway ⊖
 DAGW RM9.........................80 B5
Dagenham Park CE School
 DAGE RM10........................80 D6
Dagenham & Redbridge FC
 DAGE RM10........................80 D4
Dagenham Superbowl
 DAGE RM10........................98 D1
Dagenham Swimming Pool
 DAGE RM10........................80 C1
Daily Telegraph
 Newspaper Offices
 POP/IOD E14.....................112 D2
Dairy Meadow
 Primary School
 NWDGN UB2.......................102 E2
D'Albiac House
 HTHAIR TW6......................120 D1
Dali Universe
 STHWK SE1........................17 L1
Dallington School
 FSBYE EC1V........................6 D9
Dalmain Primary School
 FSTH SE23.......................132 B7
Dalston Junction ⊖
 HACK E8..........................74 B5
Dalston Kingsland ⊖
 IS N1............................74 A5
Damilola Taylor Centre
 PECK SE15.......................111 G6
Danegrove Primary School
 EBAR EN4.........................27 J5
Danetree School
 HOR/WEW KT19....................172 E6
Danson House
 BXLYHS DA6......................136 D3
Danson Primary School
 WELL DA16.......................136 C3
Danson Watersports Centre
 BXLYHS DA6......................136 D4
Darell Primary School
 RCH/KEW TW9.....................125 H2
Darent Industrial Park
 ERITH DA8.......................119 G4
Dartford ⇌
 DART DA1........................139 H4
Dartford Adult
 Education Centre
 DART DA1........................139 F6
Dartford Bridge Community
 Primary School
 DART DA1........................139 J1
Dartford County Court
 DART DA1........................139 H6
Dartford Grammar School
 for Boys
 DART DA1........................139 F6
Dartford Grammar School
 for Girls
 DART DA1........................139 F6
Dartford Magistrates Court
 DART DA1........................139 G5
Dartford Museum & Library
 DART DA1........................139 H6
Dartford
 Natural Health Centre
 DART DA1........................139 H6
Dartford Technology College
 DART DA1........................139 F6
Dartford West Health Centre
 DART DA1........................139 F5
Darwin Centre
 SKENS SW7........................15 G4
Datapoint Business Centre
 BOW E3...........................94 B3
Date Valley School
 MTCM CR4........................162 E2
Daubeney Primary School
 CLPT E5..........................75 G2
David Game College
 KENS W8...........................8 A8
David Ives (Erith) Stadium
 ERITH DA8.......................118 B5
David Livingstone
 Primary School
 THHTH CR7.......................149 J7
David Lloyd Leisure
 NFNCH/WDSPK N12..................39 H6
 SKENS SW7........................14 D5
David Lloyd Sports Centre
 EN EN1...........................30 C1
David Lloyd Tennis Centre
 SCUP DA14.......................155 J4
Davidson Primary School
 CROY/NA CR0.....................165 G6
Davies Laing & Dick College
 BAY/PAD W2........................8 E4
Davies Lane Primary School
 WAN E11..........................76 D1
Davies's College
 STHWK SE1........................19 C1
Dawlish Primary School
 LEY E10..........................58 A7
Days Hotel
 BETH E2..........................92 D1
 HSLW TW3........................123 G2
 MLHL NW7.........................36 E1
 RSLP HA4.........................65 G4
 STHWK SE1........................18 A4
Days Hotel London
 South Ruislip
 RSLP HA4.........................65 G3
Days Inn
 BAY/PAD W2........................9 H5
 PIM SW1V.........................16 F7
Days Lane Primary School
 BFN/LL DA15.....................136 A5
Dean College of London
 HOLWY N7.........................73 F2
Deanesfield Primary School
 RSLP HA4.........................65 H3
Deansbrook Infant School
 MLHL NW7.........................36 E5
Deansfield Primary School
 ELTH/MOT SE9....................135 F2
De Bohun Primary School
 STHGT/OAK N14....................28 B4
Delta Wharf
 GNWCH SE10......................113 G1
Denmark Hill ⇌ ⊖
 CMBW SE5........................130 E2
Denmead School
 HPTN TW12.......................142 A4
Denver Industrial Estate
 RAIN RM13........................99 H3

Department for Environment,
 Food & Rural Affairs
 CHCR WC2N........................11 J8
Department for Transport
 WEST SW1P........................17 H5
Department for
 Art & Design (London
 Metropolitan University)
 WCHPL E1.........................13 M4
Department of Economics
 (London Metropolitan
 University)
 TWRH EC3N........................13 L5
Department of Education
 STJSPK SW1H......................17 H2
Department of Health
 WHALL SW1A.......................17 J1
Department of Trade & Industry
 STJSPK SW1H......................17 H3
Deptford ⇌
 DEPT SE8........................112 D6
Deptford Bridge ⊖
 DEPT SE8........................112 D7
Deptford Business Centre
 NWCR SE14.......................112 A4
Deptford Green School
 NWCR SE14.......................112 C6
Deptford Park Business Centre
 DEPT SE8........................112 B5
Deptford Park Primary School
 DEPT SE8........................112 B6
Deptford Trading Estate
 DEPT SE8........................112 B6
Dersingham Primary School
 MNPK E12.........................77 K4
Derwentwater Primary School
 ACT W3...........................86 E7
Design Centre
 FUL/PGN SW6.....................108 B7
Design Museum
 STHWK SE1........................13 M9
Deutsche Schule
 RCHPK/HAM TW10..................124 E7
Devonshire Hospital
 MHST W1U.........................10 B2
Devonshire House School
 HAMP NW3.........................71 G4
Devonshire Primary School
 BELMT SM2.......................175 G6
Devons Road ⊖
 BOW E3...........................93 K3
Diamond College
 SOHO/SHAV W1D....................11 H4
Diana Fountain
 E/WMO/HCT KT8...................158 A1
Diana Princess of Wales
 Memorial Fountain
 BAY/PAD W2........................9 H9
Diane Matthews Clinic
 ROMW/RG RM7......................63 F3
Dilloway Industrial Estate
 NWDGN UB2.......................102 D1
Discovery Business Park
 BERM/RHTH SE16..................111 H2
Discovery Primary School
 THMD SE28........................97 F7
Docklands Medical Centre
 POP/IOD E14.....................112 D3
Docklands Sailing &
 Watersports Centre
 POP/IOD E14.....................112 D2
Dockwell's Industrial Estate
 EBED/NFELT TW14.................122 A4
Dockyard Industrial Estate
 WOOL/PLUM SE18..................114 D2
Dog Kennel Hill
 Primary School
 EDUL SE22.......................131 F2
Dokal Industrial Estate
 NWDGN UB2.......................102 D1
Dollis Hill ⊖
 WLSDN NW10.......................69 H3
Dollis Infant School
 MLHL NW7.........................38 A6
The Dolphin Leisure Centre
 ROM RM1..........................63 H3
Dolphin School
 BTSEA SW11......................128 D4
The Dominie
 BTSEA SW11......................108 E7
Dominion Business Park
 ED N9............................43 F1
Dominion Theatre
 RSQ WC1B.........................11 H4
Donhead School
 WIM/MER SW19....................146 B6
Donmar Warehouse Theatre
 LSQ/SEVD WC2H....................11 J5
Donnington Primary School
 WLSDN NW10.......................69 K6
The Dorchester Hotel
 MYFR/PKLN W1K....................10 B8
Dorchester Primary School
 WPK KT4........................161 F7
Dorma Trading Park
 LEY E10..........................57 F7
Dormers Wells High School
 STHL UB1.........................84 A5
Dormers Wells Junior School
 STHL UB1.........................84 B6
Dormers Wells Leisure Centre
 STHL UB1.........................84 B5
Dormers Wells Medical Centre
 STHL UB1.........................84 A5
Dorothy Barley Primary School
 BCTR RM8.........................79 H4
Dorset Road Infant School
 ELTH/MOT SE9....................153 J1
Douglas Bader Foundation
 PUT/ROE SW15....................126 D5
Dovers Corner
 Industrial Estate
 RAIN RM13........................99 H2
Downderry Primary School
 BMLY BR1........................152 C3
Downe Manor Primary School
 NTHLT UB5........................83 F2
Downham Health Centre
 BMLY BR1........................152 C3
Downhills Primary School
 TOTM N17.........................55 H3
Downsell Primary School
 SRTFD E15........................76 B3
Downshall Primary School
 GNTH/NBYPK IG2...................60 E6
Downsview Primary School
 NRWD SE19.......................149 J6
Downsview School
 CLPT E5..........................74 D7
Drama Centre London
 KTTN NW5.........................72 A5
Drapers Hall
 LOTH EC2R........................13 H4

The Draycott Hotel
  CHEL SW3 .... 15 M5
Drayton Green ⇌
  HNWL W7 .... 85 F6
Drayton Green Primary School
  WEA W13 .... 85 G6
Drayton Manor High School
  HNWL W7 .... 85 F6
Drayton Park ⇌
  HOLWY N7 .... 73 G4
Drayton Park Primary School
  HBRY N5 .... 73 G4
DRCA Business Centre
  BTSEA SW11 .... 109 F7
Drew Primary School
  CAN/RD E16 .... 95 J7
The Drill Hall
  GWRST WC1E 11 G2
The Drizen School
  EDGW HA8 .... 36 C6
Dr Johnson's House
  FLST/FETLN EC4A 12 B4
Dr Tripletts CE J & I School
  HYS/HAR UB3 .... 82 D5
Drury Way Industrial Estate
  WLSDN NW10 .... 69 F3
Duchess Theatre
  COVGDN WC2E 11 L6
Duff Miller College
  SKENS SW7 .... 14 F5
Duke of York Column
  STJS SW1Y 11 H9
Duke of York Theatre
  CHCR WC2N 11 J7
Dukes Hotel
  WHALL SW1A 10 E9
Dulverton Primary School
  ELTH/MOT SE9 .... 154 D1
Dulwich College
  DUL SE21 .... 131 F7
Dulwich College Pre-
  Preparatory School
  DUL SE21 .... 150 A2
Dulwich College Track
  DUL SE21 .... 150 A1
Dulwich Hamlet FC
  EDUL SE22 .... 131 F3
Dulwich Hamlet Junior School
  HNHL SE24 .... 130 E5
Dulwich Hospital
  EDUL SE22 .... 131 F3
Dulwich Leisure Centre
  EDUL SE22 .... 131 H3
Dulwich Medical Centre
  EDUL SE22 .... 131 H4
Dulwich Picture Gallery
  DUL SE21 .... 131 F6
Dulwich & Sydenham Hill
  Golf Club
  DUL SE21 .... 150 C1
Dulwich Village CE
  Infant School
  DUL SE21 .... 131 F5
Dunbar Wharf
  POP/IOD E14 .... 93 H6
Duncombe Primary School
  ARCH N19 .... 54 E7
Dundee Wharf
  POP/IOD E14 .... 93 H6
Dundonald Primary School
  WIM/MER SW19 .... 146 D6
Dundonald Road ⊖
  WIM/MER SW19 .... 146 D6
Dunraven Lower School
  STRHM/NOR SW16 .... 149 F2
Dunraven School Upper
  STRHM/NOR SW16 .... 149 F2
Durand Primary School
  BRXN/ST SW9 .... 110 A7
Durands Wharf
  BERM/RHTH SE16 .... 112 C1
Durdans Park Primary School
  STHL UB1 .... 83 K4
Durston House School
  EA W5 .... 85 K5
Dysart School
  KUTN/CMB KT2 .... 143 K3
  SURB KT6 .... 159 F6
Eaglesfield School
  WOOL/PLUM SE18 .... 115 F7
Eagle Trading Estate
  MTCM CR4 .... 162 E5
Ealdham Primary School
  ELTH/MOT SE9 .... 134 B3
Ealing Abbey
  EA W5 .... 85 J5
Ealing Abbey Scriptorium
  WEA W13 .... 85 J5
Ealing Broadway ⇌ ⊖
  EA W5 .... 85 K6
The Ealing Broadway Centre
  EA W5 .... 85 K6
Ealing Central Sports Ground
  GFD/PVL UB6 .... 85 G1
Ealing Civic Centre
  EA W5 .... 85 J6
Ealing College Upper School
  WEA W13 .... 85 H5
Ealing Common ⊖
  EA W5 .... 86 B7
Ealing Conservative
  Bowling Club
  EA W5 .... 85 J6
Ealing CC
  EA W5 .... 86 A5
Ealing Film Studios
  EA W5 .... 85 J7
Ealing Golf Club
  GFD/PVL UB6 .... 85 H2
Ealing Hammersmith &
  West London College
  WKENS W14 .... 107 G3
Ealing Hospital
  NWDGN UB2 .... 103 J1
Ealing Independent College
  EA W5 .... 85 J6
Ealing Northern Sports Centre
  GFD/PVL UB6 .... 66 D3
Ealing Park Health Centre
  EA W5 .... 104 E3
Ealing Park Health Centre
  EA W5 .... 104 E3
Ealing Road Trading Estate
  BTFD TW8 .... 104 E4
Ealing Snooker Club
  WEA W13 .... 85 H7
Ealing Sports Centre
  EA W5 .... 86 A6
Ealing & West London College
  EA W5 .... 85 J7
Eardley Primary School
  STRHM/NOR SW16 .... 148 C5
Earlham Primary School
  FSTGT E7 .... 76 D4
  WDGN N22 .... 41 F6

Earl's Court ⊖
  ECT SW5 .... 14 B7
Earl's Court Exhibition Centre
  ECT SW5 .... 14 A7
Earlsfield ⇌
  WAND/EARL SW18 .... 128 B7
Earlsfield Primary School
  WAND/EARL SW18 .... 147 G1
Earlsmead Primary School
  RYLN/HDSTN HA2 .... 65 K3
  SEVS/STOTM N15 .... 56 B3
Earth Galleries
  SKENS SW7 .... 15 H4
East Acton ⊖
  SHB W12 .... 87 H5
East Acton Primary School
  ACT W3 .... 87 G6
East Barking Centre
  BCTR RM8 .... 79 J4
East Barnet Health Centre
  EBAR EN4 .... 27 H4
East Barnet School
  EBAR EN4 .... 27 K5
East Beckton District Centre
  EHAM E6 .... 95 K5
Eastbrook
  Comprehensive School
  DAGE RM10 .... 80 E3
Eastbrook End Cemetery
  ROMW/RG RM7 .... 81 G2
Eastbrookend Country Park
  ROMW/RG RM7 .... 81 F3
Eastbury Comprehensive School
  BARK IG11 .... 79 F7
Eastbury Farm JMI School
  NTHWD HA6 .... 32 D3
Eastbury Primary School
  BARK IG11 .... 79 F6
Eastcote ⊖
  RSLP HA4 .... 47 G6
Eastcote CC
  PIN HA5 .... 47 F4
Eastcote Health Centre
  PIN HA5 .... 47 F6
Eastcote Industrial Estate
  RSLP HA4 .... 47 G6
Eastcote Lane Cemetery
  RYLN/HDSTN HA2 .... 66 C3
Eastcote Primary School
  WELL DA16 .... 135 J2
Eastcourt Independent School
  GDMY/SEVK IG3 .... 61 G2
East Croydon ⇌
  CROY/NA CR0 .... 177 K1
East Dulwich ⇌
  EDUL SE22 .... 131 F3
East End Computing &
  Business College
  WCHPL E1 .... 92 D5
Eastern Business Park
  HTHAIR TW6 .... 121 J1
East Finchley ⊖
  EFNCH N2 .... 53 J3
East Finchley Cemetery
  EFNCH N2 .... 53 F2
East Finchley Medical Centre
  EFNCH N2 .... 53 J3
East Finchley School of English
  EFNCH N2 .... 53 J2
Eastgate Business Park
  LEY E10 .... 57 G7
East Greenwich Christ Church
  CE Primary School
  GNWCH SE10 .... 113 H3
East Ham ⊖
  EHAM E6 .... 77 J6
East Ham Industrial Estate
  EHAM E6 .... 95 H4
East Ham Jewish Cemetery
  EHAM E6 .... 95 J2
East Ham Leisure Centre
  EHAM E6 .... 77 K7
East Ham Memorial Hospital
  EHAM E6 .... 77 H6
East Ham Nature Reserve
  EHAM E6 .... 95 K4
East Hill Cemetery
  DART DA1 .... 139 K6
East India ⊖
  POP/IOD E14 .... 94 B6
Eastlea Community Centre
  CAN/RD E16 .... 94 D3
Eastlea Community School
  CAN/RD E16 .... 94 C3
East London Business College
  WAN E11 .... 58 C7
East London Cemetery
  PLSTW E13 .... 94 D2
East London Christian
  Choir School
  HACK E8 .... 7 L1
East London Crematorium
  SRTFD E15 .... 94 D2
East London RFC
  EHAM E6 .... 95 K4
East London RUFC
  SRTFD E15 .... 94 D1
Eastman Dental Hospital
  FSBYW WC1X 5 L7
East Molesey CC
  E/WMO/HCT KT8 .... 157 H2
East Putney ⊖
  PUT/ROE SW15 .... 127 H4
East Sheen Cemetery
  RCHPK/HAM TW10 .... 125 H4
East Sheen Primary School
  MORT/ESHN SW14 .... 126 B3
East Thamesmead
  Business Park
  ERITHM DA18 .... 117 G1
East Wickham Primary School
  WELL DA16 .... 116 A7
Eaton Manor RFC
  WAN E11 .... 58 B1
Eaton Square Pre-
  Preparatory School
  BGVA SW1W 16 C5
Eaton Square School
  PIM SW1V 16 E6
Ebrahim Community College
  WCHPL E1 .... 92 C4
Ecclesbourne Primary School
  THHTH CR7 .... 164 D4
Eden College
  STHWK SE1 .... 18 D3
Edenham High School
  CROY/NA CR0 .... 166 B6
Eden High School
  FUL/PGN SW6 .... 107 J7
Eden Medical Centre
  WKENS W14 .... 107 J3
Eden Park ⇌
  BECK BR3 .... 166 D4

Edenvale Child Health Clinic
  MTCM CR4 .... 148 A6
Eden Walk Shopping Centre
  KUT/HW KT1 .... 159 F1
Edes Business Park
  WLGTN SM6 .... 176 A1
Edgebury Primary School
  CHST BR7 .... 154 C3
Edge Business Centre
  CRICK NW2 .... 69 K1
Edgware ⊖
  EDGW HA8 .... 36 D5
Edgware Blood
  Transfusion Centre
  EDGW HA8 .... 36 D6
Edgwarebury Cemetery
  EDGW HA8 .... 36 C1
Edgware Clinic
  EDGW HA8 .... 36 C5
Edgware College
  KIL/WHAMP NW6 .... 71 G5
Edgware Community Hospital
  EDGW HA8 .... 36 D6
Edgware FC & Wealdstone FC
  EDGW HA8 .... 36 C6
Edgware Infant School
  EDGW HA8 .... 36 C5
Edgware Jewish Girls-
  Beis Chinuch
  EDGW HA8 .... 36 C5
Edgware Jewish Primary School
  EDGW HA8 .... 36 D4
Edgware Junior School
  EDGW HA8 .... 36 D5
Edgware Road ⊖
  BAY/PAD W2 .... 9 H3
Edinburgh Primary School
  WALTH E17 .... 57 H4
Edith Neville Primary School
  CAMTN NW1 .... 5 H5
Edmonton Cemetery
  WCHMH N21 .... 41 K1
Edmonton County Court
  UED N18 .... 42 C4
Edmonton County
  Lower School
  ED N9 .... 30 A7
Edmonton Green ⇌
  ED N9 .... 42 C2
Edmonton Green
  Shopping Centre
  ED N9 .... 42 D1
Edmonton Leisure Centre
  ED N9 .... 42 C2
Edmonton Upper School
  EN EN1 .... 30 B6
Edmund Waller Primary School
  NWCR SE14 .... 132 A1
Education Centre
  WOOL/PLUM SE18 .... 115 G4
Edward Betham CE
  Primary School
  GFD/PVL UB6 .... 84 D2
Edward Pauling School
  FELT TW13 .... 140 C1
Edward Wilson Primary School
  BAY/PAD W2 .... 8 C2
Edwin Lambert School
  EMPK RM11 .... 63 J5
Effra Road Retail Park
  BRXS/STRHM SW2 .... 130 B4
The Egerton House Hotel
  CHEL SW3 .... 15 K4
Eglinton Junior School
  WOOL/PLUM SE18 .... 115 F5
Eglinton Primary School
  WOOL/PLUM SE18 .... 115 F6
Elbourne Trading Estate
  BELV DA17 .... 117 J2
Eldenwall Industrial Estate
  BCTR RM8 .... 62 A7
Eldon Infant School
  ED N9 .... 30 D7
Eldon Junior School
  ED N9 .... 30 E7
Eleanor Palmer Primary School
  KTTN NW5 .... 72 C3
Eleanor Smith School
  CAN/RD E16 .... 94 E1
Eleanor Smith Special School &
  Primary Support Service
  PLSTW E13 .... 94 E1
Electrical Trades Union College
  ESH/CLAY KT10 .... 170 A3
Electric Cinema
  NTGHL W11 .... 88 D5
Elephant & Castle ⇌ ⊖
  STHWK SE1 .... 18 D4
Elephant & Castle
  Leisure Centre
  LBTH SE11 .... 18 D5
Elephant & Castle
  Shopping Centre
  STHWK SE1 .... 18 D4
Elers Clinic
  HYS/HAR UB3 .... 101 G3
Elfrida Primary School
  CAT SE6 .... 151 K3
Eliot Bank Primary School
  FSTH SE23 .... 150 D1
Elizabeth Garrett
  Anderson Hospital
  CAMTN NW1 .... 5 H8
Elizabeth Garrett Anderson
  Language College
  IS N1 .... 5 M5
Elizabeth Selby Infant School
  BETH E2 .... 92 C2
Elizabeth Trading Estate
  NWCR SE14 .... 112 A5
Ellen Wilkinson Primary School
  CAN/RD E16 .... 95 H4
Ellen Wilkinson School for Girls
  ACT W3 .... 86 B5
Ellern Mede School
  TRDG/WHET N20 .... 26 B7
Ellerslie Square
  Industrial Estate
  BRXS/STRHM SW2 .... 129 K3
Ellingham Primary School
  CHSGTN KT9 .... 171 K6
Elliott School
  PUT/ROE SW15 .... 127 F4
Elmbridge Leisure Centre
  WOT/HER KT12 .... 156 A4
Elm Court School
  WNWD SE27 .... 149 H1
Elmers End ⇌ ⊖
  BECK BR3 .... 166 A3
The Elmgreen School
  HGT N6 .... 149 H1
Elmgrove Junior School
  KTN/HRWW/WS HA3 .... 49 G3

Elmhurst Primary School
  FSTGT E7 .... 77 F6
Elmhurst School
  SAND/SEL CR2 .... 177 K4
Elm Lea Trading Estate
  TOTM N17 .... 42 C6
Elm Park ⊖
  HCH RM12 .... 81 J3
Elm Park Primary
  HCH RM12 .... 81 H4
The Elms Football & Tennis Club
  STAN HA7 .... 35 H4
Elmstead Woods ⇌
  CHST BR7 .... 153 J5
Elmwood J & I School
  CROY/NA CR0 .... 164 C6
Elm Wood Primary School
  DUL SE21 .... 149 K2
Elsdale Street Health Centre
  HOM E9 .... 74 E6
Elsley Primary School
  WBLY HA9 .... 68 B5
Elsley School
  BTSEA SW11 .... 129 F2
Elstree Aerodrome
  BORE WD6 .... 23 F2
Elstree & Borehamwood ⇌
  BORE WD6 .... 24 B3
Elstree Golf & Country Club
  BORE WD6 .... 23 K2
Elstree Studios
  BORE WD6 .... 24 C2
Elstree Way Clinic
  BORE WD6 .... 24 D1
Eltham ⇌
  ELTH/MOT SE9 .... 134 E3
Eltham Bus Station
  ELTH/MOT SE9 .... 134 E4
Eltham CE Primary School
  ELTH/MOT SE9 .... 134 E4
Eltham College Junior School
  ELTH/MOT SE9 .... 134 C7
Eltham College Senior School
  ELTH/MOT SE9 .... 153 H1
Eltham Crematorium
  ELTH/MOT SE9 .... 135 J3
The Eltham Foundation School
  ELTH/MOT SE9 .... 134 C5
Eltham Health Clinic
  ELTH/MOT SE9 .... 134 D4
Eltham Health & Fitness Centre
  ELTH/MOT SE9 .... 135 F5
Eltham Hill Technology College
  ELTH/MOT SE9 .... 134 D5
Eltham Palace
  ELTH/MOT SE9 .... 134 D6
Eltham Pools
  ELTH/MOT SE9 .... 134 D4
Eltham Warren Golf Club
  ELTH/MOT SE9 .... 135 G4
Elthorne Park High School
  HNWL W7 .... 104 A2
Elthorne Sports Centre
  HNWL W7 .... 104 A2
Elverson Road ⊖
  LEW SE13 .... 132 E1
Elystan Business Centre
  YEAD UB4 .... 83 G6
Emanuel School
  BTSEA SW11 .... 128 C4
Embankment ⊖
  CHCR WC2N 11 K8
Embankment Pier
  CHCR WC2N 11 L8
Embassy of Afghanistan
  SKENS SW7 .... 15 G2
Embassy of Albania
  BGVA SW1W 16 D4
Embassy of Algeria
  NTGHL W11 .... 88 C7
Embassy of Angola
  MYFR/PKLN W1K 10 A7
Embassy of Argentina
  MYFR/PKLN W1K 10 C6
Embassy of Armenia
  KENS W8 .... 14 C3
Embassy of Austria
  KTBR SW1X 16 A3
Embassy of Bahrain
  SKENS SW7 .... 14 A4
Embassy of Belarus
  KENS W8 .... 14 D2
Embassy of Belgium
  KTBR SW1X 16 B4
Embassy of Bolivia
  BGVA SW1W 16 B4
Embassy of Bosnia-Herzegovina
  CAVSQ/HST W1G 10 D4
Embassy of Brazil
  MYFR/PKLN W1K 10 A6
Embassy of Bulgaria
  SKENS SW7 .... 14 F3
Embassy of Cameroon
  NTGHL W11 .... 88 C7
Embassy of China
  CAVSQ/HST W1G 10 C2
Embassy of Costa Rica
  BAY/PAD W2 .... 8 F6
Embassy of Cote d'Ivoire
  KTBR SW1X 16 B3
Embassy of Croatia
  GTPST W1W 10 D1
Embassy of Cuba
  LSQ/SEVD WC2H 11 J4
Embassy of Democratic
  Republic of The Congo
  KTBR SW1X 15 M4
Embassy of Denmark
  KTBR SW1X 15 L3
Embassy of Dominican Republic
  BAY/PAD W2 .... 8 D5
Embassy of Ecuador
  KTBR SW1X 15 L3
Embassy of Egypt
  MYFR/PICC W1J 10 C8
Embassy of Estonia
  SKENS SW7 .... 14 F2
Embassy of Ethiopia
  SKENS SW7 .... 15 H2
Embassy of Finland
  KTBR SW1X 16 A3
Embassy of France
  KTBR SW1X 15 M1
Embassy of Gabon
  SKENS SW7 .... 14 F4
Embassy of Georgia
  KENS W8 .... 14 C2
Embassy of Germany
  KTBR SW1X 16 C3
Embassy of Ghana
  HGT N6 .... 54 B7
Embassy of Greece
  NTGHL W11 .... 88 D7

Embassy of Guatemala
  WBPTN SW10 .... 14 E9
Embassy of Honduras
  MBLAR W1H 9 L2
Embassy of Hungary
  KTBR SW1X 16 B4
Embassy of Iceland
  KTBR SW1X 16 A5
Embassy of Indonesia
  MYFR/PKLN W1K 10 B7
Embassy of Iran
  SKENS SW7 .... 15 H2
Embassy of Iraq
  SKENS SW7 .... 14 F3
Embassy of Ireland
  KTBR SW1X 16 C2
Embassy of Israel
  KENS W8 .... 14 D1
Embassy of Italy
  MYFR/PKLN W1K 10 B6
Embassy of Japan
  MYFR/PICC W1J 10 D9
Embassy of Jordan
  KENS W8 .... 14 A2
Embassy of Korea
  WESTW SW1E 16 F3
Embassy of Krygyzstan
  MBLAR W1H 9 L3
Embassy of Kuwait
  KTBR SW1X 15 M1
Embassy of Latvia
  CAMTN NW1 .... 10 A1
Embassy of Lebanon
  KENS W8 .... 8 C8
Embassy of Liberia
  BAY/PAD W2 .... 8 B6
Embassy of Lithuania
  MBLAR W1H 9 L3
Embassy of Luxembourg
  KTBR SW1X 16 A2
Embassy of Mexico
  MYFR/PICC W1J 10 D9
Embassy of Mongolia
  KENS W8 .... 14 D2
Embassy of Morocco
  SKENS SW7 .... 14 C5
Embassy of Mozambique
  FITZ W1T 10 E4
Embassy of Myanmar
  MYFR/PICC W1J 10 C8
Embassy of Nepal
  KENS W8 .... 8 C8
Embassy of Netherlands
  SKENS SW7 .... 14 F2
Embassy of Norway
  KTBR SW1X 16 B3
Embassy of Paraguay
  SKENS SW7 .... 14 D4
Embassy of Peru
  KTBR SW1X 15 M3
Embassy of Philippines
  KENS W8 .... 8 C9
Embassy of Poland
  CAVSQ/HST W1G 10 C3
Embassy of Portugal
  KTBR SW1X 16 A2
Embassy of Qatar
  MYFR/PKLN W1K 10 B9
Embassy of Romania
  KENS W8 .... 14 C1
Embassy of
  Russian Federation
  KENS W8 .... 8 C9
Embassy of Saudi Arabia
  MYFR/PICC W1J 10 C8
Embassy of Senegal
  CRICK NW2 .... 70 A6
Embassy of Slovak Republic
  KENS W8 .... 8 C8
Embassy of Slovenia
  MHST W1U 10 C4
Embassy of Spain
  KTBR SW1X 16 B3
Embassy of Sudan
  WHALL SW1A 10 E9
Embassy of Sweden
  MBLAR W1H 9 L3
Embassy of Switzerland
  MBLAR W1H 9 L3
Embassy of Syria
  KTBR SW1X 16 A2
Embassy of Thailand
  SKENS SW7 .... 14 F4
Embassy of The Holy See
  WIM/MER SW19 .... 146 A2
Embassy of The US
  MYFR/PKLN W1K 10 A4
Embassy of Tunisia
  SKENS SW7 .... 15 H2
Embassy of Turkey
  KTBR SW1X 16 B2
Embassy of Turkmenistan
  FITZ W1T 10 F3
Embassy of Ukraine
  NTGHL W11 .... 88 C7
Embassy of United
  Arab Emirates
  BAY/PAD W2 .... 15 H1
Embassy of Uruguay
  SKENS SW7 .... 15 K3
Embassy of Uzbekistan
  NTGHL W11 .... 88 D7
Embassy of Venezuela
  SKENS SW7 .... 15 H4
Embassy of Vietnam
  KENS W8 .... 14 D3
Embassy of Yemen
  SKENS SW7 .... 15 G5
Emberhurst School
  ESH/CLAY KT10 .... 157 J6
Ember Sports Club
  ESH/CLAY KT10 .... 157 F6
Embroidery World
  Business Centre
  WFD IG8 .... 59 H1
Emd Walthamstow Cinema
  WALTH E17 .... 57 J3
Emery Theatre
  POP/IOD E14 .... 93 K5
Emirates Air Line
  CAN/RD E16 .... 94 D7
Emmanuel CE Primary School
  KIL/WHAMP NW6 .... 70 E4
Empire Cinema
  LSQ/SEVD WC2H 11 H7
Emperor's Gate ⊖
  NWDGN UB2 .... 102 D3
Enfield Business Centre
  PEND EN3 .... 30 E1
Enfield CC
  EN EN1 .... 30 A3
Enfield Chase ⇌
  ENC/FH EN2 .... 29 J2

Enfield County School
ENC/FH EN2 .... 29 K2

Enfield FC
ED N9 .... 42 E1

Enfield Golf Club
ENC/FH EN2 .... 29 K3

Enfield Grammar School Lower
EN EN1 .... 29 K1

Enfield Grammar School Upper
ENC/FH EN2 .... 29 K2

Enfield Town ⇌
EN EN1 .... 29 K3

English Martyrs RC Primary School
WALW SE17 .... 19 G6
WCHPL E1 .... 13 M5

Ensham Secondary School
TOOT SW17 .... 147 K4

Enterprise Business Park
POP/IOD E14 .... 112 E1

Enterprise Industrial Estate
BERM/RHTH SE16 .... 111 K4

Epsom & Ewell High School
HOR/WEW KT19 .... 172 E5

Eric Liddell Sports Centre
ELTH/MOT SE9 .... 153 H1

Eridge House Preparatory School
FUL/PGN SW6 .... 127 J1

Erith ⇌
ERITH DA8 .... 118 A4

Erith & District Hospital
ERITH DA8 .... 118 A5

Erith Health Centre
ERITH DA8 .... 118 B5

Erith Leisure Centre
ERITH DA8 .... 118 B5

Erith Library & Museum
ERITH DA8 .... 118 B4

Erith Playhouse
ERITH DA8 .... 118 C4

Erith School
ERITH DA8 .... 117 K6

Erith School Community Sports Centre
ERITH DA8 .... 117 K6

Erith Small Business Centre
ERITH DA8 .... 118 C5

Ernest Bevin College
TOOT SW17 .... 147 J2

Eros
MYFR/PICC W1J 11 G7

Esher ⇌
ESH/CLAY KT10 .... 170 D1

Esher CE High School
ESH/CLAY KT10 .... 170 A2

Esher Church Primary School
ESH/CLAY KT10 .... 170 C5

Esher College
THDIT KT7 .... 157 K6

Essendine Primary School
KIL/WHAMP NW6 .... 2 B8

Essex Primary School
MNPK E12 .... 77 J5

Ethames Graduate School
POP/IOD E14 .... 112 E1

Ethelburga GM School
BTSEA SW11 .... 108 D7

Eton Manor
OLYMPICPK E20 .... 75 K3

Euro Business Centre
SRTFD E15 .... 76 D7

Euro Freightliner Terminal ⇌
WLSDN NW10 .... 87 G2

Eurolink Business Centre
BRXS/STRHM SW2 .... 130 B3

Europa Trading Estate
ERITH DA8 .... 118 A4

European Business Centre
CDALE/KGS NW9 .... 51 F2

European Business School London
CAMTN NW1 .... 4 A9

European School of Economics
KTBR SW1X 16 B2

European Vocational College
HDTCH EC3A 13 K5

Euro Way School
CEND/HSY/T N8 .... 55 G2

Euro Way School London
FSBYPK N4 .... 55 H6

Euston ⇌ ⊖ ⊖
CAMTN NW1 .... 5 G8

Euston Centre University of Westminster
CAMTN NW1 .... 4 D9

Euston Square ⊖
CAMTN NW1 .... 4 F9

Euston Tower
CAMTN NW1 .... 4 E9

Evans Business Centre
CRICK NW2 .... 69 J2

Eveline Day School
TOOT SW17 .... 147 K1

Evelyn Grace Academy
BRXN/ST SW9 .... 130 C3

Evendine College
SOHO/SHAV W1D 11 G4

Eversley Medical Centre
CROY/NA CR0 .... 164 B5

Eversley Primary School
WCHMH N21 .... 28 E4

Everyman Baker Street
MHST W1U 9 M2

Everyman Belsize Park
HAMP NW3 .... 71 J4

Everyman Cinema
HAMP NW3 .... 71 J4

Everyman Screen on the Green
IS N1 .... 6 C4

Evolution House, Kew Gardens
RCH/KEW TW9 .... 125 F1

Ewell Athletics Track
HOR/WEW KT19 .... 173 F5

Ewell Castle Junior School
EW KT17 .... 173 H7

Ewell Castle School
EW KT17 .... 173 J7

Ewell Grove Infant School
EW KT17 .... 173 H7

Ewell West ⇌
HOR/WEW KT19 .... 173 G7

ExCeL London
CAN/RD E16 .... 95 F6

Excellence Christian School
BETH E2 .... 74 C7

Excelsior College
UED N18 .... 42 A5

Exchange Square
SDTCH EC2A 13 J2

The Exchange
IL IG1 .... 78 B1

Executive Medical & Occupational Health Centre
CROY/NA CR0 .... 177 K2

Exhibition Halls
WBLY HA9 .... 68 C3

Express by Holiday Inn
CAN/RD E16 .... 94 D5
CHING E4 .... 43 J6
CROY/NA CR0 .... 177 J1
FNCH N3 .... 52 D3
FUL/PGN SW6 .... 107 J5
GNTH/NBYPK IG2 .... 60 D5
SDTCH EC2A 7 J8
STHWK SE1 .... 12 D8
WAP E1W 93 F6
WIM/MER SW19 .... 147 H6

The Eye Clinic
NOXST/BSQ WC1A 11 H4

Faculty of Engineering & Science (University of Westminster)
FITZ W1T 10 F2

Fairbrook Medical Centre
BORE WD6 .... 24 D1

Faircharm Trading Estate
DEPT SE8 .... 112 E6
IS N1 .... 6 E6

The Faircross Complementary Medical Centre
BARK IG11 .... 78 E5

Fairfield Pool & Leisure Centre
DART DA1 .... 139 H6

Fairfield Trade Park
KUT/HW KT1 .... 159 G2

Fairholme Primary School
EBED/NFELT TW14 .... 121 G7

Fairlawn Primary School
FSTH SE23 .... 131 K6

Fairley House Junior School
STHWK SE1 .... 17 L4

Fairley House School
PIM SW1V 17 G6

Fairview Industrial Centre
RAIN RM13 .... 99 F5

Fairview Industrial Estate
HYS/HAR UB3 .... 101 J1

Fairview Medical Centre
STRHM/NOR SW16 .... 148 E7

Fairway Primary School
MLHL NW7 .... 37 J1

Fairways Business Park
LEY E10 .... 75 J1

Falconbrook Primary School
BTSEA SW11 .... 128 C1

Falcon Business Centre
BTSEA SW11 .... 128 D3

Falconer Special School
BUSH WD23 .... 21 K4

Falcon Park Industrial Estate
WLSDN NW10 .... 69 G6

The Falcon Preparatory School for Boys
RCH/KEW TW9 .... 124 E2

The Falcons Preparatory School
CHSWK W4 .... 105 J5

The Falcons School for Girls
EA W5 .... 86 B7

Falconwood ⇌
ELTH/MOT SE9 .... 135 J2

Falkner House School
SKENS SW7 .... 14 F7

Family Records Centre
FSBYW WC1X 6 A3

Fanmakers' Hall
LVPST EC2M 13 J3

The Fan Museum
GNWCH SE10 .... 113 F6

Faraday Building
BLKFR EC4V 12 D5

Faraday School
POP/IOD E14 .... 94 C6

Farm Lane Trading Estate
FUL/PGN SW6 .... 107 K5

Farnell House Medical Centre
HSLW TW3 .... 103 G7

Farnham Green Primary School
GDMY/SEVK IG3 .... 61 G5

Farringdon ⇌ ⊖
FARR EC1M 12 B2

Farrington & Stratford House School
CHST BR7 .... 154 D6

Fashion Retail Academy
FITZ W1T 11 G4

Featherstone Industrial Estate
NWDGN UB2 .... 102 D1

Featherstone Primary School
NWDGN UB2 .... 102 C3

Featherstone Road Health Clinic
NWDGN UB2 .... 102 D2

Federation of St Elpheges RC School
WLGTN SM6 .... 176 E5

Felnex Trading Estate
WLGTN SM6 .... 176 A1

Feltham ⇌
FELT TW13 .... 122 A7

Feltham Airparcs Leisure Centre
FELT TW13 .... 141 H1

Feltham Athletics Arena
EBED/NFELT TW14 .... 121 K6

Felthambrook Industrial Estate
FELT TW13 .... 141 F2

Feltham Cemetery
FELT TW13 .... 140 D2

Feltham Community College
FELT TW13 .... 141 G1

Feltham Hill Infant School
FELT TW13 .... 140 D2

Feltham Hill Junior School
FELT TW13 .... 140 D2

Feltham & Hounslow Borough FC
EBED/NFELT TW14 .... 121 K6

Feltham Superbowl
FELT TW13 .... 141 F1

Fenchurch Street ⇌
FENCHST EC3M 13 K6

Fenstanton J & I School
BRXS/STRHM SW2 .... 130 B7

Fenton House (NT)
HAMP NW3 .... 71 G2

Fern Hill Primary School
KUTN/CMB KT2 .... 144 A5

Ferrier Industrial Estate
WAND/EARL SW18 .... 128 A3

Ferry Island Retail Park
TOTM N17 .... 56 D2

Ferry Lane Industrial Estate
RAIN RM13 .... 99 J4
WALTH E17 .... 56 E3

Ferry Lane Primary School
TOTM N17 .... 56 D3

Festival Pier
STHWK SE1 .... 11 M8

Field End J & I Schools
RSLP HA4 .... 65 H1

Fielding Primary School
WEA W13 .... 104 C2

Field Junior School
WATW WD18 .... 21 G4

Fieldway ⊖
CROY/NA CR0 .... 179 K6

Film House Cinema
RCH/KEW TW9 .... 124 E4

Financial Times
STHWK SE1 .... 12 F8

Financial Times Newspaper Offices
POP/IOD E14 .... 94 A5

Finchley Catholic High School
NFNCH/WDSPK N12 .... 39 G2

Finchley Central ⊖
FNCH N3 .... 38 E7

Finchley CC
FNCH N3 .... 53 F1

Finchley Golf Club
MLHL NW7 .... 38 D5

Finchley Industrial Centre
NFNCH/WDSPK N12 .... 39 G3

Finchley Lawn Tennis Club
FNCH N3 .... 38 D5

Finchley Lido Leisure Centre
NFNCH/WDSPK N12 .... 39 H6

Finchley Memorial Hospital
NFNCH/WDSPK N12 .... 39 G6

Finchley Road ⊖
KIL/WHAMP NW6 .... 71 G5

Finchley Road & Frognal ⊖
KIL/WHAMP NW6 .... 71 F4

Finchley Youth Theatre
EFNCH N2 .... 53 J2

Finsbury Circus Medical Centre
LVPST EC2M 13 H3

Finsbury Health Centre
CLKNW EC1R 6 A9

Finsbury Leisure Centre
FSBYE EC1V 6 F8

Finsbury Park ⇌ ⊖
FSBYPK N4 .... 73 G1

Finsbury Park Track
FSBYPK N4 .... 55 H6

Finton House School
TOOT SW17 .... 147 K1

Fircroft Primary School
TOOT SW17 .... 147 K1

Fire Brigade HQ
STHWK SE1 .... 17 L5

Fire Brigade Museum
STHWK SE1 .... 18 E1

Firepower Royal Artillery Museum
WOOL/PLUM SE18 .... 115 G2

Firs Farm Primary School
PLMGR N13 .... 41 K2

Fisher Athletic FC
BERM/RHTH SE16 .... 93 F7

Fisher Industrial Estate
WATW WD18 .... 21 G4

Fishmonger's Hall
CANST EC4R 13 G7

Fitness Unlimited Leisure Centre
BOW E3 .... 93 J1

Fitzrovia Medical Centre
FITZ W1T 10 E1

Fitzroy Nuffield Hospital
MBLAR W1H 9 L4

Five Bridges
LBTH SE11 .... 17 M8

Five Elms Primary School
DAGW RM9 .... 80 B2

Five Ways Business Centre
FELT TW13 .... 141 F2

Flamsteed House Museum
GNWCH SE10 .... 113 G6

Flaxman Sports Centre
CMBW SE5 .... 130 D1

Fleecefield Primary School
ED N9 .... 42 C3

Fleet Primary School
HAMP NW3 .... 71 K4

Fleetway Business Park
GFD/PVL UB6 .... 85 H1

Fleming Lab Museum
BAY/PAD W2 .... 9 H4

Flora Gardens Primary School
HMSMTH W6 .... 106 E3

Flutters Leisure Centre
FUL/PGN SW6 .... 107 K6

Follys End Christian High School
SNWD SE25 .... 165 F5

Follys End Christian School
SAND/SEL CR2 .... 178 A3

The Foot Clinic
WIM/MER SW19 .... 146 C5

The Ford College
CONDST W1S 10 D5

Fordgate Business Park
BELV DA17 .... 117 K1

Ford Industrial Park
DAGW RM9 .... 98 D2

Fordview Industrial Estate
RAIN RM13 .... 99 J2

Foreign & Commonwealth Office
WHALL SW1A 17 H1

Foreland Medical Centre
NTGHL W11 .... 88 C6

Forest Business Park
LEY E10 .... 57 F6

Forestdale Primary School
CROY/NA CR0 .... 179 G7

Foresters Primary School
WLGTN SM6 .... 176 D5

Forest Gate ⇌
FSTGT E7 .... 76 E4

Forest Gate Community School
FSTGT E7 .... 76 E4

Forest Hill ⇌
FSTH SE23 .... 150 E1

Forest Hill Business Centre
FSTH SE23 .... 150 E1

Forest Hill Industrial Estate
FSTH SE23 .... 150 E1

Forest Hill Pools
SYD SE26 .... 150 E2

Forest Hill School
FSTH SE23 .... 151 F2

Forest House Business Centre
WAN E11 .... 58 D6

Forest Pathway College
WALTH E17 .... 57 J3

Forest Road Medical Centre
WALTH E17 .... 57 H2

Forest Trading Estate
WALTH E17 .... 57 F2

Forge Close Clinic
HAYES BR2 .... 167 K7

Forge Lane Primary School
FELT TW13 .... 141 J5

The Former Health Centre
CHARL SE7 .... 114 C3

Forster Park Primary School
CAT SE6 .... 152 C2

Fortis Green Health Clinic
EFNCH N2 .... 54 A1

Fortismere School
EFNCH N2 .... 53 K1

Fortune Theatre
HOL/ALD WC2B 11 K5

The Forum
EDGW HA8 .... 36 C5

Fossdene Primary School
CHARL SE7 .... 114 A4

Foster's Primary School
WELL DA16 .... 136 D2

Foulds School
BAR EN5 .... 26 B2

The Foundling Museum
BMSBY WC1N 5 K9

The Fountain Studios
WBLY HA9 .... 68 C2

Fountayne Business Centre
SEVS/STOTM N15 .... 56 C3

Fountayne Road Health Centre
STNW/STAM N16 .... 74 C1

Four Seasons Hotel
BERM/RHTH SE16 .... 93 H7
MYFR/PKLN W1K 16 C1

Foxfield Primary School
WOOL/PLUM SE18 .... 115 H4

Fox Primary School
KENS W8 .... 8 A9

Frances Bardsley School for Girls
ROM RM1 .... 63 J5

Franciscan Primary School
TOOT SW17 .... 148 A3

Francis Holland School
BGVA SW1W 16 B6
CAMTN NW1 .... 9 L1

Frank Barnes Primary School
STJWD NW8 .... 3 H2

Franklin Industrial Estate
PGE/AN SE20 .... 150 E7

Frederick Bremer Secondary School
WALTH E17 .... 58 A1

Frederick Hugh House
CHEL SW3 .... 15 J9

Freehold Industrial Centre
HSLWW TW4 .... 122 B4

Free Trade Wharf
WAP E1W 93 F6

The French Institute
SKENS SW7 .... 15 G5

Fresh Wharf Estate
BARK IG11 .... 78 B7

Freuchen Medical Centre
WLSDN NW10 .... 87 H1

Freud Museum
HAMP NW3 .... 71 H5

Friars Primary Foundation School
STHWK SE1 .... 18 C1

Friends House
CAMTN NW1 .... 5 G8

Friern Barnet School
FBAR/BDGN N11 .... 39 K4

Friern Bridge Retail Park
FBAR/BDGN N11 .... 40 B5

Frithwood Primary School
NTHWD HA6 .... 32 D5

Frogmore Industrial Estate
HBRY N5 .... 73 J3
HYS/HAR UB3 .... 101 H1
WLSDN NW10 .... 86 E2

Fryent Country Park
KTN/HRWW/WS HA3 .... 50 C6

Fryent Medical Centre
CDALE/KGS NW9 .... 50 E6

Fryent Primary School
CDALE/KGS NW9 .... 50 E6

Fulham Broadway ⊖
FUL/PGN SW6 .... 107 K6

Fulham Cemetery
FUL/PGN SW6 .... 107 G6

Fulham & Chelsea College
FUL/PGN SW6 .... 127 H1

Fulham Clinic
HMSMTH W6 .... 107 H5

Fulham Cross Girls School
FUL/PGN SW6 .... 107 G6

Fulham FC (Craven Cottage)
PUT/ROE SW15 .... 107 F7

Fulham Medical Centre
FUL/PGN SW6 .... 108 A6

Fulham Palace
FUL/PGN SW6 .... 127 G1

Fulham Pools
FUL/PGN SW6 .... 107 J5

Fulham Preparatory School
WKENS W14 .... 107 H5

Fulham Pre-Preparatory School
FUL/PGN SW6 .... 127 H1

Fulham Primary School
FUL/PGN SW6 .... 107 K5

Fuller Smith & Turner Sports Club
CHSWK W4 .... 106 B7

Fullwell Cross Health Centre
BARK/HLT IG6 .... 60 C1

Fullwell Cross Swimming Pool & Recreation Centre
BARK/HLT IG6 .... 60 C1

Fullwood Primary School
BARK/HLT IG6 .... 60 C3

Fulwell ⇌
WHTN TW2 .... 142 D3

Fulwell Golf Club
HPTN TW12 .... 142 D3

Furness Primary School
WLSDN NW10 .... 87 J1

Furzedown Primary School
TOOT SW17 .... 148 B5

Furze Infant School
CHDH RM6 .... 62 A5

Future Business College
CONDST W1S 10 D5

Gaflac Sports Ground Pavilion
SUN TW16 .... 140 E7

Gainsborough Clinic
PLMGR N13 .... 41 F3

Gainsborough Primary School
HOM E9 .... 75 H5
SRTFD E15 .... 94 C2

Galliard Primary School
ED N9 .... 30 C5

Gallions Mount Primary School
WOOL/PLUM SE18 .... 116 A4

Gallions Primary School
EHAM E6 .... 96 B5

Gallions Reach ⊖
EHAM E6 .... 96 B6

Gallions Reach Shopping Park
EHAM E6 .... 96 B4

Gants Hill ⊖
GNTH/NBYPK IG2 .... 60 A5

Gants Hill Medical Centre
GNTH/NBYPK IG2 .... 60 A5

Gardener Industrial Estate
SYD SE26 .... 151 G4

Garden House School
BGVA SW1W 16 A7

The Garden Museum
STHWK SE1 .... 17 K4

Garden Primary School
MTCM CR4 .... 163 J2

Garden Suburb Infant School
GLDGN NW11 .... 52 D4

Garfield Primary School
FBAR/BDGN N11 .... 40 B4
WIM/MER SW19 .... 147 G5

Garratt Park Secondary Special School
WAND/EARL SW18 .... 147 G5

Garrick Industrial Centre
CDALE/KGS NW9 .... 51 H4

Garrick Theatre
LSQ/SEVD WC2H 11 J7

Garth Primary School
MRDN SM4 .... 162 C4

The Garth Road Industrial Centre
MRDN SM4 .... 161 F6

Gascoigne Primary School
BARK IG11 .... 78 C6

Gate Cinema
KENS W8 .... 8 A8

Gatehouse School
BETH E2 .... 93 F1

The Gatehouse Theatre
HGT N6 .... 54 A8

The Gate Theatre
NTGHL W11 .... 8 A8

Gateway Business Centre
SYD SE26 .... 151 G5

Gateway Industrial Estate
WLSDN NW10 .... 87 H2

Gateway Primary School
STJWD NW8 .... 3 H9

Gateway Retail Park
EHAM E6 .... 96 B3

Gatton School
TOOT SW17 .... 147 J3

Gayhurst Primary School
HACK E8 .... 74 C6

Gazelda Industrial Estate
WAT WD17 .... 21 G4

Gearies Infant School
GNTH/NBYPK IG2 .... 60 A4

Gearies Junior School
GNTH/NBYPK IG2 .... 60 B4

Geffrye Museum
BETH E2 .... 7 K6

Gem Hampshire School
SKENS SW7 .... 15 J2

Gemini Business Estate
NWCR SE14 .... 112 A4

General Medical Clinics
WCHPL E1 .... 13 L2

Genesis Cinema
WCHPL E1 .... 92 E3

The Geoffrey Lloyd Foulkes Clinic
IL IG1 .... 78 A1

Geoffrey Whitworth Theatre
DART DA1 .... 138 D3

George Eliot Community Primary School
STJWD NW8 .... 2 F3

George Greens School
POP/IOD E14 .... 113 F4

George Mitchell Primary School
LEY E10 .... 57 K2

George Spicer Primary School
EN EN1 .... 30 B2

George Street ⊖
CROY/NA CR0 .... 177 J1

George Tomlinson Primary School
WAN E11 .... 58 C7

Germal College
FSBYPK N4 .... 55 G7

Getters Talmud Torah School
SEVS/STOTM N15 .... 55 K5

Gibbs Green Special School
WKENS W14 .... 107 J4

Gibson Business Centre
TOTM N17 .... 42 B6

Gidea Park ⇌
GPK RM2 .... 63 K3

Gidea Park College
GPK RM2 .... 63 J2

Gidea Park Primary School
GPK RM2 .... 63 H3

Gidea Park Tennis Club
GPK RM2 .... 63 J2

The Gielgud Theatre
SOHO/CST W1F 11 G6

Giffin Business Centre
DEPT SE8 .... 112 D6

Gifford Primary School
NTHLT UB5 .... 83 K1

Gilbert Collection
TPL/STR WC2R 11 M6

Gilbert Scott Primary School
SAND/SEL CR2 .... 179 G6

Gillespie Primary School
HBRY N5 .... 73 H2

Gipsy Hill ⇌
NRWD SE19 .... 150 A4

Girdlers' Hall
CITYW EC2V 12 F3

Glade Primary School
CLAY IG5 .... 45 J2

The Glades Shopping Centre
BMLY BR1 .... 167 K2

Gladstone Medical Centre
CRICK NW2 .... 69 H3

Gladstone Park Primary School
WLSDN NW10 .... 69 J4

Glaziers/Scientific Instrument Makers Hall
STHWK SE1 .... 13 G8

Glebe Primary School
  HGDN/ICK UB10 .... 64 B3
  KTN/HRWW/WS HA3 .... 49 K3
Glebe School
  WWKM BR4 .... 167 G7
Gleen Lecky Health Centre
  PUT/ROE SW15 .... 127 G3
Glenbrook Primary School
  CLAP SW4 .... 129 J5
Glencairn Sports Club
  FBAR/BDGN N11 .... 40 C6
Glenham College
  IL IG1 .... 78 B1
Glenlyn Medical Centre
  E/WMO/HCT KT8 .... 157 H4
Glenthorne High Specialist
Arts College
  CHEAM SM3 .... 161 K7
Globe Academy Lower School
  STHWK SE1 .... 19 G4
Globe Primary School
  BETH E2 .... 92 E2
Globe Wharf
  BERM/RHTH SE16 .... 93 F6
Gloucester House
  HAMP NW3 .... 71 H4
Gloucester Primary School
  PECK SE15 .... 111 F6
Gloucester Road ⊖
  SKENS SW7 .... 14 E5
Godolphin & Latymer School
  HMSMTH W6 .... 106 E3
Godwin Junior School
  FSTGT E7 .... 77 F3
Godwin Primary School
  DAGW RM9 .... 80 A6
Goethe Institute
  SKENS SW7 .... 15 H3
Golborne Medical Centre
  NKENS W10 .... 88 D3
Goldbeaters Primary School
  EDGW HA8 .... 37 F7
Golden Hinde Educational Trust
  STHWK SE1 .... 13 G7
Golden Lane Campus
  STLK EC1Y 12 F1
Golders Green ⊖
  GLDGN NW11 .... 52 E5
Golders Green Crematorium
  GLDGN NW11 .... 52 E6
Golders Green Health Centre
  GLDGN NW11 .... 53 F7
Golders Hill Health Centre
  GLDGN NW11 .... 53 G5
Golders Hill School
  GLDGN NW11 .... 52 E6
Goldhawk Industrial Estate
  SHB W12 .... 106 E2
Goldhawk Road ⊖
  SHB W12 .... 107 F1
Goldsmiths Hall
  STBT EC1A 12 E4
Goldsmiths University
of London
  BROCKY SE4 .... 132 C2
  DEPT SE8 .... 112 D5
  LEW SE13 .... 133 H3
  NWCR SE14 .... 112 B7
Gonville Academy
  THHTH CR7 .... 164 A4
Goodge St ⊖
  FITZ W1T 10 F2
Goodinge Health Centre
  HOLWY N7 .... 72 E5
Goodmayes ⇌
  GDMY/SEVK IG3 .... 61 G7
Goodmayes Retail Park
  CHDH RM6 .... 61 H6
Goodrich J & I School
  EDUL SE22 .... 131 H5
Good Shepherd RC
Primary School
  BMLY BR1 .... 152 D3
  CROY/NA CR0 .... 179 K6
The Good Shepherd RC Primary
  SHB W12 .... 106 C1
Goodwyn School
  MLHL NW7 .... 37 J4
Goose Green Primary School
  EDUL SE22 .... 131 G4
Goose Green Trading Estate
  EDUL SE22 .... 131 H3
Gordonbrock Primary School
  BROCKY SE4 .... 132 D4
Gordon Hospital
  WEST SW1P 17 C6
Gordon House Health Centre
  WEA W13 .... 85 H7
Gordon Infant School
  IL IG1 .... 78 D2
Gordon Primary School
  ELTH/MOT SE9 .... 134 E3
Goresbrook Leisure Centre
  DAGW RM9 .... 79 K7
Goresbrook Sports Centre
  DAGW RM9 .... 79 K7
The Goring Hotel
  BGVA SW1W 16 D3
Gorringe Park Primary School
  MTCM CR4 .... 148 A7
Gosai Cinema
  WEA W13 .... 85 H7
Gosbury Hill Health Centre
  CHSGTN KT9 .... 172 A3
Gosford Primary School
  REDBR IG4 .... 59 K4
Gospel Oak ⊖
  KTTN NW5 .... 72 A3
Gospel Oak Primary School
  HAMP NW3 .... 72 A3
Gove Farm Retail Park
  CHDH RM6 .... 61 J6
Government Offices
  WHALL SW1A 11 J8
Gower House School
  CDALE/KGS NW9 .... 68 E1
The Gower School
  IS N1 .... 5 M6
Grace Business Centre
  MTCM CR4 .... 162 E5
Grace Theatre at
The Latchmere
  BTSEA SW11 .... 128 E2
Graduate School
of Management
  TOTM N17 .... 42 B7
Grafton Primary School
  BCTR RM8 .... 80 A1
  HOLWY N7 .... 72 E2
Grahame Park Health Centre
  CDALE/KGS NW9 .... 37 G7
Grahame Park J & I School
  CDALE/KGS NW9 .... 37 G7

Granard Business Centre
  MLHL NW7 .... 37 G5
Granard Primary School
  PUT/ROE SW15 .... 126 E5
Granby Sports Club
  CHST BR7 .... 153 J4
Grand Avenue Primary School
  BRYLDS KT5 .... 159 K5
Grande Vitesse Industrial Centre
  STHWK SE1 .... 12 D9
Grand Union Industrial Estate
  WLSDN NW10 .... 86 C2
The Grange City Hotel
  TWRH EC3N 13 L6
Grange J & I School
  RYLN/HDSTN HA2 .... 48 B7
The Grange Museum
  CRICK NW2 .... 69 H3
Grange Park ⇌
  WCHMN N21 .... 29 H4
Grange Park Clinic
  YEAD UB4 .... 82 D3
Grange Park Junior School
  YEAD UB4 .... 82 D3
Grange Park
Preparatory School
  WCHMN N21 .... 29 H5
Grange Park Primary School
  WCHMN N21 .... 29 G3
Grange Primary School
  CAN/RD E16 .... 94 D3
  EA W5 .... 104 E1
  STHWK SE1 .... 19 J4
Grange Whitehall Hotel
  RSQ WC1B 11 J3
Grangewood
Independent School
  FSTGT E7 .... 77 H6
Grangewood School
  PIN HA5 .... 46 E4
Granton Primary School
  STRHM/NOR SW16 .... 148 C6
Granville Road Industrial Estate
  CRICK NW2 .... 70 D1
Grasmere Primary School
  STNW/STAM N16 .... 73 K3
Grasshoppers RFC
  ISLW TW7 .... 104 A5
Grassroots School
  HPTN TW12 .... 142 A7
Grasvenor Avenue
Infant School
  BAR EN5 .... 26 E5
Gravel Hill ⊖
  CROY/NA CR0 .... 179 G6
Gravel Hill Primary School
  BXLYHS DA6 .... 137 J4
Graveney School
  TOOT SW17 .... 148 B5
Graves Yard Industrial Estate
  WELL DA16 .... 136 B1
Grays Farm Primary School
  STMC/STPC BR5 .... 155 H7
Grazebrook Primary School
  STNW/STAM N16 .... 74 A1
Great Cambridge
Industrial Estate
  EN EN1 .... 30 D4
Great Chapel Street
Medical Centre
  SOHO/SHAV W1D 11 G4
Greater London Authority
Headquarters (City Hall)
  STHWK SE1 .... 13 K9
Greatham Road
Industrial Estate
  BUSH WD23 .... 21 J3
Great Jubilee Wharf
  WAP E1W 92 E7
Great Ormond Street
Hospital for Children
  BMSBY WC1N 11 K1
Great Portland Street ⊖
  GTPST W1W 10 D1
Great Scotland Yard
  WHALL SW1A 11 J8
Great Western Industrial Park
  NWDGN UB2 .... 103 G1
Great West London College
  GFD/PVL UB6 .... 66 D7
Great West Trading Estate
  BTFD TW8 .... 104 C5
Greek School of London
  ACT W3 .... 86 D6
Greenacres Primary School
  ELTH/MOT SE9 .... 154 A1
The Green CE Primary School
  TOTM N17 .... 56 B3
Green Dragon Primary School
  BTFD TW8 .... 105 F4
Greenfield Medical Centre
  CRICK NW2 .... 70 C2
Greenfields Junior School
  SHB W12 .... 87 H6
Greenfields Primary School
  OXHEY WD19 .... 33 G4
Greenfields Special School
  MUSWH N10 .... 39 K7
Greenford ⊖
  GFD/PVL UB6 .... 66 D7
Greenford Avenue
Medical Centre
  HNWL W7 .... 84 E4
Greenford Green Clinic
  GFD/PVL UB6 .... 66 E4
Greenford High School
  STHL UB1 .... 84 A2
Greenford Industrial Estate
  GFD/PVL UB6 .... 66 B7
Greenford Park Cemetery
  GFD/PVL UB6 .... 84 B4
Greenford Road Medical Centre
  GFD/PVL UB6 .... 84 D1
Greenford Sports Centre
  STHL UB1 .... 84 A2
Greengate Medical Centre
  PLSTW E13 .... 95 F2
Greengrove College
  STHGT/OAK N14 .... 40 E1
Greenheath Business Centre
  BETH E2 .... 92 D2
Greenhill College
  HRW HA1 .... 49 F4
Greenhill Park Medical Centre
  WLSDN NW10 .... 69 G7
Greenland Pier
  BERM/RHTH SE16 .... 112 C2
Green Lane Business Park
  ELTH/MOT SE9 .... 154 A1
Green Lane Primary School
  WPK KT4 .... 160 E6
Greenleaf Primary School
  WALTH E17 .... 57 H2

Greenmead Primary School
  PUT/ROE SW15 .... 126 E4
Green Park ⊖
  MYFR/PICC W1J 10 E8
The Green School
  ISLW TW7 .... 104 B6
Greenshaw High School
  SUT SM1 .... 175 G1
Greenshields Industrial Estate
  CAN/RD E16 .... 94 E7
Greenside Primary School
  SHB W12 .... 106 D1
Greenslade Primary School
  WOOL/PLUM SE18 .... 115 J5
Greenvale School
  FSTH SE23 .... 151 G2
Greenwich ⇌⊖
  GNWCH SE10 .... 112 E6
Greenwich Centre Business Park
  DEPT SE8 .... 112 E6
Greenwich Cinema
  GNWCH SE10 .... 113 F6
Greenwich Community College
  WOOL/PLUM SE18 .... 115 G5
  WOOL/PLUM SE18 .... 115 J5
Greenwich Industrial Estate
  CHARL SE7 .... 114 A3
  GNWCH SE10 .... 112 E6
Greenwich Natural
Health Centre
  GNWCH SE10 .... 113 F6
Greenwich Odeon Cinema
  GNWCH SE10 .... 113 J3
Greenwich Park
  GNWCH SE10 .... 113 J5
Greenwich Pier
  GNWCH SE10 .... 113 F4
Greenwich School
of Management
  GNWCH SE10 .... 113 F6
Greenwich Steiner School
  BKHTH/KID SE3 .... 113 K5
Greenwich Theatre & Art Gallery
  GNWCH SE10 .... 113 G6
Greenwood Primary School
  NTHLT UB5 .... 66 C4
Greenwood Theatre
  STHWK SE1 .... 19 H1
Green Wrythe Primary School
  CAR SM5 .... 162 C5
Gresham Way Industrial Estate
  WIM/MER SW19 .... 147 F2
Grey Coat Hospital CE School
for Girls
  WEST SW1P 17 G4
Grey Coat Hospital St Michaels
  WEST SW1P 17 G6
Grey Court School
  RCHPK/HAM TW10 .... 143 K2
Griffen Manor School
  WOOL/PLUM SE18 .... 115 K7
Grimsdell Mill Hill Pre-
Preparatory School
  MLHL NW7 .... 37 K4
Grims Dyke Golf Club
  PIN HA5 .... 34 A4
Grim's Dyke Hotel
  KTN/HRWW/WS HA3 .... 34 C3
Grimsdyke School
  PIN HA5 .... 33 K5
Grinling Gibbons
Primary School
  DEPT SE8 .... 112 C5
Grist Memorial Sports Club
  E/WMO/HCT KT8 .... 157 K4
Grocers' Hall
  CITYW EC2V 13 G5
The Grosvenor Hotel
  BGVA SW1W 16 D4
Grosvenor House Hotel
  MYFR/PKLN W1K 10 A7
Grove Health Centre
  KENS W8 .... 8 B1
The Grove Health Centre
  SHB W12 .... 106 E1
Grove House (Froebel College)
  PUT/ROE SW15 .... 126 C5
Grove House Primary School for
Deaf Children
  WNWD SE27 .... 149 H1
Grovelands Priory Hospital
  STHGT/OAK N14 .... 28 E7
Grovelands School
  WOT/HER KT12 .... 156 A5
Grove Medical Centre
  DEPT SE8 .... 112 B3
The Grove Medical Centre
  ARCH N19 .... 72 D1
Grove Park ⇌
  BMLY BR1 .... 152 E2
Grove Park Cemetery
  LEE/GVPK SE12 .... 153 H3
Grove Park Industrial Estate
  CDALE/KGS NW9 .... 51 F3
Grove Park Primary School
  CHSWK W4 .... 105 K5
Grove Primary School
  CHDH RM6 .... 61 H4
Grove Road Primary School
  HSLW TW3 .... 123 F3
The Groves Medical Centre
  NWMAL KT3 .... 160 B2
Grove Village Medical Centre
  EBED/NFELT TW14 .... 121 H7
Guardian Angels RC
Primary School
  BOW E3 .... 93 G2
Guardian Newspapers
  POP/IOD E14 .... 112 E1
Guards' Chapel & Museum
  STJSPK SW1H 16 F2
Gumley House Convent School
  ISLW TW7 .... 124 B2
Gunnersbury ⇌⊖
  CHSWK W4 .... 105 J4
Gunnersbury Catholic School
  BTFD TW8 .... 104 E4
Gunnersbury Cemetery
  BTFD TW8 .... 105 H3
Gunnersbury Park Museum
  ACT W3 .... 105 H2
Gurnell Leisure Centre
  WEA W13 .... 85 F2
Guru Nanak Medical Centre
  STHL UB1 .... 83 H7
Guru Nanak Sikh Academy
  YEAD UB4 .... 83 G7
Guy's Hospital
  STHWK SE1 .... 13 H9
Guys Kings & Thomas
Medical School (Kings
College London)
  STHWK SE1 .... 12 E8

Gwyn Jones Primary School
  WAN E11 .... 58 B6
GX Superbowl
  EHAM E6 .... 96 A4
Gypsy Moth IV
  GNWCH SE10 .... 113 F5
Haberdashers Askes
Crayford Academy
  DART DA1 .... 138 D3
Haberdashers Askes
Hatcham College
  NWCR SE14 .... 132 A1
Haberdashers Askes
Knights Academy
  BMLY BR1 .... 152 E3
The Haberdashers
Askes School
  BORE WD6 .... 23 H2
Haberdashers' Hall
  STBT EC1A 12 C3
Haberdashers RUFC
  BORE WD6 .... 24 B1
Hackbridge ⇌
  WLGTN SM6 .... 176 B1
Hackbridge Primary School
  WLGTN SM6 .... 163 F7
Hackney Business Centre
  HACK E8 .... 74 D5
Hackney Central ⊖
  HACK E8 .... 74 D5
Hackney City Farm
  BETH E2 .... 92 C1
Hackney Community College
  IS N1 .... 7 J6
Hackney Downs ⇌
  HACK E8 .... 74 C4
Hackney Empire Variety Theatre
  HACK E8 .... 74 D5
Hackney Free & Parochial
CE School
  HOM E9 .... 74 E5
Hackney Marshes Centre
  HACK E8 .... 75 J3
The Hackney Museum
  HACK E8 .... 74 D5
Hackney Wick ⊖
  HOM E9 .... 75 J5
The Haelan Clinic
  CEND/HSY/T N8 .... 54 E5
Haggerston ⊖
  HACK E8 .... 7 L2
Haggerston School
  BETH E2 .... 7 M5
Haggerston Swimming Pool
  BETH E2 .... 7 M4
Hague Primary School
  BETH E2 .... 92 D3
Hailey Road Business Park
  ERITHM DA18 .... 117 H1
Haimo Primary School
  ELTH/MOT SE9 .... 134 C4
Hakim Qureshi Clinic
  NWDGN UB2 .... 102 D2
The Hale Clinic
  CAMTN NW1 .... 10 D1
Half Moon Theatre
  WCHPL E1 .... 93 F3
The Halkin Hotel
  KTBR SW1X 16 B2
Halley Primary School
  POP/IOD E14 .... 93 G4
Hallfield Clinic
  BAY/PAD W2 .... 8 E5
Hallfield Primary School
  BAY/PAD W2 .... 8 E5
Hallmark Trading Estate
  WBLY HA9 .... 68 C3
Hall Place & Gardens
  BXLY DA5 .... 137 K5
The Hall Pre-Preparatory School
  NTHWD HA6 .... 32 B5
Halls Business Centre
  HYS/HAR UB3 .... 101 K2
The Hall School
  HAMP NW3 .... 71 H5
Hall School Wimbledon
  RYNPK SW20 .... 146 B7
Hall School Wimbledon
Junior Department
  PUT/ROE SW15 .... 145 J1
Hallsville Primary School
  CAN/RD E16 .... 94 E5
Halstow Primary School
  GNWCH SE10 .... 113 J4
Hambledon Clinic
  CMBW SE5 .... 130 E2
Hambrough Primary School
  STHL UB1 .... 83 J7
Hamer Indoor Market
  BOW E3 .... 93 H1
Ham Health Clinic
  RCHPK/HAM TW10 .... 143 J2
Ham House & Garden (NT)
  RCHPK/HAM TW10 .... 124 D7
Hamilton Road Industrial Estate
  WNWD SE27 .... 149 K3
Ham Lands Nature Reserve
  RCHPK/HAM TW10 .... 143 H3
Hamlet International
Industrial Estate
  ERITH DA8 .... 118 A4
Hammersmith ⊖
  HMSMTH W6 .... 107 F4
Hammersmith Apollo
  HMSMTH W6 .... 107 F4
Hammersmith Cemetery
  HMSMTH W6 .... 107 G4
Hammersmith Hospital
  SHB W12 .... 87 J5
Hammersmith Industrial Estate
  HMSMTH W6 .... 107 F5
Hammersmith New Cemetery
  RCH/KEW TW9 .... 125 J1
Hammersmith Physio & Sports
Injury Clinic
  HMSMTH W6 .... 107 F4
Hammersmith & West
London College
  WKENS W14 .... 107 H3
Hampden Gurney School
  MBLAR W1H 9 K4
Hampstead ⊖
  HAMP NW3 .... 71 H1
Hampstead Cemetery
  CRICK NW2 .... 70 D3
Hampstead College of Fine Arts
  HAMP NW3 .... 71 J5
Hampstead CC
  KIL/WHAMP NW6 .... 71 F5
Hampstead Golf Club
  GLDGN NW11 .... 53 G6

Hampstead Heath ⊖
  HAMP NW3 .... 71 J3
Hampstead Medical Centre
  HAMP NW3 .... 71 G3
Hampstead Parochial CE School
  HAMP NW3 .... 71 G3
Hampstead School
  CRICK NW2 .... 70 C3
The Hampstead School of Art
  HAMP NW3 .... 70 E3
Hampstead School of English
  KIL/WHAMP NW6 .... 70 E3
Hampstead Theatre
  .... 3 G1
Hampton ⊖
  HPTN TW12 .... 142 A7
Hampton Academy
  HPTN TW12 .... 142 A7
Hampton Cemetery
  HPTN TW12 .... 142 A6
Hampton Court ⇌
  E/WMO/HCT KT8 .... 157 K3
Hampton Court House School
  E/WMO/HCT KT8 .... 157 K1
Hampton Court Palace
  E/WMO/HCT KT8 .... 158 A2
Hampton Court Palace Golf Club
  SURB KT6 .... 158 D4
Hampton Farm Industrial Estate
  FELT TW13 .... 141 J2
Hampton FC
  HPTN TW12 .... 142 B7
Hampton Hill Junior School
  HPTN TW12 .... 142 C4
Hampton Infant School
  HPTN TW12 .... 141 K6
Hampton Junior School
  HPTN TW12 .... 142 A7
The Hampton Medical Centre
  HPTN TW12 .... 142 A6
Hampton Open Air Pool
  HPTN TW12 .... 142 C6
Hampton Road Industrial Park
  CROY/NA CR0 .... 164 D5
Hampton School
  HPTN TW12 .... 142 A4
Hampton Wick ⇌
  KUT/HW KT1 .... 143 K7
Hampton Wick Infant School
  TEDD TW11 .... 143 J6
Handball Arena
  OLYMPICPK E20 .... 75 J5
Handel's House
  MYFR/PKLN W1K 10 C5
Handsworth Health Clinic
  CHING E4 .... 44 B5
Hanger Lane ⊖
  EA W5 .... 86 B2
Hanover Primary School
  IS N1 .... 6 D5
Hanover Trading Estate
  HOLWY N7 .... 72 E4
Hanover West Industrial Estate
  WLSDN NW10 .... 86 E2
Hanwell ⇌
  HNWL W7 .... 84 E6
Hanworth Trading Estate
  FELT TW13 .... 141 J2
Harbinger Primary School
  POP/IOD E14 .... 112 D3
Harenc School
  SCUP DA14 .... 155 J4
Hargrave Park Primary School
  ARCH N19 .... 72 C1
Haringey Arts Council
  ED N9 .... 42 C1
Haringey Community
Health Clinic
  SEVS/STOTM N15 .... 56 B3
Haringey Magistrates Court
  HGT N6 .... 54 A5
Haringey Sixth Form Centre
  TOTM N17 .... 42 B6
Harkness Industrial Estate
  BORE WD6 .... 24 C3
The Harlequin Shopping Centre
  WAT WD17 .... 21 G3
Harlequins RFC & Harlequins RL
(The Stoop)
  TWK TW2 .... 123 K6
Harlesden ⊖
  WLSDN NW10 .... 87 F1
Harlesden Primary School
  WLSDN NW10 .... 87 G1
Harley Medical Centre
  CAVSQ/HST W1G 10 D4
The Harley Medical Centre
  CANST EC4R 12 F6
Harley Street Clinic
  CAVSQ/HST W1G 10 C3
The Harley Street Clinic
  CAVSQ/HST W1G 10 C2
Harlington Community School
  HYS/HAR UB3 .... 101 G3
Harlyn Primary School
  PIN HA5 .... 47 F2
The Harold Macmillan
Medical Centre
  HRW HA1 .... 48 D6
Harp Business Centre
  CRICK NW2 .... 69 J1
Harringay ⇌
  FSBYPK N4 .... 55 G5
Harringay Green Lanes ⊖
  FSBYPK N4 .... 55 H5
Harrington Hall Hotel
  SKENS SW7 .... 14 E6
Harrington Hill Primary School
  CLPT E5 .... 56 D7
Harrington Road ⊖
  SNWD SE25 .... 165 K2
Harris Academy at Peckham
  PECK SE15 .... 111 G7
Harris Academy Bermondsey
  STHWK SE1 .... 19 M5
Harris Academy Falconwood
  WELL DA16 .... 135 J3
Harris Academy Merton
  STRHM/NOR SW16 .... 163 J2
Harris Academy South Norwood
  SNWD SE25 .... 165 G2
Harris Boys Academy
East Dulwich
  EDUL SE22 .... 131 J4
Harris City Academy
Crystal Palace
  NRWD SE19 .... 150 B7
Harris Girls Academy
  EDUL SE22 .... 131 K4
Harrodian School
  BARN SW13 .... 106 C6
Harrods Store
  CHEL SW3 .... 15 L3

Harrovian Business Village
HRW HA1.............48 D6
Harrow Arts Centre
PIN HA5.............34 A6
Harrow Borough FC
RYLN/HDSTN HA2.............66 A3
Harrow Cemetery
HRW HA1.............48 D5
Harrow College
HRW HA1.............48 E6
KTN/HRWW/WS HA3.............34 E5
Harrow CC
HRW HA1.............66 E3
Harrow Crown Courts
HRW HA1.............48 D2
Harrow Driving Cycling &
Road Safety Centre
KTN/HRWW/WS HA3.............49 G2
Harrow Heritage Museum
RYLN/HDSTN HA2.............48 C2
Harrow High School
HRW HA1.............49 G5
Harrow Leisure Centre
KTN/HRWW/WS HA3.............49 F2
Harrow Magistrates Court
HRW HA1.............49 F3
Harrow-on-the-Hill ⇌ ⊖
HRW HA1.............48 E5
Harrow RFC
STAN HA7.............35 H2
Harrow Road Health Centre
BAY/PAD W2.............8 B2
Harrow School
RYLN/HDSTN HA2.............66 E1
Harrow Town CC
RYLN/HDSTN HA2.............48 A7
Harrow Weald Cemetery
KTN/HRWW/WS HA3.............34 E5
Harrow & Wealdstone ⇌ ⊖ ⊕
HRW HA1.............48 E3
Harry Gosling Primary School
WCHPL E1.............92 C5
Hartley Primary School
EHAM E6.............77 J7
Hartsbourne Primary School
BUSH WD23.............34 D1
Hartspring Industrial Park
BUSH WD23.............22 A1
Hartspring Sports Centre
BUSH WD23.............22 A1
Harvington School
EA W5.............85 J5
Haseltine Primary School
SYD SE26.............151 H3
Haslemere Business Centre
EN EN1.............30 D3
Haslemere Industrial Estate
EBED/NFELT TW14.............121 K4
WAND/EARL SW18.............147 F1
Haslemere Primary School
MTCM CR4.............162 C1
Hasmonean High School
Boys Site
HDN NW4.............52 B3
Hasmonean High School
Girls Site
MLHL NW7.............37 J7
Hasmonean Primary School
HDN NW4.............52 B4
Haste Hill Golf Club
NTHWD HA6.............46 C1
Hastings Clinic
BRXS/STRHM SW2.............130 A4
Hastingwood Trading Estate
UED N18.............43 G1
Hatcham Mews
Business Centre
NWCR SE14.............112 A6
Hatch End
PIN HA5.............34 A6
Hatch End High School
KTN/HRWW/WS HA3.............34 B6
Hatch End Swimming Pool
PIN HA5.............34 A6
Hatfield Primary School
MRDN SM4.............161 H5
Hatton Cross ⊖
HTHAIR TW6.............121 J3
Hatton School
WFD IG8.............59 H1
Havelock Primary School
NWDGN UB2.............102 E2
Haven Green Clinic
EA W5.............85 K5
Havering College of
Further & Higher Education
EMPK RM11.............63 K6
Havering Magistrates Court
ROM RM1.............63 G3
Haverstock School
HAMP NW3.............4 A1
Hawes Down Clinic
WWKM BR4.............180 B1
Hawes Down
Primary School
WWKM BR4.............167 J4
The Hawker Centre
KUTN/CMB KT2.............143 K4
Hawkesdown House School
KENS W8.............8 B9
Hawkins Clinic
PUT/ROE SW15.............127 G3
RYNPK SW20.............145 H7
Hawksmoor Primary School
THMD SE28.............97 H6
Hawley Infant School
CAMTN NW1.............4 C3
Haydon School
PIN HA5.............46 E2
Haydons Road ⇌
WIM/MER SW19.............147 G4
Hayes ⇌
HAYES BR2.............167 J7
Hayes Bridge Middle School
STHL UB1.............102 D1
Hayes Bridge Retail Park
YEAD UB4.............83 G6
Hayes CC
HYS/HAR UB3.............82 D5
Hayes FC
HYS/HAR UB3.............82 D6
Hayes Grove Priory Hospital
HAYES BR2.............180 E1
Hayes & Harlington ⇌
HYS/HAR UB3.............101 J2
The Hayes Manor School
HYS/HAR UB3.............82 B5
Hayes Park J & I School
YEAD UB4.............82 D3
Hayes Pool
HYS/HAR UB3.............82 D7
Hayes Primary School
HAYES BR2.............168 A7

Hayes School
HAYES BR2.............181 F1
Hayes Social & Sports Club
HYS/HAR UB3.............82 D6
Hayes Stadium Sports Centre
HYS/HAR UB3.............82 B5
Hay Lane School
CDALE/KGS NW9.............50 E3
Haymerle School
PECK SE15.............111 H5
Hays Galleria
STHWK SE1.............13 J8
Hayward Gallery
STHWK SE1.............11 M9
Hazelbury Junior School
ED N9.............42 A2
Hazeldene Medical Centre
WBLY HA9.............68 D5
Hazelwood Schools
PLMGR N13.............41 G3
Headstart Montessori School
TOOT SW17.............147 G2
Headstone Lane ⊖
RYLN/HDSTN HA2.............34 B7
Health & Vitality
Osteopathic Clinic
HOR/WEW KT19.............173 F4
Healy Medical Centre
CLPT E5.............56 D7
The Heart Hospital
CAVSQ/HST W1G.............10 B3
Heartlands High School
WDGN N22.............55 F1
The Heart of
Greenwich Development
GNWCH SE10.............113 J4
Heathbrook Primary School
VX/NE SW8.............129 H1
Heath Business Centre
HSLW TW3.............123 H3
Heathcote School
CHING E4.............44 C1
The Heatherley School of
Fine Art
FUL/PGN SW6.............108 B6
Heathfield College
HAYES BR2.............181 G5
Heathfield House School
CHSWK W4.............105 K4
Heathfield Primary School
WHTN TW2.............123 F7
Heathfield School
PIN HA5.............47 H6
Heath House
Preparatory School
BKHTH/KID SE3.............133 J1
Heathland School
RYLN/HDSTN HA2.............66 A2
The Heathland School
HSLWW TW4.............122 E5
Heathmere Primary School
PUT/ROE SW15.............126 D7
Heathrow Airport Central Bus &
Coach Station
HTHAIR TW6.............120 D2
Heathrow Airport Terminal 4
HTHAIR TW6.............120 E4
Heathrow Airport (Terminals
1, 2, 3)
HTHAIR TW6.............120 E1
Heathrow Air Traffic
Control Tower
HTHAIR TW6.............120 E2
Heathrow International
Trading Estate
HSLWW TW4.............122 A2
Heathrow Medical Centre
HYS/HAR UB3.............101 G4
Heathrow Primary School
WDR/YW UB7.............100 C5
Heathrow Terminal 4 ⇌ ⊖
HTHAIR TW6.............120 E4
Heathrow Terminals 1 & 3 ⇌ ⊖
HTHAIR TW6.............120 E1
Heathrow Viewing Area
HTHAIR TW6.............120 E2
Heathrow World Cargo Centre
HTHAIR TW6.............120 C4
Heathside Preparatory School
HAMP NW3.............71 G3
Heathside Preparatory
School (Upper)
HAMP NW3.............71 G3
Heathway Industrial Estate
DAGE RM10.............80 D3
Heathway Medical Centre
DAGW RM9.............80 B3
Heavers Farm Primary School
SNWD SE25.............165 G4
Heber Primary School
EDUL SE22.............131 G5
Heckford Street
Business Centre
WAP E1W.............93 F6
Hedges & Butler Estate
SRTFD E15.............94 A1
Hedgewood School
YEAD UB4.............82 C2
Helena Road Clinic
WLSDN NW10.............69 K3
Heliport Industrial Estate
BTSEA SW11.............128 C1
Helston Court Business Centre
WIM/MER SW19.............145 K4
Henderson Hospital
BELMT SM2.............174 E7
Hendon ⊖
HDN NW4.............51 J5
Hendon Cemetery
MLHL NW7.............38 B7
Hendon Central ⊖
HDN NW4.............51 K4
Hendon Crematorium
MLHL NW7.............38 B6
Hendon FC
CRICK NW2.............70 B1
Hendon Golf Club
MLHL NW7.............38 A6
Hendon Hall Hotel
HDN NW4.............52 A2
Hendon Preparatory School
HDN NW4.............52 B2
Hendon School
HDN NW4.............52 B4
Hendon Secretarial College
HDN NW4.............51 K4
Hendon Youth Sports Centre
CRICK NW2.............52 B6
Henrietta Barnett School
GLDGN NW11.............53 F4
Henry Cavendish
Primary School
BAL SW12.............129 H7

Henry Compton School
FUL/PGN SW6.............107 G7
Henry Fawcett Primary School
LBTH SE11.............18 A9
Henry Green Primary School
BCTR RM8.............61 K7
Henwick Primary School
ELTH/MOT SE9.............134 C2
Herbert Morrison
Primary School
VX/NE SW8.............109 K6
Hereward House School
HAMP NW3.............71 J5
Her Majestys' Theatre
STJS SW1Y.............11 H8
Hermitage Primary School
WAP E1W.............92 C7
Herne Hill ⇌
HNHL SE24.............130 C4
Herne Hill School
HNHL SE24.............130 D4
Herne Hill Stadium
(Cycle Centre)
HNHL SE24.............130 E5
Heron Industrial Estate
SRTFD E15.............93 K1
Heron Quays ⊖
POP/IOD E14.............93 J7
Heronsgate Primary School
THMD SE28.............115 J2
Heron Trading Estate
ACT W3.............86 D4
Hertswood School
BORE WD6.............24 E1
Heston Community School
HEST TW5.............103 F6
Heston Community Sports Hall
HEST TW5.............103 F6
Heston Industrial Mall
HEST TW5.............102 E6
Heston Infant School
HEST TW5.............103 F6
Heston Junior School
HEST TW5.............103 F6
Heston Park CC
HEST TW5.............102 E5
Heston Swimming Baths
HEST TW5.............102 E5
Heythrop College
KENS W8.............14 C3
Higgs Industrial Estate
HNHL SE24.............130 C2
Highams Lodge
Business Centre
WALTH E17.............57 F2
Highams Park ⇌
CHING E4.............44 A5
Highams Park Primary School
CHING E4.............44 B5
High Barnet ⊖
BAR EN5.............26 E3
Highbury Corner
Magistrates Court
HOLWY N7.............73 G5
Highbury Fields School
HBRY N5.............73 H3
Highbury Grove School
HBRY N5.............73 J4
Highbury & Islington ⇌ ⊖
IS N1.............73 G5
Highbury Park Clinic
HBRY N5.............73 H2
Highbury Pool
HBRY N5.............73 H5
Highbury Quadrant
Primary School
HBRY N5.............73 J3
Highbury Square Development
HBRY N5.............73 H2
High Commission of Angola
MHST W1U.............9 M3
High Commission of
Antigua & Barbuda
MHST W1U.............10 A4
High Commission of Bahamas
MYFR/PICC W1J.............10 B8
High Commission of Bangladesh
SKENS SW7.............14 F3
High Commission of Barbados
FITZ W1T.............11 G4
High Commission of Belize
CAVSQ/HST W1G.............10 D1
High Commission of Botswana
OXSTW W1C.............10 C5
High Commission of Brunei
KTBR SW1X.............16 A3
High Commission of Canada
MYFR/PKLN W1K.............10 B6
High Commission of Cyprus
MYFR/PKLN W1K.............10 A6
High Commission of Dominica
ECT SW5.............14 D6
High Commission of Fiji
SKENS SW7.............14 E2
High Commission of Guyana
BAY/PAD W2.............8 C7
High Commission of Jamaica
SKENS SW7.............15 G2
High Commission of Kenya
CAVSQ/HST W1G.............10 C2
High Commission of Lesotho
KTBR SW1X.............16 A3
High Commission of Malawi
MYFR/PKLN W1K.............10 C6
High Commission of Malaysia
KTBR SW1X.............16 B2
High Commission of Maldives
MHST W1U.............10 A2
High Commission of Malta
CONDST W1S.............10 F7
High Commission of Mauritius
SKENS SW7.............14 F4
High Commission of Namibia
CAVSQ/HST W1G.............10 D3
High Commission of
New Zealand
STJS SW1Y.............11 G8
High Commission of Nigeria
CHCR WC2N.............11 J8
EMB EC4Y.............12 B5
High Commission of Pakistan
KTBR SW1X.............15 M3
High Commission of
Papua New Guinea
STJS SW1Y.............10 F8
High Commission of
St Vincent & The Grenadines
KENS W8.............14 D2
High Commission of Seychelles
MHST W1U.............9 M2
High Commission of
Sierra Leone
REGST W1B.............10 E4

High Commission of Singapore
KTBR SW1X.............15 M2
KTBR SW1X.............16 A4
High Commission of
South Africa
CHCR WC2N.............11 J8
High Commission of Sri Lanka
BAY/PAD W2.............9 H6
High Commission of Swaziland
WESTW SW1E.............16 E3
High Commission of
The Gambia
KENS W8.............14 D2
High Commission of Tonga
MBLAR W1H.............9 K3
High Commission of Trinidad
& Tobago
KTBR SW1X.............16 A3
High Commission of Uganda
CHCR WC2N.............11 H8
High Commission of Zambia
KENS W8.............14 E2
High Commission of Zimbabwe
CHCR WC2N.............11 J7
High Cross Centre
SEVS/STOTM N15.............56 C3
Highfield Infant School
HAYES BR2.............167 H3
Highfield Junior School
HAYES BR2.............167 H3
Highfield Primary School
WCHMH N21.............29 H7
Highfield School
WAND/EARL SW18.............128 D6
Highgate ⊖
HGT N6.............54 B5
Highgate Cemetery
HGT N6.............54 A7
Highgate Golf Club
EFNCH N2.............53 J5
Highgate Junior School
HGT N6.............53 K6
Highgate Private Hospital
HGT N6.............53 K5
Highgate School
HGT N6.............53 K6
Highgate Wood School
MUSWH N10.............54 C4
Highgrove Pool
RSLP HA4.............46 E6
Highlands J & I School
IL IG1.............59 K7
Highlands Primary School
IL IG1.............59 J7
Highshore School
PECK SE15.............111 G7
High Street Kensington ⊖
KENS W8.............14 C2
High View Primary School
BTSEA SW11.............128 C3
Highview Primary School
WLGTN SM6.............176 E4
The Highway Trading Centre
WAP E1W.............93 F6
Hillbrook Primary School
TOOT SW17.............147 K3
Hillcroft College
SURB KT6.............159 F7
Hillcross Primary School
MRDN SM4.............161 J3
Hill House International
Junior School
KTBR SW1X.............15 M4
Hill House School
CHEL SW3.............15 K9
KTBR SW1X.............15 L4
Hill Mead Infant School
BRXN/ST SW9.............130 C3
Hillmead Primary School
BRXN/ST SW9.............130 C3
Hills Grove Primary School
WELL DA16.............116 D6
Hillside Infant School
NTHWD HA6.............32 E6
Hillyfield Primary School
WALTH E17.............57 G2
Hilly Fields Medical Centre
BROCKY SE4.............132 D4
Hilly Fields Medical Centre
BROCKY SE4.............132 D4
Hilton Docklands Pier
BERM/RHTH SE16.............93 H7
The Hiltongrove
Business Centre
WALTH E17.............57 J3
Hinchley Wood ⇌
ESH/CLAY KT10.............171 F2
Hinchley Wood
Primary School
ESH/CLAY KT10.............171 G1
Hinchley Wood School &
Sixth Form Centre
ESH/CLAY KT10.............171 G1
Hinley Clinic
LBTH SE11.............18 B6
Hispaniola
WHALL SW1A.............11 K2
Hitherfield Primary School
STRHM/NOR SW16.............149 G1
Hither Green ⇌
LEW SE13.............133 H1
Hither Green Cemetery
CAT SE6.............152 D1
HM Customs & Excise
HTHAIR TW6.............100 C7
HM Prison
BRXS/STRHM SW2.............129 K5
HOLWY N7.............72 E3
SHB W12.............87 J5
THMD SE28.............115 K2
WAND/EARL SW18.............128 C6
HMS Belfast
STHWK SE1.............13 K8
HMS President
EMB EC4Y.............12 B6
HM Young Offenders Institution
FELT TW13.............140 B2
Hobbayne First & Middle School
HNWL W7.............85 K5
Hobbayne Primary School
HNWL W7.............84 E5
Hockey Centre
OLYMPICPK E20.............75 J4
Hogarth Business Park
CHSWK W4.............106 B5
Hogarth Industrial Estate
WLSDN NW10.............87 J3
Hogarth's House
CHSWK W4.............106 A5
Holbeach Primary School
CAT SE6.............132 D6
Holborn ⊖
HHOL WC1V.............11 K4
Holborn College
WOOL/PLUM SE18.............114 C3

Holborn College
Independent School
HMSMTH W6.............107 F4
Holborn Medical Centre
BMSBY WC1N.............11 L1
Holborn Town Hall
HHOL WC1V.............11 K4
Holiday Inn
BMSBY WC1N.............11 J1
BORE WD6.............25 G2
BTFD TW8.............104 D6
BXLY DA5.............137 J3
CAMTN NW1.............4 C2
CHSGTN KT9.............171 J7
CRICK NW2.............52 A7
FSBYW WC1X.............5 M8
GTPST W1W.............10 D1
HYS/HAR UB3.............101 G7
MYFR/PICC W1J.............10 D7
SKENS SW7.............14 E5
SURB KT6.............158 C5
SUT SM1.............175 F4
WDR/YW UB7.............100 D4
WDR/YW UB7.............100 D7
Holiday Inn Express
ACT W3.............87 F4
HMSMTH W6.............106 E3
PIM SW1V.............16 F7
WAND/EARL SW18.............128 A3
WAT WD17.............21 F1
Holland House
WKENS W14.............107 J1
Holland House School
EDGW HA8.............36 C3
Holland Park ⊖
NTGHL W11.............88 D7
Holland Park Pre-
Preparatory School
WKENS W14.............107 J2
Holland Park School
KENS W8.............107 J1
Holland Park Theatre
WKENS W14.............107 J1
Holland Street Clinic
KENS W8.............14 B2
Hollickwood JMI School
MUSWH N10.............40 B6
Holloway Road ⊖
HOLWY N7.............73 F4
Holloway School
HOLWY N7.............72 D4
Holydale Primary School
PECK SE15.............131 K1
The Holyfield School
SURB KT6.............159 F4
Holly House Private Hospital
BKHH IG9.............45 F1
Hollymount Primary School
RYNPK SW20.............146 A2
Holly Park JMI School
FBAR/BDGN N11.............40 A4
Holly Park Montessori School
FSBYPK N4.............54 E6
Hollywood Bowl
BERM/RHTH SE16.............112 A2
The Holme
CAMTN NW1.............3 M8
The Holmewood School London
NFNCH/WDSPK N12.............39 F3
Holmleigh Primary School
STNW/STAM N16.............56 B7
Holocaust Memorial Garden
KTBR SW1X.............15 M1
The Holy Cross Catholic
Girls School
NWMAL KT3.............160 A3
Holy Cross Preparatory School
KUTN/CMB KT2.............144 E6
Holy Cross Primary School
FUL/PGN SW6.............107 K7
Holy Cross RC Primary School
CAT SE6.............133 F7
Holy Family RC Primary School
BKHTH/KID SE3.............134 A3
POP/IOD E14.............93 J6
Holy Family
Technology College
WALTH E17.............57 K3
WALTH E17.............58 A2
Holy Ghost RC Primary School
BAL SW12.............128 E6
Holy Trinity CE Junior School
WLGTN SM6.............176 C3
Holy Trinity CE Primary School
BRXS/STRHM SW2.............130 A6
DART DA1.............139 F4
EFNCH N2.............53 H2
KIL/WHAMP NW6.............71 G5
KTBR SW1X.............16 A5
NTHWD HA6.............32 A5
RCHPK/HAM TW10.............125 F3
SYD SE26.............150 E1
Holy Trinity College
BMLY BR1.............153 G7
Holy Trinity in St Silas
CAMTN NW1.............4 C1
Holy Trinity Lamorbey CE
Primary School
BFN/LL DA15.............136 B7
Holy Trinity Primary School
HACK E8.............74 B5
WIM/MER SW19.............146 E5
Holy Trinity School
CHEL SW3.............15 M5
Holywell School
WATW WD18.............20 D5
Homefield Preparatory School
SUT SM1.............174 E4
Home Office
WEST SW1P.............17 H4
Homerton ⇌
HOM E9.............75 F5
Homerton University Hospital
HOM E9.............75 F4
Homoeopathic Health Centre
PLSTW E13.............94 C2
The Homoeopathic
Health Centre
MLHL NW7.............37 H4
Honeypot Business Centre
STAN HA7.............36 A7
Honeypot Lane Centre
STAN HA7.............35 K7
Honeypot Medical Centre
STAN HA7.............50 A1
Honeywell Primary School
BTSEA SW11.............128 E5
Honor Oak Crematorium
FSTH SE23.............132 A4
Honor Oak Gallery
FSTH SE23.............132 A5
Honor Oak Health Centre
BROCKY SE4.............132 B3

Honor Oak Park ≥ ⊖
  FSTH SE23..............132 A5
Honourable Artillery
  Company HQ
  STLK EC1Y..............13 G1
Hook Lane Primary School
  WELL DA16..............136 B2
Hook Rise South
  Industrial Park
  CHSGTN KT9..............172 B2
Hopewell School
  BARK IG11..............78 D5
Horizon Business Centre
  ED N9..............43 F1
Horizon Industrial Estate
  PECK SE15..............111 H5
Horizon School
  STNW/STAM N16..............74 A3
The Horniman Museum
  & Gardens
  FSTH SE23..............131 J7
Horniman Primary School
  FSTH SE23..............131 J7
Horn Park Primary School
  LEE/GVPK SE12..............134 A6
Hornsby House School
  BAL SW12..............129 F7
Hornsey ≥
  CEND/HSY/T N8..............55 F3
Hornsey Central Hospital
  CEND/HSY/T N8..............54 C4
Hornsey Coroners Court &
  Public Mortuary
  CEND/HSY/T N8..............54 E3
Hornsey Rise Health Centre
  ARCH N19..............54 D6
Hornsey Secondary School
  for Girls
  CEND/HSY/T N8..............55 F4
Horn Stairs
  BERM/RHTH SE16..............93 H7
Horseferry Road
  Magistrates Court
  WEST SW1P..............17 H4
Horse Guards Parade
  WHALL SW1A..............11 H9
Horsenden Hill Golf Club
  GFD/PVL UB6..............65 H5
Horsenden Primary School
  GFD/PVL UB6..............66 E5
Horton Country Park
  HOR/WEW KT19..............172 C7
Horton Park Golf &
  Country Club
  HOR/WEW KT19..............172 E6
Hortus Cemetery
  NWDGN UB2..............102 E1
Hospital of St John &
  St Elizabeth
  STJWD NW8..............3 G6
Hotel Indigo
  BAY/PAD W2..............9 H5
Hotel Russell
  RSQ WC1B..............11 J1
Hotel Verta
  BTSEA SW11..............128 C1
Hotham Primary School
  PUT/ROE SW15..............127 G3
Hotspur Industrial Estate
  TOTM N17..............42 D5
Houndsfield Primary School
  ED N9..............30 C6
Hounslow ≥
  HSLW TW3..............123 H3
Hounslow Business Park
  HSLW TW3..............123 F3
Hounslow CC
  HSLW TW5..............122 E1
Hounslow Cemetery
  HSLWW TW4..............122 E6
Hounslow Central ⊖
  HSLW TW3..............123 G1
Hounslow East ⊖
  HSLW TW3..............123 H1
Hounslow Heath Infant School
  HSLWW TW4..............122 D2
Hounslow Heath Junior School
  HSLWW TW4..............122 D2
Hounslow Manor School
  HSLW TW3..............123 G2
Hounslow Manor Sports Hall
  HSLW TW3..............123 G2
Hounslow Town Primary School
  HSLW TW3..............123 H2
Hounslow West ⊖
  HSLWW TW4..............122 D1
The Household Cavalry Museum
  WHALL SW1A..............11 J9
House Mill
  POP/IOD E14..............94 A2
House of Detention
  CLKNW EC1R..............6 B9
House of St Barnabus
  SOHO/SHAV W1D..............11 C5
Houses of Parliament
  WHALL SW1A..............17 K2
Houston Business Park
  YEAD UB4..............83 G7
Howard Primary School
  SAND/SEL CR2..............177 J3
Howbury Centre
  ERITH DA8..............118 D6
Howland Quay
  BERM/RHTH SE16..............112 A2
Hoxton ≥
  BETH E2..............7 L6
Hoxton Hall Community Theatre
  IS N1..............7 J5
HQS Wellington
  (Master Mariners)
  TPL/STR WC2R..............12 A7
HSBC Sports Club
  BECK BR3..............151 G5
HSBC Tower
  POP/IOD E14..............93 K7
Hubbinet Industrial Estate
  ROMW/RG RM7..............62 E2
Hugh Myddelton
  Primary School
  CLKNW EC1R..............6 B8
The Humana
  Wellington Hospital
  STJWD NW8..............3 H7
Humber Trading Estate
  CRICK NW2..............69 K1
Hunterian Museum
  LINN WC2A..............11 M4
Hunters Hall Primary School
  DAGE RM10..............80 D4
Hunter Street Health Centre
  STPAN WC1H..............5 J9
Huntsman Sports Club
  BKHTH/KID SE3..............133 K3

Hurlingham Business Park
  FUL/PGN SW6..............127 K2
Hurlingham & Chelsea
  Secondary School
  FUL/PGN SW6..............127 K2
Hurlingham House
  FUL/PGN SW6..............127 K2
Hurlingham Private School
  PUT/ROE SW15..............127 J3
Huron University
  RSQ WC1B..............11 J2
Hurricane Trading Centre
  CDALE/KGS NW9..............37 H7
Hurstmere School
  BFN/LL DA15..............136 C7
Hurst Park Primary School
  E/WMO/HCT KT8..............157 F2
Hurst Primary School
  BXLY DA5..............136 E7
Hyatt Carlton Tower Hotel
  KTBR SW1X..............15 M4
Hyatt Regency-The Churchill
  MBLAR W1H..............9 M4
The Hyde Industrial Estate
  CDALE/KGS NW9..............51 H4
Hyde Park
  BAY/PAD W2..............9 L3
Hyde Park Corner ⊖
  KTBR SW1X..............16 A1
The Hyde School
  CDALE/KGS NW9..............51 H4
Hyland House School
  WALTH E17..............58 B1
Hylands Primary School
  EMPK RM11..............63 J5
Hyleford Leavers Unit School
  BARK/HLT IG6..............60 D1
Hythe Road Industrial Estate
  WLSDN NW10..............87 J3
Ian Mikardo High School
  BOW E3..............93 K2
  POP/IOD E14..............93 K6
Ibis Hotel
  BARK IG11..............78 B7
  BORE WD6..............24 E1
  CAMTN NW1..............4 F7
  CAN/RD E16..............94 E6
  FUL/PGN SW6..............14 A9
  GNWCH SE10..............113 F6
  HYS/HAR UB3..............101 H7
  POP/IOD E14..............94 A6
  SRTFD E15..............76 C5
  WBLY HA9..............68 C3
  WCHPL E1..............13 M4
Ibstock Place School
  PUT/ROE SW15..............126 B5
ICA Cinema
  STJS SW1Y..............11 H8
ICC London
  CAN/RD E16..............95 G6
Ickburgh School
  CLPT E5..............74 D2
Ickenham ⊖
  HGDN/ICK UB10..............64 A3
Ickenham Clinic
  HGDN/ICK UB10..............64 A2
Icon College of
  Technology & Management
  WCHPL E1..............92 C5
Ihlara Sport FC
  HBRY N5..............73 J3
Ilderton Primary School
  PECK SE15..............111 K5
Ilford ≥
  IL IG1..............78 A2
Ilford County High School
  BARK/HLT IG6..............60 C1
Ilford Golf Club
  IL IG1..............59 K7
Ilford Jewish Primary School
  BARK/HLT IG6..............60 D1
Ilford Medical Centre
  IL IG1..............78 B2
Ilford Preparatory School
  GDMY/SEVK IG3..............61 F7
Ilford Retail Park
  IL IG1..............78 C1
Ilford Swimming Pool
  IL IG1..............78 D1
Ilford Ursuline High School
  IL IG1..............78 A1
Ilford Ursuline
  Preparatory School
  IL IG1..............78 B1
Iman Zakaria Academy
  FSTGT E7..............77 F4
Imber Court Trading Estate
  E/WMO/HCT KT8..............157 J3
Immanuel CE
  Primary School
  STRHM/NOR SW16..............148 E5
Immanuel College
  BUSH WD23..............22 E6
Imperial College
  PUT/ROE SW15..............127 G1
  SKENS SW7..............15 G3
  SKENS SW7..............15 G8
Imperial College
  Athletic Ground
  HYS/HAR UB3..............101 F5
Imperial College of London
  SKENS SW7..............15 G2
Imperial College of Science
  FUL/PGN SW6..............14 A9
Imperial College of Science
  & Technology
  SKENS SW7..............15 H2
Imperial College of Science
  Technology & Medicine
  SKENS SW7..............14 F3
Imperial College School
  of Medicine
  PIM SW1V..............17 G6
Imperial War Museum
  STHWK SE1..............18 B4
Imperial War Museum Annexe
  LBTH SE11..............18 B4
Imperial Wharf ≥ ⊖
  FUL/PGN SW6..............108 B7
Inchbald School of Design
  BGVA SW1W..............16 A5
India House
  HOL/ALD WC2B..............11 L6
The Infirmary Royal Hospital
  CHEL SW3..............16 A8
Inner London Sessions House
  (Crown Court)
  STHWK SE1..............18 E3
Innholders Hall
  CANST EC4R..............13 G6
Innkeeper's Lodge
  BORE WD6..............24 E1
  CHEAM SM3..............161 K7

NTHLT UB5..............66 A5
  SAND/SEL CR2..............177 J7
Inns of Court & Chancery
  TPL/STR WC2R..............12 A5
Inns of Court Law School
  GINN WC1R..............11 M2
Insight Independent School
  WEA W13..............85 H6
Institute for Arts &
  Therapy in Education
  IS N1..............6 D3
The Institute Hampstead
  Garden Suburb
  EFNCH N2..............53 J3
Institute of Cancer Research
  ECT SW5..............14 F7
Institute of Education
  University of London
  RSQ WC1B..............11 H1
Institute of European Studies
  RSQ WC1B..............11 K2
Instituto Espanol
  Canada Blanch
  NKENS W10..............88 C4
International Broadcast Centre
  OLYMPICPK E20..............75 J4
International Business Park
  SRTFD E15..............76 B7
International
  Community School
  BAY/PAD W2..............9 J4
International Community
  School Primary
  CAMTN NW1..............10 A1
International Medical Centre
  ECT SW5..............14 B6
International School of
  Business Studies
  PIN HA5..............48 A6
International
  School of London
  ACT W3..............105 H3
International Trading Estate
  NWDGN UB2..............102 A2
International University
  BUSH WD23..............21 K3
Invicta Industrial Estate
  SRTFD E15..............94 A2
Invicta Primary School
  BKHTH/KID SE3..............113 K5
Invicta Sports Club
  DART DA1..............139 G4
Inwood Business Centre
  HSLW TW3..............123 G3
Ironmonger Row Baths
  FSBYE EC1V..............6 E8
Ironmongers Hall
  STBT EC1A..............12 E3
Islamia Girls School
  KIL/WHAMP NW6..............70 C7
Islamic College for
  Advanced Studies
  WLSDN NW10..............69 K6
The Islamic Grammar School
  WAND/EARL SW18..............127 J6
Islamic Shaksiyah
  Foundation School
  WALTH E17..............57 G4
Island Clinic
  POP/IOD E14..............113 F1
Island Gardens ⊖
  POP/IOD E14..............113 F3
Isleworth ≥
  ISLW TW7..............124 A1
Isleworth Cemetery
  ISLW TW7..............124 B1
Isleworth Recreation Centre
  ISLW TW7..............124 A3
Isleworth Crown Court
  ISLW TW7..............103 K7
Isleworth & Syon School
  for Boys
  ISLW TW7..............103 K6
Isleworth Town Primary School
  ISLW TW7..............124 A1
Islington Arts & Media School
  FSBYPK N4..............55 F7
Islington Business Centre
  IS N1..............6 F3
Islington Crematorium
  MUSWH N10..............39 K7
Islington Green Medical Centre
  IS N1..............6 C3
Islington Tennis Centre
  HOLWY N7..............72 E5
Islington Town Hall
  IS N1..............6 C1
Ismaili Centre
  SKENS SW7..............15 H5
Italia Conti Academy of
  Theatre Arts
  BRXN/ST SW9..............129 K2
  FARR EC1M..............12 E1
Italian Hospital
  PIM SW1V..............16 E5
Ivybridge Primary School
  TWK TW1..............124 A5
Ivybridge Retail Park
  ISLW TW7..............124 A4
Ivydale Primary School
  PECK SE15..............132 A3
Jack & Jill School
  HPTN TW12..............142 A5
Jack Taylor School
  STJWD NW8..............2 E3
Jack Tizard School
  FUL/PGN SW6..............107 G7
  SHB W12..............88 A6
Jacques Prevert School
  HMSMTH W6..............107 G3
James Allens Preparatory
  Girls School
  HNHL SE24..............130 E4
James Dixon Primary School
  PGE/AN SE20..............150 C7
Jamestown Mental
  Health Centre
  HAMP NW3..............3 L1
James Wolfe Primary School
  GNWCH SE10..............112 E6
Jamiah Madaniyah
  Primary School
  FSTGT E7..............77 H5
Jamiatul Ummah School
  WCHPL E1..............92 D5
Janet Adegoke Leisure Centre
  SHB W12..............87 J6
The Japanese School
  ACT W3..............86 C6
Japan Green Medical Centre
  BORE WD6..............86 D7
Jenner Health Centre
  FSTH SE23..............132 B7

Jenny Hammond
  Primary School
  WAN E11..............76 C3
Jermyn Street Theatre
  MYFR/PICC W1J..............10 F7
Jessop Primary School
  HNHL SE24..............130 C3
Jewel Tower
  WEST SW1P..............17 J3
Jewish Cemetery
  GLDGN NW11..............52 E5
Jewish Community Theatre
  HNHL SE24..............130 E2
Jewish Free School
  KTN/HRWW/WS HA3..............49 K5
  KTTN NW5..............72 D5
The Jewish Museum
  CAMTN NW1..............4 C4
  FNCH N3..............53 F1
Johanna Primary School
  STHWK SE1..............18 A2
John Ball Primary School
  BKHTH/KID SE3..............133 H1
John Betts Primary School
  HMSMTH W6..............106 D2
John Burns Primary School
  BTSEA SW11..............129 F1
John Chilton School
  NTHLT UB5..............65 J6
John Dixon Clinic
  BERM/RHTH SE16..............111 J2
John Donne Primary School
  PECK SE15..............111 J7
John F Kennedy School
  CAN/RD E16..............95 H4
John F Kennedy Special School
  SRTFD E15..............76 C7
John Keble Anglican Church
  Primary School
  WLSDN NW10..............87 H1
The John Loughborough School
  TOTM N17..............56 B1
John Lyon School
  RYLN/HDSTN HA2..............48 D7
John Nightingale School
  E/WMO/HCT KT8..............156 F2
John Orwell Sports Centre
  WAP E1W..............92 C7
John Paul II RC School
  WIM/MER SW19..............127 G6
John Perry Primary School
  ACT W3..............87 G5
John Perryn Primary School
  DAGE RM10..............81 F5
John Roan School
  BKHTH/KID SE3..............113 H6
John Ruskin College
  SAND/SEL CR2..............179 G6
John Ruskin Primary School
  WALW SE17..............18 E9
John Scott Health Centre
  FSBYPK N4..............55 J7
John Scurr Primary School
  WCHPL E1..............92 E3
John Smith House
  WALW SE17..............18 E6
Johnsons Industrial Estate
  HYS/HAR UB3..............101 K2
John Stainer Primary School
  BROCKY SE4..............132 B2
The Jo Richardson
  Community School
  DAGW RM9..............79 K7
Joseph Clarke Special School
  CHING E4..............44 B5
Joseph Hood Primary School
  RYNPK SW20..............161 H1
Jubilee Country Park
  BMLY BR1..............169 G3
Jubilee Market
  COVGDN WC2E..............11 K6
Jubilee Primary School
  BRXS/STRHM SW2..............130 B5
  THMD SE28..............97 J6
Jubilee Sports Ground
  CHING E4..............44 B3
Julians Primary School
  STRHM/NOR SW16..............149 G3
Jumeirah Carlton Tower Hotel
  KTBR SW1X..............15 M3
Jumeirah Lowndes Hotel
  KTBR SW1X..............15 M3
Juno Way Industrial Estate
  NWCR SE14..............112 A5
Jurys Inn Chelsea
  FUL/PGN SW6..............108 B7
Jurys Inn Hotel
  HTHAIR TW6..............121 J2
JVC Business Park
  CRICK NW2..............51 J7
Kaizen Primary School
  PLSTW E13..............95 F3
Kangley Business Centre
  SYD SE26..............151 H4
Katella Trading Estate
  BARK IG11..............96 E2
Katherine Road Medical Centre
  FSTGT E7..............77 G5
Keats College
  HAMP NW3..............71 H3
Keble Preparatory School
  WCHMH N21..............29 G6
Keen Students
  Supplementary School
  WCHPL E1..............92 C4
Keir Hardie Primary School
  CAN/RD E16..............94 E4
Keith Davis Cue Sports Club
  DAGW RM9..............79 K6
Kelmscott Community Centre
  WALTH E17..............57 H5
Kelmscott Leisure Centre
  WALTH E17..............57 H5
Kelmscott School
  WALTH E17..............57 H5
Kelsey Park Sports College
  BECK BR3..............166 D2
Kelvin Industrial Estate
  GFD/PVL UB6..............66 B7
Kemnal Technology College
  STMC/STPC BR5..............155 H6
Kempton Park ≥
  SUN TW16..............141 F6
Kempton Park Racecourse
  SUN TW16..............141 F6
Ken Barrington Centre
  LBTH SE11..............110 A5
Kender Primary School
  NWCR SE14..............111 K7
Kenilworth Primary School
  BORE WD6..............25 F2
Kenmont Primary School
  WLSDN NW10..............87 J2

Kenmore Park Infant School
  KTN/HRWW/WS HA3..............49 K2
Kenneth More Theatre
  IL IG1..............78 C2
Kennington ⊖
  LBTH SE11..............18 C7
Kensal Green ⊖
  WLSDN NW10..............88 A2
Kensal Green Cemetery
  WLSDN NW10..............87 K2
Kensal Rise ⊖
  WLSDN NW10..............88 A1
Kensal Rise Primary School
  KIL/WHAMP NW6..............88 B1
Kensington & Chelsea College
  NKENS W10..............88 C3
Kensington & Chelsea
  Town Hall
  KENS W8..............14 B2
Kensington Avenue
  Primary School
  THHTH CR7..............149 G7
Kensington Business Centre
  SKENS SW7..............15 K3
Kensington & Chelsea College
  CHEL SW3..............15 H9
  KENS W8..............14 A1
  NTGHL W11..............107 J1
  WBPTN W10..............108 B6
The Kensington Clinic
  KENS W8..............14 C4
Kensington College of Business
  HOL/ALD WC2B..............11 L4
Kensington House Hotel
  KENS W8..............14 C2
Kensington Leisure Centre
  NTGHL W11..............88 B6
Kensington Market
  KENS W8..............14 C2
Kensington (Olympia) ≥ ⊖ ⊖
  WKENS W14..............107 H2
Kensington Palace State
  Apartments & Royal
  Ceremonial Dress Collection
  KENS W8..............8 D9
Kensington Park School
  REGST W1B..............10 D2
Kensington Preparatory School
  FUL/PGN SW6..............107 J7
Kensington Primary School
  MNPK E12..............77 K5
Kensington School of Business
  HCIRC EC1N..............12 B2
Kensington Wharf
  WBPTN SW10..............108 C6
Kensit Memorial College
  FNCH N3..............52 C1
Kent House ≥
  BECK BR3..............151 G7
Kentish Town ≥ ⊖
  KTTN NW5..............72 C4
Kentish Town CE Primary School
  KTTN NW5..............72 C4
Kentish Town Health Centre
  KTTN NW5..............72 C5
Kentish Town Industrial Estate
  KTTN NW5..............72 B4
Kentish Town Sports Centre
  KTTN NW5..............72 A5
Kentish Town West ⊖
  KTTN NW5..............72 B5
Kenton ⊖ ⊖
  KTN/HRWW/WS HA3..............49 H5
Kenton CC
  KTN/HRWW/WS HA3..............49 J3
Kenton Clinic
  KTN/HRWW/WS HA3..............50 A3
Kent Park Industrial Estate
  PECK SE15..............111 J5
Kenwood House
  HAMP NW3..............53 J7
Kenyngton Manor
  Primary School
  SUN TW16..............140 E4
The Kerem School
  EFNCH N2..............53 H4
Keston CE Primary School
  HAYES BR2..............181 H4
Kestrel House School
  CEND/HSY/T N8..............54 E1
Kew Bridge ≥
  BTFD TW8..............105 G4
Kew Bridge Steam Museum
  BTFD TW8..............105 G4
Kew College
  RCH/KEW TW9..............105 H6
Kew Gardens ⊖ ≥
  RCH/KEW TW9..............105 H7
Kew Palace
  RCH/KEW TW9..............105 F6
Kew Retail Park
  RCH/KEW TW9..............105 J5
Kew Riverside Primary School
  RCH/KEW TW9..............125 J1
Keyplan & Roxburghe College
  FITZ W1T..............10 F1
Keyworth Primary School
  WALW SE17..............18 C8
Khalsa College London
  HRW HA1..............49 F5
Khalsa VA Primary School
  NWDGN UB2..............103 F3
Kidbrooke ≥
  BKHTH/KID SE3..............134 B2
Kidbrooke Park Primary School
  BKHTH/KID SE3..............134 B1
Kidbrooke School
  BKHTH/KID SE3..............134 C1
Kilburn ⊖
  CRICK NW2..............70 C5
Kilburn High Road ≥
  KIL/WHAMP NW6..............2 B4
Kilburn Park ⊖
  KIL/WHAMP NW6..............2 B5
Kilburn Park Junior School
  KIL/WHAMP NW6..............2 A6
  KIL/WHAMP NW6..............88 D2
Killick Street Medical Centre
  IS N1..............5 L5
Kilmorie Primary School
  FSTH SE23..............151 G1
Kimberley Industrial Estate
  WALTH E17..............43 H6
Kimpton Industrial Estate
  CHEAM SM3..............174 D1
Kinetic Business Centre
  BORE WD6..............24 B2
King Alfred School
  GLDGN NW11..............53 F7
King Athelstan Primary School
  KUT/HW KT1..............159 G2
King Edwards Road Clinic
  RSLP HA4..............46 B7

King Edward VII Hospital
for Officers
MHST W1U................10 B2
King Fahad Academy
ACT W3................87 G6
King Fahad Academy
(Girls Upper School)
EA W5................104 D3
The Kingfisher Medical Centre
DEPT SE8................112 C5
The Kingfisher Sports Centre
KUT/HW KT1................159 F1
King George Hospital
GNTH/NBYPK IG2................61 G4
King George V ⊖
CAN/RD E16................96 A7
King George VI Youth Hostel
KENS W8................107 J1
Kingham Industrial Estate
WLSDN NW10................87 F2
King Henry's Drive ⊖
CROY/NA CR0................179 K7
King Henry VIII Mound
RCHPK/HAM TW10................125 F7
King & Queen Wharf
BERM/RHTH SE16................93 F6
Kings Avenue Medical Centre
STHL UB1................84 C5
Kings Avenue School
CLAP SW4................129 K4
Kingsbury ⊖
CDALE/KGS NW9................50 C4
Kingsbury Green
Primary School
CDALE/KGS NW9................50 D4
Kingsbury High School
CDALE/KGS NW9................50 E3
Kingsbury High Upper School
CDALE/KGS NW9................50 D3
Kingsbury Hospital
CDALE/KGS NW9................50 C3
Kingsbury Trading Estate
CDALE/KGS NW9................50 E5
Kings College
(Hampstead Campus)
HAMP NW3................70 E3
King's College Hospital
CMBW SE5................130 D2
Kings College London
CMBW SE5................130 E1
HOL/ALD WC2B................11 K5
STHWK SE1................12 C8
STHWK SE1................12 F9
WEST SW1P................16 F5
Kings College London
- Humanities
TPL/STR WC2R................11 L6
Kings College London - Law
TPL/STR WC2R................11 M6
Kings College London
(Waterloo Campus)
STHWK SE1................12 A9
Kings College School
WIM/MER SW19................146 A5
Kings College School of
Medicine & Dentistry
DUL SE21................130 E5
Kings College Sports Ground
RSLP HA4................46 C5
King's Cross ⇌ ⊖
KCROSS N1C................5 J6
King's Cross St Pancras ⊖
CAMTN NW1................5 J7
Kingsdale School
DUL SE21................150 A2
Kings Estate
HCH RM12................81 J3
Kingsford Community School
PLSTW E13................95 G3
Kingsgate Business Centre
KUTN/CMB KT2................144 A7
Kingsgate Primary School
KIL/WHAMP NW6................2 A1
Kings Hall Leisure Centre
CLPT E5................74 E4
Kings Head Theatre
IS N1................6 C3
Kings House School
RCHPK/HAM TW10................125 G4
Kingsland College of
Business Studies
SRTFD E15................94 B1
Kingsland Health Centre
IS N1................7 K1
Kingsland Shopping Centre
HACK E8................74 B5
Kings Langley College
of Management
NWCR SE14................112 B6
The Kingsley Hotel
NOXST/BSQ WC1A................11 J3
Kingsley Primary School
CROY/NA CR0................164 A7
Kings Mall Shopping Centre
HMSMTH W6................107 F3
Kingsmeadow
Athletics Centre
KUT/HW KT1................159 H2
Kingsmead Primary School
CLPT E5................75 G3
Kingsmead School
EN EN1................30 C2
Kings Oak Primary School
NWMAL KT3................159 J2
King Solomon Academy
CAMTN NW1................9 J2
King Solomon High School
BARK/HLT IG6................60 D1
Kings Place
IS N1................5 K5
Kings Private Clinic
GDMY/SEVK IG3................61 F1
MHST W1U................10 A1
Kings School of English
BECK BR3................166 C1
Kings Stairs
BERM/RHTH SE16................111 J1
Kingston ⇌
KUTN/CMB KT2................144 A7
Kingston Business Centre
CHSGTN KT9................172 A2
Kingston Cemetery
KUT/HW KT1................159 G2
Kingston College
KUT/HW KT1................159 F2
Kingston College Theatre
KUT/HW KT1................158 E2
Kingston Crematorium
KUT/HW KT1................159 H2
Kingston Crown Court
KUT/HW KT1................158 E2
Kingston Grammar School
KUT/HW KT1................159 G1

Kingston Hospital
KUTN/CMB KT2................144 C7
Kingstonian FC
NWMAL KT3................159 J2
Kingston University
KUT/HW KT1................159 F2
KUT/HW KT1................159 F9
KUTN/CMB KT2................145 H4
KUTN/CMB KT2................145 H4
PUT/ROE SW15................145 H1
King Street College
HMSMTH W6................107 F3
Kingsway Business Park
HPTN TW12................141 K7
Kingsway College
CAMTN NW1................4 E9
KTTN NW5................72 B5
STPAN WC1H................5 L8
Kingswood Primary School
WNWD SE27................149 K3
Kisharon School
GLDGN NW11................52 D5
Kisimul School
SURB KT6................171 J1
K+K Hotel George
ECT SW5................14 B1
KLC School of Design
WBPTN SW10................108 B7
Knightsbridge ⊖
CHEL SW3................15 K3
Knightsbridge Barracks
SKENS SW7................15 K2
Knightsbridge Medical Centre
KTBR SW1X................15 M3
Knightsbridge School
KTBR SW1X................15 L4
Knollmead Primary School
BRYLDS KT5................172 E1
Knowledge Point School
HOLWY N7................73 F5
KP Estate
RAIN RM13................99 G6
Krishna-Avanti
Primary School
EDGW HA8................36 C3
Kubrick Business Estate
FSTGT E7................77 F3
K West Hotel
SHB W12................107 G1
Laban Centre for
Movement & Dance
DEPT SE8................112 C6
Laburnum Health Centre
DAGE RM10................80 C1
Ladbroke Grove ⊖
NKENS W10................88 C5
Lady Bankes Junior School
RSLP HA4................64 E1
The Lady Eleanor Holles School
HPTN TW12................142 B8
Lady Margaret
Primary School
STHL UB1................83 K4
Lady Margaret School
FUL/PGN SW6................107 K7
Ladywell ⇌
LEW SE13................132 E4
Ladywell Arena
BROCKY SE4................132 E5
Ladywell Cemetery
BROCKY SE4................132 C4
Ladywell Leisure Centre
LEW SE13................133 F4
Laings Sports Ground
BAR EN5................25 G3
Lake Business Centre
TOTM N17................42 C5
Laker Industrial Estate
BECK BR3................151 H4
Lambeth Academy
CLAP SW4................129 H4
Lambeth Cemetery
TOOT SW17................147 G5
Lambeth College
CLAP SW4................129 H4
STHWK SE1................13 K6
STRHM/NOR SW16................148 E1
VX/NE SW8................109 J7
Lambeth County Court
LBTH SE11................18 B7
Lambeth Crematorium
TOOT SW17................147 G3
Lambeth Hospital
BRXN/ST SW9................129 K2
Lambeth North ⊖
STHWK SE1................18 A3
Lambeth Palace
STHWK SE1................17 L4
Lambs Court
POP/IOD E14................93 G6
Lammas School
LEY E10................57 H7
Lamont Business Centre
CROY/NA CR0................163 K6
Lamorbey Swimming Centre
BFN/LL DA15................155 G1
Lampton School
HSLW TW3................103 F7
The Lanark Medical Centre
MV/WKIL W9................2 D7
Lancaster Gate ⊖
BAY/PAD W2................9 G6
Lancaster Hotel
BAY/PAD W2................9 G6
Lancaster House
WHALL SW1A................16 E1
Lancasterian Primary School
TOTM N17................42 A7
Lancaster Road
Industrial Estate
EBAR EN4................27 H4
Lancelot Medical Centre
ALP/SUD HA0................67 K4
The Landmark Hotel
CAMTN NW1................9 L2
The Lanesborough Hotel
KTBR SW1X................16 A1
Lanford Obesity Clinic
ED N9................30 D6
Langbourne Primary School
DUL SE21................150 A2
Langdon Down Centre
TEDD TW11................143 J4
Langdon Park ⊖
POP/IOD E14................93 K4
Langdon Park School
POP/IOD E14................93 K5
Langdon School
EHAM E6................96 B1
Langford Primary School
FUL/PGN SW6................128 A1
The Langham Hotel
REGST W1B................10 D3

Langhedge Lane
Industrial Estate
UED N18................42 B5
Langley Park Girls School &
Sports Centre
BECK BR3................166 E4
Langley Park Golf Club
BECK BR3................167 G5
Langley Park School for Boys
BECK BR3................166 E5
Langthorne Health Centre
WAN E11................76 B2
Langthorne Hospital
WAN E11................76 B3
Lansbury Lawrence
Primary School
POP/IOD E14................93 K5
Lansdowne College
BAY/PAD W2................8 C7
Lansdowne School
BRXN/ST SW9................130 A2
Lantern of Knowledge Boys
LEY E10................76 A1
La Retraite RC Girls School
BAL SW12................129 H6
Lark Hall Primary School
CLAP SW4................129 J1
Larkshall Business Centre
CHING E4................44 B1
Larkswood Primary School
CHING E4................43 K3
Larmenier & Sacred Catholic
Primary School
HMSMTH W6................107 G3
La Sainte Union Catholic
Secondary School
HGT N6................72 A2
La Sainte Union Convent School
KTTN NW5................72 B2
La Salette RC Primary School
RAIN RM13................99 J2
Latchmere Leisure Centre
BTSEA SW11................128 E1
Latchmere Primary School
KUTN/CMB KT2................144 B5
Lathom Junior School
EHAM E6................77 J6
Latimer Road ⊖
NTGHL W11................88 B6
Latymer All Saints CE
Primary School
ED N9................42 B1
The Latymer
Preparatory School
HMSMTH W6................106 D4
The Latymer School
ED N9................42 A1
Latymer Upper School
HMSMTH W6................106 D3
Launcelot Primary School
BMLY BR1................152 E3
Laurance Haines
Primary School
WATW WD18................20 E5
Laurel Clinic
EA W5................104 D3
Laurel Lane Primary
WDR/YW UB7................100 A3
Lauriston Primary School
HOM E9................75 F7
Lawdale Junior School
BETH E2................92 C2
Lawrence Trading Estate
GNWCH SE10................113 H3
Lawrence Wharf
SKENS SW7................14 F6
Lawrence Wharf
BERM/RHTH SE16................93 H7
Laycock Primary School
IS N1................73 G5
Lazards Sports Club
SUN TW16................141 F7
Leadenhall Market
BANK EC3V................13 J5
Lea Park Trading Estate
LEY E10................57 H6
Leaside Business Centre
PEND EN3................31 H1
Leathermarket Gardens
STHWK SE1................19 J2
Leathersellers Sports Ground
LEE/GVPK SE12................134 B6
Leathers Hall
HDTCH EC3A................13 J4
Lea Valley Primary School
TOTM N17................42 C6
Lea Valley Trading Estate
UED N18................42 E3
UED N18................43 F5
Lebanon Road ⊖
CROY/NA CR0................178 A1
L'Ecole de Battersea
BTSEA SW11................108 C7
L'Ecole des Petits
FUL/PGN SW6................108 A7
Lee ⇌
LEE/GVPK SE12................133 K5
Lee Manor Primary School
LEW SE13................133 H5
Leeside Court
BERM/RHTH SE16................93 F7
Leeside Trading Estate
TOTM N17................42 E6
Lee Valley Camping &
Caravan Park
ED N9................31 G7
Lee Valley Campsite
CHING E4................31 K1
Lee Valley Ice Centre
LEY E10................75 F1
Lee Valley Leisure Complex,
Athletics Centre & Golf Club
ED N9................31 G6
Lee Valley Watersports Centre
CHING E4................43 G5
Leicester Square ⊖
LSO/SEVD WC2H................11 H6
Leigh Close Industrial Estate
NWMAL KT3................160 A3
Leigh Technology Academy
DART DA1................139 K4
Leighton House Museum
WKENS W14................107 J2
Le Meridien Hotel
REGST W1B................10 F7
Lena Gardens Primary School
HMSMTH W6................107 F2
Leopold Primary School
WLSDN NW10................69 H6
Leopold Street Clinic
BOW E3................93 H4
Lesnes Abbey
BELV DA17................116 E3

Lessness Heath Primary School
BELV DA17................117 H4
The Levin Hotel
KTBR SW1X................15 L3
Lewin Mead Community
Mental Health Centre
STRHM/NOR SW16................148 D5
Lewis Clinic
CAR SM5................176 A3
Lewisham ⇌ ⊖
DEPT SE8................132 E1
Lewisham Bridge
Primary School
LEW SE13................132 E2
Lewisham Business Centre
NWCR SE14................112 A5
Lewisham Centre
LEW SE13................133 F3
Lewisham College
BROCKY SE4................132 D1
Lewisham Crematorium
CAT SE6................152 D1
Lewisham Lions Centre
BERM/RHTH SE16................111 K4
Lexi Cinema
WLSDN NW10................70 A7
The Leys Primary School
DAGE RM10................80 E6
Leyton ⊖
LEY E10................76 A2
Leyton Business Centre
LEY E10................75 H1
Leyton FC
LEY E10................57 H7
Leyton Industrial Village
LEY E10................57 F6
Leyton Leisure Centre
LEY E10................57 K6
Leyton Midland Road ⊖
LEY E10................58 A7
Leyton Mills Retail Park
LEY E10................76 A2
Leyton Orient FC
(Matchroom Stadium)
LEY E10................75 K2
Leyton Sixth Form College
LEY E10................58 B5
Leytonstone ⊖
WAN E11................58 C7
Leytonstone Business &
Enterprise Specialist School
WAN E11................58 C5
Leytonstone High Road ⊖ ⊖
WAN E11................76 C1
Leyton Youth Sports Ground
LEY E10................57 K7
The Liberty City Clinic
SDTCH EC2A................7 J9
Liberty II Centre
ROM RM1................63 G3
Liberty Middle School
MTCM CR4................162 D1
The Liberty
ROM RM1................63 G4
Library & Community Centre
BTSEA SW11................128 C2
The Lighthouse Group
(TLG) Centre
LBTH SE11................110 B5
L'Ile Aux Enfants
KTTN NW5................72 A4
Lilian Baylis School
VX/NE SW8................17 L9
Lilian Baylis
Technology School
VX/NE SW8................17 L9
Lillian Baylis School
LBTH SE11................17 M6
Lillian Baylis Theatre
CLKNW EC1R................6 C7
Lillian Bishop School of English
SKENS SW7................15 G5
Limehouse ⇌ ⊖
WCHPL E1................93 G5
Limehouse Hole Stairs
BERM/RHTH SE16................93 H7
Lime Trees Park Golf Club
NTHLT UB5................65 G7
Lincoln Road Clinic
EN EN1................30 C1
Lincoln's Inn
LINN WC2A................11 M4
Linden Bridge School
WPK KT4................173 G2
Linden Lodge School
WIM/MER SW19................127 H7
Linden Bennett School
FELT TW13................141 H4
Linford Christie Stadium
SHB W12................87 H4
The Link Day Primary School
CROY/NA CR0................176 E3
The Link Secondary School
CROY/NA CR0................177 F3
Links Primary School
TOOT SW17................148 A5
Linley House School
BRYLDS KT5................159 G5
Linley Sambourne House
KENS W8................14 A2
WKENS W14................107 J1
Linnet House Clinic
STJWD NW8................3 J6
Linton Mead Primary School
THMD SE28................97 H6
Lionel Road Primary School
BTFD TW8................105 F3
Lion House School
PUT/ROE SW15................127 G4
Lismarrine Industrial Park
BORE WD6................23 H5
Lisson Grove Health Centre
STJWD NW8................3 J7
Lister Community School
PLSTW E13................95 F1
The Lister Hospital
BGVA SW1W................16 C8
Lister House Clinic
CAVSO/HST W1G................10 C4
Little Danson Welfare Clinic
WELL DA16................136 B3
Little Davids School
CROY/NA CR0................179 K5
Little Hands Theatre
HDN NW4................52 A3
Little Heath School
CHDH RM6................61 H3
Little Ilford School
MNPK E12................77 K4
Little Reddings Primary School
BUSH WD23................22 B4
Little St Helens School
NTHWD HA6................32 C5

Little Venice Medical Centre
MV/WKIL W9................8 F1
Little Wandsworth School
TOOT SW17................148 A1
Liverpool Street ⇌ ⊖
LVPST EC2M................13 J2
Livesey Museum for Children
PECK SE15................111 J5
Livingstone Hospital
DART DA1................139 J6
Livingstone Primary School
EBAR EN4................27 H2
The Livity School
BRXS/STRHM SW2................129 K4
Lloyd Park ⊖
CROY/NA CR0................178 B3
Lloyd Park Centre
WALTH E17................57 J1
Lloyd's of London
HDTCH EC3A................13 J5
Lloyds Register CC
DUL SE21................130 E7
Lloyd Williamson School
NKENS W10................88 C4
Locks View Court
POP/IOD E14................93 G6
Lockwood Industrial Park
TOTM N17................56 D2
Lombard Business Centre
BTSEA SW11................128 C1
Lombard Business Park
CROY/NA CR0................164 A6
WAND/EARL SW18................128 C5
WIM/MER SW19................162 B1
Lombard Trading Estate
CHARL SE7................114 A2
Lombardy Retail Park
HYS/HAR UB3................83 F7
London 2012 Games Venues:
Aquatics Centre
OLYMPICPK E20................76 A6
Basketball Arena
OLYMPICPK E20................75 K4
BMX Track
OLYMPICPK E20................75 K4
Earl's Court
ECT SW5................14 A8
Eton Manor
OLYMPICPK E20................75 K3
ExCeL
CAN/RD E16................95 F6
Greenwich Park
GNWCH SE10................113 G5
Hampton Court Palace
E/WMO/HCT KT8................158 A2
Handball Arena
OLYMPICPK E20................75 J5
Hockey Centre
OLYMPICPK E20................75 J4
Horse Guards Parade
WHALL SW1A................11 H9
Hyde Park
BAY/PAD W2................9 J4
Lord's Cricket Ground
STJWD NW8................3 H7
The Mall
WHALL SW1A................16 F1
North Greenwich Arena
POP/IOD E14................94 C7
Olympic Stadium
OLYMPICPK E20................75 K6
Royal Artillery Barracks
WOOL/PLUM SE18................114 E5
Velodrome
OLYMPICPK E20................75 K4
Water Polo Arena
OLYMPICPK E20................75 K6
Wembley Arena
WBLY HA9................68 C3
Wembley Stadium
WBLY HA9................68 C3
Wimbledon
WIM/MER SW19................146 C2
London Academy
EDGW HA8................36 B3
London Academy of
Music & Dramatic Art
KENS W8................14 A5
London Allergy Clinic
CAVSO/HST W1G................10 C3
London Ambassador Clinic
WCHPL E1................92 C4
London Bridge ⇌ ⊖
STHWK SE1................13 H9
London Bridge City Pier
STHWK SE1................13 J8
London Bridge Hospital
STHWK SE1................13 H8
London Bridge Hotel
STHWK SE1................13 G9
London Bridge Sports Centre
CANST EC4R................13 G7
London Brookes College
HDN NW4................51 K3
London Business School
CAMTN NW1................3 L9
London Butterfly House
BTFD TW8................104 D7
The London Canal Museum
IS N1................5 K5
London Capital College
CAMTN NW1................4 D3
The London Centre for
Children with Cerebral Palsy
MUSWH N10................54 B2
London Centre of
Contemporary Music
STHWK SE1................12 F9
London Chest Hospital
BETH E2................92 C1
London Chinese Dance School
CAN/RD E16................94 A4
REGST W1B................10 D2
London Christian
Learning Centre
MNPK E12................77 H3
London Christian School
STHWK SE1................19 G2
London City Airport
CAN/RD E16................95 J7
London City Airport ⊖
CAN/RD E16................95 J7
London City College (English
Language Institute) & Schiller
International University
STHWK SE1................11 M9
London City Mission
STHWK SE1................19 K1
The London Clinic
CAVSO/HST W1G................10 B1
London College of Business &
Computer Studies
CLAP SW4................129 J3

London College of Business & Computing
BETH E2 92 D1
London College of Communication
LBTH SE11 18 D4
London College of Fashion
CAVSQ/HST W1G 10 D4
MHST W1U 10 B4
SDTCH EC2A 7 K9
London College of Further Education
LBTH SE11 18 C6
London College of Higher Education
CLAP SW4 129 G2
London College of International Business Studies
HHOL WC1V 11 K3
London Commodity Exchange
WAP E1W 13 M7
London Contemporary Dance School
PLSTW E13 94 D2
London Contemporary Dance School at The Place
STPAN WC1H 5 H8
London Cornish RFC
PUT/ROE SW15 145 H2
The London Dungeon
STHWK SE1 13 H9
London Electronics College
ECT SW5 14 C7
London Esthetique
POP/IOD E14 94 C5
London Eye
STHWK SE1 17 L1
London Eye Clinic
CAVSQ/HST W1G 10 C3
London Eye Millennium Pier
STHWK SE1 17 L1
London Fields ⇌
HACK E8 74 D6
London Fields Lido
HACK E8 74 D6
London Fields Primary School
HACK E8 74 D7
London Film Academy
FUL/PGN SW6 107 K6
London Film School
LSQ/SEVD WC2H 11 J5
London Financial Training College
FSBYPK N4 55 H4
London Foot Hospital
FITZ W1T 10 E1
London Gender Clinic
HDN NW4 51 K5
London Group Business Park
CRICK NW2 51 H7
London Heart Clinic
CAVSQ/HST W1G 10 C3
The London Industrial Estate
EHAM E6 96 A4
London Industrial Park
EHAM E6 96 B4
London International College
POP/IOD E14 94 C5
SOHO/SHAV W1D 10 F4
London Irish RFC
SUN TW16 140 E7
The London Irish Youth Theatre
HGT N6 54 B7
London Islamic School
WCHPL E1 92 D5
London Jewish Girls High School
HDN NW4 52 A4
London Ladies & Girls FC
CAT SE6 151 K4
London Lane Clinic
BMLY BR1 152 D6
London Lighthouse
NTGHL W11 88 C5
London Living Theatre
SYD SE26 151 F3
The London Make-Up Academy
UED N18 42 D4
London Marriott Hotel
HAMP NW3 3 H2
MYFR/PKLN W1K 10 B6
OXSTW W1C 9 M6
STHWK SE1 17 L1
WHTN TW2 123 K5
London Marriott West India Quay Hotel
POP/IOD E14 93 J6
London Metrocity College
BOW E3 93 J2
London Metropolitan University
HBRY N5 73 J4
HOLWY N7 73 F3
LVPST EC2M 13 H3
WCHPL E1 13 L4
WCHPL E1 92 C5
London Natural Therapy School
POP/IOD E14 94 C6
SOHO/SHAV W1F 10 F6
London Nautical School
STHWK SE1 12 B8
London Open College
FSBYE EC1V 6 D7
London Oratory School
FUL/PGN SW6 107 K6
London Road Medical Centre
CROY/NA CR0 164 B5
London School of Business & Finance
HCIRC EC1N 12 A3
London School of Economics
CLKNW EC1R 6 B8
HHOL WC1V 11 J4
STHWK SE1 12 E8
London School of Economics & Political Science
HOL/ALD WC2B 11 L5
London School of Hygiene & Tropical Medicine
GWRST WC1E 11 H2
London School of Jewish Studies
HDN NW4 52 B3
London School of Theology
NTHWD HA6 32 B5
London Scottish Golf Club
WIM/MER SW19 145 K2
London Silver Vaults
LINN WC2A 12 A3
London Soccerdome
GNWCH SE10 113 J1
London South Bank University
STHWK SE1 18 D3
London Stock Exchange
STBT EC1A 12 D4
The London Television Centre
STHWK SE1 12 A8
London Tourist Board & Convention Centre
BGVA SW1W 16 C3
London Toy & Model Museum
BAY/PAD W2 8 F6
London Transport Bus Depot
BXLYHN DA7 137 J2
London Transport Museum
HOL/ALD WC2B 11 K6
London Underwriting Centre
MON EC3R 13 J6
London Wall
BARB EC2Y 12 E3
London Weather Centre
HCIRC EC1N 12 A2
The London Welbeck Hospital
CAVSQ/HST W1G 10 B3
London Welsh FC
RCH/KEW TW9 125 F2
London West Crematorium
WLSDN NW10 87 K3
Lonesome Primary School
MTCM CR4 163 G1
Long Ditton Cemetery
SURB KT6 171 J1
Long Ditton County Infant School
SURB KT6 158 D7
Long Ditton St Marys CE Junior School
THDIT KT7 158 C7
Longfield J & I School
RYLN/HDSTN HA2 48 A5
Longford Community School
EBED/NFELT TW14 121 J6
Longford Industrial Estate
HPTN TW12 142 B5
Longlands Primary School
BFN/LL DA15 154 E2
Long Lane AFC
BKHTH/KID SE3 134 B1
Longshaw Primary School
CHING E4 44 B2
Longwood School
BUSH WD23 21 J3
Lord Chancellors Department
WEST SW1P 17 H4
Lord Lister Health Centre
FSTGT E7 76 E3
Lord's Cricket Ground
STJWD NW8 3 H7
Lordship Lane Clinic
TOTM N17 56 A1
Lordship Lane Primary School
WDGN N22 41 J7
Lord's Tour & MCC Museum
STJWD NW8 3 G8
Lorimar Business Centre
RAIN RM13 99 G5
Loughborough Junction ⇌
CMBW SE5 130 C1
Loughborough Primary School
CMBW SE5 130 C1
Lovelace Primary School
CHSGTN KT9 171 J4
Lovell's Wharf
GNWCH SE10 113 G4
Lower Clapton Health Centre
CLPT E5 74 E4
Lower Place Business Centre
WLSDN NW10 86 E1
Lower Sydenham ⇌
SYD SE26 151 H4
Lower Sydenham Industrial Estate
SYD SE26 151 H4
Lowfield Medical Centre
DART DA1 139 H6
Low Hall Sports Ground
LEY E10 57 F5
Lowther Primary School
BARN SW13 106 D5
Loxford School of Science & Technology
IL IG1 78 D4
LSE Sports Club
NWMAL KT3 160 A5
Lubavitch Boys Primary School
CLPT E5 56 B6
Lubavitch House School (Senior Girls)
STNW/STAM N16 56 A6
Lucas Vale Primary School
DEPT SE8 112 D7
Lutomer House Business Centre
POP/IOD E14 93 K7
Lux Cinema
IS N1 7 J8
Lycee Francais
SKENS SW7 15 G5
Lycee Francais Charles de Gaulle
BTSEA SW11 129 G3
Lyceum Independent School
SDTCH EC2A 13 J1
The Lyceum Theatre
COVGDN WC2E 11 L6
Lyndean Industrial Estate
ABYW SE2 116 D2
Lyndhurst House Preparatory School
HAMP NW3 71 H4
Lyndhurst Primary School
CMBW SE5 130 E1
Lyon Business Park
BARK IG11 96 E1
Lyon Park Infant School
ALP/SUD HA0 68 B6
Lyonsdown School
BAR EN5 27 G4
Lyric Theatre
SOHO/SHAV W1D 11 G6
Lyric Theatre Hammersmith
HMSMTH W6 107 F3
Mabwin Supplementary School
ED N9 42 D1
Macaulay CE Primary School
CLAP SW4 129 G2
Madame Tussauds
CAMTN NW1 10 A1
Madeira Grove Clinic
WFD IG8 45 F4
Madison Bowl
NTHWD HA6 32 C6
Madni Girls School
WCHPL E1 92 D5
Madrasah-E-Darue Qirat Majidiah School
WCHPL E1 92 D6
Mahatma Gandhi Industrial Estate
BRXN/ST SW9 130 C2
Maida Vale ⊖
MV/WKIL W9 2 D8
Maida Vale Medical Centre
MV/WKIL W9 2 C8
Malcolm Primary School
PGE/AN SE20 150 E6
The Malden Centre
NWMAL KT3 160 C3
Malden Golf Club
NWMAL KT3 160 B1
Malden Manor ⇌
NWMAL KT3 160 B6
Malden Manor Primary School
NWMAL KT3 160 B6
Malden Parochial Primary School
WPK KT4 160 B7
Malden Road Baths
CHEAM SM3 174 B3
Malham Road Industrial Estate
FSTH SE23 132 A7
The Mall Bexleyheath
BXLYHS DA6 137 H3
Mall Galleries
STJS SW1Y 11 H8
The Mall School
WHTN TW2 142 D2
The Mall
WHALL SW1A 16 F1
Malmaison Charterhouse Square Hotel
FARR EC1M 12 D2
Malmesbury Primary School
BOW E3 93 H2
MRDN SM4 162 B6
Malorees Junior School
KIL/WHAMP NW6 70 B6
Malvern Way Infant School
RKW/CH/CXG WD3 20 A4
Mandarin Oriental Hotel
KTBR SW1X 15 M1
The Mandeville Hotel
MHST W1U 10 B4
Mandeville Primary School
CLPT E5 75 G2
Mandeville Special School
NTHLT UB5 65 K5
Manford Industrial Estate
ERITH DA8 118 E5
Manor Brook Medical Centre
BKHTH/KID SE3 134 A1
Manor Drive Health Centre
WPK KT4 160 C7
Manorfield Primary School
POP/IOD E14 93 K4
Manor House ⊖
FSBYPK N4 55 J7
Manor Infant School
BARK IG11 79 F5
Manor Park ⇌
MNPK E12 77 H3
Manor Park Cemetery
FSTGT E7 77 H3
Manor Park Crematorium
FSTGT E7 77 G3
Manor Park Methodist School
MNPK E12 77 J3
Manor Park Primary School
SUT SM1 175 G4
Manor Place Industrial Estate
BORE WD6 24 E2
Manor Primary School
SRTFD E15 94 C1
Manorside Primary School
FNCH N3 39 F7
Manor Special School
WLSDN NW10 88 B1
Manor Way Business Centre
RAIN RM13 99 F4
Mansfield Infant College
IL IG1 78 A1
Mansion House ⊖
STP EC4M 12 F5
Mapledown School
CRICK NW2 52 B6
Maple Grove Business Centre
HSLWW TW4 122 B3
Maple House Independant Montessori School
THHTH CR7 164 D2
Maple Industrial Estate
FELT TW13 140 E1
Maples Business Centre
IS N1 6 B3
Maple Walk School
WLSDN NW10 69 H7
Marble Arch
MBLAR W1H 9 M6
Marble Arch ⊖
OXSTW W1C 9 M5
Marble Hill House
TWK TW1 124 D6
Maria Fidelis Convent School
CAMTN NW1 4 F8
Maria Montessori Childrens House
HAMP NW3 71 H4
Mariner Business Centre
CROY/NA CR0 177 F4
Marion Richardson Primary School
WCHPL E1 93 F5
Marion Vian Primary School
BECK BR3 166 A4
Maritime Greenwich College
DEPT SE8 112 D6
Maritime Industrial Estate
CHARL SE7 114 A3
Maritime Museum
GNWCH SE10 113 H3
Marjorie McClure School
CHST BR7 154 C7
The Marjory Kinnon School
EBED/NFELT TW14 121 H4
Market Trading Estate
NWDGN UB2 102 A3
Marks Gate Clinic
CHDH RM6 62 A2
Marks Gate Junior School
CHDH RM6 62 A2
Marlborough College of Business & Technology
FSTGT E7 76 E4
Marlborough CC
DUL SE21 131 H7
Marlborough Day Hospital
STJWD NW8 2 E5
Marlborough House
STJS SW1Y 10 F9
Marlborough Primary School
CHEL SW3 15 K6
HRW HA1 48 E3
ISLW TW7 104 B7
Marlborough School
BFN/LL DA15 136 B7
Marlborough Trading Estate
RCH/KEW TW9 105 J7
Marlowe Business Centre
NWCR SE14 112 B6
Marner Primary School
BOW E3 93 K3
Marriott Hotel
ECT SW5 14 C5
HYS/HAR UB3 101 G6
KIL/WHAMP NW6 2 C5
MBLAR W1H 9 K4
Marshalls Park School
ROM RM1 63 G1
Marsh Gate Business Centre
SRTFD E15 94 A1
Marshgate Primary School
RCHPK/HAM TW10 125 G4
Marsh Green School
DAGW RM9 98 C1
Martan College
HOL/ALD WC2B 11 K4
Martinbridge Industrial Estate
EN EN1 30 C4
Martindale Industrial Estate
EN EN1 30 A4
Martin Primary School
EFNCH N2 53 J3
Marvels Lane Primary School
LEE/GVPK SE12 153 G3
Maryland ⇌
SRTFD E15 76 C4
Maryland Industrial Estate
SRTFD E15 76 C4
Maryland Primary School
SRTFD E15 76 C4
Marylebone ⇌ ⊖
CAMTN NW1 9 K1
Marylebone Health Centre
CAMTN NW1 10 B1
Marylebone Magistrates Court
CAMTN NW1 9 K2
Marymount International School
KUTN/CMB KT2 144 E6
Mary Wallace Theatre
TWK TW1 124 B7
Maswell Park Health Centre
HSLW TW3 123 H4
Mathilda Marks Kennedy Primary School
MLHL NW7 37 F4
Matrix Business Centre
DART DA1 139 H4
Maudlin's Green
WAP E1W 13 M8
The Maudsley Hospital
CMBW SE5 130 E1
Maughan Library (Kings College)
LINN WC2A 12 A4
Mawbrey Brough Health Centre
VX/NE SW8 109 K6
The Mawney School
ROMW/RG RM7 63 F4
Mayday University Hospital
THHTH CR7 164 C5
Mayesbrook Park Arena
BARK IG11 79 G4
Mayespark Primary School
GDMY/SEVK IG3 79 G2
Mayfield Primary School
HNWL W7 84 D5
Mayfield School
BCTR RM8 61 J7
PIN HA5 47 J2
Mayflower Primary School
POP/IOD E14 93 J5
Mayplace Primary School
BXLYHN DA7 138 A3
Maytime School
IL IG1 78 A2
Mayville Junior & Primary School
WAN E11 76 C2
Maze Hill ⇌
GNWCH SE10 113 H5
McKay Trading Estate
NKENS W10 88 C3
McMillan Clinic
HYS/HAR UB3 82 A6
MDQ Majidiah School
WCHPL E1 92 D6
The Mead Infant School
WPK KT4 173 H2
Meadlands Primary School
RCHPK/HAM TW10 143 J3
Meadowgate School
BROCKY SE4 132 A2
Meadowside Leisure Centre
BKHTH/KID SE3 134 B3
The Meadow Special School
STMC/STPC BR5 155 G6
Meadow Wood School
BUSH WD23 22 C4
Mead Road Infant School
CHST BR7 154 C5
Medical Centres
CROY/NA CR0 179 G1
The Medical Centre
WAND/EARL SW18 128 A5
WAT WD17 21 F1
Medical Express Clinic
CAVSQ/HST W1G 10 C2
Mednurs Clinic
STNW/STAM N16 55 K6
Megabowl
KUTN/CMB KT2 159 F1
Melcombe Primary School
HMSMTH W6 107 G5
Melia White House Hotel
CAMTN NW1 4 D9
Mellish Industrial Estate
WOOL/PLUM SE18 114 C2
Mellow Lane School
HGDN/ICK UB10 82 A3
Melrose Special School
MTCM CR4 162 D2
Memorial Hospital
WOOL/PLUM SE18 135 F1
Menorah Grammar School
EDGW HA8 36 E6
GLDGN NW11 52 C6
Menorah High School for Girls
CRICK NW2 69 H2
Menorah Primary School
GLDGN NW11 52 C6
MERC Education
WOOL/PLUM SE18 115 G2
Mercers' Hall
LOTH EC2R 13 G5
The Merchant Taylors Hall
BANK EC3V 13 H5
Merchant Taylors School
NTHWD HA6 20 C7
Mercure London City Bankside Hotel
STHWK SE1 12 E9
Meridian Clinic
BRXN/ST SW9 130 A2
Meridian Locality Mental Health Centre
CHARL SE7 114 B5
Meridian Primary School
GNWCH SE10 113 G4
Meridian Sports Club
CHARL SE7 114 D6
Meridian Trading Estate
CHARL SE7 114 A3
Merlin Primary School
BMLY BR1 152 E2
Merlin School
PUT/ROE SW15 127 G4
Mermaid Theatre
BLKFR EC4V 12 D6
Merrielands Retail Park
DAGW RM9 80 B7
Merry Hill Infant School
BUSH WD23 22 B6
Merryhills Clinic
ENC/FH EN2 29 F2
Merryhills Primary School
ENC/FH EN2 29 F3
Merton Abbey Primary School
WIM/MER SW19 147 F7
Merton Adult College
RYNPK SW20 161 H2
Merton College
MRDN SM4 161 J5
Merton Court Preparatory School
SCUP DA14 155 J3
Merton Industrial Park
WIM/MER SW19 147 G7
Merton Park ⊖
WIM/MER SW19 146 E7
Merton Park Primary School
WIM/MER SW19 161 J1
Merton Road Industrial Estate
WAND/EARL SW18 127 K6
The Method Studio
FSBYW WC1X 11 L2
Metro Business Centre
SYD SE26 151 H5
The Metro Golf Centre
HDN NW4 38 A7
Metro Industrial Centre
ISLW TW7 123 K1
Metropolis Centre
BORE WD6 24 C2
Metropolitan Business Centre
HACK E8 7 K2
Metropolitan Hospital
STHWK SE1 18 B3
Metropolitan London Hotel
MYFR/PKLN W1K 10 C9
Metropolitan Police Bushey Sports Ground
BUSH WD23 22 A2
Metropolitan Police FC
E/WMO/HCT KT8 157 J5
Metropolitan Police Hayes Sports Club
HAYES BR2 180 D1
Metropolitan Police (Hendon) Track
CDALE/KGS NW9 51 H2
Metropolitan Police Training School, Hendon
CDALE/KGS NW9 51 H2
Metropolitan Tabernacle
STHWK SE1 18 D5
Metro Trading Centre
WBLY HA9 68 D3
Michael Faraday Primary School
WALW SE17 19 H8
Michael Manley Industrial Estate
VX/NE SW8 109 H7
Michael Sobell Sinai School
KTN/HRWW/WS HA3 50 C5
The Michael Tippett School
LBTH SE11 18 B6
Midas Business Centre
DAGE RM10 80 C3
Midas Industrial Estate
DAGE RM10 80 C3
Middle Park Primary School
ELTH/MOT SE9 134 C6
Middle Row Primary School
NKENS W10 88 C3
Middlesex Business Centre
NWDGN UB2 103 F1
Middlesex CCC (Lord's Cricket Ground)
STJWD NW8 3 H7
Middlesex Hospital Medical School
FITZ W1T 10 F2
Middlesex Hospital Nurses Home
GTPST W1W 10 E2
Middlesex Hospital School of Physiotherapy
FITZ W1T 10 F2
Middlesex Hospital Sports Ground
CHST BR7 155 F4
Middlesex School of Complementary Medicine
STAN HA7 36 A7
Middlesex University
ARCH N19 54 C7
GLDGN NW11 53 F7
PEND EN3 31 F4
WDGN N22 54 E1
Middlesex University (Cat Hill Campus)
EBAR EN4 28 A5
Middlesex University (Enfield Campus)
PEND EN3 30 D4
Middlesex University (Hendon Campus)
HDN NW4 51 K3
Middlesex University (Trent Park Campus)
EBAR EN4 28 C1
Midfield Primary School
STMC/STPC BR5 155 G6
Midway Mission Hospital
BETH E2 7 L8

Milbourne Lodge School *ESH/CLAY* KT10 170 D5
Mile End ⊖ *BOW* E3 93 H3
Mile End & Bow Business Centre *WCHPL* E1 92 D4
Mile End Hospital *WCHPL* E1 93 F2
Mile End Stadium *POP/IOD* E14 93 H4
Milehams Industrial Estate *PUR* RM19 119 K2
Miles Coverdale Primary School *SHB* W12 107 F1
Milestone Hotel *KENS* W8 14 D2
Military Barracks *WOOL/PLUM* SE18 115 F4
Millbank Millennium Pier *WEST* SW1P 17 J6
Millbank Primary School *WEST* SW1P 17 H6
Millbank Tower *WEST* SW1P 17 J6
Millennium Arena *BTSEA* SW11 109 F6
Millennium Bailey's Hotel *SKENS* SW7 14 E5
Millennium Balloon *STHWK* SE1 13 K9
Millennium & Copthorne Hotels at Chelsea FC *FUL/PGN* SW6 108 A6
Millennium Dance 2000 Theatre School *HAMP* NW3 71 J4
Millennium Gloucester Hotel *ECT* SW5 14 D6
Millennium Harbour *POP/IOD* E14 112 C1
Millennium Hotel *KTBR* SW1X 15 M2
Millennium Hotel London Mayfair *MYFR/PKLN* W1K 10 B7
Millennium Primary School *GNWCH* SE10 113 J2
Millennium Quay *DEPT* SE8 112 E5
Millennium Wharf *POP/IOD* E14 113 G2
Mill Farm Business Park *HSLWW* TW4 122 D6
Millfields Primary School *CLPT* E5 74 E3
Millfield Theatre *UED* N18 41 K3
Mill Green Business Park *MTCM* CR4 162 E6
Mill Hill Broadway ⇌ *MLHL* NW7 37 G5
Mill Hill Cemetery *MLHL* NW7 38 A5
Mill Hill County High School *EBAR* EN4 27 K6
MLHL NW7 37 G1
The Mill Hill CC *MLHL* NW7 38 A2
Mill Hill East ⊖ *MLHL* NW7 38 B6
Mill Hill Golf Club *MLHL* NW7 37 G1
Mill Hill Industrial Estate *MLHL* NW7 37 H5
Mill Hill School *MLHL* NW7 37 K3
Mill Lane Medical Centre *KIL/WHAMP* NW6 70 E4
Mill Lane Trading Estate *CROY/NA* CR0 177 F2
Mill River Trading Estate *PEND* EN3 31 G3
Millside Industrial Estate *DART* DA1 139 G3
Mill Street Clinic *STHWK* SE1 19 M1
Mill Trading Estate *WLSDN* NW10 86 D1
The Mill Trading Estate *WLSDN* NW10 86 E2
Millwall FC (The New Den) *BERM/RHTH* SE16 111 K4
Milmead Industrial Centre *TOTM* N17 56 D1
Milton Natural Health Centre *HGT* N6 54 C6
Minet Clinic *HYS/HAR* UB3 82 E7
Minet J & I Schools *HYS/HAR* UB3 83 F7
Ministry of Defence *WHALL* SW1A 11 J9
Mint Business Park *CAN/RD* E16 94 E4
Mint Hotel *WEST* SW1P 17 J5
Mirravale Trading Estate *CHDH* RM6 62 A6
Mission Grove Primary School *WALTH* E17 57 H4
Mitcham ⊖ *MTCM* CR4 162 D3
Mitcham CC *MTCM* CR4 162 D3
Mitcham Eastfields ⇌ *MTCM* CR4 163 F1
Mitcham Golf Club *MTCM* CR4 163 F4
Mitcham Industrial Estate *MTCM* CR4 148 A7
Mitcham Junction ⇌ ⊖ *MTCM* CR4 163 F4
Mitcham Vale High School *STRHM/NOR* SW16 163 H1
Mitchell Brook Primary School *WLSDN* NW10 69 F5
Mitre Bridge Industrial Park *NKENS* W10 87 K3
Mitre House Hotel *BAY/PAD* W2 9 G5
Moatbridge School *ELTH/MOT* SE9 134 C5
The Moat School *FUL/PGN* SW6 127 H1
Moberly Sports & Education Centre *WLSDN* NW10 88 B2
Molesey Cemetery *E/WMO/HCT* KT8 157 F2
Molesey Hospital *E/WMO/HCT* KT8 157 F4
Mollison Drive Health Centre *WLGTN* SM6 176 E6
Monega Primary School *MNPK* E12 77 H4
Monkfrith Primary School *EBAR* EN4 28 A6
Monks Hill Sports Centre *SAND/SEL* CR2 179 F6
Monksmead School *BORE* WD6 24 E2
Monks Orchard Primary School *CROY/NA* CR0 166 A4
The Montague on The Gardens Hotel *RSQ* WC1B 11 J2
Montbelle Primary School *ELTH/MOT* SE9 154 A3
The Montcalm Hotel *MBLAR* W1H 9 M5
Monteagle Primary School *DAGW* RM9 79 H7
Montem Primary School *HOLWY* N7 73 F2
Montpelier Primary School *EA* W5 85 K4
Monument ⊖ *MANHO* EC4N 13 H6
The Monument *CANST* EC4R 13 H6
Moore Place Golf Club *ESH/CLAY* KT10 170 A4
Moorfields Eye Hospital *FSBYE* EC1V 7 G8
Moorgate ⇌ ⊖ *BARB* EC2Y 13 G3
Moor Lane Junior School *CHSGTN* KT9 172 B4
Moor Park ⊖ *NTHWD* HA6 32 B2
Moor Park Industrial Estate *WATW* WD18 20 A6
Mora Primary School *CRICK* NW2 70 A3
Morasha Jewish Primary School *FNCH* N3 39 F5
Morden ⊖ *WIM/MER* SW19 162 A2
Morden Cemetery *MRDN* SM4 161 F5
Morden College Homes *BKHTH/KID* SE3 133 K1
Morden First School *MRDN* SM4 161 K4
Morden Hall Medical Centre *WIM/MER* SW19 162 A2
Morden Hall Park (NT) *MRDN* SM4 162 B3
Morden Mount Primary School *LEW* SE13 132 E1
Morden Park Pool *MRDN* SM4 161 J4
Morden Road ⊖ *WIM/MER* SW19 162 A1
Morden Road Clinic *WIM/MER* SW19 162 A2
Morden South ⇌ *MRDN* SM4 161 K4
Moreland Primary School *FSBYE* EC1V 6 D7
Moriah Jewish Day School *PIN* HA5 47 J7
Morley College *STHWK* SE1 18 B3
Morningside Primary School *HOM* E9 74 E5
Mornington Crescent ⊖ *CAMTN* NW1 4 E5
Mornington Sports & Fitness Centre *CAMTN* NW1 4 D3
Morpeth School *BETH* E2 92 E2
Mortimer Road Clinic *WLSDN* NW10 88 A2
Mortimer School *STRHM/NOR* SW16 148 D1
Mortlake ⇌ *MORT/ESHN* SW14 125 K2
Mortlake Cemetery *MORT/ESHN* SW14 126 B2
Mortlake Crematorium *RCH/KEW* TW9 125 J1
Moselle School *TOTM* N17 56 A1
Moselle Special School *TOTM* N17 55 K1
Mosiah Foundation Supplementary School *STNW/STAM* N16 56 A7
Mossbourne Community Academy *HACK* E8 74 C3
Mossford Green Primary School *BARK/HLT* IG6 60 C1
The Mother & Baby Clinic *HOM* E9 74 E5
Motspur Park ⇌ *NWMAL* KT3 160 E4
Mottingham ⇌ *ELTH/MOT* SE9 134 E7
Mottingham Community Health Clinic *ELTH/MOT* SE9 153 J3
Mottingham Primary School *ELTH/MOT* SE9 153 K2
Mount Carmel RC Primary School *EA* W5 104 D2
Mount Carmel RC Technical College for Girls *ARCH* N19 54 D7
Mount Medical Centre *FELT* TW13 141 J1
Mount School *MLHL* NW7 37 K4
Mount Stewart Infant School *KTN/HRWW/WS* HA3 49 K5
The Movieum of London *STHWK* SE1 17 L1
Mowlem Primary School *BETH* E2 92 E1
Mowlem Trading Estate *TOTM* N17 42 E6
MPR Eurotots School *KIL/WHAMP* NW6 70 B6
MS Business Centre *PIN* HA5 47 H2
MSP Business Centre *WBLY* HA9 68 D3
Mudchute ⊖ *POP/IOD* E14 112 E3
Mudchute City Farm *POP/IOD* E14 113 F3
Mudlands Estate *RAIN* RM13 99 G2
Mulberry Business Centre *BERM/RHTH* SE16 112 A1
Mulberry House School *CRICK* NW2 70 C4
Mulberry Primary School *TOTM* N17 56 B1
Mulberry School for Girls *WCHPL* E1 92 D5
Mulgrave Primary School *WOOL/PLUM* SE18 115 F3
Munroe Centre *STHWK* SE1 19 H1
Murky Puddle Theatre *NWMAL* KT3 160 C2
Muschamp Primary School *CAR* SM5 175 J1
Museum of Brands, Packaging & Advertising *NTGHL* W11 88 D5
Museum of Domestic Design & Architecture *EBAR* EN4 27 K4
Museum of Fulham Palace *FUL/PGN* SW6 127 G1
Museum of London *BARB* EC2Y 12 E3
Museum of London Archaeology *IS* N1 6 F4
Museum of London Docklands *POP/IOD* E14 93 J6
Museum of Richmond *TWK* TW1 124 E4
Museum of The Artillery in The Rotunda *CHARL* SE7 114 D4
Museum of The Order of St John *FARR* EC1M 12 D1
Musical Museum *BTFD* TW8 105 F5
Mustard School *IS* N1 7 K5
Muswell Hill Bowling Club *MUSWH* N10 54 A2
Muswell Hill Golf Club *MUSWH* N10 40 B7
Muswell Hill Primary School *MUSWH* N10 54 B2
Myatt Garden Primary School *BROCKY* SE4 132 C1
Myatts Field Clinic *BRXN/ST* SW9 110 C7
N1 Shopping Centre *IS* N1 6 B5
Nagi Business Centre *ALP/SUD* HA0 85 K1
Nags Head Shopping Centre *HOLWY* N7 72 E2
Naima Jewish Preparatory School *KIL/WHAMP* NW6 2 C5
Nancy Reuben Primary School *HDN* NW4 52 B3
Nash College of Further Education *WWKM* BR4 180 D2
The National Archives *RCH/KEW* TW9 105 H6
National Army Museum *CHEL* SW3 15 M9
National Gallery *LSQ/SEVD* WC2H 11 H7
National Hospital for Neurology & Neurosurgery *RSQ* WC1B 11 J1
National Maritime Museum *GNWCH* SE10 113 G5
National Physical Laboratory *TEDD* TW11 142 E5
National Portrait Gallery *LSQ/SEVD* WC2H 11 H7
National Sports Centre *NRWD* SE19 150 C5
National Temperance Hospital *CAMTN* NW1 4 E7
National Tennis Centre *PUT/ROE* SW15 126 B4
National Youth Theatre Great Britain *HOLWY* N7 72 E2
The Natural History Museum *SKENS* SW7 15 G4
Natural Therapy Clinic *TOOT* SW17 148 B4
Natwest Sports Club *BECK* BR3 151 H5
Neasden ⊖ *WLSDN* NW10 69 G4
Negus Sixth Form Centre *WOOL/PLUM* SE18 115 J5
Nelson Dock Museum *BERM/RHTH* SE16 93 H7
Nelson Hospital *RYNPK* SW20 161 J1
Nelson Primary School *EHAM* E6 96 A1
WHTN TW2 123 G5
Nelson's Column *STJS* SW1Y 11 H8
Nelson Trading Estate *WIM/MER* SW19 147 F7
Neo Clinic *PIM* SW1V 16 E5
The New Ambassadors Theatre *LSQ/SEVD* WC2H 11 H5
New Atlas Wharf *POP/IOD* E14 112 C2
The New Aylesbury Medical Centre *WALW* SE17 19 H7
New Barnet ⇌ *BAR* EN5 27 G4
New Beckenham ⇌ *BECK* BR3 151 G6
New Brentford Cemetery *HSLW* TW3 122 E1
Newbridge School *CHDH* RM6 61 H4
IL IG1 78 E3
Newbury Park ⊖ *GNTH/NBYPK* IG2 60 D5
Newbury Park Health Centre *GNTH/NBYPK* IG2 60 D5
The New Business Centre *WLSDN* NW10 87 H2
New Caledonian Wharf *BERM/RHTH* SE16 112 C2
New Chiswick Pool *CHSWK* W4 106 B6
New City Primary School *PLSTW* E13 95 G2
New Connaught Rooms *HOL/ALD* WC2B 11 K5
New Covent Garden Market *VX/NE* SW8 109 J6
New Crane Wharf *WAP* E1W 92 E7
New Cross ⇌ ⊖ *NWCR* SE14 112 C6
New Cross Gate ⇌ ⊖ *NWCR* SE14 112 B6
New Cross Sports Arena *NWCR* SE14 112 B6
New Eltham ⇌ *ELTH/MOT* SE9 135 G7
New End Primary School *HAMP* NW3 71 G3
New End Theatre *HAMP* NW3 71 G2
New England Industrial Estate *BARK* IG11 96 C1
Newfield Primary School *WLSDN* NW10 69 H6
Newham College of Further Education *EHAM* E6 95 K1
SRTFD E15 76 C6
Newham General Hospital *PLSTW* E13 95 G3
Newham Leisure Centre *PLSTW* E13 95 G4
Newham Medical Centre *PLSTW* E13 95 G1
Newham Sixth Form College *PLSTW* E13 95 F3
Newham Training & Education Centre *SRTFD* E15 76 C5
New Health Centre *TOTM* N17 42 A7
New Hope Christian School *EDUL* SE22 131 G3
New Horizons Computer Learning Centre *FSBYE* EC1V 7 G8
Newington Court Business Centre *STHWK* SE1 18 E4
Newington Green Primary School *STNW/STAM* N16 74 A4
Newington Industrial Estate *WALW* SE17 18 D6
New Kings Primary School *FUL/PGN* SW6 127 J1
Newland House School *TWK* TW1 143 F3
New London Theatre *LSQ/SEVD* WC2H 11 K4
New Malden ⇌ *NWMAL* KT3 160 B2
Newman Catholic College *WLSDN* NW10 69 J7
Newnham Junior School *RSLP* HA4 47 G7
New North Community School *IS* N1 7 G1
Newport School *LEY* E10 76 A1
New River College *ARCH* N19 72 D1
New River Sports Centre *WDGN* N22 41 H6
New River Village *CEND/HSY/T* N8 55 F2
New Rush Hall School *IL* IG1 78 C1
New School *FUL/PGN* SW6 107 J7
New Scotland Yard *STJSPK* SW1H 17 G3
News International *WAP* E1W 92 D6
New Southgate ⇌ *FBAR/BDGN* N11 40 A4
New Southgate Cemetery *FBAR/BDGN* N11 40 B2
New Southgate Crematorium *FBAR/BDGN* N11 40 B2
New Southgate Industrial Estate *FBAR/BDGN* N11 40 C4
New Southgate Pain Clinic & Medical Centre *FBAR/BDGN* N11 40 C4
New Spitalfields Market *LEY* E10 75 J3
Newton Farm J & I School *RYLN/HDSTN* HA2 65 K1
Newton Industrial Estate *CHDH* RM6 61 K3
Newton Medical Centre *BAY/PAD* W2 8 C4
Newton Preparatory School *VX/NE* SW8 109 G6
Newtons Primary School *RAIN* RM13 99 F1
New Victoria Hospital *KUTN/CMB* KT2 145 G7
New Woodlands School *BMLY* BR1 152 C3
Nightingale Academy *ED* N9 30 E6
Nightingale Clinic *PLSTW* E13 95 G1
Nightingale Primary School *CLPT* E5 74 C2
SWFD E18 59 G3
WDGN N22 41 F7
WOOL/PLUM SE18 115 G5
Nightingale School *TOOT* SW17 147 J1
No1 Poultry *MANHO* EC4N 12 F5
Noel Coward Theatre *CHCR* WC2N 11 J6
Noel Park Primary School *WDGN* N22 55 H1
Nonsuch High School for Girls *CHEAM* SM3 174 B6
Nonsuch Primary School *EW* KT17 173 K4
Noor Ul Islam Primary School *LEY* E10 76 A1
Norbiton ⇌ *KUTN/CMB* KT2 144 C7
Norbury ⇌ *STRHM/NOR* SW16 149 F7
Norbury Complementary Therapy Clinic *STRHM/NOR* SW16 149 F7
Norbury First & Middle School *HRW* HA1 48 E4
Norbury Health Centre *STRHM/NOR* SW16 164 A1
Norbury Manor Business & Enterprise College for Girls *STRHM/NOR* SW16 149 G7
Norbury Manor Primary School *STRHM/NOR* SW16 148 E7
Norbury Trading Estate *STRHM/NOR* SW16 164 A1
Norfolk House School *MUSWH* N10 54 B1
Norland Place School *NTGHL* W11 88 C7
Norlington School *LEY* E10 58 B7
Normanby College *CMBW* SE5 130 D1
Normand Croft Community School *WKENS* W14 107 J5
Normandy Primary School *BXLYHN* DA7 118 A7
Norman Park Athletics Track *HAYES* BR2 168 A5
Norman Shaw Building (MP's Offices) *WHALL* SW1A 17 J1
North Acton ⊖ *WLSDN* NW10 87 F3
North Acton Business Park *ACT* W3 87 F5
North Beckton Primary School *EHAM* E6 95 K3
North Bridge House Junior School *HAMP* NW3 71 G5
North Bridge House Preparatory School *CAMTN* NW1 4 C4
North Bridge House School *HAMP* NW3 71 H5
Northbury Primary School *BARK* IG11 78 B5
North Clinic *BMLY* BR1 152 E7
Northcote Lodge School *BTSEA* SW11 128 E5
North Croydon Medical Centre *THHTH* CR7 164 C5
North Dulwich ⇌ *HNHL* SE24 130 E4
North Ealing ⊖ *ACT* W3 86 B5
North Ealing Primary School *WEA* W13 85 H3
North East Surrey Crematorium *NWMAL* KT3 161 F5
North End Trading Estate *ERITH* DA8 118 B6
Northern Spectator Transport Mall *OLYMPICPK* E20 75 J3
North Feltham Trading Estate *EBED/NFELT* TW14 122 A3
Northfields ⊖ *WEA* W13 104 D2
Northfields Industrial Estate *ALP/SUD* HA0 68 C7
Northfields Prospect Business Centre *PUT/ROE* SW15 127 J3
Northgate Business Centre *EN* EN1 30 D2
Northgate Clinic *CDALE/KGS* NW9 51 G5
Northgate Industrial Park *CRW* RM5 62 B1
North Greenwich ⊖ *GNWCH* SE10 113 H1
North Greenwich Arena *POP/IOD* E14 94 C7
North Greenwich Pier *POP/IOD* E14 94 D7
North Harringay Primary School *CEND/HSY/T* N8 55 G3
North Harrow ⊖ *RYLN/HDSTN* HA2 48 A4
North Havering College of Adult Education *ROM* RM1 63 G3
North Kensington Video-Drama Project *NKENS* W10 88 C5
North London College *SEVS/STOTM* N15 56 B2
North London Collegiate School *EDGW* HA8 36 A5
The North London Hospice *NFNCH/WDSPK* N12 39 F2
North London International School *FBAR/BDGN* N11 39 K4
NFNCH/WDSPK N12 39 F4
North London International School (Diploma Centre) *NFNCH/WDSPK* N12 39 J4
North London International School (Lower School) *NFNCH/WDSPK* N12 39 F2
North London Nuffield Hospital *ENC/FH* EN2 29 G1
North London School of Physiotherapy *ARCH* N19 54 C7
North London Tutorial College *HDN* NW4 52 A5
North Middlesex Golf Club *NFNCH/WDSPK* N12 39 H2
North Middlesex Hospital *UED* N18 42 A4
Northolt ⊖ *NTHLT* UB5 66 A6
Northolt Aerodrome *RSLP* HA4 64 E5
Northolt High School *NTHLT* UB5 65 K5
Northolt Park ⇌ *RYLN/HDSTN* HA2 66 B3
Northolt Road Clinic *RYLN/HDSTN* HA2 66 C2
Northolt Swimarama *NTHLT* UB5 66 A5
North Pole Depot *WLSDN* NW10 87 H3
North Primary School *STHL* UB1 83 K6
North Sheen ⇌ *RCH/KEW* TW9 125 H3
Northside Primary School *NFNCH/WDSPK* N12 39 G4
The North Street Health Centre *CLAP* SW4 129 H2

Northumberland Heath Medical Centre ERITH DA8 118 A6
Northumberland Heath Primary ERITH DA8 117 J6
Northumberland Park ⇌ TOTM N17 42 D7
Northumberland Park Community School TOTM N17 42 C6
Northumberland Park Industrial Estate TOTM N17 42 D5
Northview Primary School WLSDN NW10 69 G3
Northway School MLHL NW7 37 F1
North Wembley ⊖ ⊖ ALP/SUD HA0 67 K2
North West London Jewish Day School CRICK NW2 70 C6
North West London Medical Centre MV/WKIL W9 2 E6
North Westminster Community Secondary School MV/WKIL W9 2 B9
Northwick Park ⊖ KTN/HRWW/WS HA3 49 H6
Northwick Park Hospital & Clinical Research Centre HRW HA1 49 H6
Northwold Primary School CLPT E5 74 C1
Northwood ⊖ NTHWD HA6 32 C6
Northwood Cemetery NTHWD HA6 46 D1
Northwood College NTHWD HA6 32 B6
Northwood FC NTHWD HA6 46 D1
Northwood Golf Club NTHWD HA6 32 B6
Northwood Hills ⊖ NTHWD HA6 46 E1
Northwood & Pinner Community Hospital NTHWD HA6 32 E7
Northwood Preparatory School RKW/CH/CXG WD3 32 A1
Northwood Primary School ERITHM DA18 117 F2
Northwood School NTHWD HA6 33 F7
Northwood Sports Centre NTHWD HA6 33 F7
Norwegian/British Monument BAY/PAD W2 9 J8
The Norwegian School WIM/MER SW19 146 A6
Norwood Green Infant School NWDGN UB2 102 D4
Norwood Green Junior School NWDGN UB2 102 D4
Norwood Heights Shopping Centre NRWD SE19 150 A5
Norwood Junction ⇌ ⊖ SNWD SE25 165 H3
Norwood School NRWD SE19 149 J4
Notre Dame RC Girls School STHWK SE1 18 C3
Notre Dame RC Primary School WOOL/PLUM SE18 115 G5
Notre Dame University LSQ/SEVD WC2H 11 H7
Notting Hill & Ealing High School WEA W13 85 H4
Notting Hill Gate ⊖ NTGHL W11 8 A8
Novello Theatre HOL/ALD WC2B 11 L6
Novotel
BAY/PAD W2 8 E3
CAMTN NW1 5 H7
CAN/RD E16 95 F6
GNWCH SE10 112 E6
STHWK SE1 17 L5
WDR/YW UB7 100 D3
Novotel London West HMSMTH W6 107 G4
Nower Hill High School PIN HA5 48 A3
NTGB Sports Ground EHAM E6 78 A5
Number 10 Bowling ROM RM1 63 G4
Nunhead ⇌ PECK SE15 131 K2
Nutrilife Clinic MHST W1U 10 A2
The O_2 POP/IOD E14 94 B7
Oakdale Infant School SWFD E18 59 F1
Oakdale Junior School SWFD E18 59 G1
Oakfield Preparatory School DUL SE21 149 K1
Oakfield Road Industrial Estate PGE/AN SE20 150 D6
Oak Heights Independent School HSLW TW3 123 G2
Oak Hill Health Centre SURB KT6 159 F5
Oak Hill Theological College STHGT/OAK N14 28 A5
Oakington Manor School WBLY HA9 68 D4
Oakland CP School EBAR EN4 27 K5
Oaklands College BORE WD6 24 E1
Oaklands Primary School HNWL W7 104 A1
Oaklands School ISLW TW7 123 J2
Oaklands Secondary School BETH E2 92 C2
Oak Lane Cemetery TWK TW1 124 B6
Oak Lane Medical Centre TWK TW1 124 C6
Oak Lee Montessori School PIN HA5 47 H2
Oakleigh Park ⇌ TRDG/WHET N20 27 H6
Oakleigh School TRDG/WHET N20 39 J2
Oak Lodge JMI School WWKM BR4 166 E6
Oak Lodge Medical Centre EDGW HA8 36 D6
Oak Lodge School
BAL SW12 128 E6
EFNCH N2 53 G2
Oaks Park High School GNTH/NBYPK IG2 60 D4
Oakthorpe Primary School UED N18 41 J4
Oak Tree Medical Centre GDMY/SEVK IG3 78 E1
Oakwood ⊖ STHGT/OAK N14 28 C3
Oakwood Business Park WLSDN NW10 87 F2
Oakwood Medical Centre STHGT/OAK N14 28 C4
Oakwood School BXLYHN DA7 138 A3
Oasis Academy Shirley Park CROY/NA CR0 165 J5
Oasis Sports Centre LSQ/SEVD WC2H 11 J4
Odeon Cinema
BAR EN5 26 E4
BAY/PAD W2 9 L5
BECK BR3 166 D1
BERM/RHTH SE16 112 A2
CAMTN NW1 4 D3
ED N9 31 F6
ELTH/MOT SE9 134 D3
ESH/CLAY KT10 170 B3
FITZ W1T 11 G3
HAMP NW3 3 G2
HAYES BR2 167 K1
HOLWY N7 72 E2
KENS W8 14 A4
KUT/HW KT1 159 F1
MUSWH N10 54 A3
RCH/KEW TW9 124 E4
ROM RM1 63 H4
STJS SW1Y 11 G7
STRHM/NOR SW16 148 E2
SWFD E18 58 E1
WIM/MER SW19 146 E6
Odeon Covent Garden Cinema LSQ/SEVD WC2H 11 H5
Odeon Wardour Street Cinema SOHO/SHAV W1D 11 G6
Odessa Infant School FSTGT E7 76 E4
Odyssey Business Park RSLP HA4 65 F4
Old Abbotstonians RFC YEAD UB4 82 B1
Old Actonians Sports Club EA W5 105 G1
Old Admiralty STJS SW1Y 11 H9
Old Bancroftians FC BKHH IG9 45 H3
Old Barnes Cemetery BARN SW13 126 E1
Old Beckenhamian RFC WWKM BR4 180 B2
Old Bellgate Wharf POP/IOD E14 112 C2
Old Bexley Business Park BXLY DA5 137 J6
Old Bexley CE Primary School BXLY DA5 137 G7
Old Brockleians Sports Ground LEE/GVPK SE12 134 B5
Old Bromlians CC HAYES BR2 168 A4
Old Cemetery EDUL SE22 131 J5
Old Colfeian Sports Club LEE/GVPK SE12 133 K4
Old Curiosity Shop LINN WC2A 11 L4
Old Elthamians Sports Club CHST BR7 154 E5
Oldfield House Special School HPTN TW12 141 K7
Oldfield Primary School GFD/PVL UB6 84 D1
Oldfields Trading Estate SUT SM1 174 E2
Old Ford Primary School BOW E3 93 H1
Oldhill Medical Centre STNW/STAM N16 56 B7
Old Jamaica Business Estate BERM/RHTH SE16 19 M3
Old Lyonian Sports Ground RYLN/HDSTN HA2 48 C4
Old Millhillians Sports Ground RYLN/HDSTN HA2 34 A7
Old Oak Primary School SHB W12 87 H5
Old Operating Theatre & Herb Garret Museum STHWK SE1 13 G9
Old Owens Sports Ground TRDG/WHET N20 27 H7
Old Palace Primary School BOW E3 93 K2
Old Palace School CROY/NA CR0 177 H2
Old Palace School of John Whitgift Junior Site SAND/SEL CR2 178 B5
Old Royal Naval College GNWCH SE10 113 G4
Old Royal Observatory Greenwich GNWCH SE10 113 G6
Old Spitalfields Market Hall WCHPL E1 13 L2
Old Street ⇌ ⊖ FSBYE EC1V 7 G8
Old Sun Wharf POP/IOD E14 93 G6
Old Tiffinians Sports Ground E/WMO/HCT KT8 157 K4
Old Treasury WHALL SW1A 17 J1
Old Vicarage School RCHPK/HAM TW10 125 F5
Old Vic Theatre STHWK SE1 18 B1
Old War Office WHALL SW1A 11 J9
Old Wilsonians Sports Club WWKM BR4 167 H7
Olga Primary School BOW E3 93 G1
Oliver Business Park WLSDN NW10 86 E1
Oliver Goldsmith Primary School
CDALE/KGS NW9 51 F4
CMBW SE5 111 G7
Oliver House Preparatory School CLAP SW4 129 G5
Olympia WKENS W14 107 H2
Olympia Industrial Estate WDGN N22 55 F1
Olympic Industrial Estate WBLY HA9 68 D3
Olympic Park OLYMPICPK E20 75 J6
Olympic Retail Park WBLY HA9 68 C3
Olympic Stadium OLYMPICPK E20 75 K6
Olympic Trading Estate WBLY HA9 68 D3
One Aldwych Hotel COVGDN WC2E 11 L6
One New Change CITYW EC2V 12 E5
The One Stanley Medical Centre ALP/SUD HA0 68 A6
On Sai Clinic ECT SW5 14 C6
The Open University
FSBYW WC1X 5 L7
HAMP NW3 70 E3
Ophaboom Theatre WLSDN NW10 87 K1
Optimax Laser Eye Clinic HAMP NW3 71 G5
Orange Tree Theatre RCH/KEW TW9 125 F3
Oratory RC Primary School CHEL SW3 15 J7
The Orbit Tower OLYMPICPK E20 75 K6
Orchard Business Centre BECK BR3 151 H4
The Orchard Health Centre BARK IG11 96 C1
Orchard Hill College WLGTN SM6 176 B5
Orchard House School CHSWK W4 106 A3
Orchard J & I School HOM E9 74 E6
The Orchard Junior School HSLWW TW4 123 F3
Orchard Primary School SCUP DA14 155 H4
The Orchard School
BRXS/STRHM SW2 130 A7
E/WMO/HCT KT8 157 J4
Orchard Shopping Centre DART DA1 139 H5
The Orchard Theatre DART DA1 139 H5
Orchard Way Primary School CROY/NA CR0 166 B6
Oriel Primary School FELT TW13 141 J2
Orient Industrial Park LEY E10 75 J1
Orion Business Centre NWCR SE14 112 A4
The Orion Primary School CDALE/KGS NW9 37 G7
Orleans House Gallery TWK TW1 124 C7
Orleans Infant School TWK TW1 124 C6
Orley Farm School HRW HA1 66 D2
Osidge JMI School STHGT/OAK N14 28 C7
Osier Industrial Estate WAND/EARL SW18 127 K3
Osmani Primary School WCHPL E1 92 C4
Osterley ⊖ ISLW TW7 103 J6
Osterley Park & House (NT) ISLW TW7 103 H5
Osterley RFC NWDGN UB2 103 G2
Our Lady Immaculate RC Primary School BRYLDS KT5 159 J7
Our Lady of Dolours RC Primary School BAY/PAD W2 8 C2
Our Lady of Grace RC Junior School CRICK NW2 69 K2
Our Lady of Grace RC Primary School CHARL SE7 114 A5
Our Lady of Lourdes RC Primary
FBAR/BDGN N11 40 B4
NFNCH/WDSPK N12 39 G6
Our Lady of Lourdes RC Primary School
WAN E11 58 D5
WLSDN NW10 68 E7
Our Lady of Muswell RC Primary MUSWH N10 54 A1
Our Lady of The Rosary RC Primary School ELTH/MOT SE9 135 K5
Our Lady of The Sacred Heart School HOLWY N7 73 F4
Our Lady of The Visitation RC Combined Primary School GFD/PVL UB6 84 C3
Our Lady of Victories RC Primary School
PUT/ROE SW15 127 G3
SKENS SW7 14 F6
Our Lady Queen of Heaven RC Primary School PUT/ROE SW15 127 G6
Our Lady RC Primary School
CAMTN NW1 4 F3
POP/IOD E14 93 H5
Our Lady & St Georges Catholic Primary School
WALTH E17 57 K2
WALTH E17 58 A3
Our Lady & St Johns RC Primary School BTFD TW8 104 D4
Our Lady & St Joseph Primary School IS N1 74 A5
Our Lady & St Philip Neri RC Infant School FSTH SE23 151 F2
Our Lady & St Philip Neri RC Primary School SYD SE26 151 G3
Our Ladys Catholic Primary School DART DA1 139 G5
Our Ladys Convent High School CLPT E5 56 D7
Oval ⊖ LBTH SE11 110 B5
Oval Business Centre LBTH SE11 17 M8
Oval House Theatre LBTH SE11 110 B5
Oval Primary School CROY/NA CR0 165 F7
Overton Grange School BELMT SM2 175 F7
Oxford Circus ⊖ REGST W1B 10 D4
Oxford Gardens Primary School NKENS W10 88 B5
Oxford House College SOHO/SHAV W1D 11 G4
Oxhey Park Golf Centre OXHEY WD19 21 H7
Oxhey Wood Primary School OXHEY WD19 33 G3
Oxo Tower Wharf STHWK SE1 12 B7
Paddington ⇌ ⊖ BAY/PAD W2 9 G4
Paddington Academy MV/WKIL W9 8 B1
Paddington Bowling & Sports Club MV/WKIL W9 2 C9
Paddington Community Hospital MV/WKIL W9 8 A2
Paddington Green Primary School BAY/PAD W2 9 G1
Paddington Recreation Ground Athletics Track KIL/WHAMP NW6 2 B7
Paddington Recreation Ground Pavilion MV/WKIL W9 2 C7
Paddock Primary School BTSEA SW11 129 F3
Paddock School PUT/ROE SW15 126 C3
Paines Lane Cemetery PIN HA5 47 J2
Pain Relief Clinic HDN NW4 51 K5
Paint Pots Montessori School WBPTN SW10 108 B5
Pakeman Primary School HOLWY N7 73 F2
Palace Gardens Shopping Centre ENC/FH EN2 29 K2
Palace of Westminster WHALL SW1A 17 K2
Palace Theatre
SOHO/SHAV W1D 11 H6
WAT WD17 21 F2
Palladium Theatre SOHO/CST W1F 10 E5
Palmers Green ⇌ PLMGR N13 41 F3
Palmers Green High School WCHMH N21 41 G1
Palmerston Business Centre SUT SM1 175 G4
Palm House, Kew Gardens RCH/KEW TW9 105 G7
Panorama Pier STHWK SE1 12 E7
Paradise Swimming Pools MLHL NW7 37 G4
Paragon Christian Academy CLPT E5 75 F3
Paray House School FUL/PGN SW6 127 J1
Parayhouse School WBPTN SW10 108 B6
Parchmore Medical Centre THHTH CR7 164 D2
Pardes House & Beis Yaakov School FNCH N3 52 D1
Parent Infant Clinic HAMP NW3 71 G4
Parish CE Primary School BMLY BR1 152 E6
Park Avenue Clinic WAT WD17 20 E1
Park Business Centre KIL/WHAMP NW6 2 A8
Parkfield Industrial Estate BTSEA SW11 129 F1
Parkfield JMI School HDN NW4 51 K6
Parkgate House School CLAP SW4 129 F3
Park Hall Trading Estate WNWD SE27 149 J2
Park High School STAN HA7 49 K1
Park Hill Junior School CROY/NA CR0 177 K2
Parkhill Primary School CLAY IG5 59 K2
Park Hill School KUTN/CMB KT2 144 C6
Park House Medical Centre KIL/WHAMP NW6 88 C1
Park House RFC HAYES BR2 181 G1
Park Inn
WAT WD17 21 F1
WDR/YW UB7 100 E6
Parklands Primary School ROM RM1 63 F2
Park Lane Primary School WBLY HA9 68 A3
Park Medical Centre BERM/RHTH SE16 112 A3
Park Mews Small Business Centre HNHL SE24 130 D5
Park Plaza Hotel
PIM SW1V 16 E5
STHWK SE1 17 L6
STHWK SE1 17 M1
Park Primary School SRTFD E15 76 D6
Park Road Clinic CEND/HSY/T N8 54 D4
Park Road Swimming Centre CEND/HSY/T N8 54 D4
Park Royal ⊖ EA W5 86 C3
Park Royal Business Centre WLSDN NW10 87 F3
Park School for Girls IL IG1 78 A1
Parkside Business Estate DEPT SE8 112 C5
Parkside Clinic NTGHL W11 88 C5
Parkside Health NTGHL W11 88 C5
Parkside Hospital WIM/MER SW19 146 B2
Park View School SEVS/STOTM N15 55 J3
Park Walk Primary School WBPTN SW10 108 C5
Parkway Primary School ERITHM DA18 117 F2
Parkway Trading Estate HEST TW5 102 B5
Parkwood Primary School FSBYPK N4 73 H1
Parliament Hill Fields Athletics Track HAMP NW3 71 K3
Parliament Hill Lido HAMP NW3 72 A3
Parliament Hill School KTTN NW5 72 A3
Parmiter Industrial Centre BETH E2 92 D1
Parnells Sports Ground KTN/HRWW/WS HA3 50 B5
Parsloes Primary School DAGW RM9 80 B5
Parsons Green ⊖ FUL/PGN SW6 107 K7
Parsons Green Health Clinic FUL/PGN SW6 107 K7
Pascals College BECK BR3 166 D1
Passport Language Schools BMLY BR1 153 F7
Pastoria Hotel LSQ/SEVD WC2H 11 H7
Patent Office FLST/FETLN EC4A 12 A3
The Patrick Doody Clinic & Health Centre WIM/MER SW19 146 E6
Pattinson Clinic RCH/KEW TW9 124 E4
The Paul Robeson Theatre HSLW TW3 123 G2
Pavilion Barclays Sports Ground EA W5 86 A4
The Pavilion Leisure Centre BMLY BR1 167 K1
Pavilion Restaurant RCH/KEW TW9 125 F1
Paxton Primary School NRWD SE19 150 B5
PCMS London SRTFD E15 94 B1
PDSA Hospital REDBR IG4 59 H2
Peace Pagoda CHEL SW3 108 E6
Peacock Estate TOTM N17 42 B5
Peacock Industrial Estate TOTM N17 42 B6
The Peacock Theatre HOL/ALD WC2B 11 L5
Peall Road Industrial Estate CROY/NA CR0 164 A5
Peareswood Primary School ERITH DA8 118 C7
Peckham Park Primary School PECK SE15 111 H6
The Peckham Pulse Health & Leisure Centre PECK SE15 111 H7
Peckham Rye ⇌ ⊖ PECK SE15 131 H1
Pelham Primary School
BXLYHN DA7 137 H2
WIM/MER SW19 146 E6
Pembridge Hall Preparatory School for Girls BAY/PAD W2 8 B6
Pendragon School BMLY BR1 152 E2
Penge East ⇌ SYD SE26 150 E5
Penge West ⇌ ⊖ PGE/AN SE20 150 D6
Pentavia Retail Park MLHL NW7 37 H6
Penwortham Primary School STRHM/NOR SW16 148 B5
Percival David Foundation of Chinese Art STPAN WC1H 5 H9
Perivale ⊖ GFD/PVL UB6 85 G1
Perivale Industrial Park
GFD/PVL UB6 67 G7
GFD/PVL UB6 85 G1
Perivale New Business Centre GFD/PVL UB6 85 J1
Perivale Park Athletics Track GFD/PVL UB6 84 E2
Perivale Park Golf Course GFD/PVL UB6 84 E2
Perrin Road Clinic ALP/SUD HA0 67 H3
Perrymount Primary School FSTH SE23 151 F1
The Petchy Academy HACK E8 74 B4
Peterborough & St Margarets High School STAN HA7 34 E2
Peter Hills School BERM/RHTH SE16 93 F7
Peter James Business Centre HYS/HAR UB3 101 K1
Peterley Business Centre BETH E2 92 D1
Peter Pan Statue BAY/PAD W2 9 G8
The Petersham Hotel RCHPK/HAM TW10 125 F6
Petrie Museum of Egyptian Archaeology FITZ W1T 10 F1

Petts Hill Primary School
NTHLT UB5 .... 66 B4
Petts Wood ⇌
STMC/STPC BR5 .... 169 H4
Pewterers' Hall
CITYW EC2V 12 E3
Pheasantry Welcome Centre
TEDD TW11 .... 143 H2
Phipps Bridge ⇌
WIM/MER SW19 .... 162 B4
Phoenix Academy
ED N9 .... 30 D7
Phoenix Business Centre
POP/IOD E14 .... 93 J4
Phoenix Cinema
EFNCH N2 .... 53 J3
Phoenix College
MRDN SM4 .... 162 A4
Phoenix High School
SHB W12 .... 87 J6
Phoenix Industrial Estate
HRW HA1 .... 49 F6
Phoenix Leisure Centre
CAT SE6 .... 132 E6
Phoenix Primary School
STHWK SE1 .... 111 H4
Phoenix School
HAMP NW3 .... 71 H5
Phoenix Secondary &
Primary School
BOW E3 .... 93 H2
Phoenix Theatre
LSQ/SEVD WC2H 11 H5
Phoenix Trading Estate
GFD/PVL UB6 .... 67 J7
Physical Energy Statue
BAY/PAD W2 .... 9 G9
Piccadilly Circus ⊖
MYFR/PICC W1J 11 G6
Piccadilly Theatre
SOHO/SHAV W1D 11 G6
Pickford Lane Medical Centre
BXLYHN DA7 .... 117 F7
Pickhurst Infant School
WWKM BR4 .... 167 H5
Pickhurst Junior School
WWKM BR4 .... 167 J5
Picture House Cinema
SRTFD E15 .... 76 B5
Pilgrims Way J & I School
PECK SE15 .... 111 K5
Pilot Industrial Centre
WLSDN NW10 .... 87 G3
Pilton Estate
CROY/NA CR0 .... 177 H1
Pimlico ⊖
PIM SW1V 17 G7
Pimlico Academy
PIM SW1V 16 A7
Pinkwell Primary School
HYS/HAR UB3 .... 101 F3
Pinnacles
Cricket & Squash Club
SUT SM1 .... 174 E5
Pinner ⊖
PIN HA5 .... 47 J3
Pinner Hill Golf Club
PIN HA5 .... 33 F5
Pinner Medical Centre
PIN HA5 .... 47 J3
Pinner New Cemetery
PIN HA5 .... 48 A2
Pinner Park Infant School
PIN HA5 .... 48 B2
Pinner Park Junior School
RYLN/HDSTN HA2 .... 48 B2
Pinner View Medical Centre
HRW HA1 .... 48 C4
Pinner Wood School
PIN HA5 .... 33 G4
Pioneers Industrial Park
CROY/NA CR0 .... 163 K4
Pitshanger Manor Museum
EA W5 .... 85 J7
Plaisterers Hall
STBT EC1A 12 E3
Plaistow ⇌
SRTFD E15 .... 94 D1
Plaistow Hospital
PLSTW E13 .... 95 F1
Plaistow
Jamia Islamia School
PLSTW E13 .... 95 F2
Plaistow Primary School
PLSTW E13 .... 77 G3
PLSTW E13 .... 95 F1
Plantation House
Medical Centre
LOTH EC2R 13 H4
Plashet Jewish Cemetery
MNPK E12 .... 77 H5
Plashet Road Medical Centre
FSTGT E7 .... 77 F6
Plashet School
EHAM E6 .... 77 J6
Players Theatre
CHCR WC2N 11 K8
Playgolf Northwick Park
HRW HA1 .... 49 G7
The Playhouse
CHCR WC2N 11 K8
Plaza Business Centre
PEND EN3 .... 31 H1
Plaza on the River Hotel
STHWK SE1 .... 17 L6
Pleasance Theatre
HOLWY N7 .... 72 E5
Plumcroft Primary School
WOOL/PLUM SE18 .... 115 H5
Plumstead ⇌
WOOL/PLUM SE18 .... 115 J3
Plumstead Cemetery
ABYW SE2 .... 116 C6
Plumstead Leisure Centre
WOOL/PLUM SE18 .... 116 A4
Plumstead Manor School
WOOL/PLUM SE18 .... 115 J4
The Pointer School
BKHTH/KID SE3 .... 113 K7
Police Cadet School
WAN E11 .... 58 E7
The Polish Institute &
Sikorski Museum
SKENS SW7 .... 15 H2
Polish War Memorial
RSLP HA4 .... 65 F5
Polka Theatre for Children
WIM/MER SW19 .... 147 F5
Ponders End ⇌
PEND EN3 .... 31 G4
Ponders End
Industrial Estate
PEND EN3 .... 31 H3

Pontoon Dock ⊖
CAN/RD E16 .... 95 G7
Pooles Park Primary School
FSBYPK N4 .... 73 F1
Pools on the Park
RCH/KEW TW9 .... 124 E3
Pope John Primary School
SHB W12 .... 87 K6
Pop In Business Centre
WBLY HA9 .... 68 D4
Poplar ⊖
POP/IOD E14 .... 93 K6
Poplar Business Park
POP/IOD E14 .... 112 D1
Poplar Coroners Court
POP/IOD E14 .... 93 K6
Poplar Primary School
WIM/MER SW19 .... 161 K2
Pop Up Theatre
CLKNW EC1R 6 B6
Porchester Leisure Centre
BAY/PAD W2 .... 8 C4
Portcullis House
WHALL SW1A 17 K2
Portico City Learning Centre
CLPT E5 .... 74 E3
The Portland Hospital
REGST W1B 10 D1
Portland House Medical Centre
GFD/PVL UB6 .... 84 B3
Portland Medical Centre
SNWD SE25 .... 165 J4
Portland Place School
REGST W1B 10 D2
The Portman Clinic
HAMP NW3 .... 71 H5
Portobello Market
NKENS W10 .... 88 C4
Portobello Medical Centre
NTGHL W11 .... 88 C5
Portway Primary School
SRTFD E15 .... 76 E7
The Pountney Clinic
HSLW TW3 .... 123 F2
Powergate Business Park
WLSDN NW10 .... 87 F2
Power Industrial Estate
ERITH DA8 .... 118 C7
Premier Cinema
PECK SE15 .... 131 H1
Premier Inn
BARK IG11 .... 78 B7
Prendergast Hilly Fields College
BROCKY SE4 .... 132 D3
Prendergast Ladywell
Fields College
BROCKY SE4 .... 132 D5
Preston Manor School
WBLY HA9 .... 68 B1
Preston Medical Centre
WBLY HA9 .... 68 A2
Preston Park Primary School
WBLY HA9 .... 49 K7
Preston Road ⊖
WBLY HA9 .... 50 A7
Priestmead Primary School
KTN/HRWW/WS HA3 ...... 49 H2
Primrose Hill School
CAMTN NW1 .... 4 B3
Primrose Montessori School
HBRY N5 .... 73 J2
Prince Charles Cinema
LSQ/SEVD WC2H 11 H6
Prince Edward Theatre
SOHO/SHAV W1D 11 G5
Prince of Wales Theatre
STJS SW1Y 11 G7
Prince Regent ⊖
CAN/RD E16 .... 95 G6
Princes College
NOXST/BSQ WC1A 11 J4
Princes Court Business Centre
WAP E1W 92 D6
Princes Park Stadium
DART DA1 .... 139 K7
Princes Plain Primary School
HAYES BR2 .... 168 D6
Princess Avenue School
MUSWH N10 .... 54 B2
Princess Frederica CE J &
I School
WLSDN NW10 .... 87 K1
Princess Grace Hospital
MHST W1U 10 A1
Princess Louise Hospital
NKENS W10 .... 88 A4
Princess May Primary School
STNW/STAM N16 .... 74 A4
Princess of Wales Conservatory
RCH/KEW TW9 .... 105 G6
The Princess Royal
Distribution Centre
WLSDN NW10 .... 68 D7
Priory CE Primary School
WIM/MER SW19 .... 147 F4
Priory Retail Park
WIM/MER SW19 .... 147 H6
Priory Shopping Centre
DART DA1 .... 139 G5
Priory Special School
SNWD SE25 .... 165 J4
Privy Council
STJS SW1Y 11 C9
Privy Council Office
WHALL SW1A 11 J9
Progress Business Park
CROY/NA CR0 .... 177 F1
Promised Land Academy
PLSTW E13 .... 94 E3
Pronto Trading Estate
YEAD UB4 .... 82 C4
Prospect House School
PUT/ROE SW15 .... 127 G6
Proud Gallery
CHCR WC2N 11 J7
Provident Industrial Estate
HYS/HAR UB3 .... 101 K1
PS Tattershall Castle
WHALL SW1A 11 K9
Pudding Mill Lane ⊖
SRTFD E15 .... 75 K2
Pumphouse
Educational Museum
BERM/RHTH SE16 .... 93 G7
Pump House Theatre
WATW WD18 .... 21 G4
Pump Lane Industrial Estate
HYS/HAR UB3 .... 102 A1
The Purcell School
BUSH WD23 .... 22 A1
HRW HA1 .... 66 D2
Purdy Hicks Gallery
STHWK SE1 .... 12 C8

Purfleet ⇌
PUR RM19 .... 119 K4
Purfleet Industrial Park
SOCK/AV RM15 .... 119 J1
Purfleet Primary School
PUR RM19 .... 119 K3
Purley Oaks ⇌
SAND/SEL CR2 .... 177 K7
Purley Oaks Primary School
SAND/SEL CR2 .... 177 K6
Pursuit Centre
WAP E1W 92 E6
Putney ⇌
PUT/ROE SW15 .... 127 G3
Putney Animal Hospital
PUT/ROE SW15 .... 127 G3
Putney Arts Theatre
PUT/ROE SW15 .... 127 G3
Putney Bridge ⊖
FUL/PGN SW6 .... 127 J2
Putney Exchange
Shopping Centre
PUT/ROE SW15 .... 127 G3
Putney High School
PUT/ROE SW15 .... 127 G4
Putney Leisure Centre
PUT/ROE SW15 .... 127 F3
Putney Lower
Common Cemetery
BARN SW13 .... 126 E1
Putneymead Medical Centre
PUT/ROE SW15 .... 127 F3
Putney Park School
PUT/ROE SW15 .... 126 E3
Putney School of Art & Design
PUT/ROE SW15 .... 127 H3
Putney Town Social &
Bowls Club
PUT/ROE SW15 .... 127 F1
Putney Vale Cemetery
PUT/ROE SW15 .... 145 J1
Putney Vale Crematorium
PUT/ROE SW15 .... 145 J1
Pylon Trading Estate
CAN/RD E16 .... 94 B3
Quadrant Business Park
KIL/WHAMP NW6 .... 70 C7
Quality Hotel
WBLY HA9 .... 68 C3
Quebec Industrial Estate
BERM/RHTH SE16 .... 112 B1
Queen Charlotte's &
Chelsea Hospital
SHB W12 .... 87 K5
Queen Charlotte's Cottage,
Kew Gardens
RCH/KEW TW9 .... 124 E1
Queen Elizabeth College
KENS W8 .... 14 A1
Queen Elizabeth
Conference Centre
WEST SW1P 17 H2
Queen Elizabeth Hall
STHWK SE1 .... 11 L8
Queen Elizabeth Hospital
WOOL/PLUM SE18 .... 114 E5
Queen Elizabeth II School
MV/WKIL W9 .... 88 D3
Queen Elizabeth Leisure Centre
BAR EN5 .... 26 D3
Queen Elizabeths Boys School
BAR EN5 .... 26 B2
Queen Elizabeths Girls School
BAR EN5 .... 26 D3
Queen Elizabeth Stadium
EN EN1 .... 30 B1
Queenhithe Stairs
BLKFR EC4V 12 E7
Queen Mary College
WCHPL E1 .... 93 F3
Queen Marys Hospital
SCUP DA14 .... 155 G4
Queen Mary's Hospital
HAMP NW3 .... 71 G2
Queen Mary's Hospital
for Children
SUT SM1 .... 162 B7
Queen Mary's
University Hospital
PUT/ROE SW15 .... 126 D5
Queen Mary & Westfield College
SWFD E18 .... 44 E7
Queen Mother Sports Centre
PIM SW1V 16 E5
Queensbridge Primary School
HACK E8 .... 7 M2
Queensbridge Sports Centre
HACK E8 .... 7 M1
Queen's Building
HTHAIR TW6 .... 120 E2
Queensbury ⊖
STAN HA7 .... 50 B2
Queens Business &
Secretarial College
SKENS SW7 .... 15 G5
The Queens CE Primary School
RCH/KEW TW9 .... 105 G6
Queen's Club
WKENS W14 .... 107 H4
Queens College London
CAVSQ/HST W1G 10 C3
Queens College
Preparatory School
CAVSQ/HST W1G 10 C3
The Queen's Gallery
BGVA SW1W 16 D2
Queens Gate School
SKENS SW7 .... 15 G5
Queens Hospital
ROMW/RG RM7 .... 63 G6
The Queens House
GNWCH SE10 .... 113 G5
Queens Ice Rink & Bowl
BAY/PAD W2 .... 8 D7
Queensland College London -
London Campus
ACT W3 .... 86 D7
Queens Manor Primary School
FUL/PGN SW6 .... 107 F6
Queensmead School
RSLP HA4 .... 65 H3
Queensmead Sports Centre
RSLP HA4 .... 65 H4
Queens Medical Centre
RCHPK/HAM TW10 .... 125 G4
Queensmill School
FUL/PGN SW6 .... 127 K1
Queens Park ⊖ ⇌
KIL/WHAMP NW6 .... 88 D1
Queens Park Community School
WLSDN NW10 .... 70 A7
Queens Park Health Centre
NKENS W10 .... 88 C2

Queens Park Primary School
NKENS W10 .... 88 C2
Queens Park Rangers FC
(Loftus Road Stadium)
SHB W12 .... 87 K7
Queen's Road Cemetery
CROY/NA CR0 .... 164 D5
Queen's Road Peckham ⇌
PECK SE15 .... 111 J7
Queens School
BUSH WD23 .... 21 K2
Queens Theatre
SOHO/SHAV W1D 11 G6
Queenstown Road Battersea ⇌
VX/NE SW8 .... 109 G7
Queensway ⊖
BAY/PAD W2 .... 8 C6
Queensway Business Centre
PEND EN3 .... 30 E3
Queenswell Infant School
TRDG/WHET N20 .... 39 H1
Queen Victoria Memorial
WHALL SW1A 16 E2
The Quest Academy
SAND/SEL CR2 .... 179 H1
Quest Business Training
SKENS SW7 .... 14 D6
The Questors Theatre
EA W5 .... 85 J6
Quintin Kynaston School
STJWD NW8 .... 2 F4
Quwwat UL Islam Girl's School
FSTGT E7 .... 76 E3
Radcliffe College
SOHO/SHAV W1D 10 E5
Radisson Blu Hotel
POP/IOD E14 .... 94 A4
Radisson Edwardian Hotel
MBLAR W1H 9 M4
Radisson Edwardian
Berkshire Hotel
OXSTW W1C 10 C5
Radisson Edwardian
Grafton Hotel
CAMTN NW1 .... 4 E9
Radisson Edwardian Hotel
HYS/HAR UB3 .... 101 F6
RSQ WC1B 11 H3
Radisson Edwardian
Marlborough Hotel
NOXST/BSQ WC1A 11 H4
Radisson Edwardian
Mayfair Hotel
MYFR/PICC W1J 10 D7
Radisson Edwardian
Mountbatten Hotel
LSQ/SEVD WC2H 11 J5
Radisson Edwardian
Vanderbilt Hotel
SKENS SW7 .... 14 F5
Radnor House
TWK TW1 .... 143 G7
RAF West Ruislip (University
of Maryland)
HGDN/ICK UB10 .... 64 A1
Raglan Infant School
EN EN1 .... 30 A5
Raglan Junior School
EN EN1 .... 30 A6
Raglan Primary School
HAYES BR2 .... 168 B3
Railton Road Clinic
HNHL SE24 .... 130 C4
Rainbow Clinic
BAY/PAD W2 .... 9 H1
Rainbow Industrial Estate
RYNPK SW20 .... 160 E1
Rainbow Montessori School
KIL/WHAMP NW6 .... 2 C2
Rainbow Quay
BERM/RHTH SE16 .... 112 B2
Rainbow School for
Autistic Children
WAND/EARL SW18 .... 147 G1
Raines Foundation School
BETH E2 .... 92 D2
Rainham ⇌
RAIN RM13 .... 99 J3
Rainham Hall (NT)
RAIN RM13 .... 99 J3
Rainham Marshes RSPB Reserve
RAIN RM13 .... 99 K6
Rainham Trading Estate
RAIN RM13 .... 99 G2
Rainham Village Primary School
RAIN RM13 .... 99 J3
Ramac Industrial Estate
CHARL SE7 .... 113 K4
Ramada Encore Hotel
ACT W3 .... 87 F4
Ramada Hotel
BAY/PAD W2 .... 8 C7
Ramada Hotel & Suites
CAN/RD E16 .... 95 H6
Ramada London Heathrow
HEST TW5 .... 101 K7
Rambert School of Ballet &
Contemporary Dance
TWK TW1 .... 124 C4
Randal Cremer Primary School
BETH E2 .... 7 L5
Ranelagh Gardens (site of
Chelsea Flower Show)
BGVA SW1W 16 B8
Ranelagh Primary School
SRTFD E15 .... 94 C1
Rangefield Primary School
BMLY BR1 .... 152 C4
Ransomes Dock Business Centre
BTSEA SW11 .... 108 D6
The Rathbone Education Centre
CAN/RD E16 .... 94 D4
Rathfern Primary School
FSTH SE23 .... 132 C7
Ravenor Primary School
GFD/PVL UB6 .... 84 A2
Ravensbourne
GNWCH SE10 .... 94 C7
Ravensbourne ⇌
BECK BR3 .... 152 A6
The Ravensbourne School
HAYES BR2 .... 168 B3
Ravenscourt Park ⊖
HMSMTH W6 .... 106 D3
Ravenscourt Park
Preparatory School
HMSMTH W6 .... 106 D3
Ravenscroft Medical Centre
GLDGN NW11 .... 52 D6
Ravenscroft Primary School
CAN/RD E16 .... 94 E3
Ravenscroft School
TRDG/WHET N20 .... 26 D6

Ravenside Retail Park
UED N18 .... 43 F5
Ravens Lawn Tennis Club
NFNCH/WDSPK N12 ...... 39 H3
Ravenstone
Preparatory School
SKENS SW7 .... 14 F4
Ravenstone Primary School
BAL SW12 .... 129 F7
Ravenswood Industrial Estate
WALTH E17 .... 58 A3
Ravens Wood School
HAYES BR2 .... 181 H2
Rayat London College
HEST TW5 .... 102 E6
Ray Lodge Primary School
WFD IG8 .... 45 H5
Rayners Lane ⊖
RYLN/HDSTN HA2 .... 47 K7
Raynes Park ⇌
RYNPK SW20 .... 161 F1
Raynes Park High School
RYNPK SW20 .... 160 E2
Raynes Park Sports Ground
RYNPK SW20 .... 160 D1
Raynes Park Vale FC
RYNPK SW20 .... 161 G4
Raynham Primary School
UED N18 .... 42 C4
RCA Sculpture School
BTSEA SW11 .... 108 D6
Reay Primary School
BRXN/ST SW9 .... 110 B6
Records Office
CLKNW EC1R 6 B9
Rectory Business Centre
SCUP DA14 .... 155 H3
Rectory Road ⇌
STNW/STAM N16 .... 74 C2
Red Balloon Learner Centre
HRW HA1 .... 49 F6
Redbridge ⊖
REDBR IG4 .... 59 H5
Redbridge College
CHDH RM6 .... 61 H4
Redbridge Drama Centre
SWFD E18 .... 44 E7
Redbridge Museum
IL IG1 .... 78 B2
Redbridge Primary School
REDBR IG4 .... 59 J4
Redburn Industrial Estate
PEND EN3 .... 31 F5
Redcliffe School
WBPTN SW10 .... 14 E9
Reddiford School
PIN HA5 .... 47 J3
Redford Lodge
Psychiatric Hospital
ED N9 .... 42 C1
Red Gates School
CROY/NA CR0 .... 177 G4
Redhill Primary School
CHST BR7 .... 154 B5
Red House (NT)
BXLYHS DA6 .... 137 F3
Redlands Primary School
WCHPL E1 .... 92 E4
Red Lion Business Park
SURB KT6 .... 172 B1
Redriff Primary School
BERM/RHTH SE16 .... 112 B1
Red Rose Trading Estate
EBAR EN4 .... 27 H4
Reeves Corner ⊖
CROY/NA CR0 .... 177 H1
Regal International College
ALP/SUD HA0 .... 68 A4
Regent Business Centre
HYS/HAR UB3 .... 102 A1
Regent Clinic
CAVSQ/HST W1G 10 C3
Regent College London
PIN HA5 .... 47 K6
Regent's Park ⊖
CAMTN NW1 .... 10 C1
Regent's Park Barracks
CAMTN NW1 .... 4 C6
Regent's Park Clinic
CAMTN NW1 .... 3 L9
Regent's Park Medical Centre
CAMTN NW1 .... 4 D7
Regent's Park Open Air Theatre
CAMTN NW1 .... 4 A8
Regent's Park Track
STJWD NW8 .... 3 L5
Regina Coeli RC Primary School
SAND/SEL CR2 .... 177 H6
Renaissance Hotel
HTHAIR TW6 .... 100 E7
Renoir Cinema
BMSBY WC1N 5 K9
Renwick Industrial Estate
BARK IG11 .... 97 H1
Rewards Centre
HSLW TW3 .... 123 H2
Reynard Mills Trading Estate
BTFD TW8 .... 104 D4
Reynolds Sports Centre
ACT W3 .... 105 H1
Rhodes Avenue Primary School
WDGN N22 .... 40 C7
Rhodes Farm Clinic
MLHL NW7 .... 38 A3
Rhyl Primary School
KTTN NW5 .... 72 A5
RIBA Library Drawings &
Manuscript Collection
MBLAR W1H 9 M4
Ricards Lodge High School
WIM/MER SW19 .... 146 D3
Richard Alibon Primary School
DAGE RM10 .... 80 C4
Richard Atkins Primary School
BRXS/STRHM SW2 ...... 129 K6
Richard Cloudesley School
STLK EC1Y 12 E1
Richard Cobden
Primary School
CAMTN NW1 .... 4 F4
Richdales Institute
ALP/SUD HA0 .... 67 K7
Rich Industrial Estate
PECK SE15 .... 111 J5
STHWK SE1 .... 19 L6
Richmond ⇌ ⊖ ⊖
RCH/KEW TW9 .... 125 F3
Richmond Adult &
Community College
RCH/KEW TW9 .... 124 D3
Richmond American
International University
KENS W8 .... 14 C2

Richmond American
International University
in London
RCHPK/HAM TW10 .... 125 F5
The Richmond Clinic
RCH/KEW TW9 .... 125 G3
Richmond Community College
TWK TW1 .... 124 A7
Richmond FC
RCH/KEW TW9 .... 124 E3
The Richmond Gate Hotel
RCHPK/HAM TW10 .... 125 F6
The Richmond Golf Club
RCHPK/HAM TW10 .... 144 A5
The Richmond Green
Medical Centre
RCH/KEW TW9 .... 124 E4
The Richmond Hill Hotel
RCHPK/HAM TW10 .... 125 F6
Richmond House School
HPTN TW12 .... 141 M4
Richmond Magistrates Court
RCH/KEW TW9 .... 124 E3
Richmond Park Academy
MORT/ESHN SW14 .... 126 B3
Richmond Park Golf Club
PUT/ROE SW15 .... 126 B6
Richmond Park National
Nature Reserve
RCHPK/HAM TW10 .... 145 G1
Richmond Road
Medical Centre
KUTN/CMB KT2 .... 144 A6
Richmond Theatre
RCH/KEW TW9 .... 124 E3
Richmond upon Thames College
WHTN TW2 .... 123 J5
Ridge House Clinic
WCHMH N21 .... 29 K6
Ridgeway Primary School
SAND/SEL CR2 .... 178 A7
Rio Cinema
HACK E8 .... 74 B4
Ripley Arts Centre
BMLY BR1 .... 153 H7
Ripple Primary School
BARK IG11 .... 78 E7
Rippleside Cemetery
BARK IG11 .... 79 G7
Risley Avenue Primary School
TOTM N17 .... 42 A7
The Ritz Hotel
WHALL SW1A 10 E8
Ritzy Cinema
BRXN/ST SW9 .... 130 B3
River Brent Business Park
HNWL W7 .... 103 K4
River Gardens Business Centre
EBED/NFELT TW14 .... 122 A3
River House Montessori School
POP/IOD E14 .... 93 J7
Riverley Primary School
LEY E10 .... 57 J7
River Mole Business Park
ESH/CLAY KT10 .... 157 F7
River Place Health Centre
IS N1 .... 6 E2
River Road Business Park
BARK IG11 .... 96 E2
Riversdale Primary School
WAND/EARL SW18 .... 127 M4
Riverside Business Centre
WAND/EARL SW18 .... 128 A7
Riverside Business Park
WIM/MER SW19 .... 147 G7
Riverside Community
Health Care
WKENS W14 .... 107 G2
Riverside Golf Club
THMD SE28 .... 98 A5
Riverside Industrial Estate
BARK IG11 .... 97 G2
DART DA1 .... 139 H4
Riverside Primary School
BERM/RHTH SE16 .... 111 H1
Riverside Quarter
WAND/EARL SW18 .... 127 K3
Riverside Studios Cinema
HMSMTH W6 .... 107 F4
Riverside Wandle Trading Estate
MTCM CR4 .... 162 E6
Riverston School
LEE/GVPK SE12 .... 133 K4
Riverview CE Primary School
HOR/WEW KT19 .... 172 E3
The RJ Mitchell Primary School
HCH RM12 .... 81 K5
RNLI Lifeboat Station
TWRH EC3N 13 K8
Roan Industrial Estate
MTCM CR4 .... 147 J7
Robert Blair Primary School
HOLWY N7 .... 72 E5
Robert Browning
Primary School
WALW SE17 .... 18 F7
Robert Clack School
BCTR RM8 .... 80 B1
Robin Hood Infant School
SUT SM1 .... 174 E4
Robin Hood Junior School
SUT SM1 .... 175 F4
Robin Hood Lane Health Centre
SUT SM1 .... 174 E4
Robin Hood Primary School
KUTN/CMB KT2 .... 145 F4
Robinsfield Infant School
STJWD NW8 .... 3 H5
The Roche School
WAND/EARL SW18 .... 127 K4
Rockliffe Manor
Primary School
WOOL/PLUM SE18 .... 116 A5
Rockmount Primary School
NRWD SE19 .... 149 J5
Rockware Business Centre
GFD/PVL UB6 .... 66 D7
Roding Lane Cemetery
WFD IG8 .... 45 J7
Roding Primary School
BCTR RM8 .... 79 J3
WFD IG8 .... 45 J6
Roding Valley ⊖
BKHH IG9 .... 45 H3
Roe Green Junior School
CDALE/KGS NW9 .... 50 D3
Roehampton Church School
PUT/ROE SW15 .... 126 E6
The Roehampton
Priory Hospital
PUT/ROE SW15 .... 126 C3
Roehampton Recreation Centre
PUT/ROE SW15 .... 126 C6

Roehampton University
(Digby Stuart College)
PUT/ROE SW15 .... 126 C4
Roehampton University
(Froebel College)
PUT/ROE SW15 .... 126 C5
Roehampton University
(Southlands College)
PUT/ROE SW15 .... 126 C4
Roehampton University
(Whitelands College)
PUT/ROE SW15 .... 126 C6
Roger Ascham Primary School
WALTH E17 .... 43 H7
Roger Bannister Sports Ground
KTN/HRWW/WS HA3 .... 34 C5
Rokeby School
KUTN/CMB KT2 .... 144 E6
SRTFD E15 .... 76 B6
Rokesly Junior School
CEND/HSY/T N8 .... 54 E4
Roman Bath
TPL/STR WC2R 11 M6
Roman Industrial Estate
CROY/NA CR0 .... 165 F6
Roman Road Primary School
EHAM E6 .... 95 H3
Romford ⇌
ROM RM1 .... 63 G5
Romford Cemetery
ROMW/RG RM7 .... 62 E6
Romford Clinic
ROM RM1 .... 63 H3
Romford County Court
ROM RM1 .... 63 H3
Romford Golf Club
GPK RM2 .... 63 J2
Romford Ice Arena
ROMW/RG RM7 .... 63 G6
Romford IT Learning Centre
ROM RM1 .... 63 G4
Romford Shopping Hall
ROM RM1 .... 63 G3
Ronald Rose Primary School
PUT/ROE SW15 .... 127 G6
Rood Lane Medical Centre
FENCHST EC3M 13 J6
Rooks Heath College Business
& Enterprise
RYLN/HDSTN HA2 .... 66 A2
Roosevelt Memorial
MYFR/PKLN W1K 10 B6
Ropery Business Park
CHARL SE7 .... 114 B3
Rosary Priory High School
BUSH WD23 .... 22 E5
Rosary RC Infant School
HEST TW5 .... 102 E5
Rosary RC Primary School
HAMP NW3 .... 71 J4
Rosebery Industrial Park
TOTM N17 .... 56 D1
Rose Bruford College
BFN/LL DA15 .... 136 C7
Rosedale College
HYS/HAR UB3 .... 82 B5
Roselands Clinic
NWMAL KT3 .... 159 K3
Rosemary Works School
IS N1 .... 7 H3
Rose McAndrew Clinic
BRXN/ST SW9 .... 130 A1
Rosemead Preparatory School
DUL SE21 .... 149 J1
Rosendale Primary School
DUL SE21 .... 130 D6
Rose of Kingston
(Kingston Theatre)
KUT/HW KT1 .... 158 E1
Rose Theatre Exhibition
STHWK SE1 .... 12 E8
Rosetta Primary School
CAN/RD E16 .... 95 F4
Rosewood Medical Centre
HCH RM12 .... 81 K4
Rosh Pinah Primary School
EDGW HA8 .... 36 D1
Rosslyn Park RFC
PUT/ROE SW15 .... 126 C3
Rotherfield Primary School
IS N1 .... 6 F3
Rotherhithe ⊖
BERM/RHTH SE16 .... 111 K1
Rotherhithe Civic Centre
BERM/RHTH SE16 .... 111 K1
Rotherhithe Primary School
BERM/RHTH SE16 .... 111 K1
The Rotunda
KUT/HW KT1 .... 159 F1
The Roundhouse Theatre
CAMTN NW1 .... 4 A1
Roundshaw J & I School
WLGTN SM6 .... 176 B6
Rowan Preparatory School
ESH/CLAY KT10 .... 171 F6
Rowans School
RYNPK SW20 .... 145 J6
Rowley Industrial Park
ACT W3 .... 105 J2
Roxbourne Junior School
RYLN/HDSTN HA2 .... 65 H1
Roxbourne Medical Centre
RYLN/HDSTN HA2 .... 66 B1
Roxeth Mead School
RYLN/HDSTN HA2 .... 66 D1
Roxeth Primary School
RYLN/HDSTN HA2 .... 66 D1
Roxwell Trading Park
LEY E10 .... 57 G6
Royal Academy of Arts
MYFR/PICC W1J 10 E7
Royal Academy of Dramatic Art
GWRST WC1E 11 G2
Royal Academy of Music
CAMTN NW1 .... 10 B1
Royal Air Force
Museum London
CDALE/KGS NW9 .... 51 J1
Royal Albert ⊖
CAN/RD E16 .... 95 J6
Royal Albert Hall
SKENS SW7 .... 15 G2
Royal Arsenal
WOOL/PLUM SE18 .... 115 G2
Royal Artillery Barracks
WOOL/PLUM SE18 .... 114 E5
The Royal Ballet School
(White Lodge)
RCHPK/HAM TW10 .... 126 A7
Royal Ballet Upper School
COVGDN WC2E 11 K5
Royal Blackheath Golf Club
ELTH/MOT SE9 .... 134 E6

Royal Botanic Gardens, Kew
BTFD TW8 .... 105 F6
Royal Botanic Gardens
Kew School
RCH/KEW TW9 .... 105 G6
Royal Brompton Hospital
CHEL SW3 .... 15 J7
Royal College of Anaesthetists
RSQ WC1B 11 J2
Royal College of Art
SKENS SW7 .... 14 F2
SKENS SW7 .... 14 F4
Royal College of Music
SHB W12 .... 106 D2
SKENS SW7 .... 15 G3
Royal College of Nursing
CAMTN NW1 .... 4 F9
IS N1 .... 6 C4
Royal College of Obstetricians
& Gynaecologists
CAMTN NW1 .... 3 J1
Royal College
of Ophthalmologists
CAMTN NW1 .... 10 A1
Royal College of
Paediatrics & Child Health
GTPST W1W 10 D2
The Royal College of Pathology
STJS SW1Y 11 G9
Royal College of Physicians
CAMTN NW1 .... 4 C9
Royal College of Surgeons
LINN WC2A 11 M4
Royal College of
Veterinary Surgeons
WEST SW1P 17 J5
Royal Courts of Justice
LINN WC2A 11 M5
Royal Court Theatre
BGVA SW1W 16 A4
Royal Court Young
Peoples Theatre
NKENS W10 .... 88 C4
The Royal Docks
Community School
CAN/RD E16 .... 95 G5
Royal Docks Medical Centre
EHAM E6 .... 96 A5
Royal Exchange
BANK EC3V 13 H5
Royal Festival Hall
STHWK SE1 .... 11 L9
Royal Free Hospital School
of Medicine
HAMP NW3 .... 71 J4
Royal Garden Hotel
KENS W8 .... 14 D1
Royal Geographical Society
SKENS SW7 .... 15 G2
The Royal Horseguards Hotel
WHALL SW1A 11 K9
Royal Horticultural Society
New Hall
WEST SW1P 17 G4
Royal Horticultural Society
Old Hall
WEST SW1P 17 G5
Royal Hospital
RCH/KEW TW9 .... 125 F2
Royal Hospital Chelsea
CHEL SW3 .... 16 A9
Royal Hospital for
Neuro-disability
PUT/ROE SW15 .... 127 H5
Royal Hospital & Home
PUT/ROE SW15 .... 126 E6
Royal Hospital Museum
CHEL SW3 .... 16 A8
Royal Institute of
British Architects
REGST W1B 10 D2
Royal Institution's
Faraday Museum
CONDST W1S 10 D7
The Royal London Estate
TOTM N17 .... 42 D6
Royal London
Homeopathic Hospital
BMSBY WC1N 11 K2
Royal Marsden Hospital
CHEL SW3 .... 15 H7
The Royal Mews
BGVA SW1W 16 D3
Royal Mid-Surrey Golf Club
RCH/KEW TW9 .... 124 E2
Royal Military School of Music
WHTN TW2 .... 123 J5
Royal Mint Court
TWRH EC3N 13 M7
Royal National
Orthopaedic Hospital
GTPST W1W 10 D1
STAN HA7 .... 23 H7
Royal National Theatre
STHWK SE1 .... 12 A8
Royal National
Throat Nose & Ear Hospital
FSBYW WC1X 5 L7
Royal Oak ⊖
BAY/PAD W2 .... 8 D3
Royal Opera House
COVGDN WC2E 11 K5
The Royal Oak
HAMP NW3 .... 71 H3
Royal Society of Arts
CHCR WC2N 11 K7
Royal Society of Medicine
CAVSQ/HST W1G 10 C4
The Royal Trafalgar Hotel
LSQ/SEVD WC2H 11 H7
Royal Veterinary College
CAMTN NW1 .... 5 G4
Royal Victoria ⊖
CAN/RD E16 .... 94 E6
Royal Victoria Docks
Watersports Centre
CAN/RD E16 .... 94 E6
Royal Wimbledon Golf Club
WIM/MER SW19 .... 145 K4
Royston Primary School
PGE/AN SE20 .... 151 F7
RSPCA Animal Hospital
FSBYPK N4 .... 73 F1
Rudolph Steiner Hall
CAMTN NW1 .... 3 L1
Rufus Business Centre
WIM/MER SW19 .... 147 F1
Ruislip ⊖
RSLP HA4 .... 64 C1
Ruislip Gardens ⊖
RSLP HA4 .... 64 E3
Ruislip Gardens Primary School
RSLP HA4 .... 64 C3

Ruislip Golf Club
HGDN/ICK UB10 .... 64 A1
Ruislip High School
RSLP HA4 .... 64 E2
Ruislip Manor ⊖
RSLP HA4 .... 46 C4
Ruislip Manor FC
RSLP HA4 .... 64 C1
Ruislip RFC
RSLP HA4 .... 64 C1
Ruislip Woods
National Nature Reserve
NTHWD HA6 .... 46 A2
RSLP HA4 .... 46 C4
Rushcroft School
CHING E4 .... 43 K6
Rushey Green Primary School
CAT SE6 .... 132 E7
Rush Green Primary School
ROMW/RG RM7 .... 63 F7
Rushmore Primary School
CLPT E5 .... 74 E3
Ruskin House School
HNHL SE24 .... 130 D4
The Russell School
RCHPK/HAM TW10 .... 124 E7
Russell Square ⊖
STPAN WC1H 11 J1
Rutlish School
RYNPK SW20 .... 161 J1
Ruxley Corner
Industrial Estate
SCUP DA14 .... 155 K5
Ruxley Park Golf Centre
STMC/STPC BR5 .... 155 K7
Ryefield Primary School
HGDN/ICK UB10 .... 64 B7
Ryelands Primary School
SNWD SE25 .... 165 J4
Rye Oak Primary School
PECK SE15 .... 131 J2
Saatchi Gallery
CHEL SW3 .... 15 M7
Sacred Heart Catholic
Primary School
PUT/ROE SW15 .... 126 D4
Sacred Heart High School
HMSMTH W6 .... 107 F3
Sacred Heart Language College
KTN/HRWW/WS HA3 .... 48 E1
Sacred Heart RC Infant School
BTSEA SW11 .... 128 D1
Sacred Heart RC JMI School
TRDG/WHET N20 .... 39 J1
Sacred Heart RC Primary School
NWMAL KT3 .... 160 D3
OXHEY WD19 .... 21 K5
RSLP HA4 .... 64 C1
TEDD TW11 .... 143 H6
Sacred Heart RC School
CMBW SE5 .... 110 D7
Sacred Heart School
HOLWY N7 .... 73 F4
Saddlers Hall
CITYW EC2V 12 F4
Sadler's Wells Theatre
CLKNW EC1R 6 B7
SAE Institute
HOLWY N7 .... 72 E4
Safari Cinema
CROY/NA CR0 .... 164 C7
Safari Cinema & Bingo
HRW HA1 .... 49 F4
Saffron Green Primary School
BORE WD6 .... 25 F3
Sai Medical Centre
POP/IOD E14 .... 94 A6
St Agatha's RC Primary School
KUTN/CMB KT2 .... 144 B5
St Agnes RC Primary School
BOW E3 .... 93 J2
CRICK NW2 .... 70 C2
St Aidans Primary School
FSBYPK N4 .... 55 G6
St Aidans RC Primary School
IL IG1 .... 60 D7
St Albans CE Primary School
HCIRC EC1N 12 A2
St Albans Health Clinic
HGT N6 .... 72 A2
St Albans RC Aided
Primary School
E/WMO/HCT KT8 .... 157 G4
St Albans RC Church &
School Presbytery
HCH RM12 .... 81 J4
St Albans RC JMI School
HCH RM12 .... 81 K6
St Albans Road Infant School
DART DA1 .... 139 J5
St Alfege with St Peter CE
Primary School
GNWCH SE10 .... 113 F5
St Aloysius RC College
HGT N6 .... 54 C7
St Aloysius RC Infant School
CAMTN NW1 .... 5 G7
St Aloysius RC Junior School
CAMTN NW1 .... 4 F6
St Andrew & St Francis CE
JMI School
CRICK NW2 .... 69 J5
St Andrews CE High School
CROY/NA CR0 .... 177 H2
St Andrews CE JMI School
TRDG/WHET N20 .... 38 D1
St Andrews CE Primary School
EN EN1 .... 29 K1
STHGT/OAK N14 .... 28 C6
St Andrews Greek School
CAMTN NW1 .... 72 B5
St Andrews Primary School
BRXN/ST SW9 .... 130 A1
IS N1 .... 5 M3
St Andrews & St Marks CE
Junior School
SURB KT6 .... 158 E4
St Andrews School
RYLN/HDSTN HA2 .... 48 B4
WLSDN NW10 .... 69 K6
St Angela's & St Bonaventures
Sixth Form Centre
FSTGT E7 .... 77 G3
St Angela's Ursuline School
FSTGT E7 .... 77 F5
St Annes Catholic High School
for Girls
ENC/FH EN2 .... 30 A3
PLMGR N13 .... 41 G3
St Annes CE Primary School
WAND/EARL SW18 .... 128 A4
St Annes RC Primary School
VX/NE SW8 .... 17 L9

St Anne's Special School
MRDN SM4 .... 161 K4
St Anne's Trading Estate
POP/IOD E14 .... 93 H5
St Anns CE Primary School
SEVS/STOTM N15 .... 55 K4
St Ann's General Hospital
FSBYPK N4 .... 55 J4
St Anns School
HNWL W7 .... 84 E7
St Ann's Shopping Centre
HRW HA1 .... 48 E5
St Anselms RC Primary School
DART DA1 .... 139 J4
HRW HA1 .... 48 E6
NWDGN UB2 .... 102 E2
St Anselms RC Primary School
TOOT SW17 .... 148 A2
St Anthonys Hospital
WPK KT4 .... 161 G7
St Anthonys RC Primary School
EDUL SE22 .... 131 H5
PGE/AN SE20 .... 150 D7
WATW WD18 .... 20 C4
St Anthony's School
(Junior House)
HAMP NW3 .... 71 H4
St Anthony's School
(Senior House)
HAMP NW3 .... 71 G4
St Antonys RC Primary School
FSTGT E7 .... 76 E6
WFD IG8 .... 44 E3
St Aubyns School
WFD IG8 .... 44 D6
St Augustines CE High School
KIL/WHAMP NW6 .... 2 B6
St Augustines Primary School
BELV DA17 .... 117 G2
KIL/WHAMP NW6 .... 2 B5
St Augustines Priory School
EA W5 .... 86 A4
St Augustines RC
Infant School
GNTH/NBYPK IG2 .... 60 B4
St Augustines RC
Primary School
CAT SE6 .... 151 K4
GNTH/NBYPK IG2 .... 60 B4
WKENS W14 .... 107 H5
St Barnabas CE Primary School
BGVA SW1W 16 B7
St Barnabas & St Philip's CE
Primary School
KENS W8 .... 14 A4
St Bartholomews CE
Primary School
SYD SE26 .... 150 E3
St Bartholomews Hospital
STBT EC1A 12 D3
St Bartholomews
Medical Centre
FARR EC1M 12 D1
St Bartholomews & Royal
London School of Medicine
FARR EC1M 12 E2
St Bartholomew's the Great
STBT EC1A 12 D3
St Bartholomews & The Royal
London Hospital
WCHPL E1 .... 92 D4
St Barts Hospital Sports Ground
CHST BR7 .... 154 D5
St Bedes RC Infant School
BAL SW12 .... 129 J7
St Bedes RC Primary School
CHDH RM6 .... 61 J4
St Benedicts Junior School
EA W5 .... 85 J4
St Benedicts School
EA W5 .... 85 K4
St Bernadette Catholic
Junior School
BAL SW12 .... 129 H6
St Bernadettes RC First &
Middle School
KTN/HRWW/WS HA3 .... 50 A3
St Bonaventures School
FSTGT E7 .... 76 E6
St Boniface RC Primary School
TOOT SW17 .... 147 K4
St Catherines RC Girls School
BXLYHS DA6 .... 137 J4
St Catherines RC J & I School
WDR/YW UB7 .... 100 A1
St Catherines RC School
BAR EN5 .... 26 D3
St Catherines School
TWK TW1 .... 143 F1
St Cecilias CE School
WAND/EARL SW18 .... 127 J6
St Cecilias RC Primary School
WPK KT4 .... 174 B1
St Chads RC Primary School
SNWD SE25 .... 165 F4
St Charles Hospital
NKENS W10 .... 88 B4
St Charles Primary School
NKENS W10 .... 88 B4
St Christinas RC
Preparatory School
STJWD NW8 .... 3 K5
St Christophers School
BECK BR3 .... 167 F1
HAMP NW3 .... 71 H4
WBLY HA9 .... 68 B2
St Clare Business Park
HPTN TW12 .... 142 C5
St Clement Danes CE
Primary School
HOL/ALD WC2B 11 L5
St Clement & St James CE
Primary School
NTGHL W11 .... 88 B7
St Clements Hospital
BOW E3 .... 93 H2
St Clements Primary School
EW KT17 .... 173 H7
St Columbas RC Boys School
BXLYHS DA6 .... 137 J4
St Cuthbert with St Matthias CE
Primary School
ECT SW5 .... 14 B7
St Cyprians Greek Orthodox
Primary School
THHTH CR7 .... 164 D1
St Davids College
WWKM BR4 .... 166 E6
St Davids Health Centre
STWL/WRAY TW19 .... 120 A6
St Dominics RC Primary School
HAMP NW3 .... 71 K4
HOM E9 .... 75 G5

St Dominics Sixth Form College
HRW HA1 66 E1
St Dunstans CE Primary School
CHEAM SM3 174 C5
St Dunstans College
CAT SE6 132 C7
St Ebba's Hospital
HOR/WEW KT19 172 E7
St Edmunds RC Primary School
ED N9 30 D7
POP/IOD E14 112 D3
WHTN TW2 123 G6
St Edwards CE Comprehensive School
CHDH RM6 62 C5
St Edwards CE Primary School
ROM RM1 63 F3
St Edwards RC JMI School
STJWD NW8 9 J1
St Elizabeths RC Primary School
BETH E2 92 E1
RCHPK/HAM TW10 125 G5
St Eugene de Mazenod RC Primary School
KIL/WHAMP NW6 2 B2
St Faiths CE Primary School
WAND/EARL SW18 128 A4
St Fidelis Catholic Primary School
ERITH DA8 117 K5
St Francesca Cabrini Primary School
FSTH SE23 131 K5
St Francis de Sales RC J & I School
TOTM N17 42 B6
St Francis of Assisi Primary School
NKENS W10 88 B6
St Francis RC Primary School
PECK SE15 111 H5
SRTFD E15 76 C4
St Francis Xavier College
BAL SW12 129 G5
St Gabriels CE Primary School
PIM SW1V 16 E8
St George's Cathedral
STHWK SE1 18 B3
St Georges CE Primary School
BMLY BR1 168 B1
CMBW SE5 111 F6
VX/NE SW8 109 H6
St Georges College
HOLWY N7 73 G2
St Georges Elizabethan Theatre
HOLWY N7 72 D3
St Georges Hanover Square CE Primary School
MYFR/PKLN W1K 10 B7
St Georges Hospital
TOOT SW17 147 J4
St Georges Industrial Estate
KUTN/CMB KT2 143 K4
PLMGR N13 41 H6
St Georges Medical Centre
HDN NW4 51 K2
St Georges RC Primary School
ENC/FH EN2 29 K1
HRW HA1 67 F2
St Georges RC School
MV/WKIL W9 2 D6
St Georges Shopping Centre & Cinema
HRW HA1 48 D5
St Georges University of London
TOOT SW17 147 H4
St George the Martyr CE Primary School
BMSBY WC1N 11 L1
St George Wharf
VX/NE SW8 17 J9
St Gildas RC Junior School
CEND/HSY/T N8 54 E6
St Giles College London Central
RSQ WC1B 11 K2
St Giles School
SAND/SEL CR2 177 H5
St Gregorys High School
KTN/HRWW/WS HA3 49 K4
St Gregorys RC Primary School
EA W5 85 J3
St Helens Catholic Infant School
WALTH E17 58 A4
St Helens RC Primary School
BRXN/ST SW9 130 B2
CAN/RD E16 94 D3
St Helens School
NTHWD HA6 32 C5
St Helier ≠
MRDN SM4 161 K5
St Helier Hospital
CAR SM5 162 B7
St Hildas School
BUSH WD23 22 B6
St Ignatius RC Primary School
SEVS/STOTM N15 56 A5
SUN TW16 140 E7
St James CE J & I School
BERM/RHTH SE16 111 H2
St James CE Primary School
MUSWH N10 54 A3
PEND EN3 30 E1
St James CE Junior School
FSTGT E7 76 D4
St James Hatcham CE School
NWCR SE14 112 B7
St James Independent School for Girls
NTGHL W11 8 A6
St James Junior School
WKENS W14 107 H3
St James Medical Centre
CROY/NA CR0 164 E6
St James RC Primary School
HAYES BR2 169 G4
WHTN TW2 142 E2
St James & St Michaels CE Primary School
BAY/PAD W2 8 F6
St James Senior Girls School
WKENS W14 107 H3
St James's Health Centre
WALTH E17 57 G4
St James's Hotel & Club
WHALL SW1A 10 E8
St James's Palace
WHALL SW1A 10 F9
St James's Park ⊖
STJSPK SW1H 17 G3
St James Street ≠
WALTH E17 57 G4
St James the Great RC Primary School
PECK SE15 111 G7
THHTH CR7 164 C1
St Joachims RC Primary School
CAN/RD E16 95 G5
St Joan of Arc RC Primary School
HBRY N5 73 H3
St John Fisher RC Primary School
ERITHM DA18 117 F2
GFD/PVL UB6 85 J2
PIN HA5 48 A3
RYNPK SW20 161 F4
St John of Jerusalem CE Primary School
HOM E9 74 E6
St Johns ≠
DEPT SE8 132 D1
St Johns Ambulance Station
WEA W13 85 H7
St Johns & St James CE School
UED N18 42 B4
St Johns Angell Town CE Primary School
BRXN/ST SW9 130 B1
St Johns CE Primary School
BETH E2 92 E1
CROY/NA CR0 179 F2
FBAR/BDGN N11 39 K3
KUT/HW KT1 159 F2
PGE/AN SE20 150 E6
TRDG/WHET N20 39 G1
St Johns CE School
CDALE/KGS NW9 51 G4
St John's CE Walham Green Primary School
FUL/PGN SW6 107 H7
St Johns Church of England School
STAN HA7 35 G3
St John's Concert Hall
WEST SW1P 17 J4
St Johns Highbury Vale CE Primary School
HBRY N5 73 H3
St John's Hospital Day Centre
BTSEA SW11 128 C3
St John's Lodge
CAMTN NW1 4 A7
St Johns Primary School
WEA W13 85 G6
St Johns RC Primary School
BERM/RHTH SE16 112 B1
St Johns & St Clements CE J & I School
PECK SE15 131 H2
St Johns School
NTHWD HA6 33 F5
St Johns Upper Holloway CE Primary School
ARCH N19 72 C1
St Johns Walworth CE Primary School
WALW SE17 18 E6
St Johns Way Medical Centre
ARCH N19 54 D7
St John's Wood ⊖
STJWD NW8 3 G5
St Johns Wood Pre-Preparatory School
STJWD NW8 3 J7
St John the Baptist CE Junior School
KUT/HW KT1 143 K6
St John the Baptist CE Primary School
BMLY BR1 152 A3
St John the Baptist VA CE Primary School
IS N1 7 J6
St John the Divine CE Primary School
CMBW SE5 110 C6
St John the Evangelist RC Primary School
IS N1 6 C5
St John Vianney RC Primary School
SEVS/STOTM N15 55 H3
St Joseph's Annexe
ABYW SE2 116 D5
St Josephs Catholic Infant School
LEY E10 57 H7
St Josephs Catholic Junior School
CMBW SE5 110 D6
St Josephs Catholic Primary School
BMLY BR1 153 G6
DAGW RM9 80 B3
KUT/HW KT1 159 G1
St Josephs College
STRHM/NOR SW16 149 H5
St Josephs Convent School
WAN E11 58 E5
St Josephs Primary School
WAND/EARL SW18 127 K4
St Joseph's RC College
MLHL NW7 37 H3
St Josephs RC First & Middle School
KTN/HRWW/WS HA3 49 G1
St Josephs RC Infant School
NRWD SE19 149 J5
St Josephs RC J & I School
HDN NW4 51 K3
WBLY HA9 68 B4
St Josephs RC Junior School
LEY E10 57 J7
NRWD SE19 149 J5
St Josephs RC Primary School
ARCH N19 54 B7
BARK IG11 78 C7
BERM/RHTH SE16 111 K2
CHEL SW3 15 L6
DART DA1 138 A3
DEPT SE8 112 D6
GNWCH SE10 113 H4
HNWL W7 84 E7
HOL/ALD WC2B 11 K4
MV/WKIL W9 2 E8
OXHEY WD19 33 F2
STHWK SE1 18 F1
STHWK SE1 111 H1
WLSDN NW10 69 G6
St Judes CE Primary School
HNHL SE24 130 C5
STHWK SE1 18 C4
St Judes & St Pauls CE Primary School
IS N1 74 A4
St Katharine Pier
WAP E1W 13 M8
St Katherine
TPL/STR WC2R 11 M7
St Lawrence Business Centre
FELT TW13 141 F1
St Lawrence Catholic School
FELT TW13 141 F1
St Lawrence Junior School
E/WMO/HCT KT8 157 J2
St Lawrence University
BMSBY WC1N 11 M1
St Leonards CE Primary School
STRHM/NOR SW16 148 D4
St Leonards Hospital
IS N1 7 K5
St Luke's Catholic Sixth Form College
SCUP DA14 155 F4
St Lukes Cemetery
HAYES BR2 168 E5
St Lukes CE Primary School
CAN/RD E16 94 D5
FSBYE EC1V 6 F8
KUTN/CMB KT2 144 B7
MV/WKIL W9 88 D1
POP/IOD E14 113 G3
WNWD SE27 149 J4
St Luke's Health Centre
CAN/RD E16 94 D5
St Lukes Hospital for The Clergy
FITZ W1T 10 E1
St Lukes School
THHTH CR7 164 B3
St Lukes Woodside Hospital
MUSWH N10 54 A3
St Margaret Clitherow RC Primary School
THMD SE28 97 H7
St Margaret Lee CE Primary School
LEW SE13 133 H3
St Margaret's ≠
TWK TW1 124 C5
St Margarets Business Centre
TWK TW1 124 B6
St Margarets CE Primary School
WOOL/PLUM SE18 115 H5
St Margarets Clitherow RC Primary School
WBLY HA9 68 E2
St Margarets Primary School
BARK IG11 78 B7
St Margarets School
BUSH WD23 22 A6
HAMP NW3 71 F3
St Marks Catholic School
HSLW TW3 122 E2
St Marks CE Academy
MTCM CR4 163 G1
St Marks CE Primary School
ARCH N19 72 E1
HAYES BR2 167 K2
LBTH SE11 17 M9
SNWD SE25 165 H3
St Marks Industrial Estate
CAN/RD E16 95 H7
St Marks Primary School
HNWL W7 103 K1
MTCM CR4 162 E1
St Martin-in-the-Fields
CHCR WC2N 11 J7
St Martin in the Fields High School
BRXS/STRHM SW2 130 C7
St Martin of Porres Primary School
FBAR/BDGN N11 40 C5
St Martins Hospital
MYFR/PKLN W1K 10 A6
St Martins Medical Centre
RSLP HA4 46 C6
St Martins School
MLHL NW7 37 G4
St Martins School of Art
SOHO/SHAV W1D 11 H5
St Martins Theatre
LSQ/SEVD WC2H 11 H6
St Mary Abbots CE Primary School
KENS W8 14 C2
St Mary Abbots Church Hall
KENS W8 14 C1
St Mary & St Pancras CE Primary School
CAMTN NW1 5 G6
The St Marylebone CE School
MHST W1U 10 B2
St Marylebone Crematorium
FNCH N3 53 F2
St Mary Magdalene Academy
HOLWY N7 73 G5
St Mary Magdalene CE Primary School
MV/WKIL W9 8 C1
WOOL/PLUM SE18 114 E3
St Mary Magdalen RC Junior School
CRICK NW2 69 K5
St Mary Magdalens Catholic Primary School
MORT/ESHN SW14 126 A2
St Mary of The Angels RC Primary School
NTGHL W11 8 A4
St Marys Abbey
MLHL NW7 37 J2
St Mary & St Michael Primary School
WCHPL E1 92 E5
St Mary & St Peters CE Primary School
TEDD TW11 142 E4
St Marys Bryanston Square CE Primary School
MBLAR W1H 9 K2
St Marys Catholic Primary School
HCH RM12 63 J7
St Marys CE High School
HDN NW4 51 K2
St Marys CE Infant School
CEND/HSY/T N8 55 F3
St Marys CE Junior School
CEND/HSY/T N8 54 E3
STWL/WRAY TW19 120 B5
St Mary's Cemetery
BTSEA SW11 128 D4
St Marys CE Primary School
CHSGTN KT9 172 A5
EBAR EN4 27 J5
FNCH N3 38 D7
IS N1 6 D2
LEW SE13 132 E4
STNW/STAM N16 73 K1
TWK TW1 124 B6
WALTH E17 57 K3
WLSDN NW10 69 G5
St Mary's CE Primary School
PUT/ROE SW15 127 G2
St Mary's CE School
HDN NW4 51 K2
St Marys College
TWK TW1 143 F2
St Marys Greek Cathedral
WDGN N22 41 F7
St Marys High School
CROY/NA CR0 164 D7
St Marys Hospital
BAY/PAD W2 9 H4
St Marys Hospital Medical School
BAY/PAD W2 9 H4
St Marys Infant School
CAR SM5 175 J3
St Marys Kilburn Primary School
KIL/WHAMP NW6 2 B3
St Marys Magdalens Catholic Primary School
BROCKY SE4 132 B3
St Marys Primary School
WKENS W14 107 G2
St Marys RC Infant School
CAR SM5 175 K4
St Marys RC J & I School
CROY/NA CR0 164 E7
St Marys RC Junior School
FSBYPK N4 55 K4
St Marys RC Primary School
BECK BR3 152 A6
CLAP SW4 129 H4
ELTH/MOT SE9 135 F4
ISLW TW7 124 B2
KIL/WHAMP NW6 2 A5
NKENS W10 88 C3
PEND EN3 31 F3
VX/NE SW8 109 G7
WIM/MER SW19 146 E6
St Mary's RC Primary School
CHSWK W4 106 B4
St Marys & St Johns CE Primary School
HDN NW4 51 K4
St Marys School
CEND/HSY/T N8 55 F4
HAMP NW3 71 G4
St Mary's Western Eye Hospital
MBLAR W1H 9 L2
St Matthew Academy
LEW SE13 133 G2
St Matthews CE Primary School
PEND EN3 30 E4
RYNPK SW20 145 J7
SURB KT6 159 F6
St Matthias CE Primary School
BETH E2 7 M9
STNW/STAM N16 74 A4
St Meryl JMI School
OXHEY WD19 33 J2
St Michael & All Angels CE Academy
CMBW SE5 110 C6
St Michael at Bowes CE Junior School
PLMGR N13 41 G5
St Michaels & St Martins RC Primary School
HSLWW TW4 122 E2
St Michaels Catholic College
BERM/RHTH SE16 111 H1
St Michaels Catholic Grammar School
NFNCH/WDSPK N12 39 F4
St Michaels CE Primary School
CAMTN NW1 4 E3
HGT N6 54 A6
WAND/EARL SW18 127 J6
WDGN N22 41 F7
WELL DA16 116 D7
St Michaels RC Primary School
EHAM E6 95 K1
St Michaels Sydenham CE Primary School
SYD SE26 151 G3
The St Michael Steiner School
WAND/EARL SW18 127 K4
St Monicas RC Primary School
STHGT/OAK N14 40 E2
St Monica's RC Primary School
IS N1 7 J7
St Nicholas Centre
SUT SM1 175 F4
St Nicholas Preparatory School
SKENS SW7 15 H2
St Nicholas School
BORE WD6 24 A5
CDALE/KGS NW9 68 E1
CHST BR7 154 C6
St Olaves Preparatory School
ELTH/MOT SE9 154 B1
St Pancras Hospital
CAMTN NW1 5 G4
St Pancras International ≠ ⊖
KCROSS N1C 5 J6
St Pancras International Youth Hostel
CAMTN NW1 5 H7
St Pancras & Islington Cemetery
EFNCH N2 39 J7
St Pancras Renaissance Hotel
CAMTN NW1 5 H7
St Patricks Church School
STHWK SE1 12 A9
St Patricks Infant School
WAP E1W 92 D7
St Patricks International School
SOHO/SHAV W1D 10 F4
St Patricks Primary School
KTTN NW5 72 B5
St Patricks RC Primary School
WALTH E17 57 G3
WOOL/PLUM SE18 115 J3
St Paulinus CE Primary School
DART DA1 138 B3
St Paul's ⊖
STP EC4M 12 E4
St Pauls & All Hallows Junior School
TOTM N17 42 C6
St Pauls & All Hallows CE Infant School
TOTM N17 42 C6
St Paul's Cathedral
STP EC4M 12 E5
St Pauls Catholic College
SUN TW16 140 E7
St Pauls CE Primary School
BTFD TW8 104 E5
CHSGTN KT9 172 A3
FBAR/BDGN N11 40 A4
HAMP NW3 3 K2
MLHL NW7 37 K3
WALW SE17 18 D8
WCHMH N21 29 H6
St Pauls CE Junior School
KUTN/CMB KT2 144 C6
St Pauls Girls School
HMSMTH W6 107 G3
St Paul's Primary School
HMSMTH W6 107 F4
St Pauls RC Primary School
THDIT KT7 157 K6
WDGN N22 55 F1
St Pauls RC School
ABYW SE2 116 B5
St Pauls Road Medical Centre
IS N1 73 H5
St Pauls School
BARN SW13 106 E4
St Pauls Steiner School
IS N1 73 K5
St Pauls Trust School
BOW E3 93 J4
St Pauls with St Lukes CE Primary School
BOW E3 93 H4
St Pauls with St Michaels CE Primary School
HACK E8 74 C7
St Peter Chanel RC Primary School
SCUP DA14 155 J4
St Peter In Chains RC Infant School
CEND/HSY/T N8 54 E5
St Peters Catholic Primary School
ROM RM1 63 F2
St Peters CE Primary School
HMSMTH W6 106 D4
MV/WKIL W9 8 A1
WALW SE17 19 G8
WAP E1W 92 E7
St Peter's Church
KTBR SW1X 16 C3
St Peters Eaton Square CE Primary School
BGVA SW1W 16 C4
St Peter's Hospital
COVGDN WC2E 11 K6
St Peters Primary School
SAND/SEL CR2 177 K5
St Peters RC Primary School
DAGW RM9 80 B7
WOOL/PLUM SE18 115 G4
St Peter & St Paul RC Primary School
MTCM CR4 162 E3
STMC/STPC BR5 169 K1
St Peter & St Pauls Primary School
FSBYE EC1V 6 C9
St Philips School
CHSGTN KT9 171 K5
SKENS SW7 14 F6
St Phillips Infant School
SYD SE26 150 D3
St Philomenas Catholic High School
CAR SM5 175 J4
St Quintins Health Centre
NKENS W10 88 A4
St Raphaels Hospice
WPK KT4 174 B1
St Raphaels RC Primary School
NTHLT UB5 83 F1
St Raphaels Way Medical Centre
WLSDN NW10 68 E4
St Richards with St Andrews CE Primary School
RCHPK/HAM TW10 143 H2
St Robert Southwell RC Primary School
CDALE/KGS NW9 50 E5
St Saviour & St Olaves School
STHWK SE1 19 H4
St Saviours CE Primary School
HNHL SE24 130 D2
MV/WKIL W9 8 D1
POP/IOD E14 93 K4
St Saviour's CE Primary School
WALTH E17 57 H6
St Saviours CE Infant School
EA W5 85 K7
St Saviours RC Primary School
LEW SE13 133 F3
St Scholasticas RC Primary School
CLPT E5 74 C2
St Stephens CE Junior School
TWK TW1 124 B5
St Stephens CE Primary School
BAY/PAD W2 8 B3
DEPT SE8 132 D1
SHB W12 87 K7
St Stephens CE School
VX/NE SW8 109 K6
St Stephens RC Primary School
WELL DA16 136 B2
St Stephens School & Childrens Centre
EHAM E6 77 G6
St Swithun Wells Catholic Primary School
RSLP HA4 65 G2
The St Teresa Catholic Primary School
BCTR RM8 79 J3
St Teresa RC First & Middle School
KTN/HRWW/WS HA3 34 C7
St Teresa's Catholic Primary School
KTN/HRWW/WS HA3 34 B7
St Teresa's RC Primary School
BORE WD6 24 D1
St Theresas RC Primary School
FNCH N3 52 E2
St Thomas a' Becket RC Primary School
ABYW SE2 116 B2
St Thomas Becket RC Primary School
SNWD SE25 165 H5

St Thomas CE Primary School
  NKENS W10.............................88 C3
St Thomas Childrens
  Day Hospital
  LBTH SE11............................17 M7
St Thomas' Hospital
  STHWK SE1............................17 L3
St Thomas More
  Language College
  CHEL SW3.............................15 L6
St Thomas More RC
  Primary School
  BXLYHN DA7..........................137 G5
  ELTH/MOT SE9........................134 D2
St Thomas More RC School
  ELTH/MOT SE9........................135 F5
  WDGN N22.............................41 G6
St Thomas of Canterbury
  Catholic Primary School
  FUL/PGN SW6.........................107 J6
  MTCM CR4............................163 F7
St Thomas the Apostle College
  PECK SE15...........................111 K7
St Ursulas Convent School
  GNWCH SE10..........................113 G6
St Vincent De Paul RC
  Primary School
  WEST SW1P............................16 E4
St Vincents Catholic
  Primary School
  ELTH/MOT SE9........................153 J3
St Vincents Hospital
  PIN HA5..............................46 C2
St Vincents RC Primary School
  BCTR RM8.............................79 J1
  MLHL NW7.............................37 K3
St Vincent's RC Primary School
  MHST W1U.............................10 A3
St Walter & St John
  Sports Ground
  TOOT SW17...........................128 D2
St William of York
  Primary School
  FSTH SE23...........................132 B7
St Winefrides Catholic
  Primary School
  MNPK E12.............................77 K4
St Winifreds Catholic
  Junior School
  LEE/GVPK SE12.......................133 H4
St Winifreds RC Infant School
  LEW SE13............................133 H4
Salcombe Preparatory
  Lower School
  STHGT/OAK N14........................28 C3
Salcombe Preparatory
  School (Infants)
  STHGT/OAK N14........................28 B5
Salcombe Preparatory
  School (Juniors)
  STHGT/OAK N14........................28 B6
Salesian College
  BTSEA SW11..........................108 D7
Salisbury Primary School
  MNPK E12.............................77 H4
Salusbury School
  ED N9................................30 C1
Salters' Hall
  BARB EC2Y............................12 F3
Salusbury Primary School
  KIL/WHAMP NW6........................70 C2
Salvatorian College
  KTN/HRWW/WS HA3......................48 D3
Samuel Jones Industrial Estate
  PECK SE15...........................111 F6
Samuel Rhodes School
  IS N1................................6 A3
Sanderstead ≷
  SAND/SEL CR2........................177 K7
Sanderstead Junior School
  SAND/SEL CR2........................177 K7
Sandgate Trading Estate
  BERM/RHTH SE16......................111 K4
Sandhurst Primary School
  CAT SE6.............................133 H6
Sandilands ⊖
  CROY/NA CR0.........................178 B1
Sandown Grandstand &
  Exhibition Centre
  ESH/CLAY KT10.......................170 B2
Sandown Industrial Park
  ESH/CLAY KT10.......................170 A1
Sandown Park Racecourse
  ESH/CLAY KT10.......................170 B2
Sandown Sports Club &
  Dry Ski Slope
  ESH/CLAY KT10.......................170 B2
Sandringham Primary School
  FSTGT E7............................77 G5
Sandy Lodge Golf Club
  NTHWD HA6...........................32 B1
Sapcote Trading Centre
  WLSDN NW10..........................69 H4
Sarah Bonnell School
  SRTFD E15...........................76 C6
Sarum Hall School
  HAMP NW3.............................3 K1
Satmer Trust School
  STNW/STAM N16.......................74 C1
Savoy Pier
  TPL/STR WC2R........................11 L7
The Savoy
  TPL/STR WC2R........................11 L7
Savoy Theatre
  TPL/STR WC2R........................11 L7
Saxon Business Centre
  WIM/MER SW19........................162 B1
Sayer Clinic
  CROY/NA CR0.........................177 F3
Sayer Clinics
  MBLAR W1H............................9 M5
Scargill Infant School
  RAIN RM13...........................81 J6
Scargill Junior School
  RAIN RM13...........................81 J5
Scarsdale Place
  Medical Centre
  KENS W8..............................14 C3
Schomberg House
  STJS SW1Y............................10 F9
School of English
  GLDGN NW11..........................52 E7
School of Oriental &
  African Studies
  GWRST WC1E...........................11 H1
The School of Pharmacy
  BMSBY WC1N............................5 H1
The School of St David &
  St Katharine
  CEND/HSY/T N8........................54 E3
The School of
  The Islamic Republic
  KIL/WHAMP NW6........................2 A6

Science Museum
  SKENS SW7............................15 H4
Science Museum IMAX Cinema
  SKENS SW7............................15 G4
The Science Museum Library
  SKENS SW7............................15 G3
Scotts Park Primary School
  BMLY BR1............................153 G7
Sealife London Aquarium
  WHALL SW1A...........................17 L2
Sebright Primary School
  BETH E2..............................92 C1
Secombe Centre
  SUT SM1.............................175 F5
Sedgehill School
  CAT SE6.............................151 K4
Sedgewick Centre
  WCHPL E1.............................13 M4
Selborne Primary School
  GFD/PVL UB6..........................85 F1
Selhurst ≷
  SNWD SE25...........................165 F4
The Selhurst Medical Centre
  SNWD SE25...........................165 F5
Sellincourt School
  TOOT SW17...........................147 J5
Selsdon Primary School
  SAND/SEL CR2........................178 E7
Selsdon Road Industrial Estate
  SAND/SEL CR2........................177 K6
Selwyn Primary School
  CHING E4.............................44 A6
  PLSTW E13............................76 E7
Sergeant Industrial Estate
  WAND/EARL SW18......................128 A5
Serpentine Gallery
  BAY/PAD W2...........................9 H9
Serpentine Lido & Cafe
  SKENS SW7............................15 J1
Servite RC Primary School
  WBPTN SW10...........................14 E9
Seven Islands Leisure Centre
  BERM/RHTH SE16......................111 K2
Seven Kings ≷
  GDMY/SEVK IG3........................60 E7
Seven Kings Health Centre
  GDMY/SEVK IG3........................60 E7
Seven Kings High School
  GNTH/NBYPK IG2.......................60 D6
Seven Mills Primary School
  POP/IOD E14.........................112 D1
Seven Sisters ≷ ⊖
  SEVS/STOTM N15.......................56 A4
Seven Sisters Primary School
  SEVS/STOTM N15.......................55 K4
Seymour Gardens
  Medical Centre
  IL IG1...............................59 K7
Seymour Leisure Centre
  MBLAR W1H.............................9 L3
Shaare Zedek Medical Centre
  GLDGN NW11...........................52 D5
Shacklewell Primary School
  HACK E8..............................74 B3
Shadwell ⊖
  WCHPL E1.............................92 D5
Shadwell Dock Stairs
  WAP E1W..............................93 F6
Shaftesbury Hospital
  LSQ/SEVD WC2H........................11 J5
Shaftesbury Medical Centre
  RYLN/HDSTN HA2.......................48 C7
Shaftesbury Park
  Primary School
  BTSEA SW11..........................129 F2
Shaftesbury Primary School
  FSTGT E7.............................77 G6
Shaftesbury Theatre
  LSQ/SEVD WC2H........................11 J4
Shahjalal Medical Centre
  WCHPL E1.............................92 C5
Shakespeare Business Centre
  BRXN/ST SW9.........................130 C2
Shakespeare's Globe Exhibition
  & Theatre Tour
  STHWK SE1............................12 E8
The Shamrock Sports Club
  ACT W3...............................86 E5
Shannon Corner Retail Park
  NWMAL KT3...........................160 D3
Shapla Primary School
  WCHPL E1.............................92 C6
Sharp Sports Centre
  EDGW HA8.............................36 C5
Sheen Lane Health Centre
  MORT/ESHN SW14......................125 K2
Sheen Lawn Tennis &
  Squash Club
  MORT/ESHN SW14......................125 J4
Sheen Mount Primary School
  RCHPK/HAM TW10......................125 J4
Sheen Sports Centre
  MORT/ESHN SW14......................126 B3
Shell Centre
  STHWK SE1............................11 M9
Shelley School
  CLAP SW4............................129 H2
Shenstone School
  DART DA1............................138 A4
Shepherd's Bush ≷ ⊖
  SHB W12.............................107 G1
Shepherd's Bush CC
  ACT W3...............................87 G6
Shepherd's Bush Empire
  SHB W12.............................107 F1
Shepherd's Bush Market ⊖
  SHB W12..............................88 A7
Sheraton Business Centre
  GFD/PVL UB6..........................85 J1
Sheraton Park Tower Hotel
  KTBR SW1X............................15 M1
Sheraton Skyline Hotel
  HYS/HAR UB3.........................101 G6
Sheringdale Primary School
  WAND/EARL SW18......................127 J7
Sheringham Junior School
  MNPK E12.............................77 K3
Sherington Primary School
  CHARL SE7...........................114 A5
Sherlock Holmes Hotel
  MHST W1U.............................9 M2
Sherlock Holmes Museum
  CAMTN NW1.............................9 M1
Sherwood Park Primary School
  BFN/LL DA15.........................136 C5
Sherwood Park School
  WLGTN SM6...........................176 D2
Sherwood School
  MTCM CR4............................163 H3
Shirley Clinic
  CROY/NA CR0.........................165 K7
Shirley High School
  CROY/NA CR0.........................179 F2

Shirley Oaks Hospital
  CROY/NA CR0.........................165 K6
Shirley Park Golf Club
  CROY/NA CR0.........................178 D1
Shirley Wanderers RFC
  WWKM BR4............................180 A3
Shirley Windmill
  CROY/NA CR0.........................178 E2
Shooters Hill Golf Club
  WOOL/PLUM SE18......................115 H7
Shooters Hill Post 16 Campus
  WOOL/PLUM SE18......................115 F6
Shooting Star House
  (Childrens Hospice)
  HPTN TW12...........................141 K5
Shopping City
  WDGN N22.............................55 F1
The Shopping Hall
  EHAM E6..............................77 J7
Shopping Mall
  SWFD E18.............................58 E1
Shore Business Centre
  HOM E9...............................74 E6
Shoreditch
  Comprehensive School
  IS N1................................7 K6
Shoreditch County Court
  STLK EC1Y............................7 H9
Shoreditch High Street ⊖
  WCHPL E1.............................13 L1
Shortlands ≷
  HAYES BR2...........................167 H1
Shotfield Health Clinic
  WLGTN SM6...........................176 B5
Showcase Cinema
  WDGN N22.............................55 G1
Showcase Newham Cinema
  BARK IG11............................96 C2
Shrewsbury House School
  SURB KT6............................171 K1
Shrewsbury Lodge School
  ESH/CLAY KT10.......................170 C4
Shrewsbury Road Health Centre
  FSTGT E7.............................77 H6
Sidcup ≷
  BFN/LL DA15.........................155 G1
Sidcup Cemetery
  BXLY DA5............................155 K1
Sidcup Golf Club
  BFN/LL DA15.........................155 G1
Sidcup Health Centre
  SCUP DA14...........................155 G2
Sidcup Sports Club
  SCUP DA14...........................155 F3
Sidney Russell School
  DAGW RM9.............................80 A3
Silicon Business Centre
  GFD/PVL UB6..........................85 J1
Silverdale Industrial Estate
  HYS/HAR UB3.........................101 K1
Silver Industrial Estate
  TOTM N17.............................56 B1
Silver Street ⊖
  UED N18..............................42 B3
Silver Street Medical Centre
  UED N18..............................42 A3
Silver Wing Industrial Estate
  CROY/NA CR0.........................177 F1
Simon Marks Jewish
  Primary School
  STNW/STAM N16........................56 B7
Singlegate Primary School
  WIM/MER SW19........................147 H6
Sion College
  EMB EC4Y.............................12 B6
Sion Manning RC Girls School
  NKENS W10............................88 B4
Sir Francis Drake
  Primary School
  DEPT SE8............................112 B4
Sir George Monoux College
  WALTH E17............................57 K1
Sir James Altham
  Swimming Pool
  OXHEY WD19...........................33 J4
Sir James Barrie School
  VX/NE SW8...........................109 H7
Sir John Cass Foundation &
  Redcoat CE Secondary School
  WCHPL E1.............................93 F4
Sir John Heron Primary School
  MNPK E12.............................77 K3
Sir John Lillie Primary School
  HMSMTH W6...........................107 H5
Sir John Soane's Museum
  LINN WC2A............................11 L4
Sir Thomas Abney
  Primary School
  STNW/STAM N16........................55 K6
Sir Thomas Lipton
  Memorial Hospital
  STHGT/OAK N14........................28 B6
Sir William Burrough
  Primary School
  POP/IOD E14..........................93 G5
Six Bridges Trading Estate
  STHWK SE1...........................111 H4
Skillion Business Park
  BARK IG11............................97 F2
Skinners Academy Hackney
  STNW/STAM N16........................56 A6
Slade Green ≷
  ERITH DA8...........................118 D7
Slade Green FC
  ERITH DA8...........................118 E7
Slade Green Primary School
  ERITH DA8...........................118 D6
Slade School of Fine Art
  STPAN WC1H...........................5 H8
Sleaford Industrial Estate
  VX/NE SW8...........................109 H6
Sloane Hospital
  BECK BR3............................152 B7
Sloane Square ⊖
  BGVA SW1W............................16 A6
Smallberry Green
  Primary School
  ISLW TW7............................124 B1
Smallwood Primary School
  TOOT SW17...........................147 H3
SMA Medical Centre
  LEY E10..............................57 K6
Smithy Street School
  WCHPL E1.............................92 E4
Snaresbrook ⊖
  WAN E11..............................58 E4
Snaresbrook College
  Preparatory School
  WAN E11..............................58 E3
Snaresbrook Crown Court
  WAN E11..............................58 D4
Snaresbrook Primary School
  SWFD E18.............................58 E3

Snowflake School for Children
  with Autism
  ECT SW5..............................14 A6
Snowsfields Primary School
  STHWK SE1............................19 J1
Sobell Leisure Centre
  HOLWY N7.............................73 G2
Sobell Medical Centre
  HOLWY N7.............................73 G3
Sofitel Hotel
  STJS SW1Y............................11 G8
Soho Parish CE Primary School
  SOHO/CST W1F.........................11 G6
Solent Road Health Centre
  KIL/WHAMP NW6........................70 E5
Somerset House
  COVGDN WC2E..........................11 L6
Somers Town Community
  Sports Centre
  CAMTN NW1.............................4 F3
Sorsby Health Centre
  CLPT E5..............................75 F2
South Acton ⊖
  ACT W3.............................105 K2
Southall ≷
  STHL UB1............................102 K1
Southall & West London College
  STHL UB1............................102 D1
South Bank Business Centre
  VX/NE SW8...........................109 J7
Southbank International
  School Hampstead
  HAMP NW3.............................71 G3
Southbank International
  School Kensington
  NTCHL W11............................88 D6
Southbank International
  School Westminster
  BAY/PAD W2...........................8 B7
South Bank University
  STHWK SE1............................18 C3
South Bermondsey ≷
  BERM/RHTH SE16......................111 K4
Southborough High School
  SURB KT6............................172 A2
Southborough Primary School
  HAYES BR2...........................169 F4
Southbury ≷
  EN EN1...............................30 D3
Southbury Primary School
  PEND EN3.............................30 D3
South Camden
  Community School
  CAMTN NW1.............................4 F5
South Chelsea College
  BRXN/ST SW9.........................130 A3
South Croydon ≷
  SAND/SEL CR2........................177 K6
South Croydon Medical Centre
  SAND/SEL CR2........................177 J6
South Croydon Sports Club
  CROY/NA CR0.........................178 A4
South Ealing ⊖
  EA W5...............................104 E3
South Ealing Cemetery
  EA W5...............................104 E3
South Eastern University
  HOLWY N7.............................73 F2
Southern Road Primary School
  PLSTW E13............................95 F1
Southern Spectator
  Transport Mall
  SRTFD E15............................76 A7
Southfield First & Middle School
  CHSWK W4............................106 A1
Southfield Medical Centre
  CHSWK W4............................106 A1
Southfields ⊖
  WAND/EARL SW18......................127 J7
The Southfields Clinic
  WAND/EARL SW18......................127 K5
Southfields Community College
  WAND/EARL SW18......................127 K7
Southgate ⊖
  STHGT/OAK N14........................28 D7
Southgate Cemetery
  STHGT/OAK N14........................40 C1
Southgate College
  STHGT/OAK N14........................40 C1
Southgate Compton CC
  EBAR EN4.............................27 K3
Southgate Leisure Centre
  STHGT/OAK N14........................28 D6
Southgate Road Medical Centre
  IS N1................................7 H1
Southgate School
  EBAR EN4.............................28 B4
South Greenford ≷
  GFD/PVL UB6..........................84 E2
South Grove Primary School
  WALTH E17............................57 G5
South Hampstead ≷
  KIL/WHAMP NW6........................2 E7
South Hampstead CC
  CRICK NW2............................70 D1
South Hampstead
  High School
  HAMP NW3.............................71 G5
South Harringay
  Junior School
  FSBYPK N4............................55 H4
South Harrow ⊖
  RYLN/HDSTN HA2.......................66 C2
South Herts Golf Club
  TRDG/WHET N20........................26 E7
South Kensington ⊖
  SKENS SW7............................15 H5
South Kenton ≷
  ALP/SUD HA0..........................49 J7
Southlake Primary School
  ABYW SE2............................116 E1
South Lewisham Health Centre
  CAT SE6.............................152 A3
South London Crematorium
  MTCM CR4............................163 H1
South London Gallery
  CMBW SE5............................111 F2
The South London
  Natural Health Centre
  CLAP SW4............................129 H3
South London Tamil School
  CROY/NA CR0.........................164 D6
South London Theatre
  WNWD SE27...........................149 J2
Southmead Primary School
  WIM/MER SW19........................127 H7
South Merton ≷
  RYNPK SW20..........................161 J2
South Norwood Country Park
  SNWD SE25...........................165 K3
South Norwood Hill
  Medical Centre
  SNWD SE25...........................165 F1

South Norwood Medical Centre
  SNWD SE25...........................165 F3
South Norwood Pools &
  Fitness Centre
  SNWD SE25...........................165 H4
South Norwood Primary School
  SNWD SE25...........................165 H4
South Park Business Centre
  IL IG1...............................78 E1
South Park Hotel
  SAND/SEL CR2........................178 A3
South Park Primary School
  GDMY/SEVK IG3........................78 E2
South Quay ⊖
  POP/IOD E14.........................112 E1
South Quay Plaza
  POP/IOD E14.........................112 E1
South Rise Primary School
  WOOL/PLUM SE18......................115 J4
South Ruislip ≷ ⊖
  RSLP HA4.............................65 G3
Southside Industrial Estate
  VX/NE SW8...........................109 H6
Southside Shopping Centre
  WAND/EARL SW18......................128 A5
South Thames College
  MRDN SM4............................161 J4
  PUT/ROE SW15........................126 C5
  PUT/ROE SW15........................127 G4
  TOOT SW17...........................147 J4
  WAND/EARL SW18......................128 A4
South Tottenham ≷
  SEVS/STOTM N15.......................56 B4
Southville Infant School
  EBED/NFELT TW14.....................121 J7
Southwark ⊖
  STHWK SE1............................12 C9
Southwark Bridge Stairs
  BLKFR EC4V...........................12 E7
Southwark Cathedral
  STHWK SE1............................13 G8
Southwark College
  BERM/RHTH SE16......................111 J2
  CMBW SE5............................111 F6
  STHWK SE1............................18 B1
  STHWK SE1............................19 K3
Southwark Coroners Court
  STHWK SE1............................19 G1
Southwark Crown Court
  STHWK SE1............................13 J8
Southwark Park Primary School
  BERM/RHTH SE16......................111 J2
Southwark Park Sports Centre
  BERM/RHTH SE16......................111 K3
Southwark Rose Hotel
  STHWK SE1............................12 F9
Southwark Sports Ground
  DUL SE21............................131 G7
South West
  Middlesex Crematorium
  FELT TW13...........................122 D7
South Wimbledon ⊖
  WIM/MER SW19........................147 F6
Southwold Primary School
  CLPT E5..............................74 E1
South Woodford ⊖
  SWFD E18.............................58 E1
South Woodford Health Centre
  SWFD E18.............................44 E7
Southwood Hospital
  HGT N6...............................54 A6
Southwood Primary School
  DAGW RM9.............................80 A3
Sovereign Business Centre
  PEND EN3.............................31 H2
The Space Arts Centre Cinema
  DEPT SE8............................112 C3
Sparrow Farm Infant School
  EBED/NFELT TW14.....................122 B6
Sparrow Farm Junior School
  EBED/NFELT TW14.....................122 B6
Spa School
  STHWK SE1...........................111 H3
Speakers Corner
  BAY/PAD W2...........................9 M6
The Speech & Language
  Hearing Centre
  CAMTN NW1.............................5 H8
Speedway Industrial Estate
  HYS/HAR UB3.........................101 G1
Speke's Monument
  BAY/PAD W2...........................8 F8
Spelthorne Clinic
  ASHF TW15...........................140 B5
Spelthorne Infant School
  ASHF TW15...........................140 B5
Spelthorne Sports Club
  ASHF TW15...........................140 B6
Spencer House
  WHALL SW1A...........................10 E9
The Spires Shopping Centre
  BAR EN5..............................26 C2
Spitalfields Community Farm
  WCHPL E1.............................13 M3
Spitalfields Health Centre
  WCHPL E1.............................13 M3
Spitfire Business Park
  CROY/NA CR0.........................177 G5
Splashworld Swimming Centre
  BXLYHS DA6..........................136 D3
Springfield Christian School
  CAT SE6.............................151 H2
Springfield Community
  Primary School
  SEVS/STOTM N15.......................56 C5
Springfield Hospital
  TOOT SW17...........................147 J2
Springfield Primary School
  SUN TW16............................140 C7
  VX/NE SW8...........................109 H6
Spring Grove Primary School
  ISLW TW7............................123 J1
Springhallow School
  HNWL W7..............................85 F5
Spring Park Primary School
  CROY/NA CR0.........................179 J2
Springwell Infant School
  HEST TW5............................102 D6
Springwell Junior School
  HEST TW5............................102 D6
Spurgeons College
  SNWD SE25...........................165 F1
Squirrels Heath Infant School
  GPK RM2..............................63 K4
Squirrels Heath Junior School
  GPK RM2..............................63 K4
Squirrels Trading Estate
  HYS/HAR UB3.........................101 J2
SS Peter & Pauls Catholic
  Primary School
  IL IG1...............................78 D2
St Johns Health Centre
  TWK TW1............................124 B6

The Stables Gallery & Art Centre
CRICK NW2 ....69 J3
Stadium Business Centre
WBLY HA9 ....68 D2
Stadium Industrial Estate
WBLY HA9 ....68 D4
Stadium Retail Park
WBLY HA9 ....68 C2
Stafford Cross Business Park
CROY/NA CR0 ....177 F4
The Stafford London Hotel
WHALL SW1A 10 D9
Stag Lane J & I School
EDGW HA8 ....50 C1
Stag Lane Medical Centre
CDALE/KGS NW9 ....50 E2
Staines RFC
FELT TW13 ....140 E4
Stamford Brook ⊖
CHSWK W4 ....106 C3
Stamford Clinic
HMSMTH W6 ....106 D2
Stamford Hill ⇌
SEVS/STOTM N15 ....56 A5
Stamford Hill Primary School
SEVS/STOTM N15 ....55 K5
Stanburn First School
STAN HA7 ....35 J6
Stanburn Junior School
STAN HA7 ....35 J6
Standard Industrial Estate
CAN/RD E16 ....114 C1
Stanford Primary School
STRHM/NOR SW16 ....148 D7
Stanhope Primary School
GFD/PVL UB6 ....84 C3
Stanley Park High School
CAR SM5 ....176 A5
Stanley Park Primary School
CAR SM5 ....175 K6
Stanley Primary School
TEDD TW11 ....142 E3
Stanmore ⇌
STAN HA7 ....35 K3
Stanmore College
STAN HA7 ....35 H5
Stanmore Golf Club
STAN HA7 ....35 H6
Stanmore Medical Centre
STAN HA7 ....35 C5
Stanton Square
Industrial Estate
SYD SE26 ....151 H3
Stanwell Fields CE School
STWL/WRAY TW19 ....120 B6
Staple Inn Buildings
HHOL WC1V 12 A3
Staples Corner Business Park
CRICK NW2 ....51 J7
Star Business Centre
RAIN RM13 ....99 F4
Starksfield Primary School
ED N9 ....30 A7
Star Lane
CAN/RD E16 ....94 C3
Star Primary School
CAN/RD E16 ....94 C3
Stationers Hall
STP EC4M 12 D5
Stationery Office
HOL/ALD WC2B 11 L4
Stebon Primary School
POP/IOD E14 ....93 H4
Stephen Hawking Primary
Special School
POP/IOD E14 ....93 H4
Stepney Day Hospital
WCHPL E1 ....92 E5
Stepney Green ⊖
WCHPL E1 ....93 F3
Stepney Greencoat CE
Primary School
POP/IOD E14 ....93 H5
Stepney Green Maths &
Computing College
WCHPL E1 ....93 F4
Sterling Industrial Estate
DAGE RM10 ....80 D3
Sterling Way Clinic
UED N18 ....42 B4
Stewart Fleming
Primary School
PGE/AN SE20 ....165 K2
Stewart Headlam
Primary School
WCHPL E1 ....92 D3
Stillness Primary School
FSTH SE23 ....132 B5
Stirling Industrial Centre
BORE WD6 ....25 F4
Stirling Retail Park
BORE WD6 ....25 F5
Stirling Way
Industrial Estates
CROY/NA CR0 ....163 K6
Stockley Park
Business Centre
STKPK UB11 ....82 A7
Stockley Park Golf Club
STKPK UB11 ....82 A6
Stockwell ⊖
CLAP SW4 ....129 K1
Stockwell Park School
BRXN/ST SW9 ....110 A4
Stockwell Primary School
BRXN/ST SW9 ....130 A2
Stoke Newington ⇌
STNW/STAM N16 ....74 B1
Stoke Newington School &
Sixth Form
STNW/STAM N16 ....73 K2
Stonebridge Park ⊖
ALP/SUD HA0 ....68 C6
The Stonebridge Primary
School (London Welsh School)
WLSDN NW10 ....68 B3
Stonebridge Shopping Centre
WLSDN NW10 ....69 F2
Stonehill Business Centre
UED N18 ....43 F5
Stonehill Business Park
UED N18 ....43 F5
Stone Lake Retail Park
CHARL SE7 ....114 B3
Stoneleigh ⇌
HOR/WEW KT19 ....173 H4
Stoneleigh First School
EW KT17 ....173 K3
Stoneydown Park
Primary School
WALTH E17 ....57 H2
Strand on the Green J & I School
CHSWK W4 ....105 H5

Strand Palace Hotel
COVGDN WC2E 11 K6
Stratford College
SRTFD E15 ....76 C6
Stratford High Street ⊖
SRTFD E15 ....76 B7
Stratford International ⇌ ⊖
OLYMPICPK E20 ....76 A5
Stratford Magistrates Court
SRTFD E15 ....76 B6
Stratford ⇌ ⊖
OLYMPICPK E20 ....76 A5
Stratford School
FSTGT E7 ....76 E6
Stratford Shopping Centre
SRTFD E15 ....76 B6
Strathmore School
RCHPK/HAM TW10 ....124 E7
Strawberry Fields School
NTGHL W11 ....8 B5
Strawberry Hill ⇌
WHTN TW2 ....142 E2
Strawberry Hill Golf Club
WHTN TW2 ....142 E2
Streatham ⇌
STRHM/NOR SW16 ....148 D4
Streatham Cemetery
TOOT SW17 ....147 J2
Streatham & Clapham
High School
STRHM/NOR SW16 ....148 C2
BRXS/STRHM SW2 ....130 A7
Streatham Common ⇌
STRHM/NOR SW16 ....148 D5
Streatham & Croydon RFC
THHTH CR7 ....164 B4
Streatham Hill ⇌
STRHM/NOR SW16 ....148 E1
Streatham Ice Rink
STRHM/NOR SW16 ....148 E1
Streatham Leisure Centre
STRHM/NOR SW16 ....148 E1
Streatham Modern School
STRHM/NOR SW16 ....148 E5
Streatham Park Cemetery
MTCM CR4 ....163 H1
Streatham Swimming Pool
STRHM/NOR SW16 ....148 E4
Streatham Vale Sports Club
STRHM/NOR SW16 ....148 C6
Streatham Wells
Primary School
BRXS/STRHM SW2 ....149 F1
Stroud Green Primary School
FSBYPK N4 ....55 G7
The Study Preparatory School
WIM/MER SW19 ....146 B4
The Study School
NWMAL KT3 ....160 B4
Studbourne Primary School
BRXS/STRHM SW2 ....39 A4
Sudbury Court Sports Club
ALP/SUD HA0 ....67 J2
Sudbury Golf Club
GFD/PVL UB6 ....67 J5
Sudbury & Harrow Road ⇌
ALP/SUD HA0 ....67 H4
Sudbury Hill ⊖
HRW HA1 ....66 E3
Sudbury Primary School
ALP/SUD HA0 ....67 H3
Sudbury Town ⊖
GFD/PVL UB6 ....67 H5
Suffolks Primary School
EN EN1 ....30 D1
Sulivan Primary School
FUL/PGN SW6 ....127 K1
Summerside JMI School
NFNCH/WDSPK N12 ....39 H5
Summerswood Primary School
BORE WD6 ....24 D3
Summit Business Park
SUN TW16 ....140 E6
Sunbury ⇌
SUN TW16 ....140 E7
Sunbury Business Centre
SUN TW16 ....140 C7
Sunbury Court
SUN TW16 ....156 C1
Sunbury Leisure Centre
SUN TW16 ....140 D7
Sunbury Manor School
SUN TW16 ....140 D7
Sundridge Park ⇌
BMLY BR1 ....153 F6
Sundridge Park Golf Club
BMLY BR1 ....153 G5
Sun Life Trading Estate
EBED/NFELT TW14 ....121 K2
Sunnyfields Primary School
HDN NW4 ....51 K2
Sunnyhill Primary School
STRHM/NOR SW16 ....149 F3
Sunrise School
TOTM N17 ....42 C5
Sunshine House School
NTHWD HA6 ....32 B5
Surbiton ⇌
SURB KT6 ....159 F5
Surbiton Assembly Rooms
SURB KT6 ....159 F5
Surbiton Business Centre
SURB KT6 ....158 E5
Surbiton Cemetery
KUT/HW KT1 ....159 H3
Surbiton Golf Club
CHSGTN KT9 ....171 H3
Surbiton High School
KUT/HW KT1 ....159 F3
Surbiton Hospital
SURB KT6 ....159 F5
Surbiton
Natural Health Centre
SURB KT6 ....159 F5
Surrey County CC (The Oval)
LBTH SE11 ....17 M9
Surrey Docks Farm
BERM/RHTH SE16 ....112 C1
Surrey Docks Health Centre
BERM/RHTH SE16 ....112 B1
Surrey Docks
Watersports Centre
BERM/RHTH SE16 ....112 B2
Surrey Quays ⊖
BERM/RHTH SE16 ....112 A3
Surrey Quays Leisure Park
BERM/RHTH SE16 ....112 A2
Surrey Quays Shopping Centre
BERM/RHTH SE16 ....112 A2
Surrey Square Primary School
WALW SE17 ....19 J7
Susi Earnshaw Theatre School
BAR EN5 ....26 D2

Sussex Hotel
OXSTW W1C 10 A5
Sussex House School
KTBR SW1X 15 J5
Sutcliffe Park Athletics Track
LEE/GVPK SE12 ....134 A4
Sutton ⇌
SUT SM1 ....175 G5
Sutton Alternative
Health Centre
SUT SM1 ....175 F4
Sutton Arena
CAR SM5 ....162 C6
Sutton Bowling Club
BELMT SM2 ....174 E7
Sutton Cemetery
CHEAM SM3 ....174 D1
Sutton Civic Centre
SUT SM1 ....175 F4
Sutton College of Learning
for Adults
SUT SM1 ....175 F4
Sutton Common ⇌
SUT SM1 ....174 E1
Sutton Grammar School
SUT SM1 ....175 G4
Sutton High Junior School
SUT SM1 ....175 F5
Sutton High School for
Girls GDST
SUT SM1 ....174 E5
Sutton House
HACK E8 ....74 E4
Suttons Business Park
RAIN RM13 ....99 F2
Sutton Superbowl
SUT SM1 ....175 F4
Sutton United FC
SUT SM1 ....174 E3
Sutton West Centre
SUT SM1 ....174 E4
Swaffield Primary School
WAND/EARL SW18 ....128 B5
Swaminarayan School
WLSDN NW10 ....69 F5
Swan Business Centre
CHSWK W4 ....106 A3
Swan Business Park
DART DA1 ....139 G3
Swan Lane Pier
CANST EC4R 13 G7
Swanlea School
WCHPL E1 ....92 D3
Swansmere School
WOT/HER KT12 ....156 B7
Swedish School
BARN SW13 ....106 D5
Swiss Cottage ⊖
KIL/WHAMP NW6 ....3 G1
Swiss Cottage Leisure Centre
HAMP NW3 ....3 H2
Swiss Cottage School
STJWD NW8 ....3 H2
Sybil Elgar School
EA W5 ....86 A6
The Sybil Elgar School
NWDGN UB2 ....102 E2
Sybourn Infant School
LEY E10 ....57 G7
The Sybourn Junior School
WALTH E17 ....57 H6
Sybourn Primary School
WALTH E17 ....57 H6
Sydenham ⇌
SYD SE26 ....150 E4
Sydenham Girls School
SYD SE26 ....150 D2
Sydenham High School
SYD SE26 ....150 D3
Sydenham High School
Sports Ground
CAT SE6 ....151 J4
Sydenham High
Senior School
SYD SE26 ....150 D4
Sydenham Hill ⇌
DUL SE21 ....150 A2
The Sydney Russell School
DAGW RM9 ....79 K4
Syon House
BTFD TW8 ....104 D7
Syon Lane ⇌
ISLW TW7 ....104 B6
Syon Park
BTFD TW8 ....124 D1
Syracuse University
NTGHL W11 ....88 D6
Tabard Theatre
CHSWK W4 ....106 D3
Tabernacle School
NTGHL W11 ....88 C5
Taberner House
CROY/NA CR0 ....177 J2
TA Centre
EDGW HA8 ....36 D6
HRW HA1 ....49 F4
NFNCH/WDSPK N12 ....39 H7
Tait Road Industrial Estate
CROY/NA CR0 ....165 F5
Taj Suites & Residences Hotel
WESTW SW1E 16 F1
Talmud Torah Machzikei
Hadass School
STNW/STAM N16 ....56 C6
Tamian Industrial Estate
HSLWW TW4 ....122 B3
Tandem Centre
WIM/MER SW19 ....147 H7
Tashbar of Edgware
Primary School
EDGW HA8 ....36 C3
Tate Britain
WEST SW1P 17 J6
Tate Modern
STHWK SE1 ....12 D8
Tavistock Clinic
HAMP NW3 ....71 H5
TAVR Centre
KUT/HW KT1 ....158 E3
Tavy Clinic
ABYW SE2 ....116 D1
Tawhid Boys School
STNW/STAM N16 ....74 B1
Tayyibah Girls School
STNW/STAM N16 ....56 C7
Teddington ⇌
TEDD TW11 ....143 G5
Teddington Business Park
TEDD TW11 ....143 F4
Teddington Cemetery
TEDD TW11 ....142 E3
Teddington Clinic
TEDD TW11 ....142 E5

Teddington Memorial Hospital
TEDD TW11 ....142 E5
Teddington Pool &
Fitness Centre
TEDD TW11 ....143 G4
Teddington School
TEDD TW11 ....143 K5
The Teddington Theatre Club
E/WMO/HCT KT8 ....157 J4
Telferscot Primary School
BAL SW12 ....129 H7
Temperate House, Kew Gardens
RCH/KEW TW9 ....125 G1
Temple Hill Primary School
DART DA1 ....139 K4
Temple of Bacchus
CMBW SE5 ....130 D1
Temple of Mithras
MANHO EC4N 13 G5
Tenby Road Clinic
EDGW HA8 ....50 B1
Tenterden Sports Ground
KTN/HRWW/WS HA3 ....50 A6
Terence McMillan Stadium
PLSTW E13 ....95 G3
Tetherdown Primary School
MUSWH N10 ....54 A3
Thames Barrier
CAN/RD E16 ....114 C1
Thames Barrier Information &
Learning Centre
CHARL SE7 ....114 C2
Thames Christian College
BTSEA SW11 ....128 C2
Thames College of Technology
WOOL/PLUM SE18 ....115 F3
Thames Ditton ⇌
THDIT KT7 ....157 K6
Thames Ditton & Esher
Golf Club
ESH/CLAY KT10 ....170 D1
Thames Ditton Infant School
THDIT KT7 ....158 A5
Thames Ditton Junior School
THDIT KT7 ....158 A6
Thames Gateway Park
DAGW RM9 ....98 B2
Thames House
WEST SW1P 17 J5
Thameside Industrial Estate
CAN/RD E16 ....95 H7
Thames Magistrates Court
BOW E3 ....93 J2
Thamesmead Leisure Centre
THMD SE28 ....97 H6
Thamesmead Shopping Centre
THMD SE28 ....97 G6
Thamesview Business Centre
RAIN RM13 ....99 G4
Thames View Clinic
BARK IG11 ....97 F1
Thames View J & I School
BARK IG11 ....97 G1
Thames Water Tower
NTGHL W11 ....107 G1
Theatre de l'Ange Fou
International School of
Corporeal Mime
ARCH N19 ....54 E2
Theatre for Mankind
FSBYPK N4 ....55 H7
Theatre Museum Library
& Archive
COVGDN WC2E 11 K6
Theatre Of The Dispossessed
WIM/MER SW19 ....127 G7
Theatre Royal
HOL/ALD WC2B 11 K5
SRTFD E15 ....76 B5
Theatre Royal Haymarket
STJS SW1Y 11 H7
Theodore McLeary
Primary School
EDUL SE22 ....131 G3
Therapia Lane ⊖
CROY/NA CR0 ....163 K6
Therapia Trading Estate
CROY/NA CR0 ....163 J6
Thistlebrook Industrial Estate
ABYW SE2 ....116 D3
Thistle Hotel
BAY/PAD W2 ....8 E7
CAMTN NW1 ....4 F8
FITZ W1T 10 F4
FSBYE EC1V 6 E8
WESTW SW1E 16 D1
Thistle Marble Arch Hotel
MBLAR W1H 9 M5
Thistle Piccadilly Hotel
SOHO/SHAV W1D 11 H7
Thomas Arnold Primary School
DAGW RM9 ....80 B6
Thomas Buxton Infant School
WCHPL E1 ....92 C3
Thomas Fairchild
Primary School
IS N1 ....7 G5
Thomas Francis Academy
BRXN/ST SW9 ....130 C3
Thomas Gamuel
Primary School
WALTH E17 ....57 J5
Thomas Jones Primary School
NTGHL W11 ....88 C5
Thomas London Independent
Day School
KENS W8 ....14 D3
Thomas Road Industrial Estate
POP/IOD E14 ....93 J4
Thomas's Clapham
Primary School
BTSEA SW11 ....128 E4
Thomas's Fulham
FUL/PGN SW6 ....128 A2
Thomas's London Day Schools
KENS W8 ....14 C1
Thomas's Preparatory School
BTSEA SW11 ....108 C7
Thomas Tallis School
BKHTH/KID SE3 ....134 A2
Thornhill Primary School
IS N1 ....6 A2
Thornton Heath ⇌
THHTH CR7 ....164 D3
Thornton Heath Health Centre
THHTH CR7 ....164 D3
Thornton Heath Pools &
Fitness Centre
THHTH CR7 ....164 D2
Thornton Road Industrial Estate
CROY/NA CR0 ....163 K5
Thorntree Primary School
CHARL SE7 ....114 C4

Thorpe Hall Primary School
WALTH E17 ....44 A7
Three Bridges Business Centre
NWDGN UB2 ....103 H1
Three Bridges Primary School
NWDGN UB2 ....103 G2
Three Mills Heritage Centre
BOW E3 ....94 A2
Thurston Industrial Estate
LEW SE13 ....132 E2
Tidemill Primary School
DEPT SE8 ....112 D6
Tideway Industrial Estate
VX/NE SW8 ....109 H5
Tiffin Girls School
KUTN/CMB KT2 ....144 E5
Tiffin School & Sports Centre
KUTN/CMB KT2 ....159 G1
Tiller Centre (Swimming Baths)
POP/IOD E14 ....112 D2
Tiller Leisure Centre
POP/IOD E14 ....112 D2
Timbercroft Primary School
WOOL/PLUM SE18 ....115 K6
Timbers Clinic
KTN/HRWW/WS HA3 ....34 D5
Timebridge Youth &
Community Centre
CROY/NA CR0 ....179 K4
Times Square Shopping Centre
SUT SM1 ....175 F4
Tiverton Primary School
SEVS/STOTM N15 ....55 K5
Tobacco Dock
WAP E1W 92 D6
Tokyngton Community Centre
WBLY HA9 ....68 D4
Toldos School
STNW/STAM N16 ....55 K7
Tollgate
DUL SE21 ....150 A1
Tollgate Primary School
PLSTW E13 ....95 G3
Tolworth ⇌
BRYLDS KT5 ....172 D1
Tolworth CP School
SURB KT6 ....159 G7
Tolworth Girls School
SURB KT6 ....172 B2
Tolworth Recreation Centre
SURB KT6 ....172 B2
Tooting ⇌
TOOT SW17 ....147 K5
Tooting Bec ⊖
TOOT SW17 ....148 A2
Tooting Bec Athletics Track
TOOT SW17 ....148 B3
Tooting Broadway ⊖
TOOT SW17 ....147 J4
Tooting Leisure Centre
TOOT SW17 ....147 H3
Tooting & Mitcham United FC
MTCM CR4 ....148 A7
Torah Temimah Primary School
CRICK NW2 ....69 K3
Torah Vodaas
GLDGN NW11 ....70 D1
Torat Emet Primary School
HDN NW4 ....52 B4
Torriano Junior School
KTTN NW5 ....72 C4
Torridon Primary School
CAT SE6 ....152 B1
Torrington Clinic
NFNCH/WDSPK N12 ....39 G4
Torrington Park Health Centre
NFNCH/WDSPK N12 ....39 G3
Total Health Clinic
SHB W12 ....106 E1
Tottenham Cemetery
TOTM N17 ....42 A6
Tottenham Court Road ⊖
SOHO/SHAV W1D 11 G4
Tottenham Green
Leisure Centre
SEVS/STOTM N15 ....56 A3
Tottenham Hale ⇌ ⊖
TOTM N17 ....56 D2
Tottenham Hale Retail Park
SEVS/STOTM N15 ....56 C3
Tottenham Hotspur FC
(White Hart Lane)
TOTM N17 ....42 B6
Tottenham Park Cemetery
ED N9 ....42 D2
Tottenham Sports Centre
TOTM N17 ....42 B7
Totteridge CC
TRDG/WHET N20 ....38 E1
Totteridge & Whetstone ⊖
TRDG/WHET N20 ....39 F1
Tower 42
OBST EC2N 13 J4
The Tower Bridge Exhibition
STHWK SE1 ....19 L9
Tower Bridge Primary School
STHWK SE1 ....19 L1
Tower Bridge Wharf
WAP E1W 92 C7
Tower Gateway ⊖
TWRH EC3N 13 L6
Tower Hamlets College
POP/IOD E14 ....93 K6
WCHPL E1 ....92 E4
Tower Hill ⊖
TWRH EC3N 13 L7
The Tower Hotel
WAP E1W 13 M8
Tower House School
MORT/ESHN SW14 ....125 K3
Tower Industrial Estate
SNWD SE25 ....165 H3
Tower Medical Centre
WCHPL E1 ....92 C5
Tower Millennium Pier
TWRH EC3N 13 K8
Tower of London
TWRH EC3N 13 L7
Tower Retail Park
DART DA1 ....138 C4
Towers Business Park
WBLY HA9 ....68 D3
Tower Stairs
MON EC3R 13 J7
Town Farm Primary School
STWL/WRAY TW19 ....120 A6
Townley Grammar School
for Girls
BXLYHS DA6 ....137 G3
Townmead Business Centre
FUL/PGN SW6 ....128 B3
Townsend Industrial Estate
WLSDN NW10 ....68 E7

Townsend Primary School
  WALW SE17 ....19 H5
Toynbee Hall & Curtain Theatre
  WCHPL E1 ....13 L3
Trade Union Congress
  NOXST/BSQ WC1A 11 H4
Trafalgar Business Centre
  BARK IG11 ....97 F3
Trafalgar Infant School
  WHTN TW2 ....123 J7
Trafalgar Junior School
  WHTN TW2 ....142 D1
Trafalgar Square
  STJS SW1Y 11 H8
Trafalgar Trading Estate
  PEND EN3 ....31 H1
Tramshed Theatre
  WOOL/PLUM SE18 ......115 H3
Trans Atlantic College
  BETH E2 ....7 K5
Transport for London
  Lost Property Office
  CAMTN NW1 ....9 M1
Transport House
  WEST SW1P 17 J4
Travelodge
  CAN/RD E16 ....95 H1
  FELT TW13 ....121 K7
  FSBYW WC1X 5 M8
  HEST TW5 ....102 B5
  IL IG1 ....78 B2
  SUN TW16 ....140 E6
  SURB KT6 ....159 J7
Treasury
  WHALL SW1A 17 J2
The Treaty Centre
  HSLW TW3 ....123 G2
Treehouse School
  MUSWH N10 ....54 A3
The Treehouse School
  BMSBY WC1N 5 L9
Trent CE Primary School
  EBAR EN4 ....27 K3
Trent Country Park
  EBAR EN4 ....28 A1
Trent Park Cemetery
  EBAR EN4 ....28 A2
Trent Park Golf Club
  STHGT/OAK N14 ....28 C3
Trevor Roberts School
  HAMP NW3 ....3 H1
Tricycle Theatre
  KIL/WHAMP NW6 ....70 D6
Trident Business Centre
  TOOT SW17 ....147 K4
Trinity Business Centre
  BERM/RHTH SE16 ....112 C1
Trinity Catholic High School
  WFD IG8 ....44 E3
Trinity College Centre
  PECK SE15 ....111 F6
Trinity College of Music
  GNWCH SE10 ....113 F5
  MHST W1U 10 B3
Trinity Hospital
  GNWCH SE10 ....113 G3
Trinity House
  TWRH EC3N 13 K6
Trinity RC High School Upper
  WFD IG8 ....44 E3
Trinity St Marys
  Primary School
  BAL SW12 ....129 F7
Trinity School
  DAGE RM10 ....80 C2
  LEE/GVPK SE12 ....133 H4
Trinity School Belvedere
  BELV DA17 ....117 K3
Trinity Trading Estate
  HYS/HAR UB3 ....101 K2
Tripcock Point
  Development Site
  THMD SE28 ....97 J2
Triumph Trading Estate
  TOTM N17 ....42 C5
Trocadero
  SOHO/SHAV W1D 11 G7
Trojan Business Centre
  WLSDN NW10 ....69 H5
Troy Industrial Estate
  HRW HA1 ....49 F4
True Buddha School
  IS N1 ....5 L4
TS Queen Mary
  TPL/STR WC2R 11 L7
Tudor Enterprise Park
  KTN/HRWW/WS HA3 .....48 D2
Tudor Lodge Health Centre
  WIM/MER SW19 ....127 G7
Tudor Lodge Hotel
  PIN HA5 ....47 F5
Tudor Primary School
  FNCH N3 ....39 G7
  STHL UB1 ....83 J6
Tufnell Park ⊖
  KTTN NW5 ....72 B3
Tufnell Park Primary School
  HOLWY N7 ....72 D3
Tuke School
  PECK SE15 ....111 J7
Tulse Hill ⇌
  WNWD SE27 ....149 H1
Tunnel Avenue Trading Estate
  GNWCH SE10 ....113 G1
Turney School
  DUL SE21 ....130 D6
Turnham Green ⊖
  CHSWK W4 ....106 B3
Turnham Primary School
  BROCKY SE4 ....132 B3
Turnpike Lane
  SEVS/STOTM N15 ....55 H2
Turtle Key Arts Centre
  FUL/PGN SW6 ....107 K5
Tweeddale Primary School
  CAR SM5 ....162 C6
Twenty Nevern Square Hotel
  ECT SW5 ....14 B6
Twickenham ⇌
  TWK TW1 ....124 B6
Twickenham Academy
  WHTN TW2 ....142 B1
Twickenham Cemetery
  WHTN TW2 ....123 G7
Twickenham Park Health Centre
  TWK TW1 ....124 D7
Twickenham
  Preparatory School
  HPTN TW12 ....142 B7
Twickenham Stadium
  ISLW TW7 ....123 K5
Twickenham Trading Estate
  TWK TW1 ....124 A5

Two Bridges Business Park
  SAND/SEL CR2 ....177 K5
Twyford CE High School
  ACT W3 ....86 C7
Twyford Sports Centre
  ACT W3 ....86 D7
Tyburn Infant School
  STJWD NW8 ....3 H9
Tynemouth Road Health Centre
  SEVS/STOTM N15 ....56 B3
The Type Museum
  BRXN/ST SW9 ....110 A7
Tyssen Primary School
  STNW/STAM N16 ....56 C7
UCI Cinema
  BAY/PAD W2 ....8 D5
  SUT SM1 ....175 F4
UCI Empire Cinema
  LSQ/SEVD WC2H 11 H7
UK Passport Office
  PIM SW1V 16 D5
Underhill Infant School
  BAR EN5 ....26 C4
Unicorn Primary School
  BECK BR3 ....166 E4
Unicorn School
  RCH/KEW TW9 ....105 G7
Unicorn Theatre
  STHWK SE1 ....19 K1
United Medical &
  Dental Schools
  STHWK SE1 ....17 L3
Unity Trading Estate
  WFD IG8 ....59 H2
University Church of Christ
  the King
  STPAN WC1H 11 G1
University College Hospital
  CAMTN NW1 ....4 F9
  HAMP NW3 ....71 H5
University College London
  FITZ W1T 10 F2
  STPAN WC1H 5 G9
University College London,
  Astor College
  FITZ W1T 10 F2
University College London C/O
  The Chorley Institute
  GWRST WC1E 11 G1
University College London
  Medical School
  FITZ W1T 10 F2
University College London
  Obstetrics Hospital
  GWRST WC1E 10 F1
University College London
  HAMP NW3 ....71 G4
University Hospital Lewisham
  LEW SE13 ....132 E4
University of California
  WHALL SW1A 10 G9
University of East London
  BARK IG11 ....79 G3
  CAN/RD E16 ....96 A6
  PLSTW E13 ....95 F2
  SRTFD E15 ....76 B7
  SRTFD E15 ....94 D1
University of Greenwich
  GNWCH SE10 ....113 G4
  WOOL/PLUM SE18 ......115 F2
University of Greenwich
  (Mansion Site)
  ELTH/MOT SE9 ....135 H5
University of Greenwich
  (Southwood Site)
  ELTH/MOT SE9 ....135 H6
University of Greenwich
  Sports Ground
  ELTH/MOT SE9 ....134 D3
  ELTH/MOT SE9 ....135 H6
University of London
  BAY/PAD W2 ....9 G5
  BMSBY WC1N 11 K1
  CLKNW EC1R 6 B9
  GWRST WC1E 11 H2
  MBLAR W1H 9 K4
  STHWK SE1 ....13 C9
  STPAN WC1H 5 H9
University of London
  Athletics Ground
  NWMAL KT3 ....160 D4
University of West London
  EA W5 ....85 J6
  EA W5 ....85 J7
University of Westminster
  CAMTN NW1 ....4 E9
  CAVSQ/HST W1G 10 D4
  CHSWK W4 ....105 K7
  GTPST W1W 10 D2
  HRW HA1 ....49 G6
University of Westminster
  - Environment
  MHST W1U 10 A2
Uphall Primary School
  IL IG1 ....78 B4
Upland Primary School
  BXLYHN DA7 ....137 G2
Uplands Business Park
  WALTH E17 ....57 F1
Upney ⊖
  BARK IG11 ....79 F6
Upper Holloway ⊖
  ARCH N19 ....72 D1
Upper Montagu Street Clinic
  CAMTN NW1 ....9 L2
Upper Tooting Independent
  High School
  TOOT SW17 ....147 J1
Upton Cross Primary School
  PLSTW E13 ....77 F7
Upton Day Hospital
  BXLYHS DA6 ....137 F3
Upton Lane Medical Centre
  FSTGT E7 ....77 F5
Upton Park ⊖
  PLSTW E13 ....77 G7
Upton Primary School
  BXLY DA5 ....137 F4
Upton Road School
  BXLYHS DA6 ....137 F4
The Urdang Academy
  FSBYW WC1X 6 A8
  LSQ/SEVD WC2H 11 J5
Ursuline High School
  RYNPK SW20 ....146 B6
Ursuline Preparatory School
  RYNPK SW20 ....146 B6
Uxbridge College
  HYS/HAR UB3 ....82 E6
Uxbridge County Court
  HYS/HAR UB3 ....82 C4
Uxendon Manor JMI School
  KTN/HRWW/WS HA3 .....50 A4

Vale Farm Sports Centre
  ALP/SUD HA0 ....67 H3
Vale Industrial Estate
  WATW WD18 ....20 A7
The Vale Medical Centre
  FSTH SE23 ....151 G1
Valence House Museum
  & Library
  BCTR RM8 ....79 K1
Valence Primary School
  BCTR RM8 ....79 K1
Valentine High School
  GNTH/NBYPK IG2 ....60 A5
Valentines High Lower School
  GNTH/NBYPK IG2 ....60 B4
Vale Park Industrial
  ACT W3 ....106 B1
The Vale School
  SKENS SW7 ....14 E4
Valley Link Business centre
  PEND EN3 ....31 G5
Valley Link Business Estate
  PEND EN3 ....31 G5
Valley Primary School
  HAYES BR2 ....167 J1
Valmar Trading Estate
  CMBW SE5 ....110 D7
V & A Museum of Childhood
  BETH E2 ....92 E2
Vanbrugh Theatre
  GWRST WC1E 11 G1
Vaudeville Theatre
  COVGDN WC2E 11 K6
Vaughan Primary School
  RYLN/HDSTN HA2 ....48 C5
Vauxhall ⇌⊖
  VX/NE SW8 ....17 K8
Vauxhall Primary School
  LBTH SE11 ....17 L7
Velodrome
  OLYMPICPK E20 ....75 K4
Vernon House Special School
  WLSDN NW10 ....68 E4
Vestry Hall
  MTCM CR4 ....162 E2
Vestry House Museum
  WALTH E17 ....57 K3
Vicarage Fields Health Clinic
  BARK IG11 ....78 C6
The Vicarage Field
  Shopping Centre
  BARK IG11 ....78 C6
Vicarage Primary School
  EHAM E6 ....95 K2
Vicarage Road Cemetery
  WATW WD18 ....20 E3
Vicars Green Primary School
  GFD/PVL UB6 ....85 J1
V I Components Industrial Park
  ERITH DA8 ....118 B4
Victoria ⇌⊖
  PIM SW1V 16 D5
Victoria & Albert Museum
  SKENS SW7 ....15 H4
Victoria Business Centre
  WELL DA16 ....136 B1
Victoria Bus Station
  PIM SW1V 16 D4
Victoria Chiropractic Clinic
  SKENS SW7 ....15 L2
Victoria Coach Station
  BGVA SW1W 16 C6
Victoria Hall
  FNCH N3 ....38 D7
Victoria Industrial Estate
  ACT W3 ....87 F4
Victoria Industrial Park
  DART DA1 ....139 G4
Victoria Junior School
  FELT TW15 ....122 A7
Victoria Medical Centre
  PIM SW1V 16 F6
Victoria Palace Theatre
  BGVA SW1W 16 E5
Victoria Park Industrial Centre
  HOM E9 ....75 H6
Victoria Place Shopping Centre
  BGVA SW1W 16 D5
Victoria Rail/Air Terminal
  PIM SW1V 16 D5
Victoria Retail Park
  RSLP HA4 ....65 H4
Victoria Wharf
  POP/IOD E14 ....93 G6
Victoria Wharf Industrial Estate
  DEPT SE8 ....112 B4
Victor Seymour Infant School
  CAR SM5 ....175 K2
Victory Business Centre
  ISLW TW7 ....124 A3
Victory Day School
  CRO7 ....164 D3
Victory Primary School
  WALW SE17 ....18 F5
Viking Business Centre
  ROMW/RG RM7 ....62 E6
Viking Primary School
  NTHLT UB5 ....83 H2
Village Infant School
  DAGE RM10 ....80 C6
Village Operations Support Area
  SRTFD E15 ....76 A3
The Village School
  CDALE/KGS NW9 ....50 E3
  HAMP NW3 ....71 H1
Villiers High School
  STHL UB1 ....84 A7
The Vine Clinic
  KUTN/CMB KT2 ....144 A6
Vine Medical Centre
  E/WMO/HCT KT8 ....157 H2
The Vines School
  BTSEA SW11 ....129 F6
The Vineyard Primary School
  RCHPK/HAM TW10 ....125 F4
Vinopolis, City of Wine
  STHWK SE1 ....12 F8
Vinters' Hall
  BLKFR EC4V 12 F6
VIP Trading Estate
  CHARL SE7 ....114 B3
Virginia Primary School
  BETH E2 ....7 L8
Virgo Fidelis Convent Schools
  NRWD SE19 ....149 J5
Visage School of Hair & Beauty
  ELTH/MOT SE9 ....135 H7
Vision College of Technology
  HOM E9 ....75 J5
Vita et Pax School
  STHGT/OAK N14 ....28 B4
Vittoria Primary School
  IS N1 ....6 A4

Voyager Business Estate
  BERM/RHTH SE16 ....111 H2
Vue Cinema
  ACT W3 ....86 C3
  CROY/NA CR0 ....177 F1
  DAGW RM9 ....80 A7
  FUL/PGN SW6 ....107 K6
  HAM NW3 ....71 G5
  HRW HA1 ....48 E5
  LSO/SEVD WC2H 11 H6
  NFNCH/WDSPK N12 ......39 H6
  ROMW/RG RM7 ....63 G4
  SHB W12 ....107 G1
Vulcan Business Centre
  CROY/NA CR0 ....180 C2
Waddon ⇌
  CROY/NA CR0 ....177 G3
Waddon Clinic
  CROY/NA CR0 ....177 G4
Waddon Marsh ⊖
  CROY/NA CR0 ....177 G1
Wadham Lodge Sports Centre
  WALTH E17 ....43 K7
Wadsworth Business Centre
  GFD/PVL UB6 ....85 J1
The Waldegrave Clinic
  TEDD TW11 ....143 F4
Waldegrave Girls School
  WHTN TW2 ....142 D2
Waldo Industrial Estate
  BMLY BR1 ....168 B2
Waldorf School of SW London
  BAL SW12 ....148 C1
Waldron Health Centre
  & Surgery
  NWCR SE14 ....112 C2
Walker Primary School
  STHGT/OAK N14 ....40 D1
The Wallace Centre
  DEPT SE8 ....112 C5
The Wallace Collection
  MHST W1U 10 A4
Wallbrook Business Centre
  HSLWW TW4 ....122 A2
Wall Hotel
  LOTH EC2R 13 G3
Wallington ⇌
  WGTN SM6 ....176 B5
Wallington County
  Grammar School
  WLGTN SM6 ....176 B3
Wallington High School for Girls
  WLGTN SM6 ....176 B7
Walmer Road Clinic
  NTGHL W11 ....88 C6
Walm Lane Clinic
  CRICK NW2 ....70 B4
Walnut Tree Walk
  Primary School
  LBTH SE11 ....18 A5
Waltham Forest College
  WALTH E17 ....56 E2
Waltham Forest
  Magistrates Court
  WALTH E17 ....57 K2
Waltham Forest Pool & Track
  WALTH E17 ....57 K1
Waltham Forest Theatre
  WALTH E17 ....57 H2
Walthamstow Academy
  WALTH E17 ....43 H7
Walthamstow
  Business Centre
  WALTH E17 ....58 A1
Walthamstow Central ⇌⊖
  WALTH E17 ....57 J4
Walthamstow Marsh
  Nature Reserve
  CLPT E5 ....56 D6
Walthamstow Queens Road ⊖
  WALTH E17 ....57 J4
Walthamstow School for Girls
  WALTH E17 ....57 K3
Walton Business Centre
  WOT/HER KT12 ....156 A6
Walton Casuals FC
  WOT/HER KT12 ....156 A4
Walton Swimming Pool
  WOT/HER KT12 ....156 A7
Walworth Lower
  Secondary School
  WALW SE17 ....19 H7
Walworth Town Hall
  WALW SE17 ....18 E6
Wandle Park ⊖
  CROY/NA CR0 ....177 G1
Wandle Recreation Centre
  WAND/EARL SW18 ....128 A5
Wandle Trading Estate
  MTCM CR4 ....162 E6
Wandle Valley School Sutton
  Parent Partnership
  CAR SM5 ....162 D6
Wandsworth Adult College
  BTSEA SW11 ....109 F7
Wandsworth Cemetery
  WAND/EARL SW18 ....128 B7
Wandsworth Common ⇌
  TOOT SW17 ....128 D6
Wandsworth County Court
  PUT/ROE SW15 ....127 H4
Wandsworth Road ⇌⊖
  VX/NE SW8 ....129 J1
Wandsworth Town ⇌
  WAND/EARL SW18 ....128 A3
Wandsworth Trading Estate
  WAND/EARL SW18 ....128 A6
Wanstead ⊖
  WAN E11 ....59 F5
Wanstead CC
  WAN E11 ....59 F6
Wanstead CE Primary School
  WAN E11 ....58 E4
Wanstead Golf Club
  WAN E11 ....59 G6
Wanstead High School
  WAN E11 ....59 F5
Wanstead Hospital
  WAN E11 ....59 F3
Wanstead Leisure Centre
  WAN E11 ....59 G5
Wanstead Park ⇌
  FSTGT E7 ....77 F3
Wapping ⊖
  WAP E1W 92 C7
Wapping Wharf
  WAP E1W 92 E7
War Memorial Sports Ground
  SUT SM1 ....175 J3
Warnford Industrial Estate
  HYS/HAR UB3 ....101 H1

Warren Comprehensive School
  CHDH RM6 ....62 B4
Warren Dell Primary School
  OXHEY WD19 ....33 G2
Warrender School
  RSLP HA4 ....46 D6
Warren Junior School
  CHDH RM6 ....62 B4
The Warren Medical Centre
  YEAD UB4 ....83 F5
Warren Sports Centre
  CHDH RM6 ....62 B4
Warren Street ⊖
  CAMTN NW1 ....4 E9
Warwick Avenue ⊖
  MV/WKIL W9 ....8 E1
Warwick Dubbing Theatre
  SOHO/CST W1F 11 G5
Warwick Estate
  BAY/PAD W2 ....8 D3
Warwick Leadlay Gallery
  GNWCH SE10 ....113 F5
Warwick School for Boys
  WALTH E17 ....58 A3
The Washington Mayfair Hotel
  MYFR/PICC W1J 10 D8
Waterfields Retail Park
  WAT WD17 ....21 H3
Waterfront Leisure Centre
  WOOL/PLUM SE18 ......115 F2
Watergate School
  CAT SE6 ....151 K4
  LEW SE13 ....132 E3
Waterloo ⇌
  STHWK SE1 ....18 A1
Waterloo East ⇌
  STHWK SE1 ....12 B9
Waterloo Health Centre
  STHWK SE1 ....18 A2
Watermans Arts, Cinema &
  Theatre Centre
  BTFD TW8 ....105 F5
The Watermans Hall
  MON EC3R 13 J7
Watermeads High School
  MRDN SM4 ....162 C5
Watermill Business Centre
  PEND EN3 ....31 H1
Water Polo Arena
  OLYMPICPK E20 ....75 K6
Water Rats Theatre
  STPAN WC1H 5 K7
Waterside Business Centre
  ISLW TW7 ....124 C3
Waterside Primary School
  WOOL/PLUM SE18 ......115 J4
The Waterside Trading Centre
  HNWL W7 ....103 K2
Watersports Centre
  STNW/STAM N16 ....55 J7
Watford ⇌
  WATW WD18 ....20 D2
Watford Arches Retail Park
  WAT WD17 ....21 G4
Watford Business Centre
  WAT WD17 ....21 F2
Watford County Court
  WAT WD17 ....21 F1
Watford FC & Saracens RFC
  (Vicarage Road Stadium)
  WATW WD18 ....21 G4
Watford Field School (Infant)
  WATW WD18 ....21 G4
Watford General Hospital
  WATW WD18 ....21 F4
Watford Grammar School
  for Boys
  WATW WD18 ....20 D3
Watford Grammar School
  for Girls
  WATW WD18 ....21 G4
Watford High Street ⊖
  WATW WD18 ....21 G3
Watford Junction ⇌⊖
  WAT WD17 ....21 G1
Watford Museum
  WATW WD18 ....21 G4
Watling Boys' Club
  EDGW HA8 ....36 C6
Watling Clinic
  EDGW HA8 ....37 F6
Watling Medical Centre
  EDGW HA8 ....36 E7
Wavelengths Leisure Pool
  & Library
  DEPT SE8 ....112 D6
Waverley Industrial Estate
  HRW HA1 ....48 D2
Waverley Lower
  Secondary School
  EDUL SE22 ....131 J4
Waverley School
  PEND EN3 ....30 E3
Waxchandlers' Hall
  CITYW EC2V 12 F4
Weald Junior School
  KTN/HRWW/WS HA3 .....35 F6
Wealdstone Cemetery
  KTN/HRWW/WS HA3 .....49 G2
Webber Douglas Academy of
  Dramatic Art
  SKENS SW7 ....14 F6
Webster Graduate
  Studies Center
  CAMTN NW1 ....3 M9
Welbeck Clinic
  CRICK NW2 ....70 E2
Welbourne Primary School
  SEVS/STOTM N15 ....56 C3
Welfare Clinic
  HGT N6 ....54 A5
Wellcome Institute
  CAMTN NW1 ....5 G9
Welldon Park Junior School
  RYLN/HDSTN HA2 ....66 C3
Wellesley Road ⊖
  CROY/NA CR0 ....177 J1
Well Grove School
  TRDG/WHET N20 ....27 H7
Welling ⇌
  WELL DA16 ....136 B1
The Welling Clinic
  WELL DA16 ....136 B1
Welling Medical Centre
  WELL DA16 ....136 A3
Welling School Academy
  WELL DA16 ....116 C7
Wellington Arch
  MYFR/PICC W1J 16 B1
Wellington Barracks
  WESTW SW1E 16 F2
Wellington Primary School
  BOW E3 ....93 J2

CHING E4 43 K1
HSLW TW3 122 E1
Welling United FC
WELL DA16 136 D2
Wells Primary School
WFD IG8 45 F3
Wembley Arena
WBLY HA9 68 C3
Wembley Central ⇌ ⊖ ⊖
WBLY HA9 68 A4
Wembley Commercial Centre
WBLY HA9 67 K1
Wembley Conference Centre
WBLY HA9 68 B3
Wembley FC
ALP/SUD HA0 67 H3
Wembley High Technology College
ALP/SUD HA0 67 J2
Wembley Hospital
ALP/SUD HA0 67 K5
Wembley Park ⊖
WBLY HA9 68 C2
Wembley Park Business Centre
WBLY HA9 68 D2
Wembley Primary School
WBLY HA9 68 A2
Wembley Stadium
WBLY HA9 68 C3
Wembley Stadium ⇌
WBLY HA9 68 C4
Wembley Stadium Industrial Estate
WBLY HA9 68 C2
Wendell Park Primary School
SHB W12 106 C1
Wentworth Tutorial College
GLDGN NW11 52 B5
The Wernher Collection at Ranger's House
GNWCH SE10 113 G7
Wesley's Chapel, House & Museum of Methodism
STLK EC1Y 7 G9
Wessex Gardens Primary School
GLDGN NW11 52 C7
West 12 Shopping & Leisure Centre
SHB W12 107 G1
West Acton ⊖
ACT W3 86 C5
West Acton Primary School
ACT W3 86 D5
West Beckton Health Centre
CAN/RD E16 95 G4
Westbourne Green Sports Complex
BAY/PAD W2 8 B3
Westbourne Park ⊖
NKENS W10 88 D4
Westbourne Primary School
SUT SM1 174 E2
Westbridge College
BTSEA SW11 108 D7
West Brompton ⇌ ⊖ ⊖
ECT SW5 14 B8
Westbrooke School
WELL DA16 136 E2
The Westbury Hotel
CONDST W1S 10 D6
Westbury Medical Centre
WDGN N22 55 J1
Westcombe Park ⇌
BKHTH/KID SE3 113 K4
Westcroft Leisure Centre
CAR SM5 176 A3
West Croydon ⇌
CROY/NA CR0 164 D7
West Drayton Cemetery
WDR/YW UB7 100 B2
West Drayton Primary School
WDR/YW UB7 100 B1
West Dulwich ⇌
DUL SE21 130 E7
West Ealing ⇌
WEA W13 85 H6
West Ealing Business Centre
WEA W13 85 G6
Western Avenue Business Park
ACT W3 86 D3
Western International Market
NWDGN UB2 102 A3
Western Trading Estate
WLSDN NW10 86 E3
West Ewell Infant School
HOR/WEW KT19 173 F4
Westferry ⊖
POP/IOD E14 93 H6
Westfield Community Technology College
WATW WD18 20 D4
Westfield London
SHB W12 88 A7
Westfields Primary School
BARN SW13 126 C1
Westfield Stratford City
OLYMPICPK E20 76 A5
West Finchley ⊖
FNCH N3 39 F5
Westgate Business Centre
NKENS W10 88 C3
Westgate Primary School
DART DA1 139 G6
West Green Primary School
SEVS/STOTM N15 55 J3
West Ham ⇌ ⊖ ⊖
SRTFD E15 94 C2
West Ham Church Primary School
SRTFD E15 76 D7
West Ham Lane Clinic
SRTFD E15 76 C7
West Hampstead ⇌ ⊖
KIL/WHAMP NW6 70 E5
West Hampstead ⊖
KIL/WHAMP NW6 71 F5
West Hampstead Clinic
KIL/WHAMP NW6 2 B1
West Hampstead Thameslink ⇌
KIL/WHAMP NW6 70 E5
West Ham United FC (Upton Park)
PLSTW E13 95 H1
West Harrow ⊖
HRW HA1 48 C5
West Hatch High School
WFD IG8 45 K4
West Hendon Clinic
CDALE/KGS NW9 51 H5
West Herts Business Centre
BORE WD6 24 D2
West Herts College (Watford Campus)
WAT WD17 20 E1
West Herts Golf Club
RKW/CH/CXG WD3 20 B2
West Hill Primary School
DART DA1 139 F5
WAND/EARL SW18 127 K4
West India Pier
POP/IOD E14 112 C1
West India Quay ⊖
POP/IOD E14 93 J6
West India Shopping Centre
POP/IOD E14 93 J7
West Kensington ⊖
WKENS W14 107 J4
Westland Heliport
BTSEA SW11 128 C2
West Lea School
ED N9 42 A2
West Lodge Preparatory School
BFN/LL DA15 155 F2
West Lodge Primary School
PIN HA5 47 H3
West London Academy
NTHLT UB5 65 H7
West London College
OXSTW W1C 10 A5
West London County Court
WKENS W14 107 H3
West London Magistrates Court
HMSMTH W6 107 G4
West London Tamil School
WLSDN NW10 87 H1
West Mead Clinic
RSLP HA4 65 G2
West Middlesex Golf Club
STHL UB1 84 C6
West Middlesex University Hospital
ISLW TW7 124 B1
Westminster ⊖
WHALL SW1A 17 K2
Westminster Abbey
WEST SW1P 17 J3
Westminster Abbey Choir School
WEST SW1P 17 H3
Westminster Academy
BAY/PAD W2 8 B3
Westminster Bridge Park Plaza Hotel
STHWK SE1 17 L2
Westminster Business Square
LBTH SE11 17 L8
Westminster Cathedral
WESTW SW1E 16 E4
Westminster Cathedral Choir School
WEST SW1P 16 F4
Westminster Cathedral RC Primary School
PIM SW1V 17 H7
Westminster City Hall
WESTW SW1E 16 F4
Westminster City School
WESTW SW1E 16 F3
Westminster Industrial Estate
WOOL/PLUM SE18 114 C2
Westminster Kingsway College
CAMTN NW1 4 E8
WEST SW1P 16 F5
Westminster Natural Health Centre
PIM SW1V 16 E6
Westminster Pier
WHALL SW1A 17 K2
Westminster School
WEST SW1P 17 J4
Westminster Theatre
WESTW SW1E 16 E3
Westminster Under School
WEST SW1P 17 G6
Westmoor Community Clinic
PUT/ROE SW15 126 D6
West Norwood ⇌
WNWD SE27 149 H3
West Norwood Clinic
WNWD SE27 149 J1
West Norwood Crematorium
WNWD SE27 149 J2
West One Shopping Centre
MYFR/PKLN W1K 10 B5
Weston Green School
THDIT KT7 157 K7
Weston Park Clinic
CEND/HSY/T N8 54 E4
Weston Park Primary School
CEND/HSY/T N8 55 F4
Westpoint Trading Estate
ACT W3 86 D4
West Ramp Coach Park
HTHAIR TW6 100 D7
West Ruislip ⇌ ⊖
RSLP HA4 64 A1
West Silvertown ⊖
CAN/RD E16 94 E7
West Sutton ⇌
SUT SM1 174 E3
West Thames College
ISLW TW7 103 K7
West Thamesmead Business Park
THMD SE28 116 A2
West Thornton Primary School
CROY/NA CR0 164 A6
West Twyford Primary School
WLSDN NW10 86 C1
Westway Business Centre
BAY/PAD W2 8 C3
Westway Sports Centre
NKENS W10 88 B5
West Wickham ⇌
WWKM BR4 167 F6
West Wickham Swimming Baths
WWKM BR4 167 F7
West Wimbledon Primary School
RYNPK SW20 160 E2
Westwood Language College
NRWD SE19 149 J6
Westwood Primary School
WELL DA16 135 K3
Wetherby Preparatory School
BAY/PAD W2 8 B6
Whaddon House Clinic
CMBW SE5 131 F2
Whipps Cross Hospital
LEY E10 58 B5
Whitchurch First School
STAN HA7 35 H7
Whitchurch Junior School
STAN HA7 35 K6
Whitechapel ⊖ ⊖
WCHPL E1 92 D4
Whitechapel Art Gallery
WCHPL E1 13 M4
Whitechapel Sports Centre
WCHPL E1 92 C4
White City ⊖
SHB W12 88 A6
Whitefield School
CRICK NW2 52 B6
Whitefield School & Leisure Centre
WALTH E17 44 B7
Whitefriars Community School
KTN/HRWW/WS HA3 48 E1
Whitefriars Trading Estate
KTN/HRWW/WS HA3 48 D1
Whitehall Theatre
WHALL SW1A 11 H8
White Hart Lane ⇌
TOTM N17 42 B6
Whiteheath Junior School
RSLP HA4 46 A5
Whitehorse Manor Primary School
THHTH CR7 164 E4
The White House Preparatory School
BAL SW12 129 J7
Whiteleys Shopping Centre
BAY/PAD W2 8 C5
Whiterose Trading Estate
EBAR EN4 27 J6
Whitgift Almshouses
CROY/NA CR0 177 J1
Whitgift School
SAND/SEL CR2 177 J4
Whitgift Shopping Centre
CROY/NA CR0 177 J1
Whitings Hill Primary School
BAR EN5 26 A4
Whitmore High School
RYLN/HDSTN HA2 48 C7
Whitmore Primary School
IS N1 7 H5
Whittingham Community Primary School
WALTH E17 43 G7
Whittington Hospital
ARCH N19 72 B1
Whitton ⇌
WHTN TW2 123 H6
Whitton Health Centre
WHTN TW2 123 H7
Whitton Health Clinic
WHTN TW2 123 G7
Whitton Sports & Fitness Centre
WHTN TW2 142 B1
Whybridge Infant School
RAIN RM13 81 J7
Whybridge Junior School
RAIN RM13 81 H7
Wickham Theatre
WWKM BR4 180 B2
Wide Way Health Clinic
MTCM CR4 163 J2
Widmore Centre
BMLY BR1 168 B1
Wigmore Hall
CAVSQ/HST W1G 10 C4
Wigram House (University of Westminster)
WEST SW1P 17 G4
Wilberforce Primary School
NKENS W10 88 C2
Wilbury Primary School
UED N18 41 K4
Willesden Centre for Health & Care
WLSDN NW10 69 J6
Willesden County Court
WLSDN NW10 87 G1
Willesden Green ⊖
CRICK NW2 70 A5
Willesden Junction ⊖ ⊖
WLSDN NW10 87 H1
Willesden Medical Centre
CRICK NW2 69 K5
Willesden New Cemetery
WLSDN NW10 69 H6
Willesden Sports Centre
WLSDN NW10 69 K7
Willesden Sports Stadium
WLSDN NW10 69 K7
William Bellamy J & I School
DAGE RM10 80 C1
William Booth College
CMBW SE5 130 E2
William Byrd School
HYS/HAR UB3 101 F5
William Ellis School
KTTN NW5 72 A2
William Ellis Sports Ground
EDGW HA8 36 C7
William Ford CE Junior School
DAGE RM10 80 C6
William Hogarth School
CHSWK W4 106 B5
William Morris Academy
HMSMTH W6 107 G4
William Morris Gallery
WALTH E17 57 J2
William Morris Primary School
MTCM CR4 163 J2
William Morris School
WALTH E17 43 G7
William Patten Primary School
STNW/STAM N16 74 B1
William Torbitt J & I School
GNTH/NBYPK IG2 60 E4
William Tyndale Primary School
IS N1 6 D1
Willington School
WIM/MER SW19 146 D5
Willow Brook Primary School
LEY E10 57 J7
Willow Business Centre
MTCM CR4 162 E4
Willow Business Park
SYD SE26 150 E2
Willowfield Humanities College
WALTH E17 57 F2
Willowfield School
WALTH E17 57 G2
The Willows Clinic
CHST BR7 154 A5
The Willows School
YEAD UB4 83 H3
Willow Tree Primary School
NTHLT UB5 65 J5
Wilson's School
WLGTN SM6 176 E5
Wimbledon
WIM/MER SW19 146 C2
Wimbledon ⇌ ⊖ ⊖
WIM/MER SW19 146 D5
Wimbledon Chase ⇌
RYNPK SW20 161 H1
Wimbledon Chase Primary School
RYNPK SW20 146 C7
Wimbledon College
WIM/MER SW19 146 B6
Wimbledon Common Golf Club
WIM/MER SW19 145 K4
Wimbledon Common Pre-Preparatory School
WIM/MER SW19 146 B6
Wimbledon (Gap Road) Cemetery
WIM/MER SW19 147 F3
Wimbledon High School
WIM/MER SW19 146 C5
Wimbledon House School
WIM/MER SW19 146 D7
Wimbledon Lawn Tennis Museum
WIM/MER SW19 146 C2
Wimbledon Magistrates Court
WIM/MER SW19 146 E5
Wimbledon Park ⊖
WIM/MER SW19 146 E2
Wimbledon Park Athletics Track
WIM/MER SW19 146 D1
Wimbledon Park Golf Club
WIM/MER SW19 146 D2
Wimbledon Park Primary School
WIM/MER SW19 146 E1
Wimbledon Recreation Centre
WIM/MER SW19 147 F5
Wimbledon RFC
RYNPK SW20 145 H6
Wimbledon School of Art
WIM/MER SW19 146 C7
WIM/MER SW19 146 E6
Wimbledon Squash & Badminton Club
WIM/MER SW19 146 C6
Wimbledon Stadium
WIM/MER SW19 147 F3
Wimbledon Stadium Business Centre
WIM/MER SW19 147 F2
Wimbledon Theatre
WIM/MER SW19 146 E6
Wimbledon Windmill
WIM/MER SW19 146 A2
Winchcombe Business Centre
PECK SE15 111 F5
Winchmore Hill ⇌
WCHMH N21 29 H6
Winchmore Hill Clinic
WCHMH N21 29 H7
Winchmore Hill CC
WCHMH N21 29 J7
Winchmore School
WCHMH N21 41 J1
Windmill Business Centre
NWDGN UB2 84 C7
Windmill Trading Estate
MTCM CR4 163 H4
SUN TW16 140 B7
Windrush Primary School
THMD SE28 97 H7
Winfield House
CAMTN NW1 3 K7
Wingate & Finchley FC
NFNCH/WDSPK N12 39 H6
Wingate Trading Estate
TOTM N17 42 B6
Wingfield Primary School
BKHTH/KID SE3 133 K2
Winns Primary School
WALTH E17 57 H1
Winsor Primary School
EHAM E6 96 A5
Winston Churchill's Britain at War Experience
STHWK SE1 13 H9
Winston House Preparatory School
SWFD E18 44 E7
Winston Way Primary School
IL IG1 78 A2
Winterbourne Infant School
THHTH CR7 164 B3
Winton Primary School
IS N1 5 L6
Wisdom School
SEVS/STOTM N15 55 K3
Witley Industrial Estate
NWDGN UB2 102 E3
Wolf Fields Primary School
NWDGN UB2 102 E3
Wolfson Hillel Primary School
STHGT/OAK N14 28 D5
Wolfson Medical Centre
RYNPK SW20 145 J6
Wolsey Business Park
WATW WD18 20 B6
Wolsey Junior School
CROY/NA CR0 180 B6
The Women's Library
WCHPL E1 13 L4
The Woodberry Clinic
MUSWH N10 54 B2
Woodberry Down Centre
FSBYPK N4 55 J7
Woodberry Down Community Primary School
FSBYPK N4 55 J6
Woodbridge High School
WFD IG8 45 F6
Woodcroft Primary School
EDGW HA8 37 F6
Wood End J & I Schools
GFD/PVL UB6 66 D4
Wood End Park Junior School
UX/CGN UB8 82 A6
Woodfield School
CDALE/KGS NW9 51 G7
Woodford ⊖
WFD IG8 45 F5
Woodford County High School for Girls
WFD IG8 44 D5
Woodford Golf Club
WFD IG8 44 D4
Woodford Green Preparatory School
WFD IG8 44 E5
Woodford Green Primary School
WFD IG8 44 D4
Woodford Trading Estate
WFD IG8 59 G1
Woodgrange Infant School
FSTGT E7 77 F3
Woodgrange Park ⊖
FSTGT E7 77 H4
Woodgrange Park Cemetery
MNPK E12 77 H4
Wood Green ⊖
WDGN N22 55 G1
Wood Green Crown Court
WDGN N22 41 G7
Wood Green Health Centre
WDGN N22 41 F7
Wood Green Old Boys FC
WDGN N22 41 G6
Woodhall School
OXHEY WD19 33 J3
Woodhill Primary School
CHARL SE7 114 D3
Woodhouse College
NFNCH/WDSPK N12 39 H5
Woodlands First & Middle School
KTN/HRWW/WS HA3 34 C6
Woodlands J & I School
IL IG1 78 D3
Woodlands Medical Centre
LEW SE13 133 G5
Wood Lane ⊖
SHB W12 88 A6
Wood Lane Medical Centre
RSLP HA4 46 C7
Wood Lane School
FUL/PGN SW6 108 B7
Wood Lane Sports Centre
BCTR RM8 62 D7
Woodmansterne Primary School
STRHM/NOR SW16 148 D7
Woodridge Primary School
NFNCH/WDSPK N12 38 E2
Woodside ⊖
SNWD SE25 165 J5
Woodside Childrens Centre & Infant School
CROY/NA CR0 165 H6
Woodside Health Centre
SNWD SE25 165 J4
Woodside High School
WDGN N22 41 H6
Woodside Park ⊖
NFNCH/WDSPK N12 38 E3
NFNCH/WDSPK N12 39 F3
Woodside Park Golf Club
NFNCH/WDSPK N12 38 E3
Woodside Primary School
WALTH E17 58 A2
Woodside School
BELV DA17 117 J3
Wood Street ⇌
WALTH E17 58 B3
Wood Wharf
POP/IOD E14 93 K7
Wood Wharf Business Park
POP/IOD E14 113 F1
Woolmore Primary School
POP/IOD E14 94 A6
Woolwich Arsenal ⇌ ⊖
WOOL/PLUM SE18 115 G3
Woolwich Cemetery
WOOL/PLUM SE18 116 A6
Woolwich County Court
WOOL/PLUM SE18 115 F2
Woolwich Crown Court
THMD SE28 115 K1
Woolwich Dockyard ⇌
WOOL/PLUM SE18 114 E3
Woolwich Polytechnic School
THMD SE28 97 G7
Worcester Park ⇌
WPK KT4 160 D7
World Business Centre Heathrow
HTHAIR TW6 101 F7
World Rugby Museum & Twickenham Stadium Tours
WHTN TW2 123 K5
Worlds End Place
WBPTN SW10 108 B6
World Spiritual University
WLSDN NW10 69 J6
World University Service
STLK EC1Y 13 G1
Wormholt Park Primary School
SHB W12 87 J6
Worple Primary School
ISLW TW7 124 B3
Worsley Bridge Junior School
BECK BR3 151 J6
Worton Hall Industrial Estate
ISLW TW7 123 K3
Wren Academy
NFNCH/WDSPK N12 39 H4
Wrencote House
CROY/NA CR0 177 J2
WWT London Wetland Centre
BARN SW13 106 E7
Wyborne Primary School
ELTH/MOT SE9 135 G7
Wyke Green Golf Club
ISLW TW7 104 A5
Wykeham Primary School
HCH RM12 63 J7
WLSDN NW10 69 F2
Wyndham Grand London Hotel
WBPTN SW10 108 B7
Wyndhams Theatre
CHCR WC2N 11 H6
Wyvil Primary School
VX/NE SW8 109 K6
Yale University Press
HAMP NW3 71 J3
Yardley Primary School
CHING E4 31 K5
Yavneh College
BORE WD6 24 D3
Yeading FC
YEAD UB4 83 G7
Yeading Junior School
YEAD UB4 83 G4
Yeading Medical Centre
NTHLT UB5 83 G2
Yeading Primary School
YEAD UB4 83 G4
Yerbury Primary School
ARCH N19 72 D2

Yeshivo Horomo Talmudical College *STNW/STAM* N16 ..... 55 K7
Yesodey Hatorah Jewish Boys School *SEVS/STOTM* N15 ..... 56 B6
Yesodey Hatorah School for Girls Senior Site *STNW/STAM* N16 ..... 56 B6
Yetev Lev Day School for Boys *STNW/STAM* N16 ..... 56 C7
YMCA Leisure Centre *RSQ* WC1B 11 H4
York Clinic *STHWK* SE1 ..... 13 G9
York Hall *BETH* E2 ..... 92 D1
York Road Junior School & Language Unit *DART* DA1 ..... 139 J6
York Water Gate *CHCR* WC2N 11 K8
Young Actors Theatre *IS* N1 ..... 6 A4
Young Vic Theatre *STHWK* SE1 ..... 18 B1
Zennor Road I ndustrial Estate *BAL* SW12 ..... 129 H7
Zephyr Business Centre *SEVS/STOTM* N15 ..... 56 A3
The Zetter Hotel *FARR* EC1M 12 C1
Ziam Trading Estate *CLPT* E5 ..... 56 E7
ZSL London Zoo *CAMTN* NW1 ..... 4 A5

River bus map

Map of scheduled River Bus services

Putney Pier to Blackfriars Pier
Operates Monday-Friday peak hours only
Service operated by Thames River Taxi

Embankment Pier to Woolwich Arsenal Pier
Daily
Service operated by Thames Clippers

Canary Wharf Pier to Hilton Docklands Pier
Daily
Service operated by City Cruises

Woolwich Free Ferry
Daily (except evenings)
Service operated by Serco for Transport for London

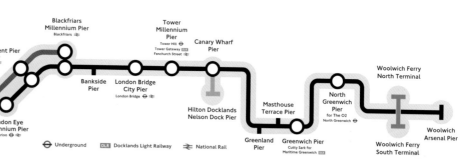

This map is a guide to services provided by the River Bus operators along the Thames on weekdays, but does not guarantee direct services between the piers shown. Some services/piers are not served outside of peak commuter hours. Please refer to tfl.gov.uk/rivers for full timetable information of scheduled River Bus services.

Reg. user No. 11/1894/P

Acknowledgements

Schools address data provided by Education Direct

Petrol station information supplied by Johnsons

Post office data provided by Post Office Limited and who accept no reponsibility for any data inaccuracies. Data accurate as of 12 July 2011

Garden centre information provided by:

Garden Centre Association Britains best garden centres

Wyevale Garden Centres

The boundary of the London Congestion Charging Zone and Low Emission Zone supplied by Transport for London

The statement on the front cover of this atlas is sourced, selected and quoted from a reader comment and feedback form received in 2004

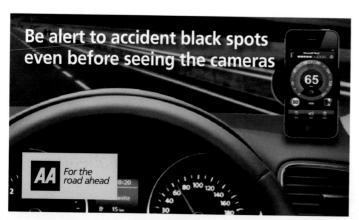

AA Travel Guides

The world at your fingertips

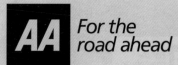